Mobil 1998
TRAVEL GUIDE®

Mid-Atlantic

**DELAWARE • DISTRICT OF COLUMBIA • MARYLAND
NEW JERSEY • NORTH CAROLINA • PENNSYLVANIA
SOUTH CAROLINA • VIRGINIA • WEST VIRGINIA**

D1385233

Fodor's Travel Publications, Inc.

Guide Staff

General Manager: Diane E. Connolly

Editorial/Inspection Coordinators: Sara D. Hauber, Doug Weinstein

Inspection Assistant: Brenda Piszczek

Editorial Assistants: Korrie Klier, Julie Raio, Kathleen Rose, Kristin Schiller, Elizabeth Schwar

Creative Director: Fabrizio La Rocca

Cover Design: John Olenyik

Cover Photograph: Ron Watts/Black Star

Acknowledgments

We gratefully acknowledge the help of our more than 100 field representatives for their efficient and perceptive inspection of every lodging and dining establishment listed; the establishments' proprietors for their coorperation in showing their facilities and providing information about them; the many users of previous editions of the *Mobil Travel Guide* who have taken the time to share their experiences; and for their time and information, the thousands of chambers of commerce, convention and visitors bureaus, city, state, and provincial tourism offices, and government agencies who assisted in our research.

Mobil

Copyright

Published in 1998 by Fodor's Travel Publications, Inc.
201 E. 50th St.
New York, NY 10022

Mid-Atlantic
ISBN 0-679-03501-X
ISSN 1090-6975

Printed in the United States of America
10 9 8 7 6 5 4 3 2 1

Contents

Mid-Atlantic

Maps

Larger, more detailed maps are available at many Mobil service stations

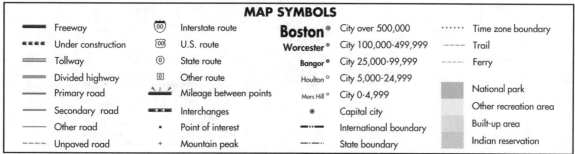

MAP SYMBOLS

▬▬ Freeway	⑩ Interstate route	**Boston**® City over 500,000	······ Time zone boundary	
◄◄◄◄ Under construction	⑩ U.S. route	**Worcester**® City 100,000-499,999	----- Trail	
▭▭▭ Tollway	⓪ State route	**Bangor**® City 25,000-99,999	----- Ferry	
▬▬ Divided highway	⓪ Other route	Houlton ° City 5,000-24,999		National park
▬▬ Primary road	▂²▂ Mileage between points	Mars Hill ° City 0-4,999		Other recreation area
▬▬ Secondary road	▬▬ Interchanges	⊛ Capital city		Built-up area
▬▬ Other road	· Point of interest	▬▪▪ International boundary		Indian reservation
---- Unpaved road	+ Mountain peak	▬··▬ State boundary		

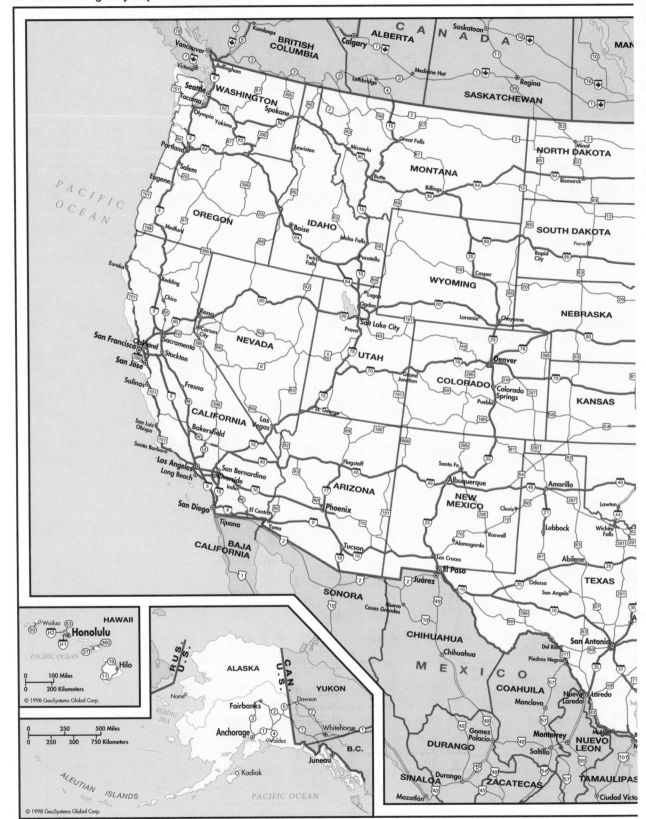

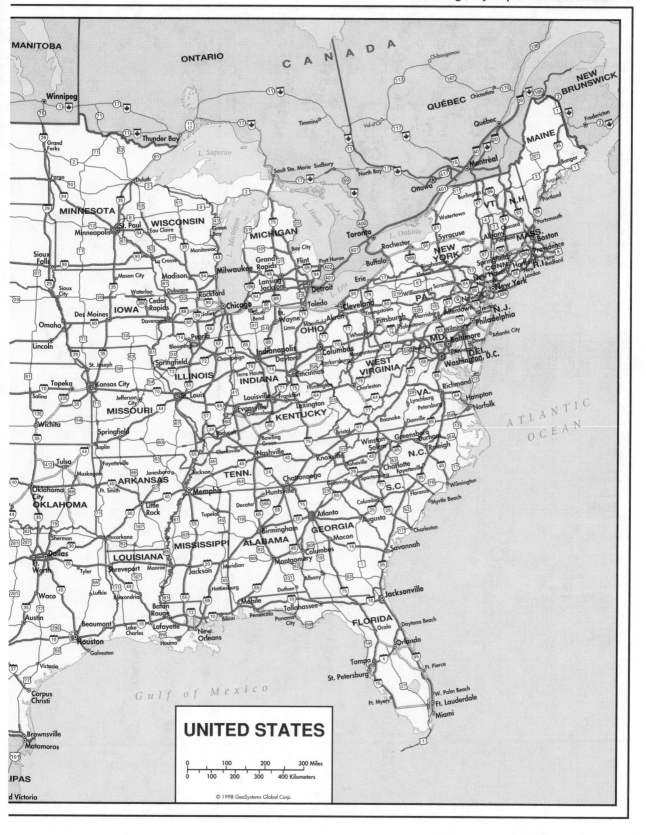

UNITED STATES

0   100   200   300 Miles

0   100   200   300   400 Kilometers

© 1998 GeoSystems Global Corp.

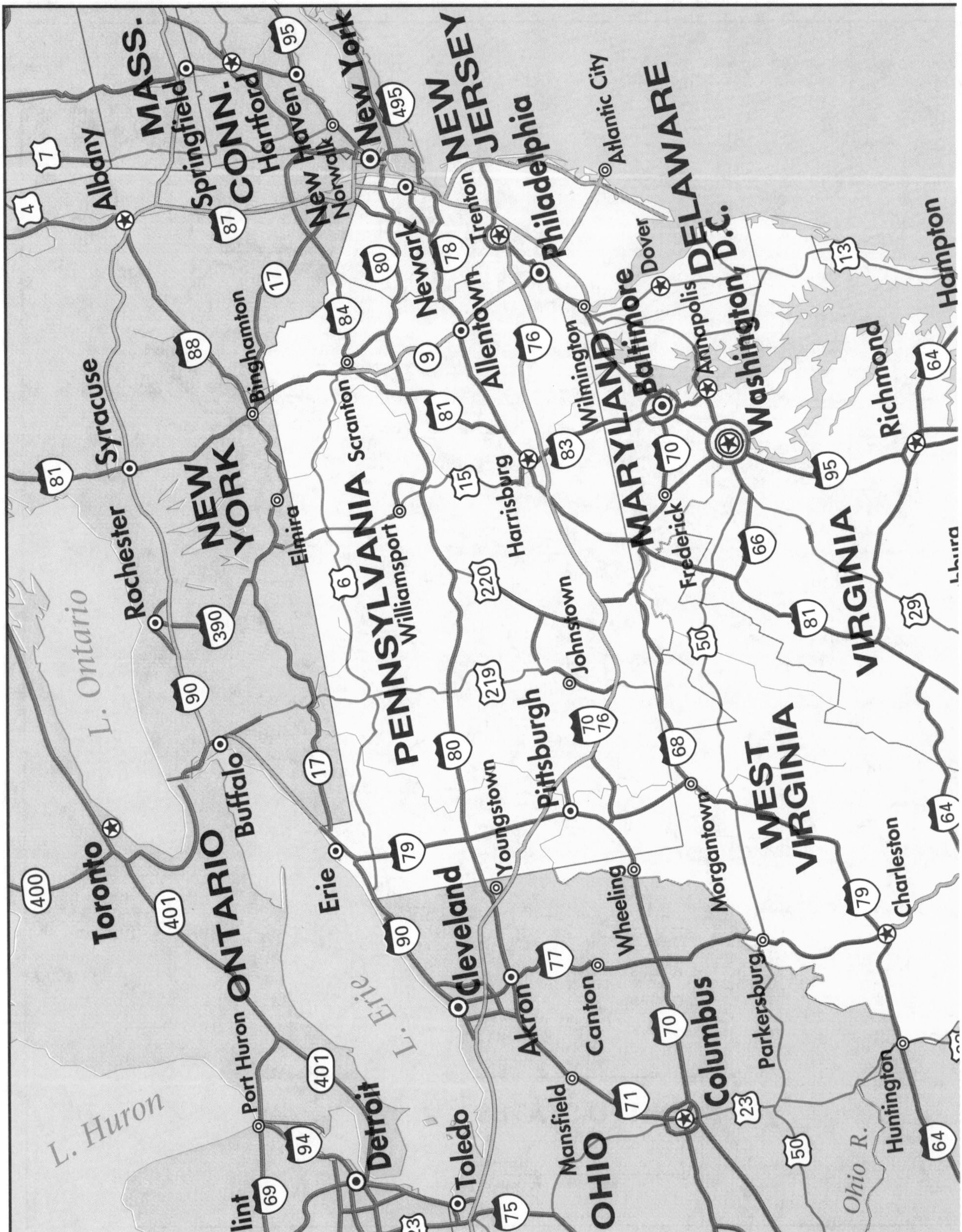

MASS.
CONN.
NEW JERSEY
NEW YORK
PENNSYLVANIA
DELAWARE
MARYLAND
D.C.
VIRGINIA
WEST VIRGINIA
OHIO
ONTARIO
L. Ontario
L. Erie
L. Huron
Ohio R.
Albany
Springfield
Hartford
New Haven
Norwalk
New York
Newark
Trenton
Philadelphia
Atlantic City
Dover
Wilmington
Baltimore
Annapolis
Washington
Richmond
Hampton
Syracuse
Binghamton
Scranton
Allentown
Harrisburg
Rochester
Elmira
Williamsport
Frederick
Johnstown
Buffalo
Toronto
Erie
Pittsburgh
Youngstown
Morgantown
Wheeling
Cleveland
Akron
Canton
Columbus
Parkersburg
Charleston
Huntington
Mansfield
Toledo
Detroit
Port Huron
Flint
4
7
87
95
495
80
78
17
84
9
76
13
88
81
83
70
15
64
95
66
6
220
29
390
50
219
90
17
80
70
76
68
400
401
79
77
70
71
23
50
94
69
75
23
64

MID-ATLANTIC REGION

© 1998 GeoSystems Global Corp.

0   50   100 Miles

0   50   100   150 Kilometers

ATLANTIC OCEAN

Hampton
Norfolk
64
13
58
64
Wilmington
17
Petersburg
85
Raleigh
40
76
Durham
Lynchburg
Greensboro
Danville
95
Myrtle Beach
Roanoke
N. CAROLINA
Charlotte
Fayetteville
Florence
Charleston
64
Winston-Salem
85
52
52
Savannah
77
S. CAROLINA
26
17
95
40
Columbia
81
Augusta
20
1
Spartanburg
77
Bristol
Asheville
26
16
23
Greenville
85
GEORGIA
Macon
Knoxville
23
75
KENTUCKY
64
Atlanta
19
75
75
20
85
80
Columbus
82

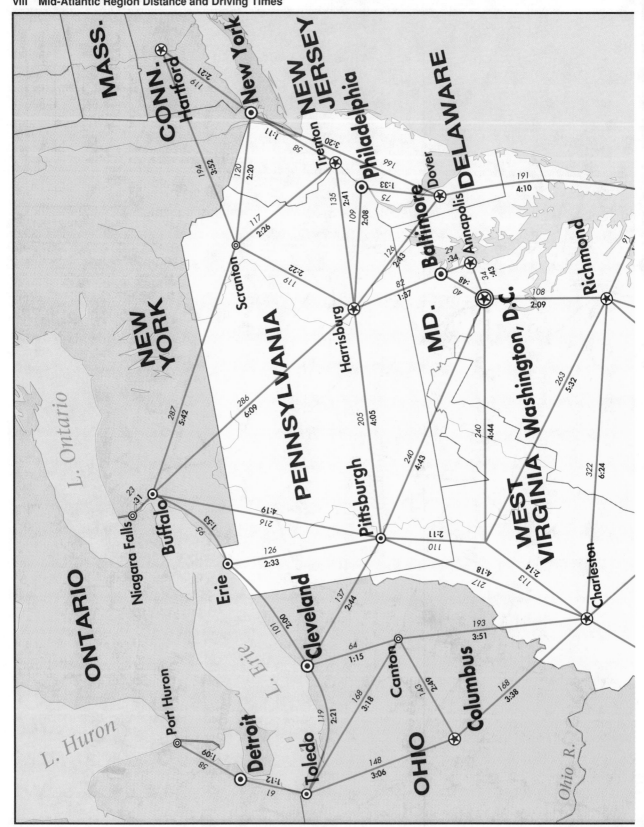

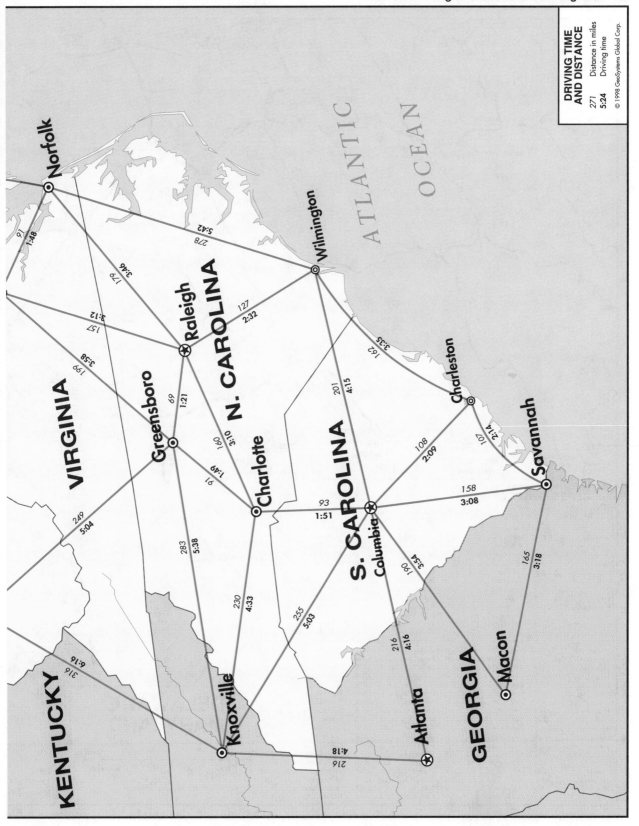

ATLANTIC

OCEAN

Norfolk

91
1:48

Wilmington

278
5:42

179
3:46

VIRGINIA

Raleigh

157
3:12

127
2:32

N. CAROLINA

Charleston

199
3:58

69
1:21

162
3:35

Greensboro

160
3:10

201
4:15

Savannah

249
5:04

91
1:49

Charlotte

108
2:09

107
2:14

S. CAROLINA

93
1:51

Columbia

158
3:08

283
5:38

N. CAROLINA

165
3:18

230
4:33

255
5:03

180
3:54

KENTUCKY

316
6:16

Macon

Knoxville

216
4:16

Atlanta

GEORGIA

216
4:18

PARTIAL INDEX TO CITIES AND TOWNS

DELAWARE

Bethany Beach	D-10
Bridgeville	D-9
Bowers Beach	C-9
Camden	C-9
Claymont	A-9
Delaware City	B-9
Dewey Beach	D-10
Dover	C-9
Ellendale	D-9
Elsmere	A-9
Felton	C-9
Fenwick Island	E-10
Frankford	D-10
Frederica	C-9
Georgetown	D-9
Harrington	C-9
Kenton	C-9
Laurel	D-9
Lewes	D-10
Middletown	B-9
Milford	C-9
Millsboro	D-10
Milton	D-10
New Castle	A-9
Newark	A-9
Odessa	B-9
Rehoboth Beach	D-10
Seaford	D-9
Selbyville	E-10
Smyrna	B-9
Talleyville	A-9
Wilmington	A-9

MARYLAND & D.C.

Aberdeen	B-8
Annapolis	C-7
Antietam	B-4
Baltimore	B-7
Bel Air	B-7
Berlin	E-10
Bethesda	C-6
Boonsboro	B-5
Bowie	C-7
Brunswick	B-5
Cambridge	D-8
Catonsville	B-7
Cecilton	B-8
Centreville	C-8
Chesapeake City	B-8
Chestertown	B-8
Clear Spring	A-4
Clinton	D-6
Cockeysville	B-7
College Park	C-6
Columbia	B-7
Crisfield	F-9
Cumberland	A-2
Damascus	B-6
Darlington	B-8
Dundalk	B-7
Easton	D-8
Edgewood	B-7
Elkton	B-9
Ellicott City	B-7
Emmitsburg	A-5
Federalsburg	D-9

Frederick	B-5
Frostburg	A-2
Gaithersburg	C-6
Germantown	C-5
Glen Burnie	C-7
Grantsville	A-1
Greenbelt	C-6
Greensboro	C-9
Hagerstown	A-4
Hampstead	B-6
Hancock	A-3
Havre De Grace	B-8
Hughesville	D-6
Huntingtown	D-7
Hurlock	D-8
Hyattsville	C-6
Jessup	C-6
Joppatowne	B-7
La Plata	D-6
La Vale	A-2
Largo	C-6
Laurel	C-6
Leonardtown	E-7
Lexington Park	E-7
Lutherville	B-7
Manchester	A-6
Mechanicsville	E-7
Mount Airy	B-6
Nanticoke	E-8
North Beach	D-7
North East	B-8
Oakland	B-1
Ocean City	E-10
Odenton	C-7
Olney	C-6
Parkville	B-7
Perry Hall	B-7

Pikesville	B-7
Pocomoke City	F-9
Preston	D-8
Prince Frederick	D-7
Princess Anne	E-9
Queen Anne	C-8
Randallstown	B-6
Reisterstown	B-6
Rock Hall	C-8
Rockville	C-6
St. Charles	D-6
St. Marys City	E-7
St. Michaels	D-8
Salisbury	E-9
Scotland	F-7
Severna Park	C-7
Sharpsburg	B-4
Silver Spring	C-6
Smithsburg	A-5
Snow Hill	E-9
Suitland	D-6
Taneytown	A-6
Taylors Island	E-7
Thurmont	B-5
Tilghman	D-7
Timonium	B-7
Toddville	E-8
Towson	B-7
Upper Marlboro	D-7
Vienna	E-8
Waldorf	D-6
Walkersville	B-5
Washington, D.C.	C-6
Wenona	E-8
Westernport	B-2
Westminster	B-6
Wheaton	C-6

DELAWARE MARYLAND

Scale: 0 – 10 – 20 – 30 Miles
0 – 10 – 20 – 30 – 40 Kilometers

© 1998 GeoSystems Global Corp.

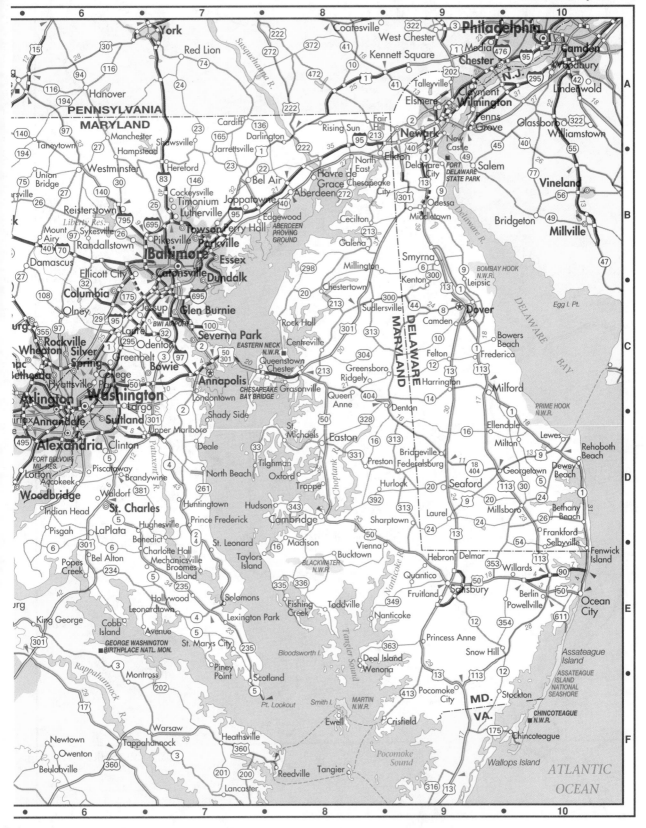

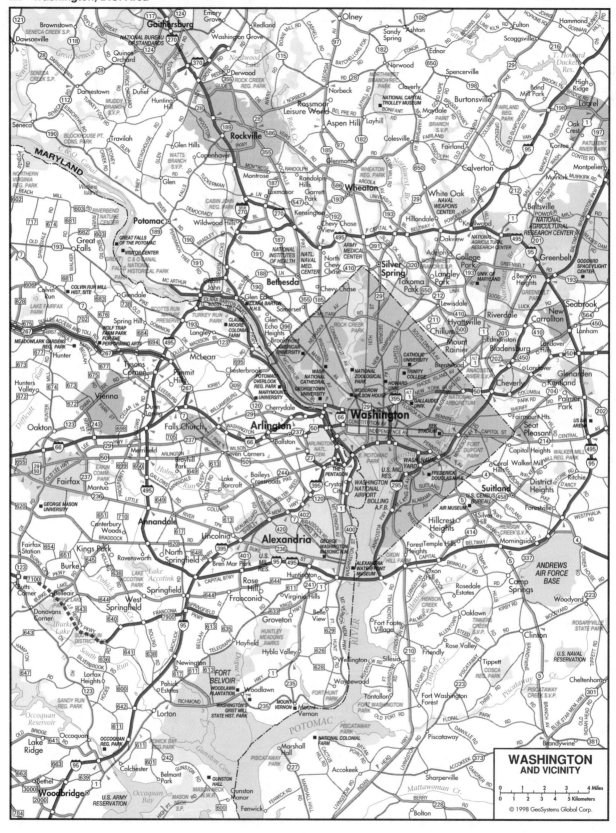

**WASHINGTON
AND VICINITY**

0   1   2   3   4 Miles
0   1   2   3   4   5 Kilometers

© 1998 GeoSystems Global Corp.

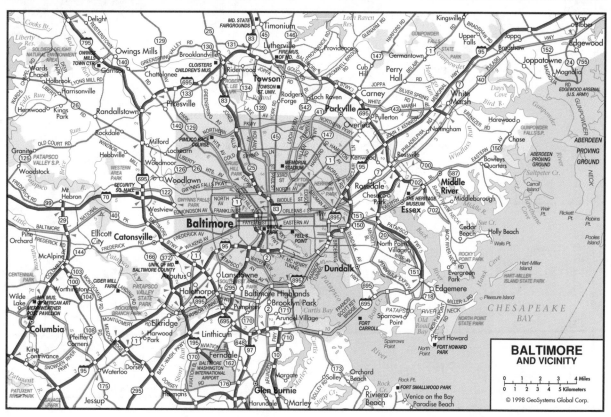

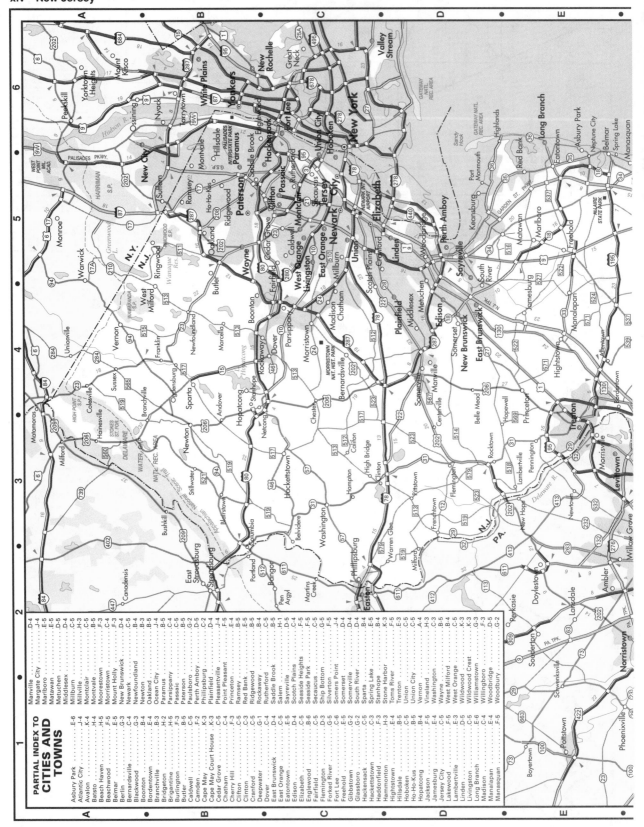

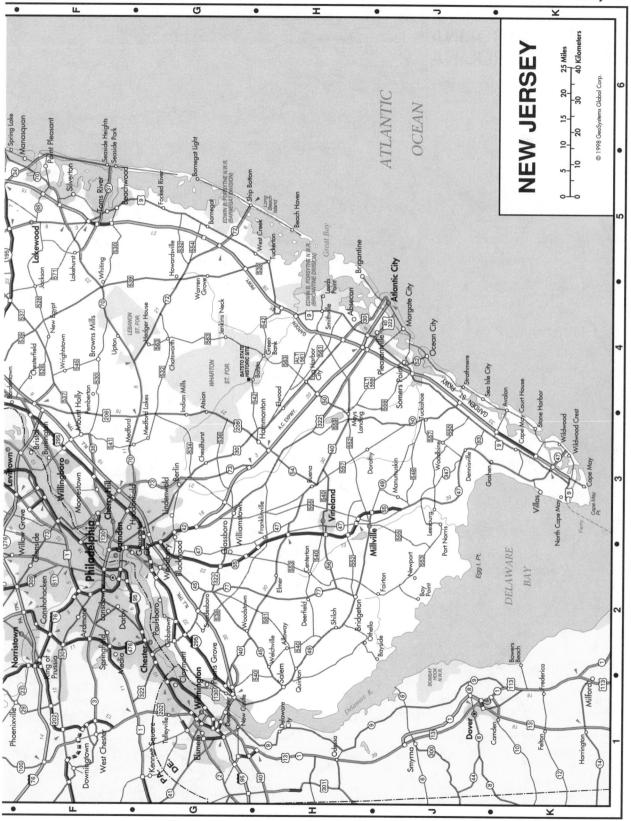

NEW JERSEY

© 1998 GeoSystems Global Corp.

25 Miles
40 Kilometers

NORTH CAROLINA
SOUTH CAROLINA

© 1998 GeoSystems Global Corp.

0 10 20 30 40 50 Miles
0 10 20 30 40 50 60 70 Kilometers

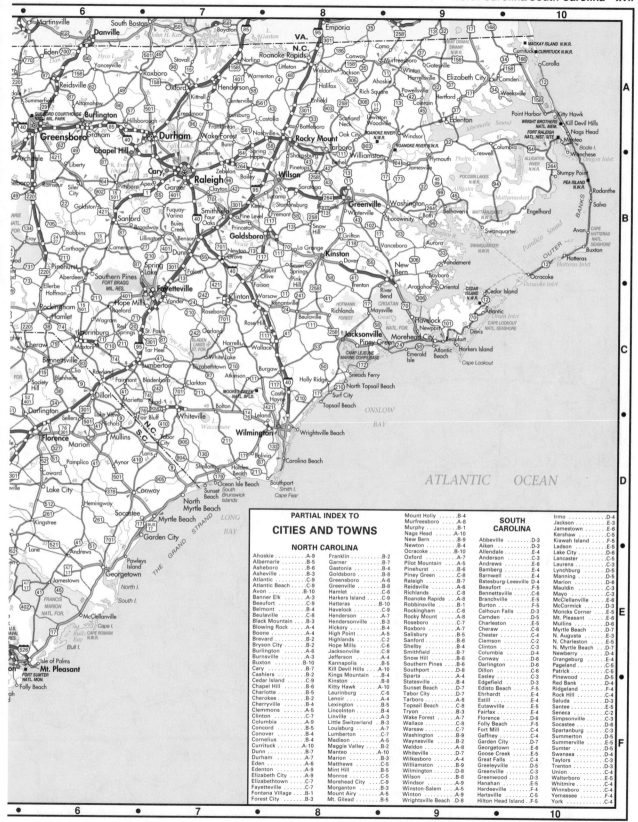

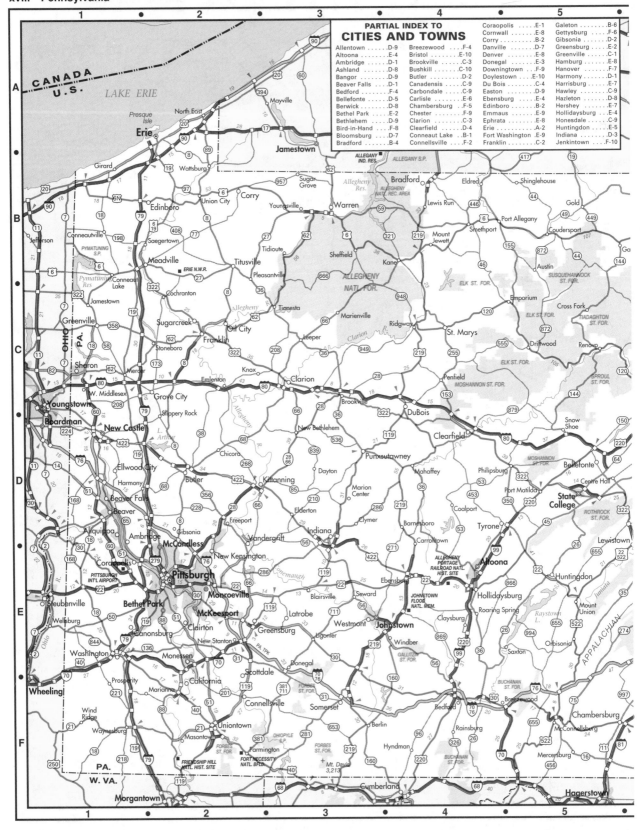

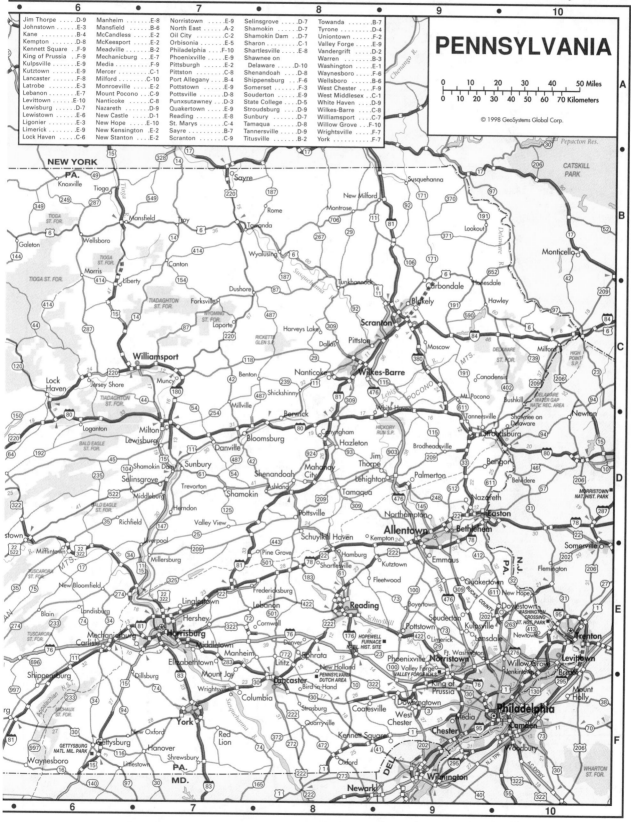

PENNSYLVANIA

0   10   20   30   40   50 Miles

0   10   20   30   40   50   60   70 Kilometers

© 1998 GeoSystems Global Corp.

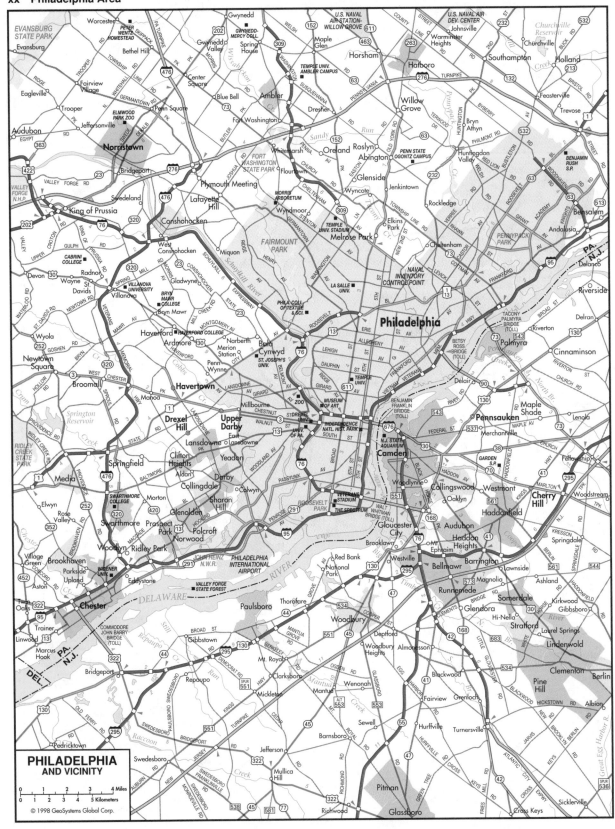

PHILADELPHIA
AND VICINITY

0 1 2 3 4 Miles
0 1 2 3 4 5 Kilometers

© 1998 GeoSystems Global Corp.

PHILADELPHIA DOWNTOWN

0   0.1   0.2 miles
0   0.1   0.2   0.3 Kilometers
© 1998 GeoSystems Global Corp.

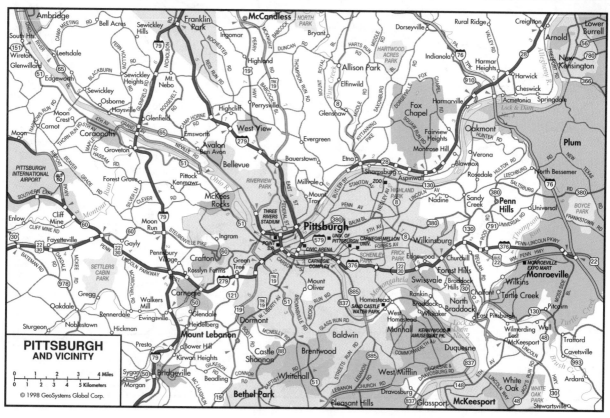

PITTSBURGH AND VICINITY

0   1   2   3   4 Miles
0   1   2   3   4   5 Kilometers
© 1998 GeoSystems Global Corp.

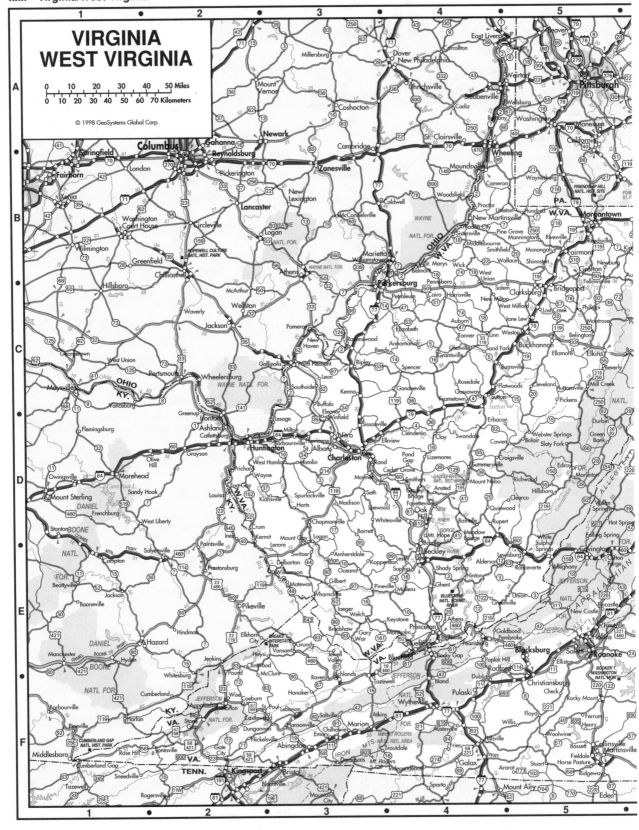

VIRGINIA
WEST VIRGINIA

0   10   20   30   40   50 Miles
0 10 20 30 40 50 60 70 Kilometers

© 1998 GeoSystems Global Corp.

PARTIAL INDEX TO CITIES AND TOWNS

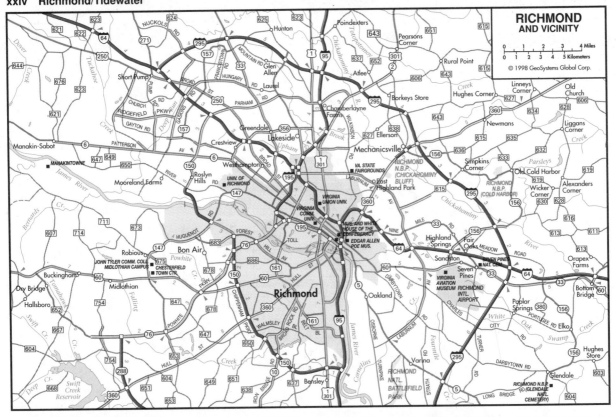

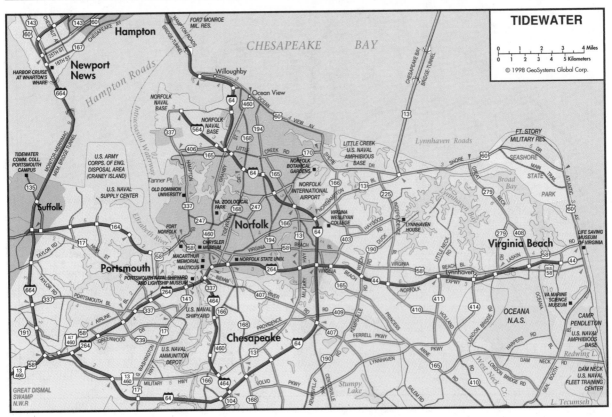

Before a long trip,
it's always smart to stop at Mobil.

On its ten-year, billion-mile mission, the International Space Station won't make pit stops, and its air system can't ever break down. So the grease for its fans and motors isn't a detail. It had to pass nearly as many tests as astronauts do, and in the end a Mobil synthetic won the job. What excites us is that we didn't create this grease for outer space. You can buy the same stuff (Mobilith SHC® 220) for your bicycle, bus or paper mill. Which, to us, shows the value of how we do research, trying to make things better than necessary. Nobody asked us to develop synthetic lubes, but we pursued it because that's how real innovation works. You aim to exceed present-day expectations so that when the future arrives, you're already there. To learn more, visit www.mobil.com.

Mobil® The energy to make a difference.

Back when racing began, our decals were a lot easier to read.

When J. Frank Duryea's race car streamed across the finish line at a breathtaking 5 mph, Mobil helped get it there. Of course, Mobil Motor Oil has protected somewhat more sophisticated engines since then. In fact, Mobil 1 is the official oil of Team Penske, the most successful team in Indy history. So whether you work in racing or race to work, call 1-800-ASK-MOBIL and find out more about any of our advanced oils. After all, we've found there's really only one place to promote our name. Under the hood.

Mobil. Changing oil for over 125 years.

A Word to Our Readers

Whether you're going on an extended family vacation, a weekend getaway, or a business trip, you need good, solid information on where to stay and eat and what to see and do. It would be nice if you could take a corps of well-seasoned travelers with you to suggest lodgings and activities, or ask a local restaurant critic for advice on dining spots, but since these options are rarely practical, the *Mobil Travel Guide* is the next best thing. It puts a huge database of information at your disposal and provides the value judgments and advice you need to use that information to its fullest.

Published by Fodor's Travel Publications, Inc., in collaboration with Mobil Corporation, the sponsor since 1958, these books contain the most comprehensive, up-to-date information possible on each region. In fact, listings are revised and ratings reviewed annually, based on inspection reports from our field representatives, evaluation by senior staff, and comments from more than 100,000 readers. These incredible data are then used to develop the *Mobil Travel Guide*'s impartial quality ratings, indicated by stars, which Americans have trusted for decades.

Space limitations make it impossible for us to include every fine hotel and restaurant, so we have picked a representative group, all above-average for their type. There's no charge to any establishment for inclusion, and only places that meet our standards are chosen. Because travelers' needs differ, we make every effort to select a variety of establishments and provide the information to decide what's right for you. If you're looking for a lodging at a certain price or location, or even one that offers 24-hour room service, you'll find the answers you need at your fingertips. Take a minute to read the next section, How to Use This Book; it'll make finding the information you want a breeze.

Also look at Making the Most of Your Trip, the section that follows. It's full of tips from savvy travelers that can help you save money, stay safe, and get around more easily—the keys to making any trip a success.

Of course, the passage of time means that some establishments will close, change hands, remodel, improve, or go downhill. Though every effort has been made to ensure the accuracy of all information when it was printed, change is inevitable. Always call and confirm that a place is open and that it has the features you want. Whatever your experiences at any of the establishments we list—and we hope they're terrific—or if you have general comments about our guide, we'd love to hear from you. Use the convenient postage-paid card near the end of this book, or drop us a line at the *Mobil Travel Guide,* Fodor's Travel Publications, Inc., 4709 W. Golf Road, Suite 803, Skokie, IL 60076.

So pack this book in your suitcase or toss it next to you on the front seat. If it gets dog-eared, so much the better. We here at the *Mobil Travel Guide* wish you a safe and successful trip.

Bon voyage and happy driving,

THE EDITORS

Welcome

For 40 years, the *Mobil Travel Guide* has provided travelers in North America with reliable advice on finding good value, quality service, and the attractions that give a destination its special character. During this time, our teams of culinary and hospitality experts have worked hard to develop objective and exacting standards. In so doing, they seek to fully meet the desires and expectations of a broad range of customers.

At Mobil, we demonstrate the energy to make a difference through a commitment to excellence that allows us to bring the best service and products to the people we serve. We believe that the ability to respond to and anticipate customers' needs is what distinguishes good companies from truly great ones.

It is our hope, whether your travels are for business or leisure, over a long distance or a short one, that this book will be your companion, dependably guiding you to quality and value in lodging and dining.

Finally, I ask that you help us improve the guides. Please take the time to fill out the customer feedback form at the back of this book or contact us on the Internet at www.mobil.com/travel.

Lucio A. Noto

Lucio A. Noto
Chairman and
Chief Executive Officer
Mobil Corporation

How to Use This Book

The *Mobil Travel Guide* is easy to use. Each state chapter begins with a general introduction that both provides a general geographical and historical orientation to the state and covers basic statewide tourist information, from state recreation areas to seat-belt laws. The balance of each chapter is devoted to the travel destinations within the state—cities and towns, state and national parks, and tourist regions—which, like the states themselves, are arranged alphabetically.

What follows is an explanation of the wealth of information you'll find within those travel destinations—information on the area, on things to see and do there, and on where to stay and eat.

Maps and Map Coordinates

The first thing you'll notice is that next to each destination is a set of map coordinates. These refer to the appropriate state map in the front of this book. In addition, there are maps of selected larger cities in the front section as well as maps of key neighborhoods within the sections on the cities themselves.

Destination Information

Because many travel destinations are so close to other cities and towns where visitors might find additional attractions, accommodations, and restaurants, cross-references to those places are included whenever possible. Also listed are addresses and phone numbers for travel-information resources—usually the local chamber of commerce or office of tourism—as well as pertinent vital statistics and a brief introduction to the area.

What to See and Do

More than 11,000 museums, art galleries, amusement parks, universities, historic sites and houses, plantations, churches, state parks, ski areas, and other attractions are described in the *Mobil Travel Guide.* A white star on a black background ★ signals that the attraction is one of the best in the state. Since municipal parks, public tennis courts, swimming pools, and small educational institutions are common to most towns, they are generally excluded.

Following the attraction's description are the months and days it's open, address/location and phone number, and admission costs (see the inside front cover for an explanation of the cost symbols). Note that directions are given from the center of the town under which the attraction is listed, which may not necessarily be the town in which the attraction is located. Zip codes are listed only if they differ from those given for the town.

Events

Events—categorized as annual, seasonal, or special—are highlighted. An annual event is one that's held every year for a period of usually no longer than a week to 10 days; festivals and fairs are typical entries. A seasonal event is one that may or may not be annual and that is held for a number of weeks or months in the year, such as horse racing, summer theater, concert or opera festivals, and professional sports. Special event listings occur infrequently and mark a certain date or event, such as a centennial or other commemorative celebration.

Major Cities

Additional information on airports and transportation, suburbs, and neighborhoods, including a list of restaurants by neighborhood, may be included for large cities.

Lodging and Restaurant Listings

ORGANIZATION

For both lodgings and restaurants, when a property is in a town that does not have its own heading, the listing appears under the town nearest its location with the address and town in parentheses immediately after the establishment name. In large cities, lodgings located within 5 miles of major, commercial airports are listed under a separate "Airport" heading, following the city listings.

LODGING CLASSIFICATIONS

Each property is classified by type according to the characteristics below. Because the following features and services are found at most motels, lodges, motor hotels, and hotels, they are not shown in those listings:

- Year-round operation with a single rate structure unless otherwise quoted
- European plan (meals not included in room rate)
- Bathroom with tub and/or shower in each room
- Air-conditioned/heated, often with individual room control
- Cots
- Daily maid service
- Phones in rooms
- Elevators

Motels and Lodges. Accommodations are in low-rise structures with rooms easily accessible to parking (usually free). Properties have outdoor room entry and small, functional lobbies. Service is often limited, and dining may not be offered in lower-rated motels and lodges. Shops and businesses are found only in higher-rated properties, as are bellhops, room service, and restaurants serving three meals daily.

Lodges differ from motels primarily in their emphasis on outdoor recreational activities and in location. They are often found in resort and rural areas rather than in major cities or along highways.

Motor Hotels. Offering the convenience of motels along with many of the features of hotels, motor hotels range from low-rise structures offering limited services to multistory buildings with a wide range of services and facilities. Multiple building entrances, elevators, inside hallways, and parking areas (generally free) near access doors are some of the features of a motor hotel. Lobbies offer sitting areas and 24-hour desk and switchboard services. Often bellhop and valet services as well as restaurants serving three meals a day are found. Expanded recreational facilities and more than one restaurant are available in higher-rated properties.

The distinction between motor hotels and hotels in metropolitan areas is minor.

Hotels. To be categorized as a hotel, an establishment must have most of the following facilities and services: multiple floors, a restaurant and/or coffee shop, elevators, room service, bellhops, a spacious lobby, and recreational facilities. In addition, the following features and services not shown in listings are also found:

- Valet service (one-day laundry/cleaning service)
- Room service during hours restaurant is open
- Bellhops
- Some oversize beds

Resorts. These specialize in stays of three days or more and usually offer American Plan and/or housekeeping accommodations. Their emphasis is on recreational facilities, and a social director is often available. Food services are of primary importance, and guests must be able to eat three meals a day on the premises, either in restaurants or by having access to an on-site grocery store and preparing their own meals.

Inns. Frequently thought of as a small hotel, an inn is a place of homelike comfort and warm hospitality. It is often a structure of historic significance, with an equally interesting setting. Meals are a special occasion, and refreshments are frequently served in late afternoon. Rooms are usually individually decorated, often with antiques or furnishings representative of the locale. Phones, bathrooms, and TVs may not be available in every room.

Guest Ranches. Like resorts, guest ranches specialize in stays of three days or more. Guest ranches also offer meal plans and extensive outdoor activities. Horseback riding is usually a feature; there are stables and trails on the ranch property, and trail rides and daily instruction are part of the program. Many guest ranches are working ranches, ranging from casual to rustic, and guests are encouraged to participate in ranch life. Eating is often family-style and may also include cookouts. Western saddles are assumed; phone ahead to inquire about English saddle availability.

Cottage Colonies. These are housekeeping cottages and cabins that are usually found in recreational areas. Any dining or recreational facilities are noted in our listing.

DINING CLASSIFICATIONS

Restaurants. Most dining establishments fall into this category. All have a full kitchen and offer table service and a complete menu. Parking on or near the premises, in a lot or garage, is assumed. When a property offers valet or other special parking features, or when only street parking is available, it is noted in the listing.

Unrated Dining Spots. These places, listed after Restaurants in many cities, are chosen for their unique atmosphere, specialized menu, or local flavor. They include delis, ice-cream parlors, cafeterias, tearooms, and pizzerias. Because they may not have a full kitchen or table service, they are not given a *Mobil Travel Guide* rating. Often they offer extraordinary value and quick service.

QUALITY RATINGS

The *Mobil Travel Guide* has been rating lodgings and restaurants on a national basis since the first edition was published in 1958. For years the guide was the only source of such ratings, and it remains among the few guidebooks to rate restaurants across the country.

All listed establishments were inspected by experienced field representatives or evaluated by a senior staff member. Ratings are based upon their detailed inspection reports of the individual properties, on written evaluations of staff members who stay and dine anonymously, and on an extensive review of comments from our readers.

You'll find a key to the rating categories, ★ through ★★★★★, on the inside front cover. All establishments in the book are recommended. Even a ★ place is above average, usually providing a basic, informal experience. Rating categories reflect both the features the property offers and its quality in relation to similar establishments.

For example, lodging ratings take into account the number and quality of facilities and services, the luxury of appointments, and the attitude and professionalism of staff and management. A ★ establishment provides a comfortable night's lodging. A ★★ property offers more than a facility that rates one star, and the decor is well planned and integrated. Establishments that rate ★★★ are professionally managed and staffed and often beautifully appointed; the lodging experience is truly excellent and the range of facilities is extensive. Properties that have been given ★★★★ not only offer many services but also have their own style and personality; they are luxurious, creatively decorated, and superbly maintained. The ★★★★★ properties are among the best in the United States, superb in every respect and entirely memorable, year in and year out.

Restaurant evaluations reflect the quality of the food and the ingredients, preparation, and presentation as well as service levels and the property's decor and ambience. A restaurant that has fairly simple goals for menu and decor but that achieves those goals superbly might receive the same number of stars as a restaurant with somewhat loftier ambitions but whose execution falls somewhat short of the mark. In general, ★ indicates a restaurant that's a good choice in its area, usually fairly simple and perhaps catering to a clientele of locals and families; ★★ denotes restaurants that are more highly recommended in their area; ★★★ restaurants are of national caliber, with professional and attentive service and a skilled chef in the kitchen; ★★★★ reflects superb dining choices, where remarkable food is served in equally remarkable surroundings; and ★★★★★ represents that rarefied group of the best restaurants in the country, where in addition to near perfection in every detail, there's that special something extra that makes for an unforgettable dining experience. A list of the four-star and five-star establishments in this region is located just before the state listings.

Each rating is reviewed annually and each establishment must work to maintain its rating (or improve it). Every effort is made to assure that ratings are fair and accurate; the designated ratings are published purely as an aid to travelers.

In general, properties that are very new or have recently undergone major management changes are considered difficult to assess fairly and are often listed without ratings.

Good Value Check Mark. In all locales, you'll find a wide range of lodging and dining establishments with a ✔ in front of a star rating. This indicates an unusually good value at economical prices as follows:

In Major Cities and Resort Areas

Lodging: average $105–$125 per night for singles; average $115–$140 per night for doubles

Restaurants: average $25 for a complete lunch; average $40 for a complete dinner, exclusive of beverages and gratuities

Local Area Listings

Lodging: average $50–$60 per night for singles; average $60–$75 per night for doubles

Restaurants: average $12 for a complete lunch; average $20 for a complete dinner, exclusive of beverages and gratuities

LODGINGS

Each listing gives the name, address, directions (when there is no street address), neighborhood and/or directions from downtown (in major cities), phone number (local and 800), fax number, number and type of rooms available, room rates, and seasons open (if not year-round). Also included are details on recreational and dining facilities on property or nearby, the presence of a luxury level, and credit-card information. A key to the symbols at the end of each listing is on the inside front cover. (Note that Mobil Corporation credit cards cannot be used for payment of meals and room charges.)

All prices quoted in the *Mobil Travel Guide* publications are expected to be in effect at the time of publication and during the entire year; however, prices cannot be guaranteed. In some localities there may be short-term price variations because of special events or holidays. Whenever possible, these price changes are noted. Certain resorts have complicated rate structures that vary with the time of year; always confirm listed rates when you make your plans.

RESTAURANTS

Listings give the name, address, directions (when there is no street address), neighborhood and/or directions from downtown (in major cities), phone number, hours and days of operation (if not open daily year-round), reservation policy, cuisine (if other than American), price range for each meal served, children's meals (if offered), specialties, and credit card information. Additionally, special features such as chef ownership, ambience, and entertainment are noted. By carefully reading the detailed restaurant information and comparing prices, you can easily determine whether the restaurant is formal and elegant or informal and comfortable for families.

TERMS AND ABBREVIATIONS IN LISTINGS

The following terms and abbreviations are used consistently throughout the listings:

A la carte entrees With a price, refers to the cost of entrees/main dishes only that are not accompanied by side dishes.

AP American plan (lodging plus all meals).

Bar Liquor, wine, and beer are served in a bar or cocktail lounge and usually with meals unless otherwise indicated (e.g., "wine, beer").

Business center The property has a designated area accessible to all guests with business services.

Business servs avail The property can perform/arrange at least two of the following services for a guest: audiovisual equipment rental, binding, computer rental, faxing, messenger services, modem availability, notary service, obtaining office supplies, photocopying, shipping, and typing.

Cable Standard cable service; "premium" indicates that HBO, Disney, Showtime, or similar services are available.

Ck-in, ck-out Check-in time, check-out time.

Coin lndry Self-service laundry.

Complete meal Soup and/or salad, entree, and dessert, plus nonalcoholic beverage.

Continental bkfst Usually coffee and a roll or doughnut.

Cr cds: A, American Express; C, Carte Blanche; D, Diners Club; DS, Discover; ER, enRoute; JCB, Japanese Credit Bureau; MC, MasterCard; V, Visa.

D Followed by a price, indicates room rate for a "double"—two people in one room in one or two beds (the charge may be higher for two double beds).

Downhill/x-country ski Downhill and/or cross-country skiing within 20 miles of property.

Each addl Extra charge for each additional person beyond the stated number of persons at a reduced price.

Early-bird dinner A meal served at specified hours, typically around 4:30–6:30 pm.

Exc Except.

Exercise equipt Two or more pieces of exercise equipment on the premises.

Exercise rm Both exercise equipment and room, with an instructor on the premises.

Fax Facsimile machines available to all guests.

Golf privileges Privileges at a course within 10 miles

Hols Holidays

In-rm modem link Every guest room has a connection for a modem that's separate from the phone line.

Kit. or kits. A kitchen or kitchenette that contains stove or microwave, sink, and refrigerator and that is either part of the room or a separate room. If the kitchen is not fully equipped, the listing will indicate "no equipt" or "some equipt".

Luxury level A special section of a hotel, covering at least an entire floor, that offers increased luxury accommodations. Management must provide no less than three of these four services: separate check-in and check-out, concierge, private lounge, and private elevator service (key access). Complimentary breakfast and snacks are commonly offered.

MAP Modified American plan (lodging plus two meals).

Movies Prerecorded videos are available for rental.

No cr cds accepted No credit cards are accepted.

No elvtr In hotels with more than two stories, it's assumed there are elevators; only their absence is noted.

No phones Phones, too, are assumed; only their absence is noted.

Parking There is a parking lot on the premises.

Private club A cocktail lounge or bar available to members and their guests. In motels and hotels where these clubs exist, registered guests can usually use the club as guests of the management; the same is frequently true of restaurants.

Prix fixe A full meal for a stated price; usually one price is quoted.

Res Reservations.

S Followed by a price, indicates room rate for a "single," i.e., one person.

Semi-a la carte Meals include vegetable, salad, soup, appetizer, or other accompaniments to the main dish.

Serv bar A service bar, where drinks are prepared for dining patrons only.

Serv charge Service charge is the amount added to the restaurant check in lieu of a tip.

Table d'hôte A full meal for a stated price, dependent upon entree selection; no a la carte options are available.

Tennis privileges Privileges at tennis courts within 5 miles.

TV Indicates color television; B/W indicates black-and-white television.

Under certain age free Children under that age are not charged for if staying in room with a parent.

Valet parking An attendant is available to park and retrieve a car.

VCR VCRs in all guest rooms.

VCR avail VCRs are available for hookup in guest rooms.

Special Information for Travelers with Disabilities

The *Mobil Travel Guide* symbol D shown in accommodation and restaurant listings indicates establishments that are at least partially accessible to people with mobility problems.

The *Mobil Travel Guide* criteria for accessibility are unique to our publication. Please do not confuse them with the universal symbol for wheelchair accessibility. When the D symbol appears following a listing, the establishment is equipped with facilities to accommodate people using wheelchairs or crutches or otherwise needing easy access to doorways and rest rooms. Travelers with severe mobility problems or with hearing or visual impairments may or may not find facilities they need. Always phone ahead to make sure that an establishment can meet your needs.

All lodgings bearing our D symbol have the following facilities:

- ISA-designated parking near access ramps
- Level or ramped entryways to building
- Swinging building entryway doors minimum 3'0"
- Public rest rooms on main level with space to operate a wheelchair; handrails at commode areas
- Elevators equipped with grab bars and lowered control buttons
- Restaurants with accessible doorways; rest rooms with space to operate wheelchair; handrails at commode areas

- Minimum 3′0″ width entryway to guest rooms
- Low-pile carpet in rooms
- Telephone at bedside and in bathroom
- Bed placed at wheelchair height
- Minimum 3′0″ width doorway to bathroom
- Bath with open sink—no cabinet; room to operate wheelchair
- Handrails at commode areas; tub handrails
- Wheelchair accessible peephole in room entry door
- Wheelchair accessible closet rods and shelves

All restaurants bearing our D symbol offer the following facilities:

- ISA-designated parking beside access ramps
- Level or ramped front entryways to building
- Tables to accommodate wheelchairs
- Main-floor rest rooms; minimum 3′0″ width entryway

- Rest rooms with space to operate wheelchair; handrails at commode areas

In general, the newest properties are apt to impose the fewest barriers.

To get the kind of service you need and have a right to expect, do not hesitate when making a reservation to question the management in detail about the availability of accessible rooms, parking, entrances, restaurants, lounges, or any other facilities that are important to you, and confirm what is meant by "accessible." Some guests with mobility impairments report that lodging establishments' housekeeping and maintenance departments are most helpful in describing barriers. Also inquire about any special equipment, transportation, or services you may need.

Making the Most of Your Trip

A few diehard souls might fondly remember the trip where the car broke down and they were stranded for a week, or the vacation that cost twice what it was supposed to. For most travelers, though, the best trips are those that are safe, smooth, and within their budget. To help you make your trip the best it can be, we've assembled a few tips and resources.

Saving Money

ON LODGING

After you've seen the published rates, it's time to look for discounts. Many hotels and motels offer them—for senior citizens, business travelers, families, you name it. It never hurts to ask—politely, that is. Sometimes, especially in late afternoon, desk clerks are instructed to fill beds, and you might be offered a lower rate, or a nicer room, to entice you to stay. Look for bargains on stays over multiple nights, in the off-season, and on weekdays or weekends (depending on location). Many hotels in major metropolitan areas, for example, have special weekend package plans, which offer considerable savings on rooms and may include breakfast, cocktails, and meal discounts. Prices change frequently throughout the year, so phone ahead.

Another way to save money is to choose accommodations that give you more than just a standard room. Rooms with kitchen facilities enable you to cook some meals for yourself, reducing restaurant costs. A suite might save money for two couples traveling together. Even hotel luxury levels can provide good value, as many include breakfast or cocktails in the price of the room.

State and city sales taxes as well as special room taxes can increase your room rates as much as 25% per day. We are unable to bring this specific information into the listings, but we strongly urge that you ask about these taxes when placing reservations in order to understand the total price to you.

Watch out for telephone-usage charges that hotels frequently impose on long-distance calls, credit-card calls, and other phone calls—even those that go unanswered. Before phoning from your room, read the information given to you at check-in, and then be sure to read your bill carefully before checking out. You won't be expected to pay for charges that weren't spelled out. (On the other hand, it's not unusual for a hotel to bill you for your calls after you return home.) Consider using public telephones in hotel lobbies; the savings may outweigh the inconvenience.

ON DINING

There are several ways to get a less-expensive meal at a more-expensive restaurant. Early-bird dinners are popular in many parts of the country and offer considerable savings. If you're interested in sampling a ★★★★ or ★★★★★ establishment, consider going at lunchtime. While the prices then are probably relatively high, they may be half of those at dinner and come with the same ambience, service, and cuisine.

PARK PASSES

While many national parks, monuments, seashores, historic sites, and recreation areas may be used free of charge, others charge an entrance fee (ranging from $1 to $5 per person to $5 to $15 per carload) and/or a "use fee" for special services and facilities. If you plan to make several visits to federal recreation areas, consider one of the following National Park Service money-saving programs:

Park Pass. This is an annual entrance permit to a specific unit in the National Park Service system that normally charges an entrance fee. The pass admits the permit holder and any accompanying passengers in a private noncommercial vehicle or, in the case of walk-in facilities, the holder's spouse, children, and parents. It is valid for entrance fees only. A Park Pass may be purchased in person or by mail from the National Park Service unit at which the pass will be honored. The cost is $15 to $20, depending upon the area.

Golden Eagle Passport. This pass, available to people who are between 17 and 61, entitles the purchaser and accompanying passengers in a private noncommercial vehicle to enter any outdoor NPS unit that charges an entrance fee and admits the purchaser and family to most walk-in fee-charging areas. Like the Park Pass, it is good for one year and does not cover use fees. It may be purchased from the National Park Service, Office of Public Inquiries, Room 1013, US Department of the Interior, 18th and C Sts NW, Washington, DC 20240, phone 202/208–4747; at any of the 10 regional offices throughout the country; and at any NPS area that charges a fee. The cost is $50.

Golden Age Passport. Available to citizens and permanent residents of the United States 62 years or older, this is a lifetime entrance permit to fee-charging recreation areas. The fee exemption extends to those accompanying the permit holder in a private noncommercial vehicle or, in the case of walk-in facilities, to the holder's spouse and children. The passport also entitles the holder to a 50% discount on use fees charged in park areas but not to fees charged by concessionaires. Golden Age Passports must be obtained in person. The applicant must show proof of age, i.e., a driver's license, birth certificate, or signed affidavit attesting to age (Medicare cards are not acceptable proof). Passports are available at most park service units where they're used, at National Park Service headquarters (see above), at park system regional offices, at National Forest Supervisors' offices, and at most Ranger Station offices. The cost is $10.

Golden Access Passport. Issued to citizens and permanent residents of the United States who are physically disabled or visually impaired, this passport is a free lifetime entrance permit to fee-charging recreation areas. The fee exemption extends to those accompanying the permit holder in a private noncommercial vehicle or, in the case of walk-in facilities, to the holder's spouse and children. The passport also entitles the holder to a 50% discount on use fees charged in park areas but not to fees charged by concessionaires. Golden Access Passports must be obtained in person. Proof of eligibility to receive federal benefits is required (under programs such as Disability Retirement, Compensation for Military Service-Connected Disability, Coal Mine Safety and Health Act, etc.), or an affidavit must be signed attesting to eligibility. These passports are available at the same outlets as Golden Age Passports.

FOR SENIOR CITIZENS
Look for the senior-citizen discount symbol in the lodging and restaurant listings. Always call ahead to confirm that the discount is being offered, and be sure to carry proof of age. At places not listed in the book, it never hurts to ask if a senior-citizen discount is offered. Two organizations provide additional information for mature travelers: the American Association of Retired Persons (AARP), 601 E St NW, Washington, DC 20049, phone 202/434–2277, and the National Council of Senior Citizens, 8403 Cosville, Ste 1200, Silver Springs, MD 20910, phone 301/528-8800.

Tipping

Tipping is an expression of appreciation for good service, and often service workers rely on tips as a significant part of their income. However, you never need to tip if service is poor.

IN HOTELS
Doormen in major city hotels are usually given $1 for getting you a cab. Bellhops expect $1 per bag, usually $2 if you have only one bag. Concierges are tipped according to the service they perform. It's not mandatory to tip when you've asked for suggestions on sightseeing or restaurants or help in making reservations for dining. However, when a concierge books you a table at a restaurant known to be difficult to get into, a gratuity of $5 is appropriate. For obtaining theater or sporting event tickets, $5–$10 is expected. Maids, often overlooked by guests, may be tipped $1–$2 per day of stay.

AT RESTAURANTS
Coffee shop and counter service wait staff are usually given 8%–10% of the bill. In full-service restaurants, tip 15% of the bill, before sales tax. In fine restaurants, where the staff is large and shares the gratuity, 18%–20% for the waiter is appropriate. In most cases, tip the maitre d' only if service has been extraordinary and only on the way out; $20 is the minimum in upscale properties in major metropolitan areas. If there is a wine steward, tip him or her at least $5 a bottle, more if the wine was decanted or if the bottle was very expensive. If your busboy has been unusually attentive, $2 pressed into his hand on departure is a nice gesture. An increasing number of restaurants automatically add a service charge to the bill in lieu of a gratuity. Before tipping, carefully review your check.

AT AIRPORTS
Curbside luggage handlers expect $1 per bag. Car-rental shuttle drivers who help with your luggage appreciate a $1 or $2 tip.

Staying Safe

The best way to deal with emergencies is to be prepared enough to avoid them. However, unforeseen situations do happen, and you can prepare for them.

IN YOUR CAR
Before your trip, make sure your car has been serviced and is in good working order. Change the oil, check the battery and belts, and make sure tires are inflated properly (this can also improve gas mileage). Other inspections recommended by the car's manufacturer should be made, too.

Next, be sure you have the tools and equipment to deal with a routine breakdown: jack, spare tire, lug wrench, repair kit, emergency tools, jumper cables, spare fan belt, auto fuses, flares and/or reflectors, flashlights, first-aid kit, and, in winter, a windshield scraper and shovel.

Bring all appropriate and up-to-date documentation—licenses, registration, and insurance cards—and know what's covered by your insurance. Also bring an extra set of keys, just in case.

En route, always buckle up!

If your car does break down, get out of traffic as soon as possible—pull well off the road. Raise the hood and turn on your emergency flashers or tie a white cloth to the roadside door handle or antenna. Stay near your car. Use flares or reflectors to keep your car from being hit.

IN YOUR LODGING

Chances are slim that you will encounter a hotel or motel fire. The ⬛ in a listing indicates that there were smoke detectors and/or sprinkler systems in the rooms we inspected. Once you've checked in, make sure that any smoke detector in your room is working properly. Ascertain the locations of fire extinguishers and at least two fire exits. Never use an elevator in a fire.

For personal security, use the peephole in your room's door.

PROTECTING AGAINST THEFT

To guard against theft wherever you go, don't bring any more of value than you need. If you do bring valuables, leave them at your hotel rather than in your car, and if you have something very expensive, lock it in a safe. Many hotels have one in each room; others will store your valuables in the hotel's safe. And of course, don't carry more money than you need; use traveler's checks and credit cards, or visit cash machines.

For Travelers with Disabilities

A number of publications can provide assistance. Fodor's *Great American Vacations for Travelers with Disabilities* ($19.50) covers 38 top U.S. travel destinations, including parks, cities, and popular tourist regions. It's available from bookstores or by calling 800/533–6478. The most complete listing of published material for travelers with disabilities is available from *The Disability Bookshop,* Twin Peaks Press, Box 129, Vancouver, WA 98666, phone 360/694–2462. A comprehensive guidebook to the national parks is *Easy Access to National Parks: The Sierra Club Guide for People with Disabilities* ($16), distributed by Random House.

The Reference Section of the National Library Service for the Blind and Physically Handicapped (Library of Congress, Washington, DC 20542, phone 202/707–9275 or 202/707–5100) provides information and resources for persons with mobility problems and hearing and vision impairments, as well as information about the NLS talking-book program (or visit your local library).

Important Toll-Free Numbers

and On-Line Information

HOTELS AND MOTELS

Adam's Mark 800/444–2326
Web www.adamsmark.com
Best Western ....800/528–1234, TDD 800/528–2222
Web www.bestwestern.com
Budgetel Inns 800/428–3438
Web www.budgetel.com
Budget Host 800/283–4678
Clarion 800/252–7466
Web www.clarioninn.com
Comfort 800/228–5150
Web www.comfortinn.com
Courtyard by Marriott 800/321–2211
Web www.courtyard.com
Days Inn 800/325–2525
Web www.travelweb.com/daysinn.html
Doubletree 800/528–0444
Web www.doubletreehotels.com
Drury Inns *800/325–8300*
Web www.drury-inn.com
Econo Lodge 800/446–6900
Web www.hotelchoice.com
Embassy Suites 800/362–2779
Web www.embassy-suites.com
Exel Inns of America 800/356–8013
Fairfield Inn by Marriott 800/228–2800
Web www.marriott.com
Fairmont Hotels 800/527–4727
Forte 800/225–5843
Four Seasons 800/332–3442
Web www.fourseasons.com
Friendship Inns 800/453–4511
Web www.hotelchoice.com
Hampton Inn 800/426–7866
Web www.hampton-inn.com
Hilton ....800/445–8667, TDD 800/368–1133
Web www.hilton.com
Holiday Inn ....800/465–4329, TDD 800/238–5544
Web www.holiday-inn.com
Howard Johnson...............800/654–4656, TDD 800/654–8442
Web www.hojo.com
Hyatt & Resorts 800/233–1234
Web www.hyatt.com
Inns of America 800/826–0778
Inter-Continental 800/327–0200
Web www.interconti.com
La Quinta ....800/531–5900, TDD 800/426–3101
Web www.laquinta.com
Loews 800/235-6397
Web www.loewshotels.com
Marriott 800/228–9290
Web www.marriott.com
Master Hosts Inns 800/251–1962

Meridien.. 800/225–5843
Motel 6 .... 800/466–8356
Nikko International 800/645–5687
Web www.hotelnikko.com
Omni 800/843–6664
Web www.omnirosen.com
Park Inn 800/437–7275
Web www.p-inns.com/parkinn.html
Quality Inn 800/228–5151
Web www.qualityinn.com
Radisson 800/333–3333
Web www.radisson.com
Ramada ....800/228–2828, TDD 800/228–3232
Web www.ramada.com/ramada.html
Red Carpet/Scottish Inns 800/251–1962
Red Lion 800/547–8010
Web www.travelweb.com/travelweb/rl/common/redlion.html
Red Roof Inn 800/843–7663
Web www.redroof.com
Renaissance 800/468–3571
Web www.niagara.com/nf.renaissance
Residence Inn by Marriott 800/331–3131
Web www.marriott.com
Ritz-Carlton 800/241–3333
Web www.ritzcarlton.com
Rodeway 800/228–2000
Web www.rodeway.com
Sheraton 800/325–3535
Web www.sheraton.com
Shilo Inn 800/222–2244
Signature Inns 800/822–5252
Web www.signature-inns.com
Sleep Inn 800/221–2222
Web www.sleepinn.com
Super 8 .... 800/848–8888
Web www.super8motels.com/super8.html
Susse Chalet 800/258–1980
Web www.sussechalet.com
Travelodge/Viscount 800/255–3050
Web www.travelodge.com
Vagabond 800/522–1555
Westin Hotels & Resorts.................................... 800/937-8461
Web www.westin.com
Wyndham Hotels & Resorts 800/822–4200
Web www.travelweb.com

AIRLINES

Air Canada 800/776–3000
Web www.aircanada.ca
Alaska 800/426–0333
Web www.alaska-air.com/home.html
Aloha 800/367–5250
American 800/433–7300
Web www.americanair.com/aahome/aahome.html

America West..800/235–9292
Web www.americawest.com
British Airways 800/247–9297
Web www.british-airways.com
Canadian 800/426–7000
Web www.cdair.ca
Continental 800/525–0280
Web www.flycontinental.com
Delta...800/221–1212
Web www.delta-air.com
Hawaiian 800/367–5320
IslandAir 800/323–3345
Mesa..800/637–2247
Northwest 800/225–2525
Web www.nwa.com
SkyWest 800/453–9417
Southwest 800/435–9792
Web www.iflyswa.com
TWA 800/221–2000
Web www.twa.com
United 800/241–6522
Web www.ual.com
USAir...800/428–4322
Web www.usair.com

TRAINS

Amtrak 800/872–7245
Web www.amtrak.com

BUSES

Greyhound..800/231–2222
Web www.greyhound.com

CAR RENTALS

Advantage..800/777–5500
Alamo 800/327–9633
Web www.goalamo.com
Allstate 800/634–6186
Avis..800/331–1212
Web www.avis.com
Budget 800/527–0700
Web www.budgetrentacar.com
Dollar 800/800–4000
Web www.dollarcar.com
Enterprise 800/325–8007
Web www.pickenterprise.com
Hertz 800/654–3131
Web www.hertz.com
National 800/328–4567
Web www.nationalcar.com
Payless...800/237–2804
Rent-A-Wreck 800/535–1391
Web www.rent-a-wreck.com
Sears 800/527–0770
Thrifty 800/367–2277
Web www.thrifty.com
Ugly Duckling 800/843–3825
U-Save 800/272–8728
Value..800/327–2501
Web www.go-value.com

Four-Star and Five-Star Establishments

in the Mid-Atlantic

DELAWARE

★★★★ Lodgings
Hotel Du Pont, *Wilmington*
Inn at Montchanin Village, *Wilmington*

DISTRICT OF COLUMBIA

★★★★ Lodgings
Four Seasons
Loews L'Enfant Plaza
Park Hyatt
Willard Inter-Continental

★★★★ Restaurants
Kinkead's
Lespinasse

MARYLAND

★★★★ Lodgings
Inn at Perry Cabin, *St Michaels*
Lighthouse Club, *Ocean City*
Mr Mole Bed & Breakfast, *Baltimore*

★★★★ Restaurant
Hampton's (Harbor Court), *Baltimore*

NEW JERSEY

★★★★ Lodgings
Bally's Park Place, *Atlantic City*
The Bernards Inn, *Bernardsville*
Hilton at Short Hills, *Millburn*
Trump's Castle Casino Resort, *Atlantic City*
Trump Taj Mahal Casino Resort, *Atlantic City*

★★★★ Restaurant
Ryland Inn, *Somerville*

NORTH CAROLINA

★★★★ Lodgings
Eseeola Lodge, *Linville*
Fearrington House, *Chapel Hill*
Grove Park Inn Resort, *Asheville*
The Park Hotel, *Charlotte*
The Swag, *Waynesville*
Washington Duke Inn & Golf Club, *Durham*

★★★★ Restaurant
Fearrington House, *Chapel Hill*

PENNSYLVANIA

★★★★★ Restaurant
Le Bec-Fin, *Philadelphia*

★★★★ Lodgings
Four Seasons Hotel Philadelphia, *Philadelphia*
Omni Hotel at Independence Park, *Philadelphia*
Park Hyatt Philadelphia at the Bellevue, *Philadelphia*
The Rittenhouse, *Philadelphia*
The Ritz-Carlton, Philadelphia, *Philadelphia*
Tara-A Country Inn, *Sharon*

★★★★ Restaurants
Brasserie Perrier, *Philadelphia*
The Dining Room (The Ritz-Carlton, Philadelphia), *Philadelphia*
Fountain (Four Seasons Hotel Philadelphia), *Philadelphia*
Striped Bass, *Philadelphia*
Susanna Foo, *Philadelphia*

SOUTH CAROLINA

★★★★ Lodgings
Charleston Place, *Charleston*
John Rutledge House, *Charleston*
Rhett House, ***Beaufort***
Woodlands Resort & Inn, *Charleston*

★★★★ Restaurant
Charleston Grill (Charleston Place), *Charleston*

VIRGINIA

★★★★★ Lodging
The Inn at Little Washington, *Washington*

★★★★★ Restaurant
The Inn at Little Washington, *Washington*

★★★★ Lodgings
Camberley's Martha Washington Inn, *Abingdon*
The Homestead, *Hot Springs*
The Jefferson, *Richmond*
Kingsmill, *Williamsburg*
Morrison House, *Alexandria*
The Ritz-Carlton, Pentagon City, *Arlington*
The Ritz-Carlton, Tysons Corner, *Tysons Corner*
Williamsburg Inn, *Williamsburg*

WEST VIRGINIA

★★★★★ Lodging
The Greenbrier, *White Sulphur Springs*
★★★★ Lodging
Bavarian Inn and Lodge, *Shepherdstown*

Delaware

Population: 666,168
Land area: 1,982 square miles
Elevation: 0-442 feet
Highest point: Ebright Road (New Castle County)
Entered Union: First state to ratify Constitution (December 7, 1787)
Capital: Dover
Motto: Liberty and independence
Nickname: First State, Small Wonder, Diamond State, Blue Hen State
State flower: Peach blossom
State bird: Blue hen chicken
State tree: American holly
State fair: July 23-August 1, 1998, in Harrington (see Dover)
Time zone: Eastern

Delaware ". . . is like a diamond, diminutive, but having within it inherent value," wrote John Lofland, the eccentric "Bard of Milford," in 1847. The state is 96 miles long and from nine to 35 miles wide. With more than half of its 1,982 square miles (excluding marshes) used for farming, Delaware produces a flood of agricultural products. Poultry contributes approximately half of the state's total farm income, with soybeans, corn, tomatoes, strawberries, asparagus, fruit and other crops bringing in about $170 million more each year. Booming industry in northern and central Delaware balances the agricultural sector of the economy. Consistent state corporate policies have persuaded more than 183,000 corporations to make their headquarters in the "corporate capital of the world." Forty major US banks alone have established lending and credit operations in the state.

Compact but diverse, Delaware has rolling, forested hills in the north, stretches of bare sand dunes in the south and mile upon mile of lonely marsh along the coast. Visitors can tour a modern agricultural or chemical research center in the morning and search for buried pirate treasure in the afternoon. The *deBraak,* which foundered off Lewes in 1798, was raised in 1986 because of the belief that it may have had a fortune in captured Spanish coin or bullion aboard. The coins that frequently come ashore at Coin Beach below Rehoboth are believed to come from the *Faithful Steward,* a passenger vessel lost in 1785.

Delaware's history started on a grim note. The first colonists, 28 men under Dutch auspices, landed in the spring of 1631 near what is now Lewes. A year later, following an argument with a Lenni-Lenape chief, the bones of all 28 were found mingled with those of their cattle and strewn over their burned fields. In 1638 a group of Swedes established the first permanent settlement, Fort Christina, at a spot now in Wilmington. This was also the first permanent settlement of Swedes in North America. Dutch, English, Scottish and Irish colonists soon followed, with German, Italian and Polish groups coming in the late 19th century.

Henry Hudson, in Dutch service, discovered Delaware Bay in 1609. A year later Thomas Argall reported it to English navigators, naming it for his superior, Lord De La Warr, Governor of Virginia. Ownership changed rapidly from Swedish to Dutch to English hands. Later the area was claimed by both Lord Baltimore and the Penn family. The Maryland-Delaware boundary was set by British court order in 1750 and surveyed as part of the Mason-Dixon Line in 1763-1767. The boundary with New Jersey, also long disputed, was confirmed by the Supreme Court in 1935.

The "First State" (first to adopt the Constitution—December 7, 1787) is proud of its history of sturdy independence, both military and political. During the Revolution, the "Delaware line" was a crack regiment of the Continental Army. After heavy casualties in 1780, the unit was reorganized. The men would "fight all day and dance all night," according to a dispatch by General Greene. How well they danced is open to question, but they fought with such gallantry that they were mentioned in nearly all of the General's dispatches.

Delaware statesman John Dickinson, "penman of the Revolution" and one of the state's five delegates to the Constitutional Convention, was instrumental in the decision to write a new document rather than simply patch up the Articles of Confederation. Later he effected the compromise on representation, a problem that had threatened to break up the convention completely.

In addition to Lofland and Dickinson, Delaware has produced many literary figures, including the 19th-century playwright and novelist Robert Montgomery Bird, writer and illustrator Howard Pyle, Henry Seidel Canby (founder of the *Saturday Review*) and novelist John P. Marquand.

A fine highway network tempts motorists to drive through diminutive Delaware without really seeing it. Those who take time to leave the major highways and explore the countryside will find much that is rewarding.

When to Go/Climate

Delaware's climate is generally mild; long Indian summers are not unusual, and there's seldom frost until late autumn. As is common in most coastal areas, temperatures at the shore can be 10°F higher in winter or lower in summer than inland temperatures.

AVERAGE HIGH/LOW TEMPERATURES (°F)

WILMINGTON

Jan 39/22	**May** 73/52	**Sept** 78/58
Feb 42/25	**June** 81/62	**Oct** 67/46
Mar 52/33	**July** 86/67	**Nov** 56/37
Apr 63/42	**Aug** 84/66	**Dec** 44/28

Parks and Recreation Finder

Directions to and information about the parks and recreation areas below are given under their respective town/city sections. Please refer to those sections for details.

Key to abbreviations: I.P. = Interstate Park; N.B.C. = National Battlefield & Cemetery; N.B.P. = National Battlefield Park; N.F. = National Forest; N.H. = National Historical Park; N.H.S. = National Historic Site; N.M. = National Monument; N.Mem. = National Memorial; N.M.P. = National Military Park; N.P. = National Park; N.Pres. = National Preserve; N.R. = National Recreational Area; N.S. = National Seashore; N.S.T. = National Scenic Trail; S.B. = State Beach; S.C.P. = State Conservation Park; S.G. = State Garden; S.H.A. = State Historic Area; S.H.P. = State Historic Park; S.N.A. = State Natural Area; S.P. = State Park; S.R. = State Reserve; S.R.A. = State Recreation Area; S.Res.P. = State Resort Park; S.R.P. = State Rustic Park.

STATE RECREATION AREAS

Place Name	Listed Under
Bellevue S.P.	WILMINGTON
Brandywine Creek S.P.	WILMINGTON
Cape Henlopen S.P.	LEWES
Delaware Seashore S.P.	REHOBOTH BEACH
Fenwick Island S.P.	FENWICK ISLAND
Fort Delaware S.P.	same
Holts Landing S.P.	BETHANY BEACH
Killens Pond S.P.	DOVER
Lums Pond S.P.	ODESSA
White Clay Creek S.P.	NEWARK

Water-related activities, hiking, riding, various other sports, picnicking and visitor centers are available in many of these areas. Delaware state parks are open all year, 8 am-sunset, except Fort Delaware (late Apr-late Sept). Most areas have fishing, boat ramps and picnicking. There is a vehicle entrance fee from Memorial Day-Labor Day, daily; May & Sept-Oct, wkends & hols. Camping is available from mid-Mar-mid-Nov at Delaware Seashore; Apr-Oct at Lums Pond, Trap Pond and Cape Henlopen; year-round at Killens Pond. There is a two-week maximum stay at campgrounds; no reservations are accepted; campsites run from $11-$21/night/site. For further information contact Department of Natural Resources & Environmental Control, Division of Parks & Recreation, PO Box 1401, Dover 19903; 302/739-4702.

FISHING & HUNTING

Both fresh and saltwater fishing are excellent. The state owns, leases or licenses 33,000 acres of game and fish lands and waters. More than 50 well-stocked state and privately owned ponds are scattered throughout the state. Many miles of ocean shoreline between Rehoboth Beach and Indian River Inlet are ideal for surf fishing. Common saltwater fish include trout, bluefish, porgie, sea bass, flounder and croaker; freshwater fish include bass, bluegill, pickerel, crappie, perch and trout.

An annual nonresident hunting license is $86; nonresident 3-day small game license $35; nonresident trapping license $25; additional single deer permit $10. An annual resident freshwater fishing license is $8.50; nonresident license $15; 7-day nonresident license $5.20. A license is not required for tidal saltwater fishing. For further information on fishing or hunting, contact the Department of Natural Resources & Environmental Control, Division of Fish & Wildlife, R & R Building, PO Box 1401, Dover 19903; 302/739-4431 or -5297.

Driving Information

Safety belts are mandatory for all persons in front seat of vehicle. Children under 4 years and 40 pounds in weight must be in an approved safety seat anywhere in vehicle; children ages 4-15 must use a regulation seat belt anywhere in vehicle. For further information phone 302/739-5901.

INTERSTATE HIGHWAY SYSTEM

The following alphabetical listing of Delaware towns in *Mobil Travel Guide* shows that these cities are within 10 miles of the indicated interstate highway. A highway map, however, should be checked for the nearest exit.

Highway Number	Cities/Towns within 10 miles
Interstate 95	Newark, New Castle, Wilmington.

Additional Visitor Information

Delaware Tourism Office, 99 Kings Highway, PO Box 1401, Dover 19903, will provide tourist information; phone 302/739-4271 or 800/441-8846.

Visitor centers also provide information and brochures on points of interest in the state. Their locations are as follows: Delaware Memorial Bridge Plaza, jct I-295 and the bridge at New Castle; I-95 rest area, Greater Wilmington Convention and Visitors Bureau, Wilmington; Delaware State Information Center, Duke of York & Federal Sts, Dover; Smyrna, 1 mi N on US 13; Bethany-Fenwick Area Chamber of Commerce, DE 1, north of Fenwick Island.

Bethany Beach (D-10)

(See also Fenwick Island, Lewes, Rehoboth Beach)

Founded 1901 **Pop** 326 **Elev** 8 ft **Area code** 302 **Zip** 19930 **E-mail** bethfnwk@dmv.com **Web** www.dmv.com/business/bethfnwk

Information Bethany-Fenwick Area Chamber of Commerce, Coastal Hwy/DE 1, PO Box 1450; 302/539-2100 or 800/962-7873.

A quiet beach town on the Atlantic Ocean, Bethany Beach was founded as a site for revival camp meetings; hence the biblical name. Surf fishing and bathing are excellent here.

What to See and Do

Holts Landing State Park. A 203-acre park located along the Indian River Bay. Fishing, crabbing, clamming; sailing, boating (launch ramp providing access to bay). Picnicking, playground, ball fields. Standard hrs, fees. 8 mi

NW via DE 26 & DE 346, N of Millville. Phone 302/539-9060 or 302/539-1055 (summer).

Annual Event

Boardwalk Arts Festival. The Boardwalk, Garfield Pkwy. Juried, original handmade works; woodcarving, photography, jewelry, batik, watercolor paintings. Sat before Labor Day wkend.

Motels

★ **BETHANY ARMS.** *99 Hollywood St, at S Atlantic Ave. 302/539-9603.* 52 units, 2-3 story, 36 kit. units. No elvtr. July-Aug: S, D $85-$135; each addl $5; under 4 free; wkly rates; lower rates rest of yr. Crib $5. TV; cable. Restaurant adj 7 am-9 pm. Ck-out 11 am. Some covered parking. Many refrigerators. Balconies. On ocean; beach. Cr cds: MC, V.

★ **BLUE SURF.** *Garfield Pkwy & Boardwalk. 302/539-7531.* 35 units, 2 story, 29 kit. units. Mid-June-Labor Day: S, D $93-$118; each addl $8; under 7 free; lower rates rest of yr. Crib $5. TV; cable. Complimentary coffee in rms. Restaurant opp 7 am-10 pm. Ck-out 11 am. Business servs avail. Refrigerators. Balconies. On beach; ocean. Cr cds: MC, V.

★ **HARBOR VIEW.** *RD 1, Box 102, 2 mi N on DE 1. 302/539-0500; FAX 302/539-5170.* 60 rms, 2 story, 8 kit. units. July-Aug: S, D $90-$100; each addl $10; kit. units $95-$115; under 14 free (off-season); wkly rates; lower rates rest of yr. Crib $5. TV; cable. Pool; lifeguard. Complimentary continental bkfst. Restaurant 5-10 pm; closed Dec-Jan. Ck-out 11 am. Coin lndry. Meeting rm. Some covered parking. Free bus depot transportation. Refrigerators. Balconies. Picnic tables, grills. On bay; swimming; crabbing and clamming. Cr cds: A, C, D, DS, MC, V.

Restaurant

✔★ **STORMALONG'S.** *210 Garfield Pkwy. 302/539-2336.* Hrs: 8 am-8 pm. Closed Thanksgiving, Dec 24, 25. Res accepted. Continental menu. Semi-a la carte: bkfst $2.95-$5.95, lunch $3.95-$6.25, dinner $4.95-$12.95. Specializes in fresh seafood, prime rib. Salad bar. Cr cds: DS, MC, V.

Dover (C-9)

(See also Odessa, Smyrna)

Founded 1717 **Pop** 27,630 **Elev** 36 ft **Area code** 302 **Zip** 19901

Information Kent County Delaware Convention & Visitors Bureau, 9 E Loockerman St, Treadway Towers, PO Box 576, 19903; 302/734-1736 or 800/233-KENT.

The capital of Delaware since 1777, Dover was laid out by William Penn around the city's lovely green. For almost 200 years there were coach houses and inns on King's Road between Philadelphia and Lewes. Circling the green north and south on State Street are fine 18th- and 19th-century houses.

Today, because of Delaware's favorable corporation laws, more than 60,000 US firms pay taxes in Dover. At Dover Air Force Base, south off US 113, the Military Airlift Command operates one of the biggest air cargo terminals in the world, utilizing the giant C5-A aircraft. Dover is also the home of Delaware State College, Wesley College and the Terry campus of Delaware Technical and Community College.

What to See and Do

Delaware Agricultural Museum and Village. Museum of farm life from early settlement to 1960. Main exhibition hall and historic structures representing a late-19th-century farming community; includes gristmill, blacksmith-wheelwright shop, farmhouse, outbuildings, one-room schoolhouse, store and train station. Gift shop. (Apr-Dec, daily exc Mon; rest of yr, Mon-Fri) 866 N du Pont Hwy (US 13). Phone 302/734-1618. ¢¢

Delaware State Museums. Complex of three buildings: **Meeting House Galleries I and II** (1790). Exhibit devoted to archaeology. **1880 Gallery.** Turn-of-the-century drugstore, blacksmith shop, general store, post office, shoemaker's shop and printer's shop; and Johnson building. (Tues-Sat; closed hols) 316 S Governors Ave. Phone 302/739-4266. **Free.**

Delaware State Visitor Center. Administered by Division of Historical and Cultural Affairs, center offers information on attractions throughout state. Exhibit galleries; audiovisual show. (Daily; closed hols) The Green. Phone 302/739-4266. **Free.**

Dover Heritage Trail. Guided walking tour of historic areas, buildings and other attractions. (By appt only) Departs from State Visitor Center. Phone 302/678-2040. ¢¢

Hall of Records. Delaware's historical public records; archive includes Royal Charter granted by King Charles II to James, Duke of York, for Delaware territory in 1682. (Mon-Fri; closed hols) Court St & Legislative Ave. Phone 302/739-5318. **Free.**

John Dickinson Plantation (1740). Restored boyhood residence of Dickinson, the "penman of the Revolution." Reconstructed farm complex. (Mar-Dec, Tues-Sat, also Sun afternoons; rest of yr, Tues-Sat; closed hols) 6 mi SE, near jct US 113 & DE 9 on Kitts Hummock Rd. Phone 302/739-3277. **Free.**

Johnson Victrola Museum. Tribute to Eldridge Reeves Johnson, founder of the Victor Talking Machine Company. Collection of talking machines, Victrolas, early recordings and equipment. (Tues-Sat; closed hols) Bank Lane & New St. Phone 302/739-4266. **Free.**

Killens Pond State Park. A 1,083-acre park with a 66-acre pond. Swimming pool; fishing; boating (rentals). Hiking, fitness trails; game fields. Picnicking. Camping (hookups, dump station). Standard hrs, fees. 13 mi S via US 13. Phone 302/284-4526.

The Old State House (1792). Second-oldest seat of government in continuous use in the US, the State House, restored in 1976, contains a courtroom, ceremonial governor's office, legislative chambers and county offices, including Levy Courtroom. A larger-than-life portrait of George Washington in the Senate Chamber was comissioned in 1802 by the legislature as a memorial to the nation's first president. Although Delaware's General Assembly moved to nearby Legislative Hall in 1934, the State House remains the state's symbolic capitol. (Daily exc Mon; closed state hols) Federal St, The Green. For information phone 302/739-4266. **Free.**

Annual Events

Old Dover Days. Tours of historic houses and gardens not usually open to the public. Crafts exhibits, many other activities. For information & tickets contact Kent County Tourism, 800/233-KENT. 1st wkend May.

Delaware State Fair. 17 mi S on US 13 in Harrington. Arts & crafts, home & trade show, carnival rides, shows; homemaking, agricultural and livestock exhibits. Phone 302/398-3269. July 23-Aug 1.

Seasonal Events

Harrington Raceway. 17 mi S on US 13, at fairgrounds in Harrington. Harness horse racing. Wagering most nights of the week. Phone 302/398-3269. Sept-Nov.

Dover Downs. 1131 N du Pont Hwy (US 13). Racing events include NASCAR Winston Cup auto racing (June, Sept); harness racing (mid-Nov-Mar). For fees and schedule, phone 302/674-4600.

Motels

✔★ **BUDGET INN.** *1426 N du Pont Hwy (US 13). 302/734-4433.* 68 rms, 2 story. May-Sept: S $42-$50; D $47-$55; each addl $5; lower rates rest of yr. Crib free. TV; cable. Pool; lifeguard. Complimentary coffee in lobby. Restaurant opp 8 am-9 pm. Ck-out 11 am. Coin lndry. Sundries. Cr cds: A, D, DS, MC, V.

⊠ ⊠ ⊠ SC

★ **COMFORT INN.** *222 S du Pont Hwy (US 13). 302/674-3300; FAX 302/674-3300, ext. 190.* 94 rms, 2 story. May-Sept: S $47-$51; D $51-$55; each addl $5; kit. units $65; family, wkly rates; higher rates NASCAR races; lower rates rest of yr. Crib free. TV; cable. Pool; lifeguard. Complimentary continental bkfst. Restaurant adj 11 am-10 pm. Ck-out noon. Sundries. Some refrigerators. Grill. Cr cds: A, C, D, DS, ER, JCB, MC, V.

⊠ ⊠ ⊠ SC

Motor Hotel

★ ★ ★ **SHERATON.** *1570 N du Pont Hwy (US 13). 302/678-8500; FAX 302/678-9073.* 152 rms, 7 story. S, D $80; each addl $10; under 18 free. TV; cable. Indoor pool; whirlpool. Restaurant 6:30 am-10 pm. Rm serv to 10:30 pm. Bars 4 pm-1 am; entertainment exc Sun. Ck-out noon. Meeting rms. Business servs avail. In-rm modem link. Bellhops. Sundries. Exercise equipt; weight machine, stair machine. Cr cds: A, D, DS, MC, V.

D ⊠ ⊁ ⊁ ⊠ SC

Restaurants

★ ★ ★ **BLUE COAT INN.** *800 N State St. 302/674-1776.* Hrs: 11:30 am-10 pm; Sat 11:30 am-3 pm, 4:30-10 pm; Sun noon-9 pm. Closed Mon; Dec 25. Res accepted. Bar. Semi-a la carte: lunch $4.25-$9.95, dinner $8.95-$24.95. Child's meals. Specializes in fresh seafood, colonial recipes. Own baking. Entertainment Sat. Early American decor. Lake setting. Cr cds: A, C, D, DS, MC, V.

★ ★ **PLAZA NINE.** *9 E Lockerman St, in Treadway Towers building. 302/736-9990.* Hrs: 11 am-2 pm, 5-10 pm; Sat from 5 pm. Closed Sun; Jan 1, Dec 25. Res accepted; required wkends & hols. Continental menu. Bar 11 am-midnight. Semi-a la carte: lunch $3.95-$7.95, dinner $10.95-$21. Child's meals. Specializes in fresh seafood, veal. Jazz Fri, Sat. Outdoor dining. Near State House and government buildings. Overlooks Mirror Lake. Cr cds: D, MC, V.

D

★ ★ **VILLAGE INN.** *(DE 9, Little Creek) E on DE 8 to DE 9. 302/734-3245.* Hrs: 11 am-2 pm, 4:30-10 pm; Sat 11 am-10 pm; Sun noon-9 pm. Closed Dec 25. Res accepted. Bar. Semi-a la carte: lunch $4.95-$9.95, dinner $12.95-$19.95. Specialties: stuffed flounder, prime rib. Colonial decor; fireplace, antiques. Cr cds: DS, MC, V.

D ⊒

Fenwick Island (E-10)

(See also Bethany Beach, Lewes, Rehoboth Beach; also see Ocean City, MD)

Pop 186 **Elev** 4 ft **Area code** 302 **Zip** 19944 **E-mail** bethfnwk@dmv.com **Web** www.dmv.com/business/bethfnwk
Information Bethany-Fenwick Area Chamber of Commerce, Coastal Hwy/DE 1, PO Box 1450, Bethany Beach 19930; 302/539-2100 or 800/962-7873.

Fenwick Island, at the southeast corner of Delaware, was named for Thomas Fenwick, a wealthy Virginia landowner who purchased the land in 1686. For a time, a dispute raged over whether Fenwick Island was part of Maryland or Pennsylvania. It ended in 1751, when the Transpeninsular Line placed Fenwick Island in Delaware. In 1775, James and Jacob Brasure, residents of the island, began extracting salt from the ocean, and until 1825, "salt making" was big business. In the latter part of the 19th century, Fenwick Island grew as a religious-oriented summer campground.

After World War I, Fenwick Island became fashionable as a summer resort.

What to See and Do

Fenwick Island Lighthouse. Historic 87-ft-tall lighthouse; light was first turned on Aug 1, 1859. (June-Aug, 2 Wed afternoons per month; also by appt) W of town via DE 54. Phone 410/250-1098.

Fenwick Island State Park. This 208-acre seashore park is located between the Atlantic Ocean and Little Assawoman Bay. Surfing, swimming, bathhouse; surf fishing; sailing (rentals). Standard hrs, fees. 1 mi N on DE 1. Phone 302/539-9060 or 302/539-1055 (summer).

Annual Event

Surf-Fishing Tournaments. Phone 302/539-2100. 1st Sat May & Columbus Day wkend.

Motel

★ **ATLANTIC BUDGET INN.** *Jct DE 54 & Ocean Hwy (DE 1). 302/539-7673; res: 800/432-8038.* 48 rms, 1-2 story, 3 kit. units. Memorial Day, July 4-Labor Day (3-day min): S, D $65-$97; each addl $8; kit. units for 2, $88; lower rates mid-Apr-June, after Labor Day-Oct. Closed rest of yr. Crib $5. TV; cable. Pool; lifeguard. Complimentary coffee in lobby. Restaurant nearby. Ck-out 11 am. Refrigerators. Beach 1 blk. Cr cds: A, D, DS, MC, V.

⊠ ⊠ ⊠

Restaurants

✔ ★ ★ **HARPOON HANNA'S.** *DE 54 at the bay. 302/539-3095.* Hrs: 11-1 am; Sun from 10 am; Sun brunch 10 am-3 pm. Bar. A la carte entrees: lunch $3.95-$7.95, dinner $7.95-$27.95. Sun brunch $3.95-$7.95. Child's meals. Specializes in fresh seafood. Entertainment Fri, Sat. Outdoor dining. Casual, contemporary decor; fireplace. On waterfront. Cr cds: A, DS, MC, V.

D

★ ★ **TOM & TERRY'S.** *DE 54 at the bay. 302/436-4161.* Hrs: 11:30 am-10 pm; early-bird dinner 5-6 pm. Closed Dec 25. Bar. Semi-a la carte: lunch $5.95-$9.50, dinner $15.95-$22.95. Specializes in fresh local seafood, prime rib. View of Ocean City & Assawoman Bay. Cr cds: MC, V.

D

Fort Delaware State Park (B-9)

(For accommodations see Newark, New Castle, Wilmington; also see Odessa)

(On Pea Patch Island, opposite Delaware City)

A must for the Civil War buff, this grim gray fort was built as a coastal defense in 1859. The fort was used as a prisoner of war depot for three years, housing up to 12,500 Confederate prisoners at a time. The damp, insect-infested terrain encouraged epidemics, leading to some 2,400 deaths. The fort remained in commission through World War II.

Restoration of the site is a continuing process. Available are nature trails, picnicking; living history programs. Museum has scale models of fort, Civil War relics. Special events throughout summer. Boat trip to island from Delaware City (mid-June-Labor Day, Wed-Sun; last wkend Apr-mid-June & Sept, Sat, Sun & hols). No pets. For further information contact the Park Superintendent, 45 Clinton St, PO Box 170, Delaware City 19706; 302/834-7941. Round trip ¢¢

Lewes (D-10)

(See also Bethany Beach, Fenwick Island, Rehoboth Beach)

Settled 1631 **Pop** 2,295 **Elev** 10 ft **Area code** 302 **Zip** 19958 **E-mail** inquiry@leweschamber.com **Web** www.leweschamber.com

Information Chamber of Commerce, Fisher-Martin House, 120 Kings Hwy, PO Box 1; 302/645-8073.

Lewes (LOO-is) has been home base to Delaware Bay pilots for 300 years. Weather-beaten, cypress-shingled houses still line the streets where privateers plundered and Captain Kidd bargained away his loot. The treacherous sandbars outside the harbor have claimed their share of ships, and stories of sunken treasure have circulated for centuries. Some buildings show scars from cannonballs that hit their mark when the British bombarded Lewes in the War of 1812. Traces of the original stockade were discovered in 1964.

What to See and Do

Cape Henlopen State Park. More than 3,000 acres at confluence of Delaware Bay and Atlantic Ocean; site of decommissioned Fort Miles, part of coastal defense system during World War II. Supervised swimming; fishing. Nature center, programs and trails. Picnicking, concession. Camping (water hookups, dump station). Standard hrs, fees. 1 mi E of ferry terminal on Cape Henlopen Dr. Phone 302/645-8983.

Lewes-Cape May, NJ, Ferry. Sole connection between US 13 (Ocean Hwy) on the Delmarva Peninsula and southern terminus of Garden State Pkwy (NJ). Trip across Delaware Bay (16 mi) takes 70 min. (Daily; 22 crossings in summer, 10 in winter, 14-18 in spring and fall) Phone 302/645-6313 or 800/643-3779 (reservations). Per person, one way ¢¢¢¢-¢¢¢¢¢

Restored buildings. Maintained by the Lewes Historical Society. Cannon Ball House and US Lifesaving Station have marine exhibits and lightship *Overfalls*. Other buildings open are Thompson country store, Plank House, Rabbit's Ferry House, Burton-Ingram House, Ellegood House, Hiram R. Burton House and old doctor's office. (June-Labor Day, Tues-Sat) Tickets at Rabbit's Ferry House. Walking tours and varied events take place during summer season. Phone 302/645-7670. Tour ¢¢

Zwaanendael Museum. Adaptation of Hoorn, Holland Town Hall was built in 1931 as memorial to original Dutch founders of Lewes (1631). Highlights the town's maritime heritage with colonial, Native American and Dutch exhibits. (Daily exc Mon; closed hols) Savannah Rd & Kings Hwy. Phone 302/645-1148. **Free.**

Annual Events

Great Delaware Kite Festival. Cape Henlopen State Park (see). Festival heralding the beginning of spring. Fri before Easter.

Zwaanendael Heritage Garden Tour. Visit hidden gardens of Lewes. Vendors. Phone 302/645-8073. 3rd Sat June.

Coast Day. University of Delaware Marine Studies Complex. Facilities and research vessel open to public; marine exhibits, research demonstrations, nautical films. Phone 302/645-4346. 1st Sun Oct.

Motel

★ **ANGLERS.** *110 Anglers Rd, 1/2 blk NE of Canal Bridge.* 302/645-2831. 25 rms, 1-2 story, 2 kits. Mid-May-mid-Sept (3-day min wkends, hols): S, D $60-$100; each addl $5; kit. units $70-$100; lower rates rest of yr. Crib free. TV; cable. Pool. Restaurant nearby. Ck-out 11 am. Refrigerators. Picnic tables, grills. Sun deck. Overlooks canal, marina opp. Boat docking. Cr cds: A, MC, V.

Hotel

★ ★ ★ **NEW DEVON INN.** *142 2nd St.* 302/645-6466; FAX 302/645-7196; res: 800/824-8754. 26 rms, 3 story. Late May-mid-Oct: S, D $110-$130; suites $155-$170; package plans; lower rates rest of yr. Restaurant 11 am-10 pm. Ck-out 11 am. Business servs avail. Shopping arcade. Built 1926. Cr cds: A, D, DS, MC, V.

Inn

★ ★ ★ **INN AT CANAL SQUARE.** *122 Market St.* 302/645-8499; FAX 302/645-7083; res: 800/222-7902. 22 rms, 4 story. Late June-early Sept: D $135-$165; each addl $15; 2-bedrm houseboat avail; wkly rates; higher rates hols, wkends (2-day min); lower rates rest of yr. Crib $15. TV; cable (premium). Complimentary continental bkfst. Restaurant nearby. Ck-out 11 am. Concierge serv. Meeting rm. Balconies. On canal. Cr cds: A, D, DS, MC, V.

Restaurants

★ **ASHBY'S OYSTER HOUSE.** *DE 24, at Peddler's Village.* 302/945-4070. Hrs: 11-1 am; Sun from 9 am. Closed Thanksgiving, Dec 25. Bar. Semi-a la carte: lunch $3.95-$6.45, dinner $11.95-$19.95. Sun bkfst buffet $6.95. Child's meals. Specializes in seafood, raw bar. Casual dining. Cr cds: A, MC, V.

★ ★ **GILLIGAN'S.** *134 Market St, at Front St.* 302/645-7866. Hrs: 11 am-11 pm. Closed Nov-Mar. Bar. A la carte entrees: lunch $6.50-$10, dinner $13-$19. Specializes in seafood, crab cakes. Outside dining deck, waterfront bar. Part of exterior resembles the "good ship Minnow." View of harbor. Cr cds: A, DS, MC, V.

★ ★ **KUPCHICK'S.** *3 East Bay Ave.* 302/645-0420. Hrs: 4:30-10 pm. Closed Dec 25; also early Jan-mid-Feb. Res accepted; required summer wkends. Continental menu. Bar. A la carte entrees: dinner $11.95-$23.95. Child's meals. Specializes in fresh seafood, Angus beef. Jazz Fri, Sat. Victorian atmosphere. Original art, antiques. Cr cds: A, C, D, DS, MC, V.

★ **LIGHTHOUSE.** *Savannah Rd at Anglers Rd, just over the drawbridge.* 302/645-6271. Hrs: 4 am-10 pm; Sept-Mar 7 am-9 pm. Closed Thanksgiving, Dec 24, 25. Bar from 11 am. Semi-a la carte: bkfst $2.25-$7.50, lunch $2.50-$15, dinner $8.95-$25. Child's meals. Specializes in fresh seafood. Entertainment wkends. Outdoor dining. Overlooks Lewes Harbor. Cr cds: A, DS, MC, V.

Newark (A-9)

(See also New Castle, Wilmington)

Settled 1685 **Pop** 25,098 **Elev** 124 ft **Area code** 302

Information Greater Wilmington Convention & Visitors Bureau-Visitors Center, 100 W 10th St, Wilmington 19801; 302/737-4059.

Newark grew up at the crossroads of two well-traveled Native American trails. The site of the only Revolutionary battle on Delaware soil is at nearby Cooch's Bridge, southeast of Newark. According to tradition, Betsy Ross's flag was first raised in battle at Cooch's Bridge on September 3, 1777.

What to See and Do

University of Delaware (1743). (18,000 students) Founded as a small private academy; stately elm trees, fine lawns and Georgian-style brick buildings adorn the central campus. Tours from Visitors Center, 196 S College Ave (Mon-Fri, also Sat mornings). Phone 302/831-8123. On campus is

University of Delaware Mineral Collection. Also fossil exhibit. Penny Hall, Academy St. (Mon-Fri, by appt only; closed hols) Phone 302/831-2569. **Free.**

White Clay Creek State Park. A 1,483-acre day park with farmlands, forest and streams. Fishing. Nature, fitness trails. Picnicking. Standard hrs, fees. 3 mi NW via DE 896. Phone 302/368-6900.

Motels

★ ★ **BEST WESTERN.** *260 Chapman Rd (DE 273 E) (19702), at I-95.* 302/738-3400. 99 rms, 2 story. S $55-$65; D $60-$75; each addl $5; under 18 free; wkend rates. Crib free. TV; cable. Pool. Restaurant 5-9 pm. Rm serv. Bar 4 pm-1 am. Ck-out noon. Meeting rms. Business servs avail. Sundries. Cr cds: A, C, D, DS, MC, V.

⊠ ⊠ 🐾 SC

✔★ ★ **COMFORT INN.** *1120 S College Ave (DE 896) (19713), Exit 1- I95 to DE 896 N.* 302/368-8715; FAX 302/368-6454. 102 rms, 2 story. S $50-$54; D $56-$60; each addl $6; under 18 free. Crib free. Pet accepted. TV; cable, VCR avail (movies). Pool; lifeguard. Complimentary continental bkfst. Ck-out 11 am. Meeting rm. Business servs avail. In-rm modem link. Some refrigerators. Cr cds: A, C, D, DS, JCB, MC, V.

D ✔ ⊠ ⊠ 🐾 SC

★ ★ **HOLIDAY INN.** *1203 Christiana Rd (19713).* 302/737-2700; FAX 302/737-3214. 144 rms, 2 story. S $71-$81; D $77-$87; each addl $6; under 18 free. Crib free. TV; cable. Pool; lifeguard. Restaurant 6:30 am-10 pm. Rm serv. Bar noon-1 am. Ck-out noon. Coin lndry. Meeting rms. Business servs avail. In-rm modem link. Valet serv. Sundries. Cr cds: A, C, D, DS, JCB, MC, V.

D ⊠ ⊠ 🐾 SC

★ ★ **HOWARD JOHNSON.** *1119 S College Ave (DE 896) (19713).* 302/368-8521; FAX 302/368-9868. 142 rms, 2 story. S $55; D $70; each addl $10; under 18 free. Crib free. Pet accepted. TV; cable. Pool. Complimentary continental bkfst. Ck-out noon. Meeting rms. Business servs avail. In-rm modem link. Valet serv. Private patios, balconies. Cr cds: A, C, D, DS, ER, JCB, MC, V.

D ✔ ⊠ ⊠ 🐾 SC

✔★ **McINTOSH INN.** *100 McIntosh Plaza (19713).* 302/453-9100; res: 800/444-2775. 108 rms. S $41.95; D $46.95; each addl $5. Crib free. TV. Restaurant adj open 24 hrs. Ck-out 11 am. Some refrigerators. Cr cds: A, D, MC, V.

D ⊠ 🐾 SC

Hotel

★ ★ ★ **HILTON INN CHRISTIANA.** *100 Continental Dr (19713), I-95 exit 4B (Stanton).* 302/454-1500; FAX 302/454-0233. 200 rms, 4 story. S $107-$125; D $117-$135; each addl $10; suites $185-$325; family plans; higher rates univ graduation. Crib free. TV; cable. Heated pool; whirlpool, poolside serv, lifeguard. Restaurant 6:30 am-10 pm. Bar 11-1 am. Ck-out 11:30 am. Meeting rms. Business servs avail. In-rm modem link. Concierge. RR station transportation. Tennis privileges. Golf privileges. Exercise equipt; treadmill, bicycles. Luxury level. Cr cds: A, C, D, DS, ER, JCB, MC, V.

D 🏋 👫 ⊠ 🏊 🚴 🐾 SC

Restaurants

✔★ **KLONDIKE KATE'S.** *158 E Main St.* 302/737-6100. Hrs: 11-1 am; Sun from 10 am. Closed Thanksgiving, Dec 25. Southwestern menu. Bar. Semi-a la carte: lunch, dinner $4.95-$12.95. Child's meals. Specializes in fresh seafood, Tex-Mex dishes. Outdoor dining. In former courthouse/jail. Cr cds: A, DS, MC, V.

★ ★ **MIRAGE.** *100 Elkton Rd (19711).* 302/453-1711. Hrs: 11:30 am-2:30 pm, 5:30-9 pm; Sat 5:30-10 pm. Closed Sun; some major hols. Res accepted. Bar. A la carte entrees: lunch $4-$7, dinner $4-$20. Specializes in fresh seafood, beef. Jazz Fri. Modern decor. Cr cds: D, DS, MC, V.

D 🍸 ♥

✔★ **SANTA FE BAR & GRILL.** *Chapman Rd at DE 273 (19713), in University Plaza Shopping Center.* 302/738-0758. Hrs: 11:30 am-10 pm; Thurs-Sat to 11 pm; Sat, Sun from noon. Closed Thanksgiving, Dec 25. Res accepted. Mexican, Amer menu. Bar. Semi-a la carte: lunch $3.95-$5.50, dinner $5.95-$12.25. Specializes in mesquite-grilled dishes, Tex-Mex dishes. Mexican decor. Cr cds: A, MC, V.

New Castle (A-9)

(See also Newark, Wilmington)

Settled 1651 **Pop** 4,837 **Elev** 19 ft **Area code** 302 **Zip** 19720

Information Mayor and Council of New Castle, 220 Delaware St; 302/322-9801.

New Castle—meeting place of the colonial assemblies, first capital of the state and an early center of culture and communication—was one of Delaware's first settlements. Its fine harbor made it a busy port in the 18th century until its commerce was taken over by Wilmington, which is closer to Philadelphia. Today, New Castle is a historian's and architect's delight—charming, mellow and relaxed. Three signers of the Declaration of Independence made their homes here: George Read, Thomas McKean and George Ross, Jr (considered a Pennsylvanian by some). New Castle lies at the foot of the Delaware Memorial Bridge, which connects with the southern end of the New Jersey Turnpike.

What to See and Do

Amstel House Museum (1730). Restored brick mansion of seventh governor of Delaware; an earlier structure was incorporated into the service wing. Houses colonial furnishings and arts; complete colonial kitchen. (Mar-Dec, daily exc Mon; rest of yr, Sat & Sun; closed major hols) Combination ticket avail with Old Dutch House. 2 E 4th St at Delaware St. Phone 302/322-2794. ¢

George Read II House (1804). Federal-style house with elegant interiors; gilded fanlights; silver door hardware; carved woodwork; relief plasterwork. Furnished with period antiques; garden design dates from 1847. (Mar-Dec, daily exc Mon; rest of yr, Sat & Sun) 42 The Strand. Phone 302/322-8411. ¢¢

Old Dutch House (late 17th century). Thought to be Delaware's oldest dwelling in its original form; Dutch colonial furnishings; decorative arts. (Mar-Dec, daily exc Mon; rest of yr, Sat & Sun; closed major hols) Combination ticket avail with Amstel House Museum. 32 E 3rd St. Phone 302/322-2794. ¢

Old Library Museum (1892). Unusual semi-octagonal Victorian building houses temporary exhibits relating to area. (Sat-Sun) 40 E 3rd St. Phone 302/322-2794. **Free.**

Old New Castle Court House (1732). Original colonial capitol and oldest surviving courthouse in the state; furnishings and exhibits on display; cupola is the center of a 12-mi circle that delineates Delaware-Pennsylvania border. (Daily exc Mon; closed hols) 211 Delaware St, on The Green. Phone 302/323-4453. **Free.**

The Green. Laid out by direction of Peter Stuyvesant, this public square of the old town is surrounded by dozens of historically important buildings. Delaware & 3rd Sts.

Annual Event

Separation Day. Battery Park. Observance of Delaware's declaration of independence from Great Britain. Regatta, shows, bands, concerts, fireworks. June.

Seasonal Event

Band concerts. Battery Park. Wed evenings, June-early Aug.

Motels

★ ★ **RAMADA INN.** *I-295 & Rte 13, Manor Branch, 1 mi S of DE Memorial Bridge at jct US 13, I-295.* 302/658-8511; FAX 302/658-3071. 131 rms, 2 story. S $67-$75; D $69-$85; each addl $6; under 18 free. Crib free. Pet accepted. TV; cable. Pool; poolside serv, lifeguard. Restaurant 6:30 am-10 pm; Sun to 9 pm. Rm serv from 7 am. Bar 4:30 pm-midnight. Ck-out noon. Meeting rms. Business servs avail. In-rm modem link. Valet serv. Sundries. RR station, bus depot transportation. Cr cds: A, C, D, DS, MC, V.

D ⚓ ⊠ ⊠ ⚒ SC

✔★ **RODEWAY INN.** *US 13/40/301.* 302/328-6246; FAX 302/328-9493. 40 rms. S $49-$59; D $55-$69; each addl $5; under 18 free. Crib $5. Pet accepted. TV; cable. Restaurant adj 11 am-10 pm. Ck-out noon. Business servs avail. Some refrigerators. Cr cds: A, C, D, DS, MC, V.

⚓ ⊠ ⚒ SC

Restaurants

★ ★ **AIR TRANSPORT COMMAND.** *143 N du Pont Hwy (US 13).* 302/328-3527. Hrs: 11 am-4 pm, 5-11 pm; Fri to midnight; Sat 4:30 pm-midnight; Sun 4-10 pm; Sun brunch 10 am-3 pm. Res accepted; required Sat. Bar to 1 am. Semi-a la carte: lunch $4.50-$8.95, dinner $9.95-$23.95. Sun brunch $14.95. Child's meals. Specialty: prime rib. Outdoor dining. Replica of WWII-era Scottish farmhouse; war memorabilia. Overlooks airfield. Cr cds: A, C, D, DS, MC, V.

D ⤓

★ ★ **ARSENAL ON THE GREEN.** *30 Market St, in historic district.* 302/328-1290. Hrs: 11:30 am-2:30 pm, 5-9 pm; Sun 11:30 am-2 pm, 4-8 pm. Closed Mon. Res accepted. Semi-a la carte: lunch $4.75-$13.95, dinner $11.95-$21.95. Specialties: Delaware crab cakes, crab imperial. Building constructed in 1809 by the Federal government; originally used as arsenal. Colonial decor. Cr cds: MC, V.

D

★ ★ ★ **LYNNHAVEN INN.** *154 N du Pont Hwy (US 13/40/301).* 302/328-2041. Hrs: 11:30 am-9:30 pm; Sat 4-10 pm; Sun 1-9 pm. Closed Dec 24, 25. Res accepted. Bar. Semi-a la carte: lunch $4.95-$11.95, dinner $10.95-$25.95. Child's meals. Specialties: imperial crab, prime rib. Early American decor. Cr cds: A, C, D, DS, MC, V.

Odessa (B-9)

(For accommodations see New Castle, Wilmington; also see Smyrna)

Settled 1721 **Pop** 303 **Elev** 50 ft **Area code** 302 **Zip** 19730

Once a prosperous grain-shipping center, Odessa tried to protect its shipping trade by haughtily telling the Delaware Railroad, in 1855, to lay its tracks elsewhere. To glorify itself that same year, the town changed its name from Cantwell's Bridge to that of the Russian grain port on the Black Sea. But the sloops and schooners that transported grain eventually found less shortsighted ports of call. Odessa was an important station on the Underground Railroad for many years before the Civil War. Now it is a crossroads town, at the junction of US 13 and DE 299. The town exhibits numerous fine examples of 18th- and 19th-century domestic architecture.

What to See and Do

Fort Delaware State Park (see). Approx 9 mi NE on Pea Patch Island, opposite Delaware City.

Historic Houses of Odessa. For full tour of houses, arrive by 2 pm. (Daily exc Mon; closed major hols; also Jan-Feb). Individual house tickets available. Main St. Phone 302/378-4069. Combination ticket ¢¢¢

Corbit-Sharp House (1774). Georgian house built by William Corbit, Odessa's leading citizen, was lived in by his family for 150 yrs. Restored and furnished with many family pieces, the interior reflects period from 1774-1818. Maintained by Winterthur Museum, Garden and Library (see WILMINGTON).

Wilson-Warner House (1769). Handsome red-brick Georgian house, with L-shape plan typical of early Delaware architecture, is accurately furnished to portray life in early 19th century. Maintained by Winterthur Museum, Garden and Library (see WILMINGTON).

Brick Hotel Gallery and Manney Collection of Belter Furniture. Federal-style, 19th-century building was a hotel and tavern for nearly a century. Gallery houses the largest private collection of Belter furniture in existence. Very high-styled Victorian furniture, Belter parlor and bedroom suites, made in New York in the mid-19th century, were famous for craftsmanship, particularly elaborate carvings. ¢¢

Lums Pond State Park. More than 1,800-acre park centered around 200-acre pond. Supervised swimming; fishing; boating (rentals). Hiking and fitness trails, game courts. Picnicking. Camping (showers, dump station; Apr-Oct). Standard hrs, fees. Approx 3 mi W on DE 299 to Middletown, then 8 mi N on US 301 & DE 71. Phone 302/368-6989. Per vehicle ¢¢

Rehoboth Beach (D-10)

(See also Bethany Beach, Fenwick Island, Lewes)

Settled 1872 **Pop** 1,234 **Elev** 16 ft **Area code** 302 **Zip** 19971 **E-mail** rehoboth@dmv.com **Web** www.dmv.com/business/rehoboth

Information Rehoboth Beach-Dewey Beach Chamber of Commerce, 501 Rehoboth Ave, PO Box 216; 302/227-2233 or 800/441-1329.

The "nation's summer capital" got its nickname by being a favorite with Washington diplomats and legislators. A two-and-one-half-hour drive from Washington, DC, the largest summer resort in Delaware began as a spot for camp meetings amid sweet-smelling pine groves. In the 1920s, real estate boomed, triggering Rehoboth Beach's rebirth as a resort town with a variety of accommodations and eateries. Deep-sea and freshwater fishing, sailing, swimming, biking and strolling along cherry tree-lined Rehoboth Avenue have kept it a favorite retreat from Washington's summer heat.

What to See and Do

Delaware Seashore State Park. Seven-mile strip of land separates Rehoboth and Indian River Bays from the Atlantic. Bay and ocean swimming, fishing, surfing and boating (marina, launch, rentals). Picnicking, concession. Primitive and improved campsites (hookups). Standard hrs, fees. 6 mi S on DE 1. Phone 302/227-2800.

Annual Events

Merchants' Attic & Public Garage Sale. State's largest indoor garage sale. Phone 800/441-1329, ext 12 or 16. Feb & Mar.

Sea Witch Halloween Festival & Fiddler's Convention. Phone 800/441-1329, ext 11. Last wkend Oct.

Seasonal Event

Bandstand concerts. Bandstand, Rehoboth Ave. Open-air concerts. Sat & Sun evenings, Memorial Day-Labor Day.

Motels

★ ★ **ADAMS OCEAN FRONT RESORT.** *(4 Read Ave, Dewey Beach) 1 mi S on DE 1. 302/227-3030; res: 800/448-8080 (exc DE).* 23 rms, 3 story, 12 villas. No elvtr. Late June-Aug: S, D $95-$115; each addl $6; villas (up to 7) $250-$295 (3-day min); lower rates mid-Mar-late June, Sept-Oct. Closed rest of yr. Crib $6. TV; cable (premium). Pool. Complimentary continental bkfst. Ck-out 11 am; villas 10 am. Refrigerators. Picnic tables, grills, On beachfront. Cr cds: MC, V.

★ ★ **ADMIRAL.** *2 Baltimore Ave. 302/227-2103; FAX 302/227-3620.* 73 rms, 5 story. Late June-late Aug: S, D $125-$190; each addl $10; wkend rates; 3-day min stay in season; lower rates rest of yr. TV. Indoor pool; whirlpool. Complimentary coffee in lobby. Restaurant adj 7 am-9 pm. Gift shop. Refrigerators. Cr cds: A, DS, MC, V.

★ **ATLANTIC BUDGET INN.** *154 Rehoboth Ave. 302/227-9446; res: 800/245-2112 (MD, OH, PA & VA).* 97 rms, 1-4 story, 10 kits. Mid-July-late Aug, hol wkends: D $95-$110; each addl $10; kits. $139; under 11 free; lower rates rest of yr. Crib $6. TV; cable, VCR avail (movies). Pool. Complimentary coffee. Restaurant nearby. Ck-out 11 am. Some refrigerators. Cr cds: A, C, D, DS, MC, V.

✔★ **ATLANTIC VIEW.** *(2 Clayton St, North Dewey Beach) 1 mi S on DE 1. 302/227-3878; res: 800/777-4162.* 35 rms, 4 story. No elvtr. Mid-June-Labor Day (2-4-day min): S, D $89-$129; each addl $10; lower rates Apr-mid-June, after Labor Day-mid-Oct. Closed rest of yr. Crib $5. TV; cable (premium). Pool; lifeguard. Complimentary coffee. Restaurant nearby. Ck-out 11 am. Coin lndry. Refrigerators. Balconies. Cr cds: A, DS, MC, V.

★ **BAY RESORT.** *Bellevue St, on the Bay. 302/227-6400; res: 800/922-9240.* 68 kit. units, 3 story. July-Labor Day: D $99-$159; each addl $10; under 12 free; wkly rates; lower rates Apr-June & Sept-Oct. Closed rest of yr. Crib $10. TV; cable (premium). Pool; lifeguard. Complimentary continental bkfst. Ck-out 11 am. Coin lndry. Some private patios, balconies. Cr cds: DS, MC, V.

★ **BEACH VIEW.** *6 Wilmington Ave. 302/227-2999; FAX 302/226-2640; res: 800/288-5962.* 38 rms, 4 story. Mid-June-early Sept: D $90-$130; each addl $7; lower rates Apr-mid-June, early Sept-mid-Oct. Closed rest of yr. Crib $5. TV; cable (premium). Pool. Complimentary continental bkfst. Restaurant adj 8 am-11 pm. Ck-out 11 am. Coin lndry. Refrigerators. Some balconies. Cr cds: A, DS, MC, V.

★ ★ **BEST WESTERN GOLD LEAF.** *(1400 DE 1, Dewey Beach) 2 mi S on DE 1. 302/226-1100; FAX 302/226-9785.* 75 rms, 4 story. July-Aug: S, D $108-$188; each addl $10; under 12 free; lower rates rest of yr. Crib $10. TV; cable (premium). Pool. Complimentary coffee in lobby. Restaurant opp 8 am-9 pm. Ck-out 11 am. Coin lndry. Meeting rms. Business servs avail. Covered parking. Refrigerators. Balconies. Ocean ½ blk; swimming beach. Cr cds: A, C, D, DS, ER, JCB, MC, V.

★ ★ **DINNER BELL INN.** *2 Christian St, off Rehoboth Ave. 302/227-2561; FAX 302/227-0323; res: 800/425-2355.* 28 rms, 2 story, 4 kit. units, 1 cottage. Late June-Aug: D $85-$135; each addl $15; kit. units $150-$200; cottage $250; under 12 free; lower rates Apr-mid-June & late Sept. Closed rest of yr. Crib free. TV; cable (premium). Complimentary continental bkfst. Restaurant 5-10 pm. Bar from 4 pm. Ck-out 11 am.

Meeting rm. Business servs avail. Individually decorated rms. Ocean 2 blks. Cr cds: A, MC, V.

✔★ **ECONO LODGE RESORT.** *4361 DE 1. 302/227-0500; FAX 302/227-2170; res: 800/553-2666.* 79 rms, 3 story. June-Aug: S, D $75-$125; each addl $5; under 16 free; lower rates rest of yr. Crib free. TV; cable (premium). Pool; lifeguard. Complimentary coffee. Restaurant nearby. Ck-out 11 am. Coin lndry. Business servs avail. Some refrigerators. Balconies. Cr cds: A, C, D, DS, ER, JCB, MC, V.

★ ★ **OCEANUS.** *6 Second St. 302/227-8200; res: 800/852-5011.* 38 rms, 3 story. No elvtr. July-Aug: D $115-$149; each addl $10; under 12 free; wkly rates; lower rates Apr-June, Sept-Oct. Closed rest of yr. Crib $7. TV; cable (premium). Pool; lifeguard. Complimentary continental bkfst. Restaurant opp 8-2 am. Ck-out noon. Coin lndry. Refrigerators. Cr cds: DS, MC, V.

★ ★ **SANDCASTLE.** *123 2nd St. 302/227-0400; res: 800/372-2112.* 60 rms, 3 story. Memorial Day-Labor Day: S, D $90-$119; each addl $10; under 11 free; lower rates Mar-Memorial Day & Labor Day-Dec. Closed rest of yr. Crib $10. TV. Indoor pool; sauna. Complimentary coffee. Ck-out 11 am. Meeting rms. Refrigerators. Balconies. Cr cds: A, DS, MC, V.

★ **SEA'ESTA MOTEL III.** *1409 DE 1, 2 mi S on DE 1, at Rodney St. 302/227-4343; res: 302/227-7299.* 33 kit. units, 3 story. July-Aug: S, D $79-$119; each addl $10; under 12 free; lower rates Apr-June & Sept-Oct. Closed rest of yr. TV; cable (premium). Complimentary coffee in lobby. Restaurant nearby. Ck-out 11 am. Covered parking. Balconies. Ocean 1 blk; swimming beach. Cr cds: A, C, D, DS, MC, V.

Motor Hotels

★ ★ **BRIGHTON SUITES.** *34 Wilmington Ave. 302/227-5780; FAX 302/227-6815; res: 800/227-5788.* 66 suites, 4 story. July-Aug: suites $129-$189; each addl $10; under 16 free; mid-wk rates; package plans; lower rates rest of yr. Crib $6. TV; cable (premium), VCR avail. Heated pool; lifeguard. Supervised child's activities (July-Sept); ages 2-12. Complimentary coffee in lobby. Restaurant opp 11 am-9 pm. Ck-out 11 am. Meeting rms. Business servs avail. Bellhops in season. Garage parking. Exercise equipt; weight machines, bicycles. Refrigerators, wet bars. Cr cds: A, C, D, DS, MC, V.

★ ★ **HENLOPEN.** *Lake Ave & Boardwalk. 302/227-2551; FAX 302/227-8147; res: 800/441-8450.* 93 rms, 8 story. July-Aug (2-day min wkends, hols): S, D $140; each addl $10; under 16 free; varied lower rates Apr-May & Sept-Oct. Closed rest of yr. Crib free. TV; cable. Coffee in rms. Restaurant 8-11 am, 5-10 pm. Ck-out 11 am. Meeting rms. Business servs avail. Some refrigerators. Balconies. On beach; ocean views. Cr cds: A, D, DS, MC, V.

Hotel

★ ★ ★ **BOARDWALK PLAZA.** *Olive Ave at the Boardwalk. 302/227-7169; FAX 302/227-0561; res: 800/332-3224.* 84 units, 4 story, 45 suites, 6 kit. units. Memorial Day-Labor Day: S, D $125-$250; each addl $20; suites $185-$350; kit. units $1,800-$2,900/wk (Memorial Day-Labor Day 1-wk min); under 6 free; lower rates rest of yr. Crib free. TV; cable (premium). VCR avail. Indoor/outdoor pool; poolside serv. Complimentary coffee in rms. Restaurant 7 am-10 pm. Rm serv. Ck-out 11 am. Meeting rms. Business servs avail. In-rm modem link. Exercise equipt; weight machines, bicycles. Minibars. Some balconies. On beach; ocean swimming. Victorian decor & architectural detail in modern structure; antiques, period furnishings; glass-encased oceanview elvtr; rooftop sun deck. Luxury level. Cr cds: A, D, DS, MC, V.

D ≋ ✗ ⊠ SC

Restaurants

★ ★ **BLUE MOON.** *35 Baltimore Ave. 302/227-6515.* Hrs: 6-11 pm; Sun brunch 11 am-2 pm. Closed Jan. Res accepted. Bar 4 pm-1 am. A la carte entrees: dinner $9-$26. Specializes in chicken, steak, seafood. Sun brunch $6.25-$9.50. Outdoor dining. Cr cds: A, C, D, DS, MC, V.

★ ★ **CHEZ LA MER.** *210 2nd St. 302/227-6494.* Hrs: 5:30-10 pm; Fri, Sat to 10:30 pm. Closed Mon-Wed off season; Thanksgiving; also Dec-Mar. Res accepted. Continental menu. Bar to 1 am. Semi-a la carte: dinner $16-$28. Child's meals. Specializes in fresh seafood, veal. Outdoor dining. Restored house with French provincial decor. Sun porch. Cr cds: A, D, DS, MC, V.

★ ★ **FRAN O'BRIEN'S BEACH HOUSE.** *59 Lake Ave. 302/227-6121.* Hrs: 5 pm-1 am. Closed Oct-Apr; also Mon-Wed in May. Res accepted. Bar. Semi-a la carte: dinner $7.95-$26.95. Child's meals. Specializes in seafood, steak. Pianist Wed-Sun. Parking. Cr cds: A, MC, V.

★ ★ **GARDEN GOURMET.** *4121 DE 1. 302/227-4747.* Hrs: 5 pm-1 am. Closed Jan, Feb. Res accepted. Continental menu. Bar. Wine list. Semi-a la carte: dinner $12.50-$30. Complete meals: dinner $26-$43. Specializes in fresh local seafood. Parking. Renovated farm homestead (1898). Cr cds: A, DS, MC, V.

⌁

★ **IRISH EYES.** *15 Wilmington Ave. 302/227-2888.* Hrs: 5 pm-1 am; Sat, Sun from noon. Closed Thanksgiving, Dec 25. Bar to 1 am. Semi-a la carte: lunch $4.75-$7.25, dinner $8.75-$19 (cover charge $5 during comedy club). Child's meals. Specializes in overstuffed sandwiches, steak, seafood. Irish music in season. Irish pub atmosphere. Cr cds: MC, V.

D

★ ★ **LA LA LAND.** *22 Wilmington Ave. 302/227-3887.* Hrs: 6-11 pm; Sun 11 am-2:30 pm (brunch), 6-11 pm. Closed Nov-Mar. Res accepted. Bar 6 pm-1 am. A la carte entrees: dinner $16.50-$24; Sun brunch $12. Specialties: grilled Thai spiced swordfish, grilled mahi mahi with corn salsa. Outdoor dining. Artistic atmosphere; hand-painted walls & chairs; bamboo garden. Cr cds: A, D, DS, MC, V.

★ ★ **LAMP POST.** *4534 DE 1. 302/645-9132.* Hrs: 7 am-9:30 pm; Fri, Sat to 10 pm. Closed Dec 25. Bar. Semi-a la carte: bkfst $3.50-$9.50, lunch $3.50-$12, dinner $8.95-$25. Child's meals. Specializes in fresh seafood, veal, salad. Parking. Rustic decor. Cr cds: A, DS, MC, V.

D ⌁

★ ★ **RUSTY RUDDER.** *113 Dickinson St, Dewey Beach, 2 mi S on DE 1. 302/227-3888.* Hrs: 11:30 am-9 pm, Fri, Sat to 10 pm; Memorial Day-Labor Day to 11 pm; Sun to 9 pm; Sun brunch 10 am-2 pm. Bar to 1 am. Semi-a la carte: lunch $3.95-$6.95, dinner $12.95-$25.95. Sun brunch $11.95. Child's meals. Specializes in prime rib, seafood. Salad bar. Entertainment. Parking. Outdoor dining. Nautical decor; on bay. Cr cds: A, D, DS, MC, V.

D SC

★ ★ **SEA HORSE.** *330 Rehoboth Ave, at State Rd. 302/227-7451.* Hrs: 11:30 am-10 pm; Fri-Sun to 11 pm. Res accepted. Bar. Semi-a la carte: lunch $4-$12, dinner $12-$22. Lunch buffet $6.95. Child's meals. Specializes in seafood, prime rib, steak. Parking. Cr cds: A, C, D, DS, MC, V.

D SC ⌁

★ ★ **SYDNEY'S SIDE STREET.** *25 Christian St. 302/227-1339.* Hrs: 4 pm-1 am; hrs vary Nov-Apr. Closed Thanksgiving, Dec 25. Res accepted. Bar. Semi-a la carte: dinner $9.50-$19.50. Specializes in New

Orleans cuisine. Own desserts. Blues, jazz evenings. Outdoor dining. Restored old schoolhouse. Cr cds: A, D, DS, MC, V.

D

Smyrna (B-9)

(For accommodations see Dover; also see Odessa)

Founded 1768 **Pop** 5,231 **Elev** 36 ft **Area code** 302 **Zip** 19977
Information Chamber of Commerce, PO Box 576, Dover 19903, phone 302/653-9291; or visit the Smyrna Visitors Center, 5500 Du Pont Hwy, phone 302/653-8910.

Named in 1806 for the chief seaport of Turkish Asia Minor, Smyrna in the 1850s was an active shipping center for produce grown in central Delaware.

What to See and Do

Bombay Hook National Wildlife Refuge. Annual fall and spring resting and feeding spot for migratory waterfowl, including a variety of ducks and tens of thousands of snow geese and Canada geese; also home for bald eagles, shorebirds, deer, fox and muskrat. Auto tour route (12 mi), wildlife foot trails, observation towers; visitor center offering interpretive and environmental education programs. (Spring and fall, daily, summer and winter, Mon-Fri) Golden Eagle, Golden Age and Golden Access passports accepted (see MAKING THE MOST OF YOUR TRIP). 5 mi E on DE 6, then 3 mi S on DE 9. Phone 302/653-6872. Per vehicle ¢¢

Smyrna Museum. Furnishings and memorabilia from early Federal to late Victorian periods; changing exhibits. (Sat, limited hrs) 11 S Main St. Phone 302/653-8844. **Free.**

Restaurants

★ ★ **THOMAS ENGLAND HOUSE.** *1165 S du Pont Blvd. (US 13). 302/653-1420.* Hrs: 4-10 pm; wkends to 11 pm; early-bird dinner to 7 pm. Res accepted; required Sat. Continental menu. Bar. Semi-a la carte: dinner $9.95-$29.95. Child's meals. Specializes in fresh seafood, prime rib. Colonial building that housed troops during Revolutionary War and was a stop on Underground Railroad. Cr cds: MC, V.

SC

✔★ **WAYSIDE INN.** *du Pont Hwy (US 13), at Mt Vernon, 1 blk S of DE 300. 302/653-8047.* Hrs: 11 am-9 pm; Fri, Sat to 9:30 pm; Sun noon-8 pm. Closed Mon; Jan 1, Dec 24, 25. Res accepted. Semi-a la carte: lunch $4.25-$8.50, dinner $9.95-$16.95. Child's meals. Specializes in seafood, prime rib. Early American decor. Cr cds: DS, MC, V.

Wilmington (A-9)

(In PA see also Chester, Kennett Square, Philadelphia)

Settled 1638 **Pop** 71,529 **Elev** 120 ft **Area code** 302
Information Greater Wilmington Convention & Visitors Bureau, 100 W 10th St, 19801; 302/652-4088.

Wilmington, the "chemical capital of the world," international hub of industry and shipping, is the largest city in Delaware. The Swedish, Dutch and British have all left their mark on the city. The first settlement was made by Swedes seeking their fortunes; they founded the colony of New Sweden. In 1655 the little colony was taken without bloodshed by Dutch soldiers under Peter Stuyvesant, governor of New Amsterdam. Nine years later the English became entrenched in the town, which grew under the influence of wealthy Quakers as a market and shipping center. Abundant water power in creeks of the Brandywine River Valley, plus accessibility to other eastern ports, stimulated early industrial growth. When Eleuthère du Pont built his powder mill on Brandywine Creek in 1802, the valley had already known a century of industry. From here come vulcanized fiber, glazed leathers, dyed cotton, rubber hose, autos and many other products.

What to See and Do

Amtrak Station. Victorian railroad station, which continues to function as such, designed by master architect Frank Furness. Restored. (Daily) Martin Luther King Blvd & French St.

Banning Park. Fishing. Tennis, playing fields. Picnicking; pavilions. (Daily) 2 mi S on DE 4. Middleboro Rd & Maryland Ave. Phone 302/323-6422. **Free.**

Bellevue State Park. Fishing. Nature and fitness trails, bicycling, horseback riding trails; tennis, game courts. Picnicking (pavilions). Standard hrs, fees. 4 mi NE via I-95, Marsh Rd exit. Phone 302/577-3390.

Brandywine Creek State Park. A 1,000-acre day-use park. Fishing. Nature, fitness trails. Cross-country skiing. Picnicking. Nature center. Standard hrs, fees. 4 mi N on DE 100. Phone 302/577-3534.

Brandywine Springs Park. Site of a once-famous resort hotel (1827-1845) for southern planters and politicos. Here, Lafayette met Washington under the Council Oak before the Battle of Brandywine in 1777. Picnicking, fireplaces, pavilions, baseball fields. Pets on leash only. (Daily) 4 mi W on DE 41, 3300 Faulkland Rd. Phone 302/323-6422. **Free.**

Brandywine Zoo and Park. Designed by Frederick Law Olmsted, the park includes Josephine Garden with fountain and roses; stands of Japanese cherry trees. The zoo, along North Park Dr, features animals from North and South America (daily). Picnicking; playgrounds. On both sides of Brandywine River, from Augustine to Market St bridges. Phone 302/571-7747. Zoo **¢¢**; Nov-Mar **Free.**

Delaware Art Museum. Expanded facility features Howard Pyle Collection of American illustrations, with works by Pyle, N. C. Wyeth and Maxfield Parrish; American painting collection, with works by West, Homer, Church, Glackens and Hopper; Bancroft Collection of English Pre-Raphaelite art, with works by Rossetti and Burne-Jones; and Phelps Collection of Andrew Wyeth works; also changing exhibits, children's participatory gallery; store. (Daily exc Mon; closed major hols) Guided tours by appt. 2301 Kentmere Pkwy. Phone 302/571-9590. **¢¢**

Delaware History Museum. Changing exhibits on history and decorative arts. (Tues-Fri afternoons & Sat; closed major hols) 504 Market St. Phone 302/656-0637. **Donation.**

Delaware Museum of Natural History. Exhibits of shells, birds, mammals; also largest bird egg and 500-pound clam. (Daily; closed major hols) 5 mi NW on DE 52 in Greenville. Phone 302/658-9111. **¢¢**

Fort Christina Monument. Monument marks location where Swedes settled in 1638. Presented in 1938 to Wilmington by the people of Sweden, monument consists of black granite plinth surmounted by pioneers' flagship, the *Kalmar Nyckel,* sculpted by Carl Milles. Complex includes nearby log cabin, moved to this location as a reminder of Finnish and Swedish contributions to our nation. Foot of E 7th St.

Fort Delaware State Park (see). Approx 15 mi S on Pea Patch Island, opp Delaware City.

Grand Opera House (1871). Historic landmark built by Masons, this restored Victorian theater now serves as Delaware's Center for the Performing Arts, home of Opera Delaware (Nov-May) and Delaware Symphony (Sept-May). Facade is fine example of style of the Second Empire interpreted in cast iron. 818 Market St Mall. Phone 302/658-7898 or 302/652-5577 (ticket box office).

Hagley Museum. Old riverside stone mill buildings, one-room schoolhouse and millwright shop highlight 19th-century explosive manufacturing and community life; 240-acre historic site of E. I. du Pont's original blackpowder mills, including exhibit building with working models and dioramas, operating water wheel, stationary steam engine and a fully operable 1875 machine shop. Admission includes bus ride along river for tour of 1803 Eleutherian Mills, residence with antiques reflecting five generations of du Ponts, a 19th-century garden and a barn with a collection of antique wagons. Museum store. (Mid-Mar-Dec, daily; rest of yr, Sat & Sun, limited

hrs Mon-Fri; closed Thanksgiving, Dec 25 & 31) 3 mi NW off DE 141. Phone 302/658-2400. **¢¢¢**

Holy Trinity (Old Swedes) Church and Hendrickson House. Founded by Swedish settlers in 1698, the church stands as originally built and still has regular services. The house, a Swedish farmhouse built in 1690, is now a museum containing 17th- and 18th-century artifacts. (Mon, Wed, Fri & Sat afternoons; closed major hols) 606 Church St. Phone 302/652-5629. **Free.**

Nemours Mansion and Gardens. Country estate (300 acres) of Alfred I. du Pont. Mansion (1910) is modified Louis XVI, by Carrère and Hastings, with 102 rooms of rare antique furniture, Oriental rugs, tapestries and paintings dating from 15th century. Formal French gardens extend one-third of a mile along main vista from house with terraces, statuary and pools. Tours (May-Nov, daily exc Mon; res required) Over 16 yrs only. Rockland Rd between DE 141 & US 202. Phone 302/651-6912. **¢¢¢**

Rockwood Museum. A 19th-century Gothic-revival estate with gardens in English-Romantic style. On grounds are manor house, conservatory, porter's lodge and other outbuildings. Museum furnished with English, European and American decorative arts of the 17th through 19th centuries. Guided tours (Mar-Dec, daily exc Mon; Jan & Feb, Tues-Sat). (See ANNUAL EVENTS) 610 Shipley Rd. Phone 302/761-4340. **¢¢**

Willingtown Square. Historic square surrounded by four 18th-century houses moved to this location between 1973 and 1976. One houses museum gift shop for the Historical Society of Delaware; others serve as office and conference space. 500 block Market St Mall. Phone 302/655-7161.

Wilmington & Western Railroad. Round-trip steam-train ride (9 mi) to and from Mt Cuba picnic grove. (May-Oct, Sun; rest of yr, schedule varies) 4 mi SW, near jct DE 2 & DE 41 at Greenbank Station. Phone 302/998-1930. **¢¢¢**

★ **Winterthur Museum, Garden and Library.** Museum houses decorative arts representing period from 1640 to 1860; collection of over 89,000 objects is displayed in two buildings. First-floor exhibition in the Galleries introduces 200 yrs of American antiques. The Period Rooms (seen on guided tours) were arranged by Henry Francis du Pont in his 9-story country house. Museum is surrounded by 60 acres of naturally landscaped garden, also arranged by du Pont, on a 980-acre estate. The Galleries at Winterthur offer self-guided tours. (Daily; closed hols) Admission varies with tour. 6 mi NW on DE 52. Phone 302/888-4600 or 800/448-3883. **¢¢¢**

Annual Events

Hagley's Irish Festival. Hagley Museum. Irish dancers, singers, bagpipes, traditional food. Phone 302/658-2400. Last Sat Apr.

Wilmington Garden Day. Tour of famous gardens and houses. 1st Sat May.

Victorian Ice Cream Festival. Rockwood Museum. Victorian festival featuring high-wheeled bicycles, hot-air balloons, marionettes, old-fashioned medicine show, baby parade, crafts; homemade ice cream. Phone 302/761-4340. Mid-July.

Delaware Nature Society Harvest Moon Festival. 3 mi NW via US 41, at Ashland Nature Center in Hockessin. Cider-pressing demonstrations, hay rides, nature walks, farm animals, arts & crafts, musical entertainment, pony rides, games. Phone 302/239-2334. 1st wkend Oct.

Seasonal Event

Horse racing. Delaware Park. 7 mi S on I-95 exit 4B. Thoroughbred racing. Phone 302/994-2521. Mid-Mar-early Nov.

Motels

✔★ ★ **BEST WESTERN BRANDYWINE VALLEY INN.** *1807 Concord Pike (US 202) (19803), I-95 exit 8. 302/656-9436; FAX 302/656-8564.* E-mail info@brandywinevalley.com; web www.brandywinevalley.com. 95 rms, 2 story, 12 kit. suites. S $77; D $92; each addl $5; kit. suites $105; under 18 free. Crib $5. Pet accepted. TV; cable (premium), VCR avail. Pool; wading pool, whirlpool, lifeguard. Complimentary coffee in rms. Restaurant adj 7 am-11 pm. Ck-out noon. Meeting rms. Business servs avail. In-rm modem link. Bellhops. Valet serv. Sundries. Gift shop. Exercise equipt; bicycles, stair machine. Microwaves avail. Cr cds: A, C, D, DS, MC, V.

⊡ ⟐ ≋ ⟅ ⋈ ⟆ SC

★ ★ **HOLIDAY INN-NORTH.** *4000 Concord Pike (US 202) (19803), I-95 exit 8.* 302/478-2222; FAX 302/479-0850. Web www.holiday inn.com. 138 rms, 2 story. S, D $79; each addl $6; under 18 free; wkend rates. Crib free. Pet accepted, some restrictions. TV; cable (premium), VCR avail. Pool; lifeguard. Restaurant 6 am-10 pm. Rm serv. Bar 4 pm-1 am. Ck-out noon. Coin lndry. Meeting rms. Business servs avail. In-rm modem link. Bellhops. Sundries. Health club privileges. Cr cds: A, C, D, DS, JCB, MC, V.

⊡ ⟐ ≋ ⋈ ⟆ SC

Hotels

★ ★ **BRANDYWINE SUITES.** *707 King St (19801).* 302/656-9300; FAX 302/656-2459. 49 suites, 4 story. S, D $109-$225; under 12 free; wkend rates. Crib free. Valet parking $7.50. TV; cable (premium), VCR avail (movies). Complimentary bkfst buffet. Complimentary coffee in rms. Restaurant 6:30 am-8:30 am, 11:30 am-2 pm, 5-10 pm; Sat, Sun 8-10 am, 5-10 pm. Bar 2-10 pm. Ck-out noon. Meeting rms. Business servs avail. In-rm modem link. Free airport, RR station, bus depot transportation. Exercise equipt; bicycles, stair machine. Bathrm phones; microwaves avail. Modern decor with European accents; atrium. Cr cds: A, C, D, MC, V.

⊡ ⟅ ⋈ ⟆ SC

★ ★ **COURTYARD BY MARRIOTT.** *1102 West St (19801).* 302/429-7600; FAX 302/429-9167. 125 rms, 10 story. S $119-$150; D $129-$150; each addl $10; wkend rates. Crib free. Garage $8.50. TV; cable (premium). Coffee in rms. Ck-out noon. In-rm modem link. Gift shop. Airport, RR station, bus depot transportation. Exercise equipt; bicycle, stair machine. Refrigerators, wet bar; some in-rm whirlpools; microwaves avail. Cr cds: A, D, DS, MC, V.

⊡ ⟅ ⋈ ⟆ SC

★ ★ ★ **HILTON.** *I-95 & Naamans Rd (19703), I-95N exit 11, or I-495S exit 6.* 302/792-2700; FAX 302/798-6182. 193 rms, 7 story. S, D $119-$159; each addl $10; suites $150-$275; under 12 free; wkend rates. Pet accepted; $60. TV; cable (premium). Pool. Playground. Coffee in rms. Restaurant 6:30 am-11 pm. Bar 3:30 pm-1 am. Ck-out noon. Meeting rms. Business center. In-rm modem link. Valet serv. Concierge. Free airport transportation. Exercise equipt; weights, bicycles. Some refrigerators; microwaves avail. Cr cds: A, C, D, DS, MC, V.

⊡ ⟐ ≋ ⟅ ⋈ ⟆ SC ⚷

✔ ★ ★ **HOLIDAY INN-DOWNTOWN.** *700 King St (19801).* 302/655-0400; FAX 302/655-5488. 217 rms, 9 story. S $79-$119; D $89-$129; each addl $10; suites $275-$395; under 18 free; wkend rates. Parking $6 wkdays; $2 wkends. Pet accepted, some restrictions. TV; cable (premium), VCR avail. Indoor pool; whirlpool. Coffee in rms. Restaurant 6:30 am-midnight; Sat, Sun from 7 am. Bar 11:30-1 am. Ck-out noon. Meeting rms. Business servs avail. In-rm modem link. Beauty shop. Exercise equipt; rower, bicycles. Some rms overlook pool. Cr cds: A, C, D, DS, JCB, MC, V.

⊡ ⟐ ≋ ⟅ ⋈ ⟆ SC

★ ★ ★ **HOTEL DU PONT.** *11th & Market Sts (19801).* 302/594-3100; FAX 302/656-2145; res: 800/441-9019. Web www.preferredhotel .com/preferred.htm. The spacious guest rooms in this renovated landmark are furnished with reproductions of 18th-century antiques. 216 rms, 12 story. S, D $139-$249; suites $395-$495; under 12 free; wkend rates, special packages. Crib free. Valet parking $13. TV; cable (premium). Restaurants (see BRANDYWINE ROOM and GREEN ROOM). Rm serv 24 hrs. Bar; entertainment. Ck-out 1 pm. Meeting rms. Business center. In-rm modem link. Concierge. Shopping arcade. Barber, beauty shop. Airport, RR station transportation. Tennis privileges. 54-hole golf privileges, greens fee, pro, putting green, driving range. Exercise rm; instructor,

weight machine, bicycles, sauna. Massage. Health club privileges. Mini-bars; microwaves avail. Cr cds: A, C, D, DS, ER, JCB, MC, V.

⊡ ⟳ ⟅ ⋈ ⟆ ⚷

★ ★ ★ **RADISSON.** *4727 Concord Pike (19803).* 302/478-6000; FAX 302/477-1492. Web www.radisson.com. 154 rms, 7 story. S $119-$139; D $129-$159; each addl $10; suites $175-$189; under 18 free. Crib $10. TV; cable (premium), VCR avail (movies). Restaurant 6:30 am-10 pm. Bar 5 pm-1 am. Ck-out noon. Meeting rms. Business servs avail. In-rm modem link. Exercise equipt; bicycle, treadmill. Health club privileges. Some refrigerators. Cr cds: A, C, D, DS, ER, JCB, MC, V.

⊡ ⟅ ⋈ ⟆ SC

★ ★ ★ **SHERATON SUITES.** *422 Delaware Ave (19801).* 302/654-8300; FAX 302/654-6036. E-mail mary_fitts@ittsheraton.com; web www.ittsheraton.com. 230 suites, 16 story. S, D $165-$185; each addl $15; under 18 free; wkend rates. Crib free. Garage $9; Fri, Sat free. TV; cable (premium), VCR avail. Indoor pool. Complimentary coffee in rms. Restaurant 6:30-10 am, 11:30 am-10:30 pm; Sun 7 am-10:30 pm. Bar. Ck-out noon. Coin lndry. Meeting rms. Business center. In-rm modem link. Airport transportation. Exercise equipt; weight machine, bicycles, sauna. Health club privileges. Refrigerators; microwaves avail. Cr cds: A, C, D, DS, ER, JCB, MC, V.

⊡ ≋ ⟅ ⋈ ⟆ SC ⚷

Inns

✔ ★ ★ ★ **THE BOULEVARD BED & BREAKFAST.** *1909 Baynard Blvd (19802).* 302/656-9700; FAX 302/656-9701. E-mail blvdbb@wserv .com. 6 rms, 2 share bath, 3 story. S $60-$75; D $65-$80; each addl $10-$15; hol wkends (2-day min). TV; cable (premium), VCR (free movies). Complimentary full bkfst. Ck-out 11 am, ck-in 2 pm. In-rm modem link. Brick house built 1913. Antiques. Cr cds: A, MC, V.

⋈ ⟆

★ ★ ★ **DARLEY MANOR.** *(3701 Philadelphia Pike, Claymont 19703) 6 mi N on I-95, exit 10.* 302/792-2127; FAX 302/798-6143; res: 800/824-4703. E-mail darley@dca.net; web www.dca.net/darley. 6 rms, 3 with shower only, 3 story. No elvtr. S, D $85-$99; each addl $10; suites $89-$99. Children over 9 yrs only. TV; cable, VCR avail. Complimentary full bkfst. Restaurant nearby. Ck-out noon, ck-in 4 pm. Business servs avail. Exercise equipt; weight machine, rower. Former residence of Felix O.C. Darley, mid-19th-century book illustrator. Totally nonsmoking. Cr cds: A, C, D, DS, MC, V.

⟅ ⋈ ⟆

★ ★ ★ ★ **INN AT MONTCHANIN VILLAGE.** *(DE 100 & Kirk Rd, Montchanin 19710) 6 mi N on DE 52, exit DE 141N, at third light.* 302/888-2133; res: 800/COWBIRD; FAX 302/888-0389. E-mail montchan@gte. com; web www.montchanin.com. This authentically restored 19th-century hamlet, nestled in the heart of Brandywine Valley, was formerly a settlement for workers at the DuPont factories along the Brandywine River. Rooms are individually decorated in period and reproduction furniture, and the multi-structure village provides unique vistas and private baths and gardens. 22 rms, 5 with shower only, 2-3 story, 16 suites. S, D $150; suites $180-$320; wkends, hols 2-3-day min. Crib free. TV; cable, VCR avail. Complimentary full bkfst. Complimentary coffee in rms. Restaurant (see KRAZY KAT'S). Rm serv Sun-Thurs. Ck-out 11 am, ck-in 3 pm. Business center. In-rm modem link. Luggage handling. Valet serv. Concierge serv. Lighted tennis privileges. 48-hole golf privileges, greens fee $65-$90. Health club privileges. Refrigerators, microwaves, wet bars; some in-rm whirlpools, fireplaces. Balconies. Picnic tables. Totally nonsmoking. Cr cds: A, C, D, MC, V.

⟳ ⟅ ⋈ ⟆ ⚷

Restaurants

★ ★ ★ **BACK BURNER.** *(425 Hockessin Corner, Hockessin 19707) DE 48 to DE 41, then N 9 mi.* 302/239-2314. Hrs: 11:15 am-2:15 pm, 5-9 pm; Fri, Sat 11:15 am-2:15 pm, 5:30-9:45 pm. Closed Sun; major hols; also wk before Labor Day. Res required. Bar. Wine cellar. Semi-a la carte: lunch $6-$12, dinner $13-$25. Specialties: black Angus beef, soft shell crabs, rack of lamb. Elegeant dining in country atmosphere; renovated barn with arched walls, display kitchen. Cr cds: A, D, DS, MC, V.

✔★ **BANGKOK HOUSE.** *104 N Union St (19805).* 302/654-8555. Hrs: 5-10 pm; Fri, Sat to 11 pm. Closed Mon; Jan 1, Dec 25. Res accepted. Thai menu. Bar. Semi-a la carte: dinner $7.95-$14.95. Child's meals. Specialties: crispy duck, sauteed shrimp and chicken. Contemporary decor; Thai artwork. Cr cds: A, DS, MC, V.

D

★ ★ ★ **BLACK TRUMPET BISTRO.** *1717 Delaware Ave (19806).* 302/777-0454. Hrs: 11:30 am-2:30 pm, 5:30-10 pm; Sat, Sun from 5:30 pm. Closed Mon; Memorial Day, Dec 25. Res required. French menu. Bar. Wine cellar. A la carte entrees: lunch $6-$12, dinner $15-$24. Specialties: exotic wild mushrooms, soft-shelled crab. Own pasta, pastries, ice creams. Intimate atmosphere; original artwork adorns walls. Totally nonsmoking. Cr cds: A, MC, V.

D

★ ★ ★ **BRANDYWINE ROOM.** *(See Hotel Du Pont)* 302/594-3156. Web www.preferredhotels.com/preferred.html. Hrs: 6-11 pm; Sun 5-10 pm. Closed Fri, Sat. Res accepted. Bar. Semi-a la carte: $16-$30. Specializes in steak, rack of lamb, seafood. Club atmosphere; Wyeth paintings. Cr cds: A, C, D, DS, ER, JCB, MC, V.

D

★ ★ ★ **COLUMBUS INN.** *2216 Pennsylvania Ave (19806), I-95 Delaware Ave exit, 3 mi W.* 302/571-1492. E-mail columbus@gim.net; web www.columbusinn.com. Hrs: 11 am-11 pm; Fri, Sat to midnight. Closed Sun; Dec 25. Res accepted. Continental menu. Bar. Wine cellar. A la carte entrees: lunch $4.95-$9.95, dinner $12-$22. Child's meals. Specializes in fresh seafood, beef. Pianist Fri, Sat. Valet parking. Early American decor in 200-yr-old house. Fireplaces. Family-owned since 1957. Cr cds: A, C, D, DS, MC, V.

D

★ ★ **CONSTANTINOU'S BEEF & SEAFOOD.** *1616 Delaware Ave (19806).* 302/652-0653. Hrs: 11 am-10 pm; Fri, Sat to 11 pm; Sun 4-9 pm. Closed Dec 25. Res accepted. Bar. A la carte entrees: lunch $5.95-$12.95, dinner $16.95-$28.95. Specializes in steak, seafood. Entertainment Thurs-Sat. Old World atmosphere; antiques, stained-glass windows. Cr cds: A, C, D, DS, MC, V.

★ ★ ★ **FOX POINT GRILL.** *321 E Lea Blvd (19802).* 302/762-5655. Hrs: 11:30 am-2:30 pm, 4:30-10 pm; Sat from 4:30 pm. Closed Sun; Dec 25. Res accepted. Regional Amer menu. Bar. Wine list. Semi-a la carte: lunch $5.75-$11.50, dinner $15.50-$22. Child's meals. Specialties: Chincoteague crab cakes, potato-crusted rockfish, grilled rack of lamb. Own baking. Elegant atmosphere. Cr cds: A, D, MC, V.

★ ★ ★ **GREEN ROOM.** *(See Hotel Du Pont)* 302/594-3154. Web www.preferredhotels.com/preferred.html. Hrs: 6:30 am-2 pm; Fri, Sat 7 am-2 pm, 6-10 pm; Sun brunch 10 am-2:15 pm. Res accepted; required Sun brunch. Continental menu. Bar. Extensive wine list. Semi-a la carte: bkfst $8.50-$14. A la carte entrees: lunch $10-$20, dinner $25-$35. Sun brunch $30.50. Child's meals. Specializes in lobster, rack of lamb, filet mignon. Harpist Fri, Sat. Valet parking. Elegant dining rm in historic hotel. Cr cds: A, C, D, DS, ER, JCB, MC, V.

D

★ ★ ★ **HARRY'S SAVOY GRILL.** *2020 Naaman's Rd (19810), I-95 Naaman's Rd exit, 2 mi on DE 92W.* 302/475-3000. E-mail dmd@harry's-savoy.com; web www.harry's-savoy.com. Hrs: 11 am-10:30 pm; Fri to 11:30 pm; Sat 4:30-11:30 pm; Sun 4-10:30 pm; Sun brunch 10:30 am-3 pm. Closed Dec 25. Res accepted. Bar to 1 am. Wine cellar. A la carte entrees: lunch $5.95-$11.95, dinner $10.95-$17.95. Sun brunch $6.95-$14.95. Child's meals. Specializes in prime rib, fresh seafood. Pianist Fri, Sat; magicians perform at tables Tues evenings. Parking. Outdoor dining. Fireplaces. Cr cds: A, D, DS, MC, V.

D

★ **INDIA PALACE.** *101 N Maryland Ave (19804).* 302/655-8772. Hrs: 11:30 am-2:30 pm, 5-10 pm; Fri, Sat to 10:30 pm. Closed Mon. Res accepted. Indian menu. Wine, beer. Semi-a la carte: lunch $5.95, dinner $6.95-$15.95. Specializes in vegetarian and tandoori meals. Native American art. Cooking observed behind glass wall. Cr cds: A, D, DS, MC, V.

★ ★ **KID SHELLEENS.** *1801 W 14th St (19810), I-95 Delaware Ave exit to PA Ave, rt on N Scott, left on W 14th St.* 302/658-4600. Hrs: 11 am-midnight; Sun brunch 10 am-2 pm. Closed Thanksgiving, Dec 25. Bar. A la carte entrees: lunch $4.95-$8.95, dinner $7.95-$13.95. Child's meals. Specializes in grilled dishes, fresh seafood. Parking. Outdoor dining. Casual atmosphere. Cr cds: A, D, DS, MC, V.

D ♥

★ ★ ★ **KRAZY KAT'S.** *(See Inn at Montchanin Village)* 302/888-2133. Hrs: 7-9 am, 11 am-2 pm, 5:30-10 pm; Sat 8-11 am, 5:30-10 pm; Sun 8 am-noon, 5:30-10 pm. Res accepted. Contemporary Amer menu. Wine cellar. Complete meal: bkfst $14.50. Semi-a la carte: lunch $5-$12, dinner $20-$26. Specialties: crab cakes, Krazy Kat's mixed grille. Restored 18th-century blacksmith shop; original fireplace and art. Totally nonsmoking. Cr cds: A, C, D, MC, V.

D

★ ★ **PICCIOTTI'S.** *3001 Lancaster Ave (19805).* 302/652-3563. Hrs: 11 am-2 pm, 5-10 pm; Sun 5-9 pm. Closed most major hols. Res accepted. Continental menu. Bar. Semi-a la carte: lunch $5.75-$13.50, dinner $12.75-$25.50. Specializes in crab cakes, filet mignon. Parking. Contemporary decor. Cr cds: A, C, D, DS, MC, V.

D

★ ★ ★ **PICCOLO MONDO.** *3604 Silverside Rd (19810), at Talleyville Towne Shoppes.* 302/478-9028. Hrs: 11:30 am-2 pm, 5-10 pm; Sat from 5 pm. Closed Sun; most major hols. Res accepted. Italian menu. Bar. Wine list. A la carte entrees: lunch $6-$9, dinner $10-$18. Specialties: risotto primavera, grilled shrimp on rosemary branch, cannelloni con frutti di mare. Own pastries. Italian decor with open hearth kitchen; wine bottles displayed. Cr cds: A, DS, MC, V.

D

★ ★ ★ **POSITANO.** *2401 Pennsylvania Ave (19806), in Devon Bldg.* 302/656-6788. Hrs: 11:30 am-2 pm, 5:30-10 pm. Closed Sun; major hols. Res required. Italian, French menu. Wine list. Semi-a la carte: lunch $8.50-$12.50, dinner $18-$32.95. Specializes in veal, fresh seafood. Parking. Elegant and intimate dining. Jacket. Totally nonsmoking. Cr cds: A, C, D, DS, MC, V.

D

★ ★ ★ **SILK PURSE & SOW'S EAR.** *1307 N Scott St (19806).* 302/654-7666. E-mail eziosilkl@aol.com. Hrs: 5:30-9:30 pm. Closed Sun, Mon; major hols. Res accepted. Eclectic menu. Wine list. A la carte entrees: dinner $13.50-$18.50. Specializes in fresh seasonal ingredients, game, fish. Own baking, pasta. In converted town house; bistro on 2nd floor. Cr cds: A, MC, V.

D

★ ★ ★ **TAVOLA TOSCANA.** *1412 N Dupont St (19806).* 302/654-8001. Hrs: 11:30 am-2 pm, 5:30-10 pm. Closed major hols. Res accepted; required wkends. Italian menu. Bar. Wine list. A la carte entrees: lunch $8-$14, dinner $12-$24. Specializes in hand-rolled pasta, shared specialty appetizers. Parking. Atmosphere of European bistro. Cr cds: A, D, DS, MC, V.

★ ★ ★ **VINCENTE'S.** *1601 Concord Pike (19803), in Independence Mall. 302/652-5142.* Hrs: 11 am-10 pm; Sat from 4 pm. Closed Sun; most major hols. Res accepted. Italian menu. Bar. Extensive wine list. Semi-a la carte: lunch $7.95-$10.95, dinner $16.95-$32.95. Child's meals. Specializes in veal, steak, seafood. Own pastries, pasta. Contemporary decor; Caesar salad made tableside. Cr cds: A, D, DS, MC, V.

★ ★ **WATERWORKS CAFE.** *16th & French Sts (19801), 4 blks N of Rodney Square. 302/652-6022.* Hrs: 11:30 am-2:30 pm, 5:30-10 pm; Sat from 5:30 pm. Closed Sun, Mon; major hols. Res accepted. Bar to 1 am. Wine list. A la carte entrees: lunch $5.95-$14.95, dinner $13.95-$26.95. Specializes in fresh seafood. Parking. Outdoor dining. Old waterworks on Brandywine River. Cr cds: A, MC, V.

District of Columbia

Population: 606,900
Land area: 63 square miles
Elevation: 1-410 feet
Highest point: Tenleytown
Flower: American Beauty rose
Bird: Wood thrush
Founded: 1790
Time zone: Eastern
Web: www.washington.org

Washington

(see C-8 VA-WV map; C-6 DE-MD map)

Area code 202

Washington, designed by Major Pierre Charles L'Enfant in about 1791, was the first American city ever planned for a specific purpose. It is a beautiful city, with wide, tree-lined streets laid out according to a design that is breathtaking in its scope and imagination. For its purpose the broad plan still works well even though L'Enfant could not have foreseen the automobile or the fact that the United States would come to have a population of more than 250 million people. Nevertheless, L'Enfant's concept was ambitious, allowing for vast growth. Washington, named for the first US president, has been the nation's capital since 1800. The city's business is centered around government and tourism; there is little heavy industry.

The District of Columbia and Washington are one and the same. Originally the District was a 10-mile square crossing the Potomac River into Virginia, but the Virginia portion (31 square miles) was turned back to the state in 1846. Residences of federal workers spill into Virginia and Maryland; so do government offices. At the beginning, in 1800, there were 130 federal employees; at the end of the Civil War there were 7,000; now there are well over half a million. Although the city was a prime Confederate target in the Civil War, it was barely damaged. The assassination of Abraham Lincoln, however, struck a blow to the nation and drove home to Americans the fact that Washington was not merely a center of government. What happened here affected everyone.

This is a cosmopolitan city. Perhaps no city on earth has a populace with so many different origins. Representatives from all nations and men and women from every state work here—and vote in their home states by absentee ballot. It is a dignified, distinguished capital. Many who visit the city go first to the House of Representatives or Senate office buildings and chat with their representatives, who receive constituent visitors when they can. At these offices visitors obtain tickets to the Senate and House galleries. From the top of the Washington Monument there is a magnificent view of the capital. The Lincoln Memorial and the Jefferson Memorial cannot fail to capture the imagination.

When to Go/Climate

DC winters are relatively mild, while summers are hot and humid. The city is alive with color in spring and fall—cherry blossoms bloom in April and May and vibrant fall foliage begins around September.

AVERAGE HIGH/LOW TEMPERATURES (°F)
WASHINGTON NATL AIRPORT

Jan 42/27	**May** 76/57	**Sept** 80/63
Feb 46/29	**June** 85/67	**Oct** 69/50
Mar 57/38	**July** 89/71	**Nov** 58/41
Apr 67/46	**Aug** 87/70	**Dec** 47/32

Visitor Information

Washington DC Convention and Visitors Association, 1212 New York Ave NW, Suite 600, Washington, DC 20005, has brochures and schedules of events; phone 202/789-7000 (Mon-Fri, 9 am-5 pm).

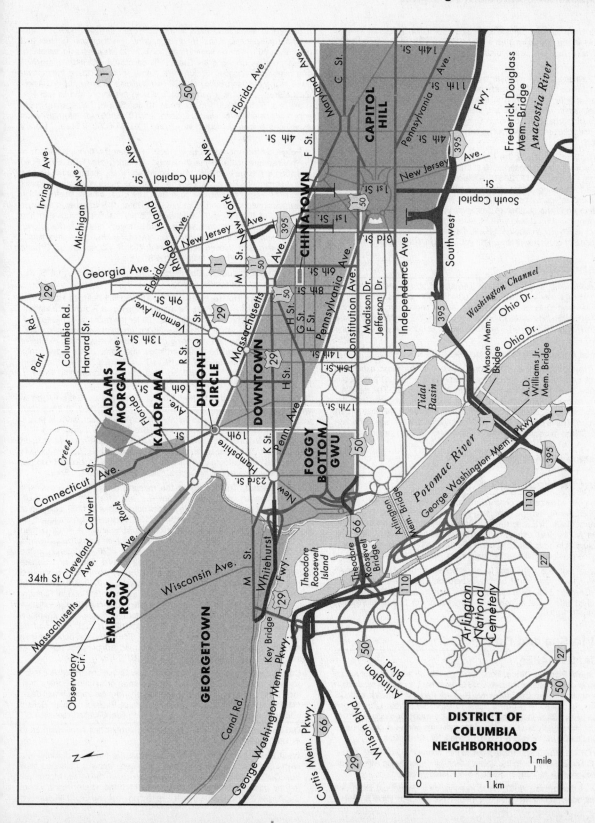

DISTRICT OF COLUMBIA NEIGHBORHOODS

CAPITOL HILL

CHINATOWN

ADAMS MORGAN

KALORAMA

DUPONT CIRCLE

DOWNTOWN

FOGGY BOTTOM/ GWU

EMBASSY ROW

GEORGETOWN

Arlington National Cemetery

Anacostia River

Potomac River

Washington Channel

Tidal Basin

Theodore Roosevelt Island

Frederick Douglass Mem. Bridge

George Washington Mem. Pkwy.

Mason Mem. Bridge

A.D. Williams Jr. Mem. Bridge

Arlington Mem. Bridge

Theodore Roosevelt Bridge

Key Bridge

0   1 mile

0   1 km

The National Park Service maintains information kiosks at several key points in the city as well as a White House Visitors Center at 1450 Pennsylvania Ave NW which distributes free tickets to tour the White House.

Note: By writing to your representative or senator ahead of time, tickets can be obtained for two Congressional Tours: a guided White House tour that differs slightly from the normal tour and begins at 8:15, 8:30 or 8:45 am (Tues-Sat; specific times are assigned); or passes to the House and Senate visitors' galleries to watch Congressional sessions in progress. Without this ticket, the chambers can only be viewed when Congress is not in session.

Write your senator at the United States Senate, Washington, DC 20510. Address your representative at the United States House of Representatives, Washington, DC 20515. All tickets are free, but in peak season, which starts in spring, White House tickets may be limited. In the letter, include the date you will be in Washington, first- and second-choice dates for the tours and the number of people in your party. Also include your home phone number, should your representative's or senator's aide need to contact you. You can also get tickets, if available, directly from the office of your senator or representative after you arrive in Washington.

Transportation

Airports: *National,* 3 mi S in Virginia (see ARLINGTON COUNTY-NATIONAL AIRPORT AREA under Virginia), phone 703/419-8000; *Dulles Intl,* 26 mi W in Virginia (see DULLES INTL AIRPORT AREA under Virginia), phone 703/419-8000; *Baltimore/Washington Intl,* 32 mi NE in Maryland (see BALTIMORE/WASHINGTON INTL AIRPORT AREA under Maryland), phone 410/859-7100.

Car Rental Agencies: See IMPORTANT TOLL-FREE NUMBERS.

Public Transportation: The Metrorail system is the least expensive means of getting around the capital. Metro (as it is called) provides a coordinated transportation system between buses and rail. The rapid rail system links the major commercial districts and neighborhoods, from the Capitol to the Pentagon and from the National Zoo to the National Airport and beyond. Trains operate every 6-12 minutes on the average: Monday-Friday, 5:30 am-midnight; Saturday & Sunday from 8 am. Phone 202/637-7000.

Rail Passenger Service: Amtrak 800/872-7245.

Driving in Washington

Since the city is divided into four quarters, or quadrants, emanating from the Capitol, driving may be confusing for the first-time visitor. The quadrants are northeast (NE), northwest (NW), southeast (SE) and southwest (SW). All Washington addresses have these designations listed after the street name. It is advisable to obtain a city map before attempting to drive through the city, especially during rush hours.

Safety belts are mandatory for all persons in front seat of vehicle. All children under 3 years must be in an approved safety seat anywhere in vehicle. Children 3-16 years must be properly restrained in either a safety belt or child safety seat anywhere in the vehicle. For further information phone 202/939-8018.

What to See and Do

THE CAPITOL AREA

Government Printing Office. Four buildings with 35 acres of floor space where most of the material issued by US Government, including production and distribution of the Congressional Record, Federal Register and US passports, is printed. (No public tours; to schedule private tours phone 202/512-1991.) Office includes the **Main Government Bookstore,** 710 N Capitol St NW. Nearly 20,000 publications available (Mon-Fri; closed hols). On N Capitol St, between G & H Sts. Phone 202/512-0132.

House Office Buildings. Pedestrian tunnel connects two of the oldest House Office Buildings with the Capitol. Along Independence Ave, S side of Capitol grounds at Independence & New Jersey Aves.

Library of Congress (1800). Treasures include a Gutenberg Bible, the first great book printed with movable metal type; the Giant Bible of Mainz, a 500-yr-old illuminated manuscript. Collection includes books, manuscripts, newspapers, maps, recordings, prints, photographs, posters and more than 30 million books and pamphlets in 60 languages. In the elaborate Jefferson Building is the Great Hall, decorated with murals, mosaics and marble carvings; exhibition halls (some sections closed for renovation). In the Madison Building, a 22-min audiovisual presentation, *America's Library,* provides a good introduction to the library and its facilities. (Daily exc Sun; closed federal hols) 10 1st St SE. For reading room schedule, calendar of events, phone 202/707-6400; for information on exhibitions & free guided tours, phone 202/707-8000. **Free.** Library complex includes

Folger Shakespeare Library (1932). Houses the finest collection of Shakespeare materials in the world, including the 1623 First Folio edition and large holdings of rare books and manuscripts of the English and continental Renaissance. The Great Hall offers year-round exhibits from the Folger's extensive collection. The Elizabethan Theatre, which was designed to resemble an innyard theater of Shakespeare's day, is the site of the Folger Shakespeare Library's series of museum and performing arts programs, which includes literary readings, drama, lectures, and education and family programs. Guided tours (mornings). (Daily exc Sun; closed federal hols) 201 E Capitol St SE. Phone 202/544-4600. **Free.** North on 1st St is the

Senate Office Buildings. Constitution Ave on both sides of 1st St NE. Linked by private subway to Capitol.

Sewall-Belmont House (1680, 1800). The Sewall-Belmont House is a living monument to Alice Paul, the author of the Equal Rights Amendment. From this house she spearheaded the fight for the passage of the amendment. The house, now a national landmark, contains portraits and sculptures of women from the beginning of the suffrage movement; extensive collection of memorabilia of the suffrage and equal rights movements; headquarters of the National Woman's Party. (Tues-Fri, also Sat afternoons; closed Jan 1, Thanksgiving, Dec 25) 144 Constitution Ave NE. Phone 202/546-3989 or 202/546-1210. **Free.**

Supreme Court of the United States. Designed by Cass Gilbert in neo-classical style. Court is in session Oct-Apr (Mon-Wed, at 2-wk intervals from first Mon in Oct) and on the first workday of each week in May & June; court sessions are open to the public (10 am & 1 pm), on a first-come basis; lectures are offered in the courtroom (Mon-Fri exc when court is in session; 20-min lectures hrly on half-hr); on ground floor are exhibits and film (23 min), cafeteria, snack bar, gift shop (Mon-Fri; closed hols). 1st St NE at Maryland Ave, E of Capitol. Phone 202/479-3211. **Free.**

★ **The Capitol.** The Capitol is the meeting place of Congress—the legislative branch of the government—as well as a symbol of the US government. George Washington laid the cornerstone in 1793, and part of the originally-planned building opened in 1800. Construction continued on and off over a number of years (including rebuilding after the British burned the Capitol in 1814) until the original building, which was crowned with a low copper-covered dome, was completed in 1826. Expansion in the 1850s and 1860s included the new wings, today's House and Senate chambers, and the cast-iron dome seen today, which was completed during the Civil War. The Rotunda, in the center, is the main ceremonial room of the Capitol, where dignitaries have lain in-state. National Statuary Hall, just to the south, houses part of the state statue collection (each state can contribute two), but was originally built for the House as its chamber. (Tour every 15 min; closed Jan 1, Thanksgiving, Dec 25) Public dining room on 1st floor of Senate wing (Mon-Fri). Summer band concerts (see SEASONAL EVENTS). Between Constitution & Independence Aves, at Pennsylvania Ave, E end of Mall. Phone 202/225-6827. **Free.**

Congress. Tickets to the House and Senate visitors' galleries can be obtained from the office of your congressman or senator. Foreign visitors can obtain passes to the Senate Gallery from the appointment desk, 1st floor, Senate Wing; and to the House of Representatives Gallery from the check stand, 3rd floor, House wing (identification required).

Old Senate Chamber. Original Senate chamber has been restored to its 1850s appearance. N of rotunda.

West Front. Along the Capitol's west front are terraces, gardens and lawns designed by Frederick Law Olmstead, who also planned New York City's Central Park. Halfway down the hill are the Peace Monument (on the north) and the Garfield Monument (on the south). At the foot of Capitol Hill is Union Square with a reflecting pool and Grant Monument.

US Botanic Gardens. The Botanic Garden, one of the oldest in the country, was established by Congress in 1820 for public education and exhibition. It features plants collected by the famous Wilkes Expedition of the South Seas. Conservatory has tropical, subtropical and desert plants; seasonal displays. Exterior gardens are planted for seasonal blooming; also here is Bartholdi Fountain, designed by sculptor of the Statue of Liberty. (Daily) Maryland Ave & 1st St SW, at base of Capitol Hill. Phone 202/225-8333. **Free.**

Union Station. Restored beaux-arts train station, designed by Daniel Burnham and completed in 1907, features lavish interior spaces under 96-ft-high, coffered, gold-leafed ceiling. Located within original station and train shed are 130 shops, restaurants and movie theater complex. Original spaces, such as the presidential suite, have been turned into restaurants without extensive alteration. Also located within the station are the Amtrak depot and Gray Line and Tourmobile Sightseeing operators (see SIGHTSEEING TOURS). (Daily) On Massachusetts Ave between 1st & 2nd Sts. **Free.**

FEDERAL TRIANGLE

The Triangle consists of a group of government buildings, of which nine were built for $78 million in the 1930s in modern classic design. The apex of the triangle is at Pennsylvania and Constitution Aves NW.

Department of Commerce Building (1932). Pennsylvania Ave, between 14th & 15th Sts NW. In the building is the

National Aquarium. The nation's oldest public aquarium was established in 1873. It now exhibits more than 1,700 specimens representing approx 260 species, both freshwater and saltwater. Touch tank; theater. Shark feeding (Mon, Wed, Sat); piranha feeding Tues, Thurs, Sun. (Daily; closed Dec 25) Phone 202/482-2826. ¢

Department of Energy, Pennsylvania Ave between 12th & 13th Sts NW; **Interstate Commerce Commission** (1934), Constitution Ave, between 12th & 13th Sts NW; **Customs Department,** Constitution Ave, between 13th & 14th Sts NW; and the **District Building,** Pennsylvania Ave, between 13th & 14th Sts NW, Washington's ornate 1908 city hall.

Department of Justice Building (1934). Pennsylvania Ave, between 9th & 10th Sts NW. (Not open to the public) Across Pennsylvania Ave is

FBI Headquarters. Tours of historical exhibits, including FBI laboratory; very large firearm collection; demonstration of firearms. J. Edgar Hoover Building, 935 Pennsylvania Ave, NW, between 9th & 10th Sts NW; tour entrance on 9th St NW. (Mon-Fri; closed major hols) Phone 202/324-3447. **Free.**

Federal Trade Commission Building (1938). (Mon-Fri; closed major hols) Pennsylvania Ave NW, between 6th & 7th Sts. Phone 202/326-2222. **Free.**

Labor Department. Lobby contains the Labor Hall of Fame, an exhibit depicting labor in United States; library on second floor is open to public. (Mon-Fri; closed major hols) Francis H. Perkins Building, 200 Constitution Ave NW. Phone 202/219-5000 or 202/219-6992 (library). **Free.**

The National Archives (1934). Original copies of the Declaration of Independence, Bill of Rights, Constitution; a 1297 version of the Magna Carta and other historic documents, maps and photographs. Guided tours by appt only; Pennsylvania Ave between 7th & 9th Sts NW; exhibition entrance on Constitution Ave, phone 202/501-5205. Archives also available to public for genealogical and historical research (daily exc Sun; closed federal hols). (Daily; closed Dec 25) Phone 202/501-5000 (recording) or 202/501-5400 (research library & exhibition hall). **Free.**

Pavilion at the Old Post Office (1899). Romanesque structure, which for years was headquarters of the US Postal Service, has been remodeled into a festival marketplace with 100 shops and restaurants, a miniature golf course and daily entertainment. In the 315-ft tower are replicas of the bells of Westminster Abbey, a Bicentennial gift from Great Britain; the tower, which is the second-highest point in DC, offers spectacular views from an open-air observation deck (free). Above the Pavilion shops is the headquarters for the National Endowment for the Arts. (Daily; closed Jan 1, Thanksgiving, Dec 25) Pennsylvania Ave, between 11th & 12th Sts NW. Phone 202/289-4224. **Free.**

United States Navy Memorial. Dedicated to those who have served in the Navy in war and in peacetime. A 100-ft diameter granite world map dominates the Plaza, where the *Lone Sailor,* a 7-ft bronze sculpture stands and the US Navy Band stages performances (Memorial Day-Labor Day, Tues evenings). Visitors Center features electronic kiosks with interactive video displays on naval history; also Navy Memorial Log Room and US Presidents Room. (Mon-Sat, also Sun afternoons) Pennsylvania Ave, at 7th & 9th Sts NW. Phone 202/737-2300. **Free.** Also here is

At Sea. Underwritten by Mobil Corp, this is an award-winning high-resolution 70mm film that conveys the experience of being at sea aboard a US Navy aircraft carrier. The 241-seat theater employs a 2-story, 52-ft-wide screen and 6-track digital audio to surround the audience with the sights and sounds of carrier operations. Showings (Mon-Sat, 4 times daily; Sun, 2 times). Arleigh and Roberta Burke Theater. ¢¢

THE MALL AND TIDAL BASIN

American Red Cross. National headquarters includes three buildings bounded by 17th, 18th, D & E Sts NW. The 17th St building includes marble busts, *Faith, Hope* and *Charity,* by sculptor Hiram Powers and three original Tiffany stained-glass windows. (Mon-Fri) 430 17th St NW. Phone 202/737-8300. **Free.**

Blair House (1824). Guest house for heads of government and state who are visiting the US as guests of the president. Not open to public. 1651 Pennsylvania Ave NW.

Bureau of Engraving and Printing. Headquarters for making US paper money; guided tours (every 10 min). (Mon-Fri; closed hols and Dec 24-Jan 3) 14th & C Sts SW, S of Mall; enter on 14th St. Phone 202/874-3019 or 202/874-3186. **Free.**

Constitution Gardens. This 45-acre park, with a man-made lake, is also the site of the Signers of the Declaration of Independence Memorial. Along Constitution Ave between 18th & 22nd Sts NW. Phone 202/426-6841. **Free.**

Corcoran Gallery of Art (1869). Oldest and largest private gallery in the city has world's most comprehensive collection of 18th-20th-century American art; Walker and Clark collections of European art; changing exhibitions (fee) of painting, sculpture and photography. (Daily exc Tues; closed major hols) 17th St between New York Ave & E St NW. For general information phone 202/639-1700. **Free.**

DAR Headquarters. Includes Memorial Continental Hall (1904) and Constitution Hall (1920); DAR Museum Gallery, located in administration building, has 33 state period rooms; outstanding genealogical research library (fee for nonmembers). Guided tours (daily exc Sat). 1776 D St NW. Phone 202/628-1776 or 202/879-3239. **Free.**

Department of the Treasury. According to legend, this Greek-revival building, one of the oldest (1836-1869) in the city, was built in the middle of Pennsylvania Avenue because Andrew Jackson, tired of endless wrangling over the location, walked out of the White House, planted his cane in the mud and said, "Here." The building has been extensively restored. Tours (90 min) include office used by President Andrew Johnson after the Lincoln assassination, and the two-story marble Cash Room (Sat; by advance reservation). Pennsylvania Ave at 15th St NW, E of White House. Phone 202/622-0896. **Free.**

Federal Reserve Building (1937). Primarily an office building, but noteworthy for its architecture; rotating art exhibits; film (20 min). Public tours (Thurs afternoons). C St between 20th & 21st Sts NW. Phone 202/452-3149. **Free.**

Lafayette Square. Statue of Andrew Jackson on horseback in center was first equestrian figure in Washington (1853). One of park benches was known as Bernard Baruch's office in 1930s and is dedicated to him. On square is

Decatur House Museum (1818). Federal town house built for naval hero Commodore Stephen Decatur by Benjamin H. Latrobe, second architect of the Capitol. After Decatur's death in 1820, the house was occupied by a succession of American and foreign statesmen and was a center of political and social life in the city. The ground floor family rooms reflect Decatur's federal-period lifestyle; the second-floor rooms retain their Victorian character. Operated by National Trust for Historic Preservation. (Daily exc Mon; closed Jan 1, Thanksgiving, Dec 25) 748 Jackson Place NW. Phone 202/842-0920. ¢¢

★ **Lincoln Memorial.** Dedicated in 1922, Daniel Chester French's Lincoln looks across a reflecting pool to the Washington Monument and Capitol. Lincoln's Gettysburg Address and Second Inaugural Address are inscribed on the walls of the temple-like structure, which is particularly impressive at night. Tours. *(Interior to remain open to the public during restoration study.)* (Daily, 24 hrs; closed Dec 25) 23rd St NW, at Daniel French & Henry Bacon Dr. Phone 202/426-6841. **Free.**

National Academy of Sciences (1924). Established in 1863 to stimulate research and communication among scientists and to advise the federal government in science and technology. A famous 21-ft bronze statue of Albert Berks by Robert Berks is on the front lawn. Art exhibits, concerts. (Schedule varies) 2101 Constitution Ave, between 21st & 22nd Sts NW. Phone 202/334-2436. **Free.**

National Gallery of Art. The West Building (1941), designed by John Russell Pope, contains Western European and American art, spanning periods between the 13th and 20th centuries: highlights include the only Leonardo da Vinci painting in the western hemisphere, *Ginevra de' Benci;* a comprehensive collection of Italian paintings and sculpture; major French Impressionists; numerous Rembrandts and examples of the Dutch school; masterpieces from the Mellon, Widener, Kress, Dale and Rosenwald collections; special exhibitions. The East Building (1978), designed by architect I. M. Pei, houses the gallery's growing collection of 20th-century art, including Picasso's *Family of Saltimbanques* and Jackson Pollock's *Lavender Mist.* (Daily; closed Jan 1, Dec 25) Constitution Ave, between 3rd & 7th Sts. Phone 202/737-4215. **Free.**

Octagon House (1798-1800). Federal town house built for Colonel John Tayloe III, based on designs by Dr. William Thornton. Served as temporary quarters for President and Mrs James Madison after White House was burned in War of 1812; also site of ratification of the Treaty of Ghent. Restored with period furnishings (1800-1828). Changing exhibits on architecture and allied arts. (Daily exc Mon; closed major hols) 1799 New York Ave NW, at 18th & E Sts NW. Phone 202/638-3105. ¢¢

Old Executive Office Building (1875). Second Empire/Victorian architecture. Built as War Office; was also home to State Department; now offices for president's staff. Guided tours by appt (Sat morning only). Pennsylvania Ave & 17th St NW. Phone 202/395-5895. **Free.**

Organization of American States (OAS). Headquarters of OAS, set up to maintain international peace and security and to promote integral development in the Americas. Tropical patio, Hall of Heroes and Flags, Hall of the Americas, Aztec Garden, Council Chamber. (Mon-Fri; closed hols) Constitution Ave & 17th St NW. Phone 202/458-3000. **Free.**

Potomac Park (East and West). On the banks of the Potomac River, park recreational activities include fishing, pedalboating; golf, tennis; picnicking. Washington's famous cherry trees can be found around the Tidal Basin. Hundreds of **Yoshino and Akebono cherry trees**, a gift from Japan in 1912, come into full bloom in a celebration of spring (see ANNUAL EVENTS), an unforgettable floral display (late-Mar-early-Apr). West Potomac park is the site of the Franklin Delano Roosevelt Memorial. NW & SE of the Jefferson Memorial. For park information phone 202/619-7222.

Renwick Gallery. American crafts from 1900 to the present. A department of the National Museum of American Art. (Daily; closed Dec 25) Pennsylvania Ave NW at 17th St NW. Phone 202/357-2700. **Free.**

★ **Smithsonian Institution.** The majority of Smithsonian museums are located on the National Mall. Smithsonian headquarters are located in the Smithsonian Institution Building, the "Castle" (1855), located at 1000 Jefferson Dr SW, on the Mall. The headquarters contain administrative offices, Smithson's crypt and the Smithsonian Information Center, which has information on all Smithsonian museums. Many visitors begin their day here. (All buildings open daily; closed Dec 25; Anacostia Museum and National Zoo hrs vary) For general information and schedule phone 202/357-2700. **Free.** Smithsonian museums on the Mall include

National Museum of Natural History. Gems (including Hope Diamond), minerals; botanical, zoological and geological materials; live insect "zoo"; Dinosaur Hall, Discovery Room, with hand-on activities for children; living coral reef; cultures of Africa, Asia, the Pacific and the Americas are explored; Western civilization is traced to its roots. Cafeteria. Special Exhibition Hall. Constitution Ave, between 9th & 12th Sts NW. **Donation.** To the west is

National Museum of American History. Cultural and technological development of the US; Star-Spangled Banner; glass exhibit; numismatic exhibit; political history exhibits; gowns of First Ladies; interactive video stations; ship models; Railroad Hall. Cafeteria, snack bar, ice cream parlor. Constitution Ave, between 12th & 14th Sts NW. **Donation.** Across the Mall is

Freer Gallery. Asian art with objects dating from Neolithic period to the early 20th century. Also works by late 19th- and early 20th-century American artists, including a major collection of James McNeill Whistler's work, highlighted by the famous Peacock Room. Jefferson Dr at 12th St SW. Phone 202/357-2700. Next to the Freer is the Smithsonian Institution Building, or "the Castle." **Free.** Connected to the Freer is the

Arthur M. Sackler Gallery. Changing exhibitions of Asian art, both Near- and Far-Eastern, from major national and international collections. Permanent collection includes Chinese and South and Southeast Asian art objects presented by Arthur Sackler. **Free.** Between the Freer Gallery and the Arts and Industries Building is the **Enid A. Haupt Garden,** four acres that comprise the "roof" of the Sackler Gallery, the International Gallery, an underground Smithsonian research and education complex and 1050 Independence Ave SW.

National Museum of African Art. Devoted to collection, study, research and exhibition of African art. The museum collection, numbering about 6,000 objects, is a primary source for the study of African art and culture; highlighted by traditional arts of sub-Saharan Africa, including collection of utilitarian ojects. Guided tours by appt. 950 Independence Ave SW. **Free.** To the east is

Arts and Industries Building. The south hall contains the Experimental Gallery, an exhibit space dedicated to innovative and creative exhibits from museums in the Smithsonian and from around the world. Discovery Theater (fee) hosts performances for children. 900 Jefferson Dr SW. **Free.** Directly to the east is

Hirshhorn Museum and Sculpture Garden. Modern, circular museum houses a collection of more than 6,000 works of art donated by Joseph H. Hirshhorn. Emphasis on contemporary art, as well as 19th- and 20th-century painting and sculpture. Sculpture garden is on the Mall, between 7th & 9th Sts SW. Independence Ave, between 7th & 9th Sts SW. **Free.** Directly east is

National Air and Space Museum. Museum presents exhibits on history of aviation and space age; artifacts include the original *Kitty Hawk Flyer, Spirit of St Louis* and *Friendship 7;* also touchable moon rocks. In honor of the 500th anniversary of Columbus' voyage to the Western Hemisphere, the exhibit *Where Next, Columbus?* looks ahead to the next 500 yrs with a study of the scientific, technological, economic, ethical and political issues of future space travel. Five-story theater shows IMAX films on air and space travel (fee; for schedule phone 202/357-1686). Museum also encompasses Albert Einstein Planetarium (fee). Independence Ave, between 7th & 4th Sts SW.

For a behind-the-scenes look at the restoration of the museum's reserve collection of approx 90 aircraft, spacecraft, engines, propellers and flight-related objects, visit the **Paul E. Garber Facility** in Suitland, MD (15 mi SE via Independence Ave to Pennsylvania Ave to Silver Hill Rd). Guided tours (daily; closed Dec 25; reservations must be made two wks in advance by contacting Tour Scheduler, Office of Volunteer Services, National Air and Space Museum, Smithsonian Institution, Washington, DC 20560; phone 202/357-1400). **Free.**

★ **Thomas Jefferson Memorial** (1943). Memorial honors the 2nd President of the United States and author of both the Declaration of Independence and Bill of Rights. Tours. (Daily; closed Dec 25) *(Site to remain open to the public during restoration study.)* S edge of Tidal Basin. Phone 202/426-6841. **Free.**

★ **US Holocaust Memorial Museum.** Interprets the story of the Holocaust through modern exhibition techniques and authentic objects, including a railroad freight car used to transport Polish Jews from Warsaw, concentration camp uniforms, photographs, diaries. Visitors are taken from Hall of Witness directly to the fourth floor, and begin a chronological journey from the roots of the Holocaust to its aftermath. Changing exhibits include "Remember the Children," which interprets Holocaust events from a child's perspective. (Daily; closed Yom Kippur, Dec 25) Permanent exhibits recommended for ages 11 and over only. Entrances at Raoul

Wallenberg Place (15th St SW) and at 14th St SW. Phone 202/488-0400. **Free.**

✪ **Vietnam Veterans Memorial.** Designed by Maya Ying Lyn, the memorial's polished black granite walls are inscribed with the names of the 58,175 US citizens who died in or remain missing from the Vietnam War (a large directory helps visitors locate names). Also Statue of Three Servicemen. Built with private contributions of American citizens. (Daily) Constitution Ave between Henry Bacon Dr & 21st St NW. Phone 202/634-1568. **Free.**

Voice of America. Live radio broadcasts to foreign countries; 45-min guided tours (Mon-Fri, res required; closed major hols). 330 Independence Ave SW between 3rd & 4th Sts SW; enter on C St. Phone 202/619-3919. **Free.**

✪ **Washington Monument.** Parking lot on N side, off Constitution Ave. The obelisk, tallest masonry structure in the world (555 ft), was dedicated in 1885 to the memory of the first US president. (Daily; extended hrs in summer; closed Dec 25) Elevator to observation room at 500-ft level. To take the 898 steps up or down, arrangements must be made in advance. Mall at 15th St NW. Phone 202/426-6839 or 202/426-6841(Visitor Center). **Free.** Directly north is

✪ **The White House** (1800). Constructed under the supervision of George Washington, the house has been lived in by every president since John Adams. It was burned by the British during the War of 1812 and reconstructed under the guidance of James Monroe (1817-1825). The West Wing, which includes the oval office, was built during Theodore Roosevelt's administration (1901-1909); before its construction, executive offices shared the second floor with the president's private quarters. The interior of the White House was gutted and rebuilt, using modern construction techniques, during the Truman administration; President Truman and family resided at Blair House for four years during the reconstruction. The Library and the Vermeil Room (on Ground Floor), the East Room, Green, Blue and Red rooms and the State Dining Room (on State Floor) are accessible to public. Tours (mid-Mar-Oct, Tues-Sat mornings; tickets avail at the new White House Visitor Center, 1450 Pennsylvania Ave NW; closed Jan 1, Dec 25 and presidential functions). 1600 Pennsylvania Ave NW. Phone 202/456-7041 (recording). **Free.**

NORTHWEST

The northwest quadrant of the city is north of the Mall and west of N Capitol St. Georgetown and Embassy Row are located within this section of Washington.

Art Museum of the Americas, OAS. Dedicated to Latin American and Caribbean contemporary art; paintings, graphics, sculpture. (Tues-Sat; closed major hols) 201 18th St NW.Phone 202/458-6016. **Free.**

B'nai B'rith Klutznick Museum. Permanent exhibition of Jewish ceremonial and folk art. Changing exhibits. (Daily exc Sat; closed major Jewish hols, some legal hols) B'nai B'rith International Center, 1640 Rhode Island Ave NW. Phone 202/857-6583. **Free.**

Chinatown. Recognizable by the Chinatown Friendship Archway at 7th and H Sts. Archway is decorated in Chinese architectural styles of Qing and Ming dynasties and is topped with nearly 300 painted dragons. G & H Streets, between 6th & 8th Sts NW.

Department of State Building. The State Department's Diplomatic Reception Rooms, furnished with 18th-century American furniture and decorative art, are used by secretary of state and cabinet members for formal entertaining. Tours (Mon-Fri; closed federal hols & special events; 3-4 wks advance reservation; children over 12 yrs preferred). 21st, 22nd, C & D Sts NW. Phone 202/647-3241. **Free.**

Department of the Interior (1938). Within is museum with exhibits and dioramas depicting history and activities of the department and its various bureaus. Photo ID required. (Mon-Fri; closed major hols) Reference library open to public. 1849 C St NW, between 18th & 19th Sts NW. Phone 202/208-4743. **Free.**

Explorers Hall. National Geographic Society headquarters. Permanent science center shows the Society's explorations and exhibits on geography; Earth Station One; also a 1,100-pound, free-standing world globe 11 ft in diameter; changing exhibits. (Daily; closed Dec 25) 17th & M Sts NW. Phone 202/857-7588 (recording). **Free.**

✪ **Ford's Theatre.** Where John Wilkes Booth shot Abraham Lincoln on Apr 14, 1865. Restored as a functioning theater with Broadway and original productions offered throughout the yr. Phone 202/347-4833 for tickets. Tours (daily; closed Dec 25). 511 10th St NW. Phone 202/426-6924. Tours **Free;** Performance tickets ¢¢¢¢-¢¢¢¢¢.   In basement is

Lincoln Museum. Exhibits and displays focus on Lincoln's life and assassination. (Daily; closed Dec 25)   **Free.** Across the street is

Petersen House (House where Lincoln died). The house to where President Lincoln was carried after the shooting at Ford's Theatre; he died here the following morning. The house has been restored to its appearance at that time. (Daily; closed Dec 25) 516 10th St NW. Phone 202/426-6924.   **Free.**

Fort Stevens Park. General Jubal Early and his Confederate troops tried to invade Washington at this point on July 11 & 12, 1864. President Lincoln risked his life at the fort during the fighting. (Daily) Piney Branch Rd & Quackenbos St NW. Phone 202/282-1063.   **Free.**

General Services Administration Building (1917). Was originally Department of Interior. 18th, 19th, E & F Sts NW.

George Washington University (1821). (20,000 students) Theater; art exhibits in Dimock Gallery (Mon-Fri; closed hols) and University Library. 19th to 24th Sts NW, F St to Pennsylvania Ave. Phone 202/994-6460.

Hillwood Museum. Opulent 25-acre estate was home of Marjorie Merriweather Post, heiress to the Post cereal fortune. Collection in 20-rm house include works of 18th- and 19th-century Russian and French decorative arts; Russian collection is the most representative outside Russia. Tearoom. Tours (Tues-Sat, reservation required; closed hols and Feb). Grounds (daily). No children under 12 admitted. 4155 Linnean Ave NW. Phone 202/686-8500.   **Donation.**

Howard University (1867). (12,000 students) Main campus: 2400 6th St NW between W & Harvard Sts NW. West Campus: 2900 Van Ness St NW. Three other campuses in area. Main campus has Gallery of Fine Art, with permanent Alain Locke African Collection; changing exhibits (Sept-July, Mon-Fri). Phone 202/806-0970.

John F. Kennedy Center for the Performing Arts. Official memorial to President Kennedy. Single structure, designed by Edward Durell Stone, incorporates opera house, concert hall, AFI movie theater, Eisenhower Theatre, Terrace Theatre and Theatre Lab; two restaurants; library. Tours (daily, limited hrs). New Hampshire Ave at F St NW. Phone 202/416-8340 (tours) or 202/467-4600 (performance tickets).

Judiciary Square. Two square blocks of judiciary buildings, including five federal and district courts and the US District Court (1820) and US Court of Appeals (1910). At D St halfway between 4th & 5th Sts is the first completed statue of Abraham Lincoln (1868). D, E, & F Sts, between 4th & 5th Sts NW.

Martin Luther King Memorial Library (1972). Main branch of DC public library was designed by architect Mies van der Rohe. Martin Luther King mural. Books, periodicals, photographs, films, videocassettes, recordings, microfilms, Washingtoniana and the *Washington Star* collection. Library for the visually impaired; librarian for the hearing impaired; black studies division; AP wire service machine; community information service. Underground parking. (Mon-Sat, also Sun afternoons; closed hols) 901 G St NW. Phone 202/727-1111.   **Free.**

MCI Center. Home of the NBA's Washington Wizards and the NHL's Washington Capitals, this 220,000-sq-ft venue also has the Discovery Channel Destination, a retail and interactive store with 3 themed floors: the earth's surface, a terrestrial level, and space and sky. *An Insiders View*, a behind-the-scenes look at Washington DC and its history, shown on high-definition screen (fee). Backstage tour of entire center (fee; includes film). Also 19,000-sq-ft sports restaurant overlooking the Wizards' practice court. (Daily) 601 F St NW. Phone 301/499-6300, ext 1830. Also here is

MCI National Sports Gallery. 25,000-sq-ft museum commemorates and showcases the best of American sports history. Includes sports memorabilia collections; participatory and technology-driven exhibits with basketball, football, hockey and baseball themes. Rotating exhibits feature special-interest sports. Home of the American Sportscasters Association Hall of Fame and Museum, honoring the memorable voices that brought us our greatest sports moments. Gallery ¢¢¢

National Building Museum. Deals with architecture, design, engineering and construction. Permanent exhibits include drawings, blueprints, models, photographs, artifacts; architectural evolution of Washington's buildings and monuments. The museum's enormous Great Hall is supported by eight of the world's largest Corinthian columns. Guided tours (afternoons: wkdays, 1 tour; wkends, 2 tours). Museum (Mon-Sat; also Sun afternoons) Housed in Old Pension Building, F St between 4th & 5th Sts NW. Phone 202/272-2448. **Free.**

National Museum of American Art. American paintings, sculpture, prints and graphic art from the 18th century to the present. (Daily; closed Dec 25) 8th & G Sts NW, Gallery Place. Phone 202/357-2700. **Free.**

National Museum of Health and Medicine. One of the most important medical collections in America. Interprets the link between history and technology; AIDS education exhibit; an interactive exhibit on human anatomy and lifestyle choices; collection of microscopes, medical teaching aids, tools and instruments (1862-1965) and famous historical icons exhibits. (Daily; closed Dec 25) Bldg #54, Walter Reed Army Medical Center. Phone 202/782-2200. **Free.**

National Museum of Women in the Arts. Focus on women's contributions to history of art. More than 1,200 works by women artists from Renaissance to present. Paintings, drawings, sculpture, pottery, prints. Library, research center by appt. Guided tours (by appt). (Daily; closed Jan 1, Thanksgiving, Dec 25) 1250 New York Ave NW. Phone 202/783-5000. **Donation.**

National Portrait Gallery. Portraits and statues of people who have made significant contributions to the history, development and culture of the US. (Daily; closed Dec 25) 8th & F Sts NW. Phone 202/357-2700. **Free.**

National Presbyterian Church and Center. Chapel of the President contains memorabilia of past US presidents; faceted glass windows depict history of man and church. Self-guided tours (daily; no tours hols). Guided tours (Sun following service). 4101 Nebraska Ave NW. Phone 202/537-0800.

New York Ave Presbyterian Church. The church where Lincoln worshipped; rebuilt 1950-1951 with Lincoln's pew. Dr. Peter Marshall was pastor 1939-1949. Mementos on display include first draft of Emancipation Proclamation. (Daily, services Sun morning; closed hols) 1313 New York Ave, at H St NW. Phone 202/393-3700.

Rock Creek Park. More than 1,700 acres with working gristmill; 18-hole golf course, hiking, exercise course, historic sites, tennis courts, picnicking, self-guided nature trails, stables, bridle paths and biking trails, ball fields. Fee for some activities. NW on Beach Dr. Phone 202/282-1063. Also here are

> **National Zoological Park.** A branch of the Smithsonian Institution, the zoo features approx 5,000 animals of 500 species, including a giant panda; lions, tigers and cheetahs; great apes; elephants and rhinos; small mammals; reptiles and invertebrates; birdhouse and wetlands; rain forest exhibit. Picnicking, refreshments. Guided tours (wkends). Metrorail (Red Line) stop. Limited parking (fee). (Daily; closed Dec 25) Main entrance at 3000 blk of Connecticut Ave NW; other entrances at Beach Dr (Rock Creek Pkwy) and jct Adams Mill Rd & Harvard St. Phone 202/673-4800. **Free.**

> **Nature Center.** Planetarium, films, exhibits, nature demonstrations. (Wed-Sun; closed hols) 5200 Glover Rd NW. Phone 202/426-6829. **Free.**

> **Carter Barron Amphitheater.** This 4,200-seat outdoor theater in wooded area is setting for summer performances of symphonic, folk, pop and jazz music (see SEASONAL EVENTS) and Shakesperean theater. Some fees. 16th St & Colorado Ave NW. Phone 202/426-6837; 202/421-6486 for tickets.

> **Art Barn.** Historic carriage house (1831). Art exhibitions. (Thurs-Sun) Tilden St & Beach Dr NW. Phone 202/244-2482. **Free.**

Shops at National Place. Tri-level marketplace—at, above and below street grade—featuring more than 100 specialty shops and restaurants. (Daily) National Press Building, F St, between 13th & 14th Sts. Phone 202/783-9090.

Theaters. Shakespeare Theatre, Lansburgh Theater 450 7th St NW, phone 202/393-2700. **The National,** E St, 1 blk N of 13th & Pennsylvania Ave, phone 202/628-6161. **Arena Stage,** 6th & Maine Ave SW, phone 202/488-3300. **The Warner,** 13th & E Sts NW, phone 703/824-1525. Also see Kennedy Center.

Theodore Roosevelt Memorial. N end of Theodore Roosevelt Island, accessible only by footbridge from George Washington Memorial Pkwy, northbound lane, in Arlington, VA. The island is an 88-acre wilderness preserve; the 17-ft statue of Roosevelt was designed by Paul Manship. (Daily; closed Dec 25) Phone 703/285-2598. **Free.**

✪ **Washington National Cathedral.** Cornerstone of the Gothic cathedral was laid in 1907; final stone was set in 1990; structure, built entirely in the manner and materials of medieval cathedrals, took 83 yrs, 5 architects and the terms of 7 bishops to complete. Details are intentionally irregular to avoid uniform features typical of machine-age building. Tombs of Woodrow Wilson, Helen Keller and others are within structure. Pilgrim Observation Gallery overlooks Washington from city's highest geographic point. Within the grounds are trees grown from a cutting of England's Glastonbury Thorne, which by legend grew from the staff of Joseph of Arimathea; museum shop; Bishop's Garden, a medieval, walled garden; Herb Cottage; greenhouse with potted herbs for sale. Shops (daily). Services (daily). Carillon recitals (Sat). Organ recitals (Sun). Tours (daily). Massachusetts & Wisconsin Aves NW. Phone 202/537-6200 (recording), 202/537-6247 or -6207 (tours). **Donation.**

GEORGETOWN

Georgetown, a neighborhood within the city's northwest quadrant, is actually older than Washington. In colonial days, it was a busy commercial center along the Potomac. Today, Georgetown is an area of fine 18th- and 19th-century residences and fashionable shops and restaurants; the commercial center radiates from the intersection of Pennsylvania Ave and M St, northwest of the White House.

Chesapeake and Ohio Canal Boat Rides. Narrated round-trip canal tours (1½ hrs) by park rangers in period clothing aboard mule-drawn boats. Ticket office adj. (Mid-Apr-Oct, Wed-Sun) Departs from Lock 3, between 30th & Thomas Jefferson Sts NW. Phone 202/653-5190. ¢¢ (Also see CHESAPEAKE AND OHIO CANAL NATIONAL HISTORIC PARK in Maryland)

Dumbarton Oaks (1800). Famous gardens (16 acres) are both formal and Romantic in design. Mansion has antiques and European art, including El Greco's *The Visitation;* galleries of Byzantine art; library of rare books on gardening and horticulture. Museum of pre-Columbian artifacts housed in structure by Philip Johnson. Garden (daily; closed major hols); house and museum (Tues-Sun afternoons; closed major hols). 1703 32nd St NW; garden entrance 31st & R Sts. Phone 202/339-6400. Garden ¢¢; Museum **Donation.**

Georgetown University (1789). (12,000 students) Oldest Catholic college in US, a Jesuit school. Campus tours (daily exc Sun, by res). Main entrance 37th & O Sts NW. Phone 202/687-3600.

Old Stone House (1765). Believed to be the oldest pre-Revolutionary building in Washington. Constructed on parcel No. 3 of the original tract of land that was then Georgetown, the house was used as both a residence and a place of business; five rooms are furnished with household items that reflect a middle-class residence of the late 18th century. The grounds are lush with fruit trees and seasonal blooms. (Daily; closed hols) 3051 M St NW. Phone 202/426-6851 (also TTY service). **Free.**

St John's Church. Oldest Episcopal congregation in Georgetown, established 1796; original design of church by William Thornton, architect of the Capitol. Many presidents since Madison have worshiped here. Francis Scott Key was a founding member. Tours (by appt). 3240 O St NW. Phone 202/338-1796.

Tudor Place (1805). Twelve-rm federal-style mansion was designed by Dr. William Thornton, architect of Capitol, for Martha Custis Peter, granddaughter of Martha Washington. Peter family lived in house for 180 yrs. All furnishings and objets d'art original. More than five acres of gardens (Mon-Sat). Guided tours (Tues-Sat, by reservation; closed hols). 1644 31st St NW. Phone 202/965-0400. Garden only ¢; House and garden ¢¢

Washington Harbour. This is a dining and shopping complex that features lavish fountains, life-size statuary and a boardwalk with a view of the Potomac River. 30th & K Sts NW. Phone 202/944-4140.

Yellow House (1733). One of Georgetown's oldest homes, typical of the area's mansions. (Private residence) 1430 33rd St NW.

EMBASSY ROW

This neighborhood, within the city's northwest quadrant, is centered around Sheridan Circle, at the intersection of Massachusetts Ave and 23rd St NW. Dozens of foreign legations can be found in the area and north along Massachusetts Ave.

Dupont-Kalorama Museum Walk. This is a joining of forces of seven museums to create an awareness of the area. Information and brochures are available at any of the museums concerned. The participating museums are

Textile Museum. Founded in 1925 with the collection of George Hewitt Myers, the museum features changing exhibits of non-Western textiles, Oriental rugs and other handmade textile art. Guided tours (Sept-May, Wed, Sat, Sun; by appt). (Daily) 2320 S St NW. Phone 202/667-0441. **Free.**

Fondo del Sol. Dedicated to presenting, promoting and preserving cultures of the Americas, the museum presents exhibitions of contemporary artists and craftsmen; holds special events; hosts traveling exhibits for museums and other institutions. (Wed-Sat afternoons; closed major hols) 2112 R St NW. Phone 202/483-2777. **¢¢**

Christian Heurich Mansion (1892). Four-story, 31-rm neo-Renaissance/late Victorian mansion has elaborate furnishings and garden; houses the Historical Society of Washington, DC, and the society's Library of Washington History; changing exhibits. House tours (Wed-Sat afternoons; closed major hols). Library (Wed, Fri, Sat; closed major hols). 1307 New Hampshire Ave NW, near Dupont Circle. Phone 202/785-2068. **¢¢**

Phillips Collection. Oldest museum of modern art in the nation. Founded in 1918, the museum continues to emphasize the work of emerging as well as established international artists. Permanent collection of 19th- and 20th-century Impressionist, Post-Impressionist and modern painting and sculpture. (Daily exc Mon; closed some major hols) Introductory tours (Wed and Sat). Concerts (Sept-May, Sun). Wkday admission by donation. 1600 21st St NW. Phone 202/387-2151 or 202/387-0961. Wkend admission **¢¢¢**

Anderson House Museum. Museum of the American Revolution and national headquarters of the Society of the Cincinnati has portraits by early American artists; 18th-century paintings; 17th-century tapestries; decorative arts of Europe and Asia; displays of books, medals and swords, silver, glass and china. (Tues-Sat; closed legal hols) Free concert series. 2118 Massachusetts Ave NW. Phone 202/785-2040. **Donation.**

Woodrow Wilson House (1915). Red-brick Georgian-revival town house to which President Wilson retired after leaving office; family furnishings and gifts-of-state. A National Trust for Historic Preservation property. (Daily exc Mon; closed Jan 1, Thanksgiving, Dec 25) 2340 S St NW. Phone 202/387-4062. **¢¢**

Meridian International Center. Housed in two historic mansions designed by John Russell Pope; hosts international exhibits, concerts, lectures and symposia promoting international understanding. Period furnishings, Mortlake tapestry; gardens with linden grove. (Daily, afternoons; closed major hols) 1630 Crescent Place NW. Phone 202/939-5544. **Donation.**

Islamic Center. Leading mosque in the US has landscaped courtyard, intricate interior mosaics. (Daily; no tours during Fri prayer service) 2551 Massachusetts Ave NW. Phone ahead for appropriate dress restrictions; 202/332-8343.

NORTHEAST

The northeast quadrant of the city is north of E Capitol St and east of N Capitol St.

Basilica of the National Shrine of the Immaculate Conception. On Metro Red Line stop. Largest Roman Catholic church in US and one of largest in the world. Byzantine and Romanesque architecture; extensive and elaborate collection of mosaics and artwork. (Daily) Carillon concerts (Sun afternoons); organ recitals (June-Aug, Sun evenings). Guided tours (daily). Phone 202/526-8300.

Capital Children's Museum. Hands-on museum where children of all ages can explore exhibits on computers, human development and Mexican culture. (Daily; closed some major hols) 800 3rd St NE. Phone 202/675-4120. **¢¢¢**

Franciscan Monastery. Within the church and grounds is the "Holy Land of America"; replicas of sacred Holy Land shrines include the Manger at Bethlehem, Garden of Gethsemane and Holy Sepulchre. Also Grotto at Lourdes and Roman catacombs. Guided tours by the friars (daily). 1400 Quincy St NE. Phone 202/526-6800. **Free.**

Kenilworth Aquatic Gardens. Water lilies, lotuses, other water plants bloom from mid-May until frost. Gardens (daily). Guided walks (Memorial Day-Labor Day, Sat, Sun & hols, also by appt). Anacostia Ave & Douglas St NE. Phone 202/426-6905. **Free.**

The Catholic University of America (1887). (6,500 students) Open to all faiths. Hartke Theatre (year-round). 620 Michigan Ave NE. Phone 202/319-5000.

US National Arboretum. Floral displays spring, summer, fall and winter on 444 acres; Japanese garden, National Bonsai and Penjing Museum (daily); National Herb Garden, major collections of azaleas (15,000), wildflowers, ferns, magnolias, crabapples, cherries, dogwoods; aquatic plantings; dwarf conifers (world's largest evergreen collection). (Daily; closed Dec 25) Under 16 yrs admitted only with adult. 3501 New York Ave NE. Phone 202/544-8733. **Free.**

SOUTHEAST

The southeast quadrant of the city is south of E Capitol St and east of S Capitol St.

Anacostia Museum, Smithsonian Institution. An exhibition and research center for black heritage in the historic Anacostia section of SE Washington. Changing exhibits. (Daily; closed Dec 25) 1901 Fort Place SE. Phone 202/357-2700. **Free.**

Eastern Market. Meat, fish and produce sold. Also crafts and farmers market on wkends. (Daily exc Mon) 225 7th St SE. Phone 202/546-2698.

Emancipation Statue. Bronze work of Thomas Ball paid for by voluntary subscriptions from emancipated slaves, depicting Lincoln presenting Emancipation Proclamation to black man, was dedicated Apr 14, 1876, the 11th anniversary of Lincoln's assassination, with Fredrick Douglass in attendance. Lincoln Park, E Capitol St NE between 11th & 13th Sts NE. Also here is

Mary McLeod Bethune Memorial. Honors the noted educator and advisor to President Lincoln and founder of the National Council of Negro Women.

Fort Dupont Park. Picnicking, hiking and bicycling in hilly terrain; cultural arts performances in summer (see SEASONAL EVENTS). Also films, slides and activities including natural science; environmental education programs; nature discovery room; Junior Ranger program; programs for sr citizens and disabled persons; garden workshops and programmed activities by reservation. Randle Circle & Minnesota Aves. Phone 202/426-7723 or 202/426-7745. **Free.** Nearby is

Fort Dupont Sports Complex. Skating, ice hockey (fee); tennis courts; basketball courts; ball fields (daily; free), jogging. E on Pennsylvania Ave SE; N on Minnesota Ave; E on Ely Pl. Phone 202/584-5007 (ice rink).

Frederick Douglass National Historic Site, "Cedar Hill." This 21-rm house on 9 acres is where Douglass, a former slave who became Minister to Haiti and a leading black spokesman, lived from 1877 until his death in 1895; visitor center with film, memorabilia. (Daily; closed Jan 1, Thanksgiving, Dec 25) 1411 W St SE. Phone 202/426-5961 or 800/365-2267 (tour reservations). **¢¢**

Navy Yard. Along the Anacostia River, at a location chosen by George Washington, the yard was founded in 1799 and was nearly destroyed during the War of 1812. Outside the yard, at 636 G St SE, is the John Phillip Sousa house, where the "march king" wrote many of his famous compositions; the house is private. M St between 1st & 11th Sts SE. One blk E is

Marine Barracks. Parade ground, more than two centuries old, is surrounded by handsome and historic structures, including the Commandant's House, facing G St, which is said to be the oldest continuously occupied public building in the city. Spectacular parade is open to public Tues & Fri evenings in summer (see SEASONAL EVENTS). Entrance to Navy Yard is at end of 9th St at M St SE. Inside is G St between 8th & 9th Sts SE.

Navy Museum. History of US Navy from the American Revolution to the space age. Dioramas depict achievements of early naval heroes; displays development of naval weapons; fully rigged foremast fighting top and gun deck from frigate *Constitution* on display; World War II guns that can be trained and elevated; submarine room has operating periscopes. Approx 5,000 objects on display include paintings, ship models, flags, uniforms, naval decorations and the bathyscaphe *Trieste*. Two-acre outdoor park displays 19th- and 20th-century guns, cannon, other naval artifacts; US Navy destroyer *Barry* located on the waterfront. (Daily; closed Jan 1, Thanksgiving, Dec 24, 25) Tours (Mon-Fri) Bldg 76, Washington Navy Yard, 901 M St SE. Phone 202/433-6897 or 202/433-4882.   **Free.**   Nearby is

Marine Corps Museum. Weapons, uniforms, maps, flags, and other artifacts describe the history of the US Marine Corps. Housed in restored 19th-century structure; also used as marine barracks from 1941 to 1975. (Daily exc Tues; closed Jan 1, Dec 25) 901 M St. Phone 202/433-3840 or 202/433-3841.   **Free.**

NEARBY—IN THE AREA

Clara Barton National Historic Site. Thirty-six-rm house (1891) of unusual architecture was both the national headquarters of the Red Cross and the home of Clara Barton for the last 15 yrs of her life. Contents include many items belonging to the founder of the American Red Cross. Period costumes worn during some special programs. Guided tours only. (Daily; closed major hols) 5801 Oxford Rd, 8 mi NW in Glen Echo, MD. Phone 301/492-6245.   **Free.**

Fort Washington National Park. Earliest defense of the city (1809), the original fort was destroyed in 1814; reconstructed by 1824. View of Potomac River; picnicking; history exhibits. (Daily) 4 mi S on MD 210, 3½ mi on Fort Washington Rd in Fort Washington, MD. Phone 301/763-4600. Per vehicle ¢¢;   per person ¢

Great Falls of the Potomac. (See CHESAPEAKE AND OHIO CANAL NATIONAL HISTORICAL PARK in Maryland)

Harness racing. (Thurs-Sat) Rosecroft Raceway. 6336 Rosecroft Dr, 8 mi SE in Oxon Hill, MD. Phone 301/567-4000.   ¢

Iwo Jima Statue. Across Theodore Roosevelt Bridge on Arlington Blvd. (See ARLINGTON COUNTY in Virginia)

★ **Mount Vernon.** 18 mi S via George Washington Memorial Pkwy. (See MOUNT VERNON in Virginia)

National Colonial Farm. Approx 150 acres in Piscataway National Park. A "living history" farm of mid-18th century; crops, herb garden, livestock, methods of the period are used; replicated farm buildings. (Daily exc Mon; closed Jan 1, Thanksgiving, Dec 25) I-95 exit 3A, then 10 mi S on MD 210, right on Bryan Point Rd, 3 mi in Accokeek, MD. Phone 301/283-2113.   ¢

Oxon Hill Farm. Living history farm circa 1898-1914 located on working farm with livestock; participation activities. (Daily; closed Jan 1, Thanksgiving, Dec 25) Entrance from Oxon Hill Rd, 300 yds W of jct MD 210 & I-95 in Oxon Hill, MD. Phone 301/839-1177.   **Free.**

★ **President Kennedy's Gravesite.** South Gate, Arlington National Cemetery. (See ARLINGTON COUNTY in Virginia)

Washington Dolls' House & Toy Museum. Splendid collection of antique doll houses, dolls, toys and games; museum shop. (Daily exc Mon; closed Jan 1, Thanksgiving, Dec 25) 5236 44th St NW. Phone 202/363-6400.   ¢¢

Wild World. Thrill rides, water attractions, children's rides; wave pool; Wild One Rollercoaster. Entertainment; game gallery. Parking fee. (Mid-May-Labor Day, schedule varies) E via Capital Beltway to exit 15A, then E on Central Ave (MD 214) in Mitchellville, MD, follow signs. Phone 301/249-1500.   ¢¢¢¢

SIGHTSEEING TOURS

Gray Line bus tours. Tours of city and area attractions depart from terminal in Union Station. For information contact 5500 Tuxedo Rd, Tuxedo, MD 20781; 301/386-8300 or 800/862-1400.

Tourmobile Sightseeing. Narrated shuttle tours to 18 historic sites on the National Mall and in Arlington National Cemetery. Unlimited reboarding throughout day (daily; no tours Dec 25). Additional tours separately or in combinations: Arlington National Cemetery; Mount Vernon (Apr-Oct) and

Frederick Douglass Home (mid-June-Labor Day). Phone 202/554-7950, -5100 or -7020.   ¢¢¢¢

PROFESSIONAL SPORTS

NBA (Washington Wizards). MCI Center, 601 F St NW. Phone 301/773-2255.

NFL (Washington Redskins). Jack Kent Cooke Stadium, Landover, MD. Phone 703/478-8900.

NHL (Washington Capitals). MCI Center, 601 F St NW. Phone 301/773-2255.

Annual Events

Cherry Blossom Festival. Celebrates the blooming Japanese cherry trees. Also Japanese Lantern Lighting ceremony and marathon run; parade. Phone 202/619-7275. Late Mar-early Apr.

Easter Egg Roll. White House Lawn. First introduced to Washington by Dolley Madison. Phone 202/456-2200 (recording). Mon after Easter.

Georgetown House Tour. Held since 1927, participants view 12 well-known and less well-known houses in Georgetown. St John's Episcopal Church members serve as hosts, guides and serve tea in the Parish Hall in the afternoon. Phone 202/338-1796. Late Apr.

Georgetown Garden Tour. Fourteen or more different gardens open to the public. Proceeds go to Georgetown Children's House; includes "Evermay" garden, which features grand expanses, fountains and sculptures. Self-guided tours. Phone 202/333-4953. Late Apr or early May.

Goodwill Industries Embassy Tour. Six to eight embassies are open to the public; only time embassies are open to public; visitors can view artifacts and design peculiar to each government's legation. Complimentary refreshments and illustrated tour booklet. Walking tour with shuttle bus between embassies. Tickets limited. No children under age 10. Phone 202/636-4225. 2nd Sat May.

Memorial Day Ceremony. Arlington National Cemetery (See ARLINGTON COUNTY in Virginia). Wreaths placed at Tomb of the Unknown Soldier. The National Symphony Orchestra gives a concert later in the evening on the lawn of the Capitol.

Festival of American Folklife. The Mall. Festival of folklife traditions from America and abroad. Sponsored by the Smithsonian Institution and National Park Service. Phone 202/357-2700 or 202/619-7222. Late June-early July.

July 4 Celebration. Washington Monument and Capitol west steps. Music, celebrations.

Washington National Cathedral Open House. Washington National Cathedral. Special tours, entertainment, food; demonstrations of cathedral arts. Only day of the year when central tower is open to the public. Phone 202/537-6200. Sat nearest Sept 29.

Taste of DC. Pennsylvania Ave NW between 9th & 14th St. Selected DC restaurants offer sample-size specialities. Phone 202/724-4093. 1st wkend in Oct.

Pageant of Peace. Ellipse, S of White House. Seasonal music, caroling, the giant Christmas tree near the White House is lit by the president. Dec.

Seasonal Events

Evening Parade. US Marine Barracks, I St between 8th & 9th Sts SE. Spectacular parade with Marine Band, US Marine Drum and Bugle Corps, Color Guard, Silent Drill Team and marching companies. Written request for reservations suggested at least 3 wks in advance. Phone 202/433-6060. Tues & Fri evenings, early-May-late Aug.

Concerts. Sylvan Theater, Washington Monument grounds, June-Aug, days vary, phone 202/619-7222. US Capitol, west terrace, June-late Aug, Mon-Wed, Fri, Sun, phone 202/619-7222. Natl Gallery of Art, west garden court, Oct-June, Sun evenings; first-come basis, phone 202/842-6941. Phillips Collection, a Dupont-Kalorama museum, Sept-May, Sun, phone 202/387-2151.

Wolf Trap Farm Park for the Performing Arts. In Vienna, VA, 14 mi NW via Washington Memorial Pkwy, VA 123, US 7, then S on Towlston Rd

(Trap Rd), (VA 676), then follow signs. Phone 703/255-1900. (See FAIRFAX in Virginia) Late May-Sept (Filene Center) & mid-Oct-mid-May (Barnes Center).

Musical programs. In Carter Barron Amphitheater, Rock Creek Park. Phone 202/619-7222. Mid-June-Aug.

Fort Dupont Summer Theatre. Fort Dupont Park. Musicals, concerts, plays, dancing. Phone 202/426-7723. Fri evenings, late June-late Aug.

Washington Area Suburbs

The following suburbs and towns in the Washington, DC, area are included in the *Mobil Travel Guide.* For information on any one of them, see the individual alphabetical listing. In Virginia: Alexandria, Arlington County (National Airport Area), Fairfax, Falls Church, McLean, Springfield, Tysons Corner. In Maryland: Bethesda, Bowie, College Park, Laurel, Rockville, Silver Spring.

Airport Areas

For additional attractions and accommodations, see ARLINGTON COUNTY (NATIONAL AIRPORT AREA) and DULLES INTL AIRPORT AREA in Virginia. Also see BALTIMORE/WASHINGTON INTL AIRPORT AREA in Maryland.

City Neighborhoods

Many of the restaurants, unrated dining establishments and some lodgings listed under Washington include neighborhoods as well as exact street addresses. Geographic descriptions of these areas are given, followed by a table of restaurants arranged by neighborhood.

Adams Morgan: North of Dupont Circle; along Columbia Rd between 18th Street NW and Kalorama, NW/Kalorama Park.

Capitol Hill: Both the Hill upon which the Capitol is built (south of Constitution Ave, west of 1st Street NE and SE, north of Independence Ave and east of 1st Street NW and SW) and the surrounding area south of F Street NW and NE, west of 14th Street NE nad SE, north of the Southwest Frwy (I-395) and east of 3rd Street NW and SW.

Chinatown: Area of Downtown along G and H Streets NW between 6th and 8th Streets NW.

Downtown: South of Massachusetts Ave, west of N Capitol Street, north of Pennsylvania Ave and east of 19th Street. **North of Downtown:** North of Massachusetts Ave. **South of Downtown:** South of Independence Ave. **West of Downtown:** West of 19th St.

Dupont Circle: On and around the circle where Massachusetts, New Hampshire, Connecticut Aves and 19th and P Streets NW intersect.

Embassy Row: Area north of Dupont Circle; along Massachusetts Ave between Observatory Circle on the north and Sheridan Circle on the south.

Foggy Bottom: Area along the Potomac River south of K Street NW (US 29), west of 19th Street NW and north of Constitution Ave and I-66 interchange.

Georgetown: Northwest of Downtown; south of the Naval Observatory and W Street NW, west of Rock Creek Park and north and east of the Potomac River; area around intersection of Wisconsin Ave and M Street NW.

Kalorama: East and west of Connecticut Ave NW, south of Rock Creek Park and Calvert Street, west of Columbia Rd and north of R Street.

DISTRICT OF COLUMBIA RESTAURANTS BY NEIGHBORHOOD AREAS
(For full description, see alphabetical listings under Restaurants)

ADAMS MORGAN
Cashion's Eat Place. 1819 Columbia Rd NW
The Grill From Ipanema. 1858 Columbia Rd NW
I Matti Trattoria. 2436 18th St NW
La Fourchette. 2429 18th St NW
Meskerem. 2434 18th St NW
Miss Saigon. 1847 Columbia Rd NW
Saigonnais. 2307 18th St NW

CAPITOL HILL
The Capitol Grill. 601 Pennsylvania Ave NW
La Colline. 400 N Capitol St NW
Monocle on Capitol Hill. 107 D St NE
Two Quail. 320 Massachusetts Ave NE

CHINATOWN
Burma. 740 6th St NW
Hunan Chinatown. 624 H St NW
Mr. Yung's. 740 6th St NW
Tony Cheng's Mongolian Barbecue. 619 H St NW

DOWNTOWN
701. 701 Pennsylvania Ave NW
Bice. Indiana between 6th & 7th Aves
Bombay Club. 815 Connecticut Ave NW
Bombay Palace. 2020 K St NW
Cafe Atlántico. 405 8th St NW
Cafe Mozart. 1331 H St NW
Coco Loco. 810 7th St NW
Fran O'Brien's (The Capital Hilton Hotel). 1001 16th St NW
Georgia Brown's. 950 15th St NW
Gerard's Place. 915 15th St NW
Haad Thai. 1100 New York Ave NW
Isabella. 809 15th St NW
Jaleo. 480 7th St NW
The Jefferson (Jefferson Hotel). 16th & M Sts
Lafayette (Hay-Adams Hotel). 800 16th St NW
Les Halles. 1201 Pennsylvania Ave NW
Lespinasse (The Carlton Hotel). 923 16th St NW
Luigino. 1100 New York Ave NW
Maison Blanche/Rive Gauche. 1725 F St NW
McCormick & Schmick's. 1652 K St NW
Morrison-Clark (Morrison-Clark Inn). 1101 11th St NW
Occidental Grill. 1475 Pennsylvania Ave NW
Old Ebbitt Grill. 675 15th St NW
The Oval Room. 800 Connecticut Ave
Prime Rib. 2020 K St NW
Primi Piatti. 2013 I St NW
Red Sage. 605 14th St NW
Taberna del Alabardero. 1776 I St NW
Thai Kingdom. 2021 K St NW
Willard Room (Willard Inter-Continental Hotel). 1401 Pennsylvania Ave NW

NORTH OF DOWNTOWN
Armand's Chicago Pizzeria. 4231 Wisconsin Ave NW
Coppi's Vigorelli. 3421 Connecticut Ave NW
Fio's. 3636 16th St
Guapo's. 4515 Wisconsin Ave NW
Krupin's. 4620 Wisconsin Ave NW
Lavandou. 3321 Connecticut Ave NW
Lebanese Taverna. 2641 Connecticut Ave NW
Murphy's of D.C. 2609 24th St NW,
New Heights. 2317 Calvert St NW
Old Europe Restaurant & Rathskeller. 2434 Wisconsin Ave NW
Petitto's Ristorante d'Italia. 2653 Connecticut Ave NW
Saigon Gourmet. 2635 Connecticut Ave NW
Sushi Ko. 2309 Wisconsin Ave NW
Thai Taste. 2606 Connecticut Ave NW

SOUTH OF DOWNTOWN
Hogate's. 9th St & Maine Ave SW
Market Inn. 200 E St SW
Phillips Flagship. 900 Water St SW

WEST OF DOWNTOWN
Goldoni. 1113 23rd St NW
Melrose (Park Hyatt Hotel). 24th & M St NW
Provence. 2401 Pennsylvania Ave NW

DUPONT CIRCLE
Anna Maria's. 1737 Connecticut Ave
Bacchus. 1827 Jefferson Place NW
Be Du Ci. 2100 P St NW
Blue Plate. 2002 P St NW
Bua. 1635 P St NW
C.F. Folks. 1225 19th St NW
Cafe Parma. 1724 Connecticut Ave NW
Gabriel (Radisson Barcelo Hotel). 2121 P St NW
Kramerbooks & Afterwords. 1517 Connecticut Ave
Lauriol Plaza. 1801 18th St NW
Nora. 2132 Florida Ave NW
Obelisk. 2029 P St NW
Palm. 1225 19th St NW
Pesce. 2016 P St NW
Pizzeria Paradiso. 2029 P St NW
Raku. 1900 Q St NW
Sam & Harry's. 1200 19th St NW
Vidalia. 1990 M St NW
Vincenzo al Sole. 1606 20th St NW

EMBASSY ROW
Jockey Club (Luxury Collection Hotel). 2100 Massachusetts Ave NW

FOGGY BOTTOM
Aquarelle (The Watergate Hotel). 2650 Virginia Ave NW
Galileo. 1110 21st St NW
Kinkead's. 2000 Pennsylvania Ave NW
Roof Terrace. 2700 F St NW
Sholl's Colonial Cafeteria. 1990 K St NW
Zuki Moon. 824 New Hampshire Ave NW

GEORGETOWN
1789. 1226 36th St NW
Aditi. 3299 M St NW
Austin Grill. 2404 Wisconsin Ave NW
Billy Martin's Tavern. 1264 Wisconsin Ave NW
Bistro Francais. 3128 M St NW
Bistrot Lepic. 1736 Wisconsin Ave NW
Busara. 2340 Wisconsin Ave NW
Cafe Milano. 3251 Prospect St NW
Citronelle (The Latham Hotel). 3000 M St NW
Clyde's. 3236 M St NW
El Caribe. 3288 M St
Filomena Ristorante. 1063 Wisconsin Ave NW
Garrett's. 3003 M St NW
Germaine's. 2400 Wisconsin Ave NW
Guards. 2915 M St NW
J Paul's. 3218 M St NW
La Chaumière. 2813 M St NW
Morton's of Chicago. 3251 Prospect St NW
Mr. Smith's. 3104 M St NW
Music City Roadhouse. 1050 30th St NW
Nathans. 3150 M St NW
Paolo's. 1303 Wisconsin Ave NW
Patisserie-Cafe Didier. 3206 Grace St NW
Sarinah Satay House. 1338 Wisconsin Ave NW
Sea Catch. 1054 31st St NW
Seasons (Four Seasons Hotel). 2800 Pennsylvania Ave NW
Sequoia. 3000 K St NW
The Tombs. 1226 36th St NW
Tony and Joe's. 3000 K St NW
Zed's Ethiopian. 3318 M St NW

Note: When a listing is located in a town that does not have its own city heading, it will appear under the city nearest to its location. In these cases, the address and town appear in parenthesis immediately following the name of the establishment.

Motor Hotels

★ ★ **CHANNEL INN.** *650 Water St SW (20024) on waterfront, south of downtown. 202/554-2400; FAX 202/863-1164; res: 800/368-5668.*

Web www.channelinn.com. 100 rms, 3 story. S, D $115-$145; each addl $10; suites $145-$175; under 13 free; wkend rates. Crib free. TV; cable (premium). Pool; lifeguard. Restaurant 7 am-11 pm; Sun to 9 pm. Rm serv. Bar 11:30-1 am; Fri, Sat to 2 am; Sun to 10 pm; entertainment. Ck-out noon. Meeting rms. In-rm modem link. Bellhops. Garage parking. Health club privileges. Balconies. Near piers. Cr cds: A, C, D, DS, JCB, MC, V.

[D] [≈] [🔥] [SC]

✔★ ★ **HOWARD JOHNSON PREMIER HOTEL.** *2601 Virginia Ave NW (20037) in Foggy Bottom. 202/965-2700; FAX 202/337-5417.* 192 rms, 8 story. Mid-Mar-Oct: S, D $89-$159; each addl $10; under 18 free; lower rates rest of yr. Crib free. TV; cable (premium). Rooftop pool; lifeguard (Memorial Day-Labor Day). Restaurant 6 am-11 pm. Fri, Sat 24 hrs. Ck-out noon. Coin lndry. Meeting rm. Business servs avail. In-rm modem link. Gift shop. Exercise equipt; rower, treadmill. Refrigerators. Some balconies. Cr cds: A, C, D, DS, JCB, MC, V.

[D] [≈] [🏃] [✈] [🔥] [SC]

★ **WINDSOR PARK.** *2116 Kalorama Rd NW (20008) off Connecticut Ave & 21st St, in Kalorama. 202/483-7700; FAX 202/332-4547; res: 800/247-3064.* 43 rms, 5 story, 6 suites. S $88-$98; D $98-$108; each addl $10; suites $125-$155; under 16 free; wkend rates (2-day min). TV; cable (premium). Complimentary continental bkfst. Restaurant nearby. Ck-out noon. Business servs avail. Refrigerators. Cr cds: A, C, D, DS, MC, V.

[✈] [🔥] [SC]

Hotels

★ ★ ★ **ANA.** *2401 M St NW (20037), west of downtown. 202/429-2400; FAX 202/457-5010; res: 800/262-4683.* 415 rms, 10 story. S, D $280-$310; each addl $30; suites $695-$1,650; under 18 free; wkend, summer rates. Crib free. Covered parking; valet $19. Pet accepted, some restrictions. TV; cable (premium), VCR avail. Indoor pool; whirlpool. Restaurant 6:30 am-11 pm. Rm serv 24 hrs. Bar 4 pm-midnight; entertainment. Ck-out 1 pm. Convention facilities. Business center. In-rm modem link. Concierge. Gift shop. Local shopping transportation. Exercise rm; instructor, weight machines, bicycles, sauna, steam rm. Massage. Squash, racquetball courts. Bathrm phones, refrigerators, minibars. Some balconies. Luxury level. Cr cds: A, C, D, DS, JCB, MC, V.

[D] [✔] [≈] [🏃] [✈] [🔥] [SC] [🚶]

★ ★ **THE CANTERBURY.** *1733 N St NW (20036), downtown, off Dupont Circle. 202/393-3000; FAX 202/785-9581; res: 800/424-2950.* 99 kit. units, 10 story. S $140-$195; D $160-$215; each addl $20; under 12 free; wkend plans. Crib free. Garage $13. TV; cable (premium), VCR avail. Complimentary continental bkfst. Complimentary coffee in rms. Restaurant 7 am-2:30 pm, 5-10 pm. wkend hrs vary. Bar 5-10 pm. Ck-out noon. Meeting rms. Business servs avail. In-rm modem link. Health club privileges. Refrigerators, microwaves. On site of "Little White House," where Theodore Roosevelt lived during his vice-presidency and first weeks of his presidency. Cr cds: A, C, D, DS, JCB, MC, V.

[✈] [🔥] [SC]

★ ★ ★ **THE CAPITAL HILTON.** *16th & K St NW (20036), downtown. 202/393-1000; FAX 202/639-5784.* Web www.hilton.com. 544 rms, 15 story. S $195-$275; D $220-$300; each addl $25; suites $495-$1,100; family, wkend rates; package plans. Crib free. TV; cable (premium). Restaurants 6:30 am-midnight (also see FRAN O'BRIEN'S). Rm serv 24 hrs. Bar 11-2 am; entertainment Tues-Sat. Ck-out noon. Convention facilities. Business center. In-rm modem link. Concierge. Shopping arcade. Barber, beauty shop. Valet parking 24 hrs. Exercise equipt; weights, bicycles, sauna. Minibars; many wet bars; some refrigerators. Luxury level. Cr cds: A, C, D, DS, JCB, MC, V.

[D] [🏃] [✈] [🔥] [SC] [🚶]

★ **CAPITOL HILL SUITES.** *200 C St SE (20003), on Capitol Hill. 202/543-6000; FAX 202/547-2608; res: 800/424-9165.* 152 kit rms, 5 story. Feb-June: S $139; D $149; each addl $20; suites $169; under 18 free; lower rates rest of yr. Crib free. Valet parking $12. TV; cable (premium), VCR avail. Complimentary continental bkfst. Coffee in rms. Restaurant nearby. Ck-out noon. Meeting rms. Business servs avail. Valet serv. Health club privileges. Refrigerators. Cr cds: A, D, DS, MC, V.

🚱 ♨ SC

★ ★ ★ **THE CARLTON.** *923 16th St NW (20006), downtown.* *202/638-2626; FAX 202/638-4231.* Web www.sheraton.com. 192 rms, 8 story. S $260-$310; D $285-$350; each addl $25; suites $550-$2,100; under 18 free; wkend rates. Crib free. Pet accepted, some restrictions. Covered valet parking $22. TV; cable (premium), VCR avail. Pool privileges. Restaurant (see LESPINASSE). Afternoon tea 3-5:30 pm. Rm serv 24 hrs. Bar. Ck-out 1 pm. Meeting rms. Business servs avail. In-rm modem link. Concierge. Gift shop. Tennis privileges. Exercise equipt; bicycles, treadmill. Health club privileges. Bathrm phones, refrigerators, minibars; microwaves avail. Italian Renaissance mansion with courtyard terrace. Cr cds: A, C, D, DS, ER, JCB, MC, V.

D 🐾 🎿 ✈ 🚱 ♨ SC

★ ★ **COURTYARD BY MARRIOTT.** *1900 Connecticut Ave NW (20009), in Kalorama.* 202/332-9300; FAX 202/328-7039; res: 800/842-4211. 147 rms, 9 story. S $69-$170; D $69-$200; each addl $15; under 18 free; wkend rates (2-day min). Crib free. Garage parking, valet $10. TV; cable (premium), VCR avail. Pool; lifeguard. Coffee in rms. Restaurant 7-10:30 am, 5-10 pm. Bar 5-11 pm. Ck-out noon. Coin lndry. Meeting rms. Business servs avail. In-rm modem link. Exercise equipt; treadmill, stair machine. Some minibars. Cr cds: A, C, D, DS, MC, V.

D ✈ 🚱 ♨ SC

✔ ★ **DAYS PREMIER-CONVENTION CENTER.** *1201 K St NW (20005), downtown.* 202/842-1020; FAX 202/289-0336. E-mail 10545. 2452@compuserve.com. 219 rms, 9 story. Mar-May, Aug-Oct: S, D $75-$175; each addl $10; family, wkend rates; higher rates Cherry Blossom Festival; lower rates rest of yr. Crib free. Garage $12. Pet accepted, some restrictions. TV; cable (premium). Pool; lifeguard. Restaurant 7 am-10 pm; Sat, Sun 7-10:30 am, 5-10 pm. Bar. Ck-out noon. Coin lndry. Meeting rms. Business servs avail. In-rm modem link. Sundries. Exercise equipt; weight machines, treadmill. Microwaves avail. Cr cds: A, C, D, DS, JCB, MC, V.

D 🐾 ✈ 🚱 ♨ SC

★ **DOUBLETREE GUEST SUITES.** *2500 Pennsylvania Ave NW (20037), in Foggy Bottom.* 202/333-8060; FAX 202/338-3818. Web www.doubletree.com. 123 kit. suites, 10 story. S $109-$169; D $109-$184; each addl $15; under 18 free. Crib free. Pet accepted; $12/day. Garage $15. TV; cable (premium). Coffee in rms. Restaurant adj 11 am-midnight. Ck-out noon. Business servs avail. In-rm modem link. Health club privileges. Microwaves. Cr cds: A, C, D, DS, MC, V.

🐾 ♨ SC

★ ★ **DOUBLETREE PARK TERRACE.** *1515 Rhode Island Ave NW (20005), in Embassy Row area.* 202/232-7000; FAX 202/332-7152. Web www.doubletreehotels.com. 220 rms, 8 story, 40 suites. S $155-$175; D $175-$195; each addl $20; suites $185-$225; higher rates Apr-June, Sept-mid Nov; under 16 free. Crib free. Valet parking $12.50. TV; cable (premium). Pool privileges. Complimentary coffee in rms. Restaurant 6 am-11 pm. Rm serv 24 hrs. Bar from 4 pm. Ck-out noon. Coin lndry. Meeting rms. Business servs avail. In-rm modem link. Gift shop. Exercise equipt; weight machine, treadmill. Health club privileges. Minibars; microwaves avail. Cr cds: A, C, D, DS, JCB, MC, V.

D ✈ 🚱 ♨ SC

★ **DUPONT PLAZA.** *1500 New Hampshire Ave NW (20036), in Dupont Circle area.* 202/483-6000; FAX 202/328-3265; res: 800/841-0003. 314 rms, 8 story. S $155-$205; D $175-$215; each addl $20; suites $205-$385; under 18 free; wkend rates. Crib free. Garage $15; valet parking. TV; cable (premium). Coffee in rms. Restaurant 6:30 am-11 pm; Fri, Sat to midnight. Bar 11-1 am. Ck-out 1 pm. Meeting rms. Business servs avail. In-rm modem link. Health club privileges. Bathrm phones, refrigerators, wet bars. Cr cds: A, C, D, DS, MC, V.

D 🚱 ♨ SC

★ ★ **EMBASSY SQUARE SUITES.** *2000 N St NW (20036), in Dupont Circle area.* 202/659-9000; FAX 202/429-9546; res: 800/424-2999.

E-mail emsgreserv@staydc.com; web www.staydc.com. 265 units, 10 story, 127 suites. Mar-mid-June, mid-Sept-mid-Nov: S $139-$250; D $159-$279; each addl $20; under 18 free; wkly, wkend rates; lower rates rest of yr. Crib free. Garage $12. TV; cable (premium). Pool; lifeguard. Complimentary continental bkfst; afternoon refreshments. Ck-out noon. Coin lndry. Meeting rms. Business servs avail. In-rm modem link. Exercise equipt; bicycles, stair machine. Health club privileges. Microwaves. Some balconies. Cr cds: A, C, D, DS, ER, JCB, MC, V.

D ≈ ✈ 🚱 ♨ SC

★ ★ **EMBASSY SUITES.** *1250 22nd St NW (20037), west of downtown.* 202/857-3388; FAX 202/293-3173. Web www.embassy dc.com. 318 suites, 9 story. S $159-$219; D $179-$239; each addl $20; 2-bedrm suites $500-$900; under 16 free; wkend rates. Crib free. Parking avail. TV; cable (premium). Indoor pool; whirlpool, lifeguard. Complimentary full bkfst. Complimentary coffee in rms. Restaurant 11 am-11 pm. Bar. Ck-out noon. Meeting rms. Business center. In-rm modem link. Concierge. Exercise equipt; weight machine, bicycles, sauna. Health club privileges. Game rm. Refrigerators, microwaves, wet bars. Cr cds: A, C, D, DS, JCB, MC, V.

D ≈ ✈ 🚱 ♨ SC 🏃

★ ★ **EMBASSY SUITES CHEVY CHASE PAVILION.** *4300 Military Rd NW (20015), north of downtown.* 202/362-9300; FAX 202/686-3405. Web www.embassy-suites.com. 198 suites, 8 story. Mar-Oct: S, D $160-$200; each addl $15; wkend rates; lower rates rest of yr. Crib avail. Garage $10. TV; cable (premium). Indoor pool. Complimentary full bkfst. Complimentary coffee in rms. Rm serv 11:30 am-10 pm. Ck-out noon. Coin lndry. Meeting rms. Business servs avail. Exercise rm; instructor, weights, stair machines. Refrigerators, microwaves, wet bars. Atrium. Connected to shopping center. Cr cds: A, C, D, DS, MC, V.

D ≈ ✈ 🚱 ♨ SC

★ ★ ★ **FOUR SEASONS.** *2800 Pennsylvania Ave NW (20007), in Georgetown.* 202/342-0444; FAX 202/944-2076. E-mail seasons @erols.com; web www.fshr.com. This highly efficient, midsize hotel on the edge of Georgetown has a strong dedication to guest service. Rooms, some of which have park views, are comfortably furnished and well-lighted. 196 rms, 6 story. S $320-$365; D $350-$395; each addl $30; suites $750-$2,400; under 18 free; wkend rates. Crib free. Pet accepted. Valet parking $22. TV; cable (premium), VCR avail (movies). Restaurant 7-2 am (also see SEASONS). Rm serv 24 hrs. Afternoon tea. Bar from 11 am. Ck-out noon. Meeting rms. Business center. In-rm modem link. Concierge. Exercise rm; instructor, weight machine, bicycles, steam rm. Spa. Bathrm phones, minibars; microwaves avail. Some balconies. Cr cds: A, C, D, ER, JCB, MC, V.

D 🐾 ≈ ✈ 🚱 ♨ 🏃

★ **GEORGETOWN DUTCH INN.** *1075 Thomas Jefferson St NW (20007), in Georgetown.* 202/337-0900; FAX 202/333-6526; res: 800/388-2410. 47 kit. suites, 7 story. Feb-mid-June, Sept-mid-Nov: S $135-$165; D $145-$180; each addl $20; suites $250-$350; under 16 free; wkly, monthly rates; higher rates Cherry Blossom season; lower rates rest of yr. Crib free. TV; cable (premium). Complimentary continental bkfst. Ck-out noon. Business servs avail. In-rm modem link. Limited free covered parking. Health club privileges. Bathrm phones. Cr cds: A, C, D, MC, V.

🚱 ♨ SC

★ ★ **GEORGETOWN INN.** *1310 Wisconsin Ave NW (20007), in Georgetown.* 202/333-8900; FAX 202/625-1744; res: 800/424-2979. 96 rms, 6 story, 10 suites. S, D $195-$225; each addl $20; suites $275-$325; under 13 free; wkend, hol rates. Crib free. Valet parking $15. TV; cable (premium), VCR avail. Restaurant 6:30 am-2 pm, 5-11 pm. Bar 11-1 am. Ck-out noon. Meeting rms. Business servs avail. In-rm modem link. Exercise equipt; treadmill, stair machine. Refrigerators avail. Cr cds: A, C, D, DS, JCB, MC, V.

D ✈ 🚱 ♨ SC

★ **GOVERNOR'S HOUSE.** *1615 Rhode Island Ave (20036), at 17th Street NW & Scott Circle, downtown.* 202/296-2100; FAX 202/331-0227; res: 800/821-4367. 149 units, 9 story, 24 kits. Mar-June, Sept-Oct: S $125-$195; D $140-$210; each addl $15; suites $175-$225; kit. units

$145-$155; under 16 free; wkend, monthly rates; higher rates Cherry Blossom Festival; lower rates rest of yr. Crib free. Valet parking $14. TV; cable (premium). Pool; lifeguard. Restaurant 7 am-midnight. Bar from 11:30 am. Ck-out noon. Meeting rms. Business servs avail. In-rm modem link. Exercise equipt; weight machine, treadmill. Health club privileges. Microwaves avail. On original site of Governor of Pennsylvania's house. Cr cds: A, C, D, DS, JCB, MC, V.

D ⊠ 🏊 🏃 ⊠ 🍴 SC

★ ★ ★ **GRAND HYATT WASHINGTON.** *1000 H St NW (20001), opp Washington Convention Center, downtown. 202/582-1234; FAX 202/637-4781.* Web www.travelweb.com/hyatt.html. 888 rms, 12 story. S $199-$239, D $224-$264; each addl $25; suites $425-$1,500; under 18 free; wkend rates. Crib free. Garage in/out $12. TV; cable (premium), VCR avail. Indoor pool; whirlpool. Restaurant 6:30-1 am. Bar; entertainment. Ck-out noon. Convention facilities. Business center. In-rm modem link. Gift shop. Exercise rm; instructor, weights, bicycles, steam rm, sauna. Minibars. 12-story atrium lobby; 3-story cascading waterfall. Luxury level. Cr cds: A, C, D, DS, JCB, MC, V.

D ⊠ 🏊 🏃 ⊠ 🔥 SC 🧖

★ ★ **HAMPSHIRE.** *1310 New Hampshire Ave NW (20036), at N & 20th St, in Dupont Circle area. 202/296-7600; FAX 202/293-2476; res: 800/368-5691.* Web www.expedia.msn.com. 82 rms, 10 story. Mid-Mar-June, early Sept-mid-Nov: S $189; D $209; each addl $20; under 12 free; wkend, monthly rates; lower rates rest of yr. Crib free. Valet parking $12. TV; cable (premium). Complimentary coffee in rms. Restaurant 7 am-10 pm. Bar. Ck-out noon. Meeting rms. Business center. In-rm modem link. Health club privileges. Refrigerators, microwaves, minibars. Some balconies. Cr cds: A, C, D, DS, JCB, MC, V.

⊠ 🔥 SC 🧖

★ ★ **HAY-ADAMS.** *800 16th St NW (20006), opp White House, downtown. 202/638-6600; FAX 202/638-2716; res: 800/424-5054.* 143 rms, 8 story. S, D $275-$475; each addl $30; suites $550-$2,250; under 13 free; wkend rates. Pet accepted, some restrictions. TV; cable (premium). Restaurant (see LAFAYETTE). Rm serv 24 hrs. Bar 4:30 pm-midnight; Fri, Sat to 1 am. Ck-out noon. Business servs avail. In-rm modem link. Meeting rms. Concierge. Valet parking $20. Health club privileges. Bathrm phones; some refrigerators, minibars, fireplaces; microwaves avail. Some balconies. Cr cds: A, C, D, ER, JCB, MC, V.

🍴 ⊠ 🔥

★ ★ ★ **HENLEY PARK.** *926 Massachusetts Ave NW (20001), 1 blk from Washington Convention Center, downtown. 202/638-5200; FAX 202/638-6740; res: 800/222-8474.* 96 rms, 8 story. Mar-May, Oct-Nov: S $165-$235; D $185-$255; each addl $20; suites $295-$875; under 16 free; wkend rates; lower rates rest of yr. Crib free. Valet parking $16. TV; cable (premium). Restaurant 7-10:30 am, 11:30 am-2 pm, 6-10 pm. Rm serv 24 hrs. Bar 11-12:30 am; entertainment. Ck-out noon. Meeting rms. Business servs avail. In-rm modem link. Health club privileges. Bathrm phones, refrigerators, minibars. Wet bar in suites. Tudor detailing; 1918 structure. Cr cds: A, C, D, DS, MC, V.

⊠ 🧖 SC

★ ★ **HILTON-EMBASSY ROW.** *2015 Massachusetts Ave (20036), in Embassy Row. 202/265-1600.* 195 rms, 9 story. Mar-mid-June, Sept-mid-Nov: S $195-$235; D $215-$255; each addl $20; suites $350-$500; under 17 free; family, wkend, wkly, hol rates; higher rates special events; lower rates rest of yr. Crib free. Valet parking $14. TV; cable (premium), VCR avail. Complimentary coffee in rms. Restaurant 6:30 am-11 pm. Rm serv 24 hrs. Bar 11:30-1 am; entertainment. Ck-out noon. Meeting rms. Business center. In-rm modem link. Concierge. Free guest lndry. Exercise equipt; bicycles, treadmills. Pool; poolside serv, lifeguard. Many bathrm phones; some refrigerators, microwaves, wet bars. Cr cds: A, C, D, DS, MC, V.

D ⊠ 🏊 🏃 ⊠ 🔥 SC 🧖

★ **HOLIDAY INN GEORGETOWN.** *2101 Wisconsin Ave NW (20007), in Georgetown. 202/338-4600; FAX 202/333-6113.* 296 rms, 7 story. S $110-$140; D $120-$149; each addl $10; suites $175; under 18 free. Crib free. Parking in/out $10. TV; cable (premium). Pool; lifeguard.

Restaurant 6:30 am-2 pm; 5-10 pm. Bar 4-11 pm. Ck-out noon. Coin lndry. Meeting rms. Business servs avail. In-rm modem link. Gift shop. Exercise equipt; weight machine, treadmill. Refrigerators avail. Cr cds: A, C, D, DS, JCB, MC, V.

D ⊠ 🏊 🏃 ⊠ 🧖 SC

✔ ★ ★ **HOLIDAY INN ON THE HILL.** *415 New Jersey Ave NW (20001), on Capitol Hill. 202/638-1616; FAX 202/638-0707.* 342 rms, 10 story. Feb-May, Sept-Nov: S, D $99-$169; each addl $10; suites $198-$475; under 18 free; wkend rates; lower rates rest of yr. Crib free. Pet accepted, some restrictions. TV; cable (premium). Rooftop pool; poolside serv, lifeguard. Supervised evening child's activities (Memorial Day-Labor Day); ages 4-14. Restaurant 6:30 am-midnight. Bar 11-2 am. Ck-out noon. Business servs avail. In-rm modem link. Sundries. Covered parking. Exercise equipt; bicycles, stair machine. Cr cds: A, C, D, DS, JCB, MC, V.

D 🏃 ⊠ 🏊 🏃 ⊠ 🧖 SC

★ ★ **HOLIDAY INN-CAPITOL.** *550 C St SW (20024), 2 blks from Mall museums, south of downtown. 202/479-4000; FAX 202/479-4353.* 529 rms, 9 story. S, D $160; suites $209-$289; under 18 free; wkend packages. Crib free. Garage $10. TV; cable (premium). Pool; lifeguard. Restaurant 6 am-10 pm. Bar 11-1 am. Ck-out noon. Coin lndry. Convention facilities. Business servs avail. In-rm modem link. Exercise equipt; bicycles, treadmill. Microwaves avail. Cr cds: A, C, D, DS, JCB, MC, V.

D ⊠ 🏊 🏃 ⊠ 🧖 SC

✔ ★ ★ **HOLIDAY INN-CENTRAL.** *1501 Rhode Island Ave NW (20005), north of downtown. 202/483-2000; FAX 202/797-1078.* E-mail holiday@inn-dc.com; web www.inn-dc.com. 213 rms, 10 story. Apr-May & Oct: S, D $89-$149; family, wkly, wkend rates; lower rates rest of yr. Crib free. Covered parking $10. TV; cable (premium). Pool; lifeguard. Coffee in lobby. Restaurant 6:30 am-5 pm. Rm serv to 10 pm. Bar to 10 pm. Ck-out noon. Free guest lndry. Meeting rms. Business servs avail. In-rm modem link. Gift shop. Exercise equipt; weight machine, stair machine. Game rm. Some refrigerators. Balconies. Cr cds: A, C, D, DS, JCB, MC, V.

D ⊠ 🏊 🏃 ⊠ 🧖 SC

✔ ★ **HOTEL HARRINGTON.** *11th & E Sts NW (20004), downtown. 202/628-8140; res: 800/424-8532; FAX 202/343-3924.* E-mail reservations@hotel-harrington.com; web www.hotel-harrington.com. 260 rms, 11 story, 29 suites. Mar-Oct: S $72-$78; D $78-$88; each addl $5; suites $109; under 16 free; family, wkend, wkly, hol rates; lower rates rest of yr. Crib free. Pet accepted, some restrictions. Garage $6.50/day. TV; cable (premium). Restaurants 7 am-midnight. Bar from 11 am. Ck-out noon. Meeting rm. Business servs avail. Gift shop. Barber. Coin lndry. Refrigerators avail. Cr cds: A, D, DS, JCB, MC, V.

D 🏃 ⊠ 🧖 SC

★ ★ ★ **HOTEL SOFITEL.** *1914 Connecticut Ave NW (20009), in Kalorama area. 202/797-2000; FAX 202/462-0944; res: 800/424-2464.* 144 units, 9 story, 40 suites. S $225-$245; D $245-$265; each addl $20; suites $275; under 12 free; wkend rates. Crib free. Pet accepted; $50 deposit. Garage parking; valet $15. TV; cable (premium). Restaurant 6:30 am-10:30 pm. Rm serv 24 hrs. Bar noon-11:30 pm; Fri, Sat to 1 am; pianist. Meeting rms. Business servs avail. In-rm modem link. Concierge. Exercise equipt; rower, treadmill. Bathrm phones, minibars, microwaves avail. Refurbished apartment building; built 1904. Cr cds: A, C, D, JCB, MC, V.

🏃 🍴 ⊠ 🔥 SC

★ ★ **HOWARD JOHNSON.** *1430 Rhode Island Ave NW (20005), downtown. 202/462-7777; FAX 202/332-3519.* 184 units, 10 story, 158 kit. units. S $109-$129; D $119-$139; each addl $10; under 18 free; wkend rates. Crib free. Garage parking; valet $10. TV; cable (premium). Pool; lifeguard. Restaurant 7 am-2:30 pm, 5-10:30 pm. Bar 5-11 pm. Ck-out noon. Coin lndry. Business servs avail. In-rm modem link. Health club privileges. Exercise equipt; weight machine, bicycle. Game rm. Microwaves avail. Cr cds: A, C, D, DS, JCB, MC, V.

D ⊠ 🏊 🏃 ⊠ 🧖 SC

★ ★ ★ **HYATT REGENCY WASHINGTON ON CAPITOL HILL.** *400 New Jersey Ave NW (20001), 2 blks N of Capitol. 202/737-1234; FAX*

202/737-5773. E-mail pr@hyattdc.com; web www.hyatt.com. 834 rms, 11 story. S $210; D $235; each addl $25; under 18 free. Crib free. Garage $16. TV; cable (premium). Indoor pool. Restaurants 6:30 am-11 pm. Bar 11-2 am. Ck-out noon. Meeting rms. Business center. In-rm modem link. Concierge. Gift shop. Barber, beauty shop. Exercise rm; instructor, weight machines, bicycles, sauna. Minibars; some refrigerators; microwaves avail. Luxury level. Cr cds: A, C, D, DS, JCB, MC, V.

D ≈ 🏊 ✗ 🏋 ➶ SC 🛶

★ ★ ★ **J.W. MARRIOTT.** 1331 Pennsylvania Ave NW (20004), at National Place, 2 blks E of White House, downtown. 202/393-2000; FAX 202/626-6991. Web www.marriott.com/marriott/dc-042.htm. 772 rms, 12 story. S, D $214-$239; each addl $20; suites $275-$1,550; Mar-June, Sept-Nov higher rates; lower rates rest of year; family, wkend rates. Crib free. Limited valet parking $16. TV; cable (premium). Indoor pool; whirlpool. Restaurant 7 am-11 pm. Rm serv 24 hrs. Bars; entertainment. Ck-out noon. Convention facilities. Business center. In-rm modem link. Concierge. Shopping arcade. Exercise rm; instructor, weights, bicycles, sauna. Massage. Game area. Bathrm phones in suites. Refrigerator in suites. Private patios on 7th, 12th floors. Luxurious hotel with elegant interior detail; extensive use of marble, mirrors; a large collection of artwork is displayed throughout the lobby. Luxury level. Cr cds: A, C, D, DS, JCB, MC, V.

D ≈ 🏊 ✗ 🏋 ➶ SC 🛶

★ ★ ★ **JEFFERSON.** 16th & M Sts NW (20036), downtown. 202/347-2200; FAX 202/331-7982; res: 800/368-5966. E-mail jefferson res@compuserve.com; web www.slh.com/slh/jefferson. 100 rms, 8 story, 32 suites. Jan-June, Sept-Nov: S $270-$305; D $285-$320; each addl $25; suites $350-$1,000; under 12 free; wkend rates; lower rates rest of yr. Crib free. Garage, valet parking $20. TV; cable (premium), VCR (movies avail). Pool privileges. Restaurant 6:30 am-10:30 pm (also see THE JEFFERSON). Rm serv 24 hrs. Afternoon tea 3-5 pm. Bar 11-1 am. Ck-out 1 pm. Business servs avail. In-rm modem link. Concierge. Health club privileges. Microwaves avail. Opened in 1923; individually decorated rms have four-poster beds, antiques. Cr cds: A, C, D, DS, JCB, MC, V.

D ≈ 🏊 ➶

★ ★ **THE LATHAM.** 3000 M St NW (20007), in Georgetown. 202/726-5000; FAX 202/337-4250; res: 800/368-5922 (exc DC), 800/LATHAM-1. 143 rms, 10 story. S $135-$190; D $165-$210; each addl $20; suites $225-$390; under 18 free; wkend rates. Valet parking $14. TV; cable (premium). Pool. Restaurant (see CITRONELLE). Bar 11-1 am; Fri, Sat to 2 am. Ck-out noon. Meeting rms. Business servs avail. In-rm modem link. Concierge. Health club privileges. Some minibars. Refrigerators avail. Sun deck. Overlooks historic Chesapeake & Ohio Canal. Cr cds: A, C, D, DS, MC, V.

D ≈ 🏊 ➶ SC

★ ★ **LINCOLN SUITES.** 1823 L St NW (20036), downtown. 202/223-4320; FAX 202/223-8546; res: 800/424-2970. 99 rms, 10 story, 24 kit. units. S, D, kit. units $175; each addl $15; under 17 free. Crib free. Garage parking $13. TV; cable (premium). Complimentary coffee in rms. Restaurant 7-10 am, 11:30 am-1:30 pm, 5-10 pm. Bar. Ck-out noon. Meeting rms. Business servs avail. Health club privileges. Refrigerators, microwaves. Cr cds: A, C, D, DS, MC, V.

D ≈ 🏊 SC

★ ★ ★ **LOEWS L'ENFANT PLAZA.** 480 L'Enfant Plaza SW (20024), south of downtown. 202/484-1000; FAX 202/646-4456. Web www.loewshotels.com/lenfanthome.html. The center piece of L'Enfant Plaza, this is an upscale hotel with a pretty lobby and pleasant rooms. The hotel is popular with travelers doing business with nearby government agencies. 370 rms on floors 11-15. S, D $190-$250; each addl $20; suites $370-$1,200; under 18 free; wkend rates. Crib free. Pet accepted. Valet parking $18. TV; cable (premium), VCR (movies avail). Pool; poolside serv, lifeguard. Restaurant 6:30 am-midnight. Bar from 11:30 am. Ck-out 1 pm. Convention facilities. Business center. In-rm modem link. Concierge. Underground shopping arcade with Metro subway stop. Gift shop. Extensive exercise rm; instructor, weights, bicycles. Refrigerators, minibars; microwaves avail. Many balconies. Cr cds: A, C, D, DS, MC, V.

D ≈ 🏊 ✗ 🏋 ➶ SC 🛶

★ ★ **LOMBARDY.** 2019 Pennsylvania Ave (20006), Foggy Bottom, west of downtown. 202/828-2600; FAX 202/872-0503; res: 800/424-5486. 125 units, 11 story. Mar-May, Sept-Oct: S $130-$150; D $150-$170; each addl $20; suites $170-$200; under 16 free; wkend rates; lower rates rest of yr. Crib free. TV; cable. Restaurant 7 am-2:30 pm, 5:30-9:30 pm; Sat, Sun 8 am-1 pm, 5-9:30 pm. Ck-out noon. Meeting rms. Business servs avail. In-rm modem link. Health club privileges. Refrigerators, minibars. Cr cds: A, C, D, DS, MC, V.

➶ SC

LUXURY COLLECTION. (New management, therefore not rated) 2100 Massachusetts Ave NW (20008), 1 blk NW of Dupont Circle, in Embassy Row Area. 202/293-2100; FAX 202/293-0641; res: 800/241-3333. 206 rms, 8 story. S, D $215-$235; suites $295-$2,100; under 18 free; wkend rates. Crib free. Valet parking $22. TV; cable (premium), VCR avail. Restaurant 6:30 am-10:30 pm (also see JOCKEY CLUB). Bar 11:30-1 am; entertainment. Ck-out noon. Meeting rms. Business center. In-rm modem link. Concierge. Tennis privileges. Golf privileges. Exercise rm; instructor, weights, stair machines, sauna. Massage. Health club privileges. Bathrm phones, minibars. Elegant ballroom. Luxury level. Cr cds: A, C, D, DS, JCB, MC, V.

D 🏊 🏋 ➶ SC 🛶

★ ★ ★ **THE MADISON.** 15th & M Sts NW (20005), downtown. 202/862-1600; FAX 202/785-1255; res: 800/424-8577. 353 rms, 14 story. S, D $230-$395; each addl $30; suites $395-$3,000; wkend packages. Crib $25. Valet, garage $14. TV; cable (premium). Restaurant 6:30 am-11 pm. Rm serv 24 hrs. Bar 11-2 am. Ck-out 1 pm. Meeting rms. Business center. In-rm modem link. Concierge. Exercise rm; instructor, weight machine, bicycles. Bathrm phones, refrigerators, minibars. Original paintings, antiques, Oriental rugs. Cr cds: A, C, D, JCB, MC, V.

D ✗ ➶ 🔥 🛶

★ ★ **MARRIOTT.** 1221 22nd St NW (20037), at M St, west of downtown. 202/872-1500; FAX 202/872-1424. 418 rms, 9 story. S, D $179-$199; suites $250-$500; under 18 free; wkend rates. Crib free. Garage $15. TV; cable (premium). Heated pool; whirlpool, poolside serv, lifeguard. Complimentary coffee in lobby. Restaurant 6:30 am-10 pm; Fri, Sat to 11 pm. Bars 11:30 am-midnight. Ck-out noon. Meeting rms. Business center. In-rm modem link. Concierge. Gift shop. Exercise equipt; weight machines, bicycles, sauna. Refrigerators avail. Luxury level. Cr cds: A, C, D, DS, JCB, MC, V.

D ≈ 🏊 ✗ ➶ SC 🛶

★ ★ **MARRIOTT AT METRO CENTER.** 775 12th St NW (20005), downtown. 202/737-2200; FAX 202/347-5886. 456 rms, 15 story. Late Feb-June, mid-Sept-mid-Nov: S, D $179-$219; wkend rates; higher rates Cherry Blossom; lower rates rest of yr. Crib free. Valet parking $16. TV; cable (premium). Indoor pool; whirlpool. Restaurant 6:30 am-2:30 pm, 5:30-10 pm; Sat, Sun 6:30 am-noon, 5:30-10 pm. Rm serv to midnight. Bar 11 am-midnight. Ck-out noon. Meeting rms. Business center. In-rm modem link. Concierge. Gift shop. Exercise rm; instructor, weight machine, treadmill, sauna. Minibars; microwaves avail. Luxury level. Cr cds: A, C, D, DS, JCB, MC, V.

D ≈ 🏊 ✗ ➶ SC 🛶

✔ ★ ★ **NORMANDY INN.** 2118 Wyoming Ave NW (20008), in Kalorama. 202/483-1350; FAX 202/387-8241; res: 800/424-3729. 75 rms, 6 story. S $103-$133; D $113-$143; each addl $10; under 12 free. Crib free. Garage $10. TV; cable (premium). Complimentary coffee in rms. Restaurant nearby. Ck-out noon. Coin lndry. In-rm modem link. Health club privileges. Refrigerators. In residential neighborhood. Cr cds: A, C, D, DS, MC, V.

D ➶ SC

★ ★ **OMNI SHOREHAM.** 2500 Calvert St NW (20008), north of downtown. 202/234-0700; FAX 202/332-1373. 771 rms, 8 story. S $215, D $245; each addl $30; suites $400-$1,600; under 18 free; wkend, hol rates. Crib free. Pet accepted, some restrictions. Garage $14. TV; cable (premium), VCR avail. Pool; wading pool, poolside serv, lifeguard. Restaurant 6:30 am-11 pm. Rm serv. Bar 11-2 am; entertainment. Ck-out noon. Meeting rms. Business center. Shopping arcade. Lighted tennis, pro.

Exercise equipt; weight machines, bicycles, sauna. Lawn games. Microwave avail in suites. Cr cds: A, C, D, DS, JCB, MC, V.

▢ ⬚ ⬚ ⬚ ⬚ ⬚ SC ⬚

★ ★ **ONE WASHINGTON CIRCLE.** *One Washington Circle NW (20037), at New Hampshire Ave, in Foggy Bottom.* 202/872-1680; FAX 202/887-4989; res: 800/424-9671. E-mail sales@onewashcirclehotel .com; web www.onewashcirclehotel.com. 151 kit. suites, 9 story. S, D $125-$275; each addl $15; under 18 free; wkend rates. Garage $15. TV; cable (premium), VCR avail. Pool. Coffee in rms. Restaurant 7 am-11:30 pm; Fri, Sat to midnight. Bar; entertainment. Ck-out noon. Meeting rms. Business servs avail. In-rm modem link. Concierge. Health club privileges. Some bathrm phones; microwaves avail. Balconies. Elegant furnishings; landscaped grounds. Cr cds: A, C, D, MC, V.

⬚ ⬚ ⬚ SC

★ ★ ★ ★ **PARK HYATT.** *24th & M St NW (20037), west of downtown.* 202/789-1234; FAX 202/457-8823. Web www.hyatt.com. An impressive collection of modern art distinguishes the interiors of this hotel, softened by touches of bronze and chinoiserie. Guest rooms are furnished with a mix of contemporary and antique pieces as well as museum reproductions of Oriental antiques. 224 units, 10 story, 133 suites. S $244-$299; D $269-$325; each addl $25; suites $270-$1,975; under 18 free; wkend rates; lower rates July, Aug. Crib free. TV; cable (premium), VCR avail. Indoor pool; whirlpool, poolside serv. Restaurant (see MELROSE). Afternoon tea 3-5 pm, Thurs-Sun. Rm serv 24 hrs. Bar 11:30-1 am; Fri, Sat to 2 am; pianist. Ck-out noon. Meeting rms. Business servs avail. In-rm modem link. Concierge. Gift shop. Barber, beauty shop. Underground valet parking. Golf privileges. Exercise rm; instructor, weight machines, bicycles, steam rm, sauna. Massage. Bathrm phones, refrigerators; microwaves avail. Cr cds: A, C, D, DS, JCB, MC, V.

▢ ⬚ ⬚ ⬚ ⬚ ⬚ SC

★ ★ **PHOENIX PARK.** *520 N Capitol St NW (20001), opp Union Station, on Capitol Hill.* 202/638-6900; FAX 202/393-3236; res: 800/824-5419. E-mail phoenixpark@worldnet.att.net. 148 rms, 9 story. S $169-$209; D $189-$229; each addl $20; suites $338-$750; under 16 free; wkend plans. Crib free. Valet parking $15. TV; cable (premium). Coffee in rms. Restaurant 7-2 am. Bar from 11 am; Fri, Sat to 3 am; entertainment. Ck-out 1 pm. Meeting rms. Business center. In-rm modem link. Exercise equipt; weight machines, bicycles. Minibars; some refrigerators. Near Capitol; traditional European decor. Cr cds: A, C, D, DS, MC, V.

▢ ⬚ ⬚ SC ⬚

★ ★ **QUALITY HOTEL DOWNTOWN.** *1315 16th St NW (20036), downtown.* 202/232-8000; FAX 202/667-9827. E-mail qualityht@ erols.com; web www.quality-suite.com/online/quality .html. 135 kit. units, 10 story. S $140; D $160; each addl $12; under 16 free; wkend rates. Crib free. Garage $10. TV; cable (premium), VCR avail. Pool privileges. Restaurant 7 am-10 pm. Rm serv 7 am-2 pm, 5-9:30 pm. Bar 5-11 pm. Ck-out noon. Guest lndry. Meeting rms. Business center. In-rm modem link. Gift shop. Exercise equipt; weight machine, bicycles. Health club privileges. Microwaves avail. Cr cds: A, C, D, DS, JCB, MC, V.

▢ ⬚ ⬚ ⬚ SC ⬚

★ ★ **RADISSON BARCELO.** *2121 P St NW (20037), in Dupont Circle area.* 202/293-3100; FAX 202/857-0134. 301 rms, 10 story. S, D $160-$180; each addl $20; suites $210-$550; under 17 free; wkend rates. Crib free. Valet parking $15. TV; cable (premium). Pool; lifeguard. Restaurant (see GABRIEL). Bar 11 am-midnight. Ck-out noon. Meeting rms. Business servs avail. In-rm modem link. Concierge. Gift shop. Exercise equipt; weights, bicycles, sauna. Bathrm phones, minibars. Cr cds: A, C, D, DS, JCB, MC, V.

▢ ⬚ ⬚ ⬚ SC

★ ★ ★ **RENAISSANCE MAYFLOWER.** *1127 Connecticut Ave NW (20036), 4 blks NW of White House, downtown.* 202/347-3000; FAX 202/466-9082. Web www.renaissancehotels.com. 660 rms, 10 story, 78 suites. S, D $250-$360; each addl $30; suites $450-$3,500; under 19 free; wkend rates. Crib free. Garage adj $11.50. TV; cable (premium), VCR avail. Complimentary coffee in rms. Restaurant 6:30 am-11:30 pm. Rm serv 24 hrs. Bar 11-1:30 am; entertainment. Ck-out 1 pm. Convention

facilities. Business center. In-rm modem link. Concierge. Exercise equipt; weight machines, bicycles. Health club privileges. Bathrm phones; refrigerators, microwaves avail. Foreign currency exchange. Opened in 1925 for Calvin Coolidge's inauguration; ornate gilded interior, stained-glass skylights. Cr cds: A, C, D, DS, ER, JCB, MC, V.

▢ ⬚ ⬚ ⬚ SC ⬚

★ ★ ★ **RENAISSANCE WASHINGTON.** *999 9th St NW (20001), near Convention Center & MCI Arena, downtown.* 202/898-9000; FAX 202/289-0947. E-mail sales@renhotels.com; web www.renaissance.com. 801 rms, 16 story. Apr-June, Sept-Nov: S, D $219-$260; each addl $25; suites $500-$2,000; under 18 free; wkend rates; lower rates rest of yr. Crib free. Pet accepted, some restrictions. Garage $15. TV; cable (premium), VCR avail. Indoor pool; whirlpool. Complimentary coffee in rms. Restaurant 6:30 am-11 pm. Rm serv 24 hrs. Bar 11-1 am. Ck-out 1 pm. Convention facilities. Business center. In-rm modem link. Concierge. Shopping arcade. Exercise rm; instructor, weight machines, bicycles, sauna. Minibars; some bathrm phones; microwaves avail. Luxury level. Cr cds: A, C, D, DS, ER, JCB, MC, V.

▢ ⬚ ⬚ ⬚ ⬚ ⬚ SC ⬚

★ ★ **RIVER INN.** *924 25th St NW (20037), 2 blks from Kennedy Center, in Foggy Bottom.* 202/337-7600; FAX 202/337-6520; res: 800/424-2741. E-mail Riverinn@erols.com. 126 kit. suites. S $125-$175; D $140-$190; each addl $15; under 18 free; wkend rates; higher rates Apr-May, Sept-Oct. Crib free. Pet accepted, some restrictions; $100. Parking $15. TV; cable (premium). Restaurant 7-10 am, 11:30 am-2 pm, 5-10 pm; Sat 8-10 am, 11 am-2 pm, 5:30-11:30 pm; Sun 8-10 am, 11 am-2 pm, 5-10 pm. Bar. Ck-out noon. Meeting rm. Business servs avail. In-rm modem link. Health club privileges. Microwaves. Cr cds: A, C, D, MC, V.

▢ ⬚ ⬚ ⬚ SC

★ ★ ★ **SHERATON.** *2660 Woodley Rd NW (20008), north of downtown.* 202/328-2000; FAX 202/234-0015. Web www.ittsheraton.com. 1,505 rms, 10 story. Mar-June: S, D $167-$220; each addl $30; suites $250-$2,250; under 12 free; lower rates rest of yr. Crib free. Pet accepted. Valet parking $17; garage $15. TV; cable (premium), VCR avail. Heated pool. Complimentary coffee in rms. Restaurants 6:30 am-11 pm. Bar 11-2 am. Ck-out noon. Convention facilities. Business center. Valet serv. Concierge. Gift shop. Barber. Exercise equipt; weight machines, bicycles, sauna. Some refrigerators. Balconies. Cr cds: A, D, DS, JCB, MC, V.

▢ ⬚ ⬚ ⬚ ⬚ ⬚ ⬚

★ ★ **SHERATON CITY CENTRE.** *1143 New Hampshire Ave NW (20037), at 21st & M Sts, west of downtown.* 202/775-0800; FAX 202/331-9491. 353 rms, 9 story. March-May, Aug-Oct: S $195-$220; D $210-$245; each addl $15; suites $250-$600; under 18 free; lower rates rest of yr. Crib free. Parking $14. TV; cable (premium). Coffee in rms. Restaurant 6 am-10 pm. Bar noon-1 am; entertainment Mon-Fri. Ck-out noon. Meeting rms. Business center. In-rm modem link. Concierge. Gift shop. Exercise equipt: stair machine, weights. Some refrigerators. Luxury level. Cr cds: A, C, D, DS, JCB, MC, V.

▢ ⬚ ⬚ ⬚ SC ⬚

★ ★ **ST JAMES.** *950 24th St NW (20037), in Foggy Bottom.* 202/457-0500; FAX 202/659-4492; res: 800/852-8512. Web www.weborgs .com. 195 kit. suites, 12 story. Feb-June, Sept-Oct: suites $139-$169; under 16 free; wkend rates; higher rates: Cherry Blossom Festival; lower rates rest of yr. Crib free. Garage parking $16; valet. TV; cable, VCR avail. Pool; lifeguard. Complimentary continental bkfst. Coffee in rms. Restaurant nearby. Ck-out noon. Coin lndry. Meeting rms. Business servs avail. In-rm modem link. Concierge. Exercise equipt; weights, treadmill. Cr cds: A, D, DS, MC, V.

▢ ⬚ ⬚ ⬚ ⬚ SC

★ ★ **STATE PLAZA.** *2117 E St NW (20037), in Foggy Bottom.* 202/861-8200; FAX 202/659-8601; res: 800/424-2859. 223 kit. suites, 8 story. S $95-$145; D $115-$165; each addl $20; under 16 free; wkend rates; higher rates Mar-June, Sept-Nov. Crib free. Garage $12. TV; cable (premium). Complimentary continental bkfst. Restaurant 7 am-11 pm. Bar from 11 am. Ck-out noon. Coin lndry. Meeting rms. Business servs avail.

In-rm modem link. Exercise equipt; bicycle, treadmills. Minibars, micro-waves. Two rooftop sun decks. Cr cds: A, C, D, DS, JCB, MC, V.

D ⚡ 🏊 🔥 SC

★✦ **TRAVELODGE-CENTER CITY.** *1201 13th St NW (20005), north of downtown.* 202/682-5300; FAX 202/371-9624. 100 rms, 8 story. Apr-Sept: S $85-$115; D $95-$125; each addl $10; under 16 free; wkend rates; lower rates rest of yr. Parking $10 in/out. TV; cable (premium). Complimentary continental bkfst. Coffee in rms. Restaurant. Ck-out 11 am. Coin lndry. Meeting rm. Business servs avail. In-rm modem link. Cr cds: A, C, D, DS, MC, V.

D 🏊 🔥 SC

★✦ **WASHINGTON.** *515 15th St NW (20004), at Pennsylvania Ave, 1 blk from White House, downtown.* 202/638-5900; FAX 202/638-4275; res: 800/424-9540. 344 rms, 11 story. S $170-$235; D $185-$235; each addl $18; suites $430-$668; under 14 free; wkend rates. Crib free. Pet accepted, some restrictions. TV; cable (premium). Restaurant 7 am-10 pm. Bar 11-1 am. Ck-out 1 pm. Meeting rms. Business center. In-rm modem link. Gift shop. Exercise equipt; weight machine, bicycles, sauna. Bathrm phones. Original Jardin D'Armide tapestry (1854). One of the oldest continuously-operated hotels in the city. Cr cds: A, C, D, DS, JCB, MC, V.

D ⚡ 🏊 🔥 SC ⛷

★★★ **THE WASHINGTON COURT ON CAPITOL HILL.** *525 New Jersey Ave NW (20001), on Capitol Hill.* 202/628-2100; FAX 202/879-7918; res: 800/321-3010. 264 rms, 15 story. S, D $175-$250; each addl $25; suites $360-$1,500; under 16 free; wkend rates. Crib free. Pet accepted, some restrictions. Valet parking $15. TV; cable (premium), VCR avail. Restaurant 6:30 am-11 pm. Bar; pianist. Ck-out noon. Meeting rooms. Business servs avail. In-rm modem link. Concierge. Exercise equipt; weight machines, bicycles, sauna. Gift shop. Bathrm phones, refrigerators. Large atrium lobby. Cr cds: A, C, D, DS, MC, V.

D ⚡ 🏊 🔥 SC

★★★ **WASHINGTON HILTON AND TOWERS.** *1919 Connecti-cut Ave NW (20009), in Kalorama.* 202/483-3000; FAX 202/265-8221. Web www.hilton.com. 1,123 rms, 10 story. S $200-$265; D $225-$285; each addl $20; suites $444-$1,400; wkend rates. Crib free. Pet accepted, some restrictions. Garage $12. TV; cable (premium), VCR avail (movies). Heated pool; poolside serv, lifeguard (in season). Supervised child's activi-ties (May-Sept). Restaurants 6:30 am-11 pm. Bar 11:30-2 am; entertain-ment. Ck-out noon. Convention facilities. Business center. In-rm modem link. Gift shop. Lighted tennis, pro. Exercise rm; instructor, weight ma-chines, bicycles, steam rm. Minibars. Resort atmosphere; on 7 landscaped acres. Luxury level. Cr cds: A, C, D, DS, JCB, MC, V.

D ⚡ 🏌 🏊 🔥 SC ⛷

★★★ **THE WATERGATE.** *2650 Virginia Ave NW (20037), adj Kennedy Center, in Foggy Bottom.* 202/965-2300; FAX 202/337-7915; res: 800/424-2736. 231 rms, 13 story. S $275-$410; D $300-$435; each addl $25; suites $400-$1,885; under 18 free; wkend, hol rates. Crib free. Pet accepted, some restrictions. Valet parking $25. TV; cable (premium), VCR avail (movies). Indoor pool; whirlpool, lifeguard. Restaurant (see AQUARELLE). Rm serv 24 hrs. Bar 11:30-1 am; pianist. Ck-out noon. Meeting rms. Business center. In-rm modem link. Concierge. Shopping arcade. Barber, beauty shop. Complimentary downtown & Capitol trans-portation. Exercise rm; instructor, weight machines, bicycles, sauna, steam rm. Massage. Health club privileges. Bathrm phones, minibars; microwaves avail. Many balconies. Kennedy Center adj. Overlooks Poto-mac River. Cr cds: A, C, D, DS, JCB, MC, V.

D ⚡ 🏊 🏌 🔥 ⛷

★★★ **WESTIN HOTEL WASHINGTON.** *2350 M St NW (20037), east of Georgetown.* 202/429-0100; FAX 202/429-9759. 262 rms. Sept-June: S $219-$279; D $249-$309; each addl $30; suites $450-$3,000; under 18 free; wkend packages; lower rates rest of yr. Crib free. Covered valet parking $18/day. TV; cable (premium), VCR avail. Heated pool; poolside serv. Restaurant 6:30 am-10:30 pm. Rm serv 24 hrs. Bar. Ck-out 1 pm. Meeting rms. Business center. In-rm modem link. Concierge. Gift shop. Exercise equipt; weight machines, bicycles. Minibars. Bathrm

phones; some fireplaces; whirlpool in suites. Some balconies. Many rms with view of landscaped interior courtyard. Luxury level. Cr cds: A, C, D, DS, JCB, MC, V.

D 🏊 🏌 🏊 🔥 SC ⛷

★★★★ **WILLARD INTER-CONTINENTAL.** *1401 Pennsylvania Ave NW (20004), 2 blks E of White House, downtown.* 202/628-9100; FAX 202/637-7326. This opulent Beaux Arts hotel was host to every president from Franklin Pierce to Dwight D. Eisenhower on the eve of their inaugura-tions. A faithful renovation has returned elegance to the stately columns, mosaic floors and turn-of-the-century decor. Guest rooms are furnished with mahogany Queen Anne-style reproductions. 341 units, 12 story, 35 suites. S $335-$450; D $365-$480; each addl $30; suites $800-$3,600; under 14 free; wkend rates. Crib free. Pet accepted, some restrictions. Covered parking, valet $20. TV; cable (premium), VCR avail. Restaurant 6:30 am-11 pm (also see WILLARD ROOM). Rm serv 24 hrs. Bar 11-1 am; Sun 11:30 am-midnight; entertainment. Ck-out noon. Convention facilities. Business center. In-rm modem link. Concierge. Shopping arcade. Exercise equipt; weight machine, treadmill. Bathrm phones, minibars; some micro-waves avail. Cr cds: A, C, D, DS, JCB, MC, V.

D ⚡ 🏌 🏊 🔥 SC ⛷

★★★ **WYNDHAM BRISTOL.** *2430 Pennsylvania Ave NW (20037), west of downtown.* 202/955-6400; FAX 202/955-5765. 240 kit. units, 8 story, 37 suites. S $179-$219; D $199-$229; each addl $20; suites $285-$850; under 17 free; monthly rates; wkend plans. Crib free. Valet garage parking $16. TV; cable (premium). Complimentary coffee in rms. Restaurant 7 am-11 pm. Rm serv 24 hrs. Bar 11-2 am. Ck-out noon. Meeting rms. Business servs avail. In-rm modem link. Concierge. Exercise equipt; stair machine, treadmills. Bathrm phones; microwaves avail. Clas-sic English furnishings, art. Cr cds: A, C, D, DS, JCB, MC, V.

D 🏌 🏊 🔥 SC

Inns

★✦ **KALORAMA GUEST HOUSE AT KALORAMA PARK.** *1854 Mintwood Place NW (20009), in Kalorama Triangle.* 202/667-6369; FAX 202/319-1262. 31 rms, some share bath, 3 story. S $45-$95; D $50-$105; each addl $5; suites $75-$125; wkly rates. TV in common rm. Complimentary continental bkfst; afternoon refreshments. Ck-out 11 am, ck-in noon. Limited parking avail. Business servs avail. Created from 4 Victorian town houses (1890s); rms individually decorated, antiques. Gar-den. Cr cds: A, D, DS, MC, V.

🏊 🔥 SC

★✦ **KALORAMA GUEST HOUSE AT WOODLEY PARK.** *2700 Cathedral Ave NW (20008), north of downtown.* 202/328-0860; FAX 202/328-8730. 19 rms, 7 share baths, 4 story, 2 suites. No rm phones. Mar-mid-June, Sept-Nov: S $45-$95; D $55-$105; each addl $5; wkly rates; lower rates rest of yr. Children over 5 yrs only. TV in sitting rm. Complimentary continental bkfst; afternoon refreshments. Restaurant nearby. Ck-out 11 am, ck-in noon. Free lndry facilities. Limited off-street parking. Sitting rm; antiques. Two early 20th-century town houses (1910). Cr cds: A, D, DS, MC, V.

🏊 🔥 SC

★★★ **MORRISON-CLARK.** *1101 11th St NW (20001), at Massa-chusetts Ave, downtown.* 202/898-1200; FAX 202/289-8576; res: 800/332-7898. 54 units, 4 story, 14 suites. Mar-June, Sept-Nov: S $135-$220; D $155-$240; each addl $20; suites $160-$220; under 12 free; wkend rates; lower rates rest of yr. Crib free. TV; cable (premium), VCR avail. Compli-mentary continental bkfst. Dining rm (MORRISON-CLARK). Rm serv. Ck-out noon, ck-in 3 pm. Bellhops. Valet serv. Business servs avail. In-rm modem link. Exercise equipt; weight machine, treadmills. Health club privileges. Underground parking. Minibars; microwaves avail. Restored Victorian mansion (1864); period furnishings. Cr cds: A, D, DS, MC, V.

🏌 🏊 🔥 SC

★✦ **TAFT BRIDGE INN.** *2007 Wyoming Ave (20009), in Kalorama.* 202/387-2007; FAX 202/387-5019. 12 rms, 7 share bath, 3 with shower only, 3 story. Mar-June, Sept-Nov: S $49-$99; D $69-$109; each addl $10; kit. unit $109-$119; wkly, hol rates; lower rates rest of yr. TV in some rms; cable, VCR avail. Complimentary continental bkfst. Restaurant nearby. Ck-out 11 am, ck-in 2 pm. In-rm modem link. Valet serv. Guest lndry. Some balconies. Georgian-style house built in 1905; eclectic antique, art collection. Totally nonsmoking. Cr cds: MC, V.

✓★ **WINDSOR.** 1842 16th St NW (20009), north of downtown. 202/667-0300; FAX 202/667-4503; res: 800/423-9111. 45 rms, 4 story, 9 suites. No elvtr. S $79-$110; D $89-$125; suites $105-$175; under 14 free; wkend rates. Crib free. TV; cable (premium). Complimentary continental bkfst; afternoon refreshments. Restaurant nearby. Ck-out noon, ck-in 2 pm. Business servs avail. Refrigerator in suites. Originally a boarding house (1922); bed & breakfast atmosphere. Cr cds: A, C, D, MC, V.

Restaurants

★ ★ ★ **1789.** 1226 36th St NW (20007), in Georgetown. 202/965-1789. Hrs: 6-10 pm; Fri, Sat to 11 pm. Closed Dec 25. Res accepted. Bar. Wine list. Semi-a la carte: dinner $18-$32. Prix fixe: pre-theater dinner $25. Specializes in seafood, rack of lamb. Own baking. Valet parking. In restored mansion; 5 dining rms on 3 levels. Federal-period decor. Fireplace. Jacket. Cr cds: A, D, DS, MC, V.

★ ★ ★ **701.** 701 Pennsylvania Ave NW (20004), across from the National Archives, downtown. 202/393-0701. Hrs: 11:30 am-3 pm, 5:30-10:30 pm; Wed, Thurs to 11 pm; Fri to 11:30 pm; Sat 5:30-11:30 pm; Sun 5-9:30 pm. Closed major hols. Res accepted. Continental menu. Bar. Wine list. Semi-a la carte: lunch $8.50-$19.50, dinner $13.50-$23.50. Specializes in seafood, lamb chops, New York strip steak. Pianist Sun-Thurs, Jazz combo Fri, Sat. Free valet parking (dinner). Outdoor dining. Overlooks fountain at Navy Memorial. Cr cds: A, C, D, MC, V.

✓★ ★ **ADITI.** 3299 M St NW (20007), in Georgetown. 202/625-6825. Hrs: 11:30 am-2:30 pm, 5:30-10 pm; Fri, Sat to 10:30 pm. Closed Thanksgiving. Res accepted. Indian menu. Serv bar. Semi-a la carte: lunch $4.95-$9.95, dinner $4.95-$13.95. Specializes in tandoori charbroiled meats, vegetarian dishes, seafood. Cr cds: A, C, D, DS, MC, V.

★ ★ **ANNA MARIA'S.** 1737 Connecticut Ave (20009), on Dupont Circle. 202/667-1444. Hrs: 11-1 am; Fri to 3 am; Sat 5 pm-3 am; Sun 5 pm-1 am. Closed most major hols. Res accepted. Italian menu. Bar. Semi-a la carte: lunch $7.95-$10.95, dinner $12.95-$19.95. Specializes in homemade pasta, veal. Atrium rm; fireplace. Cr cds: A, C, D, MC, V.

★ ★ ★ **AQUARELLE.** (See The Watergate Hotel) 202/298-4455. Hrs: 7-10:30 am, 11:30 am-2:30 pm, 5:30-10:30 pm; Sun brunch 11:30 am-2:30 pm; early-bird dinner 5:30-7 pm. Res accepted. Continental menu. Bar 11:30-1 am. Wine cellar. A la carte entrees: bkfst $7-$16, lunch $12-$20, dinner $14-$25. Complete meal: dinner $35-$65. Sun brunch $38. Specialties: quail stuffed with wild game bird mousseline, filet of sea bass in pesto broth, warm plumb tart. Own pasta. Valet parking. Panoramic view of the Potomac River. Cr cds: A, C, D, DS, JCB, MC, V.

✓★ ★ **BACCHUS.** 1827 Jefferson Place NW (20036), in Dupont Circle area. 202/785-0734. Hrs: noon-2:30 pm, 6-10 pm; Fri to 10:30 pm; Sat 6-10:30 pm. Closed Sun; most major hols. Res accepted. Lebanese menu. A la carte entrees: lunch $6.50-$10.75, dinner $11.75-$16.25. Specializes in authentic Lebanese cuisine. Valet parking (dinner). Cr cds: A, MC, V.

★ ★ **BE DU CI.** 2100 P St NW (20037), in Dupont Circle. 202/223-3824. Hrs: 11:30 am-2:30 pm, 5:30-10 pm; Fri to 10:30 pm; Sat 5:30-10:30 pm; Sun 5:30-9:30 pm. Closed late Aug; major hols. Res accepted. Mediterranean menu. Bar. Semi-a la carte: lunch $9.50-$23, dinner $10.50-$25. Specializes in game, seafood. Three dining areas. Contemporary decor. Cr cds: A, C, D, DS, MC, V.

★ ★ **BICE.** Indiana between 6th & 7th Aves (20004), downtown. 202/638-2423. E-mail bice@dcnet.com; web www.bice.washington.com. Hrs: 11:30 am-2:30 pm, 5:30-10:30 pm; Fri to 11:30 pm; Sat 5:30-11:30 pm. Closed Sun; Jan 1, Thanksgiving, Dec 25. Res accepted. Northern Italian menu. Bar. Semi-a la carte: lunch $11-$20, dinner $12-$30. Specializes in pasta, risotto, veal. Valet parking (dinner). Outdoor dining. Bright, modern Italian decor; windows on 3 sides of dining rm. Cr cds: A, C, D, MC, V.

★ **BILLY MARTIN'S TAVERN.** 1264 Wisconsin Ave NW (20007), in Georgetown. 202/333-7370. Hrs: 8-1 am; Fri, Sat to 2:30 am; Sat, Sun brunch to 5 pm. Closed Dec 25. Res accepted. Bar. Semi-a la carte: bkfst $3.95-$7.95, lunch $5.95-$8.95, dinner $6.50-$18.95. Sat, Sun brunch $5.95-$12.95. Specializes in steak, seafood, chops, pasta. Parking. Outdoor dining. Established 1933. Family-owned. Cr cds: A, D, DS, MC, V.

★ ★ **BISTRO FRANCAIS.** 3128 M St NW (20007), in Georgetown. 202/338-3830. Hrs: 11-3 am; Fri, Sat to 4 am; early-bird dinner 5-7 pm, 10:30 pm-1 am; Sat, Sun brunch 11 am-4 pm. Closed Dec 24 eve, 25. Res accepted. Country French menu. Semi-a la carte: lunch $6.95-$11.95, dinner $12.95-$19.95. Wkday brunch: $11.95. Sat, Sun brunch $13.95. Specializes in rotisserie chicken, fresh seafood. Cr cds: A, C, D, JCB, MC, V.

✓★ ★ **BISTROT LEPIC.** 1736 Wisconsin Ave NW (20007), in upper Georgetown. 202/333-0111. Hrs: 11:30 am-2:30 pm, 5:30-10 pm; Fri, Sat to 10:30 pm; Sun to 9:30 pm. Closed Mon; major hols. Res accepted. French menu. Semi-a la carte: lunch $9.75-$12.95, dinner $13.95-17.95. Specialties: roasted rack of lamb, beef tenderloin, preserved rabbit leg. Storefront restaurant. Cr cds: A, DS, MC, V.

✓★ ★ **BLUE PLATE.** 2002 P St NW (20036), in Dupont Circle. 202/293-2248. Hrs: 11:30 am-11 pm; Fri, Sat to midnight; Sun noon-10 pm. Closed most major hols. Serv bar. Semi-a la carte: lunch, dinner $8.25-$11.95. Specializes in grilled fish, steak. Own baking. Casual cafe atmosphere. Totally nonsmoking. Cr cds: MC, V.

★ ★ ★ **BOMBAY CLUB.** 815 Connecticut Ave NW (20006), across from White House, downtown. 202/659-3727. Hrs: 11:30 am-2:30 pm, 6-10:30 pm; Sat 6-11 pm; Sun 5:30-9 pm; Sun brunch 11:30 am-2:30 pm, 5-11 pm. Closed some major hols. Res accepted. Indian menu. Bar 11:30 am-3 pm, 5-11 pm. Semi-a la carte: lunch, dinner $7-$18.50. Sun brunch $16.50. Specialties: tandoori salmon, thali, lamb Roganjosh, chicken Tikka Makhani. Pianist evenings, Sun brunch. Valet parking (dinner). Outdoor dining. Extensive vegetarian menu. Elegant club-like atmosphere reminiscent of British colonial India. Cr cds: A, C, D, MC, V.

✓★ ★ **BOMBAY PALACE.** 2020 K St NW (20006), downtown. 202/331-4200. Hrs: 11:30 am-2:30 pm, 5:30-10 pm; Fri, Sat to 10:30 pm. Res accepted. Northern Indian menu. Bar. A la carte entrees: lunch, dinner $8.50-$19.95. Complete meals: lunch, dinner $16.95-$19.95. Specialties: butter chicken, gosht patiala, jumbo prawns tandoori. Indian decor and original art; 350-gallon fish tank. Totally nonsmoking. Cr cds: A, D, MC, V.

✓★ **BUA.** 1635 P St NW (20036), in Dupont Circle. 202/265-0828. Hrs: 11:30 am-2:30 pm, 5-10:30 pm; Fri to 11 pm; Sat noon-4 pm, 5-11 pm; Sun noon-4 pm. Closed Thanksgiving, Dec 25. Res accepted. Thai menu. Bar. A la carte entrees: lunch $5.85-$7.75, dinner $7.50-$12.95. Specializes in seafood. Outdoor dining on 2nd-floor balcony. In townhouse on side street; fireplace. Cr cds: A, D, DS, MC, V.

★ **BURMA.** 740 6th St NW (20001), in Chinatown. 202/638-1280. Hrs: 11 am-3 pm, 6-10 pm; Sat, Sun from 6 pm. Closed major hols. Res accepted. Burmese menu. Serv bar. Semi-a la carte: lunch, dinner

$5.95-$7.95. Specialties: green tea leaf salad, tamarind fish, mohingar. Burmese decor. Cr cds: A, C, D, DS, MC, V.

★ ★ **BUSARA.** *2340 Wisconsin Ave NW (20007), in Upper Georgetown, near the Naval Observatory.* 202/337-2340. Hrs: 11:30 am-3 pm, 5-11 pm; Fri to midnight; Sat 5 pm-midnight; Sun 5-11 pm. Closed most major hols. Res required Fri, Sat. Thai menu. Bar. Semi-a la carte: lunch $5.95-$8.50, dinner $7.25-$15.95. Specialties: panang gai, crispy whole flounder, pad Thai. Outdoor dining in a Japanese garden. New wave decor. Cr cds: A, C, D, DS, MC, V.

✔★ ★ ★ **CAFE ATLÁNTICO.** *405 8th St NW (20004), in Penn Quarter, downtown.* 202/393-0812. Hrs: 11:30 am-10 pm; Fri, Sat to 11 pm; Sun 5:30-10 pm. Closed most major hols. Res accepted. Latin Amer menu. Bar to midnight. Wine cellar. Semi-a la carte: lunch $7.95-$13.95, dinner $13.95-$16.50. Complete meal (Sun-Wed): dinner $19.95-$21.95. Specialties: Cordero a la Boliviana, Jamaican jerk chicken, quail tamal fingido. Valet parking. Outdoor dining. Contemporary decor with modern artwork; central circular stairway leads to second dining level. Cr cds: A, D, MC, V.

★ ★ **CAFE MILANO.** *3251 Prospect St NW (20007), in Georgetown.* 202/333-6183. Hrs: 11-1 am; Sun noon-11 pm. Closed Thanksgiving, Dec 25. Res accepted. Italian menu. Bar. Semi-a la carte: lunch $9-$26, dinner $13-$28. Specialties: strozzapreti moschino, costoletta di vitello. Outdoor dining. Large tie/scarf collection hanging on walls. Cr cds: A, D, MC, V.

★ **CAFE MOZART.** *1331 H St NW (20005), behind deli, downtown.* 202/347-5732. Hrs: 7:30 am-10 pm; Sat from 9 am; Sun from 11 am. Closed Jan 1, Thanksgiving, Dec 25. Res accepted. German, Austrian menu. Bar. Semi-a la carte: bkfst $3.10-$6.95, lunch $4.85-$21.50, dinner $8.95-$22.50. Child's meals. Specialties: Wienerschnitzel, pork roast, Kasseler rippchen. Entertainment Thurs-Sat. German deli on premises. Cr cds: A, C, D, DS, JCB, MC, V.

★ ★ ★ **THE CAPITOL GRILL.** *601 Pennsylvania Ave NW (20004), on Capitol Hill.* 202/737-6200. Hrs: 11:30 am-3 pm, 5-10 pm; Fri to 11 pm; Sat 5-11 pm; Sun 5-10 pm. Closed Thanksgiving, Dec 25. Res accepted. Bar. A la carte entrees: lunch $9.95-$19.95, dinner $15.95-$27.95. Specializes in steak. Club atmosphere. Cr cds: A, C, D, DS, MC, V.

★ ★ **CASHION'S EAT PLACE.** *1819 Columbia Rd NW (20009), in Adams Morgan area.* 202/797-1819. Hrs: 5:30-11 pm; Sun, Tues to 10 pm; Sun brunch 11:30 am-2:30 pm. Closed Mon; most major hols. Res accepted. Bar. Semi-a la carte: dinner $10.95-$17.95. Complete meal: dinner $25-$40. Sun brunch $3.95-$8.95. Specializes in lamb, duck, seafood. Own desserts. Valet parking. Outdoor dining. Contemporary decor; skylights. Cr cds: MC, V.

★ ★ ★ **CITRONELLE.** *(See The Latham Hotel)* 202/625-2150. Hrs: 6:30-10:30 am, 11:30 am-2 pm, 6-10 pm; Fri, Sat 5:30-10:30 pm; Sun brunch 11:30 am-2:30 pm. Res accepted. French menu. Bar. Semi-a la carte: bkfst $7.50-$12.50, lunch $15-$25, dinner $28-$45. Sun brunch $10-$18. Specialties: terrine of smoked salmon, shiitake mushroom Napoleon, shrimp wrapped in kataifi. Multi-level dining rm. Contemporary decor with modern art. Cr cds: A, C, D, DS, MC, V.

✔★ ★ **CLYDE'S.** *3236 M St NW (20007), at Wisconsin Ave, in Georgetown.* 202/333-9180. Hrs: 11:30-2 am; Fri to 3 am; Sat 10-3 am; Sun from 9 am. Closed Dec 25. Res accepted. Bars. Semi-a la carte: lunch $6.95-$10.95, dinner $9.95-$14.95. Sun brunch $4.25-$9.95. Child's meals. Specializes in seafood, crab cakes, ribs. Parking. Atrium dining. Cr cds: A, C, D, DS, MC, V.

★ ★ **COCO LOCO.** *810 7th St NW (20001), downtown, in Chinatown.* 202/289-2626. Hrs: 11:30 am-2:30 pm, 5:30-10:30 pm; Sat 5:30-11 pm. Closed Sun. Res accepted. Spanish menu. Bar. A la carte entrees: lunch $4.50-$11, dinner $5-$12. Prix fixe: $29.95. Specialties: stuffed ravioles, grilled chicken, stuffed shrimp. Salad bar. Entertainment. Outdoor dining. Modern tropical decor. Cr cds: A, D, MC, V.

✔★ ★ **COPPI'S VIGORELLI.** *3421 Connecticut Ave NW (20008), in Cleveland Park area, north of downtown.* 202/244-6437. Hrs: noon-11 pm; Fri to midnight; Sat noon-3 pm, 5 pm-midnight; Sun 5-11 pm. Closed Thanksgiving, Dec 24, 25. Northern Italian menu. Bar. Semi-a la carte: lunch, dinner $7.95-$15.95. Child's meals. Specialties: wood-oven broiled fish, baked ligurian risotto. Own pasta. Decor celebrates Italian bicycle racing. Cr cds: A, D, DS, MC, V.

★ **EL CARIBE.** *3288 M St (20007), in Georgetown.* 202/338-3121. E-mail cfearless@aol.com; web www.digitalcity.com/caribe. Hrs: 11:30 am-11 pm; Fri, Sat to 11:30 pm; Sun to 10 pm. Res accepted. South Amer, Spanish menu. Bar. Semi-a la carte: lunch $6.95-$12.95, dinner $9.95-$19.50. Specialties: fritadas con Llapingachos, paella. Spanish decor. Family-owned. Cr cds: A, C, D, DS, MC, V.

★ ★ **FILOMENA RISTORANTE.** *1063 Wisconsin Ave NW (20007), off M St on the canal, in Georgetown.* 202/338-8800. E-mail Filorest@erols.com; web www.erols.com/eire/filomena.html. Hrs: 11:30 am-11 pm; Sat, Sun brunch to 3 pm. Closed Jan 1, Thanksgiving, Dec 25. Res accepted. Italian menu. Bar. A la carte entrees: lunch $5.95-$12.95, dinner $11.95-$29.95. Lunch buffet $7.95. Sat, Sun brunch $9.95. Specializes in pasta, seafood, regional Italian dishes. Own baking, pasta. Italian garden-like atmosphere; antiques. Overlooks Chesapeake & Ohio Canal. Cr cds: A, D, DS, JCB, MC, V.

✔★ **FIO'S.** *3636 16th St (20010), in Woodner Apts, Mt Pleasant, north of downtown.* 202/667-3040. Hrs: 5-10:45 pm. Closed Mon; some major hols; last 2 wks Aug. Italian menu. Bar. Semi-a la carte: dinner $5.50-$12.50. Specializes in seafood, veal, pasta. Own bread, pasta. Free garage parking. Informal atmosphere; building overlooks Rock Creek Park. Cr cds: A, C, D, DS, MC, V.

★ ★ **FRAN O'BRIEN'S.** *(See The Capital Hilton Hotel)* 202/783-2599. Hrs: 11:30 am-11 pm; Sat, Sun from 5 pm; Sun brunch 10:30 am-3 pm (football season). Closed most major hols. Res accepted. Bar to midnight. Wine cellar. Semi-a la carte: lunch $8.25-$19.95, dinner $17.95-$29.95. Sun brunch $22-$24. Child's meals. Specialties: rib-eye steak, filet mignon, Maryland crab cakes with lobster cream sauce. Own desserts. Pianist evenings exc Sun. Valet parking (dinner). Club-like atmosphere with sport themes; large collection of football memorabilia. Cr cds: A, D, MC, V.

✔★ **FRATELLI ITALIAN.** *(5820 Landover Rd, Cheverly MD 20784) jct Baltimore Washington Pkwy & MD 202.* 301/209-9006. Hrs: 11 am-10 pm; Fri, Sat to 11 pm; Sun 2-9 pm. Italian menu. Bar. Semi-a la carte: lunch $5.95-$11.25, dinner $9.95-$13.95. Specializes in pasta, chicken, seafood. Contemporary decor. Cr cds: A, MC, V.

★ ★ **GABRIEL.** *(See Radisson Barcelo Hotel)* 202/956-6690. Hrs: 6:30 am-10 pm; Sat 7 am-11 pm; Sun to 9 pm; Sun brunch 11 am-3 pm. Closed Dec 25. Res accepted. Spanish/Latin Amer menu. Bar 11 am-midnight. Semi-a la carte: bkfst $3.50-$9.50, lunch $7.25-$15, dinner $8-$24. Sun brunch $16.75. Specialties: grilled sea scallops, grilled lamb chops, smoked black bean soup. Outdoor dining. Mediterranean decor. Cr cds: A, C, D, DS, JCB, MC, V.

★ ★ ★ **GALILEO.** *1110 21st St NW (20036), in Foggy Bottom.* 202/293-7191. E-mail roberto@robertodonna.com; web www.roberto

donna.com. Hrs: 7:30-9:30 am, 11:30 am-2 pm, 5:30-10 pm; Fri to 10:30 pm; Sat from 5:30 pm; Sun 5:30-8:30 pm. Closed some major hols. Res accepted. Northern Italian menu. Bar. Wine cellar. A la carte entrees: bkfst $3.95-$9.95, lunch $10.95-$17.95, dinner $16.95-$29.95. Specializes in game, seasonal dishes, pasta. Free valet parking (dinner) exc Sun. Outdoor dining. Mediterranean decor. Cr cds: A, C, D, DS, MC, V.

[D] [⏗]

✔★ GARRETT'S. 3003 M St NW (20007), in Georgetown. 202/333-1033. E-mail rhinorest@aol.com. Hrs: 11:30 am-10:30 pm; Fri, Sat to 11 pm. Res accepted. Bars 11:30-2 am; Fri, Sat to 3 am. Semi-a la carte: lunch $3.95-$8.50, dinner $4.75-$13.95. Specializes in steaks, pasta, seafood. 1794 landmark bldg; originally house of MD governor T.S. Lee. Cr cds: A, C, D, DS, MC, V.

[⏗]

★★★ GEORGIA BROWN'S. 950 15th St NW (20005), at McPherson Square, downtown. 202/393-4499. Hrs: 11:30 am-11 pm; Fri to midnight; Sat 5:30 pm-midnight; Sun brunch 11:30 am-3 pm, 5:30-11 pm. Closed Dec 25. Res accepted. South Carolina Low Country menu. Bar. Semi-a la carte: lunch, dinner $10.95-$19.95. Specialties: head-on Carolina shrimp with spicy sausage, frogmore stew, Southern fried chicken. Jazz & blues Sun afternoons. Valet parking (dinner). View of McPherson's Square. Cr cds: A, C, D, DS, MC, V.

[D] [⏗]

★★★ GERARD'S PLACE. 915 15th St NW (20005), at McPherson Square, downtown. 202/737-4445. Hrs: 11:30 am-2:30 pm, 5:30-10 pm; Fri to 10:30 pm; Sat 5:30-10:30 pm. Closed Sun; most major hols. Res accepted. French menu. Wine list. A la carte entrees: lunch $15.50-$19.50, dinner $16.50-$32.50. Prix fixe: dinner $58. Specializes in contemporary French cooking. Outdoor dining. Casual bistro atmosphere. Some modern art. Cr cds: A, C, D, MC, V.

[⏗]

★★ GERMAINE'S. 2400 Wisconsin Ave NW (20007), in Upper Georgetown. 202/965-1185. Hrs: 11:30 am-2:30 pm, 5:30-10 pm; Fri to 11 pm; Sat 5:30-11 pm; Sun 5:30-10 pm. Closed Jan 1, Dec 25. Res accepted. Pan-Asian menu. Bar. A la carte entrees: lunch $7.25-$12.95, dinner $12.25-$28. Specializes in grilled Asian dishes, seafood. Skylighted atrium dining rm. Cr cds: A, C, D, MC, V.

[⏗]

★★★ GOLDONI. 1113 23rd St NW (20037), west of downtown. 202/293-1511. Hrs: 11:30 am-2 pm, 5:30-10 pm; Fri 11:30 am-2 pm, 5-10:30 pm; Sat 5-10:30 pm; Sun 5-9:30 pm. Closed most major hols. Res accepted. Italian menu. Bar. Wine list. Semi-a la carte: lunch $11.95-$18.95, dinner $14.95-$26.95. Complete meal: dinner $35.95-$48.95. Specialties: grilled wild rockfish with polenta, mushrooms and cherry tomatoes; cappellacci with lobster and foie gras with white truffles. Own pasta, desserts. Validated parking nearby. Gallery setting has look and feel of Italian villa; skylights. Cr cds: A, C, D, DS, MC, V.

★ THE GRILL FROM IPANEMA. 1858 Columbia Rd NW (20009), in Adams Morgan area. 202/986-0757. Hrs: 5-11 pm; Fri to midnight; Sat noon-midnight; Sun noon to 11 pm; Sat, Sun brunch to 4 pm. Closed Jan 1, Dec 25. Res accepted. Brazilian menu. Bar. Semi-a la carte: dinner $8.95-$15.95. Sat, Sun brunch $11.95. Specialties: feijoada, moqueca, bobo de camarao. Cr cds: A, C, D, DS, MC, V.

[D] [⏗]

✔★ GUAPO'S. 4515 Wisconsin Ave NW (20016), north of downtown. 202/686-3588. Hrs: 11:30 am-11:30 pm; Fri, Sat to midnight. Res accepted. Latin Amer, Mexican menu. Bar. Semi-a la carte: lunch $3.95-$10.25, dinner $4.95-$13.95. Specializes in fajitas. Outdoor dining. Colorful dining rms with Mexican decor. Cr cds: A, DS, MC, V.

[D] [⏗]

★ GUARDS. 2915 M St NW (20007), E end of Georgetown. 202/965-2350. Hrs: 11:30 am-11 pm; Fri, Sat to midnight; Sun brunch 11:30 am-5 pm. Res accepted. Continental menu. Bar. Semi-a la carte: lunch $5.50-$12.95, dinner $13.95-$22.95. Sun brunch $5.95-$12.95.

Specializes in veal, Angus beef, fresh seafood. Valet parking $4. Atrium dining rm; country-English decor. Cr cds: A, C, D, DS, MC, V.

[SC] [⏗]

✔★ HAAD THAI. 1100 New York Ave NW (20005), downtown. 202/682-1111. Hrs: 11:30 am-2:30 pm, 5-10:30 pm; Sun from 5 pm. Closed most major hols. Res accepted. Thai menu. Bar. Semi-a la carte: lunch $5.95-$7.95, dinner $8.95-$13.95. Specialties: pad Thai, pla yang, surf-n-turf. Tropical atmosphere. Cr cds: A, D, MC, V.

[D]

★★ HOGATE'S. 9th St & Maine Ave SW (20024), on the waterfront, south of downtown. 202/484-6300. Hrs: Mon-Thurs 11 am-10 pm; Fri to 11 pm; Sat noon-11 pm; Sun 10:30 am-10 pm; Sun brunch to 2:30 pm. Closed Dec 25. Res accepted. Bar. Semi-a la carte: lunch $6-$13, dinner $13-$35. Lunch buffet $12.95. Sun brunch $18.95. Child's meals. Specialties: mariner's platter, wood grilled fish, rum buns. Brunch entertainment. Indoor parking $1.50/hr. Outdoor dining. Overlooks Potomac River. Cr cds: A, C, D, DS, MC, V.

[D] [⏗]

★★ HUNAN CHINATOWN. 624 H St NW (20001), in Chinatown. 202/783-5858. Hrs: 11 am-10 pm; Fri, Sat to 11 pm. Hunan, Szechwan menu. Serv bar. Semi-a la carte: lunch $6.50-$12, dinner $8-$23. Specialties: General Tso's chicken, tea-smoked half-duck, crispy prawns with walnuts. Parking (dinner). Modern, bi-level dining room. Cr cds: A, C, D, DS, MC, V.

[⏗] [♥]

✔★★ I MATTI TRATTORIA. 2436 18th St NW (20009), in Adams Morgan area. 202/462-8844. E-mail imatti@robertodonna.com; web www.robertodonna.com. Hrs: noon-2:30 pm, 5:30-10:30 pm; Fri to 11 pm; Sat noon-2:30 pm, 5:30-10:30 pm; Sun 5:30-10 pm. Closed Jan 1, Thanksgiving, Dec 25. Res accepted. Northern Italian menu. Bar to 11 pm Fri, Sat. A la carte entrees: lunch, dinner $10-$17. Specializes in traditional Tuscan cooking. Valet parking Tues-Sat. Upscale dining; lower dining area less formal. Cr cds: A, D, MC, V.

[D] [⏗]

★★★ ISABELLA. 809 15th St NW (20005), at McPherson Square, downtown. 202/408-9500. Hrs: 11:30 am-3 pm, 5:30-10:30 pm; Fri to 11 pm; Sat 5:30-11 pm; Sun from 5:30 pm. Closed most major hols. Res accepted. Mediterranean menu. Bar. Wine list. Semi-a la carte: lunch $9.95-$17.95, dinner $14.25-$21.50. Child's meals. Specializes in seafood, pastas, grilled meats. Own baking. Free valet parking (dinner). Outdoor dining. Contemporary Mediterranean decor; fabric wall hangings; palm trees. Cr cds: A, DS, MC, V.

[D] [⏗]

★ J PAUL'S. 3218 M St NW (20007), in Georgetown. 202/333-3450. Hrs: 11:30-1 am; Sun 10:30 am-11:30 pm; Sun brunch to 4 pm. Bar to 1:30 am. Semi-a la carte: lunch, dinner $5.25-$20.95. Sun brunch $7.95-$12.95. Child's meals. Specializes in ribs, crab cakes, burgers. Turn-of-the-century saloon decor; antique bar from Chicago's old Stockyard Inn. Cr cds: A, D, DS, MC, V.

[⏗]

★★ JALEO. 480 7th St NW (20004), downtown. 202/628-7949. E-mail tapasymas@msn.com; web dc.diningweb.com/restaurants/jaleo. Hrs: 11:30 am-11:30 pm; Sun, Mon to 10 pm; Fri, Sat to midnight. Closed Thanksgiving, Dec 24, 25. Spanish menu. Bar. Semi-a la carte: lunch $7.75-$9.95, dinner $10.50-$18. Specializes in hot & cold tapas, Spanish-style fish. Sevillanas dancers Wed nights. Valet parking $5. Murals of flamenco dancers cover the walls of this lively restaurant. Cr cds: A, D, DS, MC, V.

[D] [⏗]

★★ THE JEFFERSON. (See Jefferson Hotel) 202/833-6206. Hrs: 6:30-11 am, 11:30 am-2:30 pm, tea 3-5 pm, 6-10:30 pm. Sun brunch 10:30 am-2:30 pm. Res accepted. Bar 11-1 am. Wine list. Semi-a la carte: bkfst $4.50-$14.50, lunch $13-$22, dinner $22-$27. Sun brunch $19.50-

$25.75. Specializes in natural American cuisine. Valet parking. Jeffersonian-era cuisine and decor. Cr cds: A, C, D, DS, JCB, MC, V.

D

JOCKEY CLUB. *(New management, therefore not rated) (See Luxury Collection Hotel)* 202/659-8000. Hrs: 6:30-11 am, noon-2:30 pm, 6-10:30 pm; Sat, Sun 7-11:30 am, noon-2:30 pm, 6-10:30 pm. Res accepted. Classic French, international menu. Bar. A la carte entrees: bkfst $3.75-$16.50, lunch $11.50-$23, dinner $24.50-$34. Specializes in veal, fresh seafood, crab cakes. Own baking. Complimentary valet parking. Tableside cooking. Club-like atmosphere in 1928 landmark building. Jacket. Cr cds: A, C, D, DS, JCB, MC, V.

D

★ ★ ★ **KINKEAD'S.** *2000 Pennsylvania Ave NW (20006), at I St, in Foggy Bottom.* 202/296-7700. Chef Bob Kinkead has created two distinct but delicious dining options in this multichambered restaurant. Downstairs is a more informal and inexpensive pub-style eatery, while upstairs you can watch Kinkead and company turn out grilled dishes with an emphasis on seafood. Specialties: pepita-crusted salmon, pepper-seared tuna, grilled squid. Hrs: 11:30 am-10 pm; Fri, Sat to 10:30 pm; Sun brunch to 2:30 pm. Closed Jan 1, Thanksgiving, Dec 25. Res accepted. Bar to midnight. Semi-a la carte: lunch $12-$16, dinner $18-$22. Sun brunch $8-$12. Free valet parking (dinner). Outdoor dining. Jazz pianist Mon-Sat. Cr cds: A, C, D, DS, MC, V.

D

✔ ★ ★ **KRUPIN'S.** *4620 Wisconsin Ave NW (20016), north of downtown.* 202/686-1989. Hrs: 8 am-10 pm. Closed Dec 25. Semi-a la carte: bkfst $3.50-$15.95, lunch, dinner $5.25-$15.95. Child's meals. Specializes in smoked fish, meatloaf, beef stew. Old fashioned decor. Cr cds: A, C, D, MC, V.

D

★ ★ **LA CHAUMIÈRE.** *2813 M St NW (20007), E end of Georgetown.* 202/338-1784. Hrs: 11:30 am-2:30 pm, 5:30-10:30 pm; Sat from 5:30 pm. Closed Sun; major hols. Res accepted. Country French menu. Semi-a la carte entrees: lunch $10.95-$15.95, dinner $14.95-$24.95. Specializes in seafood, veal, game. Intimate room with beamed ceiling, open-hearth fireplace. Family-owned. Cr cds: A, C, D, MC, V.

★ ★ **LA COLLINE.** *400 N Capitol St NW (20001), on Capitol Hill.* 202/737-0400. Hrs: 7-10 am, 11:30 am-3 pm, 6-10 pm; Sat from 6 pm. Closed Sun; major hols. Res accepted. French menu. Bar. Semi-a la carte: bkfst $3.50-$8.75, lunch $9-$17, dinner $15-$22. Prix fixe: dinner $22-$27. Specializes in seasonal foods, fowl, seafood. Outdoor dining. Across from Union Station. Cr cds: A, C, D, MC, V.

D

★ ★ **LA FOURCHETTE.** *2429 18th St NW (20009), in Adams Morgan area.* 202/332-3077. Hrs: 11:30 am-10:30 pm; Sat 4-11 pm; Sun 4-10 pm. Closed major hols. Res accepted. French menu. Semi-a la carte: lunch $8.95-$19.95, dinner $10.95-$21.95. Specialties: bouillabaisse, rack of lamb, poitrine de poulet farcie au crabe. Outdoor dining. Former townhouse; painted murals on walls. Cr cds: A, C, D, MC, V.

★ ★ **LAFAYETTE.** *(See Hay-Adams Hotel)* 202/638-2570. Hrs: 6:30 am-2 pm, 5-10 pm; Sat, Sun from 7 am; Sun brunch 11:30 am-2 pm. Res accepted. Wine list. Semi-a la carte: bkfst $5.50-$15.25, lunch $14-$24, dinner $18-$29. Sun brunch $37.50. Specialties: grilled Dover sole in lobster pesto sauce, veal stuffed with asparagus and crab, sauteed big eye tuna in rice paper crust. Pianist. Overlooking Lafayette Park and the White House. Cr cds: A, D, DS, MC, V.

D ♥

★ ★ **LAURIOL PLAZA.** *1801 18th St NW (20009), in Dupont Circle.* 202/387-0035. Hrs: 11:30 am-11 pm; Fri, Sat to midnight; Sun brunch 11 am-3 pm. Res accepted wkdays. Latin Amer menu. Bar. A la carte entrees: lunch, dinner $5.95-$15. Sun brunch $5.95-$7.95. Special-

ties: paella, pollo asado, lomo saltado. Outdoor dining. Oil paintings and exotic flower arrangements. Cr cds: A, C, D, DS, MC, V.

✔ ★ **LAVANDOU.** *3321 Connecticut Ave NW (20008), north of downtown.* 202/966-3002. E-mail FD3321@aol.com; web www.dinenet.com. Hrs: 11:30 am-2:30 pm, 5-10 pm; Fri to 11 pm; Sat 5-11 pm; Sun 5-10 pm. Closed most major hols. Res accepted, required on wkends. Southern French menu. Serv bar. Semi-a la carte: lunch $9.95-$13.50, dinner $12.95-$17.95. Complete meals: dinner (to 6:30 pm) $14.95. Specialties: clam á l'ail, truite saumonnée, daube Provençale. French bistro atmosphere features country artifacts. Free parking. Cr cds: A, D, MC, V.

✔ ★ **LEBANESE TAVERNA.** *2641 Connecticut Ave NW (20008), north of downtown.* 202/265-8681. Hrs: 11:30 am-2:30 pm, 5:30-10:30 pm; Fri, Sat to 11 pm; Sun 5-10 pm. Closed major hols. Lebanese menu. Bar. Semi-a la carte: lunch $8-$12, dinner $10-$16. Specializes in falafel, shish kabob. Contemporary decor. Cr cds: A, D, DS, MC, V.

D

★ **LES HALLES.** *1201 Pennsylvania Ave NW (20004), downtown.* 202/347-6848. Hrs: 11:30 am-midnight; Sun brunch to 4 pm. Res accepted. French, Amer menu. Bar. Semi-a la carte: lunch $12.50-$19.95, dinner $15-$22.50. Sun brunch $14.95. Child's meals. Specialties: onglet, cassoulet. Outdoor dining. Three-level dining area. Cr cds: A, D, DS, JCB, MC, V.

★ ★ ★ **LESPINASSE.** *(See The Carlton Hotel)* 202/879-6900. Ornate chandeliers, French provincial furnishings and an elaborately detailed wood-beam ceiling make this elegant dining room unforgettable. Chef Troy Dupuy's entrees, featuring complex seasonings and lustrous flavors, are equally memorable. French menu. Specialties: shellfish bouillon with quinoa, sorrel and fenugreek; cauliflower-sweet pea papadum croustade with tamarind; squab breast with laratte potatoes and périgord truffles. Hrs: 7-10:30 am, noon-2 pm, 6-10 pm; Sat 7-11 am, 6-10 pm; Sun to 11 am. Closed most major hols; also Aug. Res accepted. Bar noon-midnight. Semi-a la carte: bkfst $6-$19, lunch $22-$27, dinner $27-$39. Prix fixe: lunch $36, dinner $75 or $95. Valet parking. Jacket. Cr cds: A, C, D, DS, ER, JCB, MC, V.

D

★ ★ **LUIGINO.** *1100 New York Ave NW (20005), downtown.* 202/371-0595. E-mail luigino@erols.com; web www.erols.com/luigino. Hrs: 11:30 am-2:30 pm, 5:30-10:30 pm; Fri to 11:30 pm; Sat 5:30-11:30 pm; Sun 5-10 pm. Closed major hols. Res accepted. Italian menu. Bar. Semi-a la carte: lunch $8.25-$15.50, dinner $12.50-$22.50. Child's meals. Specializes in pasta, seafood, game. Outdoor dining. Trattoria with contemporary atmosphere. Cr cds: A, D, MC, V.

D

★ ★ ★ **MAISON BLANCHE/RIVE GAUCHE.** *1725 F St NW (20006) near the White House, downtown.* 202/842-0070. Hrs: 11:45 am-2 pm, 6-9:30 pm; Sat from 6 pm. Closed Sun; major hols. Res accepted. French menu. Bar. Semi-a la carte: lunch $15-$27, dinner $26.50-$36. Prix fixe: lunch $21.95, dinner $32. Specialties: dessert souffles, Dover sole, lobster fricasée. Own pastries. Free valet parking from 5 pm. Jacket. Cr cds: A, C, D, DS, MC, V.

D

★ **MARKET INN.** *200 E St SW (20024), south of downtown.* 202/554-2100. E-mail seafrest@aol.com. Hrs: 11 am-11 pm; Fri to midnight; Sat 4:30 pm-midnight; major hols from 5 pm. Closed Thanksgiving, Dec 25. Res accepted. Bar. Semi-a la carte: lunch $6-$13.50, dinner $12.95-$24.95. Sun brunch $18.95. Child's meals. Specializes in Maine lobster, beef. Entertainment; jazz Sun brunch. Free valet parking. Outdoor dining. English pub ambience. Family-owned. Cr cds: A, C, D, DS, JCB, MC, V.

✔★ ★ **McCORMICK & SCHMICK'S.** *1652 K St NW (20006),* *downtown.* 202/861-2233. Hrs: 11 am-11 pm; Fri to midnight; Sat 5 pm-midnight; Sun 5-10 pm. Closed Dec 25. Res accepted. Seafood menu. Bar to midnight; Fri, Sat to 1 am; Sun to 11 pm. Semi-a la carte: lunch, dinner $5.95-$19.95. Child's meals. Specialties: Alaskan halibut stuffed with dungeness crab, bay shrimp and brie; cedar plank salmon with berry sauce; seared yellowfin tuna with wasabe and soy sauce. Own pastries. Valet parking (dinner). Old fashioned decor with large open grill. Cr cds: A, C, D, DS, JCB, MC, V.

D

★ ★ ★ **MELROSE.** *(See Park Hyatt Hotel)* 202/955-3899. Hrs: 6:30 am-2:30 pm, 5:30-10:30 pm; Fri, Sat to 11 pm; Sun brunch 10:30 am-2:30 pm. Res accepted. Contemporary Amer menu. Bar 11-1 am; Fri, Sat to 2 am. Wine cellar. Semi-a la carte: bkfst $8.50-$15, lunch $14-$22, dinner $19-$28. 7-course tasting dinner $55. Sun brunch $33-$36. Child's meals. Specializes in fresh fish, seafood, veal. Own baking. Pianist. Valet parking. Outdoor dining. Sunlit atrium. Italian fountain. Cr cds: A, C, D, DS, JCB, MC, V.

D

✔★ ★ **MESKEREM.** *2434 18th St NW (20009), in Adams Morgan* *area.* 202/462-4100. Hrs: noon-midnight; Fri, Sat to 1 am. Closed Thanksgiving, Dec 25. Res accepted. Ethiopian menu. Bar. Semi-a la carte: lunch, dinner $8.50-$11.95. Specializes in lamb, beef, chicken. Own Ethiopian breads. Ethiopian band Fri-Sun. Tri-level dining rm; traditional Ethiopian decor, sunny and bright. Cr cds: A, C, D, MC, V.

✔★ ★ **MISS SAIGON.** *1847 Columbia Rd NW (20009), in Adams* *Morgan area.* 202/667-1900. Hrs: noon-10:30 pm; Fri to 11 pm; Sat, Sun 5-11 pm. Closed July 4, Thanksgiving, Dec 25. Res accepted. Vietnamese menu. Bar. Semi-a la carte: lunch $5.95-$8.95, dinner $7.95-$10.95. Specialties: caramel salmon, Vietnamese steak, roast quails. Outdoor dining. Garden setting. Cr cds: A, D, MC, V.

★ ★ **MONOCLE ON CAPITOL HILL.** *107 D St NE (20002), adj* *to US Senate Office Bldg, on Capitol Hill.* 202/546-4488. Hrs: 11:30 am-midnight. Closed Sat, Sun; major hols. Res accepted. Bar. A la carte entrees: lunch $7-$16, dinner $12-$25. Child's meals. Specializes in seafood, aged beef. Valet parking. Located in 1865 Jenkens Hill building; fireplace. Close to Capitol; frequented by members of Congress and other politicians. Family-owned. Cr cds: A, C, D, MC, V.

★ ★ ★ **MORRISON-CLARK.** *(See Morrison-Clark Inn)* 202/898-1200. Hrs: 11:30 am-2 pm, 6-9:30 pm; Fri to 10 pm; Sat 6-10 pm; Sun brunch 11 am-2 pm. Closed some hols. Res accepted. Bar. Wine cellar. Semi-a la carte: lunch $13-$16, dinner $18-$24. Sun brunch $25-$27.50. Specialties: sautéed chicken breast with country ham and sage, marinated wild rockfish in citrus with fava beans and fennel, grilled rabbit with rabbit sausage and shelled beans. Own desserts. Free valet parking. Outdoor dining. Elegant Victorian dining rm; antiques; elaborately dressed floor-to-ceiling windows. Jacket. Cr cds: A, D, DS, MC, V.

★ ★ ★ **MORTON'S OF CHICAGO.** *3251 Prospect St NW (20007),* *in Georgetown.* 202/342-6258. Hrs: 5-11 pm; Sun 5-10 pm. Closed some major hols. Res accepted. Bar. Wine list. A la carte entrees: dinner $17.95-$29.95. Specializes in steak, lobster, seafood. Valet parking. Collection of Leroy Neiman paintings. Cr cds: A, C, D, JCB, MC, V.

D

✔★ **MR. SMITH'S.** *3104 M St NW (20007), in Georgetown.* 202/333-3104. E-mail mrsmith@aol.com. Hrs: 11:30-2 am; Fri, Sat to 3 am; Sat, Sun brunch 11 am-4:30 pm. Bar. Semi-a la carte: lunch, dinner $4.95-$14.95. Sat, Sun brunch $4.50-$8. Specializes in seafood, pasta, hamburgers. Pianist 9 pm-1:30 am. Old tavern atmosphere. Outdoor dining. Family-owned. Cr cds: A, C, D, MC, V.

★ **MR. YUNG'S.** *740 6th St NW (20001), in Chinatown.* 202/628-1098. Web www.menusonline.com/cities/ wash_dc/ desc/mryungs.shtml. Hrs:

11 am-10:30 pm. Chinese, Cantonese menu. Serv bar. Semi-a la carte: lunch $5.95-$7.95, dinner $6.95-$25.95. Specialties: sauteed shrimp with snow pea leaves, steamed lobster in garlic sauce. Enclosed outdoor dining. Modern Asian decor. Cr cds: A, DS, MC, V.

D

✔★ **MURPHY'S OF D.C.** *2609 24th St NW (20008), at Calvert* *St, north of downtown.* 202/462-7171. Hrs: 11-2 am. Irish, Amer menu. Beer. Semi-a la carte: lunch $5.95-$7.95, dinner $5.95-$11.95. Child's meals. Specializes in steaks, burgers, seafood. Traditional Irish music. Patio dining. Wood-burning fireplace. Cr cds: A, D, MC, V.

✔★ **MUSIC CITY ROADHOUSE.** *1050 30th St NW (20007),* *between M & K in the Foundry Building, in Georgetown.* 202/337-4444. E-mail mergm@aol.com. Hrs: 4:30 pm-2 am; Fri, Sat to 3 am; Sun 11 am-midnight; Sun brunch to 2 pm. Closed Mon; also most major hols. Res accepted. Bar. Semi-a la carte: dinner $10.95-$13.95. Sun brunch $12.95. Child's meals. Specializes in fried chicken, BBQ ribs, country fried steak. Old fashioned roadhouse with pictures of country singers. Cr cds: A, C, D, DS, MC, V.

D

★ ★ **NATHANS.** *3150 M St NW (20007), in Georgetown.* 202/338-2000. Hrs: 11 am-3 pm, 6-11 pm; Thurs-Sat to midnight; Sat, Sun brunch 10 am-3 pm. Res accepted. Northern Italian, Amer menu. Bar 11-2 am; Fri, Sat to 3 am. Semi-a la carte: lunch $5.25-$12.50, dinner $14.50-$30.50. Sat, Sun brunch $5.25-$12.50. Specializes in pasta, grilled fish. Entertainment Fri, Sat. Antiques. Family-owned. Cr cds: A, C, D, MC, V.

★ ★ ★ **NEW HEIGHTS.** *2317 Calvert St NW (20008), north of* *downtown.* 202/234-4110. Hrs: 5:30-10 pm; Fri, Sat to 11 pm; Sun brunch 11 am-2:30 pm. Closed major hols. Res accepted. New Amer cuisine. Bar from 5 pm. Semi-a la carte: dinner $15-$25. Sun brunch $8-$15. Specializes in calamari fritti, grilled salmon, fresh trout. Menu changes seasonally; some entrees offered in half-portions. Outdoor dining. Main dining rm on 2nd floor overlooks Rock Creek Park. Cr cds: A, C, D, DS, MC, V.

★ ★ ★ **NORA.** *2132 Florida Ave NW (20008), in Dupont Circle.* 202/462-5143. E-mail tthyme@erols.com; web www.noras .com. Hrs: 6-10 pm; Fri, Sat to 10:30 pm. Closed Sun; major hols; also last 2 wks Aug. Res accepted. Bar. Semi-a la carte: dinner $17.95-$24.95. Specializes in American organic cuisine with continental and Mediterranean influence. Menu changes daily. Own desserts. Atrium dining. In 1890 building with American folk art, Amish quilts on walls. Totally nonsmoking. Cr cds: MC, V.

♥

★ ★ **OBELISK.** *2029 P St NW (20036), in Dupont Circle.* 202/872-1180. Hrs: 6-10 pm. Closed Sun; major hols. Res accepted. Italian menu. Serv bar. Complete meals: dinner $40-$42. Specializes in seasonal dishes. Menu changes daily. Intimate dining rm on 2nd floor of town house. Totally nonsmoking. Cr cds: D, MC, V.

★ ★ **OCCIDENTAL GRILL.** *1475 Pennsylvania Ave NW* *(20004), downtown.* 202/783-1475. Hrs: 11:30 am-11 pm; Sun noon-9:30 pm. Closed Thanksgiving, Dec 25. Res accepted. Regional Amer menu. Bar. A la carte entrees: lunch $8-$20, dinner $13-$27. Specializes in grilled seafood, beef, lamb. Own desserts. Turn-of-the-century Victorian decor with autographed photos of celebrities; originally opened 1906. Cr cds: A, C, D, MC, V.

D

✔★ ★ **OLD EBBITT GRILL.** *675 15th St NW (20005), downtown.* 202/347-4801. Hrs: 7:30-1 am; Sat from 8 am; Sun from 9:30 am; Sun brunch to 4 pm. Res accepted. Bar to 2 am; Fri, Sat to 3 am. Semi-a la carte: bkfst $5.95-$9.95; lunch, dinner $7.95-$16.95. Sun brunch $6.95-$16.95. Specializes in fresh oysters, seafood, hamburgers. Own pasta. Valet parking (dinner, Sun brunch). In old vaudeville theater built in early

1900s. Victorian decor, gaslights; atrium dining. Cr cds: A, C, D, DS, MC, V.

[D] [symbol]

★ ★ **OLD EUROPE RESTAURANT & RATHSKELLER.** *2434 Wisconsin Ave NW (20007), north of downtown.* 202/333-7600. Hrs: 11:30 am-3 pm, 5-10 pm; Sun 4-9 pm. Closed July 4, Dec 24, 25. Res accepted. German menu. Serv bar. Semi-a la carte: lunch $5-$9, dinner $10-$20. Child's meals. Specialties: schnitzel Old Europe, Wienerschnitzel, sauerbraten. Pianist Thurs-Sun. Cr cds: A, C, D, MC, V.

[symbol]

★ ★ **THE OVAL ROOM.** *800 Connecticut Ave (20006), 1½ blocks from White House, downtown.* 202/463-8700. Hrs: 11:30 am-3:00 pm, 5:30-10:30 pm; Fri to 11 pm; Sat 5:30-11 pm. Closed Sun; some major hols. Res accepted. Bar. A la carte entrees: lunch $10.50-$22.50, dinner $13.50-$22.50. Specializes in New American cuisine. Menu changes seasonally. Pianist. Valet parking after 5:30 pm. Outdoor dining. Oval office theme is prevalent throughout this restaurant, from chandeliers to bar area. The decor and cooking style are strictly American. Cr cds: A, D, MC, V.

[D]

★ ★ **PALM.** *1225 19th St NW (20036), in Dupont Circle.* 202/293-9091. Hrs: 11:30 am-10:30 pm; Sat from 6 pm; Sun 5:30-9:30 pm. Closed major hols. Res accepted. Bar. A la carte entrees: lunch $8.50-$17, dinner $14-$30. Specializes in steak, lobster. Valet parking (dinner). 1920s New York-style steak house. Family-owned. Cr cds: A, D, MC, V.

[D] [symbol]

★ ★ **PAOLO'S.** *1303 Wisconsin Ave NW (20007), in Georgetown.* 202/333-7353. Hrs: 11:30-2 am; Fri, Sat to 3 am; Sun 11 am-2 am; Sat, Sun brunch to 4 pm. Italian menu. Bar. Semi-a la carte: lunch, dinner $7.95-$18.95. Sun brunch $6.95. Specializes in pizza, pasta, seafood. Jazz combo Sun afternoons. Patio dining; wood-burning pizza oven. Cr cds: A, C, D, DS, MC, V.

[symbol] [♥]

★ ★ **PESCE.** *2016 P St NW (20036), on Dupont Circle.* 202/466-3474. Web www.robertodonna.com. Hrs: 11:30 am-2:30 pm, 5:30-10 pm; Fri, Sat to 10:30 pm; Sun 5-9:30 pm. Closed Labor Day, Dec 25. Semi-a la carte: lunch, dinner $13.50-$22.95. Specializes in seafood. Valet parking Thurs-Sat. Modern decor. Cr cds: A, D, MC, V.

[SC]

★ ★ **PETITTO'S RISTORANTE D'ITALIA.** *2653 Connecticut Ave NW (20008), north of downtown.* 202/667-5350. Hrs: 5:30-10:30 pm; Sun to 9:30 pm. Closed major hols. Res accepted. Italian menu. Bar. A la carte entrees: dinner $11-$18. Specializes in pasta, fish, veal. Valet parking. Outdoor dining. Dessert, cappuccino rm downstairs. Turn-of-the-century Victorian townhouse overlooking Connecticut Ave; fireplaces. Cr cds: A, C, D, DS, MC, V.

[symbol]

✔★ **PIZZERIA PARADISO.** *2029 P St NW (20036), in Dupont Circle.* 202/223-1245. Hrs: 11 am-11 pm; Fri, Sat to midnight; Sun noon-10 pm. Closed some major hols. Italian menu. Wine, beer. A la carte entrees: lunch, dinner $5.50-$15.95. Specializes in pizza, salads, sandwiches. Lively, colorful atmosphere; pizza-makers visible from dining area. Totally nonsmoking. Cr cds: D, MC, V.

★ ★ **PRIME RIB.** *2020 K St NW (20006), downtown.* 202/466-8811. Hrs: 11:30 am-3 pm, 5-11 pm; Fri to 11:30 pm; Sat 5-11:30 pm. Closed Sun; major hols. Res accepted. Bar. Semi-a la carte: lunch $8-$17. A la carte entrees: dinner $15-$27. Specializes in roast prime rib, Chesapeake seafood, aged thick-cut steak. Pianist. Free valet parking (dinner). Art deco decor; 1920s lithographs. 1940s New York supper club atmosphere. Jacket. Cr cds: A, D, MC, V.

[D] [symbol]

✔★ ★ **PRIMI PIATTI.** *2013 I St NW (20006), downtown.* 202/223-3600. Hrs: 11:30 am-2:30 pm, 5:30-10:30 pm; Fri, Sat 5:30-11:30 pm. Closed Sun; most major hols. Res accepted. Italian menu. Bar. Semi-a la carte: lunch $10-$15.50, dinner $11-$20. Specializes in grilled fish, meat. Own pasta. Outdoor dining. Cr cds: A, C, D, MC, V.

[D] [symbol]

★ ★ ★ **PROVENCE.** *2401 Pennsylvania Ave NW (20037), west of downtown.* 202/296-1166. Hrs: noon-2 pm, 6-10 pm; Fri to 11 pm; Sat 6-11 pm; Sun 6-9:30 pm. Res accepted. French menu. Bar. Semi-a la carte: lunch $12-$20, dinner $17.50-$29. Specializes in French Provencal cooking. Mediterranean setting. Cr cds: A, C, D, MC, V.

[D]

✔★ **RAKU.** *1900 Q St NW (20009), in Dupont Circle.* 202/265-7258. Web www.dinersgrapevine.com/raku. Hrs: 11:30 am-midnight; Fri, Sat to 1 am; winter to 11 pm; Fri, Sat to midnight. Closed Thanksgiving, Dec 25. Pan-Asian menu. Bar. Semi-a la carte: lunch, dinner $4-$18. Specializes in noodle dishes, dumplings, satays. Street parking. Outdoor dining. Casual teahouse decor with varied Asian accents. Cr cds: MC, V.

[D] [symbol]

★ ★ **RED SAGE.** *605 14th St NW (20005), in Westory Bldg, downtown.* 202/638-4444. Web www.dinersgrapevine.com/redsage. Hrs: 11:30 am-2 pm, 5:30-10 pm; Sun from 5 pm. Closed Dec 25. Res accepted. Eclectic menu. Bar. A la carte entrees: lunch $8.50-$15.50, dinner $18.50-$31. Specializes in Western dishes with Native American influences. Validated parking. Designed as a contemporary interpretation of the American West; each of dining level's four major areas exhibits a particular style and mood. Cr cds: A, C, D, DS, MC, V.

[D] [symbol]

★ ★ **ROOF TERRACE.** *2700 F St NW (20566), within Kennedy Center, in Foggy Bottom.* 202/416-8555. Hrs: 11:30 am-3 pm only on matinee days, 5:30-9 pm on performance eves. Sun brunch 11:30 am-2:30 pm. Res accepted. Semi-a la carte: lunch $12-$16, dinner $20-$29. Sun brunch $25.95. Child's meals. Specializes in regional American cuisine. Garage parking. Summer outdoor dining. Contemporary decor; floor-to-ceiling windows offer views of Lincoln Memorial, Washington Monument, Potomac River and Virginia. Totally nonsmoking. Cr cds: A, C, D, JCB, MC, V.

[D]

★ ★ **SAIGON GOURMET.** *2635 Connecticut Ave NW (20008), north of downtown.* 202/265-1360. Hrs: 11 am-3 pm, 5-10:30 pm. Closed Thanksgiving. Res accepted. Vietnamese menu. Serv bar. Semi-a la carte: lunch $5.95-$7.95, dinner $8.95-$13.95. Specialties: Saigon roasted noodles, roasted quail, caramel chicken. Valet parking. Patio dining overlooking upper Connecticut Ave. Cr cds: A, D, DS, MC, V.

[D]

✔★ **SAIGONNAIS.** *2307 18th St NW (20009), in Adams Morgan area.* 202/232-5300. Hrs: 11 am-3 pm, 5-11 pm; Sun 5-10:30 pm. Closed Jan 1, Thanksgiving, Dec 25. Res accepted. Serv bar. Vietnamese menu. Semi-a la carte: lunch, dinner $7.95-$14.50. Specialties: lemongrass beef, shrimp on sugar cane stick. Outdoor dining. Vietnamese artwork. Cr cds: A, MC, V.

[symbol]

★ ★ ★ **SAM & HARRY'S.** *1200 19th St NW (20036), in Dupont Circle.* 202/296-4333. Hrs: 11:30 am-2:30 pm, 5:30-10:30 pm; Sat from 5:30 pm. Closed Sun; major hols. Res accepted. Bar. A la carte entrees: lunch $8.95-$22.95, dinner $17.95-$32.95. Specializes in prime-aged beef, Maine lobster, fresh seafood. Valet parking (dinner). Club-like atmosphere with mahogany paneling, paintings of jazz legends. Cr cds: A, C, D, DS, MC, V.

[D] [symbol]

★ **SARINAH SATAY HOUSE.** *1338 Wisconsin Ave NW (20007), in Georgetown.* 202/337-2955. Hrs: noon-3 pm, 6-10:30 pm; Sun from 6 pm. Closed Mon; Dec 25. Res accepted. Indonesian menu. Bar. A la carte entrees: lunch $5.95, dinner $7.90-$14.95. Specialties: gado gado, satays, rijsttafel. Two levels of dining in a lush, tropical atmosphere; Indonesian artifacts. Cr cds: A, C, D, DS, MC, V.

⌐

★ ★ **SEA CATCH.** *1054 31st St NW (20007), at M St, in Georgetown.* 202/337-8855. Hrs: noon-3 pm, 5:30-10 pm. Closed Sun. Res accepted. Bar. Semi-a la carte: lunch $4.75-$12, dinner $16-$24. Specializes in fresh seafood, lobster, crab cakes. Own pastries. Valet parking. Outdoor dining on deck overlooking historic Chesapeake & Ohio Canal. Cr cds: A, D, DS, MC, V.

D ⌐

★ ★ ★ **SEASONS.** *(See Four Seasons Hotel)* 202/342-0444. Hrs: 7-11 am, noon-2:30 pm, 6:30-10:30 pm; Sun brunch 10 am-2:30 pm. Res accepted. Bar 11-2 am. Wine list. Semi-a la carte: bkfst $9-$21, lunch $14-$23, dinner $23-$35. Child's meals. Specializes in regional and seasonal dishes. Own baking. Pianist. Valet parking. Overlooks Rock Creek Park. Cr cds: A, C, D, ER, JCB, MC, V.

D ⌐ ♥

★ ★ **SEQUOIA.** *3000 K St NW (20007), Washington Harbour complex, in Georgetown.* 202/944-4200. Hrs: 11:30 am-midnight; Fri, Sat to 1 am; Sat, Sun brunch 10:30 am-4 pm. Res accepted. Bar. Semi-a la carte: lunch, dinner $7.95-$28.95. Sun brunch $14.95. Outdoor dining. Terrace and multi-story dining rm windows overlook Kennedy Center, Potomac River and Roosevelt Bridge, Island. Cr cds: A, D, DS, MC, V.

D ⌐

★ **SUSHI KO.** *2309 Wisconsin Ave NW (20007), north of downtown.* 202/333-4187. E-mail sushiko@vni.net; web www.sushiko.com. Hrs: noon-2:30 pm, 6-10:30 pm; Mon from 6 pm; Sat 5-10:30 pm; Sun 5-10 pm. Closed July 4, Thanksgiving, Dec 25. Res accepted. Japanese menu. Semi-a la carte: lunch $6.50-$10.50, dinner $7.50-$18.50. Specializes in traditional and modern Japanese dishes. Casual decor. Cr cds: A, MC, V.

★ ★ **TABERNA DEL ALABARDERO.** *1776 I St NW (20006), entrance on 18th St, downtown.* 202/429-2200. Hrs: 11:30 am-2:30 pm, 6-10 pm; Fri to 11 pm; Sat 6-11 pm. Closed Sun; major hols. Res accepted. Basque, Spanish menu. Bar. Semi-a la carte: lunch $14-$20, dinner $16-$28. Complete meals: lunch $17.50, dinner $35. Specializes in beef, fish, paella. Tapas bar. Own baking. Flamenco dancers Mar, Oct. Garage parking (dinner). Outdoor dining. Ornate, 19th-century Spanish decor. Jacket. Cr cds: A, D, DS, MC, V.

⌐

✔★ **THAI KINGDOM.** *2021 K St NW (20006), downtown.* 202/835-1700. Hrs: 11:30 am-2:30 pm, 5-10:30 pm; Sat noon-11 pm; Sun noon-10 pm. Closed some major hols. Res accepted. Thai menu. Bar. A la carte entrees: lunch $6.50-$8.95, dinner $7.25-$9.95. Specialties: crispy chili fish, scallops wrapped in minced chicken, Thai Kingdom grilled chicken. Outdoor dining. Bi-level dining rm with full windows overlooking K St; authentic Thai decor. Cr cds: A, C, D, MC, V.

D ⌐

★ **THAI TASTE.** *2606 Connecticut Ave NW (20008), north of downtown.* 202/387-8876. Hrs: 11:30 am-10:30 pm; Fri, Sat to 11 pm. Closed some major hols. Res accepted. Thai menu. A la carte entrees: lunch, dinner $6.95-$10.95. Specializes in fish, chicken, seafood combinations. Outdoor dining. Cr cds: A, MC, V.

⌐

✔★ **THE TOMBS.** *1226 36th St NW (20007), in Georgetown.* 202/337-6668. Hrs: 11:30 am-midnight; Sat from 11 am; Sun brunch 9:30 am-3 pm. Closed Thanksgiving, Dec 24, 25. Bar. Semi-a la carte: lunch, dinner $4.95-$10.95. Sun brunch $5.25-$7.95. Specializes in chicken, pasta, burgers. Vintage crew gear and prints on walls. Cr cds: A, C, D, DS, MC, V.

★ ★ **TONY AND JOE'S.** *3000 K St NW (20007), at Washington Harbour complex, in Georgetown.* 202/944-4545. Web www.diningweb.com/restaurants/tonyandjoe's. Hrs: 11 am-11 pm; Fri, Sat to midnight;

Sun brunch to 3 pm. Closed Dec 25. Res accepted. Bar Fri, Sat to 2 am. Semi-a la carte: lunch $6.95-$22.95, dinner $14.95-$27.95. Sun brunch $17.95. Specializes in seafood. Own desserts. Entertainment Tues-Sat. Outdoor dining. Overlooks Potomac River. Cr cds: A, C, D, DS, JCB, MC, V.

D ⌐

★ ★ **TONY CHENG'S MONGOLIAN BARBECUE.** *619 H St NW (20001), in Chinatown.* 202/842-8669. Hrs: 11 am-11 pm; Fri, Sat to midnight. Res accepted. Mongolian barbecue menu. Prix fixe: lunch $8.50, dinner $13.95 (serv charge 15%). Food bar encircles Mongolian grill. Diners may select own ingredients to be stir fried, grilled or steeped tableside. Asian decor. Cr cds: A, MC, V.

⌐

★ ★ **TWO QUAIL.** *320 Massachusetts Ave NE (20002), on Capitol Hill.* 202/543-8030. Hrs: 11:30 am-2:30 pm, 5-10:30 pm; Sat, Sun from 5 pm. Closed Dec 25. Res accepted. Semi-a la carte: lunch $7-$14, dinner $11-$19. Specializes in New American cuisine, baked pork chops, seafood. Country inn atmosphere in Victorian townhouse; eclectic furnishings. Cr cds: A, C, D, DS, MC, V.

★ ★ ★ **VIDALIA.** *1990 M St NW (20036), in Dupont Circle.* 202/659-1990. Hrs: 11:30 am-2:30 pm, 5:30-10 pm; Fri to 10:30 pm; Sat 5:30-10:30 pm; Sun 5-9:30 pm. Closed most major hols. Res accepted. Bar. Semi-a la carte: lunch $11-$19, dinner $18-$25. Specialties: sauteed shrimp with creamed grits, pan roasted sweetbreads. Country manor house decor. Cr cds: A, DS, MC, V.

D

★ ★ **VINCENZO AL SOLE.** *1606 20th St NW (20009), in Dupont Circle.* 202/667-0047. Hrs: 6-10 pm. Closed Sun; major hols. Res accepted. Italian menu. Bar. Semi-a la carte: dinner $15.75-$24.75. Specializes in fresh seafood. Valet parking (dinner). Four dining rms, including atrium. Outdoor dining. Cr cds: A, C, D, MC, V.

D

★ ★ ★ **WILLARD ROOM.** *(See Willard Inter-Continental Hotel)* 202/637-7440. Hrs: 7:30-10 am, 11:30 am-2 pm, 6-10 pm; Sat, Sun from 6 pm. Res accepted. Bar 11-1 am. Wine list. European, regional Amer menu. A la carte entrees: bkfst $7.50-$12.75, lunch $10.50-$17.50, dinner $18.50-$29.50. Complete meals: breakfast $12-$17.50, lunch $24-$28, dinner $36-$65. Specializes in regional seafood, lamb, beef. Seasonal specialties. Own pastries. Pianist. Valet parking (dinner). Cr cds: A, C, D, DS, JCB, MC, V.

D ⌐

✔★ **ZED'S ETHIOPIAN.** *3318 M St NW (20007), in Georgetown.* 202/333-4710. Hrs: 11 am-11 pm. Closed most major hols. Ethiopian menu. Serv bar. Semi-a la carte: lunch $6.95-$10.75, dinner $7.75-$12.95. Specializes in seafood, beef, vegetarian dishes. No silverware is used at the restaurant; communal dining from trays. Cr cds: A, D, DS, MC, V.

⌐

✔★ ★ **ZUKI MOON.** *824 New Hampshire Ave NW (20037), 2 blks NE of Kennedy Center, in Foggy Bottom.* 202/333-3312. Hrs: 7-10 am, 11:30-2:30 pm, 5-11 pm; Sat 8-11 am, 5-11 pm; Sun 8-11 am, 5-10 pm. Closed some major hols. Res accepted. Japanese menu. Bar. A la carte entrees: bkfst $2-$4.50. Semi-a la carte: lunch, dinner $7.95-$15.50. Specializes in meal-in-a-bowl noodle soups, grilled meats and fish. Valet parking (lunch & dinner). Outdoor dining. Modern Japanese garden decor. Totally nonsmoking. Cr cds: A, D, MC, V.

D

Unrated Dining Spots

ARMAND'S CHICAGO PIZZERIA. *4231 Wisconsin Ave NW, north of downtown.* 202/686-9450. Hrs: 11:30 pm-11 pm; Fri, Sat to 1 am. Closed Thanksgiving, Dec 25. Bar. A la carte entrees: lunch, dinner $4-$7. Buffet: lunch (pizza & salad) $4.99. Specializes in Chicago-style deep-dish pizza, sandwiches, salads. Outdoor dining. Cr cds: A, DS, MC, V.

AUSTIN GRILL. *2404 Wisconsin Ave NW, in Georgetown. 202/337-8080.* Hrs: 11:30 am-11 pm; Fri, Sat to midnight; Sat brunch to 3 pm; Sun brunch 11 am-3 pm. Closed Thanksgiving, Dec 25. Tex-Mex menu. Bar. Semi-a la carte: lunch, dinner $4.95-$12.95. Sat, Sun brunch $4.95-$6.95. Specializes in enchiladas, fajitas. Southwestern decor. Cr cds: A, D, DS, MC, V.

C.F. FOLKS. *1225 19th St NW, in Dupont Circle. 202/293-0162.* Hrs: 11:45 am-3 pm. Closed Sat, Sun; major hols. Semi-a la carte: lunch $4.95-$8.95. Complete meals: lunch $7-$10. Specializes in daily & seasonally changing cuisines. Outdoor dining. Old-fashioned lunch counter. No cr cds accepted.

CAFE PARMA. *1724 Connecticut Ave NW, in Dupont Circle. 202/462-8771.* Hrs: 11:30 am-11:30 pm; Fri, Sat to midnight; Sun to 10 pm; Sat, Sun brunch to 3 pm. Italian menu. Bar. A la carte entrees: lunch, dinner $6-$13. Sat, Sun brunch $10.75. Specializes in pizza, pasta, hoagies. Cr cds: A, C, D, MC, V.

KRAMERBOOKS & AFTERWORDS. *1517 Connecticut Ave, in Dupont Circle. 202/387-1462.* Hrs: 7:30-1 am; Fri, Sat open 24 hrs; Sun brunch 9:30 am-3 pm. Closed Thanksgiving, Dec 25. Bar. Semi-a la carte: bkfst $3.95-$7.50, lunch, dinner $6.75-$12.75. Sun brunch $8.25-

$13.25. Specialties: Thai jambalaya, grilled portobello mushroom sandwich. Entertainment Thurs-Sun. Outdoor dining. In 2-story greenhouse & terrace behind Kramerbooks bookshop. Cr cds: A, DS, MC, V.

PATISSERIE-CAFE DIDIER. *3206 Grace St NW (20007), in Georgetown. 202/342-9083.* Hrs: 8 am-7 pm; Sun to 5 pm. Closed Mon; Jan 1, Dec 25. Semi-a la carte: bkfst $1.10-$7.95, lunch $5.99-$8.99. Specializes in European desserts, quiche, pizza. European-style cafe and pastry house. Cr cds: C, D, DS, MC, V.

PHILLIPS FLAGSHIP. *900 Water St SW, on waterfront, south of downtown. 202/488-8515.* Hrs: 11 am-2 pm, 5-10 pm; Fri to 11 pm; Sat, Sun 11 am-11 pm. Closed Dec 25. Bar. Buffet: lunch $14.95, dinner $19.95; Sun $19.95. A la carte bar menu: $3.50-$9.95. Specializes in seafood. Sushi bar. Garage parking. Outdoor dining. Antiques; Tiffany lamps, stained glass. Cr cds: A, C, D, DS, MC, V.

D **SC** **-**

SHOLL'S COLONIAL CAFETERIA. *1990 K St NW, in Esplanade Mall, in Foggy Bottom. 202/296-3065.* Hrs: 7 am-2:30 pm, 4-8 pm. Closed Sun; major hols. Avg ck: bkfst $3, lunch, dinner $5. Specialties: spaghetti, liver & onions, homemade pie. Family-owned. No cr cds accepted.

D

Maryland

Population: 4,917,269
Land area: 9,838 square miles
Elevation: 0-3,360 feet
Highest point: Backbone Mountain (Garrett County)
Entered Union: Seventh of original 13 states (April 28, 1788)
Capital: Annapolis
Motto: Manly deeds, womanly words
Nickname: Old Line State, Free State
State flower: Black-eyed Susan
State bird: Baltimore oriole
State tree: Wye oak
State fair: August 29-September 7, 1998, in Timonium (see Towson)
Time zone: Eastern
Web: www.mdisfun.org

Maryland prides itself on its varied terrain and diverse economy. Metropolitan life around the great cities of Baltimore and Washington, DC (the land was ceded from Maryland in 1791) is balanced by the rural atmosphere in central and southern Maryland and on the Eastern Shore, across Chesapeake Bay. Green mountains in the western counties contrast with white Atlantic beaches. A flourishing travel industry, agricultural and dairy wealth in central Maryland, the seafood industry of the Bay and its tidal rivers, manufacturing and commerce in the cities, plus federal government and defense contracts combine to make the state prosperous.

Maryland's three-and-one-half centuries of history began in March, 1634, when Lord Baltimore's brother, Leonard Calvert, solemnly knelt on tiny St Clements Island, near the wide mouth of the Potomac, and named his new province in honor of Henrietta Maria, wife of Charles I, King of England. Calvert's awkward little ships, the *Ark* and the *Dove,* then carried the 222 passengers, including religious refugees, to a Native American village a few miles away. They purchased the village and named it Saint Maries Citty (now St Mary's City). Religious toleration was practiced from the colony's founding and was assured by law in 1649. The land was cleared, tobacco was planted, and over the years, profits built elegant mansions, many of which still stand.

Maryland was one of the 13 original colonies. Its first capital was St Mary's City. In 1694 the capital was transferred to Annapolis, where it remains today.

Every war waged on US soil has seen major action by Marylanders. In 1755, British General Edward Braddock, assisted by Lt Colonel George Washington, trained his army at Cumberland for the fight against the French and Indians. In the Revolution, General William Howe invaded Maryland at the head of Chesapeake Bay, and a battle was joined at Brandywine Creek in Pennsylvania before the British moved on to capture Philadelphia. Maryland troops in the Battle of Long Island made a heroic bayonet coverage of the retreat. The courageous action of the "Old Line" gave the state one of its nicknames. The War of 1812 saw Fort McHenry at Baltimore withstand attack by land and sea, with the action immortalized in the national anthem by Francis Scott Key, a Frederick lawyer. In the Civil War, Maryland was a major battleground at Antietam; troops moved back and forth through the state for the four bloody years of destruction.

A border state with commercial characteristics of both North and South, Maryland found its original dependence on tobacco relieved by the emerging Industrial Revolution. Modern factories, mills and ironworks around Baltimore became important to the state's economy. Educational institutions were established and the port of Baltimore, at the mouth of the Patapsco River, flourished. In the mid-19th century, with the Baltimore & Ohio Railroad and the Chesapeake & Ohio Canal carrying freight to the fast-developing western states, Maryland thrived.

Sports enthusiasts have always thought well of Maryland. The state's thousands of miles of tidal shoreline allows plenty of elbow room for aquatic diversion. Maryland's race tracks include Pimlico (see BALTIMORE), featuring the nationally known Preakness Stakes, and Laurel. The "Maryland Million" is held alternately at Laurel and Pimlico. Deer hunting is allowed in most counties and goose hunting on the Eastern Shore. Historical sites cover the landscape, and more are constantly being opened up to the public by the state and National Park Service. Highways are good; reaching places in the Baltimore-Washington, DC area is simplified by direct, high-speed, four-lane highways constructed around, between and radiating from these cities.

When to Go/Climate

Spring and autumn are the best times to visit Maryland. Winter weather is unpredictable and summers are hot and humid.

AVERAGE HIGH/LOW TEMPERATURES (°F)

BALTIMORE

Jan 40/23	**May** 74/53	**Sept** 79/58
Feb 44/26	**June** 83/62	**Oct** 67/46
Mar 54/34	**July** 87/67	**Nov** 57/37
Apr 64/43	**Aug** 85/66	**Dec** 45/28

Parks and Recreation Finder

Directions to and information about the parks and recreation areas below are given under their respective town/city sections. Please refer to those sections for details.

Key to abbreviations: I.P. = Interstate Park; N.B.C. = National Battlefield & Cemetery; N.B.P. = National Battlefield Park; N.F. = National Forest; N.H. = National Historical Park; N.H.S. = National Historic Site; N.M. = National Monument; N.Mem. = National Memorial; N.M.P. = National Military Park; N.P. = National Park; N.Pres. = National Preserve; N.R. = National Recreational Area; N.S. = National Seashore; N.S.T. = National Scenic Trail; S.B. = State Beach; S.C.P. = State Conservation Park; S.G. = State Garden; S.H.A. = State Historic Area; S.H.P. = State Historic Park; S.N.A. = State Natural Area; S.P. = State Park; S.R. = State Reserve; S.R.A. = State Recreation Area; S.Res.P. = State Resort Park; S.R.P. = State Rustic Park.

NATIONAL PARK AND RECREATION AREAS

Place Name	Listed Under
Antietam National Battlefield	same
Assateague Island N.S.	OCEAN CITY
Catoctin Mountain Park	THURMONT
Chesapeake and Ohio Canal N.H.	same
Fort McHenry N.M. and Historic Shrine	BALTIMORE
Hampton N.H.S.	TOWSON

STATE RECREATION AREAS

Place Name	Listed Under
Assateague S.P.	OCEAN CITY
Cedarville State Forest	WALDORF
Cunningham Falls S.P.	THURMONT
Dans Mountain S.P.	CUMBERLAND
Deep Creek Lake S.P.	OAKLAND
Elk Neck State Forest	ELKTON
Elk Neck S.P.	ELKTON
Fort Frederick S.P.	HAGERSTOWN
Gambrill S.P.	FREDERICK
Garrett State Forest	OAKLAND
Green Ridge State Forest	CUMBERLAND
Greenbrier S.P.	HAGERSTOWN
Gunpowder Falls S.P. (Hammerman Area)	BALTIMORE
Herrington Manor S.P.	OAKLAND
Janes Island S.P.	CRISFIELD
New Germany S.P.	GRANTSVILLE
Patapsco Valley S.P.	ELLICOTT CITY
Point Lookout S.P.	ST MARY'S CITY
Potomac State Forest	OAKLAND
Rocky Gap S.P.	CUMBERLAND
Sandy Point S.P.	ANNAPOLIS
Savage River State Forest	GRANTSVILLE
Seneca Creek S.P.	GAITHERSBURG
Smallwood S.P.	LA PLATA
Susquehanna S.P.	HAVRE DE GRACE
Swallow Falls S.P.	OAKLAND
Tuckahoe S.P.	EASTON

Water-related activities, hiking, riding, various other sports, picnicking and visitor centers, as well as camping, are available in many of these areas. Most state-maintained areas have small charges for parking and special services. Camping: $2-$22/site/night; stays limited to two wks; most areas are open late Mar-early Dec, but season varies from one park to the next; ck-out 3 pm; reservations for a stay of 1 wk are available at Assateague—they may be obtained by writing directly to the park (see

OCEAN CITY). Pets allowed at the following parks (some special restrictions may apply; phone ahead): Green Ridge Forest, Elk Neck, Patapsco (Hollofield), Point Lookout, Rocky Gap, Savage River Forest, Susquehanna, Swallow Falls, Garrett Forest, Potomac Forest and Pocomoke River (Milburn Landing). Day use: 8 am-sunset; closed Dec 25; fee Mar-Oct. For complete information, including information on cabins, contact the Maryland Dept of Natural Resources, State Forest and Park Service, Tawes State Office Bldg E-3, 580 Taylor Ave, Annapolis 21401; 410/974-3771 or 800/830-3974. It is advisable to call parks before visiting, as some may be closed during the off season.

FISHING & HUNTING

Non-tidal, nonresident fishing license, $20; 5-day, $7; trout stamp, $5. Chesapeake Bay nonresident fishing license, $12; 5-day, $4.

Nonresident hunting licenses: consolidated, $83-$120.50, depending on state of residence; 3-day, $35; waterfowl stamp $6; regular deer stamp, $9.50; bow hunting deer stamp, $3.50; black powder deer stamp, $3.50; 2nd deer stamp, $10. For latest information, including *Maryland Sportfishing Guide* or the *Guide to Hunting, Trapping in Maryland,* contact Maryland Dept of Natural Resources, Licensing Division, 580 Taylor Ave B-1, Annapolis 21401; 410/974-3211.

Driving Information

Safety belts are mandatory for driver and passengers in front seat of vehicle. Children 10 years and under must be in an approved passenger restraint anywhere in the vehicle. Children under 4 years or weighing 40 pounds or less must be in an approved safety seat. For further information phone 410/486-3101.

INTERSTATE HIGHWAY SYSTEM

The following alphabetical listing of Maryland towns in *Mobil Travel Guide* shows that these cities are within 10 miles of the indicated Interstate highways. A highway map should be checked, however, for the nearest exit.

Highway Number	Cities/Towns within 10 miles
Interstate 68	Cumberland.
Interstate 70	Baltimore, Columbia, Ellicott City, Frederick, Hagerstown.
Interstate 81	Hagerstown.
Interstate 83	Baltimore, Cockeysville, Towson.
Interstate 95	Aberdeen, Baltimore, College Park, Elkton, Havre de Grace, Laurel, Silver Spring, Towson.

Additional Visitor Information

The Maryland guide to travel, *Destination Maryland,* and a calendar of events can be obtained from the Maryland Office of Tourism Development, 217 E Redwood St, Baltimore 21202; 800/543-1036.

There are several visitor information centers in Maryland; visitors who stop by will find information and brochures helpful in planning stops at points of interest. Their locations are as follows: on I-95 (N & S) near Laurel; on I-70 (E & W) between Hagerstown and Frederick; on US 15S at Emmitsburg; on I-95S near North East; on US 48E near Friendsville; on US 13N near Maryland-Virginia line; in the State House, Annapolis; Crain memorial, on US 301 N, Newburg; and in Bay Country, on US 301N/S, Centreville. (Daily; closed some major hols)

Aberdeen (B-8)

Pop 13,087 **Elev** 83 ft **Area code** 410 **Zip** 21001

This is the home of the 75,000-acre Aberdeen Proving Grounds, a federal reservation along Chesapeake Bay. Various types of army materiel, ranging from gunsights to tanks, are tested under simulated combat conditions.

What to See and Do

Peco Energy Company. Hydroelectric plant on the Susquehanna River. Limited area of plant is open for guided tours (Apr-Sept, Sat; rest of yr, by appt; closed hols). 7 mi NE on US 40 or I-95, then 11 mi NW on US 222 to Conowingo. Phone the Conowingo Information Center at 410/457-5011 for more information. **Free.** Nearby is

Recreation area with 14-mi-long man-made lake; picnicking, hiking; swimming pool (fee); boating (ramps, marinas); fishing; fishermen's gallery (over 12 yrs only). Phone 410/457-5011. **Free.**

US Army Ordnance Museum. Tanks, artillery, self-propelled artillery, extensive small arms and ammunition collection. (Daily; closed most major hols) At Aberdeen Proving Ground, off I-95 exit 85, 3 mi E on MD 22, follow signs. Phone 410/278-3602. **Free.**

Motels

✓★ **DAYS INN.** 783 W Bel Air Ave, I-95 exit 85. 410/272-8500; FAX 410/272-5782. 49 rms, 2 story. S $43; D $47; each addl $4; under 16 free. Crib free. Pet accepted; $5. TV; cable (premium). Pool. Complimentary continental bkfst. Restaurant nearby. Ck-out 11 am. Business servs avail. Refrigerators avail. Cr cds: A, C, D, DS, JCB, MC, V.

D ✓ 🏊 ✕ 🐾 SC

★★ **HOLIDAY INN-CHESAPEAKE HOUSE.** 1007 Beards Hill Rd. 410/272-8100; FAX 410/272-1714. 122 rms, 5 story. S, D $93-$99; each addl $10; suites $125; kit. units $99-$109; under 18 free; wknd rates. Pet accepted. TV; cable (premium), VCR avail. Indoor pool. Restaurant 6 am-2 pm, 5-10 pm; Sat, Sun from 7 am. Bar. Ck-out noon. Meeting rms. Sundries. Exercise equipt; stair machine, bicycle. Some refrigerators. Balconies. Cr cds: A, C, D, DS, JCB, MC, V.

D ✓ 🏊 ✕ 🏋 ✕ 🐾 SC

★ **QUALITY INN.** 793 W Bel Air Ave. 410/272-6000; FAX 410/272-2287. 124 rms, 2 story. Feb-Oct: S, D $49.95-$59.95; each addl $5; under 19 free; wkly, wknd rates; lower rates rest of yr. Crib free. TV; cable (premium), VCR avail. Pool; wading pool. Complimentary continental bkfst. Restaurant adj 6 am-2 pm, 5-10 pm. Ck-out noon. Coin lndry. Meeting rms. Business servs avail. Cr cds: A, C, D, DS, JCB, MC, V.

D 🏊 ✕ 🐾 SC

Annapolis (C-7)

(See also Baltimore, Baltimore/Washington Intl Airport Area)

Founded 1649 **Pop** 33,187 **Elev** 57 ft **Area code** 410 & 443 **Web** www.visit-Annapolis.org

Information Annapolis and Anne Arundel County Conference and Visitors Bureau, 26 West St, 21401; 410/268-TOUR. Information is also available at the Visitor Information Booth located at the city dock.

The capital of Maryland, gracious and dignified in the colonial tradition, Annapolis has had a rich history for more than 300 years. Planned and laid out as the provincial capital in 1695, it was the first peacetime capital of the United States (Congress met here November 26, 1783-August 13, 1784). In 1845 the US Naval Academy was established here, at the Army's Fort Severn. Town life centers on sport and commercial water-oriented activities, state government and the academy. Every May, at commencement time, thousands of visitors throng the narrow brick streets.

What to See and Do

Boat trips. 40-min narrated tours of city harbor, USNA and Severn River aboard *Harbor Queen* (Memorial Day-Labor Day, daily); 90-min cruises to locations aboard *Providence* and *Rebecca,* cruises to St Michaels aboard the *Annapolitan II* (Memorial Day-Labor Day); 40-min cruises up Spa Creek, residential areas, city harbor and USNA aboard the *Miss Anne* and *Miss Anne II* (Memorial Day-Labor Day). Some cruises early spring and late fall, weather permitting. Fees vary. From city dock at foot of Main St. Phone 410/268-7600, 410/269-6776 (Baltimore) or 301/261-2719 (DC).

Chesapeake Bay Bridge. The 7¼-mi link of US 50 across the Bay. Toll (charged eastbound only) ¢¢

Government House (1868). This Victorian structure was remodeled in 1935 into a Georgian country house; furnishings reflect Maryland's history and culture. Tours by appt (Jan-mid-Apr, Tues and Thurs; rest of yr, Tues-Thurs). Between State & Church Circles. Phone 410/974-3531. **Free.**

Hammond-Harwood House (1774). Georgian house designed by William Buckland; antique furnishings; garden. Matthias Hammond, a Revolutionary patriot, was its first owner. Guided tours. (Daily; closed Jan 1, Thanksgiving, Dec 25) 19 Maryland Ave, at King George St, 1 blk W of US Naval Academy. Phone 410/269-1714. ¢¢

Historic Annapolis Foundation Welcome Center and Museum Store. This ca 1815 building stands on the site of a storehouse for Revolutionary War troops that was burned in 1790. Audiocassette walking tours. Products reflecting Annapolis history. (Mon-Sat, also Sun afternoons; closed Easter, Thanksgiving, Dec 25) 18 Pinkney St. Phone 410/268-5576.

London Town (ca 1760). Once considered a site for Maryland's capital; the only surviving structure of the Lost Town is the William Brown House, a Georgian mansion on banks of South River. Has 8 acres of woodland gardens. Museum and garden shop; boat docking. Special events. Guided tours. (Mon-Sat, also Sun afternoon; closed major hols) 8 mi SE via MD 2S, (Mayo Rd) in Edgewater, at the end of Londontown Rd (#839). Phone 410/222-1919. ¢¢

Sailing tours. 2-hr narrated trips through Chesapeake Bay aboard 74-ft sailing yacht *Woodwind*. (May-Sept, Tues-Sun 4 trips daily, Mon Sunset Sail only; Apr, Oct, Nov, schedule varies) Departs from Pusser's Landing next to City Dock. Phone 410/263-8619. ¢¢¢¢

Sandy Point State Park. 786 acres. The park's location on the Atlantic Flyway makes it a fine area for bird watching; view of Bay Bridge and oceangoing vessels. Swimming in bay at 2 guarded beaches, 2 bathhouses; surf fishing, crabbing; boating (rentals, launches). Concession. Standard fees. (See ANNUAL EVENTS) 7 mi E on US 50, at W end of Chesapeake Bay Bridge. Phone 410/757-1841.

St John's College (1784). (400 students) Nonsectarian liberal arts college. This 36-acre campus, one of the oldest in the country, is a National Historic Landmark. The college succeeded King William's School, founded in 1696. George Washington's two nephews and step-grandson studied here; Francis Scott Key was an alumnus. College Ave. For information phone 410/626-2539. On campus are

> **Elizabeth Myers Mitchell Art Gallery.** Displays museum quality traveling exhibitions. (Academic yr, daily exc Mon) For schedule phone 410/626-2556. **Free.**

> **McDowell Hall** (begun 1742, finished 1789). Named for St John's first president; the main classroom building was originally built as the Governor's Mansion. Lafayette was feted here in 1824. Not open to public.

> **Charles Carroll, Barrister House** (1722). Birthplace of the author of the Maryland Bill of Rights; moved in 1955 to the campus and restored; now an administration building. Not open to public.

> **Liberty Tree.** Tulip poplar, thought to be more than 400 yrs old, under which the Sons of Liberty met during the Revolution.

State House (1772-1779). Oldest state house in continuous legislative use in US, this was the first peacetime capitol of the US. Here in 1784, a few weeks after receiving George Washington's resignation as commander-in-chief, Congress ratified the Treaty of Paris, which officially ended the American Revolution. Visitors Information Center. Guide service (exc Jan 1, Thanksgiving). (Daily; closed Dec 25) State Circle, center of town. Phone 410/974-3400. **Free.**

United States Naval Academy (1845). (4,000 students) World-renowned school for naval officers; Leftwich Visitor Center provides guided walking tours, film, exhibits, gift shop (daily; closed Jan 1, Thanksgiving, Dec 25). The remains of John Paul Jones, removed from their original burial place in France, lie here beneath the chapel in a crypt similar to Napoleon's in Paris. Naval Academy Museum exhibits 300 yrs of American naval history. Sites include Bancroft Hall, dormitory for all midshipmen, a bust of Tamanend, replica of figurehead of USS *Delaware*, renamed *Tecumseh*. Parades, concerts and other events are held annually and during "Commissioning Week" (late May), culminated by midshipmen's graduation. Enter through Gate 1, King George St. Phone 410/263-6933. Grounds **Free;** tours ¢¢¢

✪ **Walking tours.**

> **Historic Annapolis Foundation.** Self-guided audiocassette walking tours. Includes Historic District, State House, US Naval Academy and William Paca House. (Mar-Nov, daily) Tours leave from museum store, 77 Main St. Phone tour director, 410/267-7619 or 410/269-0432. ¢¢

> **Three Centuries Tours of Annapolis.** Walking tours of US Naval Academy and Historic District conducted by guides in colonial attire. Tour includes historic Maryland State House, St John's College, William Paca Garden, Naval Academy Chapel, Crypt of John Paul Jones, Bancroft Hall Dormitory and Armel-Leftwich Visitor Center. Morning tour leaves from Visitor Center at 26 West St; afternoon tour leaves from Visitor Info Booth on City Dock. (Apr-Oct, daily) Phone 410/263-5401 to confirm departure points and schedule. ¢¢¢

William Paca Garden. Restored two-acre pleasure garden originally developed in 1765 by William Paca, a signer of the Declaration of Independence and governor of Maryland during the Revolutionary War. Includes waterways, formal parterres and a garden wilderness. (Mon-Sat, also Sun afternoons; closed Thanksgiving, Dec 25) 186 Prince George St. Also here is

> **William Paca House.** Paca built this five-part Georgian mansion in 1765. (Mon-Sat, also Sun afternoons; closed Thanksgiving, Dec 25) Phone 410/263-5553. Combination ticket (includes house and garden) ¢¢¢

Annual Events

Maryland Renaissance Festival. Food, craftsmen, minstrels, dramatic productions. Phone 800/296-7304. Usually last wk Aug-3rd wkend Oct.

Maryland Seafood Festival. Sandy Point State Park. Food; entertainment. Phone 410/268-7682. Usually wkend after Labor Day.

US Sailboat Show. City dock & harbor. Features world's largest in-water display of sailboats; exhibits of related marine products. Phone 410/268-8828. Early-mid-Oct.

US Powerboat Show. City dock & harbor. Extensive in-water display of powerboats; exhibits of related marine products. Phone 410/268-8828. Mid-Oct.

Chesapeake Appreciation Days. Sandy Point State Park. Skipjack sailing festival honors state's oystermen. Usually last wkend Oct.

Annapolis by Candlelight. For information, reservations contact Historic Annapolis Foundation; for dates phone 410/267-0432. Usually early Nov.

Seasonal Event

Christmas in Annapolis. Features decorated 18th-century mansions, parade of yachts, private home tours, pub crawls, concerts, holiday meals, First Night celebration, caroling by candlelight at the State House and other events. For free events calendar phone 410/268-8687. Thanksgiving-Jan 1.

Motels

✔★ **COMFORT INN.** *76 Old Mill Bottom Rd N (21401), US 50/301 exit 28 to Bay Dale Dr.* 410/757-8500; FAX 410/757-4409. 60 rms, 2 story. Apr-Oct: S $65-$110; D $70-$120; each addl $5; under 18 free; lower rates rest of yr. Crib free. TV; cable (premium). Pool; lifeguard. Complimentary continental bkfst. Restaurant nearby. Ck-out 11 am. Coin lndry. Business servs avail. Cr cds: A, C, D, DS, ER, JCB, MC, V.

D ⊠ ⊠ ⋈ ⋈ SC

★★ **COURTYARD BY MARRIOTT.** *2559 Riva Rd (21401).* 410/266-1555; FAX 410/266-6376. Web www.courtyard.com. 149 units, 3 story. S, D $109-$119; suites $129-$149; under 12 free. Crib free. TV; cable (premium). Indoor pool; whirlpool, lifeguard. Complimentary coffee in rms. Restaurant 6:30 am-1:30 pm; Sat, Sun from 7 am. Bar 4-10 pm. Ck-out noon. Coin lndry. Meeting rms. Business servs avail. In-rm modem link. Valet serv. Sundries. Exercise equipt; weight machines, bicycles. Refrigerator in suites. Cr cds: A, C, D, DS, MC, V.

[D] [≈] [🏃] [⛷] [🔥] [SC]

✔★ ★ DAYS INN. 2520 Riva Rd (21401). 410/224-2800; FAX 410/266-5539. 152 rms, 2 story. Mid-Mar-mid-Nov: S, D $59-$119; suites $119-$129; lower rates rest of yr. Crib free. TV; cable (premium). Pool. Complimentary continental bkfst. Restaurant adj 11 am-10 pm. Bar. Ck-out 11 am. Meeting rms. Business servs avail. Coin lndry. Health club privileges. Game rm. Some refrigerators. Cr cds: A, C, D, DS, MC, V.

[D] [≈] [≈] [🔥] [SC]

Motor Hotels

★ ★ ★ HOLIDAY INN. 210 Holiday Ct at Riva Rd (21401). 410/224-3150; FAX 410/224-3413. 220 rms, 6 story. S $79-$119; D $89-$129; suites $139; under 18 free. Crib free. Pet accepted. TV; cable (premium). Pool; lifeguard. Restaurant 6:30 am-2 pm, 5-10 pm. Rm serv. Bar 4 pm-midnight. Ck-out noon. Meeting rms. Business servs avail. In-rm modem link. Bellhops. Valet serv. Sundries. Health club privileges. Microwaves avail. Cr cds: A, C, D, DS, JCB, MC, V.

[D] [🏊] [≈] [≈] [🔥] [SC]

✔★ ★ ★ WYNDHAM GARDEN. 173 Jennifer Rd (21401). 410/266-3131; FAX 410/266-6247. Web www.travelweb.com. 197 rms, 6 story. S $89-$139; D $99-$149; each addl $10; suites $109-$209; under 18 free; hol rates; higher rates special events. Crib free. TV; cable. Indoor pool; whirlpool, lifeguard. Coffee in rms. Restaurant 6:30 am-2:30 pm, 5-10 pm. Rm serv 5-10 pm. Bar 4 pm-midnight. Ck-out noon. Meeting rms. Business servs avail. In-rm modem link. Exercise equipt; bicycles, rowing machine, sauna. Health club privileges. Some refrigerators; microwaves avail. Cr cds: A, C, D, DS, MC, V.

[D] [≈] [🏃] [⛷] [🔥] [SC]

Hotels

★ ★ ★ LOEWS. 126 West St (21401). 410/263-7777; FAX 410/263-0084. Web www.loewsannapolis.com. 217 rms, 6 story, 11 suites. S, D $119-$185; each addl $15; suites $185-$350; under 17 free. Crib free. Pet accepted. Valet parking $10. TV; cable (premium). Pool privileges. Restaurant (see THE CORINTHIAN). Bar 11-2 am. Ck-out noon. Meeting rms. Business center. In-rm modem link. Concierge. Gift shop. Barber, beauty shop. Exercise equipt; weight machine, bicycles. Health club privileges. Minibars, refrigerators. Private patios, balconies. Luxury level. Cr cds: A, C, D, DS, MC, V.

[D] [🏃] [⛷] [≈] [≈] [SC] [🏌]

★ ★ ★ MARRIOTT-WATERFRONT. 80 Compromise St (21401), opp Naval Academy. 410/268-7555; FAX 410/269-5864. 150 rms, 6 story. May-Sept: S $149-$270; D $149-$290; varied rates rest of yr. Crib free. Garage $12. TV; cable (premium), VCR avail. Restaurant 6:30 am-11 pm. Bar 11-2 am. Ck-out 11 am. Meeting rms. Business servs avail. In-rm modem link. Exercise equipt; weight machines, bicycles. Some in-rm whirlpools. Refrigerators, microwaves avail. Some balconies. On waterfront; 300 ft dockage. Cr cds: A, C, D, DS, MC, V.

[D] [🏃] [≈] [≈] [🔥] [SC]

Inns

★ ★ CHESAPEAKE BAY LIGHTHOUSE. 1423 Sharps Point Rd (21401). 410/757-0248. E-mail baylight@toad.net; web 199.75.220.4/oabus/cbbb/chesbnb.htm. 5 rms, 2 story. No rm phone. S, D $99-$149; each addl $10. Children over 12 only. TV in sitting rm. Complimentary continental bkfst. Restaurant nearby. Ck-out 11 am, ck-in 3-7 pm. Working lighthouse in Chesapeake Bay. Totally nonsmoking. Cr cds: DS, MC, V.

[�] [≈] [🔥]

★ ★ GIBSON'S LODGINGS. 110 Prince George St (21401). 410/268-5555. Web www.avmcyber.com/gibson. 20 rms, 13 share baths

in 3 bldgs, 3 story. Some rm phones. S $58-$110; D $68-$125; each addl $15. TV in some rms; cable, VCR avail. Complimentary continental bkfst; afternoon refreshments. Restaurant nearby. Ck-out 11 am, ck-in 2 pm. Meeting rm. Business servs avail. Microwaves avail. Antiques; library. Totally nonsmoking. Cr cds: A, MC, V.

[D] [≈] [🔥]

★ ★ ★ GOVERNOR CALVERT HOUSE. 58 State Circle (21401). 410/263-2641; FAX 410/268-3613; res: 800/847-8882 (exc MD). 51 rms, 4 story. S $105-$135; D $105-$165; each addl $10; suites $145-$260; under 18 free; higher rates special events. Crib free. Valet parking $12. TV; cable (premium). Restaurant nearby. Ck-out noon, ck-in 3 pm. Meeting rms. Business servs avail. In-rm modem link. Lighted tennis privileges. Golf privileges. Health club privileges. Refrigerators, microwaves avail. 18th-century state house with modern addition; colonial gardens, atrium. Cr cds: A, C, D, DS, JCB, MC, V.

[D] [🏃] [⛷] [≈] [≈] [🔥] [SC]

★ ★ ★ MARYLAND. Church Circle & Main Street (21401). 410/263-2641; FAX 410/268-3813; res: 800/847-8882. 44 rms, 4 story. S $105-$135; D $105-$165; each addl $10; suites $145-$260; under 18 free; higher rates special events. Crib free. Valet parking $12. TV; cable (premium). Restaurant (see TREATY OF PARIS). Bar; entertainment. Ck-out noon, ck-in 3 pm (at Governor Calvert House). Business servs avail. In-rm modem link. Bellhops. Lighted tennis, golf privileges. Health club privileges. Some refrigerators; microwaves avail. View of bay. Historic inn built 1772; many antique furnishings. Cr cds: A, C, D, DS, JCB, MC, V.

[🏃] [⛷] [≈] [≈] [🔥] [SC]

★ ★ ★ PRINCE GEORGE INN. 232 Prince George St (21401). 410/263-6418; FAX 410/626-0009. E-mail pginn@annap.infi.net; web www.princegeorgeinn.com. 4 rms, 2 share bath, 3 story. No rm phones. S $85-$100; D $95-$110; under 8 free; wknds (2-day min). Parking $4. TV; cable, VCR. Complimentary full bkfst. Restaurant nearby. Ck-out noon, ck-in 4-6 pm. Refrigerators. Victorian townhouse built in 1884. Totally nonsmoking. Cr cds: D, MC, V.

[≈] [🔥]

★ ★ ROBERT JOHNSON HOUSE. 23 State Circle (21401). 410/263-2641; FAX 410/268-3613; res: 800/847-8882. 29 rms, 4 story. S $105-$135; D $105-$165; each addl $10; suites $260; under 18 free; higher rates special events. Crib free. Valet parking $12. TV; cable (premium). Restaurant nearby. Ck-out noon, ck-in 3 pm (at Governor Calvert House). Business servs avail. In-rm modem link. Lighted tennis privileges. Golf privileges. Health club privileges. Refrigerators, microwaves avail. Consists of 18th-century mansion plus 2 connecting townhouses of the same period. Cr cds: A, C, D, DS, JCB, MC, V.

[D] [🏃] [⛷] [≈] [≈] [SC]

✔★ ★ WILLIAM PAGE. 8 Martin St (21401). 410/626-1506; FAX 410/263-4841. E-mail wmpageinn@aol.com; web www.bbmaryland.com. 5 rms, 2 share bath, 3 story. S, D $95-$185; wkly rates. Complimentary full bkfst. Restaurant nearby. Ck-out noon, ck-in 4-6 pm. Business servs avail. Former clubhouse (1908). Totally nonsmoking. Cr cds: MC, V.

[≈] [🔥]

Restaurants

★ ★ BUSCH'S CHESAPEAKE INN. 321 Busch's Frontage Rd (US 50/301) (21401). 410/757-1717. Hrs: 11:30 am-9 pm; Fri to 10 pm; Sat to 11 pm; Sun 11 am-9 pm; early-bird dinner Mon-Fri 3-6 pm; Sun brunch to 3 pm. Closed Dec 23-26. Res accepted. Bar. Semi-a la carte: lunch $5.25-$9.95, dinner $14.95-$24.95. Lunch buffet $8.50. Sun brunch $15.95. Child's meals. Specializes in seafood. Nautical decor. Braille menu. Family-owned. Cr cds: A, C, D, DS, MC, V.

[D] [SC]

★ ★ ★ CAFE BRETTON. (849 Baltimore/Annapolis Blvd, Severna Park 21146) N on MD 2, N of College Pkwy. 410/647-8222. Hrs: 5-10 pm; early-bird dinner to 6 pm. Closed Sun, Mon; some major hols. Res required Fri, Sat. French menu. Bar. Wine list. Semi-a la carte: dinner $10.95-

$26.95. Specializes in lamb shank, seafood. Own baking. Country French atmosphere with original artwork. Totally nonsmoking. Cr cds: D, MC, V.

D

★ ★ **CAFE NORMANDIE.** *185 Main St (21401), in Historic District.* 410/263-3382. Hrs: 8 am-10 pm; Fri, Sat to 10:30 pm. French menu. Serv bar. Semi-a la carte: bkfst $3-$6, lunch $5.50-$15, dinner $8.95-$21. Specializes in seafood, Maryland crab dishes. French-style cafe. Cr cds: A, D, DS, MC, V.

D

★ ★ **CARROL'S CREEK.** *(410 Severn Ave, Eastport 21403) ¼ mi across Eastport Bridge at City Marina.* 410/263-8102. E-mail carrols cc@aol.com. Hrs: 11:30 am-4 pm, 5-10 pm; Sun brunch 10 am-2 pm. Res accepted Mon-Thurs; required hols. Bar. Semi-a la carte: lunch $4.95-$9.95, dinner $14-$22. Sun brunch $16.95. Specializes in local seafood. Own baking. Outdoor dining. On water. Cr cds: A, D, DS, MC, V.

D ▬

★ ★ **THE CORINTHIAN.** *(See Loews Hotel)* 410/263-1299. Hrs: 6:30 am-2 pm, 5-10 pm; Sun brunch from 9 am. Res accepted Sat. Bar. Wine list. Semi-a la carte: bkfst $6.50-$14.95, lunch $6.95-$15.95, dinner $18.95-$28.95. Sun brunch $16.95. Child's meals. Specializes in fresh seafood, prime beef. Valet parking. Elegant atmosphere. Cr cds: A, C, D, DS, MC, V.

D **SC** ▬

★ ★ **FRED'S.** *2348 Solomons Island Rd (21401), MD 2, 1 blk S of MD 450.* 410/224-2386. Hrs: 11 am-10 pm; Fri, Sat to 11 pm; early-bird dinner Mon-Fri 4-6 pm, Sat & Sun noon-6 pm. Closed Thanksgiving, Dec 25. Res accepted. Continental menu. Bar. Semi-a la carte: lunch $4.50-$8.95, dinner $9.95-$33.95. Child's meals. Specializes in seafood, steak, Italian dishes. Victorian decor; antiques. Family-owned. Cr cds: A, D, MC, V.

D ▬

✔★ ★ **GRIFFINS.** *24 Market Space (21401).* 410/268-2576. Web www.griffins-citydock.com. Hrs: 11 am-midnight; Fri, Sat to 1 am; Sun brunch 11 am-1 pm. Closed Dec 25. Res accepted Mon-Thurs. Bar to 1:30 am. Semi-a la carte: lunch $6.95-$8.95, dinner $8.95-$12.95. Sun brunch $6.95-$9.95. Child's meals. Specializes in seafood, steak, pasta. Salad bar. Own desserts. Cr cds: A, D, DS, MC, V.

D

★ ★ ★ **HARRY BROWNE'S.** *66 State Circle (21401).* 410/263-4332. Hrs: 11 am-3 pm, 5:30-10 pm; wkends to 11 pm; Sun brunch 10 am-3 pm. Closed Jan 1, Dec 25. Res accepted. Continental menu. Bar. Wine cellar. Semi-a la carte: lunch $6.95-$12, dinner $17-$22. Specializes in crab cakes, rack of lamb. Entertainment Mon, Fri, Sat. Valet parking Fri, Sat. Decorated with mirrors and pressed gold tin ceiling. Cr cds: MC, V.

D

✔★ ★ **INDIA PALACE.** *186 Main St (21401).* 410/263-7900. Hrs: 11:30 am-10 pm; Fri, Sat to 10:30 pm. Res accepted. Indian menu. Bar. A la carte entrees: lunch, dinner $2.95-$7.95. Complete meal: dinner $9.95-$15.95. Specializes in vegetarian, rice, chicken dishes. Cr cds: A, MC, V.

D

★ ★ **LEWNES' STEAKHOUSE.** *401 4th St (21403), at Severn Ave.* 410/263-1617. Hrs: 5-10 pm; Fri, Sat to 10:30 pm. Closed Thanksgiving, Dec 25. Res required. Bar. A la carte entrees: dinner $15-$27. Specializes in prime steak, seafood. Street parking. 1950s steakhouse atmosphere; casual fine dining. Cr cds: A, D, MC, V.

D ▬

★ ★ **MIDDLETON TAVERN.** *2 Market Space (21401).* 410/263-3323. Hrs: 11:30-2 am; Sat, Sun from 10 am. Bar. Semi-a la carte: lunch $5.95-$10.95, dinner $11.95-$23.95. Specializes in seafood, crab dishes. Oyster bar. Entertainment. Outdoor dining. Restored building (1750), tradi-

tional tavern decor. Overlooks harbor. Family-owned. Cr cds: A, DS, MC, V.

▬ ♥

★ ★ ★ **NORTHWOODS.** *609 Melvin Ave (21401).* 410/268-2609. Hrs: 5:30-10 pm; Sun 5-9 pm. Closed most major hols. Res accepted. Continental menu. Wine list. Semi-a la carte: dinner $18.95-$21.95. Complete meals: dinner $25.95. Specializes in fresh seafood, Italian dishes. Outdoor dining. Casual elegance in romantic setting. Cr cds: A, C, D, DS, MC, V.

D

★ ★ **O'LEARY'S.** *310 3rd St (21403).* 410/263-0884. Hrs: 5:30-10 pm; Fri, Sat 5-11 pm; Sun 5-10 pm. Closed Thanksgiving, Dec 24, 25. Res accepted. Bar. Semi-a la carte: dinner $10.95-$29.95. Child's meals. Specializes in seafood. Own desserts. Cr cds: A, D, MC, V.

D

★ ★ ★ **REYNOLD'S TAVERN.** *7 Church Circle (21404).* 410/626-0380. Hrs: 11:30 am-2 pm, 6-9 pm; Fri, Sat to 10 pm; Sun 5:30-8:30 pm. Closed Jan 1, July 4, Dec 25. Res accepted. Bar. A la carte entrees: lunch $5.25-$7.95, dinner $4.25-$24.95. Specializes in seafood. Entertainment. Outdoor dining. Colonial decor. Cr cds: A, MC, V.

D

★ ★ ★ **TREATY OF PARIS.** *(See Maryland Inn)* 410/263-2641. Hrs: 7 am-2:30 pm, 5:30-10:30 pm; Fri, Sat to 11:30 pm; Sun to 9:30 pm; Sun brunch 10 am-2:30 pm. Closed Jan 1. Res accepted; required Fri, Sat. Continental menu. Bar 11-2 am; Sun to 1 am. Wine cellar. Semi-a la carte: bkfst $3.50-$9, lunch $6.95-$10, dinner $14-$22. Complete meals: dinner $20, $25. Sun brunch $18.95. Specializes in New American cuisine, fresh local seafood. Salad bar (lunch). Valet parking (dinner). Early American tavern atmosphere; fireplace. Cr cds: A, C, D, DS, JCB, MC, V.

D **SC**

★ ★ ★ **VESPUCCI'S.** *87 Prince George St (21401).* 410/571-0103. Hrs: 11 am-11 pm; Sun from 10 am; Sun brunch to 4 pm. Closed Thanksgiving, Dec 25. Res accepted. Italian, Amer menu. Bar. Semi-a la carte: lunch $5-$18, dinner $8-$27. Sun brunch $12.95. Child's meals. Specializes in veal, seafood, filet mignon. Own baking, pasta. Valet parking Fri, Sat (dinner). Outdoor dining. Three distinct dining areas vary from casual bistro to formal setting; view of harbor. Totally nonsmoking. Cr cds: A, C, D, DS, MC, V.

D

Antietam National Battlefield (B-4)

(10 mi S of Hagerstown on MD 65)

On September 17, 1862, the bloodiest day in Civil War annals, more than 23,000 men were killed or wounded as Union forces blocked the first Confederate invasion of the North. A Union advantage was gained beforehand when a soldier accidentally found Lee's orders wrapped around some cigars. In spite of knowing Lee's tactical game plan, McClellan moved cautiously. The battle, critical because British aid to the Confederacy depended on the outcome, was a tactical draw but a strategic victory for the North. This victory allowed Lincoln to issue the Emancipation Proclamation, which expanded the war from simply reuniting the country to a crusade to end slavery. The rebels withdrew across the Potomac on the night of September 18, but for some reason McClellan, with twice the manpower, delayed his pursuit. Lincoln relieved him of command of the Army of the Potomac seven weeks later. Clara Barton, who was to found the Red Cross 19 years later, attended the wounded at a field hospital on the battlefield.

Approximately 350 iron tablets, monuments and battlefield maps, located on eight miles of paved avenues, describe the events of the battle.

The Visitor Center houses a museum and offers information, literature and a 26-minute orientation movie (shown on the hour). Visitor Center (daily; closed Jan 1, Thanksgiving, Dec 25); battlefield (daily); ranger-conducted walks, talks and demonstrations (Memorial Day-Labor Day, daily). Golden Age Passport (see MAKING THE MOST OF YOUR TRIP). For information phone 301/432-5124. Entrance fee per person ¢, maximum per family ¢¢

Baltimore (B-7)

Settled 1661 **Pop** 736,014 **Elev** 32 ft **Area code** 410 & 443

Information Baltimore Area Convention & Visitors Assn, 100 Light St, 12th floor, 21202; 410/659-7300 or 800/343-3468.

Suburbs Aberdeen, Cockeysville, Columbia, Ellicott City, Pikesville, Towson. (See individual alphabetical listings.)

Metropolis of Maryland and one of America's great cities, Baltimore is a city of neighborhoods built on strong ethnic foundations, a city of historic events that helped shape the nation and a city that has achieved an incredible downtown renaissance in the past 20 years. It is a major East Coast manufacturing center and, almost from its beginning, a world seaport. Several colleges and universities, foremost of which is Johns Hopkins, make their home here.

Lying midway between North and South and enjoying a rich cultural mixture of both, Baltimore is one of the nation's oldest cities. When British troops threatened Philadelphia during the Revolution, the Continental Congress fled to Baltimore, which served as the nation's capital for a little more than two months.

In October 1814, a British fleet attacked the city by land and sea. The defenders of Fort McHenry withstood the naval bombardment for 25 hours until the British gave up. Francis Scott Key saw the huge American flag still flying above the fort and was inspired to pen "The Star-Spangled Banner."

Rapid growth in the early 19th century resulted from the opening of the National Road and then the nation's first railroad, the Baltimore & Ohio.

Politics was a preoccupation in those days, and the city hosted many national party conventions. At least seven presidents and three losing candidates were nominated here. Edgar Allan Poe's mysterious death in the city may have been at the hands of shady electioneers.

Untouched physically by the Civil War, effects came later when Southerners flooded in to rebuild their fortunes, and commerce was disrupted by the loss of Southern markets. A disastrous fire in 1904 destroyed 140 acres of the business district, but the city recovered rapidly and, during the two World Wars, was a major shipbuilding and naval repair center.

In the 1950s and early 1960s, Baltimore was the victim of apathy and the general decay that struck the industrial Northeast. But the city fought back, replacing hundreds of acres of slums, rotting wharves and warehouses with gleaming new office plazas, parks and public buildings. The Inner Harbor was transformed into a huge public area with shops, museums, restaurants and frequent concerts and festivals. Millions of tourists and proud Baltimoreans flock downtown to enjoy the sights and activities.

Famous residents and native sons include Babe Ruth, Edgar Allan Poe, H.L. Mencken, Mother Elizabeth Ann Seton, Eubie Blake, Ogden Nash, Thurgood Marshall, Wallis Warfield Simpson, who became the Duchess of Windsor, and more recent sports legends Brooks Robinson, Johnny Unitas and Jim Palmer.

Transportation

Airport: See BALTIMORE/WASHINGTON INTL AIRPORT AREA.

Car Rental Agencies: See IMPORTANT TOLL-FREE NUMBERS.

Public Transportation: Bus & subway (Mass Transit Administration), phone 410/539-5000.

Rail Passenger Service: Amtrak 800/872-7245; MARC (commuter train serving Baltimore & Washington, DC) 800/325-RAIL.

What to See and Do

B & O Railroad Museum. The museum includes the Mount Clare Station (1851), site of the nation's first passenger station, and the roundhouse (1884); original tracks and wooden turntable are fully preserved. Collection includes over 120 full-sized train cars. (Daily; closed Thanksgiving, Dec 25). 901 W Pratt St, at Poppleton St. Phone 410/752-2490. ¢¢¢

Babe Ruth Birthplace/Baseball Center. Renovated house where Babe Ruth was born. Features memorabilia of Babe Ruth, Orioles and Maryland baseball; 25-min movie of the "Sultan of Swat" and many other audiovisual displays. (Daily) 216 Emory St. Phone 410/727-1539. ¢¢

Baltimore Maritime Museum. USS *Torsk*, WWII submarine, Coast Guard cutter *Taney* and lightship *Chesapeake*. (Daily) Pier 3, Pratt St, Inner Harbor area. Phone 410/396-5528. ¢¢

Baltimore Museum of Art. Variety of collections, including American paintings, period rooms; African and Oceanian art. Noted for Cone collection of French Post-Impressionists, including Matisse and Picasso; Cheney miniature rooms; modern art wing; sculpture gardens; museum cafe and shop. (Wed-Sun; closed major hols) Art Museum Dr near N Charles & 31st Sts. Phone 410/396-7100 or 410/396-7101. ¢¢¢

Baltimore Museum of Industry. Exhibits trace the growth of Baltimore as an industrial center. Turn-of-the-century machine shop, print shop and garment loft. Hands-on exhibits; children's activities. Restored tugboat on waterfront behind museum. (Thurs-Sun; limited hrs, phone ahead; closed most hols) 1415 Key Hwy. Phone 410/727-4808. ¢¢

Baltimore Streetcar Museum. Eleven electric streetcars and two horsecars used in city between 1859 and 1963; 1¼-mi rides (fee). (June-Oct, Sat & Sun afternoons; rest of yr, Sun afternoons only; also open Memorial Day, July 4, Labor Day) 1901 Falls Rd, under North Ave Bridge. Phone 410/547-0264. ¢¢

Baltimore Zoo. Main zoo has collection of more than 1,500 animals. Includes 3-acre African elephant park; 6-acre African watering hole; hippo and African flamingo exhibit; 8-acre children's zoo (daily); track train & carousel (Apr-Sept; fee). Zoo (daily exc Dec 25). Druid Hill Park. Phone 410/366-5466. ¢¢¢

Basilica of the National Shrine of the Assumption. Now a co-cathedral, this was the first Roman Catholic cathedral in the US. Bishop John Carroll, head of the diocese of Baltimore from its establishment in 1789, blessed the cornerstone in 1806. The church was dedicated in 1821. Architectural design by B. H. Latrobe. Tours (2nd & 4th Sun each month or by appt). (Daily) Cathedral & Mulberry Sts, downtown. Phone 410/727-3565.

Battle Monument (1815). Memorial to those who fell defending the city in the War of 1812. Calvert & Fayette Sts.

Carroll Mansion (ca 1810). Residence of Charles Carroll. When he died here in 1832, he was the last surviving signer of Declaration of Independence. Period furnishings. (Daily exc Mon; closed hols) 800 E Lombard St, at Front St, downtown. Phone 410/396-3523. ¢

Charles Center. Business area with European-style plazas, part of an overhead walkway system, shops, restaurants and outdoor activities. Prize-winning office building by Mies van der Rohe borders center plaza. Bounded by Charles, Liberty, Saratoga & Lombard Sts, downtown. Also here is

Baltimore Center for the Performing Arts-Morris Mechanic Theater. Hosts Broadway productions. Hopkins Plaza. For schedule, fees phone 410/752-1200.

Church Home and Hospital. Edgar Allan Poe died here in 1849. Broadway & Fairmount Ave.

City Court House (1900). On steps is statue of Cecil Calvert, brother of Leonard and founder of Maryland as the second Lord Baltimore. St Paul & Fayette Sts, downtown.

City Hall. Post-Civil War architecture, restored to original detail. 100 N Holliday St, downtown. Tours by appt, phone 410/396-3100. **Free.**

City of Baltimore Conservatory. This graceful building (ca 1885) houses a large variety of tropical plants. Special shows during Easter, Nov & Christmas. (Thurs-Sun) Druid Hill Park. Phone 410/396-0180. **Free.**

Cylburn Arboretum. Marked nature trails. Nature museum, ornithological room, horticultural library in restored mansion; shade and formal gardens,

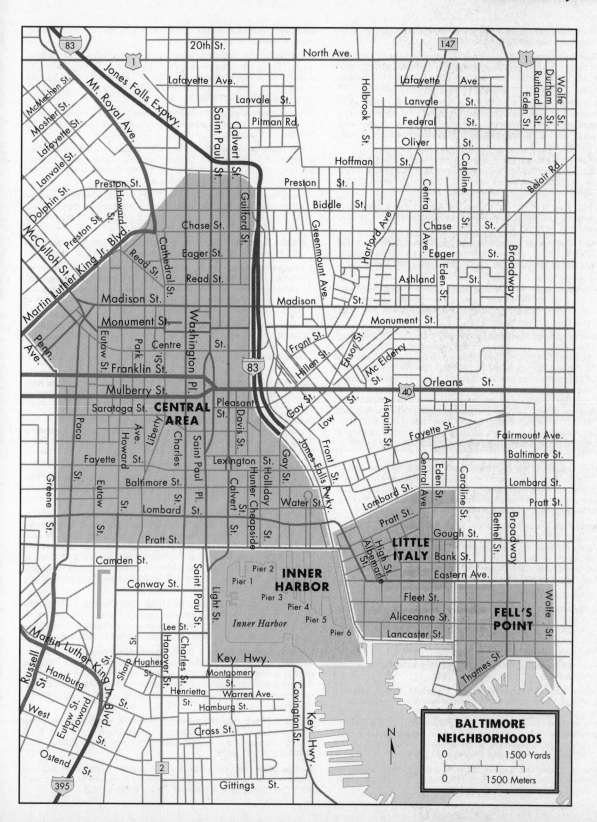

CENTRAL AREA

INNER HARBOR

LITTLE ITALY

FELL'S POINT

Inner Harbor

Pier 1
Pier 2
Pier 3
Pier 4
Pier 5
Pier 6

BALTIMORE NEIGHBORHOODS

0   1500 Yards

0   1500 Meters

All-American Selection Garden, Garden of the Senses. (Daily) 4915 Greenspring Ave. Phone 410/396-0180. **Free.**

Edgar Allan Poe Grave. Baltimore's oldest cemeteries also contain the graves of many prominent early Marylanders. Tour of catacombs by appt (Apr-Nov, 1st & 3rd Fri & Sat). At Westminster Hall & Burying Ground and Catacombs, Fayette & Greene Sts, downtown. Phone 410/706-7228. ¢¢

Edgar Allan Poe House (ca 1830). Poe's home from 1832-1835. (Apr-July & Oct-mid-Dec, Wed-Sat, afternoons; Aug & Sept, Sat afternoon only) Also offered are tours of Westminster Cemetery and Catacombs (evenings, by appt; fee). 203 N Amity St, off 900 blk W Lexington St, downtown. Phone 410/396-7932. ¢

Enoch Pratt Free Library. City's public library. H.L. Mencken & Edgar Allan Poe collections. (Oct-Apr, daily exc Fri; rest of yr, Mon-Thurs & Sat; closed hols) 400 Cathedral St, at Franklin St, downtown. Phone 410/396-5430 or -3557.

Federal Hill. View of city harbor and skyline. Named for a celebration that occurred here in 1788 to mark Maryland's ratification of the Constitution. Warren St & Battery Ave, Inner Harbor area.

Fell's Point. Shipbuilding and maritime center, this neighborhood dates back to 1730; approx 350 original residential structures. Working tugboats and tankers can be observed from docks. Broadway, S of Fleet St to the harbor.

First Unitarian Church (1817). William Ellery Channing preached a sermon here that hastened the establishment of the Unitarian denomination. Example of Classic Revival architecture. Charles & Franklin Sts, in Mt Vernon Place area. Phone 410/685-2330.

Fort McHenry National Monument and Historic Shrine. The flag flying over this five-pointed, star-shaped brick fort inspired Francis Scott Key to write the poem in 1814 that later became the lyrics to the national anthem. Named for James McHenry, Secretary of War (1796-1800). Replica flagpole on 1814 site. Restored powder magazine, guardroom, officers' quarters and barracks all contain exhibits. Cannons of War of 1812 and Civil War periods. Guided activities (mid-June-Aug, daily). The Fort McHenry Guard, in period uniform, reenacts life at the garrison (mid-June-Aug, Sat & Sun afternoons). Military ceremony (July-Aug, some Sun evenings). Visitor Center has exhibit area, film, gift shop. Special exhibits for visually and hearing impaired. (Daily; closed Jan 1, Dec 25) E end of Fort Ave. Phone 410/962-4299. ¢

> Narrated cruises on the *Baltimore Patriot* depart from Inner Harbor Finger Pier to Fort McHenry and Fells Point (Memorial Day-Labor Day). Also departures from Fort McHenry and Fells Point. For other tours contact Maryland Tours, Inc, phone ticket office 410/685-4288(Apr-Oct) or 410/745-9216 (rest of yr). Round-trip ¢¢

Gunpowder Falls State Park. Approx 17,000 acres, located in Gunpowder River Valley. **Hammerman Area**, E on US 40, right onto Ebenezer Rd, 5 mi to park entrance in Chase, is a developed day-use area. Offers swimming beach, windsurfing beach, boating, marina (Dundee Creek), picnicking, playground. Other areas offer hiking/biking trails, canoeing, trout fishing. Standard fees. Phone 410/592-2897.

Harbor cruises. Depart from Inner Harbor.

> **MV** *Lady Baltimore.* Round-trip cruises to Annapolis (June-Aug, Wed); also cruises to the Chesapeake & Delaware Canal (3 selected Sun in Oct). *Bay Lady* has lunch and dinner cruises (Apr-Oct, daily; limited schedule rest of yr). West Bulkhead, Light St. Phone 410/727-3113 or 800/695-LADY. ¢¢¢¢
>
> *Baltimore Patriot* has 90-min tours around Baltimore harbor. (Apr-Oct, daily) Phone 410/685-4288 (ticket office). ¢¢¢

Harborplace. European-style marketplace comprised of two glass-enclosed pavilions; one featuring many eateries, including waterside cafes and restaurants, the other housing dozens of specialty shops arranged in Parisian style along a colonnade. Overhead walkway leads to **The Gallery at Harborplace**, with many additional top-name shops and eateries. Free summer concerts along waterfront. (Daily; closed Thanksgiving, Dec 25) Light & Pratt Sts, Inner Harbor area. Phone 410/332-4191.

H.L. Mencken House. The "Sage of Baltimore" lived and wrote here for 68 years. Exhibits, furnishings. (Sat & Sun) 1524 Hollins St, in historic Union Square. Phone 410/396-7997. ¢

Holocaust Memorial. Simple stone memorial to the victims of the Holocaust. Water & Gay Sts, downtown.

Jewish Historical Society of Maryland. Buildings include Lloyd St Synagogue (1845), the oldest in Maryland; B'nai Israel Synagogue (1876); Jewish Museum of Maryland. (Tues-Fri & Sun afternoons; or by appt; closed Jewish hols) Research archives (Mon-Fri, by appt). 15 Lloyd St, downtown. Phone 410/732-6400. ¢

Johns Hopkins Medical Institutions (1889). Widely known as a leading medical school, research center and teaching hospital. Victorian buildings. Broadway & Monument St.

Johns Hopkins University (1876). (4,600 students) Modern buildings in Georgian style on wooded 126-acre campus. Distinguished research school founded by wealthy merchant of the city. Charles & 34th Sts, 2 mi N. Phone 410/516-8000. On grounds are

> **Lacrosse Hall of Fame Museum.** Team trophies, display of lacrosse artifacts and memorabilia; videotapes of championship games. (Mon-Fri; Sat during lacrosse season; closed hols) 113 W University Pkwy. Phone 410/235-6882. ¢
>
> **Bufano Sculpture Garden.** A wooded retreat with animals sculpted by artist Beniamino Bufano. Dunning Park, behind Mudd Hall. **Free.**
>
> **Evergreen House.** On 26 wooded acres; features Classical-revival architecture and formal garden. Contains the Library (35,000 volumes). Post-Impressionist paintings, Japanese and Chinese collections and Tiffany glass. Tours (daily). 4545 N Charles St, approx 2 mi N of Homewood campus. Phone 410/516-0341. ¢¢
>
> **Homewood House Museum.** Former country home (1801) of Charles Carroll, Jr, whose father was a signer of the Declaration of Independence; period furnishings. (Tues-Sat, also Sun afternoons) Guided tours (hourly). 3400 N Charles St near 34th St. Phone 410/516-5589. ¢¢

Joseph Meyerhoff Symphony Hall. Permanent residence of the Baltimore Symphony Orchestra. 1212 Cathedral St. Phone 410/783-8000 or 410/783-8100.

Lexington Market. In continuous operation since 1782, this famous indoor marketplace houses more than 140 stalls run by independent merchants. (Daily exc Sun; closed major hols) 400 W Lexington St, between Eutaw & Paca Sts, downtown. Phone 410/685-6169. **Free.**

Lovely Lane Museum. Permanent and changing exhibits of items of Methodist church history since 1760. Guided tours (Mon-Fri; also Sun after services and by appt; closed hols) 2200 St Paul St. Phone 410/889-4458. **Free.**

Maryland Historical Society Library of Maryland. Original manuscript of "Star-Spangled Banner" is displayed; extensive displays of Maryland silver, furniture and painting; changing exhibits; maritime museum. Also within the museum is the **Darnall Young Peoples Museum**, a gallery with "hands-on" exhibits. Museum and gallery (Oct-Apr, daily exc Mon; rest of yr, Tues-Sat). Library (Tues-Sat). Museum free on Wed. 201 W Monument St, between Park Ave & Howard St, in Mt Vernon Place area. Phone 410/685-3750. ¢¢

Maryland Institute, College of Art (1826). (880 students) Institute hosts frequent contemporary art exhibitions. Cafeteria. Campus distinguished by recycled buildings and white marble Italianate Main Building. (Daily) Main building 1300 Mt Royal Ave, at Lanvale St. Phone 410/669-9200.

Maryland Science Center & Davis Planetarium. Home of the Maryland Academy of Sciences, the oldest scientific institution in the state. Features exhibits in areas such as energy, physics, the Chesapeake Bay, optical illusions & television production. Planetarium. Includes IMAX theater. Science demonstrations. (Daily; closed Thanksgiving, Dec 25) 601 Light St, Inner Harbor area. Phone 410/685-5225 (recording). ¢¢¢

Minnie V. Chesapeake Bay skipjack built in 1906. Harbor tours under sail (mid-June-Labor Day, daily exc Mon; May-mid-June & rest of Sept, Sat & Sun). Docks near Pier 1, Pratt St, Inner Harbor area. Phone 410/522-4214 or 410/685-0295. ¢¢¢

Morgan State University (1867). (5,100 students) The James E. Lewis Museum of Art has changing exhibits (Mon-Fri; wkends by appt; closed hols). Cold Spring Lane & Hillen Rd. Phone 410/319-3333.

Mother Seton House. Home of St Elizabeth Ann Bayley Seton from 1808-1809. Here she established forerunner of the parochial school system. She also established an order of nuns here that eventually became the Daughters & Sisters of Charity in the US and Canada. (Sat & Sun afternoons, also by appt; closed Jan 1, Easter, Dec 25) 600 N Paca St, downtown. Phone 410/523-3443. **Free.**

Mount Clare Museum House (1760). Oldest mansion in Baltimore, former home of Charles Carroll, barrister. 18th-century furnishings. Guided tours on the hr. (Daily exc Mon; closed some hols) In Carroll Park at Monroe St & Washington Blvd. Phone 410/837-3262. **¢¢**

Mount Vernon Place United Methodist Church (ca 1850). Brownstone with balcony and grillwork extending entire width of house; spiral staircase suspended from 3 floors; library with century-old painting on ceiling; drawing room. (Mon-Fri; closed hols and Mon after Easter) 10 E Mt Vernon Place. Phone 410/685-5290. **Free.**

MPT (Maryland Public Television). Tours of state's television network studios. (By appt) Phone 410/356-5600 or 800/223-3MPT (surrounding states). **Free.**

⭐ **National Aquarium.** One of the most advanced facilities in US. Exhibits include a South American rain forest, Atlantic coral reef, shark tank; houses 5,000 specimens of 500 different types of mammals, fish, birds, reptiles, amphibians, invertebrates and plants. (Daily; closed Thanksgiving, Dec 25) Pier 3, 501 E Pratt St, Inner Harbor area. Phone 410/576-3800. **¢¢¢¢** Visitors cross an enclosed skywalk to reach the adj wing, which houses

Marine Mammal Pavilion. This unique structure features a 1,300-seat amphitheater surrounding a 1.2-million-gallon pool, which houses Atlantic bottlenose dolphins; underwater viewing areas enable visitors to also observe the mammals from below the surface. (Daily) Special video programs about dolphins and whales; educational arcade with computerized video screens and other participatory exhibits around the upper deck of the pavilion. A visitor service area is located in the atrium. Gift shop. Cafe. A life-size replica of a humpback whale spans two levels of the atrium. A Discovery Room houses a collection of marine artifacts. The Resource Center is designed as an aquatic learning center for school visitors; a library boasts an extensive collection of marine science material. One ticket for admission to both buildings. Pier 4.

Old Otterbein United Methodist Church (1785-1786). Fine Georgian architecture; mother church of United Brethren. Tours of historic building (Apr-Oct, Sat). Conway & Sharp Sts, Inner Harbor area. Phone 410/685-4703.

Old Town Mall. This 150-yr-old, brick-lined commercial area has been beautifully refurbished; closed to vehicular traffic. 400 & 500 blks of N Gay St. Nearby is

Stirling Street "Homesteading." First community urban "homesteading" venture in the US. Renovated homes date back to the 1830s. Original façades have been maintained; the interior rehabilitation ranges in style from the antique to the avant garde. 1000 blk of Monument St, 1 blk W of mall.

Otterbein "Homesteading." The original neighborhood dates back to 1785. Houses have been restored. Area around S Sharp St, Inner Harbor area.

Patterson Park. Defenses here helped stop British attack in 1814. Breastworks, artillery pieces are displayed. Baltimore St, Eastern & Patterson Park Aves.

Peabody Institute of the Johns Hopkins University (1857). (550 students) Founded by philanthropist George Peabody; now affiliated with Johns Hopkins. Research and reference collection in library accessible to the public (Mon-Fri; closed hols). The Miriam A. Friedberg Concert Hall seats 800. The Conservatory holds orchestra concerts, recitals and operas. In Mt Vernon Place area. Box office phone 410/659-8124.

Peale Museum (1814). Built as Rembrandt Peale's "Baltimore Museum," it is the nation's oldest museum building. Later Baltimore's first city hall, it is now a history museum housing a collection of Baltimore photographs and paintings, including many by members of the Peale family, plus an exhibit on the evolution of American museums. Walled garden. (Sat, Sun; closed hols) 225 Holliday St, downtown. Phone 410/396-3523. **¢**

Pier 6 Concert Pavilion. Summertime outdoor concerts and plays at the water's edge. Some covered seating. (June-Sept, evenings) (See SEA-SONAL EVENTS) Pier 6, Inner Harbor area. Phone 410/625-1400 for schedule. **¢¢¢¢**

Professional sports.

American League baseball (Baltimore Orioles). Camden Yards, 333 W Camden St. Phone 410/685-9800.

NFL (Baltimore Ravens). Memorial Stadium, 33rd & Greenmill. Phone 410/654-6200.

Public Works Museum & Streetscape. Museum exhibits the history and artifacts of public works. Located in historic sewage pumping station. Streetscape sculpture outside depicts the various utility lines and ducts under a typical city street, in a walk-through model. (Mid-Apr-mid-Oct, daily exc Mon; rest of yr, Wed-Sun) 751 Eastern Ave, at Inner Harbor East. Phone 410/396-5565. **¢¢**

Sherwood Gardens. More than 6 acres in size, the gardens reach their peak of splendor in late Apr & early May, when thousands of tulips, azaleas and flowering shrubs bloom. Stratford Rd & Greenway, located in the residential community of Guilford in northern Baltimore. Phone 410/366-2572.

Shot Tower (1829). Tapering brick structure (234 ft) where molten lead was dropped to form round shot that hardened when it hit water at base. Self-activated film; exhibits. (Daily) Fayette & Front Sts, downtown. Phone 410/396-3523. **Free.**

Star-Spangled Banner Flag House and 1812 Museum. The banner (30 by 42 ft) with 15 stars and 15 stripes that Key saw "by the dawn's early light" over Ft McHenry was hand-sewn here by Mary Young Pickersgill. The actual flag is in the Smithsonian. House (1793) is authentically restored and furnished in the Federal period. 1812 Museum contains relics, documents, weapons, memorabilia; audiovisual program; garden. Focal point of the garden is a stone map of the US; every state is represented by a stone native to and cut in the shape of that state. (Daily exc Sun; closed some hols) 844 E Pratt St, at Albemarle St, downtown. Phone 410/837-1793. **¢¢**

Theaters.

Vagabond Players. Oldest continuously operating "little theater" in US. Recent Broadway shows, revivals and original scripts are performed. (Fri-Sun) 806 S Broadway. Box office phone 410/563-9135.

Cockpit in Court Summer Theatre. (See SEASONAL EVENTS)

Top of the World. Observation deck and museum on the 27th floor of the World Trade Center, which was designed by I.M. Pei. Exhibits describe the city's history, famous residents and the activities of the port. (Daily) World Trade Center, Pratt St, Inner Harbor area. Phone 410/837-4515. **¢**

University of Maryland at Baltimore. (5,000 students) The 32-acre downtown campus includes 6 professional schools; the University of Maryland Medical System and the Graduate School. Davidge Hall (1812) is the oldest medical teaching building in continuous use in the Western Hemisphere. Lombard, Greene & Redwood Sts, downtown. Phone 410/706-7820.

Walters Art Gallery. City-owned fine arts collection of paintings, sculpture, arms, armor, jewelry and manuscripts from antiquity through the 19th century. (Daily exc Mon; closed major hols) 600 N Charles St, at Centre St, in Mt Vernon Place area. Phone 410/547-9000. **¢¢**

Washington Monument (1815-1842). First major monument to honor George Washington. Museum in base; view city from top. Other monuments nearby honor Lafayette, Chief Justice Roger Brooke Taney, philanthropist George Peabody, lawyer Severn Teackle Wallis and Revolutionary War hero John Eager Howard. Charles & Monument Sts, in Mt Vernon Place area.

Annual Events

ACC Crafts Fair. Convention Center. Featuring more than 800 artisans. Late Feb.

Maryland House and Garden Pilgrimage. More than 100 homes and gardens throughout the state are open. To purchase tour book contact 1105-A Providence Rd, 21286; 410/821-6933. Late Apr-early May.

Maryland Preakness Celebration. Statewide festival; events include hot air balloon festival, parade, steeplechase, celebrity golf tournament, block parties and schooner race. Phone 410/837-3030. 10 days preceding Preakness Stakes (see SEASONAL EVENTS). Early to mid-May.

Harbor Expo. Middle Branch and Canton Waterfront. Boat parades; seafood festival; entertainment; events. Phone 410/347-5225. Mid-June.

Artscape. Salute to the arts & culture. Phone 410/396-4575. 3 days July.

New Year's Eve Extravaganza. Convention Center and Inner Harbor. Parties, entertainment, big bands, fireworks.

Seasonal Events

Pimlico Race Course. Hayward & Winner Aves, 2 mi W of Jones Falls Expy.Thoroughbred racing. **The Preakness**, the $500,000 middle jewel in Thoroughbred racing's Triple Crown, has been run here yearly since 1873 and is held the 3rd Sat in May. All seats reserved Preakness Day. Phone 410/542-9400. Late Mar-early June & early Aug-early Oct.

Cockpit in Court Summer Theatre. 7201 Rossville Blvd, use Beltway (I-695) exit 34, in Baltimore County. Theater in residence at Essex Community College. Four separate theaters offer a diverse collection of plays, including Broadway productions, contemporary drama, revues and Shakespeare. Box office phone 410/780-6369. Mid-June-mid-Aug.

Pier 6 Concert Pavilion. Evening concerts featuring big names in jazz, pop, classical and country music. For schedule phone 410/625-1400. Late June-Sept.

Showcase of Nations Ethnic Festivals. Presenting the food, music and crafts of a different culture each wkend. Various downtown locations. Phone 410/752-8632. June-Sept.

Additional Visitor Information

Maps, brochures and calendars of events are available at the Baltimore Area Visitors Center, 301 E Pratt St, Constellation Pier, 21202; phone 410/837-INFO or 800/282-6632.

Baltimore/Washington Intl Airport Area

For additional accommodations, see BALTIMORE/WASHINGTON INTL AIRPORT AREA, which follows BALTIMORE.

City Neighborhoods

Many of the restaurants, unrated dining establishments and some lodgings listed under Baltimore include neighborhoods as well as exact street addresses. Geographic descriptions of these areas are given, followed by a table of restaurants arranged by neighborhood.

Central Area: South of Mt Royal Ave, west of I-83, north of the Inner Harbor and Pratt St and east of Martin Luther King Jr Blvd and Greene St. **North of Central Area:** North of Chase. **East of Central Area:** East of I-83.

Fell's Point: Waterfront area east of Inner Harbor; south of Eastern Ave, west of Wolfe St and east of Caroline St.

Inner Harbor: Waterfront area south of Central Area at Pratt St, west of Jones Fall Pkwy and east of Light St.

Little Italy: East of Inner Harbor; south of Lombard St, west of Caroline St, north of Lancaster St and the waterfront and east of Jones Fall Pkwy.

BALTIMORE RESTAURANTS BY NEIGHBORHOOD AREAS
(For full description, see alphabetical listings under Restaurants)

CENTRAL AREA
Kawasaki. 413 N Charles St
Louie's The Bookstore Cafe. 518 N Charles St
Prime Rib. 1101 N Calvert St
Ruby Lounge. 802 N Charles St
Ruth's Chris Steak House. 600 Water St
Tio Pepe. 10 E Franklin St

Water Street Exchange. 110 Water St
The Wild Mushroom. 641 S Montford Ave

NORTH OF CENTRAL AREA
Angelina's. 7135 Harford Rd
Cafe Hon. 1002 W 36th St
Jeannier's. 105 W 39th St
Morgan Millard. 4800 Roland Ave
Mt Washington Tavern. 5700 Newbury St
Polo Grill (Doubletree Inn at The Colonnade Hotel). 4 W University Pkwy
Spike & Charlie's. 1225 Cathedral St

EAST OF CENTRAL AREA
Haussner's. 3244 Eastern Ave
Ikaros. 4805 Eastern Ave
Karson's Inn. 5100 Holabird Ave

FELL'S POINT
Bertha's. 734 S Broadway
Captain Louie's. 606 S Broadway
Henninger's Tavern. 1812 Bank St
John Steven Ltd. 1800 Thames St
Obrycki's. 1727 E Pratt St
Pierpoint. 1822 Aliceanna St
Savannah (Admiral Fell Inn). 888 S Broadway
Waterfront Hotel. 1710 Thames St

INNER HARBOR
City Lights. 301 Light St
Hampton's (Harbor Court Hotel). 550 Light St
Joy America Cafe. 800 Key Hwy
Wayne's Bar-B-Que. 201 Pratt St

LITTLE ITALY
Boccaccio. 925 Eastern Ave
Chiapparelli's. 237 S High St
Dalesio's. 829 Eastern Ave
Germano's Trattoria. 300 S High St
La Scala. 411 S High St
Rocco Capriccio. 846 Fawn St
Velleggia's. 829 E Pratt St

Note: When a listing is located in a town that does not have its own city heading, it will appear under the city nearest to its location. In these cases, the address and town appear in parenthesis immediately following the name of the establishment.

Motels

(In this area I-95 is Kennedy Memorial Hwy; I-695 is the Beltway)

(Rates may be much higher Preakness wkend, mid-May)

✔★ **CHRISTLEN.** 8733 Pulaski Hwy (US 40) (21237), I-695 exit 35B, east of Central Area. 410/687-1740. 28 rms. S $32-$38; D $38-$42; each addl $5. Crib $5. TV; cable (premium). Restaurant adj open 24 hrs. Ck-out 11 am. Some refrigerators; microwaves avail. Picnic tables. Cr cds: A, D, DS, MC, V.

| D | 🖘 | 🐾 |

★ **DAYS INN-WEST.** 5801 Baltimore Natl Pike (21228), on US 40, just E of I-695 exit 15A, west of Central Area. 410/744-5000; FAX 410/788-5197. 98 rms, 3 story. S, D $55-$75; under 12 free. Crib free. TV; cable (premium). Pool; lifeguard. Complimentary continental bkfst. Restaurant 7 am-1 pm, 5-10 pm. Ck-out noon. Coin lndry. Meeting rms. Business servs avail. Cr cds: A, C, D, DS, MC, V.

| D | 🏊 | 🖘 | 🐾 | SC |

★ **HAMPTON INN.** 8225 Town Center Dr (21236), east of Central Area. 410/931-2200; FAX 410/931-2215. 127 rms, 4 story, 16 suites. S $75; D $80; suites $95; under 18 free. Crib $10. TV; cable (premium). Complimentary continental bkfst. Restaurant nearby. Ck-out noon. Meeting rms. Business center. In-rm modem link. Bellhops. Free airport transportation. Exercise equipt; bicycle, stair machine. Health club privileges. Heated pool; lifeguard. Wet bar in suites. Refrigerators, microwaves avail. Picnic tables. Cr cds: A, D, DS, MC, V.

D ≈ 🏃 🎿 ⛄ SC 🏌

★ ★ **HOLIDAY INN SECURITY/BELMONT.** *1800 Belmont Ave (21224), I-695 exit 17, north of Central Area.* 410/265-1400; FAX 410/281-9569. 135 units, 2 story. S, D $59-$83. Crib free. Pet accepted. TV; cable (premium). Pool; lifeguard. Restaurant 6 am-2 pm, 5-10 pm; Sat, Sun from 7 am. Rm serv. Bar 5 pm-midnight. Ck-out noon. Meeting rms. Business servs avail. In-rm modem link. Valet serv. Sundries. Health club privileges. Some refrigerators; microwaves avail. Cr cds: A, C, D, DS, ER, JCB, MC, V.

D 🐾 ≈ 🎿 ⛄ SC

✔★ **SUSSE CHALET.** *4 Philadelphia Court (21237), I-695 exit 34, north of Central Area.* 410/574-8100; FAX 410/574-8204. 132 rms, 5 story. S $56.70; D $61.70; each addl $3. Crib free. TV; cable (premium). Pool; lifeguard. Complimentary continental bkfst. Restaurant nearby. Ck-out 11 am. Coin lndry. Business servs avail. Sundries. Microwaves avail. Cr cds: A, C, D, DS, MC, V.

D ≈ 🎿 ⛄ SC

Motor Hotels

★ ★ **BEST WESTERN-EAST.** *5625 O'Donnell St (21224), I-95 exit 57, east of Central Area.* 410/633-9500; FAX 410/633-2812. 175 rms, 12 story. S, D $89-$94; each addl $10; suites $129-$229. Crib avail. TV; cable (premium). Indoor pool; lifeguard. Restaurant 6:30 am-10 pm. Rm serv. Bar. Ck-out noon. Coin lndry. Meeting rms. Business servs avail. In-rm modem link. Gift shop. Bus depot, downtown transportation. Exercise equipt; weight machines, bicycles, sauna. Game rm. Microwaves avail. Cr cds: A, D, DS, JCB, MC, V.

D ≈ 🏃 🎿 ⛄ SC

★ ★ **CROSS KEYS INN.** *5100 Falls Rd (21210), north of Central Area.* 410/532-6900; FAX 410/532-2403; res: 800/532-5397. 148 rms, 4 story. S $105-$175; D $115-$185; each addl $15; suites $195-$425; under 16 free; wkend rates. Crib free. TV; cable (premium). Pool; poolside serv, lifeguard. Complimentary coffee in rms. Restaurant 6:30 am-11 pm. Rm serv. Bar 11 am-midnight. Ck-out noon. Meeting rms. Business servs avail. In-rm modem link. Shopping arcade. Barber, beauty shop. Tennis privileges. Health club privileges. Bathrm phones; microwaves avail. Some private balconies. Cr cds: A, C, D, DS, MC, V.

D 🏃 ≈ 🎿 🔥 SC

★ **DAYS INN INNER HARBOR.** *100 Hopkins Pl (21201), in Central Area.* 410/576-1000; FAX 410/576-9437. 250 rms, 9 story. S $90-$120; D $100-$130; each addl $10; suites $140-$180; under 12 free; higher rates special events. Crib free. Garage $8.50. TV; cable (premium). Pool; poolside serv, lifeguard. Restaurant 6:30 am-10 pm. Rm serv. Bar. Ck-out 11 am. Meeting rms. Business center. Bellhops. Concierge. Sundries. Health club privileges. Some refrigerators, microwaves avail. Cr cds: A, D, DS, MC, V.

D ≈ 🎿 ⛄ SC 🏌

✔★ **HOWARD JOHNSON.** *5701 Baltimore Natl Pike (21228), ½ mi E of I-695 exit 15A, west of Central Area.* 410/747-8900; FAX 410/744-3522. 145 rms, 7 story. S $40-$70; D $48-$75; each addl $8; under 18 free. Crib free. TV; cable (premium), VCR avail (movies). Pool; whirlpool, lifeguard. Ck-out 11 am. Coin lndry. Meeting rms. Business servs avail. Sundries. Some refrigerators. Balconies. Cr cds: A, C, D, DS, ER, JCB, MC, V.

D ≈ 🎿 🔥 SC

Hotels

★ ★ **BROOKSHIRE INNER HARBOR SUITE HOTEL.** *120 E Lombard St (21202), Inner Harbor.* 410/625-1300; FAX 410/625-0912; res: 800/647-0013 (exc MD). 90 suites, 12 story. S $170-$305; D $190-$325; each addl $20; children free; wkend rates. Crib free. TV; cable. Coffee in

rms. Restaurant 6:30-10 am, 5-9 pm. Bar 5-10 pm. Ck-out noon. Meeting rms. Concierge. Health club privileges. Bathrm phones, refrigerators, minibars; microwaves avail. Cr cds: A, C, D, DS, MC, V.

D 🎿 🔥 SC

★ ★ ★ **CLARION.** *612 Cathedral St (21201), at Mt Vernon Place, north of Central Area.* 410/727-7101; FAX 410/789-3312; res: 800/292-5580. 103 rms, 14 story. S, D $114-$154; each addl $10; suites $189-$350; under 18 free; wkend rates; package plans. Crib free. Valet parking $12. TV; cable (premium), VCR avail (movies). Pool privileges. Restaurants 6:30 am-11 pm. Bar. Ck-out 11 am. Meeting rms. In-rm modem link. Concierge. Health club privileges. Some in-rm whirlpools. Restored hotel built in 1927. Marble floors, stairs in lobby. Period furnishings, artwork, crystal chandeliers. Cr cds: A, C, D, DS, ER, JCB, MC, V.

D 🎿 🔥 SC

★ ★ ★ **DOUBLETREE INN AT THE COLONNADE.** *4 West University Pkwy (21218), Charles St N to University Pkwy, north of Central area.* 410/235-5400; FAX 410/235-5572. Web www.doubletreehotel.com. 125 units, 3 story, 31 suites. S, D $124-$169; each addl $15; suites $149-$475; family rates; wkend plans. Crib free. Pet accepted. TV; cable (premium). Indoor pool; whirlpool, poolside serv, lifeguard. Coffee in rms. Restaurant 6 am-11 pm (also see POLO GRILL). Rm serv to 10 pm. Ck-out noon. Meeting rm. Business center. In-rm modem link. Gift shop. Barber, beauty shop. Exercise equipt; bicycles, treadmill. Some wet bars; microwaves avail. Balconies. Biedermeier-inspired furnishings; extensive collection of 18th-century European masters. Adj to Johns Hopkins University. Cr cds: A, C, D, DS, ER, JCB, MC, V.

D 🐾 ≈ 🏃 🎿 🔥 SC 🏌

★ ★ ★ **HARBOR COURT.** *550 Light St (21202), Inner Harbor.* 410/234-0550; FAX 410/659-5925; res: 800/824-0076. Web www.harbor .com 203 rms, 8 story, 25 suites. S $205-$245; D $220-$260; suites $375-$2,000; under 18 free; wkend rates; some package plans. Crib free. Covered parking: self-park $15; valet $18. TV; cable (premium), VCR avail. Heated pool; whirlpool, poolside serv, lifeguard. Restaurant 7 am-11 pm (also see HAMPTON'S). Rm serv 24 hrs. Bar 11-2 am; entertainment exc Sun. Ck-out noon. Meeting rms. Business center. In-rm modem link. Concierge. Airport transportation. Tennis. Exercise rm; instructor, weight machines, bicycles, sauna. Massage. Racquetball. Lawn games. Bathrm phones, refrigerators. Elegant retreat located on Inner Harbor; panoramic view of city. Cr cds: A, C, D, DS, ER, JCB, MC, V.

D 🏃 ≈ 🏃 🎿 🔥 SC 🏌

★ ★ ★ **HILTON AND TOWERS.** *20 W Baltimore St (21201), in Central Area.* 410/539-8400; FAX 410/625-1060. 419 rms, 23 story. S $189; D $209; each addl $15; suites $275-$400; kit. units $600-$800; under 17 free; wkend rates. Crib free. Valet parking $15. TV; cable. Restaurants 6:30 am-10 pm. Bar 11-2 am. Ck-out noon. Meeting rms. In-rm modem link. Exercise equipt; weight machines, bicycles, whirlpool, sauna. Health club privileges. Microwaves avail. Historic landmark; near harbor. Cr cds: A, C, D, DS, ER, MC, V.

D 🏃 🎿 🔥 SC

★ ★ **HOLIDAY INN BALTIMORE-INNER HARBOR.** *301 W Lombard St (21201), in Central Area.* 410/685-3500; FAX 410/727-6169. 375 rms; 10, 13 story. Apr-Sept: S $139; D $149; each addl $10; suites $275; under 13 free; lower rates rest of yr. Crib free. Pet accepted, some restrictions. Garage parking $6. TV; cable (premium). Indoor pool; lifeguard. Complimentary coffee in rms. Restaurant 6:30 am-11 pm. Bar 11-1 am. Ck-out noon. Convention facilities. Business center. Gift shop. Exercise equipt; weight machine, bicycles, sauna. Some balconies. Cr cds: A, C, D, DS, ER, JCB, MC, V.

D 🐾 ≈ 🏃 🎿 🔥 SC 🏌

★ ★ ★ **HYATT REGENCY.** *300 Light St (21202), Inner Harbor.* 410/528-1234; FAX 410/685-3362. Web www.travelweb.com/ hyatt.html. 486 rms, 14 story. S $185; D $210; each addl $25; suites $350-$900; under 18 free; wkend plan. Crib free. Valet parking $14. TV; cable (premium). Pool; whirlpool, lifeguard. Restaurant 6:30-1 am. Bar 11:30-2 am; entertainment Fri, Sat. Ck-out noon. Convention facilities. Business center. In-rm modem link. Concierge. Gift shop. Tennis. Exercise rm; instructor, weight machine, bicycles. Putting green. Basketball ½ court. Minibars; refrigerators avail. Luxury level. Cr cds: A, C, D, DS, ER, JCB, MC, V.

⟦D⟧ ⟦≈⟧ ⟦⚲⟧ ⟦✗⟧ ⟦⚲⟧ ⟦SC⟧ ⟦⚶⟧

★ ★ ★ **MARRIOTT INNER HARBOR.** *110 S Eutaw St (21201), Inner Harbor.* 410/962-0202. Web www.marriott.com. 525 units, 10 story. S, D $209; suites $195-$650; under 18 free; wkend rates. Crib free. Covered parking $8. TV; cable (premium), VCR avail. Indoor pool; whirlpool, lifeguard. Restaurant 6 am-10 pm. Bar noon-2 am; entertainment. Ck-out noon. Convention facilities. Business center. In-rm modem link. Concierge. Exercise equipt; weights, bicycles, sauna. Opp baseball stadium at Camden Yards. Luxury level. Cr cds: A, C, D, DS, ER, JCB, MC, V.

⟦D⟧ ⟦≈⟧ ⟦⚲⟧ ⟦✗⟧ ⟦⚲⟧ ⟦SC⟧ ⟦⚶⟧

★ ★ ★ **OMNI INNER HARBOR.** *101 W Fayette St (21201), Inner Harbor.* 410/752-1100; FAX 410/625-3805. 707 rms in 2 bldgs, 23, 27 story. S, D $149-$179; each addl $20; suites $200-$750; under 17 free; wkend rates. Crib free. Garage $9; valet parking $14. TV; cable (premium). Pool; poolside serv, lifeguard. Coffee in rms. Restaurant 6:30 am-midnight. Bars noon-2 am. Ck-out noon. Convention facilities. Business center. In-rm modem link. Exercise equipt; weights, bicycles. Health club privileges. Minibars; some refrigerators; microwaves avail. Cr cds: A, C, D, DS, ER, MC, V.

⟦D⟧ ⟦≈⟧ ⟦✗⟧ ⟦⚲⟧ ⟦⚲⟧ ⟦SC⟧ ⟦⚶⟧

★ ★ ★ **RENAISSANCE HARBORPLACE.** *202 E Pratt St (21202), Inner Harbor.* 410/547-1200; FAX 410/539-5780. Web www.renaissancehotels.com. 622 rms, 12 story. S $215-$285; D $235-$305; each addl $20; suites $450-$1,500; under 18 free; wkend rates. Covered parking $10; valet $14. Crib free. TV; cable (premium), VCR avail. Indoor pool; whirlpool, poolside serv, lifeguard. Coffee in rms. Restaurant 6:30 am-11 pm. Rm serv 24 hrs. Bar 11-1:30 am; entertainment. Ck-out noon. Convention facilities. Business center. In-rm modem link. Concierge. Shopping arcade. Exercise equipt; weight machines, bicycles, sauna. Minibars; bathrm phones. Luxury level. Cr cds: A, C, D, DS, ER, JCB, MC, V.

⟦D⟧ ⟦≈⟧ ⟦✗⟧ ⟦⚲⟧ ⟦⚲⟧ ⟦SC⟧ ⟦⚶⟧

★ ★ ★ **SHERATON INNER HARBOR.** *300 S Charles St (21201), in Inner Harbor.* 410/962-8300; FAX 410/962-8211. E-mail resdept @erols.com; web www.ittsheraton.com. 337 rms, 15 story. Mar-June, Sept-Dec: S, D $170-$230; each addl $15; suites $425-$1,400; under 17 free; wkly, wkend rates; lower rates rest of yr. Crib free. Covered parking $12, valet parking $19. TV; cable (premium), VCR avail (movies). Indoor pool; lifeguard. Restaurant 6:30 am-11 pm. Bar 11:30-2 am. Ck-out noon. Convention facilities. Business center. In-rm modem link. Concierge. Gift shop. Exercise equipt; bicycles, treadmill, sauna. Health club privileges. Minibars; some bathrm phones, refrigerators. Cr cds: A, C, D, DS, ER, JCB, MC, V.

⟦D⟧ ⟦≈⟧ ⟦✗⟧ ⟦⚲⟧ ⟦⚲⟧ ⟦SC⟧ ⟦⚶⟧

↙★ ★ **TREMONT.** *8 E Pleasant St (21202), in Central Area.* 410/576-1200; FAX 410/244-1154; res: 800/873-6668. 58 kit. suites, 13 story. S $89-$119; D $109-$139; each addl $20; under 16 free; wkend rates. Crib free. Pet accepted; $5. Valet parking $11. Pool privileges. TV; cable, VCR avail (free movies). Complimentary continental bkfst. Restaurant 5-9 pm. Bar to 10 pm. Ck-out noon. Meeting rms. Business servs avail. Health club privileges. Microwaves. Cr cds: A, C, D, DS, MC, V.

⟦D⟧ ⟦✓⟧ ⟦⚲⟧ ⟦⚲⟧ ⟦⚲⟧ ⟦SC⟧

Inns

↙★ ★ ★ **ABACROMBIE BADGER.** *58 W Biddle St (21201), west of Central Area.* 410/244-7227; FAX 410/244-8415. 12 rms, 4 story. S $79; D $105-$135. TV; cable. Complimentary continental bkfst. Restaurant 11 am-10 pm; Fri, Sat to midnight; closed Mon. Bar to midnight; Fri, Sat to 2 am. Ck-out 11 am, ck-in 4 pm. Business servs avail. Turn-of-the-century building; many antique furnishings. Cr cds: A, C, D, DS, MC, V.

⟦⚲⟧ ⟦⚲⟧

★ ★ ★ **ADMIRAL FELL.** *888 S Broadway (21231), in Fell's Point.* 410/522-7377; FAX 410/522-0707; res: 800/292-4667 (exc MD). E-mail admiral1@erols.com; web www.admiralfell.com. 80 rms, 5 story. S, D $105-$195; each addl $20; suites $225-$355; wkly rates. TV; cable (premium). Complimentary continental bkfst. Dining rm 11:30 am-10 pm. Bar 11-2 am. Ck-out noon, ck-in 4 pm. Meeting rms. Business servs avail. In-rm modem link. Concierge. Health club privileges. Some in-rm whirlpools; microwaves avail. Cr cds: A, D, MC, V.

⟦D⟧ ⟦⚲⟧ ⟦⚲⟧ ⟦SC⟧

★ ★ ★ **CELIE'S WATERFRONT BED & BREAKFAST.** *1714 Thames St (21231), in Fell's Point.* 410/522-2323; FAX 410/522-2324; res: 800/432-0184. E-mail celies@aol.com. 7 rms, 1 with shower only, 3 story. S $95-$175; D $115-$200; hol, wkend rates. Children over 9 yrs only. TV; cable. Complimentary continental bkfst. Complimentary coffee in rm. Restaurant nearby. Ck-out 11 am, ck-in 3-6 pm. Business servs avail. In-rm modem link. Health club privileges. Refrigerators; some in-rm whirlpools, fireplaces. On harbor; many antiques. Roof deck. Totally nonsmoking. Cr cds: A, DS, MC, V.

⟦D⟧ ⟦⚲⟧ ⟦⚲⟧

★ ★ ★ **HOPKINS INN.** *3404 St Paul St (21218), north of Central Area.* 410/235-8600; FAX 410/235-7051. 25 rms, 4 story. S, D $100-$140; wkly, monthly rates. Covered parking $6. TV. Complimentary continental bkfst. Restaurant nearby. Ck-out 11 am, ck-in 3 pm. Meeting rms. Business servs avail. 1920's Spanish-revival building. Rms individually furnished in variety of styles. Totally nonsmoking. Cr cds: A, C, D, DS, MC, V.

⟦⚲⟧ ⟦⚲⟧

★ ★ ★ **INN AT GOVERNMENT HOUSE.** *1125 N Calvert St (21202), north of Central Area.* 410/539-0566; FAX 410/539-0567. 18 rms, 4 story. S, D $125-$150; wkly rates. Preakness (2-day min). TV. Complimentary continental bkfst; afternoon refreshments. Restaurant nearby. Ck-out noon, ck-in 3-8 pm. Business servs avail. Part of complex of several Federal and Victorian mansions and town houses (1888). Totally nonsmoking. Cr cds: A, C, D, DS, MC, V.

⟦D⟧ ⟦⚲⟧ ⟦⚲⟧ ⟦SC⟧

★ ★ **THE INN AT HENDERSON'S WHARF.** *1000 Fell St (21231), in Fell's Point.* 410/522-7777; FAX 410/522-7087; res: 800/522-2088. E-mail sales@hendersonswharf.com; web www.hendersonswharf.com. 38 rms. Apr-Nov: S, D $120-$160; kit. suites $400; under 18 free; higher rates special events; lower rates rest of yr. TV; cable (premium). Complimentary continental bkfst. Restaurant nearby. Ck-out noon, ck-in 3 pm. Coin lndry. Meeting rms. Business servs avail. In-rm modem link. Valet serv. Exercise equipt; weight machine, bicycles. Some refrigerators. On waterfront; dockage avail. 19th-century tobacco warehouse. Cr cds: A, C, D, MC, V.

⟦D⟧ ⟦✗⟧ ⟦⚲⟧ ⟦⚲⟧ ⟦SC⟧

★ ★ ★ ★ **MR MOLE BED & BREAKFAST.** *1601 Bolton St (21217), north of Central Area.* 410/728-1179; FAX 410/728-3379. This restored 1870 red brick row house with oriel windows still possesses many original details, including 14-foot ceilings, plaster moldings, marble fireplaces and gilt mirrors and cornices. The large guest rooms are furnished with 18th- and 19th-century antiques and stocked with vintage books. 5 rms, 3 story, 2 suites. S $87; D $97-$125; each addl $15; suites $100-$145; 2-day min wkends Mar-Dec. Children over 12 yrs only. Complimentary bkfst. Restaurant nearby. Ck-out 11 am, ck-in 4-6 pm. Business servs avail. In-rm modem link. Health club privileges. Totally nonsmoking. Cr cds: A, C, D, DS, MC, V.

⟦⚲⟧ ⟦⚲⟧

Restaurants

★ ★ **ANGELINA'S.** *7135 Harford Rd (21214), north of Central Area.* 410/444-5545. Hrs: 11:30 am-10 pm; Fri, Sat to 11:30 pm. Closed Mon; Thanksgiving, Dec 25. Italian, Seafood menu. Bar. Semi-a la carte:

lunch $5-$16.95, dinner $9-$29. Child's meals. Specializes in crab cakes, seafood. Entertainment Fri. Cr cds: A, DS, MC, V.

⊟

★ **BERTHA'S.** 734 S Broadway (21231), in Fell's Point. 410/327-0426. E-mail berthas@ix.netcom.com. Hrs: 11:30 am-11 pm; Fri, Sat to midnight; Sun brunch to 2 pm. Closed major hols. Res required for Scottish afternoon tea (Mon-Sat). Bar. Semi-a la carte: lunch, dinner $4.95-$19.25. Sun brunch $7.95-$8.50. Specializes in mussels, seafood. Eclectic decor. Historic 19th-century building. Cr cds: MC, V.

SC

★ ★ ★ **BOCCACCIO.** 925 Eastern Ave (21231), Little Italy. 410/234-1322. Hrs: 11:30 am-2:30 pm, 5-11 pm; Sat from 5 pm; Sun 3-10 pm. Closed Thanksgiving, Dec 25. Res required eves. Italian menu. Bar. Semi-a la carte: lunch $9.75-$15.75, dinner $13.50-$28.50. Specializes in veal, seafood, pasta. Formal decor. Cr cds: A, C, D, MC, V.

D

✔★ **CAFE HON.** 1002 W 36th St (21211), north of Central Area. 410/243-1230. Hrs: 7 am-10 pm; Sat from 9 am; Sun 9 am-3 pm (brunch). Closed most major hols. Bar. Semi-a la carte: bkfst $1.25-$5.95, lunch, dinner $4.25-$13.95. Sun brunch $1.50-$6.50. Child's meals. Specialties: crab cakes, meatloaf. Eclectic cafe reminiscent of 1930s Baltimore soda fountain. Totally nonsmoking. Cr cds: A, MC, V.

D

✔★ ★ **CAPTAIN LOUIE'S.** 606 S Broadway (21231), in Fell's Point. 410/558-3600. Hrs: 11-2 am. Res accepted. Bar. A la carte entrees: lunch $6.75-$11, dinner $12-$18. Specializes in seafood, sushi bar. Cr cds: A, MC, V.

★ ★ **CHIAPPARELLI'S.** 237 S High St (21202), Little Italy. 410/837-0309. Hrs: 11 am-10 pm; Fri, Sat to midnight. Closed Thanksgiving, Dec 25. Italian menu. Semi-a la carte: lunch $7-$14, dinner $10-$25. Child's meals. Specialty: Piatto Napolitano. Valet parking after 5 pm. Built 1870; original brick walls, oak paneling. 7 dining rms on 2 levels. Family-owned. Cr cds: A, C, D, DS, MC, V.

D ⊟

★ ★ **CITY LIGHTS.** 301 Light St (21202), Light St Pavilion, Inner Harbor. 410/244-8811. Hrs: 11:30 am-10 pm; Fri to 11 pm; Sat to midnight; Sun to 9 pm. Closed Thanksgiving, Dec 24, 25. Res accepted. Bar. A la carte entrees: lunch, dinner $5-$18. Child's meals. Specializes in Chesapeake Bay seafood. Own desserts. Outdoor dining. Cr cds: A, C, D, DS, JCB, MC, V.

⊟

★ ★ ★ **DALESIO'S.** 829 Eastern Ave (21202), Little Italy. 410/539-1965. Hrs: 11:30 am-3 pm, 5-10 pm. Closed Thanksgiving. Res accepted. Northern Italian menu. Bar. A la carte entrees: lunch $5.95-$9.95, dinner $10.95-$21.95. Specializes in Northern Italian spa cuisine. Own cakes, pasta. Outdoor dining. Cr cds: A, D, MC, V.

D ⊟ ♥

★ ★ **GERMANO'S TRATTORIA.** 300 S High St (21202), Little Italy. 410/752-4515. Hrs: 11:30 am-11 pm; Fri, Sat to midnight. Closed Thanksgiving, Dec 25. Res accepted. Italian menu. Bar. Semi-a la carte: lunch $5.95-$9.95, dinner $7.50-$22. Child's meals. Specializes in Tuscan cuisine and seafood. Cr cds: A, C, D, DS, MC, V.

D ♥

★ ★ ★ **HAMPTON'S.** (See Harbor Court Hotel) 410/234-0550. This hotel dining room's setting is similar to an 18th-century mansion. Specializes in seafood, regional dishes. Own pastries. Hrs: 5:30-11 pm; Sun to 10 pm; Sun brunch 10:30 am-3 pm. Closed Mon. Res required. Serv bar. Extensive wine list. A la carte entrees: dinner $23-$36. Vegetarian prix fixe dinner: $36-$49. Sun brunch $19.95-$27.95. Valet parking. Jacket. Totally nonsmoking. Cr cds: A, C, D, DS, ER, JCB, MC, V.

D

★ ★ ★ **HAUSSNER'S.** 3244 Eastern Ave (21224), east of Central Area. 410/327-8365. Hrs: 11 am-10 pm. Closed Sun, Mon; Dec 25. German, Amer menu. Bar. Semi-a la carte: lunch, dinner $8-$24.50. Specializes in seafood. Own baking. Braille menu. Extensive dining room display of original 19th century artwork. Old-world atmosphere. Family-owned. Cr cds: A, C, D, DS, MC, V.

D

★ ★ **HENNINGER'S TAVERN.** 1812 Bank St (21231), in Fell's Point. 410/342-2172. Hrs: 5-10 pm; Fri, Sat to 11 pm. Closed Sun, Mon; Jan 1, Dec 25. Bar to 1 am. A la carte entrees: dinner $12.75-$17.95. Specializes in seafood. Late 1800s atmosphere. Cr cds: A, D, JCB, MC, V.

✔★ ★ **IKAROS.** 4805 Eastern Ave (21224), east of Central Area. 410/633-3750. Hrs: 11 am-10 pm; Fri, Sat to 11 pm. Closed Tues; Thanksgiving, Dec 25. Greek, Amer menu. Serv bar. Semi-a la carte: lunch $4-$9, dinner $8-$15. Specializes in lamb, squid, fresh whole fish. Cr cds: A, C, D, DS, MC, V.

⊟

★ ★ **JEANNIER'S.** 105 W 39th St (21211), north of Central Area. 410/889-3303. E-mail tr_ jeannier@juno.com. Hrs: noon-2:30 pm, 5:30-9:30 pm; Fri to 10 pm; Sat 5:30-10 pm; early-bird dinner 5:30-7 pm. Closed Sun; most major hols. French, continental menu. Bar noon-11 pm. A la carte entrees: lunch $6-$11, dinner $13.95-$25. Complete meals: dinner $14-$25. Specializes in seafood, country-French cuisine. Own desserts. Country chateau decor. Cr cds: A, C, D, MC, V.

⊟

★ ★ **JOHN STEVEN LTD.** 1800 Thames St (21231), in Fell's Point. 410/327-5561. Hrs: 11 am-11 pm; Fri, Sat to midnight. Res accepted. Bar to 2 am. A la carte entrees: lunch $6-$11, dinner $7-$21. Specializes in seafood, sushi. Outdoor dining. Located in building built 1838. Cr cds: A, C, D, DS, MC, V.

D

★ ★ ★ **JOY AMERICA CAFE.** 800 Key Hwy (21230), in American Visionary Art Museum, Inner Harbor. 410/244-6500. Hrs: 11:30 am-3:30 pm, 5:30-10 pm; Sun brunch 11 am-4 pm. Closed Mon; Labor Day, Thanksgiving, Dec 25. Res accepted. Contemporary Amer menu. Bar. Semi-a la carte: lunch $9-$15, dinner $19-$28.50. Sun brunch $11.50-$14. Child's meals. Specialties: chicken and dried cherry dim sum, Thai-grilled rack of lamb. Outdoor dining. View of city and Inner Harbor. Totally nonsmoking. Cr cds: A, D, MC, V.

D

★ ★ **KARSON'S INN.** 5100 Holabird Ave (21224), east of Central Area. 410/631-5400. Hrs: 11 am-9:15 pm; Sat from 4 pm; Sun 11 am-8:15 pm. Closed Mon; Thanksgiving, Dec 25. Res accepted; required hols. Bar. Semi-a la carte: lunch $6.95-$11.50, dinner $10.95-$32. Child's meals. Specializes in steak, seafood. Parking. Family-owned. Cr cds: A, DS, MC, V.

D ⊟

★ ★ **KAWASAKI.** 413 N Charles St (21201), in Central Area. 410/659-7600. Hrs: 11:30-2:30 pm, 5-11 pm; Fri to midnight; Sat 5-midnight. Closed Sun; most major hols. Japanese menu. Bar. A la carte entrees: lunch, dinner $2.50-$9. Semi-a la carte: lunch $5.95-$9.50, dinner $9.50-$18. Specializes in Japanese seafood, sushi rolls. In townhouse; Japanese decor. Cr cds: A, C, D, JCB, MC, V.

★ ★ **LA SCALA.** 411 S High St (21231), in Little Italy. 410/783-9209. Hrs: 4:30-10 pm; Fri, Sat to 11 pm; Sun 2-10 pm. Closed Jan 1, Thanksgiving, Dec 25. Res accepted. Italian menu. Bar. Semi-a la carte: dinner $9.95-$29.95. Specializes in veal, pasta. Contemporary decor. Cr cds: A, C, D, DS, MC, V.

⊟

★ ★ **MORGAN MILLARD.** 4800 Roland Ave (21210), north of Central Area. 410/889-0030. Hrs: 11:30 am-9:30 pm; Fri, Sat to 10:30 pm; Sun 11 am-8:30 pm; Sun brunch to 3 pm. Closed most major hols. Res accepted (dinner). Regional Amer menu. Bar. Semi-a la carte: lunch

$5.95-$11.50, dinner $5.95-$22. Sun brunch $6.95-$12.95. Child's meals. Specialties: pan-fried catfish, barbecued duck breast. Own baking. In historic Roland Park area; local artwork and music featured. Totally non-smoking. Cr cds: A, MC, V.

D

★★ **MT WASHINGTON TAVERN.** 5700 Newbury St (21209), I-83 N, exit Northern Pkwy E, W at Falls Rd, W onto Kelly Ave Bridge, E on Sungrave, 1 blk to Newbury, north of Central Area. 410/367-6903. Hrs: 11:30 am-10 pm; Sat to 11 pm; Sun brunch to 3 pm. Closed Dec 25. Res accepted. Bar. Semi-a la carte: lunch $5.95-$12.95, dinner $12.95-$22.95. Sun brunch $5.95-$12.95. Child's meals. Specializes in Angus beef, veal chops, steamed shrimp. Entertainment Wed, Sat. Outdoor dining. Tavern atmosphere has varied dining areas. Cr cds: A, D, MC, V.

D ♥

★★ **OBRYCKI'S.** 1727 E Pratt St (21231), in Fell's Point. 410/732-6399. Web www.obrycks.com. Hrs: noon-11 pm; Sun to 9:30 pm. Closed mid-Dec-Mar. Bar. Semi-a la carte: lunch $5.50-$17.95, dinner $13.25-$27.95. Child's meals. Specializes in crab. Family-owned. Cr cds: A, C, D, DS, MC, V.

D

★★ **PIERPOINT.** 1822 Aliceanna St (21231), in Fell's Point. 410/675-2080. Hrs: 11:30 am-2:30 pm, 5:30-9:30 pm; Fri to 10:30 pm; Sat 5:30-11 pm; Sun 4-9:30 pm. Closed Mon; Jan 1, July 4, Dec 25. Res accepted. Bar. A la carte entrees: lunch $5.95-$8.95, dinner $5.95-$24. Specializes in Maryland cuisine. Contemporary decor. Cr cds: A, MC, V.

D

★★★ **POLO GRILL.** (See Doubletree Inn at The Colonnade Hotel) 410/235-8200. Hrs: 6:30-10 am, 11:30 am-4 pm, 5:30-11 pm; Fri to midnight; Sat 7-10:30 am, 11:30 am-4 pm, 5:30 pm-midnight; Sun 7-10:30 am, 11 am-2:30 pm, 5:30-10 pm. Res accepted. Bar. A la carte entrees: lunch $5.95-$19.50, dinner $10.95-$36.95. Complete meals: bkfst $7.50-$7.95. Specializes in seafood, pasta. Valet parking. English hunt decor. Cr cds: A, C, D, DS, ER, JCB, MC, V.

D

★★★ **PRIME RIB.** 1101 N Calvert St (21202), in Central Area. 410/539-1804. Hrs: 5 pm-midnight; Sun 4-11 pm. Closed Thanksgiving. Res accepted. Bar. Wine list. A la carte entrees: dinner $20-$25. Specializes in steak, seafood, lamb. Pianist. Parking. Black laquered walls. Paintings and prints displayed. Jacket. Family-owned. Cr cds: A, C, D, MC, V.

D

★★ **ROCCO CAPRICCIO.** 846 Fawn St (21202), Little Italy. 410/685-2710. Hrs: 11:30 am-10:30 pm; Fri, Sat to 11:30 pm. Closed Thanksgiving, Dec 25. Res accepted. Northern Italian menu. Bar. Semi-a la carte: lunch $6.25-$12, dinner $9.95-$28. Child's meals. Specialties: fettucine frutta de mare (white or red), veal Capriccio. Own pasta. Cr cds: A, C, D, DS, MC, V.

★★★ **RUBY LOUNGE.** 802 N Charles St (21201), in Central Area. 410/539-8051. Hrs: 5:30-11 pm; Fri, Sat to midnight. Closed Sun, Mon; also most major hols. Res accepted. Bar. A la carte entrees: dinner $9.95-$15.95. Specializes in duck, pork, seafood. Valet parking. Casual decor. Cr cds: A, MC.

★★★ **RUTH'S CHRIS STEAK HOUSE.** 600 Water St (21202), in Central Area. 410/783-0033. E-mail serioussteaks.com. Hrs: 5-10 pm; Fri, Sat to 11 pm. Closed Thanksgiving, Dec 25. Res accepted. Bar. A la carte entrees: dinner $15.95-$28.95. Specializes in steaks, seafood. Free valet parking. Upscale furnishing. Cr cds: A, C, D, DS, ER, JCB, MC, V.

D

★★★ **SAVANNAH.** (See Admiral Fell Inn) 410/522-2195. E-mail admiral1@erols.com; web www.admiralfell.com. Hrs: 11:30 am-2 pm, 5:30-10 pm; Fri, Sat to 11 pm; Sun brunch 11 am-3 pm. Res accepted. Bar. A la carte entrees: lunch $8-$12, dinner $13-$21. Sun brunch $8-$12.

Child's meals. Specializes in southern cuisine. Free valet parking. Outdoor dining. Contemporary decor. Cr cds: A, D, MC, V.

D

★★★ **SPIKE & CHARLIE'S.** 1225 Cathedral St (21201), north of Central Area. 410/752-8144. Hrs: 5:30-10 pm; Fri, Sat to midnight. Closed Mon; most major hols. Res accepted. Bar. Semi-a la carte: dinner $8-$26. Specializes in seafood. Own baking. Contemporary decor. Cr cds: A, MC, V.

D

★★★ **TIO PEPE.** 10 E Franklin St (21202), in Central Area. 410/539-4675. Hrs: 11:30 am-2:30 pm, 5-10:30 pm; Fri to 11:30 pm; Sat 5-11:30 pm; Sun 4-10:30 pm. Closed most major hols. Res required. Spanish, continental menu. Bar. Wine cellar: Semi-a la carte: lunch $9-$14, dinner $13.75-$24. Specialties: shrimp in garlic sauce, suckling pig. Spanish casa atmosphere. Jacket. Cr cds: A, C, D, DS, MC, V.

D

★★ **VELLEGGIA'S.** 829 E Pratt St (21202), Little Italy. 410/685-2620. Hrs: 11 am-11 pm; Fri to midnight; Sat to 1 am. Closed Dec 24, 25. Res accepted. Italian menu. Bar. A la carte entrees: lunch $4.95-$9.95, dinner $9.25-$19.95. Child's meals. Specializes in veal, seafood. Own pasta. Family-owned. Cr cds: A, D, MC, V.

D

✔★ **WATER STREET EXCHANGE.** 110 Water St, in Central Area. 410/332-4060. Hrs: 11:30 am-8 pm; Mon to 3 pm; Tues to 6 pm; Sat from 5:30. Closed Sun; major hols. Res accepted. Bar to 2 am. Semi-a la carte: lunch $5.95-$13, dinner $13-$26. Specializes in pasta, seafood. Outdoor dining. Victorian decor. Cr cds: A, C, D, DS, MC, V.

★ **WATERFRONT HOTEL.** 1710 Thames St (21231), in Fell's Point. 410/327-4886. Hrs: 11 am-10 pm; Fri, Sat to 11 pm. Closed Dec 25. Res accepted. Continental menu. Bar 10-2 am. Semi-a la carte: lunch $4.50-$9.95, dinner $11.95-$20. Child's meals. Specializes in seafood, beef. Restored building (1771) located on waterfront; 3-story brick fireplace, stained-glass windows. Cr cds: A, C, D, MC, V.

✔★ **WAYNE'S BAR-B-QUE.** 201 Pratt St (21202), Inner Harbor. 410/539-3810. Hrs: 8 am-11 pm; Fri, Sat to midnight. Closed Thanksgiving. Res accepted. Bar to 2 am. A la carte entrees: bkfst $4.50-$7.95, lunch, dinner $5-$12.95. Child's meals. Specializes in barbecue dishes, desserts. Outdoor dining. View of harbor. Cr cds: A, C, DS, MC, V.

D SC

★★ **THE WILD MUSHROOM.** 641 S Montford Ave (21231), in Central Area. 410/675-4225. Hrs: 11:30-1 am. Closed Sun; Jan 1, Thanksgiving, Dec 25. Bar. A la carte entrees: lunch $4.95-$12.95, dinner $6.95-$25. Specializes in mushroom-driven dishes. Contemporary decor. Cr cds: A, C, D, DS, JCB, MC, V.

Unrated Dining Spot

LOUIE'S THE BOOKSTORE CAFE. 518 N Charles St, in Central Area. 410/962-1224. Hrs: 11:30-1 am; Mon to midnight; Fri, Sat to 2 am; Sun 10:30 am-midnight; Sun brunch to 3 pm. Closed major hols. Bar. A la carte: lunch $3.50-$10.95, dinner $3.95-$16.95. Sun brunch $3.25-$9.95. Specializes in international bistro fare. Outdoor dining. Chamber music. Original artwork. Cr cds: A, MC, V.

D

Baltimore/Washington Intl Airport Area (C-7)

(See also Baltimore; also see District of Columbia)

Services and Information

Information: 410/859-7100.

Lost and Found: 410/859-7387.

Weather: 410/936-1212.

Cash Machines: Main Terminal, Pier C.

Airlines: Air Aruba, Air Canada, Air Jamaica, America West, American, British Airways, Continental, Delta, El Al, Icelandair, Midway, Northwest, Southwest, TWA, United, USAir.

Motels

★ ★ **COURTYARD BY MARRIOTT.** *(1671 W Nursery Rd, Linthicum 21090) Approx 1 mi N on Nursery Rd.* 410/859-8855. Web www.courtyard.com. 149 rms, 3 story. Apr-Nov: S, D $104-$114; suites $123-$134; under 10 free; lower rates rest of yr. TV; cable (premium). Indoor pool, lifeguard; whirlpool. Complimentary coffee in rms. Restaurant 6:30-10:30 am, 5-10 pm; Sat, Sun 7 am-noon. Bar 4-10 pm. Ck-out noon. Meeting rms. Business servs avail. Coin lndry. Free airport transportation. Exercise equipt; bicycles, weight machine. Some refrigerators. Cr cds: A, C, D, DS, MC, V.

D ≈ ✈ ✕ ⊠ 🔥 SC

★ ★ **HAMPTON INN.** *(6617 Governor Ritchie Hwy, Glen Burnie 21061) I-695, exit 3B, in Governor Plaza Shopping Ctr.* 410/761-7666; FAX 410/761-0253. 116 rms, 5 story. S $92; D $99; suites $110; under 18 free; higher rates special events. Crib free. TV; cable (premium). Complimentary continental bkfst. Restaurant adj open 24 hrs. Ck-out noon. Meeting rms. Business servs avail. In-rm modem links. Valet serv. Sundries. Health club privileges. Microwaves avail. Cr cds: A, C, D, DS, MC, V.

D ✕ 🔥 SC

✔ ★ **HOLIDAY INN-GLEN BURNIE SOUTH.** *(6600 Ritchie Hwy, Glen Burnie 21061) I-195 to I-695, E to MD 2 (Ritchie Hwy).* 410/761-8300; FAX 410/760-4966. 100 rms, 3 story. S, D $75; each addl $10; under 18 free. Crib free. Pet accepted, some restrictions. TV; cable (premium). Pool; lifeguard. Restaurant 6 am-2 pm, 5-10 pm; Sat, Sun from 7 am. Rm serv. Bar 4 pm-midnight. Ck-out noon. Meeting rms. In-rm modem link. Valet serv. Health club privileges. Microwaves avail. Mall opp. Cr cds: A, C, D, DS, ER, JCB, MC, V.

D ✔ ≈ ⊠ 🔥 SC

Motor Hotels

✔ ★ ★ **BEST WESTERN AT BWI AIRPORT.** *(6755 Dorsey Rd, Dorsey 21227) I-295 S to MD 176.* 410/796-3300; FAX 410/379-0471. 134 rms, 4 story. S $69; D $74; each addl $5; under 18 free. Crib free. TV; cable (premium), VCR avail. Indoor pool; whirlpool. Complimentary coffee in lobby. Restaurant adj 7 am-11 pm; Sat, Sun 8 am-10 pm. Ck-out noon. Meeting rms. In-rm modem link. Valet serv. Airport transportation. Exercise equipt; weight machines, bicycles, sauna. Cr cds: A, C, D, DS, ER, MC, V.

D ≈ ✈ ✕ ⊠ 🔥 SC

★ ★ **COMFORT INN-AIRPORT.** *(6921 Baltimore Annapolis Blvd (MD 648), Baltimore 21225) N on MD 170 to Baltimore Annapolis Blvd.* 410/789-9100; FAX 410/355-2854. 188 rms, 6 story. S $79; D $89; each addl $8; suites $125-$225; studio rms $79-$89; under 12 free; wkend rates. Crib free. Pet accepted. TV; cable (premium), VCR avail. Complimentary bkfst buffet. Restaurant 7 am-11 pm. Bar 11 am-midnight. Ck-out 11 am. Meeting rms. Business servs avail. In-rm modem link. Bellhops.

Valet serv. Airport transportation. Exercise equipt; weights, bicycles, whirlpool, sauna. Game rm. Microwaves avail. Cr cds: A, C, D, DS, ER, JCB, MC, V.

D ✔ ✕ ✈ ⊠ 🔥 SC

✔ ★ **HAMPTON INN.** *(829 Elkridge Landing Rd, Linthicum 21090) From I-95 or I-295 take I-195E to exit 1A (MD 170N).* 410/850-0600; FAX 410/691-2119. 139 rms, 5 story. S $79; D $85; under 18 free. Crib free. Pet accepted. TV; cable (premium). Complimentary continental bkfst. Restaurant nearby. Ck-out noon. Meeting rms. In-rm modem link. Valet serv. Free airport transportation. Microwaves avail. Cr cds: A, C, D, DS, ER, JCB, MC, V.

D ✔ ✕ ✈ ⊠ 🔥 SC

★ ★ ★ **SHERATON INTERNATIONAL AT BWI AIRPORT.** *(7032 Elm Rd, Baltimore 21240) N of terminal.* 410/859-3300; FAX 410/859-0565. Web www.sheraton.com. 196 rms, 2 story. S $129-$139; D $129-$149; each addl $10; suites $145-$175; under 16 free; wkend rates. Crib free. TV; cable (premium). Pool; poolside serv, lifeguard. Complimentary continental bkfst. Coffee in rms. Restaurant 6:30 am-10:30 pm. Rm serv 24 hrs. Bar 11-2 am; entertainment. Ck-out noon. Meeting rms. Business servs avail. In-rm modem link. Bellhops. Sundries. Gift shop. Airport transportation. Exercise equipt; weights, bicycles. Cr cds: A, C, D, DS, MC, V.

D ≈ ✕ ✈ ⊠ 🔥 SC

★ **SUSSE CHALET.** *(1734 W Nursery Rd, Linthicum 21090)* 410/859-2333; FAX 410/859-2357. 130 rms, 5 story. S, D $68.70-$75.70; each addl $7; suites $89.70-$99.70; under 18 free. Crib free. TV; cable (premium). Pool; lifeguard. Complimentary continental bkfst. Restaurant nearby. Ck-out 11 am. Coin lndry. Business servs avail. In-rm modem link. Airport, RR station transportation. Microwaves avail. Cr cds: A, C, D, DS, MC, V.

D ≈ ✕ ⊠ 🔥 SC

Hotels

★ ★ ★ **DOUBLETREE GUEST SUITES.** *(1300 Concourse Dr, Linthicum 21090) N on MD 170 to Elkridge Landing Rd, NW 1 1/2 mi to Winterson Rd, W to Concourse Dr; or I-295 to W Nursery Rd exit, then to Winterson Rd.* 410/850-0747; FAX 410/859-0816. Web www.doubletree hotels.com. 251 suites, 8 story. S $99-$160; D $109-$170; each addl $10; under 18 free; wkend rates. Crib free. TV; cable (premium). Indoor pool; whirlpool, lifeguard. Complimentary coffee in rms. Restaurant 6:30 am-10 pm; wknds to 11 pm. Bar 11-1 am. Ck-out noon. Convention facilities. Business servs avail. In-rm modem link. Gift shop. Airport transportation. Exercise equipt; weights, bicycles, sauna. Bathrm phones, refrigerators, wet bars; microwaves avail. Cr cds: A, C, D, DS, MC, V.

D ≈ ✈ ✕ ⊠ 🔥 SC

★ ★ ★ **MARRIOTT.** *(1743 W Nursery Rd, Linthicum 21240) Approx 1 mi N on Nursery Rd.* 410/859-8300; FAX 410/691-4515. 310 rms, 10 story. S, D $149-$159; each addl $15; suites $143-$350; under 18 free. Crib free. TV; cable (premium). Indoor pool; whirlpool. Complimentary coffee in lobby. Restaurant 6:30 am-10 pm. Bar 4 pm-1:30 am. Ck-out noon. Convention facilities. Business servs avail. Free airport transportation. Exercise equipt; bicycles, weight machine. Cr cds: A, C, D, DS, ER, JCB, MC, V.

D ≈ ✈ ✕ ⊠ 🔥 SC

Bethesda (C-6)

(See also District of Columbia)

Pop 62,936 **Elev** 305 ft **Area code** 301 **Web** www.bccchamber.org
Information The Greater Bethesda-Chevy Chase Chamber of Commerce, Landow Bldg, 7910 Woodmont Ave, Suite 1204, 20814; 301/652-4900.

A suburb of Washington, DC, Bethesda is the home of both the National Institutes of Health, research arm of the Public Health Service, and Bethesda Naval Hospital.

What to See and Do

Cabin John Regional Park. This 551-acre park has playgrounds, miniature train ride; nature center; concerts (summer evenings; free); tennis courts, game fields, ice rink, nature trails, picnicking. Fee for some activities. (Daily) Approx 3 mi N on MD 355 then W on Tuckerman Lane. Phone 301/299-0024.

Clara Barton National Historic Site. 3 mi W via MD 191, Goldsboro Rd in Glen Echo (see DISTRICT OF COLUMBIA).

National Library of Medicine. World's largest biomedical library; rare books, manuscripts, prints; medical art displays. (Daily exc Sun; closed hols & Sat before Mon hols) Visitors center & guided tour (Mon-Fri, 1 departure each day). 8600 Rockville Pike. Phone 301/496-6308. **Free.**

Motor Hotel

★ ★ **AMERICAN INN OF BETHESDA.** *8130 Wisconsin Ave (20814).* 301/656-9300; FAX 301/656-2907; res: 800/323-7081. E-mail innkeeper@american-inn.com; web www.american-inn.com. 76 rms, 5 story. S $120; D $130; each addl $5; under 18 free; wkend, wkly, monthly rates. Crib free. TV; cable (premium), VCR avail. Pool; lifeguard. Complimentary continental bkfst. Restaurant 11:30 am-10 pm; Fri, Sat to midnight; Sun to 10 pm. Ck-out 12:30 pm. Coin lndry. Meeting rms. Business center. Sundries. Valet serv. Some refrigerators. Cr cds: A, C, D, DS, MC, V.

Hotels

✔ ★ ★ **HOLIDAY INN-CHEVY CHASE.** *(5520 Wisconsin Ave, Chevy Chase 20815)* S on Wisconsin Ave. 301/656-1500; FAX 301/656-5045. E-mail cornel@pop.net; web www.holidayinn.com. 215 rms, 12 story. S, D $79-$139; each addl $10; suites $115-$169; under 18 free. Crib free. Pet accepted, some restrictions; $50 deposit. TV; cable (premium), VCR avail. Pool. Complimentary coffee in rms. Restaurant 6:30 am-11 pm. Bar. Ck-out noon. Free lndry facilities. Meeting rms. Business center. In-rm modem link. Gift shop. Health club privileges. Bathrm phones; microwaves avail. Cr cds: A, C, D, DS, ER, JCB, MC, V.

★ ★ ★ **HYATT REGENCY.** *One Bethesda Metro Center (20814).* 301/657-1234; FAX 301/657-6453. Web www.hyatt.com. 381 rms, 12 story. S $195; D $220; each addl $25; suites $200-$600; under 18 free; wkend rates. Crib free. Covered parking $10; valet $12. TV; cable (premium), VCR avail. Indoor pool; lifeguard. Restaurant 6:30 am-11:30 pm. Bar 11:30-12:30 am. Ck-out noon. Convention facilities. Business center. In-rm modem link. Exercise equipt; bicycles, rower, sauna. Bathrm phones. Private patios, balconies. 12-story atrium lobby; extensive collection of artwork. Luxury level. Cr cds: A, C, D, DS, ER, JCB, MC, V.

★ ★ ★ **MARRIOTT.** *5151 Pooks Hill Rd (20814), 1 blk S of I-495 exit 34.* 301/897-9400; FAX 301/897-0192. 407 rms, 4-16 story. S $175; D $195; suites $300-$750; under 18 free; wkend plan. Crib free. TV; cable (premium), VCR avail. Indoor/outdoor pool; whirlpool, poolside serv, lifeguard. Restaurants 6:30 am-10 pm. Rm serv to 1 am. Bar 11:30 am-midnight; entertainment. Ck-out noon. Convention facilities. Business center. In-rm modem link. Gift shops. Lighted tennis. Exercise equipt: weight machines, bicycles, sauna. Game rm. Microwaves avail. Some balconies. On 18 landscaped acres. Luxury level. Cr cds: A, C, D, DS, ER, JCB, MC, V.

★ ★ ★ **MARRIOTT SUITES.** *6711 Democracy Blvd (20817).* 301/897-5600; FAX 301/530-1427. Web www.marriott.com. 274 suites, 11 story. Suites $155-$220; family rates. Crib free. TV; cable (premium), VCR avail. Indoor/outdoor pool; whirlpool, poolside serv, lifeguard. Complimentary coffee in rms. Restaurant 6:30 am-10:30 pm. Bar noon-midnight. Ck-out 11 am. Meeting rms. Business center. In-rm modem link. Metro station transportation. Exercise rm; instructor, weights, bicycles. Wet bars; microwaves avail. Balconies. Cr cds: A, C, D, DS, ER, JCB, MC, V.

★ ★ ★ **RESIDENCE INN BY MARRIOTT.** *7335 Wisconsin Ave (20814).* 301/718-0200; FAX 301/718-0679. 187 kit suites, 13 story. S, D $179-$275; under 16 free; wkend, wkly, monthly rates. Crib free. Pet accepted; $100 and $5/day. Valet parking $12. TV; cable (premium), VCR avail (movies). Pool; lifeguard. Complimentary continental bkfst. Complimentary coffee in rms. Restaurant adj 6:30 am-midnight. Ck-out noon. Coin lndry. Meeting rms. Business servs avail. Exercise equipt; weight machine, bicycles, sauna. Rec rm. Microwaves. Cr cds: A, C, D, DS, JCB, MC, V.

Restaurants

★ ★ ★ **ANDALUCIA DE BETHESDA.** *4931 Elm St (20814).* 301/907-0052. Hrs: 11:30 am-2:30 pm; Fri, Sat to 10:30 pm; Sun 5-9:30 pm. Closed some major hols. Res accepted; required Fri, Sat dinner. Spanish menu. Bar. Wine list. Semi-a la carte: lunch $7.25-$10.95, dinner $13.95-$22.95. Specialties: zarzuela Mediterraneo, mero en salsa verde. Own desserts. Classical guitar Sun-Thurs. Cr cds: A, C, D, DS, MC, V.

✔ ★ **AUSTIN GRILL.** *7278 Woodmont Ave (20814), at Elm St.* 301/656-1366. E-mail austingrill@aol.com; web www.austingrill.com. Hrs: 11:30 am-11 pm; Mon to 10:30 pm; Fri to midnight; Sat 11 am-midnight; Sun 11 am-10:30 pm; Sun brunch to 3 pm. Closed Thanksgiving, Dec 24, 25. Tex-Mex menu. Bar. Semi-a la carte: lunch $6-$9, dinner $6-$14. Sun brunch $5-$7. Child's meals. Specializes in chicken, fresh seafood, vegetarian dishes. Outdoor dining. Contemporary Southwestern motif. Totally nonsmoking. Cr cds: A, C, D, DS, MC, V.

★ ★ **BACCHUS.** *7945 Norfolk Ave (20814).* 301/657-1722. Hrs: noon-2 pm, 6-10 pm; Fri to 10:30 pm; Sat 6-10:30 pm; Sun 6-10 pm. Closed Thanksgiving. Res accepted; required Fri, Sat. Lebanese menu. Serv bar. Complete meals: lunch $8. Semi-a la carte: dinner $12.25-$16.25. Specialties: falafel, shish kebab. Valet parking. Outdoor dining. Cr cds: A, MC, V.

✔ ★ ★ **BOMBAY DINING.** *4931 Cordell Ave (20814).* 301/656-3373. Hrs: 11:30 am-2:30 pm, 5:30-10 pm; Sun noon-3 pm, 5:30-10:30 pm. Res accepted. Indian menu. Bar. Semi-a la carte: lunch, dinner $7.95-$14.95. Sat, Sun brunch $8.95. Specializes in tandoori, curries, vegetables. Salad bar. Free valet parking (dinner). Elegant decor. Cr cds: A, D, DS, MC, V.

★ ★ **BUON GIORNO.** *8003 Norfolk Ave (20814).* 301/652-1400. Hrs: 11:30 am-2:30 pm, 5:30-10 pm; Fri to 10:30 pm; Sat 5:30-10:30 pm; Sun 5:30-10 pm. Closed Mon; Jan 1, Thanksgiving, Dec 25; also mid-Aug-mid-Sept. Res accepted; required Fri, Sat. Italian menu. Serv bar. Semi-a la carte: lunch $8.95-$10.95, dinner $12.95-$19.95. Specialties:

trenette alla Genovese, pappardelle alla contadina, fresh fish. Own pasta. Valet parking (dinner). Cr cds: A, C, D, MC, V.

[D] [≛]

★ ★ ★ **CAFE BETHESDA.** *5027 Wilson Lane (20814), at Cordell Ave.* 301/657-3383. Hrs: 11:30 am-2 pm, 5-10 pm; Sat, Sun from 5 pm. Closed most major hols. Res accepted; required Fri, Sat. French menu. Wine, beer. Semi-a la carte: lunch $8-$12, dinner $14-$25. Complete meal (5-6 pm, Mon-Fri): dinner $17.50. Specializes in rack of lamb, seafood, veal. Valet parking. Outdoor dining. Atmosphere of French country inn. Totally nonsmoking. Cr cds: A, C, D, MC, V.

✔★ **CAPITAL WRAPPS.** *4733 Bethesda Ave (20814).* 301/654-0262. Hrs: 11:30 am-8 pm; Fri, Sat to 9 pm. Closed Sun; major hols. Southwestern menu. Bar. A la carte entrees: lunch, dinner $4.95-$5.95. Child's meals. Specializes in international foods wrapped in tortillas. Outdoor dining. Mediterranean open market atmosphere. Totally nonsmoking. No cr cds accepted.

[D]

★ ★ ★ **CESCO TRATTORIA.** *4871 Cordell Ave (20814).* 301/654-8333. Web www.robertdona/cesco.com. Hrs: 11:30 am-2 pm, 5:30-10 pm; Fri to 11 pm; Sat 5:30-11 pm; Sun 5:30-9 pm. Closed major hols. Res accepted; required Fri, Sat dinner. Italian menu. Bar. Wine list. A la carte entrees: lunch, dinner $12.95-$19.95. Specializes in fresh seafood, Tuscan cuisine, pasta. Own pasta. Valet parking. Outdoor dining. Contemporary Italian trattoria atmosphere. Cr cds: A, MC, V.

★ ★ **COTTONWOOD CAFE.** *4844 Cordell Ave (20814).* 301/656-4844. Web www.cottonwood-cafe.com. Hrs: 11:30 am-10 pm; Fri, Sat to 11 pm; Sun from 5:30 pm. Closed most major hols. Res accepted. Southwestern menu. Bar. Semi-a la carte: lunch $5.95-$7, dinner $12.65-$20.95. Specializes in grilled meats, seafood. Valet parking (dinner). Outdoor dining. Southwestern atmosphere. Mural of adobe village. Cr cds: A, MC, V.

[D] [≛] [♥]

✔★ ★ **FOONG LIN.** *7710 Norfolk Ave (20814).* 301/656-3427. Hrs: 11 am-10:30 pm; Fri, Sat to 11 pm. Closed Thanksgiving. Res accepted. Chinese menu. Bar. Semi-a la carte: lunch $4.50-$7.50, dinner $7.25-$19.95. Specializes in fresh fish, Peking duckling, crispy beef. Cr cds: A, MC, V.

[D] [♥]

★ ★ **FRASCATI RISTORANTE ITALIANO.** *4806 Rugby Ave (20814).* 301/652-9514. Hrs: 11 am-2:30 pm, 4-10:30 pm; Sat from 5 pm; Sun 4-9:30 pm; early-bird menu Tues-Fri, Sun 4-6:30 pm. Closed Mon; Jan 1, Easter, Dec 25. Res accepted; required Fri, Sat. Italian menu. Semi-a la carte: lunch $4.75-$6.95, dinner $9.75-$15.95. Child's meals. Specializes in fresh fish, veal, pasta. Outdoor dining. Totally nonsmoking. Cr cds: A, C, D, DS, MC, V.

[D]

★ ★ **HAANDI.** *4904 Fairmont Ave (20814).* 301/718-0121. Hrs: 11:30 am-2:30 pm, 5-10 pm; Fri, Sat to 10:30 pm; Sun from 5 pm. Res accepted. Indian menu. Bar. Semi-a la carte: lunch $4.95-$10.95, dinner $7.95-$14.95. Buffet lunch: $6.95. Specialties: tandoori dishes, vegetarian dishes, murg makhini. Totally nonsmoking. Cr cds: A, C, D, MC, V.

[D]

★ ★ **IL RITROVO.** *4838 Rugby Ave (20814).* 301/986-1447. Hrs: 11:30 am-2:30 pm, 5:30-11 pm; Sat, Sun from 5:30 pm. Closed most major hols; also Sun July-Aug. Res accepted Sat, Sun. Mediterranean menu. Bar. Semi-a la carte: lunch $2.95-$11.95, dinner $8.95-$16.95. Specializes in fresh seafood. Own baking, pasta. Outdoor dining. Mediterranean decor. Cr cds: A, C, D, DS, MC, V.

[D] [≛]

★ ★ **JEAN-MICHEL.** *10223 Old Georgetown Rd (20814).* 301/564-4910. Hrs: 11:30 am-2:30 pm, 5:30-10 pm; Sat from 5:30 pm; Sun 5:30-8:30 pm. Closed Sun (July-Aug); also most major hols. Res accepted. French menu. Serv bar. Semi-a la carte: lunch $9.50-$13.25, dinner

$12.95-$21.75. Specialties: mussels marinieres, venison with chestnut puree & cranberry jelly. French decor. Cr cds: A, C, D, MC, V.

[D]

★ ★ ★ **LA FERME.** *(7101 Brookville Rd, Chevy Chase 20815) E on MD 186.* 301/986-5255. Hrs: noon-2 pm, 6-10 pm; Sat from 6 pm; Sun 5-9 pm. Closed Mon; Dec 25. Res accepted; required Fri, Sat dinner. French menu. Serv bar. Wine cellar. Semi-a la carte: lunch $7.25-$10.75, dinner $15.75-$22.75. Specialties: duck with turnips & apple cider; lobster, shrimp, scallops and grouper in saffron broth; boneless breast of chicken. Pianist. Outdoor dining. Country inn decor. Cr cds: A, C, D, MC, V.

[D] [≛]

★ ★ **LA MICHE.** *7905 Norfolk Ave (20814).* 301/986-0707. Hrs: 11:30 am-2 pm, 6-9:45 pm; Mon, Sat from 6 pm; Sun 5:30-8 pm. Closed major hols. Res required Fri, Sat. French menu. Serv bar. A la carte entrees: lunch $6-$16, dinner $13-$24. Specialties: soufflés, fricassee of lobster, grilled breast of duck. Valet parking. Outdoor dining. French country decor. Cr cds: A, C, D, MC, V.

[D]

★ ★ ★ **LE VIEUX LOGIS.** *7925 Old Georgetown Rd (20814).* 301/652-6816. Hrs: 5:30-10 pm; Sun 5-9 pm. Closed Jan 1, Dec 25. Res accepted; required Sat. French, Amer menu. Serv bar. Wine list. Semi-a la carte: dinner $15-$21. Specialties: roasted Long Island duckling, grilled Norwegian salmon. Free valet parking. Outdoor dining. Rustic French inn atmosphere. Cr cds: A, C, D, MC, V.

[D] [♥]

✔★ **MATUBA JAPANESE.** *4918 Cordell Ave (20814).* 301/652-7449. Hrs: 11:30 am-2:30 pm, 5-10 pm; Fri to 10:30 pm; Sat noon-3 pm, 5-10:30 pm; Sun 5-10 pm. Japanese menu. Wine, beer. Semi-a la carte: lunch $4.95-$9.95, dinner $6.95-$11.95. Specialties: sushi, chicken teriyaki. Casual decor. Totally nonsmoking. Cr cds: A, MC, V.

[D]

✔★ ★ **MONTGOMERY'S GRILLE.** *7200 Wisconsin Ave (20814), 4 mi S on I-270 exit Wisconsin Ave, at Bethesda Ave.* 301/654-3595. Hrs: 11:30 am-10 pm; Thurs to 11 pm; Fri, Sat to midnight; Sun from 10 am; Sun brunch to 2 pm. Closed Thanksgiving, Dec 25. Bar to 12:30 am; Fri, Sat to 1:30 am. Semi-a la carte: lunch $5.95-$8.95, dinner $7.95-$14.95. Sun brunch $10.95. Child's meals. Specializes in pasta, fresh grilled seafood, crab cakes. Own baking. Outdoor dining. American pub atmosphere with antique bar, bronze-framed windows, hand-carved woodwork. Totally nonsmoking. Cr cds: A, C, D, DS, MC, V.

[D] [♥]

✔★ ★ **NAM'S OF BETHESDA.** *4928 Cordell Ave (20814).* 301/652-2635. Hrs: 11:30 am-2:30 pm, 5:30-11 pm; Sat 5-11 pm; Sun 5-9:30 pm. Closed Thanksgiving, Dec 25. Res accepted. Vietnamese menu. Bar. Semi-a la carte: lunch $5.50-$8.50, dinner $7.50-$10.50. Specializes in chicken, beef, pork. Contemporary decor. Cr cds: A, MC, V.

[D]

★ ★ **O'DONNELL'S.** *8301 Wisconsin Ave (20814).* 301/656-6200. Hrs: 11:30 am-10 pm; Sun noon-9 pm. Closed Dec 25. Res accepted. Bar. Semi-a la carte: lunch $5.50-$12.95, dinner $13.95-$21.95. Child's meals. Specializes in seafood. Outdoor dining on patio. Nautical theme. Family-owned. Cr cds: A, C, D, DS, MC, V.

[D] [≛]

★ **ORIGINAL PANCAKE HOUSE.** *7700 Wisconsin Ave (20814).* 301/986-0285. Hrs: 7 am-3 pm. Closed Dec 25. A la carte entrees: bkfst, lunch $3.95-$7.95. Child's meals. Specializes in crepes, waffles, pancakes. Casual dining. Cr cds: A, C, D, MC, V.

[D]

★ **RAKU.** *7240 Woodmont Ave (20814).* 301/718-8681. Hrs: 11:30 am-10 pm; Fri, Sat to 11 pm. Closed Thanksgiving, Dec 25. Pan-

Asian menu. Serv bar. Semi-a la carte: lunch $2.35-$9.25. A la carte entrees: dinner $2.35-$13.25. Child's meals. Specializes in noodles, wraps, stir fry. Own desserts. Outdoor dining. Casual decor with Oriental flair. Totally nonsmoking. Cr cds: MC, V.

★ ★ **RED TOMATO CAFE.** *4910 St Elmo Ave (20814).* *301/652-4499.* Hrs: 11:30 am-9:30 pm; Thurs to 10 pm; Fri, Sat to 11 pm; Sun 4:30-9 pm. Closed Jan 1, Thanksgiving, Dec 25. Res accepted Thurs-Sun. Italian, Amer menu. Serv bar. A la carte: lunch $3.95-$15.95, dinner $5.95-$15.95. Specializes in pasta. Valet parking. Colorful, contemporary pizzeria; large mural, wood-burning pizza oven. Totally nonsmoking. Cr cds: A, C, D, DS, MC, V.

★ ★ **ROCK BOTTOM BREWERY.** *7900 Norfolk Ave (20814).* *301/652-1311.* Hrs: 11-1 am; Fri, Sat to 2 am. Bar. Semi-a la carte: lunch $6.50-$9.95, dinner $8.50-$17.95. Specializes in enchiladas, hamburgers, pizza. Own baking. Musicians Fri, Sat. Valet parking. American brew pub atmosphere with open kitchen, wood-burning pizza oven. Cr cds: A, C, D, MC, V.

★ ★ ★ **RUTH'S CHRIS STEAKHOUSE.** *7315 Wisconsin Ave (20814).* *301/652-7877.* Hrs: 11:30 am-2 pm, 5-10:30 pm; Sat, Sun from 5 pm. Closed Thanksgiving, Dec 25. Res accepted; required Fri, Sat dinner. Bar to midnight. Extensive wine list. A la carte entrees: lunch $7.95-$29.95, dinner $16.95-$29.95. Specializes in beef, lobster, fresh seafood. Own desserts. Pianist exc Sun. Valet parking. Intimate, club-like atmosphere; artwork. Totally nonsmoking. Cr cds: A, C, D, MC, V.

★ ★ ★ **TARA THAI.** *4828 Bethesda Ave (20814).* *301/657-0488.* Hrs: 11:30 am-3 pm, 5-10 pm; Fri to 11 pm; Sat noon-3:30 pm, 5-11 pm; Sun noon-3:30 pm, 5-10 pm. Closed July 4, Thanksgiving. Thai menu. Bar. Semi-a la carte: lunch $4.95-$7.95, dinner $6.95-$15.95. Specialties: grilled whole rock fish, crispy whole flounder. Underwater theme. Totally nonsmoking. Cr cds: A, C, D, DS, MC, V.

✔★ ★ **TEL-AVIV CAFE.** *4867 Cordell Ave (20814).* *301/718-9068.* Hrs: 11:30 am-midnight; Mon to 10 pm; Sat to 1 am; Sun 4:30-10 pm. Closed Yom Kippur, Passover. Mediterranean menu. Bar to 1 am; Fri, Sat to 2 am. Semi-a la carte: lunch $4.95-$6.95, dinner $6.95-$15.95. Specializes in kabobs, vegetarian dishes, kosher dishes. Own breads, desserts. Entertainment Tues, Sat. Outdoor dining. Contemporary Mediterranean decor. Cr cds: A, C, D, DS, MC, V.

✔★ ★ **THAI PLACE.** *4828 Cordell Ave (20814).* *301/951-0535.* Hrs: 11 am-3 pm, 5-10 pm; Fri, Sat to 10:30 pm; Sun 11 am-10 pm. Thai menu. Serv bar. Semi-a la carte: lunch $5.75-$6.50, dinner $7.50-$12. Specializes in steamed fish, Thai cuisine. Cr cds: A, DS, MC, V.

★ ★ **THYME SQUARE.** *4735 Bethesda Ave (20814).* *301/657-9077.* Hrs: 11 am-10 pm; Fri, Sat to 11 pm; Sun brunch to 3 pm. Closed Dec 24, 25. Res accepted; required Thurs-Sun dinner. Bar. Semi-a la carte: lunch $5.95-$10.95, dinner $6.95-$18.95. Sun brunch $5.95-$10.95. Specializes in seasonal Amer dishes, vegetarian dishes, fresh seafood. Contemporary decor with extensive murals; open kitchen. Totally nonsmoking. Cr cds: A, MC, V.

★ ★ ★ **TRAGARA.** *4935 Cordell Ave (20814).* *301/951-4935.* Hrs: 11:30 am-2:30 pm, 5:30-10:30 pm; Sat from 5:30 pm; Sun 5-9 pm. Closed Dec 25. Res accepted; required Fri, Sat. Italian menu. Semi-a la carte: lunch $8.95-$15.95. A la carte: dinner $15.95-$25. Specialties: veal scaloppini, linguine with Maine lobster, lamb chops sauteed with herbs and mustard. Own baking, pastas. Valet parking (dinner). Italian marble, original paintings, chandelier. Cr cds: A, C, D, MC, V.

Unrated Dining Spot

BETHESDA CRAB HOUSE. *4958 Bethesda Ave.* *301/652-3382.* Hrs: 9 am-midnight. Closed Dec 25. Res accepted. Wine, beer. A la carte entrees: lunch, dinner $10-$30. Serves only spiced shrimp, steamed crab, crabcakes. Outdoor dining. Rustic decor; established 1961. No cr cds accepted.

Boonsboro (Washington County) (B-5)

(For accommodations see Frederick, Hagerstown)

Settled 1787 **Pop** 2,445 **Elev** 591 ft **Area code** 301 **Zip** 21713
Information Hagerstown/Washington County Convention and Visitors Bureau, 16 Public Sq, Hagerstown 21740; 301/791-3130.

What to See and Do

Antietam National Battlefield (see). 8 mi SW on MD 34.

Crystal Grottoes Caverns. Limestone caverns may be viewed from walkways. Picnicking. Guided tours (Apr-Oct, daily; rest of yr, by appt). 1 mi SW on MD 34. Phone 301/432-6336. ¢¢¢

Gathland State Park. 140 acres. A site once owned by George Townsend, Civil War reporter. Monument built in 1896 to honor Civil War correspondents. Visitor center contains original papers. Picnicking. Walking tour. Winter sports. 8 mi S off MD 67, then 1 mi E, W of Burkittsville off MD 17. Park schedule varies, phone ahead; 301/791-4767.

Washington Monument State Park. 147 acres. A 34-ft tower of native stone (1827) was first completed monument to honor George Washington. Views of nearby battlefields, two states (PA & WV). History Center displays firearms and Civil War mementos (by appt). The Appalachian Trail leads through the park; hiking and picnicking. 3 mi SE off US 40A. Park schedule varies, phone ahead; 301/791-4767. **Free.**

Restaurant

★ ★ **OLD SOUTH MOUNTAIN INN.** *(6132 Old National Pike, Boonsboro (Alt US 40))* *301/371-5400.* Web www.marylandrestaurants.org/ram.guide/oldsouth.html. Hrs: 5-9 pm; Sat 11:30 am-2:30 pm, 4-10 pm; Sun 10:30 am-8 pm, brunch to 2 pm. Closed Mon; Dec 25. Res accepted; required Sat, Sun. Bar. Semi-a la carte: lunch $5-$11, dinner $14-$28. Sun brunch $12.95. Child's meals. Specializes in crab cakes, prime rib. Outdoor dining. Founded in 1732; was once a stagecoach stop. Totally nonsmoking. Cr cds: A, D, MC, V.

Bowie (C-7)

(See also College Park, Silver Spring; also see District of Columbia)

Pop 37,589 **Elev** 150 ft **Area code** 301 & 204

Information Greater Bowie Chamber of Commerce, 6770 Race Track Rd, Hilltop Plaza, 20715; 301/262-0920. Information is also available from Prince George's Conference & Visitors Bureau, 9475 Lottsford Rd, #130, Landover 20785; 301/925-8300.

What to See and Do

Belair Mansion. Georgian-style home (ca 1745) was home of Governor Samuel Ogle in the 1700s; later owned by the Woodward family, prominent racehorse breeders in the first half of the 20th century. Tours. (Sun, groups by appt; closed Jan) 12207 Tulip Grove Dr. Phone 301/262-6200. **Donation.**

Belair Stable. Part of famed Belair Stud, one of the premier Thoroughbred racing stables of the '30s, '40s and '50s. Was home to two Triple Crown winners—Gallant Fox and Omaha—and the 1955 Horse of the Year, Nashua. (May, June, Sept, Oct, Sun only) 2835 Belair Dr. Phone 301/262-6200. **Free.**

Marietta Manor. A modest Federal-style plantation house built by Gabriel Duvall, an associate justice of the US Supreme Court (1811-1835). Tours. (Mar-Dec, Sun afternoons; also by appt) 3 mi W in Glenn Dale, at 5626 Bell Station Rd. Phone 301/464-5291. ¢

Annual Event

Heritage Day. Belair Mansion & Stable. Performance by Congress's Own Regiment; tour of stables and grounds; battle reenactments; demonstrations of colonial crafts. Phone 301/262-6200. 3rd Sun May.

Motel

★ **FOREST HILLS.** (2901 Crain Hwy (US 301), Upper Marlboro 20772) 8 mi S on US 301. 301/627-3969; res: 800/7932828; FAX 301/627-4058. 13 rms, shower only. Apr-Oct: S $42-$44; D $46-$49; under 13 free; lower rates rest of yr. Crib free. Pet accepted. TV. Complimentary coffee in rms. Ck-out 11 am. Some refrigerators. Picnic tables. Cr cds: A, C, D, DS, MC, V.

🅳 🐾 🐾 SC

Cambridge (D-8)

(See also Easton, Salisbury)

Founded 1684 **Pop** 11,514 **Elev** 14 ft **Area code** 410 **Zip** 21613 **Web** www.bluecrab.org/dorchester

Information Dorchester County Chamber of Commerce, 203 Sunburst Hwy; 410/228-3575 or 800/522-TOUR (Dorchester Tourism).

On the Eastern Shore, Cambridge is Maryland's second-largest deep-water port. Boating and fishing opportunities are found in the Choptank and Honga rivers and Chesapeake, Tar and Fishing bays.

What to See and Do

Blackwater National Wildlife Refuge. Over 20,000 acres of rich tidal marsh, freshwater ponds and woodlands. One of the chief wintering areas for Canada geese and ducks using the Atlantic Flyway; in fall, as many as 33,000 geese and 17,000 ducks swell the bird population. Also a haven for the bald eagle, the Delmarva fox squirrel and the peregrine falcon, all three of which are endangered species. Scenic drive, woodland trails, observation tower. Visitor center (Sept-May, daily; rest of yr, Mon-Fri; closed hols

and Labor Day wkend). Golden Age, Golden Eagle and Golden Access passports (see MAKING THE MOST OF YOUR TRIP). 12 mi S via MD 16, 335. Phone 410/228-2677. Per vehicle ¢¢; Per hiker or cyclist ¢

Old Trinity Church, Dorchester Parish (ca 1675). One of the oldest churches in US still holding regular services; faithful restoration of interior. (By appt) 8 mi SW on MD 16 in Church Creek. Phone 410/228-2940. **Free.**

Wild Goose Brewery. View the complete brewing process from brew kettle to bottling. Sample unique blends in the tasting rm. Souvenir shop. Tours (groups by appt). (Daily exc Sun; closed hols) 20 Washington St. Phone 410/221-1121. **Free.**

Annual Events

National Outdoor Show. Goose and duck calling, log sawing, crab picking, trap setting contests; entertainment. Phone 800/522-TOUR. Last wkend Feb.

Antique Aircraft Fly-In. Dorchester Heritage Museum, 5 mi W on MD 343 at 1904 Horne Point Rd. Old and new planes on display. Phone 410/228-5530 or 410/228-1899 or 800/522-TOUR. 3rd wkend May.

Inn

★★ **GLASGOW INN.** 1500 Hambrooks Blvd. 410/228-0575; res: 800/373-7890. E-mail glasgow@shorenet.net. 10 rms, 4 share bath, 3 story, 3 kit. units. 7 rm phones. Apr-Nov: S, D $75-$200; each addl $10; suites, kit. units $75-$200; hol rates; lower rates rest of yr. Crib free. TV; VCR avail. Playground. Complimentary full bkfst. Ck-out 11 am, ck-in 4-7 pm. Tennis privileges. Health club privileges. Lawn games. Riverside colonial plantation house on 7 acres. Totally nonsmoking. Cr cds: MC, V.

🅳 🐾 🐾 🔥

Chesapeake Bay Bridge Area (C-7)

The majestic twin spans of the Chesapeake Bay Bridge carry visitors to the Eastern Shore, a patchwork of small picturesque towns, lighthouses and fishing villages tucked away from the city. Scenic rivers and bays, wildlife, gardens and wildflowers fill the countryside. The main attractions of any visit, however, are the many fine inns and the restaurants specializing in local seafood.

What to See and Do

Wye Oak State Park. Official state tree of Maryland is in this 29-acre park; it is the largest white oak in the US (108 ft high, 28 ft around) and believed to be over 400 yrs old; a new tree has been started from an acorn. A restored 18th-century one-room schoolhouse and the Old Wye Mill (late 1600s) are nearby. E on US 50 to Wye Mills. Phone 410/820-1668.

Motel

(Distances given are from E end of Chesapeake Bay Bridge)

★★ **COMFORT INN.** (3101 Main St, Grasonville 21638) E via US 50, then S after Kent Narrows Bridge (exit 42). 410/827-6767; FAX 410/827-8626. 86 units, 4 story, 9 kit. suites. Apr-Nov: S $66-$126; D $76-$140; each addl $8; kit. suites $125-$200; under 18 free; higher rates special events; lower rates rest of yr. Crib free. TV; cable (premium). Indoor pool; whirlpool. Complimentary continental bkfst. Complimentary coffee in rms. Restaurant nearby. Ck-out 11 am. Coin lndry. Meeting rms. Business servs avail. Exercise equipt; weight machines, bicycles, sauna. Refrigerators, microwaves. Cr cds: A, C, D, DS, ER, JCB, MC, V.

🅳 🏊 🍴 🐾 🐾 SC

Motor Hotel

 ★ ★ **COMFORT SUITES.** *(160 Scheeler, Chestertown 21620) US 301 to Chestertown exit.* 410/810-0555. 53 suites, 3 story. Apr-Nov: S, D $69.95-$109.95, under 18 free; lower rates rest of yr. Crib avail. TV; cable. Indoor pool. Complimentary continental bkfst. Restaurant nearby. Ck-out 11 am. Meeting rms. Business servs avail. Coin lndry. Refrigerators, microwaves. Cr cds: A, C, D, DS, MC, V.

D ≈ ⚓ 🐾 SC

Inns

★ ★ **HUNTINGFIELD MANOR.** *(4928 Eastern Neck Rd, Rock Hall 21661) 2 mi S on MD 20/445.* 410/639-7779; FAX 410/639-2924. E-mail manorlord@juno; web www.kentcountry.com. 6 rms, 2 story. No rm phones. S, D $85-$125; each addl $25; under 3 free. Complimentary continental bkfst. Restaurant nearby. Ck-out noon, ck-in 2 pm. Telescope-type house on a working farm that dates back to the middle 1600s. Cr cds: A, MC, V.

D ⚓

★ ★ **IMPERIAL HOTEL.** *(208 High St, Chestertown 21620) US 301 to Chestertown exit.* 410/778-5000; FAX 410/778-9662. 13 rms, 3 story. S, D $125-$200; suites $200-$250; lower rates wkdays. Crib free. TV; cable (premium), VCR avail. Continental bkfst Tues-Sat. Dining rm 11:45 am-2:30 pm, 5:30-close; Sun brunch 11:30 am-3 pm; closed Mon. Ck-out 11 am, ck-in 3 pm. Meeting rms. Business servs avail. Refrigerator in suites. Built in 1903; Victorian furnishings. Cr cds: A, D, DS, MC, V.

D ⚓ 🐾

★ ★ ★ **INN AT MITCHELL HOUSE.** *(8796 Maryland Pkwy, Chestertown 21620) US 301 to Chestertown exit.* 410/778-6500. 6 rms, 1 shared bath, 2 story. No rm phones. S, D $75-$110; 2-day min wkends. Crib free. TV in parlor. Complimentary full bkfst. Dinner avail Fri, Sat 7 pm; res required. Ck-out noon, ck-in 3 pm. Manor house built in 1743 on 10 acres. Totally nonsmoking. Cr cds: A, MC, V.

🐾 ⚓ 🔥

★ ★ **KENT MANOR.** *(500 Kent Manor, Kent Island 21666) US 50/301, S on MD 8.* 410/643-5757; FAX 410/643-8315; res: 800/820-4511. 24 rms, 3 story. S, D $135-$215; lower rates mid-wk. Crib $15. TV. Pool. Complimentary continental bkfst. Restaurant 11:30 am-9 pm; Fri, Sat to 9:30 pm; Sun brunch 10 am-2 pm, 4:30-8 pm. Ck-out 11 am, ck-in 3 pm. Meeting rms. Business servs avail. Built in 1820, furnished with antiques. On Thompson Creek. Cr cds: A, D, MC, V.

D ≈ ⚓ 🔥 SC

★ ★ **WHITE SWAN TAVERN.** *(231 High St, Chestertown 21620) US 301 to Chestertown exit.* 410/778-2300; FAX 410/778-4543. 6 rms, 2 story, 2 suites. No rm phones. S, D $100-$130; suites $140-$150; under 3 free. Crib free. TV in sitting rm. Complimentary continental bkfst. Restaurant nearby. Ck-out noon, ck-in 3 pm. Refrigerators. Game rm. Former house and tavern built in 1733 and 1793; restored with antique furnishings; museum. No cr cds accepted.

D ⚓ 🔥

Restaurants

★ ★ **FISHERMAN'S INN & CRAB DECK.** *(US 50/301, Kent Narrows 21638) E over bridge to exit 42, turn right and continue to end of road.* 410/827-8807. Hrs: 11 am-10 pm. Closed Dec 24, 25. Bar. Semi-a la carte: lunch $4.95-$9.95, dinner $6.95-$21. Specializes in fresh seafood. 2 dining areas; fireplace; display of antique oyster plates. Scenic view of the Kent Narrows of the Eastern Bay. Family-owned. Cr cds: A, DS, MC, V.

D ⚓

★ **HARRIS CRAB HOUSE.** *(433 Kent Narrows Way N, Grasonville 21638) 4 mi E via US 50/301.* 410/827-9500. Hrs: 11 am-10 pm;

Fri, Sat to 11 pm. Closed Thanksgiving, Dec 25. Bar. Semi-a la carte: lunch, dinner $6-$21.95. Specializes in fresh seafood, barbecued ribs & chicken, steamed crabs. Outdoor dining. Gazebo. On waterfront; dockage. Cr cds: MC, V.

D SC ⚓

★ ★ **IRONSTONE CAFE.** *(236 Cannon St, Chestertown 21620) NE on US 301, N on MD 213 to Chestertown, left at 1st light to Cannon St.* 410/778-0188. Hrs: 5-8 pm; wknds to 9:30 pm. Closed Sun, Mon; some major hols; also mid-Feb-mid-Mar. Res accepted. Serv bar. Semi-a la carte: dinner $15-$21. Specializes in Maryland crab cakes, seasonal dishes. Located in the historic district, near the Chester River. Cr cds: DS, MC, V.

D ⚓

★ ★ ★ **NARROWS.** *(3023 Kent Narrows Way S, Grasonville 21638) 4 mi E via US 50/301.* 410/827-8113. Hrs: 11 am-9 pm; summer to 10 pm; Sun brunch to 2 pm. Closed Dec 24, 25. Res accepted. Regional Eastern Shore menu. Bar. Wine list. Semi-a la carte: lunch $6-$12, dinner $12.75-$25. Sun brunch $9.75. Child's meals. Specializes in seafood, traditional Maryland recipes. Waterfront dining. View of the Narrows. Cr cds: A, C, D, MC, V.

D

★ ★ **OLD WHARF INN.** *(Cannon St, Chestertown 21620) US 50 to Chestertown exit, on Chester River.* 410/778-3566. Hrs: 11 am-9 pm; Fri, Sat to 10 pm; Sun from 10 am; Sun brunch to 3 pm. Closed Dec 25. Bar. Semi-a la carte: lunch $3-$8, dinner $7.25-$19.95. Sun brunch $2.50-$12.25. Child's meals. Specializes in fresh seafood, steak, salad. Outdoor dining. View of river. Cr cds: A, MC, V.

D ⚓ ♥

✔★ **WATERMAN'S CRAB HOUSE.** *(Sharp St Wharf, Rock Hall 21661) US 301 to MD 213, N to MD 20 to Rock Hall.* 410/639-2261. Hrs: 11 am-9 pm; Fri, Sat to 10 pm. Closed Thanksgiving; also Dec-Feb. Bar. Semi-a la carte: lunch, dinner $8.99-$16.95. Child's meals. Specializes in seafood, steamed crabs, barbecued ribs. Outdoor dining. On Rock Hall Harbor. Cr cds: A, DS, MC, V.

D SC ⚓

Chesapeake and Ohio Canal National Historical Park (A-2 - C-6)

As early as 1754, the enterprising George Washington, only in his twenties, proposed a system of navigation along the Potomac River valley. His Potowmack Canal Company, organized in 1785, cleared obstructions and built skirting canals to facilitate the transportation of goods from settlements beyond the Allegheny Mountains to the lower Potomac River towns.

The eventual inadequacy of these improvements and the renowned success of the Erie Canal spurred the formation in 1828 of the Chesapeake and Ohio Canal Company, whose purpose was to connect Georgetown with the Ohio Valley by river and canal. On July 4, 1828, President John Quincy Adams led the traditional groundbreaking ceremony declaring, "To subdue the earth is preeminently the purpose of this undertaking." Unfortunately, the earth was not easily subdued. President Adams bent his shovel after several attempts before breaking into an energetic frenzy and successfully getting a shovelful of dirt.

The difficulty of the groundbreaking ceremony foreshadowed the canal's short-lived future as a major transportation artery. Completed in 1850 as far as Cumberland, MD (184 1/2 miles from Georgetown), the waterway was used extensively for the transportation of coal, flour, grain and lumber. Financial and legal difficulties, the decline of commerce after the Civil War, the Baltimore and Ohio Railroad and the advent of improved roads cut deeply into the commerce of the waterway, and it gradually faded into obsolescence. The canal still had limited commercial use as late as

1924, when a flood destroyed many of the canal locks and nothing was restored.

The unfortunate demise of the C & O Canal is now a blessing for hikers, canoeists and bikers, who can find access to the towpath along the banks of the waterway. Remaining as one of the least altered of old American canals, the Chesapeake and Ohio is flanked by ample foliage throughout most of its 20,239 acres.

Many points of interest can be seen along the waterway. Exhibits are offered in Cumberland, Georgetown, Hancock and Williamsport and at a museum near the Great Falls of the Potomac. At the Great Falls there are interpretive programs, including self-guiding trails, picnic facilities and a working lock. Although the canal at Georgetown is predominately dry, the towpath extends the entire length and many locks, lockhouses and aqueducts are still intact and extensive improvements have been made. Camping for hikers and bikers is available throughout the park.

For information about the canal contact the Chief of Visitor Services, C & O Canal National Historical Park, PO Box 4, Sharpsburg, MD 21782; 301/739-4200. Visitor centers are located in Cumberland, Georgetown, Great Falls, Hancock, and Williamsport.

Cockeysville (B-7)

(For accommodations see Baltimore, Towson)

Pop 18,668 **Elev** 260 ft **Area code** 410 **Zip** 21030
Information Baltimore County Chamber of Commerce, 102 W Pennsylvania Ave, Ste 402, Towson 21204; 410/825-6200.

What to See and Do

⭐ **Ladew Topiary Gardens.** Extensive topiary gardens on 22 acres; 15 flower gardens. Also here is the Manor House (fee), with English antiques, fox-hunting memorabilia, paintings, unusual china, reconstructed Elizabethan room; Oval Library housing more than 3,000 volumes; carriage museum; cafe; gift shop. (Mid-Apr-Oct, daily exc Mon) 3535 Jarrettsville Pike, 5 mi E on MD 143 to Sunnybrook, then 6 mi N on MD 146. Phone 410/557-9466. Gardens ¢¢¢; Combination gardens and house ¢¢¢

Annual Event

Point-to-point Steeplechase. Three well-known meets on consecutive wkends: **My Lady's Manor.** In Monkton. Mid-Apr. **Grand National.** In Butler; phone 410/666-7777. Mid-Apr. **Maryland Hunt Cup.** In Glyndon; phone 410/666-7777. Late Apr.

Motel

⭐⭐ **COURTYARD BY MARRIOTT.** *(221 International Circle, Hunt Valley)* exit 20-A from I-83. 410/584-7070; FAX 410/584-8151. 146 rms, 3 story, 12 suites. S $72; D $76; suites $92-$99. Crib free. TV; cable (premium). Complimentary coffee in rms. Restaurant 6:30-10:30 am, 5-9:30 pm. Rm serv from 5 pm. Bar 4-10 pm Mon-Fri. Ck-out noon. Meeting rms. Business servs avail. In-rm modem link. Valet serv. Sundries. Coin lndry. Exercise equipt; weight machine, treadmill. Indoor pool; whirlpool, lifeguard. Refrigerator in suites. Balconies. Cr cds: A, C, D, DS, MC, V.

D ⛱ 🏋 ✕ 🔥 SC

Motor Hotel

⭐⭐ **MARRIOTT'S HUNT VALLEY INN.** *(245 Shawan Rd, Hunt Valley 21031)* I-83 exit 20-A. 410/785-7000; FAX 410/785-0341. 390 rms, 4 story. Mar-Nov: S $129; D $149; suites $179-$350; under 18 free; wkend rates; higher rates Preakness; lower rates rest of yr. Pet accepted, some restrictions. TV; cable (premium). Complimentary coffee in rms. Restaurant 6:30 am-10 pm; Fri to 11 pm; Sat 7 am-11 pm; Sun from 7 am. Rm serv. Bar 3 pm-1 am. Ck-out noon. Convention facilities. Business center. In-rm modem link. Bellhops. Valet serv. Concierge. Sundries. Gift shop.

Coin lndry. Tennis. 4-hole golf privileges, pro, putting green, driving range. Exercise rm; instructor, weights, stair machine, sauna. Heated indoor/outdoor pool; wading pool, whirlpool, poolside serv, lifeguard. Refrigerator in suites. Luxury level. Cr cds: A, C, D, DS, JCB, MC, V.

D ⛱ 🏋 ✕ ⛱ ✕ 🔥 SC 🏊

Restaurants

⭐⭐⭐ **THE MILTON INN.** *(14833 York Rd, Sparks 21152)* 5 mi N on MD 45. 410/771-4366. Hrs: 5:30-9:30 pm; Sun 5-8 pm. Closed some major hols. Res accepted. Bar. Wine cellar. Complete meal: dinner $28. Child's meals. Specializes in seasonal dishes, fresh seafood, poultry. Outdoor dining. Main part of building ca 1820; one section was stagecoach stop ca 1740. Colonial Williamsburg-style decor. Jacket. Cr cds: A, D, DS, MC, V.

D

⭐⭐ **YORK INN.** *10010 York Rd.* 410/666-0006. Hrs: 11-2 am; Sun brunch 9 am-2 pm. Closed Dec 25. Res accepted; required major hols. Continental menu. Bar to 2 am. Semi-a la carte: lunch $5.95-$10.95, dinner $11.95-$25.95. Sun bkfst buffet $6.95. Child's meals. Specializes in seafood, steak. Casual dining. Cr cds: A, C, D, DS, MC, V.

D 🔲

College Park (C-6)

(See also Bowie, Silver Spring; also see District of Columbia)

Pop 21,927 **Elev** 190 ft **Area code** 301 **Zip** 20740
Information Prince George's Conference & Visitors Bureau, 9200 Basil Ct, #101, Largo 20774; 301/925-8300.

What to See and Do

College Park Airport Museum. World's oldest operating airport, started by Wilbur Wright in 1909 to train 2 military officers in the operation of aircraft. First airplane machine gun and radio-navigational aids tested here; first air mail and controlled helicopter flights. Museum (Wed-Sun; closed major hols). 6709 Corporal Frank Scott Dr. Phone 301/864-6029 (recording). **Free.**

Greenbelt Park. A 1,100-acre wooded park operated by the National Park Service. Nature trails. Picnicking. Camping (dump station, showers; 7-day limit Memorial Day-Labor Day; 14-day limit rest of yr). Self-registration, first come, first served. Standard fees. 6565 Greenbelt Rd, E off Kenilworth Ave, MD 201 exit 23. Phone 301/344-3948.

NASA/Goddard Visitor Center. Satellites, rockets, capsules and exhibits in all phases of space research. (Daily) SE on I-95 to Baltimore-Washington Pkwy, exit 22-A Greenbelt, then follow signs. For tour information phone 301/286-8981. **Free.**

University of Maryland (1865). (35,000 students) Tawes Fine Arts Theater has plays, musicals, concerts, dance, opera and music festivals. Tours. For information phone 301/405-1000.

Motel

⭐⭐⭐ **COURTYARD BY MARRIOTT.** *(8330 Corporate Dr, Landover 20785)* ½ mi W of I-95 exit 19B, on US 50. 301/577-3373; FAX 301/577-1780. Web www.courtyardlandover.com. 150 rms, 3-4 story. S $86; D $96; suites $105-$115; under 12 free; wkly, wkend rates. Crib free. TV; cable (premium), VCR avail. Indoor pool; whirlpool, lifeguard. Restaurant 6:30-10 am, 5-10 pm; Sat, Sun 7 am-noon, 5-10 pm. Bar. Ck-out noon. Coin lndry. Meeting rms. Business servs avail. In-rm modem link. Valet serv. Exercise equipt; weights, bicycles. Free RR station transportation. Microwaves avail. Many private patios, balconies. Cr cds: A, C, D, DS, MC, V.

D ⛱ ✕ ✕ 🔥 SC

Motor Hotel

★ ★ ★ **COURTYARD BY MARRIOTT.** (6301 Golden Triangle Dr, Greenbelt 20770) 4 mi NE on I-495, exit 23. 301/441-3311; FAX 301/441-4978. 152 rms, 4 story, 12 suites. S $95; D $109; each addl $10; suites $124-$134; under 17 free; wkend, wkly rates. Crib free. TV; cable (premium). Complimentary coffee in rms. Restaurant 6:30-10 am, 5-10 pm; wkends 7 am-midnight. Bar 4-11 pm Mon-Thurs. Ck-out noon. Meeting rms. Business servs avail. Bellhops. Valet serv. Sundries. Coin lndry. Exercise equipt; weight machine, bicycle. Indoor pool; whirlpool, lifeguard. Refrigerator in suites; microwaves avail. Some balconies. Cr cds: A, C, D, DS, MC, V.

D ⌇ 🏃 ⚡ ⛵ 🔥 SC

Hotels

★ ★ ★ **HOLIDAY INN.** 10000 Baltimore Ave (US 1), I-495/95 exit 25. 301/345-6700; FAX 301/441-4923. 222 rms in 2 bldgs, 4 story. S, D $119; under 18 free. Crib free. TV; cable (premium), VCR avail. Indoor pool; whirlpool, lifeguard. Coffee in rms. Restaurant 6:30 am-10 pm. Bar 11-2 am. Ck-out noon. Coin lndry. Meeting rms. Business servs avail. In-rm modem link. Gift shop. Exercise equipt; weights, treadmills, sauna. Refrigerators, microwaves avail. Cr cds: A, C, D, DS, ER, JCB, MC, V.

D ⌇ 🏃 ⚡ ⛵ 🔥 SC

✔ ★ ★ ★ **HOLIDAY INN-CALVERTON.** (4095 Powder Mill Rd, Beltsville 20705) I-95 exit 29B. 301/937-4422; FAX 301/937-4455. 206 rms, 9 story. S, D $109-$129; each addl $7; suites $165; under 18 free; wkend rates; higher rates Cherry Blossom. Crib free. TV; cable (premium). Pool; lifeguard. Complimentary coffee in rms. Restaurant 6:30 am-10 pm; wkends from 7 am. Bar. Ck-out noon. Coin lndry. Meeting rms. Business servs avail. In-rm modem link. Gift shop. Exercise equipt; bicycle, treadmills. Massage. Game rm. Refrigerator; microwaves avail. Cr cds: A, C, D, DS, JCB, MC, V.

D ⌇ 🏃 ⚡ ⛵ 🔥 SC

★ ★ ★ **MARRIOTT GREENBELT.** (6400 Ivy Lane, Greenbelt 20770) 2 blks N of I-95 exit 23 (Kenilworth Ave N). 301/441-3700; FAX 301/441-3995. 283 rms, 18 story. S $130-$150; D $134-$160; kit. units (min stay) $99-$136; family, wkend rates. Crib free. TV; cable (premium). VCR avail. 2 pools, 1 indoor; whirlpool, poolside serv, lifeguard. Restaurant 6:30 am-10:30 pm. Bar. Games. Ck-out noon. Coin lndry. Convention facilities. Business center. In-rm modem link. Gift shop. Free Metro transportation. Lighted tennis. Exercise equipt; weights, bicycles, sauna. Refrigerators, microwaves avail. Luxury level. Cr cds: A, C, D, DS, ER, JCB, MC, V.

D 🏃 ⌇ ⚡ ⛵ 🔥 SC 🏌

Restaurants

✔ ★ ★ **ALAMO.** (5508 Kenilworth Ave, Riverdale 20737) S on US 201; 3 mi S of I-95 exit 23. 301/927-8787. Hrs: 11 am-11 pm. Res accepted. Mexican menu. Bar. Semi-a la carte: lunch $5-$11, dinner $8.30-$12.95. Child's meals. Specializes in tostadas, tacos, enchiladas. Entertainment Fri, Sat. Mexican decor. Cr cds: A, C, D, DS, MC, V.

⤴

★ ★ **CALVERT HOUSE INN.** (6211 Baltimore Ave, Riverdale 20737) 1 mi S on US 1. 301/864-5220. Hrs: 11 am-10 pm; Sat from 3 pm; Sun 3-9 pm; early-bird dinner 4-6 pm. Closed some major hols. Res accepted; required Fri, Sat dinner. Bar. Semi-a la carte: lunch $4.50-$11.95, dinner $6.95-$19.95. Child's meals. Specializes in fresh seafood, steak, crab cakes. Jazz Fri, Sat. Tavern atmosphere. Cr cds: A, C, D, DS, MC, V.

D ⤴

★ ★ ★ **CHEF'S SECRET.** (5810 Greenbelt Rd, Greenbelt 20770) 301/345-6101. Hrs: 11:30 am-3 pm, 5-9 pm; Fri, Sat to 10 pm; Sun 4-9 pm;

early-bird dinner 5-6 pm. Closed Sun July-Aug; major hols. Res accepted. Continental menu. Serv bar. Semi-a la carte: lunch $7.95-$14.95, dinner $11.95-$17.95. Specializes in seafood, veal, steak. Own desserts. Cr cds: A, C, D, DS, MC, V.

D ⤴

✔ ★ **SANTA FE CAFE.** 4410 Knox Rd, off US 1, on Univ campus. 301/779-1345. Hrs: 11 am-midnight; Tues, Thurs-Sat to midnight. Closed Sun; Thanksgiving, Dec 25. Res accepted. Southwestern, Amer menu. Bar to 1:30 am. Semi-a la carte: lunch, dinner $3.95-$6.95. Specializes in fajitas, buffalo wings, pizzas. Entertainment Tues, Thurs-Sat. Outdoor dining. Casual Southwestern decor; murals, buffalo heads, Native American rugs. Cr cds: A, DS, MC, V.

Columbia (C-6)

(See also Baltimore)

Pop 75,883 **Elev** 402 ft **Area code** 410 & 443
Information Howard County Tourism Council, 8267 Main St, PO Box 9, Ellicott City 21041; 410/313-1900 or 800/288-TRIP.

A planned city built on a tract of land larger than Manhattan Island, Columbia is comprised of 11 villages surrounding a central downtown service area. Construction of the city began in 1966.

What to See and Do

Maryland Museum of African Art. Masks, sculptured figures, textiles, basketry, household items and musical instruments displayed in a 19th-century manor. (Tues-Fri, also Sun afternoons; closed major hols) 5430 Vantage Point Rd, in Historic Oakland at Town Center. Phone 410/730-7105. ¢

Annual Events

Wine in the Woods. Symphony Woods at Merriweather Post Pavilion. 2-day celebration featuring Maryland wines, gourmet food, entertainment, arts & crafts. Phone 410/313-PARK. 3rd wkend May.

Columbia Festival of Arts. Music, dance, theater, lakeside entertainment. Ten days in mid-June.

Symphony of Lights. Animated lighting displays along a 1½-mi park route. Late Nov-early Jan.

Hotels

★ ★ **COLUMBIA INN HOTEL AND CONFERENCE CENTER.** 10207 Wincopin Circle (21044), opp Columbia Mall. 410/730-3900; FAX 410/730-1290; res: 800/638-2817. E-mail sales@columbiainn; web www.columbiainn.com. 289 rms, 3-10 story. S $115-$130; D $130-$145; each addl $10; suites $250-$375; under 12 free; wkend plan. Crib free. Pet accepted, some restrictions; $75 refundable. TV; cable (premium). Pool; poolside serv (in season), lifeguard. Coffee in rms. Restaurant 7 am-2:30 pm, 5:30-10:30 pm. Bar 4 pm-2 am. Ck-out noon. Lndry facilities. Meeting rms. Business servs avail. In-rm modem link. Gift shop. Tennis privileges. 18-hole golf privileges, greens fee $35-$44. Health club privileges. Some bathrm phones; microwaves avail. Overlooks Lake Kittamaqundi; boat rides, entertainment on lake (summer). Cr cds: A, C, D, DS, MC, V.

D 🏃 🏌 ⌇ ⚡ ⛵ 🔥 SC

★ ★ ★ **HILTON.** 5485 Twin Knolls Rd (21045), at jct US 29 & MD 175. 410/997-1060; FAX 410/997-0169. Web www.hilton.com. 152 rms, 4 story. S, D $99-$129; each addl $10; suites $175-$250; under 18 free; wkend plans. Crib free. TV; cable (premium), VCR avail. Indoor pool; whirlpool. Coffee in rms. Restaurant 6:30 am-11 pm. Bar noon-midnight; Fri, Sat to 1 am. Ck-out 11 am. Meeting rms. Business servs avail. In-rm modem link. Exercise equipt; weights, bicycle, sauna. Microwaves avail. Cr cds: A, C, D, DS, ER, MC, V.

 D ≋ ⌧ ⋈ ⚒ SC

Restaurants

★ ★ **CLYDE'S.** *10221 Wincopin Circle (21044). 410/730-2828.* Hrs: 11:30-2 am; Sun from 10 am; early-bird dinner Mon-Fri 4:30-6 pm; Sun brunch to 4 pm. Closed Dec 25. Res accepted (dinner). Bar. Semi-a la carte: lunch $7-$13, dinner $10-$18. Sun brunch $6-$11. Child's meals. Specializes in seasonal dishes, salmon, crab. Own baking. Outdoor dining. Bistro atmosphere; etched and stained glass; view of lake. Totally nonsmoking. Cr cds: A, D, DS, MC, V.

D

★ ★ ★ **KING'S CONTRIVANCE.** *10150 Shaker Dr (21046). 410/995-0500.* Hrs: 11:30 am-2 pm, 5:30-9 pm; Fri, Sat 5:30-9:30 pm; Sun 4-8 pm. Res accepted; required Dec. Bar. Wine cellar. Semi-a la carte: lunch $8-$14, dinner $14-$26. Specializes in fresh seafood, rack of lamb. Own baking. Enclosed porch dining. Mansion built in 1900. Cr cds: A, DS, MC, V.

Crisfield (F-9)

(See also Pocomoke City)

Pop 2,880 **Elev** 4 ft **Area code** 410 **Zip** 21817
Information Crisfield Area Chamber of Commerce, PO Box 292; 410/968-2500.

What to See and Do

Janes Island State Park. These 3,147 acres are nearly surrounded by Chesapeake Bay and its inlets. Swimming; fishing; boat ramp (rentals). Cabins. Camping. Standard fees. Approx 2 mi NE via MD 413, then 1½ mi N on MD 358. Phone 410/968-1565.

Tyler's Cruises. The *Betty Jo Tyler* and the *Capt Tyler II* make approx one-hr cruises to Smith Island. Bus tour of the two villages comprising the island, with spare time to visit the rest of the island; lunch avail (fee). Tour length approx 4½ hours. (Memorial Day wkend-Oct) Somers Cove Marina. Phone 410/425-2771. ¢¢¢¢

Annual Event

National Hard Crab Derby & Fair. Cooking, crab picking, boat docking contests; crab racing; fireworks and parade. Phone 410/968-2500. Fri-Sun, Labor Day wkend.

Motel

★ ★ **PINES.** *N Somerset Ave, 3 blks E of MD 413. 410/968-0900.* 40 rms. July-Aug: S $50-$55; D $55-$70; each addl $5; kit. units $15 addl; under 11 free; higher rates: July 4, Labor Day, special events; lower rates rest of yr. TV; cable. Pool. Restaurant nearby. Ck-out 11 am. Gift shop. Picnic area. In scenic, wooded section. No cr cds accepted.

≋ ⋈ ⚒ SC

Cumberland (A-2)

Settled 1750 **Pop** 23,706 **Elev** 688 ft **Area code** 301 & 240 **Zip** 21502
E-mail Tourism@Netbiz.net **Web** www.mdmountainside.com

Information Allegany County Visitors Bureau, Mechanic & Harrison Sts; 301/777-5905 or 800/50-VISIT.

Far to the west in the state, Cumberland is nestled between Pennsylvania and West Virginia. The Potomac River and its tributary, Wills Creek, flow peaceably by this onetime western outpost of the colonies.

British General Edward Braddock was sent here to conquer the French and Native Americans in 1755; unprepared for the wilderness, he met with defeat and death. George Washington, who defended the town in that period, felt the main east-west route would pass through Cumberland eventually. In 1833 the National Road (US 40 Alternate) made the town a supply terminus for overland commerce. The road was extended farther west, the B & O Railroad reached here in 1842, and eight years later came the Chesapeake and Ohio Canal (see CHESAPEAKE AND OHIO CANAL NATIONAL HISTORICAL PARK), bringing prosperous business. Today's economy no longer depends on industry alone but includes services and recreational facilities.

What to See and Do

Dans Mountain State Park. 481 acres. Nearby Dans Rock affords a panoramic view of surrounding region from a height of 2,898 ft. Swimming pool (fee); fishing. Picnicking. Playground. Hiking. Sledding. 10 mi W on I-68, then 8 mi S on MD 36, 2 mi SE of Lonaconing. Schedule varies, phone ahead; 301/463-5564 or 301/777-2139.

Fort Cumberland Trail. Walking trail covers several city blocks downtown around the site of Ft Cumberland. Includes boundary markers, narrative plaques.

George Washington's Headquarters (ca 1755). His first military headquarters. Taped narration. In Riverside Park, downtown, on Greene St. **Free.**

Green Ridge State Forest. These 38,811 acres of forest land stretch across mountains of Western Maryland and occupy portions of Town Hill, Polish Mt and Green Ridge Mt. Abundant wildlife. Fishing. Boat launch; canoeing. Hiking trails. Camping. Winter sports. C & O Canal runs through here into 3,118-ft Paw-Paw Tunnel. 21 mi E off I-68 at exit 64. Phone 301/478-3124.

History House (ca 1867). Restored 18-rm Victorian house with nine period rooms; medical instruments, costumes; research room. (June-Oct, daily exc Mon; rest of yr, Tues-Sat) 218 Washington St, in Victorian Historic District. Phone 301/777-8678. ¢¢

Rocky Gap State Park. Mountain scenery around 243-acre lake with three swimming beaches. Swimming; fishing; boating (electric motors only; rentals). Nature, hiking trails. Picnicking, cafe. Improved camping (res accepted 1 yr in advance). Winter activities. Resort; 18-hole golf course. Standard fees. (See ANNUAL EVENTS) 6 mi E on I-68, exit 50. Phone 301/777-2138 (camping) or 301/777-2139. Per person ¢

The Narrows. Picturesque 1,000-ft gap through Alleghenies (US 40A) used by pioneers on their way to the West.

Toll Gate House (1836). Built to collect tolls from users of Cumberland Road (National Road); only remaining toll house in state; restored. (Late May-late Oct, Sat & Sun afternoons; other times by appt) Approx 6 mi W on US 40A, in La Vale. Phone 301/777-5905. ¢

Western Maryland Station Center. This 1913 railroad station houses industrial and transportation museum; art gallery; C & O Canal National Historical Park Visitors Center Allegany County Visitors Center. (Daily; closed most major hols) Canal St. Phone 301/777-5905. **Free.** This is also the departure point for

Western Maryland Scenic Railroad. Excursion train makes scenic trip 17 mi to Frostburg and back. (May-Oct, daily exc Mon; Nov-mid-Dec, wkends) For schedule and fees phone 301/759-4400 or 800/TRAIN-50.

Annual Events

Agricultural Expo & Fair. Allegany County Fairgrounds. Poultry, livestock, carnival, entertainment. Phone 301/729-1200. Mid-July.

Drumfest. Greenway Ave Stadium. Drum and bugle corps championship. Phone 301/777-8325. Last Sat July.

Rocky Gap Music Festival. Rocky Gap State Park. Features bluegrass and country music; children's activities, crafts, workshops. Phone 888/762-5942. Fri-Sun, 1st wkend Aug.

Street Rod Roundup. 6 mi S on MD 220, at fairgrounds. Hundreds of pre-1950 hot-rods on display and in competitions. Phone 301/729-5555. Labor Day wkend.

Motels

★ ★ ★ **BEST WESTERN BRADDOCK MOTOR INN.** *(1268 National Hwy, La Vale)* 6 mi W on US 40, at jct MD 53; I-68 exit 39 or 40. 301/729-3300. 108 rms, 1-2 story. S $45-$55; D $61-$75; each addl $6; suites $75-$95; under 18 free. TV; cable (premium), VCR avail (movies). Indoor pool; whirlpool, poolside serv. Restaurant 7 am-9 pm. Rm serv. Bar 4:30 pm-midnight; Fri, Sat to 1 am; closed Sun. Ck-out 11 am. Meeting rm. Business servs avail. In-rm modem link. Sundries. Airport transportation. Exercise equipt; weights, bicycles, sauna. Game rm. Cr cds: A, C, D, DS, MC, V.

D ⟼ ✕ ⊠ ⌨ SC

✔★ **SUPER 8.** *(1301 National Hwy, La Vale)* I-68 exit 39 W. 301/729-6265. 63 rms, 3 story. S, D $44.44; each addl $5; suites $39.88-$52.80; under 12 free. Crib free. TV; cable. Complimentary continental bkfst. Restaurant opp open 24 hrs. Ck-out 11 am. Meeting rms. Business servs avail. Cr cds: A, C, D, DS, JCB, MC, V.

D ⊠ ⌨ SC

Motor Hotel

★ ★ **HOLIDAY INN.** 100 S George St, I-68 exit 43C. 301/724-8800; FAX 301/724-4001. 130 rms, 6 story. S, D $79; under 18 free. Crib free. Pet accepted. TV; cable (premium), VCR avail. Pool; lifeguard. Restaurant 6:30 am-2 pm, 5-10 pm; Sun from 7 am. Rm serv. Bar noon-2 am; Sun from 1 pm; entertainment. Ck-out noon. Meeting rms. Business center. In-rm modem link. Sundries. Airport transportation. Cr cds: A, C, D, DS, JCB, MC, V.

D ⟼ ⇌ ✕ ⊠ ⌨ SC ⚂

Inn

★ ★ **INN AT WALNUT BOTTOM.** 120 Green St, I-68 exit 43A. 301/777-0003; FAX 301/777-8288; res: 800/286-9718. 12 rms, 4 share bath, 2-3 story, 2 suites. S, D $69-$99; each addl $15; suites $99-$140. Crib avail. TV; cable (premium). Complimentary full bkfst. Dining rm 7:30 am-10 pm. Ck-out 11 am, ck-in 3 pm. Business servs avail. Two buildings (1820, 1890). Rms furnished with antiques, period reproductions. Totally nonsmoking. Cr cds: A, DS, MC, V.

⊠ ⌨ SC

Restaurants

★ ★ ★ **AU PETIT PARIS.** *(86 E Main St, Frostburg)* Exit 34 off I-68. 301/689-8946. Hrs: 6-9:30 pm. Closed Sun, Mon; major hols. Res accepted. French menu. Bar 5:30 pm-midnight. Wine list. Semi-a la carte: dinner $10.50-$28.95. Child's meals. Specialties: fresh seafood, coq au vin, Dover sole. Tableside preparation. Cr cds: A, C, D, DS, MC, V.

D ➟

✔★ ★ **FRED WARNER'S GERMAN RESTAURANT.** *(Cresaptown 21505)* US 220S, off I-68. 301/729-2361. Hrs: 11 am-9 pm; Fri, Sat to 10 pm; Sun noon-7 pm. Closed Mon; Jan 1, July 4, Dec 25. German, Amer menu. Bar. Semi-a la carte: lunch $3-$7.45, dinner $5.95-$13.95.

Child's meals. Specialties: sauerbraten, bratwurst, bienenstich. Outdoor dining. Old World Bavarian atmosphere; costumed waitresses. Family-owned. Totally nonsmoking. Cr cds: A, MC, V.

Easton (D-8)

(See also Cambridge, St Michaels)

Settled 1682 **Pop** 9,372 **Elev** 28 ft **Area code** 410 **Zip** 21601
Information Talbot County Chamber of Commerce, PO Box 1366; 410/822-4606.

What to See and Do

Historical Society of Talbot County. A 3-gallery museum in a renovated early commercial building; changing exhibits, museum shop. Historic houses: 1810 Federal town house, 1700s Quaker cabinetmaker's cottage, period gardens; tours. (Daily exc Mon) 25 S Washington St. Phone 410/822-0773. Museum ¢¢; Houses ¢¢

The Academy of the Arts. Housed in renovated 1820s schoolhouse, Academy exhibits works of local & national artists in permanent collection. Also hosts over 200 visual & performing arts programs annually. (Daily exc Sun) 106 South St. Phone 410/822-0455 or -ARTS (recording). ¢

Third Haven Friends Meeting House (1682-1684). One of the oldest frame-construction houses of worship in US. (Daily) 405 S Washington St. Phone 410/822-0293. **Free.**

Tuckahoe State Park. A 60-acre lake and Tuckahoe Creek provide a secluded atmosphere in this 3,498-acre park. The Adkins Arboretum, 500 acres, propagates trees, plants and shrubs indigenous to Maryland. Fishing, hunting; boating. Hiking. Picnicking. Standard fees. 5 mi N of Queen Anne, off MD 404. For schedule phone 410/820-1668.

Annual Events

Eastern Shore Chamber Music Festival. Various locations. World-class chamber music; young people's concert. Phone 410/819-0380. 2 wks June.

Tuckahoe Steam & Gas Show and Reunion. 5 mi N via US 50, opp Woodlawn Memorial Park. Old steam and gas engines; antique tractors and cars. Demonstrations in soap and broom making; flour milling. Gas and steam wheat threshing; sawmill working; flea market, crafts, parade, entertainment. Phone 410/643-6123 or 410/820-9868 (during event). Usually wkend after July 4.

Waterfowl Festival. Downtown and various locations in and around town. Exhibits on waterfowl; pictures, carvings; food. Phone 410/822-4606. 1st or 2nd wkend Nov.

Motels

✔★ ★ **COMFORT INN.** 8523 Ocean Gateway, E on US 50. 410/820-8333; FAX 410/820-8436. E-mail bsdiggs@ix.netcom.com. 84 units, 2 story, 15 suites. Mid-Apr-Nov: S $64-$75; D $66-$95; each addl $8; under 18 free; higher rates special events; lower rates rest of yr. Crib free. Pool; whirlpool. TV; cable (premium). Complimentary continental bkfst. Restaurant nearby. Ck-out 11 am. Meeting rms. Business servs avail. In-rm modem link. Sundries. Some refrigerators; microwaves avail. Picnic tables. Cr cds: A, C, D, DS, MC, V.

D ⇌ ⊠ ⌨ SC

★ **DAYS INN.** 7018 Ocean Gateway. 410/822-4600; FAX 410/820-9723. E-mail bsdiggs@ix.netcom.com. 80 rms, 2 story. Apr-Nov: S $69-$89; D, suites $79-$99; under 18 free; higher rates Waterfowl Festival; lower rates rest of yr. Crib free. Pet accepted, some restrictions; $8. TV; cable. Complimentary continental bkfst. Ck-out 11 am. Pool; wading pool. Some refrigerators. Cr cds: A, C, D, DS, ER, JCB, MC, V.

D ⟼ ⇌ ✕ ⌨ SC

Motor Hotel

★ ★ **HOLIDAY INN EXPRESS.** 8561 Ocean Gateway. 410/819-6500. E-mail bsdiggs@ix.netcom.com; web www.holiday-inn.com. 73 rms, 4 story. Apr-Nov: S, D $89-$105; each addl $10; under 18 free; lower rates rest of yr. Crib free. TV; cable (premium). Indoor pool; whirlpool. Complimentary continental bkfst. Restaurant adj open 24 hrs. Ck-out 11 am. Meeting rms. Business servs avail. Exercise equipt; bicycles, rower. Cr cds: A, C, D, DS, MC, V.

D ≋ ⊀ ⊠ ⚑ SC

Hotel

★ ★ ★ **TIDEWATER INN.** 101 E Dover St. 410/822-1300; FAX 410/820-8847; res: 800/237-8775. 114 rms, 4 story. June-Nov: S $90-$145; D $90-$160; each addl $10; under 13 free; wkly, wkend rates; package plans; higher rates Waterfowl Festival; lower rates rest of yr. Crib free. TV; cable (premium), VCR avail. Pool; poolside serv. Restaurant (see HUNTER'S TAVERN). Bar 11-2 am; entertainment Fri, Sat, Sun brunch. Ck-out noon. Meeting rms. Business center. In-rm modem link. Free valet parking. Airport transportation. Health club privileges. Restored turn-of-the-century hotel. Cr cds: A, C, D, MC, V.

D ≋ ⊠ ⚑ SC ⊀

Inns

★ ★ ★ **ASHBY 1663.** 27448 Ashby Dr. 410/822-4235; FAX 410/822-9288. 13 rms, 3 story, 6 suites. 11 rm phones. Apr-Nov (2-day min): S, D $215-$265; suites $215-$595; lower rates rest of yr. TV; VCR avail. Pool; whirlpool, sauna. Complimentary full bkfst; afternoon refreshments. Ck-out noon, ck-in 3 pm. Luggage handling. Lighted tennis. Exercise equipt; bicycle, treadmill. Game rm. Lawn games. Some balconies. Georgian colonial manor house built in 1858; on Miles River. Totally nonsmoking. Cr cds: A, MC, V.

⊷ ⸂ ⊀ ≋ ⊀ ⊠

★ ★ **BISHOPS HOUSE.** 214 Goldsborough St. 410/820-7290; FAX 410/820-7290; res: 800/223-7290. E-mail bishopshouse@skipjack.bluecrab.org; web www.traveldata.com/inns/data/bishop.html. 5 rms, 3 story. No rm phone. No elvtr. 2-night min: S $100; D $110; lower rates mid-wk. Children over 13 only. TV in main rm. Complimentary full bkfst. Restaurant nearby. Ck-out 11 am, ck-in 4 pm. Some whirlpools. Some fireplaces. Built in 1880; antiques, toys, porcelains. No cr cds accepted.

⊠ ⚑

★ ★ **ROBERT MORRIS INN.** (314 N Morris St, Oxford 21654) 11 mi SW on MD 333. 410/226-5111; FAX 410/226-5744. 35 rms, 2-3 story, 2 kit. cottages. No rm phones. D $70-$220; kit. cottages for 2-4, $130-$170. Children over 10 yrs only. Dining rm 8-10 am, noon-9 pm; winter hrs vary. Bar noon-10 pm. Ck-out noon, ck-in 3 pm. Business servs avail. Golf privileges. Private patios, balconies. Historic house (1710) built by ships' carpenters. Private beach on river. Totally nonsmoking. Cr cds: A, MC, V.

D ⊷ ⊀ ≋ ⚑ SC

Restaurants

★ ★ **HUNTER'S TAVERN.** (See Tidewater Inn Hotel) 410/822-1300. Hrs: 7 am-10 pm; early-bird dinner Mon-Fri 4-6 pm; Sun brunch 9:30 am-2 pm. Res accepted (dinner). Bar; Fri, Sat 11-2 am. Semi-a la carte: bkfst $3.95-$9.50, lunch $6.95-$11.50, dinner $12.95-$24.95. Sun brunch $15.70-$17.80. Specializes in Chesapeake Bay seafood, prime rib, crab cakes. Valet parking. Outdoor dining. Waterfowl theme; carvings and murals. Cr cds: A, MC, V.

D SC

★ **LEGAL SPIRITS.** 42 E Dover St, at Harrison St. 410/820-0033. Hrs: 11:30 am-10 pm; Fri, Sat to 11 pm; Sun noon-9 pm. Closed

most major hols. Bar. A la carte entrees: lunch $4.25-$8.95, dinner $6.95-$17. Specializes in monster salads, crab cakes, regional seafood. Located in restored 1922 vaudeville theater. Cr cds: A, D, DS, MC, V.

D ⊣

Elkton (B-9)

(See also Havre De Grace)

Pop 9,073 **Elev** 30 ft **Area code** 410 **Zip** 21921
Information Elkton Chamber of Commerce, 101 E Main St; 410/398-1640.

What to See and Do

Elk Neck State Forest. Has 3,165 acres. Forest wildlife, particularly white-tailed deer, can be seen; food plots have been established. Hunting. Hiking, bridle trail. Picnicking. Primitive camping. Shooting range. Winter sports. Pets allowed. 4 mi W off MD 7, near North East. Phone 410/287-5675.

Elk Neck State Park. Park has 2,188 acres of sandy beaches, marshlands and heavily wooded bluffs. Swimming; fishing; boating (launch, rentals). Miniature golf (fee). Hiking and nature trails. Picnicking. Concession. Winter sports. Camping; cabins. Standard fees. 14 mi SW via US 40, MD 272, near North East. Phone 410/287-5333.

Motels

✓★ **ELKTON LODGE.** 200 Belle Hill Rd, I-95 exit 109A. 410/398-9400; FAX 410/398-9579. 32 rms, 2 story. S $32-$40; D $34-$40; each addl $4; under 15 free. Crib $5. TV; cable (premium). Restaurant nearby. Ck-out 11 am. Some refrigerators. Cr cds: A, C, D, DS, MC, V.

D ⊠ ⚑ SC

★ **SUTTON.** 405 E Pulaski Hwy. 410/398-3830. 11 rms, shower only. No rm phones. S $30; D $33-$35; each addl $2. Crib $1. Pet accepted, some restrictions. TV. Restaurant nearby. Ck-out 11 am. No cr cds accepted.

⊷ ⊠

Inns

★ ★ **INN AT THE CANAL.** (104 Bohemia Ave, Chesapeake City 21915) 7 mi S on MD 213. 410/885-5995; FAX 410/885-3585. 6 rms, 3 story. No rm phones. Apr-Nov: D $75-$105; each addl $25; 2-day min some hols; lower rates rest of yr. Children over 10 yrs only. TV; cable (premium), VCR avail (movies). Complimentary full bkfst. Restaurant nearby. Ck-out 11 am, ck-in 2 pm. Business servs avail. Lawn games. Mansion built 1870; antiques. Overlooks Chesapeake & Delaware Canal. Totally nonsmoking. Cr cds: A, C, D, DS, MC, V.

⊷ ⊠ ⚑

★ **KITTY KNIGHT HOUSE.** (MD 213, Georgetown 21930) 20 mi S on MD 213, turn right after drawbridge. 410/648-5777; FAX 410/648-5890; res: 800/404-8712. 11 rms, 3 story. No rm phones. D $75-$125; each addl $10. TV. Complimentary continental bkfst. Dining rm 11:30 am-3 pm, 5-9 pm; Fri & Sat to 10:30 pm; Sun Noon-9 pm. Ck-out 11 am, ck-in 2 pm. Built ca 1755. Antiques. Cr cds: A, MC, V.

⚑

Restaurants

★ ★ ★ **GRANARY.** (Foot of George St, Georgetown 21930) 20 mi S on MD 213, turn right before the drawbridge. 410/275-8177. Hrs: noon-9 pm; Sat 4-10 pm; Sun noon-8 pm; winter hrs vary. Closed Jan 1, Thanksgiving, Dec 25; also Mon & Tues Nov-Mar. Res accepted Sun-Fri. Bar. Extensive wine list. Semi-a la carte: dinner $15.95-$27.95. Child's meals.

Specializes in fresh seafood, steak. Entertainment Fri, Sat (Memorial Day-Labor Day). Two dining areas, one with deck overlooking river; both areas offer scenic view of Sassafras River, piers and wooded area. Cr cds: A, DS, MC, V.

★★ **SCHAEFER'S CANAL HOUSE.** *(208 Bank St, Chesapeake City 21915) 6 mi S on MD 213.* 410/885-2200. Hrs: 8 am-10 pm; wkend hrs may vary; Sun brunch 11 am-3 pm. Closed Dec 25. Res accepted Sun-Fri. Bar. Semi-a la carte: bkfst $3-$9, lunch $5-$24, dinner $18-$32. Sun brunch $12.95. Child's meals. Specializes in seafood. Outdoor dining. Nautical decor; view of canal. Cr cds: A, MC, V.

Ellicott City (B-6)

(See also Baltimore)

Settled 1772 **Pop** 41,396 **Elev** 233 ft **Area code** 410

Information Howard County Tourism Council, 8267 Main St, PO Box 9, 21041; 410/313-1900 or 800/288-TRIP.

The town was originally named Ellicott Mills for the three Quaker brothers who founded it as the site of their gristmill. Charles Carroll of Carrollton, whose Doughoregan Manor can still be seen nearby, lent financial help to the Ellicotts and the town eventually became the site of ironworks, rolling mills and the first railroad terminus in the US. The famous Tom Thumb locomotive race with a horse took place near here. Many of the town's original stone houses and log cabins, on hills above the Patapsco River, have been preserved.

What to See and Do

Cider Mill Farm. Cider press operating most days. Bushels of pumpkins, apples and other foods and produce. Hayrides, petting zoo, pony rides, storytelling, crafts, contests, apple-butter making. (Apr-May & mid-Sept-Dec, daily) 5012 Landing Rd, Elkridge, 5 mi SE via MD 29 and MD 103, Ilchester Rd to Landing Rd. Phone 410/788-9595. ¢¢

Ellicott City B & O Railroad Station Museum. Two restored buildings (ca 1830 and 1885) house historic rooms, RR displays and memorabilia, operating HO model RR of the first 13 mi of the B & O track, photographs, dioramas. Full size B & O caboose and museum store. Civil War reenactments of military and civilian life, June-Oct. (May-Sept, daily exc Tues; rest of yr, Fri-Mon) 2711 Maryland Ave, at Main St. Phone 410/461-1944 (recording). ¢¢

Patapsco Valley State Park. Four of the recreation areas located within the 15,000 acres sprawling along the Patapsco River are as follows. Area 1: Glen Artney via South St from MD 1, in Relay; Baltimore County. Picnicking, fishing. Area 2: Hilton Ave, via Rolling Rd, S of Frederick Rd, in Catonsville; Baltimore County. Picnicking, camping. Area 3: Hollofield, adj to US 40, near Ellicott City; Howard County. Scenic overlook, camping. Pets allowed (in camping area). Area 4: McKeldin Area, off Marriottsville Rd; Carroll County. Picnicking, fishing. Hiking trails & pavilions available in all areas. Golden Age Passport (see MAKING THE MOST OF YOUR TRIP). NE and SE of town; 5 mi from I-695 exits 12 and 15, 50 yds from I-195 exit 1. Phone 410/461-5005. ¢¢

Annual Events

Maryland Sheep & Wool Festival. In West Friendship. Craftsmen sell products related to sheep and wool; spinning, weaving, and sheep-shearing contests; wool dyeing; entertainment. 1st wkend May.

Howard County Fair. In West Friendship. Rides, entertainment, concessions, 4-H exhibits, horse-pulling contests and other events. Mid-Aug.

Hotel

★★ **TURF VALLEY RESORT.** *2700 Turf Valley Rd (21042), approx 8 mi W via US 40.* 410/465-1500; FAX 410/465-8280; res: 800/666-8873. Web www.turfvalley.com. 172 rms, 7 story, 6 villas. Apr-Dec: S $110; D $125; each addl $15; suites $130-$415; villas $650-$700; under 15 free; wkend packages; lower rates rest of yr. Crib free. TV; cable (premium). Pool; poolside serv, lifeguard. Restaurant 6:30 am-10 pm. Bar 4:30-11 pm; Fri, Sat to 2 am; entertainment Thurs-Sun. Ck-out noon. Convention facilities. Business servs avail. In-rm modem link. Gift shop. Lighted tennis. 54-hole golf, greens fee $35-$50, pro, putting green, driving range. Exercise equipt; weight machine, bicycles. Cr cds: A, C, D, DS, MC, V.

Restaurants

★★ **CRAB SHANTY.** *3410 Plumtree Dr & US 40W (21042).* 410/465-9660. Hrs: 11:30 am-2:30 pm, 5-10 pm; Mon, Tues to 9 pm; Sun 2-9 pm. Bar. Semi-a la carte: lunch $2.95-$9.50, dinner $8.75-$18.95. Child's meals. Specializes in seafood. Cr cds: A, C, D, DS, MC, V.

★ **SIDESTREETS.** *8069 Tiber Alley (21043).* 410/461-5577. Hrs: 11:30 am-10 pm; Fri, Sat to 11 pm; Sun 11 am-9 pm; Sun brunch to 2 pm. Closed Thanksgiving, Dec 25. Res accepted Fri, Sat dinner. Seafood menu. Bar. Semi-a la carte: lunch, dinner $5.95-$19.95. Sun brunch $2.95-$7.95. Specializes in Chesapeake Bay seafood. Eclectic decor. Totally nonsmoking. Cr cds: A, DS, MC, V.

★★★ **TERSIGUEL'S.** *8293 Main St (21043).* 410/465-4004. Hrs: 11:30 am-2:30 pm, 5-9 pm; Fri to 10 pm; Sat 11:30 am-3:30 pm, 5-10 pm; Sun 11:30 am-3:30 pm, 5-9 pm. Closed Dec 25. Res accepted. French menu. Bar. Wine cellar. Semi-a la carte: lunch $8.95-$19.95, dinner $14.95-$26.95. Prix fixe: lunch $15.95-$25.95, dinner $27.95-$37.95. Specialties: rack of lamb, châteaubriand pour deux. Historic bldg; mementos from Brittany, France. Totally nonsmoking. Cr cds: A, C, D, DS, MC, V.

Emmitsburg (A-5)

(See also Frederick, Hagerstown, Thurmont)

Settled 1785 **Pop** 1,688 **Elev** 449 ft **Area code** 301 **Zip** 21727 **Web** www.co.frederick.md.us/tour/tourpage.html

Information Tourism Council of Frederick County, 19 E Church St, Frederick 21701; 301/663-8687 or 800/999-3613.

What to See and Do

Mount Saint Mary's College and Seminary (1808). (1,800 students) Oldest independent Catholic college in US. Liberal arts and sciences. 3 mi S on US 15. Phone 301/447-6122. Near the campus is the

National Shrine Grotto of Lourdes. Replica of the French shrine is 1/3 the size of the original; oldest replica in the Western Hemisphere. Pangborn Memorial Campanile, constructed of native stone and located at the entrance, is 120 ft tall and is surmounted by a 25-ft bronze gold-leaf statue of the Blessed Virgin Mary. (Apr-Oct, daily; rest of yr, daily exc Mon; closed last 2 wks Jan) **Free.**

★ **Seton Shrine Center.** National Shrine of Saint Elizabeth Ann Seton, first US female saint, canonized 1975. Includes Stone House (1809), White House (1810), home in which Mother Seton died; slide presentation, basilica, museum and cemetery. (May-Nov, daily; rest of yr, daily exc Mon; closed Dec 25; also last 2 wks Jan) South Seton Ave. Phone 301/447-6606. **Free.**

Inn

★ ★ **ANTRIM 1844.** *(30 Trevanion Rd, Taneytown 21787)* Approx 10 mi E on MD 140. 410/756-6812; FAX 410/756-2744; res: 800/858-1844. 14 rms, 2 with shower only, 3 story, 2 suites. No rm phones. S $125-$225; D $150-$250; each addl $50; suites $300; under 3 free; ski, golf plans; 2-day min wkends, hols; higher rates Dec 31. Pet accepted, some restrictions. TV in main rm; cable, VCR. Heated pool; whirlpools. Complimentary full bkfst. Complimentary coffee in rms. Restaurant (see ANTRIM 1844). Ck-out noon, ck-in 3 pm. Luggage handling. Business servs avail. Airport transportation. Tennis. Putting green. Croquet. Downhill ski 14 mi, x-country 15 mi. Health club privileges. Lawn games. Some balconies. Antebellum plantation (1844) built on 25 acres. Elegant antique furnishings, 3-story spiral staircase, 23 fireplaces. Formal gardens and gazebo. Totally nonsmoking. Cr cds: A, C, D, DS, MC, V.

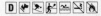

Restaurant

★ ★ **ANTRIM 1844.** *(See Antrim 1844 Inn)* 800/858-1844. Sittings: 7-7:30 pm (hors d'oeuvres served at 6:30 pm). Closed Jan 1. Res required. French, Amer menu. Bar. Wine cellar. Prix fixe: $55. Specialties: black buck antelope, black Angus tenderloin. Outdoor dining. Refined dining in elegant atmosphere; fireplace, piano. Cr cds: A, C, D, DS, MC, V.

Frederick (B-5)

(See also Hagerstown, Thurmont)

Settled 1745 **Pop** 40,148 **Elev** 290 ft **Area code** 301 & 240 **Zip** 21701 **Web** www.co.frederick.md.us/tour/tourpage.html

Information Tourism Council of Frederick County, 19 E Church St; 301/663-8687 or 800/999-3613.

Home of dauntless Barbara Fritchie, who reportedly spoke her mind to Stonewall Jackson and his "rebel hordes," Frederick is a town filled with history. Named for Frederick Calvert, 6th Lord Baltimore, it is the seat of one of America's richest agricultural counties. Francis Scott Key and Chief Justice Roger Brooke Taney made their homes here. Court House Square was the scene of several important events during the Revolutionary War, including the famed protest against the Stamp Act, in which an effigy of the stamp distributor was burned.

During the Civil War, Frederick was a focal point for strategic operations by both sides. In the campaign of 1862 the Confederacy's first invasions of the North were made at nearby South Mountain and Sharpsburg, at Antietam Creek. Wounded men by the thousands were cared for here. Troop movements continued for the duration of the war; cavalry skirmishes took place in the streets. In July, 1864, the town was forced to pay a $200,000 ransom to Confederate General Jubal Early before he fought the Battle of Monocacy a few miles south. Frederick today is an educational center, tourist attraction, location of Fort Detrick army installation and home of diversified small industry. A 33-block area has been designated an Historic District.

What to See and Do

Barbara Fritchie House and Museum. Exhibits include quilts, clothing made by Fritchie, her rocker and Bible, the bed in which she died and other items; 10-min film; also garden. (Apr-Sept, Thurs-Mon; Oct-Nov, Sat & Sun) 154 W Patrick St. Phone 301/698-0630. ¢¢

Brunswick Museum. Furnishings and clothing interpret life in turn-of-the-century railroad town; large HO model train exhibit; gift shop. Special events held on selected wkends. (June-Sept, Thurs-Sun; Apr-May & Oct-late Dec, Sat & Sun; limited hrs, phone ahead) 23 mi SW via US 340, MD 17 in Brunswick, at 40 W Potomac St. Phone 301/834-7100. ¢¢

Gambrill State Park. Park has 1,136 acres with two developed areas. Fishing. Nature, hiking trails. Picnicking. Tent & trailer sites (standard fees). Tea room. Three overlooks. (Schedule varies, phone ahead) 5 mi NW off US 40. Phone 301/271-7574.

Historical Society of Frederick County Museum. House, built in early 1800s, shows both Georgian and Federal details; leaded side and fanlights, Doric columns inside, double porches in rear and boxwood gardens. Portraits of early Frederick residents. Genealogy library (Tues-Sat). (Mon-Sat; also Sun afternoons) 24 E Church St. Phone 301/663-1188. Museum tour ¢

Horse-drawn carriage tours. (Daily, by appt) Phone Frederick Carriage Co, 301/694-RIDE.

Monocacy Battlefield. On July 9, 1864, Union General Lew Wallace with 5,000 men delayed General Jubal Early and his 23,000 Confederate soldiers for 24 hours, during which Grant was able to reinforce, and save, Washington, DC. New Jersey, Vermont, Pennsylvania and Confederate monuments mark the area. 3 mi S on MD 355. For tour information phone park ranger, 301/662-3515. **Free.**

Mt Olivet Cemetery (1852). Monuments mark graves of Francis Scott Key and Barbara Fritchie. Flag flies over Key's grave. S end of Market St.

Roger Brooke Taney Home (1799) **and Francis Scott Key Museum.** Chief Justice of Supreme Court from 1835-1864, Taney was chosen by Andrew Jackson to succeed John Marshall. He swore in seven presidents, including Abraham Lincoln, and issued the famous Dred Scott Decision. He is buried in the cemetery of St John's Catholic Church at E 3rd & East Sts. (Apr-Oct, wkends) 121 S Bentz St. Phone 301/663-8687. ¢¢

Rose Hill Manor Children's Museum. Hands-on exhibits of 19th-century family life; carriage museum; colonial herb and fragrant gardens; farm museum; blacksmith shop; log cabin. (Apr-Oct, daily; Nov, Sat & Sun only) 1611 N Market St. Phone 301/694-1648 or 301/694-1650. ¢¢

Schifferstadt (1756). Fine example of German-colonial farmhouse architecture. Tours of architectural museum. Gift shop. (Apr-mid Dec, daily exc Mon; closed Thanksgiving) Rosemont Ave & W 2nd St. Phone 301/663-3885. ¢

Trinity Chapel (1763). Graceful colonial church; Francis Scott Key was baptized here. Steeple houses town clock and ten-bell chimes; chimes play every Sat evening. W Church St, near N Market St. The chapel is now used as Sunday School for

Evangelical Reformed Church, United Church of Christ (1848). Opp Trinity Chapel. A Grecian-style building modeled after the Erechtheum, with two towers resembling Lanterns of Demosthenes. Here Stonewall Jackson slept through pro-Union sermon before Battle of Antietam; Barbara Fritchie was a member. Phone 301/662-2762.

Annual Events

Beyond the Garden Gates Tour. Downtown. Tour historic and contemporary gardens. Phone 301/663-8687. Late May.

Lotus Blossom Festival. Lilypons Water Gardens, 6800 Lilypons Rd, 10 mi S via MD 85. Endless blooms of water lilies and lotus, water garden; arts & crafts, food, entertainment, lectures. Phone 301/874-5133. First double-digit wkend July.

Great Frederick Fair. Frederick county fair. Phone 301/663-5895. Mid-late Sept.

New Market Days. 8 mi E, in New Market. Nostalgic revival of the atmosphere of a 19th-century village; costumed guides, period crafts and events; held in New Market, the town dedicated to being the "Antiques Capital of Maryland." Phone 301/831-6755. Last full wkend Sept.

Fall Festival. Rose Hill Manor. Apple-butter making, music, crafts demonstrations, tractor pull, hay rides, country cooking. Early Oct.

Motel

✔ ★ ★ **DAYS INN.** *5646 Buckeystown Pike (MD 85) (21704).* 301/694-6600; FAX 301/831-4242. 119 rms, 2 story. Apr-Oct: S, D $56-$75; under 18 free; lower rates rest of yr. Crib free. TV; cable (premium). Pool. Playground. Complimentary continental bkfst. Ck-out noon. Meeting rm. Business servs avail. Sundries. Refrigerators, microwaves avail. Cr cds: A, C, D, DS, MC, V.

D ≋ ✈ 🏋 SC

Motor Hotels

★ ★ **FAIRFIELD INN BY MARRIOTT.** *5220 Westview Dr (21703).* 301/631-2000; FAX 301/631-2100. 105 rms, 3 story. May-mid-Oct: S $62-$72; D $67-$77; higher rates special events. Crib free. TV; cable (premium). Complimentary continental bkfst. Restaurant opp 7 am-10 pm. Ck-out noon. Business servs avail. Valet serv. Sundries. Exercise equipt; bicycle, treadmill. Indoor pool; whirlpool. Some refrigerators, microwaves. Cr cds: A, D, DS, MC, V.

D ≋ ✈ 🏋 🔥

★ ★ **HAMPTON INN.** *5311 Buckeystown Pike (MD 85).* 301/698-2500; FAX 301/695-8735. 160 rms, 6 story. S, D $69-$100; suites $150; under 18 free. Crib free. Pet accepted, some restrictions. TV; cable (premium). Pool; lifeguard. Complimentary continental bkfst. Restaurant 11:30 am-9 pm. Bar; entertainment. Ck-out noon. Coin lndry. Meeting rms. Business servs avail. In-rm modem link. Sundries. Valet serv. Exercise equipt; bicycles, rowers. Health club privileges. Some refrigerators; microwaves avail. Cr cds: A, C, D, DS, MC, V.

D 🐾 ≋ ✈ 🏋 SC

Inns

★ ★ **CATOCTIN INN.** *(3613 Buckeystown Pike, Buckeystown 21717) 5 mi S on I-270, exit 31B.* 301/831-8102; res: 800/730-5550. Web www.catoctininn.fred.net. 13 rms, 3 story, 3 cottages. Mon-Thurs: S, D $85-$115; each addl $10; cottages $140; under 2 free; wkly rates; min stay hols; higher rates wkends, fall foliage. Crib free. TV; cable (premium), VCR avail (movies). Complimentary full bkfst. Complimentary coffee in rms. Restaurant nearby. Ck-out noon, ck-in by appt. Luggage handling. Business servs avail. Lawn games. Refrigerators. House built in 1780s; parlour with antique sofas, fireplaces. Cr cds: A, DS, MC, V.

D ≋ 🔥 SC

★ ★ ★ **INN AT BUCKEYSTOWN.** *(3521 Buckeystown Pike, Buckeystown 21717) 5 mi S on MD 85.* 301/874-5755; FAX 301/874-5479; res: 800/272-1190. Web www.innbrook.com/buckeystown. 5 rms, 3 story. MAP: S, D $200-$225; suite $225; cottage $250-$300. Children over 12 yrs only. TV avail; cable (premium), VCR avail (movies). Whirlpool. Restaurant (public by res) 7:30 pm sitting; closed Sun-Tue. Setups. Ck-out noon, ck-in 4 pm. Meeting rm. Business servs avail. Downhill ski 20 mi; x-country ski 1 mi. Refrigerators avail; microwaves in cottages. Restored Victorian mansion (1897). Near river. Totally nonsmoking. Cr cds: A, MC, V.

≋ ✈ 🔥

★ ★ ★ **STONE MANOR.** *(5820 Carroll Boyer Rd, Middletown 21769) US 340 W to Lander Rd exit, in Jefferson take MD 180 S, turn right on Old Middletown Rd, left on Sumantown Rd, left on Carroll Boyer Rd.* 301/473-5454; FAX 301/371-5622. Web www.ourhome.net/stonemanor. 6 rms, 2 story, 5 suites. No rm phones. S, D $200; suites $125-$250. TV in main rm; VCR. Complimentary continental bkfst. Complimentary coffee in rms. Restaurant 11 am-2 pm, 6-9 pm; Sun 11 am-2 pm (brunch), 2-7 pm; closed Mon. Rm serv 24 hrs. Ck-out 11 am, ck-in 2 pm. Business servs avail. Lawn games. Fireplaces. Balconies. Picnic tables. On pond. Stone building built in 1760s; on more than 100 acres of wooded area. Totally nonsmoking. Cr cds: A, DS, MC, V.

D 🐾 ✈ ≋ 🔥

★ ★ ★ **TURNING POINT.** *3406 Urbana Pike (21704), 9 mi S on MD 355, I-270 Ext. 26.* 301/831-8232; FAX 301/831-8092. 5 rms, 2 with shower only, 3 story, 2 kit. cottages. S, D $75-$95; kit. cottages $100-$150. TV; cable (premium). Complimentary full bkfst; afternoon refreshments. Dining rm 11:30 am-2 pm, 5:30-9 pm; wkend hrs vary; closed Mon. Ck-out

11 am, ck-in 3 pm. Business servs avail. Built in 1910; antiques. View of Sugarloaf Mt and adj farmland. Cr cds: A, DS, MC, V.

D ≋ 🔥

Restaurants

★ ★ **BROWN PELICAN.** *5 E Church St.* 301/695-5833. Hrs: 11:30 am-3 pm, 5-9:30 pm; Fri to 10 pm; Sat 5-10 pm; Sun 5-9:30 pm. Closed Jan 1, Thanksgiving, Dec 25; also Super Bowl Sun. Res accepted; required Fri, Sat. Continental menu. Bar. Semi-a la carte: lunch $5.75-$12.95, dinner $12.95-$23.95. Specializes in fresh seafood, pasta, veal. In basement of antebellum bank. Cr cds: A, D, DS, MC, V.

★ ★ **COMUS INN.** *(23900 Old Hundred Rd, Comus 20842) approx 10 mi S on I-270, S on MD 109, exit 22.* 301/253-2522. Web www.comusinn.com. Hrs: 11 am-9 pm; Sun from 9 am; Sun brunch 10:30 am-2 pm. Closed Dec 25; also wkdays in winter. Serv bar. Complete meal: lunch $6-$13.50, dinner $12-$22. Sun brunch $16. Child's meals. Specialties: mesquite-grilled chicken breast, crab cakes. Salad bar. Residence built in 1860 on family farm. View of Sugar Loaf Mt; rural setting. Cr cds: A, D, JCB, MC, V.

D SC

★ ★ **GABRIEL'S.** *(4730 Ijamsville Rd, Ijamsville 21754) E on I-70, exit 59, 2 mi S on MD 80.* 301/865-5500. Web www.gaithersburg.com. Hrs: 6-10 pm; Sun 3-9:30 pm. Closed Mon-Wed; Jan 1. Res accepted; required Fri, Sat. French menu. Serv bar. Semi-a la carte: $16.95-$24.50. Specialties: beef Wellington, salmon coulibac, stuffed breast of chicken Marengo. French provincial inn atmosphere; building constructed in 1862. Family-owned. Cr cds: MC, V.

SC ✈

★ ★ **QUAIL RIDGE INN.** *(6212 Ridge Rd, Mount Airy 21771) Approx 10 mi E on I-70, N on MD 27.* 301/831-7488. Hrs: 11:30 am-9 pm; Mon from 5 pm; Fri, Sat to 9:30 pm; Sun 11 am-8:30 pm; Sun brunch to 2 pm. Closed Mon (Apr-Sept); Dec 25. Res accepted. Italian, Amer menu. Serv bar. Semi-a la carte: lunch $3.75-$8, dinner $8.75-$20.95. Sun brunch $9-$14. Child's meals. Specializes in veal, seafood, homemade desserts. Originally a one-rm schoolhouse; intimate dining in scenic rural setting. Cr cds: A, D, DS, MC, V.

★ ★ **TAURASO'S.** *6 East St, Everedy Square.* 301/663-6600. Hrs: 11 am-10 pm; Fri, Sat to 11 pm. Closed Dec 25. Res accepted. Italian, American menu. Bar to midnight. Semi-a la carte: lunch $4.95-$8.95, dinner $7.95-$19.95. Specializes in fresh fish, veal, steak. Outdoor dining. In restored factory building (late 1800s). Cr cds: A, C, D, DS, MC, V.

D

Gaithersburg (C-6)

(See also Rockville)

Pop 39,542 **Elev** 508 ft **Area code** 301
Information Chamber of Commerce, 9 Park Ave, 20877; 301/840-1400.

What to See and Do

Seneca Creek State Park. Stream valley park of 6,109 acres with 90-acre lake. Historic sites with old mills, an old schoolhouse, stone quarries. Fishing; boating (rentals). Winter sports. Picnicking. Hiking, bicycle and bridle trails. Disk golf. Standard fees. 2¹/₂ mi W of I-270 on MD 117. Phone 301/924-2127. ¢

Annual Event

Montgomery County Agricultural Fair. One of the East Coast's leading county fairs; emphasis on agriculture, 4-H activities; animal exhibits, home arts; antique farm equipment; tractor pull, horse pull, demolition derby; rodeo; entertainment. Phone 301/926-3100. Mid-late Aug.

Motel

✔★ ★ **COMFORT INN-SHADY GROVE.** *16216 Frederick Rd (20877).* 301/330-0023; FAX 301/258-1950. 127 rms, 7 story. Apr-Oct: S, D $49-$109; each addl $10; under 18 free; monthly rates; lower rates rest of yr. Crib free. Pet accepted, some restrictions. TV; cable (premium). Pool; lifeguard. Complimentary continental bkfst. Restaurant adj 11 am-9 pm. Ck-out 11 am. Coin lndry. Meeting rms. Business center. In-rm modem link. Valet serv. Gift shop. Exercise equipt; weight machine, bicycles. Some refrigerators; microwaves. Picnic tables. Cr cds: A, C, D, DS, ER, JCB, MC, V.

D ⚓ ≈ ✗ ⚗ ⊠ SC ⚗

Motor Hotels

★ ★ **COURTYARD BY MARRIOTT.** *805 Russell Ave (20879).* 301/670-0008; FAX 301/948-4538. 203 rms, 7 story. S $105; D $115; each addl $10; suites $250. Crib free. TV; cable (premium). VCR avail. Pool; whirlpool, lifeguard. Coffee in rms. Restaurant 6-10 am, 5:30-9:30 pm; Sat 7-11 am; Sun 7 am-noon. Bar 5 pm-midnight. Ck-out noon. Coin lndry. Meeting rms. Business servs avail. In-rm modem link. Valet serv. Lighted tennis. Exercise equipt; bicycles, treadmill, steam rm. Some refrigerators, microwaves. Some balconies. Cr cds: A, C, D, DS, JCB, MC, V.

D ↗ ⚓ ≈ ✗ ⚗ ⊠ SC

✔★ ★ **HAMPTON INN-GERMANTOWN.** *(20260 Goldenrod Lane, Germantown 20876) I-270, exit 15 A.* 301/428-1300; FAX 301/428-9034. 178 rms, 6 story, 16 kit. units. S, D $95-$105; kit. units $129; suites $199; under 18 free; wknd rates. Crib free. TV; cable (premium), VCR avail. Pool; whirlpool. Complimentary continental bkfst. Restaurant 11 am-11 pm. Ck-out noon. Coin lndry. Meeting rms. Business servs avail. Valet serv. Sundries. Exercise equipt; weights, stair machine, sauna. Health club privileges. Microwaves avail. Cr cds: A, C, D, DS, MC, V.

D ≈ ✗ ⚗ ⊠ SC

★ ★ **HOLIDAY INN.** *2 Montgomery Village Ave (20879).* 301/948-8900; FAX 301/258-1940. 301 rms, 1-8 story. S $109-$124; D $119-$144; suites $300-$350; kit. units $115-$125; under 18 free. Crib free. Pet accepted, some restrictions. TV; cable (premium). Indoor pool; whirlpool, poolside serv, lifeguard. Coffee in rms. Restaurant 6:30 am-10 pm. Rm serv 6:30 am-midnight. Bar noon-midnight. Ck-out noon. Coin lndry. Convention facilities. Business servs avail. In-rm modem link. Bellhops. Gift shop. Exercise equipt; weights, bicycles. Game rm. Some refrigerators; microwaves avail. Balconies. Cr cds: A, C, D, DS, JCB, MC, V.

D ↗ ⚓ ≈ ✗ ⚗ ⊠ SC

Hotels

★ ★ **HILTON.** *620 Perry Pkwy (20877), 1 blk E of I-270 exit 11.* 301/977-8900; FAX 301/869-8597. Web www.hilton.com. 301 rms, 12 story. S, D $115-$155; suites $325; under 18 free; wkend rates. Crib free. Pet accepted. TV; cable (premium). Indoor/outdoor pool. Restaurant 6:30 am-11 pm; wkends from 7 am. Bars 11-1 am. Convention facilities. Business servs avail. In-rm modem link. Exercise equipt; weights, bicycles. Health club privileges. Refrigerators avail. Some private patios, balconies. Adj to Lake Forest shopping center. Cr cds: A, C, D, DS, ER, JCB, MC, V.

D ↗ ⚓ ≈ ✗ ⚗ ⊠ SC

★ ★ ★ **MARRIOTT WASHINGTONIAN CENTER.** *9751 Washingtonian Blvd (20878).* 301/590-0044; FAX 301/212-6155. Web www.marriott.com. 284 rms, 11 story. S $119; D $129; suites $250; under 18 free; wkend rates. Crib free. TV; cable (premium). Indoor pool; poolside serv, lifeguard. Restaurant 6:30 am-11 pm; wkend hrs vary. Bar 4 pm-midnight. Ck-out noon. Convention facilities. Business center. In-rm modem link. Concierge. Gift shop. Exercise equipt; weight machine,

stair machine, sauna. Health club privileges. Luxury level. Cr cds: A, C, D, DS, ER, JCB, MC, V.

D ≈ ✗ ⚗ ⚓ ⊠ SC ⚗

Restaurants

✔★ **ALOHA INN.** *608 Quince Orchard Rd (20878).* 301/977-0057. Hrs: 11 am-10 pm; Fri, Sat to 11 pm. Closed Thanksgiving, Dec 25. Res accepted; required Fri & Sat. Chinese menu. Serv bar. Lunch buffet $5.95. Semi-a la carte: lunch $3.95-$5.50, dinner $5.95-$9.95. Specialties: General Tso's chicken, crispy beef Szechuan-style. Polynesian floor show Fri, Sat evenings. Cr cds: A, C, D, DS, MC, V.

★ **CHRIS' STEAK HOUSE.** *201 E Diamond Ave (20877).* 301/869-6116. Hrs: 11 am-11:30 pm. Closed Sun; also most major hols. Bar. Semi-a la carte: lunch $3.25-$8, dinner $6.50-$18. Child's meals. Specializes in beef, pork, seafood. Football memorabilia. Cr cds: A, MC, V.

⊡

★ ★ **FLAMING PIT.** *18701 N Frederick Ave (20879).* 301/977-0700. Hrs: 11:30 am-10:30 pm; Fri to 11:30 pm; Sat 4-11 pm; Sun 5-10 pm. Closed some major hols. Res accepted; required Fri, Sat. Bar to midnight; Fri, Sat to 1 am. Semi-a la carte: lunch $6.95-$12.95, dinner $13.95-$29.95. Child's meals. Specializes in prime rib, lamb, fresh seafood. Pianist. Skylight; hanging baskets. Original antique fireplaces. Cr cds: A, C, D, MC, V.

★ ★ **GOLDEN BULL GRAND CAFE.** *7 Dalamar St (20877), I-270 exit 11.* 301/948-3666. Hrs: 11 am-3 pm, 4:30-10 pm; Fri, Sat to 11 pm; Sun noon-10 pm; early-bird dinner 4:30-6:30 pm; Sun noon-4 pm. Closed Dec 25. Bar 11 am-11 pm. Semi-a la carte: lunch $4.95-$10.95, dinner $7.95-$22.95. Child's meals. Specializes in beef, seafood. Salad bar. Cr cds: A, C, D, DS, MC, V.

⊡

✔★ **IL FORNO.** *8941 Westland Dr (20877).* 301/977-5900. Hrs: 11 am-10 pm; Fri, Sat to 11 pm. Closed most major hols. Italian menu. Wine, beer. A la carte entrees: lunch $4.95-$7.50, dinner $8.95-$15.95. Specializes in pizza, pasta. Outdoor dining. Casual decor. Cr cds: MC, V.

⊡

★ ★ **LE PARADIS.** *347 Muddy Branch Rd (20878).* 301/208-9493. Hrs: 11:30 am-2:30 pm, 5:30-10 pm. Closed Sun; major hols. Res accepted; required Fri, Sat. French menu. Wine list. A la carte: lunch $6.95-$12.95, dinner $15.95-$21.95. Specialties: lobster with ginger key lime sauce, black angus steak with portobello mushroom. Formal decor. Totally nonsmoking. Cr cds: A, C, D, DS, MC, V.

⊡

✔ **MR. LU'S.** *16240 Frederick Rd (20877).* 301/948-9898. Hrs: 11 am-10 pm; Fri, Sat to 10:30 pm; Sun to 9:30 pm; Sat, Sun brunch to 3 pm. Res accepted. Chinese menu. Serv bar. Semi-a la carte: lunch $4.75-$5.50, dinner $6.25-$9.95. Sat, Sun brunch $1.95-$5. Specialties: fish in hot bean sauce, hot crispy beef. Chinese decor; dragon artwork. Totally nonsmoking. Cr cds: A, MC, V.

⊡

★ ★ **OLDE TOWNE TAVERN & BREWING CO.** *227 E Diamond Ave (20877), in Olde Town.* 301/948-4200. Hrs: 4-11 pm; Fri, Sat noon-midnight; Sun from 2 pm; early-bird dinner Mon-Fri to 7 pm. Closed Thanksgiving, Dec 25. Res accepted; required Fri, Sat dinner. Bar to 12:30 am; Fri, Sat to 1:30 am; Sun to midnight. Semi-a la carte: lunch $3.95-$15.95, dinner $4.95-$17.95. Child's meals. Specializes in beef, pasta, seafood. Musicians Fri, Sat. Brew pub in historic Belt Bldg (1896); 2-level dining area. Totally nonsmoking. Cr cds: A, C, D, MC, V.

⊡

✔★ ★ **PEKING CHEERS.** *519 Quince Orchard Rd (20878).* 301/216-2090. Hrs: 11 am-10:30 pm; Fri, Sat to 11 pm. Res accepted. Chinese menu. Serv bar. Semi-a la carte: lunch $4.25-$5.50, dinner

$5.95-$11.95. Specialties: Peking duck, sesame chicken, crispy beef. Casual decor; large murals. Totally nonsmoking. Cr cds: A, DS, MC, V.

 D

✔★ PEKING SUPREME. *19204 Montgomery Village Ave (20879).* 301/963-8088. Hrs: 11:30 am-9:45 pm; Fri, Sat to 10:45 pm. Closed Thanksgiving. Chinese menu. Bar. Semi-a la carte: lunch $4.50-$5.50, dinner $6.95-$11.95. Specialties: peking style chicken, crispy beef. Art deco decor. Cr cds: A, DS, MC, V.

D

✔★ RICCIUTI'S. *(6840 Olney-Laytonsville Rd, Laytonsville 20882) 5 mi N on MD 108.* 301/921-0199. Hrs: 11 am-9 pm; Fri, Sat to 10 pm; Sun 3-9 pm. Closed major hols. Italian menu. Wine, beer. Semi-a la carte: lunch $3.25-$5.95, dinner $5.50-$10.50. Child's meals. Specialties: calzone, stromboli, chocolate pizza. Outdoor dining. Italian decor. Totally nonsmoking. Cr cds: A, DS, MC, V.

D

★ ROY'S PLACE. *2 E Diamond Ave (20877).* 301/948-5548. Hrs: 11 am-11 pm; Fri, Sat to midnight; Sun from 11:30 am. Closed Thanksgiving, Dec 24, 25. Bar. A la carte entrees: lunch, dinner $4.50-$18. Specializes in extensive sandwich selection. 1920s tavern atmosphere; Tiffany-style lamps, beamed ceiling, period posters. Family-owned. Cr cds: A, C, D, DS, MC, V.

D

✔★ ★ SIR WALTER RALEIGH. *19100 Montgomery Village Ave (20879).* 301/258-0576. Hrs: 11:30 am-2 pm, 5-9 pm; Fri to 10 pm; Sat 5-10 pm; Sun 4-8:30 pm. Closed Thanksgiving, Dec 25. Bar. Semi-a la carte: lunch $7-$11, dinner $10.95-$19.95. Child's meals. Specializes in prime rib, seafood, crab cakes. Salad bar. Brick fireplaces. Cr cds: A, C, D, DS, MC, V.

D

Grantsville (A-1)

(For accommodations see Cumberland, Oakland)

Pop 505 **Elev** 2,300 ft **Area code** 301 **Zip** 21536 **E-mail** gctourism@garrett.ncin.com **Web** www.gcnet.net/gctourism/gct.html

Information Deep Creek Lake/Garrett County Promotion Council, Courthouse Building, 200 S Third St, Oakland 21550; 301/334-1948 or 301/387-6171.

What to See and Do

New Germany State Park. A 13-acre lake built on site of a once prosperous milling center. Swimming; fishing; boating. Nature, hiking trails. Winter sports. Picnicking, playground, concession. Improved campsites, cabins (fee). 5 mi S. Phone 301/895-5453. Admission (wkends & hols) per person ¢

Savage River State Forest. Largest of Maryland's state forests comprises about 52,800 acres of near wilderness. A strategic watershed area, the northern hardwood forest surrounds the Savage River Dam. Fishing, hunting. Hiking trails. Winter sports. Primitive camping (permit required). W and S via US 40 and I-68. Phone 301/895-5759.

Springs Museum. Depicts life of settlers of Casselman Valley; 18th-century farming tools, fossil collection, other exhibits. (Memorial Day-mid-Oct, Wed-Sat afternoons) 2 mi N via MD 669, PA 669 in Springs, PA. Phone 814/662-4159. ¢

Spruce Forest Artisan Village. Original log cabins plus other historic buildings serve as studios for a potter, internationally recognized bird carver, weaver, spinner, stained-glass maker and other artisans. Buildings (Memorial Day-last Sat Oct, daily exc Sun). Special events (summer; fee). Restaurant (see). (See ANNUAL EVENTS) 1 mi E on US 40, near Penn Alps. Phone 301/895-3332. **Free.**

Annual Events

Spruce Forest Summerfest and Quilt Show. Spruce Forest Artisan Village. More than 200 quilts on display; more than 70 craftspeople demonstrate their various skills. Phone 301/895-3332. 2nd full Thurs, Fri & Sat wkend July.

Springs Folk Festival. On grounds of Springs Museum (see). Pennsylvania Dutch food, music. Phone 814/662-2051. 1st Fri & Sat Oct.

Restaurant

✔★ ★ PENN ALPS. *125 Casselman Rd, 1 mi on US 40 at Casselman River Bridge.* 301/895-5985. Hrs: 7 am-8 pm; Sun to 3 pm, brunch from 11 am. Closed Dec 24, 25. Complete meals: bkfst $2.25-$5.95, lunch $4-$6.95, dinner $5.75-$14. Sun brunch $8.95. Child's meals. Specializes in Dutch cooking. Salad bar. Colonial decor; 1818 stagecoach stop. Totally nonsmoking. Cr cds: DS, MC, V.

D ♥

Hagerstown (A-4)

(See also Boonsboro, Frederick, Thurmont)

Settled 1762 **Pop** 35,445 **Elev** 552 ft **Area code** 301 **Zip** 21740

Information Hagerstown/Washington County Tourism Office, 16 Public Sq; 301/791-3246 or 800/228-7829.

Within the city of Hagerstown, there is a walking tour with points of interest marked on downtown sidewalks and walking paths in city parks. South Prospect Street is one of the city's oldest neighborhoods, listed on the National Register of Historic Places. The tree-lined street is graced by homes dating back to the early 1800s.

What to See and Do

Antietam National Battlefield (see). 11 mi S on MD 65.

Ft Frederick State Park. Erected in 1756, during French and Indian War, the fort is considered a fine example of a pre-Revolutionary stone fort. Overlooks Chesapeake and Ohio Canal National Historical Park (see); barracks, interior and wall of fort restored; military reenactments throughout year. Fishing; boating (rentals). Nature & hiking trails. Picnicking (shelter), playground. Unimproved camping. Museum, orientation film, historical programs. Standard fees. Winter hours may vary. 18 mi W of jct I-81 & I-70 to Big Pool, then 1 mi SE via MD 56, unnumbered road. Phone 301/842-2155.

Greenbrier State Park. The Appalachian Trail passes near this 1,275-acre park and its 42-acre man-made lake. Swimming (Memorial Day-Labor Day, daily); fishing; boating (rentals; no gas motors). Nature, hiking trails. Picnicking. Standard fees. 6 mi E via US 40. Phone 301/791-4767. ¢-¢¢

Hagerstown Roundhouse Museum. Museum houses photographic exhibits of the 7 railroads of Hagerstown; historic railroad memorabilia, tools and equipment; archives of maps, books, papers and related items. Gift shop. (Fri-Sun afternoons) (See ANNUAL EVENTS) 300 S Burhans Blvd, across the tracks from City Park. Phone 301/739-4665. ¢

Jonathan Hager House and Museum (1739). Stone house in park setting; authentic 18th-century furnishings. (Apr-Dec, daily exc Mon) 110 Key St, in City Park. Phone 301/739-8393. ¢¢

Miller House. Washington County Historical Society Headquarters. Federal town house (ca 1820); 3-story spiral staircase; period furnishings; garden; clock, doll and Bell pottery collections; Chesapeake & Ohio Canal and Civil War exhibits; 19th-century country store display. (Apr-Dec, Wed-Sat; closed major hols; also 1st 2 wks Dec) 135 W Washington St. Phone 301/797-8782. ¢¢

Washington County Museum of Fine Arts. Paintings, sculpture, changing exhibits; concerts, lectures. (Daily exc Mon; closed major hols) 91 Key St in City Park, S on US 11 (Virginia Ave). Phone 301/739-5727. **Free.**

Annual Events

Hagerstown Railroad Heritage Days. Special events centered on the Roundhouse Museum. For information and schedule phone 301/739-4665. Early May.

Halfway Park Days. Helicopter rides, antique cars, dance bands, flea market, food. Late May.

Jonathan Hager Frontier Craft Day. Colonial crafts demonstrated and exhibited. Bluegrass music; food. 1st wkend Aug.

Leitersburg Peach Festival. Peach-related edibles, farmers' market, bluegrass music. 2nd wkend Aug.

Williamsport C & O Canal Days. Arts and crafts, Indian Village, National Park Service activities; food. Late Aug.

Alsatia Mummers Halloween Parade Festival. Sat, wkend closest to Halloween.

Motel

★★★ **DAYS INN.** *900 Dual Hwy (US 40), I-81 exit 6A.* 301/739-9050; FAX 301/739-8347. 140 rms, 2 story. May-Oct: S $48-$58; D $54-$65; each addl $5; under 18 free; wkend rates; lower rates rest of yr. TV; cable (premium). Pool. Restaurant 6:30 am-2 pm, 5-9 pm. Bar 4:30-9:30 pm. Ck-out noon. Coin lndry. Meeting rms. Business servs avail. Refrigerators avail. Playground. Cr cds: A, C, D, DS, JCB, MC, V.

D ≈ ⚄ ⚑ SC

Motor Hotels

★★★ **BEST WESTERN VENICE INN.** *431 Dual Hwy (US 40), I-70 exit 32B, I-81 exit 6A.* 301/733-0830; FAX 301/733-4978. 220 rms, 2-5 story. Apr-Oct: S $58-$68; D $63-$73; each addl $6; suites $125-$250; under 18 free; lower rates rest of yr. Crib $6. Pet accepted, some restrictions. TV; cable (premium), VCR (movies). Pool. Complimentary coffee in lobby. Restaurant 6 am-10:30 pm. Rm serv. Bar; entertainment Tues-Sat. Ck-out noon. Meeting rms. Bellhops. Valet serv. Beauty shop. Airport transportation. Game rm. Golf adj. Exercise equipt; bicycles, treadmill. Refrigerators, microwaves avail. Whirlpool in suites. Cr cds: A, C, D, DS, MC, V.

D ⚓ ≈ ✗ ⚄ ⚑ SC

★★★ **FOUR POINTS BY SHERATON.** *1910 Dual Hwy (US 40), I-70 exit 32B.* 301/790-3010; FAX 301/733-4559. 108 rms, 2 story. S $60-$75; D $64-$79; each addl $6; suites $150; under 18 free. Crib $6. Pet accepted; $50 deposit. TV; cable (premium). Pool; whirlpool. Complimentary continental bkfst. Restaurant 6:30 am-10 pm; Sat, Sun 7 am-9 pm. Rm serv. Bar 11-2 am. Ck-out noon. Meeting rms. Business servs avail. Bellhops. Valet serv. Sundries. Free airport transportation. Exercise equipt; weights, bicycles, sauna. Microwaves avail. Cr cds: A, C, D, DS, MC, V.

D ⚓ ≈ ✗ ⚄ ⚑ SC

★★★ **HOWARD JOHNSON PLAZA.** *Halfway Blvd, at I-81 exit 5.* 301/797-2500; FAX 301/797-6209. 164 units, 6 story. S $63; D $68; each addl $8; suites $75-$89; under 18 free. Crib free. TV; cable (premium), VCR avail. Indoor pool; whirlpool, lifeguard. Complimentary coffee in rms. Restaurant 6:30 am-9 pm. Rm serv. Bar 11 am-11 pm. Ck-out noon. Meeting rms. Business servs avail. In-rm modem link. Valet serv. Free airport transportation. Exercise equipt; weight machines, bicycles, sauna. Refrigerators. Cr cds: A, C, D, DS, JCB, MC, V.

D ≈ ✗ ⚄ ⚑ SC

★★ **RAMADA INN CONVENTION CENTER.** *901 Dual Hwy (US 40), I-70 exit 32B.* 301/733-5100; FAX 301/733-9192. E-mail dave learn@aol.com; web nfris.com/~ramada/. 210 rms, 5 story. S $62-$69; D $67-$74; each addl $5; suites $95-$200; under 18 free. Crib free. TV; cable (premium). Indoor pool. Restaurant 6:30 am-9:30 pm; Sun to 9 pm. Rm serv. Bar noon-2 am. Ck-out 11 am. Coin lndry. Meeting rms. Business servs avail. Free airport transportation. Exercise equipt; weights, rowers. Some refrigerators, in-rm whirlpools. Cr cds: A, C, D, DS, MC, V.

D ≈ ✗ ⚐ ⚄ ⚑ SC

Inn

★★★ **BEAVER CREEK HOUSE.** *20432 Beaver Creek Rd, 4 mi E on I-70, exit 32A or 35, in village of Beaver Creek.* 301/797-4764. 5 rms, 2 with shower only. No rm phones. S $75-$85; D $85-$95; lower rates mid-wk. Children over 10 yrs only. TV in sitting rm. Complimentary full bkfst; afternoon refreshments. Ck-out 11 am, ck-in 1 pm. Business servs avail. Turn-of-the-century country home located in historic village; antique furnishings and family memorabilia; parlor with fireplace; library/sitting rm; scenic view of South Mountain. Cr cds: A, DS, MC, V.

⚄ ⚑

Restaurants

★★ **RAILROAD JUNCTION.** *808 Noland Dr, at jct US 11.* 301/791-3639. Hrs: 6 am-8:30 pm. Closed Sun; also July 4, Dec 24-26. Res accepted. Semi-a la carte: bkfst $1.50-$4.95, lunch $2.50-$4.25, dinner $4.95-$10.95. Child's meals. Specializes in seafood, lasagne, Cajun steak. Own pies. Located near railroad tracks. Fun atmosphere with railroad-theme decor and tapes of actual trains; model trains circle the room at the ceiling. Totally nonsmoking. No cr cds accepted.

SC

★★ **RED HORSE STEAK HOUSE.** *1800 Dual Hwy (US 40), I-70 exit 32B.* 301/733-3788. Hrs: 4-10 pm; Sun to 9 pm. Closed major hols. Res accepted; required Fri, Sat. Bar. Semi-a la carte: dinner $9.75-$19.95. Child's meals. Specializes in prime rib, broiled seafood, steak. Open-hearth grill. Western-style atmosphere. Family-owned. Cr cds: C, D, MC, V.

D ⚑

★★ **RICHARDSON'S.** *710 Dual Hwy (US 40W).* 301/733-3660. Hrs: 7 am-10 pm; Fri, Sat to 11 pm. Closed Dec 24 evening, Dec 25. Res accepted. Bar. Semi-a la carte: bkfst $1.95-$4.95, lunch $2.95-$6.95, dinner $5.95-$14.95. Buffet: bkfst $4.95, lunch $4.99, dinner $8.95-$18.95. Child's meals. Specializes in fried chicken, seafood, crab cakes. Salad bar. Own pies, cakes. 3 dining areas; railroad theme, memorabilia. Cr cds: DS, MC, V.

D SC

Havre De Grace (B-8)

(See also Aberdeen, Elkton)

Settled 1658 **Pop** 8,952 **Elev** 52 ft **Area code** 410 **Zip** 21078

Information Chamber of Commerce, 224 N Washington St, PO Box 339; 410/939-3303 or 800/851-7756.

What to See and Do

Concord Point Lighthouse (1827). Built of granite, considered the oldest continually used lighthouse on the East Coast. It was automated in 1928. (May-Oct, wkends & hols only) At foot of Lafayette St.   **Free.**

Decoy Museum. Houses a collection of hand-carved waterfowl decoys and interprets this art form as it applies to the heritage of Chesapeake Bay. (Daily; closed Jan 1, Thanksgiving, Dec 25) (See ANNUAL EVENTS) Giles & Market Sts, at the bay. Phone 410/939-3739.   ¢

Susquehanna State Park. A 2,639-acre park. Fishing. Boat launch. Nature, riding and hiking trails. Cross-country skiing. Picknicking. Camping (May-Sept; fee). (Schedule varies, phone ahead) 3 mi N via MD 155. Phone 410/557-7994. In the park is

Steppingstone Museum. Self-guided tour of museum grounds includes sites of a once working Harford County farm; farmhouse is
furnished as a turn-of-the-century country home; nearby shops and barn
hold many displays and exhibits of the 1880-1920 period; demonstrations of rural arts and crafts of the period. Also here are blacksmith,
woodworking, cooper and dairy shops. (May-1st Sun Oct, Sat & Sun
afternoons) Special events held throughout the year (see ANNUAL
EVENTS). 461 Quaker Bottom Rd. Phone 410/939-2299. ¢-¢¢

Annual Events

Decoy Festival. Decoys on display, auction. Carving, gunning & calling
contests. Refreshments. Phone 410/939-3739. Fri-Sun 1st wkend May.

Fall Harvest Festival & Craft Show. Steppingstone Museum. Features
activities related to the harvest and preparation for winter: apple pressing,
scarecrow stuffing and other events. Entertainment. Phone 410/939-2299.
Last full wkend Sept.

Inn

★ ★ ★ **VANDIVER.** *301 S Union Ave. 410/939-5200; res:
800/245-1655.* 8 rms, 3 story. S, D $75-$105; wkly rates. TV in parlor.
Complimentary bkfst. Dining rm Fri, Sat 6-9 pm. Some fireplaces. Some balconies. Queen Anne-style mansion (1886)
with antique furnishings. Chesapeake Bay 2 blks. Cr cds: A, DS, MC, V.

D ⚲ 🐾 SC

Restaurants

✔★ ★ **BAYOU.** *927 Pulaski Hwy (US 40). 410/939-3565.* Hrs:
11:30 am-10 pm. Closed Dec 24-26. Res accepted; required hols. Semi-a
la carte: lunch $3-$6.25, dinner $7.50-$13.50. Child's meals. Specializes
in seafood, veal. Cr cds: A, C, D, MC, V.

D ⛱

★ ★ **CRAZY SWEDE.** *400 N Union Ave. 410/939-5440.* Hrs:
11-2 am; Sun brunch 10 am-2:30 pm. Closed Thanksgiving, Dec 25. Res
accepted; required Fri & Sat. Continental menu. Bar. Semi-a la carte: lunch
$4.25-$6.95, dinner $11.95-$21. Sun brunch $3.50-$9. Child's meals.
Specializes in seafood. Cr cds: A, C, D, MC, V.

D

La Plata (D-6)

(See also Waldorf; also see District of Columbia)

Pop 5,841 **Elev** 193 ft **Area code** 301 **Zip** 20646
Information Charles County Chamber of Commerce, 6360 Crain Hwy,
phone 301/932-6500; or the Dept of Tourism, 301/645-0558.

What to See and Do

Doncaster Demonstration Forest. Heavily forested with yellow poplar,
sweet gum, red and white oaks, and pine throughout its 1,477 acres.
Hunting; 13 mi of hiking trails, bridle trails; picnic area. Cross-country
skiing. 13 mi W on MD 6, near Doncaster. Phone 301/934-2282.

Port Tobacco. Infrared aerial photography and archaeological excavation
revealed the site of one of the oldest continuously inhabited English
settlements in North America. Appearing as a Native American village on
Captain John Smith's map of the area (1608), the area was colonized by
the English as early as 1638. The town was chartered in 1727, and the first
courthouse was erected in 1729. Among the remaining buildings are the
Chimney House (1765) and Stagg Hall (1732), an original colonial home
still a private residence, Burch (Catslide) House (1700), the reconstructed
Quenzel Store, house and a Federal period courthouse, with the Port
Tobacco Museum on the second floor; archeological items on display,
replicas of colonial houses; Civil War and John Wilkes Booth exhibits,

30-min audiovisual film of *The Story of Port Tobacco.* (Apr-Dec, Sat & Sun
afternoons) 3 mi SW on MD 6. Phone 301/934-4313. ¢

Smallwood State Park. Restored home of Revolutionary General William
Smallwood. Guided tour and historical program during summer. Hiking.
Picnicking. Marina. Boating (launch, rentals). Fishing. Retreat House. Park
(daily). Standard fees. 16 mi W via MD 225, 224, near Rison. Phone
301/743-7613. Wkends ¢

Motel

✔★ ★ **BEST WESTERN.** *6900 Crain Hwy (S US 301). 301/934-
4900; FAX 301/934-5389.* 73 rms, 2 story, 8 suites. S $53-$57; D $58-$62;
each addl $5; suites $65-$80; under 13 free. Crib free. TV; cable (pre-
mium), VCR avail. Pool. Complimentary continental bkfst. Restaurant adj
11 am-11 pm. Ck-out noon. Coin lndry. Meeting rm. Business servs avail.
Exercise equipt; stair machine, weights. Refrigerators. Picnic table. Cr cds:
A, C, D, DS, MC, V.

D ⚲ ✈ 🐾 SC

Laurel (C-6)

*(See also Bowie, College Park, Silver Spring; also see District of Colum-
bia)*

Pop 19,438 **Elev** 160 ft **Area code** 301
Information Corridor Information Centers, PO Box 288, Savage 20763;
301/490-2444. There are 2 information centers open daily except holidays
at the northbound and southbound rest areas on I-195 just outside of
Laurel.

What to See and Do

Montpelier Mansion (ca 1780). Built and owned for generations by Maryland's Snowden family; Georgian architecture. George Washington and
Abigail Adams were among its early visitors. On the grounds are boxwood
gardens, an 18th-century herb garden and a small summer house. Tours;
purchase ticket in gift shop. (Mar-Nov, Sun afternoons; groups by appt;
closed major hols) Candlelight tours held in early Dec. 3 mi SE on MD 197
at Muirkirk. Phone 301/953-1376. ¢¢

National Wildlife Visitor Center. 12,750-acre national wildlife refuge and
research area. Interactive exhibits focus on global environmental issues,
migratory birds, wildlife habitats and endangered species. Tram tours avail
of surrounding forests and lakes (weather permitting; fee). Trails. Gift shop.
(Daily; closed Dec 25) 10901 Scarlet Tanager Loop. Phone 301/497-5760.
Free.

Seasonal Event

Thoroughbred racing. Laurel Race Course, on MD 198. Entrances accessible from northbound or southbound on US 1, I-95 or from Baltimore-
Washington Pkwy, MD 198 exit. Phone 301/725-0400 or 800/638-1859 for
current racing schedule.

Motel

★ ★ **HOLIDAY INN.** *3400 Ft Meade Rd (20724), MD 198 &
Baltimore/ Washington Pkwy. 301/498-0900; FAX 301/498-0900, ext. 160.*
115 rms, 2 story. S $69-$84; D $74-$94; each addl $10; under 18 free. Crib
free. TV; cable (premium), VCR avail. Pool; lifeguard. Complimentary
coffee in rms. Restaurant 6:30 am-2 pm, 5-10 pm. Rm serv from 7 am. Bar
4 pm-midnight. Ck-out 11 am. Coin lndry. Meeting rms. Business servs
avail. In-rm modem link. Valet serv. Exercise equipt; weight machine,
bicycle. Health club privileges. Refrigerators, microwaves avail. Cr cds: A,
C, D, DS, ER, JCB, MC, V.

D ⚲ ✈ 🐾 SC

Motor Hotel

★ ★ **COMFORT SUITES.** *14402 Laurel Place (20707),* US 1 at Laurel Lakes Center. 301/206-2600; FAX 301/725-0056. Web www.mupages.com/washdc/comfortsuites. 119 rms, 5 story. S, D $80-$100; each addl $10; suites $95-$125; under 18 free; wkly, wkend rates; higher rates: cherry blossom, Memorial Day wkend. Crib free. Pet accepted; $50 refundable. TV; cable (premium). Indoor pool; whirlpool, lifeguard. Complimentary continental bkfst. Complimentary coffee in rms. Restaurant nearby. Ck-out noon. Coin lndry. Meeting rms. Business servs avail. Sundries. Valet serv. Airport transportation. Exercise equipt; treadmill, bicycles. Refrigerators, microwaves. Cr cds: A, C, D, DS, ER, JCB, MC, V.

Leonardtown (E-7)

(For accommodations see St Mary's City; also see District of Columbia)

Pop 1,475 **Elev** 87 ft **Area code** 301 **Zip** 20650 **E-mail** stmcdecd@mail.ameritel.net **Web** www.somd.lib.md.us/STMA/government/stmcdecd.html

Information St Mary's County Division of Tourism, PO Box 653; 301/475-4411 or 800/327-9023.

What to See and Do

Calvert Marine Museum. Museum complex with exhibits relating to the culture and marine environment of Chesapeake Bay and Patuxent River estuary; fossils of marine life; estuarine biology displays, aquariums, touch-tank; maritime history exhibits, including boat-building gallery. Also here is the restored Drum Point Lighthouse, built 1883; 1/2 mi S is the JC Lore Oyster House, with exhibits on the area's seafood industry. Gift shop. (Daily; closed Jan 1, Thanksgiving, Dec 25) 1 mi SE on MD 5, then 11 mi NE on MD 4, cross bridge and turn right on Solomons Island Rd; follow signs. Phone 410/326-2042. Main exhibit building **¢¢**

Old Jail Museum. Local historical exhibits housed in old jail; also a genealogy library for researchers. A cannon from Leonard Calvert's ship, the *Ark,* is mounted in front. (Tues-Sat; closed hols; also last wk Dec) 11 Court House Dr. Phone 301/475-2467. **Free.**

Sotterley Plantation (ca 1715). Overlooks Patuxent River. Working plantation; house in original condition. Chinese Chippendale staircase, antiques, original pine paneling in three rooms. Farming exhibit. (Grounds open May-Oct, daily exc Mon; individual tours of manor house on wkends; group tours by appt only) 9 mi E on MD 245. Phone 301/373-2280. **¢¢¢**

St Clements Island-Potomac River Museum. Maryland colonists first landed on the island in 1634. Exhibits trace 12,000 yrs of local history and pre-history. Museum includes Little Red School House (ca 1840) and country store. Picnic area; fishing and crabbing. (Late Mar-Sept, Mon-Fri, also Sat, Sun afternoons; rest of yr, Wed-Sun afternoons; closed major hols) 5 mi W via MD 234 to Clements, then 9 mi S on MD 242, in Colton Point. Phone 301/769-2222. **¢**

Annual Events

St Mary's County Fair. Midway, seafood, horse shows. Phone 301/475-2707. Late Sept.

Blessing of the Fleet & Historical Pageant. St Clements Island, Potomac River Museum. Celebration commemorates first Roman Catholic Mass held on Maryland soil and Governor Leonard Calvert's proclamation of religious freedom. Blessing of oyster and clam fishing fleets. Folk dances, historical exhibits, concerts. Boat rides to the island. Phone 301/769-2222. 1st wkend Oct.

St Mary's County Oyster Festival. County Fairgrounds. National oyster shucking contest; oyster cook-off; seafood and crafts. Phone 301/863-5015. 3rd wkend Oct.

Oakland (Garrett Co) (B-1)

Settled 1851 **Pop** 1,741 **Elev** 2,384 ft **Area code** 301 **Zip** 21550 **E-mail** gctourism@garrett.ncin.com **Web** www.gcnet.net/gctourism/gct.html

Information Deep Creek Lake/Garrett County Promotion Council, Courthouse Building, 200 S Third St; 301/334-1948 or 301/387-6171.

What to See and Do

Backbone Mt. Highest point in the state (3,360 ft). 8 mi S on US 219, then 2 mi E on US 50.

Deep Creek Lake State Park. Approx 1,800 acres with 3,900-acre man-made lake. Swimming, bathhouse; fishing, boating (rowboat rentals). Nature, hiking trails. Picnicking (shelters), playground, concession. Improved campsites (fee). From I-68, 10 mi SE off US 219. For general information and camping reservations phone 301/387-5563 (reservations accepted up to 1 yr in advance). Entrance for day-use area, per person **¢**

Garrett State Forest. Approx 6,800 acres. The forest contains much wildlife. Fishing, hunting. Hiking and riding trails. Winter activities. Primitive camping. Forestry demonstration area. 5 mi NW on County 20. Phone 301/334-2038. Within the forest are

Herrington Manor State Park. Well-developed 365-acre park with housekeeping cabins, 53-acre lake. Swimming, fishing, boating (launch, rentals). Hiking trails. Concession. Picnicking. Cross-country skiing (rentals). Interpretive programs (summer). No pets. Standard fees. Phone 301/334-9180.

Swallow Falls State Park. Surrounding 257 acres, the Youghiogheny River tumbles along the park's boundaries, passing through shaded rocky gorges and over sunny rapids. Muddy Creek produces a 52-ft waterfall. Here the last remaining stand of virgin hemlock dwarfs visitors. Fishing. Nature trails, hiking. Picnicking. Improved campsites. Pets at registered campsites only. Standard fees. Phone 301/334-9180.

Potomac State Forest. More than 10,685 acres for hiking, riding and hunting. Primitive camping. Timber is harvested regularly here and the area is important in the management of watershed and wildlife programs. 9 mi SE off MD 560, along Potomac River. Phone 301/334-2038.

Annual Events

Winterfest. Deep Creek Lake in McHenry. Ski races, parade, fireworks. Late Feb or early Mar.

McHenry Highland Festival. Deep Creek Lake. Traditional Scottish and Celtic festival. 1st Sat June.

Garrett County Fair. McHenry Fairgrounds. Early Aug.

Autumn Glory Festival. Celebrates fall foliage. Features arts and crafts, five-string banjo contest, state fiddle contest, western Maryland tournament of bands, parades, antique show. Phone 301/334-1948. Mid-Oct.

Motels

✔★ ★ **ALPINE VILLAGE.** *19638 Garrett Highway,* 7 mi N on US 219. 301/387-5534; res: 800/343-5253. 29 motel rms, 2 story, 8 kits., 14 kit. chalets. June-Sept: S, D $60-$80; each addl $5; kit. units, studio rms $70; chalets for 1-6, $550-$750/wk; lower rates rest of yr. Crib free. TV; cable. Heated pool; wading pool. Continental bkfst avail for motel rms. Restaurant 5-11 pm; Sun from 4 pm. Bar 5-11 pm. Ck-out 11 am. Downhill/x-country ski 5 mi. On lake; private sand beach; dock. Some private patios. Picnic table, grills. Cr cds: A, D, DS, MC, V.

★ **LAKE BREEZ.** *20050 Garrett Hwy,* 9 mi N on US 219. 301/387-5503. 10 rms. May-Nov 1: S, D $62; each addl $4; cottage for 2-6, $468-$900 wk; MAP avail. Closed rest of yr. Crib free. TV. Pool privileges.

Restaurant adj 7 am-2 pm, 5-9:30 pm. Ck-out 11 am. On lake; private beach, dock. Picnic tables. Cr cds: A, D, DS, MC, V.

★ **LAKE SIDE MOTOR COURT.** *19956 Garrett Hwy, 8 mi N on US 219.* 301/387-5566, ext. 2205. 10 rms, 1 cottage. Mid-June-Labor Day: S, D $64; each addl $4; cottage for 2-6, $468-$900/wk; MAP avail; lower rates weekdays; May-mid-June, after Labor Day-Oct. Closed rest of yr. TV; cable. Pool privileges. Playground. Restaurant adj 7 am-2 pm, 5-9:30 pm. Ck-out 11 am. Refrigerators. Picnic area, grills. Overlooks lake; private swimming beach; dock. Cr cds: A, D, DS, MC, V.

Restaurants

★ ★ **POINT VIEW INN.** *(Deep Creek Dr, McHenry 21541) 8 mi N on US 219.* 301/387-5555. Hrs: 8 am-10 pm; Sun to 9 pm; early-bird dinner 5-6:30 pm. Closed Easter, Dec 25. Res accepted. German, Amer menu. Bar 1 pm-2 am. Semi-a la carte: bkfst $3-$6, lunch $2.75-$6.50, dinner $6.50-$21. Child's meals. Specialities: veal Cordon Bleu, Rahmschnitzel, prime rib. Entertainment wkends. Patio dining. Elevated dining areas with view of Deep Creek Lake. Cr cds: A, MC, V.

★ ★ **SILVER TREE.** *19638 Garrett Highway, 8 blks N on Glendale Rd.* 301/387-4040. Hrs: 5-10 pm; Sat to 11 pm; summer hrs: 4-10 pm. Italian, Amer menu. Bar to 2 am. Semi-a la carte: dinner $5.95-$20. Child's meals. Specializes in pasta, seafood, steak. 1890s decor. Stone fireplaces. View of lake. Cr cds: A, C, D, DS, MC, V.

Ocean City (E-10)

Founded 1869 **Pop** 5,146 **Elev** 7 ft **Area code** 410 **Zip** 21842
Information Chamber of Commerce, 12320 Ocean Gateway; 410/213-0552.

Deep-sea fishing is highly regarded in Maryland's only Atlantic Ocean resort. The white sand beach, three-mile boardwalk, amusements, golf courses and boating draw thousands of visitors every summer.

What to See and Do

⭐ **Assateague Island National Seashore.** A 37-mi barrier strand that supports an intricate ecosystem, Assateague is also known for its population of ponies, Sika deer (miniature Oriental elk) and, in autumn, the migratory peregrine falcon. Campground (fee; phone 410/641-3030); hike-in and canoe-in campsites and day-use facilities; conducted walks and demonstrations in summer. Visitor center (daily; closed winter hols). 1 mi W on US 50, then 7 mi S on MD 611. For further information phone 410/641-1441. For camping reservations phone 800/365-2267. (See CHINCOTEAGUE, VA) Per vehicle ¢¢ Also on the island is

Assateague State Park. Has 755 acres with 2 mi of ocean frontage and gentle, sloping beaches. Swimming, fishing. Boat launch. Picnicking, concession (summer). Bicycle, hiking trails. Camping (Apr-Oct). Standard fees (summer). For reservations, contact 7307 Stephen Decatur Hwy, Berlin 21811. Phone 410/641-2120. Entrance fee (Memorial Day-Labor Day) ¢

Annual Event

Fishing contests and tournaments. Many held throughout the yr. For exact dates contact the Chamber of Commerce.

Seasonal Event

Harness racing. Ocean Downs. 4 mi W on US 50. Nightly exc Mon. Children with adult only. Phone 410/641-0600. Late July-Labor Day.

Motels

★ **BEACHMARK.** *7300 Coastal Hwy, at 73rd St.* 410/524-7300; res: 800/638-1600. 96 kit. units, 3 story. No elvtr. July-Aug: S, D $94; under 6 free; each addl $8; wkly rates; higher rates wkends & hols (3-day min); lower rates May-June & Sept. Closed rest of yr. TV; cable. Pool. Restaurant 6 am-2 pm. Ck-out 11 am. Bellhops (in season). Beach ½ blk. Cr cds: MC, V.

★ ★ **BEST WESTERN FLAGSHIP.** *2600 Baltimore Ave, 26th & Oceanfront.* 410/289-3384; FAX 410/289-1743. 93 rms, 3 story. Late June-late Aug (3-day min wkends): S, D $159-$179; under 5 free; closed 2 wks Dec & wkdays Dec 26-Feb 14; lower rates rest of yr. Crib free. TV; cable (premium), VCR (movies free). 2 pools (1 indoor); wading pool, whirlpool, poolside serv. Playground. Dinner buffet avail May-Sept. Ck-out 11 am. Guest lndry. Business servs avail. Lighted tennis. Exercise equipt; weight machine, bicycle, sauna. Game rm. Rec rm. Many kit. units. Cr cds: A, C, D, DS, MC, V.

★ ★ ★ **CASTLE IN THE SAND.** *3701 Atlantic Ave, Oceanfront at 37th St.* 410/289-6846; FAX 410/289-9446; res: 800/552-7263. 36 rms, 5 story, 27 cottages, 108 kit. units. Early July-late Aug: S, D $143-$169; each addl $8; kit. units $159-$200; cottages $750-$1,225/wk; under 12 free; lower rates mid-Apr-early July & late Aug-late Oct. Closed rest of yr. Crib $5. TV; cable (premium). Pool; lifeguard. Supervised child's activities (June-Aug); ages 3-16. Restaurant 7:30 am-midnight. Bar 11-2 am; entertainment wkends. Ck-out 11 am. Meeting rm. Business servs avail. In-rm modem link. Bellhops. Free airport transportation avail. Game rm. Refrigerators. Some balconies. Cr cds: A, D, DS, MC, V.

✔★ **EXECUTIVE.** *30th St & Baltimore Ave.* 410/289-3101; res: 800/638-1600. 47 rms, 3 story. No elvtr. Memorial Day wkend & July-Labor Day (3-day min wkends): S, D $74-$84; each addl $6; under 6 free; lower rates late May-June & after Labor Day-mid-Sept. Closed rest of yr. Crib $6. TV; cable. Restaurant nearby. Ck-out 11 am. Refrigerators. Ocean, beach ½ blk. Cr cds: MC, V.

★ **GATEWAY.** *4800 Coastal Hwy.* 410/524-6500; FAX 410/524-5374; res: 800/382-2582. 59 kit. units, 3 story. July-mid-Aug: S, D $170-$220; each addl $10; suites $1,110/wk; under 6 free; higher rates hol wkends; lower rates rest of yr. Crib $10. TV; cable (premium). Pool; wading pool, whirlpool, lifeguard (summer). Playground. Complimentary coffee in rms. Restaurant 11-2 am. Rm serv. Bar; entertainment. Ck-out 11 am. Coin lndry. Business servs avail. Lawn games. Balconies. Picnic tables. On ocean, swimming beach. Cr cds: A, C, D, DS, MC, V.

★ **NASSAU.** *6002 Coastal Hwy.* 410/524-6451. 63 rms, 3 story, 42 kits. No elvtr. July-late Aug: S, D $92-$112; each addl $6; higher rates wkends; lower rates Apr-June & late Aug-Oct. Closed rest of yr. Crib avail. TV; cable (premium). Pool. Coffee in rms. Restaurant opp 7 am-11 pm. Ck-out 11 am. Refrigerators. Sun deck. On ocean, beach. Cr cds: A, DS, MC, V.

★ ★ **QUALITY INN BEACHFRONT.** *3301 Atlantic Ave, at Oceanfront.* 410/289-1234. 73 kit. units, 5 story. Mid-July-Aug: S, D $180-$200; lower rates rest of yr. Crib free. TV; cable, VCR (movies). 2 pools, 1 indoor; wading pool, whirlpool, sauna. Restaurant 7:30 am-2 pm. Restaurant nearby. Ck-out 11 am. Sundries. Coin lndry. Business servs avail. Game rm. Balconies. Cr cds: A, C, D, DS, MC, V.

★ ★ **QUALITY INN OCEANFRONT.** *5400 Coastal Hwy, Oceanfront & 54th St.* 410/524-7200; FAX 410/723-0018. 130 kit. units, 3-5 story. Memorial Day-Labor Day: kit. units $76-$229; each addl $5; under 6 free; wkly rates; package plans; higher rates hols; varied lower rates rest of yr. Crib free. TV; cable (premium), VCR (movies). 2 pools, 1 indoor; whirlpool, wading pool. Playground. Restaurant 8 am-9 pm. Bar 11 am-11 pm. Ck-out 11 am. Free lndry facilities. Business servs avail. In-rm modem link. Bellhops (summer). Tennis. Exercise equipt; weights, bicycles, saunas. Game rm. Lawn games. Private patios, balconies. Picnic tables, grills. On ocean, swimming beach. Tropical atrium. Cr cds: A, C, D, DS, ER, JCB, MC, V.

D ⚽ ≈ ⚔ ⊠ 🐾 SC

★ ★ **RAMADA LIMITED OCEANFRONT.** *3200 Baltimore Ave, 32nd St at oceanfront.* 410/289-6444; FAX 410/289-0108. 76 kit. units, 3 story. No elvtr. July-Aug: S, D $149-$179; each addl $7; surcharge off-season wkends; lower rates rest of yr. Crib free. TV; cable (premium), VCR (movies). Pool; wading pool. Complimentary bkfst. Complimentary coffee in lobby. Ck-out 11 am. Guest lndry. Balconies overlook beach. Picnic area. Cr cds: A, C, D, DS, ER, MC, V.

D ≈ ⊠ 🐾

★ **SAFARI.** *Boardwalk at 13th St.* 410/289-6411; res: 800/787-2183. 46 rms in 2 bldgs, 3 & 4 story. July-Aug (3-day min wkends): S, D $98; under 12 free; lower rates Apr-June & Sept-Oct. Closed rest of yr. Crib free. Pet accepted, some restrictions; $7. TV; cable (premium). Restaurant opp from 8 am. Ck-out 11 am. Bellhops. Balconies. On ocean. Cr cds: A, C, D, DS, MC, V.

D ⚽ 🐾 SC

✔ ★ **SAHARA.** *19th and Baltimore Ave.* 410/289-8101; res: 800/638-1600. 161 rms in 4 bldgs, 3 & 4 story, 5 kits. Elvtr in Tower bldg. Late June-mid-Sept: S, D $72-$136; each addl $6; kit. units $88-$138; lower rates late Apr-late June & late Sept. Closed rest of yr. Crib $6. TV. 2 pools. Restaurant 6 am-3 pm. Ck-out 11 am. Refrigerators. Some balconies. On beach. Cr cds: MC, V.

D ≈ 🐾

★ ★ **SATELLITE.** *2401 Atlantic Ave, Oceanfront & 24th St.* 410/289-6401; FAX 410/289-5522. 72 units, 4 story, 26 kits. July-Aug: S, D $102-$113; each addl $8; kit. units $108-$124; under 6 free; wkly rates; varied lower rates Mar-June & Sept-Oct. Closed rest of yr. Crib $8. TV; cable (premium). Pool. Restaurant 7 am-2 pm. Ck-out 11 am. Business servs avail. Bellhops. Refrigerators. Balconies. On beach. Cr cds: A, MC, V.

D ≈ 🐾

★ ★ **SURF AND SANDS.** *Boardwalk at 23rd St.* 410/289-7161; FAX 410/289-6525. 95 rms, 2-3 story, 20 kits. July-late Aug: S, D $100-$123; each addl $8; suites $140; kit. units $110-$120; under 7 free; wkends in season (3-day min); lower rates Easter-June & late Aug-mid-Oct. Closed rest of yr. Crib $8. TV; cable (premium). Pool; wading pool. Restaurant 7 am-9 pm. Ck-out 11 am. Business servs avail. Refrigerators. Balconies. On beach. Cr cds: MC, V.

D ≈ 🐾

★ **TIDES.** *71st St & Oceanside.* 410/524-7100; res: 800/638-1600. 54 kit. units, 3 story. No elvtr. Late June-late Aug: S, D $92; each addl $8; under 6 free; higher rates: wkends & hols (3-day min), July-Aug wkdays (2-day min), Memorial Day & Labor Day; lower rates May-late June & Sept. Closed rest of yr. Crib $5. TV; cable. Pool. Restaurant nearby. Ck-out 11 am. Bellhops (in season). Some balconies. Ocean ½ blk. Cr cds: MC, V.

D ≈ 🐾

Motor Hotels

★ ★ **BRIGHTON SUITES.** *12500 Coastal Hwy.* 410/250-7600; FAX 410/250-7603; res: 800/227-5788. 57 suites. July-Aug: suites $109-$189; each addl $10; under 16 free; wkly, mid-wk rates; lower rates rest of yr. Crib $6. TV; cable (premium). Indoor pool. Complimentary coffee in lobby. Ck-out 11 am. Meeting rms. Business servs avail. Bellhops (in season). Exercise equipt; weight machine, bicycles. Refrigerators, wet bars. Balconies. Near ocean beach. Cr cds: A, C, D, DS, MC, V.

D ≈ ⚔ ⊠ 🐾 SC

★ ★ **COMFORT INN BOARDWALK.** *507 Atlantic Ave, 5th St and Boardwalk.* 410/289-5155; res: 800/282-5155. 84 kit. units in 2 bldgs, 5 story. June-Aug: S, D $135-$189; each addl $10; under 12 free; lower rates Mar-May & Sept-Nov. Closed rest of yr. Crib free. TV; cable (premium). Pool. Complimentary continental bkfst. Restaurant nearby. Ck-out 11 am. Bellhops. Balconies. On ocean. Cr cds: A, C, D, DS, ER, JCB, MC, V.

D ≈ ⊠ 🐾 SC

★ ★ ★ **HOLIDAY INN OCEANFRONT.** *6600 Coastal Hwy/Oceanfront, Oceanfront & 67th St.* 410/524-1600; FAX 410/524-1135. 216 kit. units, 8 story. Memorial Day-Labor Day: S, D $150-$239; each addl $9; under 19 free; higher rates hol wkends; golf plans; lower rates rest of yr. Crib free. TV; cable (premium). 2 pools, 1 indoor; wading pools, whirlpool, poolside serv. Supervised child's activities (June-Aug); ages 5-9. Restaurant 6:30 am-1 pm, 5-10 pm. Rm serv. Bar 5-midnight. Ck-out 11 am. Free lndry facilities. Meeting rms. Business servs avail. In-rm modem link. Bellhops. Tennis. Exercise equipt; weight machines, bicycle, sauna. Game rm. Balconies. Picnic tables. On ocean. Cr cds: A, C, D, DS, ER, JCB, MC, V.

D ⚽ ≈ ⚔ ⊠ 🐾 SC

★ ★ **HOWARD JOHNSON.** *1109 Atlantic Ave, 12th & Boardwalk.* 410/289-7251; FAX 410/289-3435. 90 rms, 7 story. Mid-June-Labor Day: S, D $109-$184; each addl $5; under 12 free; lower rates rest of yr. Crib free. TV; cable (premium). Indoor pool. Restaurant 8 am-10 pm. Rm serv in season. Ck-out 11 am. Business servs avail. Valet serv. Sundries. Gift shop. Free garage parking. Some refrigerators. Balconies. On ocean beach. Cr cds: A, D, DS, MC, V.

D ≈ ⊠ 🐾 SC

★ ★ **PHILLIPS BEACH PLAZA.** *1301 Atlantic Ave, Boardwalk at 13th St.* 410/289-9121; FAX 410/289-3041; res: 800/492-5834. 96 units, 5 story, 26 kits., 8 3-bdrm kit. suites. July-late Aug: S, D $115-$165; each addl $10; kit. units $130-$165; kit. suites $135-$170; $20 surcharge wkends; package plans; lower rates rest of yr. Crib $10. TV; cable. Restaurant 8 am-noon, 5-10 pm. Bar 5 pm-2 am; entertainment 6-11 pm. Ck-out 11 am. Business servs avail. Bellhops. Shopping arcade. On ocean. Cr cds: A, C, D, DS, MC, V.

🐾

✔ ★ **PLIM PLAZA.** *Boardwalk & 2nd St.* 410/289-6181; FAX 410/289-7686; res: 800/638-2106. 181 units, 5 story. June-Aug: S, D $79-$128; wkly rates; package plans; lower rates mid-Apr-June & Sept. Closed rest of yr. Crib free. TV; cable (premium). Pool; whirlpool. Restaurant 4:30-9 pm. Ck-out 11 am. Meeting rms. Business servs avail. Bellhops. Rec rm. Refrigerators. Some private patios. On boardwalk. Cr cds: C, D, DS, ER, MC, V.

⚽ ≈ 🐾

Hotels

★ ★ ★ **COCONUT MALORIE.** *201 60th St, on Isle of Wight Bay, 59th St exit.* 410/723-6100; FAX 410/524-9327; res: 800/767-6060. E-mail island@mv.com; web www.ocean-city.com/fagers.htm. 85 suites, 5 story. Memorial Day-Labor Day: S, D $164-$279; each addl $15; wkly rates; lower rates rest of yr. Crib $15. TV; cable (premium), VCR avail. Pool; poolside serv. Complimentary coffee in rms. Restaurant adj 11 am-11 pm. Ck-out noon. Meeting rms. Business servs avail. In-rm modem link. Concierge. Health club privileges. Refrigerators; many bathrm phones. Balconies. Original Haitian art; antique collection. Footbridge over marsh to dining facilities. Cr cds: A, C, D, MC, V.

D ≈ ⊠ 🐾

★ ★ ★ **LIGHTHOUSE CLUB.** *56th St In The Bay, on Isle of Wight Bay.* 410/524-5400; FAX 410/524-9327; res: 800/767-6060. E-mail is land@dmv.com; web www.ocean-city.com/fagers.htm. Rooms are wedge-shaped with spectacular views of the bay in this luxuriously appointed hotel, which was designed to resemble an archetypal Chesapeake Bay lighthouse. 23 rms, 3 story. No elvtr. Mid-June-Labor Day (2-day min): S, D $174-$259; each addl $15; under 6 free; wkly rates; hols 3-day min; lower rates rest of yr. Crib $15. TV; cable (premium), VCR avail. Pool privileges. Complimentary continental bkfst. Complimentary coffee in rms. Restaurant adj 11 am-11 pm. Rm serv 11 am-11 pm. Bar 11-2 am; entertainment. Ck-out noon. Meeting rm. Business servs avail. In-rm modem link. Gift shop. Airport transportation. Health club privileges. Bathrm phones, in-rm whirlpools, refrigerators, wet bars; some fireplaces. Balconies. Cr cds: A, C, D, DS, MC, V.

★ ★ ★ **PRINCESS ROYALE.** *9100 Coastal Hwy, 3 mi N on Coastal Hwy.* 410/524-7777; FAX 410/524-7787; res: 800/476-9253. 310 kit. suites, 5 story. Mid-June-Labor Day: D $109-$289; under 12 free; wkly rates; golf plans; lower rates rest of yr. Crib $10. TV; cable (premium). Indoor pool; whirlpool, poolside serv. Complimentary coffee in rms. Restaurant 7-2 am. Bar 11-2 am; entertainment. Ck-out 11 am. Coin lndry. Convention facilities. Business center. Beauty shop. Lighted tennis. 18-hole golf privileges, pro, putting green, driving range. Exercise equipt; weight machine, bicycles, sauna. Game rm. Rec rm. Balconies. On ocean; swimming beach, ocean deck, private boardwalk. All suites with ocean view. Cr cds: A, C, D, DS, MC, V.

★ ★ ★ **SHERATON FONTAINEBLEAU.** *10100 Ocean Hwy (MD 528).* 410/524-3535; FAX 410/524-3834. 250 rms, 16 story, 8 kits. June-Aug: S, D $150-$245; each addl $15; suites, kit. units $285-$315; studio rms $220-$270; condos $1,600-$2,000/wkly; under 17 free; higher rates hol wknds (3-day min); lower rates rest of yr. Crib $15. Pet accepted; $15. TV; cable (premium), VCR avail. Heated pool; whirlpool, poolside serv in season, lifeguard. Coffee in rms. Restaurant 6:30 am-11 pm. Bar to 2 am; entertainment. Ck-out 11 am. Meeting rms. Business center. In-rm modem link. Beauty shop. Airport, bus depot transportation. Exercise rm; instructor, weights, bicycles, stairs, steam rm, sauna. Tennis privileges. Golf privileges. Game rm. Refrigerators. Balconies. On ocean, beach. Cr cds: A, C, D, DS, ER, JCB, MC, V.

Inns

★ ★ ★ **ATLANTIC HOTEL.** *(2 N Main St, Berlin 21811) 8 mi W on MD 50 to MD 113, S to Berlin, right on Bay St to Main St.* 410/641-3589; FAX 410/641-4928. 17 rms, 3 story. S, D $75-$140; golf plans. Crib free. TV. Complimentary bkfst. Dining rm 6-10 pm. Bar noon-1 am. Ck-out 11 am, ck-in 3 pm. 18-hole golf privileges, greens fee $30-$35, pro, putting green. Porch on each floor. Restored Victorian hotel (1895); rms furnished with antiques. 2nd-floor parlor. Cr cds: A, MC, V.

★ ★ **MERRY SHERWOOD PLANTATION.** *(8909 Worcester Hwy, Berlin 21811) 8 mi W on US 50, then 3 mi S on MD 113.* 410/641-2112; res: 800/660-0358. 8 rms, 6 with bath. No rm phones. D $150-$175; wkly rates. Children over 8 yrs only. Complimentary full bkfst; afternoon refreshments. Restaurant nearby. Ck-out 11 am, ck-in 2 pm. Built in 1859; on grounds of former plantation; large variety of trees and shrubs. Totally nonsmoking. Cr cds: MC, V.

Restaurants

✔ ★ ★ **ANGELO'S.** *2706 Coastal Hwy.* 410/289-6522. Hrs: 4-10 pm. Closed Jan; also Tues Oct-Apr. Res accepted. Italian menu. Serv bar. Semi-a la carte: dinner $7-$15.95. Child's meals. Specializes in veal, seafood. Own pasta. Outdoor dining. Cr cds: A, C, D, DS, MC, V.

★ ★ **BONFIRE.** *71st St & Coastal Hwy.* 410/524-7171. Hrs: 5-10 pm; from 4 pm in season; early-bird dinner 5-6 pm. Closed Sun-Wed in winter. Res accepted. Bar to 2 am. Semi-a la carte: dinner $14.95-$25.95. Seafood buffet $20.95. Child's meals. Specializes in steak, prime rib, seafood. Cr cds: A, C, D, MC, V.

★ ★ **EMBERS.** *24th St & Philadelphia Ave.* 410/289-3322. Hrs: 3-10 pm; also 7:30 am-1 pm Memorial Day wkend-mid-Oct. Closed Dec-Feb. Res accepted. Bar to 2 am. Buffet: bkfst $6.99. Semi-a la carte: dinner $14-$25. Seafood buffet $20.95. Child's meals. Specializes in fresh seafood, steak, prime rib. Family-owned. Cr cds: A, MC, V.

★ ★ **FAGER'S ISLAND.** *201 60th St, in the Bay.* 410/524-5500. E-mail island@dmv.com; web www.oceancity.com/fagers.htm. Hrs: 11 am-11 pm. Res accepted. Bar. Semi-a la carte: lunch $3.75-$10.95, dinner $17-$25. Specializes in seafood, beef, roast duckling. Entertainment. View of bay. Oudoor dining in season. Cr cds: A, C, D, MC, V.

★ ★ **HANNA'S MARINA DECK.** *306 Dorchester St.* 410/289-4411. Hrs: 11 am-11 pm. Closed mid-Oct-Easter. Bar. Semi-a la carte: lunch $4.95-$7.95, dinner $7.95-$27.95. Child's meals. Specializes in fish, lobster, coconut muffins. On waterfront. Cr cds: A, DS, MC, V.

★ ★ ★ **HARRISON'S HARBOR WATCH.** *806 S. Boardwalk.* 410/289-5121. Hrs: 5-10 pm; July-Aug from 4:30 pm. Closed Mon-Thurs Nov-Mar. Res accepted. Bar. Wine list. Semi-a la carte: dinner $8.95-$24.95. Child's meals. Specializes in fresh seafood, fish. Raw bar. Own breads. View of inlet overlooking Assateague Island. Cr cds: A, C, D, DS, ER, MC, V.

★ ★ ★ **HOBBIT.** *81st St & Bay.* 410/524-8100. Hrs: 11-2 am; early-bird dinner 5-6 pm. Closed Dec 24-25. Res accepted. French, Amer menu. Bar. Wine list. Semi-a la carte: lunch $3.95-$9.95, dinner $15.95-$21.95. Child's meals. Specializes in beef, seafood. Own baking. Outdoor dining. View of bay. Cr cds: A, DS, MC, V.

★ ★ **MARIO'S.** *2204 Philadelphia Ave.* 410/289-9445. Hrs: 5-10 pm. Closed 10 days beginning mid-Dec; also Mon Oct-Memorial Day. Res accepted. Italian, Amer menu. Bar. Semi-a la carte: dinner $7.95-$23. Child's meals. Specializes in steak. Family-owned. Cr cds: A, D, MC, V.

★ ★ **OCEAN CLUB.** *49th St at Oceanfront.* 410/524-7500. Hrs: 11:30-2 am; early-bird dinner 5-7 pm; Memorial Day-Labor Day wkends from 10 am. Closed Dec 25; Tues off-season. Res accepted. Bar. Semi-a la carte: bkfst $3.25-$9.95, lunch $5-$10, dinner $9.95-$25.95. Child's meals. Specializes in seafood. Entertainment Apr-Oct; rest of yr, wkends only. Outdoor dining. On ocean. Cr cds: A, C, D, DS, MC, V.

★ ★ **PHILLIPS CRAB HOUSE.** *2004 Philadelphia Ave at 21st St.* 410/289-6821. Hrs: noon-10 pm. Closed Nov-Mar. Serv bar. Semi-a la carte: lunch, dinner $4-$25. Seafood buffet $21.95. Child's meals. Specializes in crab dishes, fresh seafood. Family-owned. Cr cds: A, C, D, DS, MC, V.

★ ★ **PHILLIPS SEAFOOD HOUSE.** *14101 Coastal Hwy, at 141st St.* 410/250-1200. Hrs: noon-10 pm; Fri, Sat to 11 pm; off-season 5-9 pm. Closed last wk Nov-Mar 1. Bar to 2 am. Semi-a la carte: lunch $4.95-$8.95, dinner $8.95-$24.95. Child's meals. Specializes in fresh seafood, crab, lobster. Entertainment exc Mon; off-season Thurs-Sun. Cr cds: A, D, DS, MC, V.

Pikesville (B-7)

(See also Baltimore)

Pop 24,815 **Area code** 410 **Zip** 21208

Motels

✓★ **COMFORT INN-NORTHWEST.** *10 Wooded Way, at I-695 exit 20. 410/484-7700; FAX 410/653-1516.* 103 rms, 2-3 story. No elvtr. S, D $59-$89; under 18 free; wkly, monthly rates. Crib free. TV; cable (premium). Pool; wading pool, lifeguard. Complimentary continental bkfst. Coffee in rms. Restaurant adj 6:30 am-11:30 pm. Ck-out 11 am. Coin lndry. Meeting rms. Business servs avail. In-rm modem link. Valet serv Mon-Fri. Health club privileges. Microwaves avail. Cr cds: A, C, D, DS, ER, JCB, MC, V.

D ≈ ⊗ 🔥 SC

★ **HOLIDAY INN.** *1721 Reisterstown Rd, at I-695 exit 20S. 410/486-5600; FAX 410/484-9377.* Web www.holiday-inn.com. 108 rms, 2 story. S, D $69; under 18 free; higher rates Preakness. Crib free. Pet accepted. TV; cable (premium). Pool; poolside serv, lifeguard. Restaurant 6 am-1 pm, 5-10 pm; Sat, Sun from 7 am. Rm serv. Bar 5 pm-midnight. Ck-out noon. Meeting rms. Business servs avail. Valet serv. Health club privileges. Some refrigerators; microwaves avail. Cr cds: A, C, D, DS, ER, JCB, MC, V.

D 🐾 ≈ ⊗ 🔥 SC

Motor Hotel

★★★ **HILTON.** *1726 Reisterstown Rd, at I-695 exit 20S. 410/653-1100; FAX 410/484-4138.* E-mail pikhi_ds@hilton.com; web www.hilton.com. 171 rms, 5 story. S $97-$150; D $97-$160; each addl $10; suites $300-$390; wkend plans; family rates. Crib $10. TV; cable (premium), VCR avail (movies). Pool; lifeguard. Coffee in rms. Restaurant 7 am-11 pm. Rm serv. Bar 11-1 am. Ck-out noon. Meeting rms. Business servs avail. Bellhops. Valet serv. Gift shop. Barber, beauty shop. Airport transportation. Tennis privileges. Exercise equipt; weight machines, stair machines. Bathrm phones; microwaves avail. Cr cds: A, C, D, DS, ER, MC, V.

D 🐾 ≈ 🏋 ⊗ 🔥 SC

Inn

★★★ **GRAMERCY.** *(1400 Greenspring Valley Rd, Stevenson 21153) I-695 exit 23N, Falls Rd to 2nd light, left on Greenspring Valley Rd. 410/486-2405.* 8 rms, 3 story, 2 suites. S, D $145-$250; each addl $25; suites $250. Crib $10. TV; VCR (movies). Pool. Complimentary full bkfst. Ck-out noon, ck-in after 3-6 pm. Business servs avail. In-rm modem link. Tennis. Lawn games. Picnic tables. Mansion (1902) on 45-acre wooded estate. Flower, herb gardens. Totally nonsmoking. Cr cds: A, DS, MC, V.

🏋 ≈ ⊗ 🔥

Restaurants

★★ **DUE.** *(25 Crossroads Dr, Owings Mills 21117) I-695, exit 20. 410/356-4147.* Hrs: 5:30-10 pm; Fri, Sat to 11 pm; Sun 5-9 pm. Closed most major hols. Res accepted. Italian menu. Bar. A la carte entrees: dinner $9.95-$24.95. Specializes in pasta, veal, chicken. Comtemporary decor. Cr cds: A, D, MC, V.

D

★★★ **LINWOOD'S CAFE.** *(25 Crossroads Dr, Owings Mills 21117) I-695, exit 20. 410/356-3030.* Hrs: 11:30 am-3 pm, 5:30-10 pm; Fri, Sat to 11 pm; Sun 5-9 pm. Closed most major hols. Res accepted; required

Fri, Sat. Bar. A la carte entrees: lunch $4.95-$14.95, dinner $9.95-$27.95. Specializes in chicken, seafood, steak. Formal decor. Cr cds: A, D, MC, V.

D

★★ **PUFFINS.** *1000 Reisterstown Rd, at Sherwood Ave. 410/486-8811.* Hrs: noon-2:30 pm, 5:30-close; Sun 5-8:30 pm. Closed most major hols. Res accepted Fri, Sat dinner. Bar. Semi-a la carte: lunch $6-$9.75, dinner $13-$21. Specializes in vegetarian, chicken, seafood dishes. Own breads. Modern decor; artwork. Totally nonsmoking. Cr cds: A, D, MC, V.

D

★★ **STIXX CAFE.** *1500 Reisterstown Rd, at Club Center. 410/484-7787.* Hrs: 11:30 am-2:30 pm, 5-10 pm; Fri to 11 pm; Sun 4-9:30 pm. Closed Thanksgiving. Res accepted Fri, Sat dinner. Continental menu. Bar. A la carte entrees: lunch, dinner $5.50-$17. Specializes in sushi. Own baking. Outdoor dining. Contemporary atmosphere. Totally nonsmoking. Cr cds: A, C, D, DS, MC, V.

D

Pocomoke City (F-9)

(See also Crisfield)

Founded 1670 **Pop** 3,922 **Elev** 22 ft **Area code** 410 **Zip** 21851
Information Pocomoke Chamber of Commerce, City Hall, 2nd floor, Clarke Ave & Vine St, PO Box 356; 410/957-1919.

Motels

★ **DAYS INN.** *1540 Ocean Hwy, on US 13S. 410/957-3000; FAX 410/957-3147.* 87 rms, 2 story. Mid-June-mid-Sept: S, D $63-$68; each addl $6; under 18 free; higher rates Pony Penning; lower rates rest of yr. Crib free. Pet accepted. TV; cable (premium). Pool. Restaurant 6:30 am-2 pm, 5-9 pm; Sun 7 am-9 pm. Rm serv. Bar 5-11 pm. Ck-out 11 am. Meeting rms. Refrigerators. Cr cds: A, C, D, DS, JCB, MC, V.

D 🐾 ≈ ⊗ 🔥 SC

✓★ **QUALITY INN.** *825 Ocean Hwy, 2½ mi S on US 13. 410/957-1300; FAX 410/957-9329.* 64 rms. S $42-$56; D $46-$70; each addl $5; under 18 free; higher rates Pony Penning. Crib free. Pet accepted. TV; cable (premium). Pool; wading pool. Restaurant 6 am-10 pm. Bar 11-1 am. Ck-out 11 am. Business servs avail. In-rm modem link. Some in-rm whirlpools, refrigerators. Picnic tables, grills. Cr cds: A, C, D, DS, ER, JCB, MC, V.

D 🐾 ≈ ⊗ 🔥 SC

Restaurant

★ **UPPER DECK.** *1245 Ocean Hwy, 2 mi S of US 113. 410/957-3166.* Hrs: 11 am-10 pm; Sun noon-9 pm. Res accepted. Bar to 2 am; Sun to 11 pm. Semi-a la carte: lunch $3.25-$5.95, dinner $7.50-$20. Child's meals. Specializes in local seafood, steak. Own desserts. Entertainment Thurs-Sat. Antiques. Cr cds: MC, V.

Rockville (C-6)

(See also Gaithersburg)

Pop 44,835 **Elev** 451 ft **Area code** 301

Information Chamber of Commerce, 600 Jefferson Plaza, Suite 101, 20852; 301/424-9300.

Second-largest city in the state of Maryland, Rockville is the seat of Montgomery County, located at the north edge of the District of Columbia. The Great Falls of the Potomac are 9 miles south off MD 189. This series of small falls was pretty but unnavigable, so the Chesapeake and Ohio Canal (see CHESAPEAKE AND OHIO CANAL NATIONAL HISTORICAL PARK) was built from Washington, DC, to Cumberland to simplify travel. Stone locks and levels are still visible. The graves of F. Scott and Zelda Fitzgerald are in St Mary's Cemetery.

What to See and Do

Beall-Dawson House (1815). Federal architecture; period furnishings; library; museum shop; 19th-century doctor's office. Tours guided by docents. (Tues-Sat; also 1st Sun of month; closed major hols) 103 W Montgomery Ave. Phone 301/762-1492. ¢

Annual Event

Hometown Holidays. Family entertainment. Memorial Day wkend.

Motels

★ ★ ★ **COURTYARD BY MARRIOTT.** *2500 Research Blvd (20850).* 301/670-6700; FAX 301/670-9023. 147 rms, 2 story, 13 suites. S $110; D $120; suites $129-$139; under 12 free; wkly rates. Crib free. TV; cable (premium). Indoor pool; whirlpool, lifeguard. Complimentary coffee. Restaurant 6:30 am-2 pm, 5-10 pm; Sat 7-11 am; Sun 7 am-2 pm. Rm serv 5-10 pm. Bar 5-11 pm. Ck-out 1 pm. Coin lndry. Meeting rms. Business servs avail. In-rm modem link. Valet serv. Sundries. Exercise equipt; weight machine, bicycles. Balconies. Refrigerators avail. Cr cds: A, C, D, DS, MC, V.

🄳 ⚊ 🏃 ⚊ 🔥 **SC**

✔★ **DAYS INN.** *16001 Shady Grove Rd (20850).* 301/948-4300; FAX 301/947-3235. 189 rms, 2 story. S, D $45-$70; each addl $5; under 18 free; wkend rates. Crib free. Pet accepted. TV; cable (premium). Pool. Playground. Restaurant 6:30 am-10 pm. Bar 10-12:30 am, Sun from 11 am. Ck-out 11 am. Business servs avail. Cr cds: A, C, D, DS, MC, V.

🄳 🐾 ⚊ ⚊ 🔥 **SC**

Motor Hotels

★ ★ **QUALITY SUITES.** *3 Research Ct (20850), 3 mi N on I-270, exit 8.* 301/840-0200; FAX 301/258-0160. 124 rms, 3 story, 66 kit. suites. S, D $109.95-$119.95; each addl $10; kit. suites $125.95-$139.95; under 18 free; wkend rates. Crib free. TV; cable (premium), VCR avail. Complimentary full bkfst. Complimentary coffee in rms. Restaurant nearby. Ck-out noon. Meeting rms. Business center. Valet serv. Sundries. Gift shop. Coin lndry. Exercise equipt; weight machine, stair machine. Pool; lifeguard. Refrigerators, microwaves, wet bars. Cr cds: A, C, D, DS, MC, V.

🄳 ⚊ 🏃 ⚊ 🔥 **SC** 🚶

★ ★ **WOODFIN SUITES.** *1380 Piccard Dr (20850), I-270 exit 8.* 301/590-9880; FAX 301/590-9614; res: 800/237-8811. 203 suites, 3 story. S, D $165-$230; each addl $15; 2-bedrm suites $275; under 12 free. Crib free. TV; cable (premium). Pool; whirlpool, lifeguard. Complimentary full bkfst. Restaurant 6-9 am, wkends 7-10 am. Bar 5-10 pm Mon-Thurs. Ck-out noon. Meeting rms. Business center. In-rm modem link. Valet serv. Sundries. Free local transportation. Exercise equipt; weight machine,

treadmill. Refrigerators, microwaves. Cr cds: A, C, D, DS, ER, JCB, MC, V.

🄳 ⚊ 🏃 ⚊ 🔥 **SC** 🚶

Hotel

★ ★ ★ **DOUBLETREE.** *1750 Rockville Pike (20852).* 301/468-1100; FAX 301/468-0163. 315 rms, 8 story. S $149; D $159; each addl $10; suites $195-$325; under 19 free; wkly, wkend rates. Crib free. TV; cable (premium). Indoor/outdoor pool; whirlpool, lifeguard. Coffee in rms. Restaurant 6:30-12:30 am. Bar from 11 am; Fri, Sat to 1 am. Ck-out noon. Convention facilities. Business center. In-rm modem link. Concierge. Gift shop. Beauty shop. Covered valet parking. Exercise equipt: weights, bicycles, sauna. Game rm. Refrigerators, microwaves avail. 8-story atrium; 20-ft waterfall. Gazebo. Luxury level. Cr cds: A, C, D, DS, ER, JCB, MC, V.

🄳 ⚊ 🏃 ⚊ 🔥 **SC** 🚶

Restaurants

✔ ★ **A & J.** *1319-C Rockville Pike (20852).* 301/251-7878. Hrs: 11:30 am-9 pm; Sat, Sun from 11 am. Chinese menu. A la carte entrees: lunch $4.50-$9, dinner $6.25-$9. Specializes in dim sum. Casual decor. Totally nonsmoking. No cr cds accepted.

🄳

✔ ★ ★ **ADDIE'S.** *11120 Rockville Pike (20852).* 301/881-0081. Hrs: 11:30 am-2:30 pm, 5:30-9:30 pm; Fri to 10 pm; Sat noon to 3 pm, 5:30-10 pm. Closed Sun; Jan 1, Thanksgiving, Dec 25. Res accepted Mon-Thurs dinner. Regional Amer menu. Bar. Semi-a la carte: lunch $6.50-$10.95, dinner $11.95-$17.50. Child's meals. Specializes in seasonal American dishes. Own pastries. Outdoor dining. Eclectic decor; collection of whimsical clocks; wood-burning grill. Cr cds: A, C, D, MC, V.

🄳

★ ★ **ANDALUCIA.** *12300 Wilkens Ave (20852).* 301/770-1880. Hrs: 11:30 am-2:30 pm, 5:30-10 pm; Sat 5:30-10:30 pm; Sun 4:30-9:30 pm. Closed Mon; Jan 1. Res accepted; required Fri, Sat dinner. Spanish menu. Serv bar. A la carte entrees: lunch $7.50-$10.95, dinner $12.50-$19.95. Specialties: paella Valenciana, zarzuela costa del sol. Own desserts. Mediterranean decor; many plants. Totally nonsmoking. Cr cds: A, C, D, DS, MC, V.

✔ ★ ★ **BENJARONG THAI.** *855-C Rockville Pike (20852).* 301/424-5533. Hrs: 11:30 am-9:30 pm; Fri, Sat to 10:30 pm; Sun 5-9:30 pm. Closed most major hols. Res accepted. Thai menu. Bar. Semi-a la carte: lunch $5.95-$7.95, dinner $7.95-$11.95. Specializes in pad thai, chicken satay, seafood. Thai decor. Cr cds: A, C, D, DS, MC, V.

🄳

✔ ★ ★ **BOMBAY BISTRO.** *98 W Montgomery Ave (20850).* 301/762-8798. Hrs: 11 am-2:30 pm, 5-9:30 pm; Fri, Sat to 10 pm; Sun noon-3 pm, 5-9:30 pm. Closed Thanksgiving. Indian menu. Wine, beer. A la carte entrees: lunch, dinner $6.95-$15.95. Buffet lunch: $6.95-$8.95. Specializes in vegetarian, tandoori dishes. Casual decor. Cr cds: A, C, D, DS, MC, V.

🄳

★ ★ **COPELAND'S OF NEW ORLEANS.** *1584 Rockville Pike (20852).* 301/230-0968. E-mail store8@vni.net. Hrs: 11 am-11 pm; Sun, Mon to 10 pm; Fri, Sat to midnight. Closed Thanksgiving, Dec 25. Bar; Semi-a la carte: lunch $6-$13.95, dinner $5.95-$19.95. Child's meals. Specializes in seafood, Creole & Cajun dishes. Art deco decor. Cr cds: A, C, D, DS, MC, V.

🄳

✔ ★ **FOUR RIVERS.** *184 Rollins Ave (20852).* 301/230-2900. Hrs: 11:30 am-10:30 pm; Fri, Sat to 11 pm; Sun to 10 pm. Res accepted; required Fri, Sat dinner. Chinese menu. Bar. Semi-a la carte: lunch $4.50-$5.95, dinner $6.95-$12.95. Specialties: golden crispy shrimp, sizzling black pepper steak. Casual decor; aquarium in lobby. Totally nonsmoking. Cr cds: DS, MC, V.

[D] [⊒]

★ ★ **IL PIZZICO.** *15209 Frederick Rd (20850). 301/309-0610.* Hrs: 11 am-2:30 pm, 5-9:30 pm; Fri to 10 pm; Sat 5-10 pm. Closed Sun; most major hols. Italian menu. Bar. Semi-a la carte: lunch $6.95-$10.95, dinner $8.95-$13.95. Specializes in pasta, seafood. Italian decor. Cr cds: A, MC, V.

[D]

★ ★ **NORMANDIE FARM.** *(10710 Falls Rd, Potomac 20854) 3¹/₂ mi SW on MD 189, I-270 exit 5. 301/983-8838.* Hrs: 11:30 am-2:30 pm, 6-10 pm; Sun 5-9 pm; Sun brunch 11 am-2 pm. Closed Mon. Res accepted. French menu. Bar. Semi-a la carte: lunch $6-$12.50, dinner $12-$23. Sun brunch $16.95. Specializes in seafood, veal. Entertainment Thur-Sat. French provincial decor. Cr cds: A, DS, MC, V.

[D]

★ ★ **OLD ANGLER'S INN.** *(10801 MacArthur Blvd, Potomac 20854) approx 8 mi S on MD 189, I-270 Exit 5. 301/299-9097.* Hrs: noon-2:30 pm, 6-10:30 pm. Closed Mon. Bar. Wine list. A la carte entrees: lunch $12-$16, dinner $22-$29. Specializes in seafood, rack of lamb. Patio dining overlooking wooded area. Stone inn (1860); fireplace. Family-owned. Cr cds: A, C, D, MC, V.

[♥]

✔ ★ **RED, HOT & BLUE.** *16811 Crabbs Branch Way (20855), in Grove Shopping Center. 301/948-7333.* Hrs: 11 am-10 pm; Fri to 11 pm; Sat noon-11 pm; Sun from noon. Closed Thanksgiving, Dec 25. Bar. Semi-a la carte: lunch, dinner $5.95-$12.95. Child's meals. Specializes in Memphis pit barbecue, ribs. Outdoor dining. Casual decor; blues memorabilia. Totally nonsmoking. Cr cds: A, MC, V.

[D]

✔ ★ **SEVEN SEAS.** *1776 E Jefferson St (20852). 301/770-5020.* Hrs: 11:30-1 am. Closed Thanksgiving. Chinese menu. Bar. Semi-a la carte: lunch $3.95-$6.50, dinner $7.25-$16.95. Specializes in Szechwan, Taiwan, Shanghai. Sushi bar. Chinese artwork. Cr cds: A, DS, MC, V.

[D] [⊒]

✔ ★ **SILVER DINER.** *11806 Rockville Pike (MD 355) (20852), in Mid-Pike Plaza. 301/770-4166.* Hrs: 7-2 am; Fri, Sat to 3 am; early-bird dinner Mon-Fri 4-6 pm. Closed Dec 25. Serv bar. Semi-a la carte: bkfst $3.95-$5.95, lunch $5.45-$7.95, dinner $5.95-$9.99. Child's meals. Specialties: meatloaf, chicken-pot pie, turkey. 1950s-style diner with jukeboxes. Servers dressed in period clothing. Cr cds: A, C, D, DS, MC, V.

[D] [SC] [⊒] [♥]

★ ★ **TASTE OF SAIGON.** *410 Hungerford Dr (20850). 301/424-7222.* Hrs: 11 am-10 pm; Fri, Sat to 11 pm; Sun 11 am-9:30 pm. Closed Thanksgiving, Dec 25. Res accepted. Vietnamese menu. Bar. A la carte entrees: lunch $5.95-$14.95, dinner $7.95-$16.95. Specialties: black pepper soft shell crab and shrimp, pepper saigon steak. Outdoor dining. Contemporary decor. Cr cds: A, C, D, DS, MC, V.

[D]

★ ★ **THAT'S AMORE.** *15201 Shady Grove Rd (20850). 301/670-9666.* Hrs: 11:30 am-10:30 pm; Fri to midnight; Sat 4 pm-midnight; Sun 4-9:30 pm. Closed Labor Day, Thanksgiving, Dec 25. Italian menu. Bar. A la carte entrees: lunch $5.95-$9.95, dinner $15-$38. Specializes in pasta, veal, chicken. Stained-glass windows. Early 20th-century mens club atmosphere. Cr cds: A, C, D, DS, MC, V.

[D]

✔ ★ ★ **WÜRZBURG HAUS.** *7236 Muncaster Mill Rd (20855), in Red Mill Shopping Center. 301/330-0402.* Hrs: 11:30 am-9 pm; Fri to 10 pm; Sat noon-10 pm; Sun noon-9 pm. German menu. Wine, beer. A la carte entrees: lunch $8.75-$12.95, dinner $9.95-$14.75. Child's meals. Specializes in schnitzel, wurst. Accordionist Fri, Sat. 2 dining areas. Ger-

man, Austrian atmosphere; collection of beer steins. Cr cds: A, C, D, DS, MC, V.

[D]

Unrated Dining Spot

HARD TIMES CAFE. *1117 Nelson St (20850), in Woodley Garden Shopping Center. 301/294-9720.* Hrs: 11:30 am-10 pm; Fri, Sat to 11 pm; Sun noon-9 pm. Closed Thanksgiving, Dec 25. Bar. A la carte entrees: lunch, dinner $4.50-$6. Child's meals. Specializes in chili, vegetarian dishes. Cr cds: A, MC, V.

[D] [⊒]

St Mary's City (E-7)

(See also Leonardtown, Waldorf; also see District of Columbia)

Settled 1634 **Pop** 1,300 (est) **Elev** 36 ft **Area code** 301 **Zip** 20686 **E-mail** stmcdecd@mail.ameritel.net **Web** www.somd.lib.md.us /STMA/government/stmcdecd.html

Information St Mary's County Division of Tourism, PO Box 653, Leonardtown 20650; 800/327-9023.

Maryland's first colonists bought a Native American village on this site upon their arrival in the New World under Leonard Calvert. The settlement was the capital and hub of the area until 1694, when the colonial capital was moved to Annapolis. The town gradually disappeared. The city and county are still rich in historical attractions.

What to See and Do

Historic St Mary's City. Outdoor museum at site of Maryland's 1st capital (1634) includes reconstructed State House (1676), replica of the original capital bldg; other exhibits include the *Maryland Dove,* replica of a 17th-century ship, and archaeological exhibits. Also seasonal living history programs, a 17th-century tobacco plantation, reconstructed 17th-century inn; visitor center, outdoor cafe. Visitor center (all yr, Wed-Sun; closed Jan 1, Thanksgiving, Dec 25); outdoor museum (4th wkend Mar-Nov, Wed-Sun). MD 5 & Rosecroft Rd. Phone 301/862-0990 or 800/SMC-1634. ¢¢¢ Also here is

Margaret Brent Memorial. Gazebo overlooking the river; memorial to the woman who, being a wealthy landowner, requested the right to vote in the Maryland Assembly in 1648, in order to settle Leonard Calvert's affairs after his death.

Leonard Calvert Monument. Monument to Maryland's first colonial governor. Trinity Churchyard.

Point Lookout State Park. Site of the Confederate Monument, the only memorial erected by the US government to honor the POWs who died in the Point Lookout Prison Camp during the Civil War (3,384 died here). Swimming, fishing, boating, hiking. Picnicking; improved camping (Apr-Oct; self-contained camping units yr round). Nature center. Civil War museum. Standard fees. (May-Sept, wkends) 13 mi S on MD 5. Phone 301/872-5688. Day-use entrance fee (May-Oct)   ¢¢

Annual Events

Maryland Days. Boat rides, seafood, 17th-century militia musters. Wkend late Mar.

Crab Festival. Steamed crabs, other seafood and nonseafood dishes. Arts and crafts, antique and classic car show. 1st Sun June.

Motel

✔ ★ ★ **DAYS INN.** *(60 Main St, Lexington Park 20653) 11 mi N on MD 235. 301/863-6666.* 165 rms, 2 story. S $54-$62; D $58-$70; each addl $4; kit. units $57-$78; under 17 free. Crib free. Pet accepted. TV; cable (premium). Pool. Complimentary continental bkfst. Restaurant 11 am-2 pm, 4:30-9 pm. Bar 11-1:30 am. Ck-out noon. Coin lndry. Some refrigerators. Cr cds: A, C, D, DS, MC, V.

 D ⛵ ≋ ⛷ 🔥 SC

Motor Hotel

✔★ ★ **PATUXENT INN.** *(MD 235, Lexington Park 20653) 11 mi NW on MD 235.* 301/862-4100; FAX 301/862-4673. 120 rms, 3 story. S, D $60; each addl $5; under 18 free; wknd rates. Crib $5. TV; cable (premium). Pool. Complimentary continental bkfst. Restaurant 11 am-9 pm; Sat, Sun from 7 am. Ck-out 11 am. Coin lndry. Business servs avail. In-rm modem link. Lighted tennis. Golf privileges. Refrigerators, some wet bars. Cr cds: A, C, D, MC, V.

D 🕺 ⛷ ≋ 🎿 ⛷ 🔥 SC

Restaurant

✔★ **ALOHA.** *(2025 Wildewood Ctr, California) 11 mi NW on MD 235, in shopping center.* 301/862-4838. Hrs: 10:30 am-10 pm; Fri to 11 pm; Sat noon-11 pm; Sun noon-9:30 pm; Sun buffet noon-3 pm. Closed Thanksgiving, Dec 25. Chinese menu. Bar. Semi-a la carte: lunch $3.95-$4.95, dinner $5.95-$19. Complete meals: lunch $4.95, dinner $7.25-$9.95. Sun buffet: $6.95. Child's meals. Specializes in Szechwan, Hunan dishes, international dishes. Polynesian atmosphere. Cr cds: A, DS, MC, V.

D

Unrated Dining Spot

EVANS SEAFOOD. *(St George Island, Piney Point 20674) N on MD 5, approx 10 mi S on MD 249.* 301/994-2299. Hrs: 4-10 pm; Sat, Sun to midnight. Closed Mon; Easter, Dec 25. Res accepted. Bar. Semi-a la carte: lunch $5.50-$13.95, dinner $8.95-$21.95. Child's meals. Specializes in steak, seafood. Outdoor dining. View of the Potomac River. Cr cds: MC, V.

D

St Michaels (D-8)

Pop 1,301 **Elev** 7 ft **Area code** 410 **Zip** 21663 **Web** internetconnection.com/talbot/

Information Talbot County Chamber of Commerce, PO Box 1366, Easton 21601; 410/822-4606.

Chartered in 1804, St Michaels has become a boating and tourist center with its many shops, marinas, restaurants, bed-and-breakfasts and country inns. It is a town with many Federal- and Victorian-period buildings.

What to See and Do

Chesapeake Bay Maritime Museum. Waterside museum consists of 9 buildings. Includes historic lighthouse, floating exhibits, boat-building shop with working exhibit, ship models, small boats; paintings; aquarium; waterfowling exhibits; workboats and mechanical propulsion. Special events throughout the year (see ANNUAL EVENT). (Daily) Mill St. Phone 410/745-2916. ¢¢¢

St Mary's Square. Public square laid out in 1770 by Englishman James Braddock. Several buildings date to the early 1800s, including the Cannonball House and Dr. Miller's Farmhouse. The Ship's Carpenter Bell was cast in 1842; across from the bell stand 2 cannons, one dating from the Revolution, the other from the War of 1812. Also here is

St Mary's Square Museum. Mid-19th-century home of "half-timber" construction; one of the earliest buildings in St Michaels. Exhibits of

historical and local interest. (1st wkend May-last wkend Oct, Sat & Sun; also by appt) Inquire about the town walking tour brochures. Contact the Town Office, phone 410/745-9535.

The Footbridge. Only remaining bridge of three that once connected the town with areas across the harbor. Joins Navy Point to Cherry St.

The *Patriot*. A 1-hr narrated cruise on Miles River. Four trips daily. (Apr-Oct) Berthed at Chesapeake Bay Maritime Museum. Phone 410/745-3100. ¢¢¢

Annual Event

Mid-Atlantic Maritime Festival. Chesapeake Bay Maritime Museum. Nautical celebration with fly-fishing demonstration, skipjack races, boat building contest, boat parade, seafood festival cooking contest. Phone 410/745-2916 or 410/822-5553. 3 days mid-May.

Motor Hotel

✔★ ★ **BEST WESTERN.** *1228 S Talbott St.* 410/745-3333; FAX 410/745-2906. 93 rms, 2 story. May-mid-Nov: S $62-$89; D $68-$99; each addl $8; under 18 free; lower rates rest of yr. TV; cable (premium). 2 pools. Complimentary continental bkfst. Restaurant adj 11 am-11 pm. Ck-out 11 am. Meeting rms. Business servs avail. Cr cds: A, D, DS, MC, V.

D ≋ ⛷ 🔥 SC

Hotel

★ ★ ★ **HARBOUR INN & MARINA.** *101 N Harbor Rd.* 410/745-9001; FAX 410/745-9150; res: 800/955-9001. E-mail harbour@friend.ly.net; web www.friend.ly/harbour/. 46 units, 3 story, 38 suites. S, D, suites $149-$419; under 18 free; higher rates wknds; 2-day min May-Oct. Crib $10. TV; cable (premium). Pool; whirlpool, poolside serv. Coffee in rms. Restaurant (see WINDOWS). Bar 11 am-10 pm. Ck-out noon. Coin lndry. Meeting rms. Business servs avail. Gift shop. Exercise equipt; bicycles, treadmill. Refrigerator in suites. Some balconies. Picnic tables. 60-slip marina. Cr cds: A, C, D, DS, MC, V.

D ≋ 🕺 ⛷ 🔥

Inns

★ **BLACK WALNUT POINT.** *(End of Black Walnut Rd, Tilghman Island 21671) 15 mi W on MD 33.* 410/886-2452; FAX 410/886-2053. 7 rms, 3 bldgs, main bldg 3 story. No rm phones. D $120; each addl $20; kit. unit $140. Adults only. TV in sitting rm. Pool; whirlpool. Complimentary continental bkfst. Ck-out 11 am, ck-in 2-7 pm. Business servs avail. Lighted tennis. Lawn games. Balconies. Picnic tables, grills. On Cheasapeake Bay. Built in 1843; hand-hewn beams. Cr cds: MC, V.

⛵ 🕺 ≋ ⛷ 🔥 SC

★ ★ ★ **CHESAPEAKE WOOD DUCK INN.** *(21490 Dogwood Harbor Rd, Tilghman Island 21671) Approx 11 mi W on MD 33.* 410/886-2070; FAX 410/886-2263; res: 800/956-2070. E-mail woodduck@skipjack.bluecrab.org; web www.woodduckinn.com. 7 rms, 3 story. No rm phones. No elvtr. Apr-Nov: S, D $125-$155; suites $165-$195; lower rates rest of yr. Children over 14 yrs only. TV in main rm; VCR. Complimentary full bkfst. Restaurant nearby. Ck-out 11 am, ck-in 4-7 pm. Business servs avail. Luggage handling. Water sport privileges. Built in 1890; antiques. Totally nonsmoking. Cr cds: MC, V.

⛵ ⛷ 🔥 SC

★ ★ ★ ★ **INN AT PERRY CABIN.** *308 Watkins Lane.* 410/745-2200; FAX 410/745-3348; res: 800/722-2949. E-mail perrycbn@friend.ly.net; web www.ashley-house.com. This white dormered farmhouse, built on the banks of the Miles River in the late 18th century, was refurbished by Sir Bernard Ashley to showcase the designs of his late wife, Laura Ashley, and has the ambience of an English country house. 41 rms, 3 story, 6 suites. S, D $195-$575; suites $475-$575. Children over 10 yrs only. TV; cable (premium), VCR avail (movies). Pool; whirlpool. Complimentary full bkfst. Dining rm (see ASHLEY ROOM). Rm serv. Ck-out noon, ck-in 3 pm.

Business center. In-rm modem link. Luggage handling. Valet serv. Concierge serv. Tennis. Golf privileges. Exercise equipt; weights, bicycles, sauna, steam rm. Massage. Health club privileges. Lawn games. Dockage. Cr cds: A, D, MC, V.

⭐ ⭐ **LAZYJACK INN.** *(5907 Tilghman Island Rd, Tilghman Island 21671)* *Approx 15 mi W on MD 33.* *410/886-2215; FAX 410/886-2215; res: 800/690-5080.* E-mail mrichards@skipjack.bluecrab.org; web www.bluecrab.org/members/mrichards. 4 rms, 2 story. No rm phone. May-mid-Nov: S, D $130-$195; lower rates rest of yr. Children over 12 yrs only. Complimentary full bkfst. TV in main rm. Restaurant nearby. Ck-out 11 am, ck-in 3-6 pm. Luggage handling. Some in-rm whirlpools. Historic waterfront bldg (1855); furnished with antiques. Totally nonsmoking. Cr cds: MC, V.

⭐ ⭐ **PARSONAGE INN.** *210 N Talbot St, edge of historic district.* *410/745-5519; res: 800/394-5519.* 8 rms, 2 story. No rm phones. May-Oct: D $110-$172; lower rates rest of yr. Crib free. TV in sitting rm and in 2 guest rms. Complimentary full bkfst, tea. Restaurant adj noon-10 pm. Ck-out 11 am, ck-in 2-7 pm. Balconies. Picnic table, grill. Built in 1883 as a private residence; later used as a parsonage. Restored and furnished with period reproductions; unique architecture. Totally nonsmoking. Cr cds: MC, V.

⭐ ⭐ **WADES POINT INN ON THE BAY.** *End of Wades Point Rd, 5 mi W via MD 33, right on Wades Point Rd, in McDaniel.* *410/745-2500; FAX 410/745-3443.* E-mail atwades@skipjack.bluecrab.org. 24 rms, 5 share bath, 12 A/C, 2-3 story, 4 kits. No rm phones. D $95-$230; each addl $10; kit. units $230; under 12 free. Crib free. Complimentary continental bkfst. Restaurant nearby. Ck-out 11 am, ck-in 2-8 pm. Business servs avail. Balconies. Picnic tables. Main building (1819) with new guest house (1989) built in same style. Both buildings surrounded by fields and Chesapeake Bay. Located on 120 acres; flower gardens, woods with nature trail. Totally nonsmoking. Cr cds: MC, V.

Resort

⭐ ⭐ **HARBOURTOWNE.** *MD 33, 3 mi W on MD 33, at Martingham Dr.* *410/745-9066; FAX 410/745-9124; res: 800/446-9066.* Web www.harbortowne.com. 111 rms, 1-2 story. Mar-Nov: S, D $135-$200; each addl $15; under 12 free; golf plans; lower rates rest of yr. TV; cable (premium), VCR avail. Crib free. Pool; poolside serv, lifeguard. Dining rm 7 am-10 pm. Ck-out 11 am, ck-in 3 pm. Grocery, package store 3 mi. Meeting rms. Business servs avail. In-rm modem link. Gift shop. Tennis. 18-hole golf, greens fee $49.50, pro, putting green, driving range. Exercise equipt; weights, treadmill. Bicycles. Paddle boats. Lawn games. Private patios, balconies. Cr cds: A, D, DS, MC, V.

Restaurants

⭐ ⭐ ⭐ **208 TALBOT.** *208 N Talbot St.* *410/745-3838.* Hrs: noon-2 pm, 5-10 pm; Sat from 5 pm; Sun 5-9 pm; Sun brunch 11 am-2 pm. Closed Mon, Tues; Dec 24, 25. Res accepted; required wkends. Bar. Semi-a la carte: lunch $8.50-$13.50, dinner $21-$26. Prix fixe: Sat dinner $43. Sun brunch $9-$15.50. Specializes in fresh seafood, rack of lamb. Own pastries, ice cream. Casual gourmet dining in a renovated mid-1800s brick house; many antiques; original fireplace. Cr cds: DS, MC, V.

⭐ ⭐ **ASHLEY ROOM.** *(See Inn At Perry Cabin)* *410/745-2200.* Hrs: 8-10:30 am, 12:30-2:30 pm, 6-10 pm; afternoon tea 3-5 pm. Res accepted. Serv bar. Wine list. Prix fixe: bkfst $17.50, lunch $27.50, 5-course dinner $59.50. High tea $9.50-$14.50. Specializes in classical cuisine. Menu changes daily. Own herb garden. Own baking. Valet parking. English country-style dining rm with fireplace; French doors open to terrace overlooking bay. Totally nonsmoking. Cr cds: A, D, MC, V.

✔ ⭐ **ST MICHAELS CRAB HOUSE.** *305 Mulberry St.* *410/745-3737.* Hrs: 11 am-10 pm; Fri, Sat to 11 pm. Closed mid-Dec-early Mar. Res accepted. Bar. Semi-a la carte: lunch $4.95-$10, dinner $9.95-$17.95. Child's meals. Specializes in steamed crab, shellfish. Outdoor dining. Overlooks harbor. Cr cds: DS, MC, V.

⭐ ⭐ **TOWN DOCK.** *125 Mulberry St, at the harbor, in public dock area.* *410/745-5577.* Hrs: 11 am-9 pm; Fri, Sat to 10 pm; early-bird dinner Sun-Fri 3:30-5:30 pm; Sun brunch to 3 pm. Closed Dec 25; also Wed Jan-Mar. Res accepted. Bar. Semi-a la carte: lunch $5.95-$10.95, dinner $15.95-$24.95. Sun brunch $13.95. Child's meals. Specializes in fresh seafood, Eastern Shore cuisine. Outdoor dining. Nightclub on 2nd floor; entertainment Sat evenings. 4-level dining; harbor view. Cr cds: A, D, DS, MC, V.

⭐ ⭐ ⭐ **WINDOWS.** *(See Harbour Inn & Marina Hotel)* *410/745-5102.* E-mail harbour@friend.ly.net; web www.friend.ly.net/harbour/. Hrs: 7 am-10 pm. Res accepted. Bar. Semi-a la carte: bkfst $4.95-$9.95, lunch $5.25-$8.75, dinner $13.95-$21.50. Specializes in seafood grill, steaks, chicken. Cr cds: A, C, D, DS, MC, V.

Salisbury (E-9)

(See also Ocean City)

Founded 1732 **Pop** 20,592 **Elev** 33 ft **Area code** 410 & 443 **Zip** 21801 **E-mail** wicotour@shore.intercom.net **Web** www.co.wicomico.md.us/tourism

Information Wicomico County Convention & Visitors Bureau, 8480 Ocean Hwy, Delmar 21875; 410/548-4914 or 800/332-TOUR. Information is also available from the Chamber of Commerce, 300 E Main St, PO Box 510, 21803; 410/749-0144.

"Central City of the Eastern Shore" and of the Delmarva Peninsula, Salisbury has a marina on the Wicomico River providing access to Chesapeake Bay. It lies within 30 miles of duck-hunting and deep-sea fishing. Gasoline pumps, hydraulic lifts, canned and frozen foods, seafood and poultry come from this area.

What to See and Do

Mason-Dixon Line Marker. Bears coats of arms of Lord Baltimore and William Penn. 5 mi N on US 13, 13A, then 7 mi W on MD 467.

Poplar Hill Mansion (ca 1805). Example of Georgian and Federal-style architecture; palladium and bull's-eye windows; large brass box locks on doors, woodwork, mantels and fireplaces. Period furniture; country garden. (Usually Sun afternoons; Tues-Sat by appt, phone ahead; closed hols) 117 Elizabeth St. Phone 410/749-1776. ¢

Princess Anne. This town was the home of Samuel Chase, signer of the Declaration of Independence. Buildings of the Colonial and Federal periods are of architectural interest. 13 mi SW on US 13.

Salisbury Zoological Park. Natural habitats for almost 400 mammals, birds and reptiles. Major exhibits include bears, monkeys, jaguars, bison, waterfowl. Also exotic plants. (Daily) 755 S Park Dr. Phone 410/548-3188. Donation.

The Nassawango Iron Furnace. One of the oldest industrial sites in Maryland and one of the earliest hot-blast mechanisms still intact. The stack was restored in 1966; archaeological excavations were made and a canal, a dike and a portion of the old waterwheel used in the manufacturing process were found. The remains of the area are undergoing restoration. (Apr-Oct, daily) 16 mi S via MD 12 to Old Furnace Rd. Phone 410/632-2032. ¢¢ Surrounding the iron furnace is

Furnace Town. This 1840s industrial village occupies 22 acres around the iron furnace and also includes six historic structures; a working

19th-century blacksmith shop and broom-making shop has demonstrations on selected days; a museum and company store; archaeological excavations; a nature trail and picnic area. Special events take place throughout the season. (Same days & fees as furnace)

Ward Museum of Wildfowl Art. Displays include the history of decoy and wildfowl carving in North America; wildfowl habitats; contemporary wildfowl art. Changing exhibits. Gift shop. (Mon-Sat, also Sun afternoons) 909 S Schumaker Dr, at Beaglin Park Dr. Phone 410/742-4988, ext 100. ¢¢

Motels

✔★ ★ **COMFORT INN.** 2701 N Salisbury Blvd, 4½ mi N on US 13. 410/543-4666; FAX 410/749-2639. 96 units, 2 story, 24 suites. Mid-May-mid-Sept: S $45.95; D $55.95; each addl $8; suites $55.95-$79.95; under 18 free; higher rates wkends; lower rates rest of yr. Crib avail. Pet accepted. TV; cable (premium). Pool privileges. Complimentary continental bkfst. Restaurant nearby. Ck-out 11 am. Meeting rm. Business servs avail. Refrigerator, wet bar in suites. Cr cds: A, C, D, DS, ER, JCB, MC, V.

★ ★ **DAYS INN.** 2525 N Salisbury Blvd, 3 mi N on US 13. 410/749-6200; FAX 410/749-7378. 98 units, 2 story. Mid-June-mid-Sept: S, D $55-$99; each addl $5; under 18 free; higher rates special events; lower rates rest of yr. Crib free. TV; cable (premium). Pool. Playground. Complimentary continental bkfst. Restaurant opp 6 am-10 pm. Ck-out 11 am. Meeting rms. Business servs avail. Some refrigerators. Cr cds: A, D, DS, MC, V.

★ ★ **HOLIDAY INN.** 2625 N Salisbury Blvd, 3 mi N on US 13. 410/742-7194; FAX 410/742-5194. 123 rms, 2 story. Mid-June-mid-Sept: S $49-$99; D $49-$107; each addl $8; under 18 free; lower rates rest of yr. Crib free. Pet accepted, some restrictions. TV; cable (premium). Pool. Complimentary bkfst buffet. Restaurant 5-10 pm. Rm serv. Bar 4:30 pm-midnight. Ck-out 11 am. Coin lndry. Meeting rms. Business servs avail. Valet serv. Cr cds: A, C, D, DS, MC, V.

Motor Hotel

★ ★ **SHERATON.** 300 S Salisbury Blvd. 410/546-4400; FAX 410/546-2528. 156 rms, 5 story. Late May-mid-Sept: S, D $98-135; each addl $10; suites $150; under 18 free; lower rates rest of yr. Crib free. TV; cable (premium), VCR avail. Indoor pool. Restaurant 6:30 am-2:30 pm, 5:30-10:30 pm; wkends from 7 am. Rm serv. Bar 4 pm-2 am; wkends from noon. Ck-out noon. Meeting rms. Business servs avail. In-rm modem link. Bellhops. Gift shop. Free airport transportation. Exercise equipt; weight machine, bicycle. Wet bar in suites. On river. Cr cds: A, C, D, DS, MC, V.

Silver Spring (C-6)

(See also Bowie, College Park, Rockville; also see District of Columbia)

Pop 76,046 **Elev** 350 ft **Area code** 301 & 240

Information Chamber of Commerce, 8601 Georgia Ave, Suite 203, 20910; 301/565-3777.

What to See and Do

Brookside Gardens. A 50-acre display garden with two conservatories; flowering displays; variety of flowering plants in eight gardens; educational programs. (Daily; closed Dec 25) N on MD 97, right on Randolph Rd, right on Glenallan Ave, in Wheaton. Phone 301/949-8230. **Free.**

National Capital Trolley Museum. Rides on old-time American and European trolleys; exhibits depict history of streetcars. Special events

during yr. (July-Aug, Sat-Sun & Wed; rest of yr, Sat & Sun only; also open Memorial Day, July 4, Labor Day) Northwest Branch Park, about 7 mi N on Bonifant Rd, just off MD 650 in Layhill. Phone 301/384-6088. Museum **Free**; Rides ¢¢

Motel

★ ★ ★ **COURTYARD BY MARRIOTT.** 12521 Prosperity Dr (20904), 6 mi NE on US 29, then E on Cherry Hill Rd to Prosperity Dr. 301/680-8500; FAX 301/680-9232. 146 units, 3 story. S $99; D $109; suites $131-$141; wkly, wkend rates. Crib free. TV; cable (premium). Indoor pool; whirlpool, lifeguard. Complimentary coffee in rms. Restaurant 6:30-10 am, 5-10 pm; Sat, Sun 7 am-1 pm. Bar 4-10 pm. Ck-out noon. Coin lndry. Meeting rms. Business servs avail. In-rm modem link. Valet serv. Sundries. Exercise equipt; weights, bicycles. Health club privileges. Refrigerators, microwaves avail. Cr cds: A, C, D, DS, ER, JCB, MC, V.

Restaurants

★ ★ **BLAIR MANSION INN.** 7711 Eastern Ave (20912). 301/588-1688. Hrs: 11:30 am-9 pm; Sat from 5 pm; Sun from 2 pm. Res accepted. Continental, Amer menu. Bar. Semi-a la carte: lunch $5.95-$9.95, dinner $9.95-$19.95. Specializes in poultry, beef, crab. Murder mystery dinners Fri, Sat, some Sun. 1890s Victorian mansion; gaslight chandelier, 7 fireplaces. Family-owned. Totally nonsmoking. Cr cds: A, C, D, DS, MC, V.

★ ★ **CRISFIELD AT LEE PLAZA.** 8606 Colesville Rd (MD 29) (20910), ground floor of high rise building, in Lee Plaza. 301/588-1572. Hrs: 11:30 am-10 pm; Fri to 11 pm; Sat 4-11 pm; Sun 2:30-9:30 pm. Closed Thanksgiving, Dec 25. Res accepted; required Fri, Sat. Bar. Semi-a la carte: lunch $4.50-$15.95, dinner $14.95-$17.95. Child's meals. Specializes in seafood, baked stuffed shrimp, crab. Art deco decor. Cr cds: A, C, D, MC, V.

★ ★ ★ **MRS. K'S TOLL HOUSE.** 9201 Colesville Rd (20910). 301/589-3500. Hrs: 11:30 am-2:30 pm, 5-9 pm; Fri, Sat to 9:30 pm; Sun 11 am-9 pm; Sun brunch to 1 pm. Closed Mon; Dec 25. Serv bar. Complete meals: lunch $11.75, dinner $17.25-$24.95. Sun brunch $15.75. Specializes in regional American cuisine. Century-old tollhouse; antique china, glass. Gardens. Totally nonsmoking. Cr cds: A, C, D, DS, MC, V.

★ **VICINO.** 959 Sligo Ave (20910). 301/588-3372. Hrs: 11:30 am-10:30 pm; Mon to 9:30 pm; Sun 1-9:30 pm. Closed some major hols; also Dec 31. Italian menu. Wine, beer. A la carte entrees: lunch, dinner $6.50-$12. Child's meals. Specializes in pizza, pasta, seafood. Outdoor dining. Casual Italian neighborhood decor. Totally nonsmoking. Cr cds: MC, V.

Thurmont (B-5)

(For accommodations see Frederick, Hagerstown)

Settled 1751 **Pop** 3,398 **Elev** 523 ft **Area code** 301 **Zip** 21788 **Web** www.co.frederick.md.us/tour/tourpage/html

Information Tourism Council of Frederick County, 19 E Church St, Frederick 21701; 301/663-8687 or 800/999-3613.

What to See and Do

Catoctin Mountain Park. A 5,770-acre area on a spur of the Blue Ridge Mountains. Self-guided nature trails; restored whiskey still; fishing, picnicking; camping (mid-Apr-mid-Nov; fee), cabins (mid-Apr-Oct; fee). Park (daily). A unit of the National Park Service. 3 mi W on MD 77. Phone 301/663-9388. **Free.**

Cunningham Falls State Park. 4,950 acres in the Catoctin Mountains. Two recreation areas: Houck, 5 mi W of town, has swimming, fishing, boating (rentals); picnicking, camping; hiking trails lead to 78-ft falls and scenic overlooks. Manor Area, 3 mi S of town on US 15, has picnicking, camping, playground. Trout fishing in Big Hunting Creek. Ruins of Iron Masters Mansion and the industrial village that surrounded it are also here. (See ANNUAL EVENTS) Standard fees. Phone 301/271-7574.

Annual Events

Maple Syrup Demonstration. At Cunningham Falls State Park. Tree tapping, sap boiling; carriage rides; food; children's storytelling corner. Usually 2nd & 3rd wknd Mar.

Catoctin Colorfest. Fall foliage; arts & crafts show. Phone 301/271-4432. 2nd wknd Oct.

Motel

★ ★ ★ **COZY COUNTRY INN.** *103 Frederick Rd. 301/271-4301.* 21 units, 3 with showers only, 2 story, 5 cottages. May-Oct: S, D $44-$130; each addl $6; cottages $44-$110; under 12 free; wkly rates. Crib free. TV; cable (premium), VCR avail. Complimentary continental bkfst Mon-Fri. Complimentary coffee in rms. Restaurant 11 am-9 pm, Sat, Sun from 8 am. Rm serv. Bar 11 am-10 pm. Meeting rms. Business servs avail. In-rm modem link. Bellhops. Valet serv. Gift shop. Downhill ski 12 mi, x-country ski 4 mi. Refrigerators; some minibars; microwaves avail. Balconies. Picnic tables. Near Camp David; visiting dignitaries have stayed here. Cr cds: A, MC, V.

D ⚡ ✕ 🔥 SC

Restaurant

✔ ★ ★ **COZY.** *105 Frederick Rd (MD 806), 3 blks E of US 15. 301/271-7373.* Hrs: 11 am-8:45 pm; Fri to 9:15 pm; Sat 8 am-9:15 pm; Sun 8 am-8:45 pm. Closed Dec 24, 25. Res accepted. Bar. Buffet: bkfst $5.99, lunch $5.59-$15.25, dinner $8.50-$15.25. Semi-a la carte: lunch $4.29-$5.99, dinner $8.19-$12.79. Child's meals. Specializes in fresh fish, poultry, rotisserie chicken. Own desserts. Patio dining (seasonal). Family-owned. Cr cds: A, MC, V.

D SC

Towson (B-7)

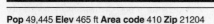

(See also Baltimore)

Pop 49,445 **Elev** 465 ft **Area code** 410 **Zip** 21204
Information Baltimore County Chamber of Commerce, 102 W Pennsylvania Ave, Ste 402; 410/825-6200.

What to See and Do

Fire Museum of Maryland. More than 60 pieces of antique fire-fighting equipment; includes motorized and hand/horse-drawn units from 1822-1957. (May, Sept-Oct, wkends; June-Aug, daily) 1301 York Rd, 1 blk N of I-695 exit 26B, in Lutherville. Phone 410/321-7500. ¢¢

Hampton National Historic Site. Includes ornate Georgian mansion (ca 1790) (tours), formal gardens and plantation outbuildings. Gift shop. (Daily; closed Jan 1, Thanksgiving, Dec 25) Tea room open for luncheon (daily exc Mon; closed 6 wks mid-Jan-early Mar). 535 Hampton Lane, ½ mi off Dulaney Valley Rd; I-695 exit 27B. Phone 410/823-1309. ¢¢

Soldiers Delight Natural Environment Area. This 1,725-acre park has 19th-century chrome mines; restored log cabin; scenic overlook; hiking, nature trails; picnicking (at visitor center only). It is the only undisturbed serpentine barren in the state. Pets must be on leash. 7 mi W on I-695, then W on MD 26, then 5 mi N on Deerpark Rd to overlook. Phone 410/922-3044.

Towson State University (1866). (15,000 students) On campus are three art galleries, including Holtzman Art Gallery, with an extensive collection of art media (Sept-May, Tues-Sat). Concerts and sporting events are held in the Towson Center. York Rd. For information on entertainment & events phone 410/830-ARTS.

Annual Event

State Fair. Timonium Fairgrounds, 3 mi N on York Rd, in Timonium. Ten-day festival of home arts; entertainment, midway; agricultural demonstrations, Thoroughbred horse racing, livestock presentations. Phone 410/252-0200. Aug 29-Sept 7.

Motor Hotel

★ ★ ★ **HOLIDAY INN SELECT.** *(2004 Greenspring Dr, Timonium 21093) I-83 exit 16. 410/252-7373; FAX 410/561-0182.* 250 rms, 5 story. S, D $119-$139; each addl $10; suites $259-$368; family, wkly, wknd, hol rates. Crib free. TV; cable (premium), VCR avail (movies). Indoor/outdoor pool; whirlpool, poolside serv. Restaurant 6 am-10 pm. Bars; entertainment. Ck-out noon. Coin lndry. Meeting rms. Business servs avail. In-rm modem link. Bellhops. Gift shop. Valet serv. Exercise equipt; weights, treadmill. Microwaves avail. Cr cds: A, C, D, DS, JCB, MC, V.

D ⚡ ✕ 🔥 SC

Hotels

✔ ★ ★ **DAYS HOTEL.** *(9615 Deereco Rd, Timonium 21093) I-83 exit 17, Padonia Rd. 410/560-1000; FAX 410/561-3918.* Web www.daysinn.com. 146 rms, 7 story. Apr-Nov: S $49.95-$85; D $55-$90; each addl $5; suites $100-$140; family, hol rates; lower rates rest of yr. Crib avail. TV; cable (premium), VCR. Pool. Complimentary continental bkfst. Restaurant open 24 hrs. Rm serv 7 am-10 pm. Bar. Ck-out noon. Guest lndry. Meeting rms. Business servs avail. In-rm modem link. Exercise equipt; weights, treadmill. Game rm. Refrigerators; microwaves avail. Cr cds: A, C, D, DS, JCB, MC, V.

D ⚡ ✕ 🔥 SC

★ ★ ★ **SHERATON BALTIMORE NORTH.** *903 Dulaney Valley Rd, I-695 exit 27A. 410/321-7400; FAX 410/296-9534.* Web www.sheraton baltimore.com. 284 units, 12 story. S, D $148-$170; each addl $12; suites $175-$350; under 17 free; wknd plans; higher rates Preakness. Crib free. TV; cable (premium). Indoor pool; whirlpool, poolside serv; lifeguard. Coffee in rms. Restaurant 6:30 am-10:30 pm. Bar 11:30-1 am; entertainment. Ck-out noon. Convention facilities. Business center. In-rm modem link. Gift shop. Free valet parking. Exercise equipt; weight machines, bicycles, sauna. Health club privileges. Refrigerators, microwaves avail. Cr cds: A, C, D, DS, MC, V.

D ⚡ ✕ 🔥 SC 🏃

Inn

★ ★ ★ **TWIN GATES.** *(308 Morris Ave, Lutherville 21093) N on MD 45 to I-695, W on I-695, exit 25. 410/252-3131; res: 800/635-0370.* Web www.innbook.com. 6 rms, 3 story. No rm phones. S, D $95-$155, each addl $30; suites $155. Children over 12 yrs only. TV in sitting rm. Complimentary full bkfst; afternoon refreshments. Restaurant nearby. Ck-out 11 am, ck-in 4-6 pm. Victorian mansion (1857), part of the underground RR during the Civil War. Totally nonsmoking. Cr cds: A, MC, V.

✕ 🔥

Restaurants

★ ★ **CAFE TROIA.** *28 W Allegheny Ave. 410/337-0133.* Hrs: 11 am-3 pm, 5-10 pm; Mon 5-10 pm; Fri to 11 pm; Sat 5-11 pm; Sun 5-9 pm. Res accepted. Italian menu. Bar. Semi-a la carte: lunch $4-$12, dinner

$9-$22. Specializes in regional Italian dishes. Outdoor dining. Cr cds: A, D, MC, V.

✔★ ★ **LIBERATORE'S RISTORANTE.** *(9515 Deereco Rd, Timonium 21093)* N on MD 45 to I-695, W on I-695, exit 25. 410/561-3300. Hrs: 11 am-10 pm; Fri, Sat to 11 pm; Sun 3-10 pm. Closed most major hols. Res accepted. Italian menu. Bar. A la carte entrees: lunch, dinner $3.95-$14.95. Specializes in pasta, chicken, seafood. Pianist Thurs-Sat. Italian decor. Cr cds: A, D, DS, MC, V.

D

★ ★ **PEERCE'S PLANTATION.** *(12460 Dulaney Valley Rd, Phoenix 21131)* 6 mi N of I-695 exit 27 N. 410/252-3100. Hrs: 11:30 am-3 pm, 5-10 pm; Fri, Sat to 11 pm; Sun 5-9 pm; Sun brunch 11:30 am-2 pm. Closed Dec 25. Res accepted. Continental menu. Bar 11:30-2 am. Semi-a la carte: lunch $6.25-$15, dinner $15.95-$25.95. Sun brunch $6.25-$12.95. Child's meals. Specialties: rack of lamb, filet Chesapeake. Valet parking. Outdoor dining. Antebellum decor. Scenic view of countryside overlooking Loch Raven Reservoir. Family-owned. Jacket. Cr cds: A, C, D, DS, MC, V.

D SC

★ ★ **ROTHWELL'S GRILLE.** *(106 W Padonia Rd, Timonium 21093)* 410/252-0600. Hrs: 11:30 am-midnight; Sat, Sun from 5 pm. Closed most major hols. Res accepted (dinner). Bar. Semi-a la carte: lunch $6-$12, dinner $9-$19. Specializes in fresh meats and fish cooked on woodburning grill. Own baking. Outdoor dining. Casual atmosphere. Cr cds: A, D, DS, MC, V.

D

★ ★ **THAT'S AMORE.** *720 Kennilworth Dr.* 410/825-5255. Hrs: 11:30 am-10:30 pm; Fri to midnight; Sat 4 pm-midnight; Sun 4-9:30 pm. Closed Labor Day, Thanksgiving, Dec 25. Italian menu. Bar. A la carte entrees: lunch $3.50-$10.95, dinner $16-$22. Specializes in seafood. Outdoor dining. Italian vineyard setting. Cr cds: A, C, D, DS, MC, V.

D

Waldorf (D-6)

(See also La Plata; also see District of Columbia)

Pop 15,058 **Elev** 215 ft **Area code** 301
Information Tourism Director, PO Box B, La Plata 20646; 301/645-0558 or 800/766-3386.

What to See and Do

Cedarville State Forest. Includes 3,697 acres of woodland, once home of the Piscataway, who settled around the Zekiah Swamp. Fishing, hunting. Nature, hiking trails. Picknicking. Standard fees. 4 mi E off US 301 on Cedarville Rd. Schedule varies, phone ahead; 301/856-8987 or 410/974-3771.

Farmer's Market and Auction. Nearby Amish farms offer fresh baked goods and produce (auction Wed) for sale; more than 90 shops. Antique dealers. (Wed & Sat) 13 mi SE on MD 5. Phone 301/884-3108.

✪ **John Wilkes Booth Escape Route.** After shooting Abraham Lincoln on Apr 14, 1865, John Wilkes Booth fled south into Maryland to rendezvous with his accomplice, David Herold at

Surratt House and Tavern (1852), where they recovered arms they had hidden there. Though she may have been innocent, Mary Surratt was hanged for conspiracy. Eight period rooms, museum; guides in period costumes; Dec candlelight tours; special events and exhibits throughout the year. (Mar-mid-Dec, Thurs-Sun) 9110 Brandywine Rd, Clinton (then Surrattsville). Phone 301/868-1121. ¢ Booth and Herold next stopped at

Dr. Samuel A. Mudd House Museum (ca 1830). Where Dr. Mudd set Booth's broken leg, unaware that Booth had just shot the president. Mudd was convicted and imprisoned for life, but pardoned four years later by President Andrew Johnson. Tours conducted by costumed docents, some of whom are Dr. Mudd's descendants. (Apr-Nov, Sat-Sun afternoons & Wed 11 am-3 pm; closed Easter Sun, Thanksgiving) From US 301, take MD 5, then left on MD 205, turn right on Poplar Hill Rd approx 4 mi, right on Dr Samuel Mudd Rd, continue to house; sign at entrance. Phone 301/934-8464 or 301/645-6870. ¢¢

Booth and Herold continued south, crossed the Potomac River and were captured at Garrett's farm, Virginia, on Apr 26; Booth was killed. (See ANNUAL EVENT)

Maryland Indian Cultural Center. Exhibits reflect diverse tribal structures, art, lodging construction and cultures of Native Americans. (Tues, Thurs, Sun afternoons) 16816 Country Ln. Phone 301/372-1932. **Free.**

Annual Event

John Wilkes Booth Escape Route Tour. Day-long bus tour of Booth's route from Ford's Theatre, Washington, through southern Maryland to site of Garrett's farm, Virginia, with expert commentary. For reservations phone 301/868-1121. Mid-Apr and early Sept.

Motels

★ **DAYS INN.** *5043 US 301 (20603).* 301/932-9200; FAX 301/843-9816. 101 rms, 3 story. S $43.95-$50; D $48.95-$80; suite $125-$150. each addl $5; under 18 free; wkly, monthly rates. Crib free. Pet accepted; $10. TV; cable (premium), VCR avail. Complimentary continental bkfst. Restaurant adj 11 am-10 pm. Ck-out 11 am. Coin lndry. Business servs avail. Game rm. Some refrigerators, in-rm whirlpools. Cr cds: A, C, D, DS, ER, JCB, MC, V.

D ✔ ≈ 🔥 SC

★ ★ **HOLIDAY INN.** *1 St Patrick's Dr (20603).* 301/645-8200; FAX 301/843-7945. 192 rms, 3 story, 8 kit. units. S, D $62-$68; each addl $6; suites, kit. units $70-$90; under 19 free. Crib free. Pet accepted; $50. TV; cable (premium). Pool; lifeguard. Complimentary coffee in rms. Restaurant 6:30 am-10 pm. Rm serv. Bar noon-11 pm. Ck-out 11 am. Coin lndry. Meeting rms. Business servs avail. In-rm modem link. Bellhops. Valet serv. Beauty shop. Health club privileges. Refrigerators avail. Cr cds: A, C, D, DS, JCB, MC, V.

D ✔ ≈ 🔥 SC

✔★ **HOWARD JOHNSON.** *3125 S Crain Hwy (US 301) (20602).* 301/932-5090; res: 800/826-4504. 109 rms. S $30-$45; D $30-$50; suites, kit. units $45-$60; under 18 free. Crib free. Pet accepted; $10. TV; cable (premium), VCR (movies). Pool. Complimentary continental bkfst. Restaurant adj 11 am-10 pm. Ck-out noon. Meeting rms. Business servs avail. Picnic tables, grills. Refrigerators avail. Cr cds: A, C, D, DS, JCB, MC, V.

D ✔ ≈ 🔥 SC

Hotel

★ ★ **COLONY SOUTH.** *(7401 Surratts Rd, Clinton 20735)* 8 mi SE on MD 5, near Andrews AFB. 301/856-4500; FAX 301/868-1439; res: 800/537-1147. 192 rms, 3 story. Mar-June: S $105; D $115; each addl $10; suites $135-$170; under 13 free; lower rates rest of yr. Crib avail. TV; cable (premium), VCR avail. Indoor pool; whirlpool. Restaurant 6 am-10 pm. Bar noon-2 am. Ck-out noon. Meeting rms. Business servs avail. Free airport transportation. Lighted tennis. Exercise rm; instructor, weights, bicycle, sauna. Some refrigerators, microwaves. Cr cds: A, C, D, DS, MC, V.

D 🏃 ≈ 🎿 🔥 SC

Westminster (B-6)

(See also Baltimore, Frederick)

Founded 1764 **Pop** 13,068 **Elev** 717 ft **Area code** 410

Westminster, a Union supply depot at the Battle of Gettysburg, saw scattered action before the battle. It is the county seat of Carroll County, first in the US to offer complete rural free delivery mail service (started in 1899 with four two-horse wagons).

Motel

★ ★ **COMFORT INN.** *451 WMC Dr (MD 140) (21158), adj to Western Maryland College.* 410/857-1900; FAX 410/857-9584. 101 rms, 1-2 story. May-June: S $69-$89; D $69-$159; each addl $10; under 18 free; wkly rates; monthly rates; higher rates: WMC parents wkend, graduation, Dec 31; lower rates rest of yr. Crib free. Pet accepted, some restrictions; $25 refundable. TV; cable. Pool; whirlpool. Complimentary continental bkfst. Ck-out 11 am. Meeting rms. Business servs avail. Valet serv. Tennis privileges. Golf privileges. Exercise equipt; bicycle, rower. Some in-rm whirlpools; microwaves avail. Cr cds: A, C, D, DS, ER, JCB, MC, V.

D 🐾 👫 ⚕ 🏊 ➤ 🎿 🔥 SC

Restaurants

✔★ **BAUGHER'S.** *289 W Main St (21158).* 410/848-7413. Hrs: 7:30 am-10 pm; Sun from 9 am; winter hrs vary. Closed most major hols. Semi-a la carte: bkfst $1.30-$3.75, lunch, dinner $1-$10.50. Specializes in Baugher's own farm-raised beef, ham, chicken. Own ice cream. Country-style restaurant; adj to farmer's market. Family-owned. Cr cds: DS, MC, V.

D ➤

★ ★ **CHAMELEON.** *32 W Main St (21157).* 410/876-9476. Hrs: 11 am-11 pm; Sun brunch from 11 am. Closed Mon; some major hols. Contemporary Amer menu. Bar to 1 am. Semi-a la carte: lunch $3.50-$7.50, dinner $9-$20. Specializes in fresh seafood, vegetarian and pasta dishes. Own baking, pasta. Outdoor dining. Contemporary cafe atmosphere; displays modern art by local artists. Cr cds: A, C, D, DS, MC, V.

D

★ ★ **JOHANSSON'S.** *4 W Main St (21157).* 410/876-0101. Hrs: 11 am-11 pm; Sat to midnight; Sun to 10 pm. Closed major hols. Res accepted; required Fri, Sat dinner. Bar to 1 am. Semi-a la carte: lunch $5.95-$8.95, dinner $11.95-$17.95. Child's meals. Specializes in veal, beef, fresh seafood. Musicians Fri. Outdoor dining. English pub atmosphere, originally a nickel-and-dime store; colored-glass artwork. Cr cds: A, DS, MC, V.

D ➤

★ ★ **RUDY'S 2900.** *(2900 Baltimore Blvd, Finksburg 21048) 8 mi E on US 140.* 410/833-5777. Hrs: 11:30 am-2:30 pm, 5:30-10 pm; Fri to 11 pm; Sat 5:30-11 pm; Sun 4-9 pm. Closed Mon; most major hols. Res accepted, required Fri, Sat dinner. Continental menu. Bar to 10:30 pm. Semi-a la carte: lunch $5.95-$11.95, dinner $9.95-$24.95. Specialties: roast duckling with plum sauce, grilled pork chop with fennel-flavored sausage, grouper in potato crust with red wine butter. Own pastries. Vocalist Wed. European decor; French impressionist oil paintings. Cr cds: A, D, DS, MC, V.

D ♥

New Jersey

Population: 7,730,188
Land area: 7,504 square miles
Elevation: 0-1,803 feet
Highest point: High Point Mountain (Sussex County)
Entered Union: Third of original 13 states (December 18, 1787)
Capital: Trenton
Motto: Liberty and prosperity
Nickname: Garden State
State flower: Purple violet
State bird: Eastern goldfinch
State tree: Red oak
State fair: Early August 1998, in Pennsauken (see Cherry Hill)
Time zone: Eastern
Web: www.state.nj.us/travel

Tree-shaded 18th-century towns and history-hallowed grounds, on which Revolutionary battles were fought, make this state one of dignified beauty and democratic tradition. More than 800 lakes and ponds, 100 rivers and streams and 1,400 miles of freshly stocked trout streams are scattered throughout its wooded, scenic northwest corner. The swampy meadows west of the New Jersey Turnpike have been reclaimed and transformed into commercial and industrial areas. The Meadowlands, a multimillion-dollar sports complex, offers horse racing, the NY Giants and the NY Jets NFL football teams, the NJ Devils NHL hockey team and the NJ Nets NBA basketball team. The coastline, stretching 127 miles from Sandy Hook to Cape May, offers excellent swimming and ocean fishing.

George Washington spent a quarter of his time here as commander-in-chief of the Revolutionary Army. On Christmas night in 1776, he crossed the Delaware and surprised the Hessians at Trenton. A few days later, he marched to Princeton and defeated three British regiments. He then spent the winter in Morristown, where the memories of his campaign are preserved in a national historical park.

New Jersey often is associated only with its factories, oil refineries, research laboratories and industrial towns. But history buffs, hunters, anglers, scenery lovers and amateur beachcombers need only to wander a short distance from its industrial areas to find whatever they like best.

When to Go/Climate

Moderate temperatures in spring and fall make these the best times to visit New Jersey. Summers can be hot and humid; winters can be bitterly cold, particularly in the inland mountain areas. Beaches are lovely, and coastal temperatures are often 5°F lower in summer and higher in winter than inland areas.

AVERAGE HIGH/LOW TEMPERATURES (°F)

ATLANTIC CITY

Jan 40/27	May 66/54	Sept 74/62
Feb 42/29	Jun 74/62	Oct 64/51
Mar 49/36	July 80/68	Nov 55/42
Apr 57/44	Aug 80/68	Dec 46/33

NEWARK

Jan 38/23	May 72/53	Sept 78/60
Feb 41/25	June 82/63	Oct 67/48
Mar 51/33	July 87/69	Nov 55/39
Apr 62/43	Aug 85/67	Dec 43/29

Parks and Recreation Finder

Directions to and information about the parks and recreation areas below are given under their respective town/city sections. Please refer to those sections for details.

Key to abbreviations: I.P. = Interstate Park; N.B.C. = National Battlefield & Cemetery; N.B.P. = National Battlefield Park; N.F. = National Forest; N.H. = National Historical Park; N.H.S. = National Historic Site; N.M. = National Monument; N.Mem. = National Memorial; N.M.P. = National Military Park; N.P. = National Park; N.Pres. = National Preserve; N.R. = National Recreational Area; N.S. = National Seashore; N.S.T. = National Scenic Trail; S.B. = State Beach; S.C.P. = State Conservation Park; S.G. = State Garden; S.H.A. = State Historic Area; S.H.P. = State Historic Park; S.N.A. = State Natural Area; S.P. = State Park; S.R. = State Reserve; S.R.A. =State Recreation Area; S.Res.P. = State Resort Park; S.R.P. = State Rustic Park.

NATIONAL PARK AND RECREATION AREAS

Place Name	Listed Under
Edison N.H.S.	WEST ORANGE
Morristown N.H.	same
Sandy Hook Unit of Gateway N.R.	same

STATE RECREATION AREAS

Place Name	Listed Under
Allaire S.P.	same
Allamuchy Mountain S.P. (Stephens Section)	HACKETTSTOWN
Barnegat Lighthouse S.P.	LONG BEACH ISLAND
Cheesequake S.P.	MATAWAN
Fort Mott S.P.	SALEM
High Point S.P.	same
Hopatcong S.P.	LAKE HOPATCONG
Island Beach S.P.	SEASIDE PARK
Liberty S.P.	JERSEY CITY
Parvin S.P.	BRIDGETON
Ringwood S.P.	same
Round Valley S.P.	CLINTON
Spruce Run S.R.A.	CLINTON
Stokes State Forest	BRANCHVILLE
Swartswood S.P.	BRANCHVILLE
Washington Crossing S.P.	TRENTON
Wharton State Forest	BATSTO

Water-related activities, hiking, riding, various sports, picnicking, camping and visitor centers are available in many of these areas. There is a $1/person (12-62 yrs) walk-in/bicycle fee in some areas; there is a parking fee ($2-$7) in many areas. In most areas, fees are collected Memorial Day wkend-Labor Day wkend; fees collected yr-round at Island Beach (see SEASIDE PARK). No pets in bathing, camping areas or buildings; in other day-use areas, pets must be attended and kept on a six-foot leash.

Bathing at inland beaches, Memorial Day-Labor Day; at ocean beaches from mid-June; cabins ($20-$100); campsites ($10-$12), lean-tos ($15); reservations accepted ($7, nonrefundable). Most areas are wildlife

sanctuaries. In addition, 1,700 acres of Palisades Interstate Parks (see) on the Hudson are in New Jersey. There are also more than 20 state-owned historic sites (clearly marked); some with museums and guides. For detailed information contact Division of Parks and Forestry, CN 404, Trenton 08625; 609/292-2797.

SKI AREAS

Place Name	Listed Under
Campgaw Mountain Ski Area	RAMSEY
Craigmeur Ski Area	NEWFOUNDLAND
Vernon Valley/Great Gorge Ski Area	VERNON

FISHING & HUNTING

Fishing opportunities abound in New Jersey's fresh and salt waters. No license is required for deep-sea or surf fishing along the 127-mile coastline; *however,* a license is required for taking shellfish. Nonresident clam license: $20; under age 14, $2. A license is required for freshwater fishing for everyone over 14 years of age. Nonresident fishing license: $25.25; nonresident trout stamp: $15.50; 7-day nonresident vacation fishing license: $16.50.

Hunting licenses are required for everyone over 10 years of age. Firearm or bow & arrow: nonresident, $100 each; small game only: nonresident, 2-day, $27.50; nonresident, 1-day, $7.75 (for commercial or semi-wild preserves only). Juveniles 10-13 with licensee over 21, $3. Woodcock stamp, $2.75; pheasant & quail stamp, $22 (for wildlife management areas only). Hunter Education Course or a previous year's resident license required to purchase license. For information contact Department of Environmental Protection, Division of Fish, Game and Wildlife, CN-400, Trenton 08625-0400; 609/292-2965.

Driving Information

Safety belts are mandatory for all persons in front seat of vehicle. Children under 5 years must be in an approved passenger restraint anywhere in vehicle: ages 18 months-5 years may use a regulation safety belt in back seat; however, in front seat, children must use an approved safety seat; children under 18 months must use an approved safety seat anywhere in vehicle. For further information phone 609/633-9300.

INTERSTATE HIGHWAY SYSTEM

The following alphabetical listing of New Jersey towns in *Mobil Travel Guide* shows that these cities are within 10 miles of the indicated Interstate highways. A highway map should be checked, however, for the nearest exit.

Highway Number	Cities/Towns within 10 miles
Interstate 78	Clinton, Plainfield, Scotch Plains, Somerville, Union.
Interstate 80	Fort Lee, Hackensack, Hackettstown, Paramus, Parsippany, Rockaway, Saddle Brook, Wayne.
Interstate 95	Elizabeth, Fort Lee, Newark, Trenton, Woodbridge.

Additional Visitor Information

The State Division of Travel and Tourism, CN-826, Trenton 08625, phone 609/292-2470 or 800/JERSEY-7, publishes a variety of materials for travelers. There are also two periodicals: *New Jersey Monthly* (write Subscription Dept, Box 936, Farmingdale, NY 11737); *New Jersey Outdoors* (write Dept of Environmental Protection & Energy, CN-402, Trenton 08625).

There are eight tourist welcome centers and numerous information centers in New Jersey. At these centers visitors will find information racks with brochures to help plan trips to points of interest. For a publication with the locations of the centers contact the State Division of Travel and Tourism.

Allaire State Park (F-5)

(For accommodations see Asbury Park, Freehold)

(On County 524 between Farmingdale and Lakewood)

Allaire State Park has more than 3,000 acres and offers a fishing pond for children under 14; bridle trails; picnic facilities; playground; camping (dump station, summer); and the opportunity to visit a historic 19th-century village (see below). Park (daily). Standard fees when village buildings are open. For more information contact PO Box 220, Farmingdale 07727; 732/938-2371. Parking fee (Memorial Day-Labor Day, wkends) ¢¢

What to See and Do

Historic Allaire Village. In 1822, James Allaire bought this site as a source of bog ore for his ironworks. Approx 500 residents turned out hollow-ware caldrons, pots, kettles and pipes for New York City's waterworks. Today, visitors can explore the enameling furnace, a bakery, carriage house, general store, blacksmith and carpentry shops, workmen's houses, the community church and other buildings still much as they were in 1835. Village grounds (all yr); village buildings (May-Labor Day, wkends); special events (Feb-Dec). For information phone village office, 732/938-2253. **Free.**

Train Rides. Narrow-gauge steam locomotive rides (mid-June-Labor Day, daily; Apr-mid-June & after Labor Day-Nov, Sat & Sun). Phone 732/938-5524. ¢

Asbury Park (E-6)

Settled 1871 **Pop** 16,799 **Elev** 21 ft **Area code** 732 **Zip** 07712
Information Greater Asbury Park Chamber of Commerce, 100 Lake Ave, PO Box 649; 732/775-7676.

This popular shore resort was bought in 1871 by New York brush manufacturer James A. Bradley and named for Francis Asbury, first American Bishop of the Methodist Episcopal Church. Bradley established a town for temperance advocates and good neighbors. The beach and the three lakes proved so attractive that, by 1874, Asbury Park had grown into a borough, and by 1897, a city. It is the home of the famous boardwalk, Convention Hall and Paramount Theatre. In September 1934, the SS *Morro Castle* was grounded off this beach and burned with a loss of 122 lives. Asbury Park became the birthplace of a favorite sweet when a local confectioner introduced "saltwater taffy" and watched the sales curve rise with the tide. Today, this is a popular resort area for swimming and fishing.

What to See and Do

Long Branch Historical Museum (Church of the Presidents). Presidents Grant, Garfield, Arthur, McKinley, Hayes, Harrison and Wilson worshiped here. Museum contains items of interest from post-Civil War to the present; also records, pictures, relics of period between the Civil War and World War I when the resort was the playground of notables. (By appt) 3 mi N at 1260 Ocean Ave in Elberon section of Long Branch. Phone 732/229-0600 or 732/222-9879. **Free.**

Annual Events

Jazz Fest. Phone 732/775-7676 or 732/502-5728. July.

Seasonal Events

Horse racing. Monmouth Park. Oceanport Ave in Oceanport via NJ 35 N to NJ 36; or via Garden State Pkwy exit 105, then E on NJ 36. Thoroughbred racing. Phone 732/222-5100. Tues, Wed, Fri-Sun, Memorial Day-Labor Day.

Metro Lyric Opera Series. At the Paramount Theater on the Boardwalk. Phone 908/531-2378 for schedule, information. Sat evenings, July-Aug.

Restaurants

★ ★ **CHRISTIE'S.** *(1 English Lane, Wanamassa)* N of Asbury Park Circle, off NJ 35. 732/776-8558. Hrs: 11:30 am-10 pm; Sat 5 pm-midnight; Sun from 1 pm; early-bird dinner 4:30-6:30 pm. Closed Mon; Thanksgiving, Dec 25. Res accepted. Italian, Amer menu. Bar. Semi-a la carte: lunch $15.95-$9.95, dinner $9.95-$18.95. Child's meals. Specialties: sea feast Fra Diavolo, duckling à l'orange, saltimbocca a la Christie. Entertainment. Valet parking. Spacious grounds with outdoor garden overlooking golf course. Family-owned. Cr cds: A, C, D, DS, MC, V.

★ **LA NONNA PIANCONE'S CAFE.** *(800 Main St, Bradley Beach 07720)* 1 mi S on NJ 71. 732/775-0906. Hrs: 11:30 am-11 pm; Fri, Sat to midnight; Sun 3-10 pm. Closed Jan 1, Thanksgiving, Dec 25. Italian menu. Bar to 1 am. A la carte entrees: lunch $5.95-$11.95, dinner $7.95-$16.95. Child's meals. Specialties: mozzarella tower, zuppa di pesce, filet mignon. Own pastries. Accordianist Fri, Sat. Outdoor dining. Casual Italian decor; open kitchen, brick archway. Cr cds: A, DS, MC, V.

★ ★ **MOONSTRUCK.** *(57 Main Ave, Ocean Grove 07756)* ½ mi S on NJ 71. 732/988-0123. Hrs: 5-10 pm; Sat to 10:30 pm; Sun to 9:30 pm. Closed Mon; some major hols; also Jan-mid-Feb. Italian, Mediterranean menu. A la carte entrees: dinner $9.95-$22.95. Specialties: Mediterranean antipasto, grilled Asian shrimp, raspberry chicken. Own pastries. Outdoor dining. Two-level dining in casual cafe atmosphere. Cr cds: MC, V.

Atlantic City (J-4)

(See also Ocean City)

Settled 1854 **Pop** 37,986 **Elev** 8 ft **Area code** 609
Information Greater Atlantic City Convention & Visitors Authority, 2314 Pacific Ave, 08401; 609/348-7100, 888/ACVISIT or 800/BOARDWALK.

Honeymooners, conventioneers, Miss America and some 37 million annual visitors have made Atlantic City the best-known New Jersey beach resort. Built on Absecon Island, it is shielded by the curve of the coast from battering northeastern storms while the nearby Gulf Stream warms its waters, helping to make it a year-round resort. A 60-foot-wide boardwalk extends along five miles of beaches. Hand-pushed wicker rolling chairs take visitors up and down the Boardwalk. Absecon Lighthouse ("Old Ab"), a well-known landmark, was first lit in 1857 and now stands in an uptown city park. The game of Monopoly uses Atlantic City street names.

What to See and Do

Amusement piers.

The Shops on Ocean One. A 900-ft, 3-deck shopping pier houses shops, food court & restaurants. (Daily) Boardwalk at Arkansas Ave. Phone 609/347-8082.

Garden Pier. Atlantic City Art Center and Atlantic City Historical Museum are located here. (Daily) Boardwalk & New Jersey Ave. Phone 609/347-5844. **Free.**

Convention Center. Seats 22,000; one of the world's largest pipe organs. Can accommodate small meetings as well as large conventions, sports events; site of the annual Miss America Pageant. Phone 609/348-7000.

Edwin B. Forsythe National Wildlife Refuge, Brigantine Division. Auto-tour route; interpretive nature trails (daily). Over the years, more than 200 species of birds have been observed at this 40,000-acre refuge. Public-use area has an 8-mi wildlife drive through diversified wetlands and uplands habitat; most popular in the spring and fall, during the course of the waterbird migration, and at sunset, when the birds roost for the evening. Refuge headquarters (Mon-Fri). 9 mi N on US 9. Contact PO Box 72, Great Creek Rd, Oceanville 08231; 609/652-1665. Per vehicle ¢¢

Fishing. Surf fishing and deep-sea fishing. License may be required, check locally. Charter boats (Mar-Nov). Many tournaments are scheduled. Contact Atlantic City Party and Charter Boat Assn. Phone 609/645-4001.

Historic Gardner's Basin. An eight-acre, sea-oriented park featuring the working lobstermen; US Coast Guard Lightship; speed boat belonging to Guy Lombardo. Educational aquarium with local species. Picnicking. (Daily) 800 New Hampshire Ave, at N end of city.Phone 609/348-2880.

Historic Town of Smithville and the Village Greene at Smithville (1787). Restored 18th-century village with specialty shops and restaurants. Also carousel, horse-drawn carriage rides, train ride, paddle boats and miniature golf (Apr-Oct, fee for some activities). Village (daily). Special events throughout the yr. 7 mi W on US 30 to Absecon, then 6 mi N on US 9, at Moss Mill Rd. Phone 609/652-7777 or -0440.

Lucy, the Margate Elephant. Only elephant in the world you can walk through and come out alive. Guided tour and exhibit inside this six-story elephant-shaped building. Built 1881; spiral stairs in Lucy's legs lead to main hall & observation area on her back. Gift shop. Concession. Free outdoor concerts (July-Aug, Thurs evenings). (Mid-June-Labor Day, daily; Apr-mid-June & Sept-Oct, Sat & Sun only) S via Atlantic Ave in Margate. Phone 609/823-6473. ¢¢

Marine Mammal Stranding Center & Museum. One of few marine mammal rescue and rehabilitation centers in US. Injured dolphins, turtles and other marine animals are brought to center for treatment. Museum offers exhibits on mammal species; recuperating animals can be viewed at center. Dolphin & whale watch tours avail (fee; res required). (Memorial Day-Labor Day, daily; rest of yr, wkends only; closed some hols) Over bridge and 2 mi N, at 3625 Atlantic-Brigantine Blvd. Phone 609/266-0538. **Donation.**

Noyes Museum. Rotating and permanent exhibits of American art; collection of working bird decoys. (Wed-Sun; closed major hols) Admission free Fri. 12 mi NW via US 9, on Lily Lake Rd in Oceanville. Phone 609/652-8848. ¢¢

Recreation areas. Beach (Memorial Day-mid-Sept; free), surfing at special areas (daily); boating. Bicycling and rolling chairs on Boardwalk (daily); golf, tennis.

Renault Winery. Guided tour (approx 1 hr) includes wine-aging cellars; press room; antique wine-making equipment; free wine tasting (daily). Restaurant (Fri-Sun; res recommended); garden cafe (daily exc Sun). 16 mi W on US 30 in Egg Harbor City. Phone 609/965-2111. Tour ¢

Storybook Land. More than 50 storybook buildings and displays depicting children's stories; live animals; rides; picnic area, playground, concession. (May-mid-Sept, daily; Mar-Apr & mid-Sept-Thanksgiving, Sat & Sun only) Christmas Fantasy with Lights and visiting with Mr. and Mrs. Santa (Thanksgiving-Dec 30, nightly). Admission includes attractions and unlimited rides. 10 mi W via US 40, 322. Phone 609/641-7847. ¢¢¢

Annual Events

Boardwalk National Professional Fine Arts Show. Phone 609/347-5844. June.

LAGA Atlantic City Classic. Phone 609/927-7888. Late June.

Miss America Pageant. Convention Center. Usually 1st or 2nd wkend after Labor Day.

Indian Summer Boardwalk Art & Craft Show. Phone 609/347-5837. Usually 3rd wkend Sept.

Atlantic City Marathon. Phone 609/822-6911. Mid-Oct.

Seasonal Event

Horse racing. Atlantic City Race Course. 14 mi NW at jct Black Horse Pike & US 40 in May's Landing. Thoroughbred racing Wed-Sat evenings. Phone 609/641-2190. June-Aug.

Motels

★ ★ **BEST WESTERN BAYSIDE RESORT.** (8029 Black Horse Pike, West Atlantic City 08232) 2 mi W on US 40, 322. 609/641-3546; FAX 609/641-4329. 110 rms, 2 story. July-mid-Sept: S, D $85-$125; each addl $10; under 12 free; lower rates rest of yr. TV; cable (premium), VCR avail. Pool; wading pool. Supervised child's activites (June-Aug; ages 8-15). Restaurant 7 am-10 pm. Serv bar. Ck-out 11 am. Coin lndry. Meeting rms. Business servs avail. Airport transportation. Indoor & outdoor tennis, pro. Exercise rm; instructor, weight machines, bicycles, sauna. On bay. Cr cds: A, C, D, DS, MC, V.

D ⤳ ≈ ✗ ⊠ 🔥 SC

✔★ ★ **FAIRFIELD INN BY MARRIOTT.** (405 E Abescon Blvd, Abescon 08201) 3 mi W on US 30. 609/646-5000; FAX 609/383-8744. Web www.fairfieldinn.com. 200 rms, 6 story. S, D $40-$129; each addl $10; suites $75-$199; under 18 free. Crib free. TV; cable (premium). Pool. Complimentary continental bkfst. Restaurant nearby. Ck-out 11 am. Meeting rms. Business servs avail. In-rm modem link. Cr cds: A, C, D, DS, MC, V.

D ≈ ⊠ 🔥 SC

★ ★ **HAMPTON INN.** (240 E White Horse Pike, Absecon 08201) 7 mi W on US 30. 609/652-2500; FAX 609/652-2212. Web www.hamptoninn.com. 129 rms, 4 story. Memorial Day-Labor Day: S, D $63-$109; suites $92-$146; under 18 free; higher rates hols; lower rates rest of yr. Crib free. TV; cable (premium), VCR avail. Pool; whirlpool, lifeguard. Complimentary continental bkfst. Restaurant adj open 24 hrs. Ck-out 11 am. Coin lndry. Meeting rms. Business servs avail. In-rm modem link. Free airport transportation. Cr cds: A, C, D, DS, MC, V.

D ≈ ⊠ 🔥 SC

★ ★ **HAMPTON INN-WEST.** (7079 Black Horse Pike, West Atlantic City 08232) 2 mi W on US 40, 322. 609/484-1900; FAX 609/383-0731. Web www.hampton-inn.com. 143 rms, 6 story. June-Sept: S, D $65-$135; family rates; higher rates: hols (2-day min), Miss America Pageant; lower rates rest of yr. Crib free. TV; cable (premium). Complimentary continental bkfst. Ck-out 11 am. Meeting rm. Business servs avail. Cr cds: A, C, D, DS, MC, V.

D ⊠ 🔥 SC

✔★ **SUPER 8-ABSECON.** (229 E US 30, Absecon 08201) 7 mi W on US 30. 609/652-2477; FAX 609/748-0666. 58 rms, 2 story. July 4-Sept 1: S, D $55-$125; suites $80-$150; under 12 free; lower rates rest of yr. TV; cable (premium). Complimentary coffee in lobby. Restaurant opp open 24 hrs. Ck-out noon. Business servs avail. Refrigerators avail. Cr cds: A, C, D, DS, MC, V.

D ⊠ 🔥 SC

Hotels

★ ★ ★ **ATLANTIC CITY HILTON.** Boston at Pacific (08404). 609/347-7111; FAX 609/340-4858; res: 800/257-8677. Web www.hilton.com. 803 rms, 22 story. Late June-Sept: S, D $125-$215; each addl $20; suites $210-$400; under 12 free; lower rates rest of yr. Crib free. TV; cable (premium), VCR avail. Indoor pool; whirlpool, poolside serv, lifeguard. Free supervised child's activities (June-Aug). Restaurant, bar open 24 hrs; entertainment. Ck-out noon. Convention facilities. Business servs avail. Concierge. Barber, beauty shop. Valet parking. Exercise rm; instructor, weights, bicycles, steam rm, sauna. Game rm. Bathrm phones. On beach. Cr cds: A, C, D, DS, MC, V.

D ≈ ✗ ⊠ 🔥

★ ★ ★ **BALLY'S PARK PLACE.** Park Place at Boardwalk (08401). 609/340-2000; FAX 609/340-4713; res: 800/225-5977 (exc NJ). Web www.bally.com. The two buildings composing this hotel are emblematic of Atlantic City present and past—there is the new hexagonal tower with a glitzy 93-foot escalator at its core, and the old Denis Hotel, built of stone, with a mansard roof and guest rooms decorated in art-deco style. 1,268 rms, 49 story. Mid-June-Sept: S, D $95-$215; each addl $15; under

18 free; lower rates rest of yr. Crib free. TV; cable (premium), VCR avail. 2 pools, 1 indoor; whirlpool, poolside serv, lifeguard. Restaurants open 24 hrs. Bars. Ck-out noon. Convention facilities. Business servs avail. In-rm modem link. Barber, beauty shop. Valet parking; self-park garage. Exercise rm; instructor, weight machines, bicycles, sauna, steam rm. Massage. Bathrm phones; refrigerators avail. On beach. Cr cds: A, C, D, DS, MC, V.

★ ★ ★ CAESARS ATLANTIC CITY HOTEL/CASINO. *Pacific & Arkansas Aves (08401).* 609/348-4411; FAX 609/347-8089; res: 800/443-0104. Web www.caesars.com. 1138 rms, 20 story. June-Labor Day: S, D $130-$300; each addl $15; lower rates rest of yr. Crib avail. TV; cable (premium), VCR avail (movies). Pool; whirlpool, lifeguard. Restaurants, bars open 24 hrs. Ck-out noon. Convention facilities. Business servs avail. Shopping arcade. Barber, beauty shop. Airport transportation. Tennis. Exercise equipt; weight machines, bicycles, steam rm, sauna. Massage. Microwaves avail. On ocean. Cr cds: A, C, D, DS, MC, V.

★ ★ CLARIDGE CASINO/HOTEL. *Indiana at Boardwalk (08401).* 609/340-3400; FAX 609/345-8909; res: 800/257-8585. 504 rms, 24 story. July-early Sept: S, D $130-$165; each addl $10; under 12 free; lower rates rest of yr. TV; cable (premium). Indoor pool; whirlpool, lifeguard. Restaurant open 24 hrs. Rm serv 24 hrs. Bar open 24 hrs. Ck-out noon. Meeting rms. Business servs avail. Concierge. Beauty shop. Exercise rm; instructor, weights, bicycles, steam rm, sauna. Refrigerators. On ocean. Cr cds: A, C, D, DS, MC, V.

✔★ ★ COMFORT INN-NORTH. *(539 Absecon Blvd, Absecon 08201) 3 mi W on US 30.* 609/641-7272; FAX 609/646-3286. 205 rms, 7 story. S, D $54-$150; each addl $10; under 12 free. Crib avail. TV; cable (premium). Complimentary continental bkfst. Ck-out noon. Meeting rms. Business servs avail. Exercise equipt; bicycle, stair machines. Cr cds: A, C, D, DS, MC, V.

★ ★ HOLIDAY INN-BOARDWALK. *Chelsea Ave at Boardwalk (08401).* 609/348-2200; FAX 609/348-0168. Web www.holiday-inn/hotels/acybw.com/hotels/acybw. 220 rms, 21 story. Mid-June-Labor Day: S, D $98-$199; each addl $15; under 19 free; lower rates rest of yr. Crib avail. TV; cable (premium). Pool; poolside serv. Restaurant 7-2 am. Bar 11:30-2 am. Ck-out 11 am. Meeting rms. Business servs avail. In-rm modem link. Health club privileges. On ocean. Cr cds: A, C, D, DS, JCB, MC, V.

★ ★ RESORTS CASINO HOTEL. *N Carolina Ave at Boardwalk (08404).* 609/344-6000; FAX 609/340-6284; res: 800/336-6378 (exc NJ). Web www.resortsac.com. 662 rms, 15 story. July-Labor Day: S, D $70-$225; each addl $10; lower rates rest of yr. Crib free. TV; cable. Indoor/outdoor pool; whirlpool. Restaurants, bars open 24 hrs. Ck-out noon. Convention facilities. Business servs avail. In-rm modem link. Concierge. Shopping arcade. Valet parking. Airport transportation. Exercise equipt; weights, bicycles, steam rm, sauna. Game rm. Bathrm phones. Some balconies. First casino in Atlantic City. Cr cds: A, C, D, DS, JCB, MC, V.

★ ★ SANDS HOTEL CASINO. *Indiana Ave at Brighton Park (08401).* 609/441-4000; FAX 609/441-4180; res: 800/257-8580. 534 rms, 21 story. July-Sept: S, D $99-$229; each addl $12; under 12 free; package plans; lower rates rest of yr. Crib free. TV; cable (premium), VCR avail. Supervised child's activities. Restaurant, bar open 24 hrs; entertainment. Ck-out noon. Convention facilities. Business servs avail. Concierge. Beauty salon. Valet, garage parking. Airport transportation. Exercise equipt; weight machines, bicycles, sauna. On ocean. Cr cds: A, C, D, DS, MC, V.

★ ★ SHOWBOAT CASINO HOTEL. *Delaware Ave at Boardwalk (08404).* 609/343-4000; FAX 609/345-2334; res: 800/621-0200. 775 rms, 24 story. July-mid-Sept: S, D $140-$180; each addl $15; suites $200-$472; under 12 free; mid-wk packages; lower rates rest of yr. Crib

free. TV; cable (premium), VCR avail. Pool; whirlpool, lifeguard. Supervised child's activities. Restaurant, bar open 24 hrs; entertainment. Ck-out noon. Convention facilities. Business servs avail. Beauty shop. Airport transportation. Bowling center. Game rm. Exercise rm; instructor, weights, stair machines, sauna. Bathrm phones. Some refrigerators. Some balconies. On ocean; ocean view from most rms. Cr cds: A, C, D, DS, MC, V.

★ ★ ★ TROPICANA CASINO. *Brighton at Boardwalk (08401).* 609/340-4000; FAX 609/343-5211; res: 800/257-6227. Web www.tropicana.com. 1,624 rms, 23 story. Mid-June-Sept: S, D $105-$225; under 16 free; lower rates rest of yr. TV; cable (premium), VCR avail. 2 pools, 1 indoor; whirlpool, poolside serv, lifeguard. Restaurants, bars open 24 hrs. Ck-out noon. Business servs avail. In-rm modem link. Shopping arcade. Barber, beauty shop. Valet, garage parking. Lighted tennis. Exercise rm; instructor, weights, bicycles, sauna. Some bathrm phones. On ocean. Cr cds: A, DS, MC, V.

★ ★ TRUMP PLAZA HOTEL & CASINO. *Mississippi & Boardwalk (08401).* 609/441-6000; FAX 609/441-2603; res: 800/677-7378. 904 rms, 38 story. June-Sept: S, D $195-$240; each addl $10; under 16 free; lower rates rest of yr. Crib avail. TV; cable (premium), VCR avail. Indoor pool; whirlpool, lifeguard. Restaurants open 24 hrs (also see IVANKA'S). Bar; entertainment. Ck-out noon. Business servs avail. In-rm modem link. Concierge. Shopping arcade. Beauty shop. Garage parking. Tennis. Golf privileges. Exercise rm; instructor, weights, bicycles, sauna, steam rm. Massage. Game rm. Bathrm phones. On ocean. Ultramodern guest rms. Cr cds: A, C, D, DS, MC, V.

★ ★ ★ TRUMP TAJ MAHAL CASINO RESORT. *1000 Boardwalk (08401), at Virginia Ave.* 609/449-1000; FAX 609/449-6818; res: 800/825-8786. Web www.trumptaj.com. As the tallest building in New Jersey, with the largest casino and most convention space of any Atlantic City hotel, this property fulfills its grand intentions. Its glittering turrets, domes and belvederes are prominent features of the local skyline. 1,250 rms, 51 story. 246 suites. July-Labor Day: S, D $165-$250; each addl $25; suites $275-$800; lower rates rest of yr. Crib free. TV; cable (premium). Indoor pool; whirlpool, poolside serv, lifeguard. Restaurant open 24 hrs. Bar; entertainment. Ck-out noon. Convention facilities. Business center. Concierge. Shopping arcade. Barber, beauty shop. Valet parking. Exercise rm; instructor, weights, bicycles, sauna, steam rm. Massage. Casino. Game rm. Bicycles avail. Refrigerators avail. Cr cds: A, C, D, DS, MC, V.

★ ★ ★ TRUMP WORLD'S FAIR CASINO. *2500 Boardwalk (08401), at Florida Ave.* 609/344-4000; FAX 609/344-1663; res: 800/234-5678. 500 rms, 22 story. Memorial Day-Labor Day: S, D $175-$195; each addl $15; suites $195-$510; under 12 free; lower rates rest of yr. Crib free. TV; cable. Indoor pool; whirlpool, lifeguard. Restaurant 7 am-midnight. Bar from 11 am. Ck-out noon. Convention facilities. Business servs avail. In-rm modem link. Concierge. Gift shop. Valet parking. Tennis. Exercise rm; instructor, weights, bicycles, sauna, steam rm. Massage. Bathroom phones; refrigerators avail. On ocean; beach. Cr cds: A, C, D, DS, MC, V.

★ ★ ★ TRUMP'S CASTLE CASINO RESORT. *1 Castle Blvd (08401), marina area.* 609/441-2000; FAX 609/441-8541; res: 800/777-8477. With its helicopter service and the state's largest marina, this hotel caters to a sophisticated clientele. Decorated with fanciful medieval motifs, it hosts major sports and entertainment events. 728 rms, 27 story. July-mid-Sept: S, D $110-$160; each addl $15; suites $150-$265; under 12 free; package plans; lower rates rest of yr. Crib free. TV; cable (premium), VCR avail. Pool; wading pool, whirlpool, poolside serv, lifeguard. Restaurants open 24 hrs. Bars; entertainment. Ck-out noon. Convention facilities. Business servs avail. In-rm modem link. Shopping arcade. Barber, beauty shop. Garage parking. Lighted tennis. Exercise rm; instructor, weights, bicycles, sauna, steam rm. Massage. Health club privileges. Basketball. Lawn games. Game rm. On ocean inlet. Cr cds: A, C, D, DS, JCB, MC, V.

Resort

★ ★ ★ **MARRIOTT'S SEAVIEW RESORT.** *(401 S New York Rd, Absecon 08201) 7 mi W on US 9, just N of Absecon. 609/748-1990; FAX 609/652-6917.* Web www.marriott.com. 300 rms; 3, 4 story. EP, May-Nov: S, D $159-$220; suites $250-$700; under 18 free; golf, package plans; lower rates rest of yr. Crib free. TV; cable (premium), VCR avail (free movies). 2 pools, 1 indoor; whirlpool, poolside serv, lifeguard. Dining rm 6:30 am-10 pm. Rm serv. Box lunches. Snack bar at pro shop. Bar noon-2 am. Ck-out 12:30 pm, ck-in 4 pm. Coin lndry. Convention facilities. Business center. In-rm modem link. Sports dir. 8 tennis courts, 4 lighted, pro. 36-hole golf, pro, 9-hole putting green; golf school. Rec rm. Game rm. Exercise equipt; weights, bicycles, sauna. Refrigerator, fireplace, private patio in suites. Located on 670-acre estate. Cr cds: A, C, D, DS, ER, JCB, MC, V.

D 🛆🏌🏊🏇🏃🏂🏄 SC ⛷

Restaurants

✔★ **BAY VIEW CAFE.** *(9707 Amherst Ave, Margate 08402) 5 mi S on Amherst Ave on the bay. 609/822-7676.* Hrs: 8-2 am. Closed Nov-Apr. Bar. Semi-a la carte: bkfst $2.75-$7.95, lunch $2.95-$8.95, dinner $10.95-$23.95. Child's meals. Specializes in fresh seafood. Entertainment Sat, Sun. Outdoor dining. Overlooks bay, marina. Cr cds: A, C, D, DS, MC, V.

D 🛆

★ ★ ★ **BRIGHTON STEAKHOUSE.** *(See Sands Hotel Casino)* 609/441-4300. Hrs: 6-10 pm; Fri, Sat to 10:30 pm; Sun brunch 10 am-2 pm. Closed Tues, Wed. Res required. Continental menu. Bar noon-midnight. Wine list. A la carte entrees: dinner $18-$48. Sun brunch $23.95. Specialties: chateaubriand, pepper-seared tuna, Brighton seafood harvest. Tropical decor. Cr cds: A, C, D, DS, MC, V.

D 🛆

★ **CAPTAIN YOUNG'S SEAFOOD EMPORIUM.** *1 Atlantic Ocean, on 3rd floor of The Shops on Ocean One Mall. 609/344-2001.* Hrs: 11:30 am-9 pm; Sat to 10 pm. Closed Thanksgiving, Dec 25. Bar. Semi-a la carte: lunch $6.25-$8.95, dinner $13.95-$19.95. Specializes in fresh fish, fresh lobster, crab legs. Overlooks beach and Boardwalk. Cr cds: A, C, D, DS, MC, V.

D 🛆 ♥

★ ★ **CHEF VOLA'S.** *111 S Albion Place (08400). 609/345-2022.* Hrs: 6-10 pm. Closed Mon; Thanksgiving, Dec 24, 25. Res required. Italian menu. A la carte: dinner $13.95-$30. Specializes in steak, veal. Italian decor. Photographs of celebrities. No cr cds accepted.

★ ★ ★ **CHINA MOON.** *(See Sands Hotel Casino)* 609/441-4100. Hrs: 6-10 pm; Fri-Sun to 10:30 pm. Closed Wed, Thurs. Res required. Chinese menu. Bar noon-midnight. Wine list. A la carte entrees: dinner $14.95-$42. Specialties: China Moon chicken, Dragon Phoenix, filet with mixed vegetables. Own baking. Elegant decor; gold Chinese script accents black walls. Cr cds: A, C, D, DS, MC, V.

D

★ ★ **DOCK'S OYSTER HOUSE.** *2405 Atlantic Ave (08400). 609/345-0092.* Hrs: 5-10:30 pm. Closed Mon; also Jan, Dec. Res accepted. Bar. Semi-a la carte: dinner $13.95-$29. Child's meals. Specialties: imperial crab, oyster stew. Pianist Thurs-Sat. Parking. Casual atmosphere in family-owned restaurant since 1897. Cr cds: A, D, MC, V.

D

★ **GRABEL'S.** *3901 Atlantic Ave (08401). 609/344-9263.* Hrs: 3 pm-7 am. Closed Dec 24. Res accepted. Continental menu. Bar. Semi-a la carte: dinner $4.95-$21.95. Child's meals. Specialties: veal rollintine, black Angus New York strip, crab cakes. Pianist Wed-Sun. Modern decor; casual dining. Family-owned. No cr cds accepted.

D

✔ ★ **HARLEY DAWN DINER.** *(1402 Blackhorse Pike, Folsom 08037) 20 mi W on US 322. 609/567-6084.* Web www.njra.com. Hrs: 6 am-10 pm. Closed Dec 25. Semi-a la carte: bkfst $1.75-$6.95, lunch $1.95-$5.75, dinner $5.25-$12.95. Child's meals. Specialties: chicken & broccoli Harley Dawn-style, broiled crab cakes, eggs Benedict. Own breads. Authentic diner atmosphere. Cr cds: A, DS, MC, V.

D 🛆

★ ★ ★ **IVANKA'S.** *(See Trump Plaza Hotel & Casino)* 609/441-6400. Hrs: 6-10:30 pm; Sat 6-11 pm; Sun 10 am-2 pm. Closed Tues-Thurs. Res accepted. Bar. Wine list. A la carte entrees: dinner $23-$36. Specialties: veal medallions, grilled loin of lamb, roast duckling. Own baking. Pianist. Valet parking. Cr cds: A, C, D, DS, MC, V.

D 🛆

★ ★ **OLD WATERWAY INN.** *1700 W Riverside Dr. 609/347-1793.* Hrs: 5-11 pm. Closed Mon, Tues Oct-Apr. Res accepted. Bar. Semi-a la carte: dinner $15-$24. Child's meals. Specializes in fresh seafood and Cajun specialities. Own pasta. Outdoor dining. Nautical decor. On waterfront; view of skyline. Cr cds: A, D, MC, V.

D

★ ★ ★ **RAM'S HEAD INN.** *(9 W White Horse Pike, Absecon 08201) on US 30 at Garden State Pkwy exit 40 S. 609/652-1700.* Hrs: noon-3 pm, 5-9:30 pm; Sat 5-10 pm; Sun 1:30-7:30 pm. Res accepted. Closed Mon; Labor Day, Dec 24. Continental menu. Bar. Semi-a la carte: lunch $7.25-$12.95, dinner $16.95-$25.95. Child's meals. Specializes in colonial Amer dishes, fresh southern New Jersey seafood, duckling. Own baking. Pianist. Valet parking. Outdoor dining. Colonial decor; gallery with paintings, plants. Jacket (dinner). Cr cds: A, C, D, DS, MC, V.

D

★ ★ ★ **RENAULT WINERY.** *(72 N Bremen Ave, Egg Harbor City) 16 mi W on US 30. 609/965-2111.* Hrs: 11:30 am-3 pm; 5-9 pm; Sun from 4:30 pm; Sun brunch 10:30 am-2:30 pm. Closed Dec 25. Res required. Wine list. Semi a la carte: lunch $5-$7. Complete meals: dinner $24-$31. Sun brunch $14.95. Specializes in fresh seafood, poultry, beef. Menu changes wkly. Pianist/guitarist. Parking. Elegant dining in eclectic Methode Champenoise rm of winery founded in 1864. Cr cds: A, C, D, MC, V.

D

★ ★ **SCANNICCHIO'S.** *119 S California Ave. 609/348-6378.* Web www.atlantic/city/online.com/scannicchios. Hrs: 4 pm-midnight. Closed most major hols. Res required wknds. Italian menu. Bar. A la carte entrees: dinner $11.95-$19.95. Specializes in veal, fresh seafood. Intimate ambiance. Cr cds: A, C, D, DS, MC, V.

D

Unrated Dining Spot

IRISH PUB AND INN. *St James Place & Boardwalk. 609/344-9063.* Open 24 hrs. Irish, Amer menu. Bar. A la carte entrees: lunch $1.95-$3.95, dinner $2.95-$6.25. Complete meals: dinner $5.50. Specialty: Dublin beef stew. Irish balladeer Thurs-Sun (summer). Patio dining. Informal, Irish pub atmosphere. No cr cds accepted.

D

Batsto (H-4)

(For accommodations see Atlantic City)

Area code 609 **Zip** 08037

(Approx 10 mi E of Hammonton)

The Batsto Iron Works, established in 1766, made munitions for the Revolutionary Army from the bog iron ore found nearby. Its furnaces shut down for the last time in 1848. Eighteen years later, Joseph Wharton, whose immense estate totaled nearly 100,000 acres, bought the land. In

1954, the state of New Jersey bought nearly 150 square miles of land in this area, including the entire Wharton tract, for a state forest.

What to See and Do

Batsto State Historic Site. Restored early 19th-century iron and glass-making community. General store, gristmill, blacksmith shop, wheelwright shop, sawmill, workers' houses and visitor center are open seasonally to the public. Guided tours of the mansion. Parking fee (Memorial Day-Labor Day, wkends & hols). For further information and hrs phone 609/561-3262. **Free.**

Wharton State Forest. Crossed by NJ 542, 563. Streams wind through 110,000 acres of wilderness. Swimming; fishing, hunting; canoeing. Limited picnicking. Tent & trailer sites, cabins. Standard fees. Along US 206 near Atsion. Phone 609/561-3262. Also here is

Atsion Recreation Area. Swimming; canoeing. Picnicking. Camping. Standard fees. For information phone the Atsion Ranger Station, 609/268-0444.

Beach Haven
(see Long Beach Island)

Bernardsville (C-4)
(See also Morristown)

Pop 6,597 **Elev** 400 ft **Area code** 908 **Zip** 07924

What to See and Do

Great Swamp National Wildlife Refuge. Nature trails, boardwalk. Observation blind; wilderness area. More than 200 species of birds, fish, reptiles, frogs, ducks, geese and fox may be seen in this 7,300-acre refuge. Headquarters (Mon-Fri; closed hols). Trails and information booth (daily, dawn-dusk). 1 mi N on US 202, W on N Maple Ave, 2 mi E on Madisonville Rd, then 1½ mi NE on Lee's Hill Rd, then right on Long Hill Rd. Phone 201/425-1222.   **Free.**

Morristown National Historical Park (see). Approx 5 mi N on US 2.

Hotel

★ ★ ★ **SOMERSET HILLS.** *(200 Liberty Corner Rd, Warren 07059)* SW on I-287 to I-78E, exit 33 (Martinsville-Bernardsville), left at top of ramp, right at 3rd light. 908/647-6700; FAX 908/647-8053; res: 800/688-0700. E-mail shhotel@aol.com; web www.shh.com. 111 units, 4 story. S $99-$165; D $99-$170; each addl $10; suites $250-$310; kits. $145-$185. Crib free. Pet accepted. TV; cable (premium). Pool; poolside serv. Restaurant 6:30 am-11 pm. Bar 11:30-1 am. Ck-out noon. Meeting rms. Business servs avail. In-rm modem link. Concierge. Gift shop. Tennis privileges. 18-hole golf privileges, pro, putting green, driving range. Exercise equipt; weight machine, bicycles. Microwaves avail. Nestled in the Watchung Mountains near the crossroads of historical Liberty Corner. Cr cds: A, C, D, MC, V.

D ⮌ 🧍 🛝 ≈ ✗ 🚭 SC

Inn

★ ★ ★ ★ **THE BERNARDS INN.** 27 Mine Brook Rd. 908/766-0002; FAX 908/766-4604; 800 888/766-0002. Web www.bernardsinn.com. This completely renovated inn, built in 1907, offers plush accommodations and gracious hospitality. 20 rms, 1 with shower only, 5 story, 4 suites. S, D $110-$175; suites $180-$205. Crib $10. TV; cable (premium). Complimentary continental bkfst. Restaurant (see THE BERNARDS INN). Rm serv Mon-Fri. Bar. Ck-out 11 am, ck-in 4 pm. Business servs avail. In-rm

modem link. Luggage handling. Concierge serv. Massage. Health club privileges. Cr cds: A, C, D, MC, V.

D 🚭 🔥

Restaurants

★ ★ ★ **THE BERNARDS INN.** *(See The Bernards Inn)* 908/766-0002. Web www.bernardsinn.com. Hrs: 11:30 am-3 pm, 5:30-10 pm; Fri, Sat to 11 pm. Closed Sun; some major hols. Res accepted, required Fri & Sat. Bar. Wine list. A la carte entrees: lunch $9-$13, dinner $21-$28. Specializes in rack of lamb, veal medallion. Pianist Tues-Sat. Outdoor dining. Elegant dining, turn-of-the-century ambiance. Jacket (dinner). Cr cds: A, C, D, MC, V.

D 🚭

★ ★ ★ **GIRAFE.** *(95 Morristown Rd, Basking Ridge)* I-287 exit 30B, W to US 202S. 908/221-0017. Hrs: 11:30 am-2 pm, 5:30-9 pm; Fri to 10 pm; Sat 5:30-10 pm. Sun 4-8 pm. Closed major hols. Res accepted. Wine cellar. A la carte entrees: lunch $6.50-$12.50, dinner $16-$28. Specializes in pasta, fresh fish, desserts. Own baking. Jacket. Cr cds: A, D, MC, V.

D 🚭

Bordentown (E-4)
(See also Trenton)

Settled 1682 **Pop** 4,341 **Elev** 72 ft **Area code** 609 **Zip** 08505
Information Historical Society Visitors Center, Old City Hall, 13 Crosswicks St, PO Box 182; 609/298-1740.

A long and honorable history has left an indelible stamp on this town. Bordentown was once a busy shipping center and a key stop on the Delaware and Raritan Canal. In January 1778, Bordentown citizens filled numerous kegs with gun powder and sent them down the Delaware River to Philadelphia hoping to blow up the British fleet stationed there. But the plan was discovered, and British troops intercepted the kegs and discharged them. In 1816, Joseph Bonaparte, exiled king of Spain and brother of Napoleon, bought 1,500 acres and settled here.

What to See and Do

Clara Barton Schoolhouse. Building was in use as a school in Revolutionary days. In 1851, Clara Barton, founder of the American Red Cross, established one of the first free public schools in the country in this building. (By appt) 142 Crosswicks St. Phone 609/298-0676.   **Free.**

Motel

★ **DAYS INN.** 1073 US 206, just N of NJ Tpke exit 7. 609/298-6100; FAX 609/298-7509. 131 rms, 2 story. S, D $85-$95; each addl $10; under 12 free; lower rates winter months. Crib free. Pet accepted. TV; cable. Pool; lifeguard. Restaurant 6:30-10 am, 5-9 pm. Rm serv. Bar 5 pm-1:30 am; entertainment Fri, Sat. Ck-out 11 am. Coin lndry. Meeting rms. Business servs avail. Sundries. Cr cds: A, C, D, DS, JCB, MC, V.

D ⮌ ≈ 🚭 🐾 SC

Branchville (B-3)

(For accommodations see Vernon)

Pop 851 **Elev** 529 ft **Area code** 201 **Zip** 07826

Information Sussex County Chamber of Commerce, 120 Hampton House Rd, Newton 07860; 201/579-1811.

This town in Sussex County is near many attractions in New Jersey's scenic northwest corner.

What to See and Do

Peters Valley. Historic buildings in the Delaware Water Gap National Recreation Area (see DELAWARE WATER GAP, PA) serve as residences and studios for professional craftspeople and summer crafts workshops in blacksmithing, ceramics, fine metals, photography, fibers and woodworking. Contemporary craft store (Thurs-Sun). Studios (June-Aug, Fri- Sat, Sun afternoons). 8 mi NW via US 206, County 560, then S on County 615. Phone 201/948-5200. **Free.**

Space Farms Zoo & Museum. Collection of more than 500 wild animals; early American museum in main building, addl museums on grounds; picnic area, concession; gift shop. Zoo and museum (May-Oct, daily). 6 mi N on County 519. Phone 201/875-5800 or 201/875-3223. ¢¢¢

Stokes State Forest. Located on the Kittatinny Ridge, this 15,482-acre forest includes some of the finest mountain country in New Jersey. Swimming; fishing, hunting. Picnicking. Camping. Scenic views from Sunrise Mt; Tillman Ravine, a natural gorge, is in the southern corner of the park. Standard fees. 4 mi N on US 206. Phone 201/948-3820.

Swartswood State Park. A 1,470-acre park on Swartswood Lake. Swimming (Memorial Day-Labor Day), bathhouse; fishing, hunting; boating (rentals, Memorial Day-Labor Day). Picnicking, concession. Camping. Standard fees. 2 mi S on County 519, then continue 2 mi on County 627, left 3 mi on County 521 to Swartswood, left 1 mi on County 622, right on County 619, ½ mi to park entrance. Phone 201/383-5230.

Annual Event

Peters Valley Craft Fair. Peters Valley. More than 150 juried exhibitors; demonstrations, music, food. Last wkend Sept.

Bridgeton (H-2)

(For accommodations see Millville)

Settled 1686 **Pop** 18,942 **Elev** 40 ft **Area code** 609 **Zip** 08302 **Web** members.aol.com/njbridge10/file.html

Information Bridgeton-Cumberland Tourist Association, 50 E Broad St; 609/451-4802 or 800/319-3379.

The city of Bridgeton has been recognized as New Jersey's largest historic district, with more than 2,200 registered historical landmarks. There are many styles of architecture here, some of which date back nearly 300 years.

What to See and Do

City Park. A 1,100-acre wooded area with swimming (protected beaches, Memorial Day-Labor Day); fishing; boating (floating dock), canoeing. Picnic grounds, recreation center. Zoo. (Daily) W Commerce St & Mayor Aitken Dr off NJ 49. Phone 609/451-9208. Also here is

New Sweden Farmstead Museum. Reconstruction of first permanent European settlement in Delaware Valley. Seven log buildings including smokehouse/sauna; horse barn, cow and goat barn, threshing barn; storage house; blacksmith shop; family residence with period furnishings. Costumed guides. (May-Labor Day, Wed-Sat, also Sun afternoons) Phone 609/455-9785. ¢¢

George J. Woodruff Museum of Indian Artifacts. Approx 20,000 local Native American artifacts, some up to 10,000 yrs old; clay pots, pipes, implements. (Mon-Fri afternoons; also by appt; closed some major hols) Bridgeton Free Public Library, 150 E Commerce St. Phone 609/451-2620. **Free.**

Gibbon House (1730). Site of New Jersey's only 18th-century tea burning party; genealogical research library (Mar-Dec, Wed & Sun). Events scheduled throughout yr. Gibbon House (early Apr-late Nov, daily exc Mon; closed Sun in July, Aug); tours (wkdays). 7 mi SW in Greenwich, on Ye Greate St. Phone 609/455-4055 or 609/451-8454. **Donation.**

Old Broad St Church (1792). Outstanding example of Georgian architecture, with Palladian window, high-backed wooden pews, wine glass pulpit, brick-paved aisles and brass lamps that once held whale oil. W Broad St & West Ave.

Parvin State Park. This 1,125-acre park offers swimming, bathhouse; fishing; boating, canoeing (rentals). Picnicking, concessions, playgrounds. Camping (dump station), cabins. Standard fees. 7 mi NE off NJ 77, near Centerton. Phone 609/358-8616.

Annual Event

Victorian Faire. Victorian Bridgeton is re-created through music, games and contests, street vendors, crafts, costumes and city tours. Phone 609/451-9208. Labor Day.

Seasonal Event

Concerts. Riverfront. Performances by ragtime, military, country & western bands and others. Sun nights. Phone 609/451-9208. Nine wks July-Aug.

Burlington (F-3)

(For accommodations see Bordentown, Mount Holly; also see Philadelphia, PA)

Settled 1677 **Pop** 9,835 **Elev** 13 ft **Area code** 609 **Zip** 08016

Information Burlington County Chamber of Commerce, Northwestern Mutual Life Bldg, 2311 Rte 541; 609/386-1012; or write to PO Box 2006, Willingboro 08046.

In 1774 Burlington, along with New York, Philadelphia and Boston, was a thriving port. A Quaker settlement, it was one of the first to provide public education. A 1682 Act of Assembly gave Matinicunk (now Burlington) Island in the Delaware River to the town with the stipulation that the revenue it generated would be used for public schools; that act is still upheld. Burlington was the capital of West Jersey; the legislature met here, and in the East Jersey capital of Perth Amboy, from 1681 until after the Revolution. In 1776, the Provincial Congress adopted the state constitution here.

What to See and Do

Burlington County Historical Society. The society maintains **D.B. Pugh Library,** in the Corson-Poley Center, genealogical and historical holdings; **James Fenimore Cooper House** (ca 1780), birthplace of the famous author, now the society headquarters; **Bard-How House** (ca 1740) with period furnishings; **Capt James Lawrence House,** birthplace of the commander of the *Chesapeake* during the War of 1812 and speaker of the immortal words "Don't give up the ship," contains 1812 objects and costume display. Tour of historic houses (Sun-Thurs afternoons). 457 High St. Phone 609/386-4773. ¢¢

Friends Meeting House (1784). (By appt) High St in 300 blk. Phone 609/387-3875. ¢¢

Historic tours. Guided walking tours of 33 historic sites (1685-1829), eight of which are open to the public. (Daily; no tours Easter, Dec 25) Leave foot of High St. Phone 609/386-3993. ¢¢

Old St Mary's Church (1703). The oldest Episcopal Church building in the state. (By appt) W Broad & Wood Sts. Phone 609/386-0902.

Thomas Revell House (1685). The oldest building in Burlington County. Included in Burlington County Historical Society home tour (see). (By appt and during Wood Street Fair; see ANNUAL EVENT) 213 Wood St. Phone 609/386-3993. **Free.**

Annual Event

Wood Street Fair. Re-creation of colonial fair; crafts, antiques exhibits; food; entertainment. 1st Sat after Labor Day.

Restaurant

★ ★ ★ **CAFE GALLERY.** *219 High St. 609/386-6150.* Hrs: 11:30 am-10 pm; Fri, Sat to 11 pm; Sun brunch 11:30 am-3 pm. Closed most major hols. Res accepted. Continental menu. Bar. Semi-a la carte: lunch $5.75-$9.75, dinner $13.50-$19.75. Sun brunch $15.75. Child's meals. Specializes in fresh seafood. Restored Colonial building overlooking Delaware River. Cr cds: A, C, D, MC, V.

Caldwell (C-5)

(For accommodations see Newark, Newark Intl Airport Area)

Pop 7,549 **Elev** 411 ft **Area code** 973 **Zip** 07006

What to See and Do

Grover Cleveland Birthplace State Historic Site. Built in 1832, this building served as the parsonage of the First Presbyterian Church. It is the birthplace of President Grover Cleveland, the only president born in New Jersey. He lived here from 1837-1841. (Wed-Sat, also Sun afternoons; closed Jan 1, Thanksgiving, Dec 25, all state hols; res recommended) 207 Bloomfield Ave. Phone 973/226-1810. **Free.**

Camden (F-2)

(For accommodations see Cherry Hill; also see Philadelphia, PA)

Settled 1681 **Pop** 87,492 **Elev** 23 ft **Area code** 609
Information Chamber of Commerce, PO Box 2017, 08101; 609/225-1400.

Camden's growth as the leading industrial, marketing and transportation center of southern New Jersey dates from post-Civil War days. Its location across the Delaware River from Philadelphia prompted large companies such as Campbell Soup (national headquarters) to establish plants here. Walt Whitman spent the last 20 years of his life in Camden.

What to See and Do

Camden County Historical Society-Pomona Hall (1726/1788). Brick Georgian house that belonged to descendants of William Cooper, an early Camden settler; period furnishings. Museum exhibits focus on regional history and include antique glass, lamps, toys and early hand tools; fire-fighting equipment; Victor Talking Machines. Library (fee) has more than 20,000 books, as well as maps (17th century-present), newspapers (18th-20th century), oral history tapes, photographs and genealogical material. (Tues, Thurs, Sun; closed major hols, also Aug) Park Blvd at Euclid Ave. Phone 609/964-3333. Museum ¢

New Jersey State Aquarium. Features one of the largest "open ocean" tanks in the country. Other highlights include an underwater research station, aquatic nursery and the opportunity to touch sharks, rays and starfish in special tanks and pools. Gift shop. Cafeteria. (Daily; closed some hols) 1 Riverside Dr, I-676 exit Mickle Blvd. Phone 609/365-3300. ¢¢¢

Tomb of Walt Whitman. The "good gray poet's" vault, designed by the poet himself, is of rough-cut stone with a grillwork door. Harleigh Cemetery, Haddon Ave & Vesper Blvd.

Walt Whitman Cultural Arts Center. Poetry readings, concerts and plays (Oct-May). Children's theater (late June-Aug, Fri). Art gallery; statuary. Center (Mon-Fri). 2nd & Cooper Sts. For schedule and fees phone 609/964-8300.

⭐ **Walt Whitman House State Historic Site.** The last residence of the poet and the only house he ever owned; he lived here from 1884 until his death on Mar 26, 1892. Contains original furnishings, books and mementos. (Wed-Sat, also Sun afternoons) 330 Mickle Blvd. Phone 609/964-5383. **Free.**

Cape May (K-3)

(See also Wildwood & Wildwood Crest)

Settled 1631 **Pop** 4,668 **Elev** 14 ft **Area code** 609 **Zip** 08204 **Web** www.capenet.com
Information Chamber of Commerce, PO Box 556, phone 609/884-5508; or the Welcome Center at 405 Lafayette St, phone 609/884-9562.

Cape May, the nation's oldest seashore resort, is located on the southern-most tip of the state surrounded by the Atlantic Ocean and Delaware Bay. Popular with Philadelphia and New York society since 1766, Cape May has been host to Presidents Lincoln, Grant, Pierce, Buchanan and Harrison, as well as notables such as John Wanamaker and Horace Greeley. The entire town has been proclaimed a National Historic Landmark because it has more than 600 Victorian homes and buildings, many of which have been restored. The downtown Washington Street Victorian Mall features three blocks of shops and restaurants. Four miles of beaches and a 1¼-mile paved promenade offer vacationers varied entertainment. "Cape May diamonds," often found on the shores of Delaware Bay by visitors, are actually pure quartz, rounded by the waves.

What to See and Do

Cape May-Lewes (DE) Ferry. Sole connection between southern terminus of Garden State Pkwy and US 13 (Ocean Hwy) on the Delmarva Peninsula. 16-mi, 70-min trip across Delaware Bay. (Daily) For schedule phone 800/64-FERRY (Cape May Terminal) or 302/645-6313 (Lewes Terminal). Per vehicle ¢¢¢¢

Emlen Physick Estate (1879). Authentically restored 18-rm Victorian mansion designed by Frank Furness. Mansion is also headquarters for the Mid-Atlantic Center for the Arts. (Apr-Nov, daily; rest of yr, Tues-Thurs & Sat-Sun) 1048 Washington St. Phone 609/884-5404. ¢¢

Historic Cold Spring Village. Restored 1870 South Jersey farm village. Craft shops; spinning, blacksmithing, weaving, pottery, broom making, ship modeling demonstrations; folk art; bakery and food shops; restaurant. (June-Sept, daily) 3 mi N via US 109. Phone 609/898-2300. ¢¢

Swimming, fishing, boating. Beaches with lifeguards (fee). Fishing is very good at the confluence of the Atlantic and Delaware Bay. A large harbor holds boats of all sizes; excellent for sailboating and other small-boat activity.

Tours. The Mid-Atlantic Center for the Arts offers the following tours. For further information contact PO Box 340; 609/884-5404.

Trolleys. Half-hr tours on enclosed trolley bus or open-air carriage; three routes beginning at Ocean St opp the Washington St Mall. (June-Oct, daily; reduced schedule rest of yr; no tours Thanksgiving) ¢¢

Mansions by Gaslight. Three-hr tour begins at Emlen Physick Estate. Visits four Victorian landmarks: Emlen Physick House (see), the Abbey (1869), Mainstay Inn (1872) and Humphrey Hughes House (1903); shuttle bus between houses. (Mid-June-Sept, Wed evenings; rest of yr, hol & special tours) ¢¢¢¢

Cape May INNteriors Tour & Tea. Features a different group of houses each week, visiting five or more bed & breakfast inns and guesthouses. Innkeepers greet guests and describe experiences. (Summer, Mon; rest of yr, Sat; no tours Dec-Jan) ¢¢¢¢

Walking Tours of the Historic District. Begin at Information Booth on Washington St Mall at Ocean St. Three 1¹/₂-hr guided tours give historical insight into the customs and traditions of the Victorians and their ornate architecture. (June-Sept, daily; reduced schedule rest of yr) ¢¢

Ocean Walk Tours. A 1¹/₂-hr guided tour of Cape May's beaches. Guide discusses marine life and history of the beaches, including legends of buried treasure. (May-Sept, Tues-Sat) Begins at Promenade & Beach Dr. ¢¢

Combination Tours. Approx 2 hrs; includes trolley tour and guided tour of Physick House. (June-Oct, daily; rest of yr, Sat & Sun) Begin at Emlen Physick Estate. (see) Phone for schedule. ¢¢¢

Annual Events

Tulip Festival. Celebrate Dutch heritage with ethnic foods and dancing, craft show, street fair, garden and house tours. Phone 609/884-5508. Apr.

Sea & Sky Festival. Sample Cape May's variety of seafood while colorful kites and blues music fill the air. Phone 609/884-5508. June.

Promenade Art Exhibit. July.

Victorian Week. Tours, antiques, crafts, period fashion shows. Mid-Oct.

Motels

★ ★ **COACHMAN'S MOTOR INN.** 205 Beach Dr. 609/884-8463; FAX 609/884-2643. Web www.capenet.com/capemay/coachman. 65 rms, 3 story, 45 kits. No elvtr. Late June-Labor Day (3-day min hols): S, D $135-$180; each addl $20; kit. units $145-$185; lower rates rest of yr. Crib free. TV. Pool; wading pool. Restaurant 7:30 am-10 pm. Bar; entertainment. Ck-out 11 am. Coin lndry. Tennis. Lawn games. Sun deck. On ocean. Cr cds: A, MC, V.

★ ★ **LA MER.** 1317 Beach Ave. 609/884-9000; FAX 609/884-5004. Web www.capenet.com/capemay/lamer. 68 rms, 2 story, 18 kits. July-Labor Day: S $118-$136; D $132-$163; each addl $15; kit. units to 5, $153-$205; lower rates May-June, after Labor Day-mid-Oct. Closed rest of yr. TV; VCR avail (movies). Pool; wading pool. Restaurant 5-10 pm. Ck-out 11 am. Coin lndry. Business servs avail. Miniature golf. Some microwaves. Bicycles. Picnic tables, grill. On ocean. Cr cds: A, C, D, DS, MC, V.

★ ★ **MT VERNON.** Beach & 1st Aves. 609/884-4665. Web www.capenet.com/capemay/mtvernon. 25 units, 2 story, 12 kits. July-Labor Day: S, D $138; each addl $12-$15; kit. units $143; lower rates Apr-June, after Labor Day-Oct. Closed rest of yr. Crib avail. TV, cable (premium). Pool; wading pool. Restaurant adj 8 am-midnight. Ck-out 11 am. Refrigerators. Some microwaves. Sun deck. Opp ocean. No cr cds accepted.

★ ★ **PERIWINKLE INN.** 1039 Beach Ave. 609/884-9200. Web www.capenet.com/capemay/prwnkl. 50 rms, 3 story, 14 kits. July-Aug: S, D $135-$148; each addl $15; suites, kit. units $141-$200; lower rates mid-Apr-June, Sept-mid-Oct. Closed rest of yr. Crib free. TV, cable (premium). Pool; wading pool. Restaurant adj 7 am-10 pm. Ck-out 11 am. Refrigerators. Some microwaves. Balconies. Grills. On ocean. No cr cds accepted.

Motor Hotels

★ ★ **MARQUIS DE LAFAYETTE.** 501 Beach Dr. 609/884-3500; FAX 609/884-0669; res: 800/257-0432. 73 units, 6 story, 43 kits. July-Labor Day: S, D $188-$260; each addl $18; kit. units $198-$274; 2 children under 8 free; package plans; wkend rates; varied lower rates rest of yr. Crib avail. Pet accepted, some restrictions; $20/day. TV. Pool; sauna, poolside serv. Complimentary full bkfst. Restaurant (see TOP OF THE MARQ). Bar; entertainment. Ck-out 1 pm. Coin lndry. Meeting rms. Business servs avail. Bellhops. Valet serv. Golf privileges. Balconies. On ocean. Cr cds: A, C, D, DS, MC, V.

★ ★ **MONTREAL.** Beach & Madison Aves. 609/884-7011; FAX 609/884-4559; res: 800/525-7011. E-mail montrealin@aol.com; web www.capemayfun.com. 70 units, 4 story, 42 kits. Mid-June-mid-Sept: S, D, suites $89-$135; each addl $6-$9; kit. units $140-$150; lower rates Mar-mid-June, mid-Sept-Dec. Closed rest of yr. Crib free. TV; cable (premium). Heated pool; wading pool, whirlpool, poolside serv, lifeguard. Restaurant 8 am-11 pm. Rm serv. Bar from 11 am. Ck-out 11 am. Coin lndry. Business servs avail. In-room modem link. Valet serv. Free airport transportation. Putting green, miniature golf. Exercise equipt; weight machine, stair machine, sauna. Game rm. Refrigerators, many microwaves. Balconies. Picnic tables, grills. On ocean. Cr cds: A, DS, MC, V.

Hotel

★ **INN OF CAPE MAY.** 601 Beach Dr. 609/884-3500; FAX 609/884-0669; res: 800/257-0432. 71 rms, 68 share bath, 5 story. No rm phones. July-Aug: S, D $98-$275; each addl $18; MAP avail; package plans; lower rates mid-May-June, Sept-mid-Nov. Closed rest of yr. Crib avail. TV; cable. Pool; poolside serv. Restaurant 8 am-noon, 5-9 pm. No rm serv. Bar 11-1 am. Ck-out 1 pm. Meeting rms. Business servs avail. On ocean. Opened 1894; antique furnishings. Cr cds: A, C, D, DS, MC, V.

Inns

★ ★ ★ **THE ABBEY.** 34 Gurney St, at Columbia Ave. 609/884-4506. 14 rms in 2 bldgs, 3 story. No rm phones. Apr-Dec: S, D $100-$275. Closed rest of yr. Children over 12 yrs only. Full bkfst; afternoon refreshments. Ck-out 11 am, ck-in after 2 pm. Beach passes, chairs, towels. Refrigerators. Gothic-style inn with 60-ft tower; main house built 1869, cottage built 1873. Stenciled and ruby glass arched windows; library, antiques. Smoking on veranda only. Cr cds: DS, MC, V.

★ ★ ★ **ANGEL OF THE SEA.** 5 Trenton Ave. 609/884-3369; FAX 609/884-3331; res: 800/848-3369. Web www.angelofthesea.com. 27 rms, 3 story. A/C July, Aug only. No elvtr. No rm phones. June-Oct: S, D $135-$285; each addl $50; lower rates rest of yr. Children over 8 yrs only. TV; cable (premium), VCR avail. Complimentary full bkfst; afternoon refreshments. Ck-out 11 am, ck-in 2 pm. Business servs avail. Concierge serv. Free airport transportation. Some balconies. Picnic tables. Authentic Victorian house (1850). Originally located in center of town, in 1891 it was relocated to the beach; because of its size, the house had to be cut in half to make the move. In 1968 the building was moved once again, from the beach to its present location and restored. Located opp ocean, swimming beach. Totally nonsmoking. Cr cds: MC, V.

✓ ★ ★ **CARROLL VILLA.** 19 Jackson St. 609/884-9619; FAX 609/884-0264. E-mail mbatter@cyberenet.com; web www.beachcomer.com/capemay. 22 rms, 3 story. Memorial Day-mid-Sept: S $90-$155; D $98-$162; each addl $20; under 2 free; wkly rates; hols, wkends (2-3-day min); lower rates rest of yr. Crib avail. TV in parlor. Complimentary full bkfst. Restaurant (see MAD BATTER). Ck-out 11 am, ck-in 2 pm.

Business servs avail. Victorian inn (1882); antiques. Cr cds: A, C, D, DS, MC, V.

★ ★ **COLUMNS BY THE SEA.** *1513 Beach Dr. 609/884-2228; FAX 609/884-4789.* 11 air-cooled rms, 3 story. No rm phones. July-Aug: S $150-$210; D $160-$275; each addl $40; wkly rates; lower rates rest of yr. Children over 10 yrs only. TV; cable. Complimentary full bkfst; afternoon refreshments. Restaurant nearby. Ck-out 11:30 am, ck-in 2 pm. Bicycles avail. Library. Refrigerators. Victorian furnishings, antiques. On beach. Totally nonsmoking. Cr cds: MC, V.

★ ★ ★ **MAINSTAY INN.** *635 Columbia Ave. 609/884-8690.* Web www.mainstayinn.com. 9 rms, 3 story, 7 suites. Mar-Dec (2-3-day min): S, D $95-$245; each addl $35. Complimentary full bkfst; afternoon refreshments. Ck-out 11 am, ck-in 2 pm. Lawn games. Some balconies. Beach passes. Built in 1872 as a gentlemen's gambling house. Victorian decor; antiques; 14-ft ceilings. Veranda. Totally nonsmoking. No cr cds accepted.

★ ★ ★ **QUEEN VICTORIA.** *102 Ocean St. 609/884-8702.* E-mail qvn@bellatlantic.com; web www.queenvictoria.com. 17 rms, 3 story, 6 suites. June-Sept: S $175-$220; D $185-$230; each addl $25; suites $235-$270; lower rates rest of yr. TV; VCR avail. Bkfst; afternoon refreshments. Ck-out 11 am. Bicycles, beach passes. Whirlpool in suites. Restored Victorian villas; rms individually decorated with Victorian antiques. Cr cds: MC, V.

★ ★ **QUEEN'S HOTEL.** *601 Columbia Ave. 609/884-1613.* Web www.queenvictoria.com. 9 rms, 3 story, 2 suites. No elvtr. Mid-June-mid-Sept: S $50-$175; D $60-$185; each addl $25; suites $115-$240; wkend, wkly rates; wkends, hols (3-day min); lower rates rest of yr. Crib free. TV; cable, VCR avail. Complimentary coffee in rms. Restaurant nearby. Ck-out 11 am. Meeting rms. Business center. Concierge serv. Refrigerators; some microwaves. Some balconies. 1 blk to ocean. Totally nonsmoking. Cr cds: MC, V.

★ ★ ★ **SOUTHERN MANSION AT THE GEORGE ALLEN ESTATE.** *720 Washington St. 609/884-7171; res: 800/381-3888; FAX 609/898-0492.* Web www.capenet.com/capemay/allen. 25 rms, 3 story. July-Dec: S $150-$295; D $175-$295; each addl $50; suite $175-$350; family, wkend, wkly, hol rates; wkends, hols (3-day min); lower rates rest of yr. Children over 12 yrs only. TV; cable, VCR avail. Complimentary continental bkfst. Restaurant 7:30 am-10 pm. Rm serv. Ck-out 3 pm, ck-in 11 am. Business servs avail. In-rm modem link. Luggage handling. Valet serv. Concierge serv. Massage. Health club privileges. Heated pool. Lawn games. Some fireplaces. Picnic tables. Built in 1863; 5,000 sq ft of verandahs, terraces & solariums; mid-19th century antiques. Totally nonsmoking. Cr cds: A, MC, V.

★ ★ **VICTORIAN LACE INN.** *901 Stockton. 609/884-1772.* 5 rms, 2 with shower only, 3 story. July-Aug: S, D $85-$180; each addl $15; lower rates Apr-June, Sept-Oct. Closed Nov-Mar. TV in sitting rm; cable. Complimentary full bkfst. Restaurant nearby. Ck-out 10 am, ck-in 2 pm. Refrigerators, microwaves. Built in 1869, decorated with antiques. Totally nonsmoking. No cr cds accepted.

★ ★ ★ **VIRGINIA.** *25 Jackson St, in historic district. 609/884-5700; FAX 609/884-1236; res: 800/732-4236.* 24 rms, 3 story. No elvtr. Memorial Day-Labor Day: S, D $120-$295; each addl $20; under 5 free; wkly rates; lower rates rest of yr. Crib free. TV; VCR (movies $2). Complimentary continental bkfst. Dining rm (see EBBITT ROOM). Rm serv. Bar 5 pm-midnight; Sat, Sun from noon. Ck-out noon, ck-in 3 pm. Meeting rms. Business servs avail. In-rm modem link. Luggage handling. Concierge serv. Health club privileges. In-rm whirlpools. Balconies. Built 1879; restored. Antique

and modern furnishing; amenities. Ocean view from veranda. Cr cds: A, C, D, DS, MC, V.

Restaurants

★ ★ **410 BANK STREET.** *410 Bank St, adj to Welcome Center. 609/884-2127.* Hrs: 5-10:30 pm. Closed Nov-Apr. Res accepted. Louisana French menu. Setups. A la carte entrees: dinner $20-$28. Child's meals. Specializes in grilled fish steaks and prime meats. Porch and garden dining. Restored 1840 Cape May residence. Island atmosphere. Cr cds: A, C, D, DS, MC, V.

★ ★ **ALEXANDER'S INN.** *653 Washington St. 609/884-2555.* Hrs: 6-10 pm; Sun brunch 10 am-1 pm. Closed Mon, Tues; Jan 1, Thanksgiving, Dec 25. Res accepted. French menu. Setups. Semi-a la carte: dinner $24.95-$29.95. Complete meals: dinner $29.95-$45.95. Specializes in sweet breads, rabbit, Angus beef. Own ice cream. Victorian decor; antiques. Totally nonsmoking. Cr cds: A, C, D, DS, MC, V.

★ ★ ★ **EBBITT ROOM.** *(See Virginia Inn) 609/884-5700.* Hrs: 5:30-9:30 pm; Fri, Sat to 10 pm. Res accepted. Bar. Semi-a la carte: dinner $18-$28. Child's meals. Specializes in seafood, fowl. Pianist in season. Valet parking. Intimate Victorian dining rm. Totally nonsmoking. Cr cds: A, D, DS, MC, V.

★ ★ **FRESCOS.** *412 Bank St, 1 blk behind Victorian Mall, adj to Welcome Center. 609/884-0366.* Hrs: 5-10:30 pm. Closed Nov-Apr. Res accepted. Italian menu. A la carte entrees: dinner $15-$22.95. Child's meals. Specializes in fresh seafood, pasta, veal. Outdoor porch dining. 3 dining areas in restored Victorian summer cottage. Cr cds: A, C, D, DS, MC, V.

★ ★ **LOBSTER HOUSE.** *Fisherman's Wharf, turn E just S of bridge at end of Garden State Pkwy. 609/884-8296.* Hrs: 11:30 am-3 pm, 4:30-10 pm; Sun from 4 pm; Sun in winter 2-9 pm. Closed Thanksgiving, Dec 24-25. Bar. Semi-a la carte: lunch $5.75-$12.50, dinner $15.95-$38.95. Child's meals. Specializes in fresh fish, lobster, crabmeat. Parking. Outdoor dining. On wharf; nautical decor. Fireplace. Cocktail lounge & lunch on fishing schooner, noon-4 pm. Raw seafood bars in main bar & dock. Cr cds: A, DS, MC, V.

★ ★ **MAD BATTER.** *(See Carroll Villa Inn) 609/884-5970.* E-mail MBatter@cyberenet.com; web www.beachcomer.com/capemay. Hrs: 8 am-2:30 pm, 5:30-10 pm; Fri, Sat to 10:30 pm. Closed Jan. Res accepted dinner only. Contemporary Amer menu. Setups. A la carte entrees: bkfst, lunch $5-$11, dinner $15-$25. Child's meals. Specializes in fresh seafood, desserts. Outdoor dining. Victorian inn (1882). Cr cds: A, C, D, DS, MC, V.

★ ★ **MERION INN.** *106 Decatur St. 609/884-8363.* Hrs: noon-2:30 pm, 5-10 pm, early-bird dinner 5-6 pm. Closed Jan-Mar; also Mon-Thurs Apr-May & mid-Oct-Dec. Res accepted. Bar. Semi-a la carte: lunch $4.50-$12.95, dinner $14.95-$32.95. Child's meals. Specializes in stuffed lobster tail, fresh grilled fish, steak. Own desserts. Outdoor dining. Turn-of-the-century Victorian decor. Built 1885. Family-owned. Cr cds: A, D, DS, MC, V.

★ ★ **PEACHES AT SUNSET.** *1 Sunset Blvd W. 609/898-0100.* Hrs: 4:30-10 pm. Closed Dec 25; also Mon-Thurs (Oct-May). Res accepted. Pacific Rim cuisine. Semi-a la carte: dinner $16.95-$27.95. Child's meals. Specialties: sea bass with mango salsa, rack of lamb. Free parking. Outdoor dining overlooking gardens. Local artwork displayed. Totally nonsmoking. Cr cds: A, D, MC, V.

★ **RUSTY NAIL BAR AND GRILL.** *205 Beach Dr. 609/884-0220.* Web www.capenet.com/capemay/coachmall. Hrs: 7:30-1 am. Closed Nov-mid-Apr. Bar. Complete meals: bkfst $5-$8.50, lunch $6.50-

$9. Semi-a la carte: dinner $9.25-$22. Child's meals. Specializes in crab cake, prime rib, lemon chicken. Beach decor. Cr cds: A, MC, V.

★ ★ **TOP OF THE MARQ.** *(See Marquis De Lafayette Motor Hotel)* 609/884-3500. Hrs: 5:30-10 pm. Closed Dec 24, 25. Res accepted. Bar. Complete meals: dinner $13.95-$43. Child's meals. Specializes in lobster, beef tenderloin. Pianist in season. Valet parking in season. Victorian setting with view of Atlantic. Cr cds: A, C, D, DS, MC, V.

★ ★ ★ **WASHINGTON INN.** *801 Washington St.* 609/884-5697. Hrs: 5-10 pm; hrs may vary wkends & off season. Closed Thanksgiving, Dec 24-25. Res accepted; required Sat. Continental menu. Bar. Wine cellar. Semi-a la carte: dinner $16.95-$25.95. Child's meals. Specializes in steak, veal, fresh seafood. Own baking. Patio dining. Former plantation house (1848). Fireside dining. Cr cds: A, C, D, DS, MC, V.

★ ★ **WATER'S EDGE.** *Beach & Pittsburgh Aves.* 609/884-1717. Hrs: July-Aug 5-11 pm; hrs vary off season. Closed Thanksgiving, Dec 25. Res accepted. Bar. A la carte entrees: dinner $18-$27. Child's meals. Specializes in fresh local seafood, free range veal, Angus steak. Contemporary decor. Patio dining, ocean view. Cr cds: A, C, D, DS, MC, V.

Cape May Court House (K-3)

(See also Cape May, Stone Harbor, Wildwood & Wildwood Crest)

Pop 4,426 **Elev** 18 ft **Area code** 609 **Zip** 08210 **Web** www.beachcomer .com

Information Cape May County Chamber of Commerce, PO Box 74; 609/465-7181.

To be accurately named, this county seat would have to be called Cape May Court Houses, for there are two of them—one is a white, 19th-century building now used as a meeting hall.

What to See and Do

Cape May County Historical Museum. Period dining room (predating 1820), 18th-century kitchen, doctor's room, military room with Merrimac flag, Cape May diamonds. Barn exhibits; whaling implements; Indian artifacts; pioneer tools; lens from Cape May Point Lighthouse. Genealogical library. (Mid-June-Labor Day wkend, daily exc Sun; after Labor Day-Nov & Apr-mid-June, Tues-Sat; Dec-Mar, Sat only) Shore Rd, 1 mi N on US 9. Phone 609/465-3535. ¢

Cape May County Park. Zoo has over 100 types of animals. Jogging path, bike trail; tennis courts. Picnicking, playground. (Daily) On US 9 at Crest Haven Rd. Phone 609/465-5271. **Donation.**

Leaming's Run Gardens. Amid 20 acres of lawns, ponds and ferneries are 25 gardens, each with a separate theme. Eighteenth-century colonial farm grows tobacco and cotton; farm animals. (Mid-May-mid-Oct, daily) Approx 4 mi N on US 9, between Pkwy exits 13 & 17 in Swainton. Phone 609/465-5871. ¢¢

Victorian houses. Fine examples of 19th-century architecture located in the area. Information can be obtained at the Chamber of Commerce Information Center, Crest Haven Rd & Garden State Pkwy, milepost 11 (Easter-mid-Oct, daily; rest of yr, Mon-Fri; closed hols).

Motel

★ **HY-LAND MOTOR INN.** *38 E Mechanic Dr (88210).* 609/465-7305; FAX 609/465-8776. 34 rms, 24 with shower only, 2 story. Mid-June-Sept: S, D $75-$85; each addl $10; suite $100-$125; kits $90-$100; under 10 free; lower rates rest of yr. Crib $5. TV; cable. Pool. Restaurant nearby. Ck-out 11 am. Business servs avail. Microwaves avail. Picnic tables, grill. Cr cds: A, MC, V.

Inn

★ ★ ★ **THE DOCTOR'S INN AT KING'S GRANT.** *2 N Main St.* 609/463-9330. 6 rms, 3 story. June-Oct: D, suites $135-$170; lower rates rest of yr. TV; cable. Complimentary full bkfst. Restaurant 11 am-2 pm, 5-9 pm. Ck-out 11 am, ck-in 1 pm. Exercise equipt; bicycles, treadmill. Some refrigerators. Built in 1854; pays tribute to physicians and teachers who ministered to the community. Totally nonsmoking. Cr cds: A, MC, V.

Chatham (C-4)

Pop 8,007 **Elev** 244 ft **Area code** 973 **Zip** 07928

Information Township of Chatham, 58 Meyersville Rd; 973/635-4600.

What to See and Do

Great Swamp National Wildlife Refuge. SW of city (see BERNARDSVILLE).

Restaurant

★ ★ ★ **RESTAURANT SERENADE.** *6 Roosevelt Ave.* 973/701-0303. Hrs: noon-2 pm, 6-9:30 pm; Sat 5:30-10 pm. Closed Sun; most major hols. Res accepted, required Sat. Bar. Wine list. A la carte entrees: lunch $8-$15, dinner $17-$28. Specializes in contemporary French cuisine. Jacket. Cr cds: A, D, DS, MC, V.

Cherry Hill (F-3)

(See also Camden, Haddonfield)

Pop 69,319 **Elev** 30 ft **Area code** 609

Information Chamber of Commerce, 1060 Kings Hwy N, Suite 200, 08034; 609/667-1600.

What to See and Do

Barclay Farmstead. One of the earliest properties settled in what is now Cherry Hill; origins traced to 1684. The township-owned site consists of 32 acres of open space; restored Federal-style farmhouse; operating forge barn; corn crib; Victorian spring house. Grounds (all yr); house tours (Tues-Fri, also Sun in fall & spring and by appt). 209 Barclay Lane. Phone 609/795-6225. ¢

Annual Event

State Fair. Garden State Park. Phone 609/646-3340. Early Aug.

Motels

★ **DAYS INN-BROOKLAWN.** *(801 US 130, Brooklawn 08030)* On US 130, 1 mi S of I-76, NJ 42 (North South Frwy). 609/456-6688; FAX 609/456-1413. 115 rms, 3 story. S $45-$65; D $49-$69; each addl $5; under 12 free. Crib free. TV; cable (premium). Pool; lifeguard. Complimentary continental bkfst. Restaurant nearby. Ck-out 11 am. Coin lndry. Business servs avail. Exercise equipt; stair machine, bicycles. In-rm modem link. Sundries. Refrigerators, microwaves avail. Cr cds: A, C, D, DS, JCB, MC, V.

★★ **HAMPTON INN.** *(121 Laurel Oak Rd, Voorhees 08043)* I-295, exit 32, 2 mi E NJ 561. 609/346-4500; FAX 609/346-2402. 122 rms, 50 with shower only, 4 story. S, D $88-$95; under 18 free. Crib avail. Pet accepted. TV; cable (premium), VCR avail. Pool. Complimentary continental bkfst. Restaurant adj 11 am-11 pm. Ck-out noon. Business servs avail. In-rm modem link. Health club privileges. Microwaves avail. Cr cds: A, D, DS, MC, V.

★★ **LANDMARK INN.** *(NJ 38 & 73, Maple Shade 08052)* at jct NJ 73, 38, ½ mi N of I-295, 1 mi N of NJ Tpke exit 4. 609/235-6400; FAX 609/727-1027; res: 800/635-5917. 150 rms, 3 story. S $49-$54; D $52-$57; each addl $3; under 18 free. Crib free. TV; VCR avail (movies). Pool; wading pool, lifeguard. Playground. Complimentary coffee in lobby. Restaurant 6:30 am-10 pm; Sat, Sun 8 am-noon, 5-11 pm. Rm serv. Bar; entertainment Thurs-Sat. Ck-out noon. Coin lndry. Meeting rms. In-rm modem link. Sundries. Exercise equipt; weights, treadmills, sauna. Refrigerators avail. Private patios, balconies. Cr cds: A, C, D, DS, MC, V.

✔★ **McINTOSH INN.** *(1132 Rte 73 S, Mount Laurel 08054)* On NJ 73, ¼ mi E of NJ Tpke exit 4. 609/234-7194; FAX 609/231-8516; res: 800/444-2775. 93 rms, 2 story. S, D $43.95-$60.95. Crib free. TV; cable (premium). Restaurant adj open 6 am-midnight. Ck-out 11 am. Business servs avail. Refrigerators, microwaves avail. Cr cds: A, C, D, MC, V.

✔★★ **QUALITY INN.** *(550 Fellowship Rd, Mount Laurel 08054)* NJ 73 at NJ Tpke exit 4. 609/235-7400; FAX 609/778-9729. 148 rms, 2 story. S, D $52-$89; each addl $10; under 12 free. Crib free. TV; cable (premium). Pool. Restaurant 7 am-11 pm. Rm serv. Bar 11-2 am. Ck-out noon. Coin lndry. Meeting rms. Business servs avail. In-rm modem link. Valet serv. Exercise equipt; bicycles, stair machine. Health club privileges. Refrigerators, microwaves avail. Cr cds: A, C, D, DS, MC, V.

Motor Hotels

★★ **HOLIDAY INN.** NJ 70 & Sayer Ave (08002), 3 mi W of I-295, 7 mi W of NJ Tpke exit 4, opp Garden State Racetrack. 609/663-5300; FAX 609/662-2913. 186 rms, 6 story. S, D $89-$105; each addl $8; under 19 free; wkend rates. Crib free. Pet accepted. TV; cable (premium), VCR avail. 2 pools, 1 indoor; wading pool. Restaurant (sec RED, HOT & BLUE). Rm serv. Bar 11 am-11 pm. Ck-out noon. Coin lndry. Meeting rms. Business servs avail. In-rm modem link. Valet serv. Exercise equipt; weights, bicycles, sauna. Microwaves avail. Cr cds: A, C, D, DS, ER, JCB, MC, V.

★★★ **RAMADA PLAZA.** *(555 Fellowship Rd, Mt Laurel 08054)* I-295, exit 36, N on NJ 73. 609/273-1900; FAX 609/273-8562. 100 rms, 5 story. S $78; D $88; each addl $10; suites $175; under 16 free. Crib avail. TV; cable (premium), VCR avail. Pool. Complimentary continental bkfst. Restaurant 6 am-10 pm. Bar 11 am-midnight. Ck-out noon. Meeting rms. Business servs avail. Valet serv. Gift shop. Exercise equipt; bicycle, weight machine. Health club privileges. Game rm. Some balconies. Cr cds: A, C, D, DS, JCB, MC, V.

Hotels

★★★ **FOUR POINTS BY SHERATON.** 1450 US 70E (08034), NJ 70 & I-295. 609/428-2300; FAX 609/354-7662. 213 rms, 4 story. S $94-$124; D $104-$149; each addl $10; under 19 free; wkend rates. Crib free. TV; cable (premium), VCR avail. Pool. Restaurant 6:30 am-11 pm. Bar 11-2 am. Ck-out noon. Meeting rms. Business servs avail. In-rm modem link. Gift shop. Airport transportation. Tennis. Exercise equipt; bicycle, weight machine. Health club privileges. Microwaves avail. Cr cds: A, C, D, DS, ER, MC, V.

★★★ **HILTON.** 2349 W Marlton Pike (08002). 609/665-6666; FAX 609/662-3676. Web www.hilton.com. 408 rms, 14 story. S $119-$189; D $139-$209; each addl $10; suites $350-$650; under 18 free. Crib free. TV; cable (premium), VCR avail. Pool; wading pool. Restaurant 6 am-11 pm. Bar 11-2 am. Ck-out noon. Convention facilities. Business center. In-rm modem link. Valet serv. Exercise equipt; weight machine, bicycles. Some refrigerators; microwaves avail. Cr cds: A, C, D, DS, JCB, MC, V.

★★★ **RADISSON AT MOUNT LAUREL.** *(NJ 73 & I-295, Mount Laurel 08054)* ½ mi N of NJ Tpke exit 4 on NJ 73N. 609/234-7300; FAX 609/866-9401. Web www.radisson.com. 283 rms, 10 story. S, D $99-$109; suites $250-$350; under 17 free. Crib free. Pet accepted. TV; cable (premium). Pool; poolside serv, lifeguard. Restaurant 6:30 am-10 pm; Sat, Sun from 7 am. Bar. Ck-out 11 am. Coin lndry. Convention facilities. Business servs avail. In-rm modem link. Gift shop. Lighted tennis. Golf privileges. Exercise equipt; bicycles, treadmill. Health club privileges. Game rm. Some in-rm whirlpools, refrigerators; microwaves avail. Picnic tables. Some private patios, balconies. Luxury level. Cr cds: A, C, D, DS, JCB, MC, V.

Restaurants

✔★ **GOLDEN EAGLE DINER.** *(NJ 73S at I-295, Maple Shade 08052)* 1 mi W of NJ Tpke exit 4. 609/235-8550. Hrs: 6 am-midnight; Fri, Sat to 4 am. Res accepted. Bar from 11 am. Semi-a la carte: bkfst $1.99-$6, lunch $5.25-$6.95, dinner $7.95-$13.95. Child's meals. Specializes in prime rib, seafood. Salad bar. Parking. Cr cds: A, DS, MC, V.

★★★ **LA CAMPAGNE.** 312 Kresson Rd (08034), US 70 to NJ 154S. 609/429-7647. Web www.lacampagne.com. Hrs: 11:30 am-2:30 pm, 5-10 pm; Sun brunch 10 am-2 pm. Closed Mon; also Dec 25. Res accepted. French menu. Semi-a la carte: lunch $7.50-$15, dinner $25-$29.50. Sun brunch $10.95-$19.95. Child's meals. Specializes in rack of lamb, seafood, duck. Outdoor dining. Country French decor. Cr cds: A, D, MC, V.

★★ **LOS AMIGOS.** *(NJ 73 & Franklin Ave, West Berlin 08091)* S on NJ 41, then 7 mi SE on NJ 561. 609/767-5216. E-mail losamigos @hotmail.com; web www.losamigos.com. Hrs: 5-10 pm; Fri to 11 pm; Sat 3-11 pm; Sun from 3 pm. Closed Mon; some hols. Southwestern menu. Bar. A la carte entrees: dinner $9.95-$20.95. Child's meals. Specialties: southwestern crab cakes, tabasco tequila shrimp. Outdoor dining. Fiesta atmosphere; Mexican cantina decor. Family-owned. Cr cds: A, C, D, MC, V.

✔★ **OLD HICKORY SMOKEHOUSE.** *(234 NJ 73, Berlin 08009)* I-295W to US 30, SE 8 mi to jct NJ 73. 609/753-1323. Hrs: 11 am-9 pm; Fri, Sat to 10 pm; Sun noon-8 pm. Closed some major hols. Res accepted. Semi-a la carte: lunch, dinner $5.25-$15.95. Child's meals. Specializes in barbecue ribs, chicken, beef. Own baking. Outdoor dining. Old-style Texas barbecue. Cr cds: A, DS, MC, V.

✔★ **RED, HOT & BLUE.** *(See Holiday Inn Motor Hotel)* *609/665-7427.* Hrs: 11 am-10 pm; Fri to 11 pm; Sat to midnight; Sun from noon. Closed Easter, Thanksgiving, Dec 25. Res accepted (dinner). Bar; Fri, Sat to 2 am. Semi-a la carte: lunch, dinner $5.50-$13. Child's meals. Specialties: pulled pork, barbecued pork ribs, beef brisket. Own baking. Blues Fri, Sat. Casual, Memphis-style barbecue. Cr cds: A, D, MC, V.

Clifton (C-5)

Pop 71,742 **Elev** 70 ft **Area code** 973 **E-mail** staff@njrcc.org **Web** www .njrcc.org

Information North Jersey Regional Chamber of Commerce, 1033 US 46E, PO Box 110, 07011; 973/470-9300.

What to See and Do

Hamilton House Museum. Early 19th-century sandstone farmhouse with period furniture; country store; exhibits. Open-hearth cooking demonstrations by costumed guides. (Mar-Dec, Sun afternoons; closed hol wkends) 971 Valley Rd. Phone 973/744-5707. **Free.**

Motel

★★ **HOWARD JOHNSON.** *680 NJ 3 W (07014), NJ Tpke exit 16W.* *973/471-3800; FAX 973/471-2125.* E-mail www.hojo.com. 116 rms, 4 story. S $84-$114, D $94-$124; each addl $10; under 18 free; wkend rates. Crib free. Pet accepted, some restrictions. TV; cable (premium). Pool; lifeguard. Complimentary continental bkfst. Restaurant 7 am-midnight. Bar 4 pm-2 am. Ck-out noon. Meeting rm. Business servs avail. In-rm modem link. Sundries. Microwaves avail. Private patios, balconies. Cr cds: A, C, D, DS, ER, JCB, MC, V.

Motor Hotel

★★ **RAMADA INN.** *265 NJ 3E.* *973/778-6500; FAX 973/778-8724.* 183 rms, 4 story. S, D $99-$149; each addl $15; suites $200; kit units $150; under 12 free; wkend rates. Crib free. TV; cable (premium). Indoor pool. Restaurant 6:30 am-10 pm; wkends from 7 am. Rm serv. Bar; entertainment. Ck-out noon. Meeting rms. Business servs avail. Concierge. Sundries. Gift shop. Exercise equipt; weights, bicycles, sauna. Some refrigerators; microwaves avail. Cr cds: A, C, D, DS, ER, JCB, MC, V.

Clinton (C-3)

(See also Flemington)

Pop 2,054 **Elev** 195 ft **Area code** 908 **Zip** 08809

What to See and Do

Clinton Historical Museum. Four-story gristmill (ca 1810). Ten-acre park houses education center, quarry and lime kilns, blacksmith shop, general store, one-room schoolhouse, log cabin, machinery sheds, herb garden. Gift shop. (Apr-Oct, daily exc Mon) Outdoor concerts some Sat evenings in summer (fee). 56 Main St, off I-78. Phone 908/735-4101. ¢¢

Round Valley State Park. A 4,003-acre park. Swimming; fishing; boating. Picnicking, concession (Memorial Day-Labor Day). Wilderness camping (access to campsites via hiking or boating only). Standard fees. Off US 22, E of jct I-78; follow signs. Phone 908/236-6355.

Spruce Run State Recreation Area. A 1,961-acre park. Swimming; fishing; boating (launch, rentals). Picnicking, concession. Camping (Apr-Oct). Standard fees. 3 mi NW off NJ 31. Phone 908/638-8572.

Motor Hotel

★★ **HOLIDAY INN SELECT.** *111 NJ 173, I-78 exit 15, then W on NJ 173.* *908/735-5111; FAX 908/730-9768.* 142 units, 5 story. S $109-$136; D $117-$142; each addl $8; suites $136-$150; under 18 free; wkend rates. Crib free. TV; cable (premium). Indoor pool. Coffee in rms. Restaurant 6:30 am-11 pm. Rm serv. Bar 3 pm-midnight; entertainment Wed-Sat. Ck-out noon. Meeting rms. Business servs avail. In-rm modem link. Sundries. Exercise equipt; weights, bicycles. Microwaves avail. Some balconies. Cr cds: A, C, D, DS, ER, MC, V.

Inn

★★ **STEWART INN.** *(708 S Main St, Stewartsville 08886) I-78 exit 4, west.* *908/479-6060; FAX 908/479-4211.* 7 rms, 2 story. S, D $95-$135; suite $125-$135. Children over 12 yrs only. TV, VCR avail. Pool. Complimentary full bkfst. Restaurant nearby. Ck-in 3 pm. Business servs avail. Picnic tables, grills. Stone manor house built in 1770s, set amidst 16 acres of lawns, gardens, woods, stream and pasture. Trout stream, barns and outbuildings with farm animals create a pastoral setting. Totally nonsmoking. Cr cds: A, MC, V.

Restaurant

★★ **CLINTON HOUSE.** *2 W Main St.* *908/730-9300.* Hrs: 11:30 am-2:30 pm, 5-9:30 pm. Closed Dec 25. Res accepted. Bar to midnight. Semi-a la carte: lunch $5.95-$13.95, dinner $15.50-$25.50. Child's meals. Specializes in beef, seafood. Built 1743; former stagecoach stop. Family-owned. Cr cds: A, D, DS, MC, V.

D

Eatontown (E-5)

(See also Red Bank)

Pop 13,800 **Elev** 46 ft **Area code** 732 **Zip** 07724

Motels

✔★ **RED ROOF INN.** *(11 Centre Plaza, Tinton Falls) Off Garden State Pkwy exit 105, turn right on Hope Rd.* *FAX 732/389-4509.* 119 rms, 3 story. May-Labor Day: S, D $75-$79; each addl $7; under 18 free; lower rates rest of yr. Crib free. Pet accepted, some restrictions. TV; cable (premium). Restaurant nearby. Ck-out noon. In-rm modem link. Cr cds: A, C, D, DS, MC, V.

★★ **RESIDENCE INN BY MARRIOTT.** *(90 Park Rd, Tinton Falls) off Garden State Pkwy exit 105, on Hope Rd, then 1st left on Park Rd.* *732/389-8100; FAX 732/389-1573.* 96 kit. suites. S, D $125-$152. Crib free. Pet accepted; $150. TV; cable (premium), VCR avail. Pool; whirlpool. Complimentary continental bkfst. Restaurant nearby. Ck-out noon. Coin lndry. Meeting rms. Business servs avail. In-rm modem link. Valet serv. Health club privileges. Microwaves. Balconies. Picnic tables, grills. Cr cds: A, C, D, DS, JCB, MC, V.

Motor Hotel

★ ★ ★ **HOLIDAY INN TINTON FALLS.** *(700 Hope Rd, Tinton Falls)* At Garden State Pkwy exit 105. 732/544-9300; FAX 732/544-0570. 171 rms, 5 story. S, D $75-$125; each addl $10; suites $115-$225; wknd rates. Crib free. TV; cable (premium). Pool; poolside serv. Restaurant 6:30 am-11 pm. Rm serv. Bar 11:30-2 am. Ck-out noon. Lndry facilities. Meeting rms. Business servs avail. In-rm modem link. Bellhops. Valet serv. Gift shop. Exercise equipt; weight machines, bicycles, sauna. Refrigerators, microwaves avail. Cr cds: A, C, D, DS, MC, V.

D ⚊ ✈ ⚊ ⚊ SC

Hotels

★ ★ ★ **HILTON-OCEAN PLACE.** *(1 Ocean Blvd, Long Branch 07740)* Garden State Pkwy exit 105, E on NJ 36. 732/571-4000; FAX 732/571-3314. Web www.hilton.com/lbrophf.shtml. 254 rms, 12 story. Memorial Day-Labor Day: S $170-$205; D $190-$225; each addl $20; suites $350-$1,000; family, wknd rates; lower rates rest of yr. Crib free. TV; cable (premium), VCR avail. 2 pools, 1 indoor; whirlpools, poolside serv, lifeguard. Supervised child's activities (mid-May-early Sept); ages 3-12. Restaurants 6:30 am-10 pm; Sat, Sun from 7 am. Rm serv 24 hrs. Bar 11-2 am; entertainment. Ck-out noon. Convention facilities. Business center. In-rm modem link. Concierge. Shopping arcade. Barber, beauty shop. Free garage parking. RR station transportation. Lighted tennis. Golf privileges. Exercise rm; instructor, weight machine, bicycles, sauna, steam rm. Massage. Balconies. On ocean. Cr cds: A, C, D, DS, ER, MC, V.

D ⚊ ⚊ ⚊ ✈ ⚊ ⚊ ⚊ SC ⚊

★ ★ ★ **SHERATON-EATONTOWN HOTEL & CONFERENCE CENTER.** 6 Industrial Way East, off Garden State Pkwy exit 105. 732/542-6500; FAX 732/542-6607. 208 rms, 6 story. May-Sept: S $134-$144; D $149-$159; each addl $15; suites $364; wknd rates; lower rates rest of yr. Crib free. TV; cable (premium). Indoor/outdoor pool; whirlpool. Restaurant 6:30 am-11 pm. Bar. Ck-out noon. Meeting rms. Business servs avail. In-rm modem link. Gift shop. Exercise equipt; bicycles, stair machine. Refrigerators, microwaves avail. Cr cds: A, C, D, DS, MC, V.

D ⚊ ✈ ⚊ ⚊ SC

Restaurant

★ ★ **MUMFORD'S.** *(45 Atlantic Ave, Long Branch 07740)* E on NJ 71. 732/222-2657. Hrs: 5-10 pm; Fri, Sat to 11 pm; Sun 4-10 pm. Closed Mon; most major hols. Res accepted. Semi-a la carte: dinner $18-$25. Child's meals. Specialties: buttermilk and pecan-crusted Northern Atlantic salmon, panchetta-wrapped shrimp, nine-spice New York sirloin. Art deco setting. Cr cds: MC, V.

D

Edison (D-4)

(See also Woodbridge)

Pop 88,680 **Elev** 95 ft **Area code** 732
Information Chamber of Commerce, PO Box 2103, 08818-2103; 732/494-0300.

Although Thomas A. Edison's house here has been destroyed, Edison State Park and the Edison Memorial Tower stand in tribute to the great American inventor. Here, on December 6, 1877, the 30-year-old Edison invented the phonograph. Two years later, he perfected the first practical incandescent light, designing and constructing various kinds of electrical equipment we now take for granted. His workshop has been moved to the Ford Museum in Dearborn, Michigan. Edison also built the first electric railway locomotive here in 1880; it ran 1½ miles over the fields of Pumptown.

What to See and Do

Edison Memorial Tower. A 131-ft tower topped by a 13-ft-high electric light bulb stands on the spot where the first incandescent bulb was made. Museum contains some of Edison's inventions (Memorial Day-Labor Day, daily exc Mon; rest of yr, Wed-Sun afternoons). Christie St, ½ mi SW of Garden State Pkwy exit 131 off NJ 27 in Edison State Park. Phone 732/549-3299. **Free.**

Motor Hotel

★ ★ ★ **CLARION HOTEL.** 2055 Lincoln Hwy (08817), ½ mi S of I-287 on NJ 27. 732/287-3500; FAX 732/287-8190. 169 rms, 5 story. S, D $99-$149; each addl $20; under 18 free; wknd rates. Crib free. TV; cable (premium), VCR avail (movies). Complimentary full bkfst. Coffee in rms. Restaurant 7 am-10:30 pm; Fri, Sat to 11 pm. Rm serv. Bar 11-1 am. Ck-out noon. Meeting rms. Business center. In-rm modem link. Bellhops. Gift shop. Exercise equipt; weights, bicycles. Refrigerators; microwaves avail. Luxury level. Cr cds: A, C, D, DS, MC, V.

D ✈ ⚊ ⚊ SC ⚊

Hotel

★ ★ ★ **CROWNE PLAZA.** 125 Raritan Center Pkwy (08837). 732/225-8300. 274 rms, 12 story. S, D $125-$140; suites $275; under 12 free; wknd rates. Crib free. Pet accepted. TV; cable (premium), VCR avail. Indoor pool; whirlpool, poolside serv. Complimentary coffee in rms. Restaurant 6 am-2 pm, 5-10 pm. Bar. Ck-out noon. Coin lndry. Convention facilities. Business servs avail. In-rm modem link. Concierge. Gift shop. Exercise equipt; weights, treadmill, sauna. Game rm. Cr cds: A, C, D, DS, ER, MC, V.

D ⚊ ⚊ ✈ ⚊ ⚊ SC

Restaurant

✔ ★ ★ **CHARLIE BROWN'S.** 222 Plainfield Ave (08820). 732/494-6135. Web www.charliebrowns.com. Hrs: 11:30 am-10 pm; Fri, Sat to 10:30 pm; Sun to 9 pm. Closed Dec 25. Bar to 2 am. Semi-a la carte: lunch $4.95-$8.45, dinner $9.75-$16.99. Child's meals. Specialties: prime rib, filet mignon, grilled salmon. Outdoor dining. Rustic American decor; stained glass windows; casual setting. Cr cds: A, MC, V.

D ⚊

Elizabeth (C-5)

(For accommodations see Jersey City, Newark, Newark Intl Airport Area)

Settled 1664 **Pop** 110,002 **Elev** 36 ft **Area code** 908
Information Union County Chamber of Commerce, 135 Jefferson Ave, PO Box 300, 07207; 908/352-0900.

More than 1,200 manufacturing industries are located in Elizabeth and Union County. Long before the Revolution, Elizabeth was not only the capital of New Jersey, but also a thriving industrial town. The first Colonial Assembly met here from 1669 to 1692. Princeton University began in Elizabeth in 1746 as the College of New Jersey. More than 20 pre-Revolutionary buildings still stand. Many noteworthy people were citizens of Elizabeth: William Livingston, first governor of New Jersey; Elias Boudinot, first president of the Continental Congress; Alexander Hamilton; Aaron Burr; General Winfield Scott; John Philip Holland, builder of the first successful submarine; and Admiral William J. Halsey. The Elizabeth-Port Authority Marine Terminal is the largest container port in the US.

What to See and Do

Boxwood Hall State Historic Site. Home of Elias Boudinot, lawyer, diplomat, president (1783) of the Continental Congress and director of the US Mint. Boudinot entertained George Washington here on Apr 23, 1789, when Washington was on his way to his inauguration. (Daily exc Sun; closed Jan 1, Thanksgiving, Dec 25) 1073 E Jersey St, 1½ blks W of US 1. Phone 201/648-4540.

First Presbyterian Church and Graveyard. The first General Assembly of New Jersey convened in an earlier building in 1668. The burned-out church was rebuilt in 1785-1787, and again in 1949. The Rev. James Caldwell was an early pastor. Alexander Hamilton and Aaron Burr attended an academy where the parish house now stands. Broad St & Caldwell Pl.

Warinanco Park. One of the largest Union County parks. Fishing; boating (rentals June-Sept, daily). Running track; parcourse fitness circuit; tennis (late Apr-early Oct); handball; horseshoes. Indoor ice-skating (early Oct-early Apr, daily). Henry S Chatfield Memorial Garden features tulip blooms each spring; azaleas and Japanese cherry trees; summer and fall flower displays. Some fees. St Georges & Linden Aves, W edge of city. Phone 908/527-4900. **Free.**

Flemington (D-3)

(See also Clinton, Somerville)

Settled 1738 **Pop** 4,047 **Elev** 160 ft **Area code** 908 **Zip** 08822

Information Hunterdon County Chamber of Commerce, 2200 Rte 31, Suite 15, Lebanon 08833; 908/735-5955.

Originally a farming community, Flemington became a center for the production of pottery and cut glass at the turn of the century.

What to See and Do

Black River & Western Railroad. Excursion ride on old steam train, 11-mi round trip to Ringoes. Picnic area; museum. (July-Aug, Thurs-Sun; Apr-June & Sept-Nov, Sat, Sun & hols) Center Shopping Area. Phone 908/782-9600. ¢¢¢

County Courthouse (1828). For 46 days in 1935, world attention was focused on this Greek-revival building where Bruno Hauptmann was tried for the kidnapping and murder of the Lindbergh baby. Main St.

Fleming Castle (1756). Typical 2-story Colonial house built as a residence and inn by Samuel Fleming, for whom the town is named. DAR headquarters. (By appt) 5 Bonnell St. Phone 908/782-6472 (days) or 908/782-4655 (evenings). **Donation.**

Kase Cemetery. John Philip Kase, Flemington's first settler, purchased a tract from William Penn. His family's crumbling gravestones date from 1774 to 1856. Kase's Native American friend, Chief Tuccamirgan, is also memorialized here. Bonnell St, W of Fleming Castle.

Volendam Windmill Museum. Named after a town in the northern Netherlands, this is an authentic reproduction of an old-time wind-driven mill used for grinding raw grain into flour. Mill stands 60 ft high with sail arms stretching 86 ft. Museum contains old milling and farm tools. (June-Sept, Sat & Sun afternoons; closed hols) Approx 21 mi NW via NJ 12, County 519 to Adamic Hill Rd in Milford, follow signs. Phone 908/995-4365. ¢¢

Annual Event

Flemington Agricultural Fair. Phone 908/782-2413. Late Aug-early Sept.

Seasonal Event

Stock-car racing. Flemington Fair Speedway. Sat, Apr-Nov.

Motel

★ **RAMADA INN.** 250 US 202, ½ mi S of jct NJ 31. 908/782-7472; FAX 908/782-1975. 104 rms, 2 story, 24 kits. S, D $90; each addl $10; suites $110; kit. units $100. Crib avail. TV; cable (premium). Pool. Complimentary coffee in lobby. Restaurant 6:30 am-10 pm. Bar. Ck-out noon. Coin lndry. Meeting rms. Microwaves avail. Cr cds: A, C, D, DS, MC, V.

Restaurants

★★★ **HARVEST MOON INN.** (1039 Old York Rd, Ringoes 08551) US 202 S to US 179. 908/806-6020. Web www.harvestmooninn.com. Hrs: 11:30 am-2:30 pm, 5-9:30 pm; Fri to 10 pm; Sat 5-10 pm; Sun 1-8 pm; early-bird dinner Tues-Fri 5-6 pm. Closed Mon; most major hols. Res accepted. Bar. Semi-a la carte: lunch $5.95-$12.95, dinner $16-$26. Complete meal: dinner $19.97. Child's meals. Specialties: grilled vegetable Napoleon with roasted peppers and goat cheese, pan-seared tuna with pea shoots, sauteed Long Island duck breast. Own baking. Piano bar Fri, Sat. Stone building (ca 1811) with two fireplaces. Cr cds: A, DS, MC, V.

D

★★ **UNION HOTEL.** 76 Main St. 908/788-7474. Hrs: 11 am-10 pm; Sun noon-8 pm. Closed some major hols. Res accepted. Bar to 2 am. Semi-a la carte: lunch $4.95-$8.95, dinner $8.95-$21.95. Child's meals. Specializes in fresh fish, steak, prime rib. Entertainment Thurs-Sat. In ornate Victorian hotel (1878) opp county courthouse. Cr cds: A, MC, V.

Forked River (G-5)

(For accommodations see Toms River)

Pop 4,243 **Elev** 19 ft **Area code** 609 **Zip** 08731

Restaurant

★★ **CAPTAIN'S INN.** East Lacey Rd, ½ mi E of US 9, Garden State Pkwy exit 74S, 69N. 609/693-3351. Hrs: 11:45 am-10 pm. Closed Dec 25. Continental menu. Bar. Semi-a la carte: lunch from $3.95, dinner $9.95-$19.95. Child's meals. Specialties: crab Imperial, steak au poivre, lobster. Entertainment Fri-Sun evenings. Docking. Built in 1831. Overlooks river. Cr cds: A, C, D, MC, V.

D

Fort Lee (C-6)

(See also Hackensack)

Pop 31,997 **Elev** 314 ft **Area code** 201 **Zip** 07024

Information Greater Fort Lee Chamber of Commerce, 2357 Lemoine Ave; 201/944-7575.

North and south of the George Washington Bridge, Fort Lee is named for General Charles Lee, who served in the Revolutionary Army under George Washington. Its rocky bluff achieved fame as the cliff from which Pearl White hung in the early movie serial "The Adventures of Pearl White." From 1907 to 1916, 21 companies and seven studios produced motion pictures in Fort Lee. Stars such as Mary Pickford, Mabel Normand, Theda Bara and Clara Kimball Young made movies here.

What to See and Do

Fort Lee Historic Park. (See PALISADES INTERSTATE PARKS)

Motor Hotel

★ **DAYS INN.** *2339 NJ 4E.* 201/944-5000; FAX 201/944-0623. 175 rms, 6 story. S $71-$85; D $81-$85; each addl $10; under 18 free. Crib free. TV; cable. Pool. Restaurant 7 am-2 pm. Rm serv. Bar 5 pm-midnight; closed Sun. Ck-out noon. Meeting rms. Business servs avail. Sundries. Cr cds: A, C, D, DS, JCB, MC, V.

Hotels

★★★ **HILTON.** *2117 NJ 4E, at jct I-95 Fort Lee exit.* 201/461-9000; FAX 201/461-6783. 235 rms, 15 story. S, D $125-$165; under 12 free. Crib free. TV; cable (premium), VCR avail. Indoor pool; whirlpool. Restaurant 6:30 am-10:30 pm. Rm serv. Bars 11-1 am. Ck-out noon. Meeting rms. Business center. In-rm modem link. Bellhops. Valet serv. Concierge. Gift shop. Covered parking. Exercise equipt; weight machine, bicycles, sauna. Cr cds: A, C, D, DS, JCB, MC, V.

★★★ **RADISSON.** *(401 S Van Brunt St, Englewood 07631)* NJ 4W exit Van Brunt St. 201/871-2020; FAX 201/871-7116. 192 rms, 9 story. Late Nov-mid Dec: S, D $145-$165; suites $185-$275; wkend rates; lower rates rest of yr. Crib free. Pet accepted, some restrictions; $25. TV; cable (premium), VCR avail. Complimentary coffee in rms. Restaurant 6:30 am-10 pm. Bar 11:30-1 am. Ck-out noon. Meeting rms. Business servs avail. Concierge. Coin lndry. Exercise equipt; treadmill, stair machine. Indoor pool. Some bathrm phones. Refrigerators, microwaves avail. Luxury level. Cr cds: A, C, D, DS, ER, JCB, MC, V.

Freehold (E-5)

(See also Eatontown, Hightstown, Lakewood)

Founded 1715 **Pop** 10,742 **Elev** 154 ft **Area code** 732 **Zip** 07728

Information Western Monmouth Chamber of Commerce, 36 W Main St; 732/462-3030.

George Washington and the Revolutionary Army defeated the British under General Sir Henry Clinton at the Battle of Monmouth near here on June 28, 1778. Molly Hays carried water to artillerymen in a pitcher and from that day on she has been known as "Molly Pitcher." Freehold is the seat of Monmouth County, and the community's principal industry is glass manufacturing.

What to See and Do

Covenhoven House. Eighteenth-century house with period furnishings; once occupied by General Sir Henry Clinton prior to the Battle of Monmouth in 1778. (May-Oct, Tues, Thur, Sat & Sun afternoons) 150 W Main St. Phone 732/462-1466. ¢

Monmouth County Historical Museum and Library. Headquarters of Monmouth County Historical Assn. Large rooms and galleries with 17th-, 18th- and early 19th-century furniture; collections of silver, ceramics, paintings; attic museum with toys, dolls, doll houses; Civil and Revolutionary War weapons. Museum (Tues-Sat, also Sun afternoons); library (Wed-Sat; both closed major hols). 70 Court St. Phone 732/462-1466. ¢

Turkey Swamp Park. An 890-acre park with fishing; boating (rentals). Hiking trails. Ice-skating. Picnicking (shelter), playfields. Camping (Mar-Nov; fee; electric & water hookups). Special events. 2 mi SW off I-195, exit 22, County 524 to Georgia Rd. Phone 732/462-7286. **Free.**

Seasonal Event

Harness racing. Freehold Raceway, jct US 9, NJ 33. Phone 732/462-3800. Daily exc Sun, mid-Aug-May.

Motor Hotels

★ **COLTS NECK INN.** *(6 NJ 537W, Colts Neck 07722)* W on NJ 537, at jct NJ 34. 732/409-1200; FAX 732/431-6640; res: 800/332-5578. 49 rms, 2 story. S $65; D $85; each addl $10; suites $135; under 12 free. Crib free. TV; cable (premium), VCR avail. Complimentary continental bkfst. Restaurant adj 11:30 am-10 pm. Bar to 1 am. Ck-out 11 am. Meeting rms. Business servs avail. Refrigerators, microwaves avail. Cr cds: A, C, D, MC, V.

★★ **FREEHOLD GARDENS.** *NJ 537 & Gibson Place,* 1 mi W on NJ 537. 732/780-3870; FAX 732/780-8725. 114 rms, 5 story. S, D $69-$90; each addl $10; under 18 free; higher rates late May-early Sept. Crib free. Pet accepted, some restrictions; $100 deposit. TV; cable. Pool. Complimentary continental bkfst. Restaurant 5-11 pm. Rm serv. Entertainment. Ck-out noon. Meeting rms. Business servs avail. Health club privileges. Refrigerators avail. Cr cds: A, C, D, MC, V.

Restaurant

★ **GOLDEN BELL.** *Adelphia Rd & US9 S.* 732/462-7259. Hrs: 6 am-midnight; Fri, Sat open 24 hrs. Italian, Amer menu. Semi-a la carte: lunch $4.95-$8.25, dinner $5.95-$23.45. A la carte entrees: lunch $2.95-$11.50, dinner $8.95-$19.95. Child's meals. Specialties: Golden Bell fisherman's platter, tropical waffle, chicken salad in pita bread. Greenhouse atrium. Cr cds: A, C, D, DS, MC, V.

Gateway National Recreation Area (Sandy Hook Unit) (D-6)

(For accommodations see Red Bank)

(5 mi E of Atlantic Highlands on NJ 36)

Sandy Hook is a barrier peninsula that was first sighted by the crew of Henry Hudson's *Half Moon* (1609). It once was (1692) owned by Richard Hartshorne, an English Quaker, but has been government property since the 18th century. Fort Hancock (1895) was an important harbor defense from the Spanish-American War through the cold war era. Among Sandy Hook's most significant features are the Sandy Hook Lighthouse (1764), the oldest operating lighthouse in the US, and the US Army Proving Ground (1874-1919), the army's first new-weapons testing site.

The park offers swimming (lifeguards in summer), fishing, guided and self-guided walks, picnicking and a concession. Visitors are advised to obtain literature at the Visitor Center (daily). There is no charge for entrance and activities scheduled by the National Park Service. Parking fee, Memorial Day wkend-Labor Day. (Daily, sunrise-sunset; some facilities closed in winter) For further information contact Superintendant, PO Box 530, Fort Hancock 07732; 732/872-5970.

What to See and Do

Twin Lights State Historic Site (1862). A lighthouse built to guide ships into New York harbor; now a marine museum operated by the State Park Service. (May-Oct, daily; rest of yr, Wed-Sun) White House Rd. Phone 732/872-1814. **Donation.**

Restaurants

★ **BAHRS LANDING.** *(2 Bay Ave, Highlands 07732)* Garden State Pkwy exit 117, then NJ 36 E to Highlands Bridge. 732/872-1245. E-mail bahr@shell.monmouth.com; web www.monmouth.com/bahrs. Hrs: 11:30 am-9:30 pm; Fri, Sat to 10:30 pm; Sun brunch 11 am-2:30 pm. Closed Dec 25. Bar. A la carte entrees: lunch, dinner $12.95-$23.95. Sun brunch $5-$9.95. Child's meals. Specializes in fresh seafood. On waterfront; scenic view of the channel. Family-owned. Cr cds: A, C, D, DS, MC, V.

★ ★ **DORIS & ED'S.** *(348 Shore Dr, Highlands 07732)* 732/872-1565. E-mail if@doris-and-eds.com; web www.doris-and-eds.com. Hrs: 5-10 pm; Sat to 11 pm; Sun 3-10 pm. Closed Mon, Tues; most major hols; also Jan-Feb. Res accepted. Semi-a la carte: dinner $19-$28. Child's meals. Specialties: grilled tuna on wasabi mayonnaise, sauteed red snapper with fresh rock shrimp, poached Atlantic salmon in a champagne mussel stew. View of Sandy Hook Bay. Cr cds: A, C, D, MC, V.

Gibbstown (G-2)

Pop 3,902 **Elev** 15 ft **Area code** 609 **Zip** 08027
Information Township of Greenwich, 420 Washington St; 609/423-1038 or 609/423-4913.

What to See and Do

Hunter-Lawrence-Jessup House (1765). Headquarters of Gloucester County Historical Society. Museum contains 16 rms of furnishings and memorabilia from 17th- to 19th-century New Jersey. (Wed & Fri afternoons, also 1st & 3rd Mon afternoon of each month; closed hols) Approx 7 mi NW via NJ 45, County 534 in Woodbury at 58 N Broad St. Phone 609/845-7881. ¢

Nothnagle Home (1638-1643). America's oldest log house. (By appt) 406 Swedesboro Rd. Phone 609/423-0916. **Free.**

Motel

 ★ ★ **DUTCH INN.** *Harmony Rd, just off I-295 at exit 17.* 609/423-6600; FAX 609/423-0757. 124 rms, 2 story. S, D $40-$54; each addl $5; under 12 free. Crib $6. Pet accepted. TV. Pool; lifeguard. Restaurant open 24 hrs; dining rm 11:30 am-2 pm, 4:30-9:30 pm; wkend hrs vary. Bar 11-2 am; closed Sun; entertainment. Ck-out noon. Meeting rms. Business servs avail. Cr cds: A, C, D, DS, MC, V.

Motor Hotel

★ ★ **HOLIDAY INN SELECT.** *(Center Square Rd, Bridgeport 08014)* 3 mi S at I-295, exit 10. 609/467-3322; FAX 609/467-3031. 149 rms, 4 story. S $59-$84; D $59-$104; each addl $10; suites $125-$170; under 19 free. Crib free. TV; cable (premium), VCR avail. Indoor pool; whirlpool, poolside serv. Restaurant 6:30 am-10 pm. Rm serv. Bar 11 am-midnight; entertainment Mon-Fri. Ck-out noon. Coin lndry. Meeting rms. Business servs avail. In-rm modem link. Bellhops. Valet serv. Sundries. Gift shop. Airport transportation. Exercise equipt; weights, bicycles. Game rm. Some refrigerators. Some balconies. Cr cds: A, C, D, DS, JCB, MC, V.

Hackensack (C-5)

(See also Fort Lee, Paterson)

Settled 1647 **Pop** 37,049 **Elev** 20 ft **Area code** 201
Information Chamber of Commerce, 190 Main St, 07601; 201/489-3700.

Hackensack was officially known as New Barbados until 1921 when it received its charter under its present name, thought to be derived from the Native American word *Hacquinsacq.* The influence of the original Dutch settlers who established a trading post here remained strong even after British conquest. A strategic point during the Revolution, the city contains a number of historical sites from that era. Hackensack is the hub for industry, business and government in Bergen County. Edward Williams College is located here.

What to See and Do

Steuben House State Historic Site (1713). Museum of the Bergen County Historical Society. Enlarged in 1752 as home of Jan and his wife, Annetie Zabriskie. The house was confiscated during the Revolutionary War because the Zabriskies were Loyalists; it was given to Baron von Steuben, by the state of New Jersey, as a reward for his military services. The baron later sold it back to the original owners. Colonial furniture, glassware, china; Native American artifacts. (Wed-Sat & Sun afternoons; closed Jan 1, Thanksgiving, Dec 25) Approx ¼ mi N of NJ 4, at 1209 Main St in River Edge, overlooking river. Phone 201/487-1739.

The Church on the Green. Organized in 1686, the original building was built in 1696 (13 monogrammed stones preserved in east wall), and rebuilt in 1791 in Stone Dutch architectural style. It is the oldest church building in Bergen County. Museum contains pictures, books and colonial items. Enoch Poor, a Revolutionary War general, is buried in the cemetery. Tours (wkdays on request). 42 Court St, NE corner of the Green, S end of Main St, opp County Court House. Phone 201/845-0957. **Free.**

USS *Ling* Submarine. Restored World War II fleet submarine; New Jersey Naval Museum. (Wed-Sun; closed most major hols) Docked at Court & River Sts. Phone 201/342-3268. ¢¢

Motel

★ ★ **BEST WESTERN ORITANI.** *414 Hackensack Ave (07601).* 201/488-8900; FAX 201/488-5456. Web www.bestwestern.com/best.html. 100 units, 4 story. S, D $81-$95. Crib $8. TV; cable (premium). Pool; sauna. Complimentary continental bkfst. Restaurant noon-2:30 pm, 5:30-10 pm. Bar noon-2:30 pm, 5:30-10:30 pm. Ck-out noon. Meeting rms. Business servs avail. Valet serv. Sundries. Exercise equipt; weight machine, treadmill. Cr cds: A, C, D, DS, MC, V.

Hotels

★ ★ ★ **CROWN PLAZA HASBROUCK HEIGHTS.** *(650 Terrace Ave, Hasbrouck Heights 07604)* At jct NJ 17N, I-80. 201/288-6100; FAX 201/288-4717. E-mail jpear@cybernex.net; web www.crownplaza.com. 355 rms, 12 story. S, D $159-$199; each addl $20; suites $220-$500; under 17 free; wkend rates. Crib free. Pet accepted. TV; cable (premium), VCR avail. Heated pool; poolside serv. Restaurant 6:30 am-11 pm; wkends from 7 am. Bars 12:30 pm-1:30 am, Sat to 2:30 am. Ck-out 1 pm. Convention facilities. Business center. In-rm modem link. Gift shop. Exercise equipt; weights, bicycles, sauna. Luxury level. Cr cds: A, C, D, DS, ER, MC, V.

★ ★ ★ **MARRIOTT GLENPOINTE HOTEL.** *(100 Frank W Burr Blvd, Teaneck 07666)* At I-80/I-95, local lanes exit 70/70B. 201/836-0600; FAX 201/836-0638. Web www.marriott.com. 341 rms, 15 story. S, D $160-$190; suites $300-$650; under 18 free; wkend rates. Crib free. TV; cable (premium), VCR avail. Indoor pool; whirlpool. Restaurant 6:30 am-midnight. Bar 11-1 am. Ck-out noon. Business center. In-rm modem link. Concierge. Exercise rm; instructor, weight machines, bicycles, sauna. Bathrm phones, refrigerators. Cr cds: A, C, D, DS, ER, JCB, MC, V.

Restaurant

★★★ **STONY HILL INN.** *231 Polifly Rd, I-80 jct NJ 17N. 201/342-4085.* Hrs: 11:30 am-3 pm, 5:30-10:30 pm; Sat from 5:30 pm; Sun 2-10 pm. Closed Dec 25. Continental menu. Bar to midnight. Wine cellar. A la carte entrees: lunch $12.95-$21, dinner $15.95-$29.95. Specializes in continental cuisine. Own pastries. Entertainment Fri, Sat. Landmark house (1818); period furnishings. Jacket. Cr cds: A, C, D, MC, V.

Hackettstown (C-3)

Settled ca 1760 **Pop** 8,120 **Elev** 571 ft **Area code** 908 **Zip** 07840
Information Town Hall, 215 Stiger St; 908/852-3130.

First called Helm's Mills and then Musconetcong, citizens renamed the town for Samuel Hackett, the largest local landowner. His popularity increased when he provided unlimited free drinks at the christening of a new hotel. Hackettstown is located in the Musconetcong Valley between Schooleys and Upper Pohatcong mountains.

What to See and Do

Allamuchy Mountain State Park, Stephens Section. Allamuchy Mountain State Park (7,263 acres) is divided into three sections. The Stephens Section (482 acres) is developed; the rest (Allamuchy) is natural. Hunting. Fishing in Musconetcong River. Hiking. Picnicking, playground. Camping. Standard fees. Willow Grove St, 1½ mi N of US 46. Phone 908/852-3790 (Stephens).

Land of Make Believe. Amusement park at foot of Jenny Jump Mountain includes the Himalaya Ride; Old McDonald's Farm; the Red Baron airplane; Santa Claus at the North Pole; a Civil War train; a maze; water activities; hayrides; picnic grove; fudge factory. (Mid-June-Labor Day, daily; Memorial Day wkend-mid-June, wkends; Sept, wkend after Labor Day) I-80 exit 12, on County 611, in Hope. Phone 908/459-5100. ¢¢¢¢

Inn

★★ **THE INN AT MILLRACE POND.** *(NJ 519, Hope 07844) off I-80 exit 12, then 1 mi S to NJ 519, then E. 908/459-4884; res: 800/746-6467.* 17 rms, 2 story, 3 bldgs. S, D $95-$165; each addl $20. TV in some rms; cable. Complimentary continental bkfst. Restaurant 5-9 pm; Sun noon-7:30 pm. Ck-out noon, ck-in 3 pm. Meeting rms. Business servs avail. Airport transportation. Tennis. Library. Colonial gristmill (1769). Rms individually decorated with colonial-style furniture and period reproductions. Cr cds: A, C, D, DS, MC, V.

Haddonfield (F-3)

(For accommodations see Cherry Hill; also see Camden)

Settled ca 1713 **Pop** 11,628 **Elev** 95 ft **Area code** 609 **Zip** 08033
Information Visitor/Information Center, 114 Kings Hwy E; 609/216-7253

Named for Elizabeth Haddon, a Quaker girl of 20 whose father sent her here from England in 1701 to develop 400 acres of land. This assertive young woman built a house, started a colony and proposed to a Quaker

missionary who promptly married her. The "Theologian's Tale" in Longfellow's *Tales of a Wayside Inn* celebrates Elizabeth Haddon's romance with the missionary.

What to See and Do

Greenfield Hall. Haddonfield's Historical Society headquarters in old Gill House (1747-1841) contains personal items of Elizabeth Haddon; furniture; costumes; doll collection. Boxwood garden; library on local history. On grounds is a house (ca 1735) once owned by Elizabeth Haddon. (Mon-Fri, mornings, other days by appt; closed Aug) 343 King's Hwy E (NJ 41). Phone 609/429-7375. ¢

Indian King Tavern Museum State Historic Site. Built as an inn; state legislatures met here frequently, passing a bill (1777) substituting "State" for "Colony" in all state papers. Colonial furnishings. Guided tours. (Wed-Sun; closed Jan 1, Thanksgiving, Dec 25; also Wed if following Mon or Tues hol) 233 King's Hwy E. Phone 609/429-6792. **Donation.**

The Site of the Elizabeth Haddon House. Isaac Wood built this house in 1842, on the foundation of Elizabeth Haddon's 1713 brick mansion, immediately after it was destroyed by fire. The original brew house Elizabeth built (1713) and the English yew trees she brought over in 1712 are in the yard. Private residence; not open to the public. Wood Lane & Merion Ave.

High Point State Park (A-4)

(7 mi NW of Sussex on NJ 23)

High Point's elevation (1,803 ft), the highest point in New Jersey, gave this 15,000-acre park its name. The spot is marked by a 220-foot stone war memorial. The view is magnificent, overlooking Tri-State—the point where New Jersey, New York and Pennsylvania meet—with the Catskill Mountains to the north, the Pocono Mountains to the west, and hills, valleys and lakes all around. Elsewhere in the forests of this Kittatinny Mountain park are facilities for swimming; fishing; boating. Nature center. Picnicking. Tent camping (no trailers). Standard fees. Phone 201/875-4800.

Hightstown (E-4)

Pop 5,126 **Elev** 84 ft **Area code** 609 **Zip** 08520

Motel

★★ **TOWN HOUSE.** *NJ Tpke exit 8, on NJ 33. 609/448-2400; FAX 609/443-0395; res: 800/922-0622.* 104 rms, 1-2 story. S $55-$125; D $58-$125; each addl $10; suites, studio rms $95-$150; under 12 free; package plans. Crib free. Pet accepted. TV; VCR avail (movies $2). Pool; wading pool, lifeguard. Complimentary continental bkfst. Restaurant 10 am-midnight. Bar 11-1 am; entertainment. Ck-out 1 pm. Meeting rms. In-rm modem link. Sundries. Refrigerators; whirlpool in some suites. Cr cds: A, C, D, DS, MC, V.

Motor Hotel

★★ **RAMADA INN.** *(399 Monmouth St, East Windsor) NJ Turnpike, exit 8. 609/448-7000.* 200 rms, 4 story. Mid-June-Aug: S $79-$109; D $85-$115; each addl $10; suite $139-$199; under 12 free; lower rates rest of yr. Crib free. Pet accepted. TV; cable (premium). Pool; sauna. Restaurant opp 7:30 am-9 pm. Bar 5 pm-1 am. Ck-out noon. Meeting rms. Business servs avai. Coin lndry. Exercise equipt; stair machine, weight machine. Cr cds: A, C, D, DS, MC, V.

Restaurant

★ ★ **FORSGATE COUNTRY CLUB.** *(Forsgate Dr, Jamesburg)* *At NJ Tpke, exit 8A. 908/521-0070.* Hrs: noon-2 pm, 6-9 pm; Sat from 6 pm. Sun brunch from 10:30 am. Closed Mon; Jan 1, Dec 25. Bar. A la carte entrees: lunch $7.50-$18, dinner $14-$26. Sun brunch $21.95. Specializes in regional American dishes. Country club atmosphere; view of golf course. Cr cds: A, D, MC, V.

Hillsdale (B-5)

(For accommodations see Montvale, Paramus)

Pop 9,750 **Elev** 83 ft **Area code** 201 **Zip** 07642

Motor Hotel

★ ★ ★ **HILTON.** *(200 Tice Blvd, Woodcliff Lake 07675) N on I-78 to exit 171, W on Glen Rd, E on Chestnut Ridge Rd, W on Tice Blvd. 201/391-3600; FAX 201/391-4572.* 334 rms, 4 story. S $125-$145; D $140-$160; each addl $15; suites $325-$400; under 18 free; wkend, wkly, hol rates. Crib free. TV; cable (premium). Complimentary coffee in rms. Restaurant 6:30 am-11:30 pm. Rm serv. Bar 11:30-12:30 am. Ck-out noon. Convention facilities. Business center. In-rm modem link. Bellhops. Concierge. Sundries. Gift shop. Coin lndry. Airport, RR station transportation. Tennis. Exercise equipt; weights, bicycle, sauna. Massage. 2 pools, 1 indoor/outdoor; whirlpool, poolside serv, lifeguard. Refrigerators, microwaves avail. Cr cds: A, DS, MC, V.

Hoboken (C-5)

(For accommodations see Jersey City, Secaucus)

Settled 1640 **Pop** 33,397 **Elev** 5 ft **Area code** 201 **Zip** 07030
Information Hoboken Community Development, 94 Washington St; 201/420-2013.

In the early 19th century, beer gardens and other amusement centers dotted the Hoboken shore, enticing New Yorkers across the Hudson. John Jacob Astor, Washington Irving, William Cullen Bryant and Martin Van Buren were among the fashionable visitors. By the second half of the century, industries and shipping began to encroach on the fun. In 1928-1929, Christopher Morley and Cleon Throckmorton presented revivals of *After Dark* and *The Black Crook* to enchanted New Yorkers. Hoboken is connected to Manhattan by the PATH rapid-transit system.

What to See and Do

Stevens Institute of Technology (1870). (3,600 students) A leading college of engineering, science, computer science management and the humanities; also a center for research. Campus tours. Castle Point, E of Hudson St between 5th & 9th Sts. Phone 201/216-5105. On campus are

Stevens Center (1962). The 14-story hub of campus. Excellent view of Manhattan from George Washington Bridge to the Verrazano Bridge.

Samuel C. Williams Library (1969). Special collections include set of facsimiles of every drawing by Leonardo da Vinci; library of 3,000 volumes by and about da Vinci; Alexander Calder mobile; the Frederick Winslow Taylor Collection of Scientific Management. (Academic yr) Phone 201/216-5198.

Davidson Laboratory. One of the largest privately owned hydrodynamic labs of its kind in the world. Testing site for models of ships, hydrofoils, the America's Cup participants and the Apollo command capsule. (Limited public access) W end of campus. Phone 201/216-5290.

Restaurants

★ **ARTHUR'S TAVERN.** *237 Washington St, at 3rd St. 201/656-5009.* Hrs: 11:30 am-11 pm; Fri, Sat to midnight; Sun 2-10 pm. Closed Thanksgiving, Dec 25. Bars. A la carte entrees: lunch $3.95-$11.95, dinner $3.95-$20.95. Specialties: 24-oz Delmonico steak, Maine lobster. Built 1850; old tavern decor, stained glass. Cr cds: A, C, D, DS, MC, V.

★ ★ **BAJA.** *104 14th St. 201/653-0610.* Hrs: 5-10:30 pm; Fri, Sat noon-11:30 pm; Sun noon-10 pm. Closed Jan 1, Thanksgiving, Dec 25. Res accepted. Mexican menu. Bar 5 pm-midnight. Semi-a la carte: lunch, dinner $3.95-$17.95. Specialties: parrillada a la baja, alambre veracruz, enchiladas a la parrilla. Southwestern decor. Cr cds: A, C, D, DS, MC, V.

✔ ★ **CAFE MICHELINA.** *423 Bloomfield St. 201/659-3663.* Hrs: 11 am-10 pm; Fri to midnight; Sat 3-11 pm; Sun 3-9:30 pm. Closed Mon; most major hols. Res accepted. Italian menu. A la carte entrees: lunch $4.50-$9, dinner $7.95-$13.95. Specialties: chicken portabella with marcella sauce, lobster ravioli, chicken Michelina. Italian decor. Cr cds: A.

✔ ★ **MARGHERITAS'S.** *740 Washington St. 201/222-2400.* Hrs: 11:30 am-10:30 pm; Fri, Sat to 11:30 pm; Sun 1-9:30 pm. Closed Mon; Easter, Thanksgiving, Dec 25. Italian menu. A la carte entrees: lunch $4.95-$7.95. Semi-a la carte: dinner $9.95-$12.95. Specialties: ravioli mondella, chicken Carol, shrimp fra diavolo. Own desserts. Italian decor. Cr cds: MC, V.

★ **ODD FELLOWS.** *80 River St. 201/656-9009.* Hrs: 11:30 am-10:30 pm; Thurs-Sat to 11 pm; Sun to 4 pm (brunch). Closed Thanksgiving, Dec 25. Bar. Semi-a la carte: lunch $7.95-$11.95, dinner $7.95-$16.95. Sun brunch $9. Child's meals. Specialties: catfish, jambalaya, crawfish etouffée. Blues Thurs, Sun. Outdoor dining. Authentic French Quarter decor; exposed brick walls, tiled tabletops. Cr cds: A, MC, V.

★ **PATSY'S.** *133 Clinton St. 201/792-0800.* Hrs: noon-11 pm; Sat, Sun from 2 pm; Tues from 5 pm. Closed Mon; Easter, Thanksgiving, Dec 25. Italian menu. Bar. A la carte entrees: lunch, dinner $11-$16. Specialties: roasted sweet red peppers, sausage pizza, mushroom pizza. Outdoor dining. Cozy, Italian atmosphere; brick fireplace; two-level dining area. Cr cds: A, MC, V.

Ho-Ho-Kus (B-5)

(For accommodations see Paramus)

Pop 3,935 **Elev** 111 ft **Area code** 201 **Zip** 07423
Information Borough of Ho-Ho-Kus, 333 Warren Ave; 201/652-4400.

In colonial times, Ho-Ho-Kus was known as Hoppertown. Its present name is derived from the Chihohokies, who also had a settlement on this spot.

What to See and Do

The Hermitage. Stone Victorian house of Gothic-revival architecture superimposed on original 18th-century house. Its span of history includes ownership by the Rosencrantz family for more than 150 yrs. Grounds consist of five wooded acres, including a second stone Victorian house. Costumed docents conduct tours of site and the Hermitage. Clothing exhibit (June-Sept). Special events held throughout the yr. Tours (phone for schedule; closed hols). 335 N Franklin Tpke. Phone 201/445-8311 for exact schedule, including events and productions. ¢¢

Jackson (F-5)

(For accommodations see Lakewood, Toms River)

Pop 33,233 **Elev** 138 ft **Area code** 908 **Zip** 08527
Information Chamber of Commerce, PO Box A-C; 908/363-1080.

What to See and Do

Six Flags Great Adventure Theme Park/Six Flags Wild Safari Animal Park. A family entertainment center, including 350-acre drive-through safari park with more than 1,200 free-roaming animals from 6 continents; 125-acre theme park featuring more than 100 rides, shows and attractions. (Late Mar-late Oct; schedule varies). On Rte 537, 1 mi S of I-195. Phone 908/928-1821. ¢¢¢¢¢

Jersey City (C-5)

(See also Newark, Newark Intl Airport Area)

Settled 1629 **Pop** 228,537 **Elev** 11 ft **Area code** 201
Information Jersey City Cultural Affairs, 1 Chapel Ave, 07305; 201/547-4305.

Jersey City's location on the Hudson River, due west of the southern end of Manhattan Island, has aided its growth to such a degree that it is now the second-largest city in New Jersey. New Yorkers across the bay tell time by the Colgate-Palmolive Clock at 105 Hudson St; the dial is 50 feet across, and the minute hand, weighing 2,200 pounds, moves 23 inches each minute. Jersey City's major links with New York are the 8,557-foot Holland Tunnel, which is 72 feet below water level; the Port Authority Trans-Hudson (PATH) rapid-transit system; and New York Waterways Ferries, which run between Exchange Place and the World Financial Center in lower Manhattan.

What to See and Do

Liberty State Park. Offers breathtaking view of New York City skyline; flag display including state, historic and US flags; swimming pool (fee); boat launch; fitness course; picnic area. Historic railroad terminal has been partially restored. The Interpretive Center houses an exhibit area; adj to the Center is a 60-acre natural area consisting mostly of salt marsh. Nature trails and observation points complement this wildlife habitat. (Daily) Off NJ Tpke, exit 14B; on the New York Harbor, less than 2,000 ft from the Statue of Liberty. Boat tours and ferry service to Ellis Island and Statue of Liberty are avail; for schedule and general information, phone 201/915-3400. Also in park is

⭐ **Liberty Science Center.** Four-story structure encompasses Environment, Health and Invention exhibit areas that feature more than 250 hands-on exhibits. Geodesic dome houses OMNI Theater with a six-story screen. (Late Apr-Labor Day, daily; rest of yr, daily exc Mon; closed Jan 1, Thanksgiving, Dec 25) 251 Phillip St. Phone 201/451-0006. Exhibits and OMNI Theater combined ticket ¢¢¢¢

Motor Hotel

★ ★ **QUALITY INN.** 180 12th St (07310), at entrance to Holland Tunnel. 201/653-0300; FAX 201/659-1963. 150 rms, 3 story. No elvtr. S $82-$87; D $86-$94; each addl $5; under 18 free. Crib free. TV; cable

(premium). Pool. Restaurant 7 am-10 pm; Sun 7 am-2 pm. Rm serv. Bar 11 am-10 pm; Sat from 5 pm; Sun noon-2 pm. Ck-out 11 am. Meeting rms. Health club privileges. Cr cds: A, C, D, DS, MC, V.

⊠ ⊠ 🛇 🔥 SC

Lake Hopatcong (B-4)

Area code 973

(Approx 15 mi N and W of Dover via NJ 15 & unnumbered road)

The largest lake in New Jersey, Hopatcong's popularity as a resort is second only to the seacoast spots. It covers 2,443 acres and has a hilly shoreline of approximately 40 miles. The area offers swimming, stocked fishing and boating.

What to See and Do

Hopatcong State Park. A 113-acre park with swimming, bathhouse; fishing. Picnicking, playground, concession. Historic museum (Sun afternoons). Standard fees. SW shore of lake, in Landing. Phone 973/398-7010.

Motel

★ ★ **DAYS INN.** (1691 Rte 46, Ledgewood 07852) On US 46E at I-80 exit 27. 973/347-5100; FAX 973/347-6356. 100 rms, 2 story. S, D $85; each addl $10; under 15 free. Crib free. TV; VCR avail (movies $5). Pool; lifeguard. Complimentary continental bkfst. Restaurant 11:30 am-9:30 pm; Sun 8 am-1 pm. Rm serv. Bar 4 pm-2 am; entertainment Fri, Sat. Ck-out 11 am. Coin lndry. Meeting rms. Business servs avail. Sundries. 2 tennis courts. Microwaves avail. Cr cds: A, DS, MC, V.

🖍 ⊠ ⊠ 🛇 🔥 SC

Motor Hotel

★ ★ ★ **FOUR POINTS BY SHERATON.** (15 Howard Blvd, Mount Arlington 07856) I-80 exit 30. 973/770-2000; FAX 973/770-1287. Web www.ITTsheraton.com. 124 rms, 5 story. S, D $120-$130; each addl $10; suites $140-$160; under 18 free; wkend rates. Crib free. Pet accepted. TV; cable (premium), VCR avail. Indoor pool. Coffee in rms. Restaurant 6:30 am-10 pm. Rm serv. Bar 11-1 am; entertainment Wed-Sat. Ck-out noon. Meeting rms. Business servs avail. Valet serv. Exercise equipt; weight machine, bicycles. Refrigerators, microwaves avail. Cr cds: A, C, D, DS, MC, V.

D 🖍 ⊠ 🛇 ⊠ 🔥 SC

Lakewood (F-5)

(See also Toms River)

Settled 1800 **Pop** 26,095 **Elev** 67 ft **Area code** 908 **Zip** 08701
Information Chamber of Commerce, PO Box 656; 908/363-0012.

A well-known winter resort in the 1890s, many socially prominent New Yorkers such as the Astors, the Goulds, the Rhinelanders, the Rockefellers and the Vanderbilts maintained large homes on the shores of Lake Carasaljo.

What to See and Do

Ocean County Park #1. The 325-acre former Rockefeller estate. Lake swimming; children's fishing lake. Tennis, platform tennis. Picnicking (grills), playground, athletic fields. (Daily) Entrance fee (July-Aug, wkends). 659 Ocean Ave, 1 mi E on NJ 88. Phone 908/370-7380. Per vehicle ¢

Motel

★★ **BEST WESTERN LEISURE INN.** *1600 NJ 70, Garden State Pkwy exit 88.* 908/367-0900; FAX 908/370-4928. 105 rms. Memorial Day-Sept: S, D $70-$104; each addl $10; lower rates rest of yr. Crib free. Pet accepted. TV; cable (premium), VCR (movies $3.50). Pool. Complimentary continental bkfst. Restaurant 7 am-10 pm. Bar 6-11 pm. Ck-out 11 am. Coin lndry. Meeting rm. Business servs avail. In-rm modem link. Refrigerators avail. Cr cds: A, C, D, DS, MC, V.

 SC

Restaurant

★ **PETERSONS SUNSET CABIN.** *105 River Rd (NJ 9).* 908/363-1135. Hrs: 11:30 am-10 pm; Sat, Sun from noon. Res accepted. Continental menu. Bar. Complete meals: lunch $5.95-$9.95, dinner $11-$18.95. Child's meals. Specializes in shrimp, steak, chicken. Casual decor. Cr cds: A, DS, MC, V.

Lambertville (E-3)

(See also Trenton)

Settled 1705 **Pop** 3,927 **Elev** 76 ft **Area code** 609 **Zip** 08530
Information Lambertville Area Chamber of Commerce, 4 S Union St; 609/397-0055.

What to See and Do

John Holcombe House. Washington stayed here just before crossing the Delaware. Privately owned residence. 260 N Main St.

Marshall House (1816). James Marshall, who first discovered gold at Sutter's Mill in California in 1848, lived here until 1834. Period furnishings; memorabilia of Lambertville; small museum collection. (May-mid-Oct, wkends or by appt) 62 Bridge St. Phone 609/397-0770. **Free.**

Inns

★★ **CHIMNEY HILL BED & BREAKFAST.** *207 Goat Hill Rd, just off NJ 179 & 29.* 609/397-1516; FAX 609/397-9353. 8 rms, 3 story. No rm phones. S, D $85-$175; wkly rates; some lower rates mid-wk. Children over 12 yrs only. Complimentary full bkfst; afternoon refreshments. Ck-out 11 am, ck-in 3 pm. Business servs avail. Downhill ski ½ mi. Picnic tables. Elegant stone and frame manor house built in 1820; furnishings are antiques and period reproductions. Cr cds: A, MC, V.

★★★ **INN AT LAMBERTVILLE STATION.** *11 Bridge St.* 609/397-4400; FAX 609/397-9744; res: 800/524-1091 (exc NJ). 45 units, 3 story. S, D $80-$115; each addl $15; suites $125. Crib avail. TV; cable (premium). Complimentary continental bkfst in rms. Dining rm 11:30 am-10 pm. Ck-out noon. Meeting rms. Business center. Fireplace in suites. View of Delaware River. Victorian antiques. Cr cds: A, C, D, MC, V.

Restaurant

★★ **LAMBERTVILLE STATION.** *11 Bridge St.* 609/397-8300. Hrs: 11:30 am-3 pm, 4-10 pm; Fri, Sat to 11 pm; early-bird dinner Mon-Thurs 4-6:30 pm, Fri to 6 pm; Sun brunch 10:30 am-3 pm. Res required. Bar. Semi-a la carte: lunch $5.95-$8.95, dinner $11.95-$21.95. Sun brunch

$5.75-$7.95. Child's meals. Specializes in rack of lamb, buffalo. Entertainment Fri, Sat. Renovated railroad station with 3 dining areas; 1 dining rm is an old station platform. Victorian-style decor. Cr cds: A, C, D, MC, V.

Livingston (C-5)

Pop 26,609 **Elev** 307 ft **Area code** 973 **Zip** 07039

This suburban community in southwestern Essex County is named for William Livingston, the first governor of New Jersey.

Restaurant

★★ **AFTON.** *(2 Hanover Rd, Florham Park) 4½ mi E of I-287 at Columbia Tpke, NJ 510.* 973/377-1871. Hrs: 11:30 am-2:30 pm, 5-9 pm; Sun noon-8 pm; Sun brunch 11 am-2 pm. Closed Mon; Dec 25. Bar to 11 pm. Complete meals: lunch $7.95-$12.95, dinner $13.50-$18.50. Sun brunch $12.50. Specializes in prime rib, seafood. Family-owned. Cr cds: A, C, D, MC, V.

Long Beach Island (G-5 - H-5)

Area code 609 **E-mail** sochamber@aol.com **Web** www.intserv.com/~lbi/soc~cc.html
Information Southern Ocean County Chamber of Commerce, 265 W 9th St, Ship Bottom 08008; 609/494-7211 or 800/292-6372.

Six miles out to sea, this island is separated from the New Jersey mainland by Barnegat and Little Egg Harbor bays. NJ 72, going east from Manahawkin on the mainland, enters the island at Ship Bottom. The island is no more than three blocks wide in some places, and extends 18 miles from historic Barnegat Lighthouse to the north. It includes towns such as Loveladies, Harvey Cedars, Surf City, Ship Bottom, Brant Beach and the Beach Havens at the southern tip. The island is a popular family resort with excellent fishing, boating and other water sports. For swimming, the bay is calm, while the ocean offers a vigorous surf.

Tales are told of pirate coins buried on the island, and, over the years, silver and gold pieces occasionally have turned up. Whether they are part of pirate treasure or the refuse of shipwrecks remains a mystery.

What to See and Do

Barnegat Lighthouse State Park. Barnegat Lighthouse, a 167-ft red and white tower, was engineered by General George G. Meade and completed in 1858; 217-step spiral staircase leading to lookout offering spectacular view. Fishing. Picnicking. Park (daily); lighthouse (Memorial Day-Labor Day, daily; May & Labor Day-Oct, wkends only). Standard fees. At N end of island. Phone 609/494-2016.

Fantasy Island Amusement Park. Family-oriented amusement park featuring rides and games; adult casino arcade. (June-Aug, daily; May & Sept, wkends; schedule varies, phone for hrs) 7th St & Bay Ave, Beach Haven. Phone 609/492-4000.

Seasonal Event

Surflight Theatre. Engleside & Beach Aves, Beach Haven. Broadway musicals nightly. Children's theater, Wed-Sat. Phone 609/492-9477. May-mid-Oct.

Motels

★ ★ ★ **ENGLESIDE INN.** *(30 Engleside Ave, Beach Haven 08008) 7 mi S of NJ 72. 609/492-1251; FAX 609/492-9175; res: 800/762-2214.* 72 units, 3 story, 37 kits. No elvtr. July-Labor Day: S, D $135-$190; each addl $12; suites $195-$254; kit. units for 2-4, $155-$200; lower rates rest of yr. Crib avail. Pet accepted, some restrictions. TV; cable, VCR (movies $2). Pool; poolside serv (in season), lifeguard. Restaurant 8 am-noon, 5-9 pm. Bar. Ck-out 11 am. Meeting rms. Business servs avail. Sundries. Refrigerators. Private patios, balconies. On beach. Cr cds: A, C, D, DS, MC, V.

★ **SANDPIPER.** *(Boulevard at 10th St, Ship Bottom 08008) NJ 72E to end. 609/494-6909.* 20 rms, shower only. July-Aug: S, D $75-$100; each addl $5; wkly rates; higher rates wkends & hols (3-day min); lower rates May-June & Sept-Oct. Closed rest of yr. TV; cable. Pool. Restaurant adj 4-10 pm. Ck-out 11 am. Refrigerators. Ocean 1 blk. Cr cds: A, MC, V.

★ **SPRAY BEACH MOTOR INN.** *(24th St at Ocean, Spray Beach 08008) 5½ mi S of NJ 72. 609/492-1501; FAX 609/492-0504.* 88 rms, 3 story, 10 kits. Late June-Labor Day: S, D $85-$155; each addl $10; kit. units $99-$165; family rates; lower rates rest of yr. Closed Jan. Crib $5. TV; cable, VCR avail. Heated pool; lifeguard. Restaurant 8 am-2:30 pm, 5-10 pm. Bar 10:30-2 am; entertainment wkends, hols in season. Ck-out noon. Business servs avail. Sundries. Refrigerators. On beach. Cr cds: A, MC, V.

Inn

★ ★ **AMBER ST INN.** *(118 Amber St, Beach Haven 08008) Garden State Pkwy, exit 63. 609/492-1611.* 6 rms, 3 story. Mid-May-mid-Sept: S, D $110-$160; each addl $10; suites $125-$160; lower rates rest of yr. Children over 12 yrs only. TV in parlor. Complimentary full bkfst. Restaurant adj 7 am-10 pm. Ck-out 11 am, ck-in 3 pm. Built in 1885; antiques. Totally nonsmoking. No cr cds accepted.

Madison (C-4)

(For accommodations see Chatham, Morristown)

Settled ca 1685 **Pop** 15,850 **Elev** 261 ft **Area code** 973 **Zip** 07940
Information Chamber of Commerce, 155 Main St, PO Box 152; 973/377-7830.

For many years, the quiet suburban town of Madison was called the "Rose City" because of the thousands of bouquets produced in its many greenhouses.

What to See and Do

Drew University (1867). (2,100 students) A 186-acre wooded campus west of town. College of Liberal Arts, Theological School and Graduate School. On campus are a Neoclassical administration building (1833), the United Methodist Archives and History Center and the Rose Memorial Library containing Nestorian Cross collection, government and UN documents and manuscripts and memorabilia of early Methodism. Tours (phone 973/408-3252 for schedule). Madison Ave, NJ 24. Phone 973/408-3000.

Fairleigh Dickinson University-Florham-Madison Campus (1958). (3,889 students) (1 of 3 campuses) On site of Twombly Estate (1895); many original buildings still in use. Friendship Library houses numerous special collections including Harry A. Chesler collection of comic art,

archives of the Outdoor Advertising Assn of America and collections devoted to printing and the graphic arts. (Academic yr, Mon-Fri; closed school hols) Tours of campus by appt. 285 Madison Ave, NJ 24. Phone 973/593-8500.

Museum of Early Trades and Crafts. Hands-on look at 18th- & 19th-century artisans. Special events include Bottle Hill Craft Festival (Oct). Tours. (Tues-Sat, also Sun afternoons; closed major hols) Main St (NJ 124) at Green Village Rd. Phone 973/377-2982. ¢¢

Seasonal Event

New Jersey Shakespeare Festival. In residence at Drew University. Professional theater company. Includes Shakespearean, classic and modern plays; special guest attractions and classic films. For schedule, reservations phone 973/408-5600. Mid-May-Sept.

Matawan (E-5)

(See also Freehold)

Pop 9,270 **Elev** 55 ft **Area code** 732 **Zip** 07747
Information Chamber of Commerce, PO Box 522; 732/290-1125.

What to See and Do

Cheesequake State Park. This 1,300-acre park offers swimming, bathhouse; fishing. Nature tours. Picnicking, playground, concession. Camping (fee; dump station). Standard fees. Garden State Pkwy, exit 120, right at 1st traffic light and right at next traffic light onto Gordon Rd, ¼ mi to entrance. Phone 732/566-2161.

Seasonal Event

Concerts. Garden State Arts Center, at Telegraph Hill Park on the Garden State Pkwy, exit 116. A 5,302-seat amphitheater; lawn area seats 4,500-5,500. Contemporary, classical, pop and rock concerts. Phone 732/442-9200. Mid-June-Sept.

Motels

★ **RAMADA INN.** *(2870 NJ 35, Hazlet 07730) 2 mi S of Garden State Pkwy exit 117. 732/264-2400; FAX 732/739-9735.* 120 rms, 2 story. S $75-$90; D $88-$119; each addl $10; under 18 free; higher rates summer wkends. Crib free. TV; cable (premium). Pool; lifeguard. Restaurant 6:30 am-10 pm. Bar 4 pm-2 am; entertainment Thurs-Sat. Ck-out noon. Meeting rms. Business servs avail. Cr cds: A, C, D, DS, JCB, MC, V.

✔★ ★ **WELLESLEY INN.** *(3215 NJ 35, Hazlet 07730) 1 mi S of Garden State Pkwy, exit 117, S on NJ 35. 732/888-2800; FAX 732/888-2902.* 89 rms, 3 story. S $63-$109; D $65-$119; each addl $5; under 18 free; higher rates summer wkends. Crib free. Pet accepted, some restrictions; $5. TV; cable (premium). Complimentary continental bkfst. Restaurant nearby. Ck-out 11 am. Business servs avail. Health club privileges. Refrigerators, microwaves avail. Cr cds: A, D, DS, JCB, MC, V.

Restaurant

★ ★ **BUTTONWOOD MANOR.** *845 Hwy 34, ½ mi N. 732/566-6220.* Hrs: 11:30 am-10 pm; Sat to 11 pm; Sun noon-9 pm. Res accepted. Bar. Semi-a la carte: lunch $5.25-$9.95, dinner $13.95-$24.95. Child's meals. Specializes in duckling, steak, fresh seafood. Entertainment Fri, Sat. Lakeside dining. Cr cds: A, MC, V.

Metuchen

(see Woodbridge)

Millburn (C-5)

(See also Newark, Newark Intl Airport Area, Union)

Settled 1720s **Pop** 18,630 **Elev** 140 ft **Area code** 201 **Zip** 07041 **E-mail** msh@rivint.com **Web** www.millburn.com

Information Chamber of Commerce, 343 Millburn Ave, PO Box 651; 201/379-1198.

Once bristling with paper mills and hat factories, Millburn today boasts a thriving downtown with a regional theater, a quiet residential area and direct access to New York City.

What to See and Do

Cora Hartshorn Arboretum and Bird Sanctuary. A 17-acre sanctuary with nature trails; guided walks. Stone House Museum with nature exhibits (late Sept-mid-June, Tues, Thurs & Sat). Grounds (daily). 2 mi W on Forest Dr in Short Hills. Phone 201/376-3587. **Free.**

Paper Mill Playhouse. State Theater of New Jersey. A variety of plays, musicals and children's theater (Wed-Sun); matinees (Thurs, Sat & Sun). Brookside Dr. Phone 201/376-4343 (box office) or 201/379-3636 (information).

Hotel

★ ★ ★ ★ **HILTON AT SHORT HILLS.** *(41 John F Kennedy Pkwy, Short Hills 07078) 3 mi W at jct NJ 24 Livingston exit, JFK Pkwy, opp Mall at Short Hills.* 201/379-0100; FAX 201/379-6870. Web www.spaatshorthills.com. Less than an hour's drive from mid-Manhattan, this elegant suburban hotel offers many facilities of a fine resort. The hotel is located across from the Mall at Short Hills with branches of many of the nation's top stores. 300 rms, 7 story, 37 suites. S $160-$256; D $160-$276; each addl $20; suites $310-$700; family, wkend rates. Crib free. TV; cable (premium), VCR avail. 2 pools, 1 indoor; whirlpool, lifeguard. Restaurant 6:30 am-10:30 pm (also see THE DINING ROOM). Rm serv 24 hrs. Bar 11:30-1:30 am; entertainment. Ck-out 1 pm. Convention facilities. Business center. In-rm modem link. Concierge. Gift shop. Beauty shop. Valet parking. Exercise rm; instructor, weight machines, bicycles, sauna, steam rm. Massage. Refrigerator in suites. Microwaves avail. Luxury level. Cr cds: A, C, D, DS, ER, JCB, MC, V.

Restaurants

★ ★ **CAFE MAIN.** *40 Main St, downtown near Paper Mill Playhouse.* 201/467-2222. Hrs: 11:30 am-11 pm. Res accepted. Bar to 2 am. Wine list. A la carte entrees: lunch $5.95-$8.95, dinner $7.95-$16.95. Specializes in seafood, steak, pasta. Own desserts. Seasonal menu; wine tasting dinners. Entertainment Thurs-Sat. Storefront location; cafe decor. Cr cds: A, D, MC, V.

★ ★ **THE DINING ROOM.** *(See Hilton At Short Hills Hotel)* 201/379-0100. Hrs: 6-10:30 pm. Closed Sun. Bar. Complete meals: 3-course dinner $58, 4-course dinner $68. Specializes in seafood, game, veal. Seasonal menu. Own pastries. Harpist. Valet parking. English drawing room atmosphere. Jacket. Cr cds: A, C, D, DS, ER, JCB, MC, V.

Millville (H-3)

(See also Bridgeton)

Pop 25,992 **Elev** 37 ft **Area code** 609 **Zip** 08332 **E-mail** chamber @cybernet.net **Web** www.cybernet.net/chamber

Information Chamber of Commerce, 415 N High St, PO Box 831; 609/825-2600.

What to See and Do

Wheaton Village. Tranquil lifestyle of an 1888 South Jersey glass town. Buildings include Museum of American Glass, which houses an extensive glass collection; working factory where demonstrations of glassmaking are given; general store; restored train station; 1876 one-room schoolhouse. Crafts demonstrations, arcade, shops. Restaurant, hotel. Self-guided tours. (Apr-Dec, daily; closed major hols) 2 mi NE via County 552. Phone 609/825-6800. ¢¢¢

Motel

★ ★ **COUNTRY INN BY CARLSON.** *1125 Village Dr.* 609/825-3100; FAX 609/825-1317; res: 800/456-4000. 100 rms, 2 story. S $66-$71; D $68-$73; each addl $5; suites $125-$130; under 18 free. Crib free. TV; cable (premium), VCR avail (movies). Heated pool. Restaurant 7 am-9 pm; Fri, Sat to 10 pm. Bar 11-1 am. Meeting rms. Business servs avail. Some refrigerators. Cr cds: A, C, D, DS, MC, V.

Montclair (C-5)

(For accommodations see Newark, Newark Intl Airport Area)

Settled 1666 **Pop** 37,729 **Elev** 337 ft **Area code** 973

Information Chamber of Commerce, 26 Park St, Suite 2025, 07042; 973/744-7660.

Originally a part of Newark, the area that includes Montclair was purchased from Native Americans in 1678 for "two guns, three coats and thirteen cans of rum." The first settlers were English farmers from Connecticut who came here to form a Puritan church of their own. Shortly after, Dutch from Hackensack arrived, and two communities were created: Cranetown and Speertown. The two communities later were absorbed into West Bloomfield.

During the Revolutionary War, First Mountain served as a lookout point and as a barrier, preventing the British from crossing into the Upper Passaic valley. In the early 1800s, manufacturing began, new roads opened and the area grew. In 1856-1857, a rail controversy arose: West Bloomfield citizens wanted a rail connection with New York City; Bloomfield residents saw no need for it. In 1868, the two towns separated and West Bloomfield became Montclair. This railroad helped to make Montclair the suburban, residential town it is today. One of the town's schools is named for painter George Inness, who once lived here.

What to See and Do

Eagle Rock Reservation. 1/2 mi W on Bloomfield Ave, then S on Prospect Ave to Eagle Rock Ave in West Orange (see).

Israel Crane House (1796). Federal mansion with period rooms; working 18th-century kitchen; school room; special exhibits during the year. Country Store & Post Office have authentic items; old-time crafts demonstrations. Research library. (Sept-June, Sun afternoons; other times by appt; costumed tours Sun only) 110 Orange Rd. Phone 973/744-1796. ¢¢

Presby Iris Gardens. Height of bloom in late May or early June. In Mountainside Park, on Upper Mountain Ave in Upper Montclair. Phone 973/783-5974.

The Montclair Art Museum. American art; Native American gallery; changing exhibits. (Daily exc Mon; closed major hols) Gallery lectures (Sun). Concerts; jazz; film series. 3 S Mountain Ave at Bloomfield Ave. Phone 973/746-5555. ¢¢

Seasonal Event

Summerfun Theater Inc. Weiss Arts Center, Montclair-Kimberley Academy, Lloyd Rd. Professional summer stock company presents six productions. Phone 973/256-0576. Tues-Sat, mid-June-mid-Aug.

Montvale (B-5)

Pop 6,946 **Elev** 187 ft **Area code** 201 **Zip** 07645

Motel

★ ★ **MONTVALE INN.** 100 Chestnut Ridge Rd. 201/391-7700; FAX 201/391-6648. 190 rms, 3 story. S, D $79-$175; each addl $10; under 18 free; wkend rates. Crib free. TV; cable (premium). Heated pool; poolside serv. Restaurant 6:30 am-2 pm. Dining rm 11:30 am-10 pm; Sat from 5:30 pm. Rm serv. Bar 11:30-2 am; entertainment. Ck-out noon. Meeting rms. Business servs avail. In-rm modem link. Bellhops. Valet serv. Gift shop. Exercise equipt; weights, bicycles. Microwaves avail. Cr cds: A, C, D, DS, MC, V.

D ⊰ 🛪 🐾 💺 SC

Hotel

★ ★ ★ **MARRIOTT-PARK RIDGE.** (300 Brae Blvd, Park Ridge 07656) Garden State Pkwy exit 172N (Grand Ave), then first 3 right turns. 201/307-0800; FAX 201/307-0859. Web www.marriott.com. 289 units, 4 story. S, D $99-$165; suites $275; under 18 free; wkly, wkend rates. Crib avail. Pet accepted, some restrictions. TV; cable (premium), VCR avail. Indoor/outdoor pool; whirlpool, poolside serv. Restaurant 6:30 am-10 pm. Bars 4:30 pm-2 am; pianist. Ck-out noon. Meeting rms. Business center. In-rm modem link. Concierge. Gift shop. Exercise equipt; weights, bicycles, sauna. Refrigerators avail. Many private patios, balconies. Extensive grounds; small lake. Luxury level. Cr cds: A, C, D, DS, JCB, MC, V.

D ✔ ⊰ 🛪 🐾 💺 SC 🏌

Restaurant

★ ★ **VALENTINO'S.** (103 Spring Valley Rd, Park Ridge) Garden State Pkwy exit 172, right on Grand Ave to 2nd light, right on Spring Valley Rd, approx 1 mi. 201/391-2230. Hrs: 11:30 am-2:30 pm, 5-10 pm; Fri to 11 pm, Sat 5-11 pm. Closed Sun; some major hols. Res accepted. Italian menu. Bar. A la carte entrees: lunch $8.95-$14, dinner $14.95-$22. Specializes in veal, pasta, fish. Jacket. Cr cds: A, C, D, DS, MC, V.

Moorestown
(see Camden)

Morristown (C-4)

(See also Madison)

Settled ca 1710 **Pop** 16,189 **Elev** 327 ft **Area code** 973

Information Historic Morris Visitors Center, 6 Court St, 07960; 973/631-5151.

Today, Morristown is primarily residential, but the iron industry, so desperately needed during the Revolutionary War, was responsible for the development of the town and the surrounding county. George Washington and his army spent two winters here, operating throughout the area until the fall of 1781. The first successful experiments with the telegraph were made in Morristown by Samuel F.B. Morse and Stephen Vail. Cartoonist Thomas Nast, writers Bret Harte and Frank Stockton and millionaire Otto Kahn all lived here. Morristown rises to a 597-foot peak at Fort Nonsense; the Whippany River runs through the town.

What to See and Do

Acorn Hall (1853). Victorian Italianate house; original furnishings; reference library; restored garden. (Mar-Dec, Thurs & Sun, limited hrs; closed major hols) 68 Morris Ave. Phone 973/267-3465. ¢¢

Fosterfields Historical Farm. Turn-of-the-century living-history farm (200 acres). Self-guided trail; displays; audiovisual presentations; workshops, farming demonstrations; restored Gothic-revival house. Visitors Center. (Apr-Oct, Wed-Sun) 73 Kahdena Rd. Phone 973/326-7645. ¢¢-¢¢¢

Frelinghuysen Arboretum. Features 127 acres of forest and open fields; natural and formal gardens; spring and fall bulb displays; labeled collections of trees and shrubs; Braille trail; gift shop. Grounds (daily). 1½ mi NE via Morris Ave, Whippany Rd; entrance from E Hanover Ave. Phone 973/326-7600. **Free.**

Historic Speedwell. Home and factory of Stephen Vail, iron master, who in 1818 manufactured the engine for the SS *Savannah,* first steamship to cross the Atlantic. In 1838, Alfred Vail (Stephen's son) and Samuel F.B. Morse perfected the telegraph and first publicly demonstrated it here in the factory. Displays include period furnishings in the mansion, exhibit on Speedwell Iron Works, exhibits on history of the telegraph; water wheel, carriage house & granary. Gift shop. Picnic area. (May-Sept, hrs vary; closed July 4) 333 Speedwell Ave. Phone 973/540-0211. ¢¢

Macculloch Hall Historical Museum. Restored 1810 house and garden; home of George P. Macculloch, initiator of the Morris Canal, and his descendants for more than 140 yrs. American, European decorative arts from the 18th and 19th centuries. Illustrations by Thomas Nast. Garden. (Wed, Thurs & Sun afternoons; closed hols) 45 Macculloch Ave. Phone 973/538-2404. ¢¢

Morris Museum. Art, science and history exhibits; permanent and changing. Musical, theatrical events; lectures and films. (Mon-Sat, also Sun afternoons; closed major hols) Free admission Thurs afternoons. 6 Normandy Heights Rd. Phone 973/538-0454. ¢¢

Morristown National Historical Park (see). Approx 3 mi S on US 202.

Schuyler-Hamilton House (1760). Former home of Dr. Jabez Campfield. Alexander Hamilton courted Betsy Schuyler here. Period furniture; colonial garden. (Tues & Sun afternoons; other times by appt; closed Easter, Dec 25) 5 Olyphant Pl. Phone 973/267-4039. ¢

Motel

★ ★ **BEST WESTERN MORRISTOWN INN.** 270 South St (07960). 973/540-1700; FAX 973/267-0241. Web www.bestwestern .com/best.html. 60 rms, 3 story, 14 kits. S $95-$115; D $105-$125; each addl $10; kit. units $100-$125; under 12 free; wkend rates. Crib $10. TV; cable (premium), VCR avail (movies). Restaurant 6:30 am-2 pm. Ck-out noon. Coin lndry. In-rm modem link. Airport transportation. Exercise equipt;

weights, bicycles, sauna. Colonial decor. Cr cds: A, C, D, DS, ER, JCB, MC, V.

D X ⚊ 🔥 SC

Motor Hotel

★ ★ ★ **HAMILTON PARK.** *(175 Park Ave, Florham Park 07932)* SE on NJ 24. 973/377-2424; FAX 973/377-9560; res: 800/321-6000. Web www.dolce.com. 219 rms, 5 story. S, D $145; family, wkend, hol rates. Crib avail. TV; cable (premium), VCR avail. Indoor/outdoor pool; whirlpool, poolside serv, lifeguard. Restaurant 6:45 am-11 pm. Rm serv. Bar; entertainment Thur-Sat. Ck-out 11 am. Convention facilities. Business center. In-rm modem link. Bellhops. Concierge. Sundries. Lighted tennis. Exercise rm; instructor, weights, treadmill, sauna. Massage. Raquetball. Rec rm. Lawn games. Microwaves avail. Cr cds: A, C, D, DS, MC, V.

D ⚊ ⚊ X 🔥 ⚊

Hotels

★ ★ ★ **HEADQUARTERS PLAZA.** 3 Headquarters Plaza *(07960)*. 973/898-9100; FAX 973/292-0112; res: 800/225-1942 (exc NJ), 800/225-1941 (NJ). Web www.travelweb.com/thisco/lri. 256 rms, 16 story. S $140-$150; D $160-$170; each addl $20; under 12 free; wkend rates. Crib free. TV; cable (premium), VCR avail. Indoor pool privileges. Supervised child's activities; ages 5-12. Restaurant 6 am-11 pm. Bar 11-1 am; entertainment Wed-Sat. Ck-out 1 pm. Meeting rms. Business center. In-rm modem link. Shopping arcade. Airport transportation. Exercise rm; instructor, treadmills, stair machines. Microwaves avail. Luxury level. Cr cds: A, C, D, MC, V.

D X X ⚊ ⚊ 🔥 SC ⚊

★ ★ ★ **MADISON.** 1 Convent Rd *(07961)*, at Madison Ave *(NJ 24)*. 973/285-1800; FAX 973/540-8566; res: 800/526-0729. 190 rms, 4 story. S $160-$200; D $180-$200; under 18 free; wkend rates. Crib avail. TV; cable (premium). Indoor pool; whirlpool, poolside serv. Complimentary continental bkfst. Coffee in rms. Restaurants 7 am-11 pm. Bar 11-2 am; entertainment. Ck-out noon. Meeting rms. Business servs avail. In-rm modem link. Concierge. Airport transportation. Tennis privileges. Golf privileges. Exercise equipt; weight machines, bicycles. Some bathrm phones; microwaves avail. Cr cds: A, C, D, DS, MC, V.

D X 🐕 ⚊ ⚊ X ⚊ SC

Restaurants

★ ★ **ROD'S 1890s RESTAURANT.** *(NJ 124, Convent Station 07961)* Approx 1½ mi E on NJ 124. 973/539-6666. Hrs: 11:30 am-11 pm; early-bird dinner 4:30-6 pm; Sun brunch 11 am-3 pm. Closed Dec 25. Bar. Semi-a la carte: lunch $7.95-$15.95, dinner $15.95-$29.95. Sun brunch $10.50-$15.95. Child's meals. Specializes in prime beef, seafood. Entertainment Wed-Sat. Valet parking. Display of authentic Victorian antiques. Large antique bar with wooden chandelier. Private dining avail in renovated railway cars by res. Family-owned. Cr cds: A, C, D, DS, MC, V.

D

★ ★ **THE STEAK HOUSE.** 142 South St *(07960)*. 973/539-8088. Hrs: 11:30 am-3 pm, 5-10 pm; Fri, Sat to 11 pm; Sun from noon. Res accepted. Bar. Semi-a la carte: lunch $5.95-$9.95, dinner $13.95-$23.95. Specializes in fresh fish, steak. Mirrors, paintings on walls. Cr cds: MC, V.

Morristown National Historical Park (C-4)

(For accommodations see Bernardsville, Morristown)

(Approx 3 mi S of Morristown on US 202)

This national historical park, the first to be established and maintained by the federal government, was created by an Act of Congress in 1933. Its three units cover more than 1,600 acres, all but Jockey Hollow and the NJ Brigade Area being within Morristown's limits. The main body of the Continental Army stayed here in the winter of 1779-1780.

Headquarters and museum (daily); Jockey Hollow buildings (summer, daily; rest of yr schedule varies, phone ahead; closed Jan 1, Thanksgiving, Dec 25). For further information contact Chief of Interpretation, Washington Pl, Morristown 07960; 973/539-2085.

What to See and Do

Ft Nonsense. Its name came long after residents had forgotten the real reason for earthworks constructed here in 1777. Overlook commemorates fortifications which were built at Washington's order to defend military supplies stored in the village. Ann St. **Free.**

Historical Museum. Contains Washington memorabilia; period weapons and 18th-century artifacts; audiovisual programs. Washington Pl, directly to the rear of Ford Mansion. ¢ Admission includes

Ford Mansion. One of the finest early houses in Morristown was built in 1772-1774 by Colonel Jacob Ford, Jr, who produced gunpowder for American troops during the Revolution. His widow rented the house to the army for General and Mrs. Washington when the Continental Army spent the winter of 1779-1780 here.

Jockey Hollow. The site of the Continental Army's winter quarters in 1779-1780 and the 1781 mutiny of the Pennsylvania Line. Signs indicate locations of various brigades. There are typical log huts and an officer's hut among other landmarks. Demonstrations of military and colonial farm life (summer). Visitor center has exhibits and audiovisual programs. 5 mi SW of Morristown. **Free.**

Wick House. Farmer Henry Wick lived here with his wife and daughter. Used as quarters by Major General Arthur St Clair in 1779-1780. Restored with period furnishings. Jockey Hollow. **Free.**

Mount Holly (F-3)

(See also Burlington)

Settled 1676 **Pop** 10,639 **Elev** 52 ft **Area code** 609 **Zip** 08060

The mountain that gives this old Quaker town its name is only 183 feet high. For two months in 1779, Mount Holly was the capital of the state; today, it is the seat of Burlington County.

What to See and Do

John Woolman Memorial (1783). John Woolman, the noted Quaker abolitionist whose *Journal* is still appreciated today, owned the property on which this small, 3-story red brick house was built; garden. Picnicking. (Fri; also by appt) 99 Branch St, ½ mi E. Phone 609/267-3226. **Donation.**

Mansion at Smithville (1840). Victorian mansion and village of inventor/entrepreneur Hezekiah B. Smith; home of the "Star" hi-wheel bicycle. Guided tours (May-Oct, Wed & Sun). Victorian Christmas tours (Dec; fee). On NJ 537, ½ mi W of US 206. Phone 609/265-5068. ¢¢

Mount Holly Library. Chartered in 1765 by King George III, the library is currently housed in Georgian mansion built in 1830. Historic Lyceum contains original crystal chandeliers, blue marble fireplaces, boxwood gardens; archives date to original 1765 collection. (July-Aug, Tues-Thurs; rest of yr, Mon-Sat, limited hrs) 307 High St. Phone 609/267-7111. **Free.**

Motel

★ ★ **HOWARD JOHNSON.** *NJ 541, on NJ 541 at NJ Tpke exit 5.* 609/267-6550; FAX 609/267-2575. 90 rms, 2 story. S $58-$90; D $60-$90; each addl $7; under 12 free. Crib free. Pet accepted. TV; cable (premium), VCR avail. Pool; lifeguard, sauna. Playground. Restaurant 6 am-midnight. Bar 5-11 pm. Ck-out noon. Meeting rms. Business center. Cr cds: A, C, D, DS, ER, MC, V.

Motor Hotel

✓★ ★ **DAYS INN.** *(Wrightstown-Cookstown Rd, Cookstown 08511) NJ 537E to McGuire Access Rd, left at 2nd light.* 609/723-6500; FAX 609/723-7895. 100 rms, 2 story. May-Sept: S $74; D $79; each addl $10; suites $125-$250; under 16 free; wkend rates; higher rates hols; lower rates rest of yr. Crib free. TV; cable. Pool; whirlpool. Complimentary full bkfst. Restaurant 6 am-10 pm. Rm serv from 10 am. Bar. Ck-out 11 am. Business servs avail. Refrigerators avail. Cr cds: A, C, D, DS, ER, JCB, MC, V.

Inn

✓★ ★ **ISAAC HILLIARD HOUSE.** *(31 Hanover St, Pemberton 08068) E on Woodlake Rd.* 609/894-0756. 4 rms, 3 with shower only, 2 story. S $45-$65; D $55-$90; each addl $20; suites $105-$130. TV; cable. Pool. Complimentary full bkfst. Restaurant nearby. Ck-out 11 am, ck-in 2 pm. Victorian house built in mid-18th century. Totally nonsmoking. Cr cds: A, MC, V.

Restaurants

★ ★ ★ **BEAU RIVAGE.** *(128 Taunton Blvd, Medford 08055) S on NJ 541, just S of Tuckerton Rd.* 609/983-1999. Hrs: 11:30 am-2:30 pm, 5:30-9:30 pm; Sat from 5:30 pm; Sun 4-8 pm. Closed most major hols; also 2 wks before Labor Day. Res accepted. French menu. Serv bar. Wine cellar. A la carte: lunch $8.50-$12.50, dinner $16-$22. Specialties: beef Wellington, pheasant. Own pastries. 2 dining areas, 1 upstairs. Sophisticated cuisine and formal service in country atmosphere. Jacket (dinner). Cr cds: A, C, D, MC, V.

★ ★ ★ **BRADDOCK'S TAVERN.** *(39 S Main St, Medford Village 08055) S on NJ 541.* 609/654-1604. Hrs: 11:30 am-2:30 pm, 5-10 pm; Sun 11 am-3 pm, 4-9 pm. Closed Jan 1, Dec 25. Res accepted. Bar to 2 am. Semi-a la carte: lunch $5.75-$8.95, dinner $14.95-$23.95. Sun brunch $13.95. Child's meals. Specializes in prime rib, fresh seafood, sauteed veal. Own baking. Cr cds: A, C, D, DS, MC, V.

✓★ ★ **CHARLEY'S OTHER BROTHER.** *NJ 537, ½ mi W of US 206.* 609/261-1555. Hrs: 11:30 am-2:30 pm, 5-9:30 pm; Fri, Sat to 10:30 pm; Sun 4-9 pm. Closed Dec 25. Res accepted. Bar; entertainment Fri-Sat. Semi-a la carte: lunch $4.50-$7.95, dinner $10.95-$16.95. Child's meals. Specializes in fresh seafood, steak, prime rib. Country setting; tiffany lamps. Cr cds: A, D, DS, MC, V.

Newark (C-5)

(See also Elizabeth, Jersey City)

Settled 1666 **Pop** 275,221 **Elev** 146 ft **Area code** 973
Information Gateway Travel & Tourism Visitors Bureau, PO Box 602, Little Perry; 201/641-7632.

Once a strict Puritan settlement, Newark has grown to become the largest city in the state and one of the country's leading manufacturing cities. Major insurance firms and banks have large offices in Newark, dominating the city's financial life. Newark was the birthplace of Stephen Crane (1871-1900), author of *The Red Badge of Courage,* and Mary Mapes Dodge (1838-1905), author of the children's book *Hans Brinker, or the Silver Skates.* Newark is also an educational center with Newark College of Rutgers University, College of Medicine and Dentistry of New Jersey, New Jersey Institute of Technology, Seton Hall Law School and Essex County College.

Transportation

Airport: See NEWARK INTL AIRPORT AREA.
Car Rental Agencies: See IMPORTANT TOLL-FREE NUMBERS.
Public Transportation: Trains, buses (NJ Transit), phone 973/762-5100.
Rail Passenger Service: Amtrak 800/872-7245.

What to See and Do

Minor Basilica of the Sacred Heart. French Gothic in design, it resembles the cathedral at Rheims. Hand-carved reredos. (Daily) 89 Ridge St, at Clifton & 6th Aves. **Donation.**

New Jersey Historical Society. Museum with collections of paintings, prints, furniture, decorative arts; period rm; special exhibitions. Reference and research library of state and local history; manuscripts, documents, maps. (Tues-Sat) 52 Park Pl. Phone 973/596-8500. **Free.**

Old Plume House. Now the rectory of the adjoining House of Prayer Episcopal Church, it is thought to have been standing as early as 1710, which would make it the oldest building in Newark. 407 Broad St. Phone 973/483-8202.

Symphony Hall (1925). A 2,811-seat auditorium; home of New Jersey State Opera and the New Jersey Symphony Orchestra; also here is the famous Terrace Ballroom. 1030 Broad St. Phone 973/643-4550 or 973/643-8009 (box office).

The Newark Museum. Museum of art and science, with changing exhibitions. American paintings and sculpture; American and European decorative arts; classical art; the arts of Asia, the Americas and the Pacific; numismatics and the natural sciences. Also here are the Junior Museum, Mini Zoo, Dreyfuss Planetarium, Garden, with its 1784 schoolhouse and the Newark Fire Museum. Special programs, lectures, concerts; cafe (lunch). (Wed-Sun, afternoons; closed some major hols) 49 Washington St. Phone 973/596-6550. **Free.**

The Wars of America. Sculptured bronze group by Gutzon Borglum features 42 human figures representing soldiers in the major conflicts in US history. Military Park, bounded by Broad St, Park Pl, Rector St, Raymond Blvd. Other works by Borglum are

Bridge Memorial. This sculpture of a Native American and a Puritan stands on the site of a colonial marketplace. N of Washington Park (Broad St, Washington Pl & Washington St).

Statue of Abraham Lincoln. Essex County Courthouse, Springfield Ave & Market St.

Newark Intl Airport Area

For additional accommodations, see NEWARK INTL AIRPORT AREA, which follows NEWARK.

Motor Hotel

★ ★ ★ **HILTON GATEWAY.** *Gateway Center (07102), Raymond Blvd, N of McCarter Hwy (NJ 21) at Raymond Blvd.* 973/622-5000; FAX 973/824-2188. 253 rms, 10 story. S, D $119-$169; each addl $10; suites $239-$350; under 18 free; wkend rates. Crib free. TV; cable (premium), VCR avail. Rooftop pool; lifeguard. Restaurant 6:30 am-10 pm; Sat, Sun 7 am-noon. Rm serv. Bar 11:30 am-midnight; Fri, Sat to 1 am. Ck-out noon. Meeting rms. Business center. Bellhops. Valet serv. Shopping arcade. Garage parking; $3. Free airport transportation. Exercise equipt; weight machine, stair machines. Covered walkways to RR station. Luxury level. Cr cds: A, D, DS, MC, V.

D 〰 ✕ ✕ 🔥 SC 🚶

Newark Intl Airport Area (C-5)

(See also Newark)

Services and Information

Information: 973/961-6000 or 800/247-7433.

Lost and Found: 973/961-6230.

Airlines: Aeroperu, Air Aruba, Air Canada, Air France, Air Jamaica, Alitalia, America West, American, Avianca, British Airways, Carnival, Colgan Air, Continental, Czech Arlns, Delta, El Al, Eva Airways, Kiwi Intl, Korean Air, Lot, Lufthansa, Mexicana, Midway Arlns, Midwest Express, Northwest, Philippine Arlns, SAS, Swissair, Tap Air Portugal, TWA, United, USAir, Virgin Atlantic, Western Pacific Arlns.

Motels

★ ★ ★ **COURTYARD BY MARRIOTT.** *(600 US 1/9, Newark 07114) NJ Tpke exit 14, S on US 1/9.* 973/643-8500; FAX 973/648-0662. 146 rms, 3 story. S, D $129-$134; suites $159-$169; children free; wkly, wkend rates. Crib free. TV; cable (premium), VCR avail. Indoor pool; whirlpool. Complimentary coffee in rms. Restaurant 6:30 am-10 pm. Rm serv Mon-Thurs. Bar 5-11 pm. Ck-out noon. Coin lndry. Meeting rms. Business servs avail. In-rm modem link. Valet serv. Sundries. Free airport transportation. Exercise equipt; weight machine, bicycles. Microwave, refrigerator in suites. Some balconies. Cr cds: A, C, D, DS, MC, V.

D 〰 ✕ ✕ 🔥 SC

✔ ★ ★ **DAYS INN-NEWARK AIRPORT.** *(450 US 1S, Newark 07114) Off NJ Tpke exit 14, S on US 1/9.* 973/242-0900; FAX 973/242-8480. 191 rms, 8 story. S, D $64.95-$89.95; each addl $5; suites $99-$120; wkend rates. TV; cable (premium). Restaurant 6:30 am-midnight. Bar. Ck-out noon. Coin lndry. Meeting rms. Business servs avail. Free airport transportation. Exercise equipt; weight machine, bicycle. Microwave avail. Cr cds: A, C, D, DS, ER, JCB, MC, V.

D ✕ ✕ ✕ 🔥 SC

✔ ★ **HOWARD JOHNSON.** *(50 Port St, Newark 07114) Off NJ Tpke exit 14, Frontage Rd.* 973/344-1500; FAX 973/344-3311. 170 rms, 3 story. S, D $59.99-$89.99; children free; wkend rates. Crib free. TV; cable (premium). Restaurant open 24 hrs; Fri, Sat 6-1 am. Ck-out noon. Coin lndry. Meeting rms. Business servs avail. In-rm modem link. Gift shop. Free airport transportation. Cr cds: A, C, D, DS, MC, V.

D ✕ ✕ 🔥 SC

Motor Hotel

★ ★ **HOLIDAY INN INTL AIRPORT-NORTH.** *(160 Frontage Rd, Newark 07114) Off NJ Tpke exit 14, opp N terminal; use Frontage Rd.*

973/589-1000; FAX 973/589-2799. 234 rms, 10 story. S, D $99-$149; under 18 free; wkend rates by res. Crib free. TV; cable (premium). Pool; lifeguard. Restaurant 6 am-midnight. Rm serv. Bar 11-2 am; entertainment. Ck-out noon. Meeting rms. Business servs avail. In-rm modem link. Bellhops. Sundries. Gift shop. Free airport transportation. Exercise equipt; weight machine, treadmills. Cr cds: A, C, D, DS, JCB, MC, V.

D 〰 ✕ ✕ 🔥 SC

Hotels

★ ★ ★ **HILTON-NEWARK AIRPORT.** *(1170 Spring St, Elizabeth 07201) Off NJ Tpke exit 13 A.* 908/351-3900; FAX 908/351-9556. Web www.hilton.com/hilton. 375 rms, 12 story. S, D $164-$209; each addl $10; suites $295-$650; under 18 free; wkend rates. Crib free. TV; cable (premium), VCR avail. Indoor pool; whirlpool. Coffee in rms. Restaurant 6:30 am-11 pm. Rm serv 24 hrs. Bar 4 pm-2 am. Ck-out noon. Convention facilities. Business center. In-rm modem link. Gift shop. Free airport, RR station transportation. Valet parking. Exercise equipt; weight machines, bicycles, sauna. Cr cds: A, C, D, DS, ER, JCB, MC, V.

D 〰 ✕ ✕ 🔥 SC 🚶

★ ★ **HOLIDAY INN.** *(1000 Spring St, Elizabeth 07201) 3 mi N on NJ Tpke, exit 13-A.* 908/355-1700; FAX 908/355-1741. 392 rms, 10 story. S $121-$145; D $131-$155; each addl $13; suites $175-$350; under 18 free; wkend, hol rates. Pet accepted, some restrictions. TV; cable (premium), VCR avail (movies). Complimentary coffee in lobby. Restaurant 6:30 am-10:30 pm. Bar; entertainment Tues, Fri, Sat. Ck-out noon. Convention facilities. Business servs avail. In-rm modem link. Gift shop. Coin lndry. Free airport, RR station transportation. Exercise equipt; bicycle, treadmill. Indoor pool; lifeguard. Some bathrm phones. Refrigerators avail. Cr cds: A, C, D, DS, JCB, MC, V.

D ✔ 〰 ✕ ✕ 🔥 SC

★ ★ ★ **MARRIOTT-AIRPORT.** *(Newark Intl Airport, Newark 07114) On airport grounds; follow signs for main terminal.* 973/623-0006; FAX 973/623-7618. 590 rms, 10 story. S, D $169-$199; suites $400-$500; under 18 free; wkend rates. Crib free. TV; cable (premium), VCR avail. Indoor/outdoor pool; whirlpool, poolside serv. Restaurants 6 am-11 pm. Rm serv 24 hrs. Bars 11:30-1:30 am. Ck-out noon. Convention facilities. Business center. Concierge. Free airport transportation. Free parking. Exercise equipt; weights, bicycles, sauna. Some refrigerators. Luxury level. Cr cds: A, C, D, DS, ER, JCB, MC, V.

D 〰 ✕ ✕ 🔥 SC 🚶

★ ★ ★ **SHERATON-NEWARK AIRPORT.** *(128 Frontage Rd, Newark 07114) Off NJ Tpke exit 14; use Frontage Rd.* 973/690-5500; FAX 973/465-7195. 502 rms, 12 story. S, D $175; each addl $10; suites $395-$495; under 18 free; wkend rates. Crib free. TV; cable (premium), VCR avail. Indoor pool; whirlpool, poolside serv, lifeguard. Coffee in rms. Restaurants 6:30 am-11 pm. Bar 2 pm-2 am; entertainment Mon-Fri. Ck-out noon. Convention facilities. Business center. In-rm modem link. Concierge. Gift shop. Free airport transportation. Exercise equipt; weights, bicycles. Game rm. Refrigerators avail. Balconies. Atrium. Luxury level. Cr cds: A, C, D, DS, MC, V.

D 〰 ✕ ✕ 🔥 SC 🚶

★ **TRAVELODGE.** *(50 Park Place, Newark 07102)* 973/622-1000; FAX 973/622-6410. 169 rms, 12 story. S $65-$85; D $75-$90; suites $275-$375; under 16 free; wkend rates. Crib avail. TV; cable (premium), VCR avail. Complimentary coffee in rms. Restaurant 7 am-11 pm. No rm serv. Bar 4 pm-midnight; entertainment Thurs. Ck-out noon. Meeting rms. Business servs avail. In-rm modem link. Gift shop. Coin lndry. Free airport, RR station transportation. Exercise equipt; weight machine, bicycles. Game rm. Bathrm phone, in-rm whirlpool, refrigerator, minibar in suites. Cr cds: A, C, D, DS, ER, JCB, MC, V.

✕ ✕ ✕ 🔥 SC

New Brunswick (D-4)

Settled 1681 **Pop** 41,711 **Elev** 42 ft **Area code** 732

Information Middlesex County Chamber of Commerce, 1 Distribution Way, Ste 101, Monmouth Junction 08852; 732/821-1700.

New Brunswick, the seat of Middlesex County, is on the south bank of the Raritan River. It is both a college town and a diversified commercial and retail city. Rutgers University, the eighth-oldest institution of higher learning in the country and the only state university with a colonial charter, was founded in 1766 as Queens College, and opened in 1771 with a faculty of one—aged 18. Livingston College, Cook College and Douglass College (for women), all part of the university, are also located here. One of New Brunswick's most important industries is Johnson and Johnson; its company headquarters are located downtown. Joyce Kilmer, the poet, was born in New Brunswick; his house, at 17 Joyce Kilmer Avenue, is open to visitors.

What to See and Do

Buccleuch Mansion. Built in 1739 by Anthony White, son-in-law of Lewis Morris, a colonial governor of New Jersey. Period rooms. (June-Oct, Sun afternoons; closed hols) Under 10 only with adult. George St & Easton Ave, in 78-acre Buccleuch Park. Phone 732/745-5094. **Free.**

Crossroads Theatre. Professional African-American theater company offering plays, musicals, touring programs and workshops. (Sept-May, Wed-Sun) 7 Livingston Ave. For schedule, information phone 732/249-5560.

George Street Playhouse. Regional theater; seven-show season of plays and musicals; touring Outreach program for students. A 367-seat house. Stage II Theater; cafe; cabaret. (Daily) 9 Livingston Ave. Phone 732/246-7717 (box office, daily exc Mon).

Hungarian Heritage Center. Museum of changing exhibits that focus on Hungarian folk life, fine and folk art; library, archives. (Daily exc Mon; closed major hols) 300 Somerset St. Phone 732/846-5777. **Donation.**

Rutgers University Display Gardens. Features extensive display of American holly. (Daily) Ryder's Lane (US 1). Phone 732/932-8451. **Free.**

Rutgers-The State University (1766). (49,000 students) Multiple campuses include 26 colleges serving students at all levels through postdoctoral studies; main campus on College Ave. Phone 732/932-1766 (general information) or 732/932-7881 (campus tours). On campus are

Jane Voorhees Zimmerli Art Museum. Paintings from early 16th century through the present; changing exhibits. (Tues-Fri, also Sat & Sun afternoons; closed major hols) George & Hamilton Sts. Phone 732/932-7237. **Donation.**

Geology Museum. Displays of New Jersey minerals; dinosaur; mammals, including a mastodon; Egyptian exhibit with mummy. (Mon-Fri; closed hols) Phone 732/932-7243. **Free.**

Annual Event

Middlesex County Fair. Cranbury-South River Rd, in East Brunswick. Aug.

Seasonal Event

Rutgers SummerFest. Rutgers Arts Center. Features music, dance, visual arts exhibits and theater performances. July.

Motel

✔★ ★ **McINTOSH INN.** (764 NJ 18, East Brunswick 08816) 6 mi S on NJ 18, 4 mi off NJ Tpke exit 9. 732/238-4900; FAX 732/257-2023. 107 rms, 2 story. S $51.95-$58.95; D $57.95-$64.95; each addl $3. TV; cable

(premium). Complimentary coffee in lobby. Restaurant adj open 24 hrs. Ck-out 11 am. Business servs avail. Cr cds: A, D, MC, V.

D ⊠ 🐾 SC

Motor Hotels

★ ★ **HOLIDAY INN-SOMERSET.** (195 Davidson Ave, Somerset 08873) Off NJ 527 at I-287 exit 6. 732/356-1700; FAX 732/356-0939. 284 rms, 6 story. S, D $75-$109; under 12 free; wkend rates. Crib free. TV; cable (premium). Heated pool; poolside serv, lifeguard. Complimentary coffee in rms. Restaurant 6:30 am-2:30 pm, 5-10:30 pm. Rm serv. Bar 11:30-1 am. Ck-out noon. Convention facilities. Business center. In-rm modem link. Bellhops. Valet serv. Sundries. Gift shop. Airport transportation. Exercise equipt; stair machine, bicycles. Health club privileges. Microwaves avail. Cr cds: A, C, D, DS, ER, MC, V.

D ≋ 🏋 ⊠ 🐾 SC 🏃

★ ★ **MADISON SUITES.** (11 Cedar Grove Lane, Somerset 08873) 1/2 mi SE of I-287, exit 6, just off Easton Ave. 732/563-1000; FAX 732/563-0352. 83 suites, 2 story. Suites $95-$120; under 17 free; wkend rates. TV; cable (premium). Complimentary continental bkfst. Ck-out noon. Meeting rms. Business servs avail. In-rm modem link. Valet serv. Health club privileges. Refrigerators, microwaves. Cr cds: A, C, D, DS, MC, V.

D ⊠ 🐾 SC

★ ★ **RAMADA INN.** (195 Hwy 18, East Brunswick 08816) NJ 18 & Eggers St, at NJ Tpke exit 9. 732/828-6900; FAX 732/937-4838. 137 rms, 4 story. S, D $75-$155; each addl $10; under 18 free. Crib free. TV; cable (premium). Pool. Coffee in rms. Restaurant 7 am-10 pm. Rm serv. Bar 11:30 am-midnight; entertainment Fri, Sat. Ck-out noon. Meeting rms. Business center. Valet serv. Exercise equipt; weights, treadmill. Health club privileges. Microwaves avail. Cr cds: A, C, D, DS, ER, MC, V.

≋ 🏋 ⊠ 🐾 SC 🏃

Hotels

★ ★ ★ **DOUBLETREE SOMERSET.** (200 Atrium Dr, Somerset 08873) Off I-287 Easton Ave exit 6, left on Davidson Ave. 732/469-2600; FAX 732/469-4617. 360 rms, 6 story. S, D $89-$149 each addl $10; suites $175-$375; family, wkend rates. Crib free. TV; cable (premium). VCR avail. 2 pools, 1 indoor; whirlpool, poolside serv, lifeguard. Restaurant 6:30 am-2 pm; dining rm 5:30-10 pm. Bar 2 pm-1:30 am; entertainment. Ck-out noon. Business center. In-rm modem link. Gift shop. Tennis. Exercise equipt; weights, bicycles. Refrigerator in suites; microwaves avail. Private patios. Cr cds: A, C, D, DS, ER, JCB, MC, V.

D 🏌 ≋ 🏋 🏊 ⊠ 🐾 SC 🏃

★ ★ ★ **EMBASSY SUITES.** (121 Centennial Ave, Piscataway 08854) off I-287 exit 5. 732/980-0500; FAX 732/980-9473. Web www .embassy-suites.com. 220 suites, 5 story. Suites $175; each addl $20; under 12 free; wkend rates. Crib free. TV; cable (premium). Indoor pool; whirlpool. Complimentary full bkfst. Coffee in rms. Restaurant 11:30 am-2 pm, 5-10 pm. Bar to midnight. Coin lndry. Meeting rms. Business servs avail. In-rm modem link. Gift shop. Exercise equipt; weight machine, bicycle, sauna. Game rm. Refrigerators, microwaves. Atrium. Cr cds: A, C, D, DS, MC, V.

D ≋ 🏋 ⊠ 🐾 SC

★ ★ ★ **HILTON AND TOWERS.** (3 Tower Center Blvd, East Brunswick 08816) off I-95 exit 9. 732/828-2000; FAX 732/828-6958. E-mail bhtsales@injersey.com; web www.hilton.com. 405 rms, 15 story. S $105-$180; D $125-$200; each addl $20; suites $250-$750; under 18 free; wkend rates. Crib free. TV; cable (premium). VCR avail. Indoor pool; whirlpool. Coffee in rms. Restaurant 6:30 am-10:30 pm. Rm serv 24 hrs. Bar 11 am-midnight; wkends to 2 am. Ck-out noon. Convention facilities. Business center. In-rm modem link. Concierge. Gift shop. Airport transportation. Exercise equipt; weight machine, bicycles, sauna. Some bathrm phones, minibars; refrigerators, microwaves avail. Luxury level. Cr cds: A, C, D, DS, ER, MC, V.

★ ★ ★ **HYATT REGENCY.** *(2 Albany St, New Brunswick NB 08901) 732/873-1234; FAX 732/873-1382.* 286 rms, 6 story. S $160; D $185; suites $250-$400; under 18 free; wkend rates. Crib free. TV; cable (premium). Indoor pool; whirlpool. Coffee in rms. Restaurant 6:30 am-11 pm. Bar 11-1 am; pianist Fri, Sat. Ck-out noon. Convention facilities. Business center. In-rm modem link. Gift shop. Garage. Tennis. Exercise equipt; weights, bicycles, sauna. Health club privileges. Refrigerators avail. Some balconies. Cr cds: A, C, D, DS, ER, JCB, MC, V.

★ ★ ★ **MARRIOTT-SOMERSET.** *(110 Davidson Ave, Somerset 08873) I-287 exit 6. 732/560-0500; FAX 732/560-3669.* Web www.marriott .com. 440 rms, 11 story. S, D $129; each addl $15; under 17 free; wkend rates. Crib free. TV; cable (premium), VCR avail. Indoor/outdoor pool; whirlpool, poolside serv (summer). Restaurant 6:30 am-10 pm. Bar 11:30 am-midnight; Fri, Sat to 2 am. Ck-out 11 am. Meeting rms. Business center. In-rm modem link. Concierge. Gift shop. Tennis. Exercise rm; instructor, weight machines, bicycles, sauna. Refrigerators, microwaves avail. Some balconies. Cr cds: A, C, D, DS, JCB, MC, V.

Restaurants

★ ★ ★ **THE FROG AND THE PEACH.** *29 Dennis St (08901),* at Hiram Square. *732/846-3216.* Hrs: 11:30 am-2:30 pm, 5:30-10:30 pm; Sat from 5:30 pm; Sun 4:30-9:30 pm. Closed most major hols. Res accepted. Bar to midnight. Wine list. A la carte entrees: lunch $9-$15.50, dinner $18.50-$32.50. Child's meals. Specialties: pastrami-cured smoked salmon, cumin-dusted swordfish, tea-marinated duck breast. Own baking. Outdoor dining. In renovated industrial bldg with antique bar, stained glass. Cr cds: A, C, D, DS, MC, V.

★ ★ ★ **LA FONTANA.** *(120 Albany St, New Brunswick NB) 732/249-7500.* Hrs: 11:30 am-2:30 pm, 5-10 pm; Fri to 11 pm; Sat 5-11 pm. Closed Sun. Res accepted. Italian menu. Bar. Wine cellar. A la carte entrees: lunch $15, dinner $22-$28. Child's meals. Specializes in aristo-cratic-style Italian cuisine. Valet parking. 1920s Old World elegance. Jacket. Cr cds: A, D, MC, V.

★ ★ **MAKEDA.** *338 George St (08901). 732/545-5115.* Hrs: 11:30 am-10:30 pm; Fri, Sat to 12:30 am; Sun 1-10 pm. Closed Mon; Jan 1, Dec 25. Res accepted. Ethiopian menu. Bar 11:30-2 am. A la carte entrees: lunch $4-$21, dinner $6-$28. Jazz Thurs-Sun. Elegant atmos-phere with authentic Ethiopian-style seating. Cr cds: A, C, D, DS, MC, V.

✔ ★ **MARITA'S CANTINA.** *1 Penn Plaza. 732/247-3840.* Hrs: 11:30-2 am; Sun 3-11:30 pm. Closed Easter, Thanksgiving, Dec 25. Res accepted. Mexican menu. Bar to 2 am. Semi-a la carte: lunch, dinner $2.95-$11.95. Child's meals. Specializes in Mexican cuisine. Own des-serts. Entertainment Thurs. Outdoor dining. Cr cds: A, C, D, MC, V.

★ **RUSTY NAIL.** *(US 130 S, North Brunswick) 4 mi S on US 130, 1 1/2 mi S of jct US 1 & US 130. 732/821-4141.* Hrs: 11:30 am-10 pm; Sun from 12:30 pm. Res accepted. Bar to 2 am. Semi-a la carte: lunch $4.25-$7.25, dinner $9.95-$16.95. Child's meals. Specializes in prime roast beef. Salad bar. Cr cds: A, C, D, DS, MC, V.

Newfoundland (B-4)

(For accommodations see Wayne; also see Paterson)

Pop 900 (est) **Elev** 756 ft **Area code** 973 **Zip** 07435

What to See and Do

Craigmeur Ski Area. Area has double chairlift, T-bar, rope tow; patrol, school, rentals; snowmaking; restaurant, cafeteria, bar. Four runs, longest run 1 1/4 mi; vertical drop 250 ft. (Dec-Mar, daily) 2 mi S on Green Pond Rd (NJ 513) off NJ 23. Phone 973/697-4500. ¢¢¢¢¢

Ocean City (J-4)

Pop 15,512 **Elev** 4 ft **Area code** 609 **Zip** 08226 **Web** www.adnetint .com/oceancity

Information Public Relations Dept, City of Ocean City, 9th & Asbury Ave; 609/525-9300 or 800/BEACH-NJ.

Families from all over the country come to this popular resort year after year, as do conventions and religious conferences. In accordance with its founder's instructions, liquor cannot be sold here. Ocean City is an island that lies between the Atlantic Ocean and Great Egg Harbor. It has eight miles of beaches, more than two miles of boardwalk, an enclosed enter-tainment auditorium on the boardwalk, and excellent swimming, fishing, boating, golf and tennis.

What to See and Do

Historic House. Furnishings and fashions circa 1920-1930. Tours. (Apr-Dec, daily exc Sun) 1139 Wesley Ave. Phone 609/399-1801. **Donation.**

Ocean City Historical Museum. Victorian furnishings and fashions; doll exhibit; local shipwreck; historical Ocean City photographic exhibit; gift shop. (Apr-Dec, Mon-Fri, also Sat afternoons; rest of yr, Tues-Sat after-noons) 1735 Simpson Ave, at 17th St. Phone 609/399-1801. **Donation.**

Annual Events

Flower Show. Music Pier. June.

Night in Venice. Decorated boat parade. Mid-July.

Baseball Card Convention. Late July.

Hermit Crab Race, Miss Crustacean Contest. 6th St Beach. Crab beauty pageant, races. Phone 609/525-9300 or 800/BEACH-NJ. Early Aug.

Boardwalk Art Show. International and regional artists. Aug.

Seasonal Event

Concerts. Music Pier. Pops orchestra and dance band. Sun-Wed. Late June-Sept.

Motels

★ ★ ★ **BEACH CLUB HOTEL.** *1280 Boardwalk, at 13th St. 609/399-8555; FAX 609/398-4379.* E-mail impbcwd@aol; web www.rocc plex.com/beach club/welcome.html. 82 rms, 3 story. Mid-June-Labor Day: S, D $170-$242; each addl $10; higher rates wkends, May-mid-June, Labor Day-Nov. Closed rest of yr. Crib free. TV; cable (premium). Pool; wading pool, lifeguard. Restaurant 7 am-9 pm. Rm serv. Ck-out 11 am. Coin lndry. Business servs avail. Bellhops. Golf privileges. Refrigerators. Balconies. Sun deck. On beach. Cr cds: A, MC, V.

★ **DAYS INN.** *7th & Boardwalk. 609/398-2200; FAX 609/391-2050.* 80 rms, 4 story, 39 kit. suites. June-Aug: S, D $55-$200; each addl $15; kit. suites $70-$205; wkly rates; higher rates sporting events; lower rates Apr-May & Sept-Oct. Closed rest of yr. Crib free. TV; cable, VCR avail (movies). Heated pool; lifeguard. Restaurant nearby. Ck-out 11 am. Coin lndry. Business servs avail. Bellhops. Balconies. Ocean ½ blk. Cr cds: A, C, D, DS, MC, V.

⧉ ⌁ ⌁ ⌁ **SC**

★★ **FORUM.** *8th St and Atlantic Ave. 609/399-8700; FAX 609/399-8704.* 60 rms, 2-3 story. July-Aug (3-day min): S, D $58-$140; each addl $8; some wkend rates; lower rates Apr-May, Sept-Oct. Closed rest of yr. Crib avail. TV; cable (premium). Heated pool; wading pool, lifeguard. Ck-out noon. Coin lndry. Business servs avail. Game rm. Rec rm. Refrigerators. Picnic tables. Sun deck. Cr cds: MC, V.

⌁ ⌁

★ **HARRIS HOUSE MOTOR INN.** *12th St & Ocean Ave. 609/399-7800.* 74 rms, 2 story. Late June-Aug: S, D $150; each addl $10; under 12 free; wkly rates; higher rates hols (3-day min); lower rates late Aug-late Oct & Apr-late June; closed rest of yr. Crib free. TV; cable. Heated pool; lifeguard. Complimentary coffee in lobby. Restaurant adj 6 am-9 pm. Ck-out 11 am. Business servs avail. Refrigerators, microwaves avail. On beach. Cr cds: A, DS, MC, V.

⧉ ⌁ ⌁ ⌁

★★ **IMPALA ISLAND INN.** *1001 Ocean Avenue, 10th St at Ocean Ave. 609/399-7500; FAX 609/398-4379.* E-mail impbcwd@aol; web www.rccplex.com/impalisland/welcome.html. 109 units in 2 bldgs, 2 story. July-Aug; S, D $117-$151; kit. units $1,075-$1,635/wk; lower rates rest of yr. Crib free. TV; cable. 2 pools, 1 heated; wading pool, lifeguard. Restaurant 7 am-9 pm. Rm serv. Ck-out 11 am. Meeting rms. Business servs avail. Refrigerators. Sun deck. Cr cds: A, MC, V.

⌁ ⌁ ⌁ **SC**

★ **PAVILION.** *801 Atlantic Ave. 609/399-2600; res: 800/523-5225.* 80 rms, 3 story. Early July-early Sept (3-day min wkends): S, D $116-$124; kit. units $150; lower rates Mar-June & early Sept-Nov; closed rest of yr. Crib avail. TV; cable (premium), VCR avail (movies). Heated pool; wading pool, poolside serv, lifeguard. Restaurant 7:30 am-9 pm. Rm serv. Ck-out 11 am. Coin lndry. Business servs avail. Refrigerators. On beach. Cr cds: A, DS, MC, V.

⌁ ⌁ ⌁ **SC**

★★ **RESIDENCE INN BY MARRIOTT.** *(900 Mays Landing Rd, Somers Point 08244) 3 mi NW on NJ 52, then W on Mays Landing Rd; E of Garden State Pkwy exits 29N, 30S. 609/927-6400; FAX 609/926-0145.* 120 kit. suites, 2 story. Memorial Day-Labor Day: S, D $160-$240; each addl $10; under 12 free; wkly rates; lower rates rest of yr. Pet accepted. TV; cable, VCR avail (movies). Heated pool; lifeguard. Complimentary continental bkfst. Ck-out 11 am. Coin lndry. Meeting rms. Business servs avail. In-rm modem link. Valet serv. Airport transportation. Golf. Health club privileges. Rec rm. Microwaves. Some private patios, balconies. Picnic tables, grills. Cr cds: A, C, D, DS, JCB, MC, V.

⧉ ⌁ ⌁ ⌁ ⌁ ⌁ **SC**

Motor Hotels

★★ **PIER 4 ON THE BAY.** *(The Bay & Broadway Ave, Somers Point 08244) 609/927-9141; res: 888/927-9141; FAX 609/653-2752.* 72 rms, 4 story, 8 suites. Apr-Dec: S, D $59-$149; each addl $15; suites $89-$149; under 14 free; wkly rates; golf plans; wkends, hols (2-day min); higher rates special events; lower rates rest of yr. Crib free. TV; cable, VCR avail (movies). Complimentary continental bkfst. Complimentary coffee in rms. Restaurant adj 11-1 am. Ck-out 11 am. Meeting rms. Business servs avail. Coin lndry. Golf privileges. Heated pool; poolside serv. Rec rm. Refrigerators, microwaves. On bay. Cr cds: A, C, D, DS, MC, V.

⧉ ⌁ ⌁ ⌁ ⌁ ⌁ **SC**

★★ **PORT-O-CALL.** *1510 Boardwalk. 609/399-8812; FAX 609/399-0387; res: 800/334-4546.* Web clever.net/wwwmall/portocall. 99 rms, 9 story. June-Sept: S, D $170-$255; each addl $15; penthouse apt $575; under 12 free; lower rates rest of yr. Crib free. TV; cable (premium). Pool; sauna, lifeguard. Free supervised child's activities (June-Aug). Coffee in rms. Restaurant 7 am-2 pm, 5-8 pm; Sun 9:30 am-1:30 pm, 5-8 pm. Rm serv. Ck-out 11 am. Coin lndry. Meeting rms. Business servs avail. In-rm modem link. Bellhops. Sundries. Airport transportation. Exercise equipt; weight machine, stair machine. Barber, beauty shop. Golf privileges. Refrigerators. Balconies. On ocean. Cr cds: A, C, D, DS, MC, V.

⧉ ⌁ ⌁ ⌁ ⌁ ⌁ **SC**

★★ **WILD DUNES INN.** *801 10th St. 609/399-2910; FAX 609/398-4379.* E-mail impbcwd@aol; web www.roccplex.com/widdunes/welcome.html. 28 suites, 2 story. S, D $155-$193; wkends, hols (3-day min). Crib free. TV; cable. Restaurant nearby. Ck-out 10 am. Coin lndry. Heated pool; wading pool, lifeguard. Refrigerators, microwaves. ½ blk opp beach. Cr cds: A, MC, V.

⧉ ⌁ ⌁ ⌁

Inn

★★★ **SERENDIPITY.** *712 9th St. 609/399-1554; res: 800/842-8544; FAX 609/399-1527.* 6 rms, 2 share bath, 3 story. No rm phones. July 4-Labor Day: S, D $75-$125; higher rates hols (3-day min); lower rates rest of yr. Children over 10 yrs only. TV; cable. Complimentary full bkfst. Restaurant opp 7 am-9 pm. Ck-out 11 am, ck-in 2 pm. Luggage handling. Picnic tables. ½ blk to ocean. Renovated inn built 1912. Totally nonsmoking. Cr cds: A, DS, MC, V.

⌁ ⌁ **SC**

Restaurants

★★ **CRAB TRAP.** *(Somers Pt Circle, Somers Point) 1 mi E of Garden State Pkwy exit 30. 609/927-7377.* Hrs: 11-2 am. Closed Dec 24, 25. Bar. Semi-a la carte: lunch $5.75-$8.95, dinner $11.25-$27.95. Child's meals. Specialties: stuffed lobster tail, prime rib. Entertainment. Nautical decor. On the bay. Family-owned. Cr cds: A, C, D, DS, MC, V.

⧉ ⌁

★★ **DEAUVILLE INN.** *(201 Willard Rd, Strathmore 08248) 6 mi E on Garden State Pkwy. 609/263-2080.* Hrs: noon-midnight; summer hrs vary; early-bird dinner 4-6 pm. Closed Dec 25, 26. Bar. Semi-a la carte: lunch $3.95-$9.25, dinner $6.95-$22.95. Child's meals. Specializes in fresh seafood, steak, veal. Valet parking. Outdoor dining overlooking bay. Cr cds: A, MC, V.

⧉ ⌁

★★ **MAC'S.** *(908 Shore Rd, Somers Point) 1 blk N of Somers Pt Circle. 609/927-4360.* Hrs: 3:30-11 pm. Closed Dec 25. Res accepted. Italian, Amer menu. Bar. Semi-a la carte: dinner $9.95-$29.95. Child's meals. Specializes in seafood, steak. Family-owned. Cr cds: A, DS, MC, V.

⧉ ⌁

Palisades Interstate Parks (B-6)

(For accommodations see Fort Lee, Hackensack)

(Reached via Palisades Interstate Pkwy, starting at New Jersey end of George Washington Bridge; US 9W, NJ/NY 17, Dewey Thrwy exit 13)

This 81,067-acre system of conservation and recreation areas extends along the west side of the Hudson River from the George Washington Bridge at Fort Lee, NJ (see), to Saugerties, NY. Its main unit is the 51,679-acre tract of Bear Mountain and Harriman (NY) state parks; the two are contiguous.

Bear Mountain (5,066 acres) extends westward from the Hudson River opposite Peekskill. Only 45 miles from New York City via the Palisades Interstate Parkway, this is one of the most popular recreation areas, with year-round facilities, mostly for one-day visits. Area includes swimming pool (Memorial Day-Labor Day; fee); bathhouse; fishing; game fields; boating on Hessian Lake. Nature trails. Cafeteria. Inn. Ice-skating (late Oct-mid-Mar; fee); square dances in July and August.

Perkins Memorial Drive leads to the top of Bear Mountain, where there is a picnic area and a sightseeing tower. Near the site of Fort Clinton, just west of Bear Mountain Bridge, is the Trailside Museum, with exhibits of local flora, fauna, geology and history (daily; fee).

Harriman (46,613 acres), southwest of Bear Mountain, includes much wilder country with several lakes. Swimming beaches (Lakes Tiorati, Welch and Sebago); fishing; boating. Hiking, biking. Picnicking. Miles of scenic drives. Tent camping (Lake Welch), cabins (Lake Sebago).

Many smaller parks are located in the New Jersey section of the park system.

Alpine Area (12 acres). This area has fishing; boat basin. Hiking. Picnicking, concession (seasonal). Outdoor concerts in summer. (Daily, weather permitting) Off Henry Hudson Dr, E of Alpine.

Englewood-Bloomers Area (13 acres). This area offers fishing; boat basin. Hiking. Picnicking, concession (seasonal). (Daily, weather permitting) Off Henry Hudson Dr, E of jct Palisades Interstate Pkwy & NJ 505 in Englewood Cliffs.

Ross Dock (14 acres). Near the southern end of the park system, this area has fishing; boat-launching ramp. Hiking. Picnicking, playgrounds. (Apr-mid-Nov, daily, weather permitting) Off Henry Hudson Dr, N of George Washington Bridge.

Fort Lee Historic Park. This 33-acre facility presents the story of Washington's retreat from Fort Lee in 1776. Visitor's Center/Museum (Mar-Dec, Wed-Sun) offers two floors of exhibits; audiovisual displays; a short film; general information; special events. On grounds (daily, daylight hrs) are 18th-century soldiers' hut, reconstructed gun batteries, a rifle parapet; overlooks with scenic views of the George Washington Bridge, the Palisades, the Hudson River and the New York skyline. Gift shop. Parking fee (May-Sept, daily; Apr & Oct-mid-Nov, wkends & hols). No pets, bicycles or fires. Hudson Ter. Phone 201/461-1776. ¢¢

There are fees for parking and special events. For further information on the New Jersey section contact Palisades Interstate Park Commission, PO Box 155, Alpine 07620; 201/768-1360. Further information on the New York section can be obtained from Palisades Interstate Park Commission, Administration Bldg, Bear Mountain, NY 10911; 914/786-2701.

Paramus (B-5)

Settled 1660 **Pop** 25,067 **Elev** 58 ft **Area code** 201 **Zip** 07652 **Web** www.paramuschamber.com

Information Chamber of Commerce, 58 E Midland Ave, PO Box 325; 201/261-3346.

This old Dutch farm community was an important hub of transportation as long ago as the Revolutionary War; western Paramus became headquarters for the Continental Army as a result. Paramus has grown as a residential community from 4,000 inhabitants in 1946, to its present size.

What to See and Do

Bergen Museum of Art & Science. Features Dwarskill and Hackensack mastodons; nature room; birds and minerals of Bergen County; Native American artifacts; galleries with changing exhibits. (Daily exc Mon; closed major hols) 327 E Ridgewood Ave at Farview Ave. Phone 201/265-1248. ¢¢

New Jersey Children's Museum. Interactive displays in 30 rms. Includes aviation, firefighting, TV studio, hospital. Gift shop. (Daily; closed some hols) 599 Industrial Ave. Phone 201/262-5151. ¢¢¢

Schoolhouse Museum. Exhibits in 1873 schoolhouse depict life from colonial times through 19th century, with emphasis on local history. Native American relics; early maps; Dutch genealogies; farm implements; doll and toy displays; clothing. Tours (by appt). (May-late Oct, Sun afternoons; closed hols) 650 E Glen Ave, at NJ 17, in Ridgewood. Phone 201/652-4584 or 201/447-3242 (recording). **Free.**

Van Saun County Park. Fishing lake. Bike trail; tennis (fee); horseshoes, shuffleboard. Ice-skating, sledding. Picnicking, concession, playgrounds, ball fields (permit). Zoo; train, pony rides (fees). Garden surrounding historic Washington Spring; farmyard. Park (daily). 216 Forest Ave, 1½ mi N of NJ 4. Phone 201/599-6124 or 201/262-3771 (zoo). **Free.**

Motor Hotel

★ ★ **RADISSON.** 601 From Rd, adj to Paramus Park Mall, Garden State Pkwy exit 165. 201/262-6900; FAX 201/262-4955. Web www.radisson.com. 119 rms, 2 story. S, D $129; each addl $10; wkend rates. Crib free. Pet accepted, some restrictions. TV; cable (premium). Pool. Complimentary coffee in rms. Restaurant 6:30 am-10 pm; Sat, Sun from 7 am. Rm serv. Bar; entertainment Sat. Ck-out noon. Coin lndry. Meeting rms. Business servs avail. In-rm modem link. Bellhops. Sundries. Health club privileges. Refrigerators. Cr cds: A, C, D, DS, ER, JCB, MC, V.

D ✉ ≈ ⊠ 🔥 SC

Parsippany (C-4)

Pop 48,478 **Elev** 282 ft **Area code** 973 **Zip** 07054

Motels

★ ★ **HOWARD JOHNSON.** (1255 NJ 10, Whippany 07981) I-80 to I-287S exit 39B (NJ 10). 973/539-8350; FAX 973/539-9338. Web www.hojo.com. 108 rms, 2 story. S $79-$89; D $89-$99; each addl $10; under 18 free; family, wkend, wkly, hol rates. Crib free. Pet accepted, some restrictions. TV; cable (premium). Complimentary continental bkfst. Restaurant 6:30 am-10 pm. Ck-out noon. Meeting rms. Business servs avail. Valet serv. Coin lndry. Pool. Refrigerators, microwaves avail. Cr cds: A, C, D, DS, JCB, MC, V.

D ✉ ≈ ⊠ 🔥 SC

✔ ★ **HOWARD JOHNSON EXPRESS INN.** 625 US 46. 973/882-8600; FAX 973/882-3493. Web www.hojo.com. 117 rms, 3 story. S $52.95-$54.95; D $59.95-$64.95; under 18 free; wkly rates. Crib free. TV; cable (premium). Complimentary continental bkfst. Restaurant nearby. Ck-out noon. Coin lndry. Meeting rm. Business servs avail. Health club privileges. Refrigerators, microwaves avail. Cr cds: A, C, D, DS, ER, JCB, MC, V.

D ⊠ 🔥 SC

Motor Hotels

★ ★ **HAMPTON INN.** 3535 US 46E, at Cherry Hill Rd. 973/263-0095; FAX 973/263-6133. Web www.hampton-inn.com. 100 rms, 4 story. 18 kits. S, D $99; kit. units $115; under 18 free; wkend rates. Crib free. TV; cable (premium). Complimentary continental bkfst. Restaurant 5-10 pm. Rm serv. Bar 4:30 pm-midnight. Ck-out noon. Meeting rm. Business servs avail. Valet serv (exc wkends). Exercise equipt; weights, bicycles, sauna. Whirlpool. Microwaves avail. Cr cds: A, C, D, DS, ER, MC, V.

D 🏋 ⊠ 🔥 SC

★ ★ **HOLIDAY INN.** 707 US 46, I-80 exit 45 (eastbound) or exit 47 (westbound). 973/263-2000; FAX 973/299-9029. Web www.holiday .com. 153 rms, 4 story. S, D $76-$89; under 18 free; lower rates wkends. Crib free. TV; cable (premium). Pool. Restaurant 7 am-11 pm. Ck-out noon. Coin lndry. Meeting rms. Business servs avail. Sundries. Exercise equipt; bicycles, weight machine. Health club privileges. Microwaves avail. Cr cds: A, C, D, DS, JCB, MC, V.

Hotel

★ ★ ★ **HILTON.** *1 Hilton Ct, jct NJ 10 & I-287. 973/267-7373; FAX 973/984-6853.* Web www.hilton.com. 508 rms, 6 story. S $135-$175; D $155-$185; each addl $20; suites $350-$675; family, wkend rates. Crib free. Pet accepted, some restrictions. TV; cable (premium), VCR avail. Indoor/outdoor pool; whirlpool. Playground. Restaurants 6:30 am-11 pm; wkends from 7 am. Rm serv Mon-Thurs 6:30-2 am. Bar 11-2 am; entertainment. Ck-out noon. Convention facilities. Business center. In-rm modem link. Airport transportation. Tennis. Exercise equipt; weights, bicycles. Some bathrm phones. Wet bar, refrigerator in suites. Cr cds: A, C, D, DS, ER, JCB, MC, V.

Restaurant

✔★ ★ **BLACK BULL INN.** *(US 46, Mountain Lakes) I-80 exit 42 (W) or 39 (E). 973/335-8585.* Hrs: 11 am-11 pm; Fri, Sat to midnight. Closed major hols. Bar. Semi-a la carte: lunch $4.95-$11.95, dinner $4.95-$17.95. Child's meals. Specializes in Delmonico steak, prime rib, fish. Entertainment Fri, Sat. Scottish atmosphere. Cr cds: A, DS, MC, V.

Paterson (B-5)

(For accommodations see Clifton, Wayne)

Settled 1711 **Pop** 140,891 **Elev** 100 ft **Area code** 973
Information Great Falls Visitor Center, 65 McBride Ave Ext, across from the Great Falls, 07501-1715, phone 973/279-9587; or the Special Events Office, 72 McBride Ave, 07501, phone 973/523-9201.

Named after Governor William Paterson, this city owes its present and historic eminence as an industrial city to Alexander Hamilton. He was the first man to realize the possibility of harnessing the Great Falls of the Passaic River for industrial purposes. As secretary of the Treasury, he helped form the Society for Establishing Useful Manufactures in 1791 and, a year later, was instrumental in choosing Paterson as the site of its initial ventures. Paterson was the country's major silk-producing town in the late 1800s. Today, it is a diversified industrial center. The area surrounding the Great Falls is now being restored and preserved as a historic district. Paterson is the seat of Passaic County.

What to See and Do

American Labor Museum-Botto House National Landmark. The history of the working class is presented through restored period rooms, changing exhibits and ethnic gardens. Tours, seminars and workshops are offered. (Wed-Sat; closed major hols exc Labor Day) N on NJ 504, at 83 Norwood St in Haledon. Phone 973/595-7953. ¢

Garret Mountain Reservation. A 570-acre woodland park on a 502-ft-high plateau. Fishing pond (stocked with trout); boat dock, rowboats, paddleboats. Trails, stables. Picnic groves. Rifle Camp Rd & Mountain Ave. Phone 973/881-4832. **Free.**

⭐ **Great Falls Historic District.** Includes 77-ft-high falls, park and picnic area, renovated raceway system, restored 19th-century buildings. McBride Ave Ext & Spruce St. For further information and tours phone 973/279-9587. ¢ Also here is

Paterson Museum. Contains shell of original 14-ft submarine invented by John P. Holland in 1878; also his second submarine (31 ft), built in 1881. Paterson-Colt gun collection (1836-1840); mineral display; exhibits on Paterson history, including the silk and locomotive industries; two

locomotives; Curtiss-Wright airplane engines; changing art exhibits. (Daily exc Mon; closed hols) Thomas Rogers Bldg, 2 Market St. Phone 973/881-3874. **Donation.**

Lambert Castle. Built by an immigrant who rose to wealth as a silk manufacturer. The 1893 castle of brownstone and granite houses a local-history museum; two restored period rooms; changing exhibits; library (by appt). *Closed for renovation until fall.* (Wed-Sun, afternoons; closed most major hols). 3 Valley Rd. Phone 973/881-2761. ¢

Rifle Camp Park. This 158-acre park is 584 ft above sea level. Includes nature and geology trails, nature center with astronomical observatory; walking paths, fitness course. Picnic areas. Rifle Camp Rd in West Paterson. **Free.**

Plainfield (D-4)

Settled 1685 **Pop** 46,567 **Elev** 118 ft **Area code** 908 **E-mail** cjcc @compuserve.com **Web** ourworld.compuserve.com/homepages/cjcc/
Information Central Jersey Chamber of Commerce, 120 W 7th St, #217, 07060; 908/754-7250.

Plainfield, directly south of the Watchung Mountains, is actually the center of a group of associated towns: Scotch Plains (see), Watchung, North and South Plainfield, Fanwood, Green Brook, Warren Township, Dunellen, Middlesex and Piscataway, all of which are mainly residential. Plainfield is also home to a number of industries.

What to See and Do

Drake House Museum (1746). General Washington's headquarters in 1777; now the Plainfield Historical Society headquarters. Period furnishings; diorama depicts Battle for the Watchungs. (Sat afternoons) 602 W Front St. Phone 908/755-5831. ¢

Motor Hotel

★ ★ **HOLIDAY INN.** *(4701 Stelton Rd, South Plainfield 07080) At jct NJ 529, I-287. 908/753-5500; FAX 908/753-5500, ext. 620.* 173 rms, 4 story. S, D $89-$109; under 19 free; wkend rates. Crib free. Pet accepted, some restrictions. TV; cable (premium). Indoor pool; whirlpool, lifeguard. Restaurant 6:30 am-10 pm. Rm serv. Ck-out 1 pm. Coin lndry. Meeting rms. Business servs avail. In-rm modem link. Valet serv. Exercise equipt; weights, bicycles, sauna. Refrigerators; microwaves avail. Cr cds: A, C, D, DS, MC, V.

Princeton (E-4)

(See also Trenton)

Settled 1685 **Pop** 12,016 **Elev** 215 ft **Area code** 609
Information Chamber of Commerce, 216 Rockingham Row PO Box 431, 08540; 609/520-1776.

In 1776, the first State Legislature of New Jersey met in Princeton University's Nassau Hall. Washington and his troops surprised and defeated a superior British Army in the 1777 Battle of Princeton. From June to November 1783, Princeton was the new nation's capital. Around the same time, Washington was staying at Rockingham in nearby Rocky Hill, where he wrote and delivered his famous "Farewell Orders to the Armies."

Princeton's life is greatly influenced by the university, which opened here in 1756; at that time it was known as the College of New Jersey. In 1896, on the 150th anniversary of its charter, the institution became Princeton University. Woodrow Wilson, the first president of the university who was not a clergyman, held the office from 1902 to 1910. Princeton is also the home of the Institute for Advanced Study, where Albert Einstein spent the last years of his life.

What to See and Do

Bainbridge House (ca 1766). Birthplace of commander of the USS *Constitution* during War of 1812. Changing exhibits on Princeton history; research library (Tues-Sat; fee), photo archives. Museum shop. Also offers walking tours of historic district (Sun). 158 Nassau St. For schedule phone 609/921-6748. **Donation.**

Kuser Farm Mansion and Park. Farm and 1890s summer mansion of Fred Kuser; more than 20 rms open; many original furnishings. Grounds consist of 22 acres with original buildings including coachman's house, chicken house; tennis pavilion; clay tennis court. Park with picnic areas; quoit courts, lawn bowling, walking trails; formal garden, gazebo. Tours (May-Nov, Thurs-Sun; Feb-Apr, Sat & Sun; limited hrs, call for schedule and hol closings); self-guided tour maps of grounds. Special programs, lectures and video evenings throughout the yr. 10 mi SE via US 206, I-295 to Olden Ave in Hamilton, then 1/2 mi W to Newkirk Ave. Phone 609/890-3630. **Free.**

Morven (1755). House of Richard Stockton, signer of the Declaration of Independence. Used as a Revolutionary headquarters; was frequently visited by General Washington and other colonial leaders. 55 Stockton St. Phone 609/683-4495 for schedule.

Princeton Battle Monument. The work of Frederick W. MacMonnies, this 50-ft block of Indiana limestone commemorates the famous 1777 battle when George Washington defeated the British. On Monument Dr, off Stockton St, near Morven.

Princeton Cemetery. Buried in the Presidents' Plot are 11 university presidents, including Aaron Burr Sr, Jonathan Edwards and John Witherspoon. Monument to Grover Cleveland and grave of Paul Tulane, in whose honor Tulane University was named. Witherspoon & Wiggins Sts.

Princeton University (1746). (4,500 undergraduate students, 1,650 graduate students) An Ivy League college that has been coeducational since 1969. A campus guide service shows the visitor points of interest on the main campus; for tour information phone 609/258-3603. (Daily; closed major hols) On campus are

Woodrow Wilson School of Public and International Affairs. Designed by Minoru Yamasaki; reflecting pool and "Fountain of Freedom" by James Fitzgerald.

Nassau Hall (1756). Provided all college facilities, classrooms, dormitories, library and prayer hall for about 50 yrs. New Jersey's first legislature met here in 1776, and the Continental Congress met here in 1783, when Princeton was the capital. During the Revolution, it served as a barracks and hospital for Continental and British troops.

The Putnam Sculptures. One of the largest modern outdoor sculpture showcases in the country, with 19 sculptures on display throughout the campus, including pieces by Picasso, Moore, Noguchi, Calder and Lipchitz.

McCarter Theatre. Professional repertory company performs classical and modern drama; concerts; ballet; other special programs yr-round. Phone 609/683-8000 (box office).

Rockingham State Historic Site. On this 5-acre site are 3 buildings: a kitchen, a wash house and the main building. This was Washington's headquarters Aug 23-Nov 10, 1783, where he wrote his "Farewell Orders to the Armies"; 10 rms with period furnishings. (Wed-Sat, also Sun afternoons; closed most major hols) 4 mi N on US 206, then 2 mi E on County 518 in Rocky Hill. Phone 609/921-8835. **Free.**

Motels

✔★ **DAYS INN.** *(4191 US 1, Monmouth Junction 08852) 2 mi N on US 1.* 908/329-4555; FAX 908/329-1041. E-mail jrczpatel@msn.com. 73 rms, 2 story, 7 suites. S $44.95-$59.95; D $59.95-$99.95; each addl $10; suites $150.95. Crib free. TV; cable, VCR avail (movies). Restaurant

6:30-10:30 am. Ck-out 11 am. Business servs avail. Refrigerators, microwaves avail. Cr cds: A, C, D, DS, JCB, MC, V.

[D] [symbols] [SC]

★★ **RESIDENCE INN BY MARRIOTT.** *4225 US 1 (08543), 4 mi NE, just S of Raymond Rd on US 1.* 732/329-9600; FAX 732/329-8422. Web www.pacpub.com/residence. 208 kit. suites, 2 story. S, D $139-$159; under 18 free; wkly, wkend rates. Crib free. Pet accepted, some restrictions; $10. TV; cable (premium). Heated pool; whirlpool. Complimentary continental bkfst. Ck-out noon. Coin lndry. Meeting rms. Business center. Valet serv. Health club privileges. Microwaves; many fireplaces. Balconies. Picnic tables, grills. Cr cds: A, C, D, DS, ER, JCB, MC, V.

[D] [symbols] [SC] [symbol]

Motor Hotels

★★★ **HOLIDAY INN.** *4355 US 1 (08540), at Ridge Rd.* 609/452-2400; FAX 609/452-2494. 242 rms, 6 story. S, D $165; each addl $15; suites from $225; under 19 free; wkend rates. Crib free. TV; cable (premium). Indoor pool. Restaurant 6 am-10 pm. Bar 11-1 am. Ck-out noon. Meeting rms. Business servs avail. Exercise equipt; bicycles, treadmills. Health club privileges. Refrigerators, microwaves avail. Cr cds: A, C, D, DS, JCB, MC, V.

[D] [symbols] [SC]

★★ **NOVOTEL.** *100 Independence Way (08540), jct NJ 522, US 1.* 609/520-1200; FAX 609/520-0594. 180 rms, 4 story. S, D $135; suites $155; under 16 free; wkend rates. Crib free. Pet accepted, some restrictions. TV; cable (premium), VCR avail. Pool; whirlpool. Restaurant 6 am-10:30 pm. Rm serv. Bar. Ck-out 1 pm. Coin lndry. Meeting rms. Business servs avail. In-rm modem link. Valet serv. Free RR station transportation. Exercise equipt; weight machine, bicycles. Microwaves avail. Cr cds: A, C, D, DS, ER, MC, V.

[D] [symbols] [SC]

Hotels

★★★ **THE FORRESTAL.** *100 College Rd E (08540), off US 1, in Princeton Forrestal Center.* 609/452-7800; FAX 609/452-7883; res: 800/222-1131. Web www.forrestal.com. 300 rms, 3-4 story. S, D $125-$175; each addl $10; suites $275-$650; under 17 free; wkend rates. Crib free. TV; cable (premium), VCR avail. Indoor pool; whirlpool. Restaurant 7 am-10 pm. Bars 11-1 am. Ck-out noon. Convention facilities. Business center. In-rm modem link. Gift shop. Free valet parking. Airport transportation. Lighted tennis. Exercise equipt; weight machines, bicycles, sauna. Lawn games. Minibars. Contemporary design and furnishings. On 25 wooded acres. Luxury level. Cr cds: A, C, D, DS, MC, V.

[D] [symbols] [SC] [symbol]

★★★ **HYATT REGENCY.** *102 Carnegie Center (08540), 2 mi E on US 1, at Alexander Rd.* 609/987-1234; FAX 609/987-2584. 348 rms, 4 story. S $79-$179; D $104-$204; suites $200-$575; under 18 free; wkend rates. Crib free. TV; cable (premium). Indoor/outdoor pool; whirlpool, poolside serv. Restaurant 6:30 am-10:30 pm. Bar 11-2 am; entertainment Fri-Sun. Ck-out noon. Business center. In-rm modem link. Gift shop. Airport transportation. Tennis. Exercise equipt; weights, bicycles, sauna. Some bathrm phones; microwaves avail. Cr cds: A, C, D, DS, ER, JCB, MC, V.

[D] [symbols] [SC] [symbol]

★★★ **MARRIOTT.** *201 Village Blvd (08540), in Forrestal Village, 8 mi S of NJ Tpke exit 9.* 609/452-7900; FAX 609/452-1123; res: 800/242-8689. 294 units, 6 story. S, D $144-$164; each addl $20; under 18 free; some wkend rates. Crib free. TV; cable (premium), VCR avail. Indoor/outdoor pool; whirlpool, poolside serv, lifeguard. Restaurant 6:30 am-11 pm. Bar noon-2 am; entertainment. Ck-out 11 am. Coin lndry. Meeting rms. Business center. In-rm modem link. Concierge. Gift shop. Exercise rm;

instructor, weights, bicycles. Refrigerators avail. Some private patios, balconies. Shopping center adj. Cr cds: A, C, D, DS, ER, JCB, MC, V.

★ ★ ★ **NASSAU INN.** *10 Palmer Sq (08542). 609/921-7500; FAX 609/921-9385; res: 800/627-7286 (exc NJ).* E-mail lorginjam@aol.com; web www.nassauinn.com. 215 rms, 5 story. S $135-$175; D $155-$195; each addl $20; suites $310-$535; under 13 free. Crib free. Pet accepted. TV; cable (premium). Restaurant 7 am-10 pm. Bar 4 pm-1 am; entertainment Fri, Sat. Ck-out noon. Business center. In-rm modem link. Exercise equipt; weight machine, treadmills. Refrigerators avail. Colonial atmosphere, beamed ceilings, fireplaces in public rms. Cr cds: A, D, MC, V.

Inn

★ ★ **PEACOCK INN.** *20 Bayard Lane (08540). 609/924-1707; FAX 609/924-0788.* 17 rms, 7 share bath, 3 story. S $90-$125; D $100-$135; each addl $15; higher rates graduation. Crib free. Pet accepted; $20. TV in some rms, lobby; cable (premium). Complimentary bkfst buffet. Dining rm 11:45 am-2:30 pm, 5:30-9:30 pm. Ck-out noon, ck-in 2 pm. Business servs avail. Historic late Georgian colonial house, built in 1775 and relocated from Nassau St to its present site. Antique furnishings; rms individually decorated. 3 blks from Princeton Univ campus. Cr cds: A, MC, V.

Restaurants

★ ★ **ALCHEMIST AND BARRISTER.** *28 Witherspoon. 609/924-5555.* Hrs: 11:30 am-2:30 pm, 5-10 pm; Fri, Sat to 10:30 pm; Sun 11:30 am-3 pm (brunch), 5-10 pm. Closed Jan 1, July 4, Dec 25. Res accepted. Bar to 2 am. Semi-a la carte: lunch $7-$13, dinner $18-$27. Sun brunch $7.95-$12.95. Specializes in seafood, steak. Outdoor dining. Colonial decor. Cr cds: A, MC, V.

★ **THE ANNEX.** *128½ Nassau St (08540). 609/921-7555.* Web www.powerpgs/#1/annex. Hrs: 11 am-10 pm; early-bird dinner Mon-Thurs 3:30-5:30 pm. Closed Sun; most major hols. Continental menu. Bar to 1 am. Semi-a la carte: lunch $4.50-$23, dinner $6.25-$23. Child's meals. Specialties: steak Diane, chicken a la cacciatori, baked stuffed sole with crabmeat. Casual atmosphere. Family-owned. Totally nonsmoking. Cr cds: A, MC, V.

★ ★ **GOOD TIME CHARLEY'S.** *(40 Main St, Kingston) 2 mi N on NJ 27. 609/924-7400.* Hrs: 11:30-1 am; Sat from 5 pm; Sun from noon. Closed Dec 25; also lunch major hols. Res accepted. Bar to 2 am. Semi-a la carte: lunch $4.95-$9.95, dinner $9.95-$21.95. Specializes in prime rib, fresh seafood. Musicians Fri, Sat. Victorian decor. Tiffany lamps; posters. Cr cds: A, C, D, DS, MC, V.

★ ★ **QUILTY'S.** *18 Witherspoon St (08540). 609/683-4771.* Hrs: 11:30 am-2:30 pm, 5:30-9:30 pm; Sat 5-10:30 pm; Sun 11 am-2 pm (brunch), 5-9 pm. Closed some major hols. Res accepted; required Fri, Sat dinner. Bar. Semi-a la carte: lunch $4-$12, dinner $14-$24. Sun brunch $7-$11. Specialties: rack of lamb in pommery mustard crust, steak au poivre, pan-roasted Chilean sea bass with port wine paprika sauce. Casual American bistro decor. Cr cds: A, C, D, DS, MC, V.

✔ ★ ★ **RUSTY SCUPPER.** *378 Alexander Rd. 609/921-3276.* Hrs: 11:30 am-2:30 pm, 5-10 pm; Fri, Sat to 11 pm; Sun 1-9 pm. Closed Dec 25. Res accepted. Bar 11:30-1 am; Sat, Sun from 1:30 pm. Semi-a la carte: lunch $6.25-$16.95, dinner $16.95-$26.95. Child's meals. Specializes in seafood, prime rib, steak. Salad bar. Outdoor dining. Cr cds: A, DS, MC, V.

Ramsey (B-5)

Pop 13,228 **Elev** 373 ft **Area code** 201 **Zip** 07446

What to See and Do

Campgaw Mountain Ski Area. Two double chairlifts, T-bar; patrol, school, rentals; snowmaking; cafeteria. Eight runs, longest run 1,760 ft; vertical drop 275 ft. (Early Dec-mid-Mar, daily) Lighted cross-country trails; half-pipe; cross-country and snowboard rentals. NJ 17 N, exit NJ 202 Suffern, 1.6 mi S on NJ 202, left on Darlington Ave 1 blk, stay to right, 1 mi on Campgaw Rd in Mahwah. Phone 201/327-7800. ¢¢¢¢

Darlington Swim Area. Two lakes provide swimming (fee); fishing (in 1 lake). Tennis, handball; shuffleboard, horseshoes. Picnicking (pavilion), playground. Park (Apr-Nov). 600 Darlington Ave in Mahwah; follow signs on NJ 17 or 208 N. For opening swim date phone 201/646-2680 or 201/327-3500. Park admission during swim season ¢¢¢

James A McFaul Environmental Center. An 81-acre wildlife sanctuary including museum with natural history displays, lectures, film programs (Tues, Sat & Sun afternoons); woodland trail; waterfowl pond; picnic area. Arboretum and perennial gardens. (Daily; closed morning wkends & major hols) 3 mi NW off NJ 208 on Crescent Ave in Wyckoff. Phone 201/891-5571. **Free.**

Motel

★ ★ **WELLESLEY INN.** *946 NJ 17 N. 201/934-9250; res: 800/444-8888.* 89 rms, 3 story. S $64-$85; D $69-$94; each addl $5; under 18 free; wkend, wkly rates; higher rates: Pathmark tennis tournament, West Point graduation. Crib free. Pet accepted, some restrictions; $3. TV; cable (premium). Complimentary continental bkfst. Complimentary coffee in rms. Restaurant adj open 24 hrs. Ck-out 11 am. Business servs avail. Health club privileges. Refrigerators, microwaves avail. Cr cds: A, C, D, DS, JCB, MC, V.

Motor Hotel

✔ ★ ★ **RAMADA INN MAHWAH.** *(180 NJ 17S, Mahwah 07430) S of US 202 on NJ 17. 201/529-5880; FAX 201/529-4767.* 128 rms, 4 story. S, D $84-$111; each addl $10; suites $99-$150; under 18 free. Crib free. TV; cable (premium). Indoor pool. Restaurant 6:30 am-11 pm. Rm serv. Bar. Ck-out noon. Coin lndry. Meeting rms. Business servs avail. In-rm modem link. Valet serv. Sundries. Exercise equipt; weight machine, bicycle. Microwaves avail. Cr cds: A, C, D, DS, JCB, MC, V.

Hotel

★ ★ ★ **SHERATON CROSSROADS.** *(Crossroads Corporate Center, Mahwah 07495) jct I-87, I-287, NJ 17. 201/529-1660; FAX 201/529-4709.* 225 units, 14-22 story. S $139-$159; D $149-$169; each addl $10; suites $260-$750; under 18 free; wkend rates. Crib free. Pet accepted, some restrictions. TV; cable (premium). Indoor pool. Restaurant 6:30 am-11 pm. Bar noon-2 am; entertainment exc Sun. Ck-out noon. Convention facilities. Business center. Concierge. Shopping arcade. Covered parking. Tennis. Exercise equipt; weights, bicycles, sauna. Refrigerators, microwaves avail. Luxury level. Cr cds: A, C, D, DS, ER, JCB, MC, V.

Red Bank (E-5)

Pop 10,636 **Elev** 35 ft **Area code** 732 **Zip** 07701

Red Bank, an historic community on the shores of the Navesink River, includes a central business area with shops, restaurants, brokerage firms and an antique center.

What to See and Do

Allen House (ca 1750). Lower floor restored as tavern of the Revolutionary period; two upstairs galleries have historical exhibits. (Days same as Holmes House) 2 mi S on NJ 35, at jct Sycamore Ave in Shrewsbury. Phone 732/462-1466. ¢

Holmes-Hendrickson House (ca 1750). A 14-rm Dutch Colonial farmhouse with period furnishings. (May-Oct, Tues, Thurs, Sat & Sun afternoons; closed hols) Longstreet Rd in Holmdel, W on NJ 520. Phone 732/462-1466. ¢

Monmouth Museum. Changing exhibits of art, science, nature and cultural history; children's hands-on wing. (Daily exc Mon; closed hols) 5 mi W on Newman Springs Rd; on campus of Brookdale Community College in Lincroft. Phone 732/747-2266. ¢¢

Motel

★ ★ **COURTYARD BY MARRIOTT.** *245 Half Mile Rd, off Garden State Pkwy exit 109.* 732/530-5552; FAX 732/530-5756. 146 rms, 3 story. S $99-$105; D $105-$119; wkend rates. Crib free. TV; cable (premium). Indoor pool; whirlpool. Complimentary coffee in rms. Restaurant 6:30-10:30 am, 6-10 pm. Bar 6-11 pm. Ck-out noon. Coin lndry. Meeting rms. Business servs avail. In-rm modem link. Valet serv. Exercise equipt; weight machines, bicycles. Some refrigerators; microwaves avail. Balconies. Cr cds: A, C, D, DS, MC, V.

[D] [≈] [✗] [⊠] [🔥] [SC]

Restaurants

★ ★ ★ **FROMAGERIE.** *(26 Ridge Rd, Rumson 07760) 7 mi E of Garden State Pkwy exit 109, east on Newman Springs Rd, turn left on Board St, turn right on Harding Rd, 4¹/₂ mi on left.* 732/842-8088. Hrs: 11:30 am-2:30 pm, 5-10 pm; Fri to 11 pm; Sat 5-11 pm; Sun from 4 pm. Closed Dec 25. Res accepted. French menu. Bar. Extensive wine cellar. Semi-a la carte: lunch $9.95-$13.95, dinner $19.50-$29.50. Specialties: smoked duck with baked lentils, grilled swordfish with roasted red pepper coulis, rack of lamb. Own baking. Valet parking. Family-owned. Jacket. Cr cds: A, C, D, MC, V.

★ ★ **MOLLY PITCHER INN.** *88 Riverside Ave, in Molly Pitcher Inn.* 732/747-2500. Web www.redbank.com-mollypitcher. Hrs: 7-10 am, 11:30 am-3 pm, 5-9 pm; Sat 8-10 am, 11:30 am-3 pm, 5-10 pm; Sun 8-10 am, 11:30 am-2:30 pm (brunch), 5-9 pm. Res accepted. Bar 11-2 am. Wine list. A la carte entrees: bkfst $2.95-$12.95, lunch $4.95-$12.95. Semi-a la carte: dinner $6-$30. Sun brunch $23.95. Child's meals. Specialties: Molly Pitcher chicken pot pie, crab cakes, coriander tuna. Pianist Fri-Sun. Elegant European decor with panoramic views of Navesink River. Jacket (dinner). Cr cds: A, D, MC, V.

[D]

★ ★ ★ **SHADOWBROOK.** *Shrewsbury, just off NJ 35, 2 mi SE of Garden State Pkwy exit 109.* 732/747-0200. Web www.shadowbrook.com. Hrs: 5:30-9 pm; Sat to 10 pm; Sun 3-9 pm. Closed Mon; Dec 24. Res accepted. Bar. Semi-a la carte: dinner $19.95-$29.95. Child's meals. Specialties: shellfish Fra Diavolo, rack of lamb, veal Francaise. Valet parking. Fireplace; in Georgian mansion; Victorian antiques. Formal gardens. Family-owned. Jacket. Cr cds: A, D, MC, V.

[D]

Ringwood State Park (B-5)

(For accommodations see Wayne)

(On the New Jersey, New York border)

Ringwood State Park lies in upper Passaic County, near the town of Ringwood, within the heart of the Ramapo Mountains. Consisting of 6,196 acres, the park is reached by Rte 23 and 511 from the west and Rte 17 and Sloatsburg Rd from the east.

Ringwood Manor Section. This section features a 51-room mansion containing a collection of Americana; relics of iron-making days (1740); formal gardens. Interpretive tours. Fishing in Ringwood River. Picnic facilities nearby. Tours (Wed-Sun).

Shepherd Lake Section. A 541-acre wooded area has trap and skeet shooting all year (fee). The 74-acre Shepherd Lake provides a swimming beach and bathhouse; fishing; boating (ramp). Also available is picnicking (tables & grills).

Skylands Section. Located here is a 44-room mansion modeled after an English baronial house (open to the public on select days). The gardens (90 acres) surrounding the manor house comprise the only botanical garden in the state park system (guided tours upon request, phone 973/962-7527). This 1,119-acre section also offers fishing, hunting. Hiking; mountain biking.

Standard fees are charged for each section Memorial Day-Labor Day. Phone 973/962-7031.

Rockaway (B-4)

Pop 6,243 **Elev** 534 ft **Area code** 973 **Zip** 07866

Motels

★ ★ **HOWARD JOHNSON.** *14 Green Pond Rd, I-80 exit 37, left.* 973/625-1200; FAX 973/625-1686. Web www.hojo.com. 64 rms, 2 story. June-Sept: S, D $79-$99; each addl $10; lower rates rest of yr. Crib free. TV; cable (premium). Pool; wading pool. Complimentary continental bkfst (Mon-Fri). Restaurant 6:30-2 am. Rm serv. Bar. Ck-out noon. Business servs avail. Downhill ski 12 mi. Some refrigerators; microwaves avail. Balconies. Cr cds: A, C, D, DS, ER, MC, V.

[D] [✗] [≈] [⊠] [🔥] [SC]

★ ★ **THE MOUNTAIN INN.** *156 NJ 46E, approx 3 mi off I-80 exit 42W.* 973/627-8310; FAX 973/627-0556; res: 800/537-3732. 86 rms, 2 story, 16 kits. (no ovens). S, D $44.50-$64.50; each addl $5; kit. units $69.50-$70; under 12 free; wkend rates. Crib free. TV; cable (premium). Pool; lifeguard. Complimentary continental bkfst. Restaurant 5-11 pm. Bar. Ck-out 11 am. Coin lndry. Meeting rms. Business servs avail. Valet serv. Microwaves avail. Cr cds: A, C, D, DS, MC, V.

[D] [≈] [⊠] [🔥] [SC]

Rutherford (C-5)

Pop 17,790 **Elev** 100 ft **Area code** 201

What to See and Do

Fairleigh Dickinson University-Rutherford Campus (1942). (2,300 students) On campus is the Kingsland House (1670), in which George Washington stayed in August 1783; and the Castle, an 1888 copy of Chateau d'Amboise in France. W Passaic & Montross Aves. Phone 201/692-7032.

Professional sports.

NBA (New Jersey Nets). Continental Airlines Arena, 50 NJ 120 in East Rutherford. Phone 201/935-8888.

NHL (New Jersey Devils). Continental Airlines Arena, 50 NJ 120 in East Rutherford. Phone 201/935-6050.

Motel

★ ★ **QUALITY INN SPORTS COMPLEX.** (10 Polito Ave, Lyndhurst 07071) Jct NJ 3 & NJ 17, Lyndhurst Serv Rd exit off NJ 17S. 201/933-9800; FAX 201/933-0658; res: 800/468-3588. 150 rms, 2 story. S $59-$85; D $65-$90; each addl $6; under 18 free; wkend rates. Crib free. TV; cable (premium), VCR (movies). Pool; lifeguard. Restaurant 6:30 am-10 pm. Rm serv. Bar 11-2 am. Ck-out noon. Coin lndry. Meeting rms. Business servs avail. In-rm modem links. Sundries. Airport transportation. Health club privileges. Microwaves avail. Stadium, racetrack opp. Cr cds: A, C, D, DS, ER, JCB, MC, V.

D ≈ ⤓ 🔥 SC

Motor Hotel

★ **FAIRFIELD INN BY MARRIOTT.** (850 NJ 120, East Rutherford 07073) On NJ 120, 1/4 mi E of NJ 17. 201/507-5222; FAX 201/507-0744. Web www.marriott.com/fairfieldinn. 140 rms, 5 story. S, D $89-$110; under 12 free; Crib avail. TV; cable (premium). Ck-out noon. Meeting rm. Business servs avail. In-rm modem link. Exercise equipt; bicycles, treadmill. Microwaves avail. Cr cds: A, C, D, DS, ER, MC, V.

D 🏋 ⤓ 🔥 SC

Hotels

★ ★ **NOVOTEL.** (1 Polito Ave, Lyndhurst 07071) NJ 17 S. 201/896-6666; res: 800/668-6735. E-mail meadmail@aol.com. 219 rms, 5 story. S $139; D $149; each addl $10; under 16 free; family, wkend, hol rates. Crib free. Pet accepted, some restrictions. TV; cable (premium), VCR avail (movies). Complimentary coffee in lobby. Restaurant 6:30 am-midnight. Bar 5 pm-1 am; entertainment Tues-Thurs. Ck-out 1 pm. Meeting rms. Business center. In-rm modem link. Coin lndry. Exercise equipt; weight machine, bicycle, sauna. Massage. Health club privileges. Indoor pool; whirlpool. Refrigerators, microwaves avail. Cr cds: A, C, D, DS, ER, JCB, MC, V.

🐾 ≈ 🏋 ⤓ 🔥 SC ⛷

★ ★ **SHERATON MEADOWLANDS.** (2 Meadowlands Plaza, East Rutherford 07073) 1/4 mi E of NJ Tpke exit 16W, opp Meadowlands Sports Complex. 201/896-0500; FAX 201/896-9696. 425 units, 21 story. S, D $130-$160; each addl $20; suites $230-$550; under 18 free; wkend rates. Crib free. Pet accepted, some restrictions. TV; cable (premium), VCR avail. Indoor pool; whirlpool, poolside serv. Restaurant 6:30 am-11 pm. Bars noon-2 am. Ck-out 1 pm. Convention facilities. Business center. In-rm modem link. Concierge. Gift shop. Exercise equipt; weights, bicycles, sauna. Bathrm phone, wet bar in suites. Cr cds: A, C, D, DS, ER, JCB, MC, V.

D 🐾 ≈ 🏋 ⤓ 🔥 SC ⛷

Restaurants

★ ★ **ROMANISSIMO.** (1 Hoboken Rd, East Rutherford) NJ 17S exit Paterson Plank Rd, follow signs. 201/939-1128. Hrs: 11:30 am-11 pm; Sat 5 pm-midnight; Sun 2-10 pm. Res accepted. Country Italian menu. Bar. A la carte entrees: lunch $10.95-$14.95, dinner $12.95-$20. Specializes in rabbit, seafood. Singer Fri, Sat. Valet parking. Glass enclosed patio. Contemporary decor. Cr cds: A, C, D, MC, V.

★ ★ ★ **SONOMA GRILL.** (64 Hoboken Rd, East Rutherford 07073) 201/507-8989. Hrs: 11:30 am-2:30 pm, 5-10 pm; Fri to 2:30 pm; Sat 5-11 pm; Sun 4-8:30 pm. Closed some major hols; Mon fall & winter, Sun spring & summer. Res accepted. Bar. Wine cellar. A la carte entrees:

lunch $7.95-$15.95, dinner $8.95-$29.95. Child's meals. Specialties: grilled fresh tuna with black olives, grilled marinated pork chop on Chinese noodles, grilled certified Angus T-bone. Jazz Fri evening. Two distinct dining areas: one casual California grill-style, one antique with stained glass and tin ceiling. Cr cds: A, C, D, MC, V.

D

Saddle Brook (B-5)

Pop 13,296 **Elev** 90 ft **Area code** 201 **Zip** 07663

Motor Hotel

★ ★ **RAMADA HOTEL.** (375 W Passaic St, Rochelle Park 07662) At Garden State Pkwy exit 160N. 201/845-3400; FAX 201/845-0412. 174 rms, 5 story. S $95-$107; D $95-$114; each addl $10; suites $150; wkend rates. Crib free. TV; cable. Indoor pool. Restaurant 6:30 am-11 pm; wkends from 7 am. Rm serv. Bar 11-2 am; entertainment Thurs-Sat. Ck-out noon. Coin lndry. Meeting rms. Business servs avail. Valet serv. Sundries. Exercise equipt; weight machine, bicycles. Cr cds: A, C, D, DS, ER, JCB, MC, V.

D ≈ 🏋 ⤓ 🔥 SC

Hotels

★ ★ **HOLIDAY INN.** 50 Kenney Place, at jct Garden State Pkwy exit 159, I-80 exit 62. 201/843-0600; FAX 201/843-2822. 144 rms, 12 story. S, D $98-$150; each addl $10; under 18 free; wkend rates. Crib free. TV; cable (premium). Pool. Coffee in rms. Restaurant 6:30 am-10 pm, wkends from 7 am. Bar 11 am-midnight. Ck-out noon. Meeting rms. Business servs avail. In-rm modem link. Exercise equipt; weight machines, bicycles. Cr cds: A, C, D, DS, JCB, MC, V.

D ≈ 🏋 ⤓ 🔥 SC

★ ★ ★ **MARRIOTT.** Garden State Parkway at I-80, Garden State Pkwy exit 159. 201/843-9500; FAX 201/843-7760. 221 rms, 12 story. S, D $130; suites $300-$450; wkend rates. Crib free. TV; cable (premium). 2 pools, 1 indoor; whirlpool, poolside serv, lifeguard. Restaurant 6:30 am-10 pm; Fri, Sat to 11 pm; Sun 7 am-10 pm. Bar 11:30-1 am. Ck-out noon. Meeting rms. Business center. Free parking. Exercise equipt; weights, bicycles, sauna. Refrigerators avail. Cr cds: A, C, D, DS, ER, JCB, MC, V.

D ≈ 🏋 ⤓ 🔥 SC ⛷

Salem (H-1)

(See also Wilmington, DE)

Founded ca 1675 **Pop** 6,883 **Elev** 19 ft **Area code** 609 **Zip** 08079
Information Salem County Chamber of Commerce, 104 Market St; 609/935-1415.

Salem is said to be the oldest English settlement on the Delaware River. The town and its surrounding area have more than sixty 18th-century houses and buildings, as well as many points of historical interest. In the Friends Burying Ground on Broadway is the 600-year-old Salem Oak, under which John Fenwick, the town's founder, signed a treaty with the Lenni-Lenape tribe.

What to See and Do

Alexander Grant House (1721). Headquarters of Salem County Historical Society. Twenty rooms with period furniture; Wistarburg glass; Native American relics; dolls; paintings; genealogy library; stone barn. (Tues-Fri afternoons; also open 2nd Sat afternoon of each month) 79-83 Market St. Phone 609/935-5004. ¢¢

Fort Mott State Park. A 104-acre park at Finns Point; established in 1837 as a defense of the port of Philadelphia. North of the park is Finns Point National Cemetery, where more than 2,500 Union and Confederate soldiers are buried. Fishing; boating. Picnicking, playground; overlook. Ft Mott Rd. Phone 609/935-3218.

Seasonal Event

Cowtown Rodeo. 12 mi NE on NJ 45, then 3 mi W on US 40, near Woodstown. PRCA sanctioned. Phone 609/769-3200. Sat evenings, late May-mid-Sept.

Inn

✔★ **BROWN'S HISTORIC HOME.** *41-43 Market St. 609/935-8595.* 6 rms, 3 with bath, 2 story. S $65, D $85; kit. unit $200/wk. Adults only. TV; cable (premium). Complimentary full bkfst. Restaurant nearby. Ck-out noon, ck-in 2 pm. Business servs avail. Refrigerators. Pre-revolutionary house (pre-1738) in historic district. Totally nonsmoking. Cr cds: A, DS, MC, V.

⊠ ⟋

Sandy Hook

(see Gateway National Recreation Area)

Scotch Plains (C-4)

(See also Plainfield)

Settled 1684 **Pop** 21,160 **Elev** 119 ft **Area code** 908 **Zip** 07076

What to See and Do

Scotch Plains Zoo. Zoo includes lions, tigers, giraffes and hippos. Pony rides. (Daily) 1451 Raritan Rd. Phone 908/322-7180. ¢¢¢

Watchung Reservation. A 2,000-wooded-acre reservation in the Watchung Mts including the 25-acre Surprise Lake. Nature trails, bridle trails. Ice-skating. Picnic areas, playground. Ten-acre nursery and rhododendron display garden. 1 mi NE. Phone 908/527-4900. Also here is

Trailside Nature and Science Center. Nature exhibits; special programs; planetarium shows (Sun; separate show for preschoolers; fee). Museum (late Mar-mid-Nov, daily; rest of yr, wkends only; closed some hols). Visitor Center with live reptile exhibit (daily, afternoons). Gift shop. Grounds (daily). 452 New Providence Rd in Mountainside. Phone 908/789-3670. **Free.**

Motel

★★ **BEST WESTERN WESTFIELD INN.** *(435 North Ave W, Westfield 07090)* 3½ mi W on NJ 28; W of Garden State Pkwy exit 137. *908/654-5600; FAX 908/654-6483.* 40 rms, 3 story, 14 kits. S $93-$115, D $103-$125; each addl $10; kit. units $115-$125; under 13 free. Crib free. TV; cable (premium), VCR avail. Complimentary continental bkfst. Restaurant noon-10 pm. Ck-out 11 am. Coin lndry. Meeting rm. Business servs avail. Valet serv. Health club privileges. Microwaves avail. Cr cds: A, C, D, DS, ER, MC, V.

⊠ ⟋ **SC**

Restaurant

★★★ **STAGE HOUSE INN.** *366 Park Ave. 908/322-4224.* Web www.powerpg.com/njl/stagehouse. Hrs: 11:30 am-2:30 pm, 5:30-10 pm; Sun 4-8 pm. Closed Mon; Dec 25. Bar. A la carte entrees: lunch $8-$17, dinner $21-$29. Specialties: charlotte of Maine crab, pan roasted cod with crispy potatoes, peas & black truffle sauce. Outdoor dining. Operated as an inn since 1737; in historic village. Cr cds: A, D, DS, MC, V.

D

Seaside Park (F-5)

Pop 1,871 **Elev** 6 ft **Area code** 908 **Zip** 08752

What to See and Do

Island Beach State Park. This strip of land (3,002 acres) is across the water, N of Long Beach Island (see) and faces Barnegat Lighthouse. There are two natural areas (Northern Area and Southern Area) and a recreational zone in the center. Excellent swimming and fishing in Atlantic Ocean (seasonal). Nature tours. Picnicking. (Daily) Standard fees. S on Central Ave. Phone 908/793-0506.

Motels

★ **ISLAND BEACH MOTOR LODGE.** *24th & Central Aves. 908/793-5400.* 72 rms, 3 story, 35 kits. Late June-Labor Day: S, D $85-$165; each addl $5; kit. units $745-$1,115/wk; lower rates rest of yr. Crib $5. TV; cable. Heated pool; wading pool, lifeguard. Restaurant nearby. Ck-out 11 am. Coin lndry. Refrigerators. Balconies. On private beach. Cr cds: DS, MC, V.

⟋ ⊠ ⟋

★★ **WINDJAMMER.** *1st and Central Ave. 908/830-2555.* 63 rms, 3 story, 24 kits. June-Sept: S, D $90-$120; each addl $10; kit. units $115; lower rates rest of yr. Crib $5. TV; cable. Heated pool; poolside serv. Restaurant 8 am-7 pm. Bar from 11 am. Ck-out 11 am. Coin lndry. Beach privileges. Cr cds: A, MC, V.

⊠ ⟋

Secaucus (C-5)

Pop 14,061 **Elev** 12 ft **Area code** 201

Motor Hotel

★★ **HOLIDAY INN.** *300 Plaza Dr (07094). 201/348-2000; FAX 201/348-6035.* 160 rms, 8 story. S, D $115-$160; each addl $10; suites $175-$200; under 18 free; wkend, monthly rates. Crib free. TV; cable (premium). Valet parking $2. Restaurant 7 am-11 pm. Rm serv. Bar. Ck-out noon. Coin lndry. Meeting rms. In-rm modem link. Bellhops. Gift shop. Exercise equipt; weights, bicycles. Refrigerators. Health club privileges. Luxury level. Cr cds: A, C, D, DS, JCB, MC, V.

D ⟓ ⊠ ⟋ **SC**

Hotels

★★★ **EMBASSY SUITES.** *455 Plaza Dr (07094). 201/864-7300; FAX 201/864-5391.* Web www.promus.comm. 261 suites, 9 story. S, D $170-$200; each addl $20; under 12 free; wkend rates. Crib free. TV; cable (premium), VCR avail. Indoor pool; whirlpool. Complimentary full bkfst. Restaurant 11:30 am-10 pm. Bar noon-midnight. Ck-out noon. Coin lndry.

Meeting rms. Business center. In-rm modem link. Gift shop. Airport transportation. Exercise equipt; bicycles, stair machines, sauna. Health club privileges. Refrigerators, microwaves. Cr cds: A, C, D, DS, JCB, MC, V.

★ ★ **HILTON-MEADOWLANDS.** 2 Harmon Plaza (07094), NJ Tpke exit 16W, Meadowlands Pkwy. 201/348-6900; FAX 201/864-0963. Web www.hilton.com. 296 rms, 14 story. S, D $89-$159; each addl $10; suites $160-$350; family, wkend rates. Crib free. TV; cable (premium). Pool; whirlpool, poolside serv. Restaurant 6:30 am-11 pm; Sat, Sun from 7 am. Bars 11-2 am. Ck-out 11 am. Convention facilities. Business servs avail. In-rm modem link. Concierge. Gift shop. Valet parking avail. Exercise equipt; weight machine, bicycles, sauna. Some refrigerators; microwaves avail. Cr cds: A, C, D, DS, ER, JCB, MC, V.

★ ★ **RADISSON SUITE.** 350 NJ 3 W (07094). 201/863-8700; FAX 201/863-6209. 151 suites, 9 story. S $179-$239; D $189-$249; each addl $20; under 12 free; wkend, wkly rates; higher rates hockey and football season. Crib avail. Pet accepted, some restrictions. TV; cable (premium), VCR avail. Complimentary coffee in rms. Restaurant 7 am-10 pm. Bar noon-midnight. Ck-out noon. Meeting rms. Business servs avail. In-rm modem link. Coin lndry. Airport, RR station transportation. Exercise equipt; weights, treadmill. Indoor pool. Refrigerators, wet bars; microwaves avail. Cr cds: A, C, D, DS, JCB, MC, V.

★ ★ ★ **RAMADA.** (500 Harbor Blvd, Weehawken 07087) 201/617-5600; FAX 201/617-5627. 244 suites, 10 story. Mar-Dec: S $189-$229; D $209-$249; each addl $20; under 18 free; family, wkly, wkend, hol rates; lower rates rest of yr. Crib free. Pet accepted. TV; cable (premium), VCR avail. Complimentary continental bkfst. Complimentary coffee in rms. Restaurant 11:30 am-10 pm. Rm serv from 7 am. Bar from noon. Ck-out noon. Meeting rms. Business center. In-rm modem link. Concierge. Gift shop. Exercise equipt; weights, bicycle. Indoor pool. Refrigerators, microwaves, wet bars. On river. Cr cds: A, C, D, DS, ER, JCB, MC, V.

Ship Bottom
(see Long Beach Island)

Somerset
(see New Brunswick)

Somerville (D-4)
(See also New Brunswick)

Pop 11,632 **Elev** 54 ft **Area code** 908 **Zip** 08876 **Web** www.somerset countychamber.org

Information Somerset County Chamber of Commerce, 64 W End Ave, PO Box 833; 908/725-1552.

What to See and Do

Duke Gardens. Features 11 gardens under glass, including colonial, desert, Italian, Oriental, English and tropical (closed Jan 1, Thanksgiving, Dec 25); 45-min guided tour (Oct-May, daily). No high heels, no cameras. On US 206, about 1¼ mi S of Somerville Circle. Res required; contact Duke Gardens Foundation (Mon-Fri), phone 908/722-3700. ¢¢-¢¢¢

Golf House—USGA Museum and Library. Georgian colonial mansion originally designed as private residence by John Russel Pope, now houses exhibits tracing the evolution of golf. Equipment and artifacts donated by golf's greatest champions, including Bobby Jones, Byron Nelson, Jack Nicklaus and Arnold Palmer. Interactive displays. Library with over 10,000 volumes on golf. USGA Research and Test Center, featuring the USGA's ball-testing robot "Iron Byron," is adj. (Daily; closed Jan 1, Easter, Thanksgiving, Dec 25) US 287 to Rte 512, in Far Hills. Phone 800/223-0041. **Free.**

Old Dutch Parsonage State Historic Site (1751). Moved from its original location, this brick building was the home of the Rev Jacob Hardenbergh from 1758 to 1781. He founded Queens College, now Rutgers University, while residing in this building. Some furnishings and memorabilia on display. (Wed-Sun; closed hols; hrs may vary; phone ahead) 65 Washington Pl. Phone 908/725-1015.

Wallace House State Historic Site. General and Mrs. Washington made their headquarters here immediately after the house was built in 1778, while the army was stationed at Camp Middlebrook. Period furnishings. (Wed-Sun; closed hols; hrs may vary, phone ahead) 38 Washington Pl. Phone 908/725-1015.

Annual Event

IBM/USET Festival of Champions. Hamilton Farm, 10 mi N on US 206 in Bedminster. Competition of 3 Olympic equestrian disciplines. Phone 908/234-1251. Mid- or late June.

Motel

★ **DAYS INN-HILLSBOROUGH.** (118 US 206, Hillsborough) 908/685-9000; FAX 908/685-0601. 100 rms, 2 story. S, D $74.95-$84.95; each addl $5; suites $100-$170; under 17 free. Crib free. TV; cable. Complimentary continental bkfst. Ck-out 11 am. In-rm modem link. Valet serv. Pool. Some refrigerators; microwaves avail. Cr cds: A, C, D, DS, MC, V.

Restaurants

★ **A LA PIETRA.** (1979 Washington Valley Rd, Martinsville 08836) 3 mi N on NJ 525. 732/469-9040. Hrs: 11 am-3 pm, 5-10 pm; Sat from 5 pm; Sun from 4 pm. Closed Jan 1, Thanksgiving, Dec 25. Res accepted Fri, Sat. Italian menu. Semi-a la carte: lunch $6-$18, dinner $10-$20. Child's meals. Specializes in pasta, veal, chicken. Outdoor dining. Trattoria atmosphere. Cr cds: A, MC, V.

★ ★ ★ **RYLAND INN.** (US 22W, Whitehouse 08888) 8 mi W on US 22. 908/534-4011. Web www.powerpg.com/njl1/ryland. Dine in one of five dining rooms of this 200-year-old Victorian manor house set on 55 sweeping acres complete with a six-acre vegetable garden. Contemporary French menu. Specialties: veal chop with asparagus and morels, warm lobster tarte, grilled foie gras with banyuls sauce. Hrs: 11:30 am-2 pm, 5:30-9 pm; Fri to 10 pm; Sat 5:30-10 pm; Sun 4-9 pm. Closed 1st wk in Jan. Res accepted. Bar. Wine cellar. A la carte entrees: lunch $10-$16, dinner $26-$34. Eight-course tasting menu: dinner $80. Child's meals. Valet parking. Jacket. Cr cds: A, D, DS, MC, V.

Spring Lake (E-5)
(See also Asbury Park)

Pop 3,499 **Elev** 25 ft **Area code** 732 **Zip** 07762

Motels

★ **BELMAR MOTOR LODGE.** (10th Ave & NJ 35, Belmar 07719) 1 mi N on NJ 35. 732/681-6600; FAX 732/681-6604; res: 800/848-

8382. 55 rms, 2 story. Memorial Day-Labor Day: S, D $90-$110; each addl $10; under 13 free; higher rates hols (3-day min); lower rates rest of yr. Crib $3. TV; cable (premium). Pool. Restaurant adj open 24 hrs. Ck-out 11 am. Coin lndry. Opp Belmar Marine Basin. Cr cds: A, D, MC, V.

≈ ⚓ ⚡ SC

★ **COMFORT INN.** 1909 NJ 35, Garden State Pkwy exit 98. 732/449-6146; FAX 732/449-6556. 70 rms, 2 story. Mid-June-Labor Day: S, D $125; each addl $10; suites from $150; lower rates rest of yr. Crib $5. TV; cable (premium). Pool; lifeguard. Complimentary continental bkfst. Meeting rm. Business servs avail. In-rm modem link. Exercise equipt; weights, bicycles. Refrigerator, microwave in suites. Cr cds: A, C, D, DS, ER, JCB, MC, V.

D ≈ 🏋 ⚓ ⚡ SC

★ **DOOLAN'S.** (700 NJ 71, Spring Lake Heights) 4 mi E of Garden State Pkwy exit 98. 732/449-3666; FAX 732/449-2601. 60 rms, 3 story. Memorial Day-Labor Day: S, D $80-$125; each addl $15; lower rates rest of yr. Crib $5. TV; cable (premium). Pool; lifeguard. Complimentary continental bkfst. Restaurant (summer) 8-10 am, noon-3 pm, 4:30-10 pm; closed for lunch Sat. Bar; entertainment Wed-Sun. Ck-out 11 am. Meeting rms. Cr cds: A, C, D, DS, MC, V.

D ≈ ⚡

★ **POINT BEACH.** (Ocean & Trenton Aves, Point Pleasant Beach 08742) Ocean Rd to NJ 35S (Main Ave), follow signs to beach. 732/892-5100. 24 rms, 2 story. July-Labor Day: S, D $124-$145; each addl $10; under 8 free; higher rates hols; lower rates rest of yr. Closed Oct-Apr. Crib $5. TV; cable. Pool; wading pool. Ck-out 11 am. Refrigerators; microwaves avail. Opp Atlantic Ocean. Cr cds: DS, MC, V.

D ≈ ⚡

★ **TRAVELODGE.** (1916 NJ 35, Wall 07719) 2 mi W on Rt 524, then N on NJ 35. 732/974-8400; FAX 732/974-8401. 52 rms, 2 with shower only. S $44-$104; D $54-$124; each addl $5-$10; under 16 free; higher rates some hol wkends. Crib free. TV; cable (premium). Pool. Complimentary continental bkfst. Complimentary coffee in rms. Ck-out 11 am. Business servs avail. Refrigerators. Cr cds: A, C, D, DS, MC, V.

D ≈ ⚓ ⚡ SC

Hotels

★★ **BREAKERS.** 1507 Ocean Ave. 732/449-7700; FAX 732/449-0161. Web wwwExit98.com/breakers.htm. 62 units. Mid-June-Labor Day (hol wkends 3-day min): S, D $150-$300; each addl $30; family, wkly rates; lower rates rest of yr. Crib free. TV; VCR avail. Pool; whirlpool, poolside serv, lifeguard. Restaurant 8 am-4 pm, 4:30-10 pm. Ck-out noon. Meeting rms. Business servs avail. Airport transportation. Refrigerators. Private beach. Restored Victorian ocean-front hotel. Cr cds: A, C, D, MC, V.

D ≈ ⚡

★★ **HEWITT WELLINGTON.** 200 Monmouth Ave. 732/974-1212; FAX 732/974-2338. 29 rms, 3 story, 17 suites. Late June-Labor Day: S, D $165-$270; each addl $40; suites $220-$270; wkly rates; higher rates: wkends (2-day min), hols (3-day min); lower rates rest of yr. Children over 12 yrs only. TV; cable. Heated pool. Complimentary continental bkfst. Coffee in rms. Restaurant 4:30-11 pm. Ck-out 11 am. Meeting rms. Business servs avail. In-rm modem link. Health club privileges. Refrigerators. Some balconies. On lake, 2 blks to ocean. Renovated Victorian hotel (1880). Cr cds: A, DS, MC, V.

≈ ⚡ SC

Inns

★★ **ASHLING COTTAGE.** 106 Sussex Ave. 732/449-3553; res: 888/274-5464; FAX 732/974-0831. E-mail ashling@longkeep.com; web www.bbbians.com/ashling/index.html. 10 rms, 5 with shower only, 2 share bath, 3 story. No rm phones. Mid-June-mid-Sept (2-day min): S $98-$169; D $103-$174; hols (3-night min); lower rates Apr-mid-June &

mid-Sept-Dec; closed rest of yr. TV in lobby, VCR avail (movies). Complimentary full bkfst. Restaurant nearby. Ck-out 11 am, ck-in 1 pm. Business servs avail. Concierge serv. Free RR station, bus depot transportation. Bicycles. Picnic tables. Victorian-style frame house (1877). Antiques. Totally nonsmoking. No cr cds accepted.

⚓ ⚡

★★★ **BAY HEAD GABLES.** (200 Main St, Bay Head 08742) S on NJ 35. 732/892-9844; FAX 732/295-2196. 11 rms, 3 story. June-Labor Day: S $110-$165; D $120-$175; wkly rates; higher rates wkends (2-3-day min); open wkends only Apr-June & Labor Day-Dec. Closed rest of yr. TV in sitting rm; cable. Complimentary full bkfst. Restaurant nearby. Ck-out 11 am, ck-in 1 pm. Designed by Stanford White in 1914. Totally nonsmoking. Cr cds: A, DS, MC, V.

⚓ ⚡

★★★ **CHATEAU.** 500 Warren Ave. 732/974-2000; FAX 732/974-0007. 38 rms, 2 story. Late June-Labor Day: S $109-$225; D $150-$165; each addl $15; suites $190-$225; lower rates rest of yr. TV; cable (premium), VCR (movies). Beach, pool privileges. Meeting rm. Business servs avail. Tennis privileges. Health club privileges. Bicycles. Refrigerators; some fireplaces; microwaves avail. Private patios. Renovated Victorian hotel (1888). Overlooks parks, lake. Cr cds: A, C, D, DS, MC, V.

🏃 ⚡ SC

★ **HOUSE BY THE SEA.** (406 Fifth Ave, Belmar 07749) N on NJ 71. 732/681-8386; res: 800/681-8386; FAX 732/681-1306. 5 rms, all share bath, 3 A/C, 3 story. No rm phones. Late May-mid-Sept: S, D $75-$85; wkly rates; hols (3-day min); lower rates early Jan-late May, mid-Sept-mid Dec. Closed rest of yr. TV in some rms; cable (premium). Complimentary continental bkfst. Ck-out 11 am, ck-in 2 pm. Luggage handling. Street parking. Lawn games. Picnic tables, grills. Built in 1884; wrap-around porch, garden, Victorian antiques. Totally nonsmoking. Cr cds: MC, V.

⚓ ⚡

★★ **INN AT THE SHORE.** (301 4th Ave, Belmar 07719) 1 mi N on NJ 35. 732/681-3762; FAX 732/280-1914. Web www.bbianj.com/innattheshore. 12 rms, 2 with shower only, 9 share baths. Memorial Day-Labor Day: S, D $55-$125; each addl $20; under 12 free; wkly rates; lower rates rest of yr. Crib free. Complimentary continental bkfst. Restaurant nearby. Ck-out noon, ck-in 2 pm. Luggage handling. Refrigerator, microwave avail. Victorian-style ambience in house built in 1888; many antiques. Cr cds: A, MC, V.

⚓ ⚡ SC

★★ **NORMANDY INN.** 21 Tuttle Ave, Garden State Pkwy exit 98. 732/449-7172; FAX 732/449-1070. Web www.bbianj.com/normandy. 19 rms, 3 story. June-Sept: S $95-$180; D $126-$310; each addl $20; lower rates rest of yr. Crib avail. TV avail; VCR avail. Complimentary full bkfst. Business servs avail. Bicycles. Some fireplaces. Porches. Garden. Built as private residence in 1888; 19th-century antiques. Cr cds: A, C, D, DS, MC, V.

⚓ ⚡

★★ **SANDPIPER.** 7 Atlantic Ave. 732/449-6060; res: 800/824-2779; FAX 732/449-8409. 15 rms, 8 with shower only, 4 story. Mid-June-early Sept: S, D $110-$220; each addl $25; wkend, wkly, hol rates; lower rates rest of yr. Children over 16 yrs only. TV; cable. Indoor pool. Complimentary continental bkfst; afternoon refreshments. Dining rm 11:30 am-2:30 pm, 5-9 pm. Ck-out noon, ck-in 2 pm. Business servs avail. Refrigerators. Opp beach. Victorian inn built 1888; casual atmosphere in elegant surroundings. Cr cds: A, DS, MC, V.

≈ ⚡

★★ **WHITE LILAC INN.** 414 Central Ave. 732/449-0211. Web www.bbianj.com/whit.lilac/. 10 rms, 2 share bath, 2½ story. No rm phones. S, D $99-$159; wkly rates; wkends (2-day min); hols (3-day min). Closed Jan. Children over 14 yrs only. TV in some rms; cable (premium), VCR avail (movies). Complimentary full bkfst. Ck-out 11 am, ck-in 2 pm. Luggage handling. Free RR station transportation. Some fireplaces. Southern accent; built in 1880. Cr cds: A, DS, MC, V.

Restaurants

✔ ★ **FAMILY TREE.** *(2420 NJ 35, Manasquan 08736) 3 mi S on NJ 71.* *732/528-5950.* Hrs: 11:30 am-11 pm. Continental menu. Bar to 2 am. Semi-a la carte: lunch $3-$7.95, dinner $11.95-$17.95. Child's meals. Specialties: coconut shrimp, chicken Elizabeth, tournedos Diane. Own pastries. Pianist Fri, Sat evenings. Casual, family atmosphere. Cr cds: A, C, D, DS, MC, V.

★ ★ **OLD MILL INN.** *(Old Mill Rd, Spring Lake Heights) Garden State Pkwy exit 98.* *732/449-1800.* Web www.powerpg.com/nji/oldmill. Hrs: 11:30 am-10 pm; Fri, Sat to 11 pm; Sun to 9 pm; early-bird dinner Sept-May, Mon-Fri 2:30-6 pm; Sun brunch 11 am-3 pm. Closed Mon; Dec 24. Res accepted. Bar. Semi-a la carte: lunch $10.95-$13.95, dinner $17.95-$35.95. Sun brunch $9.95-$19.95. Child's meals. Specializes in seafood, steak. Own baking. Entertainment Fri, Sat. Valet parking. Outdoor dining. Lakeside view. Cr cds: A, C, D, MC, V.

✔ ★ ★ **THE SANDPIPER.** *7 Atlantic Ave.* *732/449-4700.* Hrs: 11:30 am-2:30 pm, 5-11 pm; early-bird dinner to 6:30 pm; Sun brunch 11 am-2 pm. Res accepted. Continental menu. Setups. Semi-a la carte: lunch $6.50-$9.50, dinner $13-$18. Complete meal: lunch $6.50-$11.95, dinner $13.95-$21.95. Sun brunch $14.95. Child's meals. Specialties: grilled Atlantic salmon, veal and shrimp Milanese, stuffed filet mignon. Own baking. Romantic candlelit dining in Victorian setting. Cr cds: D, MC, V.

Stanhope (B-4)

(See also Lake Hopatcong, Rockaway)

Pop 3,393 **Elev** 882 ft **Area code** 973 **Zip** 07874

What to See and Do

Waterloo Village Restoration. Known as the Andover Forge during the Revolutionary War, it was once a busy town on the Morris Canal. The 18th-century buildings include Stagecoach Inn, houses and craft barns, gristmill, apothecary shop, general store. Music festival during summer (fee). (Mid-Apr-mid-Nov, Wed-Sun; closed Thanksgiving, Dec 25) I-80 exit 25; follow signs. Phone 973/347-0900. ¢¢¢

Inn

★ ★ **WOODEN DUCK.** *(140 Goodale Rd, Newton 07860) I-80 exit 25 to US 206 N, E on Goodale Rd.* *973/300-0395.* Web www.bbianj .com.woodenduck. 5 rms, 2 story, 1 guest house. S, D $100-$120; hols (2-day min). Children over 12 yrs only. TV; cable, VCR (movies). Complimentary full bkfst. Ck-out 11 am, ck-in 2 pm. Business servs avail. In-rm modem link. Luggage handling. Gift shop. Downhill ski 20 mi; x-country ski on site. Pool. Game rm. Rec rm. Lawn games. Picnic tables. On 17 acres. Totally nonsmoking. Cr cds: A, DS, MC, V.

Restaurant

★ ★ **THE BLACK FOREST INN.** *249 US 206N.* *973/347-3344.* Hrs: 11:30 am-2 pm, 5-10 pm; Sun 1-9 pm. Closed Tues; Jan 1, Dec 24, 25. Res accepted. German, continental menu. Bar. A la carte entrees:

lunch $8.75-$15.50, dinner $16.75-$22.50. Specializes in veal, seafood. Classic European elegance. Cr cds: A, D, MC, V.

Stone Harbor (K-3)

Pop 1,025 **Elev** 5 ft **Area code** 609 **Zip** 08247

Information Stone Harbor Chamber of Commerce, PO Box 422, phone 609/368-6101; or the Cape May County Chamber of Commerce, PO Box 74, Cape May Court House 08210, phone 609/465-7181.

What to See and Do

Wetlands Institute. Environmental center focusing on coastal ecology. Also includes observation tower; marsh trail; aquarium; films and guided walks (July & Aug, daily). Bookstore. (Mid-May-mid-Oct, daily; rest of yr, Tues-Sat; closed Easter, July 4, Thanksgiving; also 2 wks late Dec-early Jan) 3 mi E off Garden State Pkwy exit 10, on Stone Harbor Blvd. Phone 609/368-1211. ¢¢

Annual Events

Sail into Summer Boat Show. Pleasure boating, family entertainment, musicians, food. Phone 609/368-6101. 1st wknd May.

Wings 'n Water Festival. Arts and crafts, decoys; entertainment; seafood. Phone 609/368-1211. 3rd full wknd Sept.

Motels

★ ★ **DESERT SAND RESORT COMPLEX.** *(79th St & Dune Dr, Avalon 08202) off Garden State Pkwy exit 13.* *609/368-5133; FAX 609/368-1849; res: 800/458-6008.* 90 units, 3 story, 15 suites, 31 kits. July-Aug: S, D $110-135; each addl $10; suites $137-$150; kits. $150-$180; wkly rates; higher rates hols; lower rates mid-Apr-June, Sept-Oct. Closed rest of yr. Crib avail. TV; cable. 2 pools, 1 indoor; whirlpool, lifeguard. Restaurant 8:30 am-10 pm. Bar noon-midnight. Ck-out 11 am. Coin lndry. Meeting rms. Business servs avail. Exercise equipt; weight machine, bicycles. Refrigerators; microwaves avail. Ocean 1 blk. Cr cds: MC, V.

★ ★ ★ **GOLDEN INN.** *(7849 Dune Dr, Avalon 08202) off Garden State Pkwy exit 10.* *609/368-5155; FAX 609/368-6112.* E-mail berrire @thegoldeninn.com; web www.goldeninn.com. 160 rms, 3 story, 76 kits. June-Labor Day: S, D $169-$225; each addl $15; suites $245-$319; kit. units $194-$225; under 12 free; lower rates rest of yr. Crib avail. TV; cable (premium), VCR (movies). Heated pool; wading pool, poolside serv; lifeguard. Supervised child's activities (mid-June-late Sept). Restaurant 8 am-11 pm. Rm serv. Bar 11-2 am; entertainment wkends. Ck-out 11 am. Meeting rms. Business servs avail. In-rm modem link. Bellhops. Valet serv. Social dir. Tennis privileges. Golf privileges. Refrigerators. Balconies. Picnic tables. On beach. Cr cds: MC, V.

Restaurant

★ ★ **THE MIRAGE.** *(See Desert Sand Resort Complex Motel)* *609/368-1919.* Hrs: 8 am-1 pm, 5-9:30 pm. Closed most major hols; also Nov-Mar. Res accepted (dinner). Continental menu. Bar. A la carte entrees: bkfst $3.95-$8.95, lunch $4.95-$9.95, dinner $7.95-$25.95. Child's meals. Specialties: mixed grill, veal Bianca. Own pastries. Pianist Fri-Sun. Casual, contemporary decor. Cr cds: MC, V.

Toms River (F-5)

Pop 7,524 **Elev** 40 ft **Area code** 908

Information Toms River-Ocean County Chamber of Commerce, 1200 Hooper Ave, 08753; 908/349-0220.

What to See and Do

Cooper Environmental Center. A 500-acre facility with 3-mi bay front. Boat tours (summer; free). Ten miles of marked trails. Picnicking (grills), playground. Nature center. (Daily) 1170 Cattus Island Blvd, E on NJ 37 to Fischer Blvd, follow signs. Phone 908/270-6960. **Free.**

Motels

★ ★ **HOLIDAY INN.** 290 NJ 37E (08753). 908/244-4000. 123 rms, 4 story. Memorial Day-Labor Day: S, D $104-$114; each addl $10; higher rates wkends; lower rates rest of yr. Crib free. Pet accepted. TV; cable (premium). Indoor pool; whirlpool, sauna, poolside serv. Restaurant 6:30 am-10 pm. Rm serv. Bar 11-2 am; entertainment. Ck-out noon. Coin lndry. Valet serv. Meeting rms. Business servs avail. Game rm. Refrigerators. Cr cds: A, C, D, DS, JCB, MC, V.

D ⚓ ≈ ⊻ 🔥 SC

★ ★ **HOWARD JOHNSON.** 955 Hooper Ave (08753). 908/244-1000; FAX 908/505-3194. 96 rms, 2 story. S $75-$99, D $85-$120; each addl $6; under 18 free; higher rates some hols. Crib free. Pet accepted, some restrictions; $10. TV; cable, VCR avail (movies). Indoor/outdoor pool. Restaurant 11 am-9 pm. Bar. Ck-out noon. Meeting rms. Business servs avail. In-rm modem link. Cr cds: A, C, D, DS, MC, V.

D ⚓ ≈ ⊻ 🔥 SC

★ ★ **QUALITY INN.** 815 NJ 37W (08755), Garden State Pkwy exit 82A. 908/341-2400; FAX 908/341-6469. 100 rms, 2 story. Memorial Day-Labor Day: S, D $69-$129; each addl $10; suites $129-$179; under 18 free; lower rates rest of yr. Crib free. TV; cable, VCR avail (movies). Pool; poolside serv, lifeguard. Playground. Complimentary continental bkfst. Coffee in rms. Restaurant noon-8 pm. Rm serv. Bar; entertainment. Ck-out 11 am. Meeting rms. Business servs avail. In-rm modem link. Valet serv. Sundries. Airport transportation. Exercise equipt; weight machine, bicycles, sauna. Refrigerators avail. Cr cds: A, C, D, DS, JCB, MC, V.

D ≈ 🏋 ⊻ 🔥 SC

✔ ★ **RIVERWATCH INN.** 2 W Water St (08753). 908/341-6700; FAX 908/244-4415; res: 800/244-3631. 50 rms, 3 story. Mid-June-mid-Sept: S $59.95-$89.95; D $69.95-$89.95; each addl $5; under 16 free; lower rates rest of yr. Crib free. TV; cable. Restaurant 10-2 am. Rm serv. Bar. Ck-out 11 am. Business servs avail. Coin lndry. Some refrigerators. Cr cds: A, C, D, DS, MC, V.

⚓ ⊻ 🔥 SC

Motor Hotel

★ ★ **RAMADA HOTEL.** 2373 NJ 9 (08755), at jct NJ 70. 908/905-2626; FAX 908/905-8735. 127 rms, 3 story. Memorial Day-Labor Day: S, D $75-$125; each addl $10; under 12 free; lower rates rest of yr. Crib free. TV; cable (premium). Pool; whirlpool, lifeguard. Complimentary continental bkfst. Restaurant 7 am-10 pm. Rm serv. Bar. Ck-out noon. Coin lndry. Meeting rms. Business servs avail. In-rm modem link. Sundries. Tennis. Exercise equipt; weight machine, bicycles. Game rm. Refrigerators avail. Cr cds: A, C, D, DS, MC, V.

D ⚓ 🏋 ≈ ⊻ 🔥 SC

Restaurant

✔ ★ **THE TAVERN.** N Main St, 1 mi N on NJ 166, just N of NJ 37. 908/349-8778. Hrs: 11:30-1 am; Sun to midnight; early bird dinner 3-5 pm. Closed Dec 25. Bar. Complete meals: lunch $4.99-$9.99. A la carte: dinner $9.99-$17.99. Child's meals. Specializes in steak, seafood, selected Italian dishes. Cr cds: A, C, D, MC, V.

D ⊠

Trenton (E-3)

(See also Princeton)

Settled 1679 **Pop** 88,675 **Elev** 50 ft **Area code** 609

Information Mercer County Chamber of Commerce, 214 W State St, 08608-1002; 609/393-4143.

The capital of New Jersey since 1790, Trenton is one of the fastest-growing business and industrial areas in the country and a leading rubber-manufacturing center since colonial times. After crossing the Delaware on December 26, 1776, George Washington attacked the British-held town eight miles to the northwest.

What to See and Do

New Jersey State Museum. (Daily exc Mon). 205 W State St, adj Capitol. Phone 609/292-6464. Includes

Main Building. Fine art, cultural history, archaeology and natural science exhibits. (Daily exc Mon; closed state hols) **Free.**

Auditorium. Lectures; films; music; children's theater. Some fees. Phone 609/292-6308.

Planetarium. One of few Intermediate Space Transit planetaria (duplicates motions of space vehicles) in the world. Programs (wkends; July-Aug, daily exc Mon). Over 4 yrs only exc children's programs. Tickets one-half hr in advance. Phone 609/292-6333. ¢

Sesame Place. A family play park. 6 mi NW via NJ 29, then 8 mi SW on I-95 to Langhorne (see BRISTOL, PA).

The Old Barracks Museum. One of the finest examples of colonial barracks in the US. Built in 1758-1759, it housed British, Hessian and Continental troops during the Revolution. Museum contains restored soldiers' squad rm; antique furniture; ceramics; firearms; dioramas. Guides in period costumes. (Daily; closed most major hols & Dec 24) Barrack St, opp W Front St. Phone 609/396-1776. ¢

Trenton State College (1855). (6,150 students) A 250-acre wooded campus with 2 lakes. Tours of campus. 4 mi N on NJ 31. Phone 609/771-1855. On campus is the

College Art Gallery. (Feb-May & Sept-Dec, daily exc Sat; closed hols) Phone 609/771-2198. **Free.**

🟫 **Washington Crossing State Park.** (See WASHINGTON CROSSING STATE PARK, PA) This 841-acre park commemorates the famous crossing on Christmas night, 1776, by the Continental Army, under the command of General George Washington. Continental Lane, at the park, is the road over which Washington's army began its march to Trenton, December 25, 1776. Nature tours. Picnicking, playground. Visitor center and nature center (Wed-Sun); open-air summer theater (fee). Standard fees. (See ANNUAL EVENTS) 8 mi NW on NJ 29. Phone 609/737-0623. Also in park is

Ferry House State Historic Site. Building sheltered Washington and some of his men on Dec 25, 1776, after they had crossed the Delaware from the Pennsylvania side. It is believed that the strategy to be used for the attack on Trenton was discussed here. Restored as a living history colonial farmhouse; special programs throughout the yr. (Wed-Sun) Phone 609/737-2515.

William Trent House (1719). Trenton's oldest house is an example of Queen Anne architecture. It was the home of Chief Justice William Trent, for whom the city was named. Colonial garden; period furnishings. (Daily, limited hrs; closed major hols) 15 Market St. Phone 609/989-3027. ¢¢

Annual Events

Trenton Kennel Club Dog Show. Mercer County Central Park. Early May.

Heritage Days. 1st wkend June.

Reenactment of Crossing of the Delaware. Washington Crossing State Park. Departs PA side on the afternoon of Dec 25.

Motel

★ **HOWARD JOHNSON.** *(2995 Brunswick Pike, Lawrenceville 08648) 5 mi N on US 1.* 609/896-1100; FAX 609/895-1325. 104 rms, 2 story. S $62.50-$84.50; D $68.50-$84.50; each addl $10; under 18 free. Crib free. Pet accepted. TV; cable (premium). Pool. Complimentary continental bkfst. Restaurant open 24 hrs. Ck-out noon. Meeting rm. Business servs avail. In-rm modem link. Valet serv. Sundries. Private patios, balconies. Cr cds: A, C, D, DS, JCB, MC, V.

Restaurants

★ ★ **DIAMONDS.** *132 Kent (08611), in Chambersburg district.* 609/393-1000. Hrs: 11:30 am-2:30 pm, 4:30 pm-midnight; Sun from 5:30 pm. Closed major hols. Res accepted. Italian menu. Bar 11-2 am. Semi-a la carte: lunch $5.95-$10.95, dinner $12.95-$32.95. Specializes in seafood, steak, veal. Valet parking. Italian decor. Cr cds: A, C, D, DS, MC, V.

★ ★ **LA GONDOLA.** *762 Roebling Ave (08611).* 609/392-0600. Hrs: 11:30 am-3 pm, 4:30-10 pm; Fri to 11 pm; Sat 4:30-11 pm. Closed Sun; some major hols. Res accepted. Italian menu. Bar. Semi-a la carte: lunch $4.95-$14.95, dinner $12.95-$23.95. Child's meals. Specialties: saltimbocca alla Gondola, fettine di pollo al carciofetto. Five dining rms. Dining in wine cellar. Mediterranean decor. Cr cds: A, C, D, MC, V.

★ ★ **LARRY PERONI'S WATERFRONT.** *1140 River Rd, 7 mi NW on NJ 29, 1/2 mi N of Scudder's Falls Bridge, I-95, exit 1.* 609/882-0303. Hrs: 11:30 am-9 pm; Sat 4-11 pm. Closed Dec 25. Res accepted. Continental menu. Bar. Semi-a la carte: lunch $4.95-$8.95, dinner $9.95-$18.95. Specializes in veal, beef, seafood. Paneled dining rms, fireplaces. Spacious grounds. Cr cds: A, C, D, DS, MC, V.

★ ★ **MARSILO'S.** *541 Roebling Ave (08611), in Chambersburg district.* 609/695-1916. Hrs: 11:30 am-2 pm, 5-10 pm; Fri, Sat to 11 pm. Closed Sun; also most major hols. Res accepted. Italian menu. Bar. Semi-a la carte: lunch $5.95-$19.95, dinner $12.95-$26. Child's meals. Specializes in veal, chicken. Italian decor. Cr cds: A, MC, V.

Vernon (A-4)

Pop 1,696 **Elev** 564 ft **Area code** 201 **Zip** 07462
Information Vernon Township Municipal Bldg, 21 Church St; 201/764-4055.

What to See and Do

Action Park. Theme park includes 75 self-operative rides, shows and attractions. Action park has more than 40 water rides, including river rides and Tidal Wave Pool; also Grand Prix race cars, bungee jumping, miniature golf, children's park; food, picnic area. 3 daily shows, wkend festival series. (Mid-June-Labor Day, daily; late May-mid-June, Thurs-Sun) NJ 94. Phone 201/827-2000. ¢¢¢¢　Also here is

Vernon Valley/Great Gorge Ski Resort. Resort has 1 triple, 14 double chairlifts; 3 rope tows; school, rentals; 100% snowmaking; cafeterias, restaurants, bars, night club; nursery. 52 runs; vertical drop 1,040 ft. (Dec-Mar, daily) Night skiing. Health spa, country club (daily) NJ 94. Phone 201/827-3900 (ski conditions) or 201/827-2000 (general information & fees). ¢¢¢¢¢

Resort

★ ★ ★ **SEASONS.** *(PO Box 637, Rte 517, McAfee 07428) SW via NJ 94, at jct NJ 517.* 201/827-6000; FAX 201/827-3767; res: 800/835-2555. 560 rms, 8 story, 18 kit. units. S $100-$140; D $120-$160; each addl $10; suites, kit. units $130-$550; under 18 free. Crib $10. TV; cable. 2 pools, one indoor; wading pool, whirlpool, sauna, poolside serv, lifeguard. Playground. Supervised child's activities (Memorial Day-Labor Day, wkends). Dining rms. Box lunches. Snack bar. Picnics. Rm serv. Bar 11-2 am; entertainment wkends. Ck-out noon, ck-in 3 pm. Convention facilities. Bellhops. Concierge. Gift shop. Airport, bus depot transportation. Sports dir. Indoor and outdoor tennis, pro. 27-hole golf, greens fee $43-$63, pro, putting green, driving range. Swimming. Downhill ski 1 mi; rentals. Sleighing. Hiking. Lawn games. Social dir. Rec rm. Game rm. Health club privileges. Balconies. Scenic view of mountains and golf course. Dinner theater. Cr cds: A, C, D, DS, MC, V.

Wayne (B-5)

Pop 47,025 **Elev** 200 ft **Area code** 973 **Zip** 07470
Information Tri-County Chamber of Commerce, 2055 Hamburg Tpke; 973/831-7788.

Wayne is the home of William Paterson College of New Jersey (1855).

What to See and Do

Dey Mansion (ca 1740). Restoration of Washington's headquarters (1780); period furnishings. Guided tours. Picnic tables. (Wed-Sun; closed major hols) 199 Totowa Rd. Phone for hrs, 973/696-1776. ¢

Terhune Memorial Park (Sunnybank). Estate of the late Albert Payson Terhune, author of *Lad, a Dog* and many other books about his collies. Scenic garden; picnic area, playground. (Daily) 2 1/2 mi N on US 202N. Phone 973/694-1800. **Free.**

Van Riper-Hopper (Wayne) Museum (ca 1786). Dutch Colonial farmhouse with 18th- and 19th-century furnishings; local historical objects; herb garden; bird sanctuary. 533 Berdan Ave. Phone 973/694-7192 for schedule and fees. Also here is

Mead Van Duyne House. Restored Dutch farmhouse.

Motels

★ ★ **HOLIDAY INN.** *334 US 46E, on Service Rd, I-80 exit S Verona.* 973/256-7000; FAX 973/890-5406. 140 rms, 2 story. S, D $75-$87; under 18 free. Crib free. TV; cable (premium). Pool; poolside serv, lifeguard. Restaurant 6:30 am-11 pm. Rm serv. Bar 11-3 am; entertainment Tues-Sat. Ck-out noon. Meeting rms. Business center. In-rm modem link. Valet serv. Sundries. Health club privileges. Microwaves avail. Cr cds: A, C, D, DS, JCB, MC, V.

★ **HOWARD JOHNSON.** *1850 NJ 23 and Ratzer Rd.* 973/696-8050; FAX 973/696-0682. 149 rms, 2 story. S $63-$73; D $65-$75; each addl $10; under 16 free. Crib free. Pet accepted, some restrictions. TV; cable (premium). Pool. Complimentary full bkfst. Ck-out noon. Coin lndry. Meeting rms. Business servs avail. In-rm modem link. Valet serv. Health club privileges. Airport, RR station transportation. Some refrigerators; microwaves avail. Private patios, balconies. Cr cds: A, C, D, DS, JCB, MC, V.

Motor Hotels

★ ★ ★ **BEST WESTERN EXECUTIVE INN.** *(216 NJ 46E, Fairfield 07004)* NJ 23S, exit 53 to I-80W. 973/575-7700; FAX 973/575-4653. 170 rms, 4 story. S, D $83-$164; each addl $13; suites $112-$164; under 16 free; family, wkend, wkly, hol rates. Crib free. Pet accepted, some restrictions. TV; cable (premium), VCR avail (movies). Complimentary full bkfst. Complimentary coffee in rms. Restaurant 6 am-11 pm. Rm serv. Bar 11-1:30 am; entertainment Thurs-Sun. Ck-out noon. Meeting rms. Business center. In-rm modem link. Bellhops. Valet serv. Sundries. Coin lndry. Exercise equipt; bicycle, stair machine, sauna. Health club privileges. Indoor pool; whirlpool, poolside serv. Game rm. Rec rm. Refrigerators; some in-rm whirlpools; wet bar in suites; microwaves avail. Cr cds: A, C, D, MC, V.

★ ★ **HOLIDAY INN TOTOWA.** *(1 NJ 46W, Totowa 07512)* On US 46 just E of Union Blvd in Totowa. 973/785-9000; FAX 973/785-3031. 155 rms, 5 story. S, D $89-$109; each addl $6; under 18 free. Crib free. TV; cable (premium), VCR avail. Pool. Complimentary continental bkfst. Coffee in rms. Restaurant 7 am-11 pm. Rm serv. Ck-out noon. Meeting rms. Business servs avail. In-rm modem link. Bellhops. Valet serv. Sundries. Exercise equipt; weight machines, treadmills. Indoor parking. Movie theater. Cr cds: A, C, D, DS, MC, V.

★ ★ ★ **RADISSON FAIRFIELD.** *(690 NJ 46E, Fairfield 07004)* ¹/₂ mi W of jct NJ 23. 973/227-9200; FAX 973/227-4308. 204 rms, 5 story, 61 suites. S $150-$185; D $160-$195; each addl $10; suites $170-$375; under 18 free. Crib $10. TV; cable (premium), VCR avail. Indoor pool. Restaurant 6:30 am-10 pm. Rm serv. Bar 11-1:30 am; entertainment Fri, Sat. Ck-out noon. Meeting rms. Business center. Bellhops. Gift shop. Exercise equipt; bicycles, rower, sauna. Bathrm phones, in-rm whirlpools; some refrigerators; microwaves avail. Cr cds: A, C, D, DS, ER, JCB, MC, V.

West Orange (C-5)

(For accommodations see Newark, Newark Intl Airport Area)

Pop 39,103 **Elev** 368 ft **Area code** 973 **Zip** 07052
Information West Orange Chamber of Commerce, PO Box 83; 973/731-0360.

What to See and Do

Eagle Rock Reservation. A 644-ft elevation in the Orange Mts; visitors see a heavily populated area that stretches from the Passaic River Valley east to New York City. Hiking trails; restaurant. Picnicking. Bridle paths. (Daily) NW via Main St & Eagle Rock Ave. Phone 973/268-3500 or 973/731-3000.

Edison National Historic Site. Main St & Lakeside Ave. Phone 973/736-5050.

Edison Laboratory. Built by Edison in 1887, it was his laboratory for 44 years. During that time, he was granted more than half of his 1,093 patents (an all-time record). Here he perfected the phonograph, motion picture camera and electric storage battery. One-hr lab tour (no video cameras, strollers) includes the chemistry lab and library; demonstrations of early phonographs. Visitor center has exhibits; films (daily; closed Jan 1, Thanksgiving, Dec 25). Phone 973/736-5050. ¢

Turtle Back Zoo. This 16-acre park features animals in natural surroundings; sea lion pool; miniature train ride (1 mi). Picnicking, concessions. Gift

shop (hrs vary). (Daily; closed Jan 1, Thanksgiving, Dec 24, 25, 31; limited schedule Dec-Jan) 560 Northfield Ave, 3 mi W on I-280, exit 10, in South Mountain Reservation. Phone 973/731-5800. ¢¢¢ Adj is

South Mountain Arena. Indoor ice rink. Hockey games, special events. Phone 973/731-3828.

Restaurants

★ ★ ★ **HIGHLAWN PAVILION.** *Eagle Rock Reservation.* 973/731-3463. Web www.powerpg.com/njl/highlawn. Hrs: noon-3 pm, 5:30-10 pm; Fri to 11:30 pm; Sat 5-11:30 pm; Sun 5-10 pm. Closed Dec 24. Res accepted. Bar to midnight. A la carte entrees: lunch $8-$16.50, dinner $14.95-$28.75. Specializes in veal chop, steak, fresh seafood. Oyster bar. Pianist Thurs-Sat. Valet parking. Outdoor dining. Located in county park on top of mountain; view of NY skyline. Food preparation visible from dining rm. Jacket. Cr cds: A, C, D, DS, MC, V.

★ ★ ★ **THE MANOR.** *111 Prospect Ave, I-280 exit 8B.* 973/731-2360. E-mail information@the-manor.com; web www.the-manor.com. Hrs: noon-2:30 pm, 6-10 pm; Sat 6 pm-midnight; Sun to 8:30 pm. Closed Mon; Dec 24. Amer, continental menu. Bar to 2 am. Wine cellar. A la carte entrees: lunch $8.50-$14, dinner $23-$30. Lobster buffet Tues-Sat $36.95. Sun buffet $31.95. Wed lunch buffet $17.95. Specialties: rack of lamb, Dover sole, beef Wellington. Own baking. Pianist Tue-Sun; band, vocalist Fri, Sat. Jacket, tie. View of formal gardens. Cr cds: A, C, D, DS, MC, V.

Wildwood & Wildwood Crest (K-3)

(See also Cape May)

Pop Wildwood 4,484; Wildwood Crest 3,631 **Elev** 8 ft **Area code** 609 **Zip** 08260
Information Greater Wildwood Chamber of Commerce, PO Box 823; 609/729-4000.

Wildwood's busy boardwalk extends for approximately two miles along the five miles of protected sandy beach it shares with North Wildwood and Wildwood Crest, two neighboring resorts. The area offers swimming, waterskiing, ocean and bay fishing, boating, sailing, bicycling, golf, tennis and shuffleboard.

What to See and Do

Boat trips. Sightseeing and whale-watching cruises aboard *Big Flamingo.* (Apr-Nov, daily) Capt Sinn's Dock, 6006 Park Blvd in Wildwood Crest. For schedule, fees, phone 609/522-3934. Also aboard the *Big Blue Sightseer.* (June-Sept, daily) 4500 Park Blvd in Wildwood. Phone 609/522-2919

Motels

(Rates quoted may be for advance reservation only; holiday rates may be higher)

★ ★ **AQUA BEACH RESORT.** *(5501 Ocean Ave, Wildwood Crest)* On beach. 609/522-6507; FAX 609/522-8535; res: 800/247-4776. E-mail info@aquabeach.com; web www.aquabeach.com. 123 rms, 5 story, 113 kits. July-Aug (3-day min): S, D $108-$153; each addl $10 after 2; kits. $124-$241; under 18 free; wkly, wkend rates; lower rates Mar-June & Sept-Oct. Closed rest of yr. Crib avail. TV; cable. Heated pool; wading pool, whirlpool, lifeguard. Supervised child's activities (July-Aug). Restaurant 6 am-4 pm. Rm serv. Ck-out 11 am. Coin lndry. Meeting rms. Business servs avail. Game rm. Many microwaves. Balconies. Grills. Cr cds: DS, MC, V.

⊡ ⌁ 🔥

★ **AQUARIUS.** *(4712 Ocean Ave, Wildwood)* 609/729-0054; res: 800/982-1831. 28 rms, 4 story. S, D $99-$149; under 18 free; wkly, wkend rates; lower rates Apr-June & Sept-Oct. Closed rest of yr. Crib free. TV; cable (premium). Heated pool; wading pool. Complimentary coffee in lobby. Restaurant opp 7 am-11 pm. Ck-out 10 am. Coin lndry. Business servs avail. Refrigerators, microwaves. Balconies. Picnic tables. Opp beach. Cr cds: DS, MC, V.

⌁ 🔥 SC

★ ★ **ARMADA MOTOR INN.** *(6503 Ocean Ave, Wildwood Crest)* On beach. 609/729-3000; FAX 609/729-7472; res: 800/399-3001. 56 rms, 5 story, 40 kits. Mid-July-Aug: up to 4 persons $140-$161; each addl $10; kit. units up to 4 persons $158-$161; some lower rates rest of yr. Closed Oct-mid-Apr. Crib $5. TV; VCR avail (movies). Heated pool; wading pool, sauna. Restaurant nearby. Ck-out 11 am. Coin lndry. Meeting rms. Business servs avail. Sundries. Game rm. Refrigerators, microwaves. Balconies. Picnic tables, grill. Sun decks. Cr cds: A, DS, MC, V.

⊡ ⌁ 🔥

★ ★ **ASTRONAUT.** *(511 E Stockton Rd, Wildwood Crest)* on beach. 609/522-6981. 33 kit. units, 3 story. No elvtr. July-early Sept: up to 6 persons $133-$180; lower rates Apr-June, early Sept-mid-Oct. Closed rest of yr. Crib avail. TV. Pool; wading pool. Restaurant nearby. Ck-out 11 am. Coin lndry. Sundries. Shuffleboard. Refrigerators, microwaves. Sun decks. Picnic tables, grills. Cr cds: DS, MC, V.

⌁ 🔥

★ ★ **ATTACHE.** *(Heather Rd & Beach, Wildwood Crest)* On beach. 609/522-0241. 42 rms, 3 story, 26 kits. Mid-July-late Aug: up to 4 persons $130-$175; each addl $10; kit. units for 4 persons $130-$215; family rates; lower rates mid-Apr-mid-July, late Aug-mid-Oct. Closed rest of yr. Crib avail. TV; cable, VCR avail. Heated pool; wading pool. Restaurant nearby. Ck-out 11 am. Guest lndry. Business servs avail. Refrigerators, microwaves. Some balconies. Picnic tables, grills. Cr cds: A, MC, V.

⌁ 🔥

★ **BEACH COLONY.** *(500 E Stockton Ave, Wildwood Crest)* At Ocean Ave. 609/522-4037. 26 units, 2 story, 14 kits. Late June-Labor Day: S, D $85-$110; each addl $10; suites $128; kit. units $102; lower rates early May-late June, after Labor Day-mid-Oct. Closed rest of yr. Crib avail. TV; cable (premium); VCR (free movies). Pool; wading pool. Restaurant adj 7 am-8 pm. Ck-out 11 am. Coin lndry. Business servs avail. Rec rm. Refrigerators; microwaves avail. Picnic tables, grills. Cr cds: MC, V.

⌁ 🔥

★ ★ **CAPE COD INN.** *(6109 Atlantic Ave, Wildwood Crest)* 609/522-1177; FAX 609/729-2353. 50 units, 3 story, 27 kits. Mid-July-mid-Aug: S, D $105; each addl $10; kits. $120; family rates; higher rates wkends, hols (2-day min); lower rates May-June, mid-Aug-Sept. Closed rest of yr. TV; cable. Pool; wading pool. Restaurant nearby. Ck-out 11 am. Coin lndry. Meeting rm. Business servs avail. Sundries. Game rm. Miniature golf. Refrigerators, microwaves. Picnic tables. Cr cds: A, DS, MC, V.

⊡ ⌁ ▨ 🔥

✔★ ★ **CARIBBEAN.** *(5600 Ocean Ave, Wildwood Crest)* At Buttercup Rd. 609/522-8292; res: 800/457-7040. 30 rms, 2 story, 9 kits. July-Labor Day: up to 4 persons $93-$105; kit. units for 4 persons $112-$119; lower rates May-June, after Labor Day-Sept. Closed rest of yr. Crib avail. TV; cable. Heated pool; wading pool, lifeguard. Complimentary coffee in rms. Restaurant opp 7 am-10 pm. Ck-out 11 am. Coin lndry. Game rm. Lawn games. Refrigerators; some microwaves. Sun deck. Picnic tables, grills. Cr cds: MC, V.

⌁ 🔥

★ ★ **CARIDEON.** *(2200 Atlantic Ave, North Wildwood)* 609/729-7900. 34 rms, 3 story. July-Aug: S, D $90; each addl $10; kits. $121; higher rates wkends (3-day min); lower rates May-June & Sept. Closed rest of yr.

Crib $9. TV; cable (premium). Heated pool; wading pool, lifeguard. Complimentary coffee in rms. Restaurant nearby. Ck-out 11 am. Coin lndry. Game rm. Refrigerators. Some balconies, grills. Cr cds: A, C, D, DS, MC, V.

⌁ 🔥

✔★ **COMPASS MOTOR INN.** *(6501 Atlantic Ave, Wildwood Crest)* 609/522-6948; FAX 609/729-9363; res: 800/624-2530 Mid-Atlantic states only. 50 rms, 3 story, 25 kits. No elvtrs. July-Aug: S, D $98-$120; each addl $8; family rates; wkly, wkend rates; higher rates hols (3-day min); lower rates May-June, Sept-Oct. Closed rest of yr. Crib $8. TV; cable. Heated pool; wading pool. Complimentary coffee in rms. Restaurant nearby. Ck-out 11 am. Meeting rms. Business servs avail. Refrigerators; many microwaves. Cr cds: A, DS, MC, V.

⌁ ⌁

★ ★ **CRUSADER RESORT MOTOR INN.** *(6101 Ocean Ave, Wildwood Crest)* At Cardinal Rd, on beach. 609/522-6991; FAX 609/522-2280; res: 800/462-3260. 61 units, 3 story, 54 suites, 37 kits. July-Aug: S, D $133-$185; each addl $12; kit. units $140-$192; lower rates Apr-June & Sept-Oct. Closed Nov-Mar. Crib avail. TV; cable (premium), VCR avail. Heated pool; wading pool, sauna, lifeguard. Restaurant 7 am-8 pm. Ck-out 11 am. Coin lndry. Meeting rms. Business servs avail. Sundries. Gift shop. Game rm. Refrigerators, microwaves. Some balconies. Picnic tables. Ocean beach; boardwalk. Cr cds: A, MC, V.

⊡ ⌁ ▨ 🔥

★ ★ **FLEUR DE LIS.** *(6105 Ocean Ave, Wildwood Crest)* at Sweetbriar. 609/522-0123. Web www.BeachComber.com.southjersey. 44 rms, 3 story, 32 kits. Mid-July-late Aug: S, D $100-$116; each addl $10; kits. $140-$170; higher rates wkends (3-day min); lower rates mid-Apr-mid-July & Sept-mid-Oct. Closed rest of yr. Crib $8. TV; cable. Pool; wading pool. Restaurant adj 7 am-9 pm. Ck-out 11 am. Coin lndry. Business servs avail. Game rm. Refrigerators, microwaves. On beach. Cr cds: DS, MC, V.

⌁ ▨ 🔥

✔★ ★ **IMPERIAL 500.** *(6601 Atlantic Ave at Forget-Me-Not Rd, Wildwood Crest)* 609/522-6063; res: 800/522-1255; FAX 609/522-7643. 45 rms, 3 story, 26 kits. No elvtr. July-Labor Day: S, D for 4, $100-$105; each addl $10; kit. units $110; lower rates May-June, after Labor Day-Sept. Closed rest of yr. Crib avail. TV; cable. Heated pool; wading pool. Restaurant nearby. Ck-out 11 am. Coin lndry. Meeting rm. Business servs avail. Sundries. Shuffleboard. Rec rm. Lawn games. Refrigerators, microwaves. Sun deck. Picnic tables, grills. Cr cds: DS, MC, V.

⌁ 🔥

★ ★ **IVANHOE.** *(430 E 21st Ave, North Wildwood)* 609/522-5874. Web www.beachcomber.aladdin.html. 40 rms, 2 story. July-Sept 1: S, D $90-$150; each addl $10-$15; family, wkly rates; lower rates rest of yr. Crib $8. TV; cable (premium). Heated pools; wading pool. Coffee in rms. Restaurant nearby. Ck-out 10 am. Coin lndry. Meeting rms. Business servs avail. Refrigerators, microwaves. Some balconies. Opp beach. Cr cds: A, C, D, DS, MC, V.

⌁ ▨ 🔥 SC

★ ★ **JOLLY ROGER.** *(6805 Atlantic Ave, Wildwood Crest)* 609/522-6915; res: 800/337-5232. 74 rms, 3 story. Mid-July-mid-Aug: S, D $99-$118; each addl $7; kits. $109-$155; under 5 free; wkends, hols (3-day min); lower rates mid-May, late Aug-late Sept. Closed rest of yr. Crib $9. TV; cable. Pool; wading pool, lifeguard. Supervised child's activities (July-Aug); ages 4-16. Restaurant nearby. Ck-out 11 am. Coin lndry. Meeting rms. Tennis. Game rm. Refrigerators; some microwaves. Balconies, grills. Picnic tables. Cr cds: MC, V.

🏃 ⌁ ⌁

★ ★ **LE VOYAGEUR.** *(232 E Andrews Ave, Wildwood)* 609/522-6407; res: 800/348-0846; FAX 609/523-1834. 33 rms, 3 story, 14 kits. July-Aug: S, D $74; each addl $10; suites $96; kits. $106; under 5 free; wkly, hol rates; lower rates Apr-June, Sept-Oct. Closed rest of yr. Crib $9. TV; cable. Heated pool; wading pool. Restaurant nearby. Ck-out 10:30 am.

Coin lndry. Meeting rm. Game rm. Refrigerators; many microwaves. Balconies. Picnic tables. Cr cds: A, MC, V.

D ≈ 🔥 ⚐

★ **LONG BEACH LODGE.** *(9th Ave on Beach, North Wildwood)* 609/522-1520; FAX 609/522-0538. Web www.longbeach.com. 24 kit. units, 3 story. No elvtrs. July-late Aug: S, D $79-$89; each addl $10; under 6 free; wkend, wkly rates; golf plan; higher rates hols (3-day min); lower rates Apr-June & late Aug-Oct. Closed rest of yr. Crib $10. TV; cable. Heated pool; wading pool. Complimentary coffee in lobby. Restaurant nearby. Ck-out 11 am. Coin lndry. Business servs avail. In-rm modem link. Microwaves avail. Balconies. Swimming beach opp. Cr cds: A, DS, MC, V.

D ≈ ⚓ 🔥 SC

★ **MADRID OCEAN RESORT.** *(427 E Miami Ave, Wildwood Crest)* On beach. 609/729-1600; FAX 609/729-8483. 54 rms, 5 story, 24 kits. July-Labor Day: S, D $103-$143; each addl $10; suites $133; kit. units up to 4 persons $143; higher rates wkends; lower rates mid-May-June, after Labor Day-Sept. Closed rest of yr. Crib avail. TV. Heated pool; wading pool. Restaurant 7 am-9 pm. Ck-out 11 am. Coin lndry. Business servs avail. Sundries. Rec rm. Sun deck. Refrigerators; microwaves avail. All ocean-front rms. Cr cds: A, MC, V.

≈ 🔥

★ ★ **NASSAU INN.** *(6201 Ocean Ave, Wildwood Crest)* at Sweetbriar. 609/729-9077; FAX 609/729-2208; res: 800/336-9077. 56 rms, 5 story. July-early Sept: S, D $95-$170; each addl $10; kits. $145-$170; family, wkly, wkend, hol rates; lower rates early Sept-mid-Oct & May-June. Closed rest of yr. Crib $9. TV; cable. Heated pool; wading pool. Restaurant adj 7 am-9 pm. Ck-out 11 am. Coin lndry. Business servs avail. Game rm. Refrigerators; many microwaves. On beach. Cr cds: DS, MC, V.

≈ 🔥

★ ★ **OCEAN HOLIDAY.** *(6501 Ocean Ave, Wildwood Crest)* On beach. 609/729-2900; FAX 609/523-1024; res: 800/321-6232. Web www.beachcomber.com. 56 rms, 5 story, 40 kits. July-Aug: S, D $95-$120; each addl $10; kit. units (up to 4 persons) $100-$255; hol wkends (3-day min); lower rates Apr-June, Sept-Oct. Closed rest of yr. Crib $5. TV; cable (premium), VCR avail. Pool; wading pool. Restaurant nearby. Ck-out 11 am. Coin lndry. Meeting rms. Business servs avail. Sundries. Game rm. Refrigerators, microwaves. Some private patios, balconies. Picnic tables, grills. Cr cds: A, MC, V.

D ≈ 🔥

★ **OCEANVIEW.** *(7201 Ocean Ave, Wildwood Crest)* 609/522-6656; res: 800/647-6656; FAX 609/522-6793. 110 rms, 4 story, 36 suites, 61 kit. units. July-Aug: S, D $99-$140; each addl $10; suites $125-$145; kit. units $135-$155; family, wkend, wkly rates; lower rates May-June, Sept-Oct. Closed rest of yr. Crib $9. TV; cable (premium). Restaurant opp 7 am-9 pm. Ck-out 11 am. Business servs avail. Coin lndry. Heated pool; wading pool, lifeguard. Miniature golf. Playground. Supervised child's activities (late June-early Sept). Game rm. Refrigerators. Picnic tables, grills. On beach. Cr cds: DS, MC, V.

D ≈ 🔥

★ ★ **PAN AMERICAN HOTEL.** *(Crocus Rd & Ocean Ave, Wildwood Crest)* On beach. 609/522-6936; FAX 609/522-6937. E-mail panamericaninfo@morey-sandcastles.com; web www.morey-sandcastles.com. 78 rms, 4 story, 39 kits. Early July-early Sept: up to 4 persons $160-$170; each addl $12; suites $190-$200; kit. units (up to 4 persons) $175-$185; lower rates mid-May-early June, early Sept-mid-Oct. Closed rest of yr. Crib free. TV; VCR avail. Heated pool; wading pool, sauna, lifeguard. Playground. Free supervised child's activities (mid-June-Labor Day); ages 4-10. Restaurant 7:30 am-8 pm. Rm serv. Ck-out 11 am. Meeting rm. Coin lndry. Business servs avail. Sundries. Rec rm. Refrigerators; some microwaves. Sun deck. Balconies. Cr cds: MC, V.

≈ 🔥

★ ★ **PANORAMIC.** *(2101 Surf Ave, North Wildwood)* 609/522-1181. 25 rms, 2 story. July-Sept: S, D $98-$150; each addl $10-$15; family, wkly rates; lower rates rest of yr. Crib $8. TV; cable (premium). Heated pool; wading pool. Complimentary coffee in rms. Restaurant

nearby. Ck-out 10 am. Coin lndry. Meeting rms. Business servs avail. Refrigerators, microwaves. Some balconies. On beach. Cr cds: A, C, D, DS, MC, V.

≈ ⚓ 🔥 SC

★ **PARK LANE.** *(5900 Ocean Ave, Wildwood Crest)* 609/522-5900. 36 rms, 3 story, 14 kits. Mid-July-late Aug: S, D $110; each addl $10; kits. $116-$141; wkly rates; lower rates early July & Sept. Closed rest of yr. Crib $8. TV; cable (premium). Pool; wading pool. Complimentary coffee in rms. Restaurant opp 7 am-10 pm. Ck-out 11 am. Coin lndry. Refrigerators. Balconies. Picnic tables. Opp beach. Cr cds: MC, V.

≈ 🔥

★ ★ ★ **PORT ROYAL.** *(6801 Ocean Ave, Wildwood Crest)* On beach. 609/729-2000. E-mail portroyalinfo@morey-sandcastles.com; web www.morey-sandcastles.com. 100 rms, 6 story, 50 kits. Late June-Labor Day: S, D $160-$170; each addl $12; kit. units for 4 persons $190-$200; lower rates May-late June, after Labor Day-mid-Oct. Closed rest of yr. Crib avail. TV; VCR avail. Heated pool; wading pool, sauna. Free supervised child's activities (mid-June-Labor Day); ages 3-10. Restaurant 8 am-8 pm in season. Ck-out 11 am. Coin lndry. Meeting rm (off-season). Business servs avail. Sundries. Rec rm, game rm in season. Some microwaves. Balconies. Cr cds: MC, V.

≈ 🔥

★ ★ **ROYAL HAWAIIAN.** *(Ocean & Orchid, Wildwood Crest)* 609/522-3414; FAX 609/522-1316. 88 rms, 5 story, 58 kits. Mid-July-Aug: S, D $99-$169; suites, kit. units for 4 $136-$229; each addl $10; lower rates mid-May-mid-July, Sept-Oct. Closed rest of yr. Crib avail. TV; cable (premium). Pool; wading pool, lifeguard. Playground. Ck-out 11 am. Coin lndry. Business servs avail. Valet serv. Rec rm. Exercise equipt; bicycles, treadmills, sauna. Refrigerators, microwaves. Balconies. Sun deck. Grills. On ocean. Cr cds: A, DS, MC, V.

D ≈ 🏋 🔥

Motor Hotels

★ ★ **ADVENTURER MOTOR INN.** *(5401 Ocean Ave, Wildwood Crest)* 609/729-1200; FAX 609/523-0505; res: 800/232-7873. 104 rms, 6 story. July-early Sept: S, D $140-$210; each addl $12; under 3 free; higher rates wkends (3-day min); lower rates early-Sept-Oct & mid-Apr-June. Closed rest of yr. Crib $7. TV; cable. Heated pool; wading pool, lifeguard. Restaurant 7 am-8 pm. Rm serv. Ck-out 11 am. Coin lndry. Meeting rms. Business servs avail. Sundries. Gift shop. Game rm. Refrigerators; microwaves avail. On beach. Cr cds: DS, MC, V.

D ≈ ⚓ 🔥 SC

★ **BEACH TERRACE.** 3400 Atlantic Ave. 609/522-8100; FAX 609/729-3236; res. 800/841-8416. 78 rms, 8 story, 24 kits. July-Aug: S, D $105-$120; each addl $10; kit. units $115-$130; lower rates Apr-June, Sept. Closed rest of yr. Crib avail. TV; cable. Pool; wading pool, lifeguard. Restaurant 8 am-noon, 5-9:30 pm. Ck-out 11 am. Business servs avail. Refrigerators. Balconies. Cr cds: A, DS, MC, V.

≈ 🔥

★ ★ **BRISTOL PLAZA.** *(6407 Ocean Ave, Wildwood Crest 08260-4195)* 609/729-1234; FAX 609/729-9363; res: 800/433-9731. 55 rms, 5 story, 41 kits. Mid-July-late Aug: S, D (up to 4) $129-$181; family rates; wkly, wkend, hol rates; lower rates May-mid-July & late Aug-Oct. Closed rest of yr. Crib $9. TV; cable. Heated pool; wading pool, sauna. Complimentary coffee in rms. Restaurant nearby. Ck-out 11 am. Coin lndry. Business servs avail. Refrigerators; many microwaves. Balconies. Picnic tables. Opp ocean. Cr cds: A, DS, MC, V.

≈ ⚓ 🔥

★ ★ ★ **EL CORONADO MOTOR INN.** *(8501 Atlantic Ave, Wildwood Crest)* On beach. 609/729-1000; FAX 609/729-6557; res: 800/227-5302. Web www.elcoronado.com. 113 rms, 6 story, 63 kit. suites. July-Aug: S, D $127-$137; each addl $10; kit. suites $166-$235; under 12 free; wkly, wkend (3-night min), hol rates; lower rates May-June & Sept-Oct. Closed rest of yr. Crib avail. TV; cable (premium). Pool; wading pool, whirlpool, sauna, poolside serv, lifeguard. Supervised child's activities (July-Aug). Restaurant 8 am-4 pm. Ck-out 11 am. Coin Indry. Meeting rms. Business servs avail. In-rm modem link. Gift shop. Game rm. Refrigerators, microwaves. Balconies. Cr cds: A, DS, MC, V.

Inn

★ ★ ★ **CANDLELIGHT INN.** *(2310 Central Ave, North Wildwood) 609/522-6200; FAX 609/522-6125.* E-mail inn4pd@aol.com; web www.candlelight-inn.com. 10 rms, 8 with A/C, 4 story. No rm phones. May-Oct: S $85-$150; D $100-$260; lower rates rest of yr. Adults only. Complimentary full bkfst; afternoon refreshments. Ck-out 11 am, ck-in 1 pm. Business servs avail. Whirlpool, sun deck. Lawn games. Health club privileges. Some microwaves. Grills. Ocean, beach 3 blks. Queen Anne/Victorian-style house (ca 1905); restored. Antique furnishings include 1855 sofa and 1890 Eastlake piano. Large porch with swing and hammocks. Totally nonsmoking. Cr cds: A, DS, MC, V.

Restaurants

★ ★ **CAPTAIN'S TABLE.** *(Hollywood at Oceanfront, Wildwood Crest) 609/522-2939.* Hrs: 8 am-noon, 4:30-10 pm. Closed mid-Oct-Mother's Day. Buffet: bkfst $3.95-$8.50. Semi-a la carte: dinner $9.95-$29.95. Child's meals. Specializes in Maine lobster, steak. Nautical decor; ocean view. Family-owned. Cr cds: A, C, D, DS, MC, V.

★ ★ **GARFIELD GIARDINO.** *(3800 Pacific Ave, Wildwood) Holly Beach Station. 609/729-0120.* Hrs: 11:30-3 am; July, Aug 4-11 pm; winter hrs vary. Res accepted. Italian, seafood menu. Bar. Complete meals: lunch, dinner $6.95-$19.95. Child's meals. Specializes in fresh seafood, veal, poultry. Entertainment July, Aug. 2 dining areas in garden setting. Cr cds: A, C, D, DS, MC, V.

★ ★ **LUIGI'S.** *(4119 Pacific Ave, Wildwood) 609/522-8571.* Hrs: 4 pm-1 am; early-bird dinner to 6 pm. Closed mid-Oct-Easter. Res accepted. Italian, Amer menu. Bar. Semi-a la carte: dinner $8.95-$18.95. Child's meals. Specializes in veal, fresh fish, pasta. Valet parking. European-style dining. Family-owned. Cr cds: A, D, DS, MC, V.

★ **MENZ.** *(985 NJ 47S, Rio Grande) 5 mi NE. 609/886-5691.* Hrs: 4-9 pm; Sun from noon. Closed winter months. Res accepted. A la carte entrees: dinner $8.95-$31.95. Child's meals. Specializes in seafood. Antique decor; music boxes, clocks, stained glass. Cr cds: MC, V.

Woodbridge (D-5)

Settled 1664 **Pop** 93,086 **Elev** 21 ft **Area code** 732 **Zip** 07095
Information Chamber of Commerce Visitor Center, 52 Main St; 732/636-4040.

Here, where the first cloverleaf interchange in the US was constructed in 1929, cross two of the country's busiest roads—the Garden State Pkwy and the New Jersey Tpke. Also in Woodbridge are seaway and river port areas visited by thousands of vessels annually.

What to See and Do

Barron Arts Center. Built in 1877 in Romanesque-revival style. Originally the first free public library in Middlesex County, now an arts and cultural center with art exhibits; workshops; lectures; poetry sessions; concerts; special events. Gallery (Mon-Fri; closed hols). 582 Rahway Ave. Phone 732/634-0413. **Free.**

Motel

✔★ **BUDGET MOTOR LODGE.** *350 US 9N, off NJ Tpke exit 11 or Garden State Pkwy exit 127N. 732/636-4000; FAX 732/636-0636.* 168 rms, 5 story. S, D $53-$70; each addl $10; under 12 free. Crib free. TV; cable (premium). Bar 11:30-1 am. Coin Indry. Meeting rms. Business servs avail. In-rm modem link. Valet serv. Sundries. Cr cds: A, C, D, DS, MC, V.

Hotels

★ ★ ★ **HILTON.** *(120 Wood Ave S, Iselin 08830) W of Garden State Pkwy, exit 131A. 732/494-6200; FAX 732/603-7777.* Web www.hilton.com. 200 rms, 7-11 story. S $74-$135; D $86-$147; each addl $12; under 18 free; wkend rates. Crib free. TV; cable (premium), VCR. Indoor pool; whirlpool, lifeguard. Restaurant 6 am-midnight; dining rm 11 am-9:30 pm. Bar noon-1 am; entertainment. Meeting rms. Business center. In-rm modem link. Gift shop. Exercise rm; instructor, weights, bicycles, steam rm. Bathrm phones; refrigerator in suites. Cr cds: A, C, D, DS, MC, V.

★ ★ ★ **SHERATON AT WOODBRIDGE PLACE.** *(515 US 1S, Iselin 08830) US 1 at Gill Ln, 1/2 mi N of Garden State Pkwy exit 130. 732/634-3600; FAX 732/634-0258.* E-mail iahdecicco@aol.com. 253 rms, 7 story. S, D $140; each addl $10; suites $225; under 12 free; wkend rates. Crib free. TV; cable (premium). 2 pools, 1 indoor; whirlpool, poolside serv. Restaurants 6-11 pm. Bars 11-1 am. Ck-out noon. Convention facilities. Business center. In-rm modem link. Gift shop. RR station transportation. Exercise equipt; weights, bicycles. Health club privileges. Game rm. Microwaves avail. 40-ft atrium lobby, marble fountain. Extensive grounds. Luxury level. Cr cds: A, C, D, DS, ER, JCB, MC, V.

North Carolina

Population: 6,628,637
Land area: 48,843 square miles
Elevation: 0-6,684 feet
Highest point: Mount Mitchell (Yancey County)
Entered Union: Twelfth of original 13 states (November 21, 1789)
Capital: Raleigh
Motto: To be rather than to seem
Nickname: Tar Heel State, Old North State
State flower: American dogwood
State bird: Cardinal
State tree: Pine
State fair: October 16-25, 1998, in Raleigh
Time zone: Eastern

North Carolina, besides being a wonderful place for a vacation, is a cross section of America—a state of magnificent variety with three distinctive regions: the coast, the heartland and the mountains. Its elevation ranges from sea level to 6,684 feet atop Mt Mitchell in the Black Mountain Range of the Appalachians. It has descendants of English, German, Scottish, Irish and African immigrants. It has Quakers, Moravians, Episcopalians and Calvinists. It produces two-thirds of our flue-cured tobacco, as well as cotton, peanuts and vegetables on its farms. Fabrics, furniture and many other products are made in its factories. It also has one of the finest state university systems in the nation with campuses at Chapel Hill, Raleigh, Greensboro, Charlotte, Asheville and Wilmington.

In 1585, the first English settlement was unsuccessfully started on Roanoke Island. Another attempt at settlement was made in 1587—but the colony disappeared, leaving only the crudely scratched word "CROATOAN" on a tree—perhaps referring to the Croatan Indians who may have killed the colonists or absorbed them into their own culture, leaving behind one of history's great mysteries. Here, in the Great Smoky Mountains, lived the Cherokee before the government drove them westward to Oklahoma over the Trail of Tears, on which a third of them died. Descendants of many members of this tribe, who hid in the inaccessible rocky coves and forests, still live here. Some "mountain people," isolated, independent, still singing songs dating back to Elizabethan England, also live here. Few North Carolinians owned slaves, very few owned many, and, early on, the state accepted free blacks (in 1860 there were 30,463) as a part of the community.

Citizens take pride in being called "Tar Heels." During the Civil War, North Carolinians returning from the front were taunted by a troop from another state who had "retreated" a good deal earlier. The Carolinians declared that Jefferson Davis had decided to bring up all the tar from North Carolina to use on the heels of the other regiment to make them "stick better in the next fight." General Lee, hearing of the incident, said, "God bless the Tar Heel boys."

Individual and democratic from the beginning, this state refused to ratify the Constitution until the Bill of Rights had been added. Its western citizens strongly supported the Union in 1860. It did not join the Confederate States of America until after Fort Sumter had been fired upon and Lincoln had called for volunteers. Its independence was then challenged, and it furnished one-fifth of the soldiers of the Southern armies even though its population was only one-ninth of the Confederacy's. Eighty-four engagements (most of them small) were fought on its soil. Jealous of its rights, North Carolina resisted the authority of Confederate Army officers from Virginia and loudly protested many of the policies of Jefferson Davis; but its 125,000 men fought furiously, and 40,000 of them died for what they believed was right. For years after the Civil War North Carolina was a poverty-stricken state, although it suffered less from the inroads of carpetbaggers than did many of its neighbors.

The state seems designed for vacationers. Beautiful mountains and flowering plants, lake and ocean swimming and boating, hunting and fishing, superb golf courses, old towns, festivals, pageantry and parks are a few of the state's many attractions.

When to Go/Climate

North Carolina has the most varied climate of any state on the east coast. Subtropical temperatures on the coast are contrasted by a medium continental climate in the western mountain areas. Fall is hurricane season along the coast; winter in the western mountains can be snowy and cold. Fall foliage is magnificent in September and October; March and April are marked by blooming dogwood and azaleas.

AVERAGE HIGH/LOW TEMPERATURES (°F)

CAPE HATTERAS

Jan 52/37	**May** 74/60	**Sept** 81/68
Feb 53/38	**June** 81/68	**Oct** 72/58
Mar 60/44	**July** 85/72	**Nov** 65/49
Apr 67/51	**Aug** 85/72	**Dec** 57/41

RALEIGH

Jan 49/29	**May** 79/55	**Sept** 81/61
Feb 53/31	**June** 85/64	**Oct** 72/48
Mar 62/39	**July** 88/68	**Nov** 63/40
Apr 72/46	**Aug** 87/68	**Dec** 53/32

CALENDAR HIGHLIGHTS

APRIL

North Carolina Azalea Festival (Wilmington). Garden and home tours, horse show, celebrity entertainers, pageants, parade, street fair. Phone 910/763-0905.

Greater Greensboro Chrysler Classic Golf Tournament (Greensboro). Top golfers compete for more than $1.8 million on PGA circuit. For more information, contact Convention & Visitors Bureau, 336/274-2282 or 800/344-2282.

Springfest (Charlotte). Three-day festival in uptown, offers food, live entertainment. Phone 704/332-0126.

MAY

Gliding Spectacular (Nags Head, Outer Banks). Hang gliding competition, novice through advanced. Spectacular flying and fun events. Phone 919/441-4124.

Artsplosure Spring Jazz & Arts Festival (Raleigh). Moore Square and City Market. City-wide celebration of the arts. Showcase for regional dance, music, theater performances by nationally known artists; outdoor arts and crafts show; children's activities. Phone 919/832-8699.

JUNE

Rogallo Kite Festival (Nags Head, Outer Banks). Competition for homebuilt kites; stunt kite performances, demonstrations; kite auction. Phone 919/441-4124.

"Singing on the Mountain" (Linville). On the slopes of Grandfather Mountain. All-day program of modern and traditional gospel music featuring top groups and nationally known speakers. Concessions or bring your own food. Phone 704/733-4337.

AUGUST

Mountain Dance and Folk Festival (Asheville). Civic Center. Folk songs and ballads. Finest of its kind for devotees of the five-string banjo, gut-string fiddle, clogging and smooth dancing. Phone 704/258-6107 or 800/257-5583.

SEPTEMBER

CenterFest (Durham). Downtown. Two-day event with over 250 artists and craftsmen; musicians, jugglers and clowns; continuous entertainment from three stages. Phone 919/560-2722.

Bull Durham Blues Festival (Durham). Historic Durham Athletic Park. Celebrates the blues with performances held at the location where *Bull Durham* was filmed. Phone 919/683-1709.

OCTOBER

Southern Highland Craft Guild Fair (Asheville). Civic Center. More than 175 craftsmen from nine Southern states exhibit and demonstrate their skills. Folk and contemporary entertainment daily. Phone 704/298-7928.

State Fair (Raleigh). State Fairgrounds. Phone 919/733-2145 or 919/821-7400.

Parks and Recreation Finder

Directions to and information about the parks and recreation areas below are given under their respective town/city sections. Please refer to those sections for details.

Key to abbreviations: I.P. = Interstate Park; N.B.C. = National Battlefield & Cemetery; N.B.P. = National Battlefield Park; N.F. = National Forest; N.H. = National Historical Park; N.H.S. = National Historic Site; N.M. = National Monument; N.Mem. = National Memorial; N.M.P. = National Military Park; N.P. = National Park; N.Pres. = National Preserve; N.R. = National Recreational Area; N.S. = National Seashore; N.S.T. = National Scenic Trail; S.B. = State Beach; S.C.P. = State Conservation Park; S.G. = State Garden; S.H.A. = State Historic Area; S.H.P. = State Historic Park; S.N.A. = State Natural Area; S.P. = State Park; S.R. = State Reserve;

S.R.A. = State Recreation Area; S.Res.P. = State Resort Park; S.R.P. = State Rustic Park.

NATIONAL PARK AND RECREATION AREAS

Place Name	Listed Under
Cape Hatteras N.S.	same
Cape Lookout N.S.	BEAUFORT
Carl Sandburg Home N.H.S.	HENDERSONVILLE
Croatan N.F.	NEW BERN
Fort Raleigh N.H.S.	same
Great Smoky Mountains N.P.	same
Guilford Courthouse N.M.P.	GREENSBORO
Moores Creek National Battlefield	WILMINGTON
Nantahala N.F.	FRANKLIN
Pisgah N.F.	BREVARD
Wright Brothers N.Mem.	KILL DEVIL HILLS

STATE RECREATION AREAS

Place Name	Listed Under
Carolina Beach S.P.	WILMINGTON
Cliffs of the Neuse S.P.	GOLDSBORO
Duke Power S.P.	STATESVILLE
Fort Macon S.P.	MOREHEAD CITY
Hanging Rock S.P.	WINSTON-SALEM
Jones Lake S.P.	LUMBERTON
Kerr Reservoir	HENDERSON
Merchant's Millpond S.P.	EDENTON
Morrow Mountain S.P.	ALBEMARLE
Mt Mitchell S.P.	LITTLE SWITZERLAND
Pilot Mountain S.P.	PILOT MOUNTAIN
Raven Rock S.P.	SANFORD
Stone Mountain S.P.	WILKESBORO
William B. Umstead S.P.	RALEIGH

Water-related activities, hiking, riding, various other sports, picnicking and visitor centers, as well as camping, are available in many of these areas. Parks are open daily: June-Aug, 8 am-9 pm; Apr-May & Sept to 8 pm; Mar & Oct to 7 pm; Nov-Feb to 6 pm. Most parks have picnicking and hiking. Swimming ($3; 6-12, $2; under 3 free) and concessions open Memorial Day-Labor Day. Admission and parking free (exc reservoirs; $4); canoe and boat rentals ($3/hr first hr, $1/hr thereafter); fishing. Campgrounds: open all yr, limited facilities in winter; family of 6 for $12/day; hookups $5 more; primitive sites $8/day; youth group tent camping $1/person ($8 min). Senior citizen discounts offered. Dogs on leash only. Campgrounds are on first come, first served basis; reservations are allowed for minimum of 7 days, maximum of 14 days; write the Park Superintendent.

Information, including a comprehensive brochure, may be obtained from the Division of Parks & Recreation, Dept of Environment, Health and Natural Resources, PO Box 27687, Raleigh 27611; 919/733-7275 or 919/733-4181.

SKI AREAS

Place Name	Listed Under
Appalachian Ski Mountain	BLOWING ROCK
Cataloochee Ski Area	MAGGIE VALLEY
Fairfield Sapphire Valley Ski Area	CASHIERS
Scaly Mountain Ski Area	HIGHLANDS
Ski Beech Ski Area	BANNER ELK
Sugar Mt Ski Area	BANNER ELK
Wolf Laurel Ski Resort	ASHEVILLE

FISHING & HUNTING

Nonresident fishing license $30; daily license $10; 3-day license $15. Nonresident 6-day and basic hunting license $40. Nonresident sportsman license (includes basic hunting and fishing, trout, big game hunting, game lands and primitive weapons; excludes special device) $130. Nonresident comprehensive hunting license (includes basic hunting, big game, game lands, primitive weapons) $80. Nonresident trapping license $100. Nonresident comprehensive fishing license (includes basic fishing, trout and trout waters on gamelands) $30; 3-day license $15; daily license $10. Waterfowl stamp (mandatory) $5.

For latest regulations contact License Section, Wildlife Resources Commission, Archdale Building, 512 N Salisbury St, Raleigh 27604-1188; 919/662-4370.

Driving Information

Safety belts are mandatory for all persons in front seat of vehicle. Children under 6 years must be in an approved child passenger restraint system anywhere in vehicle; ages 3-6 may use a regulation safety belt; children under 3 years must use an approved child passenger restraint system. For further information phone 919/733-7952.

INTERSTATE HIGHWAY SYSTEM

The following alphabetical listing of North Carolina towns in *Mobil Travel Guide* shows that these cities are within 10 miles of the indicated Interstate highways. A highway map should, however, be checked for the nearest exit.

Highway Number	Cities/Towns within 10 miles
Interstate 26	Asheville, Columbus, Hendersonville, Tryon.
Interstate 40	Asheville, Burlington, Durham, Greensboro, Hickory, Maggie Valley, Marion, Morganton, Raleigh, Statesville, Waynesville, Wilmington, Winston-Salem.
Interstate 77	Charlotte, Cornelius, Dobson, Statesville.
Interstate 85	Burlington, Charlotte, Concord, Durham, Gastonia, Greensboro, Henderson, High Point, Lexington, Salisbury.
Interstate 95	Dunn, Fayetteville, Lumberton, Roanoke Rapids, Rocky Mount, Smithfield, Wilson.

Additional Visitor Information

The North Carolina Gazetteer, by William S. Powell (University of North Carolina Press, Chapel Hill, 1968) lists over 20,000 entries that will enable the reader to find any place in the state, as well as information about size, history and derivation of name. The Travel and Tourism Division, 430 N Salisbury St, Raleigh 27611, 800/VISIT-NC, has free travel information, including brochures.

North Carolina Welcome Center locations are: I-85 North, Box 156, Norlina 27563; I-85 South, Box 830, Kings Mountain 28086; I-95 North, Box 52, Roanoke Rapids 27870; I-40, Box 809, Waynesville 28786; I-95 South, Box 518, Rowland 28383; I-26, Box 249, Columbus 28722; I-77 North, Box 1066, Dobson 27017; and I-77 South, Box 410724, Charlotte 28241-0724.

Ahoskie (A-9)

Pop 4,391 **Elev** 53 ft **Area code** 919 **Zip** 27910

Motel

✔★ **TOMAHAWK.** *601 N Academy. 919/332-3194; FAX 919/332-3194, ext. 232.* 58 rms. S $32.85; D $35.85; each addl $5. TV; cable. Restaurant opp 6 am-9 pm. Ck-out 11 am. Business servs avail. Cr cds: A, C, D, DS, MC, V.

D ⬛ SC

Motor Hotel

★★ **AAHOSKIE INN.** *Rte 2, Box 3501, Jct NC 11 & 561. 919/332-4165; FAX 919/332-1632.* 98 rms, 2 story. S $47; D $56; each addl $10; suites $161; under 18 free. TV; cable. Indoor pool. Restaurant 6 am-2 pm, 5:30-9 pm. Bar; entertainment Sat. Ck-out noon. Meeting rms. Business servs avail. Valet serv. Cr cds: A, C, D, DS, MC, V.

D ⬛ ⬛ ⬛ SC

Albemarle (B-5)

(See also Concord)

Founded 1857 **Pop** 14,939 **Elev** 455 ft **Area code** 704 **Zip** 28001
Information Stanly County Chamber of Commerce, PO Box 909, 28002; 704/982-8116.

Albemarle is in the gently rolling hills of the Uwharrie Mountains, in the Piedmont section of the state. It manufactures textiles, aircraft tires, automotive parts and aluminum.

What to See and Do

Stanly Museum and Visitor Center. Originally built as a 3-rm log cabin in the 1850s, the Snuggs House has been enlarged and houses period artifacts. Research room. (Tues-Fri; also wkends by appt; closed hols) Also on lot is Marks House, town's oldest building (1850s) once used as residence/law office. 245 E Main St. Phone 704/983-7316.   **Free.**

Morrow Mountain State Park. Approx 4,700 acres of hilly forested terrain, touched on two sides by Lake Tillery. Swimming pool, bathhouse; fishing; boating (rentals, launching). Nature trails, hiking, riding. Picnic facilities, concessions. Camping (no hookups); 6 cabins, families only (Mar-Nov; advance res required). Natural history museum. Standard fees. 7 mi E off NC 740, on Morrow Mountain Rd. Phone 704/982-4402.

Town Creek Indian Mound State Historic Site. Reconstructed 14th-century Native American ceremonial center with stockade, temples and mortuary. Visitor center, audiovisual shows, exhibits (Apr-Oct, daily; rest of yr, daily exc Mon; closed hols in winter). Picnic area. 11 mi S on US 52, then 12 mi E on NC 731 to Town Creek Mound Rd. Phone 910/439-6802. **Free.**

Motel

✔★ **COMFORT INN.** *735 NC 24/27 Bypass (28002). 704/983-6990; FAX 704/983-5597.* 80 rms, 2 story. S $52.95-$54.95; D $54.95-$56.95; each addl $6; under 18 free; higher rates during races. Crib free. TV; cable (premium). Complimentary continental bkfst. Restaurant nearby. Ck-out noon. Meeting rms. Business servs avail. Pool. Some refrigerators. Cr cds: A, C, D, DS, ER, JCB, MC, V.

D ⬛ ⬛ ⬛ SC

Asheboro (B-6)

(See also Greensboro, High Point, Lexington)

Founded 1779 **Pop** 16,362 **Elev** 844 ft **Area code** 336 **Zip** 27203 **E-mail** chamber@asheboro.com **Web** www.chamber.asheboro.com

Information Asheboro/Randolph Chamber of Commerce, 317 E Dixie Dr; 336/626-2626 or 800/626-2672.

Situated in the agriculturally and industrially rich Piedmont and the timber-covered Uwharrie Mountains, Asheboro has for over a century served as the seat of Randolph County. Planked roads, covered bridges and the waters of the Deep and Uwharrie rivers provided the impetus for industrial development late in the 19th century. Asheboro is in the heart of North Carolina's pottery-making country.

What to See and Do

North Carolina Zoological Park. North American region exhibits span over 200 acres; African habitats cover over 300 acres and feature 9 outdoor exhibits; Forest Aviary; African Pavilion. (Daily) 6 mi S on NC 159. Phone 800/488-0444. ¢¢¢

Seagrove Area Potteries. Over 80 artists practice traditional hand-turning of pottery. Shops. (Daily) 10 mi S on US 73/74. Phone 336/626-2626. **Free.**

Annual Event

Randolph County Fall Festival. Arts, crafts, food, parade, music, entertainment. 1st wkend Oct.

Motel

✔★★ **DAYS INN.** *901 Albemarle Rd, at jct NC 49, US 220 Bypass.* 336/629-2101; FAX 336/626-7944. 138 rms, 2 story. S $41-$68; D $46-$72; each addl $4; suites $125. Crib free. TV; cable (premium). Pool. Ck-out 11 am. Meeting rms. Business servs avail. Valet serv. Cr cds: A, C, D, DS, MC, V.

D ⟋ ⟋ ⟋ SC

Asheville (B-3)

(See also Maggie Valley, Waynesville)

Settled 1794 **Pop** 61,607 **Elev** 2,134 ft **Area code** 704 **E-mail** cvb@ashevillechamber.org **Web** www.ashevillechamber.org

Information Convention & Visitors Bureau, 151 Haywood St, PO Box 1010, 28802-1010; 704/258-6101or 800/257-1300.

Thomas Wolfe came from Asheville, the seat of Buncombe County, as did the expression "bunkum" (nonsense). A local congressman, when asked why he had been so evasive during a masterful oration in which he said nothing, replied, "I did it for Buncombe." Wolfe wrote often of his hill-rimmed home, shrewdly observant of the people and life of Asheville.

Asheville is a vacation headquarters in the Blue Ridge Mountains, as well as a marketing and industrial city. It is the North Carolina city nearest Great Smoky Mountains National Park (see) and attracts many of the park's visitors with its annual mountain fetes, local handicrafts and summer theaters. It is the headquarters for the Uwharrie National Forest, Pisgah National Forest (see BREVARD), Nantahala National Forest (see FRANKLIN) and Croatan National Forest (see NEW BERN). The Blue Ridge Parkway brings many travelers to Asheville on their way south from the Shenandoah Valley of Virginia.

For further information about Croatan, Nantahala, Pisgah and Uwharrie national forests, contact the US Forest Service, 704/257-4202.

What to See and Do

Asheville Community Theatre. Comedies, musicals and dramas performed throughout year. 35 E Walnut St. Phone 704/254-1320 for schedule. ¢¢¢-¢¢¢¢

★ **Biltmore Estate.** The 8,000-acre country estate includes 75 acres of formal gardens, numerous varieties of azaleas and roses and the 250-rm chateau (85 rms are open for viewing), which is the largest house ever built in the New World. George W. Vanderbilt commissioned Richard Morris Hunt to design the house, which was begun in 1890 and finished in 1895. Materials and furnishings were brought from many parts of Europe and Asia; a private railroad was built to transport them to the site. Life here was lived in the grand manner. Vanderbilt employed Gifford Pinchot, later Governor of Pennsylvania and famous for forestry and conservation achievements, to manage his forests. Biltmore was the site of the first US forestry school. Much of the original estate is now part of Pisgah National Forest. Tours of the estate include greenhouses and winery facilities; tasting. Three restaurants on grounds. (Daily; closed Thanksgiving, Dec 25) Guidebook (fee) is recommended. S on US 25, 3 blks N of I-40 exit 50. Phone 704/255-1700 or 800/543-2961. ¢¢¢¢¢

Biltmore Homespun Shops. At the turn of the century, Mrs. George W. Vanderbilt opened a school to keep alive the skills of hand-dyeing, spinning and hand-weaving wool into cloth. The business still has the old machinery and handlooms. An antique automobile museum and the North Carolina Homespun Museum are in an 11-acre park adjoining Grove Park Inn Resort (see RESORTS). (Apr-Oct, daily; rest of yr, daily exc Sun; closed Jan 1, Thanksgiving, Dec 25) Grovewood Rd, near Macon Ave, 2 mi NE. Phone 704/253-7651. **Free.**

Botanical Gardens of Asheville. A 10-acre tract with thousands of flowers, trees and shrubs native to southern Appalachia; 125-yr-old "dog trot" log cabin. (Daily) On campus of University of North Carolina. Phone 704/252-5190. **Free.**

Chimney Rock Park. Towering granite monolith Chimney Rock affords 75-mi view; 3 hiking trails lead to 404-ft Hickory Nut Falls, Moonshiner's Cave, Devil's Head balancing rock, Nature's Showerbath. Trails, stairs and catwalks; picnic areas, playground; nature center; observation lounge with snack bar, gift shop. 26-story elevator shaft through granite. (Daily, weather permitting; closed Jan 1, Dec 25) 25 mi SE on US 74, just past jct US 64, NC 9. Phone 704/625-9611 or 800/277-9611. ¢¢

Folk Art Center of the Southern Highland Craft Guild. Stone and timber structure; home of Southern Highland Craft Guild, Blue Ridge Pkwy information center; craft exhibits, demonstrations, workshops, related programs. (Daily; closed Jan 1, Thanksgiving, Dec 25) 5 mi E on US 70, then 1/2 mi N on the Blue Ridge Pkwy to Milepost 382. Phone 704/298-7928. (See ANNUAL EVENTS) **Free.**

Graves of Thomas Wolfe (1900-1938) and **O. Henry** (William Sydney Porter) (1862-1910). Entrance on Birch St off Pearson Dr. Riverside Cemetery.

Mt Mitchell State Park. 27 mi NE on Blue Ridge Pkwy, then 5 mi N on NC 128 (see LITTLE SWITZERLAND).

Pack Place Education, Arts and Science Center. This 92,000 square-foot complex features multiple museums and exhibit galleries as well as a state-of-the-art theater. A permanent exhibit entitled "Here Is the Square..." describes the history of Asheville. Restaurant (lunch only); gift shop. (Tues-Sat, also some Sun afternoons; closed Jan 1, Thanksgiving, Dec 24-25) 2 S Pack Square. For general information, phone 704/257-4500. Combination ticket ¢¢ Includes

Asheville Art Museum. Permanent collection and changing exhibits. Phone 704/253-3227. ¢¢

Colburn Gem and Mineral Museum. Displays of 1,000 minerals from around the world; includes information on mineral locations in the state. Phone 704/254-7162. ¢¢

The Health Adventure. Extensive collection of imaginative, educational exhibits on the human body; includes a talking transparent woman, a bicycle-pedaling skeleton and opportunity to hear sound of your own heartbeat. Also on premises is Creative PlaySpace, a special exhibit for young children. Phone 704/254-6373. ¢¢

YMI Cultural Center. Galleries featuring permanent and rotating exhibts on African American art. Phone 704/252-4614. ¢¢

Diana Wortham Theatre. This 500-seat theater hosts local, regional and national companies. For box office information, phone 704/257-4530.

River rafting. Nantahala Outdoor Center. Offers various trips on the Nantahala, French Broad, Ocoee, Nolichucky and Chattooga rivers ranging from 1½ to 6 hrs. For information and reservations, contact 1377 US 19W, Bryson City 28713-9114; 800/232-7238. ¢¢¢¢

Thomas Wolfe Memorial. The state maintains the Wolfe boardinghouse as a literary shrine, restored and furnished to appear as it did in 1916. In Asheville it is known as the Old Kentucky Home. In *Look Homeward, Angel* it was referred to as "Dixieland"; Asheville was "Altamont." Visitor center with exhibit. (Apr-Oct; daily; rest of yr, daily exc Mon; closed major hols) 48 Spruce St, between Woodfin & Walnut Sts. Phone 704/253-8304. ¢

Western North Carolina Nature Center. Live animals, children's petting barnyard, natural history exhibits, nature trail, educational programs. (Memorial Day-Labor Day, daily; rest of yr, Tues-Sat and Sun afternoons) Gashes Creek Rd, 3 mi E on NC 81. Phone 704/298-5600. ¢¢

Wolf Laurel Ski Resort. Quad, double chairlifts, Mitey-mite; patrol, school, rentals; snow making; restaurant. Longest run ¾ mi; vertical drop 700 ft. (Mid-Dec-mid-Mar, daily) 27 mi N off US 23. Phone 704/689-4111. ¢¢¢¢

Zebulon B. Vance Birthplace State Historic Site. Log house (reconstructed 1961) and outbuildings on site where Civil War governor of North Carolina grew up. Honors Vance family, which was deeply involved with early history of state. Visitor center, exhibits. Picnic area. (Apr-Oct, daily; rest of yr, daily exc Mon; closed some hols) 9 mi N on US 19/23, exit New-Stock Rd, then 6 mi N on Reems Creek Rd in Weaverville. Phone 704/645-6706. **Free.**

Annual Events

Shindig-on-the-Green. College & Spruce Sts, in front of City Hall. Mountain fiddling, dulcimer players, singing, square dancing. Sat evenings, July-Labor Day exc last wkend July.

Southern Highland Craft Guild Fair. Civic Center, Haywood St, just off I-240. More than 175 craftsmen from 9 Southern states exhibit and demonstrate their skills. Folk and contemporary entertainment daily. Phone 704/298-7928. 3rd wkend July, 3rd wkend Oct.

World Gee Haw Whimmy Diddle Competition. Folk Art Center. Competitions, demonstrations, storytelling, music, dance. Early Aug.

Mountain Dance and Folk Festival. Civic Center. Folk songs and ballads. Finest of its kind for devotees of the 5-string banjo, gut-string fiddle, clogging and smooth dancing. 1st wkend Aug.

Seasonal Event

Shakespeare in the Park. Montford Park Players. Phone 704/254-4540. Wkends early June-late Aug.

Motels

✔★ **AMERICAN COURT.** 85 Merrimon Ave (28801). 704/253-4427; res: 800/233-3582. 22 rms. S $52; D $58-$72; each addl $3; under 12 free. TV; cable. Pool. Complimentary coffee. Restaurant nearby. Ck-out 11 am. Coin lndry. Refrigerators. Cr cds: A, C, D, DS, MC, V.

✔★ **BEST INNS OF AMERICA.** 1435 Tunnel Rd (28805). 704/298-4000. 85 rms, 3 story. Apr-Oct: S $49.88-$55.88; D $56.88-$65.88; each addl $7; under 18 free; lower rates rest of yr. Crib free. TV; cable (premium), VCR avail (movies $4). Heated pool. Complimentary continental bkfst. Complimentary coffee in lobby. Restaurant nearby. Ck-out 1 pm. Business servs avail. Some refrigerators. Cr cds: A, C, D, DS, MC, V.

★★ **COMFORT SUITES.** 890 Brevard Rd (28806), I-26 exit 2. 704/665-4000; FAX 704/665-9082. 125 suites, 5 story. May-Oct: suites $69-$99; each addl $6; under 18 free; lower rates rest of yr. Crib free. Pet

accepted; $20. TV; cable (premium). Pool; whirlpool. Complimentary continental bkfst. Coffee in rms. Restaurant nearby. Ck-out noon. Coin lndry. Meeting rms. Business servs avail. In-rm modem link. Free airport transportation. Exercise equipt; bicycles, stair machine. Refrigerators. Cr cds: A, C, D, DS, ER, JCB, MC, V.

★★ **FOREST MANOR INN.** 866 Hendersonville Rd (28803), on US 25, 1 mi S of I-40 exit 50. 704/274-3531; res: 800/866-3531; FAX 704/274-3036. Web www.ashevillechamber.org. 21 rms. July, Aug & Oct: D $79-$129; kit. units $695-$795/wk; lower rates rest of yr. Crib $5. TV; cable. Heated pool. Complimentary continental bkfst. Restaurant nearby. Ck-out 11 am. Business servs avail. Tennis privileges. Golf privileges. Lawn games. On 4 wooded acres. Cr cds: A, DS, MC, V.

★★ **HAMPTON INN.** 1 Rocky Ridge Rd (28806), jct I-26 & NC 191. 704/667-2022; FAX 704/665-9680. 121 rms, 5 story. June-Oct: S, D $64-$119; suites $145; under 18 free. Crib free. TV; cable (premium). Indoor pool; whirlpool. Complimentary continental bkfst. Coffee in rms. Ck-out noon. Meeting rms. Business servs avail. In-rm modem link. Free airport transportation. Exercise equipt; bicycles, stair machine, sauna. Refrigerator in suites. Cr cds: A, C, D, DS, MC, V.

★★ **HAMPTON INN.** 204 Tunnel Rd (28805), I-240 exit 6 & 7, US 70 to Tunnel Rd. 704/255-9220; FAX 704/254-4303. 120 rms, 5 story. June-Oct: S $65-$119; D $79-$119; suites $145-$225; under 18 free; higher rates special events; lower rates rest of yr. Crib free. TV; cable (premium). Indoor pool; whirlpool. Complimentary continental bkfst. Coffee in rms. Restaurant nearby. Ck-out noon. Meeting rms. Business servs avail. Exercise equipt; weights, bicycles, sauna. Microwaves avail. Cr cds: A, C, D, DS, MC, V.

★★ **HOWARD JOHNSON-BILTMORE.** 190 Hendersonville Rd (28803). 704/274-2300; FAX 704/274-2304. 68 rms, 2 story. Apr-Oct: S $54-$149; D $64-$149; each addl $8; higher rates: special events wkends & autumn foliage; lower rates rest of yr. Crib free. TV; cable (premium). Pool. Restaurant 6:30 am-1:30 pm, 5:30-8:30 pm; Sat, Sun from 7 am. Ck-out noon. Meeting rms. Business servs avail. Private patios, balconies. Cr cds: A, C, D, DS, JCB, MC, V.

★★ **MOUNTAIN SPRINGS.** (US 151, Candler 28715) I-40 W to exit 44, 5 mi S on US 151. 704/665-1004; FAX 704/667-1581. E-mail mtnsprings@ioa.com; web loa.com/home/mtnsprings. 12 kit. cottages, 1-2 story. S, D $90-$125; each addl $20; children $10. Crib free. TV, cable. Ck-out 10 am. Lawn games. Microwaves. Picnic tables, outdoor grills. On mountain stream. Cr cds: MC, V.

✔★ **RED ROOF INN.** 16 Crowell Rd (28806), I-40 exit 44. 704/667-9803; FAX 704/667-9810. 109 rms, 3 story. May-Oct: S $56; D $62; under 18 free; lower rates rest of yr. Pet accepted, some restrictions. TV; cable (premium). Complimentary coffee in lobby. Restaurant opp open 24 hrs. Ck-out noon. Business servs avail. Cr cds: A, D, DS, MC, V.

Motor Hotels

★★ **BEST WESTERN.** 22 Woodfin St (28801), 1 blk off I-240 at Merrimon Ave exit. 704/253-1851; FAX 704/252-9205. 150 rms, 5 story. June-Sept: S, D $65-$79; each addl $5; under 18 free; higher rates Oct; lower rates rest of yr. Crib free. TV; cable (premium). Heated pool. Complimentary coffee in rms. Restaurant 6:30-10 am; Sat, Sun 7-11 am. Bar 5 pm-1 am. Ck-out noon. Meeting rm. Business servs avail. Health club privileges. Cr cds: A, C, D, DS, MC, V.

★ ★ ★ **HOLIDAY INN SUNSPREE RESORT.** *1 Holiday Inn Dr (28806). 704/254-3211; FAX 704/254-1603.* 277 rms, 5 story. May-Oct: S $110-$135; D $122-$147; each addl $10; suites $195-$275; family rates; ski, golf plans; lower rates rest of yr. Crib free. TV; cable (premium). 2 pools; wading pool. Supervised child's activities (May-Oct); ages 3-15. Restaurant 6:30 am-10 pm. Rm serv. Bar; entertainment Tues-Sat. Ck-out noon. Convention facilities. Business servs avail. Gift shop. Bellhops. Valet serv. Indoor & outdoor tennis, pro. 18-hole golf, pro, putting green. Exercise equipt; treadmill, weights. Health club privileges. Refrigerators; some wet bars; microwaves avail. Private patios, balconies. Near shopping center. Cr cds: A, C, D, DS, ER, JCB, MC, V.

★ ★ **QUALITY INN-BILTMORE.** *115 Hendersonville Rd (28803). 704/274-1800; FAX 704/274-5960.* E-mail biltsarms@ioa.com. 160 rms, 5 story, 20 suites. Apr-Oct: S, D $95-$107; each addl $8; suites $110-$150; under 18 free; lower rates rest of yr. Crib free. TV; cable (premium). Pool. Complimentary coffee in rms. Restaurant 6:30 am-10 pm. Rm serv. Bar 5-11 pm. Ck-out noon. Meeting rms. Business servs avail. Bellhops. Valet serv. Health club privileges. Some refrigerators. Cr cds: A, C, D, DS, MC, V.

Hotels

★ ★ ★ **HAYWOOD PARK.** *One Battery Park Ave (28801). 704/252-2522; FAX 704/253-0481; res: 800/228-2522.* 33 suites, 4 story. S $130-$245; D $155-$295; each addl $15; under 18 free. TV; cable (premium), VCR avail. Complimentary continental bkfst. Restaurant 11 am-9:30 pm (also see 23 PAGE). Bar. Ck-out noon. Meeting rms. Business servs avail. In-rm modem link. Shopping arcade. Free valet parking. Exercise equipt; weights, bicycle, sauna. Bathrm phones; refrigerators. Cr cds: A, C, D, DS, MC, V.

★ ★ **RADISSON.** *One Thomas Wolfe Plaza (28801). 704/252-8211; FAX 704/254-1374.* 281 rms, 12 story. Apr-mid-Nov: S $89-$119; D $99-$139; each addl $10; suites $165-$225; under 17 free; lower rates rest of yr. Crib free. TV; cable (premium), VCR avail. Pool; poolside serv. Restaurant 6:30 am-10 pm. Bar 11-1 am. Ck-out noon. Convention facilities. Business servs avail. In-rm modem link. Concierge. Gift shop. Exercise equipt; weight machine, stair machine. Game rm. Minibars. Refrigerators avail. Cr cds: A, C, D, DS, MC, V.

Inns

★ ★ **ALBEMARLE.** *86 Edgemont Rd (28801). 704/255-0027; res: 800/621-7435.* 11 rms, 3 story. S, D $95-$160; each addl $25. Children over 13 yrs only. TV; cable. Pool. Complimentary full bkfst; afternoon refreshments. Ck-out 11 am, ck-in 3 pm. Luggage handling. Street parking. Picnic tables. Microwaves avail. Greek-revival mansion built 1909; many antiques. Totally nonsmoking. Cr cds: DS, MC, V.

★ ★ **APPLEWOOD MANOR INN.** *62 Cumberland Circle (28801), 1 mi N on I-240, exit 4-C. 704/254-2244; res: 800/442-2197; FAX 704/254-0899.* 5 rms, 2 with showers only, 1 kit. cottage, 2 story. No rm phones. S $85-$105; D $90-$110; each addl $20; kit. cottage $105-$110; hols (2-day min). Children over 12 yrs only. TV in kit. cottage; cable. Complimentary full bkfst. Complimentary coffee in rms. Ck-out 11 am, ck-in 3-7 pm. Business servs avail. Luggage handling. Lawn games. Many fireplaces. Many balconies. Colonial turn-of-the-century home built in 1910; antiques. Totally nonsmoking. Cr cds: MC, V.

★ ★ **CAIRN BRAE.** *217 Patton Mountain Rd (28804). 704/252-9219.* E-mail cairnbrae@compuserv.com. 3 rms, 1 with shower only, 2 story, 2 suites. No rm phones. S $85-$100; D $95-$110; each addl $20; suites $110. Children over 10 yrs only. TV in sitting rm; cable (premium).

Complimentary full bkfst; afternoon refreshments. Ck-out 11 am, ck-in 3 pm. Rec rm. Picnic tables. Situated along mountainside. Totally nonsmoking. Cr cds: DS, MC, V.

★ ★ ★ **CEDAR CREST.** *674 Biltmore Ave (28803). 704/252-1389; FAX 704/253-7667; res: 800/252-0310.* 9 rms, 3 story, 2 cottage suites. S, D $120-$160; each addl $20; suites $185-$210. Children over 10 yrs only. Complimentary full bkfst. Ck-out 11 am, ck-in 3-10 pm. Business servs avail. Lawn games. Balconies. Historic inn (1890); antiques. Flower gardens. Cr cds: A, D, MC, V.

★ ★ **CORNER OAK MANOR.** *53 St Dunstans Rd (28803). 704/253-3525.* E-mail vineguy@aol.com. 4 rms, 2 story, 1 kit. unit. No rm phones. S $75; D $100-$115; kit. unit $145. Children over 12 yrs only. Complimentary full bkfst. Ck-out 11 am, ck-in 3 pm. Whirlpool on terrace. Picnic tables. English Tudor home (1920); antiques. Totally nonsmoking. Cr cds: A, DS, MC, V.

✔ ★ ★ **FLINT STREET INNS.** *116 Flint St (28801). 704/253-6723.* 8 rms in 2 buildings, 2 story. S $75; D $95; each addl $25. Complimentary full bkfst; afternoon refreshments. Ck-out 11 am, ck-in noon-8 pm. In Montford Historic District. Cr cds: A, DS, ER, MC, V.

★ ★ **LAKE LURE.** *(Lake Lure 28746) 26 mi SE on US 64/74A. 704/625-2525; FAX 704/625-9655; res: 800/277-5873.* 50 rms, 3 story. Apr-Oct: S, D $85-$115; each addl $10; under 12 free; higher rates wkends; lower rates rest of yr. Crib free. TV; cable (premium). Pool. Complimentary continental bkfst. Dining rm 5-9 pm; Sun 11 am-2:30 pm; closed Mon. Bar. Ck-out 11 am, ck-in 3 pm. Business servs avail. Microwaves avail. On lake; view of Blue Ridge Mts. Mediterranean-style hostelry (1927). Cr cds: A, D, DS, MC, V.

★ ★ ★ **LION & THE ROSE.** *276 Montford (28801). 704/255-7673; res: 800/546-6988; FAX 704/285-9810.* 5 rms, 3 story. No rm phones. No elvtr. S, D $115-$155; each addl $35. Children over 12 yrs only. Complimentary full bkfst; afternoon refreshments. Restaurant nearby. Ck-out 11 am, ck-in 3 pm. Luggage handling. Health club privileges. Georgian house built in 1895; furnished with antiques. Totally nonsmoking. Cr cds: A, MC, V.

★ ★ **OLD REYNOLDS MANSION.** *100 Reynolds Heights (28804). 704/254-0496.* 10 rms, 8 with bath, 3 story. No rm phones. S, D $60-$115; cottage suite $110-$120. Pool. Complimentary continental bkfst; afternoon refreshments. Restaurant nearby. Ck-out 11 am, ck-in 3 pm. Antebellum mansion (1855) on hill overlooking mountains; antiques, verandas. No cr cds accepted.

★ ★ ★ **OWL'S NEST INN AT ENGADINE.** *(2630 Smokey Park Hwy, Candler 28715) W on I-40, exit 37. 704/665-8325; FAX 704/667-2539; res: 800/665-8868.* Web www.circle.net.owlsnest. 5 rms, 1 suite, 3 story. No rm phones. No elvtr. S $80-$135; D $95-$150; each addl $15. Children over 6 yrs only. Complimentary full bkfst. Restaurant nearby. Ck-out 11 am, ck-in 3-7 pm. Luggage handling. Victorian house built in 1885; furnished with antiques. Totally nonsmoking. Cr cds: DS, MC, V.

★ ★ ★ **RICHMOND HILL.** *87 Richmond Hill Dr (28806). 704/252-7313; FAX 704/252-8726; res: 800/545-9238.* Web richmondhillinn.com. 36 rms, 3 story, 7 cottages. S, D $140-$350; each addl $20. Crib $15. TV; cable (premium). Complimentary full bkfst; afternoon refreshments. Dining rms (see GABRIELLE'S). Ck-out 11 am, ck-in 3 pm. Business servs avail. Gift shop. Exercise equipt; treadmill, bicycle. Croquet courts. Queen Anne-style architecture; library, grand entrance hall. Former congressman's residence. Cr cds: A, MC, V.

★ ★ ★ **WRIGHT INN & CARRIAGE HOUSE.** *235 Pearson Dr (28801). 704/251-0789; FAX 704/251-0929; res: 800/552-5724.* 10 rms, 4 story. No elvtr. S, D $95-$145; cottage $215. Children over 12 yrs only. TV; cable (premium). Complimentary full bkfst. Restaurant nearby. Ck-out 11 am, ck-in 3-7 pm. Luggage handling. Victorian house built in 1898; furnished with antiques. Totally nonsmoking. Cr cds: DS, MC, V.

Resorts

★ ★ ★ **GROVE PARK INN RESORT.** *290 Macon Ave (28804). 704/252-2711; FAX 704/253-7053; res: 800/438-5800.* Web www.grovepa rkinn.com. The renovation of this inn overlooking the Blue Ridge Mountains preserves the original 1913 decor, including the fireplaces in the lobby and the terraced guest rooms. The roster of distinguished guests includes Henry Ford and F. Scott Fitzgerald. 510 rms, 5-10 story. Apr-Dec: S, D $125-$230; each addl $25; suites $450; under 16 free; golf plans; lower rates rest of yr. Crib free. TV; cable (premium), VCR avail. 2 heated pools, 1 indoor; whirlpool, lifeguard. Supervised child's activities; ages 3-16. Restaurants 6:30 am-midnight (also see HORIZONS). Rm serv. Bar from 11 am; entertainment. Ck-out noon, ck-in 4 pm. Convention facilities. Business center. Bellhops. Valet serv. Shopping arcade. 9 lighted tennis courts, 3 indoor. Golf, greens fee $65 (incl cart), nine holes $30, putting green. Rec rm. Exercise rm; instructor, weights, bicycles, sauna. Raquetball & squash courts. Massage. Luxury level. Cr cds: A, C, D, DS, JCB, MC, V.

✔ ★ **PISGAH VIEW RANCH.** *(Rte 1, Candler 28715)* Enka-Candler exit off I-40, S on US 19/23 4 mi to Candler, left on NC 151, 9 mi to ranch. *704/667-9100.* 48 units. May-Oct: AP: S $65-$125/person, $250-$625/wk; D $50-$85/person, $300-$475/wk; family rates. Closed rest of yr. Crib free. TV. Heated pool. Playground. Dining rm: bkfst 8 am, lunch 12:30 pm, dinner 5:30 pm. Ck-out 11 am, ck-in 2 pm. Coin lndry. Meeting rms. Gift shop. Airport, bus depot transportation. Tennis. Hiking trails. Rec rm. Lawn games. Entertainment. No cr cds accepted.

Restaurants

★ ★ ★ **23 PAGE.** *(See Haywood Park Hotel) 704/252-3685.* Hrs: 5:30-10 pm. Closed some major hols. Res accepted. Continental menu. Bar. Extensive wine list. A la carte entrees: dinner $14.95-$28.95. Child's meals. Specializes in seafood, desserts, pasta. Intimate dining. Cr cds: A, D, MC, V.

★ **FINE FRIENDS.** *946 Merrimon Ave, in Northland Shopping Center. 704/253-6649.* Hrs: 11:30 am-9 pm; Fri, Sat to 10 pm; Sun brunch 11:30 am-3:30 pm. Closed Thanksgiving, Dec 24, 25. Res accepted. Bar to midnight. Semi-a la carte: lunch $5.95-$10.95, dinner $10.95-$16.95. Sun brunch $6-$8. Child's meals. Specializes in seafood, beef, pasta. Own desserts. Cr cds: A, D, DS, MC, V.

★ ★ ★ **GABRIELLE'S.** *(See Richmond Hill Inn) 704/252-7313.* Hrs: 6-10 pm. Closed Tues, Wed. Res required. Wine list. Semi-a la carte: dinner $30-$40. Child's meals. Specializes in fresh fish, beef, homemade pasta. Pianist Thurs-Mon. Valet parking. Formal dining. Jacket. Totally nonsmoking. Cr cds: A, MC, V.

★ ★ **GREENERY.** *148 Tunnel Rd. 704/253-2809.* Hrs: 5-10 pm. Closed Jan 1. Res accepted. Bar. Semi-a la carte: dinner $14.95-$24.95. Specialties: Maryland crabcakes, mountain trout. Cr cds: A, MC, V.

★ ★ ★ **HORIZONS.** *(See Grove Park Inn Resort) 704/252-2711.* Web www.groveparkinn.com. Hrs: 6:30-9:30 pm. Closed Sun. Res accepted. Continental, Amer menu. Serv bar. Wine list. Semi-a la carte: dinner $21-$33. Complete meals: dinner $49-$59. Specialties: Lone star

ostrich au poivre, double breast of free range chicken, mixed grill of American wild game. Piano Tue-Sat. Valet parking. Formal dining in elegant setting with mountain views. Jacket, tie. Totally nonsmoking. Cr cds: A, C, D, DS, JCB, MC, V.

★ ★ **THE MARKET PLACE ON WALL STREET.** *20 Wall St (28801). 704/252-4162.* Hrs: 6-9:30 pm. Closed Sun; some major hols. Res accepted. Bar. A la carte entrees: dinner $12.50-$27.95. Child's meals. Specializes in seafood, veal, lamb. Outdoor dining. 3 formal dining areas. Totally nonsmoking. Cr cds: A, D, MC, V.

✔ ★ **McGUFFEY'S.** *13 Kenilworth Knoll. 704/252-0956.* Hrs: 11 am-2 am; Sun brunch to 4 pm. Closed Thanksgiving, Dec 25. Bar. Semi-a la carte: lunch $4.99-$8.99, dinner $6.99-$15. Sun brunch $4.99-$10.99. Specializes in beef, seafood, chicken. Cr cds: A, DS, MC, V.

★ ★ **VINCENZO'S.** *10 N Market St (28801). 704/254-4698.* Hrs: 11:30 am-2 pm; 5:30-11 pm; Sat from 5:30 pm; Sun 5:30-9 pm. Closed major hols. Res accepted. Italian, continental menu. Bar. Semi-a la carte: $9-$27. Child's meals. Specializes in veal, pasta, seafood. Entertainment. Cr cds: A, DS, MC, V.

★ ★ **WINDMILL EUROPEAN GRILL.** *85 Tunnel Rd, at Innsbruck Mall. 704/253-5285.* Hrs: 5:30-9:30 pm; Fri, Sat to 10 pm. Closed Sun, Mon; Jan 1, Dec 25. Res accepted. Continental menu. Bar. Complete meals: dinner $9.99-$18.99. Specializes in beef, chicken. Cr cds: A, DS, MC, V.

Unrated Dining Spot

MOUNTAIN SMOKE HOUSE. *20 Spruce St. 704/253-4871.* Hrs: June-Dec 5:30-11 pm; Fri, Sat to midnight; times vary rest of yr. Closed Jan-Mar. Res accepted. Bar. Semi-a la carte: dinner $5.95-$9.95. Child's meals. Specializes in barbecued chopped pork, herb-smoked chicken, barbecued chicken. Bluegrass band, clogging. Casual, family atmosphere. Cr cds: A, D, DS, MC, V.

Atlantic Beach

(see Morehead City)

Banner Elk (A-3)

(See also Blowing Rock, Boone, Linville)

Pop 933 **Elev** 3,739 ft **Area code** 704 **Zip** 28604 **E-mail** beacc@skybest.com **Web** www.banner-elk.com
Information Chamber of Commerce, PO Box 335; 704/898-5605.

What to See and Do

Grandfather Mountain. 3 mi SW via US 221 (see LINVILLE).

Skiing.

Ski Beech. Quad chairlift, 6 double chairlifts, J-bar, rope tow; patrol, school, rentals; snowmaking; restaurant, cafeteria; nursery, shopping. Vertical drop 830 ft. (Mid-Nov-mid-Mar, daily) Also ice-skating. 3 mi N on NC 184. Phone 704/387-2011. ¢¢¢¢¢

Sugar Mt. Five chairlifts, 2 T-bars, rope tow; patrol, school, rentals, snowmaking; children's program; lodging, cafeteria; nursery. (Mid-Nov-mid-Mar, daily) Off NC 184. Phone 704/898-4521. ¢¢¢¢¢

Motels

★ ★ **HOLIDAY INN.** *NC 184, 1 mi S on NC 184 between NC 194 and NC 105.* 704/898-4571; FAX 704/898-8437. 101 rms, 2 story. Dec-Feb: S, D $64.99-$99.99; under 18 free; ski plans; lower rates rest of yr. Crib free. TV; cable (premium). Pool. Restaurant 7 am-2 pm, 6-9 pm. Rm serv. Ck-out noon. Meeting rms. Business servs avail. Downhill/x-country ski 1 mi. Cr cds: A, C, D, DS, MC, V.

★ **PINNACLE INN.** *off NC 184.* 704/387-2231; FAX 704/387-4773; res: 800/438-2097. 242 kits, 3 story. No elvtr. Mid-Nov-mid-Mar: kit. units $75-$170; lower rates rest of yr. Crib $5. TV; cable. Indoor pool; whirlpool, sauna. Free supervised child's activities (mid-June-mid-Sept). Restaurant nearby. Ck-out 10 am. Coin lndry. Meeting rms. Business servs avail. Tennis. Downhill ski ½ mi. Game rm. Fireplaces. Balconies. Picnic tables, grills. Cr cds: A, MC, V.

Inn

✔ ★ ★ **ARCHERS INN.** *2489 Beech Mountain Pkwy.* 704/898-9004. Web www.archersinn.com. 15 rms, 2 story. Mid-Dec-mid-Mar: S, D $75-$200; each addl $10; lower rates rest of yr. Crib free. TV; cable, VCR some rms. Complimentary full bkfst. Coffee in rms. Restaurant (see JACKALOPE'S VIEW). Swimming privileges. Ck-out 11 am, ck-in 3 pm. Tennis privileges. Golf privileges. Downhill ski 2 mi. Fireplaces; many refrigerators. Many balconies. Rustic decor. Cr cds: DS, MC, V.

Restaurant

★ ★ **JACKALOPE'S VIEW.** *(See Archers Inn)* 704/899-9004. Web www.archersinn.com. Hrs: 5-9:30 pm; Fri, Sat to 10 pm. Closed Mon. Res accepted. No A/C. Continental menu. Bar. Semi-a la carte: dinner $10-$20. Child's meals. Specializes in steak, seafood, wild game. Own baking. Outdoor dining. Floor-to-ceiling windows overlook mountains, patio; artwork by local artists. Totally nonsmoking. Cr cds: DS, MC, V.

Beaufort (C-9)

(See also Morehead City)

Pop 3,808 **Elev** 7 ft **Area code** 919 **Zip** 28516 **E-mail** cctdb @bmd.clis.com **Web** www.NCcoast.com

Information Carteret County Tourism Development Bureau, PO Box 1406, Morehead City 28557; 919/726-8148 or 800/SUNNY-NC.

Beaufort, dating from the colonial era, is a seaport with more than 125 historic houses and sites.

What to See and Do

Beaufort Historic Site. Old Burying Ground, 1829 restored Old Jail, restored houses (1767-1830), courthouse (ca 1796), apothecary shop, art gallery and gift shop. Obtain additional information, self-guided walking tour map from Beaufort Historical Assn, Inc, 138 Turner St, PO Box 1709. (Daily exc Sun; closed some major hols) Phone 919/728-5225. Admission to 6 buildings open to the public ¢¢

Cape Lookout National Seashore. This unit of the National Park System, on the outer banks of North Carolina, extends 55 mi S from Ocracoke Inlet and includes unspoiled barrier islands. There are no roads or bridges; access is by boat only (fee). Ferries from Beaufort, Harkers Island, Davis, Atlantic and Ocracoke (Apr-Nov). Excellent fishing and shell collecting; primitive camping; interpretive programs (seasonal). Lighthouse (1859) at Cape Lookout is still operational. Phone 919/728-2250.

North Carolina Maritime Museum and Watercraft Center. Natural and maritime history exhibits, field trips; special programs in maritime and coastal natural history. (Daily; closed Jan 1, Thanksgiving, Dec 25) 315 Front St. Phone 919/728-7317. **Free.**

Annual Events

Beaufort by the Sea Music Festival. Late Apr.

Old Homes Tour and Antiques Show. Private homes and historic public buildings; Carteret County Militia; bus tours and tours of old burying ground; historical crafts. Sponsored by the Beaufort Historical Assn, Inc, PO Box 1709. Phone 919/728-5225. Late June.

Inns

★ ★ **CEDARS.** *305 Front St.* 919/728-7036; FAX 919/728-1685. 7 rms, 5 suites, 2 story. Mid-Apr-mid-Oct: S, D $85-$115; suites $140-$165; lower rates rest of yr. TV; cable. Complimentary full bkfst. Ck-out 11 am, ck-in 3 pm. Private patios, balconies. Historic house (ca 1770) overlooking river; antiques. Cr cds: MC, V.

★ ★ **DELAMAR INN.** *217 Turner St.* 919/728-4300; FAX 919/728-1491; res: 800/359-5823. 3 rms, 1 with shower only, 2 story. No rm phones. May-Sept: D $94; lower rates rest of yr. Children over 12 yrs only. Complimentary continental bkfst; afternoon refreshments. Restaurant nearby. Ck-out noon, ck-in 1 pm. Business servs avail. Built 1866; first and second floor porches. Many antiques. Totally nonsmoking. Cr cds: MC, V.

★ ★ **PECAN TREE INN.** *116 Queen St.* 919/728-6733. 7 rms, 6 with shower only, 2 story. No rm phones. Apr-Sept: D $85-$125; each addl $15; wkly rates; lower rates rest of yr. Children over 12 yrs only. Complimentary continental bkfst. Restaurant adj 11 am-10 pm. Ck-out 11 am, ck-in 3 pm. Game rm. Built 1866. Many antiques. Totally nonsmoking. Cr cds: DS, MC, V.

Restaurant

✔ ★ ★ **LAWRY'S LANDING.** *502 Front St, on the Waterfront.* 919/728-7541. Hrs: 11 am-9 pm; hrs may vary Nov-Feb. Bar. Semi-a la carte: lunch $6-$12, dinner $9.95-$19.95. Sun buffet: lunch, dinner $11.99. Child's meals. Specializes in fresh local seafood, prime rib. Williamsburg decor; overlooks harbor. Cr cds: DS, MC, V.

Blowing Rock (A-4)

(See also Banner Elk, Boone, Linville)

Founded 1889 **Pop** 1,257 **Elev** 4,000 ft **Area code** 704 **Zip** 28605 **E-mail** blowingrock@skybest.com **Web** www.blowingrock .com/northcarolina

Information Chamber of Commerce, PO Box 406; 704/295-7851 or 800/295-7851.

On the Blue Ridge Parkway, Blowing Rock was named, based on Native American folklore, for the cliff near town where lightweight objects thrown outward are swept back to their origin by the wind. It has been a resort area for more than 100 years; a wide variety of recreational facilities and shops can be found nearby.

What to See and Do

Blowing Rock. Cliff (4,000 ft) hangs over Johns River Gorge 2,000-3,000 ft below. Scenic views of Grandfather, Grandmother, Table Rock and Hawksbill mountains. Observation deck. Gift shop. (Apr-Nov, daily) 2 mi SE on US 321. Phone 704/295-7111. ¢¢

Julian Price Memorial Park. Boating (hand-powered only, rentals). Picnicking. Camping (trailer facilities, no hookups; June-Oct only; fee). Amphitheater; evening interpretive programs (May-Oct). Park open yr-round (weather permitting). SW via US 221 & Blue Ridge Pkwy. Phone 704/295-7591 or 704/963-5911. **Free.**

Moses H. Cone Memorial Park. Former summer estate of textile magnate. Bridle paths, 2 lakes; 25 mi of hiking and cross-country skiing trails. (May-Oct, daily) On Blue Ridge Pkwy. Phone 704/295-7591. **Free.**

Parkway Craft Center. Demonstrations of weaving, wood carving, pottery, jewelry making, other crafts. (May-Oct, daily) Handcrafted items for sale. Phone 704/295-7938. **Free.**

Mystery Hill. Educational exhibits explore science, optical illusion and natural phenoma. Features TouchTown, Mystery House, Hall of Mystery and BubbleRama. Gift shop. (Daily; closed Thanksgiving, Dec 25) N on US 321. Phone 704/264-2792. ¢¢

Skiing.

Appalachian Ski Mountain. Quad & 2 double chairlifts, 2 rope tows, 1 handle-pull tow; patrol; French-Swiss Ski College; Ski-Wee children's program; equipment rentals; 100% snowmaking; restaurant; 8 runs; longest run 2,700 ft; vertical drop 365 ft. (Thanksgiving-mid-Mar, daily & nightly; closed Dec 24 evening-Dec 25) Night skiing (all slopes lighted); half-day and twilight rates. 3 mi N on US 321, near Blueridge Pkwy intersection. Phone 704/295-7828 or 800/322-2373 (res). ¢¢¢¢

Tweetsie Railroad. A 3-mi excursion, with mock holdup and raid, on old narrow-gauge railroad; Western Town with variety show at Tweetsie Palace; country fair, petting zoo; craft village; chairlift to Mouse Mt Picnic Area. (May-Oct, limited hrs) 4 mi N on US 321. Phone 704/264-9061. ¢¢¢¢

Annual Event

Tour of Homes. 4th Fri July.

Motels

★ ★ **BLOWING ROCK INN.** N Main St, ¼ mi N on US 221/321 Business. 704/295-7921. 24 rms. July-Nov: S, D $69-$84; each addl $5; lower rates early-mid-Nov, Apr-May; also 1-bedrm villas avail. Closed Dec-Mar. TV; cable. Heated pool. Complimentary coffee on porch. Restaurant nearby. Ck-out 11 am. Picnic tables. Cr cds: A, DS, MC, V.

★ ★ **CLIFF DWELLERS INN.** 116 Lakeview Terrace, 1 mi S, Blue Ridge Pkwy exit for US 321, across from Shoppes on the Pkwy. 704/295-3121; res: 800/322-7380. E-mail cliffdwellers@boone.net. 20 rms, 3 story, 3 suites, 2 kit. units. No elvtr. Mid-May-early Nov: S, D $90-$105; each addl $5; suites, kit. units $145-$225; under 12 free; higher rates: ski season wkends, Dec 25-Jan 1; lower rates rest of yr. Closed Dec-Mar except wkends, Christmas hol. Crib $5. TV; cable. Heated pool; whirlpool. Complimentary coffee in rms. Restaurant nearby. Ck-out 11 am. Refrigerators; microwaves avail. Balconies. View of mountains. Cr cds: C, D, MC, V.

✔ ★ **HOMESTEAD INN.** 153 Morris St. 704/295-9559; FAX 704/295-7419. E-mail rvalet@aol.com. 15 rms. No rm phones. Early June-Oct: S, D $47-$62; each addl $5; family, wkday, wkly rates; lower rates rest of yr. Crib free. TV; cable. Playground. Coffee in lobby. Restaurant nearby. Ck-out 11 am. Downhill ski 4 mi. Refrigerators; microwaves avail. Picnic tables, grills. Cr cds: DS, MC, V.

Inns

★ ★ **CRIPPEN'S COUNTRY INN.** 239 Sunset Dr (28607). 704/295-3487; FAX 704/295-0388. Web www.crippen.com. 8 rms, 2 with shower only, 3 story, 1 guest house. May-Dec: S, D $99-$120; each addl $25; guest house $139-$159; under 12 free; hols (2-day min); lower rates rest of yr. TV in common rm; cable (premium). Complimentary continental bkfst. Restaurant (see CRIPPEN'S). Rm serv 6-10 pm. Ck-out 11 am, ck-in 3 pm. Business servs avail. Luggage handling. Valet serv. Built in 1931. Totally nonsmoking. Cr cds: A, DS, MC, V.

★ ★ **GREEN PARK.** 2 mi SE on US 321. 704/295-3141; res: 800/852-2462. 85 rms, 3 story. No A/C. Mid-June-mid-Nov: S $99; D $109-$139; each addl $5; suites $160-$165; under 12 free; lower rates rest of yr. Crib $10. TV; cable, VCR avail. Pool. Complimentary continental bkfst. Dining rms 5-10 pm; Sun brunch 11 am-2:30 pm. Bar 5 pm-midnight. Ck-out 11 am, ck-in 3 pm. Meeting rms. Business servs avail. Bellhops. Tennis privileges. 18-hole golf privileges. Downhill ski 2 mi. Lawn games. Many private porches. Historic building (1882); library, fireplace. Cr cds: A, DS, MC, V.

✔ ★ ★ ★ **THE INN AT RAGGED GARDENS.** 203 Sunset Dr. 704/295-9703. Web www.ragged-gardens.com. 8 rms, 2 with A/C, 3 story. S, D $105-$150. Children over 12 yrs only. Complimentary full bkfst; afternoon refreshments. Ck-out 11 am, ck-in after 3 pm. Fireplaces; some in-rm whirlpools. Some private balconies. Built in 1900; gardens. Totally nonsmoking. Cr cds: MC, V.

★ ★ **MAPLE LODGE.** 152 Sunset Dr. 704/295-3331; FAX 704/295-9986. E-mail innkeeper@maplelodge.net; web www.maplelodge .net. 11 rms, 2 story. No rm phones. No elvtr. S, D $95-$135; each addl $20; suite $135. Closed Jan, Feb. Children over 12 yrs only. Complimentary full bkfst. Restaurant opp 11 am-10 pm. Ck-out 11 am, ck-in 3-9 pm. Luggage handling. Downhill ski 5 mi; x-country ski 2 mi. Furnished with antiques. Totally nonsmoking. Cr cds: A, D, DS, MC, V.

★ ★ **MEADOWBROOK.** N Main St. 704/295-4300; res: 800/456-5456. 61 rms, 2-3 story. S, D $94-$139; each addl $10; suites $139-$259; under 12 free; ski plans. TV; cable, VCR avail. Indoor pool; whirlpool. Complimentary continental bkfst. Dining rm 11 am-2 pm, 6-9 pm; Mon-Wed from 6 pm. Bar; entertainment Thurs-Sat. Ck-out 11 am, ck-in 3 pm. Meeting rms. Business servs avail. Downhill ski 3 mi. Exercise equipt: treadmill, weights. European style country inn. Cr cds: A, D, DS, MC, V.

Resorts

★ ★ ★ **CHETOLA.** N Main St. 704/295-5500; FAX 704/295-5529; res: 800/243-8652. Web www.chetola.com. 42 rms, 1-3 story. May-Dec: S, D $125-$214; lower rates rest of yr. Crib $5. TV; cable (premium), VCR avail. Indoor pool; whirlpool. Playground. Supervised child's activities (June-Aug); ages 5-12. Dining rm (public by res) 8-10 am, 11:30 am-2 pm, 5:30-8:30 pm. Ck-out 11 am, ck-in 3 pm. Coin lndry. Meeting rms. Business servs avail. Grocery, package store ½ mi. Sports dir. Lighted tennis. Boating, fishing. Downhill/x-country ski 3 mi. Exercise equipt; weight machines, stair machine, sauna. Hiking. Bicycles. Soc dir. Entertainment. Racquetball court. Game rm. Refrigerators. Some private balconies. Picnic tables, grills. Seven-acre lake. Adj to Moses Cone Natl Park. Cr cds: A, DS, MC, V.

★ ★ ★ **HOUND EARS LODGE & CLUB.** 7 mi W, ½ mi off NC 105. 704/963-4321; FAX 704/963-8030. 29 rms in lodge & club house, 2 story. MAP, mid-June-Oct: S $150; D $270; each addl $48; suites $290; under 11, $22; lower rates rest of yr. Serv charge 17%. TV; cable (premium), VCR avail. Heated pool; poolside serv, lifeguard. Free supervised child's activities (June-Sept); ages 8-16. Dining rm 7-10 am, noon-2:30 pm, 6:30-9:30 pm (res required; jacket, tie at dinner). Rm serv. Setups; entertainment. Ck-out noon, ck-in 1:30 pm. Meeting rms. Business servs avail. Bellhops. Valet serv. 6 tennis courts, pro. 18-hole golf, greens fee $38, pro. Exercise equipt; weight machine, bicycle, sauna. Resort is named for a 4,000-ft rock outcropping that looms above it in the Blue Ridge Mountains. Cr cds: A, MC, V.

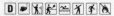

Restaurants

★ ★ **BEST CELLAR.** *On Little Springs Rd, behind Food Lion Shopping Center. 704/295-3466.* Hrs: 6-9:30 pm; Nov-mid-May, Fri, Sat only. Closed Sun. Res accepted. No A/C. Continental menu. Wine, beer. Semi-a la carte: dinner $12.95-$17.95. Specializes in roast duckling, poached salmon, banana cream pie. Valet parking. Rustic decor; pine floor, stone walls, 3 fireplaces. Cr cds: A, C, D, DS, MC, V.

★ ★ **CRIPPEN'S.** *(See Crippen's Country Inn) 704/295-3487.* Web www.crippens.com. Hrs: 6-9 pm; Fri to 10 pm; Sat 5-10 pm; summer Sat, Sun also 11:30 am-2 pm. Closed Mon; most major hols; also Super Bowl Sun. Res accepted. Continental menu. Bar 4-11 pm. Semi-a la carte: lunch $4.50-$13.50, dinner $7.95-$29. Child's meals. Specialties: grilled Maine lobster, grilled North Carolina ostrich, horseradish-encrusted salmon. Own pasta. Valet parking. Semi-formal, spacious dining area. Totally nonsmoking. Cr cds: A, DS, MC, V.

★ ★ **RIVERWOOD.** *US 321, ½ mi S of Blue Ridge Pkwy. 704/295-4162.* Web blowingrock.com/northcarolina/riverwoodrestaurant. Hrs: 6 pm-closing; Sat, Sun from 5:30 pm; winter hrs vary. Res accepted. Bar. Semi-a la carte: dinner $13.95-$23.95. Specialties: stuffed rainbow trout, marinated beef tenderloin. Own desserts. Totally nonsmoking. Cr cds: DS, MC, V.

✔ ★ **SPECKLED TROUT CAFE.** *Main St & US 221. 704/295-9819.* Hrs: 9 am-3 pm, 5-9:30 pm. Closed Dec 25. Res accepted. Bar. Semi-a la carte: bkfst $2.95-$4.95, lunch $2.95-$6.95, dinner $10.95-$16.95. Specializes in seafood. Outdoor dining. Cr cds: A, MC, V.

★ ★ **TWIG'S.** *US 321 Bypass. 704/295-5050.* Hrs: 5:30-9:30 pm; Fri, Sat to 10 pm. Closed Mon; Dec 24-25. Res accepted. No A/C. Continental menu. Bar 5:30 pm-2 am. A la carte entrees: dinner $10.95-$19.95. Specializes in crabcakes, lamb, fresh seafood. Porch dining (summer). Cr cds: A, DS, MC, V.

Blue Ridge Parkway

(see Virginia)

Boone (A-4)

(See also Banner Elk, Blowing Rock, Linville)

Settled 1772 **Pop** 12,915 **Elev** 3,266 ft **Area code** 704 **Zip** 28607 **E-mail** chamber@boone.net **Web** www.acs.appstate.edu/orgs/ec

Information Convention & Visitors Bureau, 208 Howard St, 28607-4032, 704/262-3516 or 800/852-9506; or North Carolina High Country Host, 1700 Blowing Rock Rd, 704/264-1299 or 800/438-7500.

Boone, the seat of Watauga County, was named for Daniel Boone, who had a cabin and hunted here in the 1760s. This "Heart of the High Country" sprawls over a long valley, which provides a natural pass through the hills. Watauga County boasts several industrial firms providing its economic base, in addition to tourism, agriculture and Appalachian State University. Mountain crafts are featured in a variety of craft fairs, festivals and shops.

What to See and Do

Appalachian State University (1899). (11,500 students) Offers 90 undergraduate and 12 graduate majors. Dark Sky Observatory. Atop Blue Ridge Mountains. Phone 704/262-2000 or 704/262-2179. (See SEASONAL EVENTS)

Daniel Boone Native Gardens. Native plants in informal setting; Squire Boone Cabin, wishing well, fern garden. (May-Sept, daily; Oct, wkends) Horn in the West Dr, 1 mi E off US 421, adj to Daniel Boone Amphitheatre (see SEASONAL EVENTS). Phone 704/264-6390. ¢

Seasonal Events

Horn in the West. Daniel Boone Amphitheatre, 1 mi E off US 421. Outdoor drama depicts Daniel Boone and settlers of the mountain during the Revolutionary War. Nightly exc Mon. Contact PO Box 295; 704/264-2120. Mid-June-mid-Aug.

An Appalachian Summer. Appalachian State University. Concerts, drama, art exhibits. Phone 800/841-2787.

Motels

★ **GRAYSTONE LODGE.** *2419 NC 105, 3 mi S on NC 105. 704/264-4133; res: 800/560-5942; FAX 704/262-0101.* 101 rms, 4 story. Mid-June-late Oct, late Dec-Feb: S, D $52-$79; each addl $3; under 18 free; lower rates rest of yr. Crib free. TV; cable (premium), VCR avail. Indoor pool. Complimentary continental bkfst. Restaurant nearby. Ck-out 11 am. Business servs avail. Downhill/x-country ski 8 mi. Game rm. Cr cds: A, C, D, DS, MC, V.

★ ★ **HOLIDAY INN EXPRESS.** *1855 Blowing Rock Rd. 704/264-2451; FAX 704/265-3861.* E-mail holidayinn@boone.mail.net; web www.holiday-inn.com. 138 rms, 2 story. June-Oct, ski season: S, D $69-$99; each addl $8; under 18 free; lower rates rest of yr. Crib free. TV; cable (premium), VCR avail. Heated pool. Complimentary continental bkfst. Coffee in rms. Ck-out 11 am. Coin lndry. Meeting rms. Business servs avail. In-rm modem link. Exercise equipt; treadmill, weight machine. Downhill ski 5 mi. Cr cds: A, C, D, DS, MC, V.

Motor Hotel

★ ★ **HAMPTON INN.** *1075 NC 105. 704/264-0077; FAX 704/264-4600.* 95 rms, 5 story. June-Oct: S, D $85-$117; under 18 free; golf plan; lower rates rest of yr. Crib free. TV; cable (premium), VCR avail. Indoor pool. Complimentary continental bkfst. Restaurant adj 11 am-10 pm. Ck-out 11 am. Meeting rms. Business servs avail. Health club privileges. Cr cds: A, C, D, DS, ER, JCB, MC, V.

Hotel

★ ★ ★ **QUALITY INN APPALACHIAN CONFERENCE CENTER.** *949 Blowing Rock Rd, 1 mi S at jct US 321, NC 105. 704/262-0020.* 132 rms, 7 story. Mid-June-mid-Nov: S $90; D $95; each addl $8; suites $90-$165; under 18 free; ski, golf packages; higher rates late Dec-Feb; lower rates rest of yr. TV; cable (premium). Indoor pool. Restaurant 7 am-2 pm, 5:30-10 pm. Bar 5 pm-1 am. Ck-out 11 am. Guest lndry. Meeting rms. Business servs avail. Golf privileges. Downhill ski 8 mi; x-country ski 9 mi.

Exercise equipt; weights, bicycles. Health club privileges. Refrigerator in suites. Cr cds: A, C, D, DS, JCB, MC, V.

Inn

★ ★ ★ **LOVILL HOUSE.** *404 Old Bristol Rd, just off US 421N.* 704/264-4204; res: 800/849-9466. E-mail innkeeper@lovillhouseinn.com; web www.lovillhouseinn.com. 5 rms, 2 story. No A/C. S, D $95-$160; each addl $25. Closed Mar, 2 wks Sept. Children over 12 yrs only. TV; cable. Complimentary full bkfst; afternoon refreshments. Ck-out noon, ck-in 3 pm. Concierge serv. Luggage handling. Downhill/x-country ski 8 mi. Picnic tables. Restored country farmhouse built 1875; grounds include gardens, stream with waterfall. Totally nonsmoking. Cr cds: MC, V.

Restaurants

✔★ **DAN'L BOONE INN.** *130 Hardin St, at jct US 421 & US 321.* 704/264-8657. Hrs: 11:30 am-9 pm; Sat, Sun from 8 am; Nov-May from 5 pm. Closed 2 days at Christmas. Family style: bkfst $6.95, lunch, dinner $11.95. Specializes in fried chicken. In one of oldest buildings in Boone; country atmosphere. Family-owned. No cr cds accepted.

★ ★ **MAKOTO.** *2124 Blowing Rock Rd.* 704/264-7976. Hrs: 11 am-2 pm, 5-10 pm. Closed Thanksgiving, Dec 25. Japanese menu. Serv bar. Complete meals: lunch $3.95-$9.95, dinner $8.50-$22.95. Serv charge 15%. Child's meals. Specializes in seafood, beef, poultry. Sushi bar Thurs, Sat. Tableside preparation. Cr cds: A, C, D, DS, MC, V.

Brevard (B-2)

(See also Asheville, Hendersonville)

Settled 1861 **Pop** 5,388 **Elev** 2,230 ft **Area code** 704 **Zip** 28712 **E-mail** waterfalls@citcom.net **Web** visitwaterfalls.com

Information Chamber of Commerce, PO Box 589; 704/883-3700 or 800/648-4523.

An industrial and mountain resort center near the entrance to Pisgah National Forests, Brevard has several industries, including Sterling Diagnostic Imaging, Inc, Coats American Company and the Ecusta division of P.H. Glatfelter.

What to See and Do

Mt Pisgah (5,749 ft). Blue Ridge Pkwy, US 276 to within 1 mi of summit, trail rest of way.

Pisgah National Forest. A 499,816-acre, 4-district forest. The Cradle of Forestry Visitor Center (summer, daily; fee) is at site of first forestry school in the US. The forest surrounds Mt Mitchell State Park (see LITTLE SWITZERLAND), which contains the highest point in the US east of the Mississippi (6,684 ft). Linville Gorge Wilderness is 10,975 acres of precipitous cliffs and cascading falls (permit required May-Oct for overnight camping, contact the Grandfather Ranger District in MARION). Wiseman's View looks into Linville Gorge. Shining Rock Wilderness contains 18,500 acres of rugged alpine scenery. The forest shares with Cherokee National Forest in Tennessee the 6,286-ft Roan Mountain, with its purple rhododendron and stands of spruce and fir. Offers swimming and boating sites; good fishing for trout, bass and perch; hunting for deer, bear and small game; miles of hiking and riding trails; picnic sites; campgrounds (fee). NW of town, via US 276. For further information contact the Supervisor, 100 Otis St, Box 2750, Asheville 28802; 704/257-4200.

Annual Events

Festival of the Arts. Music, crafts, art, sporting events. 2nd wk July.

Twilight Tour on Main. Horse & buggy rides, entertainment, refreshments. 1st Sat Dec.

Seasonal Event

Summer Festival of Music. Brevard Music Center. Whittington-Pfhol Auditorium. More than 50 programs presented, including symphonic, choral, chamber, recital; musical comedy and operatic performances; guest artists. Mon-Sat evenings; Sun afternoons. Contact Box 312; 704/884-2019 or 704/884-2011. Late June-early Aug.

Motels

★ **IMPERIAL MOTOR LODGE.** *1/2 mi N on US 64, 276.* 704/884-2887; FAX 708/883-9811; res: 800/869-3335. 95 rms, 1-2 story. June-Oct: S, D $45-$85; each addl $5; under 12 free; lower rates rest of yr. Crib $5. TV; cable (premium). Pool. Complimentary continental bkfst. Restaurant opp 6 am-midnight. Ck-out 11:30 am. Refrigerators. Grill. Cr cds: A, C, D, DS, MC, V.

★ **SUNSET.** *415 S Broad St.* 704/884-9106. 18 rms. June-Oct: S $50; D $60; each addl $5; lower rates rest of yr. Pet accepted, some restrictions. TV; cable. Restaurant opp 11 am-10 pm. Ck-out 11 am. Refrigerators. Cr cds: A, D, DS, MC, V.

Bryson City (B-2)

(See also Cherokee, Franklin, Waynesville)

Pop 1,145 **Elev** 1,736 ft **Area code** 704 **Zip** 28713 **E-mail** swaintda@greatsmokies.com **Web** www.greatsmokies.com

Information Chamber of Commerce, PO Box 509; 704/488-3681 or 800/867-9246.

At the confluence of the Little Tennessee and Tuckasegee rivers, Bryson City is also at the entrance to Great Smoky Mountains National Park. Fontana Lake, part of the TVA system, is nearby. Industries include textiles.

What to See and Do

Fontana Dam (see). 35 mi SW on US 19 & NC 28.

Great Smoky Mountains National Park (see). 8 mi N on US 19.

Great Smoky Mountains Railway. 4 1/2-hr rail excursions to Nantahala Gorge aboard diesel or steam locomotives. One-hr layover; view whitewater sports. Special excursions throughout yr (fees, dates vary). (Mar-Nov) For information contact PO Box 397, Dillsboro 28725-0397; 800/872-4681, ext R. ¢¢¢¢¢

Whitewater Rafting. Rolling Thunder River Co. Guided raft, canoe, kayak trips through Smoky Mountains; day and overnight. (Apr-Oct) Reservations suggested. 10 mi W on US 19S/74W, at Nantahala Gorge. For information, fees, contact Rolling Thunder River Co, Box 88, Almond 28702; 704/488-2030 or 800/344-5838. ¢¢¢¢¢

Motel

★ **ELA MOTOR COURT.** *5280 Ela Rd.* 704/488-2284. 21 rms, 1 cottage. No rm phones. Mid-June-Oct: S, D $48; kit. cottage $120; under 6 free; lower rates May-mid-June. Closed rest of yr. Crib free. TV; cable. Pool. Complimentary coffee in lobby. Ck-out 11 am. Cr cds: MC, V.

Inns

★ ★ **CHALET INN.** *(285 Lone Oak Dr, Whittier 28789) 14 mi E on US 74/441.* 704/586-0251; res: 800/789-8024; FAX 704/586-0257. E-mail chaletinn@wcu.campus.mci.net; web www.bbonline.com/nc/chaletinn. 6 rms, 2 with shower only, 2 story, 2 suites. No rm phones. S, D $70-$84; suites $120-$150; wkend rates; hols (2-day min); higher rates: hols, Oct. Children over 12 yrs only. Complimentary full bkfst. Complimentary coffee in rms. Ck-out 10:30 am, ck-in 3 pm. Luggage handling. 18-hole golf privileges, greens fee $32, pro, putting green, driving range. Playground. Lawn games. Balconies. Picnic tables, grills. European ambience in Blue Ridge Mts. Totally nonsmoking. Cr cds: MC, V.

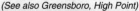

★ **FOLKESTONE.** *101 Folkestone Rd.* 704/488-2730; FAX 704/488-0722. E-mail innkeeper@folkestone.com. 10 rms, 3 story. No A/C. No rm phones. S, D $63-$90; each addl $10. Complimentary full bkfst. Ck-out 11 am, ck-in 3 pm. Business servs avail. Game rm. Lawn games. Some balconies. Picnic tables. Built 1926; restored country farmhouse. Cr cds: DS, MC, V.

★ ★ **HEMLOCK.** *Drawer EE, 3 mi NE, 1 mi N of US 19.* 704/488-2885. Web www.innbook.com/hemlock.html. 25 rms, 4 kit. units (1-3-bedrm). No A/C. MAP, mid-Apr-Oct: D $130-$148; each addl $20-$39; kit. cottage for 2, $148-$178. Closed rest of yr. Dining rm (public by res) 8:30 am & 6 pm sittings; Sun 8:30 am & 12:30 pm sittings. Ck-out 11 am, ck-in 1 pm. Game rm. Lawn games. Early Amer decor; mountain view. Cr cds: DS, MC, V.

Burlington (A-6)

(See also Greensboro, High Point)

Settled ca 1700 **Pop** 39,498 **Elev** 656 ft **Area code** 336 **E-mail** chamber@netpath.net **Web** www.netpath.net/alamance.html

Information Burlington/Alamance County Convention & Visitors Bureau, PO Drawer 519, 27216; 336/570-1444 or 800/637-3804.

In 1837, E. M. Holt converted his father's gristmill on Alamance Creek into a textile mill. The Alamance Mill produced the first commercially dyed plaids south of the Potomac, changing the face of the textile industry in the South.

What to See and Do

Alamance Battleground State Historic Site. On May 16, 1771, a two-hour battle was fought here between the colonial militia under Royal Governor Tryon and about 2,000 rebellious "Regulators." The latter were defeated. Restored log house; visitor center, exhibits, audiovisual presentation; picnic area. (Apr-Oct, daily; rest of yr, daily exc Mon; closed most major hols) 6 mi SW on NC 62. Phone 336/227-4785. **Free.**

Alamance County Historical Museum. 19th-century house-museum depicts life of textile pioneer E. M. Holt. Period rms, audiovisual presentations. Rotating exhibits feature antique clothing and toys, Native American artifacts, traditional pottery and local history pieces. Docent-guided tours. (Daily exc Mon) 5 mi S on NC 62. Phone 336/226-8254. **Free.**

Dentzel Menagerie Carousel (ca 1910). Rare hand-carved carousel; restored. (Apr-Oct, daily exc Mon) S Main, at Church St in City Park. Phone 336/222-5030. ¢

Lake Cammack Park and Marina. An 800-acre city reservoir. Waterskiing; fishing; boating. Picnic area, playground. (Daily exc Thurs; days vary winter) 6 mi N on Union Ridge Rd, off NC 62. Phone 336/421-3872. ¢

Annual Event

Hospice League Horizons Balloon Fest. Hot-air-balloon race, air show, parachuting, music. Phone 800/637-3804. May.

Seasonal Event

The Sword of Peace Summer Outdoor Drama. 18 mi SW via I-85, Liberty-49S exit, then NC 49S and NC 1005 to Snow Camp. Repertory outdoor theater (evenings) and summer arts festival; 150-yr-old and 200-yr-old buildings converted into museums, craft gallery and cane mill. Thurs-Sat. Contact PO Box 535, Snow Camp 27349; 910/376-6948 or 800/726-5115. Late June-late Aug.

Motels

★ **COMFORT INN.** *978 Plantation Dr (27215), I-85, exit 145.* 336/227-3681; FAX 336/570-0900. 127 rms, 2 story. S $57-$88; D $61-$88; each addl $4; under 18 free; higher rates Furniture Market. Crib free. Pet accepted, some restrictions. TV; cable (premium). Pool; wading pool. Complimentary continental bkfst. Complimentary coffee in rms. Restaurant adj 11 am-11 pm. Ck-out noon. Coin lndry. Meeting rms. Business servs avail. Valet serv. Exercise equipt; weight machine, stair machine. Some refrigerators; microwaves avail. Cr cds: A, C, D, DS, JCB, MC, V.

✔★ **DAYS INN.** *2133 W Hanford Rd (27215), I-85 exit 145.* 336/227-1270; FAX 336/227-1702. 122 rms, 2 story. S $44; D $49; each addl $5; under 12 free. Crib avail. TV. Pool. Complimentary continental bkfst. Restaurant adj 6 am-11 pm; Fri, Sat to 1 am. Ck-out noon. Meeting rms. Business servs avail. Valet serv. Cr cds: A, C, D, DS, ER, JCB, MC, V.

★ ★ **HAMPTON INN.** *2701 Kirkpatrick Rd (27215), I-85, exit 141.* 336/584-4447; FAX 336/721-1325. 116 rms, 4 story. S $60-$65; D $65-$70; suites $92; under 18 free; higher rates Furniture Market (Apr & Oct). Crib free. TV; cable (premium). Pool; whirlpool. Complimentary continental bkfst. Restaurant adj 5-10 pm. Ck-out noon. Meeting rms. Business servs avail. Exercise equipt; weight machine, bicycles, sauna. Cr cds: A, D, DS, MC, V.

✔★ **KIRK'S MOTOR COURT.** *1155 N Church St (27215).* 336/228-1383; FAX 336/228-9786. 102 rms, 1-2 story, 14 kits. S $28-$36; D $36-$44; each addl $6; kit. units $245-$285/wk; under 12 free. Crib $4. TV; cable. Pool; wading pool. Restaurant nearby. Ck-out 11 am. Meeting rms. Business servs avail. Valet serv. Sundries. Cr cds: MC, V.

★ ★ **RAMADA INN.** *NC 62 (27215), at jct I-85.* 336/227-5541; FAX 336/570-2701. 138 rms, 2 story. S $59; D $65; each addl $6; under 18 free; higher rates: Furniture Market, special events. Crib free. TV; cable (premium). Pool. Restaurant 6 am-2 pm. Rm serv. Bar 5-10 pm; closed Sun. Ck-out noon. Convention facilities. Business servs avail. Cr cds: A, C, D, DS, MC, V.

Restaurant

✔★ **HURSEY'S PIG PICKIN' BAR-B-Q.** *1834 S Church St (27215).* 336/226-1695. Hrs: 11 am-9 pm. Closed Sun; Dec 25. Semi-a la carte: lunch, dinner $3.50-$7.50. Child's meals. Specializes in wood-cooked pit barbecue. Rustic decor. Family-owned since 1949. No cr cds accepted.

Burnsville (A-3)

(See also Asheville, Little Switzerland)

Pop 1,482 **Elev** 2,814 ft **Area code** 704 **Zip** 28714
Information Yancey County Chamber of Commerce, 106 W Main St; 704/682-7413.

A Ranger District office of the Pisgah National Forest (see BREVARD) is located here.

Annual Event

Mt Mitchell Crafts Fair. Town Square.1st Fri & Sat Aug.

Seasonal Event

Music in the Mountains. Chamber music concerts. 3rd Sat Sept.

Inn

★ ★ **NU-WRAY.** *Town Square, on US 19E.* 704/682-2329; *res: 800/368-9729; FAX* 704/682-2661. 26 rms, 3 story. No A/C. No rm phones. S $65-$85; D $75-$95; suites $90; each addl $10; MAP avail. TV in most rms; cable (premium). Dining rm sittings (May-Oct): 8:30 am, 6 pm; Sun 1 pm; times vary rest of yr. Ck-out 11 am, ck-in after 3 pm. Inn built in 1833. Cr cds: A, DS, MC, V.

Buxton (Outer Banks) (B-10)

Pop 3,250 **Elev** 10 ft **Area code** 919 **Zip** 27920

This town is on Hatteras Island, part of the Outer Banks (see). It is surrounded by Cape Hatteras National Seashore (see).

Motels

★ **CAPE HATTERAS.** *on NC 12.* 919/995-5611; *FAX 919/995-4303; res: 800/995-0711.* 6 motel rms, 1-2 story, 29 kit. units. No rm phones. Mid June-Labor Day: S, D $105-$110; kit. units $130-$180; lower rates rest of yr. Crib $3. TV; cable (premium). Pool; whirlpool. Ck-out 11 am. Cr cds: A, DS, MC, V.

★ ★ **COMFORT INN.** *on NC 12, near Cape Hatteras lighthouse.* 919/995-6100; *FAX 919/995-5444.* 60 rms, 2 story. Mid-June-mid-Sept: S, D $92-125; each addl $5; under 18 free; lower rates rest of yr. Crib free. TV; cable (premium). Pool. Complimentary continental bkfst. Restaurant nearby. Ck-out 11 am. Business servs avail. In-rm modem link. Guest lndry. Refrigerators. Near beach. Cr cds: A, C, D, DS, JCB, MC, V.

✔★ **FALCON.** *NC 12.* 919/995-5968; *res: 800/635-6911.* 30 rms, 5 kits. No rm phones. Memorial Day-Labor Day: S, D $55-$72; kits. $70-$80; under 6 free; wkly rates; lower rates Labor Day-mid-Dec. Closed rest of yr. Crib free. TV; cable (premium). Pool. Restaurant opp 6:30 am-9:30 pm. Ck-out 11 am. Refrigerators avail. Picnic tables. Near ocean. Cr cds: MC, V.

Resort

★ **CASTAWAYS OCEANFRONT RESORT.** *(PO Box 770, Avon 27915) 6 mi N on NC 12.* 919/995-4444; *res: 800/845-6070.* 56 rms, 5 story. AP, May-Sept: S, D $68-$108; each addl $10; under 18 free; wkly rates; lower rates rest of yr. Crib free. TV; cable. Pool; whirlpool, poolside serv. Dining rm 7-10:30 am, 5-9 pm. Rm serv. Ck-out 11 am, ck-in 3 pm. Meeting rms. Swimming beach. Refrigerators, wet bars. Balconies. Picnic tables, grills. Cr cds: A, DS, MC, V.

Restaurant

✔★ **TIDES.** *NC 12.* 919/995-5988. Hrs: 6-11:30 am, 5:30-9:30 pm. Closed Jan-Mar & Dec. Wine, beer. Semi-a la carte: bkfst $2.50-$5.50, dinner $7.50-$15. Specializes in seafood, steak. Nautical decor. Cr cds: MC, V.

Cape Hatteras National Seashore (B-10)

(For accommodations see Buxton, Hatteras, Kill Devil Hills, Nags Head, Ocracoke)

(Enter from Cedar Island or Swan Quarter toll ferry. Reservations advised. Free ferry from Ocracoke Island to Hatteras Island.)

This thin strand stretches for 75 miles along the Outer Banks (see), threaded between the windy, pounding Atlantic and shallow Pamlico Sound. Nags Head (see) is the northern limit of the recreational area, which has three sections (separated by inlets): Bodie (pronounced *body*), Hatteras (largest of the barrier islands) and Ocracoke (see), the most picturesque. Bounded on three sides by the park, but separate from it, are the villages of Rodanthe, Waves, Salvo, Avon, Buxton, Frisco, Hatteras and Ocracoke. Although the area is noted for long expanses of sand beaches, wildflowers bloom most of the year. There are also stands of yaupon (holly), loblolly pine and live oak. Several freshwater ponds are found on Bodie, Hatteras and Ocracoke Islands. Many migratory and nonmigratory waterfowl winter here, including gadwalls, greater snow and Canada geese, loons, grebes and herons.

There is an information station at Whalebone Junction (Memorial Day-Labor Day, daily), south of Nags Head. Near Bodie Island Lighthouse is a bird observation platform, a nature trail and a visitor center (Good Friday-Columbus Day, daily) with natural history exhibits. There are also visitor centers with history exhibits at Ocracoke (same hours), Bodie Island Lighthouse (same hours), and the Cape Hatteras Lighthouse at Buxton (daily; closed December 25).

(Do not drive off the highways—you are likely to get stuck.)

Sport fishing, boating, sailing, swimming (recommended only at protected beaches); picnicking and camping (fee), also waterfowl hunting in season under regulation.

For further information contact the Superintendent, Rte 1, Box 675, Manteo 27954; or phone the Hatteras Island Visitor Center, 919/995-4474.

Cashiers (B-2)

(See also Franklin, Highlands)

Pop 1,200 **Elev** 3,486 ft **Area code** 704 **Zip** 28717
Information Cashiers Area Chamber of Commerce, PO Box 238; 704/743-5191.

High in the Blue Ridge Mountains, this well-known summer resort area offers scenic drives on twisting mountain roads, hiking trails, views, waterfalls, lake sports, fishing and other recreational activities.

What to See and Do

Fairfield Sapphire Valley Ski Area. Chairlift, rope tow; patrol, school, snowmaking. Longest run 2,400 ft; vertical drop 425 ft. (Mid-Dec-mid-Mar, daily) Night skiing (exc Sun). Evening, half-day rates. Other seasons: swimming, fishing, boating; hiking, horseback riding; golf, tennis; recreation center. Restaurants, inn (see RESORTS). 3 mi E on US 64. Phone 704/743-3441. ¢¢¢¢¢

Lake Thorpe. Fishing, swimming, waterskiing. Boats may be rented at Glenville (on lake) or launched from here. 5 mi N on NC 107.

Motels

★ **LAURELWOOD MOUNTAIN INN.** *NC 107 N & US 64. 704/743-9939; res: 800/346-6846; FAX 704/743-5300.* Web www.dnet.net/laurelwood. 22 rms, 10 with shower only, 3 A/C, 1-2 story. May-Oct: S, D $58-$125; under 12 free; wkly rates; wkends, hols (2-day min); lower rates rest of yr. Crib free. TV; cable. Complimentary coffee in rms. Restaurant opp 6:30 am-10 pm. Ck-out 11 am. Playground. Many refrigerators; some in-rm whirlpools, microwaves. Some balconies. Picnic tables, grills. Cr cds: A, DS, MC, V.

⊠ ⊠ SC

★ **OAKMONT LODGE.** *Rt 63, Box 71, 1/2 mi N of jct US 64. 704/743-2298; FAX 704/743-1839.* 20 rms, 2 cabins. No A/C. June-Oct: S, D $62-$69; each addl $5; kit. cottages $94-$115. Crib free. TV; cable. Restaurant 11:30 am-9 pm. Ck-out 11 am. Downhill ski 2 mi. Cr cds: MC, V.

⊠ ⊠ SC

Inns

★ ★ ★ **GREYSTONE.** *(Greystone Ln, Lake Toxaway 28747) 8 mi E on US 64. 704/966-4700; FAX 704/862-5689; res: 800/824-5766 (exc NC).* 33 rms, 3 story, 17 A/C. May-Oct: S, D $280-$420; each addl $85; family, wkly rates; higher rates wkends (2-day min); lower rates Apr, Nov, Dec. Open wkends Jan-Mar. Crib free. TV; cable (premium), VCR. Pool. Supervised child's activities (June-Aug); ages 5-14. Complimentary full bkfst; afternoon refreshments. Restaurant adj 8-10 am, 6:30-9:30 pm. Ck-out noon, ck-in 3 pm. Business servs avail. Luggage handling. Concierge serv. Tennis, pro. 18-hole golf, greens fee $45, putting green, driving range. Massage. Refrigerators, minibars. Balconies. Picnic tables. On swimming beach. Cr cds: A, MC, V.

☜ ⃯ ⃯ ⃯ ⃯

★ ★ **INNISFREE VICTORIAN INN.** *(7 Lakeside Knoll, Glenville 28736) 6 mi N on NC 107. 704/743-2946.* 10 rms, 1 & 2 story. No A/C. Some rm phones. June-Oct: S, D $150-$290; lower rates rest of yr. Adults only. TV in some rms; cable. Complimentary full bkfst; afternoon refreshments. Complimentary coffee in rms. Ck-out 11 am, ck-in 2:30 pm. Business servs avail. Luggage handling. Concierge serv. Tennis privileges. Golf privileges. Game rm. Refrigerators, minibars; some fireplaces. Balconies. 1 blk from Lake Glenville. Built 1989 in Victorian style and furnished with antiques. Totally nonsmoking. Cr cds: A, DS, MC, V.

☜ ⃯ ⃯ ⃯ ⃯

Resorts

★ ★ ★ **FAIRFIELD SAPPHIRE VALLEY.** *(4000 US 64W, Sapphire 28774) 3 mi E. 704/743-3441; FAX 704/743-2641; res: 800/533-8268.* 210 villas (summer), 160 villas (winter), 1-2 story. S, D $90; kit. villas $90-$260; wkly rates; ski, golf, tennis plans. Crib $3. TV; cable, VCR avail. Indoor/outdoor pool; whirlpool. Playground. Supervised child's activities (June-mid-Aug); ages 6-12. Dining rm 11 am-10 pm. Ck-out 10 am, ck-in 4 pm. Sports dir. Lighted tennis, pro. 18-hole golf, greens fee $38, driving range. Private beach; boats (no motors). Downhill ski 1 mi. Miniature golf. Lawn games. Soc dir; entertainment. Exercise equipt; weights, bicycles, sauna. Refrigerators, fireplaces; microwaves avail. Whirlpool in some villas. 5,700 acres in mountain setting; on lake. Gardens, extensive lawns. Cr cds: A, DS, MC, V.

⃯ ⃯ ⃯ ⃯ ⃯ ⃯ ⃯ ⃯ SC

★ ★ ★ **HIGH HAMPTON INN & COUNTRY CLUB.** *2 mi S on NC 107. 704/743-2411; FAX 704/743-5991; res: 800/334-2551.* Web www.highhamptoninn.com. 34 rms in 3-story inn, 15 cottages, 37 golf villas. No A/C. AP, July-Aug: S $93-$95; D $164-$182; each addl $57; golf villas (3-day min) $195-$356; wkly rates; golf, tennis plans; lower rates Sept-June, Oct, Nov. Closed rest of yr. Crib free. Pet accepted, some restrictions. TV rm; cable. Supervised child's activities (June-Labor Day); ages 3-12. Complimentary afternoon refreshments. Dining rm 7-9:30 am, noon-2:15 pm, 6:30-8:15 pm. Box lunches, buffets. Ck-out 1 pm, ck-in 3 pm. Coin lndry. Business servs avail. Valet serv. Gift shop. Airport transportation. Sports dir. Tennis. 18-hole golf, greens fee $26, pro, 2 putting greens, driving range. Exercise equipt; treadmill, stair machine. Boats, dockage. Archery. Trail guides. Bicycle rentals. Outdoor, indoor games. Soc dir; entertainment, movies. Rec rm, library. Lawn games. Kennels. 1,400-acre mountain estate, 2 lakes. Rustic resort; established 1924. Former hunting lodge of a Civil War general. Cr cds: A, DS, MC, V.

D ⃯ ⃯ ⃯ ⃯ ⃯ ⃯

Cedar Island (C-9)

Pop 333 (est) **Elev** 7 ft **Area code** 919 **Zip** 28520

There is daily ferry service from Cedar Island to Ocracoke (see).

Motel

✔★ **DRIFTWOOD.** *Cedar Island Beach, on NC 12 N at Cedar Island-Ocracoke ferry terminal. 919/225-4861; FAX 919/225-1113.* 37 rms. May-mid-Oct: S $40; D $50; each addl $4; under 12 free; lower rates rest of yr. Crib free. TV; cable (premium). Restaurant 6-8:30 pm. Ck-out noon. Sundries. On ocean. Cr cds: MC, V.

⃯ ⃯ ⃯ ⃯ SC

Chapel Hill (B-6)

(See also Durham, Raleigh)

Founded 1793 **Pop** 38,719 **Elev** 487 ft **Area code** 919
Information Chapel Hill-Carrboro Chamber of Commerce, PO Box 2897, 27515; 919/967-7075.

The community of Chapel Hill is centered around the University of North Carolina, the oldest state university in the US. This school has been a leader in American education for more than 170 years and is now part of a "research triangle," together with Duke University at Durham and North Carolina State University at Raleigh. Despite heavy losses of faculty and students to the Civil War, the school remained open until the years of

Reconstruction, 1870-1875. During the next decade the university was reborn.

What to See and Do

Chapel of the Cross (1842-1848). Antebellum Gothic-revival Episcopal church. (Daily, exc Sat) 304 E Franklin St, adj to Morehead Planetarium. Phone 919/929-2193.

North Carolina Botanical Garden. Approx 600 acres; variety of trees and plants of southeastern US; wildflower areas, herb gardens. Nature trails (daily). (Mid-Mar-mid-Nov, daily; rest of yr, Mon-Fri) Old Mason Farm Rd and US 15/501 Bypass. Phone 919/962-0522. **Free.**

University of North Carolina at Chapel Hill (1795). (Approx 24,000 students) This institution, the first state university in the country, is on a 720-acre campus and has more than 200 buildings. On campus are

Old Well. Long the unofficial symbol of the University, this well was the only source of water here for nearly a century. The present "Greek temple" structure dates from 1897. Cameron Ave in center of campus.

South (Main) Building. Cornerstone laid in 1798 but building not completed until 1814, during which time the boys lived inside the roofless walls in little huts. Future President James K. Polk lived here from 1814-1818. Opp Old Well.

Old East. Oldest state university building in the country; cornerstone laid in 1793. Matched by Old West (1823). Still being used as a residence hall. E of Old Well.

Davie Poplar. Ancient ivy-covered tree named for the "father of the university," William Richardson Davie; more than 200 yrs old. N of Old Well.

Memorial Hall (1930). White columns front this structure dedicated to war dead, honored alumni and university benefactors. James K. Polk, class of 1818, has a commemorative tablet here. He graduated first in his class and became the 11th President of the US. Opp New West.

Coker Arboretum. Covers 5 acres. Extensive collection of ornamental plants and shrubs. Cameron Ave & Raleigh St.

Morehead-Patterson Memorial Bell Tower (1930). A 172-ft Italian Renaissance campanile; concert chimes. The 12 bells range in weight from 300 lbs to almost 2 tons. Popular tunes are rung daily.

Kenan Stadium (1927). Seats 52,000; in wooded natural bowl. Behind Bell Tower.

Wilson Library. Houses special collections. Includes North Carolina Collection Gallery; historic rooms, texts and artifacts. Also here is the Southern Historical Collection, featuring manuscripts, rare books and photographs. (Daily) Phone 919/962-0114

Morehead Planetarium. Offers indoor star-gazing, art gallery with permanent and changing exhibits; scientific exhibits; rare Zeiss instrument. Shows (daily; closed Dec 24, 25). Rose garden has mammoth sundial showing time around the world. E Franklin St. Phone 919/549-6863. Shows ¢¢

Playmakers Theater (1851). Greek-revival temple was designed as a combination library and ballroom.

Paul Green Theater (1978). PlayMakers Repertory Company. Named for one of the first dramatic arts students at the University. Green is known as the father of American outdoor drama. (Sept-May)

(For further information on the University, phone Visitor Services at 919/962-1630.)

Motels

★ ★ **BEST WESTERN UNIVERSITY INN.** *Raleigh Rd (27515), 2 mi E on NC 54, ¼ mi E of US 15/501 Bypass. 919/932-3000; FAX 919/968-6513.* 84 rms, 1-2 story. S, D $70-$110. Crib $5. TV; cable (premium), VCR avail (movies). Pool. Complimentary continental bkfst. Ck-out noon. Business servs avail. Sundries. Cr cds: A, C, D, DS, MC, V.

D ⊠ ⊠ ⋈ SC

✔ ★ ★ **HAMPTON INN.** *1740 US 15/501 (27514). 919/968-3000; FAX 919/929-0322.* 122 rms, 2 story. S $61; D $69; under 18 free. Crib free. TV; cable (premium), VCR avail. Pool. Complimentary continental bkfst. Restaurant nearby. Ck-out noon. Meeting rms. Business servs avail. Health club privileges. Cr cds: A, C, D, DS, MC, V.

D ⊠ ⊠ ⋈ SC

★ ★ **HOLIDAY INN.** *1301 N Fordham Blvd (27514), 2 mi S of I-40 exit 270, at Eastgate Shopping Center. 919/929-2171; FAX 919/929-5736.* 135 rms, 2 story. S, D $69-$74; each addl $6; higher rates: football season (2-day min), graduation (3-day min). Crib free. TV; cable (premium), VCR avail. Pool. Restaurant 6:30-10 am, 4-9 pm. Rm serv. Bar 5-11 pm. Ck-out noon. Meeting rms. Business servs avail. In-rm modem link. Cr cds: A, C, D, DS, JCB, MC, V.

D ⊠ ⊠ ⋈ SC

Hotels

★ ★ ★ **THE CAROLINA INN.** *211 Pittsboro St (27514), on University of North Carolina's campus. 919/933-2001; FAX 919/962-3400; res: 800/962-8519.* Web www.citysearch.com. 184 rms, 3 story. S, D $125-$144; each addl $10; suites $219-$274; under 18 free; wkend rates; higher rates university events. Crib free. Valet parking $5, in/out $3. TV; cable (premium). Complimentary coffee in lobby. Restaurant 6 am-10 pm. Bar 11 am-midnight. Ck-out noon. Coin lndry. Meeting rms. Business servs avail. In-rm modem link. Concierge. Gift shop. Tennis privileges. Golf privileges. Exercise equipt; bicycle, treadmill. Game rm. Cr cds: A, C, D, DS, ER, JCB, MC, V.

D ⋈ ⋈ ⋈ ⊠ ⊠ ⋈ SC

★ ★ ★ **OMNI EUROPA.** *1 Europa Dr (27514). 919/968-4900; FAX 919/968-3520.* 168 rms, 4 story. S, D $139; each addl $10; suites $195-$275; under 16 free. Crib $10. TV; cable (premium). Pool. Restaurant 6:30 am-2 pm, 4-10 pm. Rm serv 6:30 am-10 pm. Bar 4 pm-1 am. Meeting rms. Business servs avail. Concierge. Gift shop. Airport transportation. Health club privileges. Private patios, balconies. Cr cds: A, C, D, DS, MC, V.

D ⊠ ⊠ ⋈ SC

★ ★ ★ **SIENA.** *1505 E Franklin St (27514). 919/929-4000; res: 800/223-7379; FAX 919/968-8527.* 80 rms, 4 story, 12 suites. S, D $149; each addl $10; suites $185-$200; under 17 free; higher rates: football games, graduation. Crib free. Pet accepted; $50 refundable. TV; cable (premium), VCR avail. Complimentary full bkfst. Restaurant (see IL PALIO). Bar noon-midnight; entertainment. Ck-out noon. Meeting rms. Business servs avail. In-rm modem link. Concierge. Airport transportation. Tennis privileges. Golf privileges, greens fee $60, pro, putting green, driving range. Health club privileges. Bathrm phones; some refrigerators. Picnic tables. Cr cds: A, C, D, JCB, MC, V.

D ⋈ ⋈ ⋈ ⊠ ⊠ ⋈ SC

Inns

★ ★ ★ ★ **FEARRINGTON HOUSE.** *(2000 Fearrington Village Center, Pittsboro 27312) 8 mi S on US 15/501. 919/542-2121; FAX 919/542-4202.* E-mail fci@mail.interpath.com; web www.fearrington.com. This French-style country inn on an old farm is decorated with chintz, original art and pinewood antiques. A courtyard and fountain welcome visitors at the entrance. 30 rms, 2 story. S, D $165-$200; suites $225-$275. TV; cable (premium), VCR avail. Pool; whirlpool. Complimentary full bkfst; afternoon refreshments. Dining rm (see FEARRINGTON HOUSE). Rm serv 24 hrs. Beer, wine. Ck-out noon, ck-in 3 pm. Meeting rms. Business servs avail. Tennis. Exercise equipt; weights, treadmills. Lawn games. Totally non-smoking. Cr cds: A, MC, V.

D ⋈ ⋈ ⋈ ⋈ ⋈ ⋈

★ **INN AT BINGHAM SCHOOL.** *(6720 Mebane Oaks Rd, Mebane 27302) 12 mi W on NC 54. 919/563-5583; FAX 919/563-9826; res: 800/566-5583.* E-mail fdeppez@aol.com. 5 rms, 2 with shower only, 2 story. S $75-$110; D $75-$120; each addl $15; suites $120; under 5 free. TV. Complimentary full bkfst. Restaurant nearby. Ck-out noon, ck-in 3 pm.

A combination of Greek and Federal styles; furnished with antiques. Totally nonsmoking. Cr cds: A, DS, MC, V.

Restaurants

★ ★ **AURORA.** *(200 Greensboro St, Carrboro 27510) Carr Mill Shopping Center.* 919/942-2400. Web www.citysearch.com. Hrs: 11:30 am-2 pm, 6-10 pm; Sat, Sun from 5 pm. Closed some major hols. Res accepted. Northern Italian menu. Bar. Semi-a la carte: lunch $3.95-$7.95, dinner $8.95-$17.95. Specialty: grilled lamb with garlic. Own pastas. In renovated textile mill. Cr cds: A, MC, V.

★ ★ ★ **FEARRINGTON HOUSE.** *(See Fearrington House Inn)* 919/542-2121. Each dining area in this restaurant features a different decor, from the airy garden rooms with large windows to the more formal interior room with a fireplace. Service is attentive and courteous no matter where you are seated. Specialties: lamb loin, Carolina crab cakes. Own baking. Hrs: 6-9 pm; Sun to 8 pm. Closed Mon. Res required. Wine list. Complete meals: dinner $55. Totally nonsmoking. Cr cds: A, MC, V.

★ ★ ★ **IL PALIO.** *(See Siena Hotel)* 919/929-4000. Hrs: 6:30-10 am, 11:30 am-2 pm, 6-10 pm; Sun brunch 11:30 am-2 pm. Res accepted. Continental menu. Bar. Wine cellar. Semi-a la carte: bkfst $7.50-$10, lunch $7.50-$18, dinner $17.95-$24. Sun brunch $16.95. Specialty: osso bucco. Own pasta. Entertainment. Mediterranean decor with Northern Italian emphasis; much artwork, wall ornamentation, flower arrangements. Totally nonsmoking. Cr cds: A, C, D, JCB, MC, V.

★ ★ **LA REZ.** *202 W Rosemary (27516).* 919/967-2506. Hrs: 6-9:30 pm; Sun to 8:30 pm. Closed Mon; July 4, Dec 24, 25. Res accepted. French, Amer menu. Bar. A la carte entrees: dinner $15.95-$24.95. Specializes in local seafood, duckling, wild game. Outdoor dining. Cr cds: A, C, D, MC, V.

✔★ **SQUID'S.** *1201 US 15/501 Bypass (27514).* 919/942-8757. Hrs: 5-9:30 pm; Fri, Sat to 10 pm; Sun to 9 pm. Closed Jan 1, Thanksgiving, Dec 24, 25. Bar. Semi-a la carte: dinner $9-$15. Child's meals. Specializes in fresh seafood. Oyster bar. Cr cds: A, D, DS, MC, V.

★ **THE WILD TURTLE.** *220 W Rosemary (27516).* 919/932-4841. Hrs: 6-10 pm; Closed Sun. Closed major hols. Res accepted. Continental menu. Bar. A la carte entrees: dinner $9.95-$17.95. Specializes in beef, chicken, lamb. Outdoor dining. Intimate dining in 1920 house; tapestries, fireplaces; original fixtures. Cr cds: MC, V.

Charlotte (B-5)

(See also Gastonia; also see Rock Hill, SC)

Settled 1748 **Pop** 395,934 **Elev** 700 ft **Area code** 704
Information Convention & Visitors Bureau, 122 E Stonewall St, 28202; 704/331-2700 or 800/231-4636.

The Carolinas' largest metropolis, Charlotte grew quickly as a regional retail, financial and distribution center and became the nation's leader in the textile industry. General Cornwallis occupied the town for a short time in 1780 but met such determined resistance that he called it a "hornet's nest," a name that has been applied with pride on the city seal and by several local groups. Gold was discovered here in 1799, and the region around Charlotte was the nation's major gold producer until the California gold rush in 1848. There was a US Mint here between 1837-1861. The last Confederate Cabinet meeting was held here in 1865.

Chiefly agricultural and dependent on slave labor in antebellum days, the region took eagerly to industry after Appomattox. Abundant water power for electricity from the Catawba River has been a principal reason for its rapid growth. Today, Charlotte is among the largest banking centers in the country.

Transportation

Charlotte/Douglas Intl Airport: Information 704/359-4013; lost and found 704/359-4012.

Car Rental Agencies: See IMPORTANT TOLL-FREE NUMBERS.

Public Transportation: Buses (Charlotte Transit System), phone 704/336-3366.

Rail Passenger Service: Amtrak 800/872-7245.

What to See and Do

Charlotte Coliseum. This 23,000-seat arena hosts various sports events as well as family shows and concerts. 100 Paul Buck Blvd. For schedule information phone 704/357-4700.

Discovery Place. Hands-on science museum features aquarium; also science circus, life center, rain forest, collections gallery; Omnimax theater; Space Voyager Planetarium; major traveling exhibits. (Daily; closed Thanksgiving, Dec 25) 301 N Tryon St. Phone 704/372-6261 or 800/935-0553. ¢¢¢

James K. Polk Memorial State Historic Site. Replica of log cabin and outbuildings at birthsite of 11th President of the United States. Visitor center with exhibits, film. Guided tour. (Apr-Nov, Mon-Sat, also Sun afternoons; rest of yr, Tues-Sat, also Sun afternoons; closed major hols) 12 mi S on US 521, in Pineville. Phone 704/889-7145. **Free.**

Latta Plantation Park. Approx 1,000-acre nature preserve on Mt Island Lake. Interpretive Center, Carolina Raptor Center, Audubon Sanctuary, Equestrian Center (fees for each). Bridle paths, hiking trails, fishing, picnicking, canoe access. (Daily) 12 mi NW via I-77, exit 16B (Sunset Rd W), right at Beattie's Ford Rd 5 mi, then left at Sample Rd. Phone 704/875-1391. **Free.** Also here is

Latta Place (ca 1800). Restored Federal-style plantation house, original storehouse, log slave house replica; barns, farm animals; kitchen garden, cotton field. (Daily exc Mon; closed most major hols) Phone 704/875-2312. ¢

Mint Museum of Art. First Branch US Mint operated here 1837-1861 and 1867-1913, and in 1933 it was chartered as an art museum. Collections include European and American art from Renaissance to contemporary; fine pottery and porcelain collection; maps; period costumes; survey collection of pre-Columbian and African artifacts; exhibition of coins. (Daily exc Mon; closed Jan 1, Thanksgiving, Dec 25) 2730 Randolph Rd. Phone 704/337-2000. ¢¢

Nature Museum. Live Animal Room, nature trail, puppet theater; earth science hall. (Daily; closed Thanksgiving, Dec 25) 1658 Sterling Rd. Phone 704/372-6261. ¢

Ovens Auditorium. Shows by touring Broadway companies (fall-late spring); musicals; symphony. 2700 E Independence Blvd, 5 mi E on US 74. Phone 704/372-3600 for schedule.

Paramount's Carowinds. 100-acre family theme park has over 40 rides, shows and attractions including 12-acre water entertainment complex WaterWorks; Animation Station children's area; DROP ZONE stunt tower; rollercoasters. 13,000-seat Paladium Amphitheater hosts special events. Campground (all yr). (June-late Aug, daily; Mar-May & Sept-Oct, wknds) Exit 90 off I-77, at state line. Phone 704/588-2600, 803/548-5300 or 800/888-4386. ¢¢¢¢

Professional sports.

NBA (Charlotte Hornets). Charlotte Coliseum, 100 Paul Buck Blvd. Phone 704/357-0252.

NFL (Carolina Panthers). Ericsson Stadium, 800 S Mint St. Phone 704/358-7000.

Spirit Square Center for the Arts. Exhibitions by well-known contemporary artists; studio art classes (fee); performances (fee). Parking fee. 345 N College St. Phone 704/372-9664 or 704/372-SHOW (box office).

The Charlotte Museum of History and Alexander Homesite. Includes Hezekiah Alexander House (1774), oldest dwelling still standing in Mecklenburg County; 2-story springhouse; working log kitchen. Tours (fee). (Tues-Fri, also Sat & Sun afternoons; closed major hols) 3500 Shamrock Dr. Phone 704/568-1774.   **Free.**

University of North Carolina at Charlotte (1946). (15,000 students) Beautiful landscaping and blooming plants (Mar-Nov); rhododendron garden (blooms Apr-May); ornamental garden, public greenhouse with rainforest and orchid collection. Sculpture garden. Rare Book Room and panoramic view of campus, 10th floor of library (Mon-Fri; closed hols). Walking-tour guide and map. NE off I-85. Phone 704/547-4286.

Annual Events

Springfest. Three-day festival in uptown, offers food, live entertainment. Phone 704/332-0126. Last wkend Apr.

Festival in the Park. Freedom Park. Arts and crafts, entertainment. Phone 704/338-1060. 6 days mid-Sept.

Seasonal Events

Symphony. Charlotte Symphony Orchestra, Inc. Phone 704/332-6136. Performs yr-round.

Theatre Charlotte. 501 Queens Rd. Classic and Broadway plays. Features 6 productions a yr on alternate months beginning in Sept. Thurs-Sat evenings. Phone 704/376-3777.

Opera. Opera Carolina. Phone 704/332-7177. Oct-Apr.

Auto racing. Charlotte Motor Speedway. 12 mi N on US 29 or off I-85 exit W.T. Harris Blvd. Coca-Cola 600 Winston Cup stock car race (Memorial Day wkend); Mello Yello 500 Winston Cup stock car race (early Oct); Spring AutoFair car show & flea market (mid-Apr); Fall AutoFair (mid-Sept). Phone 704/455-3200.

Motels

✔★ **COMFORT INN-AIRPORT.** *4040 I-85S (28208), exit 32 (Little Rock Rd), near Douglas Intl Airport.* 704/394-4111. 118 rms, 2 story. S $65; D $75; each addl $5; under 18 free; higher rates stock car races. Crib free. TV; cable (premium). Pool. Complimentary continental bkfst. Restaurant adj 7 am-10 pm. Bar 5-11 pm. Ck-out 11 am. Meeting rms. Business servs avail. Free airport transportation. Exercise equipt; stair machine, bicycles. Refrigerators, microwaves avail. Cr cds: A, C, D, DS, MC, V.

D 🏊 🏋 ✈ 🚫 🔥 SC

✔★ **COMFORT INN-SUGAR CREEK.** *5111 N Sugar Creek Rd (28269).* 704/598-0007. 87 rms, 2 story. S $45.95-$69.95; D $59.95-$69.95; each addl $6; under 18 free; higher rates special events. Crib free. TV; cable (premium). Pool; whirlpool. Complimentary continental bkfst. Restaurant nearby. Ck-out 11 am. Meeting rms. Business servs avail. Valet serv. Exercise equipt; weight machine, bicycles. Microwaves avail. Cr cds: A, C, D, DS, ER, JCB, MC, V.

D 🏊 🏋 🚫 🔥 SC

★★ **COURTYARD BY MARRIOTT.** *800 E Arrowwood Rd (28217), I-77 exit 3.* 704/527-5055; FAX 704/525-5848. 146 rms, 3 story. S, D $78-$88; wkend rates; under 6 free. Crib free. TV; cable (premium). Pool; whirlpool. Coffee in rms. Bar 5-10 pm. Ck-out noon. Coin lndry. Meeting rms. Business servs avail. Valet serv. Exercise equipt; stair machine, bicycles. Some refrigerators. Private patios, balconies. Cr cds: A, D, DS, MC, V.

D 🏊 🏋 🚫 🔥 SC

★★ **COURTYARD BY MARRIOTT-UNIVERSITY.** *333 W Harris Blvd (28262).* 704/549-4888; FAX 704/549-4946. 152 rms, 4 story. S $88; D $98; suites $98; under 12 free; wkend rates; higher rates special

events. Crib free. TV; cable (premium). Pool; whirlpool. Complimentary coffee in rms. Bar. Ck-out noon. Coin lndry. Meeting rms. Business servs avail. In-rm modem link. Exercise equipt; stair machine, weight machine. Health club privileges. Refrigerator in suites. Near University of NC. Cr cds: A, C, D, DS, MC, V.

D 🏊 🏋 🚫 🔥 SC

✔★ **FAIRFIELD INN BY MARRIOTT.** *5415 N I-85 Service Rd (28262), I-85 exit 41.* 704/596-2999. 133 rms, 3 story. S $48.95-$52.95; D $50.95-$54.95; under 18 free; higher rates wkends, special events. Crib free. TV; cable (premium). Pool. Complimentary continental bkfst. Restaurant nearby. Ck-out noon. Business servs avail. Cr cds: A, D, DS, MC, V.

D 🏊 🚫 🔥 SC

★★ **HAMPTON INN.** *440 Griffith Rd (28217), approx 6 mi S via I-77, Tyvola Rd exit 5.* 704/525-0747; FAX 704/522-0968. 161 rms, 4 story. S $62; D $70-$75; under 18 free. Crib free. TV; cable (premium). Pool. Complimentary continental bkfst. Ck-out noon. Meeting rms. Business servs avail. Valet serv. Airport transportation. Exercise equipt; weights, bicycles, sauna. Microwaves avail. Cr cds: A, C, D, DS, MC, V.

D 🏊 🏋 ✈ 🚫 🔥 SC

✔★ **INNKEEPER.** *305 Archdale Drive (28217).* 704/525-3033. 69 rms, 2 story. S $39.99-$44.99; D $49.99-$50.99; each addl $5; under 16 free; higher rates special events. Crib free. TV; cable (premium). Pool. Complimentary continental bkfst. Restaurant nearby. Ck-out noon. Business servs avail. Microwaves avail. Cr cds: A, C, D, DS, MC, V.

D 🏊 🚫 🔥 SC

★★ **LA QUINTA-SOUTH.** *7900 Nations Ford Rd (28217), S via I-77 to exit 4.* 704/522-7110; FAX 704/521-9778. Web www.laquinta.com. 118 rms, 3 story. S, D $57-$70; each addl $7; under 18 free; higher rates: auto race wkends, special events. Crib free. Pet accepted, some restrictions. TV; cable (premium). Heated pool. Continental bkfst. Restaurant adj open 24 hrs. Ck-out noon. Business servs avail. Valet serv. Health club privileges. Microwaves avail. Cr cds: A, C, D, DS, MC, V.

D 🐾 🏊 🚫 🔥 SC

✔★ **RED ROOF INN-COLISEUM.** *131 Red Roof Dr (28217), I-77 S to exit 4 (Nations Ford Rd).* 704/529-1020; FAX 704/529-1054. E-mail 124@redroofinn.com. 115 rms, 3 story. S $36-$41; D $41-$47; up to 5, $59; under 18 free. Crib free. Pet accepted, some restrictions. TV; cable (premium). Complimentary coffee in lobby. Ck-out noon. Business servs avail. Health club privileges. Cr cds: A, C, D, DS, MC, V.

D 🐾 🏊 🚫 🔥

★★ **RESIDENCE INN BY MARRIOTT.** *5800 Westpark Dr (28217), off I-77S at Tyvola Rd exit 5.* 704/527-8110; FAX 704/521-8282. 80 kit. suites, 1-2 story. S, D $139-$169. Crib free. Pet accepted; $100 and $5/day. TV; cable (premium). Heated pool; whirlpool. Complimentary continental bkfst. Restaurant adj 7 am-10 pm. Coin lndry. Ck-out noon. Business servs avail. Valet serv. Health club privileges. Lawn games. Microwaves. Private patios, balconies. Cr cds: A, C, D, DS, MC, V.

D 🐾 🏊 🚫 🔥 SC

✔★ **RODEWAY INN.** *1416 W Sugar Creek Rd (28213).* 704/597-5074. 56 rms, 2 story. S $40.95-$48.95; D $46.95-$54.95; each addl $5; higher rates special events; under 12 free. Crib free. TV; cable (premium). Pool. Complimentary continental bkfst. Restaurant adj open 24 hrs. Ck-out 11 am. Cr cds: A, C, D, DS, MC, V.

D 🏊 🚫 🔥 SC

Motor Hotels

★★ **HOLIDAY INN-WOODLAWN.** *212 Woodlawn Rd (28217), at I-77S exit 6A.* 704/525-8350; FAX 704/522-0671. E-mail holidaywoodlawn@travelbase.com; web www.travelbase.com/destinations/charlotte/holiday-woodlawn. 425 rms, 4 story. S, D $84-$94; suites $160; under 18 free; wkend rates; higher rates special events. Crib free. TV; cable (premium). Pool. Restaurant 6 am-10 pm. Rm serv. Bar 4 pm-1 am; entertainment. Ck-out noon. Meeting rms. Business servs avail. In-rm modem link. Bellhops. Valet serv. Sundries. Free airport transportation. Exercise equipt; weight machine, treadmill. Refrigerator in suites. Cr cds: A, C, D, DS, JCB, MC, V.

[D] [symbols] SC

★ ★ **SHERATON AIRPORT PLAZA.** *3315 S I-85 (28208), at Billy Graham Pkwy, near Douglas Intl Airport, I-85 exit 33.* 704/392-1200; FAX 704/393-2207. 222 rms, 8 story. S, D $119-$135; each addl $10; suites $150-$175; under 16 free; wkend rates. Crib free. Pet accepted. TV; cable (premium). Indoor/outdoor pool; whirlpool, poolside serv. Coffee in rms. Restaurant 6:30 am-10:30 pm. Rm serv. Bar 11 am-midnight; entertainment Thurs-Sat. Ck-out noon. Meeting rms. Business servs avail. Bellhops. Valet serv. Gift shop. Free airport transportation. Exercise equipt; weights, bicycles, sauna. Bathrm phones; microwaves avail. Cr cds: A, C, D, DS, JCB, MC, V.

[D] [symbols] SC

★ ★ **SUMMERFIELD SUITES.** *4920 S Tryon St (28217).* 704/525-2600; FAX 704/521-9932. 135 kit. suites, 5 story. Kit. suites $79-$109; under 18 free; wkends (2-day min); higher rates race wkend. Crib free. Pet accepted; $50. TV; cable (premium), VCR (movies). Complimentary continental bkfst. Complimentary coffee in rms. Ck-out noon. Meeting rms. Business center. In-rm modem link. Free airport transportation. Exercise equipt; rowers, stair machine. Pool; whirlpool. Game rm. Refrigerators, microwaves. Picnic tables, grills. Totally nonsmoking. Cr cds: A, C, D, DS, JCB, MC, V.

[D] [symbols] SC

★ ★ ★ **WYNDHAM GARDEN HOTEL.** *2600 Yorkmont Rd (28208), off Billy Graham Pkwy at Tyvola Rd & Coliseum exit.* 704/357-9100; FAX 704/357-9159. 173 rms, 3 story. S $109; D $119; each addl $10; suites $119-$129; under 12 free; wkend rates; higher rates special events. Crib free. TV; cable (premium), VCR avail. Heated pool; whirlpool. Complimentary coffee in rms. Restaurant 6:30 am-2:30 pm, 5-10 pm. Rm serv from 5 pm. Bar 4 pm-midnight. Ck-out noon. Meeting rms. Business servs avail. In-rm modem link. Bellhops. Valet serv. Free airport transportation. Exercise equipt; weight machine, bicycles. Refrigerator in some suites. Cr cds: A, C, D, DS, MC, V.

[D] [symbols] SC

Hotels

★ ★ ★ **ADAM'S MARK.** *555 S McDowell St (28204), at jct US 74 & US 77.* 704/372-4100; FAX 704/348-4645. 615 rms, 18 story. S, D $99-$145; each addl $15; suites $350-$475; under 18 free; wkend rates. Crib free. TV; cable (premium), VCR avail. Heated pools, 1 indoor; whirlpool. Restaurant (see BRAVO). Bars 11-1 am; entertainment. Ck-out noon. Convention facilities. Business center. Concierge. Gift shop. Exercise equipt; weights, bicycles, sauna. Health club privileges. Raquetball courts. Some refrigerators. Wet bar in some suites. Opp park. Cr cds: A, C, D, DS, ER, MC, V.

[D] [symbols] SC

★ ★ ★ **DOUBLETREE CLUB.** *895 W Trade St (28202).* 704/347-0070; FAX 704/347-0267. 187 rms, 8 story. S $150; D $165; each addl $15; under 12 free; wkend rates; higher rates auto races (May & Oct). TV; cable (premium). Pool; whirlpool. Coffee in rms. Restaurant 6 am-11 pm. Bar 5 pm-midnight. Ck-out 1 pm. Meeting rms. Business center. Exercise equipt; weight machine, bicycles, sauna. Health club privileges. Cr cds: A, C, D, DS, ER, JCB, MC, V.

[D] [symbols] SC

★ ★ ★ **DUNHILL.** *237 N Tryon St (28202).* 704/332-4141; FAX 704/376-4117; res: 800/354-4141. E-mail rjmj@msn.com. 60 rms, 10 story. S, D $109; each addl $10; under 16 free; wkend rates; higher rates special events. Crib free. TV; cable (premium). Restaurant 6:30 am-10:30 pm. Bar. Ck-out noon. Meeting rms. Business servs avail. In-rm modem link. Concierge. Free garage parking. Free airport transportation. Exercise equipt; stair machine, treadmill. Health club privileges. Refrigerators. Euro-

pean-style hotel built in 1929; 18th-century furnishings, original artwork. Cr cds: A, C, D, DS, MC, V.

[D] [symbols] SC

★ ★ ★ **EMBASSY SUITES.** *4800 S Tryon St (28217).* 704/527-8400; FAX 704/527-7035. Web www.embassy-charlotte.com. 274 suites, 8 story. Suites $149-$160; each addl $20; under 12 free; wkend rates; higher rates special events. Crib free. TV; cable (premium). Indoor pool; whirlpool; poolside serv. Complimentary full bkfst. Complimentary coffee in rms. Restaurant 11 am-11 pm. Bar 10-2 am; entertainment. Ck-out nooh. Coin lndry. Convention facilities. Business center. In-rm modem link. Gift shop. Covered parking. Free airport transportation. Tennis privileges. Exercise equipt; treadmill, bicycles, sauna. Refrigerators, microwaves, wet bars; some bathrm phones. Cr cds: A, C, D, DS, MC, V.

[D] [symbols] SC

★ ★ ★ **HILTON AT UNIVERSITY PLACE.** *8629 J M Keynes Dr (28262), off I-85, exit 45A (Harris Blvd).* 704/547-7444; FAX 704/549-9708. E-mail hiltonuniversity@travelbase.com; web www.travelbase.com/destinations/charlotte/hilton-univ. 243 rms, 12 story. S, D $84-$159; each addl $15; wkend rates. Crib free. Pet accepted; $50. TV; cable (premium). Heated pool; poolside serv. Restaurant 6:30 am-10 pm. Bar 11-2 am; entertainment. Ck-out noon. Meeting rms. Business servs avail. In-rm modem link. Exercise equipt; bicycles, treadmills. Health club privileges. Microwaves avail. Cr cds: A, C, D, DS, MC, V.

[D] [symbols] SC

★ ★ ★ **HILTON EXECUTIVE PARK.** *5624 Westpark Dr (28217), I-77 exit 5.* 704/527-8000; FAX 704/527-4278. 178 rms, 7 story, 34 suites. S $124; D $134; each addl $10; suites $149; under 18 free. Crib free. Pet accepted; $50 deposit, $15/day. TV; cable (premium), VCR avail. Heated pool; whirlpool. Restaurant 6:30 am-2 pm, 5-10 pm. Bar 2 pm-midnight. Ck-out noon. Meeting rms. Business servs avail. Free airport transportation. Exercise equipt; weight machine, treadmill. Microwaves avail. Refrigerator in suites. Cr cds: A, C, D, DS, MC, V.

[D] [symbols] SC

★ ★ ★ **HYATT.** *5501 Carnegie Blvd (28209), opp South Park Mall.* 704/554-1234; FAX 704/554-8319. 262 rms, 7 story. S $170; D $195; suites $350-$750; lower rates wkends; under 18 free. Crib free. Pet accepted. TV; cable (premium). Indoor pool; whirlpool, poolside serv. Restaurant 6 am-10:30 pm. Rm serv 24 hrs. Bar 2 pm-2 am. Ck-out noon. Convention facilities. Business center. Gift shop. Free valet parking. Airport transportation. Exercise equipt; weights, bicycles, sauna. Health club privileges. Refrigerators, microwaves avail. Some balconies. Luxury level. Cr cds: A, C, D, DS, ER, JCB, MC, V.

[D] [symbols] SC

★ ★ ★ **MARRIOTT-CITY CENTER.** *100 W Trade St (28202).* 704/333-9000; FAX 704/342-3419. 434 rms, 19 story. S $149; D $159; suites $200-$350; under 12 free; wkend rates. Crib free. Covered parking, valet $16. TV; cable (premium), VCR avail. Heated pool; whirlpool. Restaurant 6:30 am-10 pm. Bar 11:30-1 am. Ck-out noon. Guest lndry. Convention facilities. Business center. In-rm modem link. Concierge. Gift shop. Airport transportation. Exercise equipt; weights, bicycles. Refrigerators, microwaves avail. Shopping adj. Luxury level. Cr cds: A, C, D, DS, ER, JCB, MC, V.

[D] [symbols] SC

★ ★ ★ ★ **THE PARK HOTEL.** *2200 Rexford Rd (28211).* 704/364-8220; FAX 704/365-4712; res: 800/334-0331. Web www.theparkhotel.com. Marble, brass and traditional patterns, cast in rich colors, are used throughout the hotel's public areas and in the well-appointed guest rooms. 194 rms, 6 story. S $119-$165; D $134-$180; each addl $15; suites $325-$625; under 18 free; wkend rates. Crib free. TV; cable (premium), VCR avail. Heated pool; whirlpool, poolside serv. Restaurant (see MORROCROFTS). Rm serv 24 hrs. Bars 11-2 am; entertainment. Ck-out noon. Meeting rms. Business servs avail. In-rm modem link. Concierge. Free valet parking. Airport, RR station, bus depot transportation. Tennis privileges. Golf privileges. Exercise equipt; weight machines, bicycles, steam rm. Health club privileges. Some refrigerators; microwaves avail. Cr cds: A, C, D, DS, JCB, MC, V.

[D] [symbols] SC

★ ★ **RADISSON PLAZA.** *101 S Tryon (28280), at jct Trade & Tryon Sts.* 704/377-0400; FAX 704/347-0649. 365 rms, 15 story. S, D $135; each addl $10; suites $219-$325; under 18 free; wkend rates. Crib free. Pet accepted, some restrictions. TV; cable (premium), VCR avail. Pool; poolside serv. Coffee in rms. Restaurant 6:30 am-10:30 pm. Bar 11 am-midnight. Ck-out noon. Convention facilities. Business center. Concierge. Shopping arcade. Barber, beauty shop. Covered parking. Exercise equipt; weights, stair machine, sauna. Refrigerator, wet bar in suites. Luxury level. Cr cds: A, C, D, DS, ER, MC, V.

D 🏊 🏋 🎾 🖼 SC 🚶

★ ★ **SOUTHPARK SUITE.** *6300 Morrison Blvd (28211), near South Park Mall.* 704/364-2400; FAX 704/362-0203; res: 800/647-8483. E-mail spsh@vnet.net; web www.vnet.net/southpark. 208 kit. suites, 3-6 story. S, D $99-$169; under 18 free; wkend rates. Crib avail. TV; cable (premium). Pool; whirlpool, poolside serv. Restaurant 6:30 am-11 pm. Bar 4 pm-midnight. Ck-out noon. Lndry facilities. Meeting rms. Business center. Gift shop. Exercise equipt; weight machines, bicycles, sauna. Health club privileges. Microwaves. Private patios, balconies. Cr cds: A, C, D, DS, MC, V.

D 🏊 🎾 🖼 SC 🚶

★ ★ **WESTIN.** *222 E Third St (28202).* 704/377-1500; FAX 704/377-4143. 407 rms, 22 story. S $159-$184, D $184-$209; each addl $25; suites $195-$600; under 18 free; wkend rates. Crib free. Garage parking; valet $18. TV; cable (premium), VCR avail. Pool privileges. Restaurant 6:30 am-11 pm. Bar 11-1:30 am. Ck-out noon. Convention facilities. Business center. In-rm modem link. Shopping arcade. Airport transportation. Tennis privileges. Golf privileges. Health club privileges. Minibars; some bathrm phones; refrigerators avail. Wet bar in suites. Luxury level. Cr cds: A, C, D, DS, JCB, MC, V.

D 🏋 🏌 🎾 🖼 SC 🚶

Restaurants

★ ★ ★ **BRAVO.** *(See Adam's Mark Hotel)* 704/372-4100. Hrs: 5:30-10 pm; Fri, Sat to 10:30 pm; Sun brunch 10:30 am-2 pm. Res accepted. Italian menu. Bar. Semi-a la carte: dinner $11.75-$28. Sun brunch $16.95. Specializes in fresh seafood, pasta, chicken. Singing waiters. Italian decor. Cr cds: A, C, D, DS, ER, MC, V.

D 🔲

★ ★ ★ **EPICUREAN.** *1324 East Blvd (28203).* 704/377-4529. Hrs: 6-10 pm. Closed Sun; major hols; also 1st 2 wks July. Res accepted. Continental menu. Serv bar. Wine list. Semi-a la carte: dinner $16.95-$35.95. Child's meals. Specializes in steaks, fresh seafood, lamb. Own baking. Family-owned. Cr cds: A, C, D, MC, V.

D 🔲

★ ★ **THE FISHMARKET.** *6631 Morrison Blvd.* 704/365-0883. Hrs: 11:30 am-2 pm, 6-10 pm; Sat, Sun from 6 pm. Closed major hols. Res accepted. Bar 4 pm-midnight. Semi-a la carte: lunch $6.25-$10.95, dinner $14.95-$28.95. Specializes in seafood, pasta, desserts. Cr cds: A, D, DS, MC, V.

🔲

★ ★ **THE GINGER ROOT.** *201 E Fifth St (28202), on ground floor of office bldg.* 704/377-9429. Hrs: 11:30 am-2:30 pm, 5-9:30 pm; Fri to 10:30 pm; Sat 5-10:30 pm; Sun 5-9:30 pm. Closed most major hols. Res accepted. Chinese menu. Bar. Semi-a la carte: lunch $4.95-$6.25, dinner $6.95-$16.95. Lunch buffet $5.95. Specializes in seafood, chicken, beef. Sushi bar. Several dining areas with Oriental accents. Cr cds: A, D, MC, V.

D 🔲

★ ★ **HEREFORD BARN STEAK HOUSE.** *4320 N I-85, on service road between Sugar Creek Rd & Graham St.* 704/596-0854. Hrs: 5-10 pm; Fri, Sat to 11 pm. Closed Sun, Mon; major hols. Serv bar. Semi-a la carte: dinner $9.95-$29.95. Child's meals. Specializes in steak, prime rib, chicken. Country-barn decor; farm implements; fireplace. Family-owned. Cr cds: A, C, D, DS, MC, V.

SC 🔲

★ ★ ★ **LA BIBLIOTHEQUE.** *1901 Roxborough Rd (28211), in Morrison office bldg.* 704/365-5000. Web www.charlottenet.com/rest/labib/index.htmn. Hrs: 11:30 am-2:30 pm, 5:30-10:30 pm; Sat from 5:30 pm. Closed Sun; Jan 1, Thanksgiving, Dec 25. Res accepted. French-American menu. Serv bar. A la carte entrees: lunch $7.95-$11.95, dinner $14-$27. Specializes in seafood, beef, veal. Pianist Tues-Sun. Terrace dining. Traditional decor; oil paintings. Jacket (dinner). Cr cds: A, C, D, DS, MC, V.

D 🔲

★ ★ ★ **LAMP LIGHTER.** *1065 E Morehead St.* 704/372-5343. Hrs: 5:30-10 pm; Fri, Sat to 10:30 pm. Closed Jan 1, Thanksgiving, Dec 25. Res accepted. Continental menu. Bar. Wine list. Semi-a la carte: dinner $14.95-$29.95. Specializes in fresh seafood, wild game, ostrich. Own baking. Valet parking. In Spanish-colonial house built 1926. Jacket. Cr cds: A, C, D, MC, V.

D 🔲

★ ★ ★ **MORROCROFTS.** *(See The Park Hotel)* 704/364-8220. Hrs: 6:30 am-11 pm; early-bird dinner 5-6:30 pm; Sun brunch 10:30 am-2 pm. Res accepted. Continental menu. Bar 11-1 am. Wine list. Semi-a la carte: bkfst $2.50-$9.95, lunch $3.95-$10.95, dinner $10.95-$23.95. Sun brunch $14.95-$22.95. Child's meals. Specializes in fresh seafood, regional cuisine. Own baking. Pianist. Valet parking. Outdoor dining. English club decor. Cr cds: A, C, D, DS, JCB, MC, V.

D 🔲

★ **RANCH HOUSE.** *5614 Wilkinson Blvd (28208).* 704/399-5411. Hrs: 5-11 pm. Closed Sun; major hols. Serv bar. Semi-a la carte: dinner: $9.75-$20.75. Child's meals. Specializes in steak, seafood, chicken. Western decor. Family-owned. Cr cds: A, D, DS, MC, V.

🔲

★ ★ ★ **TOWNHOUSE.** *1011 Providence Rd.* 704/335-1546. E-mail Townhouse2@aol.com. Hrs: 6-10 pm. Closed some major hols. Res accepted. Bar from 5 pm. Wine list. Semi-a la carte: dinner $19.50-$30. Specializes in fowl, beef, seafood. Own baking, pasta. 18th-century English decor. Cr cds: A, C, D, DS, JCB, MC, V.

D 🔲

Cherokee (B-2)

(See also Bryson City, Maggie Valley, Waynesville)

Pop 8,519 **Elev** 1,991 ft **Area code** 704 **Zip** 28719
Information Cherokee Travel and Promotion, PO Box 460; 704/497-9195 or 800/438-1601.

This is the capital of the Eastern Band of the Cherokee, who live on the Qualla Reservation at the edge of Great Smoky Mountains National Park (see) and the Blue Ridge Parkway. The reservation is the largest east of the Mississippi. These descendants of members of the tribe who avoided being driven to Oklahoma over the "Trail of Tears" are progressive in their ideas, yet determined to maintain their ancient traditions.

What to See and Do

Cherokee Heritage Museum and Gallery. Interpretive center features Cherokee culture and history. Gift shop. (Daily; closed 3 wks late Dec-early Jan) On US 441 and Big Cove Rd, in Saunooke's Village. Phone 704/497-3211. ¢¢

Museum of the Cherokee Indian. Arts and crafts, audiovisual displays, portraits, prehistoric artifacts. (Daily; closed Jan 1, Thanksgiving, Dec 25) On US 441 at Drama Rd, on Cherokee Reservation. Phone 704/497-3481. ¢¢

Oconaluftee Indian Village. Replica of Native American village of more than 250 yrs ago. Includes 7-sided council house; lectures; herb garden; craft demonstrations. Guided tours (Mid-May-late Oct, daily). 1/2 mi N on US 441, adj to Mountainside Theater. Phone 704/497-2111. ¢¢¢

Santa's Land. Christmas theme park featuring Santa Claus and helpers; rides; zoo; entertainment, including magic show; lake with pedal boats; primitive crafts; snack shops, picnic area, play areas; gardens. (Early May-late Oct, daily) 3 mi E on US 19N. Phone 704/497-9191. ¢¢¢¢

Seasonal Event

Unto These Hills. Mountainside Theater. On US 441, ½ mi from jct US 19.Kermit Hunter drama re-creating the history of Cherokee Nation from 1540-1838; in natural amphitheater. Nightly exc Sun. Phone 407/497-2111. Mid-June-late Aug.

Motels

★ ★ **BEST WESTERN-GREAT SMOKIES INN.** *US 441 at Acquoni Rd.* 704/497-2020; FAX 704/497-3903. 152 rms, 2 story. Late May-Oct: S, D $85; each addl $6; under 12 free; lower rates rest of yr. Crib free. TV; cable (premium). Pool; wading pool. Restaurant 7 am-9 pm. Rm serv. Ck-out 11 am. Coin lndry. Meeting rms. Business servs avail. Sundries. Cr cds: A, C, D, DS, MC, V.

🅳 ⊠ ⋈ 🔥 🐾 SC

★ ★ **COMFORT INN.** *US 19S, ½ mi W of jct US 441 & 19.* 704/497-2411; FAX 704/497-6555. 87 rms, 2 story. Late May-Oct: S, D $59-$109; each addl $8; under 18 free; lower rates Apr-late May & Nov-Dec. Closed rest of yr. Crib $2. TV; cable (premium). Pool; whirlpool. Complimentary continental bkfst. Restaurant nearby. Ck-out 11 am. Meeting rm. Business servs avail. Some refrigerators. On river. Cr cds: A, D, DS, JCB, MC, V.

🅳 ✒ ⊠ ⋈ 🔥 🐾 SC

✔★ **COOL WATERS.** *US 19E, 1½ mi E.* 704/497-3855. 50 rms. Mid-June-Oct: S, D $42-$70; lower rates rest of yr. Crib $3. TV; cable. Pool; wading pool. Restaurant opp 6:30 am-9 pm. Ck-out 11 am. Tennis. Some patios. Picnic tables, grills. On stream; trout pond. Cr cds: DS, MC, V.

✒ 🎿 ⊠ ⋈ 🐾

★ **CRAIG'S.** *US 19.* 704/497-3821. 30 rms. S, D $49-$63; each addl $5; higher rates: hols, wkends, fall foliage season. Closed Nov-Apr. Crib $4. TV; cable (premium). Pool. Playground. Restaurant 7 am-10 pm. Ck-out 11 am. On stream; picnic tables nearby. Cr cds: A, DS, MC, V.

✒ ⊠ ⋈ 🐾 SC

★ ★ **DAYS INN.** *On US 19.* 704/497-9171; FAX 704/497-3424. 58 rms, 1-2 story. Mid-June-Labor Day, Oct: S, D $65-$90; each addl $3; lower rates Apr-mid June, after Labor Day-Sept. Crib free. TV; cable (premium). 2 pools; wading pool. Playground. Restaurant adj 7 am-noon, 5-9 pm. Ck-out 11 am. Cr cds: A, C, D, DS, JCB, MC, V.

✒ ⊠ ⋈ 🐾 SC

★ ★ ★ **HOLIDAY INN.** *US 19S, 1 mi W.* 704/497-9181; FAX 704/497-5973. 154 rms, 2 story. Mid-June-Oct: S, D $66-$100; each addl $6; under 19 free; lower rates rest of yr. Crib free. TV; cable (premium). 2 pools, 1 indoor; wading pool, whirlpool, sauna. Playground. Restaurant 7-11 am, 5-9 pm. Rm serv. Ck-out 11 am. Coin lndry. Meeting rm. Sundries. Gift shop. Game rm. Cr cds: A, C, D, DS, JCB, MC, V.

🅳 ⊠ ⋈ 🐾 SC

★ **PIONEER.** *US 19S.* 704/497-2435. 21 rms, 6 kit. cottages. Mid-June-Labor Day, Oct: S, D $48-$68; each addl $5; cottages $75-$150; under 12 free; lower rates Apr-mid-June, Sept. Closed rest of yr. Crib free. TV; cable (premium). Pool. Complimentary coffee in lobby. Restaurant nearby. Ck-out 11 am. At river. Cr cds: A, DS, MC, V.

✒ ⊠ ⋈ 🔥 SC

Cherryville (B-4)

(For accommodations see Gastonia, Shelby)

Founded 1881 **Pop** 4,756 **Elev** 960 ft **Area code** 704 **Zip** 28021
Information Chamber of Commerce, 301 E Main St, PO Box 305; 704/435-3451 or 704/435-4200.

Customs of Cherryville's original German settlers still live on in this town nestled in the rolling hills of the Piedmont.

Annual Event

Shooting in the New Year. Old rite to bring fertility to fruit trees and for good luck in the coming year. Men chant blessings and fire black-powder muzzleloaders as they go from home to home New Year's Eve until dusk, Jan 1.

Concord (Cabarrus Co) (B-5)

(See also Albemarle, Charlotte)

Pop 27,347 **Elev** 704 ft **Area code** 704 **Zip** 28026
Information Chamber of Commerce, 23 Union St N, PO Box 1029; 704/782-4111.

Concord was founded by Scottish-Irish and German-Dutch settlers and received its name when the two factions settled a dispute regarding the location of the county seat. An early textile area in the South, Concord continues to lead in dyeing, finishing and weaving of hosiery and knitted textiles.

What to See and Do

Reed Gold Mine State Historic Site. First documented discovery of gold in the United States (1799) occurred here. Panning area (Apr-Oct, daily; fee); underground mine tours, history trail; working machinery, demonstrations, exhibits, visitor center; film; picnicking. (Apr-Oct, Mon-Sat, also Sun afternoons; rest of yr, Tues-Sat, also Sun afternoons) 10 mi SE on US 601 and NC 200 to Georgeville, then 2 mi S on NC 1100. Phone 704/786-8337. **Free.**

Motels

★ **COLONIAL INN.** *1325 Hwy 29 N, ¾ mi NW on US 29/601 Concord exit.* 704/782-2146; FAX 704/786-9856. 65 rms. S $42; D $52. Crib $6. TV; cable (premium). Pool. Complimentary coffee in lobby. Restaurant adj 6 am-midnight. Ck-out 11 am. Meeting rms. Lawn games. Cr cds: A, C, D, DS, MC, V.

⊠ ⋈ 🐾 SC

✔★ ★ **COMFORT INN.** *(3100 Cloverleaf Pkwy, Kannapolis 28081)* 704/786-3100; FAX 704/784-3114. 71 rms, 2 story. S, D $58.95; each addl $5; suites $72.95; under 18 free; higher rates: auto races, horse shows. Crib $5. TV; cable (premium), VCR avail (movies). Pool. Complimentary continental bkfst. Complimentary coffee in rms. Restaurant adj 11 am-11 pm. Ck-out 11 am. Coin lndry. Meeting rms. Business servs avail. Health club privileges. Many refrigerators. Cr cds: A, C, D, DS, ER, JCB, MC, V.

🅳 ⊠ ⋈ 🔥 SC

Cornelius (B-4)

(See also Charlotte, Statesville)

Founded 1893 **Pop** 2,581 **Elev** 831 ft **Area code** 704 **Zip** 28031 **E-mail** NMeckCofCl@aol.com **Web** www.northmeck.com

Information North Mecklenburg Chamber & Visitors Center, PO Box 760; 704/892-1922.

A dispute between two cotton companies in Davidson during the late 1800s led to one of the firms relocating south of the city limits and establishing a new town. Originally called Liverpool, the community changed its name to Cornelius in honor of an investor.

What to See and Do

Lake Norman. The state's largest freshwater lake (32,510 acres); created by Cowans Ford Dam, a Duke Power project on the Catawba River. Eight public access areas. NW of town. Phone 704/382-8587.

Annual Event

LakeFest. County Park. Entertainment, dog show, Art in the Park, concessions. KidzFest, petting zoo, magic shows, face painting. Phone 704/892-1922. Wkend mid-Sept.

Motels

★ ★ **BEST WESTERN LAKE NORMAN.** *19608 Liverpool Pkwy.* 704/896-0660; FAX 704/896-8633. 80 rms, 4 story, 10 suites. S $65.95; D $72.95; each addl $7; suites $89.95-$99.95; under 15 free; higher rates special events. Crib free. TV; cable (premium), VCR avail (movies $6). Pool. Complimentary continental bkfst. Restaurant nearby. Ck-out 11 am. Meeting rms. Business servs avail. Exercise equipt; weight machine, bicycles. Refrigerators, microwaves avail. Cr cds: A, C, D, DS, MC, V.

D ☒ ✕ ☒ ☒ SC

★ ★ **COMFORT INN.** *20740 Torrence Chapel Rd, 1 mi W on I-77, exit 28.* 704/892-3500; FAX 704/892-6473. 90 rms, 2-3 story. S, D $71.95; suites $125-$175; under 18 free; wkend, hol, wkly rates; higher rates special events. Crib free. TV; cable (premium), VCR avail (movies). Pool. Complimentary continental bkfst. Complimentary coffee in rms. Restaurant nearby. Ck-out 11 am. Coin lndry. Meeting rm. Business servs avail. Health club privileges. Refrigerators. Microwaves avail. Cr cds: A, C, D, DS, ER, JCB, MC, V.

D ☒ ☒ ☒ SC

✔ ★ ★ **HAMPTON INN.** *19501 Statesville Rd, I-77 exit 28.* 704/892-9900; FAX 704/896-7488. Web www.hampton-inn.com. 117 rms, 5 story. S, D $74-$79; under 18 free; higher rates wkends, special events. Crib free. TV; cable (premium). Pool. Complimentary continental bkfst. Restaurant adj 6 am-10 pm. Ck-out noon. Meeting rm. Business servs avail. Exercise equipt; weights, treadmill. Some refrigerators. Cr cds: A, C, D, DS, MC, V.

D ☒ ✕ ☒ ☒ SC

★ ★ **HOLIDAY INN.** *19901 Holiday Ln, jct NC 73 & I-77 exit 28.* 704/892-9120; FAX 704/892-3854. 119 rms, 2 story. S, D $84; under 18 free; higher rates special events. Crib free. Pet accepted; $25. TV; cable (premium). Pool. Complimentary coffee in rms. Restaurant 6 am-10 pm. Rm serv. Bar 4:30 pm-midnight. Ck-out 11 am. Coin lndry. Meeting rms. Exercise equipt; weight machines, bicycles. Some refrigerators, microwaves. Cr cds: A, C, D, DS, JCB, MC, V.

D ✔ ☒ ✕ ☒ ☒ SC

★ ★ **HOLIDAY INN EXPRESS.** *(14135 Statesville Rd, Huntersville 28070) 5 mi S on I-77, exit 23.* 704/875-1165; FAX 704/875-1894. 60 rms, 2 story. S $66; D $71; each addl $5; suites $90; under 16 free; higher rates sports events. Crib free. TV; cable (premium). Pool. Complimentary continental bkfst. Restaurant nearby. Ck-out 11 am. Meeting rms. Business servs avail. Some refrigerators. Microwaves avail. Cr cds: A, D, DS, JCB, MC, V.

D ☒ ☒ ☒ SC

Inn

★ ★ **DAVIDSON VILLAGE.** *(117 Depot St, Davidson 28036) 1 mi N on I-77, exit 30.* 704/892-8044; FAX 704/896-2184. 18 rms, 3 story, 4 suites. S, D $100-$110; suites $115-$125; under 16 free; wkends, hols (2-day min); higher rates special events. Crib free. TV; cable (premium), VCR avail. Complimentary continental bkfst. Restaurant adj 11 am-6 pm. Rm serv to 10 pm. Ck-out 11 am, ck-in 3 pm. Business servs avail. Luggage handling. Valet serv. Health club privileges. Refrigerator, microwave, wet bar in suites; microwaves avail. Contemporary Southern atmosphere. Cr cds: A, C, D, DS, MC, V.

D ☒ ☒ SC

Restaurants

✔ ★ **CAPTAIN'S GALLEY.** *(105 J Statesville Rd, Huntersville 28070) 2 mi S on I-77, exit 23.* 704/875-6038. Hrs: 11 am-9 pm; Fri to 10 pm; Sat noon-10 pm. Closed Sun; most major hols. Semi-a la carte: lunch $3.75-$10, dinner $4.95-$16. Child's meals. Specializes in seafood. Own baking. Nautical decor; wall murals. Family-owned since 1978. No cr cds accepted.

D SC ⅃

★ ★ **KOBE JAPANESE HOUSE OF STEAK & SEAFOOD.** *20465 Chartwell Center Dr.* 704/896-7778. Hrs: 11:30 am-2 pm, 5-10 pm; Sat 5-11 pm; Sun from 5 pm; early-bird dinner Mon-Fri 5-6 pm. Closed Thanksgiving, Dec 25. Res accepted. Japanese menu. Bar. Semi-a la carte: lunch $5.95-$14.95, dinner $9.95-$24.95. Serv charge 15%. Child's meals. Specializes in teppanyaki preparation, Kobe beef, seafood. Sushi bar (dinner). Japanese decor. Cr cds: A, C, D, DS, MC, V.

D

★ ★ **LAKESIDE AT HOLIDAY MARINA.** *20210 Henderson Rd.* 704/896-8985. Hrs: 11:30 am-10 pm; Fri & Sat to 11 pm. Closed Jan 1, Thanksgiving, Dec 25. Bar. Semi-a la carte: lunch, dinner $5.95-$17.95. Child's meals. Specializes in seafood, pasta, steak. Outdoor dining overlooking Lake Norman. Marina decor. Cr cds: A, C, D, DS, MC, V.

D ⅃

★ **RAINBOW DELI & CAFE.** *8301 Magnolia Estates Dr, 5 mi S on I-77.* 704/896-0091. Hrs: 11 am-10 pm; Sun to 9 pm. Sun brunch 11 am-3 pm. Closed Thanksgiving, Dec 25. Italian, Amer menu. Bar to 2 am. Semi-a la carte: lunch $2.50-$6.95, dinner $4.95-$16.95. Sun brunch $4.75-$9.95. Child's meals. Specializes in seafood, pasta, steak. Patio dining. Art deco theme. Cr cds: A, D, MC, V.

D SC ⅃

Dunn (B-7)

(See also Fayetteville, Goldsboro)

Pop 8,336 **Elev** 213 ft **Area code** 910 **Zip** 28334

What to See and Do

Bentonville Battleground State Historic Site. Biggest battle on North Carolina soil, Mar 19-21, 1865. It was the last organized attempt to stop General William Tecumseh Sherman after he left Atlanta. A month later, the rebel cause was lost; Lee surrendered at Appomattox on Apr 9; Lincoln was shot Apr 14; and Johnston surrendered Apr 26. The restored Harper House was used as a hospital to treat wounded of both sides. Reconstructed and original trenches; history trail with exhibits. Picnic area. Visitor center, audiovisual show. (Apr-Oct, daily; rest of yr, daily exc Mon; closed Thanksgiving, Dec 24-25) 15 mi E via NC 55 to Newton Grove, 3 mi N via US 701 to NC 1008, then 3 mi E. Phone 910/594-0789. **Free.**

Motels

✔★ **BEST WESTERN.** *603 Springbranch Rd, I-95, exit 72. 910/892-2162; FAX 910/892-3010.* 146 rms, 2 story. S, D $29.99-$52.99; each addl $5; family rates. Crib $5. TV; cable (premium). Pool; wading pool. Restaurant 5:30-10 am, 5-9:30 pm. Ck-out 11 am. Business servs avail. Cr cds: A, C, D, DS, MC, V.

D ≈ ⚞ 🐾 SC

★ **RAMADA INN.** *1011 E Cumberland St, I-95 Exit 73. 910/892-8101; FAX 910/892-2836.* 100 rms, 2 story. S $39-$59; D $49-$69; each addl $6; under 18 free. Crib free. Pet accepted. TV; cable (premium). Pool. Restaurant 6:30 am-2 pm, 5-9 pm. Rm serv. Ck-out noon. Meeting rms. Business servs avail. Valet serv. Some refrigerators. Cr cds: A, C, D, DS, JCB, MC, V.

D ✔ ≈ ⚞ 🐾 SC

Durham (A-7)

(See also Chapel Hill, Raleigh)

Founded 1853 **Pop** 136,611 **Elev** 406 ft **Area code** 919 **E-mail** visit@durham-cvb.com **Web** dcvb.durham.nc.us

Information Convention & Visitors Bureau, 101 E Morgan St, 27701; 800/772-2855.

Durham's sparkle has brought it near-top national ranking in numerous livability studies. Known for excellence in medicine, education, research and industry, Durham is also a recreational and cultural center in the rolling Piedmont region.

In 1924, an endowment from James B. Duke, head of the American Tobacco Company, helped establish Duke University as a leader among the nation's institutions of higher learning. North Carolina Central University makes its home here. In the 1950s, Durham County was chosen as the site of Research Triangle Park, a planned scientific research center that includes the Environmental Protection Agency, the National Institute for Environmental Health Sciences, IBM Corporation, the Glaxo Wellcome Company and others. Duke University Medical Center, Durham Regional Hospital and several other outstanding medical institutions here have earned Durham the title "City of Medicine, USA."

What to See and Do

Bennett Place State Historic Site. Site of signing (Apr 26, 1865) of surrender of Confederate General Johnston to Union General Sherman, one of the last and most significant of the Confederate surrenders. Reconstructed Bennett homestead. Picnicking. Visitor Center, exhibits, audiovisual show. (Apr-Oct, daily; rest of yr, daily exc Mon; closed major hols) Just SW of jct I-85 exit 172 & US 70. Phone 919/383-4345. **Free.**

Duke Homestead State Historic Site (1852). Ancestral home of Duke family; first Duke tobacco factory; curing barn; outbuildings; farm crops. Tobacco Museum, exhibits, film; furnishings of period. Tours. (Apr-Oct, daily; rest of yr, daily exc Mon; closed major hols) 2828 Duke Homestead Rd, 1/2 mi N of jct I-85, Guess Rd. Phone 919/477-5498. **Free.**

Duke University (1838). (10,000 students) Two campuses, East and West, on 8,000 acres. Includes original Trinity College. The West Campus, occupied since 1930, is the showplace of the university. On campus are

Duke Chapel. Beautiful Gothic-style chapel with a carillon of 50 bells in its 210-ft tower; 5,000-pipe Flentrop organ. (Daily) Chapel Dr to main quadrangle. Phone 919/684-2572.

Duke Medical Center. Research and teaching complex. Treats more than one-half million patients annually. Phone 919/684-8111 for information.

Duke Libraries. Most comprehensive in the South, with more than 4 million volumes and more than 7 million manuscripts. Large Confederate imprint collection; Walt Whitman manuscripts. Phone 919/684-3009.

Art Museum. (Daily exc Mon; closed hols) East Campus, off W Main St. Phone 919/684-5135. **Free.**

Duke's Wallace Wade Stadium (33,941 capacity) and the 8,564-seat Cameron Indoor Stadium. Home of the Duke Blue Devils.

Sarah P. Duke Gardens. 55 acres of landscaped gardens, pine forest. Continuous display. (Daily) Main entrance on Anderson St. Phone 919/684-3698. **Free.**

Historic Stagville Center. State-owned historic property, once part of the Bennehan-Cameron plantation; several historic 18th- and 19th-century plantation buildings on 71 acres of land. (Mon-Fri; closed hols) 7 mi NE via Roxboro Rd and Old Oxford Hwy. Phone 919/620-0120. **Free.**

North Carolina Museum of Life and Science. North Carolina wildlife; hands-on science exhibits; aerospace, weather and geology collections; train ride; farmyard; science park; discovery rooms; Butterfly House. Picnic area. (Daily; closed Jan 1, Thanksgiving, Dec 25) 433 Murray Ave. Phone 919/220-5429. **¢¢¢**

West Point on the Eno. A 371-acre park along the scenic Eno River; restored farmhouse (1850); working gristmill; museum of photography; blacksmith shop. Picnicking; fishing, hiking, boating; environmental programs (fee). Park (daily). Mill, farmhouse, museum (Mar-Dec, Sat & Sun). I-85, Duke St exit then 3 1/2 mi N. Phone 919/471-1623. **Free.**

Annual Events

CenterFest. Downtown. 2-day event with over 250 artists and craftsmen; musicians, jugglers and clowns; continuous entertainment from 3 stages. Phone 919/560-2722. Sept.

Bull Durham Blues Festival. Historic Durham Athletic Park. Celebrates the blues with performances held at the location where *Bull Durham* was filmed. Phone 919/683-1709. Wkend mid-Sept.

Seasonal Event

American Dance Festival. Page Auditorium and Reynolds Industries Theater, Duke University, West Campus. Six-weeks of performances by the finest of both major and emerging modern dance companies from the US and abroad. Contact the Festival at PO Box 6097, College Station 22708; 919/684-6402. June-July.

Motels

(Rates may be higher for graduation, football wkends)

★ **BEST WESTERN SKYLAND.** *5400 US 70 (27705), Jct I-85 exit 170 & US 70W. 919/383-2508; FAX 919/383-7316.* Web www.citysearch.com. 31 rms. S $50; D $62; each addl $10; under 12 free. Crib $10. Pet accepted. TV; cable (premium). Pool. Playground. Complimentary continental bkfst. Ck-out noon. Business servs avail. Refrigerators. Picnic tables, grills. Situated atop hill. Cr cds: A, C, D, DS, ER, JCB, MC, V.

D ✔ ≈ ⚞ 🐾 SC

★★ **COMFORT INN-UNIVERSITY.** *3508 Mount Moriah Rd (27707). 919/490-4949; FAX 919/419-0535.* 138 rms, 4 story, 18 suites. S, D $67-$75; each addl $6; suites $119-$149; under 16 free; higher rates special events. Crib free. TV; cable (premium). Pool; whirlpool. Complimentary continental bkfst. Complimentary coffee in lobby. Restaurant nearby. Ck-out noon. Coin lndry. Meeting rms. Business servs avail. Exercise equipt; weight machine, stair machines, sauna. Cr cds: A, C, D, DS, ER, JCB, MC, V.

D ≈ 🏋 ⚞ 🐾 SC

✔★ **FAIRFIELD INN BY MARRIOTT.** *3710 Hillsborough Rd (27705). 919/382-3388; FAX 919/382-3388.* 135 rms, 3 story. S $56; D $61; each addl $3. Crib free. TV; cable (premium). Pool. Complimentary continental bkfst. Ck-out noon. Business servs avail. Cr cds: A, C, D, DS, MC, V.

D ⊠ ≈ ⊠ 🛇 SC

✔★ **RED ROOF INN.** *2000 I-85 Service Rd (27705), I-85 exit 175. 919/471-9882; FAX 919/477-0512.* 120 rms, 3 story. S $43.99-$52.99; D $48.99-$58.99. Crib free. Pet accepted, some restrictions. TV; cable (premium). Complimentary coffee in lobby. Restaurant nearby. Ck-out noon. Business servs avail. Cr cds: A, C, D, DS, MC, V.

D ⊅ ≈ ⊠ 🛇 SC

Motor Hotels

★★ **HAWTHORNE SUITES.** *300 Meredith Dr (27713), I-40 exit 278. 919/361-1234; FAX 919/361-1213. E-mail beaver1@bellsouth.net; web www.citysearch.com/rdu/hawthornesuites.* 100 kit. suites, 2-3 story. S, D $135; 2-bedrm suites $169. Crib free. TV; cable (premium). Pool. Complimentary full bkfst Mon-Fri; continental bkfst Sat, Sun. Ck-out noon. Meeting rms. Business servs avail. Bellhops. Free airport transportation. Health club privileges. Microwaves. Private patios. Cr cds: A, C, D, DS, ER, JCB, MC, V.

D ≈ ⊠ 🛇 SC

★★ **REGAL-UNIVERSITY.** *2800 Campus Walk Ave (27705). 919/383-8575; FAX 919/383-8495; res: 800/633-5379. Web www.regalhotels.com/durham.* 315 rms, 4 story. S $95-$185; D $95-$125; each addl $15; suites $190-$375; under 18 free. Crib $10. TV; cable (premium). Heated pool; whirlpool, poolside serv. Restaurant 6:30 am-2 pm, 5-10:30 pm. Bar 11:30 am-midnight. Ck-out noon. Meeting rms. Business servs avail. Bellhops. Concierge. Free airport transportation. Exercise equipt; weight machine, stair machine. Refrigerator in suites. Microwaves avail. Luxury level. Cr cds: A, C, D, DS, MC, V.

D ≈ ⊁ ⊠ 🛇 SC

Hotels

★★★ **DOUBLETREE GUEST SUITES.** *2515 Meridian Pkwy (27713), 1 blk N of I-40 exit 278, near Research Triangle Park. 919/361-4660; FAX 919/361-2256.* 203 suites, 7 story. Suites $155-$175; under 18 free; wkend rates. Crib free. TV; cable (premium), VCR avail. 2 heated pools, 1 indoor; whirlpool, poolside serv. Complimentary coffee in rms. Restaurant 6:30 am-10 pm. Bar 11 am-midnight. Ck-out noon. Coin lndry. Meeting rms. Business servs avail. Free airport transportation. Lighted tennis. Exercise equipt; weight machine, bicycles, sauna. Refrigerators; microwaves avail. Private patios, balconies. Small lake adj; paddleboat rentals. Cr cds: A, C, D, DS, ER, JCB, MC, V.

D ⊁ ≈ ⊁ ⊠ 🛇 SC

★★★ **HILTON.** *3800 Hillsborough Rd (27705). 919/383-8033; FAX 919/383-4287.* 152 rms, 6 story. S $99-$129; D $109-$139; each addl $10; suites $145-$270; family rates. Crib free. TV; cable (premium). Pool; whirlpool. Restaurant 6 am-10 pm. Bar 2 pm-1 am; Sun to 11 pm. Ck-out noon. Meeting rms. Business center. In-rm modem link. Exercise equipt; weights, stair machine, sauna. Bathrm phones. Cr cds: A, C, D, DS, ER, MC, V.

D ≈ ⊁ ⊠ 🛇 SC ⊁

★★★ **OMNI.** *201 Foster St (27702). 919/683-6664; FAX 919/683-2046.* 188 rms, 10 story. S $99-$148; D $99-$158; each addl $10; suites $150-$225. Crib free. TV; cable (premium). Restaurant 6:30 am-2 pm, 5-10 pm. Rm serv. Bar 3 pm-1 am. Ck-out noon. Meeting rms. Business servs avail. Gift shop. Health club privileges. Cr cds: A, C, D, DS, JCB, MC, V.

D ⊠ 🛇 SC

★★★ **SHERATON IMPERIAL HOTEL & CONVENTION CENTER.** *(4700 Emperor Blvd, Research Triangle Park 27703) 1 blk S of I-40 exit 282. 919/941-5050; FAX 919/941-5156. Web www.sheratonrtp.com.* 331 rms, 10 story. S, D $100-$175; each addl $10; suites $180-$225; under 18 free; wkend rates. TV; cable (premium). Heated pool; whirlpool, poolside serv. Coffee in rms. Restaurant 6:30 am-10 pm. Bar 11 am-midnight. Ck-out noon. Convention facilities. Business center. Concierge. Gift shop. Free valet parking. Free airport transportation. Lighted tennis. Exercise rm; instructor, weight machines, bicycles, sauna, steam rm. Massage. Some bathrm phones. Refrigerator in suites. Luxury level. Cr cds: A, C, D, DS, MC, V.

D ⊁ ≈ ⊁ ⊁ ⊠ 🛇 SC ⊁

★★★★ **WASHINGTON DUKE INN & GOLF CLUB.** *3001 Cameron Blvd (27706). 919/490-0999; FAX 919/688-0105; res: 800/443-3853. E-mail wdi@netmar.com; web www.washingtondukeinn.com.* On the campus of Duke University, this luxurious hotel overlooks the Robert Trent Jones golf course. Memorabilia belonging to the Duke family, for whom the hotel and university are named, is on display in the public rooms. The bar is called the Bull Durham. 171 rms, 5 story. S, D $160-$225; each addl $10; suites $400-$625; under 17 free; golf plans. Crib free. TV; cable (premium), VCR avail. Heated pool. Complimentary coffee in lobby. Restaurant 7 am-10 pm. Bar 11:30 am-midnight; Sun, 2 sittings: 11:30 am & 1:30 pm. Ck-out noon. Meeting rms. Business center. In-rm modem link. Concierge. Gift shop. Airport transportation. Lighted tennis, pro. 18-hole golf, greens fee $55-$80, pro, putting green, driving range. Health club privileges. Refrigerators, microwaves avail. Cr cds: A, C, D, DS, MC, V.

D ⊁ ⊁ ≈ ⊁ ⊠ 🛇 SC ⊁

★★ **WYNDHAM GARDEN HOTEL.** *4620 S Miami Blvd (27703), 10 mi SE on I-40, exit 281, near Research Triangle Park. 919/941-6066; FAX 919/941-6363.* 172 rms, 7 story. S, D $119-$149; each addl $10; suites $150-$200; under 16 free; wkend rates. Crib free. TV; cable (premium). Pool; whirlpool. Buffet bkfst. Complimentary coffee in rms. Restaurant 6-10 am, 11 am-2:30 pm, 5-10 pm; Sat from 11 am, Sun noon-2 pm, 5-10 pm. Bar. Ck-out noon. Meeting rms. Business servs avail. In-rm modem link. Free airport transportation. Exercise equipt; weight machine, bicycles, sauna. Some refrigerators, microwaves. Cr cds: A, C, D, DS, MC, V.

D ≈ ⊁ ⊠ 🛇 SC

Inns

★★ **ARROWHEAD.** *106 Mason Rd (27712), US 501, 7 mi N of I-85. 919/477-8430; res: 800/528-2207; FAX 919/471-9538.* 8 rms, 2 story, 2 suites. S, D $115; each addl $15; suites $145-$185. Crib free. TV in some rms; VCR avail (free movies). Pool privileges. Complimentary full bkfst. Ck-out 11 am, ck-in 3 pm. Business servs avail. Tennis privileges. Game rm. Lawn games. Picnic tables. In colonial house (1775) and converted carriage house; on 4 acres. Cr cds: A, D, DS, MC, V.

D ⊁ ⊠ ⊠

★ **HILLSBOROUGH HOUSE.** *(209 E Tryon St, Hillsborough 27278) 15 mi W on I-85. 919/644-1600; res: 800/616-1660.* 6 rms, 2 story. No rm phones. S $85-$95; D $95-$105; suite $175. Children over 10 yrs only. TV in sitting rm; cable (premium). Pool. Complimentary full bkfst; afternoon refreshments. Restaurant nearby. Ck-out 11 am, ck-in 3 pm. Portions of this large frame house date to circa 1790; decor includes artwork by the innkeeper. Totally nonsmoking. Cr cds: A, MC, V.

≈ ⊠ ⊠

Restaurants

✔★ **BULLOCK'S BBQ.** *3330 Quebec. 919/383-3211.* Hrs: 11:30 am-8 pm. Closed Sun, Mon; Jan 1, Dec 24, 25. Res accepted. Semi-a la carte: lunch, dinner $3.50-$9. Child's meals. Specializes in barbecued pork, seafood, chicken. Family-owned for over 50 yrs. No cr cds accepted.

D

★ ★ ★ **FAIRVIEW.** *(See Washington Duke Inn & Golf Club)* *919/490-0999.* E-mail wdi@netmar.com; web www.washingtonduke inn.com. Hrs: 7-10:30 am, 11:30 am-2 pm, 5:30-10 pm; Sun brunch sittings 11:30 am & 1:30 pm. Res accepted. Continental menu. Bar 11:30 am-midnight. Wine cellar. Semi-a la carte: bkfst $7.95-$12.95, lunch $7.95-$13.95, dinner $16.95-$26.95. Sun brunch $18.95. Child's meals. Specializes in seasonal seafood, lamb shank, game. Salad bar. Pianist Thurs-Sat, Sun brunch. Valet parking. Outdoor dining. Formal atmosphere; view of grounds and 18th green. Totally nonsmoking. Cr cds: A, C, D, DS, MC, V.

[D] ♥

★ ★ **MAGNOLIA GRILL.** *1002 9th St. 919/286-3609.* Hrs: 6-9:30 pm; Fri to 10 pm; Sat 5:30-10 pm. Closed Sun; major hols. Res accepted. Bar from 5:30 pm. A la carte entrees: dinner $12-$20. Specialties: grilled yellow fin tuna on warm green lentils with Mediterranean salsa and red pepper vinigrette; pan-seared sea scallops on fennel polenta with lobster bordelaise; grilled Black Angus strip steak with mushroom ragout. Local artwork on display. Cr cds: MC, V.

[D] ⊿

★ ★ **PAPA'S GRILL.** *1821 Hillandale Rd, in Loehmann's Plaza at Croasdaile. 919/383-8502.* Hrs: 11:30 am-2:30 pm, 5-10 pm; Fri, Sat to 10:30 pm. Closed Dec 25. Res accepted. Greek, Mediterranean menu. Bar. Semi-a la carte: lunch $5.95-$10.95, dinner $7.50-$26.95. Specializes in chicken, lamb, beef. Own baking. Cr cds: A, D, DS, MC, V.

[D] ⊿

★ ★ **PARIZADE.** *2200 W Main St (27705). 919/286-9712.* Hrs: 11:30 am-2:30 pm, 5:30-10 pm; Fri to 11 pm; Sat from 5:30 pm. Closed Sun; Dec 25. Res accepted. Mediterranean menu. Bar. Semi-a la carte: lunch $4.95-$9.50, dinner $8.95-$20. Specializes in pasta, gourmet pizza. Jazz combo (summer). Outdoor dining. Semi-formal dining in Mediterranean atmosphere. Cr cds: A, D, MC, V.

[D] ⊿

✔★ **SHANGHAI.** *3433 Hillsborough Rd, in shopping center. 919/383-7581.* Hrs: 11:30 am-2:30 pm, 5-9:30 pm; Sun from 5 pm. Closed Thanksgiving, Dec 25. Res accepted. Chinese menu. Bar. Semi-a la carte: lunch $4.75, dinner $5-$16.75. Specializes in seafood, chicken, pork. Oriental decor. Cr cds: A, DS, MC, V.

[D] [SC]

Edenton (A-9)

Settled 1658 **Pop** 5,268 **Elev** 16 ft **Area code** 919 **Zip** 27932 **Web** www.edenton.com

Information Chamber of Commerce, 116 E King St, PO Box 245, 919/482-3400; or Historic Edenton, 108 N Broad St, PO Box 474, 919/482-2637.

This is one of the oldest communities in North Carolina and was the capital of the colony for more than 22 years. The women of Edenton staged their own Revolutionary tea party on October 25, 1774, signing a resolution protesting British injustice. A bronze teapot, at the west side of the Courthouse Green, commemorates the event.

The seat of Chowan County, Edenton is now an important industrial town and marketing place. It is a charming town with the graciousness of the Old South and many houses and buildings that date back to the 1700s. Joseph Hewes, a signer of the Declaration of Independence, lived here.

What to See and Do

Historic Edenton. Tour of historic properties, which may be seen individually or as a group; allow 2½ to 3 hours for complete tour. (Apr-Dec, daily; rest of yr, daily exc Mon; closed some major hols; also day after Thanksgiving, 3 days at Christmas) Phone 919/482-2637. ¢¢

Historic Edenton Visitor Center. Audiovisual program (free), exhibits, visitor information, gift shop, tickets for guided tours of Historic Edenton. 108 N Broad St.

Chowan County Courthouse (1767). A fine example of Georgian architecture, in continuous use since built. E King & Court Sts.

St Paul's Episcopal Church (1736). A charming church with many old gravestones in its yard; three colonial governors are buried here. W Church & Broad Sts.

James Iredell House (1800/1827). Home of early attorney general of North Carolina who was appointed by George Washington to first US Supreme Court. E Church St.

Cupola House (1758). Considered an outstanding example of Jacobean architecture. Formal garden restored from 1769 map of Edenton. W Water & S Broad Sts.

Merchant's Millpond State Park. This 2,900-acre swamp forest is dominated by massive gum and cypress trees. Pond fishing, canoeing (rentals). Nature trails. Picnicking. Developed and primitive camping. Interpretive program. Standard fees. 25 mi N on NC 32, 5 mi N of Gatesville on SR 1403. Contact Superintendent, Rte 1, Box 141-A, Gatesville 27938; 919/357-1191.

Newbold-White House (1730). This brick structure was a meeting place for the proprietary government of North Carolina. (Mar-Dec, daily exc Sun) 15 mi N on US 17 Bypass to Hertford, SE on SR 1336. Phone 919/426-7567. ¢

Other historic buildings are shown in a guidebook published by the Edenton Woman's Club and sold at Historic Edenton Visitor Center ($4). Since most houses are not open to the public, we suggest calling the Historic Edenton Visitor Center for further information. Phone 919/482-2637.

Somerset Place State Historic Site. Original plantation, one of the largest in North Carolina, encompassed more than 100,000 acres. First primary crop was rice, which gave way to corn. Mansion and outbuildings built ca 1830. (Daily exc Mon; closed Jan 1, Thanksgiving, Dec 24-25) 18 mi SE via NC 32, US 64 to Creswell, then 7 mi S; on Lake Phelps in Pettigrew State Park. Phone 919/797-4560. **Free.**

Inns

✔★ **CAPTAIN'S QUARTERS INN.** *202 W Queen St. 919/482-8945; res: 800/482-8945.* 8 rms, 2 story. S $55-$65; D $80-$95; suites $80. Children over 8 only. TV; cable (premium), VCR avail. Complimentary full bkfst. Restaurant nearby. Ck-out 11 am, ck-in 3-10 pm. Built in 1907; antiques. Totally nonsmoking. Cr cds: MC, V.

[D] ⊿ 🔥

★ **GOVERNOR EDEN.** *304 N Broad St. 919/482-2072.* 4 rms, 2 story. No rm phones. S $55; D $70. TV; cable (premium). Complimentary full bkfst. Ck-out 11 am, ck-in 2 pm. Free airport transportation. Built 1906; antiques. Neoclassical design; Ionic columns, oval portals. Totally nonsmoking. Cr cds: MC, V.

⊿ 🔥

★ ★ **LORDS PROPRIETORS'.** *300 N Broad St. 919/482-3641; FAX 919/482-2432; res: 800/348-8933.* 20 rms in 3 buildings, 2 story. MAP: S, D $185-$235; each addl $20, lower rates Sun-Mon. TV; cable (premium), VCR (movies). Private pool privileges. Ck-out 11 am, ck-in 1 pm. Meeting rms. Business servs avail. Gift shop. Library. Three adj restored homes furnished with antiques. No cr cds accepted.

[D] ⊿ 🔥

★ **TRESTLE HOUSE.** *Soundside Rd, 4 mi S on NC 32, turn right on Soundside Rd. 919/482-2282.* 5 rms, 2 story. No rm phones. S $65; D $100; each addl $15; wkly rates. TV; cable, VCR avail (movies). Complimentary full bkfst; afternoon refreshments. Ck-out noon. Tennis privileges. 18-hole golf privileges. Exercise equipt; treadmill, rowing machine. Minibars. Picnic tables. Private lake fed by Albermarle Sound. Some antiques. Totally nonsmoking. Cr cds: A, MC, V.

🏊 🏃 ⚒ 🏌 ⊿ 🔥 [SC]

Elizabeth City (A-9)

Settled ca 1665 **Pop** 14,292 **Elev** 18 ft **Area code** 919 **Zip** 27909 **E-mail** ecacc@interpath.com **Web** www.elizcity.com/G-O-E/chamber

Information Elizabeth City Area Chamber of Commerce, 502 E Ehringhaus St, PO Box 426; 919/335-4365.

A town with a freshwater harbor on the Pasquotank River and accessible to the ocean, Elizabeth City has seen seafaring activity since the middle of the 17th century. The town was charterd in 1793 at the narrows of the river as Redding, and renamed Elizabeth City in 1801. The Dismal Swamp Canal, dug in 1793, provided a critical north-south transportation route and brought prosperity to Elizabeth City. Shipyards, warehouses, fisheries, tanneries, sawmills and other industries flourished along with commission merchants, artisans and navigators; trading occured with Norfolk, the West Indies, New England, New York and Charleston.

Although captured in the Civil War, Elizabeth City sustained minor damage. Today, many antebellum homes still stand alongside the historic homes and commercial buildings of the late 19th and early 20th centuries, a testament to the vitality of the community. Wood, agriculture, small specialty industries and the United States Coast Guard contribute to the area's steady economic growth. The town also welcomes boating traffic from the Intracoastal Waterway, and is a coveted location for sport fishing and hunting. It serves as a gateway to Nags Head and Cape Hatteras National Seashore (see).

What to See and Do

Historic District. A 30-blk area in the city center, contains largest number of antebellum commercial buildings in the state. Tour brochures avail at Chamber of Commerce.

Museum of the Albemarle. Regional historical displays; Native American exhibits; local artifacts, including decoys, fire engines; changing exhibits. (Daily exc Mon; closed state hols) 3 mi SW on US 17. Phone 919/335-1453. **Free.**

Annual Events

RiverSpree. Water events, arts, crafts, live entertainment. Late May.

Albemarle Craftsman's Fair. Late Oct.

Mistletoe Show. Crafts, wood carvings. 2nd wkend Nov.

Motels

★ ★ **COMFORT INN.** *306 S Hughes Blvd.* 919/338-8900; FAX 919/338-6420. 80 rms, 5 story, 28 suites. S, D $55-$95; each addl $8; suites $65-$105; under 18 free; higher rates hol wknds. Crib free. TV; cable (premium), VCR avail (movies). Pool. Complimentary continental bkfst. Restaurant nearby. Ck-out 11 am. Business servs avail. In-rm modem link. Refrigerator in suites. Cr cds: A, C, D, DS, MC, V.

D ≈ ⤴ 🐾 SC

★ ★ **HOLIDAY INN.** *522 S Hughes Blvd.* 919/338-3951; FAX 919/338-6225. 158 rms, 2 story. S $69-$75; D $71-$81; each addl $5; under 19 free. Crib free. TV; cable (premium). Pool. Restaurant 6:30-10 am, 5-10 pm. Rm serv (dinner only). Bar 5 pm-midnight. Ck-out noon. Coin lndry. Meeting rms. Business servs avail. In-rm modem link. Cr cds: A, C, D, DS, JCB, MC, V.

D ≈ ⤴ 🐾 SC

Restaurant

✔ ★ **MARINA.** *Camden Causeway, 1/2 mi E on US 158.* 919/335-7307. Hrs: 5-10 pm; Sun 11 am-9 pm. Closed Mon; Jan 1, Thanksgiving, Dec 25. Serv bar. Semi-a la carte: lunch, dinner $5-$14.95.

Child's meals. Specializes in steak, seafood. Overlooks Pasquotank River. Outdoor dining. Cr cds: MC, V.

D ⤴

Fayetteville (C-7)

(See also Goldsboro)

Founded 1739 **Pop** 75,695 **Elev** 102 ft **Area code** 910 **E-mail** facvb@foto.infi.net **Web** www.foto.com/fayettevillenc

Information Convention & Visitors Bureau, 245 Person St, 28301; 910/483-5311 or 888/NC-CHARM.

In 1783 the towns of Cross Creek and Campbellton merged and were renamed Fayetteville for the Marquis de Lafayette, becoming the first US city to thus honor him. It was the site of North Carolina's Constitutional Convention in 1787 and the capital of the state from 1789-1793. By 1831 it had become a busy commercial city.

Fayetteville is the state's farthest inland port, at the head of navigation on the Cape Fear River, with an 8-foot-deep channel connecting it to the Intracoastal Waterway. Fayetteville State University (1867) and Methodist College (1956) are located here. In 1985 Fayetteville received the All-America City Award. Today, it's a a center for retail, manufacturing and conventions, as well as the home of Ft Bragg and Pope Air Force Base.

What to See and Do

Cape Fear Botanical Garden. On 85 acres overlooking Cross Creek and the Cape Fear River. Wildflowers, oaks, native plants. Nature trails. (Mid-Dec-mid-Feb, daily exc Sun; rest of yr, daily; closed hols) Intersection of I-95 Business & US 301. Phone 910/486-0221. ¢

First Presbyterian Church. Classic Southern-colonial-style architecture and whale-oil chandeliers. Among contributors to the original building (destroyed by fire in 1831) were James Monroe and John Quincy Adams. Tours (by appt only). Bow & Ann Sts. Phone 910/483-0121.

Fort Bragg and Pope AFB. 10 mi NW on NC 24. Here are

82nd Airborne Div War Memorial Museum. Weapons, relics of the First & Second World Wars, Vietnam; library; gift shop. (Daily exc Mon; closed Jan 1, Dec 25) Ardennes St. Phone 910/432-3443. **Free.**

John F. Kennedy Special Warfare Museum. Guerrilla warfare weapons. (Daily exc Mon; closed some major hols) Ardennes St. Phone 910/432-1533. **Free.**

Parachute Jumps. For schedule infomation phone 910/396-6366.

(For further information, contact the Public Affairs Office, Fort Bragg & XVIII Airborne Corps, Fort Bragg 28307-5000; 910/396-6401.)

Museum of the Cape Fear. Retraces the regional cultural history from prehistoric Indian artifacts through 20th century. A branch of the North Carolina Museum of History. (Daily exc Mon; closed hols) 801 Arsenal Ave. Phone 910/486-1330. **Free.**

Annual Events

Dogwood Festival. Late Apr.

Pope AFB/Fort Bragg Joint Open House & Air Show. Aerial demonstrations, aircraft and equipment displays, military drill team performances. Phone 910/394-4183. 1 day late Oct.

Motels

✔★★ **COMFORT INN.** *1957 Cedar Creek Rd (28301).* 910/323-8333; FAX 910/323-3946. 120 rms, 2 story. S $52-$55; D $57-$62; each addl $6; suites $60-$63; under 18 free. Crib free. Pet accepted. TV; cable (premium). Pool. Complimentary continental bkfst. Restaurant adj 6 am-midnight. Ck-out noon. Meeting rms. Business servs avail. Valet serv. Exercise equipt; bicycles, stair machine. Refrigerators. Cr cds: A, C, D, DS, ER, JCB, MC, V.

[D] [✔] [≈] [✕] [⅄] [⚡] [SC]

★★ **COMFORT INN CROSS CREEK.** *1922 Skibo Rd (28314), off US 401 Bypass.* 910/867-1777; FAX 910/867-0325. 176 rms, 4 story. S, D $50-$65; each addl $6; suites $75-$110; under 16 free. Crib free. TV; cable (premium). Pool. Complimentary continental bkfst. Restaurant nearby. Coin lndry. Ck-out noon. Business servs avail. Health club privileges. Bathrm phone, refrigerator in suites. Cr cds: A, C, D, DS, ER, MC, V.

[D] [≈] [✕] [⚡] [SC]

✔★ **DAYS INN.** *2065 Cedar Creek Rd (28302).* 910/483-6191; FAX 910/483-4113. 122 rms, 2 story. S $39-$49; D $45-$55; each addl $6; under 12 free. Crib free. TV; cable (premium). Pool. Complimentary full bkfst 6:30-9:30 am. Restaurant 5-9 pm. Rm serv. Bar. Ck-out noon. Meeting rms. Business center. Free airport, RR station, bus depot transportation. Game rm. Cr cds: A, C, D, DS, ER, JCB, MC, V.

[D] [≈] [✕] [⚡] [SC] [⅄]

★ **ECONO LODGE.** *(28306).* Jct NC 210 & US 53; I-95 exit 49. 910/433-2100; FAX 910/433-2009. 150 rms, 2 story. S $46.95-$54.95; D $49.95-$59.95; each addl $5; under 18 free. Crib free. TV; cable (premium). Pool. Complimentary continental bkfst. Restaurant nearby. Ck-out noon. Business servs avail. Cr cds: A, C, D, DS, ER, JCB, MC, V.

[D] [≈] [✕] [⚡] [SC]

✔★ **FAIRFIELD INN BY MARRIOTT.** *562 Cross Creek Mall (28301).* 910/487-1400; FAX 910/487-1400, ext. 709. 135 rms, 3 story. S $63.95; D $55.95-$69.95; each addl $6; under 18 free. Crib free. TV; cable (premium). Pool. Complimentary coffee in lobby. Restaurant nearby. Ck-out noon. Meeting rms. Business servs avail. In-rm modem link. Valet serv. Cr cds: A, C, D, DS, MC, V.

[D] [≈] [✕] [⚡] [SC]

★★ **HAMPTON INN.** *1922 Cedar Creek Rd (28301), at I-95 exit 49.* 910/323-0111; FAX 910/323-8764. 122 rms, 2 story. S $56; D $61; under 18 free. Crib free. TV; cable (premium). Pool. Complimentary continental bkfst. Restaurant nearby. Ck-out noon. Business center. In-rm modem link. Valet serv. Cr cds: A, C, D, DS, MC, V.

[D] [≈] [✕] [⚡] [SC] [⅄]

★★ **HOLIDAY INN.** *1944 Cedar Creek Rd (28302), I-95 exit 49.* 910/323-1600; FAX 910/323-0691. 198 rms, 2 story. Mar-Nov: S, D $74-$125; each addl $5; kits. $89-$125; under 12 free; lower rates rest of yr. Crib free. TV; cable (premium). Indoor pool; whirlpool. Complimentary coffee in rms. Restaurant 6:30 am-2 pm, 5:30-10 pm. Rm serv. Bar. Ck-out noon. Coin lndry. Meeting rms. Business servs avail. In-rm modem link. Bellhops. Free airport transportation. Exercise equipt; weights, bicycles. Game rm. Cr cds: A, C, D, DS, JCB, MC, V.

[D] [≈] [✕] [⅄] [⚡] [SC]

✔★ **HORNE'S MOTOR LODGE.** *PO Box 466 (28301), 220 Eastern Blvd.* 910/483-1113; FAX 910/483-3366; res: 800/682-1919. 134 units, 2 story, 12 kits. S, D $35.95-38.95; kit. units avail; wkly rates. TV; cable. Pool. Complimentary coffee. Restaurant 6 am-9 pm. Ck-out noon. Business servs avail. In-rm modem link. Bathrm phones. Cr cds: A, C, D, MC, V.

[D] [≈] [✕] [⚡] [SC]

★★ **QUALITY INN AMBASSADOR.** *Box 64166 (28306), Jct I-95 Business, US 301S.* 910/485-8135; FAX 910/485-8682. 62 rms. S $52; D $65; each addl $6; under 18 free; golf plans. Crib $6. TV; cable (premium). Pool. Playground. Restaurant 6 am-9 pm. Ck-out noon. Meeting rms. Business servs avail. Picnic tables. Cr cds: A, D, DS, JCB, MC, V.

[≈] [✕] [⚡] [SC]

Motor Hotels

★★★ **HOLIDAY INN BORDEAUX.** *1707 Owen Dr (28304).* 910/323-0111; FAX 910/484-9444. 290 units, 6 story. S, D $78; each addl $6; suites $150-$225; under 18 free. Crib free. TV; cable (premium). Pool. Restaurant 6 am-2 pm, 5-11 pm; Fri, Sat open 24 hrs. Bar 4 pm-1 am; entertainment. Ck-out noon. Convention facilities. Business servs avail. In-rm modem link. Some covered parking. Free airport transportation. Exercise equipt; weights, treadmill. Private patios, balconies. Luxury level. Cr cds: A, C, D, DS, JCB, MC, V.

[D] [≈] [✕] [⅄] [⚡] [SC]

★★★ **HOWARD JOHNSON.** *1965 Cedar Creek Rd (28302), I-95 exit 49.* 910/323-8282; FAX 910/323-3484. 168 rms, 4 story. S $64.95-$72; D $70.95-$78; each addl $6; suites $78-$100; under 18 free; golf plans. Crib free. Pet accepted. TV; cable (premium). Indoor pool; whirlpool. Restaurant 6 am-2 pm, 5-10 pm. Rm serv 5-10 pm. Bar; dancing. Ck-out noon. Meeting rms. Business center. Bellhops. Free airport transportation. Exercise equipt; weights, bicycles, sauna, steam rm. Some private patios. Luxury level. Cr cds: A, C, D, DS, MC, V.

[D] [✔] [≈] [✕] [⅄] [⚡] [SC] [⅄]

Restaurants

✔★ **CANTON STATION.** *301 N McPherson Church Rd.* 910/864-5555. Hrs: 11 am-2:30 pm, 5-10 pm; Sat from noon; Sun noon-9 pm. Res accepted. Cantonese menu. Bar. Semi-a la carte: lunch $3.50-$4.75, dinner $6.95-$14.95. Buffet: lunch $4.75, dinner $6.95. Specializes in seafood, pork, chicken. Chinese decor. Cr cds: A, MC, V.

[D] [SC] [⅄]

★★ **DE LAFAYETTE.** *6112 Cliffdale Rd.* 910/868-4600. Hrs: 5 pm-midnight. Closed Sun, Mon; some major hols. Res accepted. Continental menu. Bar. A la carte entrees: dinner $12-$26. Specializes in French & Creole cooking. Piano, jazz quartet Fri. Formal dining rms with views of lake. French decor. Cr cds: A, C, D, DS, MC, V.

[D] [⅄]

★★ **LOBSTER HOUSE.** *448 Person St (28301).* 910/485-8866. Hrs: 11 am-2 pm, 5:30-10 pm; Fri to 11 pm; Sat 5:30-11 pm. Closed some major hols. Res accepted. Bar. Semi-a la carte: lunch $4.75-$9.95, dinner $9.95-$53.90. Specializes in lobster, seafood, steak. Intimate dining in formal atmosphere. Cr cds: A, MC, V.

[D] [⅄]

Fontana Dam (B-1)

(For accommodations see Bryson City)

Founded 1947 **Pop** 130 (est) **Elev** 2,900 ft **Area code** 704 **Zip** 28733

At the southwest corner of Great Smoky Mountains National Park, this village was originally built for the construction crew that worked on the Fontana Dam project. The 480-foot dam is crossed by the Appalachian Trail. The region is now a resort area, with swimming, fishing, boating, hiking and horseback riding centering around Fontana Lake, 30 miles long.

Fort Raleigh National Historic Site (A-10)

(For accommodations see Kill Devil Hills, Nags Head; also see Cape Hatteras National Seashore, Outer Banks)

(Off US 64, 3 mi N of Manteo)

The first English colony in America was attempted here on Roanoke Island in 1585. Virginia Dare, born here August 18, 1587, was the first child of English parents born in what is now the United States.

Governor John White left the island for England a few days after Virginia's birth, intending to return shortly with supplies. He was detained by the war with Spain and did not get back until August, 1590. The colony had disappeared, leaving behind only the mysterious word "CROATOAN" cut into a tree or post.

What happened to the colonists is unknown, though some believe that the present-day Lumbee Indians of Robeson County descend from them. Fort Raleigh has been excavated and the fort built by the colonists reconstructed. The Lindsay Warren Visitor Center has relics, an audiovisual program and exhibits. Park and Visitor Center (daily; closed Dec 25). For further information, contact Fort Raleigh National Historic Site, Rte 1, Box 675, Manteo 27954; 919/473-5772. **Free.**

Seasonal Event

The Lost Colony Outdoor Drama. Waterside Theater, 3 mi NW of Manteo on US 64/264. Outdoor drama by Pulitzer Prize winner Paul Green about the first English colony established in the New World, whose curious disappearance remains a mystery to this day. Nightly exc Sat. Reservations advised. Contact 1409 US 64, Manteo 27954; 919/473-3414 or 800/488-5012. Mid-June-late Aug.

Franklin (Macon Co) (B-2)

(See also Cashiers, Highlands)

Pop 2,873 **Elev** 2,133 ft **Area code** 704 **Zip** 28734 **E-mail** facc@franklin-chamber.com **Web** www.franklin-chamber.com

Information Chamber of Commerce, 425 Porter St; 704/524-3161 or 800/336-7829.

Home of the Cowee Valley ruby mines, Franklin attracts rockhounds who often find interesting gems in surface mines. Franklin is surrounded by waterfalls, mountain lakes and streams that offer excellent fishing for trout and bass, or boating, tubing and swimming. Around the county are 420,000 acres of the Nantahala National Forest, which offers hiking trails, camping and fishing. A Ranger District office is located here. The Appalachian Trail bisects the western part of the county through Standing Indian Wildlife Management area and over Wayah Bald Mountain.

What to See and Do

Franklin Gem and Mineral Museum. Gems & minerals; Native American artifacts, fossils; fluorescent mineral display. (May-Oct, daily) 2 W Main St, in the Old Jail. Phone 704/369-7831. **Free.**

Gem mines. There are more than a dozen mines in the area, most offering assistance and equipment for beginners. For a complete list of mines contact the Chamber of Commerce.

Macon County Historical Museum. Artifacts, documents depicting early history of Macon County; genealogical material. (Apr-Oct, Mon-Fri, also Sat mornings) 6 W Main St. Phone 704/524-9758. **Free.**

Nantahala National Forest. Nantahala, a Native American name meaning Land of the Noonday Sun, refers to Nantahala Gorge, so deep and narrow that the sun reaches the bottom only at noonday. Scenic drives through the Southern Appalachians, sparkling waterfalls, including the Whitewater Falls—a series of cascades dropping 411 ft within a distance of 500 ft—and the 17,013-acre Joyce Kilmer-Slickrock Wilderness (see ROBBINSVILLE), with more than 100 species of trees native to the region are part of this 518,560-acre forest. Hiking; swimming; fishing for bass and trout; hunting for deer, wild boar, turkey and ruffed grouse; boating; camping (fee). W of town. For further information contact the District Ranger, 100 Otis St, PO Box 2750, Asheville 28802; 704/524-6441.

Perry's Water Garden. Water park with 4½-acre sunken garden, waterfall, hundreds of water lilies and other flowers, wishing well, trails, picnicking. (Mid-May-Labor Day, daily) 8 mi NW on NC 28 to Cowee Creek Rd, then E 2 mi to Leatherman Gap Rd. Phone 704/524-3264. **Free.**

Scottish Tratans Museum. American extension of Scottish Tartans Society in Edinburgh, Scotland. Exhibits trace heritage of Scottish Tartan and traditional Scottish dress. Research library. Gift shop. (Daily; closed Jan 1, Easter, Dec 25) W. C. Burrell Bldg, 95 E Main St. Phone 704/524-7472. ¢

Annual Events

Macon County Gemboree. Jewelry and gem exhibits, ruby mining, field trips. Late July.

Macon County Fair. Mid-Sept.

Motels

✔★ **COUNTRY INN TOWN.** *277 E Main St..* 704/524-4451; res: 800/233-7555; FAX 704/524-0703. 46 rms. S $34-$37; D $42-$45; each addl $5; under 12 free; higher rates fall foliage season. Crib $5. TV; cable. Pool. Restaurant opp 11 am-8 pm. Ck-out 11 am. Sundries. On Little Tennessee River. Cr cds: A, DS, MC, V.

★ **DAYS INN.** *1320 E Main St, US 441/23N, 1 mi N.* 704/524-6491; FAX 704/369-9636. 41 rms. May-Oct: S, D $54-$85; each addl $5; higher rates: Gemboree, Labor Day wkend, Oct; lower rates rest of yr. TV; cable (premium). Pool. Complimentary continental bkfst. Restaurant opp 7 am-11 pm. Business servs avail. Microwaves avail. Scenic view of mountains. Cr cds: A, C, D, DS, MC, V.

Inn

✔★ **HERITAGE INN.** *43 Heritage Hollow Dr, ½ mi W off N Main St.* 704/524-4150; res: 888/524-4150. E-mail heritage@dnet.net; web www.intertekweb.com/heritage. 7 rms, 2 kit. units. No rm phones. Apr-Nov: S $55-$65; D $65-$75; each addl $10; kit. units $75-$85; hols (2-3-day min); lower rates rest of yr. Children over 14 yrs only. TV in common rm; cable, VCR avail (movies). Complimentary full bkfst. Restaurant adj 11 am-7 pm. Ck-out 10 am, ck-in 2 pm. Microwave, wet bar, fireplace in kit. units; microwaves avail. Southern hospitality atmosphere. Totally nonsmoking. Cr cds: MC, V.

Restaurants

★★ **FROG AND OWL KITCHEN.** *12 E Main St.* 704/349-4112. Hrs: 11 am-2 pm, 5-9 pm. Closed Sun, Mon. French menu. Semi-a la carte: lunch $5-$7, dinner $10.95-$18.95. Specializes in duck, fresh seafood, pasta. Intimate dining. Family-owned. Totally nonsmoking. Cr cds: MC, V.

✔★ **THE GAZEBO.** *103 Heritage Hollow.* 704/524-8783. Hrs: 11 am-7 pm; Sun noon-4 pm. Closed some major hols; late Oct-May. Semi-a la carte: lunch, dinner $3.95-$5.95. Child's meals. Specializes in deli and specialty sandwiches, soups. Own pasta. Entire restaurant is outdoors; three different patio levels for dining. No cr cds accepted.

Gastonia (B-4)

(See also Charlotte)

Pop 54,732 **Elev** 816 ft **Area code** 704 **Web** www.gaston.org
Information Gaston County Travel and Tourism, 2551 Pembroke, PO Box 2339, 28054; 704/867-2170 or 800/849-9994.

This is an industrial town in the Piedmont, turning out textiles, textile machinery and supplies. In addition, Gastonia produces chain saws, plastics, oil seals, lithium, automotive parts, trucks and truck parts.

What to See and Do

Gaston County Museum of Art & History. Sculpture, paintings, Gaston County artifacts and documents, carriage and sleigh collection, textile history exhibit. 19th-century parlors. Located in Hoffman Hotel (1852) and Dallas Depot (1901). (Daily exc Mon; closed hols) 6 mi N via US 321, Dallas exit. Phone 704/922-7681. **Free.**

Lake Wylie. Artificial lake formed by Duke Power Co development; fishing, swimming, waterskiing; marina. S on NC 274. Phone 803/831-2101.

Schiele Museum of Natural History and Planetarium. Habitat settings showcasing more than 75,000 mounted birds, mammals, reptiles, fish; rocks and minerals, Native American arts & crafts, forestry exhibits; 28-acre nature park. Major exhibits on the Southeast and North Carolina; special exhibits and events, films. Restored mid-1700s pioneer farm with living history programs. Hall of Natural History, Hall of Earth and Man. Also here is Catawba Indian Village, with re-created dwellings from 1500s to 1900s. Planetarium programs & Cinema 360 Wide-Screen science films (fee; phone for schedule). (Daily exc Mon; closed hols and Christmas wk) Special gallery for the visually impaired. 1500 E Garrison Blvd. Phone 704/866-6900. Museum **Free;** Planetarium ¢

Motel

★ ★ **HAMPTON INN.** *1859 Remount Rd (28054), I-85 exit New Hope Rd.* 704/866-9090. 109 rms, 5 story. S, D $61-$68; under 12 free. Crib free. TV; cable. Pool. Complimentary continental bkfst. Restaurant adj 6 am-11 pm. Ck-out noon. Meeting rm. Cr cds: A, C, D, DS, MC, V.

D ≈ ⊠ 🛦

Goldsboro (B-8)

Established 1847 **Pop** 40,709 **Elev** 121 ft **Area code** 919 **E-mail** wccc@esn.net **Web** www.entrsft.com/wayne
Information Wayne County Chamber of Commerce, PO Box 1107, 27533-1107; 919/734-2241.

Center of the bright-leaf tobacco belt, Goldsboro is also the seat of Wayne County and home of Seymour Johnson Air Force Base. Poultry production and tobacco warehousing and processing are important industries. There are also many food, wood product and textile plants here.

What to See and Do

Cliffs of the Neuse State Park. Over 700 acres on Neuse River. Swimming, bathhouse; fishing; boating (rowboat rentals). Nature trails. Picnicking. Tent & trailer sites (mid-Mar-Nov; fee). Museum, interpretive center. Standard fees. 14 mi SE, off NC 111. Contact Superintendent, 345A Park Entrance Rd, Seven Springs 28578; 919/778-6234.

Governor Charles B. Aycock Birthplace State Historic Site. Mid-1800s farmhouse and outbuildings; audiovisual presentation in one-room school (1893); exhibits in visitor center portray life of the "educational governor." Picnicking. (Apr-Oct, daily; rest of yr, daily exc Mon; closed most major hols) 12 mi N, off US 117 just S of Fremont. Phone 919/242-5581. **Free.**

Motels

★ ★ **COMFORT INN.** *909 Spence Ave (27534).* 919/751-1999; FAX 919/751-1506. 122 rms, 5 story. S $50-$70; D $54-$90; each addl $6; suites $120-$130; under 18 free. TV; cable (premium). Pool. Complimentary continental bkfst. Restaurant adj. Bar 5 pm-2 am, closed Sun; entertainment. Ck-out noon. Sundries. Business servs avail. In-rm modem link. Cr cds: A, C, D, DS, MC, V.

D ≈ ⊠ 🛦 SC

✔★ **DAYS INN.** *2000 Wayne Memorial Dr (27534).* 919/734-9471; FAX 919/736-2623. 121 rms, 2 story. S $42; D $46; each addl $4. Crib free. TV; cable. Pool. Playground. Restaurant 6 am-9 pm; Sun to 4 pm. Ck-out noon. Meeting rms. Business servs avail. Sundries. Exercise equipt; weight machine, bicycles. Some refrigerators. Cr cds: A, C, D, DS, MC, V.

D ≈ ⊀ ⊠ 🛦 SC

★ ★ **HAMPTON INN.** *905 Spence Ave (27534).* 919/778-1800; FAX 919/778-5891. 111 rms, 4 story. S, D $54-$64; each addl $10; suites $131; under 18 free. Crib free. TV; cable (premium). Pool. Complimentary continental bkfst. Restaurant adj 9 am-midnight. Ck-out noon. Meeting rms. Business servs avail. Coin lndry. Exercise equipt; bicycles, stair machine. Some refrigerators. Cr cds: A, C, D, DS, JCB, MC, V.

D ≈ ⊀ ⊠ 🛦

★ ★ **HOLIDAY INN.** *(27530). 1½ mi NE on US 13, 70 Bypass.* 919/735-7901; FAX 919/734-2946. 108 rms, 2 story. S $58; D $64; each addl $6; suites $85; under 16 free. Pet accepted. TV; cable (premium). Pool. Restaurant 6-9 am, 6-9 pm. Rm serv. Bar 5-11 pm. Ck-out noon. Meeting rms. Business servs avail. In-rm modem link. Exercise equipt; weights, bicycle. Cr cds: A, C, D, DS, JCB, MC, V.

D 🐾 ≈ ⊀ ⊠ 🛦 SC

✔★ **RAMADA INN.** *808 W Grantham St (27530), jct US 70 & US 117S.* 919/736-4590; FAX 919/735-3218. 128 rms, 2 story. S $40-$57; D $44-$62; suites from $85; under 18 free. Crib free. Pet accepted. TV; cable (premium). Pool. Restaurant 5 am-10 pm. Rm serv. Bar 5 pm-2 am; entertainment Fri-Sat. Ck-out noon. Coin lndry. Meeting rms. Business servs avail. Valet serv. Sundries. Game rm. Some refrigerators. Picnic tables, grills. Cr cds: A, C, D, DS, JCB, MC, V.

D 🐾 ≈ ⊠ 🛦 SC

Restaurant

★ **CAPTAIN BOB'S SEAFOOD.** *430 N Berkeley Blvd (27534), in Eastgate Shopping Center.* 919/778-8332. Hrs: 11 am-9 pm; Fri to 9:30 pm; Sat 4-9:30 pm; Sun 11 am-8 pm. Closed Mon; Thanksgiving, Dec 25. Res accepted Tues-Fri. Semi-a la carte: lunch $2.99-$4.25, dinner $5.95-$9.25. Child's meals. Specializes in seafood, beef, steak. Salad bar. Nautical decor. Cr cds: MC, V.

D ⤴

Great Smoky Mountains National Park (B-1 - B-2)

(For accommodations see Bryson City, Cherokee, Maggie Valley; also see Fontana Dam)

(50 mi W of Asheville off US 19)

The Appalachian Mountains, product of a slow upthrusting of ancient sediments that took place more than 200 million years ago, stand tall and regal in this 800-square-mile area. Red spruce, basswood, eastern hemlock, yellow birch, white ash, cucumber trees, silverbells, Fraser fir, tulip poplar, red maple and Fraser magnolias tower above hundreds of other species of flowering plants. Perhaps the most spectacular of these are the purple rhododendron, mountain laurel and flame azalea, in bloom from early June to mid-July.

The moist climate has helped make this a rich wilderness. From early spring to late fall the "coves" (as the open valleys surrounded by peaks are called) and forest floors are covered with a succession of flowers with colorful variety. Summer brings heavy showers, days that are warm (although 15° to 20° cooler than in the valleys below) and cool nights. Autumn is breathtaking as the deciduous trees change color. Winter brings snow, occasionally heavy, and fog over the mountains. Winter is a very good time to visit the park; but be aware of temporary road closures.

Half in North Carolina and half in Tennessee, with the Appalachian Trail following the state line along the ridge for 70 miles, this is a place to hike. In the lowlands are the cabins, barns and mills of the mountain people whose ancestors came years ago from England and Scotland. It is also a place to see the descendants of the once-mighty Cherokee Nation, whose ancestors hid in the mountains from the soldiers in the winter of 1838-1839 to avoid being driven over the Trail of Tears to Oklahoma. This is the tribe of Sequoyah, the brilliant chief who invented a written alphabet for the Cherokee people.

Stop first at one of the two visitor centers: Oconaluftee Center in North Carolina, 2 miles north of Cherokee on Newfound Gap Road, designated US 441 outside of park (daily; closed Dec 25; phone 423/436-1200); or Sugarlands, in Tennessee, 2 miles southwest of Gatlinburg (daily; closed Dec 25; phone 423/436-1200). Both have exhibits and information about the park. There are hundreds of miles of foot trails and bridle paths. Camping is popular; ask at any visitor center for locations and regulations. There are developed campgrounds (fee). For reservations at Elkmont, Cades Cove or Smokemont phone 800/365-CAMP; reservations are not taken for other sites.

The views from Newfound Gap and the observation tower at Clingmans Dome (closed in winter) are spectacular. Cades Cove is an outdoor museum reflecting the life of the original mountain people, about 25 miles west of Sugarlands. It has log cabins and barns. Park naturalists conduct campfire programs and hikes during the summer. There are also self-guided nature trails. LeConte Lodge, reached only by foot or horseback, is an accommodation within the park; phone 423/429-5704 (late Mar-mid-Nov).

Fishing is permitted with a TN or NC state fishing license. Obtain list of regulations at visitor centers and campgrounds. The park is a wildlife sanctuary; any disturbance of plant or animal life is forbidden. Dogs and cats are not permitted on trails but may be brought in if kept on leash or other physical restrictive controls. Never feed, tease or frighten bears; always give them a wide berth, as they can inflict serious injury. Watch bears from car with the windows closed. Park (daily). For the disabled, there is an all-access trail, the Sugarland Valley Nature Trail, equipped with special interpretive exhibits. Accessibility information is available at the visitor centers.   **Free.**

For information contact the Superintendent, Great Smoky Mountains National Park, 107 Park Headquarters Rd, Gatlinburg, TN 37738; 423/436-1200.

Greensboro (A-6)

(See also Burlington, High Point)

Founded 1808 **Pop** 183,521 **Elev** 841 ft **Area code** 336

Information Greensboro Area Convention & Visitors Bureau, 317 S Greene St, 27401; 336/274-2282 or 800/344-2282.

William Sydney Porter (O. Henry) was born and raised near Greensboro, a diversified Piedmont industrial city whose products are typical of North Carolina: textiles, cigarettes, machinery and electronic components. It was settled by Quakers, Germans and the Scottish-Irish with a zeal for political, religious and economic freedom. Men from this region fought in the Revolution and the War of 1812, and turned to the Confederacy in 1861. It was in Greensboro, the rebel supply depot, that Jefferson Davis met General Johnston after Richmond fell in 1865 and agreed on surrender terms. Today it is an educational, manufacturing and distribution center.

What to See and Do

Charlotte Hawkins Brown Memorial State Historic Site. North Carolina's first state historic site, honoring the achievements of African-American education in the state. In 1902, C.H. Brown, granddaughter of former slaves, founded Palmer Memorial Institute, which became one of the finest preparatory schools for blacks in the nation. Guided tours of historic campus (several buildings being restored), visitor center, audiovisual program. Picnicking. (Apr-Oct, daily; rest of yr, daily exc Mon; closed some hols) 10 mi E on I-85 to exit 135, then 1/2 mi W on US 70. Phone 336/449-4846.   **Free.**

★ **Chinqua-Penn Plantation.** English-style country house, extensive formal and rose gardens; 27 rms contain furnishings, art objects from around the world; no pets; picnic area. (Mar-Dec, Tues-Sat, also Sun afternoons; closed July 4th, Thanksgiving, Dec 25) 20 mi N on US 29, exit Hwy 14, 3 mi NW on Wentworth Rd. Phone 336/349-4576.   ¢¢¢

Greensboro Historical Museum. Housed in 19th-century church; exhibits on First Lady Dolley Madison, author O. Henry; military history, including Revolutionary Battle of Guilford Courthouse; 1960s lunch counter sit-ins; decorative arts; vintage autos; period furnishings. (Daily exc Mon; closed most hols) 130 Summit Ave. Phone 336/373-2043.   **Free.**

Guilford College (1837). (1,200 students) Oldest coed college in the South. Beautiful wooded 300-acre campus with Georgian-style buildings and a unique solar-energy fieldhouse. Quaker archives dating from 1680 (Tues-Fri, by appt; closed some hols). Official home of Eastern Music Festival (June-Aug). 5800 W Friendly Ave, 2 mi N of I-40. Phone 336/316-2000 or 336/316-2264 (archives).

Guilford Courthouse National Military Park. On Mar 15, 1781, Lord Cornwallis won a costly victory that was one link in a series of events that led to his surrender at Yorktown in Oct of the same year. After destroying a quarter of the enemy troops, General Nathanael Greene (for whom the city is named) made a successful retreat and then severely hampered the British plan of subduing the Southern colonies. The 220-acre park, established in 1917, has monuments marking important locations and honoring those who fought here; two signers of the Declaration of Independence, John Penn and William Hooper, are also buried here. Self-guided auto tour; walking trails. The visitor center has a museum housing Revolutionary War weapons, other items; 20-min film. (Daily; closed Jan 1, Dec 25) 6 mi NW and 1/4 mi E off US 220 on New Garden Rd. For additional information contact the Superintendent, 2332 New Garden Rd, 27429-0806; 336/288-1776.   **Free.**

Hagan-Stone Park. Swimming; fishing. Hiking. Picnicking, playground. Camping (hookups, dump station). Park (all yr). Some fees. Pets on leash only. 6 mi S on US 421, then 2 mi W on Hagan-Stone Park Rd. Phone 336/674-0472.

Natural Science Center of Greensboro, Inc. Natural science museum with zoo, trails and indoor exhibits including geology, paleontology and science & technology. Kid's Alley, an exploratorium for young children. Planetarium shows; inquire for schedule. Some fees. (Daily; closed major hols) 4301 Lawndale Dr, 5 1/2 mi N. Phone 336/288-3769.   ¢¢

University of North Carolina at Greensboro (1891). (12,100 students) 1000 Spring Garden St. Phone 336/334-5243. On campus is

Weatherspoon Art Gallery. Permanent collection of over 4,000 contemporary paintings, graphic arts, sculpture. (Daily exc Mon; closed school hols) Anne and Benjamin Cone Bldg. Phone 336/334-5770. **Free.**

Annual Event

Greater Greensboro Chrysler Classic Golf Tournament. Top golfers compete for more than $1.8 million on PGA circuit. Mid-late Apr.

Motels

(Rates are generally higher during Furniture Market)

★ **COMFORT INN.** *2001 Veasley St (27407). 336/294-6220; FAX 336/294-6220, ext. 199.* 123 rms, 2 story. S $57-$62; D $62-$65; each addl $5; under 16 free; higher rates special events. Crib free. TV; cable (premium). Pool. Complimentary continental bkfst. Meeting rm. Business servs avail. Cr cds: A, C, D, DS, MC, V.

⊡ ⩰ 📐 ⋈ 🐾 SC

✔★★ **DAYS INN.** *120 Seneca Rd (27406), I-85 & S Elm. 336/275-9571; FAX 336/275-9571, ext. 182.* 122 rms, 2 story. S $42-$58; D $42-$64; each addl $6; family rates. Crib free. TV; cable. Pool; wading pool. Playground. Complimentary continental bkfst. Ck-out 11 am. Cr cds: A, C, D, DS, MC, V.

⊡ ⩰ 📐 ⋈ 🐾 SC

★★ **FAIRFIELD INN BY MARRIOTT.** *2003 Athena Ct (27407). 336/294-9922; FAX 336/294-9922, ext. 709.* 135 rms, 3 story. S $49.95; D $54.95; each addl $3; under 18 free. Crib free. TV; cable (premium). Pool. Complimentary continental bkfst. Restaurant nearby. Ck-out noon. Business servs avail. Cr cds: A, D, DS, MC, V.

⊡ ⩰ 📐 ⋈ 🐾 SC

★★ **HAMPTON INN.** *2004 Veasley St (27407). 336/854-8600; FAX 336/854-8741.* 121 rms, 2 story. S $59; D $65-$73; under 18 free. Crib free. Pet accepted, some restrictions. TV; cable (premium). Pool. Complimentary continental bkfst. Meeting rm. Business servs avail. Cr cds: A, C, D, DS, JCB, MC, V.

⊡ 🐾 ⩰ 📐 ⋈ 🐾 SC

★★ **RAMADA INN-AIRPORT.** *7067 Albert Pick Rd (27409), near Piedmont Triad Airport. 336/668-3900; FAX 336/668-7012.* 170 rms, 2 story. S, D $74-$78; each addl $8; higher rates special events. Crib free. TV; cable (premium). Pool; sauna, poolside serv. Restaurant 7-10 am, 11:30 am-2 pm, 5-10 pm; Sat 7-10 am, 5-10 pm; Sun 7-10 am. Rm serv. Bar 4 pm-midnight. Ck-out noon. Meeting rms. Business servs avail. Bellhops. Valet serv. Free airport transportation. Cr cds: A, C, D, DS, JCB, MC, V.

⊡ ⩰ ✈ ⋈ 🐾 SC

✔★ **TRAVELODGE.** *2112 W Meadowview Rd (27403). 336/292-2020; FAX 336/852-3476.* 108 rms, 2 story. S, D $49-$64; each addl $5; under 17 free; higher rates golf tournament. Crib free. TV; cable (premium). Heated pool. Complimentary coffee in rms. Restaurant adj 11 am-10 pm. Ck-out noon. Meeting rms. Business servs avail. Health club privileges. Cr cds: A, D, DS, MC, V.

⊡ ⩰ 📐 ⋈ 🐾 SC

Motor Hotels

★★ **AMERISUITES.** *1619 Stanley Rd (27407). 336/852-1443; FAX 336/854-9339.* 126 suites, 6 story. S, D $80-$109; each addl $5; under 12 free; wkend rates; golf plans; higher rates special events. Crib free. TV; cable (premium), VCR. Complimentary continental bkfst. Complimentary coffee in rms. Restaurant nearby. Ck-out 11 am. Meeting rms. Business center. In-rm modem link. Free airport, RR station transportation.

Golf privileges. Exercise equipt; bicycle, stair machine. Heated pool. Refrigerators, microwaves, wet bars. Cr cds: A, C, D, DS, ER, JCB, MC, V.

⊡ 🐾 ⩰ ✈ ⋈ 🐾 SC 🚶

★★★ **HOLIDAY INN FOUR SEASONS.** *3121 High Point Rd (27407), I-40 exit 217A in Four Seasons Mall. 336/292-9161; FAX 336/292-1407.* Web www.kourycenter.com. 986 rms, 28 story. S $130-$140; D $140-$150; each addl $10; under 18 free; higher rates special events. Crib free. TV; cable (premium). Indoor/outdoor pool; whirlpool, wading pool, poolside serv. Restaurants 6 am-midnight. Rm serv. Bars 11-1 am, Sun from 1 pm; entertainment. Ck-out noon. Convention facilities. Business center. Bellhops. Valet serv. Gift shop. Free airport transportation. Golf privileges. Raquetball courts. Exercise equipt; weight machine, bicycles, sauna. Cr cds: A, C, D, DS, JCB, MC, V.

⊡ 🐾 ⩰ ✈ ⋈ 🐾 🚶

★★ **PARK LANE HOTEL AT FOUR SEASONS.** *3005 High Point Rd (27403). 336/294-4565; FAX 336/294-0572.* 161 rms, 4 story. S $70-$80; D $76-$86; each addl $10; suites $130; under 16 free. Crib free. TV; cable (premium). Pool. Complimentary continental bkfst. Restaurant 6-10 am, 5-9:30 pm; wkends 7-11 am. Rm serv. Bar 4:30-10 pm. Ck-out noon. Coin lndry. Meeting rms. Business servs avail. In-rm modem link. Sundries. Free airport transportation. Exercise equipt; weights, bicycles, sauna. Health club privileges. Some in-rm whirlpools; refrigerator, wet bar in suites; microwaves avail. Cr cds: A, C, D, DS, MC, V.

⊡ ⩰ ✈ ⋈ 🚶

Hotels

★★★ **BILTMORE.** *111 W Washington St (27401). 336/272-3474; FAX 336/275-2523; res: 800/332-0303.* 25 rms, 5 story. S, D $75-$110; under 18 free. Crib free. TV; cable (premium). Complimentary continental bkfst. Ck-out noon. Meeting rm. Business center. Concierge. Airport transportation. Refrigerators, wet bars. Built 1895. Cr cds: A, C, D, DS, MC, V.

⋈ 🐾 SC 🚶

★★★ **EMBASSY SUITES.** *204 Centreport Dr (27409), near Piedmont Triad Airport. 336/668-4535; FAX 336/668-3901.* 221 suites, 7 story. Suites $79-$214; under 16 free. Crib free. TV; cable (premium), VCR avail. Indoor pool; whirlpool. Complimentary full bkfst. Restaurant 6 am-10 pm. Bar 4 pm-midnight. Ck-out noon. Coin lndry. Meeting rms. Business center. Gift shop. Free airport transportation. Exercise equipt; weight machine, bicycles, sauna. Game rm. Refrigerators, wet bars. Microwaves avail. Balconies. Atrium lobby; glass elevators. Cr cds: A, C, D, DS, JCB, MC, V.

⊡ ⩰ ✈ ✈ ⋈ 🐾 SC 🚶

★★★ **HILTON.** *304 N Greene St (27401). 336/379-8000; FAX 336/275-2810.* Web www.hilton.com. 281 rms, 11 story. S, D $109-$139; suites $185-$450; under 17 free; wkend rates. Crib free. TV; cable (premium). Indoor pool; whirlpool. Supervised child's activities; ages 6 months-15 yrs. Restaurant 6:30 am-10 pm. Bar 4 pm-1 am. Ck-out 11 am. Convention facilities. Covered parking. Exercise rm; instructor, weight machines, bicycles, sauna. Refrigerator in suites. Luxury level. Cr cds: A, C, D, DS, JCB, MC, V.

⊡ ⩰ ✈ ⋈ 🐾 SC

★★ **MARRIOTT.** *1 Marriott Dr (27409), I-40 exit 210, at Piedmont Triad Airport. 336/852-6450; FAX 336/665-6522.* 299 rms, 5 story. S, D $114; suites $175-$250; under 16 free. Crib free. TV; cable (premium). Indoor/outdoor pool; whirlpool, poolside serv. Restaurant 6 am-10 pm. Bar 11:30-2 am. Ck-out noon. Coin lndry. Convention facilities. Business servs avail. In-rm modem link. Gift shop. Free airport transportation. Lighted tennis. Exercise equipt; weight machines, bicycles. Lawn games. Luxury level. Cr cds: A, C, D, DS, JCB, MC, V.

⊡ 🐾 ⩰ ✈ ✈ ⋈ 🐾 SC

Restaurant

★ ★ ★ **GATE CITY CHOP HOUSE.** *106 S Holden St (27407). 336/294-9977.* Hrs: 11:30 am-10 pm; Sat 4:30-10:30 pm. Closed Sun; some major hols. Res accepted. Bar. Wine list. Semi-a la carte: lunch $5.95-$8.95, dinner $13.95-$31.95. Child's meals. Specializes in Angus beef, grilled fish, chops. Salad bar. Outdoor dining. Five dining areas; circular oak bar. Cr cds: A, D, DS, MC, V.

Greenville (B-8)

(See also Washington, Williamston)

Founded 1786 **Pop** 44,972 **Elev** 55 ft **Area code** 919 **E-mail** greenvillenc@globalad.com **Web** www.globalad.com/greenvillenc

Information Greenville-Pitt County Convention and Visitors Bureau, 525 S Evans St, PO Box 8027, 27835-8027; 919/752-8044 or 800/537-5564.

An educational, cultural, commercial and medical center, Greenville is one of the towns named for General Nathanael Greene, a hero of the American Revolutionary War.

What to See and Do

East Carolina University (1907). (17,600 students) Jenkins Fine Arts Center, ECU Music School and Gray Art Gallery offer many cultural events to the public. E side of town. Medical Center campus, W side of town. Phone 919/328-6131 for information.

East Carolina Village of Yesteryear. Restoration and preservation of small-town life (1840-1940) within Pitt County and eastern North Carolina. The area contains a general store, railroad depot, museum, farmhouse, chicken house and schoolhouse. (Wkends) 2 mi N via US 264. Phone 919/758-6385. ¢

Greenville Museum of Art. Collections emphasize North Carolina contemporary fine arts and drawings, also paintings and prints of the period 1900-1945. (Tues-Fri, also Sun afternoons; closed major hols) 802 Evans St. Phone 919/758-1946. **Donation.**

River Park North Science & Nature Center. A 309-acre park with 4 lakes and 1.2 mi of Tar River water frontage. Science center near park entrance offers hands-on exhibits. Fishing, boating (ramp; no gas motors), pedal boats. Picknicking. (Daily exc Mon; closed most major hols) 5 mi N on Mumford Rd. Phone 919/830-4561. ¢

Motels

✔★ **FAIRFIELD INN.** *821 S Memorial Dr (27834). 919/758-5544; FAX 919/758-1416.* 115 rms, 2 story. S, D $39.95-$47.95; under 16 free. Crib free. TV; cable (premium), VCR avail. Pool. Complimentary continental bkfst. Restaurant adj open 24 hrs. Business servs avail. In-rm modem link. Valet serv. Free airport transportation. Health club privileges. Cr cds: A, C, D, DS, MC, V.

★ ★ **HAMPTON INN.** *3439 S Memorial Dr (27834). 919/355-2521; FAX 919/355-0261.* 121 rms, 2 story. S $46-$50; D $52-$55; under 18 free. Crib free. TV; cable (premium). Pool. Complimentary continental bkfst. Restaurant nearby. Ck-out noon. Meeting rm. Business servs avail. In-rm modem link. Cr cds: A, C, D, DS, MC, V.

✔★ **SUPER 8.** *1004 S Memorial Dr (27834). 919/758-8888; FAX 919/758-0523.* 52 rms, 2 story. S $32.99; D $37.99; each addl $5; under 12 free. Crib free. TV; cable (premium). Complimentary coffee in lobby. Ck-out 11 am. Business servs avail. Cr cds: A, C, D, DS, MC, V.

Hotels

★ ★ ★ **HILTON INN.** *207 SW Greenville Blvd (27834). 919/355-5000; FAX 919/355-5099.* 141 rms, 6 story. S, D $85-$95; each addl $10; suites $165-$250; under 18 free. Crib free. TV; cable (premium), VCR avail. Pool; whirlpool; poolside serv. Restaurant 6:30 am-10:30 pm. Bar 11-2 am. Ck-out noon. Meeting rms. Business servs avail. In-rm modem link. Airport transportation. Exercise equipt; weights, bicycles, treadmill. Refrigerator in suites. Cr cds: A, C, D, DS, MC, V.

★ ★ **RAMADA.** *203 W Greenville Blvd (27834), at jct US 264, NC 43, 11 on US 264 Bypass. 919/355-8300; FAX 919/756-3553.* 192 rms, 4 story. S, D $49-$79; each addl $6; suites $80-$100; under 12 free. Crib free. TV; cable (premium). Pool. Restaurant 6 am-10 pm. Rm serv. Bar 5 pm-2 am; entertainment. Ck-out noon. Meeting rms. Business center. Exercise equipt; bicycles, weights. Cr cds: A, C, D, DS, JCB, MC, V.

Restaurants

★ ★ **BEEF BARN.** *400 St Andrews Dr (27834). 919/756-1161.* Hrs: 11:30 am-2 pm, 5-10 pm; Sat, Sun from 5 pm. Closed some major hols. Res accepted. Bar. Semi-a la carte: lunch $3.95-$6.95, dinner $8.95-$25.95. Child's meals. Specializes in beef, steak, seafood. Salad bar. Antiques. Family-owned. Cr cds: A, D, DS, MC, V.

✔★ **PARKER'S BAR-B-QUE.** *3109 Memorial Dr (27834). 919/756-2388.* Hrs: 9 am-9 pm. Closed Thanksgiving, Dec 24, 25; also 1 wk mid-June. Res accepted. Semi-a la carte: lunch, dinner $4.75-$5.55. Child's meals. Specializes in pork barbecue, fried chicken. Outdoor dining. Family-owned. No cr cds accepted.

Hatteras (Outer Banks) (B-10)

Pop 1,660 **Elev** 2 ft **Area code** 919 **Zip** 27943

This Hatteras Island fishing village on the Outer Banks (see) was settled, it is said, by shipwrecked sailors from Devon, England. The Devon accent is indeed heard here and on the islands of Ocracoke and Manteo. There are ferries south to Ocracoke (see).

Motels

★ **HATTERAS MARLIN.** *On NC 12. 919/986-2141; FAX 919/986-2436.* 34 rms, 3 story, 5 kits. Memorial Day-Labor Day: S, D $54; each addl $5; kit. units for 1-4, $59-$64; under 6 free; lower rates rest of yr. Crib free. TV; cable. Pool. Restaurant nearby. Ck-out 11 am. Business servs avail. Sun deck. Picnic tables. Cr cds: MC, V.

★ **SEA GULL.** *On NC 12. 919/986-2550.* 45 rms, 1-2 story, 10 kits. Mar-Dec: S, D $55-$70; each addl $5; kit. units $75-$90; under 5 free. Closed rest of yr. Crib $5. TV; cable. Pool; wading pool. Restaurant opp 6 am-9 pm. Ck-out 11 am. Picnic tables. Grills. Beach adj. Cr cds: DS, MC, V.

Restaurant

★ ★ **CHANNEL BASS.** *NC 12, 8 mi S of lighthouse, 1 mi N of ferry docks.* 919/986-2250. Hrs: 5:30-9:30 pm; Sun from 5 pm. Closed Dec-Mar. Res accepted. Semi-a la carte: dinner $8.95-$24.50. Child's meals. Specializes in seafood, pies. On channel; nautical decor. Family-owned. Cr cds: DS, MC, V.

Henderson (A-7)

Founded 1840 **Pop** 15,655 **Elev** 509 ft **Area code** 919 **Zip** 27536
Information Vance County Tourism, 943 K-West Andrews Ave; 919/438-2222.

Tobacco has historically been the major crop in Vance County, of which Henderson is the seat. Manufacture and processing of textiles, hosiery, furniture, food, tobacco, mobile homes and glass containers are local industries. Tourism helps drive the economy.

What to See and Do

Kerr Reservoir. Part of the development of the Roanoke River Basin by the US Army Corps of Engineers. Approx 800 mi of shoreline and 50,000 acres of water. Swimming, waterskiing; fishing; boating, several private marinas. Picnicking. Camping (fee). Seven state recreation areas around lake, some open only Apr-Oct. (Daily) State camping areas (water and electric hookups in all exc some sites in Bullocksville; standard fees). 6 mi N off I-85. For 7-14-day reservations phone 919/438-7791.

Annual Event

Governor's Cup Regatta. Kerr Lake. 2 days mid-June.

Seasonal Event

Tobacco auctions. Held at 7 warehouses. Inquire at Chamber of Commerce. Sept-Nov.

Motels

★ **HOWARD JOHNSON.** *I-85 and Parham Rd, Parham Rd at jct US 1, 158 & I-85.* 919/492-7001; FAX 919/438-2389. 100 rms, 2 story. S $49-$60; D $54-$64; each addl $6; under 18 free. Crib free. TV; cable (premium). Pool. Restaurant 6 am-10 pm. Ck-out noon. Meeting rms. Business servs avail. In-rm modem link. Sundries. Balconies; some private patios. Cr cds: A, C, D, DS, MC, V.

★ **QUALITY INN.** *1¼ mi N on US 1, 158 at jct I-85 exit 215.* 919/492-1126; FAX 919/492-2575. 156 rms, 2 story. S $48-$61; D $49-$64; each addl $6; under 19 free. Crib free. TV; cable (premium). Pool; wading pool. Restaurant 6:30 am-2 pm, 5-10 pm. Rm serv. Bar 5-11 pm. Ck-out noon. Meeting rms. Business servs avail. In-rm modem link. Sundries. Cr cds: A, C, D, DS, JCB, MC, V.

Hendersonville (B-3)

(See also Asheville, Brevard)

Pop 7,284 **Elev** 2,146 ft **Area code** 704
Information Chamber of Commerce, 330 N King St, 28792; 704/692-1413.

The county seat of Henderson County, Hendersonville is well-known as a summer resort colony and popular retirement community. Manufacturing, agriculture and tourism help make up the county's balanced economy.

What to See and Do

✪ **Carl Sandburg Home National Historic Site** (Connemara). The famous poet's 264-acre farm residence is maintained as it was when Sandburg and his family lived here from 1945 until his death in 1967. On grounds are house and buildings for animals as well as a visitor center. (Daily; closed Dec 25) 1928 Little River Rd, 3 mi S on US 25, in Flat Rock. For further information contact the Superintendent, Flat Rock 28731; 704/693-4178. Tours ¢¢

Holmes State Forest. Managed forest designed to facilitate better understanding of the value of forests in our lives. Features "talking trees" with recorded narration about site and forest history. Picnicking. Camping (res required). (Mid-Mar-Nov, daily exc Mon) SW on Crab Creek Rd. For reservations or information contact Rte 4, Box 308; 704/692-0100.   **Free.**

Jump-Off Rock. Panoramic view from atop Jump-Off Mountain. 5th Ave, 6 mi W.

Annual Event

North Carolina Apple Festival. Labor Day wkend.

Seasonal Event

Flat Rock Playhouse. 3½ mi S on US 25 in Flat Rock. Outstanding professional theater since 1939; State Theater of North Carolina since 1961. Vagabond Players offer eight Broadway and London productions in 15 weeks. Wed-Sat evenings; Thurs, Sat, Sun matinees. For reservations phone 704/693-0731. Late May-early Sept.

Motels

★ **COMFORT INN.** *206 Mitchell Dr (28792).* 704/693-8800. 85 rms, 2 story. June-Oct: S $55.95; D $60.95; each addl $10; under 18 free; higher rates wkends; lower rates rest of yr. Crib free. Pet accepted. TV; cable, in-rm movies. Pool; whirlpool. Complimentary continental bkfst. Restaurant nearby. Ck-out 11 am. Meeting rm. Business servs avail. In-rm modem link. Refrigerators avail. Cr cds: A, C, D, DS, JCB, MC, V.

★ ★ **HAMPTON INN.** *155 Sugarloaf Rd (28792).* 704/697-2333; FAX 704/693-5280. 119 rms, 4 story. June-Oct: S $57-$67; D $62-$77; under 18 free; higher rates wkends in June, July, Aug & Oct; lower rates rest of yr. Crib free. TV; cable (premium). Pool. Continental bkfst. Ck-out noon. Business servs avail. In-rm modem link. Cr cds: A, C, D, DS, MC, V.

★ ★ **QUALITY INN AND SUITES.** *201 Sugarloaf Rd (28792), at jct I-26 & US 64.* 704/692-7231; FAX 704/693-9905. 150 rms, 2 story. June-Oct: S, D $65-$100; each addl $6; under 18 free; lower rates rest of yr. Crib free. TV; cable (premium), VCR avail. Heated pool; whirlpool; sauna. Playground. Complimentary continental bkfst. Restaurant 7-10 am, 4-9 pm. Ck-out 11 am. Meeting rms. Business servs avail. In-rm modem link. Valet serv. Sundries. Free airport transportation. Rec rm. Some refrigerators. Cr cds: A, C, D, DS, JCB, MC, V.

Inns

★ **ECHO MOUNTAIN.** *2849 Laurel Park Hwy (28739). 704/693-9626; FAX 704/697-2047.* 37 units, 2 story, 8 kits. Memorial Day-Labor Day, Oct & late Dec: S, D $65-$110; kit. suites $95-$135; each addl $10; lower rates rest of yr. Crib $10. TV; cable. Pool. Complimentary continental bkfst. Restaurant 11 am-2:30 pm, 5-9:30 pm; Sun 11:30 am-3 pm; closed Mon. Bar. Ck-out 11 am, ck-in 2 pm. Meeting rm. Business servs avail. On mountain top. Built 1896; stone & frame structure. Totally nonsmoking. Cr cds: A, MC, V.

★ ★ **WAVERLY INN.** *783 N Main St (28792). 704/693-9193; FAX 704/692-1010; res: 800/537-8195.* 15 rms, 3 story. S $80; D $89-$139; each addl $15; under 12 free. Crib free. TV; cable, VCR avail (movies free). Complimentary full bkfst; afternoon refreshments. Restaurant nearby. Ck-out 11 am, ck-in after 1 pm. Business servs avail. Golf privileges. Game rm. Restored guest house (1898); Victorian decor, upstairs sun porch. Cr cds: A, DS, MC, V.

★ ★ **WOODFIELD INN.** *(US 25, Flat Rock 28731) 3 mi S on US 25. 704/693-6016; res: 800/533-6016.* 17 rms, 3 story. No A/C. S, D $85-$125. Complimentary continental bkfst. Ck-out 11 am. Antiques. Nature trail. Built 1852. Cr cds: A, DS, MC, V.

Restaurant

★ ★ ★ **EXPRESSIONS.** *114 N Main St. 704/693-8516.* Hrs: 6-9 pm. Closed Sun; most major hols; also mid-Jan-mid-Feb. Res accepted. Bar. Wine cellar. Semi-a la carte: dinner $14.50-$24.50. Child's meals. Specializes in lamb, pork, crab cakes, fish. Fine dining in subdued atmosphere. Totally nonsmoking. Cr cds: D, MC, V.

Hickory (B-4)

(See also Statesville)

Pop 28,301 **Elev** 1,163 ft **Area code** 704
Information Catawba County Chamber of Commerce, 470 US 70 SW, PO Box 1828, 28603; 704/328-6111.

Nationally known brands of furniture and hosiery are produced here, as are ceramics and electronic equipment.

What to See and Do

Arts Center of Catawba Valley. 243 3rd Ave NE. Here are

Hickory Museum of Art. American realist 19th- & 20th-century art, including works by Gilbert Stuart; Hudson River School; Thos. Cole to Homer Martin; American Impressionists; European, Oriental and pre-Columbian pieces; changing exhibits quarterly. (Daily exc Mon; closed Easter, Dec 25) Phone 704/327-8576. **Free.**

Catawba Science Center. Interactive exhibits feature life, earth, medical and physical sciences. Also changing exhibits. (Daily exc Mon; closed hols) Phone 704/322-8169. ¢

Bunker Hill Covered Bridge. One of only two remaining covered bridges in state. Built in 1895, it spans Lyle's Creek. Nature trail, picnicking. On US 70, approx 10 mi E. Phone 704/465-0383.

Catawba County Museum of History. Exhibits include a fire engine (1919), country doctor's office (1920), Waugh Cabin (1839), Barringer Cabin (1759), blacksmith shop (1870) and an agriculture exhibit. (Sun, Tues-Fri; closed major hols) 3 mi S, Courthouse Square, in Newton. Phone 704/465-0383. **Free.**

Lake Hickory. A 4,100-acre lake with 105-mi shoreline; created by the Oxford Dam on the Catawba River. Boating, fishing, swimming, marinas. 4 mi N.

Lenoir-Rhyne College (1891). (Approx 1,700 students) Observatory (Sept-Apr, evenings, weather permitting). Concerts, athletic contests, dramatic productions, art exhibits, convocation programs and other special events throughout the academic year. 8th St & 7th Ave NE. Phone 704/328-1741.

Murray's Mill (1890). Overshot waterwheel; working machinery; milling museum and demonstrations. Country store (1890), folk art gallery (1880) (Thurs-Sun; closed major hols). Mill (Thurs-Sun; also by appt; closed major hols). 10 mi E via I-40, in Catawba. Phone 704/465-0383. ¢

Seasonal Event

Auto racing. Hickory Motor Speedway. 4 mi E on US 70. Stock car racing. For schedule, prices phone 704/464-3655. Mid-Mar-early Oct.

Motels

(Rates are generally higher during Furniture Market)

★ ★ **COMFORT SUITES.** *1125 13th Ave Dr SE (28603), off I-40 exit 125. 704/323-1211; FAX 704/322-4395.* 114 suites, 2 story, 12 kits. S $74-$100; D $81-$100; each addl $7; under 18 free. Crib free. TV; cable (premium). Pool. Complimentary full bkfst. Coffee in rms. Restaurant adj 6:30 am-11 pm. Ck-out 11 am. Coin lndry. Meeting rms. Business servs avail. In-rm modem link. Exercise equipt; weights, bicycles. Refrigerators, minibars. Cr cds: A, C, D, DS, ER, JCB, MC, V.

★ ★ **HAMPTON INN.** *1520 13th Ave Dr SE (28601). 704/323-1150; FAX 704/324-8979.* 119 rms, 2 story. S $56-$63; D $64-$71; under 18 free. Crib free. TV; cable. Complimentary continental bkfst. Restaurant adj 6 am-8 pm. Ck-out noon. Business servs avail. In-rm modem link. Cr cds: A, D, DS, MC, V.

★ ★ ★ **HOLIDAY INN SELECT.** *1385 Lenoir Rhyne Blvd SE (28601), I-40 exit 125. 704/323-1000; FAX 704/322-4275.* 201 rms, 2 story. S $89-$109; D $95-$115; each addl $6; under 19 free. Crib free. TV; cable. Indoor pool; whirlpool. Complimentary coffee in rms. Restaurant 6 am-11 pm. Rm serv. Bar 4:30 pm-1 am, Sun to midnight. Ck-out noon. Coin lndry. Meeting rms. Business servs avail. In-rm modem link. Valet serv. Exercise equipt; weights, stair machine, sauna. Some refrigerators. Balconies. Cr cds: A, C, D, DS, JCB, MC, V.

✔★ **RED ROOF INN.** *1184 Lenoir Rhyne Blvd (28602). 704/323-1500; FAX 704/323-1509.* 108 rms, 2 story. S $35-$46; D $47-$56; each addl $6; under 18 free. Crib free. Pet accepted, some restrictions. TV. Complimentary coffee in lobby. Restaurant adj. Ck-out noon. In-rm modem link. Cr cds: A, C, D, DS, MC, V.

✔★ **SLEEP INN.** *1179 13th Avenue Dr SE (28601). 704/323-1140; FAX 704/324-6203.* 100 rms, shower only, 3 story. S $49-$65; D $56-$85; each addl $7; under 18 free. Crib free. TV; cable, VCR avail (movies). Swimming privileges. Complimentary continental bkfst. Restaurant adj open 24 hrs. Ck-out noon. Business servs avail. In-rm modem link. Cr cds: A, C, D, DS, ER, JCB, MC, V.

Inn

★ ★ **HICKORY BED & BREAKFAST.** *464 7th St SW (28601). 704/324-0548; res: 800/654-2961.* 4 rms, 2 story. Phones avail. S, D $85-$90. Children over 12 yrs only. TV in sitting rm. Pool. Complimentary full bkfst; afternoon refreshments. Ck-out 11 am, ck-in 4 pm. Built in 1908;

Georgian-style architecture, antiques. Totally nonsmoking. No cr cds accepted.

Restaurant

★ ★ **1859 CAFE.** *433 2nd Ave SW (28601). 704/322-1859.* Hrs: 5-10 pm. Closed Sun; some major hols. Res accepted. Bar. Semi-a la carte: dinner $13.95-$19.50. Specializes in fresh seafood, prime beef, pasta. Entertainment Fri, Sat. Outdoor dining. 3 dining rms in converted house. Cr cds: A, C, D, DS, MC, V.

Highlands (C-2)

(See also Cashiers, Franklin)

Pop 948 **Elev** 3,835 ft **Area code** 704 **Zip** 28741
Information Chamber of Commerce, PO Box 404; 704/526-2112.

Highlands is a summer resort near the Georgia state line. Many unusual plants are part of the primeval rain forest preserve. Completely encircled by Nantahala National Forest (see FRANKLIN), the area surrounding the town is called "land of the waterfalls." A Ranger District office is located here.

What to See and Do

Bridal Veil Falls, Dry Falls. Behind Dry Falls the visitor may stand and look through to the Cullasaja River without getting wet. Also Lower Cullasaja Falls. The road here was cut from vertical cliffs and overlooks the river 250 ft below. NW of town on US 64, NC 28.

Highlands Nature Center. Cherokee artifacts, minerals of North Carolina; local flora and fauna, botanical garden; nature trail, hikes, lectures, movies. (Late May-Labor Day, daily exc Sun) E Main St (Horse Cove Rd), 1/2 mi E of jct US 64, NC 28, on grounds of Highlands Biological Station. Phone 704/526-2623.   **Free.**

Scaly Mountain Ski Area. Chairlift, rope tow; patrol, school, rentals; snowmaking; cafeteria. Longest run 2,200 ft; vertical drop 225 ft. (Mid-Dec-early Mar, daily) Half-day rates. 7 mi S on NC 106. Phone 704/526-3737. ¢¢¢¢

Motels

★ ★ **HIGHLANDS SUITE HOTEL.** *205 Main St. 704/526-4502; FAX 704/526-4840; res: 800/221-5078.* 28 suites, 2 story. Late June-early Sept, Oct-early Nov: S, D $141-$161; under 15 free; higher rates wkends, hols (2-day min); lower rates rest of yr. Crib free. TV; cable. Complimentary continental bkfst. Complimentary coffee in rms. Restaurant opp 7 am-9 pm. Ck-out noon. Meeting rms. Business servs avail. Bellhops. Minibars, microwaves, fireplaces. Balconies. Cr cds: A, MC, V.

★ ★ **MOUNTAIN HIGH.** *Main St. 704/526-2790; FAX 704/526-2750; res: 800/445-7293 (exc NC).* 55 rms, 1-2 story. June-Labor Day, Oct: S, D $93-$175; under 18 free; higher rates: wkends, hols; lower rates rest of yr. Crib $5. Pet accepted. TV; cable (premium). Complimentary continental bkfst. Restaurant opp 7:15 am-9:30 pm. Ck-out noon. Meeting rms. Business servs avail. Downhill ski 7 mi. Some bathrm phones, in-rm whirlpools, refrigerators, fireplaces; microwaves avail. Balconies. Picnic tables. Cr cds: A, DS, MC, V.

Inn

★ ★ **HIGHLANDS INN.** *Main St, near 4th St. 704/526-9380; res: 800/964-6955.* 30 rms, 3 story. Apr-Nov: S, D $89-$99; suites $99-$125; wkly rates. Closed rest of yr. TV; cable. Complimentary continental bkfst. Ck-out 11 am, ck-in 4 pm. Balconies. Built in 1880; antiques. Cr cds: A, MC, V.

Restaurants

★ ★ **NICK'S.** *NC 28 at Satulah Rd, 4 blks S on NC 28: 704/526-2706.* Hrs: 11 am-3 pm, 5:30-10 pm. Closed Jan-Feb. Res accepted. Continental menu. Semi-a la carte: lunch $5.95-$11.95, dinner $10.95-$29.95. Child's meals. Specializes in veal, prime rib, seafood, steak. Cr cds: MC, V.

★ ★ **ON THE VERANDAH.** *1536 Franklin Rd, at Sequoyah Lake. 704/526-2338.* Hrs: 6-10 pm; Sun brunch noon-2:30 pm. Closed Jan-Mar. Res accepted. No A/C. Setups. Semi-a la carte: dinner $13.50-$25. Sun brunch $18. Specializes in pasta, seafood. Pianist. Verandah dining. Vaulted ceiling; contemporary rustic decor. Cr cds: MC, V.

High Point (A-5)

(See also Burlington, Greensboro, Lexington)

Founded 1859 **Pop** 69,496 **Elev** 939 ft **Area code** 336 **E-mail** hpcvb@highpoint.org **Web** www.highpoint.org
Information Convention and Visitors Bureau, 300 S Main St, PO Box 2273, 27261; 336/884-5255 or 800/720-5255.

Furniture and hosiery are the products that make High Point prosperous. The city rests on the highest point along the North Carolina and Midland Railroad, which the state built in 1853. The plank road (finished in 1854), stretching 130 miles from Salem to Fayetteville, made it a center of trade; mileposts on this road had carved numbers instead of painted ones so travelers could feel their way at night.

What to See and Do

Furniture Discovery Center. Nation's only museum of modern day furniture manufacturing. Hands-on displays; miniatures; hall of fame; special exhibits. (Apr-Oct, daily; rest of yr, daily exc Mon; closed hols) 101 W Green Dr. Phone 336/887-3876.   ¢¢

High Point Museum. Furniture; materials reflecting the area's military, industrial, social and civic history. (Daily exc Mon; closed major hols) John Haley House (1786) contains 18th- and 19th-century furnishings; blacksmith shop (demonstrations some wkends), weaving house. 1805 E Lexington Ave, at McGuinn Ave. Phone 336/885-6859.   **Free.**

Peterson Doll and Miniature Museum. Collection of more than 2,000 dolls and related artifacts from around the world, some dating back to the 15th century. (Apr-Oct, daily; Nov-Mar, daily exc Mon; closed holidays) Main & Green Sts. Phone 336/885-3655 or 336/887-3876.   ¢¢

World's Largest Chest of Drawers. Building designed to look like a 19th-century dresser; symbolizes city's position as a furniture center. Built in 1926. 508 N Hamilton St. Phone 336/883-2016.   **Free.**

Annual Event

Gas Boat Drag Championships. Oak Hollow Lake. One of several World Series Championship races. Phone 336/883-2016. 4th wkend July.

Seasonal Event

North Carolina Shakespeare Festival. 220 E Commerce Ave, High Point Theatre. Season includes 3 productions and *A Christmas Carol*. Phone 336/841-6273 or 336/841-2273. Aug-Oct & Dec.

Motor Hotel

★★ **HOLIDAY INN-MARKET SQUARE.** *236 S Main St (27260).* 336/886-7011; FAX 336/886-5595. 165 rms, 2-6 story. S $57-$62; D $62-$67; each addl $10; suites $95-$110; under 18 free; higher rates Furniture Market. Crib free. TV; cable (premium). Pool. Restaurant 7 am-2 pm, 5-9 pm. Rm serv. Bar 5-10 pm. Ck-out noon. Coin lndry. Meeting rms. Business servs avail. Barber. Many poolside rms with balcony. Cr cds: A, C, D, DS, MC, V.

Hotel

★★ **RADISSON.** *135 S Main St (27260).* 336/889-8888; FAX 336/885-2737. 251 rms, 8 story. S, D $109-$125; each addl $10; suites $225-$275; higher rates special events. Crib free. Garage parking $3. TV; cable (premium). Restaurant 6:30 am-2:30 pm, 5-10 pm. Bar 3-11 pm. Ck-out noon. Meeting rms. Business center. In-rm modem link. Gift shop. Free airport, RR station transportation. Exercise equipt; weights, treadmill. Indoor pool; whirlpool, poolside serv. Some refrigerators, wet bars. Cr cds: A, C, D, DS, ER, JCB, MC, V.

Inn

★★ **BOULDIN HOUSE.** *4332 Archdale Rd (27263), 2 mi S on I-85, exit 111.* 336/431-4909; res: 800/739-1816; FAX 336/431-4914. E-mail lmiller582@aol.com; web www.bbonline.com/nc/bouldin. 4 rms. No rm phones. S, D $85-$95; each addl $25; higher rates Furniture Market. Children over 12 yrs only. TV in common rm; cable, VCR avail (movies). Complimentary full bkfst. Complimentary coffee in rms. Ck-out 11 am, ck-in 5-7 pm. Business servs avail. Luggage handling. Fireplaces. Grills. Built in 1918. Totally nonsmoking. Cr cds: DS, MC, V.

Restaurant

★★ **J. BASUL NOBLE.** *114 S Main St (27260).* 336/889-3354. Hrs: 6-11 pm. Closed Sun; major hols. Res accepted. French, Amer menu. Bar to midnight. A la carte entrees: dinner $10.95-$24.95. Specializes in beef, veal, seafood. Jazz combo Thurs-Sat. Cr cds: A, D, MC, V.

Jacksonville (C-8)

Pop 30,013 **Elev** 15 ft **Area code** 910

This town is on the edge of the New River Marine Base (Camp Lejeune). There is excellent fishing nearby.

Motel

★★ **HAMPTON INN.** *474 Western Blvd (28546).* 910/347-6500; FAX 910/347-6858. 120 rms, 2 story. S, D $58-$63; higher rates wkends. Crib free. TV; cable (premium). Pool. Complimentary continental bkfst. Restaurant adj 11 am-11 pm. Ck-out noon. Meeting rms. Business servs avail. In-rm modem link. Sundries. Health club privileges. Cr cds: A, C, D, DS, MC, V.

Motor Hotels

★★ **HOLIDAY INN EXPRESS.** *2115 US 17N (28546).* 910/347-1900; FAX 910/347-7593. 118 rms, 4 story. S $55; D $60; each addl $5; under 18 free. Crib free. TV; cable (premium). Pool. Coffee in rms. Complimentary full bkfst. Ck-out noon. Business servs avail. In-rm modem link. Valet serv. Some refrigerators. Cr cds: A, C, D, DS, MC, V.

↙★★ **ONSLOW INN.** *201 Marine Blvd (28540), on US 17, NC 24.* 910/347-3151; FAX 910/346-4000; res: 800/763-3151. 92 rms, 2 story. S $37-$42; D $42-$50; each addl $4; under 12 free. Crib free. TV; cable (premium). Pool; wading pool. Complimentary coffee. Restaurant 6 am-9 pm; Sun 7 am-8 pm. Rm serv. Ck-out noon. Meeting rms. Business center. In-rm modem link. Lawn games. Some private patios, balconies. Picnic tables, grills. Cr cds: A, C, D, DS, MC, V.

Jefferson (A-4)

(See also Boone)

Founded 1800 **Pop** 1,300 **Elev** 2,960 ft **Area code** 910 **Zip** 28640
E-mail ashechamber@skybest.com **Web** www.ashechamber.com
Information Ashe County Chamber of Commerce, PO Box 31, West Jefferson 28694; 910/246-9550.

What to See and Do

Ashe County Cheese Factory. North Carolina's only cheese factory. Viewing of cheese production; samples. (Daily exc Sun; closed some major hols, also Dec 26) 2 mi S on NC 194, in West Jefferson. Phone 910/246-2501 or 800/445-1378. **Free.**

Mt Jefferson State Park. National natural landmark; excellent view of Blue Ridge Mountains. Approx 500 acres. Hiking, nature trails. Picnicking. No camping avail. 1 mi S off US 221, at summit of Mt Jefferson. Phone 910/246-9653.

Motel

★★ **BEST WESTERN ELDRETH.** *US 221 & NC 88.* 910/246-8845; FAX 910/246-5620. 48 rms, 1-2 story. Mid-May-Dec: S, D $54-$68; each addl $6; higher rates wkends mid-May-late Oct; lower rates rest of yr. Crib free. TV; cable. Restaurant 6 am-9 pm. Rm serv. Ck-out 11 am. Meeting rms. Sauna. Cr cds: A, C, D, DS, MC, V.

Kill Devil Hills (Outer Banks) (A-10)

(See also Manteo, Nags Head)

Pop 4,238 **Elev** 20 ft **Area code** 919 **Zip** 27948 **E-mail** dctb-info@outer-banks.com **Web** www.outer-banks.com/visitor-info/
Information Dare County Tourist Bureau, 704 US 64/264, PO Box 399, Manteo 27954; 919/473-2138 or 800/446-6262.

Although the name Kitty Hawk is usually associated with the Wright Brothers, their early flying experiments took place on and near these dunes on the Outer Banks (see).

What to See and Do

✪ **Wright Brothers National Memorial.** Field where first powered flight took place, Dec 17, 1903, is marked showing takeoff point and landing places. The living quarters and hangar buildings used by the Wrights during their experiments have been reconstructed. The visitor center has reproductions of 1902 glider and 1903 flyer with exhibits on story of their invention. 3,000-ft airstrip. (Daily; closed Dec 25) Off US 158, between mileposts 7 & 8. Phone 919/441-7430. ¢¢

Motels

✔★ **BEACH HAVEN.** *(4104 Virginia Dare Trail, Kitty Hawk (Outer Banks) 27949) NC 12 milepost 4.* 919/261-4785. 5 rms. Early July-Labor Day: S, D $69-$95; each addl $6; wkend rates; higher rates hols (3-day min); lower rates Apr-June & Sept-Oct. Closed rest of yr. Crib free. TV; cable. Complimentary coffee in rms. Restaurant nearby. Ck-out 10 am. Coin lndry. Refrigerators. Swimming beach. Grills. Cr cds: A, MC, V.

★★ **COMFORT INN.** *401 Virginia Dare Trail, NC 12 milepost 8.* 919/480-2600; FAX 919/480-2873. 121 rms, 3 story. Memorial Day-Labor Day: S, D $89-$150; each addl $5; under 18 free; lower rates rest of yr. Crib free. TV; cable (premium). Pool. Complimentary continental bkfst. Complimentary coffee in rms. Ck-out 11 am. Coin lndry. Business servs avail. In-rm modem link. Some refrigerators. Balconies. On ocean; swimming beach. Cr cds: A, C, D, DS, ER, MC, V.

★ **DAYS INN-OCEAN FRONT.** *101 N Virginia Dare Trail, NC 12 milepost 8.5.* 919/441-7211; FAX 919/441-8080. 52 units, 2 story, 15 kits. Mid-June-early Sept: S, D $90-$105; each addl $5; kit. units $125-$150; wkly rates; higher rates: hols, wkends; lower rates mid-Jan-mid-June, early Sept-mid-Dec. Closed rest of yr. Crib free. TV; cable (premium). Pool. Complimentary continental bkfst. Ck-out 11 am. Business servs avail. In-rm modem link. On swimming beach. Cr cds: A, D, DS, JCB, MC, V.

★★ **RAMADA INN.** *1701 S Virginia Dare Trail, milepost 9.5, NC 12.* 919/441-2151; FAX 919/441-1830. 172 rms, 5 story. Memorial Day-Labor Day: D $135-$169; each addl $10; under 18 free; hol plans; lower rates rest of yr. Crib free. Pet accepted; $10. TV; cable; VCR avail (movies free). Indoor pool; whirlpool. Coffee in rms. Restaurant 7-11:30 am, 5-10 pm; summer 7 am-2 pm, 5-10 pm. Rm serv. Bar 7:30-11:30 am, 5-11 pm; entertainment wkends (in season). Ck-out 11 am. Meeting rms. Business servs avail. In-rm modem link. Refrigerators. Private balconies. Lawn games. Cr cds: A, C, D, DS, JCB, MC, V.

Motor Hotels

★★ **BEST WESTERN OCEAN REEF SUITES.** *107 Virginia Dare Trail.* 919/441-1611; FAX 919/441-1482. 70 kit. suites, 5 story. May-Sept: kit. suites (up to 6) $150-$185; each addl $10; under 17 free; lower rates rest of yr. Crib $5. TV; cable, VCR avail (movies). Heated pool; whirlpool. Complimentary coffee. Restaurant 11 am-11 pm. Ck-out 11 am. Business servs avail. Exercise equipt; weight machines, bicycles, sauna, steam rm. Private patios, balconies. Cr cds: A, C, D, DS, JCB, MC, V.

★★ **HOLIDAY INN.** *1601 Virginia Dare Trail, on US 158 Business between mileposts 9 & 10.* 919/441-6333; FAX 919/441-7779. 105 rms, 4 story. May-Sept: S, D $125-$175; each addl $10; under 19 free; lower rates rest of yr. Crib free. TV; cable. Pool; whirlpool, wading pool. Restaurant 7 am-noon, 5-9 pm. Rm serv. Bar 5:30 pm-1:30 am; entertainment. Ck-out 11 am. Coin lndry. Meeting rms. Business servs avail. In-rm modem link. Private patios, balconies. Oceanfront deck. On beach; many oceanfront rms. Cr cds: A, C, D, DS, JCB, MC, V.

★★ **THE NAGS HEAD BEACH HOTEL.** *804 N Virginia Dare Trail.* 919/441-0411; FAX 919/441-7811. 96 rms, 4 story. Mid-June-early Sept: S, D $78-$98; under 18 free; higher rates hol wknds; lower rates rest of yr. Crib free. Pet accepted. TV; cable (premium). Pool. Complimentary continental bkfst. Ck-out 11 am. Refrigerators. Many balconies. Cr cds: A, D, DS, MC, V.

Inn

✔★ **CHEROKEE INN.** *500 N Virginia Dare Trail, on NC 12, milepost 8.* 919/441-6127; FAX 919/441-1072; res: 800/554-2764. 6 rms, 2 story. No rm phones. June-Aug: S, D $95; lower rates Apr-May & Sept-Oct. Closed rest of yr. Children over 12 yrs only. TV; cable. Complimentary continental bkfst. Ck-out 11 am, ck-in 3 pm. Sitting rm. Near swimming beach. Totally nonsmoking. Cr cds: A, MC, V.

Restaurants

★ **JOLLY ROGER.** *1834 N Virginia Dare Trail, just off NC 12 between mileposts 6.5 & 7.* 919/441-6530. Hrs: 6 am-10 pm; Sun from 7 am. Bar. Semi-a la carte: bkfst $1.75-$5.95, lunch $3.95-$6.95, dinner $7.95-$16.95. Specializes in seafood, pasta, beef. Cr cds: A, C, D, DS, MC, V.

★★ **PORT O' CALL.** *504 Virginia Dare Trail.* 919/441-7484. Hrs: 5-10 pm; Sun buffet 9:30 am-1:30 pm. Closed Jan-mid-Mar. Res accepted. Bar. Semi-a la carte: dinner $9.95-$19.95. Buffet: lunch (Sun) $9.95. Child's meals. Specializes in seafood, beef, pasta. Entertainment Tues-Sun. Turn-of-the-century Victorian decor. Cr cds: A, DS, MC, V.

Kinston (B-8)

Pop 25,295 **Elev** 44 ft **Area code** 919 **Zip** 28501

What to See and Do

CSS *Neuse* State Historic Site. Remains of Confederate ironclad gunboat sunk by her crew in 1865 and not raised until 1963. Visitor center relates story of the *Neuse* through an audio show, artifacts recovered from the gunboat; photographs; memorial has exhibits on life of Caswell, first elected governor of the state of North Carolina. Picnicking. (Apr-Oct, daily; rest of yr, daily exc Mon; closed major hols) 1 mi W on US 70A. Phone 919/522-2091. **Free.**

Motels

✔★ **COMFORT INN.** 200 W Newbern Rd. 919/527-3200; FAX 919/527-3200, ext. 420. 60 rms, 2 story. Apr-Sept: S, D $52-$60; each addl $5; suites $65; under 18 free; lower rates rest of yr. Crib $5. TV; cable (premium), VCR avail. Pool; sauna. Complimentary continental bkfst. Restaurant nearby. Ck-out noon. Meeting rms. Business servs avail. Exercise equipt; bicycles, stair machine. Refrigerators. Cr cds: A, D, DS, MC, V.

D ≈ ✗ ☒ ⚒ SC

★★ **HOLIDAY INN.** 3/4 mi S on US 70, NC 58 at jct US 258. 919/527-4155; FAX 919/527-2900. 100 rms, 2 story. S, D $47-$69; each addl $6. Crib free. TV; cable (premium). Pool; wading pool. Restaurant 6 am-2 pm, 5:30-10 pm. Rm serv. Bar 5 pm-1 am. Ck-out noon. Meeting rms. Business center. In-rm modem link. Cr cds: A, C, D, DS, MC, V.

D ≈ ☒ ⚒ SC ♣

Motor Hotel

★★ **HAMPTON INN.** 1403 Richlands Rd. 919/523-1400; FAX 919/523-1326. 124 rms, 4 story. June-late Sept: S $59; D $69; each addl $5; under 17 free; lower rates rest of yr. Crib free. TV; cable (premium). Pool. Complimentary continental bkfst. Ck-out noon. Meeting rms. Business servs avail. Some refrigerators. Cr cds: A, C, D, DS, MC, V.

D ≈ ☒ ⚒ SC

Kitty Hawk (Outer Banks)

(see Kill Devil Hills)

Laurinburg (C-6)

(See also Pinehurst, Southern Pines)

Settled (ca 1700) **Pop** 11,643 **Elev** 227 ft **Area code** 910 **E-mail** scotcoc@ix-netcom.com **Web** www.NCSEorg/scotland

Information Laurinburg-Scotland County Area Chamber of Commerce, 606 Atkinson St, PO Box 1025, 28353; 910/276-7420.

Laurinburg is the seat of Scotland County, named for its early Scottish Highland settlers. Industrial development has expanded this agricultural center's economy.

What to See and Do

St Andrews Presbyterian College (1958). (800 students) Contemporary-style buildings on an 800-acre campus around a 70-acre lake. Mosaic tile wall depicts story of humankind. S city limits. Phone 910/277-5000. On campus are

Vardell Art Gallery. (Mid-Sept-May, Mon-Fri; closed school hols) Vardell Bldg. Phone 910/277-5000, ext 5023. **Free.**

Science Center. Features interdisciplinary laboratory, guides. (Sept-May and summer session, Mon-Fri; other times by appt) **Free.**

Motels

✔★★ **COMFORT INN.** 1705 US 401 S (28352), 1 mi S of US 74 on US 15/401. 910/277-7788; FAX 910/277-7229. 80 rms, 3 story. S

$53-$80; D $59-$86; each addl $6; suites $80; under 18 free; family rates; higher rates: special events, Rockingham Races. Crib free. TV; cable (premium), VCR avail. Pool. Complimentary continental bkfst. Restaurant adj 5:30-9:30 pm. Ck-out noon. Meeting rms. Business servs avail. Valet serv. Sundries. Exercise equipt; weights, bicycles. Some in-rm saunas, refrigerators. Cr cds: A, C, D, DS, ER, JCB, MC, V.

D ≈ ✗ ☒ ⚒ SC

★★ **HAMPTON INN.** 115 Hampton Circle (28352). 910/277-1516; FAX 910/277-1514. 50 rms, 3 story. S $53-$59; D $59-$65; under 18 free; higher rates race wkends (2-day min). Crib avail. TV; cable (premium), VCR avail. Pool. Complimentary continental bkfst. Restaurant nearby. Meeting rms. Business servs avail. In-rm modem link. Cr cds: A, C, D, DS, MC, V.

D ≈ ☒ ⚒

✔★ **PINE ACRES LODGE.** Rte 5, Box 135A (28352), US 15, 401 S Bypass. 910/276-1531; FAX 910/277-1481; res: 800/348-8242. 74 rms. S, D $22-$35; each addl $6. TV; cable (premium). Pool; wading pool. Complimentary continental bkfst. Restaurant nearby. Ck-out 11 am. Refrigerators. Cr cds: A, D, DS, MC, V.

D ≈ ☒ ⚒

Restaurant

✔★ **CHAMPS FINE FOODS & SPIRITS.** US 15/401 (28352). 910/276-4386. Hrs: 4 pm-2 am. Closed Easter, Dec 25. Res accepted. Bar. Semi-a la carte: dinner $9-$13. Child's meals. Specializes in ribs, seafood, beef. Salad bar. Entertainment Thur-Sat. Decorated with NC colleges memorabilia. Cr cds: A, C, D, DS, MC, V.

D SC

Lenoir (A-4)

(See also Blowing Rock)

Pop 14,192 **Elev** 1,182 ft **Area code** 704 **Zip** 28645

Motel

★★ **HOLIDAY INN EXPRESS.** 142 Wilkesboro Blvd SE. 704/758-4403; FAX 704/758-4403, ext. 179. 100 rms, 2 story. S, D $47-$59; each addl $10; under 19 free. Crib free. TV. Pool. Complimentary continental bkfst. Ck-out 11 am. Meeting rms. Cr cds: A, C, D, DS, JCB, MC, V.

D ≈ ☒ ⚒ SC

Lexington (B-5)

(For accommodations see Asheboro, High Point, Winston-Salem)

Settled 1750 **Pop** 16,581 **Elev** 809 ft **Area code** 336 **Zip** 27292 **E-mail** lexingtonnc@infoave.net **Web** web.infoave.net/~lexingtonnc

Information Chamber of Commerce, 16 E Center St, PO Box C, 27293; 336/248-5929.

In 1775, settlers learned of the battle of Lexington in Massachusetts and decided to name this town for it. Local industry is diversified and includes furniture making, textiles and clothing, food processing, electronics, ceramics, machinery and fiberglass. Native to the area is traditional pork barbecue, which can be found in many local restaurants.

What to See and Do

High Rock Lake. Its 300-mi shoreline is a center for water sports in the piedmont. 10 mi SW on US 70 or S on NC 8.

Old Davidson County Courthouse (1858). Greek-revival building facing the town square; old courtroom houses museum of local history. (Tues-Fri, also Sun afternoons; closed hols) Center of city. Phone 336/242-2035. **Free.**

Linville (A-3)

(See also Banner Elk, Blowing Rock, Boone)

Pop 244 (est) **Elev** 3,669 ft **Area code** 704 **Zip** 28646

Linville is in the heart of a ruggedly beautiful resort area. Several miles to the south, just off the Blue Ridge Parkway, is scenic Linville Falls, cascading down the steep Linville Gorge, designated a national wilderness. Visible from vantage points in this area are the mysterious Brown Mountain lights.

What to See and Do

✪ **Grandfather Mountain** (5,964 ft). Highest peak in the Blue Ridge, with spectacular views, rugged rock formations; 1-mi-high swinging bridge; bald eagles, deer, cougars and black bears, bear cubs and others in natural habitats. Hiking trails, picnic areas. Museum with exhibits on local animals, birds, flowers, geology; restaurant; gift shop. (Daily; winter, open weather permitting; closed Thanksgiving, Dec 25) 2 mi NE via US 221, 1 mi S of jct Blue Ridge Pkwy & US 221. Phone 704/733-4337. ¢¢¢

Annual Events

Grandfather Mountain Nature Photography Weekend. Grandfather Mountain. Nationally known photographers give illustrated lectures; nature photography contest; picnic dinner. Preregistration required. Early June.

"Singing on the Mountain." On the slopes of Grandfather Mountain. All-day program of modern and traditional gospel music featuring top groups and nationally known speakers. Concessions or bring your own food. 4th Sun June.

Grandfather Mountain Highland Games. MacRae Meadows, on US 221 at Grandfather Mountain. Gathering of members of over 100 Scottish clans and societies to view or participate in traditional Scottish sports, track-and-field events, mountain marathon; highland dancing, piping and drumming; ceremonies and pageantry. 2nd full wknd July.

Lodge

★ ★ ★ **ESEEOLA LODGE.** US 221 & NC 105, on US 221, NC 105, 181, 2 mi W of Blue Ridge Pkwy. 704/733-4311; FAX 704/733-3227; res: 800/742-6717. E-mail eseeola@skybest.com; web www.eseeola .com. This rustic lakeside lodge, built in the late 1880s, is the focal point of the village. Its interiors are richly detailed with chestnut paneling and stonework. 29 rms, 2 story. MAP, mid-May-mid-Oct: S $195-$225; D $245-$265; each addl $50. Closed rest of yr. Crib free. TV; cable. Pool; lifeguard. Supervised child's activities (mid-June-mid-Aug). Coffee in rms. Dining rm (public by res) 7:30-9:30 am, 11:30 am-2:30 pm, 7-9 pm (jacket, tie at dinner). Rm serv. Box lunches. Bar. Ck-out noon. Business servs avail. Tennis. 18-hole golf, greens fee $55 (incl cart), pro, putting green. Exercise rm; instructor, weights, bicycles. Croquet court. Rec rm. Soc dir. Boating, trout fishing. Cr cds: MC, V.

🏊 🎿 🧗 ⛷ 🚶 🔥

Little Switzerland (B-3)

(See also Burnsville, Linville, Morganton)

Founded 1910 **Pop** 200 (est) **Elev** 3,500 ft **Area code** 704 **Zip** 28749 **E-mail** info@mitchell-county.com **Web** www.mitchell-county.com /north-carolina

Information Mitchell County Chamber of Commerce, Rte 1, Box 796, Spruce Pine 28777; 704/765-9483 or 800/227-3912.

A restful summer resort amid the high mountains of western North Carolina, Little Switzerland is bisected by the Blue Ridge Parkway.

What to See and Do

Emerald Village. Historical area includes mines; North Carolina Mining Museum; Main Street 1920s Mining Community Museum; Gemstone Mine, where visitors can prospect for gems under shaded flumes (fee; equipment furnished); Mechanical Music Maker Museum; waterfall and scenic overlook; shops and deli. (Daily; closed some major hols) NW on County 1100 (McKinney Mine Rd), at Blue Ridge Pkwy milepost 334. Phone 704/765-6463. ¢¢

Mt Mitchell State Park. Adj Pisgah National Forest; natural national landmark. Road leads to summit (6,684 ft; highest point east of the Mississippi River) for incomparable views. Trails. Picnicking, restaurant, refreshment stands. Small tent camping area. Observation tower, museum. Standard fees. 20 mi S on Blue Ridge Pkwy, then N on NC 128. Phone 704/675-4611.

Museum of North Carolina Minerals. Mineral exhibits of the state. (May-Nov, daily; rest of yr, Wed-Sun; closed Jan 1, Thanksgiving, Dec 24-26) At jct Blue Ridge Pkwy, NC 226. Phone 704/765-2761. **Free.**

Motels

★ ★ **BIG LYNN LODGE.** 1½ mi W on NC 226A. 704/765-4257; res: 800/654-5232; FAX 704/765-0301. 26 rms, some A/C, 2 story, 4 suites, 12 cottages. MAP, Mid-Apr-early Nov: S $70-$115; D $79-$115; each addl $23; suites $115; wkly rates; EP rates rest of yr. TV in lounge. Restaurant 7:30-9 am, 6-7:30 pm. Ck-out 11 am. Coin lndry. Bellhops. Sundries. Rec rm; player piano. Lawn games. Hiking trails. Library. Cr cds: MC, V.

🏊 🔥

★ **PINEBRIDGE INN.** (101 Pinebridge Ave, Spruce Pine 28777) 3 mi S on NC 226, off Summit St. 704/765-5543; FAX 704/765-5544; res: 800/356-5059. 46 rms, 3 story. S, D $43-$68; suites $83-$125; kit. unit $125; under 12 free; ski plans, golf plans; wkly, wkend, hol rates. Crib $10. TV; cable. Ck-out noon. Meeting rm. Business servs avail. Tennis privileges. Golf privileges. Downhill/x-country ski 19 mi. Picnic tables. YMCA adj. Cr cds: A, DS, MC, V.

D 🎿 🧗 ⛷ 🏊 🔥 SC

Lodges

★ **ALPINE INN.** Blue Ridge Pkwy milepost 334, then S on NC 226A. 704/765-5380. 14 rms, 11 with shower only, 2-3 story. No A/C. No rm phones. S, D $38-$52; kit. $60; wkly rates. Closed Dec-Mar. Complimentary coffee in rms. Ck-out noon. Game rm. Balconies. Picnic tables. On Grassy Mt. Cr cds: MC, V.

🔥

★ ★ **SWITZERLAND INN.** Blue Ridge Pkwy at milepost 334. 704/765-2153; FAX 704/765-0049; res: 800/654-4026. 60 units, 8 with A/C, 2 story. May-Oct: S, D $75-$100; each addl $15; suites $110; family rates. Closed rest of yr. TV; cable (premium). Pool. Complimentary full bkfst. Dining rm 7:30-9:30 am, 11:30 am-2 pm, 5:30-9:30 pm. Ck-out 11 am. Meeting rms. Business servs avail. Sundries. Tennis. Balconies. Picnic tables. Mountain view. Cr cds: A, MC, V.

Lumberton (C-7)

Founded 1787 **Pop** 18,601 **Elev** 137 ft **Area code** 910 **Zip** 28358 **E-mail** chamber@lumberton.org

Information Chamber of Commerce & Visitors Bureau, PO Box 1008, 28359; 910/739-9999 or 910/739-4750.

Lumberton is the county seat of Robeson County and the home of many industries, including one of the largest tobacco marketing centers in the state. Hunting for quail, duck, dove and rabbit is excellent in the area. Pembroke, to the northwest, is the population center for some 30,000 Lumbee Native Americans, believed by some historians to include descendants of the "lost colonists" (see FORT RALEIGH NATIONAL HISTORIC SITE).

What to See and Do

Jones Lake State Park. More than 2,200 acres with swimming; fishing; boating. Interpretive trails. Picnicking. Primitive camping (mid-Mar-Nov). Standard fees. 25 mi E on NC 41 to Elizabethtown, then 4 mi N on NC 242. Phone 910/588-4550.

One-room schoolhouse. Restored early American furnished classroom. (Mon-Fri; closed hols) **Free.**

Annual Event

Scottish Highland Games. Celebration of Scottish heritage with music; dancing; competitions; childrens events. Phone 910/843-5000. Early Oct.

Seasonal Event

Strike at the Wind. 13 mi W of I-95, at Lakeside Amphitheater on grounds of North Carolina Indian Cultural Center. Outdoor drama about folk hero Henry Berry Lowrie & the Lumbee Native Americans of Robeson County, NC. Thurs-Sat. Phone 910/671-3088. Early July-Aug.

Motels

★ ★ **COMFORT SUITES.** 215 Wintergreen Dr. 910/739-8800; FAX 910/739-0027. 93 suites, 4 story. Suites $65-$85; each addl $5; under 18 free. Crib free. TV; cable (premium). Pool; whirlpool. Complimentary continental bkfst. Restaurant nearby. Ck-out 11 am. Coin Indry. Meeting rms. Business servs avail. In-rm modem link. Exercise equipt; weight machine, bicycles, sauna. Health club privileges. Refrigerators. Cr cds: A, C, D, DS, ER, JCB, MC, V.

✔ ★ **FAIRFIELD INN BY MARRIOTT.** 3361 Lackey St. 910/739-8444; FAX 910/739-8466. 105 rms, 3 story. May-Sept: S, D $39.95-$59.95; each addl $10; suites $59-$99; lower rates rest of yr. Crib free. TV; cable (premium). Pool. Complimentary continental bkfst. Restaurant adj 6 am-10 pm. Ck-out noon. Business servs avail. Some refrigerators. Cr cds: A, C, D, DS, MC, V.

★ ★ **HAMPTON INN.** 201 Wintergreen Dr. 910/738-3332; FAX 910/739-8671. 68 rms, 2 story. S $55-$59; D $59-$65; suites $75-$85. Crib free. TV; cable (premium), VCR avail. Pool. Complimentary continental bkfst. Restaurant adj open 24 hrs. Ck-out 11 am. Meeting rms. Business servs avail. Coin Indry. Exercise equipt; weight machine, treadmill. Refrigerators. Cr cds: A, C, D, DS, MC, V.

★ ★ **HOLIDAY INN.** 5201 Fayetteville Rd. 910/671-1166. 108 rms, 2 story. S $58; D $64; each addl $6; under 18 free. Crib free. Pet accepted. TV; cable (premium). Pool. Restaurant. Rm serv. Ck-out noon. Meeting rms. Business servs avail. In-rm modem link. Valet serv. Airport transportation. Health club privileges. Cr cds: A, C, D, DS, MC, V.

✔ ★ **QUALITY INN.** 3608 Kahn Dr. 910/738-8261; FAX 910/671-9075. 120 rms, 2 story. Late April-mid-Sept: S $45-$51; D $51-$57; suites $65-$71; under 17 free; higher rates special events; lower rates rest of yr. Crib free. TV; cable. Pool; sauna. Complimentary continental bkfst. Bar 5 pm-midnight. Ck-out noon. Meeting rms. Business servs avail. In-rm modem link. Some refrigerators. Cr cds: A, C, D, ER, MC, V.

Restaurant

★ ★ **JOHN'S.** 4880 Kahn Dr. 910/738-4709. Hrs: 5:30-10 pm. Closed Sun & Mon; major hols. Res accepted. Continental menu. Wine, beer. Semi-a la carte: dinner $9.95-$22.95. Specializes in beef, seafood, prime rib. Cr cds: A, C, D, DS, MC, V.

Maggie Valley (B-2)

(See also Asheville, Cherokee, Waynesville)

Pop 185 **Elev** 3,020 ft **Area code** 704 **Zip** 28751

Information Chamber of Commerce, 2487 Soco Rd, PO Box 87; 704/926-1686 or 800/785-8259.

In 1909, Henry Setzer decided the expanding community of Plott needed a post office. He submitted the names of his three daughters to the Postmaster General, who selected Maggie, then age 14. Lying in the shadow of the Great Smoky Mountains National Park (see), the town is four miles from the Soco Gap entrance to the Blue Ridge Parkway and has become a year-round resort area.

What to See and Do

Cataloochee Ski Area. Double chairlift, T-bar, rope tow; patrol, school, rentals; snowmaking; half-day and twilight rates; cafeteria, bar. Longest run 5,400 ft; vertical drop 740 ft. (Dec-mid-Mar, daily) 4 mi N via US 19 to Fie Top Rd. Phone 704/926-0285 or 800/768-0285. ¢¢¢¢¢

Ghost Town in the Sky. Chairlift, incline railway or shuttle to top of mountain; shows, rides, gun fights, shops; food. (Early May-late Oct, daily) On US 19. Phone 704/926-1140 or 800/GHOSTOWN. ¢¢¢¢¢

Soco Gardens Zoo. A 2½-acre zoo with more than 25 different species of animals, including exotic birds, alligators, bears, snow leopards, monkeys, jaguar and wallabies. Reptile house; poisonous and non-poisonous snake shows. Guided tours. Gift shop. (May-Oct, daily) 3578 Soco Rd. Phone 704/926-1746. ¢¢

Stompin Ground. Bluegrass and country music; clogging; exhibition dancers; square dancing (audience participation). (May-Oct, nightly) 3116 Soco Rd. Phone 704/926-1288. ¢¢¢

Annual Event

International Folk Festival. Premier folk groups from over ten countries demonstrate their cultural heritage through lively music and costumed dance. Phone 704/452-2997. 11 days late July.

Motels

★ ★ **BEST WESTERN MOUNTAINBROOK INN.** *3811 Soco Rd, on US 19.* 704/926-3962; FAX 704/926-2947. 48 rms, 2 story. May-Oct: S, D $49-$99; each addl $8; under 12 free; ski plans; higher rates special events; lower rates rest of yr. Crib free. TV; cable (premium). Pool; whirlpool. Complimentary continental bkfst. Restaurant adj 7:30 am-8 pm. Ck-out 11 am. Meeting rms. Business servs avail. Sundries. 18-hole golf privileges, greens fee $45, putting green, driving range. Refrigerators, microwaves. Picnic tables. Cr cds: A, C, D, DS, MC, V.

⊡ ⋈ ≋ ≈ ⚲ SC

★ **CARDINAL INN.** *3735 Soco Rd, on US 19.* 704/926-0422; FAX 704/926-2570; res: 800/826-0422. E-mail berg@primeline.com. 8 rms, 2 kit. units. July-Oct: S, D $30-$70; each addl $5; kits. $40-$80; under 6 free; wkly rates; 2-day min hols; higher rates special events. Crib free. TV; cable (premium), VCR avail. Complimentary coffee in lobby. Restaurant nearby. Ck-out 11 am. Picnic tables. Cr cds: A, DS, MC, V.

⊡ ≈ ⚲

★ ★ **COMFORT INN.** *3282 Soco Rd, on US 19.* 704/926-9106; FAX 704/926-9106. 68 rms, 2 story. June-Oct: S $55-$99; D $65-$99; each addl $10; under 18 free; lower rates rest of yr. Crib free. TV; cable (premium). Pool. Continental bkfst. Complimentary coffee. Restaurant opp 7 am-10 pm. Ck-out 11 am. Whirlpool in some suites. Cr cds: A, C, D, DS, ER, JCB, MC, V.

⊡ ≋ ≈ ⚲ SC

★ **JOHNATHAN CREEK INN.** *1314 Soco Rd, on US 19.* 704/926-1232; res: 800/577-7812; FAX 704/926-9751. 42 rms, 2 story. Late May-early Sept, Oct: S, D $65-$109; each addl $8; under 16 free; higher rates: Memorial Day, July 4, Labor Day; lower rates rest of yr. Crib free. TV; cable. Pool. Coffee in rms. Restaurant opp 7 am-noon. Ck-out 11 am. Refrigerators; some in-rm whirlpools; microwaves avail. Some balconies. Cr cds: A, DS, MC, V.

⊡ ≈ ≋ ≈ ⚲ SC

★ **RIVERLET.** *4102 Soco Rd (US 19), 4½ mi W on US 19.* 704/926-1900; res: 800/691-9952; FAX 704/926-0491. 21 rms. July-Labor Day & Oct: S, D $25-$90; lower rates rest of yr. Crib free. TV; cable (premium). Pool. Ck-out 11 am. Overlooks 2 streams. Cr cds: DS, MC, V.

≈ ≋ ⚲ SC

★ **ROCKY WATERS.** *4898 Soco Rd, 1½ mi W on US 19, 3 mi E of Blue Ridge Pkwy, Soco exit.* 704/926-1585. 32 rms, 2 kits. Mid-June-Labor Day, Oct: S $50; D $65; kit. units $75; lower rates May-mid-June, after Labor Day-Sept. Closed rest of yr. Crib free. TV; cable. Heated pool; wading pool. Playground. Complimentary coffee. Restaurant nearby. Ck-out 11 am. Lawn games. Some refrigerators. Picnic tables, grill. Rear porches overlook mountain brook. Cr cds: A, DS, MC, V.

≈ ≋ ⚲ SC

★ **STONY CREEK.** *4494 Soco Rd.* 704/926-1996. 20 rms, 1-2 story. June-Oct: S $40-$80; D $50-$80; each addl $5; lower rates rest of yr. Crib free. TV; cable (premium). Complimentary coffee in lobby. Restaurant nearby. Ck-out 11 am. Some refrigerators. Picnic tables. Stream runs through back of property. Cr cds: MC, V.

⊡ ≈ ≋ ⚲

Guest Ranch

★ ★ **CATALOOCHEE RANCH.** *119 Ranch Dr, 3 mi NE of US 19.* 704/926-1401; FAX 704/926-9249; res: 800/868-1401. 15 rms in two 2-story lodges, 11 cabins, 2 suites. No A/C. MAP, July, Aug, Oct & Dec: S $125-$140; D $130-$250; each addl $55-$60; suites, kit. cottages $190-$210; lower rates rest of yr. Crib free. Serv charge 17%. Supervised child's activities (June-Aug); ages 6-16. Box lunches, cookouts. Beer, wine, set-ups. Ck-out 11 am, ck-in 3 pm. Business servs avail. Tennis. Downhill ski 1 mi. Whirlpool. Lawn games. Card rm. Mountain music entertainment. Fireplace in lobby, cottages, some rms. 5,000-ft elevation. 1,000-acre

working ranch; Appalachian stone barn (1870) remodeled to ranch house. Cr cds: A, MC, V.

⊡ ➤ ⚲ ⋈ ≈ ⚲ ⚲

Restaurant

★ ★ **J ARTHUR'S.** *801 Soco Rd, on US 19S.* 704/926-1817. Hrs: 5-9:30 pm. Closed Thanksgiving, Dec 25. Bar. Semi-a la carte: dinner $9.25-$24.95. Child's meals. Specializes in steak, fresh seafood. Own desserts. Loft dining area. Cr cds: A, D, MC, V.

⊡

Manteo (A-10)

(See also Kill Devil Hills, Nags Head)

Pop 991 **Elev** 5 ft **Area code** 919 **Zip** 27954 **E-mail** dctb-info@outer-banks.com **Web** www.outer-banks.com/visitor-info/
Information Dare County Tourist Bureau, 704 US 64/264, PO Box 399; 919/473-2138 or 800/446-6262.

Fishing in the waters off Manteo is excellent. A large sport fishing fleet is available for booking at Oregon Inlet as well as on Roanoke Island.

What to See and Do

Elizabeth II **State Historic Site.** Representative 16th-century sailing vessel similiar to those that brought the first English colonists to the New World more than 400 yrs ago. Living history interpretation (summer). Visitor center with exhibits and audiovisual program. (Apr-Oct, daily; rest of yr, daily exc Mon; closed some major hols) Manteo waterfront. Phone 919/473-1144. ¢¢

Elizabethan Gardens. These 10½ acres include Great Lawn, Sunken Garden, Queen's Rose Garden, herb garden, 16th-century gazebo with thatched roof, ancient garden statuary. Plants bloom all year: spring peak (mid-Apr); summer peak (mid-July); fall peak (mid-Oct); and winter peak (mid-Feb). Gate House Reception Center displays period furniture, English portraits, coat of arms. (Daily; closed Jan 1, Dec 25) 3 mi N on US 64/264, on Roanoke Island. Phone 919/473-3234. ¢¢

Fort Raleigh National Historic Site (see). 3 mi N via US 64.

North Carolina Aquarium on Roanoke Island. Aquarium and marine-oriented educational and research facility. Public aquaria and exhibits, films and educational programs. (Daily; closed Jan 1, Thanksgiving, Dec 25) 3 mi N via US 64/264, Airport Rd exit. Phone 919/473-3493. ¢¢

Seasonal Event

The Lost Colony. Drama by Paul Green (see FORT RALEIGH NATIONAL HISTORIC SITE).

Inn

★ ★ ★ **TRANQUIL HOUSE.** *Queen Elizabeth St.* 919/473-1404; FAX 919/473-1526; res: 800/458-7069. 25 rms, 3 story. Memorial Day-Labor Day: S, D $129-$169; suites $169; wkly rates; lower rates rest of yr. Crib $10. TV; cable (premium). Complimentary continental bkfst. Restaurant 5-10 pm. Ck-out 11 am, ck-in 3 pm. Business servs avail. Library. Built in style of a 19th-century Outer Banks inn; cypress woodwork, beveled glass doors, observation tower. On bay; overlooks marina. Cr cds: A, DS, MC, V.

⊡ ≈ ⋈ SC

Restaurants

✔★ **CLARA'S SEAFOOD GRILL.** *Sir Walter Raleigh St, on the waterfront.* 919/473-1727; FAX 919/473-1723. Hrs: 11:30 am-9:30 pm. Closed Thanksgiving, Dec 25; also Jan. Bar. Semi-a la carte: lunch, dinner $3.95-$17.95. Child's meals. Specializes in fresh seafood, beef. 3 dining rms with view of bay. Art-deco decor. Cr cds: A, DS, MC, V.

★★ **QUEEN ANNE'S REVENGE.** *(1064 Old Warf Rd, Wanchese 27981) S on NC 345.* 919/473-5466. Hrs: 5-9 pm. Closed Tues; Thanksgiving, Dec 24-25. Wine, beer. Semi-a la carte: dinner $13-$25. Child's meals. Specializes in homemade pasta, fresh seafood. Artwork. Cr cds: A, C, D, DS, MC, V.

Marion (B-3)

(For accommodations see Little Switzerland, Morganton)

Founded 1843 **Pop** 4,765 **Elev** 1,395 ft **Area code** 704 **Zip** 28752

Permits for the Linville Gorge Wilderness of the Pisgah National Forest (see BREVARD) can be obtained at the Grandfather Ranger District Office (Rte 1 Box 110A; 704/652-2144), located here.

What to See and Do

Linville Caverns. Beneath Humpback Mountain. 1/2-hr guided tours. Gift shop. (Mar-Nov, daily; rest of yr, wkends only) 17 mi N on US 221. Phone 704/756-4171. ¢¢

Morehead City (C-9)

(See also Beaufort)

Founded 1857 **Pop** 6,046 **Elev** 16 ft **Area code** 919 **Zip** 28557 **E-mail** cctdb@bmd.clis.com **Web** www.NCcoast.com

Information Carteret County Tourism Development Bureau, PO Box 1406; 919/726-8148 or 800/SUNNY-NC.

Just across the Intracoastal Waterway from Beaufort, Morehead City is the largest town in Carteret County and a year-round resort town. It is involved in both sport and commercial fishing. The port accommodates oceangoing vessels and charter boats.

What to See and Do

Carteret County Museum. Paintings and artifacts from the 19th century. (Tues-Sat) 100 Wallace Rd. Phone 919/247-7533. **Free.**

Fishing. Onshore and offshore; charter boats available. Gulfstream fishing for marlin, amberjack, dolphin, mackerel, bluefish.

Fort Macon State Park. This restored fort, built in 1834, was originally used as a harbor defense. Beach (lifeguards in summer), bathhouse (fee); surf fishing; hiking, nature trails. Museum; interpretive program (summer); battle reenactments. Snack bar. 2 mi E of Atlantic Beach, on Bogue Banks. Phone 919/726-3775. **Free.**

Town of Atlantic Beach. Swimming, fishing, boating; boardwalk. Across the bridge from Morehead.

Annual Events

Big Rock Blue Marlin Tournament. Largest tournament of its kind on the East Coast. Fishing for blue marlin; cash awards; registration required. Phone 919/247-3575. Six days early June.

Atlantic Beach King Mackerel Tournament. Phone 919/247-2334. Mid-Sept.

North Carolina Seafood Festival. Seafood, arts and crafts, music. Phone 919/726-NCSF. First wkend Oct.

Motels

★★ **BEST WESTERN BUCCANEER.** *2806 Arendell St.* 919/726-3115; FAX 919/726-3864; res: 800/682-4982. 91 rms, 2 story. June-Aug: S, D $59-$82; each addl $5; under 18 free; lower rates rest of yr. Crib $5. TV; cable (premium). Pool. Complimentary full bkfst. Restaurant adj 6 am-10 pm. Ck-out noon. Meeting rms. Business center. Some in-rm whirlpools. Cr cds: A, C, D, DS, MC, V.

✔★★ **COMFORT INN.** *3100 Arendell.* 919/247-3434; FAX 919/247-4411. 100 rms, 2 story. Apr-Aug: S $45-$90; D $50-$90; each addl $5; under 18 free; lower rates rest of yr. Crib $5. TV; cable (premium), VCR avail. Pool. Complimentary continental bkfst. Restaurant adj 6 am-11 pm. Ck-out 11 am. Meeting rm. Sundries. Some refrigerators. Cr cds: A, C, D, DS, ER, JCB, MC, V.

★ **DAYS INN.** *(602 W Fort Macon Rd, Atlantic Beach 28512) S on Atlantic Beach Bridge, then 1/2 mi W on Fort Macon Rd (NC 58).* 919/247-6400; FAX 919/247-2264. 90 rms, 2 story. May-Sept: S, D $84-$121; under 12 free; fishing plans; lower rates rest of yr. Crib free. TV; cable. Pool. Complimentary continental bkfst. Restaurant nearby. Ck-out noon. Coin lndry. Business servs avail. In-rm modem link. Refrigerators. Balconies. Picnic tables. Ocean nearby. Cr cds: A, C, D, DS, MC, V.

✔★ **ECONO LODGE CRYSTAL COAST.** *3410 Bridges St, 1 blk off US 70.* 919/247-2940; FAX 919/247-4911. 56 rms, 2 story. June-Aug: S, D $48-$85; each addl $5; under 19 free; wkly rates; lower rates rest of yr. Crib $5. TV; cable (premium). Pool; wading pool. Complimentary continental bkfst. Restaurant nearby. Ck-out 11 am. Meeting rms. Business servs avail. In-rm modem link. Cr cds: A, C, D, DS, MC, V.

★★ **HAMPTON INN.** *4035 Arendell St.* 919/240-2300; FAX 919/240-2311. 120 rms, 4 story. Memorial Day-Labor Day: S, D $70-$100; suites $100-$115; under 18 free; higher rates wkends; lower rates rest of yr. Crib free. TV; cable (premium). Pool. Complimentary continental bkfst. Restaurant nearby. Ck-out 11 am. Meeting rms. Business servs avail. In-rm modem link. Cr cds: A, C, D, DS, MC, V.

✔★ **HOLLOWELL'S.** *(108 E Fort Macon Rd, Atlantic Beach 28512) S on US 70, then W on NC 58.* 919/726-5227. 29 rms, 1-2 story, 18 kits. June-Aug: S, D $40-$60; kit. cottages $85; under 19 free; lower rates Apr-June & Sept-Oct. Closed rest of yr. Crib free. TV; cable (premium). Pool. Restaurant adj 6 am-10 pm. Ck-out noon. On ocean, swimming beach. Cr cds: DS, MC, V.

★ **SEAHAWK MOTOR LODGE.** *(NC 58N, Atlantic Beach 28512) S on US 70, then W on NC 58.* 919/726-4146; res: 800/682-6898. 36 rms, 2 story. June-Labor Day: S, D $90-$100; kit. cottages $1,700/wk; under 16 free; 3-day min hol wkends; lower rates rest of yr. TV; cable (premium). Pool. Restaurant 7 am-2 pm. Rm serv. Ck-out 11 am. Refrigerators. Some balconies, patios. On ocean, swimming beach. Cr cds: MC, V.

★ **WINDJAMMER INN.** *(Atlantic Beach 28512) S on US 70, then 3 mi W on NC 58. 919/247-7123; FAX 919/247-0133; res: 800/233-6466.* 45 rms, 5 story. May-Sept: S, D $87-$112; under 12 free; wkly rates; lower rates rest of yr. Crib free. TV; cable (premium). Pool. Complimentary coffee in lobby. Restaurant nearby. Ck-out 11 am. Bathrm phones, refrigerators. Balconies. On beach. Cr cds: A, MC, V.

Motor Hotel

★ ★ **HOLIDAY INN.** *(Salter Path Rd, Atlantic Beach 28512) 3 mi W on NC 58. 919/726-2544; FAX 919/726-6570.* 114 rms, 5 story. June-Aug: S, D $89-$135; each addl $10; under 18 free; golf plans; lower rates rest of yr. Crib free. TV; cable (premium). Pool; wading pool. Restaurant 7 am-1 pm, 5:30-9 pm. Rm serv. Bar 5-10 pm. Ck-out 11 am. Meeting rms. Business servs avail. In-rm modem link. Tennis privileges. Golf privileges. Private patios, balconies. Picnic tables. On beach. Cr cds: A, C, D, DS, JCB, MC, V.

Hotel

★ ★ ★ **SHERATON RESORT & CONFERENCE CENTER.** *(2717 W Fort Macon Rd, Atlantic Beach 28512) 3 mi W on NC 58. 919/240-1155; FAX 919/240-1452.* 200 rms, 9 story. Mid-May-Labor Day: S, D $135-$165; each addl $15; suites $210; under 18 free; lower rates rest of yr. Crib free. TV; cable (premium). Indoor/outdoor pool; whirlpool, poolside serv. Supervised child's activities (Memorial Day-Labor Day). Complimentary coffee in rms. Restaurant 7 am-2 pm, 5-10 pm. Bar 5 pm-2 am; entertainment. Ck-out noon. Meeting rms. Business servs avail. Gift shop. Exercise equipt; weight machine, bicycles. Refrigerators. Balconies. On ocean. Cr cds: A, C, D, DS, MC, V.

Inns

★ ★ **EMERALD ISLE.** *(502 Ocean Dr, Emerald Isle 28594) 13 mi S US 58. 919/354-3222.* 5 rms, 2 share bath, 2 story. Memorial Day-Labor Day: S, D $75-$95; each addl $15; suites $110-$115; under 6 free. Complimentary full bkfst. Restaurant nearby. Ck-out 11 am, ck-in 3 pm. Luggage handling. On Bogue Sound. Totally nonsmoking. No cr cds accepted.

★ ★ **HARBORLIGHT GUESTHOUSE.** *(332 Live Oak Dr, Cape Carteret 28584) 20 mi S on NC 24/58. 919/393-6868; res: 800/624-8439.* 9 rms, 3 story. No rm phone. Apr-Oct: S, D $75-$90; suites $110-$175; lower rates rest of yr. Children over 16 yrs only. TV; cable. Complimentary full bkfst. Restaurant nearby. Ck-out 11 am, ck-in 3 pm. Luggage handling. Golf privileges. Tennis privileges. Some refrigerators. Some balconies. Overlooks Bogue Sound. Totally nonsmoking. Cr cds: A, MC, V.

Restaurants

★ ★ **ANCHOR INN.** *N 28th St. 919/726-2156.* Hrs: 6-11 am, 5-10 pm; Sat 6 am-noon, 5-11 pm. Closed Dec 24-25. Res accepted. Bar 5-11 pm; Fri, Sat to midnight. Semi-a la carte: bkfst $2-$6, dinner $8.95-$17.95. Child's meals. Specializes in Black Angus beef, fresh local sea-

food, chicken. Rattan furniture, ceiling fans, paintings. Cr cds: A, DS, MC, V.

★ **CAPTAIN BILL'S WATERFRONT.** *701 Evans St. 919/726-2166.* Hrs: 11 am-9 pm; Fri, Sat to 10 pm. Semi-a la carte: lunch $4.50-$17.95, dinner $5.95-$17.95. Child's meals. Specializes in seafood, lemon pie. Gift shop. On Bogue Sound; overlooks fishing fleet. Cr cds: DS, MC, V.

★ **CHARTER.** *405 Evans St. 919/726-9036.* Hrs: 11:30 am-10 pm; winter hrs vary. Closed Thanksgiving, Dec 25. Serv bar. A la carte entrees: lunch $4.95-$7.95, dinner $9.95-$29. Child's meals. Specializes in crab cakes, seafood. Salad bar. Nautical decor. View of waterfront. Cr cds: MC, V.

★ **MRS WILLIS.** *3114 Bridges St. 919/726-3741.* Hrs: 11:30 am-9:30 pm; Fri & Sat to 10 pm. Closed Dec 24-31. Res accepted. Bar 5 pm-2 am. Semi-a la carte: lunch $3-$5, dinner $5-$20. Child's meals. Specializes in fresh seafood, beef. Three dining rms. Family-owned. Cr cds: DS, MC, V.

★ **SANITARY FISH MARKET & RESTAURANT.** *501 Evans St. 919/247-3111.* Hrs: 11 am-8:30 pm; June-Aug to 9 pm. Closed Dec-Jan. Semi-a la carte: lunch $4.50-$21.95, dinner $7.95-$21.95. Child's meals. Specializes in fresh seafood, steaks, and chicken. Overlooks water, fishing fleet, state port. Family-owned. Cr cds: DS, MC, V.

Morganton (B-3)

(See also Little Switzerland, Marion)

Pop 15,085 **Elev** 1,182 ft **Area code** 704 **Zip** 28655
Information Burke County Travel & Tourism, 102 E Union St, Courthouse Sq; 704/433-6793.

This is the seat of Burke County and a manufacturing town producing furniture, textiles, shoes, chemicals, electronics, clothing and other products. In 1893, the county became a haven for the Waldenses, a religious group from the French-Italian Alps that was seeking freedom and space to expand outside their alpine homeland.

What to See and Do

Boating, fishing, swimming. Lake James. 8 mi W on NC 126. **Lake Rhodhiss.** 10 mi E off US 70.

Boat tours. Tours of Lake James on 38-ft pontoon *Harbor Queen*. Departs Mountain Harbor Marina. Phone 704/584-0666. ¢¢¢

Annual Events

Waldensian Celebration of the Glorious Return. On I-40, exit 112 in Valdese. Commemoration of the end of persecution during the reign of Louis XIV; ethnic games, arts and crafts, dances, food. Phone 704/879-2129. Mid-Aug.

Historic Morganton Festival. Downtown. Arts, crafts, ethnic foods, band concert. Phone 704/438-5280. Mid Sept.

Seasonal Event

From This Day Forward. Church St, Valdese.Outdoor historical drama depicting hardships of the Waldenses and their struggle for religious freedom. Phone 800/743-8398. Thurs-Sun evenings. Late July-mid-Aug.

Motels

★ ★ **HOLIDAY INN.** *2400 South Sterling St, 1 mi SE on NC 18, at I-40.* 704/437-0171; FAX 704/437-0171, ext. 297. 135 rms, 2 story. S, D $50-$69; each addl $7; under 19 free. Crib free. Pet accepted. TV; cable (premium). Pool. Restaurant 6 am-2 pm, 5-10 pm. Rm serv. Bar 5 pm-midnight, Sun from 6 pm. Ck-out noon. Meeting rms. Business servs avail. In-rm modem link. Valet serv. Cr cds: A, C, D, DS, JCB, MC, V.

D ✔ ⩧ ⋈ ⚞ SC

✔★ **SLEEP INN.** *2400 A South Sterling St.* 704/433-9000; FAX 704/433-9000, ext. 310. 61 rms, shower only, 2 story. S $39; D $49-$69; each addl $5; under 19 free; higher rates wknds. Crib free. TV; cable (premium). Swimming privileges. Complimentary coffee in lobby. Restaurant adj 6 am-10 pm. Ck-out noon. Business center. In-rm modem link. Valet serv. Refrigerators avail. Cr cds: A, C, D, DS, JCB, MC, V.

D ⋈ ⚞ SC ⋔ ⚷

Inn

✔★ **RICHMOND INN.** *(101 Pine Ave, Spruce Pine 28777) E on US 19.* 704/765-6993. 7 rms, 2 story. No A/C. No rm phone. Apr-Dec: S $45-$60; D $55-70; each addl $10; under 10 free; lower rates rest of yr. Complimentary full bkfst. Restaurant nearby. Ck-out 11 am, ck-in 4 pm. Luggage handling. Totally nonsmoking. Cr cds: DS, MC, V.

⋈ ⚞ SC

Nags Head (Outer Banks) (A-10)

(See also Kill Devil Hills, Manteo)

Pop 1,838 **Elev** 10 ft **Area code** 919 **Zip** 27959 **E-mail** dctd-info@outer-banks.com **Web** www.outer-banks.com/visitor-info/
Information Dare County Tourist Bureau, 704 US 64/264, PO Box 399, Manteo 27954; 919/473-2138 or 800/446-6262.

This is a year-round fishing and beachcombing town on the Outer Banks (see), just south of Kill Devil Hills. There are fishing piers and boats for rent. Swimming is good in summer. A museum is located at Jockey's Ridge State Park, which boasts one of the largest sand dunes on the East Coast.

The soft sand dunes and Atlantic breezes make this a popular area for hang gliding. Offshore, partly buried in the drifting sand, are many wrecks of both old sailing ships and more modern vessels.

Cape Hatteras National Seashore (see) is south of Nags Head.

Annual Events

Gliding Spectacular. Hang gliding competition, novice through advanced. Spectacular flying and fun events. Phone 919/441-4124. 2nd wkend May.

Rogallo Kite Festival. Competition for homebuilt kites; stunt kite performances, demonstrations; kite auction. Phone 919/441-4124. 1st wkend June.

Motels

✔★ **BEACON MOTOR LODGE.** *2617 S Virginia Dare Trail, on the oceanfront at milepost 11.* 919/441-5501; FAX 919/441-2178; res: 800/441-4804. 47 rms, 1-2 story, 20 kits. Late May-early Sept: S, D $80-$100; each addl $5; suites $700-$800/wk; kit. units $625/wk; kit. cottages $685-$1,000/wk; higher rates hols, wkends; lower rates mid-Mar-late May, early Sept-Oct. Closed rest of yr. Crib $3. TV; cable (premium). Pool; 2 wading pools. Playground. Restaurant nearby. Ck-out 11 am. Coin lndry. Business servs avail. In-rm modem link. Refrigerators. Picnic tables, grill. Sun deck. Beach. Cr cds: A, D, DS, MC, V.

✔ ⩧ ⋈ ⚞

★ **BLUE HERON.** *6811 Virginia Dare Trail.* 919/441-7447. 30 rms, 3 story, 11 kits. No elvtr. June-Labor Day: D $88-$93; each addl $5; kit. units $93; varied lower rates rest of yr. Crib $2. TV; cable. 2 pools, 1 indoor; whirlpool. Complimentary coffee in rms. Restaurant nearby. Ck-out 11 am. Refrigerators. Porches overlook private beach. Cr cds: MC, V.

D ✔ ⩧ ⚞

★ **COMFORT INN.** *8031 Old Oregon Inlet Rd.* 919/441-6315. 105 rms, 7 story. S, D $118-$165; each addl $10; under 17 free; higher rates hols (3-day min). Crib free. TV; cable. Pool; wading pool. Complimentary continental bkfst. Restaurant nearby. Bar. Ck-out 11 am. Meeting rms. Business servs avail. Some refrigerators. Balconies. Swimming beach. Cr cds: A, D, DS, MC, V.

D ✔ ⩧ ⋈ ⚞ SC

✔★ ★ **ISLANDER.** *7001 Virginia Dare Trail, on US 158 Business, near milepost 16.* 919/441-6229. 24 rms, 3 story, 6 kits. No elvtr. Mid-June-early Sept: D, kit. units $103; each addl $10; lower rates Apr-mid-June, early Sept-Oct. Closed rest of yr. TV; cable. Pool. Restaurant nearby. Ck-out 11 am. Coin lndry. Refrigerators. Private patios, balconies. Picnic table, grill. On beach. Cr cds: A, MC, V.

✔ ⩧

★ ★ **QUALITY INN SEA OATEL.** *7123 S Virginia Dare Trail, 3½ mi S on US 158 Business at milepost 16.5.* 919/441-7191; FAX 919/441-1961. 111 rms, 1-3 story. Memorial Day-Labor Day: S, D $92-$140; each addl $10; lower rates rest of yr. Crib free. TV; cable (premium), VCR avail (movies). Pool; wading pool. Ck-out 11 am. Business servs avail. Most rms with balcony overlook ocean. Some rms across street. Cr cds: A, C, D, DS, ER, JCB, MC, V.

✔ ⩧ ⋈ ⚞ SC

★ ★ **SEA FOAM.** *7111 S Virginia Dare Trail.* 919/441-7320; FAX 919/441-7324. 51 rms, 2 story, 18 kits., two 2-bedrm kit. cottages, 1 apt. Late May-early Sept: D $74-$90; each addl $5; kit. units $510-$605/wk; kit. cottages $695/wk; apt. $660/wk; under 12 free; lower rates Mar-late May, early Sept-mid-Dec. Closed rest of yr. Crib $5. TV; cable (premium). Pool. Playground. Restaurant adj 5:30 am-10 pm. Ck-out 11 am. Airport transportation. Lawn games. Refrigerators. Some private patios, balconies. Beach. Cr cds: A, MC, V.

✔ ⩧ ⚞

★ ★ **SURF SIDE.** *6701 S Virginia Dare Trail, milepost 16.* 919/441-2105; FAX 919/441-2456; res: 800/552-7873. 76 rms, 5 story, 14 suites. Mid-June-early Sept: S, D $98-$184; each addl $5; suites, kit. units $169-$184; under 12 free; higher rates hol wkends; lower rates rest of yr. Crib $5. TV; cable. 2 pools, 1 indoor; whirlpool. Complimentary continental bkfst. Restaurant nearby. Ck-out 11 am. Coin lndry. Meeting rms. Business servs avail. Rec rm. Refrigerators. Balconies. On beach. Cr cds: A, DS, MC, V.

D ✔ ⩧ ⋔ ⋈ ⚞

Motor Hotel

★ ★ **NAGS HEAD INN.** *4071 S Virginia Dare Tr.* 919/441-0454; FAX 919/441-0454; res: 800/327-8881. 100 rms, 5 story. Late May-Labor

Day: S, D $99-$175; each addl $10; suites $199; wkly rates; lower rates rest of yr. Crib $5. TV; cable (premium). Indoor/outdoor pool; whirlpool. Complimentary coffee in lobby. Restaurant nearby. Ck-out 11 am. Business servs avail. In-rm modem link. Refrigerators. Balconies. On ocean, swimming beach. Cr cds: A, DS, MC, V.

Inn

★ ★ ★ **FIRST COLONY.** 6720 S Virginia Dare Trail. 919/441-2343; FAX 919/441-9234; res: 800/368-9390. 26 rms, 3 story, 4 kits. Memorial Day-Labor Day: S, D $145-$250; each addl $30; lower rates rest of yr. Crib free. TV; cable, VCR avail (free movies). Pool. Complimentary continental bkfst; afternoon refreshments. Complimentary coffee in rms. Restaurant nearby. Ck-out 11 am, ck-in 3 pm. Business servs avail. In-rm modem link. Concierge. Picnic tables, grills. Two-story veranda; overlooks ocean. On 5 acres of landscaped grounds. Totally non-smoking. Cr cds: A, DS, MC, V.

Restaurants

★ ★ **KELLY'S.** 2316 S Croatan Hwy. 919/441-4116. Hrs: 5-10 pm. Closed Dec 24 & 25. Bar to 2 am. Semi-a la carte: dinner $10-$20. Early bird dinners. Child's meals. Specializes in seafood, prime rib. Several distinct dining areas. Nautical decor. Cr cds: A, C, D, DS, MC, V.

★ ★ **OWENS'.** 7114 S Virginia Dare Trail. 919/441-7309. Hrs: 5-10 pm. Closed Jan-mid-Feb. Bar to midnight. Semi-a la carte: dinner $12.95-$16.95. Child's meals. Specializes in crab cakes, grilled fish, whole Maine lobster. Parking. Historic artifacts of US Lifesaving Service (forerunner of US Coast Guard) on display; uniforms, log books, photographs. Family-owned. Cr cds: A, C, DS, MC, V.

★ ★ **PENGUIN ISLE.** 6708 S Croatan Hwy (US 158), milepost 16. 919/441-2637. Hrs: 5-10 pm; early-bird dinner to 6 pm. Closed Dec 24-25. Bar 5 pm-midnight. Semi-a la carte: dinner $9.95-$19.95. Child's meals. Specialties: shrimp Aristotle, mesquite-grilled tuna steak. Entertainment Fri, Sat. Nautical decor. View of sound. Cr cds: A, D, DS, MC, V.

★ ★ **WINDMILL POINT.** US 158, at Mile post 16. 919/441-1535. Hrs: 5-10 pm. Res accepted. Bar. Semi-a la carte: dinner $15.95-$18.95. Child's meals. Specializes in seafood, beef, pasta. Features memorabilia of SS United States. Cr cds: A, D, DS, MC, V.

New Bern (B-9)

(See also Kinston)

Settled 1710 **Pop** 17,363 **Elev** 15 ft **Area code** 919 **E-mail** tourism @cravencounty.com

Information Visitor Information Center, 314 Tryon Palace Dr, PO Box 1413, 28560; 919/637-9400 or 800/437-5767.

The first settlers in this, one of North Carolina's earliest towns, were Germans and Swiss seeking political and religious freedom in the New World. The name Bern came from the city in Switzerland. Many Georgian and Federal-style buildings give New Bern an architectural ambiance

unique in North Carolina. Many of these homes can be visited during April and October.

Swimming, boating and freshwater and saltwater fishing can be enjoyed on the Neuse and Trent rivers. A Ranger District office of the Croatan National Forestsis located here.

What to See and Do

Attmore-Oliver House (ca 1790). This house, headquarters for the New Bern Historical Society, exhibits 18th- and 19th-century furnishings and historical objects, including Civil War artifacts, doll collection. (Early Apr-mid-Dec, Tues-Sat; also by appt; closed July 4, Thanksgiving, Dec 25) 510 Pollock St. Phone 919/638-8558. **Free.**

Croatan National Forest. A unique coastal forest (157,724 acres), with many estuaries and waterways; northernmost habitat of the alligator. Pocosins (Native American for "swamp on a hill") have many unusual dwarfed and insect-eating plants. Swimming, boating and fishing in Neuse River; hunting for deer, bear, turkey, quail and migratory waterfowl; picnicking; camping (fee). SE via US 17, 70. For further information contact the Forest Supervisor, 100 Otis St, PO Box 2750, Asheville 28802, phone 704/257-4200; or the District Ranger, 141 E Fisher Ave, 28560, phone 919/638-5628.

New Bern Firemen's Museum. Antique firefighting equipment, relics and pictures, 1917 double-size ladder trucks and engines, 1913 pumper. (Daily; closed some major hols) 410 Hancock St, off US 17, 70 Business. Phone 919/636-4020 or 919/636-4087. ¢

★ **Tryon Palace Historic Sites & Gardens.** Built in 1767-1770 by the Royal Governor, William Tryon, this "most beautiful building in the colonial Americas" burned by accident in 1798 and lay in ruins until rebuilt between 1952-1959. It served as the colonial and first state capitol. Reconstruction, furnishings and 18th-century English gardens are beautiful and authentic. Dramas performed daily during summer. Docent-guided tours (daily; closed Jan 1, Thanksgiving, Dec 24-26). Also self-guided garden tours. 610 Pollock St, S end of George St, 1 blk S of US 17, 70 Business, NC 55.Phone 800/767-1560. Combination ticket includes admission to all historic sites and gardens that are part of the Tryon Palace. Combination ticket ¢¢¢¢ On grounds are

Dixon-Stevenson House (ca 1830). Early Federal architecture reflects maritime history of the area in its interior woodwork and widow's walk. Furnished in Federal and Empire antiques.

John Wright Stanly House (ca 1780). Georgian-style house, furnished with 18th-century American antiques. Elegant interior woodwork. Formal gardens typical of the period.

New Bern Academy (ca 1810). 4 blks from Tryon Palace complex, in the historic residential district. Major surviving landmark of an educational institution founded in the 1760s, the Academy is restored as a self-guided museum of New Bern Civil War history, early education and local architecture. Phone 919/514-4874.

Motels

★ ★ **COMFORT INN SUITES & MARINA.** 218 Front St (28560). 919/636-0022; FAX 919/636-0051. 100 rms, 4 story. Apr-Oct: S $60-$79; D $64-$89; under 18 free; lower rates rest of yr. Crib free. TV; cable (premium), VCR avail. Pool; whirlpool. Complimentary continental bkfst. Restaurant nearby. Ck-out noon. Meeting rms. Business servs avail. Tennis privileges. Exercise equipt; bicycles, weight machine. Refrigerators. Cr cds: A, C, D, DS, ER, JCB, MC, V.

✔ ★ ★ **HAMPTON INN.** 200 Hotel Dr (28562). 919/637-2111; FAX 919/637-2000; res: 800/448-8288. 101 rms, 4 story. S $54-$61; D $59-$64; under 18 free; higher rates wkends. Crib free. TV; cable (premium). Pool. Complimentary continental bkfst. Restaurant nearby. Ck-out noon. Meeting rms. Business servs avail. In-rm modem link. Exercise equipt; rowers, stair machine. Cr cds: A, C, D, DS, MC, V.

Motor Hotel

★ ★ **RAMADA INN-WATERFRONT & MARINA.** *101 Howell Rd (28562). 919/636-3637; FAX 919/637-5028.* 116 rms, 4 story. S, D $54.99-$59.99; each addl $5; suites $100; under 18 free; wkly rates. Crib free. TV; cable (premium), VCR avail. Pool. Restaurant 6:30-10:30 am, 11 am-2 pm, 5-10 pm. Rm serv. Bar 4 pm-2 am; entertainment. Ck-out noon. Business servs avail. In-rm modem link. Bellhops. Valet serv. Bathrm phones. Refrigerator, whirlpool in suites. Cr cds: A, C, D, DS, ER, JCB, MC, V.

Hotel

★ ★ ★ **SHERATON GRAND.** *1 Bicentennial Park (28560). 919/638-3585; FAX 919/638-8112.* 172 rms, 5 story. S, D $75-$104; each addl $10; suites $150; under 17 free. Crib free. Pet accepted. TV; cable (premium). Bar 10 am-2 am; entertainment Fri, Sat. Ck-out noon. Meeting rms. Business center. In-rm modem link. Free airport transportation. Golf privileges. Exercise equipt; weight machine, bicycle. Balconies. On river; marina facilities. Cr cds: A, C, D, DS, MC, V.

Inns

★ ★ **AERIE.** *509 Pollock St (28562). 919/636-5553; res: 800/849-5553.* 7 rms, 2 story. S $60; D $79-89; each addl $15; under 6 free. TV; cable. Complimentary full bkfst. Ck-out 11 am, ck-in 3 pm. Business servs avail. Airport transportation. Victorian house built in 1882; antiques. One block E of Tryon Palace. Cr cds: A, DS, MC, V.

★ ★ **HARMONY HOUSE.** *215 Pollock St (28560). 919/636-3810; res: 800/636-3113.* 10 rms, 2 story. S $60; D $85-$95; suite $130; each addl $20. TV; cable (premium). Complimentary full bkfst; afternoon refreshments. Ck-out 11 am, ck-in 3 pm. Business servs avail. In-rm modem link. Free airport transportation. Greek-revival house built in 1850; antiques, artwork. Cr cds: A, DS, MC, V.

★ **KINGS ARMS.** *212 Pollock St (28560). 919/638-4409; FAX 919/638-2191; res: 800/872-9306.* 8 rms, 3 story. S, D $55-$85. TV; cable. Complimentary continental bkfst. Rm serv. Ck-out 11 am, ck-in 3 pm. Business servs avail. In-rm modem link. Valet serv. Airport transportation. Tennis privileges. Golf privileges. In restored house built ca 1848; antiques, canopied beds. Cr cds: A, MC, V.

★ **NEW BERNE HOUSE.** *709 Broad St (28560). 919/636-2250; res: 800/842-7688.* 7 rms, 3 story. S $55; D $85. Children over 12 yrs only. TV in sitting rm; cable. Full bkfst. Restaurant nearby. Ck-out 11 am, ck-in 2 pm. Free airport transportation. Colonial-revival house (1923); porch. Totally nonsmoking. Cr cds: A, MC, V.

★ **TAR HEEL INN.** *(508 Church St, Oriental 28571) Approx 25 mi E on NC 55. 919/249-1078.* 8 rms, 2 story. No rm phones. May-Nov: S, D $65-$85; each addl $20; lower rates rest of yr. Crib free. Complimentary full bkfst. Restaurant nearby. Ck-out 11 am, ck-in 4-7 pm. Lawn games. Built in 1890; antiques. Totally nonsmoking. Cr cds: MC, V.

Restaurants

✔★ **FRED & CLAIRE'S.** *247 Craven St. 919/638-5426.* Hrs: 11 am-7 pm; Fri to 8 pm; Sat to 3 pm. Closed Sun; some major hols. Res accepted. Wine, beer. Semi-a la carte: lunch $1.50-$6.25, dinner $4.95-$7.95. Specializes in casserole dishes, quiche, soups. Housed in historic building (1870). Casual dining. No cr cds accepted.

★ ★ ★ **HARVEY MANSION.** *221 Tryon Palace Dr (28560). 919/638-3205.* Hrs: 11:45 am-2:30 pm, 5:30-10 pm; Sun brunch 10 am-2 pm. Closed Mon; Dec 25; also 1st wk of Jan. Res accepted. International menu. Bar. Semi-a la carte: lunch $3.50-$6.95, dinner $12.95-$25.95. Sun brunch $5.95-$10.95. Specializes in seafood, beef, veal. In 18th-century mansion near confluence of Trent & Neuse Rivers. Cr cds: A, C, D, DS, MC, V.

★ ★ ★ **HENDERSON HOUSE.** *216 Pollock St. 919/637-4784.* Hrs: 6-9 pm. Closed Mon, Tues; some hols. Res accepted. Semi-a la carte: dinner $17.95-$26.95. Specializes in veal, Angus beef, seafood. In restored house built in 1790. Totally nonsmoking. Cr cds: A, DS, MC, V.

★ **SCALZO'S.** *415 Broad St (28560). 919/633-9898.* Hrs: 5-10 pm. Closed Sun; Dec 25. Res accepted. Italian menu. Wine, beer. Semi-a la carte: dinner $9.95-$17.95. Child's meals. Specializes in chicken, veal, beef. Three dining areas. Prints, murals of Italian scenes. Cr cds: A, MC, V.

Ocracoke (Outer Banks) (B-10)

(See also Buxton)

Pop 658 (est) **Elev** 6 ft **Area code** 919 **Zip** 27960

Settled in the 17th century, Ocracoke was, according to legend, once used as headquarters by the pirate Blackbeard. On the Outer Banks (see), Ocracoke offers excellent fishing and hunting for wildfowl. The lighthouse, built in 1823, is still in use.

One of the visitor centers for Cape Hatteras National Seashore (see) is here.

What to See and Do

Cedar Island to Ocracoke Ferry Service. (Winter & summer, daily) **Swan Quarter to Ocracoke.** (All yr, daily) Ferries are crowded; there may be a wait. Reservations are recommended; they may be made up to one yr in advance by phone or in person at the ferry terminal: Ocracoke 919/928-3841; Cedar Island 919/225-3551; Swan Quarter 919/926-1111; or phone 800/BY-FERRY. Reservations are void if vehicle is not in loading lane at least 30 min before departure.

Ocracoke to Hatteras Ferry. Northward across Hatteras Inlet.

(For a complete list of ferry schedules and rates, contact the Ferry Division, Department of Transportation, 113 Arendell St, Morehead City 28557; 919/726-6446.)

Motels

★ ★ **ANCHORAGE INN.** *Front St. 919/928-1101; FAX 919/9286322.* 35 rms, 4 story. May-Dec: S, D $59-$99; higher rates special events; lower rates rest of yr. TV; cable (premium). Pool. Complimentary continental bkfst. Restaurant adj 7 am-9:30 pm. Ck-out 11 am. Business servs avail. Balconies. Marina. Cr cds: DS, MC, V.

★ **BLUFF SHOAL.** NC 12. 919/928-4301. 7 rms. Memorial Day-Labor Day: S, D $70-$80, each addl $8; under 12 free; lower rates rest of yr. Crib free. TV; cable (premium). Restaurant opp 6:30 am-9 pm. Ck-out 11 am. Refrigerators. On Silver Lake. Cr cds: DS, MC, V.

[M] [SC]

★ **BOYETTE HOUSE.** NC 12, 1½ blks from harbor in village. 919/928-4261. 22 rms, 3 story, 2 suites. Memorial Day-Labor Day: S, D $60-$100; suites $145-$160; each addl $5; lower rates rest of yr. Crib free. TV, cable (premium). Restaurant adj 7 am-9 pm. Ck-out 11 am. Near beach; swimming. Cr cds: DS, MC, V.

[D] [≈] [M]

✔★ **ISLAND INN.** 100 Lighthouse Rd, on NC 12. 919/928-4351. 35 rms, 2-3 story. No elvtr. Early May-late Sept: D $49-$95; each addl $5; cottages $600/wk; lower rates rest of yr. Crib free. TV; cable (premium). Heated pool. Restaurant 7 am-2 pm, 5-9 pm. Ck-out 11 am. In-room modem link. Free local airport transportation. Private patios. Near beach. Built in 1901; antiques. Cr cds: DS, MC, V.

 [≈] [M]

★ **PONY ISLAND.** ½ mi E on NC 12. 919/928-4411; FAX 919/928-2522. 50 rms, 9 kits. Memorial Day-Labor Day: S, D $73; each addl $5; kit. units $81; cottages $650-$700/wk; lower rates rest of yr. TV; cable (premium). Restaurant adj 7-11 am, 5-9 pm. Pool. Ck-out 11 am. Sundries. Bicycle rentals. Cr cds: DS, MC, V.

[D] [≈] [M] [SC]

Inn

★ **BERKLEY CENTER COUNTRY INN.** on NC 12, near south ferry docks. 919/928-5911. 9 rms in 2 bldgs, 2 story. No rm phones. S, D $70-$85; each addl $20; under 18 free. Closed Nov-Mar. Crib avail. TV in sitting rm; cable (premium). Complimentary continental bkfst. Restaurant nearby. Ck-out 11 am, ck-in 2 pm. Antiques. Library, sitting rm. No cr cds accepted.

[M]

Restaurants

★★ **BACK PORCH.** On NC 12. 919/928-6401. Hrs: 5-9:30 pm. Closed mid Oct-mid Apr. Wine, beer. Semi-a la carte: dinner $7.95-$17.95. Child's meals. Specializes in crab cakes, fresh fish. Porch dining. Cr cds: DS, MC, V.

[D] [⊐]

✔★ **ISLAND INN.** NC 12. 919/928-7821. Hrs: 7 am-2 pm, 5-9 pm. Closed Dec-Feb. Semi-a la carte: bkfst $2.95-$6.95, dinner $8.95-$15.95. Child's meals. Specialties: clam chowder, crab cakes, prime rib. Nautical decor. Cr cds: DS, MC, V.

[D] [⊐]

Outer Banks (A-10 - B-10)

E-mail chamber@outer-banks.com **Web** www.outer-banks.com /chamber
Information Chamber of Commerce, PO Box 1757, Kill Devil Hills 27948; 919/441-8144.

The Outer Banks are a chain of narrow, sandy islands stretching 175 miles from Cape Lookout to Back Bay, Virginia. Parts of the chain are 30 miles from the mainland. Cape Hatteras is about 75 miles from the southern end. The islands may be reached by bridge from Point Harbor and Manteo or by ferry from Cedar Island and Swan Quarter to Ocracoke (see).

The following Outer Banks areas are included in the *Mobil Travel Guide*. For information on any one of them, see the individual alphabetical listing: Buxton, Cape Hatteras National Seashore, Hatteras, Kill Devil Hills, Nags Head, Ocracoke.

Pilot Mountain (A-5)

Pop 1,181 **Elev** 1,152 ft **Area code** 910 **Zip** 27041

What to See and Do

Pilot Mountain State Park. More than 3,700 acres; hard-surfaced road up mountain to parking. Foot trail to base of rocky knob; extensive view. Canoeing and rafting on the Yadkin River. Nature and riding trails. Picnicking. Camping. Standard fees. 4 mi S on US 52. Phone 910/325-2355.

Motel

✔★★ **HOLIDAY INN EXPRESS.** US 52 & NC 268. 910/368-2237; FAX 910/368-1212. 68 rms, 2 story. S $51.95-$56.95; D $56.95-$64.95; each addl $5; under 12 free. Crib free. TV; cable (premium), VCR avail. Pool. Complimentary continental bkfst. Restaurant 6:30 am-9:30 pm. Ck-out 11 am. Meeting rms. Business servs avail. In-rm modem link. Valet serv. Exercise equipt: bicycle, treadmill. Microwaves avail. View of mountain. Cr cds: A, C, D, DS, MC, V.

[D] [≈] [X] [⊐] [M] [SC]

Inn

★★★ **PINE RIDGE INN.** (2893 W Pine St, Mt Airy 27030) NW on US 52 then W on NC 89. 910/789-5034; FAX 910/786-9039. 6 rms, 2 story. S, D $60-$100; each addl $10; cottage $110. Crib $10. TV; cable, VCR avail. Pool. Complimentary full bkfst; afternoon refreshments. Restaurant 7:30-8 am, 11 am-2 pm, 5-9 pm. Ck-out 11 am, ck-in 2 pm. Lawn games. English manor (1949); antique furnishings. Cr cds: A, DS, MC, V.

[≈] [⊐] [M] [SC]

Pinehurst (B-6)

(See also Southern Pines)

Founded 1895 **Pop** 5,103 **Elev** 529 ft **Area code** 910 **Zip** 28374 **E-mail** cvb4golf@mindspring.com **Web** www.sandhills.net
Information Convention & Visitors Bureau, PO Box 2270, Southern Pines 28388; 910/692-3330 or 800/346-5362.

A famous year-round resort village, Pinehurst preserves an era steeped both in tradition and golfing excellence. Its New England style was designed over 100 years ago by the firm of Frederick Law Olmsted, which also designed New York's Central Park and landscaped Asheville's Biltmore Estate. Handsome estates and other residences, mostly styled in Georgian colonial, dot the village. The Pinehurst Resort and Country Club has eight 18-hole golf courses, a 200-acre lake, 24 tennis courts and other recreational facilities that are open to members as well as to guests staying there.

What to See and Do

Sandhills Horticultural Gardens. 25 acres include Ebersole Holly Garden; Rose Garden; Conifer Garden; Hillside Garden with bridges, waterfalls and gazebo; Desmond Native Wetland Trail Garden, a nature conservancy and bird sanctuary; and Sir Walter Raleigh Garden, a one-acre formal English garden. Docent-guided group tours (by appt only). (Daily) 2200 Airport Rd, Sandhills Community College. Phone 910/695-3882. **Free.**

Motel

★ ★ **COMFORT INN.** *9801 US 15/501. 910/215-5500; FAX 910/215-5535.* 80 rms, 2 story. Mid-Feb-Nov: S $78; D $84; each addl $6; suites $118-$125; under 18 free; lower rates rest of yr. Crib free. TV; cable (premium). Pool. Complimentary continental bkfst. Restaurant nearby. Ck-out noon. Meeting rms. Free airport transportation. Exercise equipt; bicycles, weight machine. Some refrigerators. Cr cds: A, D, DS, MC, V.

D ⊗ ✗ 🔥 SC

Inns

★ ★ ★ **HOLLY INN.** *Cherokee Rd. 910/295-2300; FAX 910/295-0988; res: 800/682-6901.* 76 units, 5 story. S, D $139; each addl $20; suites $169; under 10 free. Crib free. TV; cable. Pool. Dining rm 7-10 am, 6-9:30 pm; Fri, Sat to 10 pm. Bar 5 pm-midnight. Ck-out noon, ck-in 3 pm. Business center. Tennis privileges. Golf privileges. Bicycles avail. Antique furnishings. Built in 1895. Cr cds: A, D, MC, V.

D ⊗ 🍴 🏌 ≈ 🔥 SC 🚶 ⛷

★ ★ **MAGNOLIA.** *Jct Magnolia & Chinquapin Rds. 910/295-6900; FAX 910/215-0858; res: 800/526-5562.* 12 rms, 3 story. No rm phones. MAP, Mar-May, Oct-Nov: S $85-$100; D $110-$150; family, wkly rates; golf plan; higher rates PGA tour championship; lower rates rest of yr. Crib free. TV; cable. Pool. Complimentary full bkfst. Dining rm 11:30 am-2 pm, 6-9:30 pm. Ck-out noon, ck-in 2 pm. Business servs avail. Golf privileges. Restored, turn-of-the-century inn; Victorian decor, antiques, veranda. Cr cds: A, MC, V.

🍴 ⛷ ≈ 🔥 🏌

★ **PINE CREST.** *Dogwood Rd. 910/295-6121; FAX 910/295-4880.* 40 rms, 3 story. MAP, Mar-May & early Sept-Nov: S $85-$105; D $140-$180; under 12 free; lower rates rest of yr. Crib free. TV; cable (premium). Pool. Dining rm 7-9 am, 7-9 pm. Ck-out noon, ck-in 2 pm. Tennis privileges. 18-hole golf privileges. Golf decor and artifacts in lobby. Cr cds: A, C, D, DS, MC, V.

🍴 🏌 🔥

Restaurant

★ **COVES.** *At Market Square, across from Holly Inn. 910/295-3400.* Hrs: 11:30 am-10:30 pm. Res accepted. Bar 11:30-2 am. Semi-a la carte: lunch $2.95-$8, dinner $2.95-$20. Specializes in seafood, pasta, veal. Nautical decor. Cr cds: A, MC, V.

D ⟶

Raleigh (B-7)

(See also Chapel Hill, Durham)

Founded 1792 **Pop** 207,951 **Elev** 363 ft **Area code** 919 **E-mail** visit@raleighcvb.org **Web** www.raleighcvb.org

Information Greater Raleigh Convention & Visitors Bureau, 225 Hillsborough St, Suite 400, PO Box 1879, 27602-1879; 919/834-5900 or 800/849-8499.

The capital of North Carolina, Raleigh is also known as a center of education and high-technology research. It still retains the flavor of a relaxed residential town with two centuries of history. Fine residences coexist with apartment houses and modern shopping centers; rural areas with meadows and plowed fields can be found within a few miles.

Named for Sir Walter Raleigh, the town was laid out in 1792, following a resolution by the North Carolina General Assembly that an "unalterable seat of government" should be established within 10 miles of Isaac Hunter's tavern. The founders were able to find a site just four miles from the tavern. The site was laid off in a square. Lots within and just outside the city were sold as residences, which helped finance the capitol building and the governor's residence. Both structures were subsequently destroyed (the capitol by fire in 1831, the governor's residence by Union troops during the Civil War). Their replacements remain standing today. Fortunately, many of the lovely homes and gardens of the antebellum period have survived.

Like much of North Carolina, Raleigh was sprinkled with Union sympathizers until Fort Sumter was fired upon. Lincoln's call for volunteers was regarded as an insult, and North Carolina joined the Confederacy. Raleigh surrendered quietly to General Sherman in April, 1865. During Reconstruction, carpetbaggers and scalawags controlled the Assembly, voted themselves exorbitant salaries, set up a bar in the capitol and left permanent nicks in the capitol steps from the whiskey barrels rolled up for the thirsty legislators.

Located within 15 miles of Raleigh is the Research Triangle Park, a 6,800-acre research and development center with more than 50 companies. Complementing these facilities are the resources of three major universities that form the triangle region—North Carolina State University, Duke University in Durham and the University of North Carolina at Chapel Hill.

What to See and Do

Capital Area Visitor Center. Information center; brochures. Tours may be scheduled to the State Capitol, the North Carolina Executive Mansion, the State Legislative building, historic sites and other attractions. (Daily; closed Jan 1, Thanksgiving, Dec 25 and 26) 301 N Blount St. Phone 919/733-3456. **Free.**

Falls Lake State Recreation Area. Man-made lake built as a reservoir and for flood control. Approx 38,000 acres of land and water offer swimming beach, waterskiing; fishing; boating (ramps). Hiking. Picnicking (shelters), playground. Three state recreation areas in vicinity. 12 mi N via NC 50. Phone 919/676-1027. Per vehicle **¢¢**

Mordecai Historic Park. Preserved plantation home (1785 and 1826) with many original furnishings, noted for its neoclassical architecture; early Raleigh office building, St Mark's chapel, Badger-Iredell Law Office, 1830s herb garden. Also house in which Andrew Johnson, 17th president of the United States, was born. Guided tours. (Mon, Wed-Sun; closed hols) Mimosa St & Wake Forest Rd. Phone 919/834-4844. **¢¢**

North Carolina Museum of Art. European and American painting and sculpture; Egyptian, Greek, Roman, African and pre-Columbian objects; Judaica collection; changing exhibits. Restaurant. (Daily exc Mon; closed some hols) 2110 Blue Ridge Rd. Phone 919/839-6262. **Free.**

North Carolina Museum of History. Four innovative exhibits convey the state's history. Gift shop; auditorium. (Daily exc Mon) Phone 919/715-0200. **Free.**

North Carolina State University Arboretum. Eight acres of gardens featuring more than 5,000 diverse trees and shrubs from around the world. (Daily) 4301 Beryl Rd. Phone 919/515-3132.   **Free.**

Pullen Park. Scenic 72-acre park in the heart of downtown featuring 1911 carousel, train ride, paddle boats, indoor aquatic center, ball fields, tennis courts, playground and picnic shelters. (Daily) 520 Ashe Ave. Phone 919/831-6468. Admission **Free;**   Rides **¢**

State Capitol (1840). A simple, stately Greek-revival style building. Statues of honored sons and daughters decorate the grounds. The old legislative chambers, in use until 1963, have been restored to their 1840s appearance, as have the old state library room and the state geologist's office. (Daily; closed Jan 1, Thanksgiving, late Dec) Capitol Square. Phone 919/733-4994 or 919/733-4994.   **Free.**

State Legislative Building. First building constructed to house a state general assembly (1963); designed by Edward Durell Stone in a blend of modern and classical styles. Tours of chambers may include view of legislators at work. (Daily; closed Jan 1, Thanksgiving, Dec 25) Corner of Salisbury & Jones Sts. Phone 919/733-7928.   **Free.**

State Museum of Natural Sciences. Exhibits depict natural history of state; "Freshwater Wetlands" exhibit. (Daily; closed hols) N of Capitol Sq. 102 N Salisbury St. Phone 919/733-7450.   **Free.**

William B. Umstead State Park. On 5,377 acres with a 55-acre lake. Fishing; boating. Hiking, riding. Picnicking. Camping (Mar-mid-Dec, Thurs-Sun). Nature study. **Reedy Creek Section,** 10 mi NW off I-40. Approx 1,800 acres. Fishing. Hiking, riding. Picnicking. Nature study. Crabtree Creek Section, 10 mi NW on US 70. Phone 919/787-3033 or 919/677-0062 (Reedy Creek). Hrs vary. Standard fees for boat rentals and camping.

Annual Events

Artsplosure Spring Jazz & Art Festival. Moore Square and City Market. City-wide celebration of the arts. Showcase for regional dance, music, theater performances by nationally known artists; outdoor arts and crafts show; children's activities. For further information phone 919/832-8699. Mid-May.

State Fair. State Fairgrounds. 5 mi W on US 1, then 1 mi W on NC 54. For further information contact 1025 Blue Ridge Blvd, 27607; 919/733-2145 or 919/821-7400. Oct 16-25.

Motels

★ **COMFORT INN.** 2910 Capitol Blvd (27604). 919/878-9550; FAX 919/876-5457. 149 rms, 2-4 story. S $55; D $65; each addl $5; kit. suite $115; family rates; higher rates state fair. Crib free. TV; cable (premium). Pool. Complimentary full bkfst. Restaurant nearby. Ck-out noon. Coin lndry. Meeting rms. Business servs avail. In-rm modem link. Exercise equipt; weights, rowers. Some refrigerators. Cr cds: A, C, D, DS, ER, JCB, MC, V.

[D] [≈] [✕] [⊠] [⋒] [SC]

★ ★ **COMFORT INN-SOUTH.** 1602 Mechanical Blvd (27529). 919/779-7888; FAX 919/772-4603. 60 rms, 2 story. S, D $59-$89; each addl $5; suites $89-$99; under 12 free. Crib $7. TV; cable (premium); VCR avail. Pool. Complimentary continental bkfst. Coffee in rms. Restaurant opp 11 am-10 pm. Ck-out 11 am. Meeting rms. Exercise equipt; weight machine, stair machine. Microwaves; some refrigerators. Cr cds: A, D, DS, MC, V.

[D] [≈] [✕] [⊠] [⋒] [SC]

★ ★ **COURTYARD BY MARRIOTT.** 1041 Wake Towne Dr (27609). 919/821-3400; FAX 919/821-1209. 153 rms, 4 story, 13 suites. S $83; D $93; suites $93-$97; under 12 free; wkend rates. Crib free. TV; cable (premium), VCR avail. Pool; whirlpool. Complimentary coffee in rms. Restaurant 6:30-10 am; Sat, Sun 7 am-noon. Bar 4-11 pm. Ck-out noon. Coin lndry. Meeting rms. In-rm modem link. Valet serv. Exercise equipt; weight machine, bicycles. Health club privileges. Refrigerator in suites; microwaves avail. Balconies. Cr cds: A, C, D, DS, MC, V.

[D] [≈] [✕] [⊠] [⋒] [SC]

✔★ **CRICKET INN.** 3201 Old Wake Forest Rd (27609). 919/878-9310; FAX 919/790-1451. 148 rms, 2 story. S, D $49-$59; under 18 free. Crib free. TV; cable (premium). Pool. Complimentary continental bkfst. Restaurant adj open 24 hrs. Ck-out 11 am. Meeting rm. Valet serv. Health club privileges. Cr cds: A, D, DS, MC, V.

[D] [≈] [⊠] [⋒] [SC]

★ **DAYS INN-SOUTH INN.** 3901 S Wilmington (27603). 919/772-8900; FAX 919/772-1536. 103 rms, 3 story. S $49; D $54; each addl $5; under 12 free. Crib free. TV; cable (premium), VCR avail (movies). Pool. Complimentary continental bkfst. Restaurant adj open 24 hrs. Ck-out 11 am. Business servs avail. Cr cds: A, C, D, DS, MC, V.

[D] [≈] [⊠] [⋒] [SC]

✔★ ★ **FAIRFIELD INN BY MARRIOTT.** 2641 Appliance Ct (27604). 919/856-9800. Web www.fairfieldinn.com. 132 rms, 3 story. S $52.95; D $57.95; each addl $5; under 18 free. Crib free. TV; cable (premium). Pool. Complimentary continental bkfst. Restaurant nearby. Ck-out noon. Business servs avail. In-rm modem link. Valet serv. Cr cds: A, C, D, DS, MC, V.

[D] [≈] [⊠] [⋒] [SC]

★ ★ **HAMPTON INN.** 1001 Wake Towne Dr (27609). 919/828-1813; FAX 919/834-2672. Web www.hampton-inn.com. 131 rms, 5 story. S $65-$72; D $70-$77; under 18 free; wkend rates. Crib free. TV; cable (premium). Pool. Complimentary continental bkfst. Restaurant nearby. Ck-out noon. Meeting rms. Business servs avail. In-rm modem link. Valet serv. Sundries. Health club privileges. Cr cds: A, C, D, DS, MC, V.

[D] [≈] [⊠] [⋒] [SC]

★ ★ **HAMPTON INN.** (1010 Airport Rd, Morrisville 27560) Approx 10 mi W on NC 54. 919/462-1620; FAX 919/462-3217. 102 rms, 4 story. S, D $79-$99; under 18 free. Crib free. TV; cable (premium). Pool. Complimentary continental bkfst. Restaurant nearby. Ck-out noon. Business servs avail. Valet serv. Free airport transportation. Cr cds: A, D, DS, MC, V.

[D] [≈] [✈] [⊠] [⋒] [SC]

★ ★ **THE PLANTATION INN RESORT.** 6401 Capital Blvd (27604), 9 mi NE on US 1. 919/876-1411; FAX 919/790-7093; res: 800/992-9662 (exc NC), 800/521-1932 (NC). 94 rms, 2 story. S, D $55-$75; suites $75-$100. Crib free. TV; cable (premium), VCR avail (movies). Pool; wading pool, poolside serv. Playground. Restaurant 6:30 am-10:30 pm; Sat from 7:30 am. Rm serv. Ck-out noon. Meeting rms. Business servs avail. In-rm modem link. Bellhops. Airport transportation. Putting green. Health club privileges. Some refrigerators. Greek-revival detailing. Spacious grounds; attractive landsdcaping. Cr cds: A, C, D, MC, V.

[D] [⟿] [≈] [ƒ] [⊠] [⋒] [SC]

✔★ **RED ROOF INN.** 3520 Maitland Dr (27610). 919/231-0200; FAX 919/231-0228. 115 rms, 3 story. S $41.99; D $50.99; each addl $6; under 18 free. Crib $5. Pet accepted. TV; cable (premium). Complimentary coffee in lobby. Restaurant adj 6 am-10 pm. Ck-out noon. Health club privileges. Microwaves avail. Cr cds: A, C, D, DS, MC, V.

[D] [⟿] [≈] [⊠]

★ ★ **RESIDENCE INN BY MARRIOTT.** 1000 Navaho Dr (27609). 919/878-6100; FAX 919/876-4117. 144 kit. suites, 1-2 story. S, D $120-$154; wkly, monthly rates. Crib free. Pet accepted, some restrictions; $200. TV; cable (premium). Heated pool; whirlpool. Complimentary continental bkfst. Ck-out noon. Coin lndry. Meeting rm. Business servs avail. In-rm modem link. Valet serv. Health club privileges. Microwaves; some bathrm phones. Private patios, balconies. Picnic tables, grills. Cr cds: A, C, D, DS, JCB, MC, V.

[D] [⟿] [≈] [⊠] [⋒] [SC]

Motor Hotels

★ ★ **CRABTREE SUMMIT HOTEL.** 3908 Arrow Dr (27612). 919/782-6868; FAX 919/881-9340; res: 800/521-7521. 88 rms, 4 story, 7 suites. S, D $98-$150; suites $125-$175; wkend rates. Crib free. TV; cable (premium). Pool. Complimentary full bkfst Mon-Fri; continental bkfst Sat, Sun. Restaurant nearby. Ck-out noon. Meeting rms. Business servs avail. In-rm modem link. Free airport, RR station, bus depot transportation. Health club privileges. Refrigerators, wet bars. Cr cds: A, C, D, DS, ER, JCB, MC, V.

D ⊠ ≋ ⋈ 🔥 SC

★ ★ **HAMPTON INN.** 6209 Glenwood Ave (27612). 919/782-1112; FAX 919/782-9119. 141 rms, 6 story, 17 suites. S $68; D $76; suites $99-$129; under 18 free; wkend rates; higher rates special events. Crib free. TV; cable (premium). Complimentary continental bkfst. Restaurant adj 11 am-11 pm. Ck-out noon. Meeting rms. Business servs avail. In-rm modem link. Bellhops. Valet serv. Free airport transportation. Exercise equipt; bicycle, treadmill, sauna. Pool. Some bathrm phones, in-rm whirlpools, wet bars; refrigerator, microwave in suites. Cr cds: A, C, D, DS, MC, V.

D ≋ 🍴 ⋈ 🔥 SC

★ ★ **QUALITY SUITES.** 4400 Capital Blvd (27604). 919/876-2211; FAX 919/790-1352. 114 suites, 3 story. S, D $69-$139; under 18 free; wkend rates. Crib free. TV; cable (premium), VCR (movies). Pool. Complimentary full bkfst. Complimentary coffee in rms. Restaurant adj 11 am-11 pm. Ck-out noon. Meeting rms. Business servs avail. In-rm modem link. Valet serv. Exercise equipt; weight machine, bicycles. Bathrm phones, refrigerators, microwaves, minibars. Grills. Cr cds: A, C, D, DS, ER, JCB, MC, V.

D ≋ 🍴 ⋈ 🔥 SC

★ ★ ★ **VELVET CLOAK INN.** 1505 Hillsborough St (27605), in university area, west of downtown. 919/828-0333; FAX 919/828-2656; res: 800/334-4372 (exc NC), 800/662-8829 (NC). 171 rms, 5 story. S, D $67-$107; each addl $10; suites $95-$290; under 18 free; wkend rates. Crib free. Pet accepted; $15. TV; cable (premium), VCR avail. Indoor/outdoor pool. Complimentary afternoon refreshments. Restaurant (see CHARTER ROOM). Rm serv. Bar 4:30 pm-1 am. Ck-out noon. Meeting rms. Business servs avail. Bellhops. Concierge. Sundries. Free airport transportation. Health club privileges. Bathrm phones; microwaves avail. Cr cds: A, C, D, DS, ER, JCB, MC, V.

D 🐾 ≋ ⋈ 🔥 SC

Hotels

★ ★ **BROWNESTONE.** 1707 Hillsborough St (27605). 919/828-0811; FAX 919/834-0904; res: 800/331-7919. Web www.brownstonehotel .com. 192 rms, 9 story. S $79; D $85-$105; each addl $6. Crib free. TV; cable (premium). Pool. Restaurant 6:30 am-2 pm; Sat, Sun 7-11 am. Bar 5-11 pm; closed Sun. Ck-out 1 pm. Meeting rms. Business servs avail. Free airport transportation. Microwaves avail. Balconies. Cr cds: A, C, D, DS, ER, MC, V.

D ≋ ⋈ 🔥 SC

★ ★ ★ **EMBASSY SUITES.** 4700 Creedmoor Rd (27612). 919/881-0000; FAX 919/782-7225. Web www.embassy-suites.com. 225 kit. suites, 9 story. Suites $124-$174; under 12 free; wkend rates. Crib free. TV; cable (premium), VCR avail. Indoor pool; whirlpool. Complimentary full bkfst. Restaurant 11 am-11 pm. Bar to 1 am. Ck-out noon. Meeting rms. Business servs avail. In-rm modem link. Gift shop. Free covered parking. Airport transportation. Exercise equipt; weight machines, stair machine, sauna. Microwaves. Cr cds: A, C, D, DS, JCB, MC, V.

D ≋ 🍴 ⋈ 🔥 SC

★ ★ ★ **FOUR POINTS BY SHERATON.** 4501 Creedmore Rd (27612). 919/787-7111; FAX 919/783-0024. 318 rms, 4-10 story. S $62-$120; D $95-$130; each addl $10; suites $110-$140; under 18 free; wkend rates. Crib free. TV; cable (premium), VCR avail. Indoor pool. Restaurant 6:30 am-10 pm; Sat, Sun 7-10 am. Bar 4 pm-midnight. Ck-out noon. Convention facilities. Business center. In-rm modem link. Concierge. Gift shop. Free airport transportation. Exercise equipt; weights, rower. Luxury level. Cr cds: A, C, D, DS, JCB, MC, V.

D ≋ 🍴 ✈ ⋈ 🔥 SC 🚶

★ ★ ★ **HILTON-NORTH.** 3415 Wake Forest Rd (27609). 919/872-2323; FAX 919/876-0890. 338 units, 6 story. S $99-$120; D $109-$150; each addl $10; suites $135-$450; wkend rates. Crib free. TV; cable (premium), VCR avail. Indoor pool; whirlpool. Restaurant 6:30 am-10 pm. Bars 11-2 am; entertainment. Ck-out noon. Convention facilities. Business servs avail. In-rm modem link. Gift shop. Free airport transportation. Exercise equipt; stair machine, bicycles. Luxury level. Cr cds: A, C, D, DS, ER, MC, V.

D ≋ 🍴 ⋈ 🔥 SC

★ ★ **HOLIDAY INN DOWNTOWN-STATE CAPITAL.** 320 Hillsborough St (27603). 919/832-0501; FAX 919/833-1631. 202 rms, 20 story. S, D $74-$94; each addl $5; suites $139; under 18 free; wkend rates. Crib free. TV; cable (premium). Pool. Restaurant 6:30 am-2 pm, 5:30-10 pm; Sat 7 am-1 pm; Sun 6:30 am-2 pm. Bar 4 pm-2 am. Ck-out noon. Meeting rms. Business servs avail. In-rm modem link. Free garage parking. Exercise equipt; weights, bicycle. Balconies. Cr cds: A, C, D, DS, ER, JCB, MC, V.

D ≋ 🍴 ⋈ 🔥 SC

★ ★ **HOLIDAY INN-CRABTREE.** 4100 Glenwood Ave (27612). 919/782-8600; FAX 919/781-6077. 176 rms, 12 story. S, D $99; under 12 free. Crib free. TV; cable (premium). Indoor pool. Restaurant 6:30 am-10 pm. Bar 4 pm-midnight. Ck-out noon. Meeting rms. Business servs avail. In-rm modem link. Airport, RR station, bus depot transportation. Exercise equipt; weight machine, treadmill. Some bathrm phones. Cr cds: A, C, D, DS, JCB, MC, V.

D ≋ 🍴 ⋈ 🔥 SC

★ ★ ★ **MARRIOTT CRABTREE.** 4500 Marriott Dr (27612), on US 70W opp Crabtree Valley Mall. 919/781-7000; FAX 919/781-3059. Web www.marriott.com/marriott/nc//46.htm. 375 rms, 6 story. S, D $124-$130; wkend plans. Crib free. TV; cable (premium). Indoor/outdoor pool; whirlpool, poolside serv. Restaurant 6:30 am-2 pm, 5-10 pm; Sat, Sun 7 am-2 pm, 5-11 pm. Ck-out noon. Convention facilities. Business servs avail. In-rm modem link. Gift shop. Exercise equipt; weight machines, bicycles. Balconies. Luxury level. Cr cds: A, C, D, DS, ER, JCB, MC, V.

D ≋ 🍴 ⋈ 🔥 SC

Inn

★ ★ **THE OAKWOOD INN.** 411 N Bloodworth St (27604). 919/832-9712; FAX 919/836-9263; res: 800/267-9712. 6 rms, 2 story. S $75-$110; D $85-$120. TV, cable. Complimentary full bkfst; afternoon refreshments. Ck-out 11:30 am, ck-in 3 pm. Historic district; built 1871. Cr cds: A, C, D, DS, MC, V.

⋈ 🔥 SC

Restaurants

★ ★ **42nd STREET OYSTER BAR.** 508 W Jones St. 919/831-2811. Hrs: 11:30 am-11 pm; Sat from 5 pm; Sun 5-10 pm. Closed Jan 1, Thanksgiving, Dec 24 & 25. Res accepted. Bar. Semi-a la carte: lunch $4.95-$9.95, dinner $10.95-$49.95. Child's meals. Specializes in fresh fish, beef. Rhythm & blues band Thurs-Sat. Oyster bar. Nautical decor. Cr cds: A, D, MC, V.

D ⋈

★ ★ **ANGUS BARN, LTD.** 9401 Glenwood Ave (27612), 12 1/2 mi NW on US 70. 919/787-3505. Web www.citysearch.com/rdu/angus /barn. Hrs: 5-11 pm; Sun to 10 pm. Closed Jan 1, Thanksgiving, Dec 24, 25. Res accepted Sun-Fri. Bar 4 pm-midnight. Wine list. Semi-a la carte: dinner $14.95-$47.95. Child's meals. Specializes in prime rib, charcoal-broiled steak, seafood. Own baking. Valet parking. Farm decor; fireplaces; Colt revolver display. Family-owned. Cr cds: A, C, D, DS, MC, V.

D ⋈

✔★ ★ **CASA CARBONE.** 6019-A Glenwood Ave (27612). 919/781-8750. Hrs: 5-10 pm; Sun from 4 pm. Closed Mon; also major hols. Italian menu. Wine, beer. Semi-a la carte: dinner $7-$15. Child's meals.

Specializes in veal, pasta. Own desserts. Mediterranean decor. Cr cds: A, C, D, DS, MC, V.

[D] [SC] [⌐]

★★★ **CHARTER ROOM.** (See Velvet Cloak Inn Motor Hotel) 919/828-0333. Hrs: 6:30 am-10 pm; Sat, Sun 7:30 am-10 pm; Sun brunch 11:30 am-2 pm. Res accepted. French, Amer menu. Bar 4:30 pm-1 am. Wine list. Semi-a la carte: bkfst $2-$10, lunch $6.95-$13.95, dinner $7.95-$27.95. Sun brunch $11.95. Specializes in chicken, steak, seafood. Child's meals. Valet parking. Cr cds: A, C, D, DS, ER, JCB, MC, V.

[D]

✔★ **COURTNEY'S.** 407 Six Forks Rd (27609). 919/834-3613. Hrs: 7 am-2:30 pm. Closed Thanksgiving, Dec 25. Semi-a la carte: bkst, lunch $4.25-$6.95. Child's meals. Specializes in omelettes. Cr cds: MC, V.

[D] [⌐]

✔★★ **IRREGARDLESS CAFE.** 901 W Morgan (27603). 919/833-8898. Web www.citysearch.com. Hrs: 11:30 am-2:30 pm, 5:30-9:30 pm; Fri to 10 pm; Sat 5:30-10 pm; Sun brunch 10 am-2:30 pm. Bar. Semi-a la carte: lunch $3-$8, dinner $7-$15. Sun brunch $7.95-$9.75. Specializes in chicken, seafood, vegetarian dishes. Jazz, folk, classical musician. Totally nonsmoking. Cr cds: A, DS, MC, V.

[D]

★ **JEAN CLAUDE'S CAFE.** 6112 Falls of Neuse Rd (27609), in North Ridge Shopping Center. 919/876-9025. Hrs: 11 am-2 pm, 5:30-9 pm; Fri, Sat to 9:30 pm. Closed Sun; some major hols. French, Amer menu. Wine, beer. Semi-a la carte: lunch $4.95-$7.95, dinner $8-$22. Child's meals. Specialties: beef tenderloin, salmon in puff pastry. Two dining rms with French decor. Totally nonsmoking. Cr cds: A, DS, MC, V.

[D]

✔★ **PEKING GARDEN.** 126 Millbrook Rd, in Colony Shopping Ctr. 919/848-4663. Hrs: 11:30 am-2:30 pm, 5 pm-midnight; wkends to 2 am. Chinese menu. Bar. Buffet: lunch $4.95, dinner $7.95. Specializes in Chinese cuisine. Modern decor with Chinese accents. Cr cds: A, DS, MC, V.

[D] [⌐]

★★ **SIMPSON'S.** 5625 Creedmoor Rd (27612), in Creedmore Crossing Shopping Center. 919/783-8818. Web www.citysearch.com /rdu/simpsonsbeef. Hrs: 11 am-2:30 pm, 5-10 pm; Fri, Sat to 11 pm. Closed most major hols. Res accepted. Bar. Semi-a la carte: lunch $2.95-$9.95, dinner $9.95-$39.95. Child's meals. Specializes in grilled fish, steak, prime rib. Pianist wkdays, jazz wkends. Formal dining in spacious surroundings. Cr cds: A, C, D, DS, MC, V.

[D] [⌐]

★★ **VINNIE'S STEAKHOUSE & TAVERN.** 7440 Six Forks Rd (27615). 919/847-7319. Web www.vinnies.com. Hrs: 5 pm-midnight. Closed major hols. Bar. Semi-a la carte: dinner $15-$55. Specializes in steak, seafood. Club decor. Cr cds: A, D, MC, V.

[D] [⌐]

★★ **WINSTON'S GRILLE.** 6401 Falls of Neuse Rd (27615), in Sutton Square Shopping Center. 919/790-0700. Hrs: 11 am-10 pm; Fri to 11 pm; Sat 5-11 pm; Sun brunch to 3 pm. Closed some major hols. Res accepted. Bar. A la carte entrees: lunch $4.95-$9.95, dinner $5.95-$18.95. Sun brunch $4.95-$8.95. Child's meals. Specializes in beef, seafood, pasta. Outdoor dining. Cr cds: A, D, DS, MC, V.

[D] [⌐]

Roanoke Rapids (A-8)

Pop 15,722 **Elev** 170 ft **Area code** 919 **Zip** 27870

Information Halifax County Tourism Development Authority, PO Box 144; 919/535-1687 or 800/522-4282.

What to See and Do

Historic Halifax State Historic Site. The Halifax Resolves, first formal sanction of American independence, were adopted here April 12, 1776. Buildings include Owens House (1760), Burgess Law Office, Eagle Tavern (1790), Sally-Billy House, clerk's office, jail, Montfort Archaeology Exhibit Center. Other features are Magazine Spring, garden and churchyard. Visitor center; audiovisual programs, exhibits. (Apr-Oct, daily; rest of yr, daily exc Mon; closed some hols) Historical dramas presented in summer (fee). 9 mi SE off US 301 or S on I-95 exit 168. Phone 919/583-7191. **Free.**

Lake Gaston. A 34-mi-long, 20,300-acre lake has fishing, boating (ramps); picnicking. 10 mi W via US 158 and NC 1214.

Roanoke Rapids Lake. Covers 5,000 acres. Launching facilities. NW edge of town.

Motels

✔★ **COMFORT INN.** At I-95 exit 176. 919/537-1011; FAX 919/537-9258. 100 rms, 2 story. S $38-$48; D $48-$54; each addl $5; under 18 free. Crib free. TV; cable (premium). Indoor pool. Complimentary continental bkfst. Restaurant 6:30 am-10 pm. Ck-out 11 am. Business servs avail. Gift shop. Cr cds: A, C, D, DS, MC, V.

[D] [≈] [▨] [▨] [SC]

★★ **HAMPTON INN.** 1914 Weldon Rd, I-95 exit 173. 919/537-7555; FAX 919/537-9852. 124 rms, 2 story. S $53-$70; D $59-$70; under 18 free. Crib free. TV; cable (premium). Pool. Complimentary continental bkfst. Restaurant adj 6 am-10 pm. Ck-out noon. Meeting rms. Business servs avail. In-rm modem link. Health club privileges. Cr cds: A, C, D, DS, MC, V.

[D] [≈] [▨] [▨] [SC]

★★★ **HOLIDAY INN.** 100 Holiday Dr, jct US 158, I-95. 919/537-1031; FAX 919/537-7848. 140 rms, 2 story. S $50-$68; D $56-$75; each addl $8; under 19 free. Crib free. TV; cable (premium). Pool. Playground. Complimentary continental bkfst. Restaurant 6 am-2 pm, 5-10 pm. Rm serv. Bar 5 pm-midnight. Ck-out noon. Coin lndry. Meeting rms. Business servs avail. In-rm modem link. Sundries. Health club privileges. Private patios. Cr cds: A, C, D, DS, ER, JCB, MC, V.

[D] [≈] [▨] [▨] [SC]

Robbinsville (B-1)

(See also Bryson City, Fontana Dam)

Pop 709 **Elev** 2,064 ft **Area code** 704 **Zip** 28771

A Ranger District office of the Nantahala National Forest (see FRANKLIN) is located here.

What to See and Do

Joyce Kilmer-Slickrock Wilderness. A 17,013-acre area within Nantahala National Forest (see FRANKLIN). More than 100 species of trees native to region; trails through forest to view prime specimens. Located within the area is the Joyce Kilmer Memorial Forest, a 3,840-acre stand of virgin timber dedicated to the author of the poem "Trees"; and a National Recreation Trail. 13 mi NW via US 129, SR 1116 & 1127. Inquire at District

Ranger Office (mid-Apr-Oct, wkends & hols), N off US 129; 704/479-6431. **Free.**

Motel

★ **TAPOCO LODGE RESORT.** *(Rte 72, Box A-1, Tapoco)* 15 *mi N on US 129.* 704/498-2435; res: 800/822-5083; FAX 704/479-3053. 24 rms, 3 story. MAP: S $80; D $124; each addl $40; under 3 free. Closed Dec-Mar. Crib free. TV; cable. Complimentary full bkfst. Restaurant 8 am-8 pm. Ck-out 10 am. Meeting rms. Gift shop. Lighted tennis. Playground. Game rm. Rec rm. Cr cds: A, DS, MC, V.

Lodge

★ ★ **SNOWBIRD MOUNTAIN LODGE.** *275 Santeetlah Rd, 12 mi NW, off US 129.* 704/479-3433; res: 800/941-9290; FAX 704/479-3473. E-mail snbdmtnldg@aol.com; web www.snowbirdlodge.com. 22 rms, 2 story. No A/C. No rm phones. AP, mid-Apr-early Nov: D $125-$200. Closed rest of yr. Children over 12 yrs only. Dining rm (by res only) 8-9:30 am, 6-8 pm. Setups. Ck-out 10 am, ck-in 1 pm. Hiking trails. Lawn games. 100 acres atop mountain; stone lodge with great room; adj to Joyce Kilmer Memorial Forest. Cr cds: MC, V.

Rocky Mount (A-8)

(See also Wilson)

Settled 1840 **Pop** 48,997 **Elev** 120 ft **Area code** 919
Information Chamber of Commerce, 2501 Sunset Ave, PO Box 392, 27802; 919/442-5111.

This is one of the country's largest bright-leaf tobacco marts. Cotton products in the form of yarn, bolts of fabric and ready-to-wear clothing flow from the mills. The factories produce fertilizer, furniture, chemicals, metal products, lumber and pharmaceuticals. Rocky Mount is also the home of Hardee's Food Systems.

What to See and Do

Children's Museum. Includes touch tank, greenhouse; live animal collection, exhibits. (Daily; closed Thanksgiving, Dec 25) 1610 Gay St, Sunset Park, off US 64, 301 Bypass. Phone 919/972-1167 or 919/972-1168. ¢

Seasonal Event

Tobacco auctions. Numerous warehouses. Inquire locally. Aug-mid-Nov.

Motels

★ **CARLETON HOUSE.** *215 N Church St (27804).* 919/977-0410; FAX 919/985-2115. 42 rms, 2 story. S $42-$49; D $49-$56; suites $65; under 16 free. Crib free. TV; cable (premium). Pool. Coffee in rms. Restaurant 6:30 am-9 pm; Sat 7 am-noon, 5-10 pm; Sun 7:30-10:30 am, 11:30 am-2 pm, 5-8 pm. Ck-out noon. Meeting rm. Business servs avail. Sundries. Health club privileges. Cr cds: A, D, MC, V.

✔★ **FAIRFIELD INN BY MARRIOTT.** *1200 Benvenue Rd (27804).* 919/972-9400. 104 rms, 3 story. S, D $45.95-$55.95; under 18 free. Crib free. TV; cable (premium). Pool. Complimentary continental bkfst. Ck-out noon. Business servs avail. In-rm modem link. Valet serv. Cr cds: A, C, D, DS, MC, V.

★ ★ **HAMPTON INN.** *530 Winstead Ave (27804).* 919/937-6333; FAX 919/9374333. 124 rms, 4 story. S $59; D $64; suites $85; under 18 free. Crib free. TV; cable (premium). Pool. Complimentary continental bkfst. Restaurant opp 6 am-9 pm. Ck-out noon. Meeting rms. Business servs avail. Health club privileges. Cr cds: A, D, DS, MC, V.

Motor Hotels

★ ★ **COMFORT INN.** *200 Gateway Blvd (27804), I-95 Exit 138.* 919/937-7765. 125 rms, 5 story. S, D $58-$73; each addl $5; suites $95; under 18 free. Crib free. TV; cable (premium). Pool. Complimentary continental bkfst. Restaurant adj 6 am-10 pm. Ck-out 11 am. Business servs avail. In-rm modem link. Valet serv. Exercise equipt; weight machine, bicycles. Refrigerator avail, wet bar in suites. Cr cds: A, C, D, DS, ER, JCB, MC, V.

★ ★ ★ **HOLIDAY INN.** *651 Winstead Ave (27804), 1 mi E of I-95, exit 138.* 919/937-6888; FAX 919/937-4788. 171 rms, 4 story. S, D $75-$90; each addl $6; suites $99-$125; under 12 free. Crib free. TV; cable (premium). Pool. Restaurant 6:30-11 am, 11:30 am-10 pm. Rm serv. Bar. Ck-out noon. Meeting rms. Business servs avail. Bellhops. Valet serv. Refrigerator in suites. Cr cds: A, C, D, DS, ER, JCB, MC, V.

★ ★ **HOLIDAY INN.** *5350 Dorches Rd (27801).* 919/937-6300; FAX 919/937-6300, ext. 199. 154 rms, 2 story. S, D $60-$65; under 18 free. Crib free. TV; cable (premium). Pool. Complimentary coffee in rms. Restaurant 6 am-2 pm, 5-10 pm. Bar. Ck-out noon. Meeting rms. Business servs avail. Coin lndry. Health club privileges. Some refrigerators. Cr cds: A, D, DS, MC, V.

Salisbury (B-5)

(See also Concord, Lexington, Statesville)

Founded 1753 **Pop** 23,087 **Elev** 746 ft **Area code** 704 **Zip** 28144 **Web** www.ci.salisbury.nc.us/rccvb.htm.

Information Rowan County Convention & Visitors Bureau, PO Box 4044, 28145; 704/638-3100 or 800/332-2343. Visit the Visitor Information Center at 132 E Innes for brochures, maps and audio tape tours.

A trading, cultural and judicial center since 1753, it is here that Daniel Boone spent his youth and Andrew Jackson studied law. Salisbury's wide, shady streets were twice taken over by military troops. The first time was by Lord Cornwallis during the Revolutionary War, and the Civil War brought General Stoneman. During the Civil War, Salisbury was the site of a Confederate prison for Union soldiers where 5,000 died; they are buried here in the National Cemetery. Among the dead was Robert Livingstone, Union soldier and son of African missionary David Livingstone. Livingstone College was named for the father. Catawba College and Rowan-Cabarrus Community College complete Salisbury's triad of higher learning.

What to See and Do

Dan Nicholas Park. This 330-acre park has lake with fishing; paddle boats (fee). Hiking, nature trail; tennis, miniature golf (fee). Picnicking. Camping hookups (fee). Outdoor theater; two nature museums; petting zoo. Park (all yr). 2 mi N on I-85, to exit 79, then 6 mi SE. Phone 704/636-0154 or 704/636-2089. **Free.**

Dr. Josephus Hall House (1820). Large antebellum house set amid giant oaks and century-old boxwoods; contains most of its original Federal and Victorian furnishings. House was used as Union commander's headquarters following Civil War. (Sat & Sun afternoons) 226 S Jackson. Phone 704/636-0103 or -1502. ¢¢

N.C. Transportation Museum. Once the steam locomotive repair facility for Southern Railway, now a transportation museum, railroad yards and shops. Back shop and 37-stall Bob Julian Roundhouse (1924). Rolling stock includes six engines (steam and diesel); restored luxury private cars; freight cars, trolley, passenger coaches. Train ride (seasonal; fee). Visitor Center, two exhibit buildings, audiovisual show. (Apr-Oct, daily; rest of yr, daily exc Mon; closed Jan 1, Thanksgiving, Dec 24-25) 2 mi NE via I-85, in Spencer. Phone 704/636-2889. **Free.**

Old Stone House (1766). Built of hand-laid granite with walls two feet thick. Restored (1966); authentically furnished; family burial ground opp. (Apr-Nov, Sat & Sun afternoons) 4 mi SE, off US 52 in Granite Quarry. Phone 704/633-5946. ¢¢

Poets & Dreamers Garden. Formal, Biblical and Shakespearean gardens; fountain, sundial. Tomb of founder Joseph Charles Price in garden. On campus of Livingstone College.

Rowan Museum. In Maxwell Chambers house (1819). Period rooms, authentic regional furniture; material on history of the county; 19th-century garden. (Thurs-Sun, afternoons; closed legal hols, Dec 24) 116 S Jackson St. Phone 704/633-5946. ¢¢

Waterworks Visual Arts Center. Adaptive restoration of former Salisbury Waterworks into arts center. Changing exhibits; studios, classes; courtyard; sensory garden. Guided tours. (Daily; closed legal hols). 1 Water St. Phone 704/636-1882. **Free.**

Motels

★ ★ **HAMPTON INN.** 1001 Klumac Rd, I-85 exit 75. 704/637-8000; FAX 704/639-9995. 121 rms, 4 story. S $59; D $64; suites $95; under 18 free; higher rates: Furniture Market, auto racing events. Crib free. Pet accepted, some restrictions. TV; cable (premium). Pool. Complimentary continental bkfst. Restaurant adj 11 am-11 pm. Ck-out noon. Meeting rms. Business servs avail. Health club privileges. Refrigerator in suites. Cr cds: A, C, D, DS, MC, V.

D 🐾 ⌘ ➤ 🛄 SC

★ ★ ★ **HOLIDAY INN.** 530 Jake Alexander Blvd S (28147), I-85 exit 75. 704/637-3100; FAX 704/637-9152. 181 rms, 2 story. S $63-$88; D $67-$90; each addl $6; suites $95-$125; under 18 free; higher rates special events. Crib free. Pet accepted, some restrictions. TV; cable (premium). Indoor/outdoor pool. Restaurant 7 am-2 pm, 5:30-9 pm. Rm serv. Bar 5 pm-1 am; Sat from 6 pm; entertainment Fri, Sat. Ck-out noon. Business servs avail. Bellhops. Valet serv. Exercise equipt; weights, bicycles. Refrigerator avail in suites. Cr cds: A, C, D, DS, JCB, MC, V.

D 🐾 ⌘ 🏋 ➤ 🛄 SC

Sanford (B-6)

Pop 14,475 **Elev** 375 ft **Area code** 919 **Zip** 27330

What to See and Do

House in the Horseshoe State Historic Site. House (ca 1770) was the residence of North Carolina Governor Benjamin Williams; site of a Revolutionary War skirmish. (Apr-Oct, daily; rest of yr, daily exc Mon; closed some major hols) 12 mi W on NC 42 to Carbonton, then 5 mi S on SR 1644. Phone 910/947-2051. **Free.**

Raven Rock State Park. A 2,990-acre park characterized by 152-ft outcrop of rock jutting over Cape Fear River. Fishing. Nature trails, interpretive programs. Picnicking. Primitive camping. Standard hrs, fees. 18 mi S on US 421. Phone 910/893-4888.

Motels

✔★ ★ **COMFORT INN.** 1403 N Horner Blvd. 919/774-6411; FAX 919/774-7018. 122 rms, 2 story. S $50-$54; D $54-$59; suites $80-$90;

under 18 free. Crib free. TV; cable (premium). Pool; sauna. Complimentary continental bkfst. Restaurant adj 6 am-11 pm. Bar from 5 pm. Meeting rms. Coin lndry. Exercise equipt; bicycles, weight machine. Some refrigerators. Cr cds: A, C, D, DS, MC, V.

D ⌘ 🏋 ➤ 🐾 SC

✔★ **PALOMINO.** (27331). 2¹/₂ mi on US 1, US 15/501 Bypass. 919/776-7531; FAX 919/776-9670; res: 800/641-6060. 92 rms. S $30-$38; D $35-$40; each addl $2. Crib free. Pet accepted. TV; cable (premium). Pool; whirlpool. Playground. Restaurant 6 am-10 pm. Ck-out noon. Meeting rms. Golf privileges. Exercise equipt; weight machines, stair machine, sauna. Picnic tables, grill. Cr cds: A, C, D, DS, MC, V.

D 🐾 ➤ 🏋 ⌘ 🏋 ➤ 🐾 SC

Shelby (B-4)

(See also Gastonia)

Pop 14,669 **Elev** 853 ft **Area code** 704 **Web** www.co.cleveland.nc.us
Information Cleveland County Economic Development, 311 E Marion St, PO Box 1210, 28151; 704/484-4999.

Seat of Cleveland County, this town in the Piedmont boasts of diversified industry and agriculture. It is named for Colonel Isaac Shelby, hero of the Battle of Kings Mountain in the Revolutionary War. (See KINGS MOUNTAIN NATIONAL MILITARY PARK, SC.) The town celebrates its heritage and culture with special events, fairs and historic preservation.

What to See and Do

Central Shelby Historic District Walking Tour. 2-hr self-guided tour encompasses much of original area established in 1841. Features 38 architecturally significant structures (ca 1850s). For information phone 704/481-1842.

Motel

★ ★ **DAYS INN.** Dixon Blvd and Weisler St (28150). 704/482-6721; FAX 704/480-1423. 97 rms, 2 story. S $50; D $54; each addl $5; under 18 free. Crib free. TV; cable (premium). Pool. Restaurant 6 am-2 pm, 5-10 pm; Sun 6-10:30 am, 2-11:30 pm. Rm serv. Ck-out noon. Meeting rms. Cr cds: A, D, DS, MC, V.

D ⌘ ➤ 🐾 SC

Inn

★ ★ ★ **INN AT WEBBLEY.** 403 S Washington St (28151). 704/481-1403; FAX 704/487-0619; res: 800/852-2346. 5 rms, 3 story. S, D $125-$150; children over 12 yrs only. TV; cable (premium). Complimentary full bkfst. Dining rm (guest only) 6-10 pm. Ck-out noon, ck-in 3 pm. Business servs avail. In-rm modem link. Grand piano in library. Colonial-revival house built in 1852; antiques. Landscaped grounds with gardens. Cr cds: DS, MC, V.

➤ 🐾

Smithfield (B-7)

(See also Dunn, Goldsboro, Raleigh)

Pop 7,540 **Elev** 153 ft **Area code** 919 **Zip** 27577

Motels

★ **COMFORT INN.** *(1705 Industrial Park Dr, Selma 27576) Approx 5 mi N on US 301.* 919/965-5200; FAX 919/965-5200, ext. 304. 80 rms, 2 story. S, D $49-$72; each addl $5; suites $85; under 15 free. Crib $5. TV; cable (premium). Pool; whirlpool. Complimentary continental bkfst. Restaurant nearby. Ck-out 11 am. Meeting rms. Business servs avail. Exercise equipt; bicycle, treadmill. Some refrigerators. Cr cds: A, D, DS, MC, V.

[D] [≈] [✗] [⊠] [⚹] [SC]

★ **HOWARD JOHNSON.** *1¹/₂ mi E at jct US 70 & I-95, exit 95.* 919/934-7176; FAX 919/934-6995. 60 rms, 2 story. S $40-$45; D $50-$55; each addl $5; under 18 free. Crib free. TV; cable (premium). Pool. Playground. Ck-out 11 am. Business servs avail. Lawn games. Private patios, balconies. Cr cds: A, C, D, DS, ER, JCB, MC, V.

[D] [≈] [⊠] [⚹] [SC]

✔★ **MASTERS ECONOMY INN.** *Jct US 70A & I-95.* 919/965-3771. 119 rms, 2 story. S, D $26; each addl $4; under 18 free. Crib $6. TV; cable (premium). Pool. Ck-out noon. Meeting rms. Business servs avail. Cr cds: A, C, D, DS, ER, JCB, MC, V.

[D] [≈] [⊠] [⚹] [SC]

South Brunswick Islands (D-7)

(See also Southport; also see Myrtle Beach, SC)

Web www.weblync.com/sbi_chamber

Information Chamber of Commerce, PO Box 1380, Shallotte 28459; 910/754-6644 or 800/426-6644.

The South Brunswick Islands offer wide, gently sloping beaches and beautiful scenery. Located just 50 miles from the Gulf Stream, the region has a subtropical climate and mild temperatures. Resort activities are plentiful and include fishing, swimming, tennis and golf. Shallotte is the hub of the area that includes Holden, Ocean Isle and Sunset beaches. The islands are reached by bridges across the Intracoastal Waterway.

Annual Event

North Carolina Oyster Festival. In Shallotte. Arts and crafts, music, sports, oyster-shucking contest. 3rd wkend Oct.

Motor Hotel

★★ **CLARION INN-THE WINDS OCEAN FRONT.** *(310 E First St, Ocean Isle Beach 28469) 1¹/₂ mi N of jct NC 904 & E First St.* 910/579-6275; FAX 910/579-2884. 68 units, 3 story, 45 suites, 58 kit. units, 5 houses (1-4 bedrm). No elvtr. Early June-late Aug: S, D $99-$144; each addl $15; suites, kits. $143-$223; houses $415-$469; under 19 free; lower rates rest of yr. Crib $5. TV; cable. Pool; whirlpool. Complimentary continental bkfst. Complimentary coffee in rms. Ck-out 11 am. Coin lndry. Meeting rms. Business servs avail. In-rm modem link. Airport transportation. Tennis privileges. 18-hole golf privileges, pro, putting green, driving range. Exercise equipt; weights, bicycles, sauna. Rec rm. Lawn games. Refrigerators, wet bars. Balconies. Picnic tables, grills. On beach. Cr cds: A, C, D, DS, ER, JCB, MC, V.

[D] [✈] [✗] [🛈] [≈] [✗] [⊠] [⚹] [SC]

Southern Pines (B-6)

(See also Pinehurst)

Pop 9,129 **Elev** 512 ft **Area code** 910 **Zip** 28387 **E-mail** cvb4golf@mindspring.com **Web** www.sandhills.net

Information Convention & Visitors Bureau, PO Box 2270, 28388; 910/692-3330 or 800/346-5362.

The Sandhills, among fine longleaf and loblolly pines, are famed for golf and horses. Known as "sand country," it first gained popularity as a resort in the 1880s, but the enthusiasm for golf in the 1920s fueled Southern Pines' growth as a recreational and resort area. The area is still steeped in tradition and history, with golf and equestrian activities as popular as ever.

What to See and Do

Shaw House. Antebellum house of simple and sturdy style is lightened by unusual mantels of carved cypress. Guided tours (mid-Jan-June & Sept-mid-Dec, Fri & Sat afternoons). Also on premises are Britt Sanders Cabin and Garner House. SW Broad St and Morganton Rd. Phone 910/692-2051. ¢

Weymouth Woods-Sandhills Nature Preserve. Excellent examples of Sandhills ecology. Hiking trails along pine-covered "sandridges." Natural history museum. (Daily; closed Dec 25) 3 mi SE on Indiana Ave, then N on Ft Bragg Rd. Phone 910/692-2167.   **Free.**

Annual Event

House and Garden Tour. Conducted by Southern Pines Garden Club. Mid-Apr.

Motels

★★ **HAMPTON INN.** *1675 US 1S.* 910/692-9266; FAX 910/692-9298. 126 rms, 2 story. Mar-May, Sept-Nov: S, D $69-$77; under 18 free; golf plan; higher rates: NASCAR races, PGA tournament, Stoneybrook Steeplechase races; lower rates rest of yr. Crib free. TV; cable (premium). Pool. Complimentary continental bkfst. Restaurant nearby. Ck-out noon. Coin lndry. Meeting rm. Business servs avail. Valet serv. Golf privileges. Health club privileges. Cr cds: A, C, D, DS, MC, V.

[D] [✗] [≈] [⊠] [⚹] [SC]

★★★ **HOLIDAY INN.** *On US 1 at Morganton Rd.* 910/692-8585; FAX 910/692-5213; res: 800/262-5737. 158 rms, 2 story. Mar-Oct: S $65-$75; D $75-$89; each addl $10; suites $140-$160; studio rms $65-$75; under 18 free; lower rates rest of yr. Crib free. TV; cable (premium). Pool. Restaurant 6:30 am-9:30 pm. Rm serv. Bar 4 pm-midnight. Ck-out noon. Meeting rms. Business servs avail. In-rm modem link. Valet serv. Tennis. Golf privileges. Exercise equipt; weights, bicycles. Game rm. Cr cds: A, C, D, DS, ER, JCB, MC, V.

[D] [✗] [≈] [≈] [✗] [⊠] [⚹] [SC]

Resorts

★★★ **MID PINES GOLF CLUB.** *1010 Midland Rd, W via US 1, NC 2.* 910/692-2114; FAX 910/692-4615; res: 800/323-2114. 112 rms in 3-story hotel, 6 golf villas, 10 lakeside villas. Mar-May, Sept-Nov, MAP: S, D $125; each addl $10; under 12 free; golf, tennis plans; lower rates rest of yr. TV; cable, VCR avail. Pool. Coffee in rms. Dining rm (public by res) 6:30-9 am, noon-2:30 pm, 6:30-8:30 pm. Box lunches; snack bar. Rm serv in hotel. Bar 11:30 am-11 pm. Ck-out 11 am, ck-in 2 pm. Meeting rms. Business center. Airport transportation. Lighted tennis. 18-hole golf, greens fee $30-$75, pro lessons, putting green. Lawn games. Rec rm. Minibars; some refrigerators. Cr cds: A, C, D, DS, JCB, MC, V.

[D] [✗] [✗] [≈] [⊠] [⚹] [SC] [⛳]

★ ★ ★ **PINE NEEDLES LODGE AND GOLF CLUB.** *On NC 2, 1 mi W of jct US 1.* 910/692-7111; FAX 910/692-5349; res: 800/747-7272. 71 rms in 10 lodges, 2 story. AP, mid-Mar-mid-June & mid-Sept-mid-Nov: S, D $125-$155/person; under 4 free; wkly rates; golf plans; lower rates rest of yr. Crib free. TV; cable (premium). Heated pool; whirlpool, sauna, poolside serv. Complimentary coffee in rms. Dining rm 7 am-8:30 pm. Box lunches. Snack bar. Picnics. Rm serv. Bar noon-11 pm. Ck-out 11 am, ck-in 2 pm. Meeting rms. Business servs avail. In-rm modem link. Bellhops. Valet serv. Gift shop. Lighted grass tennis. 18-hole golf, greens fee $45-$75, pro, putting green, driving range. Bicycles (rentals). Lawn games. Rec rm. Game rm. Some refrigerators. Balconies. Family-owned golf resort with course designed in 1927 by renowned golf course architect Donald Ross. Cr cds: A, MC, V.

Restaurants

★ ★ **LA TERRACE.** *270 Southwest Broad St.* 910/692-5622. Hrs: 11:30 am-2 pm, 6-10 pm. Closed Sun; Jan 1, Dec 25. Res accepted. Continental menu. Serv bar. A la carte entrees: lunch $7.50-$8.50, dinner $13.50-$19.50. Child's meals. Specializes in seafood, lamb. Outdoor dining. Intimate dining in formal atmosphere. Cr cds: MC, V.

★ **THE SQUIRE'S PUB.** *1720 US 1, S on US 1.* 910/695-1161. Hrs: 11 am-10 pm; Fri & Sat to 11 pm. Closed Sun; Thanksgiving, Dec 24 & 25. British menu. Bar. Semi-a la carte: lunch $3.95-$8.49, dinner $3.95-$16.95. Child's meals. Specializes in traditional pub fare, steak, seafood. 5 dining areas. English decor. Cr cds: DS, MC, V.

✔★ **VITO'S.** *311 SE Broad St, off US 1.* 910/692-7815. Hrs: 5-9:30 pm; Fri, Sat to 10 pm; Sun to 9 pm. Closed Mon; major hols. Italian menu. Semi-a la carte: dinner $5-$13. Child's meals. Specializes in veal, chicken. Italian decor. No cr cds accepted.

Southport (D-8)

(See also South Brunswick Islands, Wilmington)

Founded 1792 **Pop** 2,369 **Elev** 22 ft **Area code** 910 **Zip** 28461 **E-mail** chamber@southport.net **Web** www.southport.net/chamber.html

Information Southport-Oak Island Chamber of Commerce, 4841 Long Beach Rd SE; 910/457-6964 or 800/457-6964.

Saltwater and freshwater fishing are very good in the vicinity of Cape Fear. Deep-sea charter boats are available at Southport, Long Beach and Shallotte Point. There is a good yacht harbor facility for small boats and yachts, a municipal pier, three ocean piers, as well as several beaches and golf courses nearby.

Fort Johnston (1764) was the first fort built in North Carolina. With Fort Fisher and Fort Caswell (1825), it guarded the mouth of the Cape Fear River during the Civil War, making it possible for blockade runners to reach Wilmington. Fort Johnston (restored) is the residence of the Commanding Officer of the Sunny Point Military Ocean Terminal.

What to See and Do

Brunswick Town-Fort Anderson State Historic Site. Brunswick, founded in 1726, thrived as a major port exporting tar and lumber. Fearing a British attack, its citizens fled when the Revolution began; in 1776 the town was burned by British sailors. Twenty-three foundations have been excavated. Built across part of the town are the Civil War earthworks of Fort Anderson, which held out for 30 days after the fall of Fort Fisher in 1865. Visitor Center, exhibits, audiovisual show; marked historical trailside exhibits; nature trail, picnic area. (Apr-Oct, daily; rest of yr, daily exc Mon;

closed some major hols) 14 mi N on NC 133, then 5 mi S on Plantation Road. Phone 910/371-6613. **Free.**

Carolina Power & Light Company Visitors Center. Audiovisual presentations show history of energy & its use; nuclear reactor model. Picnic area. (Mon-Fri) 2 mi N on NC 87. Phone 910/457-6041. **Free.**

Ferry Service. Southport to Fort Fisher. Approx 30 min crossing. For schedule and fee information phone 910/457-6942 (local service) or 800/293-3779 (NC Dept of Transportation).

Fort Fisher State Historic Site. The largest earthworks fort in the Confederacy; until the last few months of the Civil War, it kept Wilmington open to blockade runners. Some of the heaviest naval bombardment of land fortifications took place here on Dec 24-25, 1864 and Jan 13-15, 1865. Tours. Visitor Center has exhibits, audiovisual shows. Reconstructed gun emplacement. Picnic area. (Apr-Oct, daily; rest of yr, daily exc Mon; closed some major hols) 6 mi E via US 421, ferry. Phone 910/458-5538. **Free.**

Long Beach Scenic Walkway. Crosses several important wetland communities; viewing of maritime forests, wetland birds, marsh animals and seacoast fowl. E at 20th St SE and 19th Place, across Davis Canal in Long Beach. Phone 910/278-5518.

Annual Events

Robert Ruark Chili Cook Off. Easter wkend.

US Open King Mackerel Tournament. 1st wkend Oct.

Motel

✔★ **PORT.** *4821 Long Beach Rd.* 910/457-4800. 32 units, 8 kits. Mar-Oct: S, D $33-$43; each addl $3; kit. units $400-$450/month; wkly rates; lower rates rest of yr. TV; cable (premium). Pool. Restaurant nearby. Ck-out 11 am. Refrigerators. Cr cds: D, DS, MC, V.

Inn

★ **LOIS JANE'S RIVERVIEW INN.** *106 W Bay St.* 910/457-6701; res: 800/457-1152. 4 rms (2 shared bath), 2 story. No rm phones. March-Oct: S, D $75-$90; each addl $10; lower rates rest of yr. TV; cable. Complimentary full bkfst. Restaurant opp 11:30 am-9 pm. Ck-out 11 am, ck-in 3 pm. Built in 1892; antiques. Cr cds: MC, V.

Restaurant

✔★ **SAND FIDDLER.** *On NC 211, near jct NC 87.* 910/457-6588. Hrs: 11 am-2 pm, 5-9 pm; Sat from 5 pm; Sun brunch 11:30 am-2 pm. Closed some major hols. Semi-a la carte: lunch $3-$7, dinner $6-$15. Sun brunch $6.95. Child's meals. Specializes in seafood, prime rib. Nautical decor. Cr cds: MC, V.

Statesville (B-4)

(See also Cornelius, Hickory, Salisbury)

Founded 1789 **Pop** 17,567 **Elev** 923 ft **Area code** 704 **Zip** 28677
Information Greater Statesville Chamber of Commerce, 115 E Front St, PO Box 1064, 28687; 704/873-2892.

Statesville is a community of many small, diversified industries, including furniture, apparel, metalworking and textiles. Iredell County, of which Statesville is the seat, is known for its dairy and beef cattle.

What to See and Do

Duke Power State Park. On Lake Norman (see CORNELIUS); 1,500 acres. Swimming; fishing; boating (ramp, rentals). Nature trails. Picnicking. Tent and trailer sites. Standard fees. 10 mi S via I-77, US 21. Phone 704/528-6350.

Fort Dobbs State Historic Site. Named for Royal Governor Arthur Dobbs, the now-vanished fort was built during the French and Indian War to protect settlers. Exhibits, nature trails, excavations. (Apr-Oct, daily; rest of yr, daily exc Mon; closed some major hols, also wkends Dec-Feb) N via I-40, US 21, State Rd 1930, then 1½ mi W. Phone 704/873-5866.   **Free.**

Annual Events

Carolina Dogwood Festival. Apr.

Tar Heel Classic Horse Show. Early May.

Iredell County Fair. 1 wk beginning Labor Day.

National Balloon Rally. 3rd wkend Sept.

Motels

★ **FAIRFIELD INN BY MARRIOTT.** *1505 E Broad St.* 704/878-2091; FAX 704/873-1368. 118 rms, 2 story. S $54; D $64; each addl $5; under 17 free. Crib free. TV; cable. Pool. Complimentary continental bkfst. Restaurant nearby. Ck-out noon. Business servs avail. Cr cds: A, C, D, DS, MC, V.

[D] [≈] [✕] [🖾] [SC]

✔★ **HAMPTON INN.** *715 Sullivan Rd.* 704/878-2721; FAX 704/873-6694. 122 rms, 2 story. S $54-$64; D $59-$69; under 18 free; higher rates wkends, special events. Crib free. TV; cable (premium), VCR avail. Pool. Complimentary continental bkfst. Ck-out 11 am. Meeting rm. Business servs avail. In-rm modem link. Cr cds: A, C, D, DS, MC, V.

[D] [≈] [✕] [🖾] [SC]

★ ★ ★ **HOLIDAY INN.** *1215 Garner Bagnal Blvd.* 704/878-9691; FAX 704/873-6927. 134 rms, 2 story. S, D $74-$84; under 18 free; higher rates special events. Crib free. TV; cable. Pool. Coffee in rms. Restaurant 6:30 am-2 pm, 5-9 pm. Rm serv. Bar 5 pm-2 am. Ck-out noon. Meeting rms. Business servs avail. In-rm modem link. Sundries. Cr cds: A, C, D, DS, JCB, MC, V.

[D] [≈] [✕] [🖾] [SC]

✔★ **RED ROOF INN.** *1508 E Broad St.* 704/878-2051; FAX 704/872-3885. 115 rms, 3 story. S $34.99-$40.99; D $38.99-$51.99; each addl $5; under 18 free. Crib free. TV; cable. Complimentary coffee in lobby. Restaurant nearby. Ck-out noon. Cr cds: A, C, DS, MC, V.

[D] [✕] [🖾] [SC]

Inn

★ ★ ★ **HIDDEN CRYSTAL.** *(Sulphur Springs Rd, Hiddenite 28636)* 17 mi NW on US 64. 704/632-0063; FAX 704/632-3562; res: 800/439-1639. 12 rms, 2 share bath, 2 story. S, D $75-$115; each addl $15; suites $160. Crib free. TV; cable. Pool. Complimentary full bkfst. Restaurant 11:30 am-2 pm, 5-9 pm; closed Sun. Ck-out 10:30 am, ck-in 2 pm. Luggage handling. Business servs avail. Colonial house built in 1930s. Totally nonsmoking. Cr cds: A, MC, V.

[D] [≈] [✕] [🖾] [SC]

Tryon (B-3)

(See also Hendersonville)

Pop 1,680 **Elev** 1,085 ft **Area code** 704 **Zip** 28782

Information Polk County Travel & Tourism, Visitor Information, 425 N Trade St; 800/440-7848.

On the southern slope of the Blue Ridge Mountains in the "thermal belt," almost at the South Carolina border, Tryon was named for Royal Governor William Tryon, who held office during the Revolution. The Fine Arts Center is the focal point for much of the cultural life of the community.

What to See and Do

Foothills Equestrian Nature Center (FENCE). 300-acre nature preserve has 5 mi of riding and hiking trails; wildlife programs; bird and nature walks. Host to many equestrian events. (Daily) 500 Hunting Country Rd. Phone 704/859-9021.   **Free.**

White Oak Mountain. Scenic drive around the mountain. Turn off onto Houston Rd at Columbus and take dirt road, which winds around mountain.

Inns

★ ★ ★ **IVY TERRACE.** *(Main St (SC 176), Saluda 28773)* Approx 5 mi N on US 176. 704/749-9542; FAX 704/749-2017; res: 800/749-9542. 7 rms, 2 story. No rm phone. S, D $95-$140. TV in parlor. Complimentary continental bkfst. Restaurant nearby. Ck-out 11 am, ck-in 1-6 pm. Luggage handling. Meeting rm. Business servs avail. Built in 1890; antiques. Totally nonsmoking. Cr cds: MC, V.

[D] [✕] [🔥]

★ ★ ★ **PINE CREST.** *200 Pine Crest Lane.* 704/859-9135; res: 800/633-3001. 4 rms in main building, 30 rms in 9 cottages, 1-2 story, 10 suites. S, D $125-$165; each addl $35; cottage rms $140-$185; suites $140-$435; under 12 free. Crib free. TV; cable; VCR (movies free). Complimentary continental bkfst; afternoon refreshments. Restaurant (see PINE CREST INN). Rm serv. Ck-out 11 am, ck-in 3 pm. Business servs avail. Tennis privileges. Golf privileges. Lawn games. Situated on 3 acres in the foothills of the Blue Ridge Mountains; library, stone fireplaces; some rms with equestrian, hunt club theme. Cr cds: A, DS, MC, V.

[🏃] [⛳] [✕] [🖾]

Restaurant

★ ★ ★ **PINE CREST INN.** *(See Pine Crest Inn)* 704/859-9135. Hrs: 8-9:30 am, 6-9 pm. Closed Sun. Res accepted. Continental menu. Bar. Wine cellar. Semi-a la carte: bkfst $5-$10, dinner $17-$25. Specialties: crab cakes, rack of lamb, crème brulée. Outdoor dining. Elegant, rustic decor in the style of a Colonial tavern; heavy pine tables, beamed ceiling, stone fireplace. Cr cds: A, DS, MC, V.

Warsaw (C-7)

Pop 2,859 **Elev** 160 ft **Area code** 910 **Zip** 28398

What to See and Do

Duplin Wine Cellars. Largest winery in state. Videotape, tour, wine-tasting, retail outlet. (Daily exc Sun; closed most hols) 2 mi S via US 117; off I-40 exit 380. Phone 910/289-3888.   **Free.**

Motel

★ ★ **SQUIRE'S VINTAGE INN.** *748 NC 24/50. 910/296-1831; FAX 910/296-1431.* 12 rms. S $56; D $63; each addl $15; under 12 free. TV. Complimentary continental bkfst. Restaurant 11:30 am-2 pm, 5:30-10 pm; Sat, Sun from 5:30 pm. Ck-out 11 am. Golf privileges. Nature trail. English gardens; gazebos. Cr cds: A, D, MC, V.

D ⚡ ⛷ 🏊 🔥 SC

Restaurant

★ ★ **COUNTRY SQUIRE.** *748 NC 24 & 50. 910/296-1831.* Hrs: 11:30 am-2 pm, 5:30-10 pm; Sat 5:30-11 pm; Sun noon-2 pm, 5:30-10 pm. Closed Thanksgiving, Dec 24, 25. Res accepted. Bar. Semi-a la carte: lunch $2.25-$11.25, dinner $8.95-$30.95. Child's meals. Specializes in beef, poultry. Five dining rms with historical themes. Gardens. Cr cds: A, C, D, MC, V.

D SC ➟

Washington (B-9)

(See also Greenville)

Founded 1776 **Pop** 9,075 **Elev** 14 ft **Area code** 919 **Zip** 27889
Information Chamber of Commerce, PO Box 665; 919/946-9168.

First American village named for the first president, Washington was rebuilt on the ashes left by evacuating Union troops in April, 1864. The rebels lost the town in March, 1862, and, because it was an important saltwater port, tried to retake it for two years. Evidence of the shelling and burning can be seen in the stone foundations on Water St. Water sports, including sailing, yachting, fishing and swimming, are popular.

What to See and Do

Bath State Historic Site. Oldest incorporated town in state (1705). Buildings include Bonner House (ca 1820), Van Der Veer House (ca 1790) and Palmer-Marsh House (ca 1745). (Apr-Oct, daily; rest of yr, daily exc Mon; closed some major hols) St Thomas Episcopal Church (ca 1735) (daily; free). Visitor Center, film. Picnic area. 14 mi E on US 264 & NC 92. Phone 919/923-3971. ¢

Annual Event

Washington Summer Festival. Beach music street dance, ski show, arts and crafts, children's rides, more. 3 days last full wkend July.

Motels

✔★ **COMFORT INN.** *1636 Carolina Ave, US 17N. 919/946-4444; FAX 919/946-2563.* 56 rms, 2 story. S $48; D $53; each addl $5; under 18 free. Crib free. TV; cable (premium). Pool. Complimentary continental bkfst. Restaurant adj 6 am-10 pm. Ck-out noon. Business servs avail. In-rm modem link. Exercise equipt; weight machine, stair machine. Refrigerators avail. Cr cds: A, C, D, DS, JCB, MC, V.

D 🏊 ⚡ 🏋 🔥 SC

★ ★ **DAYS INN.** *916 Carolina Ave. 919/946-6141; FAX 919/946-6167.* 76 rms, 2 story. S $49-$54; D $50-$55; each addl $5; under 18 free. Crib free. TV; cable (premium). Pool. Bar 4 pm-2 am; entertainment wknds. Ck-out noon. Business servs avail. In-rm modem link. Cr cds: A, C, D, DS, JCB, MC, V.

D 🏊 🏋 🔥 SC

Inns

★ **PAMLICO HOUSE.** *400 E Main St. 919/946-7184; FAX 919/946-9944; res: 800/948-8507.* 4 rms, 2 story. S $65-$75; D $75-$85; each addl $15. Children over 6 yrs only. TV; cable. Complimentary full bkfst. Ck-out 11 am, ck-in 3 pm. Former rector's house (1906); antiques, library. Cr cds: A, DS, MC, V.

🏋 🔥

✔★ ★ **RIVER FOREST MANOR.** *(600 E Main St, Belhaven 27810) Approx 30 mi E on US 264 at marina on Intracoastal Waterway. 919/943-2151; FAX 919/943-6628; res: 800/346-2151.* 11 rms, 2 story. S, D $50-$85. TV; cable (premium). Pool; whirlpool. Complimentary continental bkfst, coffee. Restaurant (see RIVER FOREST MANOR). Ck-out 11 am, ck-in 2 pm. Business servs avail. Gift shop. Airport transportation. Tennis. View of river. 1899 building, antique furnishings. Golf carts avail for touring town. Cr cds: A, MC, V.

D ⚡ 🎾 🏊 🔥 🏋

Restaurant

★ ★ **RIVER FOREST MANOR.** *(See River Forest Manor Inn) 919/943-2151.* Hrs: 6-8:30 pm; Sun brunch 11 am-2 pm. Bar. Dinner buffet $15.95. Sun brunch $6.95. Specialties: crabmeat casserole, pickled sausages, oyster fritters. Salad bar. Classical Greek-revival house built 1899. Cr cds: A, MC, V.

D

Waynesville (B-2)

(See also Asheville, Cherokee, Maggie Valley)

Pop 6,758 **Elev** 2,644 ft **Area code** 704 **Zip** 28786
Information Visitor & Lodging Information, 1233 N Main St, Ste I-40; 800/334-9036.

Popular with tourists, this area offers mountain trails for riding and hiking, superb scenery, golf and fishing in cool mountain streams. Waynesville is 26 miles from the Cherokee Indian Reservation (see CHEROKEE) and Great Smoky Mountains National Park (see). Maggie Valley (see), about six miles northwest, is in a particularly attractive area.

Motels

★ **ECONO LODGE.** *909 Russ Ave. 704/452-0353; FAX 704/452-3329.* 40 rms, 2 story. June-Oct: S $47; D $70; each addl $5; under 18 free; lower rates rest of yr. Crib free. TV; cable (premium). Pool. Complimentary continental bkfst. Restaurant nearby. Ck-out 11 am. Cr cds: A, C, D, DS, MC, V.

D 🏊 ⚡ 🏋 SC

✔★ **PARKWAY INN.** *2093 Dellwood Rd W. 704/926-1841; res: 800/5376394; FAX 704/926-6093.* 30 rms. June-Labor Day: S, D $79.50; higher rates Oct, special events; lower rates rest of yr. Crib $5. TV; cable. Complimentary coffee. Restaurant nearby. Ck-out 11 am. Refrigerators, microwaves avail. Picnic tables. Cr cds: A, DS, MC, V.

⚡ 🔥

Inns

★ ★ **BALSAM MOUNTAIN INN.** *(Seven Springs Dr, Balsam 28707) 7 mi W on US 74W Balsam exit. 704/456-9498; FAX 704/456-9298; res: 800/224-9498.* E-mail obi1c3po@dnet.net; web www.aski.net/ncmark/balsam.htm. 50 rms, 21 with shower only, 3 story, 8 suites. No A/C. No rm phones. June-Oct, winter wkends: S, D $95; each addl $15; suites $115-$150; wkend, hol rates (2-day min); lower rates rest of yr. Crib free. Complimentary coffee in library. Dining rm 8-9:30 am, noon-1:30 pm, 6-7:30 pm; Sun noon-2 pm; wkend hrs vary. Ck-out 11 am, ck-in 3 pm. Meeting rm. Business servs avail. Gift shop. Restored, turn-of-the-century inn nestled on scenic mountainside. Near Great Smoky Mountain Scenic Railway. Cr cds: DS, MC, V.

D ⤢ ⚓ SC

★ **GRANDVIEW LODGE.** *809 Valley View Circle Rd. 704/456-5212; FAX 704/452-5432; res: 800/255-7826.* E-mail sarnold@ haywood.main.nc.us. 9 rms, 6 with shower only, 1 A/C, 1-2 story, 2 kit. suites. No rm phones. MAP: S $80; D $105-$110; each addl $30; kit. suites $115; family, wkly rates. TV; cable, VCR avail. Dining rm, sittings: 8 am, 6 pm; also 1 pm Sun. Ck-out 10 am, ck-in 1 pm. 27-hole golf privileges. Game rm. Lawn games. Some refrigerators. Picnic tables. Built 1890; restored mountain guest lodge. Totally nonsmoking. No cr cds accepted.

👫 ⤢ ⚓

★ ★ **THE OLD STONE INN.** *109 Dolan Rd. 704/456-3333; res: 800/432-8499.* 22 rms, 1-2 story. No A/C. No rm phones. S $74-$124; D $89-$139; MAP avail. TV; cable (premium). Dining rm 8-9 am, 6-8 pm. Ck-out 11 am, ck-in 3 pm. Porches. Cr cds: DS, MC, V.

⤢ ⚓

★ ★ ★ **THE SWAG.** *2300 Swag Rd, W on US 19, then 2.3 mi N on US 276 to Hemphill Rd, then left for 4 mi, follow sign up private driveway. 704/926-0430; FAX 704/926-2036; res: 800/789-7672.* Web www.theswag.com. This mountaintop inn, decorated with early American crafts and furniture, was constructed out of six authentic log structures, including an old church, which were transported from their sites to their present setting on 250 wooded acres. 16 rms, 1-2 story, 3 cabins. AP, mid-May-Oct: S $235-$490; each addl $80; higher rates: wkends, hols (2-3-day min); fall foliage. Closed rest of yr. Children over 7 yrs only. Coffee, tea in rms. Dining rm (public by res), 2 sittings: noon & 7 pm. Ck-out 11 am, ck-in 3 pm. Business servs avail. Gift shop. Underground raquetball court. Badminton, croquet court. Sauna, whirlpool. Massage. Fireplaces. Balconies. Library, video collection. Swimming pond with swinging bridge. Walking trails. Cr cds: A, DS, MC, V.

D ⤢ 🏊 👫 ⚓

★ ★ ★ **WINDSONG.** *(459 Rock Cliffe Ln, Clyde 28721) W on I-40, exit 24, then 3 mi N on NC 209, then 2½ mi W on Riverside Dr, then 1 mi N on Ferguson Cove Loop. 704/627-6111; FAX 704/627-8080.* E-mail 100263.375@compuserv.com; web www.bbonline.com. 5 rms, 2 story. No A/C. Rm phones avail. S $99-$108; D $110-$120; guest house $150; each addl $10-$20; wkly rates. Children over 8 yrs only. TV; VCR (movies avail). Heated pool. Complimentary full bkfst. Ck-out 11 am, ck-in 3 pm. Business servs avail. Tennis. Game rm. Balconies. Grills. Contemporary log house on mountainside; fireplace and special theme decor in rms. Totally nonsmoking. Cr cds: DS, MC, V.

👫 ⤢ 🏊 ⚓

★ ★ **THE YELLOW HOUSE.** *610 Plott Creek Rd. 704/452-0991; res: 800/563-1236; FAX 704/452-1140.* Web www.bbonline .com/n.c./yellowhouse. 6 rms, 1 with shower only, 3 story, 4 suites. No A/C. S $115-$220; D $125-$230; each addl $20; suites $140-$250; golf plans; wkends, hols 2-day min; higher rates special events. Children over 12 yrs only. TV in common rm; cable. Complimentary coffee in rms. Complimentary full bkfst. Ck-out 11 am, ck-in 2 pm. Business servs avail. Luggage handling. Tennis privileges. 18-hole golf privileges, greens fee $45, pro, putting green, driving range. Fireplaces, refrigerators; some in-rm whirlpools, minibars, wet bars. Some balconies. House on 2 ½ acres of lawns and gardens built in 1885. Totally nonsmoking. Cr cds: MC, V.

👫 👟 ⤢ ⚓

Resort

★ ★ **WAYNESVILLE COUNTRY CLUB INN.** *PO Box 390, 1½ mi W on US 23/19A Bypass off I-40. 704/456-3551; FAX 704/456-3555; res: 800/627-6250.* 94 rms, eight 1-bedrm cottages, 1-2 story. MAP, May-Oct: S $110-$155; D $144-$180; cottages $180-$216; each addl $50;

lower rates rest of yr. TV; cable. Pool. Dining rm 7-9:15 am, 10 am-4 pm, 6:30-8:30 pm. Bar 4-10 pm; entertainment Tues, Wed, Fri, Sat. Ck-out noon. Meeting rms. Business servs avail. Bellhops. Airport transportation. Tennis. 27-hole golf, greens fee $20-$25, pro. Downhill ski 20 mi. Health club privileges. Balconies. Cr cds: MC, V.

👟 👫 👟 🏊 ⤢ ⚓

Wilkesboro (A-4)

(See also Jefferson)

Settled 1779 **Pop** 2,573 **Elev** 1,042 ft **Area code** 910 **Zip** 28697

What to See and Do

Stone Mountain State Park. A 13,500-acre natural landmark with waterfalls and wooded areas. The mountain, in the center of the park, is a 600-ft dome-shaped granite mass measuring 6 mi in circumference. The park is popular for mountain climbing. There are 17 mi of designated trout streams. Extensive nature, hiking trails. Picnicking. Developed and primitive camping (dump station). Interpretive program in summer. Standard fees. 25 mi NE on NC 18, SR 1002. Phone 910/957-8185.

Motels

★ ★ **ADDISON.** *2 mi N on US 421. 910/838-1000; FAX 910/667-7548; res: 800/672-7218.* 114 rms, 2 story. S $46.99-$55.99; D $51.99-$65.99; each addl $5; under 18 free. Crib free. TV; cable (premium). Pool. Coffee in lobby. Complimentary continental bkfst. Restaurant adj 6 am-11 pm; Fri, Sat to 1 am. Ck-out 11 am. Meeting rm. Business servs avail. Some refrigerators. Cr cds: A, C, D, DS, MC, V.

D 🏊 ⚓ SC

✔★ **QUALITY INN.** *US 421 & 268 Bypass. 910/667-2176; FAX 910/838-9103.* 100 rms, 2 story. S $44.95; D $49.95; each addl $5. Crib free. TV; cable. Pool. Complimentary continental bkfst. Restaurant 11 am-9:30 pm. Ck-out 11 am. Meeting rms. Valet serv. Cr cds: A, C, D, DS, JCB, MC, V.

D 🏊 ⤢ ⚓ SC

Williamston (B-9)

(See also Washington)

Pop 5,503 **Elev** 80 ft **Area code** 919 **Zip** 27892

What to See and Do

Hope Plantation. Two-hr guided tour of Georgian plantation house (ca 1800) built by Governor David Stone. Period furnishings; outbuildings; gardens. (Mar-Dec 22, Mon-Sat, also Sun afternoons) US 13 to Windsor, then 4 mi W on NC 308. Phone 919/794-3140. ¢¢¢ Included in admission is

King-Bazemore House (1763). Tour of this unique colonial-style house with gambrel roof, dormer windows and solid brick ends. Period furnishings; outbuildings; gardens.

Motels

✔★ **COMFORT INN.** *Jct US 17 & US 13/64. 919/792-8400; FAX 919/792-9003; res: 800/827-8400.* 59 rms, 2 story. S $43; D $47; each addl $5; suites $46-$51; under 18 free. Crib free. Pet accepted. TV; cable (premium). Complimentary continental bkfst. Restaurant nearby.

Ck-out noon. Business servs avail. Exercise equipt; weight machine, bicycles. Cr cds: A, C, D, DS, ER, JCB, MC, V.

★ ★ **HOLIDAY INN.** *1 mi S on US 17. 919/792-3184; FAX 919/792-9003.* 100 rms, 2 story. S, D $49; each addl $4; under 18 free. Crib free. Pet accepted. TV; cable (premium). Pool. Restaurant 6 am-9:30 pm. Rm serv. Bar 5 pm-midnight. Ck-out noon. Meeting rms. Business center. In-rm modem link. Cr cds: A, C, D, DS, JCB, MC, V.

Wilmington (D-8)

(See also Southport, Wrightsville Beach)

Settled 1732 **Pop** 55,530 **Elev** 25 ft **Area code** 910 **E-mail** info@cape-fear.nc.us **Web** www.cape-fear.nc.us
Information Cape Fear Coast Convention & Visitors Bureau, 24 N 3rd St, 28401; 910/341-4030 or 800/222-4757.

Chief port of North Carolina, Wilmington is the region's major trade and retail center. Manufacturing, tourism and port-oriented business lead the area's growth.

Patriots who defied the Crown in the Revolution were led by William Hooper, signer of the Declaration of Independence. In 1765, eight years before the Boston Tea Party, the citizens of Wilmington kept the British from unloading their stamps for the Stamp Act. Cornwallis held the town for almost a year in 1781 as his main base of operation. After the battle of Guilford Courthouse, the Lord General came back to Wilmington before heading for Yorktown and defeat.

During the Civil War, blockade runners brought fortunes in goods past Federal ships lying off Cape Fear, making Wilmington the Confederacy's chief port until January, 1865, when it fell. Wilmington was North Carolina's biggest town until 1910, when railroad-fed industries of the inland Piedmont area outgrew the limited facilities of the harbor. The channel, harbor and expanded port facilities bring goods from throughout the world to the area.

What to See and Do

Battleship *North Carolina.* World War II vessel moored on west bank of Cape Fear River. Tour of museum, gun turrets, galley, bridge, sick bay, engine room, wheelhouse. (Daily) Jct of US 74/76, 17 & 421. Phone 910/251-5797. ¢¢¢

Bellamy Mansion Museum of History and Design Arts. Restored 1859 landmark home has exhibits featuring history, restoration, southern architecture and regional design arts. Tours. (Wed-Sun) 5th & Market Sts. Phone 910/251-3700. ¢¢

Burgwin-Wright House (1770). Restored colonial town house built on foundation of abandoned town jail. British General Cornwallis had his headquarters here during April, 1781. Eighteenth-century furnishings and garden. Tours. (Tues-Sat; closed some major hols; also Jan & wk of Dec 25) 224 Market St, at 3rd St. Phone 910/762-0570. ¢¢

Cape Fear Museum. Interprets social and natural history of Lower Cape Fear. Changing exhibits. (Daily exc Mon; closed major hols) 814 Market St. Phone 910/341-7413. ¢

Carolina Beach State Park. This 700-acre park is a naturalist's delight; the rare Venus' flytrap as well as 5 other species of insect-eating plants grow here. Fishing; boating (ramps, marina). Picnicking, concession. Nature, hiking trails. Camping (dump station). Naturalist program. Standard fees. 15 mi S off US 421. Phone 910/458-8206 or marina 910/458-7770.

Cotton Exchange. Specialty shops and restaurants in historic buildings on Cape Fear River. (Daily; some stores closed Sun, closed some major hols) N Front St. Phone 910/343-9896.

Greenfield Gardens. A 150-acre municipal park with 180-acre lake, 5-mi scenic drive; canoe and paddleboat rentals (Apr-Oct); bike path; fragrance

garden; amphitheater; picnicking; nature trail. (Daily) 2½ mi S on US 421. Phone 910/341-7855. **Free.**

Moores Creek National Battlefield. In 1776 the loosely knit colonists took sides against each other—patriots versus loyalists. Colonels Moore, Lillington and Caswell, with the blessing of the Continental Congress, broke up the loyalist forces, captured the leaders and seized gold and quantities of weapons. The action defeated British hopes of an early invasion through the South and encouraged North Carolina to be the first colony to instruct its delegates to vote for independence in Philadelphia. The 86-acre park has a visitor center near entrance to explain the battle. Picnic area. (Daily; closed Jan 1, Dec 25) 17 mi N on US 421, then 3 mi W on NC 210. Phone 910/283-5591. **Free.**

North Carolina Aquarium/Fort Fisher. Fifteen aquariums of North Carolina native sea life; marine exhibits, films, workshops, programs; nature trails. (Daily; closed Jan 1, Thanksgiving, Dec 25) 21 mi S on US 421, in Kure Beach. Phone 910/458-8257. ¢¢

Orton Plantation Gardens. 20 acres. Formerly a rice plantation, now beautiful gardens with ancient oaks, magnolias, ornamental plants, lawn and water scenes; rice fields now a waterfowl refuge. Antebellum Orton House (not open), begun in 1730, can be seen from garden paths. Overlooks Cape Fear River. (Mar-Nov, daily) 18 mi S on NC 133. Phone 910/371-6851. ¢¢¢

Poplar Grove Plantation (ca 1850). Restored Greek-revival plantation; manor house, smokehouse, tenant house, blacksmith, weaver; also country store. Guided tours (daily; closed Thanksgiving, also late Dec-Jan). 14 mi NE on US 17. Phone 910/686-9989 or 910/686-4868. ¢¢¢

Sightseeing cruises.

Captain J.N. Maffitt **River Cruises.** Five-mi narrated sightseeing cruise covering Wilmington's harbor life and points of interest. Also "river taxi" service (addl fee) from Battleship *North Carolina.* (May-Sept, daily) Located at the foot of Market St. Phone 910/343-1611 or 800/676-0162. ¢¢

Henrietta II **Paddlewheel Riverboat Cruises.** One-and-one-half-hr narrated sightseeing cruise down Cape Fear River to North Carolina State Port. (June-Aug, 2 cruises daily exc Mon; Apr-May, Sept-Oct, 1 cruise daily exc Mon) Dinner cruises (Apr-Dec, Fri and Sat; June-Aug, Wed-Sat). Downtown, at riverfront. For reservations phone 910/343-1611 or 800/676-0162. ¢¢¢

St John's Museum of Art. Collection of Mary Cassatt prints; paintings and works on paper, Jugtown Pottery, sculpture. Changing exhibits; lectures; educational programs. (Daily exc Mon; closed hols) 114 Orange St. Phone 910/763-0281. ¢

Wilmington Railroad Museum. Exhibits on railroading past and present, centering on the Atlantic Coast Line and other Southeastern rail lines. HO scale regional history exhibit on 2nd floor; outside are ACL steam locomotive and caboose for on-board viewing. (Daily; closed Jan 1, Thanksgiving, Dec 25) 501 Nutt St. Phone 910/763-2634. ¢¢

Annual Events

North Carolina Azalea Festival. Garden and home tours, horse show, celebrity entertainers, pageants, parade, street fair. Early Apr.

Riverfest. Arts and crafts, music, dancing and entertainment; boat rides; raft regatta; street fair. Phone 910/452-6862. 1st full wknd Oct.

Motels

★ ★ ★ **COURTYARD BY MARRIOTT.** *151 Van Campen Blvd (28403), near New Hanover Regional Airport.* 910/395-8224; FAX 910/452-5569. 128 rms, 2 story. Mid-May-mid-Oct: S, D $79; suites $99-$129; under 18 free; wknds (2-day min); higher rates special events; lower rates rest of yr. Crib free. TV; cable (premium), VCR avail. Complimentary coffee in rms. Restaurant 6-10 am. Bar 5-11 pm. Ck-out noon. Meeting rms. Business servs avail. In-rm modem link. Valet serv. Coin lndry. Exercise equipt; bicycle, stair machine. Pool; whirlpool. Some bathrm phones, in-rm whirlpools, refrigerators, microwaves, wet bars. Some balconies. Cr cds: A, D, DS, MC, V.

✔★ **DAYS INN.** *5040 Market St (28405).* 910/799-6300; FAX 910/791-7414. 122 rms, 2 story. S $48-$85; D $54-$85; each addl $6; family rates; higher rates: Azalea Festival, summer hol wkends. Crib free. TV; cable (premium). Pool. Restaurant 6 am-9 pm. Ck-out 11 am. Business servs avail. Sundries. Cr cds: A, C, D, DS, JCB, MC, V.

D ⚊ ⚒ 🔥 SC

★★ **THE DOCKSIDER INN.** *(202 Fort Fisher Blvd, Kure Beach 28449)* 20 mi S on US 421. 910/458-4200; res: 800/383-8111; FAX 910/458-6468. 34 rms, 3 story, 15 kits. Memorial Day-Labor Day: S, D $99-$149; kits. $99-$149; under 18 free; 2-day min wkends, 3-day min hols; lower rates rest of yr. Crib free. TV; cable. Pool. Restaurant nearby. Ck-out 11 am. Refrigerators, microwaves. On beach. Cr cds: A, DS, MC, V.

D ⚊ 🔥 SC

★★ **FAIRFIELD INN BY MARRIOTT.** *306 S College Rd (28403).* 910/392-6767. 134 rms, 3 story. Apr-Sept: S, D $57.95-$95.95; each addl $6; under 18 free; lower rates rest of yr. Crib free. TV; cable (premium). Pool. Complimentary continental bkfst. Restaurant nearby. Ck-out noon. Meeting rms. Business servs avail. Cr cds: A, C, D, DS, MC, V.

D ⚊ ⚒ 🔥 SC

✔★ **FAIRFIELD INN BY MARRIOTT.** *4926 Market St (28403).* 910/791-8850; FAX 910/791-8858. 119 rms, 2 story. Apr-Sept: S, D $55-$87; each addl $5; under 18 free; lower rates rest of yr. Crib free. TV; cable (premium). Pool. Complimentary continental bkfst. Restaurant nearby. Ck-out noon. Business servs avail. In-rm modem link. Cr cds: A, C, D, DS, MC, V.

D ⚊ ⚒ 🔥 SC

✔★ **GREEN TREE INN.** *5025 Market St (28405).* 910/799-6001; res: 800/225-7666. E-mail grntreenc@aol.com. 123 rms, 2 story. Apr-Sept: S, D $55-$70; each addl $4; under 16 free; wkly rates; higher rates special events; lower rates rest of yr. Crib free. TV; cable (premium). Pool. Complimentary continental bkfst. Restaurant adj 11 am-10 pm. Bar 5 pm-2 am. Ck-out noon. Business servs avail. Cr cds: A, C, D, DS, MC, V.

D ⚊ ⚒ 🔥 SC

★★ **HAMPTON INN.** *5107 Market St (28403).* 910/395-5045; FAX 910/799-1974. 118 rms, 2 story. Apr-Sept: S $65; D $99; under 18 free; lower rates rest of yr. Crib free. TV; cable (premium). Pool. Complimentary continental bkfst. Restaurant nearby. Ck-out noon. Meeting rms. Business servs avail. In-rm modem link. Microwaves avail. Cr cds: A, C, D, DS, MC, V.

D ⚊ ⚒ 🔥 SC

★ **HoJo INN.** *3901 Market St (28403).* 910/343-1727. 80 rms. Apr-Labor Day: S, D $70; each addl $5; under 16 free; lower rates rest of yr. Crib free. TV; cable (premium). Complimentary coffee in lobby. Restaurant nearby. Ck-out 11 am. Meeting rms. Business servs avail. Microwaves avail. Cr cds: A, C, D, DS, MC, V.

D ⚒ 🔥 SC

★★ **HOLIDAY INN.** *4903 Market St (28405).* 910/799-1440; FAX 910/799-2683. 232 rms, 2 story. Mar-Oct: S, D $70-$135; under 12 free; lower rates rest of yr. Crib free. TV; cable (premium). Pool; poolside serv. Restaurant 6 am-1 pm, 5-10 pm. Rm serv. Bar 5 pm-2 am. Ck-out noon. Coin lndry. Meeting rms. Business servs avail. In-rm modem link. Valet serv. Sundries. Free airport transportation. Some in-rm whirlpools. Cr cds: A, D, DS, JCB, MC, V.

D ⚊ ⚒ 🔥 SC

✔★ **RAMADA INN CONFERENCE CENTER.** *5001 Market St (28405).* 910/799-1730; FAX 910/799-1730. 100 rms, 2 story. Apr-Sept: S, D $44-$110; under 18 free; wkly rates; golf plans; higher rates: Azalea Festival, summer, hol wkends; lower rates rest of yr. Crib free. TV; cable (premium). Pool. Playground. Complimentary full bkfst. Restaurant 6 am-2 pm, 5-10 pm. Rm serv. Bar 5 pm-2 am; entertainment. Ck-out noon.

Meeting rms. Business servs avail. Valet serv. Free airport transportation. Some refrigerators. Cr cds: A, DS, MC, V.

D ⚊ ⚒ 🔥 SC

✔★ **SLEEP INN.** *5225 Market St (28405).* 910/313-6665; FAX 910/313-2679. 104 rms, 3 story. S, D $59-$89; under 18 free; hols (2-day min). Crib free. TV; cable (premium), VCR avail. Complimentary continental bkfst. Restaurant nearby. Ck-out 11 am. Meeting rms. Business servs avail. In-rm modem link. Valet serv. Exercise equipt; bicycle, rowers. Pool. Cr cds: A, C, D, DS, JCB, MC, V.

D ⚊ 🏃 ⚒ 🔥 SC

✔★ **SUPER 8.** *3604 Market St (28403).* 910/343-9778. 62 rms, 3 story. Apr-Sept: S, D $45.98-$55.98; each addl $5; suites $70-$80; under 12 free; lower rates rest of yr. Crib free. TV; cable (premium). Complimentary coffee in lobby. Ck-out 11 am. Business servs avail. Cr cds: A, C, D, DS, MC, V.

D ⚒ 🔥 SC

Motor Hotels

★★ **COMFORT INN-EXECUTIVE CENTER.** *151 S College Rd (28403).* 910/791-4841. 146 rms, 6 story. S, D $55-$100; each addl $5; suites $110; under 18 free; golf package. Crib free. TV; cable (premium). Pool. Complimentary continental bkfst. Restaurant nearby. Ck-out noon. Meeting rms. Business servs avail. Valet serv. Cr cds: A, C, D, DS, MC, V.

D ⚊ ⚒ 🔥 SC

★★ **HOWARD JOHNSON PLAZA.** *5032 Market St (28405).* 910/392-1101. 124 rms, 5 story. S, D $89-$125; each addl $10; suites $150-$275; under 18 free; higher rates: Azalea Festival, Memorial Day, July 4, Labor Day. Crib free. TV; cable (premium). Indoor pool; whirlpool. Restaurant 6 am-2 pm, 4-10 pm. Rm serv. Bar to 11 pm. Ck-out noon. Meeting rms. Business servs avail. Bellhops. Exercise equipt; stair machine, bicycles, sauna. Refrigerator in suites. Microwaves avail. Cr cds: A, C, D, DS, MC, V.

D ⚊ 🏃 ⚒ 🔥 SC

Hotels

★★ **HAMPTON INN & SUITES-LANDFALL PARK.** *1989 Eastwood Rd (28403),* 4 mi E on US 74. 910/256-9600; FAX 910/256-1996. 120 rms, 4 story, 30 kit. suites. May-Sept: S, D $109; suites $149-$349; under 18 free; wkly rates; golf plans; wkends (2-day min); higher rates special events; lower rates rest of yr. Crib free. Pet accepted; $25. TV; cable (premium). Complimentary continental bkfst. Restaurant adj 11 am-11 pm. Bar 4:30-10 pm. Ck-out 11 am. Meeting rms. Business servs avail. In-rm modem link. Concierge. Gift shop. Drug store. Coin lndry. 18-hole golf privileges, greens fee $75, pro, putting green, driving range. Exercise equipt; bicycles, stair machine. Pool; poolside serv. Some in-rm whirlpools, fireplaces; refrigerator, microwave, wet bar in kit. suites. Picnic tables, grills. Cr cds: A, C, D, DS, MC, V.

D ✦ 🏃 ⚊ 🏃 ⚒ 🔥 SC

★★★ **HILTON.** *301 N Water St (28401).* 910/763-5900; FAX 910/763-0038. 178 rms, 9 story. S, D $99-$169; each addl $10; suites $149-$300. Crib free. TV; cable (premium). Pool; whirlpool. Restaurant 6:30 am-10:30 pm. Bar 4 pm-1 am. Ck-out noon. Meeting rms. Business servs avail. In-rm modem link. Gift shop. Free airport transporation. Exercise equipt; stair machine, bicycle. Boat dock. Luxury level. Cr cds: A, C, D, DS, ER, JCB, MC, V.

D ⚊ 🏃 🏃 ⚒ 🔥 SC

★★ **HOLIDAY INN EXPRESS.** *160 Van Campen Blvd (28403).* 910/392-3227; FAX 910/395-9907. 131 rms, 5 story. S, D $99-$139; each addl $10; suites $119-$159; under 19 free. Crib free. TV; cable (premium). Pool. Complimentary continental bkfst. Restaurant nearby. Ck-out noon. Meeting rms. Business servs avail. Coin lndry. Exercise equipt; bicycle, treadmill. Refrigerators in suites. Microwaves avail. Cr cds: A, C, D, DS, JCB, MC, V.

D ⚖ 🏃 🚭 🔥 SC

Inns

★ ★ **CATHERINE'S INN.** *410 S Front St (28401). 910/251-0863; FAX 910/772-9550; res: 800/476-0723.* 5 rms, 2 story. S $75-$85, D $85-$99; each addl $20. Children over 10 yrs only. TV; cable (premium), VCR. Complimentary full bkfst. Restaurant nearby. Ck-out 11 am, ck-in 3-6 pm. Luggage handling. Built in 1880; antiques. Totally nonsmoking. Cr cds: A, MC, V.

🚭 🔥

★ **CURRAN HOUSE.** *312 S Third St (28401). 910/763-6603; res: 800/763-6603; FAX 910/763-5116.* 3 rms, 2 story. S, D $60-$100; 2-day min hols. Children over 12 yrs only. TV; cable (premium), VCR (free movies). Complimentary full bkfst. Ck-out 11 am, ck-in 3 pm. Original building from 1837, addition made in 1885. Lawn games. Totally nonsmoking. Cr cds: MC, V.

🚭 🔥 SC

★ ★ **FRONT STREET INN.** *215 S Front St (28401). 910/762-6442; FAX 910/762-8991.* 9 rms, 2 story. S, D $89-$163; under 18 free; wkly rates. Crib free. TV; cable (premium), VCR avail. Complimentary continental bkfst. Restaurant nearby. Ck-out 11 am, ck-in 4 pm. Business servs avail. In-rm modem link. Exercise equipt; weights, bicycle. Game rm. Many refrigerators; microwaves avail. Balconies. Brick building (1923) that once housed Salvation Army. Cr cds: A, D, DS, MC, V.

🏃 🚭 🔥

★ ★ **GRAYSTONE INN.** *100 S 3rd St (28401). 910/763-2000; FAX 910/763-5555.* 7 rms, 3 story. S, D $95-$125; each addl $15; suites $125-$150. Complimentary continental bkfst. Restaurant nearby. Ck-out 11 am, ck-in 4 pm. Built in 1906; antiques. Totally nonsmoking. Cr cds: A, MC, V.

🚭 🔥 SC

★ ★ ★ **INN AT ST THOMAS COURT.** *101 S 2nd St (28401). 910/343-1800; FAX 910/251-1149; res: 800/525-0909.* 36 suites, 1-3 story. Apr-Oct: S, D $125; 2-bedrm suites $195; golf plan; lower rates rest of yr. Crib free. TV; cable (premium), VCR (free movies). Complimentary continental bkfst. Complimentary coffee in rms. Restaurant nearby. Taproom (wine, beer) noon-2 am. Ck-out 11 am, ck-in 3 pm. Meeting rm. Business center. In-rm modem link. Luggage handling. Valet serv. Concierge serv. Microwaves. Balconies. Renovated commercial building (1906) in historic district; entrance court, library, antiques. Cr cds: A, D, DS, MC, V.

D 🚭 🔥 🚶

★ ★ **TAYLOR HOUSE.** *14 N 7th St (28401). 910/763-7581; res: 800/382-9982.* 5 rms, 2 story. S, D $95-$110; wkends (2-day min). Complimentary full bkfst; afternoon refreshments. Ck-out 10:30 am, ck-in 4-7 pm. Free airport transportation. Built in 1905; many fireplaces, antiques. Totally nonsmoking. Cr cds: A, MC, V.

🚭 🔥

★ ★ **THE WORTH HOUSE.** *412 S Third St (28401). 910/762-8562; FAX 910/763-2173; res: 800/340-8559.* E-mail worthhse@wilmington.net; web www.bbonline.com/nc/north. 7 rms, 3 story. Mar-Oct: S $75-$110; D $80-$115; each addl $20; lower rates rest of yr. Children over 8 yrs only. TV in sitting rm; cable (premium). Complimentary full bkfst. Ck-out 11 am, ck-in 4-7 pm. Victorian house (1893) in historic district. Totally nonsmoking. Cr cds: A, MC, V.

🚭 🔥 SC

Restaurants

★ **BEACHES.** *2025 Eastwood Rd (28403). 910/256-4622.* Hrs: 11:30 am-2 pm, 5-10 pm; Fri to 10:30 pm; Sat 5:30-10:30 pm. Closed Jan 1, Thanksgiving, Dec 24, 25. Res accepted. Bar. Semi-a la carte: lunch $3.95-$7.95, dinner $9.95-$17.95. Child's meals. Specializes in steak, seafood. 2 dining rms. Maritime theme. Cr cds: A, C, D, DS, MC, V.

D 🍷

✔ ★ **CAFFE PHOENIX.** *9 S Front St (28401). 910/343-1395.* Hrs: 11:30 am-10 pm; Fri, Sat to 11 pm; Sun 5-10 pm. Closed most major hols. Italian menu. Bar. Semi-a la carte: lunch $5-$8, dinner $8-$16. Child's meals. Specializes in pasta, salad. Outdoor dining. Casual decor. Cr cds: A, D, DS, MC, V.

D

✔ ★ **DRAGON GARDEN.** *341-52 S College Rd (28403), Univ Commons. 910/452-0708.* Hrs: 11 am-2:30 pm, 5-9:30 pm; Fri, Sat to 10:30 pm; Sun to 9 pm. Closed Thanksgiving, Dec 24, 25. Res accepted. Chinese menu. Bar. Semi-a la carte: lunch $4-$6, dinner $5-$12. Specializes in Hunan, Szechuan, and Mandarin dishes. Chinese decor with many artifacts. Cr cds: A, DS, MC, V.

D 🍷

✔ ★ **EDDIE ROMANELLI'S.** *5400 Oleander Dr (28403). 910/799-7000.* Hrs: 11:30-2 am. Closed some major hols. Italian, Amer menu. Bar. Semi-a la carte: lunch $3.95-$7.95, dinner $8.95-$17.95. Child's meals. Specializes in marinated steak, prime rib, pasta. Parking. Beamed ceiling with skylight. Cr cds: A, MC, V.

D 🍷

★ ★ **ELIJAH'S.** *2 Ann St (28401). 910/343-1448.* Hrs: 11:30 am-3 pm, 5-10 pm; Fri, Sat 5-11 pm; Sun brunch to 3 pm. Closed Jan 1, Thanksgiving, Dec 25. Bar to midnight. Semi-a la carte: lunch $5.95-$9.95, dinner $9.95-$22.95. Sun brunch $4.95-$7.95. Child's meals. Specializes in chowder, hot crab dip, sandwiches. Pianist Sun brunch. Outdoor dining. View of river. Nautical decor; former maritime museum. Cr cds: A, DS, MC, V.

D 🍷 ♥

★ ★ **HARVEST MOON.** *5704 Oleander Dr (28403). 910/792-0172.* Hrs: 5-10 pm; Fri, Sat to 10:30 pm; Sun 5-9 pm. Closed most major hols; also Sun Nov-Apr. Res accepted. Bar. Semi-a la carte: dinner $10.95-$20.95. Child's meals. Specializes in beef, seafood, pasta. Mediterranean decor. Cr cds: A, C, D, DS, MC, V.

D

✔ ★ ★ **HIERONYMUS SEAFOOD.** *5035 Market St (28405). 910/392-6318.* Hrs: 11 am-10 pm; Fri, Sat to 11 pm. Closed Jan 1, Thanksgiving, Dec 24, 25. Res accepted. Bar to 2 am. Semi-a la carte: lunch $3.95-$7.95, dinner $4.95-$14.95. Child's meals. Specializes in seafood, prime rib. Entertainment, pianist. Outdoor dining. Oyster bar in lounge. Nautical decor. Cr cds: A, C, D, DS, MC, V.

D SC 🍷

✔ ★ **MARKET STREET CASUAL DINING.** *6309 Market St (28405). 910/395-2488.* Hrs: 5-11 pm. Closed Thanksgiving, Dec 25, Superbowl Sunday. Bar to 1 am. Semi-a la carte: dinner $4.95-$14.95. Specializes in grilled seafood & steak. Cr cds: A, DS, MC, V.

D 🍷

✔ ★ **OH! BRIAN'S.** *4311 Oleander Dr (28403). 910/791-1477.* Hrs: 11 am-11 pm; Sun to 10 pm. Closed Thanksgiving, Dec 25. Res accepted Sun-Thur. Bar to 1 am. Semi-a la carte: lunch $3.95-$6.95, dinner $4.95-$16.95. Child's meals. Specializes in barbecue ribs, chicken, salads. Atrium. Cr cds: A, D, MC, V.

D 🍷

★ ★ **PILOT HOUSE.** *2 Ann St (28401), Chandler's Wharf on waterfront. 910/343-0200.* Hrs: 11:30 am-3 pm, 5-10 pm; Fri, Sat to 11 pm; Sun brunch to 3 pm. Closed Jan 1, Dec 24, 25. Res accepted. A la carte entrees: lunch $2.95-$9.95, dinner $10.95-$22.95. Child's meals. Specialties: crab melt sandwich, Caribbean fudge pie. Own bread. Parking. Outdoor dining. Located in restored area of waterfront; built in 1870. Cr cds: A, DS, MC, V.

★★ **PORT CITY CHOP HOUSE.** *1981 Eastwood Rd (28405).* *910/256-4955.* Hrs: 11:30 am-10 pm; Fri to 10:30 pm; Sat 4:30-10:30 pm. Closed Sun; Thanksgiving, Dec 25. Res accepted. Bar. Semi-a la carte: lunch $5-$10, dinner $13.95-$33.95. Child's meals. Specializes in Angus beef, grilled fish, lamb chops. Outdoor dining. Contemporary decor with brick and light woods; open kitchen area. Cr cds: A, D, DS, MC, V.

★ **RUCKERJOHN'S.** *5511 Carolina Beach Rd (28412), on US 421.* *910/452-1212.* Hrs: 11 am-10 pm; Fri, Sat to 11 pm. Closed Thanksgiving, Dec 25. Bar. Semi-a la carte: lunch $4.50-$6.50, dinner $5.95-$14.95. Child's meals. Specializes in beef, pasta, seafood. Casual, friendly atmosphere. Cr cds: A, MC, V.

★★ **VINNIE'S.** *1900 Eastwood Rd (28403), in Lumina Station.* *910/256-0995.* Web www.vinnies.com. Hrs: from 5 pm; Sun brunch 10:30 am-3 pm. Closed Jan 1, Dec 25. Bar from 4 pm. Semi-a la carte: dinner $10.95-$49.95. Sun brunch $3.95-$17.95. Specializes in prime rib, seafood. Own pasta. Outdoor dining. Semi-formal club decor; mahogany woodwork, framed caricatures. Cr cds: A, C, DS, MC, V.

★ **WATER STREET.** *5 S Water St (28401).* *910/343-0042.* Hrs: 11-1 am. Closed Dec 25. Res accepted. Bar. Semi-a la carte: lunch $3.95-$7.95, dinner $4.95-$14.95. Specializes in seafood, sandwiches, soups. Entertainment Wed-Sun ranges from dinner theater, jazz, blues. Outdoor dining. Riverfront dining in old warehouse. Cr cds: A, MC, V.

Unrated Dining Spot

DOXEY'S MARKET & CAFE. *1319 Military Cut-Off Rd (28403).* *910/256-9952.* Hrs: 9 am-7 pm; Sun noon-6 pm. Closed most major hols. Semi-a la carte: lunch, dinner $3-$7. Specializes in soups, salads, sandwiches. Salad bar. Cr cds: A, DS, MC, V.

Wilson (B-8)

(See also Rocky Mount)

Pop 36,930 **Elev** 145 ft **Area code** 919

Located just off I-95, midway between New York and Florida, Wilson is a convenient rest stop for road-weary travelers. It is one of the Southeast's leading antique markets and is said to have one of the nation's largest tobacco markets.

Motels

✔★★ **COMFORT INN.** *4941 US 264W (27893).* *919/291-6400;* FAX 919/291-7744. 76 rms, 2 story. S, D $55-$59; each addl $6; suites $75-$125; under 18 free. Crib free. TV; cable (premium), VCR avail. Pool. Complimentary continental bkfst. Restaurant adj 6 am-10 pm. Ck-out 11 am. Meeting rms. Business servs avail. Some refrigerators. Cr cds: A, C, D, DS, MC, V.

★★ **HAMPTON INN.** *1801 S Tarboro St (27893), 6 mi E of I-95, exit 121.* *919/291-2323;* FAX 919/291-7696. 100 rms, 2 story. S $52-$57; D $57-$64; under 18 free. Crib free. TV; cable (premium). Pool. Complimentary continental bkfst, coffee. Restaurant nearby. Ck-out 11 am. Meeting rm. Business center. In-rm modem link. Health club privileges. Cr cds: A, C, D, DS, JCB, MC, V.

★ **HOLIDAY INN.** *1815 US 301 S (27893).* *919/243-5111;* FAX 919/291-9697. 100 rms, 2 story. S $57-$60; D $62-$65; each addl $5; under 12 free. Crib free. TV; cable (premium). Pool. Restaurant 6 am-2 pm, 5-10 pm. Rm serv. Bar. Ck-out noon. Meeting rms. Business servs avail. Cr cds: A, C, D, DS, JCB, MC, V.

Inn

★ **MISS BETTY'S.** *600 W Nash St (27893).* *919/243-4447;* res: *800/258-2058.* 10 rms, 3 with shower only, 2 story, 3 suites. S $50-$60; D $60-$80. Adults only. TV; cable (premium), VCR avail. Complimentary full bkfst. Restaurant opp 6 am-10 pm. Ck-out 11 am, ck-in 3 pm. Business servs avail. Three restored houses (1859 & 1900). Many antiques. Totally nonsmoking. Cr cds: A, C, D, DS, MC, V.

Winston-Salem (A-5)

(See also Greensboro, High Point, Lexington)

Founded Salem: 1766; Winston: 1849; combined as Winston-Salem: 1913 **Pop** 143,485 **Elev** 912 ft **Area code** 336

Information Convention and Visitors Bureau, PO Box 1408, 27102; 336/777-3796 or 800/331-7018.

First in industry in the Carolinas and one of the South's chief cities, Winston-Salem is a combination of two communities. Salem, with the traditions of its Moravian founders and Winston, an industrial center, matured together. Tobacco markets, large banks and arts & crafts galleries contribute to this thriving community.

What to See and Do

Hanging Rock State Park. Approx 6,200 acres in Sauratown Mts. Lake swimming, bathhouse; fishing; boating (rentals). Nature trails. Picnicking, concession. Tent & trailer sites, six family cabins (Mar-Nov, by reservation only). Observation tower. Standard fees. 32 mi N, between NC 66 & 89 near Danbury. Phone 910/593-8480.

Historic Bethabara Park. Site of first Moravian settlement in North Carolina (1753); restored buildings include Gemeinhaus (1788), Potter's House (1782), Buttner House (1803); reconstructed palisade fort (1756-1763); stabilized archaeological foundations of original settlement and God's Acre (graveyard); reconstructed community gardens (1759). Visitor center; exhibits, slide show. Nature trails. Picnicking. (Apr-Nov, daily; walking tour all yr) 2147 Bethabara Rd. Phone 336/924-8191. **Free.**

Historic Old Salem (1766). Restoration of a planned community which Moravians, with their Old World skills, made the 18th-century trade and cultural center of North Carolina's Piedmont. Many of the sturdy structures built for practical living have been restored and furnished with original or period pieces. Early crafts are demonstrated throughout the town. Here also is an original Tannenberg organ in working condition. A number of houses are privately occupied. Nine houses plus outbuildings are open to the public. Tours (self-guided) start at Visitor Center on Old Salem Rd. Special events are held during the yr. (Daily; no tours Thanksgiving, Dec 24 & 25) S of business district on Old Salem Rd. Phone 336/721-7300. Ticket to all buildings (exc museum) ¢¢¢¢ In the old village are

Salem Academy and College (1772). (1,100 women) When founded by the Moravians, it was the only school of its kind for women in the

South. The Fine Arts Center offers art exhibits, lectures, films, concerts and plays (mid-Sept-mid-May, daily; evenings during special events; some fees). Church St, on Salem Sq in Old Salem. Campus tours on request; phone 336/721-2702.

Museum of Early Southern Decorative Arts. Twenty-one period rms and six galleries (1690-1820), with decorative arts of Maryland, Virginia, Georgia, Kentucky, Tennessee and the Carolinas. (Daily; closed Thanksgiving, Dec 24 & 25) 924 S Main St. Phone 336/721-7360. Museum ¢¢¢; Combination ticket including Old Salem ¢¢¢¢¢

R.J. Reynolds Tobacco Company, Whitaker Park Cigarette Plant. Guided tours (Mon-Fri; closed hols) 1100 Reynolds Blvd. Phone 336/741-5718. **Free.**

Reynolda House, Museum of American Art. On estate of the late R.J. Reynolds of the tobacco dynasty. American paintings, original furniture, art objects, costume collection. Adj is Reynolda Gardens, 125 acres of open fields and naturalized woodlands; formal gardens, greenhouse. (Tues-Sat, also Sun afternoons; closed Jan 1, Thanksgiving, Dec 25) Approx 2 mi N on University Pkwy, then 1/2 mi E on Coliseum Dr then N on Reynolda Rd. Phone 336/725-5325. ¢¢¢

SciWorks. Hands-on exhibits of physical and natural sciences; planetarium; 31-acre outdoor environmental park and nature trails. (Daily; closed Jan 1, Easter, Thanksgiving, Dec 25) 400 W Hanes Mill Rd at US 52N. Phone 336/767-6730. ¢¢¢

Southeastern Center for Contemporary Art. Exhibits by contemporary artists from across the country with accompanying educational programs. (Daily exc Mon; closed hols) 750 Marguerite Dr. Phone 336/725-1904. ¢¢

Tanglewood Park. Swimming; fishing; boating (paddleboats, canoes); horseback riding; golf, miniature golf, tennis; nature trail. Picnicking, playgrounds. Camping (fee); accommodations. Deer park. Steeplechase (early May). (Daily) 12 mi SW off I-40, in Clemmons. Phone 336/778-6300. Per vehicle ¢

Wake Forest University (1834). (5,600 students) On campus are Fine Arts Center, Museum of Anthropology; also Reynolda Village, a complex of shops, offices & restaurants. Bowman Gray School of Medicine is on Medical Center Blvd. 3 mi NW off Reynolda Rd. Phone 336/759-5000.

Motels

(Rates are generally higher during Furniture Market)

✔★ ★ **COURTYARD BY MARRIOTT.** 3111 University Pkwy (27105). 336/727-1277; FAX 336/722-8219. 124 rms, 2 story. S, D $70; under 18 free; higher rates graduation (May). Crib free. TV; cable (premium), VCR avail. Pool; whirlpool. Complimentary coffee in lobby. Restaurant nearby. Ck-out 11 am. Coin lndry. Business servs avail. Exercise equipt; weights, stair machine. Cr cds: A, C, D, DS, MC, V.

D ≈ 🏋 🛩 🔥 SC

★ **DAYS INN.** 3330 Silas Creek Pkwy S (27103), I-40 Wake Forest exit. 336/760-4770; FAX 336/760-1085. 135 rms, 5 story. S $52-$54; D $57-$60; each addl $5; under 17 free. Crib free. TV; cable (premium). Pool; whirlpool. Complimentary continental bkfst. Ck-out noon. Meeting rms. Business servs avail. Health club privileges. Cr cds: A, D, DS, MC, V.

D ≈ 🛩 🔥 SC

✔★ ★ **HAMPTON INN.** 5719 University Pkwy (27105). 336/767-9009; FAX 336/661-0448. 117 rms, 2 story. S $60-$65; D $65-$70; under 18 free. Crib free. TV; cable (premium). Pool. Complimentary continental bkfst. Restaurant adj 6 am-10 pm. Ck-out noon. Meeting rms. Business servs avail. In-rm modem link. Cr cds: A, C, D, DS, MC, V.

D ≈ 🛩 🔥 SC

★ ★ **HAMPTON INN.** 1990 Hampton Inn Court (27103), I-40 exit 189, at Stradford Rd. 336/760-1660; FAX 336/768-9168. 131 rms, 5 story. S, D $63-$120; each addl $6; under 18 free; higher rates special events. TV; cable (premium). Pool. Complimentary continental bkfst. Ck-

out noon. Meeting rms. Business servs avail. Exercise equipt; bicycle, stair machine. Some refrigerators. Minibars. Cr cds: A, C, D, DS, MC, V.

D ≈ 🏋 🛩 🔥 SC

★ ★ **RESIDENCE INN BY MARRIOTT.** 7835 N Point Blvd (27106). 336/759-0777; FAX 336/759-9671. 88 kit. suites, 2 story. S, D $89-$129; under 18 free; wkly rates. Crib free. Pet accepted; $75-$150. TV; cable (premium). Heated pool; whirlpool. Complimentary continental bkfst. Complimentary coffee in rms. Ck-out noon. Coin lndry. Valet serv. Health club privileges. Refrigerators, microwaves. Picnic tables, grills. Cr cds: A, C, D, DS, JCB, MC, V.

D 🐾 ≈ 🛩 🔥 SC

Hotels

★ ★ ★ **ADAM'S MARK AT WINSTON PLAZA.** 425 N Cherry St (27101). 336/725-3500; FAX 336/721-2240. Web www.adamsmark.com. 315 rms, 17 story. S $140-$160; D $160-$180; each addl $20; suites $275-$550; under 18 free; wkend rates. Crib free. Garage $6. TV; cable (premium), VCR avail. Indoor pool; sauna, poolside serv. Restaurants 6:30 am-11 pm. Rm serv 24 hrs. Bar 11:30-1 am; entertainment Fri-Sat. Ck-out 1 pm. Convention facilities. Business servs avail. In-rm modem link. Concierge. Gift shop. Exercise equipt; weight machine, bicycles. Game rm. Refrigerator in suites. Local art displayed. Luxury level. Cr cds: A, C, D, DS, MC, V.

D ≈ 🏋 🛩 🔥 SC

★ ★ ★ **HOLIDAY INN SELECT.** 5790 University Pkwy (27105). 336/767-9595; FAX 336/744-1888. 150 rms, 6 story. S, D $86; suites $99; under 18 free; wkend rates. Crib free. TV; cable (premium), VCR avail. Pool. Restaurant 6:30 am-2 pm, 5:30-10 pm. Bar; entertainment. Ck-out noon. Meeting rms. Business servs avail. Exercise equipt; rower, bicycles. Health club privileges. Some refrigerators, minibars. Cr cds: A, C, D, DS, JCB, MC, V.

D ≈ 🏋 🛩 🔥 SC

★ ★ ★ **THE RADISSON MARQUE.** 460 N Cherry St (27101). 336/725-1234; FAX 336/722-9182. 293 rms, 9 story. S $115-$135; D $125-$145; each addl $10; 1-3 bedrm suites $150-$400; under 18 free; wkend rates. Crib free. Garage $6. TV; cable (premium). Heated pool; whirlpool. Restaurant 6:30 am-10 pm. Bar noon-1 am, Sun to 11 pm. Ck-out noon. Convention facilities. Business servs avail. Gift shop. Exercise equipt; weights, bicycles. Health club privileges. Microwaves avail. Built around 9-story atrium; glass-enclosed elvtrs. Luxury level. Cr cds: A, C, D, DS, JCB, MC, V.

D ≈ 🏋 🛩 🔥 SC

Inns

★ ★ **AUGUSTUS T. ZEVELY INN.** 803 S Main St (27101). 336/748-9299; res: 800/928-9299; FAX 336/721-2211. 12 rms, 3 story. S, D $80-$125; each addl $15; suite $205; higher rates special events. Children over 12 yrs only. TV; cable (premium). Complimentary continental bkfst; complimentary full bkfst on wkends. Restaurant opp 11:30 am-9 pm. Ck-out 11:30 am, ck-in 3-9 pm. Business servs avail. Some in-rm whirlpools, refrigerators, fireplaces. Some balconies. Built in 1844; restored to its mid-19th century appearance. Moravian ambience. Cr cds: A, MC, V.

D 🛩 🔥

★ ★ ★ **BROOKSTOWN INN.** 200 Brookstown Ave (27101). 336/725-1120; FAX 336/773-0147; res: 800/845-4262. Web getawaysmag .com. 71 units, 4 story. S $90-$115; D, suites $105-$125; each addl $20; under 12 free. Crib free. TV; cable (premium). Complimentary continental bkfst; afternoon refreshments. Ck-out noon, ck-in 2 pm. Business servs avail. In-rm modem link. Restored brick cotton mill (1837); antiques, handmade quilts. Cr cds: A, D, MC, V.

D 🛩 🔥 SC

★ ★ **COLONEL LUDLOW.** 434 Summit (27101), at W Fifth. 336/777-1887; FAX 336/777-1890; res: 800/301-1887. E-mail innkeeper

@bbinn.com; web www.bbinn.com. 10 rms, 2 story, 1 suite. S $75; D, suite $139-$209; higher rates special events. TV; cable (premium), VCR (movies). Complimentary full bkfst. Complimentary coffee in rms. Restaurant adj 5-10 pm. Ck-out 11:30 am, ck-in 3 pm. Business servs avail. In-rm modem link. Concierge serv. Valet serv. Exercise equipt; weights, bicycles. In-rm whirlpools, refrigerators, microwaves. Balconies. Victorian homes built in 1887 & 1895; restored and converted. Cr cds: A, DS, MC, V.

✗ ✗ 🔥

✔★ ★ **MANOR HOUSE BED & BREAKFAST.** (Clemmons 27012) 12 mi SW on US 158, I-40 exit 182, in Tanglewood Park. 336/778-6300; FAX 336/778-6379. 18 rms in lodge, 10 rms in manor house, 2 story. S $35-$95; D $45-$107. Crib $3. TV. Pool; wading pool, lifeguard. Complimentary continental bkfst. Ck-out noon, ck-in 2 pm. Meeting rms. Tennis. Golf. Facilities of Tanglewood Park avail. Cr cds: A, C, D, MC, V.

🖭 ✗ 🏃 🕴 ≈ ✗ 🔥 SC

Restaurants

★ ★ **OLD SALEM TAVERN.** 736 S Main St (27101). 336/748-8585. Hrs: 11:30 am-2 pm, 5-9 pm; Fri, Sat to 9:30 pm. Closed Jan 1, Dec 25. Serv bar. Semi-a la carte: lunch $4.75-$7.50, dinner $14-$23. Child's meals. Specializes in roast duck, fresh seafood, rack of lamb. Outdoor dining. Cr cds: A, DS, MC, V.

🖵

★ ★ **RYAN'S.** 719 Coliseum Dr (27106). 336/724-6132. Hrs: 5-10 pm; Fri & Sat to 10:30 pm. Closed Sun; Jan 1, Thanksgiving, Dec 24, 25. Res accepted. Continental menu. Bar 4:30-11:45 pm. Semi-a la carte: dinner $15.25-$34.95. Own soup, some desserts. Specializes in beef, seafood. Wooded setting. Cr cds: A, C, D, MC, V.

D 🖵

★ ★ **STALEY'S CHARCOAL STEAK HOUSE.** 2000 Reynolda Rd. 336/723-8631. Hrs: 5-10 pm; Fri, Sat to 11 pm. Closed Sun; major hols. Res accepted. Serv bar. Semi-a la carte: dinner $11.95-$39.95. Child's meals. Specializes in steak, prime rib, shish kebab. Fountain at entrance. Cr cds: A, MC, V.

D

★ ★ **THE VINEYARDS.** 120 Reynolda Village (27106). 336/748-0269. Hrs: 11 am-10 pm. Closed Sun; most major hols. Bar. Semi-a la carte: lunch $4-$10, dinner $10-$19. Child's meals. Specializes in beef, seafood, vegetarian dishes. Outdoor dining. Entertainment Thurs-Sat. Casual, contemporary atmosphere. Cr cds: A, MC, V.

D 🖵

★ ★ **ZEVELY HOUSE.** 901 W 4th St (27101). 336/725-6666. Hrs: 5:30-9 pm; Sun brunch 11 am-2 pm. Closed Mon; some major hols. Res accepted. Bar. Semi-a la carte: dinner $12.95-$21. Sun brunch $6.95-$11. Child's meals. Specialties: potato cakes with smoked salmon & caviar, chicken pie, mixed grill. Outdoor dining. Antiques, fireplace in older brick house. Cr cds: A, D, MC, V.

D 🖵

Wrightsville Beach (D-8)

(See also Wilmington)

Pop 2,937 **Elev** 7 ft **Area code** 910 **Zip** 28480

A very pleasant family-oriented resort town, Wrightsville Beach offers swimming, surfing, fishing and boating. The public park has facilities for tennis, basketball, soccer, softball, volleyball, shuffleboard and other sports.

Motels

★ **ONE SOUTH LUMINA.** 1 S Lumina Ave. 910/256-9100; res: 800/421-3255. 21 kit. suites, 3 story. Memorial Day-Labor Day: S, D $145-$160; each addl $5; wkly rates; lower rates rest of yr. Crib $3. TV; cable. Pool. Complimentary coffee in rms. Restaurant nearby. Ck-out 11 am. Guest lndry. Microwaves. Balconies. On swimming beach. Cr cds: A, C, D, DS, ER, JCB, MC, V.

🖭 ≈ ✗ 🔥 SC

★ ★ **SILVER GULL.** 20 E Salisbury St. 910/256-3728; FAX 910/256-2909; res: 800/842-8894. 32 kit. units, 3 story. June-Labor Day: S, D $125-$200; each addl $7; higher rates wkends; lower rates rest of yr. Crib $7. TV; cable. Ck-out 11 am. Coin lndry. Balconies. On ocean. Cr cds: A, DS, MC, V.

🖭 ≈

★ ★ **SURF SUITES.** 711 S Lumina Ave. 910/256-2275; FAX 910/256-1206. 45 kit. suites, 4 story. Late May-early Sept: S, D $150-$200; each addl $10; wkly rates; wkend rates; lower rates rest of yr. TV; cable. Pool. Complimentary coffee in lobby. Restaurant adj 11 am-10 pm. Ck-out 11:30 am. Coin lndry. Balconies. Swimming beach. Cr cds: A, C, D, DS, MC, V.

D 🖭 ≈ ✗ 🔥 SC

★ **WATERWAY LODGE.** 7246 Wrightsville Ave. 910/256-3771; FAX 910/256-6916; res: 800/677-3771. 42 units, 3 story. May-Sept: S, D $86-$110; each addl $5; kits. $90-$110; under 12 free; wkly rates; golf plans; higher rates wkends (2-day min); lower rates rest of yr. Pet accepted; $15. TV; cable (premium). Pool. Complimentary coffee in lobby. Restaurant opp 11 am-10 pm. Ck-out 11:30 am. Business servs avail. Refrigerators, microwaves. Cr cds: A, D, DS, MC, V.

✔ ≈ ✗ 🔥 SC

Motor Hotel

★ ★ ★ **BLOCKADE RUNNER.** 275 Waynick Blvd, ¼ mi S on US 76. 910/256-2251; FAX 910/256-5502; res: 800/541-1161. Web www.blockade-runner.com. 150 rms, 7 story. Mid-May-mid-Sept: S, D $155-$275; each addl $25; suites $300-$355; under 12 free; lower rates rest of yr. Crib free. TV; cable, VCR avail. Heated pool; whirlpool, lifeguard. Supervised child's activities (June-Labor Day); ages 5-12. Restaurant (see OCEAN TERRACE). Rm serv 24 hrs. Bar; entertainment. Ck-out 11:30 am. Meeting rms. Business servs avail. Free airport transportation. Tennis privileges. Golf privileges. Exercise rm; instructor, bicycles, sauna, steam rm. Sailboat rentals. Private patios, balconies. On ocean. Cr cds: A, C, D, DS, MC, V.

D 🖭 🕴 🏃 ≈ ✗ ✗ 🔥 SC

Inn

★ ★ **THE COTTAGE.** 225 S Lumina Ave. 910/256-2251; FAX 910/256-5502; res: 800/541-1161. Web www.blockade-runner.com. 13 rms, 2 story. Mid-May-mid-Sept: S, D $89-$225; each addl $25; under 12 free; lower rates rest of yr. Crib free. TV in sitting rm. Pool; whirlpool, sauna. Complimentary full bkfst. Restaurant adj 6:30 am-10 pm. Ck-out 11:30 am, ck-in 3 pm. Former boarding house. Totally nonsmoking. Cr cds: A, C, D, DS, MC, V.

D 🖭 ≈ ✗ 🔥 SC

Restaurants

★ ★ **BRIDGE TENDER.** 1414 Airlie Rd, at Wrightsville Beach Bridge. 910/256-4519. Hrs: 11:30 am-2 pm, 5:30-10 pm; Fri, Sat to 11 pm. Closed Jan 1, Thanksgiving, Dec 25. Bar. Semi-a la carte: lunch $4.95-$8.95, dinner $17.95-$23.95. Specializes in seafood, Angus beef. View of waterway, marina. Cr cds: D, DS, MC, V.

★ **CLARENCE FOSTER'S.** *22 N Lumina Ave. 910/256-0224.* Hrs: 5:30-10 pm. Closed Dec 25. Amer menu. Bar to 2 am. Semi-a la carte: dinner $6.75-$19.95. Specializes in seafood. Intimate dining; artwork on display. Cr cds: A, MC, V.

D 🔄

✔★ **DOCKSIDE.** *1308 Airlie Rd. 910/256-2752.* Hrs: 11 am-9:30 pm; wkends to 10 pm. Closed Thanksgiving, Dec 24-25. Bar. Semi-a la carte: lunch $1.50-$8.95, dinner $7.95-$17.95. Specializes in grilled seafood, pasta. Outdoor dining. Casual dining. Overlooks dock, waterway; docking facilities. Cr cds: DS, MC, V.

D 🔄

✔★★ **ETRUSCA.** *530 Causeway Dr, in The Landing Shopping Center. 910/256-5077.* Hrs: 5:30-10 pm; Sat to 11 pm; Sun 11:30 am- 2 pm. Closed Jan 1, Thanksgiving, Dec 24, 25. Bar. Semi-a la carte: dinner $9.95-$19.95. Child's meals. Specializes in veal, seafood, pasta. Cr cds: A, DS, MC, V.

D 🔄

★★ **KING NEPTUNE.** *11 N Lumina Ave on US 76. 910/256-2525.* Hrs: 5-10 pm; Sun 5:30-9:30 pm. Closed Thanksgiving, Dec 25. Carribean menu. Bar to 2 am. Semi-a la carte: dinner $5.25-$14.95. Child's meals. Specializes in prime rib, seafood. Nautical decor. Cr cds: A, MC, V.

D SC 🔄

★★ **OCEAN TERRACE.** *(See Blockade Runner Motor Hotel) 910/256-2251.* Hrs: 6:30 am-midnight; Sun brunch 11:30 am-3 pm. Closed wk of Dec 25. Res accepted. Bar. Semi-a la carte: bkfst $6-$10, lunch $5.95-$9.95, dinner $12.95-$24.95. Sun brunch $14.95. Child's meals. Specializes in seafood, pasta, rotating buffet dinners. Pianist Fri; jazz Sun brunch. Parking. Oceanfront outdoor dining. Cr cds: A, D, DS, MC, V.

D 🔄

★★ **OCEANIC.** *703 S Lumina Ave. 910/256-5551.* Hrs: 11:30 am-11 pm; Sun 4-11 pm, Sun brunch 10 am-4 pm. Closed Jan 1, Thanksgiving, Dec 25. Bar. Semi-a la carte: lunch $2.95-$9.95, dinner $10.95-$18.95. Sun brunch $4.75-$6.95. Child's meals. Specializes in seafood. Parking. Outdoor dining. Panoramic view of ocean. Cr cds: A, MC, V.

D 🔄

★★ **PUSSER'S LANDING AT WALLY'S.** *4 Marina Ave. 910/256-2002.* Hrs: deck dining 11:30 am-10:30 pm; upper dining level from 5:30 pm. Closed Dec 25. Res accepted (upper dining level). Bar to midnight. Semi-a la carte: lunch $4.75-$15.95, dinner (upper dining level) $13.95-$20.95. Child's meals. Specializes in seafood, grilled foods. Entertainment Fri-Sun evenings. Beach resort atmosphere; dock. Cr cds: A, DS, MC, V.

D 🔄

Pennsylvania

Population: 11,881,643
Land area: 44,892 square miles
Elevation: 0-3,213 feet
Highest point: Mt Davis (Somerset County)
Entered Union: Second of original 13 states (December 12, 1787)
Capital: Harrisburg
Motto: Virtue, liberty and independence
Nickname: Keystone State
State flower: Mountain laurel
State bird: Ruffed grouse
State tree: Eastern hemlock
State fair: (Pennsylvania State Farm Show), January 10-15, 1998, in Harrisburg
Time zone: Eastern
Web: www.state.pa.us

From its easternmost tip near Bordentown, New Jersey, to its straight western boundary with Ohio and West Virginia, Pennsylvania's 300-mile giant stride across the country covers a mountain-and-farm, river-and-stream, mine-and-mill topography. Its cities, people and resources are just as diverse. Philadelphia is a great city in the eastern part of the state, a treasure house of tradition and historical shrines; Pittsburgh is a great city in the western part, a mighty arsenal of industry. In this state are the Pennsylvania Dutch, their barns painted with vivid hex signs; here also are steel mills. Pennsylvania miners dig nearly all the anthracite coal in the US and still work some of the oldest iron mines in the country. Oil employees work more than 19,000 producing wells, and 55,000 farm families make up 20 percent of the Pennsylvania work force.

Pennsylvania, the keystone of the original 13 states, remains one of the keystones in modern America. A leader in steel and coal production, the state also is a leader in cigar leaf tobacco, apples, grapes, ice cream, chocolate products, mushrooms (nearly half of the US total) and soft drinks, plus factory and farm machinery, electronics equipment, scientific instruments, watches, textile machines, railroad cars, ships, assorted metal products and electrical machinery. This fifth most populous state is also a major factor in national politics.

Pennsylvania has been a keystone of culture. The first serious music in the colonies was heard in Bethlehem; today, it resounds throughout the state—Pittsburgh has an acclaimed symphony, as does Philadelphia. There are 140 institutions of higher learning (including the oldest medical school in the US at the University of Pennsylvania), celebrated art galleries and hundreds of museums.

Despite its size, all of Pennsylvania is within the motorist's grasp. Its 44,000 miles of state highways, including the 470-mile Pennsylvania Turnpike (pioneer of superhighways), plus 69,363 miles of other roads make up one of the largest road networks in the nation.

Swedes made the first settlement on this fertile land at Tinicum Island in the Delaware River in 1643. The territory became Dutch in 1655 and British in 1664. After Charles II granted William Penn a charter that made him proprietor of "Pennsilvania," this Quaker statesman landed here in 1682 and invested the land with his money, leadership and fellow Quakers. The Swedes, Finns and Dutch already in the new land were granted citizenship; soon came Welsh, Germans, Scots, Irish and French Huguenots. Of these, the Germans left the strongest imprint on the state's personality. Commercial, agricultural and industrial growth came quickly, and all these resources were contributed to the Revolution. In Pennsylvania, Washington camped at Valley Forge, the Declaration of Independence was signed and the Constitution drafted.

With Philadelphia the capital of the new nation, tides of pioneers pushed west and north to develop far corners of the state. The Civil War brought fresh industrial development, and for the past century Pennsylvania has continued to develop at an ever-quickening industrial pace. Today the Keystone State is an empire of industry and a storehouse of historic traditions.

When to Go/Climate

Pennsylvania's lowlands and hill country enjoy typical east-coast seasonal temperatures—hot, humid summers; relatively mild winters; crisp falls; and wet springs. The mountains, however, experience short summers and cold, snowy winters.

AVERAGE HIGH/LOW TEMPERATURES (°F)

PHILADELPHIA

Jan 38/23	**May** 73/53	**Sept** 78/59
Feb 41/25	**June** 82/62	**Oct** 66/47
Mar 52/33	**July** 86/67	**Nov** 55/38
Apr 63/42	**Aug** 85/66	**Dec** 43/28

PITTSBURGH

Jan 34/19	**May** 71/48	**Sept** 74/54
Feb 37/20	**June** 79/57	**Oct** 63/42
Mar 49/30	**July** 83/62	**Nov** 50/34
Apr 60/39	**Aug** 81/60	**Dec** 39/24

CALENDAR HIGHLIGHTS

JANUARY

Pennsylvania State Farm Show (Harrisburg). State fair. Phone 717/787-5373.

FEBRUARY

Chocolate Lovers' Extravaganza (Hershey). Hotel Hershey. Everything chocolate—tasting & sampling, chef-taught classes, decorating instruction, and more. For reservations, phone 800/533-3131.

MAY

Devon Horse Show (Philadelphia). Horse Show Grounds in Devon. One of America's leading equestrian events. More than 1,200 horses compete; country fair; antique carriage drive. Phone 610/964-0550.

JUNE

Three Rivers Arts Festival (Pittsburgh). Point State Park. Juried, original works of local and national artists; paintings, photography, sculpture, crafts and videos; artists' market in outdoor plazas. Ongoing performances include music, dance and performance art. Special art projects; film festival; food; children's activities. Phone 412/481-7040.

CoreStates US Pro Cycling Championship (Philadelphia). Longest single-day cycling event in the country—156 miles. Phone 215/973-3546.

JULY

Civil War Heritage Days (Gettysburg). Lectures by historians; Civil War collectors' show; entertainment; Civil War book show; firefighters' festival; fireworks. For information, phone Convention & Visitors Bureau 717/334-6274.

Folk Festival (Kutztown). Festival grounds. Celebration of Pennsylvania Dutch folk culture; quilts, music, dancing and food of Plain and Fancy Dutch. Craftspeople make baskets, brooms, rugs, toleware and other handcrafts. Phone 610/683-8707.

AUGUST

Das Awkscht Festival (Allentown). Macungie Memorial Park. 2,500 antique, classic and special-interest autos; arts and crafts; antique toy show, entertainment, food, fireworks. Phone 610/967-2317.

Musikfest (Bethlehem). Nine sites in downtown historic area. Nine-day festival celebrating Bethlehem's rich musical and ethnic heritage. More than 600 performances of all types of music from folk to rock. Phone 610/861-0678.

SEPTEMBER

Ligonier Highland Games and Gathering of the Clans of Scotland (Ligonier). Idlewild Park. Sports; massed pipe bands, Highland dancing competitions, Scottish fiddling; sheep dog, wool spinning and weaving demonstrations; geneology booth, Scottish fair. Phone 724/238-3666.

Wine Country Harvest Festival (North East). Gravel Pit Park and Gibson Park. Arts and crafts, bands, buses to wineries, food. Phone 814/725-4262.

DECEMBER

Army-Navy Football Game (Philadelphia). John F. Kennedy Memorial Stadium or Veterans Stadium.

The Crossing. Washington Crossing Historical Park (Bucks Co). Reenactment of George Washington's crossing of the Delaware River. Phone 215/493-4076.

Parks and Recreation Finder

Directions to and information about the parks and recreation areas below are given under their respective town/city sections. Please refer to those sections for details.

Key to abbreviations: I.P. = Interstate Park; N.B.C. = National Battlefield & Cemetery; N.B.P. = National Battlefield Park; N.F. = National Forest; N.H. = National Historical Park; N.H.S. = National Historic Site; N.M. = National Monument; N.Mem. = National Memorial; N.M.P. = National Military Park; N.P. = National Park; N.Pres. = National Preserve; N.R. = National Recreational Area; N.S. = National Seashore; N.S.T. = National Scenic Trail; S.B. = State Beach; S.C.P. = State Conservation Park; S.G. = State Garden; S.H.A. = State Historic Area; S.H.P. = State Historic Park; S.N.A. = State Natural Area; S.P. = State Park; S.R. = State Reserve; S.R.A. = State Recreation Area; S.Res.P. = State Resort Park; S.R.P. = State Rustic Park.

NATIONAL PARK AND RECREATION AREAS

Place Name	Listed Under
Allegheny N.F.	WARREN
Allegheny Portage Railroad N.H.S.	EBENSBURG
Delaware Water Gap N.R.	same
Edgar Allan Poe N.H.S.	PHILADELPHIA
Eisenhower N.H.S.	GETTYSBURG N.M.P.
Fort Necessity National Battlefield	UNIONTOWN
Friendship Hill N.H.S.	UNIONTOWN
Gettysburg N.M.P.	same
Hopewell Furnace N.H.S.	same
Independence N.H.	PHILADELPHIA
Johnstown Flood N. Mem.	JOHNSTOWN
Steamtown N.H.S.	SCRANTON
Thaddeus Kosciuszko N.Mem.	PHILADELPHIA
Valley Forge N.H.	same

STATE RECREATION AREAS

Place Name	Listed Under
Bald Eagle S.P.	LOCK HAVEN
Bendigo S.P.	KANE
Blue Knob S.P.	BEDFORD
Black Moshannon S.P.	BELLEFONTE
Caledonia S.P.	CHAMBERSBURG
Canoe Creek S.P.	ALTOONA
Chapman S.P.	WARREN
Clear Creek S.P.	BROOKVILLE
Codorus S.P.	HANOVER
Cook Forest S.P.	CLARION
Fort Washington S.P.	FORT WASHINGTON
French Creek S.P.	POTTSTOWN
Gifford Pinchot S.P.	YORK
Gouldsboro S.P.	MOUNT POCONO
Greenwood Furnace S.P.	LEWISTOWN
Hickory Run S.P.	WHITE HAVEN
Hills Creek S.P.	MANSFIELD
Kettle Creek S.P.	LOCK HAVEN
Kinzua Bridge S.P.	KANE
Kooser S.P.	SOMERSET
Laurel Hill S.P.	SOMERSET
Little Pine S.P.	WILLIAMSPORT
McConnell's Mill S.P.	NEW CASTLE
Moraine S.P.	BUTLER

Ohiopyle S.P.	UNIONTOWN
Ole Bull S.P.	GALETON
Parker Dam S.P.	CLEARFIELD
Pine Grove Furnace S.P.	CARLISLE
Presque Isle S.P.	ERIE
Prince Gallitzin S.P.	ALTOONA
Promised Land S.P.	HAWLEY
Pymatuning S.P.	CONNEAUT LAKE
Raccoon Creek S.P.	AMBRIDGE
Reeds Gap S.P.	LEWISTOWN
Ridley Creek S.P.	MEDIA
S.B. Elliott S.P.	CLEARFIELD
Shawnee S.P.	BEDFORD
Sizerville S.P.	PORT ALLEGANY
Tobyhanna S.P.	MOUNT POCONO
Whipple Dam S.P.	STATE COLLEGE
Yellow Creek S.P.	INDIANA

Water-related activities, hiking, riding, various other sports, picnicking and environmental interpretive centers, as well as camping, are available in many of these areas. More than 116 state parks and four environmental centers are scattered throughout the commonwealth. 57 campgrounds offer camping. Seven are open all year; the rest are open from 2nd Fri Apr-3rd Sun Oct or Dec. Occupancy is limited to two consecutive weeks; $9-$11 resident, $11-$13 nonresident/night (primitive areas); $11-$14 resident, $13-$16 nonresident/night (modern areas). Cabins (daily and weekly rentals spring, fall & winter; 1 wk only, Fri after Memorial Day-Fri before Labor Day). Boat launching (yearly) $10 resident, $15 nonresident. No pets allowed in overnight areas. Write to Department of Commerce, Office of Travel and Tourism, 453 Forum Bldg, Harrisburg 17120, or Bureau of State Parks, PO Box 8551, Harrisburg 17105-8551, for detailed information. Cabin reservations are made by calling the park directly. For other state park information, phone 800/63-PARKS.

SKI AREAS

Place Name	Listed Under
Alpine Mountain Ski Area	STROUDSBURG
Big Boulder Ski Area	WHITE HAVEN
Blue Mountain Ski Area	ALLENTOWN
Blue Knob Ski Area	BEDFORD
Boyce Park Ski Area	PITTSBURGH
Camelback Ski Area	TANNERSVILLE
Doe Mountain Ski Area	ALLENTOWN
Elk Mt Ski Center	CARBONDALE
Hidden Valley Ski Area	SOMERSET
Jack Frost Ski Area	WHITE HAVEN
Montage Ski Area	SCRANTON
Mount Airy Lodge Ski Area	MOUNT POCONO
Mount Tone Ski Resort	CARBONDALE
Mountain View Ski Area	EDINBORO
Seven Springs Mt Resort Ski Area	DONEGAL
Shawnee Mountain Ski Area	SHAWNEE ON DELAWARE
Ski Denton/Denton Hill Ski Area	GALETON
Ski Liberty Ski Area	GETTYSBURG
Ski Roundtop Ski Area	YORK
Ski Sawmill Resort	WELLSBORO
Spring Mountain Ski Area	LIMERICK
Tanglwood Ski Area	HAWLEY

FISHING

Pennsylvania is one of the country's leading states in the amount of waters open to public and private fishing. There are nearly 5,000 miles of trout streams stocked annually and many thousands of miles of warm-water streams plus thousands of acres of lakes with walleye, panfish, muskellunge, and bass. Nonresident fishing license is $35; 3-day tourist license is $15; 7-day tourist license is $30. A $5.50 trout/salmon stamp also is required (for trout fishing only). Write to Pennsylvania Fish and Boat Commission, PO Box 67000, Harrisburg 17106-7000, or phone 717/657-4518, for the annual "Summary of Fishing Regulations and Laws" as well as maps and other useful information.

HUNTING

A license is required to hunt, take, trap or kill any wild bird or animal in the state. Nonresident hunting license, $80.75; children 12-16, $40.75. The license tag must be displayed on the back of outer garment, between the shoulders, at all times. For big-game and turkey hunting and small-game hunting in the fall, 250 square inches of fluorescent orange must be worn on the head, chest and back combined. For the "Official Digest, Pennsylvania Hunting and Trapping Regulations," contact the Pennsylvania Game Commission, 2001 Elmerton Ave, Harrisburg 17110-9797; 717/787-6286.

Driving Information

Safety belts are mandatory for all persons in front seat of vehicle. Children under 4 years must be in an approved passenger restraint anywhere in vehicle: age 4 and older may use a regulation safety belt; ages 1-3 may use a regulation safety belt in back seat only. Children under 4 years must use an approved safety seat in front seat; under age 1 must use an approved safety seat anywhere in the vehicle. For further information phone 717/787-6853.

INTERSTATE HIGHWAY SYSTEM

The following alphabetical listing of Pennsylvania towns in *Mobil Travel Guide* shows that these cities are within 10 miles of the indicated Interstate highways. A highway map should, however, be checked for the nearest exit.

Highway Number	Cities/Towns within 10 miles
Interstate 70	Bedford, Breezewood, Donegal, Greensburg, New Stanton, Somerset, Washington.
Interstate 78	Allentown, Bethlehem, Easton, Hamburg, Kutztown, Lebanon, Shartlesville.
Interstate 79	Conneaut Lake, Edinboro, Erie, Harmony, Meadville, Mercer, Pittsburgh, Washington.
Interstate 80	Bellefonte, Bloomsburg, Brookville, Clarion, Clearfield, Danville, Du Bois, Hazleton, Lewisburg, Lock Haven, Mercer, Mount Pocono, Sharon, Shawnee on Delaware, Stroudsburg, Tannersville, White Haven.
Interstate 81	Ashland, Carlisle, Chambersburg, Harrisburg, Hazleton, Scranton, Wilkes-Barre.
Interstate 83	Harrisburg, York.
Interstate 84	Milford, Scranton.
Interstate 90	Erie, North East.
Interstate 95	Bristol, Philadelphia.

Additional Visitor Information

A free visitors guide is available by calling 800/VISIT-PA, at the Pennsylvania Office of Travel, Tourism and Film Promotion, Dept of Community & Economic Development, PO Box 61, Warrendale 15086.

There are 14 state-run traveler information centers in Pennsylvania; visitors who stop by will find information and brochures most helpful in planning stops at points of interest. Their locations are as follows: I-79

Edinboro (southbound), 1 mile south of the Edinboro exit; I-81 Greencastle (northbound), 1 mile north of the Pennsylvania/Maryland border; I-95 Linwood (northbound), 1/2 mile north of the Pennsylvania/Delaware border; I-70 Warfordsburg (westbound), 1 mile from the Pennsylvania/Maryland border; I-80 West Middlesex (eastbound), 1/2 mile east of the Pennsylvania/Ohio border; Neshaminy Welcome Center, Mile Marker 351 (westbound) on the Pennsylvania Turnpike, 7 miles west of the Pennsylvania/New Jersey border, located inside the plaza building; I-78 Easton (westbound), 1/2 mile west of the Pennsylvania/New Jersey border; Sideling Hill Welcome Center, Mile Marker 172 (eastbound and westbound) on the Pennsylvania Turnpike, 10 miles east of the Breezewood exit, located inside the plaza building; I-81 Lenox (southbound), 4 miles south of the Lenox exit 64; I-83 Shrewsbury (northbound), 1/2 mile north of the Pennsylvania/Maryland border; Zelienople Welcome Center, Mile Marker 21 (eastbound), 21 miles east of the Pennsylvania/Ohio border, located inside the plaza building; I-79 northbound, north of PA/WV line; I-70 Washington County, east of PA/WV line.

Ride with Me—Pennsylvania, Interstate 81 is a 90-minute audio cassette tape that provides information on points of interest along I-81, from New York to Maryland. Topics such as the history of the Pennsylvania Dutch, notable battlegrounds and areas related to the Civil War and anthracite coal miners are discussed. Contact RWM Associates, PO Box 1324, Bethesda, MD 20817; 301/299-7817.

Allentown (D-9)

(See also Bethlehem, Easton, Kutztown, Quakertown)

Founded 1762 **Pop** 105,090 **Elev** 364 ft **Area code** 610
Information Lehigh Valley Convention & Visitors Bureau, PO Box 20785, Lehigh Valley 18002-0785; 610/882-9200.

Allentown, situated in the heart of Pennsylvania Dutch country, is conveniently accessible via a network of major highways. Allentown was originally incorporated as Northamptontown. The city later took the name of its founder, William Allen, a Chief Justice of Pennsylvania. Allentown was greatly influenced by the Pennsylvania Germans who settled the surrounding countryside and helped the city become the business hub for a rich agricultural community.

What to See and Do

Cedar Crest College (1867). (1,700 women) An 84-acre campus that includes nationally registered William F. Curtis Arboretum (tours); chapel with stained-glass windows portraying outstanding women in history; art galleries, sculpture gardens, museum and theater. Campus tours. 100 College Dr. Phone 610/437-4471.

Dorney Park and Wildwater Kingdom. Theme park/water park featuring more than 100 rides and attractions, antique wooden carousel, four world-class roller coasters, including Steel Force—the longest, tallest, fastest steel roller coaster on the East Coast; 11 water slides; Berenstain Bear Country; midway games and entertainment; public picnic facility adjacent to the park. **Wildwater Kingdom** is one of the top seasonal water parks in the country. Dorney Park (May-Oct). Water park (mid-May-Sept). Operating hrs may vary. 3830 Dorney Park Rd. Phone 610/395-3724. ¢¢¢¢

Frank Buchman House. Constructed in 1892, this 3-story row house, typical of Allentown's inner city, is an example of Victorian architecture; period rooms. (Sat & Sun afternoons; also by appt) 117 N 11th St.Phone 610/435-4664. **Free.**

George Taylor House and Park (1768). House of a signer of the Declaration of Independence; 18th-century restoration period rooms; museum; walled garden. Guided tours. (June-Oct, Sat & Sun afternoons; also by appt) 4 mi N off US 22, at Lehigh & Poplar Sts in Catasauqua. Phone 610/435-4664. **Free.**

Haines Mill Museum (ca 1760). Operating gristmill (reconstructed 1909); exhibits portray the development and importance of the gristmill in rural

America. (May-Sept, Sat & Sun afternoons; also hols & by appt) 3 mi W via Hamilton St, at 3600 Dorney Park Rd (Cetronia). Phone 610/435-4664. **Free.**

Lehigh County Museum. Exhibits illustrate economic, social and cultural history of the county. (Mon-Sat, Sun afternoons; closed hols) Old Courthouse, 5th & Hamilton Sts. Phone 610/435-4664. **Free.**

Liberty Bell Shrine. Reconstructed Zion's church has shrine in basement area where Liberty Bell was hidden in 1777; contains a full-size replica of the original bell; a 46-ft mural depicts the journey of the bell; other historical exhibits, art collection. (Mon-Sat afternoons; closed Jan 1, Easter, Thanksgiving, Dec 25) 622 Hamilton, at Church St. Phone 610/435-4232. **Free.**

Lock Ridge Furnace Museum. Exhibits on the development of the US iron and steel industry; emphasis on the anthracite-coal-heated iron industry. Located in a reconstructed 19th-century iron furnace. (May-Sept, Sat & Sun afternoons; also by appt) 6 mi SW via US 222 in Alburtis. Phone 610/435-4664. **Free.**

Muhlenberg College (1848). (1,700 students) Founded by the Lutheran Church to honor patriarch of Lutheranism in America. On campus is the Gideon F. Egner Memorial Chapel, an example of Gothic architecture. Also here is the Center for the Arts, a dramatic building designed by renowned architect Philip Johnson, which houses the Muhlenberg Theater Association. Campus tours. Chew & 24th Sts. Phone 610/821-3230.

Saylor Park Cement Industry Museum. Exhibits on the historical development of the cement industry and its role in modern society. Located in rebuilt cement kilns. (May-Sept, Sat & Sun afternoons; also hols & by appt) 4 mi NE via MacArthur Rd, on N 2nd St in Coplay. Phone 610/435-4664. **Free.**

Skiing.

Doe Mountain. 4 chairlifts, T-bar, 2 rope tows; 15 slopes; patrol, school, rentals; snowmaking; night skiing and snowboarding; restaurant, cafeteria, bar; nursery. Longest run 1 1/2 mi; vertical drop 500 ft. (Dec-mid-Mar, daily) 12 mi SW, 4 1/2 mi off PA 100, just N of Hereford. Phone 610/682-7100 or 800/282-7107 (in PA, ski report). ¢¢¢¢¢

Blue Mountain. 7 chairlifts, T-bar; school, rentals; snowmaking; cafeteria, bar, lodge. Vertical drop 1,082 ft. Also 20 trails with day and night skiing. (Dec-Apr, daily) 17 mi N via PA 145, Treichlers exit, at "Y" turn right to Cherryville, and on to Danielsville, to top of Blue Mountain. Phone 610/826-7700 or 800/235-2226 (in PA, ski report). ¢¢¢¢¢

Trexler Memorial Park. Spring outdoor bulb display (Apr-May). **Gross Memorial Rose Garden** (at peak 2nd wk June) and **Old-Fashioned Garden,** Cedar Pkwy (June-Aug). **Trout Nursery** and Fish-for-Fun stream, Lehigh Pkwy; picnic areas. **West Park,** 16th and Turner. Band concerts (June-Aug). Cedar Crest Blvd. Phone 610/437-7628. **Free.**

Trexler-Lehigh County Game Preserve. A 1,200-acre zoo, petting farm and wilderness tour that is home to more than 350 animals. Scenic overlooks; picnic area. (Memorial Day-Labor Day, daily; April-May, Sept-Oct, wkends) 4 mi W on US 22, then 6 mi N on US 309, near Schnecksville. Phone 610/799-4171. ¢¢

Trout Hall (1770). Oldest house in city, Georgian colonial; restored. Period rooms, museum. Guided tours (Apr-Nov, Tues-Sun afternoons; also by appt; closed most major hols) 414 Walnut St. Phone 610/435-4664. **Free.**

Troxell-Steckel House and Farm Museum (1756). Stone house is an example of German medieval architecture. Period rooms; museum. Swiss-style bank barn adj has exhibits of farm implements, carriages and sleighs. Guided tours. (June-Oct, Sat & Sun afternoons; also by appt) 6 mi N on PA 145, then 1 mi W on PA 329, at 4229 Reliance St in Egypt. Phone 610/435-4664. **Free.**

Annual Events

Mayfair. Allentown parks. Family arts festival with 150 free musical performances; crafts and food. Phone 610/437-6900. Thurs-Mon, Memorial Day wkend.

Das Awkscht Fescht. Macungie Memorial Park. 2,500 antique, classic and special-interest autos; arts and crafts; antique toy show, entertainment, food, fireworks. Phone 610/967-2317. 1st wkend Aug.

Drum Corps International-Eastern Regional Championship. J. Birney Crum Stadium, 21st & Linden Sts. Drum and bugle corps competition. Phone 610/966-5344. Early Aug.

Great Allentown Fair. Fairgrounds. 17th & Chew Sts. Farm and commercial exhibits, rides, games, food, entertainment. Phone 610/435-SHOW. Late Aug-early Sept.

Super Sunday. Hamilton Street Mall. Arts and crafts, food, entertainment. Phone 610/437-7616. Mid-Sept.

Motels

★ **ALLENWOOD.** 1058 Hausman Rd (18104), E on US 22 to PA 309S to Hausman Rd. 610/395-3707. 21 rms. S, D, studio rms $40-$45; each addl $3. Crib free. Pet accepted. TV; cable. Restaurant nearby. Ck-out 11 am. Cr cds: A, DS, MC, V.

★ ★ **COMFORT SUITES.** 3712 Hamilton Blvd (18103). 610/437-9100; FAX 610/437-0221. 122 suites, 4 story. Suites $94-$104; each addl $10; under 18 free. Crib free. TV; cable, VCR avail (movies). Complimentary continental bkfst. Restaurant 7-2 am. Rm serv. Bar; entertainment Thurs-Sat. Ck-out noon. Meeting rms. Business servs avail. In-rm modem link. Sundries. Free airport, RR station, bus depot transportation. Exercise equipt; weights, bicycles. Refrigerators. Cr cds: A, C, D, DS, ER, JCB, MC, V.

✔★ **DAYS INN CONFERENCE CENTER.** 1151 Bulldog Dr (18104). 610/395-3731; FAX 610/395-9899. 282 rms, 2 story. May-Oct: S $79.95; D $85.95; each addl $6; suites $109-$129; under 18 free; wkly rates; package plans; higher rates local festivals; lower rates rest of yr. Crib free. TV; cable. Pool; poolside serv, lifeguard. Playground. Restaurant 6:30 am-10 pm. Bar 2 pm-1 am. Ck-out noon. Coin lndry. Convention facilities. Business servs avail. Sundries. Free airport, bus depot transportation. 18-hole golf privileges. Downhill ski 15 mi. Game rm. Lawn games. Some refrigerators. Some balconies. Cr cds: A, C, D, DS, MC, V.

★ ★ **HAMPTON INN.** 7471 Keebler Way (18106), I-78 exit 14A, S on PA 100. 610/391-1500; FAX 610/391-0386. 127 rms, 5 story. S $70-$78; D $75-$90; under 18 free. Crib free. TV; cable. Complimentary continental bkfst. Restaurant nearby. Ck-out noon. Meeting rms. Business servs avail. Free airport transportation. Exercise equipt; weight machine, bicycle, sauna. Cr cds: A, C, D, DS, MC, V.

✔★ **HOLIDAY INN EXPRESS.** 15th St & US 22 (18103). 610/435-7880; FAX 610/432-2555. 84 rms, 4 story. S, D $74-$95; each addl $5; under 18 free. Crib free. Pet accepted; $5. TV; cable. Complimentary continental bkfst. Restaurant nearby. Ck-out 11 am. Business servs avail. Cr cds: A, C, D, DS, MC, V.

Motor Hotel

★ ★ **SHERATON INN JETPORT.** 3400 Airport Rd (18103), 5 mi E on US 22. 610/266-1000. 147 rms, 3 story, 30 suites. S $99, D $109, each addl $10, suites $115-$130, under 13 free; higher rates NASCAR races. Crib free. Pet accepted. TV; cable (premium), VCR avail. Indoor pool; sauna, whirlpool, lifeguard. Complimentary coffee in rms. Complimentary continental bkfst. Restaurant 6:30 am-10 pm. Rm serv. Bar 11-2 am, entertainment Tues-Sun. Ck-out noon. Meeting rm. Business servs avail. In-rm modem link. Bellhops. Sundries. Valet serv. Free airport transportation. Exercise equipt; stair machine, treadmill. Some refrigerators. Cr cds: A, D, DS, MC, V.

Hotel

★ ★ ★ **HILTON.** 904 Hamilton Mall (18101), at Hamilton & 9th Sts, in center of town. 610/433-2221; FAX 610/433-6455. 224 rms, 9 story. S $80-$116; D $90-$126; each addl $10; suites $145-$250; children free; wkend rates. Crib free. TV; cable. Heated pool; lifeguard. Restaurant 6:30 am-10 pm. Bar 11-2 am. Ck-out 11 am. Meeting rms. Business servs avail. In-rm modem link. Free airport transportation. Exercise equipt; weights, bicycle, sauna. Cr cds: A, C, D, DS, ER, JCB, MC, V.

Inn

★ ★ ★ **GLASBERN.** (2141 Pack House Rd, Fogelsville 18051) Approx 10 mi W on I-78, exit PA 100 N, W on Main St, N on Church St to Pack House Rd. 610/285-4723; FAX 610/285-2862. 24 rms, 2 story, 14 suites. S $95-$135; D $105-$300; each addl $20; suites, kit. units $115-$250; 2-night min special wkends, hols. Heated pool. Complimentary full bkfst. Dining rm (public by res) 6-8 pm. Ck-out noon, ck-in 4 pm. Meeting rm. Business servs avail. Many whirlpools, fireplaces. Farmhouse, barn, gate house and carriage house built in late 1800s; antiques. Cr cds: MC, V.

Restaurant

★ ★ ★ **APPENNINO.** 3079 Willow St (18104), at Cedar Crest Blvd, 2½ mi N of PA 22 on Cedar Crest. 610/799-2727. Hrs: 11:30 am-2:30 pm, 5:30-10 pm; Sat from 5:30 pm; Closed Sun; major hols. Res accepted. Northern Italian menu. Bar. Wine list. A la carte entrees: lunch $7.75-$12.50, dinner $10-$24. Specialties: veal Valdostana, filet of sole in green sauce with shrimp. Own desserts. Restored hotel (1800s); imported Italian lamps, chandeliers and tapestry on chairs. Jacket. Cr cds: A, D, DS, MC, V.

Altoona (E-4)

(See also Ebensburg)

Founded 1849 **Pop** 51,881 **Elev** 1,170 ft **Area code** 814 **E-mail** amcvb @aol.com **Web** www.amcvb@aol.com

Information Allegheny Mountains Convention & Visitors Bureau, Logan Valley Mall, Rte 220 & Goods Ln, 16602; 814/943-4183 or 800/84-ALTOONA.

The rough, high Alleghenies ring this city, which was founded by the Pennsylvania Railroad. Altoona expanded rapidly after 1852, when the difficult task of spanning the Alleghenies with track, linking Philadelphia and Pittsburgh, was completed. The railroad shops still offer substantial employment for residents of the city and Blair County, but new and diversified industries now provide the economic base.

What to See and Do

Baker Mansion Museum (1844-1848). Stone Greek-revival house of early ironmaster; now occupied by Blair County Historical Society. Hand-carved Belgian furniture of the period; transportation exhibits, gun collection, clothing, housewares. (Memorial Day-Labor Day, daily exc Mon; mid-Apr-Memorial Day & Labor Day-Oct, Sat & Sun; closed hols) 3500 Oak Lane. Phone 814/942-3916. ¢¢

Bland's Park. More than 30 rides and attractions including antique carousel, miniature golf and pony rides. Also here are arcade games, picnic pavilions and restaurant. (May-Sept, daily exc Mon) 10 mi N, on US 220 in Tipton. Phone 814/684-3538. All-day ride pass ¢¢¢

Canoe Creek State Park. Approx 950-acre park features 155-acre lake. Swimming beach; fishing; boating (launches, rentals). Hiking. Picnicking (reservations for pavilion). Cross-country skiing, sledding, ice boating, ice-skating. Cabins. Standard fees. 12 mi E via US 22. Phone 814/695-6807.

Forest Zoo. Large collection of wild animals; contact area; picnicking, concession. (Daily) Approx 8 mi W, 3 mi off US 22 Gallitzin exit on Gallitzin-Coupon Rd in Gallitzin. Phone 814/944-4811. ¢¢

Fort Roberdeau. Reconstructed Revolutionary War horizontal log fort contains lead smelter, blacksmith shop, lead miners' hut, barracks, storehouse, officers' quarters, powder magazine. Costumed guides; wknd reenactments. Visitor's center. Picnicking, nature trails. (Mid-May-early Oct, daily exc Mon) 8 mi NE via US 220, Kettle St exit onto PA 1013. Phone 814/946-0048. ¢¢

Horseshoe Curve Visitors Center. World-famous engineering feat, carrying main-line Conrail and Amtrak trains around western grade of 91 ft per mi. Curve is 2,375 ft long and has a central angle of 220 degrees. Incline plane runs between interpretive center and observation area. Gift shop. (May-Oct, daily; rest of yr, daily exc Mon) 5 mi W via well-marked, unnumbered road. Phone 814/946-0834. ¢¢

Lakemont Park. An amusement park with more than 30 rides and attractions; home of the nation's oldest wooden roller coaster; water park, miniature golf, entertainment. (May-Sept, daily) 700 Park Ave, Frankstown Rd & I-99. Phone 814/949-7275. All-day ride pass ¢¢¢

Prince Gallitzin State Park. Approx 6,200 acres; 26 mi of shoreline on 1,600-acre lake. Swimming beach; fishing; boating (rentals, mooring, launching, marina). Hiking trails, horseback riding. Cross-country skiing, snowmobiling, ice-skating, ice fishing. Picnicking, snack bar, store, laundry facilities. Tent & trailer sites, cabins. Nature center; interpretive program. Standard fees. 8 mi NW on PA 36, then 1¼ mi NW off PA 53, then W on SR 1026. Phone 814/674-1000 or 814/674-1007 for reservations.

Railroader's Memorial Museum. Exhibits feature railroad artifacts, art and theme displays. Railroad rolling stock, steam and electric locomotive collections. (May-Oct, daily; rest of yr, daily exc Mon) 1300 9th Ave. Phone 814/946-0834. ¢¢

Wopsononock Mt. Lookout provides view of 6-county area from height of 2,580 ft; offers one of the best views in the state. 6 mi NW on Juniata Gap Rd.

Annual Events

Blair County Arts Festival. Penn State Altoona Campus. Arts, crafts, hobbies on display. Mid-May.

Keystone Country Festival. Lakemont Park. Arts & crafts, continuous music; food. Contact Convention & Visitors Bureau for details. Wkend after Labor Day.

Motor Hotel

★ ★ ★ **RAMADA.** *1 Sheraton Dr (16601), 5 mi S on US 220. 814/946-1631; FAX 814/946-0785.* 215 rms, 2-3 story. S, D $55-$85; each addl $5; suites $80-$140; under 18 free; some wknd rates; higher rates: football games, ski season. Crib $5. Pet accepted. TV; cable (premium), VCR avail. Indoor pool; wading pool, whirlpool, lifeguard. Complimentary continental bkfst. Restaurants 6:30 am-2:30 pm, 5:30-10 pm; Sat to 11 pm. Rm serv. Bar 11-2 am. Ck-out noon. Meeting rms. Business center. In-rm modem link. Bellhops. Valet serv. Gift shop. Airport transportation. 18-hole golf privileges. Downhill ski 20 mi. Exercise rm; instructor, weights, bicycles. Rec rm. Microwaves avail. Cr cds: A, C, D, DS, JCB, MC, V.

D ↙ ⟲ ✕ ≋ ✕ ⟱ SC ↗

Restaurants

★ ★ ★ **ALLEGRO.** *3926 Broad Ave. 814/946-5216.* Hrs: 4-9:30 pm; Sat to 10 pm. Closed Sun; major hols. Res accepted. Italian, Amer menu. Bar. Wine list. Semi-a la carte: dinner $10.95-$24.95. Child's meals.

Specializes in veal, seafood. Own baking, sauces, pasta. Cr cds: A, C, D, DS, MC, V.

D ↙ ♥

↙★ ★ **HOUSE OF CHANG.** *601 Logan Blvd. 814/942-3322.* Hrs: 11:30 am-10 pm; Sun to 9 pm. Closed Thanksgiving, Dec 25. Chinese menu. Bar. Semi-a la carte: lunch $4.45-$6.25, dinner $6.50-$16.50. Buffet: lunch (Sun) $7.45. Child's meals. Specialties: Peking shrimp, subgum wonton. Oriental decor. Cr cds: A, MC, V.

↙

Ambridge (D-1)

(For accommodations see Beaver Falls, Pittsburgh)

Founded 1901 **Pop** 8,133 **Elev** 751 ft **Area code** 724 **Zip** 15003
Information Beaver County Tourist Promotion Agency, 215B Ninth St, Monaca 15061-2028; 724/728-0212 or 800/342-8192.

Founded by and taking its name from the American Bridge Co, this city rests on part of the site of Old Economy Village. In 1825, under the leadership of George Rapp, the Harmony Society established a communal pietistic colony that for many decades was important in the industrial life and development of western Pennsylvania. Despite its spiritual emphasis, Old Economy Village enjoyed a great material prosperity; farms were productive, craft shops were busy and factories made textiles widely acclaimed for their quality. Surplus funds financed railroads and industrial enterprises throughout the upper Ohio Valley. After celibacy was adopted and unwise investments were made, the community's productivity decreased. Officially dissolved in 1905, the remains of the community were taken over by the Commonwealth of Pennsylvania in 1916.

What to See and Do

 Old Economy Village. Seventeen original Harmony Society buildings located on six acres, restored and filled with furnishings of the community. Included are the communal leader's 32-rm Great House, the Feast Hall, the Grotto in the Gardens, wine cellars, a 5-story granary, shops, dwellings and community kitchens. Cobblestone streets link the buildings. Special festivals and events. (Daily exc Mon; closed hols) 14th & Church Sts. Phone 724/266-4500. ¢¢

Raccoon Creek State Park. Approx 7,300 acres. Swimming beach; fishing, hunting; boating (rentals, mooring, launching). Hiking, horseback riding. Cross-country skiing, sledding, snowmobiling, ice-skating, ice fishing. Snack bar. Tent & trailer sites. Nature & historical centers. Standard fees. 9 mi W on PA 151, then 7 mi S on PA 18, near Frankfort Springs. Phone 724/899-2200.

Annual Event

Nationality Days. Ethnic cultural displays, foods; native music, dancing. Mid-May.

Ashland (D-8)

(For accommodations see Hazleton)

Pop 3,859 **Elev** 1,000 ft **Area code** 717 **Zip** 17921 **E-mail** tourism @schuylkill.org **Web** www.schuylkill.org

Information Schuylkill County Visitors Bureau, 91 S Progress Ave, Pottsville 17901; 717/622-7700 or 800/765-7282.

What to See and Do

Museum of Anthracite Mining. Museum on geology and technology of mining "hard" coal. (May-Oct, Mon-Sat, also Sun afternoons; rest of yr, Tues-Sat, also Sun afternoons; closed hols) Pine & 17th Sts. Phone 717/875-4708. ¢¢

Pioneer Tunnel Coal Mine and Steam Lokie Ride. Tour and explanation of mining in original coal mine tunnel; indoor temperature 52°F. Narrow-gauge steam train ride; picnic park. (Memorial Day-Oct, daily; May, wkends) 19th & Oak Sts. Phone 717/875-3850 or 717/875-3301. Mine tour ¢¢; Train ride ¢¢

Beaver Falls (D-1)

(See also Ambridge, Harmony)

Founded 1806 **Pop** 10,687 **Elev** 800 ft **Area code** 724 **Zip** 15010

Information Beaver County Tourist Promotion Agency, 215B Ninth St, Monaca 15061-2028; 724/728-0212 or 800/342-8192.

Founded as Brighton, the town changed its name for the falls in the Beaver River. The plates from which US currency is printed are made in Beaver Falls. Geneva College (1848) is located here.

Motels

✔★ **BEAVER VALLEY.** 7257 Big Beaver Blvd, on PA 18, ½ mi N of PA Tpke exit 2. 724/843-0630; FAX 724/843-1610; res: 800/400-8312. 27 rms. S $37-$48; D $50-$60; each addl $6; kit. units only wkly $225; under 18 free; Crib free. TV; cable (premium). Complimentary coffee in lobby. Ck-out 11 am. Business servs avail. Cr cds: A, C, D, DS, MC, V.

★ **CONLEY'S MOTOR INN.** Big Beaver Blvd, on PA 18, ¼ m S of PA Tpke exit 2. 724/843-9300. 54 rms, 4 kits. S $49; D $59; each addl $10; under 12 free; wkly, monthly rates. Pet accepted. TV; cable. Restaurant 7 am-10 pm. Bar. Ck-out 11 am. Meeting rms. Business servs avail. Refrigerators. Cr cds: A, C, D, DS, MC, V.

Motor Hotel

★ ★ ★ **HOLIDAY INN.** PA 18N at PA Tpke exit 2. 724/846-3700. 156 rms, 3 story. S, D $74-$83; each addl $8; under 18 free; wkend rates. Crib free. Pet accepted. TV. Indoor pool; whirlpool, sauna, poolside serv, lifeguard. Restaurant 6:30 am-10 pm. Rm serv. Bar 11-2 am. Ck-out noon. Meeting rms. Business servs avail. In-rm modem link. Valet serv. Miniature golf. Game rm. Cr cds: A, C, D, DS, JCB, MC, V.

Restaurant

★ ★ ★ **WOODEN ANGEL.** (308 Leopard Lane, Beaver 15009) From jct PA 51 & 68, ½ mi N on PA 51, ¼ mi W on Leopard Lane.

724/774-7880. Hrs: 11:30 am-11 pm. Closed Sun, Mon; major hols exc Mother's Day. Res accepted. Bar. Wine cellar. Semi-a la carte: lunch $6.75-$15.75, dinner $16-$28. Specializes in rack of lamb, fresh seafood. Own baking. Cr cds: A, C, D, DS, MC, V.

Bedford (F-4)

Settled 1751 **Pop** 3,137 **Elev** 1,106 ft **Area code** 814 **Zip** 15522 **E-mail** bccvb@bedford.net **Web** www.bedford.net/dtice/bedford2.htm

Information Bedford County Conference & Visitors Bureau, 141 S Juliana St; 814/623-1771 or 800/765-3331.

Fort Bedford was a major frontier outpost in pre-Revolutionary War days. After the war it became an important stopover along the route of western migration and has remained so up until the present. Garrett Pendergrass, the second settler here, built Pendergrass's Tavern, which figures in a number of novels by Hervey Allen.

What to See and Do

Bedford County Courthouse. Federal-style building constructed in 1828 has unique hanging spiral staircase. (Mon-Fri; closed hols) S Juliana St. Phone 814/623-4807. **Free.**

Blue Knob Ski Area. 2 triple, 2 double chairlifts, 3 platter pulls; patrol, school, rentals; snowmaking; bar, cafeteria; nursery. Longest run approx 2 mi; vertical drop 1,072 ft. (Dec-Mar, daily) Half-day rates avail. Phone 814/239-5111 or 800/458-3403 (snow conditions). ¢¢¢¢¢

Fort Bedford Park and Museum. Log blockhouse, erected during Bedford's bicentennial. Contains large-scale replica of original fort, displays of colonial antiques and relics, Native American artifacts. (May-late Oct, daily) Ft Bedford Dr, N end of Juliana St, park along Raystown River. Phone 814/623-8891. ¢¢

Old Bedford Village. More than 40 authentic log and frame structures (1750-1851) house historical exhibits; crafts demonstrations; operating pioneer farm. Many special events throughout the yr. (1st Sat May-last Sun Oct, daily) 1 mi N on US Business 220N. Phone 814/623-1156. ¢¢¢

State parks.

Shawnee. Approx 450-acre lake surrounded by 3,840 acres. Swimming beach; fishing, hunting; boating (rentals, mooring, launching). Cross-country skiing, snowmobiling, sledding, ice-skating, ice fishing. Picnicking, playfield, snack bar. Camping; tent & trailer sites. Standard fees. 8 mi W on US 30. Phone 814/733-4218.

Blue Knob. Approx 6,000 acres. Swimming pool; fishing, hunting. Hiking. Cross-country skiing, snowmobiling, sledding. Picnicking, playfield. Camping (mid-Apr-mid-Oct). Standard fees. 10 mi N on US 220, then 8 mi NW on PA 869. Phone 814/276-3576.

Annual Events

Civil War Reenactment. Old Bedford Village. Early Sept.

Fall Foliage Festival Days. Entertainment, ethnic foods, antique cars, craft demonstrations. 2 wkends early Oct.

Motels

✔★ ★ ★ **BEST WESTERN HOSS'S INN.** RD 2, Box 33B, 2 mi N via US 220 Business, PA Tpke exit 11. 814/623-9006; FAX 814/623-7120. Web www.bestwestern.com/best.html. 105 rms, 2 story. Apr-Oct: S $48.50; D $56.50; suites $65; each addl $8; under 18 free; lower rates rest of yr. Crib free. Pet accepted, some restrictions; $50. TV; cable (premium), VCR avail (movies). Pool; lifeguard. Restaurant 6:30-11 am, 5-10 pm; Sat, Sun 6:30 am-10 pm. Bar 5 pm-midnight. Ck-out noon. Meeting rms. Gift shop. Exercise equipt; weight machine, treadmill, sauna. Game rm. Cr cds: A, C, D, DS, MC, V.

★ **ECONOLODGE.** *US 220 Business.* 814/623-5174; FAX 814/623-5455. Web www.hotelchoice.com. 32 rms, 2 story. May-Oct: S $42; D $46-$48; each addl $6; under 18 free; ski plans; higher rates special events; lower rates rest of yr. Crib free. Pet accepted. TV; cable (premium). Restaurant 6 am-10 pm. Rm serv. Bar 4 pm-midnight. Ck-out 11 am. Downhill ski 15 mi. Game rm. Cr cds: A, C, D, DS, JCB, MC, V.

★ ★ **QUALITY INN.** *RD 2, Box 171, 2 mi N on US 220 Business, 1 blk N of PA Tpke exit 11.* 814/623-5188; FAX 814/623-0814. Web www.qualityinn.com. 66 rms. May-Nov: S $57-$63; D $63-$69; each addl $6; under 18 free; lower rates rest of yr. Crib $4. Pet accepted, some restrictions. TV; cable (premium). Pool. Restaurant 7 am-10 pm. Bar 11 am-11 pm. Ck-out 11 am. Meeting rms. Business servs avail. Downhill ski 20 mi. Cr cds: A, C, D, DS, ER, JCB, MC, V.

Restaurant

★ ★ **ED'S STEAK HOUSE.** *2 mi N on US 220 Business, ¼ mi N of PA Tpke exit 11.* 814/623-8894. Hrs: 7 am-9 pm; Fri, Sat to 10 pm. Closed Thanksgiving, Dec 25. Res accepted. Bar. Semi-a la carte: bkfst $2.29-$3.99, lunch $2.99-$5.99, dinner $5.95-$14.99. Child's meals. Specializes in steak, seafood. Family-owned. Cr cds: A, MC, V.

Bellefonte (D-5)

(For accommodations see State College)

Settled 1770 **Pop** 6,358 **Elev** 809 ft **Area code** 814 **Zip** 16823
Information Bellefonte Area Chamber of Commerce, Train Station, 320 W High St; 814/355-2917.

When the exiled French minister Talleyrand saw the Big Spring here in 1794, his exclamation—"Beautiful fountain"—gave the town its name. Bellefonte is perched on seven hills at the southeast base of Bald Eagle Mountain.

What to See and Do

Black Moshannon State Park. Approx 3,450 acres. Swimming beach; fishing, hunting; boating (rentals, mooring, launching). Hiking. Cross-country skiing, snowmobiling, ice-skating, ice fishing, ice boating. Picnicking, snack bar. Tent & trailer sites, cabins. Interpretive program. Standard fees. N via PA 144/150, SW via US 220, then approx 12 mi W on PA 504. Phone 814/342-5960.

Centre County Library and Historical Museum. Local historical museum includes central Pennsylvania historical and genealogical books, records. (Daily exc Sun; closed hols) 200 N Allegheny St. Phone 814/355-1516. **Free.**

Curtin Village. Mansion, built in 1831 by Roland Curtin; iron furnace (1848), worker's cabin, herb garden. Restored by the Pennsylvania Historical and Museum Commission. (Memorial Day-Labor Day, Wed-Sun; Labor Day-mid-Oct, wkends only) 2 mi N on PA 150 at I-80 exit 23. Phone 814/355-1982 for tours. Tours ¢¢

Restaurant

★ ★ **GAMBLE MILL TAVERN.** *160 Dunlap St, at Lamb St Bridge.* 814/355-7764. Hrs: 11:30 am-2 pm, 5-8 pm. Closed Sun; Thanksgiving, Dec 25. Res accepted. Continental menu. Bar. A la carte entrees:

lunch $6-$10, dinner $12.50-$24. Specializes in fresh seafood, veal, duck. Own desserts. Restored mill (1786); rustic early American decor. Cr cds: DS, MC, V.

Bethlehem (D-9)

(See also Allentown, Easton, Quakertown)

Founded 1741 **Pop** 71,428 **Elev** 340 ft **Area code** 610 **E-mail** BTA@itw.com **Web** info@bethtour.org
Information Bethlehem Tourism Authority, 52 W Broad St, 18018; 610/868-1513 or 800/360-8687.

The city is famous throughout the world for Bethlehem Steel products and is also well known for its Bach Festival, for Lehigh University (1865), Moravian College (1807), Musikfest, its historic district and as "America's Christmas city."

Moravians, members of a very old Protestant denomination that came here to the banks of the Lehigh River, assembled on Christmas Eve 1741 in the only building, a log house that was part stable. Singing a hymn that praised Bethlehem, they found a name for their village. The musical heritage, too, dates from this moment; string quartets and symphonies were heard here before any other place in the colonies.

The opening of the Lehigh Canal in 1829 started industrialization of the area and development of the borough of South Bethlehem (1865), which was incorporated into the city of Bethlehem in 1917.

What to See and Do

Apothecary Museum. Original fireplace (1752), where prescriptions were compounded; collection of artifacts including retorts, grinders, mortars and pestles, scales, blown-glass bottles, labels and a set of Delft jars (1743); herb and flower garden. (By appt) 424 Main St, in rear; entry gate next to book shop. Phone 610/867-0173. ¢

Brethren's House (1748). Early residence and shop area for single men of the Moravian Community. Used as a general hospital by the Continental Army during the Revolutionary War. Now serves Moravian College as its Center for Music and Art. Church & Main Sts. Phone 610/861-3916.

Central Moravian Church (1806). Federal-style with hand-carved detail, considered foremost Moravian church in the US. Noted for its music, including a trombone choir in existence since 1754. May be toured only in combination with Moravian Museum community walking tour. Main & W Church Sts.

God's Acre (1742-1910). Old Moravian cemetery following Moravian tradition that all gravestones are laid flat, indicating that all are equal in the sight of God. May be toured only in combination with Moravian Museum community walking tour. Market St.

Hill-to-Hill Bridge. Joins old and new parts of the city and provides excellent view of historic area, river and Bethlehem Steel plant. Main St, PA 378 over Lehigh River.

Historic Bethlehem Inc's 18th-Century Industrial Quarter. Guided tours (July-Aug, Sat; late Nov-late Dec, wkends). (See ANNUAL EVENTS) Ohio Rd & Main St (pedestrian entrance); Old York Rd & Union Blvd (parking lot entrance). Phone 610/691-0603. Tours ¢¢ Tour of area includes

Springhouse (1764). Reconstruction on site of original spring that served Moravian community as a water source from the time of settlement in 1741 until 1912.

Waterworks (1762) with reconstructed 18-ft wooden waterwheel and pumping mechanisms.

Tannery (1761). Exhibits Moravian crafts, trades and industries. Includes a working model of the original oil mill.

Luckenbach Mill (1869). Restored gristmill contains contemporary craft gallery and museum shop; also the offices of Bethlehem Area Chamber of Commerce and Historic Bethlehem Inc. Interpretive display here is included in guided tour.

Goundie House (1810). Restored Federal-style brick house has period-furnished rooms and interpretive exhibits. 501 Main St.

Kemerer Museum of Decorative Arts. Exhibits include art, Bohemian glass, toys, prints, china; regional German folk art from 1750-1900; Federal furniture; period room settings. (Daily exc Mon; closed hols) 427 N New St. Phone 610/691-0603. ¢¢

Lost River Caverns. Stalagmites, stalactites, other formations. Picnic area; Gilman Museum with rocks and minerals, ancient and modern armor; also jungle garden (free). 30-min guided tours. (Daily; closed Jan 1, Thanksgiving, Dec 25) Durham St, 3 mi SE via PA 412 in Hellertown. Phone 610/838-8767. Tours ¢¢¢

Moravian Museum (Gemein Haus) (1741). This five-story log building is the oldest structure in the city; docents interpret the history and culture of early Bethelehem and the Moravians. 2 tours avail: 45-min tour of museum only; a 2-hr walking tour of the community includes the museum, Old Chapel, Central Moravian Church, God's Acre and a walk down historic Church St. (Tues-Sat; closed Good Friday, Holy Saturday, most major hols & Jan) 66 W Church St. Phone 610/867-0173. Museum ¢¢; Walking tour ¢¢¢

Old Chapel (1751). Once called the "Indian chapel" because so many Native Americans attended the services, this stone structure, the second church for the Moravian congregation, is still used frequently. May be toured only in combination with Moravian Museum community walking tour. Heckeweider Place, adj Moravian Museum.

Annual Events

Shad Festival. Historic Bethlehem Inc's 18th-century Industrial Quarter. Old-fashioned planked shad bake (res required for dinner), exhibits, demonstrations. Phone 610/691-0603. 1st Sun May.

Bach Festival. Packer Church, Lehigh University campus. One of the country's outstanding musical events. Famous artists and the Bach Choir of Bethlehem participate. Phone 610/866-4382. Mid-late May.

Moravian College Alumni Association Antiques Show. Johnston Hall, Moravian College Campus. Phone 610/861-1366. Early June.

Musikfest. 9-day festival celebrating Bethlehem's rich musical and ethnic heritage. More than 600 performances (most free) of all types of music including folk, big-band, jazz, Bach, country-western, chamber, classical, gospel, rock, swing; held at 9 different sites in downtown historic area. Also children's activities. Phone 610/861-0678. Late Aug.

Christmas. Bethlehem continues more than two centuries of Christmas tradition with candlelight, music and a number of special events. Moravians sing their own Christmas songs intermingled with Mozart and Handel. A huge "Star of Bethlehem" shines from the top of South Mountain and the Hill-to-Hill Bridge has special lighting. The community "Putzes," a Moravian version of nativity scenes, are open to the public daily. Thousands of people post their Christmas cards from Bethlehem. Night Light Tours of city's Christmas displays and historical areas are offered (Dec) by the Bethlehem Tourism Authority. Reservations suggested. Phone 610/868-1513 or 800/360-8687. Thanksgiving-Jan 1.

Live Bethlehem Christmas Pageant. Scores of volunteers, garbed in biblical costumes, and live animals (including camels, horses, donkey and sheep) join together to re-create the nativity story; narrated. Phone 610/867-2893. 1st wkend Dec.

Motels

★ ★ **COMFORT INN.** *3191 Highfield Dr (18017), US 22 exit 191.* 610/865-6300. 116 rms, 2½ story. S $56-$75; D $65-$85; each addl $6; under 18 free; ski plan. Crib free. Pet accepted. TV; cable, VCR (movies $5). Complimentary continental bkfst. Restaurant adj. Bar noon-2 am; entertainment Fri, Sat. Ck-out noon. Business servs avail. Valet serv. Cr cds: A, C, D, DS, ER, JCB, MC, V.

★ ★ ★ **HOLIDAY INN.** *US 22 & PA 512 (18017).* 610/866-5800; FAX 610/867-9120. 192 rms, 2 story. S $110-$115; D $120-$125; each addl $10; under 18 free. Crib free. TV; cable. Pool; wading pool, lifeguard. Restaurant 6:30 am-10 pm. Rm serv. Bar 11-2 am. Ck-out noon. Meeting rms. Business center. In-rm modem link. Valet serv. Gift shop. Free airport, bus depot transportation. Exercise equipt; bicycle, stair machine. Cr cds: A, C, D, DS, JCB, MC, V.

Hotel

★ ★ **BETHLEHEM.** *437 Main St (18018).* 610/867-3711; FAX 610/867-0598; res: 800/545-5158. 65 rms, 9 story. S $80; D $92; each addl $10; suites $105-$162; studio rms $57; under 13 free. Crib free. TV; cable. Restaurant 6:30 am-11 pm. Bar 11:30-2 am. Ck-out 11 am. Meeting rms. Business servs avail. In-rm modem link. Shopping arcade. Beauty shop. Free garage parking. Free airport, bus depot transportation. Many refrigerators. Cr cds: A, C, D, DS, ER, MC, V.

Restaurant

★ ★ **CANDLELIGHT INN.** *4431 Easton Ave (18107), 5 mi E on US 22.* 610/691-7777. Hrs: 11 am-10 pm; Sat from 4 pm; Sun from 10 am. Closed some major hols. Res accepted. Continental menu. Bar. Semi-a la carte: lunch $5.95-$8.95, dinner $8.95-$19.95. Child's meals. Specialties: Chesapeake steak, chicken with broccoli & cheese. Contemporary decor. Cr cds: A, D, DS, MC, V.

Bird-in-Hand (F-8)

(See also Ephrata, Lancaster)

Pop 700 (est) **Elev** 358 ft **Area code** 717 **Zip** 17505

Information Pennsylvania Dutch Convention and Visitors Bureau, 501 Greenfield Rd, Lancaster 17601; 717/299-8901 or 800/PADUTCH.

This Pennsylvania Dutch farming village got its name from the signboard of an early inn.

What to See and Do

Amish Village. Reconstructed and original buildings include blacksmith shop, schoolhouse, operating smokehouse; livestock. Guided tours of Amish farmhouse. (Mid-Mar-Dec, daily; rest of yr, wkends; closed wk of Thanksgiving, also Dec 25) 1 mi W on PA 340, then 3 mi S on PA 896. Phone 717/687-8511. ¢¢¢

Bird-in-Hand Farmers' Market. Indoor market with a wide variety of Pennsylvania Dutch foods and gifts. (July-Oct, Wed-Sat; Apr-June & Nov, Wed, Fri & Sat; rest of yr, Fri & Sat; closed Jan 1, Thanksgiving, Dec 25) On PA 340 & Maple Ave. Phone 717/393-9674.

Folk Craft Center & Museum. Early 18th-century buildings display tools, household implements, stoneware pottery, toys, Stiegel glass, quilts, coverlets and early Pennsylvania Dutch memorabilia; log cabin loom house (1762); herb and ornamental gardens; turn-of-the-century woodworking and print shops; audiovisual presentation. (Apr-Nov, daily) 1½ mi W on PA 340, then N on Mt Sidney Rd, in Witmer. Phone 717/397-3609. ¢¢

The People's Place. Arts and heritage center features three-screen documentary on the Amish; interpretive museum with hands-on exhibits; Amish quilt museum. Also bookstore, art gallery. (Daily exc Sun; closed Jan 1, Thanksgiving, Dec 25) 5 mi E on PA 340, on Main St in Intercourse. Phone 717/768-7171. ¢¢-¢¢¢

Weavertown One-Room Schoolhouse. Life-size animated re-creation of activities at a one-rm schoolhouse. (Early April-Oct, daily; Mar & Nov, wkends) 1 mi E via PA 340. Phone 717/768-3976 or 717/291-1888 (winter). ¢¢

Motel

★ ★ ★ **BIRD-IN-HAND FAMILY INN.** 2740 Old Philadelphia Pike. 717/768-8271; FAX 717/768-1117; res: 800/537-2535. E-mail smucker @bird-in-hand.com; web www.bird-in-hand.com. 100 rms, 1-2 story. May-Nov: S $60-$88; D $74-$90; each addl $8; under 16 free; higher rates wkends; lower rates rest of yr. Crib $6. TV; cable, VCR avail (movies). 2 pools, 1 indoor. Playground. Complimentary coffee in rms. Restaurant 6 am-9 pm. Ck-out 11 am. Coin lndry. Meeting rms. Business servs avail. In-rm modem link. Sundries. Lighted tennis. Game rm. Refrigerators; microwaves avail. Picnic tables. Cr cds: A, D, DS, MC, V.

Inns

★ ★ ★ **GREYSTONE MANOR.** 2658 Old Philadelphia Pike, on S side of PA 340. 717/393-4233. 13 rms, 3 story, 6 suites. No rm phones. S $70-$90; D $75-$95; each addl $15; suites $95-$135; under 2 free; min stay hols, wkends. Closed Jan. Children in Carriage House only. TV. Complimentary full bkfst. Ck-out 11 am, ck-in 3 pm. Balconies. Picnic tables. Victorian mansion built in 1845; Carriage House was once a barn (1840s). Authentic antique furnishings, original woodwork, cut crystal doors. Totally nonsmoking. Cr cds: MC, V.

★ ★ ★ **THE VILLAGE.** 2695 Old Philadelphia Pike. 717/293-8369; res: 800/914-2439; FAX 717/768-1117. Web yourinfo.com/lanco/smucker /birdhand.html. 11 units, 3 story, 6 suites. Mid-June-Nov: S, D $79-$99; each addl $10; suites $109-$139; under 4 free; lower rates rest of yr. Closed early Dec-early Feb. Crib free. TV; cable. Pool privileges. Complimentary continental bkfst. Restaurant nearby. Ck-out noon, ck-in 3 pm. Tennis privileges. Built in 1734 to serve as inn on Old Philadelphia Pike. Interior Victorian in ambience. Cr cds: A, DS, MC, V.

Restaurants

✔★ ★ **AMISH BARN.** 3029 Old Philadelphia Pike. 717/768-8886. Hrs: 8 am-7 pm; summer 7:30 am-9 pm. Res accepted exc hols. Pennsylvania Dutch menu. A la carte entrees: bkfst $3-$5.25, lunch $3.95-$6, dinner $5.95-$13.95. Child's meals. Specialties: apple dumplings, shoofly pie. Courtyard patio dining. Rustic Amish decor. Braille menu. Family-owned. Cr cds: A, DS, MC, V.

★ **PLAIN & FANCY FARM.** 3121 Old Philadelphia Pike. 717/768-4400. Hrs: 11:30 am-8 pm; Sun noon-7 pm. Res accepted. Pennsylvania Dutch cuisine. Closed Dec 24, 25. Prix fixe: lunch, dinner $13.95. Child's meals. Family-style food service. Authentic Amish homestead. Buggy rides avail 8 am-dusk. Variety of specialty shops. Family-owned. Totally nonsmoking. Cr cds: A, DS, MC, V.

Bloomsburg (D-7)

(See also Danville)

Settled 1802 **Pop** 12,439 **Elev** 530 ft **Area code** 717 **Zip** 17815
Information Columbia-Montour Tourist Promotion Agency, 121 Papermill Rd; 717/784-8279 or 800/847-4810.

Situated on the north bank of the Susquehanna River, Bloomsburg is the seat of Columbia County. The town was a center of mining, transportation and industry during the 19th and early 20th centuries. Although manufacturing continues to be the largest employer here, Bloomsburg retains the relaxed atmosphere of earlier days with its lovely scenery and many covered bridges. In nearby Orangeville, nine miles west on PA 93, Fishing Creek offers trout, bass and pickerel.

The only incorporated town in the state (all the others are boroughs or cities), Bloomsburg has silk and rayon manufacturers; it also produces architectural aluminum, processed foods and electronic products. During the Civil War, Union troops came here to crush the "Fishing Creek Confederacy," a group of alleged draft dodgers who were reportedly building fortifications; no fort was found, and the men were released. One of the "Molly Maguire" murder trials was held here. (The Molly Maguires was a miners' society seeking improved conditions through force and violence.)

What to See and Do

Bloomsburg University of Pennsylvania (1839). (6,600 students) On campus are Carver Hall (1867); the Harvey A. Andruss Library (1966); Haas Center for the Arts (1967) with 2,000-seat auditorium and art gallery; McCormick Center for Human Services (1985); Redman Stadium and Nelson Field House. Tours (academic yr, Mon-Fri). E 2nd St. Phone 717/389-4316.

Columbia County Historical Society. Museum and Edwin M. Barton Library with local history exhibits, pioneer items. (Apr-Oct, Thurs-Sat; closed major hols) 6 mi N on PA 487; 410 Main St, in Orangeville. Phone 717/683-6011. Museum tour **Free;** Library research/hr ¢

Historic District. More than 650 structures spanning architectural styles ranging from Georgian to art deco. Center of town. Phone 717/784-7703.

Twin covered bridges. Believed to be only twin covered bridges in US. More than 20 other covered bridges are in the area. 10 mi N on PA 487.

Annual Events

Bloomsburg Fair. Fairgrounds, W side of town. Fair held since 1854. Agricultural and industrial exhibits; harness racing. 8 days late Sept.

Covered Bridge & Arts Festival. I-80, exit 35. Tours of covered bridges; apple butter boil, weaving; old-fashioned arts & crafts. Early Oct.

Seasonal Event

Bloomsburg Theatre Ensemble. Alvina Krause Theatre, 226 Center St. Three to four wks of performances for each of six plays. For information contact BTE, PO Box 66; 717/784-8181. Main stage Oct-June (special performances rest of yr).

Motels

✔★ **BUDGET HOST PATRIOT INN.** 6305 New Berwick Hwy (US 11). 717/387-1776; FAX 717/387-9611. 48 rms. S $42-$48; D $48-$55; each addl $6; under 18 free. Crib free. TV; cable, VCR avail (movies). Restaurant adj 11 am-9 pm. Bar from 4 pm. Ck-out noon. Meeting rms. Business servs avail. Health club privileges. Some refrigerators. Cr cds: A, C, D, DS, MC, V.

★ ★ **QUALITY INN-BUCKHORN PLAZA.** 1 Buckhorn Rd, I-80 at Buckhorn exit 34. 717/784-5300; FAX 717/387-0367. 120 rms, 2 story. S $45-$65; D $50-$70; each addl $5; under 18 free. Crib $5. Pet accepted. TV; cable. Coffee in lobby. Restaurant adj 6 am-10 pm. Bar 7-2 am, Sun from 11 am. Ck-out 11 am. Business servs avail. Sundries. Balconies. Cr cds: A, C, D, DS, ER, JCB, MC, V.

Inns

★ ★ ★ **INN AT TURKEY HILL.** 991 Central Rd, at I-80 exit 35. 717/387-1500; FAX 717/784-3718. 18 rms, 2 story. S $87, D $92; each addl $15; suites $115-$185; under 12 free. Pet accepted; $15. TV; cable. Complimentary continental bkfst. Dining rm 5-9 pm. Rm serv. Bar. Ck-out noon, ck-in 2 pm. Business servs avail. In-rm modem link. Airport, bus depot transportation. Fireplace in some rms. Elegant antiques. Old homestead (1839); guest rooms overlook landscaped courtyard; gazebo, lily pond. Cr cds: A, C, D, DS, MC, V.

★ ★ **MAGEE'S MAIN STREET.** *20 W Main St. 717/784-3200; FAX 717/784-5517; res: 800/331-9815.* 43 rms, 3 story. S $57-$79; D $66-$87; each addl $3.95-$7.95; under 6 free. Pet accepted. TV; cable. Complimentary full bkfst. Dining rm 7 am-midnight. Bar 11-1 am, Sun to 11 pm. Ck-out noon. Meeting rms. Business servs avail. Cr cds: A, C, D, DS, MC, V.

Bradford (B-4)

(See also Kane, Warren)

Settled 1827 **Pop** 9,625 **Elev** 1,442 ft **Area code** 814 **Zip** 16701
Information Bradford Area Chamber of Commerce, 10 Main St, PO Box 135; 814/368-7115.

When oil was discovered here the price of land jumped from about six cents; to $1,000 an acre; wells appeared on front lawns, in backyards, even in a cemetery. An oil exchange was established in 1877, two years after the first producing well was brought in. Diversified industry now provides the city's economic base. A Ranger District office of the Allegheny National Forest (see WARREN) is located here.

What to See and Do

Bradford Landmark Society. Headquartered in restored bakery; local history exhibits, period rms. (Mon, Wed & Fri; closed hols) 45 E Corydon St. Phone 814/362-3906. **Free.**

Crook Farm (1848). Original home of Erastus and Betsy Crook; being restored to the 1870s period. (May-Sept, Tues-Fri afternoons, also Sat by appt; closed hols) (See ANNUAL EVENT) On Seaward Ave extension near the Tuna Crossroad. Phone 814/362-3906. **¢** Includes

Old One-Room Schoolhouse #8 (1880). Authentic structure where classes are still held occasionally.

Old Barn (ca 1870). Identical to the original; moved to Crook Farm in 1981 and rebuilt on the site of the original barn.

Carpenter Shop (ca 1870). Reconstruction of original; old hand tools.

Annual Event

Crook Farm Country Fair. Crook Farm. Arts and crafts, exhibits, entertainment, food. Last wkend Aug.

Motels

★ ★ **DE SOTO HOLIDAY HOUSE.** *515 South Ave. 814/362-4511.* 70 rms, 2-3 story. No elvtr. S $37-$48; D $45-$52; each addl $4. Crib free. TV; cable. Heated pool; whirlpool, sauna. Playground. Restaurant 7 am-10 pm; Sun to 8 pm. Bar 11-2 am; entertainment. Ck-out noon. Meeting rms. Business servs avail. Sundries. Rec rm. Driving range, miniature golf. Cr cds: A, C, D, DS, MC, V.

★ ★ **HOWARD JOHNSON.** *100 S Davis St, US 219 exits Elm & Forman Sts. 814/362-4501; FAX 814/362-2709.* 120 rms, 3 story. S $64-$74; D $69-$79; each addl $10; under 12 free. Crib free. TV; cable (premium). Heated pool; lifeguard. Restaurant 6:30 am-2 pm, 5-10 pm. Bar 3 pm-1 am. Ck-out noon. Meeting rms. Valet serv. Cr cds: A, C, D, DS, JCB, MC, V.

Inn

★ ★ ★ **GLENDORN.** *1032 W Corydon St, approx 5 mi from downtown area. 814/362-6511; FAX 814/368-9923; res: 800/843-8568.* 12 units, 2 story (main lodge), 4 suites, 6 cabins. AP: S $235-$435; D $295-$495; each addl $100; cabins $295-$895; wkend rates; 2-day min hols. Closed Mar. Children over 6 yrs only in main lodge (exc bkfst and lunch). Crib free. TV. Heated pool. Playground. Sittings: 8-10 am bkfst, 1 pm lunch, 7:30 pm dinner. Ck-out 2 pm, ck-in 11 am. Luggage handling. Business servs avail. Tennis. Golf privileges. X-country ski 5 mi. Exercise equipt; weights, stair machine. Game rm. Lawn games. Some refrigerators. Cr cds: MC, V.

Breezewood (F-4)

(See also Bedford, Chambersburg)

Pop 180 (est) **Elev** 1,356 ft **Area code** 814 **Zip** 15533

Motels

★ ★ **BEST WESTERN PLAZA MOTOR LODGE.** *US 30, jct I-70, 1 blk W of PA Tpke exit 12. 814/735-4352.* Web www.bestwestern.com/best.html. 89 rms, 2 story. S $39; D $46; each addl $7. Crib $7. TV; cable (premium). Pool; lifeguard. Restaurant 7 am-11 pm. Ck-out 11 am. Meeting rm. Sundries. Cr cds: A, C, D, DS, MC, V.

★ ★ **QUALITY INN BREEZE MANOR.** *Rte 1, Box 36, E on US 30, 1 blk E of I-70 & PA Tpke exit 12. 814/735-4311; FAX 814/735-3433.* Web www.qualityinn.com. 50 rms, 1-2 story. May-Nov: S $43-$76; D $48-$76; each addl $5; family rates; lower rates rest of yr. Crib $5. TV; cable (premium). Heated pool; wading pool, lifeguard. Playground. Restaurant opp open 24 hrs. Ck-out noon. Coin lndry. Business servs avail. Sundries. Cr cds: A, C, D, DS, ER, JCB, MC, V.

★ ★ **RAMADA INN.** *I-70 & US 30. 814/735-4005; FAX 814/735-3228.* 125 rms, 2 story. Apr-Oct: S $57; D $79; under 18 free; lower rates rest of yr. Crib avail. Pet accepted, some restrictions. TV; cable (premium), VCR avail (movies). Indoor pool. Playground. Restaurant 6:30 am-10 pm. Rm serv. Bar 4 pm-midnight. Ck-out noon. Meeting rms. Business center. In-rm modem link. Gift shop. Golf privileges. Exercise equipt; weight machine, treadmill. Game rm. Lawn games. Picnic tables. Cr cds: A, C, D, DS, JCB, MC, V.

Bristol (Bucks Co) (E-10)

(For accommodations see Philadelphia)

Settled 1697 **Pop** 10,405 **Elev** 20 ft **Area code** 215 **Zip** 19007 **E-mail** bctc@bctc.org **Web** www.bctc.org

Information Bucks County Tourist Commission, 152 Swamp Rd, Doylestown 18901; 215/345-4552 or 800/836-BUCK.

Since the first forge was erected here in 1753, Bristol has been an industrial center; today it manufactures chemical products, aircraft parts, textiles and paper. An early port of call for Delaware River traffic and later for canal traffic, Bristol has been an important boat-building center since 1785.

What to See and Do

Grave of Captain John Green. Grave of US Navy captain who piloted the *Columbia* around the world in 1787-1789 on first such voyage by vessel flying American flag. St James Protestant Episcopal Church Burial Ground. Cedar & Walnut Sts.

Historic Fallsington. Restored 17th-, 18th- & 19th-century buildings. Self-guided walking tour of 17th-century log house, 18th-century schoolmaster's house, Burges-Lippincott house, tavern. Also museum store. Tours. (See ANNUAL EVENT) (Mid-May-Oct, daily; closed some hols) 4 Yardley Ave, Fallsington, 5 mi N of PA Tpke, off PA 13. Phone 215/295-6567. ¢¢

Pennsbury Manor. Reconstruction of William Penn's 17th-century country manor; formal and kitchen gardens; livestock. Craft demonstrations; hands-on workshops. (Daily exc Mon; closed some hols) 5 mi NE at 400 Pennsbury Memorial Rd, off Bordentown Rd. Phone 215/946-0400. ¢¢

Sesame Place. Family theme park combines fun with learning. More than 50 outdoor physical play activities develop skills and coordination with kid-powered units. The indoor interactive and science galleries offer games to challenge the mind. Sesame Food Factory: visible kitchen-in-the-round serves wholesome favorites. Mr. Hooper's Emporium: complete shop for all Sesame Street items. Sesame Island area with Caribbean theme; water activities include Big Bird's Rambling River and Sky Splash. Musical revue with Sesame Street characters. (May-Labor Day, daily; after Labor Day-late Oct, wkends only) Approx 7 mi N, near Oxford Valley Mall (Langhorne), just N of Philadelphia off I-95 between Philadelphia and Trenton, NJ. Phone 215/752-7070. ¢¢¢¢

Annual Event

Fallsington Day. In Fallsington. Outdoor fair; restored buildings open; colonial craft demonstrations; entertainment. 2nd Sat Oct.

Brookville (C-3)

(See also Clarion)

Settled 1830 **Pop** 4,184 **Elev** 1,269 ft **Area code** 814 **Zip** 15825
Information Brookville Area Chamber of Commerce, 70 Pickering St; 814/849-8448.

What to See and Do

Clear Creek State Park. Approx 1,600 acres. Swimming beach; fishing; canoeing. Hiking trails. Cross-country skiing. Picnicking, playing field. Camping, cabins (dump station). Nature center; interpretive activities. Standard fees. 8 mi N on PA 36, then 4 mi NE on PA 949. For information contact Park Manager, RD 1, Box 82, Sigel 15860; 814/752-2368.

Annual Event

Western Pennsylvania Laurel Festival. Phone 814/849-2024. 3rd wk June.

Motels

★ ★ **DAYS INN.** PA 36 & I-80, I-80 exit 13. *814/849-8001; FAX 814/849-8001.* 124 rms, 3 story. S $40-$60; D $45-$85; each addl $5; under 18 free; higher rates hunting season. Crib free. Pet accepted. TV; cable. Heated pool; wading pool, poolside serv, lifeguard. Restaurant 6-10 am, 4:30-10 pm; winter from 7 am. Bar 5 pm-midnight, closed Sun. Ck-out noon. Coin lndry. Business servs avail. X-country ski 17 mi. Game rm. Cr cds: A, D, DS, MC, V.

D ⮐ ⊠ ⩲ ⊠ ⊠ SC

✔★ **HOLIDAY INN EXPRESS.** *235 Allegheny Blvd, I-80 exit 13. 814/849-8381; FAX 814/849-8386.* 69 rms, 3 story. S $38-$53; D $43-$66; each addl $5; under 12 free; higher rates hunting season. Crib

free. Pet accepted. TV; cable (premium). Pool; lifeguard. Complimentary continental bkfst. Restaurant adj 11 am-11 pm. Ck-out noon. Coin lndry. Meeting rm. Business servs avail. Sundries. Private patios, balconies. Cr cds: A, C, D, DS, MC, V.

D ⮐ ⊠ ⊠ ⊠ SC

Restaurant

✔★ ★ **MEETING PLACE.** *209 Main St. 814/849-2557.* Hrs: 8 am-9 pm; Sat from 9 am; Sun 10 am-7:30 pm; early-bird dinner Mon-Sat 4-5:30 pm. Closed some major hols. Res accepted. Bar. Semi-a la carte: bkfst $2-$5, lunch $2.75-$7, dinner $4.95-$12. Child's meals. Specializes in salads, chicken, seafood. Restored Victorian building (1871); casual dining. Cr cds: A, DS, MC, V.

Bucks County (E-9 - E-10)

E-mail bctc@bctc.org **Web** www.bctc.org
Information Bucks County Tourist Commission, 152 Swamp Rd, Doylestown 18901; 215/345-4552 or 800/836-BUCK.

Bucks County's great natural resources, location and waterway transportation were known to the Leni-Lenape centuries ago. Dutch explorers, followed by Swedes, English Quakers and Germans, began to take possession of the area in the 1600s. William Penn established his country estate in this area in the 17th century.

The county's historic importance is highlighted in the central section—it was here that General George Washington crossed the Delaware River with the Continental Army during the Revolution. More recently, artists and writers have settled in and around New Hope, giving rise to the village's fame as an art center. Bucks County's scenic beauty and rich history make it a popular tourist spot.

Following are the places in Bucks County included in the *Mobil Travel Guide.* For full information on any one of them, see the individual alphabetical listing. Bristol, Doylestown, New Hope, Quakertown, Washington Crossing Historical Park.

Bushkill (C-10)

(For accommodations see Milford)

Pop 900 (est) **Elev** 365 ft **Area code** 717 **Zip** 18324
Information Pocono Mts Vacation Bureau, 1004 Main St, Stroudsburg 18360; 717/424-6050; for free brochures phone 800/POCONOS.

What to See and Do

Bushkill Falls. Largest series of falls in Pocono Mts. Main falls have 100-ft drop. Scenic gorge. Fishing; boating. Picnicking. Wildlife exhibit of mounted animals and birds of Pennsylvania. (Apr-mid-Nov, daily) 2 mi N off US 209 on local road. Phone 717/588-6682. ¢¢¢

Delaware Water Gap (see). 15 mi W on US 209.

Pocono Indian Museum. Traces history of the Delaware through displays of artifacts, weapons and tools. Gift shop. (Daily; closed Dec 25) 3 mi S on US 209. Phone 717/588-9338or 717/588-9164. ¢¢

Butler (D-2)

(See also Harmony, Pittsburgh)

Settled 1793 **Pop** 15,714 **Elev** 1,077 ft **Area code** 724 **Zip** 16003 **E-mail** chamber@isrv.com **Web** www.butlerfirst.com

Information Butler County Visitors Bureau, 201 S Main St, PO Box 1082; 724/283-2222.

This is a manufacturing city nestled amid rolling hills that were owned by Robert Morris of Philadelphia, financier of the American Revolution. The city and county are named for General Richard Butler, who died in the St Clair Indian Expedition. During the 1930s, the Butler-based American Austin Company—later called American Bantam Company—pioneered the development of small, lightweight cars in America and invented the prototype of the jeep.

What to See and Do

Jennings Environmental Education Center. Blazing Star, a relict prairie wildflower, blooms profusely here in late July-early Aug. Trails, guided walks, interpretive center; picnicking. (Memorial Day-Labor Day, daily; rest of yr, Mon-Fri, some Sun) 12 mi N, at jct PA 8, 528, 173. Phone 724/794-6011. **Free.**

Moraine State Park. A 3,225-acre lake in a 16,180-acre park. Swimming beaches; fishing, hunting; boating (rentals, mooring, launching, marina). Hiking, horseback riding. Cross-country skiing, sledding, ice-skating, ice fishing, ice boating. Picnicking, playground, snack bar, restaurant. Cabin rentals. Waterfowl observation area; interpretive programs. Standard fees. 12 mi NW on US 422. Phone 724/368-8811.

Motels

★ ★ **CONLEY'S RESORT INN.** *740 Pittsburgh Rd (PA 8) (16001), exit 4 off PA Tpke on PA SR 8N.* 724/586-7711; FAX 724/586-2944; res: 800/344-7303. 56 rms, 2-3 story, 10 kits. No elvtr. S $62-$65; D $84-$99; each addl $10; under 18 free; golf plans. Crib free. TV. Indoor pool; whirlpool, sauna, lifeguard. Restaurant 7 am-10 pm. Rm serv. Bar 11-2 am, Sun to midnight. Ck-out 1 pm. Meeting rms. Business servs avail. Sundries. Rec rm. Tennis. 18-hole golf, greens fee $18-$27, putting green. X-country ski on site. Game rm. 150-ft indoor water slide. Cr cds: A, D, DS, MC, V.

★ ★ **DAYS INN.** *139 Pittsburgh Rd (PA 8) (16001).* 724/287-6761; FAX 724/865-7240. 139 rms, 2 story. S $56-$72; D $62-$77; each addl $6; family rates; golf package plan. Crib free. TV; cable. Indoor pool; whirlpool, lifeguard. Restaurant 6 am-10 pm. Rm serv. Bar 3 pm-2 am, Sun 1 pm-midnight; entertainment. Ck-out noon. Coin lndry. Meeting rms. Business servs avail. Valet serv. Sundries. Game rm. Cr cds: A, D, DS, MC, V.

✔★ **McKEE'S.** *930 Newcastle Rd (US 422) (16001), 6 mi W of Butler on 422W.* 724/865-2272. 22 rms. S $29.68-$33.92; D $32.86-$37.10; kit. units $47.70; under 5 free; wkly rates. Crib $4. TV; cable. Ck-out 11 am. Cr cds: A, DS, MC, V.

Inn

★ ★ ★ **APPLEBUTTER.** *(152 Applewood Lane, Slippery Rock 16057) 15 mi N on US 8 to US 173, N to Slippery Rock.* 724/794-1844; FAX 724/794-3319. 11 rms, 2 story. S $59-$105; D $79-$125; each addl $15. Adults preferred. TV. Complimentary full bkfst. Ck-out 11 am, ck-in 3-8 pm; Fri, Sat 3-10 pm. Sitting rm. Massage rm. Restored brick farm-

house (1844) furnished with antiques; addition added 1988. Totally non-smoking. Cr cds: A, MC, V.

Canadensis (C-9)

Pop 1,200 (est) **Area code** 717 **Zip** 18325

What to See and Do

Holley Ross Pottery. 20-min guided tours with demonstration of pottery making (Mon-Fri). Swinging bridge, park, sawdust trails. (May-mid-Dec, daily) S on PA 390, NW on PA 447, on PA 191N in La Anna. Phone 717/676-3248. **Free.**

Inns

★ ★ ★ **BROOKVIEW MANOR.** *PA 447, 1 mi S on PA 447.* 717/595-2451; FAX 717/595-5065; res: 800/585-7974. 10 rms, 2-3 story, suite. No rm phones. MAP: S $100-$140, D $110-$150; each addl $20; suite $150; hol wkends (2-day min). Children over 12 yrs only. Complimentary full bkfst. Coffee in library. Ck-out 11 am, Ck-in 3-7 pm. Picnic tables. Totally nonsmoking. Cr cds: A, D, DS, MC, V.

★ ★ ★ **CRESCENT LODGE INN.** *(Paradise Valley, Cresco 18326) S on PA 191 to PA 447.* 717/595-7486; FAX 717/595-3452; res: 800/392-9400. 12 lodge rms, 4 motel rms, 9 suites, 6 cottages (some with kit.) Mid-June-mid-Sept: S, D $85-$185; each addl $15; suites $172-$275; kit. cottages $1,000-$1,150/wk; EP, MAP, wkly rates; ski plans; lower rates rest of yr. TV; cable. Heated pool. Complimentary continental bkfst (exc summer). Restaurant (see CRESCENT LODGE). Bar. Ck-out 11 am, ck-in 2 pm. Business servs avail. Free bus depot transportation. Gift shop. Tennis. Golf nearby. Downhill/x-country ski 5 mi. Fitness trail. Lawn games. Whirlpool in suites; some refrigerators. Varied accommodations. Private patios. Picnic tables. Same owners more than 40 yrs. Cr cds: A, D, DS, MC, V.

★ ★ **OVERLOOK INN.** *Dutch Hill Rd.* 717/595-7519; res: 800/590-3845. 20 rms, 3 story. MAP: D $160-$200; higher rates some hols (2-day min). TV in sitting rm; cable. Pool. Afternoon refreshments. Restaurant (see OVERLOOK INN). Bar. Ck-out noon, ck-in 3 pm. Downhill ski 5 mi; x-country ski on site. Lawn games. Country farmhouse; built in 1880. Antiques. Cr cds: A, MC, V.

★ ★ **PINE KNOB.** *PA 447.* 717/595-2532; FAX 717/595-6429; res: 800/426-1460. 28 units, 19 baths. No rm phones. MAP: S $79-$95; D $158-$190. TV in library; cable. Ck-out 11 am, ck-in 2 pm. Tennis. Downhill/x-country ski 5 mi. Lawn games. Pre-Civil War period inn (1847); antiques. Cr cds: A, DS, MC, V.

★ **PUMP HOUSE.** *Skytop Rd.* 717/595-7501. 8 rms, 2 story. S, D $65-$100; each addl $5; suites $85-$100. Complimentary continental bkfst. Restaurant (see PUMP HOUSE INN). Ck-out 11 am, ck-in 2 pm. Built as stagecoach stop in 1842; furnished in country decor; antiques. Cr cds: C, D, MC, V.

Resort

★ ★ **SKYTOP LODGE.** *(One Skytop, Skytop 18357) 3 mi N on PA 390.* 717/595-7401; FAX 717/595-9618. 167 rms, 1-4 story, 40 cottages. May-Oct, AP: S $190-$275; D $230-$390; each addl $45; cottages

$345-$390; under 18 free; family, wkend, hol rates; ski, golf plans; 3-day min wkends, hols; higher rates some hols; lower rates rest of yr. Crib free. 2 pools, 1 indoor; wading pool, whirlpool, poolside serv, lifeguard. Playground. Supervised child's activities; ages 4-10. Dining rm. Rm serv. Box lunches, picnics. Bar noon-midnight. Ck-out 1 pm, ck-in 3 pm. Gift shop. Grocery, coin lndry 3-5 mi. Bellhops. Valet serv. Meeting rms. Business servs avail. Sports dir. Tennis, pro. 18-hole golf, pro, greens fee $40, putting green, driving range. Boats. Downhill/x-country ski on site. Sleighing, tobogganing. Hiking. Bicycle rentals. Lawn games. Soc dir. Rec rm. Game rm. Exercise rm; instructor, weights, bicycles, sauna, steam rm. Massage. Fishing guides, clean and store. Refrigerators in cottages. Picnic tables. On beach. Cr cds: A, C, D, DS, MC, V.

Restaurants

★ ★ **CRESCENT LODGE.** *(See Crescent Lodge Inn)* 717/595-7486. Hrs: 5:30-10 pm; Sun to 9 pm. Closed Dec 25; also Mon-Tues from Jan-May. Res accepted. Continental menu. Bar 4 pm-midnight. A la carte entrees: dinner $16.95-$28.95. Specializes in seafood, veal, chicken. Pianist Sat. Family-owned. Cr cds: A, D, DS, MC, V.

★ ★ **OVERLOOK INN.** *(See Overlook Inn)* 717/595-7519. Hrs: 8-10 am, 6-9 pm; Sun 5-8:30 pm. Res accepted. Continental menu. Bar 11 am-midnight. Semi-a la carte: bkfst $8, dinner $9.50-$22. Specializes in baby rack of lamb, fresh seafood, medallions of filet mignon. Built 1880. Cr cds: A, MC, V.

★ ★ ★ **PUMP HOUSE INN.** *(See Pump House Inn)* 717/595-7501. Hrs: 5-9 pm; Sun 2:30-8:30 pm. Closed Mon; Dec 25. Res accepted. French, Amer menu. Bar. Wine list. Semi-a la carte: dinner $13.95-$24.95. Specialties: roast rack of lamb, shrimp in beer batter, chocolate mousse. Own breads. Country inn (1842). Cr cds: C, D, MC, V.

Carbondale (C-9)

(For accommodations see Hawley, Scranton)

Founded 1822 **Pop** 10,664 **Elev** 1,070 ft **Area code** 717 **Zip** 18407
E-mail pntvb@epix.net **Web** www.visitnepa.org
Information Pennsylvania Northeast Territory Visitors Bureau, 100 Terminal Rd, Ste 216, Avoca 18641; 717/457-1320 or 800/22-WELCOME.

Carbondale, located in the heart of the northeast Pocono area, has excellent sports facilities. There are 33 lakes within an 8-mile radius and 201 more lakes within 25 miles. One of the first railroad lines in the country was built to haul coal from Carbondale.

What to See and Do

Merli-Sarnoski Park. Covers 850 acres of woodlands with 40-acre lake. Swimming beach (lifeguards); fishing (seasonal); boating (launch). Hiking trails. Winter activities include cross-country skiing, ice-skating, ice fishing. Picnicking. (Daily) 1/2 mi off PA 106. Phone 717/876-1714.

Skiing.

Elk Mt Ski Center. At an elevation of 2,693 ft, this is eastern Pennsylvania's highest mountain. Five double chairlifts; patrol, school, rentals; cafeteria, restaurant, bar. Longest run 2 mi; vertical drop 1,000 ft. (Early Dec-late Mar, daily) Half-day rate. NW on PA 106, E on PA 374. Phone 717/679-2611 or 800/233-4131 (East Coast states, for snow conditions). ¢¢¢¢¢

Mount Tone Ski Resort. Triple chairlift, T-bar, double rope tow, mighty mite; school, rentals; snowmaking; cafeteria; lodge. Vertical drop 450 ft. (Late Dec-mid-Mar) Two mountains, 11 trails; also night skiing, cross-country trails. N via PA 171, E via PA 370 to Lakewood, then S on PA 247 to Lake Como, follow signs. Phone 717/798-2707. ¢¢¢¢

Carlisle (E-6)

(See also Harrisburg)

Settled 1720 **Pop** 18,419 **Elev** 478 ft **Area code** 717 **Zip** 17013
Information Greater Area Chamber of Commerce, 212 N Hanover St, PO Box 572; 717/243-4515.

In the historically strategic Cumberland Valley, Carlisle was a vital point for Native American fighting during the Revolutionary and Civil wars.

Carlisle Barracks is one of the oldest military posts in America. Soldiers mounted guard here as early as 1750 to protect the frontier. From here began British campaigns that drove the French from the Ohio Valley and, in 1763, the march to relieve Fort Pitt. In 1794 President Washington reviewed troops assembled to march against the "Whiskey Rebels." Troops went from the Barracks to the Mexican and Civil wars. The famous Carlisle Indian Industrial School, first nonreservation school, was here until 1918. The Barracks was reopened in 1920 as the Medical Field Service School. It is now the home of the US Army War College.

George Ross, James Wilson and James Smith, all signers of the Declaration of Independence, lived in Carlisle, as did Molly Pitcher.

What to See and Do

Carlisle Barracks. Army War College, senior school in US Army's educational system. Includes the US Army Military History Institute and Hessian Powder Magazine Museum (1777), built by prisoners captured at the Battle of Trenton. The Carlisle Indian Industrial School (1879-1918) was one of the first institutions of higher learning for Native Americans. Also includes the Omar Bradley Museum, containing a collection of personal and military memorabilia of the five-star general. Jim Thorpe and other famous Native American athletes studied here. Military History Institute and the Omar Bradley Museum (Mon-Fri; closed federal hols). Post/grounds (daily; closed federal hols). 1 mi N on US 11. Phone 717/245-3611. **Free.**

Cumberland County Historical Society and Hamilton Library Association. Woodcarvings, furniture, silver, tools, redware, ironware, tall-case clocks, coverlets, paintings by local artisans; mementos of the Carlisle Indian School; special exhibits and programs. Library contains books, tax lists, early photographs, genealogical material. (Daily exc Sun; closed hols) 21 N Pitt St. Phone 717/249-7610. Museum **Free;** Library (nonmembers) ¢¢

Dickinson College (1773). (1,900 students) Tenth college chartered in US; President James Buchanan was a graduate. On campus is "Old West" (1804), a building registered as a National Historic Landmark that was designed by Benjamin Henry Latrobe, one of the designers of the Capitol in Washington. Tours of campus. W High St (US 11). Phone 717/243-5121. Also here is

The Trout Gallery. Permanent and temporary exhibits. (Sept-mid-June, Tues-Sat) Emil R. Weiss Center for the Arts. Phone 717/245-1711. **Free.**

Grave of "Molly Pitcher" (Mary Ludwig Hays McCauley). Soldiers in the Battle of Monmouth (June 1778) gave Molly her nickname because of her devotion to her husband and others who were fighting by bringing them pitchers of water. When her husband was wounded, Molly took his place at a cannon and continued fighting for him. In Old Graveyard, E South St.

Huntsdale Fish Hatchery. Springs and mountain stream fill tanks and ponds of brown, rainbow and palomino trout, muskellunge and walleye; visitor center. (Daily) 10 mi SW in Huntsdale. Phone 717/486-3419. **Free.**

Pine Grove Furnace State Park. Pre-Revolutionary iron, slate and brick works were in this area. Approx 696 acres. Swimming beaches; fishing, hunting; boating (rentals, mooring, launching). Hiking, bicycling (rentals). Cross-country skiing, ice-skating, ice fishing. Picnicking, snack bar, store. Tent & trailer sites. Visitor center. Lodging avail (phone 717/486-7575). Standard fees. 10 mi SW on I-81, exit 11, then 8 mi S on PA 233. Park office phone 717/486-7174.

Annual Event

Art Festival and Octoberfest. Oct.

Motels

✔★ ★ **APPALACHIAN TRAIL INN.** *1825 Harrisburg Pike (US 11), off I-81S exit 17E.* 717/245-2242; FAX 717/258-4881; res: 800/445-6715. 200 rms, 2 story. Apr-Oct: S $42-$52; D $47-$57; each addl $5; suites $85-$125; under 12 free; higher rates car shows; lower rates rest of yr. Crib free. TV; cable (premium). Restaurant 5-2 am. Ck-out noon. Business servs avail. Downhill ski 16 mi. Picnic tables. Cr cds: A, C, D, DS, ER, MC, V.

D ⊠ ⊠ ⊠ SC

★ ★ **BEST WESTERN INN OF THE BUTTERFLY.** *1245 Harrisburg Pike (US 11).* 717/243-5411; FAX 717/243-0778. 130 rms, 2 story. S $46.50-$64.50; D $63.50-$77.50; each addl $7; suites $68.50-$140; under 18 free. Crib free. TV; cable (premium), VCR avail (movies). Pool; lifeguard. Restaurant 6:30 am-9 pm. Bar 11-1 am. Ck-out noon. Meeting rms. Valet serv. Sundries. Microwaves avail. Cr cds: A, C, D, DS, ER, MC, V.

D ⊠ ⊠ ⊠ SC

★ ★ **DAYS INN.** *101 Alexander Spring Rd, I-81 exit 13.* 717/258-4147; FAX 717/258-4147, ext. 501. Web www.daysinn.com. 130 rms, 3 story. S $55-$80; D $60-$80; suites $85-$125; each addl $5; under 18 free; higher rates special events. Crib free. TV; cable, VCR avail (movies). Pool; lifeguard. Complimentary continental bkfst. Restaurant nearby. Ck-out noon. Coin lndry. Meeting rm. Business servs avail. Sundries. Airport transportation. Exercise equipt; weights, stair machine. Game rm. Some refrigerators. Cr cds: A, C, D, DS, JCB, MC, V.

D ⊠ ⊼ ⊠ ⊠ SC

★ ★ ★ **EMBERS INN & CONVENTION CENTER.** *1700 Harrisburg Pike (US 11), I-81 exit 17, I-76 exit 16.* 717/243-1717; FAX 717/243-6648; res: 800/692-7315. 270 rms. S $62; D $67; each addl $5; suites $110-$173; under 18 free. Crib $10. Pet accepted. TV; cable (premium), VCR avail (movies). Indoor pool; wading pool, whirlpool, sauna, poolside serv, lifeguard. Restaurant 7 am-9 pm; Sat to 9:30 pm. Rm serv. Bar 11-2 am. Ck-out 11 am. Meeting rms. Business servs avail. In-rm modem link. Bellhops. Sundries. Gift shop. Airport transportation. Tennis. Putting green. Lawn games. Refrigerators; microwaves avail. Cr cds: A, C, D, DS, ER, MC, V.

D ⊬ ⊁ ⊠ ⊠ ⊠ SC

★ ★ ★ **HOLIDAY INN.** *1450 Harrisburg Pike (US 11), just off I-81, exit 17.* 717/245-2400; FAX 717/245-9070. 100 rms, 2 story. S, D $79; each addl $10; under 18 free; higher rates special events. Crib free. Pet accepted. TV; cable (premium), VCR avail. Pool; lifeguard. Restaurant 6:30 am-2 pm, 5-10 pm. Rm serv. Bar 11 am-midnight. Ck-out noon. Coin lndry. Meeting rms. Business servs avail. In-rm modem link. Valet serv. Health club privileges. Cr cds: A, D, DS, JCB, MC, V.

D ⊬ ⊠ ⊠ ⊠ SC

★ ★ **QUALITY INN.** *1255 Harrisburg Pike, US 11 at I-81.* 717/243-6000; FAX 717/258-4123. 96 rms, 2 story. S, D $59.99; each addl $5; under 18 free; higher rates special events. Crib free. Pet accepted. TV; cable (premium). Pool; wading pool. Continental bkfst. Coffee in rms. Restaurant adj open 24 hrs. Bar 5 pm-midnight. Ck-out noon. Coin lndry. Business servs avail. Valet serv. Microwaves avail. Cr cds: A, C, D, DS, MC, V.

D ⊬ ⊠ ⊠ ⊠ SC

★ **SUPER 8.** *1800 Harrisburg Pike, on US 11, N of I-81 exit 17.* 717/249-7000; FAX 717/249-9070. 112 rms, 2 story, 16 kits. S $40-$80; D $45-$90; kits. $58; under 12 free; higher rates special events. Crib free. TV; cable. Complimentary coffee in lobby. Restaurant nearby. Ck-out 11 am. Coin lndry. Microwaves avail. Cr cds: A, D, DS, MC, V.

D ⊠ ⊠ SC

Resort

★ ★ ★ **ALLENBERRY.** *(Boiling Springs 17007) 6 mi SE on PA 174.* 717/258-3211; FAX 717/258-1464. 61 rms in lodges, 1 cottage (3 bedrm). S $89; D $109; each addl $15; cottage $295; under 17 free; package plans. Crib free. TV. Pool; wading pool, whirlpool, lifeguard. Dining rm 8-10:30 am, 11 am-2 pm, 5-9 pm (also see CARRIAGE ROOM). Bar 11 am-midnight. Ck-out noon. Meeting rms. Business servs avail. Airport transportation. Lighted tennis. Professional theater. On 57 wooded acres, 200-yr-old trees; several remodeled limestone buildings date from 1785, 1812. On Yellow Breeches Creek. Cr cds: A, DS, MC, V.

⊬ ⊁ ⊠ ⊠ ⊠ SC

Restaurants

★ ★ **BOILING SPRINGS TAVERN.** *(Front & First Sts, Boiling Springs 17007) 6 mi SE on PA 174, on town square.* 717/258-3614. Hrs: 11:30 am-10 pm. Closed Sun, Mon; major hols. Res accepted. Continental menu. Bar. Semi-a la carte: lunch $4.95-$9.95, dinner $9.95-$20.95. Child's meals. Specializes in fresh seafood, aged Western steak. Old stone structure (1832), originally an inn. Colonial decor. Cr cds: A, MC, V.

D ⊣

★ ★ ★ **CALIFORNIA CAFE.** *38 W Pomfret St.* 717/249-2028. Hrs: 11 am-9 pm. Closed major hols. Res accepted; required wkends. French, California menu. Serv bar. Semi-a la carte: lunch $4.45-$9.45. Complete meals: dinner $11.95-$18.95. Specialties: escalope de veau aux artichauts, poulet grillé chasseur. 1859 fire station building; French and Florentine artwork in addition to artwork from local gallery. Cr cds: A, C, D, DS, MC, V.

D

★ ★ **CARRIAGE ROOM.** *(See Allenberry Resort)* 717/258-3211. Hrs: 5-9 pm; Wed-Sat to midnight. Closed mid-Nov-Mar. Res accepted. Bar to midnight. Semi-a la carte: dinner $16.75-$26.75. Specializes in crab cakes, prime rib. Salad bar. Pianist, guitarist Thurs-Sat. Colonial decor. Cr cds: A, DS, MC, V.

D ⊣

Chambersburg (F-5)

Settled 1730 **Pop** 16,647 **Elev** 621 ft **Area code** 717 **Zip** 17201 **E-mail** chamber@chambersburg.org **Web** www.chambersburg.org

Information Chamber of Commerce, 75 S Second St; 717/264-7101. Information is also available at the Visitors Station, 1235 Lincoln Way E; 717/261-1200.

Named for Colonel Benjamin Chambers, a Scottish-Irish pioneer, this is an industrial county seat amid peach and apple orchards. John Brown had his headquarters here. During the Civil War, Confederate cavalry burned down the town, destroying 537 buildings after the citizens refused to pay an indemnity of $100,000.

What to See and Do

Caledonia State Park. Confederate General Jubal A. Early came through here during the Civil War and destroyed an iron furnace, which had been producing arms for the Union armies. Approx 1,100 acres. Swimming pool (fee); fishing. Nature, hiking trails; bicycling, 18-hole golf course. Cross-country skiing. Picnicking, playground, snack bar. Tent & trailer sites. Standard fees. (See ANNUAL and SEASONAL EVENTS) 10 mi E on US 30. Phone 717/352-2161.

The Old Jail. Jail complex (1818) restored and renovated for use as the Kittochtinny Historical Society's Museum and Library. An 1880 cell block houses community cultural activities, art and historical exhibits; other events. Also on grounds are Colonial, Fragrance and Japanese gardens;

19th-century barn; agricultural museum. Cultural programs (May-Oct). Tours (May-Nov, Thurs-Sat). 175 E King St. Phone 717/264-6364 or 717/264-1667. **Free.**

Annual Events

ChambersFest. Caledonia State Park. Civil War festival with crafts, food, reenactments, parade of pets. Phone 717/264-7101. July.

Franklin County Fair. Arts and crafts displays, needlework, home and dairy products, state turkey-calling contest, tractor pull, agricultural and livestock exhibits, entertainment. Phone 717/369-4100. 3rd full wk Aug.

Seasonal Event

Totem Pole Playhouse. Caledonia State Park.Resident professional theater company performs dramas, comedies and musicals in 453-seat proscenium theater. Tues-Sun evenings; matinees Wed, Sat-Sun. Phone 717/352-2164. June-Aug.

Motels

✔★ **DAYS INN.** 30 Falling Spring Rd, I-81 exit 6. 717/263-1288; FAX 717/263-6514. E-mail cha33chm@attmail.com; web www.daysinn.com. 107 rms, 3 story. Apr-Oct: S $46-$60; D $51-$65; each addl $7; suites $70-$85; under 17 free; lower rates rest of yr. Pet accepted. TV; cable (premium). Complimentary continental bkfst. Restaurant adj 6 am-11 pm. Ck-out 11 am. Meeting rms. Business servs avail. Downhill ski 15 mi. Cr cds: A, C, D, DS, JCB, MC, V.

D ✦ ⌂ ⊠ ▨ SC

★★ **HAMPTON INN.** 955 Lesher Rd, ¼ mi off I-81 exit 5. 717/261-9185; FAX 717/261-1984. 124 rms, 3 story. May-Oct: S, D $62-$69; under 18 free; monthly plans; higher rates special events; lower rates rest of yr. Crib free. TV; cable (premium). Complimentary continental bkfst. Restaurant adj 6 am-11 pm. Ck-out noon. Meeting rms. Business servs avail. In-rm modem link. Sundries. Exercise equipt; weight machine, bicycles. Refrigerators. Cr cds: A, C, D, DS, MC, V.

D ⌂ ⊠ ▨ SC

★★★ **HOLIDAY INN.** 1095 Wayne Ave, I-81 exit 5. 717/263-3400. 139 rms, 2 story. Apr-Oct: S $59; D $66; each adl $7; under 19 free; wkend rates; golf plan; lower rates rest of yr. Crib free. Pet accepted, some restrictions. TV; cable; VCR avail. Pool; poolside serv, lifeguard. Restaurant 6 am-2 pm, 5-10 pm. Rm serv. Bar. Ck-out noon. Meeting rms. Business servs avail. Some in-rm modem links. Bellhops. Sundries. Valet serv. 18-hole golf privileges. Health club privileges. Cr cds: A, D, DS, JCB, MC, V.

D ✦ ⌂ ⊠ ▨ SC

★★★ **HOWARD JOHNSON INN.** 1123 Lincoln Way E (US 30), I-81 exit 6. 717/263-9191; FAX 717/263-4752. Web www.hojo.com. 132 rms, 3 story. S $49-$55; D $61-$69; each addl $7; under 18 free. Crib free. TV; cable; VCR avail (movies). Indoor pool; sauna. Complimentary coffee in rms. Restaurant 6 am-11 pm. Bar 4 pm-midnight, closed Sun. Ck-out noon. Meeting rms. Business servs avail. In-rm modem link. Valet serv. Sundries. Downhill ski 20 mi. Refrigerators. Private patios, balconies. Cr cds: A, C, D, DS, MC, V.

D ⌂ ⊠ ▨ SC

✔★ **TRAVELODGE.** 565 Lincoln Way E (US 30), I-81 exit 6. 717/264-4187; FAX 717/264-2446. 52 rms, 3 story. S $49-$51; D $53-$57; each addl $7; under 18 free. Crib free. Pet accepted, some restrictions. TV; cable (premium). Coffee in rms. Restaurant 6 am-2 pm, 4:30-9:30 pm. Rm serv. Bar 11 am-2 pm, 4:30-9:30 pm. Ck-out noon. Meeting rm. Health club privileges. Refrigerators avail. Some balconies. Cr cds: A, C, D, DS, ER, JCB, MC, V.

D ✦ ⊠ ▨ SC

Inns

★★★ **MERCERSBURG INN.** (405 S Main St, Mercersburg 17236) 13 mi S on I-81, then 11 mi W on PA 16. 717/328-5231; FAX 717/328-3403. 15 rms, 3 story. S, D $115-$210; each addl $25. TV in sitting rm. Complimentary full bkfst. Restaurant (see MERCERSBURG INN). Rm serv. Ck-out 11 am, ck-in 3 pm. Some fireplaces. Some balconies. Brick Georgian-revival mansion (1910) with double staircase in hall, mahogany paneling and beams, original lighting fixtures; period & antique furnishings. Views of Blue Ridge Mts. Totally nonsmoking. Cr cds: DS, MC, V.

★★ **PENN NATIONAL INN.** (3809 Anthony Hwy, Mont Alto 17237) E on PA 30, then S on PA 997. 717/352-2400; FAX 717/352-3926; res: 800/231-0080. 36 rms, 4 in manor house, 2 story. Mid-Apr-Oct: S $80-$100; D $90-$110; each addl $10-$15; under 18 free; golf plan; monthly rates; lower rates rest of yr. Crib free. Pet accepted, some restrictions. TV; cable. Heated pool. Playground. Complimentary full bkfst. Coffee in rms. Restaurant (Apr-Oct) 7 am-7 pm. Ck-out 11 am, ck-in 2 pm. Business servs avail. Lighted tennis. 18-hole golf; greens fee $25-$45, putting green, driving range. Refrigerators; microwaves avail. Federalist-style manor house built in 1847, additions built in 1989. Cr cds: A, MC, V.

D ✦ ⌐ ⌂ ⌐ ⊠ ⌂ ⊠ ▨ SC

Restaurants

★★ **COPPER KETTLE.** 1049 Lincoln Way E (US 30), 2 blks W of I-81 exit 6. 717/264-3109. Hrs: 5-9:30 pm; Fri, Sat to 10 pm. Closed Sun; major hols. Res accepted; required Fri, Sat. Bar to midnight. Semi-a la carte: dinner $7.95-$21. Child's meals. Specializes in seafood, steak, prime rib. Early Amer decor; antiques. Cr cds: A, C, D, DS, MC, V.

⊡

★★★ **MERCERSBURG INN.** (See Mercersburg Inn) 717/328-5231. Sitting: 6 pm, 8 pm. Closed Sun-Thur; Thanksgiving. Res required. Bar. Complete meals: 5-course dinner $45. Specialties: pan-seared venison with red currant glace de veau, cornbread crusted salmon chive ravioli, lobster ravioli. Casual elegance. Cr cds: DS, MC, V.

Chester (F-9)

(See also Kennett Square, King of Prussia, Media, Philadelphia, West Chester)

Settled 1643 **Pop** 41,856 **Elev** 20 ft **Area code** 610

Information Delaware County Convention & Tourist Bureau, 200 E State St, Suite 100, Media 19063; 610/565-3679 or 800/343-3983.

The oldest settlement in the state, Chester was established by the Swedish Trading Company as Upland. William Penn came to Upland in 1682 to begin colonization of the land granted to him by King Charles II. He renamed the settlement in honor of Chester, a Quaker center in Cheshire, England. The first Assembly here adopted Penn's Framework of Government, enacted the first laws and organized the county of Chester—from which Delaware County broke off in 1789. On the Delaware River, 15 miles southwest of Philadelphia, Chester is a busy port and home of shipyards where every type of vessel has been built for the navy and merchant marine.

What to See and Do

Caleb Pusey Home, Landingford Plantation (1683). Built for manager and agent of Penn's mill; only remaining house in state visited by William Penn. Period furniture. Also on 27 acres of original plantation are a log house (1790), stone schoolhouse-museum (1849) and herb garden. (May-Sept, Sat & Sun afternoons; also by appt; closed hols) 15 Race St, in Upland, 2 mi W. Phone 610/874-5665. ¢

Morton Homestead (ca 1655). Two-part log house built by ancestors of John Morton, signer of Declaration of Independence. Contemporary outdoor exhibits on Pennsylvania's Swedish Period, log-house construction, Morton family. (Wed-Sat) 4 mi NE on US 13, then SW on PA 420, at 100 Lincoln Ave in Prospect Park. Phone 610/583-7221. ¢

Penn Memorial Landing Stone. Marks spot where William Penn first landed Oct 28, 1682. Front & Penn Sts.

Swarthmore College (1864). (1,320 students) Coeducational; on wooded 330-acre campus are Friends Historical Library and Peace Collection; an art gallery; concert hall; performing arts center; observatory; grassy, terraced amphitheater; Friends Meeting House; Scott Arboretum, a collection of trees, shrubs and herbaceous plants throughout campus. Symposia, exhibits, music and dance programs are open to the public. 4 mi N on PA 320, in Swarthmore. Phone 610/328-8000.

Widener University (1821). (8,700 students) On campus are Old Main, a national historic landmark, and the University Art Museum, with a permanent collection of 19th- & 20th-century American Impressionist and European academic art as well as contemporary exhibits (Sept-May, Tues-Sat; June & Aug, Mon-Thurs; closed July). Also here is Wolfgram Memorial Library. Campus tours. 14th & Chestnut Sts, 1 University Pl. Phone 610/499-4000.

Clarion (C-3)

Founded 1839 **Pop** 6,457 **Elev** 1,491 ft **Area code** 814 **Zip** 16214
E-mail clarionacc@penn.com
Information Clarion Area Chamber of Commerce, 41 S Fifth Ave; 814/226-9161.

Once the forests were so thick and tall here that, according to tradition, the wind in the treetops sounded like a distant clarion. That's how the town, county and river got their names. Today many campers and sports and outdoors enthusiasts enjoy the beauty and recreation that the Clarion area offers.

What to See and Do

Clarion County Historical Society. Museum housed in mid-19th century Sutton-Ditz house. Contains exhibits on county industry and business; Victorian bedroom and parlor; genealogical and historical library (researchers may call ahead for appt other than regular hrs); changing exhibits. (Apr-Dec, Tues, Thurs & Fri afternoons; closed hols) 18 Grant St. Phone 814/226-4450. **Free.**

Cook Forest State Park. Approx 6,700 acres. Swimming pool (fee); fishing, hunting. Hiking, bicycling, horseback riding. Cross-country skiing (rentals), snowmobiling, sledding, ice-skating. Picnicking. Tent & trailer sites, cabins (rentals). Nature & historical center. Standard fees. 11 mi NE on Clarion to Cook Forest Rd, then 3 mi S on PA 36. Phone 814/744-8407.

Tionesta Reservoir. 5 mi NW on US 322, then 20 mi NW on PA 66, in Allegheny National Forest (see WARREN).

Annual Events

Summer Fun Fest. Concerts, food concessions, games, entertainment. Early June.

Autumn Leaf Festival. Parade, carnival, autorama, scholarship pageants, concerts, flea market, craft shows. Sept 25-Oct 4.

Motels

★ ★ **DAYS INN.** PA 68 & I-80, exit 9N. 814/226-8682; FAX 814/226-8372. 150 rms, 2 story. S $46-$56; D $51-$61; each addl $5; under 18 free; tennis, golf, ski plans; higher rates: Autumn Leaf Festival, hunting season. Crib free. Pet accepted. TV; cable (premium), VCR avail (movies). Heated pool; lifeguard. Complimentary continental bkfst. Restaurant 6 am-2 pm, 5-10 pm. Rm serv. Bar 4 pm-2 am; entertainment.

Ck-out noon. Coin lndry. Meeting rms. Business servs avail. Sundries. Golf privileges. Health club privileges. Cr cds: A, C, D, DS, JCB, MC, V.

D ✔ ⚷ ╬ ⇌ ⟲ 🔥 SC

★ ★ ★ **HOLIDAY INN.** I-80 at PA 68 exit 9. 814/226-8850; FAX 814/226-9055, ext. 250. 122 rms, 2 story. S, D $69-$89; suites $135; under 20 free. Crib free. TV; cable (premium), VCR avail (movies). Indoor pool; sauna, lifeguard. Restaurant 7 am-10 pm. Rm serv. Bar 4 pm-1 am. Ck-out noon. Meeting rms. Business servs avail. In-rm modem link. Airport transportation. 18-hole golf privileges, greens fee $22, putting green. Game rm. Indoor balconies. Courtyard with pool. Cr cds: A, C, D, DS, JCB, MC, V.

D ⚷ ╬ ⇌ 🔥 SC

✔ ★ **SUPER 8.** RD 3, I-80 exit 9. 814/226-4550; FAX 814/227-2337. 99 rms, 9 kits. S, D $45-$80; each addl $5; kit. units avail; wkly, monthly rates (winter); under 18 free. Crib free. Pet accepted. TV; cable (premium), VCR avail (movies). Pool; lifeguard. Complimentary continental bkfst. Restaurant adj 6 am-10 pm. Ck-out noon. Business servs avail. In-rm modem link. Cr cds: A, C, D, DS, ER, MC, V.

D ✔ ⇌ ⟲ 🔥 SC

Restaurant

✔ ★ ★ **CLARION CLIPPER.** On PA 68N, 1/2 mi N of I-80 exit 9. 814/226-7950. Hrs: 6:30 am-10 pm. Closed Thanksgiving, Dec 25. Bar noon-midnight. Semi-a la carte: bkfst $2.50-$4.75, lunch $3.50-$5.75, dinner $5.50-$13. Child's meals. Specializes in steak, seafood. Salad bar. Exterior modeled after steamboats that operated on the Allegheny and Ohio Rivers in 1848. Cr cds: A, C, D, DS, MC, V.

D SC ⌐

Clearfield (Clearfield Co) (D-4)

Settled 1805 **Pop** 6,633 **Elev** 1,109 ft **Area code** 814 **Zip** 16830
Information Clearfield Chamber of Commerce, 125 E Market St, PO Box 250; 814/765-7567.

The old and important Native American town of Chinklacamoose occupied this site until it was burned in 1757. Coal and clay mining and more than 20 diversified plants producing school supplies, firebrick, fur products, precision instruments, electronic products and sportswear now occupy what used to be cleared fields. Easy access to other parts of the state and rich river bottom land led to the establishment of the county seat here.

What to See and Do

State parks.

S.B. Elliott. Approx 300 acres in the heart of the Moshannon State Forest; entirely wooded; display of mountain laurel in season. Fishing in small mountain streams surrounding the park. Hiking. Snowmobile trails. Tent & trailer sites, cabins. Standard fees. 9 mi N, off PA 153, just N of I-80 exit 18. Phone 814/765-7271 or 814/765-0630.

Parker Dam. Approx 950 acres in Moshannon State Forest. Swimming beach; fishing; boating (launch, rentals). Hiking. Cross-country skiing, snowmobiling, sledding, ice-skating, ice fishing. Snack bar. Tent & trailer sites (electric hookups), cabins. Nature center. Standard fees. 14 mi NW on PA 153, 6 mi off I-80 exit 18, then 2 mi E on unnumbered road. Phone 814/765-0630

Annual Events

Laurel Tour. Late June-early July.

Clearfield County Fair. Phone 814/765-4629. Late July-early Aug.

Motel

★ ★ **DAYS INN.** *R R 2, PA 879 & I-80 exit 19.* 814/765-5381; *FAX 814/765-7885.* 119 rms, 2 story. S $40-$60; D $46-$80; each addl $6; under 18 free; higher rates special events. Crib free. Pet accepted. TV, VCR avail (movies). Pool; lifeguard. Complimentary continental bkfst. Bar 4 pm-2 am. Ck-out noon. Meeting rms. Business servs avail. In-rm modem link. Exercise equipt; treadmill, bicycles, weight machine. Cr cds: A, C, D, DS, MC, V.

Conneaut Lake (B-1)

(For accommodations see Edinboro, Meadville)

Pop 699 **Elev** 1,100 ft **Area code** 814 **Zip** 16316
Information Crawford County Convention & Visitors Bureau, 242½ Chestnut St, Meadville 16335; 814/333-1258.

Located on the largest natural lake in Pennsylvania (929 acres), this resort town has swimming, boating and excellent fishing for perch, muskellunge, walleye, bass and crappie.

What to See and Do

Conneaut Cellars Winery. Tours and tastings. (May-Dec, daily; rest of yr, daily exc Mon; closed Jan 1, Easter, Thanksgiving, Dec 25) 12005 Conneaut Lake Rd. Phone 814/382-3999. **Free.**

Pymatuning Spillway. Part of Pymatuning State Park. When fish are fed bread, they flock so thickly that ducks walk on them. NW via US 6 on N end of reservoir. Phone 412/932-3141. **Free.**

Pymatuning State Park. Approx 21,100 acres with 17-mi lake. Swimming beach; fishing, hunting; boating (rentals, mooring, launching, marina). Hiking. Cross-country skiing, snowmobiling, sledding, ice-skating. Picnicking, playground, snack bar. Tent & trailer areas along shore. Cabins. Waterfowl museum and refuge; fish hatchery. Standard fees. SW via US 322, 1 mi W of Jamestown. Phone 412/932-3141.

Pymatuning Visitors Center. Part of Pennsylvania Game Commission; birds and animals indigenous to Pymatuning Reservoir area; bald eagle's nest visible from museum. Educational and interpretive programs. (Mar-Oct, daily) 9 mi W on US 285, then N on Hartstown-Linesville Rd. Phone 814/683-5545. **Free.**

Connellsville (F-2)

(See also New Stanton, Uniontown)

Pop 9,229 **Elev** 885 ft **Area code** 724 **Zip** 15425
Information Greater Connellsville Chamber of Commerce, 923 W Crawford Ave; 724/628-5500.

Located in an area visited by George Washington and where he owned land, the region has many references to him in place names. The restored Crawford Cabin near the river was the home of Colonel William Crawford, surveyor of these properties and Washington's surveying pupil.

Northwest of town in Perryopolis are many historic restorations. The town square is named for Washington, who some believe planned the design of the town.

What to See and Do

⭐ **Fallingwater (Kaufmann Conservation on Bear Run).** One of the most famous structures of the 20th century, Fallingwater, designed by Frank Lloyd Wright in 1936, is cantilevered on three levels over a waterfall; interior features Wright-designed furniture, textiles, lighting, as well as sculpture by modern masters; extensive grounds are heavily wooded and planted with rhododendron, which blooms in early July. Visitor center with self-guided orientation program; concession; gift shop. Guided tours (Apr-mid-Nov, daily exc Mon; winter, Sat-Sun). No children under 10; child-care center. No pets. Res required. 8 mi E on PA 711, then 8 mi S on PA 381, near Mill Run. Phone 724/329-8501. ¢¢¢-¢¢¢¢

Linden Hall (1913). Conference and convention center in mountaintop mansion, situated in picturesque Laurel Highlands. Golf, tennis, fishing, swimming, walking trail. Guided tours of mansion (Mar-Dec, Mon-Fri; wkends by appt). 4 mi S on PA 201, then 1 mi N on PA 819, left on River Rd in Dawson. Phone 724/529-7543, 724/529-2882 or 412/461-2424. ¢¢¢

Motel

★ **MELODY MOTOR LODGE.** *1607 Morrell Ave (US 119).* 724/628-9600. 46 rms. S, D $34-$47; higher rates Labor Day wkend. Crib $5. Pet accepted, some restrictions. TV; cable. Restaurant adj 6 am-10 pm. Bar 4 pm-midnight. Ck-out 11 am. Picnic tables. Cr cds: A, DS, MC, V.

Inn

↙★ ★ **NEWMYER HOUSE.** *507 S Pittsburgh St.* 724/626-0141. 4 rms, 1 with shower only, 3 story. No rm phones. S $60; D $75; each addl $10; June-Labor Day wkends (2-day min). Children over 12 yrs only. TV in common rm; cable, VCR avail (movies). Complimentary full bkfst. Ck-out 11 am, ck-in 2 pm. Luggage handling. Downhill ski 20 mi; x-country ski 20 mi. Many fireplaces. Restored Queen Anne style mansion built in 1892; antiques. Cr cds: MC, V.

Coraopolis

(see Pittsburgh Intl Airport Area)

Cornwall (E-8)

(For accommodations see Ephrata, Hershey, Lancaster, Lebanon; also see Manheim)

Settled 1732 **Pop** 3,231 **Elev** 680 ft **Area code** 717 **Zip** 17016
Information Pennsylvania Rainbow Region Vacation Bureau, 625 Quentin Rd, PO Box 329, Lebanon 17042; 717/272-8555.

The Cornwall Ore Banks were a major source of magnetic iron ore for nearly 250 years.

What to See and Do

Cornwall Iron Furnace. In operation 1742-1883. Open pit mine; 19th-century Miners Village still occupied. Furnace building houses "great wheel" and 19th-century steam engine. Visitor center, exhibits, book store. (Daily exc Mon; closed most hols) Rexmont Rd at Boyd St. Phone 717/272-9711. ¢¢

Historic Schaefferstown. An 18th-century farm established by Swiss-German settlers. Village square with authentic log and stone and half-timber buildings; site of first waterworks in US (1758), still in operation. Schaeffer Farm Museum has Swiss Bank House and Barn (1737); early farm tools; colonial farm garden. The museum N of the Square has antiques and artifacts of settlers. (See ANNUAL EVENTS) House and museum (open during festivals; also June-Sept, by appt). 6 mi SE of Lebanon at jct PA 419, 501, 897. Phone 717/949-2244. ¢¢

Annual Events

Historic Schaefferstown Events. Events during the yr include **Cherry Fair,** 4th Sat June; **Folk Festival,** mid-July; **Harvest Fair & Horse Plowing Contest,** 2nd wkend Sept.

Danville (D-7)

(See also Bloomsburg, Lewisburg)

Pop 5,165 **Elev** 490 ft **Area code** 717 **Zip** 17821 **E-mail** danville @sunlink.net **Web** www.sunlink.net/~danville

Information Danville Area Chamber of Commerce, 206 Walnut St; 717/275-5200.

What to See and Do

Joseph Priestley House (1794). American house of the 18th-century Englishman and Unitarian theologian who, in 1774, was first to isolate the element oxygen. (By appt) SW via US 11 in Northumberland at 472 Priestley Ave. Phone 717/473-9474. **¢¢**

PP & L Montour Preserve. Fishing; boating (no gasoline motors) on 165-acre Lake Chillisquaque. Hiking and nature trails. Picnicking. Birds of prey exhibit in visitors center; scheduled programs (fee for some). From I-80 exit 33, then PA 54W to Washingtonville, and NE on local roads. Phone 717/437-3131. **Free.**

Motel

✔★ ★ **HOWARD JOHNSON.** *15 Valley West Rd, I-80 exit 33.* 717/275-5100; FAX 717/275-1886. 77 rms, 2 story. Apr-Oct: S $45-$55; D $50-$65; each addl $5; under 18 free; lower rates rest of yr. Crib free. TV; cable. Pool. Restaurant adj 6:30 am-10 pm. Ck-out noon. Coin lndry. Meeting rms. Business servs avail. In-rm modem link. Game rm. Cr cds: A, C, D, DS, ER, JCB, MC, V.

D ⌀ ⌀ ⌀ SC

Inn

★ ★ ★ **PINE BARN.** *1 Pine Barn Place.* 717/275-2071; FAX 717/275-3248; res: 800/627-2276. 65 rms, 1-2 story. S $42-$65; D $46-$75; each addl $2; under 16 free. Crib $5. TV; cable. Restaurant (see PINE BARN INN). Rm serv. Bar 11 am-midnight, Sun 1-8 pm. Ck-out 1 pm. Meeting rms. Business servs avail. Valet serv. Gift shop. Geisinger Medical Center adj. Cr cds: A, C, D, DS, MC, V.

D ⌀ ⌀

Restaurant

★ ★ **PINE BARN INN.** *(See Pine Barn Inn)* 717/275-2071. Hrs: 7 am-10 pm; Sun 8 am-8 pm; Sun brunch 11 am-2 pm. Closed major hols. Res accepted. Bar 11 am-midnight; Sun 1-8 pm. Semi-a la carte: bkfst $3.50-$6.50, lunch $4.50-$9.50, dinner $12-$26. Sun brunch $5-$13. Child's meals. Specializes in New England seafood, steak. Salad bar. Outdoor dining. Converted 19th-century barn. Fireplace. Family-owned. Cr cds: A, C, D, DS, MC, V.

Delaware Water Gap (C-10)

(For accommodations see Milford, Stroudsburg; also see Pocono Mountains)

It is difficult to believe that the quiet Delaware River could carve a path through the Kittatinny Mountains, which are nearly a quarter of a mile high at this point. Conflicting geological theories account for this natural phenomenon, which is part of a national recreation area. The prevailing theory is that the mountains were formed after the advent of the river, rising up from the earth so slowly that the course of the Delaware was never altered.

Despite the speculation about the origin of the gap, there is no doubt about the area's recreational value. A relatively unspoiled area along the river boundary between Pennsylvania and New Jersey, stretching approximately 35 miles from Matamoras to an area just south of I-80, the site of the Delaware Water Gap is managed by the National Park Service.

Trails and overlooks (year round) offer scenic views. Also here are canoeing and boating, hunting and fishing; camping is nearby at the Dingmans Campground within the recreation area. Swimming and picnicking at Smithfield and Milford beaches. Dingmans Falls and Silver Thread Falls, two of the highest waterfalls in the Poconos, are near here (see MILFORD). Several 19th-century buildings are in the area, including Millbrook Village (several buildings open May-Oct) and Peters Valley (see BRANCHVILLE, NJ). The visitors center is located off I-80 in New Jersey, at Kittatinny Point (Apr-Nov, daily; rest of yr, Sat & Sun only; closed Jan 1, Dec 25), phone 908/496-4458 or 717/588-2451. Park headquarters are in Bushkill, PA. Phone 717/588-2451.

Denver/Adamstown (E-8)

(See also Ephrata, Lancaster, Reading)

Pop Denver 2,861; Adamstown 1,108 **Elev** Denver 380 ft; Adamstown 500 ft **Area code** 717 **Zip** Denver 17517; Adamstown 19501

Information Pennsylvania Dutch Convention and Visitors Bureau, 501 Greenfield Rd, Lancaster 17601; 717/299-8901 or 800/PADUTCH.

Located near a Pennsylvania Turnpike exit, Denver and Adamstown are in the center of an active antique marketing area, which preserves its Pennsylvania German heritage.

What to See and Do

Stoudt's Black Angus. More than 350 dealers display quality antiques for sale. (Sun) Along PA 272 from PA Tpke exit 21 to just beyond Adamstown. Phone 717/484-4385.

Seasonal Event

Bavarian Summer Fest. Oom-pah bands, schuhplattler dance groups; Oktoberfest atmosphere. Includes special events, German folklore, German food, displays, shops. SW via PA 272 in Adamstown at Black Angus Bier Garten. Phone 717/484-4385 (wkends). Fri-Sun, mid-July-early Sept.

Motels

★ ★ **BLACK HORSE LODGE.** *(2180 N Reading Rd, Denver 17517) jct PA Tpke exit 21 & US 272.* 717/336-7563; FAX 717/336-1110. 74 rms, 2 story. Mid-Apr-mid-Nov: S $59-$129; D $69-$139; under 13 free; suites $100-$250; wkly, monthly rates; golf plans; lower rates rest of yr. Crib free. Pet accepted, some restrictions. TV; cable. Pool. Complimentary full bkfst. Complimentary coffee in rms. Restaurant 11:30 am-2:15 pm, 5-10 pm. Bar to 11 pm. Ck-out noon. Coin lndry. Business servs avail. Golf privileges. Many refrigerators, microwaves avail; some bathrm phones. Private patios, balconies. Picnic tables, grills. Cr cds: A, C, D, DS, MC, V.

★ ★ **HOLIDAY INN.** *(1 Denver Rd, Denver)* US 272, US 222, PA Tpke exit 21. 717/336-7541; FAX 717/336-0515. E-mail hilanc@post office.ptd.net. 110 rms, 2 story. June-Oct: S, D $89; each addl $8; under 18 free; higher rates special events; lower rates rest of yr. Crib free. TV; cable (premium), VCR avail (movies). Pool; poolside serv, lifeguard. Restaurant 6:30 am-2 pm, 5-10 pm. Rm serv. Bar 5-10 pm. Ck-out noon. Coin lndry. Meeting rms. Business servs avail. In-rm modem link. Valet serv. Golf privileges. Cr cds: A, C, D, DS, JCB, MC, V.

Inn

★ ★ **ADAMSTOWN INN.** *(62 W Main St, Adamstown 19501)* 717/484-0800; res: 800/594-4808; FAX 717/484-1384. Web www.adams town.com. 4 rms, 2 with shower only, 2 story. Rm phones avail. S $63-$94.50; D $70-$105; wkends (2-day min). Children over 12 yrs only. TV in some rms; cable. Complimentary continental bkfst; afternoon refreshments. Restaurant nearby. Ck-out 10 am, ck-in 3-6 pm. Luggage handling. Valet serv. Concierge serv. Some in-rm whirlpools, fireplaces. Patio. Picnic tables. Built in 1925; Victorian decor; antiques, family heirlooms. Totally nonsmoking. Cr cds: MC, V.

Restaurant

★ ★ ★ **BLACK HORSE.** *(2170 N Reading Rd, Denver 17517)* 1 mi N of Tpke exit 21, on PA 272. 717/336-6555. Hrs: 11:30 am-2:15 pm, 5-10 pm; Fri, Sat 11:30 am-10 pm; Sun 11:30 am-9 pm. Closed Jan 1, Dec 25. Res accepted. Bar 11 am-11 pm. Wine cellar. Semi-a la carte: lunch $5-$12, dinner $14-$30. Child's meals. Specializes in Angus beef, fresh seafood, gourmet desserts. Own pasta. Casual yet elegant decor with stained glass windows, antique chandeliers, artwork. Cr cds: A, C, D, DS, MC, V.

Donegal (E-3)

(See also Connellsville, Greensburg, Ligonier, Somerset)

Pop 212 **Elev** 1,814 ft **Area code** 724 **Zip** 15628

What to See and Do

Seven Springs Mountain Resort Ski Area. 2 quad, 7 triple, 2 double chairlifts, 7 rope tows; patrol, school, rentals; snowmaking; cafeteria, restaurant, bar; lodge. Longest run 1 1/4 mi; vertical drop 750 ft. Night skiing. (Dec-Mar, daily) Alpine slide (May-Sept, daily). Hotel and conference center; summer activities include 18-hole golf, tennis, swimming. 12 mi SE of PA Tpke exit 9 on Champion-Trent Rd. Phone 814/352-7777. Lift ¢¢¢¢¢

Motel

★ **DAYS INN.** PA 31. 724/593-7536; FAX 724/593-6165. 34 rms, 20 with shower only. S, D $59-$68; each addl $6; under 12 free; higher rates special events. TV; cable (premium). Heated pool. Complimentary continental bkfst. Restaurant nearby. Ck-out 11 am. Golf privileges. Downhill/x-country ski 9 mi. Lawn games. Picnic tables. Cr cds: A, MC, V.

Resort

★ ★ ★ **SEVEN SPRINGS.** *(RD 1, Champion 15622)* On County Line Rd, 12 mi SE of PA Tpke exit 9. 814/352-7777; FAX 814/352-7911; res: 800/452-2223. Web www.7springs.com. 385 rms in 10 story lodge; 20 kit. chalets, cabins, 1-4 bedrm, 2 story. Lodge: S $145; D $155; each addl $50; under 17 free; suites $420; kit. chalets $525; ski, golf, tennis, package plans; cabins for 6-25, $520-$895/wk; also daily rates (2-day min); wkend rates. Crib free. Maid serv avail in chalets, cabins $5/bed. TV; VCR avail. Heated indoor/outdoor pools (open to public); wading pool, whirlpool, poolside serv, lifeguard. Playground. Free supervised child's activities (ages 4-11). Dining rm 7 am-10 pm (also see HELEN'S). Snack bar; box lunches. Bar 11-2 am. Ck-out noon, ck-in 5 pm. Coin lndry. Convention facilities. Business servs avail. Bellhops. Shopping arcade. Barber, beauty shop. Airport transportation. Sports dir. Tennis. Golf, greens fee $65, pro, putting green, driving range. Miniature golf. Downhill ski on site. Outdoor games. Hay rides. Mountain bikes avail. Soc dir; dancing, entertainment. Rec rm. Bowling. Indoor roller skating. Exercise equipt; weight machine, bicycles, sauna, steam rm. Wet bar in suites. Many private patios, balconies. Cr cds: DS, MC, V.

Restaurants

★ ★ ★ **HELEN'S.** *(See Seven Springs Resort)* 814/352-7777. Web www.7springs.com. Hrs: 6-10 pm; also lunch during ski season. Res required. Continental menu. Bar. A la carte entrees: dinner $19-$30. Specialties: Dover sole, chicken Frangelica, lamb Helena. Totally nonsmoking. Cr cds: DS, MC, V.

★ ★ ★ **NINO BARSOTTI'S.** *(Star Route, Mt Pleasant 15666)* 8 mi E on PA 31. 724/547-2900. Hrs: 11 am-3 pm, 5-10 pm; Sat to 11 pm; Sun to 9 pm; Sun brunch 11:30 am-2 pm. Closed Mon; most major hols. Res accepted Fri, Sat. Italian, Amer menu. Bar. Semi-a la carte: lunch $4.95-$9.45, dinner $7.45-$23.45. Sun brunch $7.95. Child's meals. Specializes in fresh seafood, steak, homemade desserts. Salad bar. Own pasta. Valet parking. Family-owned. Cr cds: A, D, DS, MC, V.

Downingtown (F-9)

(See also King of Prussia, West Chester)

Settled 1702 **Pop** 7,749 **Elev** 244 ft **Area code** 610 **Zip** 19335 **Web** www.brandywinevalley.com
Information Chester County Tourist Bureau, 601 Westtown Rd, Ste 170, West Chester 19382; 610/344-6365 or 800/228-9933.

Settled by emigrants from Birmingham, England, Downingtown honors Thomas Downing, who erected a log cabin here in 1702. The borough was first called Milltown, after the mill built here by Roger Hunt in 1765. The town, with its many historically interesting homes, retains much of its colonial charm. Jacob Eichholtz, a leading early American portrait artist, was born here.

What to See and Do

Hibernia County Park. Once the center of an iron works community, it is now the largest of the county parks, encompassing 800 acres of woodlands and meadows. The west branch of the Brandywine Creek, Birch Run and a pond are stocked with trout; hiking trails; picnicking; tent & trailer camping (dump station). Park features Hibernia Mansion; portions of house date from 1798, period furnishings. Tours of mansion (Memorial Day-Labor Day, Sun; fee). From US 30 Bypass take PA 82 approx 2 mi N to Cedar Knoll Rd, then left 1 1/4 mi to park entrance on left. Phone 610/384-0290. **Free.**

Historic Yellow Springs. From its beginnings as a fashionable spa, this historic village has been everything from a Revolutionary hospital to an art school. Countryside covers 145 acres with buildings, medicinal herb garden and mineral springs. Events and educational programs throughout the yr (some fees). Self-guided tour. Office (Mon-Fri). 10 mi NE via PA 113, NW on Yellow Springs Rd. Phone 610/827-7414.

Valley Forge National Historical Park (see). 10 mi E on I-76.

Annual Events

Old Fiddlers' Picnic. Hibernia County Park. 2nd Sat Aug.

Hibernia Mansion Christmas Tours. Hibernia County Park. 1st wk Dec.

Motor Hotel

★ ★ **HOLIDAY INN.** *(815 N Pottstown Pike, Exton 19341)* N on PA 113 to PA 100, 1 mi S of PA Tpke exit 23. 610/363-1100; FAX 610/524-2329. 225 rms, 4 story. S, D $99; under 18 free. Crib free. Pet accepted. TV; cable (premium). 2 pools, 1 indoor; poolside serv, lifeguard. Coffee in rms. Restaurant 6:30 am-10 pm; Sat from 7 am; Sun 7 am-1 pm. Rm serv. Bar 2 pm-2 am; entertainment exc Sun. Ck-out 11 am. Coin lndry. Meeting rms. Business servs avail. In-rm modem link. Valet serv. Gift shop. Airport transportation. Health club privileges. Refrigerators, microwaves avail. Picnic tables. Cr cds: A, C, D, DS, ER, JCB, MC, V.

D ⚡ ≋ ⛷ 🐾 SC

Restaurant

★ ★ ★ **VICKERS.** *(Gordon Dr, Lionville)* PA Tpke exit 23 on Gordon Dr. 610/363-7998. Hrs: 11:30 am-2 pm, 5:30-10:30 pm. Closed Sun (exc Easter, Mother's Day). Res accepted; required Sat. French, continental menu. Bar. Semi-a la carte: lunch $6.50-$12.95, dinner $16-$26.95. Specialties: beef Wellington, Dover sole, rack of lamb. Own desserts. Pianist Fri, Sat. Authentic farmhouse, built 1823. Cr cds: A, MC, V.

D 🖼

Doylestown (Bucks Co) (E-10)

(See also Philadelphia, Quakertown)

Settled 1735 **Pop** 8,575 **Elev** 340 ft **Area code** 215 **Zip** 18901 **E-mail** bctc@bctc.org **Web** www.bctc.org

Information Bucks County Tourist Commission, 152 Swamp Rd; 215/345-4552 or 800/836-BUCK.

Doylestown is the county seat of historic and colorful Bucks County.

What to See and Do

Covered bridges. Descriptive list, map of 11 bridges in Bucks County may be obtained at Bucks County Tourist Commission.

James A. Michener Art Museum. Changing exhibitions of 20th-century American art, contemporary crafts and sculpture garden. Located in restored old Bucks County jail. (Daily exc Mon; closed major hols) 138 S Pine St. Phone 215/340-9800. ¢¢

Mercer Mile. Three reinforced-concrete structures built between 1910-1916 within a one-mi radius by Dr. Henry Chapman Mercer, archaeologist, historian, world traveler and tile maker. They include

    Mercer Museum of the Bucks County Historical Society. Collection of over 50,000 early American artifacts and tools. Changing exhibits gallery. (Daily; closed Jan 1, Thanksgiving, Dec 25) 84 S Pine St. Phone 215/345-0210. ¢¢

    Fonthill Museum. Concrete castle of Henry Chapman Mercer (1856-1930) displays his collection of tiles and prints from around the world. Guided tours (times vary; phone ahead). (Daily; closed Jan 1, Thanksgiving, Dec 25) E Court St at PA 313. Phone 215/348-9461. ¢¢

    Moravian Pottery and Tile Works. Restored and established as a living history museum; tiles are handcrafted on premises. Slide show and self-guided tour explain ceramic process and history of Mercer's work, which appears in buildings all over the country. (Daily; closed some hols) 130 Swamp Rd. Phone 215/345-6722. ¢¢

⭐ **Pearl S. Buck House** (1835). House of Pulitzer and Nobel Prize winning author Pearl S. Buck. Original furnishings include desk at which *The Good Earth* was written; memorabilia, Chinese artifacts. Picnicking on grounds. Gift shop. One-hr guided tours (Mar-Dec, daily exc Mon; closed most major hols). 520 Dublin Rd, 8 mi NW via PA 611, 313 in Hilltown Township. Phone 215/249-0100. ¢¢

Motel

★ ★ **COMFORT INN.** *(678 Bethlehem Pike/PA 309, Montgomeryville 18936)* S on US 202. 215/361-3600; FAX 215/361-7949. 84 rms, 3 story. S $82.95-$116.95; D $87.95-$122.95; each addl $5; suites $116.95-$122.95; under 18 free. Crib free. TV; cable, VCR avail (movies). Complimentary continental bkfst. Coffee in rms. Restaurant adj. Ck-out noon. Coin lndry. Meeting rm. Business servs avail. In-rm modem link. Valet serv. Health club privileges. Microwaves avail. Refrigerator, wet bar in suites. Cr cds: A, C, D, DS, ER, MC, V.

D ⛷ 🐾 SC

Inns

★ ★ ★ **HIGHLAND FARMS.** *70 East Rd, 1½ mi N on US 202, exit East Rd.* 215/340-1354. 4 rms, 2 share bath, 3 story, 2 suites. 1 rm phone. S, D $135-$195; each addl $25; suites $175-$195. Children over 12 yrs only. TV in common rm; cable, VCR avail (movies). Complimentary full bkfst. Ck-out 11 am, ck-in 3:30 pm. In-rm modem link. Tennis. Downhill ski 4 mi; x-country ski on-site. Pool. Many fireplaces. Picnic tables, grills. Built in 1800; antiques. Was home to Oscar Hammerstein, Broadway lyricist. Totally nonsmoking. Cr cds: MC, V.

🏊 🎿 ≋ 🤸 ⛷ 🐾 SC

★ ★ **THE INN AT FORD HOOK FARM.** *105 New Britain Rd.* 215/345-1766; FAX 215/345-1791. 7 rms, 2 with shower only, 2 share bath, 3 story. Many rm phones. S, D $100-$300; each addl $20; 2-day min wkends. Children over 12 yrs only. 2 TVs; VCR avail (movies). Complimentary full bkfst. Ck-out 11 am, ck-in 3 pm. Business servs avail. X-country ski on site. Lawn games. Balconies. Picnic tables. On 60 acres of woods and meadows; many antiques. Totally nonsmoking. Cr cds: A, MC, V.

🎿 ⛷ 🔥

★ ★ ★ **PINE TREE FARM.** *2155 Lower State Rd.* 215/348-0632. 4 rms, 3 story. S, D $150-$175; 2-day min wkends, 3-day min hols. Children over 16 yrs only. Pool. Complimentary continental bkfst; afternoon refreshments. Ck-out 11 am, ck-in 4 pm. Solarium. 16-acre country estate built 1730; furnished with antiques. Totally nonsmoking. No cr cds accepted.

≋ ⛷ 🔥

★ ★ **SIGN OF THE SORREL HORSE.** *4424 Old Easton Rd.* 215/230-9999; FAX 215/230-8053. 5 rms, 2 with shower only, 2 story, 2 suites. No rm phones. S, D $85-$175; wkends (2-day min). Complimentary continental bkfst. Complimentary coffee in rms. Restaurant (see SIGN OF THE SORREL HORSE). Ck-out 11 am, ck-in 4 pm. Business center. Luggage handling. Free airport, RR station transportation. Lawn games. Picnic tables. On river. Built as a grist-mill (1714). Cr cds: A, D, MC, V.

⛷ 🐾 🤸

Restaurants

★ ★ ★ **CAFÉ ARIELLE.** *100 S Main St. 215/345-5930.* Hrs: noon-2:30 pm, 6-9 pm; Sat 6-9:30 pm; Sun 6-8 pm. Closed Mon, Tues; Jan 1, Easter, Dec 25. Res required Fri, Sat. French menu. Bar. A la carte entrees: lunch $7-$12, dinner $21-$32. Specializes in duck, seafood. Own baking. Restored livery (1800s); original artwork. Open kitchen. Cr cds: A, D, MC, V.

✔ ★ **LOS SARAPES.** *(17 Moyer Rd, Chalfont 18914) 3 mi S on US 202, exit Moyer Rd. 215/822-8858.* Hrs: 11 am-9 pm; Fri, Sat to 10 pm; Sun from 4 pm. Closed Mon; major hols. Res accepted. Mexican menu. Bar. Semi-a la carte: lunch, dinner $4.50-$14. Specialties: tampiquena, mole poblano, pescado a la Veracruzana. Own desserts. Casual Mexican decor. Totally nonsmoking. Cr cds: A, DS, MC, V.

★ ★ ★ **SIGN OF THE SORREL HORSE.** *(See Sign of the Sorrel Horse Inn) 215/230-9999.* Hrs: 5:30-9:30 pm. Closed Mon, Tues; Dec 25; also 2 wks Mar. Res accepted. French, Amer menu. Bar. A la carte entrees: dinner $14.95-$28. Prix fixe: dinner $55. Specialties: Swedish elk, pheasant, game dishes. Outdoor dining. Guest rms avail. Jacket. Located in historic grist-mill (1714). Cr cds: A, C, D, MC, V.

Du Bois (C-4)

(See also Clearfield)

Settled 1865 **Pop** 8,286 **Elev** 1,420 ft **Area code** 814 **Zip** 15801
Information Du Bois Area Chamber of Commerce, 33 N Brady St; 814/371-5010.

At the entrance to the lowest pass of the Allegheny Range, Du Bois is a transportation center—once the apex of huge lumbering operations. Destroyed by fire in 1888, the town was rebuilt on the ashes of the old community and today ranks as one of the 12 major trading centers in the state.

Motels

✔ ★ ★ **BEST WESTERN INN AND CONFERENCE CENTER.** *82 N Park Place, Between I-80 exits 16 & 17 on SR 219 and SR 255. 814/371-6200; FAX 814/371-4608.* 60 rms, 3 story. S $44-$54; D $50-$60; each addl $6; under 12 free. Crib free. TV; cable. Playground. Complimentary continental bkfst in lobby. Restaurant nearby. Ck-out 11 am. Business servs avail. Sundries. Golf privileges. Picnic tables. Cr cds: A, C, D, DS, MC, V.

✔ ★ ★ **HAMPTON INN.** *PA 255 N, I-80 exit 17. 814/375-1000; FAX 814/375-4668.* 96 rms, 3 story. S $49-$54; D $54-$59; each addl $5; kit. suite $95; under 18 free; wkly, wkend, hol rates; ski, golf plans; 2-day min Penn State football games. Crib free. TV; cable (premium), VCR avail (movies). Indoor pool; whirlpool. Complimentary continental bkfst. Complimentary coffee in rms. Restaurant adj open 24 hrs. Ck-out noon. Meeting rms. Business servs avail. Valet serv. Downhill/x-country ski 1 mi. Exercise equipt; bicycle, treadmill. Refrigerators avail. Cr cds: A, C, D, DS, MC, V.

★ ★ **HOLIDAY INN.** *US 219 & I-80 exit 16. 814/371-5100; FAX 814/375-0230.* 161 rms, 2 story. S $62-$79; D $68-$85; each addl $6; studio rms $75; under 18 free. Pet accepted. TV; cable (premium), VCR avail. Pool; wading, poolside serv, lifeguard. Complimentary coffee in rms. Restaurant 7 am-2 pm, 5-10 pm. Rm serv. Bar 5 pm-1 am. Ck-out noon. Coin lndry. Meeting rms. Business servs avail. In-rm modem link. Bellhops.

Free airport transportation. Health club privileges. Cr cds: A, C, D, DS, JCB, MC, V.

★ ★ **RAMADA INN.** *Jct I-80 exit 17 & PA 255N. 814/371-7070; FAX 814/371-1055.* 96 rms, 2-3 story. No elvtr. S $53-$65; D $59-$75; each addl $10; suites $80-$150; under 18 free. Crib free. Pet accepted. TV; cable (premium); VCR avail. Indoor pool; poolside serv. Restaurant 6:30 am-2 pm, 5-10 pm. Rm serv. Bar 5 pm-2 am; entertainment exc Sun. Ck-out noon. Meeting rms. Business servs avail. Airport transportation. Golf privileges, pro. Cr cds: A, C, D, DS, JCB, MC, V.

★ ★ **TOWNE HOUSE INN.** *(138 Center St, St Mary's 15857) 27 mi NE on PA 255N. 814/781-1556; FAX 814/834-4449.* 53 rms, 3 story. S $48-$90; D $53-$97; each addl $7. Crib $7. TV; cable (premium). Complimentary coffee in rms. Complimentary continental bkfst. Restaurant 6:30 am-2 pm, 5-8:30 pm; Sat from 5 pm; closed Sun. Rm serv. Ck-out 11 am. Meeting rms. Business servs avail. In-rm modem link. Exercise equipt; weight machine, treadmill. Picnic tables. Cr cds: A, D, DS, MC, V.

Easton (D-9)

(For accommodations see Allentown, Bethlehem)

Founded 1752 **Pop** 26,276 **Elev** 300 ft **Area code** 610 **Zip** 18042
Information Two Rivers Area Chamber of Commerce, 1 S 3rd St, PO Box 637, 18044-0637; 610/253-4211.

Named by Thomas Penn, one of the proprietors, for the English birthplace of his bride, Easton today is the gateway to the great industrial Lehigh Valley. Lafayette College, with its beautiful campus, and the historic Great Square are of interest. Easton, the seat of Northampton County, is part of a larger metropolitan area, the Lehigh Valley, which also includes Allentown and Bethlehem.

What to See and Do

Canal Museum. Exhibits include photographs, models, documents and artifacts from the era of mule-drawn canal boats in the 1800s; electronic map and audiovisual programs. (Daily exc Mon; closed Jan 1, Thanksgiving, Dec 25; open Mon hols) PA 611, 1 mi S of US 22, Two Rivers Landing. Phone 610/250-6700. ¢¢¢ Admission includes

The Crayola® Factory. See how crayons & markers are created. Visit Crayola Hall of Fame; enjoy dozens of interactive exhibits featuring the wonders of light and color. Same location and schedule as Canal Museum. Phone 610/515-8000.

"The Great Square." Center of business district. Now called Center Square. Dominated by Soldiers' and Sailors' Monument. Bronze marker shows replica of Old Courthouse, which stood until 1862 on land rented from the Penns for one red rose a year. From Old Courthouse steps, the Declaration of Independence was read on July 8, 1776, when the Easton Flag, the first Stars and Stripes of the united colonies, was unfurled here.

Hugh Moore Park. Restored Lehigh Canal, locks and locktender's house; mule-drawn canal boat rides (early May-Labor Day, daily; early-late Sept, wkends) Also hiking, picnicking; boat rentals in park. Park (daily). S 25th St, 2 mi S of US 22. Phone 610/250-6700. Boat rides ¢¢

Lafayette College (1826). (2,000 students) Bronze statue of Lafayette by Daniel Chester French in front of college chapel; American historical portrait collection in Kirby Hall of Civil Rights. Tour of campus. N side of town. Phone 610/250-5000.

Northampton County Historical Society. Changing exhibits; library; museum. (By appt) 101-107 S 4th St, diagonally opp Parsons-Taylor House. Phone 610/253-1222. Museum ¢; Library ¢¢

Restaurant

★ ★ **MANDARIN TANG.** *25th St Shopping Center. 610/258-5697.* Hrs: 11:30 am-10 pm; Fri, Sat to 11 pm. Closed Thanksgiving. Res accepted Fri-Sun. Chinese menu. Semi-a la carte: lunch $3.95-$5.50, dinner $5-$16.95. Specialties: mandarin orange beef, General Tso's chicken. Chinese decor. Authentic Chinese dishes. Cr cds: A, D, MC, V.

Ebensburg (E-4)

(For accommodations see Altoona, Johnstown)

Pop 3,872 **Elev** 2,140 ft **Area code** 814 **Zip** 15931 **E-mail** chamber @ctcnet.net

Information Greater Johnstown/Cambria County Convention & Visitors Bureau, 111 Market St, Johnstown 15901-1608; 814/536-7993 or 800/237-8590.

What to See and Do

Allegheny Portage Railroad National Historic Site. Remains of railroad built 1831-1834 to link east and west divisions of the Pennsylvania Mainline Canal. Cars were pulled up 10 inclined planes by ropes powered by steam engines. Horses or locomotives pulled the cars over the level stretches of the 36-mi route across the Alleghenies from Hollidaysburg to Johnstown. The Skew Arch Bridge, an engine house exhibit, and the Lemon House, a historic tavern, help tell the story of the Allegheny Portage Railroad. A visitor center (daily; closed Dec 25) has exhibits and a 20-min film. There are ranger-led programs (summer, daily) and costumed demonstrations (summer); picnic area (daily); hiking & cross-country trails. 12 mi E on US 22. Phone 814/886-6150. **Free.**

Edinboro (B-2)

(See also Erie, Meadville)

Pop 7,736 **Elev** 1,210 ft **Area code** 814 **Zip** 16412

This is a resort town on Edinboro Lake and the home of Edinboro State College.

What to See and Do

Mountain View Ski Area. 2 T-bars, Pomalift; patrol, school, rentals; snowmaking; cafeteria. Longest run 2,800 ft; vertical drop 350 ft. (Dec-Mar, daily) Half-day and evening rates. 4 mi E on US 6N, then 3 mi S on PA 86, in Cambridge Springs. Phone 814/734-1641. **¢¢¢¢**

Motel

★ ★ ★ **RAMADA INN AND CONFERENCE CENTER.** *US 6, off I-79 exit 38, 6N.* 814/734-5650; FAX 814/734-7532. 105 rms, 2 story. S $65-$75; D $75-$85; each addl $10; wkend, ski, golf plans. Crib free. TV. Indoor pool; sauna. Restaurant 7 am-2 pm, 5-9 pm. Rm serv. Bars 11:30-2 am; entertainment. Ck-out noon. Coin lndry. Meeting rms. Business servs avail. 18-hole golf adj, greens fee $18-$24, putting green. Downhill ski 7 mi. Cr cds: A, C, D, DS, MC, V.

Inn

★ ★ **RIVERSIDE.** *(1 Fountain Ave, Cambridge Springs 16403) At US 6/19 & PA 99S.* 814/398-4645; FAX 814/398-4647; res: 800/964-5173. 74 rms, 3 story. S $40-$65; D $55-$85; each addl $10; suites $100; under 5 free. Closed Jan-mid April. TV in suites & sitting rm. Pool. Compli-

mentary full bkfst. Dining rm 11 am-2 pm, 5:30-8:30 pm; Fri, Sat to 10 pm; Sun 11 am-2 pm, 5:30-8:30 pm. Dinner theater on wkends, matinees wkdays. Bar. Ck-out 11 am, ck-in 3 pm. Business servs avail. Tennis privileges. Golf privileges. Lawn games. Victorian inn (1885) overlooking French Creek. Cr cds: DS, MC, V.

Ephrata (E-8)

(See also Bird-in-Hand, Denver/Adamstown, Lancaster, Lebanon, Reading)

Settled 1732 **Pop** 12,133 **Elev** 380 ft **Area code** 717 **Zip** 17522
Information Chamber of Commerce, 77 Park Ave, Ste 1; 717/738-9010.

What to See and Do

Ephrata Cloister. Buildings stand as a monument to an unusual religious experiment. In 1732 Conrad Beissel, a German Seventh-Day Baptist, began to lead a hermit's life here; within a few years he established a religious community of recluses, with a Brotherhood, a Sisterhood and a group of married "householders." The members of the solitary order dressed in concealing white habits; the buildings (1735-1749) were without adornment, the halls were narrow, the doorways were low and board benches served as beds and wooden blocks as pillows. Their religious zeal and charity, however, proved to be their undoing. After the Battle of Brandywine, the cloistered community nursed the Revolutionary sick and wounded, but contracted typhus, which decimated their numbers. Celibacy also contributed to the decline of the community, but the Society was not formally dissolved until 1934. Surviving and restored buildings include the Sisters' House, Chapel, Almonry and eight others. Craft demonstrations (summer). (Daily; closed some hols) 632 W Main St. Phone 717/733-6600. **¢¢**

Museum and Library of the Historical Society of Cocalico Valley. Italianate Victorian mansion contains period displays; historical exhibits; genealogical and historical research library (fee) on Cocalico Valley area and residents. (Mon, Wed, Thurs, Sat) 249 W Main St. Phone 717/733-1616. **Free.**

Annual Event

Street Fair. One of largest in state. Last full wk Sept.

Inns

★ ★ ★ **1777 HOUSE.** *301 W Main St.* 717/738-9502; FAX 717/738-9552. 12 rms, 3 story, 2 carriage house suites. S $61-$81; D $69-$89; each addl $10; suites $149-$185; package plans. Crib $8. TV in sitting rm; cable. Complimentary continental bkfst. Restaurant nearby. Ck-out 11 am, ck-in 3 pm. Health club privileges. Microwaves avail. Restored clockmaker's house (1777). Antiques. Hand-cut stenciling. Cr cds: A, C, D, DS, MC, V.

✔★ ★ ★ **DONECKERS GUEST HOUSE.** *318-324 N State St.* 717/738-9502; FAX 717/738-9554. 19 rms, 2 story. S $51-$81; D $59-$89; each addl $10; suites $149-$159. Crib $8. Complimentary continental bkfst. Restaurant (see DONECKERS). Ck-out 11 am, ck-in 3 pm. Health club privileges. Some balconies. Mansion furnished with antiques. Cr cds: A, C, D, DS, MC, V.

★ ★ **SMITHTON COUNTRY.** *900 W Main St, at S Academy Dr.* 717/733-6094. 8 rms, 2 story. S $75-$110; D $85-$150; each addl $20-$35; suites $140-$170. Complimentary full bkfst. Restaurant nearby. Ck-out noon, ck-in 3:30 pm. Concierge. Classic stone inn (1763); fireplaces, antiques. Totally nonsmoking. Cr cds: A, MC, V.

Restaurant

★ ★ ★ **DONECKERS.** *(See Doneckers Guest House Inn) 717/738-9501.* Hrs: 11 am-10 pm. Closed Wed; major hols. Res accepted. Bar. Wine list. French, Amer menu. A la carte entrees: lunch $6.95-$13.75, dinner $7.50-$29. Child's meals. Specialties: Dover sole with strawberry sauce, steak au poivre. Own baking. Elegant French decor. Cr cds: A, C, D, DS, MC, V.

Erie (A-2)

(See also North East)

Settled 1753 **Pop** 108,718 **Elev** 744 ft **Area code** 814 **E-mail** Erie-Chamber@erie.net **Web** www.erie.net/~chamber

Information Erie Area Chamber of Commerce, 1006 State St, 16501; 814/454-7191.

Third-largest city in the state and only Great Lakes port in Pennsylvania, Erie has a fine natural harbor on Lake Erie, which is protected and bounded by Presque Isle peninsula, the site of many historic events. Greater Erie is also one of the nation's mighty industrial centers, with more than 750 highly diversified manufacturing firms and several large industrial parks. The lake and city take their name from the Eriez tribe, who were killed by the Seneca about 1654.

On the south shore of Presque Isle Bay, Commodore Oliver Hazard Perry built his fleet, floated the ships across the sandbars and fought the British in the Battle of Lake Erie (1813). Fort Presque Isle, built by the French in 1753 and destroyed by them in 1759, was rebuilt by the English, burned by Native Americans and rebuilt again in 1794 by Americans.

What to See and Do

Erie Art Museum. Temporary art exhibits in a variety of media; regional artwork and lectures in the restored Greek-revival Old Customs House (1839). Art classes, concerts, lectures and workshops are also offered. (Tues-Sat, also Sun afternoons; closed major hols) Free admission Wed. 411 State St. Phone 814/459-5477. ¢

Erie Historical Museum & Planetarium. Housed in 1890s Victorian mansion. Museum features regional history and decorative arts exhibits; multimedia presentations on regional maritime history; restored period rooms; changing exhibits (Tues-Sun afternoons; closed most hols). Also planetarium with shows (Sun afternoons). 356 W 6th St. Phone 814/871-5790. Museum ¢; Planetarium ¢

Erie Zoo. Zoo houses more than 300 animals, including gorillas, polar bears and giraffes; children's zoo (May-Sept); 1-mi tour of grounds on Safariland Express Train (fee). Indoor ice rink (Sept-Mar, phone 814/868-3651). Zoo (daily). 3 mi N of I-90 State St exit 7. Phone 814/864-4091. Zoo ¢¢

Firefighters Historical Museum. More than 1,300 items of firefighting memorabilia are displayed in the old #4 Firehouse. Exhibits include fire apparatus dating from 1823, alarm systems, uniforms, badges, ribbons, helmets, nozzles, fire marks and fire extinguishers; fire safety films are shown in the Hay Loft Theater. (May-Oct, Sat & Sun) 428 Chestnut St. Phone 814/456-5969. ¢

Gridley's Grave. Final resting place of Captain Charles Vernon Gridley, to whom, at the Battle of Manila Bay in 1898, Admiral Dewey said, "You may fire when ready, Gridley." Gridley died in Japan; his body was returned here for burial. Four old Spanish cannons from Manila Harbor, built in 1777, guard the grave. Offers view of peninsula, Lake Erie and entrance to

Erie Harbor from cliff by Gridley Circle. Lakeside Cemetery, 1718 E Lake Rd. Phone 814/459-8200.

Land Lighthouse (1866). The first lighthouse on the Great Lakes was constructed on this site in 1813. Foot of Dunn Blvd. Phone 814/452-3937.

Misery Bay. State monument to Perry; named after Perry defeated British and the fleet suffered cold and privations of a bitter winter. NE corner of Presque Isle Bay.

Presque Isle State Park. Peninsula stretches 7 mi into Lake Erie and curves back toward city. Approx 3,200 acres of recreation and conservation areas. Swimming; fishing; boating (rentals, mooring, launching, marina). Hiking, birding, trails. Cross-country skiing, ice-skating, ice fishing, ice boating. Picnicking, concessions. Visitor Center, environmental education and interpretive programs. N off PA 832. Phone 814/833-7424.

Waldameer Park & Water World. Rides, midway, kiddieland, water park, picnic area, food, dance pavilion. (Memorial Day-Labor Day, daily exc Mon; open Mon hols) 220 Peninsula Drive, at entrance to Presque Isle State Park. Phone 814/838-3591. ¢¢¢¢

Wayne Memorial Blockhouse. Replica of blockhouse in which General Anthony Wayne died Dec 15, 1796, after becoming ill on a voyage from Detroit. He was buried at the foot of the flagpole; later, his son had the body disinterred and the remains moved to Radnor. (Memorial Day-Labor Day, daily) On grounds of State Soldiers' and Sailors' Home, 560 E 3rd St. Phone 814/871-4531. **Free.**

Motels

★ ★ **COMFORT INN.** *8051 Peach St (16509), I-90E exit 6. 814/866-6666; FAX 814/866-6666, ext. 309.* 110 rms, 2 story, 50 suites. Mid-May-Sept: S $80-$99; D $90-$120; each addl $6; suites $95-$125; under 18 free; higher rates hol wkends; lower rates rest of yr. Crib free. TV; cable (premium), VCR (movies). Heated pool; whirlpool, lifeguard. Complimentary continental bkfst. Restaurant adj 6 am-midnight. Ck-out noon. Meeting rm. Business servs avail. In-rm modem link. Free airport transportation. Exercise equipt; bicycles, rowers. Refrigerator, wet bar in suites. Some balconies. Cr cds: A, C, D, DS, JCB, MC, V.

★ ★ **ECONO LODGE.** *8050 Peach St (16509), I-90E exit 6. 814/866-5544; FAX 814/866-5544, ext. 142.* 97 rms, 3 story. Late May-Oct: S $69.95-$79.95; D $89.95-$109.95; each addl $6; higher rates special events; lower rates rest of yr. Crib free. TV; cable, VCR (movies). Indoor pool; whirlpool, lifeguard. Complimentary continental bkfst. Restaurant adj 7-2 am. Ck-out noon. Meeting rms. Business servs avail. In-rm modem link. Sundries. Free airport transportation. Exercise equipt; weight machine, bicycles, sauna. Some refrigerators, wet bars. Cr cds: A, C, D, DS, JCB, MC, V.

✔ ★ **GLASS HOUSE INN.** *3202 W 26th St (16506). 814/833-7751; FAX 814/833-4222; res: 800/956-7222.* 30 rms. June-Labor Day: S, D $53-$89; each addl $7; family rates; lower rates rest of yr. Crib $4. TV; cable (premium), VCR avail (movies). Heated pool. Complimentary continental bkfst. Restaurant nearby. Ck-out 11 am. In-rm modem link. Sundries. Gift shop. Downhill/x-country ski 20 mi. Cr cds: A, C, D, DS, MC, V.

✔ ★ **HAMPTON INN.** *3041 W 12th St (16505). 814/835-4200; FAX 814/835-4200.* 100 rms, 3 story. S $65-$89; D $72-$89; under 18 free. Crib (fee). TV; cable (premium). Heated pool. Complimentary continental bkfst. Restaurant nearby 7 am-10:30 pm. Ck-out noon. Business servs avail. Valet serv. Cr cds: A, C, D, DS, MC, V.

★ **HOWARD JOHNSON.** *7575 Peach St (16509), jct I-90 & US 19, exit 6. 814/864-4811.* 110 rms, 1-2 story. Late May-Sept: S $59-$65; D $69-$74; each addl $10; under 18 free; package plan; some lower rates rest of yr. Crib free. TV; cable. Indoor pool; wading pool, sauna, lifeguard. Complimentary continental bkfst. Restaurant nearby. Ck-out noon. Business servs avail. Coin lndry. Valet serv. Private patios, balconies. Cr cds: A, C, D, DS, ER, JCB, MC, V.

★ ★ ★ **RAMADA INN.** *6101 Wattsburg Rd (16509). 814/825-3100; FAX 814/825-0857.* 122 rms, 2 story. July-Sept: S, D $75-$85; each addl $8; suites $65-$95; under 16 free; ski, wkend plans; lower rates rest of yr. Crib free. Pet accepted. TV; cable (premium), VCR (movies avail). Heated pool; wading pool, lifeguard. Restaurant 6:30 am-10 pm. Rm serv. Bar 5 pm-2 am. Ck-out noon. Meeting rms. Business center. In-rm modem link. Sundries. Downhill ski 15 mi. Game rm. Cr cds: A, C, D, DS, JCB, MC, V.

✔★ **SCOTT'S.** *2930 W 6th St (PA 832) (16505). 814/838-1961; FAX 814/838-1961, ext. 161.* 58 rms, 1-2 story, 14 kits. (no equipt). June-Labor Day: S, D $65-$85; each addl $5; kit. units $75-$90; lower rates rest of yr. Crib $5. TV; cable. Playground. Heated pool; wading pool, lifeguard. Ck-out 11 am. Business servs avail. Downhill/x-country ski 20 mi. Lawn games. Cr cds: A, C, D, DS, MC, V.

Motor Hotels

★ ★ ★ **BEL AIRE.** *2800 W 8th St (16505). 814/833-1116; FAX 814/838-3242; res: 800/888-8781.* 151 rms, 3 story. Mid-June-mid-Sept: S, D $95-$100; each addl $10; suites $125-$200; under 19 free; lower rates rest of yr. Crib $10. TV; cable. Indoor pool; whirlpool, lifeguard. Complimentary coffee in rms. Restaurant 6 am-11 pm. Bar 11-2 am, Sun to midnight. Ck-out noon. Meeting rms. In-rm modem link. Valet serv. Sundries. Exercise equipt; weights, bicycles, sauna. Private patios, balconies. Cr cds: A, C, D, DS, MC, V.

★ ★ **HOLIDAY INN SOUTH.** *8040 Perry Hwy (PA 97) (16509), Exit 7 off I-90. 814/864-4911; FAX 814/864-3743.* 216 rms, 2-4 story. S, D $69-$89; each addl $6; under 18 free. Crib free. TV; cable. Heated pool; poolside serv, lifeguard. Restaurant 6:30 am-10 pm. Rm serv. Bar 11-1 am; entertainment. Ck-out noon. Meeting rms. In-rm modem link. Bellhops. Valet serv. Free airport, RR station transportation. Health club privileges. Cr cds: A, C, D, DS, JCB, MC, V.

★ ★ **HOLIDAY INN-DOWNTOWN.** *18 W 18th St (16501). 814/456-2961; FAX 814/456-7067.* 134 rms, 4 story. Memorial Day-Labor Day S, D $69-$94; each addl $6; under 19 free; lower rates rest of yr. Crib free. TV; cable (premium). Heated pool; poolside serv, lifeguard. Coffee in rms. Complimentary continental bkfst. Restaurant 6:30 am-10 pm. Rm serv. Bar 11:30-2 am; entertainment. Ck-out noon. Lndry facilities. Meeting rms. Business center. In-rm modem link. Bellhops. Valet serv. Free airport transportation. Health club privileges. Cr cds: A, D, DS, JCB, MC, V.

Restaurant

★ ★ **PUFFERBELLY.** *414 French St. 814/454-1557.* Hrs: 11 am-10 pm; Fri, Sat to midnight; Sun to 8 pm; Sun brunch to 3 pm. Closed major hols. Res accepted. Bar. Semi-a la carte: lunch $3.95-$6, dinner $8.95-$15.95. Sun brunch $9.95. Specializes in regional cuisine, steak, seafood. Outdoor dining. Restored firehouse (1907). Cr cds: A, DS, MC, V.

Fort Washington (E-9)

Pop 3,699 **Elev** 250 ft **Area code** 215 **Zip** 19034 **E-mail** vlyforge @libertynet.org **Web** www.valleyforge.org

Information Valley Forge Convention & Visitors Bureau, 600 W Germantown Pike, Suite 130, Plymouth Meeting 19462; 610/834-1550.

What to See and Do

Fort Washington State Park. Commemorates the site of Washington's northern defense line against the British in 1777. Fishing. Hiking, ball fields. Picnicking. 500 Bethlehem Pike. Phone 215/646-2942.

Hope Lodge (ca 1745). Colonial Georgian mansion; headquarters for Surgeon General John Cochran after Battle of Germantown. Historic furnishings, paintings, ceramics. (Daily exc Mon; closed most hols) 1 mi S, 553 Bethlehem Pike. Phone 215/646-1595. ¢¢

The Highlands (1796). Late-Georgian mansion on 43 acres built by Anthony Morris, active in both state and federal government. Formal gardens and crenelated walls built ca 1845. Tours (by appt). (Mon-Fri) 7001 Sheaff Lane. Phone 215/641-2687. ¢

Restaurant

✔★ ★ **PALACE OF ASIA.** *285 Commerce Dr. 215/646-2133.* Hrs: 11:30 am-11 pm; Sat, Sun to midnight; Sat, Sun brunch to 3:30 pm. Closed Dec 25. Res required Fri-Sun dinner. Indian menu. Bar. Semi-a la carte: lunch $6.25-$7.95, dinner $6.95-$14.95. Sat, Sun brunch $3.50-$8.25. Specializes in vegetarian dishes, breads, curry dishes. Own baking. Authentic Indian atmosphere. Cr cds: A, D, DS, MC, V.

Franklin (Venango Co) (C-2)

(See also Meadville, Oil City, Titusville)

Settled 1787 **Pop** 7,329 **Elev** 1,020 ft **Area code** 814 **Zip** 16323 **E-mail** chamber@franklin-pa.org **Web** www.franklin-pa.org

Information Franklin Area Chamber of Commerce, 1259 Liberty St; 814/432-5823.

A series of French and British forts was erected in this area. The last one, Fort Franklin, was razed by local settlers who used the stone and timber in their own buildings. Old Garrison took its place in 1796 and later served as the Venango County Jail. In 1859, James Evans, a blacksmith, made tools to drill an oil well that brought an oil boom to the area. For years, oil was dominant in the area's industries.

What to See and Do

DeBence Antique Music World. Features nickelodeons, band organs, calliopes, German organs, a variety of music boxes, many other items. Unique "see and hear" museum. Guided tours. (Jan-mid-Mar, Thurs-Sat; mid-Mar-Dec, daily exc Mon; closed hols) 1261 Liberty St. Phone 814/432-5668. ¢¢¢

Hoge-Osmer House (ca 1865). Museum owned by Venango County Historical Society; houses displays of materials and artifacts relating to Venango County history; period furnishings, research library. House open (May-Dec, Tues-Thurs & Sat; rest of yr, Sat; closed major hols). Inquire for genealogy library hrs. Corner of South Park & Elk Sts. Phone 814/437-2275. **Free.**

Pioneer Cemetery (1795-1879). Self-guided walking tour booklets can be purchased at the Chamber of Commerce. Otter & 15th Sts.

Venango County Court House (1868). Unique styling; contains display of Native American artifacts. (Mon-Fri; closed hols) 12th & Liberty Sts. Phone 814/432-9500.

Annual Events

Rocky Grove Fair. July.

Applefest. Apple pie baking contest; arts & crafts; enertainment; classic car show. Kids Korner. 5-km race; horse-drawn buggy rides. Phone 814/432-5823. 1st full wkend Oct.

Seasonal Event

Franklin Silver Cornet Band Concerts. City Park. Thurs, mid-June-Aug.

Motor Hotel

★ ★ **INN AT FRANKLIN.** *1411 Liberty St. 814/437-3031; FAX 814/432-7481; res: 800/535-4052.* 85 rms, 6 story. Apr-Sept: S $65; D $70; each addl $5; under 18 free; wkly, monthly rates; lower rates rest of yr. Pet accepted. TV; cable, VCR avail (movies). Complimentary continental bkfst. Restaurant 6 am-2 pm, 5-10 pm; Sun 7 am-8 pm. Bar. Ck-out 11 am. Business servs avail. Valet serv. Barber, beauty shop. Free airport, bus depot transportation. Cr cds: A, C, D, DS, MC, V.

D ⚡ ✈ ⤫ ⤰ 🖐 SC

Inns

✔★ ★ **LAMBERTON HOUSE.** *1331 Otter St (16323-1530). 814/432-7908; res: 800/481-0776.* 6 rms, 2 story, 2 share baths, 3 with shower only. No rm phones. S $45-$75, D $50-$75; each addl $10; under 8 free; wkly rates. Crib free. TV in drawing room; VCR. Complimentary full bkfst. Restaurant nearby 7 am-11 pm. Ck-out 11 am, ck-in 3 pm. Historic building (1874). Cr cds: MC, V.

🖐 ⤰ 🖐

★ ★ **QUO VADIS.** *1501 Liberty St, near Chess-Lamberton Airport, Rte 8, 15 mi N pf I-80, Exit 3. 814/432-4208; res: 800/360-6598.* 6 rms, 3 story. S, D $60-$80; each addl $10; wkly rates. TV in sitting rm. Complimentary full bkfst. Restaurant nearby. Ck-out 11 am, ck-in 4-9 pm. Victorian mansion (1867); detailed woodwork, heirloom antiques. Totally nonsmoking. Cr cds: A, MC, V.

⤰ 🖐

Galeton (B-6)

(For accommodations see Wellsboro)

Pop 1,370 **Elev** 1,325 ft **Area code** 814 **Zip** 16922

Information Potter County Recreation, PO Box 245, Coudersport 16915; 814/435-2290 or 888-POTTER2.

What to See and Do

Ole Bull State Park. At upper reaches of the Kettle Creek. Site of unsuccessful effort by the famous Norwegian violinist, Ole Bornemann Bull, to establish a colony called "New Norway." Approx 125 acres. Swimming beach; fishing, hunting. Hiking. Cross-country skiing, snowmobiling. Tent and trailer sites (electric hookups). Interpretive program. Standard fees. 18 mi SW on PA 144. Phone 814/435-5000.

Pennsylvania Lumber Museum. Exhibits on lumbering and its techniques, forest industries and products; reconstructed lumber camp and sawmill; restored locomotive and log-loader; nature trails, picnicking. Slide show in visitor center. (Apr-Nov, daily; closed hols) (See ANNUAL EVENTS) 10 mi W on US 6. Phone 814/435-2652. ¢¢

Ski Denton/Denton Hill. Triple, double chairlifts, 2 Pomalifts; patrol, school, rentals; snowmaking; cafeteria, restaurant; lodge, cabins. Longest run 1 mi; vertical drop 650 ft. (Dec-Mar, daily) 100 mi of cross-country trails; night skiing; camping. (See ANNUAL EVENTS) 10 mi W on US 6. Phone 814/435-2115. ¢¢¢¢

Annual Events

Bark Peeler's Convention. On grounds of Pennsylvania Lumber Museum. Re-creation of old-time festival held by lumber camp workers celebrating the end of the work year. Features many demonstrations, including cross-cut sawing, hewing, bark peeling; entertainment; period music; exhibits. Phone 814/435-2652. July 4-5.

Woodsmen's Carnival. Cherry Springs State Park, 12 mi SW on West Branch Rd. Horse-pulling and woodcutting competitions; food; displays. Phone 814/435-5010. First full wkend Aug.

Bowhunter's Festival. Denton Hill. Wkend late Aug.

Germania Old Home Day. 7 mi SE via PA 144 in Germania. Food, dancing, events, games, entertainment. Phone 814/435-8881. Early Sept.

Gettysburg (F-6)

(See also Hanover, York)

Founded 1798 **Pop** 7,025 **Elev** 560 ft **Area code** 717 **Zip** 17325 **Web** www.gettysburg.com

Information Gettysburg Convention & Visitors Bureau, 35 Carlisle St; 717/334-6274.

Because of the historical nature of this area and the many attractions in this town, visitors may want to stop in at the Gettysburg Convention & Visitors Bureau for complete information about bus tours, guide service (including a tape-recorded and self-guided tour) and help in planning their visit here.

What to See and Do

A. Lincoln's Place. Live portrayal of the 16th president; 45 min. (Mid-June-Labor Day, Mon-Fri) 213 Steinwehr Ave. For reservations phone 717/334-6049 or 717/334-8003. ¢¢¢

"The Conflict." A triple-screen program depicts the Civil War and battle at Gettysburg in 7 different 50-min programs. Multiple projectors blend camera, artwork of the period and modern panoramic photography with narration. Military bookshop. Abraham Lincoln performances (mid-June-Labor Day, Mon-Fri evenings). (Daily; closed Thanksgiving, Dec 25) 213 Steinwehr Ave. Phone 717/334-8003. The Conflict ¢¢; Lincoln performance ¢¢¢

Eisenhower National Historic Site (see GETTYSBURG NATIONAL MILITARY PARK).

General Lee's Headquarters. Robert E. Lee planned Confederate strategy for the Gettysburg battle in this house; contains collection of historical items from the battle. (Mid-Mar-mid-Nov, daily) 401 Buford Ave. Phone 717/334-3141. ¢

Gettysburg Battle Theatre. Miniature battlefield with 25,000 figures; 30-min multimedia program showing battle strategy. (Mar-Nov, daily) 571 Steinwehr Ave. Phone 717/334-6100. ¢¢¢

Gettysburg College (1832). (2,000 students) Liberal arts; oldest Lutheran-affiliated college in US. Pennsylvania Hall was used as Civil War hospital; Eisenhower House and statue on grounds. Tour of campus. 3 blks NW of Lincoln Sq off US 15 Business. Phone 717/337-6000.

Gettysburg National Military Park (see).

Gettysburg Railway. A 16-mi round trip to Biglerville on steam train. Also charter trips and special runs. (July-Aug, daily; May-June & Sept-Oct, Thurs-Sun; Apr, Sat & Sun) Washington St. Phone 717/334-6932. ¢¢¢

Ghosts of Gettysburg Candlelight Walking Tours. Armed with tales from Mark Nesbitt's *Ghosts of Gettysburg* books, knowledgeable guides lead 1¼-hr tours through sections of town that were bloody battlefields 130 yrs ago. (June-Oct, daily evenings; Apr, May, Nov, wkend evenings) Tours depart from gallery at 30 York St or from gallery at corner of Steinwehr Ave & Baltimore St. For reservations phone 717/337-0445. ¢¢¢

Hall of Presidents and First Ladies. Costumed life-size wax figures of all the presidents; reproductions of their wives' inaugural gowns; "The Eisenhowers at Gettysburg" exhibit. (Mid-Mar-Nov, daily) 789 Baltimore St, adj National Cemetery. Phone 717/334-5717. ¢¢¢

Land of Little Horses. A variety of performing horses—all in miniature. Continuous entertainment; indoor arena; exotic animal races. Saddle and wagon rides. Picnic area, snack bar, gift shop. (May-late Aug, daily; Apr, Sept, Oct, wkends) 5 mi W off US 30, on Knoxlyn Rd to Glenwood Dr; follow signs. Phone 717/334-7259. ¢¢¢

Lincoln Room Museum. Preserved bedroom in Wills House; collection of Lincoln items; huge plaque inscribed with Gettysburg Address, audiovisual display. (Mar-Nov, daily; rest of yr, Mon-Fri) 12 Lincoln Sq. Phone 717/334-8188. ¢¢

Lutheran Theological Seminary (1826). (250 students) Oldest Lutheran seminary in US; cupola on campus used as Confederate lookout during battle. Old Dorm, now home of Adams County Historical Society, served as hospital for both Union and Confederate soldiers. Confederate Ave, 1 mi W of Lincoln Sq on US 30. Phone 717/334-6286.

National Civil War Wax Museum. Highlights Civil War era and Battle of Gettysburg. (Mar-Nov, daily; rest of yr, Sat & Sun; closed Jan 1, Thanksgiving, Dec 25) 297 Steinwehr Ave. Phone 717/334-6245. ¢¢

National Tower. Four observation decks (two enclosed) on 300-ft-high tower permit 360° view of battlefield; 12-min sight-and-sound program, displays; landscaped grounds, picnicking. (Apr-Oct, daily; Nov, wkends only; Mar, inquire for date) 1 mi S via US 97. Phone 717/334-6754. ¢¢

Ski Liberty. 2 quad, 3 double chairlifts, J-bar, handle tow; patrol, school, rentals; snowmaking; cafeteria, restaurant, bar; nursery, lodge. Longest run approx 1 mi; vertical drop 600 ft. (Dec-Mar, daily) 9 mi W on PA 116, in Carroll Valley. Phone 717/642-8282. ¢¢¢¢¢

Soldiers' National Museum. Dioramas of major battles, with sound; Civil War collection. (Mar-Nov, daily; schedule may vary, phone ahead) 777 Baltimore St, at Gettysburg Tour Center. Phone 717/334-4890. ¢¢¢

The Lincoln Train Museum. Museum features more than 1,000 model trains and railroad memorabilia; Lincoln Train Ride—simulated trip of 20 mi. (Mar-Nov, daily) ½ mi S via US 15 on Steinwehr Ave. Phone 717/334-5678. ¢¢¢

Annual Events

Apple Blossom Festival. South Mountain Fairgrounds, 8 mi NW. 1st wkend May.

Civil War Heritage Days. Lectures by historians; Civil War collectors' show; entertainment; Civil War book show; firefighters' festival; fireworks. Late June-early July.

Apple Harvest Festival. South Mountain Fairgrounds. Demonstrations; arts and crafts; guided tours of orchard, mountain areas. 1st & 2nd wkends Oct.

Motels

★ ★ **COLLEGE.** 345 Carlisle St, opp Gettysburg College. 717/334-6731; res: 800/367-6731. Web www.gettysburg.com. 21 rms. Mid-June-Labor Day: S, D $68; each addl $5; higher rates: wkends, graduation, parents' wkend; lower rates rest of yr. TV; cable. Pool; lifeguard. Restaurant nearby. Ck-out 11 am. Cr cds: A, MC, V.

⊠ 🐾 SC

★ **COLONIAL.** 157 Carlisle St. 717/334-3126; res: 800/336-3126. Web www.gettysburg.com. 30 rms, 2 story. Early June-early Sept: S, D $64-$68; each addl $5; under 17 free; higher rates special events;

lower rates rest of yr. Crib free. TV; cable (premium). Complimentary coffee in lobby. Restaurant nearby. Ck-out 11 am. Cr cds: A, MC, V.

🐾 SC

★ ★ **COMFORT INN.** 871 York Rd. 717/337-2400; FAX 717/337-2400, ext. -399. Web www.gettysburg.com. 81 rms, 2 story. June-Aug: S $77-$82; D $87-$90; each addl $6; under 18 free; higher rates: antique car show, college events; lower rates rest of yr. Crib free. TV; cable (premium). Complimentary continental bkfst in lobby. Cafe adj. Ck-out 11 am. Business servs avail. In-rm modem link. Refrigerator in suites; some in-rm whirlpools. Cr cds: A, C, D, DS, ER, JCB, MC, V.

D ⊠ 🏊 🐾 SC

★ ★ **CROSS KEYS.** (6110 York Rd, New Oxford 17350) At jct US 30 & PA 94. 717/624-7778; FAX 717/624-7941. 64 rms, 4 story. Apr-Sept: S $37-$63; D $48-$73; each addl $5; under 12 free; wkly rates; higher rates special events; lower rates rest of yr. Crib free. TV; cable. VCR avail (movies). Restaurants 6 am-10 pm; Sat to 11 pm. Rm serv. Bar 4 pm-2 am. Ck-out 11 am. Meeting rms. Business servs avail. Gift shop. Golf privileges. Downhill ski 15 mi. Some in-rm whirlpools. Cr cds: A, DS, MC, V.

🏊 🚶 ⊠ 🐾 SC

★ ★ **HOLIDAY INN EXPRESS.** 869 York Rd (US 30). 717/337-1400; FAX 717/337-1400, ext. 301. Web gettysburg.com. 51 rms, 2 story. Apr-Oct: S $79-$99; D $89-$109; each addl $10; suites $109-$129; under 19 free; higher rates special events; lower rates rest of yr. Crib free. TV; cable (premium). Indoor pool; lifeguard, whirlpool. Complimentary continental bkfst. Restaurant adj open 24 hrs. Ck-11 am. In-rm modem link. Downhill ski 8 mi. Picnic tables. Cr cds: A, C, D, DS, MC, V.

D 🏊 🏊 ⊠ 🐾 SC

★ **HOMESTEAD MOTOR LODGE.** 1650 York Rd (US 30). 717/334-3866. 10 rms. June-Oct: S, D $45-$65; each addl $8; lower rates Apr-May, Nov. Closed rest of yr. TV. Restaurant nearby. Ck-out 10 am. Downhill ski 8 mi. Totally nonsmoking. Cr cds: A, DS, MC, V.

🏊 ⊠ 🐾

✔ ★ ★ **HOWARD JOHNSON LODGE.** 301 Steinwehr Ave. 717/334-1188. Web www.gettysburg.com. 77 rms, 2 story. Apr-Oct: S, D $59-$99; under 18 free; lower rates rest of yr. Crib free. Pet accepted, some restrictions. TV; cable (premium), VCR avail. Pool; lifeguard. Complimentary coffee in lobby. Restaurant adj 6:30 am-11 pm. Bar 4 pm-1 am, closed Sun. Ck-out noon. Sundries. Free bus depot transportation. Downhill ski 9 mi; x-country ski adj. Private patios. Sun deck. Cr cds: A, C, D, DS, MC, V.

D 🐾 🏊 🏊 ⊠ 🐾 SC

★ ★ **QUALITY INN.** 380 Steinwehr Ave. 717/334-1103. E-mail gburgqi@mail.cvn.net; web www.gettysburg.com. 109 rms, 2 story. Apr-Oct: S, D $69-$104; suite $97-$135; under 16 free; lower rates rest of yr. Crib free. Pet accepted, some restrictions. TV; cable (premium), VCR avail. 2 pools; 1 indoor, lifeguard. Coffee in rm. Restaurant opp 6 am-11 pm. Bar 6 pm-1 am. Ck-out noon. Coin lndry. Meeting rm. Gift shop. Free bus depot transportation. Putting green. Downhill/x-country ski 8 mi. Exercise equipt; weight machines, bicycle, sauna. Balconies. Cr cds: A, C, D, DS, MC, V.

D 🐾 🏊 🏊 ⊠ 🍴 ⊠ 🐾 SC

★ ★ **QUALITY INN LARSON'S.** 401 Buford Ave. 717/334-3141; FAX 717/334-1813. Web www.gettysburg.com. 41 rms. June-early Sept: S, D $69-$84; each addl $5; under 17 free; lower rates rest of yr. Crib $3. TV; VCR avail. Pool. Restaurant 7 am-9 pm. Bar from noon. Ck-out noon. Business servs avail. Downhill ski 6 mi. General Lee's Headquarters (museum) adj. Cr cds: A, C, D, DS, ER, JCB, MC, V.

D 🏊 🏊 ⊠ 🐾 SC

✔ ★ **RED CARPET INN PERFECT REST.** 2450 Emmitsburg Rd, 4 mi S on US 15 Business, at edge of National Military Park. 717/334-1345; res: 800/336-1345; FAX 717/334-5026. Web www.gettysburg.com.

25 rms. Apr-early Nov: S, D $35-$69; suites $58-$85; higher rates: spring, fall wkends, college, area events; lower rates rest of yr. Crib $5. TV; cable (premium). Pool. Complimentary coffee. Restaurant nearby. Ck-out 11 am. Microwaves avail. Picnic tables, grills. Cr cds: A, C, D, DS, MC, V.

Motor Hotel

★ ★ **DAYS INN.** 865 York Rd (US 30 E). 717/334-0030; FAX 717/337-1002. Web www.gettysburg.com. 112 rms, 5 story. Apr-Oct: S $59-$98; D $69-$108; each addl $5; under 18 free; ski plans; higher rates special events; lower rates rest of yr. Crib free. TV; cable (premium), VCR avail. Heated pool; lifeguard. Complimentary coffee in lobby. Restaurant adj 6 am-11 pm. Ck-out noon. Coin lndry. Meeting rms. Business servs avail. In-rm modem link. Valet serv. Sundries. Downhill ski 10 mi. Exercise equipt; weight machines, stair machine. Game rm. Microwaves avail. Cr cds: A, C, D, DS, JCB, MC, V.

Hotel

★ ★ ★ **BEST WESTERN.** 1 Lincoln Square, US 15 & 30. 717/337-2000; FAX 717/337-2075. Web www.apci.net/~getty. 83 rms, 6 story, 23 suites. Mid-June-Oct: S, D $88-$125; each addl $5; suites $125-$150; under 16 free; higher rates: graduation, homecoming; lower rates rest of yr. Crib free. TV; cable, VCR avail (movies). Pool; whirlpool, poolside serv, lifeguard. Restaurant 7-10:30 am, 5-9 pm. Bar from 5 pm. Ck-out 11 am. Meeting rms. Business center. In-rm modem link. Free garage parking. Tennis privileges. Downhill ski 8 mi. Some refrigerators. Established 1797. Cr cds: A, D, DS, MC, V.

Inns

★ ★ ★ **BALADERRY INN.** 40 Hospital Rd, at edge of battlefield. 717/337-1342. 8 rms, 7 with shower only, 2 story. S $71-$87; D $81-$97; each addl $15; 2-day min wkends Apr-Nov. Children over 14 yrs only. TV in common area; VCR. Complimentary full bkfst. Ck-out 11 am, ck-in 2 pm. Tennis. Golf privileges. Downhill ski 10 mi; x-country ski adj. Built in 1812; used as a field hospital during the Civil War battle of Gettysburg. Restored, furnished with antiques and reproductions. Extensive grounds. Cr cds: A, C, D, DS, MC, V.

★ ★ ★ **BATTLEFIELD.** 2264 Emmittsburg Rd. 717/334-8804; FAX 717/334-7330. Web www.gettysburg.com. 8 rms, 2 story. No rm phones. Apr-Nov: S $77-$107; D $90-$137; each addl $10; suite $149-$159; 2-day min hols, wkends; lower rates rest of yr. Crib free. TV in sitting rm; VCR. Complimentary full bkfst; afternoon refreshments. Ck-out 11:30 am, ck-in 2 pm. Luggage handling. Concierge serv. Business servs avail. Downhill ski 10 mi. Lawn games. Carriage rides. Fireplaces. Restored 1809 farmhouse famous for living history activities. Totally nonsmoking. Cr cds: A, C, D, DS, MC, V.

★ ★ **BRAFFERTON.** 44 York St. 717/337-3423; FAX 717/334-8185. Web www.gettysburg.com. 10 rms, 2 story, 2 suites. No rm phones. S, D $75-$125; each addl $10; suites $120-$125; higher rates special events. TV in suites. Complimentary full bkfst. Restaurant nearby. Ck-out 11 am, ck-in 2 pm. First house built in town (1786); antiques. Cr cds: A, DS, MC, V.

★ ★ ★ **FARNSWORTH HOUSE INN.** 401 Baltimore St, at corner of South St. 717/334-8838; FAX 717/334-5862. Web www.gettysburg address.com. 5 rms, 2 story. No rm phones. Apr-Oct: S $75; D $85; each addl $10; under 5 free. TV in sitting rm; cable. Complimentary full bkfst. Restaurant (see FARNSWORTH HOUSE). Ck-out 11 am, ck-in 3 pm. Business servs avail. Concierge serv. Luggage handling. Downhill ski 7 mi;

x-country ski ¼ mi. Historic house (1810), restored to its 1863 appearance. The uppermost level of the inn was once used by Confederate sharpshooters; more than 100 bullet holes still remain in the south wall of the inn. Daily tours. Cr cds: A, DS, MC, V.

★ ★ ★ **GASLIGHT.** 33 East Middle St. 717/337-9100; FAX 717/337-9616. 8 rms, 7 with shower only, 3 story. S, D $95-$135; each addl $20; 2-day min hol wkends. Children over 10 yrs only. TV; cable, VCR (free movies). Complimentary full bkfst; afternoon refreshments. Dining rm 6-8 pm (by res only). Restaurant nearby. Ck-out 11 am, ck-in 3 pm. Concierge serv. Luggage handling. Business servs avail. In-rm modem link. Tennis privileges. Golf privileges. Downhill ski 6 mi; x-country ski 10 mi. Health club privileges. Balconies. Italianate house (1872) with original exterior trim. Rms decorated and named in theme of flowers. Cr cds: A, DS, MC, V.

★ ★ **GETTYSTOWN INN.** 89 Steinwehr Ave. 717/334-2100; FAX 717/334-6905. E-mail info@dobbinhouse.com; web www.dobbin house.com. 5 rms, 2 story, 1 suite. No rm phones. Mar-Nov: S $79-$99, D $85-$105; each addl $6; suite $105; under 12 free; wkly rates; higher rates: hols (2-night min), special events; lower rates rest of yr. TV in some rms; cable. Complimentary full bkfst. Restaurant (see DOBBIN HOUSE). Ck-out 10 am, ck-in 2 pm. Downhill ski 7 mi; x-country ski 1 mi. Refrigerators. Renovated 1860s home; antiques. Overlooks site of Abraham Lincoln's Gettysburg Address. Totally nonsmoking. Cr cds: A, MC, V.

★ ★ ★ **HERR TAVERN & PUBLICK HOUSE.** 900 Chambersburg Rd. 717/334-4332; FAX 717/334-3332; res: 800/362-9849. 11 rms, 3 story. S, D $90-$170. Children over 12 yrs only. TV; cable, VCR (movies). Complimentary full bkfst. Coffee in rms. Restaurant (see HERR TAVERN & PUBLICK HOUSE). Rm serv. Ck-out 11 am, ck-in 4 pm. Luggage handling. Golf privileges. Downhill ski 5 mi. Exercise equipt; bicycles, treadmills. Game rm. Some in-rm whirlpools. Built in 1815, antiques; served as Confederate hospital. Totally nonsmoking. Cr cds: A, DS, MC, V.

★ ★ ★ **JAMES GETTYS HOTEL.** 28 Chambersburg Rd. 717/337-1334. 11 kit. suites, 1 with shower only, 4 story. Mid-Mar-Oct: kit. suites $115-$135; each addl $15; under 12 free; lower rates rest of yr. Crib free. TV; cable (premium), VCR avail. Complimentary continental bkfst. Complimentary coffee in rms. Restaurant 11:30 am-4:40 pm. Ck-out 11 am, ck-in 3 pm. Business servs avail. Luggage handling. Concierge serv. Gift shop. Guest lndry. Downhill ski 10 mi; x-country ski 1 mi. Refrigerators, microwaves, wet bars, fireplaces. Built in 1804. Totally nonsmoking. Cr cds: A, DS, MC, V.

★ ★ **THE OLD APPLEFORD.** 218 Carlisle St. 717/337-1711; FAX 717/334-6228; res: 800/275-3373. Web www.virtualcities.com. 10 rms, 7 with shower only, 3 story. No rm phones. Apr-Oct: S $80-$95; D $105-$120; suite $115-$150; 2-day min wkends, hols, special events; lower rates rest of yr. Children over 11 yrs only. Complimentary full bkfst; afternoon refreshments. Restaurant nearby. Ck-out 11 am, ck-in 2 pm. Concierge serv. Downhill ski 7 mi; x-country ski 15 mi. Health club privileges. Picnic tables. Victorian mansion (1867); many antiques. Totally nonsmoking. Cr cds: A, DS, MC, V.

Restaurants

★ ★ ★ **DOBBIN HOUSE.** (See Gettystown Inn) 717/334-2100. E-mail info@dobbinhouse.com; web www.dobbinhouse.com. Hrs: 11:30 am-11 pm. Closed Jan 1, Thanksgiving, Dec 25. Res accepted. Continental menu. Bar. Semi-a la carte: lunch $4.95-$15.95, dinner $15.95-$29.95. Child's meals. Specializes in 1700s recipes, fresh seafood, large selection of meats. Own baking. Oldest building in Gettysburg; built 1776. Cr cds: A, MC, V.

D **SC**

★ ★ ★ **FARNSWORTH HOUSE.** *(See Farnsworth House Inn)* *717/334-8838.* Web www.visitgettysburg address.com. Hrs: 5-9 pm. Closed Jan 1, Thanksgiving, Dec 25. Res accepted. Bar to midnight. Semi-a la carte: dinner $11.95-$18. Child's meals. Specialties: peanut soup, game pie, pumpkin fritters. Outdoor dining. Built in 1810; tour avail. Cr cds: A, DS, MC, V.

★ **GINGERBREAD MAN.** *217 Steinwehr Ave. 717/334-1100.* Hrs: 11 am-11 pm; Sun to 10 pm. Closed Jan 1, Dec 25. Varied menu. Bar. Semi-a la carte: lunch $4-$7, dinner $6.95-$12.95. Child's meals. Specializes in NY-style deli sandwiches, Mexican dishes, fresh Maryland crab-cakes. Casual, lively atmosphere. Cr cds: A, C, D, DS, MC, V.

D

★ ★ **HERR TAVERN & PUBLICK HOUSE.** *(See Herr Tavern & Publick House Inn) 717/334-4332.* Web www.cvn.net/herrtavern. Hrs: 11 am-9 pm; Sun from 5 pm. Closed Jan 1, Dec 24, 25. Res accepted. Continental menu. Bar. Semi-a la carte: lunch $3.49-$8.49, dinner $13-$20. Child's meals. Specialties: blackened prime rib, chicken Chesapeake, seafood pasta. Child's meals. Outdoor dining. Restored antebellum tavern with period art and antiques. Cr cds: A, DS, MC, V.

D

✔★ ★ **STONEHENGE.** *985 Baltimore Pike. 717/334-9227.* Hrs: 11 am-10 pm. Closed Jan 1, Dec 24, 25. Res accepted. Continental menu. Bar to 2 am. Semi-a la carte: lunch $2.95-$6.95, dinner $5.95-$19.95. Child's meals. Specialties: Cajun prime rib, crab cakes, veal Marsala. Intimate dining; fresh flowers. Cr cds: A, MC, V.

D

Gettysburg National Military Park (F-6)

(For accommodations see Gettysburg, Hanover)

The hallowed battlefield of Gettysburg, scene of one of the most decisive battles of the Civil War and immortalized by Lincoln's Gettysburg Address, is preserved by the National Park Service. The town itself is still a college community, as it was more than a hundred years ago on July 1, 2 and 3, 1863, when General Robert E. Lee led his Confederate Army in its greatest invasion of the North. The defending Northerners under Union General George Meade repulsed the Southern assault after three days of fierce fighting, which left 51,000 men dead, wounded or missing.

The Gettysburg National Military Park has more than 35 miles of roads through 5,700 acres of the battlefield area. There are more than 1,300 monuments, markers and tablets of granite and bronze; 400 cannons are also located on the field.

Visitors may wish to tour the battlefield with a Battlefield Guide, licensed by the National Park Service (two-hour tour; fee). The guides escort visitors to all points of interest and sketch the movement of troops and details of the battle. Or visitors may wish to first orient themselves at the Visitor Center-Electric Map and Cyclorama; then using the park folder, the battlefield can be toured without a guide. Audio cassettes are also available for self-guided tours.

The late President Dwight D. Eisenhower's retirement farm, a National Historic Site, adjoins the battlefield. It is open to the public on a limited-tour basis. All visitors must obtain tour tickets at the tour information center, located at the entrance of the Visitor Center-Electric Map building. Transportation to the farm is by shuttle (fee). For further information contact Visitor Services, 97 Taneytown Rd, Gettysburg 17325; 717/334-1124 or 717/334-6274.

What to See and Do

Cyclorama Center. Adj to visitor center. Instructive film and exhibits: 356-ft Cyclorama painting of Pickett's Charge. (Daily) ¢

Culp's Hill. Site of longest sustained fighting during battle.

Devil's Den. Stronghold of Confederate sharpshooters following its capture during action on the 2nd day.

East Cemetery Hill. Rallying point for Union forces on 1st day of battle. Scene of fierce fighting on evening of 2nd day.

Eisenhower National Historic Site. Farmhouse of the 34th President of the United States and his wife, Mamie. Self-guided tour (1½ hrs) of the home and grounds. Access to site only by shuttle bus from the tour information center (entrance of Visitor Center-Electric Map bldg). Tour tickets dispensed individually on a first-come, first-served basis for the next tour. Limited number of tours per day. (Apr-Oct, daily; rest of yr, Wed-Sun; closed Thanksgiving, Dec 25, also Jan) Phone 717/334-1124. Tour and shuttle bus ¢¢

Little Round Top. Key Union position during 2nd and 3rd days of battle.

Memorials to State Units. Includes Pennsylvania State Monument, with names of more than 34,500 Pennsylvanian soldiers who participated in the battle.

Seminary Ridge. Main Confederate battle line.

The Angle. Spot where Pickett's Charge was repulsed on July 3, referred to as "high water mark" of the Confederacy.

The Eternal Light Peace Memorial. On Oak Ridge. Erected in 1938 and dedicated by President Roosevelt to "peace eternal in a nation united."

The Gettysburg National Cemetery. Site of Lincoln's Gettysburg Address.

The Wheatfield and Peach Orchard. Scene of heavy Union and Confederate losses on the second day of fighting.

✠ **Visitor Center-Electric Map-Gettysburg Museum of the Civil War.** Visits to the park should begin here. Park information, including a self-guided auto tour, and guides may be obtained at the center. Story of battle told on 750-sq-ft electric map surrounded by 525 seats (every 45 min; fee). Gettysburg Museum of the Civil War has an extensive collection of Civil War relics (free). (Daily; closed Jan 1, Thanksgiving, Dec 25) On PA 134. Electric map. ¢ Obtain tickets here for

Whitworth Guns on Oak Hill. Only breech-loading cannon used here.

Gibsonia
(see Pittsburgh)

Greensburg (E-2)

(See also Connellsville, Donegal, Ligonier, New Stanton)

Founded 1785 **Pop** 16,318 **Elev** 1,099 ft **Area code** 724 **Zip** 15601
Information Laurel Highlands Visitors Bureau, 120 E Main St, Ligonier 15658; 724/238-5661.

Greensburg was named for Revolutionary General Nathanael Greene.

What to See and Do

Bushy Run Battlefield. Here Colonel Henry Bouquet defeated united Native American forces during Pontiac's War on Aug 5 & 6, 1763. The battle lifted the siege of Fort Pitt and was the turning point of the war. Picnicking, park (free); hiking trails. Visitor center exhibits depict battle (Wed-Sun; closed most hols). NW on PA 993. Phone 724/527-5584. ¢¢

Historic Hanna's Town. Costumed tour guide tells story of Hanna's Town, site of first court west of Alleghenies. Includes reconstructed courthouse, tavern, jail and stockaded fort; picnic area. (June-Aug, daily exc Mon; May, Sept & Oct, wkends only) 3 mi NE via US 119. Phone 724/836-1800. ¢

Lincoln Highway Heritage Corridor. 140-mi stretch of US 30 extending from Greensburg to Chambersburg. Pass through and explore countless historical and recreational areas. Driving guide avail (fee) from Lincoln Highway Heritage Corridor, PO Box 386; 724/668-8330. Guide ¢

Westmoreland County Courthouse. Building in style of Italian Renaissance; restored in 1982. (Mon-Fri; closed hols) Main & Pittsburgh Sts. Phone 724/830-3000.

Westmoreland Museum of American Art. 18th-, 19th- and early 20th-century American paintings, sculpture, furniture and decorative arts. 19th- and early 20th-century southwestern Pennsylvania paintings. Extensive toy collection. Lectures, guided tours. (Tues-Sat, also Sun afternoons; closed hols) 221 N Main St. Phone 724/837-1500. **Free.**

Motels

★ ★ **COMFORT INN.** *1129 E Pittsburgh St, PA Tpke exit 7, E on PA 30.* 724/832-2600; FAX 724/834-3442. Web www.comfortinn.com. 77 rms, 3 story. S $66-$99; D $71-$105; each addl $5; suites $81-$147; under 18 free; higher rates special events. Crib free. TV; cable (premium), VCR avail (movies). Heated pool. Complimentary continental bkfst. Restaurant nearby. Ck-out 11 am. Meeting rms. Business servs avail. Valet serv. Health club privileges. Some refrigerators, wet bars, in-rm whirlpools; microwaves avail. Cr cds: A, C, D, DS, ER, JCB, MC, V.

D ⊠ ≋ ⊠ SC

★ ★ ★ **FOUR POINTS BY SHERATON.** *100 Sheraton Dr (US 30E).* 724/836-6060; FAX 724/834-5640. E-mail jsupko@aol.com; web www.sheraton.com. 146 rms, 2 story. S $66-$80; D $71-$85; each addl $5; suites $110-$250; under 17 free; golf, package plans. Crib free. TV; cable (premium), VCR avail. Indoor pool; sauna. Restaurant 6:30 am-2 pm, 5-10 pm. Bar 11-2 am; entertainment. Ck-out noon. Meeting rms. Business servs avail. Bellhops. Valet serv. Sundries. Free local airport, RR station, bus depot transportation. 9-hole golf course, greens fee, pro shop, putting green. Health club privileges. Game rm. Some refrigerators. Shopping mall opp. Cr cds: A, C, D, DS, JCB, MC, V.

D ⊁ ≋ ≋ ⊠ SC

✔ ★ **KNIGHTS INN.** *1215 S Main St, at jct US 119 & US 30.* 724/836-7100; FAX 724/837-5390; res: 800/843-5644. 110 rms, 10 suites, 11 kits. May-Oct: S $41.95-$51.95; D $49.95-$70.95; each addl $7; suites, kit. units $52.95-$72.95; under 18 free; lower rates rest of yr. Crib free. TV; cable (premium), VCR avail. Pool. Complimentary coffee in lobby. Restaurant adj 6 am-11 pm. Ck-out noon. Meeting rm. Guest lndry. Refrigerators, microwaves avail. Cr cds: A, C, D, DS, MC, V.

≋ ≋ ⊠ SC

Motor Hotel

★ ★ ★ **MOUNTAIN VIEW INN.** *5 mi E on US 30, 13 mi NE of PA Tpke exit 7.* 724/834-5300; FAX 724/834-5304; res: 800/537-8739. Web www.mountainviewinn.com. 93 rms. S $55-$125; D $63-$125; suites $95-$250; ski package. TV; cable (premium), VCR avail. Pool. Complimentary continental bkfst. Coffee in rms. Restaurant 7 am-2 pm, 5-9 pm; wkend hrs vary. Rm serv 7:30 am-11 pm. Bar 11 am-midnight; Fri, Sat to 1 am; Sun noon-8 pm. Ck-out noon. Meeting rms. Business servs avail. In-rm modem link. Sundries. Exercise equipt; weights, treadmill. Antique decor; English and herb gardens; gazebo. Cr cds: A, C, D, DS, MC, V.

D ⊠ ≋ ⊁ ⊠ ⊠ SC

Restaurant

★ ★ **CARBONE'S.** *(Main St, Crabtree) 6 mi N on US 119.* 724/834-3430. E-mail carbones@westol.com; web www.westol.com/

~carbones. Hrs: 4:30-9 pm; Fri, Sat to 10 pm. Closed Sun; major hols. Res accepted. Italian, Amer menu. Bar to midnight. Semi-a la carte: dinner $8.95-$16.95. Child's meals. Specialties: angel pie, antipasto, braciole. Mediterranean decor. Family-owned. Cr cds: A, C, D, DS, MC, V.

D ⊡

Hamburg (E-8)

(For accommodations see Reading; also see Kutztown, Shartlesville)

Founded 1779 **Pop** 3,987 **Elev** 373 ft **Area code** 610 **Zip** 19526

Information Reading/Berks County Visitors Bureau, VF Factory Outlet Complex, Park Rd & Hill Ave, PO Box 6677, Reading 19610; 610/375-4085 or 800/443-6610.

Situated on the banks of the Schuylkill River, Hamburg is a center for one of the finest farming sections in Pennsylvania. The town's industries include the manufacture of brooms, iron and steel castings, knitwear and soft-drink products.

What to See and Do

Blue Rocks. Covers 90 acres; pool; fishing (stocked pond); picnicking, two pavilions; hiking, Appalachian Trail; camping, trailer facilities (fee; hookups addl). Game room. 5 mi E on I-78 to Lenhartsville, then 2 mi N on PA 143. Phone 610/756-6366. Park ¢

Hawk Mountain Sanctuary. Hawk, eagle flights visible with binoculars from lookouts mid-Aug-Nov; museum, bookstore. (Daily; closed Jan 1, Thanksgiving, Dec 25) 11 mi N via PA 61 & 895; follow signs. Phone 610/756-6961. ¢¢

Wanamaker, Kempton & Southern, Inc. A 6-mi, 40-min round trip on steam or deisel train along the Ontelaunee Creek at the foot of Hawk Mountain. Model railroad (Sun), antique shop. Snack bar, picnic area. Steam train (July, Aug, Oct, Sat & Sun afternoons; May & June, Sun afternoons). Diesel train (June & Sept, 1st & 3rd Sat afternoons only). Also special events throughout the yr. 5 mi E on I-78 to Lenhartsville exit, then 5 mi N on PA 143 to Kempton. Phone 610/756-6469. ¢¢

Hanover (F-7)

(See also Gettysburg, York)

Founded 1763 **Pop** 14,399 **Elev** 609 ft **Area code** 717 **Zip** 17331 **E-mail** lascad@netrax.net **Web** www.cvn.net/~hanoverareachamber

Information Hanover Area Chamber of Commerce, 146 Broadway; 717/637-6130.

Known in early days as "McAllisterstown" (for founder Colonel Richard McAllister) and "Rogue's Harbor" (for lack of law enforcement), Hanover is in the rich Conewago Valley. Here, on June 30, 1863, Confederate General J.E.B. Stuart's cavalry tangled with Union forces under Generals Kilpatrick and Custer. The battle prevented Stuart from reaching Gettysburg in time to function as "the eyes of Lee's army."

Among the products of the town's diversified industry are books, wirecloth, yarns, furniture, industrial machinery, textiles and foods, including snack foods.

What to See and Do

Codorus State Park. Approx 3,300 acres. Swimming pool; fishing in 1,275-acre Lake Marburg, hunting; boating (rentals, mooring, launching, marina). Hiking, bridle trails. Cross-country skiing, snowmobiling, sledding, ice-skating, ice boating, ice fishing. Picnicking, playground, snack bar. Tent & trailer sites. Standard fees. 3 mi E on PA 216. Phone 717/637-2816.

Conewago Chapel (1741). Oldest stone Catholic church in the US. Designated Sacred Heart Basilica in 1962. Cemetery dates from 1752. (Daily) 30 Basilica Dr, 2 mi W on PA 116, then 2 mi N. Phone 717/637-2721. **Free.**

Neas House Museum. Neas House (ca 1783), restored Georgian mansion, serves as local history museum. (May-Nov, Tues-Fri) Special events (spring, summer, late Dec). 113 W Chestnut St. Phone 717/632-3207. **Free.**

Utz Quality Foods, Inc. Producers of potato chips and snack foods. Glass-enclosed tour gallery overlooks production area; push-to-talk audio program and closed-circuit TV monitors. (Mon-Thurs; closed major hols) 900 High St. Phone 717/637-6644.   **Free.**

Inn

★ ★ ★ **BEECHMONT.** *315 Broadway. 717/632-3013; res: 800/553-7009.* 7 rms, 2 story, 3 suites. S, D $80-$95; suites $115-$135. Children over 12 yrs only. Complimentary full bkfst; afternoon refreshments. Restaurant nearby. Ck-out 11 am, ck-in 3 pm. Microwaves avail. Federal period house (1834); landscaped courtyard. Cr cds: A, DS, MC, V.

⊠ ⅄ SC

Harmony (D-1)

(For accommodations see Butler, Pittsburgh)

Founded 1804 **Pop** 1,054 **Elev** 925 ft **Area code** 724 **Zip** 16037 **E-mail** chamber@isrv.com **Web** www.butlerfirst.com

Information Butler County Visitors Bureau, 201 S Main St, PO Box 1082, Butler 16003; 724/283-2222.

First settlement of George Rapp's Harmony Society, Harmony served the colony only until 1814. More than 100 of the original group are buried in Harmonists Cemetery, southeast of town. Several of the Rappite Society's sturdy brick houses still stand in the village.

What to See and Do

Harmony Museum (1809). Exhibits depict early life under Harmonists and Mennonites; regional history. The Harmony Society was one of America's most successful experiments in communal living. Harmony was the society's first home (1804). Tour. (June-Sept, daily afternoons; rest of yr, Mon, Wed, Fri, also Sun afternoons) 218 Mercer St. Phone 724/452-7341.   ¢¢

Annual Events

Dankfest. Pioneer craft festival held on grounds of Harmony Museum (see). Crafts, entertainment, tours, refreshments. Contact museum for schedule. Late Aug.

Christmas Open House. Candlelight tour of Harmony Museum, Wagner House and Ziegler log house. Entertainment, refreshments. Contact museum for schedule. Early Dec.

Harrisburg (E-7)

(See also Carlisle, Hershey, York)

Settled 1718 **Pop** 52,376 **Elev** 360 ft **Area code** 717

Information Capital Region Chamber of Commerce, 114 Walnut St, PO Box 969, 17108-0969, phone 717/232-4121; or the Harrisburg-Hershey-Carlisle Tourism & Convention Bureau, phone 717/232-1377.

This midstate metropolis is graced by what many consider the finest capitol building in the nation. Its riverside park (known as City Island), Italian Lake,

unique museum and beautiful Forum are the showplaces; commerce, industry and politics keep the city going.

The site was viewed in 1615 by Etienne Brulé on a trip down the Susquehanna, but more than a century passed before John Harris, the first settler, opened his trading post here. His son established the town in 1785. It became the seat of state government in 1812; the cornerstone of the first capitol building was laid in 1819.

What to See and Do

Capitol Hill buildings. N 3rd & Walnut Sts. Phone 717/787-6810. Clustered in a 45-acre complex, the major buildings are

The Capitol (dedicated 1906). Italian Renaissance building covers two acres, has 651 rms; 26,000-ton, 272-ft dome, imitating that of St Peter's in Rome, dominates city skyline. Includes murals by Abbey and Okley. Tours (daily; closed Jan 1, Easter, Thanksgiving, Dec 25). Main entrance, 3rd & State Sts.   **Free.**

North Office Building. Map inscribed on main lobby floor shows state highways, seals of Pennsylvania cities.

South Office Building. Colorful murals by Edward Trumbull depict *Penn's Treaty with the Indians* and *The Industries of Pittsburgh.*

Forum Building. Includes auditorium below constellation-bedecked ceiling; walls review man's progress through time. Main lobby boasts a Maragliotti ceiling. General and law libraries.

Finance Building. Ceiling murals by Maragliotti, Eugene Savage; mural in south vestibule illustrates *The Collection of Taxes.* (Mon-Fri)

The State Museum of Pennsylvania. A six-story circular building housing four stories of galleries, authentic early country store, Native American life exhibit, technological and industrial exhibits, collection of antique autos and period carriages; planetarium; natural history and geology exhibits and one of world's largest framed paintings, Rothermel's *The Battle of Gettysburg.* Planetarium has public shows (Sat & Sun; fee). (Daily exc Mon; closed most hols) N of Capitol Bldg, 3rd & North Sts. Phone 717/787-4978.   **Free.**

Dauphin County Courthouse. Seven imposing courtrooms; outline map on floor in main foyer pictures borough and township boundaries. (Mon-Fri; closed hols) Front & Market Sts. Phone 717/255-2741.

Fort Hunter Park. Historic 37-acre property; site of British-built fort erected in 1754 to combat mounting threats prior to the French and Indian War. In 1787 the land was purchased and became a farm that eventually grew into a self-sufficient village. The Pennsylvania Canal runs through the park; on the grounds are historic buttonwood trees dating from William Penn's time; a 19th-century boxwood garden; herb gardens; paths along the banks of the Susquehanna River; picnic area. Also here are an ice house, springhouse (ca 1800), Centennial barn (1876), and corncrib (1880). Also on the grounds, but not open to the public because of restoration, are the old tavern (1800), blacksmith shop (1890) and stone stable. 6 mi N on N Front St. Outstanding feature of park is

Fort Hunter Mansion. Federal-style stone mansion, built in three sections. Front stone portions were built in 1786 and 1814; rear wooden portion built in 1870. Spacious mansion displays period furnishings, clothing, toys and other artifacts. Guided tours. (May-Dec, daily exc Mon) 5300 N Front St, in park. Phone 717/599-5751.   ¢¢

Indian Echo Caverns. Stalagmite and stalactite formations. Picnicking, playground. (Daily, schedule varies; closed Jan 1, Thanksgiving, Dec 25) 10 mi E on US 322, 422, in Hummelstown. Phone 717/566-8131.   ¢¢¢

Italian Lake. Bordered with flowers, shrubs and shade trees in summer. N 3rd & Division Sts.

John Harris Mansion. Home of city's founder, now Historical Society of Dauphin County headquarters. Stone house has 19th-century furnishings, library (Mon-Thurs; fee), collection of county artifacts. Tours (Tues-Sat). 219 S Front St. Phone 717/233-3462.   ¢¢¢

Museum of Scientific Discovery. Hands-on exhibits demonstrating various scientific and math principles; daily programs. (Daily exc Mon; closed most major hols) 3rd & Walnut Sts, 1st level, Strawberry Sq. Phone 717/233-7969.   ¢¢

Penn National Race Course. Live yr-round Thoroughbred racing (Wed, Fri-Sun). Nationwide simulcasts (daily). Terrace dining room; gift shop. NE via I-81, exit 28, in Grantville. Phone 717/469-2211. ¢¢

Reservoir Park. View of E end of city, five nearby counties. Walnut & N 19th Sts.

Riverfront Park. 4 mi along Susquehanna River, with park promenade flanking Front St, concrete walk along river.

Rockville Bridge (1902). A 3,810-ft stone-arch bridge; 48 spans carry four tracks of Penn Central Railroad main line. 4 mi N on US 22.

Annual Events

Kipona. Boating and water-related activites. Labor Day wkend.

(All of the following events are held in State Farm Show Building, 11th & Maclay Sts.)

Pennsylvania State Farm Show. State fair. Phone 717/787-5373. Jan 10-15.

Eastern Sports & Outdoor Show. Phone 717/630-2268. Early-mid-Feb.

Pennsylvania National Horse Show. Phone 717/975-3677. 10 days mid-Oct.

Motels

★ ★ **BEST WESTERN.** 300 N Mountain Rd (17112), I-81 exit 26. 717/652-7180; FAX 717/541-8991. Web www.bestwestern.com/best.html. 49 rms, 2 story. S $50-$80; D $50-$85; each addl $3; under 13 free. Crib $5. Pet accepted. TV; cable (premium). Restaurant 6:30 am-9 pm. Bar 11 am-11 pm. Ck-out 11 am. Business servs avail. In-rm modem link. Sundries. Microwaves avail. Cr cds: A, C, D, DS, MC, V.

★ **BUDGETEL INN.** 200 N Mountain Rd (17112), I-81 exit 26. 717/540-9339; FAX 717/540-9486. Web www.budgetel.com. 66 rms, 3 story, 8 suites. Apr-Oct: S $56.95-$64.95; D $62.95-$71.95; suites $65.95-$72.95; under 19 free; lower rates rest of yr. Crib free. Pet accepted. TV; cable (premium), VCR avail. Complimentary continental bkfst. Complimentary coffee in rms. Restaurant nearby. Ck-out noon. Coin lndry. Meeting rms. Business center. In-rm modem link. Sundries. Refrigerator in suites; microwaves avail. Cr cds: A, C, D, DS, MC, V.

★ ★ **COMFORT INN.** 4021 Union Deposit Lane (17109), I-83 exit 29. 717/561-8100; FAX 717/561-1357. 115 rms, 5 story. June-Oct: S, D $79-$99; under 18 free; higher rates car shows; lower rates rest of yr. Crib free. Pet accepted. TV; cable (premium); lifeguard. Complimentary continental bkfst. Restaurant adj 6 am-10 pm. Ck-out noon. Coin lndry. Meeting rms. Business servs avail. Free airport, RR station transportation. Health club privileges. Microwaves avail. Cr cds: A, C, D, DS, ER, JCB, MC, V.

✔ ★ **DAYS INN.** 3919 N Front St (17110), I-81, exit 22N. 717/233-1611; FAX 717/233-6415. 116 rms, 3 story. S $54.99-$69.99; D $54.99-$74.99; each addl $5; under 12 free; higher rates: car shows, farm show. Crib free. TV; cable. Pool; lifeguard. Playground. Complimentary continental bkfst. Restaurant nearby. Ck-out noon. Coin lndry. Business servs avail. In-rm modem link. Exercise equipt; weight machine, bicycle. Refrigerators, microwaves avail. Picnic tables. Cr cds: A, C, D, DS, JCB, MC, V.

★ ★ **HAMPTON INN.** 4230 Union Deposit Rd (17111), I-83 exit 29. 717/545-9595; FAX 717/545-6907. Web www.hampton-inn.com. 145 rms, 5 story. S $68-$80; D $75-$86; under 18 free; higher rates auto shows. Crib avail. TV; cable (premium). Heated pool; whirlpool, lifeguard. Complimentary continental bkfst. Restaurant adj open 24 hrs. Ck-out noon. Coin lndry. Meeting rms. Business servs avail. Valet serv. Golf privileges. Downhill ski 15 mi. Exercise equipt; bicycle, treadmill. Health club privileges. Microwaves avail. Cr cds: A, D, DS, MC, V.

★ ★ **HAMPTON INN WEST.** (4950 Ritter Rd, Mechanicsburg 17055) 8 mi SW on PA 641. 717/691-1300; FAX 717/691-9692. 129 rms, 4 story. S $75-$79; D $84-$88; under 18 free; ski plan. Crib free. TV; cable (premium), VCR avail. Heated pool; whirlpool, lifeguard. Complimentary continental bkfst. Restaurant adj 7 am-11 pm. Ck-out 11 am. Coin lndry. Meeting rms. Business center. In-rm modem link. Downhill ski 20 mi. Exercise equipt; stair machine, treadmill. Microwaves avail. Cr cds: A, D, DS, MC, V.

✔ ★ ★ **HOLIDAY INN.** (I-83 & PA Tpke, New Cumberland 17070) S on I-83, W on I-283. 717/774-2721; FAX 717/774-2485. 196 rms, 2 story. May-Oct: S, D $59-$99; each addl $10; suites $160; under 18 free; family, wknd, hol rates; ski plans; higher rates special events; lower rates rest of yr. Crib free. Pet accepted, some restrictions; $10. TV; cable (premium). Restaurant 6:30 am-2 pm, 5-9 pm; Fri, Sat to 10 pm. Rm serv. Bar 5 pm-2 am; entertainment. Ck-out 11 am. Meeting rms. Business center. In-rm modem link. Bellhops. Valet serv. Coin lndry. Free airport, RR station transportation. Exercise equipt; treadmill, stair machine. Indoor pool; whirlpool. Game rm. Some balconies. Refrigerators, microwaves avail. Picnic tables, grills. Luxury level. Cr cds: A, C, D, DS, JCB, MC, V.

★ ★ **HOLIDAY INN-WEST.** (5401 Carlisle Pike, Mechanicsburg 17055) W on I-81 exit 18 S. 717/697-0321; FAX 717/697-7594. 218 rms, 2 story. Feb-Oct: S $93; D $103; each addl $10; suites $125-$200; under 18 free; wkly rates; higher rates special events; lower rates rest of yr. Crib free. Pet accepted, some restrictions; $50 deposit. TV; cable (premium). Complimentary continental bkfst. Complimentary coffee in rms. Restaurant 6:30 am-9 pm. Rm serv. Bar 5 pm-2 am; entertainment. Ck-out noon. Meeting rms. Business servs avail. Coin lndry. Exercise equipt; weight machine, bicycle. Miniature golf. Heated indoor/outdoor pool; lifeguard. Some in-rm whirlpools; microwaves avail. Picnic tables, grills. Cr cds: A, C, D, DS, JCB, MC, V.

★ ★ **HOWARD JOHNSON.** 473 Eisenhower Blvd (17111), I-283 exit 1. 717/564-4730; FAX 717/564-4840. E-mail hkharrisburg@intereach.net. 176 rms, 2 story. S $55-$79; D $62-$89; each addl $8; under 17 free; higher rates Hershey Antique Auto Show. Crib free. TV; cable (premium). Pool; wading pool. Restaurant 5 am-midnight. Bar from 11 am. Ck-out noon. Meeting rms. Business center. Valet serv. Sundries. Free airport, RR station transportation. Exercise equipt; bicycles, treadmill. Microwaves avail. Private patios, balconies. Cr cds: A, C, D, DS, ER, MC, V.

★ ★ ★ **RADISSON PENN HARRIS.** (1150 Camp Hill Bypass, Camp Hill 17011) S on US 15, Camp Hill Bypass; 6 mi N of PA Turnpike exit 17. 717/763-7117; FAX 717/763-4518; res: 800/345-7366. 250 rms, 2-3 story. No elvtr. S $69-$119; D $79-$139; each addl $10; suites $225-$400; under 18 free. Crib free. Pet accepted. TV; cable (premium). Pool; poolside serv, lifeguard. Restaurant 6:30 am-10 pm. Rm serv. Bar 3 pm-2 am. Ck-out noon. Convention facilities. Business center. In-rm modem link. Valet serv. Bellhops. Free airport transportation. Exercise equipt; bicycles, stair machines. Cr cds: A, C, D, DS, MC, V.

✔ ★ **RED ROOF INN.** 400 Corporate Circle (17110), I-81 exit 24. 717/657-1445; FAX 717/657-2775. 110 rms, 2 story. S $40-$44; D $45-$57; under 18 free. Crib free. Pet accepted. TV; cable (premium). Complimentary coffee in lobby Mon-Fri. Restaurant nearby. Ck-out noon. Business servs avail. In-rm modem link. Cr cds: A, D, DS, MC, V.

Motor Hotels

★ ★ ★ **HOLIDAY INN EAST.** *4751 Lindle Rd (17111), jct I-283 & PA 441 exit 1.* 717/939-7841; FAX 717/939-9317. 300 rms, 4 story. S $109-139; D $121-$151; each addl $12; under 19 free. Crib free. TV; cable (premium). 2 pools, 1 indoor; whirlpool, poolside serv, lifeguard. Restaurant 7 am-2 pm, 5-10 pm. Rm serv 7 am-10 pm. Bar 11-2 am. Ck-out 11 am. Valet serv. Convention facilities. Business servs avail. Free airport transportation. Lighted tennis. Putting green. Exercise equipt; bicycles, treadmill, sauna. Health club privileges. Game rm. Private patios, balconies. Cr cds: A, C, D, DS, JCB, MC, V.

D 🚴 ⚓ ✈ 🍴 🚭 🔥 SC

★ ★ ★ **MARRIOTT.** *4650 Lindle Rd (17111), jct I-283 & PA 441.* 717/564-5511; FAX 717/564-6173. E-mail 105616.1760@compuserve.com. 348 rms, 10 story. S, D $80-$159; each addl $14; suites $225; under 18 free. Crib free. TV; cable (premium), VCR avail. Indoor/outdoor pool; whirlpool, poolside serv, lifeguard. Restaurant 6 am-midnight. Rm serv. Bar to 2 am; entertainment. Ck-out noon. Convention facilities. Business servs avail. In-rm modem link. Bellhops. Valet serv. Sundries. Gift shop. Free airport transportation. Exercise equipt; weights, bicycles, sauna. Game rm. Balconies. Luxury level. Cr cds: A, C, D, DS, ER, MC, V.

D ⚓ ✈ 🍴 🚭 🔥 SC

★ ★ ★ **SHERATON HARRISBURG EAST.** *800 East Park Dr (17111), I-83 exit 29.* 717/561-2800; FAX 717/561-8398. 174 rms, 3 story. S $86-$105; D $96-$115; each addl $10; suites $145-$165; under 18 free. Crib free. Pet accepted, some restrictions. TV; cable (premium). Heated pool; whirlpool, lifeguard. Restaurant 6:30 am-10 pm. Rm serv. Bar 11-2 am. Ck-out noon. Meeting rms. Business servs avail. In-rm modem link. Bellhops. Valet serv. Shopping arcade. Free airport transportation. Golf privileges. Exercise rm; instructor, weights, bicycles, sauna. Game rm. Cr cds: A, C, D, DS, MC, V.

D 🚴 ✈ 🍴 🚭 🔥 SC

Hotels

★ ★ ★ **HILTON AND TOWERS.** *1 N 2nd St (17101).* 717/233-6000; FAX 717/233-6271. 341 rms, 15 story. S, D $99-$164; each addl $10; suites $200-$500; wknd rates. Crib avail. TV; cable (premium). Indoor pool. Restaurant 6:30 am-11 pm. Bar 11-1 am; entertainment. Ck-out noon. Convention facilities. Business servs avail. In-rm modem link. Concierge. Shopping arcade connected to Strawberry Square Mall. Valet parking. Free airport transportation. Exercise equipt; weight machine, bicycles. Health club privileges. Minibars, refrigerators, microwaves avail. Luxury level. Cr cds: A, C, D, DS, ER, MC, V.

D ⚓ 🍴 ✈ 🚭 SC

★ ★ ★ **RAMADA HOTEL-ON MARKET SQUARE.** *23 S 2nd St (17101).* 717/234-5021; FAX 717/234-2347. Web www.ramada.com/ramada.html. 254 rms, 10 story. S $75-$95; D $85-$105; each addl $10; studio rms $78-$90; suites $145; under 19 free. TV; cable (premium), VCR avail (movies). Indoor pool. Restaurant 6:30 am-2 pm, 5-10 pm. Bar 4:30 pm-1 am. Ck-out noon. Meeting rms. Business servs avail. In-rm modem links. Gift shop. Airport transportation. Exercise equipt; bicycle, stair machine. Microwaves avail. Rooftop patio. Cr cds: A, C, D, DS, ER, JCB, MC, V.

D ⚓ 🍴 🚭 🔥 SC

★ ★ ★ **WYNDHAM GARDEN.** *765 Eisenhower Blvd (17111), I-283 exit 1.* 717/558-9500; FAX 717/558-8956. 167 rms, 6 story. May-Oct: S, D $89-$119; each addl $10; suites $150; under 19 free; ski plans; wknd rates; higher rates car shows; lower rates rest of yr. Crib free. Pet accepted. TV; cable (premium). Heated pool; lifeguard. Coffee in rms. Restaurant 6 am-10 pm. Bar 5 pm-2 am. Ck-out noon. Meeting rms. Business servs avail. In-rm modem link. Concierge. Free airport, RR station, bus depot transportation. Downhill ski 20 mi. Exercise equipt; weight machine, stair machine. Refrigerator, wet bar in suites; microwaves avail. Cr cds: A, C, D, DS, ER, JCB, MC, V.

D 🚴 ⚓ 🍴 🚭 🔥 SC

Restaurants

★ ★ ★ **ALFRED'S VICTORIAN RESTAURANT.** *(38 N Union St, Middletown)* E on I-83, then S on I-283, then SE on PA 230 to PA 441. 717/944-5373. Hrs: 11:30 am-2 pm, 5-10 pm; Sat from 5 pm; Sun 3-9 pm. Closed some major hols. Res accepted. Italian, continental menu. Bar. Wine list. Semi-a la carte: lunch $5-$12.50, dinner $9.95-$27.95. Specialties: homemade pastas, hand-cut steaks, seafood. Own baking. Tableside cooking. Patio dining. Victorian mansion; antique chandeliers, furnishings; floor-to-ceiling windows; fireplaces. Family-owned. Cr cds: A, C, D, DS, MC, V.

 SC ✍ ♥

★ ★ **MANADA HILL INN.** *128 N Hershey Rd.* 717/652-0400. Hrs: 4-9 pm; Fri-Sat to 10 pm; Sun 11 am-8 pm; Sun brunch to 2:30 pm. Closed Dec 25. Res accepted. Continental menu. Bar to 11 pm. Semi-a la carte: dinner $8.25-$19.95. Sun brunch $11.50. Child's meals. Specializes in fresh seafood, prime rib. Restored house; artwork, antique brass chandeliers. 3 dining rms. Cr cds: A, D, DS, MC, V.

D ✍

Hawley (C-9)

(See also Milford, Scranton)

Settled 1827 **Pop** 1,244 **Elev** 920 ft **Area code** 717 **Zip** 18428
Information Pocono Mts Vacation Bureau, 1004 Main St, Stroudsburg 18360; 717/424-6050; for brochures phone 800/POCONOS.

A major attraction in this Pocono resort area is man-made Lake Wallenpaupack, offering summer recreation on the lake as well as winter recreation nearby.

What to See and Do

Claws 'N Paws Wild Animal Park. A zoo in the woods with more than 100 species of exotic animals. Petting zoo with tame deer, lambs and goats. Farmyard area. Parrot, reptile shows; zookeeper talks (schedule varies). Picnicking, snack bar. (May-Oct, daily) 12 mi W via PA 590, near Lake Wallenpaupack. Phone 717/698-6154. ¢¢¢

Gravity Coach. Car used on Pennsylvania Gravity Railroad (22 inclined planes between Hawley and Scranton, 1850-1885). W of town on US 6.

Lake Wallenpaupack. One of the largest man-made lakes in state (5,600 acres), formed by damming of Wallenpaupack Creek. Swimming beach (Memorial Day-day before Labor Day; fee); fishing, boating, water sports; ice fishing; camping. Information center, 1/2 mi NW on US 6 at PA 507 (mid-May-Oct, daily; rest of yr, Thurs-Mon; closed Easter, Thanksgiving, Dec 25). Phone 717/226-2141. **Free.**

Pennsylvania Power & Light Co. Hydroelectric facilities, dam; recreation area. Visitor center near lake has exhibits. Superintendent's office has information on region (Mon-Fri); observation point. (Daily) Approx 1 1/2 mi E on US 6. 717/226-3702. **Free.**

Promised Land State Park. Approx 2,950 acres. Swimming beach; fishing; boating (rentals, mooring, launch). Hiking. Cross-country skiing, snowmobiling, ice-skating, ice fishing. Picnicking, snack bar. Tent & trailer sites, cabins. Nature center, interpretive program. 12 mi S on PA 390. Phone 717/676-3428. Camping ¢¢¢¢-¢¢¢¢¢

Skiing. Tanglwood. 2 double chairlifts, 2 T-bars, rope tow, beginner lift; patrol, school, rentals; snowmaking; cafeteria, bar; nursery. Longest run 1 mi; vertical drop 415 ft. Night skiing. (Early Dec-late Mar, daily) Half-day rates. 4 mi S via PA 390, off I-84 in Tafton. Phone 717/226-7669 or 888/226-SNOW. ¢¢¢¢

Motel

★ **GRESHAM'S LAKEVIEW.** *HC 6, Box 6150, 2 mi E on US 6. 717/226-4621.* 21 rms, 2 story. S, D $68-$73; each addl $5; under 5 free; wkly rates; ski plans; lower rates off-season. Crib free. TV; cable. Complimentary coffee in lobby. Restaurant nearby. Ck-out 11 am. Downhill/x-country ski 2½ mi. Balconies. Overlooks Lake Wallenpaupack. Cr cds: A, DS, MC, V.

[D] [icons]

Inns

★ **FALLS PORT INN.** *330 Main. 717/226-2600.* 9 rms, 5 share bath, 2 story. No rm phones. May-Labor Day: S, D $75-$95; under 2 free; wkend, hol rates (2-day min); ski plans; lower rates rest of yr. Crib free. 2 TVs; cable, VCR avail. Complimentary continental bkfst. Restaurant 11:30 am-9 pm. Rm serv. Ck-out 11 am, ck-in 1 pm. Downhill/x-country ski 9 mi. Built in 1902 as an inn. Cr cds: A, MC, V.

[D] [icons]

★★★ **ROEBLING INN ON THE DELAWARE.** *Scenic Dr (18435), 15 mi E on PA 590. 717/685-7900; FAX 717/685-1718.* 6 rms, 2 story, 4 rms with shower only, 1 rm with kit. July-Aug, AP: S $70-$90, D $75-$95, each addl $10, kit. unit $85-$105. Wkly rates. Min stay wkends, hols. Lower rates rest of yr. TV; cable. Complimentary full bkfst. Restaurant nearby 7 am-9 pm. Ck-out 11:30 am, ck-in 2:30 pm. Luggage handling. Business servs avail. Tennis privileges 1 mi. Downhill, x-country ski 5 mi. Refrigerators. On river. Cr cds: A, DS, MC, V.

[icons]

★★★ **THE SETTLERS INN.** *4 Main Ave. 717/226-2993; FAX 717/226-1874; res: 800/833-8527.* 18 rms, 2 story, 5 suites. S $58-$75; D $83-$113; each addl $15; suites $113-$153; under 12 free. Crib $10. Complimentary full bkfst. Restaurant (see THE SETTLERS INN). Ck-out noon, ck-in 1 pm. Business servs avail. In-rm modem link. Airport transportation. Downhill ski 8 mi; x-country ski 1 mi. Golf course nearby. Bingham Park opp. Tudor-revival manor (1927); stone fireplace, sitting rooms with many antiques. Totally nonsmoking. Cr cds: A, DS, MC, V.

[icons] [SC]

Resort

★★★ **CAESARS COVE HAVEN.** *Lakeville (18438), 8 mi W on PA 590. 717/226-4506; FAX 717/226-4697; res: 800/233-4141.* 282 units, 3 story. MAP: D $180-$320; wkly rates. Adults only. TV, VCR avail (movies $5). Indoor/outdoor pools; whirlpool, poolside serv. Bars 11:30-1:30 am; entertainment. Ck-out 11 am. Coin lndry. Gift shop. Free bus depot transportation. Indoor tennis; racquetball. Driving range, indoor miniature golf. Boats, waterskiing. Snowmobiling. Soc dir. Indoor ice skating and roller skating. Rec rm. Game rm. Exercise equipt; bicycles, rowers, saunas. Refrigerators, some balconies. On lake. Cr cds: A, D, DS, MC, V.

[D] [icons] [SC]

Restaurants

★ **EHRHARDT'S LAKESIDE.** *On PA 507, 1 mi S of US 6. 717/226-2124.* Hrs: 11 am-10 pm; Sun from 9 am; Sun brunch to 12:30 pm. Closed Thanksgiving, Dec 25. Res accepted. Bar. Semi-a la carte: lunch $2.50-$10, dinner $9-$20. Sun brunch $7.95. Child's meals. Specializes in steak, seafood. Tri-level dining area; overlooks lake. Cr cds: A, DS, MC, V.

[D] [♥]

★ **PERNA'S.** *1 mi SW on PA 590. 717/226-3108.* Hrs: 4:30-11 pm; Sun to 10 pm. Closed Mon, Tues, Dec-late Mar. Italian, Amer menu. Bar. Semi-a la carte: dinner $5.25-$15.95. Specializes in homemade pasta. Fireplace. Family-owned. No cr cds accepted.

[D]

★★★ **THE SETTLERS INN.** *(See The Settlers Inn) 717/226-2993.* Hrs: 11:30 am-2 pm, 5-9 pm; Sun brunch to 2 pm. Closed Dec 23-25. Res accepted wkends and July-Aug. Bar. A la carte entrees: lunch $5-$11, dinner $13-$20. Sun brunch $5.95-$10.95. Child's meals. Specializes in pheasant, seafood, trout. Pianist Fri, Sat. Dining rm of Tudor-style hotel constructed in 1920s. Cr cds: A, DS, MC, V.

[D]

Hazleton (D-8)

(See also Ashland, Bloomsburg, Jim Thorpe, Wilkes-Barre)

Settled 1809 **Pop** 24,730 **Elev** 1,660 ft **Area code** 717 **Zip** 18201 **E-mail** hazchamb@ptdprolog.net **Web** hazlechamber.org
Information Greater Hazleton Chamber of Commerce, 1 S Church St, Ste 200; 717/455-1508.

On top of Spring Mountain, Hazleton calls itself the highest city in Pennsylvania. Rich agricultural land surrounds Hazleton, and its early and rapid economic growth was spurred by the rich anthracite coal reserves found in the area. Although coal dominated the town's economy during the 19th century, today there are many diversified industries located here, producing building materials, textiles, office furniture, business forms, foods and food containers, boxes, heavy fabricated steel, plastics, electronic parts and other products.

What to See and Do

Eckley Miners' Village (Pennsylvania Anthracite Museum Complex). Mining coal patch town (1850s) portrays life in the anthracite region until about 1940. Walking tour (Memorial Day-Labor Day; fee). (Daily; closed some hols) 10 mi NE off PA 940, near Freeland. Phone 717/636-2070. ¢¢

National Shrine of the Sacred Heart. Large outdoor shrine includes stations of the cross and crucifixion scene; picnic area. (Mar-Oct, daily) 1½ mi NE on US 309, PA 940, in Harleigh section of Hazleton. Phone 717/455-1162. **Free.**

Motels

★★ **BEST WESTERN GENETTI MOTOR LODGE.** *2 mi N on PA 309. 717/454-2494; FAX 717/455-7793.* 89 rms, 3 story. June-Oct: S $55-$65; D $65-$75; each addl $7; suites $130-$150; under 12 free; higher rates special events; lower rates rest of yr. Crib free. TV; cable, VCR avail (movies). Heated pool; lifeguard. Playground. Complimentary continental bkfst. Ck-out 11 am. Coin lndry. Business servs avail. Valet serv. Sundries. Bus depot transportation. Cr cds: A, C, D, DS, MC, V.

[icons] [SC]

★★ **HOLIDAY INN.** *1½ mi N on PA 309. 717/455-2061; FAX 717/455-9387.* 107 rms, 2 story. S, D, studio rms $72; under 18 free. Crib free. Pet accepted. TV; cable. Pool; lifeguard. Restaurant 6 am-10 pm. Rm serv. Bar 5 pm-2 am. Ck-out noon. Meeting rms. Business servs avail. In-rm modem link. Bellhops. Sundries. Cr cds: A, C, D, DS, ER, JCB, MC, V.

[D] [icons] [SC]

Restaurants

★★★ **SCATTON'S.** *1008 N Vine St.. 717/455-6630.* Hrs: 5-10 pm; Thurs 11:30 am-2 pm, 5-10 pm. Closed Sun; Jan 1, Thanksgiving, Dec 25. Northern Italian menu. Bar. Semi-a la carte: lunch $3.50-$11.25, dinner $10.50-$24.75. Specializes in fresh seafood, veal, pasta. Casual; collection of antique prints. Cr cds: A, C, D, MC, V.

[D]

★ **TOM'S KITCHEN.** *(PA 93, Conyngham 18219) 6 mi NW on PA 93. 717/788-3808.* Hrs: 7 am-8 pm; Sun from 8 am. Closed most major hols. Semi-a la carte: bkfst $3.45-$4.25, lunch $2.75-$3.75, dinner $5.25-$9.95. Child's meals. Specialties: roast turkey platter, stuffed breast of chicken. Family-style restaurant. Family-owned. Totally nonsmoking. No cr cds accepted.

Hershey (E-7)

(See also Cornwall, Harrisburg, Lebanon)

Founded 1903 **Pop** 11,860 **Elev** 420 ft **Area code** 717 **Zip** 17033
Information Information Center, 300 Park Blvd; 800/HERSHEY.

One of America's most fascinating success stories, this planned community takes its name from founder M.S. Hershey, who established his world-famous chocolate factory here in 1903, then built a town around it. The streets have names like Chocolate and Cocoa, and streetlights are shaped like chocolate kisses. But there's more than chocolate here. Today, Hershey is known as one of the most diverse entertainment and resort areas in the eastern US. Hershey is also known as the "golf capital of Pennsylvania" and has a number of well-known golf courses.

What to See and Do

Founders Hall. Campus center of Milton Hershey School, noted for its striking rotunda. (Daily; closed hols) Phone 717/520-2000.

Hershey Gardens. From mid-June to first frost, 8,000 rose plants bloom on 23 acres. Tulip garden (mid-Apr-mid-May). Also chrysanthemums and annuals; 6 theme gardens. (Mid-Apr-Oct, daily) Hotel Rd. Phone 717/534-3492. ¢¢

Hershey Museum. Pennsylvania German, Native American, Eskimo collections; displays of Stiegel glass; "Apostolic Clock" depicting life of Christ; Milton Hershey history. (Daily; closed Jan 1, Thanksgiving, Dec 25) Near entrance to Hersheypark. Phone 717/534-3439. ¢¢ Adj is

Hersheypark Arena. Capacity 10,000; professional hockey, basketball, ice-skating, variety shows, concerts. Phone 717/534-3911.

★ **Hershey's Chocolate World.** Tour via automated conveyance; simulates steps of chocolate production from cacao bean plantations through chocolate making in Hershey. Also tropical gardens, shopping village. (Daily; closed Jan 1, Easter, Thanksgiving, Dec 25) Entrance adj to Hersheypark visitor information. Phone 717/534-4900. **Free.**

Hersheypark Stadium. Seats 17,000; sports and entertainment events. Phone 717/534-3911.

Hersheypark. Theme areas include Rhine Land, Tudor Square, Dutch crafts barn; more than 50 rides; Tower Plaza; live family shows. (Mid-May-Labor Day, daily; May & Sept, selected wknds) Entrance on Hersheypark Dr (PA 39). Phone 800/HERSHEY. ¢¢¢¢ Also here is

ZooAmerica. An 11-acre environmental zoo depicting 5 climatic regions of North America. (Daily; closed some major hols) Combination admission with Hersheypark avail. Phone 717/534-3860. Separate admission ¢¢

Seltzer's Lebanon Bologna Co. Outdoor wooden smokehouses since 1902. Video tours. (Daily exc Sun; closed hols) 230 N College St, 3 blks N of US 422, in Palmyra. Phone 717/838-6336. **Free.**

Annual Events

Chocolate Lovers' Extravaganza. Feb.

Antique Automobile Club. National fall rally. 2nd wkend Oct.

Christmas in Hershey. Mid-Nov-Dec.

Motels

★ **ADDEY'S.** 150 E Governor Rd (US 322E). 717/533-2591. E-mail addeysinn@aol.com; web www.go2pa.com/addeys_inn. 12 rms. May-Labor Day: S, D $65; each addl $5; lower rates rest of yr. Crib $5. TV;

cable (premium). Playground. Complimentary continental bkfst. Ck-out 11 am. Picnic tables. Cr cds: A, DS, MC, V.

★ ★ **BEST WESTERN INN.** US 422 & Sipe Ave. 717/533-5665; FAX 717/533-5675. Web www.bestwestern.com/best.html. 123 rms, 3 story. No elvtr. May-Aug: S, D $99-$159; each addl $10; under 17 free; wkly rates; higher rates special events; lower rates rest of yr. Crib $2. TV; cable (premium). Heated pool; whirlpool. Complimentary continental bkfst. Restaurant nearby. Ck-out noon. Coin lndry. Meeting rms. Business servs avail. In-rm modem link. Valet serv. Game rm. Refrigerators; microwaves avail. Cr cds: A, D, DS, ER, MC, V.

✔ ★ ★ **DAYS INN.** 350 W Chocolate Ave. 717/534-2162; FAX 717/533-6409. Web www.travelweb.com/travel. 75 rms, 4 story. Late June-Aug: S $119-$139; D $129-$149; each addl $5; under 18 free; higher rates antique car shows; lower rates rest of yr. Crib free. TV; cable, VCR avail (movies). Complimentary continental bkfst. Restaurant opp 11:30 am-10 pm. Ck-out 11 am. Valet serv. Free RR station, bus depot transportation. Health club privileges. Some refrigerators; microwaves avail. Cr cds: A, C, D, DS, JCB, MC, V.

★ ★ ★ **HERSHEY LODGE.** W Chocolate Ave, at University Dr. 717/533-3311; FAX 717/533-9642; res: 800/533-3131. Web www.800 hershey.com/~herco. 457 rms, 1-2 story. May-Labor Day: S $130-$157; D $136-$163; each addl $15; suites $250-$425; under 18 free; package plans; lower rates rest of yr. Crib free. TV; cable (premium). 2 pools, 1 indoor; wading pool, whirlpool, poolside serv, lifeguard. Playground. Free supervised child's activities (May-early Sept, late Nov-Jan 1). Complimentary coffee in rms. Restaurant 7 am-10 pm; also dining rm. Bar 11-2 am; entertainment. Ck-out 11 am. Convention facilities. Business servs avail. In-rm modem link. Valet serv. Sundries. Gift shop. Free airport transportation. Lighted tennis. 18-hole golf privileges, greens fee $60-$120, miniature golf. Exercise equipt; weights, bicycles, sauna. Rec rm. Cinema. Cr cds: A, C, D, DS, MC, V.

✔ ★ **MILTON.** 1733 E Chocolate Ave. 717/533-4533; FAX 717/533-0369. 34 rms, 2 story. Mid-May-Labor Day: S $55-$65; D $66-$79; each addl $5; wkly rates Sept-May; higher rates hol wknds; lower rates rest of yr. Crib $6. TV; cable (premium), VCR avail. Heated pool. Restaurant adj 11-2 am. Ck-out 11 am. Business servs avail. In-rm modem link. Game rm. Refrigerators; microwaves avail. Cr cds: A, D, DS, MC, V.

★ **RODEWAY INN.** 43 W Areba. 717/533-7054; FAX 717/533-3405. Web www.rodeway.com. 25 rms, 2 story, 11 kits. Mid-June-early Sept: S $75-$109; D $85-$129; each addl $5; kits. $115-$195; under 18 free; wkly rates; lower rates rest of yr. Crib free. TV; cable. Complimentary coffee in rms. Restaurant nearby. Ck-out 11 am. Business servs avail. In-rm modem link. Some refrigerators; microwaves avail. Cr cds: A, C, D, DS, JCB, MC, V.

✔ ★ **SIMMONS.** 355 W Chocolate Ave, 2 1/2 blks W of town square. 717/533-9177; FAX 717/533-3605. 32 rms, 2 story. June-Oct: S $55-$75; D $65-$95; each addl $5; apt (1-2 bedrm) $110-$185; kit. units $95-$110; wkly, family rates; higher rates antique car show; lower rates rest of yr. Crib free. TV; cable (premium), VCR avail. Complimentary coffee in lobby. Restaurant nearby. Ck-out 11 am. Business servs avail. Health club privileges. Many refrigerators; microwaves avail. Picnic tables, grills. Cr cds: A, DS, MC, V.

✔ ★ **SPINNER'S INN.** 845 E Chocolate Ave. 717/533-9157; res: 800/533-5843; FAX 717/534-1189. 52 rms, 4 with shower only, 2 story. May-mid-Oct: S $65-$95; D $69-$109; each addl $5; suites $89-$139; under 2 free; golf plans; wkends, hols (2-day min); higher rates special events; lower rates rest of yr. Crib $5. TV; cable (premium), VCR avail (movies). Complimentary continental bkfst. Restaurant (see SPIN-

NER'S). Rm serv. Bar. Ck-out 11 am. Business servs avail. Valet serv. Concierge. Heated pool; lifeguard. Game rm. Some refrigerators, microwaves. Some balconies. Picnic tables. Cr cds: A, C, D, DS, MC, V.

★ ★ **WHITE ROSE.** *1060 E Chocolate Ave.* 717/533-9876; FAX 717/533-6923. E-mail whiterose@worldnet.att.net; web www.800hershey .com. 24 rms, 2 story. July-Aug: S, D $108; under 18 free; lower rates rest of yr. Crib $5. TV; cable (premium). Heated pool; lifeguard. Restaurant nearby. Ck-out 11 am. Business servs avail. In-rm modem link. Gift shop. Health club privileges. Refrigerators. Private patios, balconies. Picnic tables. Totally nonsmoking. Cr cds: A, DS, MC, V.

Motor Hotel

★ ★ ★ **HOLIDAY INN HARRISBURG-HERSHEY.** *(604 Station Rd, Grantville 17028)* N on PA 743 to I-81, exit 28. 717/469-0661; FAX 717/469-7755. E-mail info@stayholiday.com; web www.stayholiday.com. 195 rms, 4 story. Memorial Day-mid-Oct: S $119-$149; D $129-$159; each addl $10; suites $175-$275; under 19 free; lower rates rest of yr. Pet accepted. TV; cable, VCR avail. 2 pools, 1 indoor; whirlpool, wading pool. Restaurant 6:30 am-10 pm. Rm serv. Bar 11-2 am; entertainment. Ck-out noon. Coin lndry. Meeting rms. Business center. In-rm modem link. Bellhops. Valet serv. Shopping arcade. Airport, RR station, bus depot transportation. Exercise equipt; weight machine, bicycles, sauna. Lawn games. Microwaves avail. Balconies. Cr cds: A, C, D, DS, ER, JCB, MC, V.

Inn

★ ★ **PINEHURST.** *50 Northeast Dr, on PA 743 off Hersheypark Dr & Park Ave.* 717/533-2603; FAX 717/534-2639; res: 800/743-9140. 15 rms, some share bath, 2 story. No rm phones. S, D $45-$75; each addl $5; 2-day min hols. TV in sitting rm. Complimentary full bkfst. Ck-out 11 am. Airport transportation. Health club privileges. Brick mansion built by Milton Hershey for orphaned boys. Totally nonsmoking. Cr cds: MC, V.

Resort

★ ★ ★ **HOTEL HERSHEY.** *Hotel Rd, off US 322/422.* 717/533-2171; FAX 717/534-8887; res: 800/533-3131. Web www.800hershey.com/-herco. 241 rms, 5 story. MAP, Apr-Oct: S $215-$260; D $255-$310; each addl $61; under 3 free; EP avail; package plans; lower rates rest of yr. Crib free. TV; cable, VCR avail. 2 pools, 1 indoor; whirlpool, wading pool, lifeguard. Supervised child's activities; age 3-16. Restaurants 7 am-11 pm. Rm serv 24 hrs. Bar 11-1 am; entertainment. Ck-out noon, ck-in after 4 pm. Package store 1 mi. Convention facilities. Business center. Bellhops. Valet serv. Gift shop. Airport, RR station, bus depot transportation. 3 tennis courts. 9-hole golf, greens fee $15-$17, putting green. X-country ski on site. Nature trails. Bicycle rentals. Lawn games. Basketball. Carriage rides. Exercise equipt; bicycles, treadmill, sauna. Massage. Extensive gardens, landscaping; scenic hilltop location. Cr cds: A, C, D, DS, MC, V.

Restaurants

★ ★ **DIMITRI'S.** *1311 E Chocolate Ave.* 717/533-3403. Hrs: 11 am-11 pm. Closed Jan 1, Dec 25. Res accepted. Greek, continental menu. Bar to 2 am. Semi-a la carte: lunch $3.95-$7.95, dinner $6.95-$21.95. Child's meals. Specializes in seafood, steak. Cr cds: MC, V.

★ ★ **SPINNER'S.** *(See Spinner's Inn Motel)* 717/533-9050. Hrs: 4-10 pm. Closed Sun, Mon; some major hols. Res accepted. Bar. Semi-a

la carte: dinner $10-$24. Child's meals. Specializes in steak, fresh seafood, pasta. Own baking, pasta. Elegant Colonial decor with chandelier, portraits of historical figures. Cr cds: A, D, DS, MC, V.

★ ★ **UNION CANAL HOUSE.** *107 S Hanover St, in Union Deposit Village.* 717/566-0054. Hrs: 5-10 pm. Closed Sun; major hols. Res accepted. Continental menu. Bar. Semi-a la carte: dinner $8.95-$29.95. Child's meals. Specialties: roast duckling, Angus beef, lump crab cakes. Three dining areas; fireplace, memorabilia from 1800s. Family-owned. Cr cds: A, D, MC, V.

Honesdale (C-9)

(For accommodations see Hawley, Scranton)

Founded 1826 **Pop** 4,972 **Elev** 980 ft **Area code** 717 **Zip** 18431

Information Wayne County Chamber of Commerce, 742 Main St; 717/253-1960 or 800/433-9008.

Named in honor of Philip Hone, a mayor of New York City and first president of the Delaware & Hudson Canal Co, Honesdale was for many years the world's largest coal storage center, transshipping millions of tons of anthracite. A gravity railroad brought coal here in winter; in spring it was reshipped by canal boats to tidewater. The *Stourbridge Lion,* first steam locomotive to operate in the US (1829), was used by the Delaware & Hudson Canal Co, but when the rail bed proved too weak, mule power replaced the steam engine. Today, Honesdale manufactures textile products, business forms and furniture and is surrounded by dairy farms in the beautiful rolling countryside.

What to See and Do

Replica of the Stourbridge Lion (original is in Smithsonian Institution). First steam locomotive to operate in the US (1829). Main St.

Stourbridge Rail Excursions. Scenic rail excursions from Honesdale to Lackawaxen, centering on the change of seasons, with entertainment and activities. Contact the Chamber of Commerce for schedule, fees.

Triple W Riding Stable. 181-acre horse ranch in the NE range of Pocono Mountains. Variety of trail rides for beginners or advanced riders; 1/2- and full-day trips; overnight camping trips. Hay & sleigh rides (seasonal; by appt). (Daily) US 6 through Hawley, left at post office, 3 1/2 mi to "Triple W" sign, turn right. Phone 717/226-2620. ¢¢¢¢¢

Wayne County Historical Society Museum. Dorflinger glass collection. (Apr-Dec, daily; rest of yr, Tues, Thurs, Sat; closed Jan 1, Good Friday, Thanksgiving, Dec 25) 810 Main St. Phone 717/253-3240. ¢

Annual Event

Wayne County Fair. Exhibits, livestock, horse racing. 1st full wk Aug.

Hopewell Furnace National Historic Site (E-8)

(For accommodations see Pottstown, Reading)

(15 mi SE of Reading via US 422, PA 82 to Birdsboro, then SE on Birdsboro-Warwick Rd/PA 345; 10 mi NE of Tpke Morgantown Interchange)

Hopewell, an early industrial community, was built around a charcoal-burning cold-blast furnace, which made pig iron and many other iron products from 1771 to 1883. Nearby mines and forests supplied ore and charcoal for the furnace. The National Park Service has restored the buildings, and interpretive programs emphasize the community's role in the history of American industry. Hopewell is surrounded by the approximately 7,330-acre French Creek State Park (see POTTSTOWN).

The Visitor Center has a museum and audiovisual program on iron-making and community life. Self-guided tour includes: charcoal house, where fuel for furnace was stored; anthracite furnace ruin; waterwheel and blast machinery; casting house, where 16 moulders produced up to 5,000 stoves annually; cold-blast charcoal-burning furnace; blacksmith shop; tenant houses; barn for horses and mules transporting charcoal, ore, iron products to market; office store, which was source of staples, clothing and house furnishings; springhouse, which supplied "refrigeration"; ironmaster's house, home of proprietor or manager. Stove moulding and casting demonstrations (late June-Labor Day; fee). Captioned slide program for the hearing impaired; Braille map and large-print pamphlets for the visually impaired; wheelchair access. (Daily; closed most hols) For further information contact the Superintendent, 2 Mark Bird Lane, Elverson 19520; 610/582-8773 or 610/582-2093 (TDD). ¢¢

Huntingdon (E-5)

(See also Altoona, Orbisonia)

Founded 1767 **Pop** 6,843 **Elev** 643 ft **Area code** 814 **Zip** 16652 **E-mail** rcvb@raystown.org **Web** www.raystown.org

Information Raystown County Visitors Bureau, 241 Mifflin St; 814/643-3577 or 800/269-4684.

Founded on the site of an Oneida village in the Juniata Valley, Huntingdon was first called Standing Stone—for a 14-foot etched stone pillar venerated by Native Americans.

What to See and Do

Indian Caverns. A 1-mi guided tour; extensive scenic beauty and authentic Native American history; relic room contains artifacts, tablet of picture writing; picnic area. (Apr-Oct, daily) 13 mi NW via US 22, PA 45 in Spruce Creek. Phone 814/632-7578 or 814/632-8333. ¢¢¢

Lincoln Caverns. The 1-hr tour of two caves includes Frozen Niagara, Diamond Cascade; visitors' center & gift shop. (Apr-Nov, daily; Mar & Dec, wkends only) 3 mi W on US 22. Phone 814/643-0268. ¢¢¢

Raystown Lake. Large man-made lake, with 110 mi of shoreline. Swimming; fishing, hunting; boating. Hiking. Picnicking, restaurant. Camping. Observation area. Fee for some activities. 7 mi S on PA 26, follow signs to Hesston. Phone 814/658-3405.

Swigart Auto Museum. Changing exhibits of American steam, gas, electric autos. Large collection of nameplates, license plates and auto memorabilia; picnic area. (Memorial Day-Oct, daily) 4 mi E on US 22. Phone 814/643-0885. ¢¢

Annual Event

Hartslog Day. 7 mi NW via US 22, in Alexandria. Heritage festival includes crafts, food, music, games. 2nd Sat Oct.

Motels

★ ★ **DAYS INN.** *RD 1, Box 353, 4th St at US 22. 814/643-3934; FAX 814/643-3005.* 76 rms, 3 story. S $44-$56; D $49-$61; each addl $5; under 13 free; higher rates special events. Crib free. Pet accepted; $5. TV; cable. Restaurant 6 am-10 pm; Fri, Sat to 11 pm. Bar 4:30 pm-2 am. Ck-out 11 am. Meeting rms. Business servs avail. In-rm modem link. Valet serv. Sundries. Microwaves avail. Cr cds: A, C, D, DS, MC, V.

D 🐾 🏊 🐾 SC

✔★ ★ **HUNTINGDON MOTOR INN.** *US 22 & PA 26. 814/643-1133; FAX 814/643-1331.* 48 rms, 2 story. S $37-$40; D $46-$52; each

addl $4. Crib free. Pet accepted, some restrictions. TV; cable. Restaurant 7 am-9 pm. Bar 4:30 pm-2 am. Ck-out 11 pm. Meeting rms. Business servs avail. In-rm modem link. Microwaves avail. Balconies. Cr cds: A, C, D, DS, MC, V.

🐾 🏊 🐾

Indiana (D-3)

(See also Johnstown)

Founded 1805 **Pop** 15,174 **Elev** 1,310 ft **Area code** 724 **Zip** 15701

Information Indiana County Chamber of Commerce, 1019 Philadelphia St; 724/465-2511.

Named after the Native American population in the area, this borough was established on 250 acres donated for a county seat by George Clymer of Philadelphia, a signer of the Declaration of Independence. Indiana University of Pennsylvania (1875) is located here. This is also the birthplace of actor Jimmy Stewart.

What to See and Do

County parks. Blue Spruce. Covers 420 acres. Fishing for bass, perch, catfish and crappie; boating (rowboat, canoe rentals). Winter sports area. Picnicking, grills, playground. (Daily) 6 mi N off PA 110. **Pine Ridge.** Covers 630 acres. Trout fishing. Hiking, nature study. Picnicking. (Daily) SW via US 22 near Blairsville. **Hemlock Lake.** Covers 200 acres. Fishing, small game hunting. Hiking. Ice-skating. Nature study, photography. W on PA 286 near Rossiter. (Daily) For general information phone 724/463-8636 (park commission).

Yellow Creek State Park. Approx 3,000 acres. Swimming beach; fishing, hunting; boating (rentals, launching). Hiking. Cross-country skiing, snowmobiling, sledding, ice-skating, ice fishing, ice boating. Picnicking, playground, snack bar. Standard fees. 12 mi E via US 422. Phone 724/357-7913.

Motels

★ ★ **BEST WESTERN UNIVERSITY INN.** *1545 Wayne Ave. 724/349-9620; FAX 724/349-2620.* 107 rms, 2 story. S $55-$65; D $60-$70; each addl $5; under 12 free; higher rates special university events. Crib free. TV; cable (premium). Heated pool. Coffee in rms. Restaurant 6:30 am-1:30 pm, 5-9 pm; Sun 8 am-1:30 pm. Rm serv. Bar 4 pm-midnight. Ck-out noon. Meeting rms. In-rm modem link. Cr cds: A, C, D, DS, MC, V.

D 🏊 🐾 🐾 SC

★ ★ ★ **HOLIDAY INN.** *1395 Wayne Ave. 724/463-3561; FAX 724/463-8006.* 159 rms, 2 story. S, D $79; suites $125; family, wkend rates; golf plans; higher rates university events. Crib free. Pet accepted. TV; cable (premium). Indoor pool; whirlpool, sauna, poolside serv, lifeguard. Complimentary full bkfst. Restaurant 6:30 am-10 pm; Sat, Sun from 7 am. Rm serv. Bar 2 pm-2 am; entertainment. Ck-out noon. Meeting rms. Business servs avail. In-rm modem link. Miniature golf. Game rm. Cr cds: A, C, D, DS, MC, V.

D 🐾 🏊 🐾 🐾 SC

Jenkintown (F-10)

(For accommodations see Fort Washington, Philadelphia, Willow Grove)

Pop 4,574 **Elev** 250 ft **Area code** 215 **Zip** 19046 **E-mail** vlyforge @libertynet.org **Web** www.valleyforge.org
Information Valley Forge Convention & Visitors Bureau, 600 W Germantown Pike, Suite 130, Plymouth Meeting 19462; 610/834-1550.

What to See and Do

Beth Sholom Synagogue. The only synagogue designed by Frank Lloyd Wright. (By appt) Old York & Foxcroft Rds, 1 mi S, in Elkins Park. Phone 215/887-1342. **Free.**

Restaurants

★ ★ **JOHNNY MOTT'S.** *(8460 Limekiln Pike, Cedarbrook Hill Apts, bldg #1, Wyncote 19095-2695) Jct PA 309 & Greenwood Ave. 215/887-1263.* Hrs: 11:30 am-2 pm, 4:30-10 pm; Sat 4:30-11 pm; Sun from 4:30 pm. Closed Jan 1, Dec 25. Res accepted. Continental, seafood menu. Bar. Semi-a la carte: lunch $5.95-$8.50, dinner $14.95-$23.95. Specialties: seafood pescatore, lobster diablo, trout with basil and crabmeat. Valet parking. Cr cds: A, C, D, MC, V.

✔ ★ ★ **STAZI MILANO.** *Township Line & Greenwood Ave, in Jenkintown RR station. 215/885-9000.* Hrs: 11:30 am-3 pm, 4-10:30 pm; Fri, Sat 5 pm-midnight; Sun 4-9 pm; early-bird dinner Mon-Thurs 4-6 pm. Italian menu. Bar to midnight; Fri, Sat to 2 am. Semi-a la carte: lunch $6.95-$10.95, dinner $6.95-$16.95. In 1931 RR station; mahogany railings. Cr cds: A, D, MC, V.

Jim Thorpe (D-9)

(See also Hazleton)

Settled 1815 **Pop** 5,048 **Elev** 600 ft **Area code** 717 **Zip** 18229
Information Carbon County Tourist Promotion Agency Information Center, PO Box 90; 717/325-3673 or 888/JIM-THORPE.

The twin towns, Mauch Chunk (Bear Mountain) and East Mauch Chunk, built on the sides of a narrow gorge of the Lehigh River, merged in 1954 and adopted the name of Jim Thorpe, the great Native American athlete. This, together with a "nickel-a-week" plan whereby each man, woman and child paid five cents to promote the community and attract industry, gave the area (formerly dependent on coal mining) a new lease on economic life. Little has changed in appearance after more than a century; a walking tour will reveal 19th-century architecture.

What to See and Do

Asa Packer Mansion. Former showplace home of founder of Lehigh Valley Railroad and Lehigh University, one of state's wealthiest men. Packer's house, treasures and money were left to the borough. (June-Oct, daily; Apr-May, wkends) Packer Hill. Phone 717/325-3229. ¢¢ Adj is

Jim Thorpe Memorial. A 20-ton granite mausoleum built in memory of the 1912 Olympic champion. 1 mi E on PA 903.

Stone Row. 16 townhouses built by Asa Packer for the engineers on his railroad; reminiscent of Philadelphia's Elfreth's Alley. Some are stores open to the public. Race St, downtown. Also here is

St Mark's Church. Has Tiffany windows and copy of reredos from Windsor Castle. (June-Oct, daily; Apr-May, wkends) Phone 717/325-2241. ¢¢

Whitewater rafting. On upper and lower gorges of Lehigh River.

Pocono Whitewater Adventures. Also bike tours. (Mar-Nov, daily) 8 mi NE of Jim Thorpe Bridge on PA 903. For information, reservations phone 717/325-3655. ¢¢¢¢¢

Jim Thorpe River Adventures, Inc. (Mar-Nov, daily) Coalport Rd, NE via PA 903. For information, reservations phone 717/325-2570 or 717/325-4960. ¢¢¢¢¢

Annual Events

Laurel Blossom Festival. Arts & crafts, entertainment, food, steam train rides. Early or mid-June.

Fall Foliage Festival. Arts & crafts, food, entertainment. Scenic 3-hr train rides. Mid-Oct.

Inn

★ ★ ★ **INN AT JIM THORPE.** *24 Broadway. 717/325-2599; FAX 717/325-9145; res: 800/329-2599.* 27 rms, 4 story. S $70-$90; D $70-$110; each addl $10. Crib free. TV; cable. Complimentary continental bkfst. Dining rm 11:30 am-9 pm. Bar 11:30-2 am; entertainment Sat. Ck-out 11 am, ck-in 2 pm. Business servs avail. Victorian-era hotel (1864), with ornamental-iron galleries, hosted Buffalo Bill, Thomas Edison, John D. Rockefeller, and Presidents Grant & Taft. Restored with period furnishings. Cr cds: A, D, DS, MC, V.

Johnstown (E-3)

(See also Ebensburg, Ligonier)

Settled 1800 **Pop** 28,134 **Elev** 1,180 ft **Area code** 814 **E-mail** chamber @ctcnet.net
Information Greater Johnstown/Cambria County Convention & Visitors Bureau, 111 Market St, 15901-1608; 814/536-7993 or 800/237-8590.

On May 31, 1889, a break in the South Fork Dam that impounded an old reservoir 10 miles east of the city, poured a wall of water onto the city in the disastrous "Johnstown Flood." The death toll rose to 2,209, and property damage totaled $17 million. The city has been flooded 22 times since 1850, most recently in 1977.

Founded by a Swiss Mennonite, Joseph Johns, the city today is the center of Cambria County's iron and steel industry, producing iron and steel bars, railroad cars, parts and railroad supplies.

What to See and Do

Conemaugh Gap. Gorge, 7 mi long and 1,700 ft deep, cuts between Laurel Hill Ridge and Chestnut Ridge. Located at the W end of the city.

Grandview Cemetery. 777 unidentified victims of the 1889 flood are buried under blank headstones in the "Unknown Plot." 1 mi W on PA 271, in Westmont.

Inclined Plane Railway. Joins Johnstown and Westmont. Ride is on steep (72% grade) passenger incline 500-ft ascent. Counterbalanced cable cars take 50 passengers and 2 automobiles each. (Daily; closed Jan 1, Dec 25) Vine St & Roosevelt Blvd. Phone 814/536-1816. ¢

Johnstown Flood Museum. Museum depicts history of Johnstown, with permanent exhibits on 1889 Johnstown Flood; Academy Award-winning film, photographs, artifacts, memorabilia. (Daily; closed some hols) 304 Washington St. Phone 814/539-1889. ¢¢

Johnstown Flood National Memorial. Commemorates 1889 Johnstown Flood; preserved remnants of the South Fork Dam. Visitor center with exhibits, 30-min movie (daily; closed Dec 25) Jct US 219, PA 869. Phone 814/495-4643. ¢

Motels

✔★ ★ **COMFORT INN.** *455 Theatre Dr (15904), US 219 exit Elton.* 814/266-3678; FAX 814/266-9783. 117 rms, 5 story, 27 suites. S $57-$63; D $63-$69; each addl $6; suites $84-$91; kit. units $94-$99; under 18 free; monthly rates; higher rates special events. Crib free. Pet accepted; $6. TV; cable, VCR (movies). Indoor pool; whirlpool, lifeguard. Complimentary continental bkfst. Restaurant nearby. Ck-out noon. Coin lndry. Meeting rms. Business center. In-rm modem link. Sundries. Free airport transportation. Exercise equipt; weights, bicycles. Health club privileges. Refrigerator, wet bar in suites; microwaves avail. Picnic table, grill. Cr cds: A, C, D, DS, ER, JCB, MC, V.

D ✔ ≈ 🕆 🛇 🔥 SC 🏃

✔★ **SLEEP INN.** *453 Theatre Dr (15904).* 814/262-9292; FAX 814/262-0486. 62 rms, 59 with shower only, 3 story. S $49-$55; D $55-$61; under 18 free; wkly rates; higher rates: Labor Day, sporting events. Crib free. Pet accepted, some restrictions; $6. TV; cable (premium), VCR avail. Complimentary continental bkfst. Restaurant adj 11 am-9 pm. Ck-out noon. Meeting rm. Business servs avail. In-rm modem link. Airport transportation. Microwaves avail. Cr cds: A, C, D, DS, ER, JCB, MC, V.

D ✔ ≈ 🛇 🔥 SC

Hotel

★ ★ **HOLIDAY INN-DOWNTOWN.** *250 Market St (15901), US 219 exit 56W.* 814/535-7777; FAX 814/539-1393. 164 rms, 6 story. S, D $72-$89; suites $238-$290; under 18 free. Crib free. Pet accepted, some restrictions. TV; cable (premium). Indoor pool; whirlpool, sauna, poolside serv, lifeguard. Coffee in rms. Restaurant 7 am-10 pm. Bar 4 pm-midnight. Ck-out noon. Meeting rms. Business center. In-rm modem link. Airport transportation. Exercise equipt; bicycles, treadmills. Health club privileges. Cr cds: A, C, D, DS, JCB, MC, V.

D ✔ ≈ 🕆 🛇 🔥 SC 🏃

Restaurant

★ ★ **SURF N'TURF.** *100 Valley Pike.* 814/536-9250. Hrs: 4-10 pm; Sun 11 am-8 pm. Closed Dec 25. Bar. Semi-a la carte: dinner $8.95-$32.95. Child's meals. Specializes in seafood, steak. Salad bar. Pianist Sat eve. Cr cds: A, C, D, DS, MC, V.

D

Kane (B-4)

(For accommodations see Clarion; also see Warren)

Settled 1864 **Pop** 4,590 **Elev** 2,000 ft **Area code** 814 **Zip** 16735
Information Seneca Highlands Tourist Association, Jct 770 W & US 219, PO Box H, Custer City 16725; 814/368-9370.

Situated on a lofty plateau, Kane offers hunting, fishing and abundant winter sports. Summers are cool and winters are bracing. Allegheny National Forest is to the north, west and south; there are scenic drives through 4,000 acres of virgin timber. General Thomas L. Kane of "Mormon War" fame settled here and laid out the community, which prospered as a lumber and railroad town. General Ulysses Grant was once arrested here for fishing without a license.

What to See and Do

Bendigo State Park. Approx 100 acres. Swimming pool; fishing. Sledding. Standard fees. 9 mi SE on PA 321, then 7 mi S on US 219, then 3 mi NE on unnumbered road. Phone 814/965-2646.

Kinzua Bridge State Park. An approx 300-acre park surrounds Kinzua Bridge. When built in 1882, the bridge was the highest railroad bridge in the world, taking its 2,053-ft span 301 ft above the Kinzua Creek. Overlooks, picnicking. (Daily) 12 mi E via US 6 in Mt Jewett. Phone 814/965-2646. **Free.**

Thomas L. Kane Memorial Chapel (1878). Built as a chapel for the new town under the direction of General Kane, a Civil War hero and humanitarian who championed the persecuted Mormons. Visitor center includes film of General Kane's life; small museum. (Tues-Sat) 30 Chestnut St. Phone 814/837-9729. **Free.**

Twin Lakes. Swimming (fee); fishing. Hiking. Picnicking. Camping (fee). 8 mi S of E Kane on PA 321, then 2 mi N on Forest Rd 191, in Allegheny National Forest. Phone 814/723-5150.

Kempton
(see Hamburg)

Kennett Square (F-9)

(See also West Chester; also see Wilmington, DE)

Settled 1705 **Pop** 5,218 **Elev** 370 ft **Area code** 610 **Zip** 19348 **Web** www.brandywinevalley.com
Information Chester County Tourist Bureau, 601 Westtown Rd, Ste 170, West Chester 19382; 610/344-6365 or 800/228-9933; or the Southeastern Chester County Chamber of Commerce, 206 E State St, PO Box 395; 610/444-0774.

What to See and Do

Barns-Brinton House (1714). Authentically restored 18th-century tavern, now a house museum furnished in the period. Guides in colonial costume offer interpretive tours; domestic art demonstrations. (June-Aug, Sat-Sun; also by appt) 5¹/₂ mi NE on US 1, in Chadds Ford. Phone 610/388-7376. ¢

Brandywine Battlefield. Includes Lafayette's quarters and Washington's headquarters. Here, and around Chadds Ford, the Battle of the Brandywine (1777) took place—a decisive battle for Washington. Visitor center with exhibits; tours of historic buildings; museum shop. Picnicking. (Daily exc Mon; closed some hols) 2 mi W of jct US 1, 202, near Chadds Ford. Phone 610/459-3342. House tours ¢¢; **Free.**

Brandywine River Museum. Converted 19th-century gristmill houses largest collection of paintings by Andrew Wyeth and other Wyeth family members; also collections of American illustration, still life and landscape painting. Nature trail; wildflower gardens; restaurant, museum shop, guided tours. (Daily; closed Dec 25) 7 mi NE on US 1, in Chadds Ford. Phone 610/388-2700. ¢¢

Chaddsford Winery. Tours of boutique winery, housed in renovated old barn; view of production process; tasting room. Tours; tastings. (Schedule varies) 5 mi NE on US 1, in Chadds Ford. Phone 610/388-6221. ¢¢

John Chads House. Stone building (ca 1725) is fine example of early 18th-century Pennsylvania architecture; authentically restored and furnished as a house museum. Narrated tours by guides in colonial costume; baking demonstrations in beehive oven. (May-Sept, Sat-Sun; also by appt) 7 mi NE via US 1, then ¹/₄ mi N on PA 100, in Chadds Ford. Phone 610/388-7376. ¢

🟥 **Longwood Gardens.** Longwood was the estate of Pierre S. du Pont, chairman of the board of both Du Pont Chemicals and General Motors, who designed the 1,050 acres of gardens around Peirce's Park, a grove of trees planted in 1798. Estate includes the original grove; the Peirce-du Pont House (1730); a variety of exterior gardens, including the rose, peony, wisteria, idea, hillside, heath, waterlily and topiary gardens; the Italian Water Garden, Open Air Theatre and Main Fountain Garden, which together feature more than 1,700 water jets; and the neoclassical conservatories, nearly 4 acres under glass, housing indoor gardens that are among the most spectacular in the world. Display of color-illuminated fountains (Memorial Day wkend-Sept, Tues, Thurs & Sat evenings). Organ concerts, orchestral concerts, plays, holiday displays, horticultural lectures (schedules at visitor center). Restaurant (see THE TERRACE); picnic areas; museum shop. (Daily) 3 mi NE on US 1. Phone 610/388-1000. ¢¢¢

Phillips Mushroom Museum. Museum explains history, lore and mystique of mushrooms through motion picture, diorama, slides and exhibits. Gift shop. (Daily; closed some major hols) 2 mi NE on US 1. Phone 610/388-6082. ¢

Motel

★ **LONGWOOD INN.** *815 E Baltimore Pike (US 1).* 610/444-3515; FAX 610/444-4285. 28 rms. S $74; D $80; each addl $6; under 12 free. Crib free. TV; VCR avail. Ck-out noon. Business servs avail. Cr cds: A, D, DS, MC, V.

D ⊠ 🐾 SC

Motor Hotel

★ ★ ★ **MENDENHALL HOTEL & CONFERENCE CENTER.** *(PA 52, Mendenhall 19357) 3 mi N on US 1.* 610/388-2100; FAX 610/388-1184. Web www.brandywinevalley.com. 70 rms, 3 story. S $99; D $109; each addl $15; suites $140-$195; under 12 free. Crib free. TV; cable (premium), VCR avail (free movies). Complimentary continental bkfst. Bar from 11:30 am. Ck-out noon. Meeting rms. Business center. In-rm modem link. Bellhops. Valet serv. Concierge. Airport transportation avail. Exercise equipt; weights, bicycles. Bathrm phones, minibars. Cr cds: A, C, D, DS, MC, V.

D 🏋 ⛷ 🐾 SC 🚶

Inns

★ ★ ★ **BRANDYWINE RIVER HOTEL.** *(Box 1058, US 1 & PA 100, Chadds Ford 19317) Approx 6 mi E on US 1.* 610/388-1200; FAX 610/388-1200. 40 rms, 2 story, 10 suites. S, D $119; each addl $10; suites $140. Crib free. Pet accepted, some restrictions. TV; cable. Complimentary continental bkfst. Restaurant adj 11:30 am-10 pm. Ck-out 11 am, ck-in 2 pm. Meeting rms. Business servs avail. Airport, RR station, bus depot transportation. Exercise equipt; stair machine, treadmill. Bathrm phones; refrigerator in suites. Specialty shops on site. Cr cds: A, C, D, DS, MC, V.

D 🐾 🏋 ⛷ 🐾 SC

★ ★ ★ **FAIRVILLE.** *(506 Kennett Pike, Mendenhall 19357) 2 mi S of US 1 on PA 52.* 610/388-5900; FAX 610/388-5902. 15 rms, 2 story. S, D $135-$195; each addl $15. Adults preferred. TV; cable. Complimentary bkfst. Ck-out 11 am, ck-in after 3 pm. Business servs avail. Some fireplaces. Private patios, balconies. Built in 1826; antiques, period decor. View of surrounding countryside. Totally nonsmoking. Cr cds: A, DS, MC, V.

D ⊠ 🐾

★ ★ **SCARLETT HOUSE.** *503 W State St.* 610/444-9592; res: 800/820-9592. E-mail janes10575@aol.com; web www.virtualcities.com/ons/pa/a/paa27020.htm. 4 rms, 2 with bath, 2 story, 1 suite. No rm phones. S, D $75-$125; suite $125. TV; cable (premium). Complimentary full bkfst. Restaurant nearby. Ck-out 11 am, ck-in 4 pm. Street parking. American Foursquare house built in 1910; Victorian decor. 3 sitting rms. Totally nonsmoking. Cr cds: A, DS, MC, V.

⊠ 🐾

Restaurants

★ **KENNETT SQUARE INN.** *201 E State St.* 610/444-5687. Hrs: 11:30 am-2:30 pm, 5:30-10 pm; Sun 4-8 pm; Mon, Tues to 9 pm. Closed Jan 1, Dec 25. Res accepted. Bar 11:30-2 am. Semi-a la carte: lunch $4.50-$10, dinner $10.95-$25.95. Specializes in fresh mushroom

dishes. Entertainment Wed, Sat. Restored country inn (1835). Cr cds: A, C, D, MC, V.

D ⎘

★ ★ ★ **MENDENHALL INN.** *(PA 52, Mendenhall 19357) 3 mi N on US 1 to PA 52.* 610/388-1181. Web www.brandywinevalley.com. Hrs: 11:30 am-2:30 pm, 5-10 pm; Sun 4-8 pm; Sun brunch 10 am-2 pm. Closed Dec 25. Res required. Continental menu. Bar. Wine cellar. Semi-a la carte: lunch $6-$15, dinner $18-$29. Sun brunch $21.95. Child's meals. Specializes in veal, seafood, wild game. Pianist, harpist. Valet parking. Country inn; colonial decor. Cr cds: A, C, D, DS, MC, V.

D ⎘

✔ ★ ★ ★ **THE TERRACE.** *Longwood Gardens.* 610/388-6771. Hrs: 11 am-4 pm; dinner hrs same as Longwood Gardens; wkend hrs vary; Dec to 7:30 pm. Cafeteria 10 am-4 pm; wkend hrs vary; Jan, Feb 11 am-3 pm; Dec 10 am-8 pm. Dining rm closed Jan-Mar. Res accepted. Bar. Semi-a la carte: lunch $6.95-$13.95, dinner $9.95-$18.95. Child's meals. Specialties: crab cakes, mushroom strudel, snapper soup. Salad bar. Cafeteria avg ck: lunch, dinner $7. Outdoor dining. Admission to Longwood Gardens required. Cr cds: A, MC, V.

D

King of Prussia (F-9)

(See also Norristown, Philadelphia, West Chester)

Settled early 1700s **Pop** 18,406 **Elev** 200 ft **Area code** 610 **Zip** 19406
E-mail vlyforge@libertynet.org **Web** www.valleyforge.org
Information Valley Forge Convention & Visitors Bureau, 600 W Germantown Pike, Suite 130, Plymouth Meeting 19462; 610/834-1550.

Originally named Reeseville for the Welsh family that owned the land, the town changed its name to that of the local inn, which is still standing. The area around the town is full of historic interest.

What to See and Do

Harriton House (1704). Early American domestic architecture of the Philadelphia area. Originally 700-acre estate, now 16 1/2 acres. House of Charles Thomson, Secretary of the Continental Congresses; restored to early 18th-century period. Nature park. (Wed-Sat; Sun by appt; closed hols) 6 mi SE via Old Gulph Rd to Harriton Rd, in Bryn Mawr. Phone 610/525-0201. ¢

Mill Grove (1762). Includes 175-acre wildlife sanctuary, developed around the first American home of ornithologist John James Audubon, now a museum. Prints, including complete elephant folio. Hiking trails. (Tues-Sat, also Sun afternoons; closed Jan 1, Thanksgiving, Dec 25) 5 mi NW via US 422 & Audubon Rd, N of Valley Forge National Historic Park, on Pawlings Rd, in Audubon. Phone 610/666-5593. **Free.**

Swiss Pines. Japanese gardens featuring azalea and rhododendron collection; ponds, waterfalls, winding pathway; herb and groundcover garden. Children under 12 yrs not permitted. (Mid-Apr-Nov, Mon-Fri, also Sat mornings; closed hols & inclement weather) 6 mi SW via PA 202, Great Valley exit, on Charlestown Rd in Malvern. Phone 610/933-6916. **Free.**

Valley Forge National Historical Park (see). Just W of town.

Motels

★ ★ ★ **BEST WESTERN.** *127 S Gulph Rd, jct US 202, I-76, PA Tpk.* 610/265-4500; FAX 610/337-0672. 168 units, 2 story. S, D $85-$105; each addl $10; under 12 free. Crib free. TV; cable (premium). Pool. Complimentary continental bkfst. Restaurants adj. Ck-out noon. Coin lndry. Business servs avail. In-rm modem link. Valet serv. Airport transportation. Health club privileges. Some bathrm phones. Private patios, balconies. Cr cds: A, C, D, DS, MC, V.

`D` `≈` `✕` `⊠` `SC`

★ ★ ★ **COURTYARD BY MARRIOTT.** *(1100 Drummers Lane, Wayne 19087) S on US 202, Warner Rd exit.* 610/687-6700; FAX 610/687-1149. 150 rms, 2 story. S, D $59-$144; suites $149-$159; under 16 free; wkly, wkend rates. TV; cable (premium). Indoor pool. Complimentary coffee in rms. Restaurant 6:30-10 am. Bar 5-10 pm. Ck-out 1 pm. Coin lndry. Meeting rms. Business servs avail. In-rm modem link. Valet serv. Sundries. Exercise equipt; weight machine, bicycle. Refrigerator, microwaves avail. Many balconies. Cr cds: A, D, DS, MC, V.

`D` `≈` `✕` `⊠` `⚏` `SC`

✔★ **McINTOSH INN.** *260 N Gulph Rd.* 610/768-9500; FAX 610/768-0225; res: 800/444-2775. 212 rms, 7 story. S $59.95; D $59.95-$74.95; each addl $5. Crib free. TV; cable (premium). Complimentary coffee in lobby. Restaurant adj open 24 hrs. Ck-out 11 am. Business servs avail. In-rm modem link. Valet serv Mon-Fri. Microwaves avail. Cr cds: A, C, D, MC, V.

`D` `⊠` `⚏` `SC`

Motor Hotels

✔★ ★ **COMFORT INN-VALLEY FORGE.** *550 W DeKalb (US 202N).* 610/962-0700; FAX 610/962-0218. 121 rms, 5 story. S, D $85-$129; under 18 free; wkend rates. Crib free. TV; cable (premium), VCR avail. Complimentary continental bkfst. Ck-out noon. Coin lndry. Meeting rm. Business servs avail. Concierge. Airport transportation. Exercise equipt; weights, treadmill. Some bathrm phones, minibars. Cr cds: A, C, D, DS, ER, JCB, MC, V.

`D` `✕` `⊠` `⚏` `SC`

★ ★ ★ **HOLIDAY INN.** *(260 Mall Blvd, Valley Forge) Exit 24 I-76, US 202 N to Mall Blvd.* 610/265-7500; FAX 610/265-4076. 225 rms, 5 story. S, D $119; each addl $10; under 19 free. Crib free. TV; cable (premium). Restaurant 6:30 am-9:30 pm. Rm serv. Bar 11-2 am. Ck-out 11 am. Meeting rms. Business center. In-rm modem link. Bellhops. Valet serv. Gift shop. Barber, beauty shop. Health club privileges. Microwaves avail. Cr cds: A, C, D, DS, ER, JCB, MC, V.

`D` `✦` `✕` `⊠` `⚏` `SC` `🏃`

Hotels

★ ★ ★ **HILTON VALLEY FORGE.** *251 W DeKalb Pike (PA 202N).* 610/337-1200; FAX 610/337-2224. 340 rms, 9 story. S, D $99-$119; each addl $10; suites $130-$475; under 18 free; wkend rates. Crib free. TV; cable (premium), VCR avail. Indoor/outdoor pool; whirlpool, lifeguard. Restaurants 6:30 am-11 pm. Bars 11:30-2 am; entertainment Tues-Sat. Ck-out noon. Meeting rms. Business center. In-rm modem link. Concierge. Gift shop. Garage parking. Airport, bus depot transportation. Exercise equipt; weights, bicycles, sauna. Luxury level. Cr cds: A, C, D, DS, ER, JCB, MC, V.

`D` `≈` `✕` `⊠` `⚏` `SC` `🏃`

★ ★ ★ **MARRIOTT SUITES VALLEY FORGE.** *(888 Chesterbrook Blvd, Wayne 19087) I-76 exit 26B to US 202S, at Chesterbrook exit; adj to Valley Forge Historical Park.* 610/647-6700; FAX 610/889-9420. 229 suites, 5 story. Suites $149-$189; each addl $20; under 16 free; wkend rates. Crib free. TV; cable (premium), VCR avail. Indoor pool; whirlpool, sauna, lifeguard. Coffee in rms. Restaurant (see TOWN AND COUNTRY GRILLE). Bar 11:30 am-midnight; wkends to 1 am. Ck-out noon. Meeting rms. Business servs avail. In-rm modem link. Gift shop. Airport, RR station, bus depot transportation. Tennis privileges. Exercise equipt; weights, bicycles, sauna. Refrigerators, bathrm phones; microwaves avail. Cr cds: A, C, D, DS, JCB, MC, V.

`D` `✦` `≈` `✕` `⊠` `⚏` `SC`

★ ★ ★ **SHERATON-VALLEY FORGE.** *1160 First Ave.* 610/337-2000; FAX 610/768-3222. Web www.sheratonvalleyforge.com. 489 rms,

15 story. S, D $130-$160; each addl $12; suites $145-$225. Crib. TV; cable (premium), VCR avail. Heated pool; whirlpool, poolside serv, lifeguard. Coffee in rms. Restaurant 6:30 am-11:30 pm; wkends to midnight. Bars 11-2 am; entertainment. Ck-out noon. Convention facilities. Business center. In-rm modem link. Concierge. Airport, RR station, bus depot transportation. Exercise equipt; weights, bicycles, sauna, steam rm. Microwaves avail. Wet bar in suites. Cr cds: A, C, D, DS, ER, JCB, MC, V.

`D` `≈` `✕` `✦` `✈` `⊠` `SC` `🏃`

★ ★ ★ **WAYNE.** *(139 E Lancaster Ave, Wayne 19087) S on US 202, S on PA 252 to US 30; from Blue Rte (I-476), exit 5 to US 30W.* 610/687-5000; FAX 610/687-8387; res: 800/962-5850. 37 rms, 6 story. S, D $125-$149; each addl $10; suites $159-$179; under 12 free; wkend rates. Crib free. TV; cable (premium). Pool. Complimentary continental bkfst. Restaurant (see TAQUET). Bar 11:30 am-midnight. Ck-out noon. Meeting rms. Business servs avail. In-rm modem link. Concierge. Airport, RR station transportation. Health club privileges. Microwaves avail. Restored Victorian building (1906) with ornate furnishings, antiques. Cr cds: A, D, DS, MC, V.

`D` `≈` `⊠` `⚏` `SC`

Restaurants

★ ★ ★ **LA FOURCHETTE.** *(110 N Wayne Ave, Wayne 19087) S on US 202, S on PA 252, E on US 30.* 610/687-8333. Hrs: 6-10 pm; Sat from 5:30 pm; Sun brunch 11 am-2 pm. Closed major hols. Res accepted. Classical seasonal French menu. Bar 6 pm-midnight. Wine cellar. A la carte entrees: dinner $18-$28. Sun brunch $12.50-$18.75. Specializes in seafood, lamb, game. Own pastries. Formal atmosphere. Cr cds: A, C, D, DS, MC, V.

`D` `⬑` `♥`

✔★ ★ **LOTUS INN.** *(440 W Swedesford Rd, Berwyn 19312) S on US 202, exit Devon, left on Valley Forge Rd, right on PA 252 1/2 mi.* 610/725-8888. Hrs: 11:30 am-10 pm; Fri to 11 pm; Sat noon-11 pm; Sun from noon; Sun brunch to 3 pm. Closed Thanksgiving. Res accepted; required Fri-Sun. Chinese, Japanese menu. Bar. Semi-a la carte: lunch $5.95-$14.95, dinner $5.95-$18.95. Sun brunch $9.95. Child's meals. Specialties: sushi, sashimi, General Tso's chicken. Oriental decor; sushi bar. Cr cds: A, C, D, DS, MC, V.

`D` `⬑`

★ ★ ★ **SAMUELS.** *(503 W Lancaster Ave, Wayne 19087) S on US 202, S on PA 252, E on US 30.* 610/687-2840. E-mail eaglenes@ix. netcom.com. Hrs: 11:30 am-2:30 pm, 6-10 pm. Res accepted. Contemporary Amer menu. Bar. Wine list. A la carte entrees: lunch $7-$14, dinner $17-$25. Specializes in seafood. Own desserts. Jazz Wed-Sat. Outdoor dining. Cr cds: A, C, D, DS, MC, V.

`D` `⬑`

★ ★ ★ **TAQUET.** *(See Wayne Hotel)* 610/687-5005. Hrs: 11:30 am-2:30 pm, 5:30-10 pm; Fri, Sat to 10:30 pm. Closed Sun; Jan 1, Dec 25. Res accepted. French menu. Bar. Semi-a la carte: lunch $8-$16.50, dinner $16.50-$24.50. Specializes in venison, seasonal fish, grilled duck. Outdoor dining. Victorian decor. Cr cds: A, C, D, DS, MC, V.

`D` `⬑` `♥`

★ ★ ★ **TOWN AND COUNTRY GRILLE.** *(See Marriott Suites Valley Forge Hotel)* 610/647-6700. Hrs: 7 am-2 pm, 5-10 pm; Fri, Sat to 11 pm. Res accepted. Bar. A la carte entrees: bkfst, lunch $6.95-$10.95, dinner $13.95-$22.95. Buffet: bkfst, lunch $8.95. Sun brunch $10.95. Child's meals. Specializes in pasta, grilled steak, seafood. Salad bar (lunch buffet). Country furnishings. View of Valley Forge National Park. Cr cds: A, C, D, DS, JCB, MC, V.

`D` `SC` `♥`

★ ★ ★ **VILLA STRAFFORD.** *(115 Strafford Ave, Wayne 19087) S on US 202, S on PA 252, E on US 30.* 610/964-1116. Hrs: 11:30 am-2:30 pm, 5:30-10 pm. Closed Sun; Jan 1, July 4, Dec 25. Res accepted. Continental menu. Bar. Wine cellar. A la carte entrees: lunch $9-$14, dinner $16.95-$27.95. Specialties: rack of lamb, Dover sole. Own pasta, desserts. Jazz Fri-Sat. Mansion built in 1909. Cr cds: A, D, MC, V.

[D] [символ]

✔★★ **WILD ONION.** (900 Conestoga Rd, Rosemont 19010) I-476, exit 5. 610/527-4826. Hrs: 11:30 am-11 pm. Res accepted. Bar to 2 am. Semi-a la carte: lunch $5.25-$7.95, dinner $8.95-$18.95. Child's meals. Specializes in fresh seafood, in-season produce, assorted beers. Totally nonsmoking. Cr cds: A, D, DS, MC, V.

Kulpsville (E-9)

(See also Norristown, Philadelphia)

Pop 1,200 (est) **Elev** 290 ft **Area code** 215 **Zip** 19443 **E-mail** vlyforge @libertynet.org **Web** www.valleyforge.com
Information Valley Forge Country Convention & Visitors Bureau, 600 W Germantown Pike, Suite 130, Plymouth Meeting 19462; 610/834-1550.

What to See and Do

Morgan Log House (1695). Built by the grandfather of General Daniel Morgan and Daniel Boone, this is the oldest and finest surviving medieval-style log house in the country. Partially restored; authentic early 18th-century furnishings. Guided tours (late Apr-Nov, wkends; other times by appt). E on PA 63, then N on Troxel Rd, E on Snyder Rd and N on Weikel Rd; house is on Weikel Rd, between Snyder & Allentown Rds. Phone 215/368-2480. ¢¢

Motor Hotel

★★ **HOLIDAY INN.** 1750 Sumneytown Pike, at exit 31 of PA Tpke NE extension. 215/368-3800; FAX 215/368-7824. 183 rms, 4 story. S $79-$84; D $84-$89; each addl $5; suites $89-$99; under 18 free. Crib free. Pet accepted. TV; cable (premium), VCR avail. Pool; poolside serv, lifeguard. Coffee in rms. Restaurant 6:45 am-2 pm, 5:30-10 pm. Rm serv. Bar 4 pm-2 am; entertainment Wed-Sat. Ck-out noon. Meeting rms. Business servs avail. In-rm modem link. Valet serv. Airport transportation. Exercise equipt; weights, treadmill. Cr cds: A, C, D, DS, JCB, MC, V.

[D] [símbolos] SC

Kutztown (E-9)

(For accommodations see Allentown, Reading; also see Hamburg, Pennsylvania Dutch Area)

Founded 1771 **Pop** 4,704 **Elev** 417 ft **Area code** 610 **Zip** 19530

Home of a popular folk festival, Kutztown is named for its founder, George Kutz. The town's population includes many descendants of the Pennsylvania Germans.

What to See and Do

Crystal Cave Park. Discovered in 1871; crystal formations, stalactites, stalagmites, natural bridges—all enhanced by indirect lighting. Also museum (July-Sept); nature trail; miniature golf (July-Sept; fee); theater. Cafe, rock shop, gift shop. Tours (Mar-Nov, daily). 3 mi NW off US 222. Phone 610/683-6765. ¢¢¢

Annual Event

Folk Festival. Festival grounds. Celebration of Pennsylvania Dutch folk culture; quilts, music, dancing and food of Plain and Fancy Dutch. Craftspeople make baskets, brooms, rugs, toleware and other handcrafts. Phone 610/683-8707. Late June-early July.

Restaurant

★★ **NEW SMITHVILLE COUNTRY INN.** 10425 Old Rte 22, I-78 exit 13. 610/285-2987. Hrs: 11 am-11 pm; Sun 8 am-10 pm. Closed Memorial Day, Labor Day. Res accepted. Bar. Semi-a la carte: bkfst $2.25-$6.75, lunch $4.95-$7.25, dinner $9.25-$14.50. Child's meals. Specializes in prime rib, soups, salads. Originally a post office and general store; fireplace, antiques. Cr cds: A, MC, V.

Lancaster (F-8)

(See also Bird-in-Hand, Cornwall, Ephrata, Lebanon, Reading, Wrightsville, York)

Settled 1721 **Pop** 55,551 **Elev** 380 ft **Area code** 717
Information Pennsylvania Dutch Convention & Visitors Bureau, 501 Greenfield Rd, 17601; 717/299-8901 or 800/723-8824.

Lancaster blends the industrial modern, the colonial past and the Pennsylvania Dutch present. It is the heart of the Pennsylvania Dutch Area (see), one of the East's most colorful tourist attractions. To fully appreciate the area, visitors should leave the main highways and travel on country roads, which Amish buggies share with automobiles. Lancaster was an important provisioning area for the armies of the French and Indian War and the Revolution. Its craftsmen turned out fine guns, which brought the city fame as the "arsenal of the Colonies." When Congress, fleeing from Philadelphia, paused here, September 27, 1777, the city was the national capital for one day. It was the state capital from 1799-1812.

What to See and Do

Amish Farm and House. Typical Amish farm in operation. Lecture on the Amish and tour through early 19th-century stone buildings furnished and decorated as old-order Amish household; waterwheels, windmill, hand-dug well, carriages, spring wagon, sleighs. (Daily; closed Dec 25) 4¹/₂ mi E via US 30. Phone 717/394-6185. ¢¢¢

⊠ **Bube's Brewery.** Historic brewery, built before the Civil War, is the only brewery left in the country that has remained intact since the mid-1800s; now operates as a restaurant (see THE CATACOMBS-ALOIS'S-THE BOTTLING WORKS). Guided tours take visitors 43 ft below the street into the brewery's aging vaults and passages, which were built from a cave and were part of what became known as the underground railroad; narrator tells about the history of the brewery and explains methods of producing beer in a Victorian-age brewery. Historic tours (Memorial Day-Labor Day, daily). Restaurants are open all yr (free tour included with reservations for the Catacombs restaurant). 102 N Market St, in Mount Joy. Phone 717/653-2056. **Free.**

Candy Americana Museum. Antique candy-production equipment, confectionery molds, unusual candy containers; outlet store. (Daily exc Sun; closed Labor Day, Thanksgiving, Dec 25 & 26) 5 mi N via PA 501 at Wilbur Chocolate Co, 48 N Broad St, in Lititz. Phone 717/626-1131. **Free.**

Choo-Choo Barn, Traintown, USA. A 1,700-sq-ft layout of Lancaster County in miniature, featuring 16 operating trains and more than 130 animated and automated figures and vehicles. Gift shop. Picnicking. (Apr-Dec, daily) E via US 30, then SE on PA 741, in Strasburg. Phone 717/687-7911. ¢¢

Dutch Wonderland. Family fun park with rides, botanical gardens, diving shows, shops. Monorail (fee). (Memorial Day-Labor Day, daily; Easter-Memorial Day & after Labor Day-Oct, Sat & Sun) 4 mi E via US 30. Phone 717/291-1888. ¢¢¢¢ Adj is

National Wax Museum of Lancaster County Heritage. Figures recreate Lancaster County's history from the 1700s to present. (Daily; closed Dec 25) Phone 717/393-3679. ¢¢¢

Franklin and Marshall College (1787). (1,810 students) Liberal arts college. Rothman Gallery showcases Pennsylvania-German artifacts: quilts, Fraktur and stoneware. More than 200 varieties of trees, plants and shrubs on grounds. Tours of campus. College Ave. Phone 717/291-3981. Also here are

North Museum. General science and natural history; planetarium shows (Sat & Sun, also by appt); children's Discovery Room; film series; monthly art exhibits. (Tues-Sun) Phone 717/291-3941. Planetarium shows ¢¢

Joseph R. Grundy Observatory. Holds 11-inch refractor and 16-inch reflecting telescope demonstrations. Phone 717/291-4136. **Free.**

Fulton Opera House (1852). One of the oldest American theaters, many legendary people have performed here. It is believed that more than one ghost haunts the theater's Victorian interior. Professional regional theater; home of community theater, opera and symphony organizations. 12 N Prince St. Phone 717/397-7425.

Gast Classic Motorcars Museum. Collection of 50 favorite antique & classic, cars in changing display. Self-guided tours. (Daily; closed Jan 1, Easter, Thanksgiving, Dec 24 & 25) 5 mi SE via US 30, in Strasburg. Phone 717/687-9500. ¢¢¢

Hans Herr House (1719). Example of medieval Germanic architecture; served as an early Mennonite meetinghouse and colonial residence of the Herr family. Mennonite rural life exhibit; blacksmith shop. House tours. (Apr-Dec, daily exc Sun; closed major hols) 1849 Hans Herr Dr, in Willow Street. Phone 717/464-4438. ¢¢

Heritage Center of Lancaster County (1795). Houses examples of early Lancaster County arts and crafts. Furniture, tall clocks, quilts, needlework, silver, pewter, Fraktur, rifles. (May-late Nov, Tues-Sat; late Nov-late Dec, daily) Penn Square. Phone 717/299-6440. **Free.**

Historic Rock Ford (1794). Preserved home of General Edward Hand, Revolutionary War commander, member of Continental Congress. (Apr-Oct, Tues-Fri & Sun) 2 mi S on Rock Ford Rd, off S Duke St at Lancaster County Park. Phone 717/392-7223. ¢¢ Fee includes

Kauffman Museum. Collection of folk art & crafts; antique pewter, rifles, copper and tinware collections housed in restored 18th-century barn. (Apr-Oct, Sun, also by appt)

Landis Valley Museum. Interprets Pennsylvania German rural life. Largest collection of Pennsylvania German objects in US; craft and living history demonstrations (May-Oct; see ANNUAL EVENTS); farmsteads, tavern, country store among other exhibit buildings. (Daily exc Mon; closed most hols) 2451 Kissel Hill Rd, 2½ mi N, off PA 272. Phone 717/569-0401 or -9312. ¢¢¢

Mennonite Information Center. Tourist information; interpretation of Mennonite and Amish origins, beliefs. Free video. (Daily exc Sun; closed Jan 1, Thanksgiving, Dec 25) E on US 30, 2209 Millstream Rd. Phone 717/299-0954. **Free.** Also here is

Hebrew Tabernacle Reproduction. Tours (daily exc Sun; closed Jan 1, Thanksgiving, Dec 25). ¢¢

Mill Bridge Village. Restored historic colonial mill village with operating water-powered gristmill (1738); covered bridge; country crafts including broommaking, quilting, candlemaking, blacksmithing; quilt log cabin; Amish kitchen exhibit; music boxes and nickelodeons; horse-drawn hay & carriage rides; 1890s playground; picnicking. Amish house and schoolhouse tour avail. Oktoberfest (Oct wkends). Camp resort (early Apr-Oct, daily; fee). Village (early Apr-Oct, daily; Nov-Dec, wkends only). S Ronks Rd, 4 mi E of jct US 30E, PA 462 in Strasburg. Phone 717/687-8181. ¢¢¢

Muddy Run Recreation Park of Philadelphia Electric Co. Covers 700 acres with 100-acre lake for boating (no power boats), rentals; fishing; picnicking, playgrounds, snack bar, concession; camping. Park (Apr-early Nov). 11 mi S on PA 272, then 3½ mi SW on PA 372. Phone 717/284-4325. Camping per day ¢¢¢¢ Also here is

Muddy Run Information Center of Philadelphia Electric Co. Energy and environmental center; exhibits and movies; illustrated talks periodically. (Tues-Sat) Phone 717/284-2538 for schedule. **Free.**

Robert Fulton Birthplace. Robert Fulton, a great inventor and accomplished artist, is best known for having built the steamboat *Clermont*, which, in 1807, successfully made a trip up the Hudson River against winds and strong current. This little stone house, where Fulton was born, was nearly destroyed by fire about 1822; now refurbished. (Memorial Day-Labor Day, Sat & Sun) 14 mi S via PA 222. Phone 717/548-2679. ¢

Sightseeing tours.

Historic Lancaster Walking Tour. A 90-min tour of historic downtown area. Costumed guide narrates 50 points of architectural or historic interest covering 6 sq blks. (Apr-Oct, 2 tours daily Fri & Sat, 1 tour daily Sun-Thurs; rest of yr, by appt) 100 S Queen St. Phone 717/392-1776. ¢¢

Amish Country Tours. Tours of Amish farmlands and Philadelphia. Phone 717/768-3600. ¢¢¢¢

Brunswick Tours. Private guide and auto tape tours. 2249 Lincoln Hwy E, at National Wax Museum. Phone 717/397-7541. ¢¢¢¢-¢¢¢¢¢

Abe's Buggy Rides. A tour through Amish country in an Amish family carriage. (Daily exc Sun) 6 mi E on PA 340, at 2596 Old Philadelphia Pike, Bird-in-Hand. Phone 717/392-1794. ¢¢¢

Strasburg Rail Road. Railroad runs 4½ mi to Paradise. Picnic stop. This 160-yr-old line uses late 19th-century coaches, various steam locomotives. (Apr-Oct, daily; winter, wkends) 8 mi SE via US 30, PA 896, 741, in Strasburg. Phone 717/687-7522. ¢¢¢ Adj is

Railroad Museum of Pennsylvania. More than 50 locomotives, freight and passenger cars dating from 1825; audiovisual exhibits; railroading memorabilia. Picnicking. (Mar-Oct, daily; rest of yr, daily exc Mon; closed some hols) Phone 717/687-8628. ¢¢¢

Sturgis Pretzel House. First US commercial pretzel bakery (1861), restored as museum. Early equipment (also modern plant); pretzel-making demonstrations, visitors may try twisting pretzels; outlet store. (Daily exc Sun; closed Jan 1, Thanksgiving, Dec 25) 9 mi N via PA 501, 772 at 219 E Main St, in Lititz. Phone 717/626-4354. ¢

The Watch and Clock Museum. National Association of Watch and Clock Collectors living museum of timepieces and related tools and memorabilia. Over 8,000 items representing the 1600s to the present. Extensive research library. Special exhibitions. (May-Sept, Tues-Sat, also Sun afternoons; winter schedule varies; closed major hols) 12 mi W via US 30, at 514 Poplar St in Columbia. Phone 717/684-8261. ¢¢

Toy Train Museum. Trains from the 1880s to present; 5 operating layouts; movies; rare, unusual and specialty trains. (May-Oct, daily; Apr & Nov-Dec, Sat & Sun) E via US 30, PA 896, 741, to Paradise Lane, in Strasburg. Phone 717/687-8976. ¢¢

Twin Brook Winery. Estate winery housed in a restored 19th-century barn offers wine tasting, tours of wine-making facilities, visits to the vineyard; picnic areas. Outdoor concerts (late June-mid-Sept, Sat evenings; fee); special events throughout the yr. (Apr-Dec, Mon-Sat, also Sun afternoons; rest of yr, Tues-Sat, also Sun afternoons) 17 mi E via US 30, S on PA 41, E on Strasburg Rd, located in Gap at 5697 Strasburg Rd. Phone 717/442-4915.

Wheatland (1828). Residence of President James Buchanan from 1848-1868; restored Federal mansion with period rooms containing American Empire and Victorian furniture and decorative arts. Tours by costumed guides (Apr-Nov, daily). Christmas candlelight tours (early Dec). 1120 Marietta Ave, 1½ mi W on PA 23. Phone 717/392-8721. ¢¢¢

Annual Events

Sheep Shearing. Amish Farm and House. Phone 717/394-6185. Last Thurs & Fri Apr, 1st Fri Oct.

Old Fashioned Sunday. Takes place at Wheatland. Festivities include entertainment, magic show and 19th-century activities. Phone 717/392-8721. Mid-May.

Harvest Days. Landis Valley Museum. Demonstrations of more than 80 traditional craft and harvest time activities. Phone 717/569-0401. Columbus Day wkend.

Victorian Christmas Week. On grounds of Wheatland. Phone 717/392-8721. Early Dec.

Seasonal Event

Music at Gretna. 15 mi N via PA 72, in Mt Gretna. Chamber music and jazz; well-known artists. Phone 717/964-3836. Mid-June-early Sept.

Motels

✔★★ **COUNTRY LIVING.** *2406 Old Philadelphia Pike (17602). 717/295-7295.* Web padutch.welcome.com/ctryliv.html. 34 rms, 2 story. July-Oct: S, D $78-$99; each addl $8; suite $130; higher rates hol wkends; lower rates rest of yr. Crib free. TV; cable (premium). Restaurant nearby. Ck-out noon. Whirlpool in suite. Cr cds: MC, V.

★★ **DAYS INN.** *30 Keller Ave (17601). 717/299-5700; FAX 717/295-1907.* Web www.800padutch.com/daysinnl.html. 193 rms, 2-3 story. S $76-$81; D $88-$91; each addl $10; under 12 free. Crib free. TV; cable (premium). pool, 1 indoor; wading pool, lifeguard. Playground. Restaurant 7-11 am, 5-9 pm. Bar noon-midnight. Ck-out noon. Coin lndry. Meeting rms. Business servs avail. Tennis. Game rm. Some refrigerators. Balconies. Cr cds: A, C, D, DS, MC, V.

✔★★ **GARDEN SPOT.** *2291 US 30E (17602). 717/394-4736; FAX 717/299-6339.* 18 rms. S $35-$55; D $40-$62; each addl $5; under 5 free; higher rates hols. Closed Dec-Mar. Crib $6. TV; cable. Restaurant 7:30-11 am. Ck-out 11:30 am. Gift shop. Cr cds: A, DS, MC, V.

★★ **HERSHEY FARM MOTOR INN.** *(PA 896S, Ronks 17572) 1½ mi S of US 30. 717/687-8635; res: 800/827-8635; FAX 717/687-8638.* 59 rms, 2 story. June-Aug: S $74; D $79; each addl $8; suites $104-$109; under 15 free; wkly rates; lower rates rest of yr. Crib free. TV; cable (premium). Complimentary full bkfst. Restaurant adj 8 am-8 pm; Sat, Sun to 9 pm. Ck-out 11 am. Meeting rms. Business servs avail. Gift shop. Pool. Playground. Some in-rm whirlpools; refrigerators avail. Some balconies. Cr cds: DS, MC, V.

★★★ **HILTON GARDEN INN.** *101 Granite Run Dr (17601). 717/560-0880; FAX 717/560-5400.* Web www.hilton.com. 155 rms, 2 story. May-Oct: S $119-$149; D $124-$154; family rates; lower rates rest of yr. TV; cable (premium). Indoor pool; whirlpool, lifeguard. Complimentary continental bkfst. Complimentary coffee in rms. Restaurant 6:30 am-2 pm, 5-10 pm. Bar 11:30 am-midnight. Coin lndry. Meeting rms. Business center. In-rm modem link. Sundries. Exercise equipt; weights, bicycles. Cr cds: A, C, D, DS, MC, V.

★★ **HOLIDAY INN NORTH.** *1492 Lititz Pike (PA 501) (17601). 717/393-0771; FAX 717/299-6238.* 160 rms, 2 story. May-Oct: S, D $95; under 12 free; 2-day min stay hols; lower rates rest of yr. Crib free. TV; cable. Pool. Restaurant 6 am-2 pm, 5-10 pm, Sat, Sun 7 am-2 pm. Rm serv. Bar 5 pm-midnight. Ck-out noon. Meeting rms. Business servs avail. In-rm modem link. Bellhops. Valet serv. Sundries. Health club privileges. Game rm. Some refrigerators. Balconies. Cr cds: A, C, D, DS, ER, JCB, MC, V.

★★ **HOWARD JOHNSON.** *2100 Lincoln Hwy E (17602). 717/397-7781; FAX 717/397-6340.* 112 rms, 2 story. June-Oct: S $48-$75; D $68-$88; each addl $7; higher rates major hols; lower rates rest of yr. Crib free. TV; cable (premium). Indoor pool. Restaurant 6 am-midnight. Bar from 11 am. Ck-out 11 am. Meeting rms. Business servs avail. Shopping arcade. Private patios, balconies. Cr cds: A, C, D, DS, MC, V.

★★ **RAMADA.** *2250 Lincoln Hwy E (17602), Rte 30 E. 717/393-5499; FAX 717/293-1014.* Web www.ramada .com/ramada.html. 166 rms, 5 story. Mid-June-Oct: S, D $84-$129; each addl $10; under 18 free; lower rates rest of yr. Crib free. Pet accepted, some restrictions. TV; cable. 2 pools, 1 indoor; sauna. Playground. Ck-out 11 am. Coin lndry. Meeting rms. Business servs avail. In-rm modem link. Free airport transportation. Tennis. 27-hole golf privileges, pro, putting green, driving range.

Health club privileges. Game rm. Lawn games. Refrigerators. Balconies. Picnic tables. Cr cds: A, C, D, DS, ER, JCB, MC, V.

★★ **ROCKVALE VILLAGE INN.** *24 S Willowdale Dr (17602). 717/293-9500; FAX 717/293-8558; res: 800/524-3817.* 113 rms, 2 story. Late June-Nov: S, D $79-$109; each addl $5; under 15 free; lower rates rest of yr. Crib free. TV; cable (premium). Pool; lifeguard. Restaurant 7 am-2 pm. Bar noon-midnight. Ck-out 11 am. Meeting rm. Business servs avail. Cr cds: A, C, D, DS, MC, V.

✔★★ **WESTFIELD INN.** *2929 Hempland Rd (17601), US 30W exit Centerville Rd. 717/397-9300; FAX 717/295-9240; res: 800/547-1395.* 84 rms, 2 story. S, D $49-$79; each addl $5; suites $79-$89; under 18 free. Crib free. TV; cable, VCR avail. Pool; lifeguard. Complimentary continental bkfst. Restaurant nearby. Ck-out 11 am. Coin lndry. Business servs avail. Some refrigerators; microwaves avail. Cr cds: A, C, D, DS, MC, V.

Motor Hotels

★★★ **BEST WESTERN EDEN RESORT INN.** *222 Eden Rd (17601). 717/569-6444; FAX 717/569-4208.* E-mail eden@edenresort .com; web www.edenresort.com. 274 rms, 3 story. June-Nov: S, D $125-$139; each addl $10; suites $129-$249; under 18 free; varied lower rates rest of yr. Crib free. Pet accepted. TV; cable (premium). 2 pools, 1 indoor; whirlpool, poolside serv, lifeguard. Playground. Restaurant 6:30 am-11 pm; wkends to midnight. Rm serv. Bar 11-2 am; entertainment. Ck-out noon. Meeting rms. Business center. In-rm modem link. Valet serv. Free airport transportation. Gift shop. Lighted tennis. Exercise equipt; weights, bicycles, saunas. Lawn games. Microwaves avail. Some balconies. Cr cds: A, C, D, DS, MC, V.

★★ **HOLIDAY INN VISITORS CENTER.** *521 Greenfield Rd (17601), opp Tourist Bureau. 717/299-2551; FAX 717/397-0220.* 189 rms, 4 story. Early May-Nov: S, D $79-$109; under 18 free; lower rates rest of yr. Crib free. TV; cable (premium). 2 pools, 1 indoor. Restaurant 6:30 am-2 pm, 5-10 pm. Rm serv. Bar 4 pm-2 am. Ck-out noon. Meeting rms. Business servs avail. In-rm modem link. Valet serv. Sundries. Tennis. Microwaves avail. Cr cds: A, C, D, DS, ER, JCB, MC, V.

Hotel

✔★★ **HOTEL BRUNSWICK.** *(17603), at jct Chestnut & Queen Sts. 717/397-4801; FAX 717/397-4991; res: 800/233-0182.* E-mail hblanc@lancnews.info.net; web www.hotelbrunswick.com. 222 rms, 7 story. S $62-$78; D $72-$86; each addl $6; under 17 free; monthly, wkly, wkend rates; golf plan; lower rates Nov-Apr. Crib free. Pet accepted; $100. TV; cable, VCR avail (movies). Indoor pool; lifeguard. Restaurant 7 am-1:30 pm, 5:30-9 pm. Bar; entertainment. Ck-out noon. Coin lndry. Meeting rms. Business servs avail. Free garage parking. Exercise equipt; weights, bicycles. Refrigerators avail. Cr cds: A, C, D, DS, MC, V.

Inns

★★★ **ALDEN HOUSE.** *(62 E Main St, Lititz 17543) N on PA 501. 717/627-3363; res: 800/584-0753.* E-mail aldenbb@ptd.net. 5 rms, shower only, 2 story, 3 suites. No rm phones. S $75; D $85; each addl $20; suites $100-$120; wkends (2-day min); higher rates special events. Children over 10 yrs only. TV in common rm; cable, VCR avail (movies). Complimentary full bkfst. Restaurant nearby. Ck-out 11 am, ck-in after 3 pm. Luggage handling. Concierge serv. Microwaves avail. Some balconies. Built in 1850. Totally nonsmoking. Cr cds: MC, V.

★ ★ **THE AUSTRALIAN WALKABOUT.** *(837 Village Rd, Lampeter 17537) 4 mi S on PA 741, off US 222.* 717/464-0707; FAX 717/464-2501. Web www.bbonline.com/pa/walkabout/index.html. 5 rms, 3 story, 3 suites. No rm phones. May-Nov: S $89-$135; D $99-$149; each addl $25; suites $139-$199; lower rates rest of yr. Adults only. TV; cable (premium). Whirlpools. Complimentary full bkfst. Ck-out 10 am, ck-in 3-8 pm. Lawn games. Some balconies. Picnic tables. Brick house with wraparound porch built in 1925. Totally nonsmoking. Cr cds: A, MC, V.

★ ★ **CAMERON ESTATE.** *(1855 Mansion Ln, Mount Joy 17552) 15 mi W on PA 283, Rheems exit, Colebrook Rd to Donegal Springs Rd.* 717/653-1773; res: 888/722-6376; FAX 717/653-8334. Web www.getawaysmag.com. 17 rms, 2 share bath, 3 story. No rm phones. S, D $100-$175. Children over 12 yrs only. Complimentary full bkfst. Restaurant (see CAMERON ESTATE INN). Ck-out 11 am, ck-in 3 pm. Meeting rms. Business center. Brick Federal structure (1805) on 15-acre estate, was acquired as a country house, then rebuilt and expanded by Simon Cameron, political kingmaker, US Senator and Abraham Lincoln's first Secretary of War. Cr cds: A, D, DS, MC, V.

★ ★ **GENERAL SUTTER.** *(14 E Main St, Lititz 17543) 6 mi N via PA 501, on the Square.* 717/626-2115; FAX 717/626-0992. 14 rms, 3 story. S, D $75-$100. Crib $5. Pet accepted. TV; cable. Dining rm 7 am-9 pm; Sun 8 am-8 pm. Bar 11 am-11 pm. Ck-out noon, ck-in 3 pm. Spacious brick-lined patio. Built in 1764; antique country and Victorian furniture. Fireplace in parlor. Cr cds: A, DS, MC, V.

★ ★ **GEORGE ZAHM HOUSE.** *(6070 Main St, East Petersburg 17520)* 717/569-6026. 4 rms, 3 with shower only, 2 story, 1 suite. No rm phones. S $65-$80; D $65-$85; each addl $10; suites $85; wkly rates; wkends, hols (2-day min). Children over 12 yrs only. Complimentary continental bkfst. Restaurant nearby. Ck-out 11 am, ck-in 4-7 pm. Luggage handling. Picnic tables, grills. Built in 1856; restored federal-period mansion. Totally nonsmoking. Cr cds: MC, V.

★ ★ **HISTORIC STRASBURG.** *(PA 896, Strasburg 17579) 8 mi SE via US 30, PA 896.* 717/687-7691; FAX 717/687-6098; res: 800/872-0201. Web www.800padutch.com/strasinn.html. 101 rms in 5 buildings, 2 story. Apr-Nov: S, D $119-$129; each addl $15; suites $159-$199; under 12 free; lower rates rest of yr. Crib $7. Pet accepted; $15. TV; cable, VCR avail (movies). Heated pool; whirlpool. Playground. Complimentary full bkfst. Restaurant (see WASHINGTON HOUSE). Bar 11:30 am-11 pm. Ck-out noon. Meeting rms. Business servs avail. Sundries. Gift shop. Exercise equipt; treadmill, bicycle. Lawn games. Balconies. Petting zoo and hot air balloon rides on property (58 acres). Cr cds: A, C, D, DS, MC, V.

★ ★ **KING'S COTTAGE.** *1049 E King St (17602).* 717/397-1017; FAX 717/397-3447; res: 800/747-8717. 9 rms. Rm phones avail. S, D $100-$135; suite $160-$180. Children over 12 yrs only. TV; cable in library. Complimentary full bkfst; afternoon refreshments. Restaurant nearby. Ck-out 11 am, ck-in 4 pm. Restored Spanish/mission-style house (1913); library, antiques, fireplaces. Totally nonsmoking. Cr cds: D, DS, MC, V.

★ ★ **O'FLAHERTY'S DINGELDEIN HOUSE.** *1105 E King St (17602), on PA 462.* 717/293-1723; res: 800/779-7465; FAX 717/293-1947. E-mail oflahbb@lancnews.infi.net; web www.800padutch.com/ofhouse.html. 4 rms, 2 share bath, 3 story, 1 suite. No rm phones. S, D $80-$100; each addl $15; suite $100; wkends, hols (2-3 day min). Crib free. TV in common rm; cable (premium), VCR avail (movies). Complimentary full bkfst; afternoon refreshments. Ck-out 11 am, ck-in 2:30 pm. Luggage handling. Free airport, RR station transportation. Playground.

Dutch colonial mansion built in 1912. Totally nonsmoking. Cr cds: DS, MC, V.

★ ★ ★ **SWISS WOODS INN.** *(500 Blantz Rd, Lititz 17543) N on PA 501, W on Brubaker Valley Rd, N on Blantz Rd.* 717/627-3358; res: 800/594-8018; FAX 717/627-3483. E-mail mrey88a@prodigy.com. 7 rms, 2 story, 1 suite. Apr-Dec: S $80-$130; D $95-$145; each addl $15; suite $125; wkends, hols (2-3 day min); lower rates rest of yr. Children over 12 yrs only. TV in suite and common rm; VCR avail. Complimentary full bkfst. Complimentary coffee in rms. Ck-out 11 am, ck-in 3-7 pm. Luggage handling. Concierge serv. Gift shop. Some in-rm whirlpools; refrigerator, fireplace in suite. Some balconies. Picnic tables. Built to resemble Swiss chalets. Totally nonsmoking. Cr cds: A, DS, MC, V.

Resort

★ ★ ★ **WILLOW VALLEY FAMILY RESORT & CONFERENCE CENTER.** *2416 Willow St Pike (17602), 3 mi S on Rte 222.* 717/464-2711; FAX 717/464-4784; res: 800/444-1714. Web www.travelweb.com/thisco/willow/5081/5081_b.html. 352 rms, 5 story. Mid-June-early Sept, hol wkends: S, D $109-$149; each addl $10; ages 6-11, $5; under 6 free; lower rates rest of yr. Crib free. TV; cable, VCR avail (movies). 3 pools, 2 indoor; whirlpool, lifeguard. Playgrounds. Coffee in rms. Restaurants 6 am-9 pm. Ck-out noon. Free guest lndry. Meeting rms. Business servs avail. Shopping arcade. Free airport, RR station, bus depot transportation. Lighted tennis. 9-hole golf, putting green. Exercise equipt; weight machine, bicycles, sauna. Game rm. Some private patios, balconies. Country view; large landscaped grounds. Cr cds: A, D, DS, MC, V.

Restaurants

★ ★ **CAMERON ESTATE INN.** *(See Cameron Estate Inn)* 717/653-1773. Hrs: 6-9 pm. Closed Dec 25. Res required. Bar. Semi-a la carte: dinner $19.95-$50. Daily menu featuring wild game and seafood. In mansion, dating from 1805, that was owned and rebuilt by Simon Cameron, Abraham Lincoln's first secretary of war; fireplace, sun porch. Cr cds: A, C, D, DS, MC, V.

★ ★ **THE CATACOMBS-ALOIS'S-THE BOTTLING WORKS.** *(102 N Market St, Mount Joy 17522) W on PA 283, exit Mount Joy, 2 mi W on PA 230, turn right at third light.* 717/653-2056. Web lancaster.net/bubes. Hrs: 11 am-2 pm, 5:30-9 pm; Fri, Sat to 10 pm; Sun 4:30-9 pm. Closed some major hols. Res accepted. Continental menu. Bar. Semi-a la carte: lunch $2.95-$7.45. Complete meals: dinner $15.95-$26.95. Specializes in shrimp, roast duck. Entertainment Fri, Sat. Outdoor dining. In old Victorian hotel and brewery (1876); dining areas are located in original bottling plant, original dining rms of the hotel portion (Victorian decor) and below ground, in the cellars (medieval atmosphere, costumes, entertainment). Guided tours. Cr cds: A, DS, MC, V.

★ ★ **D & S BRASSERIE.** *1679 Lincoln Hwy E (17602).* 717/299-1694. Hrs: 11:30 am-midnight; Sat 4 pm-1 am; Sun 4-10 pm. Closed Thanksgiving, Dec 25. Res accepted. Continental menu. Bar. Semi-a la carte: lunch $3.75-$8.95, dinner $8.95-$33. Specializes in prime rib, pasta, seafood. Outdoor dining. House built in 1925; original woodwork, fireplaces. Cr cds: A, D, DS, MC, V.

★ ★ ★ **GROFF'S FARM.** *(650 Pinkerton Rd, Mount Joy 17552) 11 mi SW via US 30, PA 283 (1st Mt Joy exit) and PA 772 to Pinkerton Rd, 1 mi S.* 717/653-2048. Hrs: 11:30 am-1:30 pm, 5-7:30 pm; Sat 11:30 am-1:30 pm, sittings 5 & 8 pm; Sun brunch 10 am-2 pm. Closed Dec 24-26; also wkdays Jan-mid-Feb. Res required. Serv bar. Wine list. A la carte entrees: lunch $2.50-$7.50, dinner $12.50-$25. Complete meals: dinner $16-$24. Child's meals. Specialties: chicken Stoltzfus, home-cured ham, fresh seafood. Own pastries. Located in farmhouse built in 1756. Family-owned. Cr cds: A, C, D, DS, MC, V.

★ ★ ★ **HAYDN ZUG'S.** *(1987 State St, East Petersburg)* N on PA 72. 717/569-5746. Hrs: 11:30 am-2 pm, 5-9 pm; Sat from 5 pm. Closed Sun, Mon; most major hols. Res accepted. Bar 5-9 pm. Wine cellar. A la carte entrees: lunch $4.25-$10.95, dinner $10.75-$23.50. Specialties: cheesy chowder, grilled lamb tenderloin, Norwegian chicken. Own pastries. Colonial setting. Family-operated. Cr cds: A, D, DS, MC, V.

★ ★ ★ **LOG CABIN.** *(11 Lehoy Forest Dr, Leola)* 6 mi NW off PA 272. 717/626-1181. Hrs: 5-10 pm; Sun 4-9 pm. Closed major hols. Res accepted. Bar. Wine cellar. Semi-a la carte: dinner $15-$35. Child's meals. Specializes in charcoal-broiled steak, fresh seafood. Own baking. Log cabin in woods; paintings, fireplace. Entry through covered "kissing" bridge. Cr cds: A, D, MC, V.

✔★ ★ ★ **OLDE GREENFIELD INN.** 595 Greenfield Rd (17601). 717/393-0668. Web www.find-dining.com/greenfield. Hrs: 11 am-2 pm, 5-10 pm; Mon from 5 pm; Sat 8 am-2 pm (brunch), 5-10 pm; Sun 8 am-2 pm (brunch). Closed most major hols. Res accepted. Bar. Wine cellar. Semi-a la carte: bkfst $4.95-$9.95, lunch $4.95-$8.45, dinner $10.95-$20.95. Sat, Sun brunch $4.95-$12.95. Child's meals. Specializes in steak, seafood, pasta. Own baking, pasta. Pianist Fri, Sat, hols. Outdoor dining. In restored stone farmhouse; dining avail on balcony and in wine cellar. Cr cds: A, C, D, DS, MC, V.

★ ★ **WASHINGTON HOUSE.** *(See Historic Strasburg Inn)* 717/687-9211. Hrs: 7 am-2 pm, 5-9 pm; Sun 7 am-9 pm. Res accepted. French menu. Bar 11:30 am-9 pm. A la carte entrees: lunch $5.25-$12.50, dinner $19.95-$26.95. Buffet: bkfst $5.95, lunch $9.95. Sun brunch $15.95. Child's meals. Specialties: crabcakes, medallions de filet, grillade de bouef. Outdoor dining. Colonial decor. Cr cds: A, D, DS, MC, V.

Lebanon (E-7)

(See also Cornwall, Ephrata, Hershey, Lancaster, Pennsylvania Dutch Area)

Founded 1756 **Pop** 24,800 **Elev** 460 ft **Area code** 717 **Zip** 17042

Information Pennsylvania Rainbow Region Vacation Bureau, 625 Quentin Rd, PO Box 329; 717/272-8555.

This industrial city, steeped in German traditions, is the marketplace for colorful Lebanon County. Many Hessians were confined here after the Battle of Trenton. Today, Lebanon bologna factories and food processing are important to the city's economy. Master planning for redevelopment of city and county combines with the traditional atmosphere to make this a charming community.

What to See and Do

Coleman Memorial Park. This 100-acre former estate has swimming pool (Memorial Day-Labor Day, daily; fee), tennis courts, athletic fields, picnic facilities. Fee for some activities. Park (daily). 2 mi N on PA 72, W Maple St. Phone 717/228-4470. **Free.**

Fort Zeller. One of state's oldest existing forts; originally built of logs, rebuilt of stone in 1745; has 12-ft-wide Queen Anne fireplace in kitchen. (By appt) 11 mi E on US 422, then S on PA 419, in Newmanstown. Phone 610/589-4301. **Donation.**

Middlecreek Wildlife Management Area. A 5,144-acre tract provides refuge for waterfowl, forest and farmland wildlife. Permit and open hunting areas, inquire at Visitor Center for regulations. Fishing; boating (mid-May-

mid-Sept). Hiking. Picnicking. Visitor Center (Mar-Nov, daily exc Mon). Braille trail for the visually impaired. 11 mi SE on PA 897 to Kleinfeltersville, then 1 mi S. Phone 717/733-1512. **Free.**

Stoevers Dam Recreational Area. A 153-acre park with 52-acre lake for fishing; boating (electric motors only), canoeing. A 1½-mi trail for jogging, hiking, bicycling. Primitive camping (permit only; fee). Nature trails; nature barn (Apr-Oct, daily exc Mon); winter, by appt). Community park (daily). 2 mi N on PA 343, Miller St. Phone 717/228-4470. **Free.**

Stoy Museum of the Lebanon County Historical Society. Local historical museum containing 30 permanent room and shop displays on 3 floors of house built in 1773 and used as first county courthouse; research library. Tours. (Daily exc Sat; closed Sun & Mon of hol wkends) 924 Cumberland St. Phone 717/272-1473. **¢¢**

The Daniel Weaver Company. Manufacturers, since 1885, of Weaver's Famous Lebanon Bologna and other wood-smoked gourmet meats; smoked in 100-yr-old outdoor smokehouses. Samples. Tours. (Daily exc Sun) 15th Ave & Weavertown Rd. Phone 717/274-6100 or 800/WEAVERS. **Free.**

Annual Event

Bologna Fest. Festival features Lebanon bologna, Pennsylvania Dutch food, arts & crafts, entertainment. Early Sept.

Motel

★ ★ ★ **LANTERN LODGE.** *(411 N College St, Myerstown 17067)* 7 mi E on PA 501 at US 422. 717/866-6536; FAX 717/866-6536, ext. 112; res: 800/262-5564. 80 rms, 2 story. S $54-$66; D $60-$90; each addl $10; suites $110-$225; cottage $150-$200. Crib free. TV; cable, VCR avail. Playground. Complimentary coffee in rms. Restaurant 7 am-10 pm. Rm serv. Ck-out 11 am. Meeting rms. Business servs avail. Bellhops. Barber, beauty shop. Valet serv. Sundries. Tennis. Early Amer decor. Cr cds: A, C, D, DS, MC, V.

Motor Hotel

★ ★ ★ **QUALITY INN OF LEBANON VALLEY.** 625 Quentin Rd, on PA 72. 717/273-6771; FAX 717/273-4882. 56 hotel rms, 74 motel rms, 5 story. Late May-Oct: S $78-$110; D $83-$120; each addl $7; under 18 free; lower rates rest of yr. Crib free. TV; cable. Pool; lifeguard. Restaurant 6 am-9 pm. Rm serv. Bar 11-2 am; entertainment. Ck-out noon. Meeting rms. Business servs avail. Sundries. Barber. Game rm. Microwaves avail. Cr cds: A, C, D, DS, ER, JCB, MC, V.

Inn

★ ★ **SWATARA CREEK.** *(Jonestown Rd, Annville 17003)* US 81, exit 29. 717/865-3259. 10 rms, 2 with shower only, 3 story, 1 suite. No rm phones. Apr-Nov: S $45-$70; D $55-$80; suite $115; family rates; 3-day min stay Hershey car show; lower rates rest of yr. Complimentary full bkfst. Complimentary coffee in sitting rm. Restaurant nearby. Ck-out 11 am, ck-in 3 pm. Concierge serv. Gift shop. Refrigerator on 2nd floor. Some balconies. Picnic tables. Victorian mansion built in 1860; country setting. Cr cds: A, D, DS, MC, V.

Lewisburg (D-7)

(See also Danville, Williamsport)

Settled 1785 **Pop** 5,785 **Elev** 460 ft **Area code** 717 **Zip** 17837 **E-mail** svvb@svvb.com **Web** svvb.com

Information Susquehanna Valley Visitors Bureau, RR3, 219-D Hafer Rd; 717/524-7234 or 800/525-7320.

Home of Bucknell University (1846), this college community also has light industry. The Native American village of Old Muncy Town was located nearby before the region was opened by Ludwig (Lewis) Doerr.

What to See and Do

Fort Augusta (1757). Museum collection of Northumberland County Historical Society. (Mon, Wed, Fri & Sat) 9 mi SE on PA 147, in Sunbury, at 1150 N Front St. Phone 717/286-4083. **Free.**

Packwood House Museum. A 3-story, 27-rm log and frame building begun in the late 18th century. Former hostelry houses a wide-ranging collection of Americana, period furnishings, textiles and decorative arts. Changing exhibits; museum shop. Tours. (Daily exc Mon; closed hols) 15 N Water St. Phone 717/524-0323. ¢¢

Slifer House Museum. Elaborate 3-story, 20-rm Victorian mansion. First and second floors have been restored, complete with Victorian parlor, dining room, library, 5 bedrms and the summer kitchen exhibit rm. (Apr-late Dec, daily exc Mon; rest of yr, Tues-Fri afternoons, also by appt; closed hols) 1 mi N, on grounds of Lewisburg United Methodist Homes. Phone 717/524-2245. ¢¢

Walnut Acres Organic Farms. Working organic farm; bakery; cannery; Farm Store with farm-grown items. Self-guided farm tours (daily). Guided plant tours (Mon-Fri; closed hols). (Daily; closed hols) 12 mi SW on PA 45, 7 mi S on PA 104 to Penns Creek. Phone 800/433-3998. **Free.**

Motels

★ ★ ★ **BEST WESTERN COUNTRY CUPBOARD INN.** *I-80 exit 30A, 5 mi S on US 15.* 717/524-5500; FAX 717/524-4291. 106 rms, 3 story. S $68-$99; D $75-$105; each addl $6; suites $105-$149; under 18 free; higher rates university events. Crib free. TV; cable. Heated pool; lifeguard. Complimentary continental bkfst. Restaurant adj 7 am-9 pm. Ck-out 11 am. Coin lndry. Meeting rms. Business servs avail. Exercise equipt; weight machine, bicycle. Game rm. Refrigerator in suites. Cr cds: A, C, D, DS, MC, V.

D ⊠ ✕ ⊠ 🐾 SC

★ ★ **DAYS INN-UNIVERSITY.** *On US 15, 1 blk S of jct PA 192.* 717/523-1171; FAX 717/524-4667. 108 rms, 2 story. S $55-$69; D $61-$69; each addl $6; under 16 free. Crib free. TV; cable, VCR avail (movies). Pool; lifeguard. Restaurant adj open 24 hrs. Ck-out noon. Business servs avail. In-rm modem link. Exercise equipt; weight machine, bicycles. Cr cds: A, C, D, DS, MC, V.

⊠ ✕ ⊠ 🐾 SC

Restaurant

✔ ★ ★ **COUNTRY CUPBOARD.** *Hafer Rd (US 15), 5 mi S of I-80 exit 30A.* 717/523-3211. Hrs: 7 am-9 pm. Closed Dec 25. Res accepted Mon-Fri. Semi-a la carte: bkfst $2.25-$5.50, lunch, dinner $4.99-$10.99. Buffet: bkfst (Sat, Sun), lunch (Mon-Sat) $5.99, dinner $8.99-$10.99. Child's meals. Specializes in poultry, ham. Country dining. Totally non-smoking. Cr cds: DS, MC, V.

 D

Lewistown (E-6)

Settled 1754 **Pop** 9,341 **Elev** 520 ft **Area code** 717

Information Juniata Valley Area Chamber of Commerce, 3 W Monument Sq, Suite 204, 17044; 717/248-6713.

Surrounded by rich farmland and beautiful forested mountain ranges, Lewistown lies in the scenic Juniata River Valley, in the heart of central Pennsylvania. Lewistown retains the charm of its rustic surroundings, which yearly attract thousands of sportsmen and outdoor enthusiasts to the area's fine hunting, fishing and camping facilities. A large Amish population, which thrives on the farmland of the Kishacoquillas Valley, has contributed greatly to the area's culture and heritage.

What to See and Do

Brookmere Farm Vineyards. In 19th-century stone & wood barn. Winery tour, wine tasting; picnicking. (Mar-Dec, Mon-Sat, also Sun afternoons; rest of yr, daily exc Sun; closed hols) Approx 5 mi N via US 322, then SW on PA 655, near Belleville. Phone 717/935-5380. **Free.**

Greenwood Furnace State Park. Remains of Greenwood Works, last iron furnace to operate in area (ca 1833-1904); restored stack. Approx 400 acres. Swimming beach; fishing. Hiking. Snowmobiling, ice-skating, ice fishing. Picnicking, playground, snack bar, store. Tent & trailer sites. Visitor center, interpretive program. Standard fees. 5 mi N on US 322, then 9 mi W on PA 655, then NW on PA 305. Phone 814/667-1800.

Reeds Gap State Park. Approx 200 acres. Swimming pool; fishing. Hiking. Picnicking, snack bar, store. Tent sites only. 8 mi N off US 322 & unnumbered road. Phone 717/667-3622. Camping ¢¢¢-¢¢¢¢

Motel

✔ ★ ★ **CLARION INN.** *(US 322, Burnham 17009) just off US 322 at Burnham exit.* 717/248-4961; FAX 717/242-3013. 119 rms, 2 story. S, D $59; each addl $5; under 18 free. Crib free. Pet accepted. TV; cable (premium). Pool; poolside serv, lifeguard. Restaurant 6 am-2 pm, 5-10 pm. Rm serv. Bar 4 pm-midnight. Ck-out noon. Meeting rms. In-rm modem link. Valet serv. Cr cds: A, C, D, DS, MC, V.

D 🐾 ⊠ ✕ 🐾 SC

Ligonier (E-3)

(See also Donegal, Greensburg, Johnstown)

Founded 1816 **Pop** 1,638 **Elev** 1,200 ft **Area code** 724 **Zip** 15658

Information Ligonier Valley Chamber of Commerce, Town Hall, 120 E Main St; 724/238-4200.

Fort Ligonier, built in 1758 by the British, was the scene of one of the key battles of the French and Indian War. It also served as a supply base during Pontiac's War in 1763. The town is now a center of dairying, farms, woodlands and summer and winter sports.

What to See and Do

Compass Inn Museum. A 1799 stagecoach stop; original log and stone inn authentically restored and furnished; log barn houses Conestoga wagon and stagecoach; cookhouse with beehive oven and fireplace; blacksmith shop contains working forge. (May-Oct, daily exc Mon) 3 mi E on US 30, in Laughlintown. Phone 724/238-4983. ¢¢

Fort Ligonier. Reconstructed 18th-century British fort; includes buildings with period furnishings. Museum houses outstanding French and Indian War collection, 18th-century artifacts; introductory film. (Apr-Oct, daily)

(See ANNUAL EVENTS) S Market St, on US 30, PA 711. Phone 724/238-9701. ¢¢

Idlewild Park. Amusement rides; entertainment; picnicking; children's play area; water park. (Memorial Day-late Aug, daily exc Mon) 2 mi W on US 30. Phone 724/238-3666. ¢¢¢¢ Adj is

Story Book Forest. Children's park with animals, people and buildings portraying nursery rhymes. (Memorial Day-late Aug, daily exc Mon) Phone 724/238-3666. Admission included with Idlewild Park.

St Vincent Archabbey and College (1846). (1,000 students) Includes Benedictine monastery, seminary and coeducational liberal arts college. St Vincent Theatre has performances at theater-in-the-round; for schedule phone 724/537-8900. Free self-guided tape tours. 8 mi W on US 30, in Latrobe. Phone 724/537-4560.

Annual Events

Ligonier Highland Games and Gathering of the Clans of Scotland. Idlewild Park. Sports; massed pipe bands, Highland dancing competitions; Scottish fiddling; sheep dog, wool spinning and weaving demonstrations; genealogy booth, Scottish fair. Phone 724/238-3666. 1st Sat after Labor Day.

Fort Ligonier Days. Living history program of the French and Indian War. Parade, pioneer craft demonstrations, food and special events. Usually 2nd wknd Oct.

Seasonal Event

Mountain Playhouse. 11 mi SE on US 30, then ½ mi N on US 985, in Jennerstown. Phone 814/629-9201. Broadway shows in restored gristmill (1805). Matinees and evening performances. Late May-mid-Oct.

Motels

✔★ **FORT LIGONIER MOTOR LODGE.** US 30E, 2 blks S on US 30, jct PA 711. 724/238-6677. 35 rms, 2 story. May-Oct: S, D $55-$80; each addl $6; higher rates: wknds, special events; lower rates rest of yr. Crib $4. TV; cable. Pool. Complimentary coffee. Restaurant nearby. Ck-out 11 am. Sundries. Downhill/x-country ski 7 mi. Picnic tables. Trout stream. Cr cds: A, MC, V.

★ ★ ★ **RAMADA INN-HISTORIC LIGONIER.** 216 W Loyalhanna St. 724/238-9545; FAX 724/238-9803. 66 rms, 3 story. S, D $65-$95; each addl $6; suites $95-$150; under 12 free; ski plans. Crib free. TV; cable (premium), VCR avail. Pool. Restaurant 6:30 am-10 pm. Rm serv. Bar 4 pm-2 am. Ck-out noon. Meeting rms. Business servs avail. In-rm modem link. Cr cds: A, D, DS, MC, V.

Limerick (E-9)

(For accommodations see Norristown, Pottstown, Reading)

Pop 800 (est) **Elev** 302 ft **Area code** 610 **Zip** 19468 **E-mail** vlyforge @libertynet.org **Web** www.valleyforge.org

Information Valley Forge Convention & Visitors Bureau, 600 W Germantown Pike, Suite 130, Plymouth Meeting 19462; 610/834-1550.

What to See and Do

Spring Mountain Ski Area. Triple, 3 double chairlifts, 2 rope tows; patrol, school, rentals; snowmaking; cafeteria. Longest run ½ mi; vertical drop 450 ft. Also camping avail (fee; hookups). 6 mi N, off PA 29 near Schwenksville. Phone 610/287-7900. ¢¢¢¢ (Mid-Dec-mid-Mar, daily)

Restaurant

✔★ ★ **GYPSY ROSE.** (505 Bridge Rd (PA 113), Rahns 19426) 4 mi S on US 422, exit PA 113, then N 2 mi. 610/489-1600. Hrs: 11:30 am-10 pm; Fri, Sat to 11 pm; Sun 11 am-9 pm; Sun brunch to 2 pm. Closed some major hols. Res accepted. Bar 11-2 am. Semi-a la carte: lunch $6-$11, dinner $6-$20. Sun brunch $12.50. Child's meals. Specialties: chicken Philadelphia, Maryland crab cakes. Own baking. Outdoor dining. Farmhouse (1725); views of creek and landscaped garden. Cr cds: A, D, DS, MC, V.

Lock Haven (C-6)

(See also Williamsport)

Founded 1833 **Pop** 9,230 **Elev** 564 ft **Area code** 717 **Zip** 17745
Information Clinton County Tourist Promotion Agency, Court House Annex, 151 Susquehanna Ave; 717/893-4037.

Founded on the site of pre-Revolutionary Fort Reed, the community takes its name from two sources. The lock of the Pennsylvania Canal once crossed the West Branch of the Susquehanna River here, and the town was once a "haven" for the rafts and lumberjacks of nearby logging camps. Near the geographic center of the state, the town today is a center of commerce and small industry.

What to See and Do

Bucktail Natural Area. Scenic area extends from mountain rim to mountain rim for 75 mi from Lock Haven N to Renovo and W to Emporium. Connecting the three towns and weaving through the park is PA 120, an outstanding drive through mountain scenery. Historic site W of Renovo commemorates Bucktail Trail, which served pioneers and Civil War volunteers. Fishing.

Bull Run School House (1899). Only remaining one-room schoolhouse in county; fully restored with all of its original equipment, including double desks, schoolmaster's and recitation desks, Waterbury clock, bell. (Hrs vary; phone for schedule) 12 mi S via I-80, PA 880, exit 27. Phone 717/893-4037. **Free.**

Fin, Fur & Feather Wildlife Museum. Personal collection of animals from across the globe. More than 500 animals are mounted on display. Gift shop (yr-round, daily). (Late June-Oct, daily; rest of yr, Fri-Sun, also by appt; closed Dec 25) 18 mi N via PA 664. Phone 717/769-6620 (gift shop) or 717/769-6482. ¢¢

Hyner View. At 2,000 ft, "Laurel Drive to the top of the world" provides panoramic view of valley, river, highway and forest. Site of state and national hang-gliding competitions. 22 mi NW on PA 120.

State parks.

Kettle Creek. Approx 1,600 acres. Winds through beautiful valley developed as tourist area. Swimming beach; fishing, hunting; boating (mooring, launching). Hiking. Bridle trail. Snowmobiling, sledding, ice-skating. Picnicking, playground. Tent & trailer sites (electric hookups). Standard fees. 35 mi NW on PA 120 to Westport, then 7 mi N on SR 4001. Phone 717/923-6004.

Bald Eagle. A 1,730-acre lake on approx 5,900 acres. Swimming beach; fishing, hunting; boating (rentals, mooring, launching, marina). Hiking. Sledding, ice-skating, ice boating. Picnicking, playground, snack bar, store. Tent & trailer sites. Standard fees. 13 mi SW off PA 150. Phone 814/625-2775.

The Heisey Museum. Victorian house-museum; early 1800s kitchen; ice house containing logging, farming and canal artifacts. (Tues-Fri; also by appt) 362 E Water St. Phone 717/748-7254. **Donation.**

Annual Event

Flaming Foliage Festival. 29 mi NW on PA 120, in Renovo. Includes parade, craft show and contest for festival queen. Phone 717/923-2411. 2nd wkend Oct.

Inn

★ ★ **VICTORIAN INN.** *402 E Water St. 717/748-8688.* 13 rms, 2 with shower only, 2 share bath, 2 story. S $55-$60; D $60-$65; each addl $10. Children by prior arrangement. TV. Complimentary full bkfst. Restaurant nearby. Ck-out 1 pm, ck-in 2 pm. Built in 1859; garden atrium. Cr cds: A, C, D, DS, MC, V.

Manheim (E-8)

(For accommodations see Lancaster, Lebanon; also see Cornwall)

Founded 1762 **Pop** 5,011 **Elev** 400 ft **Area code** 717 **Zip** 17545
Information Manheim Area Chamber of Commerce, 210 S Charlotte St; 717/665-6330.

Baron Henry William Stiegel founded Manheim and started manufacturing the flint glassware that bore his name. In 1770 he owned the town; by 1774 he was in debtor's prison, the victim of his own generosity and his poor choice of business associates. After his imprisonment, he made a meager living teaching here.

What to See and Do

 Mt Hope Estate & Winery. Restored sandstone mansion was originally built in the Federal style (ca 1800), then increased its size to 32 rms from an extension built in 1895, which changed the house's style to Victorian. Turrets, winding walnut staircase, hand-painted 18-ft ceilings, Egyptian marble fireplaces, grand ballroom, crystal chandeliers; greenhouse, solarium, gardens. Vineyards on grounds; wine tasting in billiards rm. (Daily; closed Jan 1, Thanksgiving, Dec 25) (See SEASONAL EVENT) ½ mi S of exit 20 at jct PA 72 & PA Tpke. Phone 717/665-7021. ¢¢

Zion Lutheran Church (1891). Victorian-Gothic structure built on site of original church; Stiegel donated the ground (1772) in exchange for one red rose from the congregation every yr. (Mon-Fri) 2 S Hazel St, 1 blk E of PA 72. Phone 717/665-5880.

Annual Event

Rose Festival. Celebration during which Stiegel decendant accepts annual rent of one red rose for church grounds. 2nd Sun June.

Seasonal Event

Pennsylvania Renaissance Faire. Mt Hope Estate & Winery. A 16th-century village is created in the acres of gardens surrounding the mansion. Eleven stages include a jousting arena with capacity of 6,000. Highlights include medieval jousting tournament, trial and dunking, human chess match, knighthood ceremonies. Wkends, Aug-mid-Oct.

Mansfield (B-6)

(See also Wellsboro)

Pop 3,538 **Elev** 1,120 ft **Area code** 717 **Zip** 16933 **E-mail** mwwacc @epix.net **Web** www.epix.net/~mwwacc/
Information Wellsboro Area Chamber of Commerce, 114 Main St, PO Box 733, Wellsboro 16901; 717/724-1926.

What to See and Do

Cowanesque Lake. Same facilities as Tioga-Hammond Lakes. (May-Sept) 15 mi N on US 15 to Lawrenceville, then 3½ mi W on Bliss Rd. Phone 717/835-5281.

Hills Creek State Park. Approx 400 acres. Swimming beach; fishing for muskellunge, largemouth bass, walleye in Hills Creek Lake; boating (rentals, mooring, launching). Hiking. Sledding, ice-skating, ice fishing. Picnicking, playground, snack bar, store. Tent & trailer sites, cabins. Interpretive program. Standard fees. 6 mi W, then N on unnumbered road. Phone 717/724-4246.

Tioga-Hammond Lakes. Twin lakes and dams for flood control and recreation. Swimming; fishing, hunting; boating. Trails. Picnicking. Camping (fee; some sites free). (Late Apr-Dec) 10 mi N on US 15, then 7 mi SW on PA 287. Phone 717/835-5281.

Motel

★ ★ **COMFORT INN.** *300 Gateway Dr. 717/662-3000; FAX 717/662-2551.* 100 rms, 2 story. S $49-$75; D $59-$85; each addl $6; under 18 free; golf plans; higher rates seasonal events. Crib avail. Pet accepted. TV; cable. Complimentary continental bkfst. Ck-out noon. Business servs avail. Exercise equipt; stair machines, bicycles. Cr cds: A, C, D, DS, ER, JCB, MC, V.

Meadville (B-2)

(See also Conneaut Lake, Franklin)

Settled 1788 **Pop** 14,318 **Elev** 1,100 ft **Area code** 814 **Zip** 16335
Information Crawford County Convention & Visitors Bureau, 242½ Chestnut St; 814/333-1258.

David Mead—Revolutionary War ensign, tavernkeeper and major-general in the War of 1812—and his brothers established Mead's Settlement in 1788. Colonel Lewis Walker started manufacture of hookless slide fasteners here; since 1923 these fasteners (now known as "zippers") have been the leading local industry. The city is also a major producer of yarn and thread and is home to many tool-and-die manufacturers.

What to See and Do

Allegheny College (1815). (1,750 students) Bentley Hall (1820) is a fine example of Federalist architecture. Also on campus are Bowman, Penelec & Megahan Art Galleries (phone 814/332-4365 for schedule). Library has colonial, Ida Tarbell and Lincoln collections. Tours of campus. N Main St. Phone 814/332-3100.

Baldwin-Reynolds House Museum (1841-1843). Restored mansion of Henry Baldwin, congressman and US Supreme Court justice. First and second floors refurbished in period; ground-level and third floors house interpretive museum with medical, dental, textile arts, military, Native American and other historical exhibits. Also on grounds is 1890 doctor's office. Elaborate landscaping. Tours (Memorial Day-Labor Day, Wed-Sun). 639 Terrace St. Phone 814/724-6080. ¢¢

Colonel Crawford Park. Within park is Woodcock Creek Lake. Swimming (fee); fishing, hunting; boating. Nature trail. Picnicking. Camping (fee). Park (Memorial Day-Labor Day, daily). 6 mi NE via PA 86, PA 198. Phone 814/724-6879. Camping per night ¢¢¢

Erie National Wildlife Refuge. Over 250 species of birds, as well as woodchuck, white-tailed deer, fox, beaver and muskrat are found on this 8,750-acre refuge. Fishing and hunting permitted; regulations at refuge office. Nature and ski trails; overlook; photo blind. Office, 1 mi E of Guys Mills on PA 198 (Mon-Fri). Refuge (daily). 10 mi E on PA 27. Phone 814/789-3585. **Free.**

Annual Event

Crawford County Fair. 3rd wk Aug.

Motel

★ ★ **DAYS INN.** 240 Conneaut Lake Rd, I-79 exit 36A. 814/337-4264; FAX 814/337-7304. 163 rms, 2 story. S $65-$85; D $70-$85; each addl $6; under 18 free; higher rates special events. Crib free. Pet accepted. TV; cable (premium), VCR avail (movies). Indoor pool; whirlpool, lifeguard. Restaurant 7 am-2 am, 5-10 pm; Sun 7 am-2 pm. Bar 3 pm-2 am. Ck-out 11 am. Coin lndry. Meeting rms. Business servs avail. Cr cds: A, D, DS, JCB, MC, V.

Media (F-9)

(For accommodations see Chester, Kennett Square, King of Prussia, Philadelphia, West Chester)

Pop 5,957 **Elev** 300 ft **Area code** 610
Information Delaware County Convention & Visitors Bureau, 200 E State St, Suite 100, 19063; 800/343-3983.

What to See and Do

Franklin Mint Museum. Houses original works by Andrew Wyeth and Norman Rockwell; collectibles are on display, including books, dolls, jewelry, furniture; artworks in porcelain, bronze, pewter, crystal and precious metals; one of the world's largest private mints. (Daily; closed major hols) 4 mi SW on US 1. Phone 610/459-6168. **Free.**

Newlin Mill Park. Park with operating stone gristmill (1704), furnished miller's house (1739), springhouse, blacksmith shop; milling exhibit. Tours, picnicking, fishing, nature trails. (Daily) 7 mi SW via US 1, in Glen Mills. Phone 610/459-2359. Guided tour ¢

Ridley Creek State Park. Approx 2,600 acres of woodlands and meadows. Hiking, bicycling. Sledding. Picnicking, playground. S on US 1, then N on PA 352. Phone 610/892-3900. Within park is

Colonial Pennsylvania Plantation. A 200-yr-old farm is a living history museum that re-creates the life of a typical farm family of the late 1700s. Period tools and methods are used to perform seasonal and daily chores. Tours (Tues-Sat, by appt). Visitors may participate in some activities. (Mid-Apr-Nov, Sat & Sun) Phone 610/566-1725. ¢¢

Tyler Arboretum. 650 acres of ornamental and native plants. Outdoor "living museum" with a 20-mi system of trails; special fragrant garden and bird garden; notable trees planted in the 1800s; bookstore. Guided walks and educational programs each wk; phone for information. (Daily) Off PA 352 via Forge & Painter Rds, adj to Ridley Creek State Park. Phone 610/566-5431. ¢¢

Restaurants

★ ★ ★ **D'IGNAZIO'S TOWNE HOUSE.** 117 Veterans Square (19063). 610/566-6141. Hrs: 11:30 am-3 pm, 4:30-10 pm; Fri, Sat to 11 pm; Sun 4-8:30 pm. Closed some major hols. Res accepted. Bar to

midnight; Fri, Sat to 1 am; Sun 4-9 pm. Wine cellar. A la carte entrees: lunch $6-$12, dinner $10-$20. Child's meals. Specializes in prime rib, seafood, Italian specialties. Pianist Tues-Sat. Many stone fireplaces; extensive collection of memorabilia, antiques and personal photographs. Family-owned. Cr cds: A, DS, MC, V.

✔ ★ **PACKY'S PUB.** 113 W State St (19063). 610/891-0810. Hrs: 11:30-2 am; Sat, Sun from noon; Sat, Sun brunch to 4 pm; Sat, Sun from 5 pm in summer. Closed some major hols. Res accepted Sun-Thurs. Bar. Semi-a la carte: bkfst $5-$7, lunch $3-$7, dinner $7-$15. Sat, Sun brunch $5-$8. Specializes in home-cooked hot roast pork, giant burgers, pub salads. Musicians Fri, Sat. Pub atmosphere. Cr cds: A, DS, MC, V.

Mercer (C-1)

(See also Franklin)

Settled 1795 **Pop** 2,444 **Elev** 1,270 ft **Area code** 724 **Zip** 16137
Information Mercer Area Chamber of Commerce, 108 N Pitt St, PO Box 473; 724/662-4185.

What to See and Do

Magoffin House Museum (1821). Houses collection of Native American artifacts, pioneer tools, furniture, children's toys, clothing; military items. Some original furnishings; memorabilia. Special collection of artifacts from John Goodsell's trip to the North Pole with Peary in 1908-1909, as well as early maps, historic records; restored print shop. Office of Mercer County Historical Society is located in the **Anderson House**, just off Court House Sq. (Tues-Sat; closed hols) 119 S Pitt St. Phone 724/662-3490. **Free.**

Wendell August Forge, Inc. Creators of hand-hammered aluminum, bronze, copper, pewter, sterling silver and glass and crystal items hand-cut on stone wheel lathe; also limited-edition collectors' items. Gift shop. Self-guided tours (15-30 min). (Daily; closed hols) 10 mi SE on PA 58, in Grove City at 620 Madison Ave. Phone 724/458-8360. **Free.**

Motel

★ ★ ★ **HOWARD JOHNSON.** 835 Perry Hwy, US 19 S, just off I-80 exit 2. 724/748-3030; FAX 724/748-3484. 102 rms, 2 story. S $67; D $71-$74; each addl $6; suites $105-$125; under 18 free; higher rates special events. Crib free. Pet accepted. TV; cable (premium), VCR avail. Heated pool; lifeguard. Playground. Restaurant 6 am-11 pm; Fri, Sat open 24 hrs. Rm serv. Bar. Ck-out noon. Coin lndry. Meeting rms. Business servs avail. In-rm modem link. Bellhops. Bus depot transportation. Exercise equipt; weights, bicycles, sauna. Private patios, balconies. Amish craft shop in lobby. Cr cds: A, C, D, DS, JCB, MC, V.

Restaurant

✔ ★ ★ **TIMBERS.** 103 Timber Village Center, on US 62. 724/662-4533. Hrs: 11:30 am-10 pm; Fri, Sat to 11 pm; Sun to 8 pm. Closed Mon; major hols. Bar. Complete meals: dinner $6.95-$13.95. Child's meals. Specializes in seafood, prime rib. Rustic atmosphere; in converted barn (1872). Cr cds: A, DS, MC, V.

Milford (C-10)

(See also Bushkill, Delaware Water Gap)

Settled 1733 **Pop** 1,064 **Elev** 503 ft **Area code** 717 **Zip** 18337
Information Pocono Mts Vacation Bureau, 1004 Main St, Stroudsburg 18360; 717/424-6050; for free brochures phone 800/POCONOS.

The borough of Milford was settled by Thomas Quick, a Hollander. Governor Gifford Pinchot, noted forester and conservationist, lived here. His house, Grey Towers, is near the town.

What to See and Do

Canoeing, rafting, kayaking and tubing. Kittatinny Canoes. Trips travel down the Delaware River. Camping. (Mid-Apr-Oct, daily) S to Dingmans Ferry via US 209, then 1/2 mi E via PA 739 S, at Dingmans Ferry toll bridge. Phone 717/828-2338 or 800/FLOAT-KC. ¢¢¢¢¢

Dingmans Falls & Silver Thread Falls. Part of Delaware Water Gap National Recreation Area (see). Two of the highest waterfalls in the Pocono Mountains; many rhododendrons bloom in July. 8 mi S & W on US 209 near Dingmans Ferry. Phone 717/588-2451. **Free.**

Grey Towers (1886). A 100-acre estate originally built as summer house for philanthropist James W. Pinchot; became residence of his son, Gifford Pinchot, "father of American conservation," governor of Pennsylvania and first chief of USDA Forest Service. Now site of Pinchot Institute for Conservation Studies. Tours. (Memorial Day wknd-Labor Day wknd, daily; after Labor Day-Veterans Day, Fri-Mon afternoons; rest of yr, by appt; occasionally closed for conferences; phone ahead) On US 6, 1/2 mi W via PA 206, 2 mi E of I-84 exit 10. Phone 717/296-6401. **Donation.**

Motels

★ ★ ★ **BEST WESTERN INN AT HUNTS LANDING.** *(900 US 6 & US 209, Matamoras 18336)* 6 mi E on I-84, exit 11. 717/491-2400; FAX 717/491-2422. 108 rms, 4 story. May-Oct: S $69-$75; D $77-$85; each addl $6; suites $115-$125; under 12 free; lower rates rest of yr. Crib free. Pet accepted. TV; cable. Indoor pool; sauna, lifeguard. Restaurant 6:30 am-9 pm; Fri, Sat to 10 pm; Sun from 7 am. Bar 4-11 pm; entertainment. Ck-out 11 am. Coin lndry. Meeting rms. Business servs avail. In-rm modem link. Sundries. Gift shop. Game rm. Lawn games. Cr cds: A, C, D, DS, MC, V.

⑃ 🐾 🏊 ≈ 🔥 SC

✔★ **MYER.** RD 4, Box 8030, 1/4 mi E on US 6, PA 209. 717/296-7223; res: 800/764-6937. 19 cottages, 1 kit. S $40-$50; D $45-$70; each addl $5; kit. unit $90. Crib free. Pet accepted, some restrictions. TV; cable. Restaurant nearby. Ck-out 11 am. Lawn games. Refrigerators. Picnic tables, grills. Cr cds: A, C, D, DS, MC, V.

🐾 🐾 ≈ 🔥 SC

Inns

★ **BLACK WALNUT.** RD 2, Box 9285 Firetower Rd, Firetower Rd, 2 mi E off US 6, I-84 exit 10, 1 mi, follow signs. 717/296-6322; FAX 717/296-7696. 12 rms, 8 with bathrm, 2 story. No A/C. D $60-$100; hols (2-day min). TV in sitting rm; movies. Dining rm 8:30-10 am; 5:30-9 pm; closed Mon-Thur. Ck-out 11 am, ck-in 3 pm. Rec rm. Tudor-style stone house; marble fireplace; some antiques. 160-acre estate on the bank of a 5-acre stocked pond; paddleboats, rowboats. Cr cds: A, MC, V.

🐾 ≈ 🔥

★ ★ **CLIFF PARK.** RR 4, Box 7200 Cliffpark Rd, 1 1/2 mi W of PA 6, on 6th St to Cliffpark Rd. 717/296-6491; FAX 717/296-3982; res: 800/225-6535. 18 rms, 1-3 story. S $82.50-$140; D $95-$205; EP, MAP avail; wknd rates. Dining rm 8-10 am, noon-3 pm, 6-9 pm. Business servs avail. In-rm modem link. 9-hole golf, greens fee $6-$13, pro, putting green,

rentals. X-country ski; rentals. Hiking trails. Near Delaware River. Classic country inn; originally a farmhouse built 1820. Some fireplaces. Screened porches. Cr cds: A, C, D, DS, MC, V.

⑃ 🐾 🏌 ≈ 🏊 SC

★ ★ **PINE HILL FARM.** 2 1/2 mi N on US 6, PA 209 (Broad St); left on Cummins Hill Rd; turn at the first Pine Hill Farm sign and continue on a 1-mi climb on a public access road. 717/296-7395. 3 rms in main house, 2 story, 2 suites in adj cottage. No rm phones. S $75-$100; D $85-$110; each addl $25; suites $100-$110; hols (2-night min). Adults only. TV in some rms and sitting rm. Complimentary full bkfst. Ck-out 11 am, ck-in 3 pm. Bellman. X-country ski on site. Main house was the original farmhouse (ca 1870); fireplace, many antique furnishings. Located atop hill overlooking the Delaware River. Includes 268 acres of fields and forests, with 5 mi of 1800s logging trails for walking, birdwatching. Cr cds: DS, MC, V.

≈ ≈ 🔥

Monroeville

(see Pittsburgh)

Mount Pocono (C-9)

(See also Pocono Mountains)

Pop 1,795 **Elev** 1,840 ft **Area code** 717 **Zip** 18344
Information Pocono Mts Vacation Bureau, 1004 Main St, Stroudsburg 18360; 717/424-6050; for brochures phone 800/POCONOS.

One of the many thriving resort communities in the heart of the Pocono Mountains, Mount Pocono offers recreation year round in nearby parks, lakes and ski areas.

What to See and Do

Gouldsboro State Park. Approx 3,000 acres; 250-acre lake. Swimming beach; fishing, hunting, boating (rentals, mooring, launching). Hiking. Ice-skating, ice fishing. Standard fees. 10 mi N on PA 611 & I-380, then NE on PA 507. Phone 717/894-8336.

Memorytown, USA. Old-time village includes hex shop, country store, store with artifacts; ice-cream parlor; paddle-boats, mini-raceway, fishing; entertainment; lodging, picnic area, restaurant and tavern. Summer festivals. Fee for some activities. (June-Sept, daily; Mar-May, Fri-Sun) 2 mi E via PA 940. Phone 717/839-1680. **Free.**

Mount Airy Lodge Ski Area. 2 double chairlifts; patrol, school, rentals; snowmaking; cafeteria, restaurant, bar; nursery, lodge. Longest run 1,800 ft; vertical drop 240 ft. Also cross-country trails. (Mid-Dec-late Mar) Just E of town via PA 940. Phone 717/839-8811. ¢¢¢¢¢

Apple Tree Farm. Petting farm. Horse-drawn wagon rides, pony rides. Bakery; country store. (Apr-Nov, daily) Grange Rd. Phone 717/839-7680. ¢¢

Pocono Knob. Excellent view of surrounding countryside. 1 1/2 mi E on Knob Rd.

Tobyhanna State Park. Approx 5,400 acres with 170-acre lake. Swimming beach; fishing, hunting, boating (rentals, mooring, launching). Hiking, biking. Cross-country skiing. Snowmobiling, ice-skating, ice fishing. Tent & trailer sites. Standard fees. 5 mi N on PA 611, then NE on PA 423. Phone 717/894-8336.

Motels

✔★ **HAMPTON COURT INN.** MCR 1, Box 4, 1/2 mi E on PA 940. 717/839-2119; FAX 717/839-6982. 14 rms. No rm phones. S $45-$50; D $55-$65; each addl $8. TV; cable. Pool. Complimentary continental bkfst. Restaurant 5-10 pm; wkends to 11 pm; closed Tues. Ck-out 11 am. Cr cds: A, C, D, MC, V.

★★ **SUPER 8.** HCR 1, Box 115, 1½ mi S on PA 611. 717/839-7728. 37 rms. May-Sept: S $58-$135; D $65-$135; each addl $5; lower rates rest of yr. Crib free. TV; cable. Pool; whirlpool. Playground. Restaurant 6 am-10 pm. Ck-out 11 am. Business servs avail. In-rm modem link. Sundries. Downhill ski 5 mi. Private patios, picnic tables. Cr cds: A, C, D, DS, MC, V.

Inns

★★★ **FRENCH MANOR.** (Huckleberry Rd, South Sterling 18460) N on PA 196, E on PA 423, then continue N on PA 191, left on Huckleberry Rd. 717/676-3244; FAX 717/676-9786; res: 800/523-8200. 9 rms, 3 story. No rm phones. S, D $165-$180. Adults only. TV in sitting rm. Indoor pool privileges. Dining rm (public by res; jacket required) 8:30-10 am, noon-2 pm, 6-9 pm. Rm serv. Ck-out 11 am, ck-in 2 pm. Airport, bus depot transportation. X-country ski on premises. French chateau-style; Spanish slate roof; patio; 38-ft high dining rm with beamed ceilings; Great Hall has 2 floor-to-ceiling fireplaces. Antiques. Cr cds: A, DS, MC, V.

★★★ **STERLING.** (PA 191, South Sterling 18460) N on PA 196, E on PA 423, N on PA 191. 717/676-3311; FAX 717/676-9786; res: 800/523-8200. 54 units, 3 story, 16 suites, 4 cottages. MAP: S $75-$95, D $140-$160; suites, cottages $190-$220; family, wkly rates; ski, golf plans; lower rates mid-wk. Crib $10. TV in some rms; cable. Indoor pool; whirlpool. Dining rm 8-10 am, noon-1:30 pm, 6-8:30 pm. Ck-out 11 am, ck-in 2 pm. Business servs avail. Airport, bus depot transportation. Tennis. Downhill ski 10 mi; x-country ski on site, rentals. Sleigh rides. Rec rm. Lawn games. On lake. Built in 1850s; country and Victorian suites. Some fireplaces. Cr cds: A, DS, MC, V.

Resorts

★★★ **CAESARS PARADISE STREAM.** 3 mi E on PA 940. 717/839-8881; FAX 717/839-1842; res: 800/233-4141. 164 rms. MAP: D $235-$320; wkly rates. Couples only. TV; cable, VCR avail (movies $5). 2 pools, 1 indoor; whirlpool, poolside serv, lifeguard. Rm serv limited hrs. Snack bar. Bar noon-2 am. Ck-out 11 am, ck-in 3 pm. Business servs avail. Grocery, package store. Sundries. Bus depot transportation. Tennis. Miniature golf. Bicycles. Boats, paddleboats. Snowmobiles available. Lawn games. Soc dir; entertainment. Game rm. Exercise equipt; weights, bicycles, sauna. Hiking trails. Archery. Fireplace in some rms. Cr cds: A, C, D, DS, MC, V.

★★★ **POCONO MANOR.** Pocono Manor (18349), On PA 314, 2 mi W of PA 611 in Pocono Manor. 717/839-7111; FAX 717/839-0708; res: 800/233-8150. 190 rms in inn, 65 in 2 lodges. MAP: S $90-$120; D $160-$200; each addl $50; under 8 free; higher rates special events. Crib $7. Serv charge. TV. Indoor/outdoor pool; poolside serv, lifeguard. Free supervised child's activities. Dining rm (public by res) 7:30-9 am, noon-1 pm, 6:30-8:30 pm. Rm serv. Box lunches, snacks. Bar 11-2 am. Ck-out 11 am, ck-in 4 pm. Business servs avail. In-rm modem link. Bellhops. Grocery, package store 2 mi. Free airport, bus depot transportation. Sports dir. Tennis, pro. 36-hole golf, pro, putting green, driving range. Trapshooting. Artificial ice rink, sleigh rides. Indoor, outdoor games. Bicycles. Soc dir. Entertainment. Rec rm; library. Exercise equipt; weights, bicycles, sauna. Extra fee for some activities. On 3,100-acre mountain estate. Cr cds: A, D, MC, V.

Restaurant

★ **TOKYO TEAHOUSE.** PA 940, 3 mi W, off I-380 exit 8. 717/839-8880. Hrs: 11:30 am-10 pm. Closed Tues in July, Aug. Res accepted. Japanese menu. Semi-a la carte: lunch $4.95-$7, dinner $7.25-$19.95. Specialties: sushi, steak takiki. Cr cds: A, D, DS, MC, V.

New Castle (D-1)

(See also Beaver Falls, Harmony)

Settled 1798 **Pop** 28,334 **Elev** 860 ft **Area code** 724 **Web** www .lawrencecounty.com/tourism

Information Lawrence County Tourist Promotion Agency, 138 W Washington St, 16101; 724/654-5593.

At the junction of the Shenango, Mahoning and Beaver rivers, this was long an important Native American trading center; the Delawares used it as their capital. Today, the fireworks and plastics industries have become an integral part of the community.

What to See and Do

Greer House. Turn-of-the-century restored mansion houses the Lawrence County Historical Society. Museum has extensive Shenango China and Castleton China collections, Sports Hall of Fame, fireworks rm. Archives; workshops and speakers. (Wed, Sun; also by appt) 408 N Jefferson. Phone 724/658-4022. **Donation.**

Hoyt Institute of Fine Arts. Cultural arts center housed in two early 20th-century mansions on four acres of landscaped grounds; permanent art collection, changing exhibits, period rms, performing arts programs, classes. Tours. (Tues-Sat; closed major hols) 124 E Leasure Ave. Phone 724/652-2882. **Donation.**

Living Treasures Animal Park. Pet and feed over 100 species from around the world. (Memorial Day-Labor Day, daily; May, Sept, Oct, wkends) On US 422. Phone 724/924-9571. ¢¢¢

McConnell's Mill State Park. Approx 2,500 acres. Century-old mill surrounded by beautiful landscape and scenery. Fishing, hunting; whitewater boating. Hiking. Picnicking, store. Historical center, interpretive program. Standard fees. 12 mi E via US 422. Phone 724/368-8091 or 724/368-8811.

Scottish Rite Cathedral. On hillside, six 32-ft columns dominate city's skyline. Large auditorium; cathedral; ballroom. Local Masonic headquarters. Tours (by appt). Highland & Lincoln Aves. Phone 724/654-6683. ¢

Motel

✔★★ **COMFORT INN.** 1740 New Butler Rd (16101), 11 mi W on US 422 Business. 724/658-7700; FAX 724/658-7727. 79 rms, 2 story, 13 suites. S $59-$69; D $64-$79; each addl $5; suites $90-$119; under 18 free. Wkly rates; higher rates July 4, Dec 31. Crib free. Pet accepted, some restrictions; $6/day. TV; cable. Complimentary continental bkfst. Restaurant nearby. Ck-out noon. Meeting rm. Business servs avail. Valet serv. Exercise equipt; weight machine, bicycle, sauna. Some refrigerators. Cr cds: A, C, D, DS, JCB, MC, V.

New Hope (Bucks Co) (E-10)

(See also Doylestown; also see Lambertville & Trenton, NJ)

Founded 1681 **Pop** 1,400 **Elev** 76 ft **Area code** 215 **Zip** 18938
Information Information Center, 1 W Mechanic St, PO Box 633; 215/862-5880.

The river village of New Hope was originally the largest part of a 1,000-acre land grant from William Penn to Thomas Woolrich of Shalford, England. In the 20th century, the area gained fame as the home of artists, literary and theatrical personalities.

What to See and Do

New Hope & Ivyland Rail Road. A 9-mi, 50-min narrated train ride through Bucks County. Reading Railroad passenger coaches from the 1920s depart from restored 1890 New Hope Station. Gift shop. (Early Apr-Nov, daily; Dec, special Santa Train Fri-Sun; rest of yr, wkends) W Bridge St, adj to Delaware Canal. Phone 215/862-2332. ¢¢¢

Parry Barn (1784). Owned by New Hope Historical Society; operated as commercial art gallery. S Main St, opp mansion. **Free.**

Parry Mansion Museum (1784). Restored stone house built by Benjamin Parry, prosperous merchant and mill owner. Eleven rooms on view, restored and furnished to depict period styles from late 18th to early 20th centuries. (May-Dec, Fri-Sun; also by appt) S Main & Ferry Sts. Phone 215/862-5652 or 215/862-5460. ¢¢

Peddler's Village. 18th-century-style village featuring over 70 specialty shops, eight restaurants, 60-rm inn (see INNS), festivals and craft competitions throughout the yr (see ANNUAL EVENTS). 42 acres with landscaped gardens and walkways. (Daily) 5 mi S on US 202 in Lahaska. Phone 215/794-4000. Also in village is

Carousel World. Learn about history of the carousel in turn-of-the-century park. Antique carousel rides. Gift shop. (Daily) Phone 215/794-8960. Carousel rides ¢

Washington Crossing Historical Park (see). 7 mi S on PA 32.

World Tubing Capital. On the Delaware River; two- to four-hour canoeing, rafting, tubing and kayaking trips; one-day outings to full vacation trips. (Apr-Oct) Bucks County River Country, PO Box 6, Point Pleasant 18950. Phone 215/297-5000. ¢¢¢¢-¢¢¢¢¢

Annual Events

Teddy Bear's Picnic. Peddler's Village. Teddy bear vendors, parades, competitions. "Bear clinic" for hurt bears. Appraisals. Music. Phone 215/794-4000. July 18-19.

Scarecrow Festival. Peddler's Village. Scarecrow making, pumpkin painting. Jack-O-Lantern & Gourd Art Contest. Square dancing, entertainment. Phone 215/794-4000. Sept 19-20.

Inns

★ ★ ★ **1740 HOUSE.** *(3690 River Rd, Lumberville 18933)* 7 mi N on PA 32. 215/297-5661. 24 rms. Wkends (Sat 2-day min), hols (3-4-day min): D $113; lower rates wkdays. Pool. Complimentary buffet bkfst. Ck-out noon, ck-in 2 pm. Meeting rms. Business servs avail. Balconies. Overlooks Delaware River. No cr cds accepted.

★ ★ ★ **AARON BURR HOUSE.** 80 W Bridge St. 215/862-2343; FAX 215/862-2343. 6 rms, 2 story, 2 suites. S, D $75-$150; each addl $20; suite $150-$195; wkly rates; lower rates mid-wk. Pet accepted. TV in sitting rm; cable, VCR avail. Complimentary full bkfst; afternoon refreshments. Restaurant nearby. Ck-out 11 am, ck-in 2 pm. Meeting rm. Business servs

avail. Concierge. Free bus depot transportation. Downhill ski 2 mi; x-country ski adj. Lawn games. Fireplace in suites. Built in 1854, some antiques. Screened flagstone patio. Totally nonsmoking. Cr cds: MC, V.

★ ★ ★ **BARLEY SHEAF FARM.** *(5281 York Rd (PA 202), Holicong 18928)* Approx 7 mi S on US 202. 215/794-5104; FAX 215/794-5332. E-mail barleysheaf@netreach.net; web www.netreach.net/n. 12 rms, 3 story. Rm phones avail. July-Oct, wkends: D $140-$255; each addl $20; lower rates rest of yr. TV in sitting rm; cable, VCR avail. Pool. Complimentary full bkfst; afternoon refreshments. Ck-out 11 am, ck-in 2 pm. Meeting rms. Business servs avail. In-rm modem link. Lawn games. Thirty-acre farm; built in 1740. Totally nonsmoking. Cr cds: A, MC, V.

★ ★ **CENTRE BRIDGE.** 2998 N River Rd, PA 32 & PA 263. 215/862-9139; FAX 215/862-9130. 9 rms, 2 story. No rm phones. D $80-$150; each addl $15. TV; cable. Complimentary continental bkfst. Restaurant (see CENTRE BRIDGE). Bar. Ck-out noon, ck-in 3 pm. Business servs avail. Sitting rm and terrace overlook river. Fireplace, antiques. Cr cds: A, MC, V.

★ ★ ★ **EVERMAY ON-THE-DELAWARE.** *(889 River Rd, Erwinna 18920)* 13 mi N on PA 32. 610/294-9100. E-mail moffly@evermay.com; web www.evermay.com. 16 rms, 4 story. No elvtrs. S $90-$150; D $95-$185; suite $235; guest house $150; wkends (2-day min). Children over 13 yrs only. TV in common rm; cable, VCR avail. Complimentary continental bkfst. Restaurant (see EVERMAY ON-THE-DELAWARE). Ck-out noon, ck-in 2 pm. Business servs avail. In-rm modem link. X-country ski on-site. Game rm. Rec rm. Lawn games. Bathrm phones; some fireplaces. On river. Built in 1790; classic Federal structure with Victorian antiques. On 25 acres. Totally nonsmoking. Cr cds: MC, V.

★ ★ ★ **THE FOX & HOUND.** 246 W Bridge St. 215/862-5082; res: 800/862-5082. Web cimarron.net/usa/pa/fx.html. 8 rms, 3 story. Some rm phones. S, D $65-$165; wkend rates. Children over 12 yrs only. TV avail; cable. Complimentary continental bkfst. Restaurant nearby. Ck-out 11 am, ck-in 1 pm. Business servs avail. Luggage handling. Health club privileges. Picnic tables. Stone manor house built in 1850. Cr cds: A, MC, V.

★ ★ ★ **GOLDEN PHEASANT INN.** *(763 River Rd, Erwinna 18920)* 13 mi N on PA 32. 610/294-9595; FAX 610/294-9882. 6 rms, 3 with shower only, 2 story, kit. suite. No rm phones. MAP: S, D $85-$155; each addl $10; suite $125-$155; wkly rates; hols (3-day min). Pet accepted; $10. Complimentary continental bkfst. Coffee in rms. Restaurant (see GOLDEN PHEASANT INN). Ck-out 11 am, ck-in 2 pm. Meeting rms. Cr cds: A, C, D, DS, MC, V.

★ ★ **GOLDEN PLOUGH.** *(US 202 & Street Rd, Lahaska 18931)* 5 mi S on US 202, in Peddler's Village. 215/794-4004; FAX 215/794-4008. Web www.peddlersuillage.com. 60 units in 6 buildings, 2-3 story, 19 suites. S, D $99-$300; each addl $15; suites $175-$300. Crib free. TV; cable. Complimentary continental bkfst. Complimentary coffee in rms. Restaurant (see SPOTTED HOG). Ck-out 11 am, ck-in 3 pm. Meeting rms. Business servs avail. In-rm modem link. Some balconies, in-rm whirlpools. Country decor, antiques. Cr cds: A, C, D, DS, MC, V.

★ ★ **HOLLILEIF.** *(677 Durham Rd (PA 413), Wrightstown 18940)* S on PA 232, approx 1/2 mi S on PA 413. 215/598-3100. 5 rms, 3 story. No rm phones. D $85-$155; each addl $20. TV in sitting rm, VCR avail (free movies). Complimentary full bkfst; afternoon refreshments. Ck-out 11:30 am, ck-in 3 pm. Business servs avail. Lawn games. 18th-century house; antiques, fireplace. Totally nonsmoking. Cr cds: A, DS, MC, V.

★ ★ **HOTEL DU VILLAGE.** *2535 N River Rd, N River Rd (PA 32) & Phillips Mill Rd.* 215/862-9911; FAX 215/862-9788. 20 rms, 2 story. No rm phones. S, D $85-$100; each addl $5; wkly rates. Pool. Complimentary continental bkfst. Dining rm 5:30-9 pm; Fri, Sat to 10:30 pm; Sun 3-9 pm; closed Mon, Tues. Bar. Ck-out 11 am, ck-in after 2 pm. Tennis. Small Tudor-style country inn on spacious grounds; former estate. Cr cds: A, D.

★ **INN AT PHILLIPS MILL.** *2590 N River Rd, 1½ mi N on PA 32.* 215/862-2984. 4 rms, 3 story, 1 suite. D $80; suite $90. Closed Jan. Pool. Dining rm (see INN AT PHILLIPS MILL). Rm serv. Ck-out 1 pm, ck-in 2 pm. Gift shop. Built in 1750 as stone barn; antiques. No cr cds accepted.

★ ★ ★ **INN TO THE WOODS.** *(150 Glenwood Rd, Washington Crossing 18977)* 6 mi S on PA 32. 215/493-1974; FAX 215/493-7592; res: 800/982-7619. E-mail intowoods@aol.com; web www.in2woods.com. 6 rms, 5 with shower only, 3 story, 1 suite. Some rm phones. S $90-$165; D $90-$185; each addl $25; suite $110-$195; wkend plans (2-day min). Children over 10 yrs only. TV; cable. VCR avail (movies). Complimentary full bkfst; afternoon refreshments. Ck-out 11 am, ck-in 2 pm. Luggage handling. Concierge serv. Business servs avail. In-rm modem link. Tennis privileges. X-country ski 1 mi. Health club privileges. Lawn games. On 10 acres of forest with hiking trails. Totally nonsmoking. Cr cds: A, MC, V.

★ **THE LOGAN.** *10 W Ferry St, at Main St.* 215/862-2300. 16 rms, 10 with shower only, 3 story. S, D $75-$150; each addl $17; under 3 free; wkly, wkday rates; 3-day min hols. Crib avail. TV; cable. Complimentary continental bkfst. Restaurant 11 am-11 pm. Ck-out noon, ck-in 3-10 pm. Downhill/x-country ski 5 mi. On canal; built in 1722. One of the oldest inns in US. Cr cds: A, D, DS, MC, V.

★ ★ **MANSION INN.** *9 S Main St, center of town.* 215/862-1231; FAX 215/862-0277. E-mail mansion@pil.net. 9 rms, 3 story, 5 suites. No elvtr. D $160-$225; suites $205-$305; min stay 2-3 days. Children over 16 yrs only. TV; cable (premium). Pool. Complimentary full bkfst. Complimentary coffee delivered to rms. Restaurant nearby. Ck-out 11 am, ck-in 2 pm. Business servs avail. In-rm modem link. Luggage handling. Concierge serv. X-country ski 15 mi. Health club privileges. Some fireplaces. Built (1865); Victorian decor. Totally nonsmoking. Cr cds: A, MC, V.

★ ★ **PINEAPPLE HILL.** *1324 River Rd, 4 mi S on PA 32.* 215/862-1790; FAX 215/862-5273. Web www.pineapple.com. 8 rms, 3 with shower only, 3 story, 3 suites. 2 rm phones. May-Dec: S $75-$130; D $85-$140; each addl $20; suites $125-$155; wkly rates; 2-day min wkends; lower rates rest of yr. TV; cable, VCR avail (movies). Pool. Complimentary full bkfst. Complimentary coffee in rms. Ck-out 11 am, ck-in 3 pm. Luggage handling. Concierge serv. Business servs avail. X-country ski on site. Health club privileges. Lawn games. Balconies. Picnic tables. On river. Built in 1790. Totally nonsmoking. Cr cds: A, MC, V.

★ ★ **TATTERSALL.** *(N River Road, Point Pleasant 18950)* 8 mi N on PA 32. 215/297-8233; FAX 215/297-5093; res: 800/297-4988. E-mail mhg17a@Progidy.com; web www.travelassist.com/neg/tall4/html. 6 rms, 2 story, 1 suite. S $60-$99; D $70-$130; each addl $15; suite $99-$115. TV in sitting rm. Complimentary full bkfst; afternoon refreshments. Restaurant nearby. Ck-out noon, ck-in 2 pm. Business servs avail. House (1740); porches, marble fireplace, antiques. Smoking in sitting rm only. Cr cds: A, DS, MC, V.

✔★ ★ ★ **WEDGWOOD.** *111 W Bridge St.* 215/862-2520; FAX 215/862-2570. 12 rms, 2 story. Some rm phones. S $75-$120; D $95-$165; each addl $20; suites $150-$210. Pet accepted. Complimentary full bkfst; afternoon refreshments. Concierge serv. Meeting rm. Business servs avail. Health club privileges. Lawn games.

Microwaves avail. Picnic tables, grills. Built 1870; antiques, many Wedgwood pieces, some fireplaces. Totally nonsmoking. Cr cds: MC, V.

★ ★ ★ **THE WHITEHALL INN.** *(1370 Pineville Rd, New Hope)* 215/598-7945; res: 888/379-4483; FAX 215/794-8078. Web www.innbook.com. 5 rms, 3 story, 1 suite. No rm phones. S, D $140-$195; suite $195; wkends, hols (2-3-day min). Complimentary full bkfst; afternoon refreshments. Ck-out 11 am, ck-in after 3 pm. Business servs avail. Luggage handling. Concierge serv. 18-hole golf privileges, pro, putting green, driving range. Downhill ski 7 mi; x-country ski on-site. Health club privileges. Pool. Lawn games. Many fireplaces. Picnic tables. Built in 1794; set on 12 rolling acres. Antiques. Totally nonsmoking. Cr cds: A, C, D, DS, MC, V.

Restaurants

★ ★ **CENTRE BRIDGE INN.** *(See Centre Bridge Inn)* 215/862-9139. Hrs: 5:30-9:30 pm; Fri, Sat to 10 pm; Sun brunch 11:30 am-2:30 pm; dinner 3:30-8:30 pm. Closed Dec 25. Res accepted Fri-Sun. Continental menu. Bar. Semi-a la carte: dinner $18.95-$28.95; brunch $28. Specializes in lamb, salmon. Entertainment Sat. Valet parking Sat. Outdoor dining. Stone fireplace. Patio overlooks canal. Cr cds: A, MC, V.

✔★ ★ **COCK 'N BULL.** *(PA 263 and US 202, Lahaska 18931)* S on US 202, in Peddler's Village. 215/794-4000. Web peddlersvillage.com. Hrs: 11 am-3 pm, 5-9 pm; Fri to 10 pm; Sat 4-10 pm; Sun 4-8 pm; Sun brunch 9:30 am-2:30 pm. Closed Jan 1, Dec 25. Res accepted (dinner only). Bar. Semi-a la carte: lunch $4.95-$8.25, dinner $11.25-$24.95. Sun brunch $14.95. Specialties: country chicken pie, beef Burgundy. Salad bar. Family-owned. Cr cds: A, D, DS, MC, V.

★ ★ ★ **CUTTALOSSA INN.** *(3498 River Rd/PA 32, Lumberville 18933)* 6 mi N on PA 32. 215/297-5082. E-mail cutta@dynanet.com; web www.ansdata.com/cutta. Hrs: 11 am-2 pm, 5:30-9 pm; Fri, Sat 5:30-10 pm. Closed Sun; Jan 1, Dec 24, 25. Bar. Complete meals: lunch $6-$15, dinner $18-$28. Specializes in seafood. Entertainment in summer exc Mon. Outdoor dining. Built 1750; overlooks waterfall and wooden bridge. Cr cds: A, MC, V.

★ ★ ★ **EVERMAY ON-THE-DELAWARE.** *(See Evermay On-The-Delaware Inn)* 610/294-9100. E-mail moffly@evermay.com; web www.evermay.com. Hrs: 7-11 pm. Closed Mon-Thurs. Res required. Bar. Wine cellar. Complete meal: $57. Specialties: grilled yellowfin tuna, roast loin of veal with lentils. Menu changes daily. Jacket. Cr cds: MC, V.

★ ★ **FORAGER.** *1600 River Rd.* 215/862-9477. E-mail forag rest@aol.com. Hrs: 5-10 pm; Fri to 11 pm; Sat noon-11 pm; Sun noon-9 pm. Closed Tues; Jan 1, Thanksgiving, Dec 25. Res accepted; required Sat dinner. Contemporary Amer menu. Bar. A la carte entrees: lunch, dinner $13.95-$21.95. Child's meals. Specialties: Thai chicken curry, grilled salmon, seared sea scallops. Own pastries, ice cream. Cabaret Fri. Outdoor dining. Contemporary decor with local artists' works; woodburning oven. Cr cds: A, D, DS, MC, V.

★ ★ ★ **GOLDEN PHEASANT INN.** *(See Golden Pheasant Inn)* 610/294-9595. Web www.goldenpheasant.com. Hrs: 5:30-10 pm; Sun 11 am-9 pm. Closed Mon. Res accepted. French menu. Bar. Wine cellar. A la carte entrees: dinner $18.95-$24.95. Sun brunch $18.95. Specialties: roast lamb, crabmeat Brittany, steak au poivre. Own baking. Restored 1857 inn; dining rm in solarium, overlooks canal. Cr cds: A, C, D, DS, MC, V.

★ ★ **HOTEL DU VILLAGE.** *2535 N River Rd (PA 32), jct Phillips Mill Rd & N River Rd (PA 32).* 215/862-9911. Hrs: 5:30-9 pm; Fri, Sat to 10:30 pm; Sun 3-9 pm. Closed Mon, Tues; Dec 25; also Jan Sun-Wed.

Res accepted. French menu. Bar. A la carte entrees: dinner $14-$20. Specialties: filet of beef Béarnaise, sweet breads. English manor house; elegant dining. Cr cds: A, D.

★ ★ **INN AT PHILLIPS MILL.** (See Inn At Phillips Mill) 215/862-9919. Hrs: 5:30-9:30 pm. Closed Dec 25; also Jan. Res accepted, required Sat. French country menu. Setups. A la carte entrees: $14-$24.50. Specialties: sole bonne femme, filet de boeuf rochambeau. Entertainment Fri, Sun. Outdoor dining in garden setting. Jacket. No cr cds accepted.

★ ★ ★ **JEAN PIERRE'S.** (101 S State St, Newtown 18940) State St & Centre Ave, 3 mi from I-95 exit 30. 215/968-6201. Hrs: 11:30 am-2 pm, 5:30-9:30 pm; Sun 4:30-8 pm. Closed Mon; Jan 1, Dec 25. Res accepted. French menu. Wine cellar. Prix fixe: lunch $19.50. A la carte entrees: dinner $22-$29. Specializes in imported fish, rack of lamb, fresh game. Own pastries. In home built in 1747. Fireplaces. Cr cds: A, C, D, DS, MC, V.

★ ★ **JENNY'S BISTRO.** (US 202 & Street Rd, Lahaska 18931) 5 mi S on US 202, in Peddler's Village. 215/794-4020. Web peddlervillage.com. Hrs: 11 am-3 pm, 4-9 pm; Mon to 3 pm; Fri, Sat to 10 pm; Sun 4:30-10 pm. Sun brunch 10 am-3 pm. Closed Dec 25. Res accepted. Continental menu. Bar. A la carte entrees: lunch $4.95-$9.95, dinner $15.95-$24.95; Sun brunch $5.25-$9.95. Specialties: lobster ravioli, filet Chesterfield, mushrooms Pennsylvania. Jazz and blues Fri, Sat. Cr cds: A, C, D, DS, MC, V.

★ ★ ★ **ODETTE'S.** S River Rd, 1 mi S on PA 32. 215/862-2432. Hrs: 11:30-2 am; Sun brunch 10:30 am-1:30 pm. Res accepted; required hols. Continental menu. Bar. Extensive wine list. A la carte entrees: lunch $6-$8, dinner $15-$22. Sun brunch $15.95. Child's meals. Specializes in veal chops, salmon. Pianist. Valet parking. Built in 1794 as bargeman's inn; overlooks Delaware River; memorabilia of Odette Myrtil Logan of South Pacific fame. Cr cds: A, MC, V.

★ **SPOTTED HOG.** (See Golden Plough Inn) 215/794-4040. Web www.peddlersvillage.com. Hrs: 7 am-11 pm; Sun to 9 pm. Closed Thanksgiving, Dec 25. Bar to midnight; Fri, Sat to 1 am; Sun to 10 pm. A la carte entrees: bkfst $2.95-$7.25, lunch, dinner $3.25-$18.95. Child's meals. Specializes in stir fry, pizza, calzones. Entertainment Thurs-Sat. Cr cds: A, C, D, DS, MC, V.

New Stanton (E-2)

(See also Connellsville, Greensburg)

Pop 2,081 **Elev** 980 ft **Area code** 724 **Zip** 15672
Information Laurel Highlands Visitors Bureau, Town Hall, 120 E Main St, Ligonier 15658; 724/238-5661.

What to See and Do

L.E. Smith Glass Co. Reproductions of several styles of antique handcrafted glass. Children under 6 yrs not admitted. (Mon-Fri; closed 1st 2 wks July) 6 mi SE via US 119, PA 31, in Mt Pleasant, 1900 Liberty St. Phone 724/547-3544 for tour schedule. **Free.**

Motels

★ ★ **DAYS INN.** 127 W Byers Ave. 724/925-3591; FAX 724/925-9859. 142 rms, 3 story. S $47-$50; D $49-$56; each addl $5; under 18 free. Crib free. TV; cable (premium). Pool; lifeguard. Restaurant

6-11 am, 4-10 pm; Sat, Sun from 7 am. Rm serv. Bar 4 pm-midnight; entertainment. Ck-out 11 am. Coin lndry. Meeting rms. Business servs avail. Sundries. Exercise equipt; bicycles, treadmill. Microwaves avail. Cr cds: A, DS, MC, V.

✔ ★ ★ **HOWARD JOHNSON.** 112 W Byers Ave, 1 blk S off US 119, 1/4 mi SW of PA Tpke exit 8. 724/925-3511. 87 rms, 2 story. Mid-May-Sept: S $38-$74; D $45-$71; each addl $5; under 18 free; lower rates rest of yr. Crib free. TV; cable (premium), VCR avail (movies). Heated pool. Playground. Complimentary continental bkfst. Restaurant adj open 24 hrs. Ck-out noon. Business servs avail. In-rm modem link. Valet serv. Refrigerators, microwaves avail. Cr cds: A, C, D, DS, MC, V.

Norristown (E-9)

(See also King of Prussia, Kulpsville, Philadelphia)

Founded 1704 **Pop** 30,749 **Elev** 130 ft **Area code** 610 **E-mail** vlyforge@libertynet.org **Web** www.valleyforge.org
Information Valley Forge Convention and Visitors Bureau, 600 W Germantown Pike, Suite 130, Plymouth Meeting 19462; 610/834-1500.

William Penn, Jr, owner of the 7,600-acre tract around Norristown, sold it to Isaac Norris and William Trent for 50¢ an acre in 1704. It became a crossroads for colonial merchants and soldiers; Washington's army camped nearby. Dutch, German, Swedish, Welsh and English immigrants left their mark on the city. Today Norristown, still a transportation hub, houses many industries and serves as a county government center.

What to See and Do

Elmwood Park Zoo. Features extensive North American waterfowl area; cougars, bobcats, bison, elk; outdoor aviary; birds of prey; children's zoo barn; museum with exhibit on animal senses. (Daily; closed Jan 1, Thanksgiving, Dec 25) Harding Blvd, off US 202. Phone 610/277-3825. ¢¢

Peter Wentz Farmstead. Restored and furnished mid-18th-century country mansion, twice used by Washington during the Pennsylvania campaign. More than 70 acres with demonstration field and orchard crops of the period. Slide presentation; costumed interpreters; reconstructed 1744 barn with farm animals. (Daily exc Mon; closed Jan 1, Thanksgiving, Dec 25, also 2nd wk Sept) 10 mi NW via US 202, W via PA 73 on Schultz Rd, in Worcester. Phone 610/584-5104. **Free.**

Valley Forge National Historical Park (see). NW on US 422 to Trooper, then S.

Inn

★ ★ ★ **WILLIAM PENN INN.** (US 202 & Sumneytown Pke, Gwynedd 19436) 5 mi N on US 202. 215/699-9277; FAX 215/699-4808. Web philanet.com/wmpenn/. 4 rms, 2 story, 3 suites. S, D $115-$135; suites $135-$165. TV; cable (premium). Complimentary continental bkfst. Restaurant (see WILLIAM PENN INN). Rm serv 5-10 pm. Ck-out 11 am, ck-in 1 pm. Business servs avail. In-rm modem link. Luggage handling. Refrigerators, minibars. Continuous operation since 1714; antiques, marble bathtubs. Totally nonsmoking. Cr cds: A, C, D, DS, MC, V.

Restaurants

★ ★ ★ **THE JEFFERSON HOUSE.** 2519 DeKalb Pike (19401). 610/275-3407. Hrs: 11:30 am-2:30 pm, 4:30-10 pm; Sun noon-8 pm; Sun brunch to 4 pm; early-bird dinner Mon-Sat 4-6 pm. Closed most major hols. Res accepted. Contemporary Amer menu. Bar to 2 am. Wine cellar. Semi-a la carte: lunch $4.95-$16.95, dinner $12.50-$32. Child's meals.

Specializes in pastas, prime meats. Jazz, blues Fri. Manor-house set on extensive, landscaped grounds; former Buckland estate. Family-owned. Cr cds: A, C, D, MC, V.

D ⟋ ♥

★ ★ **TIFFANY DINING PLACE AND GAZEBO.** *(799 DeKalb Pike, Centre Square 19422) 9 mi N on US 202, in Centre Square.* 610/272-1888. Hrs: 5-10 pm; Fri to 11 pm; Sat 4:15-11 pm; Sun 3:30-10 pm; early-bird dinner Mon-Fri 5-6:30 pm, Sat 4:15-5:30 pm; Sun brunch 10:30 am-2 pm. Closed Dec 25. Bar. Semi-a la carte: dinner $9.95-$24.95. Sun brunch $13.95. Child's meals. Specializes in New York sirloin, steak, fresh seafood. Salad bar. Also gazebo dining area. Cr cds: A, D, DS, MC, V.

D SC ⟋ ♥

★ ★ **TROLLEY STOP.** *(PA 73, Skippack) 9 mi N on US 202 to PA 73W.* 610/584-4849. Hrs: 11:30-2 am; early-bird dinner Mon-Fri 3-6 pm, Sat, Sun 2-5 pm. Closed Jan 1, Dec 25. Res accepted. Bar. Semi-a la carte: lunch $4.95-$9.95, dinner $6.95-$29.95. Sun brunch $6.95-$15.95. Child's meals. Specializes in seafood, veal, Angus beef. Pianist Wed-Sat. Dining rm in 1900s trolley. Cr cds: A, D, DS, MC, V.

D SC ⟋

★ ★ ★ **WILLIAM PENN INN.** *(See William Penn Inn)* 215/699-9272. Web www.philanet.com/wmpenn. Hrs: 11:30 am-3 pm, 5-10 pm; Fri, Sat to 11 pm; Sun 2-8 pm; early-bird dinner Mon-Fri 5-6:30 pm; Sun brunch 10:30 am-2 pm. Closed Dec 25. Res accepted. Continental menu. Bar. Semi-a la carte: lunch $5.25-$15, dinner $18-$30. Sun brunch $16.95. Specializes in seafood, roast rack of lamb, prime rib. Salad bar. Own pastries. Harpist, pianist Tues-Sat. Originally built as a tavern (1714); antiques. Guest rms avail. Cr cds: A, C, D, DS, MC, V.

D ⟋

North East (A-2)

(For accommodations see Erie)

Settled 1794 **Pop** 4,617 **Elev** 801 ft **Area code** 814 **Zip** 16428
Information North East Chamber of Commerce, 21 S Lake St; 814/725-4262.

In 1778, when Pennsylvania bought from the federal government the tract containing North East, the state gained 46 miles of Lake Erie frontage, a fine harbor and some of the best Concord-grape country in the nation.

What to See and Do

Winery tours.

Penn-Shore Vineyards and Winery. Guided tours; wine tastings. (Daily; closed some hols) 10225 E Lake Rd. Phone 814/725-8688. **Free.**

Heritage Wine Cellars. Guided tours; wine tastings. (Daily; closed some hols) 12162 E Main Rd. Phone 814/725-8015. **Free.**

Mazza Vineyards. Guided tours; wine tastings. (Daily; closed some hols) 11815 E Lake Rd. Phone 814/725-8695. **Free.**

Annual Events

Cherry Festival. Concessions, rides, games, parade. Mid-July.

Wine Country Harvest Festival. Gravel Pit Park and Gibson Park. Arts and crafts, bands, buses to wineries, food. Phone 814/725-4262. Last full wkend Sept.

Oil City (C-2)

(See also Franklin, Titusville)

Pop 11,949 **Elev** 1,000 ft **Area code** 814 **Zip** 16301

Spreading on both sides of Oil Creek and the Allegheny River, Oil City was born of the oil boom. Oil refining and the manufacture of oil machinery are its major occupations today. Nearby are natural gas fields. Seven miles northwest stood the famous oil-boom town of Pithole. In 1865 it expanded from a single farmhouse to a population of more than 10,000 in 5 months, as its first oil well brought in 250 barrels a day.

Motor Hotel

★ ★ **HOLIDAY INN.** *1 Seneca St, at State St Bridge.* 814/677-1221; FAX 814/677-0492. 103 rms, 5 story. S, D $65; each addl $5; suites $75-$99; family rates. Crib free. TV; cable. Heated pool; lifeguard. Restaurant 6:30 am-2 pm, 5-9 pm. Rm serv. Bar 5 pm-2 am, Sun from 1 pm. Ck-out noon. Meeting rms. Business servs avail. In-rm modem link. Bellhops. Valet serv. X-country ski 2 mi. Cr cds: A, C, D, DS, JCB, MC, V.

D ⟋ ≈ ⋈ ⋉ SC

Orbisonia (E-5)

(For accommodations see Chambersburg, Huntingdon)

Pop 447 **Elev** 640 ft **Area code** 814 **Zip** 17243

What to See and Do

East Broad Top Railroad. The oldest surviving narrow-gauge railroad east of the Rockies. Train ride (70 min); fascinating old equipment, buildings. Picnic area. (June-Oct, wkends only) On US 522. Phone 814/447-3011. ¢¢¢ Opp is

Rockhill Trolley Museum. Old-time trolleys; car barn and restoration shop tours. A 2-mi ride on Shade Gap Electric Railway. Gift shop. (Memorial Day-Oct, wkends) 1/2 mi W off US 522, on PA 994, in Rockhill Furnace. Phone 814/447-9576. ¢¢

Pennsylvania Dutch Area (E-8 - F-8)

(For accommodations see Allentown, Bird-in-Hand, Ephrata, Lancaster, Lebanon, Reading; also see Kutztown, Manheim)

Information Pennsylvania Dutch Convention & Visitors Bureau, 501 Greenfield Rd, Lancaster 17601; 717/299-8901 or 800/PADUTCH. There is also a downtown visitor center, at 100 S Queen St in the Lancaster Chamber of Commerce & Industry Building, which provides brochures, maps and other general information; also another on US 272 near PA Tpke exit 21.

From the Rhineland and Palatinate of Germany came great migrations of settlers to Pennsylvania in the 18th century, first near Philadelphia, and then moving west. Because they retained their customs and speech and developed beautiful and bountiful farms, the Pennsylvania Dutch (corruption of the German *Deutsch*) country is one of the state's greatest tourist attractions. There are all degrees of conservatism among these descendants of German immigrants, ranging from the Amish to the Brethren, but all share tremendous vigor, family devotion, love of the Bible and belief in thrift and hard work.

Many of the "plain people"—the Amish, Old Order Mennonites and Brethren (Dunkards)—live today much as they did a century ago. Married men wear beards, black coats and low-crowned black hats; women wear bonnets and long, simple dresses. They drive horses and buggies instead of cars, work long hours in the fields, shun the use of modern farm machinery and turn to the Bible for guidance. Despite their refusal to use machinery they are master farmers. (They were among the first to rotate crops and practice modern fertilization methods.) Their harvests are consistently among the best in the country.

Many of the Amish regard photographs as "graven images"; visitors should not take pictures of individuals without their permission.

Philadelphia (F-10)

Founded 1682 **Pop** 1,585,577 **Elev** 45 ft **Area code** 215

Information *Convention & Visitors Bureau, 1515 Market St, Ste 2020, 19102; 215/636-1666 or 800/537-7676.*

Suburbs Bristol, Chester, Fort Washington, Jenkintown, Kennett Square, King of Prussia, Media, Norristown, West Chester, Willow Grove; also Wilmington, DE and Camden, NJ. (See individual alphabetical listings.)

The nation's first capital has experienced a rebirth in the past few decades. Philadelphia has successfully blended its historic past with an electricity of modern times, all the while keeping an eye on the future. In the mid-18th century it was the second-largest city in the English-speaking world. Now, nearing the end of the 20th century, Philadelphia is the second-largest city on the East Coast and the fifth largest in the country. Here, in William Penn's City of Brotherly Love, the Declaration of Independence was written and adopted, the Constitution was molded and signed, the Liberty Bell was rung, Betsy Ross was said to have sewn her flag and Washington served most of his years as president.

This is the city of "firsts," including the first American hospital, medical college, women's medical college, bank, paper mill, steamboat, zoo, sugar refinery, daily newspaper, US Mint and public school for black children (1750).

The first Quakers, who came here in 1681, lived in caves dug into the banks of the Delaware River. During the first year, 80 houses were raised; by the following year, William Penn's "greene countrie towne" was a city of 600 buildings. The Quakers prospered in trade and commerce, and Philadelphia became the leading port in the colonies. Its leading citizen for many years was Benjamin Franklin—statesman, scientist, diplomat, writer, inventor and publisher.

The fires of colonial indignation burned hot and early in Philadelphia. Soon after the Boston tea party, a protest rally of 8,000 Philadelphians frightened off a British tea ship. In May 1774, when Paul Revere rode from Boston to Philadelphia to report that Boston's harbor had been closed, all of Philadelphia went into mourning. The first and second Continental Congresses convened here, and Philadelphia became the headquarters of the Revolution. After the Declaration of Independence was composed and accepted by Congress, the city gave its men, factories and shipyards to the cause. But British General Howe and 18,000 soldiers poured in on September 26, 1777, to spend a comfortable and social winter here while Washington's troops endured the bitter winter at Valley Forge. When the British evacuated the city, Congress returned. Philadelphia continued as the seat of government until 1800, except for a short period when New York City held the honor. The Constitution of the United States was written here and President George Washington graced the city's halls and streets.

Since those historic days, Philadelphia has figured importantly in the politics, economy and culture of the country. Here national conventions have nominated presidents. During four wars the city has served as an arsenal and a shipyard. More than 1,400 churches and synagogues grace the city. There are more than 25 colleges, universities and professional schools in Philadelphia as well. Fine restaurants are in abundance, along with an exciting nightlife to top off an evening. Entertainment is offered by the world-renowned Philadelphia Orchestra, theaters, college and professional sports, outstanding parks, recreation centers and playgrounds.

Shoppers may browse major department stores, hundreds of specialty shops and antique shopping areas.

Between the Delaware River and 9th Street for 10 blocks lies a history-rich part of Philadelphia. Here are the shrines of American liberty: Independence Hall, the Liberty Bell Pavilion and many other historical sites in and around Independence National Historical Park.

Transportation

Car Rental Agencies: See IMPORTANT TOLL-FREE NUMBERS.

Public Transportation: Subway and elevated trains, commuter trains, buses, trolleys (SEPTA), phone 215/580-7800.

Rail Passenger Service: Amtrak 800/872-7245.

Airport Information

Philadelphia Intl Airport: Information 215/492-3181; lost and found 215/937-6888; weather 215/936-1212.

What to See and Do

Academy of Music (1857). City's opera house, concert hall; home of Philadelphia Orchestra, Philly Pops, Opera Company of Philadelphia and Pennsylvania Ballet (see SEASONAL EVENTS). Broad & Locust Sts. Phone 215/893-1935.

Academy of Natural Sciences Museum (1812). Dinosaurs, Egyptian mummies, animal displays in natural habitats, live animal programs, hands-on children's museum. (Daily; closed Jan 1, Thanksgiving, Dec 25) 19th St & Benjamin Franklin Pkwy. Phone 215/299-1000. ¢¢¢

Afro-American Historical and Cultural Museum. Built to house and interpret African American culture. Changing exhibits; public events including lectures, workshops, films and concerts. (Daily exc Mon; closed Jan 1, Thanksgiving, Dec 25) 7th & Arch Sts. Phone 215/574-0380. ¢¢

American Swedish Historical Museum. From tapestries to technology, the museum celebrates Swedish influence on American life. Special exhibits on the New Sweden Colony. Research library, collections. (Daily exc Mon; closed hols) 1900 Pattison Ave. Phone 215/389-1776. ¢

Arch Street Friends Meetinghouse (1804). Perhaps the largest Friends meetinghouse in the world. Exhibits, slide show, tours. (Daily exc Sun; closed Jan 1, Thanksgiving, Dec 25) 4th & Arch Sts. Phone 215/627-2667. **Donation.**

Atwater Kent Museum—The History Museum of Philadelphia. Hundreds of fascinating artifacts, toys and miniatures, maps, prints, paintings and photographs reflecting the city's social and cultural history. (Wed-Sat; closed hols) 15 S 7th St. Phone 215/922-3031. ¢

Balch Institute for Ethnic Studies. A multicultural library, archive, museum and education center that promotes intergroup understanding using education; 300 yrs of US immigration are documented here. Features "Peopling of Pennsylvania," as well as changing exhibits. (Mon-Fri; closed hols) 18 S 7th St. Phone 215/925-8090. **Donation.**

Betsy Ross House. Where the famous seamstress is said to have made the first American flag. Upholsterer's shop, memorabilia. Flag Day ceremonies, June 14. (Daily exc Mon; closed Jan 1, Thanksgiving, Dec 25) 239 Arch St. Phone 215/627-5343. **Free.**

Burial Ground of the Congregation Mikveh Israel (1738). Graves of Haym Salomon, Revolutionary War financier, and Rebecca Gratz, probable model for "Rebecca" of Sir Walter Scott's *Ivanhoe.* Spruce & 8th Sts.

Christ Church (Episcopal). Patriots, Loyalists and heroes have worshiped here since 1695. Sit in pews once occupied by Washington, Franklin and Betsy Ross. (Mar-Dec, daily; rest of yr, Wed-Sun; closed Jan 1, Thanksgiving, Dec 25) 2nd St between Market & Arch Sts. Phone 215/922-1695.

Christ Church Burial Ground. Resting place of Benjamin Franklin, his wife, Deborah, and four other signers of the Declaration of Independence. (Mid-Apr-mid-Oct, daily) 5th & Arch Sts. Phone 215/922-1695.

City Hall. (Mon-Fri; closed hols) Broad & Market Sts.

Civil War Library and Museum. Four-story brick 19th-century town house filled with 18,000 books and periodicals dealing with events leading

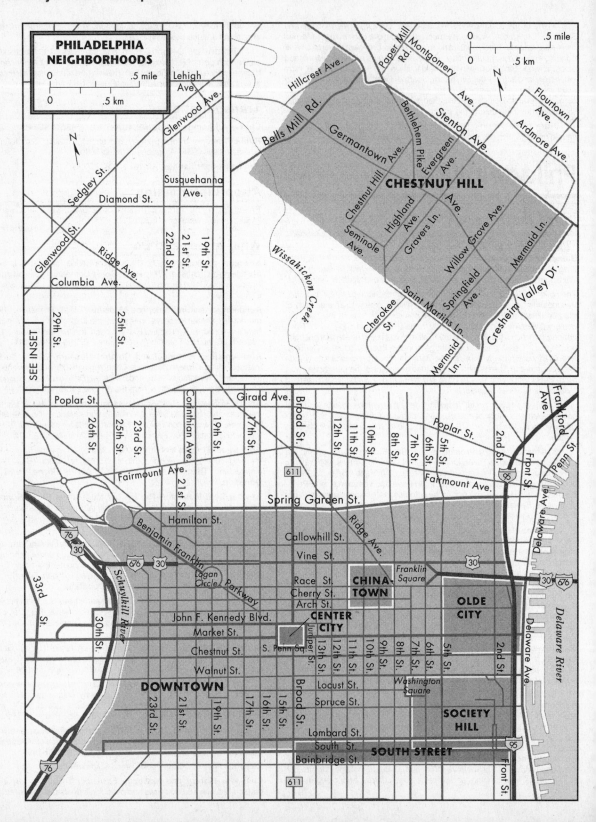

PHILADELPHIA
NEIGHBORHOODS

0   .5 mile

0   .5 km

N

CHESTNUT HILL

0   .5 mile

0   .5 km

N

Paper Mill Rd.
Montgomery Ave.
Hillcrest Ave.
Flourtown Ave.
Ardmore Ave.
Stenton Ave.
Bethlehem Pike
Germantown Ave.
Evergreen Ave.
Chestnut Hill Ave.
Highland Ave.
Gravers Ln.
Willow Grove Ave.
Mermaid Ln.
Seminole Ave.
Springfield Ave.
Bells Mill Rd.
Saint Martins Ln.
Cresheim Valley Dr.
Wissahickon Creek
Cherokee St.
Mermaid Ln.

Lehigh Ave.
Glenwood Ave.
Sedgley St.
Susquehanna Ave.
Diamond St.
Glenwood St.
Ridge Ave.
Columbia Ave.
29th St.
25th St.
22nd St.
21st St.
19th St.

SEE INSET

Poplar St.
Girard Ave.
Broad St.
Poplar St.
2nd St.
Frankford Ave.
26th St.
25th St.
23rd St.
Corinthian Ave.
19th St.
17th St.
12th St.
11th St.
10th St.
8th St.
7th St.
6th St.
5th St.
Penn St.
611
Fairmount Ave.
21st St.
Fairmount Ave.
I-95
Front St.
Delaware Ave.
Spring Garden St.
Ridge Ave.
33rd St.
Hamilton St.
Benjamin Franklin Parkway
76
30
676
30
Schuylkill River
Logan Circle
Callowhill St.
Vine St.
Franklin Square
30
676
30th St.
Race St.
Cherry St.
Arch St.
CHINA-TOWN
OLDE CITY
Delaware River
John F. Kennedy Blvd.
CENTER CITY
Market St.
S. Penn Sq.
Juniper St.
13th St.
12th St.
11th St.
10th St.
9th St.
8th St.
7th St.
6th St.
5th St.
2nd St.
Chestnut St.
Walnut St.
Locust St.
Washington Square
DOWNTOWN
23rd St.
21st St.
19th St.
17th St.
16th St.
15th St.
Broad St.
Spruce St.
SOCIETY HILL
Lombard St.
South St.
SOUTH STREET
95
Bainbridge St.
Front St.
76
611

up to the American Civil War, the war itself and early Reconstruction. Unique collection of arms, uniforms, flags of the period, memorabilia and artifacts begun in 1888 by former officers of the Union Army. Exhibits on Lincoln, Grant and Meade; also the Navy Room and the Armory. (Wed-Sun; closed hols) 1805 Pine St. Phone 215/735-8196. ¢¢

Edgar Allan Poe National Historic Site. Where Poe lived before his move to New York in 1844. The site is the nation's memorial to the literary genius of Edgar Allan Poe. Exhibits, slide show, tours and special programs. (May-Oct, daily; rest of yr, Wed-Sun; closed Jan 1, Dec 25) 532 N 7th, at Spring Garden St. Phone 215/597-8780. **Free.**

Elfreth's Alley. Oldest continuously residential street in America, with 30 houses dating from 1728-1836 (see ANNUAL EVENTS). At #126 is the mid-18th-century **Museum House;** period furnishings, historical exhibit. (Daily) Off 2nd St between Arch & Race Sts. Phone 215/574-0560. Museum ¢

★ **Fairmount Park.** Covers 8,700 acres. Begins at Philadelphia Museum of Art, extends NW on both sides of Wissahickon Creek and Schuylkill River. Phone 215/685-0000. In park are

Colonial Mansions. Handsome 18th-century dwellings in varying architectural styles, authentically preserved and furnished, include Mount Pleasant (1761) (daily exc Mon); Cedar Grove (1756) (daily exc Mon); Strawberry Mansion (1797) (daily exc Mon); Sweetbriar (1797) (daily exc Tues); Lemon Hill (1799) (Wed-Sun); Woodford (1756) (daily exc Mon); Laurel Hill (1760) (Wed-Sun). Further details and guided tours from Park Houses office at Philadelphia Museum of Art. Phone 215/684-7922. Each house ¢

Boat House Row. Used by collegiate and club oarsmen. Schuylkill River is scene of many nationally important crew competitions; crews practice all spring and summer during early morning and afternoon. On E bank of river. Phone 215/978-6919 for rowing, regatta schedules.

Japanese Exhibition House. Re-creates a bit of Japan, complete with garden, pond, bridge. (May-Labor Day, daily exc Mon; Labor Day-Oct, Sat & Sun) Fairmount Park Horticulture Center. Phone 215/878-5097. ¢

Robin Hood Dell East. (See SEASONAL EVENTS)

Philadelphia Zoo. America's first zoo. More than 1,700 animals, many in natural surroundings; TREEHOUSE (fee); waterfowl collection; bear country; five-acre African plains exhibit; reptile house; bird house; carnivore kingdom; children's zoo. Picnic areas; concession. Guided tours by appt. Main zoo (daily; closed Jan 1, Thanksgiving, Dec 24, 25, 31). 3400 W Girard Ave. Phone 215/243-1100. ¢¢¢

Fireman's Hall Museum. Collection of antique firefighting equipment; displays and exhibits of fire department history since its beginning in 1736; library. (Tues-Sat; closed hols) 149 N 2nd St. Phone 215/923-1438. **Donation.**

Fort Mifflin. Site of a 7-wk siege during the Revolutionary War. Served as a military installation until 1959. Guided tours (Apr-Nov, Wed-Sun). From the airport, follow Island Ave toward the Delaware River, follow brown and white signs. Phone 215/492-1881. ¢¢

Franklin Institute Science Museum. Science Center includes exhibits on trains, shipmaking, astronomy, bioscience, communications, aviation and electricity; highlights include a Baldwin #60000 locomotive and a giant walk-through heart. **Mandell Futures Center** is dedicated to the science and technology shaping the 21st century; it explores such areas as space, earth, health and computers. Also here are **Benjamin Franklin National Memorial, Fels Planetarium** and the four-story screen of the **Tuttleman Omniverse Theater** (30-40-min films). (Daily; closed major hols) 20th St & Ben Franklin Pkwy. Phone 215/448-1200. ¢¢¢

Free Library. Large central library with over 9 million indexed items in all fields. Rare books, maps, theater scripts and orchestral scores; automobile reference collections; changing exhibits. (Memorial Day-Labor Day, daily exc Sun; rest of yr, daily; closed hols) Logan Sq, 19th & Vine Sts. Phone 215/686-5322. **Free.**

Germantown.

Deshler-Morris House (1772-1773). Residence of President Washington in the summers of 1793, 1794; period furnishings, garden. (Apr-Nov,

Tues-Sat; rest of yr, by appt; closed most hols) 5442 Germantown Ave. Phone 215/596-1748. ¢

Stenton House (1723-1730). Mansion built by James Logan, secretary to William Penn. Excellent example of Pennsylvania colonial architecture, furnished with 18th- and 19th-century antiques. General Washington spent Aug 13, 1777, here and General Sir William Howe headquartered here for the Battle of Germantown. Colonial barn, gardens, kitchen. (Apr-Dec, Tues-Sat afternoons; rest of yr, by appt; closed hols) 18th St between Courtland St & Windrim Ave. Phone 215/329-7312. ¢¢

Cliveden (1767). A 2½-story stone Georgian house of individual design built as summer home by Benjamin Chew, Chief Justice of colonial Pennsylvania. On Oct 4, 1777, British soldiers used house as a fortress to repulse Washington's attempt to recapture Philadelphia. Used as Chew family residence for 200 yrs; many original furnishings. A National Trust for Historic Preservation property. (Apr-Dec, Thurs-Sun afternoons; closed Easter, Thanksgiving, Dec 25) 6401 Germantown Ave, between Johnson & Cliveden Sts. Phone 215/848-1777. ¢¢¢

Gloria Dei Church National Historic Site ("Old Swedes") (1700). State's oldest church. Memorial to John Hanson, president of the United States under Articles of Confederation. (Daily) Columbus Blvd & Christian St, 8 blks S of Chestnut. Phone 215/389-1513.

Haverford College (1833). (1,100 students) Founded by members of the Society of Friends. The 216-acre campus includes Founders Hall; James P. Magill Library; Arboretum; Morris Cricket Library and Collection (by appt only; phone 610/896-1162). Tours of arboretum and campus. 10 mi W on US 30, in Haverford. Phone 610/896-1000.

Historical Society of Pennsylvania. Museum exhibit features first draft of Constitution, 500 artifacts and manuscripts plus video tours of turn-of-the-century urban and suburban neighborhoods. Research library and archives house historical and genealogical collections. (Tues-Sat; closed hols) 1300 Locust St. Phone 215/732-6201. ¢¢

Historic Bartram's Garden. Pre-Revolutionary home of John Bartram, the royal botanist to the colonies under George III, naturalist and plant explorer. The 18th-century stone farmhouse (fee), barn, stable and cider mill overlook the Schuylkill River. Museum shop. (May-Oct, daily; rest of yr, Wed-Fri afternoons; closed hols) 54th St & Lindbergh Blvd. Phone 215/729-5281. House tour ¢; Combination house & garden tour ¢¢

★ **Independence National Historical Park.** The park has been called "America's most historic square mile." The Visitor Center at 3rd & Chestnut Sts has a tour map, information on all park activities and attractions and a 30-min film entitled *Independence.* An exhibit to mark the 200th anniversary of the United States Constitution, "Promise of Permanency," is composed of an interactive computer system with 16 touch-sensitive monitors that will inform visitors of the meaning of the federal Constitution, how it has endured for 2 centuries and its relevance to modern America. For information phone 215/597-8974. Unless otherwise indicated, all historic sites and museums in the park are open daily and are free. They include

Independence Square (known as State House Yard in colonial times). Bounded by Chestnut, Walnut, 5th & 6th Sts. Contains Independence Hall, Congress Hall, Old City Hall and Philosophical Hall.

Independence Mall. Extends 3 blks N of the Square. The tree-lined walks add to the ambience while viewing the Square's Georgian structures. On the mall is a glass pavilion housing the Liberty Bell.

Declaration House. Reconstructed house on site of writing of Declaration of Independence by Thomas Jefferson; two rooms Jefferson rented have been reproduced. Short orientation and movie about Jefferson, his philosophy on the common man and the history of the house. 701 Market St.

Liberty Bell Pavilion. The Liberty Bell, created to commemorate the 50th anniversary of the Charter of Privileges granted by William Penn to his colony in 1701, bears the inscription, "Proclaim liberty throughout all the land unto all the inhabitants thereof" (Leviticus, chapter 25). It was rung at public occasions thereafter, including the first reading of the Declaration of Independence on July 8, 1776, and was last rung formally on Washington's birthday in 1846. The bell got its name from 19th-century antislavery groups who adopted it as a symbol of their cause. At 12:01 am on Jan 1, 1976, it was moved across the street from its original home in Independence Hall to its own glass structure. The Liberty Bell faces

Independence Hall (1732). Site of the adoption of the Declaration of Independence. First used as the Pennsylvania State House, it housed the Second Continental Congress, 1775-1783, and the Constitutional Convention in 1787—when the Constitution of the United States was written. Admission by tour only. Chestnut St between 5th & 6th Sts. Beside Independence Hall is

Congress Hall. Congress met here during the last decade of the 18th century. House of Representatives and Senate chambers are restored. 6th & Chestnut Sts. On the other side of Independence Hall is

Old City Hall (1789). Built as City Hall, but was also home of first US Supreme Court, 1791-1800. Exterior restored. Interior depicts the judicial phase of the building. Chestnut & 5th Sts. Nearby is

Philosophical Hall (1785-1789). Home of the American Philosophical Society, oldest learned society in America (1743), founded by Benjamin Franklin. Not open to public. 5th St side of Square. Across 5th St is

Library Hall. Reconstruction of Library Company of Philadelphia (1789-1790) building is occupied by library of American Philosophical Society. Open to scholars. (Mon-Fri) 5th & Library Sts. To the E is

The Second Bank of the United States (1824-1841). Was also used as US Custom House (1845-1934). Now houses Portrait Gallery. 420 Chestnut St, between 4th & 5th Sts. One blk NE is

Franklin Court. The site of Benjamin Franklin's house has been developed as a tribute to him; area includes working printing office and bindery, underground museum with multimedia exhibits, an archaeological exhibit and the B. Free Franklin Post Office. Between Market & Chestnut Sts, in block bounded by 3rd & 4th Sts. One-half blk S is

Carpenters' Hall (1770). Constructed as guild hall; meeting site of first Continental Congress (1774). Historical museum since 1857; still operated by Carpenters Co. Contains original chairs; exhibits of early tools. (Daily exc Mon) 320 Chestnut St. Adj is

New Hall Military Museum. This reconstruction houses the US Marine Corps Memorial Museum, featuring exhibits on the early history of the Marines and the Army-Navy Museum. 4th & Chestnut Sts, in Carpenters' Court. Also in Carpenters' Court is

Museum Shop (Pemberton House). Reconstruction of Quaker merchant's house; now shop with items relating to historic sites. Nearby is

The First Bank of the United States (1797-1811). Organized by Alexander Hamilton; country's oldest bank building; exterior restored. Closed to public. 3rd St between Walnut & Chestnut Sts. Walk approx 1½ blk S to

Bishop White House (1786-1787). House of Bishop William White, first Episcopal Bishop of Pennsylvania. Restored and furnished. Tours. Free tickets at park's Visitor Center. 309 Walnut St. One blk W is

Todd House (1775). House of Dolley Payne Todd, who later married James Madison and became First Lady; 18th-century furnishings depict middle-class Quaker family life. Tours. Free tickets at park's Visitor Center. 4th & Walnut Sts. Retrace steps one blk to

The Merchant's Exchange. Designed by William Strickland, one of the East's finest examples of Greek-revival architecture. Exterior restored; now houses regional offices of the National Park Service. Closed to public. 3rd & Walnut Sts. Proceed E on Dock St.

Thaddeus Kosciuszko National Memorial. House of Polish patriot during his second visit to US (1797-1798). He was one of the 18th century's greatest champions of American and Polish freedom and one of the first volunteers to come to the aid of the American Revolutionary Army. Exterior and 2nd-floor bedroom have been restored. (Daily) 3rd & Pine Sts.

For further information about the park, contact Visitor Center, 3rd & Chestnut Sts, 19106; 215/597-8974 (voice), 215/597-1785 (TDD) or 215/597-8974 (recording).

Independence Seaport Museum. Ship models, figureheads, whaling equipment, paintings. Exhibits illustrate maritime history of Delaware Bay and River, life of a sailor; special exhibits. Waterfront facility at Penn's Landing houses boat-building workshop and small gallery. (Daily; closed hols) Delaware Ave & Walnut St. Phone 215/925-5439. ¢¢

John Heinz National Wildlife Refuge at Tinicum. Largest remaining freshwater tidal wetland in the state, protecting more than 1,000 acres of wildlife habitat. Area was first diked by Swedish farmers in 1643; Dutch farmers and the colonial government added dikes during the Revolutionary War. More than 280 species of birds and 13 resident mammal species. Hiking, bicycling, nature observation, canoeing on Darby Creek, fishing. (Daily) S via I-95, W PA 291 exit, right on Bartram Ave, left on 84th St, left on Lindbergh Blvd, at 86th & Lindbergh Blvd. Phone 215/365-3118 or 610/521-0662. **Free.**

Morris Arboretum of the University of Pennsylvania (1887). Public garden with more than 1,600 types of native and exotic trees and shrubs on 166 acres; special garden areas such as Swan Pond, Rose Garden and Japanese gardens. Tours (Sat & Sun afternoon; one each day). (Daily; closed Dec 24-Jan 1) Approx 12 mi NW in Chestnut Hill; entrance on Northwestern Ave. Phone 215/247-5777. ¢¢

Mummer's Museum. Participatory exhibits and displays highlighting the history and tradition of the Mummers Parade (see ANNUAL EVENTS). Costumes and videotapes of past parades. Free outdoor string band concerts (May-Sept, Tues evenings, weather permitting); 20 string bands, different every wk. (Sept-June, Tues-Sat, also Sun afternoons; rest of yr, daily exc Sun; closed major hols) 2nd St & Washington Ave. Phone 215/336-3050. ¢¢

Mütter Museum. In the College of Physicians of Philadelphia. Medical antiques and memorabilia; anatomical and pathological specimens and models. (Daily exc Sun; closed hols) 19 S 22nd St. Phone 215/563-3737. ¢¢

National Museum of American Jewish History. Exhibit portrays the American Jewish experience from 1654 to the present; changing exhibits; art, artifacts; audiovisual display. (Daily exc Sat; limited hrs Fri & Sun; closed Jan 1, Thanksgiving, also Jewish hols) Independence Mall East, 55 N 5th St. Phone 215/923-3811. ¢¢

Norman Rockwell Museum. Drawings, canvases, lithographs, prints and sketches covering 60 yrs of the artist's career; replica of Rockwell studio; video presentation. Gift shop. (Daily; limited hrs; closed Jan 1, Easter, Thanksgiving, Dec 25) 6th & Sansom Sts, opp Independence Hall. Phone 215/922-4345. ¢

Old Pine St Presbyterian Church (1768). Colonial church and graveyard; renovated in 1850s in Greek-revival style. 412 Pine St, at 4th St. Phone 215/925-8051.

Old St George's United Methodist Church (1769). Oldest Methodist Church in continuous service in US. Colonial architecture; collection of Methodist memorabilia; has only Bishop Asbury Bible and John Wesley Chalice Cup in America. (Daily) 235 N 4th St. Phone 215/925-7788.

Old St Mary's Church (1763). Commodore John Barry, "father of the US Navy," is interred in graveyard behind the city's first Catholic cathedral. (Daily) 252 S 4th St, between Locust & Spruce Sts. Phone 215/923-7930.

Penn's Landing. Columbus Blvd & Spruce St. Here are

USS *Olympia*. Commodore Dewey's flagship during Spanish-American War; restored. Naval museum has weapons, uniforms, ship models, naval relics of all periods. Also here is World War II submarine, **USS *Becuna*.** (Daily; closed Jan 1, Dec 25) Phone 215/922-1898. *Olympia* and *Becuna* ¢¢

Gazela of Philadelphia (1883). Portuguese square-rigger, tall ship. (June-Sept, Sat & Sun) Columbus Blvd & Chestnut St. Phone 215/923-9030. **Donation.**

Pennsylvania Academy of the Fine Arts. Oldest art museum and school in US; housed in restored Victorian building by architect Frank Furness. Outstanding permanent collection of three centuries of American art; rotating exhibits. Guided tours (daily exc Mon; closed major hols). 118 N Broad St. Phone 215/972-7600. ¢¢¢

Pennsylvania Hospital (1751). First in country, founded by Benjamin Franklin. 8th & Spruce Sts.

Philadelphia Museum of Art. Over 200 galleries with collections of paintings, graphics, sculpture; period rooms, medieval cloister, Indian temple, Chinese palace hall, Japanese teahouse; armor collection. American wing includes rural Pennsylvania Dutch crafts, Shaker furniture and paintings of early American artists, such as Gilbert Stuart and Thomas Eakins. Free guided tours. (Tues-Sun, also Wed evenings; closed legal hols) Free admission Sun mornings. 26th St & Benjamin Franklin Pkwy. Phone 215/763-8100. ¢¢¢

Please Touch Museum for Children. Unique museum, designed especially for children 1-7 yrs old. Hands-on exhibits, including "Sendak," "SuperMarket Science," "Studio PTM" and "Science Park." (Daily; closed Jan 1, Thanksgiving, Dec 25) 210 N 21st St. Phone 215/963-0667. ¢¢¢

Professional sports.

National League baseball (Philadelphia Phillies). Veterans Stadium, Broad St & Pattison Ave. Phone 215/463-6000.

NBA (Philadelphia 76ers). CoreStates Center, Broad St & Pattison Ave. Phone 215/339-7600.

NFL (Philadelphia Eagles). Veterans Stadium, Broad St & Pattison Ave. Phone 215/463-2500.

NHL (Philadelphia Flyers). CoreStates Center, Broad St & Pattison Ave. Phone 215/465-4500.

Rodin Museum. Largest collection of Rodin sculpture outside Paris. (Daily exc Mon; closed legal hols) 22nd St & Franklin Pkwy. Phone 215/563-1948. **Donation.**

Rosenbach Museum. This 19th-century town house has permanent and changing exhibits of fine and decorative arts; collection includes 18th- and 19th-century English and French prints, 18th-century American silver, historical manuscripts and American and British literature collection, including a *Canterbury Tales* manuscript. (Daily exc Mon; closed hols, also Aug) 2010 DeLancey Pl. Phone 215/732-1600. Tours ¢¢

St Peter's Church (Episcopal) (1761). Georgian colonial architecture; numerous famous people buried in churchyard. (Most Sat mornings) 3rd & Pine Sts. Phone 215/925-5968 for appt.

Schuylkill Center for Environmental Education. A 500-acre natural area with more than 7 miles of trails; discovery room; gift shop/bookstore. (Daily; closed hols) 9 mi NW, at 8480 Hagy's Mill Rd. Phone 215/482-7300. ¢¢

Sesame Place. 20 mi NE via I-95 to Levittown exit (25E). Follow signs for the Oxford Valley Mall on the US 1 Bypass. (See BRISTOL)

Shopping.

Italian Market. Historical outdoor food mall sells fresh foods, cookware and clothing. Also here are restaurants and South Philly cheesesteaks. (Daily) 9th St between Christian & Wharton Sts.

Jeweler's Row. Largest jewelry district in the country other than New York City. More than 300 shops, including wholesalers and diamond cutters. 7th & Sansom Sts.

Antique Row. Dozens of antique, third-world craft and curio shops. From 9th to 17th Sts along Pine St.

The Gallery. Concentration of 250 shops and restaurants in four-level mall with glass elevators, trees, fountains and benches. 10th & Market Sts. Phone 215/925-7162.

The Bourse (1893-1895). Restored Victorian building houses shops and restaurants. 5th St, across from Liberty Bell Pavilion.

The Shops at the Bellevue. Beaux-arts architecture of the former Bellevue Stratford Hotel has been preserved and transformed; it now contains offices, a hotel and a four-level shopping area centered around an atrium court. (Daily exc Sun) Broad St at Walnut. Phone 215/875-8350.

South St. Nearly 150 hip shops, boutiques and galleries line either side of the street.

Sightseeing tours.

Centipede Tours. Candlelight strolls (1½ hrs) through historic Philadelphia and Society Hill areas led by guides in 18th-century dress; begins and ends at City Tavern. (Mid-May-mid-Oct, Mon-Fri) Reservations preferred. 1315 Walnut St. Phone 215/735-3123. ¢¢

Philadelphia Carriage Company. Guided tours via horse-drawn carriage covering Society Hill and other historic areas; begin and end in front of Independence Hall & Liberty Bell Pavilion. (Daily, weather permitting; closed Dec 25) 500 N 13th St. Phone 215/922-6840. ¢¢¢-¢¢¢¢¢

AudioWalk & Tour/Historic Philadelphia. Recorded walking tour of the historic area with music, little-known facts, stories; rental of cassette and tape player (accommodates up to 5 people); easy-to-follow map. (Daily) Office in the Norman Rockwell museum. Phone 215/922-4345. ¢¢¢¢¢

Gray Line bus tours. For information, reservations, contact 3101 E Orthodox St, 19137; 215/569-3666 or 800/220-3133.

Society Hill Area. This historic area, the name of which is derived from the Free Society of Traders, was created by William Penn as the city's original land company and has undergone extensive renewal of its historic buildings. Area bounded approx by Front, Walnut, 7th & Lombard Sts. In this area are

Powel House (1765). Georgian town house of Samuel Powel, last colonial mayor of Philadelphia and first mayor under the new republic. Period furnishings, silver and porcelain; garden. Tours (Thurs-Sun afternoons; closed most hols) 244 S 3rd St. For tour schedule phone 215/627-0364. ¢¢

Physick House (1786). House of Dr. Philip Sung Physick, "father of American surgery," from 1815-1837. Restored Federal-style house with period furnishings; garden. (Thurs-Sun afternoons) 321 S 4th St. For tour schedule phone 215/925-7866. ¢¢

Athenaeum of Philadelphia. Landmark example of Italian Renaissance architecture (1845-1847); restored building has American neoclassical-style decorative arts, paintings, sculpture; research library; furniture and art from the collection of Joseph Bonaparte, King of Spain and older brother of Napoleon; changing exhibits of architectural drawings, photos and rare books. (Mon-Fri; closed hols) 219 S 6th St. Phone 215/925-2688. **Free.**

Temple University (1884). (33,000 students) Undergraduate, professional and research school. Walking tours of campus. Cecil B. Moore Ave & Broad St. Phone 215/204-8551.

University of Pennsylvania (1740). (23,000 students) On campus are the restored Fisher Fine Arts Library (phone 215/898-4401), Annenberg Center for performing arts (phone 215/898-6791); University Museum of Archaeology and Anthropology and Institute of Contemporary Art, located at 36th & Sansom Sts (daily exc Mon; phone 215/898-7108; fee). Chestnut to Pine Sts & 32nd to 40th Sts. For information phone 215/898-1000.

University of Pennsylvania Museum of Archaeology and Anthropology. World-famous archaeological and ethnographic collections developed from the museum's own expeditions, gifts and purchases; features Chinese, Near Eastern, Greek, ancient Egyptian, African, Pacific, and North, Middle & South American materials; library. Restaurant, shops. (Daily exc Mon; closed hols, also Sun in summer) 33rd & Spruce Sts. Phone 215/898-4000. ¢¢

US Mint. Produces coins of all denominations. Gallery affords visitors an elevated view of the coinage operations. Medal making may also be observed. Audiovisual, self-guided tours. Rittenhouse Room on the mezzanine contains historic coins, medals and other exhibits. (July-Aug, daily; rest of yr, Mon-Fri; closed Jan 1, Thanksgiving, Dec 25) On Independence Mall at 5th & Arch Sts. Phone 215/597-7350. **Free.**

Wagner Free Institute of Science. Victorian science museum with more than 50,000 specimens illustrating the various branches of the natural sciences. Dinosaur bones, fossils, reptiles and rare species are all mounted in the Victorian style. Reference library and research archives. (Tues-Fri, by appt) Montgomery & 17th Sts. Phone 215/763-6529. **Free.**

Walnut Street Theatre (1809). America's oldest theater. The Walnut Mainstage offers musicals, classical and contemporary plays. The two studio theaters provide a forum for new and avant-garde works. 9th & Walnut Sts. Phone 215/574-3550. 202/283-2646.

Washington Square. Walnut St from 6th St, where hundreds of Revolutionary War soldiers and victims of the yellow-fever epidemic are buried. Life-size statue of Washington has tomb of Revolutionary War's Unknown Soldier at its feet. Across the street is

Philadelphia Savings Fund Society Building (1816). Site of oldest savings bank in US. Not open to public. Walnut & 8th Sts.

Annual Events

Mummers Parade. An 8-hr spectacle along Broad St. Jan 1.

PECO Energy Jazz Festival. Jazz concerts around the city. Phone 800/537-7676. 4 days mid-Feb.

"The Book and the Cook." Sample fine cuisine as world-famous cookbook authors team up with the city's most respected chefs to create culinary delights. Wine tastings, market tours, film festival. Phone 215/686-3662. Early-mid-Mar.

Philadelphia Open House. House and garden tours in different neighborhoods; distinguished selection of over 150 private homes, gardens, historic sites. Many tours include lunches, candlelight dinners or high teas. Phone 215/928-1188. Late Apr-mid-May.

Devon Horse Show. Approx 20 mi NW via US 30, at Horse Show Grounds, in Devon. One of America's leading equestrian events. More than 1,200 horses compete; country fair; antique carriage drive. Phone 610/964-0550. 9 days beginning Memorial Day wknd.

Elfreth's Alley Fete Days. Homes open to public, costumed guides, demonstrations of colonial crafts; food, entertainment. Phone 215/574-0567. 1st wknd June.

CoreStates US Pro Cycling Championship. At 156 mi, it's the longest (and richest) single-day cycling event in the country. Phone 215/973-3546. Mid-June.

Thanksgiving Day Parade. Giant floats; celebrities.

Army-Navy Football Game. John F. Kennedy Memorial Stadium or Veterans Stadium. 1st Sat Dec.

Fairmount Park Historical Christmas Tours. Period decorations in 18th-century mansions. Phone 215/684-7922. Early Dec.

Seasonal Events

American Music Theater Festival. Repertory includes new opera, musical comedy, cabaret-style shows, revues and experimental works. Phone 215/567-0670. Main stage productions Mar-June.

Head House Open Air Craft Market. Pine & 2nd Sts, in Society Hill area in Head House Square. Crafts demonstrations, children's workshops. Sat & Sun, June-Aug.

Mann Music Center. 52nd St & Parkside Ave, West Fairmount Park. Philadelphia Orchestra performs late June-July, Mon, Wed & Thurs. Also popular music attractions. Phone 215/567-0707. June-Sept.

Robin Hood Dell East. 33rd & Dauphin Sts, in Fairmount Park. Top stars in outdoor popular music concerts. Phone 215/477-8810. July-Aug.

Performing arts.

Philadelphia Orchestra. Academy of Music. Phone 215/893-1900. Sept-May. Also Mann Music Center (see above), late June-late July.

Philadelphia Theatre Company. Plays and Players Theatre, 1811 Chestnut St, Ste 300. Five contemporary American plays per season. Phone 215/568-1920. Oct-Mar.

The Opera Company of Philadelphia. Academy of Music. Phone 215/928-2100. Oct-Apr.

Pennsylvania Ballet. Performs at Merriam Theatre and at Academy of Music. Phone 215/551-7000.

Horse racing. Flat racing at Philadelphia Park, Richlieu & Street Rds in Bensalem. For schedule phone 215/639-9000.

Additional Visitor Information

The Visitors Center of the Philadelphia Convention and Visitors Bureau, 16th St & John F. Kennedy Blvd, 19102, has tourist information and maps (daily; closed Thanksgiving, Dec 25). Phone 215/636-1666 or 800/537-7676.

There is also a visitor center at 3rd & Chestnut Sts, operated by the National Park Service. (Daily) Phone 215/597-8975 or 215/597-8974 for information on park attractions.

City Neighborhoods

Many of the restaurants, unrated dining establishments and some lodgings listed under Philadelphia include neighborhoods as well as exact street addresses. Geographic descriptions of these areas are given, followed by a table of restaurants arranged by neighborhood.

Center City: Area of Downtown around city hall; south of Kennedy Blvd, west of Juniper St, north of S Penn Square and east of 15th St.

Chestnut Hill: South of Stenton Ave, west and north of Cresheim Valley Dr and east of Fairmount Park; along Germantown Ave.

Chinatown: North-central area of Downtown; south of Vine St, west of 8th St, north of Arch St and east of 11th St.

Downtown: South of Spring Garden St, west of I-95, north of South St and east of the Schuylkill River. **North of Downtown:** North of Spring Garden St. **South of Downtown:** South of South St. **West of Downtown:** West of Schuylkill River.

Old City: Area of Downtown south of I-676, west of the Delaware River, north of Chestnut St and east of Independence Mall.

Society Hill: Southeast side of Downtown; south of Walnut St, west of Front St, north of Lombard St and east of 7th St.

South Street: Downtown area; South St between 10th St on the west and the Delaware River on the east; also north to Pine St and south to Bainbridge St.

PHILADELPHIA RESTAURANTS BY NEIGHBORHOOD AREAS
(For full description, see alphabetical listings under Restaurants)

CENTER CITY
Bookbinder's 15th Street Seafood House. 215 S 15th St

CHESTNUT HILL
Flying Fish. 8142 Germantown Ave
Roller's. 8705 Germantown Ave
Under The Blue Moon. 8042 Germantown Ave

CHINATOWN
Ho Sai Gai. 1000 Race St
Rangoon. 112 N 9th St
Vang's Garden. 121 N 11th St

DOWNTOWN
Bistro Bix. 114 S 12th St
Brasserie Perrier. 1619 Walnut St
Cary. 211 S 15th St
Chanterelles. 1312 Spruce St
Ciboulette. 200 S Broad St
Circa. 1518 Walnut St
Cuvee Notredame. 1701 Green St
Deux Cheminées. 1221 Locust St
The Dining Room (The Ritz-Carlton, Philadelphia Hotel). 17th & Chestnut Sts
Dock Street Brewery. 2 Logan Square
The Founders (Park Hyatt Philadelphia At The Bellevue Hotel). Broad & Walnut Sts
Fountain (Four Seasons Hotel Philadelphia). 1 Logan Square
The Garden. 1617 Spruce St
The Grill (The Ritz-Carlton, Philadelphia Hotel). 17th & Chestnut Sts
Harry's Bar & Grill. 22 S 18th St
Italian Bistro. 211 S Broad St
Le Bar Lyonnais. 1523 Walnut St
Le Bar Nostradamus. 1701 Green St
Le Bec-Fin. 1523 Walnut St
Napoleon. 1500 Locust St
Nicholas Nickolas (The Rittenhouse Hotel). 210 W Rittenhouse Square
Nick's (The Rittenhouse Hotel). 210 W Rittenhouse Square

Opus 251. 251 S 18th St
The Palm. 200 S Broad St
Peacock On The Parkway. 1700 Benjamin Franklin Pkwy
Striped Bass. 1500 Walnut St
Susanna Foo. 1512 Walnut St
Swann Cafe (Four Seasons Hotel Philadelphia). 1 Logan Square
Swann Lounge (Four Seasons Hotel Philadelphia). 1 Logan Square
Tony Clark's. 121 S Broad St
Treetops (The Rittenhouse Hotel). 210 W Rittenhouse Square
White Dog Cafe. 3420 Sansom St

NORTH OF DOWNTOWN
Berlengas. 4926 N 5th St
Fisher's Seafood. 7312 Castor Ave
Isabella's. 6516 Castor Ave
Moonstruck. 7955 Oxford Ave
Umbria. 7131 Germantown Ave

SOUTH OF DOWNTOWN
Assaggi Italiani. 935 Ellsworth St
Dmitri's. 795 S 3rd St
Famous 4th St Delicatessen. 700 S 4th St
Felicia's. 1148 S 11th St
Michael's. 824 S 8th St

WEST OF DOWNTOWN
The Marker (Adam's Mark Hotel). City Ave & Monument Rd
The Restaurant School. 4207 Walnut St
Zócalo. 3600 Lancaster Ave

OLDE CITY
Azalea (Omni Hotel At Independence Park). 4th & Chestnut
Dinardo's. 312 Race St
La Famiglia. 8 S Front St
Meiji-En. Pier 19 North
Middle East. 126 Chestnut St
New Mexico Grille. 50 S 2nd St
Ristorante Panorama (Penn's View Hotel). Front & Market Sts
Rococo. 123 Chestnut St
Sassafras. 48 S 2nd St
Serrano. 20 S 2nd St
Spirit Of Philadelphia. Pier 3

SOCIETY HILL
City Tavern. 138 S 2nd St at Walnut
Dickens Inn. Head House Square
Old Original Bookbinder's. 125 Walnut St

SOUTH STREET AREA
Bridget Foy's South Street Grill. 200 South St
Cafe Nola. 603 S 3rd St
Knave Of Hearts. 230 South St
Monte Carlo Living Room. 2nd & South Sts
Moshulu. Pier 34
Overtures. 609 E Passyunk Ave
Pompano Grille. 701 E Passyunk Ave
The Saloon. 750 S 7th St
South Street Diner. 140 South St

Note: When a listing is located in a town that does not have its own city heading, it will appear under the city nearest to its location. In these cases, the address and town appear in parenthesis immediately following the name of the establishment.

Motels

★ ★ **BEST WESTERN HOTEL-NORTHEAST.** *11580 Roosevelt Blvd (19116), north of downtown.* 215/464-9500; FAX 215/464-8511. 100 rms, 2 story. S, D $90-$125; under 18 free; wkly, wkend rates. Crib free. TV; cable (premium). Pool; lifeguard. Playground. Complimentary continental bkfst. Bar from 4 pm. Ck-out 11 am. Coin lndry. Meeting rms. Business servs avail. Exercise equipt; stair machine, bicycles. Lawn

games. Some bathrm phones, refrigerators. Many balconies. Picnic tables. Cr cds: A, C, D, DS, MC, V.

D ≈ ⚡ ✕ ➤ ⓦ SC

✔★ ★ **COMFORT INN.** *(3660 Street Rd, Bensalem 19020) N on I-95 to Street Rd W exit, 3 mi W.* 215/245-0100; FAX 215/245-1851. 141 units, 3 story. S $75-$109; D $85-$125; each addl $10; suites $125; family rates. Crib free. Pet accepted, some restrictions. TV; cable (premium). Complimentary continental bkfst. Restaurant nearby. Bar 4 pm-2 am; entertainment. Ck-out noon. Meeting rms. Business servs avail. In-rm modem link. Gift shop. Exercise equipt; weights, bicycles. Game rm. Some in-rm whirlpools. Cr cds: A, C, D, DS, ER, JCB, MC, V.

D ⚡ ✕ ➤ ⓦ SC

Motor Hotels

✔★ ★ **BEST WESTERN-CENTER CITY.** *501 N 22nd St (19130), in Center City.* 215/568-8300; FAX 215/557-0259. 183 rms, 3 story. Apr-Oct: S $99-$119.50; D $109-$129; each addl $10; suites $150; under 18 free; family rates. Pet accepted, some restrictions. TV; cable (premium), VCR avail. Complimentary coffee in lobby. Restaurant 6:30 am-10:30 pm. Bar 11-2 am. Ck-out noon. Meeting rms. Business servs avail. In-rm modem link. Bellhops. Valet serv. Gift shop. Exercise equipt; treadmill, stair machine. Pool; lifeguard. Refrigerators, microwaves avail. Cr cds: A, C, D, DS, MC, V.

D ⚡ ≈ ✕ ➤ ⓦ SC

✔★ ★ **DAYS INN-AIRPORT.** *4101 Island Ave (19153), near Intl Airport, south of downtown.* 215/492-0400; FAX 215/365-6035. 177 rms, 5 story. S $108; D $118; each addl $15; under 18 free. Crib free. TV; cable (premium), VCR avail. Pool; lifeguard. Coffee in rms. Restaurant 6 am-2 pm, 5 pm-midnight; Sat to noon. Rm serv. Bar 4 pm-midnight. Ck-out noon. Coin lndry. Meeting rms. Business servs avail. Valet serv. Free airport transportation. Refrigerators, microwaves avail. Cr cds: A, C, D, DS, MC, V.

D ≈ ⚡ ✕ ➤ ⓦ SC

★ ★ ★ **DOUBLETREE CLUB HOTEL.** *9461 Roosevelt Blvd (19114), north of downtown.* 215/671-9600; FAX 215/464-7759. 188 rms, 6 story. S $119; D $129; each addl $10; suites $175; under 17 free; wkend rates. Crib free. TV; cable, VCR avail. Indoor pool. Restaurant 6 am-11 pm. Bar 5 pm-midnight. Ck-out 11 am. Coin lndry. Meeting rms. Business center. In-rm modem link. Valet serv. Sundries. Gift shop. Exercise equipt; weight machine, bicycles. Health club privileges. Some refrigerators; microwaves avail. Cr cds: A, C, D, DS, MC, V.

D ≈ ⚡ ✕ ➤ ⓦ SC ⚡

★ ★ ★ **HILTON-PHILADELPHIA AIRPORT.** *4509 Island Ave (19153), at Intl Airport, south of downtown.* 215/365-4150; FAX 215/937-6382. 330 rms, 9 story. S, D $109-$149; suites $325; studio rms $150; under 18 free; wkend rates. Crib free. Pet accepted, some restrictions. TV; cable (premium). Indoor pool; whirlpool. Restaurant 6 am-11 pm. Rm serv 24 hrs. Bar 11-2 am. Ck-out noon. Meeting rms. Business center. In-rm modem link. Bellhops. Valet serv. Gift shop. Free airport transportation. Exercise equipt; weights, bicycles. Luxury level. Cr cds: A, C, D, DS, ER, MC, V.

D ⚡ ≈ ✕ ✈ ➤ ⓦ SC ⚡

★ ★ **HOLIDAY INN EXPRESS MIDTOWN.** *1305 Walnut St (19107), downtown.* 215/735-9300; FAX 215/732-2682. E-mail midtown@ erols.com. 166 rms, 20 story. S $110-$135; D $120-$145; each addl $10; under 19 free. Crib free. Garage $11.75. TV; cable (premium). Pool. Complimentary continental bkfst. Ck-out 1 pm. Meeting rms. Business servs avail. In-rm modem link. Bellhops. Valet serv. Concierge. Health club privileges. Cr cds: A, C, D, DS, JCB, MC, V.

D ≈ ➤ ⓦ SC

★ ★ **HOLIDAY INN-INDEPENDENCE MALL.** *400 Arch St (19106), downtown.* 215/923-8660; FAX 215/923-4633. 364 rms, 8 story. S, D $95-$169; each addl $10; suites $275-$300; under 19 free; wkend rates. Garage $10. Crib free. TV; cable (premium), VCR avail. Rooftop pool; lifeguard. Restaurant 6:30 am-10:30 pm; dining rm 11:30 am-2 pm, 5:30-10:30 pm. Rm serv. Bar 11-1 am, Sun from noon. Ck-out 11 am. Coin lndry. Meeting rms. Business center. Bellhops. Valet serv. Sundries. Gift shop. Health club privileges. Cr cds: A, C, D, DS, JCB, MC, V.

D 🏊 🗽 🏋 SC 🛶

Hotels

★ ★ ★ **ADAM'S MARK.** City Ave & Monument Rd (19131), west of downtown. 215/581-5000; FAX 215/581-5069; res: 800/444-2326. Web www.adamsmark.com. 515 rms, 23 story. S $94-$219; D $94-$235; each addl $15; suites $179-$925; under 18 free; wkend, wkly rates. Crib free. TV; cable, VCR avail. Indoor/outdoor pool; whirlpool, poolside serv. Restaurant 6 am-11 pm. Bars; entertainment. Ck-out noon. Convention facilities. Business center. In-rm modem link. Shopping arcade. Barber, beauty shop. Airport, RR station, bus depot transportation. Exercise rm; instructor, weights, bicycles, sauna, steam rm. Refrigerators. Cr cds: A, C, D, DS, MC, V.

D 🏊 🗽 🏋 🛶 🏊 SC 🛶

✔ ★ ★ **COMFORT INN.** 100 N Christopher Columbus Blvd (19106), downtown. 215/627-7900; FAX 215/238-0809. 185 rms, 10 story. S, D $99-$129; each addl $10; suites $160; under 18 free; higher rates some hols. Crib free. TV. Complimentary continental bkfst. Coffee in rms. Restaurant nearby. Bar 5 pm-2 am. Ck-out noon. Meeting rms. Business servs avail. In-rm modem link. Airport, RR station, bus depot transportation. Health club privileges. View of Delaware River. Cr cds: A, C, D, DS, ER, JCB, MC, V.

D 🗽 🛶 SC

★ ★ ★ **DOUBLETREE.** Broad St at Locust (19107), downtown. 215/893-1600; FAX 215/893-1663. Web www.doubletree.com. 427 rms, 26 story. S $160-$175; D $185-$200; each addl $15; suites $250-$500; under 18 free; wkend rates; higher rates New Year's hols. Crib free. Garage $13, valet $17. TV; cable (premium), VCR avail. Indoor pool; whirlpool. Restaurant 6:30 am-11 pm; Fri, Sat to midnight. Bar to 1 am. Ck-out noon. Convention facilities. Business servs avail. In-rm modem link. Concierge. Gift shop. Airport transportation avail. Exercise equipt; weights, bicycles, sauna, steam rm. Luxury level. Cr cds: A, C, D, DS, ER, JCB, MC, V.

D 🏊 🗽 🏋 🛶 🏊 SC

★ ★ ★ **DOUBLETREE GUEST SUITES.** (640 W Germantown Pike, Plymouth Meeting 19462) W on I-76, exit I-476N to Germantown Pike West exit, right on Hickory Rd. 610/834-8300; FAX 610/834-7813. Web www.doubletreehotels.com. 252 suites, 7 story. S, D $210-$230; family, wkend rates. Crib $10. TV; cable (premium), VCR avail. Indoor pool; whirlpool, wading pool, poolside serv. Restaurant 6:30 am-10 pm. Bar. Ck-out noon. Coin lndry. Meeting rms. Business servs avail. In-rm modem link. Gift shop. Airport, RR station, bus depot transportation. Exercise equipt; weights, bicycles, sauna. Bathrm phones, refrigerators, minibars; microwaves avail. Some private patios, balconies. Cr cds: A, C, D, DS, MC, V.

D 🏊 🗽 🏋 🛶 SC

★ ★ ★ ★ **FOUR SEASONS HOTEL PHILADELPHIA.** 1 Logan Square (19103), on Logan Circle, downtown. 215/963-1500; FAX 215/963-9506. Web www.fshr.com. This elegant eight-story hotel has a magnificent setting on Logan Circle, reminiscent of the Place de la Concorde in Paris. Guest rooms are large and uncluttered, and the spacious marble lobby has an indoor garden with a fountain that makes it easy to forget that this is the heart of a large city. 371 rms, 8 story. S $250-$325; D $280-$355; each addl $30; suites $540-$1,290; under 18 free; wkend rates. Pet accepted. Garage $12-$24. TV; cable (premium), VCR avail. Indoor pool; whirlpool, poolside serv, lifeguard. Restaurants 6:30-1 am; Sat, Sun from 7 am (also see FOUNTAIN and SWANN CAFE; and see SWANN LOUNGE, Unrated Dining). Rm serv 24 hrs. Bar 11-2 am; pianist. Ck-out 1 pm. Convention facilities. Business center. In-rm modem link. Concierge. Beauty shop.

Exercise rm; instructor, weights, bicycles, sauna. Massage. Minibars; microwaves avail. Some balconies. Cr cds: A, C, D, ER, JCB, MC, V.

D 🛶 🏊 🗽 🏋 🛶 🏊

★ ★ ★ **HOLIDAY INN SELECT-CENTER CITY.** 1800 Market St (19103), in Center City. 215/561-7500; FAX 215/561-4484. Web www.holidayinnselect-phila.com. 445 rms, 25 story. S $175-$215; D $185-$225; each addl $10; suites $450; under 19 free; wkend rates. Crib free. Garage fee. TV; cable (premium), VCR avail. Pool. Restaurant 6 am-2 am. Bar from 11 am. Ck-out noon. Coin lndry. Convention facilities. Business center. In-rm modem link. Gift shop. Airport transportation. Exercise equipt; weights, bicycles. Health club privileges. Microwaves avail. Luxury level. Cr cds: A, C, D, DS, JCB, MC, V.

D 🏊 🗽 🏋 🗽 🛶 🏊 SC 🛶

✔ ★ ★ ★ **KORMANSUITES.** 2001 Hamilton St (19130), just off the Pkwy, museum area, in Center City. 215/569-7000; FAX 215/496-0138. 125 suites, 25 story. S $129-$169, D $159-$189; under 18 free; wkend rates. Crib free. TV; cable (premium). Pool; whirlpool, poolside serv, lifeguard. Complimentary coffee. Restaurant 6:30-2 am. Bar; entertainment. Ck-out 11 am. Convention facilities. Business servs avail. In-rm modem link. Gift shop. Barber, beauty shop. Garage parking. Exercise equipt; weight machine, bicycles. Microwaves. Landscaped Japanese sculpture garden. Cr cds: A, C, D, MC, V.

D 🏊 🗽 🏋 🛶 SC

★ ★ ★ **THE LATHAM.** 135 S 17th St (19103), at Walnut St, downtown. 215/563-7474; FAX 215/563-4034; res: 800/LATHAM-1. 139 rms, 14 story. S, D $185-$235; each addl $20; suites $325 & $425; under 18 free; wkend, hol rates. Crib free. Valet parking $14. TV; cable (premium), VCR avail (movies). Pool privileges. Restaurant 6:30 am-10:30 pm. Bar 11:30-2 am. Ck-out noon. Meeting rms. Business servs avail. In-rm modem link. Concierge. Exercise equipt; treadmills, bicycles. Many minibars. European ambience in intimate, boutique-style hotel. Cr cds: A, C, D, DS, ER, JCB, MC, V.

D 🗽 🏋 🛶 🏊 SC

★ ★ ★ **MARRIOTT.** 1201 Market St (19107), in Center City. 215/625-2900; FAX 215/625-6000. E-mail 74161.1366@compuserv.com. 1,200 rms, 23 story, 56 suites. S $159-$208; D $179-$228; suites $350-$1,000; under 12 free; wkend, hol rates. Crib free. Pet accepted. Valet parking $21. TV; cable (premium), VCR avail. Indoor pool; wading pool, whirlpool, poolside serv. Restaurants 6-1:30 am. 24 hr rm serv. Bar 5 pm-2 am. Ck-out 12:30 pm. Coin lndry. Convention facilities. Business center. In-rm modem link. Concierge. Shopping arcade. Beauty shop. Exercise equipt; weight machine, stair machine, sauna. Refrigerator in suites; microwaves avail. Connected to shopping mall. Luxury level. Cr cds: A, C, D, DS, ER, JCB, MC, V.

D 🛶 🏊 🗽 🏋 🛶 🏊 SC 🛶

★ ★ ★ **MARRIOTT PHILADELPHIA WEST.** (111 Crawford Ave, West Conshohocken 19428) 11 mi W on I-76, exit 29. 610/941-5600; FAX 610/940-1060. 288 rms, 17 story. S $159-$169; D $174-$189; each addl $30; suites $375; wkend, hol rates. Crib free. TV; cable (premium), VCR avail. Indoor pool; whirlpool, poolside serv, lifeguard. Restaurant 6 am-11 pm. Bar. Ck-out 1 pm. Convention facilities. Business servs avail. In-rm modem link. Concierge. Gift shop. Airport, RR station transportation. Exercise equipt; bicycles, stair machines, sauna. Microwaves avail. 1 blk from Schuylkill River. Atrium deck. Luxury level. Cr cds: A, C, D, DS, MC, V.

D 🏊 🗽 🏋 🗽 🛶 🏊 SC

★ ★ ★ ★ **OMNI HOTEL AT INDEPENDENCE PARK.** 4th & Chestnut Sts (19106), on Independence Park, adj to Independence Hall, in Olde City. 215/925-0000; FAX 215/925-1263. Imported marble floors, fine fabrics and classical music greet you in the lobby of this elegant Philadelphia establishment. The thoughtfully detailed rooms offer soothing views of Independence Park, a peaceful oasis in the heart of the city. The pool, spa and health club have been renovated for luxury and comfort. 150 rms, 14 story. S $229; D $249; each addl $20; suites from $300; under 18 free; wkend rates. Garage, valet parking (fees). TV; cable (premium), VCR avail. Indoor pool; whirlpool. Restaurant (see AZALEA). Rm serv 24 hrs. Bar 3-11 pm; entertainment Tues-Sat. Ck-out 11 am. Meeting rms. Business center. In-rm modem link. Concierge. Gift shop. Exercise equipt; weight machine, bicycles, sauna. Massage. Bathrm phones, minibars; microwaves avail. Cr cds: A, C, D, DS, ER, JCB, MC, V.

D ⚊ 🏋 🎿 🌊 SC 🚶

★ ★ ★ ★ **PARK HYATT PHILADELPHIA AT THE BELLEVUE.** *Broad & Walnut Sts (19102), downtown. 215/893-1776; FAX 215/893-9868; res: 800/221-0833.* Web www.hyatt.com. This classic hotel, located on the Avenue of Arts, occupies the top seven stories of a landmark building. It has lavish public rooms, including the seven-story Conservatory atrium and the stained-glass-domed Barrymore Room in which high tea is served. Guest rooms are spacious and pleasant. 170 rms, 7 story. S $225-$295; D $250-$320; suites $350-$1,800; under 18 free; special plans. Crib free. Garage $14, valet $21. TV; cable (premium), VCR. Indoor pool privileges; whirlpool, sauna, lifeguard. Restaurants 7 am-11 pm (also see THE FOUNDERS). Rm serv 24 hrs. Bar 11-1 am; entertainment. Ck-out 1 pm. In-rm modem link. Concierge. Shopping arcade. Barber, beauty shop. Massage. Health club privileges. Bathrm phones, minibars. Cr cds: A, C, D, DS, ER, JCB, MC, V.

D 🎿 🌊 SC

★ ★ ★ **PENN'S VIEW.** *Front & Market Sts (19106), in Olde City. 215/922-7600; FAX 215/922-7642; res: 800/331-7634.* E-mail 74161.355. compuserve.com. 40 rms, 5 story. S, D $108-$185; under 12 free; wkend rates. Crib free. TV; cable, VCR avail. Complimentary continental bkfst. Dining rm (see RISTORANTE PANORAMA). Ck-out noon, ck-in 4 pm. Meeting rms. Business servs avail. In-rm modem link. Concierge. Airport, RR station, bus depot transportation. Health club privileges. Overlooks Delaware River. Built 1828; Old World elegance. Fireplaces, whirlpools in some rms. Cr cds: A, C, D, ER, JCB, MC, V.

D ⚊ 🔥 SC

★ ★ ★ **RADISSON.** *500 Stevens Dr (19113), at Intl Airport (US 291), south of downtown. 610/521-5900; FAX 610/521-4362.* Web www. radisson.com. 353 rms, 12 story. S $135; D $145; each addl $10; suites $165; under 18 free; wkend packages. Crib free. TV; cable. Indoor pool; whirlpool, poolside serv. Restaurant 6:30 am-2 pm, 5-11 pm. Bars 2 pm-midnight. Ck-out noon. Meeting rms. Business center. In-rm modem link. Gift shop. Free airport transportation. Exercise equipt; weight machine, bicycles. Game rm. Microwaves avail. Atrium. Cr cds: A, C, D, DS, ER, MC, V.

D ⚊ 🏋 ✈ 🌊 SC 🚶

★ ★ ★ **RADISSON-NORTHEAST.** *(2400 Old Lincoln Hwy, Trevose 19053) 16 mi N on I-95, exit 24. 215/638-8300; FAX 215/638-4377.* 282 rms, 6 story. S $119; D $130; each addl $10; suites $199-$299; under 18 free; family rates. TV; cable (premium), VCR avail. Complimentary coffee in rms. Restaurant 6:30 am-10 pm; Sun 7 am-noon, 5-10 pm. Bar noon-2 am; entertainment. Ck-out noon. Convention facilities. Business servs avail. In-rm modem link. Concierge. Gift shop. Barber, beauty shop. Coin lndry. Exercise equipt; bicycle, treadmill. Indoor/outdoor pool; poolside serv, lifeguard. Game rm. Some refrigerators; wet bars. Some balconies. Cr cds: A, C, D, DS, ER, JCB, MC, V.

D ⚊ 🏋 🎿 🌊 SC

✔ ★ ★ ★ **RADNOR.** *(591 E Lancaster, St Davids 19087) 17 mi W on US 30, ¼ mi W of Blue Rte (I-476) exit 5. 610/688-5800; FAX 610/341-3299; res: 800/537-3000.* 170 rms, 4 story. S $145-$160; D $155-$170; each addl $10; suites $220; under 16 free. Crib free. TV; cable (premium), VCR avail. Pool; wading pool, lifeguard. Restaurant (see ABBEY GRILL). Rm serv 24 hrs. Bar 11-2 am; entertainment wkends. Ck-out noon. Meeting rms. Business center. In-rm modem link. Airport transportation. Exercise equipt; weight machine, rower. Game rm. Microwaves avail. Luxury level. Cr cds: A, C, D, DS, ER, JCB, MC, V.

D ⚊ 🏋 🎿 🌊 SC 🚶

★ ★ ★ ★ **THE RITTENHOUSE.** *210 W Rittenhouse Square (19103), downtown. 215/546-9000; FAX 215/732-3364; res: 800/635-1042.* E-mail hotel@rittenhouse.com. Subdued elegance and superior, intimate service are the hallmarks of the lower floors of a residential building on fashionable Rittenhouse Square, a verdant park in central Philadelphia. The hotel is suitable for business travelers, family vacationers and honeymooners. 133

rms, 9 story. S, D $315-$340; suites $475-$1,200; wkend rates. Crib free. Pet accepted. Garage; valet parking $23. TV; cable (premium), VCR (movies avail). Indoor pool; poolside serv. Restaurants (see NICHOLAS NICKOLAS, NICK'S and TREETOPS). Rm serv 24 hrs. Bar; entertainment. Ck-out 1 pm. Meeting rms. Business center. In-rm modem link. Concierge. Barber, beauty shop. Exercise rm; instructor, weight machine, bicycles, sauna, steam rm. Massage. Bathrm phones, minibars; microwaves avail. Cr cds: A, C, D, DS, MC, V.

D ⚊ 🌊 🏋 🔥 🚶

★ ★ ★ ★ **THE RITZ-CARLTON, PHILADELPHIA.** *17th & Chestnut Sts (19103), at Liberty Place, downtown. 215/563-1600; FAX 215/567-2822.* Web www.ritzcarlton.com. The opulent decor of this contemporary hotel includes Italian mantelpieces, silk wallpaper and an art collection worth one million dollars. The fully appointed guest rooms are furnished in refined colonial style. 290 rms, 15 story. S, D $245-$305; suites $395-$1,250; wkend rates. Crib free. Garage (fee). TV; cable (premium), VCR avail. Restaurant (see THE GRILL). Rm serv 24 hrs. Bar 11-1 am; pianist. Ck-out noon. Meeting rms. Business center. In-rm modem link. Concierge. Gift shop. Airport, RR station transportation. Exercise equipt; weights, bicycles, sauna. Massage. Health club privileges. Bathrm phones, minibars. Luxury level. Cr cds: A, C, D, DS, ER, JCB, MC, V.

D 🏋 🎿 🌊 🔥

★ ★ ★ **SHERATON SOCIETY HILL.** *1 Dock St (19106), in Society Hill. 215/238-6000; FAX 215/922-2709.* Web www.ITTsheraton.com. 365 units, 4 story. S, D $175-$225; suites $375-$3,000; under 17 free; wkend rates. Crib free. Pet accepted. Covered parking (fee). TV; cable (premium), VCR avail. Indoor pool; whirlpool, wading pool, poolside serv. Coffee in rms. Restaurants 6:30 am-2 pm, 5-10 pm. Rm serv 24 hrs. Bar noon-2 am. Ck-out noon. Convention facilities. Business servs avail. In-rm modem link. Concierge. Shopping arcade. Exercise rm; instructor, weights, bicycles, sauna. Massage. Minibars; some refrigerators. Cr cds: A, C, D, DS, ER, JCB, MC, V.

D 🖐 ⚊ 🏋 🌊 🔥 SC

★ ★ **TRAVELODGE.** *2015 Penrose Ave (19145), in Packer Park subdivision, near Intl Airport, south of downtown. 215/755-6500; FAX 215/465-7517.* 208 rms, 17 story. S $79-$99; D $89-$109; each addl $6; under 18 free; wkly, wkend, hol rates; higher rates special events. Crib free. Pet accepted, some restrictions; $35. TV; cable (premium). Heated pool; wading pool, poolside serv. Complimentary continental bkfst. Complimentary coffee in rms. Restaurant 6:30 am-10 pm. Bar 7-2 am. Ck-out noon. Coin lndry. Meeting rms. Business servs avail. In-rm modem link. Gift shop. Free airport, RR station transportation. Tennis privileges. 18-hole golf privileges. Exercise equipt; weights, bicycle. Some refrigerators; microwaves avail. Cr cds: A, C, D, DS, JCB, MC, V.

D 🖐 🏋 ⛷ ⚊ 🏋 ✈ 🌊 🔥 SC

★ ★ ★ **THE WARWICK.** *1701 Locust St (19103), downtown. 215/735-6000; FAX 215/790-7766; res: 800/523-4210 (exc PA).* 180 rms, 20 story, 20 kits. S $165-$185; D $195-$200; each addl $15; suites $185-$390; studio rms $185; apt $195; under 12 free; wkend plans. Crib free. Pet accepted, some restrictions. Garage (fee). TV; cable (premium), VCR avail. Restaurant 6:30 am-midnight. Bar 11-2 am. Ck-out noon. Meeting rms. Business servs avail. In-rm modem link. Concierge. Barber, beauty shop. Health club privileges. Cr cds: A, C, D, MC, V.

D 🖐 🌊 🔥 SC

★ ★ ★ **WESTIN SUITES.** *4101 Island Ave (19153), at I-95 Island Ave exit, near Intl Airport, south of downtown. 215/365-6600; FAX 215/492-8471.* 251 suites, 8 story. S, D $170-$180; each addl $15; under 18 free; wkend rates. Crib free. TV; cable (premium), VCR avail. Indoor pool; whirlpool, lifeguard. Coffee in rms. Restaurant 6 am-11 pm. Bar noon-2 am. Ck-out noon. Meeting rms. Business center. In-rm modem link. Gift shop. Free airport transportation. Exercise equipt; weights, bicycles, sauna, steam rm. Bathrm phones, refrigerators, minibars; microwaves avail. Cr cds: A, C, D, DS, JCB, MC, V.

D ⚊ 🏋 🎿 🌊 🔥 SC 🚶

★ ★ ★ **WYNDHAM FRANKLIN PLAZA.** *2 Franklin Plaza (19103), jct 17th & Race Sts, downtown.* 215/448-2000; FAX 215/448-2864. E-mail franklinplaza@wyndham.com; web www.wyndham.com. 758 rms, 26 story. S $165-$200; D $175-$210; each addl $20; suites $300-$1,000; under 18 free; wkend rates. Crib free. Pet accepted; some restrictions. Garage $15. TV; cable (premium), VCR avail. Indoor pool; whirlpool, poolside serv. Complimentary coffee in rms. Restaurant 6 am-11 pm. Bars 11-1 am. Ck-out noon. Convention facilities. Business center. In-rm modem link. Drugstore. Barber, beauty shop. Tennis. Exercise rm; instructor, weights, bicycles, sauna, steam rm. Massage. Refrigerators; microwaves avail. Cr cds: A, C, D, DS, ER, JCB, MC, V.

Inns

✔ ★ **LA RESERVE.** *1804 Pine St (19103), in Center City.* 215/735-1137; res: 800/354-8401; FAX 215/735-0582. 8 rms, 5 share bath, 4 story, 3 suites. No rm phones. S, D $50-$95; suites $95. Crib avail. TV in common rm; cable (premium), VCR avail (movies). Complimentary full bkfst. Restaurant nearby. Ck-out, ck-in times vary. Business servs avail. Luggage handling. Concierge serv. Street parking. Many fireplaces; microwaves avail. Built in 1868. Victorian decor; antiques. Totally nonsmoking. Cr cds: A, MC, V.

✔ ★ **THOMAS BOND HOUSE.** *129 S 2nd St (19106), in Olde City.* 215/923-8523; FAX 215/923-8504; res: 800/845-2663. Web www.libertynet.org/phila-visitor. 12 rms, 4 story, 2 suites. No elvtr. S, D $90-$160; each addl $15; suites $160. TV. Complimentary continental bkfst; afternoon refreshments. Restaurants nearby. Ck-out noon, ck-in 3-9 pm. Business servs avail. Airport transportation. Health club privileges. Library/sitting rm; antiques. Restored guest house (1769) built by Dr Thomas Bond, founder of the country's first public hospital. Individually decorated rms. Totally nonsmoking. Cr cds: A, D, DS, MC, V.

★ **WALNUT STREET INN.** *1208 Walnut St (19107), in Center City.* 215/546-7000; res: 800/887-1776; FAX 215/546-7573. E-mail murrayorgn@aol.com. 25 rms, 22 with shower only, 7 story, 6 suites. S, D $95; each addl $15; suites $125. Crib free. Parking adj $9. TV; cable. Complimentary continental bkfst; afternoon refreshments. Complimentary coffee in main rm. Restaurant nearby. Ck-out noon, ck-in 3 pm. Luggage handling. Business servs avail. In-rm modem link. Built in 1890s; early American decor. Walking distance from Pennsylvania Convention Center. Cr cds: A, C, D, DS, MC, V.

Restaurants

★ ★ ★ **ABBEY GRILL.** *(See Radnor Hotel)* 610/341-3165. Hrs: 6:30 am-10 pm; wkends to 11 pm; Sun brunch 10 am-2 pm. Res accepted. Bar to 2 am. Wine list. Semi-a la carte: lunch $5.95-$12.95, dinner $12.95-$19.95. Sun brunch $17.95. Child's meals. Specializes in beef, seafood. Salad bar. Entertainment Fri. Parking. Outdoor dining. Cr cds: A, C, D, DS, ER, JCB, MC, V.

★ ★ **AMERICAN BISTRO.** *(PA 420 & Morton Ave, Morton 19070) I-95, exit 9A, N on PA 420.* 610/543-3033. Hrs: 11:30 am-2:30 pm, 5-9:30 pm; Sat from 5 pm; Sun 4-8 pm. Closed Mon; some major hols. Res accepted. American fusion menu. Semi-a la carte: lunch $5-$10, dinner $18-$28. Prix fixe $28.95. Specializes in fresh seafood. Parking. Cr cds: A, C, D, DS, MC, V.

★ ★ **ARROYO GRILLE.** *(1 Leverington Ave, Manayunk 19127) 6 mi W on I-76, exit 31, right at 1st light, left on Main St, left on Leverington.* 215/487-1400. Hrs: 11-2 am; Sun brunch to 3 pm. Closed Thanksgiving. Res accepted. Southwestern menu. Bar. A la carte entrees: lunch $5-$8, dinner $13-$16. Sun brunch $16.95. Child's meals. Specializes in smokehouse barbecue, margaritas. Own baking, pasta. Musicians Sun. Outdoor dining. Southwestern decor with woodburning fireplace; two-level dining area. Cr cds: A, DS, MC, V.

★ **ASSAGGI ITALIANI.** *935 Ellsworth St (19147), south of downtown.* 215/339-0700. Hrs: 5:30-10 pm; Fri, Sat to 11 pm. Closed Sun; most major hols. Res accepted; required Fri, Sat. Italian menu. Bar. A la carte entrees: dinner $7.50-$19. Specializes in pasta, grilled fish, veal dishes. Own baking.Casual Italian atmosphere. Cr cds: A, D, MC, V.

★ ★ ★ **AZALEA.** *(See Omni Hotel At Independence Park)* 215/931-4270. Hrs: 7 am-2:30 pm, 5:30-10 pm; wkends to 11 pm. Sun brunch 11 am-2 pm. Res accepted. Bar. Extensive wine list. A la carte entrees: bkfst $8.95-$17, lunch $8.75-$16.50, dinner $12.50-$19.50. Sun brunch $21.95. Specializes in venison, duck, seafood. Valet parking. Cr cds: A, C, D, DS, ER, JCB, MC, V.

★ **BERLENGAS.** *4926 N 5th St (19120), north of downtown.* 215/324-3240. Hrs: noon-10 pm. Closed Wed. Res required Fri-Sun dinner. Portuguese menu. Bar 9 am-midnight. A la carte entrees: lunch, dinner $11-$25. Specializes in seafood. Jacket. Intimate atmosphere. Cr cds: MC, V.

★ ★ **BIG FISH.** *(140 Moorehead Ave, Conshohocken 19428) 11 mi W on I-76, exit 29.* 610/834-7224. Hrs: 11:30 am-10 pm; Fri, Sat to 11 pm, Sun noon-9 pm. Res accepted. Bar. Semi-a la carte: lunch $6-$19, dinner $10-$23. Child's meals. Specializes in fresh seafood. Free parking. Nautical decor. Cr cds: A, C, D, DS, MC, V.

★ ★ **BISTRO BIX.** *114 S 12th St (19107), downtown.* 215/925-5336. Hrs: 11 am-3 pm, 5-10 pm; Fri, Sat to 11 pm. Closed some major hols. Res accepted. Continental menu. Bar. Semi-a la carte: lunch $7-$16, dinner $14-$22. Specialties: wild stripped bass, 13 oz. veal chops. Cr cds: A, D, MC, V.

★ ★ **BOOKBINDER'S 15TH STREET SEAFOOD HOUSE.** *215 S 15th St (19102), in Center City.* 215/545-1137. Hrs: 11:30 am-10 pm; Sat 4-11 pm; Sun 3-10 pm. Closed Thanksgiving, Dec 25. Res accepted. Bar. Semi-a la carte: lunch $6-$13.50, dinner $15.95-$24.95. Child's meals. Specializes in seafood, steak. Own pastries. Family-owned since 1893. Cr cds: A, C, D, DS, MC, V.

★ ★ ★ **BRASSERIE PERRIER.** *1619 Walnut St (19102), downtown.* 215/568-3000. E-mail saugustine@brasserieperrier.com; web www.brasserieperrier.com. Original paintings and sculpture complement the art-deco decor of this elegant restaurant. Contemporary Amer menu. Specializes in pasta, fresh seafood. Hrs: 5:30-11 pm. Closed most major hols. Res required. Bar to 1 am. Wine cellar. Semi-a la carte: dinner $19-$35. Valet parking. Totally nonsmoking. Cr cds: A, DS, MC, V.

✔ ★ ★ **BRIDGET FOY'S SOUTH STREET GRILL.** *200 South St (19147), near Head House Square, in South Street Area.* 215/922-1813. Hrs: 11:30 am-10:30 pm; Fri, Sat to midnight. Closed Thanksgiving, Dec 25. Res accepted. Bar to 2 am. A la carte entrees: lunch $6.95-$12.95, dinner $11.95-$19.95. Specializes in grilled fish, meat. Valet parking on wkends. Outdoor dining. Cr cds: A, C, D, DS, MC, V.

★ ★ **CAFE NOLA.** *603 S 3rd St (19147), in South Street Area.* 215/627-2590. Web www.cafenola.com. Hrs: noon-4 pm, 5-10 pm; Mon from 5 pm; Fri, Sat to 11 pm; Sun brunch 11 am-3 pm. Res required Fri, Sat. Bar to 2 am. A la carte entrees: lunch $8-$14, dinner $15-$26. Sun brunch $19.50. Specializes in Creole, Cajun dishes. Outdoor dining. Colorful New Orleans decor. Cr cds: A, C, D, DS, MC, V.

[D] [🍽]

★ ★ **CARY.** *211 S 15th St (19102), downtown. 215/735-9100.* Web www.caryrestaurant.com. Hrs: 11:30 am-11 pm. Res accepted. Contemporary Amer menu. Bar. A la carte entrees: lunch $4.50-$10.50, dinner $12.50-$18. Child's meals. Specializes in fresh seafood, homemade soups, salads. Valet parking. Outdoor dining. Cr cds: A, D, DS, MC, V.

[D] [🍽]

★ ★ ★ **CHANTERELLES.** *1312 Spruce St (19107), downtown. 215/735-7551.* Hrs: 5-10:30 pm; Fri, Sat to 11 pm. Closed Sun, most hols. Res accepted. French, Asian menu. Bar. Wine list. A la carte entrees: $22-$28. Complete meals: $29-$55. Child's meals. Specialties: venison cutlets, rack of lamb. French country inn decor. Totally nonsmoking. Cr cds: A, D, MC, V.

★ ★ ★ **CIBOULETTE.** *200 S Broad St (19102), downtown. 215/790-1210.* Hrs: 5:30-9 pm; Fri, Sat to 10:30 pm. Closed Sun; most major hols. Res accepted; required Sat. French Provençal menu. Bar. Wine cellar. A la carte entrees (appetizer portions): $6-$18. Specialties: roasted Maine lobster, black sea bass, loin of veal. Own desserts. Valet parking. French Renaissance-style architecture; display of local artists; original mosaic tile floor; one rm with ceiling mural. Cr cds: A, MC, V.

[D] [🍽]

★ ★ ★ **CIRCA.** *1518 Walnut St (19102), downtown. 215/545-6800.* Web circarestaurant.com. Hrs: 11:30 am-2:30 pm, 5-10 pm; Thurs, Sat to 11 pm; Mon from 5 pm; Sun 4:30-9 pm. Closed Jan 1, Dec 25. Res accepted. Bar. Wine list. Semi-a la carte: lunch $8-$13, dinner $11-$20. Child's meals. Specialties: roast Chilean sea bass, fire grilled spice-rubbed filet mignon, crazy E's BBQ pork loin chop. Valet parking. Former bank lobby, cathedral ceilings. Cr cds: A, D, MC, V.

[D] [🍽]

★ ★ **CITY TAVERN.** *138 S 2nd St at Walnut (19106), in Society Hill area. 215/413-1443.* Web www.staib.com. Hrs: 11:30 am-10:30 pm; Fri, Sat to 11:30 pm. Res accepted. Bar. Semi-a la carte: lunch $8.95-$16.95, dinner $17.95-$26.95. Child's meals. Specializes in fresh fish, poultry, meats. Entertainment Sat. Outdoor dining. Historic colonial tavern (1773). Cr cds: A, C, D, DS, ER, JCB, MC, V.

[D] [🍽]

★ ★ **COYOTE CROSSING.** *(800 Spring Mill Rd, Conshohocken 19428) 15 mi W on I-76, exit Conshohocken. 610/825-3000.* Hrs: 11:30 am-2:30 pm, 4:30-9:30 pm; Fri to 10:30 pm; Sat 4:30-10:30 pm; Sun from 4:30 pm. Closed Jan 1, July 4, Dec 25. Southwestern menu. Bar. A la carte entrees: lunch $5.75-$7.95, dinner $10.95-$18.95. Specialties: homemade stuffed crepes, filet mignon. Own baking. Classical guitarist Thurs, Sat. Modern southwestern decor. Cr cds: A, D, DS, MC, V.

[D]

★ ★ **CUVEE NOTREDAME.** *1701 Green St (19130), downtown. 215/765-2777.* Hrs: 11:30-2 am; Sun brunch 11:30 am-2:30 pm. Closed Thanksgiving, Dec 25. Res accepted. Belgian menu. Bar. A la carte entrees: lunch $5, dinner $15-$21. Sun brunch $5. Child's meals. Specializes in mussels, duck. Belgian atmosphere. Cr cds: A, DS, MC, V.

[D] [🍽]

★ ★ ★ **DEUX CHEMINÉES.** *1221 Locust St (19107), downtown. 215/790-0200.* Hrs: 5:30-8:30 pm; Sat to 9 pm. Closed Sun, Mon; major hols. Res accepted. French menu. Serv bar. Wine cellar. Prix fixe: dinner $68. Specialties: rack of lamb, crab soup. Menu changes daily. Own baking. Chef-owned. Totally nonsmoking. Cr cds: A, C, D, MC, V.

[♥]

★ ★ **DICKENS INN.** *Head House Square (19147), on 2nd St, in Society Hill. 215/928-9307.* Hrs: 11:30 am-3 pm, 5-10 pm; Sat to 10:30 pm; Sun 4:30-9 pm; Sun brunch 11 am-3 pm. Closed Mon; Jan 1, Dec 25. Res accepted. Continental menu. Bar 11:30-2 am; Mon from 5 pm. A la carte entrees: lunch $4.75-$10.75, dinner $12-$22. Sun brunch $14.75. Child's

meals. Specialties: roast beef with Yorkshire pudding, beef Wellington, fish & chips. In historic Harper House (1788); Victorian decor; artwork imported from England. Cr cds: A, D, DS, MC, V.

[D] [🍽]

★ ★ ★ **DINARDO'S.** *312 Race St (19106), in Olde City. 215/925-5115.* Web www.menusonline.com. Hrs: 11 am-10 pm; Fri, Sat to 11 pm; Sun 3-9 pm. Closed major hols. Bar. Semi-a la carte: lunch $5-$10, dinner $9-$25. Child's meals. Specializes in seafood. Historic bldg (1740). Cr cds: A, C, D, MC, V.

[D] [SC] [🍽]

★ ★ ★ ★ **THE DINING ROOM.** *(See The Ritz-Carlton, Philadelphia Hotel).* CLOSED TO PUBLIC. Web www.ritzcarlton.com. Hardwood floors, crystal chandeliers and blue cobalt stemware set an elegant stage for a traditional fine-dining experience. Chef Trish Morrissey serves up impressive New American cuisine. But arrive early—the restaurant is only open for breakfast and lunch. Specialties: fresh crab cakes, baby rack of lamb with eggplant. Hrs: 6:30 am-2:30 pm; Sun brunch from 11 am. Res accepted. Bar 11-1 am. Wine list. A la carte entrees: bkfst $7-$18, lunch $15-$30. Sun brunch $35. Child's meals. Pianist. Valet parking. Cr cds: A, C, D, DS, ER, JCB, MC, V.

[D] [🍽]

★ **DMITRI'S.** *795 S 3rd St (19047), south of downtown. 215/625-0556.* Hrs: 5:30-11 pm; Sun 5-10 pm. Closed Easter, Thanksgiving, Dec 24, 25. Mediterranean menu. Setups. A la carte entrees: $12-$20. Specializes in seafood, lamb. No cr cds accepted.

✔★ ★ **DOCK STREET BREWERY.** *2 Logan Square (19103), at 18th & Cherry Sts, downtown. 215/496-0413.* Hrs: 11:30 am-midnight; Fri to 2 am; Sat noon-2 am; Sun noon-11 pm. Closed Labor Day, Dec 25. Res accepted. Bar. A la carte entrees: lunch $5.75-$9.95, dinner $7-$17.50. Specializes in freshly brewed beer, homemade breads, grilled meats and fish. Entertainment Fri, Sat. Brewery tanks; beer brewed on premises, tours avail Wed, Sat. Dartboard and billiard tables. Cr cds: A, D, DS, MC, V.

[D] [🍽]

★ ★ **FELICIA'S.** *1148 S 11th St (19147), south of downtown. 215/755-9656.* Hrs: 11:30-2 am. Closed Mon; most major hols. Res accepted; required Sat, Sun. Italian menu. Bar. Semi-a la carte: lunch $6.95-$12.50, dinner $11.95-$21.95. Specialties: seafood ravioli, ricotta gnocci, ricotta cheesecake, veal chop. Own desserts. Valet parking. Piano in bar. Cr cds: A, C, D, DS, MC, V.

[D] [🍽]

✔★ ★ **FISHER'S SEAFOOD.** *7312 Castor Ave (19152), north of downtown. 215/725-6201.* Hrs: 11 am-9 pm; Fri, Sat to 10 pm; Sun noon-9 pm. Closed Mon; Labor Day, Thanksgiving, Dec 25. Res accepted. Bar. Semi-a la carte: lunch $3.25-$6.95, dinner $6.25-$12.95. Complete meals: lunch $4.95-$9.20, dinner $7.95-$15.95. Child's meals. Specializes in seafood, stir-fried dishes. Parking. Six large dining areas, individually decorated. Family-owned. Cr cds: DS, MC, V.

[D] [🍽] [♥]

★ ★ **FLYING FISH.** *8142 Germantown Ave (19118), in Chestnut Hill. 215/247-0707.* Hrs: 11:30 am-2:30 pm, 5:30-9 pm; Mon from 5:30 pm; Fri, Sat noon-2:30 pm, 5:30-10 pm. Closed Sun; some major hols. Bar. A la carte entrees: lunch $6.50-$8.75, dinner $13-$22. Child's meals. Specializes in seafood, clam bake (summer). Own pasta, pastries, ice cream. Totally nonsmoking. Cr cds: MC, V.

[D]

★ ★ ★ **THE FOUNDERS.** *(See Park Hyatt Philadelphia At The Bellevue Hotel) 215/790-2814.* Web www.hyatt.com. Hrs: 6:30 am-2:30 pm, 5-11 pm; Sun brunch 10:30 am-2:30 pm; Mon from 5:30 pm; pre-theater dinner 5:30-6:30 pm. Res accepted. French, Asian menu. Bar 11-2 am. Wine cellar. Complete meals: bkfst $9.50-$12.50, dinner $65. A la carte entrees: lunch $9.50-$16.50, dinner $24-$36. Sun brunch $34.50. Specialties: filet de boeuf à la Moëlle, red snapper en papillote. Entertainment. Valet parking.

Rotunda with sweeping views of city. Elegant turn-of-the-century decor. Jacket (dinner). Cr cds: A, C, D, DS, ER, JCB, MC, V.

[D] [SC]

★ ★ ★ ★ **FOUNTAIN.** *(See Four Seasons Hotel Philadelphia) 215/963-1500.* Web www.fshr.com. This quiet, luxurious restaurant, nestled in the lavish yet dignified lobby of the Four Seasons, maintains the atmosphere of a private club. Breads and pastries are made on site; entrees are predominantly local and American. Continental menu. Specialties: rack of lamb, sautéed snapper, sautéed venison medallion. Own baking, desserts. Hrs: 6:30 am-2:30 pm, 6-10:30 pm; Sun brunch 11 am-2:30 pm. Res accepted. Bar to 2 am. Wine cellar. A la carte entrees: bkfst $12-$17, lunch $22-$27.50, dinner $32-$38. Prix fixe: 4-course dinner $74. Sun brunch $31-$39. Child's meals. Entertainment. Valet parking. Jacket (dinner). Cr cds: A, C, D, DS, MC, V.

[D] [≛] [♥]

★ ★ ★ **THE GARDEN.** *1617 Spruce St (19103), downtown. 215/546-4455.* Web www.thegardenrestaurant.com. Hrs: 11:30 am-1:30 pm, 5:30-9:30 pm; Mon, Sat from 5:30 pm. Closed Sun; major hols. Res accepted. Continental menu. Bar. Extensive wine list. A la carte entrees: lunch $10.95-$24.95, dinner $16.95-$25.95. Specializes in fresh seafood, aged prime beef. Valet parking. Spacious outdoor dining. City skyline views. Cr cds: A, C, D, MC, V.

[≛]

★ ★ ★ **THE GRILL.** *(See The Ritz-Carlton, Philadelphia Hotel) 215/563-1600.* Web www.ritzcarlton.com. Hrs: 6:30 am-2:30 pm; 5:30-10:30 pm; Sat, Sun from 5:30 pm. Res accepted. Bar. Semi-a la carte: bkfst $7-$18, lunch $12-$28. A la carte entrees: dinner $19-$40. Specializes in grilled beef, seafood. Club atmosphere. Cr cds: A, C, D, DS, ER, JCB, MC, V.

[D] [≛]

★ ★ ★ **HARRY'S BAR & GRILL.** *22 S 18th St, downtown. 215/561-5757.* Hrs: 11:30 am-1:45 pm, 5:30-9 pm; Fri to 1:45 pm. Closed Sat, Sun; major hols. Res accepted. Italian, Amer menu. Bar 11:30 am-9 pm. Wine cellar. A la carte entrees: lunch $9.95-$23.95, dinner $14.95-$23.95. Specializes in fresh seafood, homemade pasta, aged prime steak. Own pastries. Parking. English club atmosphere. Cr cds: A, C, D, MC, V.

[D] [≛]

✔★ **HO SAI GAI.** *1000 Race St (19107), in Chinatown. 215/922-5883.* Hrs: 11:30-4 am; Fri, Sat to 5 am. Closed Thanksgiving. Res accepted. Chinese menu. Serv bar. Semi-a la carte: lunch $4.95-$8.95, dinner $9-$15.95. Specializes in Mandarin & Hunan cuisine. Cr cds: A, C, MC, V.

[≛]

★ ★ **HUSCH.** *(301 Woodbine Ave, Narberth 19072) 7 mi N on I-76, exit City Line, follow Montgomery Ave to Woodbine Ave. 610/668-6393.* Hrs: 11 am-2:30 pm, 5-10 pm; Fri to 11 pm; Sat 11 am-3 pm (brunch), 5-11 pm; Sun 11 am-3 pm (brunch), 5-10 pm. Closed Dec 25. Res accepted; required Fri, Sat dinner. Continental menu. Bar. A la carte entrees: lunch $6-$9, dinner $12-$25. Sat, Sun brunch $6-$11. Child's meals. Specializes in tuna, rack of lamb, sushi. Own baking. Contemporary atmosphere; blends East and West Coast styles. Cr cds: A, MC, V.

[D] [≛]

★ ★ **ISABELLA'S.** *6516 Castor Ave (19149), I-95N, exit Cottman Ave, to Castor Ave, north of downtown. 215/533-0356.* Hrs: 5:30-9 pm; Fri, Sat to 9:30 pm; Sun to 8 pm. Closed Mon; Easter, Thanksgiving, Dec 25. Res required. French, Italian menu. Bar. Semi-a la carte: dinner $13.50-$20.50. Child's meals. Specialties: shrimp and crab risotto cakes, potato gnocchi, grilled whole striped bass. Own baking. Intimate atmosphere with modern European decor. Cr cds: A, D, MC, V.

[D] [≛]

★ ★ **ITALIAN BISTRO.** *211 S Broad St (19107), downtown. 215/731-0700.* Hrs: 11:30 am-11 pm; wkends 12:30 pm-midnight. Closed Dec 25. Res accepted. Bar. Complete meals: lunch $5.50-$6.25. A la carte

entrees: dinner $8-$18. Child's meals. Specializes in Northern Italian dishes, brick oven pizza. Own pasta, desserts. Cr cds: A, D, DS, MC, V.

[D] [≛] [♥]

★ ★ ★ **JAKE'S.** *(4365 Main St, Manayunk 19127) I-76, exit 31. 215/483-0444.* Web www.jakes_restaurant.com. Hrs: 11:30 am-2:30 pm, 5:30-9:30 pm; Sun 10:30 am-2:30 pm, 5-9 pm. Closed Jan 1, Thanksgiving, Dec 25. Res accepted. Contemporary Amer menu. Bar. Extensive wine list. A la carte entrees: lunch $7-$15, dinner $18-$30. Child's meals. Sun brunch $7-$13. Specialties: crab cakes, barbecue salmon, tuna. Valet parking. Cr cds: A, D, MC, V.

★ ★ **KANSAS CITY PRIME.** *(4417 Main St, Manayunk 19127) off I-76, exit 31. 215/482-3700.* Web www.kansascityprime.com. Hrs: 5:30-11 pm; Sun 5-10 pm. Closed Thanksgiving. Res accepted. Bar to 2 am. A la carte entrees: dinner $17-$31. Specializes in aged prime beef, grilled seafood. Contemporary decor. Cr cds: A, C, D, DS, JCB, MC, V.

[D] [≛]

★ **KNAVE OF HEARTS.** *230 South St (19147), in South Street Area. 215/922-3956.* Hrs: noon-4 pm, 5:30-10:30 pm; Fri, Sat to 11:30 pm; Sun 5-10 pm. Sun brunch 11 am-4 pm. Closed Dec 25. Res accepted. Bar. A la carte entrees: lunch $5-$9, dinner $12-$20. Sun brunch $12.50-$13.50. Specialties: filet mignon, roast duckling. Intimate dining. Cr cds: A, MC, V.

[≛]

★ ★ ★ **LA FAMIGLIA.** *8 S Front St (19106), in Olde City. 215/922-2803.* Hrs: noon-2 pm, 5:30-9:30 pm; Sat 5:30-10 pm; Sun 5-9 pm. Closed Mon; major hols; also last wk Aug. Res required. Italian menu. Bar. Wine cellar. A la carte entrees: lunch $12.95-$19.95, dinner $22-$40. Specializes in veal, fresh fish, pasta. Own desserts. Built in 1878 in one of city's first blocks of buildings. Jacket. Cr cds: A, C, D, MC, V.

[≛]

★ ★ ★ **LE BAR LYONNAIS.** *1523 Walnut St (19102), downstairs at Le Bec Fin, downtown. 215/567-1000.* Web www.lebecfin.com. Hrs: 11:30-1:30 am; Sat 6-9 pm. Closed Sun; major hols. French bistro menu. Bar. A la carte entrees: lunch, dinner $12-$18. Specialties: escargots au champagne, galette de crabe, thon au poivres. Valet parking (dinner). Elegant bistro atmosphere; original art. Cr cds: A, C, D, DS, MC, V.

★ ★ **LE BAR NOSTRADAMUS.** *1701 Green St (19130), downtown. 215/765-3360.* Hrs: 5 pm-2 am. Closed Thanksgiving, Dec 25. Res accepted. Belgian steakhouse menu. Bar. A la carte entrees: dinner $15-$21. Specializes in steaks, chops. Musicians Fri. Casual atmosphere; humorous artwork, brick fireplace. Cr cds: A, D, DS, MC, V.

[≛]

★ ★ ★ ★ ★ **LE BEC-FIN.** *1523 Walnut St (19102), downtown. 215/567-1000.* Web www.lebecfin.com. There's probably no better French cuisine outside France than at this fine dining room decorated in Louis XVI style with crystal chandeliers, red silk wallpaper and gilt mirrors. The prix-fixe dinner is steep, but it includes six superb courses featuring a broad choice of delicately prepared appetizers, fish, meats and desserts. French menu. Specializes in seasonal dishes. Own baking. Sittings: lunch 11:30 am & 1:30 pm, dinner 6 & 9 pm; Fri & Sat dinner 9:30 pm. Closed Sun; major hols. Res required. Bar to 1 am. Wine cellar. Prix fixe: lunch $36, dinner $102. Valet parking (dinner). Chef-owned. Jacket. Cr cds: A, C, D, DS, MC, V.

[D]

★ ★ ★ **THE MARKER.** *(See Adam's Mark Hotel) 215/581-5010.* Hrs: 11 am-2:30 pm, 5:30-10 pm; Fri to 11 pm; Sat, Sun 5:30-11 pm; Sun brunch 10:30 am-2:30 pm. Closed some major hols. Res accepted. Contemporary Amer menu. Bar. Wine cellar. Semi-a la carte: lunch $8.95-$13.95, dinner $17.95-$25.95. Sun brunch $22.95. Specialties: lemon mint-cured salmon, wasabi and citrus-crusted tuna mignon, lavender-honey and apple cider-glazed duck. Own baking, pasta. Pianist. Formal French and English decor with stained glass, tapestries, stone fireplace and gold-plated chandelier. Jacket. Cr cds: A, C, D, DS, MC, V.

[D] [≛]

★ ★ **MEIJI-EN.** *Pier 19 North (19106), Columbus Ave at Callowhill St, Delaware River Waterfront, in Olde City.* 215/592-7100. Hrs: 5-9:30 pm; Fri, Sat to 11 pm; Sun brunch 10:30 am-3 pm. Res accepted, required for brunch. Japanese menu. Bar; wkends to 1 am. A la carte entrees: $13-$30. Sun brunch $19.95. Specializes in sushi, tempura, teppanyaki-grilled items. Jazz Fri-Sun brunch. Valet parking. Overlooks Delaware River. Cr cds: A, C, D, DS, MC, V.

D ⌐ ♥

★ ★ **MICHAEL'S.** *824 S 8th St (19147), south of downtown.* 215/922-3986. Web www.michaelsristorante.com. Hrs: 5-11 pm; Sun 3-10 pm. Closed Mon. Res accepted. Italian menu. Bar. A la carte entrees: dinner $10.95-$23.95. Child's meals. Specialties: veal chop, gnocchi. Valet parking. Exposed brick, stucco walls; statuary in alcoves. Bronze, glass chandeliers. Cr cds: A, C, D, DS, MC, V.

D ⌐

★ ★ **MIDDLE EAST.** *126 Chestnut St (19106), in Olde City.* 215/922-1003. Hrs: 5 pm-midnight; Fri, Sat to 2 am; Sun from 3 pm. Closed Thanksgiving, Dec 24, 25. Res accepted. Middle Eastern, Amer menu. Bar. Semi-a la carte: dinner $14.50-$21.50. Specialty: shish kebab. Middle Eastern band Fri-Sat. Middle Eastern decor. Cr cds: A, C, D, DS, MC, V.

D SC ⌐

★ ★ **MONTE CARLO LIVING ROOM.** *2nd & South Sts (19147), in South Street Area.* 215/925-2220. Hrs: 6-10:30 pm; Fri, Sat 5:30-11 pm; Sun 5-9 pm. Closed major hols. Res accepted. Northern Italian menu. Bar. Wine cellar. A la carte entrees: dinner $28-$40. Degustation dinner $65. Specializes in fresh fish, veal, beef. Daily menu. Own pastries. Mediterranean decor. Jacket. Cr cds: A, D, MC, V.

⌐

✔★ ★ **MOONSTRUCK.** *7955 Oxford Ave (19111), north of downtown.* 215/725-6000. Hrs: 5-9 pm; Fri, Sat to 10 pm; Sun 4:30-8 pm. Closed Jan 1, July 4, Dec 25. Italian menu. Wine cellar. Semi-a la carte: dinner $14-$20. Specializes in homemade pasta, veal dishes, seafood. Own pastries. Parking. Cr cds: A, D, MC, V.

D ⌐

★ ★ **MOSHULU.** *Pier 34 (19147), in South Street area.* 215/923-2500. Hrs: 11:30 am-3 pm, 5:30-10 pm; Sun 11 am-2 pm (brunch), 5:30-10 pm. Closed Jan 1, Dec 25. Res accepted. Continental menu. Bar to midnight. Wine cellar. Semi-a la carte: lunch $7-$14, dinner $17-$28. Sun brunch $19.95. Specializes in steak, seafood. Entertainment Wed-Sat. Valet parking. Outdoor dining. Restored 400-ft sailing ship (1904); turn-of-the-century nautical decor with mahogany paneling and brass trim. Jacket. Cr cds: A, D, DS, MC, V.

D ⌐

★ **NAIS CUISINE.** *(13-17 W Benedict Ave, Haverstown 19083) I-476, exit 3.* 610/789-5983. Hrs: 5-9 pm, wkends to 10 pm. Res accepted, required Fri, Sat. French menu with Thai influence. A la carte entrees: $13.25-$23.50. Specialties: roast duckling, steamed salmon stuffed with crab meat, snow pea salad. Cr cds: A, MC, V.

⌐

★ ★ **NAPOLEON.** *1500 Locust St (19102), downtown.* 215/893-9100. Hrs: 11:30 am-2:30 pm, 5-10 pm; Fri to 11 pm; Sun from 5 pm. Closed major hols. Res required. Continental menu. Bar. Extensive wine list. A la carte entrees: lunch $8-$15, dinner $15-$28. Specializes in beef, fish, chicken. Own pasta. Valet parking. Modern decor with old-world charm. Cr cds: A, MC, V.

D ⌐

✔★ ★ **NEW MEXICO GRILLE.** *50 S 2nd St (19106), in Olde City.* 215/922-7061. E-mail losamigos@hotmail.com; web www.losamigos.com. Hrs: 11:30 am-10 pm; Fri, Sat to 1:30 am; Sun noon-10 pm. Closed some major hols. Southwestern menu. Bar. Semi-a la carte: lunch $4.95-

$11.95, dinner $11.95-$20.95. Specializes in grilled meats, seafood. Cr cds: A, C, D, MC, V.

D ⌐

★ ★ **NICHOLAS NICKOLAS.** *(See The Rittenhouse Hotel)* 215/546-8440. Web www.harman-nickolas.com. Hrs: 5:30-10:30 pm; Fri, Sat to 11 pm. Closed Sun. Res accepted. Continental menu. Bar 11:30-2 am; Sat from 5 pm. Wine cellar. A la carte entrees: dinner $19-$46. Specialties: lobster thermidor, cioppino Raymondo, prime cowboy steak. Pianist. Valet parking. Modern decor; view of Rittenhouse Square. Totally nonsmoking. Cr cds: A, C, D, DS, MC, V.

D

✔★ ★ **NICK'S.** *(See The RittenhouseHotel)* 215/546-8440. Web www.harman-nickolas.com. Hrs: 11:30-2 am. Closed Sun. Bar from 5:30 pm. Semi-a la carte: lunch, dinner $13.50-$14.95. Specializes in portabella sandwiches, blue plate special, salads. Pianist. Valet parking. Piano and sports bar; large aquarium. Cr cds: A, C, D, DS, MC, V.

D ⌐

★ ★ ★ **OLD ORIGINAL BOOKBINDER'S.** *125 Walnut St (19106), in Society Hill.* 215/925-7027. E-mail johnny@lobsters.com; web www.oldbookbinders.com. Hrs: 11:45 am-10 pm; Sat 4:30-10 pm; Sun 3-9 pm. Closed Thanksgiving, Dec 25. Res accepted. Bars. Wine list. Complete meals: lunch $7.95-$14.95, dinner $16.95-$35. Child's meals. Specializes in lobster, snapper soup, mile high desserts. Own pastries. Valet parking. Established 1865; in historic bldg. Family-owned. Cr cds: A, C, D, DS, MC, V.

D ⌐ ♥

★ ★ ★ **OPUS 251.** *251 S 18th St (19103), downtown.* 215/735-6787. Web www.nitescene.com/opus251. Hrs: 11 am-2:30 pm, 5-10 pm; Fri, Sat to 11 pm; Sun to 9 pm; Sun brunch to 3 pm. Closed Mon; Memorial Day, Thanksgiving, Dec 25. Res required (dinner). Bar. Wine cellar. Semi-a la carte: lunch $3.75-$10.75, dinner $14-$24.50. Sun brunch $15. Specialties: Cervena venison mignonettes, eggplant pasta pillows, sun-dried tomato-dusted red snapper. Own baking, sausage, ice cream. Valet parking. Outdoor dining. Casually elegant dining in Philadelphia Art Alliance; arched windows, European garden. Cr cds: A, D, MC, V.

D ⌐

★ ★ ★ **OVERTURES.** *609 E Passyunk Ave (19147), in South Street area.* 215/627-3455. Hrs: 6-10:30 pm; Sun 5-9:30 pm. Closed Mon, hols. Res accepted. Mediterranean menu. Setups. A la carte entrees: $10-$28. Specialties: sautéed veal sweetbreads in port, roast saddle of lamb. Cr cds: A, C, D, MC, V.

⌐

★ ★ **THE PALM.** *200 S Broad St (19102), downtown.* 215/546-7256. Hrs: 11:30 am-11 pm; Sat from 5 pm; Sun 4:30-9 pm. Closed most major hols. Res accepted. Bar. A la carte entrees: lunch $7.50-$18, dinner $16.50-$40. Specializes in fresh seafood, prime aged beef, lamb chops. Valet parking. Counterpart of famous New York restaurant. Caricatures of celebrities. Cr cds: A, C, D, MC, V.

D ⌐

✔★ ★ **PEACOCK ON THE PARKWAY.** *1700 Benjamin Franklin Pkwy (19103), downtown.* 215/569-8888. Hrs: 11:30 am-3 pm, 5:30-10 pm; Sat from 5:30 pm. Closed Sun. Continental menu. Prix fixe: lunch $10, dinner $15. Semi-a la carte: dinner $11.95-$16.95. Child's meals. Specialties: lobster, shrimp and scallops over portabello mushroom; shish-kebob mix; crispy duck with wild berries. Own baking. Valet parking. Outdoor dining. Three-level dining area overlooks parkway; casual dining. Cr cds: A, C, D, MC, V.

D ⌐

★ ★ **POMPANO GRILLE.** *701 E Passyunk Ave (19147), at 5th & Bainbridge, in South Street area.* 215/923-7676. Hrs: 5 pm-2 am. Closed Dec 25. Res accepted. Caribbean fusion menu. Bar. A la carte entrees: dinner $15-$23. Complete meals: dinner $25-$50. Specializes in shrimp, crab cakes. Own baking. Musicians Fri, Sat. Valet parking. Outdoor dining.

Converted bank bldg has large windows and three dining levels. Cr cds: A, MC, V.

D ⊠

★ ★ **PROVENCE.** *(379 Lancaster Ave, Haverford 19041) 13 mi W on I-76, exit Villa Nova, to US 30E (Lancaster Ave). 610/896-0400.* Hrs: 11:30 am-2:30 pm, 5:30-10 pm; Fri, Sat to 11 pm; Sun to 9 pm; Sun brunch to 2:30 pm. Closed most major hols. Res accepted; required dinner. French Provençale menu. Bar. A la carte entrees: lunch $10-$15, dinner $17-$25. Sun brunch $10-$22. Child's meals. Specialties: marinated venison with figs, seared yellowfin tuna, shrimp and crab Napoleon. Own baking, pasta. Cr cds: A, D, MC, V.

⊠ ♥

✔ ★ ★ **RANGOON.** *112 N 9th St (19107), in Chinatown. 215/829-8939.* Hrs: 11:30 am-9 pm; Fri to 10 pm; Sat 1-10 pm; Sun from 1 pm. Closed Mon; July 4, Thanksgiving, Dec 25. Res accepted. Burmese menu. Bar. Semi-a la carte: lunch $4.50-$12.50, dinner $8.50-$12.50. Specializes in salads, curry dishes, appetizers. Authentic Burmese atmosphere. Totally nonsmoking. Cr cds: MC, V.

D

★ ★ **RISTORANTE ALBERTO.** *(1415 City Line Ave, Wynnewood 19096) I-76 W to City Line Ave exit. 610/896-0275.* Hrs: 11:30 am-2:30 pm, 5-10 pm; Fri, Sat 5-11 pm; Sun from 4 pm. Closed Jan 1, Thanksgiving, Dec 25. Res accepted; required Fri, Sat. Northern Italian menu. Bar. A la carte entrees: lunch $5.95-$11.95; dinner $12.95-$22.95. Specialties: grilled Dover sole, double veal chop. Own pasta. Valet parking. Display of wine bottles; original art. Cr cds: A, C, D, MC, V.

D ⊠

★ ★ **RISTORANTE PANORAMA.** *(See Penn's View Hotel) 215/922-7800.* Hrs: noon-2:30 pm, 5:30-10 pm; Fri, Sat 5:30-11 pm. Closed most major hols. Res accepted, required wkends. Italian menu. Bar. Extensive wine list. A la carte entrees: lunch, dinner $14.50-$22.95. Child's meals. Specializes in veal, seafood. Own pasta. Parking. Cr cds: A, C, D, ER, JCB, MC, V.

D ⊠

★ **RIVER CITY DINER.** *(3720 Main St, Manayunk 19127) 6 mi W on I-76, exit 31, at Ridge & Main. 215/483-7500.* E-mail mainstr @axs2000.net; web www.rivercitydiner.com. Hrs: 7-2 am; Fri, Sat to 4 am. Bar. A la carte entrees: bkfst, lunch, dinner $4-$12. Child's meals. Specialties: chicken-in-a-pot, grilled River City Caesar salad, Kansas City meatloaf. Outdoor dining. Dramatic diner decor with stainless steel, glass and granite. Cr cds: A, C, D, DS, MC, V.

D ⊠

★ ★ ★ **ROCOCO.** *123 Chestnut St (19106), in Olde City. 215/629-1100.* Hrs: 5-11 pm; Fri, Sat to midnight; Sun to 10 pm. Closed Dec 25. Res accepted. Eclectic menu. Bar to 2 am. Wine cellar. Semi-a la carte: dinner $12-$24. Specializes in seafood, beef, lamb. Valet parking. European decor in converted bank bldg; cathedral ceiling. Cr cds: A, D, MC, V.

D ⊠

★ ★ **THE SALOON.** *750 S 7th St (19148), in South Street area. 215/627-1811.* Hrs: 11:30 am-2 pm, 5-10 pm; Sat to midnight. Closed Sun, hols. Res accepted. Italian menu. Bar. Wine list. A la carte entrees: lunch, dinner $18-$28. Specializes in veal, steak, seafood. Pianist Wed-Sat. Parking. Family-owned. Cr cds: A.

⊠

✔ ★ ★ **SERRANO.** *20 S 2nd St (19106), in Olde City. 215/928-0770.* Hrs: 5-10:30 pm; Fri, Sat to 11:30 pm; Sun 4-10 pm. Closed major hols. Res accepted. International menu. Bar. A la carte entrees: dinner $8-$18. Specialties: chicken Hungarian, Malaysian pork chops, Korean rolled bulgogi. Own desserts. Entertainment Wed-Sat. Theatrical decor with puppets and tapestries from around the world. Cr cds: A, D, DS, MC, V.

D ⊠

★ ★ **SIGGIE'S L'AUBERGE.** *(101 Ford St, West Conshohocken 19428) 15 mi W on I-76, exit 28B. 610/828-6262.* Hrs: 11:30 am-2:30 pm, 5:30-10 pm; Fri to 11 pm; Sat 5:30-11 pm. Closed Sun; major hols. Res required. Continental menu. Bar. A la carte entrees: lunch $8.95-$11.95, dinner $19.95-$24.95. Specialties: crisp shrimp with fruit sauce, jumbo lump crab cakes, sea bass. Valet parking. Rustic French decor. Jacket. Cr cds: A, MC, V.

D

✔ ★ ★ **SONOMA.** *(4411 Main St, Manayunk 19127) 6 mi W on I-76, exit 31, at Main & Gay Sts. 215/483-9400.* Hrs: 11 am-11 pm; Fri, Sat to midnight; early-bird dinner Sun-Thurs 5-6 pm; Sun brunch to 3:30 pm. Continental menu. Bar to 2 am. Semi-a la carte: lunch, dinner $6.50-$14. Sun brunch $6-$12. Child's meals. Specialties: refried risotto, honey-lavender hickory-roasted salmon, garlic-grilled ribeye steak. Own baking, pasta. Valet parking. Outdoor dining. Modern, eclectic decor; revolving art display. Cr cds: A, C, D, DS, MC, V.

D ⊠

✔ ★ **SOUTH STREET DINER.** *140 South St (19147), in South Street area. 215/627-5258.* Open 24 hrs. Closed Dec 25. Bar. Semi-a la carte: bkfst $4.50-$7, lunch $5-$7.50, dinner $8.50-$10.50. Child's meals. Specializes in bkfst dishes, Greek dishes, meats. Own pasta. Outdoor dining. Patio and sports bar. Cr cds: A, MC, V.

⊠

★ ★ ★ ★ **STRIPED BASS.** *1500 Walnut St (19102), downtown. 215/732-4444.* This stylish, highly popular, fish-and-seafood-only restaurant is in a striking former bank building with marble columns. The creative menu is accompanied by a broad international selection of wines by the bottle and glass. Specializes in fresh seafood, shellfish. Menu changes daily. Hrs: 11:30 am-2:30 pm, 5-11 pm; Fri to 11:30 pm; Sat 5-11:30 pm; Sun 11 am-2:30 pm, 5-10 pm. Closed major hols. Res accepted. Bar. Wine cellar. A la carte entrees: lunch $14-$22, dinner $30-$50. Valet parking. Cr cds: A, D, MC, V.

D

★ ★ ★ ★ **SUSANNA FOO.** *1512 Walnut St (19102), downtown. 215/545-2666.* Fresh ingredients and cooking techniques from around the world come together here in chef Susanna Foo's unique cuisine. Silk lanterns and bouquets of orchids create a romantic setting. Chinese, French menu. Specialties: crispy duck, soft-shell crabs, hundred corner crab cake. Hrs: 11:30 am-2:30 pm, 5:30-10 pm; Fri, Sat to 11 pm; Sun 5-9 pm. Closed some major hols. Res accepted; required Sat. Bar. Wine cellar. A la carte entrees: lunch $10-$18, dinner $18-$30. Valet parking. Jacket. Cr cds: A, C, D, MC, V.

D

★ ★ ★ **SWANN CAFE.** *(See Four Seasons Hotel Philadelphia) 215/963-1500.* Web www.fshr.com. Hrs: 11:30-1 am; Sun 10 am-midnight; Sun brunch to 3 pm. Res accepted. Continental menu. Bar. Wine cellar. A la carte entrees: lunch, dinner $10-$22. Sun brunch $42. Child's meals. Specialties: minute steak with country potato; osso bucco; shrimp, crab and scallop salad. Own baking, pasta. Entertainment. Valet parking. Outdoor dining. Intimate atmosphere; luxurious decor uses mahogany, silk and large chandeliers. Cr cds: A, C, D, DS, MC, V.

D ⊠ ♥

★ ★ ★ **TONY CLARK'S.** *121 S Broad St 19107), downtown. 215/772-9238.* Hrs: 11:30 am-2:30 pm, 5:30 pm-1:30 am; Sun from 5:30 pm. Closed major hols. Res accepted. Bar. Wine cellar. A la carte entrees: lunch $13-$17, dinner $21-$29. Child's meals. Specialties: roasted rack of lamb, crisp duck with bean cassoulet, sautéed medallions of beef. Valet parking. Modern, intimate atmosphere. Cr cds: A, D, DS, MC, V.

D ⊠

★ ★ **TOSCANA CUCINA RUSTICA.** *(24 N Merion Ave, Bryn Mawr 19010) 15 mi W on I-76, exit City Ave to US 30 (Lancaster Ave) to N Merion Ave. 610/527-7700.* Hrs: 11:30 am-2:30 pm, 5:30-10 pm; Fri to 11 pm; Sat 5:30-11 pm; Sun from 5:30 pm. Closed Thanksgiving, Dec 25. Res accepted. Tuscan Italian menu. Bar. Wine cellar. A la carte entrees: lunch $7-$13, dinner $12.95-$25. Specializes in grilled meats, wafer-thin-crusted brick-oven pizza, homemade pasta. Own baking, pasta. Wine list offers over 550 selections. Totally nonsmoking. Cr cds: A.

D

★ ★ ★ **TREETOPS.** *(See The Rittenhouse Hotel)* 215/790-2534. Hrs: 6:30 am-10:30 pm; Sat, Sun from 7 pm. Res accepted. Regional Amer menu. Bar 11:30-1 am. Wine list. Semi-a la carte: lunch $15-$20, dinner $20-$35. Specializes in seafood, steak, veal. Seasonal menu. Own pastries. Valet parking. Casual decor. Overlooks park. Cr cds: A, C, D, DS, MC, V.

D

★ ★ **UMBRIA.** *7131 Germantown Ave (19119), north of downtown.* 215/242-6470. Hrs: 6-9 pm. Closed Mon; major hols. Res accepted. Eclectic menu. A la carte entrees: dinner $16.95-$24.95. Specialties: filet au poivre, curried lamb, soft shelled crabs in season. Blackboard menu changed daily. Totally nonsmoking. No cr cds accepted.

★ ★ **UNDER THE BLUE MOON.** *8042 Germantown Ave (19118), in Chestnut Hill.* 215/247-1100. Hrs: 6-9 pm; Fri, Sat to 10 pm. Closed Sun, Mon; major hols. Continental menu. Bar. A la carte entrees: dinner $19-$25. Specializes in seafood, chicken, duck. Unique modern decor. Cr cds: MC, V.

✔★ **VANG'S GARDEN.** *121 N 11th St (19107), in Chinatown.* 215/923-2438. Hrs: 10 am-10 pm. Closed Thanksgiving. Vietnamese menu. Semi-a la carte: lunch, dinner $3.75-$7.95. Specialties: lobster salad, barbecued beef on rice noodles, sautéed chicken with lemon grass. Adj to convention center. Cr cds: A, MC, V.

★ **VEGA GRILL.** *(4141 Main St, Manayunk 19127) 9 mi W on I-76, exit 31.* 215/487-9600. Hrs: 5:30 pm-1 am; Fri, Sat to 2 am; Sun, Mon to midnight; Sun brunch 11 am-3:30 pm. Closed some major hols. Contemporary Latin Amer menu. Bar 4:30 pm-2 am. A la carte entrees: dinner $12-$18. Sun brunch $7-$12. Child's meals. Specializes in South American meat and fish. Outdoor dining. Neighborhood tavern atmosphere. Cr cds: A, MC, V.

★ ★ **WHITE DOG CAFE.** *3420 Sansom St (19104), downtown.* 215/386-9224. Hrs: 11:30 am-2:30 pm, 5:30-10 pm; Fri, Sat 5:30-11 pm; Sun 5-10 pm; Sat, Sun brunch 11 am-2:30 pm. Closed Thanksgiving, Dec 25. Res accepted. Bar. A la carte entrees: lunch $7.50-$11, dinner $14-$20. Sat, Sun brunch $7-$11. Child's meals. Specializes in Contemporary Amer cuisine. Own desserts. Entertainment Wed-Sun. Outdoor dining. Former house (ca 1870) of author Madame Blavatsky, founder of the Theosophical Society. Cr cds: A, C, D, DS, MC, V.

D

✔★ ★ **ZÓCALO.** *3600 Lancaster Ave (19104), west of downtown in University City.* 215/895-0139. Hrs: noon-10 pm; Fri to 11 pm; Sat 5:30-11 pm; Sun 5-9:30 pm. Closed major hols. Res accepted. Contemporary Mexican menu. Bar. Semi-a la carte: lunch $6-$12, dinner $10-$18. Prix fixe: dinner $13.95 & $15. Specializes in handmade corn tortillas. Parking. Outdoor dining. Cr cds: A, C, D, DS, MC, V.

Unrated Dining Spots

FAMOUS 4TH ST DELICATESSEN. *700 S 4th St, south of downtown.* 215/922-3274. Hrs: 7 am-6 pm; Sun to 4 pm. Closed Rosh Hashana, Yom Kippur. Delicatessen fare. A la carte: bkfst $2-$6, lunch $3.50-$10. Specializes in chocolate chip cookies, fresh roasted turkey, corned beef. Antique telephones. Family-owned more than 70 yrs. Cr cds: A, D, MC, V.

THE RESTAURANT SCHOOL. *4207 Walnut St (19104), near University of Pennsylvania, west of downtown.* 215/222-4200. Hrs: 5:30-10 pm. Closed Sun, Mon; also during student breaks. Res accepted.

Bar. Complete meals: dinner $13.50. Seasonal menu; occasionally an extraordinary and elaborate theme dinner is offered. Own baking. Valet parking. Bakery shop on premises. Unique dining experience in a "restaurant school." Consists of 2 buildings; a restored 1856 mansion is linked by a large atrium dining area to a new building housing the kitchen and classrooms. Cr cds: A, C, D, DS, MC, V.

D

ROLLER'S. *8705 Germantown Ave, in Top-of-the-Hill Plaza, in Chestnut Hill.* 215/242-1771. Hrs: 11:30 am-2:30 pm, 5:30-9 pm; Fri to 10 pm; Sat noon-2:30 pm, 5:30-10 pm; Sun 5-9 pm; Sun brunch 11 am-2:30 pm. Closed Mon; most major hols. Bar. Semi-a la carte: lunch $6-$11, dinner $16-$24. Sun brunch $6-$10. Specializes in fresh fish, veal, duck. Parking. Outdoor dining. Modern cafe atmosphere. Totally nonsmoking. No cr cds accepted.

SASSAFRAS. *48 S 2nd St, in Olde City.* 215/925-2317. Hrs: noon-midnight; Fri, Sat to 1 am, Sun to 9 pm. Closed major hols. Bar. A la carte entrees: dinner $5-$18. Specializes in salads, omelettes, grilled fish. Cr cds: A, D, MC, V.

SPIRIT OF PHILADELPHIA. *Pier 3, on Delaware Ave, in Olde City.* 215/923-1419. Hrs: lunch cruise noon-2 pm, dinner cruise 7-10 pm; Sun brunch cruise 1-3 pm. Closed Dec 25. Res required. Bar. Buffet: lunch $16.95 (adults), $9.50 (children); dinner $28.95-$32.95 (adults), $15.95 (children). Sun brunch $18.95 (adults), $9.50 (children). Musical revue, bands, dancing. Parking. Dining and sightseeing aboard Spirit cruise liner. Cr cds: A, MC, V.

D

SWANN LOUNGE. *(See Four Seasons Hotel Philadelphia)* 215/963-1500. Hrs: 11:30 am-2:30 pm; tea 3-5 pm; Sun brunch 11 am-2:30 pm; Viennese buffet Fri, Sat 9 pm-1 am. Closed Mon. Res accepted. Bar 11:30-1 am; Fri, Sat to 2 am. Buffet: bkfst $9.75-$14, lunch $12-$21. Afternoon tea $12. Sun brunch $24. Viennese buffet $11. Specializes in English tea service with sandwiches & cakes. Valet parking. Outdoor dining (lunch). Elegant atmosphere. Cr cds: A, C, D, DS, ER, JCB, MC, V.

D

Pittsburgh (E-2)

(See also Ambridge, Beaver Falls, Connellsville, New Stanton, Washington)

Settled 1758 **Pop** 369,879 **Elev** 760 ft **Area code** 412 **E-mail** info @gpcvb.org **Web** www.pittsburgh-cvb.org

Information Greater Pittsburgh Convention & Visitors Bureau, 4 Gateway Center, 15222; 800/366-0093.

Pittsburgh has had a remarkable renaissance to become one of the most spectacular civic redevelopments in America, with modern buildings, clean parks and community pride. In fact, it has been named "all-America city" by the National Civic League. The new Pittsburgh is a result of a rare combination of capital-labor cooperation, public-private support, enlightened political leadership and imaginative, venturesome community planning. Its $1-billion international airport was designed to be the most user-friendly in the country.

After massive war production, Pittsburgh labored to eliminate the 1930s image of an unsophisticated mill town. During the 1950s and 1960s, Renaissance I began, a $500-million program to clean the city's air and develop new structures, such as Gateway Center, the Civic Arena and Point State Park. The late 1970s and early 1980s ushered in Renaissance II, a $3-billion expansion program reflecting the movement away from industry and toward high technology.

Today, Pittsburgh has completed this dramatic shift from industry to a diversified base, including high technology, health care, finance and education, and continues its transition to a services-oriented city.

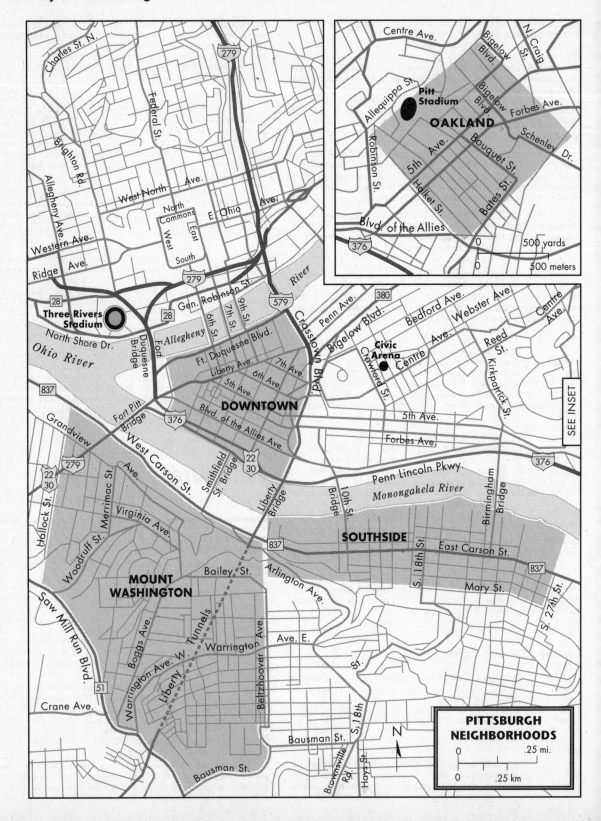

OAKLAND

Centre Ave.
Bigelow Blvd.
N. Craig St.
Allequippa St.
Pitt Stadium
Bigelow Blvd.
Forbes Ave.
Robinson St.
5th Ave.
Bouquet St.
Schenley Dr.
Halket St.
Bates St.
Blvd. of the Allies
376

0 — 500 yards
0 — 500 meters

Charles St. N.
279
Federal St.
Brighton Rd.
West North Ave.
Allegheny Ave.
North Commons
West
East
South
E. Ohio Ave.
279
Western Ave.
Ridge Ave.
28
28
Three Rivers Stadium
North Shore Dr.
Duquesne Bridge
Allegheny River
Fort
Gen. Robinson St.
6th St.
7th St.
9th St.
579
Crosstown Blvd.
380
Penn Ave.
Bigelow Blvd.
Bedford Ave.
Webster Ave.
Centre Ave.
Civic Arena
Centre Ave.
Crawford St.
Reed St.
Kirkpatrick St.
837
Ohio River
Grandview Ave.
Fort Pitt Bridge
Ft. Duquesne Blvd.
Liberty Ave.
7th Ave.
6th Ave.
5th Ave.
DOWNTOWN
Blvd. of the Allies Ave.
5th Ave.
Forbes Ave.
SEE INSET
376
West Carson St.
279
22 30
Hallock St.
Merrimac St.
Virginia Ave.
Smithfield St. Bridge
22 30
Liberty Bridge
10th St. Bridge
Penn Lincoln Pkwy
Monongahela River
Birmingham Bridge
376
Woodruff St.
Saw Mill Run Blvd.
MOUNT WASHINGTON
Bailey St.
Arlington Ave.
837
SOUTHSIDE
East Carson St.
S. 18th St.
Mary St.
S. 27th St.
837
Boggs Ave.
Warrington Ave. W. Tunnels
Warrington Ave.
Belzhoover Ave.
Ave. E.
51
Liberty Tunnels
Crane Ave.
Bausman St.
Brownsville Rd.
S. 18th St.
Hays St.
Bausman St.
N

PITTSBURGH NEIGHBORHOODS

0 — .25 mi.
0 — .25 km

Pittsburgh's cultural personality is expressed by the Pittsburgh Symphony Orchestra, Pittsburgh Opera, Pittsburgh Ballet, Phipps Conservatory and The Carnegie Museums of Pittsburgh, which include the Museum of Natural History and Museum of Art. The city has 25 parks, 45 "parklets," 60 recreation centers and 27 swimming pools.

Born of frontier warfare in the shadow of Fort Pitt, the city is named after the elder William Pitt, the great British statesman. Its militarily strategic position was an important commercial asset and Pittsburgh soon became a busy river port and transit point for the western flow of pioneers.

Industry grew out of the West's needs for manufactured goods; foundries and rolling mills were soon producing nails, axes, frying pans and shovels. The Civil War added tremendous impetus to industry, and by the end of the war Pittsburgh was producing half the steel and one-third of the glass made in the country. Such captains of industry and finance as Thomas Mellon, Andrew Carnegie and Henry Clay Frick built their industrial empires in Pittsburgh. The American Federation of Labor was born here (1881); the city has been the scene of historic clashes between labor and management.

World War I brought a fresh boom to the city, as well as changes in its industrial character. It was a vast arsenal for the Allies during World War II.

Transportation

Airport. See PITTSBURGH INTL AIRPORT AREA.

Car Rental Agencies: See IMPORTANT TOLL-FREE NUMBERS.

Public Transportation: Subway and surface trains, buses (Port Authority of Allegheny County), phone 412/442-2000.

Rail Passenger Service: Amtrak 800/872-7245.

What to See and Do

Alcoa Building. Pioneer in aluminum for skyscraper construction, exterior work was done from inside; no scaffolding was required. Draped in aluminum waffle, 30 stories high; it is considered to be one of the country's most daring experiments in skyscraper design. 425 6th Ave.

Allegheny County Courthouse. One of the country's outstanding Romanesque-style buildings, the two square-city-block structure was designed by Henry Hobson Richardson in 1884. (Mon-Fri; closed hols) Grant St & 5th Ave. Phone 412/355-5313. **Free.**

Andy Warhol Museum. The most comprehensive single-artist museum in the world. More than 500 works. (Wed-Sun) 117 Sandusky St. Phone 412/237-8300. ¢¢

Benedum Center for the Performing Arts. Expansion and restoration of the Stanley Theater, a movie palace built in 1928. Gilded plasterwork, 500,000-piece crystal chandelier and a 9-story addition to backstage area make this an exceptional auditorium with one of the largest stages in the country. The center is home to Pittsburgh Ballet Theatre, the Pittsburgh Dance Council, the Pittsburgh Opera and Civic Light Opera. Free guided tours (by appt). Penn & 7th Aves, at 719 Liberty Ave. Phone 412/456-6666.

Boyce Park Ski Area. Beginner-intermediate slopes; 2 double chairlifts; 2 Pomalifts; patrol, school, rentals; snowmaking; cafeteria. Longest run, 1/4 mi; vertical drop, 175 ft. (Dec-Feb, daily) 18 mi E on I-376 to Plum exit (16B); follow signs to park. Phone 724/733-4656 or 724/733-4665 (snow conditions; 24-hr recording). ¢¢¢¢

Carnegie Mellon University (1900). (7,900 students) Founded by Andrew Carnegie. Composed of seven colleges. Tours of campus. Adj to Schenley Park. Phone 412/268-2000 or 412/268-5052.

Civic Arena. This $22-million all-weather amphitheater accommodates 17,500 people. Retractable roof can fold up within 2½ min. In Golden Triangle.

County parks. South Park, 12 mi S on PA 88. **North Park,** 14 mi N on PA 19. **Boyce Park,** 14 mi E on I-376, US 22. **Settler's Cabin Park,** 9 mi W on I-279, US 22. Swimming; fishing; boating. Bicycling (rentals), ball fields; golf, tennis. Cross-country skiing, ice-skating (winter, daily). Picnicking. Parks open daily. Fees for activities. Attractions for each park vary; phone 412/392-8455 (permits) or 412/355-7275 (general information).

★ **Fallingwater.** 27 mi S on PA 51, 10 mi E on PA 201 to Connellsville, 8 mi E on PA 711, then 8 mi S on PA 381, near Mill Run. (See CONNELLSVILLE)

Frick Park. Covers 476 acres, largely in natural state; nature trails wind through ravines and over hills; also nature center (2005 Beechwood Blvd), tennis courts, picnic areas, playgrounds. Park (daily). Beechwood Blvd & English Lane. **Free.**

Gateway Center. Complex includes four skyscrapers of Equitable Life Assurance Society. Equitable Plaza, a 2-acre open-air garden over underground parking garage, has lovely walks, 3 fountains, more than 90 types of trees and 100 varieties of shrubs and seasonal flowers. (Mon-Fri; closed major hols) Covers 23 acres adj to Point State Park. Phone 412/392-6000.

Hartwood (1929). A 629-acre re-creation of English country estate; Tudor mansion with many antiques; formal gardens, stables. Tours (daily exc Mon; closed hols & 1 wk late Nov). Also music and theater events during summer. 12 mi N via PA 8, at 215 Saxonburg Blvd. For information and tour reservations, phone 412/767-9200. ¢¢

★ **Inclines** (hill-climbing trolleys). Travel to top of Mt Washington for excellent view of Golden Triangle, where the Allegheny and Monongahela Rivers join to form the Ohio River.

Monongahela Incline. Panoramic views from observation deck. (Daily) Station on W Carson St near Station Square & Smithfield St Bridge. Phone 412/442-2000. ¢

Duquesne Incline. Built 1877; restored and run by community effort; observation deck. (Daily) Free parking at lower station. Lower station, W Carson St, opposite the fountain, SW of Fort Pitt Bridge; upper station, 1220 Grandview Ave, in restaurant area. Phone 412/381-1665. ¢

James L. Kelso Bible Lands Museum. Artifacts and displays from the ancient Near East, especially Palestine. (Sept-May, Wed; also by appt) 616 N Highland, on grounds of Pittsburgh Theological Seminary. Phone 412/362-5610. **Free.**

Kennywood Park. Combines modern rides with rides from traditional streetcar parks, popular at the turn of the century. **Lost Kennywood,** with lagoon, Victorian-era buildings, shopping. Gardens, picnic groves. (Mid-May-Labor Day, daily) 8 mi SE on PA 837, 4800 Kennywood Blvd, in W Mifflin. Phone 412/461-0500. ¢¢¢¢¢

National Aviary in Pittsburgh. The Aviary is home to one of the world's premier bird collections and is the only indoor bird facility independent of a larger zoo in North America. A veritable jungle of colorful, amusing and exotic birds. (Daily; closed Jan 1, Thanksgiving, Dec 25) Allegheny Commons West, approx 1 mi W of downtown. Phone 412/323-7235. ¢¢

Photo Antiquities. Photo gallery and museum. Selections from 100,000 antique photographic images. (Mon-Sat; closed major hols) 531 E Ohio. Phone 412/231-7881 or 800/474-6862. ¢¢

Pittsburgh Children's Museum. Hands-on exhibits. Hands-on silkscreen studio; storytelling; regularly scheduled puppet shows; live performances; 2-story climber. (Tues-Sat, also Sun afternoons) 1 Landmarks Square. Phone 412/322-5058. Tues, Wed, Fri-Sun ¢¢; Thurs ¢

Point State Park. "Point" where the Allegheny and Monongahela rivers meet to form the Ohio; 36 acres. Giant fountain symbolizes joining of rivers. There are military drills with fifes and drums, muskets and cannon (May-Labor Day; some Sun afternoons). Foot of Ft Duquesne & Ft Pitt Blvds. Phone 412/471-0235. In the park are

Fort Pitt Museum. Built on part of original fort. Exhibits on early Pittsburgh and Fort Pitt; military struggles between France and Britain for western Pennsylvania and the Old Northwest Territory. (Daily exc Mon; closed some hols) 101 Commonwealth Place. Phone 412/281-9284. ¢¢

Block House of Fort Pitt. Last remaining building of original fort (1767). (Daily exc Mon) **Free.**

PPG Place. Designed by Philip Johnson, this is Pittsburgh's most popular Renaissance II building. PPG Place consists of six separate buildings designed in a postmodern, Gothic skyscraper style. Shopping and a food court can be found in Two PPG Place. Market Square.

Professional sports.

National League baseball (Pittsburgh Pirates). Three Rivers Stadium, 600 Stadium Circle. Phone 412/323-5000.

NFL (Pittsburgh Steelers). Three Rivers Stadium, 600 Stadium Circle. Phone 412/323-0300.

NHL (Pittsburgh Penguins). Civic Arena, 300 Auditorium Pl. Phone 412/642-1300.

Riverview Park. Covers 251 acres. Swimming pool (mid-June-Labor Day, daily, fee); tennis courts (Apr-Nov, daily); picnic shelter (May-Sept, permit required). Also playgrounds, parklet; nature, jogging trail. Fee for some activities. 2 mi N on US 19. **Free.** In the park is

Allegheny Observatory. Slides, tour of building. Maintained by University of Pittsburgh. Children under 12 yrs only with adult. Reservation required. (Apr-Oct, Thurs-Fri; closed hols) Center of park, entrance on Riverview Ave off US 19. Phone 412/321-2400. **Free.**

Rodef Shalom Biblical Botanical Garden. The natural world of ancient Israel is re-created here in settings that specialize in plants of the Bible. A waterfall, desert and stream all help simulate the areas of the Jordan, Lake Kineret and the Dead Sea. Tours (by appt). Special programs and exhibits. (June-mid-Sept, daily exc Fri; Sat hrs limited) 4905 5th Ave. Phone 412/621-6566. **Free.**

Sandcastle Water Park. The city's down-by-the-riverside water park has 15 slides, adult & kiddie pools; boardwalk; food. (1st Sat June-Labor Day, daily; closed hols) Approx 5 mi SE of downtown via I-376 & PA 837. Phone 412/462-6666. All-day slide pass ¢¢¢¢

Schenley Park. Covers 456 acres; picnic areas; 18-hole golf course, lighted tennis courts; swimming pool; ice-skating (winter); softball fields, running track; nature trails; bandstand (summer; free). Fee for some activities. (Daily) Forbes Ave, adj Carnegie-Mellon University. **Free.** Also in park is

Phipps Conservatory. Constantly changing array of flowers; tropical gardens; outstanding orchid collection. Chidren's Discovery Garden with interactive learning opportunities. Seasonal flower shows (see SEASONAL EVENTS). (Daily) Phone 412/622-6914. ¢¢

Sightseeing tours.

Small van tours. Offered through the Pittsburgh History and Landmarks Foundation. For information and reservations phone 412/471-5808. ¢¢¢

Gray Line bus tours. For information and reservations contact 110 Lenzner Ct, Sewickley 15143; 412/741-2720, 412/761-7000 or 800/342-2349.

Soldiers and Sailors Memorial Hall and Military History Museum. Auditorium has Lincoln's Gettysburg Address inscribed above stage; flags, weapons, uniforms, memorabilia from US wars. (Mon-Fri, also Sat & Sun afternoons; closed Jan 1, Labor Day, Thanksgiving, Dec 25) 5th Ave & Bigelow Blvd. Phone 412/621-4253. **Free.**

Station Square. This 40-acre area features shopping, dining and entertainment in and among the historic buildings of the P & LE Railroad (see RESTAURANTS). Shopping in warehouses that once held loaded railroad boxcars. (Daily; closed some hols) 450 Landmarks Bldg, 1 Station Sq, along Monongahela River across from downtown, via Smithfield St Bridge. Phone 412/471-5808.

The Carnegie Science Center. Learning and entertainment complex has over 40,000 sq ft of exhibit galleries that demonstrate how human activities are affected by science and technology. USS *Requin*, moored in front of the center, is a World War II diesel-electric submarine; tours (40 min) demonstrate the electronic, visual and voice communication devices on board. Henry Buhl Jr Planetarium and Observatory is a technologically sophisticated interactive planetarium with control panels at every seat. Also here are 350-seat OMNIMAX Theater and Health Sciences Amphitheater. Restaurant, gift shop. (Daily; closed Dec 25) One Allegheny Ave, adj to Three Rivers Stadium on Ohio River. For combination ticket prices and information phone 412/237-3400. Submarine ¢¢; Exhibits and planetarium ¢¢¢; OMNIMAX Theater ¢¢¢

★ **The Carnegie Museums of Pittsburgh.** Public complex built by industrialist Andrew Carnegie. (Daily exc Mon; closed hols) 4400 Forbes Ave. Phone 412/622-3360. ¢¢ Includes

Museum of Natural History. Houses one of the most complete collections of dinosaur fossils. Exhibits include Dinosaur Hall, Polar World, Hillman Hall of Minerals and Gems, the Walton Hall of Ancient Egypt; changing exhibits.

Museum of Art. Possibly America's first modern art museum, as Carnegie urged the gallery to exhibit works dated after 1896. Collection of Impressionist and Post-Impressionist paintings; Hall of Sculpture; Hall of Architecture; films, videos.

Music Hall. Home to the Mendelssohn Choir, the Pittsburgh Chamber Music Society and the River City Brass Band. Elaborate gilt and marble foyer; walls of French eschallion, 24 pillars made of green stone and a gold baroque ceiling.

Library of Pittsburgh. Central branch contains more than 4¹/₂ million books. Houses first department of science and technology established in a US public library.

★ **The Frick Art and Historical Center.** Museum complex built on grounds of estate once belonging to industrialist Henry Clay Frick; gardens, carriage house museum, greenhouse, cafe and restored children's playhouse that now serves as a visitor's center. (Daily exc Mon; closed some major hols) Between Reynolds St & Penn Ave, along S Homewood Ave. For tour schedule and information, phone 412/371-0600. **Free.** Also on grounds are

Clayton, the Henry Clay Frick Home. A restored 4-story Victorian mansion with 23 rooms; only remaining house of area in East End once known as "millionaire's row." Some original decor and personal mementos of the Fricks. Tours; reservation recommended. 7227 Reynolds St. ¢¢

The Frick Art Musuem. Collection of Helen Clay Frick, daughter of Henry Clay Frick, includes Italian Renaissance, Flemish and French 18th-century paintings and decorative arts. Italian and French furniture, Renaissance bronzes, tapestries, Chinese porcelains. Also changing exhibits; concerts, lectures. 7227 Reynolds St. Phone 412/371-0600. **Free.**

The Pittsburgh Zoo. Over 70 acres containing over 6,000 animals, children's farm (late May-Oct), discovery pavilion, reptile house, tropical and Asian forests, African savanna and aqua zoo. Merry-go-round and train rides (fee). Highland Park covers 75 acres and has tennis courts, picnic grounds, shelters (some require permit), twin reservoirs, swimming pool (fee). (Daily; closed Dec 25) NE on Highland Ave in Highland Park area. Phone 412/665-3639. ¢¢

The Senator John Heinz Regional History Center. In Chataqua Ice Warehouse (1898). Preserves 300 yrs of region's history with artifacts and extensive collection of archives, photos. Houses the Historical Society of Western Pennsylvania. Library (Tues-Sat). (Daily; closed Jan 1, Thanksgiving, Dec 25) 1212 Smallman St. Phone 412/454-6000. ¢¢¢

Tour-Ed Mine. Complete underground coal mining operation; sawmill; furnished log house (1789); old company store; historical mine museum; shelters; playground. (May-Labor Day wk, daily) 20 mi NW via PA 28 (Allegheny Valley Expy) to Tarentum, then ¹/₄ mi W via Red Belt West. Phone 724/224-4720. ¢¢¢

Two Mellon Bank Center. Formerly the Union Trust Bldg, its Flemish-Gothic style was modeled after a library in Louvain, Belgium. Interior has a glass rotunda. Grant St & 5th Ave.

University of Pittsburgh (1787). (34,000 students) Tours of Nationality Rooms in Cathedral of Learning (wkends; fee). Campus of 70 buildings on 125 acres. 5th Ave & Bigelow Blvd. Phone 412/624-4141. Buildings include

Cathedral of Learning (1935). Unique skyscraper of classrooms, stretching its Gothic-moderne architecture 42 floors high (535 ft); vantage point on 36th floor. Surrounding a 3-story Gothic commons room are an Early American Room and 24 Nationality Rooms, each reflecting the distinctive culture of the ethnic group that created and furnished it. Tours (daily; closed Jan 1, Dec 24, 25, 31). Phone 412/624-6000. Tours ¢

Heinz Chapel. Tall stained-glass windows; French Gothic architecture. (Daily exc Sat; closed hols) E of Cathedral of Learning. Phone 412/624-4157. **Free.**

Henry Clay Frick Fine Arts Building. Glass-enclosed cloister; changing exhibits; art reference library. (Sept-mid-June, daily; rest of yr, Mon-Fri; closed univ hols, also Dec 24-Jan 2) Schenley Plaza. Phone 412/648-2400. **Free.**

Stephen Foster Memorial. Auditorium/theater. Collection of the Pittsburgh-born composer's music and memorabilia. Said to be one of the most elaborate memorials ever built to a musician. (Mon-Sat, also Sun afternoons; closed hols) Phone 412/624-4100.

USX Tower. Once known as the US Steel Bldg, it is 64 stories high and the tallest building in Pittsburgh. Ten exposed triangular columns and an exterior paneling of steel make up its construction. Grant St & 7th Ave.

Annual Events

Folk Festival. Pittsburgh Expo Mart, Monroeville. Foods of many nations; arts and crafts; folk music, dancing. Phone 412/373-0123. Memorial Day wkend.

Three Rivers Arts Festival. Point State Park, Gateway Center, USX Tower, PPG Place. Juried, original works of local and national artists: paintings, photography, sculpture, crafts and videos; artists' market in outdoor plazas. Ongoing performances include music, dance and performance art. Special art projects; film festival; food; children's activities. Phone 412/481-7040. Early-mid-June.

Pittsburgh/Shop 'N Save Three Rivers Regatta. Point State Park. Water, land and air events; water shows and speedboat races. Last wkend July & 1st wkend Aug.

Pittsburgh Irish Festival. I.C. Light Amphitheatre, Station Square. Irish foods, dances and entertainment. Phone 412/422-5642. Early or mid-Sept.

Seasonal Events

Phipps Conservatory Flower Shows. Schenley Park. Phone 412/622-6914. Spring, summer, fall and hols.

Concerts. Pittsburgh Symphony Orchestra. Heinz Hall for the Performing Arts, 600 Penn Ave. Phone 412/392-4900. Sept-May.

Pittsburgh Public Theater. City's largest resident professional company. Allegheny Square, North Side. Phone 412/321-9800. Sept-June.

Additional Visitor Information

For additional information about Pittsburgh, contact the Greater Pittsburgh Convention and Visitors Bureau, 4 Gateway Center, 15222 (Mon-Fri); 412/281-7711 or 800/366-0093. A Visitor Information Center is along Liberty Ave, adj to 4 Gateway Center (Mar-Dec, daily; rest of yr, daily exc Sun). Other centers can be found in the Carnegie Library's Mt Washington branch, and on the University of Pittsburgh's campus, Log Cabin, Forbes Ave. For a schedule of events in Pittsburgh, 24-hr visitor information, phone 800/366-0093.

Pittsburgh Intl Airport Area

For additional accommodations, see PITTSBURGH INTL AIRPORT AREA, which follows PITTSBURGH.

City Neighborhoods

Many of the restaurants, unrated dining establishments and some lodgings listed under Pittsburgh include neighborhoods as well as exact street addresses. Geographic descriptions of these areas are given, followed by a table of restaurants arranged by neighborhood.

Downtown: South of the Allegheny River, west of I-579, north of the Monongahela River and east of Point State Park. **North of Downtown:** North of Allegheny River. **South of Downtown:** South of Monongahela River. **East of Downtown:** East of US 579.

Mount Washington: Across the Monongahela River south of Downtown; north of Saw Mill Run Blvd, south of West Carson St, east of Hallock and west of Beltzhoover.

Oakland: East of Downtown; centered on and around 5th Ave between Bellefield St on the north and Halket St on the south.

South Side: Across the Monongahela River south of Downtown; Station Square area east of the Liberty Bridge, west of S 27th St and north of Mary St.

PITTSBURGH RESTAURANTS BY NEIGHBORHOOD AREAS
(For full description, see alphabetical listings under Restaurants)

DOWNTOWN
1902 Landmark Tavern. 24 Market St
British Bicycle Club. 923 Penn Ave
Carlton. 1 Mellon Bank Center
Carmassi's Tuscany Grill. 711 Penn Ave
Common Plea. 308 Ross St
Del Frates. 971 Liberty Ave
Juno Trattoria. One Oxford Center, 3rd floor
Seventh Street Grille. 130 7th St
Terrace Room (Westin William Penn Hotel). 530 Wm Penn Place
Top Of The Triangle. 600 Grant St, 62nd floor

NORTH OF DOWNTOWN
The Church Brew Works. 3525 Liberty Ave
Max's Allegheny Tavern. Middle & Suisman Sts
Penn Brewery. Troy Hill, 800 Vinial St
Rico's. 1 Rico Lane

SOUTH OF DOWNTOWN
Colony. Greentree & Cochran Rds
London Grille. 1500 Washington Rd
Piccolo Mondo. 661 Andersen Dr
Samurai Japanese Steak House. 2100 Greentree Rd
Sushi Two. 2122 E Carson St
Tambellini's. PA 51

EAST OF DOWNTOWN
The Balcony. 5520 Walnut St
Bentley's. 5608 Wilkens Ave
Brandy's Place. 2323 Penn Ave
Cafe At The Frick. 7227 Reynolds St
Casbah. 229 S Highland Ave
China Palace. 5440 Walnut St
D'imperio's. 3412 Wm Penn Hwy
Jimmy Tsang's. 5700 Centre Ave
Kaya. 2000 Smallman St
Max & Erma's. 5533 Walnut St
Nina. 5701 Bryant St
Pasta Piatto. 736 Bellefonte St
Poli. 2607 Murray Ave
Primanti Bros. 46 18th St
Soba Lounge. 5847 Ellsworth Ave
Tessaro's. 4601 Liberty Ave
Thai Place. 809 Bellefonte St
Vermont Flatbread Co. 2701 Penn Ave

MOUNT WASHINGTON
Cliffside. 1208 Grandview Ave
Georgetowne Inn. 1230 Grandview Ave
Le Mont. 1114 Grandview Ave
Tin Angel. 1200 Gandview Ave

OAKLAND
Dave And Andy's Ice Cream Parlor. 207 Atwood St
India Garden. 328 Atwood St

SOUTH SIDE
Cafe Allegro. 51 S 12th St
Grand Concourse. 1 Station Square
Le Pommier. 2104 E Carson St
Station Square Cheese Cellar. #25 Freight House Shops

Note: When a listing is located in a town that does not have its own city heading, it will appear under the city nearest to its location. In these cases, the address and town appear in parentheses immediately following the name of the establishment.

Motels

★ ★ **CLUBHOUSE INN.** *5311 Campbells Run Rd (15205), jct I-279 & PA 60, west of downtown, exit Moon Run Rd.* 412/788-8400; FAX 412/788-2577; res: 800/258-2466. Web www.clubhouseinn.com. 152 rms, 3 story, 26 suites. S $85; D $95; each addl $10; suites $100; under 16 free; lower rates Fri, Sat. Crib free. TV; cable (premium). Heated pool; whirlpool. Complimentary buffet bkfst. Restaurant adj 11 am-11 pm. Ck-out noon. Coin lndry. Meeting rms. Business servs avail. In-rm modem link. Free airport transportation. Exercise equipt; treadmill, stair machine. Some microwaves; refrigerator in suites. Cr cds: A, D, DS, MC, V.

[D] [≋] [⌘] [⊠] [🐾] [SC]

✔★ ★ **HAMPTON INN.** *555 Trumbull Dr (15205), across river, west of downtown.* 412/922-0100; FAX 412/921-7631. 135 rms, 6 story. June-Nov: S $69-$75; D $79; under 18 free; wkend rates; lower rates rest of yr. Crib free. Pet accepted. TV; cable (premium). Complimentary continental bkfst. Restaurant nearby. Ck-out noon. Meeting rms. Business servs avail. In-rm modem link. Valet serv. Free airport transportation. Health club privileges. Picnic tables. Cr cds: A, C, D, DS, MC, V.

[D] [✦] [⌘] [⊠] [🐾] [SC]

✔★ ★ **HAMPTON INN-WEST MIFFLIN.** *1550 Lebanon Church Rd (15236), S on US 51, south of downtown.* 412/650-1000; FAX 412/650-1001. 70 rms, 3 story. S $79-$94; D $84-$99; under 18 free; higher rates: hols, football games. Crib free. TV; cable (premium), VCR avail (movies). Restaurant nearby. Ck-out noon. Meeting rms. Business servs avail. In-rm modem link. Valet serv. Concierge. Heated pool; lifeguard. Some in-rm whirlpools, refrigerators, microwaves. Cr cds: A, C, D, DS, JCB, MC, V.

[D] [≋] [⊠] [🐾] [SC]

★ ★ **HAWTHORN SUITES.** *700 Mansfield Ave (15205), at No-blestown Rd, or I-279 exit 4, south of downtown.* 412/279-6300; FAX 412/279-4993. E-mail tn009665@psinet.com; web www.hawthorn.com. 151 suites, 2 story. S $89-$119; D $119-$149; wkly, monthly rates. Crib free. Pet accepted, some restrictions; $50 and $6/day. TV; cable (premium). Pool; whirlpool, lifeguard. Complimentary full bkfst. Ck-out noon. Meeting rms. Business servs avail. Airport, RR station, bus depot transportation. Health club privileges. Refrigerators, microwaves, fireplaces. Private patios, balconies. Picnic tables, grills. Chalet-style buildings. Cr cds: A, C, D, DS, JCB, MC, V.

[D] [✦] [≋] [⊠] [🐾] [SC]

★ ★ **HOLIDAY INN GREENTREE-CENTRAL.** *401 Holiday Dr (15220), west of downtown.* 412/922-8100; FAX 412/922-6511. 200 rms, 4 story. S, D $104-$148; each addl $10; under 18 free. Crib free. Pet accepted. TV; cable (premium), VCR avail. Heated pool; poolside serv, lifeguard. Restaurant 6:30 am-10 pm; Fri, Sat to 11 pm. Rm serv. Bar 11-2 am, Sun from 1 pm; entertainment. Ck-out noon. Meeting rms. Business servs avail. In-rm modem link. Valet serv. Sundries. Free airport transportation. Tennis privileges. Golf privileges. Health club privileges. Exercise equipt; weight machine, bicycles. Private patios. Cr cds: A, C, D, DS, JCB, MC, V.

[D] [✦] [⛷] [🏌] [≋] [⌘] [⊠] [🐾] [SC]

★ ★ **HOLIDAY INN-ALLEGHENY VALLEY.** *180 Gamma Dr (15238), PA 28 exit 10, north of downtown.* 412/963-0600; FAX 412/963-7852. 223 rms, 2 story. S $90; D $100; each addl $10; suites $120-$150; under 18 free. TV; cable (premium). Heated pool; pooside serv, lifeguard. Restaurant 6 am-10 pm; Sat, Sun from 7 am. Rm serv. Bar 11-2 am; Sun 1 pm-1 am. Ck-out 11 am. Meeting rms. Business servs avail. In-rm modem link. Bellhops. Valet serv. Airport transportation. Exercise equipt; stair machine, bicycles. Refrigerator in suites; microwaves avail. Cr cds: A, C, D, DS, JCB, MC, V.

[D] [≋] [⌘] [⊠] [🐾] [SC]

★ ★ **HOWARD JOHNSON-SOUTH.** *5300 Clairton Blvd (PA 51) (15236), south of downtown.* 412/884-6000; FAX 412/884-6009. 95 rms, 3 story. No elvtr. S $69-$79; D $79-$89; each addl $10; under 18 free. Crib free. TV; cable (premium). Pool; lifeguard. Complimentary full bkfst; Sat, Sun continental. Restaurant nearby. Ck-out noon. Meeting rms. Business servs avail. In-rm modem link. Valet serv. Exercise equipt; weight machine, bicycles. Microwaves avail. Near Allegheny County Airport. Cr cds: A, C, D, DS, ER, MC, V.

[D] [≋] [⌘] [⊠] [🐾] [SC]

✔★ **RED ROOF INN.** *6404 Steubenville Pike (PA 60) (15205), south of downtown.* 412/787-7870; FAX 412/787-8392. 120 rms, 2 story. S, D $53.99-$59.99; under 18 free. Crib free. Pet accepted, some restrictions. TV; cable (premium). Complimentary morning coffee. Restaurant adj open 24 hrs. Ck-out noon. Business servs avail. Cr cds: A, C, D, DS, MC, V.

[D] [✦] [⊠] [🐾]

Motor Hotels

✔★ ★ ★ **BEST WESTERN-PARKWAY CENTER INN.** *875 Greentree Rd (15220), adj Parkway Center Mall, west of downtown.* 412/922-7070; FAX 412/922-4949. 138 rms, 6 story, 44 kits. S $87-$97; D $96-$106; each addl $9; kit. units $96-$106; under 12 free; wkend rates. Crib free. TV; cable (premium). Indoor pool; lifeguard. Complimentary bkfst. Ck-out noon. Coin lndry. Meeting rms. Business servs avail. In-rm modem link. Bellhops. Valet serv. Sundries. Free airport transportation. Exercise equipt; weight machine, bicycles, sauna. Rec rm. Microwaves avail. Cr cds: A, C, D, DS, ER, MC, V.

[D] [≋] [🏌] [⊠] [🐾] [SC]

★ ★ ★ **HARLEY.** *699 Rodi Rd (15235), at jct PA 791 & I-376, east of downtown.* 412/244-1600; FAX 412/829-2334; res: 800/321-2323. 152 rms, 3 story. No elvtr. S $112-$122; D $122-$132; each addl $10; under 18 free; wkend rates. Crib free. TV; cable, VCR avail. 2 heated pools, 1 indoor; whirlpool, sauna, poolside serv, lifeguard. Restaurant 6:30 am-2 pm, 5:30-10 pm; Fri, Sat 5:30-11 pm. Rm serv 7 am-11 pm. Bar 4:30 pm-midnight, Fri to 1 am, Sat noon-1 am, Sun 4:30-11 pm; entertainment Fri, Sat. Ck-out 11 am. Meeting rms. Business servs avail. In-rm modem link. Bellhops. Valet serv. Sundries. Airport transportation. Lighted tennis. Private patios, balconies. Cr cds: A, C, D, DS, JCB, MC, V.

[D] [⛷] [≋] [⊠] [🐾] [SC]

★ ★ ★ **HOLIDAY INN.** *4859 McKnight Rd (15237), 5 mi N on I-279, exit 18, north of downtown.* 412/366-5200; FAX 412/366-5682. 147 rms, 7 story, 19 suites. S, D $99-$109; each addl $10; suites $109-$139; under 18 free. Crib free. Pet accepted. TV; cable (premium). Heated pool; poolside serv, lifeguard. Restaurant 6:30 am-10 pm; Sun from 7 am. Rm serv. Bar 11 am-11 pm; entertainment Fri, Sat. Ck-out noon. Coin lndry. Meeting rms. Business servs avail. In-rm modem link. Valet serv. Sundries. Health club privileges. Refrigerator in suites; microwaves avail. Cr cds: A, C, D, DS, MC, V.

[D] [✦] [≋] [⊠] [🐾] [SC]

★ ★ ★ **HOLIDAY INN.** *164 Fort Couch Rd (15241), south of downtown.* 412/833-5300; FAX 412/831-8539. 210 rms, 8 story. S, D $75; each addl $10; suites $120-$130; under 18 free; wkend rates. Crib free. Pet accepted, some restrictions. TV; cable (premium), VCR avail. Pool; poolside serv, lifeguard. Restaurant 6:30 am-11 pm; Sat, Sun from 7 am. Rm serv. Bar 11-2 am; entertainment Tues-Sat. Ck-out noon. Meeting rms. Business servs avail. In-rm modem link. Bellhops. Valet serv. Shopping arcade. Airport transportation. Health club privileges. Game rm. Gift shop. Microwaves avail. Balconies. Cr cds: A, C, D, DS, ER, JCB, MC, V.

[D] [✦] [≋] [⊠] [🐾] [SC]

★ ★ **HOLIDAY INN-MONROEVILLE.** *(2750 Mosside Blvd, Monroeville 15146) approx 7 mi E on I-376, exit 16A, at PA 48 & US 22 Business.* 412/372-1022; FAX 412/373-4065. 189 rms, 4 story. S, D $79-$119; each addl $10; under 19 free; wkly, monthly, wkend rates. Crib free. Pet accepted. TV; cable (premium). Pool. Complimentary coffee in rms. Restaurant 6:30 am-2 pm, 5-10 pm. Rm serv. Bar 11-2 am; entertainment Wed-Sun. Ck-out noon. Coin Indry. Meeting rms. Business servs avail. In-rm modem link. Valet serv. Sundries. Exercise equipt; weight machine, stair machines. Health club privileges. Microwaves avail. Cr cds: A, C, D, DS, ER, MC, V.

★ ★ ★ **HOLIDAY INN-PARKWAY EAST.** *915 Brinton Rd (15221), east of downtown.* 412/247-2700; FAX 412/371-9619. 180 rms, 11 story. Apr-Oct: S, D $99-$119; suites $150; under 18 free; wknd, hol rates; lower rates rest of yr. Crib free. Pet accepted. TV; cable (premium). Indoor pool; lifeguard. Coffee in rms. Restaurant 6:30 am-10 pm. Rm serv. Bar 11-1 am; entertainment Fri, Sat. Ck-out noon. Coin Indry. Meeting rms. Business servs avail. Bellhops. Valet serv. Health club privileges. Some refrigerators, microwaves avail. Cr cds: A, D, DS, ER, JCB, MC, V.

★ ★ ★ **MARRIOTT GREENTREE.** *101 Marriott Dr (15205), across river, west of downtown.* 412/922-8400; FAX 412/922-8981. Web www.marriott.com. 467 rms, 7 story. S $99-$164; D $114-$179; each addl $15; suites $200-$375; under 18 free; wknd rates; package plans. Crib free. Pet accepted. TV; cable (premium), VCR avail. 3 pools, 1 indoor; whirlpool, poolside serv, lifeguard. Restaurant 6:30 am-midnight. Rm serv. Bar 11-2 am; entertainment. Ck-out noon. Meeting rms. Business servs avail. In-rm modem link. Bellhops. Valet serv. Sundries. Gift shop. Barber, beauty shop. Free airport transportation. Indoor tennis privileges. Exercise equipt; weight machines, bicycles, sauna, steam rm. Health club privileges. Rec rm. Many minibars. Luxury level. Cr cds: A, C, D, DS, ER, MC, V.

Hotels

★ ★ ★ **DOUBLETREE.** *1000 Penn Ave (15222), downtown.* 412/281-3700; FAX 412/227-4500. 616 rms, 26 story. S $125-$180; D $145-$215; each addl $20; suites $255-$1,550; family rates; wknd rates. Crib free. Pet accepted. TV; cable (premium). Indoor pool; whirlpool. Coffee in rms. Restaurants 6:30 am-10:30 pm. Rm serv 24 hrs. Bar 11-2 am. Ck-out noon. Convention facilities. Business center. In-rm modem link. Concierge. Shopping arcade. Courtesy limo downtown. Exercise rm; instructor, weights, bicycles, sauna, steam rm. Refrigerators; many bathrm phones. Cr cds: A, C, D, DS, ER, JCB, MC, V.

★ ★ ★ **HILTON.** *Gateway Center (15222), at Point State Park, downtown.* 412/391-4600; FAX 412/594-5161. 711 rms, 24 story. S $139-$196; D $159-$206; each addl $20; suites $325; studio rms $109; children free; wknd plans. Crib free. Pet accepted, some restrictions. TV; cable (premium), VCR avail. Coffee in rms. Restaurant 6:30 am-11:30 pm. 2 bars 11-2 am; entertainment. Ck-out noon. Meeting rms. Business center. In-rm modem link. Concierge. Drugstore. Barber, beauty shop. Garage avail; valet parking. Airport transportation. Exercise equipt; weights, treadmill. Minibars; some bathrm phones, refrigerators. Luxury level. Cr cds: A, C, D, DS, ER, JCB, MC, V.

★ ★ ★ **SHERATON.** *7 Station Square (15219), on South Side.* 412/261-2000; FAX 412/261-2932. 292 rms, 15 story. S $149-$170; D $164-$185; each addl $15; suites $225-$600; under 18 free; wknd rates. Crib free. TV; cable (premium), VCR avail. Indoor pool; whirlpool, lifeguard. Coffee in rms. Restaurant 6 am-midnight. Bar 11-2 am; entertainment. Ck-out noon. Meeting rms. Business center. In-rm modem link. Shopping arcade. RR station, bus depot transportation. Exercise equipt; weights, bicycles. Health club privileges. Game rm. On riverfront. Luxury level. Cr cds: A, C, D, DS, ER, JCB, MC, V.

★ ★ ★ **WESTIN WILLIAM PENN.** *530 Wm Penn Place (15219), on Mellon Square, downtown.* 412/281-7100; FAX 412/553-5252. 595 rms, 24 story. S, D $179-$189; each addl $20; suites $398-$1,200; under 18 free; wknd rates. Crib free. Pet accepted. Valet parking $19.50. TV; cable (premium), VCR avail. Restaurant 6:30 am-11 pm (also see TERRACE

ROOM, Unrated Dining). Rm serv 24 hrs. Bar 11-2 am; entertainment. Ck-out 1 pm. Convention facilities. Business center. Gift shop. Barber shop. Airport, RR station, bus depot transportation. Exercise equipt; bicycles, treadmill. Health club privileges. Historic, landmark hotel. Cr cds: A, C, D, DS, ER, JCB, MC, V.

★ ★ ★ **WYNDHAM GARDEN HOTEL.** *1 Wyndham Circle (15273-1000), off PA 60, exit Montour Run Rd, west of downtown.* 412/695-0002; FAX 412/695-7262. Web www.hyatt.com/travelweb. 140 rms, 4 story. S $104; D $114; each addl $10; suites $104-$114; under 18 free; wknd, hol rates. Crib free. TV; cable (premium). Pool; wading pool, lifeguard. Complimentary full bkfst. Complimentary coffee in rms. Restaurant 6:30 am-2 pm, 5-10 pm. Bar 4 pm-midnight. Ck-out noon. Meeting rms. Business center. In-rm modem link. Free airport transportation. Exercise equipt; stair machine, treadmill. Some refrigerators; microwaves avail. Cr cds: A, C, D, DS, ER, JCB, MC, V.

Inns

★ ★ ★ **THE APPLETREE.** *703 S Negley Ave (15232), east of downtown.* 412/661-0631; FAX 412/661-8151. Web www.appletreeb-b.com. 4 rms, 2 story, suite. MAP: S, D $99-$130; each addl $10; suite $120; wknd plans; hols (2-3 day min); children over 12 yrs only. TV in common rm; VCR. Complimentary full bkfst. Ck-out 11 am, ck-in 3-6 pm. Concierge serv. Luggage handling. Business servs avail. In-rm modem link. Health club privileges. Totally nonsmoking. Historic building (1884). Cr cds: A, DS, MC, V.

★ ★ ★ **INN AT OAKMONT.** *(Oakmont 15139) 15 mi NE on PA 28, adj to golf course.* 412/828-0410; FAX 412/828-1358. Web www.bnb.lm.com. 8 rms, 1 with shower only, 2 story. S $100-$120; D $130-$140; each addl $10. TV; VCR avail. Complimentary full bkfst. Coffee in library. Restaurant nearby. Ck-out 11 am, ck-in 2 pm. Concierge serv. Business servs avail. 18-hole golf privileges. Exercise equipt; weight machine, treadmill. Balconies. Many antiques. Totally nonsmoking. Cr cds: A, DS, MC, V.

★ ★ ★ **THE PRIORY.** *614 Pressley St (15212), north of downtown.* 412/231-3338; FAX 412/231-4838. 24 rms, 3 story. S $65-$100; D $103-$120; each addl $10; suites $110-$143; under 7 free; lower rates wknds. TV; cable. Complimentary continental bkfst; evening refreshments. Ck-out 11 am, wknds noon, ck-in 3 pm. Meeting rms. Business servs avail. Health club privileges. Previously a haven for Benedictine monks (1888); European-style inn with fountain and floral arrangements in courtyard. Cr cds: A, C, D, DS, MC, V.

★ ★ ★ **SHADYSIDE.** *5516 Maple Heights Rd (15232), east of downtown; I-279 exit 13.* 412/683-6501; FAX 412/683-7228. Web www.bnb.lm.com. 7 rms, 2 share bath, 3 story. No elvtr. No rm phones. MAP: S, D $100-$140. TV in sitting rm; cable (premium), VCR, (movies avail). Complimentary continental bkfst. Restaurant nearby. Ck-out noon, ck-in 3 pm. Concierge serv. Luggage handling. Health club privileges. Microwaves avail. Billiard rm, library. Cr cds: A, DS, MC, V.

Restaurants

★ ★ **1902 LANDMARK TAVERN.** *24 Market St (15222), downtown.* 412/471-1902. Hrs: 11:30 am-11 pm; Fri & Sat to midnight. Closed Sun; major hols. Res accepted. Italian-American menu. Bar to 2 am. Semi-a la carte: lunch $5.95-$11.50, dinner $10.95-$22. Specializes in steaks, fresh seafood, oyster bar. Restored tavern (1902); ornate tin ceiling, original tiles. Cr cds: A, D, DS, MC, V.

✔★★ **THE BALCONY.** *5520 Walnut St (15232), in Theatre Bldg, Shadyside, east of downtown.* 412/687-0110. Hrs: 11:30 am-midnight; Sun brunch 10:30 am-2:30 pm. Closed most hols. Res accepted. Bar. Semi-a la carte: lunch $5.95-$9.95, dinner $10.95-$15.95. Sun brunch $9.95. Specializes in fresh seafood, vegetarian pasta, focaccia sandwiches. Entertainment Mon-Sat. Cr cds: A, DS, MC, V.

 ♥

✔★★ **BENTLEY'S.** *5608 Wilkens Ave, east of downtown.* 412/421-4880. Hrs: 11:30 am-10 pm; Fri, Sat to 11 pm; extended hrs summer; early-bird dinner Mon-Sat 4-6 pm. Closed Thanksgiving, Dec 25. Res accepted. Continental menu. Bar. Complete meals: lunch $5.95-$6.95, dinner $8.95-$14.95. Child's meals. Specializes in seafood, veal, pasta. Parking. Outdoor dining. Cr cds: A, D, DS, MC, V.

★★ **BRANDY'S PLACE.** *2323 Penn Ave (15222), at 24th St, in Strip District, east of downtown.* 412/566-1000. Hrs: 11 am-10 pm. Closed Thanksgiving, Dec 25. Res accepted. Bar to 1 am. Semi-a la carte: lunch $3.95-$7.95, dinner $12.95-$22.95. Child's meals. Specialties: crab cakes, grilled lamb chops, veal parmigiana. Outdoor dining. Restored turn-of-the-century restaurant. Cr cds: A, C, D, DS, MC, V.

★★ **BRITISH BICYCLE CLUB.** *923 Penn Ave, downtown.* 412/391-9623. Hrs: 10 am-10 pm. Closed Sat, Sun; major hols. Res accepted. Bar. Semi-a la carte: lunch $4.75-$8.75, dinner $4.75-$15.95. Specializes in prime rib, steak salad, steaks. English pub atmosphere. Cr cds: A, C, D, DS, MC, V.

★★★ **CAFE ALLEGRO.** *51 S 12th St (15203), on South Side.* 412/481-7788. Hrs: 5-11 pm. Closed major hols. Res accepted. Italian menu. Bar. Wine list. Semi-a la carte: dinner $17-$23. Child's meals. Specialties: pasta del sole, seafood arrabbiata, grilled veal medallions. Valet parking. Ambience of Riviera cafe; artwork. Cr cds: A, D, MC, V.

★★ **CAFE AT THE FRICK.** *7227 Reynolds St (15208), at the Frick Art and Historical Center, east of downtown.* 412/371-0600. Hrs: 11 am-5:30 pm; Sun noon-6 pm; high tea from 3 pm. Closed Mon; most major hols; also Mon-Fri in Jan. Semi-a la carte: lunch $7.95-$10. High tea $9.95. Specializes in grilled chicken, desserts. Outdoor dining. View of garden and Frick estate. Totally nonsmoking. Cr cds: DS, MC, V.

★★ **CARLTON.** *1 Mellon Bank Center, on grounds of Mellon Bank Center Commercial Bldg, at Grant St, downtown.* 412/391-4099. Hrs: 11:30 am-2:30 pm, 5-10 pm; Fri to 11 pm; Sat 5-11 pm. Closed Sun; major hols. Res accepted. Continental menu. Bar. Extensive wine list. Semi-a la carte: lunch $9.95-$14.95, dinner $19.95-$25.95. Child's meals. Specializes in charcoal-grilled seafood, prime steak, veal. Own pastries. Parking. Cr cds: A, C, D, DS, MC, V.

★★ **CARMASSI'S TUSCANY GRILL.** *711 Penn Ave (15222), downtown.* 412/281-6644. Hrs: 11 am-10 pm; Sat, Sun 4:30-8 pm. Closed hols. Res accepted. Northern Italian menu. Bar. Semi-a la carte: lunch $9-$12, dinner $17-$25. Child's meals. Specialties: veal a'la lucca, penne arrabiatta. Italian art on display. Cr cds: A, C, D, DS, MC, V.

★★ **CASBAH.** *229 S Highland Ave (15206), in Shadyside, east of downtown.* 412/661-5656. Hrs: 11:30 am-2:30 pm; 5-11 pm; Sun-Tues 5-10 pm. Closed most major hols. Res accepted. Mediterranean menu. Bar. Semi-a la carte: lunch $5.50-$12, dinner $12-$22. Child's meals. Specialties: lamb mixed grill, roasted vegetable tagine, Mahi Mahi and grape leaves. Cr cds: A, D, DS, MC, V.

✔★★ **CHINA PALACE.** *5440 Walnut St (15232), in Shadyside, east of downtown.* 412/687-7423. Hrs: 11:30 am-10 pm; Fri, Sat to 11 pm; Sun 2-9 pm. Closed July 4, Labor Day, Thanksgiving. Chinese menu. Bar. Semi-a la carte: lunch $4.95-$5.50, dinner $6.95-$16.95. Specialties: crispy walnut shrimp, orange beef, lemon chicken. Cr cds: A, D, DS, MC, V.

✔★★ **THE CHURCH BREW WORKS.** *3525 Liberty Ave (15201), north of downtown.* 412/688-8200. E-mail churchbrew@juno.com; web www.churchbrew.com. Hrs: 11:30 am-midnight; Fri, Sat to 1 am; Sun noon-10 pm. Closed Jan 1, Thanksgiving, Dec 25. Regional Amer menu. Bar. Semi-a la carte: lunch $5.75-$7.95, dinner $13.95-$19.95. Specialties: buffalo steak, wood-fired oven pizza, Pittsburgh pierogie. Own pasta. Outdoor dining. Brew-pub in 1902 church; vaulted ceiling, stained-glass windows. Cr cds: A, D, DS, MC, V.

★★★ **CLIFFSIDE.** *1208 Grandview Ave, on Mount Washington.* 412/431-6996. Hrs: 5-10 pm; Fri, Sat to 11 pm. Closed major hols. Res accepted. Continental menu. Bar. Semi-a la carte: dinner $16-$22.50. Child's meals. Specializes in fresh seafood, chicken, veal. Pianist. Valet parking. Contemporary decor in older building (1897). Cr cds: A, D, DS, JCB, MC, V.

★★★ **COLONY.** *Greentree & Cochran Rds, south of downtown.* 412/561-2060. Hrs: 5-10:30 pm; Sun 4-9 pm. Res accepted. Continental menu. Bar 4 pm-1 am. Extensive wine list. Complete meals: dinner $21-$42. Specializes in fresh seafood, tournedos of veal, prime Angus steaks. Own baking. Pianist, vocalist Fri, Sat. Valet parking. Family-owned. Jacket. Cr cds: A, C, D, DS, JCB, MC, V.

★★ **COMMON PLEA.** *308 Ross St, downtown.* 412/281-5140. Hrs: 11:30 am-2:30 pm, 5-10 pm; Sat 5-10 pm. Closed Sun; major hols. Res accepted. Bar. Complete meals: lunch $6.95-$10.75, dinner $18.25-$28. Specializes in seafood, veal, chicken. Own baking. Valet parking (dinner). Courtroom decor. Family-owned. Cr cds: A, D, MC, V.

★★★ **D'IMPERIO'S.** *3412 Wm Penn Hwy (15235), east of downtown.* 412/823-4800. Hrs: 11:30 am-3 pm, 5-11 pm; Mon, Sat from 5 pm. Closed Sun; most major hols. Res accepted; required wkends. Italian, Amer menu. Bar. Semi-a la carte: dinner $13.50-$28. Child's meals. Specialties: shrimp Sorrento, lobster sausage, veal Genovese. Own bread. Pianist. Parking. Different displays of artwork in each dining rm. Cr cds: A, C, D, DS, MC, V.

★ **DEL FRATES.** *971 Liberty Ave (15222), downtown.* 412/391-2294. Hrs: 11 am-9 pm; Sat to 10 pm. Closed Sun, hols. Res accepted. Italian, Amer menu. Bar to 2 am; Sat 10 am-10 pm. Semi-a la carte: lunch $5-$8, dinner $7-$14. Specializes in pasta, steak, veal. Cr cds: A, C, D, DS, MC, V.

★★ **GEORGETOWNE INN.** *1230 Grandview Ave (15211), on Mount Washington.* 412/481-4424. Hrs: 11 am-3 pm, 5 pm-midnight; Fri, Sat to 1 am; Sun 4-10 pm. Closed most hols. Res accepted. Bar. Semi-a la carte: lunch $5.50-$15.95, dinner $15.95-$31.95. Specializes in steak, fresh seafood. Panoramic view of city. Cr cds: A, D, DS, MC, V.

★★★ **GRAND CONCOURSE.** *1 Station Square, jct Carson & Smithfield Sts, on South Side.* 412/261-1717. Hrs: 11:30 am-2:30 pm, 4:30-10 pm; Sat 4:30-11 pm; Sun 4:30-10 pm; early-bird dinner 4:30-6 pm; Sun brunch 10 am-2:30 pm. Closed Dec 25. Continental menu. Bar 11:30-2 am; Sun 11 am-10 pm. Extensive wine list. Semi-a la carte: lunch $6-$12, dinner $10-$30. Sun brunch $16.95. Child's meals. Specializes in seafood, steak, pasta. Own baking, pasta. Pianist. Converted railroad station. Braille menu. Outdoor dining. Cr cds: A, C, D, DS, MC, V.

[D] [SC] [≠]

★ ★ **INDIA GARDEN.** *328 Atwood St (15213), in Oakland.* 412/682-3000. Hrs: 11:30 am-2:30 pm, 5-10 pm. Res accepted. Northern Indian menu. Setups. A la carte entrees: $6.95-$13.95. Lunch buffet $6.95. Specialties: tandoori chicken, chicken tekka masala, vegetable korma. Indian decor, chairs. Cr cds: A, DS, MC, V.

[≠]

✔★ ★ **JIMMY TSANG'S.** *5700 Centre Ave, at Negley, in Kennilworth Bldg, east of downtown.* 412/661-4226. Hrs: 11:30 am-10 pm; Fri, Sat to 11 pm; Sun 3:30-9 pm; early-bird dinner Mon-Sat 3-6 pm. Closed July 4, Thanksgiving. Chinese menu. Bar. A la carte: lunch $4.95-$5.75, dinner $7.95-$9.95. Specialties: Peking duck, honey chicken, Mongolian beef. Oriental decor, artwork. Cr cds: A, C, D, MC, V.

[D] [≠]

★ ★ **JUNO TRATTORIA.** *One Oxford Center, 3rd floor (15282), downtown.* 412/392-0225. Hrs: 11 am-2:30 pm, 5-10 pm; Fri, Sat to 11 pm. Closed Sun, most major hols. Regional Italian, Amer menu. Bar. Semi-a la carte: lunch $6-$12, dinner $10-$16. Specializes in pastas, pizza. Cr cds: A, DS, MC, V.

[≠] [♥]

★ ★ **KAYA.** *2000 Smallman St (15222), in Strip District, east of downtown.* 412/261-6565. Hrs: 11:30 am-11 pm; Fri, Sat to midnight; Sun to 9 pm. Closed some major hols. Carribean menu. Bar. Semi-a la carte: lunch $6.25-$8.95, dinner $6.25-$16.95. Specialties: Jamaican jerk chicken wings, grilled alligator. Outdoor dining. Cr cds: A, C, D, DS, MC, V.

[D]

★ ★ **LE MONT.** *1114 Grandview Ave, on Mount Washington.* 412/431-3100. E-mail info@le-mont.com; web www.le-mont.com. Hrs: 5-11:30 pm; Sun 4-10 pm. Closed major hols. Res accepted. Contemporary Amer menu. Bar to midnight. Wine list. A la carte entrees: dinner $18.95-$46. Specialties: rack of lamb Persille, variety of wild game dishes, flaming desserts. Own baking. Pianist Fri, Sat. Valet parking. Atop Mt Washington; panoramic view of city. Cr cds: A, C, D, DS, JCB, MC, V.

[D] [≠]

★ ★ ★ **LE POMMIER.** *2104 E Carson St, on South Side.* 412/431-1901. E-mail lepommier@lepommier.com; web www.lepommier.com. Hrs: 5:30-9:30 pm; Fri, Sat to 10:30 pm. Closed Mon, Sun; some major hols. Res accepted. French menu. Bar. Wine cellar. A la carte entrees: dinner $14-$28. Specializes in seasonal French country fare. Own baking. Valet parking Fri, Sat. Located in oldest storefront in area (1863). Outdoor dining in season. Country French decor. Cr cds: A, C, D, DS, MC, V.

[D] [≠]

★ ★ **LONDON GRILLE.** *(1500 Washington Rd, Mount Lebanon 15228) US 19 S, in Galleria Mall, south of downtown.* 412/563-3400. Hrs: 11:30 am-10 pm; Fri, Sat to 11:30 pm; Sun noon-9 pm. Closed Dec 25. British menu. Bar. Wine list. Semi-a la carte: lunch $7.95-$11.95; dinner $17.95-$25.95. Specialties: prime rib, beef wellington. Valet parking. Patio dining. 4 dining rooms. Cr cds: A, C, D, DS, MC, V.

[D] [≠]

✔★ **MAX & ERMA'S.** *5533 Walnut St (15232), in Shadyside, east of downtown.* 412/681-5775. Hrs: 11:30 am-11 pm; Fri, Sat to midnight; Sun to 10 pm. Closed Thanksgiving, Dec 25. Bar. Semi-a la carte: lunch $6-$10, dinner $8-$14. Specializes in steak, ribs, pasta. Cr cds: A, D, DS, MC, V.

[D] [SC] [≠]

✔★ ★ **MAX'S ALLEGHENY TAVERN.** *Middle & Suisman Sts, north of downtown.* 412/231-1899. Hrs: 11 am-midnight; Sun to 10 pm. Closed most major hols. German menu. Bar. A la carte entrees: lunch $4.25-$7.95, dinner $5.95-$13.95. Specialties: jägerschnitzel, käse

spätzle, sauerbraten. Tavern with German memorabilia and collection of photographs. Cr cds: A, D, DS, MC, V.

[≠]

★ ★ ★ **NINA.** *5701 Bryant St (15206), east of downtown.* 412/665-9000. Hrs: 5:30-10 pm; Fri, Sat to 11 pm. Closed Sun, Mon; major hols. Res accepted. Continental menu. Bar. A la carte entrees: dinner $15.50-$23. Complete meal: 3 course dinner $19.97, 5 course dinner $49.97. Specializes in tuna, lamb, quail. Own baking, pasta. Former Highland Park Manor converted to casual yet elegant dining rm; open staircase leads to second dining level. Cr cds: A, D, MC, V.

[≠]

★ ★ **PASTA PIATTO.** *736 Bellefonte St, in Shadyside, east of downtown.* 412/621-5547. Hrs: 11:30 am-3 pm, 4:30-10 pm; Wed, Thurs to 10:30 pm; Fri, Sat to 11 pm; Sun 4-9 pm. Closed major hols. Northern Italian menu. Bar. Semi-a la carte: lunch $5-$10, dinner $10.95-$22.95. Child's meals. Specializes in homemade pasta, veal, seafood. Cr cds: A, MC, V.

[≠]

✔★ ★ **PENN BREWERY.** *Troy Hill, 800 Vinial St (15212), north of downtown.* 412/237-9402. Hrs: 11 am-midnight. Closed Sun, hols. German menu. Bar. Semi-a la carte: lunch $4.50-$8.50, dinner $8.50-$15.95. Child's meals. Specialties: weiner schnitzel, sauerbrauten, chicken berlin. Entertainment Tues-Sat. Outdoor dining. Restored 19th-century brewery, German beer hall-style communal dining. Cr cds: A, DS, MC, V.

[≠]

★ ★ ★ **PICCOLO MONDO.** *661 Andersen Dr, Bldg 7, Foster Plaza, Green Tree, south of downtown.* 412/922-0920. Hrs: 11:30 am-10 pm; Sat to 4-11 pm. Closed Sun exc Mother's Day; some hols. Res accepted. Northern Italian menu. Bar. Wine list. Semi-a la carte: lunch $7.50-$13, dinner $14-$24. Child's meals. Specializes in fresh fish, veal. Own desserts. Parking. Jacket. Cr cds: A, C, D, DS, MC, V.

[D] [≠]

★ ★ ★ **POLI.** *2607 Murray Ave (15217), east of downtown.* 412/521-6400. Hrs: 11:30 am-11 pm; Sun 11 am-9:30 pm; early-bird dinner Tues-Fri 3-5:30 pm. Closed Mon; Thanksgiving, Dec 25. Bar. Semi-a la carte: lunch $6.95-$10.50, dinner $15-$25. Child's meals. Specializes in fresh seafood, veal, pasta. Own baking. Valet parking. Family-owned. Cr cds: A, C, D, MC, V.

[D] [≠]

✔★ **PRIMANTI BROS.** *46 18th St (15222), in Strip District, east of downtown.* 412/263-2142. Hrs: open 24 hrs. Closed Dec 25. Italian, Amer menu. Wine, beer. Semi-a la carte: $3.50-$4.25. Specializes in deli sandwiches with fries and cole slaw inside, soups. Family-owned. No cr cds accepted.

★ ★ ★ **RICO'S.** *1 Rico Lane, off of Evergreen Rd in North Hills, north of downtown.* 412/931-1989. Hrs: 11:30 am-3 pm, 4-10:30 pm; Fri, Sat 4-11:30 pm. Closed Sun; most major hols. Italian, Amer menu. Bar to midnight. Wine cellar. Semi-a la carte: lunch $7.50-$12.50, dinner $15.50-$28. Specializes in fresh seafood, veal. Valet parking. Old World atmosphere; Italian lithographs. Jacket. Cr cds: A, D, DS, MC, V.

[D] [≠]

★ ★ **SAMURAI JAPANESE STEAK HOUSE.** *2100 Greentree Rd, south of downtown.* 412/276-2100. Hrs: 11:30 am-2 pm, 5:30-10 pm; Fri to 11 pm; Sat 5-11:30 pm; Sun 4:30-9 pm. Closed July 4, Thanksgiving, Dec 25. Res accepted. Japanese menu. Bar. Semi-a la carte: lunch $6.25-$9.95, dinner $12.95-$32. Child's meals. Specializes in steak, seafood. Japanese garden. Cr cds: A, C, D, DS, MC, V.

[D] [≠]

✔★ ★ **SEVENTH STREET GRILLE.** *130 7th St (15222), downtown.* 412/338-0303. Hrs: 11:30 am-10 pm. Closed most major hols. Res accepted. Continental menu. Bar. Semi-a la carte: lunch, dinner $5.95-

$16.95. Specializes in grilled seafood, prime rib, specialty beers. Cr cds: A, D, DS, MC, V.

[D] [♥]

★ ★ **SOBA LOUNGE.** *5847 Ellsworth Ave (15232), east of downtown.* 412/362-5656. Hrs: 5 pm-midnight; Sun-Tues to 11 pm;. Sat, Sun also 11:30 am-4 pm. Closed Thanksgiving. Res accepted. Pan-Asian menu. Bars. Semi-a la carte: lunch $7-$12, dinner $12-$30. Specialties: pork and vegetarian dumplings, wok-seared salmon, zaru soba noodles. Own noodles. Musicians exc Sun. Outdoor dining. Three dining levels, each with its own bar; eclectic decor with original artwork. Cr cds: A, D, DS, MC, V.

[D] [≛]

✔★ ★ **STATION SQUARE CHEESE CELLAR.** *#25 Freight House Shops, Station Square (Smithfield & Carson Sts), on South Side.* 412/471-3355. Hrs: 11:30 am-midnight; Fri & Sat to 1 am; Sun 10:30 am-11 pm. Closed Dec 25. Res accepted Sun-Thurs. Continental menu. Bar to 2 am. Semi-a la carte: Sun bkfst $5.95-$6.50, lunch, dinner $4.95-$12.95. Child's meals. Specialty: cheese and chocolate fondue. Outdoor dining. Rustic decor. Cr cds: A, C, D, DS, MC, V.

[D] [≛] [♥]

✔ ★ ★ **SUSHI TWO.** *2122 E Carson St (15203), south of downtown.* 412/431-7874. Hrs: 11:30 am-3 pm, 5-10 pm; Fri to 11:30 pm; Sat 11:30 am-11 pm; Sun 1-9 pm. Closed Labor Day. Res accepted. Japanese menu. Bar. Semi-a la carte: lunch $5.50-$10.95, dinner $9.95-$18.95. Specializes in traditional Japanese dishes. Own baking, noodles. Valet parking Fri, Sat. Contemporary Japanese decor. Cr cds: A, C, D, DS, MC, V.

[D] [≛]

★ ★ ★ **TAMBELLINI'S.** *PA 51 (15226), south of downtown.* 412/481-1118. Hrs: 11:30 am-10 pm. Closed Sun; Jan 1, Thanksgiving, Dec 25. Res accepted. Continental menu. Bar. Semi-a la carte: lunch $7.95-$8.50, dinner $12.95-$27.50. Complete meals: dinner $21.95. Child's meals. Specializes in seafood, pasta, steak. Valet parking. Modern decor. Cr cds: A, D, MC, V.

[D] [≛]

✔ ★ ★ **TESSARO'S.** *4601 Liberty Ave (15224), at Taylor St, east of downtown.* 412/682-6809. Hrs: 11 am-midnight. Closed Sun; Jan 1, Thanksgiving, Dec 25. Mexican, Amer menu. Bar. Semi-a la carte: lunch $5-$10, dinner $12-$15. Specializes in hamburgers, fresh seafood, filet mignon. Own pasta. Casual decor has pressed tin ceiling (ca early 1900s), paddle ceiling fans, fireplaces. Cr cds: A, D, DS, MC, V.

[≛]

✔ ★ ★ **THAI PLACE.** *809 Bellefonte St, in Shadyside, east of downtown.* 412/687-8586. Hrs: 11:30 am-10 pm; Fri to 10:30 pm; Sat noon-11 pm; Sun noon-9:30 pm; Mon from 4:30 pm. Thai menu. Bar. A la carte entrees: lunch $5.50-$7.50, dinner $7.50-$17.95. Specializes in authentic Thai cuisine. Outdoor dining. Asian art. Cr cds: A, D, DS, MC, V.

[≛]

★ ★ ★ **TIN ANGEL.** *1200 Gandview Ave (15221), on Mount Washington.* 412/381-1919. Hrs: 5-10 pm. Closed Sun, hols. Res accepted. Bar. Wine list. Complete meals: $26.95-$46.95. Specialties: sole baretone, black forest filet. Panoramic view of city. Jacket. Family-owned. Cr cds: A, D, MC, V.

[≛]

★ ★ ★ **TOP OF THE TRIANGLE.** *600 Grant St, 62nd floor (15219), on 62nd floor of USX Tower, downtown.* 412/471-4100. Hrs: 11:30 am-3 pm, 5:30-10 pm; Sat noon-3 pm, 5:30-11 pm; Sun 4-9 pm. Closed most major hols. Res accepted. Bar to 1 am. Wine list. Semi-a la carte: lunch $6.95-$14.95, dinner $18.95-$29.95. Child's meals. Specialties: grilled molasses glazed fresh swordfish, Colorado lamb chops. Pianist Fri, Sat. Parking (fee). Panoramic view of city. Cr cds: A, D, DS, MC, V.

[D] [≛]

✔ ★ **VERMONT FLATBREAD CO.** *2701 Penn Ave (15222), east of downtown.* 412/434-1220. Hrs: 11 am-10 pm; Fri, Sat to 11 pm. Closed Sun. Bar. Semi-a la carte: lunch $5.95-$7.50, dinner $5.95-$8.25. Child's meals. Specialties: maple-sugar flatbread, Italian grilled sandwich, sweet stuffed peppers with chorizo sausage. Own baking, pasta. Street parking. Rustic Vermont decor with skylights. Cr cds: D, DS, MC, V.

[D] [≛]

Unrated Dining Spots

DAVE AND ANDY'S ICE CREAM PARLOR. *207 Atwood St, in Oakland.* 412/681-9906. Hrs: 11:30 am-10 pm; Sat & Sun from noon. Closed major hols. Specialties: homemade ice cream (fresh daily), homemade cones. 1930s look; some counters. No cr cds accepted.

PIZZERIA UNO. *(333 Penn Center Blvd, Monroeville 15146) 15 mi E on US 376, Penn Center Blvd exit.* 412/824-8667. Hrs: 11 am-11 pm; Fri & Sat to 12:30 am; Sun noon-10 pm. Closed Thanksgiving, Dec 25. Italian, Amer menu. Bar. Semi-a la carte: lunch $3.95-$8.95, dinner $4.95-$10.95. Specialties: deep-dish pizza. Parking. Casual dining. Cr cds: A, DS, MC, V.

[D] [≛]

TERRACE ROOM. *(See Westin William Penn Hotel)* 412/281-7100. Hrs: tea time 3-6 pm. English custom tea serv. Bar. A la carte items also avail. Specializes in tea, finger sandwiches, pastries. Pianist. Parking avail opp Lobby room; Georgian decor; elaborate floral arrangements. Cr cds: A, C, D, DS, ER, JCB, MC, V.

[D] [≛]

Pittsburgh Intl Airport Area (E-1)

(See also Pittsburgh)

Services and Information

Information: 412/472-3525 or -3526.

Lost and Found: 412/472-3500.

Weather: 412/936-1212.

Cash Machines: Landside Terminal, entrance; Airside Terminal, throughout concourses in Passenger Service Centers.

Airlines: American, British Airways, Continental, Delta, Northwest, TWA, United, USAir.

(For information on this area contact Pittsburgh Airport Area Chamber of Commerce, 986 Brodhead Rd, Coraopolis 15108-2398; 412/264-6270.)

Motels

★ **HAMPTON INN-NORTHWEST.** *(1420 Beers School Rd, Coraopolis 15108) N on PA Business 60.* 412/264-0020; FAX 412/264-3220. 129 rms, 5 story. S $64; D $74; under 18 free. Crib free. Pet accepted. TV; cable (premium). Complimentary continental bkfst. Restaurant adj 6 am-10 pm. Ck-out noon. Meeting rms. Business servs avail. Valet serv. Free airport transportation. Health club privileges. Cr cds: A, C, D, DS, ER, MC, V.

[D] [✦] [✈] [⊠] [🐾] [SC]

★ ★ **LA QUINTA.** *(1433 Beers School Rd, Coraopolis 15108) N on Business PA 60.* 412/269-0400; FAX 412/269-9258. 127 rms, 3 story. S $64-$78; D $71-$85; under 19 free. Crib free. Pet accepted. TV; cable. Heated pool; lifeguard. Complimentary continental bkfst. Coffee in rms. Restaurant adj 6 am-11 pm. Ck-out noon. Coin lndry. Meeting rms. Business servs avail. In-rm modem link. Valet serv. Sundries. Free airport transportation. Exercise equipt; treadmill, rower. Cr cds: A, D, DS, MC, V.

D ✸ 🏊 🏋 ✈ 🍴 🔥 SC

✔★ ★ **PITTSBURGH PLAZA.** *(1500 Beers School Rd, Coraopolis 15108)* I-79 Bus 60 exit to Beers School Rd. 412/264-7900; FAX 412/262-3229; res: 800/542-8111. 193 rms, 2 story. S, D $49.99-$59.99; under 18 free. Pet accepted; $50 refundable. TV; cable (premium), VCR avail. Complimentary continental bkfst 5-9 am in lobby. Restaurant adj open 24 hrs. Ck-out noon. Meeting rms. Business servs avail. In-rm modem link. Valet serv. Sundries. Free airport transportation. Exercise equipt; weights, bicycles, sauna. Some refrigerators. Some balconies. Cr cds: A, C, D, DS, MC, V.

✸ 🏋 🍴 ✈ 🔥 SC

✔★ **RED ROOF INN.** *(1454 Beers School Rd, Coraopolis 15108)* N on Bus PA 60. 412/264-5678; FAX 412/264-8034. 119 rms, 3 story. S $47.99-$58.99; D $61.99-$66.99; each addl $6; under 18 free. Crib free. Pet accepted. TV; cable (premium). Coffee in lobby 6-10 am. Restaurant opp 6 am-10 pm. Ck-out noon. Coin lndry. Meeting rm. Business servs avail. Valet serv. Free airport transportation. Cr cds: A, C, D, DS, MC, V.

D ✸ 🍴 ✈ 🔥

Hotels

★ ★ ★ **CLARION-ROYCE.** *(1160 Thorn Run Rd Extension, Coraopolis 15108)* N on Bus Rte 60, exit Thorn Run Rd. 412/262-2400; FAX 412/264-9373. 193 rms, 9 story. S $69-$119; D $69-$129; each addl $10; suites $109-$139; under 18 free; wkend rates. Crib free. Pet accepted. TV; cable (premium). Pool; lifeguard. Restaurant 6 am-2 pm, 5-11 pm; Sat, Sun 7 am-11 pm. Bar 11-2 am; entertainment. Ck-out noon. Meeting rms. Business center. In-rm modem link. Concierge. Airport transportation. Exercise equipt; weight machines, bicycles. Luxury Level. Cr cds: A, C, D, DS, MC, V.

D ✸ 🏊 🏋 🏃 ✈ 🔥 SC 🎿

★ ★ ★ **MARRIOTT.** *(100 Aten Rd, Coraopolis 15108)* S on PA 60, exit Montour Run Rd. 412/788-8800; FAX 412/788-6299. 314 rms, 14 story. S, D $69-$169; each addl $15; suites $175-$425; family, wkly rates. Crib free. Pet accepted. TV; cable (premium). 2 pools, 1 indoor; whirlpool, poolside serv, lifeguard. Restaurant 6:30 am-11 pm. Bar 11-1 am; pianist Wed-Sat. Ck-out noon. Convention facilities. Business center. In-rm modem link. Concierge. Shopping arcade. Free airport, bus depot transportation. Exercise equipt; weights, bicycles, sauna. Some refrigerators. Luxury level. Cr cds: A, C, D, DS, ER, JCB, MC, V.

D ✸ 🏊 🏋 🏃 ✈ 🔥 SC 🎿

Restaurant

★ ★ ★ **HYEHOLDE.** *(190 Hyeholde Dr, Coraopolis 15108)* PA Bus N 60 to Beers School Rd, right on Beaver Grade Rd, left on Coraopolis Heights Rd. 412/264-3116. Hrs: 11:30 am-2 pm, 5-10 pm; Sat from 5 pm. Closed Sun exc Mother's Day; major hols. Res accepted. Continental menu. Serv bar. Wine list. Complete meals: lunch $9.50-$13, dinner $18.50-$36. Specializes in rack of lamb, roasted elk. Own baking. Valet parking. Patio dining. Herb garden. Country French decor; fireplaces; estate grounds. Cr cds: A, C, D, DS, MC, V.

Pocono Mountains (C-9)

(For accommodations see Canadensis, Hawley, Milford, Mount Pocono, Shawnee on Delaware; also see Bushkill)

Information Pocono Mts Vacation Bureau, 1004 Main St, Stroudsburg 18360; 717/424-6050; for free brochures phone 800/POCONOS.

(Northeast Pennsylvania resort area)

The Pocono Mountains area in northeast Pennsylvania extends north from Wind Gap and Delaware Water Gap into Pike, Carbon, Monroe and Wayne counties. Within its 2,400 square miles almost every form of recreation can be found.

This scenic country with more than 200 lakes, including Lake Wallenpaupack (see HAWLEY), has hundreds of accommodations and is a well-established resort area. Visitors, many of whom return year after year, take advantage of the large plush resorts, smaller family-run resorts, housekeeping cottage resorts, camping resorts and country and bed & breakfast inns. There is primitive, forested country for those who wish to rough it. For the hunter there are deer, bear, wildcat and fox. For the freshwater angler there are black bass, trout, pickerel and walleye.

Summer offers boating, swimming, hiking, horseback riding, mountain biking, golf, theaters and a host of other diversions. In the autumn there is a magnificent display of foliage as well as heritage festivals and country fairs. The first snowfall brings skiing, snow boarding, ice-skating, sleigh rides, tobogganing and snowmobiling.

The name "Pocono" was probably taken from the Native American "pocohanne," meaning a stream between the mountains. Settled in the mid-1700s, the Poconos yielded iron and, later, coal. The lakes and forest still retain their charm. The land "between the mountains" is as inviting as it always has been.

Port Allegany (B-4)

(See also Bradford)

Settled 1816 **Pop** 2,391 **Elev** 1,481 ft **Area code** 814 **Zip** 16743
Information Chamber of Commerce, 22 Church St; 814/642-2181.

Native Americans called this spot "canoe place" because here on the portage route between the Allegheny and Susquehanna headwaters they paused to build canoes. Early settlers followed their route. Soon after the town was established, lumbering operations reached their peak; later industrial expansion included coal mining and tanning. In the late 1890s, the borough became the center of a boom resulting from the discovery of natural gas and glass sand.

What to See and Do

Eldred World War II Museum. Exhibits include battle maps, posters, dioramas with narrative, video history. Centerpiece is "Remembering the Women Behind the Front Lines" exhibit. Library. (Tues, Thurs, Sat, Sun) 15 mi N on PA 155, 5 mi N on PA 446, in Eldred. Phone 814/225-2220. **Free.**

Sizerville State Park. Approx 385 acres. Swimming pool; fishing, hunting. Cross-country skiing, snowmobiling. Picnicking, playground, snack bar. Tent & trailer sites. Standard fees. 19 mi S on PA 155, in Sizerville. Phone 814/486-5605.

Motel

★ **MID-TOWN.** *111 Main St (PA 155). 814/642-2575.* 25 rms, 2 story. S $37-$45; D $42-$50; each addl $5. Crib $5. TV; cable (premium). Restaurant opp 6 am-11 pm. Ck-out 11 am. Cr cds: A, D, DS, MC, V.

Pottstown (E-9)

(See also Limerick, Norristown, Reading)

Settled 1701 **Pop** 21,831 **Elev** 160 ft **Area code** 610 **Zip** 19464 **E-mail** tcacc@ptdprolog.net **Web** www.tricopa.com

Information TriCounty Area Chamber of Commerce, 135 High St; 610/326-2900.

An iron forge operating in 1714 at Manatawny Creek, about three miles north of Pottstown, was the first industrial establishment in the state. The borough was established by John Potts, an ironmaster, on land William Penn had earlier deeded to his son, John. Today the community is the commercial and cultural hub for an area with a population of 130,000. Nearly 200 modern industries are located here.

What to See and Do

Boyertown Museum of Historic Vehicles. Collection of over 100 antique autos, trucks, sleighs, buggies and bicycles. Also includes the Hill, which was among the first gasoline-powered cars. (Daily exc Mon) 7 mi N via PA 100, 73, in Boyertown, on Warwick St. Phone 610/367-2090. ¢¢

French Creek State Park. Approx 7,330 acres, two lakes. Boating (rentals, mooring, launching), fishing. Swimming pool. Hiking. Ice fishing. Picnicking. Tent & trailer sites, cabins. Standard fees. 9 mi W on PA 724, then 4 mi S on PA 345. Phone 610/582-9680. Also here is

Hopewell Furnace National Historic Site (see).

Merritt's Museum of Childhood. Antique toys, costumed figures, furnishings; Native American relics; gift shop in lobby. (Daily; closed major hols) 1 mi W on US 422, in Douglassville. Phone 610/385-3408. ¢¢ Admission includes

Mary Merritt Doll Museum. Antique dolls and toys dating from 1725 to 1900. (Daily; closed major hols) Phone 610/385-3809.

Pottsgrove Manor (1752). Newly restored house of John Potts, 18th-century ironmaster and founder of Pottstown; outstanding example of early Georgian architecture and furniture. Includes recently discovered slave quarters and Potts's office. Slide orientation. Museum shop. (Daily exc Mon; closed major hols) W King St & PA 100. Phone 610/326-4014. **Free.**

Ringing Rocks Park. Roller-skating (Fri-Sun; fee); nature trails, picnicking, interesting rock formations. (Daily) 3 mi N off PA 663. Phone 610/323-6560. **Free.**

Annual Event

Duryea Day Antique & Classic Auto Show. Boyertown Community Park. Antique autos, trucks and other vehicles; displays, arts & crafts, flea market with automotive memorabilia, activities, Pennsylvania Dutch food. Labor Day wkend.

Motels

★★ **COMFORT INN.** *PA 100 & Shoemaker Rd. 610/326-5000; FAX 610/970-7230.* 121 rms, 4 story, 30 suites. S, D $59-$92; each addl $7; suites $63-$95; under 18 free; golf plans; wkend rates. Crib free. Pet accepted. TV; cable (premium). Heated pool; lifeguard. Complimentary continental bkfst. Restaurant adj 6 am-11 pm. Rm serv. Ck-out noon. Coin lndry. Meeting rms. Business servs avail. In-rm modem link. Free bus depot transportation. Refrigerator in suites. Cr cds: A, C, D, DS, ER, JCB, MC, V.

★★ **HOLIDAY INN EXPRESS.** *1600 Industrial Hwy (US 422), at Armand Hammer Blvd exit. 610/327-3300; FAX 610/327-9447.* 120 rms, 4 story. S, D $69; each addl $5; suites $122; under 19 free; wkly, hol rates; higher rates special events. Crib free. Pet accepted. TV; cable (premium), VCR avail (movies). Pool. Complimentary continental bkfst. Complimentary coffee in rms. Restaurant adj open 24 hrs. Rm serv 24 hrs. Ck-out noon. Meeting rms. Business servs avail. In-rm modem links. Sundries. Valet serv. Health club privileges. Some refrigerators; microwaves avail. Cr cds: A, D, DS, JCB, MC, V.

Inn

★★★ **TWIN TURRETS.** *(11 E Philadelphia Ave, Boyertown 19512) 7 mi N on US 100, then 1 mi W on PA 73. 610/367-4513; FAX 610/369-7898.* E-mail turrets@netjunction.com; web www.netjunction.com/twinturrets. 10 rms, 9 with shower only, 3 story. S $75; D $95-$120; each addl $15; wkly rates. Children over 12 yrs preferred. TV; cable (premium), VCR avail. Complimentary full bkfst; afternoon refreshments. Restaurant nearby. Ck-out 11 am, ck-in 1 pm. Luggage handling. Business center. Health club privileges. Original Boyer mansion built in 1850; antiques and original art. Flower gardens with fountain. Totally nonsmoking. Cr cds: A, DS, MC, V.

Restaurant

★★★ **COVENTRY FORGE INN.** *3360 Coventryville Rd (19465), 5 mi S on PA 100, 1½ mi W on PA 23 in Coventryville. 610/469-6222.* Hrs: 5:30-9 pm; Sat 5-10 pm. Res accepted. Closed Mon, Sun exc Mother's Day; Jan 1, Dec 25. French menu. Bar. Wine cellar. A la carte entrees: dinner $16.95-$25.95. Prix fixe: (Sat) dinner $39.50. Specialties: carre d'agneau Provençal, escalopes de veau. Own baking. Built in 1717; antiques. Cr cds: A, D, MC, V.

Quakertown (Bucks Co) (E-9)

(For accommodations see Allentown, Bethlehem, Doylestown, Pottstown)

Founded 1715 **Pop** 8,982 **Elev** 500 ft **Area code** 215 **Zip** 18951
Information Upper Bucks County Chamber of Commerce, 320 W Broad St; 215/536-3211.

Once a station on the "underground railroad," Quakertown today still retains some of its colonial appearance. In 1798, angered by what they considered an unfair federal tax and incited by one John Fries, Quakertown housewives started greeting tax assessors with pans of hot water. The "hot water" rebellion cooled down when federal troops arrived, but the town switched political parties (from Federalist to Jeffersonian) almost en masse.

What to See and Do

Mennonite Heritage Center. An interpretive video and exhibits including quilts, Pennsylvania German Fraktur, furniture, books, deeds and clothing show the history of local Mennonites through three centuries. (Daily exc Mon) 4 mi S of PA 309 on PA 113, in Harleysville, 565 Yoder Rd. Phone 215/256-3020. **Donation.**

Reading (E-8)

(See also Denver/Adamstown, Hamburg, Kutztown, Lancaster, Pottstown)

Founded 1748 **Pop** 78,380 **Elev** 260 ft **Area code** 610

Information Reading/Berks County Visitors Bureau, VF Factory Outlet Complex, Park Rd & Hill Ave, PO Box 6677, Wyomissing 19610; 610/375-4085 or 800/443-6610.

A city of railroads and industry famous for its superb pretzels, Reading (RED-ing) was the second community in the United States to vote a Socialist government into office; however, the city has not had such a government for many years. Love of music and the thrift and vigor of the "Dutch" are reflected in the character of this unofficial capital of Pennsylvania Dutch Land.

William Penn purchased the land now occupied by Reading from the Lenni-Lenape Native Americans and settled his two sons, Thomas and Richard, on it. They named it Reading (fern meadow) for their home in England. During the Revolution, the citizens of Reading mustered troops for the Continental army, forged cannon and provided a depot for military supplies and a prison for Hessians and British. The hundreds of skilled German craftspeople, plus canal and railroad transportation, ignited Reading's industrial development. Today some of the world's leading industries continue to headquarter here.

What to See and Do

Berks County Heritage Center. Historical interpretive complex. Here are the Gruber Wagon Works (1882), where finely crafted wagons were produced for farm and industry; Wertz's Red Bridge (1867), the longest single-span covered bridge in the state; Deppen Cemetery, with graves of Irish workers who died of "swamp fever" while building the Union Canal; C. Howard Hiester Canal Center, with its collection of canal artifacts. Tours of wagon works and canal center; orientation slide program. (May-Oct, daily exc Mon) 4 mi N via PA 183, then W onto Red Bridge Rd, in Bern Twp. Phone 610/374-8839 or 610/372-8939. ¢¢

Conrad Weiser Homestead. (1729). Restored and furnished house of colonial "ambassador" to the Iroquois nation; springhouse; gravesite; visitor center; picnicking in 26-acre park. (Wed-Sun; closed most hols) 14 mi W via US 422. Phone 610/589-2934. Homestead ¢¢; Grounds **Free.**

Daniel Boone Homestead. Birthplace of Daniel Boone in 1734. Approx 570 acres; includes Boone House, barn, blacksmith shop and sawmill. Picnicking. Nature trails. Youth camping. Visitor's center. (Daily exc Mon; closed some hols) 7 mi E on US 422 to Baumstown, then N on Boone Rd. Phone 610/582-4900. ¢¢

Historical Society of Berks County. Local history exhibits; decorative arts, antiques, transportation displays. (Tues-Sat; closed most hols) 940 Centre Ave. Phone 610/375-4375. ¢¢

Koziar's Christmas Village. Valley set aglow with over 500,000 Christmas lights; Wishing Well Lane; two barns filled with handmade items, decorations; theme exhibits, Santa's Post Office. (Thanksgiving-Dec) 12 mi N via PA 183, in Bernville, 782 Christmas Village Rd. Phone 610/488-1110. ¢¢¢

Mid-Atlantic Air Museum. Aviation museum dedicated to the preservation of vintage aircraft; planes are restored to flying condition by volunteers. Collection of 40 airplanes and helicopters; 20 on public display, including Martin 4-0-4 airliners, B-25 bomber and others. (Daily; closed Jan 1, Thanksgiving, Dec 25) Reading Regional Airport, at PA 183 & Van Reed Rd. Phone 610/372-7333. ¢¢

Outlet Shopping. More than 300 factory outlet stores can be found at five different shopping complexes. For more information, contact Visitors Bureau at 610/375-4085.

Reading Public Museum and Art Gallery. In 25-acre Museum Park with stream. Exhibits of art and science. (Tues-Sun; closed most major hols) 500 Museum Rd. Phone 610/371-5850. ¢¢ Adj is

Planetarium. For schedule and information, phone 610/371-5854. ¢¢

Motels

★ ★ ★ **BEST WESTERN DUTCH COLONY INN.** 4635 Perkiomen Ave (19606). 610/779-2345; FAX 610/779-8348; res: 800/828-2830. 71 rms, 2 story. May-Nov: S $58-$83; D $63-$88; each addl $5; under 18 free; lower rates rest of yr. Crib $5. Pet accepted, some restrictions; $5. TV; cable. Pool; lifeguard. Restaurant (see ANTIQUE AIRPLANE). Rm serv. Bar 11-2 am. Ck-out noon. Coin lndry. Meeting rms. Business servs avail. Valet serv. Sundries. Health club privileges. Lawn games. Microwaves avail. Balconies. Cr cds: A, C, D, DS, ER, MC, V.

D ✔ ⩬ ⋈ 🐾 SC

✔★ **COMFORT INN.** 2200 Stacy Dr (5th St Hwy) (19605). 610/371-0500; FAX 610/478-9421. Web www.comfortinn.com. 60 rms, 2 story. Apr-Oct: S $55-$70; D $55-$75; each addl $5; under 18 free; wkly rates; higher rates: car shows, antique shows; lower rates rest of yr. Crib free. TV; cable (premium), VCR. Complimentary continental bkfst. Restaurant nearby. Ck-out 11 am. Meeting rms. Business servs avail. In-rm modem link. Valet serv. Free airport transportation. Exercise equipt; weight machine, bicycles. Some refrigerators; microwaves avail. Cr cds: A, C, D, DS, ER, JCB, MC, V.

D 🏋 ⋈ 🐾 SC

✔ ★ **ECONO LODGE.** 635 Spring St (19610). 610/378-5105; FAX 610/373-3181. 84 rms, 4 story. Mar-Nov: S, D $48-$65; each addl $5; under 18 free; higher rates Keystone Nationals, Antique Wkends; lower rates rest of yr. Crib free. Pet accepted; $5 daily. TV; cable (premium). Complimentary continental bkfst. Restaurant adj 7 am-10 pm. Ck-out 11 am. Business servs avail. Sundries. Coin lndry. Exercise equipt; bicycles, treadmill. Many refrigerators, microwaves. Cr cds: A, DS, MC, V.

D ✔ 🏋 ⋈ 🐾 SC

★ ★ **HOLIDAY INN-NORTH.** 2545 N 5th St Hwy (19605), at Warren St Bypass. 610/929-4741; FAX 610/929-5237. 138 rms, 2 story. S $55-$175; D $60-$175; each addl $10; under 18 free; some wkend rates. Crib free. Pet accepted. TV; cable (premium), VCR avail. Pool. Restaurant 6:30 am-1 pm, 5-10 pm. Rm serv. Bar 5-11:30 pm, Sun to 11 pm. Ck-out noon. Meeting rms. Business servs avail. In-rm modem link. Valet serv. Sundries. Cr cds: A, C, D, DS, MC, V.

D ✔ ⩬ ⋈ 🐾 SC

★ ★ **INN AT READING.** (1040 Park Rd, Wyomissing 19610) 3 mi W, just off US 422 at Warren St Bypass. 610/372-7811; FAX 610/372-4545; res: 800/383-9713. 250 rms, 1-2 story. S $79-$119; D $89-$119; suites $99-$129; each addl $7; under 18 free; some wkend rates. Crib free. Pet accepted, some restrictions. TV; cable (premium). Pool; poolside serv, lifeguard. Playground. Restaurant 6:30 am-10 pm. Rm serv. Bar 11-1 am; entertainment. Ck-out 11 am. Meeting rms. Business center. In-rm modem link. Bellhops. Valet serv. Sundries. Gift shop. Free airport, bus depot transportation. Tennis privileges. Golf privileges. Exercise equipt; weight machine, bicycles. Picnic tables. Cr cds: A, C, D, DS, MC, V.

D ✔ 🏋🧍 ⩬ ⋈ 🏋 ⋈ 🐾 SC 🚶

Motor Hotels

★ ★ ★ **HOLIDAY INN.** (230 Cherry S (Rte 10), Morgantown 19543) PA Tpke exit 22. 610/286-3000; FAX 610/286-0520. 192 rms, 4 story. S $79-$99; D $89-$109; each addl $10; under 18 free. Crib free. Pet accepted, some restrictions. TV; cable (premium). Indoor pool; whirlpool. Free supervised child's activities, wkends (Jan-Mar); ages 2-12. Restaurant 6:30 am-2 pm, 5-10 pm; Sat, Sun from 5 pm. Rm serv. Bar 5 pm-1 am. Ck-out noon. Meeting rms. Business servs avail. In-rm modem link. Sundries. Exercise equipt; weight machine, bicycles. Some refrigerators. Cr cds: A, C, D, DS, JCB, MC, V.

D ✔ ⩬ 🏋 ⋈ 🐾 SC

★ ★ **SHERATON BERKSHIRE.** 1741 Papermill Rd (19610), US 422 W, Papermill Rd exit. 610/376-3811; FAX 610/375-7562. 254 rms, 5 story. S, D $79-$139; each addl $10; suites $185-$195; studio rms $140-$150; under 18 free; some wkend rates. Crib free. Pet accepted; $50.

TV; cable (premium), VCR avail. Indoor pool; whirlpool, poolside serv, lifeguard. Coffee in rms. Restaurant 6:30 am-10:30 pm. Rm serv. Bar 11:30-2 am; entertainment. Ck-out noon. Meeting rms. Business servs avail. In-rm modem link. Bellhops. Valet serv. Gift shop. Free airport, bus depot transportation. Putting green. Exercise equipt; weights, bicycles, sauna. Some bathrm phones; microwaves avail. Cr cds: A, C, D, DS, JCB, MC, V.

Restaurants

✔★ ★ **ALPENHOF BAVARIAN.** *903 Morgantown Rd (19607), 1¼ mi S of jct US 222.* 610/373-1624. Hrs: 11:30 am-2 pm, 5-8:30 pm; Mon to 2 pm; Sat to 9 pm; Sun 11:30 am-7 pm. Closed Jan 1, Dec 25. Res accepted. German menu. Bar. Semi-a la carte: lunch $3.45-$6.95, dinner $8.75-$19.95. Specializes in schnitzel, sauerbraten. Bavarian Gasthaus with authentic decor. Family-owned. Cr cds: A, MC, V.

★ ★ **ANTIQUE AIRPLANE.** *(See Best Western Dutch Colony Inn Motel)* 610/779-2345. Hrs: 7 am-3 pm, 5-9:30 pm; Sun to 1 pm. Closed Jan 1, Dec 25. Res accepted. Bar. Semi-a la carte: bkfst $2.95-$4.95, lunch $3.99-$5.95, dinner $6.95-$17.95. Child's meals. Specializes in seafood, steak. Salad bar. Casual elegance among aviation theme. Cr cds: A, C, D, DS, ER, MC, V.

★ ★ **GREEN HILLS INN.** *2444 Morgantown Rd.* 610/777-9611. Hrs: 5-9 pm. Closed Sun. Res accepted. French menu. Wine cellar. A la carte entrees: dinner $16.95-$23.95. Specialties: quenelle de brochet, boneless squab with honey ginger glaze, grilled veal chop with wild mushrooms. Family-owned. Cr cds: A, C, D, DS, JCB, MC, V.

★ ★ **MOSELEM SPRINGS INN.** *(RD 4, Box 4035, Fleetwood 19522) 12 mi N on US 222.* 610/944-8213. Hrs: 11:30 am-9 pm; Fri, Sat to 10 pm; Sun, hols to 8 pm. Closed Dec 24, 25. Res accepted. Pennsylvania Dutch menu. Bar. Semi-a la carte: lunch $6-$12.95, dinner $11.25-$20. Child's meals. Specializes in smoked meats, fresh seafood. Built in 1852; six distinct dining areas with individual decor, including the elegant Presidential Room. Cr cds: A, C, D, MC, V.

Scranton (C-9)

(See also Carbondale, Pocono Mountains, Wilkes-Barre)

Settled 1771 **Pop** 81,805 **Elev** 754 ft **Area code** 717 **E-mail** pntvb@epix .net **Web** www.visitnepa.org

Information Pennsylvania Northeast Territory Visitors Bureau, 100 Terminal Rd, Ste 216, Avoca 18641; 717/457-1320 or 800/22-WELCOME.

The first settlers here found a Monsey Native American Village on the site. In 1840, George and Seldon Scranton built five iron furnaces using the revolutionary method of firing with anthracite coal instead of charcoal. Manufacture of iron and steel remained an important industry until 1901, when the mills moved to Lake Erie to ease transportation problems.

After World War II, Scranton thoroughly revamped its economy when faced with depletion of the anthracite coal mines, which for more than a century had fired its forges. Scranton's redevelopment drew nationwide attention and served as a model for problem cities elsewhere. Today, Scranton is the home of electronic and printing industries and is host to several major trucking firm terminals.

What to See and Do

Catlin House (1912). Headquarters of Lackawanna Historical Society; period furnishings (colonial-1900s), historic exhibits, antiques; research

library (fee). (Tues-Fri, also Sat afternoons; closed hols) 232 Monroe Ave. Phone 717/344-3841. **Free.**

Lackawanna County Stadium. Open-air stadium/civic arena seats 11,000. Home of AAA baseball, high school and college football and marching band competitions. (Apr-Nov) Exit 51 off I-81, Montage Mountain Rd. For schedule phone 717/969-2255. ¢¢-¢¢¢

Montage Ski Area. Quad, double, 3 triple chairlifts; school, rentals; snowmaking; bar, restaurant; lodge. Vertical drop 1,000 ft. Night skiing. More than 130 acres of trails set in 400 acres of mountainside. (Early Dec-late Mar, daily) Summer activities include water slides, batting cages, amphitheater (late June-Labor Day). S on I-81, exit 51, follow signs. Phone 717/969-7669. ¢¢¢¢¢

Nay Aug Park. More than 35 acres with memorials to pioneer days. Picnicking, swimming pool (fee), walking trail, refreshment stands and the "Pioneer," a gravity railroad car dating back to 1850; wkend concerts (summer). (Daily) Arthur Ave & Mulberry St in E Scranton. Phone 717/348-4186. In park is

Everhart Museum. Permanent collections include 19th- and 20th-century American art; Dorflinger glass; Native American, Oriental and primitive art; natural history displays, including Dinosaur Hall. Gift shop. (Daily exc Mon; closed some hols) Phone 717/346-8370. **Donation.**

Anthracite Heritage Museum. History and culture of anthracite region. Other affiliated parts of the complex are the Iron Furnaces; Museum of Anthracite Mining (see ASHLAND), with emphasis on the technology of the industry, and the 19th-century miners' village of Eckley, near Hazleton (see). (Daily; closed some hols) Keyser Ave in McDade Park. Phone 717/963-4804. ¢¢

Lackawanna Coal Mine Tour. Underground coal mine 300 ft below ground shows world of anthracite miners. Conditions are authentic (damp, dark, slippery and cold); dress appropriately. Above-ground facilities include a "shifting shanty" exhibit room with photo-mural graphic displays, mine artifacts and video presentations; gift shop; restaurant. (Apr-Nov, daily; closed Thanksgiving) McDade Park. Phone 717/963-MINE or 800/238-7245. ¢¢¢

Scranton Iron Furnaces. Partially restored site of four anthracite-fired iron furnaces built 1848-1857 and used until 1902. Visitor center, outdoor exhibits. Self-guided tours (daily). Guided tours (late May-early Sept, Mon-Thurs). 159 Cedar Ave. Phone 717/963-3208. **Free.**

Steamtown National Historic Site. Site with large collection of steam locomotives and other memorabilia located in an authentic freight yard. Steam train ride through yard (Memorial Day-Dec; daily). 25-mi train excursion (June-Oct, Sat & Sun). 150 S Washington Ave. Phone 717/961-2033 (information) or 717/961-2035 (tickets). Excursion ¢¢¢

Motels

★ ★ **DAYS INN.** *(1226 O'Neill Hwy, Dunmore 18512) 4 mi N on I-81, exit 55A.* 717/348-6101; FAX 717/348-5064. 90 rms, 4 story. S $59.99-$83.99; D $61.99-$99.99; suites $78.99-$99.99; under 17 free; wkend, hol rates; higher rates Pocono NASCAR. Crib free. Pet accepted; $3. TV; cable (premium), VCR avail. Complimentary continental bkfst. Restaurant adj open 24 hrs. Ck-out 11 am. Business servs avail. Valet serv. Refrigerators. Cr cds: A, C, D, DS, ER, MC, V.

★ ★ **HAMPTON INN.** *Montage Mountain Rd & Davis St (18507), near Avoco Intl Airport.* 717/342-7002; FAX 717/342-7012. 129 rms, 4 story. S $72-$82; D $77-$87; suites $90-$175; under 19 free; wkend rates; ski plans; higher rates: NASCAR, hols. Crib free. TV; cable (premium). Indoor pool; whirlpool. Complimentary continental bkfst. Ck-out noon. Meeting rms. Business servs avail. Valet serv. Sundries. Free airport, bus depot transportation. Downhill ski 2 mi. Exercise equipt; bicycle, rowers. Picnic tables. Cr cds: A, C, D, DS, MC, V.

★ ★ **HOLIDAY INN-EAST.** *(200 Tigue St, Dunmore 18512) I-380 exit 1, just E of I-81.* 717/343-4771; FAX 717/343-5171. 139 rms, 2-3 story. S, D $79-$89; each addl $10; suites $145-$175; under 18 free; some wkend rates; ski plan. Crib free. Pet accepted. TV; cable. Pool. Restaurant

6:30 am-10 pm. Rm serv. Bar noon-2 am. Ck-out noon. Meeting rms. Business servs avail. In-rm modem link. Valet serv. Cr cds: A, C, D, DS, ER, JCB, MC, V.

[D] [✦] [≈] [⊁] [🖐] [SC]

Motor Hotels

★ ★ ★ **INN AT NICHOLS VILLAGE.** *(1101 Northern Blvd, Clarks Summit 18411) 3 mi N on I-81, exit 58. 717/587-1135; FAX 717/586-7140; res: 800/642-2215.* 135 rms, 4 story. S, D $98-$150; each addl $10; under 18 free. Crib free. TV; cable. Indoor pool; lifeguard. Restaurant 6 am-10 pm. Rm serv. Bar 5-11 pm. Ck-out noon. Meeting rms. Business servs avail. In-rm modem link. Sundries. Free airport transportation. Exercise equipt; weights, bicycles, sauna. Rec rm. 12 acres include over 1,000 rhododendrons; forestland. Cr cds: A, C, D, DS, MC, V.

[D] [≈] [🏋] [⊁] [🖐] [SC]

★ ★ **RAMADA INN.** *300 Meadow Ave (18505). 717/344-9811; FAX 717/344-7799.* 125 rms, 6 story. S $59-$69; D $69-$79; each addl $10; suites $135-$150; under 13 free; higher rates special events. Crib free. TV; cable (premium). Pool; lifeguard. Restaurant 6 am-10 pm. Rm serv. Bar 11-2 am; entertainment Tues-Sun. Ck-out noon. Meeting rms. Business servs avail. Valet serv. Free airport, bus depot transportation. Cr cds: A, C, D, DS, MC, V.

[D] [≈] [⊁] [🖐] [SC]

Hotel

★ ★ ★ **RADISSON LACKAWANNA STATION.** *700 Lackawanna Ave (18503), I-81 exit 53. 717/342-8300; FAX 717/347-6888.* 145 rms, 6 story. S $99; D $109; each addl $10; suites $119-$300; studio rms $109; wkend package plans. Crib free. TV; cable. Restaurant 7 am-10 pm. Bar 11-2 am. Ck-out noon. Meeting rms. Business servs avail. In-rm modem link. Free airport, bus depot transportation. Downhill/x-country ski 4 mi. Exercise equipt; weights, bicycles, sauna, steam rm. Whirlpool. Some refrigerators, in-rm whirlpools. Located in historic Lackawanna RR station building. Cr cds: A, C, D, DS, JCB, MC, V.

[D] [≋] [🏋] [⊁] [🖐] [SC]

Resort

✔ ★ ★ **SHADOWBROOK.** *(US 6, Tunkhannock 18657) 25 mi NW on US 6. 717/836-2151; FAX 717/836-5655; res: 800/955-0295.* 55 rms, 2 story. S $50-$85; D $60-$95; each addl $12; kit. units $80-$90; under 12 free. Crib $8/day. TV; cable (premium). Pool; sauna, poolside serv, lifeguard. Complimentary continental bkfst. Restaurant 6 am-10 pm. Rm serv 5-8 pm. Box lunches, picnics. Bar 11-2 am; entertainment Wed, Fri-Sun. Ck-out noon, ck-in 2 pm. Gift shop. Grocery, coin lndry 2 mi. Meeting rms. Business servs avail. Sports dir. 18-hole golf, pro. Hiking. Game rm. Exercise rm; instructor, weights, bicycles, steam rm. Some refrigerators. Balconies. Picnic tables. Cr cds: A, C, D, DS, MC, V.

[✦] [🏋] [≈] [🏋] [⊁] [🖐] [SC]

Restaurants

★ **COOPER'S SEAFOOD HOUSE.** *701 N Washington Ave (18509). 717/346-6883.* Hrs: 11 am-midnight. Closed major hols. Bar 4 pm-1 am; Sun to 11 pm. Complete meals: lunch $5.99-$9.99, dinner $9.99-$28.99. Child's meals. Specializes in seafood. Pianist, vocalist exc Mon. Nautical decor. Cr cds: A, DS, MC, V.

[D]

★ **FIREPLACE.** *(US 6, Tunkhannock) 15 mi N on US 11, W on US 6, 3 mi W of Tunkhannock. 717/836-9662.* Hrs: 11 am-10 pm; Fri, Sat to 11 pm. Closed Dec 25. Bar. A la carte entrees: lunch, dinner $2-$21.95. Child's meals. Specializes in beef, chicken. Cr cds: A, D, MC, V.

Shamokin Dam (D-7)

Settled 1790 **Pop** 1,690 **Elev** 500 ft **Area code** 717 **Zip** 17876

Motel

★ **DAYS INN.** *On US 15, 11. 717/743-1111; FAX 717/743-1190.* 151 rms, 2 story. S $50-$60; D $55-$70; each addl $5; under 18 free. Crib free. Pet accepted. TV; cable. Pool; lifeguard. Restaurant 7 am-9 pm. Bar from 5 pm; Ck-out noon. Meeting rms. Business servs avail. In-rm modem link. Valet serv. Sundries. Cr cds: A, C, D, DS, JCB, MC, V.

[D] [✦] [≈] [⊁] [🖐] [SC]

Inn

★ ★ ★ **INN AT OLDE NEW BERLIN.** *(321 Market St, New Berlin 17855-0390) 8 mi W on PA 304. 717/966-0321; FAX 717/966-9557.* Web www.newberlin-inn.com. 5 rms, 3 with shower only, 2 story. MAP: S, D $85-$175; each addl $20; higher rates special events. Crib $5. Complimentary full bkfst. Restaurant 10 am-2 pm, 4:30-8:30 pm; closed Mon, Tues. Ck-out noon, ck-in 3 pm. Gift shop. Garden setting. Cr cds: DS, MC, V.

[D] [⊁] [🖐]

Sharon (C-1)

(See also Mercer)

Settled 1802 **Pop** 17,493 **Elev** 998 ft **Area code** 724 **Zip** 16146
Information Mercer County Convention & Visitors Bureau, 835 Perry Hwy, Mercer 16137; 800/637-2370.

In the heart of the rich Shenango Valley, Sharon is a busy industrial city that started with a lonely mill on the banks of the Shenango River. Steel, fabrication of steel products and manufacture of electric transformers are a major part of the economic base. The Shenango Dam and its reservoir are northeast of town, near Sharpsville, and offer many recreational activities.

What to See and Do

Shenango Lake. Swimming, waterskiing; fishing, hunting; boating (ramps). Picnicking. More than 300 tent & trailer sites (mid-May-Labor Day; rest of Sept, reduced number of sites; electric hookups addl). 6 mi N of I-80, PA 18. Phone 724/646-1115(camping); 724/962-7746 or 724/646-1124 (general information). Camping per night ¢¢¢-¢¢¢¢

Annual Event

The Small Ships Review. Downtown. Parade of ships, entertainment, fireworks, food. Phone 724/981-3123. July.

Motel

★ **COLLINS.** *(4036 E State St, Hermitage 16148) 4 mi E on US 62. 724/981-6150.* 13 rms with shower only. S $39-$44; D $42-$55; each addl $5; higher rates special events. Crib $6. TV; cable. Restaurant nearby 11-2 am; closed Sun. Ck-out 10 am. Gift shop. 9-hole golf privileges. 2 refrigerators. Cr cds: MC, V.

[🏋] [⊁] [🖐]

Inn

★ ★ ★ ★ **TARA-A COUNTRY INN.** *(3665 Valley View Rd, Clark 16113) I-80 exit 1N, 7 mi on PA 18N exit PA 258.* 724/962-3535; FAX 724/962-3250; res: 800/782-2803. This antebellum mansion, dating from 1854, contains a library and in-room whirlpools. Its rooms are furnished with antiques and works of art. The formal gardens containing 10 Remington sculptures overlook picturesque Lake Schenago. 27 rms, 2 story. MAP: S, D $180-$355; wkly rates; package plans; higher rates Sat. Adults only. TV; cable. 3 pools, 2 indoor; whirlpool. Dining rms 11 am-8 pm. Ck-out noon, ck-in 3 pm. Meeting rm. Business servs avail. In-rm modem link. Croquet court. Some in-rm whirlpools. Cr cds: A, DS, MC, V.

Restaurants

✔★ ★ **HOT ROD CAFE AND TULLY'S GRILLE.** *101 Chestnut St* 724/981-3123. Web www.lubewings.com. Hrs: 4 pm-2 am; Sun noon-midnight. Hot Rod Cafe closed Mon. Bar. Semi-a la carte: dinner $8.99-$15.99. Child's meals. Specializes in char-grilled steak. Salad bar. Entertainment Mon, Thurs-Sat. Outdoor dining. 3 dining rooms in a converted, restored railroad depot. Family-owned. Cr cds: A, D, DS, MC, V.

★ **QUAKER STEAK & LUBE.** *101 Chestnut St.* 724/981-7221. Web www.lubewings.com. Hrs: 11-1 am; Thurs-Sat to 2 am; Sun noon-1 am. Bar. Semi-a la carte: lunch $3.99-$12, dinner $5.50-$18. Child's meals. Specializes in chicken wings, steak, hamburgers. Salad bar. Outdoor dining. Former gas station; vintage automobiles, license plates, memorabilia. Casual dining. Cr cds: A, D, DS, MC, V.

Shartlesville (E-8)

(For accommodations see Reading; also see Hamburg)

Pop 300 (est) **Elev** 560 ft **Area code** 610 **Zip** 19554

What to See and Do

Roadside America. This miniature "village" consists of O-gauge trains, villages and scenes, with 66 miniature displays re-creating 200 yrs of life in rural America. Started in 1903, displays now cover 6,000 sq ft. (Daily; closed Dec 25) Just off US 22, Shartlesville exit at I-78. Phone 610/488-6241. ¢¢

Restaurants

★ **BLUE MOUNTAIN FAMILY RESTAURANT.** *I-78 exit 8.* 610/438-0353. Hrs: 6:30 am-10 pm. Closed Jan 1, Dec 25. Res accepted. Continental menu. Bar. Semi-a la carte: bkfst $1.95-$4.95, lunch $2.75-$6.95, dinner $5.95-$12.95. Child's meals. Specializes in fresh seafood, Greek, Italian dishes. Salad bar. Own baking. Cr cds: A, MC, V.

★ **HAAG'S HOTEL RESTAURANT.** *Main & Third Sts.* 610/488-6692. Hrs: 7:30 am-7:30 pm. Closed Dec 25. Res accepted. Bar 11:00 am-midnight. Complete meals: bkfst $1.75-$6.50, lunch $4.75-$7, dinner $7-$13. Buffet: bkfst $6.50, lunch, dinner $13. Specializes in Pennsylvania Dutch cooking, family style dinners. Own pies. In former hotel (1914); early-American decor. Cr cds: MC, V.

Shawnee on Delaware (D-10)

(See also Bushkill, Stroudsburg)

Pop 400 (est) **Elev** 320 ft **Area code** 717 **Zip** 18356

Information Pocono Mts Vacation Bureau, 1004 Main St, Stroudsburg 18360; 717/424-6050; for free brochures phone 800/POCONOS.

What to See and Do

Delaware Water Gap (see). 6 mi E along Delaware River.

Shawnee Mountain Ski Area. 9 chairlifts; patrol, school, rentals; snowmaking; cafeteria, bar; nursery. 23 slopes and trails; longest run 1 mi; vertical drop 700 ft. (Dec-Mar, daily) Night skiing. Half-day rates. 6 mi N of I-80, exit 52, follow signs. Phone 717/421-7231 or 800/233-4218 (ski report). ¢¢¢¢¢

Resort

★ ★ **SHAWNEE INN.** *E on I-80, exit 52.* 717/421-1500; FAX 717/424-9168; res: 800/742-9633. 103 rms, 3 story. MAP, May-Oct: S $129; D $179; suites $50 addl; kit. units (Nov-Apr) $120; EP: S, D $89-$115; under 8 free; some wkly, wkend rates; higher rates Christmas hols; lower rates rest of yr. Crib free. Serv charge 10%. TV; cable, VCR avail. 4 pools, 1 indoor; wading pool, lifeguard. Playground. Supervised child's activities. Dining rm 7 am-9 pm. Snack bar. Picnics. Bar hrs vary. Ck-out noon, ck-in 4 pm. Coin lndry. Grocery, package store 4 mi. Meeting rms. Lighted tennis, pro (summer). 27-hole golf, pro, putting green, driving range, miniature golf. Downhill/x-country ski 3 mi. Lawn games. Soc dir; entertainment. Rec rm. Game rm. Cr cds: A, C, D, DS, MC, V.

Somerset (F-3)

(See also Johnstown, Ligonier)

Settled 1773 **Pop** 6,454 **Elev** 2,190 ft **Area code** 814 **Zip** 15501 **E-mail** somchmbr@shol.com **Web** www.shol.com/smrst/somrst.html

Information Information Center, 601 N Center Ave; 814/445-6431.

Somerset, a county seat, is also the marketing place for farms, lumber mills and coal mines in the area. James Whitcomb Riley described the countryside in his poem *'Mongst the Hills of Somerset.* The county offers fishing, boating, hiking, biking, camping and skiing.

What to See and Do

Hidden Valley Ski Area. 8 lifts; patrol, school, rentals; snowmaking; cafeteria, restaurant, bars; nursery. Longest run 5,280 ft; vertical drop 610 ft; 16 slopes (Dec-Mar, daily). 30 mi of cross-country trails (rentals). Shuttle service. Conference center, lodging. Yr-round facilities, activities. 12 mi W of PA Tpke Somerset exit 10; 8 mi E of PA Tpke Donegal exit 9, on PA 31. Phone 814/443-2600. ¢¢¢¢¢

Mt Davis. Highest point in state (3,213 ft). 26 mi S on US 219 to Salisbury, then W on unnumbered road. Phone 412/238-9533.

Somerset Historical Center. Museum exhibits on rural life; outdoor display includes log house, log barn, covered bridge, sugarhouse. Bus tour (fee). (Wed-Sun; closed most hols) 5 mi N on PA 985. Phone 814/445-6077. ¢¢

State parks.

Laurel Hill. Approx 3,900 acres. Swimming beach, snack bar; hunting; boating (mooring, launching). Hiking. Snowmobiling, ice fishing. Picnicking. Tent & trailer sites. Standard fees. 8 mi W on PA 31, then SW on unnumbered road. Phone 814/445-7725.

Kooser. Approx 220 acres. Four-acre lake with fishing; swimming beach (Memorial Day-Labor Day). Cross-country skiing, sledding. Picnicking. Tent & trailer sites, cabins. Standard fees. 9 mi NW on PA 31. Phone 814/445-8673.

Annual Events

Maple Festival. Festival Park in Meyersdale. Phone 814/634-0213. Apr.

Somerfest. Laurel Arts/Phillip Dressler Center for the Arts. German festival: dancing, competitions, entertainment, food, tours. Phone 814/443-2433. Mid-July.

Mountain Craft Days. Somerset Historical Center. More than 150 traditional craft demonstrations; antique exhibits; entertainment. Early Sept.

Farmers' and Threshermen's Jubilee. 9 mi SW via PA 281, in New Centerville. Equipment demonstrations; tractor-pulling, horseshoe-pitching, tobacco-spitting contests; antique car show and flea market; food. Early Sept.

Springs Folk Festival. On PA 669, in Springs. Crafts demonstrations include bread baking, wheat weaving, basket and broom making, candle dipping, quilt stitching; entertainment featuring banjo and fiddle music; pioneer exhibits on forest trail; maple sugaring, apple butter boiling, log hewing; museum adj with antique tools, furnishings, historical artifacts. Phone 814/662-4158 or 814/662-4298. Early Oct.

Motels

✔★ **BUDGET HOST INN.** 799 N Center Ave. 814/445-7988. 28 rms, 2 story. S $40-$50; D $45-$55; each addl $5. Crib $4. Pet accepted. TV; cable (premium). Complimentary coffee in lobby. Restaurant nearby. Ck-out 11 am. Downhill ski 10 mi; x-country ski 13 mi. Cr cds: A, C, D, DS, MC, V.

✔★ **DOLLAR INN.** 1146 N Center Ave, PA 601. 814/445-2977; FAX 814/443-6205. 15 rms. S $25-$40; D $30-$50; each addl $5; under 10 free; wkly, wkend rates; higher rates special events. Crib $5. Pet accepted, some restrictions; $5. TV; cable (premium). Complimentary coffee in lobby. Restaurant nearby. Ck-out 11 am. Business servs avail. Some refrigerators. Cr cds: A, D, DS, MC, V.

★ ★ **ECONOMY INN.** RD 2, Box 5, PA Tpke exit 10. 814/445-4144; FAX 814/445-3763. 19 rms. S $35-$45; D $40-$55; each addl $5; under 12 free; higher rates: special events, ski season. TV; cable (premium), VCR. Indoor pool. Playground. Restaurant adj. Ck-out 11 am. Coin lndry. Miniature golf. Exercise equipt; weight machines, rower. Game rm. Refrigerators, microwaves. Cr cds: A, DS, MC, V.

✔★ **KNIGHTS INN.** 585 Ramada Rd, exit 10 off I-70/76, at PA Tpke entrance. 814/445-8933; FAX 814/443-9745; res: 800/843-5644. 112 rms, 10 kit. units. S $39.95-$59.95; D $46.95-$69.95; each addl $10; kit. units $43.95-$52.95; under 18 free; wkly rates; higher rates Dec-Mar wkends. Crib free. Pet accepted, some restrictions. TV; cable (premium), VCR avail (movies). Pool. Complimentary coffee in lobby. Restaurant nearby. Ck-out noon. Coin lndry. Business servs avail. Downhill ski 15 mi. Cr cds: A, C, D, DS, MC, V.

Motor Hotel

★ ★ ★ **RAMADA INN.** At PA Tpke exit 10. 814/443-4646; FAX 814/443-7539. 152 rms, 2 story. S $64-$78; D $74-$88; suites $95-$125; under 18 free; some wkend rates. Crib free. Pet accepted. TV; cable (premium). Indoor pool; whirlpool, sauna, poolside serv, lifeguard. Restaurant 6:30 am-2 pm, 5-10 pm; Sun 7-11 am. Rm serv. Bar 2 pm-2 am; Sun to 9 pm; entertainment Tues-Sat. Ck-out noon. Meeting

rms. Business servs avail. Bellhops. Valet serv. Sundries. Downhill/x-country ski 12 mi. Health club privileges. Game rm. Cr cds: A, C, D, DS, JCB, MC, V.

Inns

★ ★ ★ **BAYBERRY.** 611 N Center Ave, on PA 601. 814/445-8471. 11 rms, shower only, 2 story. No A/C. No rm phones. S $40-$50; D $45-$55; each addl $10; suite $75; min stay some hol wkends. Children over 12 yrs only. TV in sitting rm; VCR. Complimentary continental bkfst; afternoon refreshments. Restaurant nearby. Ck-out 11 am, ck-in 3 pm. Luggage handling. Concierge serv. Downhill/x-country ski 18 mi. Brick house built 1902. Cr cds: A, DS, MC, V.

★ ★ ★ **THE INN AT GEORGIAN PLACE.** 800 Georgian Place Dr. 814/443-1043; FAX 814/443-3047. 11 rms, 3 story, 2 suites. S, D $95-$140; each addl $10; suites $165-$180. Children over 5 yrs only. Pet accepted, some restrictions. TV; cable (premium), VCR (movies). Complimentary full bkfst. Restaurant noon-4 pm. Rm serv. Ck-out noon, ck-in 3 pm. Business servs avail. Luggage handling. Valet serv. Concierge serv. Downhill/x-country ski ski 12 mi. Some fireplaces. Georgian mansion built in 1915; chandeliers, marble foyer. Cr cds: A, D, DS, MC, V.

Resort

★ ★ ★ **HIDDEN VALLEY.** (1 Craighead Dr, Hidden Valley 15502) PA Tpke exit 9, (then 8 mi E on PA 31) or exit 10 (then 12 mi W on PA 31). 814/443-6000; FAX 814/443-1907; res: 800/458-0175. Web www.hidden valleyresort.com. 206 units, some A/C, 2-3 story. Mid-Dec-mid-Mar: S $120-$180; D $222-$350; each addl $30; under 13 free; ski, golf packages; MAP avail; lower rates rest of yr. Crib free. TV; cable (premium). 4 pools, 1 indoor; whirlpool, lifeguard. Playground. Supervised child's activities (June-Sept). Dining rms 7 am-10 pm. Bars 11-1 am; entertainment. Ck-out noon, ck-in 4 pm. Grocery. Package store. Convention facilities. Business servs avail. Bellhops. Valet serv. Gift shop. Airport transportation. Sports dir. Lighted tennis, pro. 18-hole golf, greens fee $49-$59, pro, putting green, driving range. Boats. Downhill/x-country ski on site. Hiking. Soc dir. Exercise equipt; weight machine, bicycles, sauna. Fireplaces; microwaves avail. Balconies. Picnic tables. Located in scenic Laurel Highlands mountain area. Cr cds: A, C, D, DS, MC, V.

Restaurants

★ **COUNTRY COTTAGE.** (2817 New Centerville Rd, New Centerville 15557) 7 mi S on PA 281, near New Centerville. 814/926-4078. Hrs: 10:30 am-9 pm. Closed major hols. Res accepted. Semi-a la carte: bkfst $2.50-$4.25, lunch $2.50-$4.50, dinner $4.95-$6.95. Child's meals. Specialties: pot pies, roast turkey, grilled chicken salad. Own pies. Country decor; gift shop with local products and crafts. No cr cds accepted.

✔★ ★ **OAKHURST TEA ROOM.** 2409 Glades Pike, 6 mi W on PA 31. 814/443-2897. Hrs: 11 am-10 pm; Sun to 8 pm. Closed Mon; Dec 25. Bar. Semi-a la carte: lunch $3-$7. Complete meals: lunch, dinner $10.50-$26. Buffet (Tues-Sat): lunch $6.95, dinner $10.50. Sun brunch $8.95. Child's meals. Specializes in waffles, own noodles in chicken broth. Salad bar. Outdoor dining. Early Amer decor. Fireplace. Family-owned. Cr cds: A, DS, MC, V.

★ ★ **PINE GRILL.** 800 N Center Ave. 814/445-2102. Hrs: 7 am-10 pm. Closed Dec 25. Res accepted. Bar. Semi-a la carte: bkfst $1.50-$4.50, lunch $3-$14.50. Child's meals. Specializes in fresh seafood, grilled steak, gourmet pasta. Early Amer decor; artwork. Opened 1941. Cr cds: A, MC, V.

State College (D-5)

(See also Bellefonte)

Settled 1859 **Pop** 38,923 **Elev** 1,154 ft **Area code** 814 **E-mail** cccvb @visitpennstate.org **Web** www.visitpennstate.org

Information Center County Visitor & Convention Bureau, 1402 S Atherton St, 16801; 814/231-1400 or 800/358-5466.

The home of Pennsylvania State University, and principally concerned with services to this institution, this borough is near the geographic center of the state. In the beautiful Nittany Valley, State College is surrounded by farmland famous for its production of oats and swine. Iron ore was discovered just east of town in 1790, and many iron furnaces later sprang up.

What to See and Do

Columbus Chapel—Boal Mansion Museum. The mansion has been the Boal family home since 1789 and includes original furnishings, china, tools and weapons. Colonel Theodore Davis Boal, who outfitted his own troop for World War I, lived here. The 16th-century chapel belonged to the family of Christopher Columbus in Spain and was brought here in 1909 by Boal relatives. It contains religious items and Renaissance and baroque art, as well as an admiral's desk and explorer's cross that belonged to Columbus himself. Summer concerts on grounds. (Daily exc Tues) 4 mi E on US 322, in Boalsburg. Phone 814/466-6210. Mansion **¢¢**

Mount Nittany Vineyard & Winery. Stone-faced, chalet-style building nestled on southern slopes of Mt Nittany. Tasting rm offers variety of wines and view of large pond, vineyard and mountains. Group tastings (by appt). (Fri-Sun; closed major hols, also Jan) 7 mi E on US 322, E on PA 45, N on Linden Hall Rd. Phone 814/466-6373. **Free.**

Penn's Cave. A 1-hr, 1-mi boat trip through cavern; stalactites, stalagmites; plus walk-through wildlife sanctuary. Picnic area; airplane rides; visitor center; gift shop, restaurant. (Mid-Feb-Nov, daily) NE on PA 26, SE on PA 144, then 5 mi E of Centre Hall on PA 192. Phone 814/364-1664. **¢¢¢**

Pennsylvania Military Museum. On grounds of 28th Division Shrine; dioramas; battle exhibits and equipment from the Revolutionary War to the present. Audiovisual program; military bookstore. (Daily exc Mon; closed some hols) 4 mi E on US 322, in Boalsburg. Phone 814/466-6263. **¢¢**

Pennsylvania State University (1855). (39,000 students) Approx 290 major buildings on a 5,005-acre campus; it is the land-grant institution of Pennsylvania. On US 322 in University Park. Phone 814/865-4700. On campus are

Old Main (1929). Present building, on site of original Old Main (1863), uses many of the original stones; topped by lofty bell tower. Here are Henry Varnum Poor's colorful frescoes. (Mon-Fri; closed major hols) E of Mall near Pollock Rd. Phone 814/865-2501. **Free.**

Earth and Mineral Sciences Museum. Exhibitions of ores, gems and fossils; automated displays; art gallery. (Mon-Fri; closed major hols) Steidle Building on Pollock Rd. Phone 814/865-6427. **Free.**

"Ag Hill," The College of Agriculture. Showplace for state's dairy industry includes the dairy center, off Park Rd near stadium, with five herds of cows, automatic milking equipment (daily). The creamery, Curtain Rd, has retail salesroom for cheeses, milk, cream, ice cream (daily; closed major hols). Also test flower gardens off Park Rd near East Halls (July-Sept). **Free.**

Whipple Dam State Park. Approx 250 acres. Swimming beach; fishing, hunting; boating (launching, mooring). Hiking. Snowmobiling, ice-skating, ice fishing. Picnicking, snack bar. Standard fees. 10 mi S on PA 26, then 1 mi E on unnumbered road. Phone 814/667-3808.

Annual Events

Memorial Day Celebration. In Boalsburg. Celebrate the holiday in the birthplace of Memorial Day. Phone 814/231-1400.

Central Pennsylvania Festival of the Arts. Open-air display of visual and performing arts; indoor exhibits; demonstrations of arts and crafts; food booths. Phone 814/237-3682. Mid-July.

Centre County Grange Fair. PA 144S, at Grange Park in Centre Hall. Exhibits, livestock show, rides, concessions, entertainment. Phone 814/364-9674. Last wk Aug.

Motels

(Rates higher football, art festival & special wkends; may be 2-day min)

★ ★ ★ **AUTOPORT.** *1405 S Atherton St (US 322 Business) (16801).* 814/237-7666; FAX 814/237-7456; res: 800/932-7678. E-mail autoport@lazerlink; web www.autoport.statecollege.com. 86 rms, 3 story, 12 kit. units. S $55-$65; D $59-$69; each addl $5; suites $69-$85; under 16 free; wkly, wkend rates; higher rates special events. Crib free. TV; cable (premium), VCR avail (movies avail). Heated pool; lifeguard. Restaurant 6 am-11 pm; dining rm 11:30 am-3 pm, 5-10 pm. Bar 11-2 am; Sun to midnight; entertainment Wed-Sat. Ck-out 11 am. Coin lndry. Meeting rms. Business servs avail. In-rm modem link. Sundries. Downhill ski 4 mi. Rms vary. Cr cds: A, C, D, DS, MC, V.

D ⊅ ≈ ⊠ ⋈ ⋈ **SC**

★ ★ **HAMPTON INN.** *1101 E College Ave (16801).* 814/231-1590; FAX 814/238-7320. Web www.hampton-inn.com. 121 rms, 3 story. S $59-$74; D $66-$81; suites $71-$78; under 18 free; ski, golf plans. Crib free. TV; cable (premium). Heated pool; lifeguard. Complimentary continental bkfst. Restaurant adj. Meeting rm. Valet serv. Sundries. Airport transportation. Downhill/x-country ski 5 mi. Picnic tables. Cr cds: A, C, D, DS, ER, MC, V.

D ⊅ ≈ ⊠ ⋈ ⋈ **SC**

★ ★ ★ **RAMADA INN.** *1450 S Atherton St (US 322 Business) (16801).* 814/238-3001; FAX 814/237-1345. 28 rms, 2 story. S $65-$72; D $72-$79; each addl $7; suites $95; under 19 free. Crib free. Pet accepted. TV; cable (premium), VCR avail. 2 pools; lifeguard. Restaurant 7 am-2 pm, 5-10 pm. Rm serv. Bar 2 pm-2 am. Ck-out noon. Coin lndry. Meeting rms. Business servs avail. In-rm modem link. Exercise equipt; treadmill, bicycle. Health club privileges. Game rm. Microwaves avail. Cr cds: A, C, D, DS, JCB, MC, V.

D ⋈ ≈ ⋈ ⊠ ⋈ **SC**

✔ ★ **RODEWAY INN.** *1040 N Atherton St (US 322) (16803).* 814/238-6783; FAX 814/238-4519. 29 rms, 3 with shower only, 2 story. S $39-$69; D $44-$69; each addl $5; under 16 free; wkly rates; higher rates special events. Crib $6. TV; cable. Complimentary coffee in lobby. Restaurant nearby. Ck-out 11 am. Some refrigerators. Cr cds: A, C, D, DS, JCB, MC, V.

⊠ ⋈ **SC**

★ **STEVENS.** *1275 N Atherton St (US 322 Business) (16803).* 814/238-2438; FAX 814/238-7548. 18 rms, 17 with shower only, 2 story. S $33-$38; D $38-$48; each addl $4; family rates; higher rates special events (2-day min). Crib $4. TV; cable (premium). Complimentary coffee in lobby. Restaurant adj 6 am-midnight. Ck-out 11 am. Downhill ski 4 mi; x-country ski 1 mi. Cr cds: A, D, DS, MC, V.

≈ ⊠ ⋈ **SC**

Motor Hotel

★ ★ **DAYS INN-PENN STATE.** *240 S Pugh St (16801).* 814/238-8454; FAX 814/234-3377. 184 rms, 6 story. S $50-$95; D $60-$105; each addl $10; suites $150; under 18 free; some wkend rates; higher rates special events. Crib free. Pet accepted, some restrictions. TV; cable. Indoor pool; lifeguard. Complimentary continental bkfst Mon-Fri. Restaurant 6:30 am-midnight; Sun from 8 am. Rm serv. Bar 11-2 am;

entertainment. Ck-out noon. Meeting rms. Business center. In-rm modem link. Bellhops. Valet serv. Sundries. Free airport transportation. Exercise rm; instructor, weight machine, bicycles, sauna. Rec rm. Game rm. Refrigerators avail. Cr cds: A, C, D, DS, MC, V.

Hotel

★ ★ ★ **THE ATHERTON.** *125 S Atherton St (US 322 Business) (16801).* 814/231-2100; FAX 814/237-1130. E-mail atherton97@aol.com; web www.atherton.statecollege.com. 150 rms, 7 story. S $75-$95; D $85-$105; each addl $10; suites $165; under 18 free; higher rates special events. Crib free. TV; cable (premium). Restaurant 5 am-10 pm. Bar 2 pm-2 am. Ck-out noon. Meeting rms. Business servs avail. In-rm modem link. Free garage parking. Free airport, bus depot transportation. Tennis privileges. Golf privileges. Downhill ski 6 mi. Health club privileges, Some in-rm whirlpools; refrigerator in suites; microwaves avail. Cr cds: A, C, D, DS, ER, MC, V.

Inns

★ ★ ★ **CARNEGIE HOUSE.** *100 Cricklewood Dr (16803), near Penn State Univ Park Airport.* 814/234-2424; FAX 814/231-1299; res: 800/229-5033. E-mail carnhouse@aol.com; web www.cmagic.com/ch/. 22 rms, 2-3 story. S, D $125-$175; suites $250-$275; under 6 free. TV; cable (premium), VCR. Pool privileges. Complimentary continental bkfst. Dining rm 6:30-10 am, 11:30 am-1:30 pm, 5:30-9 pm. Ck-out noon, ck-in 3 pm. Business servs avail. In-rm modem link. Luggage handling. Gift shop. Free airport transportation. Tennis privileges. 18-hole golf privileges, greens fee $45-$55. Downhill ski 6 mi; x-country ski adj. Minibar; some microwaves. Decor and ambiance is reminiscent of Scotland. Cr cds: A, MC, V.

★ ★ ★ **NITTANY LION.** *200 W Park Ave (US 322 Business) (16803), on Penn State campus.* 814/231-7500; FAX 814/231-7502; res: 800/233-7505. E-mail jwp4@psu.edu. 237 rms, 3 story. S $85-$95; D $95-$105; each addl $10; suites $160-$190; under 12 free. Crib free. TV; cable, VCR avail. Dining rm 6:45 am-9 pm. Bar 11:30-1 am. Ck-out noon, ck-in 3 pm. Meeting rms. Business servs avail. In-rm modem link. Valet serv. Free airport transportation. Exercise equipt; weight machines, stair machines. Cr cds: A, C, D, DS, MC, V.

Resort

★ ★ ★ **TOFTREES.** *1 Country Club Ln (16803).* 814/234-8000; FAX 814/238-4404; res: 800/458-3602 (exc PA), 800/252-3551 (PA). 113 units, 3 story, 22 suites. Apr-mid-Oct: S $99-$150; D $125-$170; each addl $15; suites $150-$250; AP, MAP avail; golf plans; some wkend rates; lower rates rest of yr. Crib avail. TV; cable (premium), VCR avail. Heated pool; lifeguard. Dining rms 6:30 am-10 pm. Bar from 11 am; entertainment. Ck-out noon, ck-in 3 pm. Business servs avail. In-rm modem link. Free airport transportation. Tennis, pro. 18-hole golf, pro, putting green, driving range. Exercise equipt; bicycles, treadmill. Refrigerators; microwaves avail. Balconies. Mediterranean decor. Cr cds: A, C, D, DS, MC, V.

Restaurants

✔ ★ ★ **TAVERN RESTAURANT.** *220 E College Ave (16805).* 814/238-6116. Web www.thetavern.com. Hrs: 5-10:30 pm; Sun to 8:30 pm. Closed major hols. Res accepted Sun-Thurs. Bar 4 pm-12:30 am. Semi-a la carte: dinner $6.95-$16.95. Child's meals. Specializes in fresh veal dishes, fresh seafood. Classical music. Colonial decor; large collection of original Pennsylvania prints. Cr cds: A, C, D, DS, MC, V.

★ ★ ★ **VICTORIAN MANOR.** *(901 Pike St, Lemont)* 1¾ mi E on US 322, then 2 mi NE via East Branch Rd. 814/238-5534. Hrs: 5-9 pm. Closed Mon; Jan 1, Memorial Day, Labor Day, Dec 25. Res accepted; required wkends. Continental menu. Wine list. Semi-a la carte: dinner $11.95-$28.45. Prix fixe: 3-course dinner $16.50. Specialties: rack of lamb, filet of salmon. Own pastries. Historic building (1891). Victorian decor. Totally nonsmoking. Cr cds: A, C, D, DS, MC, V.

Stroudsburg (D-9)

(See also Easton, Pocono Mountains)

Settled 1769 **Pop** 5,312 **Elev** 430 ft **Area code** 717 **Zip** 18360
Information Pocono Mts Vacation Bureau, 1004 Main St; phone 717/424-6050; for free brochures phone 800/POCONOS.

This is a center for the Pocono Mountains resort area and the surrounding rural community. It is the Monroe County seat.

What to See and Do

Alpine Mountain Ski Area. 2 quad, double chairlifts; patrol, school, rentals; snowmaking; restaurant, bar; child-care center. Vertical drop 500 ft. 18 trails & slopes. (Dec-Mar, daily) 6 mi N via PA 191, 447N, just outside Analomink. Phone 717/595-2150 or 800/233-8240. ¢¢¢¢¢

Canoeing. Canoe trips on the Delaware River; equipment provided; also transportation to and from the river. (May-Oct) Contact Chamberlain Canoes, PO Box 155, Minisink Hills 18341. Phone 717/421-0180. ¢¢¢-¢¢¢¢¢

Delaware Water Gap (see). 3½ mi E on PA 611, I-80.

Quiet Valley Living Historical Farm. A log house (1765) with kitchen and parlor added 1892; 12 other original or reconstructed buildings. Demonstrations of seasonal farm activities. Guided tours with costumed guides, 1½-2 hrs. (Late June-Labor Day, daily exc Mon) 3½ mi SW on US 209 Business, then 1½ mi S (follow signs). Phone 717/992-6161. ¢¢¢

Stroud Mansion (18th century). Built by founder of city; houses Historical Society of Monroe County. Historical artifacts, genealogical records. Tours. (Tues-Fri, also Sun afternoons; closed major hols) 9th & Main Sts. Phone 717/421-7703. ¢

Motels

★ ★ **BEST WESTERN POCONO INN.** *700 Main St.* 717/421-2200; FAX 717/421-5561. 90 rms, 4 story. S, D $74-$109; each addl $10; higher rates special events. Crib free. TV; cable, VCR avail (movies). Indoor pool; whirlpools. Restaurant (see CHOP HOUSE). Rm serv. Bar 11:30-2 am; entertainment. Ck-out 11 am. Meeting rms. Business servs avail. Game rm. Cr cds: A, C, D, DS, ER, JCB, MC, V.

✔ ★ **BUDGET.** *(E Stroudsburg 18301)* E on I-80, exit 51. 717/424-5451; FAX 717/424-0389; res: 800/233-8144. 115 rms, 2-3 story. No elvtr. S $33.90-48; D $48-$66; higher rates: special events, hols, some wkends. Crib free. Pet accepted; $20 deposit. TV; cable, VCR avail (movies). Restaurant 7-11 am, 5-10 pm. Bar 4 pm-midnight. Ck-out 11 am. Business servs avail. In-rm modem link. Game rm. Cr cds: A, C, D, DS, MC, V.

★ ★ **POCONO PLAZA.** *1220 W Main St, I-80 exit 48.* 717/424-1930; FAX 717/424-5909. 133 rms, 2 story. S, D $85-$99; each addl $10; suites $120-$130; under 18 free; some wkend rates. Crib free. TV; cable. Pool; sauna, poolside serv. Restaurant 7 am-10 pm. Rm serv. Bars 11-2 am; entertainment. Ck-out 11 am. Meeting rms. Business servs avail.

In-rm modem link. Bellhops. Sundries. Game rm. Balconies. Cr cds: A, D, DS, MC, V.

⚮ ⚮ ⚮ SC

✔★ **SHANNON INN.** *(I-80, exit 52, East Stroudsburg 18301)* 4 mi E on I-80. 717/424-1951; FAX 717/424-7782; res: 800/424-8052. 120 rms, 2 story. S $60-$90; D $65-$95; each addl $5; under 18 free; 2-day min hols; higher rates NASCAR races. Crib free. TV; cable. Indoor pool. Complimentary continental bkfst. Restaurant 4 pm-2 am. Rm serv. Bar; entertainment Fri, Sat. Ck-out 11 am. Coin lndry. Meeting rms. Business servs avail. In-rm modem link. Valet serv. Sundries. Downhill/x-country ski 4 mi. Some refrigerators. Picnic tables. Cr cds: A, D, DS, MC, V.

⚮ ⚮ ⚮ ⚮ SC

Inn

★★ **INN AT MEADOWBROOK.** *(RD 7, Box 7651, Cherry Lane Rd, East Stroudsburg 18301)* I-80 exit 45 Tannersville, N on PA 715, turn right on PA 611, turn left on Cherry Lane Rd at Tannersville Inn. 717/629-0296; FAX 717/620-1754; res: 800/249-6861. 16 rms, many air-cooled, some A/C, 2 story. No rm phones. S, D $60-$95. Children over 12 yrs only. TV in sitting rm; cable. Pool; lifeguard. Complimentary full bkfst. Dining rm 5-10 pm. Ck-out noon, ck-in 2 pm. Business servs avail. Bus depot transportation. 2 tennis courts. Downhill ski 4 mi; x-country ski 2 mi. Game rm. Rec rm. Lawn games. On lake. Consists of Manor House (1842) and Mill House (1924); antiques. Equestrian Center adj. Cr cds: A, D, DS, MC, V.

⚮ ⚮ ⚮ ⚮ ⚮ ⚮ SC

Resort

★★ **CAESAR'S POCONO PALACE.** *Marshalls Creek (18335),* 6 mi N on US 209, exit 52 I-80. 717/588-6692; FAX 717/588-0754; res: 800/233-4141. 189 units, 155 suites. D, suites $195-$350; wkly rates. TV; cable, VCR avail (movies $5). 2 pools, 1 indoor; whirlpool. Complimentary full bkfst, dinner. Dining rm 8:30-11 am; 6-8 pm. Rm serv 11-2 am. Bar from 11:30 am; entertainment. Ck-out 11 am, ck in 3 pm. Business servs avail. Gift shop. 9-hole golf, pro, putting green, driving range. Marina; paddle boats, waterskiing. Downhill ski 3 mi; x-country on site. Snowmobiles, ice skating. Softball field. Volleyball. Archery. Lawn games. Rec rm. Game rm. Exercise equipt; weight machine, bicycles, sauna. Refrigerators. Some balconies. On lake. Cr cds: A, C, D, DS, MC, V.

⚮ ⚮ ⚮ ⚮ ⚮ ⚮ ⚮

Restaurants

✔★ **ARLINGTON DINER.** 834 N 9th St. 717/421-2329. Hrs: 6 am-10 pm; Fri, Sat to 11 pm; Sun 7 am-10 pm. Closed Jan 1, Thanksgiving, Dec 25. Semi-a la carte: bkfst $2.50-$6.40, lunch $3-$6, dinner $5.75-$11.50. Child's meals. Specializes in pudding, homemade pies. No cr cds accepted.

⚮

★ **BEAVER HOUSE.** 1001 N 9th St. 717/424-1020. Hrs: 11:30 am-9:30 pm; Sat to 10:30 pm; Sun noon-8 pm. Closed Dec 25. Res accepted. Bar. Complete meals: lunch $4.95-$8.95, dinner $12.50-$31.95. Specializes in seafood, prime rib. Many antiques; Tiffany lamps, trophies, bottles, stained glass, clocks. Family-owned. Cr cds: A, C, D, DS, MC, V.

D

★ **CHOP HOUSE.** *(See Best Western Pocono Inn).* 717/421-2200. Hrs: 11 am-10 pm; Fri, Sat to 11 pm. Bar. Semi-a la carte: lunch $3.95-$9.95, dinner $8.95-$23.95. Specialties: captain's seafood platter, Kansas City steak. Salad bar. Family-owned. Cr cds: A, C, D, DS, MC, V.

D SC

✔★ **LEE'S.** *(PA 611, Bartonsville)* 6 mi SE on PA 715. 717/421-1212. Hrs: noon-10 pm; Sat 1:30-11 pm; Sun 11:30-10 pm; Sun brunch to 3 pm. Closed Thanksgiving. Res required Fri-Sun. Chinese, Japanese

menu. Bar. A la carte entrees: lunch, dinner $5.25-$12.95. Lunch buffet $6.95. Specializes in steak dishes. Salad bar. Sushi bar. Oriental decor. Cr cds: A, MC, V.

D

✔★★ **YE OLDE SAYLORS INNE.** *(Old PA 115, Saylorsburg 18353)* 11 mi S off PA 33 in Saylorsburg. 717/992-5200. Hrs: 4-9 pm. Closed Sun-Tues, hols; also Jan. Bar. A la carte entrees: $4.95-$14.95. Child's meals. Specializes in steak, seafood. In historic building (1804). Totally nonsmoking. No cr cds accepted.

D

Unrated Dining Spot

THE DANSBURY DEPOT. *(50 Crystal St, East Stroudsburg)* E on I-80, exit 51. 717/476-0500. Hrs: 11 am-10 pm; Fri, Sat to 9 pm. Closed Thanksgiving, Dec 25. Continental menu. Bar. Semi-a la carte: lunch $4-$6, dinner $8-$14. Child's meals. Specializes in steak, seafood. Converted railroad station depot and freight house, built in 1864. Display of railroad memorabilia. Small trains move around the room, overhead on the walls. Cr cds: A, C, D, DS, MC, V.

D

Tannersville (D-9)

(See also Pocono Mountains, Stroudsburg)

Pop 1,200 (est) **Elev** 890 ft **Area code** 717 **Zip** 18372
Information Pocono Mts Vacation Bureau, 1004 Main St, Stroudsburg 18360; 717/424-6050; for free brochures phone 800/POCONOS.

What to See and Do

Camelback Ski Area. Quad, 2 triple, 8 double chairlifts; patrol, school, rentals; snowmaking; cafeteria, restaurant, bar; nursery. Longest run 1 mi; vertical drop 800 ft. (Mid-Dec-late Mar, daily) 27 trails. Alpine slide, water slide, swimming pool, bumper boats, entertainment (mid-June-Labor Day, daily; mid-May-mid-June & Labor Day-Oct, wkends only). Single & combination tickets. 3½ mi W off I-80, exit 45, in Big Pocono State Park. Phone 717/629-1661 or 800/233-8100 (mid-Atlantic states, ski report). ¢¢¢¢¢

Resort

★★ **CAESARS BROOKDALE.** *(PA 611, Scotrun 18355)* 3 mi N on PA 611. 717/839-8844; FAX 717/839-2414. 127 rms in 8 bldgs, 1-2 story. June-Sept, MAP: S $106-$215; D $190-$250; each addl $55; suites $230-$360; under 5 free; wkly plans; hol plans (3-day min); higher rates hols & theme wkends; lower rates rest of yr. Crib free. TV; cable, VCR avail (movies). 2 pools, 1 indoor; wading pool, whirlpool, sauna, poolside serv, lifeguard. Playground. Supervised child's activities (seasonal); from 5 yrs. Complimentary coffee in lobby. Restaurant 8:30-11:30 am, 5:30-8 pm. Rm serv. Box lunches, picnics. Bar noon-2 am; entertainment. Ck-out 11 am, ck-in 3 pm. Gift shop. Grocery. Coin lndry. Meeting rms. Business servs avail. Valet serv. Sports dir. Lighted tennis. 9-hole golf privileges, putting green, driving range. Beach, boats. Downhill ski 3 mi; x-country ski 17 mi. Snowmobiles, sleighing, tobogganing. Hiking. Bicycles. Lawn games. Soc dir. Rec rm. Game rm. Exercise rm; instructor, weights, bicycles. Massage. Some refrigerators. Balconies. Picnic tables. On lake. Cr cds: A, C, D, DS, MC, V.

D ⚮ ⚮ ⚮ ⚮ ⚮ ⚮ ⚮ ⚮ ⚮ SC

Titusville (B-2)

(See also Franklin, Meadville, Oil City)

Settled 1796 **Pop** 6,434 **Elev** 1,199 ft **Area code** 814 **Zip** 16354
Information Titusville Area Chamber of Commerce, 202 W Central Ave; 814/827-2941.

Titusville spreads from the banks of Oil Creek, so-called because of the oil that appeared on its surface. Edwin L. Drake drilled the first successful oil well in the world on August 27, 1859. Overnight, Titusville became the center of the worldwide oil industry.

What to See and Do

Drake Well Museum. Site of world's first oil well; operating replica of Drake derrick and engine house; picnic area. Museum contains dioramas, working models, life-size exhibits depicting history of oil. (May-Oct, daily; Nov-Apr, Tues-Sat, also Sun afternoons) 1 mi SE of PA 8. Phone 814/827-2797. ¢¢

Inn

✔★ ★ ★ **MCMULLEN HOUSE.** *430 E Main St. 814/827-1592.* 5 rms, 2 story, 4 rms with shower only. No elvtr. No rm phones. MAP: S $46-$48; D $56-$58. Family rates. Crib free. TV rm; cable (premium). Complimentary continental bkfst. Coffee in library. Restaurant nearby. Ck-out noon, ck-in 3:30 pm. Luggage handling. Picnic tables. Restored Italianate mansion (1870). Cr cds: D, MC, V.

Resort

★ ★ **CROSS CREEK.** *15867 Oil City-Titusville Rd, 4 1/2 mi S on PA 8. 814/827-9611; FAX 814/827-2062.* 94 rms, 1-2 story. May-Oct: S $95-$110; D $100-$120; each addl $10; suites $120-$140; under 12 free; golf plan; lower rates rest of yr. Crib free. TV; cable. Heated pool; lifeguard. Restaurant 7 am-2 pm, 6-10 pm. Bar 11-2 am; entertainment. Ck-out 2 pm. Meeting rms. In-rm modem link. Gift shop. Tennis. 27-hole golf, greens fee $28, putting green. Some private patios, balconies. Cr cds: A, D, DS, MC, V.

Towanda (B-7)

(See also Mansfield, Scranton)

Settled 1794 **Pop** 3,242 **Elev** 737 ft **Area code** 717 **Zip** 18848
Information Endless Mountains Visitors Bureau, RR 6, Box 132A, Tunkhannock 18657-9232; 717/836-5431 or 800/769-8999.

On the north branch of the Susquehanna River, Towanda takes its name from a Native American word meaning "where we bury the dead."

In 1793 the Asylum Company purchased 1,600 acres of these wild valleys as a refuge for Marie Antoinette of France, should she escape to America. "La Grande Maison," a queenly house, was built. French noblemen settled here, and a thriving community (called Azilum) was planned. The colony was unsuccessful and most of its founders returned to France. Many of their descendants, however, still live in Bradford County.

What to See and Do

David Wilmot's burial place. Congressman (1845-1851), senator (1861-1863), leader of the Free-Soil Party, Wilmot introduced the Wilmot Proviso

in Congress, which would have required the US to outlaw slavery in any lands purchased from Mexico. This was an important factor in the dissension between North and South that led to the Civil War. Riverside Cemetery, William St between Chestnut & Walnut Sts.

French Azilum. Site of colony for refugees from the French Revolution (1793-1803). Three cabins with crafts, tool exhibits; log cabin museum (1793); Laporte House (1836), built by son of one of colony's founders, reflects elegant French influence. Special events. Guided tours. (June-Aug, Wed-Sun; May, Sept-Oct, Sat & Sun) 8 mi SE via US 6, PA 187. Phone 717/265-3376. ¢¢

Tioga Point Museum. Mementos of French Azilum; Civil War, Stephen Foster and Native American exhibits; historical displays of early canals and steam railroad. (Tues, Thurs & Sat, hrs vary; closed major hols) 17 mi N off US 220, on PA 199, Spalding Memorial Bldg, 724 S Main St in Athens. Phone 717/888-7225. **Donation.**

Valley Railroad Museum. Century-old Lehigh Valley passenger station houses museum with displays of railroad memorabilia and railroad exhibit of Lehigh Valley in miniature; gift shop. (Daily exc Mon; closed major hols) 15 mi N off US 220, in Sayre on S Lehigh Ave. Phone 717/888-1881. ¢¢

Motel

✔★ **TOWANDA.** *383 York Ave (US 6). 717/265-2178; FAX 717/265-9060.* 48 rms. S $39-$65; D $43-$70; each addl $5; under 12 free. Crib $3.50. Pet accepted. TV; cable. Pool. Restaurant 6 am-9:30 pm; Sat, Sun from 7 am. Bar 3 pm-2 am. Ck-out noon. Meeting rms. Business servs avail. Sundries. Cr cds: A, C, D, DS, MC, V.

Motor Hotel

★ ★ ★ **GUTHRIE INN & CONFERENCE CENTER.** *(255 Spring St, Sayre 18840) Approx 15 mi N on US 220, E on NY 17, exit 61, S on PA 199. 717/888-7711; FAX 717/888-0541; res: 800/627-7972.* 100 rms, 4 story. S $83-$86; D $93-$96; each addl $10; suites $154; under 12 free; wkend package. Crib $10. TV; cable. Indoor pool; whirlpool, lifeguard. Complimentary coffee in rms. Restaurant 6:30 am-9 pm; Fri, Sat to 10 pm. Rm serv. Bar; entertainment Fri, Sat. Ck-out 11 am. Meeting rms. Business servs avail. In-rm modem link. Sundries. Lighted tennis. 18-hole golf privileges. Exercise rm; instructor, weights, bicycles, sauna, steam rm. Balconies. Cr cds: A, C, D, DS, MC, V.

Uniontown (F-2)

(See also Connellsville)

Settled 1768 **Pop** 12,034 **Elev** 999 ft **Area code** 724 **Zip** 15401
Information Laurel Highlands Visitors Bureau, 120 E Main St, Ligonier 15658; 724/238-5661.

Coal and its byproducts made Uniontown prosperous, but with the decline in coal mining the city has developed a more diversified economic base. First known as Union, this city has been the Fayette County seat since 1784. General Lafayette and his son, George Washington de Lafayette, came on a visit after the Revolutionary War and were welcomed by Albert Gallatin, one-time senator and secretary of the Treasury. Uniontown was a hotbed of the Whiskey Rebellion, and federal troops were sent here in 1794.

What to See and Do

Braddock's Grave. Granite monument marks burial place of British General Edward Braddock, who was wounded in battle with French and Native American forces on July 9, 1755, and died four days later. Also nearby is

Fort Necessity National Battlefield (1754). The site of Washington's first major battle and the opening battle of the French and Indian War (1754). This land was known as the Great Meadows. A portion was later purchased by Washington, who owned it until his death. A replica of the original fort was built on the site following an archaeological survey in 1953. Picnic area (mid-spring-late fall). 11 mi SE on US 40. Phone 724/329-5512. ¢ Nearby and included in the admission fee are

Visitor Center. Exhibits on battle at Great Meadows; audiovisual program. (Daily; closed Dec 25) Overlooking Fort Necessity is

Mt Washington Tavern. Restored as historic stagecoach inn; furnishings, exhibits of 1827-1855. (Daily; closed Dec 25) 1 mi W on US 40 is

Friendship Hill National Historic Site. Preserves the restored home of Albert Gallatin, a Swiss immigrant who served his adopted country, in public and private life, for nearly seven decades. Gallatin made significant contributions to our young Republic in the fields of finance, politics, diplomacy and scholarship. He is best known as the Treasury Secretary under Jefferson and Madison. Exhibits, audiovisual program, and audio tour provide information on Albert Gallatin. (Daily; closed Dec 25) 15 mi S on US 119 to PA 166. Phone 724/329-5512. **Free.**

Jumonville Glen. This is the site of the skirmish between British and French forces that led to the battle at Fort Necessity. (Mid-Apr-mid-Oct) 7 mi from Ft Necessity, 2½ mi N of US 40 on Summit Rd.

Laurel Caverns. Colored lighting; unusual formations. Indoor miniature golf. Guided tours. Exploring trips. (May-Oct, daily) 5 mi SE on US 40, then 5 mi S on marked road. Phone 724/438-3003. Tours ¢¢¢

Ohiopyle State Park. Approx 18,700 acres of overlooks, waterfalls. Fishing, hunting; whitewater boating. Hiking, bicycling. Cross-country skiing, snowmobiling, sledding. Picnicking, playground, snack bar. Tent & trailer sites. Nature center, interpretive program. Standard fees. 10 mi SE on US 40, then 6 mi NE off PA 381. Phone 724/329-8591.

River tours. Whitewater rafting on the Youghiogheny River; some of the wildest and most scenic in the eastern US. Cost includes equipment and professional guides. Age limits are imposed because of level of difficulty.

White Water Adventurers. For information contact Director, PO Box 31, Ohiopyle 15470; 800/WWA-RAFT. ¢¢¢¢¢

Laurel Highlands River Tours. For information contact PO Box 107, Dept PM, Ohiopyle 15470; 724/329-8531 or 800/472-3846. ¢¢¢¢¢

Mountain Streams & Trails Outfitters. Also on the Gauley, Big Sandy, Cheat and Tygart's Valley rivers. For information contact Manager, PO Box 106, Ohiopyle 15470; 724/329-8810. Also rentals of whitewater rafts, canoes, trail bikes; for information contact Ohiopyle Recreational Rentals, PO Box 4, Ohiopyle 15470; 800/245-4090. ¢¢¢¢¢

Motels

★ ★ **HOLIDAY INN.** *700 W Main St (US 40).* 724/437-2816; FAX 724/437-3505. 179 rms, 2 story. S $75-$97; D $77-$97; suites $145-$175; under 18 free; ski, wkend plan in winter; higher rates Labor Day wkend. Crib free. Pet accepted, some restrictions. TV; cable (premium), VCR avail. Indoor pool; whirlpool, sauna, poolside serv, lifeguard. Restaurant 6:30 am-2 pm, 4:30-10 pm. Rm serv from 7 am. Bar 11-2 am; entertainment. Ck-out 11 am. Meeting rms. Business servs avail. In-rm modem link. Valet serv. Sundries. Lighted tennis. Miniature golf. Rec rm. Game rm. Lawn games. Microwaves avail. Some balconies. Cr cds: A, C, D, DS, JCB, MC, V.

🅳 ⛵ 🎿 🏊 🌊 ⛷ SC

✓★ ★ **LODGE AT CHALK HILL.** *(Box 240, US 40E, Chalk Hill 15421)* 9 mi E on US 40. 724/438-8880; FAX 724/438-1685; res: 800/833-4283. Web it.pulsenet.com/~thelodge. 60 units, 6 suites, 6 kit. units. May-Nov: S $53.95-$70; D $64.95-$75.95; each addl $10; suites $128.95-$162.95; kit. units $69.95-$90.95; under 14 free; higher rates: July 4, Memorial Day, Labor Day, Dec 31; lower rates rest of yr. Crib free. Pet accepted, some restrictions; $5. TV; cable (premium), VCR avail. Complimentary continental bkfst. Restaurant opp 7 am-11 pm. Ck-out noon. Meeting rms. Business servs avail. Balconies. Picnic tables. On Lake Lenore. Cr cds: A, DS, MC, V.

🅳 ⛵ 🎿 🏊 🌊 ⛷ SC

Inn

★ ★ ★ **INNE AT WATSON'S CHOICE.** *RD 3, Box 363, 5 mi W on PA 21, in Village of Balsinger.* 724/437-4999. 7 rms, shower only, 2 story. S, D $89-$125; each addl $20; wkly rates; wkends, hols (2-day min). Children over 12 yrs only. TV in common rm; cable (premium), VCR avail (movies). Complimentary full bkfst. Complimentary coffee in rms. Ck-out 11 am, ck-in after 2 pm. Luggage handling. Concierge serv. Gift shop. Coin lndry. Golf privileges. Downhill ski 10 mi; x-country ski 10 mi. Many fireplaces. Picnic tables, grills. Built in 1820; German architecture. Totally nonsmoking. Cr cds: DS, MC, V.

🅳 🏊 🎿 🌊 ⛷

Resorts

★ ★ ★ **NEMACOLIN WOODLANDS.** *(US 40E, Farmington 15437)* 12 mi E on US 40. 724/329-8555; FAX 724/329-6198; res: 800/422-2736. 220 rms, 4 & 5 story, 60 condo units (1-2 bedrm). May-Oct: S, D $215; each addl $25; suites $345-$1,500; kit. condos $245; under 17 free; AP, MAP avail; wkly rates; golf plans; lower rates rest of yr. Crib free. TV; cable (premium), VCR avail. 4 pools, 2 indoor; whirlpools, poolside serv, lifeguard. Playground. Supervised child's activities; ages 4-12. Dining rm 6 am-midnight. Box lunches, snack bar, picnics. Rm serv 24 hrs. Bar noon-2 am; entertainment. Ck-out noon, ck-in 3 pm. Lndry facilities in condos. Convention facilities. Business servs avail. In-rm modem link. Bellhops. Valet serv. Concierge. Gift shop. Sports dir. Lighted tennis, pro. Two 18-hole golf courses, greens fee (incl cart) $69-$109 , pro, 2 putting greens, driving range. Boats. Downhill/x-country ski on site. Sleighing, tobogganing. Equestrian center; surrey rides all yr. Hiking. Bicycle rentals. Miniature golf. Lawn games. Social dir. Rec rm. Game rm. Exercise rm; instructor, weight machine, bicycles, saunas. Massage. Bathrm phones, minibars; many refrigerators; some wet bars. Microwave in condos. Balconies. Private collection of art and antiques. Situated on 1,250 acres with 7 lakes; landing strip. Cr cds: A, C, D, MC, V.

🅳 ⛵ 🎿 🏊 🎣 🏊 ⛳ 🎿 ⛷ 🌊 SC

★ ★ ★ **SUMMIT INN.** *(Box 2, Skyline Dr, Farmington 15437)* 6 mi E on US 40. 724/438-8594; FAX 724/438-3917. 100 rms, 3 story. No elvtr. July-Labor Day: S $65-$95; D $75-$105; suites $110-$176; family rates; golf package plan, MAP avail (2 night min); some wkend rates; lower rates mid-Apr-June, after Labor Day-early Nov. Closed rest of yr. Crib $10. TV; cable, VCR avail (movies). Indoor/outdoor pool; whirlpool, lifeguard. Dining rm (public by res) 8-11 am, noon-2 pm, 6-8:30 pm. Rm serv. Box lunches, snacks. Bar 11-1 am. Ck-out noon, ck-in 4 pm. Business servs avail. Grocery, package store 3 mi. Gift shop. Tennis. 9-hole golf, greens fee $8.50, pro, putting green. Exercise equipt; weight machine, treadmill. Rec rm. Soc dir; entertainment. Picnic tables, grills. Built in 1907. Atop Mt Summit. Cr cds: A, DS, MC, V.

🅳 🎿 🏊 🌊 🎿 🌊 SC

Restaurants

★ ★ ★ **CHEZ GERARD.** *(US 40 E Business, Hopwood 15445)* 724/437-9001. Web www.hhs.net/bedandb/. Hrs: 11:30 am-2 pm, 5:30-9 pm; Sun brunch to 2 pm. Closed Tues; most major hols. Res accepted. French menu. Bar. Wine list. Semi-a la carte: lunch $6-$10, dinner $8-$22. Prix fixe: lunch $16.50, dinner $35-$47. Sun brunch $15. Child's meals. Specialties: champagne gratined onion soup, Dover sole meuniére, créme brulée. Own baking, pasta. Outdoor dining. Renovated 1790 stone house with country French decor, fireplaces. Cr cds: DS, MC, V.

🅳

★ ★ ★ **COAL BARON.** *RD 6, 6 mi W on US 40.* 724/439-0111. Hrs: 4-11 pm; Sun noon-8 pm. Closed Mon; Dec 24-25. Res accepted. Continental menu. Bar. Wine list. Complete meals: dinner $14-$20.95. Child's meals. Specialties: veal saltimbocca, entrecôte maître d'hôtel. Own baking. Valet parking. Jacket. Cr cds: A, D, DS, MC, V.

✓★ ★ **SUN PORCH.** *(US 40E, Hopwood 15445)* 724/439-5734. Hrs: 11 am-8 pm; Sat 4-9 pm. Closed Mon; Dec 24, 25. Res accepted.

Semi-a la carte: lunch $4.50-$8, dinner $7-$12. Buffet: dinner $7.75-$10.50. Child's meals. Specializes in fresh seafood, beef, poultry, soup. Salad bar. Many plants; atmosphere of a country garden. Cr cds: C, D, DS, MC, V.

D ⌐

Valley Forge National Historical Park (E-9)

(For accommodations see King of Prussia, Philadelphia)

Web www.nps.gov/vafo/
Information Superintendent, PO Box 953, Valley Forge 19482; 610/783-1077.

(3 mi N of PA Tpke Interchange 24)

From December 19, 1777, to June 19, 1778—some of the darkest days of the American Revolution—the poorly supplied troops of Washington's army were camped here. Of those 12,000 soldiers of the Continental Army, more than 2,000 died from illness and disease brought on by weather conditions, lack of supplies and poor sanitation. The national park is a 3,600-acre memorial to their trial and success. The park itself is scenic any time of the year. A marked tour route offers the visitor a chance to see the primary encampment facilities; other roads provide a beautiful drive and a chance to view other historical features. (Daily; closed Dec 25)

What to See and Do

National Memorial Arch. Built in 1917 to commemorate Washington's army. Inscribed in the arch is a quote of General Washington: "Naked and starving as they are, we cannot enough admire the incomparable patience and fidelity of the soldiery."

Soldier Life Program. Interpreters present programs detailing camp life at Muhlenberg Brigade (offered at various times during the year).

Tours.

Auto Tape Tour. Self-guided tour dramatizes Washington's winter encampment. (2-hr tape rental, May-Oct, daily) Bookstore. Phone 610/783-5788. ¢¢¢

Bus Tour. Narrated tour (approx 90 min) includes stops at historic sites. (June-Labor Day, tour departures every half hour; Labor Day-Oct, wkends only) Tours leave from Visitor Center. Phone 610/783-5788. ¢¢¢

Visitor Center. Information, exhibits, audiovisual program, tour maps. Bus tours depart from here. (Daily) Jct PA 23 & N Gulph Rd, just inside park. Phone 610/783-1077.

Washington Headquarters. Park staff will provide information about the house where Washington lived for six months and which served as military headquarters for the Continental Army during that time. (Daily) Fee charged Apr-Nov ¢

Washington Memorial Chapel. Private property within park boundaries. Stained-glass windows depict the story of the New World, its discovery and development; hand-carved oak choir stalls, Pews of the Patriots, and Roof of the Republic bearing the State Seal of all the states. Also part of the chapel is the 58 cast-bell Washington Memorial National Carillon, with bells honoring states and territories. On PA 23. Phone 610/783-0120. Adj is

Museum of the Valley Forge Historical Society. Relics of the winter at Valley Forge. (Daily; closed Easter, Thanksgiving, Dec 25) Phone 610/783-0535. ¢

Restaurants

★ **COLUMBIA HOTEL.** *(148 Bridge St, Phoenixville 19460) 6 mi NW off PA 23. 610/933-9973.* Hrs: 11:30 am-2:30 pm, 5-10 pm. Closed most major hols. Res accepted. Bar to midnight. A la carte entrees: lunch $5.95-$12.95, dinner $13.95-$24.95. Child's meals. Specializes in fresh Maine & Florida fish, Angus beef. Own desserts. Built in 1892. Cr cds: A, C, D, MC, V.

D ⌐

★ ★ ★ **KENNEDY-SUPPLEE MANSION.** *(1100 W Valley Forge Rd (PA 23), Valley Forge 19406) opp visitors center to Valley Forge National Historical Park. 610/337-3777.* Hrs: 11:30 am-2 pm, 5:30-10:30 pm; Sat from 5:30 pm. Closed Sun; some major hols. Res accepted. Continental menu. Bar. A la carte entrees: lunch $8-$16, dinner $20-$26. Specializes in French, northern Italian cuisine. Valet parking. 8 dining rooms in mansion (1850s). Crystal chandeliers, original artwork. Jacket (dinner). Cr cds: A, D, MC, V.

D ⌐

★ ★ ★ **KIMBERTON INN.** *(Kimberton Rd, Kimberton 19442) PA 23W to PA 113S. 610/933-8148.* Hrs: 5:30-9:30 pm; Sun to 8:30 pm; Sun brunch 11 am-2 pm. Res accepted. Continental menu. Bar. Wine list. Semi-a la carte: dinner $17.95-$21.95. Sun brunch $16.95. Specializes in fresh seafood. Own desserts. Harpist or pianist. Tavern (1796) on 4½ acres of gardens. Cr cds: A, C, D, DS, MC, V.

D ⌐

★ ★ ★ **SEVEN STARS INN.** *(PA 23 & Hoffecker Rd, Phoenixville 19460) 10 mi W on PA 23. 610/495-5205.* Hrs: 4:30-10 pm; wkends to 11 pm; Sun 3-7 pm. Closed Mon; most major hols. Res accepted. Bar. Wine list. Complete meals: dinner $19.95-$27.95. Child's meals. Specializes in prime rib, seafood, veal. Colonial inn decor. Cr cds: A, C, D, MC, V.

D ⌐

Warren (B-3)

Founded 1795 **Pop** 11,122 **Elev** 1,200 ft **Area code** 814 **Zip** 16365
Information Warren County Chamber of Commerce, 315 2nd Ave, PO Box 942, 814/723-3050; or Travel Northern Alleghenies, 315 Second St, at the point, PO Box 804, 814/726-1222.

At the junction of the Allegheny and Conewango rivers, Warren is the headquarters and gateway of the famous Allegheny National Forests. Named for General Joseph Warren, American patriot killed in the Battle of Bunker Hill, the town was once the point where great flotillas of logs were formed for the journey to Pittsburgh or Cincinnati.

What to See and Do

Allegheny National Forest. More than 510,000 acres S & E on US 6, 62, located in Warren, Forest, McKean and Elk counties. Black bear, whitetail deer and wild turkey, a diversity of small birds and mammals; streams and reservoirs with trout, walleye, muskellunge, northern pike and bass; rugged hills, quiet valleys, open meadows, dense forest. These lures, plus swimming, boating, hiking, camping and picnicking facilities, draw more than 2 million visitors a year. Hundreds of campsites; fees are charged at some recreation sites. For information contact Supervisor, US Forest Service, PO Box 847, phone 814/723-5150; or Reservoir Area Office/Bradford District, phone 814/362-4613 or 814/368-8116 (TTY). In forest are

Buckaloons Recreation Area. Site of former Native American village on the banks of the Allegheny River. Boat launching. Picnicking. Camping (fee). Seneca Interpretive Trail. 6 mi W on US 6. Phone 814/362-4613 or 814/368-8116 (TTY).

Kinzua Dam and Allegheny Reservoir. Dam (179 ft high, 1,897 ft long) with 27-mi-long lake. Swimming; fishing; boating (ramps, rentals; fees). Picnicking, overlooks. Camping (fee). Kinzua Dam visitor center has displays. Kinzua Point Information Center, 4 mi NE of dam, phone 814/726-1291. Some fees. 3 mi SE on US 6, then 6 mi E on PA 59. *(It is possible that the PA 59 bridge, 1½ mi E of Kinzua Dam, will be closed; phone ahead for information.)* Phone 814/726-0661 or 814/362-4613 or 814/726-0164 (24-hr fishing hotline).

Chapman State Park. Approx 800 acres. Lake and creek stocked with trout and bass. Swimming beach; fishing, hunting; boating (rentals, mooring, launching). Hiking. Cross-country skiing, snowmobiling, sledding, ice-skating, ice fishing. Picnicking, snack bar. Tent & trailer sites avail (some with electric; fee). Interpretive program. 7 mi SE on US 6, then W at light in Clarendon. Phone 814/723-0250. Camping **¢¢¢-¢¢¢¢**

Washington (E-1)

Founded 1781 **Pop** 15,864 **Elev** 1,120 ft **Area code** 724 **Zip** 15301
E-mail tourism@pulsenet.com **Web** www.pulsenet.com/tourism
Information Washington County Tourism Promotion Agency, Franklin Mall, 1500 W Chestnut St; 724/228-5520 or 800/531-4114.

Originally a Native American village known as Catfish Camp, the village of Bassettown became Washington during the Revolution. During the Whiskey Rebellion the town was a center of protest against the new federal government's tax; arrival of federal troops quieted the rebellious farmers. Washington and Jefferson College (1781) is located here.

What to See and Do

David Bradford House (1788). Restored frontier home of a leader of the Whiskey Rebellion. (May-late Dec, Wed-Sat, limited hrs, also Sun afternoons) 175 S Main St. For fee information phone 724/222-3604.

Ladbroke at the Meadows. Harness racing. Parimutuel betting. (Tues, Thurs-Sun evenings) Simulcasts (daily). 4 mi N on US 19. Phone 724/225-9300.

LeMoyne House (1812). Abolitionist's home, built by the LeMoyne family, was a stop on the underground railroad; period furnishings, paintings, library; gardens; museum shop. Administered by Washington County Historical Society. (Feb-Dec, 1st Wed; rest of yr Wed-Fri, also Sun afternoons) 49 E Maiden St. Phone 724/225-6740. **¢¢**

Meadowcroft Museum of Rural Life. A 200-acre outdoor museum complex that preserves the history of life on the land in Western Pennsylvania. General store, restored log houses, one-room schoolhouse, blacksmith shop and archaeology exhibit. (May-Oct, Wed-Sun) 19 mi NW via PA 18, 50, in Avella. Phone 724/587-3412. **¢¢¢**

Pennsylvania Trolley Museum. Museum displays include more than 35 trolley cars dating from 1894. Scenic trolley ride; car barn and trolley-restoration shop; visitor's center and gift shop with exhibit, video presentation and picnic area. (July-Aug, daily; May-June & Sept-Oct, wkends, hols) I-79 N, exit 8 (Meadowlands), follow signs. Phone 724/228-9256. **¢¢**

Motels

★ **BEST WESTERN.** *1385 W Chestnut St, on US 40.* 724/222-6500; FAX 724/222-7671. 62 rms, 1-2 story. S $40-$60; D $48-$68; each addl $6; under 18 free; higher rates special events. Crib free. TV; cable (premium). Complimentary continental bkfst. Restaurant adj open 24 hrs. Ck-out 11 am. Business servs avail. Bellhops. Airport transportation. Picnic tables. Cr cds: A, C, D, DS, MC, V.

⊟ ⟡ ⋈ ⟡ SC

★ **MOTEL 6.** *1283 Motel 6 Dr, I-70 at US 19, exit 7A.* 724/223-8040; res: 800/843-5644; FAX 724/228-6445. 102 rms. S $35.99; D $42.39; each addl $6; under 18 free. Crib free. Pet accepted. TV; cable (premium). Pool. Complimentary coffee in lobby. Restaurant adj open 24 hrs. Ck-out noon. Cr cds: A, C, D, DS, ER, MC, V.

⊟ ⟡ ⋈ ⟡ SC

✔★ **RED ROOF INN.** *1399 W Chestnut St.* 724/228-5750; FAX 724/228-5865. 110 rms, 2 story. May-Oct: S $35.99-$45.99; D $42.99-$64.99; each addl $6; under 18 free; lower rates rest of yr. Crib free. Pet accepted, some restrictions. TV; cable (premium). Complimentary coffee in lobby. Restaurant adj open 24 hrs. Ck-out noon. Cr cds: A, C, D, DS, MC, V.

⊟ ⟡ ⋈ ⟡

Motor Hotel

★★★ **HOLIDAY INN-MEADOW LANDS.** *340 Race Track Rd, I-79 exit 8B.* 724/222-6200; FAX 724/228-1977. 138 rms, 7 story. S, D $99-$109; each addl $6; under 18 free. Crib free. Pet accepted, some restrictions. TV; cable (premium), VCR avail. Pool; whirlpool, poolside serv, lifeguard. Restaurant 6:30 am-10 pm. Rm serv. Bars 11-2 am; entertainment. Ck-out noon. Meeting rms. Business servs avail. In-rm modem link. Airport transportation. Exercise equipt; weight machines, bicycles, sauna. Microwaves avail. Private patios. Meadows Racetrack adj. Cr cds: A, C, D, DS, ER, JCB, MC, V.

⊟ ⟡ ⋈ ⟡ ⋈ SC

Washington Crossing Historical Park (Bucks Co) (E-10)

(For accommodations see Doylestown, New Hope, Philadelphia, PA; also see Trenton, NJ)

Information Superintendent, PO Box 103, Washington Crossing 18977; 215/493-4076.

(Two sections: Bowman's Hill, 2 mi S of New Hope on PA 32, and Washington Crossing, 7 mi S of New Hope on PA 32)

In a blinding snowstorm on Christmas night 1776, George Washington and 2,400 soldiers crossed the Delaware River from the Pennsylvania shore and marched to Trenton, surprising the celebrating Hessian mercenaries and capturing the city. Washington's feat was a turning point of the Revolutionary War. Park (daily exc Mon; closed some hols). Phone 215/493-4076. **¢¢**

What to See and Do

Bowman's Hill

Memorial Flagstaff. Marks graves of unknown Continentals who died during encampment.

Wildflower Preserve. Adj park; 2 mi of native wildflower trails. (Daily) Phone 215/862-2924.

Washington Crossing

Area of Embarkation. Marked by tall granite shaft supporting Washington's statue.

Concentration Valley. Where Washington assembled troops for raid on Trenton.

McConkey Ferry Inn (1752). At Washington Crossing; restored as historic house. Sold in 1777 to Benjamin Taylor, whose descendents established the 19th-century village of Taylorsville.

Memorial Building. Near Point of Embarkation. Houses copy of Emanuel Leutze's painting, *Washington Crossing the Delaware*. Movie shown five times a day. Phone 215/493-4076.

Annual Event

The Crossing. Reenactment of Washington's crossing of the Delaware River, Christmas night in 1776. Phone 215/493-4076. Dec.

Wellsboro (B-6)

(See also Galeton, Mansfield)

Settled 1799 **Pop** 3,430 **Elev** 1,311 ft **Area code** 717 **Zip** 16901 **E-mail** mwwacc@epix.net **Web** www.epix.net/~mwwacc/

Information Wellsboro Area Chamber of Commerce, 114 Main St, PO Box 733; 717/724-1926.

Wellsboro is the gateway to Pennsylvania's "canyon country." Settled largely by New Englanders, it is sustained by an assortment of industries. The area yields coal, natural gas, hardwoods, maple syrup and farm products.

What to See and Do

Auto tours. There are more than a million acres of forests, mountains and streams to be explored. The Wellsboro Area Chamber of Commerce has published a map of three tours.

   Red Arrow Tour follows PA 660 SW 10 mi from Wellsboro to Leonard Harrison State Park. Lookout Point, near the parking area, has large picnic area nearby. Path winds one mile from park to bottom of gorge, through shady glens, past waterfalls.

   Yellow Arrow Tour leads from Leonard Harrison State Park, back on PA 660, NW on PA 362, then 1/4 mi W on US 6 to Colton Point Rd for views of the canyon and Four Mile Run Country. At Colton Point State Park (observation points, picnic shelters, fireplaces) the arrows follow Pine Creek S on old lumbering railroad tracks, converted into roadways called the "Switchbacks," to Bradley Wales Park overlooking Tiadaghton, the next lookout point on Pine Creek. From here continue S on W Rim Rd to Blackwell. From Blackwell, NE on PA 414 to Morris, then N on PA 287 to Wellsboro—a circle of 65 mi.

   White Arrow Tour leads from the Switchbacks (1 1/2 mi W of Bradley Wales Park), 3 mi S to Leetonia, once a prosperous lumber village, now occupied by State Forest Rangers; then W & N to Cushman View, Wilson Point Rd, Lee Fire Tower, Cedar Run Mountain Rd & US 6; approx 75 mi.

Robinson House Museum (ca 1820). Houses turn-of-the-century artifacts; genealogical library. (Apr-Dec, Mon-Fri afternoons) 120 Main St. Contact Tioga County Historical Society, PO Box 724; 717/724-6116. **Free.**

Ski Sawmill Resort. Chairlift, 3 T-bars; patrol, school, rentals; snowmaking; cafeteria, restaurant, bar. Longest run 3,250 ft; vertical drop 515 ft. (Dec-Mar, daily) Yr-round activities. Oregon Hill Rd, 16 mi S via PA 287. Phone 800/532-SNOW. ¢¢¢-¢¢¢¢¢

Annual Event

Pennsylvania State Laurel Festival. Week-long event includes parade of floats, marching musical and precision units, antique cars, laurel queen contestants; crowning of the queen; arts and crafts; children's pet and hobby parade, exhibits and displays. Mid-June.

Motels

   ✔★ **CANYON.** 18 East Ave. 717/724-1681; FAX 717/724-5202; res: 800/255-2718. 28 rms. S $28-$45; D $32-$49; each addl $5; under 12 free; golf, ski package plans. Crib $5. Pet accepted. TV; cable. Heated pool; lifeguard. Playground. Complimentary continental bkfst. Restaurant nearby. Ck-out 11 am. In-rm modem link.

Downhill/x-country ski 17 mi. Refrigerators. Picnic tables, grills. Cr cds: A, C, D, DS, MC, V.

   ★ ★ **PENN-WELLS LODGE.** 4 Main St. 717/724-3463; FAX 717/724-2270; res: 800/545-2446. 55 rms, 2 story. S $53-$61; D $61-$69; each addl $5; under 18 free. Crib $5. TV; cable. Indoor pool; whirlpool, lifeguard. Playground. Restaurant nearby. Ck-out noon. Business servs avail. Downhill/x-country ski 17 mi. Exercise rm; instructor, weights, bicycles, sauna. Community-owned. Cr cds: A, C, D, DS, MC, V.

   ★ **SHERWOOD.** 2 Main St. 717/724-3424; FAX 717/724-5658; res: 800/626-5802. 32 rms, 1-2 story. S $37; D $49-$54; each addl $5; under 10 free; golf, ski package plans. Crib $5. Pet accepted; $5. TV; cable. Heated pool; lifeguard. Playground. Complimentary coffee. Restaurant nearby. Ck-out 11 am. Business servs avail. In-rm modem link. Downhill/x-country ski 17 mi. Refrigerators. Cr cds: A, C, D, DS, MC, V.

Hotel

   ★ **PENN-WELLS.** 62 Main St. 717/724-2111; FAX 717/724-3703; res: 800/545-2446. 73 rms. Late May-Oct, hunting season: S $30-$40; D $40-$49; each addl $5; suites $55-$60; under 18 free; golf plans; lower rates rest of yr. Crib $5. TV; cable. Indoor pool; whirlpool. Playground. Restaurant 7 am-1:30 pm, 5-10 pm. Bar 11:30-1 am; entertainment Fri, Sat. Ck-out noon. Meeting rms. Business servs avail. Downhill/x-country ski 17 mi. Exercise rm; instructor, weights, bicycles, sauna. Built in 1869; high ceilings, oak & cherry woodwork, antiques, early Americana. Community-owned. Cr cds: A, C, D, DS, MC, V.

Inn

   ★ ★ **KALTENBACH'S.** Stony Fork Rd, 2 mi W on Kelsey St, S on Stony Fork Rd. 717/724-4954; res: 800/722-4954. 10 rms, 2 suites, 1 rm with shared bath. 5 rm phones. S $35; D $70; suites $125; under age 6 free; golf, ski plans; wknds, hols (2-day min); lower rates Jan-April. TV; cable (premium). Playground. Complimentary full bkfst; afternoon refreshments. Restaurant nearby 11 am-10 pm. Ck-out 11 am, ck-in noon. 18-hole golf privileges 2 mi; greens fee $35, putting green, driving range, pro. Downhill ski 12 mi; x-country ski 20 mi. Totally nonsmoking. Cr cds: A, C, D, DS, MC, V.

West Chester (F-9)

(See also Chester, Kennett Square, King of Prussia, Media, Philadelphia)

Founded 1788 **Pop** 18,041 **Elev** 459 ft **Area code** 610 **Web** www .brandywinevalley.com

Information Chester County Tourist Bureau, 601 Westtown Rd, Suite 170, 19382; 610/344-6365 or 800/228-9933.

In the heart of three Pennsylvania Revolutionary War historic sites—Brandywine, Paoli and Valley Forge—West Chester today is a university and residential community, with fine examples of Greek-revival and Victorian architecture.

What to See and Do

Brinton 1704 House. Stone house built by Quaker farmer William Brinton, authentically restored and furnished. (May-Oct, Sat, Sun; also by appt) 5 mi S just off US 202, Oakland Rd, in Dilworthtown. Phone 302/478-2853. ¢

Motel

✔★ **ABBEY GREEN MOTOR LODGE.** *1036 Wilmington Pike (PA 202) (19382).* 610/692-3310; FAX 610/431-0811. E-mail ireland @epix.net; web www.abbeygreen.com. 18 rms. S $39-$49; D $55-$65; each addl $5; cottages with kit. $55-$65; under 12 free; wkly rates. Crib free. Pet accepted. TV; cable (premium). Restaurant nearby. Ck-out 11 am. Business servs avail. Gift shop. Airport, RR station, bus depot transportation. Refrigerators; some fireplaces; microwaves avail. Picnic tables, grill. Cr cds: A, C, D, DS, MC, V.

D ✔ ⌘ 🔥 SC

Motor Hotel

★★★ **HOLIDAY INN WEST CHESTER.** *943 S High St (19382), at US 202.* 610/692-1900; FAX 610/436-0159. 143 rms, 3 story. S, D $85-$105; each addl $10; suites $109-$129; kit. suites $129-$149; under 17 free. Crib free. TV; cable (premium), VCR avail. Pool; lifeguard. Restaurant 6:30 am-10 pm. Rm serv. Bar 4 pm-2 am. Coin lndry. Meeting rms. Business servs avail. In-rm modem link. Valet serv. Airport transportation. Lawn games. Microwaves avail. Cr cds: A, C, D, DS, MC, V.

D ⌘ ✈ ⌘ 🔥 SC

Hotel

★★★ **BEST WESTERN CONCORDVILLE.** *(US 1 & US 322, Concordville 19331) 6 mi S on US 202, then 3 mi N on US 1.* 610/358-9400; FAX 610/358-9381. Web www.concordville.com. 117 rms, 5 story. 25 suites. S $110; D $125; each addl $15; suites $150-$185; under 12 free. Crib free. TV; cable, VCR avail. Indoor pool; whirlpool, lifeguard. Complimentary continental bkfst. Restaurant (see CONCORDVILLE INN). Bar. Ck-out noon. Meeting rms. Business servs avail. In-rm modem link. Gift shop. Beauty shop. Valet serv. Exercise rm; instructor, weight machine, stair machine, sauna. Refrigerator in suites, mini bars. Cr cds: A, C, D, DS, MC, V.

D ⌘ ✈ ⌘ 🔥 SC

Inn

★★★ **DULING-KURTZ HOUSE & COUNTRY INN.** *(146 S Whitford Rd, Exton 19341) N on PA 100, ½ mi W on US 30.* 610/524-1830; FAX 610/524-6258. 15 rms, 3 story, 5 suites. S, D $55-$120; each addl $15; suites $79-$120; higher rates Fri, Sat & hols. TV; cable (premium). Complimentary continental bkfst. Restaurant (see DULING-KURTZ HOUSE). Rm serv. Ck-out 11 am, ck-in 3 pm. Business servs avail. Built in 1783; period furniture, antiques, sitting rm. Cr cds: A, C, D, DS, MC, V.

D ⌘ 🔥 🦀

Restaurants

★★ **CLEMENTE'S.** *116 E Gay St (19380).* 610/344-7644. Hrs: 11:30 am-2:30 pm, 5:30-10 pm; Sat from 5:30 pm. Closed Sun; most major hols. Res accepted. Northern Italian menu. Bar. A la carte entrees: lunch $5.50-$10, dinner $10-$28. Child's meals. Specializes in pasta, veal, seafood. Valet parking Fri, Sat. Italian decor with tapestries and artwork. Cr cds: A, C, D, DS, MC, V.

D 🔳

★★★ **CONCORDVILLE INN.** *(See Best Western Concordville Hotel)* 610/459-2230. Web www.concordville.com. Hrs: 11 am-10 pm; Sun to 8 pm. Closed Dec 25. Res accepted. Continental menu. Bar to 2 pm. Wine list. Semi-a la carte: lunch $5.50-$9.95; dinner $14.95-$24.95. Child's meals. Specialties: crab imperial, crab cakes, prime rib. Outdoor dining. Family-owned. Jacket. Cr cds: A, C, D, DS, MC, V.

D SC 🔳

★★★ **DILWORTHTOWN INN.** *1390 Old Wilmington Pike (19382), 1 mi S of PA 926.* 610/399-1390. E-mail info@dilworthtown.com; web www.dilworthtown.com. Hrs: 5:30-10 pm; Sun 3-9 pm. Closed Jan 1, Dec 25. Res required. Bar. Wine cellar. Semi-a la carte: dinner $17-$25. Specializes in seafood, game, beef. Outdoor dining. Fifteen dining rms in restored colonial house (1758). Authentic period decor. Cr cds: A, D, DS, MC, V.

D 🔳

★★★ **DULING-KURTZ HOUSE.** *(See Duling-Kurtz House & Country Inn)* 610/524-1830. Hrs: 11:30 am-11 pm; Sat from 5 pm; Sun 3-11 pm. Res accepted. French, continental menu. Bar. Wine list. A la carte entrees: lunch $5.95-$13.95, dinner $15-$29.75. Specialties: veal tenderloin chapeau, sirloin steak au poivre (flambé), crab cakes. Valet parking Fri, Sat. Formal dining in 7 dining rms. Country inn atmosphere; formal gardens with gazebo. Fireplaces. Cr cds: A, C, D, DS, MC, V.

D 🔳

★★★ **LENAPE INN.** *Jct PA 52 & 100 (19382), 5 mi S on PA 52.* 610/793-2005. Hrs: 11:30 am-10 pm; Sun 2-9 pm. Closed Mon. Res accepted. Continental menu. Bar. Wine list. Semi-a la carte: lunch $6.50-$15.95, dinner $15-$29.95. Child's meals. Specialties: wienerschnitzel, roast rack of lamb a la Bretonne, sirloin steak au Poivre. Elegant dining overlooking Brandywine River. Cathedral ceilings, chandeliers, fireplace. Cr cds: A, C, D, DS, MC, V.

D 🔳

★ **MAGNOLIA GRILL.** *971 Paoli Pike (19380), in Chester County Book Co, in West Goshen Shopping Center.* 610/696-1661. Hrs: 9 am-8:30 pm; Fri, Sat to 9 pm; Sun to 5 pm. Closed Dec 25. Semi-a la carte: bkfst $2.95-$7.95, lunch $4.95-$7.95, dinner $5.95-$14.95. Child's meals. Specializes in New Orleans cuisine. Turn-of-the-century New Orleans decor. Original artwork. Cr cds: A, C, D, DS, MC, V.

D 🔳

West Middlesex (C-1)

Pop 982 **Elev** 840 ft **Area code** 724 **Zip** 16159

Motels

★★ **HOLIDAY INN.** *(3200 S Hermitage Rd, Hermitage) N on PA 60, at jct I-80 exit 1N.* 724/981-1530; FAX 724/981-1518. 180 rms, 3 story. S, D $74; each addl $6; under 19 free; golf plans. Crib free. Pet accepted. TV; cable (premium). Heated pool; poolside serv, lifeguard. Playground. Restaurant 6:30 am-10 pm; Dec-Mar 6:30 am-2 pm, 5-10 pm. Rm serv. Bar 11-2 am; entertainment. Ck-out 11 am. Coin lndry. Meeting rms. Business servs avail. In-rm modem link. Valet serv. Sundries. Game rm. Cr cds: A, C, D, DS, ER, JCB, MC, V.

D ✔ ⌘ ⌘ 🔥 SC

★★★ **RADISSON SHARON.** *On PA 18 at I-80 exit 1N.* 724/528-2501; FAX 724/528-2306. 153 rms, 3 story. S $80-$90; D $88-$98; each addl $8; suites $150-$200; under 12 free; wkend rates. Crib free. Pet accepted. TV; cable. Indoor pool; whirlpool, poolside serv, lifeguard. Restaurant 6:30 am-10 pm. Rm serv. Bar 11-2 am; entertainment Wed, Fri, Sat. Ck-out noon. Coin lndry. Meeting rms. Business servs avail. Bellhops. Valet serv. Gift shop. Sundries. Exercise equipt; treadmill, stair machine, sauna. Game rm. In-rm whirlpools; refrigerator in suites. Cr cds: A, C, D, DS, MC, V.

D ✔ ⌘ ✈ ⌘ 🔥 SC

Restaurant

★★ **THE TAVERN.** *([B8 N Market St, New Wilmington 16142) 3 mi S on PA 60, 5 mi E on PA 208.* 724/946-2020. Hrs: 11:30 am-2 pm,

5-8 pm; Sun noon-6:30 pm. Closed Tues; July 4, Thanksgiving, Dec 25. Res required. Complete meals: lunch $9-$11, dinner $11-$18. Specialties: stuffed pork chops, creamed chicken & biscuits, baked chicken. Country decor, built in 1840. No cr cds accepted.

White Haven (D-9)

(See also Hazleton, Jim Thorpe, Pocono Mountains, Wilkes-Barre)

Pop 1,132 **Elev** 1,221 ft **Area code** 717 **Zip** 18661
Information Pocono Mts Vacation Bureau, 1004 Main St, Stroudsburg 18360; 717/424-6050; for free brochures phone 800/POCONOS.

What to See and Do

Hickory Run State Park. Approx 15,500 acres of scenic area. Swimming beach; fishing, hunting. Hiking. Cross-country skiing, snowmobiling, sledding, ice-skating, ice fishing. Picnicking, playground, snack bar, store. Tent & trailer sites. Standard fees. 6 mi S on PA 534 off I-80 exit 41. Phone 717/443-0400.

Skiing.

Jack Frost. 2 triple, 5 double chairlifts; patrol, school, rentals; snowmaking; cafeteria, restaurant, bar; nursery. Longest run approx 1/2 mi; vertical drop 600 ft. (Dec-Mar, daily) Half-day rate. 6 mi E on PA 940. Phone 717/443-8425. ¢¢¢¢¢

Big Boulder. 5 double, 2 triple chairlifts; patrol, school, rentals; snowmaking; cafeteria, bar; nursery, lodge. Night skiing. Longest run approx 3/4 mi; vertical drop 475 ft. (Dec-Mar, daily) 1 mi E off PA 903 in Lake Harmony. Phone 717/722-0100. ¢¢¢¢

Motels

★ **POCONO MOUNTAIN LODGE.** *Jct PA 940 & I-80. 717/443-8461; FAX 717/443-7988; res: 800/443-4049.* 123 rms, 6 story. S, D $70; each addl $10; under 18 free; ski plans. Crib free. TV; cable. Pool. Restaurant adj 6 am-midnight. Bar 11-2 am. Ck-out noon. Meeting rms. Business servs avail. Downhill/x-country ski 4 mi. Hiking trails. Game rm. Cr cds: A, C, D, DS, MC, V.

★ ★ ★ **RAMADA INN.** *PA 940 (18624), 4 mi E on I-80, exit 42. 717/443-8471.* 138 rms, 4 story, 2 suites. Jan-Feb & mid-June-Columbus Day: S $90-$120; D $95-$130; each addl $10; under 18 free; higher rates NASCAR races; lower rates rest of yr. Crib free. Pet accepted; $450 deposit. TV; cable. Heated indoor pool; sauna, poolside serv, lifeguard. Complimentary coffee in lobby. Restaurant 7 am-10 pm. Rm serv. Bar 4 pm-midnight. Ck-out noon. Meeting rm. Business servs avail. Gift shop. Valet serv. Coin lndry. Airport transportation. Golf privileges, greens fee $40, pro, putting green, driving range. Downhill/x-country ski 4 mi. Game rm. Lawn games. Some refrigerators. Picnic tables. Cr cds: A, C, D, DS, JCB, MC, V.

Resort

★ ★ **MOUNTAIN LAUREL.** *4 mi E on PA 940 at jct PA Tpke exit 35 & I-80 exit 42. 717/443-8411; FAX 717/443-9741; res: 800/458-5921.* 250 rms, 3 story. MAP: S $134; D $188/person; each addl $10; suites $150; under 13 free; golf plan; some wkend rates; higher rates hols. Crib free. TV; cable, VCR avail (movies). 2 pools, 1 indoor; whirlpool, poolside serv, lifeguard. Playground. Supervised child's activities. Dining rm 6-9 pm. Box lunches, snacks, picnics. Bar 11-2 am; entertainment. Ck-out noon, ck-in 4 pm. Coin lndry. Meeting rms. Business center. Airport, RR station, bus depot transportation. Sports dir. 4 lighted tennis courts. 18-hole golf, greens fee from $44 (incl cart), driving range, putting green, miniature golf.

Archery. Downhill ski 5 mi. Soc dir; entertainment. Nursery. Movies. Game rm. Exercise rm; instructor, weight machine, bicycles, sauna. Picnic tables. Cr cds: A, C, D, DS, MC, V.

Restaurant

✔ ★ ★ ★ **POWER HOUSE.** *I-80, exit 40, 1 mi E on I-80, exit 40. 717/443-4480.* Hrs: 4-10 pm; Sun noon-10 pm. Closed Dec 24, 25. Res accepted. Italian, Amer menu. Bar. Semi-a la carte: $11.95-$15.95. Specialties: veal marsala, shrimp & crab fracaise. Located in old power plant. Cr cds: A, DS, MC, V.

Wilkes-Barre (C-8)

(See also Hazleton, Pocono Mountains, Scranton, White Haven)

Founded 1769 **Pop** 47,523 **Elev** 550 ft **Area code** 717
Information Pennsylvania's Northeast Territory Visitors Bureau, 100 Terminal Rd, Ste 216, Avoca 18641; 717/457-1320.

Named in honor of two members of the British Parliament who championed individual rights and supported the colonies, Wilkes-Barre (WILKS-berry) and the Wyoming Valley were settled by pioneers from Connecticut. Pennsylvania and Connecticut waged the Pennamite-Yankee War, the first phase ending in 1771 with Connecticut in control of the valley. It was later resumed until Connecticut relinquished its claims in 1800. Wilkes-Barre was burned by the Native Americans and Tories during the Revolution and again by Connecticut settlers protesting the Decree of Trenton (1782), in which Congress favored Pennsylvania's claim to the territory. Discovery of anthracite coal in the valley sparked the town's growth after Judge Jesse Fell demonstrated that anthracite could be burned in a grate without forced draft.

Motels

★ ★ **HAMPTON INN.** *1063 PA 315 (18702). 717/825-3838; FAX 717/825-8775.* 123 rms, 5 story. May-Oct: S $55-$65; D $65-$75; under 18 free; ski plans; higher rates: car races, Dec 31; lower rates rest of yr. Crib free. Pet accepted. TV; cable. Complimentary continental bkfst. Restaurant adj 7 am-11 pm. Ck-out noon. Meeting rm. Business servs avail. In-rm modem link. Valet serv Mon-Fri. Downhill ski 10 mi. Cr cds: A, C, D, DS, ER, MC, V.

★ ★ **HOLIDAY INN.** *880 Kidder St (18702), at PA 309. 717/824-8901; FAX 717/824-9310.* 120 rms, 2 story. S, D $69-$120; each addl $10; studio rms $75; family plan; ski packages. Pet accepted. TV; cable. Pool; wading pool, poolside serv. Restaurant 6:30-1 am. Rm serv. Bar noon-2 am. Ck-out noon. Meeting rms. Business servs avail. In-rm modem link. Bellhops. Sundries. Downhill ski 10 mi. Cr cds: A, C, D, DS, ER, JCB, MC, V.

Motor Hotel

★ ★ ★ **WOODLANDS INN & RESORT.** *1073 PA 315 (18702). 717/824-9831; FAX 717/824-8865; res: 800/556-2222 (exc PA), 800/762-2222 (PA).* 179 rms, 9 story, 25 apts. S $69-$107; D $79-$107; each addl $10; package plans; wkend rates. Crib $5. TV; cable. 2 pools, 1 indoor; whirlpool, poolside serv, lifeguard. Restaurant 7 am-11 pm. Rm serv. Bar 11-2 am; entertainment, dancing. Ck-out noon. Meeting rms. Business servs avail. Bellhops. Sundries. Barber, beauty shop. Free airport transportation. Lighted tennis. Exercise rm; instructor, weights, bicycles, sauna.

Game rm. Rec rm. Lawn games. Private patios, balconies. Cr cds: A, D, DS, MC, V.

D 🏃 ≋ 🏋 ⛷ 🔥 SC

Hotels

★ ★ **BEST WESTERN GENETTI.** *77 E Market St (18701). 717/823-6152; FAX 717/820-8502; res: 800/833-6152.* 72 rms, 5 story, 16 suites. Apr-Dec: S $74-$79; D $79-$89; each addl $10; suites $89-$99; under 12 free; higher rates NASCAR races; lower rates rest of yr. Crib free. Pet accepted; $25. TV; cable, VCR avail (movies). Pool; poolside serv. Complimentary coffee in lobby. Restaurant 7 am-2 pm, 5-9 pm. Rm serv. Bar 4 pm-2 am; entertainment. Ck-out 11 am. Coin lndry. Meeting rms. Business servs avail. Bellhops. Valet serv. Downhill/x-country ski 12 mi. Cr cds: A, C, D, DS, MC, V.

D 🏃 ⛷ ≋ 🏊 🔥

★ ★ ★ **BEST WESTERN-EAST MOUNTAIN INN.** *2400 E End Blvd (PA 115) (18702), I-81 exit 47A. 717/822-1011; FAX 717/822-6072.* 156 rms, 7 story, 24 suites. S $87-$92; D $92-$97; each addl $5; suites $115-$120; under 13 free; ski, golf plans; higher rates special events. Crib free. TV; cable, VCR avail (movies). Indoor pool; whirlpool, poolside serv, lifeguard. Restaurant 6 am-11 pm. Bar 11-1 am; entertainment Tue-Sun. Ck-out noon. Coin lndry. Meeting rms. Business servs avail. In-rm modem link. Free airport, RR station, bus depot transportation. Tennis privileges. Downhill ski 10 mi. Exercise equipt; weight machine, bicycles, sauna. Game rm. Refrigerator, wet bar in suites. Balconies. Cr cds: A, C, D, DS, ER, MC, V.

D 🏃 ⛷ ≋ 🏋 ⛷ 🔥 SC

Inn

★ ★ **PONDA-ROWLAND.** *(RR 1, Box 349, Dallas 18612) 5 mi N on US 11, 10 mi N on PA 309. 717/639-3245; FAX 717/639-5531; res: 800/854-3286.* 5 rms, 2 story. No rm phones. S, D $70-$95; each addl $25; under 3 free; 2-day min hols. Crib free. 2 cable TVs. Playground. Complimentary full bkfst. Complimentary coffee in rms. Ck-out noon, ck-in 1 pm. Business servs avail. Refrigerators. Picnic tables. On 130-acre farm. Country antiques. Totally nonsmoking. Cr cds: A, DS, MC, V.

🏊 ⛷ 🔥

Restaurant

★ ★ ★ **SABER ROOM.** *94 Butler St (18702). 717/829-5743.* Hrs: 11 am-2:30 pm, 5-11 pm; Sat from 5 pm. Closed Sun, Easter, July 4. Res accepted, required hols. Continental menu. Bar. Wine list. A la carte entrees: lunch $3.95-$8.95, dinner $10.95-$21.95. Specializes in veal, seafood. Family-owned. Cr cds: A, C, D, MC, V.

D

Williamsport (C-7)

(See also Lewisburg, Lock Haven)

Settled 1795 **Pop** 31,933 **Elev** 528 ft **Area code** 717 **Zip** 17701
Information Lycoming County Tourist Promotion Agency, 454 Pine St; 800/358-9900.

Now famous as the birthplace of Little League baseball, Williamsport once was known as the "lumber capital of the world." In 1870 a log boom extended seven miles up the Susquehanna River; 300 million feet of sawed lumber were produced each year. When the timber was exhausted the city developed diversified industry and remained prosperous. The historic district of Williamsport, known as "millionaires row," includes homes of former lumber barons.

What to See and Do

Hiawatha. Sightseeing trips down Susquehanna River aboard replica of an old-fashioned paddle-wheel riverboat. Public cruises (May-Oct, daily exc Mon). I-180 Reach Rd exit, in Susquehanna State Park. For schedule and fee information, phone 800/358-9900.

Little League Baseball International Headquarters. Summer baseball camp and Little League World Series Stadium are here. (Mon-Fri; closed hols) 1 mi S on US 15. Phone 717/326-1921. **Free.** Adj is

Little League Baseball Museum. (Daily; closed Jan 1, Thanksgiving, Dec 25) 1 mi S on US 15. Phone 717/326-3607. ¢¢

Little Pine State Park. Approx 2,000 acres. Swimming beach; fishing, hunting; boating (ramps, mooring). Cross-country skiing, snowmobiling, sledding, ice-skating, ice fishing. Picnicking, playground, store. Tent & trailer sites. Interpretive program. 15 mi SW via US 220, then 13 mi N via PA 44 & Legislative Rte 4001. Phone 717/753-6000. Camping ¢¢¢-¢¢¢¢

Lycoming County Historical Museum. Exhibits on regional history from 10,000 B.C. to present. Exhibits include Native American, frontier era; canals; steam fire engine & hose cart; military history; general store; blacksmith shop; woodworker's shop; gristmill; crafts & industry; Victorian parlor and furnished period rooms; wildlife; sports & Little League; lumber business. (May-Oct, daily; rest of yr, daily exc Sun; closed major hols) 858 W 4th St. Phone 717/326-3326. ¢¢ Within museum is

Shempp Toy Train Collection. Extensive toy train collection. More than 350 train sets on display, including the entire Lionel collection. Two detailed running displays allow visitors to start trains, blow whistles. Twelve unique trains include an American Flyer #3117 and Lionel "Super #381."

Annual Events

Victorian Sunday. House tours, flower show, entertainment. 2nd Sun June.

Lycoming County Fair. 20 mi SE via US 220, at Hughesville Fairgrounds. More than 50 acres of amusements, commercial displays, livestock judging, demolition derbies, grandstand entertainment, food. Mid-July.

Little League World Series. Teams from all over the world compete. 3rd wk Aug.

Motels

✔ ★ **ECONO LODGE.** *2401 E 3rd St, at US 220. 717/326-1501; FAX 717/326-9776.* 99 rms, 2 story. S $45-$50; D $50-$55; each addl $5; higher rates Little League World Series. Crib free. Pet accepted. TV; cable (premium). Complimentary coffee in lobby. Restaurant 6 am-8 pm. Bar 6 pm-2 am; entertainment Tues-Sat. Ck-out noon. Meeting rms. Business servs avail. Valet serv. Cr cds: A, C, D, DS, ER, JCB, MC, V.

D ⛷ 🏊 🔥 SC

★ ★ **HOLIDAY INN.** *1840 E 3rd St (US 220). 717/326-1981; FAX 717/323-9590.* 170 rms, 2 story. S, D $64-$79; each addl $10; under 18 free; higher rates Little League World Series. Crib free. Pet accepted, some restrictions. TV; cable. Pool; lifeguard. Restaurant 6:30-1 am. Rm serv. Bar 11-1:30 am. Ck-out 11 am. Coin lndry. Meeting rms. Business servs avail. In-rm modem link. Cr cds: A, C, D, DS, JCB, MC, V.

D ⛷ 🏊 ≋ 🏊 SC

★ ★ **QUALITY INN.** *234 Montgomery Pike (US 15). 717/323-9801; FAX 717/322-5231.* 115 rms, 3 story. No elvtr. S $55; D $61; each addl $7; suites $85-$90; under 18 free. Crib $4. TV; cable. Pool; poolside serv, lifeguard. Restaurant 6:30 am-1:30 pm, 5-10 pm. Rm serv. Bar 4:30 pm-2 am; entertainment Wed, Fri, Sat. Ck-out noon. Business servs avail. Valet serv. Sundries. Airport, bus depot transportation. Game rm. Cr cds: A, C, D, DS, ER, JCB, MC, V.

D ≋ 🏊 🔥 SC

Motor Hotel

★ ★ ★ **SHERATON INN.** *100 Pine St, at jct PA 220 & US 15. 717/327-8231; FAX 717/322-2957.* 148 rms, 5 story. S, D $85-$95; suites $150; under 18 free. Crib free. Pet accepted. TV; cable. Indoor pool. Restaurant 6:30 am-10 pm. Rm serv. Bar 11:30-2 am; DJ Tues-Sat. Ck-out noon. Meeting rms. Business servs avail. Bellhops. Free airport transportation. Downhill/x-country ski 18 mi. Some refrigerators. Whirlpool in suites. Cr cds: A, C, D, DS, MC, V.

⊡ ⮐ ⚓ ≋ ⛷ ▨ ☃ SC

Hotel

✔ ★ ★ ★ **GENETTI HOTEL.** *200 W 4th St (17704), downtown. 717/326-6600; FAX 717/326-5006; res: 800/321-1388.* 206 rms, 10 story, 42 suites. S $29.95-$59, D $35.95-$65.95, each addl $6, suites $75.95-$139; under 10 free; higher rates Little League World Series. Wkly rates; golf plans. Crib free. Pet accepted. TV; cable (premium), VCR avail. Pool; poolside serv. Restaurant 6:30 am-10 pm. Bar 11-2 am; entertainment Fri, Sat. Ck-out 11 am. Meeting rm. Business servs avail. Barber, beauty shop. Coin lndry. Free airport transportation. Downhill ski, 20 mi. Exercise equipt; weight machine, stair machine. Some refrigerators. Cr cds: A, D, MC, V.

⊡ ⮐ ⚓ ≋ ⛷ ▨ SC

Inns

★ ★ ★ **REIGHARD HOUSE.** *1323 E 3rd St (US 220). 717/326-3593; FAX 717/323-4734; res: 800/326-8335.* 6 rms, 2 story. S $58-$68; D $58-$78; each addl $10. Closed Dec 20-Jan 1. Crib $5. TV; cable. Pool privileges. Complimentary full bkfst; afternoon refreshments. Complimentary coffee in rms. Restaurant nearby. Ck-out 11 am, ck-in 3 pm. Business servs avail. In-rm modem link. Free airport, bus depot transportation. X-country ski 8 mi. Health club privileges. Brick and stone mansion (1905); music rm, library; oak & cherry millwork, paneling. Once used as state police barracks. Cr cds: A, C, D, MC, V.

≋ ▨ ☃

★ ★ **SHADY LANE.** *(PA 42, Eagles Mere 17731) I-180 to US 220. 717/525-3394; res: 800/524-1248.* 7 rms. No AC. No rm phones. MAP: S $60; D $75; each addl $15; wkends (2-day min). Children over 12 yrs only. TV rm; cable. Complimentary full bkfst; afternoon refreshments. Restaurant nearby. Ck-out 11 am, ck-in 2 pm. Tennis privileges. 18-hole golf privileges, greens fee $44-$64, putting green, driving range. X-country ski 2 mi. Picnic tables. Totally nonsmoking. No cr cds accepted.

≋ ⛷ ▨ ☃

Willow Grove (F-10)

(See also Philadelphia)

Pop 35 (est) **Elev** 310 ft **Area code** 215 **Zip** 19090

What to See and Do

Bryn Athyn Cathedral. Outstanding example of Gothic architecture. Free guided tours (Apr-Nov, daily). 3 mi N of PA Tpke, exit 27 on PA 611N, then 4 mi E on County Line Rd to PA 232, in Bryn Athyn. Phone 215/947-0266. On grounds adj is

Glencairn Museum. Romanesque-style building features medieval sculpture and one of the largest privately owned collections of stained glass in the world; also Egyptian, Greek, Roman, ancient Near East and Native American collections. (Mon-Fri by appt) 1001 Cathedral Rd, at PA 232. Phone 215/938-2600. ¢¢

Graeme Park (1722). A fine example of Georgian architecture; stone house built by Sir William Keith, colonial governor of colony 1717-1726.

Tours. (Wed-Sun; closed some hols) 5 mi N on PA 611. Phone 215/343-0965. ¢¢

Motels

★ ★ ★ **COURTYARD BY MARRIOTT.** *2350 Easton Rd, PA Tpke exit 27. 215/830-0550; FAX 215/830-0572.* 149 rms, 3 story. S, D $134; suites $150-$160; wkly, wkend rates. Crib free. TV; cable (premium), VCR avail (movies). Indoor pool; whirlpool. Complimentary coffee in rms. Restaurant 6:30-10 am; Sat, Sun 7-11:30 am. Bar 4-11 pm Mon-Thurs. Ck-out noon. Coin lndry. Meeting rms. Business servs avail. In-rm modem link. Valet serv. Airport transportation. Exercise equipt; weight machine, bicycles. Refrigerators; microwaves avail. Cr cds: A, C, D, DS, MC, V.

⊡ ≋ ⛷ ▨ ☃ SC

★ ★ ★ **HAMPTON INN.** *1500 Easton Rd, PA Tpke, exit 27, S on PA 611. 215/659-3535; FAX 215/659-4040.* 150 rms, 5 story. S $109; D $119; under 18 free; wkend rates. Crib free. TV; cable (premium). Complimentary continental bkfst. Restaurants nearby. Ck-out noon. Meeting rms. Business servs avail. In-rm modem link. Valet. Airport transportation. Exercise equipt; bicycles, treadmill, sauna. Health club privileges. Some refrigerators; microwaves avail. Cr cds: A, C, D, DS, MC, V.

⊡ ⛷ ▨ ☃ SC

Inn

★ ★ ★ **JOSEPH AMBLER.** *(1005 Horsham Rd, Montgomeryville 19454) 2 mi N on Easton Rd, 7 mi W on Horsham Rd. 215/362-7500; FAX 215/361-5924.* 28 rms, 2-3 story. S $88-$225; D $98-$270; each addl $15. TV; VCR avail. Complimentary full bkfst. Restaurant (see JOSEPH AMBLER INN). Ck-out 11 am, ck-in 3 pm. Business center. Private parking. Three buildings built 1734-1820; antiques. Cr cds: A, D, DS, MC, V.

⊡ ▨ ☃ ⍕

Restaurants

★ ★ ★ **JOSEPH AMBLER INN.** *(See Joseph Ambler Inn)* 215/362-7500. Hrs: 6-10 pm; Sat from 5 pm; Sun 5-9 pm. Res accepted. Bar 5-11 pm. Semi-a la carte: dinner $18.95-$26.95. Specialties: rack of lamb, crab cakes, salmon en croute. Entertainment Fri. In 1820s stone barn. Cr cds: A, D, DS, MC, V.

⊡ ⊡

★ ★ **OTTO'S BRAUHAUS.** *(233 Easton Rd, Horsham) PA Tpke exit 27, 1/2 mi N on PA 611. 215/675-1864.* Hrs: 7 am-10 pm; early-bird dinner 3-5:30 pm. Closed Jan 1, Dec 25. Res accepted. German, Amer menu. Bar 11 am-midnight. Semi-a la carte: bkfst $3-$8, lunch $5-$11, dinner $9-$20. Child's meals. Specialties: sauerbraten, Wienerschnitzel. Own desserts. Outdoor dining. Large German beer garden. Cr cds: A, D, DS, MC, V.

⊡ ⊡

Wrightsville (York Co) (F-7)

(For accommodations see Bird-in-Hand, Lancaster, York; also see Pennsylvania Dutch Area)

Pop 2,396 **Elev** 306 ft **Area code** 717 **Zip** 17368
Information York County Visitors Information Center, 1618 Toronita St, York 17402; 717/843-6660.

What to See and Do

Donegal Mills Plantation & Inn (1800). Historic village and resort dating from 1736. Mansion, bake house, gardens; restaurant and lodging (yr round). Plantation tours (Mar-Dec, Sat & Sun afternoons). 5 mi N via US

30, PA 441, 772, in Mt Joy (Lancaster Co). Phone 717/653-2168. Tours ¢¢

Restaurant

★ ★ ★ **ACCOMAC INN.** *Accomac Rd. 717/252-1521.* E-mail accomac@net-works.net. Hrs: 5:30-9:30 pm; Sun 4-8:30 pm; Sun brunch 11 am-2:30 pm. Closed Dec 25. Res accepted; required wkends. Continental, French menu. Bar. Wine list. Semi-a la carte: dinner $16-$32. Sun brunch $22.95. Specialties: roast duckling, steak Diane. Own pastries. Entertainment Sat. Reconstructed historic building (1775) on banks of river. Cr cds: A, MC, V.

York (F-7)

(See also Hanover, Harrisburg, Lancaster, Pennsylvania Dutch Area, Wrightsville)

Founded 1741 **Pop** 42,192 **Elev** 400 ft **Area code** 717 **E-mail** adruck @yorkpa.org **Web** www.yorkpa.org

Information Convention and Visitors Bureau, 1 Market Way East, PO Box 1229, 17405; 800/673-2429; or the Visitors Information Center, 1618 Toronita St, 17402; 717/843-6660.

York claims to be the first capital of the United States. The Continental Congress met here in 1777 and adopted the Articles of Confederation, using the phrase "United States of America" for the first time. The first Pennsylvania town founded west of the Susquehanna River, York was and is still based on an agricultural and industrial economy. The city is dotted with 17 historical markers and 35 brass or bronze tablets marking historical events or places. There are more than 10 recreation areas in the county.

What to See and Do

Bob Hoffman Weightlifting Hall of Fame. Weightlifting section honors Olympic weightlifters, powerlifters, bodybuilders and strongmen; displays include samples of Iron Game artifacts, memorabilia and photos. (Daily exc Sun; closed hols) 4 mi N via I-83, exit 11; at York Barbell Co corporate headquarters. Phone 717/767-6481. **Free.**

Central Market House. Opened in March 1888. Over 70 vendors offer fresh produce, homemade baked goods, regional handcrafts and specialty items. (Tues, Thurs, Sat; closed hols) 34 W Philadelphia St. Phone 717/848-2243. **Free.**

Fire Museum of York County. Turn-of-the-century firehouse preserves two centuries of firefighting history; from leather bucket brigades to hand-drawn hose carts and pumps, horse-drawn equipment and finally to motorized equipment; artifacts and memorabilia; fire chief's office and firefighter's sleeping quarters are re-created, complete with brass slide pole. (Apr-Oct, Sat & 2nd Sun every month; also by appt; closed hols) 757 W Market St. Phone 717/843-0464. ¢

Friends Meeting House (1766). Original virgin pine paneling; restored. Regular meetings are still held here. (By appt) 135 W Philadelphia St. Phone 717/843-2285. **Free.**

Gifford Pinchot State Park. Approx 2,300 acres; 340-acre lake. Fishing, hunting; boating (rentals, mooring, launching). Hiking. Cross-country skiing, ice-skating, ice fishing, ice boating. Picnicking, store. Tent & trailer sites, cabins. Nature center, interpretive center. Standard fees. 14 mi NW on PA 74 to Rossville, then NE on PA 177. Phone 717/432-5011.

Harley-Davidson, Inc. Guided tour through the motorcycle assembly plant and the Rodney Gott Antique Motorcycle Museum. Children under 12 and cameras not permitted on plant tour. Plant and museum combination tour (Mon-Fri); museum tour (Sat). 1425 Eden Rd, 2 mi E on US 30. Schedule may vary; phone 717/848-1177. **Free.**

Historical Society of York County. Includes library with genealogical records (daily exc Sun; fee for nonmembers). Museum features exhibits on the history of York County. Combination ticket for all historic sites maintained by the society. (Daily; closed most major hols) 250 E Market St. Phone 717/848-1587. Museum ¢; Combination ticket ¢¢¢ Sites include

General Gates' House (1751). It was here that Lafayette gave a toast to Washington, marking the end of a movement to replace him. Also here are **Golden Plough Tavern** (1741), one of the earliest buildings in York, which reflects the Germanic background of many of the settlers in its furnishings and half-timber architecture, and the **Bobb Log House** (1811), furnished with painted and grained furniture. (Daily; closed most major hols) 157 W Market St (enter on N Pershing Ave). ¢¢

Bonham House (ca 1875). Historic house reflects life in late 19th century. (By appt; closed most hols) 152 E Market St. Phone 717/848-1587. ¢

Ski Roundtop. Triple, 5 double chairlifts, 2 J-bars, 2 pony lifts; patrol, school, rentals; snowmaking; cafeteria; nursery. Longest run 4,100 ft; vertical drop 600 ft. (Mid-Nov-mid-Mar, daily) 12 mi NW on PA 74, then 1/2 mi N on PA 177 to Mt Airy Rd, then to Roundtop Rd, follow signs. Phone 717/432-9631or 800/767-4766 (snow report). ¢¢¢¢¢

Warrington Friends Meeting House (1769; expanded in 1782). Fine example of early Quaker meetinghouse. 14 mi NW on PA 74.

York County Colonial Court House. Replica of 1754 original. Exhibits include multimedia presentation of Continental Congress's adoption of the Articles of Confederation, audiovisual story of 1777-1778 historic events; original printer's copy of Articles of Confederation, historic documents and artifacts. Tours. (Daily) W Market & Pershing Aves. Phone 717/848-1587. ¢

Annual Event

River Walk Art Festival. Along Codorus Creek at York County Colonial Court House. Late Aug.

Motels

★ **BEST WESTERN.** *1415 Kenneth Rd (17404). 717/767-6931; FAX 717/767-6938.* 105 rms, 3 story. S $57-$71; D $68-$77; each addl $5; under 18 free. Crib free. TV; cable (premium), VCR avail (movies). Complimentary continental bkfst. Restaurant adj 11-1 am; Sat, Sun to 2 am. Ck-out noon. Meeting rms. In-rm modem link. Health club privileges. Some refrigerators; microwaves avail. Cr cds: A, C, D, DS, JCB, MC, V.

🅳 🖂 ♨ 🐾 SC

✔★ **BUDGET HOST-SPIRIT OF 76.** *1162 Haines Rd (17402), I-83 exit 7. 717/755-1068; FAX 717/757-5571.* 40 rms, 1-2 story. S $34-$35; D $36-$38; each addl $4; under 12 free. Crib $2. TV; cable, VCR avail (movies $5). Restaurant adj open 24 hrs. Ck-out 11 am. Some refrigerators; microwaves avail. Cr cds: A, D, DS, MC, V.

🖂 ♨

★ ★ **HAMPTON INN.** *1550 Mt Zion Rd (17402), at US 30E, near Galleria Mall. 717/840-1500; FAX 717/840-1567.* Web www.hamptoninn.com. 144 rms, 5 story. S $75-$79; D $83-$87; suites, kit. units $92-$99; under 18 free. Crib free. TV; cable (premium), VCR avail. Heated pool; whirlpool. Complimentary continental bkfst. Restaurant adj 6 am-10 pm. Ck-out 11 am. Coin lndry. Meeting rms. Business servs avail. In-rm modem link. Sundries. Exercise equipt; bicycle, rowers. Refrigerator in suites. Picnic tables. Cr cds: A, D, DS, MC, V.

🅳 ♨ ✈ 🎿 🐾 SC

★ ★ **HOLIDAY INN.** *2600 E Market St (17402). 717/755-1966; FAX 717/755-6936.* 120 rms, 2 story. S, D, studio rms $69-$79; under 18 free; higher rates: train collectors events, hol wkends. Crib free. TV; cable (premium). Pool; lifeguard. Restaurant 6 am-2 pm, 5:30-10 pm. Rm serv 7:30 am-9:30 pm. Bar 4 pm-midnight. Ck-out noon. Business servs avail. In-rm modem link. Valet serv. Sundries. Free airport transportation. Health club privileges. Refrigerators, microwaves avail. Cr cds: A, C, D, DS, JCB, MC, V.

🅳 ♨ 🖂 🐾 SC

★ ★ ★ **HOLIDAY INN.** *334 Arsenal Rd (US 30) (17402), at Toronita St.* 717/845-5671; FAX 717/845-1898. 100 rms, 2 story. S, D $69-$79; under 18 free. Crib free. TV; cable (premium). Pool. Restaurant 6 am-2 pm, 5:30-10 pm. Rm serv. Bar 5 pm-midnight. Ck-out noon. Meeting rms. Business servs avail. Valet serv. Sundries. Microwaves avail. Cr cds: A, C, D, DS, ER, JCB, MC, V.

⬛ 🏊 🖾 🐾 SC

Motor Hotel

★ ★ ★ **HOLIDAY INN.** *2000 Loucks Rd (17404), at West Manchester Mall.* 717/846-9500. 181 rms, 2 story. S, D $72-$98; under 18 free. Crib $10. Pet accepted. TV; cable (premium). 2 pools, 1 indoor; whirlpool, poolside serv, lifeguard. Playground. Restaurant 6:30 am-9:30 pm. Rm serv. Bar 3 pm-2 am. Ck-out 11 am. Meeting rms. Business servs avail. Bellhops. Valet serv. Miniature golf. Exercise equipt; weight machine, rowers, sauna. Holidome. Cr cds: A, C, D, DS, JCB, MC, V.

⬛ 🐾 🏊 🗡 🖾 🐾 SC

Hotel

★ ★ ★ **YORKTOWNE.** *48 E Market St (17401), E Market & Duke Sts.* 717/848-1111; FAX 717/854-7678; res: 800/233-9324. 162 rms, 8 story. S $52-$89; D $59-$96; each addl $7; suites $95-$225. Crib free. TV; cable (premium). Restaurants 6:30-2 am. Bar from 11 am. Ck-out noon.

Meeting rms. Business servs avail. In-rm modem link. Gift shop. Barber. Free valet parking. Airport transportation. Exercise equipt; weight machines, stair machine. Health club privileges. Some in-rm whirlpools; microwaves avail. Cr cds: A, D, DS, MC, V.

⬛ 🗡 🖾 🐾 SC

Restaurants

★ ★ ★ **THE ALTLAND HOUSE.** *(US 30 & PA 194, Abbottstown 17301) W on US 30.* 717/259-9535. Hrs: 11 am-9 pm; Fri, Sat to 11 pm; Sun 11:30 am-9 pm; Sun brunch to 2 pm. Closed Dec 24, 25. Res accepted. American menu. Bar 5-11 pm. Semi-a la carte: lunch $4.85-$14.95, dinner $9.75-$18.95. Sun brunch $12.95. Child's meals. Specializes in seafood, veal. Own baking. Built in 1805; wall murals depict house in earlier days. Victorian setting. Guest rms avail. Family-owned. Cr cds: A, DS, MC, V.

⬛ 🍽

★ ★ **SAN CARLO'S.** *333 Arsenal Rd (US 30), I-83 exit 9E.* 717/854-2028. Hrs: 4-9:30 pm; Fri, Sat to 10 pm. Res accepted. Continental menu. Bar. Semi-a la carte: dinner $9.95-$18.95. Child's meals. Specializes in fresh seafood, prime rib, veal. Entertainment. Renovated 175-yr-old barn; original fieldstone walls. Cr cds: A, C, D, MC, V.

⬛ SC 🍽 ♥

South Carolina

Population: 3,497,800
Land area: 30,207 square miles
Elevation: 0-3,560 feet
Highest point: Sassafras Mountain (Pickens County)
Entered Union: Eighth of original 13 states (May 23, 1788)
Capital: Columbia
Motto: Prepared in mind and resources; While I breathe, I hope
Nickname: Palmetto State
State flower: Carolina yellow jessamine
State bird: Carolina wren
State tree: Palmetto
State fair: October 8-18, 1998, in Columbia
Time zone: Eastern
Web: www.prt.state.sc.us/sc

In South Carolina the modern age has neither masked the romance of the Old South nor overshadowed the powerful events of colonial and Confederate times. This state's turbulent and romantic history tells a story that remains deeply ingrained in the history of the United States.

Spanish explorers made the first attempt to settle in present-day South Carolina in 1526, less than 35 years after the Europeans discovered America. A severe winter, hostile natives and disease proved too much for the Spanish to overcome, and the settlement was abandoned. A group of French Huguenots, led by Jean Ribaut, landed near the site of present-day Parris Island Marine Corps Base in 1562. The French colony might have been a success, had not Ribaut's return to the colony from France on business been delayed. The remaining colonists, fearing they had been abandoned, built a craft and sailed for home. Light winds stranded their boat at sea, and they faced the danger of starvation until a passing English ship rescued them.

The task of settlement fell to the English, whose challenge to Spanish control of the New World eventually met with success. A land grant from England's King Charles II gave the Carolinas to eight English noblemen (still known today as the "Lords Proprietors"). In 1670, the English arrived at Albemarle Point and established Charles Towne, the first successful European settlement in the Carolinas.

During the Revolutionary War, almost 200 battles and skirmishes were fought in South Carolina. The first overt act of revolution occured at Fort Charlotte on July 12, 1775; this was the first British property seized by American Revolutionary forces. On December 20, 1860, South Carolina became the first state to secede from the Union. The initial clash of the Civil War also occured on South Carolina soil; the bombardment of Fort Sumter in 1861 resulted in its seizure by Confederate forces, which maintained possession until the evacuation of Charleston in 1865. Bloodied, impoverished and blackened by the fires of General Sherman's march to the sea, South Carolina emerged from the difficult Reconstruction days and was readmitted to the Union in 1868.

For most of the period since the Civil War, South Carolina has had economic problems, but in recent years these have eased as industry has been attracted by hospitable communities and favorable tax rates. From town to town, throughout the state, diversified industries have brought with them greater prosperity. Power projects have been created by damming the Santee, Saluda, Savannah and other rivers. Four atomic energy plants provide commercial energy. Tourism, the state's second-largest industry, continues to grow.

A temperate climate makes South Carolina an attractive all-year resort. The cool upland western area merges into a subtropical seacoast. South Carolina is a major producer of tobacco, cotton, pine lumber, corn, oats, sweet potatoes, soybeans, peanuts, peaches, melons, beef cattle and hogs.

When to Go/Climate

South Carolina enjoys a moderate climate. Summers, however, especially in the low country and along the coast, can be uncomfortably hot and humid. The barrier islands and upcountry elevations provide summer havens from the blistering heat. Early spring and late fall are good times to visit, with comfortable temperatures and moderate rainfall.

AVERAGE HIGH/LOW TEMPERATURES (°F)

CHARLESTON

Jan 56/41	**May** 80/66	**Sept** 83/71
Feb 59/43	**June** 85/72	**Oct** 75/61
Mar 65/50	**July** 88/75	**Nov** 67/52
Apr 73/58	**Aug** 87/75	**Dec** 60/45

GREENVILLE

Jan 50/30	**May** 80/56	**Sept** 81/61
Feb 54/32	**June** 86/64	**Oct** 72/49
Mar 64/40	**July** 88/68	**Nov** 63/41
Apr 72/48	**Aug** 87/67	**Dec** 53/33

CALENDAR HIGHLIGHTS

MARCH

Triple Crown (Aiken). Three events; trials (Aiken Training Track), steeplechase (Clark Field), harness race (Aiken Mile Track). For more information, phone Aiken Chamber of Commerce 803/641-1111.

Family Circle Magazine Cup Tennis Tournament (Hilton Head Island). Sea Pines Racquet Club. Phone 803/363-3500.

MAY

Spoleto Festival USA (Charleston). Internationally acclaimed counterpart to the arts festival in Spoleto, Italy, founded by Gian Carlo Menotti; includes opera, ballet, dance, visual arts, theater, chamber music, jazz, symphonic and choral performances and much more. Piccolo Spoleto, running concurrent with the main festival, has performances by local and regional artists. Phone 843/722-2764.

JUNE

Sun Fun Festival (Myrtle Beach). More than 60 seaside entertainment events, including parades. Contact Chamber of Commerce, 803/626-7444 or 800/356-3016.

JULY

Freedom Weekend Aloft (Greenville). More than 200 balloonists compete. Phone 864/232-3700.

SEPTEMBER

Southern 500 (Darlington). Darlington Raceway. 500-mile stock car classic; also beauty pageant; "Southern 500" Festival parade; golf tournament. Preceded by two days of trials. For tickets, phone 803/395-8499.

Hilton Head Island Celebrity Golf Tournament (Hilton Head Island). Palmetto Hall, Indigo Run & Sea Pines Plantation. Phone 803/842-7711.

OCTOBER

Fall Tour of Homes and Gardens (Beaufort). Contact Historic Beaufort Foundation, 803/524-6344.

South Carolina State Fair (Columbia). Fairgrounds. Agricultural, floral, home, craft, livestock and commercial exhibits. Entertainment, shows, carnival. Phone 803/799-3387.

NOVEMBER

Colonial Cup International Steeplechase (Camden). Springdale Race Course. Phone 803/432-6513.

Parks and Recreation Finder

Directions to and information about the parks and recreation areas below are given under their respective town/city sections. Please refer to those sections for details.

Key to abbreviations: I.P. = Interstate Park; N.B.C. = National Battlefield & Cemetery; N.B.P. = National Battlefield Park; N.F. = National Forest; N.H. = National Historic Park; N.H.S. = National Historic Site; N.M. = National Monument; N.Mem. = National Memorial; N.M.P. = National Military Park; N.P. = National Park; N.Pres. = National Preserve; N.R. = National Recreational Area; N.S. = National Seashore; N.S.T. = National Scenic Trail; S.B. = State Beach; S.C.P. = State Conservation Park; S.G. = State Garden; S.H.A. = State Historic Area; S.H.P. = State Historic Park; S.N.A. = State Natural Area; S.P. = State Park; S.R. = State Reserve; S.R.A. = State Recreation Area; S.Res.P. = State Resort Park; S.R.P. = State Rustic Park.

NATIONAL PARK AND RECREATION AREAS

Place Name	Listed Under
Congaree Swamp N.M.	COLUMBIA
Cowpens National Battlefield	GAFFNEY
Fort Sumter N.M.	same
Francis Marion N.F.	CHARLESTON
Kings Mountain N.M.P.	same
Ninety Six N.H.S.	GREENWOOD
Sumter N.F.	GREENWOOD

STATE RECREATION AREAS

Place Name	Listed Under
Aiken S.P.	AIKEN
Andrew Jackson S.P.	ROCK HILL
Baker Creek S.P.	GREENWOOD
Barnwell S.P.	ALLENDALE
Caesar's Head S.P.	GREENVILLE
Cheraw S.P.	CHERAW
Chester S.P.	CHESTER
Colleton S.P.	WALTERBORO
Croft S.P.	SPARTANBURG
Dreher Island S.P.	NEWBERRY
Edisto Beach S.P.	CHARLESTON
Hickory Knob Resort S.P.	GREENWOOD
Hunting Island S.P.	BEAUFORT
Huntington Beach S.P.	GEORGETOWN
Kings Mountain S.P.	KINGS MOUNTAIN NATIONAL MILITARY PARK
Lake Greenwood S.P.	GREENWOOD
Lake Hartwell S.P.	ANDERSON
Lake Wateree S.P.	CAMDEN
Landsford Canal S.P.	ROCK HILL
Lee S.P.	HARTSVILLE
Little Pee Dee S.P.	DILLON
Lynches River S.P.	FLORENCE
Myrtle Beach S.P.	MYRTLE BEACH
N.R. Goodale S.P.	CAMDEN
Oconee S.P.	CLEMSON
Old Dorchester S.P.	CHARLESTON
Paris Mountain S.P.	GREENVILLE
Poinsett S.P.	SUMTER
Rivers Bridge S.P.	ALLENDALE
Sadlers Creek S.P.	ANDERSON
Santee S.P.	SANTEE
Sesquicentennial S.P.	COLUMBIA
Table Rock S.P.	GREENVILLE
Woods Bay S.P.	FLORENCE

Water-related activities, hiking, various other sports, picnicking and visitor centers, as well as camping, are available in many of these areas. Cabins are located at Barnwell, Cheraw, Devils Fork, Edisto Beach, Givhans Ferry, Hickory Knob Resort, Hunting Island, Keowee-Toxaway, Myrtle Beach, Oconee, Poinsett, Santee and Table Rock. No pets in cabins. Cabin reservations made at individual parks. Camping: 14-day maximum; reservations accepted only at Calhoun Falls, Devils Fork, Dreher Island, Edisto Beach, Hunting Island, Huntington Beach, Lake Hartwell, Myrtle Beach, Oconee, Santee and Table Rock; $10-$20/night; pets on leash only. Not all state parks are open every day; hours of operation also vary. Contact Columbia office or individual park before making final trip plans. Daily parking fee at major coastal parks in summer, $3-$15. Swimming fee at inland parks with supervised areas & bathhouses (early June-late Aug), $2; age 3-12, $1.50; ocean swimming free. Fees subject to change. For cabin rates and further information contact Dept of Parks, Recreation & Tourism, Edgar A. Brown Bldg, 1205 Pendleton St, Columbia 29201; 803/734-0156.

FISHING & HUNTING

There is no closed fishing season; well-stocked lakes and rivers are close at hand in all parts of the state. Surf casting and deep-sea fishing can be enjoyed all along the Atlantic shore. Mountain streams offer trout fishing. Nonresident freshwater license: $35; seven-day nonresident license: $11. Saltwater stamp: $5.50. No license or permit required of children under 16. Fees subject to change.

Quail, dove, wild turkey, white-tailed deer, rabbit, squirrel and fox are all legal quarry. Nonresident annual license: $75; ten-day (consecutive) license: $50; three-day (consecutive) license: $25; wildlife management area permit: $76. Nonresident big game permit for deer, turkey and bear: $80. State duck stamp: $5.50. Fees subject to change. For further hunting and fishing information contact Wildlife and Marine Resources Department, PO Box 167, Columbia 29202; 803/734-3888.

Driving Information

Safety belts are mandatory for all persons anywhere in vehicle. Children must be in an approved safety seat or wear a safety belt. For further information phone 803/343-0734.

INTERSTATE HIGHWAY SYSTEM

The following alphabetical listing of South Carolina towns in *Mobil Travel Guide* shows that these cities are within 10 miles of the indicated Interstate highways. A highway map should, however, be checked for the nearest exit.

Highway Number	Cities/Towns within 10 miles
Interstate 20	Aiken, Camden, Columbia, Darlington, Florence.
Interstate 26	Charleston, Clinton, Columbia, Newberry, Orangeburg, Spartanburg.
Interstate 77	Columbia, Rock Hill.
Interstate 85	Anderson, Clemson, Gaffney, Greenville, Spartanburg.
Interstate 95	Darlington, Dillon, Florence, Hardeeville, Santee, Walterboro.

Additional Visitor Information

For additional information on South Carolina contact the Department of Parks, Recreation & Tourism, 1205 Pendleton St, Columbia 29201; 803/734-0122.

There are ten travel information centers in South Carolina; visitors will find the information provided at these stops useful for planning travel and making lodging reservations in the state. Their locations are: at the eastern end of the state, on I-95 on the SC/NC border; in the eastern coastal region on US 17 on SC/NC border; in the southern section on US 301 on the SC/GA border, and on I-95 on SC/GA border; in midstate center on the southbound side of I-95 near Santee; on the southwestern side on I-20 on the SC/GA border; in the western part of the state on I-85 on the SC/GA border; located in the northwestern part of the state are centers on I-85 on the SC/NC border and on I-26 on the SC/NC border; in the northern part of the state on I-77 on the SC/NC border, and also at the State House Tour and Information Center located in Columbia.

Aiken (D-31)

(See also Allendale, Orangeburg)

Founded 1834 **Pop** 19,872 **Elev** 476 ft **Area code** 803
Information Chamber of Commerce, 400 Laurens St NW, PO Box 892, 29802; 803/641-1111.

Aiken is a popular social and sports center in the winter months, providing flat-racing training, steeplechase and harness racing, polo, fox hunts, drag hunts, tennis and golf. The University of South Carolina-Aiken is located here.

What to See and Do

Aiken County Historical Museum. Period rm settings and displays in late-1800s home. Log cabin (1808) and one-room schoolhouse (1890) on grounds. Special features include an archaeology exhibit and a 1950s drug store. Museum store. (Tues-Fri, also Sat & Sun afternoons; closed hols) 433 Newberry St SW. Phone 803/642-2015. **Donation.**

Aiken State Park. Approx 1,000 acres on the South Edisto River. Swimming; fishing; boating (rentals). Nature trail. Picnicking (shelters), playground. Camping (hookups, dump station). Standard fees. 16 mi E, on unnumbered road between US 78 & SC 4. Phone 803/649-2857.

Hopeland Gardens. A 14-acre public garden on former estate; terraces, reflecting pools, continuous blooms; sculptures. Garden trail for the visually impaired. Summer concert series (May-Aug, Mon evenings). (Daily) Whiskey Rd & Dupree Pl. Phone 803/642-7630. **Free.** Also here is

Thoroughbred Racing Hall of Fame. Enshrinement of champion horses trained and wintered in Aiken. (Oct-May, daily exc Mon) Phone 803/642-7630. **Free.**

Redcliffe. On 350 acres. Built in 1850s by James Henry Hammond. Greek-revival mansion furnished with family pieces, Southern antiques, art collection, historic documents and books. Picnic area. (Thurs-Mon) 15 mi SE off US 278, near Beech Island. Phone 803/827-1473. Mansion ¢

Annual Events

Triple Crown. 3 events: trials (Aiken Training Track), steeplechase (Clark Field), harness race (Aiken Mile Track). 3 consecutive Sat Mar.

Lobster Race. Aiken restaurants provide seafood fare. Festivities include lobster races, beach music and other activities. Phone 803/648-4981. May.

Seasonal Event

Polo games. Whitney Field. Sun afternoons. Feb-July, Sept-Nov.

Motel

✔★★ **RAMADA INN.** (29802). At jct SC 19, I-20 exit 18. 803/648-4272; FAX 803/648-3933. 110 units, 2 story. S, D $49-$53; each addl $6; under 18 free; higher rates Masters Golf Tournament. Crib free. Pet accepted, some restrictions. TV; cable (premium), VCR avail. Pool; wading pool. Restaurant 6-9:30 am, 5-9:30 pm; Sat from 7 am; Sun 7-10 am. Rm serv. Bar 5-10 pm. Ck-out noon. Meeting rms. Business servs avail. Valet serv. Refrigerators, microwaves avail. Cr cds: A, C, D, DS, ER, JCB, MC, V.

D ✔ ≈ ⊅ ⊛ SC

Inn

★★★ **WILLCOX.** 100 Colleton Ave (29801). 803/649-1377; FAX 803/643-0971; res: 800/368-1047. 24 rms, 3 story, 6 suites. S, D $95; suites $115-$125; package plans; higher rates Masters Golf Tournament. TV; cable (premium), VCR avail. Restaurant 7 am-2 pm, 6-9 pm. Rm serv.

Bar; entertainment Fri, Sat. Ck-out noon, ck-in 3 pm. Meeting rm. Business servs avail. Golf privileges. Health club privileges. Refrigerators. English country decor. Built 1898; antique furnishings. Cr cds: A, D, DS, MC, V.

D 🏃 ⊠ ⊠

Allendale (E-4)

(For accommodations see Aiken, Orangeburg, Walterboro)

Pop 4,410 **Elev** 191 ft **Area code** 803 **Zip** 29810
Information Chamber of Commerce, PO Box 517; 803/584-0082.

Moved six miles in 1872 to its present site to be on the old Port Royal railroad line, Allendale is an agricultural town with access to the lush hunting and fishing areas of the Savannah River Valley. More than 130 commercial farms with an average size in excess of 1,000 acres—the largest in the state—surround the town.

What to See and Do

Barnwell State Park. Approx 300 acres preserved in natural state with an abundance of trees, flowers. Boating (rentals); fishing. Nature trails. Picnicking (shelters), barbecue pit, playground. Camping, cabins. Standard fees. 17 mi N on US 278 to Barnwell, then 7 mi N on SC 3. Phone 803/284-2212.

Rivers Bridge State Park. Approx 400 acres on site of Civil War skirmish. River fishing. Nature trails. Picnicking (shelters), playground, recreation building. Camping (hookups, dump station). Standard fees. 15 mi E off US 641. Phone 803/267-3675 or 803/267-3621.

Anderson (C-3)

(See also Clemson, Greenville, Greenwood)

Founded 1826 **Pop** 26,184 **Elev** 770 ft **Area code** 864
Information Anderson Area Chamber of Commerce, 706 E Greenville St, PO Box 1568, 29622; 864/226-3454.

Textile mills and fiberglass plants lead an array of diversified industries that team with the products of the surrounding farmland to make Anderson a lively business center. The town was created as the seat of Anderson County; both were named for Gen Robert Anderson, who fought in the Revolutionary War.

What to See and Do

Agricultural Museum. Antique farming equipment, tools, pre-Eli Whitney cotton gin. (By appt) On US 76. Phone 864/646-3782. **Free.**

Hartwell Dam and Lake. This is a 56,000-acre reservoir with a 962-mi shoreline created by a dam on the Savannah River. Swimming, waterskiing; boating (81 ramps, 5 marinas); fishing. Picnicking (shelters). Camping (Mar-Nov; some all yr; hookups, dump station). Fee for some activities. W & S of town via US 29. Phone 706/376-4788 or 888/893-0678. On lake are

Lake Hartwell State Park. Located on 680 acres along Lake Hartwell. Swimming; fishing; boating (ramps). Nature trail. Picnicking (shelter), playground, store. Camping (hookups, dump station), laundry. (Daily) Standard fees. S on I-85 exit 1. Phone 864/972-3352.

Sadlers Creek State Park. On 395 acres. Lake fishing; boating (ramps). Nature trails. Picnicking (shelters), playground. Camping (hookups, dump station). Standard fees. (Daily) 13 mi SW off I-85 & SC 187. Phone 864/226-8950.

"The Old Reformer." Cannon used by both British and Americans during Revolution; was fired in 1860, when Ordinance of Secession was signed. In front of courthouse, Main & Whitner Sts.

Pendleton Historic District. Settled in 1790, this town was the seat of what is now Anderson, Oconee and Pickens counties. There are self-guided tours (free), 2¹/₂-hr guided group tours (by appt, fee) or auto/walking tape tours (cassette, also in French; fee) of 45 historic homes and buildings. The Pendleton District Historical and Recreational Commission, 125 E Queen St, PO Box 565, phone 864/646-3782, has tour information (Mon-Fri; closed hols). Research library, Hunter's Store (ca 1850) across from village green; arts and crafts shop; visitor center (Mon-Fri; closed hols). 7 mi NW off I-85 off US 76. On Pendleton Town Square are

Pendleton Farmers' Society Building (1826). Begun as the courthouse, bought and completed by Farmers' Society. Believed to be oldest Farmers' Society building in continuous use in America.

Historic homes. Two of the many beautiful homes in the area are Ashtabula and Woodburn. (Apr-Oct, Sun; also by appt) Phone 864/646-3782. Per house ¢¢

Annual Event

Anderson Fair. Mid-Sept.

Motels

★ ★ **HOLIDAY INN.** 3025 N Main St (29621), I-85 exit 19A, on US 76. 864/226-6051; FAX 864/964-9145. 130 rms, 2 story. S $59-$64; D $65-$70; each addl $6; under 18 free; higher rates Clemson Univ football games. Crib free. Pet accepted, some restrictions. TV; cable. Pool. Complimentary coffee in rms. Restaurant 6:30 am-10 pm. Rm serv. Bar 4:30 pm-midnight; entertainment Fri, Sat. Ck-out noon. Coin lndry. Meeting rms. Business servs avail. In-rm modem link. Valet serv. Health club privileges. Refrigerators avail. Cr cds: A, C, D, DS, JCB, MC, V.

D ✎ ⊠ ⊠ 🏊 SC

✔★ ★ **LA QUINTA INN.** 3430 N Main St (29621). 864/225-3721; FAX 864/225-7789. 100 rms, 2 story. S $54-$61; D $60-$67; each addl $7; studio rms $35-$40; under 18 free. Crib free. TV; cable. Pool. Complimentary continental bkfst. Ck-out noon. Meeting rms. Business servs avail. In-rm modem link. Cr cds: A, C, D, DS, JCB, MC, V.

⊠ 🏊 SC

★ **SUPER 8.** 3302 Cinema Ave (29621). 864/225-8384. 62 rms, 3 story. No elvtr. S $34.88-$38.88; D $40.88-$48.88; each addl after 3, $4; under 12 free; higher rates: Clemson football wkends, special events. TV. Complimentary coffee. Restaurant nearby. Ck-out 11 am. Cr cds: A, C, D, DS, MC, V.

D ⊠ 🏊 SC

Beaufort (F-5)

(See also Charleston, Hardeeville, Hilton Head Island, Kiawah Island, Walterboro)

Founded 1710 **Pop** 9,576 **Elev** 11 ft **Area code** 803 **Zip** 29902
Information Greater Beaufort Chamber of Commerce, 1006 Bay St, PO Box 910, 29901-0910; 803/524-3163.

The atmosphere of antebellum days is preserved in this old town's gracious houses and churches. Second-oldest town in the state, Beaufort (BEW-fort) looks to the sea from Port Royal Island, one of 64 islands that comprise the county. Tourism and the military are major sources of income in this community.

Spanish explorers first noted the harbor in 1514-1515. In 1526, colonists from Spain made an unsuccessful attempt to settle the area. In 1562, a group of Frenchmen established the first Protestant colony on the continent, which also failed. English and Scottish attempts followed, with success finally coming when the present city was laid out and named for the Duke of Beaufort. The town was almost completely destroyed by Native Americans in 1715, captured by the British in the Revolution and menaced by British cannon in 1812. Nearly the entire population evacuated Beaufort when it was captured by Northern troops during the Civil War.

What to See and Do

Beaufort Museum. Collections of antique guns, fossils, paintings, arrowheads, Civil War relics. (Mon & Tues, Thurs-Sat; closed major hols) 703 Craven St, in the Beaufort Arsenal (1795). Phone 803/525-7077. ¢

Hunting Island State Park. A 5,000-acre barrier island in a semitropical setting; beaches, forest, marshes; lighthouse. Swimming, ocean fishing. Nature trails. Picnicking (shelters), playground, boardwalk; concession. Camping (hookups, dump station), cabins. Recreation & nature programs. Standard fees (higher rates Apr-Nov). 16 mi SE on US 21. Phone 803/838-2011.

John Mark Verdier House Museum (ca 1790). Federal-period house once known as the Lafayette Bldg; the Marquis de Lafayette is said to have spoken here from the piazza in 1825. (Daily exc Sun; closed Thanksgiving, Dec 25) 801 Bay St. Phone 803/524-6334. ¢¢

Marine Corps Air Station. Home of Marine Aircraft Groups MACS-5, MWSS-273, MALS-31 and CSSD-23. Windshield tours avail (phone ahead for availability). 6 mi NW on US 21. Phone 803/522-7201 or 803/522-7203. **Free.**

National Cemetery (1863). More than 11,000 interments, including Confederate and Union soldiers. Boundary St.

Parris Island. Famous US Marine Corps Recruit Depot. Visitor Center in Bldg 283; Museum in War Memorial Bldg. Ribaut Monument is memorial to Jean Ribaut, French Huguenot founder of Charlesfort (1562); Iwo Jima monument; monument to Spanish settlement of Santa Elena (1521). Historic driving & narrated bus tours depart from Visitor Center (driving tours, daily; bus tours, Sat-Wed). (Daily) 10 mi S. Phone 803/525-3650. **Free.**

St Helena's Episcopal Church (1712). Still in use; tombstones from surrounding burial ground became operating tables when church was used as hospital during Civil War. Silver Communion set in church was donated in 1734 by Capt John Bull in memory of his wife, who was captured by Native Americans. (Daily exc Sun) 507 Newcastle St, at North St. Phone 803/522-1712.

US Naval Hospital. On grounds are ruins of Fort Frederick (1731), one of largest "tabby" (cement & oyster shell) forts in US. 4 mi S on SC 802, between Beaufort & Port Royal, an early French settlement.

Annual Events

Beaufort Water Festival. Along waterfront at harbor. Includes parade, water show, boat races, concerts, dance. Phone 803/524-0600. Mid-July.

Fall Tour of Homes and Gardens. Contact Historic Beaufort Foundation, PO Box 11, 29901; 803/524-6334. Early Oct.

Motel

★ ★ **BEST WESTERN SEA ISLAND INN.** 1015 Bay St, in historic district. 803/522-2090; FAX 803/521-4858. 43 rms, 2 story. Mid-Feb-Nov: S, D $80-$99; each addl $10; under 12 free; higher rates special events; lower rates rest of yr. Crib free. TV; cable (premium). Pool. Complimentary continental bkfst. Restaurant nearby. Ck-out 11 am. Meeting rms. Business servs avail. In-rm modem link. Exercise equipt; bicycles, treadmills. Bicycle rentals. Opp bay. Cr cds: A, D, DS, MC, V.

🏃 🏊 🛪 🐾 SC

Motor Hotel

✔ ★ ★ **HOLIDAY INN.** 2001 Boundary St. 803/524-2144; FAX 803/524-2144, ext. 104. 152 rms, 4 story. S, D $69; each addl $8; under 19 free. Crib free. TV; cable (premium). Pool. Restaurant 6:30 am-2 pm, 5:30-9 pm. Rm serv. Bar 5-11 pm; Sat to midnight. Meeting rms. Business

servs avail. In-rm modem link. Valet serv Mon-Fri. Golf privileges. Microwaves avail. Cr cds: A, C, D, DS, JCB, MC, V.

D 🏃 🏊 🛪 🐾 SC

Inns

★ ★ ★ **BEAUFORT INN.** 809 Port Republic St. 803/521-9000; FAX 803/521-9500. 13 rms, 3 story, 4 suites. S, D $125-$150; suites $175-$195. Children over 8 yrs only. TV; cable, VCR (movies). Complimentary full bkfst. Complimentary coffee in rms. Restaurant (see BEAUFORT INN). Ck-out 11 am, ck-in 3-10 pm. Luggage handling. Concierge serv. Business servs avail. In-rm modem link. Tennis privileges. Golf privileges. Refrigerators. Some balconies. Built in 1907; double verandas. Totally nonsmoking. Cr cds: A, DS, MC, V.

D 🏃 🏊 🛪 🐾

★ ★ ★ **RHETT HOUSE.** 1009 Craven St. 803/524-9030; FAX 803/524-1310. Web www.innbook.com/rhett/html. Reminiscent of a grand plantation house, this Greek-revival townhouse, replete with galleries and gardens, is furnished with antiques and Oriental rugs. 10 rms, 3 story. S, D $125-$225; each addl $25. Children over 5 yrs only. TV; VCR avail. Swimming privileges. Complimentary full bkfst; continental bkfst avail in rms; afternoon refreshments. Ck-out 11 am, ck-in 3 pm. Business servs avail. Tennis privileges, pro. 18-hole golf privileges. Health club privileges. Some fireplaces. Bicycles. Cr cds: A, MC, V.

🏃 🏊 🛪 🐾

★ ★ **TWOSUNS INN.** 1705 Bay St, in historic district. 843/522-1122; FAX 803/5221122; res: 800/532-4244. E-mail 2suns@islc.net. 5 rms, 3 story. Mar-Nov: S $105-$120; D $120-$135; each addl $22; lower rates rest of yr. Children over 12 yrs only. TV avail. Complimentary full bkfst; afternoon refreshments. Ck-out noon, ck-in 3 pm. Business servs avail. Lawn games. Neoclassic-revival house (1917). Veranda overlooks bay. Totally nonsmoking. Cr cds: A, D, DS, MC, V.

D 🛪 🐾 SC

Restaurant

★ ★ ★ **BEAUFORT INN.** (See Beaufort Inn) 803/521-9000. Hrs: 8-10 am, 6-10 pm; Sun brunch to 2 pm. Closed Dec 24-26. Res accepted. Wine list. Semi-a la carte: dinner $17.95-$26.95. Complete meal: bkfst $9.50. Sun brunch $6.95-$12.95. Specialties: rack of lamb, jalapeno gritcakes with shrimp. Outdoor dining. Formal atmosphere. Cr cds: A, DS, MC, V.

D

Bennettsville (C-6)

(For accommodations see Florence; also see Cheraw, Darlington, Dillon, Hartsville)

Founded 1819 **Pop** 9,345 **Elev** 150 ft **Area code** 803 **Zip** 29512

Information Marlboro County Chamber of Commerce, 300 W Main St, PO Box 458; 803/479-3941.

Near the geographic center of the Carolinas, Bennettsville radiates highway spokes in every direction. Founded by Welsh settlers, and now the seat of Marlboro County, it has diversified industry including paper and electrical products, textiles and farm equipment. Agriculture is still important; cotton is the leading crop.

What to See and Do

Jennings-Brown House Restoration (1826). Served as headquarters for Union troops when Bennettsville was captured in 1865. The restored house is furnished with antiques pre-dating 1860. (Mon-Fri, also by appt; closed hols) 119 S Marlboro St. Phone 803/479-5624. ¢

Lake Wallace. A 500-acre lake with separate sections for swimming (June-Labor Day), waterskiing; fishing; boating. Waterfowl refuge. At N edge of city, off Country Club Dr. Phone 803/479-3941.

Camden (D-5)

(See also Columbia, Sumter)

Settled 1732 **Pop** 6,696 **Elev** 213 ft **Area code** 803 **Zip** 29020 **E-mail** camden@camden.net **Web** camden-sc.org
Information Kershaw County Chamber of Commerce, 724 S Broad St, PO Box 605; 800/968-4037.

The oldest inland town in the state, Camden was named after Lord Camden, defender of colonial rights. During the Revolution, General Cornwallis occupied Camden and made it the principal British garrison in the state and the interior command post for the South. Although several battles were fought in and near the town, including the Battle of Camden, the town was never recaptured by the Americans. Instead, it was evacuated and burned by the British in 1781. Camden contributed six generals to the Confederate cause and served as a storehouse, a hospital for the wounded and a haven of refuge until captured by General Sherman in 1865.

Today, Camden is famous for its history and equestrian sports—horseback riding, horse shows, hunt meets, polo and steeplechase races. There are 200 miles of bridle paths in the area and three race tracks; Springdale Course is an extremely difficult and exciting steeplechase run.

What to See and Do

Bethesda Presbyterian Church (1820). Called House of Five Porches; steeple in rear. Designed by the architect of the Washington Monument, Robert Mills; church is considered a masterpiece. (Daily exc Sun) On US 1; 502 DeKalb St. In front of church is

DeKalb Monument. German-born hero of Battle of Camden is buried here; monument consists of modest shaft with a base of 24 granite blocks, one for each state in the Union at that time. General Lafayette laid the cornerstone on Mar 9, 1825.

Camden Antique District. Offers all varieties of antiques in over 13 stores, some housing over 35 dealers. (Daily; closed hols) Downtown, bounded by King, DeKalb, Campbell & Fair Sts. Phone 803/432-2525.

Hampton Park. Named for Confederate general who later became governor. Flagstones used in crosswalks were once part of the sidewalks of old Camden and are said to have been brought over as ballast in British ships. Lyttleton St near US 1.

Historic Camden Revolutionary War Park. Archaeological site of South Carolina's oldest inland town. Visitor area includes two early 19th-century log cabins and a restored 18th-century town house. Trails lead to the reconstructed foundation of a pre-Revolutionary War powder magazine, Kershaw-Cornwallis House and two reconstructed British fortifications. Picnicking, nature trail, historical film. Self-guided and guided tours. (See ANNUAL EVENTS). (Daily exc Mon; closed some major hols) S Broad St (US 521 S). Phone 803/432-9841. ¢¢

Lake Wateree State Park. Approx 200 acres. Fishing; boating (ramp), bait shop. Nature trail. Picnicking, store. Camping (hookups, dump station). Standard fees. S on US 1, E on SC 34, then N on US 21 to SC 41, continue W. Phone 803/482-6401.

N.R. Goodale State Park. Approx 700 acres. Lake swimming; boating (rentals); fishing. 9-hole golf course. Picnicking (shelters); recreation building. Standard fees. 2 mi NW off US 1 on Old Wire Rd. Phone 803/432-2772.

Quaker Cemetery. Buried here are Richard Kirkland, who gained fame in the Battle of Marye's Hill by risking death to take water to dying Union troops; two of the three residents of the county who won Congressional Medals of Honor prior to World War II; and Dr. George Todd, brother-in-law of Abraham Lincoln. Broad & Meeting Sts, SW edge of town.

Rectory Square. Pantheon; six columns serve as memorial to Camden's six generals of the Confederacy. Chesnut & Lyttleton Sts.

Annual Events

Revolutionary War Field Days. Broad St. Historic Camden Revolutionary War Park. Two-day Revolutionary War encampment, festivities, battle re-enactments. Phone 803/432-9841. 1st wkend in Nov.

Horse racing. Springdale Race Course. 200 Knights Hill Rd. Phone 803/432-6513. Carolina Cup Steeplechase, early Apr. Colonial Cup International Steeplechase, mid-Nov.

Motels

✓★ ★ **COLONY INN.** *2020 W DeKalb St.* 803/432-5508; res: 800/356-9801; FAX 803/432-0920. 53 rms, 2 story. S $35-$39; D $45-$52; each addl $3. Crib $5. Pet accepted, some restrictions. TV; cable. Pool. Restaurant 5:30-10:30 am. Ck-out 11 am. Valet serv. Cr cds: A, C, D, DS, MC, V.

D ⛲ ≋ ⊠ 🔥 SC

★ ★ ★ **HOLIDAY INN.** *(Box 96, Lugoff 29078) 3 mi S on US 1/601.* 803/438-9441. 117 rms, 2 story. S $56-$85; D $56-$90; each addl $5; under 18 free. Crib free. TV; cable (premium). Pool; wading pool. Coffee in rms. Complimentary full bkfst. Restaurant 6:30-9 am, 5:30-10 pm. Rm serv. Bar 5 pm-midnight. Ck-out 11 am. Meeting rms. Business servs avail. In-rm modem link. Valet serv. Health club privileges. Some in-rm whirlpools; refrigerators, microwaves avail. Cr cds: A, C, D, DS, JCB, MC, V.

D ≋ ⊠ 🔥 SC

★ ★ **SHONEY'S INN.** *928 US 1S.* 803/438-4961; FAX 803/438-4961. 84 rms, 2 story. S $47; D $53; each addl $5; under 18 free. Crib free. TV; cable. Pool. Coffee. Restaurant adj 6 am-11 pm; Fri, Sat to 1 am. Ck-out noon. Meeting rm. Microwaves avail. Cr cds: A, C, D, DS, MC, V.

D ≋ ⊠ 🔥 SC

Inn

★ ★ **GREENLEAF.** *1310 Broad St.* 803/425-1806; res: 800/437-5874; FAX 803/425-5853. 11 rms, 2 story. S $55-$65; D $65-$75; each addl $10; suite $65-$75; under 12 free. TV; cable (premium). Complimentary continental bkfst. Dining rm 6-10 pm; closed Wed, Sun. Ck-out 11 am, ck-in varies. Health club privileges. Built in 1810. Cr cds: A, MC, V.

🔥 SC

Restaurants

★ ★ ★ **LILFRED'S.** *(11 Main St, Rembert)* 803/432-7063. Hrs: 6-10 pm. Closed Sun-Tues; some major hols. Res accepted. Wine cellar. Semi-a la carte: dinner $10.95-$19.95. Specializes in seafood, Black Angus beef. Rustic decor. Cr cds: MC, V.

★ ★ **LUCY'S.** *1043 Broad St.* 803/432-9096. Hrs: 11:30 am-2:30 pm, 6-10 pm; Fri to 10:30 pm; Sat 6-10:30 pm. Closed Sun, Mon; Jan 1, wk of July 4, Dec 25. Res accepted. Bar. Semi-a la carte: lunch $5.95-$8.95, dinner $13.95-$18.95. Specializes in seafood, veal, lamb. Menu changes seasonally. Historic antique bar. Cr cds: A, D, MC, V.

D ⊐

★ ★ **THE MILL POND.** *(84 Boykin Mill Rd, Boykin 29128) S on US 521, S on SC 261.* 803/424-0261. Hrs: 5-10 pm; Fri, Sat to 11 pm. Closed Sun, Mon; Jan 1, Dec 25; also first wk July. Res accepted. Regional Southern menu. Bar. Semi-a la carte: dinner $14.95-$29.95. Specializes in seafood, Angus beef. Rustic country decor; brick fireplace. Cr cds: MC, V.

⊐

Charleston (E-5)

(See also Beaufort, Kiawah Island, Walterboro)

Founded 1670 **Pop** 80,414 **Elev** 9 ft **Area code** 843
Information Visitor Reception and Transportation Center, 375 Meeting St, PO Box 975, 29402; 803/853-8000.

This aristocratic and storied American city lives up to its reputation for cultivated manners. Charleston's homes, historic shrines, old churches, lovely gardens, winding streets and intricate iron lace gateways exude charm and dignity.

Charleston enjoys international and coastal commerce in the fine harbor formed, according to local opinion, where the "Ashley and Cooper rivers unite to form the Atlantic Ocean." The strategic harbor, inlets and sea islands provide recreational retreats.

The Charleston of today is the survivor of siege, flood, hurricane and epidemic. Capital of the province until 1786, its history and that of South Carolina are almost the same. Charleston received colonists from the Old World and sent them into the wilderness. The city served as the personification of Europe's luxury and culture in the New World.

The first permanent settlement in the Carolinas, Charles Towne, as it was first called, was established as a tiny colony, westward across the Ashley River, by Anthony Ashley Cooper, Earl of Shaftesbury. At the same time, he established the only American nobility in history, with barons, landgraves (dukes) and caciques (earls), each owning great plantations.

This nobility lasted less than 50 years, but it was the foundation for an aristocratic tradition that still exists, even though the rice and indigo that made the early Charleston people rich are gone. Colonists from Barbados, England and Ireland came to enlarge the settlement in 1670, and by 1680 the colony moved across the river to become a city-state. Although many of the colonists went on to the Carolina Lowcountry and established grand plantations, every year on the traditional date of May 10, the planters and their families moved back to Charleston to escape the mosquitoes and malarial heat. From spring to frost, these planters created a season of dancing, sport, musicales, theater and socials. Commerce and plantations provided the prosperity on which the city's cosmopolitan graces were based. Charleston founded the first playhouse designed solely for presentation of drama, the first museum, the first public school in the colony, the first municipal college in America and the first fire insurance company on the continent. (It was a victim the next year of a fire that destroyed half the city.) The city became famous throughout the world as "a flourishing capital of wealth and ease."

The First Provincial Congress of South Carolina met in Charleston in 1775 and prepared the city to repulse a British attack on June 28, 1776. But in 1780 the city was captured and for two and a half years was occupied by the enemy. Charleston was almost the last point in the state to be cleared of British troops. With peace came great prosperity, but rivalry between the small farmers of the interior and the merchants and plantation owners of the Lowlands resulted in removal of the capital to Columbia.

The convention that authored the Ordinance of Secession came to Charleston to pass that declaration; the Civil War then began with the bombardment of Fort Sumter by Fort Johnson. A long siege followed, including the gallant defense of Fort Sumter (1863-1865), blockade running, the first submarine warfare, evacuation after Sherman had demolished Columbia and, finally, bombardment of the city by the Union Army.

What to See and Do

Aiken-Rhett House (1817). Home of Governor William Aiken (1833-1887). Enlarged in Greek-revival style (1833-1836); subsequent additions (1858) created some of the finest rooms in Charleston, including a Rococo-revival art gallery. Many original furnishings from 1833. (Daily; closed most hols) 48 Elizabeth St, corner of Judith St. Phone 843/723-1159. ¢¢¢ Combination ticket (addl fee) includes Nathaniel Russell House.

Boat trips.

Fort Sumter Tours. Tour (2¼ hrs) through Charleston harbor to Ft Sumter (see). (Daily; closed Dec 25) Also 2-hr Charleston harbor tour, 3-hr *Spirit of Charleston* dinner cruise. Municipal Marina, Lockwood Blvd & Patriots Point, Mt Pleasant. Phone 843/722-1691. ¢¢¢; Dinner cruise ¢¢¢¢¢

Gray Line Water Tours. Tours (approx 2 hrs) of harbor, US Naval Base, view of forts, other points of interest. City Municipal Marina, Lockwood Blvd. For information, reservations contact PO Box 861, 29402-0861; 843/723-5858. ¢¢¢

Boone Hall Plantation (1681). A 738-acre estate with nine original slave houses and ginhouse (ca 1750), pecan grove, ½-mi "Avenue of Oaks." Several rooms in the house are open to the public. (Daily; closed Thanksgiving, Dec 25) 8 mi N off US 17 on Long Point Rd in Mt Pleasant. Phone 843/884-4371. ¢¢¢

Chamber of Commerce. Building was once the South Carolina Railway Warehouse, home of one of the nation's first steam locomotives. Organized in 1773, the Chamber of Commerce (phone 843/577-2510) is one of the oldest city commercial organizations in the country. Also houses the Charleston Trident Convention & Visitors Bureau. 81 Mary St.

Charles Towne Landing. Unusual 664-acre park on site of state's first permanent English settlement (1670). Reconstructed fortifications in original settlement area; replica of *Adventure,* 17th-century trading vessel; 1670 experimental crop garden; formal gardens; nature trails; Colonial Village; 20-acre animal forest. Also featured in a 30-min movie, *Carolina.* Tram tours and bicycle rentals. Picnicking, playground; restaurant. (Daily; closed Dec 24, 25) 1500 Old Town Rd, on SC 171. Phone 843/852-4200. ¢¢

Cypress Gardens. Consists of 163 acres with giant cypresses, blackwater swamp, azaleas and camellias, dogwoods, daffodils. Boat trips. Picnic area. Free parking. Gift shop. (Daily) 24 mi N off US 52, between Goose Creek & Moncks Corner. Phone 843/553-0515. ¢¢¢

Drayton Hall. One of the oldest surviving pre-Revolutionary War plantation houses (1738) in the area, this Georgian Palladian house is surrounded by live oaks and is located on the Ashley River. Held in the Drayton family for seven generations, the mansion has been maintained in virtually its original condition. A National Trust for Historic Preservation property. Tours (hrly). (Daily; closed Jan 1, Thanksgiving, Dec 25) 9 mi NW via SC 61 (Old Ashley River Rd). Phone 843/766-0188. ¢¢¢

Edisto Beach State Park. Approx 1,200 acres. 1½ mi of beach; shell collecting is very good here. Ocean swimming, fishing. Nature trail. Picnic area (shelters), gift shop. Camping (higher fees Apr-Labor Day); cabins. Standard fees. 21 mi W on US 17, then 29 mi S on SC 174. Phone 843/869-2756.

Folly Beach County Park. Approx 4,000 ft of ocean frontage and 2,000 ft of river frontage. There is a 600-ft section of beach for swimming (Apr-Sept); lifeguards. Dressing areas, outdoor showers; picnic areas; concessions; shelter. (Daily) S via SC 171 on W end of Folly Island. Per vehicle ¢¢

Fort Sumter National Monument (see).

Francis Beidler Forest. National Audubon Society Sanctuary. Boardwalk (1½ mi) into the center of a beautiful blackwater swamp; close-up view of one of the largest stands of old-growth bald cypress and tupelo gum forest in the world. Self-guided tour. Visitor center, slide show. Canoe trips, night walks (in season, by res only; fee). (Daily exc Mon; closed Jan 1, Thanksgiving, Dec 24, 25, 31) No pets, food facilities or camping. Four Holes Swamp. 40 mi NW via I-26W to exit 187, then S on SC 27 to US 78, then W to US 178, follow signs. Phone 843/462-2150. ¢¢

Francis Marion National Forest. Early colonial settlements, plantations; lakes, moss-hung oaks, flowering trees and shrubs on 250,000 acres. Camping, picnicking, boating, fishing, hiking, horseback riding, motorcycling, rifle ranges, hunting. Fees may be charged at recreation sites. Headquarters are in Columbia (Mon-Fri). (Daily) NE via US 17 & 17A, SC 41. Phone 843/336-3248.

Hampton Park. Historic park with camellias and azaleas in spring, roses in summer; 1-mi nature trail; Charleston's mounted horse patrol stables. Rutledge Ave & Cleveland St. Phone 843/724-7321. **Free.**

Joseph Manigault House (1803). Outstanding example of Adam-style architecture. Features Charleston antiques, silver; curving staircase. (Daily; closed most hols) 350 Meeting St. Phone 843/723-2926. ¢¢¢ Combination ticket (addl fee) includes Heyward-Washington House and the Charleston Museum.

Kahal Kadosh Beth Elohim (1840). Founded in 1749; first Reform Jewish congregation in America (1824). Museum. Gift shop. (Mon-Fri mornings; closed all Jewish hols) 90 Hasell St. Phone 843/723-1090. **Donation.**

⭐ **Magnolia Plantation and Gardens.** Internationally famous gardens are America's oldest (ca 1680); now covering 50 acres with camellias, azaleas, magnolias and hundreds of other flowering species. Azaleas best mid-Mar-Apr; camellias best mid-Nov-Mar. Also on grounds is a 125-acre waterfowl refuge; tri-level observation tower, 16th-century maze, 18th-century herb garden; biblical gardens; topiary; nature trails; petting zoo; canoe and bicycle rentals; picnicking. Gift shop, snack shop; orientation theater. Plantation home and local art gallery (addl fee). (Daily) 10 mi NW on SC 61. Phone 843/571-1266. ¢¢-¢¢¢¢ Through Magnolia Plantation, enter

> **Audubon Swamp Garden.** Boardwalks, bridges and dikes make this 60-acre blackwater cypress and tupelo swamp accessible to visitors. Home to all local species of wildlife, this colorful area is planted with hundreds of varieties of local and exotic flowering shrubs. (Daily) Phone 843/571-1266. ¢¢

Medical University of South Carolina (1824). (2,200 students) Oldest medical school in the South. 171 Ashley Ave. Phone 843/792-3621. On campus is

> **Waring Historical Medical Library & Macaulay Museum of Dental History.** (Mon-Fri; closed hols) Phone 843/792-2288. **Free.**

Middleton Place Gardens, House & Stableyards. Once home of Arthur Middleton, signer of the Declaration of Independence, Middleton Place encompasses America's oldest landscaped gardens, the Plantation Stableyards, and the restored House Museum. The gardens, laid out in 1741, highlight ornamental butterfly lakes, sweeping terraces and a wide variety of flora and fauna. The Stableyards feature numerous craftspeople demonstrating skills necessary for a self-sufficient 18th-century plantation. House (addl fee). Guided tours (addl fee). Special events include Starlight Pops (May), Spoleto Finale (mid-June), Plantation Days (Nov) and Plantation Christmas (Dec). (Daily) 14 mi NW on SC 61. Phone 843/556-6020. ¢¢¢¢

Old Dorchester State Park. Congregationalists from Massachusetts established a village in 1696 at the head of the Ashley River. It grew as a trading center until 1752, when there was a general exodus of Congregationalists to Georgia in a search for plentiful land and a better climate. By 1780 the once-thriving town was occupied by the British and had only 40 houses and a church. In late 1781, Col Wade Hampton advanced against Dorchester. The British did not wait for the attack but instead destroyed the town and retreated to Charleston. Remains of the church tower and Fort Dorchester may be seen; 97-acre area has been partially excavated. Fishing. Picknicking. Drawings, artifacts in interpretive building. (Thurs-Mon) 19 mi NW on SC 642. Phone 843/873-1740. **Free.**

Palmetto Islands County Park. Nature-oriented park in tropical setting. Bicycle paths, marsh boardwalks, picnicking and grills throughout park. Two-acre pond. Canoe trails. Pedal boat, canoe & bicycle rentals. BigToy Playground. 50-ft observation tower with play area. Interpretive trails. Natural swimming facility with sand bottom. Fishing supplies; concession. (Daily; closed Jan 1, Thanksgiving, Dec 24, 25) N on US 17, 1/2 mi past Snee Farm, then left on Long Point Rd. Phone 843/884-0832. ¢

Sightseeing tours.

> **Charleston Carriage Co.** Offers narrated, horse-drawn carriage tours of Old Charleston (1 hr). Free shuttle service from visitor center. (Daily; closed Thanksgiving, Dec 25) 14 Hayne St. Phone 843/577-0042. ¢¢¢¢

> **Palmetto Carriage Tours.** One-hr tour through Old Charleston by horse- & mule-drawn carriages. Tours originate at Rainbow Market. Shuttle van from visitor center (free). (Daily; closed Dec 25) 40 N Market St. Phone 843/723-8145. ¢¢¢¢

> **Gray Line bus tours.** For information, reservations contact PO Box 219, 29402-0219; 843/722-4444.

St John's Lutheran Church (1817). Congregation established in 1742. Steeple, wrought-iron gates, churchyard fence, graves of interest. Interior restored. Pastor John Bachman (1815-1874), who coauthored *Quadrupeds of America* with Audubon, is buried beneath the altar in the church nave. (Mon-Fri; also Sun worship) Archdale & Clifford Sts. Phone 843/723-2426.

St Mary's Church (1838). Mother church for Catholic dioceses of Carolinas and Georgia. Congregation established in 1789. Stained-glass windows, paintings. (Daily) 93 Hasell St, between King & Meeting Sts. Phone 843/722-7696.

The Charleston Museum (1773). Oldest museum in US. Cultural, historical, natural history collections; children's "Discovery Me" room; decorative arts exhibits. (Daily; closed some hols) 360 Meeting St, at John St. Phone 843/722-2996. ¢¢¢ Combination ticket (addl fee) includes Heyward-Washington House and Joseph Manigault House.

The Citadel, Military College of South Carolina (1842). (2,000 uniformed cadets) Originally located near city's pre-Revolutionary War rampart, the college moved to its present site in 1922. Dress parades (academic yr, Fri). Moultrie & Rutledge Aves, near Hampton Park. Phone 843/953-5006. On campus is

> **The Citadel Archives Museum.** Exhibits depict history of the South Carolina Corps of Cadets at The Citadel. (Academic yr, afternoons) Phone 843/953-6846. **Free.**

Unitarian Church (1772). Second-oldest church in the city; under restoration. Fan tracery ceiling; interior modeled after Henry VII Chapel, Westminster Abbey. (Mon-Fri) 4 Archdale St. Phone 843/723-4617.

⭐ **Walking tour of Old Charleston.**

> **White Point Gardens.** View of harbor, city, Fort Sumter National Monument (see) and Fort Moultrie. Murray Blvd & E Battery, at foot of peninsula. Walk N on E Battery 1/2 blk to

> **Edmondston-Alston House** (ca 1825). Built by wealthy merchant and wharf owner, remodeled by next owner, an important rice planter, beginning in 1838; Greek-revival style. Uninterrupted view across harbor. Documents, engravings, portraits, original furnishings, elaborate woodwork. Guided tours (daily; closed Jan 1, Thanksgiving, Dec 25). 21 E Battery. Phone 843/722-7171. ¢¢¢ Continue N on E Battery (which becomes E Bay St) 8 blks, past Rainbow Row (14 houses dating from the mid-18th century, each painted a different color) to Broad St and the

> **Old Exchange & Provost Dungeon** (1771). Built by the British with material brought from England, this was the last building constructed by them on colonial soil in Charleston prior to the Revolutionary War; served as an exchange and a customs house. Used as a prison during the Revolutionary War. Original seawall of Charleston preserved in dungeon. Extensively restored; site of many important historical events. 122 E Bay St. Phone 843/727-2165. ¢¢ Follow Broad St to Church St and turn S; walk past Catfish Row (made famous by *Porgy and Bess*) to

> **Heyward-Washington House** (1772). Once owned by Thomas Heyward Jr, signer of Declaration of Independence and host to George Washington during his visit in 1791. Period pieces of exquisite design and craftsmanship; Charleston-made furniture; house is a classic example of a Georgian town house. Garden laid out with shrubs, plants that grew in city in Washington's time; carriage house, kitchen. (Daily; closed most hols) 87 Church St. Phone 843/722-0354. ¢¢¢ Combination ticket (addl fee) includes the Charleston Museum and Joseph Manigault House. Walk N on Church St to

> **Huguenot Church** (1845). Third building on this site; rebuilt on site of earlier structure burned in 1796. Congregation founded 1681. Only church in US using Calvinist Huguenot liturgy; services were in French until 1928. 110 Church St, at Queen St. Phone 843/722-4385. Continue N to

> **St Philip's Church** (Episcopal) (1838). Lofty steeple held mariner's light, was target for Union guns. Late Georgian architecture. Third building used by St Philip's parish. First Anglican parish (1670) south of Virginia. John C. Calhoun and other notables buried in churchyard. 142 Church St. 843/722-7734. From here walk N to Cumberland St then W to

The Powder Magazine (ca 1710). Part of city's original fortifications, oldest public building remaining. Used in Revolutionary War. Walls of this 8-gabled structure are 32 inches thick. Now houses historic colonial museum. (Mon-Sat, also Sun afternoons; closed Jan 1, Thanksgiving, Dec 25) 79 Cumberland St. Phone 843/723-1623. ¢ Walk W to Meeting St, then 1 blk S to

Gibbes Museum of Art. Permanent collection of American paintings, miniatures, Japanese wood block prints; changing exhibits. (Tues-Sat, also Sun & Mon afternoons; closed hols) 135 Meeting St. Phone 843/722-2706. ¢¢ Walk S to

City Hall Art Gallery (1801). On the site of colonial marketplace, first housed Bank of United States; became City Hall in 1818. Superb picture gallery on 2nd floor resulted from custom of commissioning artists to paint famous visitors; includes portrait of Washington by John Trumbull, considered one of the best of the general in his later yrs; painting of President Monroe by Samuel F.B. Morse. Tours. (Mon-Fri; closed hols) 80 Broad St, at Meeting St. Phone 843/724-3799. **Free.** On next blk is

St Michael's Church (1752). Steeple rises 186 ft; tower has four-faced clock in operation since 1764. Steeple bells were captured by the British, returned after the Revolution, sent to Columbia during the Civil War and partly destroyed by the fire there. Later they were sent back to England, recast in the original molds and returned in 1867. (Mon-Fri; closed hols and periodically for maintenance) Meeting & Broad Sts. Phone 843/723-0603. 2 blks S is

Nathaniel Russell House (1808). Home of wealthy merchant; example of Adam-style architecture; free-flying staircase, oval drawing rooms, period furnishings. (Daily; closed Dec 25) 51 Meeting St. Phone 843/724-8483. Combination ticket includes Aiken-Rhett House (see) ¢¢¢ Nearby are

Sword Gates. Gates represent one of the best examples of wrought-iron art, with two spears joining at center of broadsword to form cross. (Private) 32 Legare (la-GREE) St.

Annual Events

Southeastern Wildlife Exposition. Eighteen downtown historical locations. More than 500 exhibitors display wildlife art, carvings, antique collections and crafts for sale. Phone 843/723-1748. Mid-Feb.

Festival of Houses & Gardens. Many of the city's finest private residences (ca 1710-1850) and gardens are open to visitors. Afternoon and candlelight tours; res recommended. Phone 843/722-3405. Mid-Mar-mid-Apr.

Spoleto Festival USA. Internationally acclaimed counterpart to the arts festival in Spoleto, Italy, founded by Gian Carlo Menotti; includes opera, ballet, dance, visual arts, theater, chamber music, jazz, symphonic and choral performances and much more. Piccolo Spoleto, running concurrent with the main festival, has performances by local and regional artists. Phone 843/722-2764. Late May-early June.

Fall House & Garden Candlelight Tours. Evening tours of privately owned houses and gardens in the Historic District (fee). Phone 843/722-4630. Late Sept-late Oct.

Additional Visitor Information

The Charleston Visitor Reception and Transportation Center, 375 Meeting St, has information on other points of interest, tours, campsites, fishing trips, cultural, special and annual events, maps and self-guided walking tour of the city. (Daily; closed Jan 1, Thanksgiving, Dec 25) Contact PO Box 975, 29402; 843/853-8000. For city bus service information phone SCE & G at 843/747-0922; for DASH, Downtown Area Shuttle, phone 843/577-6970, ext 500.

Forever Charleston, a multimedia presentation about the city, is shown every half hr at the Visitor Center.

Motels

★ ★ **BEST WESTERN KING CHARLES INN.** *237 Meeting St (29401).* 843/723-7451; FAX 843/723-2041. 91 rms, 3 story. Mar-Oct: S, D $99-$189; each addl $10; under 12 free; lower rates rest of yr. Crib free. TV; cable. Pool. Restaurant nearby. Ck-out noon. Business servs avail. Bellhops. Valet serv. Cr cds: A, C, D, DS, MC, V.

[icons] SC

★ **DAYS INN-AIRPORT.** *2998 W Montague Ave (29418), near Intl Airport.* 843/747-4101; FAX 843/566-0378. 147 rms, 2 story. S $42-$62; D $48-$68; each addl $6; under 12 free. Crib free. Pet accepted; $6. TV; cable (premium). Pool. Playground. Restaurant 6 am-9 pm. Ck-out noon. Coin lndry. Business servs avail. Some refrigerators. Cr cds: A, D, DS, ER, MC, V.

[icons] D SC

✔★ ★ **HAMPTON INN.** *11 Ashley Pointe Dr (29407).* 843/556-5200; FAX 843/571-5499. 177 rms, 4 story. S $75-$99; D $85-$115; under 18 free; higher rates: wkends, special events. Crib free. Pet accepted. TV; cable (premium). Pool. Complimentary continental bkfst. Restaurant adj 11 am-11 pm. Ck-out noon. Coin lndry. Meeting rm. Business servs avail. In-rm modem link. Valet serv. Golf privileges. Health club privileges. Opp Ashley River; marina. Cr cds: A, C, D, DS, MC, V.

[icons] D SC

✔★ ★ **KNIGHTS INN.** *2355 Aviation Ave (29418).* 843/744-4900; FAX 843/745-0668. 242 rms, 2 story, 31 kits. S $29.95; D $41; each addl $3; suites $60-$63; kit. units $48-$53. Crib $3. TV; cable (premium). 2 pools. Complimentary continental bkfst. Ck-out noon. Coin lndry. Business servs avail. Airport transportation. Some refrigerators; microwaves avail. Lawn games. Cr cds: A, C, D, DS, MC, V.

[icons] D SC

★ ★ **LA QUINTA.** *2499 La Quinta Lane (29420), at I-26N exit 209.* 843/797-8181; FAX 843/569-1608. Web www.laquinta.com. 122 rms, 2 suites, 2 story. S $55-$66; D $65-$76; each addl $10; suites $85-$95; under 18 free; higher rates wkends. Crib free. Pet accepted. TV; cable (premium). Heated pool. Complimentary continental bkfst. Restaurant adj 6 am-11 pm. Rm serv. Ck-out noon. Business servs avail. In-rm modem link. Valet serv. Refrigerators, microwaves avail. Picnic tables, grill. Cr cds: A, D, DS, MC, V.

[icons] D SC

✔★ **MASTERS INN.** *(300 Wingo Way, Mt Pleasant 29464) 3 mi E on US 17.* 843/884-2814; FAX 843/884-2958; res: 800/633-3434. 120 units, 2 story, 26 kits. S $42.95-$55.95; D $48.95-$61.95; each addl $6; kit. units $53.95-$66.95; under 18 free; wkend rates. Pet accepted, some restrictions; $6. TV; cable (premium). Pool. Continental bkfst. Complimentary coffee. Restaurant nearby. Ck-out noon. Coin lndry. Meeting rm. Business servs avail. Cr cds: A, C, D, DS, MC, V.

[icons] D SC

★ ★ **RAMADA INN.** *W Montague Ave (29418), 7 mi NW at I-26.* 843/744-8281; FAX 843/744-6230. 155 rms, 2 story. Mid-Mar-Oct: S $59-$89; D $68-$89; each addl $10; under 18 free; lower rates rest of yr. TV; cable. Pool. Coffee in rms. Restaurant 6-10 am, 11:30 am-2 pm, 5:30-10 pm. Rm serv dinner only. Bar 4 pm-1:30 am; entertainment. Ck-out noon. Business servs avail. In-rm modem link. Valet serv. Free airport transportation. Some refrigerators. Cr cds: A, C, D, DS, MC, V.

[icons] D SC

✔★ **RED ROOF INN.** *7480 Northwoods Blvd (29406), I-26 to exit 209.* 843/572-9100; FAX 843/572-0061. 109 rms, 2 story. S $37-$51; D $43-$57; each addl $7-$8; under 18 free. Crib free. Pet accepted, some restrictions. TV; cable (premium). Complimentary coffee in lobby. Restaurant nearby. Ck-out noon. Cr cds: A, C, D, DS, MC, V.

[icons] D SC

★ ★ **SHEM CREEK INN.** *(Shem Creek at Coleman, Mt Pleasant 29464) Approx 5 mi E on US 17/701, S on US Business 17 to Mt. Pleasant.* 843/881-1000; FAX 843/849-6969; res: 800/523-4951. 50 rms, 2 story. Mid-Feb-Nov: S, D $89-$175; under 18 free; higher rates special events; lower rates rest of yr. Crib free. TV; cable. Pool. Complimentary continental bkfst. Complimentary coffee in rms. Restaurant adj 4:30 am-10 pm. Ck-out 11 am. Meeting rms. Business servs avail. Health club privileges. Microwaves avail. Cr cds: A, C, D, DS, MC, V.

D ⚡ ≈ ⛱ 🔥 SC

★ ★ ★ **TOWN AND COUNTRY INN.** *2008 Savannah Hwy (US 17) (29407). 843/571-1000; FAX 843/766-9444; res: 800/334-6660.* 122 rms, 2 story. 20 kits. Mar-Nov: S $69; D $89; each addl $7; suites $109-$189; kit. units $7 addl; under 18 free; lower rates rest of yr. Crib free. TV; cable (premium). 2 pools, 1 indoor; whirlpool. Restaurant 6:30 am-10 pm. Bar 3 pm-midnight. Ck-out noon. Coin lndry. Meeting rms. Business servs avail. In-rm modem link. Valet serv. Golf privileges, pro. Exercise equipt; weight machine, bicycles. Some refrigerators. Cr cds: A, C, D, DS, MC, V.

D 🏋 🛝 ≈ ⛱ 🔥 SC

Lodge

★ ★ **MIDDLETON.** *29414 Ashley River Rd (SC 61) (29414), 14 mi W. 843/556-0500; res: 800/543-4774.* 55 rms, 2-3 story. S, D $99-$169; each addl $20. Crib free. TV; cable. Pool. Complimentary bkfst. Meeting rms. Business servs avail. Tennis. Refrigerators, fireplaces. On 7,000 acres overlooking river, former rice fields; free admission to nearby Middleton Place Gardens. Cr cds: A, MC, V.

D 🏃 🏖 ≈ ⛱ 🔥 SC

Motor Hotels

★ ★ **BEST WESTERN NORTHWOODS ATRIUM INN.** *7401 Northwoods Blvd (29406), NW on I-26. 843/572-2200; FAX 843/863-8316.* 197 rms, 4 story. S $71-$81; D $81-$86; each addl $5; under 18 free. Crib free. TV; cable (premium). 2 pools, 1 indoor; whirlpool, poolside serv. Complimentary bkfst buffet. Restaurant 6:30 am-2 pm, 5-10:30 pm. Rm serv. Bar 5 pm-1 am; closed Sun. Ck-out 11 am. Meeting rms. Business servs avail. Bellhops. Valet serv. Free airport, RR station, bus depot transportation. Exercise equipt; bicycles, rower, sauna. Game rm. Refrigerators, microwaves avail. Cr cds: A, C, D, DS, ER, JCB, MC, V.

D ≈ ⛱ 🔥 SC

★ ★ **HAMPTON INN-HISTORIC DISTRICT.** *345 Meeting St (29403). 843/723-4000; FAX 843/722-3725.* 171 rms, 5 story. Mid-Feb-early Nov: S $89; D $99; suites $150; under 18 free; higher rates wknds, special events; lower rates rest of yr. Crib free. Garage $9. TV; cable (premium). Pool. Complimentary continental bkfst. Restaurant nearby. Rm serv. Ck-out noon. Meeting rms. Business servs avail. In-rm modem link. Bellhops. Concierge. Valet serv. Health club privileges. Some refrigerators; microwaves avail. Cr cds: A, D, DS, MC, V.

D ≈ ⛱ 🔥 SC

★ ★ **HAWTHORN SUITES.** *181 Church St (29401). 843/577-2644; FAX 843/577-2697.* E-mail hawthorne@awod.com; web www.hawthorne.com. 182 rms, 5 story, 125 kit. suites. Mar-mid-June, Sept-mid-Nov: S, D $129-$189; wkly rates; higher rates wknds; lower rates rest of yr. Crib free. Pet accepted, some restrictions; $125 and $10/day. TV; cable (premium), VCR. Complimentary full bkfst. Complimentary coffee in rms. Restaurant nearby. Ck-out noon. Coin lndry. Meeting rms. Business servs avail. In-rm modem link. Bellhops. Valet serv. Sundries. Exercise equipt; weight machine, bicycles. Whirlpool. Microwaves; some wet bars. In historic market area. Cr cds: A, C, D, DS, JCB, MC, V.

D ⚡ 🛝 ≈ ⛱ 🔥 SC

★ ★ **HOLIDAY INN-RIVERVIEW.** *301 Savannah Hwy (US 17) (29407). 843/556-7100; FAX 843/556-6176.* 181 rms, 14 story. S $79-$139; D $85-$145; under 19 free. Crib free. TV; cable (premium). Pool. Restaurant 6:30 am-2 pm, 5-10 pm. Rm serv. Bar 1 pm-1 am. Ck-out noon. Coin lndry. Business servs avail. In-rm modem link. Bellhops. Valet serv. Exercise equipt; stair machine, treadmill. Health club privileges. Balconies. On river. Cr cds: A, C, D, DS, JCB, MC, V.

D ≈ ⛱ 🔥 SC

★ ★ **QUALITY SUITES.** *5225 N Arco Lane (29418). 843/747-7300; FAX 843/747-6324.* 168 suites, 5 story. Mar-mid-June: S $89-$219;

D $99-$229; each addl $10; under 18 free; lower rates rest of yr. Crib free. TV; cable, VCR. Pool. Complimentary full bkfst. Coffee in rms. Restaurant nearby. Ck-out noon. Coin lndry. Meeting rms. Business servs avail. In-rm modem link. Gift shop. Free airport transportation. Exercise equipt; weight machine, rower. Refrigerators, microwaves, wet bars; some bathrm phones. Many balconies. Cr cds: A, C, D, DS, ER, JCB, MC, V.

D ≈ 🛝 🔥 SC

★ ★ **RADISSON INN AIRPORT.** *5991 Rivers Ave (29406), jct Aviation Ave & I-26. 843/744-2501.* 158 rms, 8 story. S $80-$104; D $90-$114; each addl $10; under 17 free. Crib free. TV; cable. Pool; whirlpool. Restaurant 6:30 am-10:30 pm. Rm serv. Bar noon-2 am; Sun 5 pm-midnight; entertainment. Ck-out noon. Meeting rms. Business servs avail. In-rm modem link. Bellhops. Valet serv. Free airport transportation. Sauna. Health club privileges. Microwaves avail. Cr cds: A, C, D, DS, ER, JCB, MC, V.

D ≈ ⛱ 🔥 SC

Hotels

★ ★ ★ ★ **CHARLESTON PLACE.** *130 Market St (29401). 843/722-4900; FAX 843/722-0728; res: 800/611-5545.* This graceful structure is in the city's historic district near a fashionable shopping area. The lobby contains antiques, a magnificent hand-blown Venetian chandelier and Italian marble floors. 440 rms, 8 story. S $295; D $315; each addl $20; suites $375-$2,000; under 17 free. Crib free. Garage $9, valet parking $13. TV; cable (premium). Indoor/outdoor pool; whirlpool, poolside serv. Supervised child's activities (June-Aug). Restaurants 6:30 am-10 pm (also see CHARLESTON GRILL). Rm serv 24 hrs. Bar 11:30-1 am; entertainment. Ck-out noon. Convention facilities. Business center. In-rm modem link. Concierge. Shopping arcade. Tennis privileges. Golf privileges. Exercise rm; instructor, weights, bicycles, sauna. Massage. Some balconies. Luxury level. Cr cds: A, C, D, DS, MC, V.

D 🏋 🛝 ≈ ⛱ 🔥 SC 🏌

★ ★ ★ **EMBASSY SUITES.** *337 Meeting St (29403). 843/723-6900; FAX 843/723-6938.* 153 suites, 5 story. Mid-Mar-early June; late Sept-late Nov: S, D $169-$269; each addl $10; under 18 free; higher rates: Southeastern Wildlife Exposition, Bridge Run; lower rates rest of yr. Crib free. Valet parking $11; garage parking $9. TV; cable (premium). Complimentary full bkfst. Restaurant nearby. Bar 4-11 pm. Ck-out noon. Meeting rms. Business servs avail. In-rm modem link. Gift shop. Coin lndry. Exercise equipt; weight machine, stair machine. Pool. Refrigerators, microwaves, wet bars; some in-rm whirlpools. Cr cds: A, C, D, DS, MC, V.

D ≈ 🛝 🔥 SC

★ ★ ★ **FRANCIS MARION.** *387 King St (29403). 843/722-0600; res: 800/433-3733; FAX 843/723-4633.* 226 rms, 12 story, 66 suites. Mid-Feb-May: S, D $119-$149; each addl $10; suites $159-$209; under 12 free; higher rates: Southeastern Wildlife Exposition, Bridge Run; lower rates rest of yr. Crib free. Garage $9, valet $12. TV; cable (premium), VCR avail. Restaurant 6:30 am-11 pm. Bar 11 am-10 pm. Ck-out noon. Meeting rms. Business servs avail. In-rm modem link. Concierge. Gift shop. Exercise equipt; bicycles, treadmill, sauna. Massage. European-style historic hotel; view of harbor. Cr cds: A, C, D, DS, MC, V.

D 🛝 ⛱ 🔥 SC

★ ★ ★ **HILTON.** *(4770 Goer Dr, North Charleston 29418) 8 mi W on I-26 exit Montague Ave. 843/747-1900; FAX 843/744-2530.* E-mail hilton@charleston.net; web www.charleston.net/com/hilton. 296 rms, 8 story. Apr-Dec: S $99-$159; D $114-$174; each addl $10; under 18 free; wkend rates; lower rates rest of yr. Crib free. TV; cable (premium). Indoor/outdoor pool; whirlpool. Restaurant 6:30 am-10 pm; Sat, Sun from 7 am. Bar; entertainment. Ck-out noon. Convention facilities. Business center. In-rm modem link. Gift shop. Free airport transportation. Tennis privileges. Golf privileges. Exercise equipt; stair machine, treadmill. Microwaves avail. Landscaped grounds. Cr cds: A, C, D, DS, ER, JCB, MC, V.

D 🏋 🏃 ≈ ⛱ 🔥 SC 🏌

★ ★ ★ **MILLS HOUSE.** *115 Meeting St (29401), at Queen St. 843/577-2400; FAX 843/722-2112; res: 800/874-9600.* 214 rms, 7 story.

Mid-Mar-mid-June, mid-Sept-mid-Nov: S, D $195; each addl $20; under 19 free; lower rates rest of yr. Crib free. Garage $9. TV; cable (premium). Pool. Restaurant (see BARBADOES ROOM). Bar 11-2 am. Ck-out 11 am. Meeting rms. Business servs avail. In-rm modem link. Concierge. Reconstruction of 19th-century inn; many antiques; reproduction furnishings. Cr cds: A, C, D, DS, MC, V.

D ≈ ⊠ 🔥 SC

Inns

★ ★ ★ **ANCHORAGE.** *26 Vendue Range, in historic district.* 843/723-8300; FAX 843/723-9543; res: 800/421-2952. 17 rms, 2 story, 2 suites. Mid-Mar-mid-June, Sept-Nov: S, D $140-$190; suites $245; lower rates rest of yr. Garage parking $6/day. Complimentary continental bkfst; afternoon refreshments. Restaurant nearby. Ck-out 11 am, ck-in 3 pm. Business servs avail. Concierge serv. Antiques. Library/sitting rm. Renovated antebellum warehouse adj to harbor, Waterfront Park; individually decorated rms. Cr cds: A, MC, V.

⊠ 🔥

★ ★ **ASHLEY.** *201 Ashley Ave (29403).* 843/723-1848; FAX 843/768-1230. 6 rms, 5 with shower only, 1 suite, 3 story. Early Mar-Nov: S, D $95-$135; suite $150; lower rates rest of yr. Children over 10 yrs only. TV; cable (premium). Complimentary full bkfst; afternoon refreshments. Ck-out 10 am, ck-in 3 pm. Business servs avail. Guest bicycles. Built 1832; antiques. Garden with fish pond, fountain. Totally nonsmoking. Cr cds: A, DS, MC, V.

⊠ 🔥

★ ★ ★ **BARKSDALE HOUSE.** *27 George St (29401), in historic district.* 843/577-4800; FAX 843/853-0482. 14 rms, 3 story. Mar-Oct: S, D $80-$180; each addl $10; lower rates rest of yr. Children over 10 yrs only. TV; cable (premium). Complimentary continental bkfst; afternoon refreshments. Restaurant nearby. Ck-out 11 am, ck-in 3 pm. Business servs avail. Townhouse built in 1778; porches, courtyard in rear. Cr cds: MC, V.

🔥 SC

★ ★ **BATTERY CARRIAGE HOUSE.** *20 S Battery (29401).* 843/727-3100; FAX 843/727-3130; res: 800/775-5575. 11 rms, 4 with shower only, 2 story. Mar-mid-June, mid-Sept-mid-Nov: S, D $149-$199; each addl $15; higher rates wkends (2-day min); lower rates rest of yr. Children over 12 yrs only. TV; cable (premium). Complimentary continental bkfst. Complimentary coffee in rms. Ck-out noon, ck-in 3 pm. Concierge serv. Street parking. Greek-revival mansion built in 1843. On Battery Park, harbor. Cr cds: A, DS, MC, V.

⊠ 🔥

★ ★ **CANNONBORO.** *184 Ashley Ave (29403).* 843/723-8572; res: 800/235-8039; FAX 843/723-9080. 7 rms, 4 with shower only, 2 story, 1 suite. Early Mar-Nov: S, D $95-$145; each addl $25; suite $165; lower rates rest of yr. Children over 10 yrs only. TV. Complimentary full bkfst; afternoon refreshments. Restaurant nearby. Ck-out 10 am, ck-in 3 pm. Business servs avail. Refrigerators avail. Guest bicycles. Second-story porch. Some Victorian furnishings; antiques. Totally nonsmoking. Cr cds: A, DS, MC, V.

⊠ 🔥

★ ★ **CHURCH STREET.** *177 Church St (29401).* 843/722-3420; FAX 843/577-0836; res: 800/552-3777. 31 kit. suites, 2 story. 1-bedrm $125-$145; 2-bedrm $225-$245; each addl (after 2nd person) $10; family rates. Crib free. Garage parking $6. TV; cable (premium). Complimentary bkfst. Restaurant adj 7 am-10 pm. Bar 5-10 pm. Ck-out noon, ck-in 3 pm. Business servs avail. Luggage handling. Valet serv. Some balconies. Antique reproductions. Courtyard. In historic market area. Cr cds: A, MC, V.

🔥 SC

★ ★ ★ **INDIGO.** *1 Maiden Lane (29401).* 843/577-5900; FAX 843/577-0378; res: 800/845-7639. E-mail IndigoInn@crabnet.net; web www.aesir.com/indigoinn. 40 rms, 3 story. Mar-June, Sept-Nov: S $140; D $155; each addl $10; under 12 free; lower rates rest of yr. Crib $10. Pet

accepted; $10. TV; cable (premium). Complimentary continental bkfst; afternoon refreshments. Restaurant nearby. Ck-out noon, ck-in 3 pm. Business servs avail. In-rm modem link. Luggage handling. Valet serv. Health club privileges. Parking. Built in 1850; antique furnishings; courtyard. Cr cds: A, D, DS, MC, V.

🐾 ⊠

★ ★ ★ **JOHN RUTLEDGE HOUSE.** *116 Broad St (29401).* 843/723-7999; FAX 843/720-2615; res: 800/476-9741. This historic inn comprises the revolutionary-era main house, built by a signer of the Constitution, and two carriage houses (each with four rooms). The guest rooms have high ceilings, wood floors, antique furnishings and four-poster beds. 19 rms, 2-3 story, 3 suites. Mid-Mar-mid-June, mid-Sept-Oct: S $180-$240; D $200-$260; each addl $20; suites $310; under 12 free; lower rates rest of yr. Crib free. TV; cable (premium). Complimentary continental bkfst; afternoon refreshments. Restaurant nearby. Ck-out noon, ck-in 3 pm. Business servs avail. In-rm modem link. Luggage handling. Valet serv. Concierge serv. Health club privileges. Stocked refrigerators, fireplaces. Cr cds: A, D, DS, MC, V.

⊠ 🔥 SC

★ ★ **KING GEORGE IV.** *32 George St (29401).* 843/723-9339; res: 888/723-1667; FAX 843/723-7749. Web www.bbonline.com/sc/kinggeorge/. 10 rms, 6 with shower only, 2 share bath, 4 story, 4 suites. No elvtr. Mid-Feb-early June, Oct-Nov: S, D $75-$135; each addl $10; suites $135-$149; wkly rates; wkends (3-day min); higher rates: Southeastern Wildlife Exposition, Festival of Houses & Gardens; lower rates rest of yr. TV. Complimentary continental bkfst. Complimentary coffee in rms. Restaurant nearby. Ck-out 11 am, ck-in 1-6 pm. Luggage handling. Refrigerators, fireplaces. Built in 1890s; Federal style. Totally nonsmoking. Cr cds: MC, V.

⊠ 🔥

★ ★ ★ **KINGS COURTYARD.** *198 King St (29401).* 843/723-7000; FAX 843/720-2608; res: 800/845-6119. 41 rms, 3 story. Mid-Mar-early June, mid-Sept-Oct: S $135-$175; D $155-$195; each addl $20; suites $230; under 12 free; lower rates rest of yr. Crib free. TV; cable (premium). Complimentary continental bkfst. Dining rm 7-10 am; Sat, Sun to 11 am. Rm serv. Serv bar. Ck-out noon, ck-in 3 pm. Meeting rms. Business servs avail. In-rm modem link. Luggage handling. Concierge serv. Whirlpool. Health club privileges. Refrigerators, fireplaces. Built in 1853; 2 inner courtyards. Cr cds: A, DS, MC, V.

D ⊠ 🔥 SC

★ ★ ★ **LODGE ALLEY.** *195 E Bay St (29401).* 843/722-1611; FAX 843/722-1611; res: 800/845-1004 (exc SC), 800/821-2791 (SC). 95 rms, 4 story, 50 kit. units. Mid-Mar-early June, early Sept-early Nov: S, D $165-$189; each addl $15; kit. suites $175-$300; under 12 free; honeymoon plans; lower rates rest of yr. Crib free. TV; cable (premium). Complimentary coffee; refreshments. Dining rm 7-10:30 am, 11:30 am-2:30 pm, 6-10 pm; closed Sun. Rm serv to 10:30 am. Bar 11:30 am-midnight; closed Sun; entertainment spring, fall. Ck-out noon, ck-in 4 pm. Business servs avail. Luggage handling. Valet serv. Health club privileges. Mini bar, refrigerators. Some balconies. Built in 1773; some fireplaces, antiques. Courtyard gardens with fountain. Cr cds: A, MC, V.

🔥

★ ★ ★ **MAISON DU PRE.** *317 E Bay St (29401).* 843/723-8691; FAX 843/723-3722; res: 800/844-INNS. 15 rms, 1-3 story, 1 kit. Early Feb-mid-June, Sept-mid-Nov: S, D $115-$165; suites $160-$200; carriage house with kit. $160; lower rates rest of yr. Crib free. TV; cable. Complimentary continental bkfst. Ck-out noon, ck-in 2 pm. Built in 1804. Composed of 3 single Charleston houses & 2 carriage houses with porches. 3 fountains. Cr cds: DS, MC, V.

⊠ 🔥

★ ★ **MEETING STREET.** *173 Meeting St (29401), in heart of downtown historic district.* 843/723-1882; FAX 843/577-0851; res: 800/842-8022. Web www.aesir.com/meetingstreet/. 56 rms, 4 story. Mid-Mar-early June & mid-Sept-Oct: S, D $109-$210; each addl $10; under 13 free; lower rates rest of yr. Crib free. Parking $6. TV; cable (premium). Complimentary continental bkfst; afternoon refreshments. Bar noon-11 pm; closed Sun. Ck-out noon, ck-in 3 pm. Business servs avail. Luggage handling. Health club privileges. Whirlpool. Walking tours. Refrigerators avail. Courtyard with fountain. Opp Old City Market. Cr cds: A, D, DS, MC, V.

[D] [🔥] [SC]

★ ★ **PLANTERS.** *112 N Market St (29401). 843/722-2345; FAX 843/577-2125; res: 800/845-7082.* Web www.plantersinn.com. 62 rms, 4 story, 21 suites. S, D $105; D $185; suites $250-$350. Crib free. TV; cable (premium). Complimentary continental bkfst; afternoon refreshments. Restaurant (see PENINSULA GRILL). Ck-out noon, ck-in 3 pm. Meeting rm. Business servs avail. In-rm modem link. Luggage handling. Concierge serv. Many antiques. Located in scenic, historic area. Cr cds: A, C, D, DS, MC, V.

[D] [🔥]

★ ★ **RUTLEDGE VICTORIAN INN.** *114 Rutledge Ave (29401). 843/722-7551; res: 888/722-7553; FAX 843/727-0065.* Web www.bbonline .com/sc/rutledge. 11 rms, 7 with shower only, 3 share bath, 4 story. No elvtr. S, D, guest house $79-$250; each addl $20. TV. Complimentary continental bkfst. Restaurant nearby. Ck-out 11 am, ck-in 2-6 pm. Luggage handling. Concierge serv. Street parking. Bathrm phones, fireplaces; some refrigerators. Built in 1880; Italianate architecture; antiques. Totally non-smoking. Cr cds: MC, V.

[📋] [📋]

★ ★ **VENDUE.** *19 Vendue Range (29401). 843/577-7970; FAX 843/577-2913; res: 800/845-7900 (exc SC), 800/922-7900 (SC).* Web www.charleston.net/com/vendueinn. 22 rms, 3 story, 23 suites. Mid-Mar-mid-June, mid-Sept-Nov: S $125-$145; D $150-$160; each addl $15; suites $170-$230; lower rates rest of yr. TV. Complimentary full bkfst; afternoon refreshments. Restaurant 6-10 pm. Bar 11:30 am-11 pm. Ck-out noon, ck-in 3 pm. Meeting rm. Business servs avail. In-rm modem link. Luggage handling. Valet serv. Concierge serv. Exercise equipt; bicycle, treadmill. Fireplace in suites. Located in 1824 structure. Rooftop terrace overlooking harbor. Cr cds: A, D, DS, MC, V.

[D] [🏃] [📋] [🔥]

★ ★ **VICTORIA HOUSE.** *208 King St (29401). 843/720-2944; FAX 843/720-2930; res: 800/933-5464.* 18 rms, 3 story, 4 suites. Mar-mid-June, Sept-Nov: S $155; D $175; each addl $20; suites $225; under 12 free; lower rates rest of yr. Crib free. TV; cable (premium). Complimentary continental bkfst; afternoon refreshments. Restaurant adj 8 am-3 pm. Ck-out noon, ck-in 3 pm. Business servs avail. In-rm modem link. Luggage handling. Concierge serv. Health club privileges. Refrigerators. Romanesque period-style building (1889). Cr cds: D, DS, MC, V.

[📋] [🔥] [SC]

★ ★ ★ **WOODLANDS RESORT & INN.** *(125 Parsons Rd, Summerville 29483) approx 20 mi N on I-26, exit 199A, 2 mi W on US 17A, N on SC 165 to Parsons Rd. 843/875-2600; FAX 843/875-2603; res: 800/774-9999.* This English country-house hotel nestled in 42 lowcountry acres offers tennis, croquet, swimming and entertainment. Guest rooms are sumptuously appointed with sitting areas, fireplaces, heated towel racks and whirlpool baths. A full-service, state-of-the-art spa offers everything from massage to mud masks and aromatherapy. 20 rms, 3 story. S, D $225-$325. TV; cable (premium), VCR (movies). Pool; poolside serv. Complimentary continental bkfst. Restaurant (see THE DINING ROOM AT WOODLANDS). Rm serv 7:30 am-10 pm. Bar 11:30 am-midnight; closed Sun. Ck-out noon, ck-in 3 pm. Luggage handling. Concierge serv. Meeting rms. Business servs avail. Lighted tennis. Golf privileges, pro. Lawn games. Bicycles. Massage. Totally nonsmoking. Cr cds: A, C, D, DS, MC, V.

[D] [🏃] [⛷] [🏊] [🔥] [📋] [📋]

Resorts

★ ★ **SEABROOK ISLAND.** *(1002 Landfall Way, John's Island 29455) 23 mi SE off US 17. 843/768-1000; FAX 843/768-4922; res: 800/845-2475.* 170 kit. villas, 1-2 story. Mid-Mar-mid Aug: 1-bedrm $150-$215; 2-bedrm $185-$285; 3-bedrm $205-$340; wkly, tennis, golf, honey-

moon, family plans; lower rates rest of yr. Crib $5. TV; cable, VCR avail. 7 pools; wading pool, lifeguard. Supervised child's activities (Memorial Day-Labor Day). Dining rm 7 am-9 pm. Bar from 11 am. Ck-out 11 am, ck-in 4 pm. Business center. Grocery. Convention facilities. Tennis, pro. 36-hole golf, greens fee $50-$90, pro, putting green, driving range. Private beach. Sailboat. Deep sea fishing. Bicycles. Health club privileges. Entertainment. Game rm. Refrigerators, microwaves; some fireplaces. Private patios, balconies. Sunset cruises avail. Cr cds: A, DS, MC, V.

[🏊] [🚤] [🏃] [⛷] [🏊] [🏊] [📋] [🚣]

★ ★ ★ **WILD DUNES.** *Box 20575 (29413), E on US 17, N on SC 703. 843/886-6000; FAX 843/886-2916; res: 800/845-8880.* E-mail wild dunes@awod.com; web www.wilddunes.com. 320 kit. villas, 1-5 story, 24 cottages. June-Sept: kit. villas, cottages $125-$375; wkly rates; golf plans; lower rates rest of yr. Crib $10. TV; cable (premium). Pools; wading pool, whirlpool, poolside serv, lifeguard. Playground. Free supervised child's activities (June-mid-Sept). Teen club. Dining rm 7 am-midnight. Box lunches, snack bar, picnics. Bar 7 am-midnight; entertainment Tues-Sat. Ck-out 11 am, ck-in 4 pm. Lndry facilities. Grocery. Package store. Convention facilities. Business center. Valet serv. Beauty shop. Gift shop. Sports dir. Lighted tennis, pro. 36-hole golf course, greens fee $39-$115, pro, putting green, driving range. Exercise rm; instructor, weight machines, treadmills. Swimming beach, boats. Bicycles (rentals). Lawn games. Soc dir. Fishing guides. Microwaves. Balconies. Picnic tables. On beach. Cr cds: A, DS, MC, V.

[🚤] [🏃] [🏊] [⛷] [🏊] [🏃] [🚣] [SC] [🚣]

Restaurants

★ ★ **82 QUEEN.** *82 Queen St. 843/723-7591.* Hrs: 11:30 am-4 pm, 5:30-10 pm; Fri, Sat to 10:30 pm. Res accepted. Bar to 2 am. Semi-a la carte: lunch $6.50-$10.95, dinner $14.95-$20.95. Specializes in seafood, regional Lowcountry dishes. Outdoor dining. Located in 1800s bldg. Cr cds: A, D, MC, V.

[📋]

★ ★ **ANSON.** *12 Anson St. 843/577-0551.* Hrs: 5:30-11 pm; Fri, Sat to midnight. Res accepted. Bar. A la carte entrees: dinner $10.95-$24.95. Child's meals. Specializes in fresh seafood, chops. Bi-level dining. Decor reminiscent of Lowcountry plantation homes. Cr cds: A, C, D, DS, MC, V.

[📋]

★ **AW SHUCKS.** *70 State St (29401). 843/723-1151.* Hrs: 11 am-10 pm; Fri, Sat to 11 pm. Closed Thanksgiving, Dec 25. Bar. Semi-a la carte: lunch $5.99-$9.99, dinner $9.99-$14.99. Specializes in seafood. Salad bar. Old fashioned decor. Cr cds: A, DS, MC, V.

[D] [📋]

★ ★ **BARBADOES ROOM.** *(See Mills House Hotel) 843/577-2400.* Hrs: 6:30 am-2 pm, 5:30-10 pm; Sun brunch 11 am-2 pm. Res accepted. Continental menu. Bar 11-2 am. Wine list. Semi-a la carte: bkfst $5.95-$8.95, lunch $5.95-$9.95, dinner $14.95-$24.95. Bkfst buffet $8.95. Sun brunch $16.95. Specializes in seafood. Own baking. Pianist evenings. Valet parking. Cr cds: A, C, D, DS, MC, V.

[📋]

★ ★ ★ **BEAUMONT'S CAFE.** *12 Cumberland St (29401). 843/577-5500.* Hrs: 11:30 am-3 pm, 5-11 pm. Closed Sun (July-Aug); Dec 25. Res accepted. French, Mediterranean menu. Bar. Semi-a la carte: lunch $5.25-$12.95, dinner $6.95-$21.75. Specialty: bouillabaisse. View of courtyard. Cr cds: A, C, D, DS, MC, V.

[D] [📋]

★ ★ **BLOSSOM CAFE.** *171 E Bay St (29401). 843/722-9200.* Hrs: 11:30 am-11 pm; Fri, Sat to 1 am; Sun 11 am-2:30 pm, 5-11 pm. Closed Jan 1, Dec 25. Res accepted. Mediterranean, American menu. Bar. Semi-a la carte: lunch, dinner $6.25-$21.95. Child's meals. Specialties: oak-roasted salmon, pizzas cooked in woodburning oven. Outdoor dining. Modern decor. Cr cds: A, D, MC, V.

[D] [□]

★ ★ **CAROLINA'S.** *10 Exchange St. 843/724-3800.* Hrs: 5:30-11 pm; Thurs-Sat to 12:30 am; Sun 5-10 pm. Res accepted. Bar from 5 pm. A la carte entrees: dinner $5.95-$20.95. Specializes in grilled seafood, pasta, regional cuisine. Own baking. Cr cds: A, D, DS, MC, V.

[□] [♥]

★ ★ ★ **CHARLESTON GRILL.** *(See Charleston Place Hotel) 843/577-4522.* The club-like atmosphere of this hotel dining room features mahogany-paneled walls, green marble floors and dim, romantic lighting. Specializes in game, beef, fresh local seafood. Own baking, soups. Hrs: 6-11 pm. Res accepted. Bar 4 pm-midnight. Wine cellar. A la carte entrees: dinner $14.50-$22.50. Jazz trio. Cr cds: A, C, D, MC, V.

[D] [□]

★ ★ ★ **THE DINING ROOM AT WOODLANDS.** *(See Woodlands Resort & Inn) 843/875-2600.* Hrs: 7-10 am, 11 am-2:30 pm, 6-10 pm. Res accepted. Regional contemporary menu. Bar noon-midnight. Wine cellar. Semi-a la carte: bkfst $4.75-$18, lunch $7-$18. Complete meals: dinner $44-$65. Specializes in seafood, lamb, beef. Valet parking. Outdoor dining. Elegant decor. View of terrace. Jacket (dinner) Cr cds: A, C, D, DS, MC, V.

[D]

★ ★ ★ **FULTON FIVE.** *5 Fulton St (29401). 843/853-5555.* Hrs: from 5:30 pm. Closed Sun; also late Aug-1st wk Sept. Res accepted. Northern Italian menu. Bar. Wine cellar. Semi-a la carte: dinner $12-$24. Specialties: risotto, antipasto spoleto, lemon sherbet with campari. Own baking. Street parking. Intimate atmosphere; European decor. Cr cds: A, D, MC, V.

[D]

★ ★ **GARIBALDI'S.** *49 S Market St. 843/723-7153.* Hrs: 6-11 pm. Closed Dec 25. Italian menu. Serv bar. Semi-a la carte: dinner $7.95-19.95. Specializes in fresh seafood, pasta, veal. Own desserts. Outdoor dining. Bistro atmosphere; in center of historic Charleston Market. Cr cds: A, MC, V.

★ ★ **J BISTRO.** *819 Coleman Blvd (29464). 843/971-7778.* Hrs: 5-10 pm; Fri, Sat to 11 pm; Sun brunch 10:30 am-2:30 pm. Closed Mon; most major hols. Bar. Semi-a la carte: dinner $6-$16. Sun brunch $10. Specializes in pork chops, seafood. Two-level dining area. Casual decor. Cr cds: A, MC, V.

★ ★ **MAGNOLIAS.** *185 E Bay St. 843/577-7771.* Hrs: 11:30 am-11 pm; Fri, Sat to midnight. Closed Jan 1, Dec 25. Res accepted. Bar. Semi-a la carte: lunch $7.50-$17.50, dinner $8.25-$21.95. Specialties: pan-fried chicken livers, spicy shrimp and sausage, veal meatloaf. Contemporary decor within historic structure; overlooks Lodge Alley. Cr cds: A, D, MC, V.

★ ★ **MARKET EAST BISTRO.** *14 N Market St (29401). 843/577-5080.* Hrs: 10:30 am-11 pm. Closed Jan 1, July 4. Res accepted. Continental menu. Bar. Semi-a la carte: lunch $6.75-$10.25, dinner $8.50-$15.95. Child's meals. Specialties: lobster ravioli with saffron sauce, sage mustard crusted rack of lamb. Outdoor dining. Bistro atmosphere. Cr cds: A, D, DS, MC, V.

[D] [□]

★ ★ ★ **McGRADY'S.** *2 Unity Alley. 843/577-0025.* Hrs: 11:30 am-3 pm, 5-11 pm; Fri, Sat to midnight. Closed Sun; also Jan 1, July 4, Dec 25. Bar. Semi-a la carte: lunch $5.95-$9.95, dinner $7.95-$19. Specializes in seafood, pasta, veal. Historic tavern (1778). Cr cds: A, MC, V.

[□]

★ **ONE EYED PARROT.** *(1130 Ocean Blvd, Isle Of Palms 29451) E on US 17B to SC 703, then S. 843/886-4360.* Hrs: 5-10 pm; Fri, Sat to 11 pm. Closed Thanksgiving, Dec 25. Caribbean menu. Bar. Semi-a la carte: dinner $6.95-$16.99. Child's meals. Specializes in seafood, beef.

Entertainment Fri-Sun. Second floor dining rm overlooking ocean; terrace dining. Cr cds: A, C, D, DS, MC, V.

[□]

✔ ★ **PAPILLON.** *32 Market St. 843/723-6510.* Hrs: 11 am-10 pm; Fri to 11 pm; Sat 8 am-11 pm; Sun 8 am-9 pm. Mediterranean menu. Semi-a la carte: lunch $6.95-$8.95, dinner $8.95-$12.95. Buffet: lunch $5.95. Specializes in pasta calzones, pizza baked in wood-burning oven. Own pastries. Trattoria atmosphere. Cr cds: A, DS, MC, V.

[□]

★ ★ ★ **PENINSULA GRILL.** *(See Planters Inn) 843/723-0700.* Hrs: 5:30-10 pm; Fri, Sat to 11 pm. Res accepted. Regional Amer menu. Bar from 4 pm. Wine cellar. Semi-a la carte: dinner $14.50-$27. Child's meals. Specialties: wild mushroom grits, spicy peach-glazed jumbo shrimp, benne seed-crusted rack of New Zealand lamb. Own pastries. Outdoor dining. Elegant atmosphere reminiscent of 1940s supper club. Cr cds: A, DS, MC, V.

[D]

★ ★ **POOGAN'S PORCH.** *72 Queen St, in historic district. 843/577-2337.* Hrs: 11:30 am-2:30 pm, 5:30-10 pm. Sun brunch 10:30 am-2:30 pm. Res accepted. Regional Lowcountry cuisine. Bar. Semi-a la carte: lunch $4.95-$6.95, dinner $9.95-$17.95. Specialties: Cajun shrimp, bread pudding, shrimp creole. Outdoor dining. Restored house (1891); fireplace, garden rm. Intimate dining. Cr cds: A, MC, V.

[□]

★ ★ ★ **RESTAURANT MILLION.** *2 Unity Alley. 843/577-3141.* Hrs: 6:30-10 pm. Closed Sun, Mon; Jan 1, July 4, Dec 25. Res accepted. French menu. Bar. Semi-a la carte: dinner $27-$33. Specializes in seafood, rack of lamb, rabbit. Tapestry, fireplaces. Jacket. Cr cds: A, D, MC, V.

★ ★ ★ **SARACEN.** *141 E Bay St (29401). 843/723-6242.* Hrs: 6-10 pm. Closed Sun, Mon; some major hols. Res accepted. Eclectic menu. Bar 5 pm-2 am. Wine cellar. Semi-a la carte: dinner $13-$25. Child's meals. Specializes in fresh seafood, beef, pork. Own baking. Jazz Fri, Sat. Street, garage parking. Former bank bldg (1853) combines Moorish, Persian, Hindu and Gothic architecture. On National Register of Historic Places. Cr cds: A, C, D, JCB, MC, V.

[□]

★ ★ **SLIGHTLY NORTH OF BROAD.** *192 E Bay St (29401). 843/723-3424.* Hrs: 11:30 am-3 pm, 5:30-10 pm; Sat, Sun from 5:30 pm. Closed maj hols. Bar. A la carte entrees: lunch $6.75-$9.95, dinner $8.50-$18.95. Child's meals. Specializes in seafood, pasta, beef. Open kitchen. Cr cds: A, D, DS, MC, V.

[D] [□]

★ ★ **SUPPER AT STACKS.** *101 Pitt St (29464). 843/884-7009.* Hrs: 6-10 pm. Closed Sun, Mon; some major hols. Res required. Regional Amer menu. Complete meals: dinner $29. Specializes in roast duck, fresh fish, beef tenderloin. Menu changes daily. Formal dining rm reminiscent of 18th-century Williamsburg, VA. Cr cds: A, MC, V.

★ ★ **THE TRAWLER.** *(100 Church St, Mt Pleasant 29464) E on US 17/701 to Mt Pleasant, at Coleman Blvd. 843/884-2560.* Hrs: 11:30 am-10:30 pm; Sun to 9 pm. Closed Dec 25. Res accepted. Bar. Semi-a la carte: lunch $6.95-$12.99, dinner $8.95-$24.50. Child's meals. Specializes in seafood, chicken, beef. Singer Fri, Sat. Outdoor dining. Overlooks creek and shrimp boats. Cr cds: A, D, DS, MC, V.

[D]

Cheraw (C-6)

(See also Bennettsville, Camden, Darlington, Florence, Hartsville)

Settled 1740 **Pop** 5,505 **Elev** 150 ft **Area code** 803 **Zip** 29520
Information Chamber of Commerce, 221 Market St; 803/537-8425 or 803/537-7681.

Profiting in commerce from both Carolinas, Cheraw grew rapidly when the Pee Dee River was opened for traffic. It is said that the town owes its many trees to an ordinance that required every person seen intoxicated in public to go out into the woods and fetch a tree for planting within the town.

What to See and Do

Carolina Sandhills National Wildlife Refuge. Approx 46,000 acres house almost 300 species of birds, mammals, reptiles and amphibians. Auto-tour route, hiking trails and observation towers avail. Fishing, hunting permitted. Interpretive displays avail at headquarters (on US 1, 4 mi NE of McBee). (Mon-Fri, during daylight) Approx 20 mi SW on US 1. Phone 803/335-8401. **Free.**

Cheraw State Park. Located on 7,361 acres of gently rolling green sandhills. Lake swimming; boating (rentals); fishing. Nature trails; 18-hole golf. Picnicking (shelters); playground; recreation building. Camping; cabins (hookups, dump station). Standard fees. Unusually cool in hot-weather periods. 4 mi SW on US 52. Phone 803/537-2215 or 800/868-9630.

⭐ **Historic District.** Comprises 214 acres downtown and contains more than 50 antebellum homes and public buildings, plus structures dating from later periods. The Town Green (ca 1768) is the site of the small Lyceum Museum (ca 1820). Other notable buildings are Town Hall (ca 1855), Market Hall (ca 1835) and the Inglis-McIver Law Office (ca 1810). Free brochures on the district are available at the Chamber office on the Green and at some local shops. Picnicking. Self-guided tours. Phone 803/537-7681.

Old St David's Episcopal Church (1768). Restored to the 1820s period; last Anglican parish established in the state prior to the Revolutionary War. Used as a hospital by British during Revolution, later by Union Army during Civil War; about 50 British soldiers are buried in the churchyard. Tours (by appt); for self-tours, pick up keys at Chamber of Commerce, 221 Market St; 803/537-7681. Front & Church Sts. Phone 803/537-8425. **Free.**

Annual Event

Spring Festival. Great Pee Dee Family Fun Run; tours; arts and crafts shows; entertainment, car show. Phone 803/537-8420. Early Apr.

Motel

★ **INN CHERAW.** 321 Second St. 803/537-2011; FAX 803/537-1398; res: 800/535-8709. 50 rms, 2 story. S $36-$60; D $40-$65; each addl $5; kit. units $45-$60; under 6 free; golf plans; higher rates NASCAR races. Crib free. Pet accepted, some restrictions. TV; cable (premium), VCR. Complimentary continental bkfst. Complimentary coffee in rms. Restaurant adj 11 am-9 pm. Ck-out 11 am. Meeting rms. Valet serv. Refrigerators; microwaves avail. Cr cds: A, D, DS, MC, V.

D ✔ 🛆 🐾 SC

Inn

★ ★ **501 KERSHAW STREET/SPEARS GUEST HOUSE.** 501 Kershaw St. 803/537-7733; res: 888/424-3729; FAX 803/537-0302. 5 rms, 2 story. S, D $50-$75; wkly, monthly rates. TV; cable (premium). Complimentary continental bkfst. Complimentary coffee in rms. Ck-out noon, ck-in

4 pm. Federal-style house built in 1845; fireplaces and antiques. Cr cds: A, MC, V.

🛆 🔥

Chester (C-4)

(For accommodations see Rock Hill)

Settled 1755 **Pop** 7,158 **Elev** 485 ft **Area code** 803 **Zip** 29706
Information Chester County Chamber of Commerce, 109 Gadsden St, PO Box 489; 803/581-4142.

Seat of Chester County, this town was named by settlers from Pennsylvania. Aaron Burr, guarded here in 1807 while under arrest for treason, broke away and climbed a high rock. After haranguing a surprised crowd, he was recaptured.

What to See and Do

Chester State Park. Approx 500 acres. Lake fishing; boating. Nature trail. Picnicking (shelters); recreation building. Camping (hookups, dump station). Equestrian show ring. Standard fees. 3 mi SW on SC 72. Phone 803/385-2680.

Clemson (C-2)

(See also Anderson, Greenville)

Founded 1889 **Pop** 11,096 **Elev** 850 ft **Area code** 864 **Zip** 29631 **E-mail** clemcham@innova.net **Web** www.clemsonchamber.org
Information Clemson Area Chamber of Commerce, PO Box 1622, 29633; 864/654-1200.

Home of Clemson University, this community also hosts vacationers attracted to the huge lake that the Hartwell Dam has formed on the Savannah River.

What to See and Do

Clemson University (1889). (17,000 students) Named for Thomas G. Clemson, son-in-law of John C. Calhoun, who bequeathed the bulk of his estate, Fort Hill, for establishment of a scientific college. 11 mi NW of I-85 at jct US 76, SC 93. Phone 864/656-3311 or 864/656-2061. On this 1,400-acre campus are

Fort Hill (1803). Mansion on 1,100 acres acquired by Calhoun during his first term as vice-president. House has many original furnishings belonging to Calhoun, Clemson. (Daily; closed some major hols) Phone 864/656-2475. **Free.**

Hanover House (1716). This French Huguenot house was moved here from its original site near Pinopolis to prevent submersion by Lake Moultrie. (Wkends). Phone 864/656-2241. **Free.**

State Botanical Gardens. This 250-acre area includes azalea and camelia trails, ornamental plantings, large collection of shrubs; dwarf conifer flower and turf display gardens; wildflower pioneer and bog garden is labeled in Braille. (Daily) E side of campus. Phone 864/656-3405. **Free.**

Oconee State Park. Approx 1,100 acres of park nestled in the foothills of the Blue Ridge and surrounded by Sumter National Forest (see GREENWOOD). Lake swimming, lifeguard (summer); boating (rentals); fishing. Nature, hiking trails; recreation building; recreation & nature programs (summer); carpet golf. Picnicking (shelters), playground, concession, restaurant. Camping (hookups, dump station), cabins. Standard fees. 20 mi NW of town, 12 mi NW of Walhalla on SC 107. Phone 864/638-5353.

Raft trips. Guided whitewater rafting trips on the Chattooga National Wild & Scenic River. Res required. Also canoe & kayak clinics and overnight trips. (Mar-Oct, daily) 34 mi NW on US 76 in Long Creek. Phone 800/451-9972.

Stumphouse Tunnel Park. Unfinished railroad tunnel, which was being cut in the 1850s, was interrupted by the Civil War. Temperature is always 50°F and the humidity 90%. It rains daily in the #1 shaft, regardless of outdoor weather. Issaqueena Falls, picnicking, shelter. Hiking along old roadbed. Park (daily). Approx 22 mi NW via US 123 & SC 28, 6 mi N of Walhalla, adj to Sumter National Forest (see GREENWOOD) in the Blue Ridge Mts. Phone 864/646-3782 or 864/646-2506.   **Free.**

World of Energy. Three-dimensional displays on the "Story of Energy," with exhibits on hydro, coal and nuclear production of electricity; also displays on radiation and supplemental energy sources. Computer games; films. Overlooks Lake Keowee and one of the world's largest nuclear generating plants. Tour of the control room training simulator. Picnic area and boat dock adj. (Daily; closed Jan 1, Thanksgiving, Dec 24, 25) 12 mi NW on SC 130, 123. Phone 864/885-4600 or 800/777-1004.   **Free.**

Annual Event

Clemson Fest. Entertainment, arts & crafts, children's activities. Boat parade & contest precedes fireworks display. Phone 864/646-6110. July 4.

Motels

✔★ **COMFORT INN.** 1305 Tiger Blvd. 864/653-3600; FAX 864/654-3123. 122 rms, 4 story. S, D $48-$54; each addl $6; suites $76-$130; under 18 free. Crib free. TV; cable. Pool; whirlpool. Complimentary continental bkfst. Restaurant nearby. Ck-out noon. In-rm modem link. Valet serv. Exercise equipt; weight machine, bicycle, sauna. Cr cds: A, C, D, DS, MC, V.

D ≈ ✕ ⊠ ⊠ SC

★ ★ **HOLIDAY INN.** 894 Tiger Blvd (29633), 1½ mi E on US 123. 864/654-4450; FAX 864/654-8451. 220 rms, 2 story. S, D $49-$54; each addl $5; suites $129; under 19 free; higher rates football wkends. Crib free. Pet accepted. TV; cable (premium). Pool. Coffee in rms. Restaurant 6:30 am-2 pm, 5:30-8:30 pm. Bar 4 pm-midnight; closed Sun. Ck-out noon. Coin lndry. Meeting rms. Business servs avail. In-rm modem link. Valet serv. Golf privileges. On lake. Cr cds: A, C, D, DS, JCB, MC, V.

D ✈ ✕ ≈ ⊠ ⊠ SC

★ ★ **RAMADA INN.** 1310 Tiger Blvd (29633), SC 76 & US 123. 864/654-7501; FAX 864/654-7301. 149 rms, 4 story. S $47-$58; D $54-$65; suites $125-$150; under 18 free; wkend rates; higher rates: football wkends, special events. Crib free. TV; cable. Indoor pool; whirlpool, sauna. Restaurant 6:30 am-2 pm, 5-10 pm. Rm serv. Bar exc Sun. Ck-out 11 am. Meeting rms. Valet serv. Golf privileges. Some refrigerators. Cr cds: A, C, D, DS, MC, V.

D ✕ ≈ ⊠ ⊠ SC

Clinton (C-3)

(See also Greenville, Greenwood, Newberry, Spartanburg)

Pop 7,987 **Elev** 680 ft **Area code** 864 **Zip** 29325
Information Laurens County Chamber of Commerce, PO Box 248, Laurens 29360; 864/833-2716.

In 1865, Clinton was "a mudhole surrounded by barrooms," according to the young Reverend William Jacobs, who not only rid the town of barrooms but founded a library, orphanage, high school and Presbyterian College (1880). A young attorney by the name of Henry Clinton Young was hired by the townspeople to help lay out the streets, hence the town came to be named for his middle name.

What to See and Do

Rose Hill (ca 1825). Forty-four acres. Located in Rose Hill State Park, this restored cotton plantation was the home of William H. Gist, known as South Carolina's secession governor. The Federal-style house with 1860 furnishings sits on a gently rising knoll amid boxwoods and roses. House (Sat & Sun; also by appt). Grounds (Thurs-Mon). Picnic area, nature trail. 15 mi E on SC 72, 2 mi N on SC 176, then W on Sardis Rd. Phone 864/427-5966. Museum ¢;   Grounds **Free.**

Motels

✔★ **DAYS INN.** Jct I-26 & SC 56, exit 52. 864/833-6600. 58 rms, 2 story. S $42-$45; D $49-$50; each addl $5; suites $80; under 12 free. Crib free. Pet accepted. TV; cable. Pool. Complimentary continental bkfst. Restaurant adj 6:30 am-10 pm. Ck-out 11 am. Coin lndry. Meeting rms. Exercise equipt; weight machine, bicycles. Some refrigerators. Cr cds: A, C, D, DS, MC, V.

D ✈ ≈ ✕ ⊠ ⊠ SC

★ ★ **HOLIDAY INN.** Jct SC 56 & I-26, exit 52. 864/833-4900; FAX 864/833-4916. 102 rms, 2 story. S, D $59; each addl $5; under 19 free. TV; cable (premium). Pool. Restaurant 6:30 am-2 pm, 5-9 pm. Rm serv. Bar 5 pm-midnight. Ck-out noon. Lndry facilities. Meeting rms. Business servs avail. Sundries. Exericise equipt; weight machine, bicycle. Cr cds: A, C, D, DS, MC, V.

D ≈ ✕ ⊠ ⊠ SC

Columbia (D-4)

(See also Camden, Newberry, Orangeburg, Sumter)

Founded 1786 **Pop** 98,052 **Elev** 213 ft **Area code** 803
Information Columbia Metropolitan Visitors Center, 1012 Gervais St, 29201; 803/254-0479 or 800/264-4884.

The broad-boulevarded capital of South Carolina is not only the state's political and governmental capital, but also its wholesale and retail trade center. Located within three miles of the geographic center of the state, Columbia was laid out as the capital as a compromise between the contending Up Country and Low Country farmers. The city rarely departs from a checkerboard pattern; the streets are sometimes 150 feet wide, planned that way originally to discourage malaria.

   The General Assembly met for the first time in the State House in Columbia on January 4, 1790. George Washington was a guest here during his Southern tour the next year. On December 17, 1860, a convention assembled in Columbia's First Baptist Church and drew up the Ordinance of Secession, setting off a chain of events that terminated, for the city, on February 17, 1865, when General William T. Sherman's troops occupied Columbia and reduced it to ashes. An area of 84 blocks and 1,386 buildings was destroyed; on Main Street only the unfinished new statehouse and the home of the French consul were spared. From these ashes, a city of stately buildings has risen.

   The economy of the city is based on trade, industry, finance and government.

   Since 1801, when the South Carolina College, now the University of South Carolina, was established here, the city has been an educational center; today it is the site of nine schools of higher education.

   Columbia is the headquarters for the Francis Marion National Forest (see CHARLESTON) and the Sumter National Forest (see GREENWOOD).

What to See and Do

Columbia Museum of Art. Galleries house Renaissance paintings from the collection of Samuel H. Kress; 19th- and 20th-century American, emphasizing the Southeast, and European paintings; changing exhibitions drawn from permanent collection and from objects on loan. Concerts, films, lectures and special events accenting exhibitions. (Daily exc Mon; closed Jan 1, Dec 25) Free admission Wed. Senate & Bull Sts. Phone 803/799-2810. ¢

Gibbes Planetarium. Changing shows dealing with various topics; tickets available on day of presentation (Sat & Sun). Phone 803/254-7827. ¢¢

Congaree Swamp National Monument. Old-growth, bottomland-hardwood forest, approximately 22,200 acres. Trees and waters teem with wildlife. Fishing, canoeing; hiking trails, boardwalks; public contact station; guided tour (Sat); primitive camping (by permit). (Daily; closed Dec 25) 20 mi SE off SC 48. Phone 803/776-4396. **Free.**

First Baptist Church (1859). First Secession Convention, which marked the beginning of the Civil War, met here Dec 17, 1860. (Daily exc Sat; closed hols) 1306 Hampton St. Phone 803/256-4251.

First Presbyterian Church (1853). First congregation organized in Columbia (1795); President Woodrow Wilson's parents are buried in churchyard. (Daily) 1324 Marion St, at Lady St. Phone 803/799-9062.

Fort Jackson. The most active entry training center for US Army, with 16,000 soldiers assigned. Museum on Jackson Blvd has displays on history of fort and of today's army. (Tues-Sat; closed hols) E edge of city, between I-20 & US 76. Phone 803/751-7419 or 803/751-7355. **Free.**

Governor's Mansion (1855). Built as officers' quarters for Arsenal Academy. Tours (Tues-Thurs). Res required. 800 Richland St. Phone 803/737-1710. **Free.**

Hampton-Preston Mansion (1818). Purchased by Wade Hampton I; occupied by the Hamptons and the family of his daughter, Mrs. John Preston. In February 1865, it served as headquarters for Union general J.A. Logan. Many Hampton family furnishings and decorative arts of the antebellum period. (Daily exc Mon; closed most major hols) 1615 Blanding St. Phone 803/252-1770. ¢¢

Lake Murray. Lake is 41 mi long, with 520-mi shoreline; impounded by Saluda Dam for hydroelectric purposes. Swimming, waterskiing; boating, fishing; picnicking; camping (fee). Marina in White Rock, 17 mi NW, phone 803/749-1554. 15 mi NW via I-26, Irmo exit. For further information phone 803/781-5940.

Lexington County Museum Complex. Historic restoration from mid-1800s; depicts life of area farmer. Period country furnishings, textiles, decorative arts. Spinning and weaving demonstrations. (Daily exc Mon; closed hols) 10 mi W via US 378 at Fox St in Lexington. Phone 803/359-8369. ¢

Riverbanks Zoological Park & Botanical Garden. Exhibits of animals in nonrestrictive natural habitat areas; aquarium-reptile complex with diving demonstrations; birdhouse with rainstorm; demonstrations at Riverbanks Farm; penguin and sea lion feedings. (Daily; closed Thanksgiving, Dec 25) 500 Wildlife Pkwy. Phone 803/779-8730 (recording) or 803/779-8717. ¢¢¢

Robert Mills Historic House (1823) **& Park.** One of a few residences designed by Robert Mills, Federal architect and designer of the Washington Monument; mantels, art, furnishings of Regency period. (Daily exc Mon; closed most major hols) 1616 Blanding St. Phone 803/252-1770. ¢¢

Sesquicentennial State Park. On 1,445 acres. Log house (1756). Interpretive center. Lake swimming, bathhouse; boating (rentals), fishing. Nature, exercise trails. Picnicking (shelters), playground. Recreation building. Camping (hookups, dump station). Swimming & boating (Memorial Day-Labor Day). Standard fees. 13 mi NE on US 1. Phone 803/788-2706.

South Carolina Archives Building. Historical and genealogical research facility with documents dating from 1671; changing exhibits. Research room (Tues-Sat, also Sun afternoons; closed state hols). Tours (by appt). 1430 Senate St. Phone 803/734-8577. **Free.**

South Carolina State Museum. Located in world's first fully electric textile mill (1894); exhibits on art, natural history, cultural history and science & technology with emphasis on contributions by South Carolinians; numerous hands-on exhibits; dioramas. Included is a center dedicated to Nobel prize winner Charles Townes, who helped develop the laser. Gift shop. (Mon-Sat, also Sun afternoons; closed Easter, Thanksgiving, Dec 25, also morning of Jan 1) 301 Gervais St. Phone 803/737-4921. ¢¢

Town Theatre. One of the oldest (since 1919) community theater groups in the US. Broadway plays and musicals. Tours (by appt). Performances (late Sept-late May; also summer show). 1012 Sumter St. For tour schedule, ticket information phone 803/799-2510.

Trinity Cathedral (Episcopal) (1846). Reproduction of Yorkminster, England; the oldest church building in Columbia and one of the largest Episcopal congregations in the US. Hiram Powers baptismal font, box pews, English stained glass. Three Wade Hamptons (a politically prominent South Carolina family) are buried in the churchyard; graves of seven governors and six bishops are also here. In 1977 it became the Cathedral Parish of the Episcopal Diocese of Upper South Carolina. (Spring & fall, Mon-Fri, limited hrs) 1100 Sumter St, at Senate St, opp statehouse. Phone 803/771-7300. **Free.**

University of South Carolina (1801). (26,000 students) Located downtown. For campus tour information stop at the University of South Carolina Visitor Center. (Daily exc Sun) Pendleton & Assemby Sts. Phone 803/777-0169 (exc SC) or 800/922-9755. Points of interest include the Thomas Cooper Library and

The Horseshoe. Original campus area. Ten of the 11 buildings on the quadrangle date back to the 19th century and are listed in the National Register of Historic Places. Monument erected in 1827 was designed by Robert Mills. Off Sumter St .

McKissick Museum. Houses Bernard M. Baruch Silver Gallery with antique European silver, J. Harry Howard gemstone collection, Laurence L. Smith Mineral Library, Catawba Native American pottery collection, Southern Folk Art, historical collections, Art Gallery, Education Museum, Broadcasting Archives. (Daily; closed most major hols, also Dec 24) At the head of the Horseshoe. Phone 803/777-7251. **Free.**

Carolina Coliseum. Houses Gamecock Basketball and other sports events, concerts, exhibitions, trade shows, circuses and other entertainment. Assembly & Blossom Sts.

Koger Center for the Arts. Contemporary structure houses center for the performing arts. Diverse musical, theatrical and dance programs. Assembly & Greene Sts.

Woodrow Wilson Boyhood Home (1872). Built by Wilson's father; items associated with Wilson's family and career. (Daily exc Mon; closed most major hols) 1705 Hampton St. Phone 803/252-1770. ¢¢

Annual Event

South Carolina State Fair. Fairgrounds, 1200 Rosewood Dr. Agricultural, floral, home, craft, livestock and commercial exhibits. Entertainment, shows, carnival. Phone 803/799-3387. Oct 8-18.

Motels

✔★ **BUDGETEL INN.** 1538 Horseshoe Dr (29223), exit 74 to Horseshoe Dr. 803/736-6400; FAX 803/788-7875. 102 rms, 3 story. S $35.95-$43.95; D $42.95-$49.95. Crib free. TV; cable (premium). Pool. Complimentary continental bkfst. Coffee in rms. Restaurant adj open 24 hrs. Ck-out noon. Coin lndry. Meeting rm. Business servs avail. In-rm modem link. Valet serv. Microwaves avail. Cr cds: A, C, D, DS, MC, V.

D ≋ ⊠ 🐾 SC

★ ★ ★ **COURTYARD BY MARRIOTT.** 347 Zimalcrest Dr (29210). 803/731-2300; FAX 803/772-6965. 149 units, 3 story. S $74.95; suites $89; under 12 free; wknd rates. Crib free. TV; cable (premium). Pool; whirlpool. Coffee in rms. Restaurant 6:30-10 am; wknds 7-11 am. Bar 4-10 pm (Mon-Fri). Ck-out noon. Coin lndry. Meeting rms. Business servs avail. In-rm modem link. Valet serv. Exercise equipt; weight machines, bicycles. Refrigerators avail. Cr cds: A, D, DS, MC, V.

D ≋ 🏋 🐾 SC

★ ★ **HAMPTON INN.** 1551 Barbara Dr (29223). 803/865-8000; FAX 803/865-8046. 111 rms, 5 story, 18 suites. Late-May-Aug: S $68; D $73; suites $92-$97; under 18 free; higher rates special events; lower rates rest of yr. Crib free. TV; cable (premium), VCR avail. Complimentary continental bkfst. Complimentary coffee in rms. Restaurant opp 11 am-11 pm. Ck-out noon. Meeting rm. Business servs avail. In-rm modem link. Exercise equipt; weight machine, bicycles. Pool. Some in-rm whirlpools; refrigerator, microwave, wet bar in suites. Cr cds: A, D, DS, MC, V.

[D] [≈] [🏃] [⛷] [🛥] [🔥] [SC]

★★ **HAMPTON INN-AIRPORT.** *I-26 & US 378 (29169).* 803/791-8940; FAX 803/739-2291. 121 rms, 4 story. S, D $57-$71; under 18 free. Crib free. TV; cable (premium). Pool. Complimentary continental bkfst. Business servs avail. In-rm modem link. Cr cds: A, C, D, DS, MC, V.

[D] [≈] [🛥] [🔥] [SC]

★★ **HOLIDAY INN EXPRESS.** *773 St Andrews Rd (29210),* I-26, exit 106. 803/772-7275; FAX 803/750-1877. 101 rms, 2 story. S, D $50-$65; family rates. Crib free. TV; cable (premium). Pool. Complimentary continental bkfst. Restaurant adj 10:30 am-10 pm. Ck-out noon. Meeting rms. Business servs avail. Valet serv. Health club privileges. Cr cds: A, C, D, DS, JCB, MC, V.

[D] [≈] [🛥] [🔥] [SC]

★★ **HOLIDAY INN-NORTHEAST.** *7510 Two Notch Rd (29223),* at I-20. 803/736-3000; FAX 803/736-6399. 253 rms, 2 story. S, D $77; each addl $6; under 12 free; wkend rates. Crib free. TV; cable (premium). Indoor/outdoor pool; whirlpool, poolside serv. Restaurant 6:30 am-2 pm, 5-10 pm. Rm serv. Bar noon-midnight. Ck-out noon. Coin lndry. Meeting rms. Business servs avail. In-rm modem link. Sauna. Health club privileges. Holidome. Game rm. Courtyard. Cr cds: A, C, D, DS, MC, V.

[D] [≈] [🛥] [🔥] [SC]

★★ **LA QUINTA.** *1335 Garner Lane (29210).* 803/798-9590; FAX 803/731-5574. 120 rms, 2 story. S $53; D $59; each addl $6; under 18 free. Crib free. TV; cable (premium). Pool. Complimentary continental bkfst. Restaurant adj 4-11 pm. Ck-out noon. Meeting rms. Business servs avail. Valet serv. Cr cds: A, C, D, DS, MC, V.

[D] [≈] [🛥] [🔥] [SC]

✔★ **RED ROOF INN.** *7580 Two Notch Rd (29223),* at I-20 Two Notch Rd exit. 803/736-0850; FAX 803/736-4270. 108 rms, 2 story. S $40.99; D $46.99; each addl $6; under 18 free. Crib free. TV; cable (premium). Complimentary coffee in lobby. Restaurant adj 6 am-10 pm. Business servs avail. In-rm modem link. Cr cds: A, C, D, DS, MC, V.

[D] [≈] [🔥]

★★ **RESIDENCE INN BY MARRIOTT.** *150 Stoneridge Dr (29210),* off I-126 Greystone Blvd exit. 803/779-7000; FAX 803/779-0408. 128 kit. suites, 2 story. S $99; D $109-$134; family rates. Crib free. Pet accepted, some restrictions. TV; cable (premium). Pool; whirlpool. Complimentary continental bkfst. Complimentary coffee in rms. Ck-out noon. Coin lndry. Meeting rms. Business servs avail. In-rm modem link. Valet serv. Exercise equipt; bicycle, stair machine. Microwaves; some fireplaces. Some grills. Cr cds: A, C, D, DS, JCB, MC, V.

[D] [🐾] [🍴] [🏃] [🛥] [🔥] [SC]

★ **TRAVELODGE COLUMBIA WEST.** *2210 Bush River Rd (29210),* at I-20. 803/798-9665. 108 rms, 3 story. S $44.95; D $49.95; each addl $5; under 18 free. Crib free. TV; cable (premium), VCR avail (movies). Heated pool. Coffee in rms. Restaurant opp 6 am-10 pm. Ck-out 11 am. Meeting rms. Business servs avail. Valet serv. Health club privileges. Refrigerators, microwaves avail. Cr cds: A, C, D, DS, ER, JCB, MC, V.

[D] [≈] [🛥] [🔥] [SC]

Motor Hotels

✔★★ **AMERISUITES.** *7525 Two Notch Rd (29223),* at I-20. 803/736-6666; FAX 803/788-6011. 112 suites, 6 story. S, D $69-$109; each addl $5; under 16 free; wkend rates. Crib free. TV; cable (premium), VCR. Pool. Complimentary continental bkfst. Coffee in rms. Restaurant nearby. Ck-out noon. Meeting rms. Business center. Valet serv. Exercise equipt; weight machine, stair machine. Microwaves. Cr cds: A, C, D, DS, MC, V.

[D] [≈] [🏃] [🛥] [🔥] [SC] [🏌]

★★★ **RAMADA PLAZA HOTEL.** *8105 Two Notch Rd (29223),* at I-77. 803/736-5600; FAX 803/736-1241. 187 units, 6 story. S $79; D $89; suites $130-$220; under 18 free; golf plan. Crib $6. Pet accepted, some restrictions. TV; cable (premium). Pool; whirlpool. Restaurant 6:30 am-10 pm. Rm serv. Bar 4:30 pm-2 am. Ck-out noon. Convention facilities. Business servs avail. In-rm modem link. Bellhops. Valet serv. Tennis privileges. 18-hole golf privileges. Exercise equipt; weight machine, bicycles, sauna. Refrigerator, microwave in suites. Cr cds: A, C, D, DS, ER, MC, V.

[D] [🐾] [🏌] [🏃] [≈] [🏃] [🛥] [🔥] [SC]

★★★ **THE WHITNEY.** *700 Woodrow St (29205).* 803/252-0845; FAX 803/771-0495; res: 800/637-4008. 74 kit. suites, 7 story. 1-bedrm $119; 2-bedrm $139. TV; cable (premium). Pool. Complimentary continental bkfst. Restaurant nearby. Ck-out noon. Meeting rms. Business servs avail. Valet serv. Free airport transportation. Exercise equipt; weight machine, treadmills. Microwaves. Balconies. In residential area. Cr cds: A, C, D, DS, MC, V.

[≈] [🏃] [🛥] [🔥]

Hotels

★★★ **ADAM'S MARK.** *1200 Hampton St (29201).* 803/771-7000; FAX 803/254-8307. 301 rms, 13 story. S $129; D $139; each addl $10; suites $225-$450; under 18 free; wkend rates. Crib free. Pet accepted; $50 deposit. TV; cable. Indoor pool; whirlpool. Restaurants 6 am-midnight. Bar 11:30-1 am. Ck-out noon. Convention facilities. Business servs avail. In-rm modem link. Airport transportation. Exercise equipt; treadmills, bicycles. Some refrigerators. Some balconies. Cr cds: A, C, D, DS, ER, JCB, MC, V.

[D] [🐾] [≈] [🏃] [🛥] [🔥] [SC]

★★★ **EMBASSY SUITES.** *200 Stoneridge Dr (29210),* on I-126 at Greystone Blvd exit. 803/252-8700; FAX 803/256-8749. 214 suites, 7 story. S $129-$159; D $134-$164; each addl $10; under 17 free; wkend rates. Crib free. TV; cable (premium). Indoor pool; whirlpool. Complimentary full bkfst. Complimentary coffee in rms. Restaurant 11 am-10 pm; Fri, Sat to 11 pm. Bar 2-11 pm; Fri, Sat to midnight. Ck-out noon. Coin lndry. Meeting rms. Business servs avail. In-rm modem link. Gift shop. Free airport transportation. Exercise equipt; weight machines, bicycles, sauna. Health club privileges. Microwaves, refrigerators. Atrium lobby; glass-enclosed elvtr. Cr cds: A, C, D, DS, MC, V.

[D] [≈] [🏃] [🛥] [🔥] [SC]

★★★ **SHERATON HOTEL & CONFERENCE CENTER.** *2100 Bush River Rd (29210).* 803/731-0300; FAX 803/731-4892. 237 rms, 5 story. S $109; D $119; each addl $10; suites $129-$350; under 17 free. Crib free. TV; cable (premium). 2 pools, 1 indoor; whirlpool. Coffee in rms. Restaurant 6:30 am-10:30 pm. Bars; entertainment. Meeting rms. Business center. In-rm modem link. Gift shop. Free airport transportation. Exercise equipt; bicycles, treadmills, sauna. Some refrigerators; bathrm phone in suites. Some balconies. Luxury level. Cr cds: A, C, D, DS, ER, MC, V.

[D] [≈] [🏃] [🛥] [🔥] [SC] [🏌]

Inns

★★★ **CLAUSSEN'S.** *2003 Greene St (29205).* 803/765-0440; FAX 803/799-7924; res: 800/622-3382. 29 units, 3 story. S $95-$115; D $103-$118; each addl $10; suites $115-$130; under 12 free. Crib free. TV; cable (premium). Complimentary continental bkfst; afternoon refreshments. Ck-out noon, ck-in 3 pm. Meeting rms. Whirlpool. Refrigerators avail. Private patios. In renovated bakery (1928). Cr cds: A, MC, V.

[D] [🛥] [🔥] [SC]

★★ **RICHLAND STREET B & B.** *1425 Richland St (29201).* 803/779-7001. 8 rms, 2 story, 1 suite. S $79-$99; D $79-$110; each addl $10; suite $135. Children over 12 yrs only. TV; cable. Complimentary continental bkfst; afternoon refreshments. Restaurant nearby. Ck-out 11 am, ck-in 4 pm. Modern building (1992) in Victorian style. Totally nonsmoking. Cr cds: A, MC, V.

Restaurants

★ ★ **AL'S UPSTAIRS.** *(304 Meeting St, West Columbia) 1 mi W on US 1, in National Register Bldg.* 803/794-7404. Hrs: 5-10 pm. Closed Sun; some major hols. Res accepted. Italian menu. Bar. Semi-a la carte: dinner $11.95-$19.95. Specializes in veal, pasta, fresh fish. Parking. Overlooks river. Views of Columbia's skyline. Cr cds: A, D, MC, V.

✔★ ★ **BLUE MARLIN SEAFOOD KITCHEN.** *1200 Lincoln St (29201).* 803/799-3838. Hrs: 11:30 am-2 pm, 5-10 pm; Sat 5-11 pm; Sun from 5 pm. Closed Jan 1, Dec 25. Regional Amer menu. Bar. Semi-a la carte: lunch $5.95-$7.45, dinner $9.95-$14.95. Child's meals. Specialties: shrimp and grits, oyster skillet bienville, blackened catfish. Own pastries. Outdoor dining. Nautical decor in former passenger train station. Cr cds: A, D, MC, V.

★ ★ **GARIBALDI'S.** *2013 Greene St.* 803/771-8888. Hrs: 5:30-10:30 pm; Fri, Sat to 11 pm. Res accepted. Italian menu. Bar. A la carte entrees: dinner $6.95-$21.95. Specializes in fish, steak, pasta. Valet parking. Art deco furnishings. Cr cds: A, MC, V.

★ ★ **HAMPTON STREET VINEYARD.** *1201 Hampton St (29201).* 803/252-0850. Hrs: 11:30 am-2 pm, 6-10 pm; Sat from 6 pm. Closed Sun; Jan 1, July 4, Dec 25. Res accepted. Bar. Semi-a la carte: lunch $6.25-$8.75, dinner $12.50-$18.75. Specializes in seafood, veal, duck. Own desserts. Street parking. In historic Sylvan Bldg (1871); bistro atmosphere; French posters adorn walls. Cr cds: A, DS, MC, V.

★ ★ **HENNESSY'S.** *1649 Main St.* 803/799-8280. Web www .scbell.com. Hrs: 11:30 am-2:30 pm, 6-10 pm; Sat from 6 pm. Closed Sun; hols. Res accepted. Continental menu. Bar. Semi-a la carte: lunch $4.95-$9.95, dinner $9.95-$23.95. Specializes in steak, poultry, fresh seafood. Converted hardware store. Cr cds: A, C, D, DS, MC, V.

★ ★ ★ **RICHARD'S.** *1109 Lincoln St (29201).* 803/212-7217. Hrs: 6-10 pm. Closed Sun; most major hols. Res accepted. Southern regional menu. Bar. Wine list. Semi-a la carte: dinner $11-$22. Specialty: bourbon barbecued strip steak. Pianist Fri, Sat. Valet parking. Local artwork. Cr cds: A, MC, V.

★ ★ **RISTORANTE DIVINO.** *4423 Devine St (29205).* 803/738-0063. Hrs: 5:30-10 pm. Closed Sun, Mon; Jan 1, Dec 25. Res accepted. Northern Italian menu. Serv bar. Semi-a la carte: dinner $12.95-$17.75. Specializes in seafood, pasta, veal. Casual, intimate dining. Totally nonsmoking. Cr cds: A, MC, V.

✔★ ★ **VISTA BREWING & BISTRO.** *936 Gervais St (29201).* 803/799-2739. Hrs: 11-1 am. Closed Sun; Dec 25. Res accepted. French bistro menu. Bar. Semi-a la carte: lunch $5.95-$6.95, dinner $14.95-$17.50. Specialties: lobster ravioli with saffron sauce, herb-encrusted salmon, honey-roasted pork loin. Jazz Tues. Brewing equipt on view; casual decor. Cr cds: A, D, DS, MC, V.

Darlington (D-6)

(For accommodations see Cheraw, Florence; also see Bennettsville, Hartsville)

Founded 1798 **Pop** 7,311 **Elev** 157 ft **Area code** 803 **Zip** 29532
Information Darlington County Chamber of Commerce, PO Box 274; 803/393-2641.

Darlington is situated in one of the most fertile sections of the state. Along with its agricultural economy, the area has diversified industry. Darlington was a pioneer in the culture and marketing of tobacco as a cash crop and has a large tobacco market. It is the home of what is said to be the nation's largest automobile auction market and is a stock car racing center.

What to See and Do

NMPA Stock Car Hall of Fame/Joe Weatherly Stock Car Museum. Museum is said to house largest collection of race cars in the world. Major automotive companies have displays tracing the evolution of the racing stock car and accessories from 1950 to present; cars, engines & trophies of famous drivers. (Daily; closed Dec 25) 1 mi W on SC 34 at Darlington Raceway, the oldest superspeedway in the country. Phone 803/395-8821. ¢¢

Annual Events

TransSouth Financial 400. Darlington Raceway. Late-model stock car race. Late Mar.

Southern 500. Darlington Raceway. 500-mi stock car classic; also beauty pageant, "Southern 500" Festival parade; golf tournament. Preceded by 2 days of trials. Labor Day wkend.

Dillon (C-6)

(See also Bennettsville, Darlington, Florence)

Settled 1887 **Pop** 6,829 **Elev** 115 ft **Area code** 803 **Zip** 29536

Industrial growth and diversification characterize this town. The county seat, Dillon also serves as a shipping center for farm produce.

What to See and Do

Little Pee Dee State Park. Approx 800 acres on Little Pee Dee River. Boating (rentals); fishing (bream). Nature trails. Picnicking (shelters); playground. Camping (hookups, dump station). Standard fees. 11 mi SE between SC 9 & 57, near I-95. Phone 803/774-8872.

Inn

★ ★ ★ **ABINGDON MANOR.** *(307 Church St, Latta 29565) S on I-95, exit 181, 6 mi E.* 803/752-5090; res: 888/752-5090. 5 rms, 2 story, 1 suite. Rm phones avail. S, D $95; each addl $25; suites $120. Children over 12 yrs only. TV; cable (premium), VCR (movies). Whirlpool. Complimentary full bkfst. Ck-out 11 am, ck-in 3 pm. Business servs avail. Luggage handling. Valet serv. Concierge serv. Exercise equipt; bicycle, rowers. Some balconies. Greek Revival mansion built in 1902. Totally nonsmoking. Cr cds: A, C, D, DS, MC, V.

Florence (D-6)

(See also Darlington, Dillon, Hartsville)

Settled 1890 **Pop** 29,813 **Elev** 149 ft **Area code** 843
Information Greater Florence Chamber of Commerce, 610 W Palmetto St, PO Box 948, 29503; 843/665-0515.

Since extensive railroad shops and yards were established here by the Atlantic coastline, this community has grown from a sparsely settled crossroads into a major retail and wholesale distribution center. The economy is no longer dependent on agriculture; a balance of farm and industry has been attained. Florence is also the home of Francis Marion College and Florence-Darlington Technical College.

What to See and Do

Air & Missile Museum. Display of 38 aircraft and missiles includes jets, cargo plane, Bomarc missile, Titan I missile, German V2 rocket, B-47 bomber; Alan Shepard's *Apollo* space suit; heat tiles from space shuttle *Columbia.* Approximately 2,000 displays in building. (Daily) Airport entrance, 2 mi E on US 76/301 or from I-95 exit 170, follow signs. Phone 843/665-5118. ¢¢

Beauty Trail. 12-mi trail within city featuring beautiful gardens (usually best in Apr). **Free.**

City parks.

Lucas Park. Picnicking, playground; tennis courts. Rose gardens, camellias, azaleas, rhododendrons; lighted fountain. Santee Dr & Azalea Ln. **Free.**

Jeffries Creek Nature Park. Fishing. Nature trails. Picnicking, playground. Deberry Blvd. **Free.**

McLeod Park. Swimming pool (fee); fishing pond. Lighted tennis; basketball courts, ball fields. Picnicking, playground. Santiago Dr.

Florence Museum. Art, history and science exhibits. Southwest Native American pottery; Oriental & African collections; Catawba pottery; furniture gallery of mixed periods; South Carolina Hall of History. (Daily exc Mon; closed major hols) 558 Spruce St, at Graham St. Phone 843/662-3351. **Free.**

Lynches River State Park. Approx 650 acres. Located on old stagecoach route. Swimming pool (fee); fishing. Nature trail, bird-watching. Picnicking; playground, community building. Primitive camping. 15 mi S off US 52. Phone 843/389-2785.

National Military Cemetery. Burial ground for Union soldiers who died here in prison. S on US 52/301 to Cherokee Rd.

Timrod Park. One-rm schoolhouse in which Henry Timrod, Poet Laureate of the Confederacy, taught. Playgrounds, picnic areas, barbecue pits; lighted tennis courts. Azalea display in spring. Test rose gardens. Nature trails; fitness station, jogging trail. Special fitness court for the disabled. (Daily) Timrod Park Dr & S Coit St. Phone 843/665-3253. **Free.**

Woods Bay State Park. Approx 1,500 acres of unique natural area with an abundance of wildlife, including alligators, in a "Carolina Bay" (an elliptical, swampy depression mostly underwater). Lake fishing, canoe trail (rentals). Picnic area (shelter). Boardwalk for nature and wildlife observation. 24 mi SW, off US 301 & I-95. Phone 843/659-4445.

Annual Event

Arts Alive. Francis Marion University. Arts, crafts, music, dance, theater, demonstrations, exhibits. Phone 843/661-1225. Apr.

Motels

★ **COMFORT INN.** *1916 W Lucas St (29502), Jct I-95 & US 52.* 843/665-4558. 163 rms, 2 story. S $47; D $53; each addl $4; under 18 free. Crib free. TV; cable (premium). Pool; whirlpool. Complimentary continental bkfst. Coffee in rms. Restaurant adj. Ck-out 11 am. Meeting rms.

Valet serv. Exercise equipt; weights, bicycles. Some in-rm whirlpools; refrigerators, microwaves avail. Cr cds: A, D, DS, MC, V.

✔★ **DAYS INN.** *2111 W Lucas St (29501), jct I-95 & US 52.* 843/665-4444. 103 rms, 2 story. S, D $38-$75; under 12 free; higher rates: race wkends, hols. Crib free. Pet accepted, some restrictions. TV; cable (premium). Pool; whirlpool. Complimentary continental bkfst. Restaurant adj 6 am-midnight. Ck-out 11 am. Meeting rms. Business servs avail. Exercise equipt; weights, bicycles, sauna. Some in-rm whirlpools, refrigerators, microwaves. Cr cds: A, C, D, DS, MC, V.

★ ★ **RAMADA INN.** *2038 W Lucas (29501).* 843/669-4241; FAX 843/665-8883. 179 rms, 2 story. S, D $54-$75; each addl $6; suites $70-$150; under 18 free; higher rates special events. Pet accepted, some restrictions. TV; cable (premium). Pool; whirlpool. Restaurant 6:30 am-2 pm, 5-10 pm. Rm serv. Bar; entertainment. Ck-out noon. Meeting rms. Business servs avail. Bellhops. Free airport transportation. Exercise equipt; weights, bicycles. Refrigerators, microwaves avail. Cr cds: A, C, D, DS, ER, JCB, MC, V.

✔★ **RED ROOF INN.** *2690 David McLeod Blvd (29501).* 843/678-9000; FAX 843/667-1267. 112 rms, 2 story. S $36.99; D $43.99-$52.99; each addl $7; under 18 free; higher rates special events. Crib free. Pet accepted. TV; cable (premium). Complimentary coffee in lobby. Restaurant adj open 24 hrs. Ck-out noon. Business servs avail. Cr cds: A, C, D, DS, MC, V.

✔★ ★ **TRAVELERS INN.** *1914 W Lucas St (29501), jct I-95 & US 52 exit 164.* 843/665-2575; FAX 843/661-0700; res: 800/847-7666. 168 rms, 2 story, 24 suites. S $35.95; D $48.95; each addl $7; suites $51.95-$59.95; under 18 free. TV; cable (premium). Pool; whirlpool. Complimentary full bkfst. Restaurant open 24 hrs. Bar 5 pm-2 am; entertainment exc Sun. Ck-out 11 am. Business servs avail. In-rm modem link. Exercise equipt; weight machine, bicycle. Refrigerators, microwaves avail. Cr cds: A, C, D, DS, MC, V.

Fort Sumter National Monument (F-6)

(For accommodations see Charleston, Kiawah Island)

On an island in Charleston harbor. Accessible by private boat or by Fort Sumter tour boat, leaving City Marina, Lockwood Blvd, Charleston (see) and from Patriots Point Naval Museum, Mt Pleasant.

The national monument includes Fort Sumter, located three miles southeast of Charleston at the harbor entrance, and Fort Moultrie, located one mile east of Fort Sumter on Sullivan's Island. Fort Moultrie is reached via US 17 to SC 703; turn right and follow signs. Fort Moultrie was originally built in 1776, of sand and palmetto logs. Colonel William Moultrie's forces drove British ships from Charleston Harbor at Fort Moultrie in June 1776. The present Fort Moultrie was completed in 1809 and was garrisoned by Union forces in late 1860, when these forces were moved to Fort Sumter.

South Carolina, first state to secede, passed its Ordinance of Secession December 20, 1860. Surrender of Fort Sumter was demanded on April 11, 1861. This demand was refused by Major Robert Anderson, in command of Union forces at the fort. At 4:30 am, April 12, Confederate firing began, and the fort was surrendered after 34 hours of intense bombardment. This attack compelled President Lincoln to call for 75,000 volunteers to put down the rebellion, thus beginning the Civil War. Fort Sumter and Fort Moultrie have been modified through the years. Both were active through World War II.

Fort Moultrie has been restored by the National Park Service; Visitor Center has an audiovisual program depicting the evolution of seacoast defense. Self-guided tour. (Daily; closed Dec 25) **Free.**

Fort Sumter's ruins have been partially excavated, and a museum has been established. (Daily; closed Dec 25) Contact the Superintendent, 1214 Middle St, Sullivan's Island 29482; 843/883-3123 or 843/883-3124. Daily tour boat (fee). **Free.**

Gaffney (C-4)

(See also Rock Hill, Spartanburg; also see Charlotte, NC)

Settled 1803 **Pop** 13,145 **Elev** 779 ft **Area code** 864 **Zip** 29340
Information Cherokee County Chamber of Commerce, 225 S Limestone St; 864/489-5721.

Once a prosperous resort town where plantation owners sought to cure malaria attacks with the supposedly therapeutic waters of the limestone springs, Gaffney is now a textile and metalworking center and the home of a variety of other industries and agricultural products, particularly peaches. On I-85, just outside of town, stands the Gaffney Peachoid (1981), an elevated tank that resembles a gigantic peach and holds a million-gallon water supply.

What to See and Do

Cowpens National Battlefield. Scene of victory of General Daniel Morgan's American Army over superior British forces on Jan 17, 1781. The British suffered 110 men killed, 200 wounded, 550 captured, while the American losses were minimal. This victory was followed by the Battle of Guilford Courthouse, and then the forces moved on to Yorktown, where Cornwallis was forced to surrender. An 843-acre tract with exhibits, Information and Visitor Center, self-guided tour road and walking trail with audio stations and restored 1830 historic house. Slide program (fee). Picnicking (shelters). (Daily; closed Jan 1, Dec 25) 11 mi NW on SC 11, 1/2 mi from jct SC 110. Phone 864/461-2828. **Free.**

Kings Mountain National Military Park (see). 20 mi NE off I-85.

Annual Event

South Carolina Peach Festival. Arts & crafts, sports events, entertainment. Mid-July.

Motel

✔★ **COMFORT INN.** *I-85 & SC 11, exit 92.* 864/487-4200. 83 rms, 2 story. S $49; D $55; each addl $5; under 18 free; higher rates special events. Crib $6. TV; cable (premium). Pool. Complimentary continental bkfst. Ck-out 11 am. Meeting rms. Exercise equipt; weight machines, bicycle. Refrigerators. Cr cds: A, C, D, DS, MC, V.

D ⩳ 🏋 ✕ 🔥 SC

Georgetown (E-6)

(See also Myrtle Beach)

Founded 1729 **Pop** 9,517 **Elev** 10 ft **Area code** 803 **Zip** 29440 **Web** myrtlebeachlive.com/tidelands/
Information Georgetown County Chamber of Commerce, PO Box 1776, 29442; 803/546-8436 or 800/777-7705.

A seaport throughout its long history, Georgetown enjoyed a resurgence of ship traffic following the deepening of the channel and the building of a new cargo dock. The shore of Winyah Bay, on which Georgetown is situated,

was the site of the first European settlement on the North American mainland outside of Mexico. In 1526 a group of Spaniards settled here, only to be driven out within a year by disease and Native American attacks. Rice and indigo plantations were established along nearby rivers about 1700. Georgetown was founded by Rev. Elisha Screven, son of the first Baptists in the South; the city was finally laid out to honor King George II of England. It became increasingly important as an export center with quantities of lumber and naval stores, rice and indigo. Lafayette landed near here to join the American cause in the Revolution. The city was later occupied by British troops. Known as a sawmill city during the first three decades of this century, Georgetown currently boasts several manufacturing industries as well as a thriving tourist economy.

What to See and Do

Brookgreen Gardens. On site of former rice and indigo plantations; more than 500 pieces of American sculpture in garden; boxwood, massive moss-hung oaks, native plants; wildlife park with native animals. Picnicking. (Daily; closed Dec 25) 18 mi N on US 17, 3 mi S of Murrells Inlet. Phone 803/237-4218. ¢¢¢

Captain Sandy's Plantation Tours. Leaves from Harborwalk Seaport. For schedule phone 803/527-4106. ¢¢¢¢

Fishing. Charter boats from docks. Channel fishing for bass or deep-sea fishing for barracuda, amberjack, albacore, bonito, mackerel. (Apr-Nov)

Hampton Plantation State Park. Restored 18th-century mansion was centerpiece of large rice plantation; ancestral home of Rutledge family. Guided tours, special programs. (Thurs-Mon) 1950 Rutledge Rd, McClellanville; 20 mi S off US 17. Phone 803/546-9361. Mansion ¢

Harold Kaminski House (ca 1760). Pre-Revolutionary house furnished with antiques. Tours. (Daily; closed legal hols) 1003 Front St. Phone 803/546-7706. ¢¢

Hopsewee Plantation (ca 1740). Preserved rice plantation house on North Santee River. Birthplace of Thomas Lynch, Jr, signer of Declaration of Independence. Grounds (daily). House (Mar-Nov, Tues-Fri; rest of yr, by appt). 12 mi S on US 17. Phone 803/546-7891. ¢¢

Huntington Beach State Park. Approx 2,500 acres. Ocean swimming; surf fishing. Hiking, nature trails; marsh boardwalk. Picnicking (shelters); playground; concession. Camping. Standard fees (higher Apr-Sept). 17 mi N on US 17, 3 mi S of Murrells Inlet. Phone 803/237-4440. ¢¢ Also here is

Atalaya. Former home and studio of the sculptress Anna Hyatt Huntington. (June-Labor Day; daily) Art festival (late Sept). ¢

Prince George Winyah Church (ca 1750). English stained-glass window behind altar was originally a part of St Mary's Chapel for Negroes at Hagley Plantation on Waccamaw. In continuous use except during Revolutionary and Civil wars. Tours. (Mar-Oct, Mon-Fri) Broad & Highmarket Sts. Phone 803/546-4358. **Free.**

Town Clock Building (rebuilt 1842). Tablet marks landing of Lafayette at North Island in 1777; Federal troops came ashore on the dock at the rear of building in an attempt to capture the town. Front & Screven Sts. Inside is

Rice Museum. Maps, dioramas, film, artifacts and exhibits depict development and production of crop that was once the basis of Georgetown's economy. (Daily exc Sun; closed hols) Phone 803/546-7423. ¢

Motel

★★ **CLARION CARRIAGE HOUSE-CAROLINIAN INN.** *706 Church St (US 17).* 803/546-5191; FAX 803/546-1514. 89 rms, 1-2 story. May-Aug: S $48-$75; D $54-$75; each addl $10; under 18 free; higher rates hols; lower rates rest of yr. Crib $5. TV; cable (premium). Pool. Complimentary full bkfst. Restaurant 6:30 am-10 pm; closed Sun. Ck-out 11 am. Meeting rms. Business servs avail. Cr cds: A, C, D, DS, JCB, MC, V.

⩳ ✕ 🔥 SC

Inns

★ ★ ★ **1790 HOUSE.** *630 Highmarket St. 803/546-4821; res: 800/890-7432.* 6 rms, 4 with shower only, 3 story, 1 suite. Mar-Nov: S, D $75-$125; each addl $15; suite $95; lower rates rest of yr. TV; cable, VCR avail (free movies). Complimentary full bkfst; afternoon refreshments. Restaurant nearby. Ck-out 11 am, ck-in 3 pm. Golf privileges. Built in 1790; West Indies-style architecture. Antiques. Gazebo. Totally nonsmoking. Cr cds: A, DS, MC, V.

🧍‍♂️ 🏌 ⛵ 🐾 SC

★ ★ **KING'S INN.** *230 Broad St. 843/527-6937; res: 800/251-8805.* Web www.bbonline.com/sc/kingsinn. 7 rms, 2 story. No rm phones. S, D $75-$115. TV in common rm; cable. Complimentary full bkfst. Restaurant nearby. Ck-out 11 am, ck-in 3 pm. Luggage handling. Street parking. Tennis privileges. Pool. Game rm. Federal style; antiques. Totally nonsmoking. Cr cds: A, MC, V.

🏌 ⛵

★ ★ **SEA VIEW INN.** *(Pawleys Island 29585) N on US 17. 803/237-4253; FAX 803/237-7909.* 20 rms, 18 air-cooled, all share bath, 2 story. No rm phones. Mid-May-Oct (2-day min); AP: S $109-$135; D $168-$220; each addl $50; wkly rates; lower rates Apr-mid-May. Closed rest of yr. Children over 3 yrs only. Complimentary full bkfst. Ck-out 11 am, ck-in noon. Built in 1930s. On beach; view of ocean. No cr cds accepted.

🦀 🐾

✔★ ★ **SHAW HOUSE INN.** *613 Cypress Court. 803/546-9663.* 4 rms, 2 story. S $55, D $65-$70. Crib free. TV; cable. Complimentary full bkfst; afternoon refreshments. Ck-out 1 pm, ck-in after 1 pm. Tennis privileges. Golf privileges. Greek-revival architecture; overlooks Willowbank Marsh. Antiques. No cr cds accepted.

🧍‍♂️ 🏌 ⛵ 🐾 SC

Restaurants

★ ★ ★ **COMMUNITY HOUSE.** *(US 17 S, Pawley's Island 29585) 20 mi S on US 17 S. 803/237-8353.* Hrs: 6-10 pm. Res accepted. Northern Italian menu. Bar. Wine list. Semi-a la carte: dinner $10.95-$21.95. Child's meals. Specializes in fresh local seafood, chicken. Own baking, pasta. In old schoolhouse bldg (1932); country decor. Cr cds: DS, MC, V.

D 🍴

★ ★ ★ **RICE PADDY.** *819 Front St. 803/546-2021.* Hrs: 11:30 am-2:30 pm, 6-10 pm. Closed Sun. Res accepted. Bar. Wine list. Semi-a la carte: lunch $5.50-$9.95, dinner $15.95-$23.95. Specializes in seafood, lamb, veal. Local art displayed. Overlooks Sampit River. Cr cds: A, DS, MC, V.

🍴

★ ★ **RIVER ROOM.** *801 Front St. 803/527-4110.* Hrs: 11 am-2:30 pm, 5-10 pm. Closed Sun; Jan 1, Thanksgiving, Dec 24, 25. Bar. Semi-a la carte: lunch $4.75-$11.95, dinner $9.95-$19.95. Child's meals. Specialties: crab cakes, shrimp and grits. Own desserts. Restored dry goods store (1880s); view of river. Cr cds: A, MC, V.

D 🍴

Greenville (C-3)

(See also Anderson, Clemson, Clinton, Spartanburg)

Founded 1797 **Pop** 58,282 **Elev** 966 ft **Area code** 864
Information Convention & Visitors Center, 206 S Main St, 29603; 864/233-0461.

Greenville has several hundred manufacturing plants producing clothing, nylon, chemicals, plastic film and machinery. It is best known for its numerous textile plants. Yet the town is also well named—beautiful trees line the streets, and there are many forested parks in the area. The Reedy River, passing over falls in the heart of Greenville, originally provided the city's power. Pleasant streets now border the twisting sylvan stream.

What to See and Do

Bob Jones University (1927). (5,000 students) During academic year, university offers vesper concerts (twice/month, Sun). Multimedia presentation (daily; closed hols). Tours. At jct US 29, SC 291. Phone 864/242-5100. On campus are

Bob Jones University Collection of Religious Art. Houses collection of rare biblical material and collection of sacred art, including works by Botticelli, Veronese, Rembrandt, Rubens. Under 6 yrs not permitted. (Daily exc Mon; closed Jan 1, July 4, Dec 20-25) **Free.**

Mack Memorial Library. Contains Archives Room and Jerusalem Chamber, display area for the university's collection of rare Bibles.

Confederate History Museum. Permanent collection of American art, featuring historical and contemporary works. Changing exhibits include painting, sculpture, photography. Lectures, tours. (Daily exc Mon; closed most hols) 420 College St. Phone 864/271-7570. **Free.**

Greenville Zoo. Picnicking, concessions. Lighted tennis courts, ball field; nature, jogging, hiking and bicycle trails; park. (Daily; closed Jan 1, Thanksgiving, Dec 25) 150 Cleveland Park Dr. Phone 864/467-4300. ¢¢

State parks.

Caesar's Head. Approx 7,000 acres. At 3,208 ft above sea level, the park overlooks a valley of almost impenetrable brush and dense forest. One side of the mountain resembles Caesar's head. Raven Cliff Falls. Scenic overlook. Hiking trails. Picnicking (shelter). Trailside camping, store, special programs. Standard fees. 30 mi NW via US 276. Phone 864/836-6115.

Paris Mountain. Approx 1,000 acres with 3 lakes. Thick forest setting with swiftly flowing streams. Lake swimming; fishing; pedal boats (rentals). Nature, hiking trail. Picnicking, playground. Camping (hookups, dump station). Standard fees. 6 mi N off US 276 & SC 253. Phone 864/244-5565.

Table Rock. Approx 3,000 acres. Extends over Table Rock Mt (elev 3,124 ft) and valleys. Lake swimming; fishing; boating, canoeing (rentals). Hiking trail; carpet golf. Picnicking, restaurant, store. Camping (hookups, dump station), cabins; recreation building. Nature center; nature & recreation programs. Standard fees. 16 mi N on US 25, then 15 mi W on SC 11. Phone 864/878-9813.

Annual Event

Freedom Weekend Aloft. More than 200 balloonists compete. Phone 864/232-3700. Memorial Day or July 4 wknd.

Motels

★ ★ ★ **COURTYARD BY MARRIOTT.** *70 Orchard Park Dr (29615).* 864/234-0300; FAX 864/234-0296. 146 rms, 3 story. S, D $78; suites $89-$99. Crib free. TV; cable (premium). Heated pool; whirlpool. Complimentary coffee in rms. Restaurant 6:30-10:30 am; Sat, Sun 7-11 am. Coin lndry. Meeting rms. Business servs avail. Valet serv. Exercise equipt; weights, bicycles. Refrigerator in suites. Cr cds: A, C, D, DS, MC, V.

D ⛵ 🏋 ⛵ 🐾 SC

✔★ **DAYS INN.** *831 Congaree Rd (29607). 864/288-6221; FAX 864/288-2778.* 124 rms, 5 story. S, D $54-$69; each addl $5; under 18 free; wkend rates; higher rates special events. Crib free. TV; cable. Pool. Complimentary continental bkfst. Restaurant adj 6 am-10 pm. Ck-out 11 am. Meeting rms. In-rm modem link. Health club privileges. Cr cds: A, C, D, DS, ER, JCB, MC, V.

D ⛵ ⛵ 🐾 SC

✔★ ★ **FAIRFIELD INN BY MARRIOTT.** *60 Roper Mountain Rd (29607), I-385 exit 37. 864/297-9996; FAX 864/297-9996, ext. 709.* 132

rms, 3 story. S $49.95; D $55.95; each addl $6; under 18 free. Crib free. TV; cable (premium). Pool. Complimentary continental bkfst. Restaurant nearby. Ck-out noon. Business servs avail. In-rm modem link. Cr cds: A, D, DS, MC, V.

D ⊠ ⊠ ⊠ ⊠ SC

★ ★ **HAMPTON INN.** 246 Congaree Rd (29607), off I-385. 864/288-1200; FAX 864/288-5667. 123 rms, 4 story. S $58-$66; D $60-$68; under 18 free. Crib free. TV; cable (premium). Pool. Complimentary continental bkfst. Ck-out noon. Meeting rm. Business servs avail. In-rm modem link. Cr cds: A, C, D, DS, MC, V.

D ⊠ ⊠ ⊠ ⊠ SC

★ ★ **LA QUINTA.** 31 Old Country Road (29607). 864/297-3500; FAX 864/458-9818. 122 rms, 2 story. S $53; D $59; under 18 free. Crib free. Pet accepted. TV; cable, VCR avail. Pool. Complimentary continental bkfst. Restaurant adj 6 am-10 pm. Ck-out noon. Coin lndry. Meeting rms. Business servs avail. Valet serv. Health club privileges. Cr cds: A, C, D, DS, MC, V.

D ✦ ⊠ ⊠ ⊠ SC

★ **QUALITY INN-HAYWOOD.** 50 Orchard Park Dr (29615). 864/297-9000; FAX 864/297-8292. 147 rms, 2 story. S $54; D $58; each addl $6; suites $75; kit. unit $80; under 18 free; higher rates Textile Show. Crib $6. TV; cable. Pool. Complimentary continental bkfst. Complimentary coffee in rms. Ck-out noon. Meeting rms. Valet serv. Health club privileges. Cr cds: A, C, D, DS, JCB, MC, V.

D ⊠ ⊠ ⊠ SC

★ ★ **RESIDENCE INN BY MARRIOTT.** 48 McPrice Ct (29615). 864/297-0099; FAX 864/288-8203. 96 kit. suites, 2 story. S, D $99-$119; wkly, monthly rates. Crib free. Pet accepted, some restrictions; $100. TV; cable (premium). Pool; whirlpool. Complimentary continental bkfst. Restaurant adj 11:30 am-11 pm. Ck-out noon. Meeting rms. Business servs avail. Private patios, balconies. Cr cds: A, C, D, DS, JCB, MC, V.

D ✦ ⊠ ⊠ ⊠ SC

Motor Hotel

★ ★ **HOLIDAY INN.** 4295 Augusta Rd (29605), I-85 exit 45-A. 864/277-8921; FAX 864/299-6066. 155 rms, 5 story. S, D $85; each addl $6; suites $95; under 18 free; higher rates special events. Crib free. TV; cable. Pool. Complimentary coffee in rms. Restaurant 7 am-2 pm, 5-10 pm. Rm serv. Bar 4 pm-midnight. Ck-out noon. Meeting rms. Business servs avail. In-rm modem link. Bellhops. Valet serv. Free airport transportation. Health club privileges. Cr cds: A, C, D, DS, ER, JCB, MC, V.

D ⊠ ⊠ ⊠ SC

Hotels

★ ★ ★ **EMBASSY SUITES.** 670 Verdae Blvd (29607). 864/676-9090; FAX 864/676-0669. 268 suites, 9 story. S $129; D $139; lower rates wkends; each addl $10; under 18 free. Crib free. TV; cable (premium). 2 pools; 1 indoor; whirlpool. Complimentary full bkfst. Complimentary coffee in rms. Restaurant 11 am-10 pm. Bar 11 am-midnight. Coin lndry. Convention facilities. Business servs avail. In-rm modem link. Gift shop. Free airport transportation. 18-hole golf privileges, greens fee $44, pro putting green, driving range. Exercise equipt; weights, bicycles, sauna. Refrigerators. Cr cds: A, C, D, DS, MC, V.

D ⅓ ⊠ ⊠ ⊠ ⊠ SC

★ ★ ★ **HILTON.** 45 W Orchard Park Dr (29615). 864/232-4747; FAX 864/235-6248. 256 rms, 9 story. S $134; D $149; suites $250-$400; family, wkend rates. Crib free. TV; cable. Indoor pool; whirlpool, poolside serv. Restaurant 6 am-11 pm. Bar 4:30 pm-2 am. Ck-out noon. Convention facilities. Business servs avail. Concierge. Gift shop. Airport, RR station, bus depot transportation. Exercise equipt; weight machines, bicycles,

sauna. Refrigerator in suites. Luxury level. Cr cds: A, C, D, DS, ER, MC, V.

D ⊠ ⅓ ⊠ ⊠ SC

★ ★ ★ **HOLIDAY INN SELECT.** I-385 & Roper Mountain Rd (29607). 864/297-6300; FAX 864/234-0747. 208 rms, 6 story. S $19.95; D $129.95; each addl $10; under 18 free; wknd rates. TV; cable (premium). Indoor pool; whirlpool, poolside serv. Coffee in rms. Restaurant 6:30 am-10 pm. Bar 11-2 am, closed Sun. Ck-out noon. Meeting rms. Business servs avail. In-rm modem link. Free airport transportation. Exercise equipt; treadmills, weight machine. Some refrigerators. Cr cds: A, C, D, DS, JCB, MC, V.

D ⊠ ⅓ ⊠ ⊠ SC

★ ★ ★ **HYATT REGENCY.** 220 N Main St (29601). 864/235-1234; FAX 864/232-7584. 327 rms, 8 story. S $135; D $160; each addl $25; suites $195-$500; under 18 free; wkend rates. Crib free. Covered parking $4. TV; cable (premium). Pool; whirlpool, poolside serv. Restaurants 6:30 am-11 pm. Bar; closed Sun. Ck-out noon. Convention facilities. Business center. In-rm modem link. Shopping arcade. Free airport transportation. Indoor tennis privileges. Golf privileges. Exercise equipt; weight machine, stair machine. Cr cds: A, C, D, DS, JCB, MC, V.

D ⅓ ✦ ⊠ ⅓ ⊠ ⊠ SC ⚲

★ ★ ★ **MARRIOTT AIRPORT.** 1 Parkway East (29615), near Greenville/Spartanburg Airport. 864/297-0300; FAX 864/281-0801; res: 800/441-1737. 204 rms, 7 story. S $125; D $129; each addl $10; under 18 free; higher rates Textile Show. Crib free. TV; cable (premium), VCR avail. 2 pools, 1 indoor; whirlpool, poolside serv. Coffee in rms. Restaurant 6:30 am-10 pm. Bar 3:30 pm-1 am; Sat to midnight; closed Sun; entertainment. Ck-out noon. Convention facilities. Business center. In-rm modem link. Concierge. Free airport transportation. Tennis privileges. 18-hole golf privileges. Exercise equipt; weight machine, bicycles, sauna. Luxury level. Cr cds: A, C, D, DS, ER, JCB, MC, V.

D ⅓ ✦ ⊠ ⅓ ⊠ ⊠ SC ⚲

Restaurants

★ ★ **858.** 18 E North St (29601). 864/242-8883. Hrs: 11 am-2:30 pm, 5-10 pm; Thur, Fri to 11 pm; Sat 5-11 pm. Closed Sun; also major hols. Res accepted. Bar. Semi-a la carte: lunch $5-$6.50, dinner $9.50-$19.99. Child's meals. Specialties: potato crusted grouper, sautéed macadamia pepper chicken. Complimentary valet parking. Grand piano in dining rm. Cr cds: A, D, DS, MC, V.

D

★ **BISTRO EUROPA.** 219 N Main St (29601). 864/467-9975. Hrs: 11:30 am-3:30 pm, 5:30-10 pm; Fri to 11 pm; Sat 11:30 am-11 pm; Sun brunch 11:30 am-2:30 pm. Closed major hols. Bar. Semi-a la carte: lunch $5.95-$7.95, dinner $5.95-$16.95. Sun brunch $5-$7.95. Specialties: pepper crusted tenderloin, salmon cakes. Outdoor dining. Bistro decor. Cr cds: A, D, DS, MC, V.

D

★ ★ **OPEN HEARTH.** (2801 Wade Hampton Blvd, Taylors) 5 mi N on US 29. 864/244-2665. Hrs: 5:30-10:30 pm. Closed Sun; major hols. Res accepted Fri, Sat. Bar. Semi-a la carte: dinner $8.95-$25.95. Child's meals. Specializes in aged steak, fresh seafood, Greek salad. Family-owned. Cr cds: A, C, D, DS, MC, V.

⊿

★ ★ ★ **SEVEN OAKS.** 104 Broadus Ave. 864/232-1895. Hrs: 6-10 pm. Closed Sun; some major hols. Res accepted. Continental menu. Serv bar. Wine cellar. A la carte entrees: dinner $15.95-$24.95. Specializes in fresh seafood, beef. Own baking. Outdoor dining. Beautifully restored 1895 mansion; eight fireplaces. Cr cds: A, D, MC, V.

D ⊿

★ ★ ★ **STAX'S PEPPERMILL.** 30 Orchard Pk Dr (29615). 864/288-9320. Hrs: 11:30 am-2 pm, 5:30-10:30 pm; Fri to 11:30 pm; Sat, Mon from 5:30 pm. Closed Sun; most major hols. Res accepted. Continental menu. Bar. Wine list. Semi-a la carte: lunch $8.50-$10.50, dinner $13.95-$31.50. Specializes in lamb, beef, fresh fish. Own baking. Pianist Tues-Sat. Outdoor dining. Tableside preparation. Cr cds: A, C, D, MC, V.

★ ★ **TAHOE SOUTH.** *1 College St. 864/235-7166.* Hrs: 11:30 am-2 pm, 6-10 pm; Fri, Sat to 11 pm. Closed Sun; also major hols. Southwestern menu. Bar from 5 pm. Semi-a la carte: lunch $3.95-$7.95, dinner $9.95-$18.95. Child's meals. Specialties: chile rellenos, pork loin tahoe supreme. Western decor. Cr cds: MC, V.

★ ★ **VINCES.** *1 E Antrim Dr. 864/233-1621.* Hrs: 11:30 am-2:30 pm, 5-10 pm; Fri, Sat to 11 pm. Closed Sun; major hols. Italian, Amer menu. Semi-a la carte: lunch $4.95-$7.95, dinner $7.95-$15.95. Child's meals. Specializes in fresh seafood, pasta, prime rib. Cr cds: A, MC, V.

★ ★ ★ **YAGOTO.** *500 Congaree Rd, in Nippon Center Yagoto. 864/288-8471.* Hrs: 6-9:30 pm. Closed Sun; major hols. Res accepted. Japanese menu. Bar. Wine cellar. A la carte entrees: dinner $13-$28. Complete meals: dinner $34.50-$39. Specializes in sushi, sashimi. Sushi bar. Tatami rm. Housed in Japanese cultural center. Tours and tea ceremonies avail by appt. Cr cds: A, D, DS, JCB, MC, V.

D

Greenwood (D-3)

(See also Clinton, Newberry)

Settled 1830 **Pop** 20,807 **Elev** 665 ft **Area code** 864
Information Chamber of Commerce, PO Box 980, 29648; 864/223-8431.

At the junction of highways and railways, Greenwood was originally the plantation of Green Wood; it later became known as the community of Woodville and finally adopted its present name. Greenwood's Main Street is one of the widest (316 feet) in the nation. The town enjoys diversified industry.

What to See and Do

J. Strom Thurmond Lake. Formed by damming of Savannah River. Fishing; boating (ramps). Picnicking (shelters). Campgrounds (fees). (Daily) 30 mi SW via US 221, 378. Phone 864/333-2476 or 706/722-3770. Free.

Ninety Six National Historic Site. Site of old Ninety Six, an early village in South Carolina backcountry, so named because of its distance of 96 miles from the Cherokee Village of Keowee on the Cherokee Path. Site of the South's first land battle of the Revolutionary War in 1775, and of the 28-day siege of Ninety Six in 1781. The earthworks of the British-built Star Fort remain, along with reconstructed siegeworks and other fortifications of the period. Visitor center; museum, video presentation. Also here are subsurface remains of two village complexes, a trading post/plantation complex and a network of 18th-century roads. (Daily; closed Jan 1, Dec 25) 9 mi E on SC 34 to present town of Ninety Six, then 2 mi S on SC 248. Phone 864/543-4068. **Free.**

State parks.

Lake Greenwood. On 914 acres bordering Greenwood Lake, which is 20 mi long, 2 mi wide. Waterskiing; lake fishing, bait shop; boating (ramps). Nature trails. Picnicking (shelters), store. Camping (hookups, dump station). Recreation building. Standard fees. 13 mi E on SC 34, then N on SC 702. Phone 864/543-3535.

Baker Creek. Approx 1,300 acres. Lake swimming, bathhouse; lake fishing; boating (ramps). Nature, bridle trails; carpet golf. Picnicking, playground. Camping (dump station). Standard fees. 28 mi SW via US 221, US 378W. Phone 864/443-2457 or 864/443-5886.

Hickory Knob Resort. On 1,091 acres. Waterskiing; lake fishing, supplies; boating (ramps, rentals). Nature trails; 18-hole golf course, putting green, field archery course, skeet range, field trial area. Playground, restaurant. Camping (hookups, dump station); lodge, cabins. Recreation and nature programs. Convention facilities. Standard fees. 32 mi SW via US 221, US 378W. Phone 800/491-1764.

Sumter National Forest. Approx 353,000 acres in the Piedmont Plateau and the Blue Ridge Mts. Miles of trails through pine and hardwood forest; canoeing, whitewater trips, swimming, trout fishing; hunting for deer, turkey, quail; picnicking, camping. Fees may be charged at recreation sites. In three sections: SW via US 221; NW via SC 28; and NE via SC 72. Phone 864/561-4000.

The Museum. Features a nostalgic "street" lined with houses, shops. Displays of minerals, mounted animal heads, Native American artifacts, ethnographic materials. Art gallery with regional art, traveling exhibits. (Tues-Fri, also Sat afternoons; closed major hols) 106 Main St. Phone 864/229-7093. **Free.**

Annual Event

South Carolina Festival of Flowers. Arts, crafts, photos, special entertainment. Phone 864/223-8411. Last wkend June.

Motels

★ **COMFORT INN.** *1215 E US 72 Bypass (29649). 864/223-2838; FAX 864/942-0119.* 83 rms, 2 story. S $44-$50; D $50-$65; suites $100; under 12 free. Crib free. TV; cable (premium). Pool; whirlpool. Complimentary continental bkfst. Complimentary coffee in rms. Restaurant nearby. Ck-out noon. Meeting rms. Business servs avail. Valet serv. Exercise equipt; bicycles, treadmill. Refrigerators. Cr cds: A, C, D, DS, ER, JCB, MC, V.

D ⊠ ✗ ⊠ 🔥 SC

✔★ ★ **DAYS INN.** *919 Montague Ave (29649), US 25N & SC 72 Bypass. 864/223-3979; FAX 864/223-3297.* 100 rms, 2 story. S $35-$44; D $40-$49; each addl $5. TV; cable (premium). Pool. Complimentary bkfst. Bar 5 am-10 pm. Ck-out noon. Meeting rms. Business servs avail. In-rm modem link. Valet serv. Cr cds: A, C, D, DS, MC, V.

D ⊠ ⊠ 🔥 SC

★ ★ **HOLIDAY INN.** *1014 Montague Ave (US 25/178) (29649). 864/223-4231; FAX 864/223-4231, ext. 145.* 100 rms, 2 story. S $58; D $64; each addl $6; under 19 free. Crib free. TV; cable. Pool. Restaurant 6-9 am, 6-9 pm; Sat, Sun 6-9 am. Rm serv. Bar 4-10 pm; closed Sun. Ck-out noon. Coin lndry. Meeting rms. Business servs avail. In-rm modem link. Valet serv. Cr cds: A, C, D, DS, MC, V.

D ⊠ ⊠ 🔥 SC

Inns

★ ★ **BELMONT.** *(106 E Pickens St, Abbeville 29620) E on SC 72. 864/459-9625.* 25 rms, 3 story. S, D $69-$109; each addl $5; higher rates wkends. Crib free. TV, cable (premium). Complimentary continental bkfst. Dining rm 11:30 am-2 pm, 6-9 pm. Bar 4:30 pm-midnight. Ck-out noon, ck-in 3 pm. Business servs avail. Historic bldg (1903); restored. Period reproduction and antique furnishings and accessories. Cr cds: A, DS, MC, V.

🔥

★ ★ ★ **INN ON THE SQUARE.** *104 Court St (29646), at Main St. 864/223-4488; FAX 864/223-7067.* 46 rms, 3 story. S, D $65.95-$75.95. Crib $15. TV; cable (premium). Pool. Complimentary refreshments. Dining rm 7-10 am, 11:30 am-2:30 pm, 5:30-10 pm; wkend hrs vary. Rm serv. Ck-out 11 am, ck-in 2 pm. Business servs avail. Atrium. Rms furnished with 18th-century reproductions. Cr cds: A, C, D, DS, MC, V.

 D ⊠ ⊠ 🔥

Restaurant

★ **BLAZER'S.** *US 221E & SC 72E, 8 mi E on SC 72. 864/223-1917.* Hrs: 5-10 pm. Closed Sun, Mon; Jan 1, Thanksgiving, Dec 24-25. Bar. Semi-a la carte: dinner $7.95-$14.95. Child's meals. Specializes in fresh seafood, steak. Overlooks Lake Greenwood. Cr cds: A, DS, MC, V.

[D] [symbol]

Hardeeville (F-4)

(See also Beaufort, Hilton Head Island)

Pop 1,583 **Elev** 80 ft **Area code** 803 **Zip** 29927

What to See and Do

Savannah National Wildlife Refuge. Approx 25,600 acres. More than half the acreage consists of bottomland hardwoods reminiscent of the great cypress/tupelo swamps that once extended along the Carolina and Georgia Lowcountry. Argent Swamp can only be reached by boat; wild azaleas, iris, spider lilies & other flowers bloom in succession, beginning in spring. Laurel Hill Wildlife Dr, open to cars, allows viewing of wildlife, especially waterfowl (Dec-Feb). Migrating songbirds are abundant in spring and fall. Tupelo-Swamp Walk (mid-Mar-Sept) is best for bird watchers and photographers. (Daily; some areas closed Oct-Nov for hunting; impoundments N of US 17 closed Nov-mid-Mar; Laurel Hill Dr hrs posted at gate) 17 mi S via US 17. Phone 912/652-4415. **Free.**

Motels

✓★★ **HOWARD JOHNSON.** *US 17 at jct I-95. 803/784-2271.* 126 rms, 2 story. S $33-$50; D $37-$55; each addl $5; under 18 free. Crib free. Pet accepted; $5. TV; cable (premium). Pool; wading pool. Restaurant 7-10 am, 11 am-2 pm, 5-9 pm. Ck-out noon. Business servs avail. Private patios, balconies. Cr cds: A, C, D, DS, MC, V.

[D] [symbols] [SC]

★ **SUPER 8.** *US 17, at I-95 exit 5. 803/784-2151; FAX 803/784-3026.* 100 rms, 2 story. S $28.95; D $35.86; each addl $5. Crib free. TV; cable. Pool. Coffee in lobby. Restaurant 5-10 pm. Bar 4:30 pm-midnight; closed Sun. Ck-out 11 am. Coin lndry. Cr cds: A, C, D, DS, MC, V.

[D] [symbols] [SC]

Hartsville (C-5)

(For accommodations see Camden, Cheraw, Florence; also see Bennettsville, Darlington)

Settled 1760 **Pop** 8,372 **Elev** 200 ft **Area code** 803 **Zip** 29550
Information Chamber of Commerce, 214 N 5th St, PO Box 578, 29551; 803/332-6401.

From a crossroads store, Hartsville has become a vigorous trading center, raising crops of cotton, soybeans, tobacco and oats, and boasts fifteen major manufacturers—including makers of consumer packaging, plastic bags, fertilizer, roller bearings, boats, brass, textiles and paper. The town developed from what was once the Hart plantation and the pioneer store established by Major James Lide Coker, a Harvard graduate who founded a series of businesses here and built a railroad to the town.

What to See and Do

H. B. Robinson Nuclear Information Center. Located at site of first commercial nuclear plant in Southeast. Exhibits explain generation of electricity, nuclear power and energy use. (Mon-Fri; closed hols) 4 mi NW at jct SC 151/23. Phone 803/857-1000. **Free.**

Hartsville Museum. Housed in restored post office; changing exhibits of local history, arts & crafts. (Daily exc Sun; closed hols) 222 N 5th St. Phone 803/383-3005. **Free.**

Kalmia Gardens of Coker College. A 30-acre botanical garden. Walking trails through blackwater swamp, mountain laurel thickets, pine-oak-holly uplands and a beech bluff. Plantings of azaleas, camellias and other ornamentals complement the native plants. (Daily) Approx 2½ mi W on Carolina Ave. Phone 803/383-8145. **Free.**

Lee State Park. Approx 2,500 acres on Lynches River. Lake swimming; river fishing, boating (pedal boat rentals). Nature trails; horse trails, show ring, stable (no rentals). Picnicking (shelters), playground. Camping (hookups, dump station). Recreation building. Standard fees. 16 mi SW via US 15, 3 mi S on SC 341, then 2 mi E off I-20 exit 123. Phone 803/428-3833.

Hilton Head Island (F-5)

(See also Beaufort, Hardeeville)

Pop 23,694 **Elev** 15 ft **Area code** 803
Information Chamber of Commerce, PO Box 5647, 29938; 803/785-3673.

This year-round resort island, the development of which began in 1956, is reached by a bridge on US 278. The island is bordered by one of the few remaining unpolluted marine estuaries on the East Coast and is the largest sea island between New Jersey and Florida. Its growth was rapid; there are 12 miles of beaches and the climate is delightful. There are numerous golf courses and tennis courts, swimming, miles of bicycle paths, horseback riding, four nature preserves and deep-sea, sound and dockside fishing. The facilities also include nine marinas and a paved 3,700-foot airstrip with parallel taxiway. There are more than 3,000 hotel and motel rooms, more than 6,000 homes/villas/condos on the rental market, more than 200 restaurants and 28 shopping centers. For the less athletic, there are many art galleries and numerous sporting and cultural events.

Annual Events

Springfest. Food, wine and seafood festivals. Sports events. Concerts, shows and house tours. Phone 803/686-4944. Mar.

Family Circle Magazine Cup Tennis Tournament. Sea Pines Racquet Club. Phone 803/363-3500. Late Mar-early Apr.

MCI Heritage Classic. Harbour Town Golf Links. Top PGA golfers. Phone 803/671-2448. Mid-Apr.

Hilton Head Island Celebrity Golf Tournament. Palmetto Hall, Indigo Run & Sea Pines Plantation. Phone 803/842-7711. Labor Day wkend.

St Luke's Tour of Homes. Tour of distinctive contemporary houses. Phone 803/785-4099. Oct.

Motels

✓★ **FAIRFIELD INN BY MARRIOTT.** *9 Marina Side Dr (29928). 803/842-4800; FAX 803/842-4800, ext. 709.* 119 rms, 3 story, 14 suites. Apr-mid-Sept: S $69.95; D $79.95; each addl $7; suites $99.95-$114.95; under 18 free; golf plans; lower rates rest of yr. Crib free. TV; cable. Heated pool. Complimentary continental bkfst. Ck-out 11 am. Business servs avail. In-rm modem link. Golf privileges. Miniature golf adj. Health club privileges. Refrigerator in suites. Picnic tables, grills. Cr cds: A, C, D, DS, MC, V.

[D] [symbols] [SC]

★ ★ **HAMPTON INN.** *1 Dillon Rd (29926). 803/681-7900; FAX 803/681-4330.* 124 rms, 2 story, 20 suites, 12 kit. units. Mar-Aug: S $76-$106; D $81-$111; suites, kit. units $101-$111; under 18 free; lower rates rest of yr. Crib free. TV; cable (premium). Pool. Complimentary continental bkfst. Restaurant nearby. Ck-out 11 am. Coin lndry. Meeting rms. Business servs avail. In-rm modem link. Free airport transportation. Tennis privileges, pro. 18-hole golf privileges. Exercise equipt; weight machine, treadmill. Some refrigerators; microwaves avail. Cr cds: A, C, D, DS, ER, JCB, MC, V.

★ ★ **HOLIDAY INN EXPRESS.** *40 Waterside Dr (29928). 803/842-8888; FAX 803/842-5948.* 92 rms, 3 story. Mar-early Sept: S, D $85; each addl $5; under 19 free; lower rates rest of yr. Crib free. TV; cable (premium). Complimentary continental bkfst. Restaurant adj 11-2 am. Ck-out 11 am. Business servs avail. In-rm modem link. Valet serv. Health club privileges. Pool. Refrigerators avail. Cr cds: A, C, D, DS, JCB, MC, V.

✔ ★ **RED ROOF INN.** *5 Regency Pkwy (29928), off US 278. 803/686-6808; FAX 803/842-3352.* 112 rms, 2 story. June-Sept: S $46.99-$57.99; D $53.99-$59.99; suites $75.99-$84.99; family rates; higher rates hols; lower rates rest of yr. Crib free. TV; cable (premium). Pool. Restaurant adj 5-10 pm. Ck-out noon. Business servs avail. Cr cds: A, C, D, DS, MC, V.

✔★ ★ **SHONEY'S INN.** *200 Museum St (29926). 803/681-3655; FAX 803/681-3655, ext. 369.* 136 rms, 3 story. Mar-Oct: S, D $72-$78; each addl $6; under 18 free; lower rates rest of yr. TV; cable (premium). Pool. Restaurant 7 am-11 pm. Bar from 5 pm. Ck-out 11 am. Coin lndry. Meeting rms. Business servs avail. In-rm modem link. Valet serv. Tennis privileges. Golf privileges. Exercise equipt; weight machine, stair machine. Cr cds: A, C, D, DS, MC, V.

Motor Hotel

★ ★ **HOLIDAY INN OCEANFRONT RESORT.** *1 S Forest Beach Dr (29938). 803/785-5126; FAX 803/785-6678.* 200 rms, 5 story. Mid-Mar-mid-Oct: S, D $139-$209; each addl $10; under 18 free; lower rates rest of yr. Crib free. TV; cable (premium). Pool; wading pool, poolside serv. Coffee in rms. Restaurant 7 am-10 pm. Rm serv. Bar 5 pm-2 am. Ck-out 11 am. Coin lndry. Meeting rms. Business servs avail. In-rm modem link. Bellhops. Tennis privileges. Golf privileges. Refrigerators avail. Patios. On beach. Cr cds: A, C, D, DS, ER, JCB, MC, V.

Hotel

★ ★ **RADISSON SUITE RESORT.** *12 Park Lane (29928), off US 278. 803/686-5700; FAX 803/686-3952.* 156 kit. suites, 3 story. Mar-Nov: S, D $119-$159; under 18 free; family rates; golf plans; lower rates rest of yr. Crib free. TV; cable (premium). Pool; whirlpool. Complimentary continental bkfst. Restaurant adj 11:30-1 am. Ck-out noon. Coin lndry. Business servs avail. Free airport transportation. Lighted tennis. Golf privileges. Bicycles. Fireplaces, microwaves. Private patios, balconies. Picnic tables. Cr cds: A, D, DS, MC, V.

Resorts

★ ★ ★ **CROWNE PLAZA RESORT.** *130 Shipyard Dr (29928), in Shipyard Plantation. 803/842-2400; FAX 803/842-9975.* 340 rms, 5 story. Early Mar-Nov: S, D $189-$269; suites $350-$495; family rates; golf plans; lower rates rest of yr. TV; cable (premium). 2 pools, 1 indoor; wading pool, whirlpool, poolside serv. Supervised child's activities (mid-Mar to late-Apr; Memorial Day-Labor Day); ages 3-19. Coffee in rms. Dining rms 6 am-midnight. Box lunches. Snack bar. Rm serv. Bar 11-2 am. Ck-out noon, ck-in

4 pm. Coin lndry. Convention facilities. Business center. In-rm modem link. Valet serv. Concierge. Gift shop. Lighted tennis, pro. 27-hole golf, greens fee $45-$72, pro, putting green, driving range. Boats, sailboats. Bicycle rentals. Entertainment, movies. Game rm. Exercise rm; instructor, weights, bicycles, sauna. Fishing guides, storage. Some refrigerators; microwaves avail. Private patios, balconies. Cr cds: A, C, D, DS, JCB, MC, V.

★ ★ ★ **DISNEY'S HILTON HEAD ISLAND.** *22 Harborside Lane (29928). 803/341-4100; FAX 803/341-4130.* 102 kit. units, 2 story. Mid-June-mid-Aug: S, D $165-$450; golf plans; lower rates rest of yr. Crib free. TV; cable (premium); VCR (movies). Pool; wading pool, whirlpool, poolside serv, lifeguard. Supervised children's activities; ages 3-16. Restaurant nearby. Ck-out 11 am, ck-in 4 pm. Gift, grocery shop. Guest lndry. Concierge. Valet serv. Lighted tennis; pro. Three 18-hole golf courses, putting green, driving range. Boats. Bicycle rental. Exercise equipt; bicycles, weights. Microwaves. Balconies. Cr cds: A, MC, V.

★ ★ ★ **HILTON.** *23 Ocean Lane (29938), on Palmetto Dunes. 803/842-8000; FAX 803/842-4988.* E-mail hiltonhh@hargray.com. 296 kit. units, 5 story, 28 suites. Apr-Aug: S, D $134-$239; each addl $15; suites $225-$375; under 18 free; golf, tennis plans; lower rates rest of yr. Crib free. TV; cable (premium). 2 pools, 1 heated; whirlpools, wading pool, poolside serv. Playground. Supervised child's activities (Mar-Oct); ages 4-11. Dining rm 6:30 am-11 pm (to 10 pm off-season). Rm serv. Bar 5 pm-2 am; entertainment exc Mon. Ck-out noon, ck-in 4 pm. Coin lndry. Convention facilities. Business center. In-rm modem link. Valet serv. Concierge. Lighted tennis, pro. Three 18-hole golf courses, greens fee $55-$89, pro. Lawn games. Exercise rm; instructor, weights, bicycles, sauna. Balconies. On ocean. Poolside entertainment (Apr-Oct). Cr cds: A, C, D, DS, MC, V.

★ ★ **HYATT REGENCY.** *(29938). On US 278, in Palmetto Dunes area. 803/785-1234; FAX 803/842-4695.* 505 rms, 10 story. Mar-mid-Nov: S, D $200-$285; each addl $25; suites $400-$975; under 18 free; golf, tennis package plans; lower rates rest of yr. Crib free. Valet parking $8/night. TV; cable (premium), VCR avail. 2 pools, 1 indoor; wading pool, poolside serv. Supervised child's activities (Memorial Day-Labor Day); ages 3-18. Dining rm (see HEMINGWAY'S). Rm serv 24 hrs. Bars 11:30-1 am, Sun from 1 pm; entertainment. Ck-out noon, ck-in 4 pm. Meeting rms. Business servs avail. In-rm modem link. Bellhops. Valet serv. Gift shops. Barber, beauty shop. Tennis. Three 18-hole golf courses, putting green. Canoes, sailboats. Bicycle rentals. Exercise rm; instructor, weights, bicycles, sauna. Massage. Private patios, balconies. Luxury level. Cr cds: A, C, D, DS, JCB, MC, V.

★ ★ ★ **PALMETTO DUNES.** *4 Queen's Folly Rd (29938), 7 mi SE of Byrnes Bridge, off US 278. 803/785-7300; FAX 803/842-4482; res: 800/845-6130.* E-mail sdmpdr@aol.com. 500 villas, 1-5 story. Mar-Labor Day: S, D $125-$436; family rates; lower rates rest of yr. Crib avail. TV; cable. 30 pools; wading pools. Playground. Supervised child's activities (June-mid-Aug); ages 4-12. Dining rms 7 am-10 pm. Rm serv. Bars to 2 am. Ck-out 10 am, ck-in 4 pm. Grocery. Package store 1 mi. Meeting rms. Business servs avail. Valet serv. Lighted tennis. 5 golf courses, greens fee $35-$85, putting green, driving range. Boats, rowboats, canoes, sailboats. Microwaves; some fireplaces. Private patios, balconies. Picnic tables. Private beach. 4,300-ft airstrip 4 mi. Cr cds: A, D, DS, MC, V.

★ ★ ★ **SEA PINES.** *32 Greenwood Dr (29938). 803/785-3333; FAX 803/842-1475; res: 800/732-7463.* Web www.seapines.com. 420 kit. suites in villas, 1-3 story, 60 houses. June-Aug: 1-3 bedrm units $145-$260; wkly rates $1500-$6500; golf, tennis packages; lower rates rest of yr. TV; cable, VCR. 19 pools, 1 indoor/outdoor; wading pools, poolside serv. Playgrounds. Supervised child's activities (June-Aug); ages 4-12. Dining rms (public by res) 7 am-10 pm. Snack bars. Cookouts. Bars. Ck-out 10 am, ck-in 4 pm. Guest lndry. Grocery, package store. Convention facilities. Business center. Bellhops. Concierge. Free beach, area transportation. Sports dir. Lighted tennis, pro. Three 18-hole golf courses, greens fee $75-$175, putting green, driving range. Exercise rm; instructor, weight machine, bicycles. Sailboat instruction, charter boats, motors, windsurfing. Bicycles. Entertainment. Microwaves; some fireplaces. Screened porch in some houses and villas. On 5,000 acres; 605-acre forest, wildlife preserve. Cr cds: A, D, DS, MC, V.

★ ★ ★ **WESTIN.** *2 Grasslawn Avenue (29928).* 803/681-4000; FAX 803/681-1087. 412 rms, 5 story; 88 villas (2-, 3- & 4-bedrm). Late Mar-early Nov: S, D $250-$350; suites from $355; villas $280-$325; under 18 free; tennis, golf plans; lower rates rest of yr. Serv charge $6/day. TV; cable (premium), VCR avail. 3 pools, 1 indoor; whirlpool, poolside serv. Playground. Supervised child's activities (Memorial Day-Labor Day, major hols). Dining rm 6:30 am-10 pm. Rm serv 24 hrs. Bars 3 pm-2 am; entertainment (seasonal). Ck-out noon, ck-in 4 pm. Meeting rms. Business center. In-rm modem link. Concierge. Valet parking. Free airport transportation. Tennis, pro. 54-hole golf, greens fee (incl cart) $38-$54, putting green, driving range. Lawn games. Exercise rm; instructor, weights, bicycles, sauna, steam rm. Massage. Bathrm phones, refrigerators. Cr cds: A, C, D, DS, ER, JCB, MC, V.

Restaurants

★ ★ **ALEXANDER'S.** *76 Queens Folly Rd, in Palmetto Dunes area.* 803/785-4999. Hrs: 5-10 pm; early-bird dinner 5-5:30 pm. Res accepted. Bar. A la carte entrees: dinner $15.95-$23.95. Child's meals. Specializes in fresh local seafood, steak, lamb. Own desserts. Parking. Garden rm decor. Overlooks lagoon. Screened porch for dining. Cr cds: A, DS, MC, V.

★ ★ **ANTONIO'S.** *Village at Wexford.* 803/842-5505. Hrs: 5-10 pm. Closed Thanksgiving, Dec 25. Res accepted. Italian menu. Bar. Semi-a la carte: dinner $9.95-$21.95. Child's meals. Specializes in pasta, seafood, veal. Parking. European cafe atmosphere. Cr cds: A, D, DS, MC, V.

★ ★ **CAFE EUROPA.** *At the lighthouse in Harbour Town.* 803/671-3399. Hrs: 10 am-2:30 pm, 5:30-10 pm. Closed late Oct-mid-Feb. Res accepted. Serv bar. Semi-a la carte: bkfst $6-$8, lunch $6-$10, dinner $12-$20. Child's meals. Specialties: baked shrimp Daufuskie, chicken Charleston. Parking. Pianist Wed-Sun. Outdoor dining. Views of boardwalk. Cr cds: A, MC, V.

★ ★ ★ **CHARLIE'S L'ETOILE VERTE.** *1000 Plantation Center (29928).* 803/785-9277. Hrs: 11:30 am-2 pm, 6-9 pm. Closed Sun, Mon; most major hols. Res accepted (dinner). French menu. Bar. Wine cellar. Semi-a la carte: lunch $7.50-$10, dinner $19-$27. Specialties: salmon in parmesan crust, rack of lamb, grilled pompano with mango vinaigrette. Own baking. Bright, eclectic decor with French artwork on walls; fresh flowers; menu changes daily. Totally nonsmoking. Cr cds: A, DS, MC, V.

★ ★ **CRAZY CRAB.** *US 278, 1/2 mi SE of Graves Bridge.* 803/681-5021. Hrs: 5-10 pm. Closed Thanksgiving, Dec 24, 25. Bar. Semi-a la carte: dinner $11.95-$18.95. Child's meals. Specializes in seafood. Own pies. Guitarist, vocalist Apr-Aug. Parking. Nautical decor; overlooks marsh. Cr cds: A, C, D, DS, MC, V.

✔ ★ **DAMON'S.** *Village at Wexford (29928), Hwy 278.* 803/785-6677. Hrs: 11:30 am-10 pm. Bar. Semi-a la carte: lunch $4.95-$13.99, dinner $7.50-$18.95. Child's meals. Specializes in barbecued ribs, onion loaf, steak. Parking. Outdoor dining (lunch). Casual atmosphere. Cr cds: A, DS, MC, V.

★ ★ ★ **GASLIGHT.** *303 Market Place.* 803/785-5814. Hrs: 11:30 am-2 pm, 6-10 pm; Sat from 6 pm. Closed Sun. Res accepted. French

menu. Serv bar. Semi-a la carte: lunch $8.95-$10.95, dinner $17.50-$24.50. Specializes in quenelles of snapper, Dover sole, beef Wellington. Own baking. Parking. Garden setting. Cr cds: A, MC, V.

★ ★ ★ **HARBOURMASTER'S.** *At Shelter Cove Harbor.* 803/785-3030. Hrs: from 5 pm. Closed Sun; Dec 25; also Jan. Res accepted. Continental menu. Bar. Wine cellar. Semi-a la carte: dinner $14.95-$24.95. Specialties: potato crusted grouper, blackened tuna mango chutney, rack of lamb. Parking. Tableside preparation. Outdoor dining. View of yacht harbor. Cr cds: A, D, MC, V.

★ ★ **HEMINGWAY'S.** *(See Hyatt Regency Hilton Head Resort)* 803/785-1234. Hrs: 5-11 pm; early-bird dinner 5-6:30 pm; Sun brunch 10 am-2 pm. Res accepted. Bar 4 pm-midnight; entertainment (exc Mon). Semi-a la carte: dinner $20.95-$26. Sun brunch $20.95. Specializes in fresh seafood, steak, fruit cobbler, fried strawberries. Valet parking. Cr cds: A, C, D, DS, JCB, MC, V.

✔ ★ ★ **HOFBRAUHAUS.** *Pope Ave & Executive Park.* 803/785-3663. Hrs: 5-9 pm, early-bird dinner 5-6:30 pm. Res accepted. German menu. Bar. Semi-a la carte: dinner $9.95-$16.95. Serv charge 15%. Child's meals. Specialties: roast young duckling, sauerbraten, Wienerschnitzel. Entertainment. Festive German decor; stained-glass windows, stein & mug collection. Cr cds: A, MC, V.

✔ ★ **HUDSON'S ON THE DOCKS.** *1 Hudson Rd, 1 mi N off US 278.* 803/342-3636. Hrs: 11 am-10 pm. Closed Jan 1, Thanksgiving, Dec 24, 25. Bar. Semi-a la carte: lunch $5.95-$11.95, dinner $12.95-$21.95. Child's meals. Specializes in fresh seafood, live Maine lobster. Magician, guitarist (Memorial Day-Labor Day). Parking. Gift shop. On Intracoastal Waterway; near boat docks. Cr cds: A, D, MC, V.

★ **KINGFISHER.** *18 Harbourside Ln (29928), off US 278, on Shelter Cove Harbour.* 803/785-4442. Hrs: 5-10 pm; early-bird dinner 5-6 pm. Closed Dec 25. Res accepted. Bar. Semi-a la carte: dinner $11-$21.95. Child's meals. Specializes in seafood. Guitarist in season. Parking. Windows overlook harbor and marshes. Cr cds: A, DS, MC, V.

★ ★ ★ **LA MAISONETTE.** *20 Pope Ave, in the Banker's Mortgage Bldg.* 803/785-6000. Hrs: 6-10 pm. Closed Dec 25. Res required. French menu. Serv bar. Wine cellar. A la carte entrees: $16.95-$21.95. Specialties: rack of lamb, filet mignon. Own desserts. Parking. Jacket. Cr cds: A, DS, MC, V.

★ ★ **LA POLA'S.** *18 Harborside Lane, in Shelter Cove Harbor.* 803/842-6400. Hrs: 5-10 pm. Closed Jan. Res accepted. Italian, Amer menu. Bar. Semi-a la carte: dinner $10.95-$22.95. Child's meals. Specializes in fresh fish, veal, Black Angus steak. Own desserts. Parking. Screened dining porch. Overlooks Shelter Cove Harbor. Cr cds: A, DS, MC, V.

★ ★ **LITTLE VENICE.** *Shelter Cove.* 803/785-3300. Hrs: noon-2:30 pm, 5-10 pm. Closed Dec 25; also Jan. Res accepted. Italian menu. Bar. Semi-a la carte: lunch $6.95-$7.95, dinner $13.95-$19.95. Specialties: veal chop, zuppa di pesce, chicken a la Fiorentina. Parking. Outdoor dining. Overlooks marina. Trattoria atmosphere. Cr cds: A, D, DS, MC, V.

✔ ★ **LONGHORN STEAK.** *841 US 278, in South Island Square.* 803/686-4056. Hrs: 11 am-10 pm; Fri to 10:30 pm; Sat noon-10:30 pm; Sun 4-10:30 pm. Closed Thanksgiving, Dec 25. Bar. Semi-a la carte: lunch $6.25-$9.99, dinner $7.95-$18.99. Child's meals. Specializes in steak, salmon, chili. Country-Western decor. Cr cds: A, C, D, DS, JCB, MC, V.

★★ **NENO IL TOSCANO.** *105 Festival Centre (29926).* *803/342-2400.* Hrs: 11:30 am-2 pm, from 6 pm; Sat from 6 pm. Closed Sun; Jan 1, Easter, Dec 25. Res accepted. Italian menu. Bar. Semi-a la carte: lunch $6.95-$8.95, dinner $13.50-$21.95. Own baking. European decor with 2-level dining area; marble-and-mahogany bar. Totally nonsmoking. Cr cds: A, DS, MC, V.

D

★★ **OLD OYSTER FACTORY.** *101 Marshland Rd.* *803/681-6040.* Hrs: 5-10 pm. Closed Thanksgiving, Dec 25. Bar. Semi-a la carte: dinner $9.95-$19.95. Child's meals. Specializes in fresh seafood, local oysters, steak. Guitarist, vocalist in season. Parking. Overlooks creek, marshes. Cr cds: A, D, DS, MC, V.

D SC

★★★ **PRIMO.** *At Orleans Plaza, Orleans Plaza.* *803/785-2343.* Hrs: from 6 pm. Closed Thanksgiving, Dec 25; Super Bowl Sun. Res accepted. Contemporary Italian menu. Bar. Semi-a la carte: dinner $10.95-$22.95. Specializes in fresh pasta, char-grilled seafood, veal. Own bread, pasta, desserts. Parking. Italian cafe atmosphere. Cr cds: A, DS, MC, V.

D

✔★ **REILLEY'S.** *7-D Hilton Head Plaza, in Gallery of Shops.* *803/842-4414.* Hrs: 11:30 am-11 pm; Sat & Sun brunch 11:30 am-2:30 pm. Closed Dec 25. Bar to 2 am. Semi-a la carte: lunch, dinner $5.95-$13.95. Sun brunch $5.75-$8.95. Child's meals. Specialties: cottage pie, corned beef & cabbage, fish & chips. Own ice cream. Irish pub atmosphere; sports memorabilia. Outdoor dining. Cr cds: A, MC, V.

D SC

★ **SCOTT'S FISH MARKET.** *At Shelter Cove Harbour.* *803/785-7575.* Hrs: 4:30-10 pm. Closed Sun; some major hols; also Jan. Bar. Semi-a la carte: dinner $13.95-$17.95. Specializes in fresh local seafood. Parking. Outdoor dining. Nautical decor. View of harbor. Cr cds: A, C, D, DS, MC, V.

D

Kiawah Island (F-5)

(See also Beaufort, Charleston)

Pop 718 **Area code** 803 **E-mail** kiawahres@aol.com **Web** kiawah-island.com
Information Kiawah Island Resort, 12 Kiawah Beach Dr, 29455; 803/768-2121 or 800/654-2924.

Kiawah Island (pronounced KEE-a-wah) is one of the richest natural environments in the Middle Atlantic states. The island is a model for maintaining the ecological balance while allowing human habitation. Named for the Native Americans who once hunted and fished here, the island is separated from the mainland by the Kiawah River and a mile-wide salt marsh.

Extensive environmental study has helped to preserve nature while also providing for human needs. Separate resort areas and private residential neighborhoods have been planned to provide a minimum of automobile traffic and leave much of the island untouched. The Kiawah Island Resort offers activities like golf, tennis and nature programs that take advantage of the island's natural beauty.

Inn

★★★ **CASSINA POINT PLANTATION.** *(1642 Clark Rd, Edisto Island 29438) SC 174, exit Indigo Hill Rd.* *803/869-2535.* Web www.bbonline.com/sc/cassina. 4 rms, 2 shared bath, 4 story. No rm phones. S $90; D $115; each addl $25. Children over 10 yrs only. TV in parlor. Complimentary full bkfst. Restaurant nearby. Ck-out 10 am, ck-in 2 pm. Canoe, kayak rentals. Plantation built in 1847 was later used by Federal troops during the Civil War. Totally nonsmoking. No cr cds accepted.

Resort

★★★ **KIAWAH ISLAND RESORT.** *12 Kiawah Beach Dr (29455), At W end of Kiawah Island, off Kiawah Beach Dr.* *803/768-2121; FAX 803/768-9339; res: 800/654-2924.* 150 rms, 3 story, 390 villas and houses (1-4 bedrms). Mar-Nov: S, D $129-$205; villas $170-$455; under 18 free; wkly rates; package plans; lower rates rest of yr. Crib free. TV; cable (premium). 4 pools, 1 heated; wading pool, poolside serv, lifeguard. Playground. Supervised child's activities (Easter-Labor Day); ages 3-19. Coffee in rms. Dining rms 6:30 am-11 pm. Snack bar, picnics. Rm serv. Bar 11-1 am; entertainment (in season). Ck-out noon, ck-in 4 pm. Grocery. Package store 3 mi. Meeting rms. Business center. Bellhops. Valet serv. Concierge. Gift shop. Lighted tennis, pro. Four 18-hole golf courses, greens fee $95-$159, pro, driving range. Swimming beach; boats. Canoe trips. Bicycle rentals. Nature walks. Lawn games. Rec rm. Game rm. Many wet bars, microwaves. On ocean; marina. Cr cds: A, C, D, DS, MC, V.

Restaurant

★★★ **THE OLD POST OFFICE.** *(1442 SC 174, Edisto Island 29438) 803/869-2339.* Hrs: 6-10 pm. Closed Sun, Mon; some major hols. Res accepted. Regional Amer menu. Bar 5-11 pm. Wine cellar. Semi-a la carte: dinner $17-$20. Specializes in seafood. Own baking. Former post office bldg; old mail boxes in entry; local artwork on walls. Cr cds: MC, V.

D

Kings Mountain National Military Park (B-4)

(For accommodations see Gaffney, Rock Hill, Spartanburg; also see Charlotte, NC)

(20 mi NE of Gaffney off I-85, near Grover, NC)

On these 3,950 rugged acres, a fierce attack by Carolina, Georgia and Virginia mountain frontiersmen in October 1780 broke up Britain's southern campaign. The mountain men and other patriots were faced with the invasion of their homes by advancing Tories. After traveling more than 200 miles, the Americans surrounded and attacked Cornwallis's left wing, which was encamped atop Kings Mountain spur and under the command of Major Patrick Ferguson. Although untrained in formal warfare, American patriots killed, wounded or captured Ferguson's entire force of 1,104 Tories. Twenty-eight patriots were killed and 62 were wounded. The battle led to renewed American resistance and American victory at Yorktown. Near the center of the park is the battlefield ridge, with several monuments, including the Centennial Monument, dedicated in 1880, and the US Monument, erected in 1909. The Visitor Center has exhibits and a film. Self-guided trail leads to main features of battlefield. (Daily; closed Jan 1, Thanksgiving, Dec 25) Contact Superintendent, PO Box 40, Kings Mountain, NC 28086; 864/936-7921. **Free.**

King's Mountain State Park on SC 161, adj to S edge of national military park, has 6,141 acres of scenic drives; living history farm; two lakes. Swimming; fishing; boating. Nature, hiking, bridle trails; carpet golf. Picnicking (shelters), store. Camping. Interpretive center. Standard fees. Phone 803/222-3209.

Myrtle Beach (D-7)

(See also Georgetown)

Pop 24,848 **Elev** 30 ft **Area code** 803 **Web** www.myrtlebeachlive.com
Information Myrtle Beach Area Chamber of Commerce, 1200 N Oak St, PO Box 2115, 29578; 803/626-7444 or 800/356-3016.

With the Gulf Stream only a few miles offshore and dunes to shelter miles of white sand, Myrtle Beach is one of the most popular seaside resorts on the Atlantic coast. Swimming, fishing, golf, tennis and boardwalk amusements combine to lure millions of vacationers each summer. The many myrtle trees in the area give this resort its name.

What to See and Do

⭐ **"The Grand Strand."** Sixty miles of beach from the North Carolina border south to Georgetown. Camping; fishing; golf, tennis; amusement parks.

Myrtle Beach State Park. Approx 300 acres. Ocean and pool swimming; surf fishing (supplies avail). Nature trail. Picnicking (shelters), playground, stores. Camping, cabins. Interpretive center. Standard fees (higher rates Apr-Sept). 3 mi S on US 17 Business. Phone 803/238-5325.

Annual Event

Sun Fun Festival. More than 60 seaside entertainment events, including parades. 1st wk June.

Motels

⭐⭐ **CHESTERFIELD INN.** *700 N Ocean Blvd (29577). 803/448-3177; FAX 803/626-4736; res: 800/392-3869.* 32 inn rms, 26 motel rms, 3 story, 6 kits. Mid-June-late Aug, MAP: S $83-$111; D $112-$140; each addl $29; kit. units $107; family rates; golf plans; lower rates Feb-mid-June, late Aug-Dec. Closed rest of yr. Crib free. TV; cable. Pool. Restaurant 7:30-10 am, 5:30-7:30 pm. Ck-out 11 am. Golf privileges. Refrigerators. Balconies. On beach. Cr cds: A, DS, MC, V.

⭐⭐ **HAMPTON INN.** *620 75th Ave N (29577). 803/497-0077; FAX 803/497-8845.* 122 rms, 5 story, 20 suites. June-Labor Day: S $109-$129; D $119-$139; suites $129-$209; golf plans; lower rates rest of yr. Crib free. TV; cable (premium), VCR avail. Complimentary continental bkfst. Complimentary coffee in rms. Restaurant adj 11-1 am. Ck-out 11 am. Meeting rms. Business servs avail. In-rm modem link. Coin Indry. Exercise equipt; weight machine, bicycle, sauna. Indoor pool; whirlpool. Refrigerators, microwaves; some in-rm whirlpools; wet bar in suites. Cr cds: A, C, D, DS, MC, V.

⭐⭐ **HAMPTON INN.** *4709 N Kings Hwy (29577). jct US 17 & 48th Ave N. 803/449-5231; FAX 803/449-1528.* Web www.mbhampton.com. 152 rms, 4 story. Memorial Day-Labor Day: S $99; D $105; higher rates: wkends, Easter, July 4; lower rates rest of yr. Crib free. TV; cable (premium). Indoor pool. Complimentary continental bkfst. Coffee in rms. Restaurant 5-10 pm. Bar 4 pm-midnight; entertainment. Ck-out 11 am. Meeting rms. Business servs avail. In-rm modem link. Valet serv. Guest Indry. Tennis privileges. Golf privileges. Health club privileges. Miniature golf adj. Some refrigerators; microwaves avail. 1½ blks to ocean. Cr cds: A, C, D, DS, MC, V.

✔ **PALM CREST.** *701 S Ocean Blvd (29577). 803/448-7141; res: 800/487-9233.* 41 units, 3 story, 38 kits. No elvtr. Early June-late Aug: S, D $57-$78; each addl $10; kit. units $78-$82; 1-2-bedrm units $89-$129; wkly rates; golf, tennis plans; lower rates rest of yr. Crib $5. TV; cable. Pool; wading pool. Restaurant adj 6:30 am-10:30 pm. Ck-out 11 am. Coin Indry. Free airport transportation. Tennis privileges. Golf privileges. Microwaves avail. Picnic tables, grills. Cr cds: DS, MC, V.

✔⭐ **VIKING.** *1811 S Ocean Blvd (29577). 803/448-4355; FAX 803/448-6174; res: 800/334-4876 (exc SC).* E-mail viking@sccoast.net; web www.seasideproperties.com. 76 units, 5 story, 67 kits. June-Aug: S, D $59-$88; each addl $7; kit. units $65-$88; 2-bedrm apts. with kit. $79-$112; family, wkly rates; higher rates: wkends, hols, special events; lower rates rest of yr. Crib free. TV; cable. Pool; wading pool. Restaurant nearby. Ck-out 11 am. Coin Indry. Business servs avail. Tennis privileges. Golf privileges. Refrigerators. Some private patios, balconies. On beach. Cr cds: A, C, D, DS, MC, V.

Motor Hotels

⭐⭐ **BEST WESTERN DAYTON HOUSE.** *2400 N Ocean Blvd (29577). 803/448-2441.* 323 kit. units, 5-16 story. June-Aug: S, D $87-$150; each addl $10; under 12 free; wkly rates; golf plans; higher rates wkends; lower rates rest of yr. Crib $5. TV; cable (premium). Complimentary coffee in lobby. Restaurant adj 6-11 am. Ck-out 11 am. Coin Indry. Golf privileges. Exercise equipt; bicycle, rowers, sauna. Heated indoor/outdoor pool; whirlpools. Refrigerators, microwaves. Balconies. On beach. Cr cds: A, C, D, DS, MC, V.

⭐⭐ **CARIBBEAN.** *3000 N Ocean Blvd (29577), at 30th Ave N. 803/448-7181; FAX 803/448-3224; res: 800/845-0883.* E-mail caribr@sccoast.net; web www.caribbeanresort.com. 278 rms, 5-14 story, 38 kits., 195 kit. suites. Early June-late Aug: D $69-$107; each addl $6; kit. units $70-$108; kit. suites $99-$135; wkly rates; golf plans; higher rates: hols, special events; lower rates rest of yr. Crib free. TV; cable (premium). Heated pool; whirlpool. Coffee in lobby. Restaurant adj 6 am-10 pm. Ck-out 11 am. Guest Indry. Business servs avail. Golf privileges. Lawn games. Game rm. Refrigerators. Balconies. On beach. Cr cds: A, C, D, DS, MC, V.

⭐⭐⭐ **HOLIDAY INN OCEANFRONT.** *415 S Ocean Blvd (29577). 803/448-4481; FAX 803/448-0086.* 311 rms, 8 story. Mid-May-Aug: S, D $99-$149; each addl $10; under 18 free; lower rates rest of yr. Crib free. TV; cable. 2 pools, 1 indoor; whirlpool, poolside serv. Supervised child's activities (Memorial Day-Labor Day); ages 3-12. Coffee in rms. Restaurant 6 am-10 pm. Bars 1 pm-midnight; entertainment. Ck-out 11 am. Coin Indry. Convention facilities. Gift shop. Tennis privileges. Golf privileges. Exercise equipt; weight machine, bicycles, sauna. Game rm. On beach. Cr cds: A, C, D, DS, ER, JCB, MC, V.

⭐⭐⭐ **PAN AMERICAN MOTOR INN.** *5300 N Ocean Blvd (29578). 803/449-7411; FAX 803/449-6031; res: 800/845-4501.* 85 kit. units, 6 story. Early June-mid-Aug: S, D $92-$155; each addl $8; 1-bedrm apts $129; golf plans; family rates; lower rates rest of yr. Crib free. TV; cable. Heated pool. Restaurant 7-11 am. Rm serv. Ck-out 11 am. Business servs avail. Bellhops. Tennis. Golf privileges. Health club privileges. Refrigerators; microwaves avail. Private patios, balconies. On beach. Cr cds: DS, MC, V.

⭐⭐⭐ **SEA ISLAND.** *6000 N Ocean Blvd (29577). 803/449-6406; FAX 803/449-4102; res: 800/548-0767.* Web www.seaislandinn.com. 112 units, 5 story, 46 kits. Early June-late Aug: D $113-$128; each addl $10; kit. units $113-$131; under 12 free; MAP avail; lower rates rest of yr. Crib free. TV; cable (premium). Heated pool; 2 wading pools. Restaurant 7:30-10 am, 5:30-8 pm. Rm serv. Ck-out 11 am. Meeting rms. Business center. Bellhops. Valet serv. Free airport transportation. Tennis privileges. Golf privileges. Refrigerators; microwaves avail. Balconies. On ocean; swimming beach. Cr cds: A, DS, MC, V.

★ ★ **ST JOHN'S INN.** *6803 N Ocean Blvd (29572).* 803/449-5251; FAX 803/449-3306; res: 800/845-0624. 90 rms, 3 story, 28 kits. June-Labor Day: D $87; each addl $5; kit. units $94; under 12 free; golf plan; higher rates hols; varied lower rates rest of yr. Crib avail. Pet accepted, some restrictions. TV; cable. Pool; whirlpool. Restaurant 7-11 am. Ck-out 11 am. Meeting rm. Lawn games. Refrigerators. Private patios, balconies. Bathrm phones. Beach opp. Cr cds: A, DS, MC, V.

◻D ⛽ ≈ ≍ ⊠ **SC**

✔ ★ **SURF & DUNES.** *2201 S Ocean Blvd (29577).* 803/448-1755; FAX 803/444-9360; res: 800/845-2109. 129 units, 3-7 story, 80 kits. Mid-May-late Oct: S, D $36-$109; each addl $5; kit. units $50-$115; under 18 free; monthly, wkly rates; golf plans; higher rates: Easter wk, all hol wkends in season; lower rates rest of yr. Crib $5. TV; cable (premium). 3 pools, 1 indoor; whirlpool, poolside serv. Restaurant nearby. Ck-out 11 am. Coin lndry. Business servs avail. Lighted tennis. Golf privileges. Exercise equipt; weight machine, treadmill. Game rm. Lawn games. Refrigerators, microwaves. Some balconies. On beach. Cr cds: A, DS, MC, V.

⚹ ⛽ ≈ ⅀ ⊠ **SC**

★ ★ **SWAMP FOX OCEAN RESORTS.** *2311 S Ocean Blvd (29578).* 803/448-8373; FAX 803/448-5444; res: 800/228-9894. 377 units, 5-16 story, 296 kits. June-late Aug: S, D $99-$119; each addl $8; kit. units $109-$134; 1-bdrm penthouses $235; under 14 free; wkly rates; golf plans; lower rates rest of yr. Crib free. TV. 7 pools, 2 indoor; wading pool, whirlpool, sauna. Supervised child's activities (mid-June-mid-Aug); ages 5-15. Restaurant 6 am-10 pm. Ck-out 11 am. Coin lndry. Meeting rms. Business servs avail. Bellhops. Tennis privileges. Golf privileges. Refrigerators; microwaves avail. Balconies. Picnic tables, grills. On beach. Cr cds: A, D, DS, ER, JCB, MC, V.

◻D ⅀ ⚹ ⛽ ≈ ⊠ **SC**

Hotels

★ ★ **BEACH COLONY.** *5308 N Ocean Blvd (29577).* 803/449-4010; FAX 803/449-2810; res: 800/222-2141. Web www.bchcolony@sccoast.net. 222 kit. suites, 22 story. Mid-June-mid-Aug: 1-bedrm $157; 2-bedrm $1,650/wk; 3-bedrm $1,900/wk; 4-bedrm $2,190/wk; lower rates rest of yr. Crib free. TV; cable. 3 pools, 1 indoor; wading pool, whirlpools, poolside serv. Free supervised child's activities (Memorial Day-Labor Day); ages 6-12. Restaurant (see FUSCO'S). Bar 5 pm-1 am. Ck-out 11 am. Coin lndry. Meeting rms. Free covered parking. Tennis privileges. Golf privileges. Exercise equipt; weight machines, bicycles, sauna. Microwaves. Balconies. On ocean, beach. Cr cds: A, C, D, DS, MC, V.

⚹ ⛽ ≈ ⅀ ⊠ **SC**

★ ★ **BEACH COVE RESORT.** *(4800 S Ocean Blvd, North Myrtle Beach 29582)* 803/272-4044; FAX 803/272-2294; res: 800/331-6533. E-mail bchcove@sccoast.net; web www.beachcove.com. 315 kit. units, 16 story. Late May-mid-Aug: kit. units for up to 6, $118-$145; each addl $10; 2-bedrm cottage $1,800/wk; under 18 free; wkly rates; lower rates rest of yr. Crib $5. TV; cable. 4 pools, 1 indoor; 3 whirlpools, sauna, poolside serv. Supervised child's activities (Memorial Day-Labor Day); ages 3-12. Restaurant 7-10:30 am, 5-10 pm. Bar. Ck-out 11 am. Meeting rms. Business servs avail. Tennis privileges. Golf privileges. Game rm. Microwaves. Private patios, balconies. On ocean; beach. Cr cds: A, DS, MC, V.

◻D ⅀ ⛽ ≈ ⊠ **SC**

★ ★ ★ **THE BREAKERS & NORTH TOWER.** *2006 N Ocean Blvd (29578).* 803/626-5000; res: 800/845-0688; FAX 803/626-5001. E-mail breakers@sccoast.net; web www.breakers.com. 391 units in 3 bldgs, 11, 15, 18 story, 98 kit. suites, 77 kits. June-Aug: D $105-$138; each addl $8; 1-, 2-bedrm kit. suites $154-$290; kit. units $113-$146; under 16 free; wkly rates; golf, tennis plans; lower rates rest of yr. Crib free. TV; cable, VCR avail. 3 pools, 1 indoor/outdoor; wading pool, whirlpool, poolside serv. Free supervised child's activities (June-Labor Day); ages 6-14. Restaurant 7-11 am, 5:30-9 pm. Bar 5 pm-2 am; entertainment. Ck-out 11 am. Coin lndry. Meeting rms. Free airport transportation. Tennis privileges. Golf privileges. Lawn games. Exercise equipt; weights, bicycles, sauna. Refrigerators.

Microwaves avail. Private patio; balconies. On ocean. Cr cds: A, C, D, DS, MC, V.

⚹ ⛽ ≈ ⅀ ⊠ **SC**

★ ★ **CARAVELLE RESORT & VILLAS.** *6900 N Ocean Blvd (29572).* 803/449-3331; FAX 803/449-0643; res: 800/845-0893. 192 rms, 4-15 story, 177 kits; 210 villas, 1-3 bedrm. June-Aug: S, D $90-$119; suites $105-$144; kit. units $92-$122; villas $79-$260; lower rates rest of yr. Crib free. TV; cable. 8 pools, 2 indoor; whirlpool, poolside serv. Free supervised child's activities (Memorial Day-Labor Day); ages 4-16. Restaurant 7-10 am, 6-9 pm. Rm serv. Ck-out 11 am. Coin lndry. Meeting rms. Business servs avail. Bellhops. Free airport, bus depot transportation. Golf privileges. Exercise equipt; stair machine, bicycles, sauna. Rec rm. Refrigerators; microwaves avail. Balconies. On beach. Cr cds: A, DS, MC, V.

⚹ ⛽ ≈ ⅀ ⊠ **SC**

★ ★ **DUNES VILLAGE RESORT.** *5200 N Ocean Blvd (29577), at 52nd Ave.* 803/449-5275; res: 800/648-3539. 93 rms, 8 story. Mid-June-mid-Aug: D $104; each addl $7; kit. apts $127; under 14 free; wkly rates; lower rates rest of yr. Crib free. TV; cable, VCR avail (movies). 2 pools, 1 indoor; whirlpool. Restaurant 7-10 am, also noon-2 pm June-Aug. Ck-out 11 am. Guest lndry. Tennis. Golf privileges. Refrigerators; microwaves avail. Balconies. On beach. Cr cds: DS, MC, V.

◻D ⅀ ⚹ ⛽ ≈ ⊠

★ ★ ★ **EMBASSY SUITES RESORT AT KINGSTON PLANTATION.** *9800 Lake Dr (29572).* 803/449-0006; FAX 803/497-1017. 255 kit. suites, 20 story. Memorial Day-Labor Day: suites $249-$289; each addl $20; condos, villas $179-$339; under 18 free; lower rates rest of yr. Crib free. TV; cable (premium), VCR. 7 pools, 1 indoor; wading pool, whirlpool, poolside serv. Supervised child's activities (June-Aug); ages 5-12. Restaurant 6 am-10 pm. Bar 10-1 am; entertainment Tues-Sat. Ck-out noon. Convention facilities. Business center. In-rm modem link. Concierge. Gift shop. Lighted tennis, pro. Golf privileges. Exercise rm; instructor, weights, bicycles, sauna. Massage. Refrigerators, microwaves. On ocean. Cr cds: A, C, D, DS, MC, V.

◻D ⅀ ⚹ ⛽ ≈ ⅀ ⊠ **SC** ⛵

★ ★ ★ **MYRTLE BEACH MARTINIQUE.** *7100 N Ocean Blvd (29578).* 803/449-4441; FAX 803/497-3041; res: 800/542-0048. E-mail marting@sccoast.net; web www.mbmartinique.com. 203 units, 17 story, 92 kits. Mid-June-late Aug: D $128; each addl $10; suites $153-$358; kit. units $138; under 18 free; lower rates rest of yr. Crib free. TV; cable. 2 pools, 1 indoor; whirlpool, poolside serv. Supervised child's activities (mid-June-mid-Aug). Complimentary coffee in rms. Restaurant 7 am-2 pm, 5-9 pm. Bar 4 pm-2 am; entertainment in season. Ck-out 11 am. Free lndry facilities. Meeting rms. Business servs avail. Golf privileges. Exercise equipt; weights, bicycles, sauna. Refrigerators, microwaves. Balconies. On ocean, beach. Cr cds: A, C, D, DS, MC, V.

◻D ⅀ ⛽ ≈ ⅀ ⊠ **SC**

★ ★ **OCEAN DUNES RESORT & VILLAS.** *201 75th Ave N (29578).* 803/449-7441; FAX 803/449-0558; res: 800/845-0635. E-mail sands@sccoast.net; web www.sandsresorts.com. 138 rms, 8-15 story, 10 townhouses, 45 villas (2-bedrm), 165 tower suites (1-bedrm). Mid-June-mid-Aug: S, D $122-$136; villas $221; suites $134; townhouses $284; advance deposit required for 1-night stay; golf plan; varied lower rates rest of yr. Crib free. TV; cable. 5 pools, 1 indoor, 1 heated; whirlpool, poolside serv. Free supervised child's activities (Memorial Day-Labor Day); ages 5-12. Restaurant 7-10 am, 6-10 pm. Bar 4 pm-1 am; entertainment. Ck-out 11 am. Coin lndry. Convention facilities. Business servs avail. Concierge. Beauty shop. Free airport transportation. Tennis privileges. Golf privileges. Exercise rm; instructor, weights, bicycle, steam rm. Game rm. Refrigerators; microwaves avail. Balconies. On beach. Cr cds: A, C, D, DS, MC, V.

◻D ⅀ ⛽ ≈ ⅀ ⊠ **SC**

★ **OCEAN FOREST PLAZA.** *5523 N Ocean Blvd (29577).* 803/497-0044; res: 800/522-0818; FAX 803/497-3051. 190 kit. suites, 23 story. Memorial Day-Labor Day: 1-bedrm $82-$139; 2-bedrm $139-$229; under 18 free; wkly rates; golf plans; higher rates hols; lower rates rest of yr. Crib free. TV; cable. 2 pools, 1 indoor; whirlpool, sauna, steam rm, poolside serv. Supervised child's activities (Memorial Day-Labor Day);

ages 5-12. Restaurant 7-10 am. Bar 5-11 pm. Ck-out 11 am. Meeting rms. Gift shop. Golf privileges. Game rm. Microwaves. Balconies. Opp beach. Cr cds: A, C, D, DS, MC, V.

★ **THE PALACE.** *1605 S Ocean Blvd (29577). 803/448-4300; FAX 803/448-6300; res: 800/334-1397.* 298 kit. units, 23 story. Late May-late Aug: 1-bedrm $75-$115; 2-bedrm $109-$159; wkly rates; lower rates rest of yr. TV; cable. 2 pools, 1 indoor; whirlpool. Restaurant 6:30 am-2 pm. Ck-out 10:30 am. Convention facilities. Guest lndry. Free covered parking. Golf privileges. Exercise equipt; bicycles, rower, sauna, steam rm. Game rm. Refrigerators, microwaves. Private patios, balconies. Resort-style hotel on ocean. Cr cds: A, DS, MC, V.

★ ★ **SAND DUNES.** *201 74th Ave N (29572). 803/449-7441; FAX 803/449-5036; res: 800/845-1011.* E-mail sands@sccoast.net; web www.sandsresorts.com. 276 units, 12 story. Mid-June-mid-Aug: S, D $136; each addl $10; suites $132-$260; kit. units $145; under 18 free; golf plans; higher rates hols; lower rates rest of yr. Crib free. TV; cable. Indoor/outdoor pool; whirlpool. Supervised child's activities (Memorial Day-Labor Day); ages 5-12. Restaurant 7 am-11 pm. No rm serv. Bar 4 pm-1 am. Ck-out 11 am. Coin lndry. Meeting rms. Business servs avail. In-rm modem link. Grocery store. Free airport transportation. Tennis privileges. Golf privileges. Exercise rm; instructor, weight machine, bicycles. Game rm. Refrigerators; microwaves avail. Balconies. On beach. Cr cds: A, C, D, DS, MC, V.

✔★ ★ **SEA MIST RESORT.** *1200 S Ocean Blvd (29577). 803/448-1551; FAX 803/448-5858; res: 800/732-6478.* E-mail seamist@sccoast.net; web www.seamist.com. 827 rms, 2-16 story, 552 kits. Mid-June-mid-Aug: S, D $78-$128.50; each addl $6; kit. units $96.50-$138; under 15 free; golf plans; lower rates rest of yr. Crib $6. TV; cable (premium). 9 pools, 1 indoor/outdoor; wading pools, whirlpool. Playground. Supervised child's activities (mid-June-mid-Aug); ages 4-12. Restaurant 5-10 am. No rm serv. Ck-out 11 am. Coin lndry. Convention facilities. Business servs avail. Gift shop. Lighted tennis. Golf privileges. Exercise equipt; bicycles, rower, sauna, steam rm. Game rm. Rec rm. Children's water park. Many refrigerators; microwaves avail. Some private patios, balconies. Picnic tables, grills. On beach. Cr cds: A, C, D, DS, MC, V.

★ ★ **SHERATON.** *2701 S Ocean Blvd (29577). 803/448-2518; FAX 803/448-1506.* 219 rms, 16 story, 57 kits. Late May-late Aug: S, D $95-$139; suites $155-$209; kits. $139; under 18 free; golf plans; lower rates rest of yr. Crib free. TV; cable (premium). 2 pools, 1 indoor. Supervised child's activities (June-Aug); ages 2-12. Restaurant 7-11 am, noon-2 pm, 5:30-10 pm. Bar. Ck-out 11 am. Guest lndry. Meeting rms. Business servs avail. Gift shop. Free airport transportation. Tennis privileges. Golf privileges. Exercise equipt; weight machine, bicycles, sauna. Massage. Game rm. Refrigerators; microwaves avail. Balconies. On oceanfront beach. Cr cds: A, D, DS, MC, V.

Inns

★ ★ **BRUSTMAN HOUSE.** *400 25th Ave S (29577). 803/448-7699; FAX 803/626-2478; res: 800/448-7699.* 5 rms, 2 story, 1 kit. suite. Memorial Day-Labor Day: S $60-$80; D $65-$100; each addl $20; kit. suite $125; under 6 free; 2-day min stay wkends, 3-day min stay hols; lower rates rest of yr. TV; cable (premium), VCR avail. Complimentary full bkfst; afternoon refreshments. Restaurant nearby. Ck-out 11 am, ck-in 2 pm. Concierge serv. Many in-rm whirlpools. Scandinavian furnishings. Totally nonsmoking. No cr cds accepted.

✔★ ★ **SERENDIPITY.** *407 71st Ave N (29572). 803/449-5268; res: 800/762-3229.* 14 rms, 2 story, 2 suites, 6 kits. June-Aug: S, D $77-$99; suites $129; kits. $99-$129; lower rates rest of yr. Crib free. TV; cable. Heated pool; whirlpool. Complimentary continental bkfst. Restau-

rant adj 6 am-2 pm, 5-10 pm. Ck-out 11 am, ck-in 2 pm. Golf privileges. Lawn games. Refrigerators; microwaves avail. Balconies. Picnic tables, grills. Library/sitting rm; antiques. Beach nearby. Cr cds: DS, MC, V.

Restaurants

★ **BISTRO.** *5101 N Kings Hwy (29577). 803/449-5125.* Hrs: 11:30 am-2 pm, 5:30-10:30 pm; Sat from 5:30 pm. Closed Sun; Jan 1, Thanksgiving, Dec 25. Continental menu. Bar from 4:30 pm. Semi-a la carte: lunch $5.25-$10, dinner $12-$25. Specializes in fresh fish, steak, snow pie. Outdoor dining. Cr cds: A, C, D, DS, MC, V.

★ **CAGNEY'S OLD PLACE.** *Kings Hwy (US 17). 803/449-3824.* Hrs: 5-11 pm. Closed Sun; also mid-Dec-2nd wk Feb. Bar to 2 am. Semi-a la carte: dinner $11.95-$18.95. Specializes in seafood, chicken, prime rib. Entertainment wkends. Nostalgic decor. Cr cds: A, DS, MC, V.

★ ★ **CAPTAIN DAVE'S DOCKSIDE.** *(US 17 Business, Murrells Inlet) 12 mi S on US 17. 803/651-5850.* Web www.webs44.com/dockside/. Hrs: 11:30 am-2:30 pm, 5-10 pm. Low country menu. Bar. Semi-a la carte: dinner $12-$25. Child's meals. Specializes in fresh seafood and aged beef. Outdoor dining. Nautical decor. View of marsh. Cr cds: A, DS, MC, V.

✔★ **DAMON'S.** *(US 17 S, North Myrtle Beach) Approx 15 mi N on US 17, in Barefoot Landing shopping center. 803/272-5107.* Hrs: 11 am-10 pm; wkends to 11 pm. Closed Dec 25. Bar. Semi-a la carte: lunch $4.50-$7.95, dinner $8.50-$15.95. Child's meals. Specializes in onion loaf, prime rib, steak. Overlooks lagoon. Cr cds: A, D, MC, V.

★ ★ **FUSCO'S.** *(See Beach Colony Hotel) 803/449-4010.* Hrs: 6-10 am, 4-10 pm; Sun 6 am-2 pm, 4-10 pm; June-Aug from 7 am. Closed 1st wk Jan. Res accepted. Italian menu. Bar from 4 pm. Semi-a la carte: bkfst $4.50-$5.25, dinner $12.95-$21.95. Child's meals. Specializes in seafood, pasta, veal. Own baking. Casual atmosphere; overlooks pool and ocean. Cr cds: A, C, D, DS, MC, V.

★ ★ **JOE'S BAR & GRILL.** *(810 Conway Ave, North Myrtle Beach 29582) Approx 15 mi N on US 17. 803/272-4666.* Hrs: 5-10 pm. Closed Thanksgiving, Dec 25. Res accepted. Bar. Semi-a la carte: dinner $13.95-$25.95. Child's meals. Specialties: steak au poivre, veal Marsala, lobster tail. Outdoor dining. Overlooks marsh. Cr cds: A, DS, MC, V.

✔★ ★ ★ **LATIF'S.** *503 61st Ave. 803/449-1716.* Hrs: 8 am-4 pm, 5-9:30 pm; Mon to 4 pm; Sun 10 am-3 pm (brunch). Continental menu. Serv bar. Semi-a la carte: lunch $5.95-$9.95, dinner $12.95-$15.95. Sun brunch $4.75-$9.95. Specialties: Chinese chicken salad, triple mocha torte. Outdoor dining. French bistro atmosphere. Cr cds: A, DS, MC, V.

★ ★ **LONGHORN STEAKHOUSE.** *7604 N Kings Hwy (US 17) (29572). 803/449-7013.* Hrs: 5-10 pm. Closed Thanksgiving; also 1 wk during Christmas season. Bar. Semi-a la carte: dinner $10.95-$36.95. Child's meals. Specializes in choice steaks, seafood. Salad bar. Western decor. Family-owned. Cr cds: A, C, D, DS, MC, V.

★ ★ **OAK HARBOR.** *(1407 13th Ave North, North Myrtle Beach 29582) 16 mi N on US 17, at Vereen's Marina. 803/249-4737.* Hrs: 5-9:30 pm. Closed Thanksgiving, Dec 25. Res accepted. Semi-a la carte: dinner $13.95-$19.25. Child's meals. Specializes in prime rib, fresh seafood, veal. Outdoor dining. Overlooks marina. Cr cds: A, D, MC, V.

✔★ **ROSA LINDA'S CAFE.** *(4635 US 17N, North Myrtle Beach)* Approx 6 mi N on US 17. 803/272-6823. Hrs: noon-10 pm. Closed Dec, Jan. Bar. Semi-a la carte: lunch $3.95-$6.95, dinner $6.50-$14.50. Child's meals. Specialties: fajitas, pasta, pizza. Mexican/Italian atmosphere. Cr cds: A, D, DS, MC, V.

★ ★ **SEA CAPTAIN'S HOUSE.** *3000 N Ocean Blvd.* 803/448-8082. Hrs: 6-10:30 am, 11:30 am-2:30 pm, 5-10 pm. Serv bar. Semi-a la carte: bkfst $4.50-$8.95, lunch, dinner $5.50-$29. Child's meals. Specializes in fresh seafood, steaks, homemade pies. Sea captain's house design, flowering shrubs. Ocean view. Cr cds: A, DS, MC, V.

★ **SHENANIGAN'S.** *10131 N Kings Hwy (US 17) (10131).* 803/272-1171. Hrs: 4-10:30 pm; Fri, Sat to 11 pm; Sun to 10:30 pm. Closed Dec 25. Bar. Semi-a la carte: dinner $7.95-$31.95. Specializes in steak, prime rib, chicken. Cr cds: A, C, D, DS, MC, V.

★ ★ **TONY'S.** *(1407 US 17, North Myrtle Beach)* 15 mi N on US 17. 803/249-1314. Hrs: 5-10 pm. Closed Dec-Jan; also Sun Sept-May. Italian menu. Bar. Semi-a la carte: dinner $8.95-$27. Child's meals. Specializes in pasta, pizza, seafood. Contemporary Mediterranean decor. Family-owned. Cr cds: A, C, D, DS, MC, V.

Newberry (D-4)

(See also Clinton, Columbia, Greenwood)

Pop 10,542 **Elev** 500 ft **Area code** 803 **Zip** 29108

What to See and Do

Dreher Island State Park. Approx 340 acres. Three islands with 12-mi shoreline. Lake swimming; fishing (supplies); boating (ramps, rental slips). Nature trail. Picnicking (shelters), playground, recreation building, store. Camping (hookups, dump station; higher fees for lakefront campsites in summer). Standard fees. 20 mi SE via US 76 to Chapin, then 9 mi SW via unnumbered road. Phone 803/364-3530 or 803/364-4152.

Sumter National Forests. N via SC 121, US 176 (see GREENWOOD).

Motels

✔★ **BEST WESTERN NEWBERRY INN.** *SC 34, at jct I-26 & Hwy 34, exit 74.* 803/276-5850. 116 rms, 1-2 story. S $37.95; D $42.95-$47.95; each addl $6; under 12 free. Crib free. TV; cable (premium). Pool. Complimentary continental bkfst. Restaurant 5-9 am. Rm serv. Bar 6 pm-midnight. Ck-out 11 am. Meeting rms. Business servs avail. Exercise equipt; weights, bicycles. Cr cds: A, C, D, DS, MC, V.

Orangeburg (E-4)

(See also Aiken, Santee)

Settled 1730s **Pop** 13,739 **Elev** 245 ft **Area code** 803 **Zip** 29115
Information Orangeburg County Chamber of Commerce, 1570 John C. Calhoun Dr, Box 328, 29116-0328; 803/534-6821.

Named for the Prince of Orange, this community is the seat of Orangeburg County, one of the most prosperous farm areas in the state. Manufacturing

plants for wood products, ball bearings, textiles, textile equipment, chemicals, hand tools and lawn mowers are all located within the county.

What to See and Do

Edisto Memorial Gardens. City-owned 110-acre site. Seasonal flowers bloom all year; more than 3,200 rose bushes, camellias, azaleas; also many flowering trees. Gardens (daily). Wetlands boardwalk park. Tennis courts, picnic areas, shelters nearby, playground. S on US 301, within city limits, alongside N Edisto River. Phone 803/533-6020. **Free.**

South Carolina State University (1896). (5,000 students) 300 College St NE. Phone 803/536-7000. On campus is

I.P. Stanback Museum and Planetarium. Museum has changing exhibits (Sept-May, Mon-Fri; closed hols). Planetarium shows (Oct-Apr, 2nd & 4th Sun; closed hols). Phone 803/536-7174 for reservations. Shows ¢

Annual Event

Orangeburg County Fair. Fairgrounds. Late Sept-early Oct.

Motels

✔★ **DAYS INN.** *3691 St Matthews Rd, on US 601N.* 803/531-2590; FAX 803/531-2829. 75 rms. S $45-$50; D $50-$60; each addl $7; under 12 free. Crib free. TV; cable (premium). Pool. Complimentary continental bkfst. Ck-out 11 am. Some refrigerators; microwaves avail. Cr cds: A, C, D, DS, MC, V.

★ ★ **HOLIDAY INN.** *1415 John C. Calhoun Dr (US 301S).* 803/531-4600; FAX 803/516-0187. 160 rms, 2 story. S $58-$66; D $70-$74; each addl $8; under 19 free. Crib free. TV; cable (premium). Pool. Restaurant 6:30 am-2 pm, 5:30-9 pm; Sat, Sun from 7 am. Bar; closed Sun. Ck-out noon. Meeting rms. Business servs avail. In-rm modem link. Valet serv. Cr cds: A, C, D, DS, JCB, MC, V.

Rock Hill (C-4)

(See also Chester, Gaffney; also see Charlotte, NC)

Founded 1852 **Pop** 41,643 **Elev** 667 ft **Area code** 803 **E-mail** yccvb@infoave.net **Web** web.infoave.net/~yccvb/index.htm
Information York County Convention & Visitors Bureau, 201 E Main St, PO Box 11377, 29731; 803/329-5200 or 800/866-5200.

Both a college and an industrial town, Rock Hill takes its name from the flint rock that had to be cut through when a railroad was being built through town.

What to See and Do

Andrew Jackson State Park. Approx 360 acres. Lake fishing; boating (rentals). Nature trail. Picnicking (shelters), playground. Camping. Recreation building, outdoor amphitheater. Log house museum contains documents, exhibits of Jackson lore. One-room school with exhibits. Standard fees. 9 mi N on US 521. Phone 803/285-3344.

Glencairn Garden. Municipally owned 6 acres of colorful azaleas, dogwood, redbud, crepe myrtle, boxwood; pool, fountain (daily). 725 Crest St. Phone 803/329-5620. **Free.**

Historic Brattonsville. Learn about local history in this restored village of over two dozen structures, including Backwoodsman Cabin, Colonel Bratton Home (ca 1780), Homestead House (ca 1823) and Brick Kitchen. Gift shop. Guided tours (by appt). Self-guided audio tour. (Mar-Nov, Tues-Sat, also Sun afternoons; closed hols) SW via SC 322, at 1444 Brattonsville Rd near McConnells. Phone 803/684-2327. ¢¢

Kings Mountain State Park. (See KINGS MOUNTAIN NATIONAL MILITARY PARK.)

Lake Wylie. Created by Duke Power Co. Dam on the Catawba River. Freshwater fishing, boating, waterskiing, swimming; 12,455 acres. N on SC 274. Phone 704/382-8587.

Landsford Canal State Park. Approx 250 acres. Site of canal built in 1820s; locks, stone bridges. Trail parallels canals. Picnicking (shelter), community building. (Thurs-Mon) 15 mi S off US 21. Phone 803/789-5800.

Museum of York County. Contains a large collection of mounted African hoofed mammals; large African artifacts collection. Hall of Western Hemisphere contains mounted animals from North and South America. Art galleries & planetarium. Catawba pottery sold here. Nature trail, picnic area. (Daily; closed Thanksgiving, Dec 25) Mt Gallant Rd, 7 mi NW, off I-77 exit 82 A. Phone 800/968-2726. ¢¢

Winthrop University (1886). (5,000 students) Coeducational; 100 undergraduate and graduate programs. Concerts, lectures, sports, plays; art galleries. Large lake and recreational area. Oakland Ave. Phone 803/323-2236.

Annual Event

"Come-See-Me." Art shows, tour of houses, entertainment, road race, concerts. 10 days early Apr.

Motels

★ ★ **COMFORT INN.** (3725 Ave of the Carolinas, Fort Mill 29715) N on I-77, exit 90. 803/548-5200; FAX 803/548-6692. 155 rms, 4 story. S $65-$95; D $75-$105; suites, kit. unit $130-$160; under 18 free. Crib free. TV; cable. Pool. Complimentary continental bkfst. Restaurant adj 6 am-10 pm. Ck-out 11 am. Meeting rms. In-rm modem link. Valet serv. Exercise equipt; stair machine, bicycles. Refrigerator in suites. Cr cds: A, C, D, DS, ER, JCB, MC, V.

D ⊠ 🛪 🛉 🐾 SC

★ **DAYS INN.** 914 Riverview Rd (29730). 803/329-6581; FAX 803/366-4472. 113 rms, 3 story. S $45-$125; D $50-$150; each addl $5. Crib free. TV; cable (premium). Pool. Complimentary continental bkfst. Restaurant 6-10 am, 4-11 pm. Ck-out 11 am. Meeting rms. Business servs avail. Cr cds: A, C, D, DS, ER, JCB, MC, V.

D ⊠ 🛪 🐾 SC

★ **DAYS INN CHARLOTTE SOUTH/CAROWINDS.** (3482 US 21, Ft Mill 29715) Approx 5 mi N on I-77 exit 90. 803/548-8000; FAX 803/548-6058. 119 rms, 2 story. Apr-Sept: S $45-$70; D $50-$75; each addl $5; higher rates special events; lower rates rest of yr. Crib free. Pet accepted. TV; cable, VCR (movies). Pool. Complimentary continental bkfst. Restaurant adj open 24 hrs. Ck-out 11 am. Cr cds: A, C, D, DS, MC, V.

D 🐾 ⊠ 🛪 🐾 SC

✔★ **ECONO LODGE.** 962 Riverview Rd (29730), I-77 exit 82B. 803/329-3232; FAX 803/328-6288. 106 rms, 2 story. S $31.46-$36.95; D $34.95-$40.95; each addl $5; under 18 free; higher rates: wknds, special events. TV; cable (premium). Complimentary coffee in lobby. Restaurant adj open 24 hrs. Ck-out 11 am. Business servs avail. Cr cds: A, C, D, DS, ER, JCB, MC, V.

D 🛪 🐾 SC

★ ★ **HOLIDAY INN.** 2640 Cherry Rd (29730), at jct I-77, US 21N. 803/329-1122; FAX 803/329-1072. 125 rms, 2 story. S, D $55; each addl $5; suites $95-$125; under 16 free. Crib free. Pet accepted, some restrictions. TV, cable (premium). Pool. Complimentary full bkfst. Coffee in rms. Restaurant 6:30 am-11 am; 5:30 pm-10 pm. Bar 3 pm-2 am, Sat to

midnight. Ck-out noon. Coin lndry. Business servs avail. In-rm modem link. Airport transportation. Cr cds: A, C, D, DS, JCB, MC, V.

D 🐾 ⊠ 🛪 🐾 SC

✔★ ★ **HOWARD JOHNSON.** 2625 Cherry Rd (29730), I-77 exit 82B, jct US 21. 803/329-3121; FAX 803/366-1043. 140 rms, 2 story. S $46-$53; D $48-$59; each addl $6; suites $125; under 12 free. Crib free. Pet accepted. TV; cable. Pool. Complimentary continental bkfst. Restaurant open 24 hrs. Rm serv 6 am-9 pm. Bar 5-10 pm, closed Sun. Ck-out noon. Meeting rm. Valet serv. Private patios, balconies. Cr cds: A, C, D, DS, JCB, MC, V.

D 🐾 ⊠ 🛪 🐾 SC

Hotels

★ ★ **RADISSON GRAND RESORT.** (9700 Regency Pkwy, Fort Mill) 5 mi I-77, exit 90. 803/548-7800. 687 rms, 4 story. Memorial Day-Labor Day: S $79-$129, D $89-$149; each addl $10; suites $219-$300; under 18 free; lower rates rest of yr. Crib free. TV; cable; VCR avail. Pool; wading pool. Supervised children's activities (Memorial Day-Labor Day). Restaurant 7 am-9 pm. Ck-out noon. Convention facilities. Business servs avail. Valet serv. Lighted tennis. 18-hole golf, greens fee $32, putting green, driving range. Exercise equipt; bicycles, weights. Some refrigerators. Cr cds: A, C, D, DS, MC, V.

D 🐾 🕴 🖈 ⊠ 🛪 🛉 🐾 SC

★ ★ **RAMADA.** (225 Carowinds Blvd, Ft Mill 29715) I-77 Carowinds exit. 803/548-2400; FAX 803/548-6382. 208 rms, 11 story. S, D $71-$85; each addl $10; under 18 free. Crib free. Pet accepted. TV; cable (premium). Pool. Complimentary bkfst. Restaurant 6:30 am-2 pm, 5-10 pm; Fri, Sat to 11 pm. Bar 4:30-11 pm. Ck-out noon. Coin lndry. Meeting rms. Business servs avail. In-rm modem link. Free airport transportation. Cr cds: A, D, DS, JCB, MC, V.

D 🐾 ⊠ 🛪 🐾 SC

Santee (E-5)

(See also Orangeburg)

Pop 638 **Elev** 250 ft **Area code** 803 **Zip** 29142 **Web** www.santee coopercountry.org

Information Santee-Cooper Country, PO Drawer 40; 803/854-2131 or 800/227-8510 outside SC.

This community serves as the gateway to the Santee-Cooper Lakes recreation area, created by the Pinopolis and Santee dams on the Santee and Cooper rivers. There are numerous marinas and campgrounds on the Santee-Cooper lakes.

What to See and Do

Eutaw Springs Battlefield Site. Site where ragged colonials fought the British on Sept 8, 1781, in what is considered to be the last major engagement in South Carolina; both sides claimed victory. Three acres maintained by state. No facilities. 12 mi SE off SC 6. **Free.**

Fort Watson Battle Site and Indian Mound. A 48-ft-high mound; site of Revolutionary War battle Apr 15-23, 1781, during which Gen. Francis Marion attacked and captured a British fortification, its garrison, supplies and ammunition. Three acres maintained by state. No facilities. Observation point has view of Santee-Cooper waters. 4 mi N, 1 mi off US 15/301, on Lake Marion. **Free.**

Santee National Wildlife Refuge. Attracts many geese and ducks during winter. Observation tower, self-guided nature trail; visitor information center with exhibits (Mon-Fri; closed hols). Seasonal hunting and fishing, wildlife observation and photography. 4 mi N on US 15/301 or exit 102 from I-95. Phone 803/478-2217. **Free.**

Santee State Park. Approx 2,500 acres. Lake swimming; fishing (supplies avail); boating (ramp, rentals, dock). Scenic lake tours. Nature trails; tennis. Picnicking (shelters), playground, restaurant, groceries. Camping, cabins (higher fees for lakefront sites), primitive camping. Interpretive center, recreation building. Standard fees. 3 mi NW off SC 6, on shores of Lake Marion. Phone 803/854-2408.

Motels

★ ★ **BEST WESTERN.** *I-95 exit 98 E.* 803/854-3089; *FAX* 803/854-3093. 108 rms. S $50-$60; D $50-$65; under 12 free. Crib $4. TV; cable (premium). Heated pool. Complimentary continental bkfst. Restaurant 5-9:30 pm. Ck-out 11 am. Business servs avail. Some in-rm whirlpools. 18-hole golf privileges. Cr cds: A, C, D, DS, MC, V.

D ⚷ ≈ ⊠ 🔥 SC

✔ ★ **DAYS INN.** *Jct I-95 & SC 6.* 803/854-2175; *FAX* 803/854-2835. 119 rms, 2 story. S $30-$50; D $40-$60; each addl $6; under 12 free; golf plans. Crib free. Pet accepted, some restrictions; $6. TV; cable (premium). Pool. Playground. Complimentary full bkfst. Restaurant 6-10 am, 5-9 pm. Ck-out noon. Guest lndry. Business servs avail. 18-hole golf privileges. Refrigerators avail. Cr cds: A, C, D, DS, MC, V.

✦ ⚷ ≈ ⊠ 🔥 SC

Spartanburg (C-3)

(See also Clinton, Gaffney, Greenville)

Founded 1785 **Pop** 43,467 **Elev** 816 ft **Area code** 864
Information Convention & Visitors Bureau, 105 N Pine St, PO Box 1636, 29304; 864/594-5050.

An array of highways and railroads feeds agricultural products into, and moves manufactured products out of, heavily industrialized Spartanburg. Textiles and peaches are the leading products. The Spartan Regiment of South Carolina militia, heroes of the Battle at Cowpens, gave both the county and its seat their names.

What to See and Do

Croft State Park. On part of old Camp Croft military area. Approx 7,000 acres. Swimming pool (fee); lake fishing. Nature, exercise trails; bridle trail (no rentals); stable, show ring; tennis. Picnicking (shelters), playground. Camping (hookups, dump station). Standard fees. 3 mi SE on SC 56. Phone 864/585-1283.

Regional Museum. Exhibits depict up-country history of state; Pardo Stone (1567), doll collections, Native American artifacts. (Daily exc Mon; closed hols) 501 Otis Blvd, at Pine St. Phone 864/596-3501. ¢

The Arts Council of Spartanburg. Permanent and changing exhibits; classes in visual and performing arts. (Daily; closed most hols) 385 S Spring St. Phone 864/583-2776.   **Free.**

Walnut Grove Plantation (1765). Restored girlhood home of Kate Moore Barry, Revolutionary heroine; period furniture; schoolhouse, kitchen, doctor's office, other buildings; family cemetery; herb gardens with "dipping well." (Apr-Oct, daily exc Mon; rest of yr, Sun only; closed some hols) 8 mi SE near jct I-26, US 221. Phone 864/576-6546.   ¢¢

Annual Event

Piedmont Interstate Fair. Art exhibit, livestock and flower shows; needlecraft and food displays; auto race. Phone 864/582-7042. 2nd full wk Oct.

Motels

★ ★ **COMFORT INN-WEST.** *2070 New Cut Rd (29303).* 864/576-2992; *FAX* 864/576-2992. 99 rms, 2 story. S $45-$55; D $55-$85;

each addl $6; suites $125; under 18 free. Crib free. TV; cable. Pool. Complimentary continental bkfst. Ck-out 11 am. Cr cds: A, C, D, DS, ER, JCB, MC, V.

D ≈ ⊠ 🐾 SC

★ ★ **HAMPTON INN.** *4930 College Dr (29301).* 864/576-6080; *FAX* 864/587-8901. 112 rms, 2 story. S $50-$54; D $58-$62; under 18 free. Crib free. TV; cable. Pool. Complimentary continental bkfst. Ck-out noon. Meeting rm. Business servs avail. Cr cds: A, C, D, DS, MC, V.

D ≈ ⊠ 🐾 SC

★ ★ **HOLIDAY INN.** *200 International Dr (29301), jct I-26 & I-85 exit 71.* 864/576-5220; *FAX* 864/574-1243. 225 rms, 3 story. S $59-$89; D $64-$94; under 18 free. Crib free. TV. Indoor pool; wading pool, whirlpool, poolside serv. Restaurant 6:30 am-2 pm, 5:30-10 pm. Rm serv. Bar; entertainment exc Sun. Ck-out noon. Coin lndry. Meeting rms. Business servs avail. In-rm modem link. Bellhops. Valet serv. Exercise equipt; weights, bicycles, sauna. Rec rm. Cr cds: A, C, D, DS, JCB, MC, V.

D ≈ ⚷ ⊠ ⊠ 🐾 SC

★ ★ **RAMADA INN.** *1000 Hearon Circle (29303), at jct I-85 & I-585.* 864/503-9048; *FAX* 864/503-0576. 138 rms, 2-3 story. No elvtr. S $58-$64; D $64-$68; each addl $7. Crib free. TV. Pool. Coffee in rms. Restaurant 6 am-1:30 pm. Rm serv. Bar 5 pm-2 am; entertainment exc Sun. Ck-out noon. Meeting rms. Business servs avail. Bellhops. Valet serv. Cr cds: A, C, D, DS, JCB, MC, V.

D ≈ ⊠ 🐾 SC

Motor Hotel

★ ★ **QUALITY HOTEL AND CONFERENCE CENTER.** *7136 Asheville Hwy (29303).* 864/503-0780. 143 rms, 6 story. S $52-$62; D $62-$75; each addl $10; under 18 free. Crib free. Pet accepted. TV; cable (premium). Pool; poolside serv. Restaurant 6:30 am-2 pm, 5-10 pm. Bar 4 pm-midnight. Ck-out noon. Meeting rms. Business servs avail. In-rm modem link. Valet serv. Exercise equipt; weight machine, treadmill. Cr cds: A, C, D, DS, JCB, MC, V.

✦ ≈ ⚷ ⊠ 🐾 SC

Restaurant

★ ★ **SPICE OF LIFE.** *100 Wood Row, Downtown, off St. John St.* 864/585-3737. Hrs: 11:30 am-2:30 pm. Closed Sun; some major hols. Res accepted. French, Italian menu. Bar. Semi-a la carte: lunch $4.95-$5.95, dinner $10.95-$29.95. Specialties: herb-crusted salmon, crab cakes Julia, veal with forest mushrooms. Terrace dining. Cr cds: A, D, MC, V.

D ⊣

Sumter (D-5)

(See also Camden, Columbia)

Settled 1785 **Pop** 36,933 **Elev** 173 ft **Area code** 803
Information Convention & Visitors Bureau, PO Box 1449, 29151; 803/778-5434.

Long the center of a prosperous agricultural area, Sumter has, in recent years, become an industrial center. Both the city and county are named for General Thomas Sumter, the "fighting gamecock" of the Revolutionary War. As a tourism spot, Sumter offers a unique contrast of antebellum mansions and modern facilities. Shaw Air Force Base, headquarters of the 9th Air Force and the 363rd Tactical Fighter Wing, is nearby.

What to See and Do

Church of the Holy Cross (1850). Built of *pise de terre* (rammed earth); unusual architectural design and construction. Also noted for stained-glass windows set to catch the rays of the rising sun. Many notable South Carolinians from the 1700s are buried in the old church cemetery, including Joel R. Poinsett. 10 mi W via US 76, exit at SC 261, in Stateburg. Phone 803/494-8101.

Poinsett State Park. Approx 1,000 acres of mountains, swamps. Named for Joel Poinsett, who introduced the poinsettia (which originated in Mexico) to the US. Spanish moss, mountain laurel, rhododendron. Lake swimming; fishing; boating (rentals). Hiking, nature trails;. Picnicking (shelters), playground. Primitive & improved camping (dump station), cabins. Nature center; programs. Standard fees. 18 mi SW via SC 763, 261. Phone 803/494-8177.

Sumter County Museum. Two-story Edwardian house depicting Victorian lifestyle; period rooms, historical exhibits, war memorabilia, economic and cultural artifacts, artwork and archives (genealogical research). Museum is surrounded by formal gardens designed by Robert Marvin; several outdoor exhibits of farm implements, rural life; carriage house. (Daily exc Mon; closed hols) 122 N Washington St. Phone 803/775-0908. **Donation.**

Sumter Gallery of Art. Regional artwork features paintings, drawings, sculpture, photography and pottery. (Tues-Sun afternoons; closed hols & July) 421 N Main St. Phone 803/775-0543. **Free.**

Swan Lake Iris Gardens. Covers 150 acres; Kaempferi and Japanese iris; seasonal plantings, nature trails; ancient cypress, oak and pine trees; 45-acre lake with several species of swan. Picnicking, playground. (Daily) W Liberty St. **Free.**

Annual Events

Sumter Iris Festival. Fireworks display, parade, art show, golf & tennis tournaments, barbecue cook-off, local talent exhibition, square dance, iris gardens display. Late May.

Fall Fiesta of Arts. Swan Lake Gardens. Features visual & performing arts, concerts & choral groups. Phone 803/436-2258. 3rd wkend Oct.

Motels

★ ★ ★ **HOLIDAY INN.** *2390 Broad St (29150). 803/469-9001; FAX 803/469-9070.* 124 rms, 2 story. S, D $59-$79; each addl $6; under 19 free. Crib free. TV; cable (premium). Pool. Complimentary bkfst buffet. Coffee in rms. Restaurant 6-9 am, 5:30-10 pm; Sat, Sun 6:30-10 am, 5:30-10 pm. Rm serv. Ck-out noon. Meeting rms. Business center. In-rm modem link. Valet serv. Tennis privileges. Exercise equipt; weight machine, treadmill. Microwaves avail. Cr cds: A, C, D, DS, JCB, MC, V.

★ ★ **RAMADA INN.** *226 N Washington St (29150), on US 76/378/521. 803/775-2323; FAX 803/773-9500.* 125 rms in 2 buildings, 2-3 story. S $49-$69; D $56-$76; each addl $9; under 18 free; golf plans. Crib free. Pet accepted, some restrictions. TV; cable (premium). Pool. Complimentary bkfst buffet. Coffee in rms. Restaurant 6:30 am-2 pm, 6-9 pm. Rm serv. Bar 5 pm-midnight; closed Sun. Ck-out noon. Meeting rms. Business servs avail. In-rm modem link. Health club privileges. Refrigerators, microwaves avail. Cr cds: A, C, D, DS, ER, JCB, MC, V.

★ **TRAVELERS INN.** *378 Broad St (29151). 803/469-9210; FAX 803/469-4306.* 104 rms. S $32.95; D $35.95-$40.95; each addl $5; higher rates: hol wkends, special events. Crib free. TV; cable (premium). Pool. Complimentary continental bkfst. Ck-out 11 am. Cr cds: A, C, D, DS, MC, V.

Inns

★ ★ **BED & BREAKFAST OF SUMTER.** *6 Park Ave (29150). 803/773-2903; res: 888/786-8372; FAX 803/775-6943.* 5 rms, 2 story. No rm phones. S $65; D $75. TV in common rm; cable. Complimentary full bkfst. Ck-out 11 am, ck-in 3-6 pm. Some fireplaces. Built in 1897; prairie home style with Victorian decor. Totally nonsmoking. Cr cds: DS, MC, V.

✔★ ★ ★ **MAGNOLIA HOUSE.** *230 Church St (29150). 803/775-6694; res: 888/666-0296.* E-mail magnoliahouse@sumter.net. 4 rms, 2 story, 1 suite. Rm phones avail. S $65; D $75; suite $125. Crib free. TV in common rm; cable, VCR avail (movies). Complimentary full bkfst; afternoon refreshments. Ck-out 11 am, ck-in 3 pm. Luggage handling. Built in 1907; Greek revival. Totally nonsmoking. Cr cds: A, D, MC, V.

Walterboro (E-5)

(See also Beaufort, Charleston)

Settled 1784 **Pop** 5,492 **Elev** 69 ft **Area code** 843 **Zip** 29488 **E-mail** chamber@lowcountry.com **Web** pride-net.com/wccc

Information Walterboro-Colleton Chamber of Commerce, 109 Benson St, PO Box 426; 843/549-9595.

Settled in 1784 by Charleston plantation owners as a summer resort area, Walterboro has retained its charm of yesterday despite its growth. The town boasts a casual pace and rural lifestyle where people can enjoy fishing and hunting, early-19th-century architectural designs, plantations and beach and recreational facilities.

What to See and Do

Colleton County Courthouse. Building designed by Robert Mills; first public nullification meeting in state was held in 1828. Hampton St & Jefferies Blvd.

Colleton State Park. On 35 acres; tree-shaded area on banks of Edisto River. Canoeing (dock); river fishing. Nature trails. Picnicking (shelters). Camping (hookups, dump station). Standard fees. 11 mi N on US 15. Phone 843/538-8206.

Old Colleton County Jail (1855). Neo-Gothic Structure resembles a castle and is home to the Colleton Museum and the Chamber of Commerce. Served as Walterboro jail until 1937. Jefferies Blvd. Phone 843/549-2303.

South Carolina Artisans Center. Features handcrafted art and gifts by regional artists. Craftspeople demonstrate their skills. Educational programs and special events also offered. (Daily; closed hols) 334 Wichman St in Hickory Valley Historic District. Phone 843/549-0011. **Free.**

Annual Event

Rice Festival. Entertainment, parade, arts & crafts; street dances, soapbox derby. Phone 843/549-1079. Last full wkend Apr.

Motels

★ **ECONO LODGE.** *1057 Sniders Hwy, I-95 & SC 63. 843/538-3830.* 100 rms, 1-2 story. S, D $31.95-$33.95; each addl $4; under 12 free. Crib free. TV, cable (premium). Complimentary continental bkfst. Restaurant opp open 6 am-11 pm. Ck-out 11 am. Cr cds: A, DS, MC, V.

★ ★ **HOLIDAY INN.** *I-95 & SC 63. 843/538-5473.* 171 rms, 2 story. S, D $65; under 18 free. Crib free. Pet accepted. TV, cable (premium). Pool; wading pool. Complimentary full bkfst. Restaurant 6 am-2 pm, 5-10 pm. Rm serv. Ck-out noon. Meeting rms. Business servs avail. Valet serv. Cr cds: A, C, D, DS, MC, V.

★ **TOWN AND COUNTRY INN.** *1139 Sniders Hwy, at jct SC 63, I-95 exit 53. 843/538-5911.* 96 rms, 2 story. S $23.95-$27.95; D $31.95; each addl $3; under 18 free. Crib free. TV; cable. Pool. Playground. Complimentary continental bkfst. Restaurant 6 am-10 pm. Ck-out 11 am. Business servs avail. Private patios, balconies. Cr cds: A, C, D, DS, MC, V.

Virginia

Population: 6,377,000
Land area: 40,815 square miles
Elevation: 0-5,729 feet
Highest point: Mt Rogers (Between Smyth, Grayson Counties)
Entered Union: Tenth of original 13 states (June 25, 1788)
Capital: Richmond
Motto: Thus always to tyrants
Nickname: Old Dominion
State flower: American dogwood
State bird: Cardinal
State fair: Late September-early October 1998, in Richmond
Time zone: Eastern
Web: www.virginia.org

Settled by Elizabethans and named for their Virgin Queen, the first of the Southern states still retains a degree of the graceful courtliness that reached its peak just before the Civil War. Evidence of strong ties with the past are apparent in the Old Dominion. More than 1,600 historical markers dot its 55,000 miles of paved roads. More than 100 historic buildings are open all year; hundreds more welcome visitors during the statewide Historic Garden Week (usually the last week in April).

Permanent English settlement of America began in Jamestown in 1607 and started a long line of Virginia "firsts": the first legislative assembly in the Western Hemisphere (1619); the first armed rebellion against royal government (Bacon's Rebellion, 1676); the first stirring debates, in Williamsburg and Richmond, which left pre-Revolutionary America echoing Patrick Henry's inflammatory "Give me liberty, or give me death!" Records show that America's first Thanksgiving was held December 4, 1619, on the site of what is now Berkeley Plantation.

To Virginia the nation owes its most cherished documents—Thomas Jefferson's Declaration of Independence, George Mason's Bill of Rights, James Madison's Constitution. From here came George Washington to lead the Revolution and to become the first of eight US presidents to hail from Virginia.

Ironically, the state so passionately involved in creating a new nation was very nearly the means of its destruction. Virginia was the spiritual and physical capital of the Confederacy; the Army of Northern Virginia was the Confederacy's most powerful weapon; General Robert E. Lee its greatest commander. More than half the fighting of the Civil War took place in Virginia; and here, in the quaint little village of Appomattox Court House, the war finally came to an end.

When chartered in 1609, the Virginia territory included about one-tenth of what is now the United States; the present state ranks 36th in size, but the remaining area is remarkably diverse. Tidewater Virginia—the coastal plain—is low, almost flat, arable land cut by rivers and bays into a magnificent system of natural harbors. It was vital to commerce and agriculture in the early days. Today it is still important commercially (the Hampton Roads port is one of the world's great naval and shipbuilding bases) and a perennial lure to vacationers as well.

Inland lies the gentle rolling Piedmont, covering about half the state. Here is Virginia's leading tobacco area; it also produces apples, corn, wheat, hay and dairy products. The world's largest single-unit textile plant is in Danville; the Piedmont also manufactures shoes, furniture, paper products, clay and glass, chemicals and transportation equipment.

West of the Piedmont rise the Blue Ridge Mountains; high, rugged upland plateaus occur to the south. Further west is the Valley of Virginia, a series of fertile valleys. Best known is the Shenandoah, which contains some of the richest—and once bloodiest—land in the nation. Civil War fighting swept the valley for four years; Winchester changed hands 72 times.

To the southwest are the Appalachian Plateaus, a rugged, forested region of coal mines. Here the splendid outdoor drama, the *Trail of the Lonesome Pine,* romanticized by the novelist John Fox, is performed.

For the vacationer today, the state offers colonial and Civil War history at every turn, seashore and mountain recreation the year round, such natural oddities as caverns in the west and the Dismal Swamp in the southeast, and the Skyline Drive (see SHENANDOAH NATIONAL PARK), one of the loveliest scenic drives in the East.

When to Go/Climate

Virginia summers can be hot and humid, marked by brief, powerful thunderstorms; winter snows are common in the mountains. Moderate temperatures, light rainfall, verdant flowering gardens, and brilliant foliage make spring and fall the best seasons to visit.

AVERAGE HIGH/LOW TEMPERATURES (°F)
RICHMOND

Jan 46/26	May 78/54	Sept 81/59
Feb 49/28	June 85/63	Oct 71/47
Mar 60/36	July 88/68	Nov 61/38
Apr 70/45	Aug 87/66	Dec 50/30

ROANOKE

Jan 44/25	May 76/53	Sept 79/57
Feb 47/27	June 83/60	Oct 68/45
Mar 58/36	July 86/65	Nov 58/37
Apr 67/44	Aug 85/64	Dec 48/29

Parks and Recreation Finder

Directions to and information about the parks and recreation areas below are given under their respective town/city sections. Please refer to those sections for details.

Key to abbreviations: I.P. = Interstate Park; N.B.C. = National Battlefield & Cemetery; N.B.P. = National Battlefield Park; N.F. = National Forest; N.H. = National Historical Park; N.H.S. = National Historic Site; N.M. = National Monument; N.Mem. = National Memorial; N.M.P. = National Military Park; N.P. = National Park; N.Pres. = National Preserve; N.R. = National Recreational Area; N.S. = National Seashore; N.S.T. = National Scenic Trail; S.B. = State Beach; S.C.P. = State Conservation Park; S.G. = State Garden; S.H.A. = State Historic Area; S.H.P. = State Historic Park; S.N.A. = State Natural Area; S.P. = State Park; S.R. = State Reserve; S.R.A. = State Recreation Area; S.Res.P. = State Resort Park; S.R.P. = State Rustic Park.

NATIONAL PARK AND RECREATION AREAS

Place Name	Listed Under
Appomattox Court House N.H.	same
Assateague Island N.S.	CHINCOTEAGUE
Blue Ridge Parkway	same
Booker T. Washington N.M.	same
George Washington Birthplace N.M.	same
Breaks I.P.	same
Cape Henry Memorial	same
Colonial N.H.	same
Colonial Parkway	same
Fredericksburg & Spotsylvania N.M.P.	same
George Washington and Jefferson N.F.	HARRISONBURG
Jamestown	same
Manassas N.B.P.	same
Petersburg National Battlefield	same
Prince William Forest Park	TRIANGLE
Richmond N.B.P.	same
Robert E. Lee Memorial	ARLINGTON COUNTY
Shenandoah N.P.	same
Wolf Trap Farm Park for the Performing Arts	FAIRFAX
Yorktown Battlefield	YORKTOWN

STATE RECREATION AREAS

Place Name	Listed Under
Chippokes Plantation S.P.	SURRY
Claytor Lake S.P.	RADFORD
Douthat S.P.	CLIFTON FORGE
Fairy Stone S.P.	MARTINSVILLE
First Landing/Seashore S.P.	VIRGINIA BEACH
Grayson Highlands S.P.	ABINGDON
Holliday Lake S.P.	APPOMATTOX COURT HOUSE N.H.
Hungry Mother S.P.	MARION
Natural Tunnel S.P.	BIG STONE GAP
Occoneechee S.P.	CLARKSVILLE
Pocahontas S.P.	RICHMOND
Sky Meadows S.P.	FRONT ROYAL
Staunton River S.P.	SOUTH BOSTON
Twin Lakes S.P.	KEYSVILLE
Westmoreland S.P.	MONTROSS
York River S.P.	WILLIAMSBURG

CALENDAR HIGHLIGHTS

FEBRUARY

Mobil Invitational Track & Field Meet (Fairfax). George Mason University campus. For more information, phone Visitors Center 703/550-2450.

APRIL

International Azalea Festival (Norfolk). Downtown & Norfolk Botanical Garden. To honor NATO. Parade, coronation ceremony, two-day air show (held at Norfolk Naval Air Station), events, concerts, fair, ball, entertainment. Phone 757/622-2312.

Garden Week (Charlottesville). Some fine private homes and gardens in the area are open. For more information, phone Garden Club of Virginia/Richmond headquarters 804/644-7776.

Garden Week in Historic Lexington (Lexington). Tour of homes and gardens in the Lexington, Rockbridge County area. Phone 540/463-3777.

MAY

Jamestown Weekend (Jamestown, Colonial National Historical Park). Original Jamestown site. Commemorates arrival of first settlers in 1607; special tours and activities. Phone 757/229-1733.

JUNE

Natural Chimneys Jousting Tournament (Harrisonburg). Natural Chimneys Regional Park. America's oldest continuous sporting event, held annually since 1821. "Knights" armed with lances charge down an 80-yard track and attempt to spear three small rings suspended from posts. Phone 540/350-2510.

JULY

Red Cross Waterfront Festival (Alexandria). Commemorates Alexandria's maritime heritage. Features "tall ships," blessing of the fleet, river cruises, races, arts & crafts, exhibits, food, variety of music; fireworks. Phone 703/549-8300.

Pony Penning (Chincoteague). The "wild" ponies are rounded up on Assateague Island, then swim the inlet to Chincoteague, where foals are sold at auction before the ponies swim back to Assateague. Carnival amusements. For more information, phone Chincoteague Chamber of Commerce, 757/336-6161.

SEPTEMBER

Publick Times (Williamsburg). Colonial Williamsburg. Re-creation of colonial market days; contests, crafts, auctions, military encampment. Phone 757/220-7645 or 800/246-2099.

OCTOBER

Virginia State Fair (Richmond). Animal and 4-H contests, music, horse show, carnival. Phone 804/228-3200.

Blue Ridge Folklife Festival (Martinsville). Blue Ridge Farm Museum. Gospel, blues and string band music; traditional regional crafts; regional foods; quilt show, antique autos, steam & gas-powered farm equipment. Sports events include horse-pulling & log-skidding contests, coon-dog swimming and treeing contests. Phone 540/365-4415.

DECEMBER

Christmas Candlelight Tour (Fredericksburg). Historic homes open to the public; carriage rides; Christmas decorations and refreshments of the colonial period. Contact Visitor Center, 540/373-1776 or 800/678-4748.

Water-related activities, hiking, various other sports, picnicking and visitor centers, as well as camping, are available in many of these areas. State park facilities and services are operated on a seasonal basis. Parking for noncampers, $1.50-$2.50/car/day, Memorial Day-Labor Day. Admission to State Historical Parks $1.25; children $1. Swimming, boat rentals, cafes and concessions, Memorial Day-Labor Day; fees for activities. Pets are allowed in camping and cabins, but must be kept inside at night. At all other times pets must be on a 6-ft leash. Facilities for the disabled at many parks.

Tent and trailer campgrounds are available in 19 state parks generally from Mar-Nov; maximum stay is two weeks. $10.50/site/night, $19.25 at Seashore (up to 6 persons, 1 vehicle); electricity and water $15/site/night where available. Reservations may be made 180 days-1 wk in advance (see below for addresses). Seven parks offer housekeeping cabins (May-Sept). Douthat (see CLIFTON FORGE) has a guest lodge for 15. Reservations for campsites are accepted beginning late March. Campsite and cabin reservations may be made by phoning 800/933-PARK or 804/225-3867. Booklets with details on each park may be obtained from the Virginia Dept of Conservation & Recreation, 203 Governor St, Ste 302, Richmond 23219. A campground directory is available from Virginia Tourism Corporation, 901 E Byrd St, Richmond 23219; 804/786-4484.

SKI AREAS

Place Name	Listed Under
Bryce Resort	BASYE
Homestead Ski Area	HOT SPRINGS
Wintergreen Resort	CHARLOTTESVILLE

FISHING AND HUNTING

Saltwater fishing on ocean, bay, river or creek is a major sport. Virginia is blessed with many miles of shoreline: 120 miles on the Atlantic Ocean, 300 miles on Chesapeake Bay, and 1,300 miles of tidal shores. There is no closed season for saltwater fishing except striped bass. There are some species size and bag limits. No license is required to fish in ocean waters or seaside of the eastern shore, but a license is required to fish in the Chesapeake and tidal tributaries. Information concerning size limits and bag limits on saltwater game fish may be obtained from the Virginia Marine Resources Commission, PO Box 756, Newport News 23607; phone 804/247-2200 or 800/937-9247. The Commonwealth of Virginia sponsors an annual Saltwater Fishing Awards Program (see VIRGINIA BEACH), open to the public. Contact Virginia Saltwater Fishing Tournament, 968 S Oriole Dr, Ste 102, Virginia Beach 23451; 757/491-5160.

Freshwater fishing is excellent in many of the state's large reservoirs and rivers for such species as largemouth and smallmouth bass, landlocked striped bass, muskie and a wide variety of pan fish. Lake Anna, Smith Mt Lake, Lake Gaston, Lake Philpott, Lake Moomaw & Buggs Island Lake are nationally known for excellent bass and landlocked striped bass fishing. Nonresident license: $30; $30 additional for license for trout in designated stocked waters. Five-day license to fish state-wide, $6; other special fees. Fishing in a national forest requires an additional fishing/hunting stamp, $3.

Hunting for upland game and migratory waterfowl in season. Nonresident license: $60; three-day license: $30; bear, deer, turkey, $60 additional; nonresident muzzle-loader license, $25; nonresident special archery license to hunt during special archery season, $25. Hunting in a national forest requires an additional fishing/hunting stamp, $3. There is a 50¢ issuance fee for all licenses. For fishing and hunting regulations and information write Department of Game and Inland Fisheries, 4010 W Broad St, Richmond 23230 or phone 804/367-1000.

Driving Information

Safety belts are mandatory for all persons in front seat of vehicle. Children under 4 years must be in an approved safety seat anywhere in vehicle. For further information phone 804/367-6400 or 800/533-1892 (VA).

INTERSTATE HIGHWAY SYSTEM

The following alphabetical listing of Virginia towns in *Mobil Travel Guide* shows that these cities are within 10 miles of the indicated Interstate highways. A highway map should, however, be checked for the nearest exit.

Highway Number	Cities/Towns within 10 miles
Interstate 64	Ashland, Charlottesville, Chesapeake, Clifton Forge, Covington, Hampton, Jamestown, Lexington, Newport News, Norfolk, Portsmouth, Richmond, Staunton, Virginia Beach, Waynesboro, Williamsburg, Yorktown.
Interstate 66	Alexandria, Arlington County, Fairfax, Falls Church, Front Royal, Manassas, McLean.
Interstate 77	Wytheville.
Interstate 81	Abingdon, Blacksburg, Bristol, Front Royal, Harrisonburg, Lexington, Marion, Natural Bridge, New Market, Radford, Roanoke, Salem, Staunton, Strasburg, Winchester, Woodstock, Wytheville.
Interstate 85	Petersburg, South Hill.
Interstate 95	Alexandria, Arlington County, Ashland, Emporia, Fairfax, Falls Church, Fredericksburg, Hopewell, McLean, Mount Vernon, Petersburg, Richmond, Springfield, Triangle.

Additional Visitor Information

Recreational and tourist information, including travel guide, brochures and maps, is available from the Virginia Tourism Corporation, 901 E Byrd St, Richmond 23219; phone 804/786-4484 or 800/932-5827. Virginia Department of Transportation, 1401 E Broad St, Richmond 23219, phone 804/786-2838, offers an official state map.

There are 10 welcome information centers in Virginia at the following locations: the northern end of the state, on I-81 in Clear Brook, and on I-66 in Manassas; at the northeastern side, on I-95 in Fredericksburg; around the bay area on the eastern side, on US 13 in New Church; around the southerly border, on I-95 in Skippers, and on I-85 in Bracey; in the southwest part of the state, on I-81 in Bristol, and I-77 in Lambsburg; and on the western side, on I-64 in Covington, and on I-77 in Rocky Gap.

Abingdon (F-3)

(See also Bristol, Marion)

Settled ca 1770 **Pop** 7,003 **Elev** 2,069 ft **Area code** 540 **Zip** 24210
Information Washington County Chamber of Commerce, 179 E Main St; 540/628-8141.

Daniel Boone passed through this area in 1760 and dubbed it Wolf Hill after a pack of wolves from a nearby cave disturbed his dogs. Wolf Hill had long been a crossing for buffalo and Native Americans; Boone later used it for his own family's westward migration. Later, Black's Fort was built here, and the community adopted that name. Now known as Abingdon, this summer resort in the Virginia Highlands, just north of Tennessee, is the Washington County seat, Virginia's largest burley tobacco market and a livestock auction center.

What to See and Do

Grayson Highlands State Park. Within this 4,935-acre park are rugged peaks, some more than 5,000 ft; alpine scenery. Hiking, horse trails, picnicking, camping, visitor center, interpretive programs, pioneer life displays (June-Aug). Adj to Mount Rogers National Recreation Area (see MARION). (Daily) Standard fees. 35 mi SE on US 58. Phone 540/579-7092.

White's Mill. Old gristmill and general store, still in operation. (Daily) 3½ mi N via VA 692, on White's Mill Rd. Phone 540/676-0285. ¢

Annual Event

Virginia Highlands Festival. Exhibits, demonstrations of rustic handicrafts; plays, musical entertainment; historical reenactments; historic house tours, antique market. Last wk July-2nd wk Aug.

Seasonal Event

Barter Theatre. Main St, on US 11 off I-81, in former Town Hall. America's oldest, longest-running professional repertory theater. Founded during the Depression on the theory that residents would barter their abundant crops for first-rate professional entertainment. Designated State Theatre of Virginia in 1946. Phone 540/628-3991 or 800/368-3240. Barter Players perform nightly exc Mon, Apr-Oct. Children's theater mid-June-Aug.

Motels

★ **ALPINE.** *882 E Main St.* 540/628-3178; FAX 540/628-4247. 19 rms. S, D $38-$56; each addl $5; higher rates special events. Crib $2. TV; cable. Restaurant nearby. Ck-out 11 am. Business servs avail. View of mountains. Cr cds: A, DS, MC, V.

✔★ ★ **COMFORT INN.** *170 Jonesboro Road, jct I-81 exit 14, VA 140.* 540/676-2222; FAX 540/676-2222, ext. 307. 80 rms, 2 story. S, D $50-$150; each addl $6; under 18 free; higher rates special events. Crib free. TV; cable (premium), VCR avail. Pool. Complimentary continental bkfst. Ck-out noon. Business servs avail. Cr cds: A, C, D, DS, ER, JCB, MC, V.

★ ★ **EMPIRE.** *887 Empire Dr, I-81 exit 19.* 540/628-7131; FAX 540/628-7158. 105 rms, 2 story. S, D $36-$48; each addl $2; under 12 free; higher rates special events. Crib $5. TV; cable (premium). Restaurant 6 am-10 pm. Ck-out 11 am. Business servs avail. Balconies. Cr cds: A, MC, V.

Inn

★ ★ ★ **CAMBERLEY'S MARTHA WASHINGTON INN.** *150 W Main St.* 540/628-3161; FAX 540/628-7652; res: 800/555-8000. Built as a private home in 1832, this historic inn became a girls' school after the Civil War and an inn in the 1930s. Today it is filled with antiques that recall its vivid past. 61 rms. S, D $140-$150; each addl $10; suites $170-$350; under 12 free. Crib free. TV; cable (premium), VCR avail. Pool privileges. Dining rm (see THE DINING ROOM). Rm serv. Bar 5 pm-midnight. Ck-out 11 am, ck-in 3 pm. Meeting rms. Business servs avail. Luggage handling. Airport transportation. Tennis privileges. Golf privileges. Health club privileges. Lawn games. Bathrm phone in suites. Cr cds: A, C, D, DS, MC, V.

Restaurants

★ ★ **THE DINING ROOM.** *(See Camberley's Martha Washington Inn)* 540/628-3161. Hrs: 5-9 pm; Fri, Sat to 10 pm; Sun brunch 11 am-2 pm. Res accepted. Bar. Semi-a la carte: dinner $15-$25. Sun brunch $16.95. Specialties: Virginia trout, tenderloin of beef. Own baking. Cr cds: A, C, D, DS, MC, V.

★ ★ **THE TAVERN.** *222 E Main St.* 540/628-1118. Hrs: 11 am-10 pm. Closed Dec 25. Res accepted. Continental menu. Bar. Semi-a la carte: lunch $5.95-$6.95, dinner $12.95-$21.95. Specialties: Kassler rippchen, Wienerschnitzel, stuffed filet mignon. Two-story building (1779); colonial decor with fireplace in each of the three dining rms. Cr cds: A, MC, V.

Alexandria (C-8)

(See also Arlington County, Fairfax, Falls Church; also see District of Columbia)

Settled 1670 **Pop** 111,183 **Elev** 52 ft **Area code** 703
Information Convention/Visitors Association, 221 King St, 22314-3209; 703/838-4200.

A group of English and Scottish merchants established a tobacco warehouse at the junction of Hunting Creek and the "Potowmack" River in the 1740s. The little settlement prospered and 17 years later John West, Jr, surveyor, and his young assistant, George Washington, arrived and "laid off in streets and 84 half-acre lots" the town of Alexandria. Among the first buyers, on the July morning in 1749 when the lots were offered for public sale, were Lawrence Washington and his brother Augustus, William Ramsay, the Honorable William Fairfax and John Carlyle. Erecting handsome town houses, these gentlemen soon brought a lively and cosmopolitan air to Alexandria, with parties, balls and horse racing. It was also the hometown of George Mason and Robert E. Lee and home to George Washington.

In 1789, Virginia ceded Alexandria to the District of Columbia, but in 1846 the still-Southern-oriented citizens asked to return to the Old Dominion, which Congress allowed.

In the Civil War, Alexandria was cut off from the Confederacy when Union troops occupied the town to protect Potomac River navigation. Safe behind Union lines, the city escaped the dreadful destruction experienced by many other Southern towns. After the war, even with seven railroads centering here for transfer of freight, Alexandria declined as a center of commerce and was in trade doldrums until about 1914, when the Alexandria shipyards were reopened and the Naval Torpedo Station was built. Today it has developed into a trade, commerce, transportation and science center. More than 250 national associations are based here.

What to See and Do

Alexandria Black History Resource Center. Photographs, letters, documents and artifacts relate history of African-Americans in Alexandria. (Tues-Sat; closed hols) 638 N Alfred St. Phone 703/838-4356. **Donation.**

Fort Ward Museum and Historic Site. Restored Union Fort from Civil War; museum contains Civil War collection. Museum (daily exc Mon; closed Jan 1, Thanksgiving, Dec 25). Park, picnicking (daily to sunset). 4801 W Braddock Rd. Phone 703/838-4848. **Free.**

George Washington Masonic National Memorial. American Freemasons' memorial to their most prominent member, this 333-ft-high structure houses a large collection of objects that belonged to George Washington, which were collected by his family or the masonic lodge where he served as the first master. Guided tours explore a replica of Alexandria-Washington Lodge's first hall, a library, museum and an observation deck on the top floor. (Daily; closed Jan 1, Thanksgiving, Dec 25) 101 Callahan Dr, Shooter's Hill, W end of King St. Phone 703/683-2007. **Free.**

Gunston Hall (1755-1759). The 550-acre estate of George Mason, framer of the Constitution, father of the Bill of Rights. Restored 18th-century mansion with period furnishings; reconstructed outbuildings; museum; boxwood gardens on grounds; nature trail; picnic area; gift shop. (Daily; closed Jan 1, Thanksgiving, Dec 25) 18 mi S on US 1, then 4 mi E on VA 242 in Lorton at 10709 Gunston Rd. Phone 703/550-9220. ¢¢

Mount Vernon (see). 9 mi S on Mt Vernon Memorial Hwy.

Pohick Bay Regional Park. Near Gunston Hall. Activities in this 1,000-acre park include swimming (Memorial Day-Labor Day); 18-hole golf; miniature and Frisbee golf; boating (ramp, rentals; fee); camping (7-day limit; electric hookups avail; fee), picnicking. Park (all yr). Fee charged for activities. 6501 Pohick Bay Dr, in Lorton. Phone 703/339-6104. Admission per vehicle (nonresidents only) ¢¢

Pohick Episcopal Church (1774). The colonial parish church of Mt Vernon and Gunston Hall. Built under supervision of George Mason and George Washington; original walls; interior fully restored. (Daily) 9301 Richmond Hwy, 16 mi S on US 1 in Lorton. Phone 703/550-9449. **Free.**

Sightseeing boat tours. Tours of Alexandria waterfront. Contact the Potomac Riverboat Co; 703/684-0580. ¢¢¢

The Athenaeum. Greek-revival house (1851) built as bank, now houses Fine Arts Assn. Art shows, dance performances. (Wed-Sat & Sun afternoons; closed hols) 201 Prince St. Phone 703/548-0035.

Torpedo Factory Arts Center. Renovated munitions plant houses artists' center with more than 160 professional artists of various media. Studios, cooperative galleries, school. Also home of Alexandria Archaeology offices, lab, museum; phone 703/838-4399. (Daily; closed most major hols) 105 N Union St. Phone 703/838-4565. **Free.**

✖ **Walking tour of historic sites.**

Start at Visitors Center in **Ramsay House** (ca 1725). Oldest house in Alexandria and later used as a tavern, grocery store and cigar factory. Here you can obtain special events information and a free visitors guide. You may also purchase "block tickets" here, good for reduced admission to five of the city's historic properties. Video shown with translations available in 18 languages. Guided walking tours, conducted by costumed guides, depart from here (spring-fall, weather permitting). The Bureau also issues free parking permits, tour and highway maps, hotel, dining and shopping information. (Daily; closed Jan 1, Thanksgiving, Dec 25) 221 King St, at Fairfax St. Phone 703/838-4200. 1 blk N on Fairfax St is

Carlyle House (1753). This stately stone mansion, built in Palladian style, was the site of a 1755 meeting between Gen Edward Braddock and five British colonial governors to plan the early campaigns of the French and Indian War. (Daily exc Mon; closed Jan 1, Thanksgiving, Dec 24, 25) 121 N Fairfax St. Phone 703/549-2997. ¢¢ 1½ blks S on Fairfax St is

Stabler-Leadbeater Apothecary Museum (1792). Largest collection of apothecary glass in its original setting in the country; more than 1,000 apothecary bottles. Original building is now a museum of early pharmacy; collection of old prescriptions, patent medicines, scales, other 18th-century pharmacy items. George Washington, Robert E. Lee and John Calhoun were regular customers. (Daily; closed Jan 1, Thanksgiving, Dec 25) 105 S Fairfax St. Phone 703/836-3713. ¢ 2 blks S on Fairfax St is

Old Presbyterian Meeting House (1774). Tomb of the unknown soldier of the Revolution is in churchyard. (Mon-Fri) 321 S Fairfax St. Phone 703/549-6670. **Free.** ½ blk N, then 3 blks W on Duke St is

Lafayette House. Fine example of Federal architecture. House was loaned to Lafayette for his last visit to America (1825). (Private) 301 St Asaph St. Walk 2 blks N to Prince St, then left on Prince St to SW corner of Prince & Washington Sts to

The Lyceum. Museum, exhibitions; Virginia travel information (limited). (Daily; closed Jan 1, Thanksgiving, Dec 25) 201 S Washington St. Phone 703/838-4994. **Free.** Go 2 blks N on Washington St to

Christ Church (1773). Washington and Robert E. Lee were pewholders. Fine Palladian window; interior balcony; wrought-brass and crystal chandelier brought from England. Structure is extensively restored but little changed since it was built. Exhibit, gift shop at Columbus St entrance. (Mon-Sat, also Sun afternoons; closed Jan 1, Labor Day,

Thanksgiving, Dec 25; also for weddings, funerals) 118 N Washington St. Phone 703/549-1450. **Donation.** 1 blk E on Cameron St is

Home of General Henry (Light Horse Harry) Lee. (Private) 611 Cameron St. 3 blks N, 1 blk W, then left on Washington St is

Lee-Fendall House (1785). Built by Phillip Richard Fendall and lived in by Lee family for 118 yrs. Both George Washington and Revolutionary War hero "Light Horse Harry" Lee were frequent visitors to the house. Remodeled in 1850, the house is furnished with Lee family belongings. (Daily exc Mon, wkend hrs may vary; closed major hols) 614 Oronoco St. Phone 703/548-1789. ¢¢ Proceed N, turn right on Oronoco St, ½ blk E to

Boyhood Home of Robert E. Lee. Federal-style architecture; antique furnishings and paintings. Famous guests included Washington and Lafayette. (Daily) 607 Oronoco St. Phone 703/548-8454. ¢¢ 3 blks E, then 3 blks S on Royal St is

Gadsby's Tavern Museum (1770, 1792). Famous hostelry, frequented by Washington and other patriots (see RESTAURANTS). Combines two 18th-century buildings; interesting architecture. (Daily exc Mon; closed major hols) 134 N Royal St. Phone 703/838-4242. ¢¢

Doorways to Old Virginia. Offers guided walking tours of historic district. (Apr-Oct, daily) Departs from Ramsay House. Phone 703/548-0100. ¢¢

Annual Events

George Washington Birthday Celebrations. Events include race, Revolutionary War reenactment; climaxed by the birthday parade on federal holiday. Feb.

House tours. Fine colonial and Federal-style houses are opened to the public: Cook's tour of kitchens (early Apr); Historic Garden Week (Apr); Hospital Auxiliary Tour of Historic Houses (Sept); Scottish Christmas Walk (Dec). Tickets, addl information at Alexandria Convention/Visitors Association; 703/838-4200.

Red Cross Waterfront Festival. Commemorates Alexandria's maritime heritage. Features "tall ships," blessing of the fleet, river cruises, races, arts & crafts, exhibits, food, variety of music; fireworks. Phone 703/549-8300. July.

Virginia Scottish Games. Athletic competition, Highland dance and music, antique cars, displays, food. Phone 703/838-4200. 4th wkend July.

Scottish Christmas Walk. Parade, house tour, concerts, greens and heather sales, dinner dance to emphasize city's Scottish origins. 1st Sat Dec.

Motels

★ ★ **BEST WESTERN MOUNT VERNON.** 8751 Richmond Hwy (22309). 703/360-1300; FAX 703/779-7713. 84 rms, 5 story. Mar-Oct: S $72-$77; D $77-$82; each addl $5; suites $100-$110; under 18 free; lower rates rest of yr. Crib free. TV; cable (premium). Complimentary continental bkfst. Restaurant nearby. Ck-out 11 am. Meeting rm. Business servs avail. Valet serv. Exercise equipt; weight machine, treadmill. Some refrigerators; microwaves avail. Cr cds: A, C, D, DS, ER, JCB, MC, V.

⊡ ✦ ≋ ⊠ SC

★ ★ **BEST WESTERN OLD COLONY INN.** 615 1st St (22314), near National Airport. 703/739-2222; FAX 703/549-2568. 151 rms, 2 story. Apr-June: S $89; D $99; each addl $10; kits. $99-$109; under 18 free; wkend, hol rates; lower rates rest of yr. Crib free. Pet accepted; $50 deposit & $10/day. TV; cable (premium). Pool; lifeguard. Complimentary continental bkfst. Restaurant adj 6:30 am-10 pm. Ck-out noon. Meeting rms. Business servs avail. In-rm modem link. Sundries. Valet serv. Free airport transportation. Health club privileges. Cr cds: A, C, D, DS, MC, V.

⊡ ✦ ≋ ✈ ≋ ⊠ SC

✦★ ★ **COMFORT INN-MT VERNON.** 7212 Richmond Hwy (US 1) (22306). 703/765-9000; FAX 703/765-2325. 92 rms, 2 story. S $50-$65; D $55-$75; each addl $7; under 17 free; wkly, wkend rates. Crib free. Pet accepted, some restrictions. TV; cable (premium), VCR avail (movies $5).

Pool; lifeguard. Complimentary continental bkfst. Restaurant nearby. Ck-out noon. Meeting rm. Business servs avail. In-rm modem link. Valet serv. Refrigerators, microwaves avail. Cr cds: A, C, D, DS, MC, V.

[D] [⌘] [≋] [⅀] [≽] [SC]

★ **ECONO LODGE OLD TOWN.** *700 N Washington St (22314). 703/836-5100; FAX 703/519-7015.* 39 rms, 2 story. S $54.95; D $64.95; each addl $5; under 18 free. Crib free. Pet accepted, some restrictions. TV; cable. Restaurant nearby. Ck-out 11 am. Business servs avail. Free airport transportation. Microwaves avail. Cr cds: A, D, DS, MC, V.

[⌘] [≽] [⅀] [SC]

★★ **HAMPTON INN.** *4800 Leesburg Pike (22302). 703/671-4800; FAX 703/671-2442.* 130 rms, 4 story. S $89; D $95-$110. Crib free. TV; cable (premium). Pool. Complimentary continental bkfst. Ck-out noon. Business servs avail. In-rm modem link. Valet serv. Exercise equipt; treadmill, stair machines. Cr cds: A, C, D, DS, MC, V.

[D] [≋] [⅄] [≽] [⅀] [SC]

✔★ **RED ROOF INN.** *5975 Richmond Hwy (US 1) (22303). 703/960-5200; FAX 703/960-5209.* Web www.redroofinn.com. 115 rms, 3 story. Apr-Oct: S, D $63.99-$75.99; each addl $7; under 18 free; higher rates special events; lower rates rest of yr. Crib free. Pet accepted, some restrictions. TV; cable (premium). Complimentary coffee in lobby. Restaurant nearby. Ck-out noon. Business servs avail. In-rm modem link. Coin lndry. Valet serv. Cr cds: A, C, D, DS, MC, V.

[D] [⌘] [≋] [⅀] [SC]

✔★★ **TRAVELERS.** *5916 Richmond Hwy (US 1) (22303). 703/329-1310; FAX 703/960-9211; res: 800/368-7378.* 30 rms. S $52.99-$65.99; D $59.99-$73.99; each addl $5. Crib free. TV; cable (premium). Pool; lifeguard. Complimentary coffee. Restaurant opp 6 am-11 pm. Ck-out 11 am. Business servs avail. Cr cds: A, C, D, DS, MC, V.

[D] [≋] [⅀] [≽] [SC]

Motor Hotels

★ **COMFORT INN-LANDMARK.** *6254 Duke St (22312). 703/642-3422; FAX 703/642-1354.* 148 rms, 7 story. Mid-Mar-early Sept: S, D $49-$88.95; under 18 free; lower rates rest of yr. Crib free. TV; cable (premium). Pool; lifeguard. Complimentary continental bkfst. Restaurant open 24 hrs. Ck-out noon. Meeting rms. Business servs avail. In-rm modem link. Valet serv. Sundries. Cr cds: A, C, D, DS, ER, JCB, MC, V.

[D] [≋] [⅀] [≽] [SC]

★★ **COURTYARD BY MARRIOTT.** *2700 Eisenhower Ave (22314). 703/329-2323; FAX 703/329-6853.* 176 rms, 8 story. Apr-May, Oct-Nov: S $109; D $119; each addl $10; suites $150; under 12 free; wkends (2-day min); higher rates Cherry Blossom Festival; lower rates rest of yr. Crib free. TV; cable (premium). Complimentary coffee in rms. Restaurant 6:30-10 am, 5-10 pm; Sat, Sun 7-11 am, 5-10 pm. Rm serv from 5 pm. Bar 4 pm-midnight. Ck-out noon. Meeting rms. Business servs avail. Valet serv. Sundries. Free RR station transportation. Exercise equipt; bicycle, stair machine, whirlpool. Some refrigerators, microwaves. Some balconies. Cr cds: A, C, D, DS, MC, V.

[D] [⅄] [⅀] [≽] [SC]

★★ **EXECUTIVE CLUB SUITES.** *610 Bashford Ln (22314). 703/739-2582; FAX 703/548-0266; res: 800/535-2582.* 78 kit. suites, 3 story. No elvtr. S, D $179-$199; wkend, hol rates. Crib free. Pet accepted, some restrictions. TV; cable (premium). Pool; lifeguard. Complimentary continental bkfst. Complimentary coffee in rms. Restaurant nearby. Ck-out noon. Coin lndry. Meeting rms. Business center. In-rm modem link. Valet serv. Sundries. Free airport transportation. Exercise equipt; weight machine, treadmill, sauna. Microwaves. Picnic tables. Cr cds: A, C, D, DS, ER, MC, V.

[⌘] [≋] [⅄] [≽] [⅀] [≽]

★★★ **HOLIDAY INN HOTEL AND SUITES-HISTORIC DISTRICT.** *625 1st St (22314), in Old Town Alexandria. 703/548-6300; FAX*

703/548-8032. 178 rms, 4 story. S, D $139; each addl $10; suites $159-$199; under 18 free; wkend rates. Crib free. TV; cable (premium). Indoor/outdoor pool; whirlpool. Restaurant 6:30 am-10 pm. Bar 11 am-midnight; entertainment. Ck-out noon. Coin lndry. Meeting rm. Business center. In-rm modem link. Bellhops. Free airport transportation. Exercise rm; instructor, weight machines, bicycles. Refrigerator, wet bar in suites; microwaves avail. Balconies. Cr cds: A, C, D, DS, JCB, MC, V.

[D] [≋] [⅄] [≽] [⅀] [SC] [≽]

★★ **HOMEWOOD SUITES.** *4850 Leesburg Pike (22302). 703/671-6500; FAX 703/671-9322.* 105 rms, 5 story. S $125-$135, D $131-$150. Crib free. TV; cable (premium). Pool; whirlpool. Complimentary continental bkfst. Restaurant nearby. Ck-out noon. Meeting rms. Business center. Valet serv. Coin lndry. Exercise equipt; bicycles, treadmill. Game rm. Gift shop. Cr cds: A, C, D, DS, MC, V.

[D] [≋] [⅄] [≽] [⅀] [≽]

★★★ **HOWARD JOHNSON-OLDE TOWNE.** *5821 Richmond Hwy (US 1) (22303). 703/329-1400; FAX 703/329-1424.* E-mail 74664.2275@compuserv. 156 rms, 7 story. Mar-June: S $55-$91; D $65-$99; each addl $10; under 18 free; lower rates rest of yr. Crib free. Pet accepted, some restrictions. TV; cable (premium), VCR avail. Indoor pool. Restaurant 6 am-10 pm; Fri, Sat to 11 pm. Rm serv. Bar. Ck-out noon. Meeting rms. Business servs avail. In-rm modem link. Valet serv. Gift shop. Beauty shop. Free airport transportation. Exercise equipt; weights, bicycles, sauna. Some in-rm whirlpools; microwaves avail. Cr cds: A, C, D, DS, JCB, MC, V.

[D] [⌘] [≋] [⅄] [≽] [⅀] [≽] [SC]

Hotels

★★ **DOUBLETREE GUEST SUITES.** *100 S Reynolds St (22304). 703/370-9600; FAX 703/370-0467.* 225 kit. suites, 9 story. Mid-Mar-Oct: S $79-$140; D $89-$180; each addl $20; under 18 free; wkend rates; lower rates rest of yr. Crib free. Pet accepted; $10/day, TV; cable. Pool; lifeguard. Complimentary continental bkfst. Restaurant 6:30-9:30 am, 11 am-3 pm, 5-10 pm. Bar from 4 pm. Ck-out noon. Coin lndry. Meeting rms. Business center. In-rm modem link. Exercise equipt; weight machine, treadmills. Health club privileges. Microwaves. Some balconies. Cr cds: A, C, D, DS, MC, V.

[D] [⌘] [≋] [⅄] [≽] [⅀] [≽]

★★★ **HOLIDAY INN SELECT OLD TOWN.** *480 King St (22314). 703/549-6080; FAX 703/684-6508.* E-mail othismta@erols.com; web www.hiselect.com. 227 rms, 6 story. S $120-$170; D $135-$190; each addl $20; suites $225-$300; under 18 free; wkend rates. Crib free. Pet accepted, some restrictions. Garage $7. TV; cable (premium). Indoor pool; lifeguard. Complimentary continental bkfst (Mon-Fri). Complimentary coffee in rms. Restaurant 6:30 am-11 pm. Bars 11 am-midnight. Ck-out noon. Coin lndry. Meeting rms. Business center. In-rm modem link. Concierge. Gift shop. Barber, beauty shop. Free airport transportation. Exercise equipt; bicycles, stair machines, sauna. Refrigerators, minibars, microwaves avail. Some balconies. Cr cds: A, C, D, DS, ER, JCB, MC, V.

[D] [⌘] [≋] [⅄] [≽] [⅀] [SC] [≽]

★★ **HOLIDAY INN TELEGRAPH ROAD.** *2460 Eisenhower Ave (22314). 703/960-3400; FAX 703/329-0953.* E-mail moli@erols.com. 201 rms, 10 story. Mar-early July, mid-Sept-mid-Nov: S $94-$120; D $104-$130; suite $250; each addl $10; under 18 free; wkend, hol rates; lower rates rest of yr. Crib free. TV; cable (premium). Indoor pool. Restaurant 6:30 am-10 pm. Bar 11 am-midnight; entertainment Fri, Sat. Ck-out noon. Coin lndry. Meeting rms. Business servs avail. In-rm modem link. Gift shop. Free airport, RR station transportation. Exercise equipt; weight machine, bicycles. Game rm. Refrigerators avail. Cr cds: A, C, D, DS, JCB, MC, V.

[D] [≋] [⅄] [≽] [⅀] [SC]

★★★ **RADISSON PLAZA AT MARK CENTER.** *5000 Seminary Rd (22311), 1 blk W of I-395 exit 4. 703/845-1010; FAX 703/845-7662.* Web www.radisson.com. 495 rms, 30 story. S, D $125-$185; each addl $20; suites $250-$575; under 18 free; wkly rates; wkend packages. Crib free. Covered parking $14, valet parking $10. TV; cable (premium), VCR avail (free movies). Indoor/outdoor pool; whirlpool. Coffee in rm. Restaurant 6 am-11 pm. Bars 11-1 am; entertainment. Ck-out noon. Convention facilities. Business center. In-rm modem link. Concierge. Gift shop. Barber, beauty shop. Free airport transportation. Tennis. Exercise equipt; weights, bicycles, sauna. Game rm. Refrigerators; some bathrm phones. Whirlpool in some suites. Located on 50 wooded acres with nature preserve. Luxury level. Cr cds: A, C, D, DS, ER, JCB, MC, V.

⊡ 🏖 🏊 🏋 🚶 🎿 🐾 SC ⛷

★ ★ **RAMADA PLAZA HOTEL-OLD TOWN.** *901 N Fairfax St (22314).* 703/683-6000; FAX 703/683-7597. 258 rms, 12 story. S, D $125-$150; each addl $10; under 18 free; wkend rates. Crib free. Pet accepted, some restrictions. TV; cable (premium). Pool; lifeguard. Coffee in rms. Restaurant 6 am-10 pm. Bar 11-1 am. Ck-out 1 pm. Business servs avail. In-rm modem link. Gift shop. Free airport transportation. Health club privileges. Refrigerators, microwaves avail. Cr cds: A, C, D, DS, MC, V.

⊡ 🏖 🏊 🐾 SC

★ ★ ★ **SHERATON SUITES.** *801 N St Asaph St (22314).* 703/836-4700; FAX 703/548-4514. Web www.ittsheraton.com. 247 suites, 10 story. Apr-May: S, D $170; under 12 free; wkend, hol rates; lower rates rest of yr. Crib free. Pet accepted. Garage parking $8. TV; cable (premium). Indoor pool; whirlpool, lifeguard. Complimentary coffee in rms. Restaurant 6:30 am-10 pm; wkends from 7 am. Bar. Ck-out 1 pm. Guest lndry. Meeting rms. Business servs avail. In-rm modem link. Gift shop. Free airport transportation. Exercise equipt; weight machine, treadmill. Health club privileges. Refrigerators; microwaves avail. Cr cds: A, C, D, DS, ER, JCB, MC, V.

⊡ 🏖 🏊 🏋 🐾 SC

Inn

★ ★ ★ **MORRISON HOUSE.** *116 S Alfred St (22314), downtown.* 703/838-8000; FAX 703/684-6283; res: 800/367-0800. Web www.morrisonhouse.com. This elegant red brick building is furnished in the style of the Federal period throughout. Public rooms include the mahogany-paneled library and a parlor with fireplace. Many of the individually decorated rooms have four-poster beds and fireplaces. 45 rms, 5 story. S, D $195-$295; suites $295-$495; wkend rates. Crib free. Covered parking $10. TV; cable (premium), VCR avail (movies $5). Dining rm (see ELYSIUM). Afternoon tea 3-5 pm. Rm serv 24 hrs. Bar 11:30 am-11 pm; entertainment Thurs-Sat. Ck-out noon, ck-in after 3 pm. Meeting rms. Business servs avail. In-rm modem link. Butlers. Health club privileges. Bathrm phones. Cr cds: A, C, D, MC, V.

⊡ 🐾 🐾

Restaurants

✔★ **THE ALAMO.** *100 King St (22314), in Old Town Alexandria, bottom of King & Union St.* 703/739-0555. E-mail fishmkt@pop.dn.net. Hrs: 11:15-2 am. Closed Thanksgiving, Dec 25. Res accepted; required Fri, Sat. Nouvelle Southwestern menu. Bar. Semi-a la carte: lunch $4.95-$8.95, dinner $8.95-$14.95. Specializes in Texas rack of ribs, steak, chicken. Entertainment. In 1871 Corn Exchange Building; luxurious, gas-lighted interior with leaded-glass windows. Cr cds: A, C, D, MC, V.

⊡ 🍽

★ ★ **BILBO BAGGINS.** *208 Queen St (22314), in Old Town Alexandria.* 703/683-0300. Hrs: 11:30 am-10:30 pm; Sun 11 am-9:30 pm; early-bird dinner Mon-Thurs 5:30-6 pm; Sun brunch 11 am-2:30 pm. Closed Dec 25. Res accepted. Continental menu. Bar. Semi-a la carte: lunch $6.95-$9.95, dinner $10.95-$17.95. Sun brunch $7.95-$9.95. Specialties: Bilbo's bread, Chicken Queen Street, Bilbo's salad. Own bread, desserts. Upstairs in 1898 structure; stained glass, skylights. Cr cds: A, C, D, DS, MC, V.

⊡

★ ★ **BLUE POINT GRILL.** *600 Franklin St (22314), in Old Town Alexandria.* 703/739-0404. Hrs: 11:30 am-10 pm; Fri, Sat to 11 pm; Sun 11 am-10 pm; Sun brunch to 2:30 pm. Closed Dec 25. Res accepted. A la carte entrees: lunch $5-$15, dinner $13.95-$20.95. Sun brunch $8.50-$11.95. Specializes in fresh seafood. Parking. Outdoor dining. Cafe atmosphere; adj to gourmet Sutton Place Market. Cr cds: A, DS, MC, V.

⊡

✔★ ★ **CALVERT GRILLE.** *3106 Mt Vernon Ave (22305).* 703/836-8425. E-mail calgrill@ids2.idsonline.com. Hrs: 11:30-12:30 am; Fri to 2 am; Sat from 9:30 am; Sun 9:30 am-9 pm; Sat, Sun brunch to 2 pm. Closed Thanksgiving, Dec 25. Bar. Semi-a la carte: bkfst $2.95-$5.75, lunch $3.95-$8.95, dinner $3.95-$11.95. Sat, Sun brunch $3.95-$8.50. Child's meals. Specializes in baby back ribs, crab cakes, regional dishes. Family-friendly atmosphere with kids' toy rm and drawing wall. Cr cds: A, DS, MC, V.

⊡ 🍽

★ ★ ★ **CHART HOUSE.** *1 Cameron St (22314).* 703/684-5080. Hrs: 5-10 pm; Fri, Sat to 11 pm; Sun 11 am-2:30 pm, 4-9 pm. Closed Dec 25. Res accepted; required Fri-Sun. Contemporary Amer menu. Bar. Semi-a la carte: dinner $14.95-$31.95. Sun brunch $16.95-$18.95. Child's meals. Specializes in grilled fresh seafood, aged beef, pasta. Views of the Capitol, Potomac River. Cr cds: A, C, D, DS, MC, V.

⊡ 🍽

★ ★ ★ **CHEZ ANDRÉE.** *10 E Glebe Rd (22305).* 703/836-1404. Hrs: 11 am-2:30 pm, 5-9:30 pm; Sat from 5 pm. Closed Sun; major hols. Res accepted; required Fri, Sat. French menu. Serv bar. Semi-a la carte: lunch $8.95-$15.50, dinner $13.95-$21.95. Prix fixe (Mon, Tues): dinner $24.95. Specialties: salmon Hollandaise, coquilles St-Jacques, duck à l'orange. Parking. French country decor. Family-owned. Cr cds: A, C, D, MC, V.

🍽

✔★ ★ **COPELAND'S OF NEW ORLEANS.** *4300 King St (22302).* 703/671-7997. Hrs: 11 am-10 pm; Fri, Sat to 11 pm; Sun brunch to 3 pm. Closed Thanksgiving, Dec 25. Cajun, Creole, American menu. Bar. Semi-a la carte: lunch $5.45-$7.95, dinner $5.95-$15.95. Sun brunch $7.95-$10.95. Child's meals. Specializes in blackened redfish, seafood. Parking. Outdoor dining. Cr cds: A, C, D, DS, MC, V.

⊡ 🍽

✔★ ★ **EAST WIND.** *809 King St (22314).* 703/836-1515. Hrs: 11:30 am-2:30 pm, 5:30-10 pm; Fri to 10:30 pm; Sat 5:30-10:30 pm; Sun 5:30-9:30 pm. Closed major hols. Res accepted. Vietnamese menu. Bar. Semi-a la carte: lunch $5.95-$7.95, dinner $7.95-$15.50. Specialties: cha gio, charbroiled shrimp & scallops. Own desserts. Original Vietnamese paintings & panels. Cr cds: A, C, D, DS, MC, V.

⊡ 🍽

✔★ ★ **ECCO CAFE.** *220 N Lee St (22314), in Old Town.* 703/684-0321. Web www.eccocafe.com. Hrs: 11 am-11 pm; Mon to 10 pm; Fri, Sat to midnight; Sun 4-10 pm; Sun brunch 11:30 am-3 pm. Closed Jan 1, Thanksgiving, Dec 25. Res accepted Sun-Thurs. Italian, Amer menu. Bar. A la carte entrees: lunch $6.95-$9.95, dinner $10.95-$15.95. Sun brunch $7.95-$11.95. Own baking, pasta. Jazz Sun. In restored 1890s warehouse bldg; eclectic decor. Cr cds: A, C, D, DS, MC, V.

⊡ 🍽 ♥

★ ★ **ELYSIUM.** *(See Morrison House Inn)* 703/838-8000. Web www.morrisonhouse.com. Hrs: 6-10 pm; Fri, Sat to 11 pm; Sun brunch noon-2:30 pm. Closed Mon; Jan 1. Res required Fri, Sat. Bar 11:30 am-11 pm. Wine list. Prix fixe: dinner $35-$55; Sun brunch $25. Specializes in new American cuisine. Formal Federal-period dining rm. Cr cds: A, C, D, MC, V.

⊡

✔★ **FACCIA LUNA.** *823 S Washington St (22314), in Old Town.* 703/838-5998. Hrs: 11:30 am-11 pm; Fri, Sat to midnight; Sun from noon. Closed some major hols. Italian menu. Bar. Semi-a la carte: lunch

$3.50-$6, dinner $7-$12. Child's meals. Specializes in pizza, fresh pasta, grinders. Own pasta. Outdoor dining. Contemporary American pizzeria with woodburning oven. Totally nonsmoking. No cr cds accepted.

🅳

★ ★ **FISH MARKET.** 105 King St (22314), at N Union St, in Old Town Alexandria. 703/836-5676. E-mail fishmkt@pop.dn.net. Hrs: 11:15-2 am; Sun to midnight. Closed Thanksgiving, Dec 25. Bar. Semi-a la carte: lunch $3.95-$12.95, dinner $4.25-$16.25. Specializes in Chesapeake Bay style seafood. Acoustic guitar Thurs-Sun. Outdoor dining. In restored 18th-century warehouse built of bricks carried to New World as ballast in ship's hold; nautical decor. Cr cds: A, C, D, MC, V.

🅳 ⊡

★ ★ **GADSBY'S TAVERN.** 138 N Royal St (22314), across from Old City Hall. 703/548-1288. Hrs: 11:30 am-3 pm, 5:30-10 pm; Sun brunch 11 am-3 pm. Closed Jan 1, Dec 24, 25. Res accepted; required Fri, Sat. Semi-a la carte: lunch $6.95-$8.95, dinner $14.95-$22.95. Sun brunch $6.75-$9.95. Child's meals. Specialties: Sally Lunn bread, George Washington's favorite duck, English trifle. Strolling minstrels. Outdoor dining. Built 1792; Georgian architecture; colonial decor & costumes. Gadsby's Tavern Museum adj. Totally nonsmoking. Cr cds: C, D, DS, MC, V.

🅳

✔★ ★ ★ **GERANIO.** 722 King St (22314), in Old Town Alexandria. 703/548-0088. Hrs: 11:30 am-2:30 pm, 6-10:30 pm; Sat from 6 pm; Sun 5:30-9:30 pm. Closed some major hols. Res accepted; required Fri, Sat. Italian menu. Serv bar. Semi-a la carte: lunch $5.95-$10.25, dinner $11.75-$15.50. Specializes in veal, seafood, pasta. Rustic Mediterranean decor. Fireplace, ceramic chandeliers. Cr cds: A, C, D, MC, V.

🅳 ⊡

★ ★ **IL PORTO.** 121 King St (22314), at N Lee St, in Old Town Alexandria. 703/836-8833. Hrs: 11:15 am-midnight. Res accepted. Northern Italian menu. Bar from 6 pm. Semi-a la carte: lunch $3.50-$8.95, dinner $9-$16.75. Child's meals. Specialties: pasta de Venezia, chicken Angelica. Extensive dessert menu. In 18th-century building originally a marine warehouse. Cr cds: A, C, D, MC, V.

⊡

★ ★ **LA BERGERIE.** 218 N Lee St (22314), 2nd floor of Crilley Warehouse, in Old Town Alexandria. 703/683-1007. Hrs: 11:30 am-2:30 pm, 5:30-10:30 pm; Fri, Sat to 11 pm. Closed Sun exc Mother's Day; major hols. Res accepted; required Fri, Sat. French, Amer menu. Serv bar. Semi-a la carte: lunch $10.95-$13.25, dinner $14.95-$23.95. Specializes in fresh seafood. Own pastries. Restored 1890s warehouse. Cr cds: A, C, D, DS, MC, V.

🅳 ⊡

★ ★ **LANDINI BROTHERS.** 115 King St (22314), in Old Town Alexandria. 703/836-8404. Hrs: 11:30 am-11 pm; Sun 3-10 pm. Closed major hols. Res accepted; required Fri, Sat. Italian menu. Bar. A la carte entrees: lunch $9-$13, dinner $13.50-$24.95. Specializes in veal, pasta, fresh fish. 1790s building. Cr cds: A, C, D, DS, MC, V.

🅳 ⊡

★ ★ **LE GAULOIS.** 1106 King St (22314), in Old Town Alexandria. 703/739-9494. Hrs: 11:30 am-10:30 pm; Fri, Sat to 11 pm. Closed Sun; major hols. Res accepted. French menu. Serv Bar. A la carte entrees: lunch $4.75-$12.50, dinner $5.75-$18.50. Specialty: pot au feu gaulois. Outdoor dining. French provincial decor; fireplace. Outdoor dining. Cr cds: A, C, D, DS, MC, V.

🅳 ⊡

★ ★ **LE REFUGE.** 127 N Washington St (22314), in Old Town Alexandria. 703/548-4661. Hrs: 11:30 am-2:30 pm, 5:30-10 pm. Closed Sun; some major hols. Res accepted; required Fri, Sat. French menu. Serv bar. Semi-a la carte: lunch $6.95-$11.95, dinner $13.95-$19.95. Complete meals: lunch $9.95. Specialties: bouillabaisse, salmon en croûte, veal Normande. Country French decor. Cr cds: A, C, D, DS, MC, V.

⊡

✔★ **MANGO MIKE'S.** 4111 Duke St (22304), 2 mi W on VA 236. 703/823-1166. Hrs: 11 am-10 pm; Thurs-Sat to 11 pm; Sun from 10 am; Sun brunch to 2 pm. Closed July 4, Thanksgiving, Dec 25. Caribbean menu. Bar to 2 am. Semi-a la carte: lunch $4.95-$10.95, dinner $9.95-$13.95. Sun brunch $9.95. Child's meals. Specialties: jerked chicken, mango barbecue ribs. Own desserts. Caribbean drummer Sun. Outdoor dining. Informal Caribbean atmosphere. Cr cds: A, C, D, DS, MC, V.

⊡

✔★ ★ **MONROE'S.** 1603 Commonwealth Ave (22301). 703/548-5792. Hrs: 5-10 pm; Fri, Sat to 11 pm; Sun 9:30 am-2 pm (brunch), 5-9 pm. Closed Jan 1, Dec 24, 25. Res accepted; required Fri, Sat dinner. Italian menu. Bar. Semi-a la carte: dinner $8.50-$16.95. Sun brunch $3.95-$6.95. Child's meals. Specialties: tonno alla livornese, bowtie pasta with crab meat. Own pastries. Outdoor dining. Contemporary trattoria with large murals, woodburning grill. Totally nonsmoking. Cr cds: A, DS, MC, V.

🅳

✔★ ★ **RT'S.** 3804 Mt Vernon Ave (22305). 703/684-6010. Hrs: 11 am-10:30 pm; Fri, Sat to 11 pm; Sun 4-9 pm. Closed some major hols. Res accepted. Bar. Semi-a la carte: lunch $5.95-$13.95, dinner $12.95-$19.95. Child's meals. Specialties: Jack Daniels shrimp, Acadian peppered shrimp, she-crab soup. Cr cds: A, C, D, DS, MC, V.

★ ★ **SANTA FE EAST.** 110 S Pitt St (22314). 703/548-6900. Hrs: 11:30 am-10 pm; Fri, Sat to 11 pm; Sun 11 am-10 pm. Closed July 4, Thanksgiving, Dec 25. Res accepted; required Fri, Sat. Southwestern menu. Bar. A la carte entrees: lunch $5.95-$9.95, dinner $8.95-$18.75. Sun brunch $5.25-$7.25. Specialties: chipotle chicken, enchilada Santa Fe, salmon a la plancha. Outdoor dining. Native American art, artifacts. Fountain in courtyard. Fireplaces. In historic (1790) building. Cr cds: A, C, D, MC, V.

🅳

★ ★ **SCOTLAND YARD.** 728 King St (22314), in Old Town Alexandria. 703/683-1742. Hrs: 6-8 pm. Closed Mon; Thanksgiving. Res accepted; required Fri, Sat. Scottish menu. Serv bar. A la carte entrees: dinner $12.95-$18.95. Complete meal: dinner $28.95. Specializes in salmon, lamb, venison. Old Scottish inn (built 1792); tin ceiling, fireplace. Fine array of single malt whiskeys. Totally nonsmoking. Cr cds: A, MC, V.

🅳

★ ★ **SEAPORT INN.** 6 King St (22314). 703/549-2341. Hrs: 11:30 am-10 pm; Fri to 11 pm; Sat 11 am-11 pm; Sun brunch to 3 pm. Closed Dec 25. Res accepted; required Fri, Sat. Bar 11:30 am-midnight; Fri, Sat to 2 am. Semi-a la carte: lunch $5.75-$10.95, dinner $11.95-$26.95. Sun brunch $5.75-$8.95. Child's meals. Specialties: shrimp & scallops in wine sauce, crab cakes, bouillabaisse. Entertainment. Fireplaces. In 1765 warehouse originally owned by George Washington's aide-de-camp; overlooks Potomac River. Cr cds: A, C, D, MC, V.

🅳 ⊡

✔★ **SOUTH AUSTIN GRILL.** 801 King St (22134), in Old Town. 703/684-8969. Web www.austingrill.com. Hrs: 11:30 am-11 pm; Mon to 10 pm; Fri to midnight; Sat 11 am-midnight; Sun 11 am-10 pm; Sat, Sun brunch to 3 pm. Closed Thanksgiving, Dec 24, 25. Tex-Mex menu. Bar. Semi-a la carte: lunch, dinner $6.95-$13.95. Sat, Sun brunch $4.95-$6.95. Child's meals. Own baking. Colorful decor with memorabilia of Austin, TX. Cr cds: A, D, DS, MC, V.

🅳

★ ★ **TAVERNA CRETEKOU.** 818 King St (22314). 703/548-8688. Hrs: 11:30 am-2:30 pm, 5-10:30 pm; Sat noon-11 pm; Sun 5-9:30 pm; Sun brunch 11 am-3 pm. Closed Mon; some major hols. Res accepted; required Fri, Sat. Greek menu. Serv bar. A la carte entrees: lunch $5.95-$8.95, dinner $10.50-$17.95. Sun brunch $11.95. Specializes in seafood, lamb. Entertainment Thurs. Outdoor dining. Mediterranean decor; brick patio, arbor. Cr cds: A, MC, V.

⊡

✔★ ★ **TEMPO.** 4231 Duke St (22304), 2½ mi W on VA 236. 703/370-7900. Hrs: 11:30 am-2:30 pm, 5:30-10 pm; Sun to 9 pm; Sun brunch to 2:30 pm. Closed most major hols. Res accepted; required Fri, Sat dinner. Italian, French menu. Bar. Semi-a la carte: lunch $7.95-$10.95, dinner $8.95-$17.95. Sun brunch $5.95-$10.95. Specialties: linguini with lobster, lamb chops with fresh herbs. Outdoor dining. Modern decor with cathedral windows, original artwork. Cr cds: A, C, D, DS, JCB, MC, V.

★ ★ **THAI HUT.** *408 S Van Dorn St (22304). 703/823-5357.* Hrs: 11 am-10 pm; Fri to 11 pm; Sat noon-11 pm; Sun noon-9:30 pm. Closed Thanksgiving, Dec 25. Thai menu. A la carte entrees: lunch, dinner $7.50-$11.95. Complete meals (Mon-Fri): lunch $5.95. Specialties: curries, pad Thai, drunken noodles. Parking. Modern decor; Thai artwork. Cr cds: A, C, D, MC, V.

★ ★ **UNION STREET PUBLIC HOUSE.** *121 S Union St (22314), between King & Prince Sts, in Old Town Alexandria. 703/548-1785.* Hrs: 11:30 am-10:30 pm; Fri, Sat to 11:30 pm; Sun brunch 11 am-3 pm. Closed Thanksgiving, Dec 25. Bar to 1:15 am. Semi-a la carte: lunch, dinner $5.50-$16.95. Sun brunch $4.95-$8.95. Child's meals. Specialties: pasta jambalya, linguine with lobster & smoked scallops, aged Angus beef. Oyster raw bar. In sea captain's house & warehouse (ca 1870). Cr cds: A, C, D, DS, MC, V.

★ ★ ★ **VILLA D'ESTE.** *818 N St Asaph St (22314), at Montgomery St. 703/549-9477.* Hrs: 11:30 am-2:30 pm, 5-10 pm; Fri, Sat to 10:30 pm; Sun 5-9 pm. Closed major hols. Res accepted; required Fri, Sat. Italian menu. Bar. Wine list. A la carte entrees: lunch $8.95-$14.95, dinner $12.95-$19.95. Specialties: osso buco, lamb shank, veal. Own baking, pasta. Elegant, modern decor. Cr cds: A, C, D, MC, V.

★ ★ **THE WHARF.** *119 King St (22314). 703/836-2836.* Hrs: 11 am-11 pm; Sun 3-10 pm. Closed Jan 1, Thanksgiving, Dec 25. Res accepted. Bar. Semi-a la carte: lunch: $5.95-$11.95, dinner $14.95-$21.95. Child's meals. Specializes in Maine lobster, Chesapeake Bay seafood. Late 18th-century building. Cr cds: A, C, D, DS, MC, V.

Unrated Dining Spot

HARD TIMES CAFE. *1404 King St. 703/683-5340.* Hrs: 11 am-10 pm; Fri, Sat to 11 pm; Sun noon-10 pm. Closed some major hols. A la carte entrees: lunch, dinner $3.95-$5.75. Specializes in Texas, Cincinnati and vegetarian-style chili, onion rings, corn bread. Country, western music on juke box. Housed in former church; rustic decor; collection of state flags. Cr cds: A, MC, V.

Appomattox Court House National Historical Park (E-7)

(For accommodations see Lynchburg)

(3 mi NE of Appomattox on VA 24)

The series of clashes between General Ulysses S. Grant and General Robert E. Lee that started with the Battle of the Wilderness (May 5, 1864) finally ended here on Palm Sunday, April 9, 1865, in the little village of Appomattox Court House.

A week earlier, Lee had evacuated besieged Petersburg and headed west in a desperate attempt to join forces with General Johnston in North Carolina. Ragged and exhausted, decimated by desertions, without sup-

plies and beset by Union forces at every turn, the once-great Army of Northern Virginia launched its last attack at dawn on April 9. By 10 am it was clear that further bloodshed was futile; after some difficulty in getting a message to Grant, the two antagonists met in the parlor of the McLean House. By 3 pm the generous surrender terms had been drafted and signed. The war was over. Three days later, 28,231 Confederate soldiers received their parole here.

The 1,743-acre park includes the village of Appomattox Court House, restored and reconstructed to appear much as it did in 1865. As visitors tour the village, uniformed park rangers or interpreters in period dress answer questions about the people who lived here and the events that took place. (Daily; closed major hols Nov-Feb) Golden Eagle Passport accepted (see MAKING THE MOST OF YOUR TRIP). Audiovisual programs, Braille guide folder, audio guide and large-print folder avail for the hearing and visually impaired. For further information contact the Superintendent, PO Box 218, Appomattox 24522; 804/352-8987. ¢

What to See and Do

✪ **Appomattox Court House Bldg.** Reconstructed building houses visitor center, museum; audiovisual slide program (every half hr, 2nd floor). Self-guided tour of village begins here and includes

Clover Hill Tavern and outbuildings (1819). Oldest structure in village; bookstore, restrooms.

Confederate Cemetery.

County jail (1870). Furnished.

Woodson Law Office. With period furnishings.

Meek's Store and Meek's Storehouse. With period furnishings.

Kelly House.

McLean House and outbuildings. Reconstruction of house where Gen. Lee and Grant met on Apr 9, 1865. East from house, past the courthouse and about 100 yards along Stage Rd past county jail, is

Stacking of Arms. On exactly the fourth anniversary of the firing on Ft Sumter, which triggered the outbreak of war, Confederate soldiers laid down their weapons here.

Holliday Lake State Park. Approx 250 acres in Buckingham-Appomattox State Forest. Swimming beach, bathhouse; fishing, boating (launch, rentals) on 150-acre lake. Hiking trails. Picnicking, concession. Tent & trailer sites. Visitor center, interpretive programs. Standard fees. Park (daily); most activities, including camping (Memorial Day-Labor Day). 9 mi NE of Appomattox on VA 24, then 6 mi SE via VA 626, 692. Phone 804/248-6308.

Arlington County (National Airport Area) (C-8)

(See also Alexandria, Fairfax, Falls Church, McLean; also see District of Columbia)

Elev 200 ft **Area code** 703 **E-mail** arlcvb@us.net **Web** www.co.arlington.va.us

Information Arlington Convention & Visitors Service, 2100 Clarendon Blvd, Suite 318, 22201, phone 703/358-3988; or the Arlington Visitors Center, 735 S 18th St, 22202, phone 703/358-5720 or 800/677-6267.

Originally a part of the District of Columbia laid out for the capital in 1791, Arlington County, across the Potomac River from Washington, was returned to Virginia in 1846. The county is the urban center of northern Virginia.

Transportation

Car Rental Agencies: See IMPORTANT TOLL-FREE NUMBERS.

Public Transportation: Subway trains and buses (Metro Transit System), phone 202/962-1234.

Rail Passenger Service: Amtrak 800/972-9245.

Airport Information

Washington National Airport: Information 703/419-8000; lost and found 703/417-8560; weather 202/936-1212; cash machines, at Main Terminal, main level near Travelers Aid, and at Interim Terminal, main level near Travelers Aid.

Airlines: America West, American, American Eagle, Continental, Delta, Midwest Express, Northwest, TWA, United, USAir.

What to See and Do

⭐ **Arlington National Cemetery.** The most famous of US national cemeteries was established in 1864. Here are interred more than 200,000 men and women who served their country; two presidents, William Howard Taft, John F. Kennedy; Sen. Robert F. Kennedy; Jacqueline Kennedy Onassis. Guided "tourmobiles" leave from visitor center (fare includes on/off privileges), phone 703/979-0690. (Daily) Tourmobiles ¢¢; Parking ¢¢ Here are

The Tomb of the Unknowns. On Nov 11, 1921, the remains of an unknown American soldier of World War I were entombed here. A memorial was erected in 1932 with the inscription "Here rests in honored glory an American soldier known but to God." On Memorial Day 1958, an unknown warrior who died in World War II and another who died in the Korean War were laid beside him. On Memorial Day 1984, an unknown soldier from the Vietnam War was interred here. Sentries stand guard 24 hrs a day; changing of the guard is every hour on the hour Oct-Mar, every 30 min Apr-Sept.

Memorial Amphitheatre. This impressive white marble edifice is used for ceremonies, such as Memorial Day, Easter sunrise and Veterans Day services.

Arlington House, the Robert E. Lee Memorial. National memorial to Robert E. Lee. Built between 1802 and 1818 by George Washington Parke Custis, Martha Washington's grandson and foster son of George Washington. In 1831, his daughter, Mary Anna Randolph Custis, married Lieutenant Robert E. Lee; six of the seven Lee children were born here. As executor of Custis's estate, Lee took extended leave from the US Army and devoted his time to managing and improving the estate. It was the Lee homestead for 30 yrs before the Civil War.

On Apr 20, 1861, following the secession of Virginia, Lee made his decision to stay with Virginia. Within a month, the house was vacated. Some of the family possessions were moved for safekeeping, but most were stolen or destroyed when Union troops occupied the house during the Civil War.

In 1864, when Mrs. Lee could not appear personally to pay property tax, the estate was confiscated by the federal government; a 200-acre section was set aside for a national cemetery. (There is some evidence that indicates that this was done to ensure that the Lee family could never again live on the estate.) G. W. Custis Lee, the general's son, later regained title to the property through a Supreme Court decision and sold it to the US government in 1883 for $150,000.

Restoration of the house to its 1861 appearance was begun in 1925. The Classic-revival house is furnished with authentic pieces of the period, including some Lee family originals. From the grand portico with its six massive, faux-marble Doric columns, there is a panoramic view of Washington, DC. (Daily; closed Jan 1, Dec 25) Phone 703/557-0613. **Free.**

Iwo Jima Statue. Marine Corps War Memorial depicts raising of the flag on Mt Suribachi, Iwo Jima, Feb 23, 1945; this is the largest sculpture ever cast in bronze. Sunset Parade concert with performances by US Marine Drum and Bugle Corps, US Marine Corps Color Guard and the Silent Drill Team (late May-late Aug, Tues evenings). On Arlington Blvd, near Arlington National Cemetery.

The Fashion Centre at Pentagon City. Upscale, 160-store shopping mall with restaurants, movie theaters and adjoining 360-rm Ritz-Carlton hotel (see HOTELS); features 115,000-sq-ft glass ceiling in atrium. Off I-395 at jct S Hayes St & Army-Navy Dr, just S of the Pentagon. Phone 703/415-2130.

⭐ **The Newseum.** 72,000-sq-ft interactive museum of news takes visitors behind the scenes to see and experience how and why news is made. Be a reporter or newscaster; relive great news stories through multimedia exhibits; and see today's news as it happens on a block-long video wall. (Wed-Sun; closed hols) 1101 Wilson Blvd. Phone 888/NEWSEUM or 703/284-3700. **Free.** On grounds is

Freedom Park. Nearly 1,000 ft in length, park occupies never-used bridge. Features memorial to journalists killed in line of duty and various icons of freedom.

The Pentagon. With some 6 million sq ft of floor area, this is one of the largest office buildings in the world; houses offices of the Department of Defense. Guided tour (1½ hr) with a walk of about 1½ miles includes movie, Hall of Heroes, Flag Corridor, Time/Life Art Collection (Mon-Fri; closed hols). Tour window located on Concourse near the Metrorail subway or by entering at Corridor One, South Parking entrance. A valid picture ID must be presented at tour registration; visitors must stay on the tour once it begins. Cameras are allowed. Accommodations for the disabled avail with 48-hr advance notice. Bounded by Jefferson Davis Hwy, Washington Blvd & I-395. Phone 703/695-1776. **Free.**

Annual Events

Memorial Day Service. Arlington National Cemetery. Presidential wreath-laying ceremony at Tomb of the Unknowns; music. Memorial Day.

Arlington County Fair. Countywide fair; arts, crafts, international foods, children's activities. Phone 703/358-6400. Aug.

Army 10-miler. America's largest 10-mi road race, attracting thousands of military and civilian runners. Phone 202/685-3361. Early Oct.

Motels

✔★ ★ **COMFORT INN BALLSTON.** *1211 N Glebe Rd (22201), at Washington Blvd.* 703/247-3399; FAX 703/524-8739. 126 rms, 3 story. Mar-Oct: S $90-$110; D $95-$125; each addl $10; suites $135; under 18 free; wknd rates; lower rates rest of yr. Crib free. TV; cable (premium). Pool privileges. Complimentary continental bkfst. Restaurant 6:30 am-10:30 pm. Rm serv. Bar 4-11 pm. Ck-out 11 am. Meeting rms. Business servs avail. In-rm modem link. Valet serv (Mon-Fri). Sundries. Gift shop. Garage parking. Refrigerators avail. Cr cds: A, C, D, DS, ER, JCB, MC, V.

[D] [≈] [🐾] [SC]

★ ★ **EXECUTIVE CLUB SUITES.** *108 S Courthouse Rd (22204).* 703/522-2582; FAX 703/486-2694. 74 kit. suites, 2-3 story. Mar-Sept: kit. suites: $159-$179; wknd, wkly, hol rates; higher rates Cherry Blossom Festival; lower rates rest of yr. Crib free. Pet accepted, some restrictions; $250 deposit ($25 nonrefundable). TV; cable (premium), VCR avail. Complimentary continental bkfst. Complimentary coffee in rms. Ck-out noon. Meeting rms. Business servs avail. Valet serv. Sundries. Coin lndry. Free airport transportation. Exercise equipt; weights, weight machine, sauna. Health club privileges. Pool; whirlpool, lifeguard. Refrigerators, microwaves. Picnic tables, grills. Cr cds: A, C, D, DS, MC, V.

[✔] [≈] [🏋] [🐾] [SC]

✔★ ★ ★ **TRAVELODGE-WASHINGTON/ARLINGTON CHERRY BLOSSOM.** *3030 Columbia Pike (22204).* 703/521-5570; FAX 703/271-0081. E-mail cherryblossom.travelodge@jung.com. 76 rms, 3 story, 12 kit. units. Mid-Mar-Nov: S, D $59-$70; each addl $7; kit. units $76; under 18 free; lower rates rest of yr. Crib free. TV; cable (premium), VCR avail. Pool privileges. Complimentary continental bkfst. Complimentary coffee in rms. Restaurant 11 am-11 pm. Ck-out noon. Coin lndry. Business servs avail. Valet serv. Exercise equipt; weight machine, stair machines. Refrigerators; microwaves avail. Cr cds: A, C, D, DS, ER, JCB, MC, V.

[D] [🏋] [≈] [🐾] [SC]

Motor Hotels

★ ★ **COURTYARD BY MARRIOTT.** *1533 Clarendon Blvd (22209).* 703/528-2222; FAX 703/528-1027. 162 rms, 10 story, 18 suites. Apr-June, Aug-Oct: S $134; D $144; each addl $10; suites $154-$164; under 12 free; wkend rates; lower rates rest of yr. Crib free. Garage parking $6 Mon-Fri; wkends free. TV; cable (premium), VCR avail. Complimentary coffee in rms. Restaurant 6-11 am, 5-10 pm. Rm serv from 5 pm. Bar from 5 pm. Ck-out noon. Meeting rms. Business servs avail. Bellhops. Valet serv. Sundries. Coin lndry. Exercise equipt; bicycle, stair machine. Health club privileges. Indoor pool; whirlpool, lifeguard. Some refrigerators; microwaves avail. Many balconies. Cr cds: A, C, D, DS, MC, V.

[D] [≈] [✗] [⇘] [🔥] [SC]

★ ★ **DAYS INN CRYSTAL CITY.** *2000 Jefferson Davis Hwy (22202).* 703/920-8600; FAX 703/920-2840. 247 rms, 8 story. Mar-June, Sept-Nov: S $120-$150; D $130-$160; each addl $10; under 16 free; wkend, hol rates; lower rates rest of yr. Crib free. TV; cable (premium). Pool; lifeguard. Complimentary coffee in rms. Restaurant 6 am-2 pm, 5-10 pm; wkends 7 am-noon, 5-10 pm. Rm serv. Bar 4:30-10 pm. Ck-out 11 am. Meeting rms. Business servs avail. In-rm modem link. Bellhops. Gift shop. Valet serv. Garage parking. Free airport transportation. Exercise equipt; weight machine, treadmills. Cr cds: A, C, D, DS, ER, MC, V.

[D] [≈] [✗] [✈] [⇘] [🔥] [SC]

★ ★ **QUALITY INN-IWO JIMA.** *1501 Arlington Blvd (Fairfax Dr) (22209),* ½ mi W of Iwo Jima Memorial. 703/524-5000; FAX 703/522-5484. 141 rms, 1-3 story. Mar-Nov: S, D $85-$110; each addl $7; wkend, family rates; higher rates special events; lower rates rest of yr. Crib free. TV; cable (premium), VCR avail. Indoor pool; poolside serv, lifeguard. Restaurant (in season) 6:30 am-10 pm; Sat, Sun from 7 am. Rm serv. Bar. Ck-out noon. Coin lndry. Meeting rms. Business servs avail. In-rm modem link. Bellhops. Sundries. Exercise equipt; bicycle, stair machine. Health club privileges. Refrigerators, microwaves avail. Some balconies. Cr cds: A, C, D, DS, ER, JCB, MC, V.

[D] [≈] [✗] [✈] [⇘] [🔥] [SC]

Hotels

★ ★ **BEST WESTERN KEY BRIDGE.** *1850 N Fort Myer Dr (22209).* 703/522-0400; FAX 703/524-5275. 178 rms, 11 story. S $113; D $123; suites $125-$155; under 12 free. Crib free. Pet accepted. TV; cable (premium). Pool. Restaurant 6:30 am-2 pm, 5-10 pm. Ck-out noon. Meeting rms. Business servs avail. Exercise equipt; bicycles, treadmill. Some refrigerators; microwaves avail. Cr cds: A, C, D, DS, MC, V.

[D] [🐾] [≈] [✗] [⇘] [SC]

★ ★ **COURTYARD BY MARRIOTT.** *2899 Jefferson Davis Hwy (22202), near National Airport.* 703/549-3434; FAX 703/549-7440. 272 rms, 14 story. S, D $139-$154; each addl $15; suites $200-$250; under 12 free. Crib free. Garage parking $8. TV; cable (premium), VCR avail. Indoor pool; whirlpool, lifeguard. Complimentary coffee in rms. Restaurant 6-10 am, 5-10 pm. Rm serv from 5 pm. Bar 4 pm-midnight. Ck-out 1 pm. Coin lndry. Meeting rms. Business servs avail. In-rm modem link. Valet serv. Sundries. Free airport transportation. Exercise equipt; weights, bicycles, treadmill. Health club privileges. Some refrigerators, wet bars; microwaves avail. Cr cds: A, C, D, DS, ER, JCB, MC, V.

[D] [≈] [✗] [✈] [⇘] [🔥] [SC]

★ ★ **DOUBLETREE.** *300 Army/Navy Dr (22202).* 703/416-4100; FAX 703/416-4126. Web www.doubletreehotels.com. 632 rms, 15 story, 265 suites. S, D $190; suites $200-$400; under 18 free; wkend rates. Crib free. Pet accepted. Garage $10; valet $12. TV; cable (premium). Indoor pool; sauna, lifeguard. Restaurant 6:30 am-11 pm. Bar 11-2 am; entertainment. Ck-out noon. Convention facilities. Business servs avail. In-rm modem link. Gift shop. Free airport transportation. Health club privileges. Bathrm phones; some refrigerators; microwaves avail. Some balconies. Luxury level. Cr cds: A, C, D, DS, ER, JCB, MC, V.

[D] [🐾] [≈] [⇘] [🔥] [SC]

★ ★ ★ **EMBASSY SUITES-CRYSTAL CITY.** *1300 Jefferson Davis Hwy (22202), entrance at 1402 S Eads St, near National Airport.* 703/979-9799; FAX 703/920-5947. 267 suites, 11 story. Feb-June, Sept-Nov: S $179-$209; D $189-$219; each addl $10; under 12 free; wkend rates; lower rates rest of yr. Crib free. TV; cable (premium). Heated pool; lifeguard. Complimentary full bkfst. Complimentary coffee in rms. Restaurant 11:30 am-10 pm; Fri, Sat to 11 pm. Bar to 11 pm. Ck-out noon. Meeting rms. Business servs avail. In-rm modem link. Gift shop. Free covered parking. Free airport transportation. Exercise equipt; weight machine, bicycles. Refrigerators. Atrium lobby. Cr cds: A, C, D, DS, JCB, MC, V.

[D] [≈] [✗] [✈] [⇘] [🔥] [SC]

★ ★ ★ **HILTON.** *950 N Stafford St (22203), at Fairfax Dr.* 703/528-6000; FAX 703/528-4386. 209 rms, 7 story. S $165-$185; D $185-$205; suites $225; under 18 free; wkend rates. Crib free. TV; cable (premium). Indoor pool; whirlpool, lifeguard. Restaurant 6:30 am-11 pm. Bar 11 am-midnight. Ck-out noon. Coin lndry. Meeting rms. Business servs avail. In-rm modem link. Concierge. Gift shop. Health club privileges. Metro stop in building. Luxury level. Cr cds: A, C, D, DS, ER, JCB, MC, V.

[D] [≈] [⇘] [🔥] [SC]

★ ★ ★ **HOLIDAY INN NATIONAL AIRPORT.** *1489 Jefferson Davis Hwy (22202).* 703/416-1600; FAX 703/416-1615. 306 rms, 11 story. S, D $145; each addl $10; suites $159-$165; under 20 free; wkend, hol rates. Crib free. Pet accepted, some restrictions. Garage $6. TV; cable (premium), VCR avail. Pool; lifeguard. Restaurant 6 am-10 pm; Sat, Sun from 7 am. Bar 11 am-midnight. Ck-out noon. Meeting rms. Business servs avail. In-rm modem link. Gift shop. Free airport transportation. Health club privileges. Game rm. Refrigerators avail. Cr cds: A, C, D, DS, JCB, MC, V.

[D] [🐾] [≈] [✗] [⇘] [🔥] [SC]

★ ★ ★ **HOLIDAY INN ROSSLYN WESTPARK.** *1900 N Ft Myer Dr (22209).* 703/807-2000; FAX 703/522-8864. 306 rms, 20 story. S, D $109-$119; suites $135-$150; under 18 free; wkly, wkend, hol rates. Crib free. Pet accepted. TV; cable (premium). Indoor pool, lifeguard. Restaurant 6:30 am-11 pm. Bar 11:30 am-midnight. Ck-out noon. Coin lndry. Convention facilities. Business center. In-rm modem link. Garage parking. Exercise equipt: stair machine, treadmill. Health club privileges. Some refrigerators. Balconies. Overlooking Potomac River. Cr cds: A, C, D, DS, ER, JCB, MC, V.

[D] [🐾] [≈] [✗] [⇘] [🔥] [SC] [⚓]

★ ★ ★ **HYATT ARLINGTON.** *1325 Wilson Blvd (22209), near Key Bridge at Nash St & Wilson.* 703/525-1234; FAX 703/875-3393. 302 rms, 16 story. S $185; D $210; each addl $25; suites $275-$575; under 12 free; wkend rates. Crib free. Pet accepted, some restrictions. Garage $10 (Sun-Thurs). TV; cable (premium), VCR avail. Restaurant 6:30 am-midnight. Bars 11 am-midnight. Ck-out noon. Free guest lndry. Meeting rms. Business center. In-rm modem link. Gift shop. Exercise equipt; bicycles, treadmill. Health club privileges. Metro adj. Cr cds: A, C, D, DS, ER, JCB, MC, V.

[D] [🐾] [✗] [⇘] [🔥] [SC] [⚓]

★ ★ ★ **HYATT REGENCY-CRYSTAL CITY.** *2799 Jefferson Davis Hwy (22202), near National Airport.* 703/418-1234; FAX 703/418-1289. E-mail wasrc1@erols.com. 685 rms, 20 story. S $185; D $210; each addl $25; suites $350-$725; under 18 free; wkend rates. Crib free. Garage; valet $9. TV; cable (premium), VCR avail. Heated pool; whirlpool, poolside serv, lifeguard. Complimentary coffee in rms. Restaurant 6-2 am. Bar 3 pm-1 am. Ck-out noon. Convention facilities. Business center. In-rm modem link. Concierge. Gift shop. Free airport transportation. Exercise equipt; weight machine, stair machine, saunas. Health club privileges. Some refrigerators, wet bars; microwaves avail. Some balconies. Cr cds: A, C, D, DS, ER, JCB, MC, V.

[D] [≈] [✗] [✈] [⇘] [🔥] [SC] [⚓]

★ ★ ★ **MARRIOTT CRYSTAL GATEWAY.** *1700 Jefferson Davis Hwy (US 1) (22202), entrance on S Eads St, between 15th & 17th Sts, near National Airport.* 703/920-3230; FAX 703/271-5212. 700 units, 16 story. S, D $192-$220; suites $199-$700; under 18 free; wkend rates. Crib free. Pet accepted, some restrictions. Garage $12. TV; cable (premium). Indoor/outdoor pool; whirlpool, lifeguard. Restaurant 6:30-2 am. Bar 11-2 am. Ck-out 1 pm. Convention facilities. Business center. In-rm modem link. Concierge. Free airport transportation. Tennis privileges. Exercise equipt; weights, bicycles, sauna. Health club privileges. Original artwork. Luxury level. Cr cds: A, C, D, DS, ER, JCB, MC, V.

★ ★ ★ **MARRIOTT KEY BRIDGE.** *1401 Lee Hwy (22209). 703/524-6400; FAX 703/524-8964.* 584 rms, 2-14 story. S, D $159; suites $225-$500; wkend rates. Crib free. Garage $8. TV; cable (premium), VCR avail. Indoor/outdoor pool; whirlpool, poolside serv, lifeguard. Restaurant (see JW'S STEAKHOUSE). Bar 11-2 am; entertainment exc Sun. Ck-out 1 pm. Convention facilities. Business center. In-rm modem link. Concierge. Gift shop. Barber, beauty shop. Exercise equipt; weights, bicycles, sauna. Health club privileges. Refrigerators, microwaves avail. Some balconies. Overlooks Washington across Potomac River. Luxury level. Cr cds: A, C, D, DS, ER, JCB, MC, V.

★ ★ ★ **MARRIOTT-CRYSTAL CITY.** *1999 Jefferson Davis Hwy (22202). 703/413-5500; FAX 703/413-0192.* 345 rms, 12 story. S $189; D $209; suites $250-$400; under 18 free; wkend rates. Crib free. Valet parking $15. TV; cable (premium), VCR avail. Indoor pool; whirlpool, lifeguard. Complimentary coffee in rms. Restaurant 6:30 am-10:30 pm; Sat, Sun from 7 am. Bar 11:30 am-midnight. Ck-out 1 pm. Coin lndry. Convention facilities. Business center. In-rm modem link. Concierge. Gift shop. Free airport transportation. Exercise equipt; weight machine, stair machines, sauna. Health club privileges. Luxury level. Cr cds: A, C, D, DS, ER, JCB, MC, V.

✔★ ★ **QUALITY HOTEL COURTHOUSE PLAZA.** *1200 N Courthouse Rd (22201). 703/524-4000; FAX 703/522-6814.* Web www.quality hotelarlington.com. 391 rms, 1-10 story. S $59.95-$125.95; D $65.95-$135.95; each addl $10; suites $109.95-$169.95; under 18 free; wkend, wkly rates. Crib free. Pet accepted, some restrictions. TV; cable (premium). Pool; lifeguard. Coffee in rms. Restaurant 6:30 am-2 pm, 5-9:30 pm. Bar 4-10 pm. Ck-out noon. Coin lndry. Convention facilities. Business servs avail. In-rm modem link. Concierge. Gift shop. Exercise equipt; weight machine, rowers, sauna. Microwaves avail. Balconies. Luxury level. Cr cds: A, C, D, DS, ER, JCB, MC, V.

★ ★ ★ **RESIDENCE INN BY MARRIOTT.** *550 Army Navy Dr (22202). 703/413-6630; FAX 703/418-1751.* 299 kit. suites, 17 story. Kit. suites $170-$235; wkend, wkly rates. Crib free. Garage parking $10/day. TV; cable (premium). Complimentary continental bkfst. Complimentary coffee in rms. Restaurant nearby. No rm serv. Ck-out noon. Meeting rms. Business servs avail. No bellhops. Concierge. Coin lndry. Free airport transportation. Exercise equipt; treadmill, stair machine. Indoor pool; whirlpool, lifeguard. Refrigerators, microwaves. Picnic tables. Cr cds: A, C, D, DS, MC, V.

★ ★ ★ ★ **THE RITZ-CARLTON, PENTAGON CITY.** *1250 S Hayes St (22202), in Pentagon City Fashion Centre Mall, near National Airport. 703/415-5000; FAX 703/415-5061.* The Persian carpets, fine art and 18th-century antiques of this quiet hotel contrast with its surroundings. Guest rooms are lavishly appointed with silk drapes and Federal-style furnishings and have panoramic views of the Capitol and the Potomac River. 345 rms, 18 story, 41 suites. S, D $184-$239; each addl $30; suites $299-$1,600; under 19 free; wkend rates. Crib free. Garage, valet parking $20. TV; cable (premium), VCR avail (movies). Indoor pool; whirlpool, lifeguard. Supervised child's activities (hols). Restaurant (see THE GRILL). Bar; entertainment. Ck-out noon. Convention facilities. Business center. In-rm modem link. Concierge. Shopping arcade. Free airport transportation. Tennis privileges. Golf privileges. Exercise rm; instructor, weight machine, bicycles, sauna, steam rm. Massage. Bathrm phones, minibars; microwaves avail. Luxury level. Cr cds: A, C, D, DS, ER, JCB, MC, V.

★ ★ ★ **SHERATON CRYSTAL CITY.** *1800 Jefferson Davis Hwy (22202), entrance on S Eads St; ½ mi S of I-395 on US 1, near National Airport. 703/486-1111; FAX 703/769-3970.* E-mail perrya@ix.netcom .com. 197 rms, 15 story. S $155-$180; D $175-$200; each addl $20; under 18 free; wkend packages. Crib $20. TV; cable (premium), VCR avail. Rooftop pool; lifeguard, sauna. Coffee in rms. Restaurant 6:30 am-10 pm; Sat, Sun from 7 am. Bar 11 am-midnight; entertainment, pianist. Ck-out 1 pm. Meeting rms. Business center. In-rm modem link. Gift shop. Free airport transportation. Exercise equipt; bicycle, rowing machine. Minibars, refrigerators; some bathrm phones. Luxury level. Cr cds: A, C, D, DS, MC, V.

Restaurants

★ ★ **ALPINE.** *4770 Lee Hwy (22207). 703/528-7600.* Hrs: 11:30 am-11 pm; Sun noon-10 pm. Closed most major hols. Res accepted. Italian, continental menu. Bar. Semi-a la carte: lunch $5.95-$10.75, dinner $10.95-$17.95. Specializes in veal, pasta dishes, seafood. Own pasta. Parking. Family-owned. Cr cds: A, C, D, MC, V.

✔★ ★ **BISTRO BISTRO.** *4021 S 28th St (22206). 703/379-0300.* Hrs: 11 am-10 pm; Fri, Sat to 11 pm; early-bird dinner Mon-Thurs 5-6:30 pm; Sun brunch 10:30 am-3 pm. Closed Thanksgiving, Dec 25. Res accepted. Bar to 1:30 am. A la carte entrees: lunch $5.75-10.95, dinner $6.95-$16.95. Sun brunch $6-$12. Specializes in pasta, seafood, oyster stew. Outdoor dining. Bistro atmosphere, eclectic decor. Cr cds: A, MC, V.

★ **CAFÉ DALAT.** *3143 Wilson Blvd (22201), at N Highland St. 703/276-0935.* Hrs: 11 am-9:30 pm; Fri, Sat to 10:30 pm. Closed Chinese New Year, July 4, Thanksgiving, Dec 25. Vietnamese menu. Serv bar. Complete meals: lunch $4.25. Semi-a la carte: dinner $7.50-$8.95. Lunch buffet $4.95. Specialties: sugar cane shrimp, grilled lemon chicken. Own desserts. Totally nonsmoking. Cr cds: MC, V.

✔★ ★ **CARLYLE GRAND CAFE.** *4000 S 28th St (22206), S on I-395, Shirlington exit. 703/931-0777.* Hrs: 11:30 am-11 pm; Fri, Sat to midnight; Sun brunch 10:30 am-2 pm. Closed Thanksgiving, Dec 25. Bar. Semi-a la carte: lunch $5.95-$11.65, dinner $8.95-$18.95. Sun brunch $4.95-$11.95. Specialties: Virginia trout, baby back ribs, smoked salmon filet. Outdoor dining. Totally nonsmoking. Cr cds: A, MC, V.

✔★ **COWBOY CAFE.** *4792 Lee Hwy (22207). 703/243-8010.* Hrs: 11 am-11 pm; Fri to midnight; Sat 9 am-midnight; Sun 9 am-9 pm. Bar to 11:30 pm; Fri, Sat to 12:30 am; Sun 11 am-8:30 pm. Semi-a la carte: bkfst $2.99-$5.95, lunch, dinner $2.75-$7.95. Specializes in hamburgers, bkfst dishes. Musicians Thurs-Sat. Casual, Western decor. Cr cds: A, C, D, DS, MC, V.

★ **FACCIA LUNA.** *2909 Wilson Blvd (22201). 703/276-3099.* Hrs: 11 am-11 pm; Fri, Sat to midnight; Sun noon-11 pm. Closed Thanksgiving, Dec 24, 25. Italian menu. Bar. Semi-a la carte: lunch $4.95-$5.95, dinner $7.75-$11.75. Child's meals. Specializes in pasta, pizza. Upscale pizzeria. No cr cds accepted.

★ ★ ★ **THE GRILL.** *(See The Ritz-Carlton, Pentagon City Hotel) 703/412-2760.* Hrs: 6:30 am-10:30 pm; Sat, Sun 7 am-11 pm; Sun brunch 11 am-2:30 pm. Res accepted. Bar. Wine list. Semi-a la carte: bkfst $5-$15, lunch $6.50-$25, dinner $20-$32. Buffet: bkfst $8.75-$12.50. Sun brunch $45. Child's meals. Seasonal, Mid-Atlantic specialties including macrobiotic daily specials and cuisine vitale. Pianist Fri, Sat evenings. Valet parking. English club-like decor and atmosphere. Fireplace. Cr cds: A, C, D, DS, ER, JCB, MC, V.

★ ★ ★ **JW'S STEAKHOUSE.** *(See Marriott Key Bridge Hotel)* *703/284-1407.* Hrs: 5-10 pm; Fri to 11 pm; Sat 6-11 pm; Sun 5:30-9:30 pm; Sun brunch 10 am-2:30 pm. Closed Jan 1. Res accepted; required July 4. Bar. Wine list. A la carte entrees: dinner $15.95-$24.95. Sun brunch $23.95-$25.95. Specializes in seafood, steak. Parking. View of Washington across Potomac. Cr cds: A, C, D, DS, ER, JCB, MC, V.

[D] [SC] [⌐]

★ ★ **KABUL CARAVAN.** *1725 Wilson Blvd (22209), in Colonial Village Shopping Ctr. 703/522-8394.* Hrs: 11:30 am-2:30 pm, 5:30-11 pm; Sat, Sun from 5:30 pm. Closed Dec 25. Res accepted. Afghan menu. Serv bar. Prix fixe dinners for 2-4: $55.95-$115.95. Semi-a la carte: lunch $7.95-$11.95, dinner $10.95-$16.95. Specialties: sautéed pumpkin with yogurt & meat sauce, orange pallow, eggplant & shish kabob. Outdoor dining. Walls covered with Afghan clothing, pictures, rugs, artifacts, jewelry. Cr cds: A, MC, V.

[D] [⌐]

★ ★ **L'ALOUETTE.** *2045 Wilson Blvd (22201). 703/525-1750.* Hrs: 11:30 am-2:30 pm, 6-10 pm; Fri to 10:30 pm; Sat 6-10:30 pm. Closed Sun; major hols. Res accepted. French menu. Serv bar. Semi-a la carte: lunch $7.50-$11.95. A la carte entrees: dinner $14.95-$19.25. Prix fixe: dinner $18.95. Specializes in seasonal dishes. Cr cds: A, C, D, DS, MC, V.

[⌐]

★ ★ **LA COTE D'OR CAFE.** *6876 Lee Hwy (22213). 703/538-3033.* Hrs: 11:30 am-3 pm, 5:30-11 pm; Sun brunch 11 am-3 pm. Closed Jan 1, Dec 25. Res accepted. French menu. Bar. Semi-a la carte: lunch $5.95-$12.75, dinner $18.25-$22.95. Sun brunch $7.50-$7.95. Specializes in seafood, veal. Pianist Wed. Outdoor dining. French decor. Cr cds: A, MC, V.

[D]

✓★ ★ **LEBANESE TAVERNA.** *5900 Washington Blvd (22205), in Westover Shopping Center. 703/241-8681.* Hrs: 11:30 am-2:30 pm, 5-10 pm; Sun 4-9 pm. Closed major hols. Res accepted Mon-Thurs. Lebanese menu. Bar. Semi-a la carte: lunch, dinner $4.50-$14. Specialties: chicken shawarma, lamb kabob, sharhat ghanam. Own baking. Lebanese decor; large windows. Family-owned. Totally nonsmoking. Cr cds: A, C, D, MC, V.

[D]

✓★ ★ **LITTLE VIET GARDEN.** *3012 Wilson Blvd (22201). 703/522-9686.* Hrs: 11 am-2:30 pm, 5-10 pm; Sat, Sun 11 am-10 pm. Closed Thanksgiving, Dec 25. Res accepted. Vietnamese menu. Bar. Semi-a la carte: lunch $4.95-$6.95, dinner $5.95-$11.95. Specialties: Viet Garden steak, grilled jumbo shrimp. Parking. Outdoor dining. Cr cds: A, C, D, DS, MC, V.

[⌐]

★ **MATUBA.** *2915 Columbia Pike (22204). 703/521-2811.* Hrs: 11:30 am-2 pm, 5:30-10 pm; Fri, Sat 5:30-10:30 pm; Sun 5:30-10 pm. Res accepted. Japanese menu. Semi-a la carte: lunch $4.95-$8.50, dinner $5.50-$11.50. Specializes in seafood, poultry. Japanese decor. Cr cds: A, MC, V.

✓★ ★ **QUEEN BEE.** *3181 Wilson Blvd (22201). 703/527-3444.* Hrs: 11 am-10 pm. Vietnamese menu. Serv bar. Semi-a la carte: lunch $3.95-$7.50, dinner $6.50-$7.95. Specialties: spring roll, Hanoi beef noodle soup, Hanoi-style grilled pork. Totally nonsmoking. Cr cds: A, MC, V.

[D]

★ **RED HOT & BLUE.** *1600 Wilson Blvd (22209). 703/276-7427.* Hrs: 11 am-10 pm; Fri, Sat to 11 pm. Closed Thanksgiving, Dec 25. Bar. Semi-a la carte: lunch, dinner $4.69-$11.99. Specializes in Memphis pit barbecue dishes. Parking. Memphis blues memorabilia. Cr cds: A, DS, MC, V.

[D] [⌐]

★ **RT'S SEAFOOD KITCHEN.** *2300 Clarendon Blvd (22201). 703/841-0100.* Hrs: 11 am-10:30 pm; Fri, Sat to 11 pm; Sun 4-9:30 pm. Closed Jan 1, Thanksgiving, Dec 25. Cajun menu. Bar to midnight. Semi-a la carte: lunch $7.95-$10.95, dinner $11.95-$17.95. Child's meals. Specializes in Cajun-style seafood. Outdoor dining. Contemporary decor. Cr cds: A, C, D, DS, MC, V.

[D]

✓★ **SILVER DINER.** *3200 Wilson Blvd (22201). 703/812-8600.* Hrs: 7 am-midnight; Thurs to 1 am; Fri, Sat to 3 am; early-bird dinner Mon-Fri 4-6 pm; Sat, Sun brunch 11 am-3 pm. Closed Dec 25. Wine, beer. Semi-a la carte: bkfst $2.99-$7.99, lunch $4.99-$7.99, dinner $4.99-$11.99. Sat, Sun brunch $5.99-$7.99. Child's meals. Specializes in meatloaf, chicken, pasta. Own desserts. Reminiscent of 1950s-style aluminum-sided diner. Cr cds: A, C, D, DS, MC, V.

[D] [SC] [⌐]

★ ★ ★ **TIVOLI.** *1700 N Moore St (22209). 703/524-8900.* Hrs: 11:30 am-2:30 pm, 5:30-10 pm; Sat from 5:30 pm. Closed Sun; major hols. Res accepted; required Fri, Sat. Italian menu. Bar 11:30 am-midnight. Semi-a la carte: lunch $8.50-$11.50; dinner $12.50-$23.50. Prix fixe: dinner $60-$65. Specializes in pasta, seafood, veal. Contemporary decor. Cr cds: A, C, D, DS, MC, V.

[D] [⌐]

★ ★ **TOM SARRIS' ORLEANS HOUSE.** *1213 Wilson Blvd (22209). 703/524-2929.* Hrs: 11 am-11 pm; Sat from 4 pm; Sun 4-10 pm. Res accepted. Bar. Semi-a la carte: lunch $4.25-$7.95, dinner $7.95-$14.95. Child's meals. Specializes in prime rib, NY steak, seafood. Salad bar. Parking. New Orleans atmosphere; fountains, iron railings, Tiffany lampshades. Family-owned. Cr cds: A, C, D, DS, MC, V.

[⌐]

★ **VILLAGE BISTRO.** *1723 Wilson Blvd (22209). 703/522-0284.* Hrs: 11:30 am-2:30 pm, 5-10:30 pm; Fri, Sat to 11 pm; Sun 5-10 pm; early-bird dinner 5-7 pm. Closed Thanksgiving, Dec 25. Res accepted; required Fri, Sat. Continental menu. Bar. Semi-a la carte: lunch $5.50-$12.95, dinner $7.95-$17.95. Specializes in seafood, pasta. Parking. Outdoor dining. Monet prints on walls. Cr cds: A, C, D, DS, MC, V.

[D] [⌐]

★ ★ **WOO LAE OAK.** *1500 S Joyce St (22202), on grounds of River House complex. 703/521-3706.* Hrs: 11:30 am-10:30 pm. Closed Jan 1. Res accepted. Korean menu. Semi-a la carte: lunch, dinner $8-$20. Specializes in barbecued dishes prepared tableside. Parking. Large, open dining rm; Korean decor. Cr cds: A, C, D, MC, V.

[⌐]

Ashland (E-8)

(See also Richmond)

Founded 1858 **Pop** 5,864 **Elev** 221 ft **Area code** 804 **Zip** 23005
Information Hanover Visitor Information Center, 112 N Railroad Ave; 804/752-6766 or 800/897-1479.

Ashland was founded when the president of the Richmond, Fredericksburg and Potomac Railroad bought land here. He dug a well, struck mineral water and started a health resort—Slash Cottage (wilderness acres were called "slashes"). A thriving village grew up and took the name of Henry Clay's Kentucky estate. In 1866, the railroad company gave land to the Methodist Church and induced the church to move Randolph-Macon College here. A section of early 1900s houses along the railroad tracks has been set aside as a historic district.

What to See and Do

Paramount's Kings Dominion. A 400-acre family theme park consisting of 6 theme areas, including Hurricane Reef water park; Days of Thunder ride simulator; the Anaconda, a looping roller coaster that passes through an underwater tunnel; also Shockwave stand-up roller coaster; The Outer

Limits roller coaster; 33-story likeness of the Eiffel Tower with panoramic view; whitewater raft ride; live entertainment; shops. (June-Labor Day, daily; late Mar-May, after Labor Day-early Oct, wkends only) 1 mi E on VA 54, then 7 mi N on I-95 in Doswell. Phone 804/876-5000. ¢¢¢¢

Patrick Henry Home "Scotchtown" (1719). Also girlhood home of Dolley Madison; fine colonial architecture. (May-Oct, Wed-Sat; Apr, wkends; also by appt) 11 mi NW via VA 54, 671, County 685 (Scotchtown Rd), left onto Chiswell Lane. Phone 804/227-3500 or 804/883-6917. ¢¢

Randolph-Macon College (1830). (1,100 students) Coeducational, liberal arts, Methodist-affiliated college. Historic buildings include Washington-Franklin Hall, Old Chapel and Pace Hall. 1 mi W of I-95. Phone 804/752-7305. Campus tours **Free.**

Motels

✔★ ★ **BEST WESTERN HANOVER HOUSE.** *10296 Sliding Hill Rd, 1 blk W of I-95 Atlee-Elmont exit 86.* 804/550-2805; FAX 804/550-3843. 93 rms, 2 story. Apr-mid-Oct: S $38-$68; D $51-$68; each addl $5; under 12 free; higher rates special events; lower rates rest of yr. Crib free. TV; cable. Pool. Restaurant 6:30 am-8:30 pm. Ck-out noon. Coin lndry. Meeting rms. Business servs avail. Some balconies. Cr cds: A, C, D, DS, MC, V.

✔★ ★ **COMFORT INN.** *101 Cottage Green Dr.* 804/752-7777; FAX 804/798-0327. 126 rms, 2 story. Memorial Day-Labor Day: S, D $59-$73; each addl $5; suites $120; under 18 free; lower rates rest of yr. Crib free. Pet accepted. TV; cable. Pool. Complimentary continental bkfst. Restaurant adj open 24 hrs. Ck-out noon. Coin lndry. Business servs avail. Exercise equipt; weight machine, bicycles, sauna. Some refrigerators. Cr cds: A, C, D, DS, JCB, MC, V.

★ ★ **HOLIDAY INN.** *810 England St, 1 blk W of I-95 exit 92, at jct VA 54.* 804/798-4231; FAX 804/798-9074. 165 rms, 2 story. S, D $45-$86; each addl $10; under 12 free; higher rates some wkends. Crib free. TV; cable (premium). VCR avail. Pool; wading pool. Restaurant 6 am-10 pm. Rm serv. Bar; entertainment. Ck-out 11 am. Coin lndry. Meeting rms. Business servs avail. Valet serv. Exercise equipt; weights, bicycles. Private patios, balconies. Cr cds: A, C, D, DS, ER, JCB, MC, V.

Inn

★ ★ ★ **HENRY CLAY.** *114 N Railroad Ave, adj to visitors center.* 804/798-3100; FAX 804/752-7555; res: 800/343-4565. 15 rms, 3 story, 1 suite. S, D $80-$90; each addl $15; suite $145; higher rates special events. Crib $15. TV; cable. Complimentary continental bkfst. Dining rm 7-9 am, 11 am-2:30 pm, 6-9 pm. Ck-out 11 am, ck-in 2 pm. Business servs avail. In-rm modem link. Gift shop. Health club privileges. Balconies. Authentic reproduction of Georgian-revival inn. Totally nonsmoking. Cr cds: A, MC, V.

Restaurants

★ ★ **IRONHORSE.** *100 S Railroad Ave.* 804/752-6410. Hrs: 11:30 am-2:30 pm, 5:30-9 pm; Mon to 2:30 pm; Fri, Sat to 10 pm. Closed Sun; some major hols; also wk after Jan 1 & wk after July 4. Res accepted. Bar to closing. Entertainment. Semi-a la carte: lunch $4.95-$8.95, dinner $13.95-$18.95. Specializes in Angus beef, barbecue shrimp, crab cakes. Railroad memorabilia. Cr cds: C, D, DS, MC, V.

★ **SMOKEY PIG.** *212 S Washington Hwy.* 804/798-4590. Hrs: 11 am-9 pm; Sun from noon. Closed Mon; major hols. Bar. Semi-a la

carte: lunch $1.75-$9.95, dinner $1.75-$15.95. Child's meals. Specializes in pit-cooked meats, seafood, ribs. Cr cds: MC, V.

Basye (C-7)

(See also Luray, New Market, Woodstock)

Pop 200 (est) **Elev** 1,354 ft **Area code** 540 **Zip** 22810 **E-mail** bryce @bryceresort.com **Web** www.bryceresort.com

Information Bryce Resort, PO Box 3; 540/856-2121.

What to See and Do

Bryce Resort. On VA 263.

Summer: Fishing, swimming, horseback riding, golf, tennis, hiking, boating, grass skiing. Fee for activities.

Winter: Skiing: 2 double chairlifts, 3 rope tows; patrol, school, rentals; snowmaking; ski shop; restaurant, cafeteria, bar. Longest run 3,500 ft; vertical drop 500 ft. (Mid-Dec-mid-Mar, daily) Phone 540/856-2121. ¢¢¢¢

Motel

✔★ ★ **BEST WESTERN-MT JACKSON.** *(250 Conicville Rd, Mt Jackson 22842) at I-81 exit 273.* 540/477-2911; FAX 540/477-2392. 98 rms, 2 story. June-Oct: S $49-$53; D $53-$61; each addl $5; lower rates rest of yr. Crib free. Pet accepted. TV; cable. Pool; wading pool. Playground. Restaurant open 24 hrs. Bar 5-10 pm. Ck-out 11 am. Meeting rms. Business servs avail. Sundries. Gift shop. Tennis. Game rm. Cr cds: A, C, D, DS, MC, V.

Inn

★ ★ ★ **WIDOW KIP'S.** *(355 Orchard Dr, Mt Jackson 22842)* approx 9 mi E via VA 263E, then S on VA 698. 540/477-2400; res: 800/478-8714. 5 rms, 2 cottages. No rm phones. S $55-$75; D $65-$85; each addl $15, lower rates mid-wk. Pet accepted in cottages. TV in sitting rm, cottages; cable (premium). Pool. Complimentary full bkfst. Picnic lunches avail. Ck-out 11 am, ck-in 3 pm. Some fireplaces. Bicycles. Grill. Federal-style saltbox house (1830) on 7 acres. Victorian furnishings. Totally non-smoking. Cr cds: MC, V.

Big Stone Gap (F-2)

(See also Breaks Interstate Park, Wise)

Founded 1888 **Pop** 4,748 **Elev** 1,488 ft **Area code** 540 **Zip** 24219

Information Lonesome Pine Tourist Information Center, E Gilley Ave, PO Box 236; 540/523-2060.

This rugged mountain country gave John Fox, Jr, his inspiration for *Trail of the Lonesome Pine* and *Little Shepherd of Kingdom Come*. The town lies at the junction of three forks of the Powell River, which cuts a pass through Stone Mountain.

What to See and Do

John Fox, Jr, House & Museum. Occupied from 1888 by the author of *Trail of the Lonesome Pine* and *Little Shepherd of Kingdom Come*, best-selling novels of the early 1900s. Memorabilia and original furnishings.

Guided tours (June-Sept, daily exc Mon; Oct, wkends). 117 Shawnee Ave. Phone 540/523-2747 or 540/523-1235. ¢¢

June Tolliver House. Heroine in *Trail of the Lonesome Pine* lived here; period furnishings; now an arts & crafts center; restored 1890 house. (June-late Dec, daily exc Mon) Jerome St and Clinton Ave, jct US 23, 58A. Phone 540/523-1235. **Free.**

Natural Tunnel State Park. Consists of 648 acres. Giant hole chiseled through Purchase Ridge by Stock Creek; pinnacles or "chimneys." Railroad and stream are accommodated in this vast tunnel—100 ft or more in diameter, 850 ft long. Tunnel, visitor center with exhibits. Swimming, pool; fishing. Hiking. Picnicking; concession. Camping, tent & trailer sites (Memorial Day-Labor Day). Interpretive programs. Chairlift. Park (daily); tunnel & most activities (Memorial Day-Labor Day; daily). Standard fees. 18 mi SE, off US 23. Phone 540/940-2674.

Southwest Virginia Museum. Four-story mansion contains exhibits dealing with life in southwestern Virginia during original coal boom of the 1890s; also Native Americans of the area and early pioneers. (Memorial Day-Labor Day, daily; Mar-late May & early Sept-Dec, daily exc Mon; closed hols) W 1st St & Wood Ave. Phone 540/523-1322. ¢

Seasonal Event

Trail of the Lonesome Pine. June Tolliver Playhouse, adj to June Tolliver House. Outdoor musical drama. For reserved seats phone 540/523-1235. Thurs-Sat, late June-Labor Day.

Blacksburg (E-5)

(See also Radford, Roanoke, Salem)

Founded 1798 **Pop** 34,590 **Elev** 2,080 ft **Area code** 540 **Zip** 24060 **E-mail** gbcc@bev.net **Web** www.guide.new-river.va.us
Information Blacksburg Regional Chamber of Commerce, 1995 S Main St, Ste 901; 540/522-4503 or 800/288-4061.

The George Washington and Jefferson National Forests, which lie to the northwest, provide a colorful backdrop: azaleas, flowering dogwood and redbud in spring and brilliant hardwoods in fall. Virginia Polytechnic Institute and State University is a source of employment for the town. The forests' Blacksburg Ranger District office is located here.

What to See and Do

Mountain Lake. A resort lake, particularly inviting in late June and early July, when azaleas and rhododendron are in bloom. 20 mi NW on US 460, VA 700.

Smithfield Plantation (1773). Restored pre-Revolutionary house; original woodwork. Home of Colonel William Preston and three governors. Architectural link between Tidewater and Piedmont plantations of Virginia and those of the Mississippi Valley. Grounds restored by the Garden Club of Virginia. (Apr-Nov, Thurs-Sun afternoons) 1/4 mi W off US 460 bypass, at VA Tech exit. Phone 540/231-3947. ¢¢

Motels

★ ★ ★ **BEST WESTERN RED LION INN.** *900 Plantation Rd (VA 685).* 540/552-7770; FAX 540/552-6346. 104 rms, 1-2 story. S $49-$54; D $64-$68; each addl $6; suites $139; under 18 free; higher rates university events. Crib free. TV; cable, VCR avail. Pool; poolside serv. Playground. Restaurant 7 am-10 pm. Rm serv. Bar 4:30 pm-2 am. Ck-out noon. Meeting rms. Business servs avail. Valet serv. Sundries. Tennis. Golf privileges. X-country ski 15 mi. Lawn games. Picnic tables, grills. On 13 acres. Cr cds: A, C, D, DS, MC, V.

D ⏰ 🏊 🎿 🏊 ≈ ✦ 🐾 🔥 SC

★ ★ **COMFORT INN.** *3705 S Main St.* 540/951-1500; FAX 540/951-1530. 80 rms, 4 story. S $57-$65; D $62-$67; each addl $5; suite

$85; under 18 free; higher rates special events. Crib free. Pet accepted. TV; cable (premium), VCR avail. Pool. Complimentary continental bkfst. Restaurant adj 6 am-10 pm. Ck-out 11 am. Business servs avail. In-rm modem link. Valet serv. Exercise equipt; weight machine, rowers. Microwaves avail. Cr cds: A, C, D, DS, ER, JCB, MC, V.

D 🐾 ≈ ✗ ➤ 🐾 SC

✔ ★ ★ **DAYS INN.** *(US 11, Christiansburg 24073) 6 mi S, 1 blk NE of I-81 exit 118.* 540/382-0261; FAX 540/382-0365. 122 rms, 2 story. S $39-$84; D $44-$84; each addl $5; under 18 free; higher rates: Radford Univ graduation, football games. Crib free. Pet accepted. TV; cable (premium). Pool. Playground. Complimentary continental bkfst. Ck-out noon. In-rm modem link. Microwaves avail. Cr cds: A, C, D, DS, JCB, MC, V.

D 🐾 ≈ ➤ 🐾 SC

★ ★ **HAMPTON INN.** *(50 Hampton Blvd, Christiansburg 24073) S via I-81, exit 118, then E.* 540/382-2055; FAX 540/382-4515. 125 rms, 2 story. S $55; D $63; under 18 free; higher rates: univ graduation, football games. Crib free. TV; cable (premium). Pool. Restaurant opp 6 am-10 pm. Ck-out 11 am. Coin lndry. Business servs avail. Microwave avail. Cr cds: A, D, DS, MC, V.

D ≈ ➤ 🐾 SC

★ ★ **HOLIDAY INN.** *3503 Holiday Ln.* 540/951-1330; FAX 540/951-4847. 98 rms, 2 story. S $55-$65; D $60-$70; each addl $5; suites $135; under 12 free; higher rates: univ graduation, football wknds. Crib free. Pet accepted. TV; cable (premium). Pool; wading pool. Restaurant 6:30 am-2 pm, 5-10 pm. Rm serv. Bar. Ck-out noon. Coin lndry. Meeting rm. Business servs avail. Valet serv. Sundries. X-country ski 20 mi. Some in-rm steam baths. Cr cds: A, C, D, DS, JCB, MC, V.

D 🐾 🎿 ≈ ➤ 🐾 SC

★ ★ ★ **MARRIOTT.** *900 Prices Fork Rd.* 540/552-7001; FAX 540/552-0827. 147 rms, 2 story. S, D $89-$139; each addl $10; suites $160; under 18 free. Crib free. TV; cable (premium), VCR avail. 2 pools, 1 indoor; wading pool, whirlpool. Playground. Complimentary coffee in lobby. Restaurant 6:30 am-10 pm. Bar noon-2 am; entertainment. Ck-out 1 pm. Meeting rms. Business servs avail. In-rm modem link. Bellhops. Valet serv. Sundries. Health club privileges. Tennis. Game rm. Microwaves avail. Cr cds: A, C, D, DS, ER, JCB, MC, V.

D 🎿 ≈ ➤ 🐾 SC

Inn

★ ★ ★ **THE OAKS.** *(311 E Main St, Christiansburg 24073) S on I-81, exit 114, turn right on Main St approx 2 mi.* 540/381-1500; FAX 540/382-1728; res: 800/336-OAKS. Web www.innbrook.com/oaks.html. 7 rms, 3 story. S $85-$125; D $115-$150; lower rates Jan-Mar. Children over 14 yrs only. TV; cable (premium). Whirlpool. Complimentary full bkfst; afternoon refreshments. Restaurant nearby. Ck-out noon, ck-in 4 pm. Business servs avail. In-rm modem link. Valet serv. Airport transportation. Refrigerators; some fireplaces. Balconies. Queen Anne/Victorian residence (1889); period furnishings. Surrounded by 300-yr-old white oak trees. Totally nonsmoking. Cr cds: A, DS, MC, V.

➤ 🔥

Blue Ridge Parkway (F-4 - D-6)

(See also Roanoke, Waynesboro)

Elev 649-6,050 ft; avg 3,000 ft

Winding 469 mountainous miles between Shenandoah and Great Smoky Mountains National Parks (about 217 miles are in Virginia), the Blue Ridge Parkway represents a different concept in highway travel. It is not an express highway (speed limit 45 MPH) but a road intended for leisurely travel. All towns are bypassed. Travelers in a hurry would be wise to take state and US routes, where speed limits are higher.

The parkway follows the Blue Ridge Mountains for about 355 miles, then winds through the Craggies, Pisgahs and Balsams to the Great Smokies. Overlooks, picnic and camp sites, visitor centers, nature trails, fishing streams and lakes and points of interest are numerous and well marked.

Accommodations are plentiful in cities and towns along the way. The parkway itself offers lodging at four spots: Peaks of Otter (86 miles south of Waynesboro, see MOTEL), Rocky Knob Cabins (174 miles south of Waynesboro), Doughton Park (241 miles south of Waynesboro) and Pisgah Inn (409 miles south of Waynesboro). Food availability is limited on the parkway; in-season food service is available at Whetstone Ridge, Otter Creek, Mabry Mill, Doughton Park, Crabtree Meadows and Mt Pisgah. Peaks of Otter Lodge provides food and lodging year-round.

The parkway is open all year, but the best time to drive it is between April and November. Some sections are closed by ice and snow for periods in winter and early spring. Fog may be present during wet weather. The higher sections west of Asheville to Great Smoky Mountains National Park and north of Asheville to Mt Mitchell may be closed January through March due to hazardous driving conditions.

For maps, pamphlets and detailed information contact Superintendent, 400 BB&T Bldg, One Pack Sq, Asheville, NC 28801; 704/298-0398.

What to See and Do

(Park visitor facilities are open May-Oct. Numbered concrete posts are located at each mile of the parkway. "Milepost 0" is at Rockfish Gap; MP 469 is just above Cherokee, NC.)

Camping. Tent and trailer sites at Otter Creek, Peaks of Otter, Roanoke Mt, Rocky Knob, Doughton Park, Julian Price Memorial Park, Linville Falls, Crabtree Meadows and Mt Pisgah. (May-Oct) 14-day limit, June-Labor Day. No electricity; pets on leash only; water is shut off with first freeze, usually late Oct. Fee/site/night. Primitive winter camping at Linville Falls when roads are passable.

Craft demonstrations and sales.

Northwest Trading Post. Country store sells native handicrafts. MP 258.6.

Parkway Craft Center. MP 294. (See BLOWING ROCK, NC)

Folk Art Center. Craft Guild Headquarters, sales, parkway travel information. Interpretive programs (daily, May-Oct). MP 382.

Fishing. Rainbow, brook, brown trout and smallmouth bass in streams and lakes. State licenses required.

Interpretive programs. Outdoor talks (mid-June-Labor Day) at Otter Creek (MP 60.8), Peaks of Otter (MP 86), Rocky Knob (MP 169), Doughton Park (MP 241.1), Price Park (MP 297.1), Linville Falls (MP 316.3), Crabtree Meadows (MP 340) and Mt Pisgah (MP 408.6). Obtain schedules at Parkway Visitor Centers.

Riding. 20 mi of trails in Moses H. Cone Memorial Park (MP 292.7). Horses for hire at Blowing Rock, NC.

Self-guided trails. Grades are not difficult. Walks take about 30 min. Trails on the parkway include

Mountain Farm Trail. Typical mountain farm, reconstructed. MP 5.8.

Greenstone Trail. Of geologic interest. MP 8.8.

Trail of the Trees. Leads to overlook of James River. MP 63.6.

Elk Run Trail. Forest, plant, animal community. MP 86.

Rocky Knob Trail. Leads to overlook of Rock Castle Gorge. MP 168.

Mabry Mill Trail. Old-time mountain industry. MP 176.

Cascades Trail. Leads to waterfall. MP 272.

Cone Park Trail. Manor house wild garden. MP 294.

Flat Rock Trail. Magnificent valley and mountain views. MP 308.3.

Linville Falls Trail. Views of falls, Linville River Gorge. MP 317.5.

Craggy Gardens Trail. Traverses high mountain "gardens." MP 364.6.

Richland Balsam Trail. Spruce-fir forests. Highest spot on parkway. MP 431.

✪ **Visitor Centers.** Exhibits, travel information, interpretive publications. Centers (daily during peak travel season) include

Humpback Rocks Visitor Center. Pioneer mountain farm, park ranger. MP 5.8.

James River Wayside. Story of James River and Kanawha Canal, park ranger. MP 63.6.

Peaks of Otter Visitor Center. Wildlife exhibits, park ranger. MP 86.

Rocky Knob Information Station. Information, exhibits, park ranger. MP 170.

Mabry Mill. Old-time mountain industry, including tannery exhibits, picturesque mill, blacksmith shop. MP 176.

Cumberland Knob Contact Station. Visitor information, publications, park ranger. MP 218.

Linn Cove Information Center. MP 304.

Museum of North Carolina Minerals. (Daily; winter hrs vary; closed hols) MP 331.

Craggy Gardens Visitor Center. 5,892-ft elevation. Natural history exhibits, naturalist. (Mid-June-Labor Day, daily; May-mid-June, early Sept-Oct, wkends) MP 364.6.

Folk Art Center. Craft Guild Headquarters, sales, parkway travel information, park ranger. (Daily) MP 382.

Motel

★ ★ ★ **PEAKS OF OTTER LODGE.** *(Bedford 24523)* on Blue Ridge Pkwy at jct VA 43 *(Milepost 86).* 540/586-1081; FAX 540/786-4420; res: 800/542-5927 (VA). Web www.1mall.com/stores/peaks. 63 rms, 2 story. Mar-Nov: S $67; D $72; each addl $6.25; suites $85-$100; under 16 free; MAP rest of yr. Crib free. TV in lobby. Restaurant (see PEAKS OF OTTER). Bar 5-11 pm. Ck-out noon. Meeting rm. Business servs avail. Sundries. Gift shop. Private patios, balconies. Located on a lake and surrounded by peaks. Scenic view. Cr cds: MC, V.

D ⇌ ⚙

Lodge

★ ★ ★ **DOE RUN.** *(Milepost 189, Fancy Gap 24328)* 1/8 mi S of Blue Ridge Pkwy. 540/398-2212; FAX 540/398-2833; res: 800/325-6189. Web www.hillsville.com/doerun. 47 kit. suites, 1-2 story. No elvtr. May-Oct: kit. suites $119-$250; each addl $18; under 15 free; wkly rates; hunting, golf plans; lower rates rest of yr. Crib free. Pet accepted; $45 deposit. TV; VCR (movies $3). Heated pool; sauna, poolside serv. Complimentary coffee in rms. Restaurant (see HIGH COUNTRY). Bar; entertainment Fri, Sat. Ck-out noon. Meeting rms. Business servs avail. Sundries. Lighted tennis. 18-hole golf privileges, greens fee, pro, putting green, driving range. Rec rm. Lawn games. Balconies. Picnic tables. Cr cds: A, MC, V.

D ⇌ ⚙ ✗ ⚙ ⚙ ⚙ ⚙ SC

Inn

★ ★ **OSCEOLA MILL COUNTRY INN.** *Steele's Tavern (24476),* 4 mi W of Blue Ridge Pkwy, Milepost 27, on VA 56. 540/377-6455. 12 rms, 1-2 story, 1 cottage. No rm phones. S, D $89-$109; each addl $20; cottage $139-$169; wkly rates. Pool. Complimentary full bkfst. Ck-out 11 am, ck-in 2 pm. Business servs avail. In renovated 1849 mill, mill store and restored 1873 miller's house. Totally nonsmoking. Cr cds: MC, V.

D ⚙ ⚙ ⚙

Restaurants

★ ★ **HIGH COUNTRY.** *(See Doe Run Lodge)* 540/398-2212. Web www.hillsville.com/doerun. Hrs: 8 am-10 pm; Sun brunch 11:30 am-3 pm. Closed Dec 25. Res accepted. Bar noon-midnight; closed Sun. Complete meals: bkfst $4.25-$12.95. Semi-a la carte: lunch $4.95-$16.95, dinner $13.95-$22.95. Entertainment Fri, Sat. Panoramic view of country-side. Cr cds: A, MC, V.

D ⊐

✔★★ **PEAKS OF OTTER.** *(See Peaks of Otter Lodge Motel)* *540/586-9263.* Web www.1mall.com/stores/peaks. Hrs: 7:30-10:30 am, 11:30 am-2:30 pm, 5-8:30 pm; Sun brunch noon-8:30 pm. Bar 5-11 pm. Semi-a la carte: bkfst $3-$7.95, lunch $4.50-$8.95, dinner $4.70-$16.95. Sun brunch $10.55. Child's meals. Specialties: prime rib of beef au jus, barbecued "little pig" ribs, whole rainbow trout. Salad bar. Panoramic view of mountains, lake. Rustic decor. Family-owned. Cr cds: MC, V.

D ⊐

Booker T. Washington National Monument (E-5)

(See also Roanoke)

(Approx 18 mi S on VA 116 from Roanoke to Burnt Chimney, then continue 6 mi E on VA 122)

The 1861 property inventory of the Burroughs plantation listed, along with household goods and farm implements, the entry "1 Negro boy (Booker)—$400." Freed in 1865, the boy and his family moved to Malden, West Virginia. There, while working at a salt furnace and in coal mines, the youngster learned the alphabet from *Webster's Blueback Spelling Book.* Later, by working at the salt furnace before school, then going to work at the mine after school, he got the rudiments of an education. When he realized that everyone else at the school roll call had two names, he chose Washington for his own.

From Malden, at 16, he started the 500-mile trip to Hampton Institute, where he earned his way. He taught at Malden for two years, attended Wayland Seminary and returned to Hampton Institute to teach. In July 1881 he started Tuskegee Institute in Alabama with 30 pupils, two run-down buildings and $2,000 for salaries. When Washington died in 1915, the Institute had 107 buildings, more than 2,000 acres and was assessed at more than $500,000.

The 224-acre monument includes most of the original plantation. A 1/4-mile self-guided plantation trail passes reconstructed farm buildings, a slave cabin, crops and animals of the period; there is also a 11/2-mile self-guided Jack-O-Lantern Branch nature trail. Picnic facilities. Visitor Center has an audiovisual program, exhibits depicting his life (daily; closed Jan 1, Thanksgiving, Dec 25). Phone 540/721-2094. **Free.**

Inn

★★ **MANOR AT TAYLOR'S STORE.** *(Rte 1, Box 533, Smith Mountain Lake 24184) 4 mi W on VA 122S. 540/721-3951; FAX 540/721-5243; res: 800/248-6267.* 9 rms, 3 story. No rm phones. S, D $85-$180. TV in sitting rm. Complimentary full bkfst. Ck-out 11 am, ck-in 4 pm. Business servs avail. Exercise equipt; rower, ski machine, whirlpool. Rec rm. Lawn games. Some balconies. Library, sun rm. On 120 acres with pond. Historic trading post built in 1799, became a post office in 1818. Totally nonsmoking. Cr cds: A, MC, V.

▸ ✗ ⊠ ✗

Breaks Interstate Park (E-3)

(See also Wise)

(8 mi N of Haysi, VA, and 7 mi SE of Elkhorn City, KY, on KY-VA 80)

The "Grand Canyon of the South," where the Russell Fork of the Big Sandy River plunges through the mountains, is the major attraction of this 4,600-acre park on the Virginia-Kentucky border. From the entrance, a paved road winds through an evergreen forest and then skirts the canyon rim. Overlooks provide a spectacular view of the Towers, a 1/2-mile-long, 1/3-mile-wide pyramid of rocks; the 5-mile-long, 1,600-foot-deep, 250-million-year-old gorge; odd rock formations; caves; springs and a profusion of rhododendron.

The visitor center houses natural and historical exhibits and a coal exhibit (Apr-Oct, daily). Laurel Lake is stocked with bass and bluegill. Picnicking, swimming pool, pedal boats, hiking and bridle trails and playground. Camping (Apr-Oct, fee); cottages (all yr), restaurant, gift shop. Motor lodge (see MOTEL). Facilities (Apr-mid-Dec, daily); park (all yr, daily). For details contact Breaks Interstate Park, PO Box 100, Breaks, 24607; 540/865-4413 or 800/982-5122 (reservations). Memorial Day-Labor Day, per car ¢; Rest of yr **Free.**

Motel

✔★★ **BREAKS MOTOR LODGE.** *(Breaks 24607) on VA 80.* *540/865-4414; FAX 540/865-5561.* 34 rms, 1-2 story. Apr-Oct: S $66.03; D $74.55; each addl $8; cottages $350/wk. Closed Dec 21-Mar. Crib free. TV; cable. Pool; wading pool, lifeguard. Restaurant 7 am-9 pm. Ck-out 11 am. Meeting rm. Sundries. Gift shop. Balconies. Picnic tables, grills. Bicycle rentals. Woodland setting; overlooks Breaks Canyon. Hiking trails, picnic shelters. Cr cds: A, DS, MC, V.

▸ ✗ ⩲ ⊠ ✗ SC

Bristol (F-3)

(See also Abingdon)

Founded 1771 **Pop** Bristol, VA: 18,426; Bristol, TN: 24,000 (est) **Elev** 1,680 ft **Area code** 540 (VA); 423 (TN) **Zip** 24201 (VA); 37620 (TN) **Web** www.bjournal.com/tourism/bristol.html

Information Chamber of Commerce, located at 20 Volunteer Pkwy, TN, or mail to PO Box 519, VA 24203; 423/989-4850.

Essentially a city in two states, Bristol is actually two cities—Bristol, TN, and Bristol, VA—sharing the same main street and the same personality. Each has its own government and city services. Together they constitute a major shopping center. Named for the English industrial center, Bristol is an important factory town in its own right. Electronics, metal goods and textiles are its major products. These carry on the pioneer tradition of an ironworks, established here about 1784, which made the first nails for use on the frontier.

What to See and Do

Bristol Caverns. Unusual rock formations, seen from lighted, paved walkways winding through caverns and along an underground river. Guided tours every 20 min. Picnic area. (Daily; closed Thanksgiving, Dec 25) 5 mi SE on US 421, off I-81. Phone 423/878-2011. ¢¢¢

Rocky Mount Historic Site. Features the 21/2-story log house (1770) that served, from 1790 to 1792, as capitol under William Blount, governor of the Territory of the United States South of the River Ohio. Restored to its original simplicity; 18th-century furniture. On grounds are restored log kitchen, slave cabin, barn, blacksmith shop and smokehouse. (Daily;

closed Thanksgiving, Dec 21-Jan 5; also wkends Jan, Feb) 11 mi SW on US 11E. Phone 423/538-7396. ¢¢

Seasonal Event

Bristol Motor Speedway. 5 mi S on US 11E. Phone 423/764-1161. Apr, June & Aug.

Motels

(Most rates higher race weekends)

★ **BUDGET HOST.** *1209 W State St.* 540/669-5187; FAX 540/466-5848. 24 rms. S, D $28.50-$80; each addl $4; under 12 free; wkly rates. TV; cable (premium). Restaurant nearby. Ck-out 11 am. Business servs avail. Cr cds: A, DS, MC, V.

★★ **COMFORT INN.** *2368 Lee Hwy.* 540/466-3881; FAX 540/466-6544. 60 rms, 2 story. Apr-Oct: S, D $63-$195; each addl $5; suites $125-$225; under 18 free; lower rates rest of yr. Crib free. TV; cable (premium). Pool. Complimentary continental bkfst. Restaurant nearby. Ck-out 11 am. Business servs avail. Cr cds: A, C, D, DS, ER, JCB, MC, V.

★★ **RAMADA INN.** *2221 Euclid Ave, at W State St.* 540/669-7171; FAX 540/669-8694. 123 rms, 2 story. S, D $49-$95; each addl $4; under 18 free; higher rates special events. TV; cable. Pool. Restaurant 7 am-2 pm, 5-10 pm. Rm serv. Bar from 5 pm. Ck-out noon. Meeting rms. Business servs avail. Sundries. Microwaves avail. Cr cds: A, C, D, DS, JCB, MC, V.

✔★ **RED CARPET INN.** *15589 Lee Hwy (24202), I-81 exit 10.* 540/669-1151. 60 rms, 2 story. June-Oct: S $35-$74; D $38-$80; each addl $8; lower rates rest of yr. Crib free. Pet accepted, some restrictions. TV; cable (premium). Pool. Ck-out noon. Business servs avail. Microwaves avail. Cr cds: A, D, DS, MC, V.

★ **SUPER 8.** *2139 Lee Hwy, I-81 exit 5.* 540/466-8800; FAX 540/466-8800, ext. 400. 62 rms, 3 story. S, D $43-$61; each addl $6; under 12 free. Crib free. Pet accepted. TV; cable. Complimentary coffee in lobby. Restaurant nearby. Ck-out 11 am. Business servs avail. Some refrigerators, microwaves. Picnic tables. Cr cds: A, C, D, DS, JCB, MC, V.

Restaurants

★ **ATHENS STEAK HOUSE.** *105 Goodson St.* 540/466-8271. Hrs: 4-10:30 pm. Closed Sun; major hols. Greek, Amer menu. Bar. Semi-a la carte: dinner $7.95-$20.45. Specializes in lobster tail, steak. Cr cds: A, MC, V.

★★ **VINYARD.** *603 Gate City Hwy.* 540/466-4244. Hrs: 7 am-10 pm; Fri, Sat to 11 pm. Closed July 4, Dec 24 (eve), 25. Res accepted wkends. Italian, Amer menu. Bar. Semi-a la carte: bkfst $3.95-$6.95, lunch $4.50-$7.50. Complete meals: dinner $8.95-$25. Specializes in fresh seafood, veal. Salad bar. Cr cds: A, C, D, DS, MC, V.

Brookneal (F-6)

(For accommodations see Lynchburg; also see South Boston)

Settled ca 1790 **Pop** 1,344 **Elev** 560 ft **Area code** 804 **Zip** 24528

What to See and Do

Patrick Henry National Memorial (Red Hill). Last home and burial place of Patrick Henry. Restoration of family cottage, cook's cabin, smokehouse, stable, kitchen. Patrick Henry's law office. Museum and gift shop on grounds. Interpretive video. (Daily; closed Jan 1, Thanksgiving, Dec 25) 3 mi E on VA 40, 2 mi S on VA 600 & 619. Phone 804/376-2044. ¢¢

Cape Charles (E-10)

(See also Hampton, Newport News, Norfolk, Portsmouth, Virginia Beach)

Pop 1,398 **Elev** 10 ft **Area code** 757 **Zip** 23310

Information Chesapeake Bay Bridge & Tunnel District, Public Relations Dept, PO Box 111; 757/331-2960, ext 20.

The Chesapeake Bay Bridge-Tunnel (17.6 miles long) leads from Cape Charles (12 miles south of the town) to Virginia Beach/Norfolk, VA. There is a scenic stop, gift shop, restaurant and fishing pier (bait avail). **Note:** Noncommercial vehicles entering with compressed gas containers are limited to **(a)** two nonpermanently mounted containers with a maximum individual capacity of 105 lbs water or 45 lbs LP-gas each, or one container with a maximum capacity of 60 lbs LP-gas; or **(b)** not more than 2 permanently mounted containers with a total capacity of 200 gallons water when LP-gas is used as a motor fuel. One-way passenger car toll ¢¢¢

Inn

★★ **BAY AVENUE SUNSET BED AND BREAKFAST.** *108 Bay Ave.* 757/331-2424; FAX 757/331-4877. E-mail sunsetb&b@aol.com. 4 rms, 3 story. No rm phones. Mar-Dec: S, D $75-$95; each addl $20; higher rates hols (2-day min); lower rates rest of yr. Children over 10 yrs only. TV; cable (premium). Complimentary full bkfst. Ck-out 11 am, ck-in 2 pm. Business servs avail. Luggage handling. Bicycles. Victorian house (1915) overlooking Chesapeake Bay. Beach. Totally nonsmoking. Cr cds: A, DS, MC, V.

Restaurants

✔★★★ **EASTVILLE MANOR.** *(6058 Willow Oak Rd, Eastville 23347)* 7 mi N on US 13, E on VA 631. 757/678-7378. Hrs: 11:30 am-2:30 pm, 5:30-9 pm. Closed Sun, Mon; also Tues Sept-May. Res accepted. Contemporary Amer menu. Wine list. A la carte entrees: lunch $3.95-$8.95, dinner $8.95-$15.95. Child's meals. Specializes in fresh seafood, beef tenderloin, pasta. Own baking. In 1886 farmhouse; polished wood floors, chandeliers, antiques; landscaped grounds. Cr cds: MC, V.

✔★ **LITTLE ITALY.** *(10027 Rogers Dr, Nassawadox 23413)* 15 mi N on US 13, E at Nassawadox stoplight. 757/442-7831. Hrs: 11 am-8 pm, Fri, Sat to 9 pm; summer Mon-Sat to 9 pm. Closed Sun; most major hols. Res accepted. Italian menu. Bar. Semi-a la carte: lunch, dinner $2.99-$12.99. Child's meals. Specialties: lasagna, cannolli, tiramisu. Street parking. Former country-style grocery store. No cr cds accepted.

Cape Henry Memorial (F-10)

(For accommodations see Norfolk, Virginia Beach)

(10 mi E of Norfolk on US 60)
The first English settlers of Jamestown landed here on April 26, 1607. They claimed the land for England, stayed four days, named their landing spot for Henry (then Prince of Wales and oldest son of King James I) and put up a cross.

A cross put up by the Daughters of the American Colonists in 1935 marks the approximate site of the first landing. An interpretive display describes the Battle of the Capes, a sea battle fought between England and France in 1781, a prelude to the Battle of Yorktown. Nearby is Cape Henry Lighthouse, first lighthouse in the United States authorized and built by the federal government (1791). The memorial is in Fort Story Military Reservation.

Charlottesville (D-7)

(See also Waynesboro)

Founded 1762 **Pop** 40,341 **Elev** 480 ft **Area code** 804 **E-mail** caccbb @comet.net
Information Charlottesville/Albemarle Convention & Visitors Bureau, jct I-64 & VA 20, PO Box 161, 22902; 804/977-1783.

Thomas Jefferson was born here, as was the University of Virginia, which he founded and designed. Ash Lawn-Highland, which was James Monroe's home, and Monticello are southeast of the city.

In the gently rolling terrain of Albemarle County, Charlottesville is almost at the center of Virginia; it is the trading center for a widespread area. In colonial times, tobacco was the dominant product. Today wheat, beef and dairy herds, riding and race horses, peaches, frozen foods, electronic products, light industry and mountains of native Albemarle pippin apples invigorate the economy.

The biggest Charlottesville employer, however, remains the university and its related enterprises.

What to See and Do

Albemarle County Court House. N wing was used in 1820s as a "common temple," shared by Episcopalian, Methodist, Presbyterian and Baptist sects, one Sunday a month to each but with all who wished attending each Sunday. Jefferson, Monroe and Madison worshiped here. Court Square.

★ **Ash Lawn-Highland** (1799). Built on a site personally selected by Thomas Jefferson, this 535-acre estate was the home of President James Monroe (1799-1823). The estate is now owned by Monroe's alma mater, the College of William and Mary. This early-19th-century working plantation offers guided tours of the house with Monroe possessions, spinning and weaving demonstrations, old boxwood gardens, peacocks, picnic spots. Special events include Summer Festival (June-Aug) of arts, evening concerts, children's shows (Sat), Plantation Days Wkend, spring and Christmas programs. (Daily; closed Jan 1, Thanksgiving, Dec 25) 4¼ mi SE on County 795. Phone 804/293-9539. ¢¢¢

Historic Michie Tavern (ca 1780). Built on land granted to Patrick Henry's father and later bought by John Michie, this is one of the oldest homesteads remaining in Virginia. Museum illustrates 18th-century tavern life; 1920s preservation perspective on colonial history. Lunch buffet in converted 200-yr-old log house. (Daily; closed Jan 1, Dec 25) 1 mi S on VA 20. Phone 804/977-1234. Museum ¢¢

★ **Monticello.** Located on a mountaintop, this is one of the most beautiful estates in Virginia and is considered a classic of American architecture.

Monticello was designed by Thomas Jefferson and built over the course of 40 yrs, symbolizing the pleasure he found in "putting up and pulling down." Jefferson moved into the first completed outbuilding of his new home in 1771, though construction continued until 1809. Most of the interior furnishings are original. Tours of the restored orchard, vineyard, 1,000-ft-long vegetable garden and Mulberry Row, once the site of plantation workshops. Jefferson died at Monticello on July 4, 1826, and was buried in the family cemetery. The Thomas Jefferson Memorial Foundation maintains the house and gardens. (Daily; closed Dec 25) 2 mi SE on VA 53. Phone 804/984-9822. ¢¢ Approx 2 mi W of here is

Monticello Visitors Center. Personal and family memorabilia; architectural models and drawings; *Thomas Jefferson: The Pursuit of Liberty,* a 35-minute film, is shown twice daily. (Daily; closed Dec 25) On VA 20S at I-64. Phone 804/984-9822. **Free.**

Monuments.

Stonewall Jackson on Little Sorrel. By Charles Keck. Adj courthouse.

Robert E. Lee Monument. Jefferson St between 1st & 2nd Sts.

Lewis and Clark Monument. Memorial to Jefferson's secretary, Meriwether Lewis, who explored the Louisiana Territory with his friend William Clark. Midway Park, Ridge & Main Sts.

George Rogers Clark Memorial. Brother of William Clark and soldier on the frontier, this intrepid explorer, who opened up the Northwest Territory, was an Albemarle County native son. W Main St, E of university.

Shenandoah National Park (see). 20 mi W on VA 250 to Afton, then N on Skyline Dr.

Sightseeing tour. The Charlottesville/Albemarle Information Center, located on VA 20S in the Monticello Visitors Center Bldg, has information for a walking tour of historic Charlottesville. Phone 804/977-1783.

Skiing. Wintergreen Resort. Five chairlifts; patrol, school, rentals; lodge (see RESORTS); nursery. 10 runs; longest run 4,200 ft; vertical drop 1,000 ft. (1st wkend Dec-3rd wkend Mar, daily) Night skiing. Summer activities include golf, tennis, fishing and boating, horseback riding. W on US 250 to VA 151, then S to VA 664, turn right, follow signs (approx 4½ mi). Phone 804/325-2200. ¢¢¢¢

University of Virginia (1819). (18,100 students) Founded by Thomas Jefferson and built according to his plans. Handsome red-brick buildings with white trim, striking vistas, smooth lawns and ancient trees form the grounds of Jefferson's "academical village." The serpentine walls, one brick thick, which Jefferson designed for strength and beauty, are famous. Room 13, W Range, occupied by Edgar Allan Poe as a student, is displayed for the public. Walking tours start at the Rotunda (daily; closed 3 wks mid-Dec-early Jan). W end of Main St. Phone 804/924-1019. Guided tours **Free.**

Annual Events

Founder's Day (Jefferson's Birthday). Commemorative ceremonies. Apr 13.

Dogwood Festival. Parade, lacrosse and golf tournaments, carnival. Nine days mid-Apr.

Garden Week. Some fine private homes and gardens in the area are open. Mid-Apr.

Motels

✔★ ★ **BEST WESTERN-MOUNT VERNON.** *1613 Emmet St (22901), Jct US 29 Business and US 250 Bypass.* 804/296-5501; FAX 804/977-6249. 110 rms, 1-2 story. Mar-Oct: S $51-$55; D $58-$65; each addl $6; under 18 free; family, wkly rates; higher rates graduation; lower rates rest of yr. Crib free. Pet accepted, some restrictions. TV; cable (premium). Complimentary coffee in rms. Restaurant adj 6-10 am. Ck-out noon. Meeting rms. Business servs avail. Bellhops. Sundries. Pool; wading pool. Microwaves, refrigerators avail. Cr cds: A, C, D, DS, ER, JCB, MC, V.

★ ★ ★ **COURTYARD BY MARRIOTT.** *638 Hillsdale Dr (22901). 804/973-7100; FAX 804/973-7128.* 150 rms, 2-3 story. Mar-late Nov: S, D $72-$85; under 18 free; wkly rates; higher rates graduation; lower rates rest of yr. Crib free. TV; cable (premium), VCR avail. Indoor pool; whirlpool. Complimentary coffee in rms. Bar 5-10 pm. Ck-out noon. Coin lndry. Meeting rms. Business servs avail. In-rm modem link. Sundries. Free airport transportation. Exercise equipt; weight machine, bicycle. Some refrigerators; microwaves avail. Balconies. Picnic tables. Cr cds: A, C, D, DS, MC, V.

D 🏊 ✕ 🏃 🔥 SC

★ ★ **HAMPTON INN.** *2035 India Rd (22901). 804/978-7888; FAX 804/973-0436.* 123 rms, 5 story. S $58-$62; D $62-$70; under 18 free; higher rates univ graduation. Crib free. TV; cable (premium). Pool. Complimentary continental bkfst, coffee. Restaurant nearby. Ck-out noon. Meeting rm. Business servs avail. Bellhops. Sundries. Free airport, RR station, bus depot transportation. Health club privileges. Cr cds: A, C, D, DS, MC, V.

D 🏊 🏃 🔥 SC

★ ★ **HOLIDAY INN.** *1600 Emmet St (22901), near jct US 29 Business & US 250 Bypass. 804/293-9111; FAX 804/977-2780.* 129 rms, 3 story. S $64-$68; D $74-$78; each addl $10; under 18 free; higher rates special univ events. Crib free. Pet accepted. TV; cable (premium), VCR avail. Pool; wading pool. Restaurant 6:30 am-10 pm; Fri, Sat to 11 pm. Rm serv. Bar 10-1 am. Ck-out noon. Meeting rms. Business servs avail. In-rm modem link. Bellhops. Valet serv. Free airport, RR station, bus depot transportation. Exercise equipt; bicycle, stair machine, sauna. Health club privileges. Cr cds: A, C, D, DS, JCB, MC, V.

D 🏄 🏊 🏃 ✕ 🔥 SC

★ ★ **HOLIDAY INN MONTICELLO.** *1200 5th St SW (22902), I-64 exit 120. 804/977-5100; FAX 804/293-5228.* 128 rms, 6 story. S $75-$85; D $75-$95; each addl $10; suites $115-$125; under 18 free; wkend rates; higher rates univ events. Crib free. TV; cable (premium). Pool; wading pool. Complimentary coffee in rms. Restaurant 6:30-10:30 am, 5-10 pm. Rm serv. Bar to 11 pm. Ck-out noon. Meeting rms. Coin lndry. Business center. Bellhops. Valet serv (Mon-Fri). Golf privileges, pro, greens fee $22, putting green, driving range. Health club privileges. Game rm. Refrigerators avail. Cr cds: A, D, DS, JCB, MC, V.

D ✕ 🏃 🏊 🏃 🔥 SC 🏌

✔ ★ **KNIGHTS INN.** *1300 Seminole Trail (22901), US 29N. 804/973-8133; FAX 804/973-1168.* 115 units. S, D $39-$58; each addl $6; kits. $63; under 18 free. Crib free. Pet accepted, some restrictions. TV; cable (premium), VCR avail (movies). Pool. Complimentary coffee in lobby. Restaurant nearby. Ck-out noon. Meeting rm. Business servs avail. Cr cds: A, C, D, DS, MC, V.

D 🏄 🏊 🏃 🔥 SC

✔★ ★ **RAMADA INN-MONTICELLO.** *2097 Inn Dr (22911), I-64, exit 124. 804/977-3300; FAX 804/979-8558.* 100 rms, 2 story. Apr-Nov: S $50-$55; D $55-$69; each addl $5; under 16 free; higher rates special events; lower rates rest of yr. Crib $5. TV; cable (premium), VCR avail. Complimentary continental bkfst. Complimentary coffee in rms. Restaurant 7 am-10 pm. Rm serv. Bar 11-2 am. Ck-out noon. Meeting rms. Business servs avail. Bellhops. Valet serv. Sundries. Coin lndry. Free airport, RR station, bus depot transportation. 18-hole golf privileges, greens fee $25, pro, putting green. Exercise equipt; weights, treadmill. Pool. Playground. Game rm. Some in-rm whirlpools, refrigerators, microwaves. Picnic tables, grills. Cr cds: A, C, D, DS, ER, JCB, MC, V.

D ✕ 🏃 🏊 ✕ 🏃 🔥 SC

Motor Hotels

★ **BEST WESTERN CAVALIER INN.** *105 Emmet St (22903), jct US Business 29, US 250. 804/296-8111; FAX 804/296-3523.* 118 rms, 5 story. S $63-$79; D $73-$89; each addl $8; suites $125; under 18 free; 2-day packages; higher rates univ events. Crib free. Pet accepted. TV; cable (premium). Pool. Complimentary continental bkfst. Coffee in rms. Restaurant 11:30 am-10 pm. Rm serv. Bar to 1 am. Ck-out 1 pm.

Meeting rms. Business servs avail. Bellhops. Valet serv. Free airport, RR station, bus depot transportation. Univ of VA opp. Cr cds: A, C, D, DS, MC, V.

D 🏄 🏊 🏃 🏃 🔥 SC

★ ★ **ENGLISH INN OF CHARLOTTESVILLE.** *2000 Morton Dr (22903). 804/971-9900; FAX 804/977-8008; res: 800/786-5400.* 88 units, 3 story, 21 suites. S $67; D $72; each addl $7; suites $73-$78; under 18 free; higher rates univ graduation, sports events. Crib free. TV; cable (premium). Indoor pool. Complimentary bkfst buffet. Ck-out noon. Meeting rms. Business servs avail. Free airport, RR station, bus depot transportation. Exercise equipt; weights, bicycles, sauna. Health club privileges. Refrigerator in suites. Cr cds: A, C, D, DS, MC, V.

D 🏊 ✕ 🏃 🔥 SC

Hotels

★ ★ ★ **DOUBLETREE.** *2350 Seminole Trail (22901), near Charlottesville-Albemarle Airport. 804/973-2121; FAX 804/978-7735.* 234 units, 9 story. S, D $65-$135; each addl $10; suites $229-$289; family, wkend rates. Crib $10. TV; cable (premium), VCR avail. Indoor/outdoor pool; whirlpool, poolside serv. Coffee in rms. Restaurant 6:30 am-10 pm. Bar 4 pm-11 pm; entertainment. Ck-out noon. Convention facilities. Business servs avail. In-rm modem link. Free airport, RR station, bus depot transportation. Tennis. Exercise equipt; weight machines, bicycles. Some bathrm phones. Refrigerators avail. Cr cds: A, C, D, DS, MC, V.

D 🏃 🏊 ✕ ✕ 🏃 🔥 SC

★ ★ **OMNI.** *235 W Main St (22902). 804/971-5500; FAX 804/979-4456.* 204 rms, 7 story. S $144-$154; D $139-$174; each addl $15; under 18 free; suites $200-$295; wkend rates; higher rates univ events. Crib free. Pet accepted, some restrictions. TV; cable (premium), VCR avail. 2 pools, 1 indoor; whirlpool, poolside serv. Coffee in rms. Restaurant 6:30 am-10 pm. Bar 11-1 am. Ck-out noon. Convention facilities. Business servs avail. Gift shop. Free covered parking. Free airport, RR station, bus depot transportation. Exercise equipt; weights, bicycles, sauna. Refrigerators avail. Ultra-modern architecture; 7-story atrium lobby. Cr cds: A, C, D, DS, JCB, MC, V.

D 🏄 🏊 ✕ 🏃 🔥 SC

Inns

★ ★ **200 SOUTH STREET.** *200 South St (22902). 804/979-0200; FAX 804/979-4403; res: 800/964-7008.* 20 rms, 4 story. S, D $100-$200; each addl $20; suites $190-$200; under 16 free. Crib free. TV in lounge. Continental bkfst 7:30-10:30 am. Restaurant nearby. Ck-out 11 am, ck-in 2 pm. Business servs avail. Health club privileges. Some in-rm whirlpools, fireplaces. Built 1853; antiques. Cr cds: A, MC, V.

D 🏃 🔥 SC

★ ★ ★ **CLIFTON-THE COUNTRY INN.** *1296 Clifton Inn Dr (22911), 5 mi E on I-64, exit 124, 2½ mi E on VA 250, S on VA 729. 804/971-1800; res: 888/971-1800; FAX 804/971-7098.* E-mail reserve @cstone.net; web www.cliftoninn.com. 14 rms, 1-2 story, 8 suites. No rm phones. Mar-June, Sept-Dec: S, D $150-$265; each addl $75-$133; suites $225-$315; wkends (2-day min); lower rates rest of yr. Complimentary bkfst. Complimentary coffee in rms. Restaurant 6:30-11 pm. Rm serv. Ck-out 11 am, ck-in 3-5 pm. Business servs avail. Luggage handling. Lighted tennis. Downhill/x-country ski 18-20 mi. Pool; whirlpool. Lawn games. Fireplaces. 18th century manor built in 1799. Totally nonsmoking. Cr cds: MC, V.

D 🏄 🏃 🏃 🏊 🏃 🔥 SC

★ ★ ★ **INN AT MONTICELLO.** *1188 Scottsville Rd (VA 20) (22902), S on VA 20, past Constitution Rte, near Monticello and Ashlawn-Highlawn. 804/979-3593; FAX 804/296-1344.* 5 rms, 2 story. No rm phones. S $115; D $120-$145; each addl $30; 2-day min wkends. Children over 12 yrs only. Complimentary full bkfst; afternoon refreshments. Ck-out 11 am, ck-in 3 pm. Business servs avail. Country manor (mid-1800s) filled with period antiques and reproductions. Totally nonsmoking. Cr cds: MC, V.

★ ★ ★ **KESWICK HALL.** *701 Club Dr (22947). 804/979-3440; FAX 804/977-4171; res: 800/274-5391.* E-mail keswick@keswick.com; web www.keswick.com. 48 rms, 1-3 story, 6 suites. Mar-June & Sept-Nov: S, D $235-$495; each addl $50; suites $545-$595; golf plan; 2-day min special events; lower rates rest of yr. Children over 8 yrs only. TV; cable (premium); VCR avail. Indoor/outdoor pool; whirlpool. Complimentary full bkfst; afternoon refreshments. Restaurant (see ASHLEY ROOM). Rm serv 24 hrs. Ck-out noon, ck-in 3 pm. Concierge serv. Luggage handling. Business servs avail. Free airport, RR station transportation. Lighted tennis privileges; pro. 18-hole golf privileges; greens fee $85, pro, putting green, driving range. Exercise equipt; weight machines, treadmill, sauna. Health club privileges. Game rm. Rec rm. Lawn games. Many balconies. Picnic tables. English country house (1912) on 600-acre estate; designs by Laura Ashley. Cr cds: A, D, MC, V.

★ ★ ★ **PROSPECT HILL PLANTATION.** *(2887 Poindexter Rd, Trevilians 23093) 15 mi E on I-64, exit 136, then right to Zion Crossroads, left onto US 250 1 mi E to VA 613, turn left and proceed 3 mi. 540/967-0844; FAX 540/967-0102; res: 800/277-0844.* Web www.innbook.com. 13 rms, 2 with shower only, 2 story, 3 suites. No rm phones. MAP: S $200-$280; D $285-$325; each addl $50; suites $325; under 5 free. Closed Dec 24 eve, Dec 25. Pool. Complimentary full bkfst; afternoon refreshments. Dining rm, 1 sitting: 7 pm; Fri, Sat 8 pm. Ck-out 11 am, ck-in 3 pm. Meeting rm. Business servs avail. Bellhop. Lawn games. Many refrigerators; some in-rm whirlpools. Plantation house built 1732; many antique furnishings; tree-shaded lawns, veranda, gazebo. Cr cds: DS, MC, V.

★ ★ ★ **SILVER THATCH INN.** *3001 Hollymead Dr (22911), near Charlottesville-Albemarle Airport. 804/978-4686; FAX 804/973-6156.* 7 rms, 4 with shower only, 2 story. No rm phones. S $100-$115; D $115-$150; each addl $25; 2-day min wkends Apr-May, Sept-Nov. Children over 5 yrs only. Pool. Complimentary bkfst; evening refreshments. Dining rm Tues-Sat 5:30-9 pm. Ck-out 11 am, ck-in 2 pm. Business servs avail. Original building dates to 1780 (built by captured Hessian soldiers), additions in 1812 & 1937. Rms are named for Virginia-born presidents. Totally nonsmoking. Cr cds: A, C, D, MC, V.

★ ★ ★ **TRILLIUM HOUSE AT WINTERGREEN.** *(VA 664, Nellysford 22958) 23 1/2 mi W on I-64 to exit 107, W on US 250, 14 mi S on VA 151, then 4 1/2 mi W on VA 664 to entry gate on grounds of Wintergreen Resort. 804/325-9126; FAX 804/325-1099; res: 800/325-9126.* E-mail Inn keeper@trilliumhouse.com; web www.trilliumhouse.com. 12 rms, 2 story. S $95-$110; D $100-$115; each addl $35; suites $130-$160. Crib $10. TV avail; cable (premium). Pool privileges. Complimentary full bkfst. Dining rm 8-9 am; Fri, Sat 7:30 pm (prix fixe dinner). Serv bar. Ck-out noon, ck-in 3 pm. Business servs avail. In-rm modem link. Tennis privileges. Golf privileges. Downhill ski on site. Health club privileges. Cr cds: MC, V.

Resorts

★ ★ ★ **BOAR'S HEAD INN.** *(22905). Ivy Rd (US 250), 2 1/2 mi W of jct US 29. 804/296-2181; FAX 804/972-6024; res: 800/476-1988.* E-mail bhi@mild.cfw.com; web www.boarsheadinn.com. 173 rms. Apr-Nov: S $140-$175; D $150-$185; each addl $10; suites $250-$300; under 18 free; lower rates rest of yr. Crib free. TV; cable (premium), VCR avail. 3 pools; poolside serv, lifeguard. Supervised child's activities (mid-June-Labor Day); ages 5-16. Dining rm (see OLD MILL ROOM). Bar 2 pm-midnight; entertainment. Ck-out noon, ck-in 4 pm. Convention facilities. Business center. In-rm modem link. Valet serv Mon-Fri. Concierge. Gift/wine shop. Free airport transportation. Lighted outdoor, indoor tennis, pro. Golf privileges adj, putting green, driving range. Bicycles. Horse stables nearby. Hot-air ballooning. Exercise equipt; weights, bicycles, sauna. Some refrigerators. Some private patios, balconies. 2 ponds with ducks, swans &

geese. Local landmark; 1834 gristmill. Flower gardens. Local winery tours. Cr cds: A, D, DS, MC, V.

★ ★ ★ **WINTERGREEN.** *(Wintergreen 22958) W on US 250 to VA 151S, follow signs. 804/325-2200; FAX 804/325-8003; res: 800/325-2200.* Web www.wintergreenresort.com. 315 kit. units, 2-3 story. Late Dec-mid-Mar: S, D $155-$195; family, golf, ski, tennis plans; lower rates rest of yr. Crib avail. TV; cable (premium), VCR avail (movies). 6 pools, 1 indoor; wading pool, whirlpools, lifeguards. Playground. Supervised child's activities (ages 3-12). Dining rm 7-10:30 am, 11 am-2 pm, 6-10 pm. Box lunches, snack bar, picnics. Bar. Ck-out noon, ck-in 4 pm. Convention facilities. Business servs avail. Shopping arcade. Airport, RR station transportation. Tennis, pro. Two 18-hole golf courses, greens fee $48-$72, pro, putting green, driving range. Rowboats, canoes. Downhill ski on site. Nature programs. Bicycles. Entertainment, movies. Exercise equipt; bicycles, treadmill. Massage. Some fireplaces. Private patios, balconies. Picnic tables. Cr cds: A, DS, MC, V.

Restaurants

★ ★ **ABERDEEN BARN.** *2018 Holiday Dr (22901). 804/296-4630.* Hrs: 5 pm-midnight; Sun noon-10 pm. Closed Thanksgiving, Dec 25. Res accepted. Bar. Semi-a la carte: dinner $14.95-$32.95. Child's meals. Specializes in prime rib, steak, seafood. Entertainment. Open charcoal hearth. Family-owned. Cr cds: A, MC, V.

★ ★ **ASHLEY ROOM.** *(See Keswick Hall Inn) 804/979-3440.* E-mail keswick@keswick.com; web www.keswick.com. Hrs: noon-3 pm, 6-10 pm; Sun to 3 pm (brunch). Res required. Continental menu. Wine cellar. Semi-a la carte: lunch $10.25-$15.50. Complete meal: dinner $58. Sun brunch $25. Specializes in bass, beef, lamb. Own baking. Entertainment Fri-Sun. Valet parking. Elegant dining in Victorian setting; murals, fireplaces, antiques. Family-owned since 1919. Jacket. Totally nonsmoking. Cr cds: A, D, MC, V.

★ ★ **BERTINES NORTH CARIBBEAN.** *(206 S Main St, Madison 22727) 27 mi N on US 29. 540/948-3463.* Hrs: 6-9 pm. Closed Tues-Thur; also Easter, Dec 25. Res accepted. Caribbean menu. Wine, beer. Semi-a la carte: dinner $6.85-$19.85. Specialties: jerk chicken, steak on a hot rock, blackened swordfish. Outdoor dining. Caribbean decor. Cr cds: C, D, DS, MC, V.

★ **BLUE RIDGE BREWING CO.** *709 W Main St. 804/977-0017.* Hrs: 11:30 am-2 pm, 5-10 pm; Sat 11:30 am-3 pm, 5-10 pm. Sun brunch 11:30 am-3 pm. Closed July 4, Dec 25. Res accepted. Bar 5-10 pm. Semi-a la carte: lunch $4.25-$5.25, dinner $9.25-$15.25. Specialties: Caribbean marinated chicken, marinated NY strip steak, West Indian seafood sauté. Within brewery in historic, turn-of-the-century building. Cr cds: A, C, D, MC, V.

★ ★ **C & O.** *515 E Water St (22602), NW of I-64, exit VA 20 N. 804/971-7044.* Hrs: 11:30-2 am; Sat, Sun from 5 pm. Closed July 4, Thanksgiving, Dec 25. Res accepted. Southwest cuisine. Bar. Wine cellar. A la carte entrees: lunch $5-$8, dinner $10-$20. Specializes in regional fresh cooking. Own baking. Cr cds: A, MC, V.

★ ★ **CARMELLO'S.** *400 Emmet St (22903). 804/977-5200.* Hrs: 5-10 pm. Closed Jan 1, Dec 25. Res accepted. Northern Italian menu. Bar. Semi-a la carte: dinner $7.95-$16.95. Specializes in veal, pasta, chicken. Cr cds: A, C, D, DS, MC, V.

★ ★ **GOODFELLAS.** *1817 Emmet St (22901). 804/977-6738.* Hrs: 4-10 pm. Closed Mon; Thanksgiving, Dec 25. Res accepted. Bar.

Semi-a la carte: dinner $6.95-$18.95. Child's meals. Specializes in pasta, steak, prime rib au jus. Own pastries. Dining area has dark woods, green and white accents. Cr cds: A, DS, MC, V.

D 🔲

★ ★ **HARDWARE STORE.** *316 E Main St (22902). 804/977-1518.* Hrs: 11 am-9 pm; Fri, Sat to 10 pm; winter hrs vary. Closed Sun; some major hols. Res accepted. Continental menu. Semi-a la carte: lunch $3.50-$9.50, dinner $7.50-$16. Specializes in seafood, chicken, gourmet deli sandwiches. Outdoor dining. In 1890s hardware store; vintage signs displayed. Cr cds: A, C, D, MC, V.

D 🔲

★ ★ **IVY INN.** *2244 Old Ivy Rd (22903). 804/977-1222.* E-mail ivyinn@aol.com. Hrs: 5-10 pm; Sun brunch 11 am-2 pm. Res accepted. Semi-a la carte: dinner $15-$24. Sun brunch $7.50-$12. Specializes in regional cuisine. Outdoor dining. Victorian-style house (1804); fireplaces. Cr cds: MC, V.

✔★ ★ **MAHARAJA.** *20 Seminole Sq (22901), off US 29N. 804/973-1110.* Hrs: noon-2 pm, 5-10 pm; Sat-Mon from 5 pm. Closed Jan 1, Dec 25. Res accepted. Indian menu. Bar. Buffet: lunch $6.99. A la carte entrees: dinner $11.90-$13.90. Specializes in chicken, lamb, seafood. Own baking. Outdoor dining. Casual decor; Indian pictures, urns. Totally nonsmoking. Cr cds: A, C, D, DS, MC, V.

D SC

★ ★ **OLD MILL ROOM.** *(See Boar's Head Inn Resort) 804/972-2220.* Hrs: 7-10 am, 11:30 am-1:30 pm, 6-9 pm; Sat, Sun 7-10:30 am, 11:30 am-1:30 pm; 6-9 pm; Sun brunch 11 am-2 pm. Res accepted. Contemporary Amer menu. Bar 4 pm-midnight. Extensive wine list. Semi-a la carte: bkfst $4.95-$9.50, lunch $6.50-$12, dinner $14-$24. Sun brunch $15.95. Child's meals. Specialties: bison carpaccio, red snapper, rack of lamb. Salad bar. Own baking. Jazz Tues-Sat evening; harpist Sun. Valet parking. Outdoor dining. 19th-century decor with mahogany woodwork, fireplaces, framed artwork. Cr cds: A, C, D, DS, MC, V.

D 🔲

★ ★ **OREGANO JOE'S.** *1252 Emmet St (22903). 804/921-9308.* Hrs: 11 am-10 pm; Fri to 11 pm; Sat 4-11 pm; Sun from 4 pm. Closed Dec 24, 25. Italian menu. Bar. Semi-a la carte: lunch $4.95-$7.25, dinner $5.95-$12.95. Child's meals. Specialties: veal Parmesan, veal piccata. Casual atmosphere. Cr cds: A, D, DS, MC, V.

D 🔲

★ ★ **ROCOCO'S.** *2001 Commonwealth Dr (22901). 804/971-7371.* Hrs: 11 am-10 pm; Fri to 11 pm; Sat 5-11 pm; Sun 10:30 am-3 pm, 5-10 pm. Closed Thanksgiving, Dec 25. Italian menu. Bar. Semi-a la carte: lunch $4.95-$7.95, dinner $7.95-$19.95. Sun brunch $5.95-$7.95. Child's meals. Specializes in pasta, pizza, mesquite-grilled seafood. Cr cds: A, DS, MC, V.

D 🔲

★ ★ **SCHNITZELHOUSE.** *2208 Fontaine Ave (22903). 804/293-7185.* Hrs: 5-9:30 pm. Closed Sun; major hols; also 1st wk Jan, 1st wk July. Res accepted. Swiss, German menu. Bar. Complete meals: dinner $7.95-$25. Child's meals. Specializes in veal. Parking. Alpine decor. Cr cds: A, MC, V.

Chesapeake (F-10)

(See also Norfolk, Portsmouth, Virginia Beach)

Pop 151,976 **Elev** 12 ft **Area code** 757
Information Public Information Dept, 306 Cedar Rd, PO Box 15225, 23320; 757/382-6241.

This city is located in the heart of the Hampton Roads area, at the northeastern boundary of the Great Dismal Swamp National Wildlife Refuge (see).

What to See and Do

Northwest River Park. Approx 8 mi of hiking/nature trails wind through this 763-acre city park. Fishing; boating, canoeing (ramp, rentals). Picnicking (shelters), playground, 9-hole miniature golf. Camping, tent & trailer sites (Apr-Dec, daily; fee; hookups, dump station). Shuttle tram. (Daily; closed Jan 1, Dec 25) Fragrance trail for the visually impaired. 1733 Indian Creek Rd, off Battlefield Blvd (VA 168). Phone 757/421-3145 or 757/421-7151. **Free.**

Annual Event

Chesapeake Jubilee. City Park. National & regional entertainment, carnival, food booths, fireworks. 3rd wkend May.

Motels

✔★ **COMFORT INN-BOWERS HILL.** *4433 S Military Hwy (23321). 757/488-7900; FAX 757/488-6152.* 93 rms, 2 story, 7 kit. units. May-Sept: S, D $65; each addl $5; kits. $70; wkly rates; higher rates major summer hols; lower rates rest of yr. Crib free. Pet accepted; $5. TV; cable (premium). Pool. Complimentary continental bkfst. Ck-out 11 am. Business servs avail. Cr cds: A, C, D, DS, ER, JCB, MC, V.

D 🐾 ⇌ ≈ 🔲 🐾 SC

★ **DAYS INN.** *1433 N Battlefield Blvd (23320). 757/547-9262; FAX 757/547-4334.* 90 rms, 2 story. May-Sept: S, D $55-$95; each addl $5; under 12 free; wkly rates (off season); lower rates rest of yr. TV; cable (premium), VCR avail (movies). Pool. Complimentary continental bkfst. Restaurant adj open 24 hrs. Ck-out 11 am. Business servs avail. Health club privileges. Some refrigerators, microwaves. Cr cds: A, C, D, DS, JCB, MC, V.

D ≈ 🔲 🐾 SC

✔★ ★ **FAIRFIELD INN BY MARRIOTT.** *1560 Crossways Blvd (23320). 757/420-1300.* 113 rms, 3 story. May-Aug: S $52-$70; D $56-$72; under 18 free; higher rates special events. Crib free. TV; cable (premium). Complimentary continental bkfst. Restaurant nearby. Ck-out noon. Meeting rm. Business servs avail. In-rm modem link. Pool. Rec rm. Cr cds: A, C, D, DS, MC, V.

D ≈ 🔲 🐾 SC

✔★ ★ **HAMPTON INN.** *701A Woodlake Dr (23320). 757/420-1550; FAX 757/424-7414.* 119 rms, 4 story. Memorial Day-Labor Day: S, D $52-$68; higher rates summer wkends; lower rates rest of yr. Crib free. TV; cable (premium). Pool. Complimentary continental bkfst. Restaurant adj 6:30 am-10 pm. Ck-out noon. Meeting rm. Business servs avail. In-rm modem link. Microwaves avail. Cr cds: A, C, D, DS, MC, V.

D ≈ 🔲 🐾 SC

★ **WELLESLEY INN.** *1750 Sara Dr (23320). 757/366-0100; FAX 757/366-0396.* 106 rms, 4 story. S $55-$70; D $60-$75; each addl $10; suites $65-$85; under 18 free. Crib free. Pet accepted; $5. TV; cable (premium). Pool. Complimentary continental bkfst. Coffee in rms. Restaurant adj 6:30 am-10:30 pm. Ck-out 11 am. Meeting rms. Business servs avail. Valet serv. Coin lndry. Health club privileges. Refrigerators, microwaves. Cr cds: A, C, D, DS, ER, JCB, MC, V.

D ✔ ≊ ⊠ 🔥 SC

Motor Hotels

★★ COMFORT SUITES-GREENBRIAR. *1550 Crossways Blvd (23320). 757/420-1600; FAX 757/420-0099.* 123 suites, 3 story. Apr-Oct: S, D $65-$95; each addl $7; under 18 free; higher rates: Labor Day, Jubilee; lower rates rest of yr. Crib free. TV; cable (premium), VCR (movies $5). Pool; whirlpool. Complimentary continental bkfst. Coffee in rms. Ck-out 11 am. Meeting rm. Business servs avail. Exercise equipt; weight machine, bicycles, sauna. Refrigerators, microwaves. Cr cds: A, C, D, DS, JCB, MC, V.

D ≊ 🏋 ⊠ 🔥 SC

★★★ HOLIDAY INN. *725 Woodlake Dr (23320), I-64 exit 289A, Greenbriar N. 757/523-1500; FAX 757/523-0683.* Web www.insiders.com/chesapeake-va/wwwads/holidaychesapk/index.htm. 230 units, 7 story. S $69-$89; D $79-$99; each addl $10; suites $89-$104; under 18 free. TV; cable (premium). Indoor pool; whirlpool. Coffee in rms. Restaurant 6:30 am-10:30 pm. Rm serv. Bar 11 am-midnight. Ck-out noon. Guest lndry. Meeting rms. Business servs avail. In-rm modem link. Bellhops. Sundries. Free airport transportation. Exercise equipt; weights, bicycles, sauna. Some refrigerators; microwaves avail. Cr cds: A, C, D, DS, JCB, MC, V.

D ≊ 🏋 ⊠ 🔥 SC

Restaurants

✔★ CARA'S. *123 N Battlefield Blvd (23320). 757/548-0006.* Hrs: 11:30 am-2:30 pm, 4-10 pm; Fri, Sat to 11 pm; Sun 11:30 am-9 pm; Sun brunch to 3 pm. Closed Thanksgiving, Dec 25. Res accepted. Contemporary Amer menu. Bar. Semi-a la carte: lunch $2.95-$8.50, dinner $9-$16. Sun brunch $4.50-$9.25. Child's meals. Specialties: sesame seed chicken with Cumberland sauce, crab cakes, steak Chesapeake. Musicians Thurs-Sat. Outdoor dining overlooking wetlands. Cr cds: C, D, DS, MC, V.

D ⊐

★★ KYOTO JAPANESE STEAK HOUSE. *1412 Greenbriar Pkwy (23320), Suite 129, Crossways center. 757/420-0950.* Hrs: 11 am-2 pm, 5-10 pm; Sun 4-9 pm. Closed July 4, Thanksgiving, Dec 25. Res accepted. Japanese menu. Bar. Semi-a la carte: lunch $4.50-$13, dinner $8.95-$20.95. Child's meals. Specialties: teppanyaki, Kyoto special, sukiyaki. Sushi bar. Original Oriental art. Cr cds: A, C, D, DS, ER, MC, V.

D ⊐

★★ LOCKS POINTE. *136 N Battlefield Blvd (23320). 757/547-9618.* Hrs: 11:30 am-3 pm, 5-10 pm; Sat from 5 pm; Sun 10:30 am-9 pm; Sun brunch to 3 pm. Closed Mon; Dec 24, 25. Res accepted. Bar 4 pm-1:30 am. Semi-a la carte: lunch $4.50-$6.95, dinner $10.50-$22.50. Sun brunch $7.95-$10.95. Child's meals. Specializes in fresh seafood. Entertainment wkends. Outdoor dining. On Intracoastal Waterway; dockage. Cr cds: A, MC, V.

D ⊐

★ TABOO. *1036 Volvo Pkwy (23320). 757/548-1996.* Hrs: 11 am-10 pm; Fri to 11 pm; Sat 4-11 pm. Closed Sun; most major hols. Res accepted. Bar. Semi-a la carte: lunch $5.95-$9.95, dinner $8.95-$21.95. Child's meals. Specializes in crab cakes, black Angus steaks, wood-fired pizzas. Own breads. Colorful, contemporary decor. Cr cds: A, DS, MC, V.

D SC

Chesapeake and Ohio Canal National Historical Park

(see Maryland)

Chincoteague (D-10)

Founded 1662 Pop 3,572 Elev 4 ft Area code 757 Zip 23336 E-mail pony@shore.intercom.net Web www.intercom.net/local/chincoteague

Information Chamber of Commerce, 6733 Maddox Blvd, PO Box 258; 757/336-6161.

Chincoteague oysters, wild ponies and good fishing are the stock in trade of this small island, connected with Chincoteague National Wildlife Refuge by a bridge and to the mainland by 10 miles of highway (VA 175, from US 13), causeways and bridges.

The oysters, many of them grown on the hard sand bottoms off Chincoteague from seed or small oysters brought from natural beds elsewhere, are among the best in the East. Clams and crabs are also plentiful. Commercial fishing has always been the main occupation of the islanders; but now, catering to those who fish for fun is also important economically.

Chincoteague's wild ponies are actually small horses; when foals no bigger than a large dog, but when full-grown somewhat larger and more graceful than Shetlands. They are thought to be descended from horses that swam ashore from a wrecked Spanish galleon, their limited growth caused by generations of marsh-grass diet.

What to See and Do

★ Assateague Island. Accessible by bridge from town. Includes Chincoteague National Wildlife Refuge and Virginia unit of Assateague Island National Seashore. A 37-mi barrier island, Assateague's stretches of ocean and sand dunes, forest and marshes create a natural environment unusual on the East coast. Sika deer, a variety of wildlife and countless birds, including the peregrine falcon (autumn), can be found here, but wild ponies occasionally roaming the marshes offer the most exotic sight for visitors. Nature and auto trails; interpretive programs. Swimming (bathhouse), lifeguards in summer; surf-fishing. Camping; hike-in and canoe-in camp sites and day-use facilities. Picnicking permitted in designated areas; cars are limited to designated roads. No pets allowed. Obtain information at Toms Cove Visitor Center (spring-fall, daily) and at Chincoteague Refuge Visitor Center (daily). Access for disabled to all facilities. For further information contact the Chief of Interpretation, Assateague Island National Seashore, Rte 611, 7206 National Seashore Lane, Berlin, MD 21811; 410/641-1441 or 410/641-3030 (camping). (See OCEAN CITY, MD) Also contact Refuge Manager, Chincoteague National Wildlife Refuge, PO Box 62, 23336; 757/336-6122. Per car 4-7 day pass ¢¢

NASA Visitor Center. Showcases world of past, present and future flight. Features Moon rock brought from *Apollo 17* mission; scale models of space probes, satellites and aircraft; displays of current and future NASA projects; full-scale aircraft and rockets; films on space and aeronotics. Model rocket demonstrations (Mar-Nov, 1st Sat; June-Aug also 3rd Sat, weather permitting). Picnic facilities. Gift shop. (July 4-Labor Day, daily; Sept-Nov & Mar-June, Thurs-Mon; closed most hols) 5 mi S on VA 175 on Wallops Island. Phone 757/824-1344 or -2298. Free.

Oyster and Maritime Museum of Chincoteague. Museum contains live marine life exhibits, details the seafood industry, shows films. Also has the Wyle Maddox Library. (May-early Sept, daily; mid-Sept-Nov, Sat & Sun) Beach Rd. Phone 757/336-6117. ¢¢

Refuge Waterfowl Museum. Rotating displays of antique decoys and hunting tools. Decoy making and waterfowl art. (Daily; closed Dec 25) 7059 Maddox Blvd. Phone 757/336-5800. ¢¢

Sightseeing tours. Captain Barry's Back Bay Cruises & Expeditions. Include Bird Watch Cruise, Back Bay Expedition, Champagne Sunset Cruise, Moonlight Excursions and Fun Cruise. Trips vary from 1-4 hrs. Reservations recommended. Phone 757/336-6508 for information. ¢¢¢-¢¢¢¢¢

Annual Events

Easter Decoy & Art Festival. Easter wkend.

Homestyle Music & Shrimp Festival. Folk & bluegrass music, workshops, crafts, kid's concerts, pony rides, food. 2nd wkend June.

Pony Penning. The "wild" ponies are rounded up on Assateague Island, then swim the inlet to Chincoteague, where foals are sold at auction before the ponies swim back to Assateague. Carnival amusements. Last Wed & Thurs July.

Oyster Festival. Columbus Day wkend.

Waterfowl Week. National Wildlife Refuge open to vehicles during peak migratory waterfowl populations. Late Nov.

Motels

★ **BIRCHWOOD.** 3650 Main St. 757/336-6133; FAX 757/336-6535. 41 rms. Apr-Nov: S, D $67-$72; each addl $5. Closed rest of yr. Crib $4. TV; cable. Pool. Playground. Ck-out 11 am. Coin lndry. Refrigerators. Cr cds: DS, MC, V.

🄳 ⊷ ≈ 🕮 🔥 SC

✔★ ★ **COMFORT INN.** (US 13, Onley 23418) Four Corner Plaza, at jct VA 179. 757/787-7787; FAX 757/787-4641. 80 units, 2 story, 10 suites. Mid-May-mid-Sept: S $56; D $62; each addl $5; suites $62-$79; under 18 free; lower rates rest of yr. Crib free. TV; cable. Heated pool. Complimentary continental bkfst. Restaurant adj 11 am-10:30 pm. Ck-out 11 am. Business servs avail. In-rm modem link. Exercise equipt; bicycles, rowers. Refrigerators. Cr cds: A, C, D, DS, ER, JCB, MC, V.

🄳 ≈ 🕮 🔥 SC

★ ★ **DRIFTWOOD MOTOR LODGE.** 7105 Maddox Blvd. 757/336-6557; FAX 757/336-6558; res: 800/553-6117. 52 rms, 3 story. Mid-June-early Sept: S, D $82; each addl $7; under 12 free; wkend, hol rates; lower rates rest of yr. Crib $6. TV; cable (premium). Pool. Complimentary coffee in lobby. Restaurant nearby. Ck-out 11 am. Business servs avail. Refrigerators. Private patios, balconies. Picnic tables. At entrance to Assateague Natl Seashore. Cr cds: A, D, DS, MC, V.

🄳 ≈ 🕮 🔥

★ ★ **ISLAND MOTOR INN.** 4391 Main St. 757/336-3141; FAX 757/336-1483; res: 800/832-2925. 60 units, 3 story, 16 suites. Mid-June-Labor Day: S, D $78-$150; suites $125-$150; under 16 free; lower rates rest of yr. Crib $5. TV; cable (premium). 2 pools: 1 indoor; whirlpool. Restaurant nearby. Ck-out 11 am. Guest lndry. Meeting rms. Business servs avail. In-rm modem link. Sundries. Exercise equipt; weight machine, bicycles. Refrigerators. Bathrm phone in suites. Balconies. Picnic tables, grills. On bay. Cr cds: A, D, DS, MC, V.

🄳 ⊷ ≈ 🕮 🔥 SC

★ **LIGHTHOUSE.** 4218 Main St. 757/336-5091; res: 800/505-5254. 25 rms, 1-2 story, 3 kits. June-Aug: S, D $57-$75; each addl $5; kit. units $57-$75; min stays summer, hols, special events; lower rates Mar-May, Sept-Nov. Closed rest of yr. Crib $5. TV; cable. Pool; whirlpool. Complimentary coffee in rms. Restaurant nearby. Ck-out 11 am. Refrigerators. Picnic tables, grill. Cr cds: A, C, D, MC, V.

≈ 🕮 🔥 SC

★ ★ **REFUGE MOTOR INN.** 7058 Maddox Blvd. 757/336-5511; FAX 757/336-6134; res: 800/544-8469. 72 units, 2 story. June-Aug: S, D $80-$190; each addl $5-$8; under 12 free; lower rates rest of yr. Crib $5.

TV; cable. Indoor/outdoor pool; whirlpool. Ck-out 11 am. Coin lndry. Business servs avail. Gift shop. Exercise equipt; weight machines, bicycles, sauna. Refrigerators. Picnic tables, grill. Near wildlife refuge. Chincoteague ponies on grounds. Cr cds: A, C, D, DS, MC, V.

🄳 ≈ 🕮 🔥

★ **SEA HAWK.** 6250 Maddox Blvd. 757/336-6527. 28 rms, 10 kit. units. Early June-mid-Sept: S, D $65-$70; each addl $5; kit. units $400-$475/wk; lower rates Mar-May, mid-Sept-Nov. Closed rest of yr. Crib $4. TV; cable (premium). Pool. Playground. Restaurant opp 5-9 pm. Ck-out 11 am. Lawn games. Refrigerators. Cr cds: A, DS, MC, V.

🄳 ≈ 🕮 🔥 SC

★ **SEA SHELL.** 3720 Willow St. 757/336-6589. 46 rms, 1-2 story. Mid-June-early Sept: S, D $60-$66; each addl $4; cottages $450-$500/wk; 2-day min wkends, 3-day min hols; lower rates Apr-mid-June, mid-Sept-Oct. Closed rest of yr. Crib $3. TV; cable. Pool. Complimentary coffee in rms. Restaurant nearby. Ck-out 11 am. Business servs avail. Refrigerators. Picnic tables. Cr cds: A, D, DS, MC, V.

🄳 ≈ 🕮 🔥

✔★ **SUNRISE MOTOR INN.** 4491 Chicken City Rd, 1/2 blk S of Maddox Blvd. 757/336-6671; FAX 757/336-1226; res: 800/673-5211. 24 units, 2 kits. Mid-June-early Sept: S $58; D $62; each addl $6; kit. units $540/wk; under 12 free; lower rates mid-Mar-mid-June, early Sept-Nov. Closed rest of yr. Crib free. TV; cable. Pool. Playground. Complimentary coffee in lobby. Restaurant nearby. Ck-out 11 am. Business servs avail. Refrigerators. Picnic tables, grills. Cr cds: A, D, DS, MC, V.

🄳 ≈ 🔥

★ ★ **WATERSIDE MOTOR INN.** 3761 S Main St. 757/336-3434; FAX 757/336-1878. 45 rms, 3 story. Mid-June-mid-Sept (2-day min): S, D $90-$145; each addl $5; under 12 free; lower rates rest of yr. Crib $5. TV; cable (premium). Pool; whirlpool. Complimentary coffee in rms. Restaurant nearby. Ck-out 11 am. Business servs avail. Sundries. Tennis. Exercise equipt; weight machine, bicycles. Refrigerators. Balconies. Picnic tables, grills. On saltwater river; marina. Cr cds: A, C, D, DS, MC, V.

🄳 ⊷ ⛹ ≈ 🕮 🔥

Inns

★ ★ **CHANNEL BASS.** 6228 Church St. 757/336-6148. 10 rms, 3 story. June-Sept: S, D $99-$175; suites $175; wkly rates; lower rates rest of yr. Children over 8 yrs only. Ck-out 11 am, ck-in 2 pm. Built 1892. Assateague Wildlife Refuge nearby. Cr cds: MC, V.

≈ 🕮 SC

★ ★ ★ **THE GARDEN & THE SEA.** (4188 Nelson Rd, New Church 23415) 12 mi NW via VA 175 to US 13, then N to VA 710 (Nelson Rd). 757/824-0672; res: 800/824-0672. 6 rms in 2 bldgs. No rm phones. July-Sept: D $75-$160; under 12 free; wkends (2-day min); wkday rates; lower rates Apr-June, Oct-Nov. Closed rest of yr. Complimentary continental bkfst; afternoon refreshments. Restaurant (see THE GARDEN & THE SEA INN). Ck-out 11 am, ck-in 3 pm. Business servs avail. Luggage handling. Concierge serv. Patio and garden. Built as Bloxom's Tavern (1803) and adj farmhouse. Cr cds: A, DS, MC, V.

🄳 ≈ 🔥

★ ★ **MISS MOLLY'S.** 4141 Main St. 757/336-6686; res: 800/221-5620. 7 rms, 2 share bath, 3 story. Memorial Day-Sept: S $79-$109; D $89-$145; each addl $20; lower rates Mar-late May, Oct-Dec. Closed rest of yr. Children over 8 yrs only wkends. Complimentary full bkfst; afternoon refreshments. Restaurant nearby. Ck-out 11 am, ck-in 2 pm. Business servs avail. On saltwater bay. In historic building (1886); library, sitting rm; antiques. Marguerite Henry stayed here while writing "Misty of Chincoteague." No cr cds accepted.

≈ 🔥

✔★ **WATSON HOUSE.** 4240 Main St. 757/336-1564; res: 800/336-6787. 6 rms, 5 with shower only, 2 story. No rm phones. Memorial Day-Labor Day: S $75-$95 D $85-$105; each addl $15; higher rates:

wkends (2-day min), holidays (3-day min); lower rates Mar-late May, early Sept-Thanksgiving. Closed rest of yr. Children over 9 yrs only. Complimentary full bkfst; afternoon refreshments. Restaurant nearby. Ck-out 11 am, ck-in 2 pm. Business servs avail. Bicycles avail. Victorian residence (1874). Totally nonsmoking. Cr cds: MC, V.

🖼️ 🔥

Restaurants

★ ★ BEACHWAY. *6455 Maddox Blvd. 757/336-5590.* Hrs: 8 am-9 pm. Closed Dec-Mar; also Tues Sept-Nov, Mar-June. Res accepted. Continental menu. Serv bar. Semi-a la carte: bkfst $3.25-$7.95, lunch $3.95-$8.95, dinner $10.25-$24.95. Child's meals. Specializes in steak, seafood, poultry. French Provincial decor; fireplace, solarium. Cr cds: A, C, D, DS, MC, V.

D SC

★ ★ ★ THE GARDEN & THE SEA INN. *(See The Garden & The Sea Inn) 757/824-0672.* Hrs: 6-9 pm. Closed Mon, Tues; also Dec-Mar. Res accepted. Wine list. A la carte entrees: dinner $15.50-$23. Complete meals: dinner $27.50-$33. Specializes in Northern French cuisine, seafood. Intimate dining rm in historic country inn. Cr cds: A, DS, MC, V.

D

★ ★ NONNIE'S. *3899 Main St. 757/336-5822.* Hrs: 6-9 pm. Closed Sun. A la carte. Italian, Amer menu. Wine, beer. Semi-a la carte: dinner $8.95-$15.95. Specializes in fresh seafood, pasta. In converted bayside cottage. Cr cds: MC, V.

✔★ STEAMERS SEAFOOD. *6251 Maddox Blvd. 757/336-5478.* Hrs: 5-9 pm. Closed Nov-Apr, May-Oct. Wine, beer. Semi-a la carte: dinner $9.95-$16.95. Child's meals. Specializes in steamed crabs & shrimp. Nautical theme. Cr cds: D, DS, MC, V.

D SC

Clarksville (F-7)

(See also South Boston, South Hill)

Pop 1,243 **Elev** 359 ft **Area code** 804 **Zip** 23927 **E-mail** clarksville@kerrlake.com **Web** kerrlake.com/clarksville

Information Clarksville Lake Country Chamber of Commerce, 105 2nd St, PO Box 1017; 804/374-2436.

What to See and Do

Occoneechee State Park. Approx 2,700 acres under development; long shoreline on John H. Kerr Reservoir (Buggs Island Lake). Fishing; boat launching. Hiking. Picnic shelters. Tent and trailer sites (hookups, season varies). Amphitheater; interpretive programs. Standard fees. (Daily) 1¹/₂ mi E on US 58. Phone 804/374-2210.

Prestwould (1795). Manor house built by Sir Peyton Skipwith; rare French scenic wallpaper; original and period furnishings; restored gardens. (May-Sept, daily; Oct, wkends; rest of yr, by appt) 2 mi N on US 15. Phone 804/374-8672. ¢¢

Annual Events

Native American Heritage Festival and Powwow. Occoneechee State Park. 2nd wkend May.

Virginia Lake Festival. Juried arts & crafts show, beach music, dancers, gymnasts. Fun Run, antique car show, sailboat race, hot air balloons. Food vendors. Phone 804/374-2436. 3rd wkend July.

Motel

✔★ LAKE. *101 Virginia Ave. 804/374-8106; FAX 804/374-0108.* 76 rms, 2 story, 3 suites. Mid-May-mid-Sept: S, D $49-$65; each addl $5; suites $65-$85; under 12 free; lower rates rest of yr. Pet accepted. TV; cable. Pool. Restaurant adj 6 am-10 pm. Bar 5 pm-1 am. Ck-out 11 am. Meeting rms. Business servs avail. Free airport transportation. Refrigerators avail. Picnic tables, grills. On lake; swimming. Cr cds: A, MC, V.

D 🐾 🚲 🏊 🔥 SC

Inn

★ SIMPLY SOUTHERN. *307 Commerce St. 804/374-9040.* 4 rms, 2 share bath, 1 with shower only, 2 story. No rm phones. S, D $50-$65. TV in sitting rm; cable. Complimentary full bkfst. Ck-out 11 am, ck-in 3 pm. Buggs Island Lake 1 blk. Built 1890; antiques. No cr cds accepted.

🖼️ 🔥

Clifton Forge (E-5)

(See also Covington, Lexington, Warm Springs)

Settled 1878 **Pop** 4,679 **Elev** 1,079 ft **Area code** 540 **Zip** 24422 **E-mail** ahchamber@aol.com **Web** www.chv.va/alleghanyhighland/

Information Alleghany Highlands Chamber of Commerce, 501 E Ridgeway St; 540/862-4969.

The town, named after a tilt-hammer forge that operated profitably for almost a hundred years, is at the southern tip of the Shenadoah Valley just west of the Blue Ridge Parkway.

What to See and Do

C & O Historical Society Archives. Includes C & O Railroad artifacts, old blueprints for cars and engines, books, models, collection of photos. (Daily exc Sun; closed hols) 312 E Ridgeway St, opp terminal bldg. Phone 540/862-2210. **Free.**

Douthat State Park. Nearly 4,500 acres, high in the Allegheny Mountains, with 50-acre lake. Swimming beach, bathhouse; trout fishing (fee/day); boating (Memorial Day-Labor Day; rentals, launching, electric motors only). Hiking, self-guided trails. Picnicking, restaurant, concession. Camping (fee), tent & trailer sites (Mar-Sept; no hookups); cabins (all yr). Visitor center, interpretive programs. Standard fees. (Daily) 8 mi N on VA 629. Phone 540/862-7200. **Free.**

Iron Gate Gorge. Perpendicular walls of rock rise from banks of Jackson River. James River Div of C & O Railroad and US 220 pass through gorge. Restored chimney of old forge is here. 2 mi S on US 220.

Inn

★ ★ LONGDALE INN. *6209 Longdale Furnace Rd, I-64 exit 35. 540/862-0892; FAX 540/862-3554.* 10 rms, 3 with shower only, 4 share bath, 3 story, 2 suites. No A/C. Rm phones avail. S, D $75-$95; each addl $25; suites $95-$120; wkly rates. Crib $25. Pet accepted. TV in common rm; VCR. Complimentary full bkfst. Ck-out 11 am, ck-in 3 pm. Business servs avail. Gift shop. X-country ski 2 mi. Playground. Game rm. Lawn games. Many fireplaces. Picnic tables, grills. Virginia countryside setting; Victorian inn built in 1873. Totally nonsmoking. Cr cds: A, DS, MC, V.

🐾 🎿 🖼️ 🔥

Colonial National Historical Park (E-9)

Made up of four independent areas—Cape Henry Memorial, Colonial Parkway, Jamestown (see all three) and Yorktown Battlefield (see YORKTOWN)—this is where America, as we know it, began. Jamestown, Yorktown and Williamsburg (not a National Park Service area) are connected by the Colonial Parkway. Each of these areas is described in this book under its own name. Abundant in natural as well as historical wealth, the park boundaries enclose more than 9,000 acres of forest woodlands, marshes, shorelines, fields and a large variety of wildlife.

Colonial Parkway (E-9)

(For accommodations see Williamsburg, Yorktown; also see Colonial National Historical Park, Jamestown)

The Colonial Parkway is a 23-mile link between the three towns that formed the "cradle of the nation"—Jamestown, Williamsburg and Yorktown. It starts at the Visitor Center at Jamestown, passes through Williamsburg (the Colonial Williamsburg Information Center is near north underpass entrance) and ends at the Visitor Center in Yorktown.

At turnouts and overlooks along the route, information signs note such historic spots as Glebeland, Kingsmill, Indian Field Creek, Powhatan's Village, Fusilier's Redoubt and others. A free picnic area is provided during the summer at Ringfield Plantation, midway between Williamsburg and Yorktown.

The parkway is free to private vehicles. Commercial vehicles are not permitted. Speed limit is 45 MPH. There are no service stations.

Covington (E-5)

(See also Clifton Forge, Hot Springs)

Founded 1833 **Pop** 6,991 **Elev** 1,245 ft **Area code** 540 **Zip** 24426 **E-mail** ahchamber@aol.com **Web** www.chv.va/alleghanyhighland/
Information Alleghany Highlands Chamber of Commerce, 501 E Ridgeway St, Clifton Forge 24422; 540/862-4969.

Named for its oldest resident, Covington developed from a small village on the Jackson River. It is located in the western part of Virginia known as the Alleghany Highlands. The James River Ranger District office of the George Washington and Jefferson National Forests is located here.

What to See and Do

Humpback Bridge. Erected in 1857, this 100-ft-long structure was made of hand-hewn oak, held together with locust-wood pins. In use until 1929, it is now maintained as part of a 5-acre state highway wayside and is the only surviving curved-span covered bridge in the US. 3 mi W just off US 60/I-64.

Lake Moomaw. The 12-mi-long lake has a rugged shoreline of more than 43 miles, set off by towering mountains. Surrounded by the Gathright Wildlife Management Area and portions of the George Washington and Jefferson National Forests. Boating, swimming, fishing and waterskiing. Picnicking. Camping (fee). Visitor center. (Apr-Oct, daily) 13 mi N via US 220, VA 687, follow signs to Gathright Dam. Phone 540/962-2214. Per vehicle ¢

Motels

✔★ ★ **BEST WESTERN-MOUNTAIN VIEW.** *820 E Madison, on US 60 at jct I-64 exit 16.* 540/962-4951; FAX 540/965-5714. 79 rms, 2 story. S $52-$69; D $66-$79; each addl $8; under 18 free. Crib free. Pet accepted; $10. TV; cable (premium). Pool; wading pool. Coffee in rms. Restaurant 6 am-2 pm, 5-10 pm. Rm serv. Ck-out 11 am. Meeting rms. Business servs avail. In-rm modem link. Bellhops. Valet serv. Some refrigerators. Cr cds: A, C, D, DS, ER, JCB, MC, V.

D ✔ ≋ ⊠ ⊠ SC

★ ★ **COMFORT INN.** *203 Interstate Dr, I-64 exit 16.* 540/962-2141; FAX 540/965-0964. 99 units, 2 story, 32 suites. S $50-$64; D $69-$74; each addl $8; suites $68-$81; under 18 free. Crib free. Pet accepted; $10. TV; cable (premium), VCR (movies $4). Pool; whirlpool. Restaurant 7 am-midnight. Bar 4 pm-2 am. Ck-out 11 am. Business servs avail. Guest lndry. Sundries. Some refrigerators. Cr cds: A, C, D, DS, ER, JCB, MC, V.

D ✔ ≋ ⊠ ⊠ SC

Inn

★ ★ ★ **MILTON HALL BED & BREAKFAST.** *207 Thorny Lane.* 540/965-0196. 6 rms, 2 with shower only, 2 story, 1 suite. Some rm phones. S $75; D $85; each addl $10; suite $130-$140; under 10 free; hunting, fishing plans. Crib free. Pet accepted. TV in some rms, sitting rm; cable (premium). Complimentary full bkfst. Ck-out noon, ck-in 2 pm. Lawn games. Historic country manor house (1874) on 44 acres adj George Washington National Forest. Cr cds: MC, V.

✔ ⊠ SC

Culpeper (D-7)

(See also Orange, Warrenton)

Founded 1748 **Pop** 8,581 **Elev** 430 ft **Area code** 540 **Zip** 22701
Information Chamber of Commerce, 133 W Davis St; 540/825-8628.

Volunteers from Culpeper, Fauquier and Orange Counties marched to Williamsburg in 1777, in answer to Governor Patrick Henry's call to arms. Their flag bore a coiled rattlesnake, with the legends "Don't Tread on Me" and "Liberty or Death."

In the winter of 1862-1863, churches, homes and vacant buildings in Culpeper were turned into hospitals for the wounded from the battles of Cedar Mountain, Kelly's Ford and Brandy Station. Later, the Union Army had headquarters here.

Today, Culpeper is a light-industry and trading center for a five-county area, with a healthy agriculture industry.

What to See and Do

Dominion Wine Cellars. Tours and tasting. (Daily; closed major hols) Winery Ave, 2 mi S on VA 3. Phone 540/825-8772.   **Free.**

Motels

★ ★ **COMFORT INN.** *890 Willis Ln.* 540/825-4900; FAX 540/825-4904. 49 rms, 2 story. Apr-Oct: S $58; D $65; each addl $8; under 18 free. Crib free. Pet accepted; $10. TV; cable (premium). Pool. Complimentary continental bkfst. Complimentary coffee in rms. Ck-out 11 am. Business servs avail. In-rm modem link. Refrigerators avail. Cr cds: A, C, D, DS, JCB, MC, V.

D ✔ ≋ ⊠ ⊠ SC

✔★ ★ **HOLIDAY INN.** *US 29, 2½ mi S on US 29.* 540/825-1253; FAX 540/825-7134. 159 rms, 2 story. S, D $59; under 19 free. Crib free.

Pet accepted, some restrictions. TV; cable. Pool; wading pool. Restaurant 6 am-2 pm, 5-10 pm. Rm serv. Bar 4 pm-12:30 am; entertainment. Ck-out noon. Coin lndry. Meeting rms. Business sersv avail. In-rm modem link. Valet serv. Sundries. Refrigerators avail. Cr cds: A, C, D, DS, JCB, MC, V.

D ⮕ ≈ ⩽ ⌦ SC

Inn

★ ★ ★ **FOUNTAIN HALL BED & BREAKFAST.** *609 S East St.* 540/825-8200; FAX 540/825-7716; res: 800/298-4748 (exc VA). 5 rms, 2 story, 1 suite. S $75-$100; D $85-$150; suite $150; Oct, some hols (2-day min). Crib $10. Complimentary continental bkfst; afternoon refreshments. Ck-out 11 am, ck-in 2 pm. Business servs avail. In-rm modem link. Lawn games. Some in-rm whirlpools. Fireplaces. Balconies. Picnic tables. Colonial-revival house (1859). Totally nonsmoking. Cr cds: A, C, D, DS, MC, V.

D ⌦

Guest Ranch

★ ★ **GRAVES' MOUNTAIN LODGE.** *(VA 670, Syria 22743)* 20 mi W via US 29, VA 609 & VA 231 to VA 670. 540/923-4231; FAX 540/923-4312. 40 rms, 13 cottages, 8 kits. AP, mid-Mar-Nov: S $57-$92; D $65-$98/person; kit. cottages $110-$230; higher rates Oct. Closed rest of yr. Crib free. Pet accepted. Pool; wading pool, lifeguard. Playground. Dining rm (public by res) 8:30-9:30 am, 12:30-1:30 pm, 6:30-7:30 pm. Box lunches. Ck-out 11 am, ck-in 3 pm. Coin lndry. Grocery 1/4 mi. Meeting rms. Business servs avail. Tennis. Golf privileges, greens fee $45. Lawn games. Rec rm. Some fireplaces. Picnic tables, grills. Cr cds: DS, MC, V.

⮕ ⮕ ⽬ ⽬ ⽬ ≈ ⩽ ⌦

Restaurant

★ ★ ★ **PRINCE MICHEL.** *(US 29S, Leon 22725)* 10 mi S on US 29. 800/800-9463. Hrs: 11:30 am-2:30 pm, 6-9 pm; Sun to 3 pm. Closed Mon-Wed; most major hols; also Jan, June. Res accepted. French menu. Serv bar. Wine list. Complete meal: lunch $20-$35, dinner $55. Specialties: venison in red wine sauce, medallions of lamb, hot foie gras with apples. Outdoor dining. Located at vineyard. Jacket. Cr cds: A, MC, V.

D

Danville (F-6)

(See also Martinsville, South Boston)

Founded 1792 **Pop** 53,056 **Elev** 500 ft **Area code** 804
Information Danville Area Chamber of Commerce, 635 Main St, PO Box 1538, 24543; 804/793-5422.

This textile and tobacco center blends the leisurely pace of the Old South with the modern tempo of industry. It is one of the nation's largest bright-leaf tobacco auction markets. Dan River Inc houses the largest single-unit textile mill in the world. Other major industries are located here. Nancy Langhorne, Viscountess Astor, the first woman to sit in the British House of Commons, was born in Danville in 1879.

What to See and Do

Chatham. Founded in 1777, this county seat of Pittsylvania County has many historically interesting houses, schools and public buildings: Hargrave Military Academy (1909) with the Owen Cheatham Chapel and Yesteryear Hall (museum); Chatham Hall (1894) with Renaissance Chapel, stained-glass windows of women, and St Francis mural in Commons Building; Old Clerk's Office (1813) restored as museum; Courthouse (1853) in Greek-revival style with delicate plaster ceiling frescoes and portraits; Emmanuel Episcopal Church (1844) with Gothic interior and signed Tiffany windows; Sims-Mitchell House (1860s). Also of interest are the Educational and Cultural Center with planetarium and museum; antique shops, restaurants, trolley diners and the many private houses, several of which offer overnight accommodations. 17 mi N via US 29. Self-guided walking tour information for town and county may be obtained at the Chamber of Commerce, 38 Main St, Chatham 24531; 804/432-1650.

Danville Science Center. Hands-on museum for the entire family. Located in a newly restored Victorian train station. (Daily; closed Thanksgiving, Dec 25) 677 Craghead St. Phone 804/791-5160. ¢¢

"Last Capitol of the Confederacy" (Danville Museum of Fine Arts and History). Home of Major W.T. Sutherlin; built 1857. President Jefferson Davis and his cabinet fled to Danville after receiving news of General Lee's retreat from Richmond. It was during this time that the Sutherlin mansion served as the last capitol of the Confederacy. Victorian restoration in historical section of house (parlor, library and Davis bedrm). Rotating art exhibits by national and regional artists. Permanent collection includes silver, textiles, costumes. (Tues-Fri, also Sat & Sun afternoons; closed major hols, also Dec 24-Jan 2) 975 Main St. Phone 804/793-5644. **Free.**

Tobacco auctions. Several huge warehouses ring with the chants of tobacco auctioneers. (Aug-early-Nov, Mon-Thurs; closed Labor Day, Columbus Day, Veterans Day) Phone 804/793-5422. **Free.**

"Wreck of the Old 97" Marker. Site of celebrated train wreck (Sept 27, 1903), made famous by a folk song. On Riverside Dr (US 58) between N Main & Locust Lane overpass.

Annual Events

Festival in the Park. Arts, crafts, entertainment. Phone 804/799-5200. 3rd wkend May.

Danville Harvest Jubilee. Celebration of tobacco harvest season. Phone 804/799-5200. Mid-Sept.

Motels

(Rates may be higher during sports car races in Martinsville)

★ **BEST WESTERN.** *2121 Riverside Dr (US 58) (24540).* 804/793-4000; FAX 804/799-5516. 98 rms, 3 story. S $53; D $59; each addl $5; under 16 free. Crib free. TV; cable (premium). Pool. Complimentary continental bkfst. Restaurant adj 6 am-10 pm. Ck-out noon. Meeting rms. Business servs avail. Health club privileges. Golf privileges. Bathrm phones; some refrigerators. Deck overlooking river. Cr cds: A, C, D, DS, ER, MC, V.

D ⮕ ⽬ ≈ ⩽ ⌦ SC

✔★ **INNKEEPER MOTOR LODGE WEST.** *3020 Riverside Dr (US 58) (24541).* 804/799-1202; FAX 804/799-9672; res: 800/822-9899. 118 rms, 2 story. S $39.99-$51.99; D $49.99-$69.99; each addl $5. Crib free. TV; cable (premium). Pool; whirlpool. Complimentary continental bkfst. Restaurant adj 6 am-midnight. Ck-out noon. Business servs avail. Valet serv. Cr cds: A, C, D, DS, MC, V.

D ≈ ⩽ ⌦ SC

✔★ **INNKEEPER NORTH.** *1030 Piney Forest Rd (24540).* 804/836-1700. 53 rms, 2 story. S $39.99-$44.99; D $43.99-$48.99; each addl $5; under 16 free. Crib free. TV; cable (premium). Pool. Complimentary continental bkfst. Restaurant adj 6 am-midnight. Ck-out noon. Business servs avail. Health club privileges. Cr cds: A, C, D, DS, MC, V.

≈ ⩽ ⌦ SC

★ ★ **STRATFORD INN.** *2500 Riverside Dr (US 58) (24540).* 804/793-2500; FAX 804/793-6960; res: 800/326-8455. 152 rms, 2 story. S $43-$48; D $48-$55; each addl $7; suites $88-$150; under 18 free. Crib free. Pet accepted. TV; cable (premium), VCR avail. Heated pool; wading pool; whirlpool. Complimentary full bkfst. Restaurant 6 am-10 pm. Rm serv. Bar to midnight. Ck-out noon. Coin lndry. Meeting rms. Business servs avail. Valet serv. Sundries. Exercise equipt; treadmill, stair machine. Cr cds: A, C, D, DS, MC, V.

D ⮕ ⮕ ⽬ ⽬ ⩽ ⌦ SC

Motor Hotel

★ ★ **HOWARD JOHNSON.** *100 Tower Dr (24540), at jct US 29N & US 58, adj Piedmont Mall.* 804/793-2000; FAX 804/792-4621. 118 rms, 6 story, 20 suites. S $52-$67; D $60-$76; each addl $8; suites $67-$82; under 18 free. Crib avail. TV; cable (premium). Pool. Restaurant 6:30 am-midnight. Rm serv. Bar from 11 am. Ck-out noon. Coin Indry. Meeting rms. Business servs avail. Valet serv. Health club privileges. Cr cds: A, C, D, DS, JCB, MC, V.

D ⚊ 🏊 ⚟ 🔥 SC

Dulles Intl Airport Area (C-8)

(See also Fairfax)

Services and Information

Information: 703/419-8000.

Lost and Found: 703/572-2954.

Weather: 703/260-0307.

Airlines: Aeroflot, Air Canada, Air France, All Nippon, American, ANA, British Airways, Continental, Continental Express, Delta, Delta Connection, Japan Airlines, KLM, Lufthansa, Northwest, Qantas, Saudi Arabia Airways, Swissair, TACA, Transbrasil, TWA, United, United Express, USAir, Western Pacific.

What to See and Do

Reston Town Center. A 20-acre urban development incorporating elements of a traditional town square. Includes more than 60 retail shops and restaurants, an 11-screen movie theater complex, office space and a 514-rm Hyatt hotel. (See ANNUAL and SEASONAL EVENTS) Adj Dulles Toll Rd (VA 267) at Reston Pkwy in Reston. Phone 703/709-8500.

Annual Events

Northern Virginia Fine Arts Festival. Reston Town Center (see). Art sale, children's activity area, barbecue. Last wkend June.

Oktoberfest. Reston Town Center (see). Biergarten with authentic German music, food. Mid-Sept.

Seasonal Events

Summer Concerts. Reston Town Center (see). Sat evenings June-Aug; also Thurs evenings July.

Fountain Square Ice Rink. Reston Town Center (see). Outdoor public ice rink. Mid-Nov-mid-Mar.

Fountain Square Holiday Celebration. Reston Town Center (see). Choral groups, puppeteers, magicians, ice shows, dancers, parade. Thanksgiving-Dec 24.

Motels

★ ★ **COMFORT INN.** *(200 Elden St, Herndon 20170)* Dulles Toll Rd exit 12, then left on Baron Cameron Ave (VA 606). 703/437-7555; FAX 703/437-7572. 103 rms, 3 story. S, D $79-$229; under 19 free; wkend plans. TV; cable (premium), VCR avail. Complimentary continental bkfst. Complimentary coffee in rms. Restaurant adj 11 am-10 pm. Rm serv. Ck-out noon. Meeting rms. Business servs avail. Valet serv. Free airport transportation. Exercise equipt; weights, bicycles. Refrigerators; microwaves avail. Cr cds: A, C, D, DS, ER, JCB, MC, V.

D 🚶 ✈ ⚟ 🔥 SC

★ ★ ★ **COURTYARD BY MARRIOTT.** *(3935 Centerview Dr, Chantilly 20151)* in Dulles Business Park. 703/709-7100; FAX 703/709-8672. 149 rms, 3 story. S $95; D $110; suites $119; under 12 free; wkly rates; higher rates special events. Crib free. TV; cable (premium). Indoor pool; whirlpool, lifeguard. Complimentary coffee in rms. Restaurant opp 11 am-midnight. Ck-out noon. Coin Indry. Meeting rms. Business servs avail. In-rm modem link. Valet serv. Sundries. Free airport transportation. Exercise equipt; treadmill, bicycle. Microwaves avail. Balconies. Picnic tables. Cr cds: A, C, D, DS, MC, V.

D ⚊ 🍴 ✈ ⚟ 🔥 SC

★ ★ **COURTYARD BY MARRIOTT.** *(533 Herndon Pkwy, Herndon 20170)* Dulles Toll Rd exit 11. 703/478-9400; FAX 703/478-3628. Web www.courtyard.com/iadhc. 146 rms, 3 story. S $110; D $120; each addl $10; suites $129-$139; under 16 free; wkend rates. Crib free. TV; cable (premium). Indoor pool; whirlpool, lifeguard. Complimentary coffee in rms. Restaurant 6-10 am, 5-10 pm; wkends 7-11 am, 5-10 pm. Bar 5-10 pm. Ck-out noon. Coin Indry. Meeting rms. Business servs avail. In-rm modem link. Sundries. Valet serv. Free airport transportation. Exercise equipt; weight machine, stair machine. Cr cds: A, C, D, DS, MC, V.

D ⚊ 🍴 ✈ ⚟ 🔥 SC

★ ★ **HOLIDAY INN EXPRESS.** *(485 Elden St, Herndon 20170)* Dulles Toll Rd exit 10, then E on Elden St. 703/478-9777; FAX 703/471-4624. E-mail disales@bfsaulco.com. 115 rms, 4 story. S, D $84-$99; each addl $6; under 19 free. Crib free. Pet accepted, some restrictions. TV; cable (premium). Complimentary continental bkfst. Complimentary coffee in rms. Restaurant nearby. Ck-out 11 am. Meeting rm. Business servs avail. Valet serv. Free airport transportation. Exercise equipt; weights, bicycles. Refrigerators, microwaves avail. Cr cds: A, C, D, DS, JCB, MC, V.

D 🐾 🍴 ✈ ⚟ 🔥 SC

★ ★ ★ **RESIDENCE INN BY MARRIOTT.** *(315 Elden St, Herndon 20170)* Dulles Toll Rd exit 12, then left on Baron Cameron Rd (VA 606). 703/435-0044; FAX 703/437-4007. Web www.marriott.com. 168 kit. units, 2 story. S, D $135-$169; wkend rates. Crib free. Pet accepted; $100 nonrefundable, $6/day. TV; cable (premium), VCR avail (movies). Pool; whirlpool, lifeguard. Playground. Complimentary continental bkfst. Complimentary coffee in rms. Restaurant opp 6:30 am-10 pm. Ck-out noon. Coin Indry. Business servs avail. In-rm modem link. Valet serv. Sundries. Lighted tennis. Health club privileges. Microwaves. Picnic tables. Cr cds: A, C, D, DS, JCB, MC, V.

D 🐾 🎾 ⚊ ⚟ 🔥 SC

Motor Hotels

✔ ★ **DAYS INN.** *(2200 Centreville Rd, Herndon 20170)* 2 mi E on Dulles Toll Rd, exit 10. 703/471-6700; FAX 703/742-8965. E-mail dullesdaysinn@daysinn.com; web www.shirenet .com\daysinn. 205 rms, 4 story. Apr-June, Sept-Oct: S, D $64-$139; each addl $10; under 18 free; wkend, monthly rates; lower rates rest of yr. Crib free. TV; cable (premium). Pool; whirlpool, lifeguard. Complimentary continental bkfst. Complimentary coffee in rms. Restaurant 6-1 am. Bar. Ck-out noon. Business servs avail. In-rm modem link. Bellhops. Sundries. Gift shop. Free airport transportation. Exercise equipt; weight machines, bicycles. Cr cds: A, C, D, DS, JCB, MC, V.

D ⚊ 🍴 ✈ ⚟ 🔥 SC

★ ★ ★ **HOLIDAY INN.** *(1000 Sully Rd, Sterling 20166)* Dulles Toll Rd exit 9B (US 28/Sully Rd), then 1 mi N. 703/471-7411. 296 rms, 2 story. S, D $125; suites $130-$160; each addl $10; under 18 free; wkend rates. Crib free. Pet accepted, some restrictions. TV; cable (premium). Indoor pool; whirlpool, lifeguard. Restaurant 6:30 am-10:30 pm. Rm serv to midnight. Bars 11-1:30 am, Sun to midnight; entertainment. Ck-out noon. Coin Indry. Meeting rms. Business center. In-rm modem link. Bellhops. Gift shop. Valet serv. Free airport transportation. Exercise equipt; weights, bicycles, sauna. Refrigerators avail. Rec rm. Cr cds: A, C, D, DS, JCB, MC, V.

D 🐾 ⚊ 🍴 ✈ ⚟ 🔥 SC 🏃

Hotels

✔✕ ★ ★ ★ **HILTON.** *(13869 Park Center Rd, Herndon 22171) On Sully Rd (VA 28), Dulles Toll Rd exit 9A, then 1 mi S to McLearen Rd.* 703/478-2900; FAX 703/834-1996. Web www.alma.net/hilton-wda. 301 rms, 5 story. S, D $110-$165; suites $360-$690; under 18 free; wkend rates. Crib free. Pet accepted, some restrictions. TV; cable (premium), VCR avail. 2 pools, 1 indoor; poolside serv, lifeguard. Coffee in rms. Restaurant 6 am-11 pm; Sat, Sun from 6:30 am. Rm serv 24 hrs. Bars 11:30 am-midnight; entertainment. Ck-out noon. Convention facilities. Business center. In-rm modem link. Gift shop. Barber, beauty shop. Free airport transportation. Tennis. Exercise equipt; weight machines, bicycles. Some bathrm phones, refrigerators. Luxury level. Cr cds: A, C, D, DS, ER, JCB, MC, V.

★ ★ ★ **HYATT.** *(2300 Dulles Corner Blvd, Herndon 20171) Dulles Toll Rd exit 9A (VA 28/Sully Rd), then S, left on Frying Pan Rd, left on Horsepen Rd, then left on Dulles Corner Blvd.* 703/713-1234; FAX 703/713-3410. Web www.hyatt.com. 317 rms, 14 story. S $179; D $204, suites $300-$700; wkly, wkend rates. Crib free. TV; cable (premium), VCR avail. Indoor pool; whirlpool, lifeguard. Restaurant 6 am-midnight. Bar from noon; pianist. Ck-out noon. Business center. In-rm modem link. Gift shop. Free airport transportation. Exercise equipt; weights, bicycles, sauna. Refrigerators, microwaves avail. Cr cds: A, C, D, DS, ER, JCB, MC, V.

★ ★ ★ **HYATT REGENCY-RESTON TOWN CENTER.** *(1800 President's St, Reston 22190) Dulles Toll Rd Reston Pkwy exit 12, at Reston Town Center.* 703/709-1234; FAX 703/709-2291. Web www.hyatt.com. 514 rms, 12 story. S $199; D $224; each addl $25; suites $275-$550; under 18 free; wkend packages. Crib free. Garage parking; valet (fee). TV; cable (premium), VCR avail. Indoor pool; whirlpool, poolside serv, lifeguard. Restaurant (see MARKET STREET BAR & GRILL). Bar 11:30-2 am; entertainment Fri-Sun. Ck-out noon. Convention facilities. Business center. In-rm modem link. Concierge. Shopping arcade. Free airport transportation. Tennis privileges. Golf privileges. Exercise rm; instructor, weights, bicycles, sauna. Luxury level. Cr cds: A, C, D, DS, ER, JCB, MC, V.

★ ★ ★ **MARRIOTT SUITES.** *(13101 Worldgate Dr, Herndon 20170) Dulles Toll Rd exit 10, in Worldgate Center.* 703/709-0400; FAX 703/709-0434. Web www.marriott.com. 254 suites, 11 story. S $175; D $190; under 18 free; wkend rates. Crib free. TV; cable (premium), VCR avail. Indoor/outdoor pool; whirlpool, lifeguard. Complimentary coffee in lobby. Restaurant 6:30 am-10:30 pm. Bar to 11 pm. Ck-out 1 pm. Free guest lndry. Meeting rms. Business servs avail. In-rm modem link. Free garage parking. Free airport transportation. Exercise equipt; weight machine, rowers, sauna. Health club privileges. Refrigerators, wet bars; microwaves avail. Cr cds: A, C, D, DS, ER, JCB, MC, V.

★ ★ ★ **MARRIOTT WASHINGTON.** *(333 W Service Rd, Chantilly 20221) Dulles Access Rd, at airport.* 703/471-9500; FAX 703/661-8714. Web www.marriott.com. 367 rms, 3 story. S $135; D $150; each addl $15; suites $275-$300; under 18 free; wkend plans. Crib free. TV; cable (premium), VCR avail. 2 pools, 1 indoor; whirlpool, poolside serv. Restaurant 6 am-midnight; Sat, Sun from 6:30 am. Bar 11:30-1 am. Ck-out noon. Coin lndry. Convention facilities. Business center. In-rm modem link. Concierge. Gift shop. Free airport transportation. Lighted tennis. Exercise equipt; weights, bicycles. Lawn games. Microwaves avail. Picnic area. On 21 acres with small lake; attractive landscaping. Luxury level. Cr cds: A, C, D, DS, ER, JCB, MC, V.

Resort

★ ★ ★ **WESTFIELDS MARRIOTT.** *(14750 Conference Center Dr, Chantilly 20151) 8 mi S on VA 28.* 703/818-0300; FAX 703/818-3655. Web www.marriott.com. 340 rms, 4 story. S $195; D $215; each addl $20; suites $295-$695; under 12 free; MAP avail; wkend rates. Crib free. Pet accepted, some restrictions. TV; cable (premium), VCR avail (movies). 2 pools, 1 indoor; whirlpool, poolside serv, lifeguard. Complimentary coffee in lobby. Restaurant (see PALM COURT). Rm serv 6-1 am. Box lunches, picnics. Bar 11-1 am; entertainment. Ck-out 1 pm, ck-in 3 pm. Bellhops. Valet serv. Concierge. Gift shop. Convention facilities. Business center. In-rm modem link. Valet parking. Free airport transportation. Sports dir. Lighted tennis, pro. 18-hole golf, greens fee $75. Hiking. Bicycles. Lawn games. Basketball. Exercise rm; instructor, weights, bicycles, sauna, steam rm. Massage. Health club privileges. Minibars. Balconies. Picnic tables. Cr cds: A, C, D, DS, JCB, MC, V.

Restaurants

★ ★ **CLYDE'S.** *(11905 Market St, Reston 20190) 4 mi E on Dulles Toll Rd, exit 12.* 703/787-6601. Hrs: 11 am-10 pm; Fri, Sat to 1 am; Sun from 10 am; early-bird dinner Mon-Fri 4:30-6 pm; Sun brunch to 4 pm. Closed Dec 25. Contemporary Amer menu. Bar to 2 am. Semi-a la carte: lunch $4.95-$10.95, dinner $4.95-$18.50. Sun brunch $4.95-$10.95. Specializes in aged beef, fresh seafood, hamburgers. Own baking, ice cream. Outdoor dining. Contemporary pub decor; toys, art and artifacts reminiscent of youth. Cr cds: A, C, D, DS, MC, V.

★ ★ **FORTUNE.** *(1428 N Point Village Ctr, Reston 22094) on VA 602 (Reston Pkwy).* 703/318-8898. Hrs: 11 am-10:30 pm; Fri, Sat to 11:30 pm. Res accepted; required Fri, Sat dinner. Chinese menu. Serv bar. A la carte entrees: lunch $1.95-$5.50, dinner $6.25-$20. Specializes in dim sum, seafood, traditional Hong Kong dishes. Chinese decor. Cr cds: A, DS, MC, V.

★ ★ **IL CIGNO.** *(1617 Washington Plaza, Reston 20190) in Lake Anne Shopping Center, off VA 606.* 703/471-0121. Hrs: 11:30 am-2:30 pm, 5:30-10 pm. Closed Sun (exc summer); most major hols. Res accepted; required Fri, Sat. Northern Italian menu. Bar. Semi-a la carte: lunch $7.95-$12.95, dinner $9.95-$18.95. Specializes in fish, veal, pasta. Outdoor dining overlooking Lake Anne. Split-level dining rm with original art. Cr cds: A, C, D, MC, V.

✔✕ ★ ★ **A LITTLE PLACE CALLED SIAM.** *(328 Elden St, Herndon 22070) Dulles Toll Rd exit 11N.* 703/742-8881. Hrs: 11:30 am-10 pm; Fri to 10:30 pm; Sat noon-10:30 pm; Sun noon-9:30 pm; early-bird dinner Sun-Thurs 4:30-6:30 pm. Closed Dec 25. Res accepted; required Fri, Sat dinner. Thai menu. Bar. Semi-a la carte: lunch $6.95-$12.95, dinner $9.95-$15.95. Specializes in pad Thai, Thai curry, seafood. Own desserts. Outdoor dining. Contemporary Thai decor with light woods, etched glass. Cr cds: A, C, D, MC, V.

★ ★ ★ **MARKET STREET BAR & GRILL.** *(See Hyatt Regency Reston Town Center Hotel)* 703/709-6262. Hrs: 11:30 am-2:30 pm, 5:30-10 pm; Fri, Sat to 11 pm; Sun 10:30 am-2:30 pm, 5-9 pm. Closed Memorial Day, July 4, Labor Day. Res accepted; required Fri, Sat. Contemporary Amer, Asian menu. Bar. A la carte entrees: lunch $6.95-$12.95, dinner $10.75-$22.75. Sun brunch $15.95. Seasonal specialties. Entertainment Fri-Sun. Valet parking. Outdoor dining. Bistro decor. Cr cds: A, C, D, DS, ER, JCB, MC, V.

★ ★ ★ **PALM COURT.** *(See Westfields Marriott Resort)* 703/818-3520. Hrs: 7 am-2 pm, 6-10 pm; Sun brunch 10 am-2 pm. Res accepted; required Fri, Sat, Sun brunch. Continental menu. Bar 11-1 am. Semi-a la carte: bkfst $4.75-$9.95, lunch $6.95-$14.95. A la carte entrees: dinner $21-$29.95. Sun brunch $30. Child's meals. Specializes in fresh seafood, game. Pianist. Valet parking. Formal decor. Cr cds: A, C, D, DS, JCB, MC, V.

★ ★ ★ **RUSSIA HOUSE.** *(790 Station St, Herndon 20170) Dulles Toll Rd exit 10.* 703/787-8880. Hrs: 11:30 am-2:30 pm, 5:30-10 pm; Sat 5:30-10:30 pm; Sun 5-9 pm. Closed most major hols. Res accepted; required Fri, Sat. Continental, Russian menu. Bar. Wine list. Semi-a la carte: lunch $8-$12.95, dinner $14-$21.95. Complete meals (wkends): dinner $25-$45. Specializes in fresh seafood, beef, veal. Pianist, violinist Fri, Sat. Parking. Modern decor highlighted by Russian artwork. Cr cds: A, C, D, DS, MC, V.

D ⌐

★ ★ **SWEETWATER TAVERN.** *(14250 Sweetwater Ln, Centreville 22020) 9 mi S on VA 28.* 703/449-1100. Hrs: 4:30-11 pm; Fri, Sat noon-1 am; Sun noon-10 pm; early-bird dinner Mon-Thurs to 6 pm. Closed Thanksgiving, Dec 25. Res accepted Sun-Thurs dinner. Bar. Semi-a la carte: lunch $4.95-$9.95, dinner $4.95-$16.95. Child's meals. Specializes in hickory-fired Angus beef, fresh seafood, chops. Own baking, desserts. Outdoor dining. Totally nonsmoking. Cr cds: A, MC, V.

D

✔ ★ **TORTILLA FACTORY.** *(648 Elden St, Herndon 20172) Off Dulles Toll Rd exit 10, Pines Shopping Center.* 703/471-1156. E-mail tortfact@aol.com. Hrs: 11 am-10 pm; Mon to 9 pm; Fri, Sat to 10:30 pm; Sun noon-9 pm. Closed most major hols. Res accepted. Mexican menu. Serv bar. Semi-a la carte: lunch $4.75-$6.50, dinner $5-$11.25. Child's meals. Specialties: carne machaca, chimichangas. Own tortillas. Folk music Tues. Cr cds: A, C, D, DS, MC, V.

D SC ⌐

★ **WINFIELD'S.** *(5127 Westfield Blvd, Centreville 20120) 7 mi S on VA 28, in Sully Station Shopping Center.* 703/803-1040. Hrs: 11 am-midnight; Fri, Sat to 1:30 am; Sun to 9 pm, brunch to 2 pm. Closed major hols. Res accepted; required Fri, Sat dinner. Bar. Semi-a la carte: lunch $5.25-$8.50, dinner $7.95-$14.95; Sat buffet $18.95. Sun brunch $14.95. Child's meals. Specializes in red salmon, seafood buffet (Sat). Outdoor dining. Sports bar; informal dining. Cr cds: A, C, D, MC, V.

D ⌐

Emporia (F-8)

Pop 5,306 **Elev** 110 ft **Area code** 804 **Zip** 23847

Motels

★ ★ **BEST WESTERN.** *1100 W Atlantic St.* 804/634-3200; FAX 804/634-5459. 97 rms, 2 story. Feb-Sept: S $50-$60; D $60-$70; each addl $5; under 18 free; lower rates rest of yr. Crib free. TV; cable (premium). Complimentary continental bkfst. Restaurant opp 6 am-10 pm. Ck-out 11 am. Meeting rms. Business servs avail. In-rm modem link. Exercise equipt; treadmill, stair machine. Some refrigerators. Cr cds: A, C, D, DS, MC, V.

D ⇲ ✕ ⋈ ⋈ SC

★ **COMFORT INN.** *1411 Skipper's Rd (10960), at I-95 exit 8.* 804/348-3282. 96 rms, 2 story. S $48.95; D 56.95; each addl $4; family rates. Crib $2. Pet accepted. TV; cable (premium). Heated pool. Playground. Complimentary continental bkfst. Restaurant adj 5:30 am-11 pm. Business servs avail. In-rm modem link. Cr cds: A, C, D, DS, ER, MC, V.

D ⇲ ⋈ ⋈ ⋈ SC

★ ★ **HAMPTON INN.** *1207 W Atlantic St, (10960), off I-95 exit 11B.* 804/634-9200; FAX 804/348-0071. 115 rms, 2 story. S $54-$65; D $62-$65; under 18 free. Crib free. Pet accepted. TV; cable (premium). Pool. Complimentary continental bkfst. Restaurant nearby. Ck-out 11 am. Cr cds: A, C, D, DS, MC, V.

D ⇲ ⋈ ⋈ ⋈ SC

Fairfax (C-8)

(See also Alexandria, Arlington County, Falls Church, McLean; also see District of Columbia)

Pop 19,622 **Elev** 447 ft **Area code** 703 **E-mail** cvbfceda@mindspring.com **Web** www.cvb.co.fairfax.va.us/fceda
Information Fairax County Convention & Visitors Bureau, 8300 Boone Blvd, Suite 450, Tysons Corner-Vienna 22182; 703/790-3329 or 703/550-2450 (visitor center).

What to See and Do

County parks. For additional information, contact Fairfax County Park Authority, 3701 Pender Dr, 22030; 703/246-5700.

Burke Lake. Consists of 888 acres. Fishing, boating (ramp, rentals). Picnicking, playground, concession; miniature train, carousel (summer, daily; early May & late Sept, wkends), 18-hole, par-3 golf course. Camping (May-Sept; 7-day limit). Beaver Cove Nature Trail; fitness trail. Fee for activities. (Daily) 6 mi S on VA 123, in Fairfax Station. Phone 703/323-6601. Day-use fee/vehicle (wkends & hols) ¢¢

Lake Fairfax. Pool; boat rentals, fishing. Picnicking; excursion boat, carousel; miniature train (late May-Labor Day, daily). Camping (Mar-Dec; 7-day limit; electric addl fee). Fee for activities. (Daily) On VA 606 near Leesburg Pike in Reston. Phone 703/471-5415. Nonresident day-use fee/vehicle (wkends & hols) ¢¢

George Mason University (1957). (24,000 students) State-supported, started as branch of University of Virginia. Fenwick Library maintains the largest collection anywhere of material pertaining to the Federal Theatre Project of the 1930s. The Research Center for the Federal Theatre Project contains 7,000 scripts, including unpublished works by Arthur Miller, sets and costume designs and an oral history collection of interviews with former Federal Theatre personnel. (Mon-Fri; closed hols) 4400 University Dr. Phone 703/993-1000.

Regional parks. Contact Northern Virginia Regional Park Authority, 5400 Ox Rd, Fairfax Station 22039; phone 703/352-5900 or 703/352-3165 (TTY).

Meadowlark Gardens. Lilac, wildflower, herb, hosta and landscaped gardens on 95 acres. Includes 3 ponds; water garden; gazebos; trails. Visitor center. (Daily) 9750 Meadowlark Gardens Ct, 6 mi N off VA 123. Phone 703/255-3631. **Free.**

Bull Run. Consists of 5,000 acres. Themed swimming pool (Memorial Day-Labor Day, daily; fee). Camping (1-4 persons, fee; electricity avail; res accepted, phone 703/631-0550). Concession; picnicking, playground; mini-golf; Frisbee golf; public shooting center; nature trail. (Mid-Mar-Dec) From Beltway I-66W, exit at Centreville, W on US 29 3 mi to park sign. Phone 703/631-0550. Admission per vehicle (nonresidents only) ¢¢

Algonkian. Located on the Potomac River, this 800-acre park offers swimming (Memorial Day-Labor Day, fee); fishing; boating (ramp); golf, miniature golf; picnicking; vacation cottages; meeting and reception areas. 6 mi NE on VA 123 to VA 7, then 9 mi NW to Cascades Pkwy N, then 3 mi N near Sterling. Phone 703/450-4655. **Free.**

Sully (1794). Restored house of Richard Bland Lee, brother of General "Light Horse Harry" Lee; some original furnishings; kitchen-washhouse, log house store, smokehouse on grounds. Guided tours. (Daily exc Tues; closed Jan 1, Thanksgiving, Dec 25) 10 mi W on US 50, then N on VA 28 (Sully Rd), near Chantilly. Phone 703/437-1794. ¢¢

Annual Events

Mobil Invitational Track & Field Meet. George Mason University campus. Early Feb.

Antique Car Show. Sully. 400 antique cars, flea market and music. June.

Quilt Show. Sully. Quilts for sale, quilting demonstrations and antique quilts on display. Sept.

Seasonal Events

Wolf Trap Farm Park for the Performing Arts. In Vienna, 8 mi NE on VA 123, then W on US 7 to Towlston Rd (Trap Rd), then follow signs. Varied programs include ballet, musicals, opera, classical, jazz and folk music. Filene Center open theater seats 3,800 under cover and 3,000 on the lawn. Picnicking on grounds, all yr. Also free interpretive children's programs, July-Aug. For schedules and prices contact Wolf Trap Foundation, 1624 Trap Rd, Vienna 22182; 703/255-1900. Late May-Sept.

Barns of Wolf Trap Foundation. 3/4 mi S of Wolf Trap Farm Park on Trap Rd. A 350-seat theater/conference center with chamber music, recitals, mime, jazz, theater and children's programs. For schedule contact the Barns, 1635 Trap Rd, Vienna 22182; 703/938-2404. Late Sept-early May.

Motels

★ ★ **COURTYARD BY MARRIOTT-FAIR OAKS.** 11220 Lee Jackson Hwy (US 50) (22030), I-66, exit 57A. 703/273-6161; FAX 703/273-3505. Web www.marriott.com/courtyard/va_197.htm. 144 rms, 3 story. S, D $71-$96; suites $89-$109; under 13 free; wkly, wkend rates. Crib free. TV; cable (premium), VCR avail. Indoor pool; whirlpool, lifeguard. Complimentary coffee in rms. Restaurant 6:30-10 am; Sat 7-11 am; Sun 7 am-noon. Bar 4-10 pm. Ck-out noon. Coin lndry. Meeting rms. Business servs avail. In-rm modem link. Valet serv. Sundries. Exercise equipt; weights, bicycles. Health club privileges. Some refrigerators; microwaves avail. Private patios, balconies. Cr cds: A, C, D, DS, JCB, MC, V.

D ≈ X ⇟ 🔥 SC

★ ★ **HAMPTON INN.** 10860 Lee Hwy (22030). 703/385-2600; FAX 703/385-2742. 86 rms, 5 story. S, D $75-$82; under 18 free. Crib free. TV; cable (premium). Complimentary continental bkfst. Complimentary coffee in rms. Restaurant adj 7 am-11 pm. Ck-out noon. Meeting rms. Business servs avail. In-rm modem link. Exercise equipt; treadmill, stair machine. Health club privileges. Some refrigerators, wet bars; microwaves avail. Cr cds: A, C, D, DS, MC, V.

D X ⇟ 🔥 SC

Hotels

★ **HOLIDAY INN.** 3535 Chain Bridge Rd (22030). 703/591-5500; FAX 703/591-7483. 127 rms, 3 story. Mar-Oct: S $79-$99; D $89-$109; each addl $10; suites $99-$129; under 18 free; lower rates rest of yr. Crib free. Pet accepted, some restrictions. TV; cable (premium). Pool. Complimentary coffee in lobby. Restaurant 6:30-10 am, 5-10 pm. Ck-out noon. Meeting rms. Business servs avail. Valet serv. Coin lndry. Health club privileges. Some refrigerators; microwaves avail. Cr cds: A, C, D, DS, JCB, MC, V.

D ✦ ≈ ⇟ 🔥 SC

★ ★ **HOLIDAY INN FAIR OAKS MALL.** 11787 Lee Jackson Hwy (22033), I-66, exit 57B. 703/352-2525; FAX 703/352-4471. E-mail hifo@erols.com. 312 rms, 6 story. S, D $129-$149; each addl $10; under 19 free; wkend, hol rates. Crib free. Pet accepted. TV; cable (premium), VCR avail. Indoor pool; lifeguard. Complimentary coffee in rms. Restaurant 6:30 am-midnight. Bar; entertainment. Ck-out noon. Coin lndry. Convention facilities. Business center. In-rm modem link. Concierge. Gift shop. Airport transportation. Exercise equipt; weight machine, bicycle, sauna. Health club privileges. Game rm. Microwaves avail. Balconies. Luxury level. Cr cds: A, C, D, DS, ER, JCB, MC, V.

D ✦ ≈ ⇟ X ⇟ 🔥 SC 🚶

★ ★ **HYATT FAIR LAKES.** 12777 Fair Lakes Circle (22033), at I-66 exit 55B. 703/818-1234; FAX 703/818-3140. 316 rms, 14 story. S, D $159-$189; each addl $25; suites $199-$475; under 18 free; wkend rates. Crib free. TV; cable (premium), VCR avail. Indoor pool; whirlpool, lifeguard. Restaurant 6:30 am-11 pm; Fri, Sat to midnight. Bar 11:30-1 am; entertainment. Ck-out noon. Convention facilities. Business center. In-rm modem link. Free airport, RR station transportation. Exercise equipt; weights, bicycles, sauna. Refrigerators avail. Cr cds: A, C, D, DS, ER, JCB, MC, V.

D ≈ ⇟ X ⇟ 🔥 SC 🚶

Inn

★ ★ ★ **BAILIWICK.** 4023 Chain Bridge Rd (VA 123) (22030). 703/691-2266; FAX 703/934-2112; res: 800/366-7666. E-mail bailiwick @erols.com. 14 rms, some with shower only, 4 story. No elvtr. S, D $130-$299. TV; VCR avail. Complimentary full bkfst. Restaurant (see BAILIWICK INN). Ck-out 11 am, ck-in 2 pm. Health club privileges. Some in-rm whirlpools, fireplaces. Restored private residence (1800); antiques. The first Civil War skirmish occured here in June of 1861. Totally nonsmoking. Cr cds: A, MC, V.

D ⇟ 🔥 SC

Restaurants

★ ★ **ARTIE'S.** 3260 Old Lee Hwy (22030). 703/273-7600. E-mail artiesrest@aol.com. Hrs: 11:30 am-midnight; Fri, Sat to 1 am; Sun 10 am-11 pm; Sun brunch to 3 pm; early-bird dinner Mon-Thurs 5-6 pm. Closed Thanksgiving, Dec 25. Bar. Semi-a la carte: lunch $6.25-$9.75, dinner $6.25-$19.95. Sun brunch $6.25-$9.95. Specializes in steak, seafood, pasta. Parking. Cr cds: A, MC, V.

D

★ ★ **BAILIWICK INN.** (See Bailiwick Inn) 703/691-2266. E-mail bailiwick@erols.com. Hrs: noon-2 pm, 6-9 pm; Tues to 2 pm; Sat, Sun from 6 pm. Closed Mon. Res required. French menu. A la carte entrees: lunch $12-$18. Complete meals: dinner $45; Fri, Sat $55. Specializes in chicken, beef, seafood. Parking. Menu changes monthly. Patio dining overlooking English garden. In restored inn (1800). Totally nonsmoking. Cr cds: A, MC, V.

✔★ **BLUE OCEAN.** 9440 Main St (22031). 703/425-7555. Hrs: 11:30 am-2:30 pm, 5-10 pm; Fri to 10:30 pm; Sat noon-2:30 pm, 5-10:30 pm; Sun from 5 pm. Closed Mon; most major hols. Res accepted. Japanese menu. Serv bar. Semi-a la carte: lunch $7.95-$9.95, dinner $5.50-$17.95. Buffet: lunch $7.95. Specialties: sushi, teriyaki, sukiaki. Salad bar. Authentic Japanese decor; sushi bar. Cr cds: A, C, D, MC, V.

D ⊿

★ ★ **BOMBAY BISTRO.** 3570 Chain Bridge Rd (22030). 703/359-5810. Hrs: 11:30 am-2:30 pm, 5-10 pm; Sun brunch noon-3 pm. Closed Thanksgiving. Indian menu. Bar. A la carte entrees: lunch, dinner $5.95-$15.95. Buffet (Mon-Fri) $6.95. Sat, Sun brunch $8.95. Specializes in tandoori, vegetarian dishes. Outdoor dining. Indian decor. Cr cds: A, C, D, DS, MC, V.

D ⊿

★ ★ **CONNAUGHT PLACE.** 10425 North St (22030). 703/352-5959. Hrs: 11:30 am-2:30 pm, 5-10 pm; Sat noon-3 pm, 5-10 pm; Sun noon-3 pm, 5-9 pm. Closed Thanksgiving, Dec 25. Res accepted. Indian menu. Bar. Semi-a la carte: lunch $5-$11, dinner $6.95-$16.95. Buffet $7.95-$8.95. Sat, Sun brunch $8.95. Specializes in seafood, vegetarian dishes. Middle Eastern decor. Cr cds: A, C, D, MC, V.

D ⊿

★ ★ **HEART-IN-HAND.** (7145 Main St, Clifton 22024) S on VA 123 to Chapel Rd, then W. 703/830-4111. Hrs: 11 am-2:30 pm, 6-9:30 pm; Sun 5-8 pm; Sun brunch 11 am-2:30 pm. Closed Jan 1, July 4, Dec 25. Res accepted. Semi-a la carte: lunch $5.95-$12.95, dinner $14.95-$22.95. Sun brunch $6.95-$12.95. Child's meals. Specializes in seafood, beef Wellington, rack of lamb. Own ice cream. Parking. Outdoor dining. Converted general store (ca 1870). Antique decor; original floors, ceiling fans, antique quilts. Totally nonsmoking. Cr cds: A, C, D, DS, MC, V.

★ ★ ★ **HERMITAGE INN.** (7134 Main St, Clifton 22024) W on US 29 to Clifton Rd (VA 645), then S. 703/266-1623. Hrs: 11:30 am-2:30 pm, 6-10 pm; Sun 11:30 am-2:30 pm, 5-9 pm. Closed Mon. Res accepted. Continental menu. Serv bar. Semi-a la carte: lunch $5.50-$12.75, dinner $13.95-$26.95. Sun brunch $17.95. Specialties: rack of lamb, Long Island duck, châteaubriand. Own pastries. Outdoor dining. Located in 1869 clapboard hotel. Country French decor. Cr cds: A, C, D, DS, MC, V.

D ⊿

★ ★ **J.R.'S STEAK HOUSE.** *9401 Lee Hwy (22030), in Circle Towers office building.* 703/591-8447. Hrs: 5:30-9:30 pm; Fri, Sat to 10:30 pm; Sun 5-9:30 pm. Closed Mon; Thanksgiving, Dec 25. Res accepted. Bar. Semi-a la carte: dinner $12.95-$18.50. Child's meals. Specializes in aged steak, grilled meat and fish. Salad bar. Parking. Patio dining. Cr cds: A, C, D, DS, MC, V.

✔★ **P.J. SKIDOO'S.** *9908 Lee Hwy (22030).* 703/591-4516. Hrs: 11-2 am; Sun 10 am-9 pm. Closed Thanksgiving, Dec 25. Bar. Semi-a la carte: lunch, dinner $5.50-$12.95. Sun brunch $8.95. Child's meals. Specializes in prime rib, fresh seafood, chicken. Entertainment Tues, Thurs-Sat. Parking. 1890s saloon atmosphere. Cr cds: A, MC, V.

✔★ ★ **SILVERADO.** *(7052 Columbia Pike, Annandale 22003) 7 mi SE on VA 244.* 703/354-4560. Hrs: 11:30 am-10:30 pm; Fri to 11:30 pm; Sat noon-11:30 pm; Sun noon-9:30 pm; early-bird dinner Mon-Thurs 5-6 pm. Closed Thanksgiving, Dec 25. Southwestern menu. Bar. Semi-a la carte: lunch $5-$9, dinner $7-$12. Child's meals. Specializes in fajitas, roasted chicken. Own desserts. Southwestern decor; stained glass, Western sculpture and mural. Totally nonsmoking. Cr cds: A, MC, V.

✔★ ★ **TASTE OF THAI.** *9534 Arlington Blvd (22031).* 703/352-4494. Hrs: 11:30 am-10:30 pm; Fri, Sat 11 am-11 pm; Sun 4-9:30 pm. Closed Dec 25. Res accepted; required Fri, Sat dinner. Thai menu. Bar. Semi-a la carte: lunch $5.50-$6.50, dinner $7.95-$11.95. Specialties: duck with basil, garlic shrimp, pad Thai. Thai decor; aquarium along one wall. Cr cds: A, DS, MC, V.

Unrated Dining Spot

THE ESPOSITOS/PIZZA 'N PASTA. *9917 Lee Hwy.* 703/385-5912. Hrs: 11 am-11 pm; Fri to midnight; Sat noon-midnight; Sun noon-10 pm. Closed Thanksgiving, Dec 24 evening, Dec 25. Southern Italian menu. Wine, beer. A la carte entrees: lunch, dinner $3.50-$11.50. Semi-a la carte: lunch $5.50-$12.95, dinner $6.25-$13.95. Specialties: pollo cardinale, fettucine alla Romano. Own pasta. Parking. Pizza baked in wood-burning oven imported from Italy. Italian trattoria decor. Cr cds: A, C, D, MC, V.

Falls Church (C-8)

(See also Alexandria, Arlington County, Fairfax, McLean; also see District of Columbia)

Pop 9,578 **Elev** 340 ft **Area code** 703

Information Greater Falls Church Chamber of Commerce, 417 W Broad St, PO Box 491, 22040-0491; 703/532-1050.

Falls Church is a pleasant, cosmopolitan suburb of Washington, DC, just over the Arlington County line, graced with many interesting old houses. This was a crossover point between the North and the South, through which pioneers, armies, adventurers and merchants passed.

What to See and Do

Fountain of Faith. Also in park is a memorial dedicated to the four chaplains—two Protestant, one Jewish, one Catholic—who were aboard the USS *Dorchester* when it was torpedoed off Greenland in 1943. They gave their life jackets to four soldiers on deck who had none. In National Memorial Park.

The Falls Church (Episcopal) (1769). This building replaced the original wooden church built in 1732. Served as a recruiting station during the

Revolution; abandoned until 1830; used during the Civil War as a hospital and later as a stable for cavalry horses. Restored according to original plans with gallery additions in 1959. (Daily exc Sat; closed some hols) 115 E Fairfax St at Washington St, on US 29. Phone 703/532-7600. **Free.**

Motel

✔★ ★ **QUALITY INN GOVERNOR.** *6650 Arlington Blvd (US 50) (22042), at I-495 exit 8E.* 703/532-8900; FAX 703/532-7121. 121 rms. Mar-Sept: S $65; D $78; each addl $5; suites $95; under 18 free; lower rates rest of yr. Crib free. TV; cable (premium). Pool; lifeguard. Restaurant 6:30 am-10 pm; Sat, Sun from 7 am. Ck-out noon. Meeting rms. Business servs avail. Some refrigerators. Cr cds: A, C, D, DS, JCB, MC, V.

Hotel

★ ★ ★ **MARRIOTT-FAIRVIEW PARK.** *3111 Fairview Park Dr (22042), at I-495 exit 8A.* 703/849-9400; FAX 703/849-8692. Web www.marriott.com. 394 rms, 15 story. S $144; D $154; suites $250-$500; under 16 free. Crib free. TV; cable (premium), VCR avail. Indoor/outdoor pool; whirlpool, poolside serv, lifeguard. Restaurant 6:30 am-10 pm; Fri, Sat 7-2 am. Bar 11-2 am. Ck-out noon. Coin lndry. Convention facilities. Business center. In-rm modem link. Concierge. Gift shop. Exercise equipt; weights, bicycles, sauna. Some bathrm phones. Some balconies. Luxury level. Cr cds: A, C, D, DS, ER, JCB, MC, V.

Restaurants

★ ★ **BANGKOK ST. GRILL AND NOODLES.** *5872 Leesburg Pike (22041).* 703/379-6707. Hrs: 11:30 am-10 pm; Fri, Sat to 10:30 pm. Closed Thanksgiving. Thai menu. Bar. A la carte entrees: lunch, dinner $6.95-$8.75. Specialties: stir fried noodles, shrimp dumplings, chicken satay. Outdoor dining. Casual Thai decor; arranged like a street scene. Totally nonsmoking. Cr cds: A, C, D, MC, V.

✔★ ★ **BANGKOK VIENTIANE.** *926A W Broad St (22046).* 703/534-0095. Hrs: 11 am-10 pm; wkends to 11 pm. Res accepted. Thai, Laotian menu. Semi-a la carte: lunch $3.95-$8.95, dinner $6.50-$9.25. Lunch buffet $5.95. Specialties: spicy Thai beef noodle, tom yam gung, kaeng seafood combo. Parking. Asian decor. Cr cds: A, C, D, DS, MC, V.

★ ★ ★ **DUANGRAT'S.** *5878 Leesburg Pike (22041), adj Glen Forest Shopping Center.* 703/820-5775. Hrs: 11:30 am-2:30 pm, 5-10:30 pm; Fri to 11 pm; Sat 11:30 am-11 pm; Sun 11:30 am-10:30 pm. Res accepted. Thai menu. Bar. Semi-a la carte: lunch $6.95-$8.95, dinner $9.95-$18.95. Specializes in pad Thai noodles, Thai curry, crispy fish with chili sauce. Parking. Display of Thai headdresses and masks. Cr cds: A, C, D, MC, V.

✔★ ★ ★ **HAANDI.** *1222 W Broad St (VA 7) (22046), in Falls Plaza.* 703/533-3501. Hrs: 11:30 am-2:30 pm, 5-10 pm; wkends to 10:30 pm. Closed Dec 25. Res accepted Sun-Thur. Northern Indian menu. Serv bar. Semi-a la carte: lunch $4.95-$10.95, dinner $6.95-$14.95. Specializes in barbecued meats, chicken, vegetarian dishes. Parking. Totally nonsmoking. Cr cds: A, C, D, MC, V.

✔★ ★ **PANJSHIR.** *924 W Broad St (22046).* 703/536-4566. Web www.enterit.com/panjshir566.htm. Hrs: 11 am-2 pm, 5-10 pm; Sun 5-9 pm. Closed July 4, Thanksgiving, Dec 25. Afghan menu. Bar. Semi-a la carte: lunch $6.50-$7.25, dinner $9.95-$13.25. Specializes in kebab, palows, vegetarian dishes. Parking. Totally nonsmoking. Cr cds: A, C, D, MC, V.

★ ★ ★ **PEKING GOURMET INN.** *6029 Leesburg Pike (22041), 4 mi SE on VA 7 (Leesburg Pike).* 703/671-8088. E-mail ftsui@aol.com. Hrs:

11 am-10:30 pm; Fri, Sat to midnight. Closed Thanksgiving. Res accepted; required Fri, Sat. Northern Chinese menu. Serv bar. Semi-a la carte: lunch $6.25-$13.45, dinner $8.45-$24.95. Specialties: Peking duck, beef Szechuan, striped bass Peking-style. Parking. Oriental antiques and screens; 300 yr-old jade Buddha; original artwork. Favorite of Washington politicians. Cr cds: A, MC, V.

★ ★ **PILIN.** 116 W Broad St (VA 7) (22046). 703/241-5850. Hrs: 11:30 am-10 pm; Fri, Sat to 11 pm; Sun 5-9 pm. Closed some major hols. Res accepted; required Fri, Sat dinner. Thai menu. Bar. Semi-a la carte: lunch $4.95-$6.95, dinner $6.95-$12.95. Specialties: spicy, crispy catfish; pad Thai; pad gra prow talay. Parking. Cr cds: A, D, DS, MC, V.

★ ★ **SECRET GARDEN BEEWON.** 6678 Arlington Blvd (22042). 703/533-1004. Hrs: 11 am-10 pm. Closed Jan 1. Res accepted; required Fri, Sat. Korean menu. Serv bar. Semi-a la carte: lunch $5.50-$8.95, dinner $8.95-$18. Complete meals: lunch (Mon-Fri) $5.95-$9.95. Specialties: bulgogi, heamul chongol. Sushi bar. Parking. Tableside preparation. Traditional Korean decor. Cr cds: A, C, D, DS, MC, V.

★ **SIR WALTER RALEIGH INN.** 8120 Gatehouse Rd (22042), I-495 exit 8W to VA 650N. 703/560-6768. Hrs: 11:30 am-2 pm, 5-9 pm; Fri to 10 pm; Sat 5-10 pm; Sun 4-8:30 pm; early-bird dinners 5-6 pm, Sun 4-5 pm. Closed Thanksgiving, Dec 25. Bar. Semi-a la carte: lunch $5.75-$10.95, dinner $7.95-$17.95. Prix fixe: early bird dinner $10.95. Child's meals. Specializes in steak, seafood. Salad bar. Parking. Cr cds: A, C, D, DS, MC, V.

Farmville (E-7)

(See also Keysville)

Pop 6,046 **Elev** 304 ft **Area code** 804 **Zip** 23901

Longwood College's Jeffersonian buildings provide architectural interest in downtown Farmville.

What to See and Do

Appomattox Court House National Historical Park (see). 26 mi NW via US 460, VA 24.

Sailor's Creek Battlefield Historic State Park. Site of last major battle of Civil War, which took place on Apr 6, 1865, preceding Lee's surrender at Appomattox by three days. Auto tour. 9 mi E on US 460, then 7 mi NE on VA 307 and 2 mi N on VA 617. Phone 804/392-3435. **Free.**

Motels

✔★ ★ **COMFORT INN.** HC 6, Box 1740, US 15 & US 460 Bypass. 804/392-8163; FAX 804/392-1966. 51 rms, 2 story. S $53-$59; D $56-$62; each addl $6; under 18 free; higher rates special events. TV; cable (premium), VCR avail. Pool. Ck-out noon. Business servs avail. Cr cds: A, C, D, DS, ER, MC, V.

✔★ **DAYS INN.** 2011 S Main St, on US 15. 804/392-6611; FAX 804/392-9774. 60 rms, 2 story. S $53; D $59; under 18 free; family, wkend, wkly rates; higher rates: homecoming wkend, graduation. Crib free. TV; cable (premium). Complimentary continental bkfst. Restaurant opp 11 am-9 pm. Ck-out 11 am. Business servs avail. Valet serv. Sundries. Pool. Picnic tables, grills. Cr cds: A, C, D, DS, ER, MC, V.

Fredericksburg (D-8)

(See also Triangle)

Settled 1727 **Pop** 19,027 **Elev** 61 ft **Area code** 540 **E-mail** fburg @illuminet.net

Information Visitor Center, 706 Caroline St, 22401; 540/373-1776 or 800/678-4748.

One of the seeds of the American Revolution was planted here when a resolution declaring independence from Great Britain was passed on April 29, 1775. Here is where George Washington went to school, where his sister, Betty, lived and his mother, Mary Ball Washington, lived and died. James Monroe practiced law in town. Guns for the Revolution were manufactured here, and four of the most savage battles of the Civil War were fought nearby.

Captain John Smith visited the area in 1608 and gave glowing reports of its possibilities for settlement. In 1727, the General Assembly directed that 50 acres of "lease-land" be laid out and the town called Fredericksburg, after the Prince of Wales.

Ships from abroad sailed up the Rappahannock River to the harbor—ampler then than now—to exchange their goods for those brought from "upcountry" by the great road wagons and river carriers. The town prospered.

The Civil War left Fredericksburg ravaged. Situated midway between Richmond and Washington, it was recurringly an objective of both sides; the city changed hands seven times, and the casualties were high.

Even so, many buildings put up before 1775 still stand. Proudly aware of their town's place in the country's history, the townspeople keep Fredericksburg inviting with fresh paint, beautiful lawns and well-kept gardens. The city's main sources of income include dairy and beef cattle, softwood timber, men's clothing and shoes, bookbinding and concrete blocks.

What to See and Do

Belmont (The Gari Melchers Estate and Memorial Gallery). Residence from 1916 to 1932 of American-born artist Gari Melchers (1860-1932), best known for his portraits of the famous and wealthy, including Theodore Roosevelt, William Vanderbilt and Andrew Mellon, and as an important impressionist artist of the period. The artist's studio comprises the nation's largest collection of his works, housing more than 1,800 paintings and drawings. The site is a registered National and State Historic Landmark and includes a 27-acre estate, frame house built in the late 18th century and enlarged over the years and a stone studio built by Melchers, which today houses his artwork. Owned by the state of Virginia, Belmont is administered by Mary Washington College. (Daily; closed Jan 1, Thanksgiving, Dec 24, 25, 31) 224 Washington St. Phone 540/654-1843. ¢¢

Fredericksburg and Spotsylvania National Military Park (see).

Mary Washington College (1908). (3,700 students) Liberal arts and sciences including historic preservation, computer science and business administration. Coeducational. Includes 275 acres of open and wooded campus; red-brick, white-pillared buildings. President of the college occupies Brompton (private), a house built in 1830 on land sold to Fielding Lewis in 1760 and expanded by a later owner, Colonel John Lawrence Marye. Campus tours. College Ave. Phone 540/654-1000 or 800/468-5614.

🗙 **Walking or driving tour of Fredericksburg.** Begin at

Visitor Center. Orientation film; information; obtain walking tour brochure and combination tickets here. 706 Caroline St. 3 blks N begin at

Hugh Mercer Apothecary Shop. This 18th-century medical office and pharmacy offers exhibits on the medicine and methods of treatment used by Dr. Hugh Mercer before he left to join the Revolutionary War as brigadier general. Authentic herbs and period medical instruments. (Daily; closed Jan 1, Thanksgiving, Dec 24, 25, 31) 1020 Caroline St. Phone 540/373-3362. ¢¢ Follow Caroline St 3 blks N to

Rising Sun Tavern (ca 1760). Washington's youngest brother, Charles, built this tavern, which became a social and political center and stagecoach stop. Restored and authentically refurnished as an 18th-century tavern; costumed tavern wenches, English and American pewter collection. (Daily; closed Jan 1, Thanksgiving, Dec 24, 25, 31) 1306 Caroline St. Phone 540/371-1494. ¢¢ W to Princess Anne St, 4 blks S is the

Fredericksburg Area Museum (Town Hall) (1814). Museum and cultural center interpret the history of Fredericksburg area from its first settlers to the 20th century. Changing exhibits. Children's events. (Daily; closed Jan 1, Thanksgiving, Dec 25) 907 Princess Anne St. Phone 540/371-3037. ¢¢ Behind Town Hall to the S on Princess Anne St is

St George's Episcopal Church and Churchyard. Patrick Henry, uncle of the orator, was the first rector. Headstones in the churchyard bear the names of illustrious Virginians. (Daily) NE corner of Princess Anne and George Sts. Phone 540/373-4133. 1 blk S to Hanover St is

Fredericksburg Masonic Lodge #4, AF and AM. Washington was initiated into this Lodge Nov 4, 1752; the building, dating from 1812, contains relics of his initiation and membership; authentic Gilbert Stuart portrait; 300-yr-old Bible on which Washington took his Masonic obligation. (Mon-Sat, also Sun afternoons; closed Jan 1, Thanksgiving, Dec 25) Princess Anne & Hanover Sts. Phone 540/373-5885. ¢ Across the street is the

Presbyterian Church (1833). Cannonballs in the front pillar and other damages inflicted in 1862 bombardment. Pews were torn loose and made into coffins for soldiers. Clara Barton, founder of the American Red Cross, is said to have nursed wounded here. A plaque to her memory is in the churchyard. Open on request (daily exc Sat). SW corner of Princess Anne & George Sts. Phone 540/373-7057. 1 blk W on George St is

Masonic Cemetery. One of nation's oldest Masonic burial grounds. George & Charles Sts. Just N on Charles St is

James Monroe Museum. James Monroe, as a young lawyer, lived and worked in Fredericksburg from 1786 to 1789 and even served on Fredericksburg's City Council. Museum houses one of the nation's largest collections of Monroe memorabilia, articles and original documents. Included are the desk bought in France in 1794 during his years as ambassador and used in the White House for signing of the Monroe Doctrine; formal attire worn at Court of Napoleon; and more than 40 books from Monroe's library. Also garden. The site is a National Historic Landmark. Owned by Commonwealth of Virginia, and administered by Mary Washington College. (Daily; closed Jan 1, Thanksgiving, Dec 24, 25, 31) 908 Charles St. Phone 540/654-1043. ¢¢ Continue N on Charles St to

Old Slave Block. Circular block of sandstone about 3 ft high, from which ladies mounted their horses, and slaves were auctioned in antebellum days. William & Charles Sts. 2 blks N on Charles St is

Mary Washington House. Bought by George for his mother in 1772. She lived here until her death in 1789. Here she was visited by General Lafayette. Some original furnishings. Boxwood garden. (Daily; closed Jan 1, Thanksgiving, Dec 24, 25, 31) 1200 Charles St. Phone 540/373-1569. ¢¢ On Charles St is

St James House. Frame house built in 1760s, antique furnishings, porcelain and silver collections; landscaped gardens. (Open Historic Garden Week in Apr and 1st week in Oct; other times by appt) 1300 Charles St. Phone 540/373-1569. ¢¢ Walk back 1 blk to Lewis St and walk 2 blks W to

Kenmore (1752). Considered one of the finest restorations in Virginia; former home of Col Fielding Lewis, commissioner of Fredericksburg gunnery, who married George Washington's only sister, Betty. On an original grant of 863 acres, Lewis built a magnificent home; three rooms have full decorative molded plaster ceilings. Diorama of 18th-century Fredericksburg. Tea and ginger cookies served free (with paid admission). (Daily; closed Jan, Feb, Thanksgiving, Dec 24, 25, 31) 1201 Washington Ave. Phone 540/373-3381. ¢¢ 2½ blks N is

Mary Washington Monument. Where Mrs Washington often went to rest and pray and where she is buried. Near "Meditation Rock." 5 blks S on Washington is

Confederate Cemetery. 2,640 Confederate Civil War soldiers are buried here, some in graves marked "Unknown." Washington Ave between Amelia & William Sts.

Annual Events

Historic Garden Week. Private homes open. Usually last wk Apr.

Market Square Fair. Entertainment, crafts demonstrations, food. Mid-May.

Quilt Show. Exhibits at various locations. Demonstrations and sale of old and new quilts. Sept.

Christmas Candlelight Tour. Historic homes open to the public; carriage rides; Christmas decorations and refreshments of the colonial period. 1st wkend Dec.

Motels

✔★★ **BEST WESTERN THUNDERBIRD.** *3000 Plank Rd (22401), I-95, exit 130B.* 540/786-7404; FAX 540/785-7415. 76 rms, 2-3 story. Mar-Oct: S $42; D $48-$55; each addl $4; under 12 free. Crib $2. Pet accepted, some restrictions. TV; cable (premium). Complimentary continental bkfst. Restaurant nearby. Ck-out noon. Coin lndry. Business servs avail. Sundries. Valet serv. Refrigerators avail. Cr cds: A, C, D, DS, ER, MC, V.

D ✔ ≈ ⚄ 🐾 SC

★ **COMFORT INN SOUTHPOINT.** *5422 Jefferson Davis Hwy (22407), I-95 exit 126.* 540/898-5550; FAX 540/891-2861. 125 rms, 5 story. Mid-Mar-Aug: S, D $59-$65; each addl $6; under 18 free; lower rates rest of yr. Crib free. TV; cable (premium). VCR (movies). Indoor pool; whirlpool. Complimentary continental bkfst. Restaurant adj 6 am-10 pm. Ck-out noon. Meeting rms. Business servs avail. In-rm modem link. Sundries. Valet serv. 18-hole golf privileges; greens fee, pro, putting green, driving range. Exercise equipt; weight machine, bicycles, sauna. Cr cds: A, C, D, DS, ER, JCB, MC, V.

D 🏌 ≈ 🏋 ⚄ 🐾 SC

★ **COMFORT INN-NORTH.** *557 Warrenton Rd (22406), jct I-95 exit 133B & US 17N.* 540/371-8900; FAX 540/372-6958. 80 rms, 3 story, 10 kit. units. S $45.95-$85.95; D $50.95-$85.95; each addl $5; kit. units $70.95; under 18 free; wkly rates. Crib free. TV; cable (premium). Indoor pool; whirlpool. Complimentary continental bkfst. Restaurant adj open 24 hrs. Ck-out 11 am. Business servs avail. In-rm modem link. Exercise equipt; weight machine, stair machine, sauna. Cr cds: A, C, D, DS, JCB, MC, V.

D ≈ 🏋 ⚄ 🐾 SC

✔★★ **DAYS INN-NORTH.** *14 Simpson Rd (22406), jct I-95 & US 17N, exit 133/133B.* 540/373-5340; FAX 540/373-5340. 120 rms, 2 story. S $38-$41; D $48-$51; each addl $5; under 12 free. Crib free. Pet accepted; $5. TV; cable (premium). Pool. Complimentary continental bkfst. Ck-out noon. Business servs avail. Cr cds: A, C, D, DS, MC, V.

✔ ≈ ⚄ 🐾 SC

★★ **HAMPTON INN.** *2310 William St (22401), E of I-95 exit 130A.* 540/371-0330; FAX 540/371-1753. 166 rms, 2 story. S $50; D $72; under 18 free; higher wknd rates. Crib free. Pet accepted, some restrictions. TV; cable (premium). Pool. Complimentary continental bkfst. Ck-out noon. Coin lndry. Meeting rms. Business servs avail. In-rm modem link. Cr cds: A, C, D, DS, MC, V.

D ✔ ≈ ⚄ 🐾 SC

★★ **HOLIDAY INN-NORTH.** *564 Warrenton Rd (22405), at jct US 17, I-95 exit 133/133B.* 540/371-5550; FAX 540/373-3641. 150 rms, 2 story. S $45; D $57; each addl $7; under 18 free. Crib free. TV; cable (premium). Pool; wading pool. Restaurant 6 am-2 pm, 5-10 pm. Rm serv. Bar 4 pm-2 am; entertainment Fri, Sat. Ck-out noon. Coin lndry. Meeting rms. Business servs avail. Valet serv. Sundries. Refrigerators avail. Cr cds: A, C, D, DS, JCB, MC, V.

D ≈ ⚄ 🐾 SC

✔★ **RAMADA INN-SPOTSYLVANIA MALL.** *2802 Plank Rd (22404), Jct I-95, VA 3W, exit 130B. 540/786-8361; FAX 540/786-8811.* 130 rms, 2 story. S $45-$57; D $50-$62; each addl $5; suites $75-$100; under 18 free. Crib free. Pet accepted. TV; cable (premium). Pool. Complimentary coffee in lobby. Restaurant 6 am-10 pm. Rm serv 11 am-9 pm. Ck-out 1 pm. Meeting rms. Business servs avail. In-rm modem link. Valet serv. Sundries. Cr cds: A, C, D, DS, ER, JCB, MC, V.

D ✦ 🏊 ✈ 🐾 SC

Motor Hotels

★★ **HOLIDAY INN SOUTH.** *5324 Jefferson Davis Hwy (22408), I-95 exit 126. 540/898-1102; FAX 540/898-2017.* 195 rms, 2 story. S, D $61-$80; each addl $6; under 18 free; golf plans. Crib free. Pet accepted. TV; cable (premium); VCR avail (movies). Indoor pool; whirlpool. Coffee in lobby. Restaurant 6:30 am-1 pm, 5-9:30 pm. Rm serv. Bar 4 pm-2 am; entertainment Wed-Sat. Ck-out noon. Coin lndry. Meeting rms. Business servs avail. In-rm modem link. Bellhops. Sundries. Valet serv. Exercise equipt; bicycles, rowers. Game rm. Cr cds: A, C, D, DS, JCB, MC, V.

D ✦ 🏊 🍴 🐾 SC

★★★ **SHERATON INN.** *2801 Plank Rd (22404), I-95 exit 130-B, jct VA 3. 540/786-8321; FAX 540/786-3957.* 195 rms, 3 story. S, D $69-$119; each addl $10; suites $150-$275; under 18 free. Crib free. TV; cable (premium). Pool; wading pool, poolside serv, lifeguard. Complimentary coffee in rms. Restaurant 6:30 am-10 pm. Rm serv. Bar 11:30-2 am; entertainment exc Sun. Ck-out noon. Meeting rms. Business servs avail. Bellhops. Valet serv. Sundries. Gift shop. Airport transportation. Tennis. Golf privileges. Exercise equipt; weight machine, stair machine. Lawn games. Private patios, balconies. Refrigerators avail. Picnic tables. Cr cds: A, C, D, DS, ER, JCB, MC, V.

D 🏃 ⛷ 🏊 🍴 ✈ 🐾 SC

Inns

★★ **FREDERICKSBURG COLONIAL.** *1707 Princess Anne St (22401). 540/371-5666; FAX 540/373-7557.* 30 rms, 2 story. S, D $55; each addl $6; suites $65-$70; under 12 free. Crib free. TV; cable. Complimentary continental bkfst. Ck-out 11 am, ck-in 2 pm. Refrigerators. Built 1928; antiques. Totally nonsmoking. Cr cds: A, MC, V.

D 🏊 🐾 SC

★★ **KENMORE.** *1200 Princess Anne St (22401). 540/371-7622; FAX 540/371-5480; res: 800/437-7622.* 12 rms, 2 story. S $75-$105; D $95-$125; each addl $10; suite $150. Crib free. TV in lounge; cable (premium). Complimentary continental bkfst. Dining rm 11:30 am-2:30 pm, 5:30-9:30 pm. Bar 11:30 am-11 pm. Ck-out noon, ck-in 2 pm. Business servs avail. In-rm modem link. Fireplace, canopy bed in some rms. Refrigerators avail. Structure built late 1700s; in historic district. Cr cds: A, C, D, MC, V.

D 🏊 🐾 SC

★★ **RICHARD JOHNSTON.** *711 Caroline St (22401). 540/899-7606.* 7 rms, 3 story, 2 suites. No rm phones. S, D $90-$115; suites $130. Complimentary continental bkfst. Ck-out 11 am, ck-in 2-8 pm. Built 1787; antiques. In historic district. Totally nonsmoking. Cr cds: A, MC, V.

🏊 🐾

Restaurants

★★ **LA PETIT AUBERGE.** *311 William St (22401). 540/371-2727.* Hrs: 11:30 am-2:30 pm, 5:30-10 pm; early-bird dinner Mon-Thurs 5:30-7 pm. Closed Sun; major hols. Res accepted. French, Amer menu. Bar. Wine list. A la carte entrees: lunch $5.50-$12.95, dinner $8.95-$19.95. Specializes in fresh seafood, seasonal specialties, beef. French café decor. Cr cds: A, C, D, MC, V.

D 🍴

★★★ **OLDE MUDD TAVERN.** *(5414 Mudd Tavern Rd, Thornburg 22565) 1/4 mi W of I-95 Thornburg exit 118. 540/582-5250.* Hrs: 4-9 pm; Sun noon-8 pm. Closed Mon, Tues; Jan 1, Dec 25; also 1st wk July. Res accepted. Serv bar. Semi-a la carte: dinner $12.95-$20. Child's meals. Specializes in fresh vegetables, seafood, steak. Own baking. Entertainment Sat. Early Amer decor. Cr cds: MC, V.

D SC 🍴

★★★ **RISTORANTE RENATO.** *422 William St (22401). 540/371-8228.* Hrs: 11:30 am-2 pm, 4:30-10 pm; Sat, Sun from 4:30 pm. Closed most major hols. Italian menu. Bar. Semi-a la carte: lunch $5.95-$9.95, dinner $9.95-$24.95. Specializes in seafood, poultry, pasta. Antique chandeliers; fireplace. Cr cds: A, MC, V.

D 🍴 ♥

Fredericksburg and Spotsylvania National Military Park (D-8)

(For accommodations see Fredericksburg)

(Visitor Center on Old US 1 in Fredericksburg)

Midway between Washington and Richmond, on a good railroad, and protected by the Rappahannock and Rapidan rivers, the Fredericksburg area represented one of the main barriers to Union invasion during the Civil War. Four major engagements—the heaviest, most concentrated fighting ever seen on this continent—were fought in and around this town between December 1862 and May 1864.

Union General A. E. Burnside, after a hard-won crossing of the Rappahannock, engaged in the Battle of Fredericksburg (December 13, 1862). Damage to the city was severe as Burnside attempted a frontal assault on Lee's Confederate forces entrenched behind a stone wall. The attempt proved suicidal. Burnside retreated across the Rappahannock River and went into winter quarters.

The Battle of Chancellorsville (April 27-May 6, 1863) was another victory for Lee, this time against Union General Joseph Hooker. Outmaneuvered, Hooker also retired across the Rappahannock, and Lee prepared his second invasion of the North. It was during this battle, on May 2, that Stonewall Jackson was mistakenly wounded by his own men; he died eight days later.

The Battle of the Wilderness (May 5-6, 1864) was the first encounter between Lee and Union general Ulysses S. Grant. When bloody fighting finally reached a stalemate, Grant elected to go around Lee, toward Richmond.

Savage fighting in the ensuing Battle of Spotsylvania Court House (May 8-21, 1864) produced no clear-cut victory; again Grant sidestepped and moved on toward Richmond. The relentless attrition of these two battles and the engagements that followed finally destroyed the offensive capabilities of Lee's Army of Northern Virginia.

Some 8,000 park acres include parts of all four battlefields, as well as Fredericksburg National Cemetery, the house at Guinea Station (where Jackson died), Old Salem Church and Chatham Manor. Miles of original trenches and gun pits remain; park roads provide ready access to many of them. (Daily) **Free.**

For further information contact the Superintendent, 120 Chatham Lane, Fredericksburg 22405; 540/371-0802.

What to See and Do

Chancellorsville Visitor Center. Slide program, museum with exhibits; dioramas. (Daily; closed Jan 1, Dec 25) 7 mi W of I-95 on Rte 3. Phone 540/786-2880. **Free.**

Chatham Manor. Georgian brick manor house, owned by a wealthy planter, was converted to Union headquarters during two of the battles of Fredericksburg. The house was eventually used as a hospital where Clara Barton and Walt Whitman nursed the wounded. (Daily; closed Jan 1, Dec 25) Phone 540/371-0802. **Free.**

Fredericksburg Visitor Center. Information and directions for various parts of park. Tours should start here. (Daily; closed Jan 1, Dec 25) Lafayette Blvd (US 1) & Sunken Rd. Phone 540/373-6122. Center includes

Museum. Slide program, diorama, exhibits. (Same days as Visitor Center) **Free.** Across Sunken Rd is

Fredericksburg National Cemetery. More than 15,000 Federal interments; almost 13,000 unknown.

Old Salem Church (1844). Building used as a field hospital and refugee center. Scene of battle on May 3-4, 1863. 1 mi W of I-95 on VA 3.

Stonewall Jackson Shrine. Plantation office where on May 10, 1863, Confederate general Jackson, ill with pneumonia and with his shattered left arm amputated, murmured, "Let us cross over the river, and rest under the shade of the trees," and died. (Mid-June-Labor Day, daily; Apr-mid-June, after Labor Day-Oct, Fri-Tues; rest of yr, Sat-Mon) 12 mi S on I-95 to Thornburg exit, then 5 mi E on VA 606 to Guinea. Phone 804/633-6076. **Free.**

Front Royal (C-7)

(See also Winchester, Woodstock)

Founded 1788 **Pop** 11,880 **Elev** 567 ft **Area code** 540 **Zip** 22630 **E-mail** coc@frontroyal.com **Web** www.frontroyal.com

Information Chamber of Commerce of Front Royal-Warren County, 414 E Main St; 540/635-3185 or 800/338-2576.

Once known as Hell Town, for all the wild and reckless spirits it attracted, Front Royal was a frontier stop on the way to eastern markets. The present name is supposed to have originated in the command, "Front the royal oak," given by an English officer to his untrained mountain militia recruits.

Belle Boyd, the Confederate spy, worked here extracting military secrets from Union officers. It is said that she invited General Nathaniel Banks and his officers, whose regiment was occupying the town, to a ball once. Later, she raced on horseback to tell General Jackson what she had learned. Next morning (May 23, 1862), the Confederates attacked and captured nearly all of the Union troops, providing Jackson one of his early victories in the famous Valley Campaign.

Front Royal was a quiet little village until the entrance to the Shenandoah National Park (see) and the beginning of the Skyline Drive opened in 1935, just one mile to the south. With millions of motorists passing through every year, the town has grown rapidly. The production of automotive finishes, limestone and cement contributes to the town's economy, but the tourism industry remains one of its largest.

What to See and Do

Belle Boyd Cottage. Relocated to its present site, the two-story cottage has been restored to reflect life in Front Royal between 1840 and 1860. For a 2-yr period during the Civil War, Belle Boyd stayed in this cottage while visiting relatives and used the opportunity to spy on Union troops occuping the town. This modest dwelling was also used to house wounded soldiers of both armies. (Mid-Apr-Oct, Mon-Fri, wkends by appt; closed hols) 101 Chester St, behind Ivy Lodge. Phone 540/636-1446. ¢

Sky Meadows State Park. A 1,862-acre park. Fishing pond. Hiking, bridle trails. Picnicking. Primitive walk-in camping. Visitor center; programs.

(Daily) Standard fees. 20 mi E on US 66, 7 mi N on VA 17. Phone 540/592-3556.

Skyline Caverns. Extensive, rare, intricate flowerlike formations of calcite (anthodites); sound and light presentation; 37-ft waterfall; clear stream stocked with trout (observation only). Electrically lighted; 54°F yr-round. Miniature train provides trip through surrounding wooded area (Mar-mid-Nov, daily, weather permitting). Snack bar; gift shop. Cavern tours start every few minutes. (Daily) 1 mi S on US 340. Phone 540/635-4545 or 800/296-4545. ¢¢¢

Warren Rifles Confederate Museum. Historic relics and memorabilia of War between the States. (Mid-Apr-Oct, daily; rest of yr, by appt) 95 Chester St. Phone 540/636-6982. ¢

Annual Events

Warren County Garden Tour. Garden Club sponsors tours of historic houses and gardens. Last wk Apr.

Virginia Mushroom and Wine Festival. Mushrooms, wine and cheese. Entertainment. 3rd Sat May.

Warren County Fair. Entertainment, livestock exhibits and sale, contests. 1st wk Aug.

Festival of Leaves. Arts and crafts, demonstrations; historic exhibits; parade. 2nd wkend Oct.

Motels

★ ★ **QUALITY INN.** *10 Commerce Ave, US 522 Bypass at end of Main St.* 540/635-3161; FAX 540/635-6624. 107 rms, 3 story. Sept-Oct: S $58-$70; D $68-$75; each addl $9; under 18 free; higher rates special events; lower rates rest of yr. Crib free. TV; cable (premium), VCR avail (movies). Pool. Restaurant 6 am-9 pm; wkends to 10 pm. Ck-out 11 am. Meeting rms. Business servs avail. In-rm modem link. Gift shop. Refrigerators avail. Cr cds: A, C, D, DS, ER, MC, V.

D ≈ ⊠ ⚡ SC

✔★ **TWIN RIVERS.** *1801 Shenandoah Ave, I-66 exit 6, 1½ mi S on US 522/340.* 540/635-4101. 20 rms. Apr-Oct: S, D $40-$50; each addl $5; lower rates rest of yr. Crib free. TV; cable. Pool. Playground. Complimentary coffee in lobby. Restaurant nearby. Ck-out 11 am. Picnic table. Cr cds: A, MC, V.

≈ ⊠ ⚡ SC

Inn

★ ★ ★ **CHESTER HOUSE.** *43 Chester St.* 540/635-3937; res: 800/621-0441. 6 rms, 2 share bath, 1 with shower only, 2 story, 1 suite. S, D $65-$110; suite $120-$150; special events (2-day min). Children over 12 yrs only. TV in lounge. Complimentary full bkfst; evening refreshments. Restaurant nearby. Ck-out 11 am, ck-in 3 pm. Business servs avail. Luggage handling. Health club privileges. Lawn games. Guest refrigerator. Picnic tables. Formal gardens with fountain and statuary. Georgian-style mansion built 1905. Cr cds: A, MC, V.

⚡

Galax (F-4)

(For accommodations see Wytheville)

Settled 1904 **Pop** 6,670 **Elev** 2,382 ft **Area code** 540 **Zip** 24333

Information Galax-Carroll-Grayson Chamber of Commerce, 405 N Main St; 540/236-2184.

Galax is named for the pretty evergreen with heart-shaped leaves that florists use in various arrangements. It grows in the mountainous regions around Galax and is gathered for sale all over the US. Nearby are three mountain passes: Fancy Gap, Low Gap and Piper's Gap. Some of the town's major industries include the production of furniture, glass and mirrors, textiles and clothing.

What to See and Do

Blue Ridge Parkway (see). 7 mi S.

Jeff Matthews Memorial Museum. Two authentically restored log cabins (1834 & 1860s). Relocated to present site and furnished with items used in the period in which the cabins were inhabited. Also houses collection of photos of Civil War veterans, artifacts and memorabilia of the area; covered wagon; farm implements. Restored log cabin used as a blacksmith's shop. (Wed-Sun, phone for hrs; closed hols) 606 W Stuart Dr, adj to Vaughan Memorial Library. Phone 540/236-7874.   **Free.**

Recreation. Swimming, boating, fishing on New River. Hunting and hiking. Canoeing and other activities can be found at

   Cliffview Trading Post. Bike rentals (Tues-Sat; closed Thanksgiving, Dec 25) and horse rentals (Apr-Nov, Tues-Sat); trail rides in New River Trail State Park. Cliffview Rd. Phone 540/238-1530.

Annual Event

Old Fiddler's Convention. Felts Park. Folk songs, bands and dancing. 2nd wk Aug.

George Washington Birthplace National Monument (D-9)

(For accommodations see Fredericksburg; also see Montross)

(38 mi E of Fredericksburg on VA 3, then 2 mi E on VA 204)

George Washington, first child of Augustine and Mary Ball Washington, was born February 11, 1732 (celebrated February 22 according to the new-style calendar) at his father's estate on Popes Creek on the south shore of the Potomac. The family moved in 1735 to Little Hunting Creek Plantation, later called Mt Vernon, then in 1738 to Ferry Farm near Fredericksburg.

   The 538-acre monument includes much of the old plantation land. (Daily; closed Jan 1, Dec 25)

What to See and Do

Family burial ground. Site of 1664 home of Colonel John Washington, first Washington in Virginia and great-grandfather of the first president. Washington's ancestors are buried here. 1 mi NW on Bridges Creek.

Memorial House. Original house burned (1779) and was never rebuilt. The Memorial House is not a replica of the original; it represents a composite of typical 18th-century Virginia plantation house. Bricks were handmade from nearby clay. Furnishings are typical of the times. Near house is

   Colonial farm. "Living" farm, designed to show 18th-century Virginia plantation life; livestock, colonial garden, several farm buildings, furnished colonial kitchen, household slave quarters and spinning and weaving room.

Picnic area. 1/4 mi N of house.

Visitor Center. Orientation film; museum exhibits. Phone 804/224-1732. ¢

Gloucester (E-9)

(For accommodations see Newport News, Williamsburg, Yorktown)

Founded 1769 **Pop** 900 (est) **Elev** 70 ft **Area code** 804 **Zip** 23061
Information Chamber of Commerce, PO Box 296; 804/693-2425.

In the spring, acres of daffodil blooms make this area a treat for the traveler. This elm-shaded village is the commercial center of Gloucester (GLOSS-ter) County. There are many old landmarks and estates nearby, including the birthplace of Walter Reed, at the jct of VA 614 & 616.

What to See and Do

County Courthouse (18th century). Part of Gloucester Court House Square Historic District. Portraits of native sons are in the courtroom; plaques memorializing Nathaniel Bacon, leader in the rebellion of 1676, first organized resistance to British authority, and Major Walter Reed, surgeon, conqueror of yellow fever. (Mon-Fri; closed hols) On US 17 Business. 804/693-4042.   **Free.**   Nearby are Debtors Prison, the pre-Revolutionary Botetourt Bldg and the

   Roswell Historic Ruins. 3-story Georgian mansion's brickwork was put in place over 250 yrs ago. Majestic ruins hint at projecting pavilions, arched windows and stone-capped chimney stacks. Tours by appt. (Apr-Oct, Sun; winter by appt) Phone 804/693-2585.   **Free.**

Virginia Institute of Marine Science, College of William and Mary. Small marine aquarium & museum display sea turtles, local fishes and invertebrates; marine science exhibits, bookstore. (Mon-Fri; closed major hols) Gloucester Point. Phone 804/642-7000.   **Free.**

Restaurant

   ★ ★ **SEAWELL'S ORDINARY.** *US 17, 5 mi N of Coleman Bridge.* 804/642-3635. Hrs: 11:30 am-3 pm, 5-9:30 pm; Sun brunch 11:30 am-3 pm. Closed Dec 25. Res accepted. Continental menu. Bar. Semi-a la carte: lunch $4-$12.95, dinner $10.95-$18.95. Sun brunch $8.95-$14.95. Specializes in regional French dishes. Outdoor dining. Built in 1712; became country tavern (1757); was frequented by Washington, Jefferson, Lafayette. Cr cds: A, C, D, MC, V.

Great Dismal Swamp National Wildlife Refuge (F-9)

(For accommodations see Chesapeake, Portsmouth)

Harriet Beecher Stowe found Virginia's Dismal Swamp a perfect setting for her antislavery novel *Dred* (1856); modern hunters, fishermen and naturalists find the area fits their ambition just as well. From its northern edge just southwest of Norfolk, the swamp stretches almost due south like a great ribbon, 25 miles long and 11 miles wide. Centuries of decaying organic matter have created layers of peat so deep that fires would sometimes smolder under the surface for weeks.

   Creation of the refuge began in 1973, when the Union Camp Corporation donated 49,100 acres of land to the Nature Conservancy, which in turn conveyed it to the Department of Interior. The refuge was officially established through the Dismal Swamp Act of 1974 and is managed for the primary purpose of protecting and preserving a unique ecosystem. The refuge now consists of over 107,000 acres of forested wetlands that have been greatly altered by drainage and logging operations.

Near the center is Lake Drummond, 3,100 acres of juniper water, which is water that combines the juices of gum, cypress and maple with a strong infusion of juniper or white cedar. The chemical mix added by the tree resins results in a water that remains sweet, or fresh, indefinitely. In the days of long sailing voyages, when ordinary water became foul after a few weeks, this "dark water" was highly valued.

The Great Dismal Swamp has also been commercially exploited for its timber, particularly cypress and cedar. A company organized by George Washington and several other businessmen bought a large piece of the swamp and used slave labor to dig the Dismal Swamp Canal, which both facilitated drainage of timber land and provided a transportation route in and out of the swamp.

Animal and bird life continues to abound in this eerie setting. There are white-tailed deer and rarely observed black bear, foxes, bobcats—and a large number of snakes, including copperheads, cottonmouths and rattlesnakes. Birding is popular in the swamp from April-June; the peak of spring migration is mid-April-mid-May.

For further information contact Refuge Manager, PO Box 349, Suffolk 23439-0349; 757/986-3705.

Hampton (F-9)

(See also Newport News, Norfolk, Portsmouth, Virginia Beach)

Settled 1610 **Pop** 133,793 **Elev** 12 ft **Area code** 757 **Web** www .hampton.va.us/tourism

Information Hampton Visitor Center, 710 Settlers Landing Rd, 23669; 757/727-1102 or 800/800-2202.

Hampton is the oldest continuously English-speaking community in the US—Jamestown, settled in 1607, is a national historical park, but not a town. The settlement began at a place then called Kecoughtan, with the building of Fort Algernourne as protection against the Spanish. In the late 1600s and early 1700s, the area was harassed by pirates. Finally, in 1718, the notorious brigand Blackbeard was killed by Lt Robert Maynard, and organized piracy came to an end here.

Hampton was shelled in the Revolutionary War, sacked by the British in the War of 1812 and burned in 1861 by retreating Confederates to prevent its occupation by Union forces. Only the gutted walls of St John's Church survived the fire. The town was rebuilt after the Civil War by its citizens and soldiers. Computer technology, manufacturing, aerospace research and commercial fishing are now big business here.

Langley Air Force Base, headquarters for the Air Combat Command, Fort Monroe, headquarters for the US Army's Training and Doctrine Command, and the NASA Langley Research Center are located here.

What to See and Do

Air Power Park and Aviation History Center. Over 50 indoor and outdoor exhibits feature real fighter aircraft, missiles and rockets; local aviation history and model aircraft exhibits. Picnicking; playground. (Daily; closed Jan 1, Thanksgiving, Dec 25) 413 W Mercury Blvd, US 258. Phone 757/727-1163. **Free.**

Bluebird Gap Farm. This 60-acre farm includes barnyard zoo; indigenous wildlife such as deer and wolves; antique and modern farm equipment and farmhouse artifacts. Picnicking; playground. (Wed-Sun; closed major hols) 60 Pine Chapel Rd. Phone 757/727-6739. **Free.**

Buckroe Beach. Swimming; public park, concerts. Lifeguards (Memorial Day-Labor Day). 4 mi E on VA 351, foot of E Pembroke Ave on Chesapeake Bay. Phone 757/727-6347. **Free.**

Fort Monroe. First fort here was a stockade called Fort Algernourne (1609); second, Fort George, though built of brick, was destroyed by hurricane in 1749; present fort was completed about 1834. 3 mi SE via Mercury Blvd, Ingalls Rd. **Free.**

Casemate Museum. Provides insight on heritage of the fort, Old Point Comfort and of the Army Coast Artillery Corps. Museum offers access to a series of casemates and a walking tour of the fort. Jefferson Davis casemate contains cell in which the Confederacy's president was confined on false charges of plotting against the life of Abraham Lincoln. Museum features Civil War exhibits, military uniforms and assorted artwork, including three original Remington drawings, along with audiovisual programs. Scale models of coast artillery guns and dioramas represent the role of the coast artillery from 1901 to 1946. (Daily; closed Jan 1, Thanksgiving, Dec 25) Phone 757/727-3391. **Free.**

Chapel of the Centurion (1858). This is one of the oldest churches on the Virginia peninsula. Woodrow Wilson worshiped here occasionally.

Hampton Carousel (1920). Completely restored in 1991, antique carousel is housed in its own pavilion and features 48 hand-carved horses. (Apr-Sept, Mon-Sat, also Sun afternoons; Oct-Nov, daily, weather permitting; Dec 1-15, wkends) 602 Settlers Landing Rd, downtown, on waterfront. Phone 757/727-6381 or 757/727-6347 (Parks & Rec Dept). **¢**

Hampton University (1868). (6,100 students) Founded by Union Brigadier General Samuel Chapman Armstrong, chief of the Freedman's Bureau, to prepare the youth of the South, regardless of color, for the work of organizing and instructing schools in the Southern states; many blacks and Native Americans came to be educated. Now Virginia's only coeducational, nondenominational, 4-yr private college. The Hampton choir is famous. It "sang up" a building, Virginia-Cleveland Hall, in 1870 on a trip through New England and Canada, raising close to $100,000 at concerts. E end of Queen St, 1/4 mi off I-64 exit 267. Phone 757/727-5253. On campus are

Emancipation Oak. The Emancipation Proclamation was read here.

Museum. Collection of ethnic art; Native American & African artifacts; contemporary African-American works; paintings by renowned artists. (Daily; closed major and school hols) Huntington Bldg. **Free.**

Miss Hampton II Boat Tours. Narrated 3-hr cruise includes a stop at Fort Wool, a Civil War island fortress. (Apr-Oct) 710 Settlers Landing Rd. Phone 757/727-1102 or 800/800-2202. **¢¢¢¢**

Settlers Landing Monument. Marks approx site of first settlers' landing near Strawberry Banks in 1607. Painting by Sidney King depicts visit to Kecoughtan by colonists en route to Jamestown. (Daily) 1/2 mi S, on grounds of the Veterans Affairs Medical Center between Hampton River and Mill Creek, off I-64 exit 268. **Free.**

St John's Church (1728) **and Parish Museum.** Fourth site of worship of Episcopal parish established in 1610. Bible dating from 1599; communion silver from 1618; Colonial Vestry Book; taped historical message. (Daily) W Queens Way & Franklin St. Phone 757/722-2567. **Free.**

Virginia Air and Space Center and Hampton Roads History Center. Exhibits show the historical link between Hampton Roads' seafaring past and spacefaring future. Exhibits include 19 full-sized air- and spacecraft, the Apollo 12 Command Module, a moon rock and rare NASA artifacts. Films shown in 283-seat IMAX theater (daily). Gift shop. (Daily; closed Thanksgiving, Dec 25) Downtown, off I-64 exit 267. Phone 757/727-0900 or 800/296-0800. **¢¢¢** During summer, take the

NASA Langley Tour. Approx 11/2-hr motor tour takes visitors to site where nation's aerospace history began. View NASA wind tunnels and Lunar Landing Research Center. Tours depart from Virginia Air and Space Center; phone for times. With paid Space Center admission **¢¢**; Tour only **¢¢¢**

Annual Events

Hampton Jazz Festival. Hampton Coliseum. Phone 757/838-4203 (box office). 4 days late June.

Hampton Cup Regatta. Inboard hydroplane races. Phone 800/800-2202. Mid-Aug.

Hampton Bay Days. Arts and crafts, rides, science exhibits; entertainment. Phone 757/727-6122. Mid-Sept.

Motels

✔★ **ARROW INN.** *7 Semple Farm Rd (23666), I-64 exit 261B or 262B, 2 mi N on VA 134, E on Semple Farm Rd. 757/865-0300; FAX*

757/766-9367; res: 800/833-2520. E-mail mb@arrowinn.com; web www.arrowinn.com. 60 rms, 3 story, 21 kit. units. No elvtr. Memorial Day-Labor Day: S $43.90-$53.90; D $47.90-$57.90; each addl $5; kit. units $51.90-$59.90; under 18 free; wkly rates; higher rates jazz festival; lower rates rest of yr. Crib free. Pet accepted; $5-$30 per day. TV; cable (premium). Complimentary coffee in lobby. Restaurant adj 6-1 am. Ck-out noon. Business servs avail. Coin lndry. Refrigerators; many microwaves. Cr cds: A, C, D, DS, MC, V.

★★ COURTYARD BY MARRIOTT. *1917 Coliseum Dr (23666).* 757/838-3300; FAX 757/838-6387. 146 rms, 3 story. June-Sept: S, D $75-$85; each addl $10; suites $90-$119; under 18 free; higher rates jazz festival; lower rates rest of yr. Crib avail. TV; cable (premium). Heated pool; whirlpool. Complimentary coffee in rms. Bar Mon-Thurs 6-10 pm. Ck-out noon. Coin lndry. Business servs avail. In-rm modem link. Valet serv. Sundries. Exercise equipt; weight machine, stair machine. Refrigerator avail in suites. Cr cds: A, C, D, DS, MC, V.

✔★★ FAIRFIELD INN BY MARRIOTT. *1905 Coliseum Dr (23666),* I-64, exit 263B. 757/827-7400. Web www.marriott.com/marriott/582N3. 134 rms, 3 story. S $49.95-$65.95; D $54.95-$70.95; under 12 free; higher rates Jazz Festival (min stay required). Crib free. TV; cable (premium). Complimentary continental bkfst. Restaurant opp open 24 hrs. Ck-out noon. Business servs avail. In-rm modem link. Health club privileges. Pool. Cr cds: A, D, DS, MC, V.

✔★ HAMPTON INN. *1813 W Mercury Blvd (23666).* 757/838-8484; FAX 757/826-0725. 132 rms, 6 story. S, D $69. Crib free. Pet accepted, some restrictions. TV; cable (premium). Pool privileges. Complimentary continental bkfst. Complimentary coffee in rms. Restaurant adj 6 am-10 pm. Ck-out noon. Business servs avail. In-rm modem link. Cr cds: A, C, D, DS, MC, V.

★★★ HOLIDAY INN HAMPTON CONFERENCE CENTER. *1815 W Mercury Blvd (23666).* 757/838-0200; FAX 757/838-4964. 320 rms, 2-4 story. S, D $89-$130; suites $125-$225; some wkend rates; higher rates Jazz Festival. Crib free. TV; cable (premium). 2 pools, 1 indoor; whirlpool. Coffee in rms. Restaurant 6 am-10 pm. Rm serv to 11 pm. Bar 11 am-midnight. Ck-out 11 am. Coin lndry. Convention facilities. Business center. In-rm modem link. Bellhops. Valet serv. Gift shop. Free airport transportation. Exercise equipt; weight machine, bicycles, sauna. Game rm. Some refrigerators. Balconies. Cr cds: A, C, D, DS, ER, JCB, MC, V.

Hotel

★★★ RADISSON. *700 Settlers Landing Rd (23669),* I-64 exit 267. 757/727-9700; FAX 757/722-4557. E-mail nossidar@aol.com; web www.radisson.com/hamptonva. 172 rms, 9 story. S, D $89-$125; each addl $10; suites $185-$450; under 18 free; wkend rates; higher rates special events. Crib free. TV; cable (premium). Pool; whirlpool, poolside serv. Restaurant 6:30 am-10 pm. Bar 11-2 am. Coffee in rms. Ck-out noon. Meeting rms. Business servs avail. In-rm modem link. Gift shop. Free airport, RR station, bus depot transportation. Exercise equipt; weight machine, bicycle. Some refrigerators. On Hampton River. Luxury level. Cr cds: A, C, D, DS, ER, JCB, MC, V.

Restaurants

★★ FIRE AND ICE. *2040 Coliseum Dr (23666),* in Coliseum Square Shopping Center. 757/826-6698. Hrs: 11 am-10 pm. Closed Sun; hols. Res accepted; required Fri, Sat. Bar. A la carte entrees: lunch

$4.95-$8.95, dinner $8.95-$18.95. Specialties: fantasy flat breads, New Orleans-style po' boy sandwiches. Cr cds: MC, V.

★ SAMMY & NICK'S. *2718 W Mercury Blvd (23666).* 757/838-9100. Hrs: 11 am-11 pm. Closed Thanksgiving, Dec 25. Res accepted. Bar. Semi-a la carte: lunch, dinner $2.95-$12.95. Child's meals. Specializes in prime rib, steak. Cr cds: A, D, DS, MC, V.

Harrisonburg (D-6)

(See also Luray, New Market, Staunton)

Founded 1780 **Pop** 30,707 **Elev** 1,352 ft **Area code** 540 **Zip** 22801
Information Harrisonburg-Rockingham Convention and Visitors Bureau, 10 E Gay St; 540/434-2319.

Originally named Rocktown due to the limestone outcroppings prevalent in the area, Harrisonburg became the county seat of Rockingham County when Thomas Harrison won a race against Mr. Keezle of Keezletown, three miles east. They had raced on horseback to Richmond to file their respective towns for the new county seat. Harrisonburg is noted for good hunting and fishing, recreational opportunities, beautiful scenery and turkeys. The annual production of more than five million turkeys, most of them processed and frozen, has made Rockingham County widely known. This is a college town with three four-year universities. Much of the George Washington and Jefferson National Forests are here.

What to See and Do

Caverns. There are several caverns within 24 mi of Harrisonburg. They include

Shenandoah Caverns. 24 mi N on US 11. (See NEW MARKET)

Grand Caverns Regional Park. Known for its immense underground chambers and spectacular formations. Visited by Union and Confederate troops during the Civil War. Unique shield formations. Electrically lighted; 54°F. Park facilities include swimming pool; tennis courts, miniature golf; picnic pavilions; hiking and bicycle trails. Guided tours. (Apr-Oct, daily; Mar, wkends) 12 mi S on I-81, then 6 mi E on VA 256 in Grottoes. Phone 540/249-5705. ¢¢¢

Eastern Mennonite University and Seminary (1917). (1,100 students) Many Mennonites live in this area. On campus is an art gallery, planetarium (shows by appt, free), natural history museum and the Menno Simons Historical Library, containing many 16th-century Mennonite volumes (school yr, daily exc Sun). Campus tours. 2 mi NW on VA 42. Phone 540/432-4000.

Fishing.

Lake Shenandoah. 3 mi E.

Silver Lake. 5 mi SW on VA 42 in Dayton.

Shenandoah River. Good bass fishing.

George Washington and Jefferson National Forests. Consist of approx 1.8 million acres. Hunting for deer, bear, wild turkey, small game; fishing for trout, bluegill and bass; riding trails; camping, picnicking, swimming. Scenic drives past Crabtree Falls, hardwood forests and unusual geologic features. Overlooks of Shenandoah Valley. Part of Appalachian Trail crosses forests. Fees are charged at some recreation sites. Trails for the visually impaired. 10 mi W on US 33. For information contact Forest Headquarters, 5162 Valleypointe Pkwy, Roanoke 24019-3050. Phone 540/265-5100. **Free.**

James Madison University (1908). (11,000 students) Interesting old bluestone buildings. Campus tours through Admissions Office. S Main St. Phone 540/568-3621. On campus is

Miller Hall Planetarium and Sawhill Art Gallery. Phone 540/568-3621 for schedules. **Free.**

Lincoln Homestead. Brick house, the rear wing of which was built by Abraham Lincoln's grandfather, and where his father was born. Main portion of the house was built about 1800 by Captain Jacob Lincoln. (Private) 9 mi N on VA 42.

Natural Chimneys Regional Park. Seven colorful and massive rock towers rise 120 ft above the plain. Picnic facilities, camping (fee; limited Nov-Feb); bicycle, nature trails; pool; playground. Park (daily). 15 mi SW off VA 42 in Mt Solon. Phone 540/350-2510. Per vehicle ¢¢

Shenandoah National Park (see). 24 mi E on US 33.

Shenandoah Valley Folk Art and Heritage Center. Featured is the Stonewall Jackson Electric Map that depicts his Valley Campaign of 1862. The 12-ft vertical relief map fills an entire wall and lets visitors see and hear the campaign, battle by battle. Also displays of Shenandoah Valley history, artifacts. (Wed-Sat, also Sun afternoons; closed mid-Dec-mid-Jan) 115 Bowman Rd. Phone 540/879-2616. ¢¢

Virginia Quilt Museum. Resource center for the study of quilts and quilting. (Mon, Thurs-Sat, also Sun afternoons; closed major hols) 3015 Main St . Phone 540/433-3818. ¢¢

Annual Events

Natural Chimneys Jousting Tournament. Natural Chimneys Regional Park. America's oldest continuous sporting event, held annually since 1821. "Knights" armed with lances charge down an 80-yard track and attempt to spear 3 small rings suspended from posts. Each knight is allowed 3 rides at the rings, thus, a perfect score is 9 rings. Ties are run off using successively smaller rings. 3rd Sat June & Aug.

Rockingham County Fair. Mid-Aug.

Motels

✔★★ **COMFORT INN.** *1440 E Market St, I-81 exit 247A, on Sheraton Access Rd.* 540/433-6066; FAX 540/433-0793. 60 rms, 2 story. S $58-$68; D $68-$78; each addl $5; under 18 free. Crib free. TV; cable (premium). Pool. Complimentary continental bkfst. Ck-out noon. Business servs avail. Cr cds: A, C, D, DS, ER, JCB, MC, V.

D ≈ ⊠ ⊠ 🔥 SC

★★ **DAYS INN.** *1131 Forest Hill Rd, I-81 exit 245.* 540/433-9353; FAX 540/433-5809. 89 rms, 4 story. June-Oct: S $55; D $68; each addl $5; under 17 free; ski plan; higher rates for special events, wkends (2-day min); lower rates rest of yr. Crib free. Pet accepted; $5 per day. TV; cable (premium). Indoor pool; whirlpool. Complimentary continental bkfst. Restaurant adj 11 am-11 pm. Ck-out 11 am. Meeting rms. Business servs avail. Sundries. Valet serv. 27-hole golf privileges; greens fee $30, pro, putting green, driving range. Downhill ski 12 mi. Health club privileges. Refrigerators avail. Cr cds: A, C, D, DS, MC, V.

D ✔ ⤡ ⋀ ≈ ⊠ 🔥 SC

✔★ **ECONO LODGE.** *1703 E Market St , ½ mi E of I-81 exit 247A.* 540/433-2576. 88 rms, 2 story. S $42.95; D $45-$55.95; each addl $5; suites $74.95; under 18 free. Crib free. Pet accepted. TV; cable (premium), VCR avail (movies). Pool. Complimentary continental bkfst. Restaurant adj open 24 hrs. Ck-out 11 am. Business servs avail. Some in-rm whirlpools. Cr cds: A, C, D, DS, JCB, MC, V.

D ✔ ≈ ⊠ 🔥 SC

★★ **HAMPTON INN.** *85 University Blvd, I-81 exit 147A.* 540/432-1111; FAX 540/432-0748. 126 rms, 4 story. May-Oct: S $52-$59; D $59-$68; under 19 free; higher rates university events; lower rates rest of yr. Crib free. TV; cable (premium). Pool. Complimentary continental bkfst. Restaurant nearby. Ck-out noon. Meeting rms. Business servs avail. In-rm modem link. Valet serv. Sundries. Refrigerators avail. Cr cds: A, C, D, DS, MC, V.

D ≈ ⊠ 🔥 SC

✔★★ **HOWARD JOHNSON.** *605 Port Republic Rd, I-81 exit 245.* 540/434-6771; FAX 540/434-0153. 134 rms, 2 story. Mar-Nov: S $44.95-$54.95; D $44.95-$59.95; each addl $5; higher rates some univ events; lower rates rest of yr. Crib free. TV; cable (premium). Pool;

wading pool. Restaurant 6 am-10:30 pm. Ck-out noon. Business servs avail. Refrigerators avail. Private patios, balconies. Cr cds: A, C, D, DS, ER, JCB, MC, V.

D ✔ ≈ ⊠ 🔥 SC

✔★★ **THE VILLAGE INN.** *Rte 1, Box 76, on VA 11, 1½ N of I-81 exit 240.* 540/434-7355; res: 800/736-7355. 36 rms. S $37; D $43-$53; each addl $5; kit. units $58. Crib $2. Pet accepted. TV; cable; VCR avail (movies). Pool. Playground. Restaurant 7-10 am, 5:30-9 pm; closed Sun. Ck-out noon. Meeting rm. Business servs avail. Sundries. Lawn games. Some in-rm whirlpools. Picnic tables. Cr cds: A, C, D, DS, MC, V.

D ✔ ≈ ⊠ 🔥

Motor Hotel

★★ **FOUR POINTS BY SHERATON.** *1400 E Market St, off I-81 exit 247A.* 540/433-2521; FAX 540/434-0253. 138 rms, 5 story. S $68-$104; D $80-$104; each addl $12; under 18 free. Crib free. Pet accepted. TV; cable (premium). 2 pools, 1 indoor; wading pool, whirlpool, sauna, poolside serv. Restaurant 6:30-11 am, 5-10:30 pm. Rm serv. Bar 11-2 am; entertainment. Ck-out noon. Meeting rms. Business servs avail. In-rm modem link. Bellhops. Valet serv. Bathrm phones; refrigerators avail. Cr cds: A, C, D, DS, ER, JCB, MC, V.

D ✔ ≈ ⊠ 🔥 SC

Hopewell (E-8)

(See also Petersburg, Richmond, Surry, Williamsburg)

Founded 1613 **Pop** 23,101 **Elev** 50 ft **Area code** 804 **Zip** 23860
Information Hopewell Area-Prince George Chamber of Commerce, 210 N 2nd Ave; 804/458-5536.

The second permanent English settlement in America has been an important inland port since early times, having a fine channel 28 feet deep and 300 feet wide. It was the birthplace of statesman John Randolph of Roanoke. Edmund Ruffin, an early agricultural chemist who fired the first shot at Fort Sumter, was born near here.

"Cittie Point," at the junction of the James and Appomattox rivers, finally became one of Virginia's big cities during World War I when an E. I. Du Pont de Nemours Company dynamite plant on Hopewell Farm supplied guncotton to the Allies.

Hopewell's industrial production includes chemicals, paper products and synthetic textiles.

What to See and Do

City Point Unit of Petersburg National Battlefield (see). Grant's headquarters during the siege of Petersburg and largest Civil War supply depot. Includes Appomattox Manor, home to one family for 340 yrs; Grant's headquarters were on the front lawn. Many other buildings. (Daily; closed Jan 1, Thanksgiving, Dec 25, also some federal hols) Jct Cedar Lane & Pecan Ave. Phone 804/458-9504. **Free.**

Flowerdew Hundred. Outdoor museum on the site of an early English settlement on the south bank of the James River. Originally inhabited by Native Americans, settled by Governor George Yeardley in 1618. Archaeological excavations are in progress. Thousands of artifacts, dating from the prehistoric period through the present, have been found and are on exhibit in the museum. A replicated 19th-century detached kitchen and working 18th-century-style windmill are open to visitors. Exhibits, interpretive tours. Picnicking. (Apr-Nov, daily exc Mon; rest of yr, by appt) 10 mi SE on VA 10. Phone 804/541-8897 or 804/541-8938. ¢¢

Merchants Hope Church (1657). Given the name of a plantation that was named for a barque plying between Virginia and England. The exterior has been called the most beautiful colonial brickwork in America. Oldest operating Protestant church in the country. (Open by request) 6 mi E on VA 10, then 1/2 mi S on VA 641. Phone 804/458-6197. **Donation.**

Annual Events

Prince George County Heritage Fair. Flowerdew Hundred. Arts and crafts; educational exhibits and demonstrations; music, food, children's rides, hayrides. Last wkend Apr.

Hooray for Hopewell Festival. Downtown. Arts and crafts, food, entertainment, children's rides. 3rd wkend Sept.

Motels

★ **DAYS INN.** 4911 Oaklawn Blvd, at jct I-295 & VA 36. 804/458-1500; FAX 804/458-9151. 115 rms, 2 story, 50 kit. suites. S $45-75; D $45-95; each addl $5; kit. suites $60-$100; under 12 free; wkly rates. Crib free. TV; cable, VCR avail (movies). Pool; whirlpool. Complimentary continental bkfst. Restaurant nearby. Ck-out 11 am. Coin lndry. Business servs avail. Exercise equipt; weight machine, bicycle, sauna. Game rm. Refrigerators. Cr cds: A, D, DS, MC, V.

✔★ **INNKEEPER.** 3952 Courthouse Rd. 804/458-2600; FAX 804/458-1915. 104 rms, 3 story. S $46.99-$79.99; D $51.99-$79.95; each addl $5. Crib free. TV; cable. Pool. Complimentary continental bkfst. Restaurant adj 6:30 am-noon. Ck-out 11 am. Coin lndry. Meeting rms. Business servs avail. In-rm modem link. Refrigerators. Cr cds: A, C, D, DS, MC, V.

Hot Springs (D-5)

(See also Clifton Forge, Covington, Warm Springs)

Pop 300 (est) **Elev** 2,238 ft **Area code** 540 **Zip** 24445

A Ranger District office of the George Washington and Jefferson National Forests is located here.

What to See and Do

Homestead Ski Area. Double chairlift, T-bar, J-bar, baby rope tow; patrol, school, rentals; snowmaking; cafeteria, bar; nursery (Nov-Mar, daily). Ice curling, ice-skating rink (Thanksgiving-Mar). On US 220. Phone 540/839-7721 (ski information) or 800/336-5771 (resort). ¢¢¢¢- ¢¢¢¢¢

Motel

✔★ **ROSELOE.** Rte 2, Box 590, 3 mi N on US 220. 540/839-5373. 14 rms, 6 kits. S $36; D $46; each addl $4; kits. $40-$53; family rates. Crib free. Pet accepted; $5. TV; cable (premium). Complimentary coffee in rms. Restaurant nearby. Ck-out noon. Business servs avail. Downhill ski 3 mi. Refrigerators; microwaves avail. Cr cds: A, D, DS, MC, V.

Resort

★ ★ ★ **THE HOMESTEAD.** US 220. 540/839-1766; FAX 540/839-7556; res: 800/838-1766. Famous for its mineral waters since 1766, this luxurious resort is on a 15,000-acre estate. Spacious guest rooms have Victorian decor. 513 units, 4-12 story. Apr-Oct: S, D $212-306; suites $372-$810; family rates; MAP avail; ski, golf, tennis plans; some seasonal rates; some lower rates rest of yr. Serv charges: 15% daily housekeeping and 15% at all dining outlets. Crib free. TV; cable. 2 pools, 1 indoor; lifeguard. Supervised child's activities; ages 3-12. Dining rm 7-10 am, noon-2:30 pm, 7-9:30 pm. Afternoon tea. Box lunches, snack bar. Rm serv

7 am-midnight. Bar 11 am-midnight. Ck-out noon, ck-in 4 pm. Convention facilities. Business center. Valet serv. Gift shops. Airport, RR station, bus depot transportation. Sports pros. Tennis. Three 18-hole golf courses, greens fee $100-$150, cart $15/person, putting greens, driving range. Downhill/x-country ski on site. Snowboarding. Skating. Hiking, horseback trails. Skeet & trap shooting. Lawn games. Game rm. Movies. Bowling. Exercise equipt; weights, bicycles. Spa, mineral pool. Microwaves avail. Cr cds: A, C, D, DS, MC, V.

Restaurants

✔★ **COUNTRY CAFE.** Rte 2, Box 2B, 2 mi S on US 220. 540/839-2111. Hrs: 7 am-9 pm; Sun to 2 pm. Closed Mon; Jan 1, Dec 25. Res accepted. Wine, beer. Semi-a la carte: bkfst $3-$6, lunch $4-$5, dinner $7-$15. Child's meals. Specializes in country cooking. Own baking. Country decor with woodburning kitchen stove. Cr cds: MC, V.

★ ★ **SAM SNEAD'S TAVERN.** Main St. 540/839-7666. Hrs: 5-10 pm. Res accepted. Semi-a la carte: dinner $7.95-$30. Specializes in fresh mountain trout, Black Angus steaks. Outdoor dining. Rustic decor. Cr cds: A, D, DS, MC, V.

Irvington (E-9)

(See also Lancaster)

Pop 496 **Elev** 31 ft **Area code** 804 **Zip** 22480

What to See and Do

Historic Christ Church (1735). Built by Robert Carter, ancestor of 8 governors of Virginia, 2 presidents, 3 signers of the Declaration of Independence, a chief justice and many others who served the country with distinction. Restored; original structure and furnishings, 3-decker pulpit. Built on site of earlier wooden church (1669); family tombs. Tours. (Apr-Nov, daily) 2 1/2 mi W, off VA 200. Phone 804/438-6855. **Free.** On the grounds is

Carter Reception Center. Narrated slide show; museum with artifacts from Corotoman, home of Robert Carter, and from the church construction; photographs of the restoration. Guides. (Apr-Nov, daily) **Free.**

Motel

★ **WHISPERING PINES.** (White Stone 22578) 1/4 mi N on VA 3. 804/435-1101. 29 rms. S, D $59-$64; each addl $5. Crib $5. TV; cable. Pool; wading pool. Restaurant nearby. Ck-out 11 am. Sundries. Picnic tables. On wooded grounds. Cr cds: A, MC, V.

Resort

★ ★ ★ **TIDES LODGE RESORT & COUNTRY CLUB.** N on VA 200, then W on VA 646, then SW on County 709, follow signs. 804/438-6000; FAX 804/438-5950; res: 800/248-4337. 60 units. Mid-Mar-Dec: S, D $108-$198; each addl $30; cottages to 2 persons $300; under 18 free; AP, MAP avail; golf packages; higher rates some wkends. Closed rest of yr. Crib free. Pet accepted, some restrictions; $10. TV; cable (premium), VCR avail (free movies). 2 pools, 1 saltwater, 1 heated; poolside serv. Playground. Free supervised child's activities (late June-Labor Day); ages 5-12. Coffee in rms. Dining rm 8-9:30 am, noon-2 pm, 6-10 pm. Bar noon-11 pm. Ck-out 1 pm, ck-in after 3:30 pm. Coin lndry. Meeting rms. Business servs avail. Bellhops. Valet serv. Gift shop. Lighted tennis. 45-hole golf, greens fee $25-$40, pro, putting greens, driving range. Exercise equipt; weight machine, bicycles. Marina, cruises, boat rental. Bicycles. Lawn games. Game rm. Rec rm. Exercise equipt; weights, bicycles, sauna. Refrigerators. Balconies. Cr cds: DS, MC, V.

Jamestown (Colonial National Historical Park) (E-9)

(For accommodations see Newport News, Williamsburg, Yorktown; also see Colonial Parkway, Surry)

Area code 757 **Zip** 23690

On May 13, 1607, in this unpromising setting, the first permanent English settlement in the New World was founded. From the beginning, characteristics of the early United States were established—self-government, industry, commerce and the plantation system. The 104 men and boys who landed here that day and the people who followed them forecast the varied origins of the American populace. There were English, Germans, Africans, French, Italians, Poles and Irish.

The *Susan Constant* (120 tons), the *Godspeed* (40 tons) and the *Discovery* (20 tons) brought the settlers here after a landing at Cape Henry. Thus, 20 years after the tragic failure to establish a colony at Roanoke Island and 13 years before the Pilgrims landed at Plymouth, Massachusetts, the English succeeded in settling in America.

The landing was not auspicious. Captain John Smith, ablest man in the group, was in chains; most of the others possessed a singular ineptitude for existing in a strange, hostile wilderness. Smith's ability and driving personality soon made him the acknowledged leader. For about a year he kept the bickering at a minimum, and the establishment of a colony was well under way.

The London Company, under whose patronage the colonists had set forth, continued to send "gentlemen" and adventurers to reinforce the colony. The second such shipment (September 1608) elicited the famous "Smith's rude answer" to company demands for gold and assorted riches. He wrote in part, "I entreat you rather send but thirty carpenters, husbandmen, gardeners, fishermen, blacksmiths, masons and diggers up of trees, roots . . . than a thousand of such as we have: for except we be able both to lodge them and feed them, the most will consume with want of necessaries before they can be made good for anything."

Good for anything or not, this little band made glass in 1608, introduced the first commercial tobacco cultivation in 1612 and produced the country's first representative legislative body in 1619. In the earliest years, clapboards (some of which were shipped back to England) were made here, and later bricks, fishing nets, pottery, a variety of tools and other items needed in the colony.

The first Africans were brought to the colony in 1619 on a Dutch privateer. They were probably indentured servants, pledged to work until their passage had been paid off. This was a common arrangement at the time.

There was not an easy day for any of the colonists for years. Crops failed, and rats ate the corn. Until John Rolfe married Pocahontas, daughter of Chief Powhatan, in 1614, the Native Americans were suspicious and unfriendly. Disease plagued the settlers. The winter of 1609-1610 was called the "starving time." The 350-person colony was reduced to about 60 emaciated, defeated survivors who decided to give up and return to England. The June 1610 arrival of Lord De la Warre with reinforcements and supplies dissuaded them. Then the colony began to build and hope returned.

When Jamestown became a Royal Colony in 1624, feeling against personal (and often high-handed) government began to mount. By 1676 there was open revolt, led by Nathaniel Bacon, the younger. Bacon's forces finally burned the town, calling it a "stronghold of oppression." It was partially rebuilt, but decline was irrevocable, in part due to the damp,

unhealthy climate of the area. The statehouse burned in 1698, and in 1699 the government moved to Middle Plantation and renamed it Williamsburg. By Revolutionary days Jamestown was no longer an active community. About the same time, the James River washed away the sandy isthmus, and the site became an island.

Nothing of the 17th-century settlement remains above ground except the Old Church Tower. Since 1934, however, archaeological exploration by the National Park Service has made the outline of the town clear. Cooperative efforts by the Park Service and the Association for the Preservation of Virginia Antiquities (which owns 22.5 acres of the island, including the Old Church Tower) have exposed foundations and restored streets, property ditches, hedgerows, fences and the James Fort site from 1607. Markers, recorded messages, paintings and monuments are everywhere. Entrance station (daily; closed Dec 25). For further information contact the Superintendent, PO Box 210, Yorktown 23690; 757/898-3400. Jamestown Island entrance fee $5/adult (over age 16); Golden Access, Age and Eagle passports accepted (see MAKING THE MOST OF YOUR TRIP).

What to See and Do

☑ **Colonial National Historical Park.** Recommended as a starting point is the

Visitor Center. Guide leaflets, introductory film and exhibits. Post office. (Daily; closed Dec 25) From here you can walk through

"New Towne." Area where Jamestown expanded around 1620 may be toured along "Back-Streete" and other original streets. Section includes reconstructed foundations indicating sites of Country House, Governor's House, homes of Richard Kemp, builder of one of the first brick houses in America, Henry Hartwell, a founder of College of William and Mary, and Dr. John Pott and William Pierce, who led the "thrusting out" of Gov John Harvey in 1635.

First landing site. Fixed by tradition as point in river, about 200 yards from present seawall, upriver from Old Church Tower.

James Fort site. Excavation of first fort (1607) can be viewed between seawall and Old Church Tower.

Old Church Tower. Only standing ruin of the 17th-century town. Believed to be part of first brick church (1639). Has 3-ft-thick walls of handmade brick.

Memorial Church. Built in 1907 by the National Society of the Colonial Dames of America over foundations of original church. Within are two foundations alleged to be of earlier churches, one from 1617 that housed first assembly.

Tercentenary Monument. Erected by US (1907) to commemorate 300th Jamestown anniversary. Other monuments include Captain John Smith statue (by William Couper), Pocahontas Monument (by William Ordway Partridge), House of Burgesses Monument (listing members of first representative legislative body in America). Located near Jamestown Visitor Center.

Confederate Fort (1861). One of two Civil War fortifications on the island. Near Old Church Tower.

Trails. Three- and 5-mi auto drives provide access to entire area. Visitor center has 45-min auto drive and town-site tape tours available.

Glasshouse. Colonists produced glass here in 1608. Demonstration exhibits, glassblowing (daily; closed Dec 25).

Dale House. Archaeological laboratory. A viewing area is open to the public.

Jamestown Settlement. Living history museum re-creates the first permanent English settlement in New World. Recalls early-17th-century Jamestown with full-scale reproductions of ships which arrived in 1607 and the triangular James Fort. Powhatan Indian Village depicts Native American culture encountered by English colonists. Museum complex features orientation film, changing gallery and three exhibit galleries focusing on the history of Jamestown and the Powhatan. Food service avail. Combination ticket with Yorktown Victory Center (see YORKTOWN) avail. (Daily; closed Jan 1, Dec 25) Adj to historic Jamestown. Phone 757/253-4838. ¢¢¢; Combination ticket ¢¢¢¢

Annual Events

Jamestown Weekend. Jamestown, the original town site. Commemorates arrival of first settlers in 1607; special tours and activities. Mid-May.

First Assembly Day. Jamestown, the original town site. Commemorates first legislative assembly in 1619. Late July.

Keysville (F-7)

Pop 606 **Elev** 642 ft **Area code** 804 **Zip** 23947

What to See and Do

Twin Lakes State Park. More than 250 acres of state forest; 2 lakes. Swimming, bathhouse; fishing; boating (rentals, launching, electric motors only). Hiking, bicycle, self-guided trails. Picnicking, playground, concession. Camping, tent & trailer sites, cabins (Mar-Dec); pavilion. Standard fees. 15 mi NE on US 360, then 1½ mi NW off VA 613. Phone 804/392-3435.

Motel

✔★ **SHELDON'S.** RFD 2, Box 189, 1½ mi N on US 15 Business. 804/736-8434; FAX 804/736-9402. 40 rms, 2 story. S $35.95-$50; D $41.95-$50; each addl $6. Crib $6. Pet accepted. TV; cable (premium). Restaurant 6:30 am-10 pm. Ck-out noon. Business servs avail. Some refrigerators; microwaves avail. Cr cds: A, DS, MC, V.

Lancaster (E-9)

(See also Irvington)

Pop 150 (est) **Elev** 89 ft **Area code** 804 **Zip** 22503

The family of Mary Ball Washington, mother of George Washington, were early settlers of this area. Washington's maternal ancestors are buried in the churchyard of St Mary's Whitechapel Church five miles west of Lancaster.

What to See and Do

Lancaster County Courthouse Historic District. Sycamore trees surround this area around the antebellum courthouse (1860). Marble obelisk is one of the first monuments erected to Confederate soldiers (1872).

Mary Ball Washington Museum and Library Complex. Contains the Old Clerk's Office (1797), the Old Jail (1819), a Native American longhouse and Lancaster House (1800), the headquarters and main museum building. Also Virginia genealogical research center. (Wed-Sat, Tues by appt) Phone 804/462-7280. Museum ¢; Research center ¢¢

St Mary's Whitechapel Church (1740-1741). Church where Mary Ball and her family worshiped; many of the tombstones bear the Ball name. 5 mi W on VA 622.

Inn

★★ **INN AT LEVELFIELDS.** 2 mi E on VA 3, beyond the Courthouse. 804/435-6887; res: 800/238-5578. 4 rms, 2 story. No rm phones. S $55; D $95; each addl $15. Pool. Complimentary bkfst. Bar. Ck-out 11 am, ck-in 2 pm. Business servs avail. Lawn games. Antiques; hand-made quilts. Antebellum landmark homestead (1857) with double-tiered portico and four massive chimneys; 1,000-ft entrance drive. Located

on 54 acres with 2 acres of lawn & 40 acres of timberland bounded by stream. Cr cds: A, MC, V.

Leesburg (C-8)

(See Arlington County, McLean; also see District of Columbia)

Founded 1758 **Pop** 16,202 **Elev** 352 ft **Area code** 703
Information Loudoun Tourism Council, 108-D South St SE, 20175; 703/777-0519 or 800/752-6118.

Originally named Georgetown for King George II of England, this town was later renamed Leesburg, probably after Francis Lightfoot Lee, a signer of the Declaration of Independence and a local landowner. Leesburg is located in a scenic area of rolling hills, picturesque rural towns and Thoroughbred horse farms, where point-to-point racing and steeplechases are popular.

What to See and Do

Ball's Bluff Battlefield. One of the smallest national cemeteries in US marks site of third armed engagement of Civil War. On Oct 21, 1861, four Union regiments suffered catastrophic losses while surrounded by Confederate forces; the Union commander, a US senator and presidential confidant, was killed here along with half his troops, who were either killed, wounded, captured or drowned while attempting to recross the Potomac River. Oliver Wendell Holmes, Jr, later to become a US Supreme Court justice, was wounded here. N via US 15.

Loudoun Museum. Century-old restored building contains exhibits and memorabilia of the area; audiovisual presentation "A Special Look at Loudoun." Brochures, information about Loudoun County; walking tours; self-guided tour booklets (fee). (Daily; closed Jan 1, Thanksgiving, Dec 25; also Jan) 16 Loudoun St SW. Phone 703/777-7427. **Donation.**

Morven Park. Originally the residence of Thomas Swann, early Maryland governor, the estate was enlarged upon by Westmoreland Davis, governor of Virginia from 1918 to 1922. The 1,200-acre park includes a 28-room mansion; boxwood gardens; Winmill Carriage Museum with more than 70 horse-drawn vehicles; Museum of Hounds and Hunting with video presentation and artifacts depicting the history of fox hunting; and Morven Park International Equestrian Center (see ANNUAL EVENTS). (Apr-Oct, Tues-Sun afternoons, also Mon hols) Old Waterford Rd, 1 mi N of Leesburg. Phone 703/777-2414. ¢¢

Oatlands (1803). A 261-acre estate; classical-revival mansion, built by George Carter, was the center of a 5,000-acre plantation; the house was partially remodeled in 1827, which was when the front portico was added. Most of the building materials, including bricks and wood, came from or were made on the estate. Interior, furnished with American, English and French antiques, reflects period between 1897 and 1965, when the house was owned by Mr and Mrs William Corcoran Eustis, prominent Washingtonians. Formal garden has some of the finest boxwood in US. Farm fields provide equestrian area for races and horse shows. (Early Apr-Dec, daily; closed Thanksgiving, Dec 25) 6 mi S on US 15. Phone 703/777-3174.

Vineyard and Winery Tours. For a list of area winery tours contact the Loudoun Tourism Council, 108-D South St SE ; 703/777-0519.

Waterford. Eighteenth-century Quaker village, designated a National Historic Landmark, has been restored as a residential community. An Annual Homes Tour (1st full wkend Oct) has craft demonstrations, exhibits, traditional music. Waterford Foundation has brochures outlining self-guided walking tours. 3 mi NW on VA 7, ¼ mi on VA 9, then 2 mi N on VA 662. Phone 703/882-3018. **Free;** Brochures ¢

Annual Events

Loudoun Hunt Pony Club Horse Trials. Held at Morven Park International Equestrian Institute, Morven Park. Competition in combined training:

dressage, cross-country and stadium jumping. Phone 703/777-2890. Late Mar.

Homes and Gardens Tour. Sponsored by Garden Club of Virginia. Late Apr.

Sheepdog Trials. Oatlands. May.

Wine Festival. Morven Park. Many wineries participate; includes seminar for home/commercial wine growers; grape-stomping, waiters' race, jousting tournament, music, wine tastings, awards presentations. Phone 202/537-0961. Mid-July.

August Court Days. Reenactment of the opening of the 18th-century judicial court. Festivities resemble a country fair with craft demonstrations, games, entertainers on the street. Phone 703/777-0519 or 800/752-6118. 3rd wkend Aug.

Draft Horse and Mule Day. Sat of Labor Day wkend.

Christmas at Oatlands. Candlelight tours, 1800s decorations, refreshments. Mid-Nov-Dec.

Motels

✔★ **DAYS INN.** 721 E Market St (20175), near Prosperity Shopping Center. 703/777-6622; FAX 703/777-4119. 81 rms, 2 story. Mar-Oct: S $49; D $53; each addl $3; under 12 free; lower rates rest of yr. Crib free. Pet accepted, some restrictions; $6. TV; cable (premium). Complimentary continental bkfst. Restaurant nearby. Ck-out noon. Coin lndry. Business servs avail. Cr cds: A, C, D, DS, JCB, MC, V.

[D] [⬚] [⬚] [⬚] [SC]

★★ **RAMADA INN-WASHINGTON DULLES.** 1500 E Market St (20175), on VA 7. 703/771-9200; FAX 703/771-1575. 126 rms, 2 story. S $59; D $63; each addl $7; suites $105; under 16 free. Crib free. TV; cable. Pool; lifeguard. Complimentary continental bkfst. Restaurant 11 am-3 pm, 5-10 pm. Bar 11:30 am-midnight; entertainment Tues-Sat. Ck-out noon. Coin lndry. Meeting rms. Business servs avail. Free airport transportation. Exercise equipt; stair machine, treadmill. Colonial mansion (1773). Cr cds: A, C, D, DS, MC, V.

[D] [⬚] [⬚] [⬚] [⬚] [⬚] [SC]

Hotel

★★★ **LANSDOWNE CONFERENCE RESORT.** (44050 Woodridge Pkwy, Lansdowne 22075) E on VA 7, left onto Lansdowne Blvd, then right onto Woodridge Pkwy. 703/729-8400; FAX 703/729-4111; res: 800/541-4801. 305 units, 9 story. S $149; D $169; suites $250-$650; under 18 free; wkend rates; golf plans. Crib free. TV; cable (premium). 2 pools, 1 indoor; whirlpool, poolside serv, lifeguard. Supervised child's activities; ages 3-12. Restaurant 6 am-midnight. Bar; entertainment Fri-Sun. Ck-out noon. Convention facilities. Business center. In-rm modem link. Concierge. Gift shop. Airport transportation. Lighted tennis. 18-hole golf, pro, greens fee $75-$85, putting green, driving range. Exercise rm; instructor, weights, bicycles, sauna. Lawn games. Bicycle rentals. Refrigerators avail. Balconies. Picnic tables. Cr cds: A, C, D, DS, MC, V.

[D] [⬚] [⬚] [⬚] [⬚] [⬚] [⬚] [⬚] [⬚] [SC] [⬚]

Inns

★★ **COLONIAL.** 19 S King St (20175). 703/777-5000; res: 800/392-1332. 10 rms, 3 story. S $58-$150; D $68-$150; under 10 free. Crib free. Pet accepted, some restrictions. TV; cable. Complimentary full bkfst; afternoon refreshments in library. Restaurant (see COLONIAL). Rm serv. Ck-out noon, ck-in 2 pm. Luggage handling. Free airport transportation. Tennis privileges. Golf privileges. Health club privileges. Picnic tables. Historic building (1759) built of same stone as Capital in DC. Fireplaces; some in-rm whirlpools. Cr cds: A, C, D, DS, MC, V.

[⬚] [⬚] [⬚] [⬚] [⬚] [SC]

✔★ **LITTLE RIVER.** (39307 John Mosby Hwy, Aldie 22001) S on VA 15, then 2 mi W on US 50. 703/327-6742. 9 units, 3 share bath, 2

story, 3 cottages. Some rm phones. S $65-$75; D $80-$90; each addl $20; cottages $115-$210. Children under 10 yrs in cottages only. Complimentary full bkfst. Pool privileges. Ck-out noon, ck-in 3 pm. Meeting rm. Private patios, balconies. Picnic tables. Built 1810; antiques. In foothills of Blue Ridge Mts. Cr cds: A, MC, V.

[D] [⬚]

★★★ **NORRIS HOUSE.** 108 Loudoun St SW (20175). 703/777-1806; FAX 703/771-8051; res: 800/644-1806. 6 rms, all share bath, 3 story. Rm phones avail. S $70-$85; D $85-$100; each addl $25; higher rates wkends (2-day min). Children wkdays only. Complimentary full bkfst; afternoon refreshments. Restaurant nearby. Ck-out noon, ck-in 4-8 pm. Business servs avail. Airport transportation. Lawn games. Picnic tables. Built 1760. Veranda overlooking gardens. Antique furnishings; most rms with fireplace. Totally nonsmoking. Cr cds: A, C, D, DS, MC, V.

[⬚] [⬚]

★★★ **RED FOX INN.** (2 E Washington St, Middleburg 22117) Approx 22 mi SW of Leesburg via US 15, 50. 540/687-6301; FAX 540/687-6053; res: 800/223-1728. 24 rms in 4 bldgs, 3 story, 9 suites. S, D $135-$155; each addl $25; suites $150-$250; under 12 free. Crib $10. TV; cable (premium). Complimentary continental bkfst. Dining rm 8 am-9:30 pm; Sun to 8 pm. Bar from 11:30 am. Ck-out noon, ck-in 3 pm. Business servs avail. Some fireplaces. Some private patios, balconies. Operated as an inn since 1728; pine floors and paneling; antique furnishings. Cr cds: A, C, D, DS, MC, V.

[D] [⬚] [⬚] [SC]

Restaurants

★★ **COLONIAL.** (See Colonial Inn) 703/777-5000. Hrs: 11:30 am-4 pm, 5-10 pm. Res accepted. Continental menu. Bar. Semi-a la carte: lunch $4.95-$10.95, dinner $5.95-$14.95. Child's meals. Specializes in beef, seafood. Entertainment. Outdoor dining. Colonial decor. Cr cds: A, C, D, DS, MC, V.

[D]

✔★★★ **GREEN TREE.** 15 S King St (20175). 703/777-7246. Hrs: 11:30 am-10 pm; Sun brunch 11:30 am-3:30 pm. Res accepted. Serv bar. Semi-a la carte: lunch $4.95-$9.95, dinner $9.95-$17.95. Sun brunch $11.95. Specialties: Robert's Delight (beef dish), Jefferson's Delight (calf's liver soaked in milk). Own baking. Authentic 18th-century recipes. Windows open to street. Fireplaces. Strolling musician Fri-Sat. Cr cds: A, C, D, DS, MC, V.

[⬚]

★★ **LAUREL BRIGADE INN.** 20 W Market St (20175). 703/777-1010. Hrs: 11:30 am-2 pm, 5:30-8:30 pm; Fri, Sat to 9 pm; Sun 8 am-11 am, noon-7 pm. Closed Mon. Res accepted; required hols. Serv bar. Semi-a la carte: lunch $4-$10. Complete meals: lunch $11-$14.50, dinner $12.50-$25. Child's meals. Specializes in chicken, beef, seafood. Outdoor dining. Oldest section dates from 1759; colonial decor, stone walls, fireplace. Family-owned. Cr cds: A, DS, MC, V.

[⬚]

Lexington (E-6)

(See also Clifton Forge, Natural Bridge)

Founded 1777 **Pop** 6,959 **Elev** 1,060 ft **Area code** 540 **Zip** 24450
E-mail lexington@rockbridge.net
Information Visitors Bureau, 106 E Washington St; 540/463-3777.

Lexington was home to two of the greatest Confederate heroes: Robert E. Lee and Thomas J. "Stonewall" Jackson. Both are buried here. Sam Houston, Cyrus McCormick and James Gibbs (inventor of the sewing machine) were born nearby.

This town, set in rolling country between the Blue Ridge and Allegheny mountains, is the seat of Rockbridge County. Lexington is known for attractive homes, trim farms, fine old mansions and two of the leading educational institutions in the Commonwealth: Washington and Lee University and Virginia Military Institute.

What to See and Do

Goshen Pass. Scenic mountain gorge formed by Maury River. Memorial to Matthew Fontaine Maury is here. 19 mi NW on VA 39.

Lexington Carriage Company. Approx 45-min narrated horse-drawn carriage tours of historic Lexington. Groups of 10 or more by appt only. (Apr-Oct, daily, weather permitting) Tours depart across street from Visitor Center, 106 E Washington St. Phone 540/463-5647. ¢¢¢

Stonewall Jackson House. Only home owned by Confederate General Stonewall Jackson, restored to its appearance of 1859-1861. Many of the furnishings were once owned by Jackson. Interpretive slide presentation and guided tours (¹/₂ hr). Restored gardens; shop. (Daily; closed Jan 1, Easter, Thanksgiving, Dec 25) 8 E Washington St. Phone 540/463-2552. ¢¢

Stonewall Jackson Memorial Cemetery. Gen Jackson and more than 100 other Confederate soldiers are buried here. E side of S Main St.

Virginia Horse Center. Sprawling across nearly 400 acres, the Center provides a versatile site for numerous horse-related functions yr-round: shows, clinics, auctions, festivals. Fees vary. VA 11N to VA 39W. For schedule of events, contact PO Box 1051; 540/463-2194.

Virginia Military Institute (1839). (1,300 cadets) State military, engineering, sciences and arts college. Stonewall Jackson taught here, as did Matthew Fontaine Maury, famed naval explorer and inventor. George Catlett Marshall, a general of the army and author of the Marshall Plan, was a graduate. Mementos of these men are on display in VMI museum (daily; closed Jan 1, Thanksgiving, Dec 24-31). Dress parade (most Fri afternoons, weather permitting). On US 11. Phone 540/464-7207. **Free.** Located on the S end of the parade ground is

> **George C. Marshall Museum** (1964). Displays on life and career of the illustrious military figure and statesman (1880-1959); World War I, electric map and recorded narration of World War II; Marshall Plan; gold medallion awarded with his Nobel Prize for Peace (1953). (Daily; closed Jan 1, Thanksgiving, Dec 25) Faces parade ground of VMI. Phone 540/463-7103. ¢¢

Washington and Lee University (1749). (1,900 students) Liberal arts university situated on an attractive campus with white colonnaded buildings; also includes Washington and Lee Law School. Founded as Augusta Academy in 1749; became Liberty Hall in 1776; its name was changed to Washington Academy in 1798, after receiving 200 shares of James River Canal Company stock from George Washington, and then to Washington College. General Robert E. Lee served as president from 1865-1870; soon after Lee's death in 1870, it became Washington and Lee University. W Washington St. Phone 540/463-8400. Within the university grounds is

> **Lee Chapel.** Robert E. Lee is entombed here. It also houses Lee family crypt and museum, the marble "recumbent statue" of Lee and some of the art collection of Washington and Lee families. Lee's office remains as he left it. (Daily; closed Jan 1, Thanksgiving & following Fri, Dec 24, 25, 31) **Free.**

Annual Events

Garden Week in Historic Lexington. Tour of homes and gardens in the Lexington, Rockbridge County area. Phone 540/463-3777. Late Apr.

"Holiday in Lexington." Parade, plays, children's events. Phone 540/463-3777. Early Dec.

Seasonal Event

Lime Kiln Arts' Theater at Lime Kiln. 14 S Randolph St. Professional theatrical productions and concerts in outdoor theater. Phone 540/463-3074. Memorial Day-Labor Day.

Motels

★ ★ ★ **BEST WESTERN INN AT HUNT RIDGE.** *Willow Springs Rd at VA 39.* 540/464-1500. 100 rms, 3 story, 10 suites. Apr-Oct: S $69-$82; D $74-$86; each addl $8, suites $81-$90; under 12 free; higher rates special events; lower rates rest of yr. Crib free. Pet accepted, some restrictions. TV; cable (premium). Indoor/outdoor pool. Complimentary coffee in rms. Restaurant 7 am-10 pm. Rm serv. Bar to midnight. Ck-out 11 am. Coin lndry. Meeting rms. Business servs avail. In-rm modem link. Refrigerator, microwave in suites. Cr cds: A, C, D, DS, JCB, MC, V.

D ✓ ≈ ⊠ ⚥ SC

✓★ ★ **DAYS INN KEYDET-GENERAL.** *325 W Midland Trail.* 540/463-2143. 53 rms, 10 kit. units. S $47.95-$57.95; D $55.95-$65.95; each addl $5. Crib free. Pet accepted, some restrictions. TV; cable (premium). Ck-out 11 am. Business servs avail. Some bathrm phones, refrigerators. Picnic tables. View of mountains. Cr cds: A, C, D, DS, ER, JCB, MC, V.

D ✓ ≈ ⊠ ⚥ SC

★ ★ **HOLIDAY INN EXPRESS.** *1 mi N on US 11.* 540/463-7351. E-mail dominion@rockbridge.net; web www.rockbridge.net/anderson/index.htp. 72 rms, 2 story. S $75; D $85; each addl $10; under 18 free. Crib free. Pet accepted. TV; cable (premium). Pool. Complimentary continental bkfst. Ck-out 11 am. Business servs avail. In-rm modem link. Valet serv. View of mountains. Cr cds: A, C, D, DS, ER, JCB, MC, V.

D ✓ ≈ ⊠ ⚥ SC

★ ★ **RAMADA INN.** *US 11N.* 540/463-6400; FAX 540/464-3639. 80 rms, 4 story. May-Oct: S $60; D $70; each addl $6; under 19 free; wkly, wkend rates; higher rates special events; lower rates rest of yr. Crib free. Pet accepted. TV; cable (premium). Indoor pool. Restaurant 6 am-2 pm, 5-10 pm. Rm serv. Bar 5-10 pm. Ck-out noon. Meeting rms. Business servs avail. Sundries. Cr cds: A, C, D, DS, ER, JCB, MC, V.

D ✓ ≈ ⊠ ⚥ SC

★ ★ **RED OAK INNS.** *US 11 & I-81, off exit 195.* 540/463-9131; FAX 540/463-7448; res: 800/521-9131. 150 rms, 3 story. May-Oct: S, D $45-$75; each addl $5; under 18 free; lower rates rest of yr. Crib free. TV; cable (premium). Pool. Restaurant adj 6 am-9 pm. Ck-out noon. Meeting rms. Microwaves avail. Cr cds: A, C, D, DS, MC, V.

D ≈ ⊠ ⚥ SC

Motor Hotels

★ ★ **COMFORT INN.** *US 11S, at I-64 exit 55, I-81 exit 191.* 540/463-7311; FAX 540/463-4590. E-mail Dominion@Rockbridge.net; web www.rockbridge.net/anderson/index.htp. 80 rms, 4 story. Apr-Nov: S, D $80-$85; each addl $5; under 18 free; lower rates rest of yr. Crib free. Pet accepted. TV; cable (premium). Indoor pool. Complimentary continental bkfst. Restaurant adj 6 am-11 pm. Ck-out 11 am. Coin lndry. Business servs avail. Sundries. Cr cds: A, C, D, DS, ER, JCB, MC, V.

D ✓ ≈ ⊠ ⚥ SC

✓★ ★ **HOWARD JOHNSON.** *US 11N, I-81 exit 195.* 540/463-9181; FAX 540/464-3448. 100 rms, 5 story. S $45-$63; D $50-$68; each addl $7; under 18 free; higher rates special events. Crib free. Pet accepted. TV; cable (premium). Pool. Restaurant 6 am-10 pm. Ck-out noon. Coin lndry. Meeting rms. Business servs avail. Gift shop. Microwaves avail. Balconies. Private patios. On hill; panoramic view of mountains. Cr cds: A, C, D, DS, ER, JCB, MC, V.

D ✓ ≈ ⊠ ⚥ SC

Inns

★ ★ **FASSIFERN.** *Rte 5, Box 87, 3 mi N at jct VA 39 & County Rd 750; just N of jct US 11 & I-64 exit 55.* 540/463-1013. 4 rms, 2 story. S, D $65-$92. Complimentary full bkfst. Restaurant nearby. Ck-out 11 am, ck-in 3 pm. Restored 1867 house; antiques. Grounds with pond, woods. Near VA Horse Center. Totally nonsmoking. Cr cds: MC, V.

★ ★ ★ **HUMMINGBIRD INN.** *(30 Wood Ln, Goshen 24439)* US 11 N to VA 39 N, turn left, S on Wood Ln. 540/997-9065; res: 800/397-3214; FAX 540/997-0289. E-mail hmgbird@cfw.com; web www.humingbird.inn.com. 5 rms, 2 story. No rm phones. May-Nov: S $75-$105; D $80-$110; wkend rates; MAP avail; wkends (2-day min); lower rates rest of yr. Children over 12 yrs only. Pet accepted; $20. TV in common rm. Complimentary full bkfst. Restaurant nearby. Ck-out 11 am, ck-in 4 pm. Business servs avail. Rec rm. Lawn games. Some in-rm whirlpools, fireplaces. Picnic tables. On river. Victorian Carpenter Gothic villa built in 1780; wraparound verandahs. Totally nonsmoking. Cr cds: A, DS, MC, V.

★ ★ ★ **THE INN AT UNION RUN.** *325 Union Run Rd, I-81 exit 191 S, or 180 N.* 540/463-9715; res: 800/528-6466; FAX 540/463-3526. 8 rms, 2 story. Apr-Nov: S $75-$90; D $85-$125; each addl $20; lower rates rest of yr. Children over 10 yrs only. TV in common rm; cable (premium). Complimentary full bkfst. Restaurant 5-9 pm; closed Sun, Mon. Rm serv. Ck-out 11 am, ck-in 3 pm. Business servs avail. Lawn games. Many in-rm whirlpools. Some balconies. Picnic tables. Federal manor house built in 1883. View of mountains. Totally nonsmoking. Cr cds: A, MC, V.

★ ★ **MAPLE HALL.** *3111 N Lee Hwy, I-81 exit 195, N on US 11.* 540/463-6693. Web www.virtualcities.com. 21 rms, 9 with shower only, 3 story. S $80-$155; D $95-$165; each addl $15; child under 12, $5. Crib avail. TV; VCR avail. Pool. Complimentary continental bkfst; afternoon refreshments. Dining rm 5:30-9 pm. Ck-out noon, ck-in 2 pm. Meeting rms. Business servs avail. Tennis. Lawn games. Plantation house built 1850; period furnishings. Cr cds: MC, V.

★ ★ **McCAMPBELL.** *11 N Main St.* 540/463-2044; FAX 540/463-7262. Web www.innbrook.com. 16 units, 4 story. S $80-$125; D $95-$140; each addl $15; family rates. Crib $5. TV; cable. Pool privileges. Complimentary continental bkfst; afternoon refreshments. Restaurant opp 5:30-9 pm. Ck-out noon, ck-in 2 pm. Business servs avail. Tennis privileges. Refrigerators. Private patios, balconies. Picnic tables. Built 1809; antiques. Cr cds: DS, MC, V.

★ ★ ★ **STEELES TAVERN MANOR.** *(US 11 & Raphine Rd, Steeles Tavern 24476)* N on US 11. 540/377-6444; res: 800/743-8666; FAX 540/377-5937. E-mail hoernlel@cfw.com; web www.steelestavern .com. 5 rms, 2 story. No rm phones. S, D $115-$145; each addl $20. Children over 13 yrs only. TV; VCR (movies). Complimentary full bkfst; afternoon refreshments. Complimentary coffee in rms. Ck-out 11 am, ck-in 3 pm. Business servs avail. Luggage handling. Valet serv. Many in-rm whirlpools. Picnic tables. Restored 1916 manor; antiques. On 55 acres. Panoramic view. Cr cds: A, DS, MC, V.

Restaurants

✔ ★ **REDWOOD.** *898 N Lee Hwy.* 540/463-2168. Hrs: 7 am-10 pm. Closed Dec 25. Semi-a la carte: bkfst $2.50-$4.50, lunch $3-$6, dinner $4.50-$9. Child's meals. Specializes in seafood, steak, chicken. Family restaurant with home-style cooking; casual atmosphere. No cr cds accepted.

★ ★ **WILLSON-WALKER HOUSE.** *30 N Main St.* 540/463-3020. Web www.webfeat-inc.com/lexington"foodanddinner". Hrs: 11:30 am-2:30 pm, 5:30-9 pm. Closed Sun, Mon; Jan 1, Thanksgiving, Dec 24, 25; also Sat lunch Dec-Mar. Res accepted. Serv bar. Wine list. Semi-a la carte: lunch $5-$8, dinner $10-$25. Child's meals. Specializes in pasta, veal, fresh seafood. Outdoor dining. In restored Greek-revival house

---

(1820) located in downtown historic district; period antiques. Cr cds: A, MC, V.

Luray (C-7)

(See also Basye, Front Royal, Harrisonburg, New Market)

Founded 1812 **Pop** 4,587 **Elev** 789 ft **Area code** 540 **Zip** 22835 **E-mail** pagecofc@shentel.net **Web** handmade-history.com/shen/page1.htm

Information Luray-Page County Chamber of Commerce, 46 E Main St; 540/743-3915.

The name of this town is of French origin; its fame comes from the caverns discovered here in 1878. Luray, at the junction of US 211 and US 340, is 9 miles away from, and within sight of, Shenandoah National Park (see) and Skyline Drive. Headquarters of the park are here. There are three developed recreation areas north and west of town in George Washington and Jefferson National Forests.

What to See and Do

★ **Luray Caverns.** One of the largest caverns in the East. Huge underground rooms (one is 300 ft wide, 500 ft long, with a 140-ft ceiling) connected by natural corridors and paved walkways, are encrusted with colorful rock formations, some delicate as lace, others massive. In one chamber is the world's only "stalacpipe" organ, which produces music of symphonic quality from stone formation. Indirect lighting permits taking color photos within caverns. Temperature is 54°F. One-hr guided tours start about every 20 min. (Daily) W edge of town on US 211. Phone 540/743-6551. ¢¢¢¢ Fee includes

Car and Carriage Museum. Exhibits include 140 restored antique cars, carriages and coaches featuring the history of transportation dating from 1625.

Luray Reptile Center and Dinosaur Park. Features large reptile collection, exotic animals and tropical birds; petting zoo; life-sized dinosaur reproductions. Gift shop. (Mid-Apr-Oct, daily) ½ mi W on US 211. Phone 540/743-4113. ¢¢

Luray Singing Tower. Houses a 47-bell carillon; largest bell weighs 7,640 lbs. Features 45-min recitals by a celebrated carillonneur. (June-Aug, Tues, Thurs, & Sun evenings; Mar-May & Sept-Oct, wkend afternoons) In park adj caverns. Phone 540/743-6551. **Free.**

Massanutten one-room school. Restored and furnished as it was in the 1800s. Period displays and pictures. (By appt) In Lawn Park. Contact Chamber of Commerce. **Free.**

Shenandoah National Park (see). 9 mi E on US 211, then S on Skyline Dr.

Annual Event

Page County Heritage Festival. Arts & crafts exhibits. Self-guided tour of churches and old homes. Columbus Day wkend.

Motels

✔ ★ **BEST WESTERN INTOWN.** *410 W Main St (US 211).* 540/743-6511; FAX 540/743-2917. 40 rms, 2 story. Apr-Nov: S, D $32.50-$73.50; each addl $5; under 18 free; higher rates foliage season; lower rates rest of yr. Crib $4. Pet accepted; $10 per day. TV; cable (premium). Pool. Playground. Restaurant 6 am-2 pm, 5-9 pm. Rm serv. Ck-out noon. Business servs avail. Lawn games. Cr cds: A, C, D, DS, MC, V.

★ ★ ★ **BROOKSIDE.** *2978 US 211E.* 540/743-5698; FAX 540/743-1326; res: 800/299-2655. 8 cottages. No rm phones. Feb-Nov: S $70-$140; D $125-$180; under 10 free; lower rates rest of yr. Crib avail.

Complimentary coffee in rms. Restaurant adj 7 am-8:30 pm. Ck-out noon. Sundries. Some refrigerators. Cr cds: A, C, D, DS, MC, V.

★ **LURAY CAVERNS MOTELS.** *US 211, opp caverns entrance.* 540/743-6551; FAX 540/743-6634. 64 rms. S, D $55-$70; each addl $7; under 16 free; TV; cable. Pools. Restaurants nearby. Business servs avail. Tennis privileges. Golf privileges. Views of Blue Ridge Mountains. Cr cds: A, DS, MC, V.

★★ **MIMSLYN INN.** *401 W Main St (US 211 Business).* 540/743-5105; FAX 540/743-2632; res: 800/296-5105. 49 rms, 2 with shower only, 3 story, 11 suites. Mid-June-Oct: S $59-$85; D $74-$95; suites $99-$139; under 18 free; lower rates rest of yr. Crib $7. Pet accepted. TV; cable. Restaurant 7-10 am, 11:30 am-2 pm, 5-9 pm. Rm serv. Ck-out noon. Business servs avail. Art gallery, antique shop. Built 1930 in style of antebellum mansion. Cr cds: A, C, D, DS, MC, V.

★★ **RAMADA INN.** *US 211 Bypass, 1 mi E on US 211 Bypass, jct VA 656.* 540/743-4521; FAX 540/743-6863. 101 rms, 2 story. Apr-Sept: S, D $75-$150; each addl $10; under 16 free; higher rates: wkends, foliage season, special events; lower rates rest of yr. Crib free. TV; cable. VCR avail (movies). Pool. Restaurant 6:30 am-2 pm, 5-9 pm. Bar 5 pm-1 am; entertainment. Ck-out noon. Meeting rms. Business servs avail. Miniature golf. Game rm. Some in-rm whirlpools. Cr cds: A, C, D, DS, JCB, MC, V.

Inns

★★★ **JORDAN HOLLOW FARM.** *(326 Hawks Bill Park Rd, Stanley 22851) 6¹/₂ mi S on US 340 Business, then E on VA 624, N on VA 689, then E on VA 626.* 540/778-2285; FAX 540/778-1759. 21 rms in 3 bldgs, 1-2 story. S $85-$130; D $110-$150; each addl $35; under 6 free. Crib free. TV in some rms; cable. Complimentary full bkfst. Dining rm 8:30-10:30 am, 6-9 pm. Bar 6-11 pm. Ck-out noon, ck-in 3 pm. Business servs avail. Some in-rm whirlpools. Converted 45-acre horse farm; sun deck with view of Blue Ridge Mts. Totally nonsmoking. Cr cds: C, D, DS, MC, V.

★★★ **MAYNE VIEW.** *439 Mechanic St.* 540/743-7921. 5 rms, 1 with shower only, 3 story. No rm phone. No elvtr. S, D $85-$130; under 4 free. Complimentary full bkfst. Restaurant nearby. Ck-out noon, ck-in 3 pm. Luggage handling. Whirlpool. Underground RR stop during the Civil War. Cr cds: A, DS, MC, V.

★★★ **SPRING FARM.** *13 Wallace Ave.* 540/743-4701; FAX 540/743-7851. 5 rms, 2 story. No rm phone. S, D $95-$150. Children over 12 only. TV in parlor. Complimentary full bkfst. Restaurant nearby. Ck-out noon, ck-in 3 pm. Underground RR stop during the Civil War. Cr cds: C, D, DS, MC, V.

★★★ **WOODRUFF HOUSE.** *330 Mechanic St.* 540/743-1494. 6 rms, 4 with shower only, 3 story. No rm phones. S, D $125-$165; each addl $25. Children over 10 only. Complimentary full bkfst. Restaurant nearby. Ck-out noon, ck-in 3 pm. Luggage handling. Health club privileges. Whirlpools. Victorian house (1830); furnished with antiques. Totally nonsmoking. Cr cds: DS, MC, V.

Restaurants

✓★ **BROOKSIDE.** *2978 US 211 E.* 540/743-5698. Hrs: 7 am-8:30 pm; Fri, Sat to 9 pm. Closed mid-Dec-mid-Jan. Res accepted. Wine, beer. Semi-a la carte: bkfst $3-$6, lunch $3.50-$7.50, dinner $6.50-$13. Buffet: bkfst (Sat & Sun) $5.95, lunch $5.95, dinner $7.50-$8.95. Child's meals. Specializes in rib-eye steak, spaghetti, seafood. Salad bar. Cr cds: A, C, D, DS, MC, V.

★★★ **PARKHURST.** *2547 US 211 W, 2 mi W on US 211.* 540/743-6009. Hrs: 4-10 pm; Fri, Sat to 11 pm. Closed some major hols. Res accepted Continental menu. Bar. Semi-a la carte: dinner $10.95-$22.95. Child's meals. Specializes in steak, fowl, seafood. View of Blue Ridge Mts. Cr cds: A, C, D, DS, MC, V.

Lynchburg (E-6)

Settled 1757 **Pop** 66,049 **Elev** 795 ft **Area code** 804 **E-mail** realva@aol.com

Information Visitors Information Center, 12th & Church Sts, 24504; 804/847-1811 or 800/732-5821.

Lynchburg is perched on hills overlooking the James River, which was for many years its means of growth. Today the city is home to more than 3,000 businesses and diversified industries. Colleges located here include Lynchburg College, Randolph-Macon Woman's College and Liberty University.

One of the first buildings in the town was a ferryhouse built by John Lynch. The same enterprising young man later built a tobacco warehouse, probably the first one in the country. During the Civil War, Lynchburg was important as a supply base and hospital town. In June of 1864, General Jubal A. Early successfully defended the town from an attack by Union forces. More than 2,200 Confederates are buried in the Confederate Cemetary, located in the Old City Cemetery.

What to See and Do

Anne Spencer House. House of noted poet, only black woman and only Virginian to be included in *Norton Anthology of Modern American and British Poetry.* On grounds is Spencer's writing cottage "Edan Kraal." Many dignitaries have visited here. Museum with artifacts, memorabilia, period antique furnishings; formal garden. (House by appt; gardens daily) 1313 Pierce St. Phone 804/846-0517. ¢

Appomattox Court House Natl Historical Park (see). 21 mi E on US 460.

Blackwater Creek Natural Area. Ruskin Freer Nature Preserve (115 acres) includes trails with plants; athletic area; bikeway winds past wildflower area and historical sites, ending downtown; Creekside Trunk Trail, natural grass trail with typical Piedmont species of plants, moist ravines, north-facing rocky bluffs. (Daily) In the center of the city. **Free.**

Fort Early. Defense earthwork for Lynchburg's closest battle during the Civil War. Confederates under General Jubal A. Early turned back forces under General David Hunter in 1864. (Daily) Memorial & Fort Aves. **Free.**

Jefferson's Poplar Forest. Designed and built by Thomas Jefferson as a personal retreat; begun in 1806. Restoration in progress; house unfurnished. (Apr-Nov, Wed-Sun & major hols) Just SW of Lynchburg on US 221, then left on VA 811 & left again on VA 661 in Bedford County. Phone 804/525-1806. ¢¢

Old Court House Museum (1855). Restored to original Greek-revival appearance. Three galleries have exhibits on early history of the area, highlighting Quaker settlement and role of tobacco; restored mid-19th-century courtroom. (Daily; closed Jan 1, Thanksgiving, Dec 24, 25) 901 Court St. Phone 804/847-1459. ¢

Pest House Medical Museum. The 1840s white frame medical office of Quaker physician Dr. John Jay Terrell, has been joined with the Pest House quarantine hospital to typify the standard of medicine during the late 1800s. Original medical instruments include an operating table, hypodermic needle, clinical thermometer and chloroform mask. Period furnishings on one side duplicate Dr. Terrell's office during the Civil War; the other represents the quarantine hospital for Confederate soldiers in which Dr.

Terrell volunteered to assume responsibility. Window displays with audio description. Tours (by appt). (Daily) Old City Cemetery, 4th & Taylor Sts. Phone 804/847-1811. **Free.**

Point of Honor (1815). Restored mansion on Daniel's Hill above the James River, built by Dr. George Cabell, Sr, physician to Patrick Henry. Federal style with octagon-bay facade and finely crafted interior woodwork; period furnishings; gardens and grounds being restored. (Daily; closed Jan 1, Thanksgiving, Dec 24, 25) 112 Cabell St. Phone 804/847-1459. **¢¢**

Randolph-Macon Woman's College (1891). (750 women) A 100-acre campus on historic Rivermont Ave near the James River. First college for women in the South granted a Phi Beta Kappa chapter. Campus is interesting mixture of architecture including the Vincent Kling design for the Houston Chapel. Tours on request. 2500 Rivermont Ave. Phone 804/947-8000. On campus is

Maier Museum of Art. Collection is representative of 19th- and 20th-century American painting. Artists include Thomas Hart Benton, Edward Hicks, Winslow Homer, James McNeil Whistler, Mary Cassatt and Georgia O'Keeffe. Changing exhibits. (Academic yr, Tues-Sun afternoons) Phone 804/947-8136. **Free.**

Riverside Park. (Daily) Rivermont Ave. **Free.** In park is

Packet Boat *Marshall.* Mounted on a stone base, this is the boat that carried the remains of Stonewall Jackson home to Lexington; for many years packets were the principal mode of transportation along the James River and Kanawha Canal.

South River Meeting House. Completed in 1798, the stone building remained the site of Quaker worship and activity until the 1840s. John Lynch, the founder of Lynchburg, and other early leaders of the community are buried in the adj historic cemetery. (Daily; closed major hols) 5810 Fort Ave. Phone 804/239-2548. **Free.**

Motels

★ ★ **BEST WESTERN.** *2815 Candlers Mt Rd (24502).* 804/237-2986; FAX 804/237-2987. 87 rms, 2-3 story. S $69; D $79; each addl $8; under 12 free; higher rates: homecoming, graduation. Crib free. TV; cable (premium). Complimentary continental bkfst. Complimentary coffee in rms. Restaurant adj 11 am-midnight. Rm serv. Ck-out 11 am. Meeting rms. Business servs avail. In-rm modem link. Valet serv. Sundries. Health club privileges. Heated pool. Microwaves avail. Cr cds: A, C, D, DS, MC, V.

D ≈ ⊠ ⋌ SC

★ ★ **DAYS INN.** *3320 Candlers Mt Rd (24502).* 804/847-8655; FAX 804/846-3297. 131 rms, 5 story. S, D $59-$79; each addl $8; under 17 free. Crib free. TV; cable (premium). Pool. Playground. Restaurant 6 am-2 pm, 5 pm-midnight. Rm serv. Ck-out noon. Meeting rms. Business servs avail. In-rm modem link. Valet serv. Sundries. Free airport, RR station, bus depot transportation. Health club privileges. Microwaves avail. Private patios, balconies. Cr cds: A, C, D, DS, JCB, MC, V.

D ≈ ⊠ ⋌ SC

✔ ★ **ECONO LODGE.** *2400 Stadium Rd (24501), US 29S Expressway City-Stadium exit.* 804/847-1045; FAX 804/846-0086. 48 rms, 2 story. S $39.95-$55; D $55-$80. Crib free. TV; cable (premium). Continental bkfst. Restaurant nearby. Ck-out 11 am. Business servs avail. Cr cds: A, C, D, DS, MC, V.

⊠ ⋌ SC

★ ★ **HAMPTON INN.** *5604 Seminole Ave (24502).* 804/237-2704; FAX 804/239-9183. 65 rms, 2 story. S $61-$67; D $71-$77; under 18 free; higher rates Randolph-Macon graduation. Crib avail. TV; cable (premium). Complimentary continental bkfst. Restaurant adj 10:30 am-midnight. Ck-out noon. Business servs avail. Health club privileges. Sundries. Cr cds: A, C, D, DS, MC, V.

D ≈ ⋌ SC

★ **HOWARD JOHNSON.** *PO Box 735 (24572), 2 mi N on US 29.* 804/845-7041; FAX 804/845-4718. 70 rms, 2 story. S, D $46-$77; each addl $7; under 18 free. Crib free. TV; cable (premium). Pool; wading pool. Restaurant 6 am-10 pm. Ck-out noon. Coin lndry. Business servs avail.

Valet serv. Sundries. Free airport transportation. Microwaves avail. Private patios, balconies. Cr cds: A, C, D, DS, MC, V.

D ≈ ⊠ ⋌ SC

✔ ★ **INNKEEPER.** *5600 Seminole Ave (24502).* 804/237-7771; FAX 804/239-0659; res: 800/466-5337. 104 rms, 3 story. S $49.99-$55.99; D $54.99-$59.99; each addl $5; under 16 free. Crib free. TV; cable (premium). Pool. Complimentary continental bkfst. Restaurant nearby. Ck-out noon. Meeting rm. Valet serv. Health club privileges. Microwaves avail. Cr cds: A, C, D, DS, MC, V.

D ≈ ⊠ ⋌ SC

Motor Hotels

★ ★ **COMFORT INN.** *3125 Albert Lankford Dr (24501), US 29, at Odd Fellows Rd.* 804/847-9041; FAX 804/847-8513. 120 rms, 5 story. S $68-$85; D $73-$90; each addl $5; suites $135-$157; under 18 free; higher rates: homecoming, graduation. Crib free. TV; cable (premium), VCR avail. Complimentary full bkfst. Complimentary coffee in rms. Restaurant nearby. Ck-out noon. Meeting rms. Business servs avail. Free airport, RR station transportation. Pool. Some refrigerators, microwaves. Balconies. Picnic tables, grills. Cr cds: A, C, D, DS, ER, JCB, MC, V.

D ≈ ⊠ ⋌ SC

★ ★ ★ **HILTON.** *2900 Candlers Mt Rd (24502).* 804/237-6333; FAX 804/237-4277. 168 rms, 5 story. S $85-$120; D $105-$140; each addl $20; suites $186; family rates. Crib free. TV; cable (premium). Indoor pool; whirlpool. Restaurant 6:30 am-2 pm, 5:30-10 pm. Rm serv. Bar 11-1:30 am; entertainment. Ck-out 11 am. Meeting rms. Business center. Bellhops. Valet serv. Sundries. Gift shop. Free airport transportation. Exercise equipt; weights, bicycles, sauna. Bathrm phone in suites. Microwaves avail. Cr cds: A, D, MC, V.

D ≈ ✕ ⋌ 🚶 SC

Hotel

★ ★ **HOLIDAY INN SELECT.** *601 Main St (24504).* 804/528-2500; FAX 804/528-4782. 243 units, 8 story. S, D $72; each addl $10; suites $85-$110; under 17 free. Crib free. Pet accepted. TV; cable (premium). Pool; poolside serv. Restaurant 6:30 am-10 pm. Bar 3 pm-1 am. Ck-out noon. Meeting rms. Business servs avail. In-rm modem link. Free airport, RR station, bus depot transportation. Exercise equipt; weights, bicycles. Some bathrm phones, refrigerators; microwaves avail. Cr cds: A, C, D, DS, ER, JCB, MC, V.

D 🐾 ≈ ✕ ⋌ SC

Inns

★ ★ ★ **DULWICH MANOR.** *(550 Richmond Hwy, Amherst 24521)* Approx 17 mi N on US 29, then 1/2 mi E on US 60. 804/946-7207. 6 rms, 4 with bath, 3 story. No rm phones. S $64-$84; D $69-$89; each addl $20; wkly rates. Complimentary full bkfst. Restaurant nearby. Ck-out 11 am, ck-in 3 pm. Whirlpool. English manor house (1912); antique furnishings. No cr cds accepted.

⊠ ⋌ SC

★ ★ ★ **MADISON HOUSE.** *413 Madison St (24504).* 804/528-1503; res: 800/828-6422; FAX 804/528-4412. E-mail madison@lynchburg.net; web www.inngetaways.com. 4 rms, 2 story. S $69-$89; D $79-$99; each addl $10; suite $99-109. TV; cable (premium). Complimentary full bkfst; afternoon refreshments. Ck-out 11 am, ck-in 3-6 pm. Free airport, RR station transportation. Victorian mansion (1880) with many antiques. Library features antiques, Civil War collection. Totally nonsmoking. Cr cds: A, MC, V.

⊠ ⋌

★ ★ ★ **MANSION INN.** *405 Madison St (24504).* 804/528-5400; res: 800/352-1199. 5 rms, 2 story. S $104-$134; D $109-$139; each addl $25; under 8 free. TV; cable. Complimentary full bkfst. Ck-out 11 am, ck-in

3-6 pm. Some refrigerators. Picnic tables. Spanish/Georgian mansion built 1914; individually decorated rms include the Gilliam Room (traditional English manor-style), and the Bowen Room (Country French-style). The back porch overlooks the landscaped grounds. Totally nonsmoking. Cr cds: A, D, MC, V.

🚳 ⚄ **SC**

Restaurants

★ ★ ★ **CAFE FRANCE.** *3225 Old Forest Rd (24501).* 804/385-8989. Hrs: 11:30 am-3 pm, 5:30-10 pm. Closed Sun, Mon; some major hols. Res accepted. Bar. Wine cellar. Semi-a la carte: lunch $4-$8.95, dinner $6-$24.95. Child's meals. Specializes in fresh seafood, lamb. Parking. Extensive beer selection. Country French decor. Gourmet retail shop adj. Cr cds: A, MC, V.

D 🔒

★ ★ **CROWN STERLING.** *6120 Fort Ave (24502).* 804/239-7744. Hrs: 5:30-10 pm. Closed Sun; major hols. Res accepted. Bar from 5 pm. Semi-a la carte: dinner $12-$24. Specializes in steak. Salad bar. Parking. Colonial decor. Cr cds: A, C, D, DS, MC, V.

D 🔒

★ ★ **JEANNE'S.** *Rte 3, Box 178 D (24504), 8 mi E on US 460.* 804/993-2475. Hrs: 11:30 am-2:30 pm, 4:30-9 pm; wkends to 10 pm; Sun noon-9 pm; Jan-Mar noon-2 pm, 5-9 pm. Closed July 4; also late Dec. Semi-a la carte: lunch $3.95-$9.95, dinner $6.95-$20.95. Child's meals. Specializes in steak, seafood. Salad bar. Own desserts. Parking. Rustic redwood overlooking lake, dining on deck. Cr cds: A, C, DS, MC, V.

D 🔒

★ ★ **LANDMARK HOUSE.** *6113 Fort Ave (24502).* 804/237-1884. Hrs: 5:30-10 pm; Sat, Sun from 5:30 pm. Closed Mon; some hols. Bar. Semi-a la carte: dinner $6.95-$25.95. Child's meals. Specialties: prime rib, filet mignon. Salad bar. Piano bar. Parking. Cr cds: A, D, MC, V.

D 🔒

★ ★ ★ **SACHIKO'S.** *126 Old Graves Mill Rd (24503).* 804/237-5655. Hrs: 5:30-10 pm. Closed Sun; some hols. Res accepted. Bar. Semi-a la carte: dinner $10.95-$25. Specializes in new American cuisine. Own baking, desserts. Parking. Fireplaces. Cr cds: A, MC, V.

D 🔒

✔★ **T.C. TROTTERS.** *2496 Rivermont Ave (24503).* 804/846-3545. Hrs: 11:30 am-10 pm. Closed Mon; Thanksgiving, Dec 25. Res accepted. Bar to 2 am. Semi-a la carte: lunch $2.25-$8.95, dinner $2.25-$16.95. Child's meals. Specializes in fajitas, steak, seafood. Entertainment Fri-Sat. Parking. Outdoor dining. Cr cds: A, MC, V.

D 🔒

Manassas (C-8)

(See also Arlington County, Fairfax, Falls Church, Triangle; also see District of Columbia)

Pop 27,957 **Elev** 321 ft **Area code** 703 **E-mail** jjensen@mnsinc.com **Web** www.visitpwc.com

Information Prince William County/Manassas Conference & Visitors Bureau, 14420 Bristow Rd, 20112; 703/792-4254 or 800/432-1792.

Though the Native Americans who had lived in this area for thousands of years were driven out under a treaty in 1722, settlement remained sparse until the coming of the railroad in 1858. The Manassas rail junction was vital to the South, and many troops were stationed along this line of communication. Control of this junction led to two major battles nearby (see MANASSAS (BULL RUN) NATIONAL BATTLEFIELD PARK).

What to See and Do

The Manassas Museum. Museum features collections dealing with Northern Virginia Piedmont history from prehistoric to modern times, with special emphasis on the Civil War. (Daily exc Mon; closed Jan 1, Thanksgiving, Dec 24, 25) 9101 Prince William St. Phone 703/368-1873. ¢

Annual Events

Prince William County Fair. Carnival, entertainment, tractor pull, exhibits, contests. Phone 703/368-0173. Mid-Aug.

Re-enactment of the Civil War Battle of Manassas. Long Park. Late Sept.

Motels

✔★ ★ **BEST WESTERN.** *8640 Mathis Ave (20110).* 703/368-7070; FAX 703/368-7292. 60 rms, 2 story. Apr-Oct: S $50-$65; D $55-$70; each addl $5; kit. units $60-$75; under 18 free; lower rates rest of yr. Crib free. TV; cable (premium). Complimentary continental bkfst. Restaurant adj 4 pm-2 am. Ck-out 11 am. Coin lndry. Business servs avail. Whirlpool, sauna. Refrigerators, microwaves. Some in-rm whirlpools. Cr cds: A, C, D, DS, ER, MC, V.

D 🚳 ⚄ **SC**

★ ★ **BEST WESTERN BATTLEFIELD INN.** *10820 Balls Ford Rd (20109), I-66 exit 47A.* 703/361-8000. 121 rms, 2 story. S $54-$69; D $64-$75; each addl $10; under 18 free. Crib free. Pet accepted, $10/day. TV; cable (premium). Pool. Complimentary continental bkfst. Restaurant 5-10 pm; closed Sun. Rm serv. Bar to midnight; Fri, Sat to 2 am; entertainment Tues-Sat. Ck-out 11 am. Meeting rms. Business servs avail. In-rm modem link. Valet serv. Sundries. Health club privileges. Refrigerators, microwaves avail. Cr cds: A, C, D, DS, MC, V.

D 🐾 ⚊ 🚳 ⚄ **SC**

★ ★ ★ **COURTYARD BY MARRIOTT.** *10701 Battleview Pkwy (20109), I-66, exit 47B.* 703/335-1300; FAX 703/335-9442. 149 rms, 3 story. S, D $86-$98; each addl $5; suites $96; under 19 free. Crib free. TV; cable (premium). Indoor pool; whirlpool. Complimentary coffee in rms. Restaurant 6:30-10 am, 5-10 pm; Sat, Sun 7 am-noon. Bar. Ck-out noon. Coin lndry. Meeting rms. Business servs avail. In-rm modem link. Valet serv. Sundries. Exercise equipt; weights, bicycles. Health club privileges. Refrigerators, microwaves avail. Balconies. Cr cds: A, C, D, DS, MC, V.

D ⚊ 🏋 🚳 ⚄ **SC**

★ ★ **DAYS INN.** *10653 Balls Ford Rd (20109).* 703/368-2800; FAX 703/368-0083. 120 rms, 2 story. S $54; D $60; each addl $6; under 18 free. Crib free. TV; cable (premium). Pool. Complimentary continental bkfst. Ck-out 11 am. Coin lndry. Business servs avail. Health club privileges. Refrigerator avail. Cr cds: A, C, D, DS, MC, V.

D ⚊ 🚳 ⚄ **SC**

✔★ **RED ROOF INN.** *10610 Automotive Dr (20109), I-66 exit 47A.* 703/335-9333; FAX 703/335-9342. 119 rms, 3 story. S $47.99-$63.99; D $53.99-$67.99; under 18 free; higher rates: Cherry Blossom, hol wkends. Crib free. Pet accepted, some restrictions. TV; cable (premium). Complimentary coffee in lobby. Restaurant adj 6-2 am. Ck-out noon. Business servs avail. Sundries. Health club privileges. Cr cds: A, C, D, DS, MC, V.

D 🐾 🚳 ⚄ **SC**

✔★ ★ **SHONEY'S INN.** *8691 Phoenix Dr (20110), off US 28.* 703/369-6323; FAX 703/369-9206. 78 rms, 3 story. S $42-$50; D $47-$55; each addl $5; under 18 free. Crib free. TV; cable (premium). Complimentary continental bkfst. Complimentary coffee in rms. Restaurant adj 6 am-11 pm. Ck-out 11 am. Meeting rm. Business servs avail. Exercise equipt; weights, bicycle, whirlpool, sauna. Some in-rm whirlpools; microwaves avail. Cr cds: A, C, D, MC, V.

D 🏋 🚳 ⚄ **SC**

Motor Hotel

★ ★ **HOLIDAY INN.** *10800 Vandor Ln (20109), I-66 exit 47B. 703/335-0000; FAX 703/361-8440.* 159 rms, 5 story. S $125; D $130; under 12 free. Crib free. Pet accepted; deposit. TV; cable (premium). Pool. Complimentary coffee in lobby. Restaurant 6-11 am, 5-10 pm; Sat, Sun 6-11 am. Rm serv. Bar 4 pm-2 am. Ck-out noon. Coin lndry. Meeting rms. Business servs avail. In-rm modem link. Valet serv. Exercise equipt; weight machines, bicycle. Health club privileges. Refrigerators, microwaves avail. Near Manassas (Bull Run) Battlefield. Cr cds: A, C, D, DS, ER, MC, V.

 D ⚡ 🏊 ✕ 🔀 ⬇ SC

Restaurants

★ ★ ★ **CARMELLO'S.** *9108 Center St (20110). 703/368-5522.* Hrs: 11:30 am-2:30 pm, 5-10 pm; Sat from 5 pm, Sun 4-9 pm. Closed most major hols. Res accepted. Northern Italian menu. Bar. Semi-a la carte: lunch $5-$10, dinner $10-$17. Child's meals. Specializes in fresh seafood, veal, chicken. Own pasta. Pianist Sat. Located in 2-story brick storefront. Cr cds: A, C, D, DS, MC, V.

D

✔ ★ ★ **HERO'S.** *9412 Main St (22110), in Old Town. 703/330-1534.* E-mail heros@look.com; web www.webasap.com/heros. Hrs: 11 am-10 pm; Thurs-Sat to 12:30 am; Sun from noon. Contemporary Amer menu. Bar to 1:30 am. Semi-a la carte: lunch, dinner $5.25-$14.95. Specializes in fresh seafood, hamburgers, sandwiches. Salad bar. Own desserts, ice cream. Jazz Thurs-Sun. Outdoor dining. Contemporary American pub; two-level dining; jazz memorabilia. Cr cds: A, C, D, DS, MC, V.

★ ★ **PANINO.** *9116 Mathis Ave (22110), 1 mi E on US 28 at Manassas Shopping Center. 703/335-2566.* Hrs: 11:30 am-2:30 pm, 5:30-10 pm; Sat from 5:30 pm. Closed Sun; major hols. Res accepted; required Fri, Sat dinner. Northern Italian menu. Serv bar. Extensive wine list. Semi-a la carte: lunch $8.50-$12.50, dinner $9-$18.50. Specialties: homemade Tuscan bread, seafood ravioli, osso bucco. Own baking. Contemporary Italian decor; extensive art collection. Cr cds: A, C, D, DS, MC, V.

 D 🔀

Manassas (Bull Run) National Battlefield Park (C-8)

(For accommodations see Falls Church, Manassas)

(26 mi SW of Washington, DC, at jct US 29, VA 234)

This 5,000-acre park was the scene of two major Civil War battles. More than 26,000 men were killed or wounded here in struggles for control of a strategically important railroad junction.

The first major land battle of the war (July 21, 1861) was fought here between poorly trained volunteer troops from both North and South. The battle finally resolved itself into a struggle for Henry Hill, where "Stonewall" Jackson earned his nickname. With the outcome in doubt, Confederate reinforcements arrived by railroad from the Shenandoah Valley and turned the battle into a rout.

Thirteen months later (August 28-30, 1862), in the second battle of Manassas, Robert E. Lee outmaneuvered and defeated Union General John Pope and cleared the way for a Confederate invasion of Maryland.

For further information contact Park Superintendent, 6511 Sudley Rd, Manassas 22110; 703/361-1339.

Park (daily; closed Dec 25). ¢

What to See and Do

Chinn House Ruins. The house served as a field hospital in both engagements and marked the left of the Confederate line at First Manassas; also the scene of Longstreet's counterattack at Second Manassas.

Dogan House. An original structure at Groveton, a village around which the battle of Second Manassas was fought.

Stone Bridge. Where Union artillery opened the Battle of First Manassas; it afforded an avenue of escape for the Union troops after both First and Second Manassas.

Stone House. Originally a tavern (ca 1825), used as field hospital in both battles. (Summer, daily)

Unfinished Railroad. Fully graded railroad bed, never completed, behind which Stonewall Jackson's men were positioned during the second battle.

Visitor Center. Hill affords view of much of battlefield. Information; self-guided tours start here (walking tour of First Manassas, directions for driving tour of Second Manassas). Markers throughout park explain various aspects of battles. Ranger-conducted tours (summer). On Henry Hill, just N of I-66 off VA 234. In same building is

Battlefield Museum. Exhibits present stories of battles; audiovisual presentations of background information. (Daily; closed Dec 25)

Marion (F-3)

(See also Abingdon, Wytheville)

Founded 1835 **Pop** 6,630 **Elev** 2,178 ft **Area code** 540 **Zip** 24354
E-mail smythcofc@netva.com **Web** www.netva.com/smythcoc
Information Smyth County Chamber of Commerce, 124 W Main St, PO Box 924; 540/783-3161.

This popular vacation spot is surrounded by George Washington and Jefferson National Forests, abounding in game and birds, near a state park and high enough to promise an invigorating climate. The seat of Smyth County, it was named for General Francis Marion, known during the American Revolution as the "Swamp Fox."

What to See and Do

George Washington and Jefferson National Forests. (See HARRISON-BURG) SE of town via VA 16 is the

Mount Rogers National Recreation Area. A 117,000-acre area that includes Mount Rogers, the state's highest point (5,729 ft), mile-high open meadows known as "balds," and a great variety of animals and plants. Swimming, fishing, hunting, camping (fee at some areas), three visitor centers, approx 400 mi of hiking, bicycle & bridle trails. Mount Rogers Scenic Byway (auto); Virginia Creeper Trail (hikers, bicycles, horses) follows an abandoned railroad grade through spectacular river gorges. Adj to Grayson Highlands State Park (see ABINGDON). (Mid-May-Mid-Sept, daily; rest of yr, Mon-Fri) Some fees. Phone 540/783-5196.

Hungry Mother State Park. More than 2,180 acres amid the mountains with a 108-acre lake; panoramic views. Swimming beach, bathhouse; fishing; boating (rentals, launching, electric motors only). Hiking, self-guided trails; horseback riding (rentals). Picnicking, cafe, concession. Tent & trailer sites (electrical hookups, late Mar-Dec), cabins (Mar-Dec). Hilltop visitor center, interpretive programs. Standard fees. 3 mi N on VA 16. Phone 540/783-3422. Parking ¢

Annual Event

Hungry Mother Arts and Crafts Festival. Hungry Mother State Park. Mid-July.

Motel

✔★★ **BEST WESTERN.** *1424 N Main St. 540/783-3193; FAX 540/783-3193, ext. 184.* 79 rms, 1-2 story. S $54-$68, D $59-$72; under 18 free. Crib free. TV; cable (premium). Pool. Complimentary continental bkfst. Restaurant 5:30-9:30 pm. Rm serv. Bar 5 pm-midnight; closed Sun. Ck-out noon. Meeting rms. Business servs avail. Valet serv. Some microwaves. Cr cds: A, C, D, DS, JCB, MC, V.

🏊 ⊠ 🐾 SC

Inn

★ **FOX HILL.** *(Rte 2, Box 1-A-1, Troutdale 24378) 20 mi S via VA 16, then follow sign. 540/677-3313; res: 800/874-3313.* 8 rms, 2 story. No A/C. No rm phones. S,D $75; each addl $5; under 18 free; wkly rates. Crib free. TV in sitting rm. Complimentary full bkfst. Restaurant nearby. Ck-out 10 am, ck-in 3 pm. X-country ski 5 mi. Situated on mountain top with panoramic view. On 70 acres of woods & pasture land; wildlife, farm animals; hiking trails. Cr cds: DS, MC, V.

🏊 ⊠ 🐾

Martinsville (F-5)

(See also Danville)

Founded 1793 **Pop** 16,162 **Elev** 1,020 ft **Area code** 540
Information Martinsville-Henry County Chamber of Commerce, 115 Broad St, PO Box 709, 24114; 540/632-6401.

Martinsville was named for Joseph Martin, a pioneer who settled here in 1773. Henry County takes its name from Patrick Henry, who lived here. When Henry County Court first opened in October 1776, 640 residents pledged an oath of allegiance to the United States; 40 refused to renounce allegiance to England. Located near the beautiful Blue Ridge Mountains, this industrial community is home to Bassett Furniture, E. I. duPont de Nemours and textile plants.

What to See and Do

Blue Ridge Farm Museum. Presents the heritage of mountain region through reconstructed farmsteads and "folklife galleries." Authentic buildings from 1800 German-heritage farm, including log house, kitchen, blacksmith shop and barn. Costumed interpreters demonstrate farm and household chores. Special events (fees). (Mid-May-mid-Aug, wknds; rest of yr, by appt) VA 40 in Ferrum. Phone 540/365-4415. ¢¢

Fairy Stone State Park. Consists of 4,570 acres, with a 168-acre lake adjoining Philpott Reservoir. Nestled in the foothills of the Blue Ridge Mountains, this park is named for the "fairy stones" (staurolites) found near the southern tip of its boundary. Swimming beach, bathhouse; fishing; boating (launch, rentals, electric motors only). Hiking, bicycle trails. Picnic shelters, concession, cafe. Tent & trailer sites (dump station, electrical hookups), cabins (Mar-Dec). Visitor center, evening programs. Standard fees. (Daily) 21 mi NW via US 220/VA 57, VA 346. Phone 540/930-2424.

Philpott Lake. State's fourth-largest lake, formed by Philpott Dam, a US Army Corps of Engineers project. Swimming, skindiving; waterskiing, boating, fishing. Hunting, hiking, picnicking; 4 camping areas (Apr-Oct) One area free; some fees. Just NE of Fairy Stone State Park. Phone 540/629-2703.

Virginia Museum of Natural History. State museum focuses on preservation, study and interpretation of Virginia's natural heritage. Features visual and hands-on exhibits; includes a computer-animated triceratops dinosaur and a life-size ground sloth model. Special events during the yr include Earth Day (Apr) and Virginia Indian Festival (Sept). (Daily exc Sun; closed most major hols) 1001 Douglas Ave. Phone 540/666-8600. **Free.**

Annual Event

Blue Ridge Folklife Festival. Held at Blue Ridge Farm Museum. Gospel, blues and string band music; traditional regional crafts; regional foods; quilt show, antique autos, steam & gas-powered farm equipment. Sports events include horse-pulling & log-skidding contests, coon-dog swimming and treeing contests. Phone 540/365-4415. Late Oct.

Seasonal Event

Stock car races. Martinsville Speedway. 3 mi S. Phone 540/956-3151. Miller Genuine Draft 300, mid-Mar. Hanes 500, late Apr. Goody's 500, late Sept. Taco Bell 300, mid-Oct.

Motels

✔★★ **BEST WESTERN.** *Business US 220N (24112).* 540/632-5611; FAX 540/632-1168; res: 800/388-3934. 97 rms, 2 story, 20 suites. S $48; D $54; each addl $10; suites $49-$59; under 12 free; wkly, monthly rates. Crib free. Pet accepted. TV, cable (premium). Pool; wading pool. Complimentary coffee in rms. Restaurant 6 am-10 pm; Sat, Sun from 7 am. Rm serv. Bar 4 pm-midnight. Ck-out noon. Coin lndry. Meeting rms. Business servs avail. In-rm modem link. Valet serv. Sundries. Exercise equipt; weight machine, treadmill. Microwave avail. Cr cds: A, C, D, DS, ER, MC, V.

D 🐾 🏊 🍴 ⊠ 🐾 SC

✔★★ **DUTCH INN.** *(2360 Virginia Ave, Collinsville 24078) 1¼ mi N on US 220 Business.* 540/647-3721; FAX 540/647-4857; res: 800/800-3996. E-mail sgrodens@neocomm.net; web www.dutch-inn.com. 150 rms, 2 story. S $48-$60; D $56-$66; each addl $6; suites $88-$125; studio rms $55-$75; under 16 free; higher rates race wks. Crib free. Pet accepted. TV; cable (premium). Pool; whirlpool, poolside serv. Restaurant 6 am-10:30 pm. Rm serv. Bar 4 pm-midnight; Fri, Sat to 2 am. Ck-out noon. Meeting rms. Business servs avail. In-rm modem link. Valet serv. Sundries. 18-hole golf privileges. Exercise equipt; bicycle, treadmill, sauna. Many bathrm phones, refrigerators; microwaves avail. Cr cds: A, C, D, DS, MC, V.

D 🐾 🎿 🏊 🍴 ⊠ 🐾 SC

McLean (C-8)

(For accommodations see Arlington County, Fairfax, Falls Church, Tysons Corner; also see District of Columbia & Rockville, MD)

Pop 38,168 **Elev** 300 ft **Area code** 703 **E-mail** cvbfceda @mindspring.com **Web** www.cvb.co.fairfax.va.us/fceda
Information Fairfax County Convention & Visitors Bureau, 8300 Boone Blvd, Suite 450, Tysons Corner 22182; 703/790-3329 or 800/VISIT-VA.

What to See and Do

Claude Moore Colonial Farm at Turkey Run. Demonstration of 1770s low-income working farm; costumed interpreters work with crops and animals using 18th-century techniques. (Apr-mid-Dec, Wed-Sun weather permitting; closed Thanksgiving) 2 mi E on VA 193 (Georgetown Pike). Phone 703/442-7557. ¢

Colvin Run Mill Park. Tours of historical gristmill. Operating general store, miller's house exhibit, barn and grounds (free). (Mar-Dec, daily exc Tues; rest of yr, wknds; closed Jan 1, Thanksgiving, Dec 25) 3 mi W via VA 123, then 5 mi NW via VA 7, on Colvin Run Rd in Great Falls. Phone 703/759-2771. Tours ¢¢

Evans Farm. Approx 25 acres of farmland. Colonial atmosphere; 18th-century-style building with restaurant (see). Collection of early American cooking utensils; Robert E. Lee memorabilia. Country store, handcraft and doll shop, old mill. Farm animals for children to feed. (Daily; closed Dec 25) Chain Bridge Rd, on VA 123, 1 mi E of I-495 McLean-VA 123N exit 11. Phone 703/356-8000. **Free.**

Restaurants

✔★ **ANGKOR WAT.** *6703 Lowell Ave (22101), at Old Dominion Dr (VA 309), in shopping center.* 703/893-6077. Hrs: 11 am-2:30 pm, 5-9:30 pm; Fri, Sat 5-10 pm; Sun from 5 pm. Closed some major hols; also Sun July-Aug. Res accepted. Cambodian menu. Wine, beer. Semi-a la carte: lunch $5.25-$6.95, dinner $6.95-$9.95. Complete meals: dinner $12.99. Specializes in soup, char-broiled dishes. Cr cds: A, C, D, DS, MC, V.

★★ **CAFE BELLA.** *6710 Old Dominion Rd (22101).* 703/448-7787. Hrs: 11:30 am-2:30 pm, 6-10 pm; Fri to 10:30 pm; Sat 5-10:30 pm; Sun 5-9 pm. Closed some major hols. Res accepted; required Fri, Sat (dinner). French, Italian menu. Serv bar. A la carte entrees: lunch $6.95-$10.95, dinner $10.95-$18.95. Complete meals: lunch $9.95. Specializes in pasta, veal, seafood. Parking. Elegant dining; oil landscapes. Cr cds: A, C, D, DS, MC, V.

[D] [⌐]

★★ **CAFE OGGI.** *6671 Old Dominion Dr (22101).* 703/442-7360. Hrs: 11:30 am-2:30 pm, 5:30-10 pm; Sat, Sun from 5:30 pm. Closed major hols. Res accepted; required Fri, Sat dinner. Italian menu. Serv bar. A la carte entrees: lunch $6.95-$9.95, dinner $9.95-$19.95. Specializes in homemade pastas, fresh seafood, veal. Own baking, pasta. Cr cds: A, C, D, DS, MC, V.

[⌐]

★★ **CAFE TAJ.** *1379 Beverly Rd (22101), in Market Place Shopping Ctr.* 703/827-0444. Hrs: 11:30 am-2:30 pm, 5:30-10 pm; Fri, Sat to 10:30 pm. Closed July 4. Res accepted. Indian menu. Bar. Semi-a la carte: lunch $6.95-$8.95, dinner $7.95-$14.95. Lunch buffet (Mon-Fri) $8.99. Specialties: tandoori chicken tikka, prawns masala. Outdoor dining. Modern decor. Cr cds: A, D, DS, MC, V.

[D]

★ **CHARLEY'S PLACE.** *6930 Old Dominion Dr (22101), jct VA 123 & VA 309/738.* 703/893-1034. Hrs: 11 am-10 pm; Fri to 10:30 pm; Sat noon-10:30 pm; Sun 10:30 am-9 pm; early-bird dinner 4-6 pm; Sun brunch 10:30 am-2 pm. Closed Dec 25. Bar to midnight. Semi-a la carte: lunch $5.99-$8.29, dinner $5.99-$18.49. Child's meals. Specializes in chicken, beef, seafood. Outdoor dining. Parking. Fireplaces. Cr cds: A, C, D, DS, MC, V.

[⌐]

★★★ **DANTE RISTORANTE.** *(1148 Walker Rd, Great Falls 22066)* 703/759-3131. Hrs: 11:30 am-2:30 pm, 5:30-10:30 pm; Sat from 5:30 pm; Sun 4-9 pm. Closed some major hols. Res accepted; required Fri, Sat. Northern Italian menu. Bar. Wine list. A la carte entrees: lunch $9.25-$13.50, dinner $14.25-$22.95. Child's meals. Specialties: grilled Dover sole, grilled veal chops. Own pasta, bread. Parking. Patio dining. Converted country house. Cr cds: A, C, D, DS, MC, V.

[D]

★★ **EVANS FARM INN.** *1696 Chain Bridge Rd (22101).* 703/356-8000. Hrs: 11:30 am-9 pm; Sat to 10 pm; Sun from 11 am, brunch to 2 pm. Closed Dec 25. Res accepted; required Fri-Sun. Semi-a la carte: lunch $7.95-$10.95, dinner $14.95-$24.95. Buffet (Mon-Sat): lunch $11.95. Sun brunch $7.25-$12.95. Child's meals. Specializes in ham, fresh seafood, colonial-era cooking. Own baking. Salad bar. Parking. 18th century-style inn on 21 acres. Family-owned. Cr cds: A, C, D, DS, JCB, MC, V.

[D] [⌐]

★★★ **FALLS LANDING.** *(774 Walker Rd, Great Falls 22066) I-495 exit 13A, 6 mi W in Village Center.* 703/759-4650. Hrs: 11:30 am-2:30 pm, 5:30-10 pm; Fri to 10:30 pm; Sat 5:30-10:30 pm; Sun 4-9 pm; Sun brunch 11:30 am-2:30 pm. Closed Mon; also most major hols. Res accepted. Serv bar. Semi-a la carte: lunch $8.95-$12.95, dinner $16.95-$24.95. Sun brunch $8-$13.95. Child's meals. Specializes in nouvelle cuisine. Outdoor dining. 18th-century colonial-style decor; beamed ceiling, century-old pine paneling. Cr cds: A, C, D, DS, MC, V.

[D] [⌐]

★★ **KAZAN.** *6813 Redmond Dr (22101).* 703/734-1960. Hrs: 11 am-2:30 pm, 5-10 pm; Sat 5-10:30 pm. Closed Sun. Res accepted. Turkish menu. Serv bar. Semi-a la carte: lunch $6.95-$11.95, dinner $11.95-$18.95. Child's meals. Specializes in seafood, lamb. Middle Eastern decor. Cr cds: A, C, D, MC, V.

[D]

★★★ **L'AUBERGE CHEZ FRANCOIS.** *(332 Springvale Rd, Great Falls) 4 mi N of jct VA 7 & 674N.* 703/759-3800. Hrs: 5:30-9:30 pm; Sun 1:30-8 pm. Closed Mon; Jan 1, July 4, Dec 25. Res required. French menu. Serv bar. Wine cellar. Table d'hôte: dinner $32-$41. Prix fixe: dinner $23.50 (Tue-Thur, Sun). Specialties: salmon soufflé de l'Auberge; le sauté gourmandise de l'Auberge; la choucroute royale garnie comme en Alsace. Own baking, ice cream. Outdoor dining. Chef-owned. Jacket. Totally non-smoking. Cr cds: A, C, D, MC, V.

[D]

★★★ **LA BONNE AUBERGE.** *(9835 Georgetown Pike, Great Falls 22066) 6 mi W on VA 193.* 703/759-3877. Hrs: 6-10 pm; Sun 5-8:30 pm. Closed Jan 1, July 4. Res accepted; required Fri, Sat. French menu. Bar. A la carte entrees: dinner $14.95-20.95. Specializes in seafood, rack of lamb. Formal decor. Cr cds: A, C, D, MC, V.

[D] [⌐]

★★ **PULCINELLA.** *6852 Old Dominion Dr (22101).* 703/893-7777. Hrs: 11:30 am-10:45 pm; Sat, Sun from noon. Closed Thanksgiving, Dec 25. Italian menu. Bar. Semi-a la carte: lunch $4.25-$13.95, dinner $6.50-$16.50. Specializes in pasta, chicken. Italian decor. Cr cds: A, C, D, MC, V.

[⌐]

★★★ **RISTORANTE IL BORGO.** *1381-A Beverly Rd (22101), in Market Place Shopping Center.* 703/893-1400. Web www.menusonline.com/cities/wash_dc/desc/ilborgoristorante.shtml. Hrs: 11 am-midnight; Fri to 1 am; Sat 5 pm-1 am; Sun 4-10:30 pm. Closed most major hols. Res accepted; required Fri, Sat dinner. Italian menu. Bar. Wine list. Semi-a la carte: lunch $4.75-$9.50, dinner $9-$19.50. Specializes in veal, pasta, seafood. Own pastas, desserts. Cr cds: A, C, D, DS, MC, V.

[D] [⌐]

★★ **SERBIAN CROWN.** *(1141 Walker Rd, Great Falls 20066) 5 mi W on VA 7, then 1/2 mi N on VA 743.* 703/759-4150. Hrs: 5:30-10 pm; Thurs, Fri noon-2:30 pm; Sun 4-9 pm. Res accepted; required Fri-Sun. Russian, Serbian, French menu. Bar. Wine list. A la carte entrees: lunch $12.50-$19.50, dinner $17.50-$26. Prix fixe: dinner $32, $40. Specialty: kulebiaka. Extensive vodka selection. Piano bar Tue, Fri, Sat. Gypsy music Wed-Sun. Parking. Intimate atmosphere; antique Russian paintings. Enclosed, heated terrace dining. Family-owned. Cr cds: A, C, D, MC, V.

[D]

★★ **SITTING DUCK PUB.** *1696 Chain Bridge Rd (22102), lower level of Evans Farm Inn Restaurant.* 703/356-8000. Hrs: 11:30 am-2 pm, 5-11 pm; Sat 5 pm-midnight; Sun 11 am-2 pm. Closed Dec 25. Res accepted. Continental, Amer menu. Bar. Semi-a la carte: lunch $7.95-$10.95, dinner $14.95-$24.95. Sun brunch $7.25-$12.95. Specializes in beef, seafood. Pianist, guitarist Fri-Sun. Parking. Large stone fireplace. Colonial-era prints. Family-owned. Cr cds: A, C, D, DS, JCB, MC, V.

[⌐]

★★ **TACHIBANA.** *6715 Lowell Ave (22101).* 703/847-1771. Hrs: 11:30 am-2 pm, 5-10 pm; Fri to 10:30 pm; Sat 5-10:30 pm. Closed Sun; some major hols. Res accepted Mon-Thurs. Japanese menu. Serv bar. Semi-a la carte: lunch $6.50-$10, dinner $8.95-$20. Complete meals: dinner $16.50-$30. Specialties: sushi, sashimi, soft shell crab tempura (in season). Parking. Circular dining rm. Totally nonsmoking. Cr cds: A, C, D, DS, MC, V.

[D]

Monterey (D-6)

(See also Staunton, Warm Springs)

Pop 222 **Elev** 2,881 ft **Area code** 540 **Zip** 24465 **E-mail** highcc@cfw.com

Information Highland County Chamber of Commerce, PO Box 223; 540/468-2550.

Annual Event

Highland County Maple Festival. Tours of sugar camps producing maple syrup and maple sugar products. Juried craft show; food, entertainment. Phone 540/468-2550. Mar 14-15 & 21-22.

Inn

★ ★ **HIGHLAND INN.** *Main St, jct of US 220, 250. 540/468-2143; res: 888/466-4682.* E-mail highinn@cfw.com; web www.highlandinn.com/. 17 rms, 3 story. No A/C. S, D $55-$95; suites $79-$95. TV; cable (premium). Dining rm Wed, Fri, Sat 6-8 pm; Sun (brunch)11:30 am-2 pm. Bar Mon, Tues, Thurs 5-9 pm; Sat noon-9 pm. Ck-out 11 am, ck-in after 2 pm. Meeting rm. Business servs avail. Gift shop. Porches. Victorian building furnished with period antiques. Built 1904. Cr cds: A, DS, MC, V.

⊠ 🐾 SC

Montross (D-9)

Pop 359 **Elev** 149 ft **Area code** 804 **Zip** 22520

What to See and Do

Stratford Hall Plantation. Boyhood home of Richard Henry Lee and Francis Lightfoot Lee and birthplace of General Robert E. Lee. Center of restored, working plantation is monumental Georgian house, built circa 1735, famous for its uniquely grouped chimney stacks. Interiors span approximately 100-yr period and feature a federal-era parlor and neoclassical paneling in the Great Hall. Flanking dependencies include kitchen, plantation office and gardener's house. Boxwood garden; 18th- & 19th-century carriages; working mill; visitor center with museum, video presentations. Plantation luncheon (daily). (Daily; closed Jan 1, Thanksgiving, Dec 25) 6 mi N on VA 3 to Lerty, then E on VA 214. Phone 804/493-8038. ¢¢¢

Westmoreland State Park. Approx 1,300 acres on Potomac River. Sand beach, swimming pool, bathhouse; fishing, boating (ramp, rentals). Hiking trails. Picnicking, playground, concession. Camping, tent & trailer sites (May-Sept; dump station, electrical hookups), cabins (May-Sept). Visitor center, evening programs. Standard fees. 5 mi NW on VA 3, then N on VA 347. Phone 804/493-8821.

Mount Vernon (C-8)

(For accommodations see Alexandria, Fairfax, Springfield; also see District of Columbia)

Area code 703 **Zip** 22121

(16 mi S of Washington, DC, on Mt Vernon Memorial Hwy)

What to See and Do

Grist Mill Historical State Park. This mill was reconstructed in 1930 on original foundation of a mill George Washington operated on Dogue Run.

Visitor center, programs. (Memorial Day-Labor Day, daily) 3 mi W on VA 235. Phone 703/780-3383. ¢

⭐ **Mount Vernon.** George Washington brought his gracious and beautiful bride here in 1759 and, with characteristic and ingenious industry, began his plan to become the leading scientific farmer in America. He kept elaborate notes, conferred with many other farmers, tried crop rotation and other new experiments, added to the house, which became a stately Georgian-colonial mansion, and planned for the family that nature unhappily denied him. He and Mrs. Washington brought up her two children by a previous marriage and raised two of her grandchildren.

The nucleus of the existing house was built in approx 1735 by Augustine Washington, George's father. George acquired it in 1754, after the death of his half-brother, Lawrence.

Family, home and farm became the focal point of Washington's life. But he was a great patriot as well as a brilliant planner, and when he was called in 1775 to lead the armies of the country he loved, he did not hesitate. When he had won freedom for his fellow Americans he returned, determined to live as he wished. But 4 yrs later he was called to preside at the Constitutional Convention in Philadelphia and in 1789 became the new nation's first president. From Mar 1797, until his death on Dec 14, 1799, he lived again at Mount Vernon. He and Martha Washington are buried here.

Mount Vernon has been accurately restored to its appearance in the last year of Washington's life, from the paint colors on the walls to the actual arrangement of the furnishings, many of which are original. The estate has been owned and maintained by the Mount Vernon Ladies' Association since 1858 and was, in effect, the nation's first tourist attraction of historic interest. Gift shop, restaurant nearby (see RESTAURANT). (Daily) Phone 703/780-2000. ¢¢¢

Potomac Spirit. Offers round-trip, Potomac River cruises from Washington, DC, to Mount Vernon. The 5-hr excursion is sufficient for a complete tour of house, gardens and tomb (late Mar-early June, 1 trip daily; early June-late Aug, 2 trips daily). Phone 202/554-7447. Excursion with admission to mansion ¢¢¢¢¢

Woodlawn Plantation (1800-1805). In 1799, George Washington gave 2,000 acres of land as a wedding present to Eleanor Parke Custis, his foster daughter, who married his nephew, Major Lawrence Lewis. Dr. William Thornton, first architect of the US Capitol, then designed this mansion. The Lewises entertained such notables as Andrew Jackson, Henry Clay and the Marquis de Lafayette. The house was restored in the early 1900s and later became the residence of a US senator; 19th-century period rooms; many original furnishings. Formal gardens. (Mar-Dec, daily; rest of yr, wkends; closed Jan 1, Thanksgiving, Dec 25) National Trust for Historic Preservation property. 3 mi W of George Washington Pkwy on US 1. Phone 703/780-4000. ¢¢¢

Frank Lloyd Wright's Pope-Leighey House (1940). Erected in Falls Church in 1940, the house was disassembled (due to the construction of a new highway) and rebuilt at the present site in 1964. Built of cypress, brick and glass, the house is an example of Wright's "Usonian" structures, which he proposed as a prototype of affordable housing for Depression-era middle-income families; original Wright-designed furniture. (Mar-Dec, daily; rest of yr, wkends only; closed Thanksgiving, Dec 25) National Trust for Historic Preservation property. Combination ticket for both houses avail. Phone 703/780-4000. ¢¢¢

Restaurant

★ ★ **MOUNT VERNON INN.** *On grounds of Mount Vernon, S end of George Washington Pkwy. 703/780-0011.* Hrs: 11 am-3:30 pm, 5-9 pm; Sun to 4 pm. Res accepted. Bar. Semi-a la carte: lunch $5.25-$8.50, dinner $12-$23.75. Child's meals. Specializes in mesquite-grilled seafood, game dishes. Own desserts. Waiters in colonial costume. Hand-painted murals of colonial scenes. Cr cds: A, DS, MC, V.

 D

Natural Bridge (E-6)

(See also Lexington)

Founded 1774 **Pop** 200 (est) **Elev** 1,078 ft **Area code** 540 **Zip** 24578 **E-mail** natbrg@aol.com **Web** www.naturalbridgeva.com/nbva/
Information Natural Bridge of Virginia, US 11 & VA 130; PO Box 57, 540/291-2121 or 800/533-1410.

Native Americans worshiped at the stone bridge that nature formed across a deep gorge; town and county were both named after it. The limestone arch, 215 feet high, 90 feet long and 150 feet wide in some places, attracted the interest of Thomas Jefferson, who purchased the bridge and 157 surrounding acres from King George III for 20 shillings, about $2.49, in 1774. Fully appreciative of this natural wonder, Jefferson built a cabin for visitors and installed caretakers. His guest book reads like a colonial "Who's Who." Surveyed by George Washington, and painted by many famous artists, the bridge easily accommodates US Highway 11. The Glenwood Ranger District of the George Washington and Jefferson National Forests has its office in Natural Bridge.

What to See and Do

Cave Mountain Lake Recreation Area. Swimming. Picnicking. Camping (fee). (May-Oct) 7 mi S via VA 130, right on VA 759, then right on Forest Service Rd 781 in George Washington and Jefferson National Forests. Phone 540/291-2189 or 540/265-6054. ¢

Natural Bridge. Self-guided tours (1 hr). (Daily) Jct US 11 & VA 130; I-81, exit 175 or 180. Phone 540/291-2121 or 800/533-1410. ¢¢¢ Ticket includes entrance to

Drama of Creation. Musical presentation, viewed from beneath Natural Bridge, includes light show cast under and across arch. (Nightly) Combination tickets can also include

Caverns of Natural Bridge. More than 300 ft below ground on three levels; streams, hanging gardens of formations, flowstone cascade, totem pole, colossal dome and more. One-mi guided tour (1 hr). (Mar-Nov, daily) ¢¢¢

Natural Bridge Wax Museum. Wax figures depicting local history; self-guided factory tours. US 11 & VA 130. (Daily). ¢¢¢

Natural Bridge Zoo. State's largest and most complete zoo with over 400 reptiles, birds and mammals. Petting area; Safari Shop; picnic grounds. (Mar-Nov, daily) I-81 between exits 175 & 180. Phone 540/291-2420. ¢¢¢

Motel

★ **WATTSTULL.** *(Rte 1, Box 21, Buchanan 24066) 8 mi S on US 11; I-81 exit 168.* 540/254-1551. 26 rms. S, D $40-$48; each addl $3. Crib $4. Pet accepted. TV. Pool; wading pool. Restaurant 6 am-10 pm. Ck-out 11 am. Panoramic view of Shenandoah Valley. Cr cds: MC, V.

Hotel

✔★ ★ **NATURAL BRIDGE INN & CONFERENCE CENTER.** *I-81 exits 175 & 180, at jct US 11, VA 130.* 540/291-2121; FAX 540/291-1551; res: 800/533-1410. E-mail natbrg@aol.com; web www.naturalbridgeva .com/nbva. 180 rms in hotel & inn. S, D $59-$139; under 18 free. Crib free. TV; cable. Indoor pool. Restaurant 7 am-9:30 pm. Bar 4-10 pm. Ck-out noon. Meeting rms. Business servs avail. Gift shop. Tennis. Miniature golf. Game rm. Cr cds: A, D, DS, MC, V.

New Market (C-7)

(See also Basye, Harrisonburg, Luray)

Settled 1761 **Pop** 1,435 **Elev** 1,060 ft **Area code** 540 **Zip** 22844 **E-mail** amy@svta.org **Web** www.svta.org
Information Shenandoah Valley Travel Association, PO Box 1040; 540/740-3132.

New Market, situated in the Shenandoah Valley, gained its niche in Virginia history on May 15, 1864, when, in desperation, Confederate General Breckinridge ordered the cadets from Lexington's Virginia Military Institute to join the battle against the forces of General Franz Sigel. The oldest was 20, but they entered the fray fearlessly, taking prisoners and capturing a battery. Their heroism inspired the Confederate defeat of Sigel's seasoned troops.

What to See and Do

Bedrooms of America. Authentic furnishings from William & Mary through Art Deco periods. Antique dolls. Gift shop. (Daily; closed Dec 25) 9386 Congress St, I-81 exit 264. Phone 540/740-3512. ¢

Endless Caverns. Lighted display of unusual rock formations; stalagmites and stalactites, columns, shields, flowstone and limestone pendants, presented in natural color. Temperature 55°F summer & winter. Camping. Guided tours (75 min). (Daily; closed Dec 25) Via I-81, exit 257 or 264, then approx 3 mi on US 11 to entrance. Phone 540/896-CAVE. ¢¢¢

New Market Battlefield State Historical Park. Site of Civil War Battle of New Market (May 15, 1864), in which 257 VMI cadets played a decisive role. Original Bushong farmhouse and outbuildings restored, period furnishings. Hall of Valor; exhibits; films. Scenic overlooks, walking tour. (Daily; closed Jan 1, Thanksgiving, Dec 25) 1 mi N of I-81 exit 264. Phone 540/740-3101. ¢¢ Also here is

New Market Battlefield Military Museum. Located on actual site of Battle of New Market, the museum houses a private collection of more than 2,000 military artifacts and genuine, personal artifacts of the American soldier from 1776 to the present. Includes uniforms, weapons, battlefield diaries, medals, mementos; film (30 min). Bookshop has more than 500 titles, some antique. Union & Confederate troop position markers are on museum grounds. (Mid-Mar-Nov, daily) Rte 305 (Collins Dr), 1/4 mi N of I-81 exit 264. Phone 540/740-8065. ¢¢

Shenandoah Caverns. Elevator lowers visitors 220 ft to large subterranean rooms, fascinating rock formations; snack bar, picnic areas. Interior a constant 56°F. (Daily; closed Dec 25) 4 mi N, off I-81 exit 269. Phone 540/477-3115. ¢¢¢

Motels

✔★ **BUDGET INN.** *2192 Old Valley Pike, 1 mi N on US 11; I-81 exit 264.* 540/740-3105; FAX 540/740-3108; res: 800/296-6835. 14 rms. Mid-Apr-mid-Nov: S $24-$34; D $28-$44; each addl $3; under 12 free; higher rates special events; lower rates rest of yr. Crib $3. TV; cable. Playground. Complimentary coffee in rms. Restaurant nearby. Ck-out 11 am. Business servs avail. Refrigerators. Picnic tables. Cr cds: A, C, D, DS, MC, V.

★ ★ **QUALITY INN SHENANDOAH VALLEY.** *Old Cross Rd, on VA 211 at I-81 exit 264.* 540/740-3141; FAX 540/740-3250. 101 rms, 2 story. May-Oct: S $51-$58; D $59-$68; each addl $6; lower rates rest of yr. Crib free. TV; cable (premium); VCR avail (movies). Pool; sauna. Playground. Restaurant 6:30 am-9 pm. Rm serv. Ck-out noon. Coin lndry. Meeting rms. Business servs avail. In-rm modem link. Gift shops. Game rm. Miniature golf. Tennis nearby. Cr cds: A, C, D, DS, ER, MC, V.

✔★ ★ **SHENVALEE.** *9660 Fairway Dr, I-81 exit 264, at jct US 11.* 540/740-3181; FAX 540/740-8931. 42 rms, 1-2 story. Apr-early Nov: S

$40-$54; D $48-$64; each addl $10; under 13 free; golf plan; lower rates rest of yr. Crib free. TV; cable. Pool; wading pool. Restaurant 6:15 am-9 pm; Sun to 8 pm. Bar 4:30 pm-midnight; wkends to 2 am. Ck-out 1 pm. Meeting rms. Business servs avail. Tennis. 36-hole golf privileges, greens fee $18-$21, putting green, driving range. Refrigerators. Balconies. Picnic tables. On 200 acres. Cr cds: A, C, D, MC, V.

D ⊁ ⛵ ⩳ 🔥 ⊠

Newport News (F-9)

(See also Hampton, Norfolk, Portsmouth, Virginia Beach, Yorktown)

Settled 1619 **Pop** 170,045 **Elev** 25 ft **Area code** 757 **Web** www .newport-news.va.us

Information Visitor Information Center, 13560 Jefferson Ave, 23603; 757/886-7777 or 888/4-WE-R-FUN.

One of the three cities (also see NORFOLK and PORTSMOUTH) that make up the Port of Hampton Roads, Newport News has the world's largest shipbuilding company, Newport News Shipbuilding Company. Hampton Roads, 14 miles long and 40 feet deep, formed by the James, York, Elizabeth and Nansemond rivers as they pass into Chesapeake Bay, is one of the world's finest natural harbors. The largest ships are accommodated at Newport News docks; huge tonnages of coal, ore, tobacco and grain are shipped from the port annually. During the two world wars it was a vitally important point of embarkation and supply. The area still has many important defense establishments.

Newport News is located on the historic Virginia Peninsula, between Williamsburg and Virginia Beach. The peninsula contains Hampton, Yorktown, Jamestown and Williamsburg. Some of the earliest landings in this country were here. The name of the town is said to derive from the good "news" of the arrival of Captain Christopher Newport, who brought supplies and additional colonists to the settlement at Jamestown.

What to See and Do

Fort Eustis. Headquarters of US Army Transportation Center. Self-guided auto tour avail; brochures at Public Affairs Office (Bldg 213). NW end of city on Mulberry Island, exit 250A off I-64. Phone 757/878-4920. **Free.** On grounds is

US Army Transportation Museum. Depicts development of army transportation from 1776 to the present; "flying saucer," amphibious vehicles, trucks, helicopters, mementos. (Daily exc Mon; closed major hols) Phone 757/878-1182. **Free.**

Harbor Cruises. Narrated sightseeing cruises (2 hrs); evening dinner cruises (4 hrs); Intracoastal Waterway cruises (8 hrs). (Apr-Oct) Located midway between Williamsburg & Virginia Beach, exit 7 off I-664. For schedule and information phone 757/245-1533 or 800/362-3046. ¢¢¢-¢¢¢¢

Historic Hilton Village. Listed on the National Register of Historic Places, this village was built between 1918-1920 to provide wartime housing for workers at Newport News Shipbuilding. Architecturally significant neighborhood features 500 English cottage-style homes and antique and specialty shops. Exit 263A off I-64, at Warwick Blvd & Main St. Phone 757/886-7777. **Free.**

Newport News Park. Facilities of this 8,330-acre park include freshwater fishing; canoes, paddleboats, boat rentals; history, nature trails; bicycle paths (bicycle rentals); archery; arboretum; interpretive center; picnicking; Civil War earthworks; 188 campsites. (All yr) Some fees. Jct VA 105, 143, exit 250B off I-64. Phone 757/888-3333 or 800/203-8322. **Free;** Camping ¢¢¢-¢¢¢¢

Peninsula Fine Arts Center. Changing bi-monthly exhibits ranging from national traveling exhibitions to regional artists; classes, workshops and special events. Children's area; museum shop. (Daily exc Mon; closed major hols) 101 Museum Dr, exit 258A off I-64. Phone 757/596-8175. **Free.**

The Mariners' Museum. Exhibits and displays represent international nautical history; ship models, figureheads, scrimshaw, paintings, decorative arts and small craft. Age of Exploration Gallery chronicles advancements in shipbuilding, ocean navigation and cartography that led to early transoceanic exploration. The Chesapeake Bay Gallery exhibits Native American artifacts, workboats, racing shells, an interactive computer game, a working steam engine, and hundreds of artifacts and photos that tell the story of this great body of water. The Crabtree Collection of Miniature Ships showcases 16 detailed miniatures that illustrate the evolution of the sailing ship. Small craft gallery showcases vessels from five continents. A short film, *Mariner,* introduces the visitor to maritime activities from around the world. Historical interpreters; research library; museum shop. A 550-acre park on the James River features the 5-mi Noland Trail, with 14 pedestrian bridges; picnic area. Special events include Community Appreciation Day (June) and Yuletide at The Mariners' (Dec). Guided tours. (Daily; closed Thanksgiving, Dec 25) Jct US 60 & J. Clyde Morris Blvd; 2½ mi off I-64 exit 258A. Phone 757/596-2222. ¢¢¢

Virginia Living Museum. Exhibits on natural science; wildlife, all native to Virginia, living in natural habitats; indoor & outdoor aviaries; aquariums; planetarium with daily shows; observatory; children's hands-on Discovery Center. (Daily; closed Jan 1, Thanksgiving, Dec 24, 25) 524 J. Clyde Morris Blvd, I-64 to exit 258A. Phone 757/595-1900. ¢¢¢

Virginia War Museum. More than 60,000 artifacts, including weapons, uniforms, vehicles, posters, insignia and accoutrements relating to every major US military involvement from the Revolution to the Vietnam War. Military history library and film collection. Civil War tours avail. (Mon-Sat, also Sun afternoons; closed Jan 1, Thanksgiving, Dec 25). 9285 Warwick Blvd in Huntington Park, on US 60, exit 263A off I-64. Phone 757/247-8523. ¢

Motels

★ ★ **COMFORT INN.** *12330 Jefferson Ave (23602), I-64 exit 255A.* 757/249-0200; FAX 757/249-4736. 124 rms, 3 story. S $64; D $71; each addl $7; under 18 free. Crib free. Pet accepted. TV; cable (premium). Pool. Complimentary continental bkfst. Complimentary coffee in rms. Restaurant adj 11 am-midnight. Ck-out noon. Coin Indry. Meeting rms. Business servs avail. In-rm modem link. Free airport transportation. Health club privileges. Some refrigerators. Cr cds: A, C, D, DS, ER, JCB, MC, V.

D ⚓ ⩳ ⊁ 🐾 SC

↩★ ★ **DAYS INN.** *14747 Warwick Blvd (23602).* 757/874-0201. 117 rms, 2 story. June-Sept: S $42-$59; D $48-$66; each addl $5; kit. units $48-$65; under 18 free; lower rates rest of yr. Pet accepted, some restrictions; $5. TV; cable (premium). Pool. Playground. Complimentary continental bkfst. Restaurant 6 am-11 pm. Ck-out 11 am. Coin Indry. Business servs avail. Free airport transportation. Refrigerators avail. Picnic tables, grills. Cr cds: A, C, D, DS, MC, V.

⚓ ⩳ ⊁ 🐾 SC

Motor Hotel

★ ★ **HAMPTON INN AND SUITES.** *12251 Jefferson Ave (23602), near Intl Airport.* 757/249-0001; FAX 757/249-3911. 120 rms, 4 story, 30 suites. Memorial Day-Labor Day: S, D $74-$79; suites $99; under 18 free; higher rates special events; lower rates rest of yr. Crib free. TV; cable (premium). Complimentary continental bkfst. Restaurant opp open 24 hrs. Ck-out noon. Meeting rms. Business center. In-rm modem link. Bellhops. Sundries. Free airport transportation. Pool. Some fireplaces; refrigerator, microwave in suites. Picnic tables, grills. Cr cds: A, DS, MC, V.

D ⩳ ✈ ⊁ 🐾 SC ⊁

Hotel

★ ★ ★ **OMNI.** *1000 Omni Blvd (23606).* 757/873-6664; FAX 757/873-1732. 183 rms, 9 story. S, D $89; each addl $10; under 17 free. Crib avail. TV; cable (premium), VCR avail. Coffee in rms. Indoor pool; whirlpool, poolside serv. Restaurant 6:30 am-11 pm. Bar 11-2 am; piano bar Mon-Sat. Ck-out noon. Meeting rms. Business center. In-rm modem link. Gift shop. Exercise equipt; weights, bicycles, sauna. Cr cds: A, C, D, DS, JCB, MC, V.

Restaurants

★ ★ **BON APPÉTITE.** *11710 Jefferson Ave (23606), at Oyster Point.* 757/873-0644. Hrs: 11 am-2:30 pm, 5-10 pm; Mon to 9 pm; Sat from 5 pm. Closed Sun; major hols. Res accepted. French, Vietnamese menu. Bar. A la carte entrees: lunch $5.25-$6.75, dinner $9.95-$18.95. Specialties: panache de mer, veal Oscar, scallops in oyster sauce. Mediterranean cafe atmosphere. Cr cds: A, DS, MC, V.

✔★ ★ **DAS WALDCAFE.** *12529 Warwick Blvd (23606).* 757/930-1781. Hrs: 11:30 am-2 pm, 5-10 pm; Sat from 4 pm; Sun 11:30 am-9 pm. Closed Mon; hols. Res accepted. German menu. Bar. Semi-a la carte: lunch, dinner $3.75-$13.50. Specialties: schnitzel, rouladen, hazelnut cake. Guest rms avail. Cr cds: A, C, D, MC, V.

★ ★ **HERMAN'S HARBOR HOUSE.** *663 Deep Creek Rd (23606).* 757/930-1000. Hrs: 11:30 am-2:30 pm, 5-10 pm; Sat from 5 pm; Sun brunch 11:30 am-3 pm. Closed Dec 25. Res accepted. Bar. Semi-a la carte: lunch $2.75-$9.95, dinner $8.95-$18.95. Specializes in local seafood, crab cakes, steak. Nautical decor. Cr cds: A, DS, MC, V.

★ ★ **PORT ARTHUR CHINESE RESTAURANT.** *11137 Warwick Blvd (23601).* 757/599-6474. Hrs: 11:30 am-10 pm; Fri, Sat to 10:30 pm; Sun noon-10 pm; Sun buffet noon-3 pm, 5:30-9 pm. Closed Thanksgiving, Dec 25. Res accepted. Chinese, Amer menu. Bar. Semi-a la carte: lunch $3.95-$5.95, dinner $5.95-$14.95. Complete meals: dinner $17.50-$63. Wkend buffet: dinner $7.95. Child's meals. Specialties: Phoenix nest, shrimp kew, Peking duck. Family-owned. Cr cds: A, C, D, DS, MC, V.

Norfolk (F-9)

Founded 1682 **Pop** 261,229 **Elev** 12 ft **Area code** 757 **Web** www .norfolk.va.us

Information Norfolk on the Virginia Waterfront, 232 E Main St, 23510; 757/664-6620 or 800/368-3097.

Suburbs Chesapeake, Hampton, Newport News, Portsmouth, Virginia Beach. (See individual alphabetical listings.)

This great seaport is part of the Port of Hampton Roads. It is a bustling trade center and has many historic and resort areas nearby to attract the tourist. Harbor tours depart from Norfolk's downtown waterfront.

In 1682, the General Assembly bought from Nicholas Wise, a pioneer settler, 50 acres on the Elizabeth River for "ten thousand pounds of tobacco and caske." By 1736 the town that developed was the largest in Virginia. During the Revolutionary War, Norfolk was shelled by the British and later burned by the colonists to prevent a British takeover. The battle between the *Merrimac* and the *Monitor* in Hampton Roads in March 1862 was followed by the fall of the city to Union forces in May of that year. In 1883, the shipment of the first coal to the port by the Norfolk and Western Railway began a new era of prosperity for the city.

Norfolk and its sister city, Portsmouth, are connected by bridge tunnels and a pedestrian ferry. Norfolk houses the largest naval facility in the world, and it is the oldest naval port in the US. It is also headquarters for the US Navy's Atlantic Fleet. Norfolk has shipbuilding and ship repair companies, consumer and industrial equipment manufacturers and food-processing plants. The city ships coal, tobacco, grain, seafood and vegetables.

Old Dominion University (1930), Virginia Wesleyan College (1967) Norfolk State University (1935) and Eastern Virginia Medical School (1973) are located here. This area is also the headquarters for year-round resort activities. Within a 50-mile radius are ocean, bay, river and marsh fishing and hunting; nearby there are 25 miles of good beaches. The 17.6-mile-long Chesapeake Bay Bridge-Tunnel, between Norfolk and the Delmarva Peninsula, opened in 1964; toll for passenger cars is $10, including passengers.

Transportation

Norfolk Intl Airport: Information 757/857-3351; lost and found 757/857-3344; weather 757/666-1212.

Car Rental Agencies: See IMPORTANT TOLL-FREE NUMBERS.

Public Transportation: Buses (Tidewater Regional Transit), phone 757/640-6300.

Rail Passenger Service: Amtrak 800/872-7245.

What to See and Do

Cape Henry Memorial (see) **and Lighthouse.** 10 mi E on US 60.

General Douglas MacArthur Memorial. Restored former city hall (1847) where MacArthur is buried. Nine galleries contain memorabilia of his life and military career. There are three other buildings on MacArthur Sq: a theater where a film biography is shown, a gift shop and the library/archives. (Daily; closed Jan 1, Thanksgiving, Dec 25) City Hall Ave & Bank St. Phone 757/441-2965. **Free.**

Hermitage Foundation Museum. Guided tours of fine arts museum in Tudor-style mansion. Collections of tapestries, Chinese bronzes and jade, ancient glass. (Daily; closed Jan 1, Thanksgiving, Dec 25) 7637 North Shore Rd. Phone 757/423-2052. **¢¢**

Hunter House Victorian Museum. Built in 1894 and rich in architectural details, the house contains the Hunter family's collection of Victorian furnishings and decorative pieces, including a Renaissance-revival bedchamber suite, a nursery with children's playthings, an inglenook and stained-glass windows; lavish period reproduction floor and wall coverings, lighting fixtures and drapery. Also exhibited is a collection of early-20th-century medical memorabilia. Tours begin every 30 min. (Apr-Dec, Wed-Sat, also Sun afternoons; closed Jan 1, Thanksgiving, Dec 25). 240 W Freemason St. Phone 757/623-9814. **¢¢**

Moses Myers House (1792). Excellent example of Georgian architecture; many pieces of original furniture, silver and china. (Apr-Dec, daily exc Mon; rest of yr, Tues-Sat; closed Jan 1, July 4, Thanksgiving, Dec 25) 331 Bank St. Phone 757/664-6283. **¢¢**

Nauticus, the National Maritime Center. Interprets aspects from marine biology and ecology to exploration, trade and shipbuilding. Interactive computer exhibits allow visitors to navigate a simulated ocean voyage, design a model ship, pilot a virtual reality submarine and view actual researchers at work in two working marine laboratories. Active US Navy ships and scientific research vessels will periodically moor at Nauticus and be open to visitors. Also 350-seat, 70mm wide-screen theater; shark-petting tank. (May-Sept, daily; rest of yr, daily exc Mon; closed Jan 1, Thanksgiving, Dec 25). One Waterside Dr. Phone 757/664-1000. **¢¢¢** Also here is

Hampton Roads Naval Museum. Interprets the extensive naval history of the Hampton Roads area; includes detailed ship models, period photographs, archaeological artifacts and a superior collection of naval prints and artwork. (Daily; closed Jan 1, Thanksgiving, Dec 25) Phone 757/444-8971. **Free.**

Norfolk Botanical Garden. Azaleas, camellias, rhododendrons, roses (May-Oct), dogwoods and hollies on 155 acres. Japanese, Colonial, Perennial and Rose Gardens; Flowering Arboretum; Hill of Nations; Fragrance Garden for the visually impaired; picnicking, restaurant and gift shop; Tropical Pavilion. Flowering displays are best from early Apr-Oct. Gardens (daily; closed special events). Information center (daily; closed Jan 1, Dec 25). Narrated boat ride (30 min) and train tours (mid-Mar-Labor Day, daily; through Oct wkends, trains only). On Azalea Garden Rd, adj Norfolk Intl Airport. Phone 757/640-6879. **¢¢**

Norfolk Naval Base and Norfolk Naval Air Station. The largest naval installation in the world. Tours of designated ships are avail (Sat & Sun); ship visitors should check in at the Naval Base Pass Office on Hampton Blvd, opp Gate 5. Naval base tours are also offered. Tour buses from Tour & Information Office, 9079 Hampton Blvd (Apr-Oct, daily; also, bus tours from downtown at the Waterside). Hampton Blvd & I-564. Phone 757/444-7955 or 757/640-6300. Bus ¢¢

Sightseeing tours.

Carrie B Harbor Tours. Replica of 19th-century riverboat takes narrated 90-min tour of naval shipyard and inner harbor (Apr-Oct, daily); narrated 2¹/₂-hr tour of naval base (Apr-Oct, daily); 2¹/₂-hr sunset cruise to Hampton Roads and naval base (June-Labor Day, daily). Departs from the Waterside. Phone 757/393-4735. (Also see PORTSMOUTH) ¢¢¢¢

American Rover. This 135-ft, 3-masted topsail passenger schooner cruises the "smooth waters" of Hampton Roads historical harbor; spacious sun decks; below-deck lounges; concessions. Tour passes historic forts, merchant and US Navy ships. Some tours pass the naval base (inquire for tour schedule). (Apr-mid-Oct, 2- and 3-hr tours daily) Waterside Marina, Waterside Dr exit off I-264. For information, reservations phone 757/627-SAIL. ¢¢¢¢-¢¢¢¢¢

Spirit of Norfolk. Harbor cruise aboard 600-passenger cruise ship. Captain's narration highlights the harbor's famous landmarks, including Waterside Festival Marketplace, Portsmouth Naval Hospital, Old Fort Norfolk, Blackbeard's hiding place, Norfolk Naval Base and downtown area's dynamic skyline. Luncheon Cruise (daily exc Mon); Evening Dinner Cruise (daily exc Mon); Moonlight Party Cruise (Fri-Sat, in season). Departs from the Waterside. For schedule, reservations phone 757/627-7771. ¢¢¢¢

St Paul's Episcopal Church (1739). Only building to survive burning of Norfolk in 1776. (Tues-Fri, also by appt) 201 St Paul's Blvd, at City Hall Ave. Phone 757/627-4353. **Donation.**

The Chrysler Museum of Art. Art treasures representing nearly every important culture, civilization and historical period of the past 4,000 yrs. Photography gallery; fine collection of Tiffany decorative arts and glass, including the 8,000-piece Chrysler Institute of Glass. (Daily exc Mon; closed some major hols) 245 W Olney Rd, at Mowbray Arch. Phone 757/664-6200. ¢¢

The Waterside Festival Marketplace. A waterfront pavilion creating a lively marketplace with more than 120 shops, restaurants. (Daily; closed Thanksgiving, Dec 25) 333 Waterside Dr. Bordering the Waterside are the city's marina and dock areas, where harbor tour vessels take on passengers. A brick promenade, skirting the marina, connects the Waterside to

Town Point Park. Home to Norfolk Festevents, the park hosts more than 100 free outdoor concerts, parties, dances, movies and festivals each year. Phone 757/441-2345.

Virginia Zoological Park. A combination zoo, park and conservatory. Playground, tennis courts, basketball courts; picnic area, concession. (daily; closed Jan 1, Dec 25). 3500 Granby St. Phone 757/441-2706 (recording) or 757/441-5227. ¢

Willoughby-Baylor House (1794). Restored town house with period furnishings; herb and flower garden adj. (By appt) inquire at Moses Myers House) 601 E Freemason St. Phone 757/664-6283. ¢¢

Annual Events

International Azalea Festival. Downtown & Norfolk Botanical Garden. To honor NATO. Parade, coronation ceremony, 2-day air show (held at Norfolk Naval Air Station), events, concerts, fair, ball, entertainment. Mid-Apr.

Virginia Waterfront International Arts Festival. 18 days of classical & contemporary music, dance, visual arts and theater performances. Phone 757/664-6492. Late Apr-mid-May.

Harborfest. Town Point Park, downtown waterfront on Wayside Dr. Sailboat and speedboat races, tall ships, ship tours, waterskiing, military demonstrations, entertainment, children's activities, fireworks, seafood. 1st full wkend June.

Virginia Children's Festival. Town Point Park. More than 200 educational, creative and interactive activities; entertainment. Early Oct.

Seasonal Events

Virginia Symphony. Chrysler Hall and other select locations. Five series. Phone 757/623-2310 (tickets). Sept-May.

Virginia Opera. Harrison Opera House & other select locations. Statewide opera company; traditional and contemporary works. Features young American artists. Phone 757/623-1223. Oct-Apr.

Virginia Stage Company, Wells Theater. Professional theater performed by nationally known artists. Phone 757/627-1234. Oct-May.

Motels

★★ **BEST WESTERN CENTER INN.** 235 N Military Hwy (23502), jct I-264 & US 13. 757/461-6600; FAX 757/466-9093. 152 rms, 2 story. Memorial Day-Labor Day: S, D $68-$77; each addl $7; suites $125-$135; under 16 free; higher rates: hols (3-day min), Jazz Festival; lower rates rest of yr. Crib free. TV; cable (premium), VCR avail (movies). 2 pools, 1 indoor; whirlpool. Complimentary coffee in rms. Restaurant 11:30 am-2 pm, 5-10 pm; wkend hrs vary. Rm serv. Bar. Ck-out noon. Coin lndry. Meeting rms. Business servs avail. In-rm modem link. Free airport transportation. Exercise equipt; weight machine, treadmill, sauna. Many refrigerators; microwaves avail. Picnic tables. Near airport. Cr cds: A, C, D, MC, V.

D ⊷ ✕ ⊼ ≈ ⊠ SC

★ **COMFORT INN.** 8051 Hampton Blvd (23505), adj naval base. 757/451-0000; FAX 757/451-8394. 120 rms, 2 story. S, D $59-$80; each addl $5; under 18 free. Crib free. TV; cable (premium). Indoor pool; whirlpool. Complimentary continental bkfst. Restaurant nearby. Ck-out 11 am. Coin lndry. Business servs avail. In-rm modem link. Refrigerators; some microwaves. Cr cds: A, D, DS, JCB, MC, V.

D ⊷ ≈ ⊠ SC

🛏★ **ECONO LODGE-OCEANVIEW BEACH.** 9601 4th View St (23503). 757/480-9611; FAX 757/480-1307. 71 units, 3 story, 22 kits. Mid-May-Labor Day: S $54.95; D $64.95; each addl $5; kit. units $69.95; under 18 free; wkly rates; higher rates: some hols, special events; lower rates rest of yr. Pet accepted, some restrictions; $50 deposit. TV; cable (premium), VCR avail (movies). Complimentary continental bkfst. Restaurant nearby. Ck-out 11 am. Business servs avail. Coin lndry. Refrigerators. Ocean; fishing pier. Beach adj. Cr cds: A, C, D, DS, JCB, MC, V.

D ⊷ ⊼ ≈ ⊠ SC

★★ **HAMPTON INN-AIRPORT.** 1450 N Military Hwy (23502). 757/466-7474; FAX 757/466-0117. 130 units, 2 story. Late May-early Sept: S $55; D $65; under 18 free; lower rates rest of yr. Crib free. TV; cable (premium). Pool. Restaurant opp 7 am-11 pm. Ck-out noon. Business servs avail. In-rm modem link. Valet serv. Free airport transportation. Health club privileges. Cr cds: A, C, D, DS, MC, V.

D ⊷ ≈ ⊠ SC

★ **HOLIDAY SANDS.** 1330 E Ocean View Ave (23503). 757/583-2621; FAX 757/587-7540; res: 800/525-5156. 101 units, 2-5 story, 76 kits. Memorial Day-Labor Day: S, D $50-$95; each addl $5; suites $85-$105; kit. units $70-$95; under 12 free; lower rates rest of yr. Crib free. TV; cable (premium). Pool. Complimentary continental bkfst. Restaurant nearby. Ck-out 11 am. Business servs avail. Coin lndry. Free airport transportation. Exercise equipt; treadmill, stair machine. Refrigerators, microwaves. Private patios, balconies. On beach. Cr cds: A, C, D, MC, V.

D ⊷ ≈ ⊼ ≈ ⊠ SC

★ **OLD DOMINION INN.** 4111 Hampton Blvd (23508). 757/440-5100; FAX 757/423-5238; res: 800/653-9030. 60 rms, 3 story. S, D $63; each addl $5; suites $88-$130; under 12 free; higher rates special events. Crib $5. TV. Complimentary continental bkfst. Restaurant nearby.

Ck-out 11 am. Meeting rms. Business servs avail. Refrigerators, microwaves avail. Cr cds: A, D, DS, MC, V.

★ ★ **QUALITY INN LAKE WRIGHT.** *6280 Northampton Blvd (23502). 757/461-6251; FAX 757/461-5925.* 304 rms, 2 story. May-Sept: S, D $74; each addl $7; suites $125; under 18 free; lower rates rest of yr. Crib $7. Pet accepted; $25. TV; cable (premium). Pool. Complimentary coffee in rms. Restaurant 6:30 am-2 pm, 5-10 pm. Bar 11:30 am-midnight. Ck-out 11 am. Meeting rms. Business servs avail. Barber, beauty shop. Coin lndry. Free airport transportation. Some refrigerators. Cr cds: A, C, D, DS, ER, MC, V.

✔★ **SUPER 8.** *7940 Shore Dr (23518). 757/588-7888.* 74 units, 3 story, 10 kit. units. June-Labor Day: S, D $46.95-$66; suites, kit. units $72.88-$89.47; higher rates: July 4, Labor Day; lower rates rest of yr. Crib free. TV; cable (premium). Complimentary continental bkfst. Restaurant nearby. Ck-out 11 am. Business servs avail. Some refrigerators. Cr cds: A, D, DS, MC, V.

Hotels

★ ★ **DOUBLETREE CLUB.** *880 N Military Hwy (23502), Military Circle Mall. 757/461-9192; FAX 757/461-8290.* 208 rms, 14 story. S $64-$115; D $74-$123; each addl $10; suites $175; under 18 free; wkend rates. Crib free. TV, cable (premium). Pool. Restaurant 6:30 am-10:30 pm. Bar 11-1 am. Ck-out noon. Meeting rms. Business center. Free airport transportation. Microwaves avail. Private balconies. Shopping mall adj. Cr cds: A, C, D, DS, ER, JCB, MC, V.

★ ★ ★ **HILTON-NORFOLK AIRPORT.** *1500 N Military Hwy (23502), at Northampton Blvd, near Intl Airport. 757/466-8000.* 250 rms, 6 story. S $89-$139; D $99-$149; each addl $15; suites $170-$360; under 18 free; wkly rates; some wkend rates. Crib free. TV; cable (premium). Pool; whirlpool, poolside serv. Coffee in rms. Restaurant 6:30 am-midnight. Bars 4 pm-1 am; entertainment. Ck-out 1 pm. Convention facilities. Business servs avail. In-rm modem link. Gift shop. Beauty shop. Free airport transportation. Lighted tennis. Exercise equipt; weights, bicycles, sauna. Minibars. Luxury level. Cr cds: A, C, D, DS, ER, JCB, MC, V.

★ ★ ★ **MARRIOTT-WATERSIDE.** *235 E Main St (23510). 757/627-4200; FAX 757/628-6466.* 404 rms, 24 story. S, D $109-$165; suites $250-$600. Crib free. Pet accepted; $35. Garage parking $8; valet $10. TV; cable (premium). Indoor pool; whirlpool, poolside serv. Restaurant 6-11 am, 5:30-11 pm. Bar 11-1 am. Ck-out noon. Coin lndry. Convention facilities. Business center. In-rm modem link. Concierge. Gift shop. Exercise equipt; weight machine, treadmill, sauna. Game rm. Refrigerator, wet bar in suites. Luxury level. Cr cds: A, C, D, DS, ER, JCB, MC, V.

★ ★ ★ **OMNI WATERSIDE.** *777 Waterside Dr (23510), at St Paul's Blvd and I-264. 757/622-6664; FAX 757/625-8271.* 446 rms, 10 story. S, D $99-$129; each addl $15; suites $150-$600; under 17 free; wkend packages. Crib free. Pet accepted. Valet parking $9.50. TV; cable (premium), VCR avail. Pool; poolside serv. Restaurant 6:30 am-10 pm. Rm serv to 12:30 am. Bars 11-2 am; entertainment wkends. Ck-out noon. Convention facilities. Business center. In-rm modem link. Gift shop. Free airport transportation. Health club privileges. Dockage. Some refrigerators. Balconies. Atrium-like lobby. On harbor. Luxury level. Cr cds: A, C, D, DS, JCB, MC, V.

✔★ ★ **RAMADA MADISON.** *345 Granby St (23510), I-264 exit 9, Waterside Dr. 757/622-6682; FAX 757/623-5949.* 124 units, 8 story. S, D $70-$150; each addl $10; under 12 free; wkend rates. Crib free. TV; cable (premium). Restaurant 6:30 am-2:30 pm, 4 pm-2 am. Bar from 4 pm.

Ck-out noon. Meeting rms. Business servs avail. In-rm modem link. Health club privileges. Cr cds: A, C, D, DS, MC, V.

Inn

★ ★ ★ **PAGE HOUSE.** *323 Fairfax Ave (23507). 757/625-5033; FAX 757/623-9451; res: 800/599-7659.* E-mail innkeeper@pagehouse inn.com. 6 rms, 1 with shower only, 3 story, 2 suites. S, D $90-$150; suites $135-$150. Children under 12 yrs only by arrangement. TV; cable (premium), VCR avail. Complimentary continental bkfst. Restaurant nearby. Ck-out 11 am, ck-in 4-6 pm. Business servs avail. In-rm modem link. Some in-rm whirlpools. Refrigerator in suites. Totally restored Georgian-revival residence (1898) in historic district. Totally nonsmoking. Cr cds: A, MC, V.

Restaurants

★ **THE BANQUE.** *1849 E Little Creek Rd (23518). 757/480-3600.* Hrs: 6 pm-2 am. Closed Mon; Thanksgiving, Dec 24-25. Res accepted. Bar. A la carte entrees: dinner $5.95-$14.95. Specializes in prime rib, seafood. Entertainment. Western decor. Cr cds: A, DS, MC, V.

✔★ ★ **THE DUMBWAITER.** *117 W Tazewell St (23510). 757/623-3663.* E-mail sydvez@aol.com. Hrs: 11 am-4 pm, 5-10:30 pm; Sat, Sun from 5 pm; early-bird dinner Tues-Sat 5-7 pm. Closed Mon; most major hols. Regional Amer menu. Bar. Semi-a la carte: lunch $2.50-$6.50, dinner $2.50-$17. Specialties: chicken and mashed potato tart, grilled portabella mushroom, sautéed crab cakes with mango chutney. Jazz Fri, Sat. Eclectic decor features modern artwork. Cr cds: A, MC, V.

★ ★ **ELLIOT'S.** *1421 Colley Ave (23517). 757/625-0259.* Hrs: 11 am-10 pm; Fri, Sat to 2 am; Sun brunch 11 am-2:30 pm. Closed Thanksgiving, Dec 25. Bar. Semi-a la carte: lunch $2.95-$7.95, dinner $2.95-$16.95. Sun brunch $5-$6.95. Child's meals. Specializes in pasta, fresh vegetables, veal. Parking. Outdoor dining. Carnival and novelty items displayed. Cr cds: A, C, D, DS, MC, V.

★ ★ **FREEMASON ABBEY.** *209 W Freemason St (23510). 757/622-3966.* Web www.cvent.net/restaurants/cvi/freemason/. Hrs: 11:30 am-10 pm; Fri, Sat to midnight; Sun brunch 11:30 am-2 pm. Closed Jan 1, Thanksgiving, Dec 25. Bar. Semi-a la carte: lunch $3.95-$9.95, dinner $9.95-$18.95. Sun brunch $5.95-$8.95. Child's meals. Specializes in whole Maine lobster, prime rib. Renovated church (1873); many antiques. Cr cds: A, DS, MC, V.

★ ★ ★ **LA GALLERIA.** *120 College Place (23510). 757/623-3939.* Hrs: 11:30 am-2:30 pm, 5:30-11:30 pm; Mon to 11 pm; Fri, Sat to midnight. Closed Sun; Thanksgiving, Dec 25. Res accepted. Italian menu. Hrs: 11:30 am-2:30 pm, 4:30 pm-2 am. Semi-a la carte: lunch $3.95-$7.95, dinner $11.95-$19.95. Child's meals. Specialty: salmon La Galleria. Own baking, pasta. Valet parking. Outdoor dining. Modern decor. Cr cds: A, D, MC, V.

★ ★ **MAGNOLIA STEAK.** *749 W Princess Anne Rd (23517). 757/625-0400.* Hrs: 11:30-1 am; Sat, Sun 4 pm-midnight; from 5 pm in summer. Closed Thanksgiving, Dec 25. Res accepted. Bar to 2 am. Semi-a la carte: lunch $4.50-$9.50, dinner $5-$23. Specialties: rib-eye magnolia steak, fresh flounder, Santa Fe chicken. Parking. Outdoor dining. In turn-of-the-century storefront building. Cr cds: A, MC, V.

★ ★ **MONASTERY.** *443 Granby St (23510). 757/625-8193.* Hrs: 11:30 am-2:30 pm, 5-10 pm; May-Labor Day from 5 pm. Closed Mon; Easter, Thanksgiving, Dec 25. Res accepted; required Fri, Sat. Czech, eastern European menu. Bar. Semi-a la carte: lunch $2.75-$8.50, dinner

$4.75-$21. Specialties: roast duck, Wienerschnitzel, goulash. Antique mirrors, original works by local artists. Cr cds: A, C, D, MC, V.

★ **PHILLIPS WATERSIDE.** *333 Waterside Dr (23510), at the Waterside.* 757/627-6600. Hrs: 11 am-10 pm. Closed Thanksgiving, Dec 25. Bar. Semi-a la carte: lunch $4.95-$9, dinner $10-$22. Specialties: spinach and crab dip, crab cakes, fresh seafood. Guitarist Fri, Sat evenings (seasonal). Tiffany glass, iron furniture, antiques. Overlooks Elizabeth River. Cr cds: A, C, D, DS, MC, V.

★ **REGGIE'S BRITISH PUB.** *333 Waterside Dr (23510), at the Waterside.* 757/627-3575. E-mail reggie's@visi.net. Hrs: 11:30 am-11 pm; Sun brunch noon-3 pm. Closed Thanksgiving, Dec 25. British menu. Bar. Semi-a la carte: lunch $5.95-$7.95, dinner $7.95-$17.95. Sun brunch $6.95-$7.95. Specialties: fish & chips, mixed grill, shepherd's pie. Outdoor dining. British Pub decor. Overlooks Elizabeth River. Cr cds: A, C, D, MC, V.

★ **SCHOONERS.** *333 Waterside Dr (23510).* 757/627-8800. Hrs: 11 am-midnight. Sun brunch 11 am-3 pm. Closed Thanksgiving, Dec 25. Res accepted. Bar to 2 am. Semi-a la carte: lunch, dinner $5.95-$15.95. Sun brunch $6.95-$7.95. Child's meals. Specializes in ribs, burgers, seafood. Outdoor dining. Overlooks river. Cr cds: A, D, DS, MC, V.

★ ★ **SHIP'S CABIN.** *4110 E Ocean View Ave (23518).* 757/362-2526. Hrs: 5:30-9:30 pm; Fri, Sat to 10:30 pm; Sun 5-9 pm. Res accepted. Bar. Wine list. Semi-a la carte: dinner $12.95-$21.95. Specializes in grilled fish & meat. Own baking. Parking. Fireplaces. View of Chesapeake Bay. Cr cds: A, C, D, MC, V.

✔★ **TODD JURICH'S BISTRO.** *210 W York St (23510).* 757/622-3210. E-mail primethyme@aol.com. Hrs: 11:30 am-2:30 pm, 5:30-10 pm; Fri to 11 pm; Sat 5:30-11 pm. Closed Sun; major hols. Bar. Semi-a la carte: lunch $5-$10, dinner $11.95-$22.95. Specializes in regional cuisine. Own pastries, pasta. Cr cds: MC, V.

✔★ ★ **UNCLE LOUIE'S.** *132 E Little Creek Rd (23505).* 757/480-1225. E-mail unclouie@erds.com. Hrs: 8 am-11 pm; Fri, Sat to midnight. Sun 8 am-10 pm. Closed Thanksgiving, Dec 25. Res accepted. Bar. Semi-a la carte: bkfst $3.50-$6.95, lunch, dinner $3.50-$16.95. Child's meals. Specializes in Angus beef, fresh fish, specialty coffees. Entertainment Wed, Sat. Cr cds: A, C, D, DS, MC, V.

Unrated Dining Spots

DOUMAR'S. *1919 Monticello Ave.* 757/627-4163. Hrs: 8 am-11 pm. Closed Sun; major hols. A la carte entrees: bkfst, lunch, dinner 70¢-$2.30. Ice cream 90¢-$3.40. Specializes in sandwiches, ice cream. Hand-rolled cones. Parking. 1950s-style drive-in with addl seating inside. Abe Doumar invented the ice cream cone in 1904; his original cone making machine is on display here. Family-owned. No cr cds accepted.

GREEN GROCER TOO. *112 Bank St.* 757/625-2455. Hrs: 7:30 am-3 pm. Closed Sat, Sun; major hols. Wine, beer. A la carte entrees: bkfst 75¢-$2.50. Semi-a la carte: lunch $3.50-$6.95. Specializes in white meat chicken salad, soups. Own baking, desserts. Cafe, wine bar and bakery. Sandwich kiosk with take-out serv, small dining area. Cr cds: MC, V.

Orange (D-7)

(See also Charlottesville, Culpeper)

Founded 1749 **Pop** 2,582 **Elev** 521 ft **Area code** 540 **Zip** 22960

This is the seat of Orange County, which was named for William, Prince of Orange, in 1734. Located in the Piedmont (foothills) of the Blue Ridge Mountains, Orange was settled by Germans under the leadership of Alexander Spotswood between 1714 and 1719.

This is riding and hunting country, drawing its livelihood from farming, livestock and light industry. There are many antebellum houses in the county.

What to See and Do

James Madison Museum. Exhibits commemorating Madison's life and his contributions to American history; also Orange County history and Hall of Agriculture that includes an 18th-century homestead. (Mar-Nov, daily; rest of yr, Mon-Fri) 129 Caroline St. Phone 540/672-1776. ¢¢

✪ **Montpelier.** Residence of James Madison, 4th president of US. Madison was the third generation of his family to live on this extensive plantation. He inherited Montpelier and enlarged it twice. After his presidency, he and Dolley Madison retired to the estate, which Mrs. Madison sold, after the president's death, to pay her son's gambling debts. In 1901, the estate was bought by William du Pont, who enlarged the house, added many outbuildings, including a private railroad station, and built greenhouses and planted gardens. Today, under the stewardship of the National Trust for Historic Preservation, a long-term research and preservation project, "The Search for James Madison," has begun. Admission includes a bus tour of the 2,700-acre estate and a guided tour of the mansion. Self-guided tours of arboretum, nature trails and formal garden. (Mar-Dec, daily; rest of yr, wkends; closed Jan 1, Thanksgiving, Dec 25; also 1st Sat Nov) 4 mi SW, on VA 20. Phone 540/672-0006. ¢¢¢

Inns

✔★ ★ ★ **HIDDEN INN.** *249 Caroline St, jct US 15, VA 20.* 540/672-3625; FAX 540/672-5029; res: 800/841-1253. 10 rms, 2 story, 4 bldgs. S $59-$79; D $79-$129; each addl $20; suites $139-$159. TV in living rm. Complimentary full bkfst; afternoon refreshments. Dining rm; dinner (guests by res). Ck-out noon, ck-in 3 pm. Business servs avail. Some in-rm whirlpools. Balconies. Each rm individually decorated; some with canopy bed, fireplace. Late 19th-century residence; on 7½ wooded acres. Totally nonsmoking. Cr cds: A, MC, V.

★ ★ **HOLLADAY HOUSE.** *155 W Main St.* 540/672-4893; FAX 540/672-3028; res: 800/358-4422. 6 rms, 3 story, 1 suite, 1 kit. unit. S, D $95-$125; each addl $25; suite $185; kit. unit $130; wkly rates. TV in some rms; cable. Complimentary full bkfst. Restaurant adj 7 am-6 pm. Ck-out 11 am, ck-in 4 pm. Business servs avail. Whirlpool. Federal-style residence (ca 1830). Totally nonsmoking. Cr cds: A, DS, MC, V.

Pearisburg (E-4)

(For accommodations see Blacksburg, Radford)

Pop 2,064 **Elev** 1,804 ft **Area code** 540 **Zip** 24134

What to See and Do

Walnut Flats. Fishing in Dismal Creek; hunting (in season). Hiking. Primitive camping. Dismal Falls and Flat Top Mt are here. 11 mi S on VA 100, then 10½ mi W on VA 42 to County 606, N 1 mi to County 201, 2½ mi.

Phone 540/552-4641. **Free.** Approx ½-mi from Walnut Flats on County 201 is

White Pine Horse Camp. Primitive camping. Horse trails. Phone 540/552-4641. **Free.**

White Rocks Recreation Area. Fishing in Big Stony Creek; hunting (in season). Hiking. Camping (fee). (Apr-Nov) 17 mi E via VA 613, 635 in George Washington and Jefferson National Forests. Phone 540/552-4641.

Pentagon City
(See Arlington County)

Petersburg (E-8)

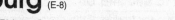

(See also Hopewell, Richmond)

Settled 1645 **Pop** 38,386 **Elev** 87 ft **Area code** 804
Information Petersburg Visitors Center, 425 Cockade Alley, 23803; 804/733-2402 or 800/368-3595.

This city, Lee's last stand before Appomattox (1864-1865), was settled in 1645 when the General Assembly authorized construction of Fort Henry at the falls of the Appomattox River. In 1784, three separate towns united to become the single city of Petersburg.

British troops under Generals Benedict Arnold and William Phillips occupied the town in 1781; the same year, on May 24, Cornwallis started the journey to his surrender at Yorktown. Between the Revolution and the Civil War, the town was a popular stopping place, with a social life that, for a time, eclipsed that of Richmond.

Physically untouched (though the town sent 17 companies to the front) during the early years of the Civil War, Petersburg in 1864 was the scene of Lee's final struggle against Grant. In April 1865, when Lee's supply routes were finally cut and he was forced to evacuate the city, the Confederacy collapsed. A week later Lee surrendered at Appomattox.

The shattered city made a new start after the war, showing amazing recuperative powers; in 1870, Petersburg had 20 more industries than there had been in 1850. Today, besides being a storehouse of colonial and Civil War history, Petersburg does a thriving business in luggage, optical lenses and ballpoint pens.

What to See and Do

Appomattox River Park. A 137-acre park with canal for canoeing or fishing; access to rapids; picnic area. (Mid-Apr-Oct, daily) W part of town, on River Rd. Phone 804/733-2394.

Blandford Church (1735) and **Cemetery** (1702). Church, since 1901 a memorial to the Confederacy, has 15 Tiffany stained-glass windows. (Daily; closed Jan 1, Thanksgiving, Dec 24, 25) 321 S Crater Rd. **¢¢**

Centre Hill Mansion (1823). Federal-style mansion visited by Presidents Tyler, Lincoln and Taft. Chandeliers, fine detail carvings; antiques, 1886 Knabe Art grand piano with holly wood inlaid on rosewood. (Daily; closed Jan 1, Thanksgiving, Dec 24, 25) Center Hill. **¢¢**

Farmers Bank (1817). Banking memorabilia includes original plates and press for printing Confederate currency. Tours depart from Visitors Center, Old Market Sq. (Apr-Oct, daily) 19 Bollingbrook St. **¢¢**

Fort Lee. Army training center in World Wars I and II. 3 mi NE on VA 36. Here is

Quartermaster Museum. Uniforms, flags, weapons, equestrian equipment from 200 yrs of military service. Civil War and Memorial Rooms. (Daily exc Mon; closed Jan 1, Thanksgiving, Dec 25) Phone 804/734-4203. **Free.**

Lee Memorial Park. Facilities of this 864-acre park include lake (launch fee); fishing (fee; license required); game fields & courts (fee); picnic area.

(Daily; lake facilities closed mid-Oct-mid-Apr) S part of town, off Johnson Rd. Phone 804/733-2394. Also here is

USSSA Softball Hall of Fame Museum. Honors outstanding persons in amateur softball. Numerous displays, exhibits, photographs; 7-min film. (Daily; closed hols) 3935 S Crater Rd, 1 mi off I-95. Phone 804/732-4099. **¢**

Lee's Retreat. 98-mi driving tour follows route of Gen Robert E. Lee's retreat from Petersburg to Appomattox. Roadside pull-overs, signs and audio interpretation at important Civil War sites. For brochures, maps and audio tapes, contact the Petersburg Visitors Center or phone 800/6-RETREAT. **Free.**

Pamplin Park Civil War Site. Site of General Ulysses S. Grant's decisive victory over Confederate forces in 1865. Battle trails, reconstructed soldier huts, plantation home Interpretive Center and museum. Guided tours available. (Daily; closed Jan 1, Thanksgiving, Dec 25) 6523 Duncan Rd. Phone 804/861-2408.

Petersburg National Battlefield (see).

Poplar Grove (Petersburg) National Cemetery. On self-guided tour of Petersburg National Battlefield (see). Of 6,315 graves, 4,110 are unidentified. S off I-85.

Siege Museum. Greek-revival building houses exhibits describing the 10-month Civil War Siege of Petersburg. Film *The Echoes Still Remain*, with Joseph Cotten, is shown every hour on the hour. (Daily; closed Jan 1, Thanksgiving, Dec 24, 25) 15 W Bank St. **¢¢**

St Paul's Episcopal Church (1856). Lee worshiped here during the siege of Petersburg (1864-1865). Open on request (Mon-Thurs). 110 N Union between W Washington & Tabb Sts. Phone 804/733-3415.

Trapezium House (1817). Built by eccentric Irish bachelor, Charles O'Hara, in the form of a trapezium, with no right angles and no parallel sides. O'Hara is said to have believed the superstition of his West Indian servant, who thought that ghosts and evil spirits inhabited right angles. Tours depart from Siege Museum, 15 W Bank St. (Apr-Oct, daily) Market & High Sts. **¢¢**

Motels

★ ★ DAYS INN. *12208 S Crater Rd (23805), I-95 exit 45.* 804/733-4400; FAX 804/861-9559. 154 rms, 2 story. S, D $44.95-$55.95; each addl $5; kit. suites $55-$59; family rates. Crib free. Pet accepted. TV; cable (premium). Pool; wading pool. Playground. Restaurant adj 5:30 am-10 pm. Ck-out 11 am. Coin lndry. Meeting rms. Business servs avail. In-rm modem link. Bellhops. Sundries. Putting green. Exercise equipt; weights, bicycles. Some refrigerators. Cr cds: A, C, D, DS, ER, JCB, MC, V.

D ⇥ ⊷ ≋ ⚡ ⟊ ⊠ ⚒ SC

✓★ ★ ★ QUALITY INN-STEVEN KENT. *12205 S Crater Rd (23805), 6 mi S, I-95 exit 45.* 804/733-0600; FAX 804/862-4549. 138 rms, 1-2 story. S $35.95-$59.95; D $37.95-$59.95; each addl $5; under 18 free. Crib $5. Pet accepted. TV; cable (premium). Pool; wading pool. Playground. Restaurant 5:30 am-10 pm. Bar noon-midnight. Ck-out 11 am. Coin lndry. Business servs avail. In-rm modem link. Sundries. Lighted tennis. Game rm. Lawn games. Miniature golf. Some refrigerators. Picnic tables. Cr cds: A, C, D, DS, ER, JCB, MC, V.

D ⇥ ⊷ ⚡ ≋ ⟊ ⊠ ⚒ SC

Restaurant

✓★ ALEXANDER'S. *101 W Bank St (23805).* 804/733-7134. Hrs: 9 am-9 pm; Mon, Tues to 3:30 pm. Closed Sun; Jan 1, wk of July 4th, Thanksgiving, Dec 25. Italian, Greek, Amer menu. Wine, beer. Semi-a la carte: bkfst $1.50-$4, lunch $4-$5.50, dinner $5.60-$8.75. Child's meals. Specialties: veal a la Greca, souvlaki, Athenian chicken. In old town storefront. No cr cds accepted.

Petersburg National Battlefield (E-8)

(For accommodations see Hopewell, Petersburg, Richmond)

The campaign that spelled doom for the Confederacy occurred in a huge 40-mile semicircle around Richmond and Petersburg, at the price of 70,000 Union and Confederate casualties.

General Grant, after his unsuccessful attempt to take Richmond by frontal assault (at Cold Harbor, June 3, 1864), withdrew and attacked Petersburg. After 4 days of fighting and failing to capture the city, Grant decided to lay siege. Petersburg was the rail center that funneled supplies to Lee and Richmond.

The siege lasted ten months, from June 15, 1864, to April 2, 1865, with the two armies in almost constant contact. When Petersburg finally fell, Lee's surrender was only a week away.

The park, more than 2,700 acres, preserves Union and Confederate fortifications, trenches and gun pits. Another unit of the battlefield, Five Forks Unit, is located 23 miles to the west. Park (daily). There are living history programs daily during summer. Access for the disabled includes several paved trails and ramps to the Visitor Center. For further information contact the Superintendent, 1539 Hickory Hill Rd, Petersburg 23803-4721; 804/732-3531. Golden Eagle, Golden Age and Golden Access Passports honored (see MAKING THE MOST OF YOUR TRIP). Per vehicle ¢¢

What to See and Do

Battery 5. Strongest original Confederate position, captured on opening day of battle. From here "the Dictator," a Union mortar, shelled Petersburg, 2¹/₂ mi away. A similar mortar is nearby.

Battery 8. Confederate artillery position captured and used by Union as Fort Friend.

Battery 9. Confederate position on original line. Site of reconstructed Union camp and living history programs.

City Point Unit. (See HOPEWELL)

Colquitt's Salient. Section of Confederate defense line.

First Maine Monument. Memorial to Maine dead in greatest regimental loss in a single action of the war.

Five Forks Unit. (1,115 acres) This road junction, beyond Lee's extreme right flank, led to the only remaining Confederate supply line, the South Side Railroad. The Battle of Five Forks (Apr 1, 1865) saw Union forces under General Philip H. Sheridan smash Confederates commanded by General George Pickett and gain access to the tracks beyond. On Apr 2, Grant ordered an all-out assault, crumbling Lee's right flank. Only a heroic stand by Confederate forces at Fort Gregg held off the Union advance while Lee evacuated Petersburg on the night of Apr 2. Visitor contact station (summer). Approx 6 mi SW via VA 613 (White Oak Rd), to jct Dinwiddie Courthouse Rd (VA 627) & Wheeler Pond Rd (VA 645). Phone 804/265-8244. **Free.**

Fort Haskell. One of the points where Union troops stopped a desperate attempt by Lee to break the siege.

Fort Stedman. Lee's "last grand offensive" concentrated here (Mar 25, 1865). The battle lasted 4 hrs; the Confederates failed to hold their breakthrough.

Gracie's Dam. Site of one of several Confederate dams intended to flood area between lines.

Harrison's Creek. First Grant (June 1864), then Lee (Mar 1865) had advances checked here.

Spring Garden. Heaviest Union artillery concentration during Battle of Crater was along this ridge.

The Crater. Hole remaining after Union troops tunneled beneath Confederate artillery position and exploded four tons of powder (July 30, 1864).

The resulting breach in Confederate lines failed as a major breakthrough. Several special monuments in vicinity.

Visitor Center. Information, exhibits; maps for self-guided tours. (Daily; closed most major hols) Off VA 36. Self-guided tour starts near center building.

Portsmouth (F-9)

(See also Chesapeake, Hampton, Newport News, Norfolk, Virginia Beach)

Founded 1752 **Pop** 103,907 **Elev** 15 ft **Area code** 757 **E-mail** p0rtscvb @aol.com

Information Portsmouth Convention and Visitors Bureau, 505 Crawford St, Suite 2, 23704; 757/393-5327 or 800/767-8782.

Connected to Norfolk by two bridge tunnels and a pedestrian ferry that cross the Elizabeth River, Portsmouth is part of the great Hampton Roads port, unrivaled for commercial shipping and shipbuilding activity. It is also the headquarters of the US Coast Guard Atlantic Fleet.

In Gosport, long a part of Portsmouth, Andrew Sprowle, a Scot, built a marine yard in 1767, which became in turn a British naval repair station and, after the Revolution, a federal navy yard. Now called the Norfolk Naval Shipyard, it is the largest naval shipyard in the world. The *Chesapeake,* sister of the *Constitution* and one of the US Navy's first warships, was built here. So was the *Merrimac,* which was seized by the Confederates, changed into an ironclad in 1861 and rechristened the CSS *Virginia.* The oldest drydock (1831) here is still in use.

What to See and Do

Carrie B Harbor Tours. Replica of 19th-century riverboat makes narrated tour (1¹/₂ hrs) of naval shipyard and inner harbor (Apr-Oct, daily); narrated tour (2¹/₂ hrs) of naval base and Hampton Roads (Apr-May & Sept-Oct, daily); sunset cruise (2¹/₂ hrs) to Hampton Roads and naval base (June-Labor Day, daily). Departs from Portside, 6 Crawford Pkwy. Phone 757/393-4735 for details. (Also see NORFOLK) ¢¢¢¢

Great Dismal Swamp National Wildlife Refuge (see). S on US 17.

Hill House. Headquarters of the Portsmouth Historical Assn. Built in early 1820s, this four-story English-basement-style house (with a raised basement) contains original furnishings collected by generations of the Hill family. In near-original condition, the house has undergone only limited renovation through the yrs. Garden restored. (Apr-Dec, Wed, Sat & Sun) 221 North St. Phone 757/393-5111. ¢

Historic houses. Portsmouth has over 300 yrs of history represented by more than 20 examples of Colonial, Federal and antebellum houses. Among them is the Nivison-Ball House (ca 1730-1750), 417 Middle St, where Andrew Jackson and General Lafayette were entertained. *These houses are private and may be viewed only from the exterior.* Obtain Olde Towne Portsmouth walking tour brochures with map and descriptions of churches, homes and old buildings from the Visitor Center at High St Landing; 757/393-5111.

Monumental United Church (Methodist) (1772). Oldest Methodist congregation in the South; history room. Guided tour (Mon-Fri, by appt; closed hols). Queen & Dinwiddie Sts, 1 blk N of High St. Phone 757/397-1297.

⭐ **The Portsmouth Museums.** Located in a 4-blk radius, the museum complex has facilities housing artistic, educational and historic exhibits. Museums (Tues-Sat; also Sun afternoons; closed Jan 1, Thanksgiving, Dec 25). Phone 757/393-8983. Key pass ¢¢ includes

Children's Museum of Virginia. More than 60 interactive activities in 12 areas; planetarium. (Mid-June-Labor Day, Mon-Sat, also Sun afternoons) 221 High St. ¢¢

Naval Shipyard Museum. Thousands of items of naval equipment, plus flags, uniforms, prints, maps and models, including models of the CSS *Virginia;* the US Ship-of-the-line *Delaware,* built in Portsmouth; and the first ship drydocked in the US. 2 High St, on Elizabeth River. ¢

Lightship Museum. Built in 1915, commissioned in 1916 as *Lightship 101,* it served 48 yrs in Virginia, Delaware and Massachusetts. Retired in 1964 and renamed *Portsmouth.* London Slip & Water St. ¢

Fine Arts Gallery. Changing exhibits. 420 High St. ¢

Trinity Church (Episcopal). Oldest church building (1762) and parish in Portsmouth. Legend says that the church bell cracked while ringing out news of Cornwallis' surrender. It was later recast. Confederate Memorial window. Commodore James Barron, many colonial patriots are buried here. Open on request (Mon-Fri); office behind church in parish hall. 500 Court St. Phone 757/393-0431.

Motel

★ ★ **HOLIDAY INN OLD TOWN-PORTSMOUTH.** *8 Crawford Pkwy (23704), on waterfront at Elizabeth River. 757/393-2573; FAX 757/399-1248.* Web www.holiday-portsmouth.com. 268 rms, 4 story. S $60-$89; D $60-$99; each addl $10; suites $130-$161; studio rms $75-$150; under 19 free; wkend rates; higher rates Harborfest. Crib free. Pet accepted; $10. TV; cable (premium). Pool. Coffee in rms. Restaurant 6:30 am-10 pm. Rm serv. Bar noon-2 am. Ck-out noon. Coin lndry. Meeting rms. Business servs avail. In-rm modem link. Exercise equipt; weights, stair machine. Refrigerators avail. Dockage, marina adj. Cr cds: A, C, D, DS, JCB, MC, V.

Restaurants

✔★ ★ **CAFE EUROPA.** *319 High St (23704). 757/399-6652.* Hrs: 11:30 am-2 pm, 5-9:30 pm; Fri, Sat to 10:30 pm. Closed Sun, Mon; most major hols; also mid-Aug-mid-Sept. Res accepted. Bar. Semi-a la carte: lunch $6.50-$12, dinner $9.50-$15.95. Specialties: salmon Russian style, snail tureen, veal Tuscany. Intimate European atmosphere; Mucha prints. Chef-owned. Cr cds: MC, V.

★ **THE CIRCLE.** *3010 High St (23707). 757/397-8196.* Hrs: 8 am-10 pm; Fri, Sat to 11 pm; Sun brunch noon-9 pm. Res accepted. Bar. Semi-a la carte: bkfst $2.50-$6.50, lunch $2.75-$14.95, dinner $7.95-$17.95. Sun brunch $10.95. Child's meals. Specializes in steak, seafood. Salad bar. Pianist Mon, Wed-Fri. Rotunda dining rm with extensive buffet. Cr cds: D, DS, MC, V.

★ ★ **THE MAX.** *425 Water St (23704). 757/397-1866.* Hrs: 11:30 am-10 pm; Sat from 5 pm. Closed Jan 1, Dec 24, 25. Res accepted. Bar. Semi-a la carte: lunch $4.50-$9.95, dinner $6.95-$16.95. Child's meals. Specializes in fresh local seafood, grilled salmon. Outdoor patio dining overlooking Elizabeth River. Cr cds: A, DS, MC, V.

★ ★ **SCALE O' DE WHALE.** *3515 Shipwright St (23703), off W Norfolk Bridge. 757/483-2772.* Hrs: 11:30 am-2:30 pm, 5-10 pm; Sat from 5:30 pm; Sun 5:30-9:30 pm. Closed major hols. Res accepted. Serv bar. Semi-a la carte: lunch $4.50-$8.25, dinner $9.95-$17.95. Child's meals. Specializes in seafood, market price lobster, steak. At end of pier, dockage. Nautical decor; ship models, antiques, scrimshaw, kerosene lights. Cr cds: A, DS, MC, V.

Radford (E-4)

(See also Blacksburg, Salem)

Settled 1756 **Pop** 15,940 **Elev** 1,820 ft **Area code** 540 **Zip** 24141 **E-mail** radford@swva.net **Web** webstation.com/radford
Information Chamber of Commerce, 1126 Norwood St; 540/639-2202.

What to See and Do

Claytor Lake State Park. Consists of 472 acres in wooded hills adjacent to 5,000-acre lake. Swimming, sand beach, bathhouse; fishing; boating (ramp, rentals, marina). Hiking, bridle trails. Picnicking, concession. Tent and trailer sites (electrical hookups, Apr-Sept); cabins (mid-May-Sept). Visitor center, interpretive programs. Standard fees. Park office and visitor center are in Howe House (1876-1879), built on land once settled by Dunkers (Dunkards), a religious sect that fled persecution in Germany in the 1720s. On VA 660, 6 mi SW, just S of I-81 exit 101. Phone 540/674-5492.

Radford University (1910). (9,500 students) Flossie Martin Gallery in Powell Hall houses visual arts with an emphasis on regional and contemporary; changing exhibits. The Corinna de la Burde Sculpture Court, adjacent to the gallery, is an open-air museum displaying large-scale sculpture through changing exhibitions and permanent installations. Archives in the McConnell Library contain pamphlets, campus information, local history, oral history of Appalachia and rare books. Greenhouse (daily). The Dedmon Center, a recreation-convocation complex, features an air-supported roof, arena seating 5,600; swimming pool; indoor tennis and handball courts. (Daily) On US 11, I-81 exit 109. Phone 540/831-5324.

Seasonal Event

The Long Way Home. Outdoor historical drama by Earl Hobson Smith depicts the true story of Mary Draper Ingles, survivor of the 1755 Draper's Meadow Massacre, and her heroic 850-mi flight to warn settlers of Native American attacks. For reservations contact PO Box 711; 540/639-0679. Thurs-Sun, evenings, Mid-June-Aug.

Motels

★ ★ ★ **BEST WESTERN RADFORD INN.** *1501 Tyler Ave. 540/639-3000; FAX 540/639-3000, ext. 412.* 72 rms, 2 story. S $75-$80; D $80-$90; each addl $5; under 12 free; higher rates univ events. Crib free. Pet accepted. TV; cable (premium). Indoor pool; wading pool, whirlpool. Restaurant 6:30 am-1:30 pm, 5-9 pm; wkends from 7 am. Ck-out noon. Business servs avail. Sundries. Exercise equipt; bicycles, stair machine, sauna. Bathrm phones; some refrigerators. Cr cds: A, C, D, DS, MC, V.

★ ★ **COMFORT INN.** *(Rte 1, Box 123F, Dublin 24084) just S of I-81 exit 98 on VA 100. 540/674-1100; FAX 540/674-2644.* 98 rms, 2 story. S $56-$75; D $61-$79; each addl $6; under 18 free; higher rates univ events. Crib free. TV; cable (premium). VCR avail. Pool. Complimentary continental bkfst. Restaurant adj 5-10 pm. Ck-out noon. Meeting rm. Business servs avail. Valet serv. Sundries. Microwaves avail. Cr cds: A, C, D, DS, ER, JCB, MC, V.

★ **DOGWOOD LODGE.** *7073 Lee Hwy, 2 mi S on US 11. 540/639-9338.* 15 rms. S $25; D $32-$34; each addl $3; higher rates univ events. Crib $5. TV; cable (premium). Restaurant nearby. Ck-out 11 am. Cr cds: DS, MC, V.

✔★ **EXECUTIVE.** *7498 Lee Hwy. 540/639-1664; res: 888/393-8483.* 27 rms, 13 with shower only, 2 story. Apr-Nov: S $32.50-$36.50; D $36.50-$46.50; under 12 free; higher rates special events; lower rates rest of yr. Crib free. Pet accepted, some restrictions; $4. TV; cable (premium),

VCR. Complimentary coffee in lobby. Restaurant adj 6 am-11 pm. Ck-out 11 am. Refrigerators. Microwaves avail. Cr cds: D, DS, MC, V.

D ✦ ⊠ 🐾 SC

Reston

(see Dulles Intl Airport Area)

Richmond (E-8)

(See also Ashland, Hopewell, Petersburg)

Settled 1607 **Pop** 203,056 **Elev** 150 ft **Area code** 804 **E-mail** mrcvbtour@aol.com **Web** www.erols.com/richmond

Information Convention and Visitors Bureau, 550 E Marshall St, 23219; 804/782-2777 or 800/370-9004.

There have been few dull moments in Richmond's history. Native Americans and settlers fought over the ground on which it now stands. In 1775, Patrick Henry made his "liberty or death" speech in St John's Church, and in 1780 the city was named capital of the state. At that time Virginia extended all the way to the Mississippi. British soldiers plundered it brutally in the Revolution. As the capital of the Confederacy from 1861 to 1865, it was constantly in danger. Finally, in 1865 the city was evacuated, and retreating Confederate soldiers burned the government warehouse; a portion of the rest of the city also went up in flames.

However, Richmond did survive. As Virginia's capital, it proudly exemplifies the modern South. It is a city industrially aggressive yet culturally aware, respectful of its own historical background yet receptive to new trends in architecture and modes of living. Richmond esteems both the oldest monuments and the newest skyscrapers.

Tobacco and tobacco products, paper and paper products, aluminum, chemicals, textiles, printing and publishing and machinery contribute to the city's economy. Richmond is also an educational center; the Virginia Commonwealth University, Virginia Union University and the University of Richmond are based here.

What to See and Do

Agecroft Hall. Half-timbered Tudor manor built in the late 15th century near Manchester, England. Disassembled, brought here and rebuilt during the late 1920s in a spacious setting of formal gardens and grassy terraces overlooking the James River. English furnishings from 16th to 17th centuries. Audiovisual presentation explains history of house. (Daily exc Mon; closed most hols) Cary St exit off I-195, turn onto N Thompson Ave, then right on Cary to Malvern, then left on Cantebury to 4305 Sulgrave Rd. Phone 804/353-4241. ¢¢

✪ **Capitol Square.** Bounded by Broad, Governor, Bank & 9th Sts, downtown.

State Capitol (1785-1788). Modeled after La Maison Carrée, an ancient Roman temple at Nîmes, France, the Capitol was designed by Thomas Jefferson. In this building, where America's oldest continuous English-speaking legislative bodies still meet, is the famous Houdon statue of Washington. The old Hall of the House of Delegates features the first interior dome in the US; here, Aaron Burr was tried for treason, Virginia ratified the Articles of Secession and Robert E. Lee accepted command of the forces of Virginia; the Confederate Congress also met in the building. (Mon-Sat, also Sun afternoons; closed Jan 1, Thanksgiving, Dec 25) 9th & Grace Sts, Capitol Sq. Phone 804/786-4344. Also on Capitol Sq are

Governor's Mansion (1813). This two-story Federal-style house was built after the capital was moved from Williamsburg. It is the oldest governor's mansion in the US still in use as a governor's residence. Tours (by appt). E of State Capitol. Phone 804/371-2642. **Free.**

Virginia State Library and Archives. Outstanding collection of books, maps, manuscripts. (Daily exc Sun; closed hols) 800 E Broad St. Phone 804/692-3500. **Free.**

Equestrian Statue of Washington. By Thomas Crawford; cast in Munich over an 18-yr period. Base features allegorical representations of six famous Revolutionary War figures from Virginia. 9th & Grace Sts.

Church Hill Historic Area. Neighborhood of 19th-century houses, more than 70 of which predate Civil War. Some Church Hill houses are open Historic Garden Week (see ANNUAL EVENTS). Bounded by Broad, 29th, Main & 21st Sts, E of Capitol Sq. In center of Church Hill is

St John's Episcopal Church (1741). Where Patrick Henry delivered his stirring "liberty or death" speech. Reenactment of Second Virginia Convention (late May-early Sept, Sun). Guided tours. (Daily; closed Jan 1, Easter, Thanksgiving, Dec 24, 25, 31) 25th & Broad Sts. Phone 804/648-5015. ¢ W of Church Hill is

Edgar Allan Poe Museum. Old Stone House portion is thought to be oldest structure in Richmond (1737). Four additional buildings house Poe mementos; James Carling illustrations of "The Raven"; scale model of Richmond of Poe's time; slide presentation of Poe's life in Richmond. Guided tours. (Daily; closed Dec 25). 1914 E Main St. Phone 804/648-5523. ¢¢ E of Church Hill is

Richmond National Battlefield Park (see). Headquarters located at 3215 E Broad St, in Chimborazo Park. Phone 804/226-1981.

City Hall Observation Deck. Eighteenth-floor observation deck offers panoramic view of the city, including Capitol grounds, James River and Revolutionary and Civil War-era buildings contrasted with modern skyscrapers. (Mon-Fri) 9th & Broad Sts, across Broad St from Capitol. Phone 804/780-7000. **Free.** Across the street is the old City Hall (1886-1894), a restored Gothic-revival building featuring an elaborate central court with arcaded galleries.

Federal Reserve Money Museum. Exhibits of currency, including rare bills; gold and silver bars; money-related artifacts. (Mon-Fri; closed hols) 701 E Byrd St, downtown, on 1st floor of bank. Phone 804/697-8000. **Free.**

Hollywood Cemetery (1847). James Monroe, John Tyler, Jefferson Davis, other notables and 18,000 Confederate soldiers are buried here; audiovisual program (Mon-Fri). (Daily) 412 S Cherry St, at Albemarle St. Phone 804/648-8501. **Free.**

Jackson Ward. Historic downtown neighborhood that was home to many famous black Richmonders, including Bill "Bojangles" Robinson. Area has numerous 19th-century, Greek-revival and Victorian buildings with ornamental ironwork that rivals the wrought iron of New Orleans. Bounded by I-95, 7th, Broad & Belvidere Sts. Within the ward are

Black History Museum and Cultural Center. Limited editions, prints, art, photographs; African memorabilia; Sam Gilliam collection. (Tues, Thurs-Sat) Clay St. Phone 804/780-9093. ¢

Bill "Bojangles" Robinson Statue. Memorial to the famous dancer, who was born at 915 N 3rd St. Corner of Leigh & Adams Sts.

Maggie Walker National Historic Site. Commemorates life and career of Maggie L. Walker, daughter of former slaves, who overcame great hardships to become successful in banking and insurance; early advocate for women's rights and racial equality. Two-story, red-brick house was home to her family 1904-1934. (Wed-Sun; closed Jan 1, Thanksgiving, Dec 25) 110-A E Leigh St. Phone 804/780-1380. **Free.**

John Marshall House (1790). Restored home of famous Supreme Court justice features original woodwork and paneling; family furnishings and mementos. (Daily exc Mon; closed most major hols) Combination ticket avail for Marshall House, Valentine Museum, Museum of the Confederacy, White House of the Confederacy. 9th & Marshall Sts, N of Capitol Sq. Phone 804/648-7998. Marshall House ¢¢; Combination ticket ¢¢¢

Kanawha Canal Locks. Impressive stone locks were part of nation's first canal system, planned by George Washington. Narrated audiovisual presentation explains workings of locks and canal. Picnic grounds. (Daily) 12th & Byrd Sts, downtown. Phone 804/281-2369. **Free.**

Meadow Farm Museum (General Sheppard Crump Memorial Park). Living history farm museum depicting rural life in the 1860s. Orientation center, farmhouse, barn, outbuildings, crop demonstration fields, 1860s doctor's office. Also a 150-acre park with picnic shelters, playground. (Mar-Dec, daily exc Mon) 12 mi NW via I-95N, I-295W, Woodman Rd S exit, at Courtney & Mountain Rds. Phone 804/672-5520. **Free;** Special events ¢

Monumental Church (1812). Located on the Medical College of VA campus of Virginia Commonwealth University. Octagonal domed building designed by Robert Mills, architect of the Washington Monument. Commemorative structure was built on site where many prominent persons, including the governor, perished in a theater fire in 1811. Interior closed. Behind the church is the distinctive Egyptian Building (1845). 1226 E Broad St, N of Capitol Sq.

Museum of the Confederacy. Contains the nation's largest collection of Confederate military and civilian artifacts, including uniforms, equipment, flags, personal belongings of Jefferson Davis, Robert E. Lee and J.E.B. Stuart, documents, manuscripts and artwork. (Daily; closed Jan 1, Thanksgiving, Dec 25) 1201 E Clay St, N of Capitol Sq. Phone 804/649-1861. ¢¢

Parks. For general information contact the Dept of Parks & Recreation; 804/780-5695.

William Byrd. Includes 287 acres of groves, artificial lakes, picnic areas. Tennis courts; softball fields; fitness course. Amphitheater (June-Aug). Virginia's World War I memorial, a 240-ft, pink brick carillon tower. Boulevard St & Idlewood Ave. Nearby is

Maymont. Dooley mansion, late Victorian in style, houses art collection and decorative arts exhibits (daily exc Mon; fee). Also here are formal Japanese and Italian gardens, an arboretum, a nature center with wildlife habitat for native species, an aviary, a children's farm and a working carriage collection. (Daily) 1700 Hampton St, at Pennsylvania Ave. Phone 804/358-7166. **Free.**

Bryan. A 279-acre park, 20 acres of which are an azalea garden with more than 55,000 plants (best view late Apr-mid-May). Picnic facilities, tennis courts. Bellevue Ave & Hermitage Rd. **Free.**

James River. Five sections. Fishing, pedestrian bridges with overlook of James River, whitewater canoe and inner-tube accesses, birdwatching, wildlife sanctuary, self-guided tours, bicycle and hiking trails, visitor center with display, information station, interpretive programs. W 22nd St & Riverside Dr. **Free.**

Lewis Ginter Botanical Garden. Victorian-era estate features the Grace Arents Garden and the Henry M. Flagler Perennial Garden; seasonal floral displays; emphasis on daffodils, daylilies, azaleas and rhododendrons. (Daily) 1800 Lakeside Ave, in Lakeside. Phone 804/262-9887. ¢¢

Pocahontas State Park. More than 7,000 acres; Swift Creek Lake. Swimming, pool, bathhouse; fishing; boating (launch, rentals, electric motors only). Hiking trails, bicycle path (rentals). Picnicking, concession. Tent and trailer sites (seasonal), group cabins. Nature center; evening interpretive programs (summer). Standard fees. (Daily) S on US 10, then W on VA 655.Phone 804/796-4255.

Richmond Children's Museum. Exhibits on arts, nature and the world around us designed for children 2-12 yrs old; many hands-on exhibits. (July-Aug, daily; rest of yr, daily exc Mon; closed hols) 740 Navy Hill Dr, downtown. Phone 804/643-5436 or 804/788-4949. ¢¢

Shopping.

6th Street Marketplace. Restored area of shops, restaurants, entertainment. 6th St between Coliseum & Grace St, downtown.

Shockoe Slip. Restored area of historic buildings and gaslit cobblestone streets; shopping, restaurants, galleries. E Cary St between 12th & 14th Sts, downtown.

Carytown. Eight blks of shops, restaurants, theaters adjacent to historic Fan neighborhood. W Cary St, between Boulevard St & I-95.

17th Street Market. Farmers market built on site of Native American trading village. Seasonal produce, flowers, holiday greens. (Daily) 17th St between E Main & E Market Sts.

Sightseeing.

Paddlewheeler *Annabel Lee.* Departs from Intermediate Terminal. Triple-decked, 350-passenger, 19th-century-style riverboat cruises the James River. Narrated tour; entertainment. Lunch, brunch, dinner and plantation cruises. (Apr-Dec, at least one cruise daily exc Mon) Phone 804/644-5700 or 800/752-7093. ¢¢¢¢

Historic Richmond Tours. Offers guided van tours with pickup at Visitors Center and major hotels (daily); res required. Also guided walking tours (Apr-Oct, daily; fee). For details, reservations phone 804/780-0107. Van tours ¢¢¢; Walking tours ¢¢

Plantation tours. The Richmond-Petersburg-Williamsburg area has many fine old mansions and estates. Some are open most of the yr; others only during Historic Garden Week (see ANNUAL EVENTS). The Metro Richmond Visitors Center has maps, information folders, suggestions. (Daily) 1710 Robin Hood Rd. Phone 804/358-5511.

St Paul's Church (Episcopal). Established in 1843, the church survived the Civil War intact. It was here that Jefferson Davis received news of Lee's retreat from Petersburg to Appomattox. Beginning in 1890, the church added many fine stained-glass windows, including eight from the Tiffany studios. Sanctuary ceiling features decorative plasterwork, interweaving Greek, Hebrew and Christian motifs around a central panel. A Tiffany mosaic of da Vinci's *Last Supper* surmounts the altar. (Daily; closed hols) 9th & Grace Sts, W of Capitol Sq. Phone 804/643-3589.

★ **The Fan** and **Monument Avenue.** Named for the layout of streets that fan out from Monroe Park toward the western part of town. Historical neighborhood has restored antebellum and turn-of-the-century houses, museums, shops, restaurants and famed Monument Ave. The fashionable boulevard, between Lombard and Belmont Sts, is dotted with imposing statues of Generals Lee, Stuart and Jackson, of Jefferson Davis and of Commodore Matthew Fontaine Maury, inventor of the electric torpedo. Bounded by Franklin St & Monument Ave, Boulevard, Main & Belvidere Sts. Within the area are

Virginia Museum of Fine Arts. America's first state-supported museum of art. Collections of paintings, prints, sculpture from major world cultures; Russian Imperial Easter eggs and jewels by Fabergé decorative arts of the art nouveau and art deco movements; sculpture garden; changing exhibitions. Cafeteria. (Daily exc Mon; closed Jan 1, July 4, Thanksgiving, Dec 25) Boulevard St & Grove Ave. Phone 804/367-0844. ¢¢

Virginia Historical Society. Comprehensive collection of Virginia history housed in Museum of Virginia History, with permanent and changing exhibits, and Library of Virginia History, with historical and genealogical research facilities. (Mon-Sat, museum also Sun afternoons; closed hols) Kensington & Boulevard Sts. Phone 804/358-4901. ¢¢

Science Museum of Virginia. Hands-on museum. Major exhibits include aerospace, computers, electricity, visual perception, physical phenomena and astronomy, giant analemmic sundial and Foucault pendulum. The Ethyl Universe Planetarium Space Theater features Omnimax films and planetarium shows (inquire for schedule). (Mon-Sat, also Sun afternoons; closed Thanksgiving, Dec 25) 2500 W Broad St, N of Monument Ave. Phone 804/367-6552. Museum ¢¢; Museum & planetarium ¢¢¢

Valentine Museum. Traces history of Richmond. Exhibits focus on city life, decorative arts, costumes and textiles, industrial and social history; tour of restored 1812 Wickham House. Lunch served in walled garden (Apr-Oct). (Daily; closed some hols) 1015 E Clay St, N of Capitol Sq. Phone 804/367-6552. ¢¢

Virginia Aviation Museum. Exhibits and artifacts on the history of aviation, with emphasis on Virginia pioneers. (Daily; closed Dec 25) 5701 Huntsman Rd in Sandston, at Richmond Intl Airport. Phone 804/236-3622. ¢¢

Virginia House. A Tudor building constructed of materials from Warwick Priory (built in England in 1125 and rebuilt in 1565 as a residence); moved here in 1925. West wing is modeled after Sulgrave Manor, at one time the home of Lawrence Washington. Furniture, tapestries and paintings from 15th to 20th centuries. Formal gardens. Tours by appt only exc during Historic Garden Week (see ANNUAL EVENTS). (Daily exc Mon; closed major hols) 4301 Sulgrave Rd, 1/2 mi off VA 147 (Cary St), in Windsor Farms. Phone 804/353-4251. ¢

Virginia War Memorial. Honors Virginians who died in WW II, Korean and Vietnam Wars. Mementos of battles; eternal flame; more than 12,000

names engraved on glass and marble walls. (Daily) 621 S Belvidere St, downtown at N end of Robert E. Lee Bridge. **Free.**

White House of the Confederacy. Classical-revival house (1818) used by Jefferson Davis as his official residence during period when Richmond was capital of the Confederacy. Abraham Lincoln met with troops here during the Union occupation of the city. Restored to pre-wartime appearance; original furnishings. (Daily; closed Jan 1, Thanksgiving, Dec 25) 12th & E Clay Sts, N of Capitol Sq. Phone 804/649-1861. ¢¢

Wilton (1753). Georgian mansion built by William Randolph III. Fully paneled, authentic 18th-century furnishings. Headquarters of National Society of Colonial Dames in Virginia. (Daily exc Mon; closed hols) Open during Historic Garden Week (see ANNUAL EVENTS). S Wilton Rd off Cary St, 8 mi W. Phone 804/282-5936. ¢¢

Annual Events

Historic Garden Week in Virginia. Many private houses and gardens of historic or artistic interest are opened for this event, which includes more than 200 houses and gardens throughout the state. Tours. Contact 12 E Franklin St, 23219; 804/644-7776. Apr 19-27.

June Jubilee. Downtown. Performing and visual arts festival with ethnic foods, African folk dances, music, crafts. 2nd wknd in June.

Virginia State Fair. Animal and 4-H contests, music, horse show, carnival. Phone 804/228-3200. Late Sept-early Oct.

Richmond Newpapers Marathon. Last Sun Oct.

Motels

★ ★ **AMERISUITES.** (4100 Cox Rd, Glen Allen 23060) 804/747-9644; FAX 804/346-9320. 126 suites, 6 story. S, D $99; under 18 free. Crib free. TV; cable (premium), VCR. Pool. Complimentary continental bkfst. Restaurant nearby. Ck-out noon. Meeting rms. Business center. Coin Indry. Exercise equipt; weight machine, bicycle. Microwaves. Cr cds: A, C, D, DS, MC, V.

D ⌘ 🏋 📶 🔥 SC 🚶

★ ★ **COURTYARD BY MARRIOTT.** 6400 W Broad St (23230). 804/282-1881; FAX 804/288-2934. 145 rms, 3 story. S, D $96; suites $119; under 19 free; wknd rates. Crib free. TV; cable (premium). Pool; whirlpool. Coffee in rms. Bar. Ck-out noon. Coin Indry. Business servs avail. In-rm modem link. Valet serv. Sundries. Exercise equipt; weight machines, stair machines. Some refrigerators. Cr cds: A, C, D, DS, MC, V.

D ⌘ 🏋 📶 🔥 SC

★ **FAIRFIELD INN BY MARRIOTT.** 7300 W Broad St (23294). 804/672-8621; FAX 804/755-7155. 124 rms, 2 story. S $61-$89; D $66-$89; each addl $5; suite $129; under 18 free. Crib free. TV; cable (premium). Complimentary continental bkfst. Restaurant adj 11-2 am. Ck-out noon. Business servs avail. In-rm modem link. Health club privileges. Pool. Refrigerator, microwave in suite. Picnic tables. Cr cds: A, D, DS, MC, V.

D ⌘ 📶 🔥 SC

★ **LA QUINTA.** 6910 Midlothian Pike (US 60W) (23225), at VA 150. 804/745-7100; FAX 804/276-6660. 130 rms, 3 story. S $52-$59; D $59-$66; each addl $7; under 18 free. Crib free. Pet accepted, some restrictions. TV; cable (premium). Heated pool. Complimentary continental bkfst. Restaurant adj 6 am-11 pm. Ck-out noon. Meeting rms. Business servs avail. In-rm modem link. Cr cds: A, C, D, DS, ER, JCB, MC, V.

D 🐾 ⌘ 📶 🔥 SC

✔★ **RED ROOF INN.** 4350 Commerce Rd (23234), south of downtown. 804/271-7240; FAX 804/271-7245. 108 rms, 2 story. S $33.99-$49.99; D $39.99-$49.99; under 18 free; higher rates race wknds. Pet accepted. TV; cable (premium). Complimentary coffee in lobby. Restaurant nearby. Ck-out noon. Business servs avail. Some refrigerators. Cr cds: A, C, D, DS, MC, V.

D 🐾 📶 🔥

★ ★ **RESIDENCE INN BY MARRIOTT.** 2121 Dickens Rd (23230). 804/285-8200; FAX 804/285-2530. 80 kit. suites, 2 story. S, D $109-$159; monthly, wkly, wknd rates. Crib free. Pet accepted, some restrictions; $50 and $5/day. TV; cable (premium), VCR avail (movies). Pool. Complimentary continental bkfst. Ck-out noon. Coin Indry. Meeting rm. Business servs avail. In-rm modem link. Valet serv. Health club privileges. Microwaves; many fireplaces. Private patios, balconies. Picnic tables, grills. Cr cds: A, C, D, DS, ER, JCB, MC, V.

D 🐾 ⌘ 📶 🔥 SC

Motor Hotels

★ ★ **HAMPTON INN.** 10800 W Broad St (23060). 804/747-7777; FAX 804/747-7069. 136 rms, 5 story. S $77-$98; D $84-$98; each addl $7; under 18 free. Crib free. TV; cable (premium). Complimentary continental bkfst. Restaurant nearby. Ck-out noon. Meeting rms. Business servs avail. In-rm modem link. Bellhops. Exercise equipt; bicycle, treadmill. Pool. Picnic table. Cr cds: A, C, D, DS, ER, JCB, MC, V.

D ⌘ 🏋 📶 🔥 SC

★ ★ **HILTON AIRPORT.** (5501 Eubank Rd, Sandston 23150) near Intl Airport. 804/226-6400; FAX 804/226-1269. 160 rms, 5 story, 122 suites. S, D $79-$155; each addl $15; family, wknd rates. Crib free. TV; cable (premium). Pool; whirlpool. Coffee in rms. Restaurant 6:30 am-10 pm. Rm serv to midnight. Bar 11-2 am. Ck-out noon. Meeting rms. Business servs avail. In-rm modem link. Bellhops. Valet serv. Sundries. Gift shop. Free airport transportation. Exercise equipt; treadmill, stair machine. Some balconies. Cr cds: A, C, D, DS, ER, JCB, MC, V.

D ⌘ 🏋 🍽 📶 🔥 SC

★ ★ **HOLIDAY INN AIRPORT.** (5203 Williamsburg Rd, Sandston 23150) near Intl Airport. 804/222-6450; FAX 804/226-4305. 230 rms, 3-6 story. S, D $76-$90; suites $86-$101; under 12 free. Pet accepted, some restrictions. TV; cable (premium). Pool; lifeguard. Complimentary continental bkfst. Restaurant 6 am-3 pm, 5-10:30 pm. Rm serv noon-1 am; entertainment. Ck-out noon. Meeting rms. Business servs avail. In-rm modem link. Bellhops. Free airport transportation. Refrigerators, microwaves avail. Cr cds: A, C, D, DS, JCB, MC, V.

D 🐾 ⌘ 🏋 🍽 🔥 SC

★ ★ **HYATT.** 6624 W Broad St (23230). 804/285-1234; FAX 804/288-3961. 372 rms, 3-8 story. S, D $145-$160; suites $175-$450; under 18 free; wknd rates. Crib free. TV; cable (premium), VCR avail. Indoor/outdoor pool; poolside serv. Playground. Coffee in rms. Restaurant 6-10 pm. Rm serv 6 am-midnight. Bar noon-2 am; entertainment. Ck-out noon. Meeting rms. Business center. In-rm modem link. Bellhops. Valet serv. Gift shop. Airport transportation. Lighted tennis. Exercise equipt; weight machine, stair machine. Some private patios. Luxury level. Cr cds: A, C, D, DS, ER, JCB, MC, V.

D 🚶 ⌘ 🏋 🤽 🍽 🔥 SC 🚶

✔★ **QUALITY INN.** 8008 W Broad St (23294). 804/346-0000; FAX 804/346-4547. 194 rms, 6 story. Apr-Oct: S $59-$99; each addl $10; under 16 free; lower rates rest of yr. Crib free. TV; cable (premium). Pool. Coffee in rms. Complimentary continental bkfst. Restaurant nearby. Ck-out 11 am. Meeting rms. Business servs avail. In-rm modem link. Health club privileges. Microwaves avail. Cr cds: A, C, D, DS, ER, JCB, MC, V.

D ⌘ 📶 🔥 SC

★ ★ **SHERATON INN-AIRPORT.** 4700 S Laburnum Ave (23231), near Intl Airport. 804/226-4300; FAX 804/226-6516. 151 rms, 4 story. S $98-$118; D $105-$125; each addl $10; suites $115-$205; under 17 free; wknd rates. Crib free. Pet accepted. TV; cable (premium), VCR avail. Indoor pool; whirlpool. Restaurant 6-1 am. Rm serv. Bar 11-2 am. Ck-out noon. Business servs avail. In-rm modem link. Bellhops. Valet serv. Gift shop. Barber, beauty shop. Free airport transportation. Exercise equipt; weights, bicycles, sauna. Bathrm phones. Some private patios, balconies. Cr cds: A, C, D, DS, ER, JCB, MC, V.

D 🐾 ⌘ 🏋 🛫 📶 🔥 SC

Hotels

★ ★ ★ **BERKELEY.** *1200 E Cary St (23219), in Shockoe Slip area, downtown.* 804/780-1300; FAX 804/648-4728. 55 rms, 6 story. S $115-$154; D $128-$164; each addl $15; under 12 free; wkend rates. Crib free. TV; cable (premium), VCR avail. Pool privileges. Coffee in rms. Restaurant 7 am-2 pm, 6-10 pm; Fri, Sat to 11 pm; Sun to 9 pm. Bar 11:30 am-2 pm, 4:30 pm-midnight. Ck-out noon. Meeting rms. Business servs avail. In-rm modem link. Concierge. Free valet parking. Airport transportation. Health club privileges. Bathrm phones. Cr cds: A, C, D, DS, MC, V.

D 🏊 🏋 🐾 SC

★ ★ **CROWNE PLAZA.** *555 E Canal St (23219), downtown.* 804/788-0900; FAX 804/788-0791. 299 rms, 16 story. Apr-June, Sept-Oct: S, D $119-$149; each addl $10; suites $175-$500; under 12 free; wkend rates; lower rates rest of yr. Crib free. TV; cable (premium). Indoor pool; whirlpool. Coffee in rms. Restaurant 6:30 am-11 pm. Bar 4 pm-1:30 am. Ck-out noon. Convention facilities. Business servs avail. In-rm modem link. Concierge. Gift shop. Exercise equipt; weights, bicycles. Cr cds: A, C, D, DS, JCB, MC, V.

D 🏊 🏋 🏊 🔥 🐾 SC

★ ★ ★ **EMBASSY SUITES.** *2925 Emerywood Pkwy (23294), Commerce Center.* 804/672-8585; FAX 804/672-3749. 225 suites, 8 story. Suites $109-$170; each addl $20; under 18 free. Crib free. TV; cable (premium). Indoor pool; whirlpool. Complimentary full bkfst. Restaurant 11 am-10 pm. Bar to midnight. Ck-out noon. Coin lndry. Meeting rms. Business servs avail. In-rm modem link. Gift shop. Exercise equipt; weight machine, bicycles, sauna, steam rm. Refrigerators, microwaves; wet bar in suites. Cr cds: A, C, D, DS, JCB, MC, V.

D 🏊 🏋 🏊 🐾 SC

★ ★ ★ ★ **THE JEFFERSON.** *Franklin & Adams Sts (23220).* 804/788-8000; FAX 804/325-0334; res: 800/424-8014. E-mail sales@jefferson.hotel.com; web www.jefferson.hotel.com. This twin-towered landmark about one-half mile from downtown is an immaculately restored illustration of Richmond's rich history. Some guest rooms are small, but they are well furnished with reproductions and have large, lighted closets and all other facilities necessary for a comfortable stay. 274 rms, 9 story. Apr-mid-June & mid-Sept-early Dec: S $140-$180; D $155-$195; each addl $15; suites $225-$825; under 18 free; special packages; lower rates rest of yr. Crib free. Valet parking $10. TV; cable (premium), VCR avail. Pool privileges. Restaurant 6:30 am-midnight (also see LEMAIRE). Rm serv 24 hrs. Bar 11-2 am. Ck-out noon. Meeting rms. Business center. In-rm modem link. Concierge. Shopping arcade. Exercise equipt; weights, bicycles. Bathrm phones, refrigerators, minibars. Some balconies. Cr cds: A, C, D, DS, ER, JCB, MC, V.

D 🏋 🏊 🔥 SC 🚶

★ ★ **MARRIOTT.** *500 E Broad St (23219), downtown.* 804/643-3400; FAX 804/788-1230. 400 rms, 17 story. S $109; D $119; each addl $10; suites $200-$700; under 18 free; wkend packages. Crib free. TV; cable (premium). Indoor pool; whirlpool, poolside serv, lifeguard. Restaurant 6:30 am-10 pm. Bar 11-1 am. Ck-out noon. Coin lndry. Convention facilities. Business servs avail. In-rm modem link. Concierge. Exercise equipt; weights, bicycles, sauna. Game rm. Some bathrm phones, refrigerators. Luxury level. Cr cds: A, C, D, DS, JCB, MC, V.

D 🏊 🏋 🏊 🐾 SC 🚶

★ ★ ★ **OMNI.** *100 S 12th St (23219), in Shockoe Slip area, downtown.* 804/344-7000; FAX 804/648-6704. 363 units, 19 story. Mid-Apr-mid-June, mid-Sept-mid-Nov: S $134; D $149; each addl $15; suites $209-$450; under 18 free; wkly, wkend rates; lower rates rest of yr. Crib free. TV; cable (premium). Indoor pool; poolside serv. Restaurant 6:30 am-11 pm. Bar noon-1 am; entertainment. Ck-out 1 pm. Convention facilities. Business servs avail. In-rm modem link. Concierge. Shopping arcade. Health club privileges. Minibars. Luxury level. Cr cds: A, C, D, DS, ER, JCB, MC, V.

D 🏊 🏊 🔥 🐾 SC

Inns

★ ★ **EMMANUEL HUTZLER HOUSE.** *2036 Monument Ave (23220).* 804/353-6900; FAX 804/355-5053. Web www.bensonhouse.com. 4 rms, 3 story. S $85-$115; D $95-$145. Children over 12 yrs only. TV; cable. Complimentary continental bkfst; full bkfst wkends. Complimentary coffee in library. Restaurant nearby. Ck-out noon, ck-in 4 pm. Luggage handling. Built 1914; antiques. Totally nonsmoking. Cr cds: A, D, DS, MC, V.

🏊 🐾

★ ★ ★ **LINDEN ROW INN.** *100 E Franklin St (23219), entrance at 101 N 1st St, downtown.* 804/783-7000; FAX 804/648-7504; res: 800/348-7424. 70 rms, 4 story, 7 suites. S, D $109-$159; each addl $10; suites $129-$209. TV; cable (premium). Complimentary continental bkfst. Dining rm (public by res) 11 am-2:30 pm, 5:30-10 pm. Rm serv. Ck-out noon, ck-in 3 pm. Business servs avail. In-rm modem link. Bellhops. Valet serv. Concierge. Health club privileges. In block of Greek-revival rowhouses (1847) and around courtyard thought to be boyhood playground of Edgar Allan Poe; antique and period furnishings and decor. Cr cds: A, C, D, DS, ER, MC, V.

D 🏊 🐾 SC

★ ★ **MR. PATRICK HENRY'S.** *2300-02 E Broad St (23223), in Church Hill Historic District.* 804/644-1322; res: 800/932-2654. 4 rms. Apr-June, Oct-Nov: S $95-$125; D $115-$135; each addl $10; family, wkly, wkend rates; 2-day min hol wkends; higher rates special events; lower rates rest of yr. TV; cable. Complimentary full bkfst. Complimentary coffee in rms. Restaurant (see MR. PATRICK HENRY'S INN). Rm serv. Ck-out noon, ck-in 3 pm. Luggage handling. Street parking. Refrigerators. Greek revival antebellum row house (ca 1855); garden patio, carriage house. Cr cds: A, C, D, DS, MC, V.

🐾 SC

✔ ★ ★ **WILLIAM CATLIN HOUSE.** *2304 E Broad St (23223), in Church Hill Historic District.* 804/780-3746. 5 rms, 2 share bath, 3 story. No elvtr. S $85, D $95; suites $150. Complimentary full bkfst; afternoon refreshments. Ck-out 11 am, ck-in 3 pm. Balconies. Greek revival town house (1845) furnished with antiques, family heirlooms; fireplaces. Spacious veranda overlooks courtyard. Cr cds: DS, MC, V.

🔥

Restaurants

★ **AMICI.** *3343 W Cary St (23221).* 804/353-4700. Hrs: 11:30 am-2:30 pm, 5:30-10 pm; Fri, Sat to 11 pm; Sun from 5:30 pm. Closed major hols. Res accepted. Northern Italian menu. Bar. A la carte entrees: lunch $4-$8.95, dinner $5.95-$18.95. Specializes in pasta, game, seafood. Own breads. Outdoor dining. Cr cds: A, MC, V.

🍴

★ **BYRAM'S LOBSTER HOUSE.** *3215 W Broad St (23230).* 804/355-9193. Hrs: 11:30 am-10 pm; Fri, Sat to 11 pm; early-bird dinner Mon-Fri 3:30-6 pm. Closed Jan 1, Dec 25. Res accepted. Continental menu. Bar. Semi-a la carte: lunch $2-$24.95, dinner $7.95-$24.95. Specializes in Maine lobster, crab. Parking. Local artwork, Greek reproductions. Family-owned. Cr cds: A, C, D, DS, MC, V.

D SC 🍴

★ **CAFFE DI PAGLIACCI.** *214 N Lombardy St (23220).* 804/353-3040. Hrs: 5-10 pm; Fri, Sat to 11 pm. Closed Sun; major hols. Res accepted. Italian menu. Bar. Semi-a la carte: $6.95-$14.95. Specializes in pasta, veal. Own desserts. Casual decor. Cr cds: A, DS, MC, V.

🍴

✔ ★ **FAROUK'S HOUSE OF INDIA.** *3033 W Cary St (23221), west of downtown.* 804/355-0378. Hrs: 11:30 am-3 pm, 5:30-10:30 pm. Res accepted. Indian menu. Bar. Semi-a la carte: lunch $4.50-$7.50, dinner $6.95-$12. Lunch buffet: $5.99. Specialties: curries, biryanies, tandoori. Cr cds: MC, V.

★ ★ ★ **THE FROG AND THE REDNECK.** *1423 E Cary St (23219).* 804/648-3764. E-mail frogneck@mindspring.com; web www.frog andredneck.com. Hrs: 5:30-10 pm; Sat 5-10:30 pm. Closed Sun; major hols. Res accepted. Regional American menu. Bar. Wine list. Semi-a la carte: dinner $9.75-$26.25. Specializes in soft shell crab, jumbo lump crab cakes, buffalo. Contemporary decor, with a touch of art deco. Muraled walls. Totally nonsmoking. Cr cds: A, C, D, DS, MC, V.

★ ★ **HALF WAY HOUSE.** *10301 Jefferson Davis Hwy (Petersburg Tpke) (23237), 13 mi S on US 1.* 804/275-1760. Hrs: 11:30 am-2 pm, 5:30-9 pm; Sat, Sun from 5:30 pm. Res accepted. Bar. Wine list. Semi-a la carte: lunch $7-$15, dinner $17-$30. Specialties: lobster Von Grinegan, filet mignon, colonial chicken & beef pies. Parking. Antique-furnished manor house (1760) was stop on Petersburg stagecoach line until late 19th century; hosted Washington, Lafayette, Patrick Henry, Jefferson, among others. Used as a Union headquarters during 1864 siege of Richmond. Cr cds: A, D, DS, MC, V.

✔ ★ **INDOCHINE.** *2923 W Cary St (23221).* 804/353-5799. Hrs: 11:30 am-3 pm, 5-10 pm; Sat from 5 pm. Closed Sun; Memorial Day, Dec 25. Res required Fri, Sat dinner. Vietnamese menu. Bar. Semi-a la carte: lunch $7.95, dinner $12.95-$17.95. Specialties: crispy softshell crab; scallops and shrimp in curry sauce; crispy salmon filet with spicy apple-cognac sauce. Own baking. French Colonial atmosphere; greenery throughout. Totally nonsmoking. Cr cds: A, D, DS, MC, V.

★ ★ **JAMES RIVER WINE BISTRO.** *1520 W Main St (23220).* 804/358-4562. Hrs: 4-11 pm; Sun brunch 11:30 am-2:30 pm. Closed Dec 25. Res accepted. Regional Amer menu. Bar. Wine cellar. Semi-a la carte: dinner $11-$22.95. Sun brunch $15.95. Child's meals. Specializes in seafood, wood-grilled meats. Own baking. Outdoor dining. Old schoolhouse (ca 1891) complete with brick archways and frosted windows. Cr cds: A, DS, MC, V.

★ ★ **KABUTO STEAK HOUSE.** *8052 W Broad St (23294).* 804/747-9573. Hrs: 11:30 am-2 pm, 5:30-10 pm; Fri to 10:30 pm; Sat 5-10:30 pm; Sun noon-2:30 pm, 5:30-9:30 pm. Closed Thanksgiving, Dec 25. Res accepted. Japanese menu. Bar. Complete meals: lunch $6-$10.25, dinner $11.50-$22. Child's meals. Specializes in Teppanyaki cooking. Sushi bar. Parking. Japanese-style building. Cr cds: A, C, D, DS, MC, V.

★ ★ ★ **LA PETITE FRANCE.** *2108 Maywill St (23230).* 804/353-8729. Hrs: 11:30 am-2 pm, 5:30-10 pm; Sat 5:30-11 pm. Closed Sun, Mon; major hols; also last 2 wks Aug. Res accepted. French menu. Serv bar. Wine list. A la carte entrees: lunch $7.95-$10.95, dinner $17.95-$22.50. Child's meals. Specializes in seafood, veal. Family-owned. Jacket. Cr cds: A, C, D, DS, MC, V.

★ ★ ★ **LEMAIRE.** *(See The Jefferson Hotel)* 804/788-8000. E-mail sales@jefferson.hotel.com; web www.jefferson.hotel.com. Hrs: 6:30 am-2 pm, 5:30-10:30 pm. Closed Memorial Day. Res accepted. Bar. A la carte entrees: bkfst $2.25-$10.50, lunch $3.50-$13.95, dinner $3.75-$25.95. Child's meals. Specializes in regional cuisine, venison, pheasant. Valet parking. Seven small dining rms. Cr cds: A, C, D, DS, ER, JCB, MC, V.

★ ★ **MR. PATRICK HENRY'S INN.** *(See Mr. Patrick Henry's Inn)* 804/644-1322. Hrs: 11:30 am-2:30 pm, 5:30-10 pm. Closed Sun (exc hols); Jan 1, Dec 24-25. Res accepted. Continental menu. Bar. Semi-a la

carte: lunch $6-$12, dinner $17-$24. Specializes in duckling, crabcakes. Own soups. Outdoor dining. In Greek-revival antebellum row house (ca 1855); many antique furnishings. Cr cds: A, C, D, DS, MC, V.

✔ ★ **O'TOOLE'S.** *4800 Forest Hill Ave (23225).* 804/233-1781. Hrs: 11-2 am; Sun to midnight. Closed Dec 24, 25. Bar. Semi-a la carte: lunch $3.75-$8, dinner $4.25-$12.95. Child's meals. Specializes in seafood, steak, barbecued dishes. Pianist. Parking. Irish pub decor. Family-owned. Cr cds: A, DS, MC, V.

★ ★ **PEKING PAVILION.** *1302 E Cary St (23219), in Shockoe Slip historic district, downtown.* 804/649-8888. Hrs: 11:30 am-2:15 pm, 5-9:30 pm; Fri to 10:30 pm; Sat 5-10:30 pm; Sun brunch 11:30 am-2 pm. Closed Thanksgiving. Res accepted. Chinese menu. Bar. Semi-a la carte: lunch $4.25-$6.95, dinner $6.50-$22.50. Sun brunch $8.95. Specialties: Peking duck, seafood delight, chicken imperial. Oriental antiques; teakwood sculpture. Cr cds: A, MC, V.

★ ★ ★ **RUTH'S CHRIS STEAK HOUSE.** *11500 Huguenot Rd (23113), at Bellgrade Plantation House.* 804/378-0600. E-mail rcsh30@aol.com. Hrs: 5-10 pm; Fri, Sat to 11 pm; Sun to 9 pm. Closed some major hols. Res accepted. Bar. A la carte entrees: dinner $16-$29. Specializes in steak, lobster. Organist Tues-Sun. Parking. Outdoor dining. Cr cds: A, C, D, DS, MC, V.

★ ★ **SAM MILLER'S WAREHOUSE.** *1210 E Cary St (23219), in Shockoe area of downtown.* 804/643-1301. Hrs: 11 am-11 pm; Sun brunch 10 am-5 pm. Res accepted. Bar to 1:30 am. Semi-a la carte: lunch $4.95-$10.95, dinner $15-$25. Sun champagne brunch $6-$13.95. Child's meals. Specializes in fresh seafood, live Maine lobster, prime Western beef. Lobster tank. In historic district; display of antique mirrors. Cr cds: A, D, MC, V.

★ ★ **SKILLIGALEE.** *5416 Glenside Dr (23228).* 804/672-6200. Web www.skilligalee.com. Hrs: 11:30 am-4 pm, 5-10 pm; Fri to 10:30 pm; Sat 5-10:30 pm; Sun 5-9 pm. Closed Thanksgiving, Dec 25. Bar. A la carte entrees: lunch $5.95-$11.95, dinner $13.95-$25.95. Child's meals. Specializes in fresh seafood, soups. Raw bar. Own salad dressing. Parking. Nautical decor with fireplace. Family-owned. Cr cds: A, D, MC, V.

★ ★ **SORRENTO.** *5604 Patterson Ave (23226).* 804/282-9340. Hrs: 5:30-10 pm; Sun to 9 pm. Closed Mon; major hols; also 1st 2 wks July. Res accepted. Italian menu. Bar. Semi-a la carte: dinner $8.75-$19.95. Child's meals. Specializes in veal dishes. Own pasta. Cr cds: A, MC, V.

✔ ★ **TANGLEWOOD ORDINARY.** *(2210 River Rd W, Maidens 23102) 16 mi W on VA 6 (Patterson Ave).* 804/784-7011. Web www.ordinary.com. Hrs: 5:30-9 pm; Sun noon-6 pm. Closed Mon-Tues; some major hols. Res accepted; required Wed. Traditional Southern menu. Bar. Complete meals: dinner $9. Specializes in fried chicken, catfish, ham. Casual dining in log cabin building. Collection of The Saturday Evening Post dating from 1913. Totally nonsmoking. No cr cds accepted.

★ ★ ★ **TOBACCO COMPANY.** *1201 E Cary St (23219), in Shockoe Slip area, downtown.* 804/782-9431. Hrs: 11:30 am-2:30 pm, 5:30-10:30 pm; Sat 5-11 pm; Sun 10:30 am-2:30 pm, 5:30-10 pm. Closed Jan 1, Dec 25. Res accepted. Bar 11:30-2 am. A la carte entrees: lunch $2.99-$7.95, dinner $12.95-$25.95. Sun brunch $4.95-$15.95. Specializes in prime rib, fresh fish. Own baking. Band exc Sun. In former tobacco warehouse (ca 1880); built around skylighted atrium with antique cage elevator; many unusual antiques. Cr cds: A, D, MC, V.

✔ ★ **WINNIE'S.** *200 E Main St (23219).* 804/649-4974. Hrs: 11 am-10 pm; Fri to 10:30 pm; Sat 5-10:30 pm. Closed Sun; major hols. Res accepted Fri, Sat dinner. Caribbean menu. Wine, beer. Semi-a la carte: lunch $3.99-$7.99, dinner $5.99-$16.50. Child's meals. Specializes in Jamaican jerk chicken, roti, goat. Street parking. Bright Caribbean decor with posters, bamboo chairs. Totally nonsmoking. Cr cds: MC, V.

SC

★ ★ YEN CHING. 6601 Midlothian Tpke (23225). 804/276-7430. Hrs: 11:30 am-10 pm; Sat, Sun to 11 pm. Closed Thanksgiving. Res required. Chinese menu. Bar. Semi-a la carte: lunch $5-$22, dinner $7-$22. Specializes in Hunan and Szechuan dishes. Parking. Chinese tapestries and art. Cr cds: A, C, D, MC, V.

D ➤

Richmond National Battlefield Park (E-8)

(For accommodations see Ashland, Richmond)

A total of seven Union drives on Richmond, the symbol of secession, were made during the Civil War. Richmond National Battlefield Park, 770 acres in 10 different units, preserves sites of the two efforts that came close to success—McClellan's Peninsula Campaign of 1862 and Grant's attack in 1864.

Of McClellan's campaign, the park includes sites of the Seven Days' Battles at Chickahominy Bluffs, Beaver Dam Creek, Gaines' Mill (Watt House) and Malvern Hill. Grant's campaign is represented by the battlefield at Cold Harbor, where on June 3, 1864, Grant hurled his army at fortified Confederate positions, resulting in 7,000 casualties in less than one hour. Confederate Fort Harrison, Parker's Battery and Drewry's Bluff (Fort Darling) and Union-built Fort Brady are also included. Park (daily).

What to See and Do

Main Visitor Center. Information, exhibits, film, slide program. (Daily; closed Jan 1, Thanksgiving, Dec 25) In Chimborazo City Park. 3215 E Broad St, on US 60E in Richmond. Phone 804/226-1981. **Free.** From here start

Self-guided tour. Auto drive (60 mi) with markers, maps, recorded messages providing background, detailed information for specific places. Visitors may select own route, including all or part of the drive.

Other Visitor Centers. Cold Harbor, 16 mi NE on VA 156 (daily, unstaffed) and Fort Harrison, 10 mi SE on VA 5 & Battlefield Park Rd (June-Aug, daily). **Free.**

Roanoke (E-5)

(See also Salem)

Settled 1740 **Pop** 96,397 **Elev** 948 ft **Area code** 540 **E-mail** rvcvb@rbnet **Web** www.visitroanokeva.com
Information Roanoke Valley Convention & Visitors Bureau, 114 Market St, 24011; 540/342-6025 or 800/635-5535.

Roanoke was incorporated in 1882, when it became a junction of the Norfolk and Western Railway and the Shenandoah Valley Railroad. Before that, the town was called Big Lick (salt marshes in the area attracted big game).

It is the cultural, industrial, commercial, convention and medical center for western Virginia. Manufactured products include railroad cars, fabricated steel, fabrics, apparel, furniture, flour, wood products, electronic equipment, plastics, cosmetics and locks.

Set in the Shenandoah Valley, between the Blue Ridge and the Allegheny Mountains, it is near the outdoor attractions of the huge George Washington and Jefferson National Forests (see HARRISONBURG) and the Blue Ridge Parkway (see).

What to See and Do

Blue Ridge Pkwy (see). Runs on crest of mountains both N and S of Roanoke. Narrow in parts; limited restaurants. Beautiful seasonal views from overlooks. 6 mi E on US 460 or 3 mi S on US 220.

Center in the Square. Restored 20th-century furniture warehouse housing five independent cultural organizations: three museums, including Art Museum of Western Virginia, and two professional theater companies (see SEASONAL EVENT). (Daily exc Mon; closed major hols) One Market Sq, downtown. Phone 540/342-5700. Art museum **Free.** Also here are

Science Museum of Western Virginia. Museum contains hands-on exhibits in the natural and physical sciences: animals of land & ocean, computers, TV weather station. Workshops, programs and classes for children & adults; special exhibits. Hopkins Planetarium shows films. (Daily; closed hols) Phone 540/342-5710 or 540/343-7876 (recording). ¢¢

Roanoke Valley History Museum. Permanent exhibits deal with Roanoke history from days of Native Americans to present. Archives, library (by appt). (Daily exc Mon; closed most hols) Phone 540/342-5770. ¢

George Washington and Jefferson National Forests (see HARRISONBURG).

Mill Mountain Zoological Park. Zoo sits atop Mill Mt; offers picnic areas with magnificent views of city and valley. (Daily; closed Dec 25) Off US 220/I-581 & Blue Ridge Pkwy. Phone 540/343-3241. ¢¢

Virginia Museum of Transportation. Vehicles from the past and present. Large steam, diesel and electric locomotive collection. Aviation exhibits; model of miniature traveling circus. Hands-on exhibits. (Mar-Dec, daily; rest of yr, daily exc Mon; closed major hols) 303 Norfolk Ave, downtown. Phone 540/342-5670. ¢¢

Virginia's Explore Park. 1,300-acre living history museum and nature center features re-created frontier settlement with interpreters demonstrating 19th-century life. Tutelo Native American Village; 19th-century structures; visitor participation exhibits. 6 mi of hiking trails. Picnic areas. (Apr-Oct, Fri-Mon) Milepost 115 on Blue Ridge Pkwy. Phone 540/427-1800. ¢¢¢

Annual Events

Virginia State Championship Chili Cookoff. City Market. Teams compete to represent Virginia in World Cook-off. Samples, entertainment. For information contact Roanoke Special Events Committee, 210 Reserve Ave SW, 24016; 540/342-2028. 1st Sat May.

Festival in the Park. Art exhibits, crafts, sports, food, parade, entertainment. 2 wkends beginning Fri before Memorial Day.

Seasonal Event

Mill Mountain Theatre. Center in the Square. Musicals, comedies, dramas. Nightly exc Mon; Sat, Sun matinees. For res phone 540/342-5740. Regular season, Oct-Aug.

Motels

✔ ★ **COLONY HOUSE.** 3560 Franklin Rd SW (24014). 540/345-0411; res: 800/552-7026. 69 rms, 2 story. S $46; D $58-$68; each addl $5; under 13 free. Crib avail. TV; cable. Complimentary continental bkfst. Restaurant adj 11 am-10 pm. Ck-out 11 am. Meetng rms. Business servs avail. Valet serv. Health club privileges. Pool. Bathrm phone, in-rm whirlpool, refrigerator in suites. Cr cds: A, C, D, DS, MC, V.

D ≈ ≈ ⚒ SC

✔ ★ ★ **DAYS INN-AIRPORT/INTERSTATE.** 8118 Plantation Rd (24019), I-81 exit 146. 540/366-0341; FAX 540/366-3935. 123 rms, 2 story. S $45-$60; D $55-$65; each addl $6; suites $80; under 12 free. Crib avail. TV; cable (premium), VCR avail. Pool. Restaurant 6-10:30 am, 5-10 pm.

Bar 4:30-11 pm. Ck-out noon. Meeting rms. Business servs avail. In-rm modem link. Valet serv. Free airport transportation. Cr cds: A, C, D, DS, JCB, MC, V.

[D] [≈] [⊠] [▨] [SC]

★ ★ **HAMPTON INN-AIRPORT.** 6621 Thirlane Rd (24019), near Regional Airport. 540/265-2600; FAX 540/366-2091. 79 rms, 2 story. S $70-$72; D $76-$80; suites $103; under 18 free; higher rates: graduation, sporting events. Crib free. Valet parking $20. TV; cable (premium), VCR. Complimentary coffee in lobby. Restaurant nearby. Ck-out 11 am. Meeting rms. Business servs avail. Valet serv. Sundries. Coin lndry. Free airport transportation. Exercise equipt; weight machine, treadmill. Heated pool. Refrigerators, microwaves; some bathrm phones; in-rm whirlpool in suites. Cr cds: A, C, D, DS, MC, V.

[D] [≈] [⊀] [✈] [⊠] [▨] [SC]

★ **HAMPTON INN-TANGLEWOOD.** 3816 Franklin Rd SW (24014). 540/989-4000; FAX 540/989-0250. 59 rms, 2 story. May-Nov: S $58-$62; D $68-$72; family rates; higher rates special events. Crib free. TV; cable (premium), VCR avail. Complimentary continental bkfst. Restaurant adj 10:30 am-9 pm; wkends from 8 am. Ck-out 11 am. Coin lndry. Meeting rm. Business servs avail. In-rm modem link. Valet serv. Health club privileges. Some refrigerators, microwaves. Cr cds: A, C, D, DS, MC, V.

[D] [⊠] [▨] [SC]

★ ★ **HOLIDAY INN-AIRPORT.** 6626 Thirlane Rd (24019), near Municipal Airport. 540/366-8861; FAX 540/366-1637. 163 rms, 2 story. S, D $74-$85; under 18 free; wkend, special event rates. Crib free. TV; cable (premium), VCR avail. Pool; wading pool, lifeguard in summer. Complimentary coffee in rms. Restaurant 6 am-10 pm. Rm serv. Bar. Ck-out noon. Coin lndry. Meeting rms. Business servs avail. In-rm modem link. Bellhops. Valet serv. Sundries. Airport, bus depot transportation. Tennis privileges. Golf privileges. Some bathrm phones. Cr cds: A, C, D, DS, ER, JCB, MC, V.

[D] [⊀] [✈] [≈] [✕] [⊠] [▨] [SC]

★ ★ **QUALITY INN-CIVIC CENTER.** 501 Orange Ave at Williamson Rd (24016). 540/342-8961; FAX 540/342-3813. 152 rms, 2 story. S, D $60-$80. Crib free. TV; cable (premium), VCR avail. Pool; wading pool. Complimentary bkfst buffet. Coffee in rms. Restaurant 6 am-10 pm. Rm serv from 7 am. Bar from 5 pm. Ck-out noon. Business servs avail. In-rm modem link. Bellhops. Valet serv. Microwaves avail. Cr cds: A, C, D, DS, ER, JCB, MC, V.

[D] [≈] [⊠] [▨] [SC]

★ ★ **RAMADA INN.** 1927 Franklin Rd SW (24014). 540/343-0121; FAX 540/342-2048. 127 rms, 4 story. S $58; D $64; each addl $7; under 18 free; higher rates special events. Pet accepted. Pool. Complimentary full bkfst. Coffee in rms. Restaurant 11:30 am-2:30 pm, 4:30-9:30 pm. Bar 4:30 pm-2 am. Ck-out noon. Coin lndry. Meeting rms. Business servs avail. In-rm modem link. Health club privileges. Sundries. Near river. Cr cds: A, C, D, DS, ER, JCB, MC, V.

[D] [✦] [≈] [⊠] [▨] [SC]

★ **SLEEP INN.** 4045 Electric Rd (24014). 540/772-1500. 103 rms, shower only, 2 story. No elvtr. S $55.95-$60.95; D $60.95-$65; each addl $6; under 18 free. Crib free. TV; cable (premium), VCR. Complimentary continental bkfst. Restaurant nearby. Ck-out noon. Meeting rm. Business servs avail. In-rm modem link. Valet serv. Health club privileges. Microwaves avail. Cr cds: A, C, D, DS, ER, JCB, MC, V.

[D] [⊠] [▨] [SC]

✔ **TRAVELODGE-NORTH.** (2444 Lee Hwy S, Troutville 24175) I-81 exit 150-A. 540/992-6700; FAX 540/992-3991. 109 rms. S $45; D $52; each addl $6; kit. units $45; under 18 free; wkly rates. Crib free. Pet accepted; $6. TV; cable (premium). Pool. Playground. Complimentary continental bkfst. Coffee in rms. Restaurant nearby. Ck-out 11 am. Meeting rms. Business servs avail. Cr cds: A, D, DS, MC, V.

[D] [✦] [≈] [⊠] [▨] [SC]

Motor Hotels

★ ★ ★ **CLARION-AIRPORT.** 2727 Ferndale Dr (24017), near Municipal Airport. 540/362-4500; FAX 540/362-4506. 154 rms, 5 story. S $89-$109; D $99-$115; each addl $10; under 18 free; wkend rates. Crib free. Pet accepted; $50 deposit. TV; cable (premium). Indoor/outdoor pool; whirlpool. Restaurant 6 am-10:30 pm. Rm serv. Complimentary coffee in rms. Bar 11:30 am-11 pm. Ck-out noon. Meeting rms. Business servs avail. In-rm modem link. Bellhops. Valet serv. Sundries. Free airport transportation. Lighted tennis. 18-hole golf privileges. Exercise equipt; weight machine, bicycles. Bathrm phones. Picnic tables, grills. Cr cds: A, C, D, DS, ER, JCB, MC, V.

[D] [✦] [⊀] [⌕] [≈] [✕] [✈] [⊠] [▨] [SC]

★ ★ ★ **HOLIDAY INN-TANGLEWOOD.** 4468 Starkey Rd SW (24014). 540/774-4400; FAX 540/774-1195. 196 rms, 5 story. S, D $88-$102; suites $128-$153; under 18 free; wkend rates. Crib free. Pet accepted; $10. TV; cable (premium). Pool; poolside serv. Restaurant 6:30 am-10 pm. Rm serv. Bar 4 pm-2 am; entertainment. Ck-out noon. Meeting rms. Business servs avail. In-rm modem link. Bellhops. Valet serv. Concierge. Free airport, bus depot transportation. Golf privileges. Health club privileges. Some wet bars; microwaves avail. Luxury level. Cr cds: A, C, D, DS, JCB, MC, V.

[D] [✦] [⊀] [≈] [▨] [SC]

Hotels

★ ★ ★ **DOUBLETREE HOTEL ROANOKE & CONFERENCE CENTER.** 110 Shennandoah Ave (24016). 540/985-5900; FAX 540/345-2890. 332 rms, 7 story. S $119-$145; D $129-$155; each addl $10; suites $165-$450; under 18 free; wkend, hol rates; higher rates: graduation, football. Crib free. Valet parking $5. TV; cable (premium). Complimentary coffee in lobby. Restaurant 6:30 am-10 pm; Sat from 7 am; Sun 7 am-9 pm. Bar 11 am-midnight; Fri, Sat to 1 am; entertainment Fri, Sat. Ck-out noon. Convention facilities. Business center. In-rm modem link. Gift shop. Free airport, RR station transportation. Tennis privileges. Golf privileges, pro, putting green, driving range. Exercise equipt; treadmill, stair machine. Pool; whirlpool. Some refrigerators, fireplaces. Cr cds: A, C, D, DS, ER, JCB, MC, V.

[D] [⊀] [⌕] [≈] [✕] [⊠] [▨] [SC] [⛷]

★ ★ ★ **MARRIOTT-ROANOKE AIRPORT.** 2801 Hershberger Rd NW (24017), I-581 exit 3W, near Municipal Airport. 540/563-9300; FAX 540/366-5846. Web www.swva.net/roanoke.marriott/. 320 rms, 8 story. S, studio rms $74-$134; D $84-$150; each addl $10; suites $210-$250; under 18 free; golf, wkend rates. Crib free. Pet accepted, some restrictions; $10. TV; cable (premium), VCR avail. 2 pools, 1 indoor; whirlpool, poolside serv. Restaurant 6:30 am-10 pm. Bars 11-1 am. Ck-out noon. Convention facilities. Business servs avail. Concierge. Gift shop. Free airport transportation. Lighted tennis. Exercise equipt; weights, bicycles, sauna. Some refrigerators. Private patios, balconies. Luxury level. Cr cds: A, C, D, DS, ER, JCB, MC, V.

[D] [✦] [≈] [⊀] [✕] [✈] [⊠] [▨] [SC]

★ ★ ★ **RADISSON PATRICK HENRY.** 617 S Jefferson St (24011). 540/345-8811; FAX 540/342-9908. E-mail phhotel13@aol.com. 117 kit. units, 10 story. S $99; D $109; each addl $10; suites $125-$250; under 18 free; monthly rates. Crib avail. TV; cable (premium). Complimentary continental bkfst. Restaurant 11:30 am-11 pm. Bar 4 pm-2 am. Ck-out noon. Guest lndry. Meeting rms. Business servs avail. In-rm modem link. Barber, beauty shop. Free airport transportation. Health club privileges. Refrigerators; microwaves avail. Cr cds: A, C, D, DS, ER, JCB, MC, V.

[D] [⊠] [▨] [SC]

Inn

★ ★ **CLAIBORNE HOUSE.** (185 Claiborne Ave, Rocky Mount 24151) US 220 S, W on VA 40. 540/483-4616. 5 rms, 2 story. Some rm phones. S, D $75-$125. TV in some rms; cable (premium). Complimentary full bkfst. Complimentary coffee in rms. Ck-out 11 am, ck-in 3 pm. Business servs avail. Game rm. Built in 1895; Victorian-style decor. Totally non-smoking. Cr cds: MC, V.

⊠ ⊠

Restaurants

★ ★ **BILLY'S RITZ.** *102 Salem Ave SE (24011), at Market St. 540/342-3937.* E-mail britz@roanoke.infi.net. Hrs: 5-10:30 pm; Fri, Sat to midnight. Closed most major hols; Jan 1-16. Bar. Semi-a la carte: dinner $8.50-$16. Specializes in steak, pork chops, seafood. Outdoor dining. Three dining areas with eclectic decor. Cr cds: A, D, DS, MC, V.

D ⊡

★ ★ **CHARCOAL STEAK HOUSE.** *5225 Williamson Rd (24012). 540/366-3710.* Hrs: 11 am-10 pm, Mon, Sat from 5 pm; Sun brunch 10:30 am-3 pm. Closed most major hols. Res accepted. Bar. Semi-a la carte: lunch $4.95-$11.50, dinner $9.95-$24. Child's meals. Specializes in prime rib, steak, seafood. Entertainment. Parking. Cr cds: A, C, D, DS, MC, V.

D ⊡

★ ★ **KABUKI.** *3503 Franklin Rd SW (24014). 540/981-0222.* Hrs: 5-10:30 pm; Fri, Sat 4:30-11 pm. Closed some major hols; also Jan 2, Super Bowl Sun. Res accepted; required Fri, Sat. Japanese menu. Bar. Complete meals: dinner $10.45-$24.45. Child's meals. Specializes in Teppanyaki cooking. Parking. Japanese antique display. Cr cds: A, C, D, DS, MC, V.

D ⊡

★ ★ ★ **LIBRARY.** *3117 Franklin Rd (24014), in Piccadilly Square Shopping Ctr. 540/985-0811.* Hrs: 6 pm-midnight. Closed Sun; major hols. Res accepted. French, Amer menu. Bar. Wine cellar. Semi-a la carte: dinner $12.95-$24.95. Specialties: roast rack of lamb, Dover sole. Own pastries. Parking. Antique books on display. Jacket. Cr cds: A, C, D, MC, V.

D ⊡

↙★ **SUNNYBROOK INN.** *7342 Plantation Rd NW (24019). 540/366-4555.* Hrs: 7 am-8 pm; Fri, Sat to 9 pm; Sun to 7 pm. Closed Dec 25. Res accepted. Wine, beer. Semi-a la carte: bkfst $3-$6, lunch $4-$8, dinner $6-$18. Buffet: (Fri & Sat) dinner $12.99-$18.99; (Sun) lunch & dinner $9. Child's meals. Specializes in oysters, country ham, fresh mountain trout. Salad bar. Parking. Outdoor dining. In colonial-revival farmhouse (1912). Cr cds: C, D, DS, MC, V.

D SC ⊡

Salem (E-5)

(See also Roanoke)

Founded 1802 **Pop** 23,756 **Elev** 1,060 ft **Area code** 540 **Zip** 24153

Information Salem/Roanoke County Chamber of Commerce, 9 N College Ave, PO Box 832; 540/387-0267.

Salem, part of the industrial complex of the Roanoke Valley, shares with Roanoke the beautiful setting between the Blue Ridge and Allegheny Mountains. Historic markers throughout Salem indicate the city's colonial heritage.

What to See and Do

Dixie Caverns. Stalactites in lofty chambers; modern lighting system makes 45-min tour comfortable as well as interesting. Pottery shop and mineral shop (all yr). Camping facilities (fee). (Daily; closed Dec 25) Off I-81 at exit 132. Phone 540/380-2085. ¢¢¢

Roanoke College (1842). (1,600 students) One of the few Southern colleges to remain open during Civil War. Many historic buildings, some

antebellum. Olin Hall, fine arts building, has theater, art gallery and sculptures. Excellent exhibit of paintings, photographs and other items concerning Mary, Queen of Scots (by appt only; phone 540/375-2487). Tours. College Ave, off I-81. Phone 540/375-2282.

Motels

★ ★ **HOLIDAY INN.** *1671 Skyview Rd, I-81 exit 137. 540/389-7061; FAX 540/389-7060.* 102 rms, 3 story. S, D $52-$89; each addl $6; under 19 free. Crib free. TV; cable (premium). Pool; wading pool. Continental bkfst. Restaurant 6:30 am-2 pm, 5-10 pm. Rm serv. Ck-out noon. Meeting rms. Business servs avail. In-rm modem link. Bellhops. Valet serv. Sundries. Cr cds: A, C, D, DS, ER, JCB, MC, V.

D ⧆ ⊠ ⊠ SC

★ ★ **HOLIDAY INN EXPRESS.** *1535 E Main St. 540/986-1000; FAX 540/986-0355.* 70 rms, 3 story. S $55; D $60-$65; each addl $7; under 19 free. Crib free. TV; cable (premium), VCR avail (movies). Complimentary continental bkfst. Ck-out 11 am. Business servs avail. In-rm modem link. Sundries. Exercise equipt; bicycle, treadmill. Refrigerators, microwaves. Cr cds: A, D, DS, MC, V.

D ⅄ ⊠ ⊠ SC

↙★ **QUALITY INN.** *179 Sheraton Dr. 540/562-1912; FAX 540/562-0507.* 120 rms, 2 story. S $48; D $52; each addl $6; under 18 free. Crib free. TV; cable (premium), VCR avail. Pool. Complimentary continental bkfst. Coffee in rms. Restaurant 5-9 pm. Bar 5 pm-11 pm. Ck-out 11 am. Meeting rms. Coin lndry. Business servs avail. Airport transportation. Putting green. Exercise equipt; weight machine, bicycle. Balconies. Cr cds: A, C, D, DS, ER, JCB, MC, V.

D ⧆ ⅄ ⊠ ⊠ SC

Restaurant

★ **SHANGHAI.** *1416 Colorado St. 540/389-4151.* Hrs: 11:30 am-10 pm; Fri to 10:30 pm; Sat 5-10:30 pm; Sun from noon; Sun brunch to 2:30 pm. Closed Thanksgiving, Dec 25. Chinese menu. Bar. Semi-a la carte: lunch $2.95-$4.95, dinner $4.95-$8.95. Buffet: lunch $4.50, dinner $6.95. Sun brunch $4.50. Child's meals. Specialties: beef imperial, General Tso's chicken. Chinese decor with mural, vases. Cr cds: A, DS, MC, V.

D ⊡

Shenandoah National Park (C-7 - D-7)

(See also Front Royal, Luray, New Market, Waynesboro)

About 450 million years ago the Blue Ridge was at the bottom of a sea. Today it averages about 2,000 feet above sea level; some 300 square miles of the loveliest Blue Ridge area are included in Shenandoah National Park.

The park is 80 miles long and from two to 13 miles wide. Running its full length is the 105-mile Skyline Drive. Main entrances are the North Entrance (Front Royal), from I-66, US 340, US 522 and VA 55; Thornton Gap Entrance (31.5 miles south), from US 211; Swift Run Gap Entrance (65.7 miles south), from US 33; and the South Entrance (Rockfish Gap), from I-64, US 250 and the Blue Ridge Parkway (see). The Drive, twisting and turning along the crest of the Blue Ridge, is one of the finest scenic trips in the East. Approximately 70 overlooks give views of the Blue Ridge, the Piedmont and, to the west, the Shenandoah Valley and the Alleghenies.

The Drive offers much, but the park offers more. Exploration, on foot or horseback, attracts thousands of visitors who return again and again. Most of the area is wooded, predominantly in white, red and chestnut oak, with hickory, birch, maple, hemlock, tulip poplar and nearly 100 other species scattered here and there. At the head of Whiteoak Canyon are hemlocks more than 300 years old. The park bursts with color and contrast in the fall, which makes this season particularly popular with visitors. The park is a sanctuary for deer, bear, fox and bobcat, along with more than 200 varieties of birds.

Accommodations are available in the park, with lodges, motel-type units and cabins at Big Meadows and Skyland, and housekeeping cabins at Lewis Mountain. For reservations and rates (which vary), contact ARA MARK Virginia Sky-Line Co, Inc, PO Box 727, Luray 22835-9051; 800/999-4714. Nearby communities provide a variety of accommodations, also. There are restaurants at Panorama, Skyland and Big Meadows; light lunches and groceries are available at Elkwallow, Big Meadows, Lewis Mountain and Loft Mountain Waysides.

The park is open all year; lodge and cabin accommodations, usually Mar-Dec; phone ahead for schedule. Skyline Drive is occasionally closed for short periods during Nov-Mar. As in all national parks, pets must be on a leash. The speed limit is 35 miles per hour. $10/car/week, annual permit $20; Golden Age, Golden Access and Golden Eagle passports accepted (see MAKING THE MOST OF YOUR TRIP).

Park Headquarters is five miles east of Luray on US 211. Detailed information and pamphlets may be obtained by contacting Superintendent, Shenandoah National Park, 3655 US 211E, Luray 22835; 540/999-3500.

What to See and Do

Camping. First-come, first-serve tent and trailer sites (no hookups) at Lewis Mountain and Loft Mountain. Big Meadows requires reservations (phone DESTINET, 800/365-CAMP). 14-day limit. Campers must register and check out. (Spring-fall) Write Park Superintendent, 3655 US 211E, Luray 22835, for information. ¢¢¢¢

Fishing. Trout. Regulations and directions at entrance stations, Panorama, Big Meadows and Loft Mt. State or 5-day nonresident license necessary. ¢¢¢-¢¢¢¢

Hiking. The 500 mi of trails include 101 mi of Appalachian Trail. Along the trail, which winds 2,100 mi from Maine to Georgia, are numerous side trails to mountain tops, waterfalls and secluded valleys. Trail crosses Skyline Drive at several points and can be entered at many overlooks. Overnight backcountry use requires a permit. No open fires are allowed. Regulations and permits may be obtained at any park entrance station, visitor center or at Park HQ. Backcountry may be closed during periods of high fire danger.

Visitor Centers and lodges post schedules of evening programs and ranger-led hikes. Self-guided walks, ranging from 1/2 to 2 hrs, are at Dickey Ridge (mi 4.6), Skyland (mi 41.7), Big Meadows (mi 51.1), Lewis Mt (mi 57.5) and Loft Mt (mi 79.5).

Interpretive program. Guided walks, illustrated campfire talks. (Usually mid-June-mid-Oct; rest of yr, on a limited basis) Obtain schedule at Park HQ, entrance stations, visitor centers and concessions.

Picnicking. Near Dickey Ridge Visitor Center, Elkwallow, Pinnacles, Big Meadows, Lewis Mountain, South River, Loft Mountain.

★ **Points of special interest on Skyline Drive.** (Mileposts are numbered north to south, starting at Front Royal. Periods of operation are estimated—phone ahead.)

Dickey Ridge Visitor Center. Exhibits, programs, information, book sales; picnic grounds. (usually Apr-Nov, daily) Mile 4.6.

Elkwallow (2,445 ft). Picnic grounds; food. (May-Oct, daily) Mile 24.1.

Panorama (2,300 ft). Dining room, gift shop. Trail to Marys Rock. Closed in winter. Mile 31.5, at jct US 211.

Marys Rock Tunnel (2,545 ft). Drive goes through 600 feet of rock (clearance 13 ft). Mile 32.4.

Pinnacles (3,500 ft). Picnic grounds. Mile 36.7.

Skyland (3,680 ft). Accommodations, restaurant; guided trail rides; Stony Man Nature Trail. Mile 41.7.

Byrd Visitor Center. Exhibits, information, book sales, orientation programs, maps. (Usually Apr-Nov, daily) Mile 51.

Big Meadows (3,500 ft). Accommodations, restaurant; store, gas; tent and trailer sites; picnic grounds; nature trail. (Usually Apr-Nov) Mile 51.1.

Lewis Mountain (3,390 ft). 1-2 bedroom cabins with heat; tent and trailer sites; picnic grounds. (Usually late May-Oct) Mile 57.5.

South River (2,940 ft). Picnic grounds, 2 1/2-mi round trip trail to falls. Mile 62.8.

Loft Mountain (3,380 ft). Picnicking, camping (May-Oct); wayside facility; gas, store (May-Oct). Mile 79.5.

Riding. Many mi of horseback trails. Trail rides (ponies for children) for rent at Skyland.

Motels

★★ **BIG MEADOWS LODGE.** *(Box 727, Luray 22835) 19 mi S of US 211, 15 mi N of US 33 on Skyline Dr. 540/999-2211; FAX 540/999-2011; res: 800/999-4714.* 92 units: 62 motel rms, 20 lodge rms, 10 cabins. No A/C. Apr-Nov 2: lodge S, D $60-$75; motel S, D $81-$91; cabins $65-$74; suites $90-$120; each addl $5; under 16 free. Closed rest of yr. Crib free. TV in some rms. Playground. Restaurant 7:30-10 am, noon-2 pm, 5:30-8:30 pm. Box lunches. Bar 4-11 pm; entertainment. Ck-out noon. Business servs avail. Gift shop. Private patios, balconies. Panoramic view of Shenandoah Valley. Cr cds: A, C, D, DS, MC, V.

D ⊠ 🌲

✔★★ **SKYLAND LODGE.** *(Box 727, Luray 22835) 10 mi S of US 211, 25 mi N of US 33 on Skyline Dr. 540/999-2211; FAX 540/999-2231; res: 800/999-4714.* 177 rms. No A/C. Apr-Nov: S, D $77-$97; each addl $5; suites $110-$152; under 16 free. Closed rest of yr. Crib free. TV avail. Playground. Restaurant 7:30-10:30 am, noon-2:30 pm, 5:30-8:30 pm. Box lunches avail. Bar 2:30-11:30 pm. Ck-out noon. Meeting rms. Business servs avail. Sundries. Gift shop. Private patios. Balconies. Cr cds: A, D, DS, MC, V.

D ⚡ ⊠ 🌲

Skyline Drive
(see Shenandoah National Park)

South Boston (F-6)

(For accommodations see Clarksville, Danville)

Pop 6,997 **Elev** 407 ft **Area code** 804 **Zip** 24592

What to See and Do

Staunton River State Park. Approx 1,300 acres of woods, meadows and lengthy shoreline on John H. Kerr Reservoir (Buggs Island Lake). Swimming pool, wading pool, bathhouse; fishing; boating (ramp). Hiking, nature trails; tennis courts. Picnic facilities, shelters; children's playground; concession. Tent & trailer sites, 7 cabins (Mar-Dec). Visitor center, interpretive programs. Standard fees. 8 mi NE on VA 304, then 11 mi SE on VA 344. Phone 804/572-4623.

South Hill (F-7)

(See also Clarksville)

Pop 4,217 **Elev** 440 ft **Area code** 804 **Zip** 23970

Motels

★ ★ **BEST WESTERN.** *Box 594, Jct I-85, US 58. 804/447-3123; FAX 804/447-4237.* 152 rms, 2 story. S $52-$59; D $58-$65; each addl $6; under 19 free. Crib free. Pet accepted. TV; cable (premium). Heated pool; wading pool. Restaurant adj open 24 hrs. Bar 5 pm-1 am. Ck-out 11 am. Coin lndry. Meeting rms. Valet serv. Free airport, bus depot transportation. Health club privileges. Game rm. Cr cds: A, C, D, DS, JCB, MC, V.

D ⛟ ≋ ⋈ 🛇 SC

✔ ★ **COMFORT INN.** *918 E Atlantic St, I-85 exit 12. 804/447-2600; FAX 804/447-2590.* 50 rms, 2 story. S $39.95-$68.95; D $42.95-$68.95; under 12 free. Crib $6. TV; cable (premium). Continental bkfst. Complimentary coffee. Restaurant opp 6 am-10 pm. Ck-out 11 am. Business servs avail. Cr cds: A, C, D, DS, MC, V.

D ⋈ 🛇 SC

Springfield (C-8)

(See also Alexandria, Arlington County, Fairfax, Mount Vernon; also see District of Columbia)

Pop 23,706 **Elev** 300 ft **Area code** 703

Motels

★ ★ **COMFORT INN.** *6560 Loisdale Court (22150), I-95 exit 169A. 703/922-9000; FAX 703/971-6944.* 112 rms, 5 story. S, D $69-$89; each addl $6; under 18 free. Pet accepted. TV; cable (premium). Complimentary continental bkfst. Ck-out noon. Meeting rms. Business servs avail. In-rm modem link. Valet serv. Health club privileges. Microwaves avail. Cr cds: A, C, D, DS, MC, V.

D ⛟ ≋ 🛇 SC

★ ★ **DAYS INN-POTOMAC MILLS.** *(14619 Potomac Mills Rd, Woodbridge 22192) 10 mi S on I-95, exit 156. 703/494-4433; FAX 703/385-2627.* E-mail daysinn@pwcweb.com; web www.pwcweb.com/daysinn. 176 rms, 9 story. S $68-$78; D $75-$85; each addl $7; suites $89; under 13 free. Crib free. Pet accepted, some restrictions. TV; cable; Pool; lifeguard. Complimentary continental bkfst. Restaurant adj 6 am-midnight. Ck-out noon. Coin lndry. Meeting rms. Business servs avail. In-rm modem link. Valet serv. Sundries. Exercise equipt: stair machine, bicycle. Some refrigerators, minibars. Cr cds: A, C, D, DS, MC, V.

D ⛟ ≋ 🏋 ⋈ 🛇 SC

✔ ★ **DAYS INN-SPRINGFIELD MALL.** *6721 Commerce St (22150), I-95 exit 169A. 703/922-6100; FAX 703/922-0708.* 179 rms, 6 story. Apr-Oct: S, D $62-$94; each addl $6, under 19 free; wkly, monthly rates; lower rates rest of yr. Crib free. TV; cable (premium). Pool; lifeguard. Restaurant 6 am-1 pm, 5-8 pm; Sun to 1 pm. Ck-out noon. Meeting rms. Business servs avail. In-rm modem link. Valet serv. Health club privileges. Refrigerators avail. Cr cds: A, C, D, DS, ER, MC, V.

D ≋ 🛇 SC

★ ★ **HAMPTON INN.** *6550 Loisdale Ct (22150). 703/924-9441; FAX 703/924-0324.* 153 rms, 7 story. Apr-June: S, D $89-$99; each addl $10; under 18 free; lower rates rest of yr. Crib free. TV; cable (premium). Pool. Complimentary continental bkfst. Restaurant nearby.

Ck-out noon. Valet serv. Health club privileges. Some refrigerators. Cr cds: A, C, D, DS, MC, V.

D ⛟ ≋ ⋈ 🛇 SC

Hotel

★ ★ ★ **HILTON.** *6550 Loisdale Rd (22150), I-95 exit 169 A. 703/971-8900; FAX 703/971-8527.* E-mail guest@springfieldhilton.com. 246 rms, 12 story. Mar-July: S $117; D $127; each addl $10; suites $270; under 18 free; wkend rates; lower rates rest of yr. Crib free. TV; cable (premium), VCR avail. Indoor pool; lifeguard. Complimentary coffee in rms. Restaurant 6:30 am-10 pm. Bar 2 pm-2:30 am; entertainment Thurs-Sat. Ck-out 1 pm. Meeting rms. Business servs avail. In-rm modem link. Concierge. Gift shop. Health club privileges. Some refrigerators. Cr cds: A, C, D, DS, MC, V.

D ≋ ⋈ 🛇 SC

Restaurant

★ ★ **MIKE'S AMERICAN GRILL.** *6210 Backlick Rd (22152). 703/644-7100.* Hrs: 11:30 am-10:30 pm; Fri, Sat noon-midnight; Sun to 10 pm. Closed Thanksgiving, Dec 25. Bar. Semi-a la carte: lunch, dinner $8.95-$17.95. Specializes in grilled meats, seafood, vegetarian cuisine. Warehouse decor. Cr cds: A, MC, V.

D

Staunton (D-6)

(See also Harrisonburg, Waynesboro)

Settled 1736 **Pop** 24,461 **Elev** 1,385 ft **Area code** 540 **Zip** 24401
Information Travel Information Center, 1250 Richmond Rd; 540/332-3972 or 800/332-5219.

To historians, Staunton (STAN-ton) is known as the birthplace of Woodrow Wilson, and to students of government, as the place where the city-manager plan was first conceived and adopted. Set in fertile Shenandoah Valley fields and orchards, between the Blue Ridge and Allegheny mountain ranges, the area around Staunton produces poultry, livestock and wool. Manufacturing firms in the city make air conditioners, razors, candy and clothing.

A Ranger District office of the George Washington and Jefferson National Forests is located here.

What to See and Do

Augusta Stone Church (1747). Oldest Presbyterian church in continuous use in state. Once used as fort during Native American raids. Museum of early church artifacts (by appt). 7 mi N on US 11 in Ft Defiance. Phone 540/248-2634.

Gypsy Hill Park. Lake stocked with fish; swimming (late May-Labor Day, fee); lighted softball field with concession stand, outdoor basketball courts; tennis; 18-hole golf; picnicking; miniature train ride, playgrounds; fairgrounds. (Daily) Off Churchville & Thornrose Aves. Phone 540/332-3945.

McCormick Memorial Wayside. Cyrus McCormick's first reaper is displayed here. Picnic grounds. (Daily) 16 mi SW via US 11, I-81; 1 mi E of I-81 on VA 606 near Steeles Tavern. Phone 540/377-2255. **Free.**

Museum of American Frontier Culture. Living history museum consists of working farms brought together from England, Germany, Northern Ireland and an American farm. The European farms represent what America's early settlers left; the American farm, from the Valley of Virginia, reflects the blend of the various European influences. Visitors are able to see and take part in life as it was lived on these 17th-, 18th- and 19th-century farmsteads. Costumed interpreters demonstrate daily life at all four sites. Visitor center. (Daily; closed 1st wk Jan, Thanksgiving, Dec 25) I-81 exit 222, US 250 W, first left after stoplight. 1250 Richmond Rd. Phone 540/332-7850. ¢¢¢

Trinity Episcopal Church (1855). Founded as Augusta Parish Church (1746), original building on this site served as Revolutionary capitol of state for 16 days in 1781. Open on request (Mon-Fri). 120 W Beverley St. Phone 540/886-9132.

⭐ **Woodrow Wilson Birthplace and Presidential Museum.** Restored Greek-revival manse with period furnishings and Wilson family mementos from 1850s; museum building on grounds houses seven-gallery presidential exhibit, "The Life and Times of Woodrow Wilson," and his 1919 Pierce-Arrow limousine. Victorian gardens. (Daily; closed Jan 1, Thanksgiving, Dec 25) 24 N Coalter St, near I-81, I-64 & US 11. Phone 540/885-0897. ¢¢¢

Seasonal Event

Jazz in the Park. Gypsy Hill Park. Thurs nights. July-Aug.

Motels

⭐⭐ **BEST WESTERN.** *260 Rowe Rd, I-81, exit 222.* 540/885-1112. 80 rms, 4 story. May-Oct: S $62-$75; D $72-$85; each addl $8; under 18 free; family rates; higher rates: graduation, fall foliage; lower rates rest of yr. Crib free. TV; cable. Complimentary continental bkfst. Complimentary coffee in rms. Restaurant adj 6:30 am-9 pm. Ck-out 11 am. Business servs avail. Valet serv. Sundries. Indoor pool. Some refrigerators. Cr cds: A, C, D, DS, JCB, MC, V.

⭐⭐ **COMFORT INN.** *1302 Richmond Ave.* 540/886-5000; FAX 540/886-6643. 98 rms, 5 story. May-Oct: S $49-$75; D $57-$75; each addl $8; under 18 free; higher rates special events; lower rates rest of yr. Crib avail. Pet accepted, some restrictions. TV; cable (premium). Pool. Complimentary continental bkfst. Complimentary coffee in rms. Restaurant adj open 24 hrs. Ck-out 11 am. Business servs avail. Some refrigerators. Cr cds: A, C, D, DS, ER, JCB, MC, V.

✔⭐ **ECONO LODGE-HESSIAN HOUSE.** *Rte 2, Box 364, ½ mi S of jct I-81 & 64 exit 213/213A Greenville.* 540/337-1231; FAX 540/337-0821. 32 rms, 2 story. May-Nov: S $32-$35.95; D $35.95-$55; each addl $5; under 12 free; wkly rates; lower rates rest of yr. Crib free. Pet accepted, some restrictions; $5. TV; cable (premium). Pool; wading pool. Playground. Complimentary continental bkfst. Restaurant nearby. Ck-out 11 am. Refrigerators. Private patios, balconies. Picnic tables. Cr cds: A, DS, MC, V.

⭐⭐ **SHONEY'S INN.** *Rte 4, Box 99E, jct US 250 & I-81 exit 222.* 540/885-3117; FAX 540/885-5620. 91 rms, 2 story. S $48; D $55; each addl $6; under 18 free. Crib free. TV; cable (premium). Indoor pool; whirlpool. Continental bkfst. Restaurant 6 am-11 pm; Fri, Sat to 1 am. Ck-out noon. Business servs avail. Valet serv. Sundries. Exercise equipt; weights, bicycles, sauna. Some in-rm whirlpools. Cr cds: A, C, D, DS, ER, MC, V.

Motor Hotel

⭐⭐⭐ **HOLIDAY INN GOLF & CONFERENCE CENTER.** *I-81 exit 225, at Woodrow Wilson Pkwy.* 540/248-6020; FAX 540/248-2902. E-mail higcc@cfw.com. 116 rms, 4 story. Mid-Mar-mid-Nov: S, D $75-$85; each addl $6; suites $95-$125; under 17 free; golf plans; lower rates rest of yr. Crib free. TV; cable (premium). Indoor/outdoor pool; poolside serv. Restaurant 6 am-10 pm. Rm serv. Bar 4 pm-11 pm; entertainment. Ck-out noon. Meeting rms. Business servs avail. In-rm modem link. Valet serv. Sundries. Free airport transportation. Lighted tennis. 18-hole golf, greens fee $25, pro, putting green, driving range. Exercise equipt; treadmill, stair

machine. Refrigerator, wet bar in suites. Some balconies. Cr cds: A, C, D, DS, ER, JCB, MC, V.

Inns

⭐⭐ **BELLE GRAE.** *515 W Frederick St.* 540/886-5151; FAX 540/886-6641. Web www.virginia.org/bellegrae. 14 rms, 2 story. Some rm phones. S, D $95-$150; each addl $25; suites $140-$170; higher rates wkends. Children over 12 yrs only. TV in most rms. Complimentary full bkfst; afternoon refreshments. Dining rm 7:30-9:30 am, 6-9 pm. Ck-out 11 am, ck-in 3 pm. Meeting rms. Business servs avail. Airport, RR station, bus depot transportation. Tennis privileges. Golf privileges. Fireplaces. Private patios, balconies. 1870s restored Victorian mansion. Each rm individually decorated; antiques. Cr cds: A, MC, V.

✔⭐⭐ **BUCKHORN.** *(HCR 33, Box 139, Churchville 24421) 12 mi W on US 250.* 540/337-6900; res: 800/693-4242. 6 rms, 3 story. No rm phones. S $35-$45; D $55-$65; each addl $10. Closed Dec 24, 25. Crib free. Complimentary full bkfst. Restaurant (see BUCKHORN INN). Ck-out 11 am, ck-in 1 pm. Located in Shenandoah Valley of the George Washington National Forest. Restored 1811 inn. Cr cds: DS, MC, V.

⭐⭐ **FREDERICK HOUSE.** *28 N New St.* 540/885-4220; res: 800/334-5575. Web www.marketplace.stauton.va.us/frdrkhs.html. 18 units, 2 story, 8 suites. S, D $75-$150; each addl $25; suites $85-$115; wkly rates. Crib $10. TV; cable. Complimentary full bkfst. Ck-out 11 am, ck-in 3 pm. Tennis privileges. Golf privileges. Private patios, balconies. Picnic tables. Encompasses 6 adj townhouses built 1810-1919. Antiques and period furnishings. Mary Baldwin College adj. Totally nonsmoking. Cr cds: A, D, DS, MC, V.

⭐⭐⭐ **SAMPSON EAGON.** *238 E Beverly St.* 540/886-8200; FAX 540/886-8200; res: 800/597-9722. 5 rms, 1 with shower only, 2 story. S, D $89-$110; each addl $20; 2-day min wkends. Children over 12 yrs only. TV; cable, VCR (free movies). Complimentary full bkfst; afternoon refreshments. Ck-out 11 am, ck-in 4 pm. Business servs avail. Antiques. Restored antebellum home (1800) adj to Woodrow Wilson birthplace; antiques. Cr cds: A, MC, V.

⭐⭐ **THORNROSE HOUSE.** *531 Thornrose Ave.* 540/885-7026; res: 800/861-4338; FAX 540/885-6458. Web www.shenwebworks.com:8001/thornrose. 5 rms, 2 story. No rm phones. S $50-$70; D $60-$80. Complimentary full bkfst. Ck-out 11 am, ck-in 3 pm. Georgian-revival house (1912); wrap-around veranda. Antiques; four poster and brass beds. Opp park with swimming, tennis, golf. Totally nonsmoking. No cr cds accepted.

Restaurants

✔⭐⭐ **BUCKHORN INN.** *(See Buckhorn Inn)* 540/337-6900. Hrs: 11 am-8 pm; Fri, Sat to 9 pm. Closed Mon; Dec 24, 25; also Tues in Jan, Feb. Semi-a la carte: lunch $3.50-$7.95. Complete meals: lunch, dinner $4.50-$7.95. Sun brunch $10.95. Child's meals. Specializes in regional country dishes. Salad bar. Located in colonial-era country inn in Shenandoah Valley. Cr cds: DS, MC, V.

⭐ **McCORMICK'S PUB.** *41 N Augusta St.* 540/885-3111. Hrs: 5 pm-midnight; Fri, Sat to 1 am. Closed some major hols. Res accepted. Bar. Semi-a la carte: dinner $5.25-$14.95. Child's meals. Specializes in prime rib, seafood, pasta. In old YMCA building (1915) funded by Cyrus Hall McCormick family. Cr cds: A, DS, MC, V.

★ **MRS. ROWE'S.** *Rte 4, Box 88, at I-81 exit 222. 540/886-1833.* Hrs: 6:30 am-9 pm; Sun 7 am-7 pm. Closed some major hols. Res accepted. Wine, beer. Semi-a la carte: bkfst $2-$5, lunch $3-$6, dinner $5-$13. Child's meals. Specializes in country ham, chicken, catfish. Country atmosphere. Family-owned since 1947. Cr cds: DS, MC, V.

Strasburg (C-7)

(See also Front Royal, Winchester, Woodstock)

Founded 1761 **Pop** 3,762 **Elev** 578 ft **Area code** 540 **Zip** 22657
Information Chamber of Commerce, PO Box 42; 540/465-3187.

Lying at the base of Massanutten Mountain and on the north fork of the Shenandoah River, Strasburg was founded in 1761 by German settlers. Prospering in the early 19th century as a center of trade and flour milling, the village later became identified with the manufacture of high quality pottery, earning the nickname "Pottown" after the Civil War. The town's location on the Manassas Gap Railroad and the Shenandoah Valley Turnpike gave Strasburg a pivotal role in Stonewall Jackson's Campaign of 1862. The first western Virginia town to be served by two railroads, Strasburg became prominent after 1890 as a railroad town, manufacturing center and home of printing and publishing businesses.

Today, Strasburg, located near the entrance to the Skyline Drive, offers historical and cultural museums. It attracts visitors with its antebellum and Victorian architecture and its burgeoning art community. The town calls itself the "antique capital of Virginia" because of its many antique shops.

What to See and Do

Belle Grove (1794). The design of this limestone mansion reflects the influence of Thomas Jefferson. Used as Union headquarters during the Battle of Cedar Creek, Oct 19, 1864. Unusual interior woodwork; herb garden in rear. Guided tours. (Apr-Oct, daily) National Trust for Historic Preservation property. (See ANNUAL EVENTS) 4 mi N on US 11. Phone 540/869-2028. ¢¢

Hupp's Hill Battlefield Park and Study Center. Former campsite for six different Civil War generals' troops, now a museum and hands-on learning center. Artifacts, documents, exhibits. Guided battlefield tours (by appt; fee). (Daily; closed major hols) I-81 to exit 298, S 1 mi on US 11. Phone 540/465-5884. ¢¢

Strasburg Museum. Blacksmith, cooper and potter shop collections; displays from colonial homes; relics from Civil War and railroad eras; Native American artifacts. Housed in Southern Railway Depot. (May-Oct, daily) E King St. Phone 540/465-3175. ¢

Annual Events

Mayfest. Celebration of town's German heritage with parade, entertainment and arts, crafts, antiques and foods fairs. 3rd wkend May.

Battle of Cedar Creek Re-Enactment. Belle Grove. Mid-Oct.

Seasonal Event

Wayside Theatre. On US 11, I-81 exit 302. Professional performances. Wed-Sun. Res required. Phone 540/869-1776. Late May-mid-Oct & Dec.

Inns

★ ★ ★ **HOTEL STRASBURG.** *213 S Holliday St, 2 mi E of I-81 exit 298. 540/465-9191; FAX 540/465-4788; res: 800/348-8327.* 29 rms, 17 with shower only, 3 story. S, D $74; suites $109-$165; under 16 free. Crib free. TV; cable. Complimentary continental bkfst (Mon-Fri). Restaurant (see HOTEL STRASBURG). Bar. Ck-out 11 am, ck-in 2 pm. Business servs avail. Health club privileges. Some in-rm whirlpools. Beach nearby;

swimming privileges. Victorian building; antiques. Cr cds: A, C, D, DS, MC, V.

★ ★ **WAYSIDE INN.** *(7783 Main St (US 11), Middletown 22645) I-81 exit 302. 540/869-1797; FAX 540/869-6038.* 24 rms, 3 story. S, D $95-$145; each addl $20; suites $145; under 12 free. Crib free. TV; cable. Restaurant (see WILKINSON'S TAVERN). Bar 11 am-midnight. Ck-out 11 am, ck-in 2 pm. Meeting rms. Business servs avail. Boating, swimming nearby. Restored colonial-era bldg; antiques. An inn since 1797. Cr cds: A, C, D, DS, MC, V.

Restaurants

★ ★ ★ **HOTEL STRASBURG.** *(See Hotel Strasburg Inn) 540/465-9191.* Hrs: 11:30 am-2:30 pm, 5-9 pm; Fri, Sat 8 am-2:30 pm, 5-10 pm; Sun 8 am-9 pm. Res accepted; required Sat. Continental menu. Bar from 11 am. Semi-a la carte: bkfst $4.95, lunch $5.25-$6.95, dinner $7.95-$18.95. Buffet lunch Mon-Fri: $5.95. Buffet bkfst Sat, Sun: $4.95. Sun brunch $8.95. Child's meals. Specialties: Tournados Jack Daniels, chicken Shenandoah. Cr cds: A, C, D, DS, MC, V.

★ ★ **WILKINSON'S TAVERN.** *(See Wayside Inn) 540/869-1797.* Hrs: 7 am-3 pm, 5-9 pm; Sat to 10 pm; Sun 7 am-8 pm. Res accepted; required Sat. Bar 11 am-midnight. Semi-a la carte: bkfst $2.75-$6.95, lunch $4.95-$7.95, dinner $14.95-$23.95. Child's meals. Specializes in fresh seafood, chicken, veal. Entertainment Sun Brunch. In restored Colonial-style inn; many antiques. Cr cds: A, C, D, DS, MC, V.

Suffolk
(see Portsmouth)

Surry (E-9)

(For accommodations see Newport News, Williamsburg; also see Colonial Parkway, Jamestown)

Pop 192 **Elev** 122 ft **Area code** 757 **Zip** 23883

What to See and Do

Chippokes Plantation State Park. Plantation continuously operated since 1619. Approx 1,600 acres. Swimming pool; fishing; Hiking, bicycle paths; interpretive tour road. Picnicking, concession. Visitor center, programs. Tours of mansion, carriage house, kitchen and formal gardens (Memorial Day-Labor Day, Sat, Sun). (See ANNUAL EVENT) Farm & Forestry Museum (Memorial Day-Labor Day, Wed-Sun; Apr-Oct, wkends). Standard fees. 6 mi E via VA 10, 634. Across James River from Jamestown. Phone 757/294-3625 (park) or 757/294-3439 (museum). Farm & Forestry Museum ¢

Annual Event

Pork, Peanut and Pine Festival. Chippokes Plantation. Pork products, peanuts, crafts, pine decorations. 3rd wkend July.

Tangier Island (E-10)

Settled 1666 **Pop** 659 **Elev** 3 ft **Area code** 757 **Zip** 23440

Bought from Native Americans for two overcoats, Tangier was first settled by a mainland family named West. In 1686 John Crockett moved here with his four sons and four daughters. They were later joined by a few other families. Descendants of these families now populate the island. Life is simple and lacks most urban complexities. Most of the men are fishermen, oystering and clamming in one season, crabbing in another.

This tranquil little island (approximately four miles long) is 12 miles out in Chesapeake Bay. The island offers good duck hunting, fishing, swimming and relaxation. There is an airfield here, and there are excursion boats from Reedville and Onancock, Virginia, and Crisfield, Maryland. Accommodations include a boarding house, Chesapeake House, with seven rooms, family-style meals. Contact PO Box 194; 757/891-2331 for reservations.

Tappahannock (D-9)

(See also Lancaster, Montross, Richmond)

Founded 1680 **Pop** 1,550 **Elev** 22 ft **Area code** 804 **Zip** 22560
Information Chamber of Commerce, PO Box 481; 804/443-5241.

Bartholemew Hoskins patented the first land here in 1645. Following his lead, others came and a small village soon sprang up, known at that time as Hobbes His Hole. Formally chartered in 1682 as New Plymouth, the town was to experience yet another name change. Built around the Rappahannock River, which means "running water," the town port became known as Tappahannock or "on the running water." Four hundred men gathered here in 1765 to protest the Stamp Act.

Today, the area around Prince and Duke streets and Water Lane of Tappahannock has been declared a historic district. Highlights include the beautifully renovated Ritchie House; the Anderton House, once used for the prizing of tobacco into hogsheads; and Scot's Arms Tavern.

Motels

✔★ **DAYS INN.** *Jct US 17, 360.* 804/443-9200; FAX 804/443-2663. 60 rms, 2 story. S, D $44-$49; each addl $6; under 12 free. Crib free. TV; cable. Complimentary continental bkfst. Ck-out 11 am. Business servs avail. Cr cds: A, D, DS, MC, V.

★ **SUPER 8.** *Jct US 360 & US 17.* 804/443-3888. 43 rms, 2 story. Apr-Sept: S $49.88; D $55.88; each addl $5; under 12 free; lower rates rest of yr. TV; cable. Complimentary coffee in lobby. Restaurant opp 6 am-11 pm. Ck-out 11 am. Meeting rms. Business servs avail. Some refrigerators. Cr cds: A, C, D, DS, ER, JCB, MC, V.

Restaurant

★★ **LOWERY'S.** *On US 17.* 804/443-4314. Hrs: 7:30 am-9 pm. Closed Dec 25. Semi-a la carte: bkfst $1.75-$6.75, lunch $3.25-$19, dinner $7-$19. Specializes in fresh local seafood. Own salad dressing. Antique cars on display. Cr cds: A, DS, MC, V.

Triangle (D-8)

(For accommodations see Alexandria, Fredericksburg; also see District of Columbia)

Pop 4,740 **Elev** 150 ft **Area code** 703 **Zip** 22172 **E-mail** jjensen@mnsinc.com **Web** www.visitpwc.com
Information Prince William County/Manassas Conference & Visitors Bureau, 14420 Bristow Rd, Manassas 20112; 703/792-4254 or 800/432-1792.

Quantico Marine Corps Base is three miles east of town.

What to See and Do

Marine Corps Air-Ground Museum. Chronological presentation of the Marine Corps Air-Ground Team's role in American history; artifacts on exhibit include aircraft, engines, armor, tracked & wheeled vehicles, artillery, small arms, uniforms, dioramas and photographs in pre-World War II aviation hangars. (Apr-late Nov, daily exc Mon) 2 mi E, in OCS area on Quantico Marine Corps Base. Phone 703/640-7965. **Free.**

Prince William Forest Park. Consists of 17,000 acres. Hiking, bicycling. Picnicking. Camping (14-day limit; no hookups; fee; group cabins by res only); trailer campground off VA 234 (fee; hookups, showers, lndry). Naturalist programs. (Daily) From I-95, 1/4 mi W on VA 619. Phone 703/221-7181. Per vehicle ¢¢

Tysons Corner (C-8)

(See also Arlington County, Fairfax, Falls Church, McLean; also see District of Columbia)

Pop 13,124 **Area code** 703 **E-mail** cvbfceda@mindspring.com **Web** www.cvb.co.fairfax.va.us/fceda
Information Fairfax County Convention & Visitors Bureau, 8300 Boone Blvd, Suite 450, Tysons Corner 22182; 703/790-3329 or 800/VISIT-VA.

This Virginia suburban area of Washington, DC, is the location of one of the largest shopping centers in the nation.

Motels

★★ **COMFORT INN.** *(1587 Spring Hill Rd, Vienna 22182)* 1½ mi W of I-495, exit 10B. 703/448-8020; FAX 703/448-0343. 250 rms, 3 story. S, D $89-$109; each addl $5; suites $109-$114; under 18 free. Crib free. Pet accepted, some restrictions. TV; cable (premium). Pool; lifeguard. Complimentary continental bkfst. Coffee in rms. Ck-out noon. Coin lndry. Meeting rms. Business servs avail. In-rm modem link. Valet serv. Free airport transportation. Health club privileges. Refrigerators, microwaves avail. Cr cds: A, C, D, DS, ER, JCB, MC, V.

★★ **RESIDENCE INN BY MARRIOTT.** *(8616 Westwood Center Dr, Vienna 22182)* I-495 exit 10B to VA 7, then 2 mi W. 703/893-0120; FAX 703/790-8896. 96 kit. suites, 2 story. Kit. suites $149-$199; each addl $10; under 18 free; wkend rates. Crib free. Pet accepted; $85 and $5/day. TV; cable (premium), VCR avail (movies). Pool; whirlpool, lifeguard. Complimentary continental bkfst 6:30-9 am; Sat, Sun 7:30-10 am. Restaurant nearby. Ck-out noon. Coin lndry. Meeting rm. Business servs avail. In-rm modem link. Valet serv. Lighted tennis. Health club privileges. Many fireplaces. Picnic tables, grills. Cr cds: A, C, D, DS, MC, V.

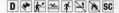

Hotels

★ ★ ★ **EMBASSY SUITES.** *(8517 Leesburg Pike, Vienna 22182) I-495 exit 10B to VA 7, then 2 mi W.* 703/883-0707; FAX 703/883-0694. Web www.embassysuites.com. 232 suites, 8 story. S, D $169-$189; each addl $10; under 12 free; wkend rates. Crib free. TV; cable (premium). Indoor pool; whirlpool. Complimentary full bkfst. Restaurant 11:30 am-11 pm. Bar. Ck-out noon. Business servs avail. In-rm modem link. Gift shop. Exercise equipt; bicycles, treadmill, sauna. Refrigerators, microwaves, wet bars. Cr cds: A, C, D, DS, JCB, MC, V.

D 🐾 🏋 🖾 🔥 SC

✔ ★ ★ ★ **HOLIDAY INN OF TYSONS CORNER.** *(1960 Chain Bridge Rd, McLean 22102) 2 blks W of I-495 exit 11B.* 703/893-2100; FAX 703/356-8218. 316 rms, 9 story. S, D $144-$159; each addl $15; family rates; wkend rates. Crib free. TV; cable (premium). Indoor pool; whirlpool. Restaurant 6:30 am-10 pm. Bar; entertainment. Ck-out 1 pm. Conference facilities. Business center. In-rm modem link. Gift shop. Airport transportation. Exercise equipt; weights, bicycles. Balconies. Cr cds: A, C, D, DS, JCB, MC, V.

D 🖾 🏋 🖾 🔥 SC 👟

★ ★ ★ **MARRIOTT.** *(8028 Leesburg Pike, Vienna 22182) 1 blk W of I-495 exit 10W.* 703/734-3200; FAX 703/442-9301. 390 units, 15 story. S, D $154-$174; suites $250; family rates; wkend packages. Crib free. TV; cable (premium). Indoor pool; whirlpool, poolside serv, lifeguard. Restaurant 6:30 am-11 pm. Bar 4:30 pm-1 am, Fri to 2 am, Sat 7 pm-2 am, closed Sun. Ck-out noon. Convention facilities. Business servs avail. In-rm modem link. Gift shop. Coin lndry. Some covered parking. Exercise equipt; weights, bicycle, sauna. Refrigerators avail. Luxury level. Cr cds: A, C, D, DS, ER, JCB, MC, V.

D 🖾 🏋 🖾 🔥 SC

★ ★ ★ **McLEAN HILTON AT TYSONS CORNER.** *(7920 Jones Branch Dr, McLean 22102-3308) S on VA 123, turn right at Tysons Blvd, right on Galleria Dr/Westpark Dr, then right on Jones Branch Dr.* 703/847-5000; FAX 703/761-5100. E-mail mclean_hilton@hilton.com; web www .hilton.com. 458 units, 9 story. S $150-$210; D $170-$230; each addl $20; suites $375-1750; wkly, wkend rates. Crib free. TV; cable (premium), VCR avail (free movies). Indoor pool; lifeguard. Restaurant 6:30 am-11 pm. Rm serv 6-2 am. Bar 11-2 am; entertainment. Ck-out noon. Convention facilities. Business center. In-rm modem link. Gift shop. Exercise equipt; weights, bicycles, sauna. Minibars. Atrium lobby; marble floors, fountain. Luxury level. Cr cds: A, C, D, DS, ER, JCB, MC, V.

D 🖾 🏋 🖾 🔥 SC 👟

★ ★ ★ ★ **THE RITZ-CARLTON, TYSONS CORNER.** *(1700 Tysons Blvd, McLean 22102) N via I-495 exit 11B, adj Tysons II Mall.* 703/506-4300; FAX 703/506-4305. A keynote of this hotel is its superb service. The lobby, furnished with antiques and 18th-century oil paintings, sets a tone of comfort and elegance that is carried through in the generously appointed guest rooms. 399 units, 24 story. S, D $170-$250; suites $375-$1,400; under 16 free; monthly rates; wkend family rates; lower rates some wkends. Crib free. Garage parking $12; valet $4. TV; cable (premium), VCR avail (movies $4). Indoor pool; whirlpool, lifeguard. Supervised child's activities (wkends only). Restaurant (see THE RESTAURANT). Afternoon tea in lounge. Rm serv 24 hrs. Bar 11:30-1 am; entertainment. Ck-out noon. Convention facilities. Business center. In-rm modem link. Concierge. Gift shop. Beauty shop. Tennis privileges. 18-hole golf privileges, greens fee $75, pro, putting green, driving range. Exercise rm; instructor, weight machine, bicycles, sauna. Massage. Bathrm phones, minibars; microwaves avail. Luxury level. Cr cds: A, C, D, DS, JCB, MC, V.

D 👤 ⛳ 🖾 🏋 🖾 🔥 👟

★ ★ ★ **SHERATON PREMIERE.** *(8661 Leesburg Pike, Vienna 22182) I-495 exit 10B, then 2¹/₂ mi W on VA 7.* 703/448-1234; FAX 703/893-8193. E-mail jkennedy@sptc.com; web www.sptc.com. 437 rms, 24 story. S $155-$170; D $175-$195; each addl $15; suites $375-$2,000; under 17 free; wkly rates. Crib free. TV; cable (premium), VCR avail. 2 pools, 1 indoor; whirlpool, poolside serv, lifeguard. Complimentary coffee in rms. Restaurant 6:30 am-midnight. Rm serv 24 hrs. Bars 11-1 am.

Ck-out noon. Convention facilities. Business center. In-rm modem link. Concierge. Gift shop. Drugstore. Free airport transportation. Lighted tennis privileges. 18-hole golf privileges, pro, greens fee. Racquetball. Exercise equipt; weights, bicycles, sauna. Massage. Health club privileges. Bathrm phones; some refrigerators. Cr cds: A, C, D, DS, ER, JCB, MC, V.

D 👤 ⛳ 🖾 🏋 🖾 🔥 SC 👟

Restaurants

★ ★ **AARATHI INDIAN CUISINE.** *(409 Maple Ave E, Vienna 22180-4722) approx 2 mi S on VA 123, in Danor Plaza.* 703/938-0100. Hrs: 11:30 am-2:30 pm, 5:30-10 pm; Fri, Sat to 10:30 pm. Closed July 4, Dec 25. Res accepted; required Fri, Sat dinner. Indian menu. Serv bar. Semi-a la carte: lunch $4.95-$8.50, dinner $4.95-$12.95. Lunch buffet $6.95. Specializes in curry and vegetarian dishes. Cr cds: A, C, D, DS, MC, V.

D 🗡

★ ★ **BONAROTI.** *(428 Maple Ave E, Vienna 22180) 3 mi W on I-495 on VA 123, in Wolf Trappe Shopping Center.* 703/281-7550. Hrs: 11:30 am-3 pm, 5-10:30 pm; Sat 5-11 pm. Closed Sun; some major hols. Res accepted. Italian menu. Bar. Semi-a la carte: lunch $8.95-$13.95, dinner $13.95-$22.95. Child's meals. Specializes in veal, pasta, seafood. Own pastries, pasta. Italian art. Cr cds: A, C, D, MC, V.

✔ ★ ★ **CLYDE'S.** *(8332 Leesburg Pike, Vienna 22182) 10 blks W of I-495 exit 10B on VA 7, then right.* 703/734-1901. Hrs: 11-2 am; Sun brunch 10 am-4 pm. Res accepted. Bar. A la carte entrees: lunch $4.95-$10.95, dinner $6.50-$15.50. Child's meals. Specializes in pasta, seafood, sandwiches. Entertainment Thurs-Sat. Parking. Original art collection. Cr cds: A, C, D, DS, MC, V.

D SC 🗡

★ ★ **DA DOMENICO.** *(1992 Chain Bridge Rd, McLean 22102) 2 blks W of I-495 exit 11B.* 703/790-9000. Hrs: 11:30 am-11 pm; Sat from 5 pm. Closed Sun; major hols. Res accepted; required Fri, Sat. Northern Italian menu. Bar. Semi-a la carte: lunch $7.95-$9.95, dinner $9.95-$23.95. Specializes in veal chop, seafood, fresh pasta. Parking. Italian garden decor. Cr cds: A, C, D, DS, MC, V.

🗡

★ ★ **FEDORA CAFE.** *(8521 Leesburg Pike, Vienna 22180)* 703/556-0100. Web fedora@erols.com. Hrs: 11:30 am-10:30 pm; Fri, Sat to 11 pm; Sun 10:30 am-2 pm, 4:30-9:30 pm. Res accepted. Bar to 12:30 am. Semi-a la carte: lunch $6.95-$11.95, dinner $8.95-$22.95. Specializes in rotisserie chicken, spit-roasted duck, fresh fish. Own pasta, desserts. Pianist Wed-Fri, Sun brunch. Valet Wed-Fri. Cr cds: A, C, D, DS, MC, V.

D 🗡

★ **HUNAN LION.** *(2070 Chain Bridge Rd, Vienna 22182) S of I-495 on VA 123, I-495 exit 11B, third light on right.* 703/734-9828. Hrs: 11:30 am-10:30 pm; Fri, Sat to 11 pm. Closed Thanksgiving. Res accepted. Chinese menu. Bar. Semi-a la carte: lunch $6-$8, dinner $6-$10.50. Specialties: triple delicacy prawns, orange beef, General Tso's chicken. Parking. Cr cds: A, C, D, DS, MC, V.

D 🗡

★ ★ **J.R.'S STOCKYARDS INN.** *(8130 Watson St, McLean 22102) ¹/₂ mi W of I-495 exit 10B.* 703/893-3390. E-mail steaks@jrsbeef.com; web www.jrsbeef.com. Hrs: 11:30 am-3 pm, 5-10:30 pm; Fri to 11 pm; Sat 5-11 pm; Sun 5-9 pm. Closed July 4, Thanksgiving, Dec 24, 25. Res accepted; required Fri, Sat. Bar. Semi-a la carte: lunch $4.50-$8.95, dinner $12.95-$19.95. Child's meals. Specializes in marinated sirloin, prime aged beef, fresh seafood. Parking. Western-style chop house. Cr cds: A, C, D, DS, MC, V.

🗡

★ ★ ★ **LA PROVENCE.** *(144 W Maple Ave, Vienna 22180) 2¹/₂ mi W on VA 123.* 703/242-3777. Hrs: 11:30 am-2:30 pm, 5:30-10 pm. Closed Sun; most major hols. Res accepted; required Fri, Sat dinner. French Provençal menu. Bar. Extensive wine list. Semi-a la carte: lunch $6.95-$12.95, dinner $15.95-$22.95. Specialties: bouillabaisse, duck confit. Own baking. Open bistro atmosphere; large flower murals. Totally nonsmoking. Cr cds: A, C, D, DS, MC, V.

★ ★ ★ **LE CANARD.** *(132 Branch Rd, Vienna 22180)* VA 123 at Branch Rd, in Danor Shopping Center. 703/281-0070. E-mail tiger spaw.com/bite/lecanard.htm; web www.erols.com/bitebyte/lecanard.htm. Hrs: 11:30 am-2:30 pm, 5:30-10:30 pm; Fri to 11 pm; Sat 6-11 pm. Res accepted; required Fri, Sat. French menu. Bar to 2 am. Wine list. Semi-a la carte: lunch $4.75-$10, dinner $13.95-$22.95. Specializes in fresh seafood, veal, beef. Own pastries. Piano bar. Cr cds: A, C, D, DS, MC, V.

★ ★ **MARCO POLO.** *(245 Maple Ave W, Vienna 22180)* 2½ mi N of I-66 exit 62. 703/281-3922. Hrs: 11:30 am-10:30 pm; Fri, Sat to 11 pm; early-bird dinner Thurs 5:30-7:30 pm. Closed Sun exc Mother's Day. Res accepted. Continental, Northern Italian menu. Serv bar. Semi-a la carte: lunch $6-$9, dinner $11-$18. Buffet: lunch (Tues-Fri) $8.25, dinner (Thurs) $14.50. Child's meals. Specializes in fresh seafood, fresh pasta, veal. Parking. Cr cds: A, C, D, MC, V.

✔★ **MASQUERADE.** *(8601 Westwood Center Dr, Vienna 22180)* I-495 exit 10B, then 2½ mi W on VA 7. 703/848-9476. E-mail kabaudan@aol.com. Hrs: 11 am-11 pm; Fri, Sat to 1 am; Sun from 10:30 am; Sun brunch to 2:30 pm. Res accepted. Contemporary American menu. Bar. Semi-a la carte: lunch $6.50-$12.95, dinner $8.95-$16.95. Sun brunch $6.95-$10.95. Child's meals. Specializes in salads, sandwiches, grilled dishes. Parking. Patio dining. Take-out gourmet market. Cr cds: A, C, D, DS, MC, V.

★ ★ **MORTON'S OF CHICAGO.** *(8075 Leesburg Pike, Vienna 22182)* I-495 exit 10W, then 1/4 mi W on VA 7 (Leesburg Pike) on left. 703/883-0800. Hrs: 11:30 am-2:30 pm, 5:30-11 pm; Sat from 5:30 pm; Sun 5-10 pm. Closed major hols. Res accepted; required Thurs-Sat. Bar. Wine list. A la carte: lunch $7.95-$18.95, dinner $19.95-$29.95. Specializes in steak, seafood. Valet parking. Jacket. Cr cds: A, C, D, JCB, MC, V.

★ ★ **NIZAM'S.** *(523 Maple Ave W, Vienna 22180)* In Village Green Shopping Ctr. 703/938-8948. Hrs: 11 am-3 pm, 5-10 pm; Sat 5-11 pm; Sun 4-9 pm. Closed Jan 1, Thanksgiving, Dec 25. Res accepted, required Fri, Sat. Turkish menu. Serv bar. Semi-a la carte: lunch $5.25-$10.50, dinner $11.95-$17.50. Specializes in beef, lamb, chicken. Turkish artwork. Totally nonsmoking. Cr cds: A, DS, MC, V.

✔★ ★ **PANJSHIR II.** *(224 W Maple Ave, Vienna 22180)* 3 mi W on I-495, exit 10B; on VA 123. 703/281-4183. Hrs: 11:30 am-2 pm, 5-10 pm; Sun 5-9 pm. Closed Jan 1, July 4, Thanksgiving. Res accepted. Afghan menu. Bar. Semi-a la carte: lunch $5.95-$7.25, dinner $9.95-$13.25. Specializes in kebabs, saffron rice, vegetarian dishes. Parking. Cr cds: A, C, D, MC, V.

★ ★ **PHILLIPS SEAFOOD GRILL.** *(8330 Boone Blvd, Vienna 22182)* approx 2 mi S on VA 123, I-495 exit 10A. 703/442-0400. Hrs: 11:30 am-9:30 pm; wkends to 10 pm; early-bird dinner Mon-Fri 5-6 pm. Closed Dec 25. Res accepted; required Fri, Sat dinner. Bar. Semi-a la carte: lunch $5.95-$9.95, dinner $8.95-$19.95. Child's meals. Specialties: crab cakes, free-range chicken, raw bar. Parking. Outdoor dining. Hickory wood-burning grills. Family-owned. Cr cds: A, C, D, DS, MC, V.

★ ★ **PIERRE ET MADELEINE.** *(246 E Maple Ave, Vienna 22180)* 2 mi N of I-66 exit 62. 703/938-4379. Hrs: 11:30 am-2 pm, 5:30-10 pm; Fri to 10:30 pm; Sat 5:30-10:30 pm. Closed Sun. Res accepted. French menu. Bar. Semi-a la carte: lunch $4.75-$11.95, dinner $15-

$21.95. Complete meals: dinner $34.95. Specialties: fresh Maine lobster with vanilla sauce, ravioli with snails. Parking. Cr cds: A, C, D, MC, V.

★ ★ ★ **PRIMI PIATTI.** *(8045 Leesburg Pike, Vienna 22182)* W of I-495 exit 10 W B. 703/893-0300. Hrs: 11:30 am-2:30 pm, 5:30-10 pm; Fri to 10:30 pm; Sat 5:30-10:30 pm. Closed Sun; most major hols. Res accepted; required Fri, Sat. Italian menu. Bar. Semi-a la carte: lunch $9.95-$14, dinner $11-$18. Specializes in contemporary Italian cuisine. Valet parking. Outdoor dining. Cr cds: A, C, D, MC, V.

★ ★ ★ **THE RESTAURANT.** *(See The Ritz-Carlton, Tysons Corner Hotel)* 703/506-4300. Hrs: 6:30 am-10 pm; Sun 6:30-11 am, 5-10 pm; Sun brunch 11 am-2:30 pm. Res accepted. Wine list. Semi-a la carte: lunch $12-$24. Complete meals: dinner $32, $39, $45, $60. Sun brunch $37. Child's meals. Specializes in seafood, lamb chops, prime aged beef. Harpist. Valet parking. Cr cds: A, C, D, DS, JCB, MC, V.

★ ★ **TARA THAI.** *(226 Maple Ave W, Vienna 22180)* approx 2 mi S on VA 123, 2 mi N I-66 exit 62. 703/255-2467. Hrs: 11:30 am-3 pm, 5-10 pm; Fri to 11 pm; Sat noon-3:30 pm, 5-11 pm; Sun noon-3:30 pm, 5-10 pm. Closed July 4. Res accepted; required Fri, Sat dinner. Thai menu. Bar. Semi-a la carte: lunch $4.95-$7.95, dinner $6.95-$12.95. Specializes in pad Thai, fresh seafood, grilled fish. Parking. Underwater ocean decor. Cr cds: A, C, D, DS, MC, V.

★ **THAT'S AMORE.** *(150 Branch Rd SE, Vienna 22180)* approx 2 mi S on VA 123, I-495 exit 11B. 703/281-7777. Hrs: 11:30 am-10:30 pm; Fri to midnight; Sat 4 pm-midnight; Sun 4-9:30 pm. Closed Labor Day, Thanksgiving, Dec 25. Italian menu. Bar. A la carte: lunch $5.95-$9.95, dinner $15-$38 (dinner entrees serve 2 people). Specializes in pasta, seafood, chicken. Parking. Cr cds: A, C, D, DS, MC, V.

✔★ **WU'S GARDEN.** *(418 Maple Ave E, Vienna 22180)* 3 mi W off I-495 exit 11A. 703/281-4410. Hrs: 11:30 am-10 pm; Sat noon-11 pm. Closed Thanksgiving. Res accepted. Chinese menu. Bar. Semi-a la carte: lunch $4-$7, dinner $7.95-$12. Specialties: kung pao chicken, crispy shrimp with walnuts. Parking. Oriental screens and artwork. Cr cds: A, D, DS, MC, V.

Virginia Beach (F-10)

(See also Chesapeake, Hampton, Newport News, Norfolk, Portsmouth)

Pop 393,069 **Elev** 12 ft **Area code** 757 **Web** www.virginia-beach.va.us
Information Visitor Information Center, 2100 Parks Ave, 23451; 757/437-4882 or 800/446-8038.

For those who seek year-round recreation, Virginia Beach is the answer. A renovated resort area with a three-mile boardwalk and 28 miles of oceanfront and bay beaches offer visitors myriad activities: surfing, swimming, superb fishing, boating, waterskiing, in-line skating; bowling, tennis, golf, bicycling; amusement park and arcade games.

After a full day, there's nothing like dinner and a night out. Virginia Beach delivers with many fine restaurants serving fresh seafood, and nightclubs, concerts and theaters catering to all musical tastes. With activities for all ages and hundreds of places to stay in all price ranges, Virginia Beach is one of the most popular resorts on the East Coast.

What to See and Do

Adam Thoroughgood House (ca 1680). One of the oldest remaining brick houses in US; restored, furnished; restored gardens. (Apr-Dec, daily exc Mon; rest of yr, Tues-Sat; closed some major hols) 1636 Parish Rd. Phone 757/460-0007. ¢¢

Association for Research and Enlightenment. Headquarters for study and research of work of psychic Edgar Cayce. Visitor Center has bookstore, library, displays, ESP-testing machine, movie and daily lecture. (Daily; closed Thanksgiving, Dec 25) 67th St & Atlantic Ave. Phone 757/428-3588. **Free.**

Contemporary Art Center of Virginia. This 32,000-sq-ft facility is devoted to presentation of 20th-century art through exhibitions, education, performing arts and special events. (Daily; closed major hols) 2200 Parks Ave. Phone 757/425-0000. **Free.**

***Discovery* Sightseeing Cruise.** Lunch, dinner and sightseeing cruises aboard 80-foot luxury yacht. Reservations required. (May-Oct, daily) 600 Laskin Rd. Phone 757/491-8090 or 757/422-2900. ¢¢¢¢

First Landing/Seashore State Park. More than 2,700 acres with lagoons, cypress trees and sand dunes. Swimming at own risk; fishing; boating (ramp). Hiking, bicycle and self-guided nature trails. Picnicking. Tent & trailer sites (Mar-Nov; fee); 20 cabins (May-Sept). Visitor center, interpretive programs. Access for disabled to nature trail. (Daily) Standard fees. 5 mi N on US 60 at Cape Henry. Phone 757/481-2131. Seasonal parking fee ¢¢

Fishing. In the Lynnhaven and Rudee Inlets for channel bass, speckled trout, spots, croakers, flounder and whiting in season; in the Back Bay area, 18 mi S on VA 615, for largemouth black bass, pickerel and perch. Pier fishing and surf casting from piers jutting into the Atlantic and piers in the Chesapeake Bay. Reef, deep-sea and Gulf Stream fishing from charter boats, for sea bass, weakfish, flounder, cobia, bonito, tuna, marlin, false albacore, blue and dolphin. Lake and stream fishing at Lake Smith, Lake Christine and the inland waterways of the Chesapeake and Albemarle Canal. Crabbing for blue crabs in Lynnhaven waters, Linkhorn Bay and Rudee Inlet. (No license or closed season for saltwater fishing.)

Francis Land House Historic Site and Gardens. Late-18th-century-plantation home features period rooms, special exhibits, gardens and museum gift shop. (Tues-Sat, also Sun afternoons; closed major hols) 3131 Virginia Beach Blvd, on the S side of the boulevard, just E of the Princess Anne Plaza Shopping Center. Phone 757/431-4000. ¢¢

Lynnhaven House (ca 1725). This stately story-and-a-half masonry structure is a well-preserved example of 18th-century architecture and decorative arts. (Limited hrs, phone ahead) 4405 Wishart Rd, intersects with Independence Blvd (US 255), exit 3 on Virginia Beach-Norfolk Expy (Rte 44). Phone 757/460-1688. ¢¢

Norwegian Lady Statue. A gift to Virginia Beach from the people of Moss, Norway. The statue commemorates the tragic wreck of the Norwegian bark *Dictator* off the shores of Virginia Beach in 1891. 25th St & Boardwalk.

Ocean Breeze Fun Park. Family fun park includes MotorWorld, with various driving tracks; Wild Water Rapids, a water park with slides, wave pool, rapids, and children's water amusements (late May-early Sept); Shipwreck Golf miniature-golf course; Strike Zone batting cages. (Memorial Day-Labor Day, daily; mid-Apr-May & Sept-Oct, wkends) 849 General Booth Blvd. Phone 757/422-4444 (recording) or 800/678-WILD. Combination ticket ¢¢¢¢¢

Old Cape Henry Lighthouse and Memorial Park. First US-government-built lighthouse (ca 1791). On Fort Story, an active army base. 6 mi N on US 60 .

Old Coast Guard Station. Former Life-Saving/Coast Guard Station (1903); visual exhibits of numerous shipwrecks along the Virginia coastline tell of past bravery and disaster. "The War Years" exhibit relates United States Coast Guard efforts during World Wars I and II. Photographs, ship models, artifacts. Gift shop. (Memorial Day-Sept, daily; rest of yr, daily exc Mon; closed Jan 1, Thanksgiving, Dec 25, 31) 24th St & Atlantic Ave. Phone 757/422-1587. ¢¢

Virginia Marine Science Museum. Live animals, interactive exhibits, 6-story screen, 300-seat **IMAX 3-D** theater. Exhibits include ocean aquarium with sharks, large fish; sea turtle aquarium; seal and other habitats;

aviary; salt-marsh preserve; touch tank; river room; garden. (Daily; closed Thanksgiving, Dec 25) 717 General Booth Blvd, 2 mi S of resort area. Phone 757/425-FISH. ¢¢¢

Annual Events

Pungo Strawberry Festival. Sat & Sun of Memorial Day wkend.

Boardwalk Art Show. Works by more than 350 artists from US and abroad. 10 days mid-June.

East Coast Surfing Championship. 4th wkend Aug.

Neptune Festival. Last 2 wks Sept.

Seasonal Events

Winter whale-watching boat trips. Phone 757/437-4882. Daily exc Tues, Thurs. Jan-Mar.

Virginia Saltwater Fishing Tournament. The Commonwealth of Virginia sponsors this annual Saltwater Fishing Awards Program. No entry fee or registration requirements; open to everyone who fishes in tournament waters and complies with tournament rules. For information about this program contact Virginia Saltwater Fishing Tournament, 968 S Oriole Dr, Suite 102, 23451; 757/491-5160. Mar-Dec.

Motels

★ ★ ★ **COURTYARD BY MARRIOTT.** *5700 Greenwich Rd (23462). 757/490-2002; FAX 757/490-0169.* 146 rms, 3 story. Memorial Day-Labor Day: S, D $75-$99; suites $110-$120; under 12 free; wkly, wkend rates; lower rates rest of yr. Crib free. TV; cable (premium). Pool; whirlpool. Coffee in rms. Bar. Ck-out noon. Business servs avail. In-rm modem link. Valet serv. Exercise equipt; weight machine, bicycles. Some refrigerators. Cr cds: A, C, D, DS, JCB, MC, V.

D ⟆ ✕ ⊠ ⊠ SC

✔ ★ ★ **FAIRFIELD INN BY MARRIOTT.** *4760 Euclid Rd (23462). 757/499-1935.* 134 rms, 3 story. Mid-May-Labor Day: S, D $62-$85; under 18 free; lower rates rest of yr. Crib free. TV; cable (premium). Pool. Complimentary continental bkfst. Restaurant nearby. Ck-out noon. Business servs avail. In-rm modem link. Cr cds: A, D, DS, MC, V.

D ⟆ ⊠ ⊠ SC

✔ ★ ★ **HAMPTON INN.** *5793 Greenwich Rd (23462). 757/490-9800; FAX 757/490-3573.* 122 rms, 4 story. June-Aug: S $62-$74; D $64-$74; under 18 free; higher rates special events; lower rates rest of yr. Crib free. TV; cable (premium). Pool. Complimentary continental bkfst. Restaurant adj 6:30 am-11 pm. Ck-out noon. Meeting rm. Business servs avail. In-rm modem link. Exercise equipt; weights, bicycles. Microwaves avail. Cr cds: A, C, D, DS, MC, V.

D ⟆ ✕ ⊠ ⊠ SC

★ ★ **SEA GULL.** *Atlantic Ave at 27th St (23451), on oceanfront. 757/425-5711; FAX 757/425-5710; res: 800/426-4855.* E-mail seagull motel@worldnet.att.net; web www.vgnet.com/vabeach/sponsor/seagull. 51 units, 4 story, 9 kit. units. Memorial Day-Labor Day: S, D $120-$138; each addl $10; kit. units $115-$140; family, wkly rates; lower rates rest of yr. Crib $5. TV; cable (premium). Indoor pool; whirlpool, poolside serv. Restaurant 7 am-10 pm. Rm serv. Bar. Ck-out 11 am. Business servs avail. Refrigerators. On ocean, swimming beach. Cr cds: DS, MC, V.

⟆ ⊠ ⊠ SC

Motor Hotels

★ ★ **COMFORT INN.** *2800 Pacific Ave (23451). 757/428-2203; FAX 757/422-6043.* E-mail comfortinn@Va-Beach.com; web www.va beach.com/comfortinn. 135 rms, 7 story. Memorial Day-Labor Day: S, D $104-$154; each addl $8; under 15 free; family rates; lower rates rest of yr. Crib free. TV; cable (premium). Indoor/outdoor pool; whirlpool. Complimentary continental bkfst. Restaurant opp 11 am-11 pm. Ck-out 11 am. Coin lndry. Meeting rms. Business servs avail. In-rm modem link. Bellhops.

Valet serv. Exercise equipt; weight machine, bicycle. Game rm. Some refrigerators; microwaves avail. Cr cds: A, C, D, DS, ER, JCB, MC, V.

D ≋ 🏃 ✈ ⚒ 🔥 SC

★ ★ COMFORT INN-OCEANFRONT. *2015 Atlantic Ave (23451). 757/425-8200; FAX 757/425-6521.* Web www.vbeach.com/hotels /comfort.html. 83 kit. suites, 10 story. Memorial Day-Labor Day: S, D $169-$180; each addl $10; under 12 free; lower rates rest of yr. Crib free. TV; cable (premium). Indoor pool; whirlpool. Continental bkfst. Restaurant adj 6:30 am-10 pm. Ck-out 11 am. Business center. In-rm modem link. Bellhops. Exercise equipt; weights, bicycles. Private patios. On ocean. Cr cds: A, C, D, DS, ER, JCB, MC, V.

D ≋ 🏃 ⚒ 🔥 SC 🚶

★ ★ DAYS INN-OCEANFRONT. *32nd St & Atlantic Ave (23451). 757/428-7233; FAX 757/491-1936.* 121 units, 8 story. Late June-early Sept: S, D $135-$225; each addl $10; under 12 free; golf plans; lower rates rest of yr. Crib free. Pet accepted; $10. TV; cable (premium). Indoor pool; whirlpool. Restaurant 7-11 am, noon-2 pm, 6-10 pm. Rm serv. Bar from 5 pm. Ck-out 11 am. Coin lndry. Meeting rms. Business servs avail. In-rm modem link. Golf privileges. Game rm. Some refrigerators; micro-waves avail. Balconies. On ocean; beach. Cr cds: A, C, D, DS, MC, V.

D 🐾 🏃 ≋ ⚒ 🔥 SC

★ ★ ★ HILTON INN. *8th St & Atlantic Ave (23451). 757/428-8935; FAX 757/425-2769.* 120 rms, 6 story. Memorial Day-Labor Day: S $165; D $175; each addl $10; under 18 free; lower rates rest of yr. Crib free. TV; cable (premium), VCR avail. Indoor/outdoor pool; whirlpool, sauna, pool-side serv. Restaurant 7 am-midnight. Rm serv to 10 pm. Bar noon-1:30 am. Ck-out 11 am. Meeting rms. Business servs avail. In-rm modem link. Bellhops. Valet serv. Lawn games. On ocean; beach. Cr cds: A, C, D, DS, ER, MC, V.

≋ ⚒ 🔥 SC

★ ★ ★ HOLIDAY INN. *2607 Atlantic Ave (23451). 757/491-6900; FAX 757/491-2125.* E-mail surfside@vabeach.com; web www.infi.net /~beachnet/surfside. 143 rms, 10 story, 18 kit. suites. Mid-June-Labor Day: S, D $159-$199; each addl $10; kit. suites $199-$219; under 17 free; family rates; wkly rates; higher rates special events. Crib free. TV; cable (premium). Complimentary coffee in lobby. Restaurant 7 am-10 pm. Rm serv. Bar 5-10 pm. Ck-out 11 am. Meeting rms. Business servs avail. In-rm modem link. Bellhops. Valet serv. Coin lndry. Indoor pool; whirlpool. Refrigerators; some in-rm whirlpools, microwaves. Balconies. On beach. Cr cds: A, C, D, DS, ER, JCB, MC, V.

D 🐾 ≋ ⚒ 🔥 SC

★ ★ ★ HOLIDAY INN EXECUTIVE CENTER. *5655 Greenwich Rd (23462), near Norfolk Intl Airport. 757/499-4400; FAX 757/473-0517.* 336 rms, 6 story. S, D $99-$119. Crib free. TV; cable (premium). 2 pools, 1 indoor; whirlpool. Complimentary coffee in rms. Restaurant 6:30 am-10 pm. Rm serv. Bar 11 am-10 pm. Ck-noon. Convention facilities. Business servs avail. In-rm modem link. Bellhops. Concierge. Valet serv. Gift shop. Free airport transportation. Exercise equipt; weight machine, bicycle, sauna. Cr cds: A, C, D, DS, ER, JCB, MC, V.

D ≋ 🏃 ✈ ⚒ 🔥 SC

✔★ ★ ★ HOLIDAY INN SUNSPREE RESORT. *39th St & Ocean-front (23451). 757/428-1711; FAX 757/425-5742.* E-mail sunspree@va beach.com/ web www.infi.net/~beachnet/sunspree. 266 rms, 7 story, 55 kits. Mid-June-Labor Day: S, D $149-$189; suites $184-$249; each addl $10; under 19 free. Crib free. TV; cable (premium). Indoor/outdoor pool; poolside serv (summer). Free supervised child's activities (Memorial Day-Labor Day); ages 2-8. Complimentary coffee in rms. Restaurant 6:30 am-2 pm, 4-11 pm (in season), to 10 pm rest of yr. Rm serv. Bar 4-11 pm. Ck-out 11 am. Meeting rms. Business servs avail. Bellhops. Gift shop. Refrigerators. Balconies. On ocean. Cr cds: A, C, D, DS, JCB, MC, V.

D ≋ ⚒ 🔥 SC

★ ★ ★ HOLIDAY INN-OCEANSIDE. *Atlantic Ave & 21st St (23451). 757/491-1500; FAX 757/491-1945.* E-mail oceansid@va beach.com; web www.vabeach.com/oceansid. 138 rms, 12 story. June-Sept: S, D $85-$179; each addl $10; under 18 free; lower rates rest of yr.

TV; cable (premium). Indoor pool; whirlpool. Restaurant 7 am-10 pm. Rm serv. Bar 11 am-11 pm. Ck-out 11 am. Meeting rms. Business servs avail. In-rm modem link. Bellhops. Refrigerators; microwaves avail. Balconies. On ocean; swimming beach. Cr cds: A, D, DS, JCB, MC, V.

D 🐾 ≋ ⚒ 🔥 SC

Hotels

★ ★ BEST WESTERN-OCEAN FRONT. *1101 Atlantic Ave (23451). 757/422-5000; FAX 757/425-2356.* 110 rms, 8 story. Memorial Day-Labor Day: S, D $120-$180; each addl $10; suites $157-$225; under 12 free; lower rates rest of yr. Crib free. TV; cable (premium). Pool; whirlpool. Coffee in rms. Restaurant 7 am-11 pm (seasonal). Bar 11-1:30 am. Ck-out 11 am. Business servs avail. Valet parking. Some refrigerators. Balconies. On ocean; swimming beach. All rms with ocean view. Cr cds: A, C, D, DS, MC, V.

D ≋ ⚒ 🔥 SC

★ ★ ★ CLARION-PEMBROKE CORPORATE CENTER. *4453 Bonney Rd (23462), VA 44 exit Independence 3B, right on Bonney Rd. 757/473-1700; FAX 757/552-0477.* 149 rms, 8 story. Memorial Day-Labor Day: S, D $89-$149; each addl $10; suites, studio rms $109-$159; under 12 free; lower rates rest of yr. Crib free. TV; cable (premium). Indoor pool; whirlpool, poolside serv. Complimentary coffee in rms. Restaurant 6:30-10:30 am. Bars 3 pm-1 am. Meeting rms. Business center. In-rm modem link. Exercise equipt; weight machine, treadmills, sauna. Some refrigerators, microwaves. Cr cds: A, C, D, DS, ER, JCB, MC, V.

D ≋ 🏃 ✈ ⚒ 🔥 SC 🚶

★ ★ ECONO LODGE-OCEANFRONT. *2109 Atlantic Ave (23451). 757/428-2403; FAX 757/422-2530.* E-mail econo-lodge@va beach.com/ web www.va-beach.com/econo-lodge. 52 rms, 10 story. Memorial Day-Labor Day: S, D $120-$169; each addl $8; kit. units $149-$189; under 18 free; lower rates rest of yr. Crib free. TV; cable (premium). Indoor pool; poolside serv. Restaurant 6 am-11 pm. Ck-out 11 am. Meeting rm. Business servs avail. In-rm modem link. Free garage parking. Cr cds: A, C, D, DS, ER, JCB, MC, V.

D 🐾 ≋ ⚒ 🔥 SC

★ ★ ★ FOUNDERS INN CONFERENCE CENTER. *5641 Indian River Rd (23463). 757/424-5511; FAX 757/366-0613; res: 800/926-4466.* Web www.foundersinn.com. 249 rms: 27 rms in Founders Inn, 222 rms in 2 lodge buildings located on grounds. Memorial Day-Labor Day: S, D $89-$119; each addl $15; suites $200-$950; lower rates rest of yr; family, wkly rates; golf plans. Crib free. TV; cable (premium), VCR avail (movies). 2 pools, 1 indoor; poolside serv, lifeguard (summer). Playground. Super-vised child's activities (Memorial Day-Labor Day); ages 3-17. Complimen-tary coffee in rms. Restaurant 6 am-10 pm; dinner theatre (Thurs-Sat). Rm serv to midnight. Ck-out noon. Meeting rms. Business center. In-rm mo-dem link. Concierge. Shopping arcade. Free valet parking. Free airport, RR station, bus depot transportation. Lighted tennis, pro. Golf privileges, greens fee $29-39, pro. Exercise rm; instructor, weights, bicycles, sauna. Indoor racquetball court. Lawn games. Bicycle rentals. Bathrm phones, refrigerators, minibars. Balconies. Picnic tables, grills. Cr cds: A, C, D, DS, MC, V.

D 🐾 🎾 ≋ ⚒ 🏃 ✈ ⚒ 🔥 SC 🚶

✔★ ★ ★ PAVILION TOWERS. *1900 Pavilion Dr (23451). 757/422-8900; FAX 757/425-8460.* 293 rms, 12 story. Late May-early Sept: S, D $155; each addl $10; suites $165-$395; under 17 free; wkend rates; lower rates rest of yr. Crib free. TV; cable (premium). Indoor pool; whirlpool. Restaurant 6:30 am-2 pm, 5-10 pm. Bar from 4 pm; entertainment. Ck-out 11 am. Convention facilities. Business servs avail. In-rm modem link. Gift shop. Oceanfront transportation (in season). Tennis. Exercise equipt; weights, bicycles, sauna, steam rm. Some refrigerators. Cr cds: A, C, D, DS, ER, JCB, MC, V.

D 🎾 ≋ 🏃 ✈ ⚒ 🔥 SC

★ ★ ★ QUALITY INN-OCEAN FRONT. *2207 Atlantic Ave (23458). 757/428-5141; FAX 757/422-8436.* 111 rms, 14 story. Late May-Labor Day: S, D $125-$141; each addl $8; under 12 free; higher rates

Memorial Day wkend; lower rates rest of yr. Crib free. TV; cable (premium). Heated pool; whirlpool. Restaurant 7 am-11 pm (seasonal). Bar 11-2 am. Ck-out 11 am. Business servs avail. In-rm modem link. Coin lndry. Airport transportation. Refrigerators; some microwaves. Private patios; balconies. On beach. Cr cds: A, C, D, DS, ER, JCB, MC, V.

D ⚐ ≋ ⋈ ⚒ **SC**

★ ★ **RAMADA PLAZA RESORT.** *57th & Ocean Front (23451). 757/428-7025; FAX 757/428-2921.* 215 rms, 17 story. May-Sept: S, D $135-$180; suites $230-$280; each addl $8; under 18 free; lower rates rest of yr. TV; cable (premium), VCR avail. Indoor/outdoor pool; whirlpool, poolside serv, lifeguard in season. Supervised child's activities (mid-June-Labor Day); ages 5-11. Coffee in rms. Restaurant 7 am-10 pm. Bar 3 pm-1 am. Ck-out 11 am. Meeting rms. Business center. In-rm modem link. Concierge. Gift shop. Exercise equipt; weights, bicycles, sauna. Some refrigerators, microwaves. Balconies. On ocean; oceanfront deck, swimming beach. Most rms with ocean view. Luxury level. Cr cds: A, C, D, DS, ER, JCB, MC, V.

D ⚐ ≋ ⚡ ⚒ ≋ ⚒ **SC** ⚒

★ ★ **VIRGINIA BEACH RESORT & CONFERENCE CENTER.** *2800 Shore Dr (23451). 757/481-9000; FAX 757/496-7429; res: 800/468-2722 (exc VA), 800/422-4747 (VA).* E-mail vb-resort@vabeach.com; web www.vabeach.com/varesort. 295 suites, 8 story. Memorial Day-Labor Day: S, D $159-$329; each addl $10; under 18 free; lower rates rest of yr. Crib free. TV; cable (premium). Indoor/outdoor pool; whirlpool, poolside serv. Supervised child's activities (Memorial Day-Labor Day); ages 4-14. Restaurant 6:30 am-11 pm. Bar. Ck-out 11 am. Coin lndry. Convention facilities. Business center. In-rm modem link. Gift shop. Airport, bus depot transportation. Tennis privileges. Golf privileges. Exercise equipt; weights, sauna. Private beach. Boat, jet ski. Bicycles. Refrigerators, microwaves. Balconies. On bay. Cr cds: A, C, D, DS, MC, V.

D ⚐ ⚡ ⚡ ≋ ⚡ ⚒ ≋ ⚒ **SC** ⚒

Inn

★ ★ **CHURCH POINT MANOR HOUSE.** *4001 Church Point Rd (23455). 757/460-2657; FAX 757/460-2845.* E-mail cpmanor@aol.com; web www.symweb.com/churchpoint. 10 rms, 6 with shower only, 3 story. Mid-May-mid-Oct: S, D, guest house $125-$175; each addl $25; lower rates rest of yr. Crib free. TV; cable, VCR avail (movies). Pool. Complimentary full bkfst. Ck-out 11 am, ck-in 3 pm. Luggage handling. Tennis. Game rm. Lawn games. Some fireplaces. Some balconies. Picnic tables, grills. Farmhouse built in 1860s; art and antiques. On 30 acres of private trails and parks. Totally nonsmoking. Cr cds: A, D, DS, MC, V.

D ⚡ ≋ ⋈ ⚒

Restaurants

★ ★ **ALDO'S RISTORANTE.** *1860 Laskin Rd (23454), at La Promenade shopping center. 757/491-1111.* Hrs: 11 am-11 pm; Fri, Sat to 12:30 am; Sun 4-11 pm. Closed Thanksgiving, Dec 25. Res accepted. Italian menu. Bar. A la carte entrees: lunch, dinner $2.99-$19.95. Child's meals. Specializes in seafood, pizza, filet mignon. Entertainment Tues-Sat. Outdoor dining. Contemporary decor. Cr cds: A, MC, V.

D ⚒

★ ★ **BLUE PETE'S SEAFOOD & STEAK.** *1400 N Muddy Creek Rd (23456). 757/426-2005.* Web www.bluepetes.com. Hrs: 6-10 pm. Closed Tues off season. Bar. Semi-a la carte: dinner $7.50-$29.95. Child's meals. Specializes in fresh seafood, sweet potato biscuits, Angus steak. Own desserts. Parking. Outdoor dining. Located on creek in wooded area. Cr cds: A, D, MC, V.

D ⚒

★ ★ **COASTAL GRILL.** *1427 N Great Neck Rd (23454). 757/496-3348.* Hrs: 5:30-11 pm; Sat 5 pm-midnight; Sun 5-9:30 pm. Closed most major hols. Bar. A la carte entrees: dinner $3.95-$15.95.

Child's meals. Specializes in fresh fish, roast chicken. Parking. Cr cds: A, DS, MC, V.

D

★ ★ **HENRY'S SEAFOOD.** *3319 Shore Dr (23451), at US 60 & E end of Lessner Bridge. 757/481-7300.* Hrs: 11-2 am; Nov-Mar 5-11 pm; Sun brunch 10 am-2 pm. Res accepted. Bar. Semi-a la carte: lunch $3.95-$9.95, dinner $9.95-$19.95. Sun brunch $9.95. Child's meals. Specializes in fresh seafood. Lobster tank. Raw bar. Valet parking. Outdoor dining. On Lynnhaven Inlet; 2-story saltwater aquarium in dining area. Cr cds: A, C, D, DS, MC, V.

D ⚒

★ ★ **IL GIARDINO.** *910 Atlantic Ave (23451), at 10th St. 757/422-6464.* Hrs: 5-11:30 pm; Fri, Sat to midnight. Closed Thanksgiving, Dec 25. Res accepted. Italian menu. Bar. Semi-a la carte: dinner $9.95-$22.95. Child's meals. Specializes in seafood, veal. Entertainment nightly in season. Valet parking. Outdoor dining. Wood-burning pizza oven. Cr cds: A, D, DS, MC, V.

D ⚒

★ ★ ★ **LA CARAVELLE.** *1040 Laskin Rd (23451), 5 blks W of oceanfront. 757/428-2477.* Hrs: 5:30-10:30 pm. Res accepted; required Fri, Sat. French, Vietnamese menu. Bar. Wine list. Semi-a la carte: dinner $4.95-$19.95. Specializes in seafood, fowl. Pianist Fri, Sat. Parking. Country French decor. Cr cds: A, C, D, DS, MC, V.

⚒

★ ★ ★ **LE CHAMBORD.** *324 N Great Neck Rd (23454). 757/498-1234.* Hrs: 11:30 am-3 pm, dinner from 6 pm. Closed Jan 1, Dec 25. Res accepted; required wkend. French, continental menu. Bar. Wine list. Semi-a la carte: lunch $4.95-$8.95, dinner $4.95-$22.95. Specialties: rack of lamb, poached salmon, veal chops. Jazz pianist Fri-Sat. Modern Mediterranean-style decor; fireplaces in lounge area, dining rm. Cr cds: A, C, D, DS, MC, V.

D

★ ★ **THE LIGHTHOUSE.** *1st St & Atlantic Ave (23451). 757/428-7974.* Hrs: noon-9:30 pm; Sat, Sun from 10 am; Sun brunch to 3 pm; early-bird dinner 5-6:30 pm. Res accepted. Bar. Semi-a la carte: lunch $4.95-$18.95, dinner $6.95-$25.95. Sun brunch $17.95. Child's meals. Specialties: she-crab soup, whole lobster, prime rib. Patio dining. View of ocean or inlet. Family-owned. Cr cds: A, C, D, DS, MC, V.

D **SC** ⚒

✔ ★ **LUCKY STAR.** *1608 Pleasure House Rd (23455). 757/363-8410.* Hrs: 5:30-10 pm. Closed Sun; some major hols. Res accepted; required Fri, Sat. Bar. A la carte entrees: dinner $5.50-$22. Specialties: tuna Stremberg, Chesapeake Bay crab cakes (in season), bayou banana split. Parking. Local artwork. Totally nonsmoking. Cr cds: A, MC, V.

D

★ ★ **LYNNHAVEN FISH HOUSE.** *2350 Starfish Rd (23451), next to Westminster Canterbury. 757/481-0003.* Hrs: 11:30 am-10:30 pm. Closed Thanksgiving, Dec 25. Bar. A la carte entrees: lunch $5.95-$10.95, dinner $13.95-$21.95. Child's meals. Specializes in seafood. Lobster tank. Valet parking. On Lynnhaven fishing pier. Cr cds: A, C, D, DS, MC, V.

D ⚒

✔ ★ **PUNGO GRILL.** *1785 Princess Anne Rd (23456). 757/426-6655.* Hrs: 11 am-9 pm; Fri, Sat to 10 pm. Closed Mon; Thanksgiving, Dec 24, 25; also Jan-Feb. Res accepted. Regional Amer, continental menu. Bar. Semi-a la carte: lunch $4.50-$12.50, dinner $8.95-$16.95. Child's meals. Specializes in Cajun soups, homemade desserts. Parking. Outdoor dining. Dining rm on enclosed porch of 1919 Aladdin house. Cr cds: DS, MC, V.

D ⚒

★ ★ **RUDEE'S.** *227 Mediterranean Ave (23451). 757/425-1777.* Web www.rudees.comm. Hrs: 11 am-midnight. Closed Thanksgiving, Dec

25. Bar. Semi-a la carte: lunch, dinner $4.95-$18.95. Sun brunch $4.95-$9.95. Child's meals. Specializes in fresh seafood, steamed shrimp, hand-cut steak. Raw bar. Valet parking. Outdoor dining. Nautical decor; casual atmosphere. On inlet; transient slips avail for boats. Cr cds: A, C, D, DS, MC, V.

⊡ ⊡

✔★ **SAN ANTONIO SAM'S.** *604 Norfolk Ave (23451).* *757/491-0263.* Hrs: 4-11 pm. Closed Dec 24, 25. Tex-Mex menu. Bar. Semi-a la carte: dinner $3.95-$11.99. Child's meals. Specializes in fajitas, ribs, chili. Parking. Casual dining rm in renovated 1898 ice house. Cr cds: A, C, D, DS, MC, V.

⊡

★★ **TANDOM'S PINE TREE INN.** *2932 Virginia Beach Blvd (23452).* *757/340-3661.* E-mail tandoms@msn.com; web www.tandoms.com. Hrs: 11:30 am-2:30 pm, 5-9 pm; Fri, Sat to 10 pm; Sun 10:30 am-9 pm; Sun brunch to 2:30 pm. Closed Memorial Day, Labor Day. Res accepted. Bar. Semi-a la carte: lunch $3.95-$7.95, dinner $9.95-$19.95. Sun brunch $7.95-$10.95. Child's meals. Specializes in fresh seafood, prime rib, veal Oscar. Salad bar. Pianist. Parking. 1930s style. Cr cds: A, C, D, DS, MC, V.

⊡

★ **WATERMAN'S.** *415 Atlantic Ave (23451).* *757/428-3644.* Hrs: 11 am-10 pm; Fri, Sat to 11 pm. Closed Thanksgiving, Dec 24 evening, 25. Res accepted. Bar to midnight. A la carte entrees: lunch $5.95-$12.95, dinner $5.95-$21.95. Child's meals. Specializes in seafood, beef. Outdoor dining. Two dining areas, with ocean view. Cr cds: A, C, D, DS, MC, V.

⊡ SC ⊡

Unrated Dining Spot

CUISINE AND COMPANY. *3004 Pacific Ave.* *757/428-6700.* Hrs: 9 am-8 pm; summer 9 am-9 pm. Closed Jan 1, Thanksgiving, Dec 25. Continental menu. Wine, beer. A la carte entrees: lunch, dinner $1.25-$12. Specializes in pasta, salads, specialty desserts. Parking. Cr cds: A, DS, MC, V.

⊡ ♥

Warm Springs (D-5)

(See also Clifton Forge, Covington, Hot Springs, Monterey)

Pop 425 (est) **Elev** 2,260 ft **Area code** 540 **Zip** 24484

Nestled at the foot of Little Mountain (3,100 ft), the spring wildflowers or groves of fall foliage make Warm Springs a very scenic spot for sightseeing, hiking or taking the waters. Visitors also enjoy walking tours to view the many historic buildings.

Inn

★★★ **INN AT GRISTMILL SQUARE.** *2 blks W of US 220.* *540/839-2231;* *FAX 540/839-5770.* E-mail grist@va.tds.net; web www.vainns.com/grist.htm. 17 units, 1 & 2 bedrm. Rms: S, D $80-$100; inn apt: S $120; D $140; each addl $10; under 12 free. Crib free. TV; cable. Pool; sauna. Complimentary continental bkfst. Restaurant (see WATERWHEEL). Bar 5-10 pm. Ck-out noon, ck-in 2 pm. Business servs avail. In-rm modem link. Airport transportation. Tennis. 18-hole golf privileges, pro. Downhill ski 5 mi. Refrigerators, some fireplaces. Private patios. Picnic tables. Consists of 5 restored 19th-century buildings. Cr cds: DS, MC, V.

Restaurant

★★★ **WATERWHEEL.** *(See The Inn at Gristmill Square)* *540/839-2231;* *FAX 540/839-5770.* E-mail grist@va.tds.net; web www.vainns.com/grist.htm. Hrs: 6-9 pm; Fri, Sat to 10 pm; Sun brunch 11 am-2 pm. Res accepted. Continental menu. Bar. Wine list. Semi-a la carte: dinner $18-$24. Specializes in fresh local trout, veal, homegrown vegetables. Own baking. Parking. In gristmill dating from turn of the century. Cr cds: DS, MC, V.

Warrenton (C-8)

(See also Culpeper, Fairfax, Front Royal, Manassas)

Pop 4,830 **Elev** 560 ft **Area code** 540 **Zip** 20186 **E-mail** visctr@crosslink.net
Information Warrenton-Fauquier County Visitor Center, 183A Keith St; 800/820-1021.

The seat of Fauquier County, Warrenton was named for General Joseph Warren, who fought at Bunker Hill in the Revolutionary War. The town is situated in the valley of the Piedmont near the foothills of the Blue Ridge Mountains and is known for its cattle and Thoroughbred horse farms. Many old buildings and houses provide for an interesting walking tour of the town.

Seasonal Event

Flying Circus. Flying shows of the barnstorming era, from comedy acts to precision and stunt flying. Rides, picnic area. 7 mi S on US 15/29, then 7 mi SE on US 17 near Bealeton. Phone 540/439-8661. Sun. May-Oct.

Motels

★★ **COMFORT INN.** *7379 Comfort Inn Dr (20187),* *US 29 Bypass N.* *540/349-8900;* *FAX 540/347-5759.* 97 rms. May-Oct: S, D $59-$79; each addl $8; suites $99-$125; under 18 free; mid-wk rates; lower rates rest of yr. Crib free. Pet accepted, some restrictions; $10/day. TV; cable (premium). Pool. Complimentary continental bkfst. Coffee in rms. Ck-out 11 am. Coin lndry. Meeting rm. Business servs avail. In-rm modem link. Exercise equipt; weight machine, treadmill. Refrigerators; microwaves avail. Whirlpool in some suites. Cr cds: A, C, D, DS, MC, V.

⊡ ⊡ ⊡ ⊡ ⊡ ⊡ SC

★★ **HAMPTON INN.** *501 Blackwell Rd.* *540/349-4200;* *FAX 540/349-0061.* Web www.hampton-inn.com. 100 rms, 2 story. S, D $59-$75; under 18 free. Crib free. TV; cable (premium), VCR (movies). Pool. Complimentary continental bkfst. Ck-out noon. Meeting rms. Business servs avail. Coin lndry. Exercise equipt; bicycle, stair machine. Refrigerators, microwaves avail. Picnic tables, grill. Cr cds: A, C, D, DS, MC, V.

⊡ ⊡ ⊡ ⊡ ⊡ SC

Restaurants

★★★ **FANTASTICO RISTORANTE ITALIANO.** *251 W Lee Hwy, Ste 640, 2 mi NW jct US 29 Business & US 17, in shopping center.* *540/349-2575.* E-mail fantast@erols.com. Hrs: 11:30 am-2 pm, 5-9:30 pm; Fri to 10 pm; Sat 5-10 pm. Closed Sun; most major hols. Res accepted. Northern Italian menu. Wine list. Bar. Semi-a la carte: lunch $5.50-$8.95, dinner $9.95-$16.50. Child's meals. Specializes in seafood, veal. Own baking, pasta. Cr cds: A, C, D, DS, MC, V.

⊡ ⊡

★★ **FIDDLER'S GREEN.** *(4244 Loudoun Ave, The Plains 20198)* *11 mi NE on US 17 to VA 245 & I-66W, exit 31.* *540/253-7022.* Hrs: 11:30 am-2 pm, 6-9 pm; Sun 11:30 am-2 pm (brunch), 5:30-9 pm. Closed Mon; Jan 1, Dec 25. Res accepted; required Fri-Sun. Contemporary Amer menu. Bar to 10 pm. Semi-a la carte: lunch $6.50-$10, dinner $13-$22.

Sun brunch $6.50-$10. Specialties: pan-roasted chicken with mustards and shallots; salmon salad; seared jumbo scallops with crab meat and caviar. Own baking, pasta. Entertainment Thurs. Outdoor dining. Two-level dining rm with contemporary decor; flagstone patio with waterfall, fish pond. Cr cds: A, DS, MC, V.

✔★★ **NAPOLEON'S.** *67 Waterloo St.* 540/347-1200. Hrs: 11 am-midnight; Fri, Sat to 1 am. Closed Dec 25. Res accepted. Continental menu. Bar. Semi-a la carte: lunch $5.75-$7.95, dinner $9.95-$15.95. Specializes in veal, fresh fish, hand-cut beef. Outdoor dining. Historic 1838 mansion owned by Confederate General Eppa Hunton. Attractive flower gardens. Cr cds: DS, MC, V.

Washington (C-7)

(See also Warrenton)

Founded 1796 **Pop** 198 **Elev** 690 ft **Area code** 540 **Zip** 22747

The oldest of more than 25 American towns to be named after the first president, this town was surveyed in 1749 by none other than George Washington himself. The streets remain laid out exactly as surveyed, and still bear the names of families who owned the land on which the town was founded. It is romantically rumored that Gay St was named by the 17-year-old Washington after the lovely Gay Fairfax.

The town, seat of Rappahannock County, is situated in the foothills of the Blue Ridge Mountains, which dominate the western horizon.

Inns

★★★ **BLEU ROCK.** *12567 Lee Hwy, On US 211.* 540/987-3190; FAX 540/987-3193; res: 800/537-3652. Web www.innsandouts.com \bleu_rock_inn. 5 rms, 2 story. No rm phones. S, D $109-$195. Closed Mon, Tues. Complimentary full bkfst. Restaurant (see BLEU ROCK INN). Ck-out 11 am, ck-in 3 pm. Business servs avail. Balconies. Restored farmhouse (1899) on lake; rustic setting; vineyard. Cr cds: A, DS, MC, V.

★★★★★ **THE INN AT LITTLE WASHINGTON.** *Middle & Main Sts.* 540/675-3800; FAX 540/675-3100. The staff at this immaculate, meticulously orchestrated English-style inn, with superb decor and details, spares no effort in pampering guests. What makes a getaway truly memorable is dinner at the restaurant here—one of the country's finest. 14 rms in 2 bldgs, 2 story. D $290-$450; each addl in suite $50; suites $440-$580; higher rates: Fri, Sat, hols & Oct. Inn closed Tues (exc May & Oct); also Dec 24, 25. Complimentary continental bkfst. Restaurant (see THE INN AT LITTLE WASHINGTON). Rm serv. Bar. Ck-out noon, ck-in 3 pm. Business servs avail. Luggage handling. Gift shop. Airport transportation. Minibars. Some balconies. Cr cds: MC, V.

★★★ **MIDDLETON.** *176 Main St.* 540/675-2020; FAX 540/675-1050; res: 800/816-8157. E-mail middleinn@shentel.net. 4 rms, 2 with shower only, 2 story, 1 cottage. S, D $235-$360; 2-day min hol wkends, Oct; higher rates Oct. Children over 12 yrs only. TV; cable (premium), VCR avail (movies). Complimentary full bkfst; afternoon refreshments. Restaurant nearby. Ck-out 11 am, ck-in 3 pm. Luggage handling. Business servs avail. Lawn games. Federal house built in 1850; rural setting. Totally nonsmoking. Cr cds: A, MC, V.

★★★ **SYCAMORE HILL HOUSE & GARDENS.** *110 Menefee Mt Ln, On US 211, adj to Rappahannock Library.* 540/675-3046. 3 rms, 2 story. No rm phones. S, D $115-$165; higher rates: wkends, hols, month of Oct (2-day min). Closed Tues. Children over 12 yrs only. Complimentary full bkfst; afternoon refreshments. Ck-out 11 am, ck-in 2 pm. Business

servs avail. Luggage handling. Lawn games. On top of hill, view of mountains. Gardens. Totally nonsmoking. Cr cds: MC, V.

Restaurants

★★★ **BLEU ROCK INN.** *(See Bleu Rock Inn)* 540/987-3190. Web www.menusonline.com. Hrs: 5:30-9 pm; Sun brunch 11 am-3 pm. Closed Mon, Tues; Dec 25. Res accepted. French, Amer menu. Serv bar. Semi-a la carte: dinner $16-$23. Sun brunch $6.25-$23. Specialties (seasonal): Tempura soft shell crab, fresh seafood. Outdoor dining. French provincial decor; fireplaces, antiques. Family-owned. Totally nonsmoking. Cr cds: A, DS, MC, V.

★★★ **FOUR & TWENTY BLACKBIRDS.** *(US 522 & VA 647, Flint Hill 22627) S on US 522.* 540/675-1111. Hrs: 5:30-9 pm; Sun brunch 10 am-2 pm. Closed Mon, Tues; July 4, Dec 25; also 1st 2 wks of Jan and Aug. Res accepted dinner; required Fri, Sat dinner. Serv bar. Semi-a la carte: dinner $13-$22. Sun brunch $6-$10. Specialties: vegetarian dishes, eclectic regional dishes. Entertainment. Originally built in 1910 as a carpenter's shop. Totally nonsmoking. Cr cds: MC, V.

★★★★★ **THE INN AT LITTLE WASHINGTON.** *(See The Inn At Little Washington Inn)* 540/675-3800. Owner/chef Patrick O'Connell demonstrates great creative culinary versatility, utilizing many products of the nearby Virginia countryside. Impeccable service, striking old-world decor, and artful food preparation are found in three dining salons, all with a view of the beautifully landscaped garden. Eclectic regional cuisine. Specialties: local rabbit braised in pressed apple cider, native wild rockfish panroasted. Hrs: 6-9:30 pm; Sat 5:30-10 pm; Sun from 4 pm. Closed Tues (exc May & Oct); also Dec 24, 25. Res accepted; required Fri, Sat. Wine cellar. Prix fixe: dinner $95, Fri $105, Sat $115. Valet parking. Chef-owned. Cr cds: MC, V.

Waynesboro (D-6)

(See also Charlottesville)

Settled ca 1739 **Pop** 18,549 **Elev** 1,300 ft **Area code** 540 **Zip** 22980 **E-mail** chamber@cfw.com **Web** www.cfw.com/~chamber

Information Waynesboro Augusta County Chamber of Commerce, 301 W Main St; 540/949-8203.

Waynesboro is at the southern end of the Skyline Drive and the northern end of the Blue Ridge Parkway.

What to See and Do

P. Buckley Moss Museum. Museum's exhibits and programs examine the symbolism and aesthetic ideas of one of America's most notable living artists. (Daily; closed hols) 150 P. Buckley Moss Dr. Phone 540/949-6473. **Free.**

Shenandoah National Park (see). 1 mi E to Skyline Dr.

Shenandoah Valley Art Center. Art galleries, studios. Working artists; performing arts. (Daily exc Mon) 600 W Main St. Phone 540/949-7662. **Donation.**

Sherando Lake Recreation Area. Facilities include 21-acre lake with sand beach and bathhouses. Swimming, fishing. Picnicking. Camping (Apr-Oct, fee). Amphitheater, campfire programs. (Apr-Nov, daily) 16 mi SW on Blue Ridge Pkwy, in George Washington and Jefferson National Forests. Phone 540/942-5965 (summer) or 540/261-6105. Day use ¢¢

Annual Event

Fall Foliage Festival. 1st & 2nd wkend Oct.

Motels

✔★★ **COMFORT INN.** *640 W Broad St. 540/942-1171; FAX 540/942-4785.* 75 rms. S $45-$59; D $52-$69; each addl $5; under 18 free. Crib free. Pet accepted, some restrictions. TV; cable (premium). Pool; wading pool. Coffee in rms. Ck-out noon. Business servs avail. Valet serv. Downhill ski 20 mi. Health club privileges. Microwaves avail. Cr cds: A, C, D, DS, ER, JCB, MC, V.

[D] [icons] SC

★ **DAYS INN.** *2060 Rosser Ave, I-64 exit 94. 540/943-1101; FAX 540/949-7586.* 98 rms, 2 story. May-Oct: S $45-$75; D $50-$85; each addl $5; higher rates fall foliage, graduation; lower rates rest of yr. Crib free. Pet accepted; $6. TV; cable (premium). Pool. Restaurant adj 6 am-midnight. Ck-out 11 am. Meeting rms. Business servs avail. Valet serv. Game rm. Lawn games. Microwaves avail. Picnic tables. Cr cds: A, C, D, DS, MC, V.

[D] [icons] SC

★★ **INN AT AFTON.** *US 250 & I-64, 4 mi E on US 250 at jct Skyline Dr & I-64 exit 99. 540/942-5201; res: 800/860-8559; FAX 540/943-8746.* Web www.comet.net/nelsoncty. 118 rms, 2-3 story. No elvtr. May-Oct: S $60-$76; D $63-$81; each addl $7; under 18 free; higher rates special events; lower rates rest of yr. Crib free. Pet accepted. TV. Heated pool. Restaurant 7 am-2 pm, 5-10 pm. Rm serv. Bar 5 pm-12:30 am; entertainment Fri, Sat. Ck-out noon. Meeting rms. Business servs avail. Valet serv. Downhill ski 18 mi. Cr cds: A, C, D, DS, JCB, MC, V.

[D] [icons] SC

Inn

★★★ **THE IRIS INN.** *191 Chinquapin Dr. 540/943-1991.* 9 rms, 2 story. Rm phone avail. S $75-$90; D $80-$100; each addl $20; suites $130-$140; wknd rates (2-day min). TV. Complimentary full bkfst. Ck-out 11 am, ck-in 3:30 pm. Balconies. Wooded setting overlooking Shenandoah Valley. Totally nonsmoking. Cr cds: A, MC, V.

[D] [icons]

Williamsburg (E-9)

(See also Colonial Parkway, Jamestown, Newport News, Surry, Yorktown)

Settled 1633 **Pop** 11,530 **Elev** 86 ft **Area code** 757 **E-mail** wacc@williamsburgcc.com **Web** www.williamsburgcc.com

Information Chamber of Commerce, 201 Penniman Rd, PO Box 3620, 23187; 757/229-6511.

After the Native American massacre of 1622, this Virginia colony built a palisade across the peninsula between the James and York rivers. The settlement that grew up around the palisade was called Middle Plantation and is now the site of Colonial Williamsburg.

Middle Plantation figured prominently in Bacon's Rebellion against Governor Berkeley. In 1693, it was chosen as the site of the College of William and Mary, and in 1699, the seat of Virginia government was moved here. The capitol was built to replace the Jamestown statehouse, which had burned the year before. Renamed in honor of William III of England, the new capital gradually became a town of about 200 houses and 1,500 residents. For 81 years, Williamsburg was the political, social and cultural capital of Virginia.

The colony's first successful printing press was established here by William Parks, and in 1736 he published Virginia's first newspaper. The capitol was the scene of such stirring colonial events as Patrick Henry's Stamp Act speech (1765).

The First Continental Congress was called from here by the dissolved House of Burgesses in 1774. Two years later, the Second Continental Congress was boldly led by delegates from Virginia to declare independence; George Mason's Declaration of Rights, which became the basis for the first ten amendments to the Constitution, was adopted here.

Williamsburg's exciting days came to an end in 1780, when the capital was moved to Richmond for greater safety and convenience during the Revolution. For a century and a half it continued as a quiet little college town, its tranquility interrupted briefly by the Civil War. In 1917, when a munitions factory was built near the town and cheap housing for the factory's 15,000 workers was hastily erected, Williamsburg seemed destined to live out its days in ugliness.

In 1926, however, John D. Rockefeller, Jr, and Dr. W.A.R. Goodwin, rector of Bruton Parish Church, who saw the town as a potential treasure house of colonial history, shared the broad vision that inspired the restoration of Williamsburg. For more than 30 years, Rockefeller devoted personal attention to the project and contributed funds to accomplish this nonprofit undertaking.

Today, after many years of archaeological and historical research, the project is near completion. The Historic Area, approximately a mile long and a half-mile wide, encompasses most of the 18th-century capital. Eighty-eight of the original buildings have been restored; 50 major buildings, houses and shops and many smaller outbuildings have been reconstructed on their original sites; 45 of the more historically significant buildings contain more than 200 exhibition rooms, furnished either with original pieces or reproductions and open to the public on regular seasonal schedules.

Visitors stroll Duke of Gloucester Street and mingle with people in 18th-century attire. Craftsmen at about 20 different shops ply such trades as wigmaking and blacksmithing, using materials, tools and techniques of pre-Revolutionary times.

Williamsburg is beautiful year-round. November through March is an excellent time to visit, when it is less crowded and the pace is more leisurely; some holiday weekends may be busy. The Historic Area is closed to private motor vehicles 8 am-10 pm.

What to See and Do

(Please note that Colonial Williamsburg is only a part of the town of Williamsburg. Other attractions are listed for which there are separate admission fees.)

America's Railroads on Parade. More than 4,000-sq-ft of model train layouts. Hands-on exhibits, gift shop. (Daily; closed Jan 1, Thanksgiving, Dec 25) 1915 Pocahontas Trail, in Village Shops at Kingsmill. Phone 757/220-8725. ¢¢

Busch Gardens Williamsburg. European-style themed park on 360 acres features re-created 17th-century German, English, French, Italian, Scottish and Canadian villages. Attractions include more than 30 thrill rides, including Drachen Fire roller coaster, one of the nation's largest; 3-D movie *Haunts of the Olde Country*, with in-theater special effects; live shows, antique carousel, celebrity concerts, miniature of Le Mans racetrack, rides for small children. Themed restaurants; shops. Transportation around the grounds by sky ride or steam train. A computer-operated monorail links the park with the Anheuser-Busch Hospitality Center; brewery tour. Park (mid-May-Labor Day, daily; late Mar-mid-May, wknds; after Labor Day-Oct, Fri-Tues). 3 mi E on US 60. Phone 757/253-3000. ¢¢¢¢

Carter's Grove (part of Colonial Williamsburg). This James River site includes the Winthrop Rockefeller Archaeology Museum, the partially reconstructed Wolstenholme Towne and an early-18th-century slave quarter. Also a 1755 mansion, located on 80-ft bluff overlooking the James River, that has been restored to its 1930s splendor. A one-way country road begins here and winds through woods, meadows and marshes back to Williamsburg, or visitors may return via US 60. (Mid-Mar-Dec, daily exc Mon) 7 mi SE. ¢¢¢¢

College of William and Mary (1693). (7,000 students) America's second-oldest college (only Harvard is older). Initiated honor system, elective system of studies, schools of law, modern languages; second to have school of medicine (all in 1779). Phi Beta Kappa Society founded here (1776). W end of Duke of Gloucester St. Phone 757/221-4000. On campus are

Wren Building. Oldest (1695-1699, restored 1928) academic building in America; designed by the great English architect Sir Christopher Wren. Tours (daily). **Free.**

Earl Gregg Swem Library. Houses College Museum. Large display honoring the college's 300th anniversary. (Mon-Fri; closed most hols)

Muscarelle Museum of Art. Traveling displays and exhibitions from an extensive collection. (Mon-Fri & wknd afternoons; closed Jan 1 & 2, also Easter Sun) Phone 757/221-2700. **Free.**

⭐ **Colonial Williamsburg.**

Colonial Williamsburg Visitor Center. Ticket sales, sightseeing information; orientation film; lodging and dining assistance; bookstore; transportation. Center (daily). Colonial Pkwy & VA 132. Contact the Colonial Williamsburg Foundation, PO Box 1776, 23187; 757/220-7645 or 800/246-2099.

Ticket information. An admission ticket is necessary to enjoy the full scope of Colonial Williamsburg. Three types of general admission tickets are available: The **Basic Ticket** provides admission on the Colonial Williamsburg transportation system and entrance to the exhibits in the Historic Area for one day. (This ticket does *not* provide admission to the Governor's Palace, the DeWitt Wallace Decorative Arts Gallery, Carter's Grove or the Abby Aldrich Rockefeller Folk Art Center.) The **Patriot's Pass** (valid one yr) provides admission on the transporation system and entrance to all historic buildings, colonial houses, craft shops, Governor's Palace, Carter's Grove, DeWitt Wallace Decorative Arts Gallery, Abby Aldrich Rockefeller Folk Art Center and historical film. Ticket prices vary. Phone 800/246-2099 for exact prices.

Disabled Visitor Information. Efforts are made to accommodate the disabled while still retaining the authenticity of colonial life. Many buildings have wheelchair access once inside, but it should be noted that most buildings are reached by steps. Visitor Center has a list detailing accessibility of each building; wheelchair ramps may be made avail at some buildings. In addition, there are wheelchair rentals and parking. A hands-on tour of several historic trades may be arranged for the visually impaired and sign language tours are avail with advance notice. Phone 800/246-2099.

Exhibition buildings.

The Capitol. House of Burgesses met here (1704-1779); scene of Patrick Henry's speech against Stamp Act. E end of Duke of Gloucester St. N of capitol, across Nicholson St is

Public Gaol. Where debtors, criminals and pirates (including Blackbeard's crew) were imprisoned. A few steps W and back to Duke of Gloucester St is

Raleigh Tavern. Frequent meeting place for Jefferson, Henry and other Revolutionary patriots; a social center of the Virginia Colony. Opp is

Wetherburn's Tavern. One of the most popular inns of the period.

Governor's Palace and Gardens. Residence of Royal Governor, one of the most elegant mansions in colonial America; set in 10-acre restored gardens. N end of Palace Green. Included in all admission tickets, or by separate ticket ¢¢¢¢¢

Brush-Everard House. Home of early mayor, with programs on slave life. SE is

Peyton Randolph House (1716). Home of president of First Continental Congress. Rochambeau's headquarters prior to Yorktown campaign. SW is

James Geddy House. Once home of a prominent silversmith with working brass, bronze, silver and pewter foundry. Across Palace Green at corner of Prince George St is

Wythe House. Home of George Wythe, America's first law professor, teacher of Jefferson, Clay and Marshall. This was Washington's headquarters before siege of Yorktown, Rochambeau's after.

The Magazine. Arsenal and military storehouse of Virginia Colony; authentic arms exhibited. Duke of Gloucester St, 1 blk E of Palace Green.

Abby Aldrich Rockefeller Folk Art Center. Outstanding collection of American folk art. Items in this collection were created by artists not trained in studio techniques, but who faithfully recorded aspects of everyday life in paintings, sculpture, needlework, ceramics, toys and other media. York St ½ blk SE of capitol. ¢¢¢

Historic trades. Craftsmen in 18th-century costume pursue old trades of apothecary, printer, bookbinder, silversmith, wigmaker, shoemaker, blacksmith, harnessmaker, cabinetmaker, miller, milliner, gunsmith, wheelwright, basketmaker, cook, cooper and carpenter.

Public Hospital. Reconstruction of first public institution in the English colonies devoted exclusively to treatment of mental illness.

DeWitt Wallace Decorative Arts Gallery. Modern museum adjoining Public Hospital, features exhibits, lectures, films and related programs centering on British and American decorative arts of the 17th to early 19th centuries. ¢¢¢

Bruton Parish Church. One of America's oldest Episcopal churches, in continuous use since 1715. Organ recitals (Mar-Dec, Tues & Sat). (Daily; no tours during services) Duke of Gloucester St, just W of Palace Green. Phone 757/229-2891.

Courthouse. County and city business was conducted here from 1770 until 1932. The interior has been carefully restored to its original appearance. Visitors often participate in scheduled re-enactments of court sessions. Duke of Gloucester St, E of Palace Green.

Play Booth Theater. Scenes from 18th-century plays in open-air theater. Open to all Colonial Williamsburg ticket holders. (Spring-fall, daily)

Special focus and orientation tours. Orientation tours (30 min) for first-time visitors; special tours (90 min), called history walks, include African American life, gardens, religion and women of Williamsburg. Reservations are avail at any ticket sales location.

Carriage and wagon rides. A drive through Historic Area in carriage or wagon driven by costumed coachman. General admission ticket holders may make reservations on day of ride at Lumber House ticket office. (Daily, weather permitting) ¢¢¢

Lanthorn Tour. A costumed interpreter conducts evening walking tour of selected shops that are illuminated by candlelight. Tickets may be purchased at any sales location or by phone 800/246-2099. (Mar-Dec, daily) ¢¢¢

Children's Tours. Special programs, tours and experiences exclusively for children and families are offered in the summer.

Evening entertainment. Colonial Williamsburg presents "rollicking 18th-century plays" throughout the yr; wide variety of cultural events, concerts and historical reenactments (fees vary). Chowning's Tavern offers colonial "gambols" (games), music, entertainment and light food and drink (evenings).

Shopping. Superior wares typical of the 18th century are offered in nine restored or reconstructed stores and shops; items include silver, jewelry, herbs, candles, hats and books. Two craft houses sell approved reproductions of the antiques on display in the houses and museums.

Ride with Me to Williamsburg. Informative and entertaining 90-min audiocassette describes events from Williamsburg's colorful colonial, revolutionary and Civil War past. The town's famous restoration is summarized by one of the architects who worked on the project. Contact RWM Associates, PO Box 1324, Bethesda MD 20817; 301/299-7817 or 800/840-7433. ¢¢¢¢

York River State Park. A 2,500-acre park along the York River and its related marshes. Includes the Taskinas Creek National Estuarine Research Reserve. Fishing; boating (launch), canoe trips. Hiking, bridle trails. Picnicking. Interpretive center, programs; nature walks. (Daily) Standard fees. 8 mi NW via I-64, exit 231B, then 1 mi N on VA 607 to VA 606E. Phone 757/566-3036.

Annual Events

Antiques Forum. Colonial Williamsburg. Mid-Feb.

Washington's Birthday Celebration. Colonial Williamsburg. President's Day wknd.

Learning Weekend. Colonial Williamsburg. Family-oriented wknd of discovery on a single topic. Mar.

Garden Symposium. Colonial Williamsburg. Lectures and clinics. Last wk Apr.

Prelude to Independence. Colonial Williamsburg. May 15.

Publick Times. Colonial Williamsburg. Re-creation of colonial market days; contests, crafts, auctions, military encampment. Labor Day wkend.

Traditional Christmas Activities. Colonial Williamsburg. Featuring grand illumination of city; fireworks. Dec.

Seasonal Events

Colonial Weekends. Package wkends on 18th-century theme, features introductory lecture, guided tours, banquet at Colonial Williamsburg. Jan.-early Mar.

18th-Century Comedy. Williamsburg Lodge Auditorium. Sat nights. Mar.-Dec.

Military Drill. On Market Square Green. Costumed wkly drill by Williamsburg Independent Company. Mid-Mar-Oct.

Fife-and-Drum Corps. Colonial Williamsburg. Performances in the Historic Area. Sat. Apr-Oct.

Living History Programs at Colonial Williamsburg. Include *An Assembly, Cross or Crown* and *Cry Witch!* Varying schedule wkly. Spring, summer & fall.

Motels

(Rates may be higher holiday seasons)

★ **GOVERNOR'S INN.** *506 N Henry St (23185). 757/229-1000, ext. 6000; FAX 757/220-7019; res: 800/447-8679.* 200 rms, 3 story. May-Aug: S, D $89; family rates; lower rates rest of yr. Closed Jan-mid-Mar. Crib $8. Pet accepted. TV; cable (premium). Pool. Complimentary coffee. Restaurant nearby. Business servs avail. Sundries. Gift shop. Tennis privileges. Golf privileges. Game rm. Cr cds: A, D, DS, MC, V.

⊡ 🖬 🛅 🛅 🛅 🛅 SC

★ ★ **HAMPTON INN.** *201 Bypass Rd (23185). 757/220-0880; FAX 757/229-7175.* 122 rms, 4 story. Mid-June-early Sept: S, D $89-$99; lower rates rest of yr, higher rates July 4, Labor Day. Crib free. TV, cable (premium). Indoor pool; whirlpool, sauna. Complimentary continental bkfst. Coffee in rms. Ck-out 11 am. Meeting rm. Business servs avail. Game rm. Cr cds: A, C, D, DS, MC, V.

⊡ 🛅 🛅 🛅 SC

★ **HERITAGE INN.** *1324 Richmond Rd (23185). 757/229-6220; FAX 757/229-2774; res: 800/782-3800.* 54 rms, 3 story. Mid-June-Labor Day: S, D $74; 2-day min hols, special events; lower rates rest of yr. Crib avail. Pet accepted. TV; cable. Pool. Continental bkfst. Ck-out noon. Business servs avail. Cr cds: A, C, D, DS, MC, V.

🛅 🛅 🛅 🛅 SC

★ ★ **HOLIDAY INN 1776.** *725 Bypass Rd (23185). 757/220-1776; FAX 757/220-3124.* Web www.holiday-inn1776.com/. 202 rms, 2 story. Mid-June-late Aug: S, D $89-$129; each addl $6; suite $129-$150; under 18 free; lower rates rest of yr. TV; cable (premium). Pool; wading pool, poolside serv. Playground. Supervised child's activities (Memorial Day-Labor Day); ages 4-12. Restaurant 7 am-2 pm, 5-10 pm. Rm serv. Bar from 4 pm; Sat, Sun from 1 pm. Ck-out 11 am. Coin lndry. Meeting rms. Business servs avail. Bellhops. Valet serv. Concierge (in season). Sundries. Gift shop. Lighted tennis. Game rm. Lawn games. Picnic tables. Cr cds: A, C, D, DS, JCB, MC, V.

⊡ 🛅 🛅 🛅 🛅 SC

★ **HOLIDAY INN EXPRESS-HISTORIC AREA.** *119 Bypass Rd (23185). 757/253-1663; FAX 757/220-9117.* Web www.holiday-express.com. 132 rms, 2 story. Mid-June-Labor Day: S, D $72-$94; each addl $6; under 19 free; lower rates rest of yr. Crib free. TV; cable (premium). Pool. Complimentary continental bkfst. Ck-out 11 am. Meeting rms.

Business servs avail. In-rm modem link. Cr cds: A, C, D, DS, ER, JCB, MC, V.

⊡ 🛅 🛅 🛅 SC

★ ★ ★ **MARRIOTT'S MANOR CLUB.** *101 St Andrews Dr (23188). 757/258-1120; FAX 757/258-5705.* 111 kit. suites, 3 story. Memorial Day-Labor Day: kit. suites $249/day, $1358/wk; family rates; lower rates rest of yr. Crib free. TV; cable (premium), VCR (movies). Complimentary coffee in rms. Restaurant 7 am-7 pm. Ck-out 10 am. Meeting rms. Business servs avail. In-rm modem link. Concierge. Sundries. Gift shop. Lighted tennis. 45-hole golf, greens fee $50-$100, pro, putting green, driving range. Exercise rm; instructor, weights, bicycles. Massage. 2 pools, 1 indoor; whirlpools. In-rm whirlpools, refrigerators, microwaves, fireplaces. Balconies. Grills. Cr cds: A, C, D, DS, MC, V.

⊡ 🛅 🛅 🛅 🛅 🛅 🛅 🛅

✔★ ★ **QUALITY INN LORD PAGET.** *901 Capitol Landing Rd (23185). 757/229-4444; FAX 757/220-9314; res: 800/537-2438.* 94 rms, 1-2 story. May-Oct: S, D $59-$89; suites $89-$109; lower rates rest of yr. Crib $7. TV; cable (premium). Pool; wading pool. Restaurant 7 am-10 pm. Ck-out 11 am. Coin lndry. Bellhops. Putting green. Refrigerators, microwaves avail. On 7½ wooded acres with small fishing lake. Cr cds: A, C, D, DS, ER, JCB, MC, V.

⊡ 🛅 🛅 🛅 🛅 SC

★ **QUARTERPATH INN.** *620 York St (23185). 757/220-0960; FAX 757/220-1531; res: 800/446-9222.* 130 rms, 2 story. Apr-Oct: S, D $62-$75; each addl $6; packages avail; lower rates rest of yr. Crib free. Pet accepted, some restrictions. TV, cable (premium). Pool. Restaurant adj 4-10 pm. Ck-out noon. Meeting rm. Business servs avail. Some in-rm whirlpools. Cr cds: A, C, DS, MC, V.

⊡ 🛅 🛅 🛅 🛅 SC

★ ★ ★ **WILLIAMSBURG WOODLANDS.** *Box 1776 (23185), 1 mi SE of I-64, exit 238, opp Visitor Ctr. 757/229-1000; FAX 757/565-8942; res: 800/447-8679.* 315 rms. Apr-Dec: S, D $91-$125; each addl $8; golf, tennis packages; lower rates rest of yr. Crib free. TV. 2 pools, wading pool, lifeguard. Playground. Supervised child's activities (mid-June-Aug); ages 5-12. Restaurant (see THE CASCADES). Ck-out 11 am. Meeting rms. Business servs avail. Bellhops. Valet serv. Sundries. Barber, beauty shop. Tennis. Golf privileges, putting green. Health club privileges. Lawn games. Miniature golf. Picnic tables. Cr cds: A, D, DS, MC, V.

⊡ 🛅 🛅 🛅 🛅 🛅 SC

Motor Hotels

★ ★ **COURTYARD BY MARRIOTT.** *470 McLaws Circle (23185). 757/221-0700; FAX 757/221-0741.* 151 rms, 4 story. Memorial Day-Labor Day: S, D $119-129; suites $165-185; lower rates rest of yr. Crib free. TV; cable (premium). Indoor/outdoor pool; whirlpool. Complimentary coffee in rms. Bar 4-10 pm. Ck-out noon. Coin lndry. Meeting rms. Business servs avail. In-rm modem link. Valet serv. Concierge. Sundries. Exercise equipt; weight machine, bicycles. Game rm. Refrigerator in suites. Balconies. Cr cds: A, C, D, DS, MC, V.

⊡ 🛅 🛅 🛅 🛅 SC

★ ★ ★ **FORT MAGRUDER INN & CONFERENCE CENTER.** *6945 Pochanontas Trail (US 60E) (23187). 757/220-2250; FAX 757/220-3215; res: 800/582-1010.* 303 rms, 4 story. Apr-Oct: S $79-$129; D $99-$148; each addl $10; suites $145-$250; under 18 free; lower rates rest of yr. Crib free. TV; cable (premium). 2 pools, 1 indoor; whirlpool, wading pool. Playground. Coffee in lobby. Restaurant 6:30 am-10 pm. Rm serv. Bar 11:30-1 am; entertainment. Ck-out 11 am. Coin lndry. Convention facilities. Business center. Bellhops. Concierge. Gift shop. Lighted tennis. Golf privileges, greens fee $65-$115. Exercise equipt; weights, bicycles, sauna. Game rm. Bicycles. Minibars, some in-rm whirlpools. Balconies; many private patios. Cr cds: A, C, D, DS, MC, V.

⊡ 🛅 🛅 🛅 🛅 🛅 🛅 SC 🛅

★ ★ **HOLIDAY INN-DOWNTOWN.** *814 Capitol Landing Rd (23185). 757/229-0200; FAX 757/220-1642.* 139 rms, 3 story. Apr-Oct: S,

D $79-$95; each addl $6; under 18 free; wkend rates; golf plan; lower rates rest of yr. Crib free. TV; cable (premium). Indoor pool; whirlpool, poolside serv. Restaurant 7 am-10 pm. Rm serv. Bar 5-11 pm. Ck-out noon. Coin lndry. Meeting rms. Business servs avail. Bellhops. Gift shop. Exercise equipt; weights, bicycles, sauna. Holidome. Game rm. Refrigerators, microwaves avail. Cr cds: A, D, DS, JCB, MC, V.

★ ★ **HOWARD JOHNSON-HISTORIC AREA.** *7135 Pocahontas Trail (US 60E) (23185).* 757/229-6900; FAX 757/220-3211. E-mail hojohst@erols.com; web www.erols.com/hojohst. 100 rms, 4 story. Mid-June-Labor Day: S, D $89-$140; under 12 free; 2-day min stay in season wkends; lower rates rest of yr. Crib free. TV; cable (premium). Pool; wading pool, poolside serv. Complimentary coffee in lobby. Restaurant adj 7 am-2 pm. Ck-out noon. Coin lndry. Meeting rms. Business servs avail. Valet serv. Sundries. Health club privileges. Game rm. Cr cds: A, C, D, DS, JCB, MC, V.

★ ★ ★ **MARRIOTT.** *50 Kingsmill Rd (23185).* 757/220-2500; FAX 757/221-0653. Web www.marriott.com. 295 rms, 6 story. Apr-mid-Nov: S, D $109-$169; suites $250-$500; family rates; package plans; lower rates rest of yr. Crib free. TV; cable (premium). Indoor/outdoor pool; whirlpool, poolside serv. Restaurant 6:30 am-10:30 pm. Rm serv. Bar. Ck-out noon. Convention facilities. Business center. In-rm modem link. Bellhops. Concierge. Gift shop. Tennis. Exercise equipt; weights, bicycles, sauna. Game rm. Rec rm. Refrigerators avail. Private patios, balconies. Cr cds: A, C, D, DS, ER, JCB, MC, V.

Hotels

★ ★ ★ **WILLIAMSBURG HOSPITALITY HOUSE.** *415 Richmond Rd (23185).* 757/229-4020; FAX 757/220-1560; res: 800/932-9192. E-mail wcorp52554@aol.com. 297 rms, 4 story. Mid-Mar-Dec: S, D $143-$153; each addl $10; suites $250-$500; under 18 free; wkend rates; golf plan; lower rates rest of yr. Crib free. TV; cable (premium). Heated pool; poolside serv. Restaurant 6:30 am-11 pm. Bar 11:30-1 am. Ck-out noon. Meeting rms. Business servs avail. In-rm modem link. Concierge. Gift shop. Indoor parking. Health club privileges. Cr cds: A, C, D, DS, MC, V.

★ ★ ★ ★ **WILLIAMSBURG INN.** *Francis St (23185), in historic area.* 757/229-1000; FAX 757/220-7096; res: 800/HISTORY. E-mail sales@cwf.org; web www.history.org. This inn provides elegant English Regency-style accommodations and a wide range of recreational facilities. Rooms are comfortable; furnishings are antiques or Williamsburg reproductions. Public areas are spacious and appealing, and, perhaps best of all, the inn is an easy walk from the 18th-century historic area that made Williamsburg famous. 91 rms, 2 story. S, D $245-$345; suites $410-$750; package plans. Crib $12. TV; cable (premium), VCR avail. 3 pools, 1 indoor; wading pool, whirlpool, poolside serv, lifeguard. Supervised child's activities (Memorial Day-Labor Day); ages 4-12. Restaurant 7 am-10 pm (also see REGENCY ROOM). Afternoon tea 4 pm. Rm serv 24 hrs. Bar 11:30 am-11 pm; entertainment. Ck-out noon, ck-in 3 pm. Meeting rms. Business center. In-rm modem link. Airport transportation. Concierge. Tennis, pro. 9-hole & two 18-hole golf courses, greens fee $95, pro, putting green. Exercise equipt; weights, bicycles, sauna, steam rm. Massage. Lawn games. Bicycle rentals. Card rm. Some refrigerators. Balcony, fireplace in suites. Cr cds: A, D, DS, MC, V.

★ ★ ★ **WILLIAMSBURG LODGE.** *S England St (23185).* 757/229-1000; FAX 757/220-7799; res: 800/447-8976. E-mail conference sales@cwf.org; web www.history.org. 315 rms, 3 story. Mar-Dec: S, D $175-$225; each addl $12; suites $225-$450; lower rates rest of yr. TV, VCR avail. 3 pools; wading pool, whirlpool, poolside serv, lifeguard. Supervised child's activities (Memorial Day-Labor Day); ages 4-12. Complimentary coffee in lobby. Restaurant 7 am-10 pm. Bar; pianist. Ck-out 11 am. Meeting rms. Business servs avail. In-rm modem link. Gift shop. Beauty shop. Tennis, pro. 45-hole golf, greens fee $95, pro, putting green. Exer-

cise equipt; weights, bicycles, steam rm, sauna. Lawn games. Bicycle rentals. Some fireplaces. Some private patios. Lounge, verandas. Gardens; at edge of Colonial Williamsburg historic district. Cr cds: A, D, DS, MC, V.

Inns

★ ★ **COLONIAL CAPITAL.** *501 Richmond Rd (23185).* 757/229-0233; FAX 757/253-7667; res: 800/776-0570. E-mail ccbb@widomaker.com; web www.ccbb.com. 5 rms, 3 story. No elvtr. Mid-Mar-Dec: S $75-$95; D $95-$115; each addl $20; suite $135; lower rates rest of yr. Children over 8 yrs only. Complimentary full bkfst. Restaurant adj 6:30 am-10 pm. Ck-out 11 am, ck-in 2 pm. Built in 1926; antiques. Totally nonsmoking. Cr cds: A, DS, MC, V.

★ ★ ★ **COLONIAL HOUSES.** *302 Francis St (23185), in historic area.* 757/229-1000; FAX 757/565-8444; res: 800/447-8679. E-mail conferencesales@crw.org.com; web www.history.org. 82 rms in 25 colonial houses and taverns, 1-2 story. Apr-Dec: S, D $155-$245/rm; 2-8 persons $285-$625/house; lower rates rest of yr. Crib $12. TV, cable (premium). Pool privileges. Supervised child's activities (Memorial Day-Labor Day); ages 4-12. Dining facilities. Ck-out noon, ck-in 3 pm. Business center. In-rm modem link. Recreational facilities avail at Williamsburg Lodge (see). Some of the houses are more than 200 yrs old; furnished in the period. Cr cds: A, D, DS, MC, V.

★ ★ ★ **EDGEWOOD.** *(4800 John Tyler Hwy, Charles City 23030) 28 mi W on VA 5.* 804/829-2962; res: 800/296-3343. 8 rms, 3 with shower only, 3 story. S, D $120-$198. Children over 12 yrs only. TV; VCR. Pool. Complimentary full bkfst. Restaurant nearby. Ck-out 11:30 am, ck-in 3 pm. Microwaves avail. Once part of the Berkeley Plantation; it has served as a church, post office, and nursing home. Cr cds: A, MC, V.

★ ★ **INDIAN SPRINGS.** *330 Indian Springs (23185).* 757/220-0726; res: 800/262-9165. E-mail Indianspgs@tni.net. 4 rms, 2 story. Rm phone in cottage only. Mid-Mar-Dec: S, D $85-$130; lower rates rest of yr. Crib free. TV; cable. Complimentary full bkfst. Restaurant nearby. Ck-out 11 am, ck-in 3-6 pm. Gardens. Near William & Mary College. Totally nonsmoking. Cr cds: MC, V.

★ ★ **LEGACY OF WILLIAMSBURG.** *930 Jamestown Rd (23185).* 757/220-0524; FAX 757/220-4722. 4 rms, 2 story, 3 suites. Mar-Dec: S, D $100-$108; suites $150; lower rates rest of yr. Adults only. TV in sitting rm; cable, VCR (free movies). Complimentary full bkfst. Restaurant nearby. Ck-out 10:30 am, ck-in noon. Business servs avail. Rec rm. Billiards. Some balconies. Built in 18th-century style; period antiques, furnishings; library. Large rear deck overlooks small ravine. Totally nonsmoking. Cr cds: A, MC, V.

★ ★ ★ **LIBERTY ROSE.** *1022 Jamestown Rd (23185).* 757/253-1260; res: 800/545-1825. Web www.libertyrose.com. 4 rms, 2 story. S, D $135-$205; each addl $40. Children over 12 yrs only. TV; VCR (free movies). Complimentary full bkfst; afternoon refreshments. Restaurant nearby. Ck-out 11 am, ck-in 3 pm. Picnic tables. Built 1920; many antiques. Wooded grounds. Totally nonsmoking. Cr cds: A, MC, V.

★ ★ **NORTH BEND PLANTATION.** *(12200 Weyanoke Rd, Charles City 23030) 19 mi W on VA 5.* 804/829-5176. 4 rms, 2 story. S $105-$140; D $115-$140; each addl $40. TV. Pool. Complimentary full bkfst. Restaurant nearby. Ck-out 11 am, ck-in 3 pm. Fireplaces. Greek revival house (1819); furnished with antiques. Cr cds: MC, V.

★ ★ **PINEY GROVE AT SOUTHALL'S PLANTATION.** *(16920 Southall Plantation Ln, Charles City 23030) US 5W to VA 623N. 804/829-2480.* 4 rms, 2 story, 1 suite. No rm phones. S, D $125-$150; suite $160; hols (2-day min). TV avail in some rms; cable, VCR avail (movies) in common rm. Complimentary full bkfst. Ck-out noon, ck-in 4 pm. Luggage handling. Pool. Lawn games. Refrigerators. 2 historic farmhouses (ca 1800). Totally nonsmoking. No cr cds accepted.

✔ ★ **WAR HILL.** *4560 Long Hill Rd (23188). 757/565-0248; res: 800/743-0248.* Web www.ngetaway.com/va/warhill. 5 rms, 2 suites. No rm phones. S, D $75-$95; each addl $15; suites $95-$120. Crib free. TV; cable. Playground. Complimentary full bkfst. Restaurant nearby. Ck-out noon, ck-in 4 pm. On a working farm; built 1969 in colonial style. Totally nonsmoking. Cr cds: MC, V.

★ ★ ★ **WILLIAMSBURG SAMPLER.** *922 Jamestown Rd (23185). 757/253-0398; FAX 757/253-2669; res: 800/722-1169.* E-mail wbgsampler@aol.com. 4 rms, 3 story. Rm phones avail. S, D $95-$140. TV; cable (premium). Complimentary full bkfst. Restaurant nearby. Ck-out 11 am, ck-in 1 pm. Business servs avail. Picnic tables. Plantation-style house; fireplaces, antiques, colonial-style furnishings; gardens. Near William and Mary College; walking distance to historic area. Totally nonsmoking. Cr cds: MC, V.

Resort

★ ★ ★ ★ **KINGSMILL.** *1010 Kingsmill Rd (23185). 757/253-1703; FAX 757/253-3993; res: 800/832-5665.* The weathered-grey buildings and steep, shingled roofs of this resort are typical of those seen frequently in this part of Virginia. 407 rms, 2 story. Mar-Nov: S, D $155-$255; 1-bedrm suites $191-$275; 2-bedrm suites $330-$490; 3-bedrm suites $470-$705; family rates; golf, tennis plans; lower rates rest of yr. Crib free. TV; cable (premium), VCR avail. Indoor/outdoor pools; whirlpool. Supervised child's activities (Memorial Day-Labor Day); ages 5-12. Dining rm 6 am-10 pm. Rm serv to midnight. Bar from 10 am. Ck-out 11 am, ck-in 4 pm. Meeting rms. Business center. In-rm modem link. Concierge. Lighted tennis, pro. Three 18-hole golf courses (1 par 3), pro, driving range, putting green. Paddle boats. Marina privileges. Racquetball courts. Entertainment. Exercise rm; instructor, weights, bicycles, sauna. Massage. Some refrigerators, fireplaces. Microwave in suites. Picnic tables, grills. Cr cds: A, C, D, DS, JCB, MC, V.

Restaurants

★ ★ **ABERDEEN BARN.** *1601 Richmond Rd (23185). 757/229-6661; FAX 757/229-4440.* Web www.aberdeen-barn.com. Hrs: 5-9:30 pm; Fri, Sat to 10 pm. Closed Thanksgiving, Dec 25; also first 2 wks Jan. Res accepted. Bar. Semi-a la carte: dinner $12.95-$36.95. Child's meals. Specializes in roast prime rib, seafood, baby back ribs. Parking. Open-hearth grill. Barn-like atmosphere; farm implements. Cr cds: A, DS, MC, V.

★ ★ **BERRET'S.** *199 S Boundary St (23185), on Merchant's Square. 757/253-1847.* Hrs: 11:30 am-10 pm. Closed Jan 1, Dec 25; also Mon in Jan & Feb. Res accepted. Regional Amer menu. Bar. Semi-a la carte: lunch $2.50-$7.95, dinner $3.50-$19.50. Child's meals. Specialties: Virginia crab cakes, lobster & crabmeat combo, seafood & herbs baked in parchment. Raw bar. Parking. Outdoor dining. Casual dining rm; fireplace, nautical decor. Cr cds: A, DS, MC, V.

★ **THE CASCADES.** *(See Williamsburg Woodlands Motel) 757/229-1000.* Hrs: 7:30-10 am, 11:30 am-2 pm, 5:30-9 pm; Sun brunch 8 am-2 pm. Res accepted. Bar. Semi-a la carte: bkfst $3-$7, lunch $6-$9, dinner $7-$19. Buffet: bkfst $7.25, lunch $5.95. Sun brunch $10.95. Child's

meals. Specializes in Chesapeake Bay seafood. Parking. Overlooks ravine with cascading brook; contemporary decor. Cr cds: A, D, DS, MC, V.

★ ★ **COACH HOUSE TAVERN.** *(12604 Harrison Landing Rd, Charles City 23030) Approx 25 mi W on VA 5. 804/829-6003.* Hrs: 11 am-4 pm; Fri-Sat 6-9 pm; Sun brunch 11 am-5 pm. Closed Dec 25. Res accepted; required Fri-Sat. Bar. Semi-a la carte: lunch $3.95-$14.95. Complete meals: dinner $14-$26. Sun brunch $3.95-$14.95. Child's meals. Specializes in seafood, game, desserts. Parking. In coach house of Berkeley Plantation; view of grounds and plantation house. Cr cds: A, D, MC, V.

★ ★ **DYNASTY.** *1621 Richmond Rd (23185). 757/220-8888.* E-mail dynasty@wmbg.com; web www.wmbq.com/dynasty. Hrs: noon-midnight; to 10 pm off-season. Res accepted. Chinese menu. Bar. Semi-a la carte: lunch $3.95-$5.95, dinner $5.95-$18.95. Child's meals. Specialties: steamed whole fish, General Zuo's chicken, Peking duck. Parking. Outdoor dining. Large dining area decorated with Chinese screens and art objects. Gift shop. Fish pond. Oriental karaoke. Cr cds: A, C, D, DS, JCB, MC, V.

★ ★ ★ **FORD'S COLONY COUNTRY CLUB.** *240 Ford's Colony Dr (23188), 4 mi W on Long Hill Dr, then left, in clubhouse. 757/258-4100.* Hrs: 6-9:30 pm; Sun brunch 11:30 am-2:30 pm. Closed Mon; also early Jan. Res accepted. Regional Amer menu. Bar. Wine cellar. Semi-a la carte: dinner $16-$28. Sun brunch $15.95. Child's meals. Specializes in fresh seafood, rack of lamb. Outdoor dining. Large floral centerpiece, original artwork, fine china and glassware. Jacket (dinner). Cr cds: A, MC, V.

★ **GAZEBO.** *409 Bypass Rd (23185). 757/220-0883.* Hrs: 6 am-2 pm. Res accepted. A la carte entrees: bkfst $3.75-$7.50, lunch $2.50-$8.50. Child's meals. Specializes in pancakes, omelets. Casual decor. Cr cds: C, D, DS, MC, V.

✔ ★ **GIUSEPPE'S.** *5601 Richmond Rd (23188). 757/565-1977.* E-mail dkenn@erols.com; web www.giuseppes.com. Hrs: 11:30 am-2 pm, 5-9 pm; Fri, Sat to 9:30 pm. Closed Sun; major hols. Italian menu. Bar. Semi-a la carte: lunch, dinner $4.25-$15.95. Child's meals. Specialties: pasta primavera, chicken Provençale. Parking. Patio dining. Cr cds: DS, MC, V.

★ ★ **INDIAN FIELDS TAVERN.** *(9220 John Tyler Memorial Hwy, Charles City 23030) Approx 25 mi W on VA 5. 804/829-5004.* Hrs: 11 am-4 pm, 5-9 pm; Fri, Sat to 10 pm. Sun brunch to 4 pm. Closed Dec 24, 25; also Mon in Jan. Res accepted. Bar. Semi-a la carte: lunch $5.50-$11.95, dinner $13.95-$21.95. Sun brunch $7-$14.95. Child's meals. Specialties: crab cakes Harrison, venison, bread pudding. Parking. Screened porch dining area. Turn-of-the-century farmhouse on working farm. Cr cds: A, DS, MC, V.

★ ★ **JEFFERSON INN.** *1453 Richmond Rd (23185). 757/229-2296.* Hrs: 4-11 pm. Closed Thanksgiving, Dec 24, 25. Res accepted. Italian, continental menu. Semi-a la carte: dinner $6.95-$19.95. Child's meals. Specializes in steak, fresh seafood, Southern favorites. Family-owned. Cr cds: A, C, D, MC, V.

★ ★ **KING'S ARMS TAVERN.** *Duke of Gloucester St (23185). 757/220-7010.* Hrs: 11:30 am-2:30 pm, 5-9:30 pm. Closed mid-Feb-mid-Mar; also Tues Nov-Dec. Res required dinner. Bar. Semi-a la carte: lunch $1.95-$8.50, dinner $17.75-$25.95. Child's meals. Specialties: game pie, peanut soup, Virginia ham. Garden bar serv. Own apple cider. Garden dining. Colonial balladeers. Restored 18th century tavern; colonial decor. Cr cds: A, D, DS, MC, V.

★ ★ ★ **KITCHEN AT POWHATAN.** *3601 Ironbound Rd (23188), on grounds of Powhatan Plantation.* 757/220-1200. Hrs: 5:30-10 pm. Closed Mon. Res accepted. Bar. Semi-a la carte: dinner $13-$24. Prix fixe: dinner $35. Specializes in game, seafood, regional cuisine. Parking. In 1737 structure near James River. Cr cds: C, D, MC, V.

⊡

★ ★ ★ **LE YACA.** *1915 Pocohantas Trail (23185), US 60E in Kingsmill Village shops.* 757/220-3616. Hrs: 11:30 am-2 pm, 6-9:30 pm. Closed Sun. Res accepted. Southern French menu. Bar. Wine cellar. Semi-a la carte: lunch $6.50-$13.50. Complete meals: dinner $21-$47. Specialties: open-spit leg of lamb, marquise au chocolat. Salad bar (lunch). Own pastries. Cr cds: A, C, D, MC, V.

⊡ ⊡

★ **LOBSTER HOUSE.** *1431 Richmond Rd (23185).* 757/229-7771. Hrs: 4:30-10 pm; Fri, Sat to 11 pm. Res accepted. Continental menu. Bar. A la carte entrees: $11.95-$19.95. Child's meals. Specializes in pasta, seafood. Nautical decor. Cr cds: A, MC, V.

⊡ SC ⊡

★ **MR LIU'S.** *Village Shops Kingsmill (23185).* 757/253-0990. Hrs: 11:30 am-10 pm. Closed Jan 1, Thanksgiving, Dec 25. Chinese menu. Bar. Semi-a la carte: lunch $3.95-$6.95, dinner $5.95-$11.95. Child's meals. Specialties: General Liu chicken, mongolian spicy beef. Chinese art. Cr cds: A, C, D, DS, MC, V.

⊡ SC

✔★ **OLD CHICKAHOMINY HOUSE.** *1211 Jamestown Rd (23185), at jct VA 199 & 31.* 757/229-4689. Hrs: 8:30-10:15 am, 11:30 am-2:15 pm. Closed Thanksgiving, Dec 25; also 2 wks mid-Jan. Wine, beer. Semi-a la carte: bkfst $.95-$7.50, lunch $2-$6.50. Specialties: ham on hot biscuits, Brunswick stew, chicken & dumplings. Gift shop. 18th-century stagecoach stop atmosphere. Totally nonsmoking. Cr cds: MC, V.

✔★ ★ **PEKING.** *122-A Waller Mill Rd (23185).* 757/229-2288. Hrs: 11:30 am-10 pm; Fri, Sat to 11 pm; brunch 11:30 am-2:30 pm; dinner buffet 5:30-8:30 pm. Closed Thanksgiving. Res accepted; required wkends. Chinese menu. Bar. A la carte: $6.95-$9.95; buffet: lunch $4.95, dinner $6.95. Sun brunch $4.95. Specialties: General Tso's chicken, Emperor's shrimp, Peking chicken. Cr cds: A, D, DS, MC, V.

⊡ ⊡ ♥

★ ★ **PRIME RIB HOUSE.** *1433 Richmond Rd (23185).* 757/229-6823. Hrs: 4:30-10 pm; Fri, Sat to 11 pm. Southwestern menu. Bar. A la carte entrees: dinner $9.95-$17.95. Child's meals. Specializes in prime rib, fresh seafood, Angus steak. Casual decor. Cr cds: A, MC, V.

⊡ SC ⊡

★ ★ ★ **REGENCY ROOM.** *(See Williamsburg Inn Hotel)* 757/229-2141. E-mail conferencesales@cwf.org; web www.history.org. Hrs: 7-10 am, noon-2 pm, 6-9:30 pm; Sun brunch noon-2 pm. Res accepted. Continental menu. Bar. Wine list. Semi-a la carte: bkfst $9-$14, lunch $9-$15. A la carte entrees: dinner $22-$35. Sun brunch $24-$29.50. Specialties: snapper or veal with crabmeat, rack of lamb. Own baking. Valet parking. Jacket. Cr cds: A, D, DS, MC, V.

⊡

★ ★ **SEASON'S CAFE.** *110 S Henry (23185).* 757/259-0018. Hrs: 11 am-10 pm; Fri, Sat to 11 pm. Sun brunch 11 am-3 pm. Closed Dec 25. Res accepted. Continental menu. Bar. Semi-a la carte: lunch $6-$10, dinner $9-$19. Sun brunch $10.95. Child's meals. Specializes in steak, prime rib, pasta. Salad bar. Outdoor dining. Located in former post office. Cr cds: A, D, DS, MC, V.

⊡

★ ★ **SHIELDS TAVERN.** *Duke of Gloucester St (23185).* 757/220-7677. Hrs: 8:30-10 am, 11:30 am-3 pm, 5-9:30 pm; Sun brunch 10 am-2:30 pm. Closed Jan. Res accepted. Bar. Semi-a la carte: bkfst $2.75-$8.75, lunch $3.50-$12.95, dinner $6.75-$24. Sun brunch $6.25-$10.95. Child's meals. Specialties: filet mignon, cream of crayfish soup.

18th-century balladeers. Outdoor dining. Eight dining rms in authentically restored Colonial building. Totally nonsmoking. Cr cds: A, DS, MC, V.

⊡

★ ★ **THAT SEAFOOD PLACE.** *1647 Richmond Rd (23185).* 757/220-3011. Hrs: 11:30 am-2:15 pm, 4:30-9 pm; Fri, Sat 4:30-10 pm; Sun noon-9 pm; summer hrs vary. Closed Dec 25. Res accepted. Bar. Semi-a la carte: lunch $4.95-$6.95, dinner $8.25-$13.95. Child's meals. Specialties: shrimp sampler, sautéed shrimp & scallops. Salad bar. Parking. Outdoor dining. Nautical decor. Cr cds: A, C, D, DS, MC, V.

SC ⊡

★ ★ ★ **TRELLIS.** *403 Duke of Gloucester St (23185), in Merchant's Square.* 757/229-8610. Hrs: 11 am-9:30 pm; Sun brunch to 3 pm. Closed some major hols. Res accepted. Bar 11:30 am-10:30 pm. Semi-a la carte: lunch $5.50-$9.95, dinner $14.50-$24. Sun brunch $5.50-$14.95. Specializes in fresh seafood, mesquite grilling. Own ice cream, pasta. Entertainment wkends. Outdoor dining under trees. Cr cds: A, MC, V.

⊡ ⊡

★ **VICTORIA'S FIRE.** *264 AB McLaws Circle (23185).* 757/220-2511. Hrs: 11 am-2:30 pm, 5-9 pm; Fri, Sat to 10 pm. Closed Jan 1, Thanksgiving, Dec 25. Res accepted. Bar. A la carte entrees: lunch $3.95-$7.95, dinner $7.25-$19.95. Specialties: salmon struedel, lamb chops. Waterpainting by local artists. Cr cds: A, MC, V.

⊡

★ ★ **WHALING COMPANY.** *494 McLaw Circle (23185).* 757/229-0275. Hrs: 4:30-10 pm; early-bird dinner Sun-Fri 4:30-6 pm. Res accepted. Bar. Semi-a la carte: dinner $9.95-$18.95. Child's meals. Specializes in fresh fish, steaks, homemade bread. Parking. Nautical decor. Cr cds: A, C, D, MC, V.

⊡ SC ⊡

★ ★ **YORKSHIRE STEAK & SEAFOOD HOUSE.** *700 York St (23185).* 757/229-9790. Web yorkshire-wmbg.com. Hrs: 4-10 pm; summer to 10:30 pm. Closed Dec 25. Res accepted. Bar. Semi-a la carte: dinner $10.95-$22.95. Child's meals. Specializes in shish kebab, prime rib, seafood. Parking. In Colonial-style building. Totally nonsmoking. Cr cds: A, MC, V.

SC

Winchester (C-7)

(See also Front Royal)

Settled 1732 **Pop** 21,947 **Elev** 720 ft **Area code** 540
Information Winchester-Frederick County Visitor Center, 1360 S Pleasant Valley Rd, 22601; 540/662-4135.

This is the oldest colonial city west of the Blue Ridge, a Civil War prize that changed hands 72 times (once, 13 times in a day). Sometimes called the "apple capital of the world," it is located at the northern approach to the Shenandoah Valley.

George Washington, a red-haired 16-year-old, blithely headed for Winchester and his first surveying job in 1748. He began a decade of apprenticeship for the awesome military and political responsibilities he would later assume as a national leader. During the French and Indian Wars, Colonel Washington made the city his defense headquarters while he built Ft Loudoun in Winchester. Washington was elected to his first political office as a representative from Frederick County to the House of Burgesses.

At the intersection of travel routes, both east-west and north-south, Winchester grew and prospered. By the time of the Civil War, it was a major transportation and supply center, strategically located to control both Union approaches to Washington and Confederate supply lines through the Shenandoah Valley. More than 100 minor engagements and 6 battles took place in the vicinity. General Stonewall Jackson had his headquarters here during the winter of 1861-1862. From his headquarters in Winchester, Union General Philip Sheridan started his famous ride to rally his troops at Cedar Creek, 11 miles away, and turn a Confederate victory into a Union rout.

Approximately 3.5 million bushels of apples are harvested annually in Frederick County and are one of Winchester's economic mainstays today. The world's largest apple cold storage plant and one of the world's largest apple processing plants are here.

What to See and Do

Abram's Delight and Log Cabin (1754). Oldest house in city, restored, furnished in 18th-century style; boxwood garden; log cabin, basement kitchen. (Apr-Oct, daily; rest of yr, by appt, weather permitting) Inquire about combination ticket. 1340 S Pleasant Valley Ave. Phone 540/662-6519 or 540/662-6550. ¢¢

First Presbyterian Church of Winchester (1788). Bulding has been used as a church, a stable by Union troops in Civil War, a public school and an armory; restored in 1941. (Daily) 116 S Loudoun St. Phone 540/662-3824.

Stonewall Jackson's Headquarters. Jackson's headquarters Nov 1861-Mar 1862; now a museum housing Jackson memorabilia and other Confederate items of the war years. (Apr-Oct, daily; rest of yr, by appt, weather permitting) Inquire about combination ticket. 415 N Braddock St. Phone 540/667-3242 or 540/662-6550. ¢¢

The Handley Library and Archives. Completed in 1913, the public library was designed in the Beaux-arts style. The rotunda is crowned on the outside with a copper-covered dome and on the inside by a dome of stained glass. Interesting features of the interior include wrought iron staircases and glass floors. Historical archives are housed on the lower level (non-resident fee). (Daily exc Sun; closed hols) 100 W Piccadilly St. Phone 540/662-9041.

Washington's Office-Museum. Building used by George Washington in 1755-1756 during erection of Ft Loudoun. Housed in this museum are French and Indian, Revolutionary and Civil War relics. (Apr-Oct, daily; rest of yr, by appt, weather permitting) Jct Cork & Braddock Sts. Phone 540/662-4412 or 540/662-6550. ¢

Annual Events

Historic Garden Tour. Open house and gardens in historic Winchester. Phone 540/662-6550. Mid-Apr.

Shenandoah Apple Blossom Festival. Apple Blossom Queen, parades, arts & crafts, band contests, music, food and attractions. Phone 540/662-3863. Apr 29-May 3.

Apple Harvest Arts & Crafts. Jim Barnett Park. Pie contests, apple-butter making, music, arts & crafts. 3rd wkend Sept.

Motels

(Rates may be higher during Apple Blossom Festival)

★ ★ **BEST WESTERN LEE-JACKSON MOTOR INN.** 711 Millwood Ave (22601). 540/662-4154; FAX 540/662-2618. 140 rms, 2 story. Apr-Oct: S $48.50; D $53.50; each addl $5; suites $60-$65; kit. units $35 (14-day min); under 13 free; lower rates rest of yr. Crib avail. Pet accepted. TV; cable (premium). Pool. Restaurant 6 am-10 pm. Rm serv. Bar 4-10:30 pm. Ck-out noon. Coin lndry. Meeting rms. Business servs avail. Valet serv. Free airport transportation. Health club privileges. Some refrigerators. Picnic tables, grills. Cr cds: A, C, D, DS, MC, V.

★ ★ **COMFORT INN STEPHENS CITY.** *(167 Town Run Ln, Stephens City 22655)* I-81 exit 307. 540/869-6500; FAX 540/869-2558. 58 rms, 2 story. S $43-$70; D $49-$80; each addl $6; under 18 free. Crib free. TV; cable (premium), VCR avail (movies). Pool. Complimentary continental bkfst. Restaurant adj 11 am-9 pm. Ck-out noon. Business servs avail.

✔★ **ECONO LODGE-NORTH.** 1593 Martinsburg Pike (VA 11) (22603), I-81 exit 317. 540/662-4700; FAX 540/665-1762. 50 rms, 2 story. S $44; D $49; each addl $5; under 19 free. Crib free. TV; cable (premium). Complimentary continental bkfst. Restaurant adj. Ck-out 11 am. Business servs avail. In-rm modem link. Cr cds: A, C, D, DS, JCB, MC, V.

★ ★ **HAMPTON INN.** 1655 Apple Blossom Dr (22601), I-81 exit 313, Apple Blossom Mall (US 50 W). 540/667-8011; FAX 540/667-8033. 103 rms, 4 story. S, D $50-$58; under 18 free. Crib free. TV; cable (premium). Pool. Complimentary continental bkfst. Restaurant nearby. Ck-out noon. Meeting rms. Business servs avail. In-rm modem link. Valet serv. Golf privileges. Health club privileges. Cr cds: A, C, D, DS, MC, V.

★ ★ **HOLIDAY INN.** 1017 Millwood Pike (22602), at jct I-81 & US 50E, exit 313. 540/667-3300; FAX 540/722-2730. 175 rms, 2 story. S, D $49-$69; each addl $6; under 18 free. Crib free. Pet accepted, some restrictions. TV; cable. Pool. Restaurant 6:30 am-10 pm. Rm serv. Bar 5:30 pm-midnight. Ck-out noon. Meeting rms. Business servs avail. In-rm modem link. Bellhops. Valet serv. Sundries. Tennis. Health club privileges. Some refrigerators. Balconies. Cr cds: A, C, D, DS, JCB, MC, V.

★ ★ **SHONEY'S INN.** 1347 Berryville Ave (22601), jct I-81 & VA 7, exit 315. 540/665-1700; FAX 540/665-3037. 98 rms, 4 with shower only, 3 story. May-Oct: S $45-$50; D $50-$55; each addl $5; under 18 free; lower rates rest of yr. Crib free. TV; cable (premium). Indoor pool; whirlpool. Restaurant 6 am-11 pm. Ck-out noon. Meeting rm. Business servs avail. Sundries. Valet serv. Exercise equipt; weight machine, rowers, sauna. Some refrigerators. Cr cds: A, C, D, DS, ER, MC, V.

✔★ ★ **TRAVELODGE.** 160 Front Royal Pike (22602), I-81 exit 313. 540/665-0685; FAX 540/665-0689. 149 rms, 3 story. S $41-$57; D $47-$63; each addl $5; suites $95; under 17 free. Crib free. Pet accepted. TV; cable (premium), VCR avail (movies). Heated pool. Complimentary continental bkfst. Complimentary coffee in rms. Restaurant nearby. Ck-out 11 am. Coin lndry. Business servs avail. In-rm modem link. Health club privileges. Refrigerators avail. Cr cds: A, C, D, DS, ER, JCB, MC, V.

Inns

★ ★ ★ **ASHBY.** *(692 Federal St, Paris 20130)* 18 mi SE on US 50, exit VA 759. 540/592-3900; FAX 540/592-3781. 10 rms, 8 with bath, 3 story. Rm phones avail. S, D $100-$220; each addl $30. Children over 10 yrs only. TV in some rms. Complimentary full bkfst. Restaurant (see ASHBY INN). Ck-out noon, ck-in 3 pm. Business servs avail. Tennis privileges. Golf privileges. Lawn games. Library/sitting rm. Converted residence (1829) and one-rm schoolhouse; stone fireplace; antique furnishings. Totally nonsmoking. Cr cds: MC, V.

★ ★ ★ **L'AUBERGE PROVENÇALE.** *(Rt 1, Box 203, Boyce 22663)* 9 mi E on US 50, then 1 mi S on VA 340. 540/837-1375; FAX 540/837-2004; res: 800/638-1702. 11 rms, 2 story. S $120-$175; D $145-$195; suite $225; each addl $25. Children over 10 only. Closed Jan. Complimentary full bkfst. Restaurant (see L'AUBERGE PROVENÇALE). Rm serv to 11 pm. Ck-out 11 am, ck-in 3 pm. Free airport transportation. Tennis privileges. 36-hole golf privileges. Health club privileges. Balcony. Originally a sheep farm (1753) owned by Lord Fairfax. Victorian decor. Cr cds: A, C, D, MC, V.

★ ★ **THE RIVER HOUSE.** *(US 50E & Shennandoah River, Boyce 22620)* 15 mi E on US 50 opp County 622. 540/837-1476; FAX

540/837-2399. E-mail rvrhouse@visuallink.com. 5 rms, 2 with shower only, 3 story. D $90-$125; higher rates Sat. Crib $15. TV lounge. Playground. Complimentary brunch. Ck-out noon, ck-in by arrangement. Business servs avail. Tennis privileges. Golf privileges. Fireplaces. On 17-acres at Shenandoah River. Original part of house built 1780 as slave quarters; used as field hospital during Civil War. Cr cds: MC, V.

Restaurants

★ ★ ★ **ASHBY INN.** *(See Ashby Inn)* 540/592-3900. Hrs: 6-9 pm; Sun noon-2:30 pm. Closed Mon, Tues; Jan 1, July 4, Dec 25. Res required. Serv bar. A la carte entrees: dinner $15-$23.95. Sun brunch $19. Specializes in roasted lamb, fresh and smoked seafood, crab cakes. Menu changes daily. Outdoor dining. Virginia hunt country atmosphere; antiques. Plank flooring dates back to original inn (1829). Cr cds: MC, V.

★ ★ ★ **L'AUBERGE PROVENÇALE.** *(See L'auberge Provençale Inn)* 540/837-1375. Hrs: 6-10:30 pm; Sun 5-9 pm. Closed Mon, Tues; July 4, Dec 25. Res accepted; required Fri-Sun. French Provençal menu. Bar. Wine cellar. Prix fixe: dinner $55. Specialties: ris de veau au porto, le lapin fume aux champignons, game dishes. Outdoor dining. Country inn with extensive art collection. Totally nonsmoking. Cr cds: A, C, D, MC, V.

[D]

Wise (F-2)

(For accommodations see Big Stone Gap, Breaks Interstate Park)

Pop 3,193 **Elev** 2,454 ft **Area code** 540 **Zip** 24293

What to See and Do

Recreation Areas. In George Washington and Jefferson National Forests (see HARRISONBURG). **High Knob,** 4 mi S on US 23 to Norton, then 3 mi S via VA 619, 1½ mi E on FS Road 238. Camping, swimming, picnicking. Parking fee. **Bark Camp,** 4 mi S on US 23 to Norton, then 6 mi E on US 58A to Tacoma, then 4 mi S off VA 706, 3 mi S on VA 822. Camping, boating, fishing, picnicking. Parking fee. **Cave Springs,** 7 mi W of Big Stone Gap on US 58A, then 1 mi N on VA 622, then 3 mi W on VA 621. Camping (fee). Swimming. Parking fee. **North Fork of Pound Lake,** US 23 to Pound, then W on VA 671. Camping (fee), picnicking, swimming, boat ramp, hiking. Clinch Ranger District office is in Wise. Phone 540/328-2931.

Woodstock (C-7)

(See also Basye, Front Royal, Luray, New Market)

Founded 1761 **Pop** 3,182 **Elev** 780 ft **Area code** 540 **Zip** 22664 **Web** www.woodstockva.com/chamber
Information Chamber of Commerce, PO Box 605; 540/459-2542.

A German immigrant, Jacob Müller, received a land grant from Lord Fairfax and came here in 1752 with his wife and six children. A few years later he set aside 1,200 acres for a town, first called Müllerstadt, later Woodstock. In a small log church here, John Peter Gabriel Mühlenberg, in January 1776, preached his famous sermon based on Ecclesiastes 3:1-8: "There is a time to every purpose . . . a time to war and a time to peace," at the end of which he flung back his vestments to reveal the uniform of a Continental colonel and began to enroll his parishioners in the army that was to overthrow British rule.

The *Shenandoah Valley-Herald,* a weekly newspaper established in 1817, is still published here.

What to See and Do

Shenandoah County Court House (1792). Oldest courthouse still in use west of the Blue Ridge Mountains; interior restored to original design. (Mon-Fri) Main St.

Shenandoah Vineyards. Valley's first winery. Premium wines; hand-picked and processed in the European style. Picnic area. Tours, free tastings available. (Daily; closed Jan 1, Thanksgiving, Dec 25) From I-81 exit 279 at Edinburg, W on VA 675, make first right on VA 686, go 1½ mi to winery. Phone 540/984-8699. **Free.**

Woodstock Tower. Panoramic view of seven horseshoe bends of the Shenandoah River. 4 mi E on Mill Rd, crest of Massanutten Mt.

Annual Event

Shenandoah County Fair. One of the oldest county fairs in the state. Harness racing last 4 days. Late Aug-early Sept.

Seasonal Event

Shenandoah Valley Music Festival. Symphony pops, classical, folk, jazz, country and big band concerts. Pavilion and lawn seating. Outdoor pavilion on grounds of historic Orkney Springs Hotel in Orkney Springs. Contact Festival, PO Box 12; 540/459-3396. 4 wkends, mid-July-Labor Day wkend.

Motels

✔★ **BUDGET HOST INN.** *US 11 S & I-81, I-81 exit 283.* 540/459-4086; FAX 540/459-4043. 43 rms, 1-2 story. S $30; D $34-$40; each addl $4; under 6 free; wkly rates. Crib $5. Pet accepted, some restrictions. TV; cable. Pool. Restaurant 6:30 am-9 pm; Sun from 7 am. Ck-out 11 am. Coin lndry. Business servs avail. Downhill ski 20 mi. Picnic tables. Cr cds: A, C, D, DS, MC, V.

[D]

★ ★ **RAMADA INN.** *1130 Motel Dr, I-81 exit 283.* 540/459-5000; FAX 540/459-8219. 124 rms, 3 story. May-Oct: S $58; D $66; each addl $8; under 18 free; lower rates rest of yr. Crib free. TV; cable (premium). Heated pool. Restaurant 7 am-2 pm, 5-9 pm. Rm serv. Bar 5 pm-midnight. Ck-out noon. Meeting rms Business servs avail. Valet serv. Sundries. Some refrigerators. Cr cds: A, C, D, DS, JCB, MC, V.

[D] [SC]

Inn

★ ★ ★ **INN AT NARROW PASSAGE.** *30 Chapman Landing Rd, US 11S, 2 mi S of I-81 exit 283.* 540/459-8000; FAX 540/459-8001; res: 800/459-8002. 12 rms, 10 with bath, 2 share bath, 2 story. Rm phones avail. S $75; D $85-$110; each addl $10. Crib $10. TV. Complimentary full bkfst. Ck-out 11 am, ck-in 2 pm. Business servs avail. On river; canoeing. Historic inn (1740), used as a headquarters by Gen. Stonewall Jackson during Civil War. Totally nonsmoking. Cr cds: MC, V.

Restaurant

★ ★ **SPRING HOUSE.** *325 S Main St (US 11).* 540/459-4755. Hrs: 9 am-9 pm; Fri, Sat 8:30 am-10 pm; Sun 8:30 am-9 pm; Sun brunch 10 am-1:30 pm. Closed Jan 1, Dec 25. Res accepted. Bar from 4 pm. Semi-a la carte: bkfst $3.75-$5.25, lunch $3.75-$7.75, dinner $9.99-$16.99. Sun brunch $5.99. Child's meals. Salad bar. 5 dining rms include a log lounge. Early American antiques, artifacts. Cr cds: A, C, D, MC, V.

[D] [SC]

Wytheville (F-4)

(See also Marion)

Founded 1792 **Pop** 8,038 **Elev** 2,284 ft **Area code** 540 **Zip** 24382
E-mail chamber@naxs.com **Web** www.wytheville.org/chamber
Information Wytheville-Wythe-Bland Chamber of Commerce, 150 Monroe St, PO Box 563; 540/223-3365.

With lead mines and the only salt mine in the South nearby, Wytheville was a Union target during the Civil War. One story states a detachment of Union Cavalry attempted to take the town in July, 1863, only to be thwarted by Molly Tynes, who rode 40 miles over the mountains from Rocky Dell to tell the countryside that the Yankees were coming. The alerted home guard turned them away. A transportation center today, Wytheville is a vacationland nestled between the Blue Ridge and Allegheny mountains. Rural Retreat Lake is nearby. Wythe Ranger District office for the George Washington and Jefferson National Forests (see HARRISONBURG) is located here.

What to See and Do

Big Walker Lookout. A 120-ft observation tower at 3,405-ft elevation; swinging bridge. Gift shop; snack bar. (Apr-late May, Thurs-Sun; Memorial Day-Oct, daily exc Mon) 12 mi N on US 52; on Big Walker Mountain Scenic Byway. Phone 540/228-4401. ¢¢

Shot Tower Historical Park (1807). On bluff overlooking New River. One of three shot towers still standing in US; fortress-like stone shaft has 2½-ft-thick walls, rising 75 ft above ground and boring 75 ft below to a water tank. Molten lead was poured through sheet-iron colanders from the tower top; during the 150-ft descent it became globular before hitting the water. Pellets were then sorted by rolling them down an incline; well-formed shot rolled into a receptacle; faulty ones zig-zagged off and were remelted. Visitor center, programs; hiking trails, picnicking. (Memorial Day-Labor Day, daily) Standard fees. At Jackson's Ferry, 6 mi E on I-81, then 7 mi S on US 52; or I-77 S, Poplar Camp exit. Phone 540/699-6778 (New River Trail State Park). Tower ¢

Wytheville State Fish Hatchery. Approx 150,000 lbs of rainbow trout produced annually. Five-tank aquarium; displays. Self-guided tours. (Daily) 12 mi SE on US 52 to VA 629. Phone 540/637-3212 or 804/525-FISH. **Free.**

Annual Event

Chautauqua Festival. Held over a 5-day period. Includes parade, educational events, performing arts, art shows, children's activities, music, food, entertainment. 3rd wk June.

Motels

★★ **BEST WESTERN WYTHEVILLE INN.** *355 Nye Rd, I-77N exit 41 & I-81 exit 72. 540/228-7300; FAX 540/228-4223.* 99 rms, 2 story. Apr-Oct: S $45-$60; D $50-$66; each addl $6; under 18 free; higher rates special events; lower rates rest of yr. Crib free. TV, cable (premium). Pool. Complimentary continental bkfst. Ck-out noon. Business servs avail. Valet serv. Microwaves avail. Sundries. Cr cds: A, C, D, DS, MC, V.

⊡ ⊠ ⊠ ♨ SC

✔★★ **COMFORT INN.** *315 Holston Rd, I-81 exit 70. 540/228-4488; FAX 540/228-4092.* 80 rms, 2 story. S $46, D $55; each addl $5; under 18 free. Crib free. TV; cable (premium). Pool. Complimentary continental bkfst. Restaurant nearby. Ck-out 11 am. Business servs avail. Cr cds: A, C, D, DS, ER, JCB, MC, V.

⊡ ⊠ ⊠ ♨ SC

✔★★ **DAYS INN.** *150 Malin Dr. 540/228-5500; FAX 540/228-6301.* 118 rms, 1-3 story. Apr-Oct: S, D $48-$58; each addl $5; under 17 free; higher rates: hols, Bristol auto races; lower rates rest of yr. Crib free.

TV; cable (premium). Complimentary coffee in lobby. Restaurant adj 6 am-midnight. Ck-out noon. Business servs avail. Microwaves avail. View of mountains. Cr cds: A, C, D, DS, MC, V.

⊡ ⊠ ♨ SC

★★ **ECONO LODGE.** *1160 E Main St. 540/228-5517.* 72 rms, 2 story. Apr-Oct: S $35.95-$55.95; D $38.99-$58.99; each addl $5; under 18 free; higher rates special events; lower rates rest of yr. Crib free. TV; cable. Complimentary coffee in lobby. Restaurant adj 11 am-9:30 pm. Ck-out 11 am. Business servs avail. Cr cds: A, C, D, DS, MC, V.

⊡ ⊠ ♨ SC

★★ **HOLIDAY INN.** *1800 and Main St, I-81 exit 73. 540/228-5483; FAX 540/228-5417.* 199 rms, 1-4 story. Mar-Oct: S $49-$70; D $54-$70; each addl $5; suites $104-$150; under 18 free; higher rates auto races; lower rates rest of yr. Crib free. Pet accepted. TV; cable (premium). Pool; wading pool. Restaurant 6 am-2 pm, 5-9 pm. Rm serv. Bar. Ck-out 11 am. Meeting rms. Business servs avail. Cr cds: A, C, D, DS, JCB, MC, V.

⊡ ⤙ ⊠ ⊠ ♨ SC

★★ **RAMADA INN.** *955 Pepper's Ferry Rd, I-77 exit 41 & I-81 exit 72. 540/228-6000.* Web www.naxs.com/wytheville/ramada. 154 rms, 2 story. S $64-$70; D $69-$75; each addl $5; under 18 free. Crib free. Pet accepted. TV; cable (premium). Pool. Coffee in rms. Restaurant 6 am-10 pm. Rm serv. Bar 5-11 pm; Sun 5 pm-midnight. Ck-out noon. Coin lndry. Meeting rms. Business servs avail. Cr cds: A, C, D, DS, ER, JCB, MC, V.

⊡ ⤙ ⊠ ⊠ ♨ SC

★ **THE SHENANDOAH.** *140 Lithia Rd. 540/228-3188; FAX 540/228-6458; res: 800/273-0935.* 100 rms, 1-2 story. S $35-$45; D $43-$60; each addl $6; under 16 free; wkly, wkend, hol rates; higher rates some special events. Crib free. Pet accepted; $5. TV; cable. Complimentary coffee in lobby. Restaurant nearby. Ck-out 11 am. Balconies. Cr cds: A, C, D, DS, MC, V.

⊡ ⤙ ⊠ ♨ SC

Inn

★★ **BOXWOOD.** *460 E Main St, I-81 exit 73. 540/228-8911.* 8 rms, 2 story. No rm phones. S $54-$64; D $64-$74; each addl $10. TV in some rms; cable. Complimentary full bkfst. Restaurant adj 11 am-10 pm. Ck-out 11 am, ck-in 4 pm. Built 1845 by local businessman as a wedding gift for his daughter. Antiques and period furnishings. Totally nonsmoking. Cr cds: MC, V.

⊡ ⊠ ♨

Restaurant

★ **LOG HOUSE.** *520 E Main St. 540/228-4139.* Hrs: 11 am-10 pm. Closed Sun; Dec 25. Res accepted. Wine, beer. Semi-a la carte: lunch $2.99-$15.50, dinner $5.55-$16.95. Child's meals. Specialties: beef stew, stuffed chicken breast, tenderloin steak. Outdoor dining. Colonial motif; built in 1776. Cr cds: A, DS, MC, V.

⊡ ⊣

Yorktown (E-9)

(See also Colonial Parkway, Gloucester, Jamestown, Newport News, Williamsburg)

Founded 1691 **Pop** 390 (est) **Elev** 54 ft **Area code** 757
Information Colonial National Historical Park, PO Box 210, 23690; 757/898-3400.

Free land offered in 1630 to those adventurous enough "to seate and inhabit" the 50-foot bluffs on the south side of the York River "formerly known by ye Indyan name of Chiskiacke," brought about the beginning of settlement. When the Assembly authorized a port, built there in 1691, the town quickly expanded and in the following years became a busy shipping center, with prosperity reaching a peak about 1750. From then on, the port declined along with the Tidewater Virginia tobacco trade.

Yorktown's moment in history came in 1781. British commander Cornwallis, after raiding up and down Virginia almost without resistance (and almost without effect), was sent here to establish a port in which British ships-of-the-line could winter. The Comte de Grasse's French fleet effectively blockaded the British, however, by controlling the mouth of the Chesapeake Bay. At the Battle of the Capes on September 5, 1781, a British fleet sent to relieve Cornwallis was defeated by the French. Cornwallis found himself bottled up in Yorktown by combined American and French forces under Washington, which arrived on September 28.

Shelling began October 9. The siege of Yorktown ended on October 17 with Cornwallis requesting terms of capitulation. On October 19, Cornwallis' troops marched out with flags and arms cased, their band playing. Then they laid down their arms, bringing the last major battle of the American Revolution to a close.

Yorktown Battlefield, part of Colonial National Historical Park, surrounds the village. Though Yorktown itself is still an active community, many surviving and reconstructed colonial structures supply an 18th-century atmosphere.

What to See and Do

Grace Episcopal Church (1697). Walls of local marl (a mixture of clay, sand and limestone); damaged in 1781, gutted by fire in 1814. A 1649 communion service is still in use. (Daily) Church St. Phone 757/898-3261.

York County Courthouse. Reconstructed in 1955 to resemble 1733 courthouse. Clerk's office has records dating from 1633. (Mon-Fri; closed hols) Main St. **Free.**

✪ **Yorktown Battlefield.** Surrounds and includes part of town. Remains of 1781 British fortifications, modified and strengthened by Confederate forces in Civil War. Reconstructed American and French lines lie beyond. Roads lead to headquarters, encampment areas of Americans, French. Admission fee includes access to Visitor Center, battlefield tour, Moore House and Nelson House. ¢¢ Golden Access, Age and Eagle passports honored (see MAKING THE MOST OF YOUR TRIP). Stop first at

Visitor Center. Information; special exhibits, General Washington's field tents. (Daily; closed Dec 25) E side of town, at end of Colonial Pkwy. Phone 757/898-3400.

Self-guided battlefield tour. Markers, displays aid in visualizing siege. Highlights include headquarters sites of Lafayette, von Steuben, Rochambeau, Washington; American Battery #2; Grand French Battery; a key point is

Moore House. In this 18th-century house, the "Articles of Capitulation" were drafted. These were signed by the Americans and French in the captured British Redoubt #10 on Oct 19. (Mid-June-mid-Aug, daily; spring & fall, wkends) Located along battlefield tour road. Phone 757/898-3400. W of here on VA 238 is

Yorktown National Civil War Cemetery. 2,183 interments (1,436 unknown).

Yorktown Victory Monument. Elaborately ornamented 95-ft granite column memorializes American-French alliance in Revolution. E end of Main St. Then proceed to

Nelson House. Original restored mansion built by "Scotch Tom" Nelson in the early 1700s. Home of his grandson, Thomas Nelson, Jr, a signer of the Declaration of Independence. Impressive example of Georgian architecture. (Mid-June-mid-Aug, daily) Nelson & Main Sts.

Yorktown Victory Center. Museum of the American Revolution chronicles the struggle for independence, from the beginnings of colonial unrest to the formation of the new nation. Exhibit galleries, living history Continental Army encampment, and late-18th-century farm. (Daily; closed Jan 1, Dec 25) Combination ticket with Jamestown Settlement (see JAMESTOWN COLONIAL NATIONAL HISTORICAL PARK) avail. 1/2 mi W on VA 238. Phone 757/253-4838. Museum ¢¢¢; Combination ticket ¢¢¢¢

Annual Event

Yorktown Victory Weekend. Observance of America's Revolutionary War victory at Yorktown in 1781. Oct 19.

Motels

★ ★ **DUKE OF YORK.** *508 Water St (23690), 1 blk E of bridge.* 757/898-3232; FAX 757/898-5922. 57 rms, 2-3 story. Memorial Day-Labor Day: S, D $73; each addl $10; lower rates rest of yr. TV. Pool. Restaurant (hrs vary). Ck-out noon. Business servs avail. Some refrigerators. Balconies. Opp beach; overlooks river. Cr cds: A, C, D, DS, MC, V.

⊠ ⊠ ⊠

★ **YORKTOWN MOTOR LODGE.** *8829 George Washington (23692).* 757/898-5451; FAX 757/895-1766; res: 800/950-4003. 42 rms, 1 story. Memorial Day-Labor Day: S $37-$45; D $45-$65; each addl $5; under 12 free; lower rates rest of yr. Crib $5. TV; cable (premium). Pool. Playground. Restaurant adj 7 am-9 pm. Ck-out 11 am. Business servs avail. Refrigerators, microwaves. Cr cds: A, D, DS, MC, V.

⊠ ⊠ ⊠ SC

Restaurants

★ ★ **NICK'S SEAFOOD PAVILION.** *(23690). On VA 238 (Water St) at S end of bridge.* 757/887-5269. Hrs: 11 am-10 pm. Closed Dec 25. Continental menu. Semi-a la carte: lunch, dinner $7-$35. Child's meals. Specializes in lobster, seafood kebab. Grecian atmosphere; art collection. Family-owned. Cr cds: A, C, D, MC, V.

D ⊠

★ ★ **RIVER'S INN.** *(8109 Yacht Haven Dr, Gloucester Point 23062) 2 1/2 mi N on US 17.* 804/642-9942. Hrs: 11:30 am-3 pm; 5:30-9 pm; Fri, Sat to 10 pm. Closed Dec 25. Res accepted. Seafood menu. Bar. Semi-a la carte: lunch $5-$8, dinner $15-$21. Child's meals. Specialties: pan-fried crab cakes, Chesapeake "blue plate," steamed lobster. Outdoor dining. View of marina and York River; nautical decor and artwork. Cr cds: A, MC, V.

West Virginia

Population: 1,793,477
Land area: 24,282 square miles
Elevation: 240-4,863 feet
Highest point: Spruce Knob (Pendleton County)
Entered Union: June 20, 1863 (35th state)
Capital: Charleston
Motto: Mountaineers are always free
Nickname: Mountain State
State flower: Rhododendron
State bird: Cardinal
State tree: Sugar maple
State fair: August 14-22, 1998, in Lewisburg
Time zone: Eastern
Web: wvweb.com

The wild, rugged topography that made settlement of this area difficult in the early days has today made West Virginia a paradise for outdoor enthusiasts. The state's ski industry has taken advantage of the highest total altitude of any state east of the Mississippi River by opening several alpine and nordic ski areas. Outfitters offer excellent whitewater rafting on the state's many turbulent rivers. Rock climbing, caving and hiking are popular in the Monongahela National Forests, and West Virginia also boasts an impressive state park system, as well as extensive hunting and fishing areas.

The nickname "mountain state" gives only a hint of West Virginia's scenic beauty, which is unsurpassed in the East. West Virginia is also a land of proud traditions, with many festivals held throughout the year as tributes to the state's rich heritage. These events include celebrations honoring the state's sternwheel riverboat legacy, its spectacular autumn foliage and even its strawberries, apples and black walnuts.

The occupation of West Virginia began with the Mound Builders, a prehistoric Ohio Valley culture that left behind at least 300 conical earth mounds that challenge the imagination. Many have been worn away by erosion, but excavations in some have revealed elaborately adorned human skeletons and artifacts of amazing beauty and utility.

Pioneers who ventured into western Virginia in the 18th century found fine vistas and forests, curative springs and beautiful rivers. George Washington and his family frequented the soothing mineral waters of Berkeley Springs (see); and White Sulphur Springs (see) later became a popular resort among the colonists. But much of this area was still considered "the wild West" in those days, and life here was not easy.

The Commonwealth of Virginia largely ignored its western citizens—only one governor was elected from the western counties before 1860. When the counties formed their own state during the Civil War, it was the result of many years of strained relations with the parent state. The move had been debated during those years, and the war finally provided the opportunity the counties needed to break away from Virginia. Although many sentiments in the new state remained pro-South, West Virginia's interests were best served by staying with the Union.

The first land battle of the Civil War took place in the western counties (see PHILIPPI) soon after Fort Sumter was fired upon in April 1861. Through the rest of 1861 and into 1862, Union forces under Generals George McClellan and William S. Rosecrans chased the Confederates back toward rebel Virginia. Succeeding battles were fought farther and farther south until major Confederate resistance became impossible. For the rest of the war, Confederate Army activity in the state was limited to destructive lightning raids designed to wreck railroad lines and damage Union supply sources.

The war left West Virginia a new state, but, like other war-ravaged areas, it had suffered heavy losses of life and property. The recovery took many years, but West Virginians eventually rebuilt their state; new industry was developed, railroads were built, and resources like coal, oil and natural gas brought relative prosperity.

Today, West Virginia still is an important source of bituminous coal and a major producer of building stone, timber, glass and chemicals. The state is also the home of such technological wonders as the National Radio Astronomy Observatory (see MARLINTON), where scientists study the universe via radio telescopes, and the New River Gorge Bridge (see GAULEY BRIDGE), the world's longest steel span bridge.

When to Go/Climate

West Virginia summers are hot and humid, although temperatures in elevated areas rarely top 90°F. Snowfall can range from 10 to 15 feet in some areas. The best time to visit is in spring or fall.

AVERAGE HIGH/LOW TEMPERATURES (°F)

CHARLESTON

Jan 41/23	**May** 76/52	**Sept** 79/57
Feb 45/26	**June** 83/60	**Oct** 68/44
Mar 57/35	**July** 86/64	**Nov** 57/36
Apr 67/43	**Aug** 84/63	**Dec** 46/28

ELKINS

Jan 38/16	May 71/44	Sept 74/50
Feb 41/18	June 78/52	Oct 64/37
Mar 52/27	July 80/57	Nov 53/30
Apr 62/35	Aug 79/56	Dec 43/21

Parks and Recreation Finder

Directions to and information about the parks and recreation areas below are given under their respective town/city sections. Please refer to those sections for details.

Key to abbreviations: I.P. = Interstate Park; N.B.C. = National Battlefield & Cemetery; N.B.P. = National Battlefield Park; N.F. = National Forest; N.H. = National Historical Park; N.H.S. = National Historic Site; N.M. = National Monument; N.Mem. = National Memorial; N.M.P. = National Military Park; N.P. = National Park; N.Pres. = National Preserve; N.R. = National Recreational Area; N.S. = National Seashore; N.S.T. = National Scenic Trail; S.B. = State Beach; S.C.P. = State Conservation Park; S.G. = State Garden; S.H.A. = State Historic Area; S.H.P. = State Historic Park; S.N.A. = State Natural Area; S.P. = State Park; S.R. = State Reserve; S.R.A. = State Recreational Area; S.Res.P. = State Resort Park; S.R.P. = State Rustic Park.

NATIONAL PARK AND RECREATION AREAS

Place Name	Listed Under
Gauley River N.R.	SUMMERSVILLE
Harpers Ferry N.H.	HARPERS FERRY
Monongahela N.F.	ELKINS
New River Gorge National River	HINTON

STATE RECREATION AREAS

Place Name	Listed Under
Audra S.P.	BUCKHANNON
Babcock S.P.	BECKLEY
Beartown S.P.	HILLSBORO
Beech Fork S.P.	HUNTINGTON
Berkeley Springs S.P.	BERKELEY SPRINGS
Blackwater Falls S.P.	DAVIS
Blennerhassett Island Historical S.P.	PARKERSBURG
Bluestone S.P.	HINTON
Cacapon Resort S.P.	BERKELEY SPRINGS
Camp Creek S.P.	PRINCETON
Canaan Valley Resort S.P.	DAVIS
Carnifex Ferry Battlefield S.P.	SUMMERSVILLE
Cass Scenic Railroad S.P.	MARLINTON
Cathedral S.P.	AURORA
Cedar Creek S.P.	WESTON
Droop Mountain Battlefield S.P.	HILLSBORO
Grave Creek Mound S.P.	WHEELING
Hawks Nest S.P.	GAULEY BRIDGE
Holly River S.P.	WEBSTER SPRINGS
Lost River S.P.	MOOREFIELD
North Bend S.P.	PARKERSBURG
Pinnacle Rock S.P.	BLUEFIELD
Pipestem Resort S.P.	HINTON
Prickett's Fort S.P.	FAIRMONT
Stonewall Jackson Lake S.P.	WESTON
Tomlinson Run S.P.	WEIRTON
Twin Falls Resort S.P.	BECKLEY
Tygart Lake S.P.	GRAFTON
Watoga S.P.	HILLSBORO
Watters Smith Memorial S.P.	CLARKSBURG

CALENDAR HIGHLIGHTS

MAY

Webster Springs Woodchopping Festival (Webster Springs). Southeastern World Woodchopping Championships; state championship turkey calling contest, draft horse pull, horse show, fireman's rodeo; arts & crafts; music, parades, concessions. Phone 304/847-7666.

Vandalia Gathering (Charleston). A festival of traditional arts; craft demonstrations, clogging, gospel music, fiddling, banjo picking, special exhibits. Phone 304/558-0220.

JUNE

Mountain Heritage Arts and Crafts Festival (Harpers Ferry). More than 190 craftspeople and artisans demonstrate quilting, wool spinning, pottery throwing, vegetable dyeing and other crafts; concerts. Also in Sept. Phone 304/725-2055.

JULY

Jamboree in the Hills (Wheeling). A 4-day country music festival featuring more than 30 hours of music; top country stars. Camping is available. Phone 800/624-5456.

AUGUST

State Fair (Lewisburg). Fairgrounds. Exhibitors from a number of other states; horse shows, harness racing. Phone 304/645-1090.

SEPTEMBER

Sternwheel Regatta Festival (Charleston). Sternwheeler and towboat races, parades, contests, hot-air balloon race, fireworks; nationally known entertainers nightly; arts & crafts. Phone 304/348-6419.

Stonewall Jackson Heritage Arts & Crafts Jubilee (Weston). Jackson's Mill State 4-H Conference Center. Mountain crafts, music, dance and food. Phone 304/269-1863.

OCTOBER

Mountain State Forest Festival (Elkins). Some events on campus of Davis & Elkins College. Queen Silvia is crowned; carnival, parades; entertainment; tilting at rings on horseback; sawing and woodchopping contests; marksmanship tests; State Championship Fiddle and Banjo Contest; juried craft fair and art exhibit. Phone 304/636-1824.

Mountaineer Balloon Festival (Morgantown). Morgantown Municipal Airport. Hot-air balloon races, carnival, music, food. Phone 304/296-8356.

Bridge Day (Gauley Bridge). New River Gorge Bridge. Bridge is opened to pedestrians; parachutists test their skills by jumping off the bridge and floating to the bottom of the gorge. Contact Upper Kahawha Valley Chamber of Commerce, 304/442-5756.

Water-related activities, hiking, riding, various other sports, picnicking and visitor centers, as well as camping, are available in many of these areas. There is a small fee for swimming and game court use. Campgrounds with picnic facilities are available in 22 state parks and forests; all have drinking water and sanitary facilities; some have showers, coin laundries, utility hookups; 2-wk limit; $6-$14/night for 6 persons or less, $1 each addl person. Camping season runs from mid-April-October in all parks except Canaan Valley and Pipestem resorts, which are open year round. Campground reservations may be made at Babcock, Beech Fork, Blackwater Falls, Bluestone, Canaan Valley Resort, Cedar Creek, Chief Logan, Holly River, North Bend, Pipestem Resort, Stonewall Jackson Lake, Tomlinson Run, Twin Falls Resort, Tygart Lake and Watoga state parks and at Greenbrier and Kanawha state forests. There is a $5 handling fee; reservations must be made 7-14 days in advance. Camping at all other state parks is on a first-come, first-served basis. Pets on leash only. Many cabins and lodges are available for seasonal or year-round use; 7-day minimum second Monday in June-Labor Day. Most parks are open daily, 8 am-sunset. For information and reservations contact individual parks or phone 800/225-5982 (exc AK and HI).

SKI AREAS

Place Name	Listed Under
Alpine Lake Ski Resort	AURORA
Canaan Valley Resort State Park	DAVIS
Elk River Touring Center	MARLINTON
Oglebay Resort Park	WHEELING
Snowshoe Mt Resort	MARLINTON
Timberline Four Seasons Resort	DAVIS
White Grass Touring Center	DAVIS
WinterPlace Ski Resort	BECKLEY

FISHING & HUNTING

In addition to a million acres of prime federal hunting and fishing land, West Virginia has 48 wildlife management areas. Nonresident statewide fishing license $30; 3-day license $5. Nonresident (exc KY, OH, PA) hunting, basic license, $100; archery deer, muzzleloader deer and turkey stamps $25; 6-day, small-game license $20. Nonresident migratory waterfowl stamp $5. A conservation stamp is required in addition to all regular hunting and fishing licenses (nonresident $5). For further information contact the Division of Natural Resources, Wildlife Resources Section, State Capitol Complex, Building 3, Charleston 25305; 304/558-2771.

Driving Information

Children under 9 must be in an approved passenger restraint anywhere in vehicle: ages 3-8 may use a regulation safety belt; children under 3 yrs must use an approved safety seat. For further information phone 304/746-2121.

INTERSTATE HIGHWAY SYSTEM

The following alphabetical listing of West Virginia towns in *Mobil Travel Guide* shows that these cities are within 10 miles of the indicated interstate highways. A highway map, however, should be checked for the nearest exit.

Highway Number	Cities/Towns within 10 miles
Interstate 64	Beckley, Charleston, Huntington, Lewisburg, Nitro, White Sulphur Springs.
Interstate 70	Wheeling.
Interstate 77	Charleston, Parkersburg, Princeton, Ripley; also see WV Tpke.
Interstate 79	Charleston, Clarksburg, Fairmont, Morgantown, Sutton.
Interstate 81	Martinsburg.

Additional Visitor Information

Travel materials, including information on accommodations, skiing, caving, rock climbing, whitewater rafting and other activities, are available from the West Virginia Division of Tourism, State Capitol Complex, 2101 Washington St E, Charleston 25305; 800/225-5982. The Information & Education Section, Department of Natural Resources, State Capitol, Charleston 25305, publishes a monthly magazine, *Wonderful West Virginia*.

Information on hiking along the completed portion of the Allegheny Trail, including a hiking guide (fee), is available from the West Virginia Scenic Trails Association, 633 West Virginia Ave, Morgantown 26505. The trail runs north-south from the Pennsylvania state line near Coopers Rock State Forest to Peters Mountain, southeast of Lindside, at the Virginia state line.

There are several welcome centers in West Virginia; visitors who stop by will find information and brochures most helpful in planning stops at points of interest. Their locations are as follows: on I-64, westbound near White Sulphur Springs and eastbound near Huntington; on I-81, southbound by the West Virginia/Maryland border and

northbound near the West Virginia/Virginia border; on I-79, southbound north of Morgantown; on I-77, southbound near Mineral Wells; on I-70, westbound near the West Virginia/Pennsylvania border. The West Virginia Information Center is located at Harpers Ferry. All centers are open (daily; closed Jan 1, Thanksgiving, Dec 25). Personnel at any of these locations will also assist visitors in making lodging reservations. In addition, information may be obtained at the Capitol Guides Desk in the rotunda of the State Capitol at Charleston (Memorial Day-Labor Day, Mon-Sat, also Sun afternoons).

Aurora (C-6)

(For accommodations see Davis, Grafton)

Settled 1787 **Pop** 150 (est) **Elev** 2,641 ft **Area code** 304 **Zip** 26705

Located at the summit of Cheat Mountain, Aurora offers visitors clean air and high altitude.

What to See and Do

Alpine Lake Ski Resort. 2 Pomalifts, 1 pony lift, T-bar; patrol, rentals; snowmaking; restaurant, bar; lodging. Longest run 2,200 ft; vertical drop 700 ft. Half-day rates. (Late Nov-Mar, Mon, Fri-Sun & hols) 18 mi of cross-country trails (late Dec-Mar, daily). Summer activities include boating, fishing on 145-acre lake; also 18-hole golf (fee). 10 mi N on unnumbered road to Terra Alta, then approx 1 mi E on WV 7, follow signs. Phone 800/752-7179. ¢¢¢¢

Cathedral State Park. Hiking trails through 132 acres of deep, virgin hemlock forest. Cross-country skiing. Picnicking. Standard hrs. 1 mi E on US 50. Phone 304/735-3771.

Beckley (E-4)

(See also Gauley Bridge, Hinton)

Founded 1838 **Pop** 18,296 **Elev** 2,416 ft **Area code** 304 **E-mail** captjim @citynet.net **Web** www.swvcvb.com

Information Southern West Virginia Convention & Visitors Bureau, PO Box 1799, 25802; 304/252-2244or 800/VISIT-WV (outside WV).

The "smokeless coal capital of the world" is a center for more than 200 small mining and farming towns. Beckley is situated on a high plateau surrounded by fertile valleys. During the Civil War, the village was held at various times by both armies; Union troops shelled it in 1863. Coal was found here in 1774, but was not mined until 1890. Smokeless coal became the standard bunker fuel during World War I, and the demand continued for years thereafter. Beckley now serves as a commercial, medical and tourist center.

What to See and Do

Babcock State Park. More than 4,100 acres of rugged mountain scenery with trout stream and waterfalls, views of New River Canyon, rhododendrons (May-July); restored operating gristmill. Swimming pool; lake and stream fishing; boating (rowboat, paddleboat rentals). Hiking trails, horseback riding; game courts (equipment rentals). Cross-country skiing. Picnicking, playground, concession; restaurant (seasonal). Camping (electrical hookups), 26 cabins (rentals, spring & fall). Nature and recreation programs (summer). Standard hrs, fees. (Mid-Apr-Oct) 23 mi NE via US 19 to WV 41, near Landisburg. Phone 304/438-3003 or 800/CALL-WVA.

Beckley Exhibition Coal Mine. Riding tours in coal cars through 1,500 feet of underground passageways; constant 56°F temperature; museum, coal company house, superintendent of coal mines house, campground. (Apr-Oct, daily) 1½ mi SE off I-77, exit 44 on Ewart Ave in New River Park. Phone 304/256-1747. ¢¢

Grandview Unit of New River Gorge National River. Nearly 900 wooded acres at the northern end of the New River Gorge National River area (see HINTON); offers spectacular overlooks of New River Gorge and Horseshoe Bend; rhododendron gardens. Hiking trails, game courts (some fees). Cross-country skiing. Picnicking, playgrounds, concession. Outdoor dramas (June-Labor Day, daily exc Mon). 5 mi SE on US 19, then 5 mi NE via Airport, Glen Hedrick & Grandview Rds. Contact Superintendent, PO Box 246, Glen Jean 25846; 304/763-3715 or 304/465-0508.

Lake Stephens. A 303-acre lake with swimming; fishing; boating. Trailer camping (hookups). W of town. Phone 304/934-5323.

Plum Orchard Lake Wildlife Management Area. More than 3,200 acres with rabbit, grouse, squirrel hunting. Also 202-acre lake with more than 6 mi of shoreline; boating; fishing for bass, channel catfish, crappie and bluegill. Picnicking, playground, camping. 11 mi N on I-77 to Pax exit, then E on RR 23. Phone 304/469-9905.

Twin Falls Resort State Park. Approx 4,000 acres with restored pioneer house and farm. Swimming pool. Hiking trails; 18-hole golf course, clubhouse; tennis, game courts. Picnicking, playground, restaurant, lodge. Camping, 13 cabins (equipment rentals). Recreation center, programs. Standard hrs, fees. (Daily) 25 mi SW via WV 16 & WV 54, then W on WV 97, near Maben. Phone 304/294-4000.

Whitewater rafting. Many outfitters offer guided trips on the New and Gauley rivers. For a list of outfitters contact the Southern West Virginia Convention & Visitors Bureau, PO Box 1799, 25802; 304/252-2244 or 800/VISIT-WV (outside WV).

WinterPlace Ski Resort. On southern West Virginia's highest peak. 2 quad, 3 triple, double chairlifts, 2 surface lifts; school, rentals; snowmaking; cafeteria, lounge; restaurants; entertainment; children's program; sporting goods shops. 27 trails. Night skiing. 24 runs; longest run 1¼ mi; vertical drop 603 ft. Snowboard park. (Thanksgiving-late Mar, daily) 17 mi S via I-77 exit 28 (Ghent/Flat Top), follow signs. Phone 304/787-3221 or 800/607-SNOW. ¢¢¢¢¢

Youth Museum of Southern West Virginia. Hands-on exhibits, planetarium, log house; John Henry exhibit features more than 100 carved figures depicting railroad work in the 1880s. (May-Labor Day, daily; rest of yr, Tues-Sat) Ewart Ave, in New River Park. Phone 304/252-3730.

Annual Event

Appalachian Arts and Crafts Festival. Tamarack. Exhibitions and demonstrations of native crafts; entertainment, food. Phone 304/252-7328. Late Aug.

Seasonal Event

Theatre West Virginia. Cliffside Amphitheatre. Outdoor musical dramas. Grandview Park, W on I-64, exit 129B, follow signs. Contact PO Box 1205, 25802; 304/256-6800 or 800/666-9142. Mid-June-mid-Aug.

Motels

✔★ **COMFORT INN.** *1909 Harper Rd (WV 3) (25801). 304/255-2161.* Web wvweb.com/www/cibeckley.html. 130 rms, 3 story. S $56-$84; D $61-$89; under 19 free. Crib free. Pet accepted; $10. TV; cable (premium), VCR avail (movies). Complimentary continental bkfst. Restaurant nearby. Ck-out noon. Coin lndry. Business servs avail. Sundries. Downhill ski 15 mi. Exercise equipt; weights, bicycle. Some refrigerators, microwaves. Cr cds: A, C, D, DS, ER, JCB, MC, V.

D ★ ≋ ✕ ≈ 🐾 SC

★ **HAMPTON INN.** *110 Harper Park Dr (25801), just off I-77. 304/252-2121; FAX 304/255-6238.* 108 rms, 5 story. S, D $64-$85; each addl $7; under 18 free; higher rates Bridge Day. Crib free. TV; cable (premium). Pool. Complimentary continental bkfst. Restaurant adj. Ck-out

noon. Business servs avail. Downhill ski 15 mi. Microwaves avail. Cr cds: A, C, D, DS, MC, V.

D ★ ≋ ≈ 🐾 SC

★★ **HOLIDAY INN.** *1924 Harper Rd (WV 3) (25801). 304/255-1511.* Web wvweb.com/www/holiday-inn-beckley. 105 rms, 3 story. No elvtr. Apr-Oct: S, D $85-$90; under 19 free; lower rates rest of yr. Crib free. TV; cable. Pool. Restaurant 6 am-2 pm, 5-10 pm. Rm serv. Bar 3 pm-3 am; Sun to 1 am. Ck-out 1 pm. Free guest lndry. Meeting rms. Business servs avail. In-rm modem link. Downhill ski 15 mi. Some refrigerators, microwaves. Cr cds: A, C, D, DS, JCB, MC, V.

D ★ ≋ ≈ 🐾 SC

Berkeley Springs (B-7)

(See also Martinsburg)

Founded 1776 **Pop** 735 (est) **Elev** 612 ft **Area code** 304 **Zip** 25411 **Web** wvweb.com/www/BERKELEY-SPRINGS

Information Berkeley Springs-Morgan County Chamber of Commerce, 304 Fairfax St; 304/258-3738 or 800/447-8797.

Popularized by George Washington, who surveyed the area for Lord Fairfax in 1748, Berkeley Springs is the oldest spa in the nation. Fairfax later granted the land around the springs to Virginia. The town is officially named Bath, for the famous watering place in England, but the post office is Berkeley Springs. The waters, which are piped throughout the town, are fresh and slightly sweet, without the medicinal flavor of most mineral springs. Washington and his family returned again and again. The popularity of the resort reached its peak after the Revolution, becoming something of a summer capital for Washingtonians in the 1830s. But like all resort towns, Berkeley Springs declined as newer, more fashionable spas came into vogue. The Civil War completely destroyed the town's economy. Today, the town is again visited for its healthful waters, spas and charming downtown.

What to See and Do

Berkeley Springs State Park. Famous resort with health baths of all types (fees); five warm springs. Main bathhouse (daily; closed Jan 1, Dec 25). Roman bathhouse with second-floor museum (Memorial Day-mid-Oct, daily). Swimming pool (Memorial Day-Labor Day, daily; fee). Center of town. Phone 304/258-2711 or 304/258-5860. Overlooking park is

The Castle (1886). English-Norman castle, built by Colonel Samuel Taylor Suit for his fiancee, has the flavor of England's famous Berkeley Castle, where King Edward II was murdered in 1327. The battlement tower walls are indented with the cross of St George. The castle is furnished with 17th- and 18th-century antiques and contains a pine-paneled library, carved staircase, interesting collections. Gift shop. Tours. (Daily) Phone 304/258-3274. ¢¢¢

Cacapon Resort State Park. More than 6,100 acres with swimming, sand beach; fishing, boating (rowboat and paddleboat rentals). Hiking, bridle trails, horseback riding; 18-hole golf course, tennis, game courts. Cross-country skiing. Picnicking, playground, concession, restaurant, lodge (see RESORTS). No camping; 30 cabins. Nature, recreation programs. Arts & crafts center. Standard hrs, fees. 10 mi S off US 522. Phone 304/258-1022.

Sleepy Creek Wildlife Management Area. Approx 23,000 acres of rugged forest offer wild turkey, deer, grouse and squirrel hunting. Boating, bass fishing on 205-acre lake. Primitive camping (fee). Also 70 miles of hiking trails crossing 2 mountains, several valleys. 15 mi SE, E of US 522. Phone 304/754-3855.

View from Prospect Peak. Potomac River winds through what the National Geographic Society has called one of the nation's outstanding vistas. On WV 9, near town.

Annual Event

Apple Butter Festival. Crafts demonstrations, music, contests. Columbus Day wkend.

Motel

★ **ECONOLODGE.** *(118 Limestone Rd, Hancock MD 21750) 7 mi NE on US 522.* 301/678-6101. 50 rms, 2 story. S, D $60; under 18 free. Crib free. TV; cable (premium). Complimentary continental bkfst. Restaurant nearby. Ck-out noon. Cr cds: A, C, D, DS, ER, JCB, MC, V.

D ⊁ ⚲ SC

Inns

★ ★ ★ **THE COUNTRY INN & RENAISSANCE SPA.** *207 S Washington St.* 304/258-2210; FAX 304/258-3986; res: 800/822-6630. Web wvweb.com/www/country_inn/html. 70 rms, 13 share bath, 3 story. S, D $37-$85; each addl $15; suites $80-$145; hol wkends 2-night min; some wkday rates. TV; cable, VCR avail (movies). Dining rm 7-11 am, 11:30 am-2 pm, 5-9 pm; Fri, Sat to 10 pm. Private club 11 am-11 pm; entertainment Sat, Sun. Ck-out noon, ck-in 3 pm. Meeting rms. Business servs avail. Gift shop. Massage. Colonial design. Mineral baths & spa. Cr cds: A, C, D, DS, MC, V.

D ⊁ ⚱ SC

★ ★ ★ **HIGHLAWN.** *304 Market St.* 304/258-5700. Web www.virtualcities.com. 12 rms in 4 bldgs, 2-3 story. No rm phones. S, D $85-$185; whirlpool suite $135. Adults only. TV; cable. Complimentary full bkfst; afternoon refreshments. Ck-out noon, ck-in 2 pm. Victorian mansion; built 1897. Antiques. Cr cds: MC, V.

D ⊁ ⚱

Resorts

✔★ ★ **CACAPON LODGE.** *Rte 1, Box 304, On US 522, in Cacapon Resort State Park.* 304/258-1022; res: 800/225-5982; FAX 304/258-5323. Web wvweb.com/www/cacapon.html. 49 rms, 2 story, 30 kit. cabins. Apr-Oct: S $31-$59; D $65; each addl $6; kit. cabins for 1-8, $330-$621/wk; some wkend rates; lower rates rest of yr. Crib free in cabins, $4 in cabins. Some TV; cable. Dining rm 7 am-9 pm; winter 8 am-7 pm. Ck-out noon, ck-in 3 pm. Gift shop. Tennis. 18-hole golf, greens fee $13-$22, putting green, driving range. Rec rm. Picnic tables. Near lake; boat rentals, sandy beach. Hiking trails. Naturalist program (Apr-Oct). State-operated. Cr cds: C, D, MC, V.

D ⛵ ⚜ ⚿ ⚲ SC

★ ★ **COOLFONT RESORT.** *1777 Cold Run Valley Rd, 4 mi W on WV 9, then left on Cold Run Valley Rd.* 304/258-4500; FAX 304/258-5499; res: 800/888-8768 (exc WV). Web www.coolfont.com. 22 rms in main bldg, 2 story, 34 cottages. MAP, Oct: S $107-$119; D $168-$188; each addl $84-$94; cottages $198-$238; family, wkend rates; fitness plan; wkends, hols (2-3 day min); lower rates rest of yr. Crib $10. Indoor pool; whirlpool. Playground. Supervised child's activities (June-Aug; wkends only rest of yr); ages 5-12. Complimentary coffee in rms. Dining rm 8 am-2 pm, 5:30-8:30 pm; Fri, Sat to 9:30 pm; Sun 8 am-3 pm, 5:30-8 pm. Snacks. Picnics. Bar; entertainment Sat. Ck-out noon, ck-in 4 pm. Gift shop. Coin lndry. Meeting rms. Tennis. Swimming beach; boats. X-country ski on site. Sleighing. Hiking. Lawn games. Exercise equipt; weight machine, bicycles, sauna. Massage. Refrigerators; microwaves avail. Some balconies. Picnic tables. Secluded woodland resort on 1,350 acres. Cr cds: DS, MC, V.

D ⛵ ⚜ ⚛ ⚿ ≋ ⚟ ⚑ ⚲ ⚱

Bethany (A-5)

(For accommodations see Wheeling; also see Weirton)

Pop 1,139 **Elev** 932 ft **Area code** 304 **Zip** 26032

What to See and Do

Bethany College (1840). (800 students) Founded by Alexander Campbell, the leading influence in the 19th-century religious movement that gave rise to the Disciples of Christ, Churches of Christ and Christian Churches. Historic buildings on 300-acre campus include Old Main, styled after the University of Glasgow in Scotland; Pendleton Heights, a 19th-century house used as the college president's residence; Old Bethany Meeting House (1852), Delta Tau Delta Founder's House (1854) and the

Campbell Mansion. A 24-rm house where Campbell lived; antique furnishings. On property is hexagonal brick study, one-room schoolhouse and smokehouse. The Campbell family cemetery, "God's Acre," is across from the mansion. (Apr-Oct, daily exc Mon; rest of yr, by appt) For tour of all buildings, phone 304/829-7285 or 304/829-7000. ¢¢

Bluefield (E-4)

(See also Princeton)

Founded 1889 **Pop** 12,756 **Elev** 2,611 ft **Area code** 304 **Zip** 24701
E-mail bcvb@bluestonecvb.com **Web** www.bluestonecvb.com
Information Convention & Visitors Bureau, 500 Bland St, PO Box 4099; 304/325-8438 or 800/221-3206.

Named for the bluish chicory covering the nearby hills, Bluefield owes its existence to the Pocahontas Coal Field. The town came to life in the 1880s, when the railroad came through to transport the coal. This commercial and industrial center of southern West Virginia is known as nature's "air-conditioned city" because of its altitude—one-half mile above sea level. Bluefield has a sister city by the same name in Virginia, directly across the state line.

What to See and Do

Eastern Regional Coal Archives. Center highlights the history of West Virginia coal fields; exhibits, photographs, mining implements; films, research material. (Mon-Fri afternoons; closed most hols) In Craft Memorial Library, 600 Commerce St. Phone 304/325-3943. **Free.**

Panther State Forest. More than 7,800 acres of rugged hills. Swimming pool (Memorial Day-Labor Day); fishing, hunting. Hiking trails. Picnicking, playground, concession. Camping. Standard hrs, fees. 50 mi NW off US 52 near Panther. Phone 304/938-2252.

Pinnacle Rock State Park. The approx 250-acre park contains a 15-acre lake and interesting sandstone formations, which resemble a giant cockscomb. Hiking. Picnicking. Standard hrs, fees. 7 mi NW on US 52. Phone 304/589-5307.

Motels

✔★ **ECONO LODGE.** *3400 Cumberland Rd.* 304/327-8171. 48 rms, 2 story. S $39; D $45; each addl $5; under 18 free. Crib free. Pet accepted; $5. TV; cable. Coffee in lobby. Restaurant nearby. Ck-out 11 am. Business servs avail. Cr cds: A, C, D, DS, MC, V.

D ⚟ ⊁ ⚲ SC

★ ★ **HOLIDAY INN.** *US 460/52 Bypass, 3 mi W of I-77, Bluefield exit 1, via US 460/52.* 304/325-6170. Web www.com.holidayinnonthehill.com. 118 rms, 2 story. S, D $85; each addl $10; suites $170; under 18 free. Crib free. Pet accepted. TV; cable (premium), VCR avail. Heated pool; poolside serv. Saunas. Restaurant 6 am-10 pm. Ck-out noon. Meeting rms. In-rm modem link. Gift shop. Valet serv Mon-Fri. Golf privileges. Cr cds: A, C, D, DS, JCB, MC, V.

★★ **RAMADA INN.** *3175 E Cumberland Rd. 304/325-5421; FAX 304/325-6045.* 98 rms, 2 story. May-early Sept: S $63; D $68; each addl $5; under 18 free; wkend, wkly rates; ski plans; wkends (2-day min); lower rates rest of yr. Crib free. TV; cable (premium); VCR avail. Restaurant 6 am-10 pm. Rm serv. Bar 5 pm-1 am; entertainment Fri, Sat. Ck-out noon. Meeting rms. Business servs avail. Bellhops. Valet serv. Sundries. Exercise equipt; bicycles, weight machine, saunas. Indoor pool; whirlpool, poolside serv. Game rm. Rec rm. Some refrigerators; microwaves avail. Cr cds: A, C, D, DS, MC, V.

Restaurant

✔★ **MAYFLOWER I.** *105 Hockman Pike (24605). 540/322-4575.* Hrs: 3-8:30 pm; Sat 1-9:30 pm; Sun from 11:30 am. Closed Mon; Jan 1, July 4, Dec 25. Seafood menu. Semi-a la carte: lunch, dinner $5.75-$11. Child's meals. Specializes in seafood platters. Casual atmosphere with nautical decor. Cr cds: MC, V.

Buckhannon (C-5)

(See also Elkins, Philippi, Weston)

Settled 1770 **Pop** 5,909 **Elev** 1,433 ft **Area code** 304 **Zip** 26201

Information Buckhannon-Upshur Chamber of Commerce, 16 S Kanawha St, PO Box 442; 304/472-1722.

What to See and Do

Audra State Park. Approx 360 acres offer swimming in a natural mountain stream surrounded by tall timber; bathhouse. Hiking trails. Picnicking, playground, concession. Tent & trailer camping. Standard hrs, fees. 8 mi N on US 119, then 6 mi E on WV 11. Phone 304/457-1162.

West Virginia State Wildlife Center. Fenced-in habitats of approx 50 species of birds and animals native to West Virginia, including deer, elk, buffalo, timber wolf, mountain lion and black bear. Loop walkway (1¼ mi). Trout pond. Picnicking, concession. (May-Oct, daily; Apr & Nov, wkends & hols only; Dec-Mar, days vary) 12 mi S on WV 4, 20. Phone 304/924-6211. Apr-Nov ¢

West Virginia Wesleyan College (1890). (1,600 students) An 80-acre campus featuring Georgian architecture. Wesley Chapel, the largest place of worship in the state, contains a Casavant organ with 1,474 pipes. College Ave & Meade St. Phone 304/473-8000.

Annual Event

West Virginia Strawberry Festival. Parades, dances, exhibits, air show, arts & crafts, other activities. Phone 304/472-9036. Usually wk before Memorial Day.

Motels

★★ **BICENTENNIAL.** *90 E Main St. 304/472-5000; res: 800/762-5137.* 55 rms, 2 story. S $39.95-$45.95; D $45.95-$51.95; each addl $6; under 12 free. Crib free. TV; cable (premium). Pool; wading pool, lifeguard. Playground. Restaurant 6 am-9 pm. Rm serv. Private club 5 pm-1 am. Ck-out noon. Meeting rms. Business servs avail. Sundries. Gift shop. Some refrigerators. Picnic tables, grills. Cr cds: A, C, D, DS, MC, V.

✔★ **CENTENNIAL.** *22 N Locust St. 304/472-4100.* 24 rms. S $27.95-$39.95, D $39.95; each addl $6; apt. $175/wk; under 12 free. Crib free. Pet accepted. TV; cable. Complimentary coffee. Restaurant nearby. Ck-out noon. Cr cds: A, C, D, DS, MC, V.

Charleston (D-3)

(See also Nitro)

Settled 1794 **Pop** 57,287 **Elev** 601 ft **Area code** 304

Information Convention & Visitors Bureau, Charleston Civic Center, 200 Civic Center Dr, 25301; 304/344-5075 or 800/733-5469.

Charleston, capital of the state, is the trading hub for the Great Kanawha Valley, where deposits of coal, oil, natural gas and brine have greatly contributed to this region's national importance as a production center for chemicals and glass. Two institutions of higher learning, West Virginia State College and the University of Charleston, are located in the metropolitan area. Charleston is also the northern terminus of the spectacular West Virginia Turnpike.

Daniel Boone lived around Charleston until 1795. During his residence he was appointed a lieutenant colonel in the county militia in 1789 and was elected to the Virginia assembly the same year. The area became important as a center of salt production in 1824, when steam engines were used to operate brine pumps. After Charleston became the capital of West Virginia in 1885, following a dispute with Wheeling, the town came into its own. During World War I, an increased demand for plate and bottle glass, as well as for high explosives, made Charleston and the nearby town of Nitro (see) boom.

What to See and Do

Coonskin Park. Recreation area includes swimming; fishing for bass and catfish; pedal boating. Hiking trails; 18-hole golf, miniature golf; tennis. Picnicking, playground, concession. (Daily; closed Dec 25; some activities seasonal) Fees for activities. ¾ mi N off WV 114. Phone 304/341-8000.

Elk River Scenic Drive. Beautiful drive along the Elk River from Charleston northeast to Sutton (approx 60 mi). Begins just north of town; take US 119 NE to Clendenin, then WV 4 NE to Rte 19 in Sutton.

Kanawha State Forest. Approx 9,300 acres with swimming pool, bathhouse (Memorial Day-Labor Day); hunting. Hiking, interpretive trail for the disabled. Horseback riding. Cross-country skiing. Picnicking, playground, concession. Camping. Standard hrs, fees. 7 mi S off US 119. Phone 304/558-3500.

State Capitol (1932). One of America's most beautiful state capitols, the building was designed by Cass Gilbert in Italian-Renaissance style. Within the gold-leaf dome, which rises 300 ft above the street, hangs a 10,080-piece, hand-cut imported chandelier weighing more than 2 tons. Guided tours avail. (Daily exc Sun) On river at E Kanawha Blvd between Greenbrier St & California Ave. Phone 304/558-3456 or 800/225-5982. **Free.** Across the grounds is the

Governor's Mansion (1925). Beautiful Georgian structure of red Harvard brick with white Corinthian columns. Tours (Thurs & Fri, also by appt). 1716 Kanawha Blvd E. Phone 304/558-3809. **Free.**

Sunrise Museum. On 16 acres of wooded grounds with gardens and trails, the museum is housed in two historic mansions built by William MacCorkle, ninth governor of West Virginia. Guided tours by appt. (Wed-Sun; closed major hols) 746 Myrtle Rd, across South Side Bridge. Phone 304/344-8035. ¢¢

Art Museum. American paintings, graphics and sculpture from 19th through 20th centuries; rotating exhibits; films and lectures. ¢¢

Science Museum. Exhibits in natural sciences and technology; nature center with animals; planetarium, programs, lectures. Interactive exhibits, demonstrations. ¢¢

The Cultural Center. The Center houses the Division of Culture and History and Library Commission; West Virginia crafts shop (daily); archives library (daily exc Sun); state museum; special events, changing exhibits. (Daily; closed hols) Next to state capitol, on Greenbrier St. Phone 304/558-0220. **Free.** Also here is

Mountain Stage. Live public radio show heard on more than 115 stations nationwide; features jazz, folk, blues and rock. Visitors may watch show; afternoon performances (Sun). Phone Ticketmaster at 304/342-5757. ¢¢¢

West Virginia State College (1891). (4,635 students) On campus are Davis Fine Arts Bldg with periodic exhibits (daily exc Sun; closed hols); Asian art collection in library (daily; closed hols); and East Hall (1895), formerly president's residence. Tours. 8 mi W via I-64 exit 50, in Institute. Phone 304/766-3000.

Whitewater rafting. Many outfitters offer guided rafting, canoeing and fishing trips on the New and Gauley rivers. For a list of outfitters contact the West Virginia Division of Tourism, Research & Development, 2101 Washington St E, Bldg 17, 25305; 800/225-5982.

Annual Events

Vandalia Gathering. A festival of traditional arts; craft demonstrations, clogging, gospel music, fiddling, banjo picking, special exhibits. Phone 304/558-0220. Memorial Day wkend.

Sternwheel Regatta Festival. Sternwheeler and towboat races, parades, contests, hot-air balloon race, fireworks; nationally known entertainers nightly; arts & crafts. Phone 304/348-6419. Late Aug-early Sept.

Motels

★ **KANAWHA CITY MOTOR LODGE.** *3103 MacCorkle Ave SE (25304).* 304/344-2461; FAX 304/345-1419. 50 rms, 2 story. S $51-$55; D $56-$60; each addl $5; kit. units $61; under 18 free. Crib free. TV; cable (premium). Complimentary coffee in lobby. Restaurant nearby. Ck-out noon. Business servs avail. Charleston Memorial Hospital opp. Cr cds: A, C, D, DS, MC, V.

D ≈ 🖼 SC

✔★ **RED ROOF INN.** *6305 MacCorkle Ave SE (25304).* 304/925-6953; FAX 304/925-8111. E-mail i0059@redroof.com; web www.redroofinns.com. 108 rms, 2 story. Apr-Oct: S $49.99; D $59.99; each addl $7; under 18 free; higher rates special events; lower rates rest of yr. Crib free. Pet accepted. TV; cable (premium). Complimentary coffee in lobby. Restaurant adj 6 am-10:30 pm. Ck-out noon. Business servs avail. Cr cds: A, C, D, DS, MC, V.

D 🖼 ≈ 🖼

Motor Hotels

★★ **HAMPTON INN.** *1 Preferred Place (25309).* 304/746-4646; FAX 304/746-4665. 104 rms, 6 story. S $70-$85; D $75-$90; each addl $5; under 18 free; higher rates: basketball tournament, Sternwheel Regatta Festival. Crib free. TV; cable (premium). Complimentary continental bkfst. Restaurant adj 10-1 am. Ck-out noon. Meeting rms. Business center. In-rm modem link. Sundries. Coin lndry. Free airport transportation. Exercise equipt; bicycle, stair machine. Indoor pool; whirlpool. Some in-rm whirlpools, refrigerators, microwaves. Cr cds: A, D, DS, MC, V.

D ≈ 🖼 🖼 🖼 SC 🖼

★★ **HAMPTON INN.** *1 Virginia St W (25302).* 304/343-9300; FAX 304/342-9393. 112 rms, 5 story. S $73-$83; D $78-$88; each addl $5; under 18 free; higher rates basketball tournament. Crib free. TV; cable (premium). Complimentary continental bkfst. Restaurant nearby. Ck-out noon. Meeting rm. Business servs avail. Sundries. Free airport, RR station transportation. Heated pool. Cr cds: A, D, DS, MC, V.

D ≈ 🖼 🖼 SC

★★ **HOLIDAY INN-CIVIC CENTER.** *100 Civic Center Dr (25301).* 304/345-0600; FAX 304/343-1322. 197 rms, 6 story. S, D $68-

$89; under 18 free; wkend rates (Nov-Feb). Crib free. TV; cable, VCR avail. Pool. Restaurant 6 am-2 pm, 5-10 pm; Sat, Sun from 6:30 am. Rm serv. Bar. Ck-out noon. Coin lndry. Meeting rms. Business servs avail. Bellhops. Valet serv. Free airport transportation. Some refrigerators. Cr cds: A, C, D, DS, JCB, MC, V.

D ≈ 🖼 🖼 SC

Hotels

★★★ **HOLIDAY INN-CHARLESTON HOUSE.** *600 Kanawha Blvd E (25301).* 304/344-4092; FAX 304/345-4847. Web wvweb.com/www/holiday_inn_charleston_house. 256 rms, 12 story. S, D $99-$109; each addl $6; under 18 free; suites $200-$375; 4-day min Labor Day wkend; wkend rates; package plans. Crib free. Pet accepted. TV; cable (premium), VCR avail. Heated pool. Restaurant 6:30 am-2 pm; dining rm 5-10 pm. Bar 4 pm-2 am, closed Sun; pianist. Ck-out noon. Convention facilities. Business servs avail. In-rm modem link. Barber, beauty shop. Gift shop. Garage. Free airport transportation. Exercise equipt; weights, bicycles. Some wet bars. Some rms with river view. Cr cds: A, C, D, DS, JCB, MC, V.

D 🖼 ≈ 🖼 🖼 🖼 SC

★★★ **MARRIOTT TOWN CENTER.** *200 Lee St E (25301).* 304/345-6500; FAX 304/353-3722. 352 rms, 16 story. S, D $89-$140; suites from $250-$275; under 18 free; wkend rates. Crib free. TV; cable (premium), VCR avail. Indoor pool; whirlpool, poolside serv. Restaurant 6:30 am-11 pm; dining rm 5:30-11 pm. Bar 11-1 am. Ck-out noon. Coin lndry. Meeting rms. Business center. Gift shop. Exercise equipt; weights, bicycles, sauna. Game rm. Some refrigerators. Luxury level. Many balconies. Cr cds: A, C, D, DS, ER, JCB, MC, V.

D 🖼 ≈ 🖼 🖼 🖼

Restaurants

★★ **ALADDIN.** *3024 Chesterfield Ave (25304).* 304/345-0052. Hrs: 4-10 pm. Closed Sun; also most major hols. Res accepted. Middle Eastern menu. Bar. Semi-a la carte: dinner $10-$19. Specialties: mussafa'ah, falafel, shish kabob. Entertainment Fri, Sat. Middle Eastern atmosphere. Cr cds: A, D, DS, MC, V.

D 🖼

★★★ **CAGNEY'S.** *400 Court St (25301).* 304/345-3463. Hrs: 11 am-10 pm; Fri, Sat to 11 pm. Closed Thanksgiving, Dec 25. Res accepted. Continental menu. Bar. Semi-a la carte: lunch $6.25-$14.95, dinner $9.95-$21.95. Child's meals. Specialties: cajun chicken pasta, prime rib. Early 1900s decor. Cr cds: A, C, D, DS, MC, V.

D 🖼

★ **CHEF DAN'S.** *222 Broad St (25301).* 304/344-2433. Hrs: 11 am-9 pm; Fri, Sat to 10 pm. Closed Sun; major hols. Continental menu. Wine, beer. Semi-a la carte: lunch, dinner $3.95-$15.95. Child's meals. Specializes in pasta, pizza. Bistro decor. Totally nonsmoking. Cr cds: A, C, D, DS, MC, V.

D

★ **FIFTH QUARTER.** *201 Clendenin St (25301).* 304/345-2726. Hrs: 11 am-4 pm, 5-10 pm; Fri & Sat to 11 pm; Sun 11 am-9 pm. Closed Dec 25. Bar. Semi-a la carte: lunch $5.49-$12.99, dinner $8.69-$19.99. Child's meals. Specializes in prime rib. Salad bar. Entertainment Tues-Sat. Parking. Rustic decor. Cr cds: A, C, D, DS, MC, V.

D SC 🖼

★★★ **JOE FAZIO'S.** *1008 Bullitt St (25301).* 304/344-3071. Hrs: 5-10:30 pm. Closed Mon; Jan 1, Easter, Dec 24, 25. Res accepted. Italian, Amer menu. Serv bar. Semi-a la carte: dinner $10.95-$19.95. Child's meals. Specializes in veal, chicken, steak with an Italian accent. Parking. Family-owned. Cr cds: A, D, MC, V.

D 🖼

★ ★ ★ **LAURY'S.** *350 McCorkle Ave SE (25314). 304/343-0055.* Hrs: 11 am-2 pm, 5-11 pm. Closed Sun; major hols. Res accepted. Continental menu. Bar. Semi-a lå carte: lunch $4.95-$10.95, dinner $11.95-$35. Specialties: châteaubriand, veal, rack of lamb. Entertainment Fri, Sat. Near Kanawha River. Renovated train depot. Cr cds: A, C, D, DS, MC, V.

D ⊡

★ **STEAK & ALE.** *320 McCorkle Ave SE (25314). 304/344-3455.* Hrs: 11 am-10 pm; Fri, Sat to 11 pm; Sun to 9 pm. Res accepted. Bar. Semi-a la carte: lunch $5-$9, dinner $8-$18. Child's meals. Specialty: herb crusted prime rib. Salad bar. Casual decor. Cr cds: A, C, D, DS, ER, MC, V.

D ⊡

Charles Town (C-8)

(See also Harpers Ferry, Martinsburg, Shepherdstown; also see Winchester, VA)

Founded 1786 **Pop** 3,122 **Elev** 530 ft **Area code** 304 **Zip** 25414

Information Jefferson County Chamber of Commerce, 201 Frontage Rd, PO Box 426; 304/725-2055.

Charles Town is serene, aristocratic and full of tradition, with orderly, tree-shaded streets and 18th-century houses. It was named for George Washington's youngest brother, Charles, who laid out the town and named most of the streets after members of his family. The Charles Washingtons lived here for many years. Charles Town is also famed as the place where John Brown was jailed, tried and hanged in 1859 after his raid on Harpers Ferry.

What to See and Do

Horse racing. Charles Town Races. Thoroughbred racing; clubhouse, dining rm. (Wed, Fri-Sun; closed major hols) 1 mi E on US 340. Phone 304/725-7001 or 800/795-7001. **Free.**

Jefferson County Courthouse (1836). This red-brick, Georgian-colonial structure was the scene of John Brown's trial, one of three treason trials held in the US before World War II. The courthouse was shelled during the Civil War but was later rebuilt; the original courtroom survived both the shelling and fires and is open to the public. In 1922, leaders of the miners' armed march on Logan City were tried here; one, Walter Allen, was convicted and sentenced to 10 yrs. (Mon-Fri; closed hols) Corner of N George & E Washington Sts. Phone 304/725-9761. **Free.**

Jefferson County Museum. Houses John Brown memorabilia, old guns, Civil War artifacts. (Apr-Nov, daily exc Sun) N Samuel & E Washington Sts. Phone 304/725-8628. **Donation.**

Site of the John Brown Gallows. Marked by pyramid of three stones supposedly taken from Brown's cell in Charles Town jail. At execution, 1,500 troops were massed around the scaffold. Some were commanded by Major Thomas "Stonewall" Jackson; among them was John Wilkes Booth, Virginia militiaman. S Samuel & Hunter Sts.

Tours of Charles Town. Historical walking tours; candlelit tours of Jefferson County Courthouse (evenings); carriage rides. All tours by appt. Phone 304/728-7713. **Free.**

Zion Episcopal Church (1852). Buried in cemetery around church are about 75 members of Washington family, as well as many Revolutionary and Confederate soldiers. (Interior, by appt) E Congress between S Mildred & S Church Sts. Phone 304/725-5312.

Annual Event

Jefferson County Fair. Livestock show, entertainment, amusement rides, exhibits. Late Aug.

Motels

✔★ **TOWNE HOUSE.** *549 E Washington St. 304/725-8441; FAX 304/725-5484; res: 800/227-2339.* 115 rms, 2-3 story. Mar-mid-Nov: S $35; D $40; each addl $5; suites $90; higher rates wkends; lower rates rest of yr. Crib free. TV; cable (premium). Pool. Restaurant adj 7 am-8 pm; Fri, Sat to 9 pm. Ck-out 11 am. Meeting rm. Business servs avail. Refrigerators. Cr cds: A, C, D, MC, V.

D ⊠ ⋈ ⚙

★ **TURF.** *608 E Washington St, 1 mi E on WV 51. 304/725-2081; FAX 304/728-7605; res: 800/422-8873.* 46 rms, 2 story, 6 kits. June-Labor Day: S $32-$56; D $46-$56; each addl $2-$5; suites $75-$150; kit. units $55-$75; lower rates rest of yr. Crib $5. Pet accepted. TV; cable (premium). Pool. Restaurant 6:30 am-9 pm; Fri, Sat to 10 pm. Rm serv. Bar 10-2 am. Ck-out noon. Meeting rms. Business servs avail. Free RR station transportation. Microwaves avail. Cr cds: A, C, D, DS, MC, V.

D ✦ ⊠ ⋈ ⚙ SC

Inns

★ ★ ★ **HILLBROOK.** *Rte 2, Box 152, 5 mi SW on WV 13 (Summit Point Rd). 304/725-4223; FAX 304/725-4455; res: 800/304-4223.* 6 rms, 2 story. S, D $130-$290. Dining rm (public by res) dinner (1 sitting) 8 pm. Ck-out noon, ck-in 3 pm. Meeting rm. Business servs avail. Lawn games. Some balconies, fireplaces. Manor house surrounded by English garden. English country manor-decor; eclectic collection of antiques, Oriental rugs, original art. Cr cds: A, DS, MC, V.

⚙

★ ★ **WASHINGTON HOUSE INN.** *216 S George St. 304/725-7923; res: 800/297-6957; FAX 304/728-5150.* E-mail mnvogel@intrepid .net; web www.bbonline.com/wv/washington. 6 rms, shower only, 3 story. S, D $75-$125; each addl $25; Oct wkends (2-day min). Complimentary full bkfst; afternoon refreshments. Restaurant nearby. Ck-out 11 am, ck-in 3-6 pm. Business servs avail. Luggage handling. Valet serv. Gift shop. Airport transportation. Health club privileges. Lawn games. Grills. Built in 1899 by George Washington's descendants; turn-of-the-century Victorian architecture. Totally nonsmoking. Cr cds: A, DS, MC, V.

⋈ ⚙ SC

Chesapeake and Ohio Canal National Historical Park

(see Maryland)

Clarksburg (C-5)

(See also Fairmont, Grafton, Weston)

Settled 1773 **Pop** 18,059 **Elev** 1,007 ft **Area code** 304 **Zip** 26301 **E-mail** visit@northnap.citynet.net **Web** www.bridgeport-clarksburg.com

Information Bridgeport-Clarksburg Convention & Visitors Bureau, 158 Thompson Dr, Bridgeport 26330; 304/842-7272 or 800/368-4324.

Clarksburg, in the heart of the West Virginia hills, is the trading center for an area of grading lands, coal mines and oil and gas fields. The Criminal Justice Information Services Division of the FBI is located here. During the Civil War it was an important supply base for Union troops. The famous

Civil War General "Stonewall" Jackson was born in Clarksburg in 1824. His statue stands before the courthouse.

What to See and Do

North Bend Rail Trail. 71 mi of scenic countryside trails featuring 13 tunnels, numerous bridges and several historic sites. Bike, hike or horse-back ride trail from nearby Wilsonburg to North Bend State Park (see PARKERSBURG). I-79, exit 119 to US 50. Phone 304/643-2500 or 800/899-6278. **Free.**

Salem-Teikyo University (1888). (750 students) On campus is the Jennings Randolph Center (by appt; fee), which houses papers and memorabilia of the former senator. 12 mi W in Salem. Phone 304/782-5011 or 304/782-5378. Also here is

Fort New Salem. Collection of 20 log houses from throughout the state were relocated to campus; pioneer history is re-created through crafts and folklore. Special events throughout the year (fee); summer concerts (mid-June-July, Sat evenings). (Memorial Day wkend-Oct, Wed-Sun; Apr-mid-May, Mon-Fri) Phone 304/782-5245. ¢¢

Stealey-Goff-Vance House (1807). House restored by Harrison County Historical Society as museum with period rooms, antique furniture, tools, Native American artifacts. (May-Sept, Fri, limited hrs) 123 W Main St. Phone 304/842-3073 or 304/624-6512. ¢

Watters Smith Memorial State Park. More than 500 acres on Duck Creek with visitor center/museum and 19th-century pioneer homestead. Swimming pool (seasonal). Hiking, game courts. Picnicking, playground, concession. Recreation building. Standard hrs, fees. 8 mi S on US 19, then SE on unnumbered road. Phone 304/745-3081.

Annual Event

West Virginia Italian Heritage Festival. Italian arts, music, contests, entertainment. Phone 304/622-7314. Labor Day wkend.

Motels

✔★ ★ **DAYS INN.** *(112 Tolley Dr, Bridgeport 26330) 1 mi E of I-79 exit 119.* 304/842-7371; FAX 304/842-3904. 62 rms, 2 story. S $53; D $61; each addl $8; family rates; higher rates: Buckhannon Festival, graduation, Italian Festival, football games. Crib free. TV; cable (premium). Indoor pool; whirlpool. Complimentary full bkfst. Restaurant 6:30-10:30 am. Bar 5 pm-midnight; entertainment Fri, Sat. Ck-out 11 am. Meeting rms. Business servs avail. Cr cds: A, C, D, DS, MC, V.

D ⊠ ⇌ 🐾 SC

★ ★ **HOLIDAY INN.** *(100 Lodgeville Rd, Bridgeport 26330) 2½ mi E on US 50E, just E of I-79 exit 119.* 304/842-5411; FAX 304/842-7258. 160 rms, 2 story. S, D $60-$75; suites $85; under 19 free; wkend rates. Crib free. TV; cable. Pool; wading pool. Restaurant 6 am-2 pm, 5-10 pm; Sat, Sun 6:30 am-2 pm, 5-10 pm. Rm serv. Private club 2 pm-1 am, Sun 5-11 pm. Ck-out noon. Meeting rms. Business servs avail. Valet serv. Sundries. Airport transportation. Cr cds: A, C, D, DS, JCB, MC, V.

D ⊠ ⇌ 🐾 SC

Restaurants

★ ★ **JIM REID'S.** *(1422 Buckhannon Pike, Nutter Fort) US 50 W to Joyce St exit, then ½ mi S on WV 20.* 304/623-4909. Hrs: 11 am-2 pm, 5-10 pm; Sun noon-8 pm. Closed Mon; Jan 1, Dec 24-26. Res accepted. Bar. Wine list. Complete meals: lunch $4.25-$6.50, dinner $8.95-$16.95. Child's meals. Specializes in fresh seafood, prime rib, steak. Family-owned. Cr cds: A, MC, V.

D ⇌

★ ★ **MINARD'S SPAGHETTI INN.** *813 E Pike St.* 304/623-1711. Hrs: 11:30 am-10 pm; Fri, Sat to 11 pm. Closed major hols. Res accepted. Italian menu. Wine, beer. Semi-a la carte: lunch $3.50-$6.75,

dinner $6.75-$13. Child's meals. Specializes in steak, spaghetti. Italian decor. Cr cds: A, MC, V.

D SC

Davis (C-6)

(See also Aurora, Elkins)

Founded 1883 **Pop** 799 **Elev** 3,099 ft **Area code** 304 **Zip** 26260
Information Potomac Highland Travel Council, 1200 Harrison Ave, Lower Level, Suite A, Elkins 26241; 304/636-8400.

Davis, the highest town in the state, was founded by Henry Gassaway Davis, US senator between 1871 and 1883. Senator Davis established the first night train in America (1848). He and his son-in-law, Senator Stephen B. Elkins, became wealthy from coal, lumber and railroading.

What to See and Do

Blackwater Falls State Park. This 1,688-acre park includes deep river gorge with 66-ft falls of dark, amber-colored water. Swimming in lake (fee); bath houses (Memorial Day-Labor Day); fishing; boating (rowboat and paddleboat rentals). Nature trails, horseback riding. Cross-country ski trails, center (rentals; school); sledding. Picnicking, playground, concession, lodge, cabins (see RESORTS). Tent & trailer campground. Nature, recreation programs and tours. Paved falls viewing area for the disabled. Standard hrs, fees. 2 mi W off WV 32. Phone 304/259-5216.

Canaan Valley Resort State Park. Approx 6,000 acres includes valley 3,200 ft above sea level, which is surrounded by spectacular mountain peaks. Swimming pool, bathhouse; fishing; boating. Hiking trails; 18-hole golf course, tennis courts. Skiing, ice rink. Playground, lodge, cabins (see RESORTS). Camping (dump station). Nature, recreation programs. Standard hrs, fees. 9 mi S on WV 32. Phone 304/866-4121.

Skiing.

Canaan Valley Resort State Park. Quad, 2 triple chairlifts, Pomalift; patrol, school, SKIwee program, rentals; snowmaking; restaurant, cafeteria; lodging, nursery; night skiing (Thurs-Sun). 22 trails, 34 slopes; vertical drop 850 ft. (Dec-Mar, daily) 18 mi of cross-country trails. Chairlift rides (early May-Oct, daily). Special programs for the disabled. Phone 304/866-4121 or 800/622-4121. ¢¢¢¢

Timberline Four Seasons Resort. Triple, 2 double chairlifts; patrol, school, SKIwee program, rentals; snowmaking; restaurant, bar; nursery; lodging, night skiing and special events. 35 slopes and trails; longest run 2 mi, vertical drop 1,000 ft. (Thanksgiving-mid-Apr, daily) Cross-country skiing. Chairlift rides (July-Oct, Sat & Sun, also Mon hols). 8 mi S off WV 32. Phone 304/866-4801 or 800/SNOWING. ¢¢¢¢

White Grass Touring Center. 36 mi of cross-country trails, some machine-groomed; patrol, school, rentals; snowmaking; restaurant, beer; night skiing; telemark slopes, guided tours. (Late Nov-Mar, daily) 9 mi S on WV 32 to Freeland Rd; ½ mi N of Canaan Valley Resort State Park. Phone 304/866-4114. ¢¢

Whitewater rafting. Many outfitters offer guided trips on the Cheat River. For a list of outfitters contact the West Virginia Division of Tourism, Research & Development, 2101 Washington St E, Bldg 17, Charleston 25305; 800/225-5982.

Annual Event

Tucker County Alpine Winter Festival. Governor's Cup ski races. Phone 304/866-4121. 1st wkend Mar.

Motel

✔★ ★ **BEST WESTERN ALPINE LODGE.** *Box 520, On WV 32, near Blackwater Falls State Park entrance.* 304/259-5245; FAX 304/259-5168. 46 rms, 1-2 story. S $48-$52; D $52-$56; each addl $5. Crib $5. TV;

cable. Pool; whirlpool. Restaurant 6 am-9 pm. Ck-out 11 am. Coin lndry. Meeting rms. Business servs avail. Sundries. Downhill ski 10 mi; x-country ski 2 mi. Refrigerators. Cr cds: A, D, DS, MC, V.

Resorts

★ ★ **BLACKWATER LODGE.** Box 490, 3 mi SW off WV 32 in Blackwater Falls State Park. 304/259-5216; FAX 304/259-5881. 54 rms in lodge, 1-2 story, 25 kit. cabins (1, 2 & 4 bedrm). S $55; D $63; each addl $6; cabins for 2-8, $88-$116 (1st night), $66-$101 (addl nights), $418-$621/wk. Crib $4; free in lodge. TV in lodge; cable (premium). Playground. Dining rm 7 am-9 pm. Lodge: ck-out noon, ck-in 3 pm. Cabins: ck-out 10 am, ck-in 4 pm. Coin lndry. Meeting rms. Business servs avail. Tennis. Downhill ski 10 mi; x-country ski on site. Lawn games. Game rm. Picnic tables, grills. All state park facilities avail. Lake swimming. Cr cds: A, MC, V.

★ ★ ★ **CANAAN VALLEY RESORT.** HC 70, Box 330, via WV 33, then 10 mi N on WV 32 in Canaan Valley Resort State Park. 304/866-4121; FAX 304/866-2172; res: 800/622-4121. 250 rms, 2 story. Mid-May-mid-Oct, mid-Dec-mid-Mar: S $73; D $79; each addl $6; suites $119; 2-4 bedrm cabins $565-$879/wk; family rates: ski, golf, tennis plans; lower lodge rates rest of yr. Deposit required. Crib $6; free in lodge. TV; cable (premium). 2 pools, 1 indoor; whirlpool, lifeguard (outside). Playground. Supervised child's activities. Dining rm 7:30 am-10 pm. Snack bars; box lunches, picnics. Private club 4 pm-midnight. Ck-out noon, ck-in 4 pm. Grocery 2 mi. Coin lndry. Convention facilities. Business servs avail. Sports dir. Lighted tennis, pro. 18-hole golf, greens fee $27, pro, putting green, driving range, miniature golf. Downhill/x-country ski on site. Naturalist program. Bicycles. Lawn games. Entertainment, movies. Rec rm. Game rm. Exercise equipt; weight machine, bicycles, sauna. Fishing privileges. Some refrigerators. Fireplace in cabins. Picnic tables. Camping sites avail. Cr cds: A, D, DS, MC, V.

Elkins (C-5)

(See also Buckhannon, Davis, Philippi)

Founded 1890 **Pop** 7,420 **Elev** 1,830 ft **Area code** 304 **Zip** 26241
Information Potomac Highland Travel Council, 1200 Harrison Ave, Lower Level, Suite A; 304/636-8400.

Elkins was named for US Senator Stephen B. Elkins, an aggressive politician and powerful industrial magnate who was Secretary of War under Benjamin Harrison (1888-1892). This town is in a coal and timber region, and is also a railroad terminus and trade center. Some of the finest scenery in the state can be seen in and around Elkins.

What to See and Do

Bowden National Fish Hatchery. Produces brook, brown and rainbow trout for stocking in state and national forest streams; also striped bass for Chesapeake Bay restoration project. Hatchery (daily). Visitor center (Memorial Day-mid-Oct, daily). 10 mi E on Old US 33. Phone 304/636-2823. **Free.**

Monongahela National Forest. This 901,000-acre forest, in the heart of the Alleghenies, has some of the loftiest mountains in the East. Spruce Knob (4,862 ft) is the highest point in the state. Headwaters of the Ohio and Potomac rivers are here. The forest is a meeting ground of northern and southern plant life, with stands of red spruce and northern hardwoods joining with oak, hickory and other southern hardwoods. There are also many interesting secondary and tertiary plants and wildflowers. Several recreation areas, including five wilderness areas, Spruce Knob/Seneca Rocks National Recreation Area, near Petersburg (see), and Blue Bend

and Lake Sherwood recreation areas, near White Sulphur Springs (see), are all located within the forest. Swimming; fishing, hunting; boating. Hiking, rock climbing, spelunking. Picnicking. Camping (fee). Fees charged at the more developed recreation sites. Part of the Greenbrier River Trail (see MARLINTON) runs through the southern section of the forest. Forest headquarters are in Elkins; the Cranberry Mountain Visitor Center is near Marlinton (see); and the Seneca Rocks Visitor Center is in Seneca Rocks (see PETERSBURG). Entrance is E of town on US 33. For further information contact Supervisor, US Department of Agriculture Building, 200 Sycamore St; 304/636-1800.

The Old Mill (1877). A gristmill powered by water turbines rather than a waterwheel. It was also used for planing wood and for producing white flour. Today it still uses water power to grind corn, wheat, rye and buckwheat. Observation hive has live bees. West Virginia crafts shop includes rug weaving. (Memorial Day-Labor Day, daily exc Sun) 25 mi E via US 33 to WV 32 N, in Harman. Phone 304/227-4466. **Donation.**

Annual Events

Augusta Festival. On campus of Davis & Elkins College, 100 Sycamore St. Celebration of traditional folk life and arts, featuring local and national performers, dances, juried craft fair, storytelling sessions, children's activities and homemade foods. Phone 304/637-1209. Mid-Aug.

Mountain State Forest Festival. Some events on campus of Davis & Elkins College. Queen Silvia is crowned; carnival, parades; entertainment; tilting at rings on horseback; sawing and woodchopping contests; marksmanship tests; State Championship Fiddle and Banjo Contest; juried craft fair and art exhibit. Phone 304/636-1824. Late Sept-early Oct.

Motels

★ ★ **BEST WESTERN.** PO Box 1878, US 219/250S. 304/636-7711. 63 rms, 2 story. S $38-$42; D $45-$49; each addl $5; suites, kit. suites $67-$77; under 12 free. TV; cable, VCR avail (movies $2). Indoor pool. Complimentary coffee in lobby. Restaurant nearby. Ck-out noon. Business servs avail. Sundries. Cr cds: A, C, D, DS, MC, V.

★ ★ **ECONO LODGE.** 4533 US 33E, near Randolph County Airport. 304/636-5311; res: 800/797-0014. 72 rms, 1-2 story. S $36-$50; D $40-$53; each addl $5; suites $49-$55; kit. units $53-$58; under 18 free; wknd & wkly rates; higher rates: college graduation, Forest Festival. Crib free. TV; cable (premium), VCR avail. Indoor pool; whirlpool. Complimentary continental bkfst. Ck-out 11 am. Coin lndry. Meeting rms. Business servs avail. Some bathrm phones. Picnic tables. Cr cds: A, C, D, DS, MC, V.

✔ ★ ★ **ELKINS MOTOR LODGE.** Box 46, Harrison Ave, 5 blks W. 304/636-1400; FAX 304/636-6318. 54 rms. S $35-$41; D $38-$44; each addl $3; suites $50-$60. Crib $3. TV; cable. Restaurant 5-10 pm, Sun to 8 pm. Rm serv. Private club 4:30 pm-1 am. Ck-out noon. Meeting rms. Business servs avail. Free airport transportation. Cr cds: A, D, DS, MC, V.

★ **FOUR SEASONS.** 1091 Harrison Ave, on US 33 & 250. 304/636-1990; res: 800/367-7130. 14 rms, 1-2 story. S $26-$28; D $30-$34; each $3; under 12 free; wkly rates. Crib free. TV; cable (premium), VCR avail. Complimentary coffee in lobby. Restaurant nearby. Ck-out 11 am. Cr cds: DS, MC, V.

✔ ★ **SUPER 8.** 350 Beverly Pike, 2 mi S on US 219/250, near Randolph County Airport. 304/636-6500; FAX 304/636-6500, ext. 300. 43 rms, 2 story. S $38.88-$44.88; D $44.88-$52.88; each addl $6; under 12 free; higher rates: Forest Festival, graduation, ski wk. Crib free. TV; cable (premium). Complimentary coffee in lobby. Restaurant opp 7 am-10 pm. Ck-out 11 am. Business servs avail. Cr cds: A, C, D, DS, JCB, MC, V.

Restaurant

★ **CHEAT RIVER INN.** *US 33E. 304/636-6265.* Hrs: 4-10 pm. Closed Mon. Res accepted. Bar. Semi-a la carte: dinner $8.95-$17. Specializes in seafood. Outdoor dining. Mounted fish on display. Cr cds: MC, V.

Fairmont (B-5)

(See also Clarksburg, Morgantown)

Settled 1793 **Pop** 20,210 **Elev** 883 ft **Area code** 304 **Zip** 26554 **E-mail** mm@westvirginia.com **Web** www.westvirginia.com/marion

Information Convention & Visitors Bureau of Marion County, 110 Adams St, PO Box 58, 26555-0058; 304/368-1123.

Fairmont was a Union supply depot plundered by Confederate cavalry in April 1863. General William Ezra Jones's division swept through town, took 260 prisoners, destroyed the $500,000 bridge across the Monongahela River and raided the governor's residence. After the war, resources in the region were developed, and coal became the mainstay. Today Fairmont manufactures aluminum, mine machinery and other products.

What to See and Do

Fairmont State College (1867). (7,000 students) On campus is a one-room schoolhouse with original desks, books and other artifacts related to early era of education (Apr-Oct, schedule varies; free). Locust Ave. Phone 304/367-4000.

Marion County Museum. Displays of B & O china, five furnished rooms covering 1776-1920s, doll, train and toy collection. (Daily exc Sun; closed hols) Adams St, adj to courthouse. Phone 304/367-5398. **Free.**

Prickett's Fort State Park. Approx 200 acres with reconstructed 18th-century log fort, colonial trade and lifestyle demonstrations by costumed interpreters, outdoor historical drama (July, Wed-Sat). Boating (ramps). Picnicking. Visitor center. Fort and museum (mid-Apr-Oct, daily). Museum (fee). I-79 exit 139, then 2 mi W. Phone 800/CALL-WVA or 304/363-3030 (museum).

Annual Event

Three Rivers Festival and Regatta. Palatine Park. Entertainment, parade, clipper ship cruises, carnival, games. Phone 304/363-2625. 3rd wkend May.

Motels

★ ★ **DAYS INN.** *1185 Airport Rd. 304/367-1370; FAX 304/367-1806.* 98 rms, 2 story. S $43-$60; D $48-$65; each addl $5; suites $57-$100; wkly rates; higher rates: WVU football games, graduation. Crib free. TV; cable (premium). Pool. Complimentary continental bkfst. Restaurant nearby. Ck-out noon. Meeting rms. Business servs avail. Sundries. Game rm. Cr cds: A, C, D, DS, MC, V.

★ ★ **HOLIDAY INN.** *I-79 & Old Grafton Rd, 1½ mi E on I-79 exit 137. 304/366-5500; FAX 304/363-3975.* 106 rms, 2 story. S, D $50-$80; under 18 free; higher rates: WVU football games, graduation. Crib free. TV; cable, VCR avail. Pool. Restaurant 6 am-2 pm, 5-10 pm. Rm serv. Private club. Ck-out noon. Meeting rms. Business servs avail. In-rm modem link. Bellhops. Valet serv. Sundries. Cr cds: A, C, D, DS, ER, JCB, MC, V.

✔★ **RED ROOF INN.** *50 Middletown Rd, Jct I-79 & US 250. 304/366-6800; FAX 304/366-6812.* 108 rms, 2 story. S $29.99-$39.99; D $40.99-$50.99; each addl $3; under 12 free. Crib free. TV. Complimentary coffee in lobby. Restaurant nearby. Ck-out noon. Business servs avail. Cr cds: A, C, D, DS, MC, V.

Restaurants

✔★ ★ **MURIALE'S.** *(1742 Fairmont Ave, South Fairmont) 2 mi S on US 250; 2 mi N of I-79 exit 132. 304/363-3190.* Hrs: 11 am-9 pm; Sun from 10 am. Closed Dec 25. Italian, Amer menu. Beer. Semi-a la carte: lunch $3-$5.25, dinner $5-$15.50. Sun bkfst buffet $7.85. Child's meals. Specializes in lasagne, ravioli, steak. Own pasta. Family-owned. Cr cds: A, D, DS, MC, V.

★ ★ **TIFFANY'S CONTINENTAL KEY CLUB.** *N Bellview Blvd, 1½ mi N of US 19N. 304/363-7859.* Hrs: 11 am-11 pm; early-bird dinner 4:30-6:30 pm. Closed Sun; major hols. Italian, French continental menu. Res accepted. Serv bar. Wine list. Semi-a la carte: lunch $2.95-$6.95, dinner $5.95-$18.95. Child's meals. Specialties: beef Wellington, veal parmigiana, whole Maine lobster. Own baking. Valet parking. Braille menu. Family-owned. Cr cds: A, C, D, DS, MC, V.

Franklin (C-6)

(For accommodations see Petersburg; also see Harrisonburg, VA)

Settled 1794 **Pop** 914 **Elev** 1,731 ft **Area code** 304 **Zip** 26807

Information Potomac Highland Travel Council, 1200 Harrison Ave, Lower Level, Suite A, Elkins 26241; 304/636-8400.

What to See and Do

Seneca Caverns. Caves, which contain magnificent stalagmites and stalactites, were used as a refuge by the Seneca people. (Daily) Approx 17 mi NW on US 33 to Riverton, then 3 mi E. Phone 304/567-2691. ¢¢¢

Annual Event

Treasure Mountain Festival. Square dancing, clogging; parade; gospel and mountain music, drama; rifle demonstration, cross-cut sawing contest; children's contests, games; trail rides; craft exhibits; country food. Phone 304/249-5422. 3rd wkend Sept.

Gauley Bridge (D-4)

(See also Beckley, Charleston, Summersville)

Pop 691 **Elev** 680 ft **Area code** 304 **Zip** 25085

Information Upper Kahawha Valley Chamber of Commerce, PO Box 831, Montgomery 25136; 304/442-5756.

This town, at the junction of the New and Gauley rivers, was the key to the Kanawha Valley during the Civil War. In November 1861, Union General W.S. Rosecrans defeated Confederate General John B. Floyd, a victory that assured Union control of western Virginia. Stone piers of the old bridge, which was destroyed by retreating Confederates in 1861, can be seen near the present bridge.

What to See and Do

Contentment Museum Complex (ca 1830). Former residence of Confederate Colonel George W. Imboden contains original woodwork, period furniture, toy collection. Adjacent Fayette County Historical Society Museum features displays of Native American relics, local artifacts, Civil War items; restored one-room schoolhouse. (June-Sept, daily; May, Sun; rest of yr, by appt) 7 mi E on US 60, 1 mi E of Hawks Nest State Park. Phone 304/658-5695 or 304/465-0165. Or contact Fayette County Chamber of Commerce, 800/927-0263. ¢

Hawks Nest State Park. Approx 280 acres on Gauley Mt, with fine views of New River Gorge from rocks 585 ft above the river. A 600-ft aerial tramway carries passengers to canyon floor. Swimming pool; fishing. Hiking trails; tennis. Picnic area, playground, concession, restaurant, lodge (see LODGE). Log museum with early West Virginia artifacts (May-Nov, daily; free). Standard hrs, fees. 6 mi E on US 60. Phone 304/658-5212 or 304/658-5196.

New River Gorge Bridge. A masterpiece of engineering, this four-lane, single-arch, steel-span bridge rises 876 ft above the New River Gorge National River (see HINTON), making it the second-highest bridge in the US, and at 3,030 ft, the longest bridge of its type in the world. Just north of the bridge, on US 19, is the Canyon Rim Visitors Center (daily; closed Dec 25). The visitors center provides 2 overlooks of the bridge and river, a 70-ft descending boardwalk, slide presentation, exhibits and ranger-guided walks (May-Oct). 13 mi SE on US 60, then 6 mi SW on US 19, near Fayetteville. Phone 304/574-2115.

Whitewater rafting. Many outfitters offer guided trips on the New and Gauley rivers. For a list of outfitters contact the West Virginia Division of Tourism, Research & Development, 2101 Washington St E, Bldg 17, Charleston 25305; 800/225-5982; or the Fayette County Chamber of Commerce, 310 Oyler Ave, Oak Hill 25901; 800/927-0263.

Annual Event

Bridge Day. New River Gorge Bridge. Bridge is opened to pedestrians; parachutists test their skills by jumping off the bridge and floating to the bottom of gorge. 3rd Sat Oct.

Lodge

★ ★ **HAWKS NEST LODGE.** *(PO Box 857, Ansted 25812) 8 mi E on US 60, in Hawks Nest State Park.* 304/658-5212; FAX 304/658-4549. 31 rms, 4 story. Late May-early Sept: S, D $60; each addl $6; suites $66-$80; under 13 free; lower rates rest of yr. Crib free. TV; cable. Pool. Dining rm 7 am-9 pm; Dec-Feb to 8 pm. Ck-out noon. Meeting rm. Business servs avail. Tennis. Golf privileges. Balconies. View of mountains. 1,100-ft vertical tramway to marina. Cr cds: A, D, MC, V.

Inn

★ ★ **GLEN FERRIS.** *(PO Box 128, Glen Ferris 25090) 1½ mi W on US 60.* 304/632-1111; FAX 304/632-0113; res: 800/924-6093 (WV). 16 rms. S, D $61-$75; suite $130. TV; cable (premium). Dining rm 6 am-9 pm; Sun from 7 am. Ck-out 11 am. Meeting rm. Business servs avail. Renovated 1840s inn, originally Federal style in design; built by grandson of one of signers of Declaration of Indepedence. Overlooks Kanawha Falls. Cr cds: A, DS, MC, V.

Grafton (B-5)

(See also Clarksburg, Fairmont, Morgantown, Philippi)

Founded 1856 **Pop** 5,524 **Elev** 1,004 ft **Area code** 304 **Zip** 26354
Information Grafton-Taylor County Convention & Visitors Bureau, 214 W Main St, Rm 205; 304/265-3938.

Mother's Day started in Grafton in 1908 when Anna Jarvis observed the anniversary of her mother's death during a religious service. The idea caught on nationally, and in 1914 President Woodrow Wilson issued a proclamation urging nationwide observance. The International Shrine to Motherhood in the original Mother's Day church is located at 11 E Main Street.

During the Civil War, Grafton was an important railroad center; 4,000 Union troops camped here before the Battle of Philippi in 1861. General McClellan also had his headquarters in the town. The first land soldier killed in the war, T. Bailey Brown, fell at Grafton. He is buried in the Grafton National Cemetery.

What to See and Do

Tygart Lake State Park. This scenic 2,100-acre park contains one of the largest concrete dams east of the Mississippi (1,900 ft by 209 ft). Swimming, waterskiing; fishing; boating (ramp, rentals, marina). Hiking, game courts. Picnic area, playground, concession, lodge (see MOTELS). Tent and trailer camping, 10 cabins. Nature and recreation programs, dam tours (summer; phone 304/265-1760). Standard hrs, fees. 2 mi S off US 119, 250. Phone 304/265-3383.

Annual Event

Taylor County Fair. Fairgrounds, US 50. Horse racing, livestock shows, auctions, carnival, crafts. Phone 304/265-4155. Last wk July.

Motels

✔ ★ **CRISLIP MOTOR LODGE.** *300 Moritz Ave, 1 mi NE on US 50, 1 blk W of jct US 119.* 304/265-2100. 40 rms, 2 story. S $34; D $43; each addl $5; bridal suites $38-$40. Crib $8. TV; cable. Pool. Complimentary coffee in rms. Restaurant nearby. Ck-out 11 am. Business servs avail. Sundries. Cr cds: A, D, DS, MC, V.

★ ★ **TYGART LAKE STATE PARK LODGE.** *Rte 1, Box 260, 4 mi S off US 119.* 304/265-3383; res: 800/225-5982. 20 rms, 1 story. May-Oct: S $52; D $58; each addl $6; cabins $418-$540/wk; under 13 free; golf plans. Closed rest of yr. Crib free. TV; cable. Free supervised child's activities (Memorial Day-Labor Day). Restaurant 8 am-8 pm. Ck-out noon. Meeting rm. Rec rm. Lawn games. Picnic tables. Rms overlook lake. Cr cds: A, MC, V.

Harpers Ferry (C-8)

(See also Charles Town, Martinsburg, Shepherdstown; also see Frederick, MD)

Settled 1732 **Pop** 308 **Elev** 247 ft **Area code** 304 **Zip** 25425
Information Jefferson County Chamber of Commerce, 201 Frontage Rd, PO Box 426, Charles Town 25414; 304/725-2055.

Harpers Ferry, the scene of abolitionist John Brown's raid in 1859, is at the junction of the Shenandoah and Potomac rivers, where West Virginia, Virginia and Maryland meet. A US armory and rifle factory made this an important town in early Virginia; John Brown had this in mind when he began his insurrection. He and 16 other men seized the armory and arsenal the night of October 16 and took refuge in the engine house of the armory when attacked by local militia. On the morning of the 18th, the engine house was stormed, and Brown was captured by 90 marines from Washington under Brevet Colonel Robert E. Lee and Lt J.E.B. Stuart. Ten of Brown's men were killed, including two of his sons. He was hanged in nearby Charles Town (see) for treason, murder and inciting slaves to rebellion.

When war broke out, Harpers Ferry was a strategic objective for the Confederacy, which considered it the key to Washington. "Stonewall" Jackson captured 12,693 Union prisoners here before the Battle of Antietam in 1862. The town changed hands many times in the war, during which many buildings were damaged. In 1944, Congress authorized a national monument here, setting aside 1,500 acres for that purpose. In 1963, the same area was designated a National Historical Park, now occupying more than 2,200 acres.

What to See and Do

⭐ **Harpers Ferry National Historical Park.** Here the old town has been restored to its 19th-century appearance; exhibits and interpretive presentations explore the park's relation to the water-power industry, the Civil War, John Brown and Storer College, a school established for freed slaves after the war. A Visitor Center is located just off US 340. Visitors should park there; a bus will take them to Lower Town. Contact the Visitor Center, PO Box 65; 304/535-6298. Park entrance fee: per person ¢¢; per vehicle ¢¢ A walking tour of the park follows.

Information Center. Restored federalist house built in 1859 by US government as residence for the master armorer of the US Armory. During the Civil War it was used as headquarters by various commanding officers. Also on this street is the site of the US Armory that John Brown attempted to seize; it was destroyed during the Civil War. Farther down Shenandoah St and right under the trestle is S side of Shenandoah St near High St.

The Point. Three states, West Virginia, Virginia and Maryland, and two rivers, the Shenandoah and Potomac, meet at the Blue Ridge Mountains. Back under the trestle is

John Brown's Fort. Where John Brown made his last stand; rebuilt and moved near original site. On Arsenal Square. Across the street is the

John Brown Museum. Contains an exhibit and film on John Brown and a 10-min slide presentation on the history of the park. Exiting the museum to the right is High St, which has two Civil War museums and two black history museums. Up the stone steps from High St is

Harper House. Three-story, stone house built between 1775 and 1782 by founder of town; both George Washington and Thomas Jefferson were entertained as overnight guests. Restored and furnished with period pieces. Behind this house is

Marmion Row. Four restored, private houses built 1832-1850. Continue up the hill to the

Ruins of St John's Episcopal Church. Used as a guardhouse and hospital during the Civil War. Approx 100 yards farther is

Jefferson's Rock. From here Thomas Jefferson, in 1783, pronounced the view "one of the most stupendous scenes in nature." Farther along, above the cemetery, is

Lockwood House (1848). Greek-revival house used as a headquarters, barracks and stable during Civil War; later used as a classroom building by Storer College (1867), which was founded to educate freed men after the war.

Other buildings open to the public during the summer are the dry goods store, provost office and blacksmith shop.

John Brown Wax Museum. Sound and animation depict Brown's exploits, including the raid on Harpers Ferry. (Mid-Mar-early Dec, daily; Jan-Mar, Sat & Sun) High St. Phone 304/535-6342 or 304/535-2792. ¢¢

Whitewater rafting. Many outfitters offer guided trips on the Shenandoah and Potomac rivers. For a list of outfitters contact the West Virginia Division of Tourism, Research & Development, 2101 Washington St E, Bldg 17, Charleston 25305; 800/225-5982.

Annual Events

Mountain Heritage Arts and Crafts Festival. More than 190 craftspeople and artisans demonstrate quilting, wool spinning, pottery throwing, vegetable dyeing and other crafts; concerts. 2nd full wkend June & last full wkend Sept.

Election Day 1860. More than 100 people in 19th-century clothing reenact the 1860 presidential election. 2nd Sat Oct.

Old Tyme Christmas. Caroling, musical programs, children's programs, taffy pull, candlelight walk. 1st 2 wkends Dec.

Motel

★★ **COMFORT INN.** *Union St & US 340. 304/535-6391; FAX 304/535-6395.* 50 rms, 2 story. Apr-Oct: S, D $60-$85; each addl $6; under 18 free; lower rates rest of yr. Crib free. TV; cable, VCR avail (movies). Complimentary continental bkfst. Coffee in rms. Restaurant nearby. Ck-out 11 am. Meeting rms. Business servs avail. Refrigerators avail. Cr cds: A, C, D, DS, JCB, MC, V.

D ⊠ 🐾 SC

Hillsboro (D-5)

(See also Marlinton)

Settled 1765 **Pop** 188 **Elev** 2,303 ft **Area code** 304 **Zip** 24946
Information Potomac Highland Travel Council, 1200 Harrison Ave, Lower Level, Suite A, Elkins 26241; 304/636-8400.

Civil War troops marched through Hillsboro, and Confederates camped in town before the decisive Battle of Droop Mountain. Novelist Pearl S. Buck was born in her grandparents' house while her parents, missionaries on leave from China, were visiting.

What to See and Do

Beartown State Park. Approx 110 acres of dense forest with unique rock formations created by erosion; boardwalk with interpretive signs winds through park. Standard hrs. 5 mi S off US 219. Phone 304/653-4254.

Droop Mountain Battlefield State Park. Encompasses approx 285 acres on site where, on Nov 6, 1863, Union forces under General William W. Averell defeated Confederates under General John Echols, destroying the last major rebel resistance in the state. Park features graves, breastworks and monuments. Hiking. Picnic areas, playground. Museum. Battle reenactments (2nd wk Oct, every even yr). Standard hrs. 3 mi S on US 219. Phone 304/653-4254.

⭐ **Pearl S. Buck Birthplace Museum** (Stulting House). Birthplace of Pulitzer and Nobel Prize-winning novelist, restored to its 1892 appearance; original and period furniture; memorabilia. Exhibit of antique tools and farm implements in restored barn. Sydenstricker House, home of Buck's father and his ancestors, was moved 40 mi from its original site and restored here. Guided tours. (May-Oct, Mon-Sat, also Sun afternoons) ½ mi N on US 219. Phone 304/653-4430. ¢¢

Watoga State Park. More than 10,100 acres make this West Virginia's largest state park. Watoga, derived from the Cherokee term *watauga*, means "river of islands." It aptly describes the Greenbrier River, which forms several miles of the park's boundary. Swimming pool, bathhouses; fishing; boating on 11-acre Watoga Lake (rentals). Hiking, bridle trails, horseback riding; tennis, game courts. Cross-country skiing. Picnicking, playground, concession, restaurant (seasonal). Tent and trailer camping, 33 cabins. Brooks Memorial Arboretum; nature, recreation programs (summer). Standard hrs, fees. 1 mi N on US 219, then SE. Phone 304/799-4087. Adj to the park is

Calvin Price State Forest. This vast, undeveloped forest has more than 9,400 acres for fishing, deer and small-game hunting, hiking and primitive camping (fee). Phone 304/799-4087.

Hinton (E-4)

(See also Beckley)

Founded 1873 **Pop** 3,433 **Elev** 1,382 ft **Area code** 304 **Zip** 25951
E-mail sccc@inetone.com
Information Summers County Chamber of Commerce, 221 Temple St, PO Box 231; 304/466-5332 or 304/466-5420.

Hinton, a railroad town on the banks of the New River, is the seat of Summers County, where the Bluestone and Greenbrier rivers join the scenic and protected New River.

What to See and Do

Bluestone State Park. More than 2,100 acres on Bluestone Lake, which was created by the Bluestone Dam. Swimming pool (Memorial Day-Labor Day), wading pool, bathhouses, waterskiing; fishing; boating (ramps, marina nearby; canoe, rowboat and motorboat rentals). Hiking trails; game courts. Picnicking, playground. Gift shop. Tent & trailer camping (dump station), 25 cabins. Nature, recreation programs (summer). Standard hrs, fees. 5 mi S on WV 20. Phone 304/466-2805.

New River Gorge National River. One of the oldest rivers on the continent, the New River rushes northward through a deep canyon with spectacular scenery. The 52-mi section from Hinton to Fayetteville is popular among outdoor enthusiasts, especially whitewater rafters and hikers. The Hinton Visitor Center is located along the river at WV 3 Bypass (Memorial Day-Labor Day, daily); phone 304/466-0417. A yr-round visitor center is located on US 19 near the New River Gorge Bridge (see GAULEY BRIDGE). For further information and a list of whitewater outfitters contact Superintendent, PO Box 246, Glen Jean 25846; 304/465-0508.

Pipestem Resort State Park. More than 4,000 acres with 3,600-ft aerial tramway to Bluestone River complex. Swimming, bathhouses; fishing; canoeing, paddleboating. Hiking trails, horseback riding; 9- and 18-hole golf courses, miniature golf, tennis, archery, lighted game courts. Cross-country skiing, sledding. Playground, 2 lodges (see RESORT), 4 restaurants. Tent & trailer camping (dump station), 25 cabins. Visitor center; nature, recreation programs. Aerial tramway, arboretum, observation tower. Amphitheater; dances. Standard hrs, fees. 12 mi SW on WV 20. Phone 304/466-1800.

Inn

✔★ **PENCE SPRINGS HOTEL.** *(Pence Springs 24962)* 14 mi E on WV 3. 304/445-2606; FAX 304/445-2204; res: 800/826-1829. 15 units, 3 story, 1 cottage. Apr-Dec: S $59.50-$89.50; D $69.50-$99.50; cottage $350; under 3 free; wkly rates; lower rates rest of yr. Crib $10. Complimentary full bkfst. Dining rm 8-10 am, 5-9 pm; wkend hrs vary. Bar 5 pm-midnight. Ck-out 11 am, ck-in 1 pm. Meeting rms. Business servs avail. Lawn games. Picnic tables. Resort hotel, built in 1918 for guests who came to "take the waters" of Pence Springs, was closed in 1935 due to the Depression. In 1947, resort was turned into a women's prison, which was closed in 1985. Restored structure retains flavor of rambling country house; sunroom, portico, gallery. On high plateau overlooking Greenbrier River valley. Cr cds: A, C, D, DS, MC, V.

D ⚡ 🏊 🛶 SC

Resort

★★★ **PIPESTEM.** *(Pipestem 25979)* 12 mi SW via WV 20, in Pipestem Resort State Park, 3 mi from park entrance. 304/466-1800; FAX 304/466-5679; res: 800/225-5982. 143 units in 2 bldgs, 7 story, 30 lodge rms, 25 kit. cottages. May-Sept: S $62; D $68; lodge rms (Nov-Mar only): S $46; D $52; each addl $6; under 13 free; suites $72-$94; 2-4 bedrm cottages $575-$754/wk; varied lower rates rest of yr. Crib free. TV; cable (premium), VCR avail (movies $4). 2 pools, 1 indoor; wading pool, sauna, lifeguard. Playground. Restaurants (see BLUESTONE DINING ROOM and MOUNTAIN CREEK). Bar (seasonal). Snack bars. Ck-out noon, ck-in

4 pm; cottages ck-out 10 am, ck-in 4 pm. Business servs avail. Grocery 3 mi. Lighted tennis. 18-hole golf. X-country ski on site; sleighing, tobogganing. Exercise equipt; bicycles, treadmill. Lawn games. Soc dir. Rec rm; entertainment in summer. Many balconies. Picnic tables. Mt Creek Lodge (open May-Oct) located at foot of Bluestone Canyon; accessible only by aerial tram. Resort state-owned, operated; all state park facilities avail to guests. Cr cds: A, D, MC, V.

D 🚣 🏌 🎿 🚵 🏇 🎣 🏊 🎯 ⛳ 🏃 SC

Restaurants

✔★★ **BLUESTONE DINING ROOM.** *(See Pipestem Resort)* 304/466-1800, ext. 360. Hrs: 7 am-2 pm, 5:30-9 pm. Wine, beer. Semi-a la carte: bkfst $3.95-$7.95, lunch $5.95-$7.95, dinner $9.95-$15.95. Buffet: bkfst $5.50, lunch $6.95, dinner $9.95. Child's meals. Specializes in seafood, steak, country dishes. Outdoor dining. View of gorge and mts. Cr cds: D, DS, MC, V.

D 🛶

✔★ **KIRK'S.** HC 75 Box 3, WV 20 just below Bluestone Dam. 304/466-4600. Hrs: 6:30 am-9 pm; Sun brunch 11 am-2 pm. Closed Thanksgiving, Dec 25. Semi-a la carte: bkfst, lunch $3-$5, dinner $5-$12.25. Sun brunch $6.25. Specialties: Kirk's hot dogs, fried chicken, stuffed baked potatoes. Own pastries. Outdoor dining. On New River near Bluestone Resort Park; patio overlooks river. No cr cds accepted.

D

★★ **MOUNTAIN CREEK.** *(See Pipestem Resort)* 304/466-1800, ext. 387. Hrs: 7 am-2 pm, 5:30-9 pm; Tues, Thurs 7-11 am, 5:30-9 pm; Sat to 10 pm. Closed May-Oct. Res accepted (dinner). French, Amer menu. Bar. Semi-a la carte: bkfst $2.25-$4.50, lunch $4.95, dinner $14.95-$23.95. Child's meals. Specialties: roasted pork filet, rack of lamb, prime rib of beef. Own pastries. Park in Pipestem Resort State Park. Dining rm at 1,000-ft-deep gorge; accessible by tram only. Totally nonsmoking. Cr cds: A, MC, V.

★★ **OAK SUPPER CLUB.** *(Just N of Pipestem Park entrance, in Pipestem)* 12 mi SW on WV 20. 304/466-4800. Hrs: 5:30-9 pm. Closed Thanksgiving, Dec 25. Res accepted. Bar. Semi-a la carte: dinner $10.95-$24.95. Child's meals. Specializes in barbecued pork, duckling, fresh mountain trout, country cooking. Named for 800 year-old white oak on grounds. Dining rm overlooks mountains. Family-owned. Cr cds: MC, V.

D

Huntington (D-2)

Founded 1871 **Pop** 54,844 **Elev** 564 ft **Area code** 304 **E-mail** htgncvb @marshall.edu **Web** wvweb.com/Greater_Huntington_CVB
Information Cabell-Huntington Convention & Visitors Bureau, PO Box 347, 25708; 304/525-7333 or 800/635-6329.

The millionaire president of the Chesapeake & Ohio Railroad, Collis P. Huntington, founded this city and named it for himself. Originally a rail and river terminus, commerce and industry have made it the second-largest city in the state. Thoroughly planned and meticulously laid out, Huntington is protected from the Ohio River by an 11-mile floodwall equipped with 17 pumping stations and 45 gates. Glass, railroad products and metals are important city industries.

What to See and Do

Beech Fork State Park. Nearly 4,000 acres on 720-acre Beech Fork Lake. Fishing; boating (ramp, marina). Hiking trails, physical fitness trail; tennis, game courts. Picnicking. Camping; store. Visitor center; nature, recreation programs (summer). Meeting rms. Standard hrs, fees. Approx 15 mi SE via WV 10, then 7 mi W on Hughes Branch Rd, near Bowen. Phone 304/522-0303.

Camden Park. Amusement park with 27 rides, games, concession; boat and train rides, log flume, miniature golf, roller rink, picnicking. (Mid-Apr-Memorial Day, Sat, Sun; Memorial Day-Labor Day, daily exc Mon) Rides individually priced; also unlimited ride plan. US 60 E. Phone 304/429-4231. ¢¢¢

East Lynn Wildlife Management Area. Almost 23,000 acres used primarily by sportsmen; trails, primitive camping (fee). 15 mi SE via WV 152 & WV 37, near East Lynn. Phone 304/675-0871.

Heritage Village. Restored Victorian B & O Railroad yard surrounding brick courtyard. Restaurant (see RESTAURANTS) in original passenger station (1887), restored Pullman car, shops in renovated freight and box cars, warehouses. (Daily exc Sun) 11th St & Veterans Memorial Blvd. Phone 304/696-5954. **Free.**

Huntington Museum of Art. Museum with American and European paintings, prints and sculpture; Herman P. Dean Firearms Collection; Georgian silver; Oriental prayer rugs; pre-Columbian art; Appalachian folk art; Ohio Valley historical and contemporary glass. Complex includes exhibition galleries, library, studio workshops, amphitheater, auditorium, sculpture garden, observatory, art gallery for young people, nature trails. Free admission Wed. (Tues-Sat, also Sun afternoons; closed some major hols) 2033 McCoy Rd; I-64 exit 8. Phone 304/529-2701. **Donation.**

Industrial tours.

Blenko Glass Co, Inc. Famous glass factory; makers of Country Music Award, presidential gifts and original supplier to Colonial Williamsburg. Visitor center (daily; closed hols) has stained glass from nine leading studios; observation gallery for viewing hand-blown glassmaking and blown stained glass. (Mon-Fri; closed hols; also 1st 2 wks July, Dec 25-Jan 1) Museum of Historical Glass; Garden of Glass beside three-acre lake. 16 mi E via US 60, in Milton; I-64 exit 28. Phone 304/743-9081. **Free.**

Pilgrim Glass Corp. Observation deck to watch making of hand-blown glassware, including cranberry, cobalt and crystal glass. Gift shop. (Mon-Fri; closed hols, also last wk June & 1st wk July) 5 mi W off I-64 exit 1, adj to Tri-State Airport on Airport Rd, in Ceredo. Phone 304/453-3553. **Free.**

Seasonal Event

Tri-State Fair & Regatta. Various events held in tri-state area of Kentucky, Ohio and West Virginia. Highlights include Regattafest, Central Park Festival, Budweiser Jet Ski Races, Huntington Miller Classic Power Boat Races and the Industrial Fun O-Limp-ics. Phone 304/525-8141. Last wk July.

Motels

★ ★ ★ **GATEWAY.** *6007 US 60E (25726).. 304/736-8974; FAX 304/736-8974, ext. 726.* 208 rms, 1-2 story. S, D $70-$90; under 19 free; wkend rates; higher rates special events. Crib free. TV; cable, VCR avail. Indoor pool. Playground. Restaurant 6 am-10 pm. Rm serv. Bar; entertainment. Ck-out noon. Coin lndry. Meeting rms. Business servs avail. Bell-hops. Valet serv. Barber, beauty shop. Sundries. Lighted tennis. Exercise equipt; weights, bicycles, sauna. Game rm. Cr cds: A, C, D, DS, JCB, MC, V.

D ⚷ ≈ ✕ ⊠ ⊠ SC

✔★ **RED ROOF INN.** *5190 US 60E (25705). 304/733-3737; FAX 304/733-3786.* 108 rms, 2 story. S $45-$55; D $52-$57; each addl $7; under 18 free. Crib free. Pet accepted. TV; cable. Business servs avail. Microwaves avail. Cr cds: A, C, D, DS, MC, V.

D ⚷ ⊠ ⊠

★ **TRAVELODGE.** *5600 US 60E (25705). 304/736-3451; FAX 304/736-3451, ext. 706.* 120 rms, 3 story. S $42-$54; D $47-$60; each addl $5; suites $54; under 18 free. Crib free. Pet accepted. TV; cable (premium). Pool. Restaurant 5-9 pm. Private club 5 pm-2 am. Ck-out noon. Meeting rms. Business servs avail. Sundries. Free airport transportation.

Exercise equipt; weight machine, stair machines. Private patios, balconies. Cr cds: A, C, D, DS, JCB, MC, V.

D ⚷ ≈ ✕ ⊠ ⊠ SC

Motor Hotel

★ ★ **UPTOWNER INN.** *1415 4th Ave (25701). 304/525-7741; res: 800/828-9016; FAX 304/525-3508.* 138 rms, 4 story. S, D $63-$70; each addl $5; suites $90-$100; under 18 free. Crib free. Pet accepted. TV; cable. Pool; wading pool. Restaurants 6:30 am-10 pm. Rm serv. Bar 4 pm-midnight, Fri, Sat to 1 am. Ck-out noon. Meeting rms. Business servs avail. In-rm modem link. Free airport transportation. Exercise equipt; weights, bicycle. Cr cds: A, C, D, DS, JCB, MC, V.

D ⚷ ≈ ✕ ⊠ ⊠ SC

Hotel

★ ★ ★ **RADISSON.** *1001 3rd Ave (25701). 304/525-1001; FAX 304/525-1048.* 200 rms, 11 story. S, D $88-$108; each addl $5; suites $160-$377; under 18 free; wkend rates. Crib free. TV; cable (premium), VCR avail. Heated pool; poolside serv. Coffee in rms. Restaurant 6:30 am-11 pm; Fri, Sat to midnight. Bar 3 pm-midnight. Ck-out noon. Meeting rms. Business servs avail. In-rm modem link. Shopping arcade. Valet parking. Airport, RR station, bus depot transportation. Exercise equipt; weight machines, stair machines, sauna. On Ohio River. Cr cds: A, C, D, DS, ER, JCB, MC, V.

D ≈ ✕ ⊠ ⊠ SC

Restaurants

★ ★ ★ **REBELS & REDCOATS TAVERN.** *412 W 7th Ave (25701). 304/523-8829.* Hrs: 11:30 am-2:30 pm, 5:30-10 pm; Sat 5:30-11:30 pm. Closed Sun; major hols; also wk of July 4. Res accepted. Continental menu. Bar. Wine cellar. Semi-a la carte: lunch $6-$9, dinner $11-$25. Specialties: veal Oscar, châteaubriand bouquetière. Colonial decor; fireplace. Family-owned. Cr cds: A, C, D, DS, MC, V.

D ⊠

✔★ ★ **THE STATION AT HERITAGE VILLAGE.** *11th St & Veterans Memorial Blvd (25701). 304/523-6373.* Hrs: 11:30 am-9 pm. Closed Sun; Jan 1, Thanksgiving, Dec 25. Res accepted. Bar. Semi-a la carte: lunch, dinner $5.99-$16.99. Specializes in seafood, pasta, steak. Outdoor dining. Former railroad station built in 1887; memorabilia, antiques. Cr cds: A, D, DS, MC, V.

D ⊠

Lewisburg (E-5)

(See also White Sulphur Springs)

Founded 1782 **Pop** 3,598 **Elev** 2,099 ft **Area code** 304 **Zip** 24901 **Web** wvweb.com/www/LEWISBURG
Information Lewisburg Visitors Center, 105 Church St; 304/645-1000 or 800/833-2068.

At the junction of two important Native American trails, the Seneca (now US 219) and the Kanawha (now US 60), Lewisburg was the site of colonial forts as well as a Civil War battle. The town's 236-acre historic district has more than 60 buildings from the 18th and 19th centuries, in a variety of architectural styles.

What to See and Do

Lost World Caverns. Scenic trail over subterranean rock mountain; prehistoric ocean floor; stalagmites, stalactites; flow stone, ribbons, hex stones. Guided tours (daily; closed some major hols). 1 mi N on Fairview Rd. Phone 304/645-6677. ¢¢¢

North House Museum. Colonial and 19th-century objects and artifacts. (Tues-Sat) 101 W Church St, at Washington. Phone 304/645-3398. ¢¢

Old Stone Presbyterian Church (1796). Original log church (1783) was replaced by present structure. (Daily) 200 Church St. Phone 304/645-2676. **Free.**

Annual Event

State Fair. Fairgrounds, 2 mi S on US 219. Exhibitors from a number of other states; horse shows, harness racing. Phone 304/645-1090. Aug 14-22.

Motels

(Rates are generally higher during state fair)

★ ★ **BRIER INN.** *540 N Jefferson, jct US 219 & I-64 exit 169.* 304/645-7722; FAX 304/645-7865. 162 units, 2 story. S $42; D $47; each addl $5; suites $70-$75; kit. units $62-$67; under 12 free; higher rates state fair. Crib $5. Pet accepted, some restrictions; $10. TV; cable, VCR avail (movies). Pool. Restaurant 11 am-10 pm; Fri, Sat to 11 pm. Rm serv. Bar 10-2 am; entertainment Fri. Ck-out 11 am. Meeting rms. Business servs avail. In-rm modem link. Health club privileges. Cr cds: A, D, DS, MC, V.

✔ ★ **BUDGET HOST-FORT SAVANNAH INN.** *204 N Jefferson St.* 304/645-3055; FAX /; res: 800/678-3055. E-mail omb00827.@mall .wunit.edu. 66 rms, 2 story. S $36-$50; D $42-$65; each addl $5; under 18 free. Crib free. Pet accepted; $5. TV; cable. Pool; whirlpool. Restaurant 6 am-10 pm. Rm serv. Ck-out noon. Business servs avail. Airport transportation. Balconies. Cr cds: A, C, D, DS, MC, V.

★ **DAYS INN.** *635 N Jefferson St.* 304/645-2345; FAX 304/645-5501; res: 800/325-2525. 26 rms. S $48-$65; D $48-$85; each addl $5; higher rates special events. Crib free. Pet accepted, some restrictions; $10. TV; cable (premium). Complimentary coffee in lobby. Restaurant nearby. Ck-out 11 am. Business servs avail. Airport transportation. Cr cds: A, D, DS, MC, V.

Inn

★ ★ ★ **GENERAL LEWIS.** *301 E Washington St.* 304/645-2600; FAX 304/645-2600; res: 800/628-4454. Web www.innbook.com. 25 rms, 2 story. S $74-$94; D $85-$105; each addl $12; higher rates special evnts; package plans. Crib free. TV; cable. Dining rm 7 am-9 pm. Rm serv. Bar 11 am-9 pm. Ck-out 11 am. Part of building dates from 1834. Antiques; gardens. Totally nonsmoking. Cr cds: A, DS, MC, V.

Marlinton (D-5)

(See also Hillsboro)

Settled 1749 **Pop** 1,148 **Elev** 2,130 ft **Area code** 304 **Zip** 24954

Information Potomac Highland Travel Council, 1200 Harrison Ave, Lower Level, Suite A. Elkins 26241; 304/636-8400.

Marlinton is the seat of Pocahontas County, an area known for its wide variety of outdoor recreational opportunities. A Ranger District office of the Monongahela National Forest (see ELKINS) is located in the town.

What to See and Do

Cass Scenic Railroad State Park. Steam train makes 8-mi round trip (1¹/₂ hr) up the mountain to Whittaker (daily) and 22-mi round trip (4¹/₂ hr) to top of Bald Knob (daily exc Mon); picnic stopover; dinner trains (some Sat; call for reservation). On 1,089-acre property are 2 museums, a country store and 12 renovated logging camp houses now serving as tourist cottages. Picnicking. Camping. Standard hrs, fees. 5 mi E on WV 39, then 19 mi N on WV 28 to WV 66 in Cass. Phone 304/456-4300. Train ride ¢¢¢¢-¢¢¢¢¢

Cranberry Mountain Visitor Center-Monongahela National Forests. Exhibits, videos and publications on conservation and forest management. (June-Labor Day, daily; Jan-Apr, Oct-Nov, Sat-Sun; May & Sept, Fri-Sun) Approx 7 mi NW of Mill Point via US 219 & WV 39. Phone 304/653-4826 or 304/846-2695 (off-season). **Free.** 2 mi W is

Cranberry Glades. A USDA Forest Service botanical area. Approx 750 acres featuring open bog fringed by forest and alder thicket. Boardwalk with interpretive signs. Guided tours leave from visitor center (June-Labor Day, wkends). Glades (all-yr, weather permitting). **Free.**

Greenbrier River Trail. Part of the state park system, this 76-mi trail runs along the Greenbrier River from the town of Cass, on the north, through Marlinton to North Caldwell, on the south; passes through small towns, over 35 bridges and through 2 tunnels. Originally the trail was part of the Chesapeake & Ohio RR. Activities include backpacking, bicycling and cross-country skiing; trail also provides access for fishing and canoeing. No developed sites. Phone 304/799-4087.

National Radio Astronomy Observatory. Study of universe by radio telescopes. Slide show, exhibits and 1-hr bus tour of site. (Mid-June-Labor Day wkend, daily; Memorial Day wkend-mid-June & after Labor Day-Oct, Sat & Sun) 5 mi SE on WV 39, then 21 mi N on WV 28, 92 in Green Bank. Phone 304/456-2209. **Free.**

Pocahontas County Historical Museum. Displays on history of the county from its beginnings to present. Extensive photo collection. (Early June-Labor Day, daily) On US 219 S, at WV 39. Phone 304/799-4973. ¢

Seneca State Forest. Approx 12,000 acres with fishing and boating on 4-acre lake; hunting. Hiking trails. Picnicking, playground. Camping, 7 rustic cabins. Standard hrs, fees. 5 mi E via WV 39, then 10 mi NE on WV 28. Phone 304/799-6213.

Skiing.

Snowshoe Mountain Resort. 2 quad, 8 triple, double chairlifts; patrol, school, rentals; snowmaking; restaurants, lodging, nursery, health club, 4 pools. 53 slopes and trails; longest run 6,200 ft; vertical drop 1,500 ft. (Mid-Nov-mid-Apr, daily) Summer activities include horseback riding, fishing, hiking. 26 mi N on US 219, near Slatyfork. Phone 304/572-1000 or 304/572-4636 (ski report). ¢¢¢¢

Elk River Touring Center. Features 34 mi of cross-country trails in the Monongahela National Forests; patrol, school, rentals; restaurant; lodging. Night skiing. Guided tours. (All yr, daily) Also guided mountain bike tours, cave tours in season. 16 mi N on US 219, follow signs, near Slatyfork. Phone 304/572-3771. Skiing ¢¢¢¢

Annual Event

Pioneer Days. Craft exhibits and demonstrations; horse-pulling contests, frog and turtle races; bluegrass and mountain music shows; "4-by-4" pulling; parade; antique car show. Phone 304/799-4315. Early-mid-July.

Martinsburg (B-7)

(See also Berkeley Springs, Charles Town, Harpers Ferry, Shepherdstown; also see Hagerstown, MD)

Settled 1732 **Pop** 14,073 **Elev** 457 ft **Area code** 304 **Zip** 25401 **E-mail** chamber@intrepid.net **Web** wvweb.com/www/berkeley_chamber

Information Martinsburg-Berkeley County Chamber of Commerce, 198 Viking Way; 304/267-4841 or 800/332-9007.

Martinsburg is located in the center of an apple- and peach-producing region in the state's eastern panhandle. Because of its strategic location at the entrance to the Shenandoah Valley, the town was the site of several battles during the Civil War. The famous Confederate spy Belle Boyd was a resident. Officially chartered in 1778, Martinsburg is recognized for the preservation of its many 18th- and 19th-century houses and mercantile and industrial buildings.

What to See and Do

General Adam Stephen House (1789). Restored residence of Revolutionary War soldier and surgeon Adam Stephen, founder of Martinsburg. Period furnishings; restored smokehouse and log building. (May-Oct, Sat & Sun, limited hrs; also by appt) 309 E John St. Phone 304/267-4434. **Free.** Adj is

Triple-Brick Building. Completed in three sections just after the Civil War, the structure was used to house railroad employees. A museum of local history is located on the top two floors. (May-Oct, Sat & Sun, limited hrs; also by appt) **Free.**

Annual Event

Mountain State Apple Harvest Festival. Parade, celebrity breakfast, contests, entertainment, Apple Queen coronation, square dancing, grand ball, arts & crafts show. Phone 304/263-2500. 3rd wkend Oct.

Motels

★ ★ **COMFORT INN.** 2800 Aikens Center, exit 16E. 304/263-6200; FAX 304/263-6200, ext. 113. Web wvweb.com/www/comfort_inn_mtsbg.html. 110 rms, 4 story, 11 suites. Apr-Oct: S, D $69; each addl $10; suites $98; under 18 free; wkend, hols rates; lower rates rest of yr. Crib free. TV; cable. Pool. Complimentary continental bkfst. Restaurant adj 11 am-10 pm. Ck-out noon. Coin lndry. Meeting rms. Business servs avail. In-rm modem link. Sundries. Gift shop. Valet serv. Exercise rm: rower, bicycles. Game rm. Some refrigerators, microwaves, minibars. Cr cds: A, C, D, DS, JCB, MC, V.

D ⊠ ✕ ⊠ ⏁ SC

★ ★ **COMFORT SUITES.** US 9E & Short Rd, I-81 exit 12, E on US 9. 304/263-8888; FAX 304/263-1540. Web wvweb.com/www/comfort_suites. 76 rms, 3 story. May-Oct: S, D $65-$80; each addl $5; under 18 free; lower rates rest of yr. Crib free. TV; cable. Pool; whirlpool. Complimentary continental bkfst. Restaurant nearby. Ck-out 11 am. Meeting rms. Business servs avail. Coin lndry. Golf privileges. Exercise equipt; bicycles, weight machine. Refrigerators, microwaves. Cr cds: A, C, D, DS, ER, MC, V.

D ⏁ ✕ ⊠ ⏁ SC

★ **KNIGHTS INN.** 1599 Edwin Miller Blvd, I-81 exit 16E. 304/267-2211; FAX 304/267-9606. 59 rms, 1-2 story, 6 kits. Apr-Dec: S $46.95; D $55; each addl $5; kits. $46.95-$55; under 17 free; lower rates rest of yr. Crib free. Pet accepted. TV; cable (premium), VCR avail. Complimentary coffee in lobby. Restaurant adj 6 am-11 pm. Ck-out noon. Meeting rms. Business servs avail. Sundries. Refrigerators, microwaves avail. Cr cds: A, C, D, DS, MC, V.

D ➤ ⊠ ⏁ SC

★ **SUPER 8.** 1602 Edwin Miller Blvd, I-81, exit 16E. 304/263-0801. 43 rms, 3 story. June-Sept: S, D $43.88-$49.88; each addl $6; under 16 free; wkly, wkend rates; higher rates special events; lower rates rest of yr. Crib free. Pet accepted; $20 deposit. TV; cable (premium). Complimentary continental bkfst. Restaurant adj 6 am-11 pm. Ck-out 11 am. Meeting rms. Cr cds: A, C, D, DS, JCB, MC, V.

D ➤ ⊠ ⏁ SC

Hotel

★ ★ **HOLIDAY INN.** 301 Foxcroft Ave, I-81 exit 13. 304/267-5500; FAX 304/264-9157. 120 rms, 5 story. Apr-Oct: S, D $79-$90; each addl $10; under 17 free; lower rates rest of yr. Crib free. Pet accepted, some restrictions. TV; cable (premium), VCR avail. 2 pools, 1 indoor; whirlpool, lifeguard. Restaurant 6:30 am-10 pm; Sun 7 am-9 pm. Bar 4 pm-1 am. Ck-out noon. Meeting rms. Business servs avail. In-rm modem link. Lighted tennis, pro. Exercise rm; instructor, weight machines, bicycles, saunas. Lawn games. Some refrigerators. Cr cds: A, C, D, DS, ER, JCB, MC, V.

D ➤ ➤ ⊱ ✕ ✕ ⊠ ⏁ SC

Inn

★ ★ ★ **EDGEWOOD MANOR.** (Rte 2, Box 329, Bunker Hill 25413) 10 mi S on I-81, exit 5, 3 mi S on US 11. 304/229-9353; FAX 304/229-9379. Web www.wvweb.com/www/edgewood. 6 rms, 2 share bath, 3 story. No rm phones. S, D $95-$145; wkend, wkly, hol rates. Children over 12 yrs only. Complimentary full bkfst; afternoon refreshments. Complimentary coffee in rms. Ck-out noon, ck-in 3 pm. Luggage handling. Rec rm. Lawn games. Fireplaces. Some balconies. Picnic tables. Built in 1839; used as headquarters for Lt Gen Thomas J. "Stonewall" Jackson and Gen Robert E. Lee. Also used as hospital for both sides in Civil War. Totally nonsmoking. Cr cds: A, MC, V.

⊠ ⏁ SC

Resort

★ ★ ★ **THE WOODS RESORT & CONFERENCE CENTER.** (, Hedgesville 25427) 10 1/2 mi W of I-81 exit 16W via WV 9, then left on Mt Lake Rd 2 1/2 mi. 304/754-7977; FAX 304/754-8146; res: 800/248-2222. Web www.thewoodsresort.com. 60 rms in 3-bldg lodge, 14 kit. cabins. MAP: D $91.50-$111.50/person; EP: S, D $94-$127; each addl $11; kit. cabins $138; under 5 free; wkends 2-night min. Crib free. TV; cable (premium), VCR avail. 3 pools, 1 indoor; wading pools, whirlpool, lifeguard. Supervised child's activities (June-Aug); ages 5-18. Complimentary coffee in lobby. Dining rm 7 am-3 pm, 5-9 pm; Fri 5-10 pm; Sat 3-10 pm; Sun 3-9 pm. Box lunches, picnics. Bar noon-midnight; entertainment Sat. Ck-out noon, ck-in 4 pm. Grocery 2 1/2 mi. Coin lndry. Package store 12 mi. Meeting rms. Business servs avail. Indoor/outdoor lighted tennis. 27-hole golf privileges, greens fee, pro. Exercise equipt; weights, bicycles, sauna. Lawn games. Refrigerators; some fireplaces. Whirlpools in lodge rms. Private patios. Cr cds: A, C, D, DS, MC, V.

D ➤ ⏁ ⊱ ⊠ ✕ ⏁ ⏁

Moorefield (C-6)

(For accommodations see Petersburg)

Settled 1777 **Pop** 2,148 **Elev** 821 ft **Area code** 304 **Zip** 26836

Information Potomac Highland Travel Council, 1200 Harrison Ave, Lower Level, Suite A, Elkins 26241; 304/636-8400.

What to See and Do

Lost River State Park. More than 3,700 acres where Lee's White Sulphur Springs was once a famous resort; an original cabin still stands; museum.

Swimming pool, wading pool (Memorial Day-Labor Day). Hiking trails, horseback riding; tennis, game courts. Picnicking, playground, restaurant; 24 cabins. Recreation building; nature programs (summer); scenic overlooks. Standard hrs, fees. 18 mi E on WV 55 to Baker, then 13 mi S on WV 259, near Mathias. Phone 304/897-5372 or 800/CALL-WVA.

Annual Event

Hardy County Heritage Weekend. Tours of antebellum houses, medieval jousting, crafts, traditional events. Phone 304/538-6560. Last full wknd Sept.

Morgantown (B-5)

(See also Fairmont)

Settled 1776 **Pop** 25,879 **Elev** 892 ft **Area code** 304 **Zip** 26505 **Web** www.mgtn.com

Information Greater Morgantown Convention & Visitors Bureau, 709 Beechurst Ave, 304/292-5081 or 800/458-7373.

Morgantown is both an educational and industrial center. West Virginia University was founded here in 1867, the Morgantown Female Collegiate Institute in 1839. Known internationally for its glass, Morgantown is home to a number of glass plants, which produce wares ranging from lamp parts to decorative paper weights and crystal tableware. The town is also home to a number of research laboratories that are maintained by the federal government.

What to See and Do

Coopers Rock State Forest. More than 12,700 acres. Trout fishing, hunting. Hiking trails to historical sites; Henry Clay iron furnace (1834-1836). Cross-country ski trails. Picnicking, playground, concession. Tent & trailer camping. Standard hrs, fees. 10 mi E on I-68. Phone 304/594-1561. Adj is

Chestnut Ridge Regional Park. Swimming beach; fishing. Tent & trailer camping (hookups, dump station), rustic cabins, lodge (fees). Hiking. Picnicking. Cross-country ski trails (Dec-Feb). Nature center. Park (daily). Phone 304/594-1773.

West Virginia University (1867). (22,712 students) University has 15 colleges. Tours (daily exc Sun; for reservation phone 304/293-3489). The Visitors Center in the Communications Bldg on Patterson Dr has touch-screen monitors and video presentations about the university and upcoming special events (phone 304/293-6692 for 24-hr event information). Of special interest on the downtown campus are Stewart Hall and the university's original buildings, located on Woodburn Circle. In the Evansdale area of Morgantown are the Creative Arts Center, the 75-acre Core Arboretum, the 63,500-seat Coliseum and the

Cook-Hayman Pharmacy Museum. Re-creates pharmacy of yester-year with old patent medicines. (Mon-Fri; wknds by request; closed hols) Health Sciences Center North, Rm 1136. Phone 304/293-5101. **Donation.**

Personal Rapid Transit System (PRT). A pioneering transit system, the PRT is the world's first totally automated system. Operating without operators or ticket takers, computer-directed cars travel between university campuses and downtown Morgantown. (Daily exc Sun; may not operate certain hols and univ breaks) Phone 304/293-5011. One-way ¢

Whitewater rafting. Many outfitters offer guided trips on the Cheat and Tygart rivers. For a list of outfitters contact the West Virginia Division of Tourism, Telemarketing Dept, State Capitol Complex, Bldg 6, Rm 564, 1900 Kanawha Blvd E, Charleston 25305; 800/225-5982.

Annual Events

Mountaineer County Glass Festival. More than 50 glass companies present shows and exhibits; arts, entertainment. Mid-June.

Mason-Dixon Festival. Morgantown Riverfront Park. River parade, boat races, arts & crafts, concessions. Mid-Sept.

Mountaineer Balloon Festival. Morgantown Municipal Airport. Hot-air balloon races, carnival, music, food. Phone 304/296-8356. Mid-Oct.

Motels

★ ★ **COMFORT INN.** *Rte 9, Box 225, At jct US 68, US 119.* 304/296-9364; FAX 304/296-0469. 81 rms, 2 story. S $45-$100; D $49-$100; each addl $6; suites $80-$125; kit. units $45-$100; under 18 free; higher rates: football wkends, graduation. Crib free. TV; cable (premium), VCR avail. Heated pool; whirlpool. Complimentary continental bkfst. Restaurant adj 11:30 am-10:30 pm; Fri, Sat to 2 pm; Sun to 4 pm. Ck-out noon. Meeting rm. Business servs avail. Valet serv. Sundries. Exercise equipt; weights, bicycles. Cr cds: A, C, D, DS, ER, JCB, MC, V.

[D] [≈] [X] [⊗] [🔥] [SC]

★ **DAYS INN.** *(366 Boyers Ave, Star City) 1 mi N on US 19, WV 7.* 304/598-2120; FAX 304/598-3272. 102 rms, 3 story. Apr-Oct: S $53; D $61; each addl $8; under 12 free; higher rates: football games, graduation; lower rates rest of yr. Crib free. TV; cable (premium), VCR avail. Indoor pool; whirlpool. Complimentary full bkfst. Restaurant 6:30 am-9 pm. Rm serv. Bar 5 pm-midnight; entertainment. Ck-out 11 am. Coin lndry. Meeting rm. Business servs avail. Exercise equipt; weight machines, bicycles, steam rm. Cr cds: A, C, D, DS, JCB, MC, V.

[D] [≈] [X] [⊗] [🔥] [SC]

★ **ECONO LODGE.** *(15 Commerce Dr, Westover) I-79 exit 152.* 304/296-8774. 81 rms, 2 story. S $42; D $48; each addl $5; under 18 free. Crib free. TV, VCR avail (movies $5). Restaurant nearby. Ck-out noon. Business servs avail. Cr cds: A, C, D, DS, JCB, MC, V.

[D] [⊗] [🔥] [SC]

✔ ★ **ECONO LODGE-COLISEUM.** *3506 Monongahela Blvd.* 304/599-8181; FAX 304/599-4866. 71 rms, 2 story. S, D $59; each addl $5; higher rates: football wkends, graduation. Crib $5. Pet accepted. TV; VCR avail. Restaurant adj 6 am-midnight. Ck-out 11 am. Meeting rm. Business servs avail. Sundries. Cr cds: A, D, DS, MC, V.

[D] [✔] [⊗] [🔥] [SC]

✔ ★ **FRIENDSHIP INN-MOUNTAINEER.** *452 Country Club Rd, near University Medical Center.* 304/599-4850; FAX 304/599-4866. 30 rms, 1-2 story. S, D $34-$44; each addl $5; higher rates: football wkends, graduation. Crib $5. Pet accepted. TV; cable. Restaurant adj 7 am-11 pm. Ck-out 11 am. Business servs avail. Cr cds: A, D, DS, MC, V.

[D] [✔] [⊗] [🔥] [SC]

★ ★ **HAMPTON INN.** *1053 Van Voorhis Rd, I-79 exit 155.* 304/599-1200; FAX 304/598-7331. 108 rms, 5 story. S $59-$68; D $63-$75; suites $100; under 18 free; higher rates special events. Crib free. TV; cable. Complimentary continental bkfst. Restaurant nearby. Ck-out noon. Meeting rms. Business servs avail. In-rm modem link. Valet serv. Cr cds: A, C, D, DS, MC, V.

[D] [⊗] [🔥] [SC]

★ ★ **HOLIDAY INN.** *1400 Saratoga Ave.* 304/599-1680; FAX 304/598-0989. 147 rms, 2 story. S, D $45-$66; under 18 free; higher rates: graduation, athletic events. Crib free. Pet accepted. TV; cable. Pool. Restaurant 6 am-2 pm, 5-10 pm. Rm serv. Bar 4 pm-2 am. Ck-out noon. Meeting rms. Business servs avail. Balconies. Cr cds: A, C, D, DS, ER, MC, V.

[D] [✔] [≈] [⊗] [🔥] [SC]

Motor Hotel

★ ★ **RAMADA INN.** *Box 1242, 3 mi S on US 119 at jct US 68 & I-79 exit 148.* 304/296-3431. 159 rms, 4 story. S $55-$85; D $60-$85; each addl $5; suites, studio rms $100-$185; under 18 free; higher rates: special events, football games, Dec 31, Memorial Day wkend, graduation. Crib free. TV; cable (premium). Pool; lifeguard. Restaurant 6 am-10 pm. Private club 11-2 am; entertainment, dancing exc Sun. Ck-out noon. Meeting rms. Business servs avail. In-rm modem link. Sundries. Gift shop. Free airport transportation. Exercise equipt; weights, stair machine. Game rm. Cr cds: A, C, D, DS, JCB, MC, V.

Hotel

✔★ **MORGAN.** *127 High St.* 304/292-8401; FAX 304/292-8200. 40 rms, 7 story, 27 kit. suites. S, D $40-$45; kit. suites $60-$100; under 12 free; wkly, monthly rates; higher rates: football season, graduation. TV; cable. Ck-out 11 am. Meeting rms. Business servs avail. Some refrigerators. Historic brick hotel (1925). Cr cds: A, DS, MC, V.

Resort

★ ★ ★ **LAKEVIEW RESORT AND CONFERENCE CENTER.** *1 Lakeview Dr, 7 mi N, 1/4 mi S off WV 857; 1/4 mi N of US 68 exit 10.* 304/594-1111; FAX 304/594-9472; res: 800/624-8300. 187 rms, 1-3 story. Apr-Nov: S $135; D $145; each addl $10; suites $225-$375; under 18 free; summer, winter rates; golf plans; lower rates rest of yr. Crib free. TV; cable. 4 pools, 2 indoor; wading pool, whirlpool, poolside serv, lifeguard. Dining rms 6:30 am-10 pm. Bar 11-1 am, Sun from 1 pm; entertainment, dancing exc Sun. Ck-out 2 pm, ck-in 4 pm. Meeting rms. Business servs avail. Valet serv. Gift shop. Free airport transportation. Indoor/outdoor tennis. Two 18-hole golf courses, greens fee $20-$40, pro. Rec rm. Exercise rm; instructor, weight machines, weights, sauna. Massage. Some refrigerators. On 400 acres. Cr cds: A, C, D, DS, MC, V.

Restaurants

★ ★ **BACK BAY.** *1869 Mileground, near airport.* 304/296-3027. Hrs: 11 am-9:30 pm; Fri to 10:30 pm; Sat 4-10:30 pm; Sun noon-9 pm. Closed major hols. Bar. Semi-a la carte: lunch $3.95-$7.95, dinner $5.95-$19.95. Specializes in fresh seafood, prime rib, Cajun dishes. Nautical atmosphere. Cr cds: A, DS, MC, V.

★ ★ **THE FLAME STEAK HOUSE.** *76 High St.* 304/296-2976. Hrs: 5-11 pm. Closed major hols. Res accepted. Private club. Complete meals: dinner $6.45-$21.95. Child's meals. Specializes in steak, fresh seafood, Italian dishes. Colonial decor. Family-owned. Cr cds: A, D, DS, MC, V.

Nitro (D-3)

(See also Charleston)

Founded 1918 **Pop** 6,851 **Elev** 604 ft **Area code** 304 **Zip** 25143 **Web** www.newwave.net/~putcochamber

Information Putnam County Chamber of Commerce, PO Box 553, Teays 25569; 304/757-6510.

Nitro experienced explosive growth around a huge smokeless powder plant during World War I, when the town's population reached 35,000 overnight and some 3,400 buildings were erected. When the war ended, the demand for smokeless powder fizzled, and the town dried up; factory buildings were scrapped, and whole houses were shipped down the river. Now a western suburb of Charleston, Nitro produces chemicals.

What to See and Do

Tri-State Greyhound Park. Indoor grandstand, clubhouse, concessions. (Mon-Sat evenings; matinees Sat, Sun & hols) Must be 18 to wager. E via I-64 exit 47a to Goff Mountain Rd, then to Greyhound Dr in Cross Lanes. Phone 304/776-1000.

Waves of Fun. Water park featuring three water slides, wave pool, swimming areas; bathhouse, tube rentals (fee), lockers, concessions. (Memorial Day-early June, wkends; early June-Labor Day, daily) W via I-64 exit 39, then 3 mi S on WV 34, at Valley Park in Hurricane. Phone 304/562-0518. ¢¢¢

Motels

✔★ **BEST WESTERN MOTOR INN.** *4115 1st Ave.* 304/755-8341; FAX 304/755-2933. 42 rms, 1-3 story. No elvtr. S $42-$55; D $44-$60; each addl $5; under 12 free. Crib $6.50. TV; cable (premium). Restaurant adj open 24 hrs. Ck-out 11 am. Business servs avail. Cr cds: A, C, D, DS, MC, V.

★ **COMFORT INN.** *(102 Racer Dr, Cross Lanes 25313) E on I-64 exit 47 to Goff Mountain Rd.* 304/776-8070; FAX 304/776-6460. 112 rms, 2 story. S $52-$66; D $62; each addl $5; under 18 free. Crib free. TV; cable (premium). Pool; whirlpool. Coffee in rms. Complimentary continental bkfst. Restaurant adj 7 am-midnight. Bar 4 pm-1 am; Fri, Sat to 2 am. Ck-out noon. Meeting rms. Business servs avail. Sundries. Microwaves avail. Cr cds: A, C, D, DS, ER, MC, V.

✔★ ★ **RAMADA LIMITED.** *(419 Hurricane Creek Rd, Hurricane 25526) W on US 60.* 304/562-3346; FAX 304/562-7408. 147 rms, 2 story. Apr-Sept: S, D $45-$55; each addl $5; under 16 free; wkly rates; higher rates special events; lower rates rest of yr. Crib free. Pet accepted, some restrictions; $5. TV; cable (premium). Complimentary continental bkfst. Restaurant adj 7 am-10 pm. Ck-out noon. Meeting rms. Business servs avail. Sundries. Pool. Some refrigerators. Microwaves avail. Picnic tables, grills. Cr cds: A, C, D, DS, JCB, MC, V.

Restaurant

★ **DIEHL'S.** *152 Main Ave.* 304/755-9353. Hrs: 10:30 am-9 pm. Closed Mon. Semi-a la carte: lunch $3-$6, dinner $3.50-$7. Specializes in home cooked meals. Casual decor. Cr cds: DS, MC, V.

Parkersburg (C-3)

Settled 1785 **Pop** 33,862 **Elev** 616 ft **Area code** 304 **Zip** 26101 **E-mail** Parkersburg@citynet.net **Web** wvweb.com/www/PARKERSBURG

Information Parkersburg/Wood Co Convention & Visitor's Bureau, 350 7th St; 304/428-1130 or 800/752-4982.

In 1770, George Washington came to this area to inspect lands awarded to him by Virginia for his military services. After the Revolution, Blennerhassett Island, in the Ohio River west of Parkersburg, was the scene of the alleged Burr-Blennerhassett plot. Harman Blennerhassett, a wealthy Irishman, built a lavish mansion on this island. After killing Alexander Hamilton in a duel, Aaron Burr came to the island, allegedly with the idea of seizing the Southwest and setting up an empire; Blennerhassett may have agreed to join him. On December 10, 1806, the plot was uncovered. Both men were acquitted of treason but were, in the process, ruined financially. The Blennerhassett mansion burned in 1811, but was later rebuilt.

Today, Parkersburg is the center for many industries, including glass, chemicals, petrochemicals and ferrous and other metals. Fishing is popular in the area, especially below the Belleville and Willow Island locks and dams on the Ohio River.

What to See and Do

Actors Guild Playhouse. Musical, comedic and dramatic performances. (Fri-Sun) 8th & Market Sts. Phone 304/485-1300. ¢¢¢

Blennerhassett Island Historical State Park. A 500-acre island accessible only by sternwheeler. There are self-guided walking tours of the island; horse-drawn wagon rides; tours of the Blennerhassett mansion. Bicycle rentals. Picnicking, concession. (May-Labor Day, daily exc Mon, also hols; Sept-Oct, Thurs-Sun) Tickets avail for boat ride, mansion tour and Blennerhassett Museum. 2 mi S in Ohio River. Phone 304/420-4800. Mansion tour ¢¢

Blennerhassett Museum. Features archaeological and other exhibits relating to history of Blennerhassett Island and Parkersburg area; includes artifacts dating back 12,000 yrs. Theater with video presentation. (May-Oct, daily exc Mon; rest of yr, Sat & Sun; closed Jan 1, Thanksgiving, Dec 25) 2nd & Juliana Sts. Phone 304/420-4800. ¢

City Park. A 55-acre wooded area with the Cooper Log Cabin Museum, which dates from 1804. Swimming pool; fishing; paddle boats. Miniature golf, tennis. Shelters and picnic facilities. Park Ave & 23rd St.

Industrial tour. Middleton Doll Company. Tour of vinyl and porcelain doll factory (20 min). Factory store (daily exc Sun). (June-Aug, Tues-Sat; rest of yr, Mon-Fri; closed hols) 2 mi W via US 50, at 1301 Washington Blvd in Belpre, OH. Phone 614/423-1481or 800/233-7479. **Free.**

Mountwood Park. Wooded area with fishing, boating (no gasoline motors); hiking, mountain biking and OHV trails, nature trails; picnic area. 12 mi E via US 50 to Volcano Rd. Phone 304/679-3611. **Free.**

North Bend State Park. Approx 1,400 acres in the wide valley of the North Fork of the Hughes River; scenic overlooks of famous horseshoe bend. Swimming pool, bathhouse; fishing. Miniature golf; tennis, game courts. Hiking, bicycle, bridle trail; 71-mi North Bend Rail Trail (see CLARKSBURG). Picnicking, playground, concession, restaurant, lodge (see MOTELS). Tent & trailer camping (dump station), eight cabins. Nature, recreation programs. Nature trail for disabled. Standard hrs, fees. 22 mi E on US 50, then 7 mi SE on WV 31, near Cairo. Phone 304/643-2931 or 800/CALL-WVA.

Parkersburg Art Center. Changing exhibits. (Daily exc Mon; closed hols) 220 8th St. Phone 304/485-3859. ¢

Ruble's Sternwheelers Riverboat Cruises. To Blennerhassett Island. (Early May-early Sept, daily exc Mon; early Sept-Oct, Thurs-Sun) Depart from Point Park, 2nd & Ann Sts. Phone 614/423-7268. ¢¢

Annual Events

Parkersburg Homecoming. Point Park, just off WV 68 at foot of 2nd St. Riverfront celebration features entertainment, parade, stern-wheeler races, waterskiing show, miniature car races, fireworks. Phone 304/422-3588. 3rd wkend Aug.

West Virginia Honey Festival. City Park. Honey-related exhibits, baking, food, arts and crafts. Mid-Sept.

Motels

★ ★ ★ **HOLIDAY INN.** *US Rte 50 & I-77, 3¹/₂ mi E on US 50, at jct I-77.* 304/485-6200; FAX 304/485-6200, ext. 350. 148 rms, 2 story. S, D $59-$70; under 18 free; wkend packages. Crib free. TV. Indoor pool; whirlpool, sauna. Restaurant 7 am-2 pm, 5-10 pm. Rm serv. Bar 11-2 am; entertainment. Ck-out noon. Coin lndry. Meeting rms. Business servs avail. Bellhops. Game rm. Some refrigerators. Some balconies. Cr cds: A, D, DS, JCB, MC, V.

D ⚊ ⚊ ⚊ SC

★ ★ **NORTH BEND LODGE.** *(US 1, Box 221, Cairo 26337) 22 mi E on US 50, then 7 mi SE on WV 31, in North Bend State Park.* 304/643-2931; FAX 304/643-2970; res: 800/225-5982. 29 rms, 2 story, 8 cabins. Memorial Day wkend-Labor Day: S $53; D $59; each addl $6; 2-3 bedrm cabins $517-$592/wk; under 12 free; lower rates rest of yr. TV, VCR avail. Pool. Playground adj. Free supervised child's activities (June-Aug). Restaurant 7 am-9 pm. Ck-out noon (lodge), 10 am (cabins). Business servs avail. Sundries. Tennis. Picnic tables, grills. On river. View of mountains. State owned, operated. Cr cds: A, MC, V.

D ⚊ ⚊ ⚊ ⚊ ⚊ SC

★ **RED ROOF INN.** *3714 7th St.* 304/485-1741; FAX 304/485-1746. 107 rms, 2 story. S $36.99-$45.99; D $41.99-$48.99; each addl $5; under 18 free. Crib free. Pet accepted. TV; cable (premium). Ck-out noon. Meeting rms. Business servs avail. In-rm modem link. Cr cds: A, C, D, DS, MC, V.

D ⚊ ⚊ ⚊ SC

Hotel

★ ★ ★ **CLARION CARRIAGE HOUSE INN-BLENNERHASSETT.** *4th & Market Sts.* 304/422-3131; FAX 304/485-0267. 103 rms, 5 story. S, D $69-$74; each addl $6; suites $75-$95; under 18 free. Crib free. TV; cable (premium), VCR avail. Coffee in rms. Restaurant 6 am-10 pm. Bar 11-1 am. Ck-out noon. Meeting rms. Business center. In-rm modem link. Gift shop. Valet parking. Free airport transportation. Health club privileges. Restored Victorian hotel built in 1889. Cr cds: A, C, D, DS, ER, MC, V.

D ⚊ ⚊ SC ⚊

Restaurants

✔★ **MOUNTAINEER.** *4006 Seventh St, at jct US 50 & I-77.* 304/422-0101. Open 24 hrs. Closed Dec 25. Semi-a la carte: bkfst $1.95-$4.95, lunch $1.95-$5.95, dinner $3.95-$11.95. Child's meals. Specializes in steak, seafood, chicken. No cr cds accepted.

D SC ♥

★ ★ **POINT OF VIEW.** *Blennerhassett Heights Rd, 3 mi SW via WV 68, Star Ave exit.* 304/863-3366. Hrs: 11:30 am-2:30 pm, 5-9:30 pm. Closed major hols. Semi-a la carte: lunch $4-$8, dinner $9-$22. Child's meals. Specializes in prime rib, fresh seafood, steak. Own baking. Open-hearth grill; fireplace. View of Blennerhasset Island. Family-owned. Cr cds: A, D, DS, MC, V.

⚊

Petersburg (C-6)

(See also Franklin, Moorefield)

Settled 1745 **Pop** 2,360 **Elev** 937 ft **Area code** 304 **Zip** 26847

Information Potomac Highland Travel Council, 1200 Harrison Ave, Lower Level, Suite A, Elkins 26241; 304/636-8400.

A Ranger District office (phone 304/257-4488) of the Monongahela National Forest (see ELKINS) is located in Petersburg.

What to See and Do

Monongahela National Forest. Recreation area is popular for canoeing, hiking and other outdoor sports. Camping (fee). USDA Forest Service, H659, PO Box 240. Phone 304/257-4488. **Free.**

Smoke Hole Caverns. Caverns were used centuries ago by the Seneca both for shelter and the smoking of meat. During the Civil War, they were used by troops on both sides for storing ammunition. Later, they hid the illegal distillation of corn whiskey. It is claimed the caverns contain the longest ribbon stalactite and the second-highest cave room in the world. Guided tours. Large gift shop with wildlife exhibits; concessions. (Daily; closed Thanksgiving, Dec 25) 8 mi S on WV 28 & 55. Phone 304/257-4442. ¢¢¢

Motels

★ ★ **HERMITAGE MOTOR INN.** *203 Virginia Ave. 304/257-1711; FAX 304/257-4330; res: 800/437-6482.* 39 rms, 2 story. S $33-$41; D $39-$47; each addl $6; under 12 free. Crib $10. TV; cable (premium). Pool; whirlpool. Restaurant 11 am-9 pm; Fri-Sat to 10 pm. Ck-out noon. Business servs avail. In-rm modem link. Airport transportation. Craft shop, bookstore in 1840s inn. Cr cds: A, C, D, DS, MC, V.

★ **SMOKE HOLE CAVERNS MOTEL.** *(HC 59, Box 39, Seneca Rocks 26884) 12 mi S on WV 28/55. 304/257-4442; FAX 304/257-2745; res: 800/828-8478.* 13 rms, 3 suites, 18 cottages. S $25-$45; D $45-$55; each addl $10; kit. cottages $69.50-$109.50; family, wkly rates; varied lower rates. TV; cable. Pool. Playground. Ck-out 11 am. Gift shop. Lawn games. Refrigerators in cabins. Adj Smoke Hole Caverns. Cr cds: A, DS, MC, V.

Philippi (C-5)

(See also Buckhannon, Clarksburg, Grafton)

Settled 1780 **Pop** 3,132 **Elev** 1,307 ft **Area code** 304 **Zip** 26416
Information Philippi-Barbour County Chamber of Commerce, PO Box 5000; 304/457-1958.

The first land battle of the Civil War, a running rout of the Confederates known locally as the Philippi Races, was fought here on June 3, 1861. An historical marker on the campus of Alderson-Broaddus College marks the site. The Union attacked to protect the Baltimore & Ohio Railroad, whose main line between Washington and the West ran near the town.

What to See and Do

Barbour County Historical Society Museum. This B & O Railroad station (1911), used until 1956, is now restored as a museum; also local arts & crafts. (May-Oct, daily; rest of yr, by appt) 146 N Main St. For further information contact the Chamber of Commerce.

Covered bridge. Spanning Tygart River since 1852; restored in recent years; believed to be the only two-lane bridge of its type still in daily use on a federal highway (US 250).

Annual Events

Blue & Gray Reunion. Commemorates the first land battle of the Civil War; reenactment, parade, crafts. 1st wkend June.

Barbour County Fair. Fairgrounds, 5 mi SE on US 250. Horse and antique car shows, quilt and livestock exhibits, carnival rides, nightly entertainment, parade and more. Phone 304/457-3254. Wk before Labor Day.

Motel

★ **SUPER 8.** *US 250. 304/457-5888.* 40 rms, 2 story. S $41.88-$47.88; D $49.88-$57.88; each addl $6; under 12 free. Crib free. TV; cable (premium). Complimentary coffee in lobby. Restaurant adj 6 am-9 pm. Ck-out 11 am. Business servs avail. Some refrigerators. Cr cds: A, C, D, DS, MC, V.

Restaurant

✔ ★ **PHILIPPI INN.** *On US 250S. 304/457-1733.* Hrs: 6 am-9 pm; Fri, Sat to 9:30 pm; Sun 7 am-9 pm. Closed Dec 25. Res accepted. Semi-a la carte: bkfst, lunch $1.95-$5.95, dinner $3.95-$7.95. Child's meals. Specializes in prime rib, steak. Own pies. Family-owned. Cr cds: MC, V.

Point Pleasant (C-3)

(See also Ripley)

Settled 1774 **Pop** 4,996 **Elev** 569 ft **Area code** 304 **Zip** 25550
Information Mason County Area Chamber of Commerce, 305 Main St; 304/675-1050.

On October 10, 1774, British-incited Shawnees under Chief Cornstalk fought a battle here against 1,100 frontiersmen. The colonists won and broke the Native American power in the Ohio Valley. Historians later argued that this, rather than the battle at Lexington, Massachusetts, was the first battle of the Revolutionary War. In 1908, the US Senate rewrote history by recognizing this claim.

What to See and Do

Krodel Park and Lake. A 44-acre park with a replica of Fort Randolph (ca 1775). Fishing (license required); paddle boats (fee). Miniature golf (fee). Playground. Camping (mid-Apr-Oct; fee). 1 mi SE via WV 62/2. Phone 304/675-1068 (seasonal). **Free.**

McClintic Wildlife Management Area. Approx 2,800 acres with primitive camping (fee). Also hunting, fishing (licenses required). 7 mi NE off WV 62. Phone 304/675-0871.

Point Pleasant Battle Monument State Park. An 84-ft granite shaft was erected here in 1909, after the US Senate agreed to a claim made by historians that the first battle of the Revolutionary War was fought here. Park also contains a marker where Joseph Celeron de Bienville buried a leaden plate in 1749, claiming the land for France, and the graves of Chief Cornstalk and "Mad Anne" Bailey, noted pioneer scout. 1 Main St, in Tu-Endie-Wei Park (Native American for "where two rivers meet"). Phone 304/675-0869. **Free.** Also here is

Mansion House (1796). Oldest log building in Kanawha Valley, restored as a museum. (May-Oct, daily) Phone 304/675-0869. **Free.**

West Virginia State Farm Museum. Contains more than 30 farm buildings depicting early rural life, including a log church, one-room schoolhouse, kitchen, scale house and 4-unit stable. Barn contains mount of one of the largest horses in the world; also animals. (Apr-Nov, daily exc Mon) 4 mi N via WV 62, adj to county fairgrounds. Phone 304/675-5737. **Free.**

Annual Event

Mason County Fair. County Fairgrounds. Livestock show, arts & crafts, contests, Nashville entertainers. Phone 304/675-5463. Mid-Aug.

Motel

★ ★ **LOWE.** *401 Main St. 304/675-2260; res: 800/280-8489.* 30 rms, 3 story. S $38; $42; suites $48-$54. Crib free. TV; cable (premium); VCR avail. Complimentary coffee in lobby. Restaurant nearby. Ck-out noon. Meeting rms. Business servs avail. Some refrigerators. Cr cds: A, C, D, DS, MC, V.

Princeton (E-4)

(See also Bluefield)

Settled 1826 **Pop** 7,043 **Elev** 2,446 ft **Area code** 304 **Zip** 24740
Information Princeton-Mercer County Chamber of Commerce, 910 Oakvale Rd; 304/487-1502.

Princeton is the southern terminus of the spectacular 88-mile West Virginia Turnpike and a trade center for an agricultural, industrial and coal mining area.

What to See and Do

Camp Creek State Park. Approx 500 acres. Fishing. Hiking trails, game courts. Picnicking, playgrounds. Camping. Standard hrs, fees. 13 mi N on I-77, exit 20, then 2 mi NW, near Camp Creek. Phone 304/425-9481.

Motels

✔★★ **COMFORT INN.** *1909 Harper Rd, Ambrose Lane & US 460W.* 304/487-6101; FAX 304/425-7002. 51 rms, 2 story. S, D $60-$90; each addl $6; under 18 free. Crib free. TV; cable (premium). Complimentary continental bkfst. Restaurant nearby. Ck-out noon. Business servs avail. Downhill ski 20 mi. Whirlpool. Cr cds: A, D, DS, MC, V.

★ **DAYS INN.** *347 Meadowfield Ln.* 304/425-8100; FAX 304/487-1734. 122 rms, 2 story. S $58-$63; D $63-$68; kit. units $67-$75; under 16 free. Crib free. Pet accepted. TV; cable. Indoor pool; whirlpool. Complimentary continental bkfst. Restaurant adj 6 am-10 pm. Ck-out 11 am. Business servs avail. Sundries. Downhill ski 15 mi. Cr cds: A, C, D, DS, JCB, MC, V.

Restaurant

★ **JOHNSTON'S INN.** *On US 460 (Old Oakvale Rd).* 304/425-7591. Hrs: 6:30 am-10:30 pm; Sun to 10 pm. Closed Thanksgiving, Dec 25. Res accepted. Bar from 11:30 am; Sun 3-10 pm. Semi-a la carte: bkfst $2-$5.50, lunch $5-$7, dinner $8-$15.95. Child's meals. Specializes in steak, seafood, desserts. Salad bar. Own salad dressings. Tiffany lamps, artwork, antiques. Family-owned. Cr cds: A, C, D, DS, MC, V.

SC ⬛

Ripley (C-3)

(See also Point Pleasant)

Settled 1768 **Pop** 3,023 **Elev** 616 ft **Area code** 304 **Zip** 25271

What to See and Do

Washington's Lands Museum and Park. Housed in converted river lock building and restored Sayre Log House; exhibits trace the pioneer and river history of the area. Park, on the Ohio River, has picnicking and boat launching facilities. Museum (by appt). 6 mi N via I-77 exit 146 to Ravenswood, then 2½ mi S on WV 68. Phone public library, 304/372-5343. **Donation.**

Annual Events

Mountaineer State Art & Craft Fair. Cedar Lakes Conference Center. Features traditional crafts, art, folk music and foods. Phone 304/372-7860 or 304/372-7866. Early July.

West Virginia Black Walnut Festival. 25 mi E on US 33/119 in Spencer. Parade, carnival, band festival, car show, contests, livestock show, arts & crafts. Phone 304/927-1780. Mid-Oct.

Motels

★★ **BEST WESTERN McCOYS.** *701 W Main St (US 33), I-77 exit 138.* 304/372-9122; FAX 304/372-4400. 127 rms, 2 story. S, D $50-$56; each addl $4; under 12 free. Crib $3. TV; cable. Pool. Complimentary continental bkfst. Restaurant 5-10 pm; Sun 10 am-3 pm. Rm serv. Private club. Ck-out 11 am. Coin lndry. Meeting rms. Business servs avail. Sundries. Cr cds: A, C, D, DS, ER, JCB, MC, V.

🐾 ≈ ⊠ ⬛ SC

✔★ **HOLIDAY INN EXPRESS.** *1 Hospitality Dr, I-77 exit 138N, near hospital.* 304/372-5000; FAX 304/372-5600. 43 rms, 2 story. S $50-$55; D $55-$60; each addl $4; under 18 free; higher rates Mountain State Arts & Crafts Fair. TV; cable. Complimentary continental bkfst. Restaurant adj 6:30 am-11 pm. Ck-out 11 am. Business servs avail. Cr cds: A, C, D, DS, ER, JCB, MC, V.

D ⊠ ⬛ SC

Shepherdstown (B-8)

(See also Charles Town, Harpers Ferry, Martinsburg; also see Frederick, Hagerstown, MD)

Settled ca 1730 **Pop** 1,287 **Elev** 406 ft **Area code** 304 **Zip** 25443
Information Jefferson County Chamber of Commerce, 201 Frontage Rd, PO Box 426, Charles Town 25414; 304/725-2055.

In 1787, Shepherdstown was the site of the first successful public launching of a steamboat. James Rumsey, inventor of the craft, died, however, before he could exploit his success. Rival claims by John Fitch, and Robert Fulton's commercial success with the *Clermont* 20 years later, have beclouded Rumsey's achievement.

The state's first newspaper was published here in 1790, and Shepherdstown almost became the national capital. (George Washington considered it as a possible site, according to letters in the Library of Congress.) Shepherdstown is also the location of one of the early gristmills, which is believed to have been constructed around 1739 and finally ceased production in 1939. This is the oldest continuously settled town in the state.

What to See and Do

Historic Shepherdstown Museum. Artifacts dating to 1700s, including many items concerning the founding of the town. Guided tours (by appt). (Apr-Oct, daily) In old Entler Hotel (1786), German & Princess Sts. Phone 304/876-0910. **Free.** Also avail here are

Guided walking tours of historic sites in Shepherdstown. Phone 304/876-0910. ¢¢

Inns

★★★★ **BAVARIAN INN AND LODGE.** *WV 480, ¼ mi N on WV 480 at the Potomac Bridge.* 304/876-2551; FAX 304/876-9355. Web www.intrepid.net/bavarian_inn. Situated above the Potomac, this inn includes a grey stone main lodge and chalets reminiscent of old Bavarian inns. The luxurious guest rooms have canopy beds. 71 rms, 2 in main bldg, 1-3 story, 4 chalets. S, D $85-$165; each addl $10; suites $195-$275; under 12 free; wkday package rates; golf plan. Crib $10. TV; cable (premium), VCR avail. Pool. Complimentary coffee, tea. Dining rm (see

BAVARIAN INN AND LODGE RESTAURANT). Bar 5 pm-midnight; Sun from 1 pm. Ck-out noon, ck-in 3 pm. Meeting rms. Business servs avail. In-rm modem link. Tennis. Golf privileges, putting green. Exercise equipt; weight machine, bicycles. In-rm whirlpools, fireplaces. Balconies. Cr cds: A, C, D, DS, MC, V.

⬚🖬🏃‍🕉‍🌊🍴🌊🔥

★ ★ ★ **THOMAS SHEPHERD INN.** *300 W German St.* 304/876-3715; res: 888/889-8952; FAX 304/876-3313. Web www.intrepid.net/thomas_shepherd. 7 rms, 2 story. S, D $85-$95; higher rates wkends. Children over 8 yrs only. TV, VCR in sitting rm (movies). Complimentary full bkfst. Restaurant nearby. Ck-out 11 am, ck-in 3 pm. Business servs avail. Tennis privileges. Golf privileges. Fireplaces. Federal-style house (1868) on land originally owned by town founder Thomas Shepherd. Totally nonsmoking. Cr cds: A, MC, V.

🏃‍🕉‍🌊🔥 SC

Restaurants

★ ★ ★ **BAVARIAN INN AND LODGE.** *(See Bavarian Inn and Lodge)* 304/876-2551. Hrs: 7:30-10:30 am, 11:30 am-2:30 pm, 5-10 pm; Sat from 4 pm; Sun noon-9 pm. Res accepted. German, continental menu. Bar 5 pm-midnight; Sun from 1 pm. Wine list. Semi-a la carte: bkfst $4.50-$9.75, lunch $5.50-$12, dinner $13.50-$22.50. Child's meals. Specializes in sauerbraten, vegetarian dishes. Own baking. Entertainment. Fireplaces. Antiques. Overlooks Potomac River. Family-owned. Cr cds: A, C, D, DS, MC, V.

⬚🖬

★ **OLD PHARMACY CAFÉ.** *138 E German St.* 304/876-2085. Hrs: 11 am-9 pm; Fri, Sat to 10 pm. Closed Jan. Res accepted. Wine, beer. Semi-a la carte: lunch $4.95-$7.95, dinner $9.95-$14.95. Child's meals. Specializes in gourmet sandwiches, vegetarian dishes, soup. In former pharmacy (1911); many original pieces including a marble soda fountain. Totally nonsmoking. Cr cds: A, C, D, DS, MC, V.

⬚

★ ★ ★ **YELLOW BRICK BANK & LITTLE INN.** *201 German at Princess St, downtown.* 304/876-2208. Hrs: 11:30 am-10 pm; Sun brunch 11 am-4 pm. Closed Thanksgiving, Dec 25. Res accepted. Bar. A la carte entrees: lunch $5-$14, dinner $12-$20. Sun brunch $5-$14. Specializes in seafood, pasta, regional cuisine. Own baking. In 1910 bank building in historic commercial district. Overnight stays avail. Cr cds: C, D, MC, V.

⬚🖬

Summersville (D-4)

(See also Gauley Bridge)

Founded 1824 **Pop** 2,906 **Elev** 1,894 ft **Area code** 304 **Zip** 26651
Information Chamber of Commerce, 411 Old Main Dr, PO Box 567; 304/872-1588.

Twenty-year-old Nancy Hart led a surprise Confederate attack on Summersville in July of 1861, captured a Union force and burned the town. She was captured, but her jail guard succumbed to her charms. The guard was then disarmed and killed by the young woman. She escaped to Lee's lines. After the war, she returned to Summersville.

What to See and Do

Carnifex Ferry Battlefield State Park. Here on Sept 10, 1861, 7,000 Union troops under General William S. Rosecrans fought and defeated a lesser number of Confederates under General John B. Floyd. The 156-acre park includes Patteson House Museum (Memorial Day-wkend after Labor Day, Sat, Sun, hols), which displays Civil War relics. Hiking trails. Picnicking; game courts, playgrounds; concession. Civil War reenactment

(wkend after Labor Day). Park (daily). 12 mi W on WV 39, then SE on WV 129, near Kesslers Cross Lanes. Phone 304/872-0825.   **Free.**

Gauley River National Recreation Area. Designated a federally protected area in Oct 1988, the 25-mi stretch of the Gauley from the Summersville Dam west to just above the town of Swiss is famous for whitewater rafting. There are no developed sites. Large tracts of land along river are privately owned. For further information and a list of whitewater outfitters contact Superintendent, New River Gorge National River, PO Box 246, Glen Jean 25846; 304/465-0508.

Summersville Lake. A 2,700-acre lake. Swimming, waterskiing; fishing; boating. Hiking. Picnicking. Battle Run Campground is 3 mi W on WV 129 (fee). (May-Oct, daily) Fee for some activities. 5 mi S on US 19. Phone 304/872-3459

Annual Events

Nicholas County Fair. 3 mi N at Nicholas County Memorial Park. Midway; flower show; agricultural and crafts exhibits. July.

Nicholas County Potato Festival. Citywide. Includes parades, entertainment, volleyball tournament, arts & crafts show, bed races. 1st full wk Sept.

Motels

✔★ **BEST WESTERN SUMMERSVILLE LAKE.** *1203 Broad St.* 304/872-6900; FAX 304/872-6908. 59 rms, 3 story. April-Oct: S $42-$48; D $47-$53; each addl $5; under 12 free; lower rates rest of yr. Crib free. Pet accepted, some restrictions. TV; cable, VCR avail (movies avail). Complimentary continental bkfst. Restaurant 11 am-10 pm. Rm serv. Bar. Ck-out 11 am. Business servs avail. Microwave avail. Cr cds: A, C, D, DS, ER, JCB, MC, V.

⬚🖬🌊🌊 SC

★ ★ **COMFORT INN.** *903 Industrial Dr, 2 mi N on US 19 at jct WV 41.* 304/872-6500; FAX 304/872-3090. Web wvweb.com/www/comfort.inn-summersville. 99 rms, 2 story. June-Oct: S $47-$62; D $52-$69; each addl $5-$7; suites $62-$114; under 18 free; lower rates rest of yr. Crib free. Pet accepted, some restrictions; $5. TV; cable (premium), VCR avail (movies avail). Heated pool; wading pool. Complimentary continental bkfst. Restaurant nearby. Ck-out 11 am. Coin lndry. Meeting rms. Bellhops. Exercise equipt; weight machine, bicycles, sauna. Refrigerator in suites. Microwave avail. Picnic tables. Cr cds: A, C, D, DS, ER, JCB, MC, V.

⬚🖬🌊🍴🌊🌊 SC

★ **SLEEP INN.** *701 Professional Park Dr, off US 19.* 304/872-4500; FAX 304/872-0288; res: 800/872-1751. 97 rms, 2 story. June-Oct: S $40-$53; D $45-$65; each addl $5; under 18 free; higher rates special events; lower rates rest of yr. Crib free. Pet accepted, some restrictions; $5. TV; cable (premium), VCR avail (movies). Heated pool. Complimentary continental bkfst. Restaurant adj 11 am-10 pm. Ck-out 11 am. Coin lndry. Meeting rms. Business servs avail. Sundries. Lawn games. Refrigerators, microwaves avail. Cr cds: A, C, D, DS, ER, JCB, MC, V.

⬚🖬🌊🌊🔥 SC

Restaurant

★ **COUNTRY ROAD INN.** *Country Rd, 8 mi W on WV 39.* 304/872-1620; res: 800/439-8852 (WV). Hrs: 5-8 pm; Fri, Sat to 8:30 pm; Sun 2-6 pm. Closed major hols. Res required. Italian menu. Wine. Complete meals: dinner $14.95-$24.95. Child's meals. Specialties: shrimp scampi, fettucine, lasagne. Own pasta. In restored 19th-century farmhouse; country setting. Cr cds: A, DS, MC, V.

Sutton (C-4)

Settled 1826 **Pop** 939 **Elev** 840 ft **Area code** 304 **Zip** 26601

What to See and Do

Sutton Lake. Dam is one mi E. Swimming in designated areas. Boat launch (fee). Camping (May-Dec; some electric hookups; fees) at Gerald R. Freeman Campground, 16 mi E on WV 15; and at Mill Creek-Bakers Run Area, 16 mi SE on WV 17. Phone 304/765-2816 or 304/765-2705 (recording).

Motel

✔★ **SUTTON LANE.** 4 mi N on US 19 (WV 4), just off I-79, Flatwoods exit 67. 304/765-7351. 31 rms, 2 story. S $28.50; D $33; each addl $5; higher rates: hols, special events. TV; cable (premium). Restaurant open 24 hrs. Ck-out 11 am. Meeting rm. Sundries. Private patios, balconies. Cr cds: A, D, MC, V.

[🔥] [SC]

Motor Hotel

★ ★ ★ **DAYS INN.** 2000 Sutton Lane, I-79 exit 67. 304/765-5055; FAX 304/765-2067. 201 units, 5 story. Mar-Nov: S $49.95-$54.95; D $54.95-$59.95; each addl $5; suites $100-$105; under 13 free; lower rates rest of yr. Crib free. TV; cable. Indoor Pool. Restaurant 5-10 pm. Bar 5 pm-midnight. Ck-out 11 am. Meeting rms. Business servs avail. In-rm modem link. Sundries. Gift shop. Exercise equipt; weights, treadmill, sauna. Many balconies. Cr cds: A, C, D, DS, MC, V.

[D] [≈] [🏃] [🎣] [🐾] [SC]

Webster Springs (D-5)

Settled 1860 **Pop** 990 (est) **Elev** 1,509 ft **Area code** 304 **Zip** 26288
Information Mayor's Office, 146 McGraw Ave; 304/847-5411.

Once a resort famed for its medicinal "lick" or spring, the town is now a trading center and meeting place for sportsmen.

What to See and Do

Holly River State Park. More than 8,000 acres of heavy forest with excellent trout fishing in Laurel Fork. Swimming pool, bathhouse. Hiking trails to waterfalls and Potato Knob; tennis, game courts. Picnicking, playground; restaurant (seasonal). Camping (dump station), 9 cabins. Nature, recreation programs (summer). Standard hrs, fees. 20 mi N on WV 20 to Hacker Valley, then 1 mi E. Phone 304/493-6353.

Kumbrabow State Forest. More than 9,400 acres of wild, rugged country with trout fishing and deer, turkey and grouse hunting. Hiking trails. Cross-country skiing. Picnicking, playground. Tent & trailer camping, 5 rustic cabins. Standard hrs, fees. 25 mi NE on WV 15, then 5 mi N, near Monterville. Phone 304/335-2219.

Annual Events

Webster Springs Woodchopping Festival. Southeastern World Woodchopping Championships; state championship turkey calling contest, draft horse pull, horse show, fireman's rodeo; arts & crafts, music, parades, concessions. Phone 304/847-7666. Memorial Day wkend.

Webster County Fair. 11 mi S on WV 20 to 4-H Camp Caesar. Rides, agricultural exhibits, entertainers, horse show. Labor Day wk.

Weirton (A-5)

(For accommodations see Wheeling; also see Pittsburgh, PA)

Founded 1910 **Pop** 22,124 **Elev** 760 ft **Area code** 304 **Zip** 26062
Information Chamber of Commerce, 3200 Maine St; 304/748-7212.

Weirton has been a steel-producing town since its founding in 1910 by Ernest T. Weir, who also founded the Weirton Steel Company. In 1984, Weirton Steel became the largest employee-owned steel company in the world. Modern plants produce tin plate and hot-rolled, cold-rolled and galvanized steels for containers, automobiles, appliances and other products.

What to See and Do

Horse racing. Mountaineer Racetrack & Resort. Thoroughbred racing on one-mile track; three restaurants. (Thurs-Mon) 12 mi N on WV 2. Phone 304/387-2400.

Industrial tours. Weirton Steel Corp and Half Moon Industrial Park. Tours of Weirton Steel Corp, Alpo and others. Contact Chamber of Commerce for details, 304/748-7212.

Tomlinson Run State Park. Approx 1,400 acres. Swimming pool, bathhouse; fishing; boating on 27-acre lake (rowboat and paddleboat rentals). Hiking trails; miniature golf, tennis. Picnicking, playground. Tent & trailer camping (dump station). Nature, recreation programs (summer). Standard hrs, fees. 15 mi N off WV 8. Phone 304/564-3651.

Weston (C-5)

(See also Buckhannon, Clarksburg)

Settled 1784 **Pop** 4,994 **Elev** 1,009 ft **Area code** 304 **Zip** 26452
Information Lewis County Convention & Visitors Bureau, PO Box 379; 304/269-7328.

Surveyed originally by "Stonewall" Jackson's grandfather, Weston today is a center for coal, oil and gas production, as well as the manufacture of glass products. The Weston State Hospital, completed in 1880 and said to be the largest hand-cut stone building in the nation, is located in town.

What to See and Do

Cedar Creek State Park. More than 2,400 acres. Swimming pool, bathhouse; fishing; boating (rentals). Hiking trails; miniature golf; tennis, game courts. Picnicking, playground, concession. Tent & trailer camping (dump station). Park office in restored log cabin. Standard hrs, fees. 31 mi SW off US 33/119, near Glenville. Phone 304/462-7158.

Jackson's Mill State 4-H Conference Center. First camp of its kind in US; with 43 buildings, gardens, swimming pool, amphitheater, interfaith chapel. Picnicking. 4 mi N off US 19. Phone 304/269-5100. Also here is

Jackson's Mill Historic Area. Includes Blaker's Mill, an operating water-powered grist-mill; blacksmith shop; McWharten cabin (ca 1700s); Mary Conrad's cabin (ca 1800s); and **Jackson's Mill Museum**, where "Stonewall" Jackson lived and worked as a boy. Museum represents grist and saw milling agriculture and home arts of the area as practiced 100 yrs ago. (Memorial Day-Labor Day, daily exc Mon; May & after Labor Day-mid-Oct, wkends only) Historic area ¢¢

Stonewall Jackson Lake & Dam. Approx 2,500-acre lake, with over 82 mi of shoreline, created by impounding the waters of the West Fork River. Swimming, scuba diving, waterskiing; fishing; boating (ramps, rentals, marinas). Picnicking. Camping. Visitor center. Just S off I-79 exit 96, follow signs to dam. Phone 304/269-4588 or -0523.

Stonewall Jackson Lake State Park. Approx 3,000 acres. Fishing; boating (launch, marina). Nature, fitness trails. Picnicking; playground. Camping (hookups). Visitor center. Standard hrs, fees. 11 mi S on US 19. Phone 304/269-0523.

Annual Events

Horse show. Trefz Farm, 3 mi E on US 33. Saddle, walking, harness, pony, western and Arabian riding. Phone 304/269-3257. Usually July.

Stonewall Jackson Heritage Arts & Crafts Jubilee. Jackson's Mill State 4-H Conference Center. Mountain crafts, music, dance and food. Phone 304/269-1863. Labor Day wkend.

Motel

✔★ ★ **COMFORT INN.** *Box 666, At jct US 33 & I-79. 304/269-7000.* 60 rms, 2 story. S $40-$52; D $46-$58; each addl $6; under 18 free. Crib free. Pet accepted. TV; cable. Heated pool. Restaurant 6 am-9 pm. Bar 5-11 pm. Ck-out noon. Meeting rm. Balconies. Cr cds: A, C, D, DS, ER, JCB, MC, V.

Wheeling (A-4)

Settled 1769 **Pop** 34,882 **Elev** 678 ft **Area code** 304 **Zip** 26003 **E-mail** whcvb-wv@worldnet.ah.net **Web** wvweb.com/www/wheeling.html

Information Convention & Visitors Bureau, 1310 Market St; 304/233-7709 or 800/828-3079.

Wheeling stands on the site of Fort Henry, built in 1774 by Colonel Ebenezer Zane and his two brothers, who named the fort for Virginia's Governor Patrick Henry. In 1782, the fort was the scene of the final battle of the Revolutionary War, a battle in which the valiant, young pioneer Betty Zane was a heroine. The fort had withstood several Native American and British sieges during the war. However, during the last siege (after the war was officially ended), the defenders of the fort ran out of powder. Betty Zane, sister of the colonel, volunteered to run through the gunfire to the outlying Zane cabin for more. With the powder gathered in her apron, she made the 150-yard trek back to the fort and saved the garrison. Zane Grey, a descendant of the Zanes, wrote a novel about Betty and her exploit.

Today, Wheeling is home to many industries, including producers of steel, iron, tin, chemical products, pottery, glass, paper, tobacco, plastics and coal.

What to See and Do

Grave Creek Mound State Park. Features nation's largest prehistoric Adena burial mound—79 ft high, 900 ft around, 50 ft across the top. Some excavating was done in 1838; exhibits in Delf Norona Museum & Cultural Center (daily; fee). 9 mi S via WV 2, on Jefferson Ave in Moundsville. Phone 304/843-1410.

Jamboree, USA. Live country music shows presented by WWVA Radio since 1933. (Sat) Capitol Music Hall, 1015 Main St. Phone 304/234-0050 or 800/624-5456. ¢¢¢¢¢

Oglebay Resort Park. A 1,500-acre municipal park. Indoor, outdoor swimming pools; fishing, boating on 3-acre Schenk Lake. Three 18-hole golf courses, miniature golf; tennis courts. Picnicking, restaurant, snack shop. Cabins, lodge (see RESORT). Miniature train ride; 65-acre Good Children's Zoo (fee) with animals in natural habitat. Benedum Natural Science Theater; garden center; arboretum with 4 mi of walking paths; greenhouses; observatory. Fee for most activities. 3 mi NE of I-70, on WV 88. Phone 304/243-4000 or 800/624-6988. (See ANNUAL and SEASONAL EVENTS) Also in park are

Ski area. 3 Pomalifts; rentals, snowmaking; snack shop. (Dec-Mar, daily) Phone 304/243-4000. ¢¢¢¢

Mansion House Museum. Period rms, exhibits trace history from 1835 to present. (Daily) Phone 304/242-7272. ¢¢

Site of Fort Henry. Bronze plaque marks location of fort that Betty Zane saved. Main St, near 11th St.

The Artisan Center. Restored 1890s Victorian warehouse houses Nail City Brewing Co, West Virginia's largest brew pub. Wymer's General Store Museum, "Made in Wheeling" crafts and exhibits; artisan demonstrations. (Daily) Heritage Square, 1400 Main St. Phone 304/232-1810. Center **Free;** Museum ¢¢

West Virginia Independence Hall-Custom House (1859). Site of meeting at which Virginia's secession from the Union was declared unlawful, and the independent state of West Virginia was created. The building, used as a post office, custom office and federal court until 1912, has been restored. It now houses exhibits and events relating to the state's cultural heritage, including an interpretive film and rooms with period furniture. (Mar-Dec, daily; rest of yr, daily exc Sun; closed state hols) 16th & Market Sts. Phone 304/238-1300. **Free.**

Wheeling Park. Approx 400 acres. Swimming pool, water slide; boating on Good Lake. Golf, miniature golf, indoor/outdoor tennis. Ice-skating (rentals). Picnicking, playground, refreshment area with video screen and lighted dance floor. Aviary. Fees for activities. (Daily; some facilities seasonal) 5 mi E on US 40. Phone 304/242-3770.

Annual Events

Jamboree in the Hills. 15 mi W off I-70 exit 208 or 213, in St Clairsville, OH. A 4-day country music festival featuring more than 30 hours of music; top country stars. Camping avail. Phone 800/624-5456. 3rd wkend July.

Oglebayfest. Oglebay Resort Park. Country fair, artists' market, fireworks, parade, ethnic foods, contests, square & round dancing, entertainment. Phone 304/243-4000. 1st wkend Oct.

Seasonal Event

City of Lights. Oglebay Resort Park. A 350-acre lighting display featuring lighted buildings, holiday themes with more than 500,000 lights, including 28-foot candy canes and giant swans on Schenk Lake. Winter Fantasy in Good Zoo. Nov-Jan.

Motel

(Rates are usually higher for Jamboree in the Hills)

★ ★ **DAYS INN.** *(RD 1, Box 292, Triadelphia 26059) 9 mi E, at I-70 exit 11. 304/547-0610; FAX 304/547-9029.* 106 rms, 2 story. S, D $45-$55; each addl $6; under 18 free. Crib free. Pet accepted. TV; cable (premium), VCR avail. Pool. Bar 5 pm-1 am, closed Sun. Ck-out noon. Meeting rm. Business servs avail. Valet serv. Some in-rm whirlpools. Cr cds: A, C, D, DS, MC, V.

Motor Hotel

★ ★ **HAMPTON INN.** *795 National Rd, I-70, exit 24. 304/233-0440; FAX 304/233-2198.* 104 rms, 5 story. S $57-$68; D $62-$73; suites $68-$81; under 18 free; wkends (2-day min). Crib free. TV; cable (premium), VCR avail. Complimentary continental bkfst. Restaurant adj 6:30 am-11 pm. Rm serv. Ck-out noon. Meeting rms. Business servs avail. In-rm modem link. Valet serv. Exercise equipt; stair machine, rowers. Refrigerator, wet bar in suites. Cr cds: A, C, D, DS, MC, V.

Hotel

✔★ **BEST WESTERN WHEELING INN.** *949 Main St. 304/233-8500; FAX 304/233-8500, ext. 345.* 80 rms, 5 story. S $46.75-$57.75; D $53.75-$62.75; each addl $8; suites $110.50; under 12 free; higher rates wkends, special events. Crib free. TV; cable (premium). Complimentary continental bkfst. Restaurant 11 am-10 pm; Sat, Sun from 7 am. Bar 11-2 am. Ck-out 11 am. Business servs avail. Free valet parking. Exercise equipt; treadmill, stair machine; sauna. Whirlpool. Cr cds: A, C, D, DS, JCB, MC, V.

Resort

★ ★ **OGLEBAY'S WILSON LODGE.** *WV 88, 3 mi NE of I-70 exit 2A.* 304/243-4000; FAX 304/243-4070; res: 800/624-6988. 204 rms in 2-story lodge, chalets; 49 kit. cabins (2-6 bedrm). S $69-$122; D $110-$150; suites $145-$170; kit. cabins $625-$1,350/wk; golf plans. Crib $5. TV; cable (premium), VCR avail (movies avail). 2 pools, 1 indoor; wading pool, whirlpool, poolside serv, lifeguard. Playground. Supervised child's activities (June-Aug); ages 6-12. Dining rm 6:30-10:30 am, noon-2 pm, 5-9 pm. Box lunches, snack bar. Lounge noon-midnight. Rm serv. Ck-out noon, ck-in 3 pm. Grocery 1/2 mi. Package store 2 mi. Meeting rms. Business center. In-rm modem link. Airport, bus depot transportation. 11 lighted tennis courts, pro. Two 18-hole golf courses, greens fee $26-$50, par-3 golf, pro, driving range, miniature golf. Downhill ski 1/2 mi. Stocked lake. Paddleboats. Lawn games. Children's zoo. Stables. Exercise rm; instructor, weight machine, stair machine. Some fireplaces. Some private patios, balconies. Picnic tables, grills. Mansion museum, garden center. Rustic setting in Oglebay Park. Cr cds: A, D, DS, MC, V.

Restaurants

★ ★ **CORK'N BOTTLE.** *39 12th St.* 304/232-4400. Hrs: 11-3:30 am; major hols from 5 pm. Closed Dec 25. Res accepted. Bar 11-2 am; Sun 5 pm-midnight. Semi-a la carte: lunch $2.95-$7.95, dinner $5.95-$12.95. Child's meals. Specialties: coquille, Greek kebab. Salad bar. Entertainment. New Orleans decor; paddle fans. Family-owned. Cr cds: A, C, D, DS, MC, V.

★ ★ **ERNIE'S ESQUIRE.** *1 W Bethlehem Blvd, 11/4 mi off I-70 on WV 88S.* 304/242-2800. Hrs: 11 am-midnight; Fri to 1 am; Sat to 2 am; Sun to 10:30 pm; Sun brunch to 2 pm. Closed Dec 25. Res accepted. Continental menu. Bar. Wine list. Semi-a la carte: lunch $3.75-$8.95, dinner $8.95-$26.95. Sun brunch $8.95. Child's meals. Specializes in fresh seafood, beef. Own baking. Entertainment Fri, Sat. Valet parking. 6 rms, each with different decor. Family-owned. Cr cds: A, C, D, DS, MC, V.

White Sulphur Springs (E-5)

(See also Lewisburg; also see Covington, VA)

Settled 1750 **Pop** 2,779 **Elev** 1,923 ft **Area code** 304 **Zip** 24986
Information Chamber of Commerce, PO Box 11; 304/536-2500.

In the 18th century, White Sulphur Springs became a fashionable destination for rich and famous colonists, who came for the "curative" powers of the mineral waters. It has, for the most part, remained a popular resort ever since. A number of US presidents summered in the town in the days before air conditioning made Washington habitable in hot weather. The John Tylers spent their honeymoon at the famous "Old White" Hotel. In 1913 the Old White Hotel gave way to the present Greenbrier Hotel (see RESORT), where President Wilson honeymooned with the second Mrs. Wilson. During World War II the hotel served as an internment camp for German and Japanese diplomats and, later, as a hospital.

The first golf course in America was laid out near the town in 1884, but the first game was delayed when golf clubs, imported from Scotland, were held for three weeks by customs men, who were suspicious of a game played with "such elongated blackjacks or implements of murder."

What to See and Do

Fishing, swimming, boating, camping, hiking. In Monongahela National Forest (see ELKINS): Blue Bend Recreation Area, 6 mi N on WV 92, then 4 mi W on WV 16/21; Lake Sherwood Recreation Area, 23 mi N via WV 92, then 11 mi NE on WV 14. Phone 304/536-2144. Camping ¢¢¢-¢¢¢¢

Greenbrier State Forest. More than 5,100 acres. Swimming pool (Memorial Day-Labor Day); bass fishing in Greenbrier River; hunting. Hiking trails. Picnicking, playground. Tent and trailer camping, 12 cabins. Nature, recreation programs (summer). Standard hrs, fees. 3 mi W on US 60, then 11/2 mi S on Harts Run Rd. Phone 304/536-1944.

Memorial Park. Swimming pool (Memorial Day-Labor Day; fee). Tennis courts, ball fields, track, horseshoe pits, playground. (Daily) Greenbrier Ave. **Free.**

National Fish Hatchery. Rainbow trout in raceways and ponds. Visitor center has display pool, aquariums and exhibits. (Memorial Day-Labor Day, daily) 400 E Main St, on US 60. Phone 304/536-1361. **Free.**

Motel

(Rates are generally higher during state fair)

✔★ ★ **OLD WHITE.** *865 E Main St.* 304/536-2441; res: 800/867-2441. 26 rms. S $36; D $44; each addl $3; higher rates special events. Crib free. Pet accepted, some restrictions. TV; cable (premium). Pool. Coffee in lobby. Restaurant adj 7:30 am-9 pm. Ck-out noon. Cr cds: A, C, D, DS, MC, V.

Resort

★ ★ ★ ★ ★ **THE GREENBRIER.** *300 W Main St, 1/2 mi W on US 60.* 304/536-1110; FAX 304/536-7854; res: 800/624-6070. E-mail tjkbrier@aol.com; web www.greenbrier.com. This elegant, immaculately maintained, 7,000-acre resort has been a popular watering spot for more than 200 years. A huge selection of recreational opportunities is available—even falconry—and no two guest rooms are alike. 699 rms in hotel, 6 story, 103 guest house rms. MAP, Apr-Oct: S, D, guest rms, cottages $229-$281/person; each addl $125; wkend, family rates; tennis, golf plans; lower rates rest of yr. Serv charge $20/person/day. Crib free. TV; cable, VCR avail (movies $2.50). 2 pools, 1 indoor; whirlpool, wading pool, poolside serv, lifeguard. Playground. Supervised child's activities. Dining rms 7:30 am-9:30 pm (see THE GREENBRIER MAIN DINING ROOM and THE TAVERN ROOM). Box lunches, snack bar. Rm serv 24 hrs. Private club noon-1 am; entertainment. Ck-out noon, ck-in 3 pm. Convention facilities. Business center. In-rm modem link. Extensive shopping arcade. Airport, RR station, bus depot transportation. Sports dir. 5 indoor, 15 outdoor tennis courts, pro. Lighted, heated platform tennis. Three 18-hole golf courses, greens fee $120, pro, 2 putting greens, driving range. Canoeing; rafting (seasonal). Ice-skating (seasonal). Horse-drawn sleighing & carriage rides. Stables, English saddles. Fitness trail. Bicycling. Lawn games. Trap & skeet shooting. Hunt club and game preserve. British regulation croquet court. Soc dir; movies, dancing, entertainment. Bowling; indoor games. Extensive exercise rm; instructor, weight machines, bicycles, sauna, steam rm. Spa. Some refrigerators; microwaves avail; fireplace in cottages. Private patios, balconies. Cr cds: A, C, D, DS, MC, V.

Restaurants

★ ★ ★ **THE GREENBRIER MAIN DINING ROOM.** *(See The Greenbrier Resort)* 304/536-1110. E-mail tjkbrier@aol.com; web www.greenbrier.com. Hrs: 7:30-10 am, 6:30-9 pm. Res required. Continental menu. Private club noon-1 am. Wine cellar. Prix fixe: bkfst $20-$25, dinner $75-$80. Serv charge 15%; addl serv charge for alcoholic beverages. Child's meals. Specialties: veal medallions with creamed morrels, roast Long Island duckling, fresh North Carolina seafood. Own baking.

Chamber music at dinner. Valet parking. Jacket, tie (dinner). Cr cds: A, C, D, DS, MC, V.

[D] [↵]

★ ★ ★ **THE TAVERN ROOM.** *(See The Greenbrier Resort)* *304/536-1110.* E-mail tjkbrier@aol.com; web www.greenbrier.com. Hrs: 7-9:30 pm. Closed Nov-Mar. Res required. Continental menu. Bar 7 pm-1 am. Wine cellar. Prix fixe: $100-$105. Serv charge 15%. Child's meals. Specializes in fresh salmon, lobster, veal. Pianist. Valet parking. Jacket. Cr cds: A, C, D, DS, MC, V.

[D]

Williamson (E-3)

Founded 1892 **Pop** 4,154 **Elev** 665 ft **Area code** 304 **Zip** 25661
Information Tug Valley Chamber of Commerce, 45 E 2nd Ave, PO Box 376; 304/235-5240.

The center of the "billion-dollar coal field," Williamson is truly a coal town; the walls of the local Chamber of Commerce building, at the west corner of Courthouse Square, are made of coal. The surrounding Tug River Valley was the scene of the bitter Hatfield-McCoy mountaineer family feud.

What to See and Do

Cabwaylingo State Forest. Approx 8,100 acres. Swimming pool (Memorial Day-Labor Day); fishing, hunting. Hiking trails; game courts. Picnicking, playground, concession. Tent & trailer camping (dump station), 13 cabins. Standard hrs, fees. 38 mi N off US 52, WV 152 near Wilsondale. Phone 304/385-4255.

Matewan. This tiny hamlet was the site of the famous feud between the West Virginia Hatfields and the Kentucky McCoys. On Election Day, Aug 7, 1882, three McCoy sons stabbed and shot Ellison Hatfield. Devil Anse Hatfield avenged his brother by executing the three McCoys. Soon Kentucky bounty hunters made raids into West Virginia to capture the Hatfields, who retaliated in 1888 by attacking a McCoy homestead. By 1890 the killings had ended but the feud continued to be sensationalized. Later, in 1920, Matewan was the scene of a shootout between union organizers and coal company operators that left 10 dead, including the mayor. 12 mi SW via WV 49. For a walking tour of the area phone 304/426-4239.

Annual Event

King Coal Festival. Entertainment, exhibits; theatrical presentation; country music, square dancing. Mid-Sept.

Index

Establishment names are listed in alphabetical order followed by a symbol identifying their classification, and then city, state and page number. Establishments affiliated with a chain appear alphabetically under their chain name, followed by the state, city and page number. The symbols for classification are: [H] for hotel; [I] for inns; [M] for motels; [L] for lodges; [MH] for motor hotels; [R] for restaurants; [RO] for resorts, guest ranches, and cottage colonies; [U] for unrated dining spots.

THE DOCKSIDER INN [M] *Wilmington NC*, 189

THE DOCTOR'S INN AT KING'S GRANT [I] *Cape May Court House NJ*, 95

DOE RUN [L] *Blue Ridge Parkway VA*, 346

DOGWOOD LODGE [M] *Radford VA*, 392

DOLLAR INN [M] *Somerset PA*, 281

DONECKERS GUEST HOUSE [I] *Ephrata PA*, 217

DONECKERS [R] *Ephrata PA*, 218

DOOLAN'S [M] *Spring Lake NJ*, 123

DORIS & ED'S [R] *Gateway National Recreation Area (Sandy Hook Unit) NJ*, 101

DOUBLETREE
District of Columbia
    Washington, [H] 25
Maryland
    Baltimore/Washington Intl Airport Area, [H] 53; Baltimore, [H] 49; Rockville, [H] 76
New Jersey
    New Brunswick, [H] 112
North Carolina
    Charlotte, [H] 148; Durham, [H] 153
Pennsylvania
    Philadelphia, [MH] 257, [H] 258; Pittsburgh, [H] 271
Virginia
    Alexandria, [H] 336; Arlington County (National Airport Area), [H] 341; Charlottesville, [H] 350; Norfolk, [H] 388; Roanoke, [H] 399

DOUMAR'S [U] *Norfolk VA*, 389

DOXEY'S MARKET & CAFE [U] *Wilmington NC*, 191

DRAGON GARDEN [R] *Wilmington NC*, 190

DRIFTWOOD [M] *Cedar Island NC*, 144

DRIFTWOOD MOTOR LODGE [M] *Chincoteague VA*, 354

DUANGRAT'S [R] *Falls Church VA*, 362

DUE [R] *Pikesville MD*, 75

DUKE OF YORK [M] *Yorktown VA*, 422

DULING-KURTZ HOUSE [R] *West Chester PA*, 290

DULING-KURTZ HOUSE & COUNTRY INN [I] *West Chester PA*, 290

DULWICH MANOR [I] *Lynchburg VA*, 378

THE DUMBWAITER [R] *Norfolk VA*, 388

DUNES VILLAGE RESORT [H] *Myrtle Beach SC*, 324

DUNHILL [H] *Charlotte NC*, 148

DUPONT PLAZA [H] *Washington DC*, 25

DUTCH INN [M] *Gibbstown NJ*, 101

DUTCH INN [M] *Martinsville VA*, 381

DYNASTY [R] *Williamsburg VA*, 417

EAST WIND [R] *Alexandria VA*, 337

EASTVILLE MANOR [R] *Cape Charles VA*, 348

EBBITT ROOM [R] *Cape May NJ*, 94

ECCO CAFE [R] *Alexandria VA*, 337

ECHO MOUNTAIN [I] *Hendersonville NC*, 163

ECONO LODGE
Delaware
    Rehoboth Beach, [M] 8
North Carolina
    Fayetteville, [M] 156; Morehead City, [M] 171; Waynesville, [M] 186
Pennsylvania
    Bedford, [M] 202; Erie, [M] 218; Reading, [M] 277; Williamsport, [M] 292
South Carolina
    Rock Hill, [M] 327; Walterboro, [M] 329
Virginia
    Alexandria, [M] 336; Harrisonburg, [M] 370; Lynchburg, [M] 378; Norfolk, [M] 387; Staunton, [M] 403; Virginia Beach, [H] 409; Winchester, [M] 419; Wytheville, [M] 421
West Virginia
    Berkeley Springs, [M] 427; Bluefield, [M] 427; Elkins, [M] 432; Morgantown, [M] 440; Ripley, [M] 444

ECONOMY INNS OF AMERICA
Pennsylvania
    Somerset, [M] 281

ED'S STEAK HOUSE [R] *Bedford PA*, 202

EDDIE ROMANELLI'S [R] *Wilmington NC*, 190

EDGEWOOD [I] *Williamsburg VA*, 416

EDGEWOOD MANOR [I] *Martinsburg WV*, 439

EHRHARDT'S LAKESIDE [R] *Hawley PA*, 228

EL CARIBE [R] *Washington DC*, 31

EL CORONADO MOTOR INN [MH] *Wildwood & Wildwood Crest NJ*, 129

ELA MOTOR COURT [M] *Bryson City NC*, 141

ELIJAH'S [R] *Wilmington NC*, 190

ELKINS MOTOR LODGE [M] *Elkins WV*, 432

ELKTON LODGE [M] *Elkton MD*, 63

ELLIOT'S [R] *Norfolk VA*, 388

ELYSIUM [R] *Alexandria VA*, 337

EMBASSY SUITES
District of Columbia
    Washington, [H] 25
New Jersey
    New Brunswick, [H] 112; Secaucus, [H] 121
North Carolina
    Charlotte, [H] 148; Greensboro, [H] 160; Raleigh, [H] 179
South Carolina
    Charleston, [H] 305; Columbia, [H] 312; Greenville, [H] 317; Myrtle Beach, [H] 324
Virginia
    Arlington County (National Airport Area), [H] 341; Richmond, [H] 396; Tysons Corner, [H] 406

EMBERS [R] *Ocean City MD*, 74

EMBERS INN & CONVENTION CENTER [M] *Carlisle PA*, 209

EMERALD ISLE [I] *Morehead City NC*, 172

EMMANUEL HUTZLER HOUSE [I] *Richmond VA*, 396

EMPIRE [M] *Abingdon VA*, 334

ENGLESIDE INN [M] *Long Beach Island NJ*, 106

ENGLISH INN OF CHARLOTTESVILLE [MH] *Charlottesville VA*, 350

EPICUREAN [R] *Charlotte NC*, 149

ERNIE'S ESQUIRE [R] *Wheeling WV*, 448

ESEEOLA LODGE [L] *Linville NC*, 168

THE ESPOSITOS/PIZZA 'N PASTA [U] *Fairfax VA*, 362

ETRUSCA [R] *Wrightsville Beach NC*, 194

EVANS FARM INN [R] *McLean VA*, 382

EVANS SEAFOOD [U] *St Mary's City MD*, 78

EVERMAY ON-THE-DELAWARE [I] *New Hope (Bucks Co) PA*, 247

EVERMAY ON-THE-DELAWARE [R] *New Hope (Bucks Co) PA*, 248

EXECUTIVE [M] *Ocean City MD*, 72

EXECUTIVE [M] *Radford VA*, 392

EXECUTIVE CLUB SUITES [MH] *Alexandria VA*, 336

EXECUTIVE CLUB SUITES [M] *Arlington County (National Airport Area) VA*, 340

EXPRESSIONS [R] *Hendersonville NC*, 163

FACCIA LUNA [R] *Alexandria VA*, 337

FACCIA LUNA [R] *Arlington County (National Airport Area) VA*, 342

FAGER'S ISLAND [R] *Ocean City MD*, 74

FAIRFIELD INN BY MARRIOTT
Maryland
    Frederick, [MH] 66
North Carolina
    Charlotte, [M] 147; Durham, [M] 153; Fayetteville, [M] 156; Greensboro, [M] 160; Greenville, [M] 161; Lumberton, [M] 169; Raleigh, [M] 178; Rocky Mount, [M] 181; Statesville, [M] 185; Wilmington, [M] 189
South Carolina
    Greenville, [M] 316; Hilton Head Island, [M] 319
Virginia
    Chesapeake, [M] 352; Hampton, [M] 369; Richmond, [M] 395; Virginia Beach, [M] 408

FAIRFIELD SAPPHIRE VALLEY [RO] *Cashiers NC*, 144

FAIRVIEW [R] *Durham NC*, 154

FAIRVILLE [I] *Kennett Square PA*, 234

FALCON [M] *Buxton (Outer Banks) NC*, 143

FALLS LANDING [R] *McLean VA*, 382

FALLS PORT INN [I] *Hawley PA*, 228

FAMILY TREE [R] *Spring Lake NJ*, 124

FAMOUS 4TH ST DELICATESSEN [U] *Philadelphia PA*, 265

FANTASTICO RISTORANTE ITALIANO [R] *Warrenton VA*, 411

FARNSWORTH HOUSE INN [I] *Gettysburg PA*, 222

GRAYSTONE INN [I] *Wilmington NC,* 190
GRAYSTONE LODGE [M] *Boone NC,* 140
GREEN GROCER TOO [U] *Norfolk VA,* 389
GREEN HILLS INN [R] *Reading PA,* 278
GREEN PARK [I] *Blowing Rock NC,* 139
GREEN ROOM [R] *Wilmington DE,* 12
GREEN TREE [R] *Leesburg VA,* 374
GREEN TREE INN [M] *Wilmington NC,* 189
THE GREENBRIER [RO] *White Sulphur
   Springs WV,* 448
THE GREENBRIER MAIN DINING ROOM
   [R] *White Sulphur Springs WV,* 448
GREENERY [R] *Asheville NC,* 137
GREENLEAF [I] *Camden SC,* 301
GRESHAM'S LAKEVIEW [M] *Hawley PA,*
   228
GREYSTONE [I] *Cashiers NC,* 144
GREYSTONE MANOR [I] *Bird-in-Hand PA,*
   204
GRIFFINS [R] *Annapolis MD,* 43
THE GRILL [R] *Philadelphia PA,* 262
THE GRILL [R] *Arlington County (National
   Airport Area) VA,* 342
THE GRILL FROM IPANEMA [R]
   Washington DC, 32
GROFF'S FARM [R] *Lancaster PA,* 239
GROVE PARK INN RESORT [RO] *Asheville
   NC,* 137
GUAPO'S [R] *Washington DC,* 32
GUARDS [R] *Washington DC,* 32
GUTHRIE INN & CONFERENCE CENTER
   [MH] *Towanda PA,* 285
GYPSY ROSE [R] *Limerick PA,* 242
HAAD THAI [R] *Washington DC,* 32
HAAG'S HOTEL RESTAURANT [R]
   Shartlesville PA, 280
HAANDI [R] *Bethesda MD,* 55
HAANDI [R] *Falls Church VA,* 362
HALF WAY HOUSE [R] *Richmond VA,* 397
HAMILTON PARK [MH] *Morristown NJ,*
   109
HAMPSHIRE [H] *Washington DC,* 26
HAMPTON COURT INN [M] *Mount Pocono
   PA,* 245
HAMPTON INN
   Maryland
      *Baltimore/Washington Intl Airport
         Area,* [M] 53, [MH] 53; *Baltimore,* [M]
         48; *Frederick,* [MH] 66; *Gaithersburg,*
         [MH] 67
   New Jersey
      Atlantic City, [M] 87; *Cherry Hill,* [M]
         96; *Parsippany,* [MH] 115
   North Carolina
      Asheville, [M] 135; *Boone,* [MH] 140;
         Burlington, [M] 142; *Chapel Hill,* [M]
         145; *Charlotte,* [M] 147; *Cornelius,*
         [M] 151; *Fayetteville,* [M] 156;
         Gastonia, [M] 158; *Goldsboro,* [M]
         158; *Greensboro,* [M] 160; *Greenville,*
         [M] 161; *Hendersonville,* [M] 162;
         Hickory, [M] 163; *Jacksonville,* [M]
         165; *Kill Devil Hills (Outer Banks),*
         [MH] 166; *Kinston,* [MH] 167;

Laurinburg, [M] 167; *Lumberton,* [M]
   169; *Morehead City,* [M] 171; *New
   Bern,* [M] 174; *Raleigh,* [M] 178, [MH]
   179; *Roanoke Rapids,* [M] 180;
   Rocky Mount, [M] 181; *Salisbury,* [M]
   182; *Southern Pines,* [M] 183;
   Statesville, [M] 185; *Wilmington,* [M]
   189, [H] 189; *Wilson,* [M] 191;
   Winston-Salem, [M] 192
Pennsylvania
   Allentown, [M] 199; *Chambersburg,*
      [M] 210; *Du Bois,* [M] 216; *Erie,* [M]
      218; *Harrisburg,* [M] 226; *Pittsburgh
      Intl Airport Area,* [M] 274; *Pittsburgh,*
      [M] 270; *Scranton,* [M] 278; *State
      College,* [M] 282; *Wilkes-Barre,* [M]
      291; *Willow Grove,* [M] 293; *York,* [M]
      294
South Carolina
   Charleston, [M] 304, [MH] 305;
      Columbia, [M] 311, 312; *Greenville,*
      [M] 317; *Hilton Head Island,* [M] 320;
      Myrtle Beach, [M] 323; *Spartanburg,*
      [M] 328
Virginia
   Alexandria, [M] 336; *Blacksburg,* [M]
      345; *Charlottesville,* [M] 350;
      Chesapeake, [M] 352; *Emporia,* [M]
      360; *Fairfax,* [M] 361; *Fredericksburg,*
      [M] 364; *Hampton,* [M] 369;
      Harrisonburg, [M] 370; *Lynchburg,*
      [M] 378; *Newport News,* [MH] 385;
      Norfolk, [M] 387; *Richmond,* [MH]
      395; *Roanoke,* [M] 399; *Springfield,*
      [M] 402; *Virginia Beach,* [M] 408;
      Warrenton, [M] 411; *Williamsburg,*
      [M] 415; *Winchester,* [M] 419
West Virginia
   Beckley, [M] 426; *Charleston,* [MH]
      429; *Morgantown,* [M] 440;
      Wheeling, [MH] 447
HAMPTON STREET VINEYARD [R]
   Columbia SC, 313
HAMPTON'S [R] *Baltimore MD,* 51
HANNA'S MARINA DECK [R] *Ocean City
   MD,* 74
HARBOR COURT [H] *Baltimore MD,* 49
HARBOR VIEW [M] *Bethany Beach DE,* 3
HARBORLIGHT GUESTHOUSE [I]
   Morehead City NC, 172
HARBOUR INN & MARINA [H] *St Michaels
   MD,* 78
HARBOURMASTER'S [R] *Hilton Head
   Island SC,* 321
HARBOURTOWNE [RO] *St Michaels MD,* 79
HARD TIMES CAFE [U] *Rockville MD,* 77
HARD TIMES CAFE [U] *Alexandria VA,* 339
HARDWARE STORE [R] *Charlottesville VA,*
   352
HARLEY
   Pennsylvania
      Pittsburgh, [MH] 270
HARLEY DAWN DINER [R] *Atlantic City NJ,*
   89

HARMONY HOUSE [I] *New Bern NC,* 175
HARPOON HANNA'S [R] *Fenwick Island
   DE,* 4
HARRIS CRAB HOUSE [R] *Chesapeake
   Bay Bridge Area MD,* 58
HARRIS HOUSE MOTOR INN [M] *Ocean
   City NJ,* 114
HARRISON'S HARBOR WATCH [R] *Ocean
   City MD,* 74
HARRY BROWNE'S [R] *Annapolis MD,* 43
HARRY'S BAR & GRILL [R] *Philadelphia
   PA,* 262
HARRY'S SAVOY GRILL [R] *Wilmington
   DE,* 12
HARVEST MOON [R] *Wilmington NC,* 190
HARVEST MOON INN [R] *Flemington NJ,* 99
HARVEY MANSION [R] *New Bern NC,* 175
HATTERAS MARLIN [M] *Hatteras (Outer
   Banks) NC,* 161
HAUSSNER'S [R] *Baltimore MD,* 51
HAWKS NEST LODGE [L] *Gauley Bridge
   WV,* 434
HAWTHORN SUITES
   North Carolina
      Durham, [MH] 153
   Pennsylvania
      Pittsburgh, [M] 270
   South Carolina
      Charleston, [MH] 305
HAY-ADAMS [H] *Washington DC,* 26
HAYDN ZUG'S [R] *Lancaster PA,* 240
HAYWOOD PARK [H] *Asheville NC,* 136
HEADQUARTERS PLAZA [H] *Morristown
   NJ,* 109
HEART-IN-HAND [R] *Fairfax VA,* 361
HELEN'S [R] *Donegal PA,* 214
HEMINGWAY'S [R] *Hilton Head Island SC,*
   321
HEMLOCK [I] *Bryson City NC,* 142
HENDERSON HOUSE [R] *New Bern NC,*
   175
HENLEY PARK [H] *Washington DC,* 26
HENLOPEN [MH] *Rehoboth Beach DE,* 8
HENNESSY'S [R] *Columbia SC,* 313
HENNINGER'S TAVERN [R] *Baltimore MD,*
   51
HENRY CLAY [I] *Ashland VA,* 344
HENRY'S SEAFOOD [R] *Virginia Beach VA,*
   410
HEREFORD BARN STEAK HOUSE [R]
   Charlotte NC, 149
HERITAGE INN [I] *Franklin (Macon Co) NC,*
   157
HERITAGE INN [M] *Williamsburg VA,* 415
HERMAN'S HARBOR HOUSE [R] *Newport
   News VA,* 386
HERMITAGE INN [R] *Fairfax VA,* 361
HERMITAGE MOTOR INN [M] *Petersburg
   WV,* 443
HERO'S [R] *Manassas VA,* 380
HERR TAVERN & PUBLICK HOUSE [I]
   Gettysburg PA, 222
HERR TAVERN & PUBLICK HOUSE [R]
   Gettysburg PA, 223

Notes

Notes

Notes

Notes

Notes

Notes

Notes

Notes

Mobil Travel Guide

Please check the guides you would like to order:

☐ 0-679-03506-0
America's Best Hotels & Restaurants
$11.00 (Can $14.95)

☐ 0-679-03498-6
California and the West (Arizona, California, Nevada, Utah)
$15.95 (Can $21.95)

☐ 0-679-03500-1
Great Lakes (Illinois, Indiana, Michigan, Ohio, Wisconsin, Canada: Ontario)
$15.95 (Can $21.95)

☐ 0-679-03501-X
Mid-Atlantic (Delaware, District of Columbia, Maryland, New Jersey, North Carolina, Pennsylvania, South Carolina, Virginia, West Virginia)
$15.95 (Can $21.95)

☐ 0-679-03502-8
Northeast (Connecticut, Maine, Massachusetts, New Hampshire, New York, Rhode Island, Vermont, Canada: New Brunswick, Nova Scotia, Ontario, Prince Edward Island, Québec)
$15.95 (Can $21.95)

☐ 0-679-03503-6
Northwest and Great Plains (Idaho, Iowa, Minnesota, Montana, Nebraska, North Dakota, Oregon, South Dakota, Washington, Wyoming, Canada: Alberta, British Columbia, Manitoba)
$15.95 (Can $21.95)

☐ 0-679-03504-4
Southeast (Alabama, Florida, Georgia, Kentucky, Mississippi, Tennessee)
$15.95 (Can $21.95)

☐ 0-679-03505-2
Southwest & South Central (Arkansas, Colorado, Kansas, Louisiana, Missouri, New Mexico, Oklahoma, Texas)
$15.95 (Can $21.95)

☐ 0-679-03499-4
Major Cities (Detailed coverage of 45 major U.S. cities)
$17.95 (Can $25.00)

☐ 0-679-00047-X
Southern California (Includes California south of Lompoc, with Tijuana and Ensenada, Mexico)
$12.00 (Can $16.95)

☐ 0-679-00048-8
Florida
$12.00 (Can $16.95)

☐ 0-679-03548-6
On the Road with Your Pet (More than 3,000 Mobil rated Lodgings that Welcome Travelers with Pets)
$12.00 (Can $16.95)

☐ My check is enclosed.

☐ Please charge my credit card

☐ VISA ☐ MasterCard ☐ American Express

Total cost of book(s) ordered $ _____

Shipping & Handling (please add $2 for first book, $.50 for each additional book) $ _____

Add applicable sales tax (In Canada and in CA, CT, FL, IL, NJ, NY, TN and WA.) $ _____

TOTAL AMOUNT ENCLOSED $ _____

Credit Card # _____

Expiration _____

Signature _____

Please ship the books checked above to:

Name _____

Address _____

City _____ State _____ Zip _____

Please mail this form to: Mobil Travel Guides, Random House, 400 Hahn Rd., Westminster, MD 21157

M⊙bil Travel Guide

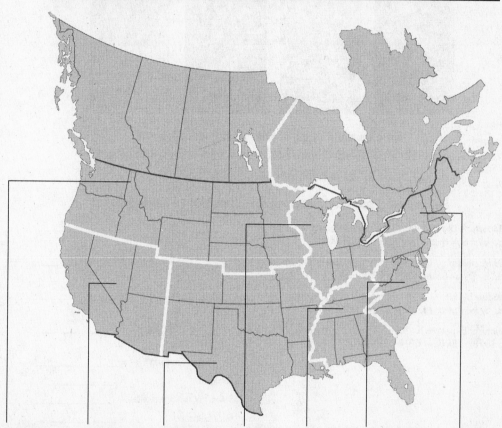

Northwest & Great Plains

Idaho
Iowa
Minnesota
Montana
Nebraska
North Dakota
Oregon
South Dakota
Washington
Wyoming

Canada:
Alberta
British Columbia
Manitoba

California & the West

Arizona
California
Nevada
Utah

Southwest & South Central

Arkansas
Colorado
Kansas
Louisiana
Missouri
New Mexico
Oklahoma
Texas

Great Lakes

Illinois
Indiana
Michigan
Ohio
Wisconsin

Canada:
Ontario

Southeast

Alabama
Florida
Georgia
Kentucky
Mississippi
Tennessee

Mid–Atlantic

Delaware
District of Columbia
Maryland
New Jersey
North Carolina
Pennsylvania
South Carolina
Virginia
West Virginia

Northeast

Connecticut
Maine
Massachusetts
New Hampshire
New York
Rhode Island
Vermont

Canada:
New Brunswick
Nova Scotia
Ontario
Prince Edward Island
Quebec

MAKE THE MOST OF YOUR TRAVELING TIME . . .

with Random House AudioBooks.

WITH MORE THAN 500 TITLES TO CHOOSE FROM, LISTEN TO GREAT BOOKS WHILE STILL ADMIRING THE SCENERY . . . YOU'LL REACH YOUR DESTINATION IN NO TIME.

 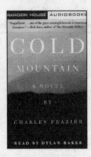  

For a complete listing of Random House AudioBooks,
Fax: (212) 572-6074; call (212) 572-6004; write: Random House Audio, Dept. CC,
201 East 50th Street, New York, NY 10022

Please send me the following Random House AudioBooks:

A Reporter's Life by Walter Cronkite (abridged, 4 hours) _____ @ $24.00 = _____
Read by the Author • ISBN: 0-679-45814-X

Cold Mountain by Charles Frazier (abridged, 3 hours) _____ @ $18.00 = _____
Read by Dylan Baker • ISBN: 0-679-46069-1

Paradise by Toni Morrison (abridged, 6 1/2 hours) _____ @ $25.95 = _____
Read by the Author • ISBN: 0-375-40179-2

Unnatural Exposure by Patricia Cornwell (abridged, 4 hours) _____ @ $24.00 = _____
Read by Blair Brown • ISBN: 0-679-44509-9 (Quantity)

Shipping/Handling* = _____

Subtotal = _____

Sales Tax (where applicable) = _____

Total Enclosed = _____

*Please enclose $4.00 to cover shipping and handling (or $6.00 if total order is more than $30.00).
☐ If you wish to pay by check or money order, please make it payable to Random House Audio Publishing.
☐ To charge your order to a major credit card, please fill in the information below.

Charge to ☐ American Express ☐ Visa ☐ MasterCard

Account No._____ Expiration Date_____

Signature_____

Name_____

Address_____

City_____ State_____ Zip_____

Also available wherever books are sold.

Send your payment with the order form above to:
Random House Audio Publishing, Dept. CC, 23-2, 201 East 50th Street, New York, NY 10022.
Prices subject to change without notice. Please allow 4-6 weeks for delivery.

HELP US GET TO KNOW YOU AND RECEIVE A FREE KEY CHAIN!

Please complete and return this postage paid card to Mobil Travel Guide. The information on you and your travel habits will help us improve the Guide to better serve you in the future. The first 500 respondents who successfully complete and return this questionnaire will receive a free Mobil key chain with our thanks and appreciation. The information supplied herein will be treated in confidence; names and addresses will not be released to mailing list houses or any other associations or organizations.

Please circle the appropriate letter or number, or fill in the blank, as necessary.

1. 1.__Mr.   2.__Mrs.   3.__Ms.   4.__Miss

_____
First Name   Initial   Last Name

_____
Street   Apt. No.

_____
City   State   Zip Code

2. Date of Purchase: Month___ Date___ Year___

3. How many round trips of 200 miles or more via any method of transportation have you taken in the last year?
a) How many of these were for leisure/pleasure? _____
b) How many of these were for business? _____

4. What is the duration of your average trip?
a) Leisure/pleasure travel? _____
b) Business travel? _____

5. How many of these trips were by car?
a) Leisure/pleasure travel? _____
b) Business travel? _____

6. Do you use the Mobil Travel Guide in your car?
a) Yes   b) No

7. What cities/towns/states or regions were your destinations for your last three (3) leisure/pleasure trips?
_____ _____ _____

8. What cities/towns/states or regions were your destinations for your last three (3) business trips?
_____ _____ _____

9. What kinds of activities do you prefer when you travel for leisure/pleasure? Circle all that apply.
a) Sightseeing-Historical
b) Sightseeing-Scenic
c) Camping/hiking
d) Sports and recreation
e) Shopping
f) Rest and relaxation
g) Visiting museums/galleries
h) Fine dining
i) Going to the beach

10. How much do you typically spend (on a per-night basis) for your accommodations when you travel for leisure/pleasure?
$_____ per night

11. How much do you typically spend (on a per-night basis) for your accommodations when you travel for business?
$_____ per night

12. What are your restaurant preferences when you travel for leisure/pleasure?
a) 4 or 5 Star   c) Family
b) Moderately priced   d) Fast food chain

13. What are your restaurant preferences when you travel for business?
a) 4 or 5 Star   c) Family
b) Moderately priced   d) Fast food chain

14. What kind of resources are used to plan your trips?
a) Leisure/pleasure travel?
   i) Travel books/guides
   ii) Magazines
   iii) Internet
   iv) Friends/family recommendations
   v) Travel agent
   vi) Other _____
b) Business travel?
   i) Travel books/guides
   ii) Magazines
   iii) Internet
   iv) Friends/family recommendations
   v) Travel agent
   vi) Other _____

15. If your vacation/business travel requires you to rent an automobile, how likely would you be to buy a travel guide of the area if offered (1: Not likely 5: Very likely)
1 2 3 4 5

16. Did you purchase the Mobil Travel Guide primarily for (choose one)?
a) Leisure/pleasure travel
b) Business travel
c) Maps
d) Coupons
e) Other _____

17. How did you hear about the Mobil Travel Guide?
a) Advertisement
b) Friends and family
c) Colleague
d) Point of sale (bookstore, service station)
e) Other _____

18. Where did you purchase the Mobil Travel Guide?
a) Furnished by employer
b) It was a gift
c) Chain bookstore Which? _____
d) Independent bookstore Which? _____
e) Travel store Which? _____
f) Department store
g) Drug store
h) Gift shop
i) Newsstand
j) Service station
k) Other _____

19. When was the last time you purchased a Mobil Travel Guide?
a) Never   d) Three to five years ago
b) Last year   e) More than five years ago
c) Two years ago

20. Why did you choose the Mobil Travel Guide in lieu of other options (choose three)?
a) Price
b) Quality ratings of accommodations
c) Quality ratings of restaurants
d) Factual information on accommodations
e) Factual information on restaurants
f) Information on things to see and do in the area
g) Maps
h) Discount coupons
i) Background information on states, cities and towns
j) Other _____

004

FOLD AND TAPE (OR SEAL) FOR MAILING—PLEASE DO NOT STAPLE

CUT ALONG DOTTED LINE

86

21. What three (3) features would you like to see more of?
a) Accommodation choices
b) Details/comments on accommodations
c) Restaurant choices
d) Details/comments on restaurants
e) Things to see and do in the area
f) State/city background information
g) Maps
h) Icons/Easy-to-use symbols
i) Discount Coupons
j) Other_____

22. In your opinion, does the Mobil Travel Guide improve Mobil Corporation's image?
a) Yes   c) Not sure
b) No

23. You are:
a) Female   b) Male

24. Your age is:
a) 18–24   d) 45–54
b) 25–34   e) 55–64
c) 35–44   f) 65+

25. You are:
a) Single/never married   c) Separated/divorced
b) Married   d) Widowed

26. The ethnic group that best describes you is:
a) African-American   d) Caucasian/White
b) Asian   e) Hispanic
c) Other_____

27. Highest level of education:
a) Some High School
b) High School Graduate
c) Some College
d) Technical Certification
e) College Degree (2- or 4-Year)
f) Some Post College Study
g) Advanced Degree

28. Your occupation is:
a) Professional
b) Executive, Managerial, Administrative
c) Military
d) Clerical, Sales, Technical
e) Precision, Crafts, Repair
f) Retired
g) Other_____

29. Your spouse/significant other's occupation is:
a) Professional
b) Executive, Managerial, Administrative
c) Military
d) Clerical, Sales, Technical
e) Precision, Crafts, Repair
f) Retired
g) Other

30. How many children do you have living at home in the following age groups?
a) None   f) 10–11 Years
b) < 1 Year   g) 12–14 Years
c) 1–2 Years   h) 15–18 Years
d) 3–5 Years   i) Over 18
e) 6–9 Years

31. Which choice best describes your household income level?
a) Under $10,000
b) $10,000–$19,999   g) $60,000–$69,999
c) $20,000–$29,999   h) $70,000–$79,999
d) $30,000–$39,999   i) $80,000–$89,999
e) $40,000–$49,999   j) $90,000–$99,999
f) $50,000–$59,999   k) >$100,000

32. Which types of credit cards do you use most for travel?
a) American Express, Diners Club, Discover, Carte Blanche
b) Bank Card (Mastercard, Visa)
c) Gas, Department Store
d) None of the Above

33. What type of vehicle do you drive on your trips?
a) Luxury   d) Mini Van
b) Mid Size   e) Sport Utility
c) Compact   f) RV

34. Do you belong to an automobile club?
a) Yes Which? _____
b) No

35. What other products/services do you purchase specifically for travel?
a) Tire/Auto Service
b) Luggage
c) Travel Store Items
d) Maps
e) Other_____

YOU CAN HELP MAKE THE *MOBIL TRAVEL GUIDE* MORE ACCURATE AND USEFUL

ALL INFORMATION WILL BE KEPT CONFIDENTIAL

Your Name_____
(Please Print)

Street_____

City, State, Zip_____

Were children with you on trip? ☐ Yes ☐ No

Number of people in your party _____

Your occupation_____

1.

Establishment name_____

Hotel ☐ Resort ☐ Other ☐
Motel ☐ Inn ☐ Restaurant ☐

Street_____ City_____ State _____

Do you agree with our description? ☐ Yes ☐ No; if not, give reason _____

Please give us your opinion of the following:

DECOR	CLEANLINESS	SERVICE	FOOD
☐ Excellent	☐ Spotless	☐ Excellent	☐ Excellent
☐ Good	☐ Clean	☐ Good	☐ Good
☐ Fair	☐ Unclean	☐ Fair	☐ Fair
☐ Poor	☐ Dirty	☐ Poor	☐ Poor

1998 *GUIDE* RATING _____ ★

CHECK YOUR SUGGESTED RATING BELOW:
☐ ★ good, satisfactory ☐ ★★★★ outstanding
☐ ★★ very good ☐ ★★★★★ one of best
☐ ★★★ excellent in country
☐ ✓ unusually good value

Comments:_____

Date of visit_____

First ☐ Yes visit? ☐ No

2.

Establishment name_____

Hotel ☐ Resort ☐ Other ☐
Motel ☐ Inn ☐ Restaurant ☐

Street_____ City_____ State _____

Do you agree with our description? ☐ Yes ☐ No; if not, give reason _____

Please give us your opinion of the following:

DECOR	CLEANLINESS	SERVICE	FOOD
☐ Excellent	☐ Spotless	☐ Excellent	☐ Excellent
☐ Good	☐ Clean	☐ Good	☐ Good
☐ Fair	☐ Unclean	☐ Fair	☐ Fair
☐ Poor	☐ Dirty	☐ Poor	☐ Poor

1998 *GUIDE* RATING _____ ★

CHECK YOUR SUGGESTED RATING BELOW:
☐ ★ good, satisfactory ☐ ★★★★ outstanding
☐ ★★ very good ☐ ★★★★★ one of best
☐ ★★★ excellent in country
☐ ✓ unusually good value

Comments:_____

Date of visit_____

First ☐ Yes visit? ☐ No

3.

Establishment name_____

Hotel ☐ Resort ☐ Other ☐
Motel ☐ Inn ☐ Restaurant ☐

Street_____ City_____ State _____

Do you agree with our description? ☐ Yes ☐ No; if not, give reason _____

Please give us your opinion of the following:

DECOR	CLEANLINESS	SERVICE	FOOD
☐ Excellent	☐ Spotless	☐ Excellent	☐ Excellent
☐ Good	☐ Clean	☐ Good	☐ Good
☐ Fair	☐ Unclean	☐ Fair	☐ Fair
☐ Poor	☐ Dirty	☐ Poor	☐ Poor

1998 *GUIDE* RATING _____ ★

CHECK YOUR SUGGESTED RATING BELOW:
☐ ★ good, satisfactory ☐ ★★★★ outstanding
☐ ★★ very good ☐ ★★★★★ one of best
☐ ★★★ excellent in country
☐ ✓ unusually good value

Comments:_____

Date of visit_____

First ☐ Yes visit? ☐ No

FOLD AND TAPE (OR SEAL) FOR MAILING—PLEASE DO NOT STAPLE

CUT ALONG DOTTED LINE

Revised editions are now being prepared for publication next year:

California and the West: Arizona, California, Nevada, Utah.

Northeast: Connecticut, Maine, Massachusetts, New Hampshire, New York, Rhode Island, Vermont; Eastern Canada.

Mid-Atlantic: Delaware, District of Columbia, Maryland, New Jersey, North Carolina, Pennsylvania, South Carolina, Virginia, West Virginia.

Southeast: Alabama, Florida, Georgia, Kentucky, Mississippi, Tennessee.

Great Lakes: Illinois, Indiana, Michigan, Ohio, Wisconsin; Ontario, Canada.

Northwest and Great Plains: Idaho, Iowa, Minnesota, Montana, Nebraska, North Dakota, Oregon, South Dakota, Washington, Wyoming; Western Canada.

Southwest and South Central: Arkansas, Colorado, Kansas, Louisiana, Missouri, New Mexico, Oklahoma, Texas.

Major Cities: Detailed coverage of 45 Major Cities.

The Mobil Travel Guide is available at Mobil Service Stations, bookstores, or by mail from the Mobil Travel Guide, Random House, 400 Hahn Rd., Westminster, MD 21157, or call toll-free, 24 hours a day, 1-800/533–6478.

HOW CAN WE IMPROVE *THE MOBIL TRAVEL GUIDE*?

Mobil Travel Guides are constantly being revised and improved. All attractions are updated and all listings are revised and evaluated annually. You can contribute to the accuracy and usefulness of the guides by sending us your reactions to the places you have visited. Your suggestions for improving the guides are also welcome. Just complete this prepaid mailing form or address letters to: *Mobil Travel Guide*, 4709 W. Golf Rd., Suite 803, Skokie, IL 60076. The editors appreciate your comments.

Have you sent us one of these forms before?   ☐ Yes   ☐ No

Please make any general comment here. Thanks! _____

_____

_____

_____

Mobil Travel Guide®

The Guide That Saves You M[...] When You Travel!

Please note: All offers may not be available in Canada. Call **(410) 825-3463** if you are unable to use an 800 number listed on the coupon.

Mobil Travel Guide®

The Guide That Saves You Money When You Travel!

Audio Diversions

$25.00 VALUE

FREE 1ST YEAR MEMBERSHIP IN THE "LITERATURE FOR LISTENING CLUB™."

Membership gives you 10% off on all purchases and rentals. When renting you get twice as long (30 days) to listen to your selections with over 2,600 titles to choose from. You will never run out of choices. Call 800-628-6145.

OFFER EXPIRES JUNE 30, 1999

Budget All The Difference In The World.™

15% OFF

TAKE 15% OFF WEEKLY OR WEEKEND STANDARD RATES.

Valid on Economy through Full-Size Cars. For reservations call: 800-455-2848. Be sure to mention **BCD#: T445311**.

OFFER EXPIRES JUNE 30, 1999

Empire State Building Observatories

UP TO FOUR ADMISSIONS

ENJOY $1.00 OFF ADULT ADMISSIONS AND $1.00 OFF CHILDREN ADMISSIONS.

Offer good for up to four admissions upon presentation of coupon at ticket office. Open daily 9:30 am - midnight. Last elevator to the top at 11:30 pm.

OFFER EXPIRES JUNE 30, 1999

DAYS INN Follow the Sun™

10% SPECIAL DISCOUNT

FOLLOW THE SUN TO DAYS INNS.

Now you can save even more at any of our more than 1,700 Days Inns throughout the United States and internationally. Just present this coupon upon check-in and we'll take 10% off our regular room rate for your entire length of stay! Advance reservations recommended so call now! For reservations and location information call **800-DAYS-INN**.

OFFER EXPIRES JUNE 30, 1999

FREE CAMPING STAY

CAMP FREE WHEN YOU RENT A KOA DEAL MOTOR HOME FROM CRUISE AMERICA.

Call **800-327-7778** and request a KOA DEAL Motor Home rental and learn how to camp free at participating KOA Kampgrounds.

OFFER EXPIRES JUNE 30, 1999

UP TO $21.00 OFF

BUSCH GARDENS WILLIAMSBURG AND WATER COUNTRY USA INVITE YOU TO ENJOY $3.50 OFF THE ONE-DAY REGULAR OR CHILD'S ADMISSION PRICE.

For information on opening schedule call **800-343-SWIM**. See reverse for details.

OFFER EXPIRES JUNE 30, 1999

UP TO $20.00 OFF

SAVE FROM $10.00 TO $20.00 ON A WEEKEND RENTAL.

Rent an Intermediate through Full Size 4-Door car for a minimum of two consecutive weekend days and you can save $5.00 per day, up to a total of $20.00 off for four weekend rental days, when you present this coupon at a participating Avis location in the U.S. Subject to complete Terms and Conditions on back. For information and reservations, call the special Avis reservation number: **800-831-8000**. Be sure to mention the special Avis Worldwide Discount (AWD) number for this offer A291814. Avis features GM cars.

Offer cannot be used in conjunction with any other coupon, promotion or offer.

Coupon #MUGD717 for a 2 day rental • Coupon #MUGD718 for a 3 day rental • Coupon #MUGD719 for a 4 day rental

OFFER EXPIRES JUNE 30, 1999

Taste Publications International, The Mobil Travel Guide, and Fodor's Travel Publications, Inc., will not be responsible if any establishment breaches its contract or refuses to accept coupons. However, Taste Publications International will attempt to secure compliance. If you encounter any difficulty, please contact Taste Publications International. We will do our best to rectify the situation to your satisfaction. ©1998 Taste Publications International

TASTE PUBLICATIONS INTERNATIONAL • 1031 CROMWELL BRIDGE ROAD • BALTIMORE, MD 21286

Budget
All The Difference In The World.

TERMS AND CONDITIONS
Be sure to mention BCD# T445311 when reserving an economy through full-size car and present this certificate at participating U.S. Budget locations (except in the New York metro area) to receive your member savings discount. This offer requires a one-day advance reservation, and is subject to vehicle availability. Vehicle must be returned to the original renting location except where intra-inter metro area drop-offs are permitted. Local age and rental requirements apply. Locations that rent to drivers under 25 may impose an age surcharge. Offer is not available with CorpRate, government or tour/wholesale rates, or with any other promotion. Refueling services, taxes, surcharges, and optional items are extra. Blackout dates may apply. Limit one certificate per rental.

TASTE PUBLICATIONS INTERNATIONAL

Audio Diversions
Good Books are for listening too!

More than 2,600 titles carefully drawn from among the best in travelbooks, adventure, biographies, business, children's, classics, education, how to's, foreign language, inspirational, literature, motivational, mystery, and self help books, Audio Diversions is sure to have what you need. Rentals are 10% off plus come with addressed and stamped packages for easy return.
10 % off everything.

TASTE PUBLICATIONS INTERNATIONAL

DAYS INN
Follow the Sun™

Available at participating properties. This coupon cannot be combined with any other special discount offer. Limit one coupon per room, per stay. Not valid during blackout periods or special events. Void where prohibited. No reproductions accepted.

TASTE PUBLICATIONS INTERNATIONAL

Empire State Building Observatories
Managed by:
Helmsely Spear, Inc.

Built in 1931, this 1,454 foot high skyscraper was climbed by King Kong in the movie classic. View Manhattan from the 86th floor observatory with outdoor promenade. Also enjoy the enclosed 102nd floor and exhibits of the eight wonders of the world.

TASTE PUBLICATIONS INTERNATIONAL

BUSCH GARDENS

Present this coupon when purchasing your ticket at any Busch Gardens Williamsburg or Water Country USA General admission price. Children two and under are admitted FREE. Admission price includes all regularly scheduled rides, shows and attractions. This coupon has no cash value and cannot be used in conjunction with any other discount. Prices and schedule subject to change without notice. Busch Gardens Williamsburg and Water Country USA have a "no solicitation" policy. Limit six tickets per coupon.

1   2   3   4   5   6

Please circle number of admissions.

PLU #R364 C365

TASTE PUBLICATIONS INTERNATIONAL

KOA has over 550 locations throughout the U.S. and Canada. Cruise America and Cruise Canada have over 100 rental centers.

TASTE PUBLICATIONS INTERNATIONAL

AVIS
We try harder®

TERMS AND CONDITIONS (*Save up to $20.00 on a Weekend Rental*) Offer valid on an Intermediate (Group C) through a Full Size 4-door (Group E) car for a 2-day minimum rental. Coupon must be surrendered at time of rental; one per rental. Coupon valid at Avis corporate and participating licensee locations in the continental U.S. Weekend rental period begins Thursday noon, and car must be returned by Monday 11:59 p.m. or a higher rate will apply. Offer not available during holiday and other blackout periods. Offer may not be available on all rates at all times. An advance reservation is required. Cars subject to availability. Taxes, local government surcharges and optional items, such as LDW, additional driver fee and refueling, are extra. Renter must meet Avis age, driver and credit requirements. Minimum age is 25. Offer expires June 30, 1999.

RENTAL SALES AGENT INSTRUCTION AT CHECKOUT: 1. In AWD, enter A291814. **2.** For a 2 day rental, enter MUGD717 in CPN. **3.** For a 3 day rental, enter MUGD718 in CPN. **4.** For a 4 day rental, enter MUGD719 in CPN. **5.** Complete this information:
RA#_____ Rental Date ___/___/___ **6.** Attach to COUPON tape.

TASTE PUBLICATIONS INTERNATIONAL

Mobil Travel Guide®

The Guide That Saves You Money When You Travel!

FREE FANNY PACK

YOURS FREE WHEN YOU JOIN NPCA NOW!

Join NPCA and save our national treasures! We are offering a special one-year introductory membership for only $15.00! Enjoy the many benefits of a NPCA membership and receive: a free National Parks and Conservation Association Fanny Pack, a free PARK-PAK, travel information kit, an annual subscription to the award-winning National Parks magazine, the NPCA discount photo service, car rental discounts and more.

See reverse for order form. MTG98

OFFER EXPIRES JUNE 30, 1999

Ripley's Believe It or Not!®

BUY ONE GET ONE FREE!*

(Limit 6 people)

Receive one complimentary admission with purchase of an equal value ticket.

Not valid with any other offers. Not for resale.
Valid only at locations listed. Coupon non-relinquishable.

Ripley's and Believe It or Not! are registered trademarks of Ripley Entertainment Inc.

PLU-MOBIL

OFFER EXPIRES JUNE 30, 1999

ADVENTURE WORLD THE GREAT ESCAPE.

$7.00 OFF

SAVE $7.00 OFF EACH REGULAR ADMISSION (UP TO 6 PEOPLE) WHEN YOU PRESENT THIS COUPON AT ANY ADVENTURE WORLD TICKET WINDOW.

One (1) coupon good for up to six people and cannot be combined with any other discount, sold, or be redistributed, and not valid with Junior or Senior admission. Valid 1998/1999 season. Call for details 301-249-1500, for dates and time.

Code: 1017

OFFER EXPIRES JUNE 30, 1999

CHOICE HOTELS INTERNATIONAL

10% OFF

ENJOY A 10% DISCOUNT AT PARTICIPATING COMFORT, QUALITY, CLARION, SLEEP, ECONO LODGE AND RODEWAY INN HOTELS AND SUITES.

The next time you're traveling call 800-4-CHOICE and request Mobil discount #00052333. Advance reservations required. Kids 18 and under stay free and 1,400 hotels will provide free continental breakfast.

OFFER EXPIRES JUNE 30, 1999

Travel Discounters

UP TO $100.00 OFF

RECEIVE UP TO $100.00 OFF WHEN YOU BUY AN AIRLINE TICKET FROM TRAVEL DISCOUNTERS. CALL 800-355-1065 AND MENTION CODE MTG IN ORDER TO RECEIVE THE DISCOUNT.

Savings are subject to certain restrictions and availability. Valid for flights on most major airlines. See reverse for discount chart.

OFFER EXPIRES JUNE 30, 1999

General Cinema · LOEWS THEATRES SONY THEATRES · UNITED ARTISTS

THEATER DISCOUNT

Valid at all participating theatres.

Please send me:

_____ Sony/Loews at $4.50 each = _____
_____ United Artists at $4.50 each = _____
_____ General Cinema at $5.00 each = _____

Add $1.00 for handling. Allow 2-3 weeks for delivery. Orders over $75.00 will be sent via certified mail and may require additional processing time.

Limit 20 tickets per order.

OFFER EXPIRES JUNE 30, 1999

American Tourister · Samsonite · COMPANY STORE

SAVE 20% OFF

SHOPPING SPREE!

20% off selected merchandise when you visit any American Tourister or Samsonite Company Store. All stores carry first quality luggage, accessories and gifts to fit all your travel needs at 35%-50% off comparable prices.

Call 1-800-547-BAGS for a location nearest you.

OFFER EXPIRES JUNE 30, 1999

CAREERS
IN PUBLISHING

BLYTHE CAMENSON

VGM Career Books

Chicago   New York   San Francisco   Lisbon   London   Madrid   Mexico City
Milan   New Delhi   San Juan   Seoul   Singapore   Sydney   Toronto

Library of Congress Cataloging-in-Publication Data

Camenson, Blythe.
    Careers in publishing / Blythe Camenson.
        p.   cm. — (VGM professional careers series)
    Includes bibliographical references.
    ISBN 0-658-00114-0 (hardcover) — ISBN 0-658-00116-7 (paperback)
     1. Publishers and publishing—Vocational guidance—United States.   2. Book industries
and trade—Vocational guidance—United States.   3. Authorship—Vocational guidance—
United States.   I. Title.   II. Series.

Z471 .C36   2002
070.5'023—dc21   2001056903

VGM Career Books

A Division of The **McGraw·Hill** *Companies*

1 2 3 4 5 6 7 8 9 0 LBM/LBM 1 0 9 8 7 6 5 4 3 2

ISBN 0-658-00114-0 (hardcover)
ISBN 0-658-00116-7 (paperback)

This book was set in Times
Printed and bound by Lake Book Manufacturing

Cover photograph copyright © Eyewire

McGraw-Hill books are available at special quantity discounts to use as premiums and sales
promotions, or for use in corporate training programs. For more information, please write to the
Director of Special Sales, Professional Publishing, McGraw-Hill, Two Penn Plaza, New York, NY
10121-2298. Or contact your local bookstore.

This book is printed on acid-free paper.

CONTENTS

ABOUT THE AUTHOR

Blythe Camenson is a full-time writer. In addition to extensive writing on the subject of careers—with more than four dozen books in print—she has also written several books to help new writers learn how to get published. *Your Novel Proposal: From Creation to Contract* (Writer's Digest Books), coauthored with Marshall J. Cook, has been particularly well received. She is also the author of *Careers in Writing* and *How to Sell, Then Write Your Nonfiction Book.*

Camenson is also director of Fiction Writer's Connection (FWC), an organization dedicated to helping new writers improve their craft and learn the many steps toward publication. She maintains an informational website at fiction writers.com and is a frequent speaker at national conferences and bookstores.

She earned her bachelor of arts degree with a double major in English and psychology from the University of Massachusetts, Boston, and her master of education degree (M.Ed.), majoring in counseling, from Northeastern University, also in Boston.

Camenson also spent eight years working in the Persian Gulf, teaching English at various universities. Her many travel articles have appeared in both national and international publications.

ACKNOWLEDGMENTS

The author would like to thank the following professionals for providing information and advice on careers in publishing:

Andrea Au, associate editor, Simon & Schuster
Dianna Bacchi, meeting planner, McGraw-Hill
Victoria Harnish Benson, author/owner, Silver Dove Publishing Company
Joan Marie Bledig, typographer, JDA Typesetting Corporation
Wendy Butler, editor, *About.com Publishing Guide*
Carolyn Campbell, author
Stephanie Dooley, event planner, Enchantment Events
Jessica Faust, literary agent, BookEnds
Miranda Garza, publisher and editor, *Kids' Highway* magazine
Sara Goodman, publishing law attorney
Joseph Hayes, freelance features writer
Tracey Hessler, managing editor, *Somniloquy* magazine
Nancy Zoole Kenney, director of contracts, Henry Holt and Company
Tanya Lochridge, freelance medical/health care writer
Rod Mitchell, literary and entertainment publicist, Adventures in Media, Inc.
Mark Ortman, author, director, The Self-Publishing Resource Center
Kathy Ptacek, publisher and editor, *Gila Queen's Guide to Markets* newsletter
Linda L. Roghaar, literary agent, former sales rep
Marilyn and Tom Ross, authors, self-publishing consultants
Kelly Boyer Sagert, managing editor, *Over the Back Fence* magazine
Doug Schmidt, senior editor, David C. Cook Publishing Company
Ellen Urban, freelance editor and proofreader
Nancy Yost, literary agent, Lowenstein Associates

CAREERS
IN PUBLISHING

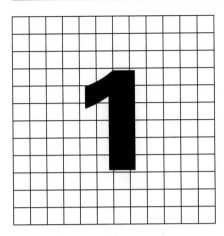

CAREERS IN PUBLISHING

"There are only two or three human stories, and they go on repeating themselves as fiercely as if they had never happened before."—Willa Cather

The field of publishing is exciting and competitive. There are risks and surprises, and sometimes, disappointments. Those working in this industry have a great deal of power. They determine which books and stories will see print, and to some extent, help to shape the tastes of the reading public.

In the publishing industry there are many sectors in which to pursue careers. This chapter will give you an overview of the different arenas; subsequent chapters examine these fields in more depth.

BOOK PUBLISHING

Although there are many sectors in the publishing industry, book publishing leads the field. Last year book sales totaled more than $25 billion, a 3.4 percent increase over the previous year, according to sales figures released by the Association of American Publishers (AAP). Book publishing is big business.

What sells the most? Although overall trade sales dropped 3.7 percent—adult hardbound book sales experienced the largest drop, down $2.69 billion—juvenile book sales showed positive figures in both hardbound (up 13.2 percent, $1.20 billion in sales) and paperbound (up 16.4 percent, $753.1 million in sales).

Educational book sales were strong, up a significant $3.88 billion, and sales of professional and scholarly books were also positive, up $5.13 billion. Religious book sales were up slightly, 2.5 percent with sales of $1.25 billion. But university press sales joined the adult trade category and dropped 2.4 percent ($402.0 million).

Mail-order publications sales showed positive numbers for the first time in two years. Book club sales were up 1.5 percent, with sales of $1.29 billion. Mass-market paperback sales remained fairly even, totaling $1.56 billion.

Financial concerns often determine which books get published. When those books do well, then everyone is happy, from bookstore owners to the sales team and distributors. But there are only ten to fifteen slots on the various bestseller lists, and with thousands of books published each year, the odds are against producing a blockbuster. Although some books have steady sales and can stay on the publisher's backlist for years, others can disappear from bookstore shelves after only a month.

TYPES OF BOOK PUBLISHERS

Between 75 and 85 percent of all books published in North America today are produced by about eight megacorporations and a dozen or so of the largest independent publishers. After the big guys, another 2,200 publishers or so are listed by the U.S. Commerce Bureau. *Literary Marketplace*, the industry reference published by R. R. Bowker, lists another 18,000 to 20,000 smaller and independent publishers.

Book publishers can be categorized as follows:

National/International Publishers

The eight megaconglomerates that rule book publishing in North America, with some of their major imprints in parentheses, are these:

1. Hearst Corporation (Avon, William Morrow)

2. News Corporation/Rupert Murdoch (HarperCollins)

3. Pearson PLC (Penguin, G. P. Putnam, Berkley)

4. Viacom (Simon & Schuster, Pocket Books)

5. Advance/Newhouse (Random House, Knopf, Modern Library, Ballantine)

6. Bertelsmann AG (Bantam, Doubleday, Dell; Dial)

7. Time Warner/Ted Turner (Little Brown, Book of the Month)

8. Holtzbrinck (Farrar, Straus and Giroux; St. Martin's Press; Henry Holt)

Because of their sheer size, these large publishers require the biggest staffs.

Regional/Small Presses

There are thousands of independent book publishers, most of who never see the light of the *New York Times Book Review* or the bestseller list. But these small presses can take chances; they don't need megahits to survive. They know how to reach specialty and special-interest markets and specific regions of the country. They choose to publish the books that will appeal to those markets.

Small-press and regional publishers release fewer titles a year; print runs are smaller, and so are sales. Staff might consist of one or two people wearing many hats, from editor and publisher to errand runner and mail clerk.

University Presses

Most university presses specialize in particular subjects, often educational in nature, but many also publish mainstream books. Most enjoy fine reputations and give each project professional care.

**Organizational/
Sponsored Presses**

Many organizations have their own publishing section, putting into print books that would interest their constituents. A professional association dealing with adoption, for example, might produce a nonfiction how-to or a novel with adoption as its theme. The first publisher for Tom Clancy's book *The Hunt for Red October* was the Naval Institute Press.

Subsidy Publishers

While traditional publishers are always overrun with manuscript submissions, subsidy publishers have to advertise their need for manuscripts. It's the writers, not the reading public, who pay the subsidy publishers.

Subsidy publishers are also known as vanity presses because they prey on new writers who have not been able to break in yet—and on new writers who just don't know any better. They present themselves as if they are commercial publishers, offering to evaluate your manuscript (all manuscripts are accepted) and offering a publishing contract. But when it comes time for payment, it's the writers' money that goes to the publisher, instead of advances and royalties that should be going to the writers.

Subsidy publishers do put a manuscript into print. Some offer minimal help with marketing. But libraries and book reviewers recognize subsidy publishing when they see it and won't buy or review those books.

Cooperative Publishers

Some publishers ask authors to share the cost of producing the book. The author might pay for part of the cost of printing and binding, for example, or provide the typeset, camera-ready copy. Writers who participate in cooperative publishing are sharing the risk that is usually the publishers' alone.

Some small publishers work in three categories, publishing some books on a commercial basis, some through a co-op arrangement, and others through author subsidy. The stigma of vanity publishing still attaches itself to some cooperative publishers—especially those that also work on a subsidy basis.

**Book Packagers/
Producers**

This fairly new breed of publishing is on the rise. Book packagers, or book producers as they are sometimes called, act as go-betweens, selling a concept to a publisher and then contracting with a writer to create the book. More often than not the author works for a set, work-for-hire fee rather than receiving royalties. Often the book packager holds the copyright to the book.

In an article previously published on the Authorlink website, former book packager Jessica Faust says, "A book packager is a cross between an agent and an editor, and more. A book packager often works with agents, authors, editors, designers, illustrators, photographers, and printers—all of the people who make a book possible. By working with such a variety of people, a book packager has the ability to deliver a printer-ready manuscript to the publisher. That means that once the publisher receives the final product it has already been written and edited, pictures have been supplied, production people have been called in to lay out the book, and the entire project is ready to be sent to the printer.

"Much like an agent, a book packager submits manuscripts to an editor at a publishing house. These manuscripts are usually prepared in either of two ways:

"One. The project has been requested by the publisher. The book packager puts together an outline and finds a writer interested in authoring the book.

"Two. The concept is developed 'in-house' (within the book-packaging company), an outline and sample materials are put together—with or without an author—and the material is sent to the publisher.

"Then, just as if a writer or his or her agent were to submit a proposal to a publisher, the packager waits for that fateful phone call and checks the mailbox for rejections.

"Once an editor agrees to buy or publish a project, the process starts from the top. The packager works with the author to develop a well-written book and turns in the edited manuscript to the publisher."

Currently Jessica Faust acts as a literary agent and is profiled in Chapter 3.

Self-Publishers

Self-publishers are responsible for every aspect of the publication of their own material: writing and editing, designing page layout, choosing the cover copy and colors, getting the printing done, arranging for distribution, and handling publicity and sales. It can be very risky business, and it can carry the same sort of stigma that attaches itself to vanity and cooperative publishing.

There are a handful of self-publishing success stories (see Chapter 9), but compared to the billions of dollars of books published each year, a handful is pretty small.

Electronic Publishing

Electronic publishing is emerging as an alternative delivery system for books. Or so they say. The options mentioned here do exist, but nobody knows if anyone is making any money at them.

In theory, people pay for and then download material. Then they either read the material on their computer screen or handheld device designed just for this purpose or print out individual copies of the work. This print-on-demand is carried out at some bookstores or in the customer's own home.

Some electronic publishers act as the online equivalent to subsidy and cooperative publishers, charging writers for web space and uploading fees and not providing any marketing help per se. Many of these do not edit the material and accept every manuscript that comes their way. Other online publishers are trying to be selective and publish only books they feel are worthy.

Many traditional publishing houses have created websites to promote their traditionally published books. One such traditional publisher tried an experiment, providing a Stephen King serial only to online customers. Another followed suit—but then the fad rolled to a halt. The question is will these cyberbooks ever become more than a fad? Again, no real figures are available to back up the claims electronic publishers may make.

For writers electronic publishing might seem an easy avenue to publication, one that is less expensive than working with a vanity press. And they can eliminate the stacks of books sitting in the garage. But again, there's that stigma.

The National Writers Union (NWU) offers guidelines to help writers as they navigate their way through this rapidly changing industry. They assert that the right to publish the electronic version of any book should be negotiated. These rights should be retained by the creator of the work unless specifically stated in the contract. The NWU is aware that some publishers claim that electronic versions of a book are simply extensions of print rights. The NWU's position, recently reinforced by the Supreme Court decision in *Tasini v. NY Times*, is that electronic versions of any book are not extensions of print rights; an E-book is a different version altogether (as with movie rights, audio rights, etc.) and should be a separate item negotiated for in the contract. For more on this issue visit nwu.org.

Most job opportunities resulting from electronic publishing include editing and web design and troubleshooting. Are there enough online entities to provide work? In a survey of 546 publishing professionals conducted by Book Zone, a website hosting and marketing firm specializing in book publishing, nearly 79 percent of the respondents' firms currently had websites, and 36 percent of those firms had had sites for three years or more.

According to Mary Westheimer, president of Book Zone, only 56 percent of all U.S. companies sell or promote their products online. Of the 8,596 publishing professionals the survey was distributed to, 546 responded—a 6.4 percent response rate. The respondents appear to be mostly smaller firms, reporting revenues of under $2 million. About 6.9 percent reported sales of more than $10 million.

The responding publishers report using their sites for promotion and for direct sales (73 percent). The sites use linking campaigns from other sites, online advertising, and strategic alliances such as associate programs to promote their sites. However, the survey reveals that more than half the sites are dissatisfied with the traffic they receive, and 43 percent see fewer than five hundred Web visitors a month. Westheimer noted that those using newsgroups and mailing lists for promotion were the most pleased with the traffic level at their sites.

For an extensive list of online publishers, see Appendix E.

SAMPLE JOB ADVERTISEMENT

The following is a sample advertisement. The employer has not been identified because the job has already been filled. Other sample jobs are highlighted throughout this book in subsequent chapters.

Position: Electronic Publishing Specialist

Location: An independent investment management firm in Boston

Responsibilities: The electronic publishing specialist will report to the production manager and will provide publishing support for the production, updating, and maintenance of prospect- and client-presentation books.

Qualifications: Proficiency with Macintosh OS 9.0 or above is required (PC knowledge a plus). Proofreading experience would be helpful. Publishing software knowledge: PageMaker 6.5, DeltaGraph 4.0, Microsoft Word, Microsoft Excel, Adobe Acrobat. Graphics software knowledge a plus: Illustrator, Photoshop. Must be detail-oriented with the ability to prioritize projects, meet strict deadlines, and communicate effectively with internal clients. Ability to work well under pressure cooperatively and within a highly structured corporate electronic publishing environment is critical.

LITERARY AGENCIES

Literary agents act as go-betweens for writers and editors. These days most of the big New York publishing houses refuse to consider manuscripts unless they are sent by an agent. Many publishers credit agents with the ability to screen out inappropriate submissions. An agent is expected to be familiar with the different kinds of books publishers prefer to take on.

Agents spend their time reading manuscripts, choosing which ones to work with, and then trying to sell them to publishers. Agents free a writer to concentrate on writing instead of marketing. The agents' job is to find the right house for their clients' work and, once successful, to negotiate the best financial deal for the writer.

Agents also handle film rights for feature or TV movies and foreign rights, selling books to publishers overseas. See Chapter 3 for more information on the role of the agent.

OTHER PUBLISHING AVENUES

Other publishing avenues include magazines and newspapers, professional association newsletters, and corporate publications. Within publishing there are, of course, the writers (see Chapter 2); editors (see Chapter 4); book and other print-production personnel (see Chapter 5); marketing and sales specialists (see Chapter 6); publicists, event planners, and advertising managers (see Chapter 7); and lawyers and contract specialists (see Chapter 8).

PREPARING FOR A CAREER IN PUBLISHING

The field is so broad, a generalized discussion of career preparation would be difficult. The path an editor would take would be different from the path of a sales rep or contract director. One obvious piece of advice is to have at least a bachelor's degree in a major related to the intended career goal. Finance majors work in accounting departments. Paralegals or lawyers work in contracts departments. English, journalism, or communications majors work as editors.

Other important preparation would include any kind of work in the field of publishing. Those seeking a newspaper career should land employment in that setting to familiarize themselves thoroughly with the type of work they would be doing. Gaining this background preparation helps candidates land jobs when the time comes.

FINDING JOBS IN PUBLISHING

To learn about openings, job candidates must take a proactive approach. While in college, investigate the obvious sources—career placement offices, the English department job board, job fairs, and so on. Read *Publishers Weekly*. Regularly search the Internet and bookmark sites that feature posted jobs. Build up your resume with internships, work-study positions, and other "get-a-foot-in-the-door" types of jobs.

The get-a-foot-in-the-door approach is a very viable strategy for this field. In the world of newspapers, magazines, and book publishing, experts advise you to take any job you can to get started. If you want to be an editor, for example, you could start out as a contract assistant, then move into an editorial position, and then move up the ladder to senior editor or higher.

If you get yourself in the door and get to know the people in the department for which you prefer to work, your chances are better than are the chances of an unknown candidate hoping to go immediately into an editorial position. The same holds true of internships. Any related internship allows for networking and making contacts. Even if the student is hoping for a sales and promotions posting, an internship in the book-production department of a publishing house, for example, will provide fodder for a resume, along with a host of important contacts. And that student will be one of the first to hear about any new job openings.

SALARIES IN PUBLISHING

Salaries vary widely depending upon the type of job, the rank within that position, the employer's size and budget, and the region of the country in which the job is located. In general, though, salaries in publishing are not the most glamorous aspect of the work. Yes, you hear about the seven-figure advances some writers can pull in, but that's not the norm—and the people paying those salaries seldom earn anything anywhere near that.

In the chapters ahead, salaries for each publishing sector are provided.

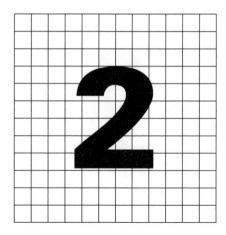

WRITERS, ILLUSTRATORS, AND PHOTOGRAPHERS

"Writing is the only profession where no one considers you
ridiculous if you earn no money."—Jules Renard

"Only a fool would write for nothing."—Samuel Johnson

Before editors and agents, before book-production workers and sales staff, before promotion and advertising, must come writers and illustrators. For without the written word or a graphic to accompany it, there would be no use for any of the careers covered in this book.

Writers have the widest opportunities in this career field. Writers write for magazines, newspapers, advertising agencies, and PR firms. Writers write novels and nonfiction books. They write travel brochures and technical manuals. They write obituaries and garden columns. Here's a listing of areas a writer can consider:

MAGAZINES

Visit any bookstore or newsstand and you will see hundreds of magazines covering a variety of topics—from sports and cars to fashion and parenting. There are also many you won't see there, the hundreds of trade journals and magazines written for businesses, industries, and professional workers in as many different careers. These publications all offer information on diverse subjects to their equally diverse readership. They are filled with articles and profiles, interviews and editorials, letters and advice, as well as pages and pages of advertisements.

The Different Kinds of Articles

Articles fall into two broad categories: those that educate and those that entertain. Here is a sampling of the topics that articles for magazines cover:

Art	Humor
Aviation	Military
Business and finance	Nature
Careers	Parenting
Child care	Pets
Computers	Photography
Contemporary culture	Politics
Entertainment	Psychology and self-help
Food	Retirement
Gardening	Science
General interest	Sports
Health	Travel
Hobbies	

Although the subject matter can be very different, most magazine articles include many of the same elements. They all start with an interesting "hook," that first paragraph that grabs the reader's (and the editor's) attention. They use quotes from experts, cite important facts, and sometimes include amusing anecdotes or experiences.

NEWSPAPERS

There are different kinds of newspapers—large-city dailies or small-town weeklies—but whatever the size or location, the job of a newspaper and its writers is to cover local, state, national, and international events and put all this news together to keep the reading public informed.

Writers, copyeditors, and photojournalists cover a range of topics, depending on the newspaper. Most are given assignments and cover stories such as a downtown riot or a car accident. Some get to travel abroad and might find themselves on the front line in a war zone or witnessing flood rescues or criminal activity. Reporters gather information by visiting the scene, interviewing people, following leads and news tips, and examining documents. While some reporters might rely on their memories, most take notes or use a tape recorder while collecting facts. Back in the office, they organize their material, decide what the focus or emphasis should be, and then write their stories, generally using a computer. Because of deadlines, while away from the office, many reporters use portable computers to file stories, which are then sent by telephone modem directly to the newspaper's computer system.

The departments within newspapers vary from location to location, but most include some, if not all, of the following sections:

Art	Health
Books	International news
Business	Lifestyles/features
Consumer affairs	Local news
Courts	National news
Crime	Religion
Education	Science
Entertainment	Social events
Fashion	Sports
Finance	State news
Food	Travel
Foreign affairs	Weather

FICTION

Fiction writers are creative, imaginative people. After all, they have to be; they make up stories for a living. Whether writing short stories or full-length novels, fiction writers have to be able to create imaginary characters and events and make them seem real to their readers. Fiction writers have to be troublemakers, too, inventing all sorts of problems for their characters. They have to make their characters' conversations and thoughts entertaining and fill their lives with action. Finally, fiction writers have to be expert problem solvers, helping their heroes find satisfying solutions to their troubles by the end of the story.

If you love to read fiction and you find yourself stopping in the middle of a book and saying out loud, "I could do that better," then maybe you can.

But few new fiction writers have the luxury of working at their craft full time. Most need to maintain some other sort of employment to help pay the bills until they are able to support themselves through their writing. Because of this, dedicated writers use every spare minute they have to work on their books or stories. John Grisham, for example, wrote a good deal of *The Firm* on yellow legal pads while taking the train to and from work as a full-time attorney in a law firm. Others get up an hour earlier, stay up an hour later, turn down invitations to parties or other social events, or let the housework go—whatever they can do to find the time to write.

Successful authors who support themselves through their writing treat it as a full-time job. Most report learning how to discipline themselves to put in a certain number of hours each day. Every writer chooses a schedule that is comfortable to him or her. Some work in the early hours of the morning, take afternoon naps, and then go back to the computer in the evenings. Others write for eight or ten or twelve hours straight each day for a period of months until the book is finished. Still others might take years to complete one volume.

There is no set formula how a writer should work. The only rule is that you have to write. Author James Clavell said that even if you write only one page every day for a year, at the end of that time you'll have 365 pages. And that's a good-sized book.

THE MANY CATEGORIES OF FICTION

Next time you visit a bookstore, take note of where the different books are shelved and what the signs in each section say. Here is an example of some of the different genres or categories you'll encounter, with a few of their subgenres also included:

Action/adventure

Children's

Fantasy

General/mainstream

Historical

Horror

Literary

Mystery (cozy, crime, detective, police procedural)

Romance (contemporary, gothic, historical, regencies, sensuous, sweet)

Science fiction

Suspense (legal, medical, psychological, woman-in-jeopardy)

Thriller

Western

Young adult

NONFICTION BOOKS

Writers of nonfiction have a distinct advantage over fiction writers. There are more than twice the number of nonfiction titles published each year than there are fiction titles. This means that there are more than twice as many opportunities for the beginning nonfiction book writer to break in and get published. In fact, it's probably safe to say that any competent writer with a little market savvy can find a home for his or her writing.

But you might be thinking that a nonfiction writer needs to be experienced in a specialized field of knowledge before he or she could even think about writing a nonfiction book. After all, a fiction writer can rely on imagination; nonfiction writers have to be experts. Right?

Wrong.

Nonfiction book writers do not have to start out as experts, though many of them end up that way by the time they've finished.

GETTING PUBLISHED

Freelance Magazine or Newspaper Articles

Before starting, read as many magazines and newspapers as you can, and in particular, read those you would like to write for. It's never a good idea to send an article to a publication you have not seen before. Being familiar with the different magazines or newspapers will also help you to come up with future article ideas.

Once you have decided what you want to write about, there are two ways you can proceed. You can write the entire article "on spec," send it off to appropriate editors, and hope they like your topic. Or, you can write a query letter—a miniproposal—to see if there is any interest in your idea first. Query letters will save you the time of writing articles you might have difficulty selling. Only once you're given a definite assignment do you proceed.

There are three important keys to keep in mind to get your articles published:

1. Make sure your writing is polished and that your article includes all the important elements.

2. Make sure your letter and manuscript are neatly typed and mistake-free.

3. Make sure you are sending your articles to the right publication. A magazine that features stories only on "Planning the Perfect Wedding" will not be interested in your piece on "Ten Tips for the Perfect Divorce."

You can find out about different publications and the kinds of materials they prefer to publish in the market guides listed in Appendix D.

Payment for Magazine and Newspaper Freelancers

Most new writers are thrilled to see their "byline," that is, their name in print, giving them credit for the article. And to writers, nothing is more exciting than the finished product, getting to see their stories in print. Getting a check or a salary for your efforts can be rewarding as well, but sadly, for new freelancers, the checks might not come often enough and are not always large enough to live on comfortably.

While staff writers are paid a regular salary (the average wage for staff positions ranges from $35,270 for news reporters to $45,500 for staff writers, plus benefits, according to the Bureau of Labor Statistics), a freelancer gets paid only when he or she sells an article. Fees could range from as low as $5 to $1,000 or more per article, depending upon the publication. Some pay per word—from 1 cent to $1 or $2 or more. But even with a high-paying magazine, writers often have to wait until their stories are published before they are paid. Because publishers work so far ahead, planning issues six months or more in advance, payment could be delayed from three months to a year or more.

Recently, the National Writers Union (NWU) Delegates Assembly appointed a committee to study pay rates for freelance writers to determine a minimum recommended pay rate. Their research was motivated by a sense among members that freelance rates don't provide freelancers with even a moderate income. The NWU believes that rates have not kept up with staff salaries in recent years. They had also heard claims that freelance rates had not increased since the 1960s.

The NWU discovered that the situation is even worse than they had thought. In real dollars, freelance rates have gone down by more than 50 percent since the 1960s. And while rates have gone down, publishers are getting more for their money. As an example of the pay decrease, the NWU report cited that in 1966 *Cosmopolitan* reported offering 60 cents a word; in 1998 they reported offering $1 a word. But, during this time, the buying power of the dollar fell by a factor of five. So *Cosmopolitan*'s real rates fell by a factor of three. *Good Housekeeping* reported offering $1 a word in 1966 and the same $1 a word in 1998—an 80 percent decline in real pay. Another way of looking at these figures is to translate them into 2001 dollars. Under those terms, *Good Housekeeping* was paying the equivalent of $5 a word in 1966.

How much do freelancer writers need to work to make a decent living? This is something the NWU report tried to answer. They state: "Freelance writers spend a tremendous amount of time looking for work (researching and pitching articles) and revising. While some articles can be done in a week and others may take three months, for most full-time freelance writers, selling and writing 3,000 or 4,000 words a month is about the best that they can expect to do—two feature articles or the equivalent in smaller pieces. (This is more than most magazine staff writers write—which is about 2,500 words a month.)

"At this level of output, a rate of a dollar a word means a gross income of $36,000 to $48,000 a year, out of which has to be taken expenses, insurance, and other benefits. This is the equivalent of earning a salary, with benefits, of about $30,000 to $40,000 a year. So for a college graduate working as a full-time freelance writer to bring in even a moderate income that includes benefits requires at least $1 a word.

"The median income of full-time, college-educated workers in the U.S. is around $50,000, plus benefits. So to earn as much as the average college graduate would require somewhat more, between $1.25 and $1.60 a word."

The NWU report also studied what publications could afford to pay, based on their ad rates. They compared publication income with words of text published "to get an estimate of income per word and to determine what fraction of total revenue is paid to writers. For example, for *Discover* magazine, five hundred pages of ads a year at $50,000 per full-page ad gives $25 million a year in gross revenue. (This underestimates their income, because half-page ads cost two-thirds as much as full-page ads). Since the magazine has one million subscriptions at $25 per year, it has another $25 million a year. (This ignores newsstand sales, which make the total even larger.) Divide by five hundred pages of text a year at eight hundred words per text page and *Discover*'s income is more than $125 per word. *Discover* pays its writers $1 a word. So they pay their writers less than 1 percent of their gross income. If they paid writers 15 percent of gross income, the way book publishers manage to and still turn handsome profits, they would be paying at least $19 a word."

The numbers are the same for magazines such as *Forbes*. The gap is even larger with the larger magazines. *Good Housekeeping* and *Women's Day* have ad rates of $200,000 a page and more and as many as eight million readers, earning something like $500 a word. Yet they pay freelancers $1 to $2 a word, less than 0.5 percent of revenues. "If they paid the writers 15 percent of revenue," states the NWU report, "freelancers would be getting $75 a word at these publications."

The National Writer's Union report also covers newspapers. "*The New York Times* takes in about $40,000 per ad page or about $2 million per issue, about comparable to *Discover*, *Forbes*, and *Good Housekeeping*. The *Times* metro edition hits about a million readers. With $1 million or more in subscriptions per issue, not counting newsstand sales, and thirty pages of text in a daily edition, this works out to at least $38 a word. So at 15 percent of income, the *Times* could afford at least $6 a word, not the 30 cents to a dollar it normally pays freelancers."

The report asks publications to consider that a minimum rate of $1 a word is no hardship and would be the first step to recovering the ground writers have lost over the past thirty-five years.

To learn what specific publications pay, check the *Writer's Market*. (It's listed as a resource in Appendix D.)

To the freelancers' advantage, sometimes the same article can be sold to more than one magazine or newspaper. These "resales" help to increase salaries. And you can also be paid additional money if you can provide your own photographs to illustrate your articles.

Fiction

Writing a short story or a full-length novel is only half the battle. In addition to honing your skills as an expert storyteller, you also have to be a knowledgeable salesperson. That means you must learn which publishers you should approach and how to approach them. There are several market guides, which are mentioned in Appendix D, that will tell you what categories of fiction the different publishers buy. The guides will also list the different magazines that purchase short stories. You can also check your own book collection to learn who the publishers are.

Once you've made a list of possible markets, you need to make sure your approach is appropriate. Your manuscript needs to be typed and double-spaced, with your name at the top of each page. There are several sources that can give you the information you need to format your manuscript properly. One such source is Fiction Writer's Connection. Go to fictionwriters.com and click on Tip Sheets for some helpful information.

Before you send in your completed manuscript, you should write the editor a brief query letter describing your project. Don't forget to enclose a self-addressed stamped envelope (SASE). The editor will use this to send you a reply. If the editor likes what he or she sees so far, you'll probably receive a request to send more. Alternatively, you can look for an agent first, following the same steps you'd use to make your initial approach to a publisher. But this time, you are asking that the agent consider you as a possible client.

At this point, after the query letters are in the mail, many new writers just sit back and wait for responses. The smart writer puts that manuscript out of his head and gets to work on the next one. And the next one. And the next one.

In the end, the key to getting published can be summed up in one word: *persistence*.

Advances and Royalties   Even if you manage to break in and sell your first novel, you should expect to receive only about $2,500 or $5,000. The six-figure advances that some superstar authors receive are not the norm. Zebra Books senior editor John Scognamiglio says, "That kind of stuff like with John Grisham doesn't really have anything to do with the rest of us. There are 110,000 new titles a year, and there are only fifteen on the *NY Times* Bestseller List at a time. Most of the rest of us are going to make a moderate income and do a civilized business if we work very, very hard. There's not that much room at the top. And there isn't much of a middle class in publishing. You either make a little bit of money, which the grand majority will do, or you make a lot."

If you do manage to land that first book contract, you will receive an advance against royalties. A royalty is a percentage, usually 6 to 10 percent, of the money your book earns in sales. The advance is paid half on signing the contract, half on delivery and acceptance of the manuscript.

But money is not the only reason writers write. For some, the profession is almost an obsession—a burning desire to put words to paper, to start a book and see it to its finish. They wouldn't be happy doing anything else. Other perks include recognition and publicity, though some might view the attention as a downside. Many writers report that the nicest perk is being able to go to work in their bathrobe.

Nonfiction Books As with any book, you must start with an idea, a topic that interests you and that you would like to learn more about. The topics that nonfiction writers write about cover everything under the sun. Here is just a small sampling of general categories that publishers are interested in:

Autobiography	Investing/making money
Biography	New age
Career/finding a job	Parenting
Child care	Politics
Cooking	Relationships
Dieting	Self-help/psychology
Health/fitness	Spiritual
History	Textbooks
Hobbies	Travel
How-to	

At this writing, among the current top fifteen bestselling nonfiction books are three autobiographies, two biographies, one cookbook, one fitness, one history, two politics, one relationship, and four spiritual/New Age. Most of these books have been written by famous people, but that doesn't mean that an unknown, competent writer can't get a foot in the door.

What to do with your idea. First you have to check what's already been written on the subject. You won't get your book published if it only duplicates the information of a hundred other books. However, if your book idea will provide additional or different information from what is currently available—in other words, if your book will fill a gap in the marketplace—then you have a shot at getting it published.

Go to the library and the bookstore and see what's already out there. Note the publishers, because they might be the ones who will be interested in your book, too. Once you have examined the competing books, you can decide if your idea is still a good one.

The next step. Before you write your proposal, which is your entry into a literary agency or a publishing house, you have to make sure you can collect the information you will need to write your book. If you already are an expert in a particular area, a hobby or form of cooking, for example, then you have a head start. But you still will need factual information to complete your book. Most nonfiction writers use two sources for information: books, articles, and documents on the subject; and interviews with professionals or experts in the field. If you are writing a biography of a famous person, for example, you can study other books written about that person's life, and you can track down and interview people who know that person. If you want to write about gardening, you interview gardeners. If you want to write about money matters, you interview investment counselors, and so on.

Query letters and book proposals. After you've done your initial research—you have your idea, you know what the competition is, and you know how to gather the information you'll need to write the book—you are ready to compose a query letter. This is basically a miniproposal, telling an editor or agent about your book idea, why you think it should be published, who the readers will be, and why you should be the person to write this book. You end your letter by offering to send a full proposal and sample chapters.

The proposal is a longer version of your query letter. It should include a table of contents that shows you know how to organize and present the material for your book, and one or two sample chapters. If the editor or agent likes your proposal, he or she will probably ask to see the completed manuscript. Few first-time writers can land a book contract without a finished book, but it does happen that a good proposal can get you a sale.

Your proposal could also save you the time of writing a book that will never get published. You might learn from the editors or agents that there is no interest in your idea for a number of reasons. Some possible reasons for lack of interest are (1) there are too many similar books on the same subject; (2) there aren't any current books on the subject, but that's because earlier ones did not sell well; (3) the audience for your book is too narrow—not enough people would be interested in it to make publishing it financially worthwhile; (4) your book doesn't cover enough ground; or (5) your book covers too much ground.

If your book idea is turned down, don't get discouraged. The feedback you get from agents and editors can give you an idea how to revise your book or might even lead you to a new topic altogether.

The rewards for the nonfiction book writer. If you do receive that exciting phone call or letter in the mail informing you that your book has been accepted, you can expect to receive a book contract that will spell out all the terms. Usually an advance for a nonfiction book could be from $1,000 on up, to even a million dollars or more, depending on how big the publishing house is, how timely and important your book topic is, and how many books the publishers believe they'll be able to sell. First-time writers should expect to fall somewhere at the bottom of the scale.

You will also be paid royalties, a percentage of the price of each book that sells. But while you're waiting for your advance or first royalty check, it would be a good idea to get started on that next book, then the next one, and the next one. Few people can retire after one book; most writers have to write many in order to support themselves. But writing a complete book, then getting it published, no matter the amount you're paid, is an accomplishment to be proud of, a reward unto itself.

FREELANCING

Freelance writers can find satisfying and financially rewarding work writing for others. There are many people, business owners or politicians, for example, who, because they do not have either the skill or the time, hire the services of professional writers to do their writing for them. You can keep busy writing magazine ads, travel brochures, political speeches, or press releases. The possibilities are as wide as the number of clients you can develop.

If you have an interest in writing, with a good command of English grammar, a grasp of the political process, or knowledge of sales and marketing techniques—or you are willing to learn—then a career writing for others might be for you. When you write for others, you either work in a client or employer's office or you can work from home as a freelance writer.

You will meet with your client or employer and listen to what he or she needs. Your project might be a brochure describing a resort hotel or a magazine ad to sell a new product. You will then have to estimate the amount of time the job will take you and what additional expenses, such as photography or artwork, you will have. When you have calculated your time and the cost, you then give an exact price to the client. Even if your estimate was short and it takes you more time than you had initially planned for, you still have to stick by your initial fee.

You most likely will be working on your own, and this means that you have to be self-motivated and disciplined. The client will want the project finished by a certain date, and he or she will expect you to deliver on time. That could mean you're working weekends and nights as well as days to get the job done.

When you write for others you could be involved in a variety of different projects. Here is a selected list:

Advertising copywriters write all the words for magazine ads and radio and TV commercials. To describe a business's services or a client's product, they design and write the copy for brochures or pamphlets. They write all the copy for direct mail packages, which are used to sell products or services such as magazine subscriptions or memberships in a book club through the mail.

Ghostwriters write books for people who don't have the necessary skill to do it themselves. The client could be a famous person such as a former president or a movie star who has a story to tell but needs help doing it. Ghostwriters sometimes get credit for their writing (you might see "as told to" on the book jacket cover), but many times they stay anonymous, writing behind the scenes.

Press secretaries work for government officials, actors and actresses, or big corporations that are concerned with relations with the press. They schedule public appearances and read prepared statements to reporters. They also write press releases, which are announcements of an event or service or product. The press releases are sent to various newspapers and TV and radio shows in the hopes of receiving some free publicity.

Speechwriters work with politicians and other public figures, listening to what they want to say, then writing the speeches they will deliver. When you listen to the president on television or see the mayor or governor speaking to a group of voters, you can make a good bet that the speech was written by someone else.

Technical writers can freelance or work for a particular company. They frequently write manuals or other instructional material.

ILLUSTRATORS AND PHOTOGRAPHERS

Illustrators and photographers (some photographers are known as photojournalists) can work for the same establishments that attract writers: magazines, newspapers, book publishing companies, advertising agencies, PR firms, corporations, private clients, print shops, professional associations, and so on.

As with writers, some illustrators or photographers work on staff; others freelance their services. For illustrators and photojournalists, there are a few different routes to take in the job hunting process, but they all include putting together a professional portfolio. Some photojournalists identify the papers they would like to work for and, at their own expense, fly out on spec to talk to the different editors—even when they know there are currently no openings. This approach, though a bit costly for someone just starting out, can often work. The job applicant makes him- or herself known, and when an opening does occur, potential employers will remember the top-quality portfolio.

Job hunting through the mail can be just as effective. Send out your portfolio with a good cover letter, and don't be afraid to mention any story ideas you might have. Newspapers aren't looking for robots; they appreciate a photojournalist who does more than stand behind the camera and click his or her shutter. Then follow up a week or so later as a reminder. You can make up your own picture postcards, using your best work. This helps to jog the editor's memory—and shows how creative you are.

Internships

College programs and internships can give the job candidate an opportunity to get a portfolio started. Another successful job-hunting method is to take more than the one required college internship. If you can get involved in two or even three internships, you'll make more contacts and have a better chance of lining up full-time employment when you graduate. At the same time you'll be adding to your portfolio and creating impressive specifics to include on your resume.

Payment

Payment for illustrators and photographers can vary by the publication or the employers. One well-placed photo in a newspaper cover story on a hot topic could land the photographer a hefty sum. A photo in a small publication could pull in $25 to $50. A travel spread could earn the photographer more money than the writer earns. The bigger the publication's budget, the better the chances of a comfortable paycheck.

FINDING CLIENTS

Many writers and illustrators work for ad agencies, gaining experience and making contacts, before striking out on their own. Others might start with just one client, a big corporation, for example, that will send enough work their way. And through building a reputation of being a good worker who delivers on time, you will receive recommendations from your clients, and that will lead you to new clients. Word-of-mouth is how most writers build up business.

For whatever sector you choose to work in, each has its own protocol. For example, press secretary jobs for politicians are usually filled outside the civil service system; the congressman (or other officeholder or candidate) hires directly. Knowing a congressman personally is the best way to go about getting a job, but most people aren't in that position. If you don't have an inside contact, you would have to go to the politicians' offices (at your own expense), walk the hallways, go door-to-door, and ask about openings. Someone just out of college might try for an assistant press secretary position or volunteer his or her time as a student intern.

SAMPLE JOB ADVERTISEMENTS

The following are real advertisements, but the hiring employers are not identified because the positions have already been filled. They are meant as examples to give you an idea of the types of positions you'll see advertised.

> **Position:** Copywriter
> **Location:** Large independent ad agency in Michigan
> **Description:** Seeking a copywriter with experience managing client relations as well as managing a team and major accounts, including attending meetings, developing and presenting concepts, and writing copy for all media, especially collateral. As a seasoned, dynamic copywriter you manage

other copywriters and are able to work independently, but also within a new design department that focuses on collateral. Your book contains extremely high-end copy. You can sell solutions, not products. You are team-oriented, upbeat, and averse to seclusion to your own cubicle. Your work will include interface with the client as needed, the brainstorming of fresh ideas with the art director and creative director, writing your own concepts complete with strategic foundation, and finishing with a flawless piece that tells a story in a confined amount of real estate.

Position: Copywriter
Location: Large travel-industry corporation based in South Florida
Description: Seeking a copywriter for the creative-services department. Must have excellent attention to detail and be organized and able to work under tight deadlines. Individual must have solid editing skills as well as creative writing. This position will be 50 percent editing and 50 percent writing. Must have solid Quark skills as well as proficiency in using the Mac. Bilingual a must (English and Spanish)! Portuguese a plus.

Position: Freelance Writer
Location: New trade magazine in Colorado
Description: We need freelance writers to write articles on business subjects and trends along with technical articles on such subjects as metal cutting, metal fabricating, tools, applications, etc. Payment is by article. $200–$300.

Position: Technical Writer
Location: Web-based company in California
Description: Looking for technical writers to create Web copy, data sheets, and FAQs. Candidates must have background in one of the following areas: component manufacturing, enterprise software/Web infrastructure software/CRM, managed services (ISPs, VSPs, ASPs, Internet applications solutions/iBuilders, Exchanges), communication services and infrastructure (including wireless data services). Component manufacturing audience is typically going to be product engineers (mechanical/electrical). Enterprise software audience is going to be CIOs, IT directors, engineers, or business line managers. Managed services and communication services audience is going to be C-level business line managers, CIOs, IT directors, or engineers.

Position: Illustrator
Location: Toy company based on Long Island
Description: Seeking an experienced, high-end illustrator. You should have five-plus years of experience and proficiency in Photoshop, heavy retouching, package design, production, bleeds, designing logos on packaging, and the ability to work in dimensions. The ability to execute package die strikes is extremely important. This is a freelance position.

Position: Illustrator
Location: Educational online company based in northern Virginia
Description: This illustrator will be producing simple line illustrations, photo-realistic (not cartoony) for online curriculums for K–2 grades. Can work in Freehand or Illustrator. Will be working closely with Flash Scripters who will be animating illustrations. Flash experience is a plus but not necessary. Submit resume outlining skills and qualifications and illustration samples.

Position: Assistant Art Director
Location: Leading magazine based in New York City
Description: Must have at least one to two years of magazine experience. Responsibilities will include designing front-of-the-book columns and dealing with still photographers and illustrators for these pages; calling in stock film; returning film and issues to photographers; and coding and keeping track of the department bills; plus any other departmental needs (pasting up boards, ordering supplies, etc.). Qualifications include college degree. QuarkXPress 3.3 or higher is a must! Photoshop and Illustrator are a plus. Excellent organizational and communication skills required. Must be able to work in a fast-paced environment.

Position: Art Director
Location: Leading publisher of newspapers and magazines to the fashion and retail trade and consumer audience/book division
Description: Seeking an art director for our books division, which publishes fashion and interior design college textbooks. The art director will be responsible for designing and scheduling book projects from heavily illustrated manuscript through the production process. Other responsibilities include supervision of freelance designers and illustrators, budgeting, estimating, and interfacing with editorial and production

departments. Three to five years' experience in textbooks is required. The ideal candidate will be detail-oriented, organized, and able to manage multiple projects and will have strong communication and supervisory skills. Expert knowledge in QuarkXPress, Illustrator, and Photoshop is a must.

FIRSTHAND ACCOUNTS

Tanya Lochridge, Freelance Medical/Health Care Writer

Tanya Lochridge writes medical/health care magazine articles, patient education materials, and presentation materials primarily for the consumer/patient audience. In addition, she does some annual reports for managed care organizations and pharmaceutical companies. Her clients also include magazines, websites, medical associations, nonprofit associations, and hospitals. She has been freelancing since 1984.

Getting Started

"I knew that writing was always in my soul. I was just not sure a person could actually make a living at it. I grew up in a blue-collar world, and writing was not an option that was ever discussed as a career. After teaching for several years, I knew that wasn't for me, so I landed my first job by coincidence at the only pharmaceutical company at the time in Southern California. I spent about a year working in market research—designing, implementing, and writing various market research studies. I realized at that point that I could make a living writing.

"While working in market research, I started talking with copywriters and other writers to see what was required for that job and how they reached the position they had. It's strange—all work from that point in some way led to my freelance status and success now. I wandered around in the pharmaceutical industry for several years working in sales, marketing, and education. That experience provided a much broader background than that of most writers—giving me a slight edge."

The Realities of the Work

"Freelance writing has many positives and many negatives. For me the positives far outweigh the negative qualities of the work. Freelancing is not a job for someone who likes the social atmosphere supplied by an office environment.

"My day begins about 10:00 or 11:00, checking E-mail for assignment updates, and then I write until about 3:00 in the afternoon, taking short breaks to stretch in between. At 3:00 I return calls, check with editors or directors on assignments, and then back to writing until about 9:00 in the evening—although many nights I am up writing until 2:00 or 3:00 in the morning, depending on the work flow. This schedule is the one I keep when I have plenty of work in the pipeline. If I see assignments slowing, and just on a regular basis, I send out a lot of promo materials to existing clients and potential new clients. So basically, if I am not working on a specific assignment, I am working on promotion/marketing. Eighty percent of my time is actually spent researching the topic, and the remaining 20 percent is spent writing.

"Sometimes to clear my head, I grab the dog and head for the park—what appears to be play to the innocent passerby is really a time for structuring and solving problems in a current assignment."

The Upsides and Downsides

"I like that some days I can work in my jammies, or a T-shirt and shorts, with my dog keeping me company. I like that I get to use my talents to help consumers/patients at a time when they might be experiencing fear about their health. I like knowing that I can possibly have an effect on someone's life, because they took the time to read the material I produced, and then took action to seek medical advice. I like that, being a night person, I can work into the wee hours of the morning. I like that I can pick and choose the projects on which I work, although it wasn't always that way.

"What I like least is being the bill collector. Some clients are great and pay invoices promptly, while others make me chase my money. Although, over the years this has become less of a problem since I have weeded out the slow payers by turning down their assignments. Sometimes I find it too easy to work around the clock, throwing the balance off in my life. But as a freelancer, you almost have to take all assignments when they come, because there is no guarantee that they will come again next month. So living on a strict budget is a must—no matter how much you earn in a month.

"I don't know how working as a freelancer would work if I had a family to care for—I think that would make it much more difficult. One problem that I had to solve was making friends understand that just because I am home, doesn't mean I'm not busy working."

Earnings

"My annual earnings range between $90K and $125K. However, keep in mind that I have been doing this for years and work in a specialty area in which few writers succeed. It takes a certain skill to be able to take 'medicalese' and make it consumer-friendly without talking down to the reader. I believe I could be earning more after all these years—but I am at a point in my life where I am trying to strike a balance between my work and my personal life."

Advice

"First of all, you've got to be a good writer. So many people today come out of school without writing skills. So be sure that your skills are tops. I believe that part of being a great writer is being an avid reader. Read anything you can get your hands on that fits into the category in which you are interested. And, read all the stuff you can that just gives you joy.

"Education opens the door, but once you're there you must prove yourself, again and again. It takes a while to establish a reputation in an industry. So be patient, but be persistent. Having the tenacity of a terrier certainly helps in this profession! You also need good researching skills. And, don't take rejection or criticism to heart. Use it constructively to improve your skills.

"Develop a promotional package that lists your education, clients, skills, and so on. Also include samples of previous work. If you are starting out and don't have previous work, then write some samples that can be included. Don't expect that one promo package will get you the job. Do regular mailings every few weeks (even after all these years, I still mail once a month to all clients and include samples of projects recently completed). I would suggest you work in-house with a company or agency for a period of time—this lends more credibility to your credentials.

"Always continue to learn and upgrade your skills. For example, I started by writing brochures, added newsletters and magazine articles, and now write content for the Web as well. Each of these requires a slightly different set of skills. So, it's best to stay current. Never, ever, miss a deadline—that will be your undoing. Everything you did before will be forgotten, and the missed deadline will long be remembered.

"If you want to freelance because you think it is easier than working in an office—think again. As a freelancer, in most cases, you are working in a vacuum and do not have the luxury of bouncing ideas off colleagues or just complaining to colleagues about a current project—which can be a relief at times.

"As a freelance writer, you not only complete projects for clients, you also have to complete projects for yourself on a regular basis. There are no paid holidays, paid vacations, or paid sick days. Every day you must get up and write."

Joseph Hayes, Freelance Features Writer

Joseph Hayes writes features for a variety of magazines and newspapers. His articles cover people, food, computers and technology, travel, music, and writing about writing. His work has appeared in the following publications: *Fiction Writers Guideline, Gila Queen's Guide to Markets, Inklings/Inkspot, iUniverse.com Nonfiction Industry Newsletter, January Magazine, Jerusalem Report, MaximumPC, Moments Aboard Spirit Airlines, MyMatcher.com, Orlando Magazine, Orlando Sentinel, Poets & Writers, savvyHEALTH, Venture Woman*, and *Writer's Journal*. His first article was published in January 1997.

Getting Started

"It began as an outgrowth of my 'other' profession: I was a corporate sales trainer for many years, and as such, I developed a skill at taking complicated technical terms and processes and putting them down on paper so they were understandable to ordinary people. My first love will always be fiction writing, but I've been able to take those talents and use them to create what is called creative nonfiction.

"I got started by calling up the local newspaper and speaking to a regional editor. I suggested several concrete story ideas about the community I live in. She liked one, told me to write it, and I've been writing steadily ever since."

The Realities of the Work

"My first duty involved personal accountability—weighing the necessities of getting paying assignments with social responsibility. Will I take any assignment as long as it pays? So far the answer is no.

"Then the duties of the professional writer come in—meeting deadlines, being obligated to deliver the best work you are capable of regardless of the subject matter, and being in contact with editors once they give you assignments so they know what you're up to.

"I love my job. Not only do I get to (and *have* to) set my own schedule, but I have the opportunity to meet incredible people, people whom I wouldn't ordinarily get to know. The hours are long, and there can sometimes be long gaps between paydays, but I'm getting paid for doing something I've always wanted to do.

"Mostly I write about people—about life. I like to tell stories about ordinary people who do extraordinary things: the guy who sells UFO abduction insurance, the woman who takes photographs of people's auras, the former police officer who teaches the bagpipes. My travel articles are about places a tourist wouldn't normally go; my technology pieces are based on helping people understand what on earth modern technology means to them. Bottom line—I'm a storyteller, whether I'm doing it in a piece of fiction or a newspaper.

"Ninety-five percent of my work is generated by ideas I send out. This is called the query process. If it's an editor I know or have worked with before, I will pick up the phone and give my idea a quick pitch. If it's a new editor or a new publication, I send a letter with a detailed but brief summary of the idea, along with copies of similar articles that I've published before—these are called clips.

"In either case, it means that you have to have a very clear and specific idea of what story you want to do. Saying 'I'd really like to do an interview with a band' isn't an idea; it's a daydream. 'I've met the drummer for Backstreet Boys, and he'll talk to me about the band' is a legitimate article pitch.

"How you decide whom to approach depends on what you write. By looking at guidebooks such as the *Writer's Market* and visiting your local newsstands, you get to see which magazines print articles on topics you can write about, which magazines pay, and which ones accept pieces from freelancers.

"A freelancer's life goes through cycles: periods of waiting for work followed by frantic episodes of meeting deadlines. A query can go unanswered for months, but when an editor finally decides he wants the work, he wants it yesterday. This year I had enough time to go on a two-week vacation . . . and when I got back home, there were six contracts waiting for me, all due in a month!

"I truly believe the job is what you make it. You can be as busy (and successful) as you want to be. Even at this stage, I'm still learning to pace myself when it comes to getting work, and I think I could be doing twice as much writing as I'm doing now if I wanted to, but at the risk of doing less quality work than I demand from myself. As it is, I will often put in a twelve-hour day, between writing, researching, and interviewing."

The Upsides and Downsides

"The best part is the freedom, working for myself. Of course, I don't work for myself; I work for magazines and newspapers and editors, but each job has a different boss, and I know if I have a bad experience with one boss, I need not work for him or her again.

"The thrill of stepping up to a magazine rack and seeing your name on the stands is one that I hope will never wear off.

"The bad side is waiting—waiting for an assignment, then waiting for a check. Keeping track of your submissions, your billing, even your expenses, can be tiring and overwhelming, but it's part of the job. A writer writes only part of the time. The rest of the time is spent with details and selling yourself.

"It can also get lonely—most of the time you are in your office, facing a screen, talking to yourself. And there are times when you have to convince your friends and family that you are actually working even though you are home, and they must respect that."

Earnings

"Someone just starting out can expect to earn very little, if anything. Most freelance writers do it as a part-time thing and very often get no pay at all for their work. It's part of establishing yourself in the business and getting experience.

"Once your reputation and skill warrant it, a freelance feature writer can expect to find widely varying pay rates—everything from 5 cents to $1 a word (and some lower than that) is typical, while the big, national magazines will pay thousands of dollars an article . . . but that's a tough group to join."

Advice

"First of all, love language. Love to write. Some writers say they love having written, but hate writing. Such a waste of time! Enjoy every part of the process, of sitting in front of the computer or typewriter or notepad, and you'll never suffer from what is called writer's block.

"The article writer should be, first and foremost, an article reader—be aware of styles of writing, of how things are said. Be a reader; be voracious. Devour facts. Some people keep journals or diaries and jot down observations of people and places. Learn how to put those observations on paper; it's called finding your voice. Writer and teacher Larry Bloom says that voice, the personal voice of the writer, is the most important part of any story; that is, what you yourself add to the article. Remember that only you can tell the story you are telling.

"To start out, find a discussion group at your library or local bookstore or online, and talk about your daily encounters. Learn to listen. Call your local newspaper or church, check the clubs you belong to, ask at local businesses, and see if they have newsletters you can write for. The more words you put in print, the better your words get. And most important, never give up! I've been very lucky, being as successful as I've been in such a short time. Some writers take several years of hard work before they see real success. It can be very discouraging, but it's also very rewarding."

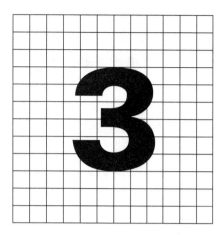

LITERARY AGENTS

"Having an agent is the difference between being published and not being published."—John Grisham

Literary agents provide a valuable service to writers. They represent writers and act as go-betweens with editors at publishing houses. They free a writer to concentrate on writing instead of marketing. They provide the new writer with credibility—if an agent likes the writer's work, then that writer has made the first step toward publication. These days most of the big New York publishing houses refuse to consider a manuscript from a new, unpublished writer unless an agent has sent it to them.

Many publishers credit agents with the ability to screen out inappropriate submissions, and rightfully so. An agent is expected to be familiar with the different kinds of books publishers prefer to take on. New writers don't always take the time to research this information. A knowledgeable agent won't send a romance novel to a publisher who handles only science fiction, although a new writer might make that mistake.

Agents are trained to recognize good or bad writing and can also spot a diamond in the rough. Some agents will work with their clients to get almost-ready manuscripts to a salable level. Others expect the writer to have his or her manuscript in market-ready condition before the writer approaches them. In any event, an agent will not submit to publishers a manuscript that isn't ready, while new writers often rush to send out their work before taking the time to polish and edit.

Agents also work with writers with a track record to help them find the best house for new work and to negotiate the best financial package. In addition to having a good eye for marketable writing and topics, an agent must be versed in legalese. Agents handle contracts and rights and must understand the different clauses and what best suits their clients. In addition to literary rights, agents also handle film rights for feature or TV movies and foreign rights, selling their clients' books to publishers overseas.

Agents must also keep good financial records and maintain separate bank accounts for each client. Agents generally receive advances and royalty checks from the publishers for their clients and must disburse those funds as they come into the office.

Most of an agent's time is spent reading manuscripts, choosing which ones to work with, and then trying to sell them to publishers. Agents also attend writers' conferences in search of new talent. They meet with writers and discuss their work. If an idea seems appealing or marketable, the agent will ask the writer to send his or her manuscript to the agent's office after the conference. (Most agents prefer not to carry dozens of manuscripts home with them on the plane.)

TRAINING FOR AGENTS

Most agents have at least a bachelor's degree in communications, English, journalism, or any relevant liberal arts or humanities major. It is also helpful to be knowledgeable about publishing law and contracts and to know how to do word processing.

Needless to say, a love of reading must come above all else. As agent Nancy Yost says, "The truth is, I have always been a reader, and once I started actually working with books and authors, I realized I would be able to do something I would be proud of at the end of the day." Nancy Yost earned her B.A. in comparative literature from the University of Nevada at Las Vegas in the early 1980s before entering the New York publishing arena.

In publishing it's rare for someone to start out as an agent without any prior experience. Many agents work for publishing houses first, becoming familiar with the editorial process and contracts, before moving into a literary agency. "My training came from my experience as an editor," says agent Jessica Faust. "As an acquisitions editor for six years I learned the ins and outs of what makes a good book, the importance of marketing potential, and how much is too much competition. I also learned one of the most important aspects of agenting: how to negotiate and understand a publishing contract."

Nancy Yost followed a similar path. "My first job in publishing was as a contracts assistant at Random House, then later I worked as an editor at Avon. During that time I was approached by my current boss, who had lost an agent and needed fresh blood. She had gotten my name from several editors and agents as a likely candidate."

Some agents start as assistants and work their way up. This sample advertisement gives you an idea of what the workload for an assistant is like:

"Our small (seven full time), dynamic, and fast-paced office seeks an assistant to two literary agents. One year's office, publishing experience preferred. Duties include evaluating queries and manuscripts, reviewing contracts, handling heavy phone, tracking submissions to publishers here and in foreign markets, dealing with authors and editors, and generally assisting in the sale of authors' work to book publishers and magazines. Experience in foreign rights and contracts a plus. Candidates should demonstrate ability to work in a fast-paced environment and organize a steady flow of material."

HOW LITERARY AGENCIES ARE STRUCTURED

Some literary agents choose to work on their own, with little more than secretarial assistance. They can rent space in an office building or work from a home office. Other agents prefer to work within an established literary agency, either as the owner or as one of the associates. They can still function independently, choosing the writers and book projects they want to work with. Usually in an agency, agents must contribute a percentage of their income to cover the office's operating expenses.

LOCATION, LOCATION, LOCATION

At one time agents worked only in New York City, which is where most of the major publishing houses are. But this is fast changing. Agents are now located all over the country. Phone calls, E-mail, and commuter flights make business possible, no matter where the agent hangs his or her shingle.

Although there still is some stigma attached to non–New York locations, it's important not to confuse a "Podunk" location with a "Podunk" agent. If an agent is up on current publishing trends, knows his or her business, and is well read and well informed, the location isn't important. But if the agent's practices reflect something less than professionalism—submitting substandard manuscripts or submitting manuscripts to the wrong houses, for example—the agent rather than the location is to blame.

In truth, there are good agents and not-so-good agents. And some of those not-so-good agents work and live right there in New York City.

CHOOSING A CAREER IN AGENTING OVER EDITING

While both professions can be satisfying, an editor might face some restrictions an agent doesn't have to encounter. Nancy Yost had a few reasons to switch roles from editing to agenting. "Publishing houses are organized by lists—they have certain kinds of books that they're good at, and they have certain kinds of books that they don't do. For example, Avon is very good with romances, very good with original mysteries; they have great science fiction and fantasy editors. But if you ever wanted to work with a big picture book or a cookbook you couldn't. You were limited by the list. Basically, it seemed to me that if I became an agent I'd be able to play in everyone's backyard instead of just one.

"And the money is better, of course; the more you sell, the more you earn. And you work only with the people you want to work with and the projects you like. You don't have to work in a bureaucratic sort of environment. Even in the best of houses you have salespeople, marketing people, and production people who are all many times at odds with your vision of a book or your enthusiasm for a book. The only limit on my enthusiasm now is what I think the market can do. If one editor doesn't like it, I can go to six other editors—or twenty other editors—until I sell it or until I've been beaten down and realize I'm not going to be able to sell it."

EARNINGS FOR AGENTS

Although editors are generally paid a set salary, agents must sell their clients' manuscripts to publishers to earn any income. The salary structure varies from agency to agency. Some beginning agents might work partly for salary and partly for commission, earning between beginning $20,000 and $30,000 per year to start—more as the number of sales increase. Other agents generally work on a commission basis only, getting 10 to 15 percent of the money the writer earns. Nancy Yost, as an example, makes between 25 and 75 sales a year.

If an agent has a lot of market savvy, carefully chooses which manuscripts to represent, and has success bargaining for big advances and royalty percentages, then he or she can make a very good living, often much more than the editors to whom he or she is selling.

The downside for agents is that the marketplace is fickle, fads come and go, and publishing houses merge with each other and often decrease the number of books they will let see print. In a bad year, an agent might have to struggle to make a living.

For those starting their own business, initial expenses are fairly light. Says Jessica Faust, "All you really need besides a computer, a phone line, and office supplies are business cards. Of course, once you start acquiring clients you must budget for mailing costs, photocopying, envelopes, and stationery."

CHARGING FEES

Can agents charge their clients for expenses? It depends. The Association of Authors' Representatives (AAR) has a Canon of Ethics that member agents are expected to follow. It states, in part, "The practice of literary agents charging clients or potential clients for reading and evaluating literary works (including outlines, proposals, and partial or complete manuscripts) is subject to serious abuse that reflects adversely on our profession. For that reason, members may not charge clients or potential clients for reading and evaluating literary works and may not benefit, directly or indirectly, from the charging for such services by any other person or entity. The term 'charge' in the previous sentence includes any request for payment other than to cover the actual cost of returning materials."

In other words, the job of an agent is to sell the work of a writer to a publisher. If the agent makes his or her income from editing or evaluating work, then a conflict of interest enters into the equation. Why should the agent successful at earning evaluation fees bother to expend the energy looking for a publisher for the work?

Having said that, editing or suggesting changes is often an important part of an agent's job. This is something that agents do when they decide to take on a project but the project still needs some work. They work directly with the writer making notes and suggesting changes and improvements. This is not a conflict of interest; it's only a conflict if the agent charges for this service. Some unscrupulous "agents" (anyone can hang out a shingle and call him- or herself an agent) have even made false promises to writers: "Pay for my editing service and I'll agree to take you on as a client. I'll get you published if you pay for the editing."

For every rule there is an exception—and there is an exception to the policy of charging fees. Also stated in the AAR Canon of Ethics is the following: "In addition to the compensation for agency services that is agreed upon between a member and a client, a member may, subject to the approval of the client, pass along charges incurred by the member on the client's behalf, such as copyright fees, manuscript retyping, photocopies, copies of books for use in the sale of other rights, long-distance calls, special messenger fees, etc. Such charges shall be made only if the client has agreed to reimburse such expenses." Some agents pass these charges on to a client only after they've made a sale for the client. No sale? No charges. Others charge for photocopying right up front; still other agents might allow clients to make their own manuscript copies.

It boils down to what overhead expenses an agency believes it's responsible for and what should be charged individually to the client. AAR member agents must act ethically in all professional matters and avoid any conflict of interest.

BECOMING A MEMBER OF THE AAR

The Association of Authors' Representatives was formed in 1991 as a result of the merger of the Society of Authors' Representatives (founded in 1928) and the Independent Literary Agents Association (founded in 1977). The AAR is the sole professional association specifically attending to the agenting profession. The AAR's objectives include "keeping agents informed about conditions in publishing, the theater, the motion picture and television industries, and related fields; encouraging cooperation among literary organizations; and assisting agents in representing their author-clients' interests."

It takes two years of active agenting before an agent can become a member of the AAR. Says the AAR: "To qualify for membership, the applicant for membership in the literary branch of the AAR must have been the agent principally responsible for executed agreements concerning the grant of publication, translation, or performance rights in ten different literary properties during the eighteen-month period preceding application.

"Member agents must conduct their business in such a manner as to be in compliance with the agents' legal and fiduciary duties to their clients, and each member agent must agree, in writing, to adhere to the AAR's Canon of Ethics."

Associate members of AAR are full-time employees of an agency member. They do not themselves qualify yet for full membership but are actively engaged in the selling of rights and are working toward qualifying.

The full requirements are available in the Bylaws of the Association of Authors' Representatives, Inc. Contact the Association of Authors' Representatives, Inc., at P.O. Box 237201, Ansonia Station, New York, NY 10023, or visit their website at publishersweekly.com/aar/homepage.html. You'll find the complete AAR Canon of Ethics at the website.

WHAT A WRITER LOOKS FOR IN AN AGENT

An agent is only as good as his or her word. An agent's reputation—both good and bad—can spread quickly through the writers' community. With more and more writers' associations and Internet connections, writers are not as isolated as they once were. They talk to each other and exchange information. New writers learn what to look for in an agent. As a prospective agent, it's important to have a sense of what writers would expect from you.

Here's a list of questions a writer might ask a prospective agent who has agreed to take him or her on as a client:

1. Do you have agents at your agency or subagents working in Hollywood or overseas who handle movie and television rights? Foreign rights?

2. Will you be solely responsible for my work, or will another associate in your firm handle my work?

3. Do you have an agent-author agreement or contract?

4. How do you keep clients up-to-date on your activities on their behalf? Will you let me know whom you are sending my work to and what their responses are? Do you call with rejections? Do you mail copies of all correspondence?

5. Do you confer with your clients on all offers that are made?

6. What percentage commission do you charge? What are your policies about charging for normal overhead expenses such as photocopying and messengers?

7. What is your policy for ending the author-agent relationship? Is this stated in your author-agent contract?

FIRSTHAND ACCOUNTS

Nancy Yost, Literary Agent

Nancy Yost has been a literary agent with Lowenstein Associates in New York City since 1990. Before that she worked in publishing as a contracts assistant and then as an editor since 1985.

What the Job's Really Like

"In the very broadest terms, my job is to represent an author's interests. This includes being able to recognize good writers; to help them refine and market their books in all areas (foreign countries, films, etc.); to act as adviser and advocate through all aspects of the publishing process, from editing to final cover up through the publicity and promotion; and to help authors set and achieve career goals.

"Specific duties will vary from author to author—and indeed from agent to agent. My duty is to help the author's career, and that mandate takes all kinds of forms. For some, it will be editorial input: working on perfecting proposals and manuscripts; finding the right project, the right voice, the best way to present the writing; developing plotlines; and so on.

"Then an agent would try to match the writer/project with the right editor and publisher, and that requires that the agent know well what's being bought and published by all the various publishing houses. Everyone thinks that 'lunching' with editors is just for fun!

"Agenting also requires knowing what's going on in national events and reading current books to get a sense of tone and subject matter.

"Once we've found the right place for the author, there are all kinds of details that need to be tracked, from making sure the contract is right, to making sure the editor reads the manuscript in a timely fashion, to making sure payments are received, to staying on top of the in-house publishing plans—art, copy, publicity, and so on.

"On top of that, there's pursuing all sorts of other avenues that spring from the book, including foreign publication, film possibilities, and magazine excerpts. And this is just the tip of the iceberg, really. No wonder I'm on the phone all day!

"What I like about my job is that there's really no typical day. However, mostly I spend the day talking, talking, talking! I'm talking about a manuscript I'm sending out, finding out who's read it and what they're doing, telling all the other people who are supposed to be reading it what the others are doing, finding out when manuscripts are going to be read, nagging people to read faster, chasing after overdue payments, relaying all this info to the author—you get the idea.

"When I'm not talking, I'm reading through contracts or writing submission letters. I save the weekends for reading and editing manuscripts; it's hard to concentrate when you're constantly being interrupted by the phone."

Types of Projects   "I represent different kinds of books because I like variety. The majority of the
titles, though, are commercial fiction—lots of crime novels, thrillers, suspense,
mysteries—also women's novels. I also love historical fiction. In terms of nonfiction, I'm interested in human issues (but not politics!), interesting history,
and adventure. The other agents in this office do more nonfiction than I do, so
among us all we cover the shelves."

The Upsides and   "The thing I like most about my job is sharing a good book with others! There's
Downsides   still nothing that equals the thrill of finding an author whose books you will
look forward to reading the rest of your life. And there's nothing as thrilling as
actually helping that come to fruition.

"I also love working with publishing people, whom I find (mostly) to be intelligent, informed, thoughtful, and witty. It's a treat to call them colleagues. I also
like the everyday challenges the job brings, the chances to be inventive and
smart.

"What I like least about my work is when everyone's best efforts fail. I also
am disappointed by the lack of common courtesy displayed by the few people
who won't return a phone call—or even have an assistant do it for them. And
sometimes, it's disheartening to know that no matter how hard you work you'll
probably still be a bit behind."

Advice   "The best advice I could give someone wanting to get involved in any aspect of
publishing is to read a lot. So much of your career is based on knowing whether
a book is salable, and you can't know that if you don't know what's been or is
being published."

Jessica Faust, Literary Agent

Jessica Faust is cofounder of BookEnds agency. She earned her B.A. in journalism from Marquette University in Milwaukee, Wisconsin, in 1993. She then
went to work at Berkley as an acquisitions editor. She acquired and edited books
ranging from romance, mysteries, and young adult to various kinds of
nonfiction.

As an acquisitions editor, Faust had the opportunity to not only acquire books
but to create ideas for a number of books that were later published in-house.
Her work has ranged from nonfiction titles such as *Practical Aromatherapy*, *The
Good Beer Book*, and *The Wedding Guide for the Grownup Bride* to the Edgar-
nominated mass-market mystery series Gaslight Mysteries, which are set in
early 1900s New York City.

After five years at Berkley, Faust moved on to Macmillan, where she became
senior editor, handling more than one hundred Complete Idiot's Guide titles.

Upon Macmillan's sale to IDG Worldwide, Jessica moved over to acquire for the Dummies guides and The Unofficial Guide series.

Faust first met her partner Jacky Sach in 1994 while working for the Berkley Publishing Group, now a division of Penguin Putnam Inc. In 1999 these Book-Ends cofounders decided it was time to leave their corporate publishing jobs to make a new start in book packaging. (See Chapter 1 for information on book packaging.) With a little help and guidance, they put together BookEnds LLC, an editorial book-packaging company focusing primarily on developing fiction and nonfiction books for adult audiences, including handling titles on a for-hire basis.

A year and many successes later, including the publication of *The Complete Idiot's Guide to Throwing a Great Party*, *The Ten-Minute Guide to Performance Appraisals*, *For My Daughter on Her Wedding Day*, and *For My Daughter on the Birth of Her First Child*, BookEnds decided to embark on yet another endeavor—agenting.

The agents at BookEnds represent writers in all fields but have special interest in romance, mystery, suspense, and women's fiction. On the nonfiction side, they handle books in the areas of spirituality, self-help, health, general nonfiction, business, parenting, and books geared to women.

What the Job's Really Like

"I consider my primary duty as agent is to be the best representative for the author that I can be. That includes submitting his or her manuscript as often as necessary until the appropriate publishing house and editor take an interest and make an offer, negotiating a contract that is in the best interest of my client, and being there whenever needed to provide moral support or advice.

"I am an authors' advocate, and my job is not only to see that they are getting the best deal possible, but to ensure that they are happy and pleased with the final outcome of the book.

"My job can be filled with great joy, tremendous disappointment, and incredible stress all in one day. The typical day is often spent answering E-mails and phone calls, looking through the mail to get an idea of the submissions coming in, reading *Publisher's Lunch* and *Publishers Weekly* to keep up on publishing trends, and checking on submissions as well as calling authors to see that everything is on track.

"One of the hardest things about this job is its unpredictability. Too often I'll walk into the office with a plan to catch up on an author's manuscript, clean out the files, or just read through my submissions pile, when one phone call throws all of those plans out the window.

"Each day is so different that there is no set schedule. One of the most important things to know about being an agent, or working in almost any job in publishing, is that it is not nine to five. Agents often get fifty to a hundred submissions a week and rarely have time to read any of them while in the office. And that includes the latest book from any of your already-published authors.

This means that a great deal of submission reading must be done at home during the night or on weekends.

"In addition to that, it is important to keep up with the latest mystery author, bestselling diet book, or big new romance, and equally important to know what the hottest trends are if you plan on covering any sort of nonfiction. In other words, an agent must be reading all of the time.

"There is no doubt that agenting is both busy and exciting. However, it can also be incredibly stressful. After all, you have a list of people who have put their careers in your hands. You'll find that being an agent is a big responsibility. Your authors want nothing more in this world than to be published, and they are depending on you to get this job done. That means that you have to know exactly what editor at what house is looking for the kind of book that you are selling, and you have to convince them that they want to buy it.

"Keeping up with contacts is often the most important part of an agent's job. This means calling editors just to check in, attending cocktail parties, and meeting over lunch. While this may sound like lots of fun, it is also work. Remember, every cocktail party and lunch you attend cuts into all of the other things you need to be getting done that day. So often, one little lunch means an afternoon of catching up on missed phone calls. It also means calling to check in with authors to make sure their writing is going smoothly or just to lend moral support and to let them know they are not alone.

"Another key component to the job is acting as an editor. While it isn't your primary job to edit the author's material, you'll often find that a tweak here or a revision there can make all the difference in whether or not you can sell the book. Therefore, you need to make sure the author does the work needed to shape the book into what it needs to be before you send it off to the publisher.

"I often describe agenting as a cross between an editor and therapist. Because you are the author's advocate, you are also the middleman between her or him and the editor. That means that you will be called upon to ask for extensions, fight for a new cover design, or even just ask if the book is acceptable. You might also need to comfort authors after rejections, assure them that their writing is still terrific, and just lend an ear when a deadline is looming and they aren't sure if they can still meet it."

The Hard Part of the Job

"Rejecting a good author is the hardest part of my job. So often you'll read a manuscript that is either very well written but just doesn't have a good story, or a manuscript that has a terrific story or idea, but the execution just isn't there. Either way, you know in your heart that this is a not a book you will be able to sell. It is so hard to say no to these people."

Advice

"I really think that the best agents either have experience working for a reputable publishing company or started out as assistants to already-established agents. Learning how to be an agent can't be done simply by reading a book. One of the most important things you need to become an agent is contacts.

"My advice would be to get an entry-level job with either a publishing house or a literary agency (preferably a literary agency) and learn, learn, learn. This is the only way you really understand how to negotiate a contract, determine the marketability of a book, and learn where to make contacts. While you don't necessarily have to go to NYC to do this, I really believe it is the best way."

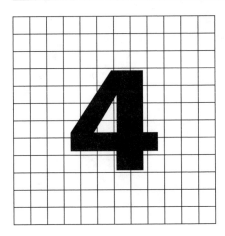

EDITORS

"An editor is a person who knows precisely what he wants, but isn't quite sure."—Walter Davenport

There are more than 340,000 editors working in the field nationwide. Nearly one-third of salaried editors work for newspapers, magazines, and book publishers. Other editors work in educational facilities, in advertising agencies, in radio and television broadcasting, in public relations firms, and on journals and newsletters published by business and nonprofit organizations, such as professional associations, labor unions, and religious organizations. Some develop publications and technical materials for government agencies or the military; others write for motion picture companies.

Jobs with major book publishers, magazines, broadcasting companies, advertising agencies, public relations firms, and the federal government are concentrated in New York, Chicago, Los Angeles, Boston, Philadelphia, San Francisco, and Washington, DC. Jobs with newspapers, business and professional journals, and technical and trade magazines are more widely dispersed throughout the country.

TYPES OF EDITORS AND THEIR DUTIES

Editors review, edit, and frequently rewrite the work of writers. An editor's specific responsibilities vary depending on the employer and editorial position held. In the publishing industry, an editor's primary duties are to plan the contents of books, technical journals, trade magazines, newsletters, and general-interest publications.

Editors decide what material will appeal to readers, review and edit drafts of books and articles, offer comments to improve the work, and suggest possible titles. Additionally, they oversee the production of the publications.

Job titles for the most part are the same, no matter the setting—magazines as well as publishing houses will employ executive or senior editors—although the duties might vary. For an example, let's take a look at the masthead of *Publishers Weekly*, the well-known trade publication for the publishing field, and a list of editor ranks at the publishing house McGraw-Hill. You'll see a good range of editor job titles employed by both a magazine and a book publishing house.

PUBLISHERS WEEKLY

Vice president

Editor-in-chief

Editorial director

Executive editor

Executive editor, bookselling

Senior managing editor

Managing editor

Department senior editors, editors, and associate editors (New, Book News, Bookselling, Children's Books, Forecasts, Religion, *PW* Interview, Fiction, Nonfiction, Lifestyle, Mass Market, Audio, Notables)

Art

Production editor

Research librarian

Research manager

Executive assistant

Assistant to the editor-in-chief

Contributing editors

Correspondents

MCGRAW-HILL

Vice president

Editor-in-chief

Editorial director

Executive editor

Developmental editors

Editorial coordinator

Executive assistant

Editorial assistant

Freelance copyeditors

In smaller organizations, such as small daily or weekly newspapers or membership newsletter departments, a single editor may do everything or share responsibility with only a few other people. The larger the company, the more editors are required. Some job definitions follow.

Executive Editors

In book, magazine, and newspaper publishing the executive editor generally oversees senior editors, editors, associate editors, and assistant editors. Executive editors usually have the final say about what stories or books get published and how they should be covered or approached.

Managing Editors

In the news industry, the managing editor usually is responsible for the daily operation of the news department. Executive and managing editors typically hire writers, reporters, or other employees. They also plan budgets and negotiate contracts with freelance writers, sometimes called "stringers."

Editors (Senior, Editor, Assistant)

Editors can be responsible for particular subjects, for example, romance fiction for a book publisher or local news, international news, feature stories, or sports for a magazine or newspaper.

Assignment Editors

Assignment editors work for magazines or newspapers and determine which staff writer, freelance writer, or reporter will cover a given story.

Publication Assistants/ Assistants to Editors

Editors often have assistants. Many assistants, such as copyeditors or production assistants, hold entry-level jobs. They review copy for errors in grammar, punctuation, and spelling and check copy for readability, style, and agreement with editorial policy. They add and rearrange sentences to improve clarity; they delete incorrect and unnecessary material. They also do research for writers and verify facts, dates, and statistics.

At magazines and newspapers, production assistants arrange page layouts of articles, photographs, and advertising; compose headlines; and prepare copy for printing. On small papers or at radio stations, assistants may clip stories that come from the wire services, answer phones, and make photocopies.

Assistants who work for publishing houses may be the first readers, screening and evaluating manuscripts submitted by writers or agents and passing the approved ones on to their editors. They might also proofread printers' galleys or answer letters about published material.

Copyeditors

Copyeditors at news organizations mostly review and edit a reporter's copy for accuracy, content, grammar, and style. They may be employed in-house or work independently as freelancers.

Associate Editor

Associate editor (a rank usually placed between assistant editor and editor) and acquisitions editor are other jobs titles encountered in the field of publishing. Certainly there are others, and investigations into job openings will reveal more.

SAMPLE JOB ADVERTISEMENTS

The following are real advertisements, but the hiring employers are not identified because the positions have already been filled. They are meant as examples to give you an idea of the types of positions you'll see advertised.

Position: Acquisitions Editor
Location: University press at a New England university
Description: Award-winning university press seeks energetic candidates to acquire twenty to twenty-five new titles per year of exceptional merit addressed to targeted audiences in academic and general marketplaces. Ideal candidate will have graduate training in relevant fields and three or more years' experience in editorial acquisitions or related publishing. Competitive salary/benefits. May be filled at senior level. This press concentrates in American cultural studies, art and material culture, ethnic studies, nature/environment, international studies, civil society, and new fiction. Applicants should send a letter stating their interests, salary requirements, titles acquired, resume, and references.

Position: Copy/Production Editor
Location: East Coast art museum
Description: Small art museum seeks full-time copy/production editor to assist in editing, proofing, and production of books, magazines, brochures, labels, etc. B.A. plus three to five years' editorial experience required. Superior knowledge of English language, eye for detail, and consistency. Familiarity with *Chicago Manual of Style* a must. Ability to handle multiple priorities in deadline-driven environment. Send cover letter and resume.

Position: Home Page Editor
Location: Major bookstore chain based in NYC
Description: A major bookstore is currently searching for a website home page editor. The home page editor will be responsible for ensuring the top-flight merchandising and editorial effort on the Internet. Will run weekly planning meetings. The home page editor will also act as the key liaison with production and other departments involved in the daily publication of the page. Will take charge of the home page, making it a dynamic and compelling example of the best we have.

The ideal candidate will have an editorial background with a love for books and experience in book publishing or sales. As this person will function much like a news editor, the successful candidate may very well come from a newsroom environment. The candidate must have a proven record of handling multiple tasks and be able to thrive in an environment where priorities and needs change frequently. The home page editor has to be cool under pressure, diplomatic, and creative. Please submit writing samples/clips along with resume.

Position: News and Media Person
Location: United States Navy
Description: History owes a debt of gratitude to the men and women who have documented the triumphs and conflicts of the United States Navy. Sailors in the news and media field are the eyes and ears of the fleet and often the rest of the world. This specialty is an intricate part of the Navy's delivery of visual, audio, and written information, both internally and to the public. Your ability to handle deadlines as well as your ability to communicate ideas creatively, artistically, and effectively might make this the perfect career choice for you.

As a videographer with a combat photography unit, you might develop a training video for an Explosive Ordnance Disposal team. As a photojournalist, your images of a humanitarian operation in a foreign country could open the eyes of the world. Or maybe you'll keep your fellow sailors informed on what's happening in the fleet as a news anchor for the Navy/Marine Corps News.

Your skills of gathering and creatively communicating information will be used on a daily basis. Some other duties you might encounter in the news and media field include: gather facts and write articles for publications; write, edit, and proofread news for radio and TV; write and produce radio and TV programs; prepare layouts and content for papers, magazines, and websites; maintain and repair interior communications systems; operate various types of still and video equipment. On-the-job training in this field is extensive, and there are a number of opportunities for intermediate and advanced schooling in the news and media disciplines, depending on the career path you choose.

Position: Editor
Location: Leading trade book publisher
Description: Publisher of award-winning picture books and children's novels is looking for an editor to acquire and develop twelve to fifteen books per year. Job requirements: two-plus years of children's book editing experience (include a full list of books edited with your resume and cover letter), computer fluency (Word, Excel).

Position: Editorial and Research Assistant
Location: Corporate marketing and communications company
Description: This long-term, part-time temporary position (twenty-four-plus hours per week) provides support to the manager of corporate publications for various projects, including the company's annual review. Exposure to a wide variety of creative marketing communications activities. Researches, checks, and verifies content via phone, E-mail, Internet, etc., for key marketing communication projects. Writes, edits, processes, and proofs manuscripts. Helps coordinate the production process for various projects. Handles extensive communication with personnel across the nation and worldwide. Provides administrative support as needed. Qualifications: bachelor's degree in communications/journalism/English with focus on creative feature writing; excellent written and oral communications skills; meticulous eye for detail; proficiency in PC MS Word, MS Outlook, Excel, and online research; motivated self-starter who is creative and has an investigative mind and an excellent command of language.

Position: Freelance Proofreaders
Location: Global management consulting firm specializing in human resources
Description: Seeking talented individuals to work as freelancers in our expanding communication practice office in New Jersey. Job responsibilities: proofread corporate communication materials for grammatical errors, consistency, clarity, basic layout/design, and client style. Work with communication consultants and designers to incorporate edits.

Assist one specific client team in managing the proofreading process through all stages of production. Create client-specific style sheets and update them to reflect client needs as they arise. Requirements: strong grammar/editing skills; good eye for detail; organization/project management skills; strong interpersonal/communication skills (can speak comfortably with clients/designers/printers, etc.); ability to juggle multiple tasks and handle projects of different scopes; assertive/able to suggest alternatives (both written and visual) to the existing content/appearance of a piece; ability to work under pressure and provide quick turnaround on rush projects; task-oriented; flexible/able to work with a variety of personalities and work styles; good sense of humor; personal maturity.

Position: Online Associate Editor
Location: Major financial publisher
Description: The successful candidate will edit feature articles, write headlines, research to support new and existing features, write news briefs, keep content partners on deadline, lay out and translate copy into appropriate format, and perform other assignments. Qualifications: strong, proven copyediting skills are requisite. Must possess good writing and reporting skills and have experience in a deadline-driven news organization. Must be able to use Microsoft Office and have practical knowledge of the Internet and electronic publishing. Would prefer someone with HTML and FrontPage2000 experience. We require a detail-oriented, hands-on, proactive individual comfortable in a PC environment.

Position: Editorial Assistant (Entry Level)
Location: Scientific publisher of books, journals, and electronic media
Description: Seeking organized, detail-oriented individuals with an interest in medicine or life sciences to provide support to acquisitions editors. Responsibilities include interacting with publishers, authors, and in-house staff concerning permissions; drafting and editing back cover copy and book marketing plans; acting as liaison between authors and in-house departments; attending exhibits (two to three times a year); and preparing manuscripts for production. Requirements for this position include a bachelor's degree with a minimum six months' general office experience. Excellent verbal and written communication skills with MS Word and Windows required.

Position: Assistant Editor
Location: Educational publisher
Description: This position is responsible for providing support in manuscript preparation, as well as administrative and clerical support, to an acquisitions editor or manager. Requirements: B.A. or B.S. degree in education. Two years' experience in publishing preferred. Solid computer skills; knowledge of Excel and Word. Quark helpful but not necessary. Excellent written and verbal communication and interpersonal skills. Excellent organizational skills with close attention to detail.

ADVERTISEMENTS TO AVOID

Just as in every industry, publishing sees its share of scam notices. If you've seen ads for readers, pass them by. Publishing houses have their own readers and never need to advertise for additional help. The people who advertise these bogus positions claim to have a booklet you can buy that will teach you how to get a reader job. Whatever the cost of the booklet, you can assume you'll be out that amount of money.

An editor at Tor Books reveals: "Contrary to certain reports, we aren't on the lookout for slush readers, and neither is any other publishing house we know of. Tor is fairly typical in that we handle most of our unsolicited manuscripts ourselves. We do have a few freelancers who sometimes read manuscripts for us, but they have industry experience and could use more work as it is.

"We're acutely aware of the common scam whereby intelligent and enthusiastic readers are sold expensive books that promise to teach them all about the lucrative world of slush reading. We're constantly hearing from them. Unfortunately, that market for freelance readers doesn't exist. The only really lucrative gig consists of selling fraudulent guidebooks. Here's the truth: manuscript reading is poorly paid and only sporadically available, and publishing houses don't use inexperienced readers. We've heard of one or two cases where an industry veteran got paid a barely three-figure sum to evaluate a manuscript, but that was freelance editorial work, not slush reading."

If you're a hopeful writer, there are a lot of scams to avoid as well. Steer clear of "literary agents" who charge fees and hint or out-and-out promise to get you published if you pay their fee. Ditto for book doctors who make the same claims. Reading manuscripts is a part of an agent's job. Agents get paid by the publishers when they sell your work. See Chapter 3 on literary agents for more information.

TRAINING FOR EDITORS

A college degree generally is required for a position as an editor. Although some employers look for a broad liberal arts background, most prefer to hire people with degrees in communications, journalism, or English. For those who specialize in a particular area, such as science, fashion, or legal issues, additional background in the chosen field is helpful.

Editors must be able to express ideas clearly and logically and should love to write. Creativity, curiosity, a broad range of knowledge, self-motivation, and perseverance also are valuable. Editors must demonstrate good judgment and a strong sense of ethics in deciding what material to publish. They also need tact and the ability to guide and encourage others in their work.

For some jobs, the ability to concentrate amid confusion and to work under pressure is essential. Familiarity with electronic publishing, graphics, and video production equipment increasingly is needed. Online newspapers and magazines require knowledge of computer software used to combine online text with graphics, audio, video, and 3-D animation.

High school and college newspapers, literary magazines, community newspapers, and radio and television stations all provide valuable, but sometimes unpaid, practical writing experience. Many magazines, newspapers, and broadcast stations have internships for students. Interns write short pieces, conduct research and interviews, and learn about the publishing or broadcasting business. In small firms, editors hired as assistants may actually begin editing material right away. Opportunities for advancement can be limited, however. In larger businesses, jobs usually are more formally structured. Beginners generally do research, fact checking, or copyediting. They take on full-scale writing or editing duties less rapidly than do the employees of small companies.

MOVING UP THE LADDER

Within a publishing house there is a distinct ladder most editors climb as they gain experience and develop a successful track record. They usually start out as editorial assistants, answering the phone, opening and distributing the mail, and typing correspondence. Some editorial assistants are first readers for their editors; they'll read a manuscript and then write a reader's report. If it's a good report then the editor will take a look at the manuscript. Most editorial assistants learn the editing process from the editor they work for, and over time they move up into editorial positions with more and more responsibility.

SALARIES FOR EDITORS

According to the *Occupational Outlook Handbook*, the middle 50 percent of editors earn between approximately $30,000 and $50,000 a year. The lowest 10 percent earn less than $21,000, and the highest 10 percent earn more than $77,000.

Median annual earnings in the industries employing the largest numbers of editors of nontechnical material are as follows:

Advertising	$38,100
Periodicals	$35,900
Books	$35,200
Newspapers	$28,500
Radio and television broadcasting	$26,300

The following statistics are culled from the 2001 Association of American Publishers (AAP) Compensation Survey. They reflect average annual salaries.

Position (Area)	Average Base	Average Total
Top editorial executive (college)	$142,500	$203,100
Top editorial executive (mass market)	$194,400	$280,100
Top editorial executive (adult)	$228,100	$284,200
Top editorial executive (children)	$215,800	$297,400
Top editorial executive (technical)	$174,900	$191,200
Editorial director (college)	$103,100	$129,600
Editorial director (mass market/trade)	$119,100	$136,400
Editorial director (adult trade)	$103,600	$126,800
Editorial director (children)	$117,800	$166,000
Editorial director (technical)	$118,200	$142,800
Executive editor (college)	$103,300	$143,300
Executive editor (mass market/adult trade)	$114,000	$148,800
Executive editor (children trade)	$102,500	$126,600
Executive editor (technical)	$93,000	$112,800
Senior editor (mass market/adult trade)	$74,900	$82,800
Senior editor (children)	$62,500	$77,300
Senior editor (technical)	$68,500	$96,600
Editor (mass market/adult trade)	$52,100	$60,600

Position (Area)	Average Base	Average Total
Editor (technical)	$56,400	$72,700
Editor (children)	$44,900	$49,000
Developmental editor (college)	$48,500	$57,400
Developmental editor (technical)	$70,100	$85,200
Acquisitions editor (college)	$59,100	$79,800
Associate editor (college)	$42,500	$54,000
Associate editor (mass market/adult trade/children)	$38,000	$41,000
Associate editor (technical)	$44,800	$52,200
Assistant editor	$31,900	$35,400
Executive managing editor	$96,900	$99,700
Managing editor	$59,200	$68,300
Associate managing editor	$48,400	$50,900

Senior production editor	$46,300	$49,100
Production editor (mass market/adult trade/children)	$39,400	$39,600
Copyeditor	$39,100	$39,800

Doug Schmidt, senior editor for the Bible-in-Life Curriculum at David C. Cook Publishing Company, points out: "Salaries depend on the type of editor you become, your education level, and the geographic location of the company. Many companies do compensation studies to determine the market value of the positions they offer. Every editorial position has a labor grade, and every grade has a salary range, and publishers tend to hire toward the middle of those ranges. Depending on how a company is doing and how well you're doing, it's reasonable to expect a 3 percent to 5 percent raise each year."

For additional editorial salary information, see the firsthand accounts featured later in this chapter.

EMPLOYMENT OUTLOOK

Employment of editors is expected to increase faster than the average for all occupations through the year 2008. Employment of salaried editors for newspapers, periodicals, book publishers, and nonprofit organizations is expected to increase as demand grows for their publications. Magazines and other periodicals increasingly are developing market niches, appealing to readers with special interests. Also, online publications and services are growing in number and sophistication, spurring the demand for writers and editors. Businesses and organizations are developing Internet websites, and more companies are experimenting with publishing materials directly for the Internet. Advertising and public relations agencies, which also are growing, should be another source of new jobs.

Despite projections of fast employment growth and high turnover, the outlook for most writing and editing jobs is expected to be competitive. Many people with writing or journalism training are attracted to the occupation. Opportunities should be best for technical writers because of the growth in the high-technology and electronics industries and the resulting need for people to write users' guides, instruction manuals, and training materials. This work requires people who are not only technically skilled as writers but are able to keep pace with changing technology. Also, individuals with the technical skills for working on the Internet may have an advantage finding a job as a writer or editor.

Opportunities for editing positions on small daily and weekly newspapers and in small radio and television stations, where the pay is low, should be more numerous than opportunities in larger media markets. Some small publications hire freelance copyeditors as backup for staff editors or as additional help with special projects.

People preparing to be writers and editors benefit from academic preparation in another discipline as well, either to qualify them as writers specializing in that discipline or as a career alternative if they are unable to get a job in writing.

FIRSTHAND ACCOUNTS

Andrea Au, Associate Editor, Simon & Schuster

Andrea Au is an associate editor with Simon & Schuster, a major publishing house located in New York City. She acquires nonfiction titles, edits manuscripts, supervises the production process for books, and assists in the marketing of the books. She has been working in the field since 1996, when she graduated from Princeton with a bachelor's degree in history.

Getting Started

"I had begun my senior year interviewing with management consultants, because that's what my classmates were doing. I realized halfway through the interview process, though, that that was not what I wanted to do. I had always worked on student publications (I was the editor of my high school and college yearbook) and enjoyed it, so I then began doing informational interviews with people in publishing to see if that was something I might want to do.

"At the same time, Prentice Hall sent a recruiter to campus, one of the few nonconsulting or investment banking recruiters; I interviewed with him and was offered a job at Prentice Hall starting that summer.

"My first job in publishing was for the engineering division of Prentice Hall, and while I loved the people I worked with, I realized fairly early on that I wasn't interested in working on engineering textbooks for the rest of my life. Around this time, my college roommate, then working as an editorial assistant at Random House, told me about a position she'd heard about at Simon & Schuster. I applied for the job and got it. It was an assistant editor position, working with two editors at the illustrated book imprint of Simon & Schuster.

"About a month after I started, the illustrated book imprint was folded into the main hardcover imprint of Simon & Schuster, where I worked for almost two years.

"In late 1999, Simon & Schuster created a new unit called Simon & Schuster Reference. It was a separate department devoted to series and brand-name publishing. One of my editors was transferred to S&S Reference, and I followed her there. Shortly afterward, both my editor and the assistant to the director of S&S Reference left the company, and I moved into my current position, which combines parts of both their jobs.

"In the meantime, S&S Reference as a unit was reorganized to become part of The Free Press imprint, changed its name to Simon & Schuster Source, and broadened its focus to become a more general nonfiction imprint.

"So I am now formally an associate editor with The Free Press/Simon & Schuster Source/Wall Street Journal Books . . . which means that I can acquire titles for any of the above imprints. In addition, I still work as an assistant to the director of S&S Source and edit a number of the books he acquires."

What the Job's Really Like

"As an associate editor, I'm in a transitional stage, so I have a two-part job. One part of my job is as assistant to the director of S&S Source. Since his job is both administrative and editorial, I serve as both an administrative assistant (I answer calls, keep his schedule, and sometimes take notes for him at meetings) and an editorial assistant.

"The duties of an editorial assistant vary widely depending upon the editor; my current boss does all of his own editing and writes most of his own marketing material (tip sheets for the sales force, catalog copy, flap copy, etc.), but I handle almost everything once the manuscripts go to production. That involves making sure that the manuscripts are in the proper form for copyediting (one-sided, double-spaced, numbered consecutively), tracking and labeling art for illustrated books, making comments on the design and layout of pages, and working with production to make sure that everything stays on schedule and that the author has ample time to review each stage.

"I also work with the publisher (who is our liaison with the sales force) and publicist to make sure they have whatever materials they need to sell the book.

"The other part of my job is as an acquiring editor myself. In this role, I talk with literary agents to let them know what sorts of proposals I'm interested in, review proposals as they come in, and decide whether or not they are worthy projects (which means not just being well written or well organized, but being of the right subject matter for the imprint and having a well-connected author).

"If I think a project is worthy, I'll circulate it to our editorial board, consisting of all the other editors in the imprint and our publisher. (I also am obliged to read my colleagues' proposals and comment on them.) If they all agree with me that the project is worthy, then the publisher will authorize me to offer a certain amount of money to acquire the book. After acquisition, I'll work with the author to make sure the book comes in on time . . . and I'll edit it, of course, and prepare it for production. I will also be responsible for presenting the book initially to our sales force—which we do about a year before the scheduled publication at positioning meetings.

"It's my job to be the in-house champion for the book and the author's advocate in-house. It's also my job to explain to the authors why their ideas (whether it's their choice of words or their plans for publicity) may not be realistic or prudent or commercially wise. I also need to oversee the production budget for the book, together with the production manager.

"Because I work for an imprint that does almost exclusively nonfiction titles, I do only nonfiction titles at the moment. My editor works on history, politics, business, sports, health, home improvement, pop reference, and cookbooks—

so I work on all of these. But as an editor, I'm looking for books on history, health, self-help, spirituality, and pop reference.

"One of my primary responsibilities is with the Harvard Medical School series of books. The first book in the series was the *Harvard Medical School Family Health Guide*, a big home medical reference, which we published in 1999. We have since begun to spin off single-subject health books featuring proprietary Harvard research—on new fertility treatments, for example, or the latest arthritis drugs.

"I've also done some work on two cookbook series (though mostly in my administrative assistant capacity only)—the Joy of Cooking: All About series and the Williams-Sonoma Collection. Both of these are series of single-subject cookbooks, with such luscious photographs that I always get hungry looking at them.

"I've also been fortunate to have the opportunity to work on some original electronic books we've done with the *Wall Street Journal*. The most ambitious of these was *The Wall Street Journal Guide to Business Schools*. The *Wall Street Journal*, together with Harris Interactive, conducted for the first time in its history a thorough ranking of business schools based on corporate recruiters' input. It's been very interesting to see both the possibilities and limitations of E-books in action throughout this process.

"My workday usually runs from 10:00 A.M. to 8:00 P.M. (this is very flexible, however), and I always take work home on the weekends. Most of my day is taken up by meetings, phone calls, and all the little production or publicity or scheduling details. I very rarely have the opportunity to read proposals or edit manuscripts at work; that almost always happens in the evenings or on weekends.

"I also spend a lot of time reading magazines and newspapers—to keep track of what competing titles are in the workplace, to keep up on popular trends in the world, and to keep an eye out for talented writers or interesting people who might be interested in writing a book. So it's a lot of work, and a job where one never feels quite caught up. There's always more that can be done . . . which can be hugely frustrating but is never boring.

"Most people are very helpful if you approach them for advice or help, however, and over time I've found it a more and more collegial place to work. It's pretty informal, too, and not that hierarchical, which is nice."

Upsides and Downsides "I've always loved books, and I love having a say in what books get made and how. The free books are a great perk as well, of course. I don't work in the most glamorous side of the business, but I have had the opportunity to meet so many interesting and accomplished people, it's amazing. I like the flexibility, as well, of being able to pursue whatever project strikes my fancy (within certain limits, of course) and of perhaps one day having a sideline writing myself.

"Because I work at a large publishing house owned by a media conglomerate, there is a lot of pressure for editors to acquire more and more profitable books—which inevitably means that everyone is overworked and never has all the time they'd like to spend on any one book.

"Also, I've had to turn down a few really great books because they're simply geared toward a niche market that makes it just not lucrative enough for us. One was a self-help book wrapped around the story of a young girl growing up in Hawaii and learning life lessons from her grandmother. I found it moving and powerful and useful, but self-help is such a crowded market that we really require an author to have a built-in publicity platform before we publish them.

"Another that I liked very much was originally called *Mothers' Night Out*, a collection of stories and advice from mothers to mothers. With this one, many editors felt that most mothers would turn more readily to the Internet for the sort of advice and support that the book would offer.

"Yet another was an illustrated book celebrating interracial relationships and families. While it was very well done, it was luxurious and expensive enough (by the nature of the illustrations) that most consumers would simply not buy it for themselves. It would have to work as a gift book—and I would be leery of buying such a gift for my friends in interracial relationships, because there's unfortunately still a taboo of sorts hovering over the subject.

"I've also seen many very practical reference books that were very well done but just too narrowly focused: one on homeschooling children with AD/HD and/or gifted children; one on uncovering the environmental dangers that may be lurking in your home; one on starting a business using a pick-up truck.

"As with any large company, there are office politics at work. Also, because you are working on your own projects (or your editor's own projects), there's very little need for you to work with other editors (though you do need to work closely with people in other parts of the company), which I found rather isolating when I first began working at S&S.

"It's a bureaucracy, as well, with any number of senseless procedures and lots and lots of paperwork. I also feel rather divorced from the sales reps who actually are seeing what the reaction of the public is to these books that we've worked so hard on. And, of course, I'm not paid nearly enough for the hours I work."

Salaries

"I currently earn $33,000, which is slightly on the high side for an associate editor. I started out earning $20,500; these days starting salaries are, on average, still only about $25,000."

Advice

"First of all, be prepared for a lot of grunt work. This is not the glamorous and luxurious business you might think it is. Publishing still works by the apprenticeship system, so you almost always have to start at the bottom and work your way up.

"Second, make sure you find an editor who is nice and willing to give you some of his or her work. It's crucial that you find an editor who will allow you to read some proposals, write some flap copy, and talk to you about why they do what they do (in specifics, not generalities). You might be able to find a mentor who is not your boss, but it's rare, so if you find yourself with a very controlling boss who won't let you do anything more than photocopying, start looking elsewhere.

"There are no real prerequisites to being in publishing, though it helps to be able to write well, to read quickly, and to socialize regularly. There are publishing institutes and classes that can help teach specific skills, but the best way to get started is probably to temp or intern at publishing houses. I wish I had done that, because it allows you to get to know people in different departments in different imprints in different companies."

Doug Schmidt, Senior Editor, Bible-in-Life Curriculum, David C. Cook Publishing Co.

Doug Schmidt is a senior editor at the Colorado Springs, Colorado–based Christian publisher, supervising a group of editors who produce David C. Cook's Bible-in-Life curriculum. In 1984 he earned his bachelor of arts in biblical studies at Wheaton College in Illinois and in 1988 his master of arts at the Trinity Evangelical Divinity School in Deerfield, Illinois. He has been working in the field since 1989.

Getting Started

"I was interested in theological education but didn't really want to teach in a traditional Bible college or seminary setting. I didn't feel called to be a pastor or teacher but felt strongly pulled to support people in these roles.

"Christian publishing turned out to be the perfect fit for me. I discovered an opening for a youth curriculum editor at Cook through Wheaton College's career center (four years after I graduated from Wheaton). I got the job, in part, because all of my future coworkers had English or journalism degrees, and the department was looking for someone who had a theological background. So I came to Cook as a theologian; I learned how to be an editor on the job. My senior editor decided to do freelance work full time, and I was offered his position."

What the Job's Really Like

"We produce and distribute Sunday school curriculum and books; Cook has been in business for 125 years.

"My job as a senior editor at Cook is to coordinate the production of thirty-eight cyclical curriculum products. At one time there were three senior editors doing what I do, so I could not be successful in my job without a team of exceptionally competent editors who are also great team players. They must work well not only with each other but also with their respective designers.

"Seventy to 80 percent of my time is spent reading and reviewing the products that my team works on. I check the material for structure, tone, content, clarity, and theological accuracy. Unless something raises a red flag for me, I go with the editors' decisions on most content matters. I have found that the best way to manage self-motivated people (like those on my team) is to make sure they have what they need to do their jobs—and then to stay out of their way!

"Twenty to 30 percent of my time is spent in meetings that generally focus on issues that can have an impact on product development: customer feedback, quality control, marketing support, and so on.

"When I was an editor, I really enjoyed the creative aspects of the job. When I became a manager, I found that I was doing less product-related creative work and focusing more on people-related issues. For me, the trade was worth it; I really enjoy managing creatives. However, many editors and designers who move into management find that they have been promoted 'beyond their competency' and find that they hate the lack of product-related creative challenges.

"One outlet for these creative urges is freelance work. As long as there's no conflict of interest with your employer, publishing creatives (and managers) can often do well on freelance projects. Of course the drawback is that you have to do those jobs in the evenings and on weekends, so they can take a toll on the rest of your life. Balance is key here."

Upsides and Downsides

"One thing I like about my workload is that it ebbs and flows—it's not a constant barrage of products that never seem to end. There are periods when the work flow slows down just enough so I can catch my breath and get organized. And if I plan well enough, the next wave of product packages is conquered with little or no pain.

"Schedules are a necessary evil in the publishing industry. Each of our products has anywhere from seventy to one hundred deadlines associated with it, and we have two full-time people to make sure all those deadlines are met. As a manager, I often have to explain why certain deadlines are being missed and what we're going to do to make up the time. Keeping up with the schedules is the most unpleasant part of my job, but I'd be floundering without them."

Advice

"If someone asked me how to best prepare for a job in publishing, this is what I would tell him or her: (1) pursue a liberal arts education and major in something for which you have a lot of passion; (2) read with a critical eye—look for things that the publisher did well and for things where somebody dropped the ball; (3) develop a thick skin for criticism by having your work critiqued by knowledgeable people; (4) practice critiquing the work of others—be sure to point out what was done well as well as make suggestions for improvement; (5) put yourself on teams in which you have to work with people with divergent personalities, interests, and skills; (6) seek out internships with publishers—you'll get a great picture of what it takes to enjoy a career in publishing."

Kelly Boyer Sagert, Managing Editor, Back Fence Publishing, Inc.

Kelly Boyer Sagert is the managing editor of *Over the Back Fence* magazine, based in Ohio. She is also the editor of the company's business directories, travel guides, and monthly trade magazine. She earned her B.A. in psychology from Bowling Green State University in Bowling Green, Ohio, in 1983 with a concentration in speech and communications. She has worked in the field of publishing since 1990 and has been the editor of *Over the Back Fence* since 1997. In addition, she is a freelance writer.

Getting Started

"My great-grandmother claimed a kinship to First Lady 'Lemonade' Lucy Hayes. While no one knows how true this claim is, I became interested in this fascinating woman, and I researched her life. Then I consulted the *Writer's Market* for a suitable market for an article. I discovered that *Over the Back Fence* of Chillicothe, Ohio, was looking for historical profiles of local people—and Lucy was a Chillicothe native.

"I sent them a query, along with a clip. The clip was of a piece I'd written on the Underground Railroad. On the editor's 'wish list' was an article about Lucy Hayes and another about the Underground Railroad in Southern Ohio. So, I began writing for them. When *Over the Back Fence* decided to expand and encompass a Northern Ohio edition of the magazine, they called and offered me the job. Serendipity."

What the Job's Really Like

"While I work only about forty hours per week (not counting any freelance writing that I do), the scope of my job is wide. For *Over the Back Fence* magazine I decide which stories will go into each issue, choosing ones that will appeal to our readers, and I discuss the angles and lengths with the freelance writers. I also have to reject some of the writers' queries. I hire the writers and photographers and negotiate their contracts. I also write some of the articles for the magazine myself.

"When the assigned articles are completed, I edit them, both in a copyediting sense and to ensure that the article fits the tone and focus of *Over the Back Fence*. I then pass the articles and photographs to our design team and let them know how much space is available for each. I fact check each of the pieces, as well.

"Once the design team has created the magazine, there are a few days of intense proofing and tweaking. We then send the document to the printer. A few days later, we receive a blueline (or final proof), and about a week later we have the magazine in hand.

"I am also responsible for the budget for the magazine, and I turn invoices in for payment. Besides that, I generate the publicity for the magazine by sending out press releases, appearing on TV/radio, and speaking at writer's conferences, libraries, civic groups, and so on.

"Back Fence Publishing also publishes business directories, travel planners, and two monthly trade magazines. I do the hiring, editing, and photo gathering for those as well. The company also publishes a Southern Ohio edition of *Over the Back Fence* magazine, and the editor of that edition forwards me her articles for a second opinion, and I do the same with my articles. She's terrific, and we bounce ideas off each other all of the time. Her workload is similar to mine.

"My job is truly interesting, and I love working with creative people. Our pace is hectic, and there are plenty of last-minute details and crises, but, near the end of a particular publication, the energy is high. My coworkers are intelligent people with terrific senses of humor.

"I'm the mother of two active boys, and I work about 50 percent of the time in the magazine office and about 50 percent at home. The owner of the publishing company is also the mother of young children, and she allows me great freedom."

Upsides and Downsides   "I adore the creative end of the business. Writing is one of my passions, and public speaking is the other—and this job allows plenty of room for both. I'm blessed to be working with wonderful and talented people, and I genuinely look forward to working with them every day. Besides that, the flexibility of my job is a big plus.

"I'm in a business I love, one where I receive plenty of praise and recognition for my work.

"The downside would be the tight deadlines. And what I like least is having to tell a writer that a particular story isn't working or that it needs to be reduced in scope. I know what that's like, and so I hate doing that to someone else."

Salaries   "With my writing and editing combined, I earn about $35,000. I'm paid at an hourly rate, which I understand isn't the standard."

Advice   "Read, both critically and for sheer pleasure. Learn all that you can about grammar and punctuation, and practice your writing and communication skills whenever possible. Ask to apprentice somewhere if you have no writing or editing resume, or work as a stringer at your local newspaper. Get started in the field!

"Respect accuracy, cultivate curiosity, and honor deadlines—and add to, rather than take away from, the creativity and ideas of those around you. Mentally slap yourself on the wrist whenever you catch yourself saying, 'I'm sure this is accurate—no use checking it out further.' Be concise. Work on your people skills.

"Strive for perfection, but realize its impossibility; strive for each project to be better than the last, but don't be hard on yourself when it doesn't happen. It won't—at least not always.

"Associate with others in the field by joining writing and editing organizations. Know your librarians. Search out your ideal job, but be willing to take on lesser jobs along the way—if they're in the direction you'd like to take. Don't expect to start out at the top, but intend to get there—at least your own definition of what the top really is."

Ellen Urban, Freelance Editor and Proofreader

Ellen Urban is a freelance editor and proofreader based in Connecticut. In 1976 she earned a B.A. in English literature from Loyola University, Chicago, and in 1984 she earned her M.A. in English literature from DePaul University, Chicago. She has been in the publishing field since 1978 and has been a freelance editor since 1991.

Getting Started

"Many people I know in publishing didn't actively pursue it as a career. Like me, they were English lit majors who didn't know what they were going to do with this degree. Some decided on teaching. Others fell into publishing by happenstance—someone needed someone to proofread something and an English lit grad seemed like a good person to do the job. I belong to the latter category. A friend told me about an opening in a small publishing house, and I got the job. It certainly wasn't something I purposely went after. I just needed work.

"A year later when the company folded, I worked for two more publishers before landing a job with a publishing giant, where I used my editorial skills in producing educational software. Instead of working with paper and pencil, I then worked with a keyboard and computer.

"My current job is with paper and pencil again as a freelance editor/proofreader. I started freelancing in 1991 when my husband and I moved to the East Coast for his job. We had a two-year-old and an infant at the time, so I didn't want to work outside the house. Freelancing was the perfect solution for me. Since then we've had two more kids, so freelancing is still the perfect solution for me.

"These days, though, I rarely work at home—which may seem like a ridiculous thing to say given that I decided to freelance so I could stay at home. But it's tough to concentrate with four—shall we say active—children about. The youngest one hasn't started kindergarten yet, so he's around for most of the day. Next year, when he does start school, working at home will seem like such a treat. But for now, when my husband comes home from work and on weekends, I pack up my "homework" and head for the library where it's quiet and where there is a lot of reference material available for checking facts. Editing is a portable job. It can be done anywhere—as long as you have a dictionary and a manual of style with you."

What the Job's Really Like

"I work for several different publishers. One is McGraw-Hill's VGM Career Books line, my bread-and-butter publisher. I have a regular gig with them that keeps me busy about eight months of the year. I fill in the rest of the time with odd jobs from other publishers.

"I edit new or revised manuscripts, checking for grammatical errors and proper word usage and sentence and paragraph construction. I also proofread typeset manuscripts for typographical errors and to ensure that the style of the book is consistent throughout.

"I always have questions for an author when I'm done, and it's my responsibility to talk with him or her and resolve these queries. Another duty is to typemark the manuscript—which provides a blueprint for the typesetter to follow. I mark which parts of the manuscript are plain vanilla text, label the headings and how they should be set (i.e., major heads, subheads, etc.), show where numbered lists and bulleted lists occur, identify elements of the front matter (table of contents, foreword, preface, etc.) and back matter (glossary, appendixes, etc.), and in short, label and identify all the disparate elements of the book.

"I typically work on a line of books about careers—welding, medicine, sales, law, public relations, plumbing, real estate, biotechnology, metalworking, horticulture. You name it and there's a book about it. All the books look the same; only the subject matter is different. Some books are on obvious careers; others are not so obvious. At first, anybody—as I was—might be amused that someone could write an entire book about, oh, working in a summer camp, for example, but the day-to-day details of various careers are always richer and more complicated than the uninitiated could possibly guess. That's the value of these books; they offer details instead of gloss and a realistic assessment of the opportunities, salaries, and life cycle a career has to offer.

"It's hard to gauge how long a job will take to complete because each one is different. So much depends on how long the book is; whether it is a new manuscript or a revision, meaning that it has already been edited one or more times; how good a writer the author is; and how technical or easy the material is. Generally, though, by the time you've gotten through the first chapter or two, you have a good idea what you're up against.

"Once I've edited and typemarked a book and checked for seemingly hundreds of little details, it is typeset. That done, I'll get a copy of the galleys— the typeset pages—and I'll read them against the original manuscript to make sure that all the changes I asked for were made and that nothing from the copy has been dropped. I also check to make sure that all the stylistic elements are set correctly and consistently. When I'm done, all the changes I've made to the galleys will be marked either as typesetter's errors or editor's errors, which are changes or corrections that I missed or didn't make at the manuscript stage.

"Finally, I'll talk with the author and incorporate his or her changes into my master set of galleys. From there it's back to the typesetter, who makes the final changes and sends it back so that the corrections can be checked. The last stop on the journey of a book in progress is the printer.

Upsides and Downsides   "Reading is one of my most favorite things to do, so it's satisfying to have a job that requires that I do a lot of it. Of course the mind-set is different and I'm not reading for pleasure. Nonetheless, it's always interesting to see how people think—which comes through in their style of writing and how they express themselves. Also, as I mentioned earlier, this is a job that I can do anywhere, anytime—even 3:00 A.M.

"As far as the downsides are concerned, there aren't many. I've heard some people say that editors are wanna-be writers who can't write. I don't know if this is true, but for the most part, it seems that in this profession you're either one or the other but not usually both.

"One more thing that comes to mind is that editing is an imprecise science. Of course, there are definite grammatical rules to follow and the correct spelling of words is indisputable. Nonetheless, give five different editors the same copy to edit, and they'll each produce something slightly different. Some would consider this problematic. I know of editors who switched to computer science because they craved the precision and clarity computer languages offer—as opposed to the sometimes-ambiguous style and prose of the English language.

"Finally, the editor is often an unsung hero. One never knows in what condition a book will arrive and what 'magic' the editor will have to perform to make it readable. But if you like working behind the scenes, this won't be a problem."

Salary   "Salary is a difficult thing to discuss only because the salary scales from one publisher to the next can be very different, particularly if you are a freelancer. Some publishers pay a flat fee per book. Others have you bill them for the hours you worked for a set per-hour dollar amount. The type of publisher you work for—a publisher of highly technical material, a small house that publishes corporate newsletters, a trade publisher, or an educational publisher—will also affect what you can expect in terms of salary. I've made anywhere from $120 to $1,200 on a book, depending on complexity, length, and other factors."

Advice   "It goes without saying, but I'll say it anyway. You should love to read to do this work. And you shouldn't mind working alone, because for the most part it'll be just you and your manuscript for great blocks of time. It would help if you enjoy solving puzzles, enjoy working things out, and are a little obsessed with precision and details. All these can be applied to turning a rough manuscript into a readable and coherent book.

"The best way to get started is to get work with a publisher, perhaps beginning as a proofreader. You'll see what seasoned editors do with manuscripts, and this will be a marvelous education for you. Eventually, you'll be ready to tackle your first editing assignment. You don't need to have a degree in English, but taking an editing and/or proofreading course would be a good idea. Many universities offer courses (see Appendix B). I took one at the University of Chicago in basic manuscript editing, as well as a course in writing picture books for children. Any such courses you can take will be very helpful.

"If you want to go the freelance route, you'll have an extremely difficult time finding work unless you've had several years of experience working for one or more publishers. There are a great many people out there who enjoy the freelance life, and publishers typically have dozens of good, experienced people from which to choose."

Kathy Ptacek,
Newsletter Editor
and Publisher

Kathy Ptacek is the publisher and editor of the popular writers' newsletter *The Gila Queen's Guide to Markets*. She earned her B.A. with a major in journalism and a minor in history from the University of New Mexico in Albuquerque in 1974. She has been in the publishing field since 1988 and is currently based in Newton, New Jersey.

Getting Started

"I always seemed to find various bits of market information, and I would pass along to my friends—all writers—what I had heard about anthologies or magazines currently reading. For some time I had been joking that I should start a market newsletter. Eventually I joked less and thought more seriously about it.

"The newsletter comes out about every six weeks. I charge $45 for ten issues."

What the Job's Really Like

"I'm not being immodest to say that I *am* the newsletter. I have folks who do various things—contribute columns and some proofreading—but I do everything else. I contact markets, format files, lay out the newsletter using a computer program, proof, reproof, and so on. I also maintain the subscriber file and take care of all correspondence.

"It's a job with lots and lots of details. It's a never-ending one. Some days I'll start off by checking out various markets on the Internet. Those files—if I've found any—have to be formatted to fit my newsletter. Other days I may only proofread. And still other days it'll be simply a matter of catching up on E-mail and sending out new requests for guidelines.

"Most of my correspondence is now done via E-mail. I still fax a number of editors, particularly when I'm sending market report forms out for the big issues I publish. Those annual issues are devoted to romance, mystery/suspense, and science fiction, fantasy, and horror.

"Sometimes I'm quite busy; at other times, I have a lot of idle time—time that seems to get used for a lot of other things. It's never boring. I have worked for companies and I have worked for myself, and I will tell you that I work far harder and far longer hours than I ever did for an outside job. Sometimes I'm still working at midnight—but that's all right. I enjoy it."

Upsides and Downsides

"The nice thing about working from home—and having no employees—is that I don't have to worry about dress codes and such. I can wear shorts and T-shirts and no shoes in the summer; I can bundle up in the winter. I can take as long as I want for lunch, too. But no matter how much I goof off, I know if I don't buckle down and get the work done, no one else is going to do it.

"One of the things I like the most about my job is meeting new people, discovering new markets. I have made so many friends and acquaintances through this newsletter—it's truly amazing. I was always shy and it was difficult for me to talk to people, particularly over the telephone (that's one of the reasons I went into journalism—to force myself to get over my shyness). Now I find myself calling folks in foreign countries—and not thinking anything about it. Of course, faxes and E-mail make it a lot simpler, especially for someone who is shy.

"What I like least about my job is this: waiting and waiting and waiting for folks to get back to me. I query them about guidelines, then sometimes wait; then I have to ask them again. All in all, though, that's not too terribly negative."

Salaries

"What do I earn? Not enough. I don't give myself a salary, per se. Someone just starting out can expect to not earn very much. I think for a business like this, it helps to have been in the business (I have been a writer for many years), because you have some contacts. And contacts mean more business, which means more money for you."

Advice

"Be sure this is what you really want to do. It's a lonely business, as is writing. Be sure that you're at least halfway organized—or can get that way.

"I think having a writing or editing background would help. Someone starting out this way should be detail-oriented—there's a lot to making a newsletter look good. The best thing to do if you're going to start a newsletter is check out the books on various newsletters. Determine what kind of newsletter it will be, who will be the target audience—and above all, make sure that the field needs your newsletter. There's no sense in starting a newsletter in a field in which dozens already exist—unless you can do it quite differently."

Tracey Hessler, Managing Editor, *Somniloquy* Magazine

Tracey Hessler is managing editor for Dreamwalker Press, which publishes *Somniloquy* magazine out of Orlando, Florida. The magazine is sold throughout the United States and in the United Kingdom. She started in the field in 1995.

Getting Started

"As a writer, I realized the need for a magazine willing to breach the genre barrier and willing to judge material on its own merits rather than publish only authors with salable names. I also wanted to produce a medium that provided entertainment without an accompanying flood of advertising.

"I started the magazine myself on a shoestring, paying for everything out-of-pocket until it began to pay for itself. I advertised on the Internet and with flyers, posters, and word of mouth. I offered other writers the type of product that I wanted for myself."

What the Job's Really Like

"My duties? It would be easier to describe what aren't my duties. I receive, compile, and forward all submissions to the appropriate editors, then begin setting up the layout. I have three editors who help me choose the material that goes in each issue. They also go over the proof copy for errors prior to final printing.

"I spend a great deal of time choosing the right cover art, something applicable to the content if possible. I try to keep the magazine simple so I can remove the contents of the previous issue (on the computer) and replace it with the upcoming copy.

"A typical day will find me reading and answering my E-mail, transferring material into the correct category, and deleting what I won't need. Since I also run a writers' group, host two online chats, and run a web design service, as well as networking with other magazines, I have an intricate filing system to keep track of the constant influx of mail. I check my post office box daily and also spend at least two hours on my personal writing projects.

"Then I work for a few hours, compiling the magazine. In short I am busy, busy, but I am satisfied with that. Of course there is a lot of hard work involved in running a publishing company with its accompanying responsibilities, but it is also rewarding. The financial benefits are not very good at first, but as you develop readership, that improves."

Upsides and Downsides

"I enjoy the challenge of providing a unique service to my readers, choosing the right material, then putting it together in an attractive package. I compile, print, and bind the entire magazine.

"There's nothing I don't like, except that most times everything, including family and friends, must come in second."

Salaries

"The magazine comes out quarterly and costs subscribers $22 per year, including postage, in the United States and Canada; $30 abroad. Last count I had about 150 subscribers. And very little advertising (by design). With self-employment the salary varies as the readership increases. Most of my employees are volunteers, and the money I receive just barely covers the expenses I incur."

Advice

"If you want to start your own magazine or publishing company, first make sure you have the funds to finance it. Keep your day job until everything starts to fall into place.

"Above all, the desire to present the best writing available (even if it's not your own) must be first and foremost in your mind. You have to have drive, stamina, and the unconditional support of your family and friends.

"Carefully study the publications that are similar to the one you desire to produce, then just start. Set up your format and start compiling the information you'll need. You can have your publication printed and bound if you have the funds to do it. And set up a web page, send E-mail to your acquaintances online, and frequent writers' chatrooms and offer them a chance to submit (with pay if you can, comp copies and subscriptions if you can't). You'll be amazed how many beginning writers have real talent."

Miranda Garza, Publisher and Editor, *Kids' Highway* Magazine

Miranda Garza is the publisher and nonfiction, poetry, and book reviews editor for *Kids' Highway*, a home-based family business she runs with her brother. She started the magazine in 1999 when she had just turned seventeen.

Getting Started

"I like to write fiction and poetry that leaves people with a smile. I strongly believe that fiction should be entertaining and enjoyable, not a way of showing how hard life is. It was difficult to find a market that catered to this kind of work. So, my brother and I decided to create a magazine that would entertain with fiction as well as nonfiction. We made it a family magazine to show that adult fare and children's reading can coexist. With assistance from the adults in our life, it has been a great success and a lot of fun.

"My brother, Hector Cole, has a keen imagination that complements his ability to make quick decisions on what's perfect for our magazine's fiction. When he finds it, he revels in it, and this makes him a better fiction/video reviews editor and webmaster.

"The job I have fell upon me because of my love for poetry, my insatiable desire to read books, and a well-defined idea of what type of nonfiction I knew should go into *Kids' Highway*. It could be informative; educational; new and improved; a goal to strive for; something to do, see, hear, or feel; but it also had to be fun.

"In essence, our different personalities created our own niches in the building of *Kids' Highway.*"

**What the Job's
Really Like**

"*Kids' Highway* is the family magazine where the kids are at the wheel. The finished product is twenty-four pages at eight and one-half by eleven inches, saddle stitched with a card stock cover. The color is different with each issue. Each issue costs $5.95. Subscriptions cost $29. Our circulation is about 100. To get subscribers we advertise on our website and through direct mail campaigns.

"Our business is totally supported by our subscribers, because we carry no advertisements. We target grown-ups with our 'Grown-Ups' Tug-Out Pages' and kids ages seven and up.

"I love my job! *Kids' Highway* is one of my top priorities every day. I work from one to six hours a day, depending on how close we are to our deadline. There's always something to do or a decision to make.

"As the nonfiction/poetry/book reviews editor, my job is to review all submissions that fall under these categories. And I do read the fiction that my brother wants to accept as a means of fortifying his decision. (He does the same for nonfiction.)

"As soon as a submission comes in (via E-mail or post), we label and date it. We read submissions in the order in which they come in. Because we know what should go in the magazine, we never disagree about what should or shouldn't be included.

"Naturally, I read submissions by E-mail at my computer, but I don't like to do that with the submissions by post. The dining room table is a necessity for me. I prefer a relaxed atmosphere where I can have a clear head and no distractions when I read work from writers.

"Sometimes, I won't read past the first paragraph because I can tell that the piece is not right for us. A poem about deformities at birth, African poverty, or death by concentration camp may be about a worthy topic, but not in our magazine. This is frustrating! We are not the type of market that insists writers buy a copy of the magazine, but we would like writers to read our guidelines at least—which we make readily available (through writing publications, E-mail, website, or post), and we are thorough in explaining what we want. When writers can't make that effort, I don't feel guilty not going on.

"I have total say in what gets accepted or rejected (in my editorial areas), but there are times when I will consult our other editors. We will discuss the piece to see if it is worth editing. This is the time when I might suggest rewrites or word cuts to the writers.

"If I find a piece that is perfect for our magazine, I contact the writer via phone, E-mail, or post and let him or her know when it will be published, how much the compensation will be, and when it will get sent.

"If I find a piece that is attractive but isn't perfect for us, I will suggest other markets. It takes time and a lot of concentration to consider submissions. An editor needs to be focused on the work at hand to give fair consideration to all the writers. If I'm worried or sick I can't give the attention they deserve, so I have to wait until I feel better, I'm relaxed, and I'm not distracted.

"When our decisions are made for the upcoming issue, we start to build the pages. More decisions. We want to present the stories and articles in the best possible light with the technology we have available to us. We add pictures and have different column widths and fonts. Again the premise here is fun. Sometimes it takes a month to achieve the look we want.

"Then, there is the business end of publishing a magazine: balancing the checkbook, paying our writers and the printers, updating technology, and so on. This also includes seeing to it that our writers have copies of their work and sending them out."

Upsides and Downsides   "The greatest feeling in the world for a writer comes when she reads those five wonderful words: 'your work has been accepted.' The bulk of our writers send us thank-you cards or notes telling us how thrilled they are about getting accepted. To be able to help writers get published while introducing our readers to the kind of fiction we feel should be published is extremely satisfying.

"It's enjoyable reading how different writers handle old ideas and plots. I love the enthusiasm a writer gets across in his cover letter. It's so exciting to discover a piece that I just can't keep to myself or that I'm still thinking about days after I've read it.

"When a writer has been rejected and he writes us to 'tell us off' or let us know how 'appalled' he is that we didn't accept his work, this is hard to swallow.

"It also gets frustrating when there's a mound of submissions to review and most of them scream that the writers didn't even read the guidelines. This wastes my time and the writers' time as well.

"It's also difficult to discard a submission because the writer failed to include a SASE or at least a valid E-mail address. But we can't waste the time reading the submission if there's no way to contact the writer with our decision. We don't have the extra resources to pay for a writer's postage.

"But the good definitely outweighs the bad because this is something I really enjoy doing. I've always wanted to publish my own magazine, and to be able to do it is literally a dream come true. Not many have such a privilege."

Salaries   "When you publish and edit a magazine, how much you make depends largely on how much advertising you do. At first, you shouldn't expect a lot because people don't know you or your work. But as you establish yourself and tell more people about your magazine, you can expect a better response.

"*Kids' Highway* has made money for us, but we put it straight back into the business. So none of us earns a salary as yet. What we're doing is building a good reputation for ourselves and the magazine. We have the reputation of paying our writers on time and giving them the utmost respect. And too, we have the reputation of publishing entertaining fiction and nonfiction that parents can trust. We intend to cash in on that reputation."

Advice

"I think you have to be a writer yourself to appreciate how hard the process of submitting is. Only then could you give the writer his due. Sure, writing is like singing. Everyone thinks he can do it. But it takes a special kind of person and fluidity of thought to keep a reader's attention. Appreciate those people because they are the ones who'll keep you in business.

"Be a trendsetter, not a trend-wagoneer (jumping on the bandwagon to cash in with copycat manuscripts) or follower.

"A publisher must have patience. She deals with people every day, sometimes with angry, stupid, misunderstood, or lazy people who don't care about quality control. To deal with these people and still have high publishing standards takes a great deal of patience.

"You must know how to work and act under the pressure of deadlines.

"And, you must love this mode of communication or you'll find it too easy to give up."

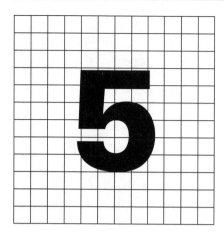

BOOK PRODUCTION

"I cannot live without books."—Thomas Jefferson

The printing industry, like many other industries, continues undergoing technological change as computers and technology alter the manner in which work is performed. Many of the processes that were once done by hand are becoming more automated.

Technology's influence can be seen in all three stages of printing:

1. Prepress—the preparation of materials for printing

2. Press—the actual printing process

3. Postpress or finishing—the folding, binding, and trimming of printed sheets into final form

The most notable changes are occurring in the prepress stage. Instead of cutting and pasting articles by hand, it is now common to produce an entire publication on a computer, complete with artwork and graphics. Columns can be displayed and arranged on the computer screen exactly as they will appear in print, and then printed. Nearly all prepress work is expected to be computerized by 2008, and workers will need more training in electronics, computers, and mathematics.

ELECTRONIC PUBLISHING

There is another method of production: many segments of the publishing industry now produce their products electronically. For example, many periodicals, books, and promotional materials can be found on the Internet, on CD-ROM, and on audio- and videotapes. This expansion into nonprint media is expected to continue as the Internet heralds a new era in the printing and publishing industry. Individuals are now designing their own work on the Web and, consequently, have a potential reader base of millions. As a result, the market for the design and development of Internet pages and publications is growing significantly.

PREPRESS

Prepress workers prepare material for printing presses. They perform a variety of tasks involved with transforming text and pictures into finished pages and making printing plates of the pages.

Advances in computer software and printing technology continue to change prepress work. Customers, as well as prepress workers, use their computers to produce camera-ready material that looks like the desired finished product. Customers, using their own computers, increasingly do much of the typesetting and page layout work formerly done by prepress workers. This process, called "desktop publishing," poses new challenges for the printing industry. Instead of receiving simple typed text from customers, prepress workers get the material on a computer disk. Because of this, customers are increasingly likely to have already settled on a format on their own, rather than relying on suggestions from prepress workers. Furthermore, the printing industry is rapidly moving toward complete "digital imaging," by which customers' material received on computer disks is converted directly into printing plates. Other innovations in prepress work are digital color page-makeup systems, electronic page-layout systems, and off-press color-proofing systems.

Typesetting and page layouts have also been affected by technological changes. The old "hot type" method of text composition—which used molten lead to create individual letters, paragraphs, and full pages of text—is nearly extinct. Today, composition work is done with computers and "cold type" technology. Cold type, which is any of a variety of methods creating type without molten lead, has traditionally used "phototypesetting" to prepare text and pictures for printing. Although this method has many variations, all use photography to create images on paper. The images are assembled into page format and rephotographed to create film negatives from which the actual printing plates are made. However, newer cold-type methods are becoming more common. These automate the photography or make printing plates directly from electronic files. In one common form of phototypesetting, text is entered into a computer programmed to hyphenate, space, and create columns of text. Typesetters or data-entry clerks may do keyboarding of text at the printing establishment, or, increasingly, authors do this work before the job is sent out for composition. The coded text is then transferred to a typesetting machine, which uses photography, a cathode-ray tube, or a laser to create an image on typesetting paper or film. Once it has been developed, the paper or film is sent to a lithographer who makes the actual printing plate.

Desktop-publishing specialists use a keyboard to enter and select the size and style of type, the column width, and appropriate spacing and to store it in the computer. The computer then displays and arranges columns of type on a screen resembling a television screen. An entire newspaper, catalog, or book page, complete with artwork and graphics, can be made up on the screen exactly as it will appear in print. Operators transmit the pages for production into film and then into plates or directly into plates. Preflight technicians edit the work of the desktop-publishing specialists and ensure the overall quality of the finished product before it is delivered to the customer. In small shops, job printers may be responsible for composition and page layout, reading proofs for errors and clarity, correcting mistakes, and printing.

New technologies also affect the roles of other composition workers. Improvements in desktop-publishing software allow customers to do more of their own typesetting. "Imagesetters" read text from computer memory and then "beam" it directly onto film, paper, or plates, bypassing the slower photographic process traditionally used.

With traditional photographic processes, the material is arranged and typeset and then passed on to workers who further prepare it for the presses. Camera operators are usually classified as line-camera operators, halftone operators, or color-separation photographers. Line-camera operators start the process of making a lithographic plate by photographing and developing film negatives or positives of the material to be printed. They adjust light and expose film for a specified length of time and then develop film in a series of chemical baths. They may load exposed film in machines that automatically develop and fix the image. The use of film in printing will decline as electronic imaging becomes more prevalent. With decreased costs and improved quality, electronic imaging has become the method of choice in the industry.

The lithographic printing process requires that images be made up of tiny dots coming together to form a picture. Photographs cannot be printed without them. When normal "continuous-tone" photographs need to be reproduced, halftone-camera operators separate the photograph into pictures containing the dots. Color-separation photography is more complex. In this process, camera operators produce four-color separation negatives from a continuous-tone color print or transparency. Most of this separation work is done electronically on scanners. Scanner operators use computerized equipment to create film negatives or positives of photographs or art. The computer controls the color separation of the scanning process, and with the help of the operator, corrects for mistakes or compensates for deficiencies in the original color print or transparency. Each scan produces a dotted image, or halftone, of the original in one of four primary printing colors—yellow, magenta, cyan, and black. The images are used to produce printing plates that print each of these colors, with transparent colored inks, one at a time. These produce "secondary" color combinations of red, green, blue, and black, which can be combined to produce the colors and hues of the original photograph.

Scanners that can perform color correction during the color-separation procedure are rapidly replacing lithographic dot etchers, who retouch film negatives or positives by sharpening or reshaping images. They work by hand, using chemicals, dyes, and special tools. Dot etchers must know the characteristics of all types of paper and must produce fine shades of color. Like camera operators, they are usually assigned to only one phase of the work and may have job titles such as dot etcher, retoucher, or letterer.

New technology is also lessening the need for film strippers, who cut the film to the required size and arrange and tape the negatives onto "flats"—or layout sheets used by platemakers to make press plates. When completed, flats resemble large film negatives of the text in its final form. In large printing establishments such as newspapers, arrangement is done automatically.

Platemakers use a photographic process to make printing plates. The film assembly or flat is placed on top of a thin metal plate, which is coated with a light-sensitive resin. Exposure to ultraviolet light activates the chemical in parts not protected by the film's dark areas. The plate is then developed in a solution that removes the unexposed nonimage area, exposing bare metal. The chemical on the areas of the plate that were exposed to the light hardens and becomes water-repellent. The hardened parts of the plate form the text.

A growing number of printing plants use lasers to directly convert electronic data to plates without any use of film. Entering, storing, and retrieving information from computer-aided equipment require technical skills. In addition to operating and maintaining the equipment, lithographic platemakers must make sure that plates meet quality standards.

PRINTING

During the printing process, the plate is first covered with a thin coat of water. The water adheres only to the bare metal nonimage areas and is repelled by the hardened areas that were exposed to light. Next, the plate comes in contact with a rubber roller covered with oil-based ink. Because oil and water do not mix, the ink is repelled by the water-coated area and sticks to the hardened areas. The ink covering the hardened text is transferred to paper.

Although computers perform a wider variety of tasks, printing still involves text composition, page layout, and platemaking, so printing will still require prepress workers. As computer skills become increasingly important, these workers will need to demonstrate a desire and an ability to benefit from the frequent retraining required by rapidly changing technology.

Duties of press operators vary according to the type of press they operate— offset lithography, gravure, flexography, or letterpress. Offset lithography, which transfers an inked impression from a rubber-covered cylinder to paper or other material, is the dominant printing process. With gravure, the recesses on an etched plate or cylinder are inked and pressed to paper. Flexography is a form of rotary printing in which ink is applied to the surface by a flexible rubber printing plate with a raised image area. Gravure and flexography should increase in use, but letterpress, in which an inked, raised surface is pressed against paper, will be phased out.

In addition to the major printing processes, plateless or nonimpact processes are coming into general use. Plateless processes—including electronic, electrostatic, and ink-jet printing—are used for copying, duplicating, and document and specialty printing, usually by quick and in-house printing shops.

POSTPRESS BINDERY WORKERS

The process of combining printed sheets into finished products such as books, magazines, catalogs, folders, directories, or product packaging is known as "binding." Binding involves cutting, folding, gathering, gluing, stapling, stitching, trimming, sewing, wrapping, and other finishing operations. Bindery workers operate and maintain the machines that perform these various tasks.

Job duties depend on the kind of material being bound. In firms that do edition binding, for example, workers bind books produced in large numbers, or "runs." Job-binding workers bind books produced in smaller quantities. In firms specializing in library binding, workers repair books and provide other specialized binding services to libraries. Pamphlet-binding workers produce leaflets and folders, and manifold-binding workers bind business forms such as ledgers and books of sales receipts. Blankbook-binding workers bind blank pages to produce notebooks, checkbooks, address books, diaries, calendars, and notepads.

Some types of binding and finishing consist of only one step. Preparing leaflets or newspaper inserts, for example, requires only folding. Binding of books and magazines, on the other hand, requires a number of steps.

Bookbinders assemble books and magazines from large, flat, printed sheets of paper. Skilled bookbinders operate machines that first fold printed sheets into "signatures," which are groups of pages arranged sequentially. Bookbinders then sew, stitch, or glue the assembled signatures together, shape the book bodies with presses and trimming machines, and reinforce them with glued fabric strips. Covers are created separately and then glued, pasted, or stitched onto the book bodies. The books then undergo a variety of finishing operations, often including wrapping in paper jackets.

A small number of bookbinders work in hand binderies. These highly skilled workers design original or special bindings for limited editions or restore and rebind rare books. The work requires creativity, knowledge of binding materials, and a thorough background in the history of binding. Hand bookbinding gives individuals the opportunity to work in the greatest variety of jobs.

Bindery workers in small shops may perform many binding tasks, while those in large shops are usually assigned only one or a few operations, such as operating complicated manual or electronic guillotine paper cutters or folding machines. Others specialize in adjusting and preparing equipment and may perform minor repairs as needed.

EMPLOYMENT FIGURES

The printing and publishing industry have about 1.6 million wage and salary jobs in addition to 125,000 self-employed workers, ranking it among the largest manufacturing industries. Nearly two-thirds of wage and salary jobs are in establishments employing fewer than ten workers; nearly 70 percent are in the two largest sectors: commercial printing and newspapers.

Prepress workers. Prepress workers hold about 135,000 jobs. Employment is distributed as follows:

Desktop publishing specialists	26,000
Film strippers, printing	23,000
Job printers	17,000
Platemakers	15,000
Compositors and typesetters	14,000
Camera operators	9,200
Pasteup workers	9,000
Photoengravers	2,700
All other precision printing workers	17,000
Typesetting- and composing-machine operators	13,000
Photoengraving- and lithographic-machine operators	6,800

Most prepress jobs are found in firms that handle commercial or business printing and in newspaper plants. Commercial printing firms print newspaper inserts, catalogs, pamphlets, and advertisements, while business-form establishments print material such as sales receipts. A large number of jobs are also found in "in-plant" operations and printing-trade-service firms. Establishments in printing trade services typically perform custom compositing, platemaking, and related prepress services.

Printing-press operators. Press operators hold about 253,000 jobs. Employment is distributed as follows:

Printing-press-machine setters and operators	142,000
Offset-lithographic-press operators	63,000
Screen-printing-machine setters and setup operators	28,000
Letterpress operators	10,000
All other printing-press setters and setup operators	9,500

Most press-operator jobs are in newspaper plants or in firms handling commercial or business printing. Commercial printing firms print newspaper inserts, catalogs, pamphlets, and the advertisements found in mailboxes, and business-form establishments print items such as business cards, sales receipts, and paper used in computers. Additional jobs are in the "in-plant" section of organizations and businesses that do their own printing—such as banks, insurance companies, and government agencies.

The printing and publishing industry is one of the most geographically dispersed industries in the United States, and press operators can find jobs throughout the country. However, jobs are concentrated in large printing centers such as New York, Los Angeles, Chicago, Philadelphia, Washington, DC, and Dallas.

Bindery workers. Bindery workers hold about 96,000 jobs, including about 6,600 working as skilled bookbinders and approximately 90,000 working as lesser-skilled bindery machine operators. Although large libraries and book publishers employ some bindery workers, the majority of jobs are in commercial printing plants. Other large employers of bindery workers are bindery trade shops, which specialize in providing binding services for printers without binderies or whose printing production exceeds their binding capabilities. Few publishers maintain their own manufacturing facilities, so most contract out the printing and assembly of books to commercial printing plants or bindery trade shops.

Bindery jobs are concentrated near large metropolitan areas such as New York, Chicago, Washington, DC, Los Angeles, Philadelphia, and Dallas.

TRAINING

Prepress workers. Most prepress workers train on the job; the length of training varies by occupation. Some skills, such as typesetting, can be learned in a few months, but they are the most likely to be automated in the future. Other skills, such as stripping (image assembly), require years of experience to master. However, these workers should also expect to receive intensive retraining.

Workers often start as helpers who are selected for on-the-job training programs after demonstrating their reliability and interest in the occupation. They begin with instruction from an experienced craft worker and advance based on their demonstrated mastery of skills at each level. All workers should expect to be retrained from time to time to handle new, improved equipment. As workers gain experience, they advance to positions with greater responsibility. Some move into supervisory positions.

Apprenticeship is another way to become a skilled prepress worker, although few apprenticeships have been offered in recent years. Apprenticeship programs emphasize a specific craft—such as camera operator, film stripper, lithographic etcher, scanner operator, or platemaker—but apprentices are introduced to all phases of printing.

Most employers prefer to hire high school graduates who possess good communication skills, both oral and written. Prepress workers should be able to deal courteously with people, because in small shops they may take customer orders. They may also add, subtract, multiply, divide, and compute ratios to estimate job costs. Persons interested in working for firms using advanced printing technology need to know the basics of electronics and computers. Mathematical skills are also essential for operating many of the software packages used to run modern, computerized prepress equipment. Prepress workers need good manual dexterity, and they must be able to pay attention to detail and work independently. Good eyesight, including visual acuity, depth perception, field of view, color vision, and the ability to focus quickly, are also assets. Artistic ability is often a plus. Employers also seek persons who are even-tempered and adaptable, important qualities for workers who often must meet deadlines and learn how to operate new equipment.

Printing. Although completion of a formal apprenticeship or a postsecondary program in printing-equipment operation continue to be the best ways to learn the trade, most printing-press operators are trained informally on the job while working as assistants to experienced operators. Beginning press operators load, unload, and clean presses. With time, they move up to operating one-color sheetfed presses and eventually advance to multicolor presses. Operators are likely to gain experience on many kinds of printing presses during the course of their career.

Apprenticeships for press operators in commercial shops take four years. In addition to on-the-job instruction, apprenticeships include related classroom or correspondence-school courses. Once the dominant method for preparing for this occupation, apprenticeships are becoming less prevalent.

In contrast, formal postsecondary programs in printing-equipment operation offered by technical and trade schools and community colleges are growing in importance. Some postsecondary school programs require two years of study and award an associate degree, but most programs can be completed in one year or less. Postsecondary courses in printing are increasingly important because they provide the theoretical knowledge needed to operate advanced equipment.

People who wish to become printing-press operators need mechanical aptitude to make press adjustments and repairs. Oral and written communication skills are also required. Operators should possess the mathematical skills necessary to compute percentages, weights, and measures and to calculate the amount of ink and paper needed to do a job. Because of technical developments in the printing industry, courses in chemistry, electronics, color theory, and physics are helpful.

Technological changes have had a tremendous effect on the skills needed by press operators. New presses now require operators to possess basic computer skills. Even experienced operators periodically receive retraining and skill updating. For example, printing plants that change from sheetfed-offset presses to web-offset presses have to retrain the entire press crew because skill requirements for the two types of presses are different. Web-offset presses, with their faster operating speeds, require quicker decisions, monitoring of more variables, and greater physical effort. In the future, workers are expected to need to retrain several times during their career.

Formal graphic arts programs, offered by community and junior colleges and some four-year colleges, are a good way to learn about the industry. These programs provide job-related training, which will help when you are seeking full-time employment. Bachelor's degree programs in graphic arts are usually intended for students who may eventually move into management positions, and two-year associate degree programs are designed to train skilled workers.

Bindery workers. Most bindery workers learn the craft through on-the-job training. Inexperienced workers are usually assigned simple tasks such as moving paper from cutting machines to folding machines. They learn basic binding skills, including the characteristics of paper and how to cut large sheets of paper into different sizes with the least amount of waste. As workers gain experience, they advance to more difficult tasks and learn to operate one or more pieces of equipment. Usually, it takes one to three months to learn to operate the simpler machines, but it can take up to one year to become completely familiar with more complex equipment, such as computerized binding machines.

Formal apprenticeships are not as common as they used to be, but they are still offered by some employers. Apprenticeships provide a more structured program that enables workers to acquire the high levels of specialization and skill needed for some bindery jobs. For example, a four-year apprenticeship is usually necessary to teach workers how to restore rare books and to produce valuable collectors' items.

Employers will often train workers with some basic knowledge of binding operations. High school students interested in bindery careers should take shop courses or attend a vocational-technical high school. Occupational skill centers, usually operated by labor unions, also provide an introduction to the bindery career. To keep pace with ever-changing technology, retraining will become increasingly important for bindery workers.

Bindery workers need basic mathematics and language skills. Bindery work requires careful attention to detail, so accuracy, patience, neatness, and good eyesight are also important. Manual dexterity is essential in order to count, insert, paste, and fold. Mechanical aptitude is needed to operate the newer, more automated equipment. Artistic ability and imagination are necessary for hand bookbinding. Training in graphic arts can also be an asset. Also, vocational-technical institutes offer postsecondary programs in the graphic arts, as do some skill-updating or retraining programs and community colleges. Some updating and retraining programs require students to have bindery experience; other programs are available through unions for members. Four-year colleges also offer programs, but their emphasis is on preparing people for careers as graphic artists, educators, or managers in the graphic arts field.

Without additional training, advancement opportunities outside of bindery work are limited. In large binderies, experienced bookbinders may advance to supervisory positions.

JOB OUTLOOK

Employment growth will differ among the various occupations in the printing and publishing industry, largely due to technological advances. Processes currently performed manually will be automated in the future, causing a shift from craft occupations to related occupations that perform the same function using electronic equipment. For example, employment of desktop-publishing specialists is expected to increase much faster than average as the elements of print production, including layout, design, and printing, are increasingly performed electronically. In contrast, demand for workers who perform these tasks manually, including pasteup workers, photoengravers, camera operators, film strippers, and platemakers, is expected to decline.

Overall employment of prepress workers is expected to decline through 2008. Demand for printed material should continue to grow, spurred by rising levels of personal income, increasing school enrollments, higher levels of educational attainment, and expanding markets. However, increased use of computers in desktop publishing should eliminate many prepress jobs.

Technological advances will have a varying effect on employment among the prepress occupations. Employment of desktop-publishing specialists is expected to grow much faster than average. This reflects the increasing proportion of page layout and design that will be performed using computers. In contrast, a decline in prepress machine operators is expected as the duties these workers perform manually become increasingly automated. Pasteup, composition and typesetting, photoengraving, platemaking, film-stripping, and camera-operator occupations are expected to experience declines as handwork becomes automated.

Compositors and typesetters should find competition extremely keen in the newspaper industry. Computerized equipment allowing reporters and editors to specify type and style and to format pages at a desktop computer terminal has already eliminated many typesetting and composition jobs; more may disappear in the years ahead.

Many new jobs for prepress workers are expected to emerge in commercial printing establishments. New equipment should reduce the time needed to complete a printing job and allow commercial printers to make inroads into new markets that require fast turnaround. Because small establishments predominate, commercial printing should provide the best opportunities for inexperienced workers who want to gain a good background in all facets of printing.

Employment in printing trade services is expected to decline because more companies are preparing printing and postpress in-house. Employment in newspapers is also expected to decline as more people choose to receive their news from nonprint sources. Newspapers will also continue to face strong competition for advertising dollars from direct-mail advertising, which targets specific types of consumers in a more cost-effective manner. Many newspapers are responding by featuring specialized products and services for niche markets.

Slow employment growth is expected in periodicals, spurred by increasing interest in professional, scientific, and technical journals as well as special interest publications, such as health and fitness magazines. Similarly, employment in book publishing and greeting cards should also see slow growth, spurred by an increasing and aging population.

Employment in miscellaneous publishing is expected to grow slowly. The popularity of catalogs and mail-order shopping fuel this sector. However, increased paper costs, changing consumer preferences, and the growth of online catalogs will result in fewer jobs than in years past.

With increasing use of computers that do typesetting and composing electronically, the number of typesetting- and composing-machine operators will decline sharply. Declines among precision typesetters and compositors will occur in the newspaper industry, because news analysts and editors can perform these tasks themselves. Of other prepress occupations, job printers, desktop publishers, and other printing workers who perform a variety of printing tasks are expected to experience growth.

Employment of press operators is expected to decline. People seeking jobs as printing-press operators are likely to face keen competition from experienced operators and prepress workers who have been displaced by new technology, particularly those who have completed retraining programs. Opportunities to become printing-press operators are likely to be best for those who qualify for formal apprenticeship training or who complete postsecondary training programs. Employment of offset-press operators and letterpress operators should decrease rapidly.

Employment of bookbinders will decline in response to the growth of electronic printing; however, bindery machine operators will increase. Employment of bindery workers is expected to grow about as fast as the average for all occupations through 2008 as demand for printed material grows but productivity in bindery operations increases. Most job openings for bindery workers will result from the need to replace experienced workers who change jobs or leave the labor force.

As the industry continues to modernize, a greater diversity of workers will be needed, including engineers, marketing specialists, graphic artists, and computer specialists. New equipment will require workers to update their skills to remain competitive in the job market. For example, pasteup workers will have to learn how to lay out pages using a computer. The concepts and principles behind page layout and design are the same, but the workers will have to learn how to perform their work using different tools. Employment of marketing and sales workers in the printing and publishing industry is expected to experience little to no growth as a result of increased competition from nonprint media and advances in printing technologies.

SALARIES

According to the 2001 Association of American Publishers (AAP) Compensation Survey, the average annual base earnings for these selected positions are as follows:

Top art/design executive	$134,600
Art director (educational publishing)	$71,700
Art director (trade, mass market and technical)	$80,500
Design director	$71,600
Senior designer	$50,800
Designer	$39,900
Image researcher	$43,100
Top production executive	$129,300
Director, production	$84,800
Manager, production	$58,000
Associate, production	$42,500
Coordinator, production	$36,700
Director, electronic publishing	$90,600
Manager, electronic publishing	$55,400
Specialist, electronic publishing	$39,900
Director, new-technology development	$110,900
Senior producer, new technology	$75,500
Producer, new technology	$52,600
Director, audio production	$126,200
Producer, audio	$59,800

According to the *Occupational Outlook Handbook*, average weekly earnings for production workers in the printing and publishing industry are $515, compared to $563 for all production workers in manufacturing. Weekly wages in the printing and publishing industry range from $414 in bookbinding to $671 in printing trade services. Wage rates for prepress workers vary according to occupation, level of experience, training, location and size of the firm, and union membership.

The following table shows the range of median hourly earnings of workers in various prepress occupations:

Film strippers, printing	$15.53
All other printing workers, precision	$14.63
Desktop-publishing specialists	$14.00
Platemakers	$13.75
Photoengravers	$13.67
Camera operators	$11.72
Job printers	$11.58
Photoengraving- and lithographic-machine operators and tenders	$11.52
Typesetting- and composing-machine operators and tenders	$11.08
Compositors and typesetters, precision	$10.85
Pasteup workers	$9.53

Of the unionized prepress workers, scanner operators earn an hourly wage of approximately $23.20, and film strippers earn $19.45 per hour, according to the Graphic Communications International Union, the principal union for prepress workers.

The basic wage rate for a press operator depends on the type of press being run and the geographic area in which the work is located. Workers covered by union contracts usually have higher earnings. The following table shows the range of median hourly earnings of various press operators:

Offset-lithographic-press operators	$14.91
Letterpress operators	$13.76
All other printing-press setters and setup operators	$13.33
Printing-press-machine setters, operators, and tenders	$12.51
Screen-printing-machine setters and setup operators	$9.08

According to the *Occupational Outlook Handbook*, median hourly earnings of bookbinders are about $9.95. The middle 50 percent earn between $7.65 and $13.94 an hour. The lowest 10 percent earn less than $6.35, and the highest 10 percent earn more than $17.56.

Median hourly earnings of bindery machine and setup operators are $9.91. The middle 50 percent earn between $7.55 and $13.39 an hour. The lowest 10 percent earn less than $6.26, and the highest 10 percent earn more than $17.25. Workers covered by union contracts usually have higher earnings.

SAMPLE JOB ADVERTISEMENTS

The following are real advertisements, but the hiring employers are not identified because the positions have already been filled. They are meant as examples to give you an idea of the types of positions you'll see advertised.

Position: Bindery Shift Supervisor
Description: Looking for a very experienced saddle-stitch and perfect-stitch supervisor for daytime operation for 150-plus-employee bindery including cutters, fulfillment, direct mail, etc. We need someone with hands-on experience to oversee, schedule, evaluate, motivate, and prioritize work. Looking for someone with growth potential, someone who could be the bindery manager someday. Salary: $55,000–65,000.

Position: Production Coordinator (Second Shift)
Description: Busy commercial printer has an opening for a production person. Must understand print production and the full print and finishing processes. Most clients involve high-end advertising and annual reports. You must be able to analyze quotes and work with outside vendors and various printers throughout Los Angeles. You will be required to write purchase orders, do press layouts, schedule outside services, and follow deadlines—basic trafficking involved in printing. Three years' experience required. Salary: $55,000–65,000.

Position: Mac Retouchers (Two Openings, First and Second Shifts)
Description: Seeking qualified Mac operators for commercial printing prepress departments. You must know trapping *within* the applications, i.e., trapping within Photoshop or trapping within QuarkXPress. Must know Freehand and Illustrator also. You will be tested. Two to three years' experience required. Must know printing aspects and troubleshooting as related to the printing industry. Salary: $24–$32 per hour.

Position: Electronic Prepress Manager

Description: Electronic prepress manager needed for a high-volume commercial printing company. Macintosh and PC environment. DTP technical knowledge of networks and imagesetting equipment desired. Must have printing background and be able to troubleshoot and solve typical print-production-related problems occurring in prepress production. High-volume, heavy-work-flow, high-production facility. Must have at least five years of supervisory experience. The position requires a self-motivated, quality-conscious person with a thorough knowledge of electronic work flow in a printing environment. The successful candidate will have proven success in improving efficiencies and quality. Strong staff- and project-management skills a must. The right individual will have excellent problem-solving skills, be able to communicate technical issues to laypersons, and be able to train and motivate staff members. This is a hands-on position that requires experience in all of the major software packages. Salary: $75,000–$110,000, depending on experience level.

FIRSTHAND ACCOUNT

Joan Marie Bledig, Typographer

Joan Marie Bledig is president and cofounder of JDA Typesetting Corporation in Chicago. She earned her B.A. from the University of Illinois in 1968 with a major in anthropology and a minor in geology. She has been working in the book-production field since 1967.

Getting Started

"I learned the basic rudiments of typesetting when I took a part-time job with a small type house during my last year and a half in college. I never expected to become a typographer. A couple of years after graduation, I was job hunting for a computer-programmer-trainee position without success. The woman I had worked for while I was in college told me I could always get a job as a typesetter. She was right. I had six interviews in two days and was working full time the following Monday.

"On my first day I was shown that there are different type sizes and styles and how to change them and how to set copy flush left, flush right, centered, justified, and with leaders. The woman who hired me then gave me a four-panel invitation with envelopes and reply card to set while she went out to make her deliveries and pickups. Yes, that invitation used all those formats, and it was done when she returned!

"Two close friends, Debbie and Andy Tranchita, and I started JDA as a part-time business back in 1977. We dissolved the partnership about six months later and are still the best of friends today. About September of 1978, JDA business occupied more hours of my day than my day job did, so I decided it was time to make JDA the day job and get some sleep at night."

What the Job's Really Like

"I generally refer to myself as a typographer, not a typesetter. There used to be a difference between these terms. Nowadays the differences are virtually nonexistent.

"My official title is president of the corporation, which really means I pay the bills. However, the majority of the work I do is production, that is, typesetting, more often today called page building. I capture keystrokes and format them according to the customer's design. In book production, I style the raw copy into chapter titles, introductions, heads, subheads, text, footnotes, sidebars, etc., to follow the designer's model. I decide where each page will end, governed by rules established by my customer. I place sidebars, figure text, or artwork on the pages where these elements are referenced so they look pleasing to the eye but do not interfere with text flow. The object of book page building is to maintain a steady flow for the reader. I make sure that happens, thus encouraging the reader to continue to the next page and beyond.

"I may discover certain design elements do not work. I may then be asked to modify the design to create a more pleasing look. I also have to remain aware that book pagination is based on the signature. (A signature is sixteen contiguous pages printed eight per side on one sheet of paper in a pattern so when it is folded three times and trimmed on three sides it results in sixteen pages arranged in proper sequence.) I sometimes have to go back and restructure pages by increasing or decreasing the number of lines on each page in order to come as close as possible to a page count evenly divisible by sixteen.

"As a trade typographer, I work on just about everything imaginable, from as small as a #10 envelope corner cut (return address) to four- and six-color advertising materials to large-scale projects such as textbooks and trade publications several hundred pages in length.

"I recently worked on a college-level text dealing with business marketing. It was a two-color book, meaning that some elements of the design were in a second color, in this case a teal green. I had to make sure that these elements were selected and colored green. In addition, there were sidebar elements having gradient backgrounds in green. I discovered a basic flaw in the design when facing pages each contained a sidebar. The design called for sidebars to always start at the top of the page and end wherever. No problem. But the color gradient flowed from 60 percent green at the top to white at the bottom. Two facing sidebars of differing lengths looked terrible next to each other. Turning the gradient 90 degrees and having the color taper off to white on the right was a much better arrangement and less jarring to the reader.

"The page building was further complicated by the large number of figures and diagrams illustrating various points in the text. Most of these figures were supplied using design specs from an earlier version of this title. I had to modify each figure to match this edition's design. I had to place these art elements as close to their text references as possible. Students don't want to be turning two or three or four pages to find the graphic example illustrating what they read in their text. They want that diagram or figure right there to look at. It is easier for students to assimilate the point the author is making if they don't have to break their train of thought because they need to leaf through many pages to find that piece of art.

"After initial page building, I supplied my client with laser copies of each page. In addition, I sent a laser copy of just those page elements appearing in the second color so the client could check to make sure color separations were correct. These proofs were returned to me with editor and designer changes indicated. I corrected the pages and supplied new composite and second-color proofs for final checking. A few additional changes were requested. These changes were made, new printouts (composite and color separated) were made, and final files were copied to a zip disk for delivery to my customer.

"The project was behind schedule before I received the initial copy and design specs. I worked extra hours evenings and weekends on the project and was able to deliver it ahead of schedule. My customer was very pleased with that.

"In any one day I may work on a PC or Mac platform or move copy from one platform to another and from one program to another, because the end user of the material I am preparing for my customer needs PageMaker on a PC or QuarkXPress on a Mac.

"Deadlines are everything in this business. I like to challenge myself, seeing how many days in advance of a deadline I can finish a project. My customer base appreciates getting materials ahead of schedule. Some days can be boring and slow. For instance, statistical jobs are tedious if the customer is unable to supply raw keystrokes in some kind of word-processing or text file. Keyboarding numbers all day is just not my idea of an exciting time.

"Typography requires attention to minute details of context, grammar, and format. The ability to spot inconsistencies in the material is extremely helpful. I have always felt that a call to the customer to clear up an inconsistency before I turn in the job is good business sense. The customer sees that you are paying close attention to his job and giving him that personal service so important in a good business relationship. He also realizes that you make him look good to his superiors or his customer by catching possibly embarrassing mistakes. He gets the opportunity to correct those errors before he has to turn in those first proofs you give him.

"If I have questions about the job I try to finish as much of it as I can and then make one call to the customer to resolve any apparent discrepancies. One call is not an interruption to the customer; three or four in the same day about the same job is! Their time is just as valuable as yours. You don't want to get six calls about the same thing in one day. Neither does your customer. If the issues cannot be clarified immediately, I put their job on hold till they get back to me. Back to the pile of jobs and on to the next one, all the while fielding phone calls to and from customers and arranging pickups of new work that cannot be transmitted via E-mail. Sometimes I arrange for a messenger service to handle the running for me."

Upsides and Downsides   "Possibly the greatest advantage to this job is exposure to information on just about everything in the world, from the basics of plumbing to high finance to organic chemistry. We have the potential to be the kings of trivia! I have often thought that typographers must be the most knowledgeable people in the world. We get exposed to an awful lot of information in a wide variety of fields. Good typographers remember as much as they can because five years down the road they benefit from that knowledge while working on some other project in an allied field. Every job is different and therefore challenging.

"The downside is that every job is different and therefore challenging. There are days when you're just not up to being challenged. Or the customer calls and puts the job on hold after you've just finished it. Or the customer calls and changes the major parameters of the job after you've just finished it. That's the nature of the business.

"The other downside is that it's either feast or famine—you have too much to do or you don't have enough to keep you busy for the entire day. After all, you really can't work at 120 percent every day.

"But, all things considered, too much is always better than not enough."

Salaries   "My monthly salary varies, being dependent on the number of jobs I've done and what I billed for them. Most jobs are priced by time. In the case of books, however, I bill the customer a mutually agreed-upon per-page price.

"After receiving design specs and template files from the customer, I prepare a sample chapter, usually the first chapter in the book. I take the amount of time it took to prepare the sample chapter, multiply it by my hourly rate, then divide that figure by the number of pages in the chapter. This gives me a per-page price. I have worked on books where the per-page price was $5.50 and others where the per-page price was more than $35 because of the difficulty of the design!

"Books are priced by the page because the customer doesn't always know how many pages the finished project will be. Last winter I worked on a book that was expected to have only 432 pages. The actual page count was 464. A per-page price allows the letter of agreement (LOA, a type of purchase order) to have flexibility, so it can be increased or decreased when the book is finished. Another project I worked on was expected to have approximately 528 pages. The finished book was significantly less, only 448.

"Other projects are governed by page count. I worked on a series of titles that had a 96-page format. When copy exceeded the prearranged page count for each section in the book, the editor had to cut copy. In those cases, the LOA had a provision for overset copy, based on a dollar amount for each extra inch of copy.

"A per-page price makes my bookkeeping for this kind of project simple. I don't have to worry about starting and stopping my stopwatch to field phone calls or work with customers who stop by to pick up or drop off their jobs. When the job is finished I need only the number of pages to figure my bill.

"Typesetters in small companies can make as little as $12 per hour to start or as much as the market will bear, upward of $30 per hour, or anywhere in between.

"Freelance designers often bill their time at $100 per hour or more. Freelance typesetters and proofreaders currently bill around $25 to $35 per hour for their services. One downside to working in a job shop or electronic prepress department is that the number of hours worked per week varies with the workload. If the company is slow, daily hours may be cut from a full eight-hour day to six hours or even less. Conversely, working overtime during peak busy periods is expected and usually compensated at time-and-a-half. Many employers will have second and third shifts, and new hires usually find themselves placed on one of these shifts."

Advice

"The most important piece of advice: be consistent in what and how you do something. Try to train yourself to do a particular procedure the same way every time. For example, always use a tab to start a paragraph or always use a preset paragraph indent. That way, if you have to go in and modify the parameters of this indent, you know that you always used one procedure or another and can use your automatic formatting to easily and quickly change that parameter. If you are not consistent, you may have to go back and change each paragraph individually! And that's a waste of your time and the customer's money.

"Second, hone your typing skills. Unless you are strictly doing design work, you need to be able to type accurately and rapidly. Train yourself to pay attention to the smallest detail. Don't rely on spellcheckers to fix your copy— spellcheckers do not know the difference between *from* and *form*, *except* and *expect*, or *their* and *they're*!

"Training in this field is available from many community colleges through either degree programs or continuing adult education. Or, you can buy any of a number of computer programs specifically designed for page makeup and design and teach yourself, with or without OEM help books. All major programs come with tutorials. A number of books explaining typography are available and are formatted so you can read a page or two to get a quick history of a particular aspect of typography and how it is now accomplished via the personal computer.

"Currently, it doesn't matter whether you learned your skills through a degree program, continuing adult education, or on-the-job training. I'm sure in the future it will."

FOR MORE INFORMATION

Information on apprenticeships and other training opportunities may be obtained from local employers such as newspapers and printing shops, local offices of the Graphic Communications International Union, local affiliates of the Printing Industries of America, or local offices of the state employment service.

See Appendix A for union and professional association addresses and websites.

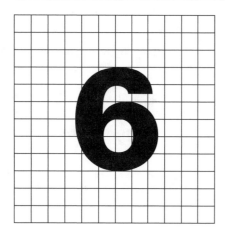

MARKETING AND SALES

"There can hardly be a stranger commodity in the world than books. Printed by people who don't understand them; sold by people who don't understand them; bound, criticized, and read by people who don't understand them; and now even written by people who don't understand them."

—Georg Christoph Lichtenberg

Marketing is often defined as the umbrella category that encompasses sales, advertising, publicity, public relations, and promotion (see Chapter 7). In simple terms, marketing experts help decide toward which audiences the advertising and promotion campaign should be aimed. To aid in the advertising and sales endeavor, marketing professionals poll public opinion or analyze the demographics and buying patterns of specific audiences. They play the role of researcher, statistician, social psychologist, and sociologist.

MARKET RESEARCH

Professionals working in market research departments are tuned in to the consumer—what he or she worries about, desires, thinks, believes, and holds dear. Market researchers conduct surveys or one-on-one interviews, utilize existing research, test consumer reactions to new products or advertising copy, track sales figures and buying trends, and become overall experts on consumer behavior.

Agency research departments can design questionnaires or other methods of studying groups of people, implement the surveys, and interpret the results. Sometimes, research departments hire an outside market research firm to take over some of the workload. For example, a market researcher could come up with a procedure to test the public's reaction to a television commercial; the outside firm would put the procedure into action.

Assistants report directly to a research executive and are responsible for compiling and interpreting data and monitoring the progress of research projects. An entry-level assistant research executive has strong quantitative skills and a good aptitude for analyzing data. In addition, computer skills and the ability to write and speak effectively are a must. In this field a bachelor's degree is the basic requirement, but it is becoming more and more common to find master's and Ph.D. holders. A graduate of a college program that emphasizes research would have an edge over the competition.

Publishers usually rely on the results of marketing research for their advertising and sales campaigns but don't usually hire marketers directly. Those interested in a career in marketing should approach research firms or advertising or public relations agencies.

SALES

The field of sales is easy to understand. A salesperson has a product or service he or she must sell. Within the field of publishing you'll see salespeople working in four main settings:

Publishing houses

Book distributors

Book wholesalers

Bookstores

PUBLISHERS' SALES REPRESENTATIVES

Publisher reps are responsible for making sure every customer (bookstore or chain, for example) they are assigned to cover is informed of the publisher's offerings of frontlist books. These are the books that will be coming out that season. They are also responsible for taking that customer's order and delivering the order to the publisher. In addition, reps are responsible for seeing that the publisher's backlist (already published) titles are well represented in the account.

Reps usually travel to the customer, then follow up when necessary by phone. Appointments can last anywhere from twenty minutes to a full day, depending on the number of books, the time available, the attention span of the buyer, and so on.

Former sales rep Linda Roghaar says, "Larger publishers have their own, 'house' reps, who are usually salaried and paid expenses and are responsible for their time as well as for their sales. Smaller publishers hire independent reps to do the same thing. However, independent reps are paid straight commission, pay their own expenses, and are not accountable for their time, only their sales."

Finding a Sales Rep Job Publishers usually divide the country into sales territories, and there is usually some sort of open slot available. To find openings, try various online avenues such as About.com's job boards at http://freelancewrite.about.com/cs/job

boards/index.htm or job opportunities listed with professional associations, such as the AAP. *Publishers Weekly* (publishersweekly.com) is another good source, as is networking with bookstore staff. You can also try sending your resume to a publisher.

BOOK WHOLESALERS AND DISTRIBUTORS

The two terms *wholesaler* and *distributor* are often used interchangeably, but there is a difference. Generally wholesalers purchase books outright, and distributors take books on a commission basis, paying the publisher as books are sold. Bookstores and other outlets such as supermarket and airport bookstands are accustomed to dealing with wholesalers, both local and national ones. (Refer to Appendix C for some names of wholesalers and distributors.)

Jobs Within Wholesalers and Distributors

Visit Ingram's website at ingrambook.com, and you'll see an extensive listing of job openings. These are just a sampling:

Position: Collection Development Specialist
Description: Degreed librarian responsible for creating Opening Day Collection lists for libraries.

Position: Manager of Bids and Contracts
Description: Directs process and associates responsible for producing proposals to libraries.

Position: Shift Order Pullers
Description: $8.55 plus 10 percent shift differential.

Position: Warehouse Positions
Description: $8.55 to $9.20 per hour, including quality control, order pullers, stockers, receivers, shipping, supply distribution tech.

BOOKSTORES

Chances are if you're reading this book you love bookstores. Browsing the shelves, reading excerpts from books, listening to snatches of music, sipping an iced coffee at the pastry bar—all of these experiences make bookstore browsing a pleasant experience. For those who want to keep the experience going on a full-time (and sometimes part-time) basis, consider the four main jobs bookstores have to offer:

Managers/supervisors

Bookstore clerks/sales

Buyers

Events coordinators

Managers supervise the day-to-day activity within bookstores. Clerks stock shelves, wait on customers, update the database, and handle the cash register. Buyers meet with sales reps and sometimes with authors to order books. Event coordinators arrange for book signings, speaking engagements, and other activities that will bring in the public.

Finding Work in Bookstores

One of the first avenues to explore would be to visit your local bookstores in person and ask to speak to the managers. You can also do a web search for specific bookstores and the chains and click on their "job opportunity" links. Sometimes *Publishers Weekly* will list higher-level bookstore jobs, and local papers will also run help-wanted ads.

Salaries

A 2000 study jointly conducted by the International Association of Business Communicators and the Public Relations Society of America shows that the average annual base salary for communicators such as sales and marketing professionals is $69,000, with an average bonus of $10,000.

Bookstores in general are known for low hourly wages. Many sales and clerk positions are filled by students working part time.

Consultants' salaries are considerably higher than salaries of those with a corporate position ($110,000 vs. $63,000). Consultants' cash bonuses are higher, too ($20,000 vs. $9,000 for those in corporate).

Median and Average Salaries by Job Title

	Median	Average
President/executive director/CEO	$75,000	$135,000
Manager/assistant manager	$56,000	$56,000
Director	$65,000	$79,000
Specialist	$39,000	$41,000
Coordinator	$35,000	$37,500
Consultant	$52,000	$153,000
Vice president	$95,000	$149,000
Writer	$45,000	$50,000
Editor	$51,000	$48,000
Managing director	$60,000	$65,500

	Median	Average
Independent/self-employed	$56,000	$57,000
Group manager	$60,000	$60,000
Supervisor	$51,000	$45,000
Account executive	$36,500	$36,000
Senior account executive	$50,000	$48,000
Senior/executive vice president	$100,000	$125,864
Partner/principal/associate	$150,000	$97,000
Educator/professor	$44,000	$52,000

Salary by Industry

	Median	Average
Education	$43,000	$53,000
Consulting firm	$61,000	$79,650
Public relations	$62,500	$123,500
Advertising	$52,500	$50,500
Retail sales	$69,000	$67,500

According to the 2001 Association of American Publishers (AAP) Compensation Survey, these are the average annual base salaries of the following positions:

Top sales and marketing executive (educational)	$135,400
Top sales and marketing executive (noneducational)	$144,800
Top marketing executive (educational)	$130,400
Top marketing executive (noneducational)	$158,000
Director, marketing (educational)	$85,200
Director, marketing (noneducational)	$84,200
Senior marketing manager (educational)	$70,800
Senior marketing manager (noneducational)	$67,000
Marketing manager (mass market/adult trade/ children)	$55,100
Marketing manager (college and technical)	$58,400
Top sales executive (educational)	$173,200
Top sales executive (noneducational)	$204,300
Director, sales (noneducational)	$97,400

Regional sales manager (educational)	$88,300
Regional sales manager (noneducational)	$76,900
District sales manager (college)	$64,300
Senior sales representative (educational)	$53,100
Senior sales representative (mass market/ adult trade/children)	$60,000
Senior sales representative (technical)	$64,300
Sales representative (educational)	$41,500
Sales representative (mass market/trade)	$44,900
Sales representative (technical)	$50,400
National account manager	$74,900
Telemarketing manager	$50,000
Telemarketing representative	$30,200
Consultant (educational publishing)	$52,200
Top international sales executive	$115,000
Manager, international sales	$65,100
Manager, retail special sales	$75,900
Manager, wholesale special sales	$65,300
Director, mass merchandising sales	$210,000
Director, premium and promotional sales	$90,500
Director, advertising and promotion (educational)	$80,500
Director, advertising and promotion (mass market/ adult trade/children)	$112,900
Director, advertising and promotion (technical)	$105,500
Manager, advertising and promotion (educational)	$47,600
Manager, advertising and promotion (mass market/ adult trade/children)	$53,700
Manager, advertising and promotion (technical)	$74,300

Magazine Ad Sales Salaries

A recent ad sales salary survey conducted by *Folio* shows that despite growth in ad sales, salaries are flat or are dropping. In answer to why, Jeff Ward, publisher of Southern Progress Corporation's *Weight Watchers Magazine*, suggests an answer: "Lately, inflation has been basically nonexistent, which is probably why companies are not providing significant percentages on base salaries. But while business has been good at the same time, publishers have been more aggressive with bonuses."

According to the same survey, ad sales directors reported bonus increases of nearly 6 percent, while ad sales managers took in almost 11 percent. But regional/branch ad managers and ad salespersons/account executives both experienced decreases in their bonuses. This could be because when salaries are assessed by job title and category, business publishing is generous with ad directors and ad sales representatives/account executives, but ad managers and regional managers are compensated the best by consumer magazines.

"Titles can mean different things in different industries," says publisher E. Patrick Weisner. "An ad director for a trade title might not be equivalent to one at a mass-market magazine."

Although there are still more men than women in most of the job categories, women, on average, earn more. Among ad directors, for example, women average $5,000 a year more than men, although men hold 83 percent of the ad director jobs.

SAMPLE JOB ADVERTISEMENTS

The following are real advertisements, but the hiring employers are not identified because the positions have already been filled. They are meant as examples to give you an idea of the types of positions you'll see advertised.

Position: Single-Copy Sales Analyst
Location: Publisher of special-interest magazines and books for master craftspeople
Description: Detail-oriented individual with strong financial, analytical, and communication skills needed to analyze all distribution, promotional, and marketing strategies for our magazines. This individual will work closely with distributors, wholesalers, and various departments within the company. Must be proficient in Excel, Word, and PowerPoint.

Position: Sales Operations Assistant
Location: Publisher of books and textbooks in the sciences
Description: Sales assistant wanted to assist international marketing director. Responsibilities include day-to-day operations of international sales group, including approving all orders, managing consignment accounts, sending promotional information to agents and distributors, liaising with warehouse staff on orders and billing. Also analyze sales figures and determine commission payments, handle all customer service

issues, provide up-to-date product information to sales representatives and managers. Must be able to prioritize and work independently as international marketing director travels frequently. Salary: mid- to high 20s.

Position: Ad Sales Assistant
Location: National magazine for women
Description: A national women's magazine is now hiring an ad sales assistant. Will support three account managers by performing the following duties: answer phones, type, and file; manage the complimentary magazine list; handle mass mailings, issue mailings, etc.; coordinate entertainment functions; prepare media kits and presentation materials. Job requirements: college degree; knowledge of Word, Excel, and PowerPoint. Ability to prioritize work a must when working for three managers.

Position: Marketing Associate
Location: Independent publisher in Chicago suburb
Description: An independent publisher seeks someone with one to two years' experience in marketing. Must have excellent communication skills and general knowledge and interest in a variety of subjects. Terrific, unique workplace in suburb of Chicago.

Position: Key Account Manager
Location: Large travel publisher
Description: The key account manager will identify and implement sales strategy to meet revenue and unit objectives; identify, select, and direct alternative distribution channels; create annual territory business plan; prepare motivating sales presentations; create and execute communications plan; as well as analyze competitive merchandising programs. Candidates must have a minimum of three years' book industry experience; B.A./B.S.; and working knowledge of cooperative advertising, merchandising, and buying procedures. Candidates should enjoy travel and have extensive travel experiences within the United States and Europe. French language skills a plus.

Position: Special Sales Manager
Location: Independent publisher, Boston office
Description: An independent publisher seeks an experienced special sales manager for its Boston office. This is an excellent opportunity for candidates who have a desire to sell out-

side of the traditional book market. A dynamic, analytical, aggressive personality is a necessity. Be part of a team that identifies and pursues new markets. Responsibilities include preparing sales materials, making presentations, following up on sales calls, and creating programs to maximize sell-through.

Position: Sales Director
Location: Spirituality trade publisher in Vermont
Description: Innovative and experienced salesperson wanted to lead high-energy team in rapid-growth environment. Position to be filled immediately.

Position: Marketing Director
Location: National child health care association
Description: Direct the marketing and sales of our publications and programs. Qualified candidates must have demonstrated abilities in developing and implementing marketing and business plans and promotional strategies, forecasting and analyzing revenue/expense projections, generating revenues, and maintaining strong relationships with book distributors. This position requires at least seven years' proven experience in product and marketing management in a medical and/or consumer publishing environment and a B.S. in marketing/business (master's desired). Previous association experience and medical/consumer publishing is highly preferred. Excellent interpersonal, supervisory, organizational, communication, and presentation skills are necessary. Travel and some weekend work are required.

Position: Sales Rep
Location: Educational publisher
Description: Educational publisher seeks aggressive salesperson with three-plus years' book trade experience for the southwestern states. You will call on trade and nontraditional markets with our highly regarded products. We offer a competitive salary and performance program, comprehensive benefits, and company car.

Position: Sales Representative
Location: Major educational publisher in Seattle, Washington
Description: This position is responsible for the selling of our educational books, software, and multimedia products to the K–12, higher-ed, and adult markets. In addition, this person will be responsible for gathering marketing and editorial leads

and supplying feedback on established products. Responsibilities: achieve assigned quantitative sales goals; design and implement individual sales and marketing strategies in assigned territory.

Requirements: Bachelor's degree and a minimum of one to three years' sales experience preferred. Professional selling experience and territory-management skills required. Experience or background in the English as a secondary language discipline preferred. Candidate must possess the ability to present and connect to audience and to positively influence customers. Excellent organizational, time-management, and verbal/written communications skills required. Must be self-motivated and disciplined with the ability to prioritize. Travel required.

Position: Marketing Manager—Trade
Location: Major magazine and book publisher
Description: Act as liaison with New York publishing house to ensure sales reps have all the materials and information they need on a timely basis. Responsible for sales conference presentations, display materials, conference booths, and regional book trade show. Create the trade catalog, including managing the design and production schedule; acting as liaison among the freelance designer, copywriter, editorial groups, and production; and creating rep-only version of the catalog. Monitor all co-op advertising, including keeping track of expenditures, promotion run-dates, and materials needed. Act as library marketing specialist that includes working with the library sales reps to expand sales and marketing efforts into this area. Act as Spanish-language marketing specialist that includes finding marketing avenues and accounts that sell into the Spanish market. Acquire in-depth knowledge of the content areas and assist in the development of marketing campaigns for these content groups. Must have two or more years of marketing and/or publishing experience; some knowledge of advertising and promotion; strong oral and writing skills; and strong organizational and computer skills.

Position: Internet Marketing Manager
Location: Large trade publishing house in New York City
Description: We are seeking a marketing manager who will manage Internet marketing initiatives. Responsible for the initial planning and execution of promotions for division titles online, including author-specific sites and the corporate site. Will evaluate online advertising opportunities and work with

the advertising and promotions department to execute new online outreach programs. Candidates must have strong communication skills, strong HTML and computer skills, and a four-year college degree.

Position: Sales Manager
Location: Family-owned book wholesaler
Description: Book wholesaler seeks experienced, entrepreneurial individual to lead our retail sales division. You will sell directly to national accounts and manage the inside sales force. You must love books and have retail book sales experience.

Position: Warehouse Supervisor
Location: Major book distributor
Description: Supervisory experience needed to accomplish goals in this fast-paced distribution center. You will report to the manager of an assigned department and have responsibility for ensuring all department productivity and quality goals are met. Must have good communication and leadership skills. Ability to maintain productivity and quality standards. Recommend and identify solutions as needed. Analyze staffing and scheduling and manage work flow. Prefer three to five years of warehouse experience.

Position: Bookstore General Merchandise Department Clerk
Location: University bookstore
Description: Must have the ability to lift approximately thirty to forty pounds. Must have prior cash register experience. Duties include operating cash register; recording all sales transactions on proper register key; processing Visa/MasterCard/American Express charges; assisting customers; stocking, straightening, and cleaning shelves. Will also assist with merchandise inventories. $6.75 per hour.

Position: Bookstore Salesperson
Location: Museum collection and independent bookstore
Description: We are seeking applicants who are friendly and outgoing, with a positive attitude. Valued qualities include a professional and courteous manner when dealing with customers and coworkers and enthusiasm when dealing with any aspect of the job, from customer service to stock work. Ability to work evenings and weekend shifts (at least one weekend shift per week). Starting salary range $6.25–$6.75 per hour, depending on experience.

FIRSTHAND ACCOUNT

Linda Roghaar, Former Independent Publishers' Sales Rep

From 1979 to 1997, Linda Roghaar was the owner of Roghaar Associates, a regional publishing sales organization based in Nashville, Tennessee. She earned her bachelor's degree in religion from Miami University in Ohio and her master's degree in liberal studies from Vanderbilt University in Nashville. She currently is a literary agent based in Massachusetts.

Getting Started

"I had worked in a bookstore and fell in love with the book business. Later, I had a job traveling to bookstores as a field rep for a franchise book chain. I couldn't believe that I was being paid to do this! I loved seeing all the different stores and loved the travel as well—becoming a publishers' rep was the next logical step.

"Because I always worked as an independent rep, I had no formal training. I learned from other reps, my accounts, and, most of all, from experience.

"A couple of publishers hired me, and I was off on the road. It grew from there."

What the Job's Really Like

"The publishers' rep is never bored! The job is cyclical, and a typical cycle is six months, and goes about like this:

"The first two weeks of December are spent in sales conferences in New York City. We go at our own expense and meet with most of the publisher clients we represent. At these meetings, which are a few hours for the small houses and up to three days for the large ones, we are formally presented with all the new, forthcoming titles for the next six months (books that will ship from March through August of the next year).

"We sit and listen to editors and publishers describe why they are publishing each book and talk about the author and the market for each one. This is much harder than it seems. First of all, there's so much information to absorb in so little time (perhaps you've seen the T-shirts: 'So many books, so little time'; this is an apt description of a rep's life). Second, we are people who spend most of our time working independently, and sitting still and not being in charge are not our strong suits. So, sales conferences are exhilarating and exhausting. We leave New York with bags of information on the books of the upcoming season.

"The publishers provide us with their catalogs, order forms, book covers, book-by-book information, and promotion plans for each book. These are the tools of the trade, and their quality is important.

"We return home, sort through the piles of mail, begin to sort out all the information, and often get together with our colleagues to discuss the goals for the season ahead. Then, we create the sales kit that will stay with us all season.

This includes a brief presentation of every book, often with a mock-up of a cover. Also, we reacquaint ourselves with the special deals/discounts that we'll be offering accounts that season.

"We begin to make appointments for the next four months. We map out our itinerary. In the Southeast, where I worked, all of us were traveling almost every week, as our territories often included two or three states and lots of driving. We call on the biggest accounts first and then begin the serious traveling.

"By the time all the publishers' material arrives and we've sorted it and have all our appointments, it's the middle of January, sometimes a bit later. We hit the road and call on accounts until mid-April.

"We handle all kinds of accounts that sell books. This includes the independent bookstores, the wholesalers, and the specialty stores. Independent bookstores were the mainstay of our accounts in the past, but that's no longer true. Specialty stores and wholesalers now provide much of the business. This includes museum stores, parenting/school stores, regional wholesalers (which carry only books about the region and often place the books in airports and hotels), and anyone else we can find. For the most part, our accounts are wonderful, informed, and interesting people. Often they become friends.

"In an appointment with a bookstore buyer, we are trying to get them to buy as many of our books as we can—as many as they think they can sell in their store. In the old days, you would sell a season's (three to four months) worth of every title, but now with almost instant restocking options through wholesalers, you are selling information as well as books. It's important to get a title's information into a store's database, so that when the one or two copies they order sell, they can reorder easily. There's always a haggle over the amount: the owner wants fewer, the rep wants more. And, of course, the customer is always right!

"A rep will present one catalog at a time. Each book has unique qualities, and it's up to the rep to point out these unique factors and explain why customers need the selection. For example, a rep can carry two different travel lines. One focuses on budget travel, another on quaint inns and B&Bs. Even though both have guides to New York, the rep points out the differences, not the similarities. And the prevailing wisdom has always been that these books will be sold to every bookstore, and as long as they're represented correctly, it doesn't matter what else the rep is selling. That said, however, reps try to avoid carrying lines that do really directly compete with one another, such as the Complete Idiot's Guides and Dummies Guides.

"By the middle of April, we've made our rounds and take two weeks off before we start with sales conferences again in May.

"On a daily basis, a sales day might look like this: wake up in a medium-priced hotel, arrive at the appointment when the store opens at 10:00 A.M. Have lunch with the buyer, finish the sales call, and arrive at the second appointment at 2:30 or 3:00 P.M. Finish about 6:00.

"Big accounts are an all-day appointment; seldom do we see more than three accounts a day."

Upsides and Downsides

"What I liked most is the personal independence of this job. It's my schedule—no one checking on me, no one to report to.

"When I started as a rep, one of the more experienced reps told me the two most difficult parts of the job are driving out the driveway and knowing when to stop. I've found this to be true!

"After fifteen years I decided to leave repping for one simple reason: I was burned out and needed a new challenge and a change of venue. The business was thriving (still is, in fact, with my company's new owner), but after fifteen years I was ready for a change!"

Salaries

"An independent rep works on straight commission, so the income varies widely depending on the season, the sales of the various books, and the returns to publishers, which are deducted from the commissions.

"Commissions are paid on net sales, less returns. So, a $10 retail book is sold to a store for $6. The rep makes 60 cents, which is 10 percent. For wholesale sales, the percentage is less, 2 to 5 percent, depending on the account.

"Usually in a group of reps (which I had), reps operate on a draw against commission. This includes enough to cover all expenses as well and can range from $800 to $1,200 per week. Because you are paying your own expenses, you have a much greater choice about your final paycheck: if you like really nice places to stay and fancy restaurants, you'll make less in the end, but you'll be happy while you travel.

"A beginning rep ends up making about $35,000 (net), but there's no limit with commission work. Often an established rep makes $80,000 to $100,000 per year. The salary/bonus/commission structure differs with every group, but the basis is almost always commission. (The exception is that some publishers will pay a group a flat fee.)"

Advice

"You must be highly motivated and organized to do this job. Key ingredients for hiring a rep include an ability to work independently and manage time well and a willingness to travel and work long hours.

"The best training is to work for a major publisher in an 'in-house' job; they train you and provide much more structure—and also lots more paperwork!"

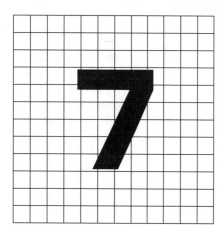

PUBLICITY, EVENT PLANNING, AND ADVERTISING

"Our greatest weakness lies in giving up. The most certain way to succeed is always to try just one more time."

—Thomas Edison

In the dictionary you'll find the following definitions for the word *publicity*:

Publicity: 1. Public notice or exposure resulting from mention through any means of communication, including advertising, and popularizing by word of mouth. 2. The business or technique of attracting public attention to a person, product, or company. 3. The material used for this purpose.

Publicity is one of the most important weapons in a publisher's arsenal. The success of a book or new magazine, for example, depends heavily on publicity. If a bookstore has never heard of the publication, then chances are the store's buyers won't be tracking down the publishers to make sure its shelves are well stocked. If it's not available in the marketplace, it won't end up in people's homes—and that translates to insignificant sales.

On the other hand, if customers come in with tongues wagging—where's that wonderful new book everyone's been talking about?—it's likely the bookstore will take immediate action to order in a good supply. This can translate to healthy sales. Word of mouth can help propel a book to stardom.

Publicists can help make that happen. Within the publishing industry publicists generally work in two major settings: (1) for publishers and (2) for authors.

Most of the big publishing houses have publicity departments or a publicity staff associated with the sales and marketing department. Within a publishing department the budget for a particular book is discussed and decided across several departments—editorial, sales, accounting. What makes a book a bestseller is still a mystery—no one has the answer to that. But, the amount of attention and money a publisher will put behind any particular title can go a long way to ensuring bestseller status.

Of course, well-known writers such as Danielle Steel or Stephen King don't need much publicity. Millions of fans eagerly wait for each new book to come out. Publishers have a pretty good idea in advance how many copies will be needed, and they're ready to meet the demand.

But the scenario is different with an unknown author with an unknown product. Publishers first have to decide (guess) that this new writer will be a breakout writer. In other words, they must feel they've discovered the next John Grisham or Tom Clancy. And if they feel that way, they then get behind the book 100 percent. In varying degrees, other new books by midlist writers earn publicity from their publishers with a range of a million-dollar budget to no budget (and no publicity) at all.

When the publishing house provides the money, it also provides the staff. With a no-publicity budget authors can provide publicity on their own. In each case the services of a publicist are vital.

WHAT A PUBLICIST DOES

The primary goal of literary publicists is to work with the media, setting up interviews and TV or radio appearances. They can also arrange book signings at bookstores both locally and nationally.

In Wendy Butler's About.com publishing guide (http://publishing.about .com), she quotes publicists Phenix & Phenix's article "Why Does Any Author Need a Publicist?": "Today, there are more than 700,000 books in print. Sixty percent of all trade titles lose money for their publishers. Americans are besieged with 2,700 marketing messages every day. To penetrate potential consumers' information-boggled minds, you must get a message in front of him at least nine times."

Even authors published by large publishing companies should consider taking part in their own publicity campaign. Says Joanna Hurley of Booksavvy .com, "Each of their many divisions or imprints alone publishes dozens of books per year. While their publicists are generally able and competent, they simply cannot pay attention to every book on their list. When I was director of publicity at Vintage, for example, my department was responsible for the publicity for some two hundred books per year, and we had a staff of three, including me. There was no way we could read, much less promote, them all. And at Vintage we were lucky: many of our titles fell into series so we could promote some of them together. This is not true for most publishers."

Wendy Butler goes on to explain that a good publicist must have the right contacts and knowledge of the topic and genre of the writer's book.

Rod Mitchell, the author of *Hiring a Publicist? Get Your Money's Worth!* and founder and president of Adventures in Media, Inc., a Houston-based literary and entertainment publicity and promotions agency, says, "Many first-time authors do not understand the reason or importance of retaining a publicist. If the public do not hear about an author's book, they will not know that the book exists, and consequently very few sales will result.

"Also, those authors who purchase a 'publicize-your-own-book' promotion kit are in for the surprise of their life. The media lists provided in these kits are often outdated, as there is vast turnover with the media. They are also bound to receive a cold shoulder from many in the media, since wrangling the media is a relationship business and takes years to develop. Authors and others unknown to them are not very high on their reception list."

Mitchell goes on to explain, "Professional publicists purchase expensive but current media data lists and are constantly updating their media files. Because they maintain regular dialogue with news desks, TV and radio talk show producers, and newspaper and magazine editors, they are a 'known' contact and their calls are taken, and their faxes and E-mail messages are read, and bookings result.

"Though most major trade publishers maintain a publicity department, in-house publicists are often overworked and regularly assigned to handle up to a dozen titles, which are released simultaneously. The average promotion period for a trade publisher is only forty-five days, so for longevity, trade publishers normally suggest that authors retain an outside publicist.

"Also, in-house publicists do not have the time and luxury to place multiple calls to media outlets, and they depend greatly on the power of their publishing house name for response. The media are always on deadline and have a very short attention span. That is why it takes a publicist an average of six phone calls (or communications) to book and schedule an interview or appearance."

Earnings for Publicists

Publicists who work in-house for publishing companies usually are paid a set yearly salary. According to the *Occupational Outlook Handbook*, average yearly salaries for promotions managers are about $58,000. Those with nonsupervisory roles average about $35,000 annually.

The earnings of publicists who freelance can vary widely. Some charge by the hour—from $50 to $200 is the usual range. Some charge a flat fee for each venue or event they book for the author. Some charge a flat monthly fee, and others charge a set rate for each city tour that's booked. Still others require a retainer.

Publicist Rod Mitchell says, "Publicists operate very similarly to an attorney. They require a retainer, and from that retainer, fees and expenses are charged and deducted. There is much confusion over the retainer/fee issue, because retainers and fees are all over the map, varying from $1,000 to $25,000, depending on the size and reputation of the firm. When retainers are not collected, publicists are too often left holding the bag and end up spending more time as a collector than as a publicist.

"The larger firms often charge greater per-venue fees. For example, while smaller firms charge $1,000 for an *Oprah* booking, larger firms feel this booking is worth $5,000. Even though the outcome from an *Oprah* booking can be phenomenal, the cost for the appearance is not always relative."

According to the 2001 Association of American Publishers (AAP) Compensation Survey, here are the average annual base salaries of the following positions:

Director, publicity	$107,800
Manager, publicity	$56,200
Senior publicist	$42,500
Publicist	$34,600

Accountability

One of the major concerns authors have when working with a publicist is the publicist's accountability. In other words, are they doing what they say they will do—and what they charge their clients for? As an ethical publicist, you will need to keep a performance log, listing which media outlets were contacted and the outcome.

Says Rod Mitchell, "Authors have the right to question accountability—what they have received in exchange for their money. This seems to be especially true when authors are charged by the hour, or a flat monthly rate, in instances when they do not net the number of bookings they had anticipated.

"It is a harsh fact that, despite the best efforts of any publicist, first-time, uncredentialed authors releasing a unique, 'niche,' nonfiction, or concept fiction book will not net as many interviews, reviews, or feature articles as mainstream topics. Normally, nonfiction authors who are experts on the topic about which they have written draw the greatest attention from the media. This rule does not always apply, and surprises do happen, when books are based on true incidents (*Civil Action*) or stories that can be tied in with high-profile (current) news stories.

"When a publicist accepts a first-timer with a ho-hum book, it is probably best that the publicist require a lower retainer amount and not oversell the outcome. By focusing more on local print and radio media and scheduling book signings and appearances that match the audience they can still perform well for their client and leave the author smiling."

Mitchell concludes, "As more and more authors release books, and as the literary publicity and promotion industry becomes more competitive, there is a cry for us to be fair and equitable in what we charge and more accountable for what we do. This is a good thing for our industry and can be a win-win for everyone."

EVENT AND MEETING PLANNING

Within the realm of publicity falls event planning. A planned event can help promote a person or product—although not every event planner has publicity as a goal.

Planners organize conferences and meetings, weddings, parties, and book signings and other events for bookstores. In the publishing field most event planners work on professional writers' conferences or publishing and library book fairs and the like. Most work as freelancers, as publishers tend not to want to pay a full-time yearly salary for an event that occurs only occasionally.

Event planner Stephanie Dooley says, "My company specializes in writing conferences and events. In proposals we present to prospective clients, I cover everything from how the sessions will be laid out and whom will be invited to speak to how many banquets there will be and budget planning. Once the concept is firm, I go about planning the event. I make the calls, work the registration, and take care of every detail.

"When the big day arrives, depending on the size of the event, one or more of my partners and I will be on-site to make sure the day goes smoothly, working the registration desk, troubleshooting, and so on."

Earnings for Event Planners

"Salary structure is all over the place in this industry," explains Dooley. "A new planner working at a midsized hotel can probably expect to earn around $20,000 to $30,000 a year. An independent planner like myself will get paid per event. Because of the work involved, most independent planners should expect between $10,000 and $20,000 per event. This would be for larger conferences with a large faculty and multiple subevents.

"A basic standard would be to estimate a proposal based on $50 to $100 per hour, depending on your experience and years in the industry. But again, that depends on the location. A Chicago or New York City market would bear a higher hourly wage than say, Albuquerque or Little Rock."

Working on staff for a publishing house is a different story. Says McGraw-Hill meeting planner Dianna Bacchi, "No matter what your yearly salary is, divide it by the number of hours you actually work and you will see you make about $1.50 an hour."

WHAT PUBLIC RELATIONS IS

The practice of public relations is a relatively young field, formally founded less than a hundred years ago. Early definitions emphasized public relations as press agentry and publicity. As the profession evolved, those aspects became less the work of the PR professional, falling more into the realm of publicists and advertising and marketing professionals.

Today, public relations is a huge umbrella under which a variety of job titles and professional responsibilities exist. Modern public relations embraces the consultant, the corporate communicator, the investor-relations specialist, the public-information officer, the community liaison, the government mediator, the troubleshooter, the spokesperson, and the media coordinator.

The number of professionals doing public relations work is estimated to be as high as 160,000. Public relations professionals work in every sector, from the corporate publishing world to the sporting world, from government departments to health and medical facilities. And though the settings might vary, their main responsibility usually doesn't. The backbone of every PR professional's job description is his or her role as communicator.

Effective communications are recognized as vital to the success of every organization or cause. Every organization has a series of "publics" to which it must answer. Let's take for an example a large movie theater concern that we'll call National Cinema Corporation. The publics that National Cinema Corporation must stay sensitive to include nutritionists and other health professionals who insist that consumers be informed about the fat content of movie theater popcorn; environmentalists who insist that the containers used for the popcorn and cold drinks be biodegradable or that the tickets be printed on recycled paper; city and town planners who are concerned about parking facilities and traffic patterns near the movie theater as well as signage and lighting; civic groups that are lobbying for improved movie rating systems; zoning officials; school officials—the list can go on and on. However, excluded from the list are customers or consumers. This public is attended to or reached by professionals involved in advertising, marketing, opinion research, publicity, and promotion and is categorized separately.

The public relations professional is concerned with how the company is perceived by the various publics. He or she can also help shape a company and the way it performs. The PR practitioner, by research and evaluation, finds out the expectations and concerns of the various publics and reports back to the organization on his or her findings. A good public relations program needs the support of the organization and the publics it is involved with.

The Public Relations Society of America (PRSA) offers accreditation to PR professionals who have been in the field, either in practice or teaching in an accredited college or university, for a period of time not less than five years. After candidates pass a written and oral examination to demonstrate their competence and knowledge, they are given the right to use the designation "PRSA Accredited" or "APR." This adds to their professional credibility and personal confidence. See Appendix A for the Public Relations Society of America's address and website.

ADVERTISING

The goal of advertising (and marketing—see Chapter 6) is to reach the consumer—to motivate or persuade a potential buyer; to sell a product, service, idea, or cause; to gain political support; or to influence public opinion. In the words of the American Association of Advertising Agencies (known as the four A's): "Advertising is an indispensable part of our economic system. It is the vital link between businesses and consumers.

"The business of advertising involves marketing objectives and artistic ingenuity. It applies quantitative and qualitative research to the creative process. It is the marriage of analysis and imagination, of marketing professional and artist.

"Advertising is art and science, show business and just plain business, all rolled into one. And it employs some of the brightest and most creative economists, researchers, artists, producers, writers, and businesspeople in the country today."

With an idea of the specific audience to target, advertising professionals assess the competition, set goals and a budget, design an advertisement—whether a simple three-line ad or a full-blown campaign—and determine what vehicle is best utilized to reach that audience.

Most large publishing houses maintain their own in-house advertising departments, often closely linked with the sales departments. Some contract with outside ad agencies for big projects. Advertising agencies are organized into the following departments (although within smaller agencies, departments can be combined or services contracted out to independent subcontractors): agency management, account management, creative services, traffic control and production, media services, publicity and public relations, sales promotion, direct response, television production, and personnel.

Job Titles in Advertising   To work within all of the various departments, advertising agencies employ a number of professionals to perform a variety of duties. Selected job titles are described here:

Agency manager. In a small agency, the manager could be the president, owner, or a partner. In giant agencies, the manager could be the chief executive officer reporting to a board of directors or an executive committee, in much the same way any corporation functions. The agency manager is responsible for establishing policies and planning, developing, and defining goals to ensure growth and economic viability.

Account manager/executive. An agency's client is generally known as an "account." The account manager supervises all the activity involved with a specific account and is ultimately responsible for the quality of service the client receives. The account manager functions as a liaison between the advertising agency and the client's organization. He or she must be thoroughly familiar with the client's business, the consumer, the marketplace, and all the aspects of advertising such as media, research, creative design, and commercial production.

Small agencies might function with just one account manager; large megaagencies could have hundreds or thousands, each handling a multitude of accounts. Account managers usually reach their position after working up through the ranks.

Assistant account manager/executive. Commonly, the assistant account manager reports directly to an account manager and can be assigned a wide range of duties. Some of these include analyzing the competition, writing reports, and coordinating creative, media, production, and research projects.

Candidates should possess at least a bachelor's degree, but a specific major in advertising or marketing is not a prerequisite.

Account-management departments, along with media departments, hire the greatest number of entry-level candidates. Entry-level positions within the field of advertising often quickly lead to more senior roles.

Creative/art director. The creative department of an advertising agency develops the ideas, images, words, and methods that contribute to the ultimate product—the commercial, ad, or campaign. Within an agency's creative department, a host of different professionals work together to meet the needs of the client. The creative or art director supervises and works with writers, artists, and producers, from conceptualization of the advertisement to its final production.

Assistant/junior art director. The assistant art director reports to one or more art directors and is commonly responsible for preparing pasteups and layouts for television storyboards and print ads. The assistant can also be involved in developing visual concepts and designs and supervising commercial production and photo sessions.

Employers expect job candidates to have at least a two-year associate's degree from an art or design school, but they of course appreciate a bachelor's-level communications major with strong graphic arts experience. Even more important, though, is being able to show a top-quality portfolio that displays skill and creativity.

The four A's reports that entry-level opportunities in art departments are very limited for those without some related business experience such as an internship or practicum spent in a retail advertising department or some other related setting.

Copywriter and assistant/junior copywriter. Copywriters write body copy for print advertising and develop sales promotional materials. Assignments could range from creating names for companies and products to writing television commercial dialogue, scripts for radio spots, or copy for direct-mail packages. Junior copywriters assist the copywriter and also edit and proofread.

Although a bachelor's degree is not required—someone with a strong portfolio could beat out a degree holder—majors that are sought after are communications, English, journalism, advertising, or marketing. Even though some of the largest advertising agencies offer copywriting training programs, opportunities are limited for those with no writing experience.

Entry into the creative department of an advertising agency, as a copywriter, designer, or assistant art director, is particularly competitive. Having a good portfolio to present to the creative director will be a plus. Submitting freelance work can also help you get a foot in the door.

Print-production managers and assistants. Personnel who work in the print-production department of an agency are responsible for the final creation of the advertisement. After the creative team has specified the different elements it wants incorporated into an ad, the print-production team must see to it that the instructions are carried through. They are responsible for two-color, four-color, and black-and-white printing, color separations, and the preparation of mechanicals. The print-production department works closely with the traffic department and the creative staff and is also responsible for quality control.

Some experience with production work is the usual requirement to enter this department. Not considered a highly competitive area, it is still a good place for someone to break in and move up.

Assistant media planner. The media department is responsible for making sure the advertising is presented to the right audiences, at the right time, and at the right place. As mentioned earlier, media departments are usually open to hiring entry-level candidates. The assistant media planner reports to a senior planner. His or her usual duties are to gather and study information about people's viewing and reading habits; evaluate programming and editorial content of different media vehicles; calculate reach and frequency for specific target groups and campaigns; and become completely familiar with the media in general, with specific media outlets, and with media databanks and information and research sources.

Media buyer. Media buyers and their assistants keep track of where and when print space and airtime is available for purchase. They verify that agency orders actually appear or run and calculate costs and rates. They are familiar with all media outlets and are skilled at negotiations. Other skills that media buyers possess include the ability to work under pressure, excellent communications skills, and strong general business skills. They are also adept at working with numbers and are familiar with basic computer programs such as spreadsheet software.

Candidates for entry-level positions are expected to have earned a four-year degree. Some of the large agencies offer training programs for new hires.

Traffic managers and assistants. People working in the traffic department make sure that the various projects are conceived, produced, and placed as specified. This department is in charge of scheduling and record keeping. The traffic department is an excellent place for those with more interest than experience to get a foothold.

TRAINING AND QUALIFICATIONS

The best course of study to pursue in this arena has been an issue of some debate. There are those who believe that a straight degree in advertising is the best preparation, but they are usually shouted down by those who recognize the importance of a broader curriculum. To some extent, the answer is determined by the area of this career path that you intend to pursue. If you are aiming for a title of account manager, courses in marketing, business and finance, and speech communications are as important as advertising theory. Potential art directors obviously need technical training in drawing, illustration, and graphic design. Courses in publishing—and especially internships in publishing houses—would be an important component of any course of study.

SAMPLE JOB ADVERTISEMENTS

The following are real advertisements, but the hiring employers are not identified because the positions have already been filled. They are meant as examples to give you an idea of the types of positions you'll see advertised.

Position: Senior-Level Publicist
Location: Major New York publishing house
Description: Publicist needed to work on special projects and publishing programs, especially J.R.R. Tolkien's *The Lord of the Rings* and forthcoming movie tie-in books. Looking for creative idea person to initiate and execute nontraditional campaigns. Work closely with marketing/sales team and film company. Salary commensurate with experience.

Position: Associate Publicist
Location: Subsidiary press of large New York publishing house
Description: Publicist needed to manage publicity campaigns and author tours. This is a wonderful opportunity for an associate publicist or someone with two years of publicity experience in book publishing. Requirements: excellent communication/organization skills, knowledge of media, and the ability to manage publicity of own books.

Position: Assistant Publicist
Location: Children's book publisher
Description: We are seeking two dynamic individuals to fill assistant publicist positions in our children's book publicity department. Under moderate supervision this key individual prepares review sheets and publication slips; processes and types labels for review copies; arranges distribution of these copies with our other offices; answers telephones and queries; redirects calls as necessary; processes bills; assists with publicity for high-profile authors; writes press releases; prepares responses to correspondence; and assists with press release typing as requested. Requirements: must possess college degree or equivalent work experience; at least one year's rel-

evant work experience, including booking experience, and thorough familiarity with the media; and college-level understanding and use of English language. Must be detail-oriented, well organized, and able to set priorities under pressure.

Position: Publicity and Marketing Associate
Location: On guide series produced by major publisher
Description: With great interpersonal and organizational skills, the associate will drive through the marketing/promotions for guides; create an extensive network to publicize the books; act as liaison between our New York and London office while promoting the books in the United States; and assist with events and marketing efforts on the magazine side as needed. This position demands a motivated self-starter to build and develop it. Being part of an energetic and successful marketing team, the associate will have boundless opportunities to grow and succeed. Candidates must have one to two years' experience in publicity/PR and marketing in book publishing. Excellent communication and writing skills are a must. Please fax writing samples (press release preferred) along with a cover letter, resume, and salary.

Position: VP, Public Relations and Promotions
Location: Major men's magazine
Description: Under the direction of the senior vice president/chief marketing officer, this position is accountable for overseeing all national/international press relations and promotional activity for the company's businesses (primarily publishing and entertainment). This position is responsible for evaluating all activities company-wide as they relate to attaining a positive image in the media and among trade constituencies. This position interacts with various levels of management internally and with the press, trade, and clients/potential clients externally. College degree in communications, journalism, marketing, or equivalent, with a minimum of ten years' overall work experience and a minimum of seven years in public relations, in either an agency or publishing company, required. Experience in high-level media contact and promotional planning required. Excellent writing skills and the ability to interact with high-level corporate executives a must.

Position: Advertising Manager
Location: Major New York publishing house

Description: Handle ninety books a year! Seeking an advertising manager to manage all phases of advertising print production for approximately ninety titles a year. Duties include supplying the outside advertising agency with creative direction and materials with which to create ads, critiquing advertising layouts and designs, and supervising all phases including final proofreading of mechanicals and release of ad materials. Job requirements: bachelor of arts, preferably in English; at least five years' experience in advertising/promotion department of a major publishing house (those with magazine publishing, ad agency, and other business experience need not apply). Excellent proofreading and copywriting skills a must. Ability to communicate effectively and work well with outside ad agency as well as with in-house personnel. Good eye for typography and overall ad design needed, as is the ability to work autonomously.

Position: Advertising Sales Assistant
Location: Major women's magazine
Description: Our sales assistant was just promoted to marketing coordinator, so we are currently looking for someone to fill her shoes. Will support three account managers by performing the following duties: answer phones; type and file; manage the complimentary magazine list; handle mass mailings, issue mailings, etc.; coordinate entertainment functions; and prepare media kits and presentation materials. Requirements: college degree. Familiarity with Word, Excel, and PowerPoint. Ability to prioritize work a must when working for three managers.

FIRSTHAND ACCOUNTS

Rod Mitchell, Literary and Entertainment Publicist

Rod Mitchell is the founder and president of Adventures in Media, Inc., located in Spring, Texas. He has been working in public relations since 1979 and serving as a publicist since 1987.

Getting Started

"I began working with the media at a Des Moines, Iowa, radio station, in the news department. It was my introduction to the media and how important and effective publicity was for a news department. We were regularly briefed by public affairs directors, who controlled the content of the stories that we were reporting.

"I have always been fascinated with both news and publicity, and from my radio days, I clearly understood the difference. This was engraved in my mind by my radio station news director after every assignment session. He would close by saying, 'now go out there and get the story, and remember, we don't make the news, we only report it.'

"Every time he said that I always thought, wouldn't it be grand if I could create news instead of just reporting it! I remembered how I felt when I queried a public affairs director to complete a news assignment. That's what led me to my present career. Now I do create the news, and reporters come to me.

"When I quit college and got married, I discovered that I could not support my new financial obligations on a radio reporter's salary, so I answered an ad in 1971 and took a job in the public affairs and marketing department of a large international insurance conglomerate. It was my job to write copy for newspaper ads, product brochures, and sales presentations. When our company purchased a new company, or if there was news of significant public interest, I created press releases and circulated them to the media.

"As our company grew, it was time to take advantage of the popular new forum, TV-direct-response advertising. At the time, a former carnival hawker by the name of Ron Popeil was selling gizmos and gadgets on the airways, and word had it that telemarketing switchboards were jammed after one of his TV ads aired.

"Our company had salespeople who faced cold rejection as they went door-to-door, and turnover was off the charts. Possibly we could develop prospect leads via the same medium that was making Ron Popeil a household name. We would have to give people an incentive to pick up the phone—a free gift in exchange for their valuable time.

"We hired some unemployed but somewhat popular TV and film actors as our spokespeople and went to the airways. It worked, but it also created an unexpected role for the marketing department: a publicist to represent the celebrities for personal-appearance requests generated by the commercials. Guess who got that assignment.

"In 1980, I was promoted and assigned to open up the country of Canada. I already knew which celebrity I would approach: Lorne Greene of the *Bonanza* television series. Canadians loved him, and whatever the Western star said was taken as gospel by Canadians. The response was incredible.

"My role as national director of marketing was again taking on an entirely different look. In addition to my regular duties, I was finding myself serving as publicist for our spokespeople, writing press releases and scheduling personal and public appearances. I quickly determined that working as a publicist was fun and it would be my future.

"In 1984, after fourteen years' serving the insurance company, I left to open my own consulting firm—Direct Response Resources. I relocated from Sioux City, Iowa, to Omaha, Nebraska, to the world's busiest telemarketing hub and the ideal place to set up a direct-response-marketing business. It was more work and less money than I expected, but the celebrity spokespeople that I hired and served as publicist for generated a secondary source of revenue that set the stage for a career adjustment. I would focus solely on publicity and promotion and represent celebrities and authors who wanted to bring attention to themselves or their work.

"In 1990, I moved my family to Texas and formed Adventures in Media. I immediately began establishing myself with local print and electronic media and representing local celebrities, authors, and events. From 1990 to 1992, I represented a colorful furniture mogul named Mattress Mack. That opened many doors with both local and national media. When he produced a feature film (*Sidekicks*, starring Chuck Norris and Beau Bridges), major doors in the entertainment industry opened.

"Then, in 1992, word of my work had spread to an author located in Las Vegas. She was releasing a little 120-page self-published book. The title and topic were a bit provocative, and I was unsure if I could promote a former New York record producer who went to work in a Las Vegas brothel and after four years wrote a book about her experience. The title of her book: *The Brothel Bible*.

"By that time I had established relationships with national news desks and radio and TV talk show producers. I pitched my new client to national media. To my pleasant surprise, despite the fact that this book was cheaply and poorly printed and was self-published, national media was fascinated with my client. I booked my client with Sally Jesse, Rolonda Watts, Maury Povich, Montel Williams, Geraldo Rivera, and Howard Stern. My client was interviewed on more than thirty major-market TV programs and news segments and got picked up by such TV tabloids as *Hard Copy*, *Extra*, and *Inside Edition*. A cable network also called and wanted to produce a documentary about life as a legal prostitute. Her story appeared in more than a dozen newspapers and magazines.

"The publicity that surrounded that little book generated tens of thousands of sales. My client was elated, and I had become even better established with TV news and talk show outlets and the hundreds of local-market and syndicated radio shows where I had scheduled my client. My reputation as an effective publicist also grew, leading to many new client solicitations."

What the Job's Really Like

"Since that 1992 book promotion, I have gone on to represent more than forty authors, three of which have become bestsellers. I have been honored to work as an outside freelancer for such major trade publishers as HarperCollins, Morrow, Regan Books, Simon & Schuster, and Wiley Publishing.

"Unlike the larger agencies, which maintain a large staff of publicists and represent dozens of clients, our small boutique agency represents only three to four clients at any given time. We provide each client with close personal service and accept their calls around the clock (one of the downsides of operating a home-office business).

"On the literary side, our agency represents only nonfiction authors and experts who operate in a variety of fields. From those early days as a news journalist, I work very closely with news desks and TV news magazine producers and tie in the agency's clients with current or breaking news stories.

"My work as a publicist is fun, exciting, and different every day. The majority of my time is spent representing authors, but it is split with assignments for celebrities, film and TV projects, and major events. On entertainment projects it is my job to bring major TV and print entertainment media to the set (programs such as *Entertainment Tonight* and *Access Hollywood* and magazines such as *People* and *Entertainment Weekly*).

"The variety of my work is incredible, and I truly love that I have the power and ability to pick and choose what I do every day."

Finding Clients

"In the past five years I find that I depend more and more on the Internet in my work. The Web has become a major ingredient to both marketing and the distribution of press materials. In 1996, I pioneered Internet News Blasts. I was a bit ahead of my time, but today more and more media outlets not only accept press materials via the Internet—they prefer it.

"On the marketing side, the Internet has delivered my last twelve out of fifteen clients. My website (aimpress.com) is found on most major search engines when people are seeking a literary publicist."

Salaries

"In our agency we traditionally charge on a per-venue basis and provide free telephone and fax services; our retainer averages $5,000."

Advice

"If you are a people person, like being in the spotlight, are a news junkie, like to write and create, or would enjoy the adrenaline rush that comes after seeing something in the national news that you have taken to the media, then you will love being a literary publicist. It is also best that you enjoy reading, because you will be doing a lot of it.

"I suggest you pursue an education in journalism and creative writing. Today many colleges and trade schools also offer public relations courses. If you want to determine if this is going to be your lifeblood, then I suggest seeking an internship with a local public relations firm—preferably one that handles literary publicity.

"As is the case in any job, you must love it to be most effective. In a short period of time you will discover if it's either in your blood or it is not."

Stephanie Dooley, Event Planner

Stephanie Dooley is director of events for Enchantment Events, a division of Author's Venue, LLC, based in Albuquerque, New Mexico. She is one semester away from a B.A. in English and has been working in the field since 1998.

Getting Started

"I had never considered an event planning profession until after I became a writer. Writers' conferences are a huge component to the overall publishing industry. Writing is a solitary profession, so the meetings, conferences, seminars, and retreats have played a large part in information exchange, connections, networking, and learning.

"Once I organized the SouthWest Writers Conference in Albuquerque, I was hooked. I found an untapped talent within myself for organization and overall meeting conception. I was good at it! And I enjoyed being able to merge my love for writing with the detail-intensive meeting planning.

"Before I founded Enchantment Events, I worked with the writers' organization SouthWest Writers in Albuquerque, New Mexico, in their outreach program. I organized workshops and other programs for a year. When the opportunity arose to become the director for the 1999 SouthWest Writers Conference I took it.

"In January 1999 I founded Enchantment Events, an event-planning company specializing in writers' events. However, I soon found other agencies coming to me to plan their events. Some were arts or writing related, but I had clients from government agencies, private companies, and others.

"After two years with Enchantment Events I began negotiations with my current business partners to create a new company of writers' services, bringing Enchantment Events in as the event planning component. I still do what I did before, but I have the opportunity to be a part of the publishing industry in a direct way. The events my company produces internally are designed to help writers get published, and I have complete control over the quality of those events. It's extremely gratifying to see the result in helping other writers."

What the Job's Really Like

"I plan workshops, seminars, retreats, and conferences. Most of the events are writing-related events. However, we can serve any company or organization that requires event planning. The process is the same, only the content changes.

"The work is definitely not boring! I spend anywhere from sixteen to eighteen hours a day working on the computer, making calls, going to meetings, developing plans. It requires constant attention, particularly since it's my own company. The buck stops with me, so I have to make sure everything is running like clockwork. I have a wonderful staff that keeps the details in line. That frees up a lot of my time that can be spent on more development- and concept-oriented tasks. As both industries constantly fluctuate (hospitality and publishing), I have to be on top of the new trends.

"I have a home office with roughly five large file cabinets—not to mention shelves and a full closet of supplies. Basically my office is overflowing with things I need every day to make the business run. I keep a file on each state in the United States and some foreign countries with hotel portfolios. That way, if I have an event in a particular city, I can have a place to start.

"I also keep files on possible speakers and speakers' bureaus. Even though requests come in for particular speakers I have to track down, for the most part my database keeps quality instructors in the events I plan. Working with the faculty of any given event is also a challenge. A single conference can hold anywhere from ten to sixty faculty members. While some of the tasks can be turned over to the contracted travel agent, members of the faculty must be kept informed of conference developments, and biographies, photos, session descriptions, and other material must be obtained by the faculty. All of this takes an enormous amount of time.

"Working with the venue is another task altogether. The hospitality industry is a whole new world, with its own language, set of rules, and duties. Extensive knowledge of hotel contracts is a must. Once a good contract is determined, most of the hotel contact is just maintenance. But one wrinkle can send the whole deal into a big mess. A date off or unanticipated attrition (a hotel term that basically means penalties) can mean a struggle.

"All in all, it's the details that are the biggest part of my job—making sure nothing falls through the cracks."

Upsides and Downsides   "I like the concept stage. I do constant research to see what's out there, what other meeting planners are doing. If there's anything I can incorporate into my own meetings to make them run more smoothly, give the attendees more than they bargained for, I'll try it at least once. Dreaming up what your final product will look like, feel like, what the attendees will come away with, is exciting and fun.

"While planning the actual event isn't a drag, it can become overwhelming. When I look at the calendar and realize I have four or five events coming up in the next three months, and I've had two or three cancellations, and my events manager is on vacation, well, it can become quite tiresome. There are so many details to keep on top of, and when there are multiple conferences to maintain, it's like throwing fifteen or twenty lead balls in the air and making sure they all stay up."

Advice   "Organization skills are a must. You must like details and be good at multitasking. Joining a local meeting planners' group is a good place to get basic information. MPI (Meeting Planners International) is a huge organization that is known for keeping up with global trends and information. There are degree programs in hospitality, or you can become certified."

See Appendix A for MPI's address and website.

Dianna Bacchi, Meeting Planner

Dianna Bacchi is a meeting planner with McGraw-Hill, a large publishing house in New York City, where she works in the Professional Books Division. In 1997, she earned her B.A. in media and communications at the State University of New York College at Old Westbury. She has been working in the field since 1999.

Getting Started

"I first realized I had the skills to be a professional meeting planner at my wedding. Looking back at my life, it seems I was always planning events in one form or another. I realized that I had what it took to do this sort of thing and I actually enjoyed it. My first job planning events was in college. I coordinated all rush and alumni events for the sorority I was in.

"After college I worked for McGraw-Hill in the publicity department. I created press releases and contacted reviewers for the training, careers, outdoor, and aviation titles. I also created two newsletters named *Beyond Flight* and *Training News* that helped our books reach target publications. When my current position became available I applied for it and got it. I knew I could plan the meetings and do a good job."

What the Job's Really Like

"I handle every detail of the meetings for our sales division, from picking the hotels and selecting the menus to reconciling and paying the bill and a few thousand things that fall in between.

"I think you need to have three things before becoming a meeting planner. You need to be detail-oriented to a fault, you need to be quick on your feet and able to troubleshoot problems, and you need to be a mom. The last one sounds a little funny, but believe me when I say you have to baby your attendees. They will change their minds a hundred times about room reservations, meal invitations, AV equipment—anything and everything; you can never do enough. One time an international attendee at one of our meetings got something in his eye, and I had to find him a clinic in NYC that would take his insurance.

"My job is very broad. I plan three sales conferences a year with about 130 attendees at each. I also handle a majority of the work for the BookExpo America, which is the largest trade show in publishing. The space we exhibit in is approximately 1,200 square feet. To top it all off, I am the assistant to the vice president of sales. A typical day starts off with about thirty E-mails and ten voice mails, each one with a request. There is never a time when you can say 'I have done all my work.' Even after your meeting you need to go through the bill with a fine-tooth comb. Every conference I find thousands of dollars in mistakes."

Upsides and Downsides

"The greatest thing about meeting planning is the way hotels treat you. You have the ability to spend hundreds of thousands of dollars at a hotel or convention, and these places know it. They will always give you the penthouse suite and the treatment to go with it.

"The most frustrating thing about my job is that if you are a good meeting planner everyone thinks it is so easy. Most people don't see how hard you work; it is one of those things you physically have to do to know what it is really like.

"I spend countless hours outside of work thinking about every little detail, and I never enjoy the beautiful places we go. I am always on the clock, 24/7."

Salaries

"Unless your boss has done your job and fully knows what it takes to be a meeting planner, expect not to make much money. Because many people see this job as easy, the chances are you will do the work of several people."

Advice

"The best advice I can give anyone is know someone. And make sure you're detail-oriented and a troubleshooter. Be careful before signing contracts with the hotels or other venues. I'd recommend taking a course in contract law.

"Meeting planning sounds glamorous, but it is a very difficult job."

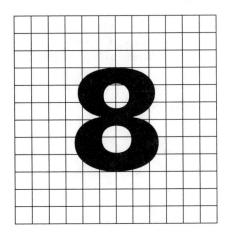

PUBLISHING LAW

"Most writers regard the truth as their most valuable possession, and therefore are most economical in its use."—Mark Twain

Among other things, the relationship an author has with a publishing house is a legal one. For every book that gets published, a legal contract is drawn up, discussed, negotiated, agreed upon, and executed. In addition, some books require preparation of licensing agreements in connection with the exercise of subsidiary rights. Some books also might need to be vetted for legally objectionable or libelous material.

But if you're getting ready to skip over this chapter because you think you'd have to go to law school to work in this field, feel free to stay put. The field of publishing has many uses for publishing law professionals, and not all these professionals need to have law degrees.

CONTRACTS AND LEGAL DEPARTMENTS

In general, publishing companies, especially the large ones, maintain two distinct law-related departments to function efficiently. One is the contracts department. This employs the people who draft the contracts, help the editors come up with wording that makes sense for any special provisions, negotiate the fine points of the deal, propose compromises, file copyrights, disburse the contracts information to the rest of the company, get the authors or their agents their checks quickly, and other related duties.

Some publishing companies also have a legal department. Here work the people who protect the company from getting sued. They go through manuscripts and work with the authors to make sure they haven't written anything libelous; they settle claims or bring in outside lawyers when things get serious.

While in most cases legal departments are run by and staffed with attorneys, the same isn't necessarily true of contracts departments.

Nancy Zoole Kenney, director of contracts at Henry Holt and Company, a well-known midsized publisher of trade books in New York City, is not a lawyer. She earned a bachelor's in English from Syracuse University in 1967 and started in the contracts arena working as an assistant to a literary agent. There she learned the fundamentals of contract negotiation and the basics of subsidiary rights. She has thirty-three years' experience in publishing, twenty-three of those years writing publishing contracts.

She says, "I'd like to think that the heads of publishing companies tend to hire people without law degrees to run their contracts departments because there's a general appreciation of the fact that the ability to write a good publishing contract has more to do with a person's understanding of how the business works than with the theory of contract law.

"In fact, it's probably mostly about salaries. A publisher can save money by hiring a nonlawyer with enough experience to know when a real lawyer should be called in for advice. Every job I've held since 1968 has given me some element of the overall experience in publishing that has become my foundation.

"On the other hand, I'm sure that many publishing companies would hire a person with a law degree to manage a contracts department. In fact, the person I replaced here at Holt had a law degree . . . but she didn't have much experience in publishing. She tended to be much too rigid in her negotiations, and she started alienating both the authors and their agents. An agent expects the contracts manager to take the needs of her particular client seriously, and this usually has absolutely nothing to do with the law.

"For example, we have a provision in our contract boilerplate that specifies that an author must read, correct, and return his page proofs within fourteen days. But an agent might argue that her author couldn't possibly do that in less than twenty-one days. The contracts manager cannot simply refuse to make the change; the contract boilerplate is not the absolute final word on the subject. Instead, she should find out from the managing editor how long the production department can really wait for page proofs to be returned and how long it takes authors, in general, to deal with this particular responsibility. Then she can come up with a compromise that makes everyone happy. As I look back on the contracts managers I've known with law degrees, I realize that the best of them were in publishing before they went to law school."

Kenney does not look for law graduates when she hires assistants. "When our human resources department recently placed an ad in *The New York Times* for a contracts assistant, an overwhelming number of responses were from recent law school graduates claiming they were willing to take an entry-level position in the contracts department to get a foot in the door. That's not what I'm looking for in an assistant.

"I want someone right out of college with little or no publishing experience . . . the idea being that (1) I can teach that kind of person the idea of good publisher/author relations, that is, the possibility that a contract can be created that gives the author every possible concession but does not inhibit the publisher's way of doing business; and (2) I'll have someone who will stay for a while and do the photocopying and filing and record keeping and general grunt work that needs to be done."

WHAT IF YOU HAVE A LAW DEGREE?

If the company is big enough to have a separate legal staff, a lawyer with experience in some form of entertainment or intellectual property law can apply for a position on that legal staff. At some publishing houses, the general counsel would not hire a lawyer without litigation experience for the legal staff. Lawyers aren't necessary to write contracts, but they are necessary to handle lawsuits and make court appearances. Starting out in a law firm that handles a wide range of legal areas would be helpful to gain all the necessary experience.

Says Nancy Zoole Kenney, "If you're just out of law school with no experience whatsoever, and you want to be in publishing, either apply for a position as a contracts administrator—that is, start as assistant to an experienced contracts manager—or try to get into a law firm that specializes in intellectual property or entertainment law and get experience that way."

The main point to keep in mind is that to work in law in publishing, the job candidate must have a thorough knowledge of the publishing field—it's not just about the law; it's about the particular context in which law is practiced.

But as intellectual property/publishing law attorney Sara Goodman advises, "Make sure you're burning up with love for the practice of law before going to law school, because law is not an easy profession to be in these days. Even though I really liked law school and actually like what I do, many lawyers don't enjoy law school and eventually leave the practice of law.

"In fact, most law students have no notion about what they really want to do with their law degree. So, unfortunately, young lawyers will find a lot of unhappiness and burnout among their colleagues. Although, I think this is more common among litigators because the judicial system is often a frustrating arena in which to solve problems for clients."

HOW TO BECOME A LAWYER

Formal educational requirements for lawyers include a four-year college degree, three years in law school, and successful completion of a written bar examination. To practice law in the courts of any state or other jurisdiction, a person must be licensed, or admitted to its bar, under rules established by the jurisdiction's highest court. All states require that applicants for admission to the bar pass a written bar examination; most jurisdictions also require applicants to pass a separate written ethics examination.

Lawyers who have been admitted to the bar in one jurisdiction may occasionally be admitted to the bar in another without taking an examination, if they meet that jurisdiction's standards of good moral character and have a specified period of legal experience. Federal courts and agencies set their own qualifications for those practicing before them.

To qualify for the bar examination in most states, an applicant must usually obtain a college degree and graduate from a law school accredited by the American Bar Association (ABA) or the proper state authorities. ABA accreditation signifies that the law school—particularly its library and faculty—meets certain standards developed to promote quality legal education. ABA currently accredits 183 law schools; others are approved by state authorities only. With certain exceptions, graduates of schools not approved by the ABA are restricted to taking the bar examination and practicing in the state or other jurisdiction in which the school is located; most of these schools are in California.

In 1997, the latest figures available, seven states accepted the study of law in a law office or in combination with study in a law school; only California accepts the study of law by correspondence as qualifying for taking the bar examination. Several states require registration and approval of students by the State Board of Law Examiners, either before they enter law school or during the early years of legal study.

Although there is no nationwide bar examination, forty-seven states, the District of Columbia, Guam, the Northern Mariana Islands, Puerto Rico, and the Virgin Islands require the six-hour Multistate Bar Examination (MBE) as part of the bar examination; the MBE is not required in Indiana, Louisiana, and Washington. The MBE covers issues of broad interest and is sometimes given in addition to a locally prepared state bar examination. The three-hour Multistate Essay Examination (MEE) is used as part of the state bar examination in several states. States vary in their use of MBE and MEE scores.

Many states have begun to require Multistate Performance Testing (MPT) to test the practical skills of beginning lawyers. This program has been well received, and many more states are expected to require performance testing in the future. Requirements vary by state, although the test usually is taken at the same time as the bar exam and is a one-time requirement.

The required college and law school education usually takes seven years of full-time study after high school—four years of undergraduate study followed by three years in law school. Although some law schools accept a very small number of students after three years of college, most require applicants to have a bachelor's degree. To meet the needs of students who can attend only part time, a number of law schools have night or part-time divisions that usually require four years of study; about one in ten graduates from ABA-approved schools attends part time.

Although there is no recommended "prelaw" major, prospective lawyers, especially those interested in pursuing publishing law, should develop proficiency in writing and speaking, reading, researching, analyzing, and thinking logically—skills needed to succeed both in law school and in the profession. Regardless of major, a multidisciplinary background is recommended. Courses in English, foreign languages, public speaking, government, philosophy, history, economics, mathematics, and computer science, among others, are useful.

Acceptance by most law schools depends on the applicant's ability to demonstrate an aptitude for the study of law, usually through good undergraduate grades, the Law School Admission Test (LSAT), the quality of the applicant's undergraduate school, any prior work experience, and sometimes a personal interview. However, law schools vary in the weight they place on each of these and other factors.

All law schools approved by the ABA, except for those in Puerto Rico, require applicants to take the LSAT. Nearly all law schools require applicants to have certified transcripts sent to the Law School Data Assembly Service, which then sends applicants' LSAT scores and their standardized records of college grades to the law schools of their choice. Both this service and the LSAT are administered by the Law School Admission Council.

Competition for admission to many law schools is intense, especially for the most prestigious schools. Enrollments in these schools rose very rapidly during the 1970s, as applicants far outnumbered available seats. Although the number of applicants decreased markedly in the 1990s, the number of applicants to most law schools still greatly exceeds the number that can be admitted.

During the first year or year and a half of law school, students usually study core courses such as constitutional law, contracts, property law, torts, civil procedure, and legal writing. In the remaining time, they may elect specialized courses in fields such as publishing, intellectual property, tax, labor, or corporate law. Law students often acquire practical experience by participation in school-sponsored legal clinic activities, in the school's moot court competitions in which students conduct appellate arguments, in practice trials under the supervision of experienced lawyers and judges, and through research and writing on legal issues for the school's law journal.

A number of law schools have clinical programs in which students gain legal experience through practice trials and law school projects under the supervision of practicing lawyers and law school faculty. Law school clinical programs might include work in legal aid clinics, for example, or on the staff of legislative committees. Part-time or summer clerkships in law firms, government agencies, and publishing legal departments also provide valuable experience. Such training can lead directly to a job after graduation and help students decide what kind of practice best suits them.

Law students in fifty-two jurisdictions are required to pass the Multistate Professional Responsibility Examination (MPRE), which tests knowledge of the ABA codes on professional responsibility and judicial conduct. In some states, the MPRE may be taken during law school, usually after completing a course on legal ethics.

Law school graduates receive the degree of juris doctor (J.D.) as the first professional degree. Advanced law degrees may be desirable for those planning to specialize, research, or teach. Some law students pursue joint degree programs, which usually require an additional semester or year. Joint degree programs are offered in a number of areas, including law and business administration or public administration.

After graduation, lawyers must keep informed about legal and nonlegal developments that affect their practice. Currently, thirty-nine states and jurisdictions mandate Continuing Legal Education (CLE). Many law schools and state and local bar associations provide continuing-education courses that help lawyers stay abreast of recent developments. Some states allow CLE credits to be obtained through participation in seminars on the Internet.

SAMPLE JOB ADVERTISEMENTS

The following are real advertisements, but the hiring employers are not identified because the positions have already been filled. They are meant as examples to give you an idea of the types of positions you'll see advertised.

Position: Contracts Assistant
Location: Publisher of film and nonfiction books
Description: Publishing professional with minimum two years in subsidiary rights or contract administration wanted to assist subsidiary rights manager of thirty to forty titles annually for growing, fast-paced publisher of film books (*Traffic*, *Gladiator*, *Crouching Tiger*, etc.), self-help, parenting, and some fiction. Must be familiar with contracts and rights procedures, detail-oriented, and skilled in communication and organization. Administrative duties related to contracts include sending contracts out for signature, tracking contracts, handling check requests, etc. Facility with computers, Word, Excel, FileMaker Pro a must. Salary commensurate with experience.

Position: Foreign Rights Associate
Location: Major publishing house in New York City
Description: Assist VP/director of foreign rights; perform secretarial duties including answering phones, screening calls, taking messages, scheduling appointments, making travel arrangements, and prioritizing correspondence. Qualifications: six months to one year of experience in subsidiary or foreign rights and familiarity with production terms and processes. Excellent communication skills with an emphasis on written correspondence and telephone manner. Excellent typing with knowledge of word processing. Must be able to work under pressure to meet deadlines and be detail-oriented.

Position: Subsidiary Rights Assistant
Location: Large general trade book publisher

Description: Seeking a subsidiary rights assistant whose time will be divided equally between the domestic and foreign rights departments. Domestic rights responsibilities will include many facets of sublicensing such as the sale of book club, serial, audio, electronic, and other domestic subsidiary rights. Will learn to build and maintain relationships with rights contacts and act as liaison with in-house departments as well as literary agents and authors. Foreign rights responsibilities will include handling rights inquiries, drawing and tracking foreign licenses, communicating with international publishers and subagents, creating a monthly sales log, reporting to agents on foreign sales, maintaining files, answering phones, and providing general administrative support. Candidate should be self-starter, well organized, with ability to prioritize. Strong written and verbal communication skills, with a strong interest in reading and a willingness to learn. Proficiency in Word, Excel, and Outlook essential.

Position: Copyright and Permissions Assistant
Location: Large general trade book publisher
Description: Seeking an assistant to respond to inquiries regarding permissions and assist in acquiring and licensing permissions. Customer service attitude a must for variety of telephone requests, combined with the ability to research and understand agreements with attention to detail. Must have excellent communication, organization, research, and time-management skills. College degree, prior office experience, and a desire to be in publishing required as well as the ability to work under pressure on time-sensitive projects.

Position: Business Affairs Counsel
Location: Legal department of major magazine publisher
Description: Actively participate in the evaluation of transactions and business opportunities. Provide legal and business affairs advice to senior management. Draft and negotiate legal documents including, among others, talent, content licensing, copyright, and business development. Develop "state-of-the-art" standardized contracts for publishing operations. Respond to and evaluate requests for structuring, optimizing, and terminating business ventures. Negotiate and advise management regarding joint venture contracts (involving multiple alliances/partners) pertaining to intellectual knowledge, networks, and technologies. Review and provide counsel regarding Internet-

related transactions/contracts. The position will be project-oriented, entailing exposure to a variety of diverse business issues associated with the continuing transition into a content-driven, multimedia business. Requirements: J.D. degree and bar membership; five to eight years of experience in a corporate legal department or law firm specializing in the entertainment or publishing industries; solid track record in basic contracts review and drafting abilities; strong negotiation and communications skills, both written and oral; sophisticated and professional presentation skills; highly developed and reasoned business perspective to complement legal skills; resourcefulness and ability to create structure from concept, taking ideas and crystallizing into term sheets and legal documents; ability to interact effectively with internal executives and business managers as well as with external consultants, authors, and other service providers; excellent analytical skills; ability to identify business and financial risks. Must be a "big-picture" thinker and strategist who can analyze and decipher complex business agreements but also be attuned to critical details relevant to success.

JOB OUTLOOK FOR LAW CAREERS

If you're interested in pursuing a law career in a publishing company or any aspect of law, there is no doubt you'll encounter some stiff competition. The *Occupational Outlook Handbook* has predicted this competition will last through the year 2008. The number of law school graduates is expected to continue to strain the economy's capacity to absorb them.

Employment of lawyers grew very rapidly from the early 1970s through the early 1990s but has started to level off recently. Through 2008, employment is expected to grow about as fast as the average for all occupations. Continuing demand for lawyers will result primarily from growth in the population and the general level of business activities. Demand will also be spurred by the growth of legal action in such areas as health care, international law, elder law, environmental law, sexual harassment, and, most significant in the publishing industry, intellectual property.

However, employment growth is expected to be slower than in the past. In an effort to reduce the money spent on legal fees, many businesses are increasingly utilizing large accounting firms and paralegals to perform some of the same functions lawyers might have performed in the past. For example, accounting firms may provide employee benefit counseling, process documents, or handle various other services previously performed by the law firm. And, as stated earlier, publishing contracts departments will hire nonlawyers to write contracts.

SALARIES IN PUBLISHING LAW

Salaries of experienced attorneys vary widely according to the type, size, and location of their employer. Lawyers who own their own practices usually earn less than those who are partners in law firms. Lawyers starting their own practices may need to work part time in other occupations to supplement their income until their practice is well established.

According to the National Association for Law Placement, median annual earnings of all lawyers is about $78,170. The middle half of the occupation earns between $51,450 and $114,520. The bottom 10 percent earns less than $37,310. Median annual earnings in the industries employing the largest numbers of lawyers are shown here:

Legal services	$78,700
Federal government	$78,200
Fire, marine, and casualty insurance	$74,400
State government	$59,400
Local government	$49,200

Median salaries of lawyers six months after graduation from law school vary by type of work, as indicated by the following table:

Private practice	$60,000
Business/industry (including publishing)	$50,000
Academe	$38,000
Judicial clerkship	$37,500
Government	$36,000
Public interest	$31,000

In general, publishing law is not listed among the highest-paying fields. Leaving a position in a big law firm to join a publishing house could mean a cut in pay. One lawyer working for Von Holtzbrinck, Henry Holt's parent company, was not distressed at her lower salary. She had left a prestigious law firm and was happy with her new job doing work that was "more fun and diversified." And she didn't have to worry about the number of hours she was billing.

"A contracts director without a law degree can probably make between $50,000 and $100,000 a year," Nancy Zoole Kenney says, "depending upon the size of the publishing company."

According to the 2001 Association of American Publishers (AAP) Compensation Survey, average annual salaries for selected job titles are as follows:

Top division finance executive	$150,700
Business manager	$79,000
Top rights executive	$112,200
Rights manager	$57,600
Royalty manager	$80,500
Royalty accountant	$41,500
Manager, copyrights and/or permissions	$69,000
Manager, contracts	$54,000

FIRSTHAND ACCOUNTS

Nancy Zoole Kenney, Director of Contracts

Nancy Zoole Kenney is director of contracts at Henry Holt and Company, a trade book publisher of both adult and children's titles.

Getting Started

"I think that I probably wanted to be in publishing in general because I really wanted to be a writer, and I had the fantasy that if I hung around writers, something would rub off on me.

"My first job in publishing was as assistant to the managing editor/acting editor-in-chief of *McCall's* magazine. This was way back when *McCall's* was still one of the top magazines for women. The daughter of some old friends of my parents had been a magazine editor, and I thought it all sounded terribly glamorous. When I was a senior in college, I consulted her about getting a job at a magazine, and it was she who suggested that I take a course at Katharine Gibbs and apply as an executive secretary. In those days, "editorial assistants" were a dime a dozen and were paid about $90 a week, but college graduates who could type and take dictation were in great demand.

"In fact, I finished my Gibbs course on a Friday and started working at *McCall's* the next Tuesday (that Monday was Memorial Day) at the grand salary of $110 per week. And so, with an unimpressive grade point average from Syracuse and virtually no prior office experience, I got my foot in the door of the publishing world.

"After a year at *McCall's* and a few false starts (for example, I spent some time in the advertising production department at *Redbook* magazine), I became the assistant to a literary agent (one of the very grand old ladies of the literary world), where I dug in and remained for three and a half years, learning the fundamentals of contract negotiation and the basics of subsidiary rights. After I realized that I was not particularly interested in becoming a literary agent myself, I made what could be considered a lateral move into the subsidiary rights department at Bantam Books. I refer to this as a lateral move, because I was still doing basically the same thing . . . but I was working on behalf of the publisher rather than the author. While my years with the agency gave me valuable insight into (and an appreciation of) the relationship between the author and agent, I must admit that I much preferred being on the publishing end of the business.

"In 1973, Bantam was still considered primarily a 'reprint' house, by which I mean that many of our books were paperback reprint editions of works that had already been published in hardcover elsewhere; but Bantam had also begun to publish its share of noteworthy original fiction and nonfiction in paperback, so the subsidiary rights department was becoming increasingly active. It was there that I began to realize my affinity to contracts and began to channel my 'creative writing' skills into the preparation of customized licensing agreements. I remained in the subsidiary rights department for five years, at which time Bantam hired a new general counsel to run the legal/contracts department . . . one who believed that there was no such thing as a standard 'fill-in-the-blanks' acquisition agreement and that her assistants should be trained to prepare contracts from scratch. I asked for a transfer into her department.

"During the next sixteen years, I wrote contracts and worked my way up to the head of the department, as Bantam grew in size and prominence and merged with Doubleday and Dell. In 1991, I became vice president and director of the combined BDD contracts department, and then in 1994, when I found myself writing fewer and fewer contracts and having to deal with more and more administrative and personnel issues, I left the company. For the next few years, I worked on a part-time basis as the contracts manager for two small publishing companies, and then in 1999, the new president and publisher of Henry Holt and Company was looking for an experienced contracts director, and my former colleagues at BDD suggested he call me."

What the Job's Really Like

"As director of contracts, I'm primarily responsible for the drafting of our acquisition agreements (in other words, contracts with authors and other publishers), including the negotiation of deal points (other than the basic terms; for example, I wouldn't negotiate such things as the advance, delivery date, description of the work, etc.) and the transmittal of contractual information to the appropriate departments. I also oversee the preparation of licensing agreements in connection with the exercise of subsidiary rights.

"As with most people in this business, my day varies depending upon the crisis of the moment and which author or agent is being the most insistent. Whether or not the job can be considered stressful depends upon the personality of the individual. The job is not suitable for a person who becomes agitated simply because there's too much to do and too little time in which to do it. For the most part, there are few real emergencies, and overanxious agents, authors, and editors can be cajoled into calming down and waiting until you're finished.

The job can be boring at times, for example, when there's nothing new to negotiate . . . when the agents ask the same old questions and want the same old alterations in the boilerplate. On the other hand, it never stays that way for long.

"When I receive an official request for a contract, I prepare a first draft and send it to the author or his agent for review. If the agent has objections to provisions in our boilerplate contract, I'm usually able to determine which are reasonable or unreasonable and which can be worked out with some compromise language. If I don't know an answer, I consult with the appropriate authority in that particular area. Part of being a good contracts manager is in knowing who is best able to give advice and who has the authority to make decisions in each area.

"When all of the deal points have been worked out, I prepare final copies of the agreement for the author's signature. When a contract has been signed by an author, I see that it is countersigned on behalf of the publisher and that any payment due the author is properly issued. As part of this, I convey to the accounting department any special provisions we have with that author, and I am responsible for updating that information as situations change (for example, if an author fires his agent). If anyone has a question regarding an aspect of the contract, it is up to me to render an interpretation.

"If the original deal with the author changes, it falls to me to prepare an amendment to the contract. If a book is out of print and an author wants us to terminate our agreement with him, it is up to me to review the sales history and get a consensus as to whether it would be worth our while to have that title reissued.

"At the moment, I am fortunate enough to have a manager of copyrights and permissions who has at least as much experience in the business as I have, but in the absence of such a person, I would be responsible for registering copyrights in all of the new books (and, in the old days, would have handled renewals) and handling all permissions requests.

"I advise editors on such subjects as whether or not the author's use of a quotation from someone else's work requires permission; if a previously published work is still protected by copyright; how many advance installments are still payable to an author; what is the best royalty we can offer an author on sales of his book through nontraditional markets; how the sell-off of excess inventory is handled; and so forth.

"A contracts director with a law degree would also be responsible for making sure that the manuscripts are legally acceptable. In large publishing companies, there may be a sufficient staff of lawyers so that this would be handled in-house. Otherwise, the lawyer/contracts director would be the one to hire an outside expert to read a manuscript for liability, accuracy, etc., and then to work with the author and the author's editor to ensure that any changes recommended by the outside lawyer are properly made.

"Likewise, if a claim is made against a book, the lawyer/contracts director will take the first stab at making it go away (usually via a flurry of correspondence) and then, as a last resort, will hire the outside law firm to handle the litigation.

"A lawyer/contracts director might also be called upon to handle other legal matters for the publisher; such as the lease on the office space or the registration of a trademark, including the trademark search."

Sara Goodman, Intellectual Property Specialist

Sara Goodman is a solo practitioner concentrating in intellectual property law, publishing matters, contracts, copyright, libel, and defamation. She received her B.A. with honors in history from Rice University in Houston in 1978 and her J.D. with honors from New York University School of Law in New York City in 1982. She is a member of the New York and Florida bars.

Getting Started

"I decided to go to law school because, as corny or nostalgic as it may seem, my father had, from as long as I can remember, always told everyone that I was going to go to law school and follow in his footsteps. He was a unique and perhaps in some ways an anachronistic lawyer—a solo practitioner with a lot of sophisticated appellate work in a small city, educated at Harvard Law School in the 1930s, interested in helping his clients solve personal and professional problems, and, more often than not, not billing them for his services. This has become a repeated theme in my own life!

"When I was very young, in the early 1960s, he argued a case before the U.S. Supreme Court—my whole family went down to hear the argument—and I remember being in awe of the pomp and ceremony at the court, of the respect given to the law and to the justices and to the entire court system. Interestingly, his opponent, who won the case, was a female attorney working for the New York Attorney General's Office, and my father went out of his way to impress on me that being a girl would in no way stop me from being a successful lawyer.

"He also had two to three women lawyers clerking for him over the years, and while these facts might seem insignificant now, they were not insignificant in the 1960s and early 1970s when female attorneys were still very few and very far between, particularly in small cities.

"I worked in his office during summers when I was about twelve to fifteen, acting as a general office gopher and helper, and I was always introduced to people as his youngest child, the one who was going to go to law school.

"In my senior year of college, my father learned he had advanced colon cancer and had only a few months to live. He wanted me to go to law school so badly; I remember him telling me just a few weeks before he died about some of the schools he thought I should consider.

"In the end, I think the decision was influenced a lot by my emotions at the time, as well as an inability at that time in my life—I was only twenty-one—

to figure out how to pursue other interests I had. Also, everyone I knew said something to the effect that going to law school would always be helpful 'no matter what else you decided to do.' I don't know any lawyer who wasn't told the same thing. Actually, that was good advice, but I wouldn't repeat the advice now. Law school is too costly, too time-consuming, and too difficult to merely use as a stepping-stone to something else."

What the Job's Really Like

"When I was at Sullivan & Cromwell, a huge Wall Street firm with more than two hundred lawyers worldwide (this is the law firm hired by Bill Gates to defend Microsoft from antitrust attack by the U.S. Justice Department), the atmosphere was more formal and hierarchical, although I think S&C was more progressive and laid back than other firms of its kind. As a junior associate, I spent hours in the law library doing lots of legal research and drafting memos and briefs in cases for huge corporate clients mostly. I also spent a lot of time doing discovery and motion practice in big litigation matters—which meant I spent a lot of time reviewing reams of documents and deciding which ones had to be turned over to our clients' adversaries.

"After just a short stint at Sullivan & Cromwell, I knew that I didn't want to stay in a big firm representing the largest corporations in America, and I knew I didn't want to stay in litigation. The lawyers at the firm were so impressive, but their personal lives were so drained by the long, long hours.

"I actually got into publishing law accidentally. During a period of time when I was particularly frustrated with the tortuous history and slow progress of the cases I was working on, I applied to a blind ad in my law school's alumni job newsletter for an in-house counsel position at a publishing company. I had no idea where I was sending my resume, and I even had forgotten about the ad by the time I eventually got a call from the general counsel of Simon & Schuster. But after my initial interview was over, I knew I would really love working in-house, doing publishing law.

"At Simon & Schuster and later at Bantam Doubleday Dell, my in-house work was totally different than at S&C. I was on the 'front line' with my clients, helping them make practical decisions all day long and anticipating legal problems that I was able to help them avoid through careful planning. I worked on a lot of contracts and manuscripts. I also really liked working on books—they're probably the nicest type of product I can think of working with, as opposed to something like widgets, soap, or toilet paper—not that we don't need widgets, soap, and toilet paper!

"I worked with a lot of interesting and famous authors—some of whom were really wonderful and some of whom were kind of a pain in the neck. Publishing is a very egocentric business. Only in Hollywood are the players more egocentric.

"Now, in my own practice, which I would characterize as a 'part-time' practice at this point in time, I do a lot of the same things that I did in-house, because

I prefer to stay away from litigation matters (referring them to others) and taking things on that for the most part help people avoid legal problems with others.

"I represent writers and publishers who want help with their publishing contracts or their collaboration or work-for-hire agreements. I help authors plan ahead of time if they are taking on a project that will necessarily raise lots of legal flags.

"I sometimes represent my former employer, Bantam Doubleday Dell, on a freelance basis, helping their legal department with their overflow of manuscript reviews. This means that I read a book before it gets published and work with the author and editor to help ensure that the publisher and author do not get any successful legal claims against them on publication—for example, claims for libel, invasion of privacy, and copyright infringement mostly.

"I like the area of law that I practice in a lot. I also like helping people solve problems in connection with something that matters to them. Unlike most attorneys I know, I honestly think that the law—at least intellectual property law—is fascinating. This area of the law has also taken on new significance in light of the Internet. People generally understand today, for example, that copyright is a live issue that can affect them every day, at least in their businesses.

"What I like least is the billing of clients—I hate keeping track of my time, and I find it difficult to bill clients for all of my time. I just want to do a really good job for people even if it takes a lot of time that I don't want to charge the client for. I really disliked this aspect of lawyering when I was an associate in a large law firm."

Advice

"The litigation system is mind-boggling to most laypeople—it's extremely expensive, it's extremely time-consuming, we have so few really outstanding judges, and, unfortunately, the really frivolous cases give many good lawyers an undeserved bad reputation. I tell everyone I know that 'if you're in court, you're in trouble,' and this is true no matter what the case is about and no matter what side you're on.

"Certainly anyone who is happy and content with his current career should not seek out a law degree simply to improve his economic standing—it's a circuitous and very unsteady path.

"I think the most important qualities you need to be a good lawyer are integrity and compassion—and it also definitely helps to be an excellent writer."

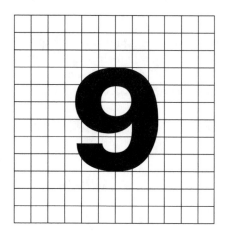

SELF-PUBLISHING

"No author is a man of genius to his publisher."—Heinrich Heine

Currently there are approximately 700,000 books in print. Somewhere in the neighborhood of 60,000 books are printed annually in the United States. That's more than 160 different titles a day! How many of those are self-published? It's hard to say. We only really hear about the ones that make a splash. *The Joy of Sex*, *The Celestine Prophecy*, *The Christmas Box*, *Chicken Soup for the Soul*, and *What Color Is Your Parachute?* are all bestselling books—and they were all originally self-published.

That's five.

True, these aren't the only five. *Tarzan* author Edgar Rice Burroughs self-published. So did Mark Twain, Zane Grey, Stephen Crane, Virginia Woolf, Edgar Allen Poe, and James Joyce. They took their work to a printer and brought home cartons full of books. But those were different times.

Self-publishing is risky business. Only a handful of books make it; all the others can end up suffering from the same sort of stigma that attaches itself to subsidy and cooperative publishing ventures. (See Chapter 1.) Stigma aside, most self-published books end up collecting cobwebs in garages, basements, and spare rooms.

Can it ever work? Yes. In some situations. It can work if you're an expert on a particular subject, if you're writing nonfiction (self-published fiction is notoriously hard to impossible to sell), and if you know who your readers will be and how to reach them.

IS SELF-PUBLISHING FOR YOU?

"It depends," says Mark Ortman, author of *A Simple Guide to Self-Publishing* and director of the online Self-Publishing Resource Center (wiseowlbooks.com/ publish).

"To help you decide," says Ortman, "answer the following five questions:

"1. What is my motivation and purpose for publishing my book? Writing a book is a lot of work. Publishing one is even more work. Is your purpose clear and well enough conceived to sustain you through the experience? If profit is a motive, this venture must be treated as a business. Keep your purpose clear!

"2. Is my book written for a specific market niche or group of people? It is more expensive to promote a book to a wide, general audience. Marketing costs are less when the target audience is specific, definable, and accessible.

"3. Do I have a way to sell books direct? Selling books direct (at retail price to your target audience) is the most profitable way to recover your initial self-publishing investment. The standard heavy discounts to wholesalers and book-stores can be costly for slow-moving books. In fact, without a solid marketing plan, selling books to bookstores can be the least profitable way to distribute your book. Think of alternative ways to distribute your book: organizations, associations, corporations, conventions, fund-raisers, back-of-the-room sales after lectures or workshops, to list a few.

"4. Am I willing to go out and promote my book? A general rule for authors: a book stops selling when the author does. No matter who publishes your book, the author is responsible for creating the demand. A book will not sell well sit-ting on a bookstore's shelf unless interest is created in the book. Typically, from start to finish, a writer will spend 10 percent of his or her time writing the book, 15 percent publishing it, and 75 percent marketing and promoting the finished book.

"5. Can I sell at least five hundred copies? Beyond friends and family, who will be interested in your book? It is important to know your market and how to reach those people before investing in self-publishing. If profit is your motive, the initial cost of producing and printing (fewer than five hundred copies) may be higher than a realistic retail price. Of course, the more you print, the less they cost. However, that decision must be weighed against the possibility of many unsold books sitting in your garage. The fact is that 95 percent of all books published sell fewer than 7,500 copies. Most self-publishers initially print five hundred to three thousand copies. Develop a solid marketing plan to give you a more accurate estimate of how many books may sell."

Your answers to the previous questions should help you determine if self-publishing is a viable option. The next step is to read books on this subject before you make a final decision.

THE COMPLETE GUIDE TO SELF-PUBLISHING

One book, *The Complete Guide to Self-Publishing*, by Tom and Marilyn Ross is a must for anyone considering self-publishing. It is not self-published. It is published by Writer's Digest Books. That aside, *The Complete Guide to Self-*

Publishing covers everything you need to know to write, publish, promote, and sell your own book. The authors are the gurus on the subject of self-publishing. Their bio states: "After self-publishing six books, Tom and Marilyn Ross began giving nationwide writing and publishing seminars to share what they had learned about the process. A flood of requests for individual guidance led to the creation of their consulting service. . . .

"In the eighties they decided to put their knowledge in print to be made available to even larger numbers than they could personally reach."

The Rosses have generously allowed the reprinting of their article, called "Self-Publish Your Own Book and Keep All the Profits!" for this book. It shows the can-do side of self-publishing.

"Self-Publish Your Own Book and Keep All the Profits!"

by Marilyn and Tom Ross

How does a person bridge the enormous gap between a manuscript and a book? There are three options: trade (commercial) publishing, subsidy (vanity) publishing, or self-publishing.

Commercial publishers are the so-called giants in the industry. Unfortunately, they're so big they no longer hear the voice of the little person. Continuing corporate mergers and takeovers compound the problem. Unless you are famous (or infamous), your manuscript has little chance of making it through the corporate front door. And even if it does, this can be more of a curse than a blessing.

Trade publishers typically offer a $2,000 to $10,000 advance against royalties. Yet industry statistics show that only one in ten books ever earns back that advance. That's a 90 percent failure rate! It means you're unlikely to ever get any more than that paltry initial payment.

Those who sign with commercial houses have no guarantee their book will be properly presented to the public. A disproportionate chunk of advertising dollars is spent on authors with established track records or well-known names. We hear many horror stories about authors who make media appearances to promote their work . . . yet customers can't find their books in bookstores.

In desperation, many novices turn to subsidy (vanity) presses. Beware! Here the ink hits the paper only when the author underwrites the cost of the entire venture. But despite the investment, the author is expected to sign away all rights and receives only a partial royalty in return. Plus the vanity publisher's name on your book stigmatizes it, causing it to be shunned by important reviewers. Last, marketing efforts by vanity houses are dismal to nonexistent.

Self-publishing is a viable option for many. This "do-it-by-yourself" method places you in complete control of the entire process. Critical decisions concerning the title, cover design, content, marketing, and distribution are made by you—not by some executive sitting in a remote New York office. Yes, you invest in your project. Done properly, however, this is a prudent investment in your future.

In the past ten years, overall quality in the industry has skyrocketed. Well-edited manuscripts, eye-catching covers, and high-tech marketing techniques are the norm. Privately published titles typically command respect—and profits—for their authors. We know that many busy professionals want to control their destinies—but they don't have time to handle the myriad details involved. To meet this need, About Books, Inc. [editor's note: About Books, Inc., is the name of the Rosses' consulting business] offers a turnkey service to oversee the entire editing, design, printing, and marketing process.

Here's the approach many savvy people are taking today: they self-publish initially and promote their book to success. Then they leverage this successful track record by "allowing" a trade publisher to buy the rights to their proven product. This way they have the clout to command a higher advance and can negotiate more favorable terms. By removing the risk for the commercial publisher, you put yourself in a more powerful position. Success can be yours. Self-publishing your book is often the profitable alternative.

Many dramatic success stories have left their imprint on the entire self-publishing movement. Such was the case of Louise Hay, author of a phenomenally successful line of books, who chose self-publishing to launch her works. She began with a forty-eight-page staple-bound edition of *Heal Your Body*; her second venture, *You Can Heal Your Life,* captured the number nine spot on the trade paperback bestseller list for 1988! Her books and resulting tapes and seminars have helped hundreds of thousands to discover the pathway to well-being. And they've helped Louise to wealth.

Consider the example of self-publisher Ted Nicholas. His *How to Form Your Own Corporation Without a Lawyer for Under $50* started its journey with $5,000 borrowed from a life insurance policy. The result? Over 800,000 copies sold to date. Entrepreneurs of America, a service for independent businesspeople, is just one of his latest spin-offs. Capitalizing on his direct-mail wizardry, Nicholas recently published *The Golden Mailbox*, a how-to guide for selling books through the mail.

The classic career counseling handbook *What Color Is Your Parachute?* began its climb to bestsellerdom as a self-published title. Author and clergyman Richard Nelson Bolles eventually sold it to Ten Speed Press, where the book continues to move at a rate of 300,000 copies a year. The total number of copies sold so far is over five million!

Another author to join the ranks of the elite with several million books sold is Peter McWilliams. This self-publishing all-star has written on amazing topics. Starting with poetry and transcendental meditation, he quickly moved into the exploding computer market with *The Personal Computer Book*. McWilliams's latest title, *You Can't Afford the Luxury of a Negative Thought*, is representative of his popular self-help style.

These dramatic success stories have left their imprint on the entire self-publishing movement. Today, more and more people are deciding to publish their own books and keep all the profit!

THE OTHER SIDE

So far, you've been getting a positive perspective—honest, but perhaps overly optimistic. In fact, very few books make money; even fewer are taken up by traditional publishers; hardly any go on to be well known.

Although Richard Paul Evans's *The Christmas Box* is a success story—his book made history as the only self-published novel to hit number one on the *New York Times* bestseller list—he cautions would-be self-publishers. In an interview with author Carolyn Campbell, Evans says, "Don't start by considering self-publishing. Becoming self-published is not the easy way to become a published book author, but it is sometimes the only way. In studying self-publishing, you will see both history and the law of chance aren't on your side. When I decided to self-publish *The Christmas Box*, no publisher wanted it, yet I sensed that readers wanted it very much. I would definitely begin by submitting the book to traditional publishers through an agent rather than trying to send it to publishers directly."

Be wary of the people who would tell you otherwise. It is fine to use a consulting service, just make sure they don't encourage every project that comes their way. Those who want to collect their commissions, knowing full well your project will never leave the garage, are doing you a disservice. Be wary of vanity presses, too. Vanity presses are so-called because they do cater to a new writer's strong desire to see his or her work between the covers of a book. They are no more than subsidy presses, taking the writers' money and printing books but not selling or distributing them—and in many cases keeping a percentage of the profits.

Look around to get an honest and unbiased opinion of your work and its marketability. If you've submitted your work to major publishers or agents already and they've turned it down, reread the rejection letters. The clues might be there. If they don't think they can sell the book, chances are you won't be able to either.

But, if you can reach a target audience they can't, then you might have a shot. Ultimately, if you choose to self-publish, learn what's involved and what steps to take. This way you'll save yourself a lot of money and frustration.

The Rosses have also contributed the following article:

"Eleven Tips to Avoid Self-Publishing Traps"

Self-publishing used to be the Rodney Dangerfield of book publishing. It didn't get "no respect." Today that's all changed. With originally self-published books such as *The Celestine Prophecy*, *Mutant Message Down Under*, *The Christmas Box*, and *What Color Is Your Parachute?* monopolizing bestseller lists, do-it-yourself publishing is very much in vogue.

To be successful, however, it's mandatory that you adhere to certain guidelines. By following the tips below, you'll avoid the pitfalls and enhance your chances of flourishing.

1. *Educate yourself.* Self-publishing is a business. Approach it as such. There are informative books on the subject, seminars offered, and associations where you can learn the ropes and network with the more experienced. This can be very lucrative if properly approached. Conversely, you can waste thousands of dollars by blundering along without knowledge or a plan.

2. *Study the competition.* Don't add more to a subject that's already glutted. Be sure the topic hasn't been overdone. Just checking a local library or bookstore is not adequate research. Look in *Books in Print Subject Guide* and *Forthcoming Books in Print Subject Guide*. You'll be amazed at how many books there are on the topic. Yours must be better than what's already available. Make it shorter, longer, easier to use, more informative, funnier, richer in content, or better organized. For fiction, try to tie into a hot topic so you have a "hook" for publicity.

3. *Write what other people want.* Catering to your personal desires often makes for lackluster books nobody buys. The fact is, few care about your life history or your deep-felt opinions. Personal journals and impassioned tirades are best saved for family and friends, not foisted upon the general public.

4. *Think "marketing" from the very beginning.* The time to generate marketing ideas is before you write the book, not after you have three thousand copies in your garage. Identify and target your market. How can you reach them? Start folders of ideas: what catalogs might be interested, which associations reach your potential readers, what magazines and newsletters are relevant? Can you sell the book as a premium to companies that would give it away as a gift to entice new customers or would use it internally for training? Think about who else reaches your potential customer and how you can partner with them. Do you have

contacts who have national name recognition and might write an advance endorsement?

5. *Get professional editing.* No, we repeat, no author should edit or proofread his or her own work. You'll miss the forest for the trees, overlooking things that are obvious to you but unclear to your reader. And it's so easy to pass by the same typo time after time.

6. *Create a snappy title.* The right title can make a book, just like an uninspired one can be a death peal. Short is best. While clever is nice, don't sacrifice clarity. For nonfiction, be sure to include a subtitle as it gives you extra mileage in helping readers know what the book is about.

7. *Include all the vital components.* Just as a cake falls flat if you don't add the right ingredients, so do books. Yours needs an ISBN, LCCN, EAN Bookland Scanning Symbol, subject categories on the back cover, etc. (If you don't know what these are, refer back to #1!)

8. *Have a dynamite cover.* The cover is your book's salesperson in bookstores. Get it designed by a professional who understands cover design . . . not just somebody who does nice logos or pretty brochures. You have enormous competition—and a wonderful opportunity to stand out.

9. *Make the interior inviting.* Go to a bookstore and study the insides of books. Find one with clean, "user-friendly" pages. Use this as your model. It may not make sense to purchase and learn typesetting software if you're only doing one book, however. In that case, consider hiring an outside vendor.

10. *Use a book manufacturer for printing.* Don't expect your corner print shop to have the knowledge or technical capabilities to turn out a quality book. Book manufacturers specialize in this type of printing and can save you enormous grief and considerable money.

11. *Publicize, promote, publicize, promote.* Eat, sleep, and talk your book. Nobody cares about it as much as you do. Ongoing, enthusiastic marketing is the real key to success. Never quit. Keep your antenna out for new review opportunities, freelancers who write articles on your topic, etc. We have books that have been in print since 1979 because we're tireless promoters.

THE FINANCES INVOLVED

Every project is different, and costs (and profits and losses) will vary greatly. Self-publisher Victoria Harnish Benson, profiled later in this chapter, reveals some of her expenses for the book she self-published:

Editing fee (I was able to have an editor friend give me a discount):	$200
Typesetting and cover work (adapted from my own design):	$320
Printing and shipping costs for 500 books:	$2,188
Total cost for 500 books:	**$2,708**
Cover price per book:	$14.95
Cost per book ($2,708 divided by 500):	$5.42
Net profit per book:	**$9.53**

"We set the cover price of each book at $14.95, which is standard for a trade paperback of two hundred pages. Deducting the per-book cost of $5.42 leaves us with a potential profit of $9.53 per book sold at full price. Multiply that by five hundred books, and the potential income is $4,765 net.

"However, self-publishers, like traditional publishers, do not sell all their books at cover price. Heavy discounts (anywhere from 30 to 55 percent) are taken by bookstores and distributors. Many copies are given away to media reviewers, friends, and family, and discounts of all types are given to any number of other groups or individuals. You, as the publisher, may set any price for any individual book you sell.

"We have given away about seventy books, and about one hundred and forty were sold at an average 40 percent discount to bookstores, museums, and a Latvian organization for resale.

"Our gross income from the full and discounted price of 480 books was about $5,100. After deducting the publishing costs of $2,700, our net income, or profit, on these sales was approximately $2,400. This is a highly satisfactory sum for us to collect in royalties in one year of sales.

"Remember, you will spend additional funds on promoting and marketing your book. This amount can be as small or as large as meets your purposes, and some of these expenses can be considered business expenses and deducted.

"Check with your state to see if there is a requirement for you to buy a business license to market your self-published book. You then must file the appropriate tax returns for your business . . . another factor to consider in deciding whether to self-publish."

Costs will vary depending on the number of pages your book has, whether you use color or black-and-white illustrations, whether you use a four-color cover, how many copies you print, and where you get the books printed. Generally speaking, it's less expensive to use printers in the northern part of the country—that's where most of the trees are—but the shipping costs could be more, depending on where you live.

Other expenses include postage, mailers, labels, long-distance phone calls to promote your book, advertisements, and office supplies.

DISTRIBUTION

Some bookstores will take small-press books (and self-published books fall into that category); others will not. The bookstores' main concern is whether the book sells. Visits to local bookstores can result in outright purchases or a consignment arrangement. While there, offer to sit for a book signing.

For wider distribution, consider distributors and wholesalers. Investigate what Ingrams, Baker & Taylor, and the like can offer. Appendix C has a list of distributors and their websites.

If you do distribute your books to bookstores, be prepared to take a 40 to 55 percent discount off the cover price of all books sold to them. Although the amount of your profit is reduced, you have the chance to sell more books.

Victoria Benson says, "Research your market, the shelf life of a first-time author's book, and any other factors relevant to your book before setting up distribution. I know an author who has seen a large success in using a publicist and a distributor for his self-published book. The subject matter of his work is of interest to a large segment of Americans, and he wisely took that into consideration before making his decision. Because my book appeals to a smaller market, I chose not to undertake such a large expenditure."

FIRSTHAND ACCOUNT

Victoria Harnish Benson, Author and Self-Publisher

Victoria Harnish Benson is the coauthor of *To No Man's Glory: A Child's Journey from Holocaust to Healing*, a book she wrote with her husband. It's her husband's true story about his childhood as an orphan in Latvia. She started writing the book in 1997, then published and sold it in 2000 and 2001. To do so, she formed the Silver Dove Publishing Company.

Benson earned her B.A. in English literature from the University of Colorado-Boulder in 1969. She currently lives in Oregon.

Getting Started

"I decided to self-publish for several reasons:

1. I wanted this book to be available as a finished product sooner than traditional publishing would allow. Because it is my husband's true story, I wanted his grown children to have it right away. There were also many of our friends who were interested in reading it, and many of them are elderly. The time it takes to send queries, send manuscripts, receive rejections, get an acceptance, and then actually publish can stretch out for two years or more. I was not that patient in this case.

2. We purchased the copyright and an ISBN so that any bookstore can order our book for a customer who requests it, and we are in charge of negotiating our discounts. I didn't feel we needed a publisher for these services.

3. The major burden of marketing and promotion of this type of book would fall into our laps even if it were traditionally published, so it was no more work for us to self-publish. Because we keep all the royalties, which are about 65 percent of the cover price, we feel that our profit more than compensates for the smaller arena of exposure.

4. Our book crosses genres, falling in both historical and spiritual categories, which sends publishers into a tizzy. They didn't have a prefab niche for our book, so it wasn't going to easily find a home with one of them.

"Once I decided to self-publish, I went to my local library and read some of the more popular books on self-publishing. Then I took an online course in pre-publishing. These are invaluable sources to learn about the nitty-gritty details of self-publishing. Rather than attempting to persuade you to self-publish, they present the facts, the hard work, and the commitment involved in the entire process, from preparing your manuscript for publishing to marketing and promoting your published work."

What Self-Publishing Is Really Like

"Self-publishing one book would not be considered a regular job or career. However, if one is serious about making a profit on that book, it will be a full-time job for a good six months to a year of manuscript preparation and publishing, then marketing and promoting the book. There is a timetable to follow, and there are steps to take.

"After making the decision to self-publish, I hired a professional editor to go over my manuscript, something all writers ought to do. At least one more rewrite followed, then I hired a typesetter to prepare the entire book, cover to cover, in camera-ready format for the printer. At this point I made the decision not to buy galleys of my book for reviewers. I didn't feel that my book would reach the number of readers that would make the cost of galleys reasonable. Also, I chose not to hire a publicist, nor to hire a distributor.

"If you have a desire to do either of these things, you need to follow a publication release schedule that allows several months' notice to these people for them to get word out to bookstores, reviewers, and media before publication. Because I opted not to go that route, my publishing date was moved up to the immediate future. I then requested quotes from various short-run printers (also called on-demand printers) whom I located online. After comparing their per-book costs, I selected one and placed my order for five hundred books.

"As soon as I ordered my books from the printer and knew what the cost per book would be, I began advertising for discounted presales to my friends. I also contacted various organizations and museums interested in Latvian history or Holocaust survivor stories. I set up a web page specifically for this book, with a sample chapter to be offered each month. By the time my books arrived a few weeks later, I had collected enough money in presales to cover the printing cost. More sales covered the editing and typesetting costs, and nearly 50 percent of my total sales income has been profit."

Upsides and Downsides   "What I enjoyed most about self-publishing was my total involvement in what became of my book. I didn't have to wait to find a publisher who liked it, and then wait while their bureaucratic policies ate up precious time before seeing my book in print. I love learning and putting what I learn to use, and this was a rewarding challenge.

"I kept copious notes on my computer, dated and saved to both hard drive and floppy disk with zip disk backup. Nothing ruins recordkeeping like a hard-drive crash.

"Additionally, I was able to design my own book cover, choose my title, and make all decisions concerning the presentation of the contents. Call it control if you prefer, but it was most satisfying.

"Perhaps the least enjoyable part was the physical work of mailing books—the grunt work. All books mailed from my house were autographed by both my husband and myself. Some were personally inscribed as well. I wrapped each order in bubble wrap, placed it inside a mailing envelope or a box, then drove a carload to the post office.

"When my books first arrived, I had about a hundred of them to mail at once, and it seemed I was wrapping books for days. Yet there was a degree of satisfaction even in that, knowing that someone was going to be reading my book and a message would be spread somewhere new."

The Future   "This is the only book I have planned to self-publish. I now have an agent who is representing me for this book, and I hope to turn over all the publishing details to someone else. I imagine I'll have to do much of the promotion myself, as I did when I first published it, but that's part of the fun.

"I didn't make the decision not to self-publish again because the effort was not profitable. On the contrary; I believe it was highly successful in that I exceeded my expectations in sales and the book received high praise. But the commitment in time spent on the business end kept me from doing the writing that I wanted to do. That's my main reason not to do it again in the near future. But I still have a block of ISBNs and a company name, so I don't rule out the possibility at some later date."

Advice   "Believe in your work, have a message to tell, tell it well, then have it professionally edited. This should be done even if you are submitting it to an agent or publisher.

"Research the requirements for self-publishing before making a decision. It's not for everyone. You must be willing to dig in to the business side of the project after finishing the creative side. Do you enjoy running a business? If not, this will not appeal to you.

"And if you still wish to self-publish? In that case, I hope you have a friend or family member who is dying to help you run your business free of charge!

"Are you shy? Are you willing to contact strangers in order to promote your book? Can you write jacket material for your book? Can you summarize your book in one sentence? These are the tasks that are normally handled by your publisher, and in this case, that means you. If you don't feel comfortable writing your own promotional material, can you afford to hire someone?

"Make sure your book follows the same guidelines and requirements for marketability as would any other published work. Would you buy your book if you saw it on a shelf? Compare how you envision your book with other published books. Can it compete? Check your final proof from the printer in the same way.

"Order as many books as you can reasonably expect to sell. You don't want a garage full of books you will never sell. You might start with a few hundred and order more if you need them. Estimate how many books you will need to sell to cover your costs of publishing. Then you will have an idea what your profit can be, realistically considering giveaways and discounts.

"Be willing to give up most of your writing time to market and promote your self-published book for at least six months. Fill orders promptly and politely with a thank you. Autographed copies are a nice touch. Network your book like crazy. Mention it in conversations. My husband used to be shy about his past, and now he tells everyone he meets that he survived the Holocaust and has a book about the experience. You'd be surprised how many people ask to buy his book right then and there. I spend a good deal of time online, and I mention our book in writers' chats and in E-mail, and I've been a guest speaker in several chats.

"I even contacted local radio stations and our newspaper, and to our surprise, the title of our book made the headlines of our city paper! Take advantage of small publishing associations, writers' associations, and writers' conferences. They are all opportunities to market your book.

"Set aside a few dozen complimentary copies for organizations interested in your topic, book reviewers, even interviewers. Many online book reviewers will publish a review of your book if you send them a complimentary copy. Reach for the stars and send them to radio and TV personalities. You can assemble press packages to send to the media. Many how-to books on self-publishing will outline these points for you.

"Most of all, have a commitment to your project. You can't sell something you aren't 100 percent proud of."

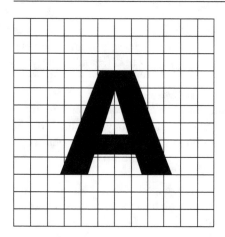

PROFESSIONAL ASSOCIATIONS

Most professional associations provide career information, and many offer job-locating services. A letter, an E-mail, or a visit to a website will bring you in contact with a wealth of leads in your areas of interest.

The following is just a sampling of key associations. Your own Internet search will bring you hundreds more:

Books

American Booksellers Association
Information Service Center
828 South Broadway
Tarrytown, NY 10591
info@bookweb.org
ambook.org

American Society of Business Publication Editors
710 East Ogden Avenue, Suite 600
Naperville, IL 60563
asbpe.org

Association of American Publishers (AAP)
50 F Street NW, Fourth Floor
Washington, DC 20001
publishers.org

Association of American University Presses (AAUP)
71 West Twenty-third Street, Suite 901
New York, NY 10010
http://aaup.princeton.edu

The Association of Authors' Representatives, Inc. (AAR)
P.O. Box 237201 Ansonia Station
New York, NY 10003
publishersweekly.com/aar

The Audio Publishers Association
627 Aviation Way
Manhattan Beach, CA 90266
audiopub.org

Electronic Publishing Coalition
P.O. Box 35
Ellsworth, ME 04605
epccentral.org/members.html

National Association of Independent Publishers
P.O. Box 430
Highland City, FL 33846-0430
NAIP@aol.com
http://lcweb.loc.gov/loc/cfbook/coborg/nai.html

National Association of Independent Publishers Representatives
111 East Fourteenth Street
New York, NY 10003
naipr.org

Publishers Marketing Association
627 Aviation Way
Manhattan Beach, CA 90266
pma-online.org

Publishers Weekly
245 West Seventeenth Street, Sixth Floor
New York, NY 10011
publishersweekly.com

Small Publishers Association of North America (SPAN)
P.O. Box 1306
425 Cedar Street
Buena Vista, CO 81211
spannet.org

Society of National Association Publications
1150 Connecticut Avenue NW, Suite 1050
Washington, DC 20036
snaponline.org
Offers seminars and resource networks, publications, and job listings

Event Planning, Promotion, Advertising, Sales, and Marketing

American Advertising Federation
1101 Vermont Avenue NW, Suite 500
Washington, DC 20005-6306
aaf.org

American Association of Advertising Agencies
405 Lexington Avenue, Eighteenth Floor
New York, NY 10174-1801
aaaa.org

American Marketing Association
311 South Wacker Drive, Suite 5800
Chicago, IL 60606
ama.org

Association of National Advertisers
708 Third Avenue
New York, NY 10017-4270
ana.net

Meeting Professionals International (MPI)
4455 LBJ Freeway, Suite 1200
Dallas, TX 75244-5903
mpiweb.org

National Association of Sales Professionals (NASP)
8300 North Hayden Road, Suite 207
Scottsdale, AZ 85258
http://216.119.96.39/index.html

Point of Purchase Advertising Institute
1600 L Street NW, Tenth Floor
Washington, DC 20036
popai.com

Public Relations Society of America
33 Irving Place
New York, NY 10003-2376
prsa.org

Sales and Marketing Executives International
P.O. Box 1390
Sumas, WA 98295-1390
smei.org

Magazines

Council of Literary Magazines and Presses
CLMPNYC@aol.com
litline.org/html/clmp.html

Magazine Publishers of America
919 Third Avenue
New York, NY 10022
1211 Connecticut Avenue NW
Washington, DC 20036
http://publishing.about.com/business/publishing/msub1a.htm

Society of National Association Publications
1595 Spring Hill Road, Suite 330
Vienna, VA 22182
snaponline.org
Publications owned or operated by professional associations and societies

For magazine jobs
http://publishing.about.com/business/publishing/msubmagazinejobs.htm

Newspapers and Newsletters

American Society of Media Photographers
150 North Second Street
Philadelphia, PA 19106
asmp.org

American Society of Newspaper Editors
P.O. Box 4090
Reston, VA 22090-1700
asne.org

The Dow Jones Newspaper Fund, Inc.
P.O. Box 300
Princeton, NJ 08543-0300
dowjones.com

International Newspaper Marketing Association (INMA)
10300 North Central Expressway, Suite 467
Dallas, TX 75231
inma.org
A nonprofit association dedicated to the promotion of advanced marketing
    principles within the newspaper industry

National Press Photographers Association (NPPA)
3200 Cloasdaile Drive, Suite 306
Durham, NC 27705
http://metalab.unc.edu/nppa
nppa.org

Newsletter & Electronic Publishers Association
1501 Wilson Boulevard, Suite 509
Arlington, VA 22209
newsletters.org

Newspaper Association of America
1921 Gallows Road, Suite 600
Vienna, VA 22182
naa.org

The Newspaper Guild
501 Third Street NW, Suite 250
Washington, DC 20001
newsguild.org

Production

The Graphic Arts Technical Foundation
200 Deer Run Road
Sewickley, PA 15143
gatf.org

Graphic Communications Council
1899 Preston White Drive
Reston, VA 20191
npes.org/edcouncil/index.htm

Graphic Communications International Union
1900 L Street NW
Washington, DC 20036
gciu.org

Printing Industries of America, Inc. (PIA)
100 Daingerfield Road
Alexandria, VA 22314
printing.org

Publishing Law

Information on law schools and a career in law may be obtained from the following:

American Bar Association
750 North Lake Shore Drive
Chicago, IL 60611
abanet.org

Information on the LSAT, the Law School Data Assembly Service, applying to law school, and financial aid for law students may be obtained from the following:

Law School Admission Council
P.O. Box 40
Newtown, PA 18940
lsac.org

Writers

American Association for the Advancement of Science (AAAS)
1200 New York Avenue NW
Washington, DC 20005
aaas.org
For information on technical writing

American Medical Writers' Association (AMWA)
9650 Rockville Pike
Bethesda, MD 20814
amwa@amwa.org
amwa.org

American Society of Journalists and Authors
1501 Broadway, Suite 302
New York, NY 10036
asja.org

American Translators Association (ATA)
1800 Diagonal Road, Suite 220
Alexandria, VA 22314
atanet.org

Association for Business Communication (ABC)
Box G-1326, Baruch College
17 Lexington Avenue
New York, NY 10010
MyersABC@compuserve.com
theabc.org

Association for Computing Machinery's Special Interest Group on
    Documentation (ACM/SIGDOC)
1515 Broadway, Seventeenth Floor
New York, NY 10036
acm.org/sigdoc

Association for Educational Communications and Technology
1025 Vermont Avenue NW, Suite 820
Washington, DC 20005
aect.org

Association for Women in Communications (AWC)
780 Ritchie Highway, Suite 28-S
Severna Park, MD 21146
womcom.org

Association of Teachers of Technical Writing (ATTW)
Department of Rhetoric and Writing Studies
San Diego State University
San Diego, CA 92182-4452
http://rhet.agri.umn.edu/~tcq

Authors Guild, Inc.
31 East Twenty-eighth Street, Tenth Floor
New York, NY 10016
authorsguild.org

Copywriter's Council of America
Communications Building
102 Seven Putter Lane
Middle Island, NY 11953

Council for Programs in Technical and Scientific Communication (CPTSC)
New Mexico State University
English Department, Box 3E
Las Cruces, NM 88003

Council for the Advancement of Science Writing
Abbotts Building, Room 100
Philadelphia, PA 19104

Council of Biology Editors (CBE)
60 Revere Drive, Number 500
Northbrook, IL 60062

Editorial Freelancers Association (EFA)
71 West Twenty-third Street
New York, NY 10010

Education Writers Association
1331 H Street NW, Number 307
Washington, DC 20005
ewa.org

Fiction Writer's Connection (FWC)
P.O. Box 72300
Albuquerque, NM 87195
Bcamenson@aol.com
fictionwriters.com

Freelance Editorial Association
P.O. Box 835
Cambridge, MA 02238

Health Sciences Communications Association
6728 Old McLean Village Drive
McLean, VA 22101

IEEE Professional Communication Group
345 East Forty-seventh Street
New York, NY 10017

Institute of Electrical and Electronics Engineers' Professional
Communication Society (IEEE/PCS)
IEEE Operations Center, Admission and Advancement Department
445 Hoes Lane
P.O. Box 459
Piscataway, NJ 08855-0459
ieee.org/society/pcs

National Association of Agricultural Journalists
c/o Audrey Mackiewitz
312 Valley View Drive
Huron, OH 44839

National Association of Black Journalists
P.O. Box 17212
Washington, DC 20041

National Association of Government Communicators
609 South Washington Street
Alexandria, VA 22314
nagc.com

National Association of Hispanic Journalists
National Press Building
Washington, DC 20045

National Association of Science Writers
P.O. Box 294
Greenlawn, NY 11740
http://nasw.org

National Conference of Editorial Writers
6223 Executive Boulevard
Rockville, MD 20852

National Federation of Press Women
P.O. Box 99
Blue Springs, MO 64013

National Writer's Union
National Office East
113 University Place, Sixth Floor
New York, NY 10003
nwu@nwu.org
nwu.org

National Writer's Union
National Office West
337 Seventeenth Street, Number 101
Oakland, CA 94612
nwu@nwu.org
E-mail for Job Hotline: hotline@nwu.org
nwu.org

Science Fiction Writers of America
Five Winding Brook Drive, Number Eighteen
Guilderland, NY 12084
sfwa.org

Society for Technical Communication, Inc.
901 North Stuart Street, Suite 904
Arlington, VA 22203
stc-va.org

Society of American Travel Writers
1155 Connecticut Avenue, Suite 500
Washington, DC 20006

Writers Guild of America (WGA) East, Inc.
555 West Fifty-seventh Street
New York, NY 10019
wgaeast.org

Writers Guild of America (WGA) West, Inc.
8955 Beverly Boulevard
West Hollywood, CA 90048
wga.org

Canadian and International Associations for Writers

The Association of Canadian Publishers
110 Eglinton Avenue W, Suite 401
Toronto, ON M4R 1A3
Canada
info@canbook.org
publishers.ca

Canadian Authors Association
275 Slater Street, Suite 500
Ottawa, ON K1P 5H9
Canada

Canadian Magazine Publishers Association
130 Spadina Avenue, Suite 202
Toronto, ON M5V 2L4
Canada
cmpa.ca

Canadian Publishers' Council
250 Merton Street, Suite 203
Toronto, ON M4S 1B1
pubcouncil.ca

Societe Quebecoise de la Redaction Professionelle (SQRP) (Canada)
C.P. 126
Succursale Roxboro
Roxboro, Quebec H8Y 3ES
Canada

Writers Union of Canada
24 Ryerson Avenue
Toronto, ON M5R 2G3
Canada

Australia Society for Technical Communication (ASTC) (Australia)
68 Holmes Road
Moonee Ponds
Victoria
Australia 3039
+61-3365-2272
vicnet.net.au/~astc

Conseil des Redacteurs Techniques (CRT) (France)
5, Villa des Carrieres
F-94120 Fontenay-sous-Bois
France
http://ourworld.compuserve.com/homepages/bardez_cristina

DANTEKOM (Denmark)
P.O. Box 146
DK-3600
Frederikssund
Denmark
toc@foss-electric.dk

Foreningen Teknisk Information (FTI) (Sweden)
Skansgatan 19
S-27231
Simrishamn
Sweden
nts.mh.se/~fti/FTI-intr.htm

Gesellschaft fuer Technische Kommunikation (TEKOM) (Germany)
Markelstrasse 34
D-70193 Stuttgart
Germany
tekom.de

Gesellschaft fur Technische Kommunikation Schweize (TECOM Schweiz)
    (Switzerland)
Kirchbergstrasse 30
CH-5024 Kuttigen
Switzerland

Institute of Scientific and Technical Communicators (ISTC) (United
    Kingdom)
Blackhorse Road
Letchworth
Herts SG6 1YY
England
istc.org.uk

International Association of Audiovisual Communicators (IAAVC)
9531 Jamacha Boulevard, Number 263
Spring Valley, CA 91977
cindys.com

International Association of Business Communicators (IABC)
One Hallidie Plaza, Number 600
San Francisco, CA 94102
iabc.com

International Communication Association (ICA)
P.O. Box 9589
Austin, TX 78766-9589
icahdq@uts.cc.utexas.edu

International Council for Technical Communication
106 South Airmont Road
Suffern, NY 10901-7731
nts.mh.se/~fti/Intecom.htm

International Interactive Communications Society (IICS)
10160 Southwest Nimbus Avenue, Suite F2
Portland, OR 97223
iics.org

International Society for Performance Improvement (ISPI)
1300 L Street NW, Suite 1250
Washington, DC 20005
ispi.org

International Television and Video Association (ITVA)
6311 North O'Connor Road, Suite 230
Irving, TX 75039
itva.org

Israel Society for Technical Communication (ETTY) (Israel)
8 Spinoza Street, Apartment Three
Ra'anana IL-43588
Israel
zelenko@shani.co.il

Norsk Forening for Teknisk Informasjon (NFTI) (Norway)
ComText AS
Gjerdrums vei 12G
N-0486 Oslo
Norway
tove.ostberg@comtext.no

Studiekring voor Technische Informatie and Communicatie (STIC) (The
Netherlands)
Punselie Communication Services
St.Adrianusstr. 1
NL-5614 EL
Eindhoven
The Netherlands
tutornet.com

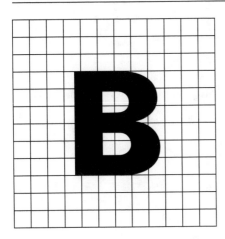

PREPARATORY PROGRAMS FOR THE BOOK TRADE

The following is a sampling of the many institutions offering courses and programs in the different areas of the publishing field. To locate current addresses, phone numbers, and websites, do an Internet search or refer to any of the college directories, available in public libraries.

Arizona State University
Creative Writing Program

Arkansas State University
Printing Program

Association of Graphic Communications
Graphic Arts Education Center

Baylor University
Writing Program

Binghamton University
Writing Program

Boston University
Graduate Creative Writing Program

Bowling Green State University
Creative Writing Program

Center for Book Arts
Bookbinding, printing, and papermaking workshops

Chicago Book Clinic Seminars
Seminars for publishers

Childworks Agency
White Pines National Conference for Writers and Illustrators of Children's
    Books

Columbia University School of the Arts
Writing Division

Dynamic Graphics Educational Foundation
Professional workshops and seminars

Emerson College
Writing and Publishing Program

Fiction Writer's Connection
Writing for Publication Program

Fordham University
Graduate School of Business Administration

George Washington University
Center for Career Education

Graphic Arts Guild New York
Business workshops and seminars

H. H. Herbert School of Journalism and Mass Communication
Professional Writing Program

Hamilton College
English/Creative Writing

Harvard University
Radcliffe Publishing Course

Hofstra University
English Department

Hollins College
Writing Program

Louisiana State University
Writing Program

Massachusetts College of Art
Writing Children's Literature

McNeese State University
Writing Program

Mississippi Review/University of
    Southern Mississippi
Center for Writers

Mystery Writers of America Inc.
Writing Workshops

The National Writer's Voice Project
The Writer's Voice of New York, New York

New York City Technical College
Center for Advertising, Printing, and Publishing

New York University
Center for Publishing

Oberlin College
Creative Writing Program

Ohio University
English Department, Creative Writing Program

Pace University
Master of Science in Publishing

Parsons School of Design
Design courses

Rice University Continuing Studies
Rice University Publishing Program

Rochester Institute of Technology
School of Printing

School of Visual Arts
New York

Stanford University
Stanford Professional Publishing Course

Syracuse University
Creative Writing Program

Syracuse University
S. I. Newhouse School of Public Communications

University of Alabama
Program in Creative Writing

University of Baltimore–Yale Gordon College of Liberal Arts
Institute for Language, Technology, and Publications Design

University of California Extension
Certificate Program in Publishing and Professional Sequence in Copyediting

University of Chicago
Graham School of General Studies

The University of Connecticut
The Realities of Publishing

University of Denver
Publishing Institute

University of Hawaii
Manoa Writing Program

University of Houston
Creative Writing Program

University of Illinois at Chicago
Program for Writers

University of Illinois
Department of Journalism

University of Iowa
Writer's Workshop, Graduate Creative Writing Program

University of Missouri–Kansas City
New Letters Weekend Writers Conference

University of Montana
Environmental Writing Institute

University of Pennsylvania
College of General Studies Special Programs

University of Southern California
Professional Writing Program

University of Texas at Austin
Writing Program

University of Texas at El Paso
Writing Program

University of Virginia
Publishing and Communications Program

University of Wisconsin
Madison Communication Programs

Vermont College
MFA Writing Program

Warren Wilson College
MFA Program for Writers

Washington University
The Writing Program

Writer's Digest School
Correspondence Courses

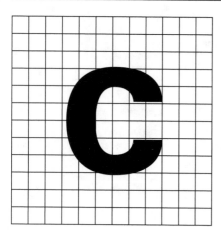

BOOK DISTRIBUTORS

Baker & Taylor
2709 Water Ridge Parkway
Charlotte, NC 28217
btol.com
A leading full-line distributor of books, videos, and music products

BookPeople
603 North Lamar
Austin, TX 78703
bookpeople.com
Books, magazines, books on tape, cards and stationery, jewelry, and arts and
    crafts from around the world; includes searchable database, book reviews,
    and special-events calendar

Christianbook.com
P.O. Box 7000
Peabody, MA 01961-7000
christianbook.com
Bibles, homeschooling products, software, videos, and other products

Educational Paperback Association
P.O. Box 1399
East Hampton, NY 11937
edupaperback.org
Association of publishers and distributors who supply paperback books,
    prebound books, and other materials to schools and libraries

Independent Publishers Group
814 North Franklin Street
Chicago, IL 60610
ipgbook.com
Book distributor for a large number of independent publishers and small
  presses throughout the United Sates and worldwide

Ingram Book Group
One Ingram Boulevard
P.O. Box 3006
La Vergne, TN 37086-1986
ingrambook.com
Wholesaler of trade books and related products

LEA Book Distributors
170-23 Eighty-third Avenue
Jamaica Hills, NY 11432
leabooks.com
Spanish and Latin American book import-export service

Seven Hills Book Distributors
1531 Tremont Street
Cincinnati, OH 45214
sevenhillsbooks.com
Major distributor to the book trade of international publishers and small
  domestic presses

SPB & Associates Inc.
411 Wesley Drive, Suite 200
Chapel Hill, NC 27516
soprobooks.com
Books and reference material acquisitions for special librarians worldwide

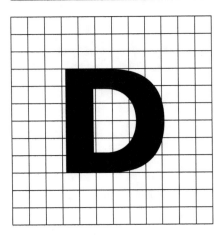

RESOURCES

Broadcasting and Cable Marketplace
R. R. Bowker
121 Chanlon Road
New Providence, NJ 07974

Encyclopedia of Associations
Gale Research, Inc.
P.O. Box 33477
Detroit, MI 48232

Gale Directory of Publications and Broadcast Media
Gale Research, Inc.
P.O. Box 33477
Detroit, MI 48232-5477

Guide to Literary Agents & Art/Photo Reps
Photographer's Market
Writer's Market
Writer's Digest Books
F & W Publications
1507 Dana Avenue
Cincinnati, OH 45207

The Literary Marketplace
R. R. Bowker
121 Chanlon Road
New Providence, NJ 07974

Novel and Short Story Writer's Market
Writer's Digest Books
F & W Publications
1507 Dana Avenue
Cincinnati, OH 45207

The Self-Publishing Resource Center
wiseowlbooks.com/publish

Trade Book Publishing 2001 Report: Analysis by Category
Simba Information Inc.
P.O. Box 4234
11 River Bend Drive South
Stamford, CT 06907-0234
info@simbanet.com
simbanet.com/products/pr_bp.html
Comprehensive source of data, analysis, and statistics for the $11 billion
    trade book publishing industry. This report breaks down consumer book
    sales by category, segment, distribution channels, and publishers.

Writer's Digest Magazine
Writer's Digest Books
F & W Publications
1507 Dana Avenue
Cincinnati, OH 45207
https://commerce.cdsfulfillment.com/WRD/
    subscriptions.cgi?IN_Code=IYAG000

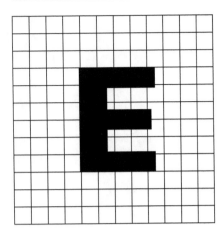

ELECTRONIC PUBLISHERS

The following is a list of electronic publishers from the Electronic Publishing Coalition. Visit epccentral.org/members.html for more information.

Abby the Troll Publications

Allstory.com

Antelope Publishing

Athina Publishing

Atlantic Bridge Publishing

Author-Network

Awe-Struck E-Books

Belgrave House

BookBooters.com

BookMice

Booksurge.com

Boson Books

CityScape Books

Clock Tower Fiction

Cloudy Mountain Books

Dancing Willow Publications

Denlinger's Publishers, Ltd.

Digitz.net

Disk Us Publishing

DLSIJ Press

Dreams Unlimited

Durksen Enterprises

eBookAd.com

eBooksOnThe.Net

eboox.co.uk

eKIDna eBooks

ElectricStory

eNovel.com

Gemini Books

Hard Shell Word Factory

Hidden Knowledge

Intellectua.com

Iumix Ltd.

Jacobyte Books

Kripgans.de-Publishing Services

Kudlicka Publishing

LTD Books

Mystic-Ink Publishing

Online Originals

RSVP Press

Salvo Press

SeeSpotBooks.com

Shoppes At Home

Silver Lake Publishing

Sirius Publications

SMC Publishing

Stinky Dog Press

SynergEbooks

Truefire.Com, Inc.

23 House

VanGoach Books

Virtual Publishing Group, Inc.

whidbeybooks.com

Word Wrangler Publishing, Inc.

Wordbeams

Write Words, Inc.

Writers Exchange E-Publishing

XC Publishing

Yellow Creek Publishing

Zander eBooks

Zeus Publications